The American V[ision]
Modern Tim[es]

Features and Benefits

Dynamic Instructional Structure

. . . presents a clear and comprehensive coverage of American history.
- Each engaging section introduction includes a Connection, Main Ideas, Content Vocabulary, Academic Vocabulary, People and Terms to Identify, Places to Locate, Reading Objectives, a Reading Strategy, and a Preview of Events.
- The Chapter Summaries offer concise synopses of important chapter topics and can be used to preview, review, or summarize chapter content.
- The Skillbuilder Handbook teaches students the skills they need to be successful in their study of history.

A Strong Reading Strand

. . . encourages active reading and learning for students of all reading levels.
- The Reading Skills Handbook provides students with vital strategies to improve their reading comprehension.
- The American Literature features ask students to analyze poems and excerpts from literature tied to each unit.
- Reading Checks help students check their reading comprehension.
- Reading Strategies in the Teacher Wraparound Edition provide a wealth of activities designed to involve students of all reading levels.

Universal Access

. . . makes *The American Vision: Modern Times* accessible to students of all learning levels.
- Universal Access activities and strategies are designed for students of varying ability levels and learning styles.
- A variety of question types and strategies provide students of differing ability levels and learning styles with a variety of assessment activities that cater to their strengths.
- The comprehensive Teacher Wraparound Edition indicates which activities are suitable for various ability levels.

Standards Practice

. . . gives students the opportunity to monitor their grasp of the California standards.
- Chapter Assessments and a Standards Practice question at the end of each chapter provide a variety of ways to check students' command of the California standards, including multiple choice questions, open-ended short response, and open-ended extended response.
- Section Assessments allow students to check mastery of the concepts keyed to the standards.

A Variety of History Activities and Features

. . . are essential for student success and get students excited about history.
- Different Viewpoints features challenge students to interpret opposing views on events in history.
- You're the Historian features provide students with opportunities to explore various views of historical events.
- The Primary Sources Library provides students with examples of sources vital to understanding American history.
- What If? features examine what might have happened if certain historical events had turned out differently.
- National Geographic Geography and History features show students how geography has affected key events in American history.

Teacher Resources

. . . provide convenient strategies to help new and experienced teachers.
- Unit and Chapter Resources provide background and extension material to help in lesson preparation.
- Fast File™ Unit Resource Books contain important reproducible masters.
- Reading and Study Skills Foldables help students organize and process key concepts as they read.

Technology

. . . provides time-saving software products to help you reduce preparation time and engage students creatively.
- *The American Vision: Modern Times* Video Programs offer interesting and diverse content extension.
- TeacherWorks™ includes an Interactive Teacher Edition as well as an Interactive Lesson Planner that contains all resources available with the program on a CD-ROM.
- StudentWorks™ includes an electronic version of the Student Edition, along with all of the program's workbooks.
- History Online at tav.mt.glencoe.com provides resources and activities designed for your book.

Improving Active Reading and Study Skills

Dinah Zike's

FOLDABLES™

Foldables are easy-to-make, three-dimensional, interactive graphic organizers that students create out of simple sheets of paper. The Teacher Classroom Resources include *Dinah Zike's High School American History Reading and Study Skills.* This booklet provides you with step-by-step instructions for using Foldables in your classroom. Each Foldable is designed to be used as a study guide for the main ideas and key points presented in a chapter. Foldables can also be used for a more in-depth investigation of a concept, idea, opinion, or event, or people or places studied in a chapter. These unique hands-on tools for study and review were created exclusively for Glencoe by education specialist Dinah Zike.

Why Use Foldables in Social Studies?

Because they:

- organize, display, and arrange information, making it easier for students to grasp social studies concepts, theories, facts, opinions, questions, research, and ideas.

- are student-made study guides that students themselves create as they listen for main ideas, read their textbook, or conduct research.

- provide a multitude of creative formats in which students can present projects, research, interviews, and inquiry-based reports.

- replace teacher-generated writing or photocopied sheets with student-generated print.

- incorporate the use of such skills as comparing and contrasting, recognizing cause-and-effect relationships, and understanding similarities and differences.

- reinforce previously learned vocabulary, concepts, information, generalizations, ideas, and theories, providing students with a strong foundation that they can build upon with new observations, concepts, and knowledge.

- can be used by students or teachers to easily communicate data through graphs, tables, charts, models, and diagrams, including Venn diagrams.

- allow students to make their own journals for recording observations, information, primary and secondary source data, surveys, and so on.

- can be used as alternative assessment tools by teachers to evaluate student progress or by students to evaluate their own progress.

- integrate language arts, the sciences, and mathematics into the study of social studies.

- provide a sense of student ownership or investment in the social studies curriculum.

Teacher Wraparound Edition

The American Vision

Modern Times

CALIFORNIA EDITION

Joyce Appleby, Ph.D.

Alan Brinkley, Ph.D.

Albert S. Broussard, Ph.D.

James M. McPherson, Ph.D.

Donald A. Ritchie, Ph.D.

NATIONAL GEOGRAPHIC

McGraw Hill Glencoe

New York, New York   Columbus, Ohio   Chicago, Illinois   Peoria, Illinois   Woodland Hills, California

Authors

Joyce Appleby, Ph.D., is Professor of History at UCLA. Dr. Appleby's published works include *Inheriting the Revolution: The First Generation of Americans; Capitalism and a New Social Order: The Jeffersonian Vision of the 1790s; and Ideology and Economic Thought in Seventeenth-Century E...*, both won the Berkshire Prize. She served as president of the Organization of American Historians and the ... of Early American History and Culture at Williamsb... and the American Academy to the American Philosophical ...esponding Fellow of the British of Arts and Sciences, and i...

Alan Brinkley ...is Allan Nevins Professor of American ...versity. His published works include *Voices ..., Father Coughlin, and the Great Depression,* History at Col... National Book Award; *The End of Reform:* of Protest:...lism in Recession and War; The Unfinished which w...cise History of the American People;* and *Liberalism Newcontents.* He received the Levenson Memorial Teaching ...Harvard University.

...ert S. Broussard, Ph.D.,** is Professor of History and ...raduate Coordinator at Texas A&M University. Before joining the Texas A&M faculty, Dr. Broussard was Assistant Professor of History and Director of the African American Studies Program at Southern Methodist University. Among his publications are the books *Black San Francisco: The Struggle for Racial Equality in the West, 1900–1954* and *African American Odyssey: The Stewarts, 1853–1963.* Dr. Broussard has also served as president of the Oral History Association.

James M. McPherson, Ph.D., is George Henry Davis Professor of American History at Princeton University. Dr. McPherson is the author of 11 books about the Civil War era. These include *Battle Cry of Freedom: The Civil War Era,* for which he won the Pulitzer Prize in 1989, and *For Cause and Comrades: Why Men Fought in the Civil War,* for which he won the 1998 Lincoln Prize. He is a member of many professional historical associations, including the Civil War Preservation Trust.

Donald A. Ritchie, Ph.D., is Associate Historian of the United States Senate Historical Office. Dr. Ritchie received his doctorate in American history from the University of Maryland after service in the U.S. Marine Corps. He has taught American history at various levels, from high school to university. He edits the Historical Series of the Senate Foreign Relations Committee and is the author of several books, including *Doing Oral History, The Oxford Guide to the United States Government,* and *Press Gallery: Congress and the Washington Correspondents,* which received the Organization of American Historians Richard W. Leopold Prize. Dr. Ritchie has served as president of the Oral History Association and as a council member of the American Historical Association.

The National Geographic Society, founded in 1888 for the increase and diffusion of geographic knowledge, is the world's largest nonprofit scientific and educational organization. Since its earliest days, the Society has used sophisticated communication technologies, from color photography to holography, to convey knowledge to its worldwide membership. The School Publishing Division supports the Society's mission by developing innovative educational programs—ranging from traditional print materials to multimedia programs including CD-ROMs, videodiscs, and software. "National Geographic Geography & History," featured in each unit of this textbook, and "National Geographic Moment in Time," featured in chapters 8–29 of this textbook, were designed and developed by the National Geographic Society's School Publishing Division.

About the Cover See page 1096 for a complete explanation of the cover images.

Glencoe

The *McGraw-Hill* Companies

National Geographic Geography & History and Moment in History © 2006 by the National Geographic Society. The name "National Geographic Society" and the "Yellow Border Rectangle" are trademarks of the Society, and their use without prior written permission is strictly prohibited.

TIME Notebook © by TIME, Inc. Prepared by TIME School Publishing in collaboration with Glencoe/McGraw-Hill.

Send all inquiries to: Glencoe/McGraw-Hill, 8787 Orion Place, Columbus, OH 43240-4027

ISBN 0-07-867851-X (Student Edition), ISBN 0-07-867852-8 (Teacher Wraparound Edition)

Printed in the United States of America.

1 2 3 4 5 6 092/055 08 07 06 05

Contributing Authors, Consultants, and Reviewers

Contributing Authors

Stephen F. Cunha
Humboldt State University
Arcata, CA

Douglas Fisher
San Diego State University
San Diego, CA

Nancy Frey
San Diego State University
San Diego, CA

Robin C. Scarcella
University of California, Irvine
Irvine, CA

Emily M. Schell
San Diego State University
San Diego, CA

David Vigilante
National Center for History in the Schools
San Diego, CA

Ruben Zepeda II
Los Angeles Unified School District
Los Angeles, CA

Academic Consultants

Richard G. Boehm
Southwest Texas State University
San Marcos, Texas

Gloria Contreras
University of North Texas
Denton, Texas

Frank de Varona
Florida International University
Miami, Florida

Larry Elowitz
Georgia College and State University
Milledgeville, Georgia

Susan Hartmann
The Ohio State University
Columbus, Ohio

Cole C. Kingseed
United States Military Academy at West Point
West Point, New York

Barbara Lindemann
Santa Barbara City College
Santa Barbara, CA

David E. Maas
Wheaton College
Wheaton, Illinois

William E. Nelson, Jr.
The Ohio State University
Columbus, Ohio

Bernard Reich
George Washington University
Washington, D.C.

Calbert A. Seciwa
Arizona State University
Tempe, Arizona

Dale Steiner
California State University, Chico
Chico, CA

Athan Theoharis
Marquette University
Milwaukee, Wisconsin

Mark Van Ells
Queensborough Community College
New York, New York

Reading Consultants

Maureen D. Danner
Project CRISS
Kalispell, MT

ReLeah Cossett Lent
University of Central Florida
Orlando, FL

Steve Qunell
Montana Academy
Kalispell, MT

Carol M. Santa
Montana Academy
Kalispell, MT

Bonnie Valdes
Project CRISS
Largo, FL

Teacher Reviewers

Ann T. Ackerman
Nashua High School
Nashua, New Hampshire

Edward Brickner
Woodbury High School
Prescott, Wisconsin

David Doris
North Salinas High School
Salinas, California

Christine Johnson
Herbert Hoover High School
San Diego, California

Tom Laichas
Crossroads School
Santa Monica, California

James Wolfe
Suitland High School
Forrestville, Maryland

California Advisory Board

Helen Ligh
Social Studies and
Language Arts Teacher
Macy Intermediate
Montebello Unified School District
Monterey Park, CA

Barbara S. Lindemann, Ph.D.
Professor of History and
Ethnic Studies
History Department Chair
Santa Barbara City College
Santa Barbara, CA

Reynaldo Antonio Macías
World History Teacher
Mark Twain Middle School
Los Angeles Unified School District
Los Angeles, CA

Jennifer Metherd
Program Coordinator
Tehama County
Department of Education
Red Bluff, CA

Derrick K. Neal
Social Studies Department Chair
Patrick Henry Middle School
Los Angeles Unified School District
Los Angeles, CA

Robin C. Scarcella, Ph.D.
Professor and Director
Academic English/ESL
University of California, Irvine
Irvine, CA

Emily M. Schell, Ed.D.
Visiting Professor,
San Diego State University
Social Studies Education Director
SDSU City Heights
Educational Collaborative
San Diego, CA

Dale Steiner, Ph.D.
Professor of History
California State University, Chico
Chico, CA

Roy Sunada
Social Studies Teacher/
AP Coordinator
Marshall Fundamental
Secondary School
Pasadena Unified School District
Pasadena , CA

David Vigilante
Associate Director
National Center for History
in the Schools
San Diego, CA

Ruben Zepeda II, Ed.D.
Adviser, Instructional
Support Services
Los Angeles Unified School District
Los Angeles, CA

Contents

NATIONAL GEOGRAPHIC Reference Atlas

NATIONAL GEOGRAPHIC Geography Handbook

UNIT 1

A Nation is Born   92
Beginnings–1900

Contents

A Changing Society   844
1968–Present

Appendix

Features

Features

Primary Sources Library

Documents of American History

SKILLBUILDER Handbook

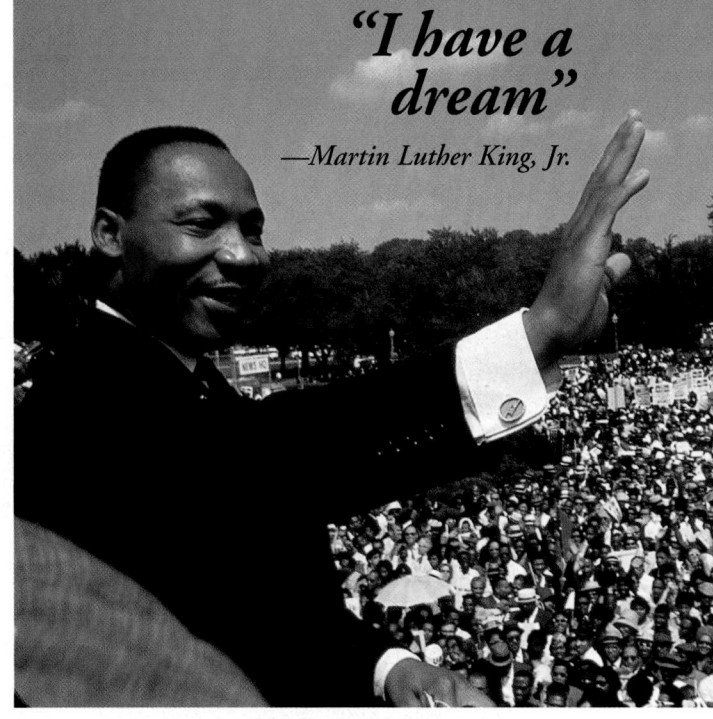

"I have a dream"
—*Martin Luther King, Jr.*

Primary Source Quotes

A variety of quotations and excerpts throughout the text express the thoughts, feelings, and life experiences of people, past and present.

Primary Source Quotes

Primary Source Quotes

Primary Source Quotes

Primary Source Quotes

NATIONAL GEOGRAPHIC Maps

NATIONAL GEOGRAPHIC — Battles of World War I, 1914–1918

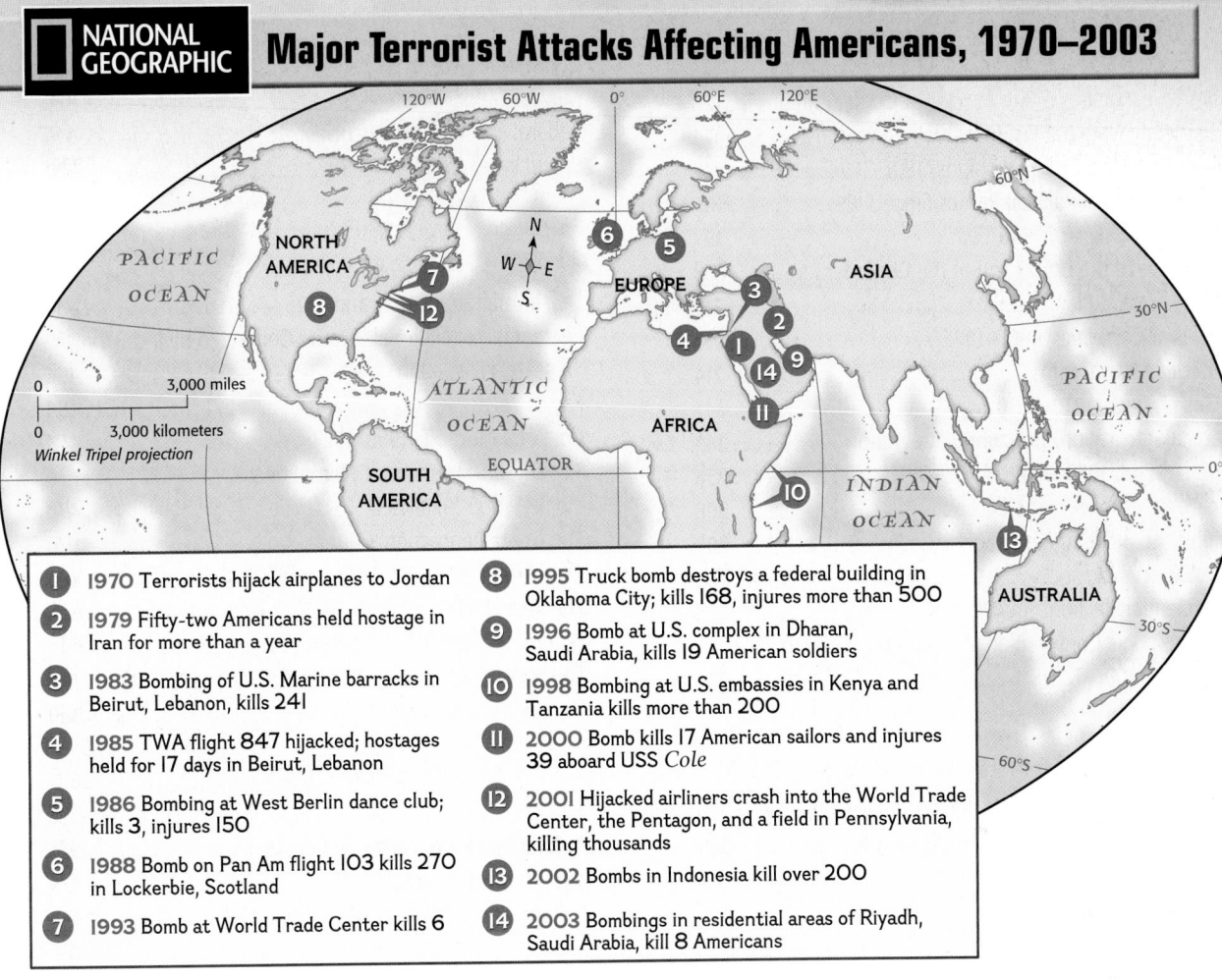

NATIONAL GEOGRAPHIC **Major Terrorist Attacks Affecting Americans, 1970–2003**

① **1970** Terrorists hijack airplanes to Jordan

② **1979** Fifty-two Americans held hostage in Iran for more than a year

③ **1983** Bombing of U.S. Marine barracks in Beirut, Lebanon, kills 241

④ **1985** TWA flight 847 hijacked; hostages held for 17 days in Beirut, Lebanon

⑤ **1986** Bombing at West Berlin dance club; kills 3, injures 150

⑥ **1988** Bomb on Pan Am flight 103 kills 270 in Lockerbie, Scotland

⑦ **1993** Bomb at World Trade Center kills 6

⑧ **1995** Truck bomb destroys a federal building in Oklahoma City; kills 168, injures more than 500

⑨ **1996** Bomb at U.S. complex in Dharan, Saudi Arabia, kills 19 American soldiers

⑩ **1998** Bombing at U.S. embassies in Kenya and Tanzania kills more than 200

⑪ **2000** Bomb kills 17 American sailors and injures 39 aboard USS *Cole*

⑫ **2001** Hijacked airliners crash into the World Trade Center, the Pentagon, and a field in Pennsylvania, killing thousands

⑬ **2002** Bombs in Indonesia kill over 200

⑭ **2003** Bombings in residential areas of Riyadh, Saudi Arabia, kill 8 Americans

Unit 3
European Immigration Totals, 1890–1920 409
Dust Bowl, 1930s 477
The TVA, 1940 509

Unit 4
Axis Expansion, 1935–1941 545
Jewish Losses, 1939–1945 555
Pearl Harbor, Hawaii, December 7, 1941 560
Nazi Concentration and Extermination Camps,
    1933–1945. 567
Battle of Midway, 1942 582
Migration in the United States, 1940–1950 589
Island-Hopping in the Pacific, 1942–1945 604
World War II in Europe and Africa, 1939–1945 610
Rise and Fall of Axis Powers 611
Battle of the Bulge, December 1944–January 1945 . . . 621
Divided Europe, 1948 631
NATO and the Warsaw Pact, 1955 638
Korean War, 1950–1953 635

The Occupation of Berlin after World War II, 1945 661
The Election of 1948 669
The Interstate System, 2000 672

Unit 5
The Election of 1960 735
Route of the Freedom Riders, 1961 767
Indochina, 1959 774
The Tet Offensive, 1968 790
The Vietnam War 801
ERA Ratification, 1972–1982 843

Unit 6
The Election of 1968 852
Rise of the Sunbelt, 1950–1980 889
Revolution in Eastern Europe, 1989–1993 916
War in the Persian Gulf, 1991 921
The Election of 1992 925
The Election of 2000 950
Major Terrorist Attacks Affecting Americans,
    1970–2003 958

T21

Charts & Graphs

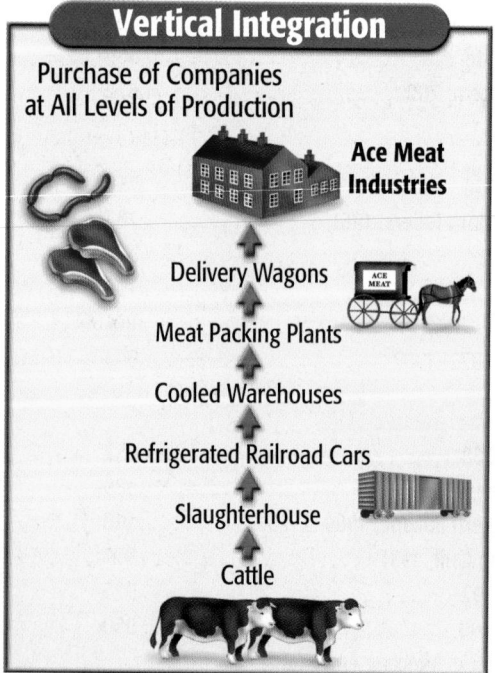

Vertical Integration

Purchase of Companies
at All Levels of Production

Ace Meat Industries

Delivery Wagons

Meat Packing Plants

Cooled Warehouses

Refrigerated Railroad Cars

Slaughterhouse

Cattle

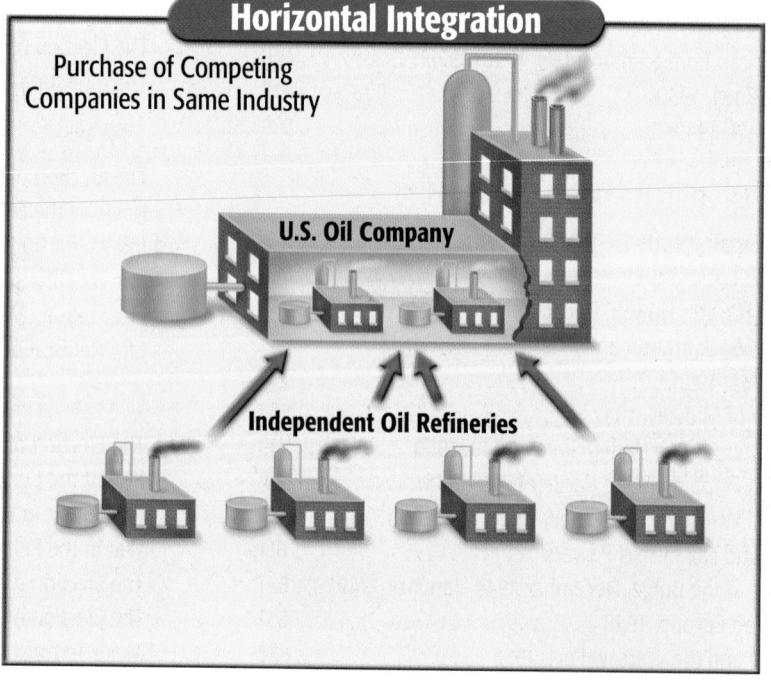

Horizontal Integration

Purchase of Competing
Companies in Same Industry

U.S. Oil Company

Independent Oil Refineries

The Florida Election, 2000

Bars represent the number of votes by which Bush led in Florida, in 15-minute intervals.

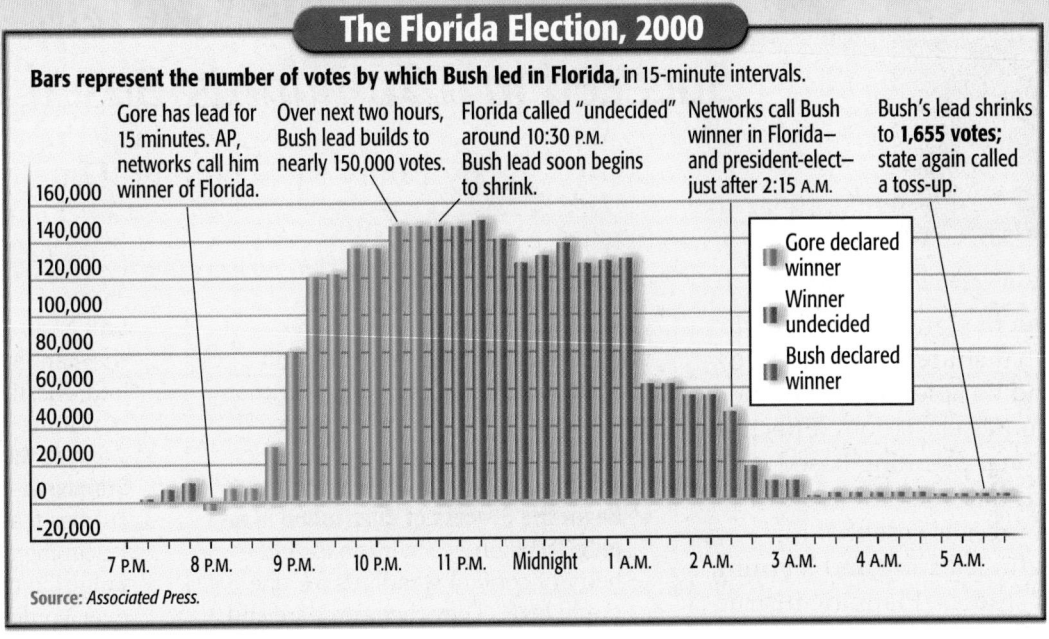

Gore has lead for 15 minutes. AP, networks call him winner of Florida.

Over next two hours, Bush lead builds to nearly 150,000 votes.

Florida called "undecided" around 10:30 P.M. Bush lead soon begins to shrink.

Networks call Bush winner in Florida— and president-elect— just after 2:15 A.M.

Bush's lead shrinks to **1,655 votes;** state again called a toss-up.

Gore declared winner

Winner undecided

Bush declared winner

Source: Associated Press.

One-Stop Internet Resources

This textbook contains one-stop Internet resources for teachers, students, and families. Log on to tav.mt.glencoe.com for more information. Online study tools include Study Central, ePuzzles and Games, Self-Check Quizzes, Vocabulary E-Flashcards, and multi-language glossaries. Online research tools include Student Web Activities, Current Events, Beyond the Textbook Features, Web Resources, and State Resources. The interactive online student edition includes the complete Interactive Student Edition. Especially for teachers, Glencoe offers an online Teacher Forum, Web Activity Lesson Plans, and Literature Connections.

Backward Mapping

How Can My Instruction Help Students Succeed in a Standards-Based System?

by Emily M. Schell, Ed.D.

Content standards articulate what students should know and be able to do in every social studies classroom. Effective instructional planning based in the standards and maximizing available resources is essential for meaningful teaching and learning of social studies. Planning instruction with educational goals in mind makes for the most effective teaching.

How Do I Map My Curriculum?

Mapping the curriculum from beginning to end, and from the end to the beginning—**backward mapping**—makes for solid instruction.

Mapping out the curriculum allows teachers to achieve several goals. These goals include a better understanding of the standards and content-specific objectives, organization and pacing of the curriculum, and focused assessment related to specific goals and objectives.

✔ **Begin the Process of Curriculum Mapping** To begin, teachers analyze the body of content standards for one grade level. They then compare and contrast these standards to additional sources of information that support effective teaching and learning at that grade level and in that subject area. This process works best with same-grade colleagues who bring varying perspectives and expertise to teaching this subject. As a result of this collaboration, strengths and weaknesses of the standards become apparent. Teachers will have a better understanding of the standards and identify concerns and questions for follow-up while mapping.

✔ **Analyze the Organization of the Standards-Based Content** Most social studies teachers agree with researchers that history is best taught in chronological order. However, some grade-level standards either do not or cannot present the content in chronological order. Rich discussions about themes and concepts tend to emerge, and teachers identify meaningful methods for presenting complex and overlapping information. In this way students will see the connections that transcend chronology.

✔ **Identify the Content and Order of Teaching** A plan is developed to present certain content first, then second, then third and so on. Folding in content that is either missing from the standards or essential in building background knowledge with students enters the curriculum map as well. Outside resources brought into the classroom are good supplements.

✔ **Separate Overlapping Units** Identify areas of instruction for the topics, themes, big ideas, or concepts. It is at this stage that backward planning is introduced for the development of instructional units, which will support the grade-level curriculum map. The instruction must support the planned assessment.

Robin Nelson/PhotoEdit

✔ **Map Curriculum at Each Grade Level**
Curriculum planning should be shared among grade levels. Teachers will have a better understanding of what knowledge and skills students bring to their coursework if they take into consideration what has been learned previously.

How Do I Use Backward Mapping?

After a year-long course of study is mapped out, each unit must be further developed through backward mapping. You will start with the end in mind—knowing your curricular goals and objectives at the outset, which are often found in the content standards and articulated in the curriculum maps.

Once goals have been determined, teachers develop assessments that will show progress toward those goals and objectives. In the final step of this backward mapping process, teachers determine meaningful teaching and learning strategies and identify useful resources that support the assessment.

To use backward mapping in developing your units of instruction, consider the following steps:

Step One: Know Your Targets

First, identify exactly what students must know and do in this unit. Analyze content standards and any other resources that support curricular goals and objectives for this unit. As you plan, ask yourself:

✔ What do I want my students to know as a result of this unit?
✔ What skills will students develop during the course of this unit?
✔ How do I describe these goals clearly and concisely to my students so they understand where we should be at the end of this unit?
✔ What essential knowledge will students need to access to make sense of this information?
✔ Do my instructional goals align with strategies identified in the curriculum map?

✔ Have I introduced any Big Ideas that are pertinent to this content?

Step Two: Identify and Develop Assessments

Second, consider the multiple forms of formal and informal assessments that will help you determine to what degree each student has achieved the stated goals and objectives seen in Step One. Some assessments are embedded throughout the instructional unit, while others come at the end of the unit. Some assessments are performance-based, while others are not. Some are authentic applications of information and skills, while others require the formal recall of information. Ask yourself:

✔ What do I want to know and see from each student?
✔ What are the best methods for students to demonstrate what they know and can do based on the goals and objectives?
✔ How many assessments do I need to determine what students know and can do?
✔ How will I balance informal and formal assessments?
✔ How will I assess students with diverse learning styles, skills, and abilities?
✔ How can I prepare and support students?
✔ How will these assessments promote student progress in social studies?
✔ At what time(s) during the unit will I administer these assessments?

Step Three: Develop Meaningful Instruction

After the assessments for the unit have been determined, consider the meaningful and effective teaching strategies that will support learning and student achievement on assessments. While developing lesson plans for instruction, ask yourself:

✔ How will students learn what they are expected to know?
✔ How will I engage students in the studies of this unit?

✔ In what ways might students relate or connect to this information?
✔ What research-based strategies will be most effective with my students and in these studies?
✔ How will I differentiate my instruction to meet the diverse needs of my students?
✔ How will I scaffold or provide access to the curriculum for my English learners?
✔ What vocabulary requires attention in this unit?
✔ How much time will I have to effectively teach this unit?
✔ How will I use the textbook and other resources to support the goals and objectives for this unit?
✔ What lessons will I develop?
✔ In what sequence will I teach these lessons during this unit?
✔ How will these lessons support the assessments from Step Two?

Step Four: Locate and Manage Resources

Effective teaching and learning of social studies requires the use of multiple forms of text and varied resources. Consider what you have available in your classroom, including your textbook, and identify resources you will add in order to teach this unit successfully. Ask yourself:

✔ What parts of the textbook are required for the lessons determined in Step Three?
✔ What ancillary materials are needed for the lessons in this unit?
✔ What Web sites will I recommend to students to support these lessons?
✔ Do I need to contact guest speakers or obtain outside resources?
✔ What literature resources are available to support this unit?

Emily Schell is Visiting Professor, San Diego State University; and Social Studies Education Director, SDSU City Heights Educational Collaborative, San Diego, CA

Meeting the Diverse Needs of Our Students

by Douglas Fisher, Ph.D.

Today's classroom contains students from a variety of backgrounds with a variety of learning styles, strengths, and challenges. As teachers we are facing the challenge of helping each student reach their educational potential. With careful planning, you can address the needs of all students in the social studies classroom. The basis for this planning is **universal access**. When classrooms are planned with universal access in mind, fewer students require specific accommodations.

What Is a Universal Access Design for Learning?

Universal design was first conceived in architectural studies when business people, engineers, and architects began making considerations for physical access to buildings. The idea was to plan the environment in advance to ensure that everyone had access. As a result, the environment would not have to be changed later for people with physical disabilities, people pushing strollers, workers who had injuries, or others for whom the environment would be difficult to negotiate. The Center for Universal Design **www.design.ncsu.edu/cud** defines Universal Design as:
The design of products and environments to be usable by all people, to the greatest extent possible, without the need for adaptation or specialized design.

Universal Design and Access in Education

Researchers, teachers, and parents in education have expanded the development of built-in adaptations and inclusive accommodations from architectural space to the educational experience, especially in the area of curriculum.

In 1998, the National Center to Improve the Tools of Educators (NCITE), with the partnership of the Center for Applied Special Technology (CAST), proposed an expanded definition of universal design focused on education:
In terms of learning, universal design means the design of instructional materials and activities that allows the learning goals to be achievable by individuals with wide differences in their abilities to see, hear, speak, move, read, write, understand English, attend, organize, engage, and remember.

How Does Universal Design Work in Education?

Universal design and access, as they apply to education and schooling, suggest the following:

✔ **Inclusive Classroom Participation** Curriculum should be designed with all students and their needs in mind. The Glencoe/McGraw-Hill Social Studies texts and materials were designed with a wide range of students in mind. For example, understanding that English learners and students who struggle with reading would be using this textbook, vocabulary is specifically taught and

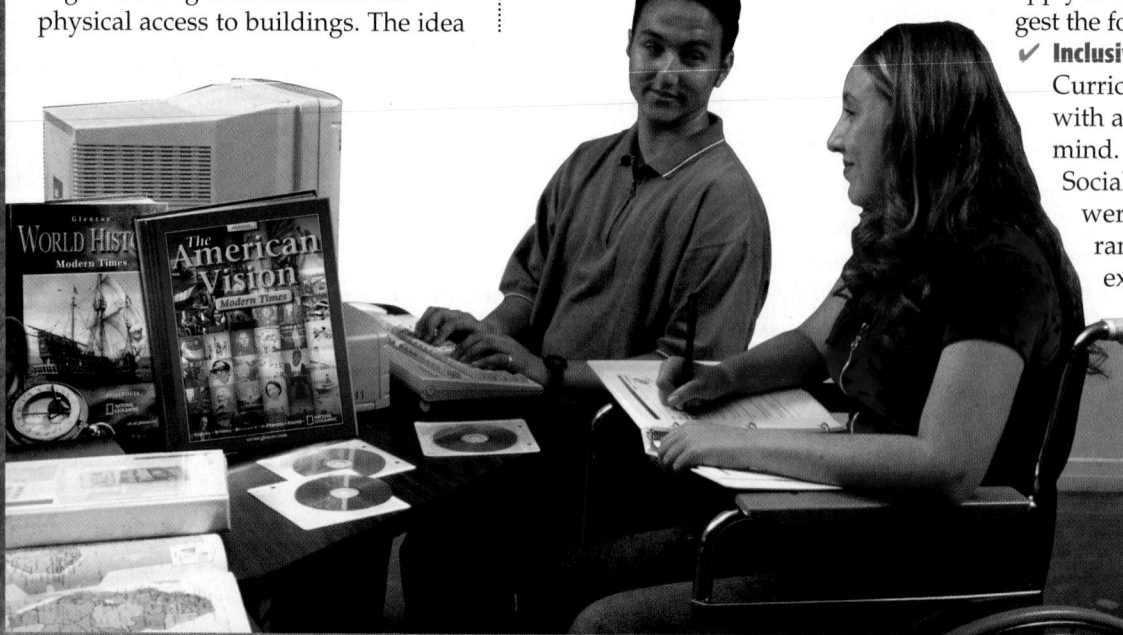

Jonathan Nourok/PhotoEdit

reinforced. Similarly, the teacher-support materials provide multiple instructional points to be used depending on the needs of the students in the class. Further, the text is written such that main ideas are identified for all learners. Throughout the text there are multiple opportunities to activate students' prior knowledge. Connections between what students know and think about are made within the text.

✔ **Maximum Text Readability** In universally designed classrooms that provide access for all students, texts use direct language, clear noun-verb agreements, and clear construct-based wording. In addition to these factors, the Glencoe Social Studies text uses embedded definitions for difficult terms, provides for specific instruction in reading skills, uses a number of visual representations, and includes note-taking guides.

✔ **Adaptable and Accommodating** The content in this textbook can be easily translated, read aloud, or otherwise changed to meet the needs of students in the classroom. The section and end-of-chapter assessments provide students with multiple ways of demonstrating their content

knowledge while also ensuring that they have practice with thinking in terms of multiple-choice questions. Critical thinking and analysis skills are also practiced.

How Is Differentiated Instruction the Key to Universal Access?

To differentiate instruction, teachers must acknowledge student differences in background knowledge and current reading, writing, and English language skills. They must also consider student learning styles and preferences, interests, and needs, and react accordingly. There are a number of general guidelines for differentiating instruction in the classroom to reach all students, including:

✔ **Link Assessment With Instruction** Assessments should occur before, during, and after instruction to ensure that the curriculum is aligned with what students do and do not know. Using assessments in this way allows you to plan instruction for whole groups, small groups, and individual students. Backward planning, where you establish the assess-

ment before you begin instruction, is also important.

✔ **Clarify Key Concepts and Generalizations** Students need to know what is essential and how this information can be used in their future learning. In addition, students need to develop a sense of the **Big Ideas**— ideas that transcend time and place.

✔ **Emphasize Critical and Creative Thinking** The content, process, and products used or assigned in the classroom should require that students think about what they are learning. While some students may require support, additional motivation, varied tasks, materials, or equipment, the overall focus on critical and creative thinking allows for all students to participate in the lesson.

✔ **Include Teacher- and Student-Selected Tasks** A differentiated classroom includes both teacher- and student-selected activities and tasks. At some points in the lesson or day, the teacher must provide instruction and assign learning activities. In other parts of the lesson, students should be provided choices in how they engage with the content. This balance increases motivation, engagement, and learning.

Classroom Activity	To differentiate this activity:
Display a map of imperialism that includes North America, the Caribbean, and the Pacific in 1898. Be sure your map notes the European countries that controlled other countries in the Caribbean, Central America, and Asia. Discuss with students the general information on the map. Then have them list each country under the correct European country that controlled it.	• Ask students to imagine they are living at the time of the Spanish-American War. Have students write an editorial to a local newspaper regarding the war with Spain. • Have students tabulate the number of countries controlled by European countries. Have them take the data and create a bar graph that shows who were the most active imperialistic powers at the time in these regions. • Have students write a poem about the Spanish-American War from the point of view of a Cuban. • Have students create and present a dialog that might have taken place between a Filipino and an American after the United States decided to annex the Philippines. • Have students create a map—using whatever material they choose—that shows the major physical features of the Caribbean or the Pacific. • Have students research one of the countries that came under American dominance after the Spanish-American War. Ask them to write a three-page paper discussing the effects of U.S. control on the country's history. • Have students list each city they see on the map and write in which country these cities are located.

Classroom Solutions

How Do I Support Individual Students?

The vast majority of students will thrive in a classroom based on universal access and differentiated instruction. However, wise teachers recognize that no single option will work for all students and that there may be students who require unique systems of support to be successful.

Tips For Instruction

The following tips for instruction can support your efforts to help all students reach their maximum potential.

✔ Survey students to discover their individual differences. Use interest inventories of their unique talents so you can encourage contributions in the classroom.

✔ Be a model for respecting others. Adolescents crave social acceptance. The student with learning differences is especially sensitive to correction and criticism, particularly when it comes from a teacher. Your behavior will set the tone for how students treat one another.

✔ Expand opportunities for success. Provide a variety of instructional activities that reinforce skills and concepts.

✔ Establish measurable objectives and decide how you can best help students who meet them.

✔ Celebrate successes and make note of and praise "work in progress."

✔ Keep it simple. Point out problem areas if doing so can help a student effect change. Avoid overwhelming students with too many goals at one time.

✔ Assign cooperative group projects that challenge all students to contribute to solving a problem or creating a product.

How Do I Reach Students With Learning Disabilities?

✔ Provide support and structure. Clearly specify rules, assignments, and responsibilities.

✔ Practice skills frequently. Use games and drills to help maintain student interest.

✔ Incorporate many modalities into the learning process. Provide opportunities to say, hear, write, read, and act out important concepts and information.

✔ Link new skills and concepts to those already mastered.

✔ If possible, allow students to record answers on audiotape.

✔ Allow extra time to complete assessments and assignments.

✔ Let students demonstrate proficiency with alternative presentations, including oral reports, role plays, art projects, and musical presentations.

✔ Provide outlines, notes, or tape recordings of lecture material.

✔ Pair students with peer helpers, and provide class time for pair interaction.

How Do I Reach Students With Behavioral Challenges?

✔ Provide a structured environment with simple and clearly defined schedules, rules, seat assignments, and safety procedures.

✔ Reinforce appropriate behavior and model it for students.

✔ Cue distracted students back to the task through verbal signals and teacher proximity.

✔ Set very small goals that can be achieved in the short term. Work for long-term improvement in the big areas.

How Do I Reach Students With Physical Challenges?

✔ Openly discuss with the student any uncertainties you have about when to offer aid.

✔ Ask parents or therapists and students what special devices or procedures are needed and whether any special safety precautions need to be taken.

✔ Welcome students with physical challenges into all class activities, including field trips, special events, and classroom and community projects.

✔ Provide information to assist class members and adults in their understanding of support needed.

How Do I Reach Students With Visual Impairments?

✔ Facilitate independence. Modify assignments as needed.

✔ Teach classmates how and when to serve as visual guides.

✔ Limit unnecessary noise in the classroom if it distracts the student with visual impairments.

✔ Provide tactile models whenever possible.

✔ Foster a spirit of inclusion. Describe people and events as they occur in the classroom. Remind classmates that the student with visual impairments cannot interpret gestures and other forms of nonverbal communication.

- ✔ Provide taped lectures and reading assignments for use outside the classroom.
- ✔ Team the student with a sighted peer for written work.

How Do I Reach Students With Hearing Impairments?

- ✔ Seat students where they can see your lip movements easily and where they can avoid any visual distractions.
- ✔ Avoid standing with your back to the window or light source.
- ✔ Use an overhead projector so you can maintain eye contact while writing information for students.
- ✔ Seat students where they can see speakers.
- ✔ Write all assignments on the board, or hand out written instructions.
- ✔ If the student has a manual interpreter, allow both student and interpreter to select the most favorable seating arrangements.
- ✔ Teach students to look directly at each other when they speak.

How Do I Reach English Learners?

- ✔ Remember, students' ability to speak English does not reflect their academic abilities.
- ✔ Try to incorporate the students' cultural experience into your instruction. The help of a bilingual aide may be effective.
- ✔ Avoid any references in your instruction that could be construed as cultural stereotypes.
- ✔ Preteach important vocabulary and concepts.
- ✔ Encourage students to preview text before they begin reading, noting headings.
- ✔ Remind students not to ignore graphic organizers, photographs, and maps since there is much information in these visuals.

- ✔ Use realia and photographs whenever possible to build background knowledge and understanding. An example of this would be coins in a foreign currency or a raw cotton ball to reinforce its importance in history.

How Do I Reach Gifted Students?

- ✔ Make arrangements for students to take selected subjects early and to work on independent projects.
- ✔ Ask "what if" questions to develop high-level thinking skills. Establish an environment safe for risk taking in your classroom.
- ✔ Emphasize concepts, theories, ideas, relationships, and generalizations about the content.

- ✔ Promote interest in the past by inviting students to make connections to the present.
- ✔ Let students express themselves in alternate ways such as creative writing, acting, debates, simulations, drawing, or music.
- ✔ Provide students with a catalog of helpful resources, listing such things as agencies that provide free and inexpensive materials, appropriate community services and programs, and community experts who might be called upon to speak to your students.
- ✔ Assign extension projects that allow students to solve real-life problems related to their communities.✦

Douglas Fisher is a professor at San Diego State University, San Diego, CA

Getty Images

Academic Vocabulary

How Can I Help My Students Learn Academic Vocabulary?

by Robin Scarcella, Ph.D.

What Is Academic English?

Academic English is the language used by the educated and by leaders in business, academic, and other professional disciplines. It is the language used in courts of law and in professional books, including textbooks. This type of English contains specific linguistic features that are associated with academic disciplines like social studies. Proficiency in reading and using academic English is especially related to long-term success in all parts of life.

Academic vocabulary is the basis for academic English. By reinforcing academic vocabulary and academic English, teachers can help learners to access authentic, academic texts—not simplified texts that dummy down the content. In this way, they can provide information that will help build their students' background knowledge rapidly.

What Is Academic Vocabulary?

By the time children have completed elementary school, they must have acquired the knowledge needed to understand academic vocabulary. How many words should they acquire to be able to access their textbooks? A basic 2,000-word vocabulary of high-frequency words makes up 87% of the vocabulary of academic texts. Eight hundred other academic words comprise an additional 8% of the words. Three percent of the remaining words are technical words. The remaining 2% are low-frequency words. There may be as many as 123,000 low-frequency words in academic texts.

Why Should Students Learn Academic Vocabulary?

English learners who have mastered a basic 2,000-word vocabulary are ready to acquire the majority of general words found in their academic texts.

Knowledge of academic words combined with continued acquisition of general words can significantly boost an English learner's comprehension level of academic texts. English learners who learn and practice these words before they graduate from high school are likely to be able to master academic material with more confidence and speed. They waste less time and effort in guessing words or consulting dictionaries than those who only know the basic 2,000 words that characterize general conversation.

Also, consider academic success in terms of measurement and assessment—state standards-based assessments, the SAT, the ACT, and the GRE—with regards to word mastery. All demand an understanding of academic vocabulary.

How Do I Include Academic Vocabulary and Academic English in My Teaching?

Teachers can provide their students with rich samples of academic vocabulary and help students understand and attend to the academic English of their text.

To develop academic English, learners must have already acquired a large amount of basic proficiency in the grammar of everyday English.

Will Hart/ PhotoEdit

Academic English should not be taught overtly but rather within contexts that make sense. In terms of instruction, teaching academic English includes providing students with access to core curriculum—in this case Social Studies.

Academic English arises not only from knowledge of a linguistic code and cognition but also from social practices in which academic English is used to accomplish communicative goals. The acquisition of academic vocabulary and grammar is necessary to advance the development of academic English.

Tips for Teaching Academic Vocabulary:

✔ **Expose Students to Academic Vocabulary** Do not teach it. You do not need to call attention to words students are learning because they will acquire them subconsciously.

✔ **Do Not Correct Students' Mistakes When Using the Vocabulary Words** All vocabulary understanding and spelling errors are developmental and will disappear once the student reads more.

✔ **Help Students Decode the Words Themselves** Once they learn the alphabet, they should be able to decode words. Decoding each word they don't recognize will help them more than trying to focus on sentence structure. Once they can recognize the words, they can read "authentic" texts.

✔ **Do Not Ignore the English Learner in This Process** They can learn academic vocabulary before they are completely fluent in oral English.

✔ **Helping Students Build Academic Vocabulary Leads to Broader Learning** Students who have mastered the basic academic vocabulary are ready to continue acquiring words from the rest of the groups. To help determine which words are in the 2,000-word basic group, refer to *West's General Service List of English Words, 1953.* The list is designed to

serve as a guide for teachers and as a checklist and goal list for students. For additional information about the list, visit:

http://www.vuw.ac.nz/research/awl/info.html or you can check http://www.uni-trier.de/uni/tb2/anglistik/projekte/stubbs/awl.htm

There are a number of guidelines that teachers can follow when teaching academic English and vocabulary:

Guidelines for Teaching Academic Vocabulary

1. Direct and planned instruction
2. Models—that have increasingly difficult language
3. Attention to form—pointing out linguistic features of words
4. Practice
5. Motivation
6. Instructional feedback
7. Assessment—on a regular basis

Robin Scarcella is professor and Director Academic English/ESL, University of California at Irvine; Irvine, CA

Classroom Activity: Writing About Modern America

Advice from Robin Scarcella

Give students an impromptu writing assignment. Ask them to write a short essay about one of the topics listed below in the left column. Have students use as many of the academic vocabulary words in the right column as they can in their essay. Give students a time limit for their writing. When completed, ask student volunteers to share their writing. Note what academic vocabulary words they use.

Topic	Academic Vocabulary
The challenges of reducing poverty	impoverished
in America	housing
	health insurance
	income
Recent technological advances	computers
	technology
	laptop
	desk station
	compact disc player
	transmit

Project CRISS

How Can I Teach My Students How to Learn Social Studies?

by Carol M. Santa, Ph.D.

We all know that teaching social studies involves far more than teaching just course content. We understand that students need to become engaged, confident learners. Achieving that goal means helping them to understand, organize, and retain information.

Teaching Both Content and Skills

In other words, we want our students to have the skills and confidence to be lifelong learners. With its rich content, social studies offer an ideal arena for teaching both content and skills.

✔ **A Dual Responsibility** Let's take a moment to consider why the dual responsibility of teaching both content and skills is so important. Think back to your own middle and high school years. What do you remember about the content

you learned? If I recall my experiences, I find I remember remarkably little content. What did I learn in biology or history? What did my textbooks look like? As the years go by, I don't even remember the names of most of my teachers.

✔ **An Inspiring Teacher** Yet I have vivid memories of my eighth-grade social studies teacher, who came out of retirement to fill in for a history teacher who left on maternity leave. I remember how fascinated I became with ancient history; I recall giving oral reports and how she helped me become comfortable speaking before a group. In fact, I remember more from her class than any other I took during high school.

✔ **Teach How to Learn** More important, I now understand that she taught me how to learn to learn. She showed me how to underline, how to organize information using different note-taking formats, and how to write coherent

answers on essay tests. She taught me the need to test myself on what I knew. And during that vulnerable, adolescent year, I went from being a mediocre student to being an excellent one.

This inspirational teacher did something else for me. At some point during that eighth-grade year, I decided to become a teacher. Later I realized that she had launched me on my professional mission—to spread her wisdom to others. Eventually this led to Project CRISS.

What Is CRISS?

CRISS stands for **CR**eating Independence through **S**tudent-owned **S**trategies. It is a staff development program that I created in collaboration with middle and high school teachers in Kalispell, Montana.

✔ **Origin of CRISS** CRISS had its start 20 years ago in a lunchtime conversation in a teachers' lounge. One of the social studies teachers said, "My students aren't doing a good job of answering chapter questions. In fact, I don't think they even read my assignments. My reading assignments are becoming a waste of time!" His words struck a chord. "My students don't have a clue about how to study, and they don't write very well either," another teacher lamented.

✔ **Evolving Strategies** Supported by a state grant, we started working together to find practical ways to help students read, write, and learn content. We met in teams, read professional literature, and designed studies to test classroom strategies. From these efforts, we evolved a project

Tom & DeeAnn McCarthy/CORBIS STOCK MARKET

to help students become better readers, writers, and learners. Once the project took shape, we shared our discoveries with other teachers by offering a two- or three-day CRISS workshop to schools and districts in the state.

✔ **Constant Growth** Over the last two decades, Project CRISS has spread from teacher to teacher across this country, into Canada, and to several European countries. The project seems to sell itself. Teachers who use CRISS principles and strategies find that their students attain a deeper understanding of course content and become better readers, writers, and learners at the same time. In fact, data from numerous quantitative studies shows that using CRISS strategies improves student learning. (For the most recent data and for information on CRISS workshops, see www.projectcriss.com)

CRISS Strategies in the Teacher Edition

When the editors of Glencoe/McGraw-Hill asked me and my colleagues to help them integrate CRISS strategies into their social studies texts, we welcomed the opportunity. In this teacher wraparound edition, we offer many references to CRISS strategies. We have packed the pages with strategies that help students gain a deeper understanding of specific content.

CRISS Training

We have one word of caution, however: the integration of CRISS strategies within this teacher wraparound edition does not take the place of a Project CRISS workshop, which provides an in-depth knowledge of CRISS. So, if you haven't yet participated in a CRISS workshop, we encourage you to do so. During a workshop, CRISS trainers take you step-by-step through the philosophy and instructional strategies.

Participants are actively involved in all aspects of the program—practicing, adapting, and applying strategies to meet teaching needs.

Long-lasting change occurs when teachers and administrators work together to share, extend ideas, and problem solve. The most effective implementations occur when the initial workshop is supported by follow-up sessions, including a specific follow-up day. At this session, teachers bring examples of strategies they have used since the initial training. Part of this time may be spent in review and in learning new strategies. The rest of the time is for sharing applications. Additional ongoing support can occur in teacher planning periods.

In any case, for those of you unfamiliar with Project CRISS, let's begin with a little background knowledge. In this way you will have some context for the various activities suggested throughout the teacher wraparound edition.

The CRISS Philosophy

The first thing to know is that Project CRISS is more than a collection of learning strategies. Its underlying power rests not on the individual strategies but on the teaching philosophy behind them. This philosophy integrates work from cognitive psychology, social learning theory, and neurological research about how the brain learns. It includes these overlapping principles:

✔ background knowledge and purposeful reading
✔ author's craft
✔ active involvement
✔ discussion
✔ organization
✔ writing
✔ teacher modeling

Let's look at each of these principles in more detail, along with examples of instructional strategies that illustrate them.

Background knowledge and purposeful reading are powerful determinants of reading comprehension.

Teachers involved in Project CRISS often talk about the importance of background knowledge. Readers are far more likely to learn new information when they have some previous knowledge and have a purpose in mind before they read or listen.

✔ **More Than Simply Reading** We warn students not to simply begin reading. We ask them, *"What might you already know about the topic? What questions do you have about the topic?"* We also remind them to preview the assignment and think about their goals for reading. We often have to be very explicit about the goals. For example, we might tell students, *"After reading this selection, you should be able to . . . ,"* or, *"After viewing the video, you should be able to identify . . ."*

✔ **KWLH** In the teaching strategies included for each chapter in this book, we offer ideas for helping students tap into their background knowledge. For example, we suggest that students preview their reading assignment and consider what they already know about a topic. Or, we might develop a whole-class **KWLH** chart (**K**now, **W**ant to learn, **L**earned, **H**ow to learn more), where students work on this task together. They can generate questions about what they want to learn, and then, after completing the assignment, they can list the new information they have learned and how they can learn more.

What I **Know**	What I **Want** to Find Out	What I **Learned**	**How** I Can Learn More

✔ **Reading Goals** We also suggest ways to make sure your students have clear goals for their reading. Each section

(Continued on next page)

Project CRISS

opener lists reading strategies and main ideas that outline reading goals. Most students will skip over this material and simply start reading. Teachers need to help students understand that the reading goals are important tools for understanding. We tell students, *"Don't ignore your purposes for reading. Take time to think about them before delving into your reading."* Project CRISS also provides hints about how to get students to use these purpose statements to evaluate whether they have understood their reading.

Reading social studies materials has its own special considerations. CRISS specialist Malla S. Kolhoff shares this advice: "As educators, it is our responsibility to set a purpose for historical reading. Students often must struggle to connect history with their own lives. To compare and contrast, establish cause and effect, and sequence events in chronological order presents a challenge for even the best reader. CRISS strategies allow students to move beyond words to the real significance for their society. With CRISS, my students are able to become engaged in the learning process through:

a. background knowledge
b. active reading, listening, and learning
c. discussion
d. metacognition
e. writing
f. organization
g. understanding

I have found that these strategies help my students attain a higher level of historical thinking and understanding."

Good readers have an intuitive understanding of the author's craft.

When students know how authors craft their writing, they can more readily understand and remember what they read.

✔ **Pay Attention** Good readers and writers know that paying attention to how text is organized—its headings and paragraphs, for example—makes it easier to comprehend its content. Good readers will analyze the author's style of presentation as they read. They might ask themselves, *"What is this author doing to help me learn key concepts? How does the writer lead me from one idea to the next?"* When students become aware of what the author is doing to impart content, they have a clearer idea of what the author is saying.

✔ **The Walk Through** In the sample lesson on the following pages, we offer advice about "walking through" the text to discover the author's style of presentation. Our suggestions go beyond examining the surface structure (headings, bold print, color coding of topical headings, italicized words) to analyzing how the author elaborates on key topics.

Effective learners are actively involved when they listen and read.

We learn best when we act on the information presented. We can do this by using a variety of organizing activities that require us to write, talk, and transform the information we are absorbing. None of us learns much from reading alone—it's far too passive.

CRISS strategies encourage active engagement in learning. We might ask students to read a section and describe what they are learning to a partner, or we might be more elaborate and have students develop concept maps or write summaries.

Students need many opportunities to talk with one another about what they are learning.

Discussion is critical to learning. The discussions we advocate are different from those in which the teacher remains the authority figure, with students simply reciting answers to questions. If discussion becomes mere recitation and there is little interaction among students, little learning occurs. Thus we focus on how to get students to lead their own discussions about a topic. We want them to understand that it is their discussing, their oral grappling with meaning—not ours—that leads to deeper understanding.

(Continued on next page)

Jose L. Pelaez/CORBIS STOCK MARKET

Competent readers know several ways to organize information for learning.

Learning depends on organization. We show students different ways to organize information. They can take notes, underline selectively, develop concept maps, and summarize ideas in charts. Once we have taught students these techniques, we tell them, *"You have to do more than just read this assignment. How are you going to organize the information from this assignment? You have to change it, to transform it so that it becomes your own."*

For each chapter of this text, we offer ideas for assisting students in organizing information. Once students have learned a variety of organizing systems, we suggest ways to help them apply these structures independently.

Students deserve opportunities to write about what they are learning.

Writing is an integral part of the CRISS project. Writing lets us figure out what we know and what we still need to know. We cannot write about something we do not understand. While we teach students how to write expository papers and essay exams, we also encourage students to write more informally by questioning, speculating, and writing explanations in learning logs. We make sure that students are writing continually about what they are learning.

For each chapter of this text, we offer ideas for assisting students in writing about what they are learning. Once students have practiced a variety of techniques for writing about their learning, including formal and informal writing, we suggest ways to help them apply these strategies independently.

Teaching involves explanation and modeling.

Our final principle has to do with our own teaching. Students learn to think strategically when we use these processes as part of our instruction. Our demonstrations are especially critical for struggling readers. Most have never been taught how to learn. We have to show them how.

✔ **Take Center Stage** When you introduce a new strategy, you should take the center stage: showing, telling, modeling, demonstrating, and explaining not only the content but the process of active reading. As students learn, gradually release responsibility to them. Strategy instruction involves two overlapping steps. First, we explain what the strategy is and why students should use it. If students do not know why they are performing an activity, they will rarely use the activity on their own. Next, we demonstrate and talk about procedures for carrying out the strategy. We discuss, demonstrate, and think aloud while modeling. Then, students practice under our guidance and feedback.

✔ **A Systematic Approach** Project CRISS is a valuable basis for instruction. It provides a systematic approach for using what we now know about teaching and learning. The following chart lists questions we need to continually ask ourselves while we are teaching. Use this chart to monitor your efforts to incorporate CRISS principles into your teaching.

CRISS Principles	The CRISS Philosophy	Yes	No	Somewhat
Background knowledge:	Did I assist students in thinking about what they already knew about the topic before beginning the unit? Did I develop necessary concepts before students read?			
Purpose setting:	Did my students have a clear purpose about what they were going to learn before beginning the lesson?			
Author's craft:	Can my students use the author's style of presentation to facilitate their understanding?			
Active involvement:	Were my students engaged in the topic? Did I help students become actively involved in their learning?			
Discussion:	Did my students have opportunities to talk about what they were learning?			
Organization:	Did my students organize information in a variety of ways?			
Writing:	Did my students write about what they were learning?			
Teacher modeling:	Did I do enough teacher modeling of learning strategies so that students could begin doing them on their own?			

Project CRISS

How Do I Use Project CRISS to Teach The American Vision: Modern Times?

When students know how authors structure their writing, they can better understand and remember what they read. For the first several chapters of this book, show students how to analyze the author's craft by "walking through" the chapter. Then show students how to use the author's organization to develop two-column notes.

To demonstrate these strategies, make transparencies of pages 288–299 of Chapter 4, *Becoming a World Power*. Then organize students into small groups to complete the following activities.

Introducing the Chapter

Place the transparencies of pages 288–289 on the overhead and begin modeling.

Tell students: *"Before reading a text, I take time to figure out how the author has presented the information. If I understand the author's craft, I can do a better job of reading and learning. The authors of this book have a consistent plan for organizing and presenting information. Let's discover what it is."*

Ask students to preview the introductory pages of Unit 2. Then say: *"Why do you think the authors have included the Why It Matters, the photo, and the quote? How might this help you gain an overview of what this unit is about? What resources are available for learning more about the people and events of the time period you will be studying?"*

Place the transparencies of pages 290–291 on the overhead and ask students to turn to Chapter 4: *"Look at the chapter Big Ideas. Read the brief summaries of each of the sections. Why do you think the authors have told you information before you read? Notice the time line and how it highlights key events during the time period discussed in the chapter. How might you use History Online to expand your understanding of the chapter?"*

Introducing the Section
Guide to Reading

Place a transparency of page 294 on the overhead and ask students to turn to that page in their textbooks. *"Notice how this page is organized. Let's take a moment and talk about how these features might help you."* (It begins with a Guide to Reading that includes a Connection, Main Ideas, Content Vocabulary, Academic Vocabulary, People and Terms to Identify, Reading Objectives, a Reading Strategy, and Preview of Events.) It is followed by a Big Idea.

Connection

"Why have the authors provided a connection at the beginning of the section?" (Learning occurs when we are able to make connections between what we already know and new concepts.)

Main Idea

"Why have the authors included the main idea at the beginning of the section?" (to let readers know what they are going to learn, help them think about what they might already know about the topic, and help them set goals.)

Content Vocabulary and Academic Vocabulary

"Now look at the list of content and academic vocabulary words and skim the first several pages of the chapter. What do you notice about how the vocabulary words are sequenced and highlighted in this section?" (The vocabulary words are highlighted in yellow and presented in the same order in the section as listed here.)

People and Terms to Identify; Places to Locate

"How might these features help you prepare to read this section?" (helps readers build a context for people, terms, and places mentioned in the section)

Reading Objectives

"How might you use the reading objectives while you read?" (They help readers identify what they should learn in the section.)

Reading Strategy

"Notice the reading strategy suggested for this section. How could you use it to organize the information for learning?" (The graphic organizer helps readers organize the information in the section.)

Preview of Events

"How might the time line help you comprehend the information in this section?" (provides an overview of the time period for this section and helps to organize information)

The Big Idea

"How does the Big Idea prepare you to read this section?" (It helps readers to focus on the most important concepts to be learned and helps them to see thematic connections across time.)

Walking Through the Narrative

As you talk aloud about the narrative, point out each of the features on the chapter transparencies of pages 295–299. *"Now let's see how the* authors have helped us figure out the main topics covered in this chapter. Notice the bold-print heading. The main topics are printed in larger red print, and the subtopics are printed in smaller blue print. This organization and color coding should help me figure out what is important."

"The first heading includes an American Story. I wonder what the purpose of this story is?" (to provide background knowledge and generate interest in reading the section)

"At the end of each subsection, I notice a Reading Check. The Reading Check questions will help me know if I have comprehended each subsection. When I come to a Reading Check, I will stop and try to answer the question. If I can't, I will reread the subsection. I should also read through these questions before I begin reading a section. In this way, I will know what I am supposed to get out of this section."

"As I continue my walk-through, I notice the visuals on the pages of the chapter. Why did the author include these references? Why should I pay attention to them? It's a good idea to look through these references before reading the chapter." (makes the topics more interesting, provides background knowledge, includes important information for understanding the content, and so on)

"There are also assessments at the end of each section (page 299). The questions in this assessment will help me make sure that I understand everything I have read and that I can identify the Big Idea, the Main Ideas, and the Reading Objectives outlined in the Guide to Reading."

Reading the Chapter

Ask students to read the first section of the chapter. Tell them to keep in mind the Reading Check questions for the section as they read.

Main Idea-Detail Notes

Ask students to divide their notebook paper into two columns to create a graphic organizer similar to the one on the right. Explain that they will record key points in the left column and details about the key points in the right column. Main points should be questions or key words. Students then use their notes as a study guide. They can use the key words or questions to quiz themselves.

✔ Demonstrate how to use the author's clues (headings, bold-print vocabulary) to develop main idea-detail notes. On a blank transparency, develop two-column notes about the first section of the chapter while students write down their own notes at their desks. In the left column, model how to include main topics and vocabulary essential to understanding the content. In the right column, record details that elaborate on the main points. Talk about being brief and using your own words. Explain why making the author's message your own ensures better comprehension and retention.

✔ Continue modeling notes on the rest of this section. Then ask students to work in pairs or small groups to develop two-column notes about the remaining chapter. Ask students to share their notes in a class discussion.

✔ Demonstrate how to use the notes to test themselves. Show students how you cover the right column with a sheet of paper and recite what you can remember. Talk about why testing yourself is important for learning. "You are the only one who knows if you know. Testing yourself is an excellent way to learn and to check your understanding."

✔ Take time for reflection. After students have completed their notes, allow time for discussion about reading and learning strategies. Ask students to write and then talk about how analyzing the author's craft and developing two-column notes helped them read and learn content, and how they might use these strategies in the future.

SAMPLE ORGANIZER

Main Ideas	Details
Why did interest in imperialism arise?	interest in new markets following industrialization and settlement of the West
Anglo-Saxonism	idea that the English race is destined to spread its civilization to other people
military might in Japan	Commodore Matthew C. Perry takes four warships to force Japan to open up to trade; Japan begins to Westernize and build an empire
annexing Hawaii	geographic location and U.S. sugar plantations lead to strong U.S. interest in Hawaii; planters force Hawaii to grant them powers and limit those of the king; United States adds new territory outside North America
cooperation with Latin America	desire to be dominant trading partner and power in the region; Latin American nations reject idea of a customs union and a common system to settle disputes; Latin American delegates reject both but agree to the Commercial Bureau of the American Republics to promote cooperation
Why did the United States build a modern navy?	need to defend American interests in foreign markets against European interests; European imperialism seemed to threaten the United States; a modern navy required overseas naval bases

Reading in the Content Areas

How Can I Use Jamestown Education Products to Help Struggling Readers?

For over 30 years, Jamestown Education has made its primary focus helping older readers become better readers. The Jamestown products shown on this page support the basic elements of reading cited by the National Reading Panel. Each of them can help your struggling readers become better readers.

Timed Readings Plus in Social Studies

✔ **Reading Levels:** 4–13+
✔ **Benefits:**

This ten-book series will help your students increase both reading rate and comprehension. The nonfiction passages cover current social studies topics and are similar to those found on both state and national tests. Each of the two-part lessons focuses on reading rate, factual recall, comprehension strategies, and higher-level critical thinking skills.

Reading in the Content Areas: Social Studies

✔ **Reading Levels:** 4–12+
✔ **Benefits:**

This book concentrates on six essential reading skills that will help your students better comprehend what they read. Seventy-five high-interest nonfiction passages written at increasing levels of difficulty, followed by consistent, targeted skills, teach the techniques needed to organize, understand, and apply information.

Reading Fluency

✔ **Reading Levels:** 1–10
✔ **Benefits:**

This seven-book series will help your students read smoothly, accurately and expressively. Students work in pairs to provide immediate feedback and self-assessment. Author Camille Blachowicz states that "the ability to read fluently is highly correlated with many other measures of reading competence."

Jamestown's Reading Improvement

✔ **Reading Levels:** 4–10
✔ **Benefits:**

Authored by renowned reading expert Edward Fry, this eight-book series focuses on helping build your students' comprehension, vocabulary, and skimming and scanning skills. Repeated practice with targeted exercises ensures mastery of valuable reading skills.

Critical Reading Series

✔ **Reading Levels:** 2–8
✔ **Benefits:**

This 24-book high-interest series, written at three reading spans, encourages your reluctant readers to build a love for nonfiction while focusing on critical reading skills. Topics ranging from Fateful Journeys to Weird Science to Heroes draw students in, while giving students ample opportunities to master important skills found on both state and national tests.

To order Jamestown products, call 1-800-334-7344.

In addition to the Project CRISS Reading Strategies, you may find it effective to implement some of the following instructional methods. They help *your* struggling students take increasing ownership of the reading process.

Reciprocal Teaching

Reciprocal teaching is characterized by a dialogue between you and your student, and ultimately among students in a group, in which students take the role of dialogue reader. Construction of meaning is built upon four reading strategies:

✔ **Summarizing** Readers identify the most important information in a segment of text and state that information in their own words. Summarizing involves students in recognizing and communicating the significant ideas in a text. Reviewing other reading strategies such as "Finding the Main Idea" might also be helpful.

✔ **Questioning** Readers ask themselves questions about the text segment. These questions should be asked periodically after students have completed "chunks" of the reading. Self-questioning aids comprehension by helping students identify where their understanding of the text has broken down and what they still need to know in order to understand what they have read.

✔ **Clarifying** Readers try to find answers to the questions they have raised and to make sense of parts of the text that have caused confusion. They seek clarification by rereading, reading ahead, or by seeking outside help, such as through a peer or a reference source. Clarifying can work well if students are reading with partners.

✔ **Predicting** Readers tell what they think will happen next, basing their predictions on evidence from the text they have already read. Predicting can take place at the beginning, middle, or end of a reading selection. Readers should later revisit and evaluate their predictions.

✔ **Assessment** The following advice from educator Dr. Sara Wartenberg presents how CRISS strategies can help in assessing student understanding: "Help your students achieve testing success by combining CRISS strategies with the Jamestown Readers. The stories appeal to students of all reading levels. The stories are interesting and informative for students and teachers alike. Implementing CRISS strategies as students read the selections will help them respond with greater success to the questions that accompany each selection. Students will gain confidence and thus work for greater skill in reading comprehension and critical thinking."

Modeling

An important element of strategic instruction is teacher modeling. As a part of the modeling process, think aloud as you apply a strategy to solve a reading problem, putting words to the inner voice that successful readers have with text, and demonstrating the strategy used for understanding. To construct a "think-aloud," read aloud a passage, stopping at pertinent points to talk about what you are thinking. A think-aloud demonstrates the cognitive process and allows students to observe how a proficient reader approaches a problem with reading.

"Fix-Up" Strategies

Explain that readers perform certain tasks. Guide them through these following steps:

✔ **Stop** Tell students to stop and fix the problem when they do not understand.

✔ **Identify the Problem** Have students ask themselves when they stopped understanding and what they do not understand.

✔ **Apply a Fix-Up Strategy** Encourage students to try these strategies:

✔ **Reread**

✔ **Read Ahead**

✔ **Alter** the pace or voice

✔ **Ask** for help

Test-Taking Strategies

How Can I Help My Students Succeed on Tests?

It's not enough for students to learn social studies facts and concepts—they must be able to show what they know in a variety of test-taking situations.

How Can I Help My Students Do Well on Objective Tests?

Objective tests may include multiple choice, true/false, and matching questions. Applying the following strategies can help students do their best on objective tests.

Multiple-Choice Questions

✔ Students should read the directions carefully to learn what answer the test requires—the best answer or the right answer. This is especially important when answer choices include "all of the above" or "none of the above."

✔ Advise students to watch for negative words in the questions, such as *not, except, unless, never,* and so forth. If the question contains a negative, the correct answer choice is the one that does not fit.

✔ Students should try to mentally answer the question before reading the answer choices.

✔ Students should read all the answer choices and cross out those that are obviously wrong. Then they should choose an answer from those that remain.

True/False Questions

✔ It is important that students read the entire question before answering. For an answer to be true, the entire statement must be true. If

one part of a statement is false, the answer should be marked *False.*

✔ Remind students to watch for words like *all, never, every,* and *always.* Statements containing these words are often false.

Matching Questions

✔ Students should read through both lists before they mark any answers.

✔ Unless an answer can be used more than once, students should cross out each choice as they use it.

✔ Using what they know about grammar can help students find the

right answer. For instance, when matching a word with its definition, the definition is often the same part of speech (noun, verb, adjective, and so forth) as the word.

How Can I Help My Students Do Well on Essay Tests?

Essay tests require students to provide thorough and well-organized written responses, in addition to telling what they know. Help students use the following strategies on essay tests.

Analyze:	To **analyze** means to systematically and critically examine all parts of an issue or event.
Classify or Categorize:	To **classify** or **categorize** means to put people, things, or ideas into groups, based on a common set of characteristics.
Compare and Contrast:	To **compare** is to show how things are similar, or alike. To **contrast** is to show how things are different.
Describe:	To **describe** means to present a sketch or impression. Rich details, especially details that appeal to the senses, flesh out a description.
Discuss:	To **discuss** means to systematically write about all sides of an issue or event.
Evaluate:	To **evaluate** means to make a judgment and support it with evidence.
Explain:	To **explain** means to clarify or make plain.
Illustrate:	To **illustrate** means to provide examples or to show with a picture or other graphic.
Infer:	To **infer** means to read between the lines or to use knowledge and experience to draw conclusions, make a generalization, or form a prediction.
Justify:	To **justify** means to prove or to support a position with specific facts and reasons.
Predict:	To **predict** means to tell what will happen in the future, based on an understanding of prior events and behaviors.
State:	To **state** means to briefly and concisely present information.
Summarize:	To **summarize** means to give a brief overview of the main points of an issue or event.
Trace:	To **trace** means to present the steps or stages in a process or event in sequential or chronological order.

Read the Question

The key to writing successful essay responses lies in reading and interpreting questions correctly. Teach students to identify and underline key words in the questions, and to use these words to guide them in understanding what the question asks. Help students understand the meaning of some of the most common key words, listed in the chart on the previous page.

Plan and Write the Essay

After students understand the question, they should follow the writing process to develop their answer. Encourage students to follow the steps below to plan and write their essays.

 1. Map out an answer. Make lists, webs, or an outline to plan the response.

 2. Decide on an order in which to present the main points.

 3. Write an opening statement that directly responds to the essay question.

 4. Write the essay. Expand on the opening statement. Support key points with specific facts, details, and reasons.

 5. Write a closing statement that brings the main points together.

6. Proofread to check for spelling, grammar, and punctuation.

How Can I Help My Students Prepare for Standardized Tests?

Students can follow the steps below to prepare for standardized assessments they are required to take.

✔ **Read About the Test** Students can familiarize themselves with the format of the test, the types of questions that will be asked, and the amount of time they will have to complete the test. Emphasize that it is very important for students to budget their time during test-taking.

✔ **Review the Content** Consistent study throughout the school year will help students build social studies knowledge and understanding. If there are specific objectives or standards that are tested on the exam, help students review these facts or skills to be sure they are proficient.

✔ **Practice** Provide practice, ideally with real released tests, to build students' familiarity with the content, format, and timing of the real exam. Students should practice all the types of questions they will encounter on the test—multiple choice, short answer, true or false, and extended response.

✔ **Pace** Students should pace themselves differently depending on how the test is administered. If the test is timed, students should not allow themselves to become stuck on any one question. As students practice, they should try to increase the number of questions they can answer correctly. If the test is untimed, students should work slowly and carefully. If students have trouble with an item, they should mark it and come back to it later.

✔ **Analyze Practice Results** Help students improve test-taking performance by analyzing their test-taking strengths and weaknesses. Spend time discussing

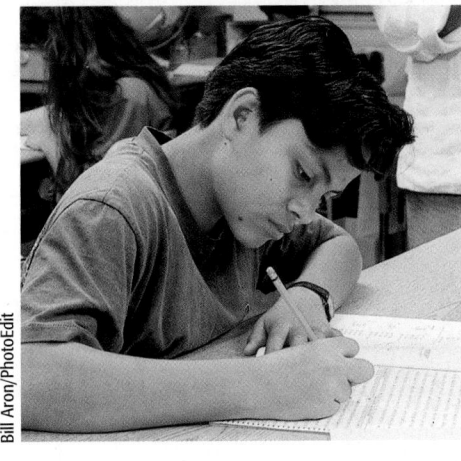

Bill Aron/PhotoEdit

students' completed practice tests, explaining why particular answers are right or wrong. Help students identify what kinds of questions they had the most difficulty with. Look for patterns in errors and then tailor instruction to review the appropriate test-taking skills or social studies content.

Below is an example of an activity to incorporate assessment review in the classroom from experienced instructor Tara Musslewhite. Frequently reviewing graded tests is a great way for students to assess their test-taking skills. It also gives teachers the opportunity to teach test-taking strategies and review content. As the class rereads each test question, guide students to think logically about their answer choices. Show students how to:

1. Read each question carefully to determine its meaning.
2. Look for key words in the question to support their answers.
3. Recognize synonyms in the answer choices that may match phrases in the question.
4. Narrow down answer choices by eliminating ones that don't make sense.
5. Anticipate the answer before looking at the answer choices.
6. Circle questions of which they are unsure and go back to them later. Sometimes a clue will be found in another question on the test.◆

Alternative Assessment Strategies

How Can I Go Beyond Tests to Assess Students' Understanding of Social Studies Facts and Concepts?

In response to the growing demand for accountability in the classroom, educators must use multiple assessment measures to accurately gauge student performance. In addition to quizzes, tests, essay exams, and standardized tests, assessment today incorporates a variety of performance-based measures and portfolio opportunities.

Performance assessment is a way of teaching and learning that involves both process and product. It is not just a testing strategy. Performance assessment activities provide hands-on approaches to learning concepts. Through activities students are able to actually experience these concepts rather than just reading and listening about them. These activities also help students become aware of diverse audiences for their work.

Students are also involved in developing the process that leads to the finished product.

Performance assessment tasks are based on what is most essential in the curriculum and what is interesting to the student.

What Are Some Typical Performance-Based Assessments?

There are many kinds of performance-based assessments. They all share one common characteristic—they challenge students to create products that demonstrate what they know. One good way to present a performance assessment is in the form of an open-ended question.

Writing

Performance-based writing assessments challenge students to apply their knowledge of social studies concepts and information in a variety of written ways. Writing activities are most often completed by one student, rather than by a group.

- ✔ **Journals** Students write from the perspective of a historical character or a citizen of a particular historical era.

- ✔ **Letters** Students write a letter from one historical figure to another or from a historical figure to a family member or other audience.
- ✔ **Position Paper or Editorial** Students explain a controversial issue and present their own opinion and recommendations, supported with strong evidence and convincing reasons.
- ✔ **Newspaper** Students write a variety of stories from the perspective of a reporter living in a particular historical time period. This could also involve the writing of editorials or letters to the editor.
- ✔ **Biographies and Autobiographies** Students write about historical figures either from the third person point of view (biography) or from the first person (autobiography).
- ✔ **Creative Stories** Students integrate historical events into a piece of fiction, incorporating the customs, language, and geography of the period.
- ✔ **Poems and Songs** Students follow the conventions of a particular type of song or poem as they tell about a historical event or person.
- ✔ **Research Reports** Students synthesize information from a variety of sources into a well-developed research report.

Oral Presentations

Oral presentations allow students to demonstrate their social studies literacy before an audience. Oral presentations are often group efforts, although this need not be the case.

Jonathan Nourok/Photo Edit

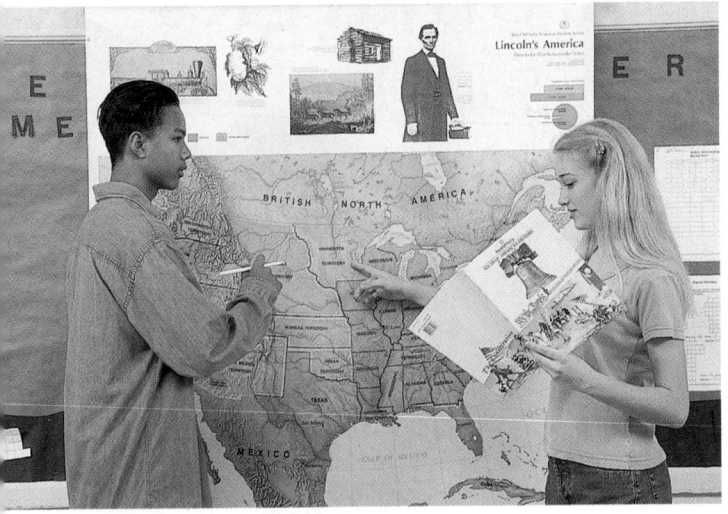

Simulations Students hold simulations, or reenactments, of actual events, such as trials, acts of civil disobedience, battles, speeches, and so forth.

Debates Students debate two or more sides of a historical policy or issue. Students can debate from a contemporary perspective or in a role play in which they assume a viewpoint held by a historical character.

Interview Students conduct a mock interview of a historical character or bystander.

Oral Reports Students present the results of research efforts in a lively oral report. This report may be accompanied by visuals.

Skits and Plays Students use historical events as the basis for a play or skit. Details should accurately reflect customs, language, and the setting of the period.

Visual Presentations
Visual presentations allow students to demonstrate their social studies understandings in a variety of visual formats. Visual presentations can be either group or individual projects.

Model Students make a model to demonstrate or represent a process, place, event, battle, artifact, or custom.

Museum Exhibit Students create a rich display of materials around a topic. Typical displays might include models, illustrations, photographs, videos, writings, and audio-taped explanations.

Graph or Chart Students analyze and represent historical data in a line graph, bar graph, table, or other chart format.

Drawing Students represent or interpret a historical event or period through illustration, including political cartoons.

Posters and Murals Posters and murals may include maps, time lines, diagrams, illustrations, photographs, collages, and written explanations that reflect students' understandings of historical information.

Quilt Students sew or draw a design for a patchwork quilt that shows a variety of perspectives, events, or issues related to a key topic.

Videotapes Students film a video to show historical fiction or to preserve a simulation of a historical event.

Multimedia Presentation or Slide Show Students create a computer-generated multimedia presentation containing historical information and analysis.

How Are Performance Assessments Scored?

There are a variety of means used to evaluate performance tasks. Some or all of the following methods may be used.

Scoring Rubrics A scoring rubric is a set of guidelines for assessing the quality of a process and/or product. It sets out criteria used to distinguish acceptable responses from unacceptable ones, generally along a scale from excellent to poor. Rubrics clearly outline expectations for behaviors and outcomes. Rubrics may be used as guidelines as the students prepare their products. They are also commonly used for self-assessment.

Models of Excellent Work Teacher-selected models of excellent work concretely illustrate expectations and help students set goals for their own projects.

Student Self-Assessment Common methods of self-assessment include ranking work in relation to the model, using a scoring rubric, and writing their own goals and then evaluating how well they have met the goals they set for themselves. Regardless of which method or methods students use, they should be encouraged to evaluate their behaviors and processes, as well as the finished product.

Peer or Audience Assessment Many of the performance tasks target an audience other than the classroom teacher. If possible, the audience of peers should give the student feedback. Have the class create rubrics for specific projects together.

Observation As students carry out their performance tasks, you may want to formally observe students at work. Start by developing a checklist, identifying all the specific behaviors and understandings you expect students to demonstrate. Then observe students as they carry out performance tasks and check off the behaviors as you observe them.

Interviews As a form of ongoing assessment, you may want to conduct interviews with students, asking them to analyze, explain, and assess their participation in performance tasks. When projects take place over an extended period of time, you can hold periodic interviews as well as exit interviews. In this way the interview process allows you to gauge the status of the project and to guide students' efforts along the way.◆

Primary Source Strategies

How Do I Use Primary Sources in My Classroom?

A primary source is direct evidence of an event, idea, period, or development. It is an oral or written account obtained from actual participants in an event. Examples of primary sources include the following:

- ✔ official documents (records, statistics)
- ✔ political declarations, laws, and rules for governance
- ✔ speeches and interviews
- ✔ diaries, memoirs, and oral histories
- ✔ autobiographies
- ✔ recipes and cookbooks
- ✔ advertisements and posters
- ✔ letters

Physical objects, such as tools and dishes, can be primary sources; so can visual evidence in the form of fine art, photographs, maps, films, and videotapes. Primary sources can also include songs and audio recordings.

Why Use Primary Sources in Your Classroom?

Using primary sources to teach transforms the study of social studies from a passive process to an active one. Students become investigators—finding clues, formulating hypotheses and drawing inferences, making judgments, and reaching conclusions. Bringing primary sources into the classroom stimulates students to think critically about events, issues, and concepts rather than just memorizing dates, names, and generalizations reached by others. Thinking critically then becomes a habit that can work towards making students good citizens.

Choosing Primary Sources

- ✔ Provide exposure to a variety of source types, including historic photographs, folk or popular music, financial records or household accounts, as well as letters, journals, and historic documents.
- ✔ When choosing print sources, consider the interests and reading levels of your students. Many texts contain challenging vocabulary and unfamiliar sentence structure. You may need to create a reader's guide that defines key vocabulary and paraphrases the main points of the reading.
- ✔ Some documents may be too long. Decide whether using an excerpt will provide enough information for students to draw conclusions.
- ✔ Depending upon the topic and your instructional objectives, you may need to provide several different primary sources to expose students to a variety of perspectives.
- ✔ Decide how students will access the primary sources: through the Internet, the library, a museum, or other print resources. Consider the possibility of an Internet virtual field trip for students. Moving from URL to URL, students can visit museum sites and other Web pages to view artifacts; interpret economic or census data; and read journals, letters, and official documents.

How Do I Introduce Students to Primary Sources?

Carefully explain the nature of primary sources when you introduce them to students. Although primary sources contain valuable clues, be sure to alert students that primary sources contain biases and prejudices and must be approached with caution. Every primary source reflects the creator's point of view to some degree. Students must consider the authorship and why the primary source was written.

Using Primary Sources in the Classroom

Primary sources provide a rich source of inspiration for a variety of instructional strategies. They can be used to spark interest in a new topic, foster deeper exploration into a historical era, or assess students' understanding of social studies concepts and facts.

Interpreting a Primary Source

Before students interpret a primary source, they need to know the context into which the source fits. Then they can use questions and guidelines, such as those below, to help them analyze and interpret the primary source.

Print Sources

- Who created the source, and what was the purpose for doing so?
- Did the writer personally experience or witness the event(s)?
- At what point did the writer record the information—as it happened or afterward? How long after?
- Who was the intended audience?
- Was the writer trying to record facts, express an opinion, or persuade others to take action?
- What is the author's main message?
- What values does the document convey?
- What bias does it reflect?
- What information about the topic can you gather from this document?
- Compare this document with what you know about the topic. Does it confirm those ideas or introduce a new perspective?
- How might other accounts about this topic support or modify the message this source delivers?

Visual Sources

- Who created the source, and what was the purpose for doing so?
- What does the image show?
- What mood does the image convey?
- Who or what dominates the image or catches your eye?
- How does the view impact the message?
- What details can you learn from the image?
- What is excluded from view?
- What bias does the visual reflect?
- What information about the topic can you gather from this visual?
- How might other visuals about this topic support or modify the message this one delivers?

Audio Sources

- Who created the source? What was the purpose for creating this source?
- What is the main idea of the audio?
- What mood does the recorder's voice convey?
- What bias does the audio text reflect?
- What information about the topic can you gather from this audio source?
- Compare the information in this source with what you already know about the topic. Does it confirm those ideas or introduce a new perspective?
- How might other sources about this topic support or modify the message that this one delivers?

✔ **Prereading Activities** Present a primary source for students to study at the beginning of a new chapter or topic. Have students analyze the source, using the questions and guidelines presented above. Then have students make predictions about what they might learn in the upcoming lessons. A primary source that presents a point of view or information that conflicts with students' prior knowledge can be a powerful motivator to learn new material.

✔ **Exploring Information** Provide a variety of primary sources related to a topic or time period. Have students compare and contrast the items, analyzing the information, making inferences, and drawing conclusions about the period.

✔ **Evaluation Activities** Have students evaluate a primary source and tell how it supports or refutes what they learned in the textbook, or have students read a primary source document that provides one perspective on a topic and have students write their own account, presenting another perspective or opinion. Below is a specific, step-by-step activity suggested by educator Leslie Espinosa. This activity is

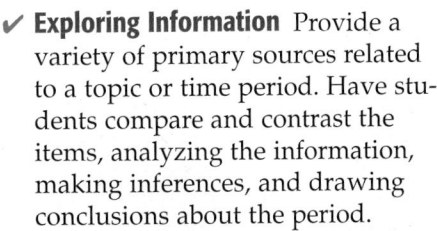

especially beneficial when a less-proficient reader is paired with a more-proficient reader.

1. Before class make a list of student reading partners. Make sure one of the two is a good reader.
2. Have students read a primary source document (or part of a primary source document), taking turns as they go. They should "mark" any words that they do not understand.
3. After each paragraph, the student pair should stop and paraphrase what it says in their own words.
4. Students should look up unfamiliar words they've marked and create an illustrated dictionary entry for each term (over the course of the year or semester).
5. Ask student pairs to present their paraphrased primary source to the rest of the class.◆

To Teachers

Welcome to the Teacher Wraparound Edition of *The American Vision: Modern Times*. We have created this teacher edition based on input from experienced teachers and educational consultants. Our goal is to provide you with standards-based teaching strategies and activities, which are labeled for you at point-of-use.

Standards-Based Instruction

Point-of-Use
- Strategies and activities apply directly to student content.
- Brackets and guide letters on your reduced student edition pages show you where and when to teach.

Universal Access
- Leveled activities and options for differentiated instruction help meet the needs of all your students, including English learners.

Review and Reinforcement
- Scaffolding—the introduction and reinforcement of skills and content—is incorporated throughout the lessons.

Assessment and Intervention
- Lessons provide standards practice.
- Assessments gauge student mastery of standards.
- Additional resources provide intervention options.

Lesson Structure

Each lesson in *The American Vision: Modern Times* is presented in a structured lesson plan: **Focus, Teach, Assess,** and **Close.**

FOCUS

Includes a *Bellringer* activity to get your class thinking about the lesson topic

GUIDE TO READING

Provides pre-reading strategies to improve content literacy

UNPACKING THE STANDARDS

Presents a step-by-step approach for teaching the California content standards

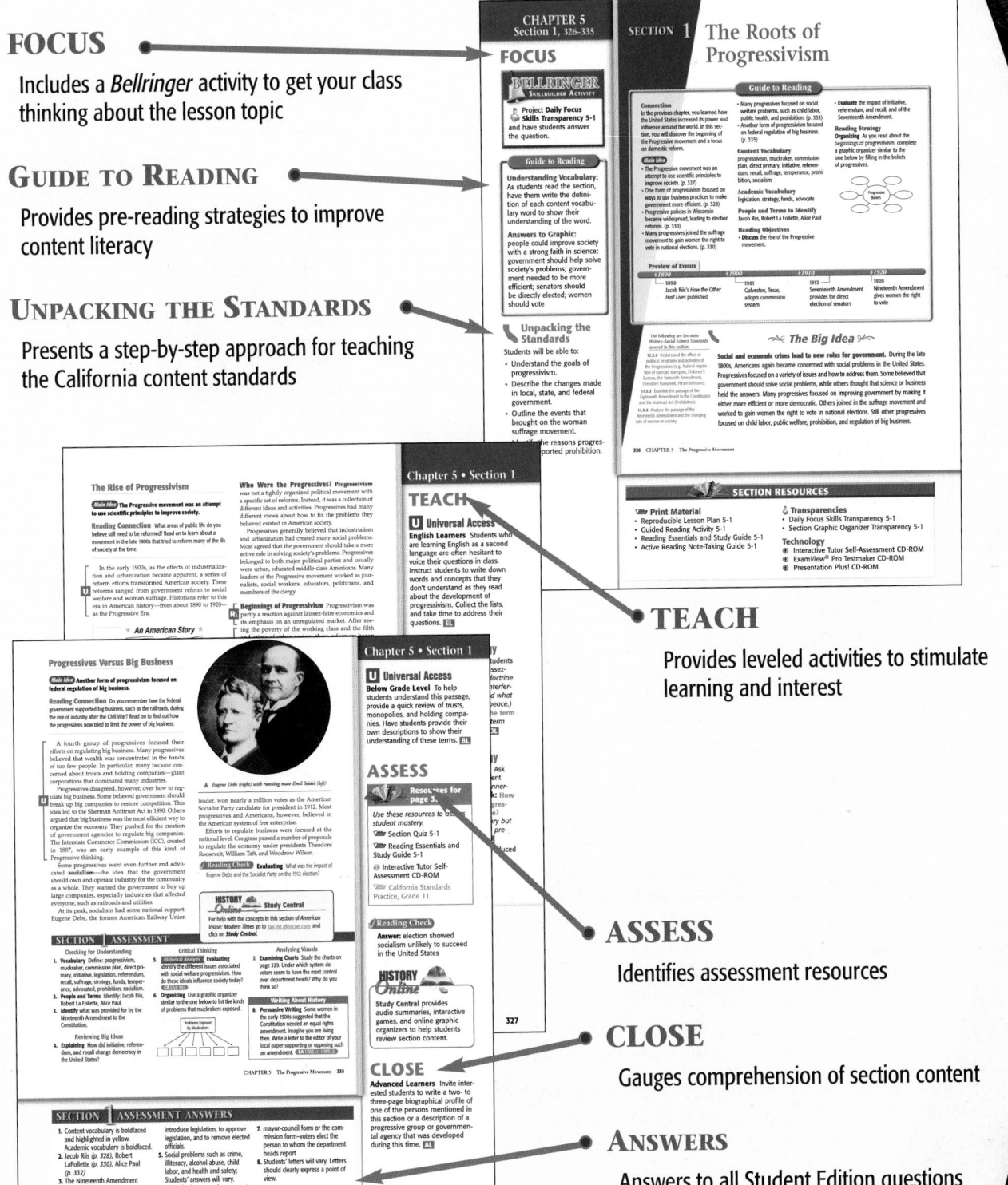

TEACH

Provides leveled activities to stimulate learning and interest

ASSESS

Identifies assessment resources

CLOSE

Gauges comprehension of section content

ANSWERS

Answers to all Student Edition questions

Understanding the Brackets and Letters

BRACKETS

Brackets on the reduced Student Edition page correspond to teaching strategies and activities in the Teacher Wraparound Edition. As you teach the lesson, the brackets show you <u>exactly</u> where to teach these strategies and activities.

LETTERS

The letters on the reduced Student Edition page identify the type of strategy or activity. See the key below to learn about the different types of strategies and activities.

Chapter 5 • Section 2

C Critical Thinking
Determining Cause and Effect
President Roosevelt was not afraid to use the power of the government to shape the operations of the economy. **Ask:** How do you think President Roosevelt's victory over Northern Securities would affect the attempts of other businesses to create trusts? *(Businesses would be less likely to form trusts after witnessing Roosevelt's aggressive approach toward violators of the Sherman Antitrust Act.)* **AL**

R Reading Strategy
Scaffolding—Academic Vocabulary The word *violate* was introduced in Chapter 4, Section 2. Ask a student to define the word. **OL**

W Writing Support
Research Report Writing
Using library or Internet resources, instruct students to research the types of health problems that were common to coal workers. Have students write a summary of their findings. **OL**
CA 11WA2.4d; 11WA3.2b

Answers and Additional Support

could have plunged the nation into a recession. The three men ultimately compromised by creating a giant new holding company called **Northern Securities.**

The formation of the Northern Securities Company alarmed many Americans, including Roosevelt. The stock battle that led to its creation seemed a classic example of private interests acting in a way that threatened the nation as a whole. Roosevelt decided that the company was in violation of the Sherman Antitrust Act. In early 1902, he ordered his attorney general to file a lawsuit against Northern Securities.

In 1904 in *Northern Securities v. United States*, the Supreme Court ruled five to four that Northern Securities had violated the Sherman Antitrust Act. The dissenting justices argued that the Sherman Antitrust Act did not stop companies from buying or selling stock in each other. They observed that Northern Securities had not hurt commerce. It had

not tried to keep other companies from competing, and it had not tried to raise railroad rates. In fact, rates had fallen on railroads owned by Northern Securities, although the court was sharply divided, Roosevelt declared the decision a great victory. Newspapers hailed Roosevelt as a "trustbuster," and his popularity soared. (*See page 1006 for more information on Northern Securities v. the United States.*)

The Coal Strike of 1902 As president, Roosevelt regarded himself as the nation's head manager. He believed it was his job to keep society operating efficiently, preventing conflict between the nation's different groups and their interests. In the fall of 1902, he put these beliefs into practice.

The previous spring, the **United Mine Workers** (UMW) union had called a strike of the miners who dug anthracite, or hard coal. Nearly 150,000 workers walked out of eastern Pennsylvania's anthracite mines demanding a pay increase, a reduction in work hours, and recognition for their union.

As the months passed and the strike continued, coal prices began to rise. To Roosevelt it was another example of groups pursuing their private interests at the expense of the nation. If the strike dragged on too long, the country would face a coal shortage that could shut down factories and leave many people's homes cold with winter fast approaching.

Roosevelt urged the union and the owners to accept **arbitration**—a settlement imposed by an outside party. The union agreed. The mine owners, determined to destroy the UMW, did not. One owner, George Baer, declared, "The rights and interests of the laboring man will be protected and cared for not by the labor agitators, but by the Christian men to

Analyzing Political Cartoons
Corporate Giants This 1904 cartoon portrays Roosevelt as "Jack the Giant-Killer," but he actually restrained very few trusts. *Why do you think the scene is set on Wall Street?*

John D. Rockefeller

J.P. Morgan

James J. Hill

T. Roosevelt

342   CHAPTER 5   The Progressive Movement

Analyzing Political Cartoons
Answer: Wall Street was the major financial center of the nation.
Ask: How did the artist make his point of view known? *(by choosing a familiar story and by the relative size of the components of the drawing)*

More Skill Practice
Connecting Have students look up the meaning of *arbitration* in the dictionary. *(the settlement of a dispute by an appointed person)* **Ask:** How might a teacher arbitrate a disagreement between two students who are accusing each other of copying test answers? *(Students' answers will vary.)* **BL**

342

---

whom God in His infinite wisdom has given the control of the property interests of the country."

The mine owners' stubbornness infuriated Roosevelt, as it did much of the public. Roosevelt threatened to order the army to run the mines. Fearful of this, the mine owners finally accepted arbitration. By intervening in the dispute, Roosevelt had taken the first step toward establishing the federal government as an honest broker between powerful groups in society.

The Bureau of Corporations Despite his lawsuit against Northern Securities and his role in the coal strike, Roosevelt was not opposed to big business. He believed most trusts benefited the economy and that breaking them up would do more harm than good. Instead, Roosevelt proposed the creation of a new federal agency to investigate corporations and publicize the results. He believed the most effective way to keep big business from abusing its power was through knowledge and providing the public with the facts.

In 1903 Roosevelt convinced Congress to create the Department of Commerce and Labor. G.B. Cortelyou was appointed the first secretary of the new department. Within this department would be a division called the Bureau of Corporations, with the authority to investigate corporations and issue reports on their activities.

The following year, the Bureau of Corporations began investigating U.S. Steel. Created in 1901, U.S. Steel was a gigantic holding company. Worried about a possible antitrust lawsuit, the company's leaders met privately with Roosevelt and offered a deal. They would open their account books and records to the Bureau of Corporations. In exchange, if the Bureau found anything wrong, the company would be advised privately and allowed to correct the problem without having to go to court.

Roosevelt accepted this "gentlemen's agreement," as he called it. Shortly afterward he made similar deals with other companies. These arrangements gave Roosevelt the ability to regulate big business and continue the economic benefit of big business without having to sacrifice economic efficiency by breaking up the trusts.

Congress Follows In addition to creating the Department of Commerce and Labor, Congress passed the Expedition Act, which gave federal antitrust suits precedence on the dockets of circuit courts. Then, in 1906, Roosevelt pushed the **Hepburn Act** through Congress. This act was intended to strengthen

Picturing History
Miner's Lot In the early 1900s, miners worked long hours under dangerous conditions for little pay. In an effort to obtain better compensation, reduction in work hours, and recognition of their union, many workers went on strike. *How did Roosevelt respond when they went on strike?*

the Interstate Commerce Commission (ICC). An early effort to regulate the railroad industry, the ICC had been ineffective because it lacked sufficient authority.

The Hepburn Act tried to strengthen the ICC by giving it the power to set railroad rates. The agency originally was intended to regulate rates to ensure that companies did not compete unfairly. At first, railroad companies were suspicious of the ICC and tied up its decisions by challenging them in court. Eventually, the railroads realized that they could work with the ICC to set rates and regulations that limited competition and prevented new competitors from entering the industry. Over time the ICC became a supporter of the railroads' interests, and by 1920 it had begun setting rates at levels intended to ensure the industry's profits.

✓ Reading Check **Comparing** What was the purpose of the Interstate Commerce Commission, and how successful was it?

CHAPTER 5   The Progressive Movement   **343**

Chapter 5 • Section 2

C Critical Thinking
Drawing Conclusions Have students create a table showing the advantages and disadvantages of a gentlemen's agreement. **Ask:** Do you think this is the best way to resolve conflicts between the government and industry? *(Supportive students may point out that this type of agreement helps achieve quick resolutions to problems by eliminating formal legal action. Critical students might state that these private deals do not educate the public to the problems existing in society.)* **OL**

U Universal Access
Verbal/Linguistic Individually ask each student in the class to verbally restate his or her understanding of the Hepburn Act. Help students to state clearly the act's purpose, and then have them transfer their answers into sentences. **OL**

✓ Reading Check
Answer: regulated railroad rates so that companies did not compete unfairly; not very—lacked authority

343

Picturing History
Answer: He worked to get the labor union and mine owners to accept arbitration as a way to settle the strike.
Ask: Why did mine owners finally accept arbitration as a way to settle the strike? *(Roosevelt threatened to bring in the military to run the mines.)*

KEY for Using the Teacher Wraparound Edition

R Reading Strategies activities help you teach reading skills and vocabulary.

C Critical Thinking strategies help students apply and extend what they have learned.

U Universal Access activities provide differentiated instruction for students learning to speak English, along with suggestions for teaching various types of learners.

S Skill Practice strategies help students practice historical analysis and geography skills.

W Writing Support activities provide writing opportunities to help students comprehend the text.

BRACKETS AND LETTERS

Letters are followed by a number when there is more than one of the same type of strategy or activity on the page.

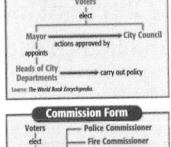

ANSWERS AND ADDITIONAL SUPPORT

Along the bottom of the Teacher Wraparound Edition, you will find Student Edition answers, more general strategies and activities, and additional content information.

ACTIVITY LEVELING

Teaching strategies and activities have been coded for ability level appropriateness. A competency level is given for each activity using the following code.

AL Activities for students working above grade level
OL Activities for students working on grade level
BL Activities for students working below grade level
EL Activities for English learners

Planning the Unit

Planning pages appear at the beginning of each unit.

STANDARDS

Use this chart to identify the California standards covered in each chapter.

PREVIEW FROM THE AUTHORS

A personal note from one of the authors tells you about the main themes found in the unit.

Unit 2 Resources

Teaching the Unit

Use the information on these pages to help you teach Unit 2.

History–Social Science Standards Covered in Unit 2

Standard	Chapter 4	5	6
11.2 Students analyze the relationship among the rise of industrialization, large-scale rural-to-urban migration, and massive immigration from Southern and Eastern Europe.	✔	✔	
11.3 Students analyze the role religion played in the founding of America, its lasting moral, social, and political impacts, and issues regarding religious liberty.	✔		
11.4 Students trace the rise of the United States to its role as a world power in the twentieth century.	✔		✔
11.5 Students analyze the major political, social, economic, technological, and cultural developments of the 1920s.			✔

Pacing Your Lessons

This pacing chart provides time management suggestions for teaching Unit 2.

	Days
Unit 2 Introduction	1
Chapter 4	
• **Reading Skill:** Cause and Effect	
• **Historical Analysis Skill:** Evaluating Past Events	
• **Sections 1–3**	7
• **You're the Historian:** Who Sank the *Maine*?	
• **Why It Matters:** The Panama Canal	
• **Eyewitness to History:** Primary Source Documents	
Chapter 5	
• **Reading Skill:** Making Inferences	
• **Historical Analysis Skill:** Interpreting Events	
• **Sections 1–4**	
• **American Literature:** *The Jungle* by Upton Sinclair	8
• **National Geographic:** Geography & History: The Story of Yosemite	
• **Eyewitness to History:** Primary Source Documents	
Chapter 6	
• **Reading Skill:** Using Problem/Solution	
• **Historical Analysis Skill:** Distinguishing Valid and Fallacious Arguments	
• **Sections 1–4**	9
• **TIME Notebook:** A War to End All Wars: 1914–1918	
• **Eyewitness to History:** Primary Source Documents	

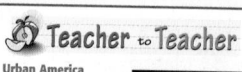

Teacher to Teacher

Urban America

Select 10 to 15 images from Jacob Riis's *How the Other Half Lives* (available online at http://www.cis.yale.edu/amstud/inforev/riis/title.html and in most libraries). Images of children are particularly effective for this exercise. Show these pictures to the students (slides, scanned images, or photocopies).

Heather Pang
Castilleja School
Palo Alto, California

Organize the students into small groups and assign each group one of the following roles: city police, local school board, charitable organization, philanthropic guild, schoolchildren, garment district workers, and a merchants' association. Each group should use the pictures as evidence to prepare a report titled "Poverty in the City: What Is to Be Done?" Remind the students that each of these groups will have different reactions to the Riis images depending on their own backgrounds. Each report should list the most significant problems shown in the images and provide suggestions for solutions.

It might be helpful to start the lesson with a short introduction to Riis and the tradition of muckraking journalism.

288A

Unit 2 Resources

Previewing the Chapters

Dear American History Teacher:

As you begin to teach this unit, there are themes that recur throughout the chapters that you will want to point out to students.

The expansion of the American economy and its projection beyond the borders of the United States are hallmarks of this period. By the 1890s, with little potential for territorial growth in North America, the United States sought to acquire colonies beyond its borders.

This expansion in turn thrust the nation into the sphere of Great Powers at a time of increasing international tensions that led to World War I. American entry into the war in 1917 created a new era of American power in the world, with its attendant responsibilities.

At home, the growing pains of industrialism spawned many reform movements that came to be called Progressivism. These reforms addressed some of the worst social and economic problems, but did not overcome all of the injustices in American society.

You may want to use the following information at the beginning of each chapter as a lesson launcher to help students begin to focus on what they will be studying.

James M. McPherson

Chapter 4: Becoming a World Power, 1872–1912

(pages 290–321)

During the last decades of the nineteenth century, the United States began involving itself more and more in global affairs. Whether for economic, missionary, or military reasons, Americans balanced the tradition of American isolation versus American imperialism. The Spanish-American War involved the United States for all of these reasons.

Chapter 5: The Progressive Movement, 1890–1919

(pages 322–361)

The Progressive Era defines a period of social change. Progressive reformers began their efforts to improve local and state governments, making them more efficient and equitable. Reforms at state levels, especially the woman suffrage movement, soon became issues for the federal government. Presidents Roosevelt, Taft, and Wilson all supported federal progressive reform, attempting to use the power of government to regulate private industry and systematize the interaction between public and private organizations.

Chapter 6: World War I and Its Aftermath, 1914–1920

(pages 362–399)

President Woodrow Wilson's opposition to imperialism and belief in democracy guided his foreign policy in the years leading up to World War I. Though initially neutral, the United States eventually entered into the European conflict. Once committed, American politicians used many progressive ideas to organize the wartime economy and mobilize the armed forces. President Wilson's Fourteen Points represented his desire to create a just peace after World War I and to build international organizations to prevent similar wars in the future. The U.S. Senate rejected his peace efforts as the nation turned inward and the economy shifted back to peacetime production. The nation, tired of domestic and international struggles, sought normalcy in the 1920s, signaling an end to the Progressive Era.

288B

PACING CHART

Provides time management suggestions for teaching the unit

TEACHER IDEAS

Activities from the classrooms of successful teachers

LESSON LAUNCHERS

Chapter summaries help you launch the lesson.

Teaching the Unit

STANDARDS

The California History–Social Science Content Standards are listed to help you plan your instruction.

SKILL PRACTICE

Provides opportunities to interpret primary source materials

Introducing UNIT 2

FOCUS

History–Social Science Standards

This unit addresses the following main standards:

11.2 Students analyze the relationship among the rise of industrialization, large-scale rural-to-urban migration, and massive immigration from Southern and Eastern Europe.

11.3 Students analyze the role religion played in the founding of America, its lasting moral, social, and political impacts, and issues regarding religious liberty.

11.4 Students trace the rise of the United States to its role as a world power in the twentieth century.

11.5 Students analyze the major political, social, economic, technological, and cultural developments of the 1920s.

Connecting to Past Learning

In Unit 1, students learned about the formation of the United States and its development from the Revolutionary War through the Civil War and Industrialization. In Unit 2, the development of the United States as a world power will be presented.

Unit Launch Activity

Remind students of George Washington's warning to stay away from foreign alliances. Tell them that after the Civil War, the United States developed into a world power. Discuss in class why Americans might have become interested in foreign affairs.

Why It Matters Activity

Tell students that the Pure Food and Drug Act of 1906 regulated standards on food and drugs. **Ask:** How does passage of this act affect us today? (Students should mention such things as ingredient lists on food products and quality inspections performed on such food.) **OL**

288

UNIT 2 Imperialism and Progressivism

1890–1919

"It is hard to fail, but it is worse never to have tried to succeed."

—Theodore Roosevelt, 1899

Why It Matters

As the United States entered the twentieth century, it grew to become a world power. While the nation was expanding its territory into other parts of the world, conditions at home gave rise to a widespread Progressive movement. This movement worked for various reforms in government, business, and society. While Americans focused on their own country, Europe slid into a devastating world war that eventually involved the United States as well. These crucial years of domestic change and foreign conflict provided important foundations for the world you live in today. The following resources offer more information about this period in American history.

Primary Sources Library

See pages 974–975 for primary source readings to accompany Unit 2.

Use the American History Primary Source Document Library CD-ROM to find additional primary sources about imperialism and progressivism.

World War I pin

OVER ★ THERE

American Troops Arriving in Paris July 14, 1918 by J.F. Boucher

Introducing UNIT 2

TEACH

Skill Practice

Recognizing Point of View Instruct students to read Theodore Roosevelt's quote on the top of this page. **Ask:** What does this quote indicate about Roosevelt's personality? As students read through the unit, instruct them to look for actions Roosevelt took as president that supported this point of view. **OL**
CA HR4

Skill Practice

Visual Literacy Although the war itself was devastating to Europe, fanfare often accompanied American troops marching into large cities such as Paris. The United States' involvement in the war was brief compared to that of European powers, but the European people often viewed Americans as heroes who had saved Allied countries from complete destruction. **Ask:** What is the mood and tone of this painting? (Students should use descriptive words to describe what they see in the painting and how they feel about the painting.) **BL**

NCLB NO CHILD LEFT BEHIND

Teaching Tip The NCLB Act emphasizes reading. Ask students to write down events and people they will encounter in this unit and keep the list with them as they read. When students find a person or item on the list, they should note the page number and write a brief summary. Students can use this list while studying.

TEAM TEACHING ACTIVITY

SOCIOLOGY Read to students the following lines written by poet Sarah Cleghorn in the early 1900s: *The golf links lie so near the mill/That almost every day/The laboring children can look out/And see the men at play.* **Ask:** What does this quote tell you about economic conditions and child labor in the United States in the early 1900s? (Students should mention that child labor was common during this era, unlike the present day.) Have the sociology teacher explain the evolution of child labor laws in the United States and protections for children today. **OL**

288

UNIVERSAL ACCESS

Below Grade Level: Have students write the term "world power" on a piece of paper. Underneath the term, ask them to write what they think this term means in their own words. As students study the unit, have them add information and explanations to help them fully understand the term's meaning. **BL**

Advanced Learners: Ask students to pick one event in Unit 2 they think had a major impact on U.S. history. Have them prepare a two-page paper in which they explain why their chosen event was important. **AL**

289

CONNECTING TO PAST LEARNING

Activates prior knowledge and provides a chronological framework for students

UNIVERSAL ACCESS

Activities for diverse learners, including English learners

NCLB

Provides suggestions for meeting No Child Left Behind requirements

T51

Planning the Chapter

Planning pages appear at the beginning of each chapter.

RESOURCE LIST

Resources needed to teach each section

STANDARDS

Use this chart to identify the California standards covered in each section.

Chapter 4 Planning Guide

SECTION RESOURCES

MAIN IDEAS	PRINT MATERIALS	TECHNOLOGY RESOURCES
Section 1: The Imperialist Vision 1. A desire for world markets and belief in the superiority of white culture led the United States to assert itself as a world power. 2. The desire for new markets led to trade with Japan and the annexation of Hawaii. 3. The United States worked to increase trade with Latin America. 4. The United States began constructing a large navy to protect its international interests.	• Reproducible Lesson Plan 4-1* • Daily Lecture and Discussion Notes 4-1 • Active Reading Note-Taking Guide 4-1 • Guided Reading Activity 4-1 • Section Quiz 4-1 • Reading Essentials and Study Guide 4-1	♦ Daily Focus Skills Transparency 4-1 ♦ Section Graphic Organizer Transparency 4-1 ⊕ Interactive Tutor Self-Assessment CD-ROM ⊕ ExamView® Pro Testmaker CD-ROM ⊕ Presentation Plus! CD-ROM ♦ California Standards Practice Transparencies
Section 2: The Spanish-American War 1. In support of the Cuban rebellion and in retaliation for the loss of the USS *Maine*, the United States declared war on Spain. 2. The United States fought Spain in both the Pacific and the Caribbean. 3. Victory in the Spanish-American War allowed the United States to expand its holdings in the South Pacific and to control Puerto Rico and Cuba.	• Reproducible Lesson Plan 4-2* • Daily Lecture and Discussion Notes 4-2 • Active Reading Note-Taking Guide 4-2 • Guided Reading Activity 4-2 • Section Quiz 4-2 • Reading Essentials and Study Guide 4-2	♦ Daily Focus Skills Transparency 4-2 ♦ Section Graphic Organizer Transparency 4-2 ⊕ Interactive Tutor Self-Assessment CD-ROM ⊕ ExamView® Pro Testmaker CD-ROM ⊕ Presentation Plus! CD-ROM ♦ California Standards Practice Transparencies
Section 3: New American Diplomacy 1. Theodore Roosevelt went from governor of New York to president in a few short years and supported the country's rise to a world power. 2. The United States pursued an Open Door policy in China to allow all nations access to China's markets. 3. Theodore Roosevelt pushed for construction of the Panama Canal and declared the intent of the United States to act as a police force in Latin American nations.	• Reproducible Lesson Plan 4-3* • Daily Lecture and Discussion Notes 4-3 • Active Reading Note-Taking Guide 4-3 • Guided Reading Activity 4-3 • Section Quiz 4-3 • Reading Essentials and Study Guide 4-3	♦ Daily Focus Skills Transparency 4-3 ♦ Section Graphic Organizer Transparency 4-3 ⊕ Interactive Tutor Self-Assessment CD-ROM ⊕ ExamView® Pro Testmaker CD-ROM ⊕ Presentation Plus! CD-ROM ♦ California Standards Practice Transparencies

⏱ PACING YOUR LESSONS

Chapter Introduction	Section 1	Section 2	Section 3	Chapter Assessment
½ Day	2 Days	2 Days	2 Days	½ Day

0:00 OUT OF TIME? Assign the Chapter 4 *Reading Essentials and Study Guide.*

*Available on TeacherWorks™ CD-ROM

290A

Chapter 4 Planning Guide

Standards-Based Lesson Plan

🖊 **History–Social Science Standards Covered in Chapter 4**

The standards covered in the chapter are listed below. Use the accompanying activity as you teach the chapter to ensure student mastery of these standards. This activity can be used in combination with the program's print and technology assessment materials.

Standard	Section 1	Section 2	Section 3
11.2.7 Analyze the similarities and differences between the ideologies of Social Darwinism and Social Gospel (e.g., using biographies of William Graham Sumner, Billy Sunday, Dwight L. Moody).	✔		
11.3.2 Analyze the great religious revivals and the leaders involved in them, including the First Great Awakening, the Second Great Awakening, the Civil War revivals, the Social Gospel Movement, the rise of Christian liberal theology in the nineteenth century, the impact of the Second Vatican Council, and the rise of Christian fundamentalism in current times.	✔		
11.4 Students trace the rise of the United States to its role as a world power in the twentieth century.		✔	✔
11.4.1 List the purpose and effects of the Open Door policy.			✔
11.4.2 Describe the Spanish-American War and U.S. expansion in the South Pacific.		✔	
11.4.3 Discuss America's role in the Panama Revolution and the building of the Panama Canal.	✔	✔	✔
11.4.4 Explain Theodore Roosevelt's Big Stick diplomacy, William Taft's Dollar Diplomacy, and Woodrow Wilson's Moral Diplomacy, drawing on relevant speeches.			✔

Cumulative Standards-Assessment Activity

The Cumulative Standards-Assessment Activity will help students organize and learn the important information from the chapter. Begin teaching the chapter with this activity, and have students complete it as they read the chapter.

CREATING A MAIN IDEA AND SUPPORTING DETAILS CHART

Purpose Reviewing how to locate main ideas throughout the chapter will help students continue to refine their reading skills. This type of organizer aids students in identifying main ideas and their supporting details. It helps them develop the skill of knowing what is important and what is supportive of the main ideas. Students will need to use information about how the text is structured and combine it with what they know about the topic. Identifying main ideas and details can give students practice in logical and systematic thinking.

Introduction to Modeling

1. Begin the discussion with a brainstorming session. Ask students to list what they know or believe they know about American imperialism. Write the information on an overhead transparency. Have them identify some key main ideas about this period of American expansionism from the list. You might also want to model how certain comments are, in fact, details that support a main idea.

2. Ask students to copy this chart into their notebooks.

Supporting Details

Main Ideas

As students read each section, ask them to search for a main idea, and have them fill in the chart with as many supporting details as necessary. Encourage them to create more charts as they encounter important concepts during their reading.

3. As part of your chapter review, have students share their charts. Consider asking them to do a final chart with a single main idea for the entire chapter. Encourage them to use their charts as study aids.

290B

PACING CHART

Provides time management suggestions for teaching the chapter

CUMULATIVE STANDARDS-ASSESSMENT ACTIVITY

Front-loaded assessment allows you to monitor student understanding throughout the chapter.

READING SUPPORT

Reading resources for students at all levels

ASSESSMENT

Diagnostic and prescriptive resources for identifying standards proficiency

SPANISH RESOURCES

Resources for English learners

INTERVENTION

A complete list of intervention resources for students at all levels

PROFESSIONAL DEVELOPMENT

Extra support for beginning and experienced teachers

Chapter 4 Planning Guide

READING SUPPORT
- Content Vocabulary Activity 4
- Academic Vocabulary Activity 4
- Reading Skills Activity 4
- Chapter 4 Active Reading Note-Taking Guide
- Chapter 4 Guided Reading Activities
- Chapter 4 Reading Essentials and Study Guide
- *The American Vision: Modern Times* Video Program
- Vocabulary PuzzleMaker CD-ROM
- American History Primary Source Document Library CD-ROM

CRITICAL THINKING
- Critical Thinking Skills Activity 4
- Primary Source Reading 4
- Cause-and-Effect Transparency 4 Strategy and Activity
- Presentation Plus! CD-ROM

UNIVERSAL ACCESS
- Universal Access Activity 4
- English Learner Activity 4
- American Art Prints
- StudentWorks™ Plus CD-ROM
- American Music: Hits Through History
- School-to-Home Connection Activity 4

SKILL PRACTICE
- Map Overlay Transparency 4 Strategy and Activity
- Historical Analysis Skills Activity 4
- Time Line Activity 4
- Reading Skills Activity 4
- Reinforcing Skills Activity 4
- Linking Past and Present Activity 4
- Interpreting Political Cartoons 4
- MindJogger Videoquiz

WRITING SUPPORT
- Chapter 4 Active Reading Note-Taking Guide
- Writer's Guidebook
- High School Writing Process Transparencies

ASSESSMENT
- Chapter 4 Section Quizzes
- Chapter 4 Tests, Forms A and B
- Authentic Assessment Activity 4
- ExamView® Pro Testmaker CD-ROM
- Interactive Tutor Self-Assessment CD-ROM
- California Standards Practice, Grade 11
- Succeeding on …™ the California Standards: Grade 11 History–Social

290C

Chapter 4 Planning Guide

TECHNOLOGY
- StudentWorks™ Plus CD-ROM
- TeacherWorks™ CD-ROM
- ExamView® Pro Testmaker CD-ROM
- Interactive Tutor Self-Assessment CD-ROM
- Presentation Plus! CD-ROM
- Vocabulary PuzzleMaker CD-ROM
- American History Primary Source Document Library CD-ROM
- MindJogger Videoquiz
- *The American Vision: Modern Times* Video Program
- Professional Development in High School Social Studies Video Series
- Teach, Use, and Succeed With *The American Vision: Modern Times*
- American Music: Hits Through History
- Succeeding on …™ the California Standards: Grade 11 History–Social Science CD-ROM

SPANISH RESOURCES
- Spanish Activities and Assessment
  - Spanish Vocabulary Activities
  - Spanish Guided Reading Activities
  - Spanish Quizzes and Tests
  - Spanish Reteaching Activities
- Spanish Reading Essentials and Study Guide
- Spanish School-to-Home Connection Activities

TEACHER PLANNING
- Daily Lecture and Discussion Notes
- English Learner Handbook
- Building Academic Vocabulary
- *The American Vision: Modern Times* Reading and Study Skills Foldables
- Reading Strategies and Activities for the Social Studies Classroom
- Universal Access for the American History Classroom
- NGS United States Desk Map
- NGS World Atlas
- Chapter 4 Reproducible Lesson Plans on TeacherWorks™ CD-ROM
- California Guide to Daily Intervention

PROFESSIONAL DEVELOPMENT
- Building Academic Vocabulary
- Strategies for Success
- Research Based Strategies Used to Develop *The American Vision: Modern Times*
- Character Education in the High School Classroom
- Professional Development in High School Social Studies Video Series
- Teach, Use, and Succeed With *The American Vision: Modern Times*

UNIVERSAL ACCESS

Resources for differentiated instruction

Chapter 4 Planning Guide

NATIONAL GEOGRAPHIC — TEACHER'S CORNER

Index to National Geographic Magazine:
The following articles relate to this chapter:
- "Alone Across the Arctic Crown," April 1993
- "Remember the Maine," February 1998

National Geographic Society Products:
To order the following, call National Geographic at 1-800-368-2728
- Hawaii: Strangers in Paradise (Video)
- Historical Atlas of the United States (Atlas)

NGS ONLINE
Access National Geographic's new dynamic MapMachine Web site and other geography resources at:
www.nationalgeographic.com
www.nationalgeographic.com/maps

MASTERING THE STANDARDS
The content and assessment in the Student Edition, Teacher Wraparound Edition, teacher planning materials, and the print and technology products are all standards-based. The use of these products during instruction leads to mastery of the standards.

PRACTICE
- California Standards Practice, Grade 11
- California Standards Practice Transparencies
- School-to-Home Connection

BENCHMARK ASSESSMENT
- Section Quizzes, Chapter Tests, and Authentic Assessment
- ExamView® Pro Testmaker CD-ROM
- Succeeding On …™ the California Standards: Grade 11 History–Social Science CD-ROM

REMEDIATION
- California Guide to Daily Intervention
- Interactive Tutor Self-Assessment CD-ROM
- ExamView® Pro Testmaker CD-ROM
- California Standards Practice, Grade 11
- Reading Essentials and Study Guide

History Online

Use our Web site for additional resources. All essential content is covered in the Student Edition.

You and your students can visit tav.mt.glencoe.com, the Web site companion to the *American Vision: Modern Times*. This innovative integration of electronic and print media offers your students a wealth of opportunities. The student text directs students to the Web site for the following options:
- Chapter Overviews
- Self-Check Quizzes
- Student Web Activities
- Textbook Updates

Answers to the student Web activities are provided for you in the Web Activity Lesson Plans. Additional Web resources and ePuzzles and games are also available.

FOLDABLES — Study Organizer
Dinah Zike's Foldables

Foldables are three-dimensional, interactive graphic organizers that help students practice basic writing skills, review key vocabulary terms, and identify main ideas. Every chapter has a foldable activity in the *Dinah Zike's Reading and Study Skills Foldables* booklet. You can use the foldables as they are presented or modify them to suit the needs of your individual class.

A&E — Biography — THE HISTORY CHANNEL
A variety of videotape programs are available from A&E Television and The History Channel to provide teaching assistance. To order, call Glencoe at 1-800-334-7344.

290E

Reading List Generator CD-ROM

GLENCOE BOOKLINK CD-ROM

The Glencoe BookLink CD-ROM is a database that allows you to search more than 15,000 titles to create a customized reading list for your students.
- Reading Lists can be organized by students' reading level, author, genre, theme, or area of interest.
- The database provides Degrees of Reading Power™ (DRP) and Lexile™ readability scores for all selections.
- A brief summary of each selection is included.

Leveled reading suggestions for this chapter:
For students at a Grade 8 reading level:
- *Theodore Roosevelt: 26th President of the United States*, by Rebecca Stefoff

For students at a Grade 9 reading level:
- *William McKinley: 25th President of the United States*, by David R. Collins

For students at a Grade 10 reading level:
- *The Path Between the Seas: The Creation of the Panama Canal 1870–1914*, by David McCullough

READING SUPPORT FROM JAMESTOWN EDUCATION

- *Timed Readings Plus in Social Studies* help students increase their reading rate and fluency while maintaining comprehension. The 400-word passages are similar to those found on state and national assessments.
- *Reading in the Content Area: Social Studies* concentrates on six essential reading skills that help students better comprehend what they read. The book includes 75 high-interest nonfiction passages written at increasing levels of difficulty.
- *Reading Fluency* helps students read smoothly, accurately, and expressively.
- *Jamestown's Reading Improvement*, by renowned reading expert Edward Fry, focuses on helping build your students' comprehension, vocabulary, and skimming and scanning skills.
- *Critical Reading Series* provides high-interest books, each written at three reading levels.

  For more information about these products, see the Jamestown Education materials in the Classroom Solutions in the front of this Teacher Wraparound Edition. To order these products, call Glencoe at 1-800-334-7344.

KEY for Using the Teacher Wraparound Edition

Use this key to help you identify the different types of prompts found in the Teacher Wraparound Edition

- **R** Reading Strategies activities help you teach reading strategies and vocabulary.
- **C** Critical Thinking strategies help students apply and extend what they have learned.
- **U** Universal Access activities provide differentiated instruction for students learning to speak English, along with suggestions for teaching various types of learners.
- **S** Skill Practice strategies help students practice historical analysis and geography skills.
- **W** Writing Support activities provide writing opportunities to help students comprehend the text.

Teaching strategies and activities have been coded for ability level appropriateness.
- **AL** Activities for students working above grade level
- **OL** Activities for students working on grade level
- **BL** Activities for students working below grade level
- **EL** Activities for English learners

290F

ADDITIONAL RESOURCES

Resources for supplementing the chapter

MORE READING SUPPORT

Additional resources for intervention and enrichment

Teaching the Chapter

The Big Ideas and Essential Questions at the beginning of the chapter help you teach the standards.

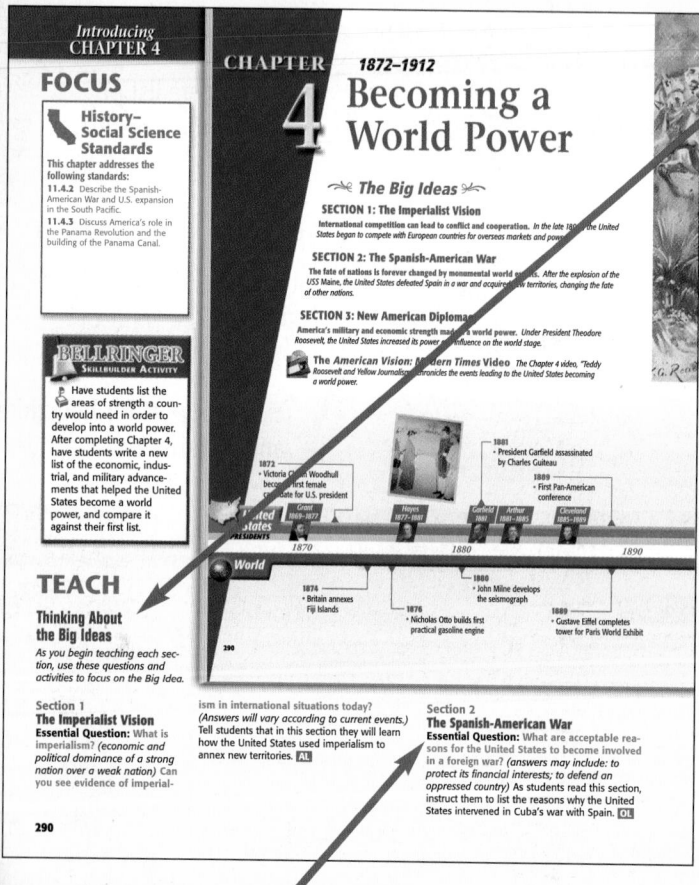

BIG IDEAS

Big Ideas are major themes, issues, concepts, questions, or ideas. They help students organize information and understand historical themes. The *Big Ideas* allow students to not only see the "big picture" but also the relevancy of what they are learning.

Big Ideas for Grade 11:

1. Political philosophies and major events influence the formation of constitutional governments.

2. A written contract between the people and their government can preserve natural rights and allow for change over time.

3. Differences in economic, political, and social beliefs and practices can lead to division within a nation and have lasting consequences.

4. The Industrial Revolution changed the face of America.

5. America's military and economic strength made it a world power.

6. People react to periods of breathtaking social and cultural change in different ways.

7. Social and economic crises lead to new roles for government.

8. The fate of nations is forever changed by monumental world events.

9. International competition can lead to conflict and cooperation.

10. The quest for equality is eternal.

11. Societies change over time.

ESSENTIAL QUESTIONS

Essential Questions lead to an understanding of the Big Ideas. They are broad and have no right or wrong answers. *Essential Questions* are thought-provoking, challenge old assumptions, and stimulate discussion.

Teaching the Standards

All content and assessment in *The American Vision: Modern Times* is standards-based. As you develop your lesson plans, you will be able to incorporate the following:

- California History–Social Science Content Standards
- California Historical and Social Sciences Analysis Skills
- California English–Language Arts Content Standards

History–Social Science Standards

11.3.2 Analyze the great religious revivals and the leaders involved in them, including the First Great Awakening, the Second Great Awakening, the Civil War revivals, the Social Gospel Movement, the rise of Christian liberal theology in the nineteenth century, the impact of the Second Vatican Council, and the rise of Christian fundamentalism in current times.

11.3.3 Cite incidences of religious intolerance in the United States (e.g., persecution of Mormons, anti-Catholic sentiment, anti-Semitism).

11.3.4 Discuss the expanding religious pluralism in the United States and California that resulted from large-scale immigration in the twentieth century.

11.3.5 Describe the principles of religious liberty found in the Establishment and Free Exercise clauses of the First Amendment, including the debate on the issue of separation of church and state.

11.4 Students trace the rise of the United States to its role as a world power in the twentieth century.

11.4.1 List the purpose and the effects of the Open Door policy.

11.4.2 Describe the Spanish-American War and U.S. expansion in the South Pacific.

11.4.3 Discuss America's role in the Panama Revolution and the building of the Panama Canal.

11.4.4 Explain Theodore Roosevelt's Big Stick diplomacy, William Taft's Dollar Diplomacy, and Woodrow Wilson's Moral Diplomacy, drawing on relevant speeches.

11.4.5 Analyze the political, economic and social ramifications of World War I on the home front.

11.4.6 Trace the declining role of Great Britain and the expanding role of the United States in world affairs after World War II.

▼ **Death Valley National Park**

WHAT ARE THE STANDARDS?

A complete list of all the standards is provided on pages 4–19.

WHERE ARE THE STANDARDS COVERED?

Each type of standard is correlated by page number. See pages T62–T73.

Correlation to the History–Social Science Standards

Standards	Student Edition Pages	Teacher Edition Pages
11.2.5 Discuss corporate mergers that produced trusts and cartels and the economic and political policies of industrial leaders.	246, 248, 249, 252, 253, 341–343	246, 248, 249, 252, 253, 341–343, 355
11.2.6 Trace the economic development of the United States and its emergence as a major industrial power, including its gains from trade and the advantages of its physical geography.	197, 198, 237–240, 244–251	197, 198, 237–240, 243, 244–251, 290, 291
11.2.7 Analyze the similarities and differences between the ideologies of Social Darwinism and Social Gospel (e.g., using biographies of William Graham Sumner, Billy Sunday, Dwight L. Moody).	266–270, 296	266–270, 296
11.2.8 Examine the effect of political programs and activities of Populists.	275–279	275–279
11.2.9 Understand the effect of political programs and activities of the Progressives (e.g., federal regulation of railroad transport, Children's Bureau, the Sixteenth Amendment, Theodore Roosevelt, Hiram Johnson).	327–335, 341–345, 349–351, 353–355, 356, 357	322, 327–335, 341–347, 349–351, 353–357
11.3 Students analyze the role religion played in the founding of America, its lasting moral, social, and political impacts, and issues regarding religious liberty.	102–108, 111, 112, 145, 159, 185–189, 266–270, 407–410, 416, 417, 424, 425, 809, 810, 872, 873, 887–891	102–108, 111, 112, 145, 159, 185–189, 266–270, 407–410, 416, 417, 424, 425, 809, 810, 872, 873, 887–891
11.3.1 Describe the contributions of various religious groups to American civic principles and social reform movements (e.g., civil and human rights, individual responsibility and the work ethic, antimonarchy and self-rule, worker protection, family-centered communities).	102–108, 111, 112, 186–189, 266–270	102–108, 111, 112, 186–189, 266–270
11.3.2 Analyze the great religious revivals and the leaders involved in them, including the First Great Awakening, the Second Great Awakening, the Civil War revivals, the Social Gospel Movement, the rise of Christian liberal theology in the nineteenth century, the impact of the Second Vatican Council, and the rise of Christian fundamentalism in current times.	112, 186–189, 424, 425, 887–891	112, 186–189, 424, 425, 887–891
11.3.3 Cite incidences of religious intolerance in the United States (e.g., persecution of Mormons, anti-Catholic sentiment, anti-Semitism).	185, 187, 407–410, 416, 417	185, 187, 407–410, 416, 417
11.3.4 Discuss the expanding religious pluralism in the United States and California that resulted from large-scale immigration in the twentieth century.	809, 810, 872, 873	809, 810, 872, 873
11.3.5 Describe the principles of religious liberty found in the Establishment and Free Exercise clauses of the First Amendment, including the debate on the issue of separation of church and state.	145, 159, 424, 425	145, 159, 424, 425
11.4 Students trace the rise of the United States to its role as a world power in the twentieth century.	295–298, 300–319, 367, 368, 371–381, 397, 399, 457–459, 463, 627, 634–636	290, 291, 295–298, 300–319, 322, 323, 354, 362, 363, 367, 368, 370–383, 388–397, 399, 457–459, 463, 627, 634–636

T63

Where Are the History–Social Science Standards Found?

CHAPTER STANDARDS

The History–Social Science Content Standards covered in the chapter are listed at the beginning of the chapter.

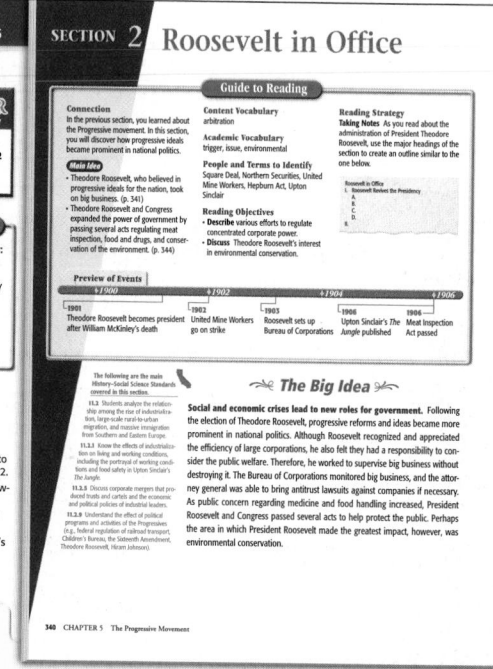

SECTION STANDARDS

The learning goals for the content standards covered in each specific section are listed in the section opener.

FEATURE STANDARDS

The History–Social Science Content Standards covered in features are listed at the start of each feature spread.

Where Are the Historical and Social Sciences Analysis Skills Found?

HISTORICAL AND SOCIAL SCIENCES ANALYSIS SKILLS

The Historical and Social Sciences Analysis Skills are introduced on pages 13–14.

SKILLS REINFORCEMENT

Opportunities to reinforce the Historical and Social Sciences Analysis Skills are found throughout the lessons.

Chapter 5 • Section 1

S Skill Practice

Historical Interpretation Instruct students to list the reforms that were directly or indirectly a result of Robert La Follette's democratic philosophies. (direct primary, initiative, referendum, and recall) Have students write an essay explaining the importance of these reforms to our democratic process today. **AL CA CS1**

R Reading Strategy

Using Context Clues Unfamiliar phrases can prevent students from understanding the deeper meaning of a statement. Ask: What did Charles Edward Russell mean when he said that the Senate had become "only a chamber of butlers for industrialists and financiers"? (Senators served wealthy businessmen rather than the people of their state.) **OL CA 11RC2.5**

Reading Check

Answer: because government could not carry out reforms unless it was reformed first.

Reading Check

Answer: Allowing the public to elect senators made the Senate more democratic. It was intended to end corruption but instead removed one of the state government's checks on federal power.

Answers and Additional Support

---

commissioner. These progressives argued that a board of commissioners or a city manager with expertise in city services should hire the specialists to run city departments. Galveston, Texas, adopted the commission system in 1901. Other cities soon followed.

Reading Check **Explaining** Why did progressives want to reorganize city government?

Democracy and Progressivism

Main Idea Progressive policies in Wisconsin became widespread, leading to election reforms.

Reading Connection Do you remember how candidates were nominated for office during the early years of the nation? Read on to discover the progressives' new method for choosing candidates.

Not all progressives agreed with the efficiency progressives. Many believed that society needed more democracy, not less. They wanted to make elected officials more responsive to voters.

"Laboratory of Democracy" Political reform first came to the state level when Wisconsin voters elected Republican **Robert La Follette** to be governor. La Follette used his office to attack the way political parties ran their conventions. Because party bosses controlled the selection of convention delegates, they also controlled which candidates were chosen to run for office. La Follette pressured the state legislature to require each party to hold a **direct primary**, in which all party members could vote for a candidate to run in the general election.

La Follette's great reform success gave Wisconsin a reputation as the "laboratory of democracy." La Follette claimed, "Democracy is based upon knowledge. . . . The only way to beat the boss . . . is to keep the people thoroughly informed."

Inspired by La Follette, progressives in other states pushed for similar electoral changes. To force state legislators to respond to voters, three new reforms were introduced in many states. The **initiative** allowed a group of citizens to introduce **legislation** and required the legislature to vote on it. The **referendum** allowed proposed legislation to be submitted to the voters for approval. The **recall** allowed voters to demand a special election to remove an elected official from office before his or her term had expired.

Direct Election of Senators
Another reform the progressives favored affected the federal government—the direct election of senators. As originally written, the United States Constitution directed each state legislature to elect two senators from that state. Political machines or large trusts often influenced the election of senators, who then repaid their supporters with federal contracts and jobs. By the early 1900s, muckraker Charles Edward Russell charged that the Senate had become "only a chamber of butlers for industrialists and financiers."

To counter Senate corruption, progressives called for the direct election of senators by all state voters. In 1912 Congress passed a direct-election amendment. Although the direct election of senators was intended to end corruption, it also removed one of the state legislatures' checks on federal power. In 1913 the amendment was ratified, becoming the Seventeenth Amendment to the Constitution.

Reading Check **Evaluating** What was the impact of the Seventeenth Amendment? What was it intended to solve?

The Suffrage Movement

Main Idea Many progressives joined the suffrage movement to gain women the right to vote in national elections.

Reading Connection How would you feel if you were unable to vote for your country's leaders because of your gender? Read on to find out how women defeated that bias in 1920.

In July 1848, Elizabeth Cady Stanton and Lucretia Mott organized the first women's rights convention in Seneca Falls, New York. Stanton proposed to the delegates that their first priority should be getting women the right to vote. The movement for women's voting rights became known as the women's **suffrage** movement. **Suffrage** is the right to vote.

Woman suffrage was an important issue for progressives. Although the suffrage movement began well before progressivism emerged, many progressives joined the movement in the late 1800s and early 1900s.

Early Problems The suffrage movement got off to a slow start. Women suffragists were accused of being unfeminine and immoral. Several were physically attacked. The movement also remained weak because many of its supporters were abolitionists as

well. In the years before the Civil War, they preferred to concentrate on abolishing slavery and spent less time working for woman suffrage.

After the Civil War, the Republicans in Congress introduced the Fourteenth and Fifteenth Amendments to the Constitution to protect the voting rights of African Americans. Several leaders of the woman suffrage movement had wanted these amendments worded to give women the right to vote as well. They were bitterly disappointed when Republicans refused.

The debate over the Fourteenth and Fifteenth Amendments split the suffrage movement into two groups: the National Woman Suffrage Association, led by Elizabeth Cady Stanton and Susan B. Anthony, and the American Woman Suffrage Association, led by Lucy Stone and Julia Ward Howe. The National Woman Suffrage Association wanted to focus on passing a constitutional amendment allowing woman suffrage. The American Woman Suffrage Association believed that the best **strategy** was to convince state governments to give women the right to vote before trying to amend the Constitution.

This split reduced the movement's effectiveness. In 1878 a constitutional amendment granting woman suffrage was introduced in Congress, but it

failed to pass. Few state governments granted women the right to vote either. With the woman suffrage movement divided between goals, it was difficult for the movement to be successful. By 1900 only Wyoming, Idaho, Utah, and Colorado had granted women full voting rights.

The Movement Builds Support In 1890 the two groups united to form the National American Woman Suffrage Association (NAWSA). The movement still did not make significant gains, however, until about 1910. Part of the problem was convincing women to become politically active. As the Progressive movement began, however, many middle-class women concluded that they needed the vote to promote the social reforms they favored. Many working-class women also wanted the vote to ensure passage of labor laws protecting women.

As the suffrage movement grew, members began lobbying lawmakers, organizing marches, and delivering speeches on street corners. By the end of 1912, Washington, Oregon, California, Arizona, and Kansas had granted women full voting rights. On March 3, 1913, the day before President Wilson's inauguration, suffragists marched in Washington, D.C., to draw attention to their cause.

330 CHAPTER 5 The Progressive Movement

Chapter 5 • Section 1

S Skill Practice

Identifying Point of View Instruct students to write a speech from the perspective of a suffragist who is against the effort to pass a constitutional amendment granting women the right to vote. The speech should explain why she disagrees with this particular tactic and describe what method of gaining woman suffrage she prefers. Allow students to present their speeches to the class. **OL CA11W**

U Universal Access

Below Grade Level Students struggling to understand the meaning of the text's words may gain insight through activities that involve elements of role playing. Have students create a poster or a sign that suffragists could have carried during one of their protests or marches. **BL**

Did You Know?

Well before the suffrage movement, Abigail Smith Adams, the wife of President John Adams, was a vocal supporter of women's rights. In 1776 she wrote to her husband: "Remember the ladies, or we will not hold ourselves bound by any laws in which we have no voice or representation."

Profiles IN HISTORY

Susan B. Anthony
1820–1906

Susan B. Anthony was born in Adams, Massachusetts, to Quaker parents. Quakers were generally more supportive of women's rights than some other groups, and so Anthony was able to receive a good education. She finished her schooling at the age of 17. Anthony then worked as a teacher in New York, but she was fired after protesting that her pay was only the amount of her male colleagues. She found another job, however, as a principal at New York's Canajoharie Academy. Between 1848 and 1863, Anthony was involved in both the temperance and abolitionist movements.

Her involvement in the drive for women's equality began in 1851 after she met Elizabeth Cady Stanton. Between 1854 and 1860, the duo

attempted to change discriminatory laws in New York. In 1869 Anthony and Stanton organized the National Woman Suffrage Association and began promoting an amendment to grant woman suffrage. Anthony even cast votes in the presidential election of 1872. They were arrested and convicted, but the court feared that the jury would rule in Anthony's favor. He dismissed the jury and fined Anthony instead. She refused to pay the $100 fine, but the judge decided to let her go, afraid that appealing the case might generate sympathy for the suffrage movement.

In 1883 Anthony traveled to Europe, and she helped form the International Council of Women in 1888. This organization represented the rights of women in 48 countries. She died in Rochester, New York, in 1906. Though Anthony did not live to see her dream of woman

suffrage become reality, the United States government honored her by placing her portrait on a one dollar coin in 1979.

CHAPTER 5 The Progressive Movement 331

More Skill Practice

Determining the Main Idea One goal of progressives was to make government more responsive to the voters. Ask: What is a political initiative? (the right of a group of citizens to introduce a matter for legislation) What does it mean to take initiative in a situation? (to take the first step; originating a new idea) **OL**

TURNING POINT

In addition to being allowed to own and run their own ranches and farms, Western women were the first to win the right to vote. Based on the information from the map on page 332, where did women first receive the right to vote? (territory of Wyoming in 1869) **BL**

Profiles IN HISTORY

Chapter 5 • Section 4

R Reading Strategy

Activating Prior Knowledge Have students recall what they learned about the Sherman Antitrust Act (p. 275) and compare it with the Clayton Antitrust Act. Ask: How did the two acts differ? (While both acts sought to break up big business trusts, the Clayton Antitrust Act went further and banned tying agreements and price discrimination.) **OL**

S Skill Practice

Scaffolding—Relating Current Events Ask students to summarize the reforms initiated by President Wilson in the section "Federal Aid and Social Welfare." Ask: Why might the Supreme Court ruling that child labor could not be nationally regulated be considered only a temporary setback? (eventually laws were written to protect children; today many child labor laws exist) **OL CA CS4**

This *Historical Analysis* skill was introduced in Chapter 2.

Reading Check

Answer: The Sixteenth Amendment made it legal for the federal government to directly tax the income of individuals.

Reading Check

Answer: created an eight-hour workday for railroad workers

Answers and Additional Support

Progressives in Congress responded by passing the Clayton Antitrust Act. The act banned tying agreements, which required retailers who bought from one company to stop selling a competitor's products. It also banned price discrimination, and manufacturers could no longer give wholesale discounts to chain stores and other retailers.

Before the act passed, labor unions lobbied Congress to exempt unions from the antitrust laws. The Clayton Antitrust Act specifically declared that unions were not unlawful combinations in restraint of trade. When the bill became law, Samuel Gompers, head of the American Federation of Labor, called the Clayton Antitrust Act the worker's "Magna Carta," because it gave unions the right to exist.

Reading Check What was the impact of the passage of the Sixteenth Amendment?

Federal Aid and Social Welfare

Main Idea Wilson continued to support progressive reforms as he faced reelection in 1916.

Reading Connection What strategies did previous presidents use to secure their reelection? Read on to discover President Wilson's actions as he tried to win voters.

By the fall of 1914, Wilson believed that his New Freedom program was essentially complete. As a result, he began to retreat from activism.

The congressional elections of 1914, however, shattered the president's complacency. Democrats suffered major losses in the House of Representatives, and voters who had supported the Bull Moose Party in 1912 began returning to the Republicans. Realizing that he would not be able to rely on a divided opposition when he ran for reelection in 1916, Wilson began to support further reforms.

In 1916, for example, Wilson signed the first federal law regulating child labor. The Keating-Owen Child Labor Act prohibited the employment of children under the age of 14 in factories producing goods for interstate commerce. The Supreme Court declared the law unconstitutional on the grounds that child labor was not interstate commerce and therefore only states could regulate it. Wilson's effort, however, helped his reputation with progressive voters.

Two other acts Wilson supported were the Adamson Act and the Federal Farm Loan Act. The Adamson Act established the eight-hour workday for railroad workers and provided for additional compensation for any time worked over eight hours. The Federal Farm Loan Act created 12 Federal Land Banks to provide farmers with long-term loans at low interest rates. Farmers were able to borrow up to 50 percent of the value of their land. The act enabled small farmers to be more competitive with larger farms and businesses. Both acts were passed by Congress in 1916.

Reading Check **Examining** How did the Adamson Act improve labor conditions in the United States?

Picturing History

Factory Girls
The young girls pictured in this photo worked in a hosiery factory. The young girl in front must stand on a stool to see what she is knitting. Factory jobs were often dangerous and required long, tiring hours. Why did the Supreme Court find the Keating-Owens law unconstitutional?

356 CHAPTER 5 The Progressive Movement

Picturing History

Answer: The Supreme Court ruled that child labor was not interstate commerce and could not be federally regulated.

Ask: Why was the Keating-Owen Child Labor Act important? (the first federal law regulating child labor; helped Wilson get a good reputation with progressives)

More Skill Practice

Drawing Conclusions Many presidents have experienced a shift in political influence due to the mid-term congressional elections, just as Wilson did in 1914. Ask: What are some of the challenges a president faces when the House or Senate has a majority in the opposing party? (lack of support for his policies; voting party line) **OL**

Where Are the English–Language Arts Standards Found?

STANDARDS-BASED ACTIVITY

The ovals show the English–Language Arts Content Standards covered by these activities.

Chapter 4 • Section 1

W Writing Support

Letter Writing Have students imagine they live during the late 1800s. Ask them to write a letter to a relative in another country, explaining to them the idea of Anglo-Saxonism and why they think it is popular in the United States. **OL** **CA 11WS1.1**

W Writing Support

Response to Literature Writing Have students use the Internet to locate a copy of *Our Country* by Josiah Strong. Instruct students to read the text and then write a paragraph explaining Strong's connection of Anglo-Saxonism to Christian missionary actions. **OL** **CA 11RLS.2; 11WA2.2**

R Reading Strategy

Scaffolding—Academic Vocabulary The word *commission* was introduced in Chapter 3, Section 3. Ask a student to define the word. **BL**

Reading Check

Answer: More people believed it was the American destiny to spread its civilization overseas.

Answers and Additional Support

A Feeling of Superiority In addition to economic concerns, other key ideas convinced many Americans to encourage expansion overseas. Many supporters of Social Darwinism argued that nations competed with each other politically, economically, and militarily, and that only the strongest would ultimately survive. They used this idea to justify expanding the power of the United States overseas.

Many Americans, such as the well-known writer and historian John Fiske, took this idea even further. Fiske argued that English-speaking nations had superior character, ideas, and systems of government, and were destined to dominate the planet:

> The work which the English race began when it colonized North America is destined to go on until every land ... that is not already the seat of an old civilization shall become English in its language, in its religion, in political habits and traditions, and to a predominant extent in the blood of its people.
>
> —quoted in *Expansionists of 1898*

This idea, known as **Anglo-Saxonism**, was popular in Britain and the United States. Many Americans saw it as part of the idea of Manifest Destiny. They believed that after reaching the Pacific Ocean it was the nation's destiny to expand overseas and spread its civilization to other people.

Another influential advocate of Anglo-Saxonism was Josiah Strong, a popular American minister in the late 1800s. Strong linked Anglo-Saxonism to

U.S. Foreign Investments at the Turn of the Century

Graph Skills

1. **Interpreting Graphs** By how many millions of dollars did U.S. investment in foreign countries increase between 1897 and 1908?
2. **Analyzing** How did the expansionist economic policies depicted here affect U.S. diplomacy?

296 CHAPTER 4 Becoming a World Power

Christian missionary ideas. His ideas influenced many Americans. "The Anglo-Saxon," Strong declared, "[is] divinely commissioned to be, in a peculiar sense, his brother's keeper." By linking missionary work to Anglo-Saxonism, Strong convinced many Americans to support imperialism and an expansion of American power overseas.

Reading Check **Summarizing** How did Americans' opinions on overseas expansion begin to change in the 1800s?

Expansion in the Pacific

Main Idea The desire for new markets led to trade with Japan and the annexation of Hawaii.

Reading Connection What products do you use that have been manufactured in Japan? Read on to learn how the United States and Japan became trade partners.

From the earliest days of the Republic, Americans had expanded their nation by moving west. When Americans began looking overseas for new markets in the 1800s, therefore, they naturally tended to look westward. Even before imperialist ideas became popular, Americans had begun expanding across the Pacific Ocean toward East Asia. By the early 1800s, dozens of ships were making the long trip to China every year.

Perry Opens Japan Many American business leaders believed that the United States would benefit from trade with Japan as well as with China. Japan's rulers, however, believed that excessive contact with the West would destroy their culture and only allowed the Chinese and Dutch to trade with their nation.

In 1852, after receiving several petitions from Congress, President Millard Fillmore attempted to persuade Japan to trade with the United States. He ordered Commodore **Matthew C. Perry** to take a naval expedition to Japan to negotiate a trade treaty.

On July 8, 1853, four American warships under Perry's command entered Yedo Bay (today known as Tokyo Bay). The Japanese had never seen steamships before and were impressed by the display of American technology and firepower. Perry's arrival in Japan forced the Japanese to make changes internally. Realizing that they could not compete against modern Western technology and weapons, the Japanese signed a treaty opening the ports of Simoda and Hakodati to American trade on March 31, 1854.

The American decision to force Japan to open trade played an important role in Japanese history. Many Japanese leaders concluded that the time had come to remake their society. In 1868, after a long internal power struggle, Japanese leaders began to Westernize their country. They adopted Western technology and launched their own industrial revolution. By the 1890s, the Japanese had built a powerful modern navy, and they set out to build their own empire in Asia.

R Annexing Hawaii As trade with China and Japan grew in the 1800s, many Americans became interested in Hawaii. Ships traveling between China and the United States regularly stopped in Hawaii to allow their crews to rest and to take on supplies. In 1820 a group of missionaries from New England settled in Hawaii. At about the same time, American whaling ships operating in the North Pacific began using Hawaii as a base.

The American settlers in Hawaii quickly discovered that the climate and soil of the islands were suitable for growing sugarcane. By the mid-1800s, many sugarcane plantations had been established in the islands. In 1872 a severe recession struck Hawaii's economy. Worried that the economic crisis might force the Hawaiians to turn to the British or French for help, the United States Senate ratified a trade treaty in 1875 that exempted Hawaiian sugar from tariffs. Several years later, when the treaty came up for renewal, the Senate insisted that the Hawaiians grant the United States exclusive rights to a naval base at Pearl Harbor.

The trade treaty led to a boom in the Hawaiian sugar industry and wealth for the planters. In 1887 prominent planters pressured Hawaiian King Kalakaua into accepting a new constitution that limited the king's authority and increased the planters' power. These developments angered the Hawaiian people, who feared they were losing control of the country.

Tensions between the planters and the Hawaiians mounted. Congress passed the McKinley Tariff in 1890. Although the tariff eliminated all duties on sugar, it also gave subsidies to sugar producers in the United States. Hawaiian sugar was now more expensive than American sugar, despite the lack of tariffs. As sales of Hawaiian sugar declined, the islands' economy went into a tailspin.

In 1891 **Queen Liliuokalani** ascended the Hawaiian throne. Liliuokalani disliked the influence that American settlers had gained in Hawaii. In January 1893, she unsuccessfully attempted to impose a new constitution that would have reasserted her authority as ruler of the Hawaiian people.

Faced with the economic crisis and the queen's actions, the planters backed an attempt to overthrow the monarchy. Supported by the marines from the USS *Boston*, a group of planters forced the queen to give up power and set up a provisional government. They then requested that the United States annex Hawaii. President Cleveland strongly opposed imperialism. He withdrew the annexation treaty from the Senate and tried to restore Liliuokalani to power. Hawaii's new leaders refused to restore Liliuokalani, and they decided to wait until a new president took office who favored annexation. Five years later, the United States annexed Hawaii. (*See page 997 for more text on Hawaiian annexation.*)

Reading Check **Explaining** How did the desire to expand into new markets help push the United States to extend its influence into the Pacific?

CHAPTER 4 Becoming a World Power 297

Picturing History

American Imperialism To open Japan to American trade, Commodore Matthew Perry led the U.S. Navy into what is now Tokyo Bay on July 8, 1853. This lithograph shows Perry's forces arriving in Yokohama in March 1854. *How did Perry's action affect Japan?*

Chapter 4 • Section 1

R Reading Strategy

Summarizing Instruct students to make a list of all the steps the United States took to annex Hawaii. **BL**

R Reading Strategy

Sequencing Information An important aspect of understanding history is understanding how the order of events affect other events. **Ask:** How did the McKinley Tariff affect the economy of Hawaii? *(It provided U.S. sugar producers with subsidies that allowed them to sell sugar at a cheaper rate. Hawaii then sold less sugar to the U.S. and it severely hurt the economy.)* **AL** **CA HI2**

R Reading Strategy

Organizing Information Have students look up *monarchy* and *democracy* in the dictionary. Working in pairs, have them list ways the two forms of government are different. **OL**

Resources for page 297

Have students read more about the transformation of Hawaii in *Linking Past and Present Activity 4.*

Reading Check

Answer: It led them to annex Hawaii and open trade with Japan.

Graph Skills

Answers:
1. by $1,800 million
2. caused the U.S. to have greater trade and diplomatic contacts with Asia and Latin America

Graphs Skills Practice
Ask: How would such an increase in foreign investment affect the standing of the United States? *(showed its growing power in the world)*

More Skill Practice

Historical and Social Sciences Analysis Skill Instruct students to use the Internet to expand the information on U.S. foreign investments found in the graph, showing the increases in 1925, 1950, 1975, and 2000. They should analyze the data and determine where the largest period of growth was, and what events contributed to the growth. **OL** **CA HI1**

Did You Know?

Queen Liliuokalani was the last reigning monarch of Hawaii before it was annexed to the United States. She possessed musical ability and is better known for writing the song "Aloha Oe" than for her role as queen. After abdicating her throne, she withdrew from public life and died in Honolulu in 1917.

Picturing History

Answer: The Japanese could not compete against Western technology and weapons. They adopted Western technology, launched their own industrial revolution, and built a modern navy.

Ask: What objection did the Japanese have in the early 1850s to trading with the United States? *(The Japanese believed contact with the West would destroy their culture.)*

296

297

Scaffolding: Reinforcing Content

Skills that aid student comprehension are introduced and reinforced throughout the text.

SKILLS

Reading Skills and *Historical Analysis Skills* are introduced at the beginning of each chapter and reinforced throughout the textbook.

Chapter 5 • Section 4

R Reading Strategy

Activating Prior Knowledge Have students recall what they learned about the Sherman Antitrust Act (p. 275) and compare it with the Clayton Antitrust Act. **Ask:** How did the two acts differ? *(While both acts sought to break up big business trusts, the Clayton Antitrust Act went further and banned tying agreements and price discrimination.)* **OL**

S Skill Practice

Scaffolding—Relating Current Events Ask students to summarize the reforms initiated by President Wilson in the section "Federal Aid and Social Welfare." **Ask:** Why might the Supreme Court ruling that child labor could not be nationally regulated be considered only a temporary setback? *(eventually laws were written to protect children; today many child labor laws exist)* **OL CA CS1**

This **Historical Analysis** skill was introduced in Chapter 2.

✓ Reading Check

Answer: The Sixteenth Amendment made it legal for the federal government to directly tax the income of individuals.

✓ Reading Check

Answer: created an eight-hour workday for railroad workers

Answers and Additional Support

Progressives in Congress responded by passing the Clayton Antitrust Act. The act banned tying agreements, which required retailers who bought from one company to stop selling a competitor's products. It also banned price discrimination, and manufacturers could no longer give wholesale discounts to chain stores and other retailers.

Before the act passed, labor unions lobbied Congress to exempt unions from the antitrust laws. The Clayton Antitrust Act specifically declared that unions were not unlawful combinations in restraint of trade. When the bill became law, Samuel Gompers, head of the American Federation of Labor, called the Clayton Antitrust Act the worker's "Magna Carta," because it gave unions the right to exist.

✓ Reading Check Evaluating What was the impact of the passage of the Sixteenth Amendment?

Federal Aid and Social Welfare

Main Idea Wilson continued to support progressive reforms as he faced reelection in 1916.

Reading Connection What strategies did previous presidents use to secure their reelection? Read on to discover President Wilson's actions as he tried to win voters.

By the fall of 1914, Wilson believed that his New Freedom program was essentially complete. As a result, he began to retreat from activism.

The congressional elections of 1914, however, shattered the president's complacency. Democrats suffered major losses in the House of Representatives, and voters who had supported the Bull Moose Party in 1912 began returning to the Republicans. Realizing that he would not be able to rely on a divided opposition when he ran for reelection in 1916, Wilson began to support further reforms.

In 1916, for example, Wilson signed the first federal law regulating child labor. The Keating-Owen Child Labor Act prohibited the employment of children under the age of 14 in factories producing goods for interstate commerce. The Supreme Court declared the law unconstitutional on the grounds that child labor was not interstate commerce and therefore only states could regulate it. Wilson's effort, however, helped his reputation with progressive voters.

Two other acts Wilson supported were the Adamson Act and the Federal Farm Loan Act. The Adamson Act established the eight-hour workday for railroad workers and provided for additional compensation for any time worked over eight hours. The Federal Farm Loan Act created 12 Federal Land Banks to provide farmers with long-term loans at low interest rates. Farmers were able to borrow up to 50 percent of the value of their land. The act enabled small farmers to be more competitive with larger farms and businesses. Both acts were passed by Congress in 1916.

✓ Reading Check Examining How did the Adamson Act improve labor conditions in the United States?

Picturing **History**

Factory Girls
The young girls pictured in this photo are knitters in a hosiery factory. The young girl in front must stand on a stool to see what she is knitting. Factory jobs were often dangerous and required long, tiring hours. Why did the Supreme Court find the Keating-Owen law unconstitutional?

336 CHAPTER 5 The Progressive Movement

Picturing **History**

Answer: The Supreme Court ruled that child labor was not interstate commerce and could not be federally regulated.

Ask: Why was the Keating-Owen Child Labor Act important? *(the first federal law regulating child labor; helped Wilson get a good reputation with progressives)*

More Skill Practice

Drawing Conclusions Many presidents have experienced a shift in political influence due to the mid-term congressional elections, just as Wilson did in 1914. **Ask:** What are some of the challenges a president faces when the House or Senate has a majority in the opposing party? *(lack of support for his policies; voting party line)* **OL**

ACADEMIC VOCABULARY

New academic vocabulary is introduced in each section and is reinforced in later chapters.

The Election of 1912

Main Idea Woodrow Wilson's "New Freedom" campaign won him the White House after progressive voters split over Taft and Roosevelt.

Reading Connection What political slogans have you heard during campaigns for office or school elections? Read on to learn about the "New Freedom" and "New Nationalism" of the 1912 election.

The 1912 presidential campaign featured a current president, a former president, and an academic who had entered politics only two years earlier.

★ An American Story ★

On September 15, 1910, in the Taylor Opera House in Trenton, New Jersey, a young progressive named Joseph Patrick Tumulty watched as a lean man with iron-gray hair made his way toward the stage. The man was Thomas Woodrow Wilson, the Democratic Party's nominee for governor.

Wilson was the choice of the party bosses. As Tumulty recalled, progressives were "feeling sullen, beaten, and hopelessly betrayed." To Tumulty's astonishment, Wilson announced: "I shall enter upon the duties of the office of governor, if elected, with absolutely no pledge of any kind to prevent me from serving the people of the state with singleness of purpose."

Tumulty knew that Wilson was declaring his independence from the New Jersey political machine. It brought the progressives at the convention roaring to their feet. From one came the cry, "Thank God, at last, a leader has come!"

Two years later, Woodrow Wilson was the Democrats' nominee for the presidency, an office they had won only twice since the Civil War. This time they were confident of victory, for Wilson, a committed progressive, faced a Republican party wracked by division.

—adapted from *Wilson: The Road to the White House*

The election's outcome determined the path of the Progressive movement and helped shape the nation's path in the 1900s.

The Republican Party Splits Believing that President Taft had failed to live up to Progressive ideals, Theodore Roosevelt informed seven state governors that he was willing to accept the Republican nomination. "My hat is in the ring!" he declared. "The fight is on."

The struggle for control of the Republican Party reached its climax at the national convention in Chicago in June. Conservatives rallied behind Taft. Most of the progressives lined up for Roosevelt. When it became clear that Taft's delegates controlled the nomination, Roosevelt decided to leave the party and campaign as an independent. "We stand at Armageddon," he told his supporters, "and we battle for the Lord."

Declaring himself "fit as a bull moose," Roosevelt became the presidential candidate for the newly formed Progressive Party, nicknamed the Bull Moose Party. Because Taft had alienated so many groups, the election of 1912 became a contest between two progressives: the Bull Moose Roosevelt and the Democrat Wilson.

Wilson's Character and Background Woodrow Wilson entered politics as a firm practical. As governor of New Jersey, he pushed one Progressive reform after another through the statehouse. He revamped election laws, established utility regulatory boards, and allowed cities to change to the commissioner form of government. In less than two years, New Jersey became a model of Progressive reform.

A Woodrow Wilson election poster ▼

FOR GOVERNOR

WOODROW WILSON

CHAPTER 5 The Progressive Movement 353

Chapter 5 • Section 4

TEACH

R Reading Strategy

Scaffolding—Academic Vocabulary The word *academic* was introduced in Chapter 2, Section 2. Ask a student to define the word. **BL**

C Critical Thinking

Making Inferences Remind students that Theodore Roosevelt's Bull Moose Party competed with President Taft's support in the Republican Party. **Ask:** Without a split in the Republican Party, do you think Woodrow Wilson still would have won the presidency? *(Students should give reasons to support their opinions. These opinions should be based upon information provided in the text.)* **AL**

S Skill Practice

Visual Literacy Instruct students to examine the portrait of Woodrow Wilson. **Ask:** What descriptive words come to mind about Wilson as you observe his dress and demeanor? *(Answers may include: formal, stern, intellectual, precise, purposeful, or determined.)* **BL**

Review the Big Idea

Review the Big Idea for this section, "Social and economic crises lead to new roles for government." As students read this section, have them note the policies President Wilson put into place in a graphic organizer similar to the one below. **BL**

Economy	
Welfare	

Did You Know?

Prior to the 1912 election, the last time either the Republican or Democratic party split because it was unable to decide on a single candidate was in the 1860 election that preceded the Civil War. The Democrats nominated a Northern and a Southern candidate. Abraham Lincoln won the election with less than forty percent of the total popular vote.

353

Assessment and Intervention: Sections

Student activities and questions throughout the book provide opportunities for standards assessment and intervention.

CORRELATIONS

Lozenges appear next to questions and writing activities that are correlated to the California Historical Analysis Skills and the English–Language Arts Standards.

QUESTIONS

Assessment questions are closely tied to the section Guide to Reading.

ANSWERS

The Teacher Wraparound Edition provides answers to all assessment questions.

INTERVENTION

This resource lets students test their content knowledge and identifies areas that need reinforcement.

The Legacy of Progressivism

Main Idea Progressivism changed the view many people had about the government's role in social issues.

Reading Connection Do you believe that groups of people have been left out of "the American dream"? Read on to find out about the failures and successes of progressivism.

During his presidency, Wilson had built upon Roosevelt's **foundation**. He expanded the role of the federal government and of the president.

A New Kind of Government Progressivism made important political changes in the United States. Most Americans did not expect the government to pass laws protecting workers or regulating big business. In fact, many courts had previously ruled that it was unconstitutional for the government to do so.

By the end of the Progressive era, however, both legal and public opinion had shifted. Increasingly, Americans expected the government, particularly the federal government, to play a more active role in regulating the economy and solving social problems.

The Limits of Progressivism The most conspicuous limit to progressivism was its failure to address African American and religious issues. African Americans themselves were absorbing the reform spirit, fueling their desire for advancement.

In 1905 W.E.B. Du Bois and 28 other African American leaders met at Niagara Falls to demand full

political rights for African Americans. They met on the Canadian side because no hotel on the American side would accept them. There they launched the Niagara Movement. This meeting was one of many steps leading to the founding of the **National Association for the Advancement of Colored People** (NAACP) in 1909. Du Bois and other NAACP founders believed that the vote was essential to bring about an end to lynching and racial discrimination. "The power of the ballot we need in sheer self-defense," Du Bois said, "else what shall save us from a second slavery?"

Progressivism also did not address anti-Semitism. Lawyer Sigmund Livingston founded the Anti-Defamation League (ADL) in 1913 to fight for civil liberties for Jews and to protect Jews against discrimination in housing, employment, education.

Despite the failure of most progressives to focus on racial and religious issues, Progressive reform helped change American society. Although many groups were excluded, the progressives expanded democracy and improved the quality of life for millions. As the country entered World War I, however, Americans soon turned from reforming their own society to a crusade to "make the world safe for democracy."

Reading Check **Evaluating** How did progressivism change American beliefs about the federal government?

HISTORY Online **Study Central**
For help with the concepts in this section of *American Vision: Modern Times* go to tav.mt.glencoe.com and click on **Study Central**.

SECTION 4 ASSESSMENT

Checking for Understanding
1. **Vocabulary** Define: capacity, levying, income tax, unfair trade practices, labor, foundation.
2. **People and Terms** Identify: Progressive Party, New Nationalism, New Freedom, Federal Trade Commission, National Association for the Advancement of Colored People.
3. **Explain** why President Wilson proposed the establishment of the Federal Reserve System.

Reviewing Big Ideas
4. **Identifying** What new federal agencies increased the government's power to regulate the economy?

Critical Thinking
5. **Analyzing** Which of Wilson's reforms do you consider most important? Why?
6. **Organizing** Use a graphic organizer similar to the one below to list the effects progressivism had on American society.

Effects of Progressivism

Analyzing Visuals
7. **Analyzing Photographs** Study the photograph on page 356. What details do you see in the image that might have contributed to the Keating-Owen Child Labor Act?

Writing About History
8. **Expository Writing** Imagine that you are a newspaper editor during the Wilson administration. Write an article on the shortcomings of the Progressive movement in terms of racial issues. Provide ideas about how the movement might have addressed discrimination and segregation. **CA 11WS1.1**

CHAPTER 5 The Progressive Movement 357

SECTION 4 ASSESSMENT ANSWERS

1. Content vocabulary is boldfaced and highlighted in yellow. Academic vocabulary is boldfaced.
2. Progressive Party (p. 353), New Nationalism (p. 354), New Freedom (p. 354), Federal Trade Commission (p. 355), National Association for the Advancement of Colored People (p. 357)
3. to restore public confidence in the banking system
4. the Federal Reserve System and the Federal Trade Commission
5. Students' answers will vary but should include a reasonable argument.
6. expanded democracy, improved quality of life, expanded government role
7. Small children are operating dangerous equipment.
8. Students' editorials will vary. Students should point out specific shortcomings and suggest ways that the progressives could have addressed the social problem.

Chapter 5 • Section 4

S Skill Practice

Historical Interpretation Instruct students to create a database of Presidents Roosevelt, Taft, and Wilson. Have them list the progressive policies each president initiated while in office. Then have students write a paragraph identifying which president they feel made the greatest contribution to progressivism and why. **OL** **CA HI1**

ASSESS

Resources for page 357

Use these resources to assess student mastery.

📖 Section Quiz 5-4
📖 Reading Essentials and Study Guide 5-4
💿 Interactive Tutor Self-Assessment CD-ROM
📖 California Standards Practice, Grade 11

Reading Check

Answer: expanded democracy and raised expectations of the federal government's role in the economy and society

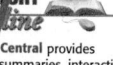

Study Central provides audio summaries, interactive games, and online graphic organizers to help students review section content.

CLOSE

Drawing Conclusions Ask students to reread the paragraph on Wilson's character and background on page 353. Then have them write a one-page report that describes how Wilson carried his progressive ideas into the White House. **OL** **CA 11WA2.4**

357

Assessment and Intervention: Chapters

ADDITIONAL ASSESSMENT RESOURCES

Additional California standards practice and assessment resources.

STANDARDS PRACTICE

Questions to help practice the standards are answered in the Teacher Wraparound Edition.

DOCUMENT-BASED QUESTIONS

Answers to questions based on primary sources are provided.

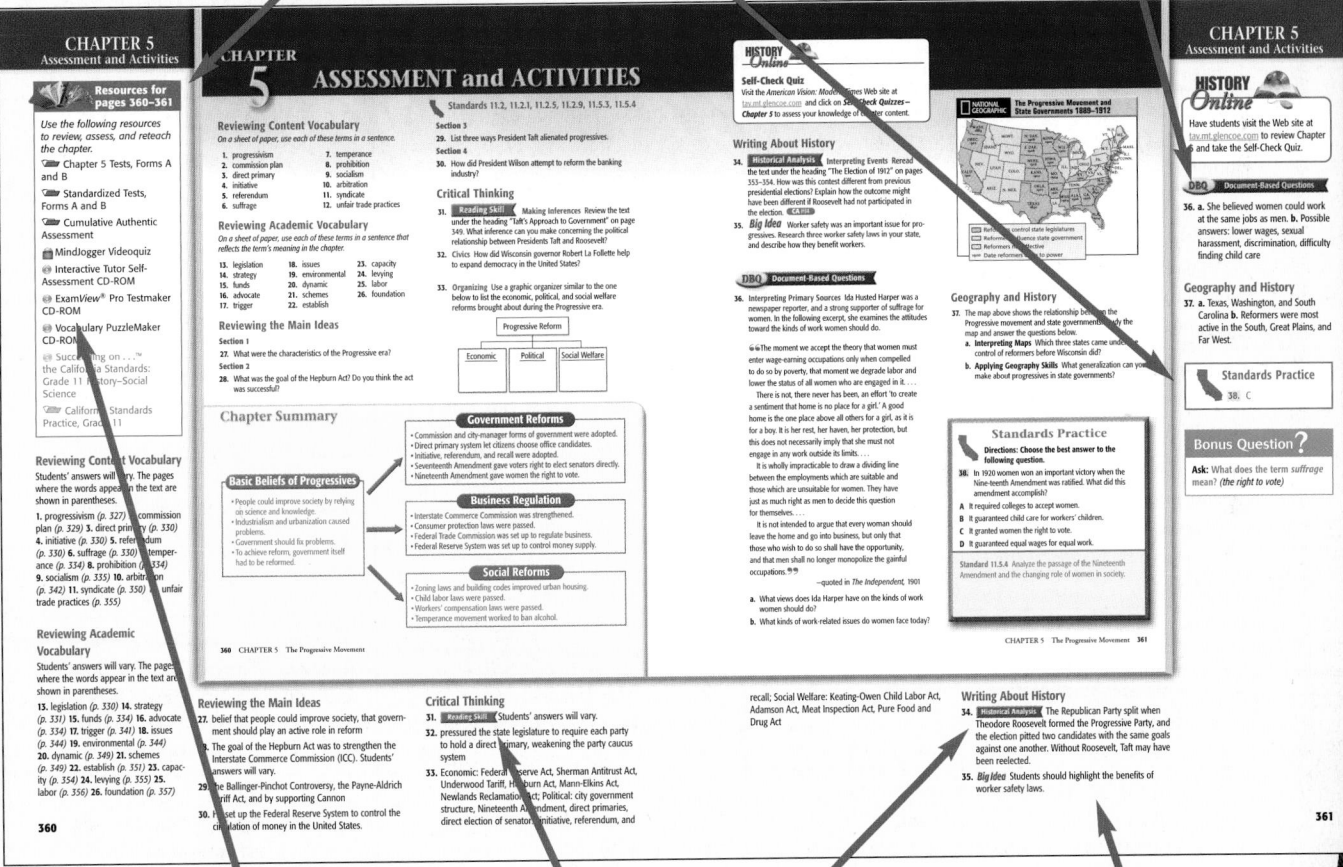

INTERVENTION

This resource provides opportunities for intervention.

READING SKILLS AND HISTORICAL ANALYSIS SKILLS

Answers to questions that reinforce skills introduced in the chapter are provided.

BIG IDEA

Answers to questions that reinforce the Big Idea are provided.

Grade Eleven

United States History and Geography: Continuity and Change in the Twentieth Century

Standards	Student Edition Pages	Teacher Edition Pages
11.1 Students analyze the significant events in the founding of the nation and its attempts to realize the philosophy of government described in the Declaration of Independence.	111–134, 136–167, 173–189, 192–201, 206–225, 228, 229, 231, 238–240, 244, 247, 248, 265, 276, 284, 285, 424, 425, 518, 519, 640, 641, 730, 731, 919, 952, 953	111–134, 136–167, 169, 173–189, 192–226, 228, 229, 231, 238–240, 244, 247, 248, 265, 276, 284, 285, 424, 425, 518, 519, 640, 641, 730, 731, 919, 952, 953
11.1.1 Describe the Enlightenment and the rise of democratic ideas as the context in which the nation was founded.	111, 112, 124–130, 134, 424, 425	111, 112, 124–130, 134, 424, 425
11.1.2 Analyze the ideological origins of the American Revolution, the Founding Fathers' philosophy of divinely bestowed unalienable natural rights, the debates on the drafting and ratification of the Constitution, and the addition of the Bill of Rights.	113–123, 125–133, 136–167, 173, 174, 216, 217, 640, 641, 730, 731, 952, 953	113–133, 136–167, 173, 174, 216, 217, 518, 519, 640, 641, 730, 731, 952, 953
11.1.3 Understand the history of the Constitution after 1787 with emphasis on federal versus state authority and growing democratization.	145–147, 159–167, 173–189, 192–201, 206–225, 228, 229, 231, 518, 519, 919	145–147, 159–167, 173–189, 192–225, 228, 229, 231, 518, 519, 919
11.1.4 Examine the effects of the Civil War and Reconstruction and of the industrial revolution, including demographic shifts and the emergence in the late nineteenth century of the United States as a world power.	207–215, 218, 225, 238–240, 244, 247, 248, 265, 276, 284, 285	169, 206–215, 218, 225, 226, 238–240, 244, 247, 248, 265, 276, 284, 285
11.2 Students analyze the relationship among the rise of industrialization, large-scale rural-to-urban migration, and massive immigration from Southern and Eastern Europe.	175–180, 197, 198, 237–240, 244–253, 255–263, 266–270, 272–281, 284, 285, 296, 327–338, 341–345, 349–351, 353–357, 407–410, 450, 451	175–180, 197, 198, 232, 237–240, 243–253, 255–263, 266–270, 272–281, 283–285, 290, 291, 296, 322, 327–339, 341–347, 349–351, 353–357, 407–410, 450, 451
11.2.1 Know the effects of industrialization on living and working conditions, including the portrayal of working conditions and food safety in Upton Sinclair's *The Jungle.*	244, 249–251, 255–263, 267–270, 284, 285, 336–338, 344, 345, 356, 357, 450, 451	243, 244, 249–251, 255–263, 267–270, 283–285, 336–339, 344, 345, 356, 357, 450, 451
11.2.2 Describe the changing landscape, including the growth of cities linked by industry and trade, and the development of cities divided according to race, ethnicity, and class.	179, 180, 255–263, 284, 285	179, 180, 232, 255–263, 283–285
11.2.3 Trace the effect of the Americanization movement.	175–180, 257, 258, 407–410	175–180, 257, 258, 407–410
11.2.4 Analyze the effect of urban political machines and responses to them by immigrants and middle-class reformers.	272–274, 280, 281	272–274, 280, 281

Correlation to the History–Social Science Standards

Standards	Student Edition Pages	Teacher Edition Pages
11.2.5 Discuss corporate mergers that produced trusts and cartels and the economic and political policies of industrial leaders.	246, 248, 249, 252, 253, 341–343	246, 248, 249, 252, 253, 341–343, 355
11.2.6 Trace the economic development of the United States and its emergence as a major industrial power, including its gains from trade and the advantages of its physical geography.	197, 198, 237–240, 244–251	197, 198, 237–240, 243, 244–251, 290, 291
11.2.7 Analyze the similarities and differences between the ideologies of Social Darwinism and Social Gospel (e.g., using biographies of William Graham Sumner, Billy Sunday, Dwight L. Moody).	266–270, 296	266–270, 296
11.2.8 Examine the effect of political programs and activities of Populists.	275–279	275–279
11.2.9 Understand the effect of political programs and activities of the Progressives (e.g., federal regulation of railroad transport, Children's Bureau, the Sixteenth Amendment, Theodore Roosevelt, Hiram Johnson).	327–335, 341–345, 349–351, 353–355, 356, 357	322, 327–335, 341–347, 349–351, 353–357
11.3 Students analyze the role religion played in the founding of America, its lasting moral, social, and political impacts, and issues regarding religious liberty.	102–108, 111, 112, 145, 159, 185–189, 266–270, 407–410, 416, 417, 424, 425, 809, 810, 872, 873, 887–891	102–108, 111, 112, 145, 159, 185–189, 266–270, 407–410, 416, 417, 424, 425, 809, 810, 872, 873, 887–891
11.3.1 Describe the contributions of various religious groups to American civic principles and social reform movements (e.g., civil and human rights, individual responsibility and the work ethic, antimonarchy and self-rule, worker protection, family-centered communities).	102–108, 111, 112, 186–189, 266–270	102–108, 111, 112, 186–189, 266–270
11.3.2 Analyze the great religious revivals and the leaders involved in them, including the First Great Awakening, the Second Great Awakening, the Civil War revivals, the Social Gospel Movement, the rise of Christian liberal theology in the nineteenth century, the impact of the Second Vatican Council, and the rise of Christian fundamentalism in current times.	112, 186–189, 424, 425, 887–891	112, 186–189, 424, 425, 887–891
11.3.3 Cite incidences of religious intolerance in the United States (e.g., persecution of Mormons, anti-Catholic sentiment, anti-Semitism).	185, 187, 407–410, 416, 417	185, 187, 407–410, 416, 417
11.3.4 Discuss the expanding religious pluralism in the United States and California that resulted from large-scale immigration in the twentieth century.	809, 810, 872, 873	809, 810, 872, 873
11.3.5 Describe the principles of religious liberty found in the Establishment and Free Exercise clauses of the First Amendment, including the debate on the issue of separation of church and state.	145, 159, 424, 425	145, 159, 424, 425
11.4 Students trace the rise of the United States to its role as a world power in the twentieth century.	295–298, 300–319, 367, 368, 371–381, 397, 399, 457–459, 463, 627, 634–636	290, 291, 295–298, 300–319, 322, 323, 354, 362, 363, 367, 368, 370–383, 388–397, 399, 457–459, 463, 627, 634–636

Correlation to the History–Social Science Standards

Standards	Student Edition Pages	Teacher Edition Pages
11.4.1 List the purpose and the effects of the Open Door policy.	310, 312, 313, 315	310, 312, 313, 315
11.4.2 Describe the Spanish-American War and U.S. expansion in the South Pacific.	295–298, 300–309, 312, 313, 318, 319	290, 291, 295–298, 300–309, 312, 313, 318, 319
11.4.3 Discuss America's role in the Panama Revolution and the building of the Panama Canal.	311, 314, 316, 317	311, 314, 316, 317
11.4.4 Explain Theodore Roosevelt's Big Stick diplomacy, William Taft's Dollar Diplomacy, and Woodrow Wilson's Moral Diplomacy, drawing on relevant speeches.	313–315, 367, 368, 388, 389	310, 313–315, 322, 323, 354, 367, 368, 388, 389
11.4.5 Analyze the political, economic, and social ramifications of World War I on the home front.	371–381, 390–397, 399, 457, 463	362, 363, 370–383, 390–397, 399, 457, 463
11.4.6 Trace the declining role of Great Britain and the expanding role of the United States in world affairs after World War II.	458, 459, 627, 634–636	458, 459, 627, 634–636
11.5 **Students analyze the major political, social, economic, technological, and cultural developments of the 1920s.**	327, 330–332, 334, 358, 359, 361, 408–413, 419–422, 427–434, 436, 437, 439, 445–448, 450–455, 457–461, 463, 469–472, 477	327, 330–332, 334, 358, 359, 361, 392, 400, 402, 403, 408–413, 416, 417, 419–422, 427–434, 436, 437, 439, 441, 445–448, 450–455, 457–461, 463, 465, 469–472, 477, 480, 481, 483, 751
11.5.1 Discuss the policies of Presidents Warren Harding, Calvin Coolidge, and Herbert Hoover.	445–448, 455, 457–459, 469–472	445–448, 455, 457–459, 465, 469–472, 483
11.5.2 Analyze the international and domestic events, interests, and philosophies that prompted attacks on civil liberties, including the Palmer Raids, Marcus Garvey's "back-to-Africa" movement, the Ku Klux Klan, and immigration quotas and the responses of organizations such as the American Civil Liberties Union, the National Association for the Advancement of Colored People, and the Anti-Defamation League to those attacks.	408–412, 429, 430, 431, 439	408–412, 416, 417, 429–432, 439, 751
11.5.3 Examine the passage of the Eighteenth Amendment to the Constitution and the Volstead Act (Prohibition).	334, 412, 413, 436, 437	334, 412, 413, 436, 437
11.5.4 Analyze the passage of the Nineteenth Amendment and the changing role of women in society.	327, 330–332, 358, 359, 361, 452	327, 330–332, 358, 359, 361, 452
11.5.5 Describe the Harlem Renaissance and new trends in literature, music, and art, with special attention to the work of writers (e.g., Zora Neale Hurston, Langston Hughes).	419, 420, 422, 427–429, 432–434, 439	392, 400, 402, 403, 419, 420, 422, 427–429, 432–434, 439
11.5.6 Trace the growth and effects of radio and movies and their role in the worldwide diffusion of popular culture.	421, 428, 453, 477	392, 420, 421, 428, 453, 460, 461, 477, 480, 481
11.5.7 Discuss the rise of mass production techniques, the growth of cities, the impact of new technologies (e.g., the automobile, electricity), and the resulting prosperity and effect on the American landscape.	450–455, 460, 461, 463	441, 450–455, 460, 461, 463

Correlation to the History–Social Science Standards

Standards	Student Edition Pages	Teacher Edition Pages
11.6 Students analyze the different explanations for the Great Depression and how the New Deal fundamentally changed the role of the federal government.	249–251, 287, 470–481, 483–487, 490–493, 501–517, 520–529, 828, 829	249–251, 287, 400, 465, 470–481, 483–495, 501–517, 520–529, 828, 829
11.6.1 Describe the monetary issues of the late nineteenth and early twentieth centuries that gave rise to the establishment of the Federal Reserve and the weaknesses in key sectors of the economy in the late 1920s.	470–473	470–473, 475
11.6.2 Understand the explanations of the principal causes of the Great Depression and the steps taken by the Federal Reserve, Congress, and Presidents Herbert Hoover and Franklin Delano Roosevelt to combat the economic crisis.	471–473, 483–485, 487, 492, 493, 501–507, 510–517, 520–529	400, 465, 471–473, 475, 483–485, 487, 492–495, 501–507, 510–517, 520–529
11.6.3 Discuss the human toll of the Depression, natural disasters, and unwise agricultural practices and their effects on the depopulation of rural regions and on political movements of the left and right, with particular attention to the Dust Bowl refugees and their social and economic impacts in California.	474–481, 485–487, 490, 491	474–481, 485–487, 490, 491
11.6.4 Analyze the effects of and the controversies arising from New Deal economic policies and the expanded role of the federal government in society and the economy since the 1930s (e.g., Works Progress Administration, Social Security, National Labor Relations Board, farm programs, regional development policies, and energy development projects such as the Tennessee Valley Authority, California Central Valley Project, and Bonneville Dam).	501–509, 513, 514, 516, 517, 521–528	488, 489, 501–509, 513, 514, 516, 517, 521–528
11.6.5 Trace the advances and retreats of organized labor, from the creation of the American Federation of Labor and the Congress of Industrial Organizations to current issues of a postindustrial, multinational economy, including the United Farm Workers in California.	249–251, 287, 514–516, 524, 828, 829	249–251, 287, 514–516, 524, 828, 829
11.7 Students analyze America's participation in World War II.	537–541, 543–548, 550–555, 557–565, 567, 573–578, 580–585, 587–596, 599–607, 609–615, 621, 628, 629, 634–636, 639, 672, 673	532, 533, 537–555, 557–565, 567, 568, 573–575, 577, 578, 580–585, 587–596, 599–607, 609–615, 618, 619, 621, 628, 629, 634–636, 639, 672, 673
11.7.1 Examine the origins of American involvement in the war, with an emphasis on the events that precipitated the attack on Pearl Harbor.	537–541, 543–548, 557–565, 567, 621	532, 533, 537–548, 557–565, 567, 573, 621
11.7.2 Explain U.S. and Allied wartime strategy, including the major battles of Midway, Normandy, Iwo Jima, Okinawa, and the Battle of the Bulge.	580–585, 599–607, 609–615	568, 580–585, 599–607, 609–615
11.7.3 Identify the roles and sacrifices of individual American soldiers, as well as the unique contributions of the special fighting forces (e.g., the Tuskegee Airmen, the 442nd Regimental Combat team, the Navajo Code Talkers).	577, 578, 581, 588, 591, 600, 602–605, 612, 613	577, 578, 581, 587–591, 600, 602–605, 612, 613, 618, 619

Standards	Student Edition Pages	Teacher Edition Pages
11.7.4 Analyze Roosevelt's foreign policy during World War II (e.g., Four Freedoms speech).	539–541, 543, 557–563, 599, 601, 628, 629	539–541, 543, 557–563, 599, 601, 628, 629
11.7.5 Discuss the constitutional issues and impact of events on the U.S. home front, including the internment of Japanese Americans (e.g., *Fred Korematsu* v. *United States of America*) and the restrictions on German and Italian resident aliens; the response of the administration to Hitler's atrocities against Jews and other groups; the roles of women in military production; the roles and growing political demands of African Americans.	550–555, 576–578, 587–591, 594–596, 609	533, 549–555, 576–578, 587–591, 594–596, 609
11.7.6 Describe major developments in aviation, weaponry, communication, and medicine and the war's impact on the location of American industry and use of resources.	547, 548, 554, 573–575, 591–593, 600, 603–605, 614, 615, 672, 673	547, 548, 554, 573–575, 591–593, 600, 603–605, 614, 615, 672, 673
11.7.7 Discuss the decision to drop atomic bombs and the consequences of the decision (Hiroshima and Nagasaki).	614, 615	614, 615
11.7.8 Analyze the effect of massive aid given to Western Europe under the Marshall Plan to rebuild itself after the war and the importance of a rebuilt Europe to the U.S. economy.	634–636, 639	634–636, 639
11.8 Students analyze the economic boom and social transformation of post–World War II America.	648, 649, 651–654, 666, 668–673, 675–679, 681–687, 689, 690, 697, 707–709, 716–718, 720, 721, 724–729, 735, 778–780, 784, 785, 801, 828, 829, 833–838, 853, 871–877, 889, 890, 894–896, 903–905, 907–909, 918, 919, 931–934	648, 649, 651–654, 662, 663, 666–673, 675–691, 694, 695, 697, 707–709, 712, 713, 716–718, 720, 721, 724–729, 735, 778–780, 784, 785, 801, 828, 829, 833–838, 847, 853, 871–877, 889, 890, 894–896, 903–905, 907–911, 918, 919, 922, 931–934
11.8.1 Trace the growth of service sector, white collar, and professional sector jobs in business and government.	675–677	662, 675–677
11.8.2 Describe the significance of Mexican immigration and its relationship to the agricultural economy, especially in California.	690, 828, 829	690, 828, 829, 910, 911
11.8.3 Examine Truman's labor policy and congressional reaction to it.	668–670	667–670
11.8.4 Analyze new federal government spending on defense, welfare, interest on the national debt, and federal and state spending on education, including the California Master Plan.	651–654, 666, 670–673, 689, 690, 707–709, 724–729, 735, 853, 894–896, 918, 919	651–654, 663, 666, 670–673, 688–691, 694, 695, 707–709, 724–729, 735, 853, 894–896, 918, 919, 922
11.8.5 Describe the increased powers of the presidency in response to the Great Depression, World War II, and the Cold War.	652–654, 716–718, 778–780, 784, 785, 801	652–654, 716–718, 778–780, 784, 785, 801

Correlation to the History-Social Science Standards

Standards	Student Edition Pages	Teacher Edition Pages
11.8.6 Discuss the diverse environmental regions of North America, their relationship to local economies, and the origins and prospects of environmental problems in those regions.	833–837, 889, 890	833–837, 889, 890
11.8.7 Describe the effects on society and the economy of technological developments since 1945, including the computer revolution, changes in communication, advances in medicine, and improvements in agricultural technology.	648, 649, 652, 653, 672, 673, 678, 679, 697, 716, 720, 721, 836–838, 904, 905, 907–909, 931–934	648, 649, 652, 653, 662, 672, 673, 675–679, 697, 716, 720, 721, 836–838, 904, 905, 907–909, 931–934
11.8.8 Discuss forms of popular culture, with emphasis on their origins and geographic diffusion (e.g., jazz and other forms of popular music, professional sports, architectural and artistic styles).	648, 649, 681–687, 871–877, 903–905	648, 649, 663, 680–687, 712, 713, 847, 871–877, 903–905
11.9 Students analyze U.S. foreign policy since World War II.	616, 617, 624, 627–631, 633–639, 643–649, 651–657, 661, 715–718, 732, 733, 773–785, 787–791, 793–799, 807–812, 828, 829, 854–856, 866, 867, 869, 870, 888, 896–899, 915, 916, 918–921, 925, 941, 943, 944, 954–960, 962, 963	616, 617, 622–624, 627–639, 643–649, 651–659, 661, 700, 714–718, 732, 733, 768, 769, 773–799, 807–812, 828, 829, 854–856, 866, 867, 869, 870, 882, 883, 888, 896–899, 915, 916, 918–921, 925, 941, 943, 944, 954–960, 962, 963
11.9.1 Discuss the establishment of the United Nations and International Declaration of Human Rights, International Monetary Fund, World Bank, and General Agreement on Tariffs and Trade (GATT) and their importance in shaping modern Europe and maintaining peace and international order.	616, 617, 628, 629, 634, 635, 638	616, 617, 628, 629, 634, 635, 638
11.9.2 Understand the role of military alliances, including NATO and SEATO, in deterring communist aggression and maintaining security during the Cold War.	624, 630, 631, 635, 636, 774–776	624, 630, 631, 635, 636, 774–776
11.9.3 Trace the origins and geopolitical consequences (foreign and domestic) of the Cold War and containment policy, including the following: • The era of McCarthyism, instances of domestic Communism (e.g., Alger Hiss) and blacklisting • The Truman Doctrine • The Berlin Blockade • The Korean War • The Bay of Pigs Invasion and the Cuban Missile Crisis • Atomic testing in the American West, the "mutual assured destruction" doctrine, and disarmament policies • The Vietnam War • Latin American policy	627–631, 633–639, 643–649, 651–657, 661, 715–718, 732, 733, 773–785, 787–791, 793–799, 854–856, 866, 867, 869, 897–899, 916	622, 623, 627–639, 643–649, 651–659, 661, 700, 714–718, 732, 733, 768, 769, 773–799, 854–856, 866, 867, 869, 897–899, 916
11.9.4 List the effects of foreign policy on domestic policies and vice versa (e.g., protests during the war in Vietnam, the "nuclear freeze" movement).	627, 643–649, 652, 656, 657, 787–791, 793–799, 807–812, 888, 898	627, 643–649, 652, 656, 657, 787–799, 807–812, 888, 898

Standards	Student Edition Pages	Teacher Edition Pages
11.9.5 Analyze the role of the Reagan administration and other factors in the victory of the West in the Cold War.	896–898, 916, 925	882, 883, 896–898, 916, 925
11.9.6 Describe U.S. Middle East policy and its strategic, political, and economic interests, including those related to the Gulf War.	869, 870, 897, 898, 915, 918–921, 941, 954–960, 962, 963	869, 870, 897, 898, 915, 918–921, 941, 954–960, 962, 963
11.9.7 Examine relations between the United States and Mexico in the twentieth century, including key economic, political, immigration, and environmental issues.	828, 829, 943, 944	828, 829, 943, 944
11.10 Students analyze the development of federal civil rights and voting rights.	199, 211, 212, 214, 215, 220, 221, 223, 224, 226, 227, 279–281, 576, 577, 588, 589, 668, 677, 678, 684, 690, 708–710, 741–747, 749–756, 758–767, 789, 791, 814–819, 825–831, 840, 841, 843, 872, 873, 896, 897, 908	199, 211, 212, 214, 215, 220, 221, 223, 224, 226, 227, 279–281, 301, 576, 577, 588, 589, 668, 677, 678, 684, 690, 708–710, 741–767, 789, 791, 803, 814–819, 825–831, 840, 841, 843, 872, 873, 896, 897, 908
11.10.1 Explain how demands of African Americans helped produce a stimulus for civil rights, including President Roosevelt's ban on racial discrimination in defense industries in 1941, and how African Americans' service in World War II produced a stimulus for President Truman's decision to end segregation in the armed forces in 1948.	576, 577, 588, 589, 668, 684, 690	576, 577, 588, 589, 668, 684, 690
11.10.2 Examine and analyze the key events, policies, and court cases in the evolution of civil rights, including *Dred Scott* v. *Sandford, Plessy* v. *Ferguson, Brown* v. *Board of Education, Regents of the University of California* v. *Bakke,* and California Proposition 209.	199, 211, 212, 214, 215, 220, 221, 223, 224, 226, 227, 279–281, 709, 710, 741–743, 766, 826	199, 211, 212, 214, 215, 220, 221, 223, 224, 226, 227, 279–281, 709, 710, 741–743, 752, 766, 826
11.10.3 Describe the collaboration on legal strategy between African American and white civil rights lawyers to end racial segregation in higher education.	742, 745, 747, 750–753	742, 745, 747, 750–753
11.10.4 Examine the roles of civil rights advocates (e.g., A. Philip Randolph, Martin Luther King, Jr., Malcom X, Thurgood Marshall, James Farmer, Rosa Parks), including the significance of Martin Luther King, Jr.'s "Letter from Birmingham Jail" and "I Have a Dream" speech.	588, 741, 742, 744, 745, 749, 750, 752–756, 758–765, 767, 789, 791, 825, 827–829	301, 588, 741, 742, 744, 745, 749, 750, 752–765, 767, 789, 791, 825, 827–829
11.10.5 Discuss the diffusion of the civil rights movement of African Americans from the churches of the rural South and the urban North, including the resistance to racial desegregation in Little Rock and Birmingham, and how the advances influenced the agendas, strategies, and effectiveness of the quests of American Indians, Asian Americans, and Hispanic Americans for civil rights and equal opportunities.	741–747, 749–756, 758–760, 764, 765, 825–831	741–747, 749–756, 758–760, 764, 765, 803, 825–831
11.10.6 Analyze the passage and effects of civil rights and voting rights legislation (e.g., 1964 Civil Rights Act, Voting Rights Act of 1965) and the Twenty-Fourth Amendment, with an emphasis on equality of access to education and to the political process.	747, 753–756, 763	747, 748, 753–756, 763

Correlation to the History–Social Science Standards

Standards	Student Edition Pages	Teacher Edition Pages
11.10.7 Analyze the women's rights movement from the era of Elizabeth Cady Stanton and Susan B. Anthony and the passage of the Nineteenth Amendment to the movement launched in the 1960s, including differing perspectives on the roles of women.	677, 678, 708, 709, 814–819, 840, 841, 843, 872, 873, 896, 897, 908	677, 678, 708, 709, 803, 814–819, 840, 841, 843, 872, 873, 896, 897, 908
11.11 Students analyze the major social problems and domestic policy issues in contemporary American society.	578, 587, 670, 675–678, 707–709, 712, 724–729, 751–756, 814–819, 828, 829, 833–837, 840, 841, 852–854, 857–862, 866, 868, 873, 874, 878, 879, 881, 882, 894–898, 905–908, 918, 919, 922, 923, 936–940, 945, 946, 950, 951, 965	346, 347, 578, 587, 670, 675–678, 707–709, 712, 724–729, 751–756, 803, 814–821, 828, 829, 833–837, 840, 841, 846, 852–854, 857–862, 866, 868, 873, 874, 878, 879, 881, 890, 894–898, 900, 905–908, 918, 919, 922, 923, 936–940, 945, 946, 950, 951, 965
11.11.1 Discuss the reasons for the nation's changing immigration policy, with emphasis on how the Immigration Act of 1965 and successor acts have transformed American society.	727, 728, 751–756, 828, 829	727, 728, 751–756, 828, 829
11.11.2 Discuss the significant domestic policy speeches of Truman, Eisenhower, Kennedy, Johnson, Nixon, Carter, Reagan, Bush, and Clinton (e.g., with regard to education, civil rights, economic policy, environmental policy).	670, 707–709, 712, 725, 852, 853, 866, 868, 878, 879, 881, 894–896, 922, 923, 936–938, 940, 950, 951, 965	670, 707–709, 712, 725, 852, 853, 866, 868, 878, 879, 881, 894–896, 922, 923, 936–938, 940, 950, 951, 965
11.11.3 Describe the changing roles of women in society as reflected in the entry of more women into the labor force and the changing family structure.	578, 587, 677, 678, 708, 709, 814–819, 840, 841, 873, 874, 897, 908	578, 587, 677, 678, 708, 709, 814–821, 840, 841, 873, 874, 897, 908
11.11.4 Explain the constitutional crisis originating from the Watergate scandal.	857–860, 866, 881, 882	846, 857–862, 866, 878, 879
11.11.5 Trace the impact of, need for, and controversies associated with environmental conservation, expansion of the national park system, and the development of environmental protection laws, with particular attention to the interaction between environmental protection advocates and property rights advocates.	833–837, 896, 906, 907, 945, 946	346, 347, 803, 833–837, 896, 906, 907, 945, 946
11.11.6 Analyze the persistence of poverty and how different analyses of this issue influence welfare reform, health insurance reform, and other social policies.	724, 725, 853, 854, 895	724, 725, 853, 854, 895
11.11.7 Explain how the federal, state, and local governments have responded to demographic and social changes such as population shifts to the suburbs, racial concentrations in the cities, Frostbelt-to-Sunbelt migration, international migration, decline of family farms, increases in out-of-wedlock births, and drug abuse.	675–677, 724–729, 815, 817–819, 834–836, 853, 854, 898, 890, 905–907, 918, 919, 937, 939	675–677, 724–729, 815, 817–819, 834–836, 853, 854, 898, 890, 900, 905–907, 918, 919, 937, 939

Grades Nine Through Twelve Historical and Social Sciences Analysis Skills

The intellectual skills noted below are to be learned through, and applied to, the content standards for grades nine through twelve. They are to be assessed *only in conjunction with* the content standards in grades nine through twelve.

In addition to the standards for grades nine through twelve, students demonstrate the following intellectual, reasoning, reflection, and research skills.

Standards	Student Edition Pages	Teacher Edition Pages
Chronological and Spatial Thinking		
CS1. Students compare the present with the past, evaluating the consequences of past events and decisions and determining the lessons that were learned.	216, 217, 252, 253, 262, 263, 284, 285, 293, 320, 490, 491, 640, 641, 693, 735, 771, 800, 878, 879, 951	173, 187, 275, 283, 293, 304, 330, 378, 387, 407, 455, 470, 522, 543, 552, 648, 673, 750, 771, 798, 815, 837, 852, 875, 887, 917
CS2. Students analyze how change happens at different rates at different times; understand that some aspects can change while others remain the same; and understand that change is complicated and affects not only technology and politics but also values and beliefs.	97, 135, 180, 226, 227, 665, 696, 697, 734	97, 116, 173, 186, 220, 411, 445, 518, 538, 545, 561, 619, 665, 676, 689, 931, 953, 974
CS3. Students use a variety of maps and documents to interpret human movement, including major patterns of domestic and international migration, changing environmental preferences and settlement patterns, the frictions that develop between population groups, and the diffusion of ideas, technological innovations, and goods.	235, 247, 256, 262, 263, 287, 567, 621, 638, 639, 697, 735, 885, 900, 901, 924	100, 185, 193, 198, 235, 239, 241, 245, 255, 260, 263, 283, 304, 312, 355, 370, 371, 379, 386, 546, 589, 706, 811, 828, 885, 889, 950, 960
CS4. Students relate current events to the physical and human characteristics of places and regions.	171, 488, 489, 929	88, 171, 356, 864, 877, 929, 950
Historical Research, Evidence, and Point of View		
HR1. Students distinguish valid arguments from fallacious arguments in historical interpretations.	130, 132, 133, 228, 229, 308, 309, 318, 319, 321, 358, 359, 365, 396, 397, 436, 437, 460, 461, 484, 526, 527, 564, 565, 614, 615, 617, 637, 658, 659, 735, 764, 765, 780, 781, 894, 934	197, 319, 365, 381, 478, 514, 537, 591, 670, 692, 760, 825, 829, 856, 945, 1016
HR2. Students identify bias and prejudice in historical interpretations.	284, 285, 308, 309, 318, 319, 321, 358, 359, 396, 397, 416, 417, 436, 437, 484, 526, 527, 564, 565, 614, 615, 618, 619, 625, 637, 658, 659, 661, 694, 695, 703, 764, 765, 780, 781, 878, 879, 894	118, 130, 142, 166, 199, 213, 214, 215, 265, 441, 478, 484, 503, 571, 592, 625, 633, 645, 703, 717, 808, 829, 894, 960

Standards	Student Edition Pages	Teacher Edition Pages
HR3. Students evaluate major debates among historians concerning alternative interpretations of the past, including an analysis of authors' use of evidence and the distinctions between sound generalizations and misleading oversimplifications.	116, 252, 253, 308, 309, 321, 358, 359, 380, 396, 397, 436, 437, 484, 526, 527, 614, 615, 637, 711, 764, 765, 798, 799	130, 142, 157, 161, 176, 183, 197, 222, 241, 265, 280, 319, 368, 401, 471, 484, 500, 545, 558, 571, 613, 615, 633, 692, 717, 718, 784, 825, 829, 856, 918
HR4. Students construct and test hypotheses; collect, evaluate, and employ information from multiple primary and secondary sources; and apply it in oral and written presentations.	201, 230, 252, 253, 308, 309, 417, 467, 493, 548, 564, 565, 618, 619, 658, 659, 694, 695, 784, 785, 878, 879, 934, 962, 963	90, 99, 105, 110, 111, 122, 123, 131, 144, 147, 152, 157, 164, 184, 187, 196, 223, 224, 237, 257, 259, 269, 273, 289, 311, 332, 408, 446, 467, 470, 489, 502, 505, 522, 523, 551, 558, 560, 582, 590, 592, 600, 609, 616, 629, 643, 692, 710, 760, 784, 789, 790, 825, 829, 869, 890, 901, 907, 918, 940, 949, 1029

Historical Interpretation

Standards	Student Edition Pages	Teacher Edition Pages
HI1. Students show the connections, causal and otherwise, between particular historical events and larger social, economic, and political trends and developments.	180, 181, 226, 227, 231, 252, 253, 258, 374, 399, 424, 425, 443, 541, 567, 571, 621, 649, 697, 739, 767, 797, 805, 821, 843, 856, 891, 922, 923, 951	99, 110, 122, 127, 159, 176, 177, 187, 193, 194, 198, 200, 203, 212, 223, 224, 255, 260, 268, 272, 296, 301, 341, 357, 369, 407, 409, 411, 430, 443, 446, 458, 461, 470, 476, 486, 499, 500, 503, 512, 514, 524, 537, 540, 558, 588, 589, 599, 601, 610, 633, 636, 649, 739, 750, 784, 805, 825, 833, 837, 865, 877, 887, 896, 917, 938, 956, 957, 960
HI2. Students recognize the complexity of historical causes and effects, including the limitations on determining cause and effect.	114, 115, 200, 201, 225, 268, 292, 393, 470, 535, 658, 659, 694, 695, 756, 776, 840, 841, 878, 879, 894, 922, 923, 951	114, 185, 224, 255, 265, 272, 297, 301, 303, 513, 521, 524, 530, 535, 543, 545, 547, 573, 582, 601, 602, 609, 611, 655, 692, 784, 917, 960
HI3. Students interpret past events and issues within the context in which an event unfolded rather than solely in terms of present-day norms and values.	114, 115, 126, 132, 133, 190, 191, 202, 203, 204, 214, 216, 217, 225, 228, 229, 252, 253, 258, 284, 285, 287, 361, 405, 416, 417, 439, 563, 564, 565, 618, 619, 620, 637, 649, 776, 780, 781, 784, 785, 798, 799, 840, 841, 962, 963	100, 114, 127, 173, 176, 177, 181, 195, 207, 214, 216, 223, 224, 241, 255, 268, 272, 308, 318, 368, 389, 405, 453, 500, 503, 504, 515, 526, 543, 546, 550, 551, 577, 583, 592, 612, 613, 615, 629, 633, 636, 643, 644, 645, 690, 743, 751, 784, 788, 789, 816, 860, 865, 877, 916, 917
HI4. Students understand the meaning, implication, and impact of historical events and recognize that events could have taken other directions.	114, 115, 215, 216, 217, 325, 361, 555, 566, 602, 603, 605, 620, 849, 880, 951	110, 114, 115, 127, 145, 175, 195, 207, 215, 241, 268, 298, 306, 325, 331, 378, 380, 388, 401, 516, 540, 543, 573, 582, 583, 599, 601, 602, 610, 611, 636, 646, 655, 690, 784, 788, 837, 849, 887, 916, 917, 957
HI5. Students analyze human modifications of landscapes and examine the resulting environmental policy issues.	259, 346, 347, 488, 489, 497, 508, 509, 529, 837, 900, 901, 965	88, 89, 100, 489, 497, 509, 782, 833, 834, 835, 901, 921
HI6. Students conduct cost-benefit analyses and apply basic economic indicators to analyze the aggregate economic behavior of the U.S. economy.	176, 209, 251, 296, 344, 345, 353, 354, 450, 451, 454, 470, 471, 472, 473, 501, 502, 503, 504, 505, 506, 507, 513, 514, 515, 516, 517, 524, 525, 708, 836, 864, 865, 895, 896, 918, 919, 936, 937	186, 275, 276, 306, 307, 443, 452, 524, 592, 839, 865, 898, 922, 943

Eleventh Grade and Twelfth Grade English–Language Arts Content Standards

The following English-Language Arts standards are addressed in the Student Edition and the Teacher Wraparound Edition of *The American Vision: Modern Times*.

Standards	Student Edition Pages	Teacher Edition Pages
Reading		
11RC2.4 Make warranted and reasonable assertions about the author's arguments by using elements of the text to defend and clarify interpretations.	204, 321, 596, 621, 631, 735, 781, 822, 912, 925, 965	117, 189, 252, 261, 282, 469, 472, 473, 475, 499, 500, 513, 564, 576, 581, 595, 633, 651, 724, 741, 746, 751, 851, 866, 868, 874, 978
11RC2.5 Analyze an author's implicit and explicit philosophical assumptions and beliefs about a subject.	204, 231, 321, 338, 399, 439, 735, 781, 912, 925	93, 185, 203, 234, 240, 249, 253, 265, 301, 314, 330, 349, 358, 359, 457, 559, 564, 571, 581, 614, 633, 746, 773, 841, 855, 879, 1021
11RL3.2 Analyze the way in which the theme or meaning of a selection represents a view or comment on life, using textual evidence to support the claim.	434	117, 296, 306, 314, 344, 409, 432, 433, 434, 457, 460, 501, 539, 651, 977
11RL3.4 Analyze ways in which poets use imagery, personification, figures of speech, and sounds to evoke readers' emotions.	204, 434, 439	104, 432–434, 653, 689, 755, 977
11RL3.8 Analyze the clarity and consistency of political assumptions in a selection of literary works or essays on a topic (e.g., suffrage, women's role in organized labor). (Political approach)	567, 631	282, 855, 978
Writing		
11WS1.1 Demonstrate an understanding of the elements of discourse (e.g., purpose, speaker, audience, form) when completing narrative, expository, persuasive, or descriptive writing assignments.	108, 119, 181, 189, 201, 225, 287, 335, 351, 357, 399, 431, 493, 541, 578, 593, 617, 621, 639, 649, 661, 671, 729, 783, 891, 941	122, 129, 151, 193, 200, 212, 213, 215, 229, 244, 272, 302, 314, 349, 419, 499, 546, 553, 577, 633, 654, 709, 745, 778, 779, 874, 909, 921, 945
11WS1.2 Use point of view, characterization, style (e.g., use of irony), and related elements for specific rhetorical and aesthetic purposes.	215, 242, 261, 270, 307, 315, 335, 389, 395, 421, 439, 487, 563, 578, 621, 776, 856, 862	101, 174, 212, 303, 393, 410, 451, 458, 485, 497, 511, 539, 553, 619, 628, 712, 745
11WS1.3 Structure ideas and arguments in a sustained, persuasive, and sophisticated way and support them with precise and relevant examples.	131, 299, 315, 525	85, 87, 115, 180, 184, 198, 207, 245, 253, 274, 296, 299, 337, 345, 359, 394, 437, 447, 472, 491, 517, 519, 552, 561, 562, 575, 615, 638, 646, 652, 658, 671, 710, 729, 754, 779, 787, 860, 868, 897, 908, 941, 945, 950, 1010
11WS1.5 Use language in natural, fresh, and vivid ways to establish a specific tone.	381, 593, 639	282, 314, 499, 502, 629, 690

Correlation to the English–Language Arts Standards

Standards	Student Edition Pages	Teacher Edition Pages
11WS1.6 Develop presentations by using clear research questions and creative and critical research strategies (e.g., field studies, oral histories, interviews, experiments, electronic sources).	201, 399, 417, 548, 605, 661, 693, 735	104, 144, 196, 282, 382, 422, 451, 457, 530, 580, 584, 595, 616, 731, 733, 762, 784, 798, 933
11WA2.1 Write fictional, autobiographical, or biographical narratives:	108, 119, 215	174, 179, 199, 509, 678, 716
a. Narrate a sequence of events and communicate their significance to the audience.	231, 473, 555, 617, 621, 661, 719, 797, 831, 837, 899, 919, 961	103, 106, 176, 186, 191, 238, 255, 279, 369, 386, 481, 521, 533, 581, 587, 613, 619, 635, 718, 727, 730, 741, 764, 872, 895, 963, 978
b. Locate scenes and incidents in specific places.	307, 320, 797, 870, 961	191, 279, 581, 587, 596, 599, 746, 764, 822, 872
c. Describe with concrete sensory details the sights, sounds, and smells of a scene and the specific actions, movements, gestures, and feelings of the characters; use interior monologue to depict the characters' feelings.	389, 395, 479, 487, 517, 555, 756	90, 101, 186, 195, 211, 238, 239, 255, 303, 396, 477, 485, 491, 595, 613, 618, 727, 742, 746, 781, 977
e. Make effective use of descriptions of appearance, images, shifting perspectives, and sensory details.	479, 585, 617, 719, 812, 875, 934	193, 211, 239, 383, 822
11WA2.2 Write responses to literature:		104, 203, 296, 301, 306, 433, 527, 823
a. Demonstrate a comprehensive understanding of the significant ideas in works or passages.	345, 909	107, 120, 689, 741, 821, 879
c. Support important ideas and viewpoints through accurate and detailed references to the text and to other works.	507, 657	107, 573, 689, 723, 741, 821
11WA2.3 Write reflective compositions:		145, 293
a. Explore the significance of personal experiences, events, conditions, or concerns by using rhetorical strategies (e.g., narration, description, exposition, persuasion).	459, 541, 555, 649, 747, 819, 919, 946	104, 140, 166, 388, 460, 531, 618, 836, 963
b. Draw comparisons between specific incidents and broader themes that illustrate the writer's important beliefs or generalizations about life.	251, 671, 946	88, 105, 115, 142, 154, 160, 315, 461, 544, 554, 557, 765, 811, 819, 828, 936, 959
c. Maintain a balance in describing individual incidents and relate those incidents to more general and abstract ideas.	455, 679	274, 665, 809, 819, 939, 953
11WA2.4 Write historical investigation reports:	108, 119, 201, 261, 270	132, 173, 224, 227, 239, 248, 316, 334, 355, 357, 436, 600, 750, 774, 908, 923
a. Use exposition, narration, description, argumentation, exposition, or some combination of rhetorical strategies to support the main proposition.	181, 225, 320, 374, 413, 439, 448, 493, 685, 711, 735, 791, 801, 925	112, 113, 123, 128, 153, 156, 196, 223, 244, 272, 295, 342, 347, 354, 377, 383, 385, 387, 392, 394, 423, 511, 604, 665, 790, 810, 855, 866, 903, 904, 961
b. Analyze several historical records of a single event, examining critical relationships between elements of the research topic.	548, 605	117, 142, 158, 176, 185, 280, 283, 305, 342, 377, 607, 641, 656, 720, 956, 1027
d. Include information from all relevant perspectives and take into consideration the validity and reliability of sources.	548, 925	87, 112, 157, 161, 176, 223, 269, 313, 347, 429, 451, 491, 720, 746, 828, 855, 860, 866, 891, 944, 955

Scope and Sequence

Chapter	1	2	3	4	
Big Ideas					
Political philosophies and major events influence the formation of constitutional governments.	Section 2				
A written contract between the people and their government can preserve natural rights and allow for change over time.	Section 3				
Differences in economic, political, and social beliefs and practices can lead to division within a nation and have lasting consequences.		Sections 2, 3, 4			
The Industrial Revolution changed the face of America.			Sections 2, 3		
America's military and economic strength made it a world power.				Section 3	
People react to periods of breathtaking social and cultural change in different ways.			Sections 4, 5		
Social and economic crises lead to new roles for government.		Section 5			
The fate of nations is forever changed by monumental world events.				Section 2	
International competition can lead to conflict and cooperation.				Section 1	
The quest for equality is eternal.					
Societies change over time.	Section 1	Section 1	Section 1		

5	6	7	8	9	10
		Sections 1, 2, 3			
Sections 1, 2, 3, 4				Section 3	Sections 1, 2, 3
	Sections 1, 2, 3, 4				
			Sections 1, 2, 3	Sections 1, 2	

Chapter	11	12	13	14	15
Big Ideas					
People react to periods of breathtaking social and cultural change in different ways.					
A written contract between the people and their government can preserve natural rights and allow for change over time.					
Differences in economic, political, and social beliefs and practices can lead to division within a nation and have lasting consequences.					
The Industrial Revolution changed the face of America.					
America's military and economic strength made it a world power.					
People react to periods of breathtaking social and cultural change in different ways.		Sections 1, 3			
Social and economic crises lead to new roles for government.			Section 3		
The fate of nations is forever changed by monumental world events.	Sections 2, 3, 4	Sections 2, 4, 5	Sections 2, 4	Section 1	Section 2
International competition can lead to conflict and cooperation.			Section 1		
The quest for equality is eternal.					
Societies change over time.	Section 1			Sections 2, 3, 4	Sections 1, 3

16	17	18	19	20	21
Sections 1, 3	Section 3				
Section 2		Section 2	Section 3		
	Sections 1, 2, 4				Section 5
			Section 1	Sections 2, 4	Section 3
		Section 3			
		Sections 1, 4	Sections 2, 4	Sections 1, 3	Sections 1, 2, 4

A Guide to Students and Families

How do I Succeed in United States History?

Welcome to United States History and Geography: Continuity and Change in the Twentieth Century and to Glencoe's *The American Vision: Modern Times*. The content of this course focuses on the major turning points in the shaping of the modern United States, from 1900 to the present. You will be viewing and interpreting periods in United States history from various perspectives, including historical, geographic, political, economic, and cultural. Together, these perspectives can help you to understand how the past has led to our present and to appreciate your role in shaping our future.

Your textbook includes a variety of tools designed to help you be successful as you study modern United States history. One of the most valuable of these is a list of the standards and objectives that you will be expected to master by the end of the school year. These are called the California Grade 11 Content Standards for United States History and Geography: Continuity and Change in the Twentieth Century, and are listed on pages 4–12 of this book. This book also includes a list of the California Historical and Social Sciences Analysis Skills that you will be expected to master. These are listed on pages 13–14.

Knowing what you are expected to learn from the very beginning of the year will help focus your study of United States history. It will also help you and your family see when you might need extra help in mastering the concepts of a particular unit of study. Such extra help will ensure that your study of United States history will be both enjoyable and successful.

▼ **California State Capitol, Sacramento**

What are the California History–Social Science Standards?

The California State Board of Education approved the History–Social Science Framework, with Content Standards, on October 11, 2004. The purpose of the History–Social Science Framework and the Content Standards is to provide you, the student, with expectations for achievement in California. These standards spell out what you should learn in social sciences from kindergarten through grade twelve. These Content Standards represent the knowledge and skills you need to achieve in order to succeed in the world of work or college.

Why do the California History–Social Science Standards matter to me?

The California History–Social Science Standards are the things you should learn and be able to do as you take the course. The standards are specific for each grade and subject. Your teachers base their lessons and tests on the California History–Social Science Standards. Teachers also pay special attention to the Historical and Social Sciences Analysis Skills. Unlike the Content Standards, the analysis skills are the same for grades nine through twelve.

So, to be successful in this course, you may want to read over the Content Standards and Analysis Skills with your family. (These Content Standards and Analysis Skills are listed on pages 4–12.) Although some of the names and terms may not be familiar to you at first, you and your family can outline some steps to take to achieve proficiency. As you take this course, review the standards from time to time to help the things you are learning fall into place.

What is included on the following pages?

California History–Social Science Standards for Grade 11: United States History and Geography: Continuity and Change in the Twentieth Century and Grades Nine Through Twelve Historical and Social Sciences Analysis Skills

- Pages 4–12 include a listing of all of the California Content Standards for this course.

- Pages 13–14 include a listing of the Historical and Social Sciences Analysis Skills for grades nine through twelve.

- Turn to page 15 to see how Glencoe's *The American Vision: Modern Times* will help you learn the Content Standards, the Analysis Skills, and how to be successful in this course.

▼ Joshua Tree National Park

The California Grade 11 Content Standards tell you what you need to learn and be able to do as you complete your course in United States History and Geography: Continuity and Change in the Twentieth Century. The course is designed to cover important events that have shaped the United States, from 1900 to the present. Reading through these standards with your parents or family will help you understand the goals for your course—and help you to achieve them.

Grade Eleven

United States History and Geography: Continuity and Change in the Twentieth Century

11.1 Students analyze the significant events in the founding of the nation and its attempts to realize the philosophy of government described in the Declaration of Independence.

11.1.1 Describe the Enlightenment and the rise of democratic ideas as the context in which the nation was founded.

11.1.2 Analyze the ideological origins of the American Revolution, the Founding Fathers' philosophy of divinely bestowed unalienable natural rights, the debates on the drafting and ratification of the Constitution, and the addition of the Bill of Rights.

11.1.3 Understand the history of the Constitution after 1787 with emphasis on federal versus state authority and growing democratization.

11.1.4 Examine the effects of the Civil War and Reconstruction and of the industrial revolution, including demographic shifts and the emergence in the late nineteenth century of the United States as a world power.

▼ **Lake Tahoe**

11.2 Students analyze the relationship among the rise of industrialization, large-scale rural-to-urban migration, and massive immigration from Southern and Eastern Europe.

11.2.1 Know the effects of industrialization on living and working conditions, including the portrayal of working conditions and food safety in Upton Sinclair's *The Jungle*.

11.2.2 Describe the changing landscape, including the growth of cities linked by industry and trade, and the development of cities divided according to race, ethnicity, and class.

11.2.3 Trace the effect of the Americanization movement.

11.2.4 Analyze the effect of urban political machines and responses to them by immigrants and middle-class reformers.

11.2.5 Discuss corporate mergers that produced trusts and cartels and the economic and political policies of industrial leaders.

11.2.6 Trace the economic development of the United States and its emergence as a major industrial power, including its gains from trade and the advantages of its physical geography.

11.2.7 Analyze the similarities and differences between the ideologies of Social Darwinism and Social Gospel (e.g., using biographies of William Graham Sumner, Billy Sunday, Dwight L. Moody).

11.2.8 Examine the effects of political programs and activities of Populists.

11.2.9 Understand the effect of political programs and activities of the Progressives (e.g., federal regulation of railroad transport, Children's Bureau, the Sixteenth Amendment, Theodore Roosevelt, Hiram Johnson).

11.3 Students analyze the role religion played in the founding of America, its lasting moral, social and political impacts, and issues regarding religious liberty.

11.3.1 Describe the contributions of various religious groups to American civic principles and social reform movements (e.g., civil and human rights, individual responsibility and the work ethic, antimonarchy and self-rule, worker protection, family-centered communities).

11.3.2 Analyze the great religious revivals and the leaders involved in them, including the First Great Awakening, the Second Great Awakening, the Civil War revivals, the Social Gospel Movement, the rise of Christian liberal theology in the nineteenth century, the impact of the Second Vatican Council, and the rise of Christian fundamentalism in current times.

11.3.3 Cite incidences of religious intolerance in the United States (e.g., persecution of Mormons, anti-Catholic sentiment, anti-Semitism).

11.3.4 Discuss the expanding religious pluralism in the United States and California that resulted from large-scale immigration in the twentieth century.

11.3.5 Describe the principles of religious liberty found in the Establishment and Free Exercise clauses of the First Amendment, including the debate on the issue of separation of church and state.

11.4 **Students trace the rise of the United States to its role as a world power in the twentieth century.**

11.4.1 List the purpose and the effects of the Open Door policy.

11.4.2 Describe the Spanish-American War and U.S. expansion in the South Pacific.

11.4.3 Discuss America's role in the Panama Revolution and the building of the Panama Canal.

11.4.4 Explain Theodore Roosevelt's Big Stick diplomacy, William Taft's Dollar Diplomacy, and Woodrow Wilson's Moral Diplomacy, drawing on relevant speeches.

11.4.5 Analyze the political, economic and social ramifications of World War I on the home front.

11.4.6 Trace the declining role of Great Britain and the expanding role of the United States in world affairs after World War II.

▼ **Death Valley National Park**

6

11.5 Students analyze the major political, social, economic, technological, and cultural developments of the 1920s.

11.5.1 Discuss the policies of Presidents Warren Harding, Calvin Coolidge, and Herbert Hoover.

11.5.2 Analyze the international and domestic events, interests, and philosophies that prompted attacks on civil liberties, including the Palmer Raids, Marcus Garvey's "back-to-Africa" movement, the Ku Klux Klan, and immigration quotas and the responses of organizations such as the American Civil Liberties Union, the National Association for the Advancement of Colored People, and the Anti-Defamation League to those attacks.

11.5.3 Examine the passage of the Eighteenth Amendment to the Constitution and the Volstead Act (Prohibition).

11.5.4 Analyze the passage of the Nineteenth Amendment and the changing role of women in society.

11.5.5 Describe the Harlem Renaissance and new trends in literature, music, and art, with special attention to the work of writers (e.g., Zora Neale Hurston, Langston Hughes).

11.5.6 Trace the growth and effects of radio and movies and their role in the worldwide diffusion of popular culture.

11.5.7 Discuss the rise of mass production techniques, the growth of cities, the impact of new technologies (e.g., the automobile, electricity), and the resulting prosperity and effect on the American landscape.

11.6 Students analyze the different explanations for the Great Depression and how the New Deal fundamentally changed the role of the federal government.

11.6.1 Describe the monetary issues of the late nineteenth and early twentieth centuries that gave rise to the establishment of the Federal Reserve and the weaknesses in key sectors of the economy in the late 1920s.

11.6.2 Understand the explanations of the principal causes of the Great Depression and the steps taken by the Federal Reserve, Congress and Presidents Herbert Hoover and Franklin Delano Roosevelt to combat the economic crisis.

11.6.3 Discuss the human toll of the Depression, natural disasters, and unwise agricultural practices and their effects on the depopulation of rural regions and on political movements of the left and right, with particular attention to the Dust Bowl refugees and their social and economic impacts in California.

11.6.4 Analyze the effects of and the controversies arising from New Deal economic policies and the expanded role of the federal government in society and the economy since the 1930s (e.g., Works Progress Administration, Social Security, National Labor Relations Board, farm programs, regional development policies, and energy development projects such as the Tennessee Valley Authority, California Central Valley Project, and Bonneville Dam).

11.6.5 Trace the advances and retreats of organized labor, from the creation of the American Federation of Labor and the Congress of Industrial Organizations to current issues of a postindustrial multinational economy, including the United Farm Workers in California.

11.7 **Students analyze America's participation in World War II.**

11.7.1 Examine the origins of American involvement in the war, with an emphasis on the events that precipitated the attack on Pearl Harbor.

11.7.2 Explain U.S. and Allied wartime strategy, including the major battles of Midway, Normandy, Iwo Jima, Okinawa, and the Battle of the Bulge.

11.7.3 Identify the role and sacrifices of individual American soldiers, as well as the unique contributions of the special fighting forces (e.g., the Tuskegee Airmen, the 442nd Regimental Combat team, the Navajo Code Talkers).

11.7.4 Analyze Roosevelt's foreign policies during World War II (e.g., Four Freedoms speech).

▼ **Redwood National Forest**

11.7.5 Discuss the constitutional issues and impact of events on the U.S. home front, including the internment of Japanese Americans (e.g., *Fred Korematsu* v. *United States of America*) and the restrictions on German and Italian resident aliens; the response of the administration to Hitler's atrocities against Jews and other groups; the roles of women in military production; the roles and growing political demands of African Americans.

11.7.6 Describe major developments in aviation, weaponry, communication, and medicine and the war's impact on the location of American industry and use of resources.

11.7.7 Discuss the decision to drop atomic bombs and the consequences of the decision (Hiroshima and Nagasaki).

11.7.8 Analyze the effect of massive aid given to Western Europe under the Marshall Plan to rebuild itself after the war, and the importance of a rebuilt Europe to the U.S. economy.

11.8 **Students analyze the economic boom and social transformation of post–World War II America.**

11.8.1 Trace the growth of service sector, white collar, and professional sector jobs in business and government.

11.8.2 Describe the significance of Mexican immigration and its relationship to the agricultural economy, especially in California.

11.8.3 Examine Truman's labor policy and congressional reaction to it.

11.8.4 Analyze new federal government spending on defense, welfare, interest on the national debt, and federal and state spending on education, including the California Master Plan.

11.8.5 Describe the increased powers of the presidency in response to the Great Depression, World War II, and the Cold War.

11.8.6 Discuss the diverse environmental regions of North America, their relationship to local economies, and the origins and prospects of environmental problems in those regions.

11.8.7 Describe the effects on society and the economy of technological developments since 1945, including the computer revolution, changes in communication, advances in medicine, and improvements in agricultural technology.

11.8.8 Discuss forms of popular culture, with emphasis on their origins and geographic diffusion (e.g., jazz and other forms of popular music, professional sports, architectural and artistic styles).

11.9 Students analyze the U.S. foreign policy since World War II.

11.9.1 Discuss the establishment of the United Nations and International Declaration of Human Rights, International Monetary Fund, World Bank, and General Agreement on Tariffs and Trade (GATT), and their importance in shaping modern Europe and maintaining peace and international order.

11.9.2 Understand the role of military alliances, including NATO and SEATO, in deterring communist aggression and maintaining security during the Cold War.

11.9.3 Trace the origins and geopolitical consequences (foreign and domestic) of the Cold War and containment policy, including the following: the era of McCarthyism, instances of domestic Communism (e.g., Alger Hiss) and blacklisting; the Truman Doctrine; the Berlin Blockade; the Korean War; the Bay of Pigs Invasion and the Cuban Missile Crisis; atomic testing in the American West, the "mutual assured destruction" doctrine, and disarmament policies; the Vietnam War; Latin American policy.

11.9.4 List the effects of foreign policy on domestic policies and vice versa (e.g., protests during the war in Vietnam, the "nuclear freeze" movement).

11.9.5 Analyze the role of the Reagan administration and other factors in the victory of the West in the Cold War.

11.9.6 Describe U.S. Middle East policy and its strategic, political, and economic interests, including those related to the Gulf War.

11.9.7 Examine relations between the United States and Mexico in the twentieth century, including key economic, political, immigration, and environmental issues.

▼ **San Diego**

11.10 Students analyze the development of federal civil rights and voting rights.

11.10.1 Explain how demands of African Americans helped produce a stimulus for civil rights, including President Roosevelt's ban on racial discrimination in defense industries in 1941, and how African Americans' service in World War II produced a stimulus for President Truman's decision to end segregation in the armed forces in 1948.

11.10.2 Examine and analyze the key events, policies, and court cases in the evolution of civil rights, including *Dred Scott* v. *Sanford, Plessy* v. *Ferguson, Brown* v. *Board of Education, Regents of the University of California* v. *Bakke,* and California Proposition 209.

11.10.3 Describe the collaboration on legal strategy between African American and white civil rights lawyers to end racial segregation in higher education.

11.10.4 Examine the roles of civil rights advocates (e.g., A. Philip Randolph, Martin Luther King, Jr., Malcolm X, Thurgood Marshall, James Farmer, Rosa Parks), including the significance of Martin Luther King, Jr.'s "Letter from Birmingham Jail" and "I Have a Dream" speech.

11.10.5 Discuss the diffusion of the civil rights movement of African Americans from the churches of the rural South and the urban North, including the resistance to racial desegregation in Little Rock and Birmingham, and how the advances influenced the agendas, strategies, and effectiveness of the quests of American Indians, Asian Americans, and Hispanic Americans for civil rights and equal opportunities.

11.10.6 Analyze the passage and effects of civil rights and voting rights legislation (e.g., 1964 Civil Rights Act, Voting Rights Act of 1965) and the Twenty-Fourth Amendment, with an emphasis on equality of access to education and to the political process.

11.10.7 Analyze the women's rights movement from the era of Elizabeth Cady Stanton and Susan B. Anthony and the passage of the Nineteenth Amendment to the movement launched in the 1960s, including differing perspectives on the roles of women.

History–Social Science Standards

11.11 Students analyze the major social problems and domestic policy issues in contemporary American society.

11.11.1 Discuss the reasons for the nation's changing immigration policy, with emphasis on how the Immigration Act of 1965 and successor acts have transformed American society.

11.11.2 Discuss the significant domestic policy speeches of Truman, Eisenhower, Kennedy, Johnson, Nixon, Carter, Reagan, Bush, and Clinton (e.g., with regard to education, civil rights, economic policy, environmental policy).

11.11.3 Describe the changing roles of women in society as reflected in the entry of more women into the labor force and the changing family structure.

11.11.4 Explain the constitutional crisis originating from the Watergate scandal.

11.11.5 Trace the impact of, need for, and controversies associated with environmental conservation, expansion of the national park system, and the development of environmental protection laws, with particular attention to the interaction between environmental protection advocates and property right advocates.

11.11.6 Analyze the persistence of poverty and how different analyses of this issue influence welfare reform, health insurance reform, and other social policies.

11.11.7 Explain how the federal, state, and local governments have responded to demographic and social changes such as population shifts to the suburbs, racial concentrations in the cities, Frostbelt-to-Sunbelt migration, international migration, decline of family farms, increases in out-of-wedlock births, and drug abuse.

▼ **Orange Grove and Sierra Nevada**

The California Content Standards also address the skills you need in order to master the study of United States history. Read over these skills standards so you can be familiar with them. This will give you a good idea of what skills you will acquire as you complete your course in United States history.

Historical and Social Sciences Analysis Skills

The intellectual skills noted below are to be learned through, and applied to, the content standards for grades nine through twelve. They are to be assessed *only in conjunction with* the content standards in grades nine through twelve.

In addition to the standards for grades nine through twelve, students demonstrate the following intellectual, reasoning, reflection, and research skills.

Chronological and Spatial Thinking

CS 1 Students compare the present with the past, evaluating the consequences of past events and decisions and determining the lessons that were learned.

CS 2 Students analyze how change happens at different rates at different times; understand that some aspects can change while others remain the same; and understand that change is complicated and affects not only technology and politics but also values and beliefs.

CS 3 Students use a variety of maps and documents to interpret human movement, including major patterns of domestic and international migration, changing environmental preferences and settlement patterns, the frictions that develop between population groups, and the diffusion of ideas, technological innovations, and goods.

CS 4 Students relate current events to the physical and human characteristics of places and regions.

▼ **Golden Gate Bridge, San Francisco**

13

Historical Research, Evidence, and Point of View

HR 1 Students distinguish valid arguments from fallacious arguments in historical interpretations.

HR 2 Students identify bias and prejudice in historical interpretations.

HR 3 Students evaluate major debates among historians concerning alternative interpretations of the past, including an analysis of authors'

use of evidence and the distinctions between sound generalizations and misleading oversimplifications.

HR 4 Students construct and test hypotheses; collect, evaluate, and employ information from multiple primary and secondary sources; and apply it in oral and written presentations.

Historical Interpretation

HI 1 Students show the connections, causal and otherwise, between particular historical events and larger social, economic, and political trends and developments.

HI 2 Students recognize the complexity of historical causes and effects, including the limitations on determining cause and effect.

HI 3 Students interpret past events and issues within the context in which an event unfolded rather than solely in terms of present-day norms and values.

HI 4 Students understand the meaning, implication, and impact of historical events and recognize that events could have taken other directions.

HI 5 Students analyze human modifications of landscapes and examine the resulting environmental policy issues.

HI 6 Students conduct cost-benefit analyses and apply basic economic indicators to analyze the aggregate economic behavior of the U.S. economy.

▼ **Fisherman's Wharf, Monterey Bay**

How does Glencoe's *The American Vision: Modern Times* Help Me Practice the Standards?

Glencoe's *The American Vision: Modern Times* has been carefully organized to ensure that the textbook's content, features, maps, and activities provide comprehensive coverage of all History–Social Science Standards for Grade Eleven. To further help you, Glencoe has reproduced these History–Social Science Standards in the previous pages to help you relate the major concepts that you should know to the textbook. For example, if you turn back to page 8 and examine the first portion of Standard 11.7, you will find the following:

11.7 Students analyze America's participation in World War II.

11.7.1 Examine the origins of American involvement in the war, with an emphasis on the events that precipitated the attack on Pearl Harbor.

11.7.2 Explain U.S. and Allied wartime strategy, including the major battles of Midway, Normandy, Iwo Jima, Okinawa, and the Battle of the Bulge.

Each History–Social Science Standard begins with a general statement that will help you identify the broad historical time period and subject matter to which that standard refers. For example, Standard 11.7 is concerned with the participation of the United States in World War II. By understanding that, you know in which chapters of the textbook you will find information relevant to this History–Social Science Standard.

Standards are further divided into more supporting standards that relate to the topic and help you learn more about the historical context. Standard 11.7 is divided into eight supporting standards, two of which are listed above.

    Supporting Standard 11.7.1 Examine the origins of American involvement in the war, with an emphasis on the events that precipitated the attack on Pearl Harbor.
    Supporting Standard 11.7.2 Explain U.S. and Allied wartime strategy, including the major battles of Midway, Normandy, Iwo Jima, Okinawa, and the Battle of the Bulge.

How should you use these standards? Try the following strategies:

- Read through the standards before you begin your study of each chapter. Based on the content of that chapter, decide which standards relate to the material you are about to read. Make it your goal to understand the standards by the end of the chapter.

- Keep these standards in mind as you read the chapter and take notes on the relevant information you find.

- Review these standards after you complete the chapter to see if you have indeed learned what you need to know.

A Guide to Students and Families

How do I succeed in United States History?

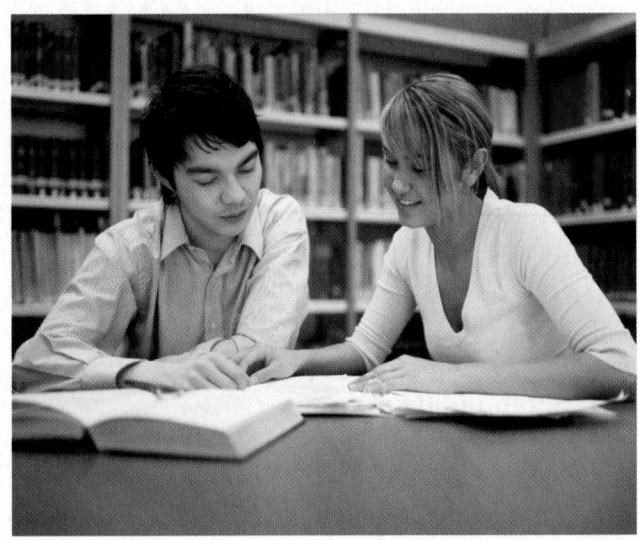

As you study the history of the United States in the twentieth century, you are building your understanding of our nation today. At the same time, you are learning many other skills that you will need in order to succeed after you graduate from high school.

Reading is one of the skills you have been learning and honing throughout your school years. Learning the alphabet and making sense of words was one of the first skills you learned. Writing also has been an integral part of your learning over the past years. Writing has allowed you to put your thoughts on paper and has helped you show your teachers what you have learned.

These skills serve you well because they make it possible for you to do many other things. While reading and writing are essential skills for the English and Language Arts classrooms, they are equally important in other classrooms. Without the ability to read, you cannot learn math, history, or sciences. Without the ability to write, you cannot take a math test, write a paper about the Great Depression, or create a lab report in biology.

▼ **Big Sur**

How are the English–Language Arts Standards Addressed in My Textbook?

Your textbook addresses all of the History–Social Science Standards for grade eleven. It also covers many of the English–Language Arts Standards. Reading the textbook helps you with your reading skills. You will find a Reading Skill in each chapter that introduces a specific strategy to improve your reading. You can also practice your writing and presentation skills with the many writing activities offered in the section and chapter assessments.

What are the English–Language Arts Standards?

The California English–Language Arts Standards for eleventh grade continue the English Language Arts curriculum in California. You should build on what you have learned in previous grades. The English–Language Arts Standards include Reading, Writing, and Listening and Speaking.

Why do English–Language Arts Standards Matter to Me?

The English–Language Arts Standards address essential skills that help you succeed not only in school, but also in life after you graduate. Almost all jobs require basic reading and writing skills. These skills also are essential in college or other post-secondary education. Because of their importance, reading and writing have become a major focus of education not only in the English and Language Arts classroom, but also in other curriculum areas. Glencoe's *The American Vision: Modern Times* provides many opportunities to practice reading, writing, and speaking skills.

Glencoe's **The American Vision: Modern Times** *will help you practice many of the California English–Language Arts Standards for eleventh grade. The standards which are addressed in your textbook are listed below and can be found throughout this textbook. Become familiar with these standards as you take this course. This knowledge will help you master the English–Language Arts Standards for eleventh grade.*

Reading

11RC2.4 Make warranted and reasonable assertions about the author's arguments by using elements of the text to defend and clarify interpretations.

11RC2.5 Analyze an author's implicit and explicit philosophical assumptions and beliefs about a subject.

11RL3.2 Analyze the way in which the theme or meaning of a selection represents a view or comment on life, using textual evidence to support the claim.

11RL3.4 Analyze ways in which poets use imagery, personification, figures of speech, and sounds to evoke readers' emotions.

11RL3.8 Analyze the clarity and consistency of political assumptions in a selection of literary works or essays on a topic (e.g., suffrage, women's role in organized labor). (Political approach)

Writing

11WS1.1 Demonstrate an understanding of the elements of discourse (e.g., purpose, speaker, audience, form) when completing narrative, expository, persuasive, or descriptive writing assignments.

11WS1.2 Use point of view, characterization, style (e.g., use of irony), and related elements for specific rhetorical and aesthetic purposes.

11WS1.3 Structure ideas and arguments in a sustained, persuasive, and sophisticated way and support them with precise and relevant examples.

11WS1.5 Use language in natural, fresh, and vivid ways to establish a specific tone.

11WS1.6 Develop presentations by using clear research questions and creative and critical research strategies (e.g., field studies, oral histories, interviews, experiments, electronic sources).

11WA2.1 Write fictional, autobiographical, or biographical narratives:
a. Narrate a sequence of events and communicate their significance to the audience.
b. Locate scenes and incidents in specific places.
c. Describe with concrete sensory details the sights, sounds, and smells of a scene and the specific actions, movements, gestures, and feelings of the characters; use interior monologue to depict the characters' feelings.
e. Make effective use of descriptions of appearance, images, shifting perspectives, and sensory details.

11WA2.2 Write responses to literature:
  a. Demonstrate a comprehensive understanding of the significant ideas in works or passages.
  c. Support important ideas and viewpoints through accurate and detailed references to the text and to other works.

11WA2.3 Write reflective compositions:
  a. Explore the significance of personal experiences, events, conditions, or concerns by using rhetorical strategies (e.g., narration, description, exposition, persuasion).
  b. Draw comparisons between specific incidents and broader themes that illustrate the writer's important beliefs or generalizations about life.
  c. Maintain a balance in describing individual incidents and relate those incidents to more general and abstract ideas.

11WA2.4 Write historical investigation reports:
  a. Use exposition, narration, description, argumentation, exposition, or some combination of rhetorical strategies to support the main proposition.
  b. Analyze several historical records of a single event, examining critical relationships between elements of the research topic.
  d. Include information from all relevant perspectives and take into consideration the validity and reliability of sources.

How Does Glencoe's *The American Vision: Modern Times* Help Me Practice the Standards?

When you study American history with Glencoe's *The American Vision: Modern Times,* you are also practicing many of the English–Language Arts Standards for eleventh grade. Your textbook includes many opportunities to practice reading, writing, and speaking skills. Those standards that are addressed in Glencoe's *The American Vision: Modern Times* appear on pages 18–19.

- Each Section Assessment includes a writing prompt in the Writing About History box. The writing prompts can be short journal entries, letters, or brief reports.
- Each Chapter Assessment contains a Writing About History component with several activities. Many of these activities require you to do research either on the Internet or in the library and ask you to give a presentation about your research to your class.
- The American Literature feature in each unit, along with other features in your textbook, gives you the opportunity to practice your reading skills. These features also present you with additional activities that include writing.
- The SkillBuilder Handbook on pages 1008–1029 provides additional opportunity to practice your reading and interpreting skills. It also includes activities that let you practice what you have learned.

Introduction

The California *At-Home Standards Practice* on pages 21–42 has been designed to help your students check their mastery of the California History–Social Science Standards for Grade Eleven.

Format

The Standards Practice consists of 22 weeks of questions, with every 2 weeks and 10 questions focusing on one of the California History–Social Science Standards for eleventh grade. All questions are in a multiple-choice format. Each week also includes a question based on a primary source quote or a visual, such as a map or graph.

Students can easily use this Standards Practice at home with their families because it provides all the information they need. Each question shows the standard and supporting standard it addresses. Questions also are correlated to the sections of the textbook in which the material is covered. This helps students review the material or gather more information to gain a better understanding of the topic. The Answer Key on page 43 provides the answers for all questions.

Each page in your Teacher Wraparound Edition includes the answers and several tips on how to find the right answer for particular questions. The box at the bottom of each page provides the supporting standards for the History–Social Science Standard that is addressed on that page.

A Guide to Glencoe's Standards Practice for Your United States History Course

The History-Social Science Standards adopted by the California State Board of Education highlight the most important developments in modern United States history. That is why you are expected to master these standards by the time you have finished your United States history course.

Glencoe's *At-Home Standards Practice* is designed to help you become familiar with the content of the California standards. If you use this Standards Practice as you are taking the course, you will be able to know whether you are learning the material of your United States History course.

How does the Standards Practice work?

- For each two-week period, the *At-Home Standards Practice* focuses your attention on a single standard. On each day of the school week, you can try to answer a question on the standards. By the end of the course, you will have completed a practice session on every standard!
- You will notice that each question tells you which standard you are covering as you practice. This will increase your familiarity with the standards and the content they refer to.
- After each question, the Standards Practice provides a reference to the Chapter and Section of your textbook where you can find the answer. This will help you review material quickly.
- Each practice session includes questions based on primary quotes, maps, charts, and illustrations. These questions will help you acquire the history and analysis skills you need to master United States history.
  - Finally, you can check your understanding by consulting the Answer Key at the back of the Standards Practice pages.

FRIDAY 11.1.2

5 The purpose of the so-called Three-Fifths Compromise was to determine *(Section 1.3)*

A how senators would be elected to Congress from each state.

B how power would be divided between an upper house and lower house in Congress.

C how African Americans would be counted for representation in Congress and for taxation.

D how power would be shared between the federal government and the states.

Teacher Notes

After working through the Standards Practice, Students should be able to:
- master the California History–Social Science standards.
- understand all material introduced in the textbook.
- interpret documents, maps, graphs, charts, and other visuals and relate them to the material they have studied during the course.

WEEK 1

Standard 11.1 Students analyze the significant events in the founding of the nation and its attempts to realize the philosophy of government described in the Declaration of Independence.

MONDAY
11.1.1, 11.1.2

1 Both Enlightenment ideas and the Great Awakening *(Section 1.2)*

A encouraged the development of a mercantile society.

B led to the growth of cities.

C gave rise to the idea of no taxation without representation.

D emphasized individualism in a way that supported political independence.

TUESDAY
11.1.1, 11.1.2

2 The Founders' ideas of divinely bestowed unalienable natural rights derived in large part from the works of Enlightenment thinkers, especially *(Section 1.2)*

A Jonathan Edwards.

B John Locke.

C Jean Jacques Rousseau.

D Baron Montesquieu.

WEDNESDAY
11.1.1

That to secure these rights, Governments are instituted among Men, deriving their just powers from the consent of the governed,

That whenever any Form of Government becomes destructive of these ends, it is the Right of the People to alter or to abolish it, and to institute a new Government, . . ."

—Declaration of Independence

3 What Enlightenment principle is reflected in this passage? *(The Declaration of Independence)*

A republicanism

B limited government

C federalism

D the social contract

THURSDAY
11.1.2

4 Ratification of the Constitution occurred as a result of *(Section 1.3)*

A the election of George Washington as president.

B the promise to add a bill of rights.

C the defeat of the Antifederalists in elections in Virginia and New York.

D the addition of a system of checks and balances to the Constitution.

FRIDAY
11.1.2

5 The purpose of the so-called Three-Fifths Compromise was to determine *(Section 1.3)*

A how senators would be elected to Congress from each state.

B how power would be divided between an upper house and lower house in Congress.

C how African Americans would be counted for representation in Congress and for taxation.

D how power would be shared between the federal government and the states.

21

Standard 11.1

Answers

1 **MONDAY – D**
Standards 11.1.1, 11.1.2
Emphasize that the Enlightenment and the Great Awakening dealt with ideas about the power of traditional authority and the individual. Thus, students can rule out answer B.

2 **TUESDAY – B**
Standards 11.1.1, 11.1.2
Eliminate the wrong answers with students: Jonathan Edwards was a spiritual philosopher and the leader of the Great Awakening but not an Enlightenment thinker; Rousseau defined the social contract; Montesquieu put forth the idea of separation of powers.

3 **WEDNESDAY – D**
Standard 11.1.1

4 **THURSDAY – B**
Standard 11.1.2

5 **FRIDAY – C**
Standard 11.1.2

History–Social Science Standards Grade Eleven

11.1.1	Describe the Enlightenment and the rise of democratic ideas as the context in which the nation was founded.
11.1.2	Analyze the ideological origins of the American Revolution, the Founding Fathers' philosophy of divinely bestowed unalienable natural rights, the debates on the drafting and ratification of the Constitution, and the addition of the Bill of Rights.

Standard 11.1

Answers

1 MONDAY – D
Standard 11.1.3
Be sure students understand the important elements of the Fourteenth Amendment. Remind them that the amendment addressed citizenship issues. Students therefore can eliminate answer B, which mentions voting rights.

2 TUESDAY – C
Standard 11.1.3

3 WEDNESDAY – C
Standards 11.1.3, 11.1.4

4 THURSDAY – A
Standard 11.1.4

5 FRIDAY – B
Standard 11.1.4
Encourage students to use the line graph's key to identify what each line represents. Students should then identify the trend of each line. They will notice that there is a downward trend in the Native American population from 1860 to 1900.

WEEK 2

Standard 11.1 Students analyze the significant events in the founding of the nation and its attempts to realize the philosophy of government described in the Declaration of Independence.

MONDAY ⟍ 11.1.3

1 Which of the following is true of the Fourteenth Amendment, which guarantees "equal protection of the laws"? *(Section 1.3)*

A It increased civil rights and increased states' rights.

B It granted voting rights and limited states' rights.

C It decreased civil rights and increased the power of the federal government.

D It guaranteed civil rights and limited the power of the states.

TUESDAY ⟍ 11.1.3

2 Calhoun's idea of nullification *(Section 1.2)*

A threatened states' rights.

B ended the threat of secession.

C challenged the authority of the federal government and the Constitution.

D led to the Tariff of Abominations and an amendment to the Constitution.

WEDNESDAY ⟍ 11.1.3, 11.1.4

3 Before the Civil War ended, Republicans and antislavery Democrats began working together to pass the *(Section 1.3)*

A Congressional Reconstruction Plan.

B Wade-Davis Bill.

C Thirteenth Amendment.

D Civil Rights Act.

THURSDAY ⟍ 11.1.4

4 The purpose of the alliance between Northern financiers and Southern leaders after the Civil War was to *(Section 1.3)*

A industrialize the South.

B finance old-style plantation agriculture.

C tie African Americans to the land as sharecroppers.

D control Southern legislatures.

FRIDAY

5 Use the graph to answer the following question. ⟍ 11.1.4

Which statement is BEST supported by the information on the graph? *(Section 3.1)*

A The expansion of the railroad had a positive impact on the Native American population.

B The expansion of the railroad had a negative impact on the Native American population.

C The expansion of the railroad had little impact on the Native American population.

D The expansion of the railroad impacted the ability of Native Americans to find food.

22

History–Social Science Standards Grade Eleven

| 11.1.3 | Understand the history of the Constitution after 1787 with emphasis on federal versus state authority and growing democratization. | 11.1.4 | Examine the effects of the Civil War and Reconstruction and of the industrial revolution, including demographic shifts and the emergence in the late nineteenth century of the United States as a world power. |

WEEK 3

Standard 11.2 Students analyze the relationship among the rise of industrialization, large-scale rural-to-urban migration, and massive immigration from Southern and Eastern Europe.

MONDAY 11.2.1

1 In *The Jungle*, author Upton Sinclair exposed the dangers and horrors of *(Section 5.2)*

A organized industrial labor unions.

B the meatpacking industry.

C the patent medicine industry.

D conditions in the nation's coal mines.

TUESDAY 11.2.2

2 The large influx of immigrants and people from rural areas into the cities resulted in *(Section 3.3)*

A neighborhoods in which people from different backgrounds mixed.

B all residents being squeezed into tenements.

C rapid development of water and sewage systems to keep up with demand.

D a separation by class.

WEDNESDAY 11.2.3

3 The main purpose of the Americanization movement was to *(Section 3.4)*

A teach English to immigrants.

B prevent the spread of disease through instruction in hygiene.

C preserve cultural traditions.

D assimilate immigrants into American culture.

THURSDAY 11.2.4

4 Tammany Hall is an example of a political machine because *(Section 3.3)*

A it adopted nativist policies.

B it attacked urban problems like crime and violence in a machine-like way.

C party bosses provided favors in return for votes.

D its leaders were appointed rather than voted into office.

FRIDAY

5 Use the diagram to answer the following question. 11.2.5

Purchase of Competing Companies in Same Industry

U.S. Oil Company

Independent Oil Refineries

Which title completes the diagram? *(Section 3.2)*

A Holding Company

B Vertical Integration

C Horizontal Integration

D Monopoly

23

Standard 11.2

Answers

1 MONDAY – B
Standard 11.2.1

2 TUESDAY – D
Standard 11.2.2

3 WEDNESDAY – D
Standard 11.2.3
Make sure students understand that they should look for the answer choice that best matches the question. Point out to them that while the Americanization movement did aim to teach English to immigrants, this was not its main purpose.

4 THURSDAY – C
Standard 11.2.4
Remind students that political machines were in part successful because they helped solve problems of recent immigrants who now lived in American cities. Students can therefore rule out answer A.

5 FRIDAY – C
Standard 11.2.5

History–Social Science Standards Grade Eleven

11.2.1	Know the effects of industrialization on living and working conditions, including the portrayal of working conditions and food safety in Upton Sinclair's *The Jungle*.	11.2.3	Trace the effect of the Americanization movement.
		11.2.4	Analyze the effect of urban political machines and responses to them by immigrants and middle-class reformers.
11.2.2	Describe the changing landscape, including the growth of cities linked by industry and trade, and the development of cities divided according to race, ethnicity, and class.	11.2.5	Discuss corporate mergers that produced trusts and cartels and the economic and political policies of industrial leaders.

Standard 11.2

Answers

1 MONDAY – B
Standard 11.2.6

2 TUESDAY – A
Standard 11.2.7

3 WEDNESDAY – D
Standard 11.2.7

4 THURSDAY – C
Standard 11.2.8
Remind students that the Populists and the People's Party were the same, and that the money supply was a key issue for farmers, their main supporters. This was especially the case after the economic crisis of 1893. Remind students that the Populists thought a focus on the gold standards was hurting the economy and worsening the economic problems of farmers. They can therefore rule out answer B.

5 FRIDAY – A
Standard 11.2.9
Students should remember that Roosevelt earned his nickname for one particular action. Even though he gained the nickname of trustbuster, he actually took a moderate stance in relation to trusts and often worked with big business to protect a range of interests, including those of big business. Students should identify each choice before deciding on an answer.

At-Home Standards Practice

WEEK 4

Standard 11.2 Students analyze the relationship among the rise of industrialization, large-scale rural-to-urban migration, and massive immigration from Southern and Eastern Europe.

MONDAY — 11.2.6

1 The United States was able to industrialize quickly because of *(Sections 3.1 and 3.2)*

A its lack of labor unions.

B its abundance of natural resources.

C its low tariffs on imports.

D the depressed price of agricultural products.

TUESDAY — 11.2.7

2 Dwight L. Moody is best known for *(Section 3. 4)*

A heading the Chicago YMCA in the late 1860s.

B establishing settlement houses in New York.

C putting forth the idea of philanthropy.

D developing the idea of Social Darwinism.

WEDNESDAY — 11.2.7

3 Use the passage to answer the following question.

. . . [T]he whole effort of nature is to get rid of such as are unfit, to clear the world of them, and make room for better.

—Herbert Spencer

This passage reflects Spencer's attempt to adapt the theory of evolution to society. His ideas are known as *(Section 3.4)*

A the Gospel of Wealth.

B Pragmatism.

C the Social Gospel.

D Social Darwinism.

THURSDAY — 11.2.8

4 After the economic crisis of 1893, the Populists focused their efforts on *(Section 3.5)*

A a graduated income tax.

B a gold standard.

C the free coinage of silver.

D a general strengthening of the role of government.

FRIDAY — 11.2.9

5 Which of these progressive reforms secured the nickname of "trustbuster" for Theodore Roosevelt? *(Section 5.2)*

A the success of *Northern Securities v. United States*

B the Hepburn Act

C the Newlands Reclamation Act

D the establishment of the Bureau of Corporations

24

History—Social Science Standards Grade Eleven

11.2.6 Trace the economic development of the United States and its emergence as a major industrial power, including its gains from trade and the advantages of its physical geography.

11.2.7 Analyze the similarities and differences between the ideologies of Social Darwinism and Social Gospel (e.g., using biographies of William Graham Sumner, Billy Sunday, Dwight L. Moody).

11.2.8 Examine the effect of political programs and activities of Populists.

11.2.9 Understand the effect of political programs and activities of the Progressives (e.g., federal regulation of railroad transport, Children's Bureau, the Sixteenth Amendment, Theodore Roosevelt, Hiram Johnson).

At-Home Standards Practice

WEEK 5

Standard 11.3 — Students analyze the role religion played in the founding of America, its lasting moral, social, and political impacts, and issues regarding religious liberty.

MONDAY — 11.3.1

1 Use the excerpt to answer the following question.

[T]he Awakening nurtured a subtle change in values that crossed over into politics and daily life. . . . People assumed new responsibilities in religious affairs and became skeptical of dogma and authority.

—from The American People

One result of the Great Awakening was that (Section 1.2)

A it served as a basis for revolutionary thought.
B people tended to rejoin traditional religions.
C many Americans turned away from religion.
D Americans accepted the authority of the Anglican Church.

TUESDAY — 11.3.1

2 African American ministers came together to end segregation by forming the (Section 16.1)

A NAACP.
B SCLC.
C SNCC.
D EEOC.

WEDNESDAY — 11.3.1, 11.3.2

3 The settlement house movement was like the Social Gospel movement because both (Section 3.4)

A were based on the belief that the duties of a Christian involved helping the poor.
B organized revival meetings in American cities.
C were forms of Reform Darwinism.
D restricted their mission to the plight of the urban poor.

THURSDAY — 11.3.2

4 One of the leaders of the Great Awakening was (Sections 1.2, 2.2, 3.4, and 20.1)

A Walter Rauschenbusch.
B Jonathan Edwards.
C Joseph Smith.
D Billy Graham.

FRIDAY — 11.3.2

5 The movement called the Moral Majority was part of a larger phenomenon that is best described as (Section 20.1)

A the resurgence of liberalism.
B the social rise of suburban conservatism.
C the political rise of Christian fundamentalism.
D the resurgence of political activism.

At-Home Standards Practice

Standard 11.3

Answers

1 MONDAY – A
Standard 11.3.1
Tell students to carefully read the excerpt and pay special attention to the last words. They will learn of a change in the way people viewed values and authority. Students can assume that people would tend to reject traditional religion or the authority of the church of England.

2 TUESDAY – B
Standard 11.3.1
Suggest to students that they spell out the meaning of each of the acronyms for the organizations listed. They can then easily rule out answers A (National Association for the Advancement of Colored People) and D (Equal Employment Opportunity Commission).

3 WEDNESDAY – A
Standards 11.3.1, 11.3.2

4 THURSDAY – B
Standard 11.3.2

5 FRIDAY – C
Standard 11.3.2

History–Social Science Standards Grade Eleven

11.3.1	Describe the contributions of various religious groups to American civic principles and social reform movements (e.g., civil and human rights, individual responsibility and the work ethic, antimonarchy and self-rule, worker protection, family-centered communities).
11.3.2	Analyze the great religious revivals and the leaders involved in them, including the First Great Awakening, the Second Great Awakening, the Civil War revivals, the Social Gospel Movement, the rise of Christian liberal theology in the nineteenth century, the impact of the Second Vatican Council, and the rise of Christian fundamentalism in current times.

25

Standard 11.3

Answers

1 MONDAY – C
Standard 11.3.3

2 TUESDAY – D
Standard 11.3.3
Remind students that John F. Kennedy was the first presidential candidate of his faith. This engendered much discussion during the election campaign of 1960.

3 WEDNESDAY – D
Standard 11.3.4

4 THURSDAY – C
Standard 11.3.5

5 FRIDAY – C
Standard 11.3.5
Be sure students recognize the establishment and free exercise clauses of the First Amendment. Although these clauses clearly establish religious liberty, their interpretation has engendered enormous debate.

At-Home Standards Practice

WEEK 6

Standard 11.3 Students analyze the role religion played in the founding of America, its lasting moral, social, and political impacts, and issues regarding religious liberty.

MONDAY `11.3.3`

1 Where did the Mormons of the Midwest settle before their final move west to Utah territory? *(Section 2.2)*

A New York

B Ohio

C Illinois

D Missouri

TUESDAY `11.3.3`

2 One issue that surfaced in the presidential election of 1960 between Kennedy and Nixon was *(Section 15.1)*

A the separation of church and state.

B the emergence of a Moral Majority.

C anti-Semitic sentiment.

D anti-Catholic sentiment.

WEDNESDAY `11.3.4`

3 What is the reason for the increase in religious pluralism today? *(Section 20.1)*

A Many Americans choose to no longer belong to a religion.

B Americans are turning away from traditional religions.

C Many Americans have become adherents of transcendentalism.

D More and more immigrants are moving to the United States, bringing with them their religions.

THURSDAY `11.3.5`

4 During the 1960s, the Supreme Court under Chief Justice Earl Warren ruled that *(Section 15.1)*

A states could mandate prayer in school.

B the federal government could force states to mandate prayer in school.

C states would not be allowed to mandate Bible readings in school.

D states would have to prohibit all prayer in school.

FRIDAY `11.3.5`

Congress shall make no laws respecting an establishment of religion, or prohibiting the free exercise thereof; . . .

—Constitution of the United States

5 This quotation from the beginning of the First Amendment is widely interpreted to mean that *(Constitution Handbook)*

A the state has only limited authority over religion.

B religion takes precedence over the state.

C religion and the state are separate.

D government can protect the religion of the state.

26

History–Social Science Standards Grade Eleven

11.3.3 Cite incidences of religious intolerance in the United States (e.g., persecution of Mormons, anti-Catholic sentiment, anti-Semitism).	**11.3.5** Describe the principles of religious liberty found in the Establishment and Free Exercise clauses of the First Amendment, including the debate on the issue of separation of church and state.
11.3.4 Discuss the expanding religious pluralism in the United States and California that resulted from large-scale immigration in the twentieth century.	

WEEK 7

Standard 11.4

Students trace the rise of the United States to its role as a world power in the twentieth century.

MONDAY   11.4.1

1 U.S. interest in trade with China resulted in the *(Section 4.3)*

A Open Door Policy.

B Roosevelt Corollary.

C leasehold strategy.

D "big stick" approach to foreign policy.

TUESDAY   11.4.1

2 After the Boxer Rebellion in China, the United States *(Section 4.3)*

A divided China into several colonies.

B lost all influence in Asia.

C shared power in China with Great Britain.

D convinced European nations to let all countries trade with China.

WEDNESDAY

3 Use the diagram to answer the following question.   11.4.2

Yellow journalism

Jingoism

?

De Lôme letter

"Remember the *Maine*"

Which title best completes the diagram? *(Section 4.2)*

A The War in Cuba

B The Spanish-American War

C U.S. Response to the War for Cuban Independence

D Causes of the Spanish-American War

THURSDAY   11.4.2

4 Which of these resulted from the American decision to annex the Philippines? *(Section 4.2)*

A resistance from Spain

B a Filipino revolt

C the passage of the Platt Amendment

D the end of American imperial power

FRIDAY   11.4.3

5 In order to build the Panama Canal, the United States *(Section 4.3)*

A sent Matthew Perry to Colombia with a fleet of warships.

B supported Panama's fight for independence from Colombia.

C sent George Dewey to Panama with a fleet of warships.

D signed a treaty with Colombia to build the canal in Panama.

27

Standard 11.4

Answers

1 **MONDAY – A**
Standard 11.4.1
Tell students to consider that there were many different approaches to foreign policy during the late 1800s and early 1900s. Only one describes the foreign policy used exclusively in China. Have students eliminate those answer choices that imply more general terms.

2 **TUESDAY – D**
Standard 11.4.1

3 **WEDNESDAY – D**
Standard 11.4.2

4 **THURSDAY – B**
Standard 11.4.2
Suggest to students that they eliminate answer choices that do not make sense. For example, the United States had gained the Philippines after defeating Spain, so Spain would not have resisted annexation. In addition, gaining territory would mark the beginning of imperial power, not the end of it.

5 **FRIDAY – B**
Standard 11.4.3

History–Social Science Standards Grade Eleven

11.4.1 List the purpose and the effects of the Open Door policy.	11.4.3 Discuss America's role in the Panama Revolution and the building of the Panama Canal.
11.4.2 Describe the Spanish-American War and U.S. expansion in the South Pacific.	

Standard 11.4

Answers

1 MONDAY – B
Standard 11.4.4

2 TUESDAY – D
Standard 11.4.4

3 WEDNESDAY – C
Standard 11.4.5
Point out to students that despite many volunteers, the United States instituted a draft during World War I. This rules out answer A.

4 THURSDAY – C
Standard 11.4.6

5 FRIDAY – A
Standard 11.4.6
Remind students that Afghanistan was not one of the three countries President Bush included in his "axis of evil." Students can therefore eliminate choices B and D.

WEEK 8

Standard 11.4   Students trace the rise of the United States to its role as a world power in the twentieth century.

MONDAY

1 Use the cartoon to answer the following question.   11.4.4

This cartoon illustrates President Theodore Roosevelt's *(Section 4.3)*

A career as a Rough Rider.

B approach to foreign policy.

C views on conservation policy.

D loan policy for Latin America.

TUESDAY   11.4.4

2 Taft's efforts in Latin America to place less emphasis on military force and more emphasis on business development was referred to as *(Section 4.3)*

A yellow imperialism.

B sphere of influence policy.

C laissez-faire.

D dollar diplomacy.

WEDNESDAY   11.4.5

3 During World War I *(Section 6.2)*

A no draft was needed because so many Americans volunteered for military service.

B women served in combat positions in the military.

C many African Americans migrated to Northern cities to take wartime factory jobs.

D the War Industries Board sold Liberty Bonds to pay for the war.

THURSDAY   11.4.6

4 The peace treaty known as the Camp David Accords reflected the importance of the Middle East in U.S. foreign policy. It also demonstrated *(Section 19.3)*

A the failure of the Carter administration in Iran.

B the collapse of détente.

C U.S. status as a world power.

D the economic problems of the Carter administration.

FRIDAY   11.4.6

5 In the war in Afghanistan, the United States took leadership of a coalition *(Section 21.5)*

A in response to the September 11 bombing.

B to send a message to the government of Saddam Hussein.

C to respond to anthrax attacks on American citizens.

D to combat the "Axis of Evil."

28

History–Social Science Standards Grade Eleven

11.4.4 Explain Theodore Roosevelt's Big Stick diplomacy, William Taft's Dollar Diplomacy, and Woodrow Wilson's Moral Diplomacy, drawing on relevant speeches.	11.4.6 Trace the declining role of Great Britain and the expanding role of the United States in world affairs after World War II.
11.4.5 Analyze the political, economic, and social ramifications of World War I on the home front.	

WEEK 9

Standard 11.5
Students analyze the major political, social, economic, technological, and cultural developments of the 1920s.

MONDAY
11.5.1

The chief business of the American people is business. The man who builds a factory builds a temple. The man who works there worships there.

1 This quote best describes the presidency of *(Section 8.1)*

A Herbert Hoover.

B Calvin Coolidge.

C Franklin D. Roosevelt.

D Warren G. Harding.

TUESDAY
11.5.1

2 Which of the following badly damaged Americans' opinion of President Hoover? *(Section 9.3)*

A the army's eviction of the Bonus Army from Washington, D.C.

B establishment of the Reconstruction Finance Corporation

C Hoover's opposition to the Emergency Relief and Construction Act

D newsreel scenes of farmers destroying their crops

WEDNESDAY
11.5.2

3 The leader who introduced the "back to Africa" movement was *(Sections 7.3 and 16.3)*

A Marcus Garvey.

B Oscar DePriest.

C Paul Robeson.

D Malcolm X.

THURSDAY
11.5.2

4 Which group was the main target of the Palmer Raids of the 1920s? *(Section 6.4)*

A African Americans

B Jewish Americans

C trade union leaders

D foreign residents and immigrants

FRIDAY
11.5.3

5 The Volstead Act is important because it *(Section 9.1)*

A led to the Eighteenth Amendment and created Prohibition.

B ended Prohibition.

C gave the federal government police powers.

D shut down secret bars called speakeasies.

29

At-Home Standards Practice

Standard 11.5

Answers

1 MONDAY – B
Standard 11.5.1

2 TUESDAY – A
Standard 11.5.1
Remind students that while people generally did not approve of President Hoover, especially with regard to his policies at the beginning of the Great Depression, it was one specific event that hurt his presidency. Ask students to recall which of the events listed hurt his reelection the most.

3 WEDNESDAY – A
Standard 11.5.2

4 THURSDAY – D
Standard 11.5.2

5 FRIDAY – C
Standard 11.5.3
Tell students to consider each of the answer choices carefully. While government officials tried to put an end to all alcohol production and consumption, students should remember that the officials were not successful in their attempts. Therefore, students can eliminate answer choice D.

History–Social Science Standards Grade Eleven

11.5.1 Discuss the policies of Presidents Warren Harding, Calvin Coolidge, and Herbert Hoover.	tions such as the American Civil Liberties Union, the National Association for the Advancement of Colored People, and the Anti-Defamation League to those attacks.
11.5.2 Analyze the international and domestic events, interests, and philosophies that prompted attacks on civil liberties, including the Palmer Raids, Marcus Garvey's "back-to-Africa" movement, the Ku Klux Klan, and immigration quotas and the responses of organiza-	**11.5.3** Examine the passage of the Eighteenth Amendment to the Constitution and the Volstead Act (Prohibition).

Answers

1 MONDAY – B
Standard 11.5.4

2 TUESDAY – D
Standard 11.5.5
Encourage students to identify what each of the persons listed in the answer choices is known for. Langston Hughes was a poet, while Bessie Smith became known for her interpretations of the blues. Students can thus cross out answer choices A and C.

3 WEDNESDAY – C
Standard 11.5.6

4 THURSDAY – B
Standard 11.5.7
Ask students to remember why the assembly line made a difference in how cars were produced. Remind students that it sped up the way in which cars were put together. This would increase the efficiency of workers, who could now produce many more cars in a given time period than before.

5 FRIDAY – A
Standard 11.5.7

WEEK 10

Standard 11.5 — Students analyze the major political, social, economic, technological, and cultural developments of the 1920s.

MONDAY   11.5.4

1 After a long battle for suffrage, women finally gained the right to vote when *(Section 5.1)*

A the Senate finally passed the Nineteenth Amendment in June 1919.

B three-fourths of the states ratified the Nineteenth Amendment on August 20, 1920.

C the House of Representatives passed the Nineteenth Amendment in 1918.

D President Wilson finally supported woman suffrage in the individual states.

TUESDAY   11.5.5

2 The Harlem Renaissance author who wrote the first major stories to feature African American females as central characters was *(Section 7.3)*

A Langston Hughes.

B Claude McKay.

C Bessie Smith.

D Zora Neale Hurston.

WEDNESDAY

3 Use the list to answer the following question.   11.5.6

- Radio
- Movies
- Newspapers
- Magazines

In the 1920s, the items in the list helped to *(Section 7.2)*

A foster regional ties.

B create informed consumers.

C unify the nation and shape a national identity.

D encourage minority rights.

THURSDAY   11.5.7

4 As a result of Henry Ford's introduction of the assembly line, *(Section 8.2)*

A the price of his Model T's increased.

B the price of his Model T's decreased.

C the number of Model T's produced in his factories remained the same.

D the efficiency of workers producing his Model T's declined.

FRIDAY   11.5.7

5 Higher wages, a booming economy, technical inventions, and a change in traditional attitudes all contributed to a new consumer society in which *(Section 6.2)*

A consumers became willing to buy on credit.

B there was little need for advertising.

C more and more workers joined labor unions.

D managers were no longer required in businesses.

30

History–Social Science Standards Grade Eleven

11.5.4 Analyze the passage of the Nineteenth Amendment and the changing role of women in society.	**11.5.6** Trace the growth and effects of radio and movies and their role in the worldwide diffusion of popular culture.
11.5.5 Describe the Harlem Renaissance and new trends in literature, music, and art, with special attention to the work of writers (e.g., Zora Neale Hurston, Langston Hughes).	**11.5.7** Discuss the rise of mass production techniques, the growth of cities, the impact of new technologies (e.g., the automobile, electricity), and the resulting prosperity and effect on the American landscape.

WEEK 11

Standard 11.6

Students analyze the different explanations for the Great Depression and how the New Deal fundamentally changed the role of the federal government.

MONDAY 🔔 11.6.1

1 To restore public confidence in the banking system in the 1910s, President Woodrow Wilson favored *(Section 5.4)*

A passage of the Clayton Antitrust Act.

B the repeal of the Underwood Tariff.

C the establishment of the Federal Reserve System.

D the creation of the Federal Trade Commission.

TUESDAY 🔔 11.6.1

2 The "quiet depression" of the 1920s refers to the *(Section 8.2)*

A decline in prices paid for U.S. farm products.

B damage done to U.S. manufacturers by high U.S. tariffs.

C decrease in real wages among U.S. workers.

D lack of well-paying jobs for African Americans.

WEDNESDAY

3 Use the passage to answer the following question. 🔔 11.6.2

The second step we have taken in the restoration of normal business enterprise has been to clean up thoroughly unwholesome conditions in the field of investment. . . . I sincerely hope that as a result people will be discouraged in unhappy efforts to get rich quick by speculating. . . .

—*Franklin D. Roosevelt, fireside chat, 1934*

In this fireside chat, President Roosevelt was referring to *(Section 10.2)*

A the Home Owners' Loan Corporation.

B the Securities and Exchange Commission.

C Social Security.

D the Emergency Farm Mortgage Act.

THURSDAY 🔔 11.6.2

4 Two causes of the Depression were *(Section 9.1)*

A overproduction and high tariffs.

B high unemployment and the crash of the stock market in 1929.

C high tariffs and high unemployment.

D mistakes by the Federal Reserve and too much immigration.

FRIDAY 🔔 11.6.3

5 What happened to many farmers in the Great Plains when they lost their farms during the Dust Bowl and headed to California to find work? *(Section 9.2)*

A They were welcomed because they filled a severe labor shortage.

B They had to turn back because California refused to let them enter the state.

C Many faced hostility because they competed with Californians for job.

D They were all sent to the Central Valley where jobs were plentiful.

31

Standard 11.6

Answers

1 MONDAY – C
Standard 11.6.1
Have students review the issues surrounding trusts and tarriffs. Remind them that these dealt with big business and trade and did not relate to any problems with the banking system in the United States. Students therefore can rule out answers A and B.

2 TUESDAY – A
Standard 11.6.1

3 WEDNESDAY – B
Standard 11.6.2

4 THURSDAY – A
Standard 11.6.2
Encourage students to cross out any item that was not a cause of the Depression. Since the question stem asks for two causes, any item that is crossed out eliminates that entire choice. For example, unemployment was not high before the Depression. Therefore, answers B and C can be eliminated.

5 FRIDAY – C
Standard 11.6.3

History–Social Science Standards Grade Eleven

11.6.1	Describe the monetary issues of the late nineteenth and early twentieth centuries that gave rise to the establishment of the Federal Reserve and the weaknesses in key sectors of the economy in the late 1920s.
11.6.2	Understand the explanations of the principal causes of the Great Depression and the steps taken by the Federal Reserve, Congress, and Presidents Herbert

Hoover and Franklin Delano Roosevelt to combat the economic crisis.

11.6.3 Discuss the human toll of the Depression, natural disasters, and unwise agricultural practices and their effects on the depopulation of rural regions and on political movements of the left and right, with particular attention to the Dust Bowl refugees and their social and economic impacts in California.

Standard 11.6

Answers

1 MONDAY – C
Standard 11.6.3
Remind students to read the labels and the data of the table carefully. They should then use their knowledge of history, in addition to the table, to select their answer choice. For example, students should be able to eliminate answer B because while federal revenue increased, the federal debt increased more rapidly.

2 TUESDAY – A
Standard 11.6.4

3 WEDNESDAY – B
Standard 11.6.4

4 THURSDAY – D
Standard 11.6.5
Briefly review the early history of labor unions by reminding students that craftworkers began to form the first unions in the 1830s. The first nationwide industrial union, the Knights of Labor, was formed in the 1870s. None of these included all workers within an industry.

5 FRIDAY – C
Standard 11.6.5

WEEK 12

Standard 11.6   Students analyze the different explanations for the Great Depression and how the New Deal fundamentally changed the role of the federal government.

MONDAY

1 Use the table to answer the following question.   11.6.3

Year	Federal Revenue (in billions of dollars)	Federal Debt (in billions of dollars)
1932	2.0	19.5
1933	2.1	22.5
1934	3.1	27.1
1935	3.8	28.7
1936	4.2	33.8
1937	5.6	36.4
1938	7.0	37.2
1939	6.6	40.4
1940	6.9	43.9

During the New Deal, President Roosevelt was criticized by those on the political right for (Section 10.3)

A   not increasing revenue enough to keep up with spending.

B   balancing the budget.

C   using deficit spending to pay for government programs.

D   maintaining the same ratio of revenue and debt.

TUESDAY   11.6.4

2 When it was first passed, the Social Security Act of 1935 did not include (Section 10.3)

A   farmworkers.

B   people with disabilities.

C   unemployed workers.

D   retired workers.

WEDNESDAY   11.6.4

3 As a result of the New Deal, many Americans came to believe that (Section 10.4)

A   states, not the federal government, should provide a safety net for Americans.

B   providing a safety net for Americans is a duty of the federal government.

C   there is no need for a safety net for Americans.

D   Congress, not the president, should set policies for the federal government.

THURSDAY   11.6.5

4 After passage of the National Labor Relations Act of 1935, increased union activity led to the formation of the Congress for Industrial Organizations. Unlike earlier unions, the CIO became (Section 10.3)

A   the nation's first trade union.

B   the first nationwide labor union.

C   the first union to use strikes to achieve its goals.

D   the first union to organize all workers in a particular industry.

FRIDAY   11.6.5

5 When farmworkers under the leadership of César Chávez and Dolores Huerta went on strike against California growers in the 1960s, (Section 18.3)

A   it involved a national boycott of vegetables.

B   the growers quickly agreed to raise wages and improve working conditions.

C   it resulted in huge losses for California growers.

D   the AFL-CIO refused to support the strike.

32

History–Social Science Standards Grade Eleven

11.6.3	Discuss the human toll of the Depression, natural disasters, and unwise agricultural practices and their effects on the depopulation of rural regions and on political movements of the left and right, with particular attention to the Dust Bowl refugees and their social and economic impacts in California.
11.6.4	Analyze the effects of and the controversies arising from New Deal economic policies and the expanded role of the federal government in society and the economy since the 1930s (e.g., Works Progress

Administration, Social Security, National Labor Relations Board, farm programs, regional development policies, and energy development projects such as the Tennessee Valley Authority, California Central Valley Project, and Bonneville Dam).

11.6.5	Trace the advances and retreats of organized labor, from the creation of the American Federation of Labor and the Congress of Industrial Organizations to current issues of a postindustrial, multinational economy, including the United Farm Workers in California.

WEEK 13

Students analyze America's participation in World War II.

Standard 11.7

MONDAY
11.7.1

1 Lend-lease was one of President Roosevelt's efforts to help Great Britain in the beginning days of World War II in spite of *(Section 12.1)*

A the objections of internationalists.

B the objections of isolationists.

C German submarine warfare.

D the economic problems of the Depression.

TUESDAY
11.7.2

2 The Battle of Midway was a turning point for the Allies in the war in the Pacific because *(Section 12.2)*

A it showed that the United States could reach Japan.

B by then the United States had finally learned to decode Japanese messages.

C the Japanese Navy lost four of its largest carriers and the heart of its fleet.

D it led to the Bataan Death March.

WEDNESDAY

3 Use the map to answer the following question.
11.7.2

This map shows plans for *(Section 12.4)*

A the invasion of North Africa.

B the D-Day invasion.

C the Battle of the Coral Sea.

D the assault on Iwo Jima.

THURSDAY
11.7.3

4 The Tuskegee Airmen *(Section 12.1)*

A created the Double "V" campaign.

B proved invaluable by using a special code to relay messages during combat.

C filled important wartime jobs in aircraft factories.

D distinguished themselves in combat but were not allowed to serve in integrated units.

FRIDAY
11.7.4

5 Well before the end of the war, President Roosevelt gained approval from Joseph Stalin for an international peace organization at a meeting in *(Section 12.4)*

A Tehran.

B Dumbarton Oaks.

C Yalta.

D Potsdam.

33

Standard 11.7

Answers

1 MONDAY – B
Standard 11.7.1

2 TUESDAY – C
Standard 11.7.2
Point out that the Bataan Death March involved American prisoners of war in the Philippines. Rather than a turning point for the Allies, it was a low point for the United States in the Pacific. Therefore, students can rule out answer D.

3 WEDNESDAY – B
Standard 11.7.2
Suggest to students that they carefully read the labels on the map. They should then use their geography skills to determine which part of the world is depicted on the map. This will quickly help them to rule out events in the Pacific, which are represented by answers C and D.

4 THURSDAY – D
Standard 11.7.3

5 FRIDAY – A
Standard 11.7.4

History–Social Science Standards Grade Eleven

11.7.1	Examine the origins of American involvement in the war, with an emphasis on the events that precipitated the attack on Pearl Harbor.	11.7.3	Identify the roles and sacrifices of individual American soldiers, as well as the unique contributions of the special fighting forces (e.g., the Tuskegee Airmen, the 442nd Regimental Combat team, the Navajo Code Talkers).
11.7.2	Explain U.S. and Allied wartime strategy, including the major battles of Midway, Normandy, Iwo Jima, Okinawa, and the Battle of the Bulge.	11.7.4	Analyze Roosevelt's foreign policy during World War II (e.g., Four Freedoms speech).

Answers

1 MONDAY – A
Standard 11.7.5
Remind students to carefully read the excerpt. They should determine the key phrases in the excerpt, which help them focus on "exclusion of large groups of citizens from their homes." This phrase should help students focus on the internment of Japanese Americans during the war.

2 TUESDAY – D
Standard 11.7.5

3 WEDNESDAY – B
Standard 11.7.6
Suggest to students that they rule out any answer choices that don't make sense. For example, riveted ships proved much more vulnerable when hit by torpedoes than welded ships. Since liberty ships were welded and thus safer, it is not likely that they would have been replaced by riveted ships. Students can therefore rule out answer C.

4 THURSDAY – B
Standard 11.7.7

5 FRIDAY – C
Standard 11.7.8

Standard 11.7
Students analyze America's participation in World War II.

MONDAY

1 Use the excerpt to answer the following question. *11.7.5*

Compulsory . . . exclusion of large groups of citizens from their homes, except under circumstances of direst emergency and peril, is inconsistent with our basic governmental institutions. But when under conditions of modern warfare our shores are threatened by hostile forces, the power to protect must be commensurate with the threatened danger.
—*U.S. Supreme Court*

This quote from a Supreme Court decision from December 1944 *(Section 12.3)*

A confirmed the right of the federal government to relocate Japanese Americans.

B ruled that the migration of Americans to the South and West during the war was constitutional.

C dealt with Jewish immigrants during the Holocaust.

D limited the right of African Americans to demand jobs in defense plants.

TUESDAY *11.7.5*

2 During the war, Rosie the Riveter became a symbol for *(Section 12.3)*

A people working on the home front, especially in defense plants.

B thanking women on the home front for their contributions to the war effort.

C promoting increases in wages for women, minorities, and other wartime workers.

D encouraging the work of women in defense plants.

WEDNESDAY *11.7.6*

3 As part of the conversion to a wartime economy, *(Section 12.1)*

A the government created a faster bidding process for companies.

B the Reconstruction Finance Corporation provided loans to help companies convert to wartime production.

C riveted ships replaced liberty ships.

D new factories were built to produce tanks and airplanes.

THURSDAY *11.7.7*

4 Which of the following best explains why Truman decided to use the atomic bomb? *(Section 12.5)*

A He believed that Japanese civilians would not die in large numbers.

B He believed that the United States would suffer massive casualties if forced to invade Japan.

C He believed that it would be necessary to drop only one bomb.

D He was not fully aware of the use and power of the atomic bomb.

FRIDAY *11.7.8*

5 Both the Truman Doctrine and the Marshall Plan *(Section 13.2)*

A offered aid only to Western European nations.

B provided military rather than economic aid to anti-Communist nations.

C provided economic aid in the hopes of fighting Communist aggression.

D refused aid to Germany.

34

History–Social Science Standards Grade Eleven

11.7.5 Discuss the constitutional issues and impact of events on the U.S. home front, including the internment of Japanese Americans (e.g., *Fred Korematsu* v. *United States of America*) and the restrictions on German and Italian resident aliens; the response of the administration to Hitler's atrocities against Jews and other groups; the roles of women in military production; the roles and growing political demands of African Americans.	**11.7.6** Describe major developments in aviation, weaponry, communication, and medicine and the war's impact on the location of American industry and use of resources.
	11.7.7 Discuss the decision to drop atomic bombs and the consequences of the decision (Hiroshima and Nagasaki).
	11.7.8 Analyze the effect of massive aid given to Western Europe under the Marshall Plan to rebuild itself after the war and the importance of a rebuilt Europe to the U.S. economy.

WEEK 15

Standard 11.8 Students analyze the economic boom and social transformation of post–World War II America.

MONDAY — 11.8.1

1 The economic boom after World War II resulted in significant changes to business, including *(Section 14.2)*

A an increase in the number of smaller stores.

B a growth of blue-collar jobs.

C the increase of free-thinking in middle management.

D the creation of multinational corporations.

TUESDAY — 11.8.2

2 The Bracero program *(Section 14.4)*

A provided farm jobs for Mexicans.

B ended during the 1950s.

C brought nearly 5,000 Mexicans to the Southwest.

D guaranteed a minimum wage and a 40-hour work week.

WEDNESDAY — 11.8.3

3 Which of these Fair Deal proposals by President Truman was enacted? *(Section 14.1)*

A national health insurance

B federal aid to schools

C an increase in the minimum wage

D farm subsidies

THURSDAY — 11.8.4

4 In addition to national educational legislation, California passed a law to improve education that *(Section 15.3)*

A brought educational opportunities to preschoolers.

B targeted adult education.

C provided college preparation for low-income teenagers.

D helped residents graduating in the top percentages of their high school classes to attend a state university.

FRIDAY

5 Use the chart to answer the following question. — 11.8.4

Major Great Society Programs		
Health and Welfare	**Education**	**War on Poverty**
Medicare	The Elementary and Secondary Education Act	The Office of Economic Opportunity
Medicaid	Higher Education Act	Housing and Urban Development Act
Child Nutrition Act	Project Head Start	Demonstration Cities and Metropolitan Development Act

The most accurate assessment of the Great Society based on the items in the chart and your knowledge is that *(Section 15.3)*

A most Great Society programs did not succeed or last.

B the Great Society had the same aims as the New Deal.

C the Great Society mainly was focused on economic reforms that would trickle down to help society as a whole.

D the Great Society created massive growth in the federal government.

35

Standard 11.8

Answers

1 MONDAY – D
Standard 11.8.1

2 TUESDAY – A
Standard 11.8.2

3 WEDNESDAY – C
Standard 11.8.3

4 THURSDAY – D
Standard 11.8.4
Remind students to make a careful distinction between programs that applied to the entire nation and those that were specifically enacted in the state of California. Students should realize, for example, that preschoolers were targeted with Project Head Start, one of the Great Society programs of President Johnson. They can therefore eliminate answer A.

5 FRIDAY – D
Standard 11.8.4
Students should carefully study the chart and compare it to the answer choices. For example, they should recognize a lack of programs geared toward farmers, one of the groups on which the New Deal focused. Students can thus rule out answer B.

History–Social Science Standards Grade Eleven

11.8.1	Trace the growth of service sector, white collar, and professional sector jobs in business and government.	11.8.3	Examine Truman's labor policy and congressional reaction to it.
11.8.2	Describe the significance of Mexican immigration and its relationship to the agricultural economy, especially in California.	11.8.4	Analyze new federal government spending on defense, welfare, interest on the national debt, and federal and state spending on education, including the California Master Plan.

Standard 11.8

Answers

1 MONDAY – B
Standard 11.8.5
Suggest to students that they recall the major legislation that came out of the Vietnam era with regard to war powers. Then ask students the purpose of each of these pieces of legislation. They should remember that it was the the War Powers Act of 1973 that restricted executive power, so they can rule out answer D.

2 TUESDAY – A
Standard 11.8.6

3 WEDNESDAY – A
Standard 11.8.7
Tell students to carefully read the question and the answer choices and to identify if they are related. They should be able to determine that while the rise of the Internet paralleled the development of computers, it was not brought about by the microchip.

4 THURSDAY – B
Standard 11.8.7

5 FRIDAY – D
Standard 11.8.8

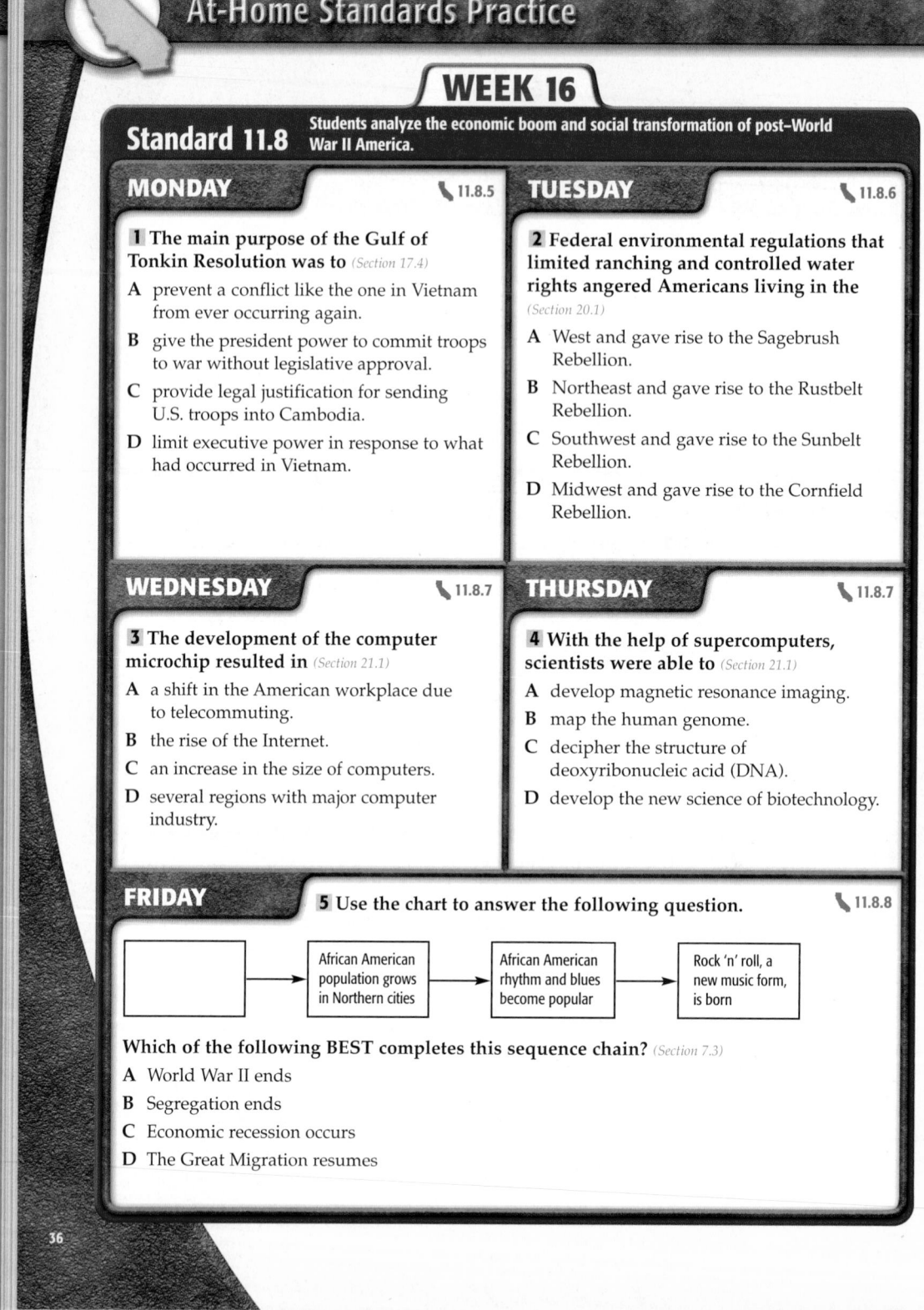

At-Home Standards Practice

WEEK 16

Standard 11.8 Students analyze the economic boom and social transformation of post–World War II America.

MONDAY ☎ 11.8.5

1 The main purpose of the Gulf of Tonkin Resolution was to *(Section 17.4)*

A prevent a conflict like the one in Vietnam from ever occurring again.

B give the president power to commit troops to war without legislative approval.

C provide legal justification for sending U.S. troops into Cambodia.

D limit executive power in response to what had occurred in Vietnam.

TUESDAY ☎ 11.8.6

2 Federal environmental regulations that limited ranching and controlled water rights angered Americans living in the *(Section 20.1)*

A West and gave rise to the Sagebrush Rebellion.

B Northeast and gave rise to the Rustbelt Rebellion.

C Southwest and gave rise to the Sunbelt Rebellion.

D Midwest and gave rise to the Cornfield Rebellion.

WEDNESDAY ☎ 11.8.7

3 The development of the computer microchip resulted in *(Section 21.1)*

A a shift in the American workplace due to telecommuting.

B the rise of the Internet.

C an increase in the size of computers.

D several regions with major computer industry.

THURSDAY ☎ 11.8.7

4 With the help of supercomputers, scientists were able to *(Section 21.1)*

A develop magnetic resonance imaging.

B map the human genome.

C decipher the structure of deoxyribonucleic acid (DNA).

D develop the new science of biotechnology.

FRIDAY **5** Use the chart to answer the following question. ☎ 11.8.8

| | → | African American population grows in Northern cities | → | African American rhythm and blues become popular | → | Rock 'n' roll, a new music form, is born |

Which of the following BEST completes this sequence chain? *(Section 7.3)*

A World War II ends

B Segregation ends

C Economic recession occurs

D The Great Migration resumes

36

History–Social Science Standards Grade Eleven

11.8.5	Describe the increased powers of the presidency in response to the Great Depression, World War II, and the Cold War.	11.8.7	Describe the effects on society and the economy of technological developments since 1945, including the computer revolution, changes in communication, advances in medicine, and improvements in agricultural technology.
11.8.6	Discuss the diverse environmental regions of North America, their relationship to local economies, and the origins and prospects of environmental problems in those regions.	11.8.8	Discuss forms of popular culture, with emphasis on their origins and geographic diffusion (e.g., jazz and other forms of popular music, professional sports, architectural and artistic styles).

WEEK 17

Students analyze U.S. foreign policy since World War II.

Standard 11.9

MONDAY 11.9.1

1 Senate approval of U.S. membership in the United Nations was assured because *(Section 12.5)*

A the new organization received its charter in San Francisco.

B each member nation would have one vote in the General Assembly.

C the United States would have veto power as a permanent member of the Security Council.

D the General Assembly was responsible for international peace and security.

TUESDAY 11.9.2

2 The two major alliances that opposed one another in Europe during the Cold War were *(Section 13.2)*

A NATO and SEATO.

B SEATO and OAS.

C OAS and the Warsaw Pact.

D the Warsaw Pact and NATO.

WEDNESDAY

3 Use the graph to answer the following question. 11.9.3

Loyalty Review Program — Trial of Alger Hiss — Red Scare — Rosenbergs — ( )

Which term belongs in the empty oval?
(Section 13.3)

A Cold War

B Nuclear Fallout

C McCarthyism

D The Long Telegram

THURSDAY 11.9.3

4 The Truman Doctrine stipulated that *(Section 13.2)*

A the United States would fight Communist aggression worldwide.

B the United States would prevent any European influence in Latin America.

C the United States would threaten to use nuclear weapons to fight Communist threats.

D the president could take any action necessary to fight armed attacks against U.S. forces.

FRIDAY 11.9.3

5 Which of the following best describes the Bay of Pigs invasion? *(Section 15.2)*

A It was Kennedy's first foreign policy triumph.

B It was a failed invasion of Cuba by armed Cuban exiles.

C It was an attempt by the Soviet Union to place long-range missiles in Cuba.

D It was Kennedy's attempt to prevent the construction of the Berlin Wall.

37

Standard 11.9

Answers

1 MONDAY – C
Standard 11.9.1
Ask students to remember why the Senate refused to sign the Treaty of Versailles, particularly the clauses that dealt with the League of Nations. Students should note that those opposed to the treaty feared that the United States would lose its autonomy.

2 TUESDAY – D
Standard 11.9.2

3 WEDNESDAY – C
Standard 11.9.3
Suggest to students that they think carefully about the events and issues associated with the Red Scare. While the Red Scare was a direct response to communism and the threat associated with it, it was limited to the United States. Students should identify the answer choices that address domestic or foreign policy issues.

4 THURSDAY – A
Standard 11.9.3

5 FRIDAY – B
Standard 11.9.3

History–Social Science Standards Grade Eleven

11.9.1	Discuss the establishment of the United Nations and International Declaration of Human Rights, International Monetary Fund, World Bank, and General Agreement on Tariffs and Trade (GATT) and their importance in shaping modern Europe and maintaining peace and international order.
11.9.2	Understand the role of military alliances, including NATO and SEATO, in deterring communist aggression and maintaining security during the Cold War.

11.9.3 Trace the origins and geopolitical consequences (foreign and domestic) of the Cold War and containment policy, including the following: the era of McCarthyism, instances of domestic Communism (e.g., Alger Hiss) and blacklisting; the Truman Doctrine; the Berlin Blockade; the Korean War; the Bay of Pigs Invasion and the Cuban Missile Crisis; atomic testing in the American West, the "mutual assured destruction" doctrine, and disarmament policies; the Vietnam War; Latin American policy.

Standard 11.9

Answers

1 MONDAY – A
Standard 11.9.3

2 TUESDAY – B
Standard 11.9.4
Have students think about the items listed in the answer choices and identify what they mean. Students should realize that Vietnamization meant handing the war over to South Vietnam. Since this would limit, and eventually end, U.S. involvement in Vietnam, it is not likely that students at Kent State University would have protested this policy. Therefore, answer D can be eliminated.

3 WEDNESDAY – B
Standard 11.9.5

4 THURSDAY – D
Standard 11.9.6

5 FRIDAY – A
Standard 11.9.7
Ask students to recall the member nations of NAFTA. They should know that three countries fall under this trade agreement: the United States, Mexico, and Canada. They can thus rule out answer choice C.

WEEK 18

Standard 11.9 — Students analyze U.S. foreign policy since World War II.

MONDAY   11.9.3

1 Use the quote to answer the following question.

You have a row of dominoes set up, you knock over the first one, and what will happen to the last one is the certainty that it will go over very quickly.

Which president and country are associated with this quote? *(Section 17.1)*

A   Eisenhower and Vietnam

B   Kennedy and Cuba

C   Johnson and Vietnam

D   Truman and Poland

TUESDAY   11.9.4

2 The event that sparked a deadly student protest at Kent State University was *(Section 17.4)*

A   the publication of the Pentagon Papers.

B   President Nixon's announcement of the invasion of Cambodia.

C   news reports about the My Lai massacre.

D   the new policy of Vietnamization.

WEDNESDAY   11.9.5

3 Agreements between the United States and the Soviet Union during the Reagan presidency, especially the Intermediate-Range Nuclear Forces (INF) Treaty, helped lead to *(Section 20.2)*

A   the Strategic Defense Initiative (SDI), or "Star Wars."

B   the end of the Cold War.

C   the Iran-Contra Scandal.

D   the buildup of the U.S. military.

THURSDAY   11.9.6

4 The Iraqi invasion of Kuwait resulted in *(Section 20.4)*

A   the fall of the government of Saddam Hussein.

B   the ousting of the Taliban from Afghanistan.

C   the Iran-Iraq War.

D   Operation Desert Storm.

FRIDAY   11.9.7

5 In 1994 the United States joined Mexico in the North American Free Trade Agreement (NAFTA) in order to *(Section 21.3)*

A   increase trade with Mexico.

B   prevent the establishment of the European Union (EU).

C   keep Canada from interfering with U.S.-Mexican trade.

D   limit its trade surplus.

38

History–Social Science Standards Grade Eleven

11.9.3 Trace the origins and geopolitical consequences (foreign and domestic) of the Cold War and containment policy, including the following: the era of McCarthyism, instances of domestic Communism (e.g., Alger Hiss) and blacklisting; the Truman Doctrine; the Berlin Blockade; the Korean War; the Bay of Pigs Invasion and the Cuban Missile Crisis; atomic testing in the American West, the "mutual assured destruction" doctrine, and disarmament policies; the Vietnam War; Latin American policy.	**11.9.5** Analyze the role of the Reagan administration and other factors in the victory of the West in the Cold War.
	11.9.6 Describe U.S. Middle East policy and its strategic, political, and economic interests, including those related to the Gulf War.
11.9.4 List the effects of foreign policy on domestic policies and vice versa (e.g., protests during the war in Vietnam, the "nuclear freeze" movement).	**11.9.7** Examine relations between the United States and Mexico in the twentieth century, including key economic, political, immigration, and environmental issues.

WEEK 19

Standard 11.10

Students analyze the development of federal civil rights and voting rights.

Standard 11.10

MONDAY

1 Use the excerpt to answer the following question. 🔍 11.10.1, 11.10.4

. . . [T]here shall be no discrimination in the employment of workers in defense industries or government because of race, creed, color, or national origin.

—Executive Order 8802

This excerpt from Executive Order 8802 was largely the result of a threatened march on Washington and other efforts led by *(Section 12.3)*

A A. Philip Randolph.
B Martin Luther King, Jr.
C Eleanor Roosevelt.
D Mary McLeod Bethune.

TUESDAY 🔍 11.10.2

2 In *Plessy* v. *Ferguson,* the Supreme Court ruled that *(Section 3.5)*

A private organizations could not be held accountable for discriminatory practices.
B states could be sued for alleged discriminatory laws.
C the Civil Rights Act of 1875 was unconstitutional.
D separate but equal facilities for African Americans were legal.

WEDNESDAY 🔍 11.10.2, 11.10.4

3 Civil rights workers who were beaten and firebombed in their quest to integrate interstate buses in the South *(Section 16.2)*

A were called Black Panthers.
B belonged to the Nation of Islam.
C were known as Freedom Riders.
D were members of SNCC.

THURSDAY 🔍 11.10.3

4 When Thurgood Marshall prepared for the lawsuits that became known as *Brown* v. *Board of Education,* he

A worked only with local African American lawyers.
B prepared the cases by himself.
C was limited to assistance from his legal staff at the NAACP's Legal Defense and Education Fund.
D sought the advice of many experts.

FRIDAY 🔍 11.10.4, 11.10.5

5 After the successful end of the Montgomery bus boycott, African American ministers continued to fight segregation by forming the Southern Christian Leadership Conference (SCLC). As their first president they chose *(Section 16.2)*

A James Farmer.
B Martin Luther King, Jr.
C Malcom X.
D Jesse Jackson.

39

Answers

1 **MONDAY – A**
Standards 11.10.1, 11.10.4
Tell students to carefully read a passage when a question is based on an excerpt. This passage mentions workers in defense industries. Of the people listed, which one would most likely be interested in ending discrimination in defense industries?

2 **TUESDAY – D**
Standard 11.10.2

3 **WEDNESDAY – C**
Standards 11.10.2, 11.10.4

4 **THURSDAY – D**
Standard 11.10.3

5 **FRIDAY – B**
Standards 11.10.4, 11.10.5
Make sure students remember when the Montgomery bus boycott and the formation of SCLC occurred. They should then be able to eliminate people who did not come to prominence until later, such as Jesse Jackson.

History–Social Science Standards Grade Eleven

11.10.1 Explain how demands of African Americans helped produce a stimulus for civil rights, including President Roosevelt's ban on racial discrimination in defense industries in 1941, and how African Americans' service in World War II produced a stimulus for President Truman's decision to end segregation in the armed forces in 1948.

11.10.2 Examine and analyze the key events, policies, and court cases in the evolution of civil rights, including *Dred Scott* v. *Sanford, Plessy* v. *Ferguson, Brown* v. *Board of Education, Regents of the University of California* v. *Bakke,* and California Proposition 209.

11.10.3 Describe the collaboration on legal strategy between African American and white civil rights lawyers to end racial segregation in higher education.

11.10.4 Examine the roles of civil rights advocates (e.g., A. Philip Randolph, Martin Luther King, Jr., Malcolm X, Thurgood Marshall, James Farmer, Rosa Parks), including the significance of Martin Luther King, Jr.'s "Letter from Birmingham Jail" and "I Have a Dream" speech.

11.10.5 Discuss the diffusion of the civil rights movement of African Americans from the churches of the rural South and the urban North, including the resistance to racial desegregation in Little Rock and Birmingham, and how the advances influenced the agendas, strategies, and effectiveness of the quests of American Indians, Asian Americans, and Hispanic Americans for civil rights and equal opportunities.

Standard 11.10

Answers

1 MONDAY – C
Standard 11.10.5

2 TUESDAY – A
Standard 11.10.5

3 WEDNESDAY – B
Standard 11.10.6
Have students review the amendments to the Constitution, specifically the two amendments mentioned in the question. They will learn that these deal with voting rights rather than segregation issues. Students therefore can rule out answers C and D.

4 THURSDAY – B
Standard 11.10.7

5 FRIDAY – A
Standard 11.10.7
Suggest to students that they identify what each of the answer choices mean. They will then recognize that only one of the items listed deals with women's rights at work.

WEEK 20

Standard 11.10 — Students analyze the development of federal civil rights and voting rights.

MONDAY 11.10.5

1 When Mexican American students and teachers protested racism by walking out of classrooms in East Los Angeles in 1968, they were *(Section 18.3)*

A part of a larger movement called AIM.

B protesting the policies of *La Raza Unida*.

C using the protest techniques of the civil rights era.

D advocating the end of bilingualism in schools.

TUESDAY 11.10.5

2 Similar to African Americans, Native Americans used the federal court system to gain rights. The cases resulted in *(Section 16.3)*

A being able to perform certain sovereign functions on reservations, such as taxing business.

B the return of approximately half of their original lands.

C having complete sovereignty on their reservations.

D busing Native American students to local white schools to achieve racial balance.

WEDNESDAY 11.10.6

3 The legislation that finally gave all citizens equal access to restaurants, parks, libraries, and theaters, as well as more power to the attorney general to bring lawsuits to force school desegregation, was *(Section 16.2)*

A the Civil Rights Act of 1957.

B the Civil Rights Act of 1964.

C the Fifteenth Amendment.

D the Twenty-Fourth Amendment.

THURSDAY 11.10.7

4 The president of the National American Woman Suffrage Association, who led the movement in its final effort to support state voting initiatives and gain passage of the Nineteenth Amendment, was *(Section 5.1)*

A Alice Paul.

B Carrie Chapman Catt.

C Susan B. Anthony.

D Elizabeth Cady Stanton.

FRIDAY

5 Use the list to answer the following question. 11.10.7

- Civil Rights Act of 1964
- *Roe* v. *Wade* Decision
- Title IX
- Publication of *The Feminine Mystique*

Which of the items in the list represented an advancement for women in the workplace? *(Section 18.2)*

A the Civil Rights Act of 1964

B the *Roe* v. *Wade* decision

C Title IX

D the publication of *The Feminine Mystique*

40

History–Social Science Standards Grade Eleven

11.10.5 Discuss the diffusion of the civil rights movement of African Americans from the churches of the rural South and the urban North, including the resistance to racial desegregation in Little Rock and Birmingham, and how the advances influenced the agendas, strategies, and effectiveness of the quests of American Indians, Asian Americans, and Hispanic Americans for civil rights and equal opportunities.

11.10.6 Analyze the passage and effects of civil rights and voting rights legislation (e.g., 1964 Civil Rights Act, Voting Rights Act of 1965) and the Twenty-Fourth Amendment, with an emphasis on equality of access to education and to the political process.

11.10.7 Analyze the women's rights movement from the era of Elizabeth Cady Stanton and Susan B. Anthony and the passage of the Nineteenth Amendment to the movement launched in the 1960s, including differing perspectives on the roles of women.

WEEK 21

Standard 11.11 Students analyze the major social problems and domestic policy issues in contemporary American society.

MONDAY   11.11.1

1 The Immigration Reform Act of 1965 was a turning point in U.S. immigration policy because *(Section 15.3)*

A it helped eliminate the national origins system of the 1920s.

B it nearly stopped all immigration from the Western Hemisphere.

C it halted immigration from the Eastern Hemisphere.

D for the first time, the United States closed its doors to all immigrants.

TUESDAY   11.11.2

2 When President Reagan said, "government is not the solution to our problem. Government is the problem," he referred to *(Section 20.2)*

A increasing tensions with China and other Communist nations.

B increasing concerns about the arms race.

C the policy called Reaganomics.

D earlier domestic policies, including the legacy of the New Deal.

WEDNESDAY   **3** Use the excerpt to answer the following question.   11.11.2

In a land of great wealth, families must not live in hopeless poverty. In a land rich in harvest, children just must not go hungry. In a land of healing miracles, neighbors must not suffer and die untended. In a great land of learning and scholars, young people must be taught to read and write.

—Lyndon Johnson

In this excerpt of his Inaugural Address, **President Johnson** *(Section 15.3)*

A described how he would continue the policies of President Kennedy.

B outlined his ideas for a Great Society.

C recalled details of his policy initiatives as senator.

D referred to the policies President Kennedy had initiated.

THURSDAY   11.11.3

4 One of the changes for women brought about by the 1960s women's rights movement includes *(Section 18.2)*

A the elimination of the income gap.

B a dramatic gain in professional jobs.

C a move back to one-career families.

D the passage of the Equal Rights Amendment.

FRIDAY   11.11.4

5 The legislative effect of Watergate was *(Section 19.2)*

A proposed legislation to eliminate the executive branch.

B an amendment to the Constitution redefining impeachment.

C Congress's increased control and oversight of the FBI.

D a series of laws intended to limit the power of the executive.

41

Standard 11.11

Answers

1 MONDAY – A
Standard 11.11.1

2 TUESDAY – D
Standard 11.11.2

3 WEDNESDAY – B
Standard 11.11.2

4 THURSDAY – B
Standard 11.11.3
Suggest to students that they consider the current situation of women and families as they read the question. For example, rather than decreasing, the number of two-career families is increasing. Therefore, students can rule out answer C.

5 FRIDAY – D
Standard 11.11.4
Remind students that the executive branch has been established by the Constitution of the United States. Changes to the Constitution can only be made with amendments, not legislation. In addition, the executive branch of government is one of the three cornerstones of the republic and would not be considered for elimination. Students can safely rule out answer A.

History–Social Science Standards Grade Eleven

11.11.1 Discuss the reasons for the nation's changing immigration policy, with emphasis on how the Immigration Act of 1965 and successor acts have transformed American society.

11.11.2 Discuss the significant domestic policy speeches of Truman, Eisenhower, Kennedy, Johnson, Nixon, Carter, Reagan, Bush, and Clinton (e.g., with regard to education, civil rights, economic policy, environmental policy).

11.11.3 Describe the changing roles of women in society as reflected in the entry of more women into the labor force and the changing family structure.

11.11.4 Explain the constitutional crisis originating from the Watergate scandal.

Answers

1 MONDAY – B
Standard 11.11.5
Have students recall the topic of Rachel Carson's book and the effects its publication had on the United States. They will quickly realize that the environment was the main focus of early efforts.

2 TUESDAY – C
Standard 11.11.5

3 WEDNESDAY – D
Standard 11.11.6

4 THURSDAY – A
Standard 11.11.7

5 FRIDAY – A
Standard 11.11.7
Suggest to students that they look carefully at the graphic organizer and the events listed. They should then choose the answer choice that best fits as the next step. For example, while welfare reform helped relieve poverty, it did not have a direct impact on the decline of the inner city.

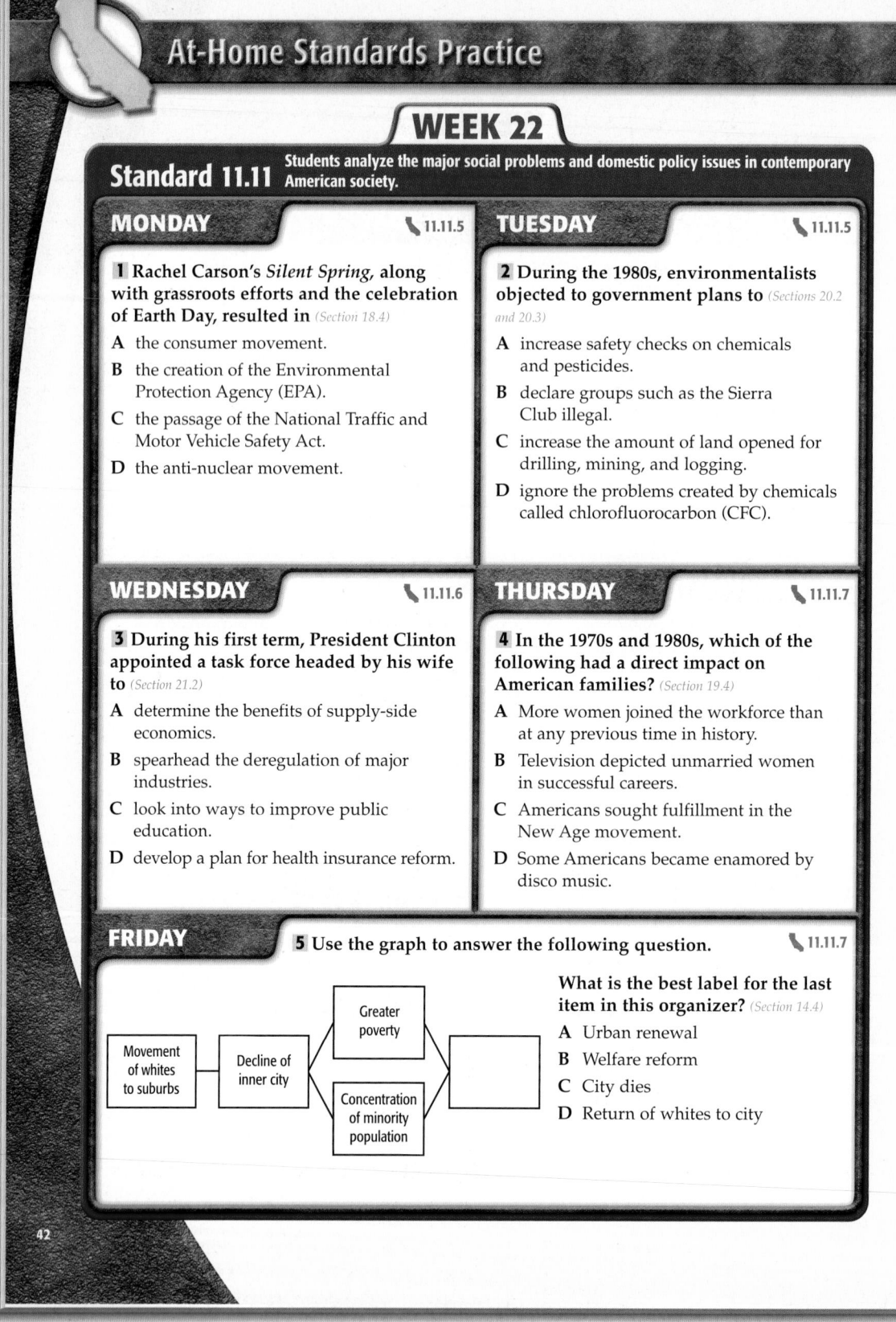

At-Home Standards Practice

WEEK 22

Standard 11.11 Students analyze the major social problems and domestic policy issues in contemporary American society.

MONDAY 📞 11.11.5

1 Rachel Carson's *Silent Spring,* along with grassroots efforts and the celebration of Earth Day, resulted in *(Section 18.4)*

A the consumer movement.

B the creation of the Environmental Protection Agency (EPA).

C the passage of the National Traffic and Motor Vehicle Safety Act.

D the anti-nuclear movement.

TUESDAY 📞 11.11.5

2 During the 1980s, environmentalists objected to government plans to *(Sections 20.2 and 20.3)*

A increase safety checks on chemicals and pesticides.

B declare groups such as the Sierra Club illegal.

C increase the amount of land opened for drilling, mining, and logging.

D ignore the problems created by chemicals called chlorofluorocarbon (CFC).

WEDNESDAY 📞 11.11.6

3 During his first term, President Clinton appointed a task force headed by his wife to *(Section 21.2)*

A determine the benefits of supply-side economics.

B spearhead the deregulation of major industries.

C look into ways to improve public education.

D develop a plan for health insurance reform.

THURSDAY 📞 11.11.7

4 In the 1970s and 1980s, which of the following had a direct impact on American families? *(Section 19.4)*

A More women joined the workforce than at any previous time in history.

B Television depicted unmarried women in successful careers.

C Americans sought fulfillment in the New Age movement.

D Some Americans became enamored by disco music.

FRIDAY

5 Use the graph to answer the following question. 📞 11.11.7

Movement of whites to suburbs → Decline of inner city → Greater poverty / Concentration of minority population →

What is the best label for the last item in this organizer? *(Section 14.4)*

A Urban renewal

B Welfare reform

C City dies

D Return of whites to city

42

History–Social Science Standards Grade Eleven

11.11.5 Trace the impact of, need for, and controversies associated with environmental conservation, expansion of the national park system, and the development of environmental protection laws, with particular attention to the interaction between environmental protection advocates and property rights advocates.

11.11.6 Analyze the persistence of poverty and how different analyses of this issue influence welfare reform, health insurance reform, and other social policies.

11.11.7 Explain how the federal, state, and local governments have responded to demographic and social changes such as population shifts to the suburbs, racial concentrations in the cities, Frostbelt-to-Sunbelt migration, international migration, decline of family farms, increases in out-of-wedlock births, and drug abuse.

Answer Key

Week 1
1. D
2. B
3. D
4. B
5. C

Week 2
1. D
2. C
3. C
4. A
5. B

Week 3
1. B
2. D
3. D
4. C
5. C

Week 4
1. B
2. A
3. D
4. B
5. A

Week 5
1. A
2. B
3. A
4. B
5. C

Week 6
1. C
2. D
3. D
4. C
5. C

Week 7
1. A
2. D
3. D
4. B
5. B

Week 8
1. B
2. D
3. C
4. C
5. A

Week 9
1. B
2. A
3. A
4. D
5. C

Week 10
1. B
2. D
3. C
4. B
5. A

Week 11
1. C
2. A
3. B
4. A
5. C

Week 12
1. C
2. A
3. B
4. D
5. C

Week 13
1. B
2. C
3. B
4. D
5. A

Week 14
1. A
2. D
3. B
4. B
5. C

Week 15
1. D
2. C
3. C
4. D
5. D

Week 16
1. B
2. A
3. A
4. B
5. D

Week 17
1. C
2. D
3. C
4. A
5. B

Week 18
1. A
2. B
3. B
4. D
5. A

Week 19
1. A
2. D
3. C
4. D
5. B

Week 20
1. C
2. A
3. B
4. B
5. A

Week 21
1. A
2. D
3. B
4. B
5. D

Week 22
1. B
2. C
3. D
4. A
5. A

Additional Resources

Your textbook program provides many opportunities for students to practice the History–Social Science Standards.

- The California Standards Practice, Grade 11 is a print ancillary that will help you teach your students the standards.
- The Succeeding on the End-of-Course Test CD-ROM provides questions in a format similar to the actual test and helps you manage student progress.
- You can find additional questions in the ExamView® Pro Testmaker CD-ROM to help prepare your students for a variety of test question formats.
- The Self-Check Quizzes and the Interactive Tutor on the Web at tav.mt.glencoe.com are additional tools for your students to check their mastery of the material.

Textbook Tips

As your students practice the History–Social Science Standards and prepare for tests, provide them with these tips for the best results:

- Students should read each question carefully, making sure they understand all of the text.
- Tell students to use the process of elimination to narrow down the possible answer choices.
- Students should try to remember everything they know about a particular standard that is relevant to a particular question.

Previewing Your Textbook

Your textbook has been organized to help you learn about the significant events and people that make up United States history. Before you start reading, though, here is a road map to help you understand what you will encounter in the pages of this textbook. Follow this road map before you read so that you can understand how this textbook works.

Units

Your textbook is divided into 6 units. Each unit begins with two pages of information to help you start your study of the topics.

WHY IT MATTERS

Each unit begins with *Why It Matters.* This is a short summary about the important topics and what you will study in the unit.

QUOTATION

A short quotation gives a glimpse of the ideas of a key figure from the unit's era.

UNIT

2 Imperialism and Progressivism

1890–1919

"It is hard to fail, but it is worse never to have tried to succeed."

–Theodore Roosevelt, 1899

Why It Matters

As the United States entered the twentieth century, it grew to become a world power. While the nation was expanding its territory into other parts of the world, conditions at home gave rise to a widespread Progressive movement. This movement worked for various reforms in government, business, and society. While Americans focused on their own country, Europe slid into a devastating world war that eventually involved the United States as well. These crucial years of domestic change and foreign conflict provided important foundations for the world you live in today. The following resources offer more information about this period in American history.

Primary Sources Library
See pages 974–975 for primary source readings to accompany Unit 2.

Use the American History Primary Source Document Library CD-ROM to find additional primary sources about imperialism and progressivism.

288

World War I pin

OVER ★ THERE

American Troops Arriving in Paris July 14, 1918 by J.F. Boucher

PRIMARY SOURCES LIBRARY

This tells you where to find the *Primary Sources Library* readings that accompany the unit.

VISUALS

A photograph or painting shows you what life was like during the time period of the unit.

Chapters

Each unit in *The American Vision: Modern Times* is made up of chapters. Each chapter starts by providing you with background information to help you get the most out of the chapter.

CHAPTER TITLE

The chapter title tells you the main topic you will be reading about.

THE BIG IDEAS

The Big Ideas identify major themes in history for each section of the chapter.

CHAPTER

5

1890–1919

The Progressive Movement

❧ *The Big Ideas* ❧

SECTION 1: The Roots of Progressivism

Social and economic crises lead to new roles for government. As Americans became more aware of the social problems affecting the United States, progressives began to look to the government to help solve these problems and regulate big business.

SECTION 2: Roosevelt in Office

Social and economic crises lead to new roles for government. When Theodore Roosevelt, a progressive, won the presidency in 1901, progressivism entered national politics.

SECTION 3: The Taft Administration

Social and economic crises lead to new roles for government. William Howard Taft was a more moderate progressive than Theodore Roosevelt, but he still continued several progressive reforms.

SECTION 4: The Wilson Years

Social and economic crises lead to new roles for government. When the Progressive era ended, the role of the federal government had changed, and people expected the government to take action in regulating the economy and solving social issues.

The *American Vision: Modern Times* Video The Chapter 5 video, "The Stockyard Jungle," portrays the horrors of the meatpacking industry first investigated by Upton Sinclair.

Women marching for the vote in New York City, 1912

1889
• Hull House opens in Chicago

1890
• Jacob Riis's *How the Other Half Lives* published

1902
• Maryland workers' compensation laws passed

1904
• Ida Tarbell's *History of the Standard Oil Company* published

1905
• Industrial Workers of the World founded

1906
• Pure Food and Drug Act passed

1910
• Mann-Elkins Act passed

1913
• Seventeenth Amendment ratified

1920
• Nineteenth Amendment ratified, guaranteeing women's voting rights

VOTE YES NOV. 2

United States PRESIDENTS

B. Harrison 1889–1893 | Cleveland 1893–1897 | McKinley 1897–1901 | T. Roosevelt 1901–1909 | Taft 1909–1913 | Wilson 1913–1921

1890 | 1900 | 1910 | 1920

World

1884
• Toynbee Hall, first settlement house, established in London

1900
• Freud's *Interpretation of Dreams* published

1902
• Anglo-Japanese alliance formed

1903
• Russian Bolshevik Party established by Lenin

1905
• Einstein's theory of relativity formulated

1910
• Mexican Revolution

1914
• World War I begins in Europe

HISTORY Online

Chapter Overview
Visit the *American Vision: Modern Times* Web site at tav.mt.glencoe.com and click on *Chapter Overviews– Chapter 5* to preview chapter information.

322

323

TIME LINE

The time line shows you when and where events happened during the period of time covered in the chapter.

VISUALS

A photograph or painting depicts a scene from the chapter's era.

WEB SITE

History Online directs you to the Internet, where you can find activities, quizzes, and additional information about the chapter's topic.

Previewing Your Textbook

Sections

A section is a division, or part, of the chapter. The first page of the section, the section opener, helps you set a purpose for reading.

CONNECTIONS

The *Connection* sums up what you have learned in the previous chapter and introduces you to the section.

MAIN IDEA

Learn how each major heading ties to the *Big Idea* for the section.

THE BIG IDEA

Read a summary of how the section relates to the *Big Idea* outlined in the chapter opener.

CALIFORNIA STANDARDS

The main California content standards covered in the section can be found here.

VOCABULARY

The *Content Vocabulary* words are the section's key terms and will be defined in the text. *Academic Vocabulary* consists of words you should know to be successful in school and life.

READING STRATEGY

Completing the *Reading Strategy* activity will help you organize information as you read the section.

SECTION 1

The Roots of Progressivism

Guide to Reading

Connection
In the previous chapter, you learned how the United States increased its power and influence around the world. In this section, you will discover the beginning of the Progressive movement and a focus on domestic reform.

Main Idea
• The Progressive movement was an attempt to use scientific principles to improve society. (p. 327)
• One form of progressivism focused on ways to use business practices to make government more efficient. (p. 328)
• Progressive policies in Wisconsin became widespread, leading to election reforms. (p. 330)
• Many progressives joined the suffrage movement to gain women the right to vote in national elections. (p. 330)

• Many progressives focused on social welfare problems, such as child labor, public health, and prohibition. (p. 333)
• Another form of progressivism focused on federal regulation of big business. (p. 335)

Content Vocabulary
progressivism, muckraker, commission plan, direct primary, initiative, referendum, recall, suffrage, temperance, prohibition, socialism

Academic Vocabulary
legislation, strategy, funds, advocate

People and Terms to Identify
Jacob Riis, Robert La Follette, Alice Paul

Reading Objectives
• **Discuss** the rise of the Progressive movement.

• **Evaluate** the impact of initiative, referendum, and recall, and of the Seventeenth Amendment.

Reading Strategy
Organizing As you read about the beginnings of progressivism, complete a graphic organizer similar to the one below by filling in the beliefs of progressives.

Preview of Events

♦1890	♦1900	♦1910	♦1920
1890 Jacob Riis's *How the Other Half Lives* published	**1901** Galveston, Texas, adopts commission system	**1913** Seventeenth Amendment provides for direct election of senators	**1920** Nineteenth Amendment gives women the right to vote

The following are the main History–Social Science Standards covered in this section.

11.2.9 Understand the effect of political programs and activities of the Progressives (e.g., federal regulation of railroad transport, Children's Bureau, the Sixteenth Amendment, Theodore Roosevelt, Hiram Johnson).

11.5.3 Examine the passage of the Eighteenth Amendment to the Constitution and the Volstead Act (Prohibition).

11.5.4 Analyze the passage of the Nineteenth Amendment and the changing role of women in society.

∾ *The Big Idea* ∾

Social and economic crises lead to new roles for government. During the late 1800s, Americans again became concerned with social problems in the United States. Progressives focused on a variety of issues and how to address them. Some believed that government should solve social problems, while others thought that science or business held the answers. Many progressives focused on improving government by making it either more efficient or more democratic. Others joined in the suffrage movement and worked to gain women the right to vote in national elections. Still other progressives focused on child labor, public welfare, prohibition, and regulation of big business.

326 CHAPTER 5 The Progressive Movement

Reading Roadmap

You will get more out of your textbook if you recognize the different elements that help you understand what you read.

AN AMERICAN STORY

Think of *An American Story* as a moment in time. It introduces you to an important event that you will read about.

OUTLINE

The headings in each section form an outline. The red titles are the main headings. The blue titles that follow are the subheadings.

READING CHECK

The *Reading Checks* allow you to check your understanding of the main ideas.

MAIN IDEA

The *Main Idea* ties the text under the heading to the Big Idea for the section.

READING CONNECTION

The *Reading Connections* help you connect to what you are about to read.

SECTION ASSESSMENT

Completing the *Section Assessments* can help you evaluate your comprehension of section material.

VISUAL AIDS

Photographs, maps, and charts provide visual information about the section. Questions help you interpret them and relate them to content.

The Rise of Progressivism

Main Idea The Progressive movement was an attempt to use scientific principles to improve society.

Reading Connection What areas of public life do you believe still need to be reformed? Read on to learn about a movement in the late 1800s that tried to reform many of the ills of society at the time.

In the early 1900s, as the effects of industrialization and urbanization became apparent, a series of reform efforts transformed American society. These reforms ranged from government reform to social welfare and woman suffrage. Historians refer to the era in American history—from about 1890 to 1920—as the Progressive Era.

★ An American Story ★

In 1917 suffragist Rose Winslow and several other women, including Alice Paul, founder of the National Woman's Party, were arrested for obstructing traffic and blocking sidewalks. The women had been picketing the White House to draw attention to the fact that women did not yet have the right to vote in federal elections. After being sentenced to seven months in jail, Paul, Winslow, and other women prisoners went on a hunger strike. Prison authorities forced the prisoners to eat. Winslow smuggled details of their treatment out to the public:

❝We have been in solitary for five weeks. . . . I felt quite feeble the last few days—faint, so that I hardly get my hair brushed, my arms ached so. But today I am well again. . . . [Alice Paul] dreaded forcible feeding frightfully, and I hate to think how she feeling. . . . I am really all right. If this continues long I perhaps won't be. All the officers here know we are making this hunger strike [so] that women for liberty may be considered political prisoners. [W]e don't want women ever to have to do this again.❞

—quoted in *Jailed for...*

Progressive reform efforts were not [limited to] women's voting rights. Progressives came [from] different backgrounds, focused on a variety [of issues] and did not always agree on solutions [to the] nation's problems.

One reason progressives believed people could improve society was because they had a strong faith in science and technology. The application of scientific knowledge had produced the lightbulb, the telephone, the automobile, and the airplane. It had built skyscrapers and railroads. Science and technology had benefited people, thus progressives believed using scientific principles could also produce solutions for society.

The Muckrakers Among the first people to articulate Progressive ideas was a group of crusading journalists who investigated social conditions and political corruption. These writers became known as **muckrakers** after a speech by President Theodore Roosevelt:

❝Now, it is very necessary that we should not flinch from seeing what is vile and debasing. There is filth on the floor and it must be scraped up with the muck-rake; and there are times and places where this service is the most needed of all the services that can be performed. . . .❞

—Washington, D.C., April 14, 1906

Picturing **History**

Muckrakers *McClure's* published Ida Tarbell's exposé on Standard Oil. What issues particularly concerned the muckrakers?

By the early 1900s, American publishers were competing to expose the most corruption and scandal. A group of aggressive 10¢ and 15¢ magazines grew in popularity at this time, including *McClure's*, *Collier's* and *Munsey's*.

Muckrakers uncovered corruption in many areas. Some concentrated on what they considered the unfair practices of large American corporations. In *McClure's*, for example, Ida Tarbell published a series of articles critical of the standard Oil Company. In *Everybody's Magazine*, Charles Edward Russell attacked the beef industry.

Other muckrakers targeted government. David Graham Philips described how money influenced the Senate, while Lincoln Steffens, another *McClure's* reporter, reported on vote stealing and other corrupt practices of urban political machines. These were later collected into a book, *The Shame of the Cities*.

Still other muckrakers concentrated on social problems. In his influential book *How the Other Half Lives*, published in 1890, **Jacob Riis** described the poverty, disease, and crime that afflicted many immigrant neighborhoods in New York City. The muckrakers' articles led to a general public debate on social and economic problems and put pressure on politicians to introduce reforms.

Reading Check **Describing** How did the muckrakers help spark the Progressive movement?

Making Government Efficient

Main Idea One form of progressivism focused on ways to use business practices to make government more efficient.

Reading Connection In what ways do you try to use your time and resources wisely and efficiently? Read on to find out about political programs the progressives designed to make the government more efficient.

There were many different types of progressivism. Different causes led to different approaches, and progressives even took opposing positions on how to solve some problems.

HISTORY *Online*

Student Web Activity Visit the *American Vision: Modern Times* Web site at tav.mt.glencoe.com and click on **Student Web Activities—Chapter 5** for an activity on the Progressive movement.

---

everyone, such as railroads and [...] At its peak, socialism had some national support. Eugene Debs, the former American Railway Union

Online

...or help with the concepts in this section of *American Vision: Modern Times* go to tav.mt.glencoe.com and click on **Study Central**.

SECTION 1 ASSESSMENT

Checking for Understanding

1. **Vocabulary** Define: progressivism, muckraker, commission plan, direct primary, initiative, legislation, referendum, recall, suffrage, strategy, funds, temperance, advocated, prohibition, socialism.

2. **People and Terms** Identify: Jacob Riis, Robert La Follette, Alice Paul.

3. **Identify** what was provided for by the Nineteenth Amendment to the Constitution.

Reviewing Big Ideas

4. **Explaining** How did initiative, referendum, and recall change democracy in the United States?

Critical Thinking

5. **Historical Analysis** **Evaluating** Identify the different issues associated with social welfare progressivism. How do these ideals influence society today? **CA CS1: H11**

6. **Organizing** Use a graphic organizer similar to the one below to list the kinds of problems that muckrakers exposed.

Analyzing Visuals

7. **Examining Charts** Study the charts on page 329. Under which system do voters seem to have the most control over department heads? Why do you think so?

Writing About History

8. **Persuasive Writing** Some women in the early 1900s suggested that the Constitution needed an equal rights amendment. Imagine you are living then. Write a letter to the editor of your local paper supporting or opposing such an amendment. **CA 11WS1.1; 11WS1.2**

Special Features

A variety of special features will help you as you study *The American Vision: Modern Times.*

READING SKILL

Use the *Reading Skills* to learn strategies for reading and to improve your reading and comprehension skills.

HISTORICAL ANALYSIS SKILL

Historical Analysis Skills teach you valuable skills to help you understand and interpret historical events.

PRIMARY SOURCES

The *Primary Sources* provide additional primary sources about one specific topic in each chapter.

AMERICAN LITERATURE

American Literature analyzes poems and excerpts from biographies, American fiction, and other writings, and describes the excerpts' historical lessons.

Preparing to Read Chapter 5

Reading Skill — **Making Inferences**

When people read a text, they do not just read the text itself. They also use a skill called making inferences to understand the meaning of the text. This is sometimes called "reading between the lines." It means that readers look for clues that might explain what is occurring in a passage even though it may not be openly stated. Readers think about what they already know and draw conclusions based on this knowledge. Authors rely on a reader's ability to infer. They usually cannot include all the details in a text, because it would make passages needlessly long and repetitive.

As you read a text and make inferences, you must think about your own background knowledge. You will also use several reading strategies you learned earlier, including predicting and questioning. When you combine all of this information, you can understand the greater message the author

---

Historical Analysis Skill — **Interpreting Events**

Analysis Skill Standard H14

Historical Interpretation When you learn to interpret events, it helps you understand their meaning, implication, and impact. One way to interpret is by recognizing and examining how events could have taken other directions.

As you complete your high school education, you might be considering a job in a specific industry. Consider how your lif...

Primary Sources
Eyewitness to History

For most of the history of the United States, women did not have the right as the head of his household, and he voted as the representative of his fa became more involved outside the home, they started to demand a voice The battle became increasingly heated until women finally won the vote i

Source 1:

Abigail Scott Duniway became the sole supporter of her six children after her husband was disabled in an accident. She earned a living as a writer and led the fight for woman suffrage in Oregon. In 1899 she gave a speech promoting women's right to vote before the annual meeting of the National American Woman Suffrage Association in Michigan.

The first fact to be considered, when working to win the ballot, is that there is but one way by which we may hope to obtain it, and that is by and through the affirmative votes of men. We may theorize, organize, appeal, argue, coax, **cajole**[1] and threaten men till doomsday; we may secure their pettings, praises, flattery, and every appearance of **acquiescence**[2] in our demands; we may believe with all our hearts in the sincerity of their promises to vote as we dictate, but all of this will avail us nothing unless they deposit their affirmative votes in the ballot box.

Every man who stops to argue the case, as an opponent, tells us that he "loves women," and, while wondering much that he should consider such a declaration necessary, I have always admired the loyal spirit that prompts his utterance. But, gentlemen, . . . there is another side to this expression of loyalty. Not only is our movement not instigated in a spirit of warfare between the sexes, but it is engendered, altogether in the spirit of harmony, and interdependence between men and women. . . . In order

▲ Abigail Scott Duniway

Source 2:

Mrs. Arthur M. Dodge led the National Assoc She believed that allo the family. In 1913 sh the New York Times.

That is a sad state the woman's busine turies. It is the foun morals. Without the and without morals

To offset the sus frage means destru the movement are otherwise. Watch t recent days and th and you will find a leaders with their against the velvet have decided that

[1] **cajole:** persuade
[2] **acquiescence:** passive acceptance

American LITERATURE

Born in Maryland in 1878, **Upton Sinclair** spent his life writing about and trying to change what he saw as wrong in the United States. One of his most famous novels, *The Jungle*, deals with working conditions and the rights of immigrants. The novel tells the story of Jurgis Rudkus, a Lithuanian immigrant who comes to the United States with his family in the early 1900s, dreaming of wealth and freedom. What he finds is "Packingtown," the bustling, filthy stockyards of Chicago. In the following excerpt, Sinclair describes the system Jurgis comes to know after gaining his first job in a meatpacking plant.

Read to Discover
What qualities did Sinclair believe a person must have to succeed in Packingtown?

Reader's Dictionary
killing-beds: areas where cattle were slaughtered

dismayed: alarmed, disheartened

universality: the state of including all

pitted: set against each other

caldron: a large kettle or pot for boiling

knave: a tricky, deceitful person

trice: short period of time

from The Jungle
by Upton Sinclair

This was the first time in his life that he had ever really worked, it seemed to Jurgis; it was the first time that he had ever had anything to do which took all he had in him. Jurgis had stood with the rest up in the gallery and watched the men on the killing-beds, marveling at their speed and power as if they had been wonderful machines; it somehow never occurred to one to think of the flesh-and-blood side of it— that is, not until he actually got down into the pit and took off his coat. Then he saw things in a different light, he got at the inside of them. The pace they set here, it was one that called for every faculty of a man—from the instant the first steer fell till the sounding of the noon whistle, and again from half-past twelve till heaven only knew what hour in the late afternoon or evening, there was never one instant's rest for a man, for his hand or his eye or his brain. Jurgis saw how they managed it; there were portions of the work which deter-

mined the pace of the rest, and for these they had picked men whom they paid high wages, and whom they changed frequently. You might easily pick out these pace-makers, for they worked under the eye of the bosses, and they worked like men possessed. This was called "speeding up the gang," and if any man could not keep up with the pace, there were hundreds outside begging to try.

Yet Jurgis did not mind it; he rather enjoyed it. It saved him the necessity of flinging his arms about and fidgeting as he did in most work. He would laugh to himself as he ran down the line, darting a glance now and then at the man ahead of him. It was not the pleasantest work one could think of, but it was necessary work; and what more had a man the right to ask than a chance to do something useful, and to get good pay for doing it?

So Jurgis thought, and so he spoke, in his bold, free way; very much to his surprise, he found that it had a

Scavenger Hunt

T*he American Vision: Modern Times* contains a wealth of information. The trick is to know where to look to access all the information in the book. If you go through this scavenger hunt, either alone or with your teachers or family, you will quickly learn how the textbook is organized and how to get the most out of your reading and study time. Let's get started!

1. How many units and chapters are in the book?
6 units and 21 chapters

2. Where do you find the glossary? appendix

3. Most sections of a chapter open with a primary source—a document or other testimony dating from the period. Where else can you find primary sources in the textbook?
Eyewitness to History feature; Primary Sources Library

4. In what special feature can you find the definition of a physical map, a political map, and a special-purpose map? Geography Handbook

5. If you want to quickly find all the maps, charts, and graphs about World War II, where in the front do you look? Table of Contents

6. How can you find information about civil rights activist Martin Luther King, Jr.? Index

7. Where can you find a graphic organizer that summarizes the major events of the Vietnam War discussed in Chapter 17?
Chapter Summary

8. Where and how do you find the content vocabulary for Chapter 15, Section 3? listed in Guide to Reading and Section Assessment, bold-faced and highlighted in text

9. The Web site for the book is listed four times in Chapter 20. After finding all four, list how the Web site can help you.
provides overviews, practice tests, and additional activities and resources

10. Which of the book's main features will give you practice for improving your historical analysis skills?
Different Viewpoints feature

How Do I Study History?

As you read *The American Vision: Modern Times,* you will be given help in sorting out all the information you encounter. This textbook organizes the events of your nation's past and present around 11 Big Ideas. The Big Ideas are the keys that will help you unlock the most important concepts of our nation's history. By recognizing these Big Ideas and how they relate to different events over time, you will better understand events of the past and how they affect you today.

Big Ideas in *The American Vision: Modern Times*

Political philosophies and major events influence the formation of constitutional governments.

Ideas have power. Philosophies and movements that emphasized people's natural rights and consent to be governed inspired American colonists to declare and win independence from Britain. These ideas shaped the new government created after the revolution. Such events can, in turn, inspire similar revolutions and the creation of new governments elsewhere around the world.

A written contract between the people and their government can preserve natural rights and allow for change over time.

People are often advised to get important agreements "in writing." A written document approved by both the people and their government clearly spells out each side's rights and responsibilities. Such a contract, like the U.S. Constitution, defines and protects citizens' rights, but can be amended over time to meet the changing needs of society.

Differences in economic, political, and social beliefs and practices can lead to division within a nation and have lasting consequences.

Different regions of the United States developed unique ways of life. Sometimes, these differences have erupted in violence, such as the Civil War. The diversity in political and social life that makes the United States great can also lead to conflict. Whatever the nature of the dispute, divisions within a nation can take a long time to heal.

The Industrial Revolution changed the face of America.

The United States was founded as a rural, agricultural nation. With the Industrial Revolution, many people moved to the cities. New industries and technologies changed the way people lived and worked. As millions of rural Americans and immigrants poured into the cities, new challenges—and solutions—associated with urban life arose.

America's military and economic strength made it a world power.

For many years, the United States avoided involvement in world affairs. Following two world wars in the twentieth century, however, the nation emerged as the dominant international power. Its role as a military and economic force has been accompanied by the responsibility to serve as a leader in promoting cooperation among and prosperity for all nations.

People react to periods of breathtaking social and cultural change in different ways.

Everyone responds differently to change. Some people actively promote change, while other people fight against it. During periods of dramatic change in our society, such as the industrial age, the Roaring Twenties, or the civil rights era, people's various reactions have had a powerful impact on society.

Social and economic crises lead to new roles for government.

The role of the government evolves over time in response to important events and changing conditions in society. President Roosevelt redefined the role of the government during the Great Depression. Later presidents responded to other crises in the United States. One of the greatest strengths of our government is its ability to respond and adapt to the needs of society.

The fate of nations is forever changed by monumental world events.

At times, world events have brought about pivotal changes within and among nations. Various revolutions, wars, and acts of terrorism have altered the way people think and live. In today's globally interdependent world, it is difficult for a nation *not* to be affected by the events that take place elsewhere in the world.

International competition can lead to conflict and cooperation.

Nations compete for wealth and influence. Sometimes competition erupts in aggression and conflict. Many nations, however, have realized that they benefit more by partnering and cooperating than by competing for dominance.

The quest for equality is eternal.

Although our nation was founded on the premise that "all men are created equal," there has been an enduring struggle to achieve this ideal. Women and minorities have made significant progress toward greater equality. However, the search for equality is an ongoing journey as our nation becomes ever more diverse.

Societies change over time.

Change—political, social, economic—is inevitable in a society. Societies change in response to events and conditions at home as well as in other parts of the world. These changes influence the way Americans think and act.

Using the Big Ideas

You will find Big Ideas at the beginning of every section of your text. You are asked questions that help you better understand how ideas and themes are connected across time—and to see why history is important to you today.

Reading for Information

Think of your textbook as a tool that helps you learn more about the world around you. It is an example of nonfiction writing—it describes real-life events, people, ideas, and places. Here is a menu of reading strategies that will help you become a better textbook reader. As you come to passages in your textbook that you don't understand, refer to these reading strategies for help.

✔ Before You Read

Set a purpose
- Why are you reading the textbook?
- How does the subject relate to your life?
- How might you be able to use what you learn in your own life?

Preview
- Read the chapter title to find what the topic will be, and then look over the section titles to see how the topic will be organized.
- Skim the photos, charts, graphs, or maps. How do they support the topic?
- Look for words and terms that are bold-faced and highlighted in yellow. These include content vocabulary words and important people, terms, and places.
- Find the words that are boldfaced only. Knowing these academic vocabulary words will help you read and write in all subjects.

Draw From Your Own Background
- What have you read or heard concerning new information on the topic?
- How is the new information different from what you already know?
- How will the information you know help you understand the new information?

Question

- What is the main idea?
- How do the photos, charts, graphs, and maps support the main idea?

Connect

- Think about people, places, and events in your own life. Are there any similarities with those in your textbook?
- Can you relate the textbook information to other areas of your life?

Predict

- Predict events or outcomes by using clues and information that you already know.
- Change your predictions as you read and gather new information.

Visualize

- Pay careful attention to details and descriptions.
- Create graphic organizers to show relationships that you find in the information.

Look For Clues As You Read

Comparison and Contrast Sentences

- Look for clue words and phrases that signal comparison, such as *similarly, just as, both, in common, also,* and *too.*
- Look for clue words and phrases that signal contrast, such as *on the other hand, in contrast to, however, different, instead of, rather than, but,* and *unlike.*

Cause-and-Effect Sentences

- Look for clue words and phrases such as *because, as a result, therefore, that is why, since, so, for this reason,* and *consequently.*

Chronological Sentences

- Look for clue words and phrases such as *after, before, first, next, last, during, finally, earlier, later, since,* and *then.*

✓ After You Read

Summarize

- Describe the main idea and how the details support it.
- Use your own words to explain what you have read.

Assess

- What was the main idea?
- Did the text clearly support the main idea?
- Did you learn anything new from the material?
- Can you use this new information in other school subjects or at home?
- What other sources could you use to find more information about the topic?

Why Should I Teach Reading to My Social Studies Students?

For many social studies teachers, helping students develop reading skills is a low priority—nice to do if there is time, but not necessary. After all, there is scarcely time to meet many of the state-mandated standards. Why add reading instruction to the list? The answer is that reading skills are essential to the learning of all subjects. In the social studies, students must read to learn. Struggling readers risk learning less than those who are proficient in reading.

Teachers who infuse literacy strategies with social studies content actively engage students in learning. Once students internalize reading strategies such as visualizing, predicting, questioning, and making connections, they inevitably become better social studies students.

Reading Skills Handbook

READING TO LEARN

This handbook focuses on skills and strategies that can help you understand the words you read. The strategies you use to understand whole texts depend on the kind of text you are reading. In other words, you do not read a textbook the way you read a novel. You read a textbook mainly for information; you read a novel for the story and the characters. To get the most out of your reading, you need to choose the right strategy to fit the reason you are reading. This handbook can help you learn about the following reading strategies:

- how to identify new words and build your vocabulary;
- how to adjust the way you read to fit your reason for reading;
- how to use specific reading strategies to better understand what you read;
- how to use critical thinking strategies to think more deeply about what you read; and
- how to understand text structures to identify an author's ideas.

TABLE OF CONTENTS

Professional Development: Teaching Reading

The following sources will help you teach reading skills:

- *Subjects Matter: Every Teacher's Guide to Content-Area Reading* by Harvey Daniels and Steven Zemelman. Portsmouth, NH: Heinemann, 2004.
- *Improving Adolescent Literacy: Strategies at Work* by Douglas Fisher and Nancy Frey. Upper Saddle River, NJ: Merrill Education, 2004.
- *I Read It But I Don't Get It: Comprehension Strategies for Adolescent Readers* by Cris Tovani. Portland, ME: Stenhouse Publishers, 2000.
- *Readers, Teachers, and Learners: Expanding Literacy Across the Content Areas (4th Edition)* by William G. Broze and Michele L. Simpson. Upper Saddle River, NJ: Merrill Prentice Hall, 2002.

Identifying Words and Building Vocabulary

What do you do when you come across a word you do not know as you read? Do you skip over the word? If you are reading a novel, you use the context to understand the meaning of the word. But if you are reading for information, an unfamiliar word may get in the way of your understanding. When that happens, follow the strategies below to learn how to say the word and what it means.

Reading Unfamiliar Words

Sounding Out the Word One way to figure out how to say a new word is to sound it out, syllable by syllable. Look carefully at the word's beginning, middle, and ending. For example, in the word *coagulate,* what letters make up the beginning sound or beginning syllable of the word? *Co* rhymes with *so.* Inside *coagulate,* do you see a word you already know how to pronounce? The syllable *ag* has the same sound as the *ag* in *bag,* and the syllable *u* is pronounced like the letter *u.* What letters make up the ending sound or syllable? *Late* is a familiar word you already know how to pronounce. Now try pronouncing the whole word: **co ag u late.**

Determining a Word's Meaning

Using Syntax Like all languages, the English language has rules and patterns for the way words are arranged in sentences. The way a sentence is organized is called the syntax. If English is your first language, you have known this pattern since you started using sentences. If you are learning English now, you may find that the syntax is different from the patterns you know in your first language.

In a simple sentence in English, someone or something (the subject) does something (the predicate or verb) to or with another person or thing (the object): *The soldiers attacked the enemy.* Sometimes adjectives, adverbs, and phrases are added to add details to the sentence: *The courageous young soldiers fearlessly attacked the well-entrenched enemy shortly after dawn.*

Knowing about syntax can help you figure out the meaning of an unfamiliar word. Just look at how syntax can help you figure out the following nonsense sentence: *The blizzy kwarkles sminched the flerky fleans.* Your experience with English syntax tells you that the action word, or verb, in this sentence is *sminched.* Who did the *sminching?* The *kwarkles.* What kind of *kwarkles* were they? *Blizzy.* Whom did they *sminch?* The *fleans.* What kind of *fleans* were they? *Flerky.* Even though you don't know the meaning of the words in the nonsense sentence, you can make some sense of the entire sentence by studying its syntax.

Using Context Clues You can often figure out the meaning of an unfamiliar word by looking at its context, the words and sentences that surround it. To learn new words as you read, follow these steps for using context clues.

- Look before and after the unfamiliar word for a definition or a synonym, a general topic associated with the word, a clue to what the word is similar to or different from, or an action or a description that has something to do with the word.
- Connect what you already know with what the author has written.
- Predict a possible meaning.
- Use the meaning in the sentence.
- Try again if your guess does not make sense.

Identifying Words and Building Vocabulary

Why It's Important

Research documents the relationship between a strong vocabulary and the ability to read and write proficiently. Vocabulary may be the most important factor in comprehension, showing that ongoing, specific vocabulary instruction must be an integral part of every lesson.

Providing instructional support while students are reading is not enough to ensure they are learning the content. For this reason, this handbook provides skills for before reading, during reading, and after reading.

Before Reading

Activating Prior Knowledge Distribute index cards with a key word from the chapter written on each card. Organize students into groups of four, and give them time to discuss their words. After the group discussion, ask each group to write what they think the word means on the back of the card. Then have groups present the words to the class by writing their words and definitions on the board. Other students should help confirm or revise the definitions. Use pictures or graphs to enhance or correct the students' definitions. **OL**

UNIVERSAL ACCESS

Below Grade Level One way to help students increase their vocabularies is to have them play word games before they read the chapter. Give students a word from the chapter that they do not know, and allow them to ask questions about its definition. When a student correctly guesses its meaning, he or she can then be "it," choosing a new word for the class to question. This type of game demonstrates that there are often many definitions for a word, and it allows students to learn from each other. **BL**

During Reading

Learning Vocabulary Post a chart on the wall listing the steps for learning new vocabulary. Students may refer to the chart as they read. Steps include: sound out the word; look at prefixes, suffixes, and roots; look at how the word is used in the sentence; use context clues in surrounding sentences; use reference materials such as dictionaries and thesauruses; ask someone the meaning of the word. Encourage students to experiment with different steps to find the one that works best for them. **OL**

After Reading

Understanding Vocabulary Students should use graphic organizers and web diagrams to explain the definition of a word. Have students write the word in the center of a sheet of notebook paper. Then have them write *What it is* at the top left of the page, *What it is like* at the top right, *Examples of its meaning* at the bottom left of the page, and *What it is not* at the bottom right. Have students write the appropriate information under each head. **OL**

Checking Your Understanding Answers

1. graled
2. shabs
3. the mul-bulowed rotfabs

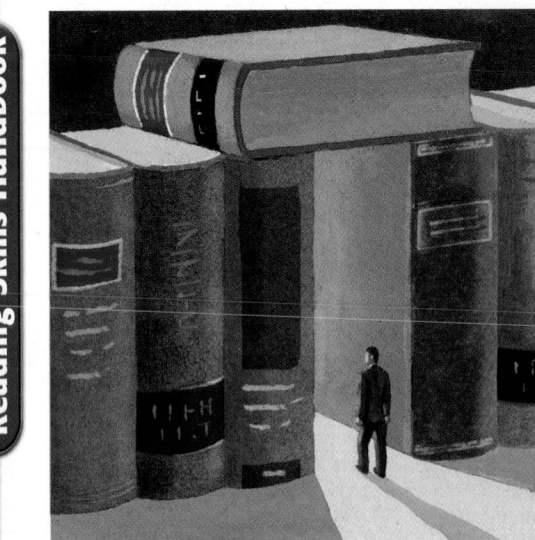

Using Types of Reference Materials Dictionaries and other reference sources can help you learn new words and how to use them. Check out these reference sources. You can find these in your local public or school library as well as on the Internet.

- A **dictionary** gives the pronunciation, the meaning or multiple meanings, and often examples of how to use the words. Some dictionaries also provide illustrations or diagrams to help define words, other forms of words, their parts of speech, and synonyms. You might also find the historical background of a word, such as its Greek, Latin, or Anglo-Saxon origins.
- A **glossary** is a word list that appears at the end—or Appendix—of a book or other written work and includes only words that are in that work. Like dictionaries, glossaries include the pronunciation and definitions of words.
- A **thesaurus** lists groups of words that have the same, or almost the same, meaning. Words with similar meanings are called synonyms. Seeing the synonyms of words can help you build your vocabulary.

Recognizing Word Meanings Across Subjects

Have you ever learned a new word in one class and then noticed it in your reading for other subjects? The word probably will not mean exactly the same thing in each class. But you can use what you know about the word's meaning to help you understand what it means in a different subject area. Look at the following example from three different subjects:

- **Social studies:** One *product* manufactured in the southern part of the United States is cotton cloth.
- **Math:** After multiplying the numbers five and five, explain how you arrived at the *product*.
- **Science:** One *product* of photosynthesis is oxygen.

CHECKING YOUR UNDERSTANDING

The following sentence does not include real English words, but you can use what you have learned about English syntax to decode the sentence. First read the sentence. Then answer the questions that follow.

The shabs smatously graled the mul-bulowed rotfabs.

1. What is the verb in the sentence?
2. What is the subject?
3. What is the object?

MORE ABOUT THE READING STRATEGY

How can teachers help students understand word concepts instead of just learning simple definitions? One way is to use words often and in a variety of ways. Teams of teachers can choose common vocabulary words which they will present in various content area classes. Teachers should provide opportunities for integrating the words into meaningful contexts. The goal is for students to develop full knowledge of the words so that they become fixed parts of their vocabularies. For example, the word *prime* may mean different things in math, social studies, and science. Students need to understand all of these uses.

Reading for a Reason

Why are you reading that paperback mystery? What do you hope to get from your American history textbook? And are you going to read either of these books in the same way that you read a restaurant menu? The point is, you read for different reasons. The reason you are reading something helps you decide on the reading strategies you use with a text. In other words, how you read will depend on why you are reading.

Reading Skills Handbook

Knowing Your Reason for Reading

In school and in life, you will have many reasons for reading, and those reasons will lead you to a wide range of materials:

- **To learn and understand new information,** you might read news magazines, textbooks, news on the Internet, books about your favorite pastime, encyclopedia articles, primary and secondary sources for a school report, instructions on how to use a calling card, or directions for a standardized test.
- **To find specific information,** you might look at the sports section for the score of last night's game, a notice on where to register for a field trip, weather reports, bank statements, or television listings.
- **To be entertained,** you might read your favorite magazine, e-mails or letters from friends, the Sunday comics, or even novels, short stories, plays, or poems!

Adjusting How Fast You Read

How quickly or how carefully you should read a text depends on your purpose for reading it. Because there are many reasons and ways to read, think about your purpose and choose the strategy that works best. Try out these strategies:

- **Scanning** means quickly running your eyes over the material, looking for key words or phrases that point to the information you are looking for. Scan when you need to find a particular piece or type of information. For example, you might scan a newspaper for movie show times.
- **Skimming** means quickly reading a piece of writing to find its main idea or to get a general overview of it. For example, you might skim the sports section of the daily newspaper to find out how your favorite teams are doing. Or you might skim a chapter in your textbook to prepare for a test.
- **Careful reading** involves reading very slowly and paying close attention with a purpose in mind. Read carefully when you are learning new concepts, following complicated directions, or preparing to explain information to someone else.

CHECKING YOUR UNDERSTANDING

If you were working on a research paper on the American Revolution, how would you adjust the speed at which you were reading for each of the following cases?

1. You have just found a 1,200-page work that covers the entire colonial and revolutionary era of the British colonies in North America.

2. You have discovered an article in a leading history magazine that supports every point that you are trying to make.

Reading Skills Handbook

Reading for a Reason

Why It's Important

When students have a reason or purpose for reading, the task becomes relevant and meaningful, both of which are necessary for comprehension. Good readers inherently set purposes for themselves, but less-proficient readers might need help finding a reason for reading.

Before Reading

Skimming Help students establish a reason for reading by skimming the text. Point out section headings, illustrations, and boldfaced words. Tell students that these text features can help establish a purpose for reading. **OL**

During Reading

Identifying a Reason for Reading Give students a specific task to perform while they read, such as looking for a specific piece of information, summarizing content, finding details to support a position, or writing a response to what they have read. **BL**

After Reading

Paraphrasing When students finish reading, have them work with a partner to paraphrase what they have read. Encourage them to reread sections of text or share notes and answers to questions in order to clarify the reading. **OL**

Checking Your Understanding Answers

1. scanning
2. careful reading

UNIVERSAL ACCESS

Below Grade Level Students need practice with establishing a reason for reading. Encourage students to read news magazines, newspapers, historical novels, nonfiction books, or Internet articles. Before reading, have students write a rationale for why they have chosen that type of reading. Students should describe what they will do after they read, such as present an oral report or post a response on a discussion board. **BL**

Understanding What You Read

Why It's Important

Students who read but don't "get it" or who simply will not read at all cannot adequately master the content of their courses. Helping students learn to use a variety of reading strategies as tools for comprehension will lead to long-term benefits in school and everyday life.

Before Reading

Predicting On index cards, write important words from the chapter—one word per card. Place the cards on various desks around the room. Allow students to move from desk to desk until they find a word that they think they may know something about. Have students use the word to make predictions about what they will learn in the chapter. **OL**

Understanding What You Read

*R*eading without understanding is like trying to drive a car on an empty gas tank. Fortunately, there are techniques you can use to help you concentrate on and understand what you read. Skilled readers adopt a number of strategies before, during, and after reading to make sure they understand what they read.

Preparing to Read

It is important to set the stage before you read. Following these steps will make the reading process more rewarding.

Previewing If you were making a preview for a movie, you would want to let your audience know what the movie is like. When you preview a piece of writing, you are trying to get an idea about the piece. Follow these steps to preview your reading assignments.

- Look at the title and any illustrations that are included.
- Read the headings, subheadings, and anything in bold letters.
- Skim the passage to see how it is organized.
- Set a purpose for your reading.

Using What You Know You already know quite a bit about what you are going to read. You bring knowledge and personal experience to a selection. Drawing on what you learned in a previous class is called *activating prior knowledge,* and it can help you create meaning in what you read. Ask yourself, *What do I already know about this topic?*

Predicting *Predicting* requires using background and prior knowledge, as well as the ability to make educated guesses. Make educated guesses before you read and while you read to figure out what might happen in the story or article you are reading.

Reading the Text

Following these suggestions while you read will help ensure that you get the most out of your reading.

Visualizing Creating pictures in your mind as you read—called *visualizing*—is a powerful aid to understanding. As you read, set up a movie theater in your imagination. Picture the setting—city streets, the desert, or the moon. If you can visualize, selections will be more vivid, and you will recall them better later on.

Identifying Sequence When you discover the logical order of events or ideas, you are identifying *sequence*. Do you need to understand step-by-step directions? Are you reading a persuasive speech with the reasons listed in order of importance? Look for clues and signal words that will help you find the way information is organized.

Determining the Main Idea When you look for the *main idea* of a selection, you look for the most important idea. The examples, reasons, and details that further explain the main idea are called *supporting details*. Some main ideas are clearly stated within a passage—often in the first sentence of a paragraph, or sometimes in the last sentence of a passage. Other times, however, an author does not directly state the main idea. Instead, he or she provides details that help readers figure out what the main idea is.

MORE ABOUT THE READING STRATEGY

What does it mean to read? What do we know about how the brain processes the written word? Consider forming a study group with other teachers interested in learning more about the process of reading. There are books available through several educational presses that focus on new research about the learning process and comprehension.

Reading Skills Handbook

Questioning By learning how to analyze questions, you will quickly learn where to look for information as you read. Questions vary in many ways. One of the ways that questions vary is by how explicit or implied the question is compared with the text. These types of questions fall into four categories:

- **Right there** questions can be answered based on a line from the text.
- **Think and search** questions can be answered by looking in a few different places in the text.
- **Author and you** questions can be answered by thinking about the text but that also require your prior knowledge.
- **On your own** questions cannot be answered by the text and rely on the reader.

Clarifying Clear up, or clarify, confusing or difficult passages as you read. When you realize you do not understand something, try these techniques to help you clarify the ideas. *Reread* the confusing parts slowly and carefully. *Look up* unfamiliar words. Simply *talk out* the part to yourself.

Monitoring Your Comprehension As you read, check your understanding by using the following strategies.

- **Summarize** what you read by pausing from time to time and telling yourself the main ideas of what you have just read. Answer the questions *Who? What? Where? When? Why?* and *How?* Summarizing tests your comprehension by encouraging you to clarify key points in your own words.
- **Paraphrase** what you have just read to see whether you really got the point. Paraphrasing is retelling something in your own words. If you cannot explain it clearly, you should probably reread the text.

CHECKING YOUR UNDERSTANDING

1. How does visualizing help you understand what you read in your textbook or when you read for pleasure?

2. How can you determine the main idea of a selection if the author never explicitly explains what it is?

3. Why is clarifying an important skill for you to develop?

Reading Skills Handbook   **59**

During Reading

Questioning Encourage students to write questions or mark confusing parts of the text with a sticky note as they read. Organize students into groups and allow them to discuss the comments they made on their notes. Have a member of the group record common difficulties. Discuss as a class the sections of the reading that were difficult or confusing, and help clarify the material for the students. **OL**

After Reading

Reviewing Remind students to use the following strategies after each section or chapter to ensure greater comprehension:

- Readers should summarize the most important parts of the text in their own words.
- Readers should clarify confusing content by rereading, asking questions, or seeking outside help.
- Readers should predict what might happen next.
OL

Checking Your Understanding Answers

1. Visualizing helps make readings more vivid and thus easier to recall later on.

2. Answers will vary, but students should point out that the details in the passage provide a clue about the author's main idea.

3. It helps clear up confusing passages.

UNIVERSAL ACCESS

Below Grade Level Prediction guides (often called anticipation guides) are an effective way of setting a purpose for reading, engaging students during reading, and monitoring comprehension after reading. Create statements related to the upcoming section or chapter. Write some statements that are true, some that are false, and some that are outrageous or funny. Have students write *True* or *False* beside each statement. Students should then check and make corrections to their predictions as they read. **BL**

Thinking About Your Reading

Why It's Important

While many students are capable of reading the text and answering specific comprehension questions about what they have read, understanding subtleties of meaning or thinking critically may be more difficult. Students become better readers, writers, and thinkers when they know how to use critical thinking skills.

Before Reading

Modeling When teaching critical thinking skills, it is best to focus on teaching only one or two skills prior to reading. Explain the skill, and model how you, as a reader, use it to comprehend the reading. OL

Thinking About Your Reading

Sometimes it is important to think more deeply about what you have read so you can get the most out of what the author says. These critical thinking skills will help you go beyond what the words say and get at the important messages of your reading.

Interpreting

When you listen to your best friend talk, you do not just hear the words he or she says. You also watch your friend, listen to the tone of voice, and use what you already know about that person to put meaning to the words. In doing so, you are interpreting what your friend says. Readers do the same thing when they interpret as they read. *Interpreting* is asking yourself *What is the writer really saying here?* and then using what you know about the world to help answer that question.

Inferring

You may not realize it, but you make inferences every day. Here is an example: You run to the bus stop a little later than usual. No one is there. "I have missed the bus," you say to yourself. You might be wrong, but that is the way our minds work. You look at the evidence (you are late; no one is there) and come to a conclusion (you have missed the bus).

When you read, you go through exactly the same process because writers do not always directly state what they want you to understand. They suggest certain information by providing clues and interesting details. Whenever you combine those clues with your own background and knowledge, you are making an inference.

Drawing Conclusions

Skillful readers are always *drawing conclusions,* or figuring out much more than an author says directly. The process is like a detective solving a mystery. You combine information and evidence that the author provides to come up with a statement about the topic. Drawing conclusions helps you find connections between ideas and events and gives you a better understanding of what you are reading.

Making Connections

One way that you can remember what you have read is by making connections with the text. Your teacher often expresses these connections aloud so that you and your classmates have a model. Your teacher may also ask you to make connections with the text and share them with the class. The most common connections include:

MORE ABOUT THE READING STRATEGY

Have students evaluate their proficiency with using different types of critical thinking skills. Draw a continuum on the board for each skill, with 0 representing great difficulty using the skill and 10 indicating mastery of it. Have students rate their abilities by answering questions such as: Am I usually able to infer and understand what the author is suggesting, even if it is not stated? Can I usually draw conclusions when I read? Can I easily tell facts from opinions?

- **Text-to-self** connections, in which you remember something from your own life that serves as a connection with what is being read. *(While reading about the Civil War, you think about a fight you had with a relative.)*
- **Text-to-world** connections, in which you remember something that is happening or has happened in the world that serves as a connection with what is being read. *(While reading about the Civil War, you remember reading a newspaper article about the civil war in Somalia.)*
- **Text-to-text** connections, in which you remember something you have read elsewhere that serves as a connection with what is being read. *(While reading about the Civil War, you recall the novel* Red Badge of Courage.*)*

Analyzing

Analyzing, or looking at separate parts of something to understand the entire piece, is a way to think critically about written work. In analyzing persuasive *nonfiction,* you might look at the writer's reasons to see if they actually support the main point of the argument. In analyzing *informational text,* you might look at how the ideas are organized to see what is most important.

Distinguishing Fact From Opinion

Distinguishing between fact and opinion is an important reading skill. A *fact* is a statement that can be proved. An *opinion,* on the other hand, is what a writer believes on the basis of his or her personal viewpoint. Writers can support their opinions with facts, but an opinion is something that cannot be proved.

Evaluating

When you form an opinion or make a judgment about something you are reading, you are *evaluating.* If you are reading informational texts or something on the Internet, it is important to evaluate how qualified the author is to be writing about the topic and how reliable the information is that is presented. Ask yourself whether the author seems biased, whether the information is one-sided, and whether the argument presented is logical.

Synthesizing

When you *synthesize,* you combine ideas (maybe even from different sources) to come up with something new. It may be a new understanding of an important idea or a new way of combining and presenting information. For example, you might read a manual on coaching soccer, combine that information with your own experiences playing soccer, and come up with a winning plan for coaching your sister's team this spring.

CHECKING YOUR UNDERSTANDING

1. How does making connections with what you have read help you remember more?

2. How do analyzing and synthesizing differ?

3. How do facts and opinions differ? Why is it important to differentiate between the two as you study history?

During Reading

Thinking Critically Students who interact with the text can think more critically about it. Organize students into small groups, and assign a section of text for each group to read. Have students discuss questions such as, "Why was the *Dred Scott* decision seen differently in the North and the South?" or "Is the reason why this event occurred based on fact or opinion?" Encourage students to examine the questions from different perspectives. Have students share their discussions with the class. **OL**

After Reading

Understanding Question/Answer Relationships Tell students that after they read, they will write one question that reflects each type of the thinking skills described in this handbook. Knowing that they will have to write questions about the text will help students think more about it as they read. **OL**

Checking Your Understanding Answers

1. Relating the reading to prior knowledge or to personal experience helps integrate new learning into what has already been learned.

2. Analyzing involves looking at separate parts of the reading in order to understand the entire text. Synthesizing involves combining ideas to come up with a new conclusion.

3. Facts can be proven; opinions are simply points of view. Differentiating is important in history because you need to separate events that happened from historians' interpretations of them.

UNIVERSAL ACCESS

Below Grade Level When students find connections to their own lives in the text, their ability to comprehend it improves. Offer projects that build upon these connections. Projects may include: debating issues presented in the text; writing articles for the school or local paper; conducting interviews with others who have knowledge of the subject; role playing; finding relevant poetry, art, or music to share with the class; and reading and reporting on books or magazine articles related to the subject. **BL**

Understanding Text Structure

Why It's Important

Students who begin reading without understanding text structures may have difficulty with comprehension and retention. Students can categorize information better and make sense of the text more easily when they learn how authors organize the text.

Before Reading

Skimming Before students read the chapter, walk them through it. For each page, note photos, charts, diagrams, maps, headings, and boldfaced words. Ask students questions such as: Why did the author choose this particular photograph to illustrate this topic? How does this map relate to the topic described in the title? What do you think the author intends for you to learn in the section? **OL**

Understanding Text Structure

Good writers do not just put together sentences and paragraphs in any order. They structure each piece of their writing in a specific way for a specific purpose. That pattern of organization is called text structure. When you know the text structure of a selection, you will find it easier to locate and recall an author's ideas. Here are four ways that writers organize text.

Comparison and Contrast

Comparison-and-contrast structure shows the *similarities* and *differences* among people, things, and ideas. Maybe you have overheard someone at school say something like "He is better at throwing the football, but I can run faster than he can." This student is using comparison-and-contrast structure. When writers use comparison-and-contrast structure, they often want to show you how things that seem alike are different or how things that seem different are alike.
Signal words and phrases: *similarly, on the one hand, on the other hand, in contrast to, but, however*

Cause and Effect

Just about everything that happens in life is the cause or the effect of some other event or action. Sometimes what happens is pretty minor: You do not look when you are pouring milk *(cause);* you spill milk on the table *(effect).* Sometimes it is a little more serious: You do not look at your math book before the big test *(cause);* you mess up on the test *(effect).*

Writers use cause-and-effect structure to explore the reasons for something happening and to examine the results of previous events. This structure helps answer the question that everybody is always asking: *Why?* A historian might tell us why an empire rose and fell. Cause-and-effect structure is all about explaining why things are as they are.
Signal words and phrases: *so, because, as a result, therefore, for the following reasons*

MORE ABOUT THE READING STRATEGY

Why should students understand the different types of text structure? Knowledge about the different types of text structure helps students remember content. It also helps students make sense out of unfamiliar text. Students who internalize the process of cause and effect or problem and solution are developing thinking processes that will serve them for the rest of their lives.

Problem and Solution

How did scientists overcome the difficulty of getting a person to the moon? How will I brush my teeth when I have forgotten my toothpaste? These questions may be very different in importance, but they have one thing in common: Each identifies a problem and asks how to solve it. *Problems and solutions* are part of what makes life interesting. Problems and solutions also occur in fiction and nonfiction writing.

Signal words and phrases: *how, help, problem, obstruction, difficulty, need, attempt, have to, must*

Sequence

Take a look at three common forms of sequencing, the order in which thoughts are arranged.

- **Chronological order** refers to the order in which events take place. First, you wake up; next, you have breakfast; then, you go to school. Those events do not make much sense in any other order.
  Signal words: *first, next, then, later, finally*

- **Spatial order** tells you the order in which to look at objects. For example, consider this description of an ice-cream sundae: *At the bottom of the dish are two scoops of vanilla. The scoops are covered with fudge and topped with whipped cream and a cherry.* Your eyes follow the sundae from the bottom to the top. Spatial order is important in descriptive writing because it helps you as a reader to see an image the way the author does.
  Signal words: *above, below, behind, next to*

- **Order of importance** is going from most important to least important or the other way around. For example, a typical news article has a most important to least important structure.
  Signal words: *principal, central, important, fundamental*

CHECKING YOUR UNDERSTANDING

Read the following paragraph and answer the questions about the selection's text structure below.

The Huntington City Council recently approved an increase in the city sales tax. Recognizing the need to balance the city's budget, the council president Matt Smith noted that the council had no choice. The vote ended more than a year of preparing voters for the bad news. First, the council notified citizens that there would be a public discussion last April. Then, the council issued public statements that the vote would take place in November. Finally, the council approved the increase last week even though many residents opposed it. On one hand, the increase will increase revenues. On the other hand, more taxes could lead to fewer shoppers in the city's struggling retail stores.

1. How does the writer use comparison and contrast text structure?

2. How does the writer use problem and solution text structure?

3. What signal words show that the write is setting the chronological order of events?

During Reading

Identifying Text Structure
Organize students into groups of four, and assign different sections of the text to each group. Have groups choose a facilitator, a reader, a recorder, and a reporter. As the reader reads a section aloud, have the recorder note all the signal words. The facilitator will help the group identify the section's text structure based on the categories listed in the *Reading Skills Handbook*. The reporter will describe to the class the signal words and the text structure that the group identified. OL

After Reading

Organizing Information Graphic organizers help students organize and comprehend ideas and events. Have a variety of blank graphic organizers available for students to choose from to help them organize text information, including flow charts, time lines, and Venn diagrams. OL

Checking Your Understanding Answers

1. points out that on one hand the increase will make money but on the other hand it might hurt businesses

2. uses the word *need* when explaining why the council felt it necessary to increase taxes

3. *first, then, finally*

UNIVERSAL ACCESS

Below Grade Level Students who are not proficient readers may get little practice at the skill. As a result, they may be unfamiliar with some of the features of a book that they can use as aids. Review with students how to use the table of contents to locate major divisions in the book, the glossary to find the definitions of new words, and the index to locate the coverage of particular topics. Then review with them the heads within a section so they can see how headings structure the text and provide clues to content. BL

REFERENCE ATLAS

NATIONAL GEOGRAPHIC

ATLAS KEY

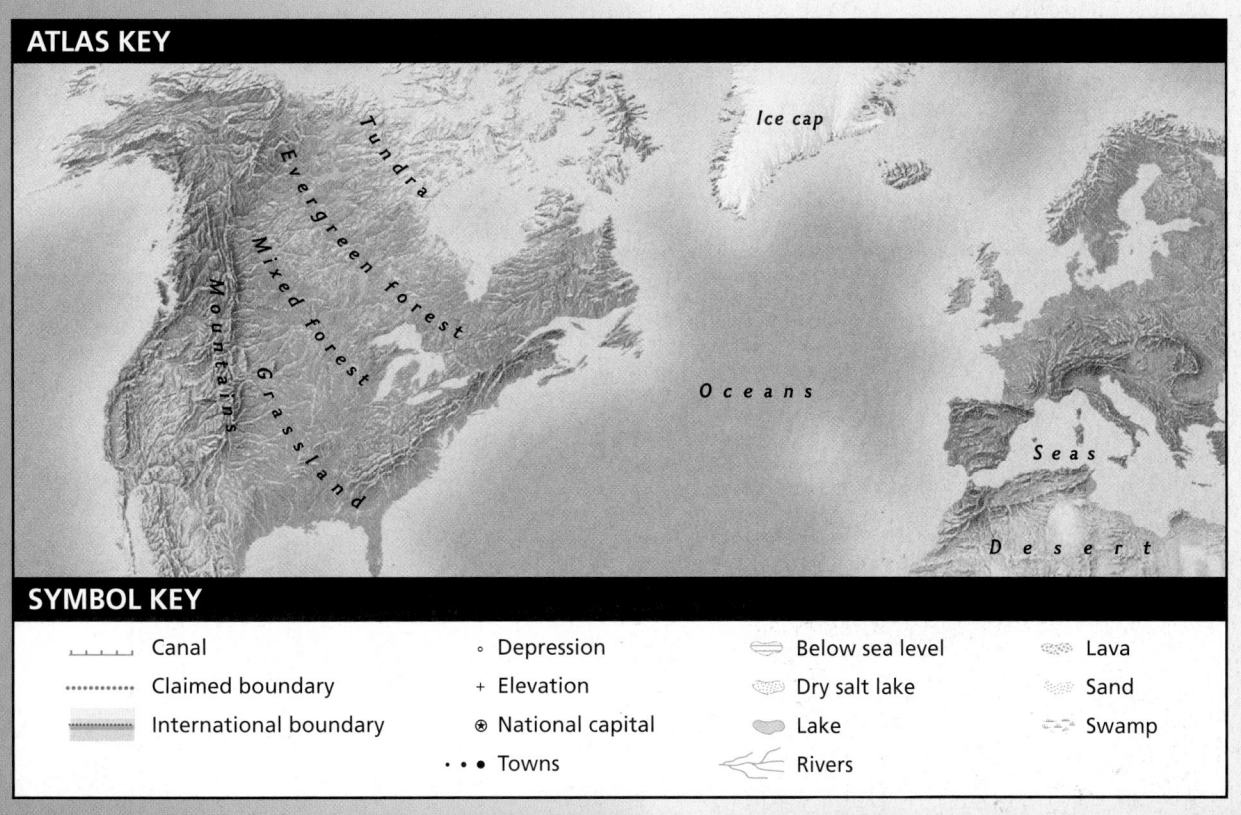

Tundra · Evergreen forest · Mixed forest · Mountains · Grassland · Ice cap · Oceans · Seas · Desert

SYMBOL KEY

⊥⊥⊥⊥ Canal	∘ Depression	⬱ Below sea level	⬭ Lava
⋯⋯⋯ Claimed boundary	+ Elevation	⬭ Dry salt lake	⬭ Sand
▥▥▥ International boundary	⊛ National capital	⬭ Lake	⬭ Swamp
	• • Towns	⋘ Rivers	

UNITED
STATES
POLITICAL

0 mi   600

0 km   600

OBLIQUE AZIMUTHAL EQUIDISTANT PROJECTION

NATIONAL
GEOGRAPHIC

Column numbers (top): 1 2 3 4 5 6 7 8
Row letters (left): A B C D E F G H J K

130°W   125°W   50°N   120°W   115°W   110°W   105°W   100°W

Cape Flattery
Mt. Olympus+
7,965 ft
2,428 m
•Seattle

C A N A D A

45°N

COAST RANGES

CASCADE RANGE

COLUMBIA PLATEAU

Columbia

Blue Mts.

Clearwater Mts.

Bitterroot Range

ROCKY

Missouri

GREAT

130°W
40°N

Cape Mendocino

Great Sandy Desert

Salmon River Mts.

Snake

Snake River Plain

Shoshone Falls

Absaroka Range

Bighorn Mts.

Wind River Range

Laramie Mts.

Black Hills

Missouri

PACIFIC

SIERRA NEVADA

Central Valley

Lake Tahoe

Great Salt Lake

GREAT BASIN

Wasatch Range

Uinta Mts.

14,433 ft
4,399 m+ Mt. Elbert

•Denver

N. Platte

Sand Hills

Platte

35°N

OCEAN

San Francisco

Mt. Whitney
14,494 ft
4,418 m

Death Valley
-282 ft, -86 m

Lake Mead

Lake Powell

Colorado

Sangre de Cristo Mts.

San Juan Mts.

High Plains

Arkansas

Point Conception

Mojave Desert

Lake Mead

Grand Canyon

Colorado Plateau

MOUNTAINS

Los Angeles

Channel Islands

Salton Sea

San Diego•

Phoenix•

Colorado

Sonoran Desert

Rio Grande

Sacramento Mts.

Llano Estacado

Red

Dallas•

Brazos

30°N

125°W   120°W   115°W

Edwards Plateau

Rio Grande

C O

25°N

TROPIC OF CANCER

M E X I C O

Alaska inset:

ARCTIC OCEAN

Point Barrow

Beaufort Sea

68°N
180°

Chukchi Sea

North Slope

Brooks Range

RUSSIA

ARCTIC CIRCLE

68°N

Bering Strait

Seward Pen.

St. Lawrence Island

ALASKA

CANADA

172°W
60°N

Nunivak Island

Yukon

Kuskokwim

Tanana

Alaska Range

+Mt. McKinley (Denali)
20,320 ft, 6,194 m

•Anchorage

110°W

60°N

Bering Sea

Bristol Bay

Alaska Peninsula

Gulf of Alaska

Kodiak I.

Alexander Archipelago

25°N

PACIFIC OCEAN

ALASKA

0 mi   300
0 km   300

52°N

52°N

164°W   156°W   148°W   140°W   132°W   105°W   100°W

UNITED STATES
PHYSICAL

0 mi   300

0 km   300

ALBERS CONIC EQUAL-AREA PROJECTION

NATIONAL GEOGRAPHIC

Lake of the Woods

Isle Royale
Lake Superior

Upper Peninsula

Minneapolis

Mississippi

Milwaukee

Lake Michigan

Lower Peninsula

Chicago

Lake Huron

Detroit

CENTRAL
LOWLAND

Indianapolis

Ohio

St. Louis

Wabash

Flint
Hills

Ozark Plateau

Boston Mts.

Memphis

Tennessee

Ouachita Mts.

Mississippi

Red

Black Belt

Houston

New Orleans

Mississippi
River Delta

Gulf of Mexico

Lake Champlain

Adirondack Mts.

Green Mts.

White Mts.

Gulf of Maine

Boston

Cape Cod

Lake Ontario

Niagara Falls

Lake Erie

Cleveland

Pittsburgh

Hudson

Connecticut

Long Island

New York City

Philadelphia

Baltimore

Delaware Bay

Washington

Chesapeake Bay

ATLANTIC

OCEAN

Appalachian Plateau

Allegheny Mts.

Cumberland

Cumberland Plateau

Blue Ridge

APPALACHIAN MOUNTAINS

Mt. Mitchell
6,684 ft
2,037 m

Piedmont

Cape Hatteras

Atlanta

Savannah

Jacksonville

Cape Canaveral

Lake Okeechobee

The Everglades

Miami

Florida Keys

Straits of Florida

TROPIC OF CANCER

CUBA

CANADA

A

Niihau

Kauai

Honolulu

Oahu

Molokai

Lanai

Kahoolawe

Maui

Hawaii

PACIFIC OCEAN

Mauna Kea
13,796 ft
4,205 m

PRINCIPAL HAWAIIAN
ISLANDS

0 mi   100

0 km   100

UNITED STATES

2000 CONGRESSIONAL REAPPORTIONMENT

0 mi.   300

0 km   300

ALBERS CONIC EQUAL-AREA PROJECTION

NATIONAL GEOGRAPHIC

Map labels

CANADA

MAINE 2   ⊙Augusta

MINNESOTA 8

WISCONSIN 8   Milwaukee, Madison

MICHIGAN 15   Lansing, Detroit

Montpelier   **VT.** 1   **N.H.** 2   ⊙Concord

NEW YORK 29   Albany   Boston   **MASS.** 10

Buffalo   Hartford   **CONN.** 5   Providence   **RHODE ISLAND** 2

IOWA 5   ⊙Des Moines

ILLINOIS 19   Chicago   Springfield⊙

INDIANA 9   Fort Wayne   Indianapolis⊙

OHIO 18   Cleveland   Columbus⊙   Cincinnati

PENNSYLVANIA 19   Harrisburg   Pittsburgh

N.J. 13   New York City   Trenton⊙   Philadelphia

MARYLAND 8   Washington, D.C. 1   Annapolis⊙   **DELAWARE** 1   Dover

WEST VIRGINIA 3   Charleston⊙

VIRGINIA 11   Richmond⊙   Virginia Beach

KENTUCKY 6   Frankfort⊙   Louisville

MISSOURI 9   St. Louis   Jefferson City⊙

Omaha   Kansas City   Topeka⊙

TENNESSEE 9   Nashville⊙   Memphis

NORTH CAROLINA 13   Raleigh⊙   Charlotte

SOUTH CAROLINA 6   Columbia⊙

ARKANSAS 4   Little Rock⊙   Tulsa

MISSISSIPPI 4   Jackson⊙

ALABAMA 7   Birmingham   Montgomery⊙

GEORGIA 13   Atlanta⊙   Savannah

LOUISIANA 7   Baton Rouge⊙   New Orleans   Houston

FLORIDA 25   Tallahassee⊙   Jacksonville   Tampa   Miami

Mobile

MINNESOTA St. Paul   Minneapolis

ATLANTIC OCEAN

Gulf of Mexico

CUBA

Lake Superior   Lake Michigan   Lake Huron   Lake Erie   Lake Ontario

Mississippi   Ohio   Tennessee   Savannah

N

Inset: Principal Hawaiian Islands

159°W   156°W

Niihau   Kauai   Oahu   Honolulu⊙   Molokai   Maui — 21°N   Lanai   Kahoolawe   **Hawaii** 2

PACIFIC OCEAN

PRINCIPAL HAWAIIAN ISLANDS

0 mi.   100   0 km   100   156°W

TROPIC OF CANCER

90°W   80°W   70°W   50°N   40°N   30°N   20°N

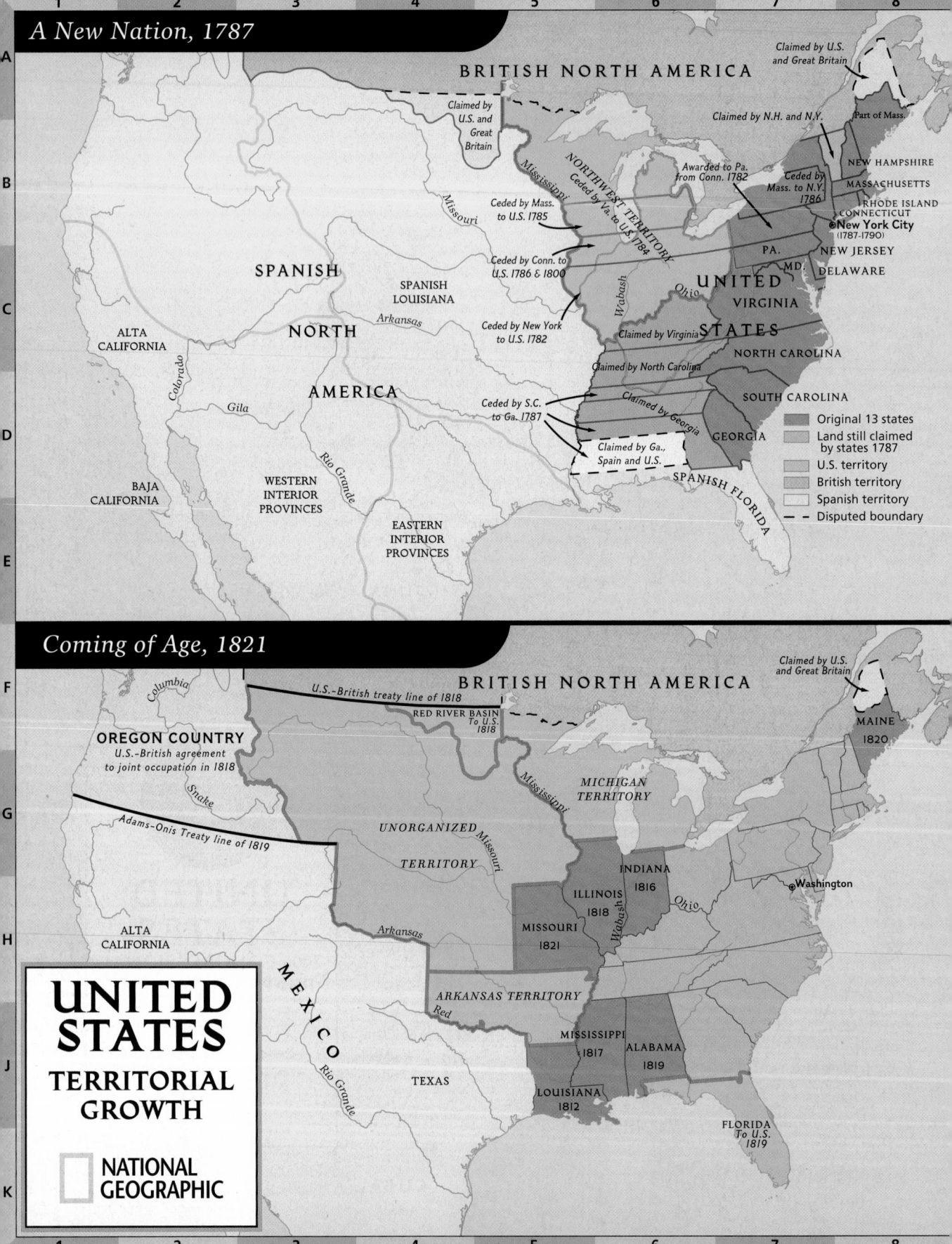

A New Nation, 1787

BRITISH NORTH AMERICA

Claimed by U.S. and Great Britain

Claimed by U.S. and Great Britain

Claimed by N.H. and N.Y.

Part of Mass.

NEW HAMPSHIRE

Awarded to Pa. from Conn. 1782

Ceded by Mass. to N.Y. 1786

MASSACHUSETTS

RHODE ISLAND

CONNECTICUT

New York City (1787-1790)

NORTHWEST TERRITORY Ceded by Va. to U.S. 1784

Ceded by Mass. to U.S. 1785

PA.

NEW JERSEY

DELAWARE

MD.

Mississippi

Missouri

SPANISH

Ceded by Conn. to U.S. 1786 & 1800

Wabash

Ohio

UNITED

LOUISIANA

Arkansas

Ceded by New York to U.S. 1782

VIRGINIA

STATES

NORTH

Claimed by Virginia

NORTH CAROLINA

ALTA CALIFORNIA

Colorado

AMERICA

Claimed by North Carolina

SOUTH CAROLINA

Gila

Ceded by S.C. to Ga. 1787

Claimed by Georgia

GEORGIA

Rio Grande

BAJA CALIFORNIA

WESTERN INTERIOR PROVINCES

Claimed by Ga., Spain and U.S.

SPANISH FLORIDA

EASTERN INTERIOR PROVINCES

Original 13 states

Land still claimed by states 1787

U.S. territory

British territory

Spanish territory

Disputed boundary

Coming of Age, 1821

Columbia

U.S.-British treaty line of 1818

BRITISH NORTH AMERICA

Claimed by U.S. and Great Britain

RED RIVER BASIN To U.S. 1818

MAINE 1820

OREGON COUNTRY

U.S.-British agreement to joint occupation in 1818

Snake

MICHIGAN TERRITORY

Mississippi

Adams-Onis Treaty line of 1819

UNORGANIZED

Missouri

TERRITORY

INDIANA 1816

Washington

ALTA CALIFORNIA

ILLINOIS 1818

Ohio

Wabash

Arkansas

MISSOURI 1821

M E X I C O

ARKANSAS TERRITORY

Red

MISSISSIPPI 1817

ALABAMA 1819

Rio Grande

TEXAS

LOUISIANA 1812

FLORIDA To U.S. 1819

UNITED STATES

TERRITORIAL GROWTH

NATIONAL GEOGRAPHIC

Expanding West of the Mississippi, 1803

BRITISH NORTH AMERICA

Claimed by U.S. and Great Britain

OREGON COUNTRY
Claimed by Great Britain, Russia, Spain, and United States

Claimed by U.S. and Great Britain

VERMONT 1791

Mississippi

Missouri

INDIANA

TERRITORY

LOUISIANA PURCHASE
Purchased by U.S. in 1803 from France

OHIO 1803

Wabash

Ohio

⊕ Philadelphia (1790-1800)
⊕ Washington (new capital 1800)

NEW SPAIN (SPANISH MEXICO)

Arkansas

KENTUCKY 1792

TENNESSEE 1796

Red

Ceded by Georgia to U.S. 1802

MISSISSIPPI TERR.

Rio Grande

Claimed by U.S. and Spain

BAJA CALIFORNIA

SPANISH FLORIDA

Claimed by U.S. and Spain

☐ States previously in the Union
☐ States newly admitted

Coast to Coast, 1850 and beyond

Treaty line of 1846

BRITISH NORTH AMERICA

Treaty line of 1842

Treaty line of 1842

WASHINGTON 1889

MONTANA 1889

NORTH DAKOTA 1889

MINNESOTA 1858

OREGON TERRITORY
Added to U.S. in 1846

Snake

OREGON 1859

IDAHO 1890

MINNESOTA TERRITORY

MICHIGAN 1837

WISCONSIN 1848

WYOMING 1890

SOUTH DAKOTA 1889

NEVADA 1864

UNORGANIZED

Missouri

IOWA 1846

UTAH TERRITORY

TERRITORY

NEBRASKA 1867

W. VA. 1863

Wabash

Ohio

⊕ Washington

CALIFORNIA 1850

UTAH 1896

COLORADO 1876

KANSAS 1861

Colorado

ARIZONA 1912

Arkansas

Gila

NEW MEXICO TERRITORY

OKLAHOMA 1907

ARKANSAS 1836

GADSDEN PURCHASE
To U.S. 1853

NEW MEXICO 1912

Red

Mississippi

Rio Grande

RUSSIA

ALASKA 1959
Purchased by U.S. 1867

TEXAS 1845

MEXICO

FLORIDA 1845

······ States admitted after 1850

HAWAII 1959
Annexed by U.S. 1898

MIDDLE AMERICA
PHYSICAL/POLITICAL

0 mi   400
0 km   400

AZIMUTHAL EQUIDISTANT PROJECTION

NATIONAL GEOGRAPHIC

UNITED STATES

Tijuana
Mexicali
Sonoran Desert
30°N
Gulf of California
BAJA CALIFORNIA
SONORA
Ciudad Juárez
CHIHUAHUA
Chihuahua
COAHUILA
Rio Grande
BAJA CALIFORNIA SUR
Sierra Madre Occidental
DURANGO
Nuevo Laredo
NUEVO LEON
Monterrey
Matamoros
La Paz
ZACATECAS
False Cape
Mazatlan
SINALOA
20°N
NAYARIT
SAN LUIS POTOSI
TAMAULIPAS
Gulf of Mexico
AGUASCALIENTES
San Luis Potosí
Ciudad Madero
Tampico
QUERETARO
Guadalajara
JALISCO
Leon
VERACRUZ
Revillagigedo Islands
Mex.
GUANAJUATO
HIDALGO
TLAXCALA
Merida
YUCATAN
Yucatan Peninsula
COLIMA
MICHOACAN
Mexico City
Orizaba
18,855 ft
5,747 m
Bay of Campeche
CAMPECHE
QUINTANA ROO
DISTRITO FEDERAL
Popocatepetl
17,802 ft
5,426 m
PUEBLA
Veracruz
TABASCO
Belize City
MEXICO
MORELOS
Sierra Madre del Sur
GUERRERO
OAXACA
Isthmus of Tehuantepec
Belmopan
BELIZE
Gulf of Honduras
Acapulco
CHIAPAS
Sierra Madre
HO
10°N
Gulf of Tehuantepec
GUATEMALA
Guatemala City
Tegucigalpa
EL SALVADOR
San Salvador
Leo
CENTRA
AMERICA
PACIFIC
OCEAN
Cocos Islar
C.R.
0°
110°W
100°W
90°W

CANADA
PHYSICAL/POLITICAL

0 mi   400
0 km   400

AZIMUTHAL EQUIDISTANT PROJECTION

NATIONAL GEOGRAPHIC

N

ICELAND

Ellesmere Island

GREENLAND
(KALAALLIT NUNAAT)
Den.

Devon Island

Baffin Bay

Baffin Island

Melville Peninsula

Foxe Basin

N U N A V U T

Southampton Island

Davis Strait

◉Iqaluit

Hudson Strait

Labrador Sea

Ungava Bay

Hudson Bay

Belcher Islands

N E W F O U N D L A N D A N D L A B R A D O R

•Cartwright

Schefferville•
Smallwood Reservoir
Happy Valley-
Goose Bay•
"Churchill Falls

Island of Newfoundland

James Bay

Q U E B E C

Manicouagan Reservoir
Sept-Iles•

Anticosti I.

St. John's⊙
Avalon Peninsula

S H I E L D

O N T A R I O

Lake Nipigon

Gaspe Pen.

Gulf of St. Lawrence

St.-Pierre & Miquelon
Fr.

PRINCE EDWARD ISLAND

Cape Breton I.

Chicoutimi•

Thunder
Bay•
Lake Superior

•Rouyn-Noranda

Quebec City⊙

NEW
BRUNSWICK

Charlottetown⊙

NOVA
SCOTIA

A T L A N T I C

Sudbury•

Montreal•

St. Lawrence

Fredericton•
Saint John•
Bay of Fundy

⊙Halifax

O C E A N

Ottawa⊛

Lake Huron

Lake Michigan

Toronto•
Niagara Falls
London•
L. Ontario
L. Erie

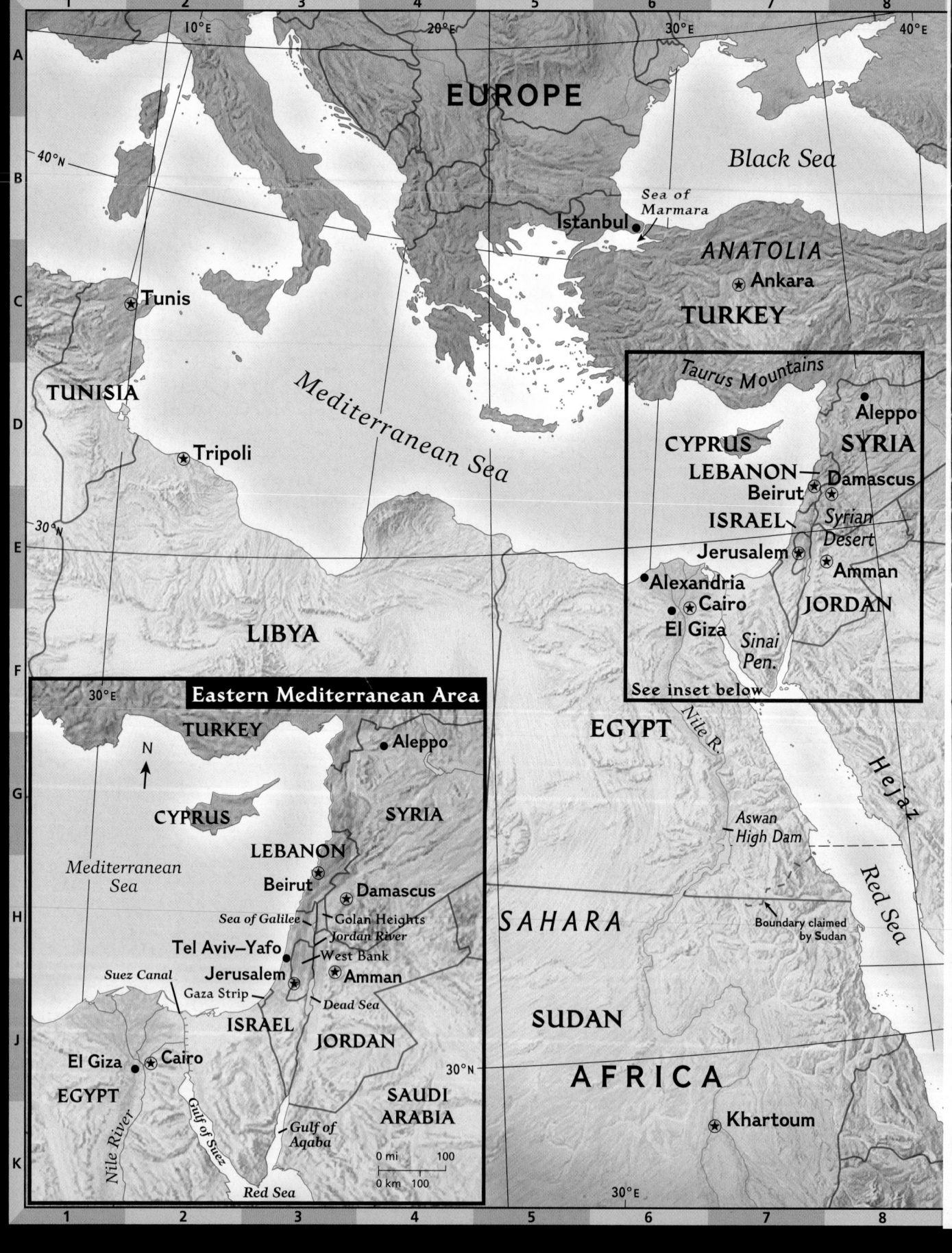

A 1 | 2 | 3 | 4 | 5 | 6 | 7 | 8

10°E   20°E   30°E   40°E

EUROPE

Black Sea

40°N

*Sea of
Marmara*

Istanbul

ANATOLIA

Ankara

TURKEY

Tunis

Taurus Mountains

Aleppo

CYPRUS   **SYRIA**

TUNISIA

Tripoli

Mediterranean Sea

LEBANON
Beirut   Damascus

30°N

ISRAEL   *Syrian
Desert*

Jerusalem

Amman

Alexandria

Cairo   **JORDAN**

El Giza

*Sinai
Pen.*

LIBYA

See inset below

EGYPT

Nile R.

Hejaz

Eastern Mediterranean Area

30°E

TURKEY

N

CYPRUS

*Mediterranean
Sea*

Aleppo

SYRIA

LEBANON
Beirut   Damascus

Sea of Galilee
Golan Heights

Tel Aviv–Yafo   *Jordan River*
West Bank

Suez Canal
Jerusalem   Amman
Gaza Strip   *Dead Sea*

ISRAEL

El Giza   Cairo

JORDAN

SAHARA

*Aswan
High Dam*

Boundary claimed
by Sudan

*Red
Sea*

EGYPT

Nile River

Gulf of Suez

*Gulf of
Aqaba*

**SAUDI
ARABIA**

SUDAN

30°N

AFRICA

Khartoum

0 mi   100

0 km   100

Red Sea

30°E

78   Reference Atlas

MIDDLE EAST
PHYSICAL / POLITICAL

0 mi — 500
0 km — 500
AZIMUTHAL EQUIDISTANT PROJECTION

NATIONAL GEOGRAPHIC

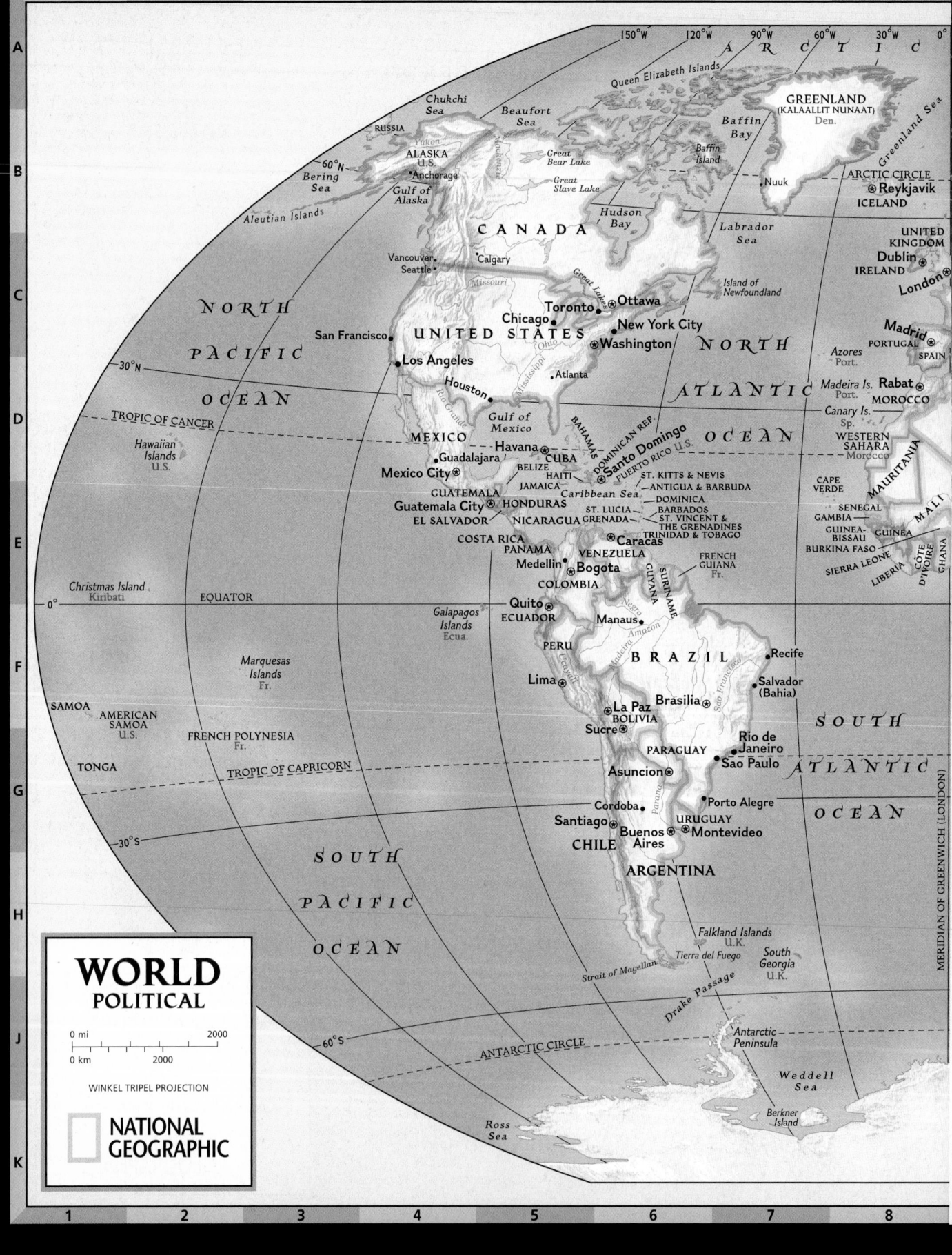

WORLD
POLITICAL

0 mi — 2000

0 km — 2000

WINKEL TRIPEL PROJECTION

NATIONAL GEOGRAPHIC

United States Facts

Washington, D.C.
Population: 572,059
Land area: 61 sq. mi.

U.S. Territories

Puerto Rico
Population: 3,808,610
Land area: 3,425 sq. mi.

Guam
Population: 155,000 (est.)
Land area: 209 sq. mi.

U.S. Virgin Islands
Population: 121,000 (est.)
Land area: 134 sq. mi.

American Samoa
Population: 65,000 (est.)
Land area: 77 sq. mi.

The states are listed in the order they were admitted to the Union.

Population figures are based on U.S. Bureau of the Census for 2000. House of Representatives figures are from the Clerk of the House of Representatives. States are not drawn to scale.

1 Delaware
Year Admitted: 1787
Population: 783,600
Land area: 1,955 sq. mi.
Representatives: 1
★ Dover

2 Pennsylvania
Year Admitted: 1787
Population: 12,281,054
Land area: 44,820 sq. mi.
Representatives: 19
Harrisburg ★

3 New Jersey
Year Admitted: 1787
Population: 8,414,350
Land area: 7,419 sq. mi.
Representatives: 13
Trenton ★

9 New Hampshire
Year Admitted: 1788
Population: 1,235,786
Land area: 8,969 sq. mi.
Representatives: 2
Concord ★

10 Virginia
Year Admitted: 1788
Population: 7,078,515
Land area: 39,598 sq. mi.
Representatives: 11
Richmond ★

11 New York
Year Admitted: 1788
Population: 18,976,457
Land area: 47,224 sq. mi.
Representatives: 29
★ Albany

17 Ohio
Year Admitted: 1803
Population: 11,353,140
Land area: 40,953 sq. mi.
Representatives: 18
★ Columbus

18 Louisiana
Year Admitted: 1812
Population: 4,468,976
Land area: 43,566 sq. mi.
Representatives: 7
★ Baton Rouge

19 Indiana
Year Admitted: 1816
Population: 6,080,485
Land area: 35,870 sq. mi.
Representatives: 9
Indianapolis ★

25 Arkansas
Year Admitted: 1836
Population: 2,673,400
Land area: 52,075 sq. mi.
Representatives: 4
Little Rock ★

26 Michigan
Year Admitted: 1837
Population: 9,938,444
Land area: 56,809 sq. mi.
Representatives: 15
Lansing ★

27 Florida
Year Admitted: 1845
Population: 15,982,378
Land area: 53,997 sq. mi.
Representatives: 25
★ Tallahassee

33 Oregon
Year Admitted: 1859
Population: 3,421,399
Land area: 96,003 sq. mi.
Representatives: 5
★ Salem

34 Kansas
Year Admitted: 1861
Population: 2,688,418
Land area: 81,823 sq. mi.
Representatives: 4
Topeka ★

35 West Virginia
Year Admitted: 1863
Population: 1,808,344
Land area: 24,087 sq. mi.
Representatives: 3
★ Charleston

36 Nevada
Year Admitted: 1864
Population: 1,998,257
Land area: 109,806 sq. mi.
Representatives: 3
★ Carson City

42 Washington
Year Admitted: 1889
Population: 5,894,121
Land area: 66,582 sq. mi.
Representatives: 9
★ Olympia

43 Idaho
Year Admitted: 1890
Population: 1,293,953
Land area: 82,751 sq. mi.
Representatives: 2
★ Boise

44 Wyoming
Year Admitted: 1890
Population: 493,782
Land area: 97,105 sq. mi.
Representatives: 1
Cheyenne ★

45 Utah
Year Admitted: 1896
Population: 2,233,169
Land area: 82,168 sq. mi.
Representatives: 3
★ Salt Lake City

4 Georgia
Year Admitted: 1788
Population: 8,186,453
Land area: 57,919 sq. mi.
Representatives: 13
★ Atlanta

5 Connecticut
Year Admitted: 1788
Population: 3,405,565
Land area: 4,845 sq. mi.
Representatives: 5
★ Hartford

6 Massachusetts
Year Admitted: 1788
Population: 6,349,097
Land area: 7,838 sq. mi.
Representatives: 10
Boston ★

7 Maryland
Year Admitted: 1788
Population: 5,296,486
Land area: 9,775 sq. mi.
Representatives: 8
Annapolis ★

8 South Carolina
Year Admitted: 1788
Population: 4,012,012
Land area: 30,111 sq. mi.
Representatives: 6
Columbia ★

12 North Carolina
Year Admitted: 1789
Population: 8,049,313
Land area: 48,718 sq. mi.
Representatives: 13
Raleigh ★

13 Rhode Island
Year Admitted: 1790
Population: 1,048,319
Land area: 1,045 sq. mi.
Representatives: 2
★ Providence

14 Vermont
Year Admitted: 1791
Population: 608,827
Land area: 9,249 sq. mi.
Representatives: 1
★ Montpelier

15 Kentucky
Year Admitted: 1792
Population: 4,041,769
Land area: 39,732 sq. mi.
Representatives: 6
Frankfort ★

16 Tennessee
Year Admitted: 1796
Population: 5,689,283
Land area: 41,220 sq. mi.
Representatives: 9
★ Nashville

20 Mississippi
Year Admitted: 1817
Population: 2,844,658
Land area: 46,914 sq. mi.
Representatives: 4
★ Jackson

21 Illinois
Year Admitted: 1818
Population: 12,419,293
Land area: 55,593 sq. mi.
Representatives: 19
★ Springfield

22 Alabama
Year Admitted: 1819
Population: 4,447,100
Land area: 50,750 sq. mi.
Representatives: 7
Montgomery ★

23 Maine
Year Admitted: 1820
Population: 1,274,923
Land area: 30,865 sq. mi.
Representatives: 2
★ Augusta

24 Missouri
Year Admitted: 1821
Population: 5,595,211
Land area: 68,898 sq. mi.
Representatives: 9
Jefferson City ★

28 Texas
Year Admitted: 1845
Population: 20,851,820
Land area: 261,914 sq. mi.
Representatives: 32
Austin ★

29 Iowa
Year Admitted: 1846
Population: 2,926,324
Land area: 55,875 sq. mi.
Representatives: 5
Des Moines ★

30 Wisconsin
Year Admitted: 1848
Population: 5,363,675
Land area: 54,314 sq. mi.
Representatives: 8
Madison ★

31 California
Year Admitted: 1850
Population: 33,871,648
Land area: 155,973 sq. mi.
Representatives: 53
Sacramento ★

32 Minnesota
Year Admitted: 1858
Population: 4,919,479
Land area: 79,617 sq. mi.
Representatives: 8
Saint Paul ★

37 Nebraska
Year Admitted: 1867
Population: 1,711,263
Land area: 76,878 sq. mi.
Representatives: 3
Lincoln ★

38 Colorado
Year Admitted: 1876
Population: 4,301,261
Land area: 103,730 sq. mi.
Representatives: 7
Denver ★

39 North Dakota
Year Admitted: 1889
Population: 642,200
Land area: 68,994 sq. mi.
Representatives: 1
Bismarck ★

40 South Dakota
Year Admitted: 1889
Population: 754,844
Land area: 75,898 sq. mi.
Representatives: 1
Pierre ★

41 Montana
Year Admitted: 1889
Population: 902,195
Land area: 145,556 sq. mi.
Representatives: 1
★ Helena

46 Oklahoma
Year Admitted: 1907
Population: 3,450,654
Land area: 68,679 sq. mi.
Representatives: 5
Oklahoma City ★

47 New Mexico
Year Admitted: 1912
Population: 1,819,046
Land area: 121,365 sq. mi.
Representatives: 3
★ Santa Fe

48 Arizona
Year Admitted: 1912
Population: 5,130,632
Land area: 113,642 sq. mi.
Representatives: 8
Phoenix ★

49 Alaska
Year Admitted: 1959
Population: 626,932
Land area: 570,374 sq. mi.
Representatives: 1
Juneau ★

50 Hawaii
Year Admitted: 1959
Population: 1,211,537
Land area: 6,432 sq. mi.
Representatives: 2
Honolulu ★

FOCUS

Handbook Objectives

After studying this handbook, students should be able to:

1. Understand the themes and elements associated with the study of geography.
2. Understand the purpose and uses of globes and map projections.
3. Identify the most commonly used geographic terms.
4. Analyze geographic factors that have shaped the course of historic events.

Vocabulary Pre-Check

Survey students' knowledge of geographic terms. Create three columns on the board with the headings *Landforms, Map Elements,* and *Bodies of Water.*

List one term that fits each column, such as "canyon," "meridian," and "bay." Ask students to list as many other terms for each column as they can. Then have students turn to the geographic dictionary on pages 90–91 and identify additional terms for each column. Write the terms on the board in the appropriate columns of the chart.

NATIONAL GEOGRAPHIC

Geography Handbook

The story of the United States begins with geography–the study of the earth in all of its variety. Geography describes the earth's land, water, and plant and animal life. It is the study of places and the complex relationships between people and their environments.

The United States is a land of startling physical differences. Within the borders of the United States is a rich variety of landscapes–dense forests, hot deserts, rolling grasslands, and snow-capped mountains. It is also a nation of diverse groups of people. With a total land area of 3,537,441 square miles (9,161,930 sq. km)–the United States is the world's fourth largest country in size. Only Russia, Canada, and China are larger. Because of its size and diversity, the United States has offered people from Europe, Africa, Asia, and other parts of the Americas many opportunities. Today more than 287 million people make the United States their home.

▲ Makapuu Point, Hawaii

◀ Mount Hood, Oregon

GEOGRAPHY HANDBOOK RESOURCES

Print Material
- Glencoe Social Studies Outline Map Resource Book
- Building Geography Skills for Life Workbook

Transparencies
- NGS Focus on Geography Literacy

- NGS PicturePack Transparencies: Midwest, Southeast, Southwest, West

Multimedia
- Student Desk Map
- NGS Picture Show: Midwest, Northeast, Southeast
- ZipZapMap! USA

Globes and Maps

Globes

Photographs from space show the earth in its true form—a great ball spinning around the sun. The most accurate way to depict the earth is as a globe, or a round form. A globe gives a true picture of the earth's relative size and the shape of its landmasses and bodies of water. Globes are proportionally correct, thus showing the true distances and directions between places.

Maps

A map is a flat drawing of the earth's surface. People use maps to locate places, plot routes, and judge distances. Maps can also display useful information about the nation's peoples, such as political boundaries, population densities, or even voting results by city and state.

What advantages does a map have over a globe? Unlike a globe, a map allows you to see all areas of the world at the same time. Maps also show much more detail and can be folded and more easily carried.

Types of Maps

This text uses many different kinds of maps to help you see the connection between geography and the history of the United States.

General-Purpose Maps Maps that show a wide range of general information about a particular area are called **general-purpose maps.** Two of the most common general-purpose maps are physical maps and political maps. **Physical maps** show the location and the shape, or **topography,** of the earth's physical features. **Political maps** show the boundaries between different countries.

Special-Purpose Maps **Special-purpose maps,** also called **thematic maps,** show information on specific topics, such as climate, land use, or vegetation. Human activities, such as exploration routes, territorial expansion, or battle sites, also appear on special-purpose maps. Colors and map key symbols are very important on these maps.

LANDSAT Maps LANDSAT maps are made from photographs taken by camera-carrying LANDSAT satellites in space. The cameras record millions of energy waves invisible to the human eye. Computers then change this information into pictures of the earth's surface. With LANDSAT images, scientists can study whole mountain ranges, oceans, and geographic regions. Changes to the earth's environment can also be tracked using the satellite information.

◄ Special-purpose map

U.S. forces
British forces
German forces
Front line at date shown.

0   15 miles
0   15 kilometers
Albers Conic Equal-Area projection

NETH.
Aachen
January 16
BELGIUM
Liège
Meuse R.
December 25
December 16
Namur   Huy
Ourthe R.
Stavelot
Dinant   Ciney
Celles   Vielsalm
La Roche   Prüm
Rochefort
GERMANY
St. Hubert   Houffalize   Clervaux
            Bastogne
Libramont   Wiltz   Vianden
Neufchâteau   Echternach
American units at Bastogne were encircled on Dec. 19, and relieved on Dec. 26.
LUXEMBOURG
Arlon   Luxembourg
FRANCE

▲ LANDSAT map

TEACH

U Universal Access

English Learners Have each student bring an orange to class. Ask students to draw a face on the orange. Then have them carefully peel the orange so that the peel lies flat. Ask students to describe what happened to the face. Then ask students to explain what this activity illustrates about the difficulty of transferring information about the earth's surface to a map. **EL**

W Writing Support

Expository Writing Have students conduct research on how computers have revolutionized cartography. Suggest that students select one area of focus, such as how computers gather, process, and store data about elevation, or how computer technology has changed the way storm movement is tracked and mapped. Students should present their findings in an essay. **OL**
CA 11WS1.3

EXTENDING THE CONTENT

Geographic Information Systems (GIS) Geographic Information Systems are computer hardware and software systems that can store, display, analyze, and map information. Geographers, urban planners, engineers, and utility companies are just a few of the groups of people that use these systems. GIS are vital to planning because they enable geographers, scientists, and others to combine data and look at layers of information at the same time. One GIS, for example, may begin with a digitized base map. A retailer wishing to make an informed decision about where to build a store may need to consider a combination of data such as population distribution, traffic movement, land availability, and real estate prices.

Using Maps

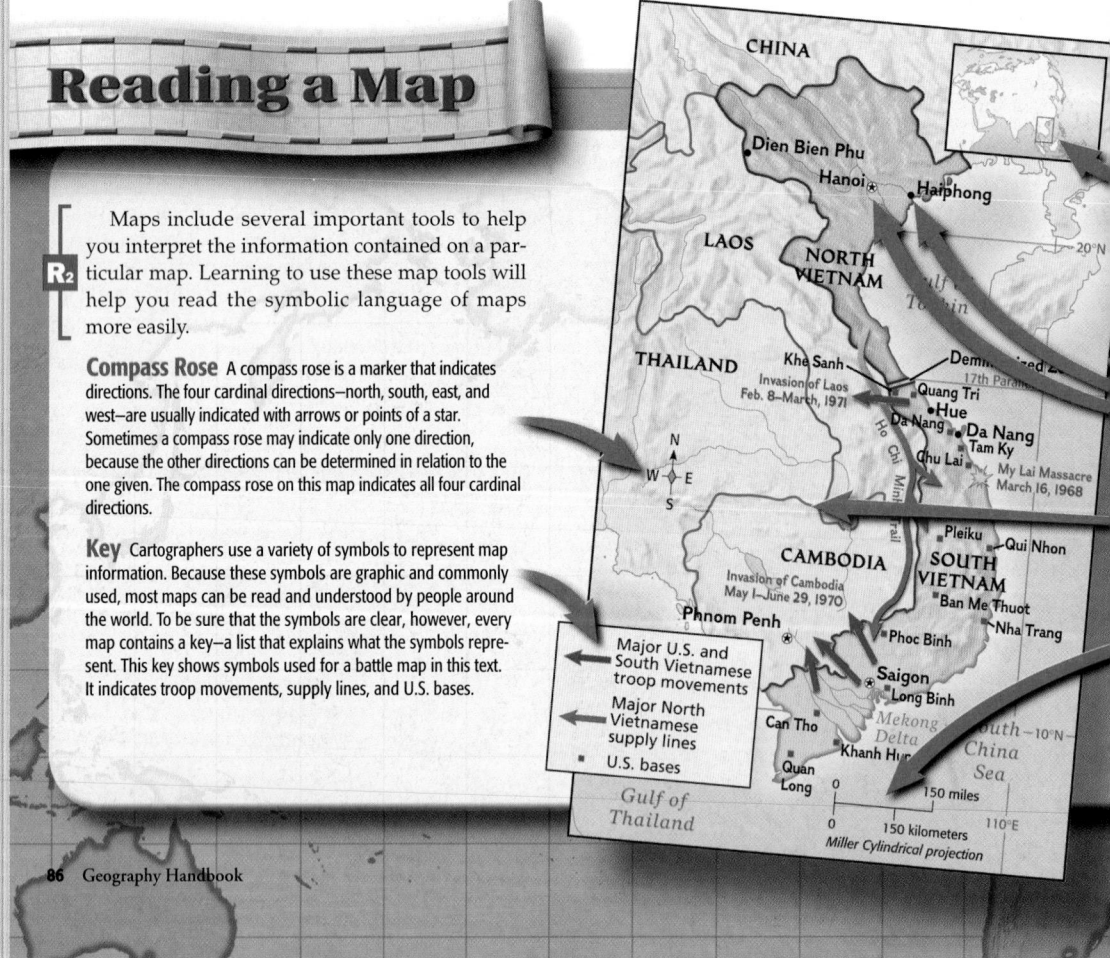

▲ Most general reference maps use the Winkel Tripel projection. Adopted by the National Geographic Society in 1998, this projection provides a better balance between the size and shape of land areas as they are shown on the map.

R₁ Reading Strategy

Organizing Information Have students create a four-column chart and label the columns *Winkel Tripel, Robinson, Goode's Interrupted Equal-Area,* and *Mercator.* As students read about the four map projections described on these pages, have them note the characteristics, advantages, and disadvantages of each type of projection. Ask students to use the information in their charts to write a brief summary that compares and contrasts the four different projections. **OL**

R₂ Reading Strategy

Reading Maps, Graphs, and Charts Have students look at some of the maps in this textbook and identify the map projections used for this book. Instruct them to read the section on these two pages titled "Reading a Map." Ask students to look at two or three maps in the book and locate the compass rose, key, cities, capitals, relative location, absolute location, boundary lines, and scale bar. Students should note whether each map they looked at has all these features. **OL**

Map Projections Maps, however, do have their limitations. As you can imagine, drawing a round object on a flat surface is very difficult. **Cartographers,** or mapmakers, have drawn many projections, or kinds of maps. Each map projection is a different way of showing the round earth on a flat map.

R₁ Different map projections include the Winkel Tripel, Robinson, Goode's Interrupted Equal-Area, and Mercator projections. It is impossible to accurately represent the round earth on a flat surface without distorting some part of the earth. Thus, map projections typically distort distance, direction, shape, or area.

Reading a Map

R₂ Maps include several important tools to help you interpret the information contained on a particular map. Learning to use these map tools will help you read the symbolic language of maps more easily.

Compass Rose A compass rose is a marker that indicates directions. The four cardinal directions—north, south, east, and west—are usually indicated with arrows or points of a star. Sometimes a compass rose may indicate only one direction, because the other directions can be determined in relation to the one given. The compass rose on this map indicates all four cardinal directions.

Key Cartographers use a variety of symbols to represent map information. Because these symbols are graphic and commonly used, most maps can be read and understood by people around the world. To be sure that the symbols are clear, however, every map contains a key—a list that explains what the symbols represent. This key shows symbols used for a battle map in this text. It indicates troop movements, supply lines, and U.S. bases.

More Skill Practice

Interpersonal Organize students into small groups of three or four. Have each group make a large map of the school. Tell students that their maps should include a title, a compass rose, a scale bar, and a key. Have each student attach six index cards to the map. On each card, they should list one of the six essential elements for the study of geography. Students can refer to pages 88 and 89 of this handbook to review these elements. Then have them fill out each card with information that pertains to their school. **OL**

Robinson Projection

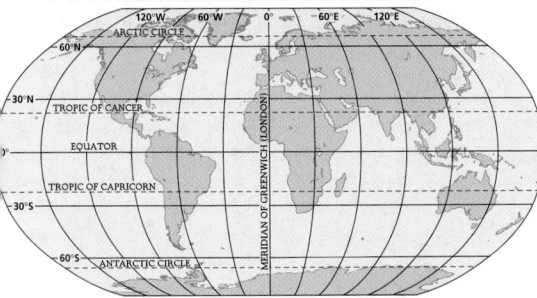

▲ The Robinson projection has minor distortions. The sizes and shapes near the eastern and western edges of the map are accurate, and the outlines of the continents appear much as they do on the globe. The shapes of the polar areas, however, are somewhat flat.

W

Goode's Interrupted Equal-Area Projection

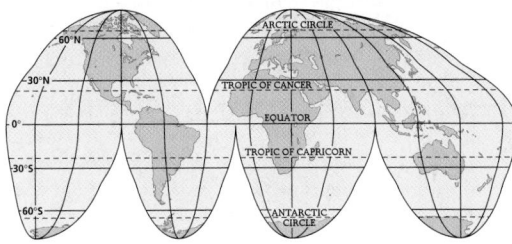

▲ An interrupted projection looks something like a globe that has been cut apart and laid flat. Goode's Interrupted Equal-Area projection shows the true size and shape of the earth's landmasses, but distances are distorted.

Relative Location Relative location is the location of one place in relation to another, while absolute location indicates the exact position of a place on the earth's surface. On this map, the relative location of where the Vietnam War took place is given in relation to the rest of Asia.

Cities and Capitals Cities are symbolized by a solid circle. Sometimes the relative sizes of cities are shown with circles of different sizes. Capitals are represented by a star within a circle.

Boundary Lines On political maps of large areas, boundary lines highlight the borders between different countries, states, or counties.

Scale Bar Every map is a representation of a part of the earth. The scale bar shows the relationship between map measurements and actual distance. Scale can be measured with a ruler to calculate actual distances in standard or metric measurements. On this map, 5/8 inch represents 150 miles (241 km).

Mercator Projection

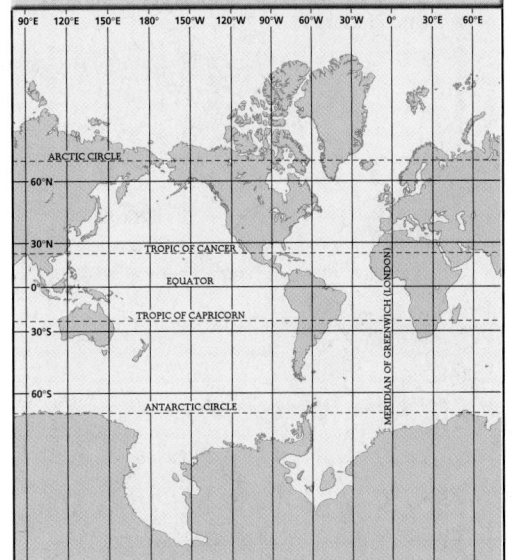

▲ The Mercator projection increasingly distorts size and distance as it moves away from the Equator. However, Mercator projections accurately show true directions and the shapes of the landmasses.

C

Geography Handbook **87**

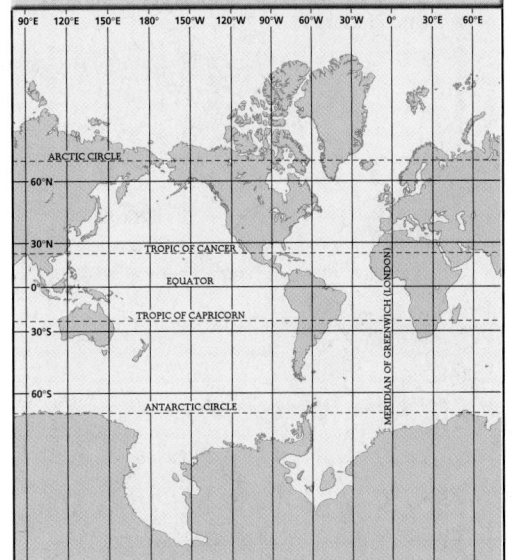
EXTENDING THE CONTENT

The Work of Geographers Geographers work for the federal government in the Defense Mapping Agency, United States Geological Survey, Central Intelligence Agency, Army Corps of Engineers, National Science Foundation, Smithsonian Institution, and Office of the Geographer in the Department of State. State environmental and transportation agencies hire geographers and analysts, planners, and cartographers. In the private sector, geographers work as professors, researchers, and cartographers for high-tech mapping companies. Businesses as varied as fast-food chains and ski resorts consult geographers about optimal locations for new restaurants and effects of pollution on the ski slopes.

The Elements of Geography

R

R Reading Strategy

Connecting Ask students to write definitions for the five themes of geography. For each definition, have them write a sentence that describes a personal connection with that term. To prompt students, use location as an example and identify the town where you were born. Invite students to share with the class their personal connections with the themes and essential elements of geography. **OL** **CA** 11WA2.3b

C Critical Thinking

Analyzing Information Ask students to identify the physical and human characteristics of place. *(Students should identify each place as having distinctive landforms, bodies of water, climate, soils, vegetation, people with particular languages and political beliefs.)* Then ask students to describe the characteristics of places that distinguish their neighborhood, city, or town from others nearby. **OL**

R To understand how our world is connected, some geographers have broken down the study of geography into five themes. The **Five Themes of Geography** are (1) location, (2) place, (3) human/environment interaction, (4) movement, and (5) regions.

Six Essential Elements

Recently, as suggested in the **Geography Skills for Life**, geographers have broken down the study of geography into **Six Essential Elements**. Being aware of these elements will help you sort out what you are learning about geography.

Element 1

The World in Spatial Terms Geographers first look at where a place is located. **Location** serves as a starting point by asking, "Where is it?" Knowing the location of places helps you develop an awareness of the world around you. For example, the surrender of Confederate General Robert E. Lee took place at Appomattox Courthouse, located in Virginia.

Element 2

Place and Regions **Place** has a special meaning in geography. It means more than where an area is located. It also describes what features a place includes. These features may be physical characteristics, such as landforms, climate, and plant or animal life. They may also be human characteristics, including language and way of life. For example, the English settlement of Jamestown was located in a swampy area with mosquitoes and high humidity. This made the way of life difficult for the new settlers.

To help them organize their study, geographers often group places into regions. **Regions** are united by one or more common characteristics. The original thirteen colonies, for instance, were divided into three regions—New England Colonies, Middle Colonies, and Southern Colonies.

88 Geography Handbook

More Skill Practice

Historical and Social Sciences Analysis Skill As students read this textbook, have them keep a journal in which they record significant geographic information. Ask students to record at least five major events in U.S. history. Then have them select one of these events and write an essay analyzing the effects of physical and human geographic factors on this event. As part of their analysis, students should find and use historical and contemporary maps related to the event they selected. Ask students to interpret these maps to identify geographic factors and show the connections between these factors and the historical event and people affected. Have students share their findings in an oral and visual presentation. **AL** **CA** CS4; HI5

Element 3

Physical Systems When studying places and regions, geographers analyze the ways in which **physical systems**—such as hurricanes, volcanoes, and glaciers—shape the earth's surface. They also look at communities of plants and animals that depend upon one another and their surroundings for survival. Glaciers are an example of a physical system. Near the end of the Ice Age, glaciers melted, raising ocean levels and covering a land bridge that once connected Asia and North America.

Element 4

Human Systems Geographers also examine an area's **human systems,** or how people have shaped our world. They look at how boundary lines are determined and analyze why people settle in certain places and not in others. A key theme in geography is the continual **movement** of people, ideas, and goods. An example of such movement occurred in the 1820s, when Stephen F. Austin organized a group of Americans to settle in the Mexican territory of Texas.

R

Element 5

Environment and Society "How does the relationship between people and their natural surroundings influence the way people live?" This is one of the questions that the geographic element of **environment and society** answers. This element also shows how people use the environment and how their actions affect it. One example was when some people in the South established large plantations to take advantage of the warm climate and fertile soil.

Element 6

The Uses of Geography Knowledge of geography helps people understand the relationships between people, places, and environment over time. Understanding geography and knowing how to use the tools and technology available to study it prepares you for life in our modern society. Early European explorers, for example, relied on their knowledge of geography to discover lands never seen before by Europeans.

Geography Handbook **89**

W Writing Support

Persuasive Writing Ask students to imagine that they work for an advertising agency and have landed a contract for a series of travel brochures. Have each student create a travel brochure for the destination of his or her choice. Students should include in their brochures information about latitude and longitude and physical and cultural features. They should also describe in detail at least three geographic features listed in the dictionary that are unique or important to the destinations they have selected. **AL**

U Universal Access

Verbal/Linguistic Have students select any geographic location illustrated in the diagram and use that as their starting point for a "walking tour." Ask students to write a description of their walking tour that includes characteristics of the different geographic features they see along the way. Challenge students to include ten different terms from the geographic dictionary. **BL**

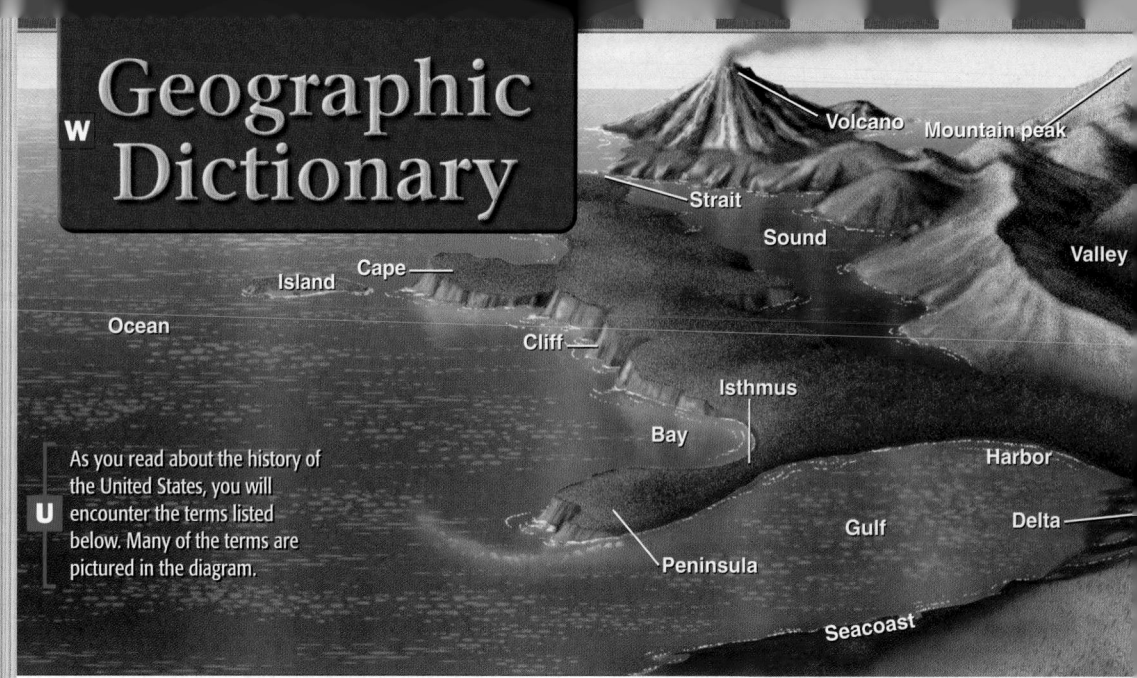

W Geographic Dictionary

U As you read about the history of the United States, you will encounter the terms listed below. Many of the terms are pictured in the diagram.

absolute location exact location of a place on the earth described by global coordinates

basin area of land drained by a given river and its branches; area of land surrounded by lands of higher elevations

bay part of a large body of water that extends into a shoreline, generally smaller than a gulf

canyon deep and narrow valley with steep walls

cape point of land that extends into a river, lake, or ocean

channel wide strait or waterway between two landmasses that lie close to each other; deep part of a river or other waterway

cliff steep, high wall of rock, earth, or ice

continent one of the seven large landmasses on the earth

cultural feature characteristic that humans have created in a place, such as language, religion, housing, and settlement pattern

delta flat, low-lying land built up from soil carried downstream by a river and deposited at its mouth

divide stretch of high land that separates river systems

downstream direction in which a river or stream flows from its source to its mouth

elevation height of land above sea level

Equator imaginary line that runs around the earth halfway between the North and South Poles; used as the starting point to measure degrees of north and south latitude

glacier large, thick body of slowly moving ice

gulf part of a large body of water that extends into a shoreline, generally larger and more deeply indented than a bay

harbor a sheltered place along a shoreline where ships can anchor safely

highland elevated land area such as a hill, mountain, or plateau

hill elevated land with sloping sides and rounded summit; generally smaller than a mountain

island land area, smaller than a continent, completely surrounded by water

isthmus narrow stretch of land connecting two larger land areas

lake a large inland body of water

latitude distance north or south of the Equator, measured in degrees

longitude distance east or west of the Prime Meridian, measured in degrees

lowland land, usually level, at a low elevation

map drawing of the earth shown on a flat surface

meridian one of many lines on the global grid running from the North Pole to the South Pole; used to measure degrees of longitude

---

More Skill Practice

Historical and Social Sciences Analysis Skill Ask students to imagine that they are creating a documentary series called *Through the Eyes of the Great Mapmakers.* Have students work in groups to collect information from multiple sources about Lewis and Clark's exploration of the West, an upcoming episode in their documentary series. Have students use this information to re-create a historical enactment of Lewis and Clark's exploration and mapping of the West, narrating some of the hardships these two men went through to describe and map the West. Within each group, students should take responsibility for an individual role, such as director, researcher, maker of props, script writer, or actor. Have each group present their documentary episode to the class. **OL** **CA** HR4

Mountain range

Source of river

Glacier

Channel

Highland

Lake

Plateau

Hills

Canyon

Mouth of river

Desert

River

Upstream

Downstream

Lowland

Plain

Basin

Tributary

mesa broad, flat-topped landform with steep sides; smaller than a plateau

mountain land with steep sides that rises sharply (1,000 feet or more) from surrounding land; generally larger and more rugged than a hill

mountain peak pointed top of a mountain

mountain range a series of connected mountains

mouth (of a river) place where a stream or river flows into a larger body of water

ocean one of the four major bodies of salt water that surround the continents

ocean current stream of either cold or warm water that moves in a definite direction through an ocean

parallel one of many lines on the global grid that circle the earth north or south of the Equator; used to measure degrees of latitude

peninsula body of land jutting into a lake or ocean, surrounded on three sides by water

physical feature characteristic of a place occurring naturally, such as a landform, body of water, climate pattern, or resource

plain area of level land, usually at a low elevation and often covered with grasses

plateau large area of flat or rolling land at a high elevation, about 300–3,000 feet high

Prime Meridian line of the global grid running from the North Pole to the South Pole at Greenwich, England; starting point for measuring degrees of east and west longitude

relief changes in elevation over a given area of land

river large natural stream of water that runs through the land

sea large body of water completely or partly surrounded by land

seacoast land lying next to a sea or ocean

sea level position on land level with surface of nearby ocean or sea

sound body of water between a coastline and one or more islands off the coast

source (of a river) place where a river or stream begins, often in highlands

strait narrow stretch of water joining two larger bodies of water

tributary small river or stream that flows into a larger river or stream; a branch of the river

upstream direction opposite the flow of a river; toward the source of a river or stream

valley area of low land between hills or mountains

volcano mountain created as ash or liquid rock erupts from inside the earth

Geography Handbook **91**

Unit 1 Resources

Teaching the Unit

Use the information on these pages to help you teach Unit 1.

History–Social Science Standards Covered in Unit 1

Standard	Chapter 1	2	3
11.1 Students analyze the significant events surrounding the founding of the nation and its attempts to realize the philosophy of government described in the Declaration of Independence.	✔	✔	✔
11.2 Students analyze the relationship among the rise of industrialization, large-scale rural-to-urban migration, and massive immigration from Southern and Eastern Europe.		✔	✔
11.3 Students analyze the role religion played in the founding of America, its lasting moral, social, and political impacts, and issues regarding religious liberty.	✔	✔	✔

Pacing Your Lessons

This pacing chart provides time management suggestions for teaching Unit 1.

	Days
Unit 1 Introduction	1
Chapter 1 • **Reading Skill:** Predicting • **Historical Analysis Skill:** Understanding Change • **Sections 1–3** • **Eyewitness to History:** Primary Source Documents	6
Chapter 2 • **Reading Skill:** Questioning • **Historical Analysis Skill:** Relating Current Events • **Sections 1–5** • **What Life Was Like:** Old-Fashioned School Days • **American Literature:** *Narrative of the Life of Frederick Douglass* by Frederick Douglass • **Why It Matters:** The Fourteenth Amendment • **Eyewitness to History:** Primary Source Documents	11
Chapter 3 • **Reading Skill:** Comparing and Contrasting • **Historical Analysis Skill:** Interpreting Maps • **Sections 1–5** • **You're the Historian:** Investigating Standard Oil • **National Geographic:** Geography & History: Immigrants Arrive in Chicago • **Eyewitness to History:** Primary Source Documents	11

 Teacher to Teacher

The Influence of the East on the West

The wave of European exploration of the Americas following the voyages of Columbus had its origin in the Crusades, begun by Pope Urban II. The Crusades brought Europeans into contact with Muslims and Byzantine civilizations in the Middle East. Traders followed the European armies eastward and brought back spices and silk. They also brought back the concept of paying with money instead of trading goods. Later the search for new routes east launched the age of exploration.

**Karen O'Connor
San Diego Unified
School District
San Diego, California**

Gather students into small groups and ask them to research other areas where the contact between the East and West during this time period influenced European culture. Assign each group one of the following areas: architecture, art, literature, science, or language.

Give them one week to prepare an oral presentation. Their written reports should be due one week later.

Previewing the Chapters

Dear American History Teacher:

As you begin to teach this unit, there are themes that recur throughout the chapters that you will want to point out to students.

Important nation-building acts defined the United States during this period. The significant political developments, like declaring independence, winning the revolution, securing a fair peace treaty, and writing a new constitution, constituted high politics, but ordinary people also engaged in migration from the Atlantic coastline and across the Appalachian Mountains. American ingenuity led to an expansion of manufacturing and, with it, the growth of cities.

Not everyone benefited from these decades of growth and innovation. Native Americans were forced further into the West as white settlers continued to push toward new land to cultivate. A cotton culture dependent on slavery spread across the Southeast. By 1801, however, all the Northern states had abolished slavery, dividing the country between free and enslaved labor. Students should understand that this division generated tensions that led to the Civil War and recognize the moral force of the antislavery movement that grew after 1830.

You may want to use the following information at the beginning of each chapter as a lesson launcher to help students begin to focus on what they will be studying.

Joyce Appleby

Chapter 1: Creating a Nation, Beginnings to 1789

(pages 94–167)

When colonists came to the Americas seeking goods to trade and religious freedom, life changed for the Native Americans. European colonies grew and established governments. Eventually, many people in the British colonies demanded independence. When the Americans won the Revolutionary War, Britain was forced to recognize the United States as an independent nation. The Constitution, written to define the new government and the rights of its people, marked a great success, but not everyone was given equal rights.

Chapter 2: Growth and Conflict, 1789–1877

(pages 168–231)

The United States continued to expand its territory and solidify its political system. As growth transformed the United States, social, political, and economic divisions became apparent. Disagreement over slavery separated North and South and led Southern states to secede from the Union and declare themselves a separate nation, the Confederate States of America. Soon after, the Civil War began. It lasted four years, ending when the Confederate forces surrendered in 1865. The challenge of rebuilding the country followed.

Chapter 3: The Birth of Modern America, 1877–1900

(pages 232–287)

Reconstruction required dealing with social conflicts, the new roles of African Americans, and economic crises. Industry was gaining importance in the country. Many people moved West to take advantage of the mining and agricultural resources available. Increased settlement in the West further impacted Native Americans. Industrialization led to new jobs, transportation, and migration. In addition, many people immigrated to the United States from other countries. Urban populations grew rapidly, and with the advantages of industrialization came new challenges.

FOCUS

History– Social Science Standards

This unit addresses the following main standards:

11.1 Students analyze the significant events in the founding of the nation and its attempts to realize the philosophy of government described in the Declaration of Independence.

11.2 Students analyze the relationship among the rise of industrialization, large-scale rural-to-urban migration, and massive immigration from Southern and Eastern Europe.

11.3 Students analyze the role religion played in the founding of America, its lasting moral, social, and political impacts, and issues regarding religious liberty.

Connecting to Past Learning

In Unit 1, students will learn about the formation of the United States and its development from the Revolutionary War through the Civil War and industrialization.

Unit Launch Activity

Ask students to name some of the core values that they believe all Americans share and explain how they think colonists shaped these values. Students should evaluate their answers after they have completed the unit. **OL**

Why It Matters Activity

Point out to students that the United States was shaped by many different events in its first century and a half of existence. **Ask:** What do you think is the most important event that occurred during this period? *(Students may mention several different events, such as the writing of the Declaration of Independence or the Civil War. Make sure students defend their choice with a clear argument.)* **OL**

UNIT 1

A Nation is Born

Beginnings–1900

Why It Matters

The history of the United States of America begins with the decision of the thirteen English colonies to rebel against Britain. After emerging victorious from the Revolutionary War, the United States created a new form of government. The new republic struggled to balance federal versus states' rights as the nation grew in size and the North and South divided over the issue of slavery. Unable to reconcile these differences, the country fought the Civil War. After a difficult period of reunification, the United States expanded across the continent and developed its industrial economy. As the twentieth century approached, a modern United States prepared to face a new century. The following resources offer more information about this period in American history.

Declaration of Independence

Primary Sources Library

See pages 974–975 for primary source readings to accompany Unit 1.

Use the **American History Primary Source Document Library CD-ROM** to find additional primary sources about events in early America.

Washington's Inauguration at Independence Hall by Jean Leon Gérôme Ferris, 1793

92

TEAM TEACHING ACTIVITY

ECONOMICS Have the economics teacher compare and contrast small entrepreneurial businesses with big businesses, and family farms with large agricultural enterprises. After the presentation, have a class discussion using the following questions: How are workers treated differently in different types of enterprises? How is family life affected by the various enterprises? How does the type of enterprise in which your family is involved affect where and how you live? What effect do economic changes such as recessions have on these types of enterprises? **AL**

"The country shall be independent, and we will be satisfied with nothing short of it."

—Samuel Adams, 1774

TEACH

Skill Practice

Recognizing Point of View
Instruct students to read Samuel Adams's quote on the top of this page. **Ask:** What other quotes might also serve to capture this period of American history? As students read through the unit, instruct them to look for statements that might work to encapsulate this period of American history. **OL** **CA** 11RC2.5

Skill Practice

Visual Literacy George Washington faced many challenges as the first American president. He understood that many things which he did would serve as a guide to all presidents that followed him. **Ask:** How does the inauguration depicted in this painting differ from presidential inaugurations today? *(Students should use descriptive words to describe what they see in the painting and how this image is different from modern inaugurations. They might point out that the president is significantly closer to the people than modern presidents often get.)* **EL**

NC LB **No Child Left Behind**

Teaching Tip The NCLB Act emphasizes reading. Ask students to write down events and people they will encounter in this unit and keep the list with them as they read. When students find a person or item on the list, they should note the page number and write a brief summary. Students can use this list while studying.

UNIVERSAL ACCESS

English Learners Have students write down on index cards any unfamiliar words that they find on these unit opener pages. Then have pairs of students look up these terms in the glossary in the back of the book or in a dictionary. **EL**

Verbal/Linguistic Ask students to organize a geography bee in which they name a significant event that occurred during the decades of this unit. The class should locate in an atlas where the chosen event took place, either in the United States or in another country. **BL**

Chapter 1 Planning Guide

SECTION RESOURCES

MAIN IDEAS	PRINT MATERIALS	TECHNOLOGY RESOURCES
Section 1: Converging Cultures 1. Native Americans adapted to their environments and developed diverse cultures. 2. European countries began to explore the world and established colonies in the Americas. 3. The French and English settled in North America, and English colonists began their own local governments. 4. As English settlements grew, colonists developed different forms of government to regulate life in their communities. 5. The different colonies created new social structures that were more open than those of aristocratic Europe.	• Reproducible Lesson Plan 1-1* • Daily Lecture and Discussion Notes 1-1 • Active Reading Note-Taking Guide 1-1 • Guided Reading Activity 1-1 • Section Quiz 1-1 • Reading Essentials and Study Guide 1-1	• Daily Focus Skills Transparency 1-1 • Section Graphic Organizer Transparency 1-1 • Interactive Tutor Self-Assessment CD-ROM • ExamView® Pro Testmaker CD-ROM • Presentation Plus! CD-ROM • California Standards Practice Transparencies
Section 2: Dissent and Independence 1. The colonists learned about the ideas of natural rights and justified revolutions, while British mercantilist policies limited their freedom. 2. The ideas of the Enlightenment and the Great Awakening made the colonists question their role as subjects of the English monarch. 3. Unpopular British laws and taxes led to colonial protests and violence. 4. When Britain introduced new laws to assert its authority, the colonists decided to declare their independence. 5. With the help of their allies, the Americans defeated the British in the Revolutionary War.	• Reproducible Lesson Plan 1-2* • Daily Lecture and Discussion Notes 1-2 • Active Reading Note-Taking Guide 1-2 • Guided Reading Activity 1-2 • Section Quiz 1-2 • Reading Essentials and Study Guide 1-2	• Daily Focus Skills Transparency 1-2 • Section Graphic Organizer Transparency 1-2 • Interactive Tutor Self-Assessment CD-ROM • ExamView® Pro Testmaker CD-ROM • Presentation Plus! CD-ROM • California Standards Practice Transparencies
Section 3: The Constitution 1. The states created constitutions that gave people more rights, but the national framework could not address all the problems of the new nation. 2. American leaders created a new constitution based on compromise. 3. The promise of a Bill of Rights guaranteed the ratification of the Constitution.	• Reproducible Lesson Plan 1-3* • Daily Lecture and Discussion Notes 1-3 • Active Reading Note-Taking Guide 1-3 • Guided Reading Activity 1-3 • Section Quiz 1-3 • Reading Essentials and Study Guide 1-3	• Daily Focus Skills Transparency 1-3 • Section Graphic Organizer Transparency 1-3 • Interactive Tutor Self-Assessment CD-ROM • ExamView® Pro Testmaker CD-ROM • Presentation Plus! CD-ROM • California Standards Practice Transparencies

PACING YOUR LESSONS

Chapter Introduction	Section 1	Section 2	Section 3	Chapter Assessment
½ Day	1 Day	2 Days	2 Days	½ Day

0:00 OUT OF TIME? Assign the Chapter 1 *Reading Essentials and Study Guide.*

*Available on TeacherWorks™ CD-ROM

Chapter 1 Planning Guide

Standards-Based Lesson Plan

 History–Social Science Standards Covered in Chapter 1

The standards covered in the chapter are listed below. Use the accompanying activity as you teach the chapter to ensure student mastery of these standards. This activity can be used in combination with the program's print and technology assessment materials.

Standard	Section 1	2	3
11.1 Students analyze the significant events in the founding of the nation and its attempts to realize the philosophy of government described in the Declaration of Independence.	✔		✔
11.1.1 Describe the Enlightenment and the rise of democratic ideas as the context in which the nation was founded.		✔	✔
11.1.2 Analyze the ideological origins of the American Revolution, the Founding Fathers' philosophy of divinely bestowed unalienable natural rights, the debates on the drafting and ratification of the Constitution, and the addition of the Bill of Rights.		✔	✔
11.3 Students analyze the role religion played in the founding of America, its lasting moral, social, and political impacts, and issues regarding religious liberty.	✔		
11.3.1 Describe the contributions of various religious groups to American civic principles and social reform movements (e.g., civil and human rights, individual responsibility and the work ethic, antimonarchy and self-rule, worker protection, family-centered communities).	✔		
11.3.2 Analyze the great religious revivals and the leaders involved in them, including the First Great Awakening, the Second Great Awakening, the Civil War revivals, the Social Gospel Movement, the rise of Christian liberal theology in the nineteenth century, the impact of the Second Vatican Council, and the rise of Christian fundamentalism in current times.		✔	

Cumulative Standards-Assessment Activity

The Cumulative Standards-Assessment Activity will help students organize and learn the important information from the chapter. Begin teaching the chapter with this activity, and have students complete it as they read the chapter.

CREATING A CAUSE-AND-EFFECT CHART

Purpose Studying history in the context of cause and effect will enable students to see how prevailing attitudes and ideas are related to political and social events and how historical events are related to each other. Making cause-and-effect connections will also help students to understand the importance of studying history and can lead to lessons on individual responsibility, comprehending interconnectedness, and applying lessons of the past to the present and future.

Introduction to Making Connections

1. Begin by choosing a cause and effect from current events. Ask students to explain how the effect resulted from the cause. In addition, see if they can list other effects of the cause. Then encourage students to relate this current event to their own lives. What effect might it have on them, their families, friends, or neighbors?

2. Explain to students how they can use the same skill to understand the significance of historical events.

3. Ask students to copy this chart into their notebooks.

Causes	Effects

Ask the class to chart causes and effects from the chapter as they read. Remind them that one cause may have several effects.

4. As part of the chapter review, have students share their charts of causes and effects. Allow discussion to develop around items about which the students disagree. Encourage the class to use their charts as study aids.

Chapter 1 Planning Guide

READING SUPPORT

- Content Vocabulary Activity 1
- Academic Vocabulary Activity 1
- Reading Skills Activity 1
- Chapter 1 Active Reading Note-Taking Guide
- Chapter 1 Guided Reading Activities
- Chapter 1 Reading Essentials and Study Guide
- *The American Vision: Modern Times* Video Program
- Vocabulary PuzzleMaker CD-ROM
- American History Primary Source Document Library CD-ROM

SKILL PRACTICE

- Map Overlay Transparency 1 Strategy and Activity
- Historical Analysis Skills Activity 1
- Time Line Activity 1
- Reading Skills Activity 1
- Reinforcing Skills Activity 1
- Linking Past and Present Activity 1
- Interpreting Political Cartoons 1
- Economics and History Activity, Unit 1
- MindJogger Videoquiz

CRITICAL THINKING

- Critical Thinking Skills Activity 1
- Primary Source Reading 1
- Cause-and-Effect Transparency 1 Strategy and Activity
- Presentation Plus! CD-ROM

WRITING SUPPORT

- Chapter 1 Active Reading Note-Taking Guide
- Writer's Guidebook
- High School Writing Process Transparencies

ASSESSMENT

- Chapter 1 Section Quizzes
- Chapter 1 Tests, Forms A and B
- Authentic Assessment Activity 1
- Exam*View*® Pro Testmaker CD-ROM
- Interactive Tutor Self-Assessment CD-ROM
- California Standards Practice, Grade 11
- Succeeding on . . .™ the California Standards: Grade 11 History–Social Science CD-ROM

UNIVERSAL ACCESS

- Universal Access Activity 1
- English Learner Activity 1
- American Art Prints
- StudentWorks™ Plus CD-ROM
- American Music: Hits Through History
- School-to-Home Connection Activity 1

- CD-ROM
- DVD
- Print Material
- Poster

- Transparency
- Music Program
- Videocassette

Chapter 1 Planning Guide

TECHNOLOGY

- StudentWorks™ Plus CD-ROM
- TeacherWorks™ CD-ROM
- ExamView® Pro Testmaker CD-ROM
- Interactive Tutor Self-Assessment CD-ROM
- Presentation Plus! CD-ROM
- Vocabulary PuzzleMaker CD-ROM
- American History Primary Source Document Library CD-ROM
- MindJogger Videoquiz
- *The American Vision: Modern Times* Video Program
- Professional Development in High School Social Studies Video Series
- Teach, Use, and Succeed With *The American Vision: Modern Times*
- American Music: Hits Through History
- Succeeding on . . .™ the California Standards: Grade 11 History–Social Science CD-ROM

SPANISH RESOURCES

- Spanish Activities and Assessment
  - Spanish Vocabulary Activities
  - Spanish Guided Reading Activities
  - Spanish Quizzes and Tests
  - Spanish Reteaching Activities
- Spanish Reading Essentials and Study Guide
- Spanish School-to-Home Connection Activities

TRANSPARENCIES

- Daily Focus Skills Transparencies
- Section Graphic Organizer Transparencies
- Map Overlay Transparencies
- Cause-and-Effect Transparencies
- Unit Time Line Transparencies
- Why It Matters Transparencies
- American Art and Architecture Transparencies
- High School Writing Process Transparencies
- California Standards Practice Transparencies

TEACHER PLANNING

- Daily Lecture and Discussion Notes
- English Learner Handbook
- Building Academic Vocabulary
- *The American Vision: Modern Times* Reading and Study Skills Foldables
- Reading Strategies and Activities for the Social Studies Classroom
- Universal Access for the American History Classroom
- NGS United States Desk Map
- NGS World Atlas
- Chapter 1 Reproducible Lesson Plans on TeacherWorks™ CD-ROM
- California Guide to Daily Intervention

PROFESSIONAL DEVELOPMENT

- Building Academic Vocabulary
- Strategies for Success
- Research-Based Strategies Used to Develop *The American Vision: Modern Times*
- Character Education in the High School Classroom
- Professional Development in High School Social Studies Video Series
- Teach, Use, and Succeed With *The American Vision: Modern Times*

MOMENTS IN TIME

The following resource can help you teach the content of this chapter.

- Unit 1 George Washington (1777–1789)

94D

Chapter 1 Planning Guide

TEACHER'S CORNER

Index to National Geographic Magazine:

The following articles relate to this chapter:

- "1491: America Before Columbus," October 1991
- "Dawn of Humans: The First Americans," December 2000
- "La Salle's Last Voyage," May 1997
- "Thomas Jefferson: Architect of Freedom," February 1976
- "Two Revolutions," July 1989

National Geographic Society Products:

To order the following, call National Geographic at 1–800–368–2728

- *American Indians: A Brief History* (Video)
- *Historical Atlas of the United States* (Atlas)

NGS ONLINE

Access National Geographic's new dynamic MapMachine Web site and other geography resources at:

www.nationalgeographic.com

www.nationalgeographic.com/maps

MASTERING THE STANDARDS

The content and assessment in the Student Edition, Teacher Wraparound Edition, teacher planning materials, and the print and technology products are all standards-based. The use of these products during instruction leads to mastery of the standards.

PRACTICE
- California Standards Practice, Grade 11
- California Standards Practice Transparencies
- School-to-Home Connection

BENCHMARK ASSESSMENT
- Section Quizzes, Chapter Tests, and Authentic Assessment
- Exam*View*® Pro Testmaker CD-ROM
- Succeeding On . . . ™ the California Standards: Grade 11 History–Social Science CD-ROM

REMEDIATION
- California Guide to Daily Intervention
- Interactive Tutor Self-Assessment CD-ROM
- Exam*View*® Pro Testmaker CD-ROM
- California Standards Practice, Grade 11
- Reading Essentials and Study Guide

Use our Web site for additional resources. All essential content is covered in the Student Edition.

You and your students can visit tav.mt.glencoe.com, the Web site companion to the **American Vision: Modern Times.** This innovative integration of electronic and print media offers your students a wealth of opportunities. The student text directs students to the Web site for the following options:

- **Chapter Overviews**
- **Self-Check Quizzes**
- **Student Web Activities**
- **Textbook Updates**

Answers to the student Web activities are provided for you in the **Web Activity Lesson Plans.** Additional Web resources and ePuzzles and games are also available.

FOLDABLES™ Study Organizer

Dinah Zike's Foldables

Foldables are three-dimensional, interactive graphic organizers that help students practice basic writing skills, review key vocabulary terms, and identify main ideas. Every chapter has a foldable activity in the *Dinah Zike's Reading and Study Skills Foldables* booklet. You can use the foldables as they are presented or modify them to suit the needs of your individual class.

A variety of videotape programs are available from A&E Television and The History Channel to provide teaching assistance. To order, call Glencoe at 1-800-334-7344.

Chapter 1 Planning Guide

KEY for Using the Teacher Wraparound Edition

Use this key to help you identify the different types of prompts found in the Teacher Wraparound Edition.

R — **Reading Strategies** activities help you teach reading skills and vocabulary.

C — **Critical Thinking** strategies help students apply and extend what they have learned.

U — **Universal Access** activities provide differentiated instruction for students learning to speak English, along with suggestions for teaching various types of learners.

S — **Skill Practice** strategies help students practice historical analysis and geography skills.

W — **Writing Support** activities provide writing opportunities to help students comprehend the text.

Teaching strategies and activities have been coded for ability level appropriateness.

AL — Activities for students working above grade level
OL — Activities for students working on grade level
BL — Activities for students working below grade level
EL — Activities for English learners

FOCUS

History–Social Science Standards

This chapter addresses the following main standards:

11.1 Students analyze the significant events in the founding of the nation and its attempts to realize the philosophy of government described in the Declaration of Independence.

11.3 Students analyze the role religion played in the founding of America, its lasting moral, social, and political impacts, and issues regarding religious liberty.

BELLRINGER
SKILLBUILDER ACTIVITY

This chapter introduces the foundation of many rights of American citizens.
Ask: What are some of the important rights and freedoms that you enjoy as citizens of the United States? Have students write their responses to this question. Then have students share what they have written with the class.

TEACH

Thinking About the Big Ideas

As you begin teaching each section, use these questions and activities to focus on the Big Idea.

Section 1
Converging Cultures
Essential Question: What impact have the cultures in North America had on each other over time? Divide the class into two groups: one representing Native Americans and the other representing European settlers.

Ask each group to respond to this question. Remind students to think about positive as well as negative impacts when constructing their answers. Using these responses, ask students to write a short paragraph reflecting on how North American culture changed over time. **OL**

CHAPTER
1

Beginnings to 1789
Creating a Nation

~≈ *The Big Ideas* ≈~

SECTION 1: Converging Cultures
Societies change over time. *European settlers established colonies in lands inhabited by Native Americans and developed new forms of government.*

SECTION 2: Dissent and Independence
The quest for equality is eternal. *American colonists developed an independent spirit, began to resent Britain's mercantilist policies and tightening control, and fought a war for independence.*

SECTION 3: The Constitution
A written contract between the people and their government can preserve natural rights and allow for change over time. *When the Articles of Confederation proved to be too weak, Americans crafted a new constitution based on compromise and flexibility.*

The *American Vision: Modern Times* Video *The Chapter 1 video, "The Power of the Constitution," discusses one of the nation's most important documents.*

c. 28,000–13,000 B.C.
• First humans migrate to North America from Asia

1492
• Christopher Columbus lands in America

1607
• Jamestown Colony is founded

1619
• Virginia House of Burgesses meets for first time

1630
• Massachusetts Bay Colony is established

1639
• Fundamental Orders of Connecticut adopted

United States
PRESIDENTS

28,000 BC   *1500*   *1600*

World

1517
• Protestant Reformation begins

1600
• Tokugawa period of feudal rule begins in Japan

1642
• English Civil War begins

1660
• Charles II becomes king of England

1689
• English Bill of Rights issued

94

Section 2
Dissent and Independence
Essential Question: Have you ever had to follow a rule or law that you felt was unfair? What was it? Did you follow the rule, or did you rebel against it? After students have discussed these questions, tell them that just as they resent unfair rules, the colonists considered the laws and policies of the British to be unfair and as a result, went to war. **BL**

This painting by Dutch artist Adam Willaerts is believed to depict the Plymouth Colony.

Section 3
The Constitution
Essential Question: Who should hold the most power in a nation, the government or the people? What rights or freedoms should be guaranteed to citizens? Organize students into groups of four. Tell the groups that they are responsible for writing a new constitution governing a fictional nation and they must decide whether to govern as a democracy, a monarchy, or another form of government. After the groups have taken turns describing their new governments to the class, tell them that the original founders of the United States faced similar questions when writing the U.S. Constitution. OL

Cultural Perspectives

The Framers of the Constitution extended citizenship rights only to white male landowners. Discuss with students the reasons why the Framers did not grant citizenship rights to groups such as women, Native Americans, and African Americans. **Ask: What might members of these groups have felt or said about the new Constitution?** Have students work in small groups to list ways some of the specific rights of citizens outlined in the Bill of Rights were not extended to these groups of people. What problems could this denial of rights create for a new nation? OL

Timeline

1775
• The first shots of the Revolutionary War fired at Lexington and Concord in Massachusetts

1776
• Declaration of Independence signed

1765
• Parliament passes the Stamp Act, triggering protests throughout the colonies

1781
• Cornwallis surrenders at Yorktown
• Articles of Confederation ratified

1787
• Constitutional Convention begins in Philadelphia

Washington 1789–1797

1700   *1800*

1748
• Montesquieu's *Spirit of the Laws* published

1751
• Chinese invade Tibet and control succession to the throne

1776
• Adam Smith's treatise *The Wealth of Nations* published

1787
• Freed Africans found colony in Sierra Leone

1789
• French Revolution begins

HISTORY
Online
Chapter Overview
Visit the *American Vision: Modern Times* Web site at tav.mt.glencoe.com and click on *Chapter Overviews— Chapter 1* to preview chapter information.

95

FOLDABLES™
Study Organizer

Dinah Zike's Foldables are three-dimensional, interactive graphic organizers that help students practice basic writing skills, review key vocabulary terms, and identify main ideas. Have students complete the foldable activity in the *Dinah Zike's Reading and Study Skills Foldables* booklet.

HISTORY
Online

Go to tav.mt.glencoe.com for student activities, lesson plans, and links to additional Web resources to help students learn about the the creation of the United States.

Reading Skill

Why It's Important

Predictions help people identify the logical consequences of decisions or actions. Explain to students that predictions are not based on random guesses but are based on extending knowledge of facts, events, patterns, and trends.

1. Introducing the Skill

Have students brainstorm how they use prediction every day. Then ask students to offer examples of how this skill is used in business and government as well as personal situations. Record their answers in a two-column, three-row chart like the one below. *(Students' answers will vary. For example, a business has to predict consumer behavior before a product is launched.)* **OL**

Personal situations	
Business	
Government	

2. Extending the Skill

Have students read several newspaper articles about a current event. Ask students to write a one-page paper where they predict what will happen and explain their reasoning. **OL**

Answers and Additional Support

Preparing to Read Chapter 1

Reading Skill — Predicting

Good readers make predictions before they read and while they read. Predictions are educated guesses, based on what you already know or what the author has already told you. Even though your prediction may not always be correct, predicting is a valuable tool because it gives you a chance to think about what you already know about the topic. In addition, reviewing your predictions will help you remember the information and improve your ability to predict.

One way to make predictions is to read the headings and subheadings in a section or chapter before reading the entire selection. As you read each heading, think about the story you believe the chapter will tell you about this time in history. What do you already know about this time? What do you expect to find out?

Read these headings from Section 1 and the predictions about them.

The Earliest Americans (*I think this heading will tell me about the first inhabitants of the Americas. They came here thousands of years ago.*)

European Explorations (*I expect that I will learn about the first Spanish explorers in the Americas.*)

Early French and English Settlement (*I wonder if I will learn about Jamestown and the Plymouth Colony?*)

The Thirteen Colonies (*What do I know about the original colonies? I know that they later formed the United States of America.*)

A Diverse Society (*Will I learn about enslaved Africans? What else is unique to colonial society?*)

PREDICTING
Use headings and subheadings like signposts to guide your reading. They let you know where you're going!

Apply the Skill

Before you read each section in this chapter, look at the headings and subheadings. Write down your predictions for each. You can think about information you already have on the topic from previous classes or from other sources. Based on the heading or subheading, you can also make a connection to a current event. After you have finished reading, review your predictions and note any differences between your predictions and the text.

96

UNIVERSAL ACCESS

Below Grade Level If students have trouble understanding how to assess information to make accurate predictions, provide them with these five steps: (1) Review what they already know about a situation by listing facts, events, and people's responses; (2) Analyze patterns and try to determine what the patterns show; (3) Ask themselves if similar decisions or actions have occurred in the past, and what their consequences were; (4) Analyze each of the potential consequences by asking, "How likely is it that this will occur?"; and (5) Make a prediction. **BL**

Historical Analysis Skill ▸ Understanding Change

Chronological and Spatial Thinking As you study the history of the United States in the twentieth century, you will analyze how change happens at different rates at different times; understand that some aspects can change while others remain the same; and understand that change is complicated and affects not only technology and politics, but also values and beliefs.

Do you recall a time when a major event changed your community forever? It may have been a national tragedy, like the terrorist attacks of September 11, 2001. It might have been a positive event, like the opening of a major business in your town that provided new employment opportunities for the many people. In either case, some changes seemed to occur overnight, while other changes evolved more slowly. Historians understand that change is complex and that change occurs at different rates.

When historians study events, they consider the time frame in which these events occur. Sometimes events occur quickly, in a matter of hours, days or weeks. Other times, events can occur over much longer periods, such as years or even decades. Historians also analyze how the events lead to changes, and what changes occur as a result of events. These changes can happen in the environment or in the societies in which the events take place. Some changes are barely noticeable, while others can have a profound effect.

A major event occurred centuries ago when European explorers first landed on the American continent. The impact on Native Americans was immediate, especially the effects of war and disease on their populations. Other changes occurred more slowly as European settlers arrived to colonize the land. In some cases, Native Americans and Europeans engaged in violent conflict.

Apply the Skill

As you read this chapter, consider how change occurred in the societies that developed in America. What changes happened to Native American societies? What new societies grew out of the arrival of European settlers, and how did their lives differ from or remain the same as that in Europe? How did life change for Africans who were enslaved and forcibly brought to the American colonies?

97

FOCUS

SKILLBUILDER ACTIVITY

🖥 Project **Daily Focus Skills Transparency 1-1** and have students answer the question.

Guide to Reading

Understanding Vocabulary: Ask students to write each vocabulary word in a blank grid. Read off the definitions and have students mark off the corresponding vocabulary words on their grids.

Answers to Graphic: Students should complete the outline by including all heads in the section.

⬥ Unpacking the Standards

Students will be able to:
- Explain how the Americas became home to diverse cultures.
- Identify the main areas of Spanish, French, and English settlement.
- Describe the reasons for English colonization.

Answers and Additional Support

SECTION 1 Converging Cultures

Guide to Reading

Connection
In this section, you will discover how societies in North and Middle America changed over time and how European colonies developed.

Main Idea
- Native Americans adapted to their environments and developed diverse cultures. (p. 99)
- European countries began to explore the world and established colonies in the Americas. (p. 101)
- The French and English settled in North America, and English colonists began their own local governments. (p. 102)
- As English settlements grew, colonists developed different forms of government to regulate life in their communities. (p. 103)

- The different colonies created new social structures that were more open than those of aristocratic Europe. (p. 107)

Content Vocabulary
civilization, joint-stock company, Pilgrim, subsistence farming, proprietary colony, indentured servant, triangular trade, slave code

Academic Vocabulary
culture, immigrate, hierarchy

People and Terms to Identify
Christopher Columbus, William Penn

Places to Locate
Jamestown

Reading Objectives
- **Explain** how the Americas were populated and became home to diverse cultures.

- **Identify** the main areas of Spanish, French, and English settlement and the reasons for English colonization.

Reading Strategy
Taking Notes As you read about the early settlements of America, use the section headings to create an outline similar to the one below.

Discovery and Settlement
I. The Earliest Americans
 A. Early Civilizations in America
 B.
 C.
II. European Exploration
 A.
 B.
 C.
III.
IV.
V.

Preview of Events

⬥30,000 — ⬥1500 — ⬥1675 — ⬥1750

c. 28000 B.C.–13000 B.C.
First humans migrate to North America

1492
Columbus claims American lands for Spain

1607
English found Jamestown

1639
Fundamental Orders of Connecticut adopted

The following are the main History–Social Science Standards covered in this section.

11.1 Students analyze the significant events surrounding the founding of the nation and its attempts to realize the philosophy of government described in the Declaration of Independence.

11.3 Students analyze the role religion played in the founding of America, its lasting moral, social and political impacts, and issues regarding religious liberty.

11.3.1 Describe the contributions of various religious groups to American civic principles and social reform movements (e.g., civil and human rights, individual responsibility and the work ethic, antimonarchy and self-rule, worker protection, family-centered communities).

⚜ The Big Idea ⚜

Societies change over time. A shift to agriculture in Middle and North America led to the development of civilizations and Native American cultures. At the same time these cultures were flourishing in the Americas, Europeans began looking for trade routes to Asia to obtain desired goods. Their search brought Europeans into contact with the Americas. Contact between Native Americans and Europeans brought the exchange of foods and ideas but also introduced new diseases. Many Native Americans died, and cultures were destroyed from disease and war between the groups. France and England focused on settling eastern North America, straining relationships with Native Americans. As the colonies continued to develop and expand, so did different forms of government and the dependency on slave labor. Trade, the growth of cities, and the increase in African Americans and immigrants led to additional changes in colonial society.

98 CHAPTER 1 Creating a Nation

SECTION RESOURCES

📁 **Print Material**
- Reproducible Lesson Plan 1-1
- Guided Reading Activity 1-1
- Reading Essentials and Study Guide 1-1
- Active Reading Note-Taking Guide 1-1

🖥 **Transparencies**
- Daily Focus Skills Transparency 1-1
- Section Graphic Organizer Transparency 1-1

Technology
- Interactive Tutor Self-Assessment CD-ROM
- ExamView® Pro Testmaker CD-ROM
- Presentation Plus! CD-ROM

The Earliest Americans

Main Idea Native Americans adapted to their environments and developed diverse cultures.

Reading Connection Do you remember when you started at a new school and had to get used to new ways of doing things? Read on to learn how the first American settlers adapted to their new environments.

No one knows exactly when the first people arrived in America. Scientists have pieced together many clues by studying the earth's geology and the items left by early humans.

★ An American Story ★

In 1925 an African American cowboy named George McJunkin was riding along a gully near the town of Folsom, New Mexico, when he noticed something gleaming in the dirt. He began digging and found a bone and a flint arrowhead. J.D. Figgins of the Colorado Museum of Natural History knew the bone belonged to a type of bison that had been extinct for 10,000 years. The arrowhead's proximity to the bones implied that human beings had been in America at least 10,000 years, which no one had believed at that time.

The following year, Figgins found another arrowhead embedded in similar bones. In 1927 he led a group of scientists to the find. Anthropologist Frank H.H. Roberts, Jr., wrote, "There was no question but that here was the evidence. . . . The point was still embedded . . . between two of the ribs of the animal skeleton." Further digs turned up more arrowheads, now called Folsom points. Roberts later noted: "The Folsom find was accepted as a reliable indication that man was present in the Southwest at an earlier period than was previously supposed."

—adapted from *The First American: A Story of North American Archaeology*

The Folsom discoveries proved that people were here at least 10,000 years ago. More recent research, however, suggests that our ancestors may have arrived much earlier—between 15,000 and 30,000 years ago.

These newcomers to America were probably nomads, people who continually move from place to place. As time passed, Native Americans learned how to plant and raise crops. The shift to agriculture led to the first permanent villages and to new building methods. As early village societies became more complex, civilizations emerged. A **civilization** is a highly organized society marked by advanced knowledge of trade, government, the arts, science, and, often, written language.

Early Civilizations in America Anthropologists think the earliest civilization in the Americas arose between 1500 B.C. and 1200 B.C. among the Olmec people in southern Mexico. The Maya and the Aztec later developed their own civilizations in Central America, building impressive temples and pyramids and establishing trade networks. Many anthropologists believe that the agricultural technology of Mesoamerica eventually spread north into the American Southwest and beyond. Around A.D. 300, the Hohokam began farming in what is today Arizona. They and another nearby people, the Anasazi, were able to grow crops in the dry Southwest by building elaborate irrigation systems.

About the time that the Olmec civilization began in Mesoamerica, the people in North America's eastern woodlands were developing their own **cultures.** The Hopewell built huge geometric earthworks that served as ceremonial centers, observatories, and burial places. Between A.D. 700 and 900, the Mississippian people in the Mississippi River valley created Cahokia, one of the largest cities early Americans ever built.

Native American Cultural Diversity In the Eastern Woodlands, most Native Americans combined hunting and fishing with farming. Many different groups lived in the Eastern Woodlands, but most spoke either Algonquian or Iroquoian languages.

In the Southeast, the Cherokee were the largest group. They, along with the Creek, Choctaw, Natchez, and others, generally built wooden stockades around their villages for protection. Women did most of the farming, while men hunted deer, bear, and alligator.

This Folsom point, lying between animal bones, was one of a number of arrowheads found near the town of Folsom, New Mexico.

TEACH

S Skill Practice

Historical Interpretation Have students write a short newspaper article describing the finding of the first Folsom points in 1925. Tell them to include details of the find, the significance of the points, and eyewitness accounts from George McJunkin and J.D. Figgins. Invite students to illustrate their articles with a drawing or photograph. **OL** **CA HI1**

R Reading Strategy

Evaluating Tell students that early explorers and settlers did not view the Native Americans as being a "civilized" people. **Ask:** How many words can you think of that can be associated with the word "civilized?" Keep track of the list on the board and use it to write a definition. Have students use the information from the textbook and the definition on the board to write a paragraph explaining why the Europeans were wrong in their assessment of the Native American lifestyle. **OL**

U Universal Access

Below Grade Level Understanding the culture of Native Americans might be difficult for some students. Invite the class to use library and Internet resources to locate photographs or drawings of the earthworks built by the Hopewell. Ask students to lay out their collection of images on a large piece of poster board and provide an informative caption for each picture. Display the posters in your classroom. **BL**

More Skill Practice

Conducting Research Divide the class into groups of five. Have the groups use library or Internet resources to research specific topics of Cherokee culture, such as farming or hunting methods, art, or village life. Each group should prepare a short oral report, possibly with illustrations. **OL** **CA HR4**

Did You Know?

Beginning around 1130, Chaco Canyon suffered at least 50 years of drought, probably driving out the Anasazi. Attacks by hunter-gatherers or epidemics may also have contributed to the collapse of Anasazi civilization.

Geography Skills

In the Southwest, the Hohokam and the Anasazi eventually disappeared, but their descendants, including the Zuni and the Hopi, continued to farm corn, beans, and cotton. Around the 1500s, two other groups—the Apache and the Navajo—came to the Southwest. The Navajo settled in farming villages, but many of the Apache remained nomadic hunters.

Hunting also sustained the Sioux and other peoples who lived on the western Great Plains. They followed buffalo herds and camped in tepees that they could easily set up, dismantle, and carry.

Along the Pacific Coast, the Northwest was home to fishing peoples like the Kwakiutls and the Chinook. They caught the plentiful salmon, built

R Reading Strategy

Reading Maps, Graphs, and Charts Have students use the information from the map on page 100 to create a three-column chart. The chart should list the name of each group, the region in which the group lived, and the type of culture the group had. Using the photographs inside the map as an example, invite students to select one of the groups listed on their chart and draw a picture of one aspect of life in that group. **BL** **CA CS3**

S Skill Practice

Scaffolding—Predicting
Students might have difficulty understanding the very different lifestyle of historical Native Americans. Beginning a discussion on the topic might help them understand. **Ask: How do you think the fishing peoples of the Pacific Coast might have spent their time during a typical day?** *(Possible answers might include: hunted, fished, repaired nets, made boats, made clothes, talked)* Discuss what people might have eaten, how families might have interacted with one another, and the various roles people might have had in this early society. **OL** **CA HI3; HI5**

This **Reading Skill** is introduced in this chapter.

Answers and Additional Support

NATIONAL GEOGRAPHIC
Native American Cultures, Including Mesoamerica,
500 B.C.–A.D. 1500

Map legend:
- Agriculture
- Fishing
- Hunting
- Hunting-Gathering
- Uninhabited

Northeastern longhouse

Southwest pueblo

Geography *Skills*

1. **Interpreting Maps** What was the main food source for the Northwest?
2. **Applying Geography Skills** Why were Great Plains peoples nomadic?

Did You Know?

The Iroquois were a mighty and warlike people given to fighting among themselves. During the 1500s, a tribal elder named Dekanawidah urged the Iroquois to unite against common enemies. Dekanawidah's ideas led to the formation of the Iroquois Confederation of the Five Nations, commonly known as the Iroquois League.

Geography *Skills*

Answers:
1. fish
2. They hunted migrating buffalo herds.

Geography Skills Practice
Ask: What type of culture do you think each picture represents? *(Southwest pueblo: agricultural; Northeastern longhouse: agricultural)*

wooden houses and canoes, and crafted ceremonial totem poles from the trunks of redwood and cedar trees. To the south, in what is today central California, groups such as the Pomo trapped small game and gathered acorns. Farther inland lived other hunter-gatherer groups like the Nez Perce, the Yakima, the Ute, and the Shoshone.

Meanwhile, in the Far North region from Alaska to Greenland, the Inuit and the Aleut hunted seals, walruses, whales, polar bears, and caribou. They adapted to their harsh environment by inventing tools such as the harpoon, kayak, dogsled, and oil lamp.

By the 1500s, Native Americans had established a wide array of cultures and languages. They had also developed economies and lifestyles suited to their particular environments.

Reading Check **Explaining** How did climate and food sources help shape Native American lifestyles?

European Explorations

Main Idea **European countries began to explore the world and established colonies in the Americas.**

Reading Connection Have you tried new foods from other parts of the country or the world? Read on to learn about the exchange of foods after European explorers came to America.

As the people of Europe emerged from the Middle Ages, they became interested in Asia, the source of spices, perfumes, fine silks, and jewels. The hope to find a sailing route to Asia that would bypass merchants and traders from Italy and the Middle East motivated the rulers of Portugal, Spain, France, and England. Equipped with new navigational tools and newly designed ships, the Portuguese took the lead in exploration in the late 1400s.

Columbus's Voyages The Spanish monarchs, meanwhile, had agreed to fund an expedition by **Christopher Columbus,** an Italian sea captain. Columbus was convinced that he could reach Asia by sailing west across the Atlantic Ocean. In August 1492, Columbus and his crew set off in three ships—the *Niña,* the *Pinta,* and the *Santa Maria.* After a harrowing voyage, they probably landed on present-day San Salvador Island.

Christopher Columbus was not the first European to set foot in the Americas. A group of Vikings from Scandinavia, led by Leif Ericsson, had visited northeastern Canada around A.D. 1000. It was Columbus, however, who launched a wave of European exploration and settlement. Columbus made three more voyages, sailing to the Caribbean and along the Central and South American coasts. He claimed the new lands for Spain, believing all the time that he was in Asia.

Continuing Expeditions Europeans soon realized that Columbus had not reached Asia but a part of the globe unknown to Europeans. They named the new continent America in honor of Amerigo Vespucci, who explored the South American coastline for Portugal.

The 1494 Treaty of Tordesillas had confirmed Spain's right to most of the newly discovered lands of America, and now explorers paved the way for the Spanish Empire in the Americas. With their superior weapons, the Spanish began to conquer the local peoples and build settlements. Hernán Cortés defeated the Aztec in Mexico in 1521. Francisco Pizarro conquered the Inca in Peru eleven years later. Other Spaniards led forces into what is now the United States. Juan Ponce de Leon, for example, claimed Florida, and Francisco Vásquez de Coronado explored the Southwest, while Hernando de Soto traveled through the Southeast and became the first European to see the Mississippi River.

The Spanish soon controlled an immense territory that stretched from the Florida peninsula to California and down into South America. Settlers farmed the land, established mines and cattle ranches, and tried to spread the Catholic faith. Adobe missions, where priests lived alongside Native American converts in the 1600s and 1700s, still stand in the American Southwest today.

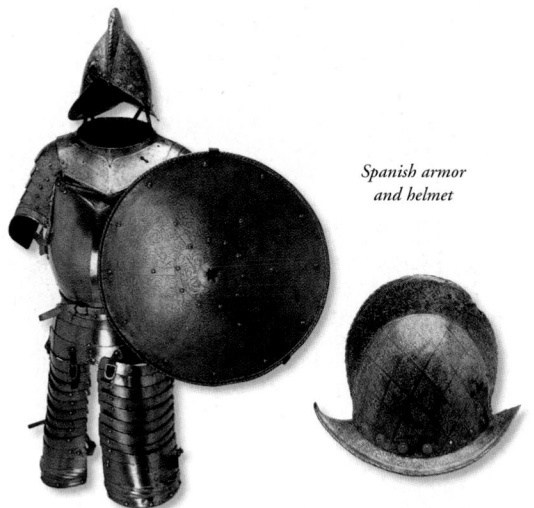

Spanish armor and helmet

CHAPTER 1   Creating a Nation   **101**

W **Writing Support**

Narrative Writing Tell students to pretend that they are Christopher Columbus and have just landed in what they think is Asia. Ask students to write a diary entry describing what their journey was like and what their feelings were as they set foot in this new place. Invite volunteers to share what they have written with the class.
BL **CA** 11WA2.1c

U₁ **Universal Access**

Interpersonal Organize the class into groups of four to research the battle between the Aztec and Hernán Cortés's Spanish troops, making sure that Aztec and Spanish points of view are equally represented in the research. **Ask each group: What are the motivations and goals of the Spanish? The Aztec?** Tell students to use their findings to write and perform a short skit depicting the battle. Students may use photographs to help them create authentic costumes for their performance. **AL**
CA 11WS1.2

U₂ **Universal Access**

Visual/Spatial To help visual learners remember Spain's various navigators and expeditions to the Americas, have them research, trace and label the voyages of Cortés, Pizarro, Ponce de Leon, Vásquez de Coronado, and de Soto on a map. **OL**

Reading Check

Answer: determined hunting, fishing, and agricultural practices; influenced tool invention and animal domestication

Did You Know?

For six years Columbus tried to persuade the rulers of Portugal, England, France, and Spain to fund his voyage across the Atlantic to Asia. He promised Spain's King Ferdinand and Queen Isabella that his scheme would bring them wealth, empire, and converts to Catholicism. Finally, in 1492, after it became clear that Portugal was about to reach Asia by going east around Africa, the Spanish rulers agreed to finance his expedition.

R **Reading Strategy**

Organizing Information Tell students that the cultural interactions between European colonists and Native Americans was called the Columbian Exchange. Have students make a chart showing the advantages and disadvantages of the Columbian Exchange for the Native Americans and the Europeans. **Ask: Did humanity, as a whole, benefit or suffer from the Columbian Exchange?** Have students write a paragraph explaining their answer. **OL**

C **Critical Thinking**

Determining Cause and Effect Have students make a time line of French and English exploration and colonization of North America. Students should note that France and England did not succeed in establishing colonies until a century after they began to explore North America. Have students brainstorm answers to the following question: **What do you think finally caused France and England to establish colonies in the Americas?** *(Answers may vary, but students should mention competition with Spain for wealth and resources.)* **OL**

✓ Reading Check

Answer: They contracted diseases and were killed by European troops.

Answers and Additional Support

Cultural Changes The arrival of Europeans in the Americas altered life for everyone. Native Americans introduced the Europeans to new farming methods and foods like corn, potatoes, squash, pumpkins, beans, and chocolate, as well as tobacco and chewing gum. Europeans also adopted many Native American inventions, including canoes, snowshoes, and ponchos.

Meanwhile, the Europeans introduced Native Americans to wheat, rice, coffee, bananas, citrus fruits, and domestic livestock such as chickens, cattle, pigs, sheep, and horses. In addition, Native Americans acquired new technologies, including firearms and better metalworking and shipbuilding methods. Along with these beneficial imports, however, came invisible and deadly ones—germs that cause diseases. Native Americans had never before been exposed to influenza, measles, chicken pox, mumps, typhus, or smallpox. With no immunity, millions of Native Americans died in widespread epidemics. Military conquests also devastated Native Americans, costing them their lands and their traditional ways of life.

✓ Reading Check **Identifying** Why did millions of Native Americans die as a result of contact with Europeans?

Picturing **History**

Critical Leadership Captain John Smith helped save early Jamestown by trading with local Native Americans. Sidney King painted its fort as it might have appeared around 1607. Why do you think the fort was set up with only three sides?

Early French and English Settlement

Main Idea The French and English settled in North America, and English colonists began their own local governments.

Reading Connection Some people today dream about settling new frontiers such as oceans or other planets. Read on to learn what brought the first French and English settlers to North America.

Soon after Columbus made his historic voyage, France and England began exploring the new lands. These countries directed their efforts to the eastern part of North America. England sent John Cabot on expeditions in 1497 and 1498. France funded trips by Giovanni da Verrazano and Jacques Cartier in the early 1500s. Yet it was not until the 1600s that the French and the English succeeded in establishing colonies.

New France In 1608 French geographer Samuel de Champlain founded the outpost of Quebec. Instead of having settlers clear land and build farms, the backers of New France sought profits from fur. Frenchmen began a brisk trade with Native Americans. Quebec eventually became the capital of New France, a sparsely settled colony of fur traders and Jesuit missionaries.

In the late 1600s, France focused on increasing the population and size of the colony. Explorers Louis Joliet and Jacques Marquette found the Mississippi River, and René-Robert Cavalier de La Salle followed the Mississippi to the Gulf of Mexico. The French claimed the region and named it Louisiana. Settlers founded the towns of New Orleans, Biloxi, and Mobile, and they began growing sugar, rice, and tobacco. The French also began importing enslaved Africans to do the hard field work that these labor-intensive crops required.

Jamestown A year before the French founded Quebec, the English established their first lasting settlement in Virginia. The colony, **Jamestown**, was funded by a **joint-stock company,** a group of private investors who pooled their money to support big projects. These investors, along with many others in business and government, saw colonies as vital sources of raw materials and as markets for English goods.

Despite early troubles, the settlers persevered with the help of the Powhatan Confederacy, a group of local Native Americans. Within a few years, they began to prosper by growing tobacco. Newcomers

Did You Know?

Most of Jamestown's colonists were townspeople who did not know how to raise livestock, cultivate crops, or make use of the area's abundant fish and game. The upper-class "gentlemen" among them refused to do manual labor. Sickness and food shortages resulted, and only 53 of the original 190 settlers lived to the end of 1608.

Picturing **History**

Answer: Possible answer: It was easier to build and defend three sides than four.
Ask: The fort is constructed of what material? *(wood)*

History *Through Art*

Solemn Signing Tompkins Matteson painted his vision of the Mayflower Compact signing. By signing this document, the Pilgrims wanted to set up a legal basis for their colony. How did the artist try to suggest the seriousness of the occasion? 📖 *(See page 985 for an excerpt from the Mayflower Compact.)*

arrived, attracted by the promise of land ownership. In 1619 colonists formed an assembly, the House or Burgesses, to make their own laws.

With encouragement of the Virginia Company, by 1622 more than 4,500 settlers **immigrated** to Virginia. This expansion alarmed Native Americans, who attacked Jamestown in 1622. An English court blamed the Company's policies for the high death rate and revoked its charter. Virginia became a royal colony run by a governor appointed by the king.

The Pilgrims in Plymouth Colony Not all settlers came for economic gain. King James was persecuting a group of Puritans who were called Separatists because they wanted to form their own congregations separate from the Anglican Church, the official church of England. These Separatists hoped to be able to worship freely in America.

In 1620 a small band of Separatists, who came to be known as **Pilgrims,** headed for Virginia on the *Mayflower.* During the voyage, a storm blew the ship off its course. The Pilgrims finally dropped anchor off the coast of Cape Cod. Since they would be landing in territory without an English government, they drew up a plan for self-government called the Mayflower Compact. 📖 *(See page 985 for an excerpt from the Mayflower Compact.)*

The settlers quickly built homes and befriended the local Wampanoag people. The following autumn, the Pilgrims joined with the Wampanoag in a harvest celebration—the first Thanksgiving.

Ten years later, as the persecution of Puritans increased, another group of Puritans arrived in Massachusetts Bay with a charter for a new colony. They founded several towns, including Boston. A depression of England's wool industry encouraged more people to leave, and Massachusetts expanded rapidly.

The people of Massachusetts set up a representative government, with an elected assembly to make laws. Government and religion were closely intertwined. The government collected taxes to support the church, and the Puritan leaders of the colony set strict rules for behavior.

✓ Reading Check **Explaining** Why did English colonists come to America?

The Thirteen Colonies

Main Idea As English settlements grew, colonists developed different forms of government to regulate life in their communities.

Reading Connection Have you ever been a part of a new group or organization? What rules did you draw up? Read on to learn about new colonies and their new kinds of government.

The Jamestown, Plymouth, and Massachusetts Bay colonies were only the beginning of English settlements in the Americas. Although slow at first, over the next century the English began establishing colonies all along the eastern shore of the Atlantic Ocean.

New England Puritan efforts in the Massachusetts Bay Colony to suppress other religious beliefs led to the growth of other New England colonies. One early dissenter was a young minister named Roger Williams. He challenged many Puritan beliefs as well as the authority of the king to claim Native American lands. In 1636, after being banned from Massachusetts, Williams headed south, purchased land from the Narragansett people, and founded the town of Providence. There the government had no authority in religious matters, and different beliefs were tolerated rather than suppressed.

Like Roger Williams, Anne Hutchinson was also exiled from Massachusetts because of her religious views. Hutchinson and a few followers ended up settling near Providence, as did other free-thinking Puritans over the following years. In 1644 Providence joined with neighboring towns to become the colony of Rhode Island and Providence Plantation. Religious freedom, with a total separation of church and state, was a key feature of the new colony.

Identifying Central Issues Have students assume the role of a Puritan and write a letter to a friend or relative explaining their decision to move to America. **OL** **CA** 11WA2.1a

U **Universal Access**

Logical/Mathematical Have students use a map to locate two points: the original destination of the *Mayflower* and the area where the *Mayflower* actually landed. Students should identify the latitude and longitude of these two locations and calculate the approximate distance between the two. **EL**

R **Reading Strategy**

Visualizing Have students create a set of fashion sketches for the typical wardrobe of the Puritans. The sketches should include an ensemble for a woman and one for a man. Encourage students to use library and Internet resources to learn more about clothing and fashion in colonial times. Then ask students to use their sketches to write a short paragraph answering the following question: How were Puritan values exhibited in the clothing of the time? *(Answers will vary. Possible answers: clothing was simple because Puritans did not believe in being frivolous; clothing was not revealing because Puritans had strict rules governing their behavior.)* **AL**

✓ Reading Check

Answer: economic gain and religious freedom

 History *Through Art*

Answer: dark clothing and surroundings except for the Compact; faces are serious and intent on the speaker
Ask: How does the portrait of John Winthrop indicate his status in the community? *(possible answer: His more formal dress and well-groomed hair and beard show that he is wealthy.)*

Chapter 1 • Section 1

Answers and Additional Support

W Writing Support

Persuasive Writing Ask students to brainstorm a list of groups whose rights were not included in the Fundamental Orders of Connecticut. Have students choose one of the groups and write a newspaper editorial explaining why this group should also be guaranteed the right to vote and hold office. **OL**
CA 11WA2.3a

Review the Big Idea

Review the Big Idea for this section, "Societies change over time." **Ask: How did the Puritan town meetings evolve into a form of local governance?** *(They changed from meetings to discuss problems into people voting to create laws.)* **How would this change affect the colonial attitude?** *(It established a tradition of self-government.)* **OL**

U Universal Access

Advanced Learners Have students examine the photograph of the manuscript for Anne Bradstreet's "The Tenth Muse" on page 104. Ask them to write a three-page paper on how documents have been preserved in the past and to explain the scientific innovations that are currently used in preservation. **AL**
CA 11WS1.6

Answers and Additional Support

Religion also played a part in the founding of Connecticut. In 1636 the Reverend Thomas Hooker moved his entire congregation from Massachusetts to the Connecticut River valley. The group needed more land to raise cattle, and Hooker disagreed with the political system that allowed only church members to vote. The new colony came to be called Connecticut. Three years later, the people adopted America's first written constitution, the Fundamental Orders of Connecticut. It allowed all adult men to vote and hold office. 📖 *(See page 986 for more on the Fundamental Orders of Connecticut.)*

Not everyone who left Massachusetts headed for Rhode Island or Connecticut. Some religious dissenters, along with fishers and fur traders, went north instead. In 1679 a large area north of Massachusetts became the royal colony of New Hampshire.

New England Puritans valued religious devotion, hard work, and obedience to strict rules regulating daily life. Puritan society revolved around town life. Towns included a meetinghouse (church), a school, and a marketplace around an open public area called the town common. At town meetings, New Englanders would gather to discuss local problems and issues. These meetings evolved into the local government, with landowners voting on laws and electing officials to oversee town matters. Yet even residents without property could attend a town meeting and express an opinion. For a peasant back in England, this would have been unthinkable. The colonists in New England—and indeed throughout America—grew used to managing their own affairs, and they came to believe strongly in their right to self-government.

New England's thin and rocky soil was ill suited for cash crops. Instead, on small farms from Connecticut to Maine, colonists practiced **subsistence farming,** raising only enough food to feed their families. The main crop was corn, but farmers also grew other grains, vegetables, apples, and berries, and they raised dairy cattle, sheep, and pigs.

It was maritime activity, however, that brought prosperity to New England. Fishers sold their catch of cod, mackerel, halibut, and herring to other colonists, Southern Europeans, and people in the Caribbean. Whaling also played a major role in New England's economy, providing blubber for making candles and lamp oil.

A thriving lumber industry developed too. Timber was plentiful, and lumber was in high demand for furniture, building materials, and the barrels that were used to store and ship almost everything in the colonial era. Lumbering led to another successful industry: shipbuilding. With forests and sawmills close to the coast, ships could be built quickly and cheaply. By the 1770s, one out of every three British ships had been built in America.

Profiles IN HISTORY

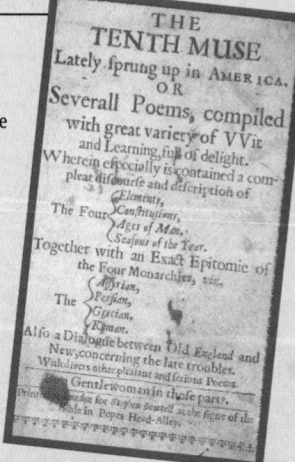

Anne Bradstreet
c. 1612–1672

Anne Dudley was born about 1612 in Northampton, England. At the age of 16 she married Simon Bradstreet, and two years later she accompanied her husband to America. The Bradstreets, traveling with John Winthrop's party, were among the first settlers of the Massachusetts Bay Colony.

In America Anne Bradstreet faced the difficult task of building a home in the wilderness. Despite the hard work of raising eight children, she found time to write poetry. In 1650 the first edition of her poetry was published in England as *The Tenth Muse Lately Sprung Up in America.* Bradstreet had not anticipated this recognition. Her brother-in-law had secretly taken a copy of her manuscript to a London publisher.

Anne Bradstreet was a devoted supporter of her husband, who became a leading political figure in Massachusetts, serving two terms as governor. During the period of the Dominion of New England, he spoke out against the harsh rule of Edmund Andros. In a poem, *To My Dear Loving Husband,* published after her death, Anne described their relationship:

If ever two were one, then
* surely we.*
If ever man were loved by
* wife, then thee;*
If ever wife was happy in
* a man,*
Compare with me ye
* women if you can.*

Profiles IN HISTORY

Have students use library and Internet resources to learn more about Anne Bradstreet and her poetry. Then have them compose a short poem describing some aspect of their own lives. **CA** 11RL3.4; 11WA2.2

Relations of the English settlers with their Native American neighbors were peaceful most of the time. In 1636 war broke out with the Pequot over the killing of two Massachusetts traders. For almost the next 40 years, good relations continued. By the 1670s, however, new conflict arose when colonial governments demanded that Native Americans follow English laws and customs. Tensions touched off what came to be called King Philip's War. After the colonists won the war in 1678, very few Native Americans were left in New England.

The Middle Colonies While the English focused their early settlements on Virginia and New England, the Dutch had claimed much of the land south of Connecticut. In 1609 Henry Hudson, a navigator hired by Dutch merchants, had discovered what is now the Hudson River valley in New York. The Dutch called the region New Netherland and established their main settlement of New Amsterdam on Manhattan Island. Dutch policies encouraged immigration, and by 1664 New Netherland had become England's main rival in North America.

Charles II, who had become king of England in 1660 after the English Civil War, decided to act. He seized New Netherland from the Dutch and granted the land to his brother, James, the Duke of York. James held onto the largest portion of the land, which he renamed New York. The rest of the land became New Jersey, a colony which offered generous land grants, religious freedom, and the right to have a legislative assembly.

In 1681 King Charles agreed to let **William Penn** create a new colony south of New York. Penn regarded Pennsylvania as a "holy experiment" where settlers would have religious freedom and a voice in government. He particularly wanted to help his fellow Quakers escape persecution in England. Quakers objected to all political and religious authority, including obligatory taxes and military service. They also opposed war or violence as a means to settle disputes. In Pennsylvania, people of all faiths found a safe haven. A treaty Penn signed in 1682 assured peace with a local group of Native Americans. To give his colony access to the Atlantic Ocean, Penn soon acquired a strip of coastal land to the southeast. This land later became a colony in its own right—Delaware.

The Middle Colonies were blessed with fertile land and a long growing season. Farmers produced bumper crops of rye, oats, barley, and potatoes. Most important, however, was wheat, which rapidly became the region's main cash crop.

Picturing **History**

Bethlehem, Pennsylvania Laid out along a river with farmsteads on the village outskirts, this town is typical of many in the Middle Colonies. What was the region's main cash crop?

In the early and mid-1700s, the demand for wheat soared, thanks to a population explosion in Europe. Between 1720 and 1770, wheat prices more than doubled in the Middle Colonies, bringing a surge of prosperity. Europe's population growth also brought a new wave of immigrants to America, particularly to the Middle Colonies where land was still available.

Some people who grew wealthy from the wheat boom invested in new businesses. They established glass and pottery works and built large gristmills that produced vast quantities of flour for export.

The Southern Colonies Farther south, tobacco helped Virginia to thrive. The colony had been joined by Maryland, a **proprietary colony** which began in the 1630s. A proprietary colony was one owned by an individual who could govern it any way he wanted, appointing government officials, coining money, imposing taxes, and even raising an army. The owner of the colony was George Calvert, also known as Lord Baltimore. He hoped to make the colony a refuge for Catholics, because they, like the Puritans, were persecuted in England. Most settlers, however, were Protestants. Maryland passed the Toleration Act in 1649, granting religious toleration to all Christians in the colony.

In the meantime, Virginia continued to thrive. After the end of the English Civil War, though, new colonies sprang up south of Virginia. In 1663 King Charles II gave eight friends and political allies a vast tract of land that had been named Carolina. From the start, Carolina developed as two separate regions. North Carolina was home to a small and scattered population of farmers who grew tobacco. Because North Carolina's coastline made the colony hard to reach, many more settlers came to South Carolina.

CHAPTER 1 Creating a Nation **105**

Picturing **History**

Answer: wheat
Ask: Why was growing wheat so prosperous in the early and mid-1700s? *(A population explosion in Europe caused the demand for wheat in the colonies to soar.)*

C Critical Thinking

Predicting Consequences
Have students write a one-page description of what they think life in the colonies would have been like if the settlers and Native Americans had collaborated more effectively. Encourage volunteers to share with the class what they have written. OL CA 11WA2.3b

U Universal Access

English Learners Have students create flyers advertising the benefits of immigrating to the Middle Colonies. Display the flyers around the classroom and have students discuss which ones are the most convincing, and why. EL

R Reading Strategy

Questioning One of the most important reading strategies students can learn is monitoring their reading comprehension. Tell students that they can do this by questioning themselves as they read. If they do not understand an important idea, they need to reread, review, or read on to clarify what is unclear. Have students practice this strategy by defining the term *proprietary colony* based on information in the text. Ask students to share their definitions with the class, and provide explanations for anything that seems unclear. EL

S Skill Practice

Conducting Research Have students prepare a two-minute oral presentation about George Calvert (also known as Lord Baltimore). Encourage students to use library and Internet resources to locate information about Calvert that is not found in the textbook. OL CA HR4

105

106

W Writing Support

Persuasive Writing Have students write an advertisement for recruiting indentured servants. The advertisement should include information about what the landowner is willing to provide, what the servant must agree to do, and the length of service required. **OL**

C₁ Critical Thinking

Comparing and Contrasting To help students understand the significance of geography, economics, and agriculture in the Southern Colonies, have students create a table to compare and contrast wealthy planters, backcountry farmers, and tenant farmers. The table should list types of crops grown by each and the geographic location of each. **OL**

C₂ Critical Thinking

Identifying Central Issues Have students imagine that they are reporters for a British newspaper. Ask them to write an informative article for the magazine explaining the causes and results of Bacon's Rebellion. Tell them to be sure to include enough information that readers in England will clearly understand the situation in Virginia. **OL** **CA 11WA2.1a**

Answers and Additional Support

History *Through Art*

The Ideal Plantation This painting depicts the well-structured plantation as a world unto itself. Centered around the family home, the plantation's fields, support houses, and merchant ships unite to serve the needs of the plantation. *What influence did large landholders have on life in the South?*

There they established the community of Charles Town (Charleston), exported deerskins, and grew rice in the tidal swamps.

The last Southern colony, Georgia, arose south of the Carolinas in 1733, based on an idea of James Oglethorpe, a wealthy member of Parliament. Oglethorpe had been horrified to learn that many people in English prisons were jailed simply because they could not pay their debts. Oglethorpe asked King George II for a colony where the poor could start over. The king agreed, realizing that in addition to helping those in need, a new Southern colony would keep Spain from expanding north of Florida. Georgia soon attracted settlers from all over Europe.

As in Jamestown, agriculture was the focus of the Southern economy. In early colonial days, there was plenty of land for farmers, but not enough labor to work it. England had the opposite problem—not enough land and high unemployment. The situation led many poor English people to come to America as **indentured servants.** They signed contracts with American colonists, agreeing to work for four or more years in return for paid passage to America and free food, clothing, and shelter. Southern farmers also relied on the labor of enslaved Africans, a practice that grew dramatically as time passed.

The hard lives of enslaved workers and indentured servants contrasted sharply with the privileged lives of the elite. A small number of wealthy colonists

bought most of the land along the rivers and established large plantations. These large landholders had enormous economic and political influence. They served in the governing councils and assemblies, commanded the local militias (citizen armies), and became county judges. With few towns or roads in the region, their plantations functioned as self-contained communities.

Although they dominated Southern society, large landowners were few in number. Most Southerners were small farmers living inland in the backcountry. They owned modest plots devoted mostly to subsistence farming. Another group of colonists were tenant farmers—landless settlers who worked fields that they rented from the well-to-do.

By the 1660s, Virginia's government was dominated by wealthy planters led by the governor, Sir William Berkeley. Berkeley arranged to restrict voting to property owners, cutting the number of voters in half. Berkeley also exempted himself and his councilors from taxation. These actions angered the backcountry farmers and tenant farmers. Yet it was the governor's policies toward Native American lands that led to a rebellion.

Crisis Over Land Over time, the most important issue for most colonists was acquiring land. Many indentured servants and tenant farmers wanted to own farms eventually. Backcountry farmers wanted to expand their holdings. By the 1670s, most land left was in areas claimed by Native Americans in the Piedmont, the region of rolling hills between the coastal plains and the Appalachians. Most wealthy planters, who lived near the coast, opposed expanding Virginia's territory because they did not want to endanger their plantations by risking war with the Native Americans.

In 1675 war broke out between settlers and a Susquehannock group, but Governor Berkeley refused to support further military action. Nathaniel Bacon, a well-to-do but sympathetic planter, took up the cause of outraged backcountry farmers. After organizing a militia to attack the Native Americans, he ran for office and won a seat in the House of Burgesses. The assembly immediately authorized another attack. It also restored the right to vote to all free men and took away tax exemptions Berkeley had granted to his supporters. Not satisfied with these reforms, Bacon challenged Berkeley, and a civil war erupted. Bacon's Rebellion ended suddenly the next month, when Bacon, hiding in a swamp, became sick and died. Without his leadership, his army rapidly disintegrated, and Berkeley returned to power.

History *Through Art*

Answer: The cash crops of the South required the right kind of conditions and techniques to be cultivated. As large landowners gained more land and many laborers on their estates, plantations came into being.

Ask: What differences do you note between the family home and the support houses? *(Students should note differences in size and style.)*

Did You Know?

The contract of an indentured servant was indented (folded) and torn along the indenture. Each party to the contract kept half.

Bacon's Rebellion convinced many wealthy planters that land should be made available to back-country farmers. From the 1680s onward, Virginia's government generally supported expanding the colony westward, regardless of the impact on Native Americans.

Bacon's Rebellion also helped increase Virginia's reliance on enslaved Africans rather than indentured servants to work their plantations. Enslaved workers did not have to be freed and, therefore, would never need their own land. In addition, in 1672 King Charles II granted a charter to the Royal African Company to engage in the slave trade. Planters now found it easier to acquire enslaved people because they no longer had to go through the Dutch or the Portuguese. Earlier purchases had been difficult because English laws limited trade between the English colonies and other countries. Planters also discovered another economic advantage to slavery. Because enslaved Africans, unlike indentured servants, were considered property, planters could use them as collateral to borrow money and expand their plantations.

✓ **Reading Check** **Analyzing** How did the types of settlements influence the way each was governed?

A Diverse Society

Main Idea The different colonies created new social structures that were more open than those of aristocratic Europe.

Reading Connection Think about the social structure in your school, from the principal down to you, the student. Read on to learn about the social structure that developed in the growing English settlements.

The increasing population of enslaved Africans, along with a rise in trade, changed colonial society. This brought with it a growth of cities, increased immigration, and changes in status for women and Africans.

Trade and the Rise of Cities In the early colonial period, settlers produced few goods that England wanted in exchange for the goods they purchased. Instead, colonial merchants developed systems of **triangular trade** involving exchanges of goods among the colonies, England, Caribbean sugar planters, and Africa.

This trade brought great wealth for merchants, who began to build factories. It also fostered the growth of cities in the North. By 1760 the Middle Colonies

boasted the two largest cities in America: Philadelphia, with 30,000 people, and New York with 25,000.

In these cities, a new society with distinct social classes developed. At the top of the **hierarchy** were a small number of wealthy merchants who controlled trade. Below them, artisans, or skilled workers, made up nearly half of the urban population in colonial times. Innkeepers and retailers with their own businesses held a similar status. The lower class consisted of people without skills or property. Below them in status were indentured servants and enslaved Africans. Although relatively few enslaved people lived in the North, many dwelled in the cities there, making up 10 to 20 percent of the urban population.

Enslaved Africans No group in the American colonies endured lower status or more hardship than enslaved Africans. Africans had arrived in Virginia as early as 1619, when they were regarded as "Christian servants." By about 1775, these unwilling immigrants and their descendants numbered about 540,000 in all colonies, roughly 20 percent of the colonial population. Throughout the colonies, laws called **slave codes** kept African captives from owning property, receiving an education, moving about freely, or meeting in large groups.

Most enslaved Africans lived on Southern plantations, where they worked long days and were subjected to beatings and brandings by planters. Planters also controlled enslaved Africans by threatening to sell them away from their families. Family and religion

Port of Boston As one of the main cities in the colonies, Boston was a center of activity in colonial America. It was a central point for the anger over the creation of the Dominion of New England.

CHAPTER 1 Creating a Nation **107**

R Reading Strategy

Reading Primary Sources The voyage of enslaved Africans from Africa to the Americas was called the Middle Passage. Olaudah Equiano, a West African shipped to America in the 1760s, later wrote about this journey. Have students use library and Internet resources to locate and read *The Interesting Life of Olaudah Equiano, or Gustav Vassa the African.* Then have students write a summary report of reactions to the book. **AL**

CA 11WA2.2a; 11WA2.2c

U Universal Access

Visual/Spatial Historians estimate that 10–12 million Africans were enslaved and sent to the Americas between 1450 and 1870. Have students use the following information to make a pie chart illustrating the distribution of enslaved persons in the Americas. **BL**

Died at sea during voyage from Africa	2 million
Brazil	3.6 million
Spanish colonies	1.5 million
British, French, and Dutch Caribbean	3.7 million
British North America	427,000

✓ **Reading Check**

Answer: Settlements of religious people were governed largely by those associated with the church. Less religious settlements were governed using the principle of separation of church and state, either by land owners or by a governing council.

Did You Know?

When the first Africans arrived in Virginia in 1619, they were treated much like indentured servants. English law did not recognize chattel slavery—the actual ownership of one human being by another. Many English settlers, however, found it acceptable to enslave Africans if they were not Christians.

ASSESS

 Resources for page 108

Use these resources to assess student mastery.

📁 Section Quiz 1-1

📁 Reading Essentials and Study Guide 1-1

💿 Interactive Tutor Self-Assessment CD-ROM

📁 California Standards Practice, Grade 11

 Geography *Skills*

Answers:
1. four
2. Savannah, Plymouth

 Reading Check

Answer: enslaved Africans, Jews, and women

HISTORY
Online

Study Central provides audio summaries, interactive games, and online graphic organizers to help students review section content.

CLOSE

Summarizing Have students summarize the reasons that the English colonies succeeded. **OL**

Answers and Additional Support

---

helped enslaved Africans maintain their dignity. Some resisted by escaping to the North, where slavery was not as widespread as in the South; others refused to work hard or lost their tools.

Immigrants While enslaved Africans were brought to America against their will, Europeans came eagerly. Between 1700 and 1775, hundreds of thousands of free white immigrants streamed in. Most settled in the Middle Colonies, especially Pennsylvania. Among them were Germans fleeing religious wars back home and Scotch-Irish escaping high taxes, poor harvests, and religious discrimination in Ireland. Jews migrated to America for religious reasons too. By 1776 approximately 1,500 Jews lived in the colonies, mainly in the cities of New York, Philadelphia, Charleston, Savannah, and Newport. They were allowed to worship freely, but they could not vote or hold public office.

Women Like Jews, women did not receive equal rights in colonial America. At first, married women could not legally own property or make contracts or wills. Husbands were the sole guardians of the children and were allowed to physically discipline both their children and their wives. Single women and widows had more rights. They could own and manage property, file lawsuits, and run businesses. In the 1700s, the status of married women improved. Despite legal limitations, many women worked outside their homes.

☑ **Reading Check** **Identifying** What groups faced discrimination in colonial times?

NATIONAL GEOGRAPHIC **The Thirteen Colonies, 1750**

 Geography *Skills*

1. **Interpreting Maps** How many colonies were in New England in 1750?
2. **Applying Geography Skills** Which town or city is located the farthest west? Which town or city is located the farthest east?

HISTORY *Online* **Study Central**

For help with the concepts in this section of *American Vision: Modern Times* go to tav.mt.glencoe.com and click on **Study Central.**

SECTION 1 ASSESSMENT

Checking for Understanding

1. **Vocabulary** Define: civilization, culture, joint-stock company, immigrate, Pilgrim, proprietary colony, indentured servant, subsistence farming, triangular trade, hierarchy, slave code.
2. **People and Terms** Identify: Christopher Columbus, William Penn.
3. **Places** Locate: Jamestown.
4. **Summarize** why settlers came to Jamestown and Plymouth colony.

Reviewing Big Ideas

5. **Describing** What are the different ways in which early settlers in the English colonies developed new and unique forms of government?

Critical Thinking

6. **Analyzing** What role did religion play in the founding of English colonies?
7. **Historical Analysis** **Evaluating** How did geography influence the way the English colonies developed? **CA CS3; CS4**
8. **Organizing** Use a graphic organizer similar to the one below to briefly explain how the English colonies came into being.

Colony	Description of Founding

Analyzing Visuals

9. **Examining Art** Study the painting of the signing of the Mayflower Compact on page 103. Do you think the artist's depiction of the people and the ship is accurate, considering that they have just completed a long journey? Why or why not?

Writing About History

10. **Descriptive Writing** Take on the role of a settler in Jamestown. Write a letter to someone back in England describing the hardships you faced after arriving at the colony. **CA** 11WS1.1; 11WA2.1; 11WA2.4

108 CHAPTER 1 Creating a Nation

SECTION 1 ASSESSMENT ANSWERS

1. Content vocabulary is boldfaced and highlighted in yellow. Academic vocabulary is boldfaced.
2. Christopher Columbus (p. 101), William Penn (p. 105)
3. Jamestown (p. 102)
4. to make money to own land
5. New England developed communal towns. Middle colonists had

religious freedom. Southern colonists were proprietary.
6. New England's settlers wanted Puritan religious freedom. Middle colonists welcomed all faiths.
7. Varying conditions for growing cash crops affected the economy in each colonial region.
8. MA/RI: escape intolerance; CN:

separating church and state; NH and ME: split two grants; NY/NJ: raw materials; PN: repay debt; VA, Carol.: cash crops; GA: home for debtors
9. Answers should discuss how the voyage affected passengers.
10. Letters should discuss hardships suffered.

SECTION 2 Dissent and Independence

Guide to Reading

Connection
In the previous section, you learned about the colonial development of North America. In this section, you will discover why American colonists became dissatisfied with Britain's rule and fought to gain independence.

Main Idea
- The colonists learned about the ideas of natural rights and justified revolutions, while British mercantilist policies limited their freedom. (p. 110)
- The ideas of the Enlightenment and the Great Awakening made the colonists question their role as subjects of the English monarch. (p. 111)
- Unpopular British laws and taxes led to colonial protests and violence. (p. 113)

- When Britain introduced new laws to assert its authority, the colonists decided to declare their independence. (p. 114)
- With the help of their allies, the Americans defeated the British in the Revolutionary War. (p. 117)

Content Vocabulary
mercantilism, Enlightenment, Great Awakening, customs duty, committee of correspondence, minuteman

Academic Vocabulary
logic, exports, communicate

People and Terms to Identify
John Locke, Stamp Act, Townshend Acts, Intolerable Acts, George Washington, Declaration of Independence

Places to Locate
Lexington, Concord, Yorktown

Reading Objectives
- **Explain** how the Enlightenment and the Great Awakening influenced American thinking.
- **Discuss** how the growing tensions between England and the colonies led to a revolution and independence.

Reading Strategy
Organizing Complete a graphic organizer similar to the one below to describe the causes that led the colonies to declare their independence.

Causes → Declaration of Independence

Preview of Events

♦1690　　　　♦1720　　　　♦1750　　　　♦1780

1690
Two Treatises of Government published

c. 1740
Great Awakening peaks

1765
Stamp Act passed

1776
Declaration of Independence drafted and signed

The following are the main History–Social Science Standards covered in this section.

11.1.1 Describe the Enlightenment and the rise of democratic ideas as the context in which the nation was founded.

11.1.2 Analyze the ideological origins of the American Revolution, the Founding Fathers' philosophy of divinely bestowed unalienable natural rights, the debates on the drafting and ratification of the Constitution, and the addition of the Bill of Rights.

11.3.2 Analyze the great religious revivals and the leaders involved in them, including the First Great Awakening, the Second Great Awakening, the Civil War revivals, the Social Gospel Movement, the rise of Christian liberal ideology in the nineteenth century, the impact

≈ The Big Idea ≈

The quest for equality is eternal. Frustrated by British policies and limited rights, American colonists began demanding greater freedom. Fueled by the Enlightenment and the Great Awakening, many colonists protested the English monarch's policies. Angered by the protests, Britain increased its control over the colonies. Many colonists responded by declaring independence, while others remained loyal to Britain. The Americans won the Revolutionary War, and Britain recognized the United States of America as an independent nation.

of the Second Vatican Council, and the rise of Christian fundamentalism in current times.

BELLRINGER
SKILLBUILDER ACTIVITY

Project **Daily Focus Skills Transparency 1-2** and have students answer the question.

Guide to Reading

Understanding Vocabulary:
Provide students with blank note cards. On one side of each note card, have students write a content vocabulary word or an academic vocabulary word. On the other side, have them write the definition. Organize students into pairs and have them quiz each other on vocabulary words using the flash cards they just created.

Answers to Graphic:
British attempts to pay for French and Indian War debt—Stamp Act, Townshend Acts, Intolerable Acts.

Unpacking the Standards

Students will be able to:

- Explain how the Enlightenment and the Great Awakening influenced American thinking.

- Discuss how the growing tensions between England and the colonies led to a revolution and independence.

SECTION RESOURCES

🗀 Print Material
- Reproducible Lesson Plan 1-2
- Guided Reading Activity 1-2
- Reading Essentials and Study Guide 1-2
- Active Reading Note-Taking Guide 1-2

🖳 Transparencies
- Daily Focus Skills Transparency 1-2
- Section Graphic Organizer Transparency 1-2

Technology

- ⊕ Interactive Tutor Self-Assessment CD-ROM
- ⊕ Exam*View*® Pro Testmaker CD-ROM
- ⊕ Presentation Plus! CD-ROM

TEACH

S Skill Practice

Evaluating Evidence Have students create a chart that lists the advantages and disadvantages of mercantilism for England and for the American colonies. Then have students write a paragraph explaining their answer to the following question: **Do you think that mercantilism was a fair policy for the colonies? Why or why not?** Tell students to refer to their charts when writing their responses. **OL** **CA HI1; HI4**

R Reading Strategy

Sequencing Some students may not be able to understand the impact of Charles II's decision to create the Dominion of New England. It is helpful to draw out students' thoughts on the topic with some discussion. **Ask: Was the Dominion of New England a positive or negative step toward freedom for the American colonies? Why?** *(negative; Dominion was a royal province, levied new taxes, upheld Navigation Acts, and undermined Puritan Church's authority)* Have students create a time line of events leading up to the establishment of the Dominion of New England. **OL**

Answers and Additional Support

Mercantilism and the Glorious Revolution

Main Idea **The colonists learned about the ideas of natural rights and justified revolutions, while British mercantilist policies limited their freedom.**

Reading Connection What rights do you have under the Bill of Rights? Read on to learn about the English Bill of Rights.

The triangular trade had allowed colonists to expand their trade and their colonies. Soon, however, the English Parliament enacted laws that limited the colonies while furthering England's economic interests.

★ An American Story ★

In the second half of the 1600s and the early 1700s, the British Parliament passed a series of laws that restricted and controlled colonial manufacturing. One of these laws affected the hat industry and another affected the iron industry. These laws annoyed many colonists, including Benjamin Franklin, who argued:

❝The hatters of England have prevailed to obtain an act in their own favor restraining that manufacture in America. . . . In the same manner have a few nail makers and a still smaller body of steelmakers (perhaps there are not half a dozen of these in England) prevailed totally to forbid by an act of Parliament the erecting of slitting mills or steel furnaces in America; that Americans may be obliged to take all their nails for their buildings and steel for their tools from these artificers [craft workers].❞

—quoted in *The Rise of American Civilization*

◄ *Benjamin Franklin*

England's policies were based on the idea that the purpose of colonies was to help the country increase its wealth. The colonists soon grew frustrated with such limits, but at the same time were encouraged by events in England that granted the colonies more freedoms.

Mercantilism **Mercantilism** is a set of ideas about the world economy, which were popular in the 1600s and 1700s. Mercantilists believed that to become wealthy and powerful, a country had to accumulate gold and silver by selling more goods to other countries than it bought from them. Mercantilists also argued that a country should be self-sufficient in raw materials. It would buy raw materials from its colonies and sell them manufactured goods in return.

Mercantilism gave colonies a reliable market for some of their raw materials and was an eager supplier of manufactured goods. At the same time, it prevented colonies from selling goods to other nations, even if they could get a better price. Furthermore, if a colony produced nothing the home country needed, it could not acquire gold or silver to buy manufactured goods.

When Charles II assumed the throne in 1660, he and his advisers were determined to use the colonies to generate wealth for England. Charles asked Parliament to pass the Navigation Acts of 1660, requiring that all goods shipped to and from the colonies be carried on English ships. Specific products, including the major products that earned money for the colonies, could be sold only to England or other English colonies. Three years later, in 1663, Parliament passed another navigation act, the Staple Act. It required all colonial imports to come through England. Merchants bringing foreign goods to the colonies had to stop in England, pay taxes, and then ship the goods out again on English ships. This increased the price of the goods in the colonies.

Frustration with the Navigation Acts encouraged colonial merchants to break the laws. New England merchants routinely smuggled goods to Europe, the Caribbean, and Africa. To control the colonies, in 1684 Charles II deprived Massachusetts of its charter and declared it a royal colony. James II, who succeeded his brother Charles on the English throne in 1685, went even further by creating a new royal province called the Dominion of New England. At first it included Massachusetts, Plymouth, and Rhode Island, but later Connecticut, New Jersey, and New York were added. Sir Edmund Andros, the Dominion's first governor-general, quickly made himself unpopular by levying new taxes, rigorously enforcing the Navigation Acts, and attempting to undermine the authority of the Puritan Church.

Did You Know?

Major products that could be sold only to England or other English colonies under the Navigation Acts included sugar, tobacco, lumber, cotton, wool, and indigo.

More Skill Practice

Conducting Research Massachusetts resisted the Navigation Acts because the acts negatively affected its ports. Have students use library and Internet resources to locate colonial pictures of Boston and present their findings on a poster with descriptive captions. Students should also write a one-page report on colonial Boston. **AL**
CA HR4

The Glorious Revolution of 1688 While Andros was angering New England colonists, King James II was offending many in England by disregarding Parliament, revoking the charters of many English towns, and converting to Catholicism. The birth of James's son in 1688 triggered protests against a Catholic heir. To prevent a Catholic dynasty, Parliament invited James's Protestant daughter Mary and her Dutch husband, William of Orange, to claim the throne. James fled, and William and Mary became the new rulers. This bloodless change of power is known as the Glorious Revolution.

Before assuming the throne, William and Mary had to swear their acceptance of the English Bill of Rights. This document, written in 1689, said monarchs could not suspend Parliament's laws or create their own courts, nor could they impose taxes or raise an army without Parliament's consent. The Bill of Rights also guaranteed freedom of speech within Parliament, banned excessive bail and cruel and unusual punishments, and guaranteed every English subject the right to an impartial jury in legal cases. 📖 *(See page 987 for an excerpt from the English Bill of Rights.)*

The English Bill of Rights later influenced American government. Almost immediately Boston colonists ousted Governor-General Andros. William and Mary then permitted Rhode Island and Connecticut to resume their previous forms of government, and they issued a new charter for Massachusetts in 1691. The new charter combined Massachusetts Bay Colony, Plymouth Colony, and Maine into the royal colony of Massachusetts. The king retained the power to appoint a governor, but he restored the colonists' right to elect an assembly. Voters no longer had to belong to a Puritan congregation, and Anglicans there were granted freedom of worship.

John Locke's Political Theories The Glorious Revolution had another important legacy. It suggested there were times when revolution was justified. In 1690 **John Locke's** *Two Treatises of Government* was published on this subject. 📖 *(See page 988 for an excerpt from the* Two Treatises.*)* Locke argued that a monarch's right to rule came from the people. All people, he said, were born with certain natural rights, including the right to life, liberty, and property. Because their rights were not safe in the state of nature in which people originally lived, people had come together to create a government. In effect, they had made a contract—they agreed to obey the government's laws, and the government agreed to uphold their rights. If a ruler violated those rights, the people were justified in rebelling. Locke's ideas struck

a chord with American colonists. When Thomas Jefferson drafted the Declaration of Independence in 1776, he relied upon the words and ideas of John Locke. The colonists understood Locke's "natural rights" to be the specific rights English people had developed over the centuries and that were referred to in documents such as the Magna Carta and the English Bill of Rights. 📖 *(See page 984 for an excerpt from the Magna Carta.)*

✓ **Reading Check** **Examining** In what ways did the Navigation Acts affect trade in the colonies?

The Enlightenment and the Great Awakening

Main Idea The ideas of the Enlightenment and the Great Awakening made the colonists question their role as subjects of the English monarch.

Reading Connection Have you ever read a book that changed the way you think about a subject? Read on to learn how two cultural movements influenced the colonists.

The English Bill of Rights was not the only set of ideas that influenced the colonists. During the 1700s, America saw the emergence of two great cultural movements. One championed human reason and science as a means of learning truth, while the other stressed an intense, personal relationship with God. Both challenged traditional authorities.

▼ *John Locke*

CHAPTER 1   Creating a Nation   **111**

More Skill Practice

Activating Prior Knowledge Review why the English Bill of Rights was developed and what fundamental rights were granted under the bill. Then explain the influence that John Locke had on the political thinking of his time. Ask students to list the rights they believe all Americans should have today. Then have them identify which items on their list relate to items that are found in the English Bill of Rights or in the theories of John Locke. **OL**

Answers and
Additional Support

W Writing Support

Summary Writing Have each
student write a one-page essay
about the continuing influence of
Montesquieu on our government.
Tell students to address the following question as they are writing: **Why are Montesquieu's
ideas important to preserving
citizens' freedom?** *(Students
should recognize that Montesquieu helped provide the basis
for the separation of powers in
our government. This separation
has held the overall power of
the federal government in
check.)* **OL** **CA** 11WA2.4a

C Critical Thinking

Comparing and Contrasting
Invite interested students to use
library and Internet resources to
research present-day religious
revivals. Have students make a
chart comparing the attendance,
affiliation, goals, and methods of
today's revivals with those that
took place in the American
colonies in the 1700s. Then tell
students to write a short paragraph describing what has
changed about revivals, as well
as what has remained the
same. **OL** **CA** 11WA2.4d

✓ Reading Check

Answer: It split churches
into various factions. It also
reinforced the concept of
individualism.

The Great Awakening George Whitefield, pictured here standing, was one of the most famous ministers of the colonial religious
revival. What effect did the Great Awakening have on
Americans?

branches would provide checks and balances
against each other and would prevent the
government from abusing its authority.
Montesquieu's ideas influenced many of the
leaders who wrote the American Constitution.

The Great Awakening While some Americans turned away from a religious worldview
in the 1700s, others renewed their Christian
faith. Throughout the colonies, ministers held
revivals—large public meetings for preaching
and prayer—where they stressed piety and
being "born again," or emotionally uniting with
God. This widespread resurgence of religious
fervor is known as the **Great Awakening.**

The Great Awakening reached its height
around 1740 with the fiery preaching of Jonathan
Edwards and George Whitefield. Churches soon
split into factions over a movement called pietism,
which stressed an individual's devoutness. Those
who embraced the new ideas—including Baptists,
Presbyterians, and Methodists—won many converts,
while older, more traditional churches lost members.

In the South, the Baptists gained a strong following among poor farmers. Baptists also welcomed
enslaved Africans at their revivals and condemned
the brutality of slavery. Hundreds of Africans joined
Baptist congregations and listened to sermons that
taught that all people were equal before God. Despite
violent attempts by planters to break up Baptist
meetings, about 20 percent of Virginia's whites and
thousands of enslaved Africans had become Baptists
by 1775.

A Powerful Legacy The Enlightenment and the
Great Awakening had different origins and directions. Both movements, though, emphasized an individualism that inclined American colonists toward
political independence. The Enlightenment provided
the supporting arguments against British rule. The
Great Awakening undermined allegiance to traditional authority.

The Enlightenment During the late 1600s and
1700s in Europe, a period known as the age of
Enlightenment, philosophers put forth the theory
that both the physical world and human nature operated in an orderly way according to natural laws.
Furthermore, they believed anyone could figure out
these laws by using reason and **logic.**

One of the leading Enlightenment writers was
John Locke. His contract theory of government is an
example of Enlightenment thinking. Locke's views of
human nature also appealed to many Americans. In
his *Essay on Human Understanding,* Locke argued that
contrary to what the Church taught, people were not
born sinful. Instead their minds were blank slates
that society and education could shape for the better.
These ideas that all people have rights and that society can be improved became core beliefs in American
society.

French thinker Jean Jacques Rousseau carried
these ideas further. In *The Social Contract,* he argued
that a government should be formed by the consent
of the people, who would then make their own laws.
W Another influential Enlightenment writer was Baron
Montesquieu. In his work *Spirit of the Laws,* published in 1748, Montesquieu suggested that there
were three types of political power—executive, legislative, and judicial. These powers should be separated into different branches of the government to
protect the liberty of the people. The different

✓ Reading Check **Determining Cause and Effect**
How did the Enlightenment and the Great Awakening affect the
established order?

History *Through Art*

Answer: emphasized individualism, undermined
traditional authority, laid groundwork for revolutionary ideas
Ask: Why did Baptists gain a strong following
in the South? *(They were supported by poor
farmers, welcomed Africans at their revivals,
and condemned slavery.)*

**Resources for
page 112**

*Have students read more about the
Great Awakening in the **Primary Source
Reading 1–1.***

Growing Rebelliousness

Main Idea Unpopular British laws and taxes led to colonial protests and violence.

Reading Connection Have you ever read letters to the editor of your local newspaper protesting some local policies? Read on to learn how the colonists began to protest against unpopular taxes.

Britain and France struggled for dominance on the North American continent. Whenever the two countries were at war, their colonies went to war as well. In 1754 such a conflict began in America.

The French and Indian War In the 1740s, Great Britain became interested in the Ohio River valley. So did their long-standing rivals, the French. Before long, fighting broke out, and the French, with help from their Native American allies, took temporary control of the region.

From 1754 to 1759, the so-called French and Indian War raged along the North American frontier. The fighting between Great Britain and France also spread to Europe, where it was known as the Seven Years' War. In the end, the British triumphed. The Treaty of Paris of 1763 made Great Britain the dominant power in North America. Its empire now included New France and all of Louisiana east of the Mississippi, except New Orleans. Britain also gained Florida from Spain, which had allied itself with France. However, to make up for Spain's loss, France gave the Spanish western Louisiana and New Orleans.

Unpopular Regulations Great Britain's victory left it with steep debts to repay and new territories to govern and defend. Many British leaders thought that the colonies should share in these costs. The American colonists did not like the policies Britain adopted to solve its financial problems.

The first troubles came with passage of the Proclamation Act of 1763. This act tried to halt colonial expansion into Native American lands west of the Appalachian Mountains. King George III wanted to avoid another costly war with the Native Americans, but the colonists who had fought the French and Indian War to secure access to the Ohio River valley were enraged.

While western farmers denounced the Proclamation Act, eastern merchants objected to new tax policies. The British government had discovered that the colonists were smuggling goods without paying **customs duties**—taxes on imports and **exports.** Britain tightened customs control and began introducing other unpopular measures. To bring in new revenue, the Sugar Act of 1764 raised taxes on imports of raw sugar and molasses. It also placed new taxes on silk, wine, coffee, and indigo. To make the colonists contribute to their own defense, the Quartering Act of 1765 obligated them to provide shelter for British troops.

Nothing, however, outraged the colonists more than the **Stamp Act** of 1765. The act required stamps to be bought and placed on most printed materials, from newspapers and legal documents to diplomas and playing cards. Unlike taxes on trade, this was a direct tax—the first Britain had ever placed on the colonists. Opposition was swift. Editorials, pamphlets, and speeches poured out against the tax. Groups calling

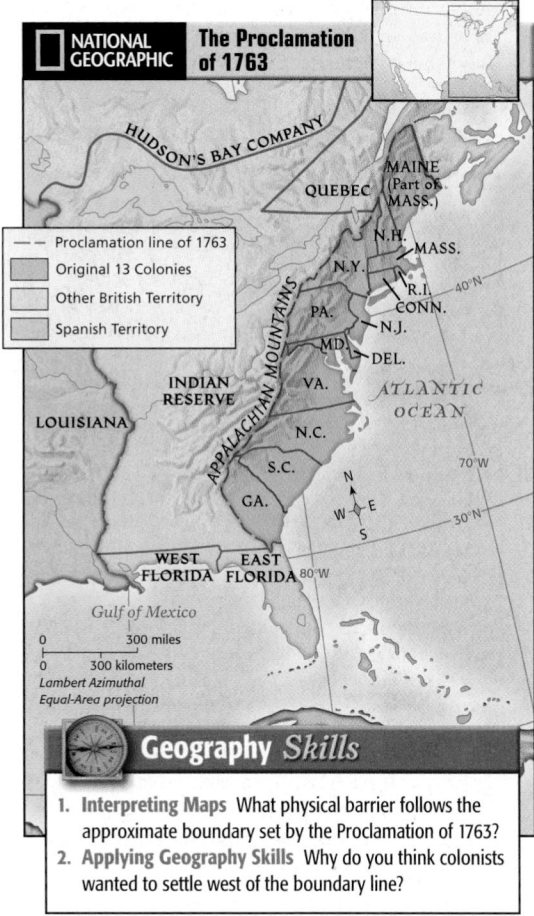

NATIONAL GEOGRAPHIC The Proclamation of 1763

- - - Proclamation line of 1763
Original 13 Colonies
Other British Territory
Spanish Territory

HUDSON'S BAY COMPANY

QUEBEC
MAINE (Part of MASS.)
N.H.
MASS.
N.Y.
R.I.
CONN.
PA.
N.J.
MD.
DEL.
VA.
ATLANTIC OCEAN
INDIAN RESERVE
LOUISIANA
N.C.
S.C.
GA.
WEST FLORIDA
EAST FLORIDA
Gulf of Mexico

40°N
70°W
30°N
80°W

0   300 miles
0   300 kilometers
Lambert Azimuthal
Equal-Area projection

Geography *Skills*

1. **Interpreting Maps** What physical barrier follows the approximate boundary set by the Proclamation of 1763?
2. **Applying Geography Skills** Why do you think colonists wanted to settle west of the boundary line?

C Critical Thinking

Determining Cause and Effect Identifying causes for events and evaluating their effects helps students understand these events in their historical context. Ask students to work in pairs to summarize the causes of the French and Indian War. (*English competition with France over the Ohio River valley*) **Ask: Do you agree with Great Britain's opinion that the colonists should share in the costs of the war? Why or why not?** Have students work independently to write a short paragraph explaining their answer. Then invite volunteers to share what they have written with the class. **OL**

U Universal Access

English Learners Have students create a thematic map showing the area controlled by France in 1754 and after the Treaty of Paris was signed in 1763. Remind students to include an appropriate title and legend for the map. **EL**

Review the Big Idea

Review the Big Idea for this section, "Political philosophies and major events influence the formation of constitutional governments." Review British mercantilism polices with the class. (*Great Britain bought raw materials from its colonies and sold them manufactured goods in return. The colonies could only trade with Great Britain.*) Ask students to write a one-page paper explaining why colonists opposed the Sugar Act of 1764 and how this act and other regulations fostered a sense of rebellion in the colonies. **OL** **CA 11WA2.4a**

Geography *Skills*

Answers:
1. Appalachian Mountains
2. possible answers—to have more land for farming, to trap furs for trading

Geography Skills Practice
Ask: How was most of the British territory west of the Proclamation Line used? (*as an Indian reserve*)

themselves the Sons of Liberty organized outdoor meetings and protests and tried to intimidate stamp distributors. In October 1765, representatives from nine colonies met for what became known as the Stamp Act Congress. Together, they issued the Declaration of Rights and Grievances, arguing that only the colonists' political representatives, and not Parliament, had the right to tax them. "No taxation without representation" became a popular catch-phrase.

R On November 1, when the Stamp Act took effect, the colonists ignored it. They began to boycott all goods made in Britain, refusing to drink British tea or buy British cloth. Their strategy paid off. Merchants in England saw sales plunge, and thousands of workers lost their jobs. Under pressure, British lawmakers repealed the Stamp Act in 1766.

The Townshend Acts During the Stamp Act crisis, Britain's financial problems worsened. To raise more money from the colonies, Parliament passed new measures in 1767. These came to be called the **Townshend Acts,** after Charles Townshend, the head

of Britain's treasury. The Townshend Acts put new customs duties on glass, lead, paper, paint, and tea imported into the colonies. They also gave customs officers new powers to help them arrest smugglers.

The Townshend Acts stirred a heated outcry. In Massachusetts, Sam Adams and James Otis led the resistance; in Virginia, the leading protestors included George Washington, Patrick Henry, and Thomas Jefferson. When the assemblies of both colonies passed statements challenging Britain's right to tax them, Parliament dissolved their assemblies. The colonists remained undeterred. Merchants in Boston, New York, and Philadelphia united in a boycott against British goods. In 1769 colonial imports from Britain declined sharply from what they had been in 1768.

S On March 5, 1770, anger turned to violence in Boston. A crowd of colonists began taunting and throwing snowballs at a British soldier guarding a customs house. He called for help, and as jostling and shoving ensued, the British fired shots and five colonists lay dead. The Boston Massacre, as the incident became known, might well have initiated more violence. Within weeks, though, tensions were calmed by news that the British had repealed almost all of the Townshend Acts. Parliament kept one tax—on tea—to uphold its right to tax the colonies. At the same time, it allowed the colonial assemblies to resume meeting. Peace and stability returned to the colonies, at least temporarily.

✓**Reading Check** **Summarizing** What disagreements arose between Britain and the colonies in the 1700s?

The Road to War

Main Idea When Britain introduced new laws to assert its authority, the colonists decided to declare their independence. ⌐TURNING**POINT**⌐

Reading Connection Have you ever wondered how the colonists must have felt as they decided to defy Parliament? Read on to learn about the growing discontent of the colonists.

The repeal of the Townshend Acts in 1770 brought calm to the colonies for a time. Soon, however, new British policies again enraged American colonists and led them to declare their independence.

The Colonists Defy Britain After trade with England had resumed, so had smuggling. When some 150 colonists seized and burned the stranded

Causes and Effects of Tensions With Britain

Causes
- 1764, Sugar Act
- 1765, Stamp Act
- 1767, Townshend Acts
- 1773, Tea Act
- 1774, Coercive Acts

Effects
- Colonists protest that their rights have been violated.
- Nine colonies hold Stamp Act Congress.
- Colonists boycott British goods.
- Sons and Daughters of Liberty formed.
- Tea dumped into Boston Harbor during the "Boston Tea Party."
- Twelve colonies attend the Continental Congress.

TEA THROWN INTO BOSTON HARBOR DEC 16 1773.

Graphic Organizer → Skills

Parliament's efforts to tax the colonists led to growing protests in the colonies.

Analyzing Information If you had been a colonist, how would you have reacted to these taxes? Why?

⌐TURNING**POINT**⌐

Great Britain's taxing regulations served to unite the diverse American colonies in ways not seen before. This sense of colonial unity and a feeling of being unrepresented by the British Parliament led to colonial rebellion.

customs ship *Gaspee,* the British gave investigators the authority to bring suspects back to England for trial. Colonists thought this denied them the right to a trial by a jury of their peers. Following a suggestion by Thomas Jefferson, they created **committees of correspondence** to **communicate** with the other colonies about British activities. The committees of correspondence helped unify the colonies and shape public opinion. They also helped colonial leaders coordinate strategies for resisting the British.

In May 1773, Parliament passed the Tea Act, further igniting the flames of rebellion. The Tea Act created favorable business terms for the struggling British East India Company. American merchants, who feared they would be squeezed out of business, were outraged. That fall, when new shipments of British tea arrived in American harbors, colonists in New York, Philadelphia, and Charleston blocked its delivery. Bostonians went one step further. On the night before the tea was to be unloaded, approximately 150 men boarded the ships. They dumped 342 chests of tea overboard as several thousand people on shore cheered. The raid came to be called the Boston Tea Party.

The Boston Tea Party outraged the British. In the spring of 1774, Parliament passed new laws that came to be known as the Coercive Acts to punish Massachusetts and dissuade other colonies from challenging British authority. One law shut down Boston's port until the city paid for the destroyed tea. Other laws banned most town meetings and expanded the powers of the royally appointed governor, General Thomas Gage. To enforce the acts, the king stationed 2,000 troops in New England.

A few months later the British introduced the Quebec Act, which extended Quebec's boundaries to include much of what is today Ohio, Illinois, Michigan, Indiana, and Wisconsin. If colonists moved west into that territory, they would have no elected assembly. The Quebec Act, coming so soon after the Coercive Acts, seemed to signal Britain's desire to seize control of colonial governments.

Colonists wasted no time in protesting the **Intolerable Acts,** as they came to be known. In June 1774, after the Virginia governor had suspended the House of Burgesses, the Massachusetts assembly suggested that representatives from all the colonies gather to discuss how to proceed. The First Continental Congress met in Philadelphia on September 5. The 55 delegates, who came from each of the 12 colonies except Georgia, debated a variety of ideas. Finally they approved a plan to boycott British goods. They also agreed to hold a second Continental Congress in May 1775 if the crisis remained unresolved.

Picturing **History**

Tea Tantrum In December 1773, colonists in Boston took matters into their own hands and dumped hated British tea into Boston Harbor. Why did Boston tea merchants object so strongly to the Tea Act?

The Revolution Begins Meanwhile, Great Britain had suspended the Massachusetts assembly. Massachusetts lawmakers responded by regrouping and naming John Hancock as their leader. He became, in effect, a rival governor to General Gage. A full-scale rebellion was now under way. The Massachusetts militia began to drill and practice shooting. The town of Concord created a special unit of **minutemen** who were trained and ready to "stand at a minute's warning in case of alarm." Through the summer and fall of 1774, colonists prepared for a fight.

Not everyone favored resistance. Although many colonists disagreed with Parliament's policies, they still felt a strong sense of loyalty to the king and believed British law should be upheld. Americans who backed Britain came to be known as Loyalists, or Tories. On the other side were the Patriots, or Whigs, who believed the British had become tyrants. The Patriots dominated in New England and Virginia, while the Loyalists had a strong following in Georgia, the Carolinas, and New York.

In April 1775, General Gage decided to seize Patriot arms and ammunition being stored in

CHAPTER 1   Creating a Nation   **115**

Sidebar (right column)

C **Critical Thinking**

Predicting Consequences As students read about the Boston Tea Party, ask if reconciliation would have been possible between the British and the colonists at this point. Students should explain their views. **BL**
CA HI4

W₁ **Writing Support**

Expository Writing To help students better understand the position of the colonists after the Boston Tea Party, have students identify a law with which they disagree. Ask them to write an essay expressing the reasons for their disagreement and arguing for their point of view. **OL**
CA 11WA2.3b

R **Reading Strategy**

Connecting Ask students if they or anyone they know has ever participated in a boycott. If someone has, **ask: Based on your experience, do you think that a boycott was an effective way for the colonists to fight the Intolerable Acts? Why or why not? If not, what would have been a better method?** If no one has participated in a boycott, have students consider these questions in a class discussion. **OL**

W₂ **Writing Support**

Persuasive Writing Tell students that they may choose to be a Loyalist or a Patriot. Encourage them to research both their chosen position and the opposing position. Have students create pamphlets that express their point of view and urge readers to join their cause. Have students share their pamphlets with the class.
OL **CA 11WS1.3**

Bottom box

Picturing **History**

Background: The East India Company held a seven-year tea surplus at the time and faced financial ruin if the tea was not sold.
Answer: It took away their business.
Ask: What tactics did the colonists in other places use to prevent the East India Company from selling tea in the colonies? *(Colonists blocked its delivery in New York, Philadelphia, and Charleston.)*

115

U₁ Universal Access

English Learners Have students use a map of Massachusetts to draw and label the routes taken by both armies after the fighting at Lexington, ending with the arrival of the armies in Boston. Remind students to provide a legend and title for their maps. **EL**

U₂ Universal Access

Visual/Spatial Have students locate a picture of Percy Moran's *Battle of Bunker Hill* or John Trumbull's *Battle of Bunker's Hill.* Direct them to use these pictures to write a paragraph describing the battle. **BL**

S Skill Practice

Creating a Time Line The early stages of the Revolutionary War involved several events that occurred in rapid succession, pushing a disagreement into a war. Tell students to create a time line that includes the events from the fighting in Lexington to the signing of the Declaration of Independence. **BL** **CA CS2**

Answers and Additional Support

What If...

The Declaration of Independence Had Condemned Slavery?

In 1776 the Continental Congress chose a committee to draft the Declaration of Independence. The committee included Thomas Jefferson, John Adams, Roger Sherman, Benjamin Franklin, and Robert Livingston. Jefferson later recalled the following in his memoirs: "[The committee members] unanimously pressed on myself alone to undertake the draught. I consented; I drew it; but before I reported it to the committee I communicated it separately to Dr. Franklin and Mr. Adams requesting their corrections. . . ."

Franklin and Adams urged Jefferson to delete his condemnation of King George's support of slavery. The two realized that the revolution needed support from all the colonies to succeed, and condemning slavery would alienate pro-slavery colonists and force them to support the king. Jefferson modified the draft accordingly. If the Declaration of Independence had included Jefferson's condemnation of slavery, which is excerpted below, the history of the United States might have been very different.

❝He [King George] has waged cruel war against human nature itself, violating its most sacred rights of life and liberty in the persons of a distant people who never offended him, captivating and carrying them into slavery in another hemisphere, or to incur miserable death in their transportation thither. . . . He has [stopped] every legislative attempt to prohibit or to restrain this execrable commerce determining to keep open a market where [people] should be bought and sold. . . .❞

Concord. On the night of April 18, about 700 British troops secretly set out from nearby Boston. Patriot leaders heard about the plan and sent messengers, including Paul Revere, to spread the alarm. When the British reached **Lexington,** a town on the way to Concord, they found 70 minutemen lined up waiting for them. No one knows who fired the first shot, but when the smoke cleared, 8 minutemen lay dead and 10 more were wounded.

The British then headed to **Concord,** only to find most of the military supplies already removed. When they were forced to retreat by 400 colonial militiamen, militia members and farmers in the area fired at them from behind trees, stone walls, barns, and houses on their way back to Boston. As news spread of the fighting at Lexington and Concord, militia raced from all over New England to help. By May 1775, militia troops had surrounded Boston, trapping the British inside.

Three weeks after the battles, the Second Continental Congress met again and voted to "adopt" the militia surrounding Boston. **George Washington** became general and commander in chief of this Continental Army. Before Washington could reach his troops, though, the militia was tested again. In the Battle of Bunker Hill it turned back two British advances before running out of ammunition. The situation returned to a stalemate, with Boston still under siege. Yet the battle helped to build American confidence. It showed that the largely untrained colonial militia could stand up to one of the world's most feared armies.

The Decision for Independence Despite the onset of fighting, many colonists were still not prepared to break away from Great Britain. In July 1775, the Continental Congress sent King George III a document known as the Olive Branch Petition. The petition asserted the colonists' loyalty to the king and urged him to resolve their grievances peacefully. King George not only rejected the petition, but he declared the colonies to be "open and avowed enemies."

With no compromise likely, the fighting spread. The Continental Congress established a navy and began seizing British merchant ships. Patriots invaded Canada and faced off against British and

Did You Know?

Many citizens of Boston had a bird's-eye view of the Battle of Bunker Hill. Some climbed onto rooftops and church steeples to watch the fighting.

Did You Know?

At the beginning of the Revolutionary War, the colonists had no navy, so they began to commission private ships to attack British vessels. Captain Jonathan Haraden hid his ship's gun ports with canvas. When an unsuspecting British ship neared what it thought was a vulnerable merchant vessel, it was met with gunfire.

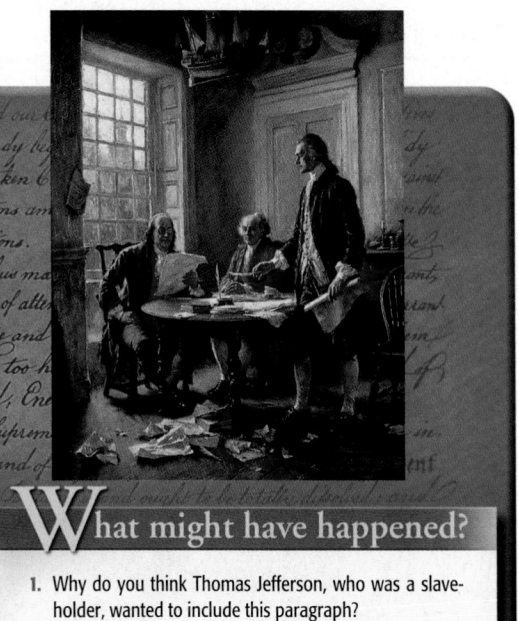

What might have happened?

1. Why do you think Thomas Jefferson, who was a slaveholder, wanted to include this paragraph?
2. **Historical Analysis** Would the course of American history have changed significantly if the Declaration of Independence had included Jefferson's statement? If so, how? If not, why not? **CA HI2, HI3, HI4**

Loyalist troops in Virginia and the Carolinas. As the conflict dragged on, more and more colonists began to favor a break with Britain.

Thomas Paine helped sway public opinion with his pamphlet called *Common Sense*, published in January 1776. Paine persuasively argued that King George III, and not Parliament, was responsible for British actions against the colonies. In his view, monarchies had been established by seizing power from the people. George III was a tyrant, he proclaimed, and it was time to declare independence:

> 66Everything that is right or reasonable pleads for separation. The blood of the slain, the weeping voice of nature cries, 'Tis Time To Part.... Every spot of the old world is overrun with oppression. Freedom hath been hunted round the globe ... [and] England hath given her warning to depart.99
>
> —from *Common Sense*

In early July, a committee of the Continental Congress approved a document that Thomas Jefferson had drafted in which the colonies dissolved ties with Britain. On July 4, 1776, the full Congress issued this **Declaration of Independence.** The colonies now proclaimed themselves the United States of America, and the American Revolution formally began.

Reading Check **Explaining** Why did the colonies declare their independence?

Fighting for Independence

Main Idea With the help of their allies, the Americans defeated the British in the Revolutionary War.

Reading Connection Do you remember trying something new without having time for practice? Read on to learn how the Americans fought a war without proper training or equipment.

The Continental Army could not match the British Army in size, funding, discipline, or experience. American soldiers often were poorly equipped and went without food, pay, or adequate clothing. The Americans did have several advantages. The Continental Army was fighting on home ground. In every state it also had help from local militias that used unconventional tactics. Moreover, British support for the war was only half-hearted. Britain already faced threats to other parts of its empire from the French, Spanish, and Dutch, and it could not afford a long and costly struggle in America.

The Northern Campaign The British under the command of General William Howe were quickly able to seize New York City. Then, in October, Howe led his troops south toward Philadelphia, where the Continental Congress was meeting. George Washington raced to meet him, but both armies were surprised by the early onset of winter weather and set up camp. Nevertheless, Washington decided to try a surprise attack. On the night of December 25, 1776, he led some 2,400 men across the icy Delaware River from Pennsylvania to New Jersey. There they achieved two small victories before they camped for the winter.

By the spring of 1777, both sides were on the move again. General Howe revived his plan to capture Philadelphia and the Continental Congress. On September 11, 1777, he defeated Washington at the Battle of Brandywine Creek. Howe captured Philadelphia but the Continental Congress escaped before the city fell.

R₁ Reading Strategy

Summarizing Within three months of its publication, Thomas Paine's *Common Sense* had sold over 150,000 copies. Ask students to read the document and write a one-page summary of the main ideas. **AL** **CA 11RC2.4; 11RL3.2**

R₂ Reading Strategy

Organizing Information Have students create a chart listing the advantages and disadvantages faced by the British and Continental Armies in the Revolutionary War. Ask students to use their charts to write the answers to the following question: **Why was fighting on home ground considered an advantage for the colonists?** *(closer to resources, family; not surrounded by hostile population)* **OL**

U Universal Access

English Learners Have students use library or Internet resources to view paintings of the crossing of the Delaware by artists George Caleb Bingham and Thomas Sully. Ask them which one seems closest to historical accounts. Tell students to write a short paragraph explaining their answer. **EL** **CA 11WA2.4b**

Reading Check

Answer: because of laws and taxes imposed on the colonies without direct government representation in return

What If...

Answers:
1. Answers may vary. Students may realize that Jefferson's rhetoric did not always match his actions.
2. Answers may vary. Possible reasons: the colonies may not have united to throw off British rule, individual colonies may have struggled for their own independence, or slavery may have ended sooner than it actually did.

Ask: Why do you think one person was asked to make the original draft? (*possible answer: to create a working document that others could respond to*)

117

R Reading Strategy

Visualizing Invite an art teacher or artist to speak to your class about the artwork related to the War of Independence. Ask the speaker to give examples of works that inspired patriotism during the war and works that illustrate historical events. Encourage the speaker to talk about how artists learned about the historical events they depicted. Have students draw their own scenes of the Battle of Saratoga based on the information they have learned. **EL**

S Skill Practice

Identifying Point of View Have students consider what it would have been like to be one of the following people in the South during the Revolutionary War: a Continental soldier, a Loyalist, a wife waiting for news of her soldier husband, a merchant smuggling supplies to the troops, or a woman serving as a spy for the Continental army. Have students write a letter about the dangers they faced and the reasons for their commitment to their cause. **OL** **CA HR2**

Answers and Additional Support

NATIONAL GEOGRAPHIC **The Revolutionary War, 1776–1781**

← British forces
← American and allied forces
✷ British victory
✷ American victory
✷ Indecisive battle

❸ Burgoyne surrenders at Saratoga, 1777

❶ British capture New York City, 1776

❼ Washington and Rochambeau rush toward Virginia, August, 1781

❷ Americans attack British at Trenton and Princeton, 1776

❹ Howe captures Philadelphia, 1777

❾ Cornwallis is trapped; the British surrender at Yorktown, 1781

❽ French Admiral De Grasse keeps British ships away

❻ British capture Charles Town and win the battle of Camden, but are defeated at Kings Mountain in 1780 and at Cowpens in 1781

❺ British capture Savannah, 1778

N
W ◆ E
S

0   200 miles
0   200 kilometers
Albers Conic Equal-Area projection

De Grasse (From West Indies)

ATLANTIC OCEAN

Geography *Skills*

1. **Interpreting Maps** Name two sites of colonial victories in New Jersey.
2. **Applying Geography Skills** Approximately how far apart were the northernmost and southernmost battles shown on the map?

While General Howe remained in Philadelphia, another British force, led by General John Burgoyne, was marching south from Quebec. Burgoyne expected to link up with Howe in New York but failed to coordinate with him. When he and his 5,000 men reached Saratoga in upstate New York, they were surrounded by a far bigger American army. On October 17, 1777, they surrendered—a stunning victory for the Americans. Not only did it improve morale dramatically, but it also convinced the French to commit troops to the American cause.

While both Spain and France had been secretly aiding the Americans, the French now agreed to fight openly. On February 6, 1778, France signed an alliance, becoming the first country to recognize the United States as an independent nation. In 1779 Spain entered the war as an ally of France.

Fighting on Other Fronts After losing the Battle of Saratoga, the British changed their strategy. Instead of campaigning in the North, they decided to attack in the South, where they expected to find more Loyalist support. They certainly weren't doing well on the western frontier. In 1779 George Rogers Clark secured American control of the Ohio River valley.

 Geography *Skills*

Answers:
1. Trenton and Princeton
2. approximately 1,100 miles

Geography Skills Practice
Ask: What British victory was farthest south?
(Savannah)

 Resources for page 118

*Have students read more about George Washington's experiences leading the war effort in **Moments in Time, Unit 1: George Washington (1777–1789).***

History *Through Art*

A Savage Winter William B.T. Trego's painting, *The March to Valley Forge*, depicts the difficult conditions that led to almost 2,500 deaths during the winter encampment of 1777 to 1778. Where did the Americans and the British fight the last battle of the war?

American troops also took control of western Pennsylvania, western New York, and Cherokee lands in western Virginia and North Carolina.

In the South, though, the British at first held the upper hand. In December 1778, they captured Savannah, Georgia, and seized control of Georgia's backcountry. Then a massive British force led by General Charles Cornwallis moved on to Charles Town, South Carolina. On May 8, 1780, they forced the surrender of nearly 5,500 American troops, the greatest American defeat in the war. The tide finally turned on October 7, 1780, at the Battle of Kings Mountain. Patriot forces crushed Loyalists there and then drove the British out of most of the South.

The Americans also fought the British at sea. Since they did not have the resources to assemble a large navy, Congress issued letters of marque, or licenses, to about 2,000 privately owned ships. In addition to winning some naval battles, the Americans were able to seriously harm British trade by attacking merchant ships.

The American Victory The last major battle of the Revolutionary War was fought in **Yorktown,** Virginia, in the fall of 1781. General Cornwallis became trapped there, with George Washington closing in on land and the French navy blocking the possibility for escape by sea. On October 19, 1781, Cornwallis and approximately 8,000 British troops surrendered.

After learning of the American victory at Yorktown, Parliament voted to end the war. Peace talks began in early April 1782, and the final settlement, the Treaty of Paris, was signed on September 3, 1783. In this treaty, Britain recognized the United States of America as an independent nation with the Mississippi River as its western border. The British kept Canada, but they gave Florida back to Spain and made other concessions to France. On November 24, 1783, the last British troops left New York City. The Revolutionary War was over, and a new nation began to take shape.

 Reading Check **Analyzing** Which major battle during the war was a turning point for the Americans?

HISTORY *Online* **Study Central**

For help with the concepts in this section of *American Vision: Modern Times* go to tav.mt.glencoe.com and click on *Study Central.*

SECTION 2 ASSESSMENT

Checking for Understanding

1. **Vocabulary** Define: mercantilism, Enlightenment, logic, Great Awakening, customs duty, exports, committee of correspondence, communicate, minuteman.

2. **People and Terms** Identify: John Locke, Stamp Act, Townshend Acts, Intolerable Acts, George Washington, Declaration of Independence.

3. **Places** Locate: Lexington, Concord, Yorktown.

Reviewing Big Ideas

4. **Analyzing** Which ways did the Great Awakening contribute to the independent spirit of American colonists?

Critical Thinking

5. **Evaluating** What effect did the Glorious Revolution have on the American colonies?

6. **Organizing** Use a graphic organizer similar to the one below to indicate ways in which colonists defied Britain's attempts at regulation and taxation.

Colonists' Acts of Defiance

Analyzing Visuals

7. **Analyzing Charts** Study the chart on page 114 of causes and effects of tensions with Britain. Then make your own similar chart.

Writing About History

8. **Persuasive Writing** Imagine you are a colonist in 1767, unhappy about Britain's policies toward the colonies. Write a pamphlet explaining your position and urging other colonists to support resistance efforts.
   CA 11WS1.1; 11WA2.1; 11WA2.4

 Resources for page 119

Use these resources to assess student mastery.

📁 Section Quiz 1-2

📁 Reading Essentials and Study Guide 1-2

💿 Interactive Tutor Self-Assessment CD-ROM

📁 California Standards Practice, Grade 11

 History *Through Art*

This painting, like much of Trego's work, illustrates the artist's talent for showing detail. In Trego's case the talent is even more remarkable because the artist had limited use of his fingers.
Answer: Yorktown, Virginia

 HISTORY *Online*

Study Central provides audio summaries, interactive games, and online graphic organizers to help students review section content.

✓ **Reading Check**

Answer: Battle of Saratoga

CLOSE

Summarizing Ask students to explain the terms of the Treaty of Paris.
OL

SECTION 2 ASSESSMENT ANSWERS

1. Content vocabulary is boldfaced and highlighted in yellow. Academic vocabulary is boldfaced.

2. John Locke *(p. 111),* Stamp Act *(p. 113),* Townshend Acts *(p. 114),* Intolerable Acts *(p. 115),* George Washington *(p. 116),* Declaration of Independence *(p. 117)*

3. Lexington *(p. 116),* Concord *(p. 116),* Yorktown *(p. 119)*

4. encouraged individualism and undermined authority

5. justified revolt against Andros, led to the English Bill of Rights

6. Boston Tea Party, boycotts, *Gaspee* burning, committees of correspondence

7. Effects should be linked to Britain's aims.

8. Pamphlets should discuss British policies and why colonists should protest.

The Declaration of Independence

The Declaration
of Independence

FOCUS

History–Social Science Standards

This feature addresses the following standards:

11.1 Students analyze the significant events in the founding of the nation and its attempts to realize the philosophy of government described in the Declaration of Independence.

11.1.2 Analyze the ideological origins of the American Revolution, the Founding Fathers' philosophy of divinely bestowed unalienable natural rights, the debates on the drafting and ratification of the Constitution, and the addition of the Bill of Rights.

TEACH

U Universal Access

English Learners Choose a student to read aloud the first paragraph under "Declaration of Natural Rights" on this page. Discuss with students any unfamiliar terms such as *self-evident* and *inalienable.* Then have students close their textbooks and write a paraphrase of the first paragraph. **EL** **CA 11WA2.2a**

Answers and Additional Support

What It Means
The Preamble The Declaration of Independence has four parts. The Preamble explains why the Continental Congress drew up the Declaration.

impel *force*

What It Means
Natural Rights The second part, the Declaration of Natural Rights, states that people have certain basic rights and that government should protect those rights. John Locke's ideas strongly influenced this part. In 1690 Locke wrote that government was based on the consent of the people and that people had the right to rebel if the government did not uphold their right to life, liberty, and property. The Declaration calls these rights *unalienable rights.* Unalienable means nontransferable. An unalienable right cannot be surrendered.

endowed *provided*
despotism *unlimited power*

What It Means
List of Grievances The third part of the Declaration lists the colonists' complaints against the British government. Notice that King George III is singled out for blame.

usurpations *unjust uses of power*

120   The Declaration of Independence

In Congress, July 4, 1776. The unanimous Declaration of the thirteen united States of America,

[Preamble]

When in the Course of human events, it becomes necessary for one people to dissolve the political bands which have connected them with another, and to assume among the Powers of the earth, the separate and equal station to which the Laws of Nature and of Nature's God entitle them, a decent respect to the opinions of mankind requires that they should declare the causes which **impel** them to the separation.

[Declaration of Natural Rights]

We hold these truths to be self-evident, that all men are created equal, that they are **endowed** by their Creator with certain unalienable Rights, that among these are Life, Liberty, and the pursuit of Happiness.

That to secure these rights, Governments are instituted among Men, deriving their just powers from the consent of the governed,

That whenever any Form of Government becomes destructive of these ends, it is the Right of the People to alter or to abolish it, and to institute new Government, laying its foundation on such principles and organizing its powers in such form, as to them shall seem most likely to effect their Safety and Happiness. Prudence, indeed, will dictate that Governments long established should not be changed for light and transient causes; and accordingly all experience hath shown, that mankind are more disposed to suffer, while evils are sufferable, than to right themselves by abolishing the forms to which they are accustomed. But when a long train of abuses and usurpations, pursuing invariably the same Object evinces a design to reduce them under absolute **Despotism,** it is their right, it is their duty, to throw off such Government, and to provide new Guards for their future security.

[List of Grievances]

Such has been the patient sufferance of these Colonies; and such is now the necessity which constrains them to alter their former Systems of Government. The history of the present King of Great Britain is a history of repeated injuries and **usurpations,** all having in direct object the establishment of an absolute Tyranny over these States. To prove this, let Facts be submitted to a candid world.

He has refused his Assent to Laws, the most wholesome and necessary for the public good.

EXTENDING THE CONTENT

Real Title Strictly speaking, the title of this famous document is not the "Declaration of Independence," but rather "The Unanimous Declaration of the Thirteen United States of America." The document was not the act by which independence was declared. That had been done on July 2, when the Continental Congress adopted Lee's resolution.

He has forbidden his Governors to pass Laws of immediate and pressing importance, unless suspended in their operation till his Assent should be obtained; and when so suspended, he has utterly neglected to attend to them.

He has refused to pass other Laws for the accommodation of large districts of people, unless those people would **relinquish** the right of Representation in the Legislature, a right **inestimable** to them and formidable to tyrants only.

He has called together legislative bodies at places unusual, uncomfortable, and distant from the depository of their Public Records, for the sole purpose of fatiguing them into compliance with his measures.

He has dissolved Representative Houses repeatedly, for opposing with manly firmness his invasions on the rights of the people.

He has refused for a long time, after such dissolutions, to cause others to be elected; whereby the Legislative Powers, incapable of **Annihilation,** have returned to the People at large for their exercise; the State remaining in the mean time exposed to all the dangers of invasion from without, and **convulsions** within.

He has endeavoured to prevent the population of these States; for that purpose obstructing the Laws for **Naturalization of Foreigners;** refusing to pass others to encourage their migrations hither, and raising the conditions of new Appropriations of Lands.

He has obstructed the Administration of Justice, by refusing his Assent to Laws for establishing Judiciary Powers.

He has made Judges dependent on his Will alone, for the **tenure** of their offices, and the amount and payment of their salaries.

He has erected a multitude of New Offices, and sent hither swarms of Officers to harass our people, and eat out their substance.

relinquish *give up*
inestimable *priceless*

annihilation *destruction*

convulsions *violent disturbances*

Naturalization of Foreigners *process by which foreign-born persons become citizens*

tenure *term*

C Critical Thinking

Comparing and Contrasting
The Declaration lists many accusations against King George.
Ask: Why would Britain have been opposed to allowing more immigrants to come to the colonies? *(An influx of immigrants would increase the power of the colonies; by restricting immigration, Britain could control the size of the colonial army.)* Ask students to research the current U.S. policy on immigration. Have them write a one-page report explaining how today's immigration regulations compare with the restrictions placed on immigration to the American colonies by the British before the Revolutionary War. **AL**
CA 11WA2.4c

The Declaration of Independence **121**

More Skill Practice

Identifying Central Issues Refer students to the painting on this page. Mention that the painting includes many of the delegates who also signed the Constitution. Discuss differences and similarities between this group and the current members of the United States Congress. The discussion can include observations about numbers, gender, ethnicity, age, style of dress, and so on. Point out that in the eyes of the British government, each of these representatives was guilty of treason. **Ask: How does the artist convey the serious mood of the event?** *(Answers will vary and may include the somber expressions on the men's faces, the dark clothing, the lack of light, or the lack of decorations.)* **OL**

The Declaration of Independence

S Skill Practice

Conducting Research Organize students into small groups. Assign each group one or two of the grievances listed in the Declaration of Independence. Have the groups find specific events, acts, or statements made by the king or Parliament that relate to the grievance. Have the groups read aloud the grievances that they were assigned and state the information that relates to the grievance. **OL** **CA HR4**

W Writing Support

Persuasive Writing Tell students to write an editorial about the Declaration of Independence for an influential Loyalist newspaper in Boston. Point out that their editorials should support the position of the newspaper and therefore should explain why the colonists should remain loyal to Great Britain. **AL** **CA 11WS1.1**

Answers and Additional Support

---

quartering *lodging*

render *make*

abdicated *given up*

perfidy *violation of trust*

insurrections *rebellions*

petitioned for redress *asked formally for a correction of wrongs*

unwarrantable jurisdiction *unjustified authority*

consanguinity *originating from the same ancestor*

He has kept among us, in times of peace, Standing Armies without the Consent of our legislature.

He has affected to render the Military independent of and superior to the Civil Power.

He has combined with others to subject us to a jurisdiction foreign to our constitution, and unacknowledged by our laws; giving his Assent to their acts of pretended legislation:

For **quartering** large bodies of troops among us:

For protecting them, by a mock Trial, from Punishment for any Murders which they should commit on the Inhabitants of these States:

For cutting off our Trade with all parts of the world:

For imposing taxes on us without our Consent:

For depriving us in many cases, of the benefits of Trial by Jury:

For transporting us beyond Seas to be tried for pretended offences:

For abolishing the free System of English Laws in a neighbouring Province, establishing therein an Arbitrary government, and enlarging its Boundaries so as to **render** it at once an example and fit instrument for introducing the same absolute rule into these Colonies:

For taking away our Charters, abolishing our most valuable Laws, and altering fundamentally the Forms of our Governments:

For suspending our own Legislature, and declaring themselves invested with Power to legislate for us in all cases whatsoever.

He has **abdicated** Government here, by declaring us out of his Protection and waging War against us.

He has plundered our seas, ravaged our Coasts, burnt our towns, and destroyed the lives of our people.

He is at this time transporting large armies of foreign mercenaries to compleat the works of death, desolation and tyranny, already begun with circumstances of Cruelty & **perfidy** scarcely paralleled in the most barbarous ages, and totally unworthy the Head of a civilized nation.

He has constrained our fellow Citizens taken Captive on the high Seas to bear Arms against their Country, to become the executioners of their friends and Brethren, or to fall themselves by their Hands.

He has excited domestic **insurrections** amongst us, and has endeavoured to bring on the inhabitants of our frontiers, the merciless Indian Savages, whose known rule of warfare, is an undistinguished destruction of all ages, sexes and conditions.

In every stage of these Oppressions We have **Petitioned for Redress** in the most humble terms: Our repeated Petitions have been answered only by repeated injury. A Prince, whose character is thus marked by every act which may define a Tyrant, is unfit to be the ruler of a free People.

Nor have We been wanting in attention to our British brethren. We have warned them from time to time of attempts by their legislature to extend an **unwarrantable jurisdiction** over us. We have reminded them of the circumstances of our emigration and settlement here. We have appealed to their native justice and magnanimity, and we have conjured them by the ties of our common kindred to disavow these usurpations, which, would inevitably interrupt our connections and correspondence. They too have been deaf to the voice of justice and of **consanguinity**. We must, therefore, acquiesce in the necessity, which denounces our Separation, and hold them, as we hold the rest of mankind, Enemies in War, in Peace Friends.

More Skill Practice

Connecting Organize students into groups of four. Point out that the Declaration has been a force for change in the United States. People have used words and ideas like the principle of "unwarrantable jurisdiction" to promote such measures as the abolition of slavery and equal rights for women. Have each group use library and Internet resources to research three examples in which an individual or a group used the words and ideas expressed in the Declaration to promote change or reform. **AL** **CA HI1**

[Resolution of Independence by the United States]

We, therefore, the Representatives of the united States of America, in General Congress, Assembled, appealing to the Supreme Judge of the world for the **rectitude** of our intentions, do, in the Name, and by Authority of the good People of these Colonies, solemnly publish and declare, That these United Colonies are, and of Right ought to be Free and Independent States; that they are Absolved from all Allegiance to the British Crown, and that all political connection between them and the State of Great Britain, is and ought to be totally dissolved; and that as Free and Independent States, they have full Power to levy War, conclude Peace, contract Alliances, establish Commerce, and to do all other Acts and Things which Independent States may of right do.

And for the support of this Declaration, with a firm reliance on the Protection of Divine Providence, we mutually pledge to each other our Lives, our Fortunes and our sacred Honor.

John Hancock
    President from
    Massachusetts

Georgia
Button Gwinnett
Lyman Hall
George Walton

North Carolina
William Hooper
Joseph Hewes
John Penn

South Carolina
Edward Rutledge
Thomas Heyward, Jr.
Thomas Lynch, Jr.
Arthur Middleton

Maryland
Samuel Chase
William Paca
Thomas Stone
Charles Carroll
    of Carrollton

Virginia
George Wythe
Richard Henry Lee
Thomas Jefferson
Benjamin Harrison
Thomas Nelson, Jr.
Francis Lightfoot Lee
Carter Braxton

Pennsylvania
Robert Morris
Benjamin Rush
Benjamin Franklin
John Morton
George Clymer
James Smith
George Taylor
James Wilson
George Ross

Delaware
Caesar Rodney
George Read
Thomas McKean

New York
William Floyd
Philip Livingston
Francis Lewis
Lewis Morris

New Jersey
Richard Stockton
John Witherspoon
Francis Hopkinson
John Hart
Abraham Clark

New Hampshire
Josiah Bartlett
William Whipple
Matthew Thornton

Massachusetts
Samuel Adams
John Adams
Robert Treat Paine
Elbridge Gerry

Rhode Island
Stephen Hopkins
William Ellery

Connecticut
Samuel Huntington
William Williams
Oliver Wolcott
Roger Sherman

What It Means
Resolution of Independence
The Final section declares that the colonies are "Free and Independent States" with the full power to make war, to form alliances, and to trade with other countries.

rectitude *rightness*

What It Means
Signers of the Declaration The signers, as representatives of the American people, declared the colonies independent from Great Britain. Most members signed the document on August 2, 1776.

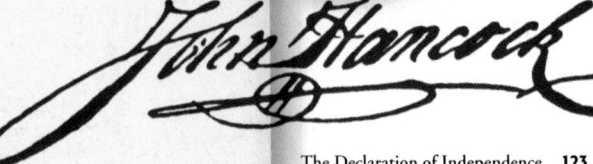

The Declaration of Independence **123**

More Skill Practice

Identifying Central Issues Ask students to identify what they believe to be the most important idea expressed in the Declaration of Independence. Have students write a paragraph stating the idea and explaining their choice. **OL**

CA 11WA2.4a

The Declaration of Independence

ASSESS

C Critical Thinking

Analyzing Primary Sources
Have students create a three-column chart that lists each of the four sections of the Declaration of Independence, provides a brief summary of each section, and explains the purpose of each section. *(Preamble: explains Declaration's purpose; Declaration of Natural Rights: government should protect people's inalienable rights; List of Grievances: colonial justification for revolutionary action; Resolution of Independence: declares powers of newly independent nation)* **OL**

S Skill Practice

Making Oral Presentations
Tell students that the Declaration of Independence had significant influence on independence movements in other countries whose citizens felt that their leaders were unfit to rule. Organize the class into groups of four. Assign each group one of the following: the French Revolution, Latin American independence movements, Tiananmen Square demonstrations, or the breakup of the Soviet Union. Have the groups use library and Internet resources to learn about their assigned movement and the effects that the Declaration of Independence had on the movement. Have the groups prepare an oral report on their findings. **OL** **CA HR4**

CLOSE

Organizing Information Have students list the powers that the newly independent states planned to claim. **OL**

123

FOCUS

SKILLBUILDER ACTIVITY

Project **Daily Focus Skills Transparency 1-3** and have students answer the question.

Guide to Reading

Understanding Vocabulary: Pair students to list the section's vocabulary words and write a definition for each. Ask them to see if their definitions match each word's usage in this section.

Answers to Graphic: Federalists—supported by landowners, merchants; Goals: strengthen central government. Antifederalists—supported by small farmers; Goals: strengthen state governments

Unpacking the Standards

Students will be able to:

• Describe the features of the governments set up under the Articles of Confederation and the Constitution.

• Identify key events leading up to ratification of the Constitution.

Answers and Additional Support

SECTION 3 · The Constitution

Guide to Reading

Connection
In the previous section, you learned how the American colonists defeated the British in the Revolutionary War. In this section, you will discover how America's founders authored the United States Constitution.

Main Idea
• The states created constitutions that gave people more rights, but the national framework could not address all the problems of the new nation. (p. 125)
• American leaders created a new constitution based on compromise. (p. 126)
• The promise of a Bill of Rights guaranteed the ratification of the Constitution. (p. 129)

Content Vocabulary
republic, recession, popular sovereignty, federalism, separation of powers, checks and balances, veto, amendment, ratification

Academic Vocabulary
framework, interpret, revise

People and Terms to Identify
Articles of Confederation, Northwest Ordinance, Shays's Rebellion, Constitutional Convention, Great Compromise, Three-Fifths Compromise, Federalists, Antifederalists

Reading Objectives
• **Describe** features of the governments set up under the Articles of Confederation and the Constitution.
• **Identify** key steps and events leading up to ratification of the Constitution.

Reading Strategy
Categorizing As you read about the efforts to ratify the Constitution, complete a graphic organizer similar to the one below by listing the supporters and goals of the Federalists and Antifederalists.

	Federalists	Antifederalists
Source of Support		
Goals		

Preview of Events

♦1777	♦1782	♦1787	♦1792

November 1777
Articles of Confederation adopted

May 1787
Constitutional Convention opens in Philadelphia

September 1787
Final draft of Constitution signed

May 1790
Constitution ratified by all thirteen states

The following are the main History–Social Science Standards covered in this section.

11.1 Students analyze the significant events surrounding the founding of the nation and its attempts to realize the philosophy of government described in the Declaration of Independence.

11.1.1 Describe the Enlightenment and the rise of democratic ideas as the context in which the nation was founded.

11.1.2 Analyze the ideological origins of the American Revolution, the Founding Fathers' philosophy of divinely bestowed unalienable natural rights, the debates on the drafting and ratification of the Constitution, and the addition of the Bill of Rights.

⫷ The Big Idea ⫸

A written contract between the people and their government can preserve natural rights and allow for change over time. States adopted individual constitutions that called for a government with powers divided among three different branches. Lawmakers stressed individual liberty and separation of church and state, but women and African Americans continued to be denied political rights. The states finally ratified the national Constitution after many compromises and the proposal of a Bill of Rights.

124 CHAPTER 1 Creating a Nation

SECTION RESOURCES

📁 Print Material
• Reproducible Lesson Plan 1-3
• Guided Reading Activity 1-3
• Reading Essentials and Study Guide 1-3
• Active Reading Note-Taking Guide 1-3

📇 Transparencies
• Daily Focus Skills Transparency 1-3
• Section Graphic Organizer Transparency 1-3

Technology
🔘 Interactive Tutor Self-Assessment CD-ROM
🔘 ExamView® Pro Testmaker CD-ROM
🔘 Presentation Plus! CD-ROM

The Young Nation

Main Idea The states created constitutions that gave people more rights, but the national framework could not address all the problems of the new nation.

Reading Connection If you had lived in the colonies under British rule, what kind of government would you have created? Read on to learn how the American leaders at first created a weak central government.

The democratic spirit burned stronger than ever after the Revolution. Notions of equality and freedom, which had inspired the fight for independence, now took firmer root.

★ *An American Story* ★

In 1781 an enslaved Massachusetts man named Quock Walker took an extraordinary step: He took legal action against his slaveholder who had assaulted him. Given the times, this was a bold step, but Walker believed he had the law on his side. Massachusetts's new constitution referred to the "inherent liberty" of all men. The judge, William Cushing, agreed:

66 Our Constitution [of Massachusetts] sets out with declaring that all men are born free and equal—and that every subject is entitled to liberty, and to have guarded by the laws, as well as life and property—and in short totally repugnant to the idea of being born slaves. This being the case, I think the idea of slavery is inconsistent with our own conduct and Constitution. 99

While the Quock Walker case did not abolish slavery, it demonstrated that the Massachusetts courts would not support the institution. As a result of this ruling and various antislavery efforts, slavery ceased to exist in Massachusetts.

—adapted from *Founding the Republic*

Wooden statue of an African American breaking his chain

The Walker case showed that republican ideas began to change American society.

New State Constitutions When American leaders created the United States of America, they made a deliberate choice to replace royal rule with a republic. In a **republic**, power resides with citizens who are entitled to vote, and elected leaders must govern according to laws or a constitution.

Before the war ended, each state had drawn up its own written constitution. Virginia's, written in 1776, and Massachusetts's, drafted in 1780, became models for other states to follow. Their constitutions called for a government with a separation of powers among the executive, legislative, and judicial branches. They set up bicameral, or two-house, legislatures, with a senate to represent people of property and an assembly to protect the rights of the common people. They also included a list of rights guaranteeing essential freedoms.

Other states varied in their constitutions. Perhaps most democratic was that of Pennsylvania. Rather than simply limiting the power of the governor, the Pennsylvania constitution eliminated the position entirely, along with the upper house. Instead, the state would be governed by a one-house legislature in which representatives would be elected annually.

The Revolution Changes Society

The concern for individual liberty led, among other things, to greater separation of church and state. For example, the Virginia Statute of Religious Freedom, passed in 1786, declared that Virginia no longer had an official church and that the state could not collect taxes to support churches.

Voting rights also expanded in the post-war years. Many states allowed any white male taxpayer to vote, whether or not he owned property. Property restrictions on running for office were also relaxed, and more people of modest means became eligible to serve in government.

Women and African Americans, however, continued to be denied political rights. At the same time, they made some advances. Women gained greater access to education and could more easily obtain

CHAPTER 1 Creating a Nation **125**

U Universal Access

Kinesthetic Have students work together in groups of three to create a piece of antislavery art, using the picture of the statue on this page as an example. Invite representatives from each group to share their art project with the entire class. Display projects in the classroom. **BL**

C₁ Critical Thinking

Identifying Central Issues Write the words *Monarchy* and *Republic* on the board. Have students list words that describe each of these forms of government. Review the lists and ask students to identify pairs of opposite words. **BL**

C₂ Critical Thinking

Comparing and Contrasting Organize students into groups of four and assign each group a different state. Have groups use library and Internet resources to learn about the constitution of their assigned state. Have the groups learn when the constitution was ratified and identify its basic provisions. Conduct a class discussion comparing and contrasting the various constitutions with each other. **AL**

Did You Know?

Suffrage is another term for the right to vote. For example, you can say that suffrage was extended to more citizens after the Revolutionary War.

U₁ Universal Access

Visual/Spatial Provide the data shown below. Ask students to select one of the states and create three circle graphs, one for each year, showing the number of enslaved persons as a segment of the total population. **OL**

Number of Enslaved Persons

	1790	1800	1810
New York	21,193	20,613	15,017
Pennsylvania	3,707	1,706	795
Rhode Island	958	380	108

Total Population

	1790	1800	1810
New York	340,241	586,182	959,049
Pennsylvania	433,611	602,365	810,019
Rhode Island	69,112	69,122	76,931

U₂ Universal Access

Advanced Learners Tell students that English clergyman Josiah Tucker claimed that once the British were gone, "the Americans will have no center of union among them, and no common interest to pursue." Ask:
Was Tucker's prediction accurate for the 1780s? *(Answers will vary.)* Have the class write a one-page story demonstrating the difficulties in forming a union. **AL**

✓ Reading Check

Answer: could not control national trade or commerce, could not enforce treaties

Answers and Additional Support

divorces. African Americans still faced discrimination, but opposition to slavery began to mount. Thousands of enslaved Africans achieved freedom during the Revolution in return for their military service. Several Northern states, such as Massachusetts, even took steps to end slavery entirely, albeit gradually. In the South enslaved labor remained the backbone of the economy, and little changed for African Americans.

A Weak National Government While the states wrote their individual constitutions, American leaders worked to plan a central government that could hold the new nation together. On March 2, 1781, the **framework** they created took effect. The **Articles of Confederation** loosely unified the states under a single governing body, the Confederation Congress. There were no separate branches of government, and Congress had only limited powers. After fighting to free themselves from Britain's domineering rule, the states did not want to create a new government that might become tyrannical.

Some Weaknesses of the Articles of Confederation

Provision	Problem Created
Congress has no power to tax	Weak currency and growing debt
	Inability to pay army leads to threats of mutiny
Congress has no power to enforce treaties	Foreign countries angry when treaties are not honored; for example, Britain keeps troops on American soil
Every state, despite size, has one vote	Populous states not equally represented
Congress has no power to regulate commerce	Trade hindered by states imposing high tariffs on each other
Amendment requires unanimous vote of states	Difficult to adapt articles to changing needs

Chart *Skills*

1. **Interpreting Charts** What was the problem with requiring a unanimous vote of the states to create changes in the Articles of Confederation?
2. **Analyzing** Why did the states approve a government with so many weaknesses?

Under the Articles, each state had one vote in Congress. Congress could act only in certain arenas, however. It could negotiate with other nations, raise armies, and declare war, but it had no authority to regulate trade or impose taxes.

One of Congress's achievements was the **Northwest Ordinance** of 1787, a plan for selling and then governing the new lands west of the Appalachian Mountains and north of the Ohio River. The ordinance spelled out how states would be created from the Northwest Territory. It also guaranteed residents certain rights, including freedom of religion and freedom from slavery.

Congress lacked the power to effectively handle other challenges. Trade problems arose because states did not have uniform trade policies and Congress had no authority to intervene. Foreign relations suffered because Congress could not compel the states to honor its agreements with other countries. The country sank into a severe **recession,** or economic slowdown, because without the power to tax, Congress could not raise enough money to pay its war debts or its expenses. It could not even stop the states from issuing their own currency, which sent the economy spinning further out of control.

Among those hardest hit by the recession were poor farmers. Their discontent turned violent in January 1787, when a bankrupt Massachusetts farmer named Daniel Shays led some 1,200 followers in a protest of new taxes. **Shays's Rebellion** was put down by the state militia, but the incident raised fears about the direction in which the country was heading. As the weaknesses of the Confederation Congress became clear, people began to call for a stronger central government.

✓ Reading Check
Explaining In what ways was the Confederation Congress ineffective?

A New Constitution

Main Idea American leaders created a new constitution based on compromise.

Reading Connection Have you ever come up with new rules to a game because the old ones did not work? Read on to learn how the Constitution replaced the Articles of Confederation.

In May 1787, every state except Rhode Island sent delegates to Philadelphia "for the sole purpose of revising the Articles of Confederation." Instead of

Chart *Skills*

Answers:
1. It was virtually impossible to adapt the Articles to changing needs.
2. Possible answer: They wanted to retain power.

changing the Articles, though, the delegates quickly decided to abandon the Articles and write a brand-new framework of government. The meeting, attended by 55 of America's most distinguished leaders, is therefore known as the **Constitutional Convention.** The delegates chose George Washington as their presiding officer. Other notable delegates included Benjamin Franklin, Alexander Hamilton, and James Madison.

Debate and Compromise All the delegates supported a stronger national government with the power to levy taxes and make laws that would be binding upon the states. The delegates also accepted the idea of dividing the government into executive, legislative, and judicial branches.

On other points, the delegates found themselves split. One contentious question was whether each state should have an equal vote in Congress. Small states favored such a plan, but the larger states insisted that representation in Congress should be based on population. The convention appointed a special committee to find a compromise. Ben Franklin, one of the committee members, warned the delegates what would happen if they failed to agree:

66 [You will] become a reproach and by-word down to future ages. And what is worse, mankind may hereafter, from this unfortunate instance, despair of establishing governments by human wisdom, and leave it to chance, war, and conquest. 99

—quoted in *American History*

The committee's solution was based on a suggestion by Roger Sherman from Connecticut. Congress would be divided into two houses. In one, the House of Representatives, the number of a state's representatives would depend on its population. In the other house, the Senate, each state would have equal representation. The eligible voters in each state would elect members to the House of Representatives, but the state legislatures would choose senators. This proposal came to be known as the **Great Compromise** or the Connecticut Compromise.

The Connecticut Compromise sparked a fresh controversy: whether to count enslaved people when determining how many representatives a state could elect to the House. The matter was settled by the **Three-Fifths Compromise.** Every five enslaved people in a state would count as three free persons for determining both representation and taxation.

S Skill Practice

Historical Interpretation Have students imagine that they are delegates to the Constitutional Convention. Have them list the freedoms they want to be included in the new constitution. Instruct students to write a paragraph explaining why they feel it is important to guarantee these rights. OL CA HI1; HI3; HI4

C Critical Thinking

Conducting a Debate Divide the class into three equal groups. Assign one group to research the small states' position of equal representation in Congress. Ask the second group to research the large states' argument that representation should be based on population. Tell each group to prepare arguments that present their position favorably while critiquing the other group's position. The third group should listen to and judge the effectiveness of each debating group's argument. OL

". . . to form a more perfect union . . ."

—*Preamble to the Constitution*

 History *Through Art*

We the People The delegates at Philadelphia devised a new government that tried to balance national and state power. What compromises were necessary to complete the Constitution?

CHAPTER 1 Creating a Nation **127**

History *Through Art*

Answer: determining state representation, how to count enslaved persons, how to regulate trade
Ask: Why was George Washington chosen to be the presiding officer? (*He was a widely respected war hero.*)

Resources for page 127

Have students read more about one man's effort to eliminate enslaved labor during the early Constitution period in the **Primary Source Reading 1-2.**

U₁ Universal Access

English Learners Have students work in pairs or small groups to create posters that explain the principles of federalism. Invite the groups to share their posters with the class. Display the posters and use them as a starting point to discuss the importance of federalism in shaping the new nation. **EL**

U₂ Universal Access

Visual/Spatial Have students create a diagram that shows the powers granted to each branch of government and how each branch can limit the power of the other two branches. **Ask:** Do you think that a system of checks and balances is important to maintaining a democracy? Why or why not? Have students write a short paragraph explaining their answer. Remind them to refer to specific examples when constructing their responses. **OL** **CA 11WA2.4a**

Answers and Additional Support

Picturing History

Historic Landmark The Philadelphia Statehouse, the site of the Constitutional Convention, was later renamed Independence Hall. How did the Framers preserve the rights of the states?

In another compromise, the delegates dealt with the power of Congress to regulate trade. Delegates agreed that the new Congress could not tax exports. They also agreed that it could not ban the slave trade until 1808 or impose high taxes on the import of enslaved persons.

A Framework for Limited Government With the major disputes behind them, the delegates now focused on the details of how the new government would operate. The new Constitution they crafted was based on the principle of **popular sovereignty** (SAH·vuhrn·tee), or rule by the people. Rather than a direct democracy, it created a representative system of government in which elected officials speak for the people.

U₁ To strengthen the central government but still preserve the rights of the states, the Constitution created a system known as **federalism.** Under federalism, power is divided between the federal, or national, government and the state governments.

The Constitution also provided for a **separation of powers** among the three branches of the federal government. The two houses of Congress made up the legislative branch of the government. They would make the laws. The executive branch, headed by a president, would implement and enforce the laws Congress passed. The president would perform other duties as well, such as serving as commander in chief of the armed forces. The judicial branch—a system of federal courts—would **interpret** federal laws and render judgment in cases

HISTORY Online

Student Web Activity Visit the *American Vision: Modern Times* Web site at tav.mt.glencoe.com and click on **Student Web Activities— Chapter 1** for an activity on the Constitution.

involving those laws. To keep the branches separate, no one serving in one branch could serve in either of the other branches at the same time.

Checks and Balances In addition to giving each of the three branches of government separate powers, the framers of the Constitution created a system of **checks and balances**—a means for each branch to monitor and limit the power of the other two.

For example, the president could check Congress by deciding to **veto,** or reject, a proposed law. The legislature would need a two-thirds vote in both houses to override a veto. The Senate also had the power to approve or reject presidential appointees to the executive branch and treaties the president negotiated. Congress also could impeach the president **U₂** and other high-ranking officials in the executive or judicial branch; that is, the House could formally accuse such officials of misconduct. If the officials were convicted during trial in the Senate, they would be removed from office.

Members of the judicial branch of government could hear all cases arising under federal laws and the Constitution. The powers of the judiciary were counterbalanced by the other two branches. The president would nominate judges, including a chief justice of the Supreme Court, but the Senate had to confirm or reject such nominations. Once appointed, federal judges, including the chief justice, would serve for life to ensure their independence from both the executive and the legislative branches.

Amending the Constitution The delegates in Philadelphia recognized that the Constitution they wrote in the summer of 1787 might need to be **revised** over time. To allow this to happen, they created a clear system for making **amendments,** or

Picturing History

Answer: A system known as federalism divided power between the federal government and the states.
Ask: How long did the Constitutional Convention last? *(about 4 months, from May to September 1787)*

HISTORY Online

Objectives and answers to the student activity can be found in the **Web Activity Lesson Plan** at tav.mt.glencoe.com.

changes, to the Constitution. To prevent frivolous changes, however, they made the process difficult.

Amending the Constitution would require two steps: proposal and ratification. An amendment could be proposed by a vote of two-thirds of the members of both houses of Congress. Alternatively, two-thirds of the states could call a constitutional convention to propose new amendments. To become effective, the proposed amendment would then have to be ratified by three-fourths of the state legislatures or by conventions in three-fourths of the states.

✓ **Reading Check** **Summarizing** What compromises did the delegates agree on during the convention?

The Fight for Ratification

Main Idea The promise of a Bill of Rights guaranteed the ratification of the Constitution.

Reading Connection Have you ever had to convince a friend to agree to something? Read on to learn how the states agreed to ratify the Constitution.

On September 28, the Confederation Congress voted to submit the Constitution to the states. Each state would hold a convention to vote on it. To go into effect, the Constitution required the **ratification**, or approval, of 9 of the 13 states.

Delaware became the first state to ratify the Constitution, on December 7, 1787. Pennsylvania, New Jersey, Georgia, and Connecticut quickly followed suit. The most important battles still lay ahead. Arguments broke out among Americans debating whether the Constitution should be ratified.

Debating the Constitution In fact, debate over ratification began at once—in state legislatures, mass meetings, newspapers, and everyday conversations. Supporters of the Constitution called themselves **Federalists.** They chose the name to emphasize that the Constitution would create a federal system—one with power divided between a central government and state governments.

Many Federalists were large landowners who wanted the property protection that a strong central government could provide. Supporters also included merchants and artisans in large coastal cities and farmers who depended on trade. They all believed that an effective federal government that could impose taxes on foreign goods or regulate interstate trade consistently would help their businesses.

Opponents of the Constitution were called **Antifederalists,** although they were not truly against federalism. They accepted the need for a national government, but they were concerned about whether the federal or state governments would be supreme. Some Antifederalists also believed that the new Constitution needed a bill of rights.

U **Universal Access**

Visual/Spatial Have students create a political cartoon that supports the Federalist position. Remind students that political cartoons often convey their message by attacking the opposite point of view. Display political cartoon in and around your classroom, and have students vote on which one is the most effective. **OL**

W **Writing Support**

Persuasive Writing Have students review the arguments of the Federalists and Antifederalists about the Constitution. Then ask them to write a newspaper editorial that might have been published during that time, either supporting or opposing the Constitution. Students can write their editorials from the viewpoint of one of the colonists, such as a western farmer, a merchant in a coastal city, or a large landowner. **AL** **CA** 11WS1.1

✓ **Reading Check**

Answer: the Connecticut Compromise, the Three-Fifths Compromise, and compromises limiting the federal government's power to impose certain types of taxes and to regulate slavery

Profiles IN HISTORY

James Madison
1751–1836

Although many individuals contributed to the framing of the United States Constitution, the master builder was James Madison. An avid reader, the 36-year-old Virginia planter spent the better part of the year preceding the Philadelphia Convention with his nose in books. Madison read volume after volume on governments throughout history. He scoured the records of ancient Greece and Rome and delved into the administrations of Italian city-states such as Florence and Venice. He even looked at the systems used by federal alliances like Switzerland and the Netherlands. "From a spirit of industry and application," said one colleague, Madison was "the best-informed man on any point in debate."

Bringing together his research and his experience in helping to draft Virginia's constitution, Madison created the Virginia Plan. His proposal strongly influenced the final document.

Perhaps Madison's greatest achievement was in defining the true source of political power. He argued that all power, at all levels of government, flowed ultimately from the people.

At the Constitutional Convention, Madison served his nation well. The ordeal, he later said, "almost killed" him. As one of the authors of *the Federalist,* he helped get the Constitution ratified. In the years to come, the nation would call on him again. In 1801 he became President Thomas Jefferson's secretary of state. In 1808 he was elected the fourth president of the United States.

Profiles IN HISTORY

Have students review the profile of James Madison and write down three questions about his life that cannot be answered by the profile. Instruct the class to use library and Internet resources to find the answers. Use these questions and answers as a basis for a discussion about Madison.

S Skill Practice

Identifying Point of View Write the word *Democracy* on the board. Have students review the arguments of James Madison and Thomas Jefferson on this page. **Ask: In your opinion, does Jefferson or Madison best defend the principles of democracy? Why?** Instruct students to write a short paragraph explaining their answer. `OL` `CA HR2; HR3`

Review the Big Idea

Review the Big Idea for this section, "A written constitution between the people and their government can preserve natural rights and allow for change over time." Organize the class into groups of five, and have each group create a classroom bill of rights. Then lead students in a discussion of the various classroom rights proposed and have them vote on which ones they feel are most important. Point out that the Bill of Rights was the first occurrence of a change to the Constitution. **Ask: Why did the addition of a Bill of Rights encourage Antifederalists to ratify the Constitution?** *(Students may note that a Bill of Rights guaranteed individual freedoms and supported states' rights.)* `OL`

Answers and Additional Support

As the states prepared to vote on ratification, both sides knew the decision could go either way. Those in favor of the Constitution summarized their arguments in *The Federalist*—a collection of 85 essays written by James Madison, Alexander Hamilton, and John Jay. The essays were extremely influential. Even today, judges, lawyers, legislators, and historians rely upon *The Federalist* papers to help interpret the intention of the framers of the Constitution. 📖 *(See page 990 for an excerpt from Federalist Paper No. 10.)*

Ratification in Massachusetts In Massachusetts opponents of the proposed Constitution held a clear majority. They included Samuel Adams, who had signed the Declaration of Independence but now strongly believed the Constitution endangered the independence of the states and failed to safeguard Americans' rights.

Federalists quickly promised to attach a bill of rights to the Constitution once it was ratified. They also agreed to support an amendment that would reserve for the states or the people all powers not specifically granted to the federal government. These Federalist promises and the support of artisans guaranteed Massachusetts's approval. In 1791 the promises led to the adoption of the first ten amendments to the Constitution, which came to be known as the Bill of Rights. The amendments guaranteed the

Different Viewpoints

Should the Majority Rule?

James Madison argued persuasively for the Constitution's ratification. In *The Federalist #10,* Madison explained that the Constitution would prevent the effects of *faction*—the self-seeking party spirit of a democracy. In contrast, Thomas Jefferson argued that the will of the majority would thwart the tyranny of oppressive government.

James Madison opposes majority rule:

"When a majority is included in a faction, the form of popular government . . . enables it to sacrifice to its ruling passion or interest both the public good and the rights of other citizens.

. . . [A] pure democracy . . . can admit of no cure for the mischiefs of faction [and has always] been found incompatible with personal security or the rights of property. . . .

A republic, by which I mean a government in which the scheme of representation takes place . . . promises the cure for which we are seeking. . . .

The effect of [a republic] is, on the one hand, to refine and enlarge the public views, by passing them through the medium of a chosen body of citizens, whose wisdom may best discern the true interest of their country, and whose patriotism and love of justice will be least likely to sacrifice it to temporary or partial considerations."

Thomas Jefferson defends majority rule:

"I own I am not a friend to a very energetic government. It is always oppressive. The late rebellion in Massachusetts has given more alarm than I think it should have done. Calculate that one rebellion in 13 states in the course of 11 years, is but one for each state in a century & a half. No country should be long without one.

. . . After all, it is my principle that the will of the Majority should always prevail. If they approve the proposed [Constitution] in all its parts, I shall concur in it chearfully, in hopes that they will amend it whenever they shall find it works wrong. . . . Above all things I hope the education of the common people will be attended to; convinced that on their good sense we may rely with the most security for the preservation of a due degree of liberty."

Learning From History

1. What were the "mischiefs" that Madison believed republican government could prevent?
2. **Historical Analysis** Was Jefferson correct in believing the voice of the common people would preserve liberty? Explain. `CA HR1`

Different Viewpoints

Learning from History
Answers:
1. the majority or a large faction making decisions in its own interest to the detriment of all others
2. Students should note that the United States today is still based on the same freedoms that were articulated by the Founders.

Ask: Do you think that Thomas Jefferson supported Shays's rebellion? *(He did not necessarily support the rebellion; rather, he supported the idea that people have the right to protest against their government or against laws that oppress them.)*

freedoms of speech, press, and religion; protection from unreasonable searches and seizures; and the right to a trial by jury.

Maryland easily ratified the Constitution in April 1788, followed by South Carolina in May. On June 21, New Hampshire became the ninth state to ratify the Constitution. The Federalists had now reached the minimum number of states required to put the new Constitution into effect. Virginia and New York, however, still had not ratified. Together, Virginia and New York represented almost 30 percent of the nation's population. Without the support of these states, many feared the new government would not succeed.

Virginia and New York At the Virginia convention in June, George Washington and James Madison presented strong arguments for ratification. Patrick Henry, Richard Henry Lee, and other Antifederalists argued against it. Madison's promise to add a bill of rights won the day for the Federalists—but barely. The Virginia convention voted 89 in favor of the Constitution and 79 against.

In New York, two-thirds of the members elected to the state convention were Antifederalists. The Federalists, led by Alexander Hamilton and John Jay, managed to delay the final vote until news arrived that New Hampshire and Virginia had both voted to ratify the Constitution and that the new federal government was now in effect. If New York refused to ratify, it would have to operate independently of all of the surrounding states that had accepted the Constitution. This argument convinced enough Antifederalists to change sides. The vote was very close, 30 to 27, but the Federalists won.

By July 1788, all the states except Rhode Island and North Carolina had ratified the Constitution. Because ratification by nine states was all that the Constitution required, the members of the Confederation Congress prepared to proceed without them. In mid-September 1788, they established a timetable for electing the new government. The new Congress would hold its first meeting on March 4, 1789.

The two states that had held out finally ratified the Constitution after the new government was in place. North Carolina waited until November 1789 after a bill of rights had actually been proposed. Rhode Island, still nervous about losing its independence, did not ratify the Constitution until May 1790.

The United States now had a new government, but no one knew if the Constitution would work any better than the Articles of Confederation. Many expressed great confidence, however, because George Washington had been chosen as the first president under the new Constitution.

✓ Reading Check Examining Why was it important for Virginia and New York to ratify the Constitution, even after the required nine states had done so?

HISTORY Online Study Central
For help with the concepts in this section of *American Vision: Modern Times* go to tav.mt.glencoe.com and click on *Study Central.*

SECTION 3 ASSESSMENT

Checking for Understanding

1. **Vocabulary** Define: republic, framework, recession, popular sovereignty, federalism, separation of powers, interpret, checks and balances, veto, revise, amendment, ratification

2. **People and Terms** Identify: Articles of Confederation, Northwest Ordinance, Shays's Rebellion, Constitutional Convention, Great Compromise, Three-Fifths Compromise, Federalists, Antifederalists.

3. **Explain** why the Antifederalists opposed the Constitution.

Reviewing Big Ideas

4. **Describing** How was the Constitution written as a flexible framework of government?

Critical Thinking

5. **Evaluating** Did the Articles of Confederation or the Constitution provide a better way to solve the problems facing the nation? Explain.

6. **Categorizing** Use a graphic organizer similar to the one below to list the compromises the Founders reached at the Constitutional Convention.

Compromises Reached

Analyzing Visuals

7. **Analyzing Paintings** Examine the painting of the Constitutional Convention on page 127. How does the tone of the painting compare with the text's description of differences and difficulties at the convention? What purpose do you think the artist had that might account for any difference?

Writing About History

8. **Persuasive Writing** Take on the role of a Federalist or an Antifederalist at a state ratifying convention. Write a speech in which you try to convince your audience to either accept or reject the new Constitution. **CA 11WS1.3**

SECTION 3 ASSESSMENT ANSWERS

1. Content vocabulary is boldfaced and highlighted in yellow. Academic vocabulary is boldfaced.

2. Articles of Confederation (*p. 126*), Northwest Ordinance (*p. 126*), Shays's Rebellion (*p. 126*), Constitutional Convention (*p. 127*), Great Compromise (*p. 127*), Three-Fifths Compromise (*p. 127*), Federalists (*p. 129*), Antifederalists (*p. 129*)

3. disliked strong central government

4. representation in Congress was based on two formulas; could be amended without unanimity

5. Students should recognize that Constitutional government had powers that Confederation government lacked.

6. Great Compromise, Three-Fifths Compromise, compromises on trade and the slave trade

7. painting shows no division among delegates; artist may have wanted to show positive image

8. Speeches will vary but should be based on logical arguments.

S Skill Practice
Conducting Research Invite interested students to use library and Internet resources to learn the order in which the first nine states ratified the Constitution. Have students use this information to create a time line. **EL**
CA HR4

ASSESS

Resources for page 131

Use these resources to assess student mastery.

📁 Section Quiz 1-3

📁 Reading Essentials and Study Guide 1-3

💿 Interactive Tutor Self-Assessment CD-ROM

📁 California Standards Practice, Grade 11

✓ Reading Check

Answer: Without the support of these two large, influential states, many feared that the new government would not succeed.

HISTORY Online

Study Central provides audio summaries, interactive games, and online graphic organizers to help students review section content.

CLOSE

Evaluating Have students explain the major changes in American society following the War for Independence. **OL**

Primary Sources
Eyewitness to History

FOCUS

History–Social Science Standards

This feature addresses the following standard:

11.1.2 Analyze the ideological origins of the American Revolution, the Founding Fathers' philosophy of divinely bestowed unalienable natural rights, the debates on the drafting and ratification of the Constitution, and the addition of the Bill of Rights.

Understanding Vocabulary

Before students begin reading, point out that difficult or unfamiliar words are footnoted throughout the text.

TEACH

C Critical Thinking

Analyzing Primary Sources
Ask students to review the statements made by Ben Franklin in the document and state in their own words the main point of this speech. (*Students' answers will vary, but all students should recognize that Franklin was unsure of the future but determined that unanimous acceptance of this new government was the best choice the convention delegates could make.*) **AL**

Primary Sources
Eyewitness to History

The leaders of the new United States wanted to limit the power of the federal government. Their plan for government, the Articles of Confederation, had many weaknesses, and the need for a strong central government soon became evident. In May 1787, a small group of men met in Philadelphia to write the Constitution. The adoption of the Constitution became a topic of heated debate.

SOURCE 1:

Benjamin Franklin was the oldest delegate at the Constitutional Convention. He proved one of the most influential delegates because of his ability to end arguments and encourage compromise. In a speech on the last day of the convention, Franklin urged his colleagues to unanimously support the new plan.

Mr. President, I confess that there are several parts of this constitution which I do not at present approve, but I am not sure I shall never approve them. For having lived long, I have experienced many instances of being **obliged**[1] by better information, or fuller consideration, to change opinions even on important subjects, which I once thought right, but found to be otherwise. . . .

. . . I doubt . . . whether any other Convention we can obtain, may be able to make a better Constitution. For when you assemble a number of men to have the advantage of their joint wisdom, you inevitably assemble with those men, all their prejudices, their passions, their errors of opinion, their local interests, and their selfish views. From such an assembly can a perfect production be expected? It therefore astonishes me, Sir, to find this system approaching so near to perfection as it does; and I think it will astonish our enemies, who are waiting with confidence to hear that our councils are confounded like those of the Builders of Babel; and that our States are on the point of separation, only to meet hereafter for the purpose of cutting one another's throats. Thus I consent, Sir, to this

▲ *George Mason*

Constitution because I expect no better, and because I am not sure, that it is not the best. The opinions I have had of its errors, I sacrifice to the public good. . . . If every one of us in returning to our Constituents were to report the objections he has had to it, and endeavor to gain partizans in support of them, we might prevent its being generally received, and thereby lose all the **salutary**[2] effects and great advantages resulting naturally in our favor among foreign Nations as well as among ourselves, from our real or apparent unanimity. Much of the strength and efficiency of any Government in procuring and securing happiness to the people, depends, on opinion, on the general opinion of the goodness of the Government, as well as well as of the wisdom and integrity of its Governors. I hope therefore that for our own sakes as a part of the people, and for the sake of posterity, we shall act heartily and unanimously in recommending this constitution (if approved by Congress and confirmed by the Conventions) wherever our influence may extend, and turn our future thoughts and endeavors to the means of having it well administred.

SOURCE 2:

George Mason, a planter and a delegate from Virginia, opposed the Constitution. While he supported a stronger national government, he wanted the states to be more powerful than the national government. Mason's speech to the convention summarized the arguments of many opponents.

---

[1] **oblige:** commit

[2] **salutary:** producing a beneficial effect

132 CHAPTER 1 Creating a Nation

UNIVERSAL ACCESS

Verbal/Linguistic Have students use library and Internet resources to write a two-page report on a key figure from this time period. The report should discuss the person's stance on the Constitution. Some suggestions include: George Washington, James Madison, John Jay, Benjamin Rush, Patrick Henry, Benjamin Franklin, and George Mason. **OL** **CA** 11WA2.4

132

▲ *James Wilson*

The Judiciary of the United States is so constructed and extended, as to absorb and destroy the judiciaries of the several States; . . .

The President of the United States has no Constitutional Council, a thing unknown in any safe and regular government. He will therefore be unsupported by proper information and advice; and will generally be directed by **minions**[3] and favorites; or he will become a tool to the Senate. . . . From this fatal defect has arisen the improper power of the Senate in the appointment of public officers, and the alarming dependence and connection between that branch of the legislature and the supreme Executive. . . .

By declaring all treaties supreme laws of the land, the Executive and the Senate have in many cases, an exclusive power of legislation; . . .

By requiring only a majority to make all commercial and navigation laws, the five Southern States, whose produce and circumstances are totally different from that of the eight Northern and eastern states, may be ruined; . . . Whereas requiring two-thirds of the members present in both Houses would have produced mutual moderation, promoted the general interest, and removed an **insuperable**[4] objection to the adoption of this Government.

There is no declaration of any kind, for preserving the liberty of the press, or the trial by jury in civil causes; nor against the danger of standing armies in time of peace.

➤ [3]**minion:** subordinate
[4]**insuperable:** incapable of being overcome

This government will set out a moderate aristocracy; it is at present impossible to forese whether it will, in its operation, produce a monarchy, or a corrupt, tyrannical aristocracy. . . .

SOURCE 3:

James Wilson, a lawyer and Pennsylvania delegate, is best known for the legal advice he gave to the Constitutional Convention. When Pennsylvania began to debate the Constitution, Wilson replied to critics.

After all, my fellow-citizens, it is neither extraordinary or unexpected that the constitution offered to your consideration should meet with opposition. It is the nature of man to pursue his own interest in preference to the public good . . . I will confess, indeed, that I am not a blind admirer of this plan of government, and that there are some parts of it which, if my wish had **prevailed**,[5] would certainly have been altered. But when I reflect how widely men differ in their opinions, and that every man (and the observation applies likewise to every State) has an equal pretension to assert his own, I am satisfied that anything nearer to perfection could not have been accomplished. If there are errors, it should be remembered that the seeds of reformation are sown in the work itself, and the concurrence of two-thirds of Congress may at any time introduce alterations and amendments. Regarding it, then, in every point of view, with a candid and disinterested mind, I am bold to assert that it is the best form of government which has ever been offered to the world.

➤ [5]**prevail:** persist

DBQ   Document-Based Questions

Historical Analysis   CA HR4; HI2; HI3

Source 1: Why does Franklin believe that the delegates should approve the Constitution?

Source 2: What are Mason's main concerns about the Constitution?

Source 3: Why does Wilson think that the Constitution will work?

Comparing and Contrasting Sources
How do Franklin, Mason, and Wilson differ in their views about concerns over apparent shortfalls of the Constitution?

Primary Sources
Eyewitness to History

C Critical Thinking

Analyzing Primary Sources
George Mason was concerned that the president would not receive adequate advice from a Constitutional Council that was not created by the Constitution. **Ask:** *Has the president, in your opinion, suffered from not receiving adequate advice? (Students should note that George Washington and every president since can rely on cabinet members and other staff for advice. These positions were not part of the Constitution.)* OL

R Reading Strategy

Summarizing Divide the class into four groups of equal size and tell each group to read the statement by James Wilson on this page. **Ask:** *Is Wilson's view similar to the views of Franklin and Mason, or does he view the Constitution differently than they did? (Wilson, like Franklin and Mason, was not entirely convinced that the Constitution was a perfect system of government, but he was confident that nothing near to perfection was possible.)* OL

ASSESS/CLOSE

Have students answer the Document-Based Questions.

DBQ   Document-Based Questions

1. He believes that the states need to approve the Constitution to defy the country's enemies, who are waiting for this effort to fail. He also thinks the convention created the best Constitution possible.

2. no Declaration of Rights, federal government superior to state governments, people not properly represented in the House, no advisory council for the president, too much power for the Senate

3. It provides a good way for Congress to make changes if necessary.

Comparing and Contrasting Sources: Franklin and Wilson both stress the strength of the Constitution, arguing it presents the best possible framework of government. Mason's criticism focuses on the weaknesses of the document, stating that there are too many weaknesses to be overcome.

Resources for pages 134–135

Use the following resources to review, assess, and reteach the chapter.

📂 Chapter 1 Tests, Forms A and B

📂 Standardized Tests, Forms A and B

📂 Cumulative Authentic Assessment

🔒 MindJogger Videoquiz

◉ Interactive Tutor Self-Assessment CD-ROM

◉ Exam*View*® Pro Testmaker CD-ROM

◉ Vocabulary PuzzleMaker CD-ROM

◉ Succeeding on . . .™ the California Standards: Grade 11 History–Social Science

📂 California Standards Practice, Grade 11

Reviewing Content Vocabulary

Students' answers will vary. The pages where the words appear in the text are shown in parentheses.

1. civilization *(p. 99)* **2.** joint-stock company *(p. 102)* **3.** Puritan *(p. 103)* **4.** proprietary colony *(p. 105)* **5.** indentured servant *(p. 106)* **6.** subsistence farming *(p. 104)* **7.** triangular trade *(p. 107)* **8.** slave code *(p. 107)* **9.** mercantilism *(p. 110)* **10.** Enlightenment *(p. 112)* **11.** Great Awakening *(p. 112)* **12.** customs duty *(p. 113)* **13.** committee of correspondence *(p. 115)* **14.** minutemen *(p. 115)* **15.** republic *(p. 125)* **16.** recession *(p. 126)* **17.** popular sovereignty *(p. 128)* **18.** federalism *(p. 128)* **19.** separation of powers *(p. 128)* **20.** checks and balances *(p. 128)* **21.** veto *(p. 128)* **22.** amendment *(p. 128)* **23.** ratify *(p. 129)*

Reviewing Academic Vocabulary

Students' answers will vary. The pages where the words appear in the text are shown in parentheses.

134

Reviewing Content Vocabulary

On a sheet of paper, use each of these terms in a sentence.

1. civilization
2. joint-stock company
3. Puritan
4. proprietary colony
5. indentured servant
6. subsistence farming
7. triangular trade
8. slave code
9. mercantilism
10. Enlightenment
11. Great Awakening
12. customs duty
13. committee of correspondence
14. minuteman
15. republic
16. recession
17. popular sovereignty
18. federalism
19. separation of powers
20. checks and balances
21. veto
22. amendment
23. ratify

Chapter Summary

Discovery and Early Settlements

- Spain, France, and England settled a new continent inhabited by many different peoples
- English colonies arose in three distinct areas of North America, with the beginnings of self government in each
- Diverse societies developed within the thirteen colonies

The Road to Independence

- Enlightenment ideas and the Great Awakening stirred colonists' first thoughts of dissent to British rule
- Unpopular laws by Parliament after the French and Indian War led to protests by colonists; colonists began to organize
- Colonists declared their independence
- In the Treaty of Paris, the defeated British recognize the United States of America

The Constitution

- States drafted individual written constitutions and set up a weak national government governed by the Articles of Confederation
- Leaders of the Constitutional Convention drafted a new constitution based on flexibility and compromise, which strengthened the central government
- States ratified the Constitution after promises of a bill of rights and shared power between the federal government and the states

134 CHAPTER 1 Creating a Nation

Reviewing Academic Vocabulary

On a sheet of paper, use each of these terms in a sentence that reflects the term's meaning in the chapter.

24. culture	27. logic	30. framework
25. immigrate	28. export	31. interpret
26. hierarchy	29. communicate	32. revise

Reviewing the Main Ideas

Section 1

33. Why did the Pilgrims leave England?
34. Why did William Penn regard his colony as a "holy experiment"?

Section 2

35. How did the Great Awakening influence the American colonies?
36. What made the Stamp Act different from other legislation that Parliament enacted?

Section 3

37. How did the Founders provide for a separation of powers in the federal government?
38. What convinced Massachusetts to ratify the Constitution?

Critical Thinking

39. **Reading Skill** **Predicting** Select one of the sections in this chapter and rewrite the headings. How could you phrase the headings so other students could make better predictions?

40. **Civics** What rights did the colonists want from Britain?

41. **Evaluating** What do you think would have happened if New York and Virginia had not ratified the Constitution?

42. **Categorizing** Use a graphic organizer similar to the one below to list the events that led to the American Revolution.

Events that led to the American Revolution

24. culture *(p. 99)* **25.** immigrate *(p. 103)* **26.** hierarchy *(p. 107)* **27.** logic *(p. 112)* **28.** export *(p. 113)* **29.** communicate *(p. 115)* **30.** framework *(p. 124)* **31.** interpret *(p. 128)* **32.** revise *(p. 128)*

Reviewing the Main Ideas

33. The Pilgrims sought religious freedom.

34. He wanted a colony in which settlers had religious freedom and a voice in government.

35. The Great Awakening undermined allegiance to traditional authority.

36. The Stamp Act was the first direct tax on colonists.

37. They specified three branches—executive, legislative, and judicial—each with specific powers. The legislative branch would make laws; the executive branch would implement and enforce laws; and the judicial branch would interpret laws. No one is allowed to serve in more than one branch at a time.

HISTORY Online

Self-Check Quiz
Visit the *American Vision: Modern Times* Web site at
tav.mt.glencoe.com and click on *Self-Check Quizzes—
Chapter 1* to assess your knowledge of chapter content.

Writing About History

43. **Historical Analysis** **Understanding Change** Select one aspect of the changes brought by European colonization and describe the change in a paragraph. Make sure you include a topic sentence and three or four descriptive sentences. **CA CS2**

44. *Big Idea* Write an editorial for a local newspaper discussing the laws the British Parliament enacted after the French and Indian War. Express your opinion about the laws and the colonists' reactions. In your editorial, include information you have gathered while studying this chapter. **CA 11WS1.1**

45. **Descriptive Writing** Take on the role of an American at the time the Constitution was ratified. Write a letter to a friend in Britain describing the kind of government provided for by the Constitution. In your letter, explain why you support or oppose ratification and what you think life will be like under the new government. **CA 11WS1.1, 11WA2.4**

DBQ Document-Based Questions

46. **Interpreting Primary Sources** In his 1789 textbook *American Geography,* Reverend Jedidiah Morse discusses the defects of the Articles of Confederation. Read the excerpt and answer the questions that follow.

66[The Articles of Confederation] were framed during the rage of war, when a principle of common safety supplied the place of a coercive power in government. . . .

When resolutions were passed in Congress, there was no power to compel obedience. . . . Had one state been invaded by its neighbor, the union was not constitutionally bound to assist in repelling the invasion. . . .99

—quoted in *Readings in American History*

a. What defects in the Articles of Confederation does Morse see?

b. Why does Morse think the Articles were effective during the American Revolution but not afterward?

NATIONAL GEOGRAPHIC **Land Claims in North America, 1783**

Hudson Bay
BRITISH NORTH AMERICA
SPANISH LOUISIANA
UNITED STATES
NEW SPAIN
PACIFIC OCEAN
ATLANTIC OCEAN
Gulf of Mexico

0 1,000 miles
0 1,000 kilometers
Azimuthal Equal-Area projection

British | Spanish
French | United States
Russian | Disputed

Geography and History

47. The map above shows the land claims in North America as a result of the 1783 Treaty of Paris. Study the map and answer the questions below.

a. **Interpreting Maps** What were the borders for the United States after the war for independence?

b. **Applying Geography Skills** Which countries shared a border with the United States?

Standards Practice

Directions: Choose the best answer to the following question.

48. Which of the following quotations best expresses the complaint of colonists who had to pay British taxes but could not vote for members of the British Parliament?

A "Give me liberty or give me death."

B "Taxation without representation is tyranny."

C "These are the times that try men's souls."

D "Don't fire until you see the whites of their eyes."

Standard 11.1.2 Analyze the ideological origins of the American Revolution, the Founding Fathers' philosophy of divinely bestowed unalienable natural rights, the debates on the drafting and ratification of the Constitution, and the addition of the Bill of Rights.

HISTORY Online

Have students visit the Web site at
tav.mt.glencoe.com to review Chapter 1 and take the Self-Check Quiz.

44. *Big Idea* Editorials should reflect a strongly held opinion supported by examples from the text.

45. Students' letters will vary. Remind students that they should explain their views on ratification and describe their expectations.

DBQ Document-Based Questions

46. **a.** They had no power to compel obedience. **b.** They were effective during the Revolution when states had a common goal.

Geography and History

47. **a.** Mississippi River to the west, Canada to the north, and original colonies in the East; **b.** British-owned Canada, Spanish-owned Spanish Louisiana and New Spain

Standards Practice

48. B

Bonus Question ?

Ask: What is the system by which the Constitution can be revised? *(The delegates provided for changes to the Constitution through the amendment process.)*

---

38. Federalists promised to add a bill of rights and to support an amendment reserving to the states all powers not specifically granted to the federal government.

41. They would have joined later or formed a separate union, or the union would have crumbled.

42. Proclamation of 1763, Sugar Act, Quartering Act, Stamp Act, Townshend Acts, Tea Act, Intolerable Acts

Critical Thinking

39. **Reading Skill** Students' phrases will vary.

40. right to tax themselves, trial by jury, protection against home searches without a warrant, and government seizing property without court proceedings

Writing About History

43. **Historical Analysis** Students' paragraphs may vary but should clearly describe the change.

The Constitution Handbook

The Constitution Handbook

FOCUS

History–Social Science Standards

This section addresses the following main standards:

11.1 Students analyze the significant events in the founding of the nation and its attempts to realize the philosophy of government described in the Declaration of Independence.

11.3 Students analyze the role religion played in the founding of America, its lasting moral, social, and political impacts, and issues regarding religious liberty.

Unpacking the Standards

Students will be able to:

• Identify the key provisions of the United States Constitution.

• Describe the responsibilities of the three branches of government.

• Describe the rights and responsibilities of American citizens.

Answers and Additional Support

EXTENDING THE CONTENT

Constitutions The United States has the oldest written national constitution still in effect. Compared to other written constitutions, it might be characterized as succinct. The average federal constitution contains about 26,500 words, while the United States Constitution with its 27 amendments has fewer than 7,500 words.

Guide to Reading

Connection
In the previous chapter, you learned about the ratification of the Constitution. In this section, you will study the Constitution in depth.

Main Idea
- The Constitution is based on several principles that assure people's rights and provide for a balance among the different branches of government. (p. 138)
- The legislative branch of government makes the nation's laws and appropriates funds. (p. 141)
- As the nation's leader, the president carries out laws with the help of executive offices, departments, and agencies. (p. 143)

- The judicial branch consists of different federal courts that review and evaluate laws and interpret the Constitution. (p. 144)
- The Constitution and the Bill of Rights provide Americans with protection and freedoms. (p. 145)
- When Americans fulfill their rights and responsibilities, they help protect the basic ideas of democracy. (p. 146)

Content Vocabulary
popular sovereignty, federalism, enumerated powers, reserved powers, concurrent powers, override, appropriate, impeach, constituent, bill, standing committee, select committee, joint committee, conference committee, cabinet, judicial review, due process

Academic Vocabulary
consent, define

Reading Objectives
- **Identify** the branches of the federal government and their separate areas of power.
- **Understand** and describe the responsibilities that American citizens share.

Reading Strategy
Taking Notes As you read about the Constitution, use the major headings of the handbook to fill in an outline similar to the one below.

I. Major Principles
  A.
  B.
  C.
  D.
  E.
  F.
  G.
II.

Preview of Events

♦1786	♦1787	♦1788	♦1789	♦1790	♦1791	♦1792

September 1786 Annapolis Convention begins

May 1787 Constitutional Convention begins

September 1787 Constitution signed and Convention adjourns

June 1788 New Hampshire ratifies Constitution, making it the new form of government

December 1791 The Bill of Rights becomes part of the Constitution

---

The following are the main History–Social Science Standards covered in this section.

11.1 Students analyze the significant events in the founding of the nation and its attempts to realize the philosophy of government described in the Declaration of Independence.

11.1.2 Analyze the ideological origins of the American Revolution, the Founding Fathers' philosophy of divinely bestowed unalienable natural rights, the debates on the drafting and ratification of the Constitution, and the addition of the Bill of Rights.

11.1.3 Understand the history of the Constitution after 1787 with emphasis on federal versus state authority and growing democratization.

The Big Idea

A written contract between the people and their government can preserve natural rights and allow for change over time. The Framers of the Constitution created a document based on seven major principles: popular sovereignty, republicanism, limited government, federalism, separation of powers, checks and balances, and individual rights. The Constitution divides the government into three main branches—legislative, executive, and judicial. These three branches work in conjunction to provide a democratic government for the people. By creating a system of checks and balances and separation of powers, the Framers ensured that power would be divided and that no one group would become too powerful. The principles on which the Constitution is based guarantee all citizens their natural rights. Citizens also have responsibilities, such as obeying laws, being familiar with the government, and voting.

The Constitution Handbook **137**

BELLRINGER
SKILLBUILDER ACTIVITY

Provide pairs of students with board games, such as chess or checkers. Have pairs play the game, but tell them there are no rules. They are to make up their own rules as they go along. After a few minutes, initiate a discussion about the needs for rules and organization. Conclude by asking students to consider why the Constitution might be regarded as a rule book for government.

Guide to Reading

Understanding Vocabulary: Provide students with blank note cards. On one side of each note card, have students write a new content or academic vocabulary word. On the other side, have them write the definition. Organize students into pairs and have them quiz each other on the vocabulary words using the flash cards they have just created.

Answers to Graphic:
I. Major Principles
  A. Popular Sovereignty
  B. Republicanism
  C. Limited Government
  D. Federalism

Students should complete the outline by including all heads in the section.

EXTENDING THE CONTENT

Historic Building The red brick building in which the Framers met to draw up the Constitution is now known as Independence Hall. Several important events took place there, including the meeting of the First and Second Continental Congresses and Jefferson's reading of the Declaration of Independence. On July 4, 2003, the National Constitution Center opened a few blocks from Independence Hall. This museum explains the importance of the Constitution and its role in the history of the United States.

TEACH

C Critical Thinking

Identifying Central Issues
Have students read through and define in their own words each of the Constitution's major underlying principles. Students should then locate at least one part of the Constitution that addresses that principle. **Ask:** Which constitutional principle affects your life the most today? *(Students' answers will vary.)* **OL**

R Reading Strategy

Activating Prior Knowledge
Have groups of students recall aspects of self-government with which American colonists had experimented. *(Answers include the Mayflower Compact, the Articles of Confederation, and organizations such as the Virginia House of Burgesses and the Continental Congress.)* Explain that this handbook will help them see how those early forms of self-government helped shape the American system of government. **OL**

Answers and Additional Support

Major Principles

Main Idea The Constitution is based on several principles that assure people's rights and provide for a balance among the different branches of government.

Reading Connection If you had to create the rules for a new organization, would you give all members an equal voice? Read on to learn how the Constitution reflects representative government.

The Founders of the Constitution wanted to create a framework for government that would not only reflect the present, but also would be flexible enough to work in the future.

★ *An American Story* ★

In 1987 the United States began a four-year celebration commemorating the Constitution's bicentennial. In a series of ceremonies that lasted to 1991, the nation reflected on the writing and ratifying of the document providing the country's foundation of government. Proclaiming the creation of Citizenship Day and Constitution Week in August 1990, President George Bush quoted the words of Daniel Webster:

'We may be tossed upon an ocean where we can see no land—nor, perhaps, the sun or stars. But there is a chart and a compass for us to study, to consult, and to obey. That chart is the Constitution.'

Serving as the framework of national government and the source of American citizens' basic rights, the Constitution is the United States's most important document. As President Bush reminded the nation in his proclamation:

[I]f we are to continue to enjoy the blessings of freedom and self-government, each of us must understand our rights and responsibilities as citizens.

—adapted from the Citizenship Day and Constitution Week Proclamation

The principles outlined in the Constitution were the Framers' solution to the complex problems of a representative government. The Constitution rests on seven major principles of government: (1) popular sovereignty, (2) republicanism, (3) limited government, (4) federalism, (5) separation of powers, (6) checks and balances, and (7) individual rights.

Popular Sovereignty The opening words of the Constitution, "We the people," reinforce the idea of **popular sovereignty**, or "authority of the people." In the Constitution, the people **consent** to be governed. The Constitution lists the rules by which the people shall be governed and specifies how powers are distributed.

Under the Articles of Confederation, the government had few powers, and it was unable to cope with the many challenges facing the nation. The new Constitution gave the government greater powers and influence. At the same time, it provided specific limitations. A system of interlocking responsibilities kept any one branch of government from becoming too powerful.

▼ *Daniel Webster and George Bush*

Did You Know?

Constitutionally Speaking Students may hear so much grumbling about governmental issues today that they may wonder why we say that the government is based on popular sovereignty. Point out that *popular* comes from the Latin word *populus,* meaning "the people." The same Latin word also gives us *population* and *populate.*

Republicanism Voters hold sovereign power in a republican system. The people elect representatives and give them the responsibility to make laws and conduct government. For most Americans today, the terms *republic* and *representative democracy* mean the same thing: a system of limited government where the people are the final source of authority.

Limited Government Although the Framers agreed that the nation needed a stronger central authority, they feared misuse of power. They wanted to prevent the government from using its power to give one group special advantages or to deprive another group of its rights. By creating a limited government, they restricted the government's authority to specific powers granted by the people.

The members of the Constitutional Convention wished to list the range of powers granted to the new government as specifically as possible. Their decision to write down the governmental outline also served as a clear record of what they intended. Article I of the Constitution states the powers that the government has and does not have. Other limits on government appear in the Bill of Rights, which guarantees certain rights and liberties to the people.

Federalism In establishing a strong central government, the Framers did not deprive states of all authority. The states would give up some powers to the national government while retaining others. States could no longer print their own money or tax items imported from other states, but mostly, each state continued to govern itself much as it had in the past.

The Right to Vote The voting booth is a symbol of one of the Constitution's major principles—popular sovereignty. What does popular sovereignty mean?

This principle of shared power is **federalism.** Our federal government allows the people of each state to deal with their needs in their own way. At the same time, it lets the states act together to deal with matters that affect all Americans.

The Constitution defines three types of government powers. Certain powers belong only to the federal government. These **enumerated powers** include the power to coin money, regulate interstate and foreign trade, maintain the armed forces, and create federal courts (Article I, Section 8).

The second kind of powers are those retained by the states, known as **reserved powers,** including the power to establish schools, pass marriage and divorce laws, and regulate trade within a state. Although specific reserved powers are not listed in the Constitution, the Tenth Amendment says that all powers not specifically granted to the federal government "are reserved to the States."

The third set of powers defined by the Constitution are **concurrent powers**—powers the

The Federal System

Enumerated Powers
Powers *enumerated* to national government; for example, declaring war

Concurrent Powers
Powers *concurrent* to national and state governments; for example, the power to tax

Reserved Powers
Powers *reserved* for state governments; for example, setting up educational system

The Constitution Handbook **139**

U Universal Access

Visual/Spatial Federalism can be graphically illustrated in many ways. After reading the section on federalism, ask students to graphically represent federalism. Encourage them to clearly reflect in their graphics the enumerated powers specific to the federal government, the reserved powers that are specific to the states, and the concurrent powers that the states and the federal government share. **BL**

C Critical Thinking

Making Inferences Write the enumerated powers of the federal government on the board. **Ask:** Why do you think the Framers thought it was important to list the powers of the federal government? *(Students may suggest that the Framers wanted to avoid confusion over what the federal government could and could not do.)* **OL**

Picturing **History**

Answer: the authority of the people
Ask: How is the concept of limited government a reflection of popular sovereignty? *(The central government is not all powerful; it is limited. The people give consent to be governed.)*

Constitution Handbook

U Universal Access

English Learners Students learning English as a second language may have difficulty understanding uncommon English phrases. Pair students and ask each group of two to write for five minutes on what they believe the phrase "the supreme Law of the Land" means. Once each pair is finished, ask students to read one another's writing and discuss their opinions with each other.

EL **CA** 11WA2.3a

R Reading Strategy

Organizing Information Ask students to create a table listing the following presidents: Ulysses S. Grant, Franklin D. Roosevelt, Harry S. Truman, Richard M. Nixon, and Ronald Reagan. Have students research the following information for each president and add it in separate columns of their table: the total number of vetoes, the number of overturned vetoes, and the number of "pocket" vetoes. Then have students compare each president's acts and offer possible explanations for any differences they see. *(Answers will vary but should provide plausible explanations for the data.)* **OL**

Answers and Additional Support

state and federal governments share. They include the right to raise taxes, borrow money, provide for public welfare, and administer criminal justice.

Conflicts between state law and federal law must be settled in a federal court. The Constitution declares that it is "the supreme Law of the Land."

Separation of Powers To prevent any single group or institution in government from gaining too much authority, the Framers divided the federal government into three branches: legislative, executive, and judicial. Each branch has its own **functions** and powers. The legislative branch, Congress, makes the laws. The executive branch, headed by the president, carries out the laws. The judicial branch, consisting of the Supreme Court and other federal courts, interprets and applies the laws.

In addition to giving separate responsibility to separate branches, the membership of each branch is chosen in different ways. The president nominates federal judges and the Senate confirms the appoint-

ments. People vote for members of Congress. Voters cast ballots for president, but the method of election is indirect. On Election Day the votes in each state are counted. Whatever candidate receives a majority receives that state's electoral votes, which total the number of senators and representatives the state has in Congress. Electors from all states meet in December after the November election to formally elect a president. A candidate must receive at least 270 of 538 electoral votes to win.

Checks and Balances The Framers also established a system of checks and balances in which each branch of government can check, or limit, the power of the other branches. This system helps balance the power of the three branches. For example, imagine that Congress passes a law. Then the president can reject the law by vetoing it. However, Congress can **override,** or reverse, the president's veto if two-thirds of the members of both the Senate and the House of Representatives vote again to approve the law.

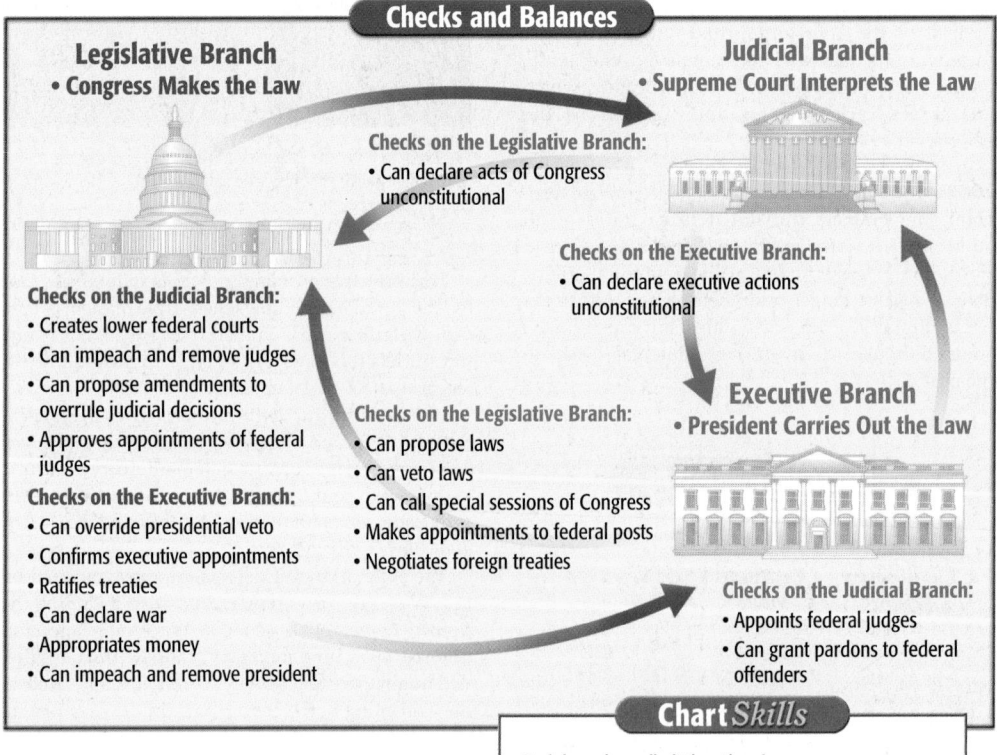

Checks and Balances

Legislative Branch
• Congress Makes the Law

Judicial Branch
• Supreme Court Interprets the Law

Checks on the Legislative Branch:
• Can declare acts of Congress unconstitutional

Checks on the Executive Branch:
• Can declare executive actions unconstitutional

Executive Branch
• President Carries Out the Law

Checks on the Judicial Branch:
• Creates lower federal courts
• Can impeach and remove judges
• Can propose amendments to overrule judicial decisions
• Approves appointments of federal judges

Checks on the Executive Branch:
• Can override presidential veto
• Confirms executive appointments
• Ratifies treaties
• Can declare war
• Appropriates money
• Can impeach and remove president

Checks on the Legislative Branch:
• Can propose laws
• Can veto laws
• Can call special sessions of Congress
• Makes appointments to federal posts
• Negotiates foreign treaties

Checks on the Judicial Branch:
• Appoints federal judges
• Can grant pardons to federal offenders

Chart *Skills*

Each branch can limit the others' power.

Analyzing Information How can the president help control the judiciary?

Chart *Skills*

Answer:
The president nominates federal judges and can grant federal pardons.

Chart Skills Practice
Ask: Of the three branches of government, which one interprets the law? *(the judicial branch)*

Did You Know?

Check The term *check* comes from Persian and is related to the royal title *shah.* It is also a sports term, relating to a blocking action in hockey.

The Bill of Rights: The First Ten Amendments

Amendment 1	Guarantees freedom of religion, of speech, and of the press, and the right to assemble peaceably and to petition the government
Amendment 2	Guarantees the right to organize state militias and bear arms
Amendment 3	Prohibits quartering soldiers in private homes in peacetime and limits it in time of war
Amendment 4	Prohibits the unreasonable search and seizure of persons and property without a valid warrant
Amendment 5	Requires a grand jury for serious criminal charges; prohibits double jeopardy; prohibits forcing accused persons to testify against themselves; guarantees that no one may be deprived of life, liberty, or property, without due process of law; prohibits government taking private property for public use without just compensation
Amendment 6	Guarantees suspects the right to a speedy trial by jury in criminal cases; to know all charges; to question and obtain witnesses; and to have counsel
Amendment 7	Guarantees a jury trial in most civil cases
Amendment 8	Prohibits excessive bail and fines and cruel and unusual punishment
Amendment 9	Assures people that they may have other basic rights in addition to those mentioned in the Constitution
Amendment 10	Guarantees that rights not given to the federal government, nor denied to the states, are reserved to the states or to the people

Individual Rights The Bill of Rights became part of the Constitution in 1791. These first 10 amendments protect basic liberties and rights that some Americans may take for granted—including freedom of speech, freedom of the press, freedom of assembly, freedom of religion, and the right to a trial by jury.

The 17 amendments that follow the Bill of Rights expand the rights of Americans and adjust certain provisions of the Constitution. Included among them are amendments that abolish slavery, **define** citizenship, guarantee voting rights, authorize an income tax, and set a two-term limit on the presidency.

Student Web Activity
Visit the *American Vision: Modern Times* Web site at tav.mt.glencoe.com and click on *Student Web Activities—Constitution Handbook* for an activity on the principles of the Constitution.

Chart *Skills*

Antifederalists demanded a specific list of individual rights and freedoms.

Analyzing Information Why did the Framers include Amendment 4, prohibiting unreasonable searches?

The Legislative Branch

Main Idea The legislative branch of government makes the nation's laws and appropriates funds.

Reading Connection Have you written to your representative to express support for or opposition to a bill? Read on to find out how Congress proposes and enacts laws.

The legislative branch includes the two houses of Congress: the House of Representatives and the Senate. Congress's two primary roles are to make the nation's laws and to control federal spending.

The Role of Congress The government cannot spend any money unless Congress **appropriates,** or sets aside, funds. All tax and spending bills must originate in the House of Representatives and gain

U Universal Access

English Learners Divide the class into groups of three and assign each group one of the 17 amendments that follow the Bill of Rights. Tell each group to create a poster illustrating the key provisions of their assigned amendment. Display the posters around the classroom in the order in which the amendments were ratified and use the visuals to help discuss how the Constitution has changed throughout American history. EL

Resources for page 141

Refer to The Living Constitution ancillary for student activities and information related to the Constitution.

Objectives and answers to the student activity can be found in the **Web Activity Lesson Plan** at tav.mt.glencoe.com.

Chart *Skills*

Answer:
to protect individual rights by limiting the powers of the police

Chart Skills Practice
Ask: Why do you think a higher degree of approval is needed to ratify an amendment than to propose one? *(Students may suggest that this is one way in which the Framers sought to discourage minor or frequent changes to the Constitution.)*

approval in both the House and the Senate before moving on to the president for signature.

Congress also monitors the executive branch and investigates possible abuses of power. The House of Representatives can **impeach**, or bring formal charges against, any federal official it suspects of wrongdoing or misconduct. If an official is impeached, the Senate acts as a court and tries the accused official. Officials who are found guilty may be removed from office.

The Senate also holds certain special powers. Only the Senate can ratify treaties made by the president and confirm presidential appointments of federal officials such as department heads, ambassadors, and federal judges.

All members of Congress have the responsibility of representing their **constituents**, the people of their home states and districts. As a constituent, you can expect your senators and representative to promote national and state interests.

Congress at Work Thousands of **bills**—proposed laws—are introduced in Congress every year. Because individual members of Congress cannot possibly study all these bills carefully, both houses use committees of selected members to evaluate proposed legislation.

Standing committees are permanent committees in both the House and the Senate that specialize in a particular topic, such as agriculture, commerce, or veterans' affairs. These committees are usually divided into subcommittees that focus on a particular aspect of an issue.

The House and the Senate sometimes form temporary **select committees** to deal with issues requiring special attention. These committees meet only until they complete their task.

Occasionally the House and the Senate form **joint committees** with members from both houses. These committees meet to consider specific issues, such as the system of federal taxation. One type of joint committee, a **conference committee,** has a special function. If the House and the Senate pass different versions of the same bill, a conference committee tries to work out a compromise bill acceptable to both houses.

Once a committee in either house of Congress approves a bill, it is sent to the full Senate or House for debate. After debate the bill may be passed, rejected, or returned to the committee for further changes.

When both houses pass a bill, it goes to the president. If the president approves the bill and signs it, the bill becomes law. If the president vetoes the bill, it does not become law unless Congress overrides the veto.

How a Bill Becomes Law

1. A legislator introduces a bill in the House or Senate, where it is referred to a committee for review.

2. After review, the committee decides whether to shelve it or to send it back to the House or Senate with or without revisions.

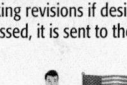

3. The House or Senate then debates the bill, making revisions if desired. If the bill is passed, it is sent to the other house.

4. If the House and Senate pass different versions of the bill, the houses must meet in a conference committee to decide on a compromise version.

5. The compromise bill is then sent to both houses.

6. If both houses pass the bill, it is sent to the president to sign.

7. If the president signs the bill, it becomes law.

8. The president may veto the bill, but if two-thirds of the House and Senate vote to approve it, it becomes law without the president's approval.

Chart *Skills*

The legislative process is complex.

Analyzing Information What is the role of a conference committee?

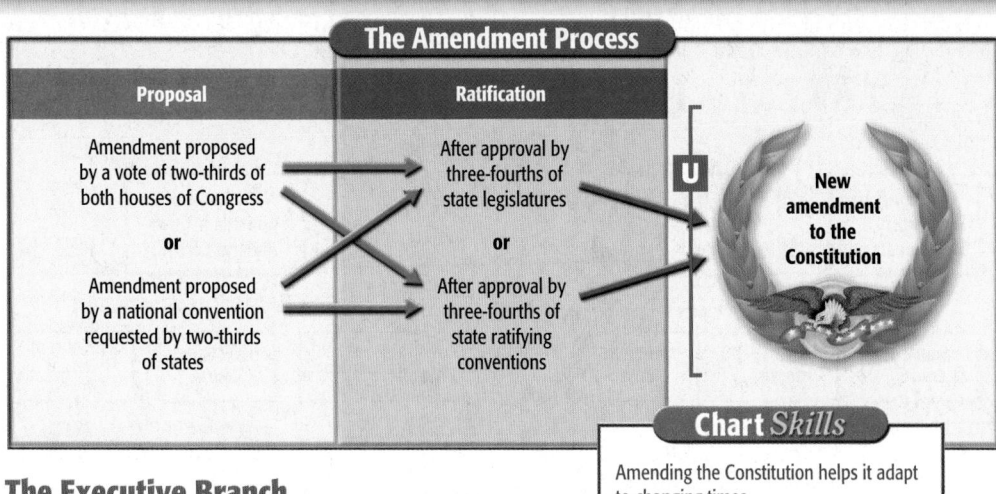

The Amendment Process

Proposal

Amendment proposed by a vote of two-thirds of both houses of Congress

or

Amendment proposed by a national convention requested by two-thirds of states

Ratification

After approval by three-fourths of state legislatures

or

After approval by three-fourths of state ratifying conventions

New amendment to the Constitution

Chart Skills

Amending the Constitution helps it adapt to changing times.

Analyzing Information What role do the states play in the amendment process?

The Executive Branch

Main Idea As the nation's leader, the president carries out laws with the help of executive offices, departments, and agencies.

Reading Connection What would you do if you were the student council president? Read on to learn about the different roles of the U.S. president.

The executive branch of government includes the president, the vice president, and various executive offices, departments, and agencies. The executive branch carries out the laws that Congress passes. The president plays a number of different roles in government, each of which has specific powers and responsibilities. These roles include the nation's chief executive, chief diplomat, commander in chief of the military, chief of state, and legislative leader.

The President's Roles

- **Chief Executive and Chief Diplomat** As chief executive, the president is responsible for carrying out the nation's laws. As chief diplomat, the president directs foreign policy, appoints ambassadors, and negotiates treaties with other nations.
- **Commander in Chief** As commander in chief of the armed forces, the president can use the military to intervene or offer assistance in crises at home and around the world. The president cannot declare war; only Congress holds this power. The president can send troops to other parts of the world for up to 60 days but must notify Congress when doing so. The troops may remain longer only if Congress gives its approval or declares war.

- **Chief of State** As chief of state, the president serves a symbolic role as the representative of all Americans. The president fulfills this role when receiving foreign ambassadors or heads of state, visiting foreign nations, or honoring Americans.
- **Legislative Leader** The president serves as a legislative leader by proposing laws to Congress and working to see that they are passed. In the annual State of the Union address, the president presents goals for legislation.

The Executive Branch at Work Many executive offices, departments, and independent agencies help the president carry out and enforce the nation's laws. The Executive Office of the President (EOP) is made up of individuals and agencies that directly assist the president. Presidents rely heavily on the EOP for advice and for gathering information needed for decision making.

The executive branch also includes 15 executive departments, each responsible for a different area of government. For example, the Department of State plans and carries out foreign policy, and the Department of the Interior manages and protects the nation's public lands and natural resources. The new Department of Homeland Security is responsible for the nation's internal security. The heads of these departments, who have the title of secretary, are members of the president's **cabinet.** This group helps the president make decisions and set government policy.

The Constitution Handbook **143**

R Reading Strategy

Evaluating Have students review the key roles of the president: chief executive and chief diplomat, commander in chief, chief of state, and legislative leader. Students should be able to describe each of these roles. **Ask:** Which of these roles is most important, and why? Then ask students to write a paragraph answering this question. *(Answers will vary, but students should cite evidence or examples to logically support their opinion.)* **OL**

C Critical Thinking

Analyzing Information The Constitution gives no specific authorization for the president's department heads known as the cabinet. However, every president has established a cabinet. **Ask:** Why has the cabinet assumed such an important role in the executive branch? *(The amount of responsibility involved in overseeing the extremely large and complex government cannot be given to a single individual.)* **BL**

Chart Skills

Answer:
Two-thirds of the states can request a national convention to propose amendments. States must approve amendments before they can be added to the Constitution. They can do so in one of two ways. Legislatures in three-fourths of the states may approve the amendment, or conventions in three-fourths of the states may approve the amendment.

Chart Skills Practice
Ask: How can Congress propose an amendment to the Constitution? *(with a two-thirds majority in both houses of Congress)*

S Skill Practice

Conducting Research Organize students into nine groups. Assign each group to use library and Internet resources to research one of the current Supreme Court justices. Have students present their findings in one-page reports that include each justice's background information, political stance, and role in important or controversial court decisions. Tell students to present their reports to the class. **OL** **CA HR4** **CA 11WS1.6**

C Critical Thinking

Drawing Conclusions Supreme Court justices hold lifetime appointments. The Supreme Court is described in the textbook as "the least public of the government's branches." The Court is like this because it was hoped this would remove the justices from the competing passions of politics and outside points of view. **Ask: Do you believe that today's Supreme Court sees itself as outside of politics and operates in such a manner?** *(Students may agree that the justices see themselves as above politics, but students may also state that the justices make decisions that are political in nature. Other opinions will vary.)* **AL**

Answers and Additional Support

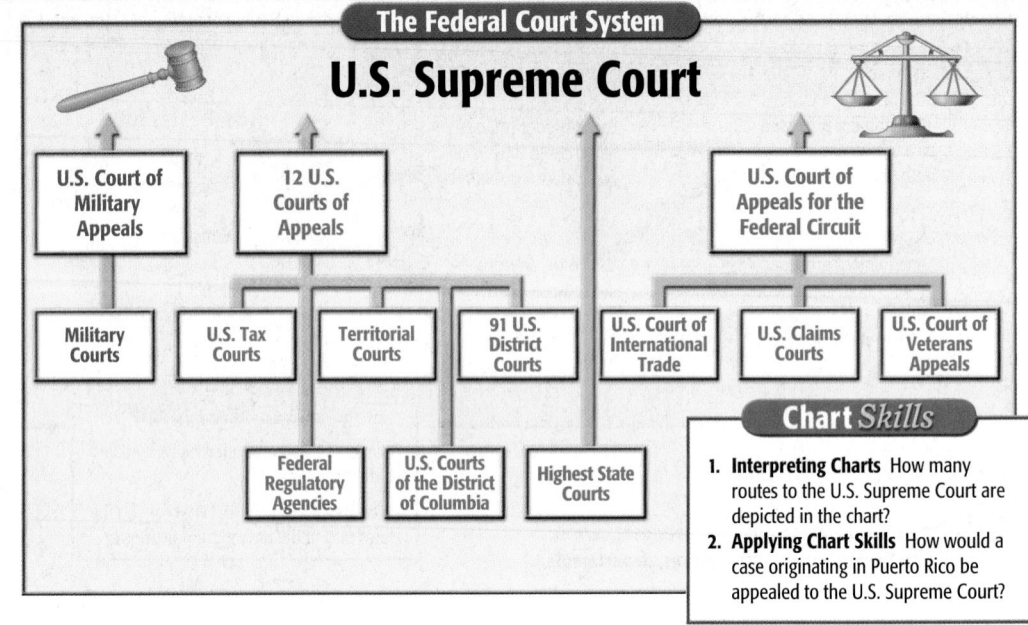

The Federal Court System

U.S. Supreme Court

- U.S. Court of Military Appeals
- 12 U.S. Courts of Appeals
- U.S. Court of Appeals for the Federal Circuit

- Military Courts
- U.S. Tax Courts
- Territorial Courts
- 91 U.S. District Courts
- U.S. Court of International Trade
- U.S. Claims Courts
- U.S. Court of Veterans Appeals

- Federal Regulatory Agencies
- U.S. Courts of the District of Columbia
- Highest State Courts

Chart *Skills*

1. **Interpreting Charts** How many routes to the U.S. Supreme Court are depicted in the chart?
2. **Applying Chart Skills** How would a case originating in Puerto Rico be appealed to the U.S. Supreme Court?

The Judicial Branch

Main Idea The judicial branch consists of different federal courts that review and evaluate laws and interpret the Constitution.

Reading Connection The Constitution did not give the judicial branch the power to review laws. Do you think it is a reasonable task? Read on to learn about the role of federal judges and the Supreme Court.

Article III of the Constitution calls for the creation of a Supreme Court and "such inferior [lower] courts as Congress may from time to time ordain and establish." Today the judicial branch consists of three main categories of courts, including:

- **District Courts** United States district courts are the lowest level of the federal court system. These courts consider criminal and civil cases that come under federal authority, including such criminal offenses as kidnapping and federal tax evasion. Civil cases cover claims against the federal government and cases involving constitutional rights, such as free speech. There are 91 district courts, with at least one in every state.
- **Appellate Courts** The appellate courts, or appeals courts, consider district court decisions in which the losing side has asked for a review of the verdict. If an appeals court disagrees with the lower

144 The Constitution Handbook

court's decision, it can either overturn the verdict or order a retrial. There are 14 appeals courts in the United States, one for each of the 12 federal districts, a military appeals court, and an appellate court for the federal circuit.

- **The Supreme Court** The Supreme Court, the final authority in the federal court system, consists of a chief justice and eight associate justices. Most of the Supreme Court's cases come from appeals of lower court decisions. Only cases involving foreign ambassadors or disputes between states can begin in the Supreme Court.

Supreme Court Independence The Supreme Court is the least public of the government's branches. The president appoints the Court's justices for life, and the Senate confirms the appointments. The public has no input. The Framers hoped that because judges were appointed rather than elected, they would be free to evaluate the law with no consideration of pleasing a group of electors.

Judicial Review The role of the judicial branch is not described in very much detail in the Constitution, but the role of the courts has grown as powers implied in the Constitution have been put into practice. In 1803 Chief Justice John Marshall expanded the powers of the Supreme Court by striking down an act of Congress in the case of *Marbury* v. *Madison*.

Chart *Skills*

Answer:
1. 4
2. A case originating in Puerto Rico would be appealed through one of the 12 U.S. Courts of Appeals.

Chart Skills Practice
Ask: Cases that are appealed in U.S. Tax Courts go to which court? *(the U.S. Court of Appeals)*

Did You Know?

Careful Selection Of the approximately 7,000 cases that get sent to the U.S. Supreme Court each year, the Court agrees to hear only 160 or so. Many cases are rejected simply because they were improperly filed.

Although not mentioned in the Constitution, **judicial review** has become a major power of the judicial branch. Judicial review gives the Supreme Court the ultimate authority to interpret the meaning of constitutional provisions and explain how the words of this 200-year-old document apply to our modern nation. *(See page 1005 for more information on Marbury v. Madison.)*

The Rights of American Citizens

Main Idea The Constitution and the Bill of Rights provide Americans with protection and freedoms.

Reading Connection How do you think the Constitution protects your rights as a student? Read on to find out about the major rights of Americans.

The rights of Americans fall into three broad categories: the right to be protected from unfair actions of the government, to receive equal treatment under the law, and to retain basic freedoms.

Protection from Unfair Actions Parts of the Constitution and the Bill of Rights protect all Americans from unfair treatment by the government or the law. Among these rights are the right to a lawyer when accused of a crime and the right to trial by jury when charged with a crime. In addition, the Fourth Amendment protects us from unreasonable

searches and seizures. This provision requires police to have a court order before searching a person's home for criminal evidence. To obtain this, the police must have a very strong reason to suspect the person of committing a crime.

Equal Treatment All Americans, regardless of race, religion, or political beliefs, have the right to be treated the same under the law. The Fifth Amendment states that no person shall "be deprived of life, liberty, or property, without due process of law." **Due process** means that the government must follow procedures established by law and guaranteed by the Constitution, treating all people equally. The Fourteenth Amendment requires every state to grant its citizens "equal protection of the laws."

Basic Freedoms The basic freedoms involve the fundamental liberties outlined in the First Amendment—freedom of speech, freedom of religion, freedom of the press, freedom of assembly, and the right to petition. In a democracy, power rests in the hands of the people. Therefore, citizens in a democratic society must be able to exchange ideas freely. The First Amendment allows citizens to criticize the government, in speech or in the press, without fear of punishment.

In addition, the Ninth Amendment states that the rights of Americans are not limited to those mentioned in the Constitution. This has allowed basic freedoms

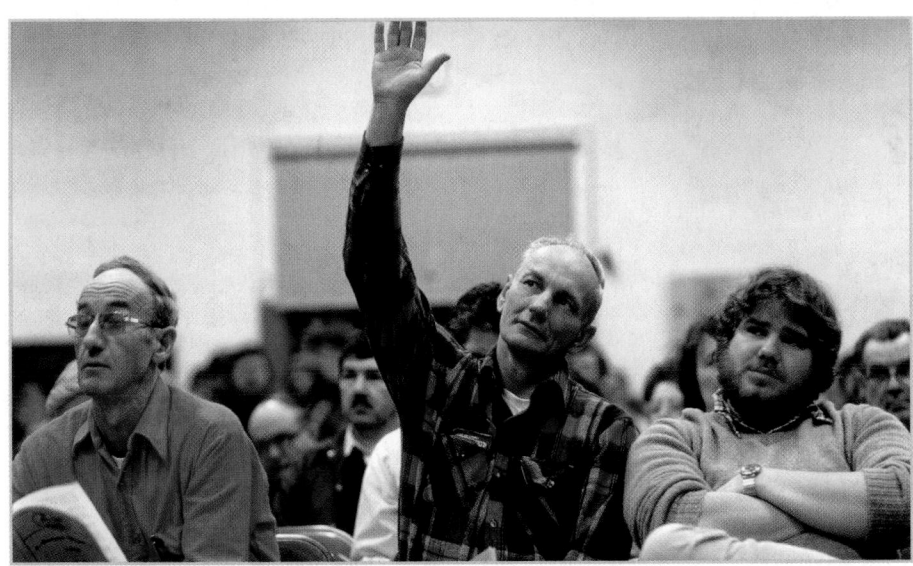

Democracy in Action Town meetings in New England give local residents the chance to express their views. It is a responsibility of American citizens to remain informed about the actions of their local, state, and national government.

The Constitution Handbook **145**

S Skill Practice

Identifying Point of View Have students use library and Internet resources to research the exclusionary rule. *(a rule that keeps improperly or illegally obtained evidence from being admissible in a court of law)* Use the information students have found to discuss the exclusionary rule as a class. Then ask students to write two paragraphs: one in favor of the exclusionary rule, and one opposed to it. *(Answers will vary but may include the following. Pro: protects Fourth and Fourteenth Amendment rights; Con: criminals may go free based on "technicalities")* **AL** **CA HI4**

W Writing Support

Expository Writing Remind students that while the First Amendment guarantees an individual's right to free speech, it does not give individuals the right to shout "fire" in a crowded theater. Have students write a two-page paper that discusses the government's need to balance an individual's constitutional rights with society's need for order and safety. **OL** **CA 11WA2.3**

More Skill Practice

Interpersonal Organize the class into five groups, one for each of the five rights incorporated in the First Amendment. Tell students that they will have 10 minutes to prepare an outline about the right assigned to their group. Also tell them that they will have five minutes to persuade the class that the right they represent is more important than the other four. Students should include as many factual details and real-life scenarios as possible. After each group has presented, have the class vote on which right they think is most important. **OL**

C Critical Thinking

Making Generalizations Ask students to write a short paragraph in which they answer the following questions: **Should communities permit rallies by unpopular groups such as the KKK, even though such rallies may upset some members of the community or could possible incite violence? Why or why not?** Organize students into small groups to discuss their opinions, and then invite one representative from each group to summarize the group's opinions for the class. **OL**

R Reading Strategy

Questioning The textbook states that "one of the fundamental duties of all Americans is to obey the law." **Ask: Can you think of times when people have not obeyed the law?** *(abolitionists during the antebellum period, civil rights protests of the 1960s)* **Must all laws be obeyed?** *(Students may say that some laws are wrong and must be disobeyed to publicize the need to correct them.)* **OL**

Answers and Additional Support

---

to expand over the years through the passage of other amendments and laws. The Nineteenth Amendment, for example, granted the right to vote to all qualified women in federal and state elections. The Twenty-sixth Amendment extends the right to vote to American citizens who are at least 18 years of age.

Limits on Rights

Limits on Rights Although Americans enjoy a broad range of rights, these rights are not absolute. There are certain limitations on these rights, which are based on the principle that everyone's rights should be respected equally. For example, many cities and towns have passed laws that require groups to obtain a permit to march on city streets. While such a law does limit free speech, it also protects the community by allowing the police to make provisions so that the march will not disturb the lives of other people. However, a law banning all marches would be unreasonable and would violate the First Amendment rights of free speech and assembly. Similarly, a law preventing only certain groups from marching would be unfair because it would not apply equally to everyone.

In this and other cases, the government balances an individual's rights, the rights of others, and the community's health and safety. Most Americans are willing to accept some limitations on their rights to gain these protections as long as the restrictions are reasonable and apply equally to all.

Duties of Citizenship All males age 18 or over are required to register for military duty. In July 2001, David Edmond Lucitt, 18, of Haymarket, Virginia, became the one-millionth man to register online. Why do males over age 18 need to register?

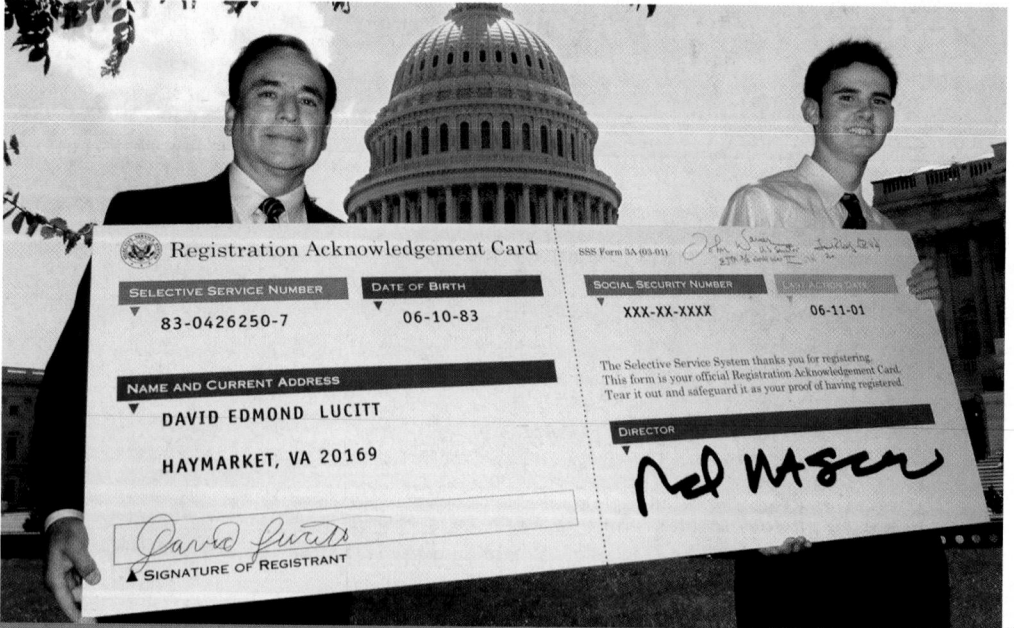

Citizens' Responsibilities

Main Idea When Americans fulfill their rights and responsibilities, they help protect the basic ideas of democracy.

Reading Connection Have you thought about a political candidate for whom you would vote in the next election? Read on to learn about the rights and responsibility you will gain at the age of 18.

Participation in a democratic society involves certain duties and responsibilities. Duties are actions required by law. Responsibilities are voluntary actions. Fulfilling both your duties and your responsibilities helps ensure good government and protects your rights.

R Duties One of the fundamental duties of all Americans is to obey the law. Laws serve three important functions. They help maintain order; they protect the health, safety, and property of all citizens; and they make it possible for people to live together peacefully. If you disobey laws, for example, you endanger others and interfere with the smooth functioning of society. If you believe a law needs to be changed, you can work through your electoral representatives to improve it.

Americans also have a duty to pay taxes. The government uses tax money to defend the nation, provide health insurance for people over 65, and build roads and bridges. Americans benefit from services provided by the government.

Picturing **History**

Answer: It is a duty of all male 18-years-old citizens to register in case the government needs to call on them for military service.

Another duty of citizens is to defend the nation. All males aged 18 and older must register with the government in case the nation needs to call on them for military service. Military service is not automatic, but a war could make it necessary.

The Constitution guarantees all Americans the right to a trial by a jury of their equals. For this reason, you should be prepared for jury duty when you become eligible at the age of 18. Having a large group of jurors on hand is necessary to guarantee the right to a fair and speedy trial. You also have a duty to serve as a trial witness if called to do so.

S Most states require you to attend school until a certain age. School is where you gain the knowledge and skills needed to be a good citizen. In school you learn to think more clearly, to express your opinions more accurately, and to analyze the statements and ideas of others. These skills will help you make informed choices when you vote.

Responsibilities The responsibilities of citizens are not as clear-cut as their duties. Responsibilities are as important as duties, however, because they help maintain the quality of government and society.

One important responsibility is to become well informed. You need to know what is happening in your community, your state, your country, and the world. Knowing what your government representatives are doing and expressing your feelings about their actions can help keep the government responsive to the wishes of the people.

You also need to be informed about your rights and to exercise them when necessary. Knowing your rights helps preserve them. Other responsibilities include respecting diversity, accepting responsibility for your actions, and supporting your family.

Vote, Vote, Vote! Perhaps your most important responsibility as an American citizen will be to vote when you reach the age of 18. Voting allows you to participate in government and guide its direction. When you vote for people to represent you in government, you will be exercising your right of self-government. If you disapprove of the job your representatives are doing, it will be your responsibility to help elect other people in the next election. You can also let your representatives know how you feel about issues through letters, telephone calls, and petitions and by taking part in public meetings or political rallies.

To enjoy your rights to the fullest, you must be prepared to respect the rights of others. Respecting the rights of others also means respecting the rights of people with whom you disagree. Respecting and accepting others regardless of race, religion, beliefs, or other differences is essential in a democracy.

HISTORY *Online* **Study Central**

For help with the concepts in this section of the *American Vision: Modern Times* go to tav.mt.glencoe.com and click on *Study Central.*

Citizenship Handbook Assessment

★ ★ ★ ★ ★ ★ ★ ★ ★ ★ ★ ★ ★ ★ ★ ★ ★

Checking for Understanding

1. **Vocabulary** Define: popular sovereignty, consent, federalism, enumerated powers, reserved powers, concurrent powers, function, override, define, appropriate, impeach, constituent, bill, standing committee, select committee, joint committee, conference committee, cabinet, judicial review, due process.

2. **Summarize** the provisions of the First Amendment.

Reviewing Big Ideas

3. **Explaining** What is the difference between a duty and a responsibility?

Critical Thinking

4. **Comparing** Some people want a limit on the number of terms one can serve in the legislature. What are some of the advantages of the present system, which does not limit the number of terms? What are some of the disadvantages? How would one make term limits an official part of the Constitution?

5. **Organizing** Use a graphic organizer like the one below to list reasons why the Framers of the Constitution provided for separation of powers.

Separation of Powers

Analyzing Visuals

6. **Analyzing Photographs** Study the photograph on page 139. How does the democratic voting process reflect our national identity?

Writing About History

7. **History and Government** Working with a partner, choose one of the constitutional rights listed below. Write a report that traces the right's historical development, from the time the Constitution was ratified to the present.

suffrage
freedom of speech
freedom of religion
equal protection of law

The Constitution Handbook **147**

Constitution Handbook

S **Skill Practice**

Evaluating Evidence Remind students that most states have laws requiring children to attend school until a certain age. Have students use library and Internet resources to research your state's laws about school attendance. Summarize key findings on the board. **Ask:** Should the government have the right to force you to go to school? Why or why not? Invite students to share their answers with the class. Use student responses to begin a discussion on the role of school in shaping responsible citizens in a democracy. **BL** **CA HR4**

ASSESS

Assign the Constitution Handbook Assessment as homework or as an in-class activity.

CLOSE

Using Context Clues Have students identify 10 vocabulary words from the Handbook and offer one-sentence definitions of the terms. Examples could include *legislative, executive, judicial, checks and balances,* and *amendments.* Have students use their definitions to create a Constitution Dictionary to use as a future reference. **EL**

HISTORY *Online*

Study Central provides audio summaries, interactive games, and online graphic organizers to help students review section content.

The Constitution of the United States

The Constitution of the United States is a truly remarkable document. It was one of the first written constitutions in modern history. The entire text of the Constitution and its amendments follow. For easier study, those passages that have been set aside or changed by the adoption of amendments are printed in blue. Also included are explanatory notes that will help clarify the meaning of important ideas presented in the Constitution.

A burst of fireworks celebrating the 200-year anniversary of the Constitution highlights Independence Hall in Philadelphia.

Preamble

We the People of the United States, in Order to form a more perfect Union, establish Justice, insure domestic Tranquility, provide for the common defence, promote the general Welfare, and secure the Blessings of Liberty to ourselves and our Posterity, do ordain and establish this Constitution for the United States of America.

Article I

Section 1

All legislative Powers herein granted shall be vested in a Congress of the United States, which shall consist of a Senate and House of Representatives.

Section 2

[1.] The House of Representatives shall be composed of Members chosen every second Year by the People of the several States, and the Electors in each State shall have the Qualifications requisite for Electors of the most numerous Branch of the State Legislature.

[2.] No person shall be a Representative who shall not have attained to the Age of twenty five Years, and been seven Years a Citizen of the United States, and who shall not, when elected, be an Inhabitant of that State in which he shall be chosen.

[3.] Representatives and direct Taxes shall be apportioned among the several States which may be included within this Union, according to their respective Numbers, which shall be determined by adding to the whole Number of free Persons, including those bound to Service for a Term of Years, and excluding Indians not taxed, three fifths of all other Persons. The actual Enumeration shall be made within three Years after the first Meeting of the Congress of the United States, and within every subsequent Term of ten Years, in such Manner as they shall by Law direct. The Number of Representatives shall not exceed one for every thirty Thousand, but each State shall have at Least one Representative; and until such enumeration shall be made, the State of New Hampshire shall be entitled to chuse three; Massachusetts eight, Rhode-Island and Providence Plantations one, Connecticut five, New-York six, New Jersey four, Pennsylvania eight, Delaware one, Maryland six, Virginia ten, North Carolina five, South Carolina five, and Georgia three.

[4.] When vacancies happen in the Representation from any State, the Executive Authority thereof shall issue Writs of Election to fill such Vacancies.

[5.] The House of Representatives shall chuse their Speaker and other Officers; and shall have the sole Power of Impeachment.

The Preamble introduces the Constitution and sets forth the general purposes for which the government was established. The Preamble also declares that the power of the government comes from the people.

The printed text of the document shows the spelling and punctuation of the parchment original.

Article I. The Legislative Branch

The Constitution contains seven divisions called articles. Each article covers a general topic. For example, Articles I, II, and III create the three branches of the national government—the legislative, executive, and judicial branches. Most of the articles are divided into sections.

> ### Section 1. Congress
> **Lawmaking** The power to make laws is given to a Congress made up of two chambers to represent different interests: the Senate to represent the states and the House to be more responsive to the people's will.

> ### Section 2. House of Representatives
> **Division of Representatives Among the States** The number of representatives from each state is based on the size of the state's population. Each state is entitled to at least one representative. The Constitution states that each state may specify who can vote, but the Fifteenth, Nineteenth, Twenty-fourth, and Twenty-sixth Amendments have established guidelines that all states must follow regarding the right to vote. *What are the qualifications for members of the House of Representatives?*

Vocabulary

preamble: *introduction*
constitution: *principles and laws of a nation*
enumeration: *census or population count*
impeachment: *bringing charges against an official*

The Constitution Handbook **149**

Constitution Handbook

TEACH

U Universal Access

Advanced Learners Committing the Preamble of the Constitution to memory provides a useful language model for students' spoken language development. To aid in this memory task, structure the activity by asking students to write the words *who, why,* and *what* in their notebooks. Have students write the various phrases of the Preamble under the words to which they are most closely related. **AL**

> **Answer:** A member of the House of Representatives must be at least 25 years old, be a United States citizen for at least seven years, and be an inhabitant of the state from which he or she was elected.

C Critical Thinking

Analyzing Information Have students research data from the 1990 and 2000 censuses. Students should create a chart that identifies the populations of each state and the number of representatives each state had in 1990. Then students should list the populations each state had in 2000 and whether that state lost or gained representation in the House of Representatives. Have students identify which states gained the most seats and speculate as to why those states are gaining populations. **OL**

Did You Know?

Female Representatives Republican and pacifist Jeannette Rankin of Montana was the first woman elected to the House of Representatives in 1916. In 1917 she and 49 House colleagues voted against entering World War I. In 1941 she was the only member of Congress to vote against declaring war on Japan.

ABCNEWS INTERACTIVE™

▐▌▌ **VIDEOCASSETTE**
Historic America Electronic Field Trips
View **Tape 1, Chapter 7:** "Independence Hall"

Constitution Handbook

C₁ Critical Thinking

Analyzing Primary Sources
Write on the board the following, which George Washington supposedly said to Thomas Jefferson in defense of the Senate: "We pour legislation into the senatorial saucer to cool it." Have students speculate on what Washington meant by this. (*The Senate was seen as the more deliberative of the two houses of Congress.*) **OL**

Answer: The Senate has the power to remove impeached officials from office and disqualify them from holding office in the future.

C₂ Critical Thinking

Making Generalizations Call on students to list the qualifications for serving in Congress as set forth in the Constitution. Then ask students what other qualifications, if any, they think should be applied to members of Congress. Discuss with students whether they would like to serve in Congress. (*Note: For information on serving in the House, see Article I, Section 2 on page 149.*) **OL**

Answers and Additional Support

Section 3. The Senate
Voting Procedure Originally, senators were chosen by the legislators of their own states. The Seventeenth Amendment changed this, so that senators are now elected by their state's people. There are 100 senators, 2 from each state.

What Might Have Been
Electing Senators South Carolina delegate Charles Pinckney suggested during the Convention that the members of the Senate come from four equally proportioned districts within the United States and that the legislature elect the executive every seven years.

Section 3. The Senate
Trial of Impeachments One of Congress's powers is the power to impeach—to accuse government officials of wrongdoing, put them on trial, and, if necessary, remove them from office. The House decides if the offense is impeachable. The Senate acts as a jury and, when the president is impeached, the Chief Justice of the United States serves as the judge. A two-thirds vote of the members present is needed to convict impeached officials. *What punishment can the Senate give if an impeached official is convicted?*

Vocabulary

president pro tempore: *presiding officer of Senate who serves when the vice president is absent*
quorum: *minimum number of members that must be present to conduct sessions*

150 The Constitution Handbook

Section 3

[1.] The Senate of the United States shall be composed of two Senators from each State, chosen by the Legislature thereof, for six Years; and each Senator shall have one Vote.

[2.] Immediately after they shall be assembled in Consequence of the first Election, they shall be divided as equally as may be into three Classes. The Seats of the Senators of the first Class shall be vacated at the Expiration of the second Year, of the second Class at the Expiration of the fourth Year, and of the third Class at the Expiration of the sixth Year, so that one third may be chosen every second Year; and if Vacancies happen by Resignation, or otherwise, during the Recess of the Legislature of any State, the Executive thereof may make temporary Appointments until the next Meeting of the Legislature, which shall then fill such Vacancies.

[3.] No Person shall be a Senator who shall not have attained to the Age of thirty Years, and been nine Years a Citizen of the United States, and who shall not, when elected, be an Inhabitant of that State for which he shall be chosen.

[4.] The Vice President of the United States shall be President of the Senate, but shall have no Vote, unless they be equally divided.

[5.] The Senate shall chuse their other Officers, and also a President pro tempore, in the Absence of the Vice-President, or when he shall exercise the Office of the President of the United States.

[6.] The Senate shall have the sole Power to try all Impeachments. When sitting for that Purpose, they shall be on Oath or Affirmation. When the President of the United States is tried, the Chief Justice shall preside: And no Person shall be convicted without the Concurrence of two thirds of the Members present.

[7.] Judgment in Cases of Impeachment shall not extend further than to removal from Office, and disqualification to hold and enjoy any Office of honor, Trust or Profit under the United States: but the Party convicted shall nevertheless be liable and subject to Indictment, Trial, Judgment and Punishment, according to Law.

Section 4

[1.] The Times, Places and Manner of holding Elections for Senators and Representatives, shall be prescribed in each State by the Legislature thereof; but the Congress may at any time by Law make or alter such Regulations, except as to the Places of chusing Senators.

[2.] The Congress shall assemble at least once in every Year, and such Meeting shall be on the first Monday in December, unless they shall by Law appoint a different Day.

Section 5

[1.] Each House shall be the Judge of the Elections, Returns and Qualifications of its own Members, and a Majority of each shall constitute a Quorum to do

---

Did You Know?

Experience, Not Age The title Senior Senator refers to the senator from each state who has more experience as a senator. A senior senator may actually be younger than the other senator from his or her state.

Did You Know?

Quorum When the first Congress was called to assemble in New York City in 1789, it took nearly a month for enough members to arrive to make a quorum.

Business; but a smaller Number may adjourn from day to day, and may be authorized to compel the Attendance of absent Members, in such Manner, and under such Penalties as each House may provide.

[2.] Each House may determine the Rules of its Proceedings, punish its Members for disorderly Behaviour, and, with the Concurrence of two thirds, expel a Member.

[3.] Each House shall keep a Journal of its Proceedings, and from time to time publish the same, excepting such Parts as may in their Judgment require Secrecy; and the Yeas and Nays of the Members of either House on any question shall, at the Desire of one fifth of those Present, be entered on the Journal.

[4.] Neither House, during the Session of Congress, shall, without the Consent of the other, adjourn for more than three days, nor to any other Place than that in which the two Houses shall be sitting.

Section 6

[1.] The Senators and Representatives shall receive a Compensation for their Services, to be ascertained by Law, and paid out of the Treasury of the United States. They shall in all Cases, except Treason, Felony and Breach of the Peace, be privileged from Arrest during their Attendance at the Session of their respective Houses, and in going to and returning from the same; and for any Speech or Debate in either House, they shall not be questioned in any other Place.

[2.] No Senator or Representative shall, during the Time for which he was elected, be appointed to any civil Office under the Authority of the United States, which shall have been created, or the Emoluments whereof shall have been encreased during such time; and no Person holding any Office under the United States, shall be a Member of either House during his Continuance in Office.

Section 7

[1.] All Bills for raising Revenue shall originate in the House of Representatives; but the Senate may propose or concur with Amendments as on other Bills.

[2.] Every Bill which shall have passed the House of Representatives and the Senate, shall, before it become a Law, be presented to the President of the United States; If he approve he shall sign it, but if not he shall return it, with his Objections to that House in which it shall have originated, who shall enter the Objections at large on their Journal, and proceed to reconsider it. If after such Reconsideration two thirds of that House shall agree to pass the Bill, it shall be sent, together with the Objections, to the other House, by which it shall likewise be reconsidered, and if approved by two thirds of that House, it shall become a Law. But in all such Cases the Votes of both Houses shall be determined by yeas and Nays, and the Names of the Persons voting for and against the Bill shall be entered on the Journal of each House respectively. If any Bill shall not be returned by the President within ten Days (Sundays excepted) after it

Vocabulary

Section 6. Privileges and Restrictions

Pay and Privileges To strengthen the federal government, the Founders set congressional salaries to be paid by the United States Treasury rather than by members' respective states. Originally, members were paid $6 per day. In 2002, all members of Congress received a base salary of $150,000.

Section 7. Passing Laws

Revenue Bill All tax laws must originate in the House of Representatives. This ensures that the branch of Congress that is elected by the people every two years has the major role in determining taxes.

Section 7. Passing Laws

W
How Bills Become Laws A bill may become a law only by passing both houses of Congress and by being signed by the president. The president can check Congress by rejecting–vetoing–its legislation. *How can Congress override the president's veto?*

The Constitution Handbook **151**

Constitution Handbook

R Reading Strategy

Using Context Clues Have students work in pairs to create a study card for each vocabulary word listed on this page. Instruct students to write the term on one side of a blank note card. On the other side, have students write an explanation for how this word relates to the Constitution. Have students take turns quizzing each other using their study cards. **OL**

W Writing Support

Letter Writing Point out that because of the heavy volume of legislation, both houses of Congress have committees that do much of the work in preparing bills. Each committee deals with a particular issue, such as banking, foreign affairs, or natural resources. Encourage students to write letters asking representatives and senators from your state about the committees on which they serve. Invite volunteers to share the replies they receive. **BL**
CA 11WS1.1

Answer: A bill can become law, despite not being signed by the president, if two-thirds of the House of Representatives and two-thirds of the Senate approve the bill.

Did You Know?

The Capitol The interior of the Capitol, the seat of Congress, is a combination of new and old. Many of the furnishings and works of art date from the mid-1800s. However, signs of modern technology are everywhere. Roll-call votes are counted electronically. In addition, members of both houses have access to computers and other electronic information services. There are even electric subways connecting many of the office buildings on Capitol Hill.

Constitution Handbook

C Critical Thinking

Drawing Conclusions Organize students into groups of five to consider one of the expressed powers of Congress: taxing and spending; regulating commerce, foreign policy, and national defense; and providing for the nation's growth. Have each group discuss why the power it selected was delegated to Congress rather than to the executive branch. Then ask each group to share their discussion results with the entire class. **AL**

Answer: Article 1, Section 8, Clause 11

S Skill Practice

Conducting Research Have students work in pairs to research the naturalization process. Each pair should present the information in a flow chart or other graphic organizer. **Ask each pair: Why is the process of becoming a U.S. citizen so difficult? Do you think it should be easier? Why or why not?** Have the pairs copy their paragraphs onto a poster board along with their flow chart or graphic organizer and display the posters around your classroom. **AL** **CA HR4**

Answers and Additional Support

C

Section 8. Powers Granted to Congress

Expressed Powers Expressed powers are those powers directly stated in the Constitution. Most of the expressed powers of Congress are itemized in Article I, Section 8. These powers are also called enumerated powers because they are numbered 1 to 18. *Which clause gives Congress the power to declare war?*

Though Congress has many specific powers, the people have the right of protest.

Vocabulary

resolution: *legislature's formal expression of opinion*

naturalization: *procedure by which a citizen of a foreign nation becomes a citizen of the United States.*

152 The Constitution Handbook

---

shall have been presented to him, the Same shall be a Law, in like Manner as if he had signed it, unless the Congress by their Adjournment prevent its Return, in which Case it shall not be a Law.

[3.] Every Order, Resolution, or Vote to which the Concurrence of the Senate and House of Representatives may be necessary (except on a question of Adjournment) shall be presented to the President of the United States; and before the Same shall take Effect, shall be approved by him, or being disapproved by him, shall be repassed by two thirds of the Senate and House of Representatives, according to the Rules and Limitations prescribed in the Case of a Bill.

Section 8

[1.] The Congress shall have the Power to lay and collect Taxes, Duties, Imposts and Excises, to pay the Debts and provide for the common Defence and general Welfare of the United States; but all Duties, Imposts and Excises shall be uniform throughout the United States;

[2.] To borrow Money on the credit of the United States;

[3.] To regulate Commerce with foreign Nations, and among the several States, and with the Indian Tribes;

S [4.] To establish an uniform Rule of Naturalization, and uniform Laws on the subject of Bankruptcies throughout the United States;

[5.] To coin Money, regulate the Value thereof, and of foreign Coin, and fix the Standard of Weights and Measures;

[6.] To provide for the Punishment of counterfeiting the Securities and current Coin of the United States;

[7.] To establish Post Offices and post Roads;

[8.] To promote the Progress of Science and useful Arts, by securing for limited Times to Authors and Inventors the exclusive Right to their respective Writings and Discoveries;

[9.] To constitute Tribunals inferior to the supreme Court;

[10.] To define and punish Piracies and Felonies committed on the high Seas, and Offences against the Law of Nations;

[11.] To declare War, grant Letters of Marque and Reprisal, and make Rules concerning Captures on Land and Water;

[12.] To raise and support Armies, but no Appropriation of Money to that Use shall be for a longer Term than two Years;

[13.] To provide and maintain a Navy;

[14.] To make Rules for the Government and Regulation of the land and naval Forces;

[15.] To provide for calling forth the Militia to execute the Laws of the Union, suppress Insurrections and repel Invasions;

[16.] To provide for organizing, arming, and disciplining, the Militia, and for governing such Part of them as may be employed in the Service of the United States, reserving to the States respectively, the Appointment of the Officers, and the Authority of training the Militia according to the discipline prescribed by Congress;

Did You Know?

Sergeants-at-Arms House and Senate sergeants-at-arms are the police officers of Congress. They enforce the rules and maintain order. When they walk down the aisle of the legislature, carrying a ceremonial staff called a mace, Congress must be orderly. Any member of Congress who persists in disorderly conduct is guilty of contempt. The sergeants-at-arms also maintain security within the Capitol and associated buildings and supervise the Capitol police force. Sometimes the sergeants-at-arms round up members for floor votes, personally escorting any member who refuses to attend.

[17.] To exercise exclusive Legislation in all Cases whatsoever, over such District (not exceeding ten Miles square) as may, by Cession of particular States, and the Acceptance of Congress, become the Seat of Government of the United States, and to exercise like Authority over all Places purchased by the Consent of the Legislature of the State in which the Same shall be, for the Erection of Forts, Magazines, Arsenals, dock-Yards, and other needful Buildings; And

[18.] To make all Laws which shall be necessary and proper for carrying into Execution the foregoing Powers, and all other Powers vested by this Constitution in the Government of the United States, or in any Department or Officer thereof.

Section 9

[1.] The Migration or Importation of such Persons as any of the States now existing shall think proper to admit, shall not be prohibited by the Congress prior to the Year one thousand eight hundred and eight, but a Tax or duty may be imposed on such Importation, not exceeding ten dollars for each Person.

[2.] The Privilege of the Writ of Habeas Corpus shall not be suspended, unless when in Cases of Rebellion or Invasion the public Safety may require it.

[3.] No Bill of Attainder or ex post facto Law shall be passed.

[4.] No Capitation, or other direct, Tax shall be laid, unless in Proportion to the Census or Enumeration herein before directed to be taken.

[5.] No Tax or Duty shall be laid on Articles exported from any State.

[6.] No Preference shall be given by any Regulation of Commerce or Revenue to the Ports of one State over those of another: nor shall Vessels bound to, or from, one State, be obliged to enter, clear, or pay Duties in another.

[7.] No Money shall be drawn from the Treasury, but in Consequence of Appropriations made by Law; and a regular Statement and Account of the Receipts and Expenditures of all public Money shall be published from time to time.

[8.] No Title of Nobility shall be granted by the United States: And no Person holding any Office of Profit or Trust under them, shall, without the Consent of the Congress, accept of any present, Emolument, Office, or Title, of any kind whatever, from any King, Prince, or foreign State.

Section 10

[1.] No State shall enter into any Treaty, Alliance, or Confederation; grant Letters of Marque and Reprisal; coin Money; emit Bills of Credit; make any Thing but gold and silver Coin a Tender in Payment of Debts; pass any Bill of Attainder, ex post facto Law, or Law impairing the Obligation of Contracts, or grant any Title of Nobility.

[2.] No State shall, without the Consent of the Congress, lay any Imposts or Duties on Imports or Exports, except

Section 8. Powers Granted to Congress

Elastic Clause The final enumerated power is often called the "elastic clause." This clause gives Congress the right to make all laws "necessary and proper" to carry out the powers expressed in the other clauses of Article I. It is called the elastic clause because it lets Congress "stretch" its powers to meet situations the Founders could not have anticipated.

What does the phrase "necessary and proper" in the elastic clause mean? It was a subject of dispute from the beginning. The issue was whether a strict or a broad interpretation of the Constitution should be applied. The dispute was first addressed in 1819, in the case of *McCulloch v. Maryland,* when the Supreme Court ruled in favor of a broad interpretation. The Court stated that the elastic clause allowed Congress to use its powers in any way that was not specifically prohibited by the Constitution.

Section 9. Powers Denied to the Federal Government

Original Rights A writ of habeas corpus issued by a judge requires a law official to bring a prisoner to court and show cause for holding the prisoner. A bill of attainder is a bill that punishes a person without a jury trial. An "ex post facto" law is one that makes an act a crime after the act has been committed. *What does the Constitution say about bills of attainder?*

Section 10. Powers Denied to the States

Limitations on Powers Section 10 lists limits on the states. These restrictions were designed, in part, to prevent an overlapping in functions and authority with the federal government.

U Universal Access

Interpersonal Organize students into groups of five. Have each group write a statement answering these questions: **What does the phrase "necessary and proper" in the elastic clause mean? How much should members of Congress be able to "stretch" the powers of the Constitution?** Ask a volunteer from each group to present their group's statement, inviting the rest of the class to respond. OL
CA 11WA2.4a

Answer: No bills of attainder shall be passed.

R Reading Strategy

Evaluating Article I, Section 9 prohibits the suspension of the writ of habeas corpus. Discuss with students the protection this offers. **Ask: Is this an outdated principle today or still necessary to the Constitution?** *(Most students will see this as a major principle of our legal system.)*
OL

The Constitution Handbook **153**

Did You Know?

Bills of Attainder Bills of attainder were first used in England in 1459 and gave the government the power to imprison people, take their property, and even order their execution, all without allowing them the benefit of a jury trial.

Constitution Handbook

C Critical Thinking

Analyzing Information Point out that one of the difficult questions for the Framers of the Constitution concerned the Chief Executive—exactly how much power should the president have? Have students discuss why the Framers set up an office of president with limited powers. *(Discussion should focus on the Framers' fear of a single leader with uncontrolled powers.)* **OL**

R Reading Strategy

Evaluating Tell students that the Constitution originally did not limit the number of terms the president could serve. George Washington set a precedent by serving only two terms. Until Franklin D. Roosevelt, no president had served more than two terms. Many people opposed Roosevelt's four terms in office. This opposition eventually led to the ratification of the Twenty-second Amendment in 1951, which limited presidents to two terms. **Ask: Do you think that presidents should be limited to two terms in office? Why or why not?** As a class, use the board to make a list of pros and cons to a two-term limit for presidential office. Have students write a paragraph explaining their opinion. **BL** **CA 11WA2.3b**

Answers and Additional Support

Article II. The Executive Branch

C Article II creates an executive branch to carry out laws passed by Congress. Article II lists the powers and duties of the president, describes qualifications for office and procedures for electing the president, and provides for a vice president.

What Might Have Been
Term of Office Alexander Hamilton also provided his own governmental outline at the Constitutional Convention. Some of its most distinctive elements were that both the executive and the members of the Senate were "elected to serve during good behaviour," meaning there was no specified limit on their time in office.

Section 1. President and Vice President
Former Method of Election In the election of 1800, the top two candidates received the same number of electoral votes, making it necessary for the House of Representatives to decide the election. To eliminate this problem, the Twelfth Amendment, added in 1804, changed the method of electing the president stated in Article II, Section 3. The Twelfth Amendment requires that the electors cast separate ballots for president and vice president.

what may be absolutely necessary for executing it's inspection Laws: and the net Produce of all Duties and Imposts, laid by any State on Imports and Exports, shall be for the Use of the Treasury of the United States; and all such Laws shall be subject to the Revision and Controul of the Congress.
[3.] No State shall, without the Consent of Congress, lay any Duty of Tonnage, keep Troops, or Ships of War in time of Peace, enter into any Agreement or Compact with another State, or with a foreign Power, or engage in War, unless actually invaded, or in such imminent Danger as will not admit of delay.

Article II
Section 1
R **[1.]** The executive Power shall be vested in a President of the United States of America. He shall hold his Office during the Term of four Years, and, together with the Vice-President, chosen for the same Term, be elected, as follows
[2.] Each State shall appoint, in such Manner as the Legislature thereof may direct, a Number of Electors, equal to the whole Number of Senators and Representatives to which the State may be entitled in the Congress: but no Senator or Representative, or Person holding an Office of Trust or Profit under the United States, shall be appointed an Elector.
[3.] The Electors shall meet in their respective States, and vote by Ballot for two Persons, of whom one at least shall not be an Inhabitant of the same State with themselves. And they shall make a List of all the Persons voted for, and of the Number of Votes for each; which List they shall sign and certify, and transmit sealed to the Seat of the Government of the United States, directed to the President of the Senate. The President of the Senate shall, in the Presence of the Senate and House of Representatives, open all the Certificates, and the Votes shall then be counted. The Person having the greatest Number of Votes shall be the President, if such Number be a Majority of the whole Number of Electors appointed; and if there be more than one who have such Majority, and have an equal Number of Votes, then the House of Representatives shall immediately chuse by Ballot one of them for President; and if no person have a Majority, then from the five highest on the List the said House shall in like Manner chuse the president. But in chusing the President, the Votes shall be taken by States, the Representation from each State having one Vote; A quorum for this Purpose shall consist of a Member or Members from two thirds of the States, and a Majority of all the States shall be necessary to a Choice. In every Case, after the Choice of the President, the Person having the greatest Number of Votes of the Electors shall be the Vice-President. But if there should remain two or more who have equal Votes, the Senate shall chuse from them by Ballot the Vice President.

Did You Know?

Electoral College The electors in the Electoral College almost always vote as expected. Exceptions are rare: there have been only a small number of "faithless electors" among the more than 17,000 electors chosen since 1789. For example, in 1988 Democratic nominee Michael Dukakis was denied one of his 112 electoral votes when a West Virginia elector cast her ballot for Dukakis's running mate, Lloyd Bentsen. She gave her vice presidential vote to Dukakis. In 2004 Democratic nominee John Kerry received one electoral vote less than the expected 252 when a Minnesota elector cast a ballot for his running mate, John Edwards.

[4.] The Congress may determine the Time of chusing the Electors, and the Day on which they shall give their Votes; which Day shall be the same throughout the United States.

[5.] No Person except a natural born Citizen, or a Citizen of the United States, at the time of the Adoption of this Constitution, shall be eligible to the Office of President; neither shall any Person be eligible to that Office who shall not have attained to the Age of thirty five Years, and been fourteen Years a Resident within the United States.

[6.] In Case of the Removal of the President from Office, or of his Death, Resignation, or Inability to discharge the Powers and Duties of the said Office, the Same shall devolve on the Vice-President, and the Congress may by Law provide for the Case of Removal, Death, Resignation or Inability, both of the President and Vice-President, declaring what Officer shall then act as President, and such Officer shall act accordingly, until the Disability be removed, or a President shall be elected.

[7.] The President shall, at stated Times, receive for his Services, a Compensation, which shall neither be encreased nor diminished during the Period for which he shall have been elected, and he shall not receive within that Period any other Emolument from the United States, or any of them.

[8.] Before he enter on the Execution of his Office, he shall take the following Oath or Affirmation—"I do solemnly swear (or affirm) that I will faithfully execute the Office of President of the United States, and will to the best of my Ability, preserve, protect and defend the Constitution of the United States."

Section 2

[1.] The President shall be Commander in Chief of the Army and Navy of the United States, and of the Militia of the several States, when called into the actual Service of the United States; he may require the Opinion, in writing, of the principal Officer in each of the executive Departments, upon any Subject relating to the Duties of their respective Offices, and he shall have Power to grant Reprieves and Pardons for Offences against the United States, except in Cases of Impeachment.

[2.] He shall have Power, by and with the Advice and Consent of the Senate, to make Treaties, provided two thirds of the Senators present concur; and he shall nominate, and by and with the Advice and Consent of the Senate, shall appoint Ambassadors, other public Ministers and Consuls, Judges of the supreme Court, and all other Officers of the United States, whose Appointments are not herein otherwise provided for, and which shall be established by Law: but the Congress may by Law vest the Appointment of such inferior Officers, as they think proper, in the President alone, in the Courts of Law, or in the Heads of Departments.

Section 1. President and Vice President
Qualifications The president must be a citizen of the United States by birth, at least 35 years of age, and a resident of the United States for 14 years.

What Might Have Been
Qualifications At the Constitutional Convention, the New Jersey Amendments, sponsored by the smaller states, raised the possibility of making the executive a committee of people rather than a single individual. Also, executives were not allowed to run for a second term of office under this plan.

Section 1. President and Vice President
Vacancies If the president dies, resigns, is removed from office by impeachment, or is unable to carry out the duties of the office, the vice president becomes president.

Section 1. President and Vice President
Salary Originally, the president's salary was $25,000 per year. The president's current salary is $400,000 plus a $50,000 nontaxable expense account per year. The president also receives living accommodations in two residences—the White House and Camp David.

Section 2. Powers of the President
Cabinet Mention of "the principal officer in each of the executive departments" is the only suggestion of the president's cabinet to be found in the Constitution. The cabinet is an advisory body, and its power depends on the president. Section 2, Clause 1 also makes the president the head of the armed forces. This established the principle of civilian control of the military.

Section 2. Powers of the President
Treaties With Foreign Nations The president is responsible for the conduct of relations with foreign countries. *What role does the Senate have in approving treaties?*

The Constitution Handbook **155**

C₁ Critical Thinking
Analyzing Information Ask students to discuss why the Framers of the Constitution made the president commander in chief of the armed forces and any state militias called to serve the United States. *(The Framers wanted to ensure civilian control of the military.)* **OL**

C₂ Critical Thinking
Determining Cause and Effect Discuss examples showing the increase in presidential power during this century. For example, increasing globalization has expanded the president's foreign relations responsibilities, such as negotiating internal treaties, military policing interventions, and waging "undeclared wars." Write the following statement on the chalkboard: "The increase in presidential power during this century has been largely related to crises, whether domestic or foreign." **Ask:** Do you think this is the true cause of the increase in presidential power? Why or why not? If not, what do you think caused the increase? *(Students' answers will vary. Some may agree that globalization is the cause of increased presidential importance. Others may point to the role of the media focusing attention on one governing individual.)* **AL**

Answer: Two-thirds of the Senators must concur in order for a treaty to be approved.

Did You Know?
Incapacitated Presidents The United States has had a disabled president several times in its history. In the 1880s James Garfield remained bedridden for 79 days before dying from injuries sustained by an assassin's bullet. Woodrow Wilson had a stroke and was incapacitated for the last several months of his presidency.

155

Constitution Handbook

156

★ ★ ★ ★ ★ ★ ★ ★ ★ ★ ★

C Critical Thinking

Identifying Central Issues Ask students to consider the meaning of the phrase "respect for the law." Guide their discussion by asking the following questions: **What is the law? How can the law affect individuals and society? Why is respect for the law necessary to good government?** (Students' answers will vary.) **OL**

R Reading Strategy

Questioning The judicial branch is the least public branch of the federal government. **Ask: What does it mean when the Constitution states "The judges . . . shall hold their Offices during good Behaviour . . . ?"** (Judges would not be elected but appointed to lifetime positions.) **BL**

Answers and Additional Support

Section 3. Duties of the President

Executive Orders An important presidential power is the ability to issue executive orders. An executive order is a rule or command the president issues that has the force of law. Only Congress can make laws under the Constitution, but executive orders are considered part of the president's duty to "take care that the laws be faithfully executed." This power is often used during emergencies. During the Civil War, for example, President Lincoln issued an order suspending writs of habeas corpus. Over time the scope of executive orders has expanded, increasing the president's power. Decisions by federal agencies and departments are also considered to be executive orders.

Section 4. Impeachment

Reasons for Removal From Office This section states the reasons for which the president and vice president may be impeached and removed from office. Only Andrew Johnson and Bill Clinton have been impeached by the House. Richard Nixon resigned before the House could vote on possible impeachment.

Article III. The Judicial Branch

C The term *judicial* refers to courts. The Constitution set up only the Supreme Court but provided for the establishment of other federal courts. The judiciary of the United States has two different systems of courts. One system consists of the federal courts, whose powers derive from the Constitution and federal laws. The other includes the courts of each of the 50 states, whose powers derive from state constitutions and laws.

Section 2. Jurisdiction

General Jurisdiction Federal courts deal mostly with "statute law," or laws passed by Congress, treaties, and cases involving the Constitution itself.

Vocabulary

original jurisdiction: *authority to be the first court to hear a case*

appellate jurisdiction: *authority to hear cases that have been appealed from lower courts*

Section 2. Jurisdiction

The Supreme Court A court with "original jurisdiction" has the authority to be the first court to hear a case. The Supreme Court generally has "appellate jurisdiction" in that it mostly hears cases appealed from lower courts.

156 The Constitution Handbook

[3.] The President shall have Power to fill up all Vacancies that may happen during the Recess of the Senate, by granting Commissions which shall expire at the End of their next Session.

Section 3

He shall from time to time give to the Congress Information of the State of the Union, and recommend to their Consideration such Measures as he shall judge necessary and expedient; he may, on extraordinary Occasions, convene both Houses, or either of them, and in Case of Disagreement between them, with Respect to the Time of Adjournment, he may adjourn them to such Time as he shall think proper; he shall receive Ambassadors and other public Ministers; he shall take Care that the Laws be faithfully executed, and shall Commission all the Officers of the United States.

Section 4

The President, Vice-President and all civil Officers of the United States, shall be removed from Office on Impeachment for, and Conviction of, Treason, Bribery, or other high Crimes and Misdemeanors.

Article III

Section 1

The judicial Power of the United States, shall be vested in one supreme Court, and in such inferior Courts as the Congress may from time to time ordain and establish. The Judges, both of the supreme and inferior Courts, shall hold their Offices during good **R** Behaviour, and shall, at stated Times, receive for their Services, a Compensation, which shall not be diminished during their Continuance in Office.

Section 2

[1.] The judicial Power shall extend to all Cases, in Law and Equity, arising under this Constitution, the Laws of the United States, and Treaties made, or which shall be made, under their Authority;—to all Cases affecting Ambassadors, other public Ministers and Consuls;—to all Cases of admiralty and maritime Jurisdiction;—to Controversies to which the United States shall be a Party;—to Controversies between two or more States; —between a State and Citizens of another State;— between Citizens of different States,—between Citizens of the same State claiming Lands under Grants of different States, and between a State, or the Citizens thereof, and foreign States, Citizens or Subjects.

[2.] In all Cases affecting Ambassadors, other public Ministers and Consuls, and those in which a State shall be Party, the supreme Court shall have original Jurisdiction. In all the other Cases before mentioned, the supreme Court shall have appellate Jurisdiction, both as to Law and Fact, with such Exceptions, and under such Regulations as the Congress shall make.

More Skill Practice

Expository Writing The first African American Supreme Court justice, Thurgood Marshall, was named to the Court by President Lyndon Johnson in 1967. President Ronald Reagan nominated the first woman justice, Sandra Day O'Connor, in 1981. Ask students to write a paragraph speculating on why more minorities and women have not been appointed to the Supreme Court. Invite volunteers to share their answers with the class. **OL** **CA** 11WA2.4a

[3.] The Trial of all Crimes, except in Cases of Impeachment, shall be by Jury; and such Trial shall be held in the State where the said Crimes shall have been committed; but when not committed within any State, the Trial shall be at such Place or Places as the Congress may by Law have directed.

Section 3

[1.] Treason against the United States, shall consist only in levying War against them, or in adhering to their Enemies, giving them Aid and Comfort. No Person shall be convicted of Treason unless on the Testimony of two Witnesses to the same overt Act, or on Confession in open Court.

[2.] The Congress shall have Power to declare the Punishment of Treason, but no Attainder of Treason shall work Corruption of Blood, or Forfeiture except during the Life of the Person attainted.

Article IV

Section 1

Full Faith and Credit shall be given in each State to the public Acts, Records, and judicial Proceedings of every other State. And the Congress may by general Laws prescribe the Manner in which such Acts, Records and Proceedings shall be proved, and the Effect thereof.

Section 2

[1.] The Citizens of each State shall be entitled to all Privileges and Immunities of Citizens in the several States.

[2.] A Person charged in any State with Treason, Felony, or other Crime, who shall flee from Justice, and be found in another State, shall on Demand of the executive Authority of the State from which he fled, be delivered up, to be removed to the State having Jurisdiction of the Crime.

[3.] No Person held to Service of Labour in one State, under the Laws thereof, escaping into another, shall, in Consequence of any Law or Regulation therein, be discharged from such Service or Labour, but shall be delivered up on Claim of the Party to whom such Service or Labour may be due.

Section 3

[1.] New States may be admitted by the Congress into this Union; but no new State shall be formed or erected within the Jurisdiction of any other State; nor any State be formed by the Junction of two or more States, or Parts of States, without the Consent of the Legislatures of the States concerned as well as of the Congress.

[2.] The Congress shall have Power to dispose of and make all needful Rules and Regulations respecting the Territory or other Property belonging to the United States; and nothing in this Constitution shall be so construed as to Prejudice any Claims of the United States, or of any particular State.

Section 2. Jurisdiction
Jury Trial Except in cases of impeachment, anyone accused of a crime has the right to a trial by jury. The trial must be held in the state where the crime was committed. Jury trial guarantees were strengthened in the Sixth, Seventh, Eighth, and Ninth Amendments.

Article IV. Relations Among the States

Article IV explains the relationship of the states to one another and to the national government. This article requires each state to give citizens of other states the same rights as its own citizens, addresses the admission of new states, and guarantees that the national government will protect the states.

Section 1. Official Acts
Recognition by States This provision ensures that each state recognizes the laws, court decisions, and records of all other states. For example, a marriage license issued by one state must be accepted by all states.

Vocabulary

treason: *violation of the allegiance owed by a person to his or her own country, for example, by aiding an enemy*

Section 3. New States and Territories
New States Congress has the power to admit new states. It also determines the basic guidelines for applying for statehood. Two states, Maine and West Virginia, were created within the boundaries of another state. In the case of West Virginia, President Lincoln recognized the West Virginia government as the legal government of Virginia during the Civil War. This allowed West Virginia to secede from Virginia without obtaining approval from the Virginia legislature.

The Constitution Handbook **157**

R Reading Strategy

Evaluating Have students underline the definition of treason in Section 3 of the Constitution (Article III, Section 3, Clause 1). Tell students that this specific definition cannot be modified by Congress and can only be changed by a constitutional amendment. Have students use library and Internet resources to research United States citizens who have been found guilty of treason. **Ask:** Do you think the person was guilty of treason? Did the person's crime fit the definition presented in the Constitution? Invite students to share their findings and responses with the class. **OL**
CA HR3

S Skill Practice

Conducting Research Have students use library and Internet resources to research a current United States territory, including the history of the territory's relationship with the United States. Tell them to present their findings in three-page reports. Encourage the class to supplement the reports with photographs, maps, and drawings that provide information about the territory. **AL**
CA HR4 **CA 11WA2.4d**

More Skill Practice

Predicting Have students discuss the pros and cons of federal judges being elected rather than appointed. Direct them to list the possible outcomes they foresee if the federal judiciary was subject to the electoral process. Encourage students to share and compare their lists. **AL**

Vocabulary

amendment: *a change to the Constitution*
ratification: *process by which an amendment is approved*

Article V. The Amendment Process

Article V explains how the Constitution can be amended, or changed. All of the 27 amendments were proposed by a two-thirds vote of both houses of Congress. Only the Twenty-first Amendment was ratified by constitutional conventions of the states. All other amendments have been ratified by state legislatures. *What is an amendment?*

Article VI. Constitutional Supremacy

Article VI contains the "supremacy clause." This clause establishes that the Constitution, laws passed by Congress, and treaties of the United States "shall be the supreme Law of the Land." The "supremacy clause" recognizes the Constitution and federal laws that conform to the Constitution as supreme when in conflict with those of the states.

Article VII. Ratification

Article VII addresses ratification and states that, unlike the Articles of Confederation, which required approval of all thirteen states for adoption, the Constitution would take effect after it was ratified by nine states.

Section 4
The United States shall guarantee to every State in this Union a Republican Form of Government, and shall protect each of them against Invasion; and on Application of the Legislature, or of the Executive (when the Legislature cannot be convened) against domestic Violence.

Article V
The Congress, whenever two thirds of both Houses shall deem it necessary, shall propose Amendments to this Constitution, or, on the Application of the Legislatures of two thirds of the several States, shall call a Convention for proposing Amendments, which, in either Case, shall be valid to all Intents and Purposes, as Part of this Constitution, when ratified by the Legislatures of three fourths of the several States, or by Conventions in three fourths thereof, as the one or the other Mode of Ratification may be proposed by the Congress; Provided that no Amendment which may be made prior to the Year One thousand eight hundred and eight shall in any Manner affect the first and fourth Clauses in the Ninth Section of the first Article; and that no State, without its Consent, shall be deprived of its equal Suffrage in the Senate.

Article VI
[1.] All Debts contracted and Engagements entered into, before the Adoption of this Constitution, shall be as valid against the United States under this Constitution, as under the Confederation.
[2.] This Constitution, and the Laws of the United States which shall be made in Pursuance thereof; and all Treaties made, or which shall be made, under the Authority of the United States, shall be the supreme Law of the Land; and the Judges in every State shall be bound thereby, any Thing in the Constitution or Laws of any State to the Contrary notwithstanding.
[3.] The Senators and Representatives before mentioned, and the Members of the several State Legislatures, and all executive and judicial Officers, both of the United States and of the several States, shall be bound by Oath or Affirmation, to support this Constitution; but no religious Test shall ever be required as a Qualification to any Office or public Trust under the United States.

Article VII
The Ratification of the Conventions of nine States, shall be sufficient for the Establishment of this Constitution between the States so ratifying the same.
Done in Convention by the Unanimous Consent of the States present the Seventeenth Day of September in the Year of our Lord one thousand seven hundred and Eighty seven and of the Independence of the United States of America the Twelfth. In witness whereof We have hereunto subscribed our Names,

Did You Know?

Ratification The first five states to ratify the Constitution—Delaware, Pennsylvania, New Jersey, Georgia, and Connecticut—did so quickly and by large majorities.

Signers

George Washington,
President and Deputy
from Virginia

New Hampshire
John Langdon
Nicholas Gilman

Massachusetts
Nathaniel Gorham
Rufus King

Connecticut
William Samuel Johnson
Roger Sherman

New York
Alexander Hamilton

New Jersey
William Livingston
David Brearley
William Paterson
Jonathan Dayton

Pennsylvania
Benjamin Franklin
Thomas Mifflin
Robert Morris
George Clymer
Thomas FitzSimons
Jared Ingersoll
James Wilson
Gouverneur Morris

Delaware
George Read
Gunning Bedford, Jr.
John Dickinson
Richard Bassett
Jacob Broom

Maryland
James McHenry
Daniel of St. Thomas
    Jenifer
Daniel Carroll

Virginia
John Blair
James Madison, Jr.

North Carolina
William Blount
Richard Dobbs Spaight
Hugh Williamson

South Carolina
John Rutledge
Charles Cotesworth
    Pinckney
Charles Pinckney
Pierce Butler

Georgia
William Few
Abraham Baldwin

Attest:
William Jackson,
    Secretary

Amendment I

Congress shall make no law respecting an establishment of religion, or prohibiting the free exercise thereof; or abridging the freedom of speech, or of the press; or the right of the people peaceably to assemble, and to petition the Government for a redress of grievances.

Amendment II

A well regulated Militia, being necessary to the security of a free State, the right of the people to keep and bear Arms, shall not be infringed.

Amendment III

No Soldier shall, in time of peace be quartered in any house, without the consent of the Owner, nor in time of war, but in a manner to be prescribed by law.

Amendment IV

The right of the people to be secure in their persons, houses, papers, and effects, against unreasonable searches and seizures, shall not be violated, and no Warrants shall issue, but upon probable cause, supported by Oath or affirmation, and particularly describing the place to be searched, and the persons or things to be seized.

Amendment V

No person shall be held to answer for a capital, or otherwise infamous crime, unless on a presentment or indictment of a Grand Jury, except in cases arising in the

The Bill of Rights

The first 10 amendments are known as the Bill of Rights (1791). These amendments limit the powers of the federal government. The First Amendment protects the civil liberties of individuals in the United States. The amendment freedoms are not absolute, however. They are limited by the rights of other individuals. *What freedoms does the First Amendment protect?*

Amendment 2

Bearing Arms This amendment is often debated. Originally it was intended to prevent the national government from repeating the actions of the British, who tried to take weapons away from the colonial militia, or armed forces of citizens. This amendment seems to support the right of citizens to own firearms, but the Supreme Court has ruled that it does not prevent Congress from regulating the interstate sale of weapons.

Vocabulary

quarter: *to provide living accommodations*
warrant: *document that gives police particular rights or powers*
probable cause: *police must have a reasonable basis to believe a person is linked to a crime*

The Constitution Handbook **159**

Did You Know?

Signers of the Constitution Of the 55 delegates who attended the Constitutional Convention, only 38 signed the document. A thirty-ninth signature—that of John Dickinson—was written by George Read at Dickinson's request. Elbridge Gerry of Massachusetts and Edmund Randolph and George Mason of Virginia refused to sign, while 13 other delegates left the Convention early.

Constitution Handbook

Answer: The Grand Jury evaluates whether there is enough evidence to bring the accused person to trial.

Answer: The requirement of a "speedy" trial ensures that an accused person will not be held in jail for a lengthy period as a means of punishing the accused without a trial.

C Critical Thinking

Making Generalizations

Supply students with the following information: Some lawyers maintain that the mass media threaten a defendant's Sixth Amendment rights. These lawyers argue that extensive coverage of a crime on television and in the newspapers makes it difficult to find jurors who are truly impartial. **Ask: Should the mass media be allowed to cover trials if doing so interferes with a defendant's Sixth Amendment rights? Why or why not? What is an acceptable role for the media in jury trials?** Encourage students to write down their responses, and then use these written responses to generate discussion. **OL**

CA 11WA2.3b

Answers and Additional Support

Amendment 5

Rights of the Accused This amendment contains important protections for people accused of crimes. One of the protections is that government may not deprive any person of life, liberty, or property without due process of law. This means that the government must follow proper constitutional procedures in trials and in other actions it takes against individuals. *According to Amendment V, what is the function of a grand jury?*

Amendment 6

Right to Speedy and Fair Trial A basic protection is the right to a speedy, public trial. The jury must hear witnesses and evidence on both sides before deciding the guilt or innocence of a person charged with a crime. This amendment also provides that legal counsel must be provided to a defendant. In 1963, in *Gideon* v. *Wainwright*, the Supreme Court ruled that if a defendant cannot afford a lawyer, the government must provide one to defend him or her. *Why is the right to a "speedy" trial important?*

Vocabulary

common law: *law established by previous court decisions*

bail: *money that an accused person provides to the court as a guarantee that he or she will be present for a trial*

Amendment 9

Powers Reserved to the People This amendment prevents government from claiming that the only rights people have are those listed in the Bill of Rights.

Amendment 10

Powers Reserved to the States This amendment protects the states and the people from the federal government. It establishes that powers not given to the national government and not denied to the states by the Constitution belong to the states or to the people. These are checks on the "necessary and proper" power of the federal government, which is provided for in Article I, Section 8, Clause 18.

Amendment 11

Suits Against States The Eleventh Amendment (1795) provides that a lawsuit brought by a citizen of the United States or a foreign nation against a state must be tried in a state court, not in a federal court. The Supreme Court had ruled in *Chisholm* v. *Georgia* (1793) that a federal court could try a lawsuit brought by citizens of South Carolina against a citizen of Georgia.

land or naval forces, or in the Militia, when in actual service in time of War or public danger; nor shall any person be subject for the same offence to be twice put in jeopardy of life or limb; nor shall be compelled in any criminal case to be a witness against himself, nor be deprived of life, liberty, or property, without due process of law; nor shall private property be taken for public use without just compensation.

Amendment VI

C

In all criminal prosecutions, the accused shall enjoy the right to a speedy and public trial, by an impartial jury of the State and district wherein the crime shall have been committed, which district shall have been previously ascertained by law, and to be informed of the nature and cause of the accusation; to be confronted with the witnesses against him; to have compulsory process for obtaining Witnesses in his favor, and to have the assistance of counsel for his defence.

Amendment VII

In Suits at common law, where the value in controversy shall exceed twenty dollars, the right of trial by jury shall be preserved, and no fact tried by a jury, shall be otherwise reexamined in any Court of the United States, than according to the rules of common law.

Amendment VIII

Excessive bail shall not be required, nor excessive fines imposed, nor cruel and unusual punishments inflicted.

Amendment IX

The enumeration in the Constitution, of certain rights, shall not be construed to deny or disparage others retained by the people.

Amendment X

The powers not delegated to the United States by the Constitution, nor prohibited by it to the States, are reserved to the States respectively, or to the people.

Amendment XI

The Judicial power of the United States shall not be construed to extend to any suit in law or equity, commenced or prosecuted against one of the United States by Citizens of another State, or by Citizens or Subjects of any Foreign State.

Did You Know?

Constitutional Roots The right to a "speedy and public trial" was one of the first procedural rights to develop in English law. The Magna Carta states in Article 40: "To no one will we sell, to none will we refuse or delay, right or justice."

Amendment XII

The electors shall meet in their respective states and vote by ballot for President and Vice-President, one of whom, at least, shall not be an inhabitant of the same state with themselves; they shall name in their ballots the person voted for as President, and in distinct ballots the person voted for as Vice-President, and they shall make distinct lists of all persons voted for as President, and of all persons voted for as Vice-President, and of the number of votes for each, which lists they shall sign and certify, and transmit sealed to the seat of the government of the United States, directed to the President of the Senate;—The President of the Senate shall, in the presence of the Senate and House of Representatives, open all the certificates and the votes shall then be counted;—The person having the greatest number of votes for President, shall be the President, if such number be a majority of the whole number of Electors appointed; and if no person have such majority, then from the persons having the highest numbers not exceeding three on the list of those voted for as President, the House of Representatives shall choose immediately, by ballot, the President. But in choosing the President, the votes shall be taken by states, the representation from each state having one vote; a quorum for this purpose shall consist of a member or members from two-thirds of the states, and a majority of all the states shall be necessary to a choice. And if the House of Representatives shall not choose a President whenever the right of choice shall devolve upon them, before the fourth day of March next following, then the Vice-President shall act as President, as in the case of the death or other constitutional disability of the President. The person having the greatest number of votes as Vice-President, shall be the Vice-President, if such number be a majority of the whole number of Electors appointed, and if no person have a majority, then from the two highest numbers on the list, the Senate shall choose the Vice-President; a quorum for the purpose shall consist of two-thirds of the whole number of Senators, and a majority of the whole number shall be necessary to a choice. But no person constitutionally ineligible to the office of President shall be eligible to that of Vice-President of the United States.

Amendment XIII

Section 1

Neither slavery nor involuntary servitude, except as a punishment for crime whereof the party shall have been duly convicted, shall exist within the United States, or any place subject to their jurisdiction.

Amendment 12

Election of President and Vice President The Twelfth Amendment (1804) corrects a problem that had arisen in the method of electing the president and vice president, which is described in Article II, Section 1, Clause 3. This amendment provides for the Electoral College to use separate ballots in voting for president and vice president. *If no candidate receives a majority of the electoral votes, who elects the president?*

Vocabulary

majority: *more than half*

Amendment 13

Abolition of Slavery Amendments Thirteen (1865), Fourteen, and Fifteen often are called the Civil War amendments because they grew out of that conflict. The Thirteenth Amendment outlaws slavery.

Answer: the House of Representatives

S Skill Practice

Conducting Research Point out that the Electoral College has been criticized as being obsolete, and various reforms have been suggested for changing it or abolishing it altogether. Ask students to research some of these suggestions or reforms. Lead a discussion about the 2000 and 2004 presidential elections, which continued the debate over the role of the Electoral College, and discuss how any potential reforms might or might not have affected the elections' outcomes. **OL** **CA HR3**

The Constitution Handbook **161**

More Skill Practice

Researching the Constitution Ask students to research the number of amendments to the California state constitution, a relatively easy constitution to amend. Have them write three-page papers discussing California as an example of what happens when a constitution is easily amended. Encourage students to consider in their reports whether they think the national Constitution would work better if it were easier to amend. **AL** **CA 11WA2.4d**

Constitution Handbook

Amendment 14
Rights of Citizens The Fourteenth Amendment (1868) originally was intended to protect the legal rights of the freed slaves. Its interpretation has been extended to protect the rights of citizenship in general by prohibiting a state from depriving any person of life, liberty, or property without "due process of law." In addition, it states that all citizens have the right to equal protection of the laws in all states.

Amendment 14. Section 2
Representation in Congress This section reduced the number of members a state had in the House of Representatives if it denied its citizens the right to vote. Later civil rights laws and the Twenty-fourth Amendment guaranteed the vote to African Americans.

Vocabulary

abridge: *to reduce*
insurrection: *rebellion against the government*

Amendment 14. Section 3
Penalty for Engaging in Insurrection The leaders of the Confederacy were barred from state or federal offices unless Congress agreed to remove this ban. By the end of Reconstruction, all but a few Confederate leaders were allowed to return to public service.

Amendment 14. Section 4
Public Debt The public debt acquired by the federal government during the Civil War was valid and could not be questioned by the South. However, the debts of the Confederacy were declared to be illegal. *Could former slaveholders collect payment for the loss of their slaves?*

Section 2

Congress shall have power to enforce this article by appropriate legislation.

Amendment XIV

Section 1

All persons born or naturalized in the United States, and subject to the jurisdiction thereof, are citizens of the United States and of the State wherein they reside. No State shall make or enforce any law which shall abridge the privileges or immunities of citizens of the United States; nor shall any State deprive any person of life, liberty, or property, without due process of law; nor deny to any person within its jurisdiction the equal protection of the laws.

Section 2

Representatives shall be apportioned among the several States according to their respective numbers, counting the whole number of persons in each State, excluding Indians not taxed. But when the right to vote at any election for the choice of electors for President and Vice-President of the United States, Representatives in Congress, the Executive and Judicial officers of a State, or the members of the Legislature thereof, is denied to any of the male inhabitants of such State, being twenty-one years of age, and citizens of the United States, or in any way abridged, except for participation in rebellion, or other crime, the basis of representation therein shall be reduced in the proportion which the number of such male citizens shall bear to the whole number of male citizens twenty-one years of age in such State.

Section 3

No person shall be a Senator or Representative in Congress, or elector of President and Vice-President, or hold any office, civil or military, under the United States, or under any State, who, having previously taken an oath, as a member of Congress, or as an officer of the United States, or as a member of any State legislature, or as an executive or judicial officer of any State, to support the Constitution of the United States, shall have engaged in insurrection or rebellion against the same, or given aid or comfort to the enemies thereof. But Congress may by a vote of two-thirds of each House, remove such disability.

Section 4

The validity of the public debt of the United States, authorized by law, including debts incurred for payment of pensions and bounties for service, in suppressing insurrection or rebellion, shall not be questioned. But neither the United States nor any State shall assume or pay any debt or obligation incurred in aid of insurrection or rebellion against the United States, or any

EXTENDING THE CONTENT

Civil War Amendments The Thirteenth, Fourteenth, and Fifteenth Amendments represent attempts to use the Constitution to end slavery, to extend citizenship to formerly enslaved persons, and to guarantee male African Americans the right to vote. Literacy tests, poll taxes, and grandfather clauses, however, continued to keep large numbers of African Americans from voting in many Southern states until after Reconstruction.

claim for the loss or emancipation of any slave; but all such debts, obligations and claims shall be held illegal and void.

Section 5
The Congress shall have power to enforce, by appropriate legislation, the provisions of this article.

Amendment XV

Section 1
The right of citizens of the United States to vote shall not be denied or abridged by the United States or by any State on account of race, color, or previous condition of servitude.

Section 2
The Congress shall have power to enforce this article by appropriate legislation.

Amendment XVI

The Congress shall have power to lay and collect taxes on incomes, from whatever source derived, without apportionment among the several States and without regard to any census or enumeration.

Amendment XVII

Section 1
The Senate of the United States shall be composed of two Senators from each State, elected by the people thereof, for six years; and each Senator shall have one vote. The electors in each State shall have the qualifications requisite for electors of the most numerous branch of the State legislatures.

Section 2
When vacancies happen in the representation of any State in the Senate, the executive authority of such State shall issue writs of election to fill such vacancies: *Provided,* That the legislature of any State may empower the executive thereof to make temporary appointments until the people fill the vacancies by election as the legislature may direct.

Section 3
This amendment shall not be so construed as to affect the election or term of any Senator chosen before it becomes valid as part of the Constitution.

Amendment XVIII

Section 1
After one year from ratification of this article, the manufacture, sale, or transportation of intoxicating liquors within, the importation thereof into, or the

R | **Amendment 15**
Voting Rights The Fifteenth Amendment (1870) prohibits the government from denying a person's right to vote on the basis of race. Despite the law, many states denied African Americans the right to vote by such means as poll taxes, literacy tests, and white primaries.

Amendment 16
Income Tax The origins of the Sixteenth Amendment (1913) date back to 1895, when the Supreme Court declared a federal income tax unconstitutional. To overturn this decision, this amendment authorizes an income tax that is levied on a direct basis.

Amendment 17
Direct Election of Senators The Seventeenth Amendment (1913) states that the people, instead of state legislatures, elect United States senators. *How many years are in a Senate term?*

Vocabulary

apportionment: *distribution of seats in House based on population*
vacancy: *an office or position that is unfilled or unoccupied*

C | **Amendment 18**
Prohibition The Eighteenth Amendment (1919) prohibited the production, sale, or transportation of alcoholic beverages in the United States. Prohibition proved to be difficult to enforce. This amendment was later repealed by the Twenty-first Amendment.

The Constitution Handbook **163**

R **Reading Strategy**
Categorizing Information Have students work together in three groups to research one of the following: poll taxes, literacy tests, or white primaries. Remind students to pay particular attention to how their provision was used to keep African Americans from voting. Then ask the groups to combine their information and present it in a chart or graphic organizer that lists the provisions, a definition or explanation for each, and the impact of each on African American voting rights. **OL**

Answer: six years

C **Critical Thinking**
Predicting Consequences Inform students that Prohibition successfully reduced the consumption of alcohol in the United States, thus decreasing the number of alcohol-related deaths and accidents. **Ask:** What do you think happened to this number after Prohibition was repealed in 1933? Have students check their predictions by using library and Internet resources to locate statistics on alcohol-related deaths and accidents during the early twentieth century. **AL**

More Skill Practice

Visualizing Help visual learners to remember unfamiliar vocabulary words by encouraging them to draw pictures illustrating the definition of the word. Instruct students to write each vocabulary word on one side of a note card and to draw their picture on the other side. Then have students quiz themselves using the note cards they have created. **EL**

★ ★ ★ ★ ★ ★ ★ ★ ★ ★

Amendment 19
Woman Suffrage The Nineteenth Amendment (1920) guaranteed women the right to vote. By then women had already won the right to vote in many state elections, but the amendment made their right to vote in all state and national elections constitutional.

Amendment 20
"Lame Duck" The Twentieth Amendment (1933) sets new dates for Congress to begin its term and for the inauguration of the president and vice president. Under the original Constitution, elected officials who retired or who had been defeated remained in office for several months. For the outgoing president, this period ran from November until March. Such outgoing officials, referred to as "lame ducks," could accomplish little. *What date was fixed as Inauguration Day?*

Amendment 20. Section 3
Succession of President and Vice President This section provides that if the president-elect dies before taking office, the vice president-elect becomes president.

Vocabulary

president-elect: *individual who is elected president but has not yet begun serving his or her term*

---

exportation thereof from the United States and all territory subject to the jurisdiction thereof for beverage purposes is hereby prohibited.

Section 2
The Congress and the several States shall have concurrent power to enforce this article by appropriate legislation.

Section 3
This article shall be inoperative unless it shall have been ratified as an amendment to the Constitution by the legislatures of the several States, as provided in the Constitution, within seven years from the date of the submission hereof to the States by the Congress.

Amendment XIX

Section 1
The right of citizens of the United States to vote shall not be denied or abridged by the United States or by any state on account of sex.

Section 2
Congress shall have power by appropriate legislation to enforce the provisions of this article.

Amendment XX

Section 1
The terms of the President and Vice President shall end at noon on the 20th day of January, and the terms of the Senators and Representatives at noon on the 3rd day of January, of the years in which such terms would have ended if this article had not been ratified; and the terms of their successors shall then begin.

Section 2
The Congress shall assemble at least once in every year, and such meeting shall begin at noon on the 3rd day of January, unless they shall by law appoint a different day.

Section 3
If, at the time fixed for the beginning of the term of the President, the President elect shall have died, the Vice President elect shall become President. If a President shall not have been chosen before the time fixed for the beginning of his term, or if the President elect shall have failed to qualify, then the Vice President elect shall act as President until a President shall have qualified; and the Congress may by law provide for the case wherein neither a President elect nor a Vice President elect shall have qualified, declaring who shall then act as President, or the manner in which one who is to act shall be selected, and such person shall act accordingly until a President or Vice President shall have qualified.

Section 4

The Congress may by law provide for the case of the death of any of the persons from whom the House of Representatives may choose a President whenever the right of choice shall have devolved upon them, and for the case of the death of any of the persons from whom the Senate may choose a Vice President whenever the right of choice shall have devolved upon them.

Section 5

Sections 1 and 2 shall take effect on the 15th day of October following the ratification of this article.

Section 6

This article shall be inoperative unless it shall have been ratified as an amendment to the Constitution by the legislatures of three-fourths of the several States within seven years from the date of its submission.

Amendment XXI

Section 1

The eighteenth article of amendment to the Constitution of the United States is hereby repealed.

Section 2

The transportation or importation into any State, Territory, or possession of the United States for delivery or use therein of intoxicating liquors, in violation of the laws thereof, is hereby prohibited.

Section 3

This article shall be inoperative unless it shall have been ratified as an amendment to the Constitution by conventions in the several States, as provided in the Constitution, within seven years from the date of the submission hereof to the States by the Congress.

Amendment XXII

Section 1

No person shall be elected to the office of the President more than twice, and no person who had held the office of President, or acted as President, for more than two years of a term to which some other person was elected President shall be elected to the office of the President more than once. But this Article shall not apply to any person holding the office of President when this Article was proposed by the Congress, and shall not prevent any person who may be holding the office of President, or acting as President, during the term within which this Article becomes operative from holding the office of President or acting as President during the remainder of such term.

Amendment 21

Repeal of Prohibition The Twenty-first Amendment (1933) repeals the Eighteenth Amendment. It is the only amendment ever passed to overturn an earlier amendment. It is also the only amendment ratified by special state conventions instead of state legislatures.

Amendment 22

Presidential Term Limit The Twenty-second Amendment (1951) limits presidents to a maximum of two elected terms. The amendment wrote into the Constitution a custom started by George Washington. It was passed largely as a reaction to Franklin D. Roosevelt's election to four terms between 1933 and 1945. It also provides that anyone who succeeds to the presidency and serves for more than two years of the term may not be elected more than one more time.

The Constitution Handbook **165**

Constitution Handbook

U Universal Access

Visual/Spatial Have students create political cartoons illustrating the Twenty-first Amendment. Remind them to include titles and captions, if necessary. Then ask students to write paragraphs explaining their cartoons. Display the cartoons around your classroom as you discuss the Twenty-first Amendment. **EL**

R Reading Strategy

Evaluating Have students list advantages and disadvantages of the two-term limit for presidents. Ask volunteers to present and defend their lists. Then have students discuss the following: Should there be presidential term limits? If so, to how many terms should the president be limited? **OL**

Did You Know?

Presidential Term Limits The Framers were concerned about giving the executive branch of the new government too much power. They originally considered having the president serve a seven-year term with no opportunity for reelection. However, many delegates thought that a seven-year term was too long. The final decision set the presidential term of office at four years and allowed presidents to run for reelection.

W Writing Support

Expository Writing Write the following statement on the board: "That the people of Washington, D.C., have no representation in Congress is a violation of their democratic rights." Ask all students to write a one-page paper expressing their feelings and point of view on this statement. **OL** **CA 11WA2.3a**

S Skill Practice

Identifying Point of View
Have students write two newspaper editorials. The first editorial should be written from the perspective of someone in favor of the Twenty-third Amendment, and the second from the perspective of someone who is against the amendment. Provide present-day examples of how to set up an editorial. **OL** **CA HR2**

Answer: the president pro tempore of the Senate (the vice president) and the Speaker of the House of Representatives

Vocabulary

District of Columbia: *site of nation's capital occupying an area between Maryland and Virginia*

W Amendment 23

D.C. Electors The Twenty-third Amendment (1961) allows citizens living in Washington, D.C., to vote for president and vice president, a right previously denied residents of the nation's capital. The District of Columbia now has three presidential electors, the number to which it would be entitled if it were a state.

Amendment 24

Abolition of the Poll Tax The Twenty-fourth Amendment (1964) prohibits poll taxes in federal elections. Prior to the passage of this amendment, some states had used such taxes to keep low-income African Americans from voting. In 1966 the Supreme Court banned poll taxes in state elections as well.

Amendment 25

Presidential Disability and Succession The Twenty-fifth Amendment (1967) established a process for the vice president to take over leadership of the nation when a president is disabled. It also set procedures for filling a vacancy in the office of vice president.

This amendment was used in 1973, when Vice President Spiro Agnew resigned from office after being charged with accepting bribes. President Richard Nixon then appointed Gerald R. Ford as vice president in accordance with the provisions of the Twenty-fifth Amendment. A year later, President Nixon resigned during the Watergate scandal, and Ford became president. President Ford then had to fill the vice presidency, which he had left vacant upon assuming the presidency. He named Nelson A. Rockefeller as vice president. Thus individuals who had not been elected held both the presidency and the vice presidency. *Who does the president inform if he or she cannot carry out the duties of the office?*

Section 2

This article shall be inoperative unless it shall have been ratified as an amendment to the Constitution by the legislatures of three-fourths of the several States within seven years from the date of its submission to the States by the Congress.

Amendment XXIII

Section 1

The District constituting the seat of Government of the United States shall appoint in such manner as the Congress may direct:

S A number of electors of President and Vice President equal to the whole number of Senators and Representatives in Congress to which the District would be entitled if it were a State, but in no event more than the least populous State; they shall be in addition to those appointed by the States, but they shall be considered, for the purposes of the election of President and Vice President, to be electors appointed by a State; and they shall meet in the District and perform such duties as provided by the twelfth article of amendment.

Section 2

The Congress shall have power to enforce this article by appropriate legislation.

Amendment XXIV

Section 1

The right of citizens of the United States to vote in any primary or other election for President or Vice President, for electors for President or Vice President, or for Senator or Representative in Congress, shall not be denied or abridged by the United States or any State by reason of failure to pay any poll tax or other tax.

Section 2

The Congress shall have power to enforce this article by appropriate legislation.

Amendment XXV

Section 1

In case of the removal of the President from office or his death or resignation, the Vice President shall become President.

Section 2

Whenever there is a vacancy in the office of the Vice President, the President shall nominate a Vice President who shall take the office upon confirmation by a majority vote of both Houses of Congress.

Section 3

Whenever the President transmits to the President pro tempore of the Senate and the Speaker of the House of

Did You Know?

The Poll Tax After the Civil War, poll taxes were levied in many Southern states. Although the poll tax kept many low-income white males from voting, its major purpose was to keep African Americans away from the polls. Not until the 1960s did Congress take firm action to enforce the Fifteenth Amendment and end this kind of racial discrimination.

Representatives his written declaration that he is unable to discharge the powers and duties of his office, and until he transmits to them a written declaration to the contrary, such powers and duties shall be discharged by the Vice President as Acting President.

Section 4

Whenever the Vice President and a majority of either the principal officers of the executive departments or of such other body as Congress may by law provide, transmit to the President pro tempore of the Senate and the Speaker of the House of Representatives their written declaration that the President is unable to discharge the powers and duties of his office, the Vice President shall immediately assume the power and duties of the office of Acting President.

Thereafter, when the President transmits to the President pro tempore of the Senate and the Speaker of the House of Representatives his written declaration that no inability exists, he shall resume the powers and duties of his office unless the Vice President and a majority of either the principal officers of the executive department or of such other body as Congress may by law provide, transmit within four days to the President pro tempore of the Senate and the Speaker of the House of Representatives their written declaration that the President is unable to discharge the powers and duties of his office. Thereupon Congress shall decide the issue, assembling within forty-eight hours for that purpose if not in session. If the Congress, within twenty-one days after receipt of the latter written declaration, or, if Congress is not in session, within twenty-one days after Congress is required to assemble, determines by two-thirds vote of both Houses that the President is unable to discharge the powers and duties of his office, the Vice President shall continue to discharge the same as Acting President; otherwise, the President shall resume the power and duties of his office.

Amendment XXVI

Section 1

The right of citizens of the United States, who are eighteen years of age or older, to vote shall not be denied or abridged by the United States or by any State on account of age.

Section 2

The Congress shall have power to enforce this article by appropriate legislation.

Amendment XXVII

No law, varying the compensation for the services of Senators and Representatives, shall take effect, until an election of representatives shall have intervened.

Amendment 26
Voting Age of 18 The Twenty-sixth Amendment (1971) lowered the voting age in both federal and state elections to 18.

Amendment 27
Congressional Salary Restraints The Twenty-seventh Amendment (1992) makes congressional pay raises effective during the term following their passage. James Madison offered the amendment in 1789, but it was never adopted. In 1982 Gregory Watson, then a student at the University of Texas, discovered the forgotten amendment while doing research for a school paper. Watson made the amendment's passage his crusade.

The Constitution Handbook **167**

C Critical Thinking

Analyzing Information Inform students that people age eighteen to twenty-five have historically low voter turnout (the lowest of any age group). **Ask:** Why don't many young people vote? (Answers will vary. Students may note that young people are not interested or do not feel connected to political issues.) Organize students into small groups to answer the following question: What can be done to increase voter turnout among eighteen- to twenty-five-year-olds? Have the groups come up with plans to increase voter turnout in this age group and present their findings to the class. OL

U Universal Access

Visual/Spatial Have students work in pairs to create a poster informing eighteen-year-olds of their right and responsibility to vote. Remind them to include illustrations on their posters, as well as information about how, when, and where to register to vote. Display the posters in a high-traffic area of the school, such as the lunch room or the hallway outside your classroom. BL

Did You Know?

The Twenty-sixth Amendment Many people used the Vietnam War to justify the adoption of the Twenty-sixth Amendment. These people argued that those old enough to fight and die for their country were also old enough to vote.

167

Chapter 2 Planning Guide

SECTION RESOURCES

MAIN IDEAS	📁 PRINT MATERIALS	TECHNOLOGY RESOURCES
Section 1: The New Republic 1. The United States established a federal government, created the Bill of Rights, and witnessed the first political parties. 2. During the Jefferson administration, the Supreme Court established judicial review, and the country doubled in size. 3. After the War of 1812, nationalism united the country. 4. New industries and railroads transformed the North in the early 1800s, while slavery expanded in the South.	• Daily Lecture and Discussion Notes 2-1 • Active Reading Note-Taking Guide 2-1 • Section Quiz 2-1 • Reading Essentials and Study Guide 2-1	🖥 Daily Focus Skills Transparency 2-1 💿 Interactive Tutor Self-Assessment CD-ROM 💿 ExamView® Pro Testmaker CD-ROM 💿 Presentation Plus! CD-ROM 🖥 California Standards Practice Transparencies
Section 2: Growing Division and Reform 1. Sectionalism increased after the War of 1812, while voting rights expanded for American citizens. 2. The Second Great Awakening brought an era of reform.	• Daily Lecture and Discussion Notes 2-2 • Active Reading Note-Taking Guide 2-2 • Section Quiz 2-2 • Reading Essentials and Study Guide 2-2	🖥 Daily Focus Skills Transparency 2-2 💿 Interactive Tutor Self-Assessment CD-ROM 💿 ExamView® Pro Testmaker CD-ROM 💿 Presentation Plus! CD-ROM 🖥 California Standards Practice Transparencies
Section 3: Manifest Destiny and Crisis 1. In the 1840s, the nation expanded as settlers moved west. 2. Continuing disagreements over the westward expansion of slavery increased sectional tensions between the North and South. 3. The slavery controversy shook up political parties and accelerated the crisis between North and South. 4. The election of Abraham Lincoln led the Southern states to secede from the Union.	• Daily Lecture and Discussion Notes 2-3 • Active Reading Note-Taking Guide 2-3 • Section Quiz 2-3 • Reading Essentials and Study Guide 2-3	🖥 Daily Focus Skills Transparency 2-3 💿 Interactive Tutor Self-Assessment CD-ROM 💿 ExamView® Pro Testmaker CD-ROM 💿 Presentation Plus! CD-ROM 🖥 California Standards Practice Transparencies
Section 4: The Civil War 1. The plan to resupply Fort Sumter started the Civil War. 2. The North and South each had distinct advantages and disadvantages at the beginning of the Civil War. 3. With Union casualties rising, President Lincoln issued the Emancipation Proclamation. 4. With the help of key victories at Vicksburg and Gettysburg, the North defeated the South after four long years of fighting.	• Daily Lecture and Discussion Notes 2-4 • Active Reading Note-Taking Guide 2-4 • Section Quiz 2-4 • Reading Essentials and Study Guide 2-4	🖥 Daily Focus Skills Transparency 2-4 💿 Interactive Tutor Self-Assessment CD-ROM 💿 ExamView® Pro Testmaker CD-ROM 💿 Presentation Plus! CD-ROM 🖥 California Standards Practice Transparencies
Section 5: Reconstruction 1. After the Civil War, the nation began rebuilding. 2. Radical Republicans, angered with President Johnson's actions, designed their own policies. 3. As African Americans entered politics, some Southerners began to resist Republican reforms. 4. Reconstruction came to an end as Democrats regained power in the South and in Congress.	• Daily Lecture and Discussion Notes 2-5 • Active Reading Note-Taking Guide 2-5 • Section Quiz 2-5 • Reading Essentials and Study Guide 2-5	🖥 Daily Focus Skills Transparency 2-5 💿 Interactive Tutor Self-Assessment CD-ROM 💿 ExamView® Pro Testmaker CD-ROM 💿 Presentation Plus! CD-ROM 🖥 California Standards Practice Transparencies

PACING YOUR LESSONS

Chapter Introduction	Section 1	Section 2	Section 3	Section 4	Section 5	Chapter Assessment
½ Day	2 Days	2 Days	2 Days	2 Days	2 Days	½ Day

`0:00` OUT OF TIME? 📁 Assign the Chapter 2 *Reading Essentials and Study Guide.*

Chapter 2 Planning Guide

Standards-Based Lesson Plan

 ## History–Social Science Standards Covered in Chapter 2

standards covered in the chapter are listed below. Use the accompanying activity as you teach the chapter to ensure student stery of these standards. This activity can be used in combination with the program's print and technology assessment materials.

Standard	Section 1	2	3	4	5
1.1 Students analyze the significant events in the founding of the nation and its attempts to realize the philosophy of government described in the Declaration of Independence				✔	✔
1.1.3 Understand the history of the Constitution after 1787 with emphasis on federal versus state authority and growing democratization.	✔	✔	✔	✔	✔
1.1.4 Examine the effects of the Civil War and Reconstruction and of the industrial revolution, including demographic shifts and the emergence in the late nineteenth century of the United States as a world power.				✔	✔
1.3.2 Analyze the great religious revivals and the leaders involved in them, including the First Great Awakening, the Second Great Awakening, the Civil War revivals, the Social Gospel Movement, the rise of Christian liberal theology in the nineteenth century, the impact of the Second Vatican Council, and the rise of Christian fundamentalism in current times.		✔			
1.3.3 Cite incidences of religious intolerance in the United States (e.g., persecution of Mormons, anti-Catholic sentiment, anti-Semitism).		✔	✔		
1.10.2 Examine and analyze the key events, policies, and court cases in the evolution of civil rights, including *Dred Scott* v. *Sanford*, *Plessy* v. *Ferguson*, *Brown* v. *Board of Education*, *Regents of the University of California* v. *Bakke*, and California Proposition 209.			✔	✔	✔

Cumulative Standards-Assessment Activity

Cumulative Standards-Assessment Activity will help students organize and learn the important information from the chapter. in teaching the chapter with this activity, and have students complete it as they read the chapter.

CREATING A CHART FOR MAKING GENERALIZATIONS

urpose Explain that generalizations—broad statements that should e based on observable or accurate information—are useful when ey want to summarize large amounts of information. Even before ey read the chapter, students can probably think of several gener-izations about the Civil War. As they read this chapter, students ill learn many facts about the problems leading up to the Civil ar. Studying the facts in order to support a broader generalization in focus students as they read and help them retain information.

ntroduction to Reading with Purpose

Review with the class the steps in making valid generalizations:
• Identify the subject matter.
• Collect related facts.
• Identify similarities among these facts.
• Make a generalization that is consistent with most of the facts gathered.

2. Ask students to list what they know or believe they know about this period of American history.

3. Have students copy this chart into their notebooks.

Supporting Facts

Generalization

As they read, students should identify facts that support their generalizations. Have them choose five facts supporting their generalization.

4. As part of the chapter review, have students share their general-ization charts. Guide the class in constructive criticism until the group is satisfied that the generalizations are supported by the facts. Encourage the class to use their charts as study aids.

Chapter 2 Planning Guide

READING SUPPORT

- Content Vocabulary Activity 2
- Academic Vocabulary Activity 2
- Reading Skills Activity 2
- Chapter 2 Active Reading Note-Taking Guide
- Chapter 2 Guided Reading Activities
- Chapter 2 Reading Essentials and Study Guide
- *The American Vision: Modern Times* Video Program
- Vocabulary PuzzleMaker CD-ROM
- American History Primary Source Document Library CD-ROM

CRITICAL THINKING

- Critical Thinking Skills Activity 2
- Primary Source Reading 2
- Cause-and-Effect Transparency 2 Strategy and Activity
- Presentation Plus! CD-ROM

UNIVERSAL ACCESS

- Universal Access Activity 2
- English Learner Activity 2
- American Art Prints
- StudentWorks™ Plus CD-ROM
- American Music: Hits Through History
- School-to-Home Connection Activity 2

SKILL PRACTICE

- Map Overlay Transparency 2 Strategy and Activity
- Historical Analysis Skills Activity 2
- Time Line Activity 2
- Reading Skills Activity 2
- Reinforcing Skills Activity 2
- Linking Past and Present Activity 2
- Interpreting Political Cartoons 2
- History Simulations and Problem Solving, Unit 1
- MindJogger Videoquiz

WRITING SUPPORT

- Chapter 2 Active Reading Note-Taking Guide
- Writer's Guidebook
- High School Writing Process Transparencies

ASSESSMENT

- Chapter 2 Section Quizzes
- Chapter 2 Tests, Forms A and B
- Authentic Assessment Activity 2
- Exam*View*® Pro Testmaker CD-ROM
- Interactive Tutor Self-Assessment CD-ROM
- California Standards Practice, Grade 11
- Succeeding on . . .™ the California Standards: Grade 11 History–Social Science CD-ROM

- CD-ROM
- DVD
- Print Material
- Poster

- Transparency
- Music Program
- Videocassette

Chapter 2 Planning Guide

TECHNOLOGY

- StudentWorks™ Plus CD-ROM
- TeacherWorks™ CD-ROM
- ExamView® Pro Testmaker CD-ROM
- Interactive Tutor Self-Assessment CD-ROM
- Presentation Plus! CD-ROM
- Vocabulary PuzzleMaker CD-ROM
- American History Primary Source Document Library CD-ROM
- MindJogger Videoquiz
- *The American Vision: Modern Times* Video Program
- Professional Development in High School Social Studies Video Series
- Teach, Use, and Succeed With *The American Vision: Modern Times*
- American Music: Hits Through History
- Succeeding on . . .™ the California Standards: Grade 11 History–Social Science CD-ROM

SPANISH RESOURCES

- Spanish Activities and Assessment
  - Spanish Vocabulary Activities
  - Spanish Guided Reading Activities
  - Spanish Quizzes and Tests
  - Spanish Reteaching Activities
- Spanish Reading Essentials and Study Guide
- Spanish School-to-Home Connection Activities

TRANSPARENCIES

- Daily Focus Skills Transparencies
- Section Graphic Organizer Transparencies
- Map Overlay Transparencies
- Cause-and-Effect Transparencies
- Unit Time Line Transparencies
- Why It Matters Transparencies
- American Art and Architecture Transparencies
- High School Writing Process Transparencies
- California Standards Practice Transparencies

TEACHER PLANNING

- Daily Lecture and Discussion Notes
- English Learner Handbook
- Building Academic Vocabulary
- *The American Vision: Modern Times* Reading and Study Skills Foldables
- Reading Strategies and Activities for the Social Studies Classroom
- Universal Access for the American History Classroom
- NGS United States Desk Map
- NGS World Atlas
- Chapter 2 Reproducible Lesson Plans on TeacherWorks™ CD-ROM
- California Guide to Daily Intervention

PROFESSIONAL DEVELOPMENT

- Building Academic Vocabulary
- Strategies for Success
- Research-Based Strategies Used to Develop *The American Vision: Modern Times*
- Character Education in the High School Classroom
- Professional Development in High School Social Studies Video Series
- Teach, Use, and Succeed With *The American Vision: Modern Times*

MOMENTS IN TIME

The following resources can help you teach the content of this chapter.

- Unit 1 George Washington (1777–1789)
- Unit 2 Territorial Expansion (1834–1859)
- Unit 3 The Road to Civil War (1850–1861)

TEACHER'S CORNER

Index to National Geographic Magazine:

The following articles relate to this chapter:

- "Daniel Boone: First Hero of the Frontier," December 1985
- "Ghost Ships from the War of 1812: Hamilton and Scourge," March 1983
- "Lewis and Clark," October 1998
- "The Underground Railroad," July 1984

National Geographic Society Products:

To order the following, call National Geographic at 1–800–368–2728

- *Historical Atlas of the United States* (Atlas)
- *Millennium in Maps Series: Battlefields of the Civil War*
- *Steal Away: The Harriet Tubman Story* (Video)

NGS ONLINE

Access National Geographic's new dynamic MapMachine Web site and other geography resources at:

www.nationalgeographic.com

www.nationalgeographic.com/maps

MASTERING THE STANDARDS

The content and assessment in the Student Edition, Teacher Wraparound Edition, teacher planning materials, and the print and technology products are all standards-based. The use of these products during instruction leads to mastery of the standards.

PRACTICE
- California Standards Practice, Grade 11
- California Standards Practice Transparencies
- School-to-Home Connection

BENCHMARK ASSESSMENT
- Section Quizzes, Chapter Tests, and Authentic Assessment
- *ExamView®* Pro Testmaker CD-ROM
- Succeeding On . . . ™ the California Standards; Grade 11 History–Social Science CD-ROM

REMEDIATION
- California Guide to Daily Intervention
- Interactive Tutor Self-Assessment CD-ROM
- *ExamView®* Pro Testmaker CD-ROM
- California Standards Practice, Grade 11
- Reading Essentials and Study Guide

History Online

Use our Web site for additional resources. All essential content is covered in the Student Edition.

You and your students can visit tav.mt.glencoe.com, the Web site companion to the **American Vision: Modern Times.** This innovative integration of electronic and print media offers your students a wealth of opportunities. The student text directs students to the Web site for the following options:

- **Chapter Overviews**
- **Student Web Activities**
- **Self-Check Quizzes**
- **Textbook Updates**

Answers to the student Web activities are provided for you in the **Web Activity Lesson Plans.** Additional Web resources and ePuzzles and games are also available.

Dinah Zike's Foldables

Foldables are three-dimensional, interactive graphic organizers that help students practice basic writing skills, review key vocabulary terms, and identify main ideas. Every chapter has a foldable activity in the *Dinah Zike's Reading and Study Skills Foldables* booklet. You can use the foldables as they are presented or modify them to suit the needs of your individual class.

A variety of videotape programs are available from A&E Television and The History Channel to provide teaching assistance. To order, call Glencoe at 1-800-334-7344.

Chapter 2 Planning Guide

The Glencoe BookLink CD-ROM is a database that allows you to search more than 15,000 titles to create a customized reading list for your students.

- Reading Lists can be organized by students' reading level, author, genre, theme, or area of interest.
- The database provides Degrees of Reading Power™ (DRP) and Lexile™ readability scores for all selections.
- A brief summary of each selection is included.

Leveled reading suggestions for this chapter:

For students at a Grade 8 reading level:
- *Not for Ourselves Alone,* by Geoffrey Ward and Ken Burns

For students at a Grade 9 reading level:
- *The Bill of Rights: How We Got It and What It Means,* by Milton Meltzer

For students at a Grade 10 reading level:
- *American Sphinx: The Character of Thomas Jefferson,* by Joseph J. Ellis

- *Timed Readings Plus in Social Studies* help students increase their reading rate and fluency while maintaining comprehension. The 400-word passages are similar to those found on state and national assessments.

- *Reading in the Content Area: Social Studies* concentrates on six essential reading skills that help students better comprehend what they read. The book includes 75 high-interest nonfiction passages written at increasing levels of difficulty.

- *Reading Fluency* helps students read smoothly, accurately, and expressively.

- *Jamestown's Reading Improvement,* by renowned reading expert Edward Fry, focuses on helping build your students' comprehension, vocabulary, and skimming and scanning skills.

- *Critical Reading Series* provides high-interest books, each written at three reading levels.

For more information about these products, see the Jamestown Education materials in the Classroom Solutions in the front of this Teacher Wraparound Edition. To order these products, call Glencoe at 1-800-334-7344.

KEY for Using the Teacher Wraparound Edition

Use this key to help you identify the different types of prompts found in the Teacher Wraparound Edition.

R   **Reading Strategies** activities help you teach reading skills and vocabulary.

C   **Critical Thinking** strategies help students apply and extend what they have learned.

U   **Universal Access** activities provide differentiated instruction for students learning to speak English, along with suggestions for teaching various types of learners.

S   **Skill Practice** strategies help students practice historical analysis and geography skills.

W   **Writing Support** activities provide writing opportunities to help students comprehend the text.

Teaching strategies and activities have been coded for ability level appropriateness.

AL   Activities for students working above grade level
OL   Activities for students working on grade level
BL   Activities for students working below grade level
EL   Activities for English learners

FOCUS

History–Social Science Standards

This chapter addresses the following main standards:

11.1 Students analyze the significant events in the founding of the nation and its attempts to realize the philosophy of government described in the Declaration of Independence.

11.3 Students analyze the role religion played in the founding of America, its lasting moral, social, and political impacts, and issues regarding religious liberty.

BELLRINGER
SKILLBUILDER ACTIVITY

Have students create time lines of events in the United States from 1861 through 1877 using the time lines found in the chapter. Instruct them to include months for all events.

TEACH

Thinking About the Big Ideas

As you begin teaching each section, use these questions and activities to focus on the Big Idea.

Section 1
The New Republic
Essential Question: What words do you associate with nationalism? Tell students that in Section 1 they will discover how Americans developed a sense of nationalism in the early years of the republic. `OL`

Section 2
Growing Division and Reform
Essential Question: Have you ever had a disagreement with a

CHAPTER **1789–1877**

2 Growing and Conflict

⌁ *The Big Ideas* ⌁

SECTION 1: The New Republic
Societies change over time. *The young republic saw the growth of the federal government and nationalism. Industry prospered in the North, while Southern agriculture depended on slavery.*

SECTION 2: Growing Division and Reform
Differences in economic, political, and social beliefs can lead to division within a nation. *Sectional disputes increasingly gripped the nation, while reformers sought to improve society.*

SECTION 3: Manifest Destiny and Crisis
Differences in economic, political, and social beliefs can lead to division within a nation. *During the mid-1800s, the United States expanded westward and sectional conflict escalated.*

SECTION 4: The Civil War
Differences in economic, political, and social beliefs can lead to division within a nation. *Unable to reach a compromise in the controversy over slavery, the North and South resorted to civil war.*

SECTION 5: Reconstruction
Social and economic crises lead to new roles for government. *Republicans introduced many reforms during Reconstruction but some of these failed, creating new hardships for newly freed African Americans.*

The *American Vision: Modern Times* Video *The Chapter 2 video, "The Battle of New Orleans," focuses on this important event of the War of 1812.*

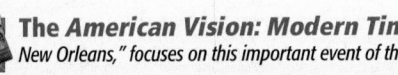

1789
• Washington elected president

1808
• Congress bans international slave trade

1820
• Missouri Compromise proposed by Henry Clay

1832
• Democrats hold their first presidential nominating convention

United States
PRESIDENTS

| Washington 1789–1797 | J. Adams 1797–1801 | Jefferson 1801–1809 | Madison 1809–1817 | Monroe 1817–1825 | J.Q. Adams 1825–1829 | Jackson 1829–1837 | Van Buren 1837–1841 | W. Harrison 1841 | Tyle 1841–18 |

1790   *1820*

World

1794
• Polish rebellion suppressed by Russians

1812
• Napoleon's invasion and retreat from Russia

1821
• Mexico and Greece declare independence

1832
• Male voting rights expanded in England

1842
• China opened by force to foreign trade

168

---

friend, parent, or sibling? What caused the dispute? Why were the issues involved so important? How was the disagreement resolved? *(Students' answers will vary based on their own experiences.)* Explain that disputes over issues such as slavery, which are discussed in Section 2, caused divisions between regions of the United States in the years leading up to the Civil War. `OL`

Section 3
Manifest Destiny and Crisis
Essential Question: Why do you think the expansion into the West would create sectional problems? *(Students should note the issue of slavery.)* Point out to students that the early sectional differences intensified as settlers moved West. They will study these issues in Section 3. `OL`

Charge by Don Troiani, depicts the advance of the English Pennsylvania Cavalry during the Battle of Chancellorsville.

Section 4
The Civil War
Essential Question: What are the modern differences between regions of the United States? Explain that because the different regions of the country fought against each other in the Civil War, families were sometimes divided, pitting brother against brother. Tell students they will learn more about the Civil War in Section 4. **OL**

Section 5
Reconstruction
Essential Question: What do you remember about the impeachment of President Clinton? Tell students that heated political battles between Congress and the president led to the impeachment of President Andrew Johnson. They will find out about problems during Reconstruction in Section 5. **OL**

Cultural Perspectives

Manifest Destiny was the belief that Americans had a calling to expand their country's border westward to the Pacific Ocean. Cultures clashed, however, as white settlers moved westward onto lands already occupied by Native American groups. Locate a copy—in print or online—of John Gast's painting *American Progress.* Have students work in small groups to analyze the painting and list their observations. What perspective does the painting reveal? Ask students to consider what a painting from the same time period by a Native American artist might depict. What might a painting from a Native American perspective be titled? **BL**

1846
• United States begins war with Mexico

1850
• Compromise of 1850 adopted in an attempt to ease sectional tensions

1861
• Fort Sumter bombarded by Confederate forces; the Civil War begins

1865
• Lee surrenders to Grant at Appomattox Courthouse; John Wilkes Booth assassinates Lincoln

1877
• Compromise of 1877 ends Reconstruction efforts

1848
• Karl Marx and Frederich Engels's *The Communist Manifesto* published

1859
• Darwin's *Origin of Species* published

1868
• Meiji Restoration begins Japanese modernization

| olk −1849 | Taylor 1849–1850 | Fillmore 1850–1853 | Pierce 1853–1857 | Buchanan 1857–1861 | Lincoln 1861–1865 | A. Johnson 1865–1869 | Grant 1869–1877 | Hayes 1877–1881 |

1850   *1880*

HISTORY Online
Chapter Overview
Visit the *American Vision: Modern Times* Web site at tav.mt.glencoe.com and click on *Chapter Overviews— Chapter 2* to preview chapter information.

169

Study Organizer

Dinah Zike's Foldables are three-dimensional, interactive graphic organizers that help students practice basic writing skills, review key vocabulary terms, and identify main ideas. Have students complete the foldable activity in the *Dinah Zike's Reading and Study Skills Foldables* booklet.

HISTORY Online

Go to tav.mt.glencoe.com for student activities, lesson plans, and links to additional Web resources to help students learn about the early national period and the Civil War era.

Preparing to Read Chapter 2

Reading Skill

Why It's Important

Tell students that when they are reading new material, they may encounter ideas and events they do not immediately understand. One way to overcome this difficulty is to formulate educated questions while they are reading, putting the material into their own words, and then identifying the parts they do not understand.

1. Introducing the Skill

Write a popular topic on the board, such as "pop music" or "football." Ask students to brainstorm questions they could ask to stimulate discussion of the topic. Record students' responses in a graphic organizer similar to the one below. **BL**

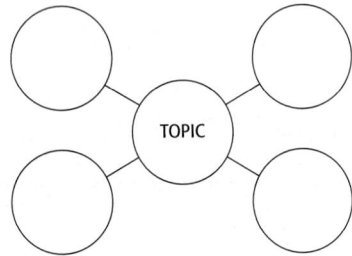

TOPIC

2. Extending the Skill

Instruct students to look at a newspaper photograph and read the caption, but not the accompanying article. Ask them to develop questions based on the photo and caption. Then have students read the newspaper article to find answers to as many of the questions as possible. **OL**

Answers and Additional Support

Reading Skill · Questioning

When authors write books, they try to anticipate the questions their readers are likely to ask and to provide the information that answers those questions. One way to make sure you understand what you are reading is to ask questions of the text. This means that you think about questions you would like answered. By formulating questions in your mind as you read, you increase your ability to understand and remember.

An easy way to practice asking questions during reading is to turn the headings into questions. For example, a heading that reads "John Brown's Raid" can be turned into "What was John Brown's raid?" When you turn the heading into a question, you can expect that it will be answered in the passage. You can ask more than one question. For instance, another good question would be "Why was John Brown's raid important?"

Read the following passage and note how the questions from above were answered.

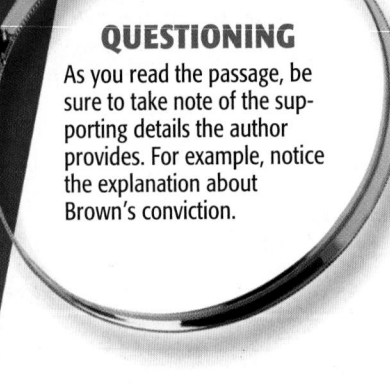

QUESTIONING
As you read the passage, be sure to take note of the supporting details the author provides. For example, notice the explanation about Brown's conviction.

Brown developed a plan to incite an insurrection, or rebellion, against slaveholders. To obtain weapons, he and about 18 followers seized the federal arsenal at Harpers Ferry, Virginia (now West Virginia) on the night of October 16, 1859. A contingent of U.S. Marines, commanded by Colonel Robert E. Lee, rushed from Washington, D.C., to Harpers Ferry. Outnumbered, Brown surrendered, and a Virginia court tried and convicted him and sentenced him to death.
Many Northerners viewed Brown as a martyr in a noble cause. For most Southerners, Brown's raid offered all the proof they needed that Northerners were actively plotting the murder of slaveholders. (page 199)

The first highlighted area answers the first question by telling what the raid was about: a raid on a federal arsenal to obtain weapons. The second highlighted area explains the importance of the raid, the second question posed. The raid was one more instance pitting Northerners against Southerners.

Apply the Skill

Read the following headings with a partner and turn them into questions. What do you expect to discover?

The Civil War (Section 4)
The Opposing Sides
The Opposing Economies
The Political Situation
The First Modern War

Reconstruction (Section 5)
Reconstruction Begins
Lincoln and the Radical Republicans
The Wade-Davis Bill
The Freedman's Bureau

170

UNIVERSAL ACCESS

Below Grade Level Jeopardy is a game that provides answers and requires contestants to come up with the questions. Assign students one of the sections from the chapter and ask each student to come up with five questions and answers. Provide students with note cards and have them write the questions on one side of the cards and the answers on the other side. Before a quiz or test, review by using the questions and answers that students have written to play classroom Jeopardy. **BL**

Historical Analysis Skill

Analysis Skill Standard CS4

Relating Current Events

Chronological and Spatial Thinking To better understand historical events both in the past and the present, you should learn to relate current events to the physical and human characteristics of places and regions.

The events of the past can have a long-lasting impact, extending even to the present day. For example, the work of the framers of the Constitution is a continued topic of interpretation and debate. Lawyers, legislators, and citizens regularly debate the intent of the Constitution, especially regarding issues such as the right to bear arms, the purpose of the electoral college, or the balance between personal freedoms and national security.

In the decades leading up to the Civil War, a number of events had a long-range impact on the United States. During this volatile time in our nation's history, decisions were made about the removal of Native Americans from their ancestral lands. In addition, a war with Mexico resulted in the vast expansion of American territories in the West. Finally, a Supreme Court ruling declared that African Americans could never become citizens.

Read the following passages about how Presidents Jackson and Van Buren moved Native Americans from their homelands to the West.

In 1830 Jackson signed the Indian Removal Act, which helped the states relocate Native Americans to largely uninhabited regions west of the Mississippi River. (page 185)

In 1838 Martin Van Buren, Jackson's successor, sent in the army to forcibly move the Cherokee. Roughly 2,000 Cherokee died in camps while waiting for the westward march to begin. On the journey, known to the Cherokee as the Trail of Tears, about 2,000 others died of starvation, disease, and exposure. (page 185)

With the passage of the Indian Removal Act and the forced removal of the Cherokee, by 1838 most Native Americans had left the eastern part of the United States. They now lived on government reservations west of the Mississippi River.

Apply the Skill

As you read this chapter, consider how the seeds of unrest were sown during this critical period. What human characteristics motivated some Americans to seek the physical and political isolation of Native Americans and African Americans? What is the impact today of this legacy of separation? How has a Mexican history influenced western states, particularly those bordering on Mexico, such as California?

171

Historical Analysis

Why It's Important
Understanding the historical roots of present-day laws and policies helps students make informed opinions and judgments about present-day actions.

1. Introducing the Skill
Have students brainstorm ways that the past affects their everyday lives. Then ask them to offer examples of how the past affects the present in business and government as well as in personal situations. Record their answers in a chart similar to the one below. *(Students' answers will vary. For example, a business may look at how a product performed in the past before launching a similar product.)* **OL**
CA CS4

Business				
Government				
Personal				

2. Extending the Skill
Using library and Internet resources, have students locate news articles from the year they were born. **Ask: How has the event described in the article affected your life? How would your life have been different if the event had never occurred?** *(Students' answers will be determined by their own examples and experiences.)* Encourage students to present their articles and paragraphs to the class. **BL**

UNIVERSAL ACCESS

Auditory/Musical Have students use the library and Internet to locate songs and rituals performed by Native American groups of the Great Plains. **Ask: Did these rituals help Native Americans cope with the pressure put on them by European settlers?** Next, have students research songs and rituals performed by Native American groups today. Ask students to use their research to write one-page essays explaining this topic: **How do events of the past influence the present-day lives of Native American groups?** Remind students to consider such issues as economics, religion, and family life when formulating their responses. **AL** **CA** CS4

FOCUS

SKILLBUILDER ACTIVITY

Project **Daily Focus Skills Transparency 2-1** and have students answer the question.

Guide to Reading

Understanding Vocabulary: Have students skim Section 1 to glean the meaning or significance of each of the vocabulary words.

Answers to Graphic: creation of new national bank, imposition of protective tariff, Supreme Court decisions established dominance of the nation over states, invasion of Florida, proclamation of the Monroe Doctrine

Unpacking the Standards

Students will be able to:

- Describe the challenges faced by the young United States while adjusting to its constitutional government.
- Analyze the growth of national pride.
- Discuss the results of United States's territorial expansion.

Answers and Additional Support

SECTION 1 The New Republic

Guide to Reading

Connection
In the previous chapter, you studied the development of state constitutions and the national Constitution. In this section, you will discover how the new nation continued to develop and how Americans developed a sense of nationalism.

Main Idea
- The United States established a federal government, created the Bill of Rights, and witnessed the first political parties. (p. 173)
- During the Jefferson administration, the Supreme Court established judicial review, and the country doubled in size. (p. 175)
- After the War of 1812, Americans focused on policies that brought the nation together. (p. 176)

- New industries and railroads transformed the North in the early 1800s, while slavery expanded in the South. (p. 178)

Content Vocabulary
cabinet, enumerated powers, implied powers, judicial review, nativism, labor union

Academic Vocabulary
clause, ambiguous

People and Terms to Identify
Bill of Rights, Louisiana Purchase, *McCulloch* v. *Maryland,* Monroe Doctrine, Industrial Revolution, Eli Whitney

Places to Locate
District of Columbia, Louisiana Territory

Reading Objectives
- **Describe** the rise of political parties, nationalism, and the Supreme Court.
- **Explain** why industrialization thrived in the North and cotton dominated the Southern economy.

Reading Strategy
Organizing As you read about the early years of the American republic, complete a graphic organizer by listing actions that strengthened the federal government at home and abroad.

Government Actions

Preview of Events

♦1785	♦1800	♦1815	♦1830
1789 George Washington becomes president	**1793** Eli Whitney invents the cotton gin	**1803** *Marbury* v. *Madison* case decided; Louisiana Purchase made	**1812** United States declares war on Britain	**1823** Monroe Doctrine announced

The following are the main History–Social Science Standards covered in this section.

11.1.2 Analyze the ideological origins of the American Revolution, the Founding Fathers' philosophy of divinely bestowed unalienable natural rights, the debates on the drafting and ratification of the Constitution, and the addition of the Bill of Rights.

11.1.3 Understand the history of the Constitution after 1787 with emphasis on federal versus state authority and growing democratization.

11.2 Students analyze the relationship among the rise of industrialization, large-scale rural-to-urban migration, and massive immigration from Southern and Eastern Europe.

❧ The Big Idea ❧

Societies change over time. During this time of change, the federal government became stronger, political parties developed, and the Supreme Court established judicial review. The country expanded westward with the Louisiana Purchase. Nationalism increased after the War of 1812 as the government focused on national policy. Great change also came during the Industrial Revolution.

172   CHAPTER 2   Growth and Conflict

SECTION RESOURCES

📁 Print Material
- Reproducible Lesson Plan 2-1
- Guided Reading Activity 2-1
- Reading Essentials and Study Guide 2-1
- Active Reading Note-Taking Guide 2-1

📖 Transparencies
- Daily Focus Skills Transparency 2-1
- Section Graphic Organizer Transparency 2-1

Technology
- 💿 Interactive Tutor Self-Assessment CD-ROM
- 💿 ExamView® Pro Testmaker CD-ROM
- 💿 Presentation Plus! CD-ROM

The Early Years of the Republic

Main Idea The United States established a federal government, created a Bill of Rights, and witnessed the first political parties.

Reading Connection Of all the freedoms that are granted to Americans, which do you consider most precious, and why? Read on to learn about the ratification of the Bill of Rights, which guarantees basic freedoms to all Americans.

The newly elected members of Congress met even before the Constitution had been ratified. Americans were confident, though, because they knew George Washington would be the first president.

★ An American Story ★

On April 6, 1789, the ballots of the presidential electors were officially counted in the new United States Senate. As expected, George Washington became the first president of the United States under the new Constitution. Americans everywhere greeted the news with great joy, but Washington remained unexcited. Calling his election "the event which I have long dreaded," he described his feelings as "not unlike those of a culprit who is going to the place of his execution."

Although Washington had high hopes for the new Constitution, he did not know if it would work as intended. "I am . . . [bringing] the voice of the people and a good name of my own on this voyage; but what returns will be made of them, Heaven alone can foretell." Despite his doubts and frustrations with the "ten thousand embarrassments, perplexities and troubles of the presidency," the new president retained his faith in the American people. He explained that "nothing but harmony, honesty, industry and frugality are necessary to make us a great and happy people. . . . We are surrounded by the blessings of nature."

—adapted from
Washington: The Indispensable Man

When President Washington and the newly elected Congress took office, one of their first tasks was to organize the government itself. In the summer of 1789, Congress created three executive departments: the Department of State, the Department of the Treasury, and the Department of War, along with the Office of the Attorney General. Washington then chose his **cabinet**—the individuals who would head these departments and advise him. His appointments included Thomas Jefferson as Secretary of State and Alexander Hamilton as Treasury Secretary.

Congress also organized the judicial branch. The Judiciary Act of 1789 outlined the makeup of the Supreme Court and established lower federal courts. As the first Chief Justice of the United States, Washington chose John Jay.

The Bill of Rights One of the most important acts of Congress in 1789 was to propose amendments to the Constitution. During the campaign to ratify the Constitution, the Federalists had promised to add a bill of rights detailing the rights of American citizens. In December 1791, the **Bill of Rights**—the first 10 amendments to the Constitution—were ratified. Eight of the amendments protect the rights of individuals against the government. The Ninth Amendment states that the people have other rights that are not listed in the Constitution. The Tenth Amendment adds that any powers not specifically given to the federal government are reserved for the states.

Tackling Financial Troubles With the bureaucracy up and running, the most pressing concerns involved the economy. The federal government had inherited a huge debt from the Continental Congress. As Secretary of the Treasury, Alexander Hamilton proposed a plan to pay off all debts. He also wanted the federal government to accept responsibility for the states' outstanding debts. Hamilton called for the creation of a national bank to manage the country's finances.

George Washington ▼

TEACH

S Skill Practice

Historical Interpretation Have students write job descriptions for the position of president of the United States in 1789. The job descriptions should include lists of duties and qualifications. Encourage students to use help wanted ads in local newspapers or on the Internet as references.
AL **CA** CS1; HI3

C Critical Thinking

Comparing and Contrasting Have students use library and Internet resources to research what positions make up the present-day presidential cabinet, as well as who is currently filling those positions. Then ask students to write paragraphs comparing and contrasting Washington's cabinet with the cabinet of today. **OL** **CA** CS2

More Skill Practice

Interpersonal Organize the class into ten groups. Have each group research a different amendment of the Bill of Rights and create an oral presentation answering the following question: Why was this amendment important to citizens of the United States in 1789? *(Answers should be based on each group's research.)* **OL** **CA** 11WA2.4

 ### Resources for page 173

Have students read more about the development of the constitutional government in:

📂 *Moments in TIME, Unit 1: George Washington (1777–1789)*

📂 *Primary Source Reading 2-1*

U Universal Access

Below Grade Level Have students create political cartoons that either support or oppose the Bank of the United States. Encourage them to look at styles of political cartoons from the era and to use the types of tools that a satirist of the era may have used. Have students display their cartoons around the class. **BL**

S Skill Practice

Historical Interpretation Have students use library and Internet resources to research the Whiskey Rebellion. Remind them to pay particular attention to key individuals and events connected with the rebellion. Then organize the class into groups of four and have each group write a brief skit about the Whiskey Rebellion. Allow groups to take turns presenting their skits to the class. **OL** **CA** 11WS1.2; 11WA2.1

R Reading Strategy

Scaffolding–Predicting Before students read about the administration of John Adams, have them think about the political views of the Federalists. Which policies do they predict Adams will support? **OL**

This **Reading Skill** was introduced in Chapter 1.

Answers and Additional Support

Thomas Jefferson, James Madison, and others favored less government interference in the economy. They also pointed out that establishing a bank was not one of the federal government's **enumerated powers**—the powers specifically mentioned in the Constitution. Hamilton rebuffed this criticism by citing Article I, Section 8, which gives the federal government the power "to make all laws which shall be necessary and proper" to fulfill its responsibilities. The "necessary and proper" **clause**, he said, created **implied powers**—powers not explicitly listed in the Constitution but necessary for the government to do its job. A national bank, Hamilton argued, was needed to collect taxes, regulate trade, and provide for the common defense.

Hamilton eventually won approval for his financial program after promises to Southern congressmen that the nation's capital would be moved to the **District of Columbia** on land donated by Virginia and Maryland. With that settled, the Bank of the United States was established in 1791 for a 20-year period.

The same year, Congress enacted a high tax on whiskey. The new tax brought in needed revenue, but it proved extremely unpopular among Western farmers who resisted the tax by terrorizing tax collectors, robbing mail, and destroying whiskey-making stills of those who paid the tax. In August 1794, President Washington sent nearly 13,000 troops to crush the Whiskey Rebellion.

Competing National Visions

Hamilton and the Federalists	Jefferson and the Democratic-Republicans
Strong national government	Strong state government
Ruling power given to wealthy, educated	Ruling power given to *all* landowners
Government should promote manufacturing	Government should promote agriculture
Loose interpretation of the Constitution	Strict interpretation of the Constitution
Protective tariffs protect domestic industries	Protective tariffs burden farmers

Chart *Skills*

1. **Interpreting Charts** Which party did not support tariffs, and why?
2. **Making Generalizations** Which party usually attracted bankers and manufacturers?

174 CHAPTER 2 Growth and Conflict

The Rise of Political Parties The handling of the Whiskey Rebellion intensified the tensions that had arisen over Hamilton's financial program. By 1794 the factions in Congress had solidified into rival political parties.

Hamilton's supporters called themselves Federalists. They favored a strong national government led by the "rich, well born, and able." The Federalist Party included many manufacturers, merchants, and bankers, especially in the urban Northeast who believed that manufacturing and trade were the basis of national wealth and power.

Their opponents, led by Madison and Jefferson, took the name Democratic-Republicans, although most people at the time referred to them as Republicans. They favored strict limits on the federal government's power and protection of states' rights and supported agriculture over commerce and trade. The party had a strong base among farmers in the rural South and West.

Tough Times for Adams After two terms as president, a weary George Washington stepped down from office. His Farewell Address to the American people warned of the dangers of party politics and sectionalism—pitting North against South, or East against West. Washington also urged Americans "to steer clear of permanent alliances with any portion of the foreign world."

Washington's successor as president was a fellow Federalist, John Adams. One of Adams's most urgent challenges was averting war with France. France was enraged by a treaty between the United States and Britain and had begun seizing American ships at sea. The two nations soon were fighting an undeclared war at sea until negotiations finally brought an end to hostilities in 1800.

Meanwhile, the division between the two political parties had been deepening. The Federalists resented the harsh Republican criticism. Using their majority in Congress, they passed the Alien and Sedition Acts in 1798. One of these laws made it a crime to utter or print anything "false, scandalous, and malicious" against the federal government or any federal official. The other laws were directed at aliens—foreigners living in the country—who often were anti-British and tended to vote Republican once they became citizens. The new laws made it harder for them to gain citizenship and left them vulnerable to deportation without trial.

Many Americans denounced the Alien and Sedition Acts as an infringement on people's freedoms. In 1798 and 1799, Kentucky and Virginia

---

Chart *Skills*

Answers:
1. Democratic-Republicans, because tariffs hurt farmers
2. Federalists

Chart Skills Practice
Ask: What example indicates the Federalists' support for a loose interpretation of the Constitution? *(the Bank of the United States, which was not specifically described in the Constitution)*

passed resolutions challenging the laws' constitutionality. At the time, few states accepted the premise behind the resolutions that states had a right to decide on the validity of federal laws. Many years later, states used these ideas to defend their interests.

The Election of 1800 When he ran for reelection in 1800, John Adams could not overcome public anger over the Alien and Sedition Acts and a new tax the Federalists had passed. The winner, however, was not clear. Thomas Jefferson had unexpectedly tied with Aaron Burr, his running mate for vice president.

The Constitution specified that citizens would vote for electors who would then vote for president and vice president. Collectively known as the Electoral College, the electors—a fixed number from each state—would vote for two persons. The candidate receiving the most votes would become president; the runner-up would become vice president. Ties would be decided by the House of Representatives. The election results of 1800 revealed a flaw in this system for selecting the president, because no one expected a tie between political allies.

The divided House took days to reach a decision, but the members finally voted to make Jefferson president and Burr vice president. The Federalists, who controlled both the army and the government, stepped down. The election of 1800 established that power could be peacefully transferred despite disagreements between political parties. It also led to the Twelfth Amendment in 1804, providing for separate ballots for the president and vice president.

Reading Check Examining What is the difference between enumerated powers and implied powers?

The Republicans Take Power

Main Idea During the Jefferson administration, the Supreme Court established judicial review, and the country doubled in size.

Reading Connection Are there times when you feel especially patriotic? Read on to learn about the War of 1812, which generated a new spirit of patriotism.

Tumultuous times continued with President Jefferson's attempts to limit the federal government and the power of the judiciary. At the same time, the country greatly expanded in size and faced another war with Great Britain.

Analyzing *Political Cartoons*

War Between the Parties This cartoon reveals the emotions of American politics in the 1790s. Republican Matthew Lyon and Federalist Roger Griswold are shown fighting in the House of Representatives. How did Federalists respond to Republican attacks?

Jefferson in Office Thomas Jefferson came to Washington committed to limiting the scope of government. He began paying off the federal debt, cut government spending, did away with the hated whiskey tax, and trimmed the armed forces.

Weakening the Federalists' control of the judiciary was another aim of the new administration. On his last day in office, President Adams had appointed dozens of new Federalist judges and court officers. Jefferson asked the incoming Republican Congress to abolish some of the new positions and to withhold the paperwork confirming other appointments. One of those who didn't receive his documents, William Marbury, took the matter to the Supreme Court. The Court sympathized with Marbury but ruled in 1803 that it could not issue an enforcement order. According to Chief Justice John Marshall and his colleagues, the law that authorized the Court to write such orders actually was unconstitutional and invalid.

With the case of *Marbury* v. *Madison,* the Court asserted its right of **judicial review,** the power to decide whether laws are constitutional and to strike down those that are not. John Marshall remained as Chief Justice for more than 30 years, continuing to build the Supreme Court into a powerful independent branch of the federal government.

Westward Expansion Under Jefferson, the size of the country increased considerably. The Treaty of Paris of 1783 had already established the Mississippi as the western border of the United States. After the defeat of Native Americans in the Northwest Territory and the Treaty of Greenville in 1795, more

U Universal Access

Logical/Mathematical Ask students to create a bar graph showing the presidential election results in 1800. **Ask:** *Why was the Twelfth Amendment created? (to avoid a tie vote in the future by requiring separate ballots for the president and vice president)* OL

Candidate	Electoral Vote	Political Party
Jefferson	73	Democratic Republican
Adams	65	Federalist
Burr	73	Democratic Republican
Pinckney	64	Federalist
Jay	1	Federalist

R Reading Strategy

Determining Importance Point out to students that the right of judicial review was a new concept. **Ask:** *Why is judicial review so important? (It confirms the power of the judiciary.)* OL
CA HI4

Reading Check

Answer: Enumerated powers are specifically mentioned in the Constitution; implied powers are not specifically mentioned in the Constitution but necessary for the government to do its job.

Analyzing *Political Cartoons*

Answer: They pushed the Alien and Sedition Acts through Congress.
Ask: How would the Alien Acts harm the Republicans? *(They targeted recent immigrants, who tended to vote Republican.)*

Did You Know?

Thomas Jefferson was the first president to begin his term at the new capital, Washington, D.C. He used this opportunity to break with his predecessors' formal style. He rode on horseback rather than in carriages, and he substituted intimate dinners for formal receptions.

U₁ Universal Access

English Learners Provide students with an outline map of the U.S. Have them mark the states that were created from the Louisiana Purchase. **EL**

S Skill Practice

Identifying Point of View Ask students to research the British burning of Washington, D.C., in 1814. Have them write diary entries recounting the event from the point of view of either an American citizen or a British soldier. **OL** **CA HR3; HI1; HI3** **CA 11WA2.1a**

U₂ Universal Access

Advanced Learners Have students work in pairs to research and present arguments for the case *McCulloch v. Maryland*. Each pair should pretend to argue their case before the Supreme Court, represented by the class. The "court" may ask questions of each lawyer. **AL**

✓ Reading Check

Answer: It established the Court's right of judicial review, the power to decide whether laws passed by Congress are constitutional.

Answers and Additional Support

settlers poured into the region. During Washington's term, Kentucky and Tennessee had become new states, and Ohio followed suit in 1803.

In 1800 Spain had given Louisiana back to France. To finance his plans for European conquest, the French leader, Napoleon Bonaparte, now offered to sell all of the **Louisiana Territory,** as well as New Orleans, to the United States. Congress overwhelmingly approved the **Louisiana Purchase** of April 30, 1803. The United States paid $11.25 million and also agreed to take on French debts of about $3.75 million owed to American citizens. The United States had more than doubled its size and gained control of the entire Mississippi River.

The War of 1812 A foreign relations crisis loomed when Republican James Madison became president in 1809. The British regularly seized American ships at sea and often practiced impressment, kidnapping sailors to serve in the British navy. Americans in the West also accused Britain of inciting Native Americans to attack white settlers. President Jefferson had tried economic sanctions with the Embargo Act of 1807, but the actions mostly hurt the United States.

Like Jefferson, President Madison first responded with economic measures. After several attempts, the measures finally began to have the desired effect. Unfortunately, word of British cooperation came too late—Congress had already declared war.

At the beginning of the War of 1812, conquering Canada was the primary objective of the United States. American forces on Lake Erie and Lake Champlain were victorious but they could not prevent the British from marching into Washington, D.C. and setting fire to both the White House and the Capitol. In Baltimore, though, the British encountered a strong defense. After bombarding the city's harbor throughout the night of September 13, the British abandoned their attack early the next morning. The sight of the American flag still flying at dawn inspired Francis Scott Key to pen "The Star-Spangled Banner," which later became the national anthem.

With battles still raging, peace talks began in the European city of Ghent. The Treaty of Ghent, signed on December 24, 1814, restored prewar boundaries but did not mention neutral rights or impressment. Still, it increased the nation's prestige overseas and generated a new spirit of patriotism. The American victory also destroyed the Federalist Party, which had strongly opposed the war.

✓ Reading Check Explaining Why is the Supreme Court decision *Marbury v. Madison* important?

The Growth of American Nationalism

Main Idea After the War of 1812, Americans focused on policies that brought the nation together.

Reading Connection Do you know of any Supreme Court decisions that had a significant national impact? Read on to learn about Supreme Court decisions that strengthened the power of the federal government.

After the war of 1812, a sense of nationalism swept the United States. More and more Americans began to consider themselves to be part of a whole, rather than identifying with a state or region. Riding this wave of nationalism was Republican James Monroe, the nation's fifth president. Harmony in national politics reached a new high, mostly because only one party, the Republicans, had any power. At the same time, the war had taught Americans that a stronger federal government was advantageous. In the postwar years, Republican leaders shifted their focus from world affairs to national growth.

Economic Nationalism As Monroe's presidency began, Congress prepared an ambitious economic program that included creating a new national bank. The charter of the First Bank of the United States had not been renewed, and the results had been disastrous. State-chartered banks and other private banks greatly expanded their lending with bank notes that were used as money. Without the regulatory presence of the national bank, prices rose rapidly during the War of 1812.

Other legislation included the Tariff of 1816, aimed at protecting American manufacturers by taxing imports. The Republicans also wanted to build roads and canals. President Madison vetoed this legislation, arguing that the Constitution did not empower Congress to improve transportation. Nevertheless, road and canal construction soon began with support from private businesses and state and local governments.

Judicial Nationalism The judicial philosophy of the Chief Justice of the United States, John Marshall, provided another boost to postwar nationalism. In several important cases between 1816 and 1824, Marshall interpreted the Constitution broadly to support federal power.

The 1819 case of *McCulloch v. Maryland* involved Maryland's attempt to tax the Baltimore branch of the

---

More Skill Practice

Identifying Point of View Have students imagine that they are legislators and write speeches to give before Congress, either in favor of or against the Louisiana Purchase. Encourage students to use outlines to organize their key points before writing their speeches. **AL** **CA HR3** **CA 11WA2.4b; 11WA2.4d**

Major Supreme Court Decisions, 1801–1824

Marbury v. *Madison* (1803)	Declared congressional act unconstitutional; Court asserts power of judicial review
Fletcher v. *Peck* (1810)	Protected contracts from legislative interference; Court could overturn state laws that opposed specific provisions of Constitution
Martin v. *Hunter's Lessee* (1816)	Court can accept appeals of state court decisions and review state decisions that involve federal statutes or treaties; asserted the Supreme Court's sovereignty over state courts
McCulloch v. *Maryland* (1819)	Upheld constitutionality of the Bank of the United States; doctrine of "implied powers" provided Congress more flexibility to enact legislation
Cohens v. *Virginia* (1821)	Reasserted federal judicial authority over state courts; argued that when states ratified Constitution, they gave up some sovereignty to federal courts
Gibbons v. *Ogden* (1824)	Revoked an existing state monopoly; Court gave Congress the right to regulate interstate commerce

Source: *The Oxford Companion to the Supreme Court of the United States*

Chart *Skills*

1. **Interpreting Charts** In which case did Chief Justice Marshall assert the Court's right of judicial review?
2. **Analyzing** Was Marshall a strict interpreter of the Constitution? Use a case to support your answer.

Second Bank of the United States. Before addressing Maryland's right to tax the national bank, the Supreme Court first ruled on the federal government's right to create a national bank in the first place. In the Court's opinion, written by John Marshall, the Constitution gave the federal government the power to collect taxes, to borrow money, to regulate commerce, and to raise armies and navies. The national bank helped the federal government exercise these powers. Marshall concluded that the "necessary and proper" clause allowed the federal government to use its powers in any way not specifically prohibited by the Constitution. 📖 *(See page 1005 for more information on* McCulloch v. Maryland*.)*

Marshall then went on to argue that the federal government was "supreme in its own sphere of action." This meant that a state government could not interfere with an agency of the federal government exercising its specific constitutional powers within a state's borders.

In another case, *Gibbons* v. *Ogden,* the Court ruled that states could regulate commerce only within their borders, but that control of interstate commerce was a federal right. Defenders of states' rights attacked many of Marshall's decisions, which helped make the "necessary and proper" clause and the interstate commerce clause vehicles for expanding federal power. 📖 *(See page 1005 for more information on* Gibbons v. Ogden*.)*

Nationalist Diplomacy Postwar nationalism also influenced foreign affairs. During the early 1800s, Spanish-held Florida was a source of frustration for Southerners. Many runaway slaves hid there, and the Seminole, a Native American group, often clashed with American settlers across the border in Georgia.

When Spain was unable to control the border, Secretary of War John C. Calhoun sent troops under the command of Andrew Jackson into Florida. President Adams then put pressure on Spain in ongoing border questions. Occupied with problems throughout its Latin American empire, Spain gave in and ceded all of Florida to the United States in the Adams-Onís Treaty of 1819.

Spain had good reason to worry about Latin America. Many of Spain's colonies there were declaring their independence. Meanwhile, some European monarchies expressed their interest in helping Spain suppress these Latin American revolutions. Neither Great Britain nor the United States wanted Spain to regain control of its colonies.

The Monroe administration also had concerns at this time about Russia's growing interest in the American northwest. In 1821 Russia had announced that its empire extended south from Alaska to the Oregon territory.

R Under these circumstances, Monroe decided to issue a statement in December 1823. In the **Monroe Doctrine,** the president declared that the American continents should no longer be viewed as open to colonization. He specifically advised Europe to respect the sovereignty of new Latin American nations. 📖 *(See page 994 for more information on the Monroe Doctrine.)*

✓ **Reading Check** **Analyzing** How did the decisions of the Marshall Court strengthen the federal government?

Review the Big Idea

Review the Big Idea for this section, "Societies change over time." Note to students that the Marshall Court expanded the powers of the federal government and the judiciary at the same time. **Ask:** Do you agree with Chief Justice Marshall's loose construction of the Constitution? Why or why not? *(Students should explain their position with specific examples.)* `OL`

R Reading Strategy

Evaluating The Monroe Doctrine was announced in 1823, less than 50 years after the nation declared its independence and just 23 years after Washington's Farewell Address. **Ask:** How does the Monroe Doctrine show the continued independence of the United States? *(It reaffirmed the desire to keep European influence away from the United States.)* `OL` `CA HI1; HI3`

✓ Reading Check

Answer: The Supreme Court interpreted the Constitution broadly to support federal power.

More Skill Practice

Analyzing Primary Sources Tell students that a Seminole named Kinache warned Americans to stay out of Florida: "You charge me with killing your people, stealing your cattle and burning your houses; it is I that have cause to complain. . . ." Have each student evaluate Kinache's statement in a paragraph. `OL`

Chart *Skills*

Answers:
1. *Marbury* v. *Madison*
2. possible answer: No; *McCulloch* v. *Maryland* emphasized the idea of implied powers.

U Universal Access

Visual/Spatial Provide students with an outline map of the United States without state borders. Instruct students to draw in the Ohio and Mississippi Rivers and their major tributaries. Tell them that they are planning a steamboat trip in 1850 from Wheeling, West Virginia, to New Orleans, Louisiana. Have students draw in the state borders that surround their route of travel and locate and label the major cities along the route. **OL**

R Reading Strategy

Evaluating Instruct students to write short paragraphs or journal entries that agree or disagree with the bracketed sentence. *(Students' answers will vary, but students should note that trains could travel more quickly than stagecoaches or wagons and could go anywhere that track could be laid.)* **OL**

Answers and Additional Support

NATIONAL GEOGRAPHIC Roads, Canals, and Railroads, 1820–1840

- — Canal
- —— Railroad
- — Road

500 miles
500 kilometers
Lambert Azimuthal Equal-Area projection

Geography *Skills*

1. **Interpreting Maps** Which Southern state had the most miles of railroad track?
2. **Applying Geography Skills** Why do you think canals were more common in the North than in other areas?

A Growing Nation

Main Idea New industries and railroads transformed the North in the early 1800s, while slavery expanded in the South.

Reading Connection What kinds of businesses generate the most wealth in the United States today? Read on to learn about the critical role that farming and industry played during the early 1800s.

The early 1800s were a time of rapid change in the United States. Transportation greatly improved access to different regions, while the Industrial Revolution turned the North into a manufacturing center. The South, meanwhile, continued to rely on agriculture.

178 CHAPTER 2 Growth and Conflict

A Revolution in Transportation With the United States expanding rapidly, Americans sought new ways to connect the distant regions of the country. The first steps came in 1806, when Congress funded the building of a major east-west highway. The National Road turned out to be the only great U.S.-funded transportation project of its time. American leaders disagreed on whether the Constitution permitted such internal improvements. Instead, states, localities, and private businesses took the initiative by laying hundreds of miles of toll roads.

Rivers offered a more efficient and cheaper way to move goods than did early roads. Loaded boats and barges, however, could usually travel only downstream, as trips against the current with heavy cargoes were impractical. The steamboat changed all that. The first successful such vessel, the *Clermont*, was developed by Robert Fulton and promoted by Robert R. Livingston. By 1850 more than 700 steamboats, also called riverboats, traveled the Mississippi, the Great Lakes, and other waterways.

Railroads also appeared in the early 1800s. A wealthy, self-educated industrialist named Peter Cooper built the *Tom Thumb*, a tiny but powerful locomotive based on engines originally developed in Great Britain. Perhaps more than any other kind of transportation, trains helped settle the West and expand trade among the nation's different regions.

Industrialization Sweeps the North Along with dramatic changes in transportation, a revolution occurred in business and industry. The **Industrial Revolution**, which began in Britain in the middle 1700s, brought large-scale manufacturing using complex machines and organized workforces in factories. Manufacturers sold their wares nationwide or abroad instead of just locally. By the early 1800s, these innovations had reached the United States. They transformed not only the economy, but society as well.

 Geography *Skills*

Answers:
1. Georgia
2. The North had more industry and more money to invest in canal building.

Geography Skills Practice
Ask: What modes of transportation could you have used to travel from New York to Baltimore in 1840? *(by rail, road, or sea)*

Did You Know?

New York Commissioner Samuel Young explains the importance of the Erie Canal project in the following quote: "... By this great highway, unborn millions will easily transport their surplus productions to the shores of the Atlantic, procure their supplies, and hold a useful and profitable intercourse with all the maritime nations of the earth."

The United States industrialized quickly for several reasons. Perhaps the key factor was the American system of free enterprise based on private property rights. People could acquire and use capital without strict governmental controls while competition between companies encouraged them to try new technologies. The era's low taxes also meant that entrepreneurs had more money to invest. In addition, beginning in the 1830s, many states encouraged industrialization by passing general incorporation laws that greatly eased the forming of businesses.

Industrialization began in the Northeast, where many swift-flowing streams provided factories with waterpower. The region was also home to many entrepreneurs who were willing to invest in British technology. Soon textile mills sprung up throughout the Northeast. The use of interchangeable parts, or standard components, popularized by a New Englander named **Eli Whitney,** led to factories producing lumber, shoes, leather, wagons, and other products. The sewing machine allowed inexpensive clothes to be mass produced, and canning allowed foods to be stored and transported without fear of spoilage.

In 1832 a major improvement in communications took place when Samuel F.B. Morse began perfecting the telegraph and developing Morse code. Journalists began using the telegraph to speedily relay news. By 1860 more than 50,000 miles of telegraph wire connected most parts of the country.

Urban Growth and Immigration The industrialization of the United States drew thousands of people from farms and villages to towns in search of higher-paying factory jobs. Many city populations doubled or tripled. In 1820 only New York boasted more than 100,000 residents. By 1860 eight other cities had reached that size.

Immigrants hoping for a better life in the United States also contributed to urban growth. Between 1815 and 1860, over 5 million foreigners journeyed to America. While thousands of newcomers, particularly Germans, became farmers in the rural West, many others settled in cities, providing a steady source of cheap labor. A large number of Irish—over 44,000—arrived in 1845, after a devastating potato blight caused widespread famine in their homeland.

The presence of people from different cultures, with different languages and different religions, produced feelings of **nativism,** a preference for native-born people and a desire to limit immigration. Several societies sprang up to keep foreign-born persons and Catholics—the main religion of the Irish and many Germans—from holding public office. In 1854 delegates from some of these groups formed the American Party. This party came to be called the Know-Nothings because its members, when questioned about their activities, were supposed to answer, "I know nothing."

By 1860, factory workers numbered roughly 1.3 million. They included many women and children, who would accept lower wages than men. Not even men were well paid, however, and factory workers typically toiled for 12 or more drudgery-filled hours a day. Hoping to gain higher wages or shorter workdays, some workers began to organize in **labor unions**—groups of workers who press for better working conditions and member benefits. During the late 1820s and early 1830s, about 300,000 men and women belonged to these organizations. Early labor unions had little power. Most employers refused to bargain with them, and the courts often saw them as unlawful conspiracies that limited free enterprise. Decades would pass before organized labor achieved real influence.

Factory Worker This young girl worked in the new factories of the Northeast.

CHAPTER 2 Growth and Conflict **179**

Chapter 2 • Section 1

C Critical Thinking

Determining Cause and Effect Write *Industrial Revolution* on the board. Ask students to list the causes and effects of the Industrial Revolution. For example, one cause was "division of labor" and its effect was "the rise of labor unions." Have students discuss whether they think these effects would have happened without industrialization. **OL**

U Universal Access

Logical/Mathematical Have students create graphs using the following U.S. Census Bureau data about the six largest cities in 1860. **OL**

City	Population in 1860	Population in 1820
New York, NY	813,669	123,706
Philadelphia, PA	565,529	63,802
Brooklyn, NY	266,661	7,175
Baltimore, MD	212,418	62,738
Boston, MA	177,840	43,298
New Orleans, LA	168,675	27,176

R Reading Strategy

Scaffolding—Academic Vocabulary The word *culture* was introduced in Chapter 1, Section 1. Ask a student to define the word. **BL**

More Skill Practice

Response to Literature Writing Organize students into groups of four. Have each group research the lives of children who worked in the textile mills and then write a script of an event that might have occurred in the life of such a child. Examples include an encounter between a foreman and a worker who has fallen asleep, a dialogue with another worker as they are on their way home from a day's work, or a monologue of the child's thoughts as he or she walks to work on a hot summer's day. Encourage groups to perform the script for the class. **OL** **CA 11WA2.1**

Visualizing Provide students with a map of the Southern states. Have students list the crops grown in each state. As a class, identify various regions based on the crops grown and explain the reasons that certain crops grow better in certain states. **BL**

S Skill Practice

Identifying Point of View Use free writing to explore students' background knowledge and check their reading comprehension. Ask students to play one of the following roles: a plantation owner, an enslaved person, a ship's captain, a textile mill owner, or a textile mill worker. Have students write letters to Eli Whitney describing to the inventor the impact of the cotton gin on their lives. Have students exchange their letters and write responses, playing the role of Eli Whitney. **OL** **CA 11WS1.3**

Answers and Additional Support

180

The Continuing Importance of Agriculture
Despite the trend toward urban and industrial growth, agriculture remained the country's leading economic activity. Until the late 1800s, farming employed more people and produced more wealth than any other kind of work.

Farming was even more important in the South, which had few cities and less industry. The South thrived on the production of several major cash crops, including tobacco, rice, and sugarcane. No crop, however, played a greater role in the South's fortunes during this period than cotton, which was grown in a wide belt stretching from inland South Carolina west into Texas.

In 1793 Eli Whitney invented the cotton gin—"gin" being short for engine—that quickly and efficiently removed cotton seeds from bolls, or cotton pods. Cotton production soared, and by 1860 Southern cotton accounted for nearly two-thirds of the total export trade of the United States. Southerners began saying, rightly, "Cotton is King."

While agriculture brought prosperity to Southern states, they lagged behind the North in industrial-ization. Compared to the many textile mills and factories in the North, the Southern region had only scattered iron works, textile mills, and coal, iron, salt, and copper mines. Together, these accounted for only 16 percent of the nation's total manufacturing.

Enslaved and Free African Americans The spread of cotton plantations boosted the Southern economy, but it also made the demand for slave labor skyrocket. Congress had outlawed the foreign slave trade in 1808, but a high birthrate among enslaved women—encouraged by slaveholders—kept the population growing. Between 1820 and 1850, the number of slaves in the South rose from about 1.5 million to nearly 3.2 million, to account for almost 37 percent of the total Southern population.

The overwhelming majority of enslaved African Americans toiled in the fields on small farms. Some became house servants, while others worked in trades. All enslaved persons, no matter how well treated, suffered indignities. State slave codes forbade enslaved men and women from owning property, leaving a slaveholder's premises without permission,

---

TECHNOLOGY & History

The Cotton Gin

While visiting Catherine Greene's Georgia plantation in 1793, Eli Whitney had an inspiration. He built a device that removed the seeds of the "green-seed" cotton variety that grew in abundance throughout the South. Whitney devised a "gin" (short for *engine*) that combed the seeds out of the cotton. This simple cotton gin was easy to mass produce, and it increased cotton's profitability for many Southern farmers. *How did the invention of the cotton gin affect the South's economy?*

1 Cotton bolls are dumped into the **hopper.**

2 A **crank** turns the cylinder with wire teeth. The teeth pull the cotton past a grate.

3 Slots in the **grate** allow the cotton, but not its seeds, to pass through.

4 A second cylinder with **brushes** pulls the cotton off the toothed cylinder and sends it out of the gin.

crank   grate   hopper

brushes

cylinder

Did You Know?

In 1840 President Martin Van Buren showed his gratitude for labor's political support by reducing the workday for federal employees to 10 hours. In 1842 in the case of *Commonwealth* v. *Hunt,* the Massachusetts Supreme Court ruled that union strikes were a legal bargaining tactic.

TECHNOLOGY & History

Background: Eli Whitney showed mechanical skill when he built a violin at the early age of 12. He never made much money from his cotton gin. It was so easy to build that few planters bothered to buy one.
Answer: It created a boom in cotton production in the South.

or testifying in court against a white person. Laws even banned them from learning to read and write. Frederick Douglass, who rose from slavery to become a prominent leader of the anti-slavery movement, recalled how life as an enslaved person affected him:

" . . . the dark night of slavery closed in upon me . . . "

—*Frederick Douglass*

66My natural elasticity was crushed; my intellect languished; the disposition to read departed; the cheerful spark that lingered about my eye died out; the dark night of slavery closed in upon me, and behold a man transformed to a brute.99

–from *Narrative of the Life of Frederick Douglass*

Music helped many African Americans endure the horrors of slavery. Songs also played a key role in religion, one of the most important parts of African American culture.

Many enslaved men and women found ways to actively resist the dreadful lifestyle forced on them. Some quietly staged work slowdowns. Others broke tools or set fire to houses and barns. Still others risked beatings or mutilations by running away. Some enslaved persons turned to violence, killing their owners or plotting revolts.

Free African Americans occupied an **ambiguous** position in Southern society. In cities like Charleston and New Orleans, some were successful enough to become slaveholders themselves. Almost 200,000 free African Americans lived in the North, where slavery

had been outlawed, but they were not embraced there either. Still, in the North free African Americans could organize their own churches and voluntary associations. They also were able to earn money from the jobs they held.

 Reading Check **Describing** How did the Industrial Revolution change American society?

HISTORY Online Study Central

For help with the concepts in this section of *American Vision: Modern Times* go to tav.mt.glencoe.com and click on *Study Central.*

SECTION 1 ASSESSMENT

Checking for Understanding

1. **Vocabulary** Define: cabinet, enumerated powers, clause, implied powers, judicial review, nativism, labor union, ambiguous
2. **People and Terms** Identify: Bill of Rights, Louisiana Purchase, *McCulloch v. Maryland*, Monroe Doctrine, Industrial Revolution, Eli Whitney
3. **Places** Locate: District of Columbia, Louisiana Territory

Reviewing Big Ideas

4. **Discussing** Does the Monroe Doctrine represent a continuation or a change in President Washington's foreign policy? Why or why not?

Critical Thinking

5. **Synthesizing** Name at least three key moments in the early 1800s when federal authority clashed with state authority. What trend developed in the resolution of these disputes?
6. **Organizing** Use a graphic organizer similar to the one below to list examples of nationalism in the United States after the War of 1812.

Examples of Nationalism		
Economic	Judicial	Diplomatic

Analyzing Visuals

7. **Posing Questions** Study the chart of Supreme Court decisions on page 177. Use the information to construct a 10-question quiz to give to your classmates to assess their understanding of the Marshall Court.

Writing About History

8. **Expository Writing** Imagine you are a newspaper editor in Georgia or Spanish-held Florida. Write an editorial in which you criticize or defend the Alien and Sedition Acts. **CA** 11WS1.1; 11WA2.4a

CHAPTER 2 Growth and Conflict **181**

SECTION 1 ASSESSMENT ANSWERS

1. Content vocabulary is boldfaced and highlighted in yellow. Academic vocabulary is boldfaced.
2. Bill of Rights *(p. 173)*, Louisiana Purchase *(p. 176)*, *McCulloch* v. *Maryland (p. 177)*, Monroe Doctrine *(p. 177)*, Industrial Revolution *(p. 178)*, Eli Whitney *(p. 179)*

3. District of Columbia *(p. 174)*, Louisiana Territory *(p. 176)*
4. continuation, because it upheld policy of avoiding European entanglements
5. creation of the Second Bank of the United States, *McCulloch* v. *Maryland, Gibbons* v. *Ogden;* loose interpretation of the

Constitution allowed for expanded national powers
6. economic: protective tariffs; judicial: the court strengthened federal power; diplomatic: Monroe Doctrine
7. Students' quizzes will vary.
8. Editorials should clearly support one side of the issue or the other.

S **Skill Practice**

Conducting Research Tell students that the nation's best-known slave revolt was led by Nat Turner on August 22, 1831. Have students use library and Internet resources to research the revolt and present their findings in a written report. **OL** **CA HI3**

ASSESS

 Resources for page 181

Use these resources to assess student mastery.

📁 Section Quiz 2-1

📁 Reading Essentials and Study Guide 2-1

💿 Interactive Tutor Self-Assessment CD-ROM

📁 California Standards Practice, Grade 11

Reading Check

Answer: The North became a manufacturing center, transportation revolution, growth of cities and immigration, increased demand for slave labor, increasing sectional division

 HISTORY Online

Study Central provides audio summaries, interactive games, and online graphic organizers to help students review section content.

CLOSE

Determining Importance Have students explain which event they consider most important in the early years of the nation, and why. **OL**

FOCUS

BELLRINGER
SKILLBUILDER ACTIVITY

Project **Daily Focus Skills Transparency 2-2** and have students answer the question.

Guide to Reading

Understanding Vocabulary: Have students identify a person discussed in the section who could be used in describing the meaning of each content vocabulary word.

Answers to Graphic:
early 1800s: Second Great Awakening begins;
1820: Missouri Compromise;
1824: Jackson elected;
1828: Nullification crisis;
c. 1835: creation of Whig Party;
1848: Seneca Falls convention

Unpacking the Standards

Students will be able to:

- Describe the increased sectional conflicts that developed during this time period.
- Analyze how the Second Great Awakening spurred a renewed interest in reforming American society.

Answers and Additional Support

SECTION 2 — Growing Division and Reform

Guide to Reading

Connection
In the previous section, you learned how changes in politics, territory, and production methods changed the United States. In this section, you will discover how growing sectional disputes affected the nation and how reformers sought to improve society.

Main Idea
- Sectionalism increased after the War of 1812, while voting rights expanded for American citizens. (p. 183)
- The Second Great Awakening brought an era of reform. (p. 186)

Content Vocabulary
spoils system, caucus, secede, nullification, temperance, abolition, emancipation

Academic Vocabulary
item, academic

People and Terms to Identify
Missouri Compromise, John C. Calhoun, Trail of Tears, Whig, Second Great Awakening, Elizabeth Cady Stanton, Frederick Douglass

Places to Locate
Missouri, Seneca Falls

Reading Objectives
- **Discuss** the issues surrounding the Missouri Compromise.
- **Explain** the goals of the temperance movement, the women's movement, and the abolition movement.

Reading Strategy
Sequencing As you read about growing division and reform in the early 1800s, complete a time line similar to the one below to record key events.

early 1800s	1820	1828	1848
	1824	c.1835	

Preview of Events

◆1820	◆1830	◆1840	◆1850
1820 Missouri Compromise proposed	**1830** Jackson signs Indian Removal Act	**1833** American Antislavery Society founded	**1848** Seneca Falls Convention
			1851 Maine passes first state prohibition law

The following are the main History–Social Science Standards covered in this section.

11.1.3 Understand the history of the Constitution after 1787 with emphasis on federal versus state authority and growing democratization.

11.3.1 Describe the contributions of various religious groups to American civic principles and social reform movements (e.g., civil and human rights, individual responsibility and the work ethic, anti-monarchy and self-rule, worker protection, family-centered communities).

11.3.2 Analyze the great religious revivals and the leaders involved in them, including the First Great Awakening, the Second Great Awakening, the Civil War revivals, the Social Gospel Movement, the rise of Christian liberal theology in the nineteenth century, the impact of the Second Vatican Council, and the rise of Christian fundamentalism in current times.

11.3.3 Cite incidences of religious intolerance in the United States (e.g., persecution of Mormons, anti-Catholic sentiment, anti-Semitism).

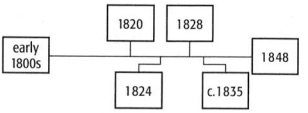

⚜ The Big Idea ⚜

Differences in economic, political, and social beliefs can lead to division within a nation. Sectional differences increased as new states joined the Union and issues over slavery continued to divide free and slave states. Adding to the tensions, South Carolina threatened to leave the Union over high tariffs that raised the price of needed goods. President Jackson initiated the effort to move Native Americans west. Many protested his decision to dissolve the Second Bank of the United States. In response, a new party, the Whigs, organized. During this time, reformers began to work to improve society. Religious reformers focused on reviving Americans' commitment to religion in what became known as the Second Great Awakening. Social reformers were involved in different reform efforts focusing on women's rights, educational reform, and the abolition of slavery.

11.10.7 Analyze the women's rights movement from the era of Elizabeth Stanton and Susan Anthony and the passage of the nineteenth Amendment to the movement launched in the 1960s, including differing perspectives on the roles of women.

182 CHAPTER 2 Growth and Conflict

SECTION RESOURCES

📁 Print Material
- Reproducible Lesson Plan 2-2
- Guided Reading Activity 2-2
- Reading Essentials and Study Guide 2-2
- Active Reading Note-Taking Guide 2-2

📠 Transparencies
- Daily Focus Skills Transparency 2-2
- Section Graphic Organizer Transparency 2-2

Technology
- ⊚ Interactive Tutor Self-Assessment CD-ROM
- ⊚ ExamView® Pro Testmaker CD-ROM
- ⊚ Presentation Plus! CD-ROM

The Resurgence of Sectionalism

Main Idea Sectionalism increased after the War of 1812, while voting rights expanded for American citizens.

Reading Connection What do you see as the defining characteristics of your state and region? Read on to learn why conflicts between different sections of the United States arose in the early and mid-1800s.

The Louisiana Purchase and improved transportation spurred new settlement in the West. Soon some of the territories grew large enough to apply for statehood.

★ *An American Story* ★

C As May approached in 1820, Thomas Jefferson should have been enjoying his retirement from public life. Instead, a bitter political controversy had him feeling deeply troubled. After more than a year of debate, Congress had finally crafted a plan to allow the Missouri Territory to enter the Union as a slave state while Maine came in as a free state. This arrangement preserved the delicate balance in the number of free and slave states. The arrangement, known as the Missouri Compromise, highlighted the growing dispute over slavery's expansion into the Western territories—a dispute that Jefferson feared could tear the nation apart:

❝This momentous question, like a firebell in the night, awakened and filled me with terror. I considered it at once as the knell [funeral bell] of the Union. It is hushed, indeed, for the moment. But this is a reprieve only, not a final sentence.❞

—quoted in *The Annals of America*

The matter of statehood for **Missouri** stirred up passionate disagreements. Increasingly, sectional disputes came to divide Americans.

The Missouri Compromise In 1819 the Union consisted of 11 free and 11 slave states. Admitting any new state, either slave or free, would upset the balance of political power in the Senate. Many Northerners opposed extending slavery into the western territories because they believed that human bondage was morally wrong. The South feared that if

slavery could not expand, new free states would eventually give the North enough votes in the Senate to outlaw slaveholding.

Missouri's territorial government requested admission into the Union as a slave state in 1819. The next year, Maine, then a part of Massachusetts, sought statehood. The Senate voted to admit Maine as a free state and Missouri as a slave state. The Senate added an amendment to prohibit slavery in the rest of the Louisiana Territory north of Missouri's southern boundary. Southerners agreed, viewing this Northern region as unsuitable for farming anyway.

Henry Clay carefully steered the **Missouri Compromise** through the House of Representatives, which passed it by a close vote in March 1820. The next year, Missouri became the twenty-fourth state, and the Missouri Compromise temporarily settled the dispute over the westward expansion of slavery. Like Jefferson, however, many leaders feared more trouble ahead.

A Disputed Election Although the Republicans remained the only official political party, sectionalism was strong in the election campaign of 1824. On Election Day, four Republicans ran for president. Andrew Jackson of Tennessee led in the popular vote and in the Electoral College, but he did not win the necessary majority of electoral votes. In accordance with constitutional procedure, the decision went to the House of Representatives, whose members would select the president from the top three with the most votes.

U Henry Clay of Kentucky, who had placed fourth, was eliminated. As the Speaker of the House, Clay enjoyed tremendous influence, and he threw his support to John Quincy Adams of Massachusetts. On February 9, 1825, Adams won the House election easily, with 13 votes to Jackson's 7 and William Crawford's 4.

Upon taking office, the new president named Clay as his secretary of state. Jackson's supporters immediately accused the pair of striking a "corrupt bargain," whereby Clay had secured votes for Adams in return for a cabinet post. Adams and Clay denied

▲ *Thomas Jefferson*

CHAPTER 2   Growth and Conflict   **183**

TEACH

C **Critical Thinking**

Drawing Conclusions Ask students to use library and Internet resources to research Thomas Jefferson's own position on slavery. **Ask: Was Jefferson in favor of the system of slavery? How do you know?** Tell students to consider Jefferson's public record, as well as his personal life when constructing their answers. *(In 1806 Jefferson urged Congress to pass a law prohibiting the importation of enslaved people; however, Jefferson himself was a slaveholder.)* **OL** **CA HR3**

U **Universal Access**

Below Grade Level Have students work in pairs to create two political cartoons that might have appeared in newspapers in 1820. One cartoon should be in support of the Missouri Compromise, and the other should oppose it. **Ask: Why was the issue of slavery in Missouri so controversial?** *(Admitting Missouri upset the even balance of 11 slave and 11 free states.)* **BL**

More Skill Practice

Analyzing Information Tell students to review the main provisions of the Missouri Compromise. **Ask: Do you think the Missouri Compromise adequately settled the dispute over the expansion of slavery?** *(The Missouri Compromise only temporarily settled the problem.)* **OL**

Did You Know?

Other U.S. leaders recognized that the Missouri Compromise would not be a permanent resolution to the debate over slavery. "I take it for granted," wrote John Quincy Adams, President Monroe's secretary of state, "that the present question is a mere preamble—a title page to a great tragic volume."

Writing Support

Persuasive Writing Have students imagine they live in one of the states that is considering changing the voting requirements, but they do not own property. Tell them to write a letter to their state representative explaining why the requirements should be changed so that they have the right to vote. **OL** **CA 11WS1.3**

Skill Practice

Conducting Research Have students select one of the candidates in the 1828 election and use library and Internet resources to create and present an oral biography of that political figure. Encourage students to use quotes that express their figure's political views. **OL** **CA HR4**

Answers and Additional Support

The Missouri Compromise, 1820

Geography *Skills*

1. **Interpreting Maps** The Missouri Compromise allowed which two states to enter the Union?
2. **Applying Geography Skills** Why did the South readily agree to making slavery illegal in the unorganized Louisiana Territory?

any wrongdoing, and no evidence of a deal ever emerged. Still, Jackson's outraged supporters decided to break with the faction of the party allied with Adams. The Jacksonians called themselves Democratic Republicans, later shortened to Democrats. Adams and his followers became known as National Republicans.

A New Era in Politics Throughout the first decades of the 1800s, hundreds of thousands of white males gained the right to vote. This was largely because many states lowered or eliminated property ownership as a voting qualification. They did so partly to reflect the ideals of the Declaration of Independence and the social equality of frontier life. In addition, as cities and towns grew, the percentage of working people who did not own property increased. These people paid taxes and had an interest in the political affairs of their communities, and so they wanted a say in electing those who represented them. The expansion of voting rights was very much in evidence by 1828. That year, more than 1.13 million citizens voted for president, compared with about 355,000 in 1824.

The campaign that year pitted John Quincy Adams against Andrew Jackson, who believed that the presidency had been unjustly denied him four years earlier. The candidates resorted to mudslinging, attacking each other's personalities and morals. When the results came in, Jackson had 56 percent of the popular vote and 178 of the 261 electoral votes, a clear victory. Much of his support came from the West and South, where rural and small-town residents, many voting for the first time, saw Jackson as the candidate most likely to represent their interests.

As president, Jackson actively tried to make the government more inclusive. In an effort to strengthen democracy, he vigorously utilized the **spoils system,** the practice of appointing people to government jobs based on party loyalty and support. In his view, he was getting rid of a permanent office-holding class and opening up the government to more ordinary citizens.

Jackson's supporters also moved to make the political system—specifically, the way in which presidential candidates were chosen—more democratic. At that time, political parties used the caucus system to select presidential candidates. The members of the party who served in Congress would hold a closed meeting, or **caucus,** to choose the party's nominee. Jackson's supporters believed that such a method restricted access to office to mainly the elite and well connected. The Jacksonians replaced the caucus with the national nominating convention, where delegates from the states gathered to decide on the party's presidential nominee.

The Nullification Crisis Jackson had not been in office long before he had to focus on a national crisis. It centered on South Carolina but highlighted the growing rift between the nation's northern and southern regions.

During the early 1800s, South Carolina's economy had been growing increasingly weak. Many residents blamed their troubles on the nation's tariffs. With little state industry, South Carolina purchased many of its manufactured goods from England. Tariffs made

 Geography *Skills*

Answers:
1. Missouri and Maine
2. They believed the land was unsuitable for farming.

Geography Skills Practice
Ask: At what latitude is the Missouri Compromise line? *(36°30′N)*

Did You Know?

Andrew Jackson's determined character made him a man not to be crossed. He once killed a man in a duel, which was a common way to settle disputes in his day. When he considered something a matter of honor, there was no compromising.

these **items** extremely expensive. When Congress levied a new tariff in 1828—which critics called the Tariff of Abominations—many South Carolinians threatened to **secede,** or withdraw, from the Union.

The growing turmoil particularly troubled Vice President **John C. Calhoun,** who was from South Carolina. To pave the way for his home state to legally resist the tariff, Calhoun had put forth the idea of **nullification** in 1828. He argued that because the states had created the federal union, they had the right to declare a federal law null, or not valid.

The issue of nullification intensified in January 1830, when Senators Robert Hayne of South Carolina and Daniel Webster of Massachusetts confronted each other on the Senate floor. Hayne, asserting that the Union was no more than a voluntary association of states, advocated "liberty first and Union afterward." Webster, perhaps the greatest orator of his day, countered that neither liberty nor the Union could survive without binding federal laws. He ended his speech with a stirring call: "Liberty *and* Union, now and for ever, one and inseparable!"

The war of words erupted into an explosive situation in 1832 when Congress passed yet another tariff law. South Carolinians stepped up their call for secession, while a special session of the state legislature voted to nullify the law. President Jackson considered nullification an act of treason and sent a warship to Charleston. As tensions rose, Senator Henry Clay managed to defuse the crisis. At Clay's insistence, Congress passed a bill that would lower tariffs gradually until 1842. South Carolina then repealed its nullification of the tariff law.

Native American Removal Slavery remained a divisive question, but President Jackson decided to focus on other matters, including Native Americans. Although Jackson wanted to ensure the survival of Native American peoples, he accelerated an effort that had been going on for years—moving them out of the way of white settlers. In 1830 Jackson signed the Indian Removal Act, which helped the states relocate Native Americans to largely uninhabited regions west of the Mississippi River.

The Cherokee in Georgia fought back by appealing to the Supreme Court, hoping that their territorial rights would be legally recognized. Chief Justice Marshall supported the Cherokees' right to control their land in two decisions, *Cherokee Nation* v. *Georgia* (1831) and *Worcester* v. *Georgia* (1832). Jackson refused to carry out the Court's decision. "Marshall has made his opinion," the president reportedly said, "now let him enforce it." 📖 *(See page 1007 for more information on Worcester v. Georgia.)*

In 1838 Martin Van Buren, Jackson's successor, sent in the army to forcibly move the Cherokee. Roughly 2,000 Cherokee died in camps while waiting for the westward march to begin. On the journey, known to the Cherokee as the **Trail of Tears,** about 2,000 others died of starvation, disease, and exposure.

Missionary-minded religious groups and a few members of Congress, like Henry Clay, declared that Jackson's policies toward Native Americans stained the nation's honor. Most citizens, however, supported them. By 1838 the majority of Native Americans still living east of the Mississippi had been forced onto government reservations.

Profiles IN HISTORY

John C. Calhoun
1782-1850

John C. Calhoun of South Carolina had a great impact on the history of the United States. As an influential member of Congress, he had urged war with Great Britain in 1812. He also was an ardent nationalist in his early career. After the War of 1812, Calhoun helped introduce congressional bills for a new Bank of the United States, a permanent road system to bind the nation together, and a tariff to protect the nation's industries. In the 1830s Calhoun abandoned his nationalist stance in favor of states' rights and sectional interests. Fearing that the North intended to dominate the South, Calhoun spent the rest of his career trying to prevent the federal government from weakening states' rights and from interfering with the Southern way of life.

Review the Big Idea

Review the Big Idea for this section, "Differences in economic, political, and social beliefs can lead to division within a nation." Then write the two quoted statements from Senators Robert Hayne and Daniel Webster on the board. Tell students to write a paragraph or journal entry explaining whether they agree or disagree with the statement of their choice. Use these responses to begin discussion of growing sectionalism and the nullification crisis. **OL** **CA HI2** **CA 11RC2.5**

S Skill Practice

Using Geography Skills Have students use library and Internet resources to research the Indian Removal Act and its outcomes. Ask them to use maps of the United States in 1830 to trace the movement of various Native American groups as a result of the Removal Act. Encourage students to clearly color code and label their maps and to provide a key. Display the posters in your classroom. **BL** **CA CS3**

W Writing Support

Research Report Writing Tell the class that John Ross was the elected leader of the eastern Cherokee during the legal struggle to avoid relocation to the western Indian Territory. Ask students to write a two-page report on Ross, highlighting his leadership roles before and after the Cherokee were forced to take the Trail of Tears. **AL** **CA 11WA2.4b**

Profiles IN HISTORY

John C. Calhoun served in both Houses of Congress, as secretary of state, and as vice president. **Ask:** Why did Calhoun abandon his nationalist position in favor of a states' rights point of view? *(Calhoun was a sectionalist who worried that weakened states' rights would allow the North to dominate the Southern way of life.)*

Did You Know?

Prior to the 1800s, the Cherokee had no written language. It took Native American scholar Sequoya about 12 years to break down every Cherokee word into syllables, represented by 86 symbols. He introduced the writing system in 1821, and within four years the majority of Cherokee adults had mastered it.

S Skill Practice

Scaffolding—Understanding Change Point out to students that since ratification of the Constitution, there have been several major parties, but only two have continued until today. **Ask: Why do you think so many changes in political parties occurred during this particular time?** *(Students may note that this was a turbulent time in which parties had to face new issues and may not have responded to these changes quickly enough.)* `AL` `CA CS2` `CA` 11WA2.1a; 11WA2.1c; 11WA2.1d

This `Historical Analysis` skill was introduced in Chapter 1.

C Critical Thinking

Determining Cause and Effect Before discussing the Panic of 1837, ask the economics teacher to explain the conditions that can cause a bank panic. Include the problems caused by individual banks printing their own money and the results of bank panics, such as bank collapses. Based on the discussion, have students create cause-and-effect charts to explain the economic impact of bank panics. `AL` `CA HI6`

✓ Reading Check

Answer: the imposition of tariffs that hurt an already struggling South Carolina economy

Answers and Additional Support

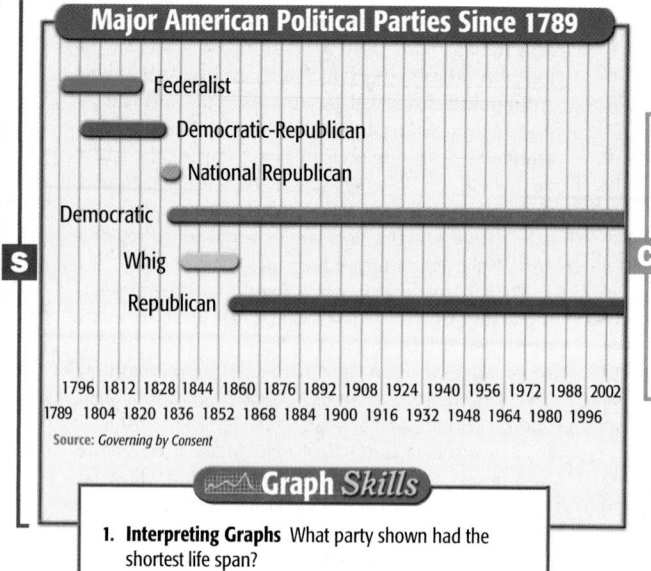

Major American Political Parties Since 1789

Federalist
Democratic-Republican
National Republican
Democratic
Whig
Republican

1789 1796 1804 1812 1820 1828 1836 1844 1852 1860 1868 1876 1884 1892 1900 1908 1916 1924 1932 1940 1948 1956 1964 1972 1980 1988 1996 2002

Source: *Governing by Consent*

📈 Graph Skills

1. **Interpreting Graphs** What party shown had the shortest life span?
2. **Comparing** How long have Republicans and Democrats been major political rivals?

A New Party Emerges President Jackson also decided to dismantle the Second Bank of the United States. He resented the power that its wealthy stockholders exercised. Jackson vetoed a bill that would have extended the Bank's charter for 20 years. Then, by withdrawing the government's deposits, he forced the Bank to end.

By the mid-1830s, those who criticized Jackson's decision had formed a new political party, the **Whigs.** Led by former National Republicans like Henry Clay, John Quincy Adams, and Daniel Webster, the Whigs wanted to expand the federal government, encourage industrial and commercial development, and create a centralized economy. Such policies differed from those of the Democrats, who favored a limited federal government. The Whigs ran three candidates for president in the election of 1836. Jackson's continuing popularity, however, helped assure victory for his handpicked successor, Democrat Martin Van Buren.

Shortly after Van Buren took office, a crippling economic crisis hit the nation. The roots of the crisis stretched back to the end of Jackson's term, a period in which investment in roads, canals, and railroads boomed, prompting a wave of land speculation and bank lending. This heavy spending pushed up inflation, which Jackson feared eventually would render the nation's paper currency worthless. Just before

leaving office, therefore, Jackson issued the Specie Circular, which ordered that all payments for public lands must be made in the form of silver or gold.

Jackson's directive set off the Panic of 1837. With easy paper credit no longer available, land sales plummeted and economic growth slowed. In addition, the National Bank, which could have helped stabilize the economy, no longer existed. As a result, many banks and businesses failed and thousands of farmers lost their land through foreclosures. Van Buren, a firm believer in his party's philosophy of limited federal government, did little to ease the crisis.

With Van Buren clearly vulnerable, the Whigs easily won the 1840 election by nominating General William Henry Harrison, a hero of the battle against Native Americans at Tippecanoe in 1811. Harrison, who spoke at his inauguration for two hours in bitter cold without coat or hat, died one month later of pneumonia. Vice President John Tyler, a Southerner and former Democrat who had left his party in protest over the nullification issue, then took over.

Tyler's ascendancy to the presidency dismayed Whig leaders. Tyler sided with the Democrats on numerous key issues, refusing to support a higher tariff or a new national bank. The new president did win praise, however, for the 1842 Webster-Ashburton Treaty, which established a firm boundary between the United States and Canada.

✓ **Reading Check** **Summarizing** What caused the nullification crisis?

The Reform Spirit

Main Idea **The Second Great Awakening brought an era of reform.**

Reading Connection Identify a local, national, or world issue that you believe citizens and lawmakers need to address. Why is this issue important to you? Read on to find out about the issues that attracted the attention of reformers during the mid-1800s.

During the mid-1800s, many citizens worked to reform various aspects of American society. The reform movement stemmed in large part from a revival of religion that began at the turn of the century.

Did You Know?

John Tyler, a Southerner and former Democrat who had left his party in protest over the nullification issue, joined Harrison's ticket as the vice presidential candidate. Campaigning with the slogan "Tippecanoe and Tyler Too," the Whigs won a decisive victory in 1840.

📈 Graph Skills

Answers:
1. National Republican
2. since the mid-1850s

Graph Skills Practice
Ask: In what year did the Whig party begin?
(1836)

The Second Great Awakening Many church leaders sensed that the growth of scientific knowledge and rationalism were challenging the doctrine of faith. In the early 1800s, religious leaders organized to revive Americans' commitment to religion. The resulting movement came to be called the **Second Great Awakening.** Various Protestant denominations—most often the Methodists, Baptists, and Presbyterians—held camp meetings where thousands of followers sang, prayed, and participated in emotional outpourings of faith. One of the most successful ministers was Charles G. Finney, a former lawyer. Using some methods he learned in court, Finney pioneered many methods of revivalism evangelists still use today.

As membership in many Protestant churches swelled, other religious groups also flourished. Among them were Unitarianism, Universalism, and the Church of Jesus Christ of Latter-day Saints, whose followers are commonly known as Mormons. Joseph Smith began preaching the Mormon faith in New York in the 1820s. After enduring much harassment in New York, Ohio, Missouri, and elsewhere, Mormons across the Midwest moved to Illinois. There the group prospered, and their settlement of Nauvoo grew to about 15,000 in 1844. Persecution continued, however, and following the murder of Joseph Smith, the Mormons headed west, finally putting down permanent roots in the Utah Territory.

Revivalists preached the power of individuals to improve themselves and the world. Lyman Beecher, one of the nation's most prominent Presbyterian ministers, insisted that the nation's citizenry, more than its government, was responsible for building a better society.

Associations known as benevolent societies sprang up in cities and towns across the country. At first, they focused on spreading the word of God and attempting to convert nonbelievers. Soon, they sought to combat a number of social problems. One of the most striking features of the reform effort was the overwhelming presence of women. Young women in particular had joined the revivalist movement in much larger numbers than men. One reason was that many unmarried women with uncertain futures discovered in religion a foundation on which to build their lives. As more women turned to the church, many of them also joined religious-based reform groups.

Social Reform The optimism and emphasis on the individual found in religion gave rise to dozens of utopian communities in which people wanted to find a better life. While only a few chose that path, many more attempted to reform society instead. A number of these reformers, many of them women, argued that no social vice caused more crime, poverty, or family damage than the excessive use of alcohol.

Although advocates of **temperance,** or moderation in the consumption of alcohol, had been active since the late 1700s, the new reformers energized the campaign. Temperance groups formed across the country, preaching the evils of alcohol and urging heavy drinkers to give up liquor. In 1833 a number of groups formed a national organization, the American Temperance Union, to strengthen the movement.

While persuading people not to drink, temperance societies pushed to halt the sale of liquor. In 1851 Maine passed the first state prohibition law, an example a dozen other states followed by 1855. Other states passed "local option" laws, which allowed towns and villages to prohibit liquor sales within their boundaries.

Other reformers focused on prisons and education. Around 1816 many states began replacing overcrowded prisons with new penitentiaries where prisoners were to be rehabilitated rather than simply

History *Through Art*

Religious Zeal J. Maze Burban's *Religious Camp Meeting* shows a charismatic preacher reaching many in the audience. From studying the image, can you suggest other reasons people might want to attend?

CHAPTER 2   Growth and Conflict   **187**

U Universal Access

English Learners Organize the class into groups of four, and make sure that at least one student in each group is an English learner. If you only have a few English learners in your class, you may want to assign students who read below grade level. To make it easier for students having trouble reading in English, tell students to create posters encouraging people to attend a camp meeting. **EL**

R Reading Strategy

Connecting Inform students that many communities throughout the United States do not sell or serve alcohol. Have students use the library and Internet to research a "dry" community near you. Create a bulletin board with information about the community, including maps, history, and photographs. **OL** **CA CS1**

S Skill Practice

Conducting Research Have students use library and Internet resources to research Dorothea Dix, a schoolteacher and prison reformer. Tell them to write a report that contains information about Dix's personal life as well as her participation in the prison reform movement. Students should include at least two quotes from Dix in their reports. **OL** **CA HR4; HI1**

 ### History *Through Art*

Answer: It was a social gathering where people could enjoy meeting and being part of a crowd.
Ask: What is seen in the background that helps you understand the name of these meetings? *(tents)*

Did You Know?

The phrase "on the wagon," referring to a recovering alcoholic, originated during the temperance movement. To publicize their cause, reformers pulled a water wagon through the streets and urged people to climb on. Over time "going on the wagon" came to mean accepting the temperance cause and staying sober.

187

U Universal Access

Gifted and Talented Invite interested students to take on the role of an abolitionist and prepare a speech, poster, or pamphlet supporting the abolition of slavery. Compile students' creations on a bulletin board in your classroom entitled "Abolition." **AL**

R Reading Strategy

Sequencing Information
Divide students into groups of five. Assign each group one of the following female abolitionists: Prudence Crandall, Lucretia Mott, Sarah Grimké, or Angelina Grimké. Have the members of each group work together to create a time line of important events in the abolitionist's life. Encourage students to use library and Internet resources, as well as their textbook, to locate information. **OL**

Answers and Additional Support

locked up. States also began funding schools in which students would become better-educated workers and voters.

The Women's Movement Since women had no vote in the 1800s and did not need to become educated voters, they were largely left out of the education reform. In addition, with the rise of factories and other work centers in the 1800s, men left home to go to work, while women tended the house and children.

Most people believed the home was the proper place for women, partly because the outside world was seen as dangerous and partly because of the era's ideas about the family. For many parents, raising children was treated as a solemn responsibility because it prepared young people for a proper Christian life. Women were viewed as better able to serve as models of piety and virtue for their families. At that time, most women did not feel that their role in life was too limited. Instead, the era's ideas implied that wives were partners with their husbands, and, in some ways, morally superior.

Nonetheless, a number of women took advantage of the reform movement to create more educational opportunities for girls and women. The early 1800s saw the funding of schools for girls that taught **academic** subjects. In 1837 the first higher education institution for women, Mount Holyoke Female Seminary in Massachusetts, opened.

The idea that women had an important role in building a virtuous home was soon expanded to society. As women became involved in reform movements, some argued for the right to promote their ideas. In 1848 activists Lucretia Mott and **Elizabeth Cady Stanton** organized the **Seneca Falls** Convention in New York. This gathering of women reformers marked the beginning of an organized woman's movement. The convention issued the Declaration of Sentiments and Resolutions, better known as the Seneca Falls Declaration. It began with words expanding the Declaration of Independence: "We hold these truths to be self-evident: that all men and women are created equal. . . ." 📖 *(See page 994 for more information on the Seneca Falls Declaration.)*

Although Stanton shocked the women present when she proposed a focus on suffrage, or the right to vote, the convention narrowly passed her proposal. Throughout the 1850s, women organized conventions to promote greater rights for themselves.

The Abolitionist Movement Of all the reform movements that began in the early 1800s, the movement calling for **abolition,** or the immediate end to

slavery, was the most divisive. By pitting North against South, it polarized the nation and helped bring about the Civil War.

Opposition to slavery in the United States had actually begun as early as the Revolutionary War era. Quakers and Baptists in the North and South agreed not to enslave people, viewing the practice as a sin that corrupted both slaveholder and slave. In Virginia in 1789, the Baptists recommended "every legal measure to [wipe out] this horrid evil from the land."

One notable antislavery effort in the early 1800s was the formation of the American Colonization Society (ACS) in December 1816. This group, supported by such prominent figures as President James Monroe and Chief Justice John Marshall, encouraged African Americans to resettle in Africa. The privately funded ACS chartered ships and helped relocate between 12,000 and 20,000 African Americans along the west coast of Africa in what became the nation of Liberia. Still, there were more than 1.5 million enslaved persons in the United States in 1820. Many of them, already two or three generations removed from Africa, strongly objected to the idea of resettlement.

The antislavery movement gained new momentum in the 1830s, thanks largely to William Lloyd Garrison. In his newspaper, the *Liberator,* Garrison called for the immediate **emancipation,** or freeing, of enslaved persons. Garrison attracted enough followers to found the New England Antislavery Society in 1832 and the American Antislavery Society in 1833.

Many women also gave their efforts to the abolitionist cause. Prudence Crandall worked as a teacher and abolitionist in Connecticut. Lucretia Mott also spoke out in favor of abolition. Some Southern women, such as the South Carolina sisters Sarah and Angelina Grimké, also joined the crusade.

African American Abolitionists Not surprisingly, free African Americans took a prominent role in the abolitionist movement. The most famous was **Frederick Douglass,** who had escaped from slavery in Maryland. He published his own antislavery newspaper, the *North Star,* and an autobiography. Another important African American abolitionist was Sojourner Truth. She gained freedom in 1827 when New York freed all remaining enslaved persons in the state. In the 1840s her eloquent and deeply religious antislavery speeches attracted huge crowds.

While many Northerners disapproved of slavery, some objected to abolitionism even more. They regarded the movement as a dangerous threat to the existing social system. Some whites, including many prominent businesspeople, warned that it would

ABCNEWS INTERACTIVE™

▭ VIDEOCASSETTE
Historic America Electronic Field Trips
View **Tape 2, Chapter 6:** "Seneca Falls."

Did You Know?

In the early 1800s, a strict code of behavior governed relationships between unmarried men and women. In 1839 English novelist Frederick Marryat toured the United States and was surprised by Americans' obsession with modesty. When visiting a girls' school, he found a grand piano on which each piano "leg" had been covered with a frilly trouser.

produce a destructive war between the North and the South. Others feared it might bring a great influx of freed African Americans to the North, overwhelming the labor and housing markets. Many Northerners also had no desire to see the South's economy crumble. If that happened, they might lose the huge sums Southern planters owed to Northern banks as well as the Southern cotton that fed Northern textile mills.

To most Southerners, slavery was a "peculiar institution," one that was distinctive and vital to the Southern way of life. The South had remained mostly agricultural, becoming increasingly tied to cotton and the enslaved people who planted and picked it. Southerners responded to the growing attacks against slavery by vehemently defending the institution. South Carolina's governor called it a "national benefit," while Thomas Dew, a leading academic of the South, claimed that most slaves had no desire for freedom, as they enjoyed a close and beneficial relationship with their slaveholders. "We have no hesitation in affirming," he declared, "that . . . the slaves of good [slaveholders] are his warmest, most constant, and most devoted friends."

R

In 1831, when a slave rebellion left more than 50 white Virginians dead, Southerners were outraged. They cracked down on slaves throughout the region and railed against the North. Further, they demanded the suppression of abolitionist material as a condition for remaining in the Union. Southern postal workers refused to deliver abolitionist newspapers. In 1836, under Southern pressure, the House of Representatives passed a "gag rule" providing that all abolitionist petitions be shelved without debate.

▲ *Frederick Douglass (center left) attending an abolitionist rally in Cazenovia, New York, in August 1850*

Such measures did not deter the foes of slavery. Although the abolitionist movement was still relatively small, it continued to cause an uproar, and the North-South split continued to widen.

✓ **Reading Check** **Comparing** How did Northerners' views on abolition differ from those of Southerners?

HISTORY *Online* **Study Central**

For help with the concepts in this section of *American Vision: Modern Times* go to tav.mt.glencoe.com and click on *Study Central.*

SECTION 2 ASSESSMENT

Checking for Understanding

1. **Vocabulary** Define: spoils system, caucus, item, secede, nullification, temperance, academic, abolition, emancipation.
2. **People and Terms** Identify: Missouri Compromise, John C. Calhoun, Trail of Tears, Whig, Second Great Awakening, Elizabeth Cady Stanton, Frederick Douglass.
3. **Places** Locate: Missouri, Seneca Falls.
4. **Describe** the changes President Jackson instituted in order to make government more inclusive and democratic.

Reviewing Big Ideas

5. **Explaining** What were the issues behind the Missouri Compromise?

Critical Thinking

6. **Historical Analysis** **Understanding Change** How did the Second Great Awakening affect the reform spirit of the mid-1800s? **CA HI2**
7. **Categorizing** Use a graphic organizer similar to the one below to identify key facts about the political parties active in the 1830s.

Party	Leaders	Policies
Democrats		
Whigs		

Analyzing Visuals

8. **Examining Art** Study the painting on page 187 of the camp meeting. What elements of the image suggest that the revival attracted many working-class people?

Writing About History

9. **Persuasive Writing** Imagine that you are active in one of the reform movements of the early 1800s. Write a speech to persuade others to support your cause. Make sure you clearly describe your cause and include at least three reasons why others should support it. **CA 11WS1.1**

SECTION 2 ASSESSMENT ANSWERS

1. Content vocabulary is boldfaced and highlighted in yellow. Academic vocabulary is boldfaced.
2. Missouri Compromise (p. 183), John C. Calhoun (p. 185), Trail of Tears (p. 185), Whig (p. 186), Second Great Awakening (p. 187), Elizabeth Cady Stanton (p. 188), Frederick Douglass (p. 188)
3. Missouri (p. 183), Seneca Falls (p. 188)
4. He used the spoils system and replaced the caucus system with a national nominating convention.
5. Missouri's request for statehood would upset the balance of free and slave states.
6. belief in the power of individuals;

many sought social reform
7. Democrats: Jackson, Van Buren/limit federal government; Whigs: Clay, Adams/expand federal government and industry, centralizing the economy
8. people were camping in tents; their clothes were not fancy
9. Speeches should be persuasive.

R **Reading Strategy**

Evaluating Read aloud the bracketed passage. **Ask:** Do you agree with Dew's beliefs? Why or why not? How do you know? *(Students' answers will vary.)* **OL**
CA 11RC2.4

ASSESS

 Resources for page 189

Use these resources to assess student mastery.

📂 Section Quiz 2-2

📂 Reading Essentials and Study Guide 2-2

🔘 Interactive Tutor Self-Assessment CD-ROM

📂 California Standards Practice, Grade 11

✓ **Reading Check**

Answer: In the North, there was some support, some opposition, and some indifference. Abolition was widely opposed in the South.

HISTORY *Online*

Study Central provides audio summaries, interactive games, and online graphic organizers to help students review section content.

CLOSE

Drawing Conclusions Have students describe how nullification intensified the sectional division. **OL**

189

What *Life* Was Like...

FOCUS

History– Social Science Standards

This feature addresses the following standard:

11.1.3 Understand the history of the Constitution after 1787 with emphasis on federal versus state authority and growing democratization.

Reading Connection

Tell students that in order for democracy to flourish, the new republic required an informed and educated electorate. One way to educate people was to establish public schools.

TEACH

R Reading Strategy

Connecting Ask students to compare their own educational experiences with what is depicted in this feature. Invite two students to record the comparison on the board or on flip charts. **BL**

Answers and Additional Support

Old-Fashioned School Days

R Public schools in the early to mid-1800s were rough-and-ready affairs. Students came in all ages and sizes, teachers often had little training, and books and supplies were hard to obtain.

● **School Desk**

● **Hand Bell**
In a lot of schools, teachers rang the hand bell to call their students to class. Most districts could not afford an expensive bell tower, so teachers stood in the doorway or school-yard to ring the bell.

● **First Readers**
Generations of students used McGuffey's Readers, first produced in the 1830s by William McGuffey. His readers—the first Eclectic Reader is pictured here—ranged from simple to advanced and aimed to give students a happy, positive feeling. A college president at the end of his life, McGuffey began teaching in frontier Ohio schools when he was only 13.

EXTENDING THE CONTENT

Black Law In 1831 Prudence Crandall was running a successful school for girls in Canterbury, Connecticut, when Sara Harris, the daughter of a prominent African American farmer, sought admission. When Crandall agreed to let her in, local parents objected, and many withdrew their children from the school. Crandall then reorganized her school as a teacher-training institution for African American women. The state legislation passed the "Black Law," which forbade Connecticut schools from admitting out-of-state African American students and severely limited the type of schools that in-state African Americans could attend. Crandall was arrested in 1833; her school was terrorized until its close in 1834.

One-Room Schoolhouse
The painting *New England School* by Charles Frederick Bosworth tells the tale of teachers' challenges in early public schools. With a mixed-aged class, the teacher had to teach a few students at a time, leaving the others to their own education—or entertainment.

School Ink Jar

School Lunch Pail

U **Universal Access**

Interpersonal Have students conduct interviews with teachers in your school. Instruct them to ask questions about the teachers' training and certification, as well as challenges they face as teachers today. Remind students to bring tape recorders or notebooks to record the teachers' answers. Ask students to present their findings in one-page reports. The reports should close with paragraphs comparing and contrasting the challenges teachers faced in the mid-1800s with the challenges they face today. **OL**

W **Writing Support**

Narrative Writing Have students pretend that they are living in the mid-1800s. Ask them to write diary entries in which they describe a typical day at school. Encourage interested students to use quills or fountain pens to make their diary entries look authentic. **OL**
CA 11WA2.1a; 11WA2.1b

ASSESS/CLOSE

Have students answer the Understanding the Time questions.

UNDERSTANDING THE TIME

Checking for Understanding
1. **Explaining** Why would an increase in voting rights be a reason for broader public education?

Critical Thinking
2. **Synthesizing** What could you have done to minimize the distractions in a one-room schoolhouse?

ANSWERS TO UNDERSTANDING THE TIME

1. As the political responsibilities of citizens increased, the need for education became more important.

2. Answers will vary. Students might suggest having different groups of students working together or having older students help educate the younger classmates.

FOCUS

BELLRINGER
SKILLBUILDER ACTIVITY

 Project **Daily Focus Skills Transparency 2-3** and have students answer the question.

Guide to Reading

Understanding Vocabulary: Have students learn about one of the vocabulary terms so that they can teach the meaning to the class.

Answers to Graphic: Settlement of Texas: war between Texas and Mexico; Texas's fight for independence: gains independence; War with Mexico: United States gains territory and sets Rio Grande as border; Oregon's division: compromise with Britain to establish border at 49th parallel

Unpacking the Standards

Students will be able to:

- Explain the belief in Manifest Destiny.
- Discuss the deepening sectional crisis in the 1850s.
- Describe the events that led to the secession of the Southern states.

Answers and Additional Support

SECTION 3 Manifest Destiny and Crisis

Guide to Reading

Connection
In the previous section, you learned about social reform and growing tensions between states. In this section, you will discover how slavery continued to divide the country and how the election of Abraham Lincoln as president resulted in the secession of Southern states.

Main Idea
- In the 1840s, the nation expanded as settlers moved west. (p. 193)
- Continuing disagreements over the westward expansion of slavery increased sectional tensions between the North and South. (p. 195)
- The slavery controversy shook up political parties and accelerated the crisis between North and South. (p. 198)
- The election of Abraham Lincoln led the Southern states to secede from the Union. (p. 199)

Content Vocabulary
Manifest Destiny, annexation, popular sovereignty, secession, Underground Railroad, transcontinental railroad, insurrection, Confederacy

Academic Vocabulary
adjacent, prospect

People and Terms to Identify
John C. Frémont, Bear Flag Republic, Wilmot Proviso, Harriet Tubman, Republican Party, Dred Scott, Crittenden's Compromise, Jefferson Davis

Places to Locate
Harpers Ferry

Reading Objectives
- **Describe** the issues surrounding the War with Mexico and the statehood of Texas and California.
- **Evaluate** how the Fugitive Slave Act and the transcontinental railroad heightened sectional tensions.
- **Analyze** the significance of the *Dred Scott* decision and John Brown's raid on Harpers Ferry.
- **Explain** how the election of Abraham Lincoln as president led to the secession of the South.

Reading Strategy
Organizing Complete a graphic organizer similar to the one below to describe the outcomes of disputes that arose during this period.

Dispute	Outcome

Preview of Events

♦1845	♦1850	♦1855	♦1860
1846 Oregon boundary dispute settled	**1854** Kansas-Nebraska Act adopted	**1857** Supreme Court announces *Dred Scott* decision	**1860** South Carolina secedes from the Union

The following are the main History–Social Science Standards covered in this section.

11.1.3 Understand the history of the Constitution after 1787 with emphasis on federal versus state authority and growing democratization.

11.2.6 Trace the development of the United States and its emergence as a major industrial power, including its gains from trade and the advantages of its physical geography.

11.10.2 Examine and analyze the key events, policies, and court cases in the evolution of civil rights, including *Dred Scott v. Sanford, Plessy v. Ferguson, Brown v. Board of Education, Regents of the University of California v. Bakke,* and California Proposition 209.

 The Big Idea

Differences in economic, political, and social beliefs can lead to division within a nation. As the United States continued to expand even farther west, sectionalism and disagreements over slavery in the new territories continued to plague the nation. The crisis between free states and slave states resulted in the destruction of the Whig Party and division within other political parties. After the raid on Harpers Ferry, Southern Democrats became convinced that Northerners and Republicans would stop at nothing to end slavery. Spurred by failing compromises and the election of Abraham Lincoln as president, Southern states seceded from the Union, proclaimed themselves a separate nation known as the Confederate States of America, and appointed Jefferson Davis as their president.

192 CHAPTER 2 Growth and Conflict

SECTION RESOURCES

Print Material
- Reproducible Lesson Plan 2-3
- Guided Reading Activity 2-3
- Reading Essentials and Study Guide 2-3
- Active Reading Note-Taking Guide 2-3

Transparencies
- Daily Focus Skills Transparency 2-3
- Section Graphic Organizer Transparency 2-3

Technology
- Interactive Tutor Self-Assessment CD-ROM
- ExamView® Pro Testmaker CD-ROM
- Presentation Plus! CD-ROM

Manifest Destiny

Main Idea In the 1840s, the nation expanded as settlers moved west.

Reading Connection To which country did California and Texas belong before they became part of the United States? Read on to learn how the two states entered the Union.

With the Louisiana Purchase opening up the West, thousands of people began pushing into the Midwest and beyond, journeying all the way to California and the Oregon Territory.

★ An American Story ★

In July 1821, Stephen F. Austin set off from Louisiana for the Texas territory in the northeastern corner of Mexico. The Spanish government had promised to give his father, Moses, a huge tract of Texas land if the elder Austin settled 300 families there from the United States. Moses died before he could fulfill his end of the deal. On his deathbed, his dying wish was that Stephen take his place in Texas.

Stephen Austin was favorably impressed with the region. As he surveyed the land grant between the Brazos and Colorado Rivers, he noted its natural abundance:

66 The Prairie comes bluff to the river . . . and affords a most beautiful situation for a Town or settlement. . . . The country . . . is as good in every respect as man could wish for, Land all first rate, plenty of timber, fine water, beautifully rolling. 99

—quoted in *Stephen F. Austin: Empresario of Texas*

Between the late 1830s and early 1860s, more than 250,000 Americans braved great obstacles to venture west along overland trails.

Pushing West The opportunity to farm fertile soil, enter the fur trade, or trade with foreign nations across the Pacific lured farmers, adventurers, and merchants alike. Most emigrants, like the majority of Americans, believed in **Manifest Destiny.** Manifest Destiny was the idea that the nation was meant to spread to the Pacific.

Latecomers to the Midwest set their sights on California and Oregon, although other nations had already claimed parts of these lands. The United

States and Great Britain had agreed in 1818 to occupy the Oregon land jointly. The British dominated the region until about 1840, when the enthusiastic reports of American missionaries began to attract large numbers of would-be farmers to the region.

California was a frontier province of Mexico. Because few Mexicans wanted to make their homes in California, the local government welcomed foreign settlers. By 1845 more than 700 Americans lived in and around the Sacramento Valley. Though the central government in Mexico City relied on these American settlers, it was suspicious about their national loyalties.

By the 1840s, several east-to-west routes had been carved, including the Oregon Trail, the California Trail, and the Santa Fe Trail. As the overland traffic increased, the Plains Indians came to resent the threat it posed to their way of life. They feared that the buffalo herds, on which they relied for food, shelter, clothing, and tools, would die off or migrate elsewhere. Hoping to ensure peace, the federal government negotiated the Treaty of Fort Laramie in 1851. Eight Plains Indian groups agreed to specific geographic boundaries, while the United States promised that the defined territories would belong to the Native Americans forever. White settlers still streamed across the plains, however, provoking Native American hostility.

Stephen F. Austin ▼

TEACH

W Writing Support

Narrative Writing Have students pretend that they are farmers traveling west to settle in California or Oregon. Ask them to write letters to friends back home describing what route they are taking, what they have seen, and some of the obstacles they have faced along the way. Invite students to read their letters aloud to the class. **BL**
CA 11WS1.1; 11WA2.1e

U Universal Access

Visual/Spatial Provide students with an outline map of the United States with all of the current state boundaries. Have students use the map to locate and label one of the following: the Oregon Trail, the California Trail, or the Santa Fe Trail. Instruct students to name the current states and major geographic landmarks along the trail. **OL** **CA CS3**

Review the Big Idea

Review the Big Idea for this section, "Differences in economic, political, and social beliefs can lead to division within a nation." As students read this section, have them create time lines on which they mark the major events that led to a deepening of sectional division. **OL** **CA HI1**

Did You Know?

The name *Texas* comes from a Native American word meaning "friend" or "ally." Spanish settlers used the word to refer to the Native Americans who were occupying the area when they arrived.

Did You Know?

Some of the first pioneers were called squatters, because they settled on lands they did not own. In 1841, however, Congress passed the Pre-emption Act. This law allowed squatters to buy up to 160 acres before the land went up for public sale.

Picturing **History**

Independence for California In June 1846, John C. Frémont and other California settlers declared their independence from Mexico. When did California become part of the United States?

War With Mexico Texas's entry into the Union outraged the Mexican government, which promptly broke diplomatic relations with the United States. Matters worsened when the two countries disputed Texas's southwestern border.

President Polk's designs on California added to the conflict. In November 1845, he sent John Slidell as an envoy to Mexico City to try to purchase California and resolve other differences. Mexico's new president, José Joaquín Herrera, refused even to meet with Slidell.

With no realistic chance of a diplomatic solution, the president ordered General Zachary Taylor in January 1846 to lead troops across the Nueces River into territory claimed by both the United States and Mexico. Polk wanted Mexican troops to fire the first shot. If he could say Mexico was the aggressor, he could more easily win support for a war. Finally, on May 9, news reached him that a force of Mexicans had attacked Taylor's men. Four days later, the Senate and House both overwhelmingly voted in favor of the war.

Even before war with Mexico was officially declared, settlers in northern California, led by American general **John C. Frémont,** had begun an uprising. The official Mexican presence in the territory had never been strong, and the settlers had little trouble overcoming it. On June 14, 1846, they declared California independent and renamed the region the **Bear Flag Republic.** Within a month, American navy forces arrived to occupy the ports of San Francisco and San Diego and claim the republic for the United States.

Despite the loss of California and defeat in several battles, Mexico refused to surrender. Polk decided to send General Winfield Scott to seize Mexico City. After a 6-month campaign beginning in the Gulf Coast city of Veracruz, Scott's forces captured Mexico's capital in September 1847.

Defeated, Mexico's leaders signed the Treaty of Guadalupe Hidalgo on February 2, 1848. Mexico gave the United States more than 500,000 square miles (1,295,000 sq. km) of territory—what are now the states of California, Nevada, and Utah, as well as most of Arizona and New Mexico and parts of Colorado and Wyoming. Mexico also accepted the Rio Grande as the southern border of Texas. In return, the United States paid Mexico $15 million and took over $3.25 million in debts the Mexican government owed to American citizens.

With Oregon and the former Mexican territories now under the U.S. flag, the dream of Manifest Destiny had been realized, but this expansion had cost more than 12,000 American lives. Furthermore, the question of whether the new lands should allow slavery would soon lead the country into another bloody conflict.

✓ **Reading Check** **Explaining** What is the idea of Manifest Destiny?

Slavery and Western Expansion

Main Idea Continuing disagreements over the westward expansion of slavery increased sectional tensions between the North and South.

Reading Connection Under what circumstances, if any, do you believe that citizens are justified in disobeying a law? Read on to learn how some Northerners responded to the Fugitive Slave Act of 1850, which required them to aid in the capture of runaway slaves.

When California applied for statehood, attempts by Congress to find a compromise further heightened opposing viewpoints on slavery.

CHAPTER 2 Growth and Conflict **195**

C **Critical Thinking**

Predicting Consequences
Present the following situation to students: **What if James K. Polk had not won the presidential election of 1844? Would the war with Mexico have taken place? Why or why not? How would this have affected the U.S. acquisition of western lands?** Encourage students to write their answers to these questions in paragraph form. Call on volunteers to read and discuss their paragraphs. **AL** **CA HI4**

S **Skill Practice**

Identifying Point of View Have students write diary entries from the point of view of a Mexican living in Nevada at the time that the Treaty of Guadalupe Hidalgo was signed by the United States. Remind students that it should be clear to the audience whether the individual is in favor of or against the Treaty. Invite students to share what they have written with the class. **OL** **CA HI3** **CA 11WA2.1c**

✓ **Reading Check**

Answer: that the nation was meant to spread to the Pacific Ocean

More Skill Practice

Visualizing Inform students that San Diego is still a large port for the U.S. Navy today. Have students use library and Internet resources to research the military bases at San Diego and present their findings in a travel brochure. Encourage students to use photographs, maps, and statistical and historical information to complete their brochures. **OL**

Picturing **History**

Answer: became part of the United States with the Treaty of Guadalupe Hidalgo on February 2, 1848
Ask: **What happened during the two years before this treaty?** *(Californians revolted, declared independence, and renamed California the Bear Flag Republic.)*

C Critical Thinking

Analyzing Primary Sources
Organize the class into eight groups. Read the following quote made in 1844 by Sidney George Fisher, a Philadelphia lawyer: "Every day the difference between the North and the South is becoming more prominent and apparent. The difference exists in everything which forms the life of the people—in institutes, laws, opinions, manners, feelings, education, pursuits, climate and soil." Assign each group one item Fisher mentions to prepare a brief oral presentation about the growing differences between the North and South. **AL** **CA** 11WS1.6

S Skill Practice

Visual Literacy Have students examine the poster for the antislavery meeting that appears on this page. **Ask:** Do you think the poster is effective? Would it convince you to attend an antislavery meeting? Why or why not? *(Students may note that the large number of words makes it difficult to find important information on the poster.)* Have students work in pairs to create new posters advertising an antislavery meeting. **OL** **CA** HR4

Answers and Additional Support

196

Impact of the War With Mexico In August 1846, Representative David Wilmot, a Democrat from Pennsylvania, proposed that in any territory the United States gained from Mexico, "neither slavery nor involuntary servitude shall ever exist." Despite fierce Southern opposition, a coalition of Northern Democrats and Whigs passed the **Wilmot Proviso** in the House of Representatives. The Senate refused to vote on it. Senator John C. Calhoun of South Carolina argued that Americans settling in the territories had the right to bring along their property, including enslaved laborers, and that Congress had no power to ban slavery in the territories.

Senator Lewis Cass of Michigan suggested that the citizens of each new territory should be allowed to decide for themselves if they wanted to permit slavery. This idea, which came to be called **popular sovereignty,** appealed strongly to many members of Congress because it removed the slavery issue from national politics. It also appeared democratic, since the settlers themselves would make the decision. Abolitionists, however, argued that it still denied African Americans their right to be free.

As the 1848 election approached, both major candidates—Democrat Lewis Cass and General Zachary

▼ *Poster calling for antislavery meeting*

196 CHAPTER 2 Growth and Conflict

Taylor, the Whig nominee—sidestepped the slavery issue. Many Northern opponents of slavery decided to join with members of the abolitionist Liberty Party to form the Free-Soil Party, which opposed the spread of slavery onto the "free soil" of the western territories. Adopting the slogan "Free soil, free speech, free labor, and free men," they chose former president Martin Van Buren as their candidate. On Election Day, support for the Free-Soilers pulled votes away from the Democrats. When the ballots were counted, the Whig candidate, Zachary Taylor, had won a narrow victory.

Congress Struggles for a Compromise Within a year of President Taylor's inauguration, the issue of slavery took center stage. A year earlier, in January 1848, a carpenter named James Marshall found traces of gold in a stream near a sawmill in Sacramento, California. Word of the find leaked out, and San Franciscans abandoned their homes and businesses to pile into wagons and head to the mountains in search of gold. During the summer, news of the find swept all the way to the East Coast and beyond, and the California Gold Rush was on.

By the end of 1849, over 80,000 "Forty-Niners" had arrived in California hoping to make their fortunes. Mining towns sprang up overnight, and the frenzy for gold led to chaos and violence. Needing a strong government to maintain order, Californians decided to seek statehood. With the encouragement of President Taylor, California applied to enter the Union as a free state in December 1849.

At the time, there were 15 free states and 15 slave states. If California tipped the balance, the slaveholding states would become a minority in the Senate. Southerners dreaded losing power in national politics, fearful it would lead to limits on slavery. A few Southern politicians began to talk of **secession**—taking their states out of the Union.

In early 1850, one of the most senior and influential leaders in the Senate, Henry Clay of Kentucky, tried to find a compromise that would enable California to join the Union and resolve other sectional disputes. Among other resolutions, Clay proposed allowing California to come in as a free state and organizing the rest of the Mexican cession without any restrictions on slavery. Clay further proposed that Congress would be prohibited from interfering with the domestic slave trade and would pass a stronger law to help Southerners recover African American runaways. These measures were intended to assure the South that the North would not try to abolish slavery after California joined the Union.

Did You Know?

John C. Calhoun died on March 31, 1850. Earlier that year, he predicted the dissolution of the Union "within twelve years or three presidential terms."

More Skill Practice

Identifying Central Issues Have students write editorials explaining why slaveholding would be the major issue of the 1848 presidential election in spite of the major parties' efforts to ignore it. Provide students with present-day newspaper editorials to serve as examples. Have students read their editorials aloud to the class. **OL**
CA 11WA2.4a

Clay's proposal triggered a massive debate in Congress. When President Taylor, who opposed the compromise, died unexpectedly of cholera in July 1850, Vice President Millard Fillmore succeeded him and quickly threw his support behind the measure. By September, Congress had passed all parts of the Compromise of 1850, which had been divided into several smaller bills.

The Fugitive Slave Act To Northerners, one of the most objectionable components of the Compromise of 1850 was the Fugitive Slave Act. Under this law, a slaveholder or slavecatcher had only to point out alleged runaways to have them taken into custody. The accused would then be brought before a federal commissioner. With no right to testify on their own behalf, even those who had earned their freedom years earlier had no way to prove their case. An affidavit asserting that the captive had escaped from a slaveholder, or testimony by white witnesses, was all a court needed to order the person sent South. Furthermore, federal commissioners had a financial incentive to rule in favor of slaveholders: such judgments earned them a $10 fee, while judgments in favor of the accused paid only $5.

In addition, the act required federal marshals to assist slavecatchers. Marshals could even deputize citizens to help them. It was this requirement that drove many Northerners into active defiance. The abolitionist Frederick Douglass, himself an escapee from slavery, would work crowds into a furor over this part of the law. Northerners justified their defiance of the Fugitive Slave Act on moral grounds. In his 1849 essay "Civil Disobedience," Henry David Thoreau wrote that if the law "requires you to be the agent of injustice to another, then I say, break the law."

A key to many African Americans' escape from the South was the **Underground Railroad.** This informal but well-organized network of abolitionists helped thousands of enslaved persons flee north. "Conductors" transported runaways in secret, gave them shelter and food along the way, and saw them to freedom in the Northern states or Canada with some money for a fresh start. The most famous conductor was **Harriet Tubman,** herself a runaway. Again and again, she risked journeys into the slave states to bring out men, women, and children.

New Territorial Troubles The opening of the Oregon country and the admission of California to the Union brought further problems. Many people became convinced of the need for a **transcontinental**

The Compromise of 1850	
Legislative Item	**Victory for?**
• California admitted to the Union as free state	Clear victory for the North
• Popular sovereignty to determine slavery issue in Utah and New Mexico territories	Moderate victory for both sides
• Texas border dispute with New Mexico resolved • Texas receives $10 million	Moderate Southern victories
• Slave trade, but not slavery itself, abolished in the District of Columbia	Moderate Northern victory
• Strong federal enforcement of new Fugitive Slave Act	Clear victory for the South

Chart *Skills*

1. **Interpreting Charts** Did the new Fugitive Slave Act appeal to the North or the South?
2. **Generalizing** Which side, North or South, achieved more of its goals in the Compromise of 1850?

railroad to promote growth in the territories along the route. The choice of the railroad's eastern starting point, though was contentious.

Many Southerners favored the southern route, from New Orleans to San Diego. Since part of that route would lead through northern Mexico, the United States purchased the necessary land for $10 million. Democratic Senator Stephen A. Douglas of Illinois, though, wanted the eastern starting point to be in Chicago. He knew that any route from the north would run through the unsettled lands west of Missouri and Iowa and prepared a bill to organize the region into a new territory to be called Nebraska. Key Southern committee leaders prevented this bill from coming to a vote in the Senate. These senators made it clear that before Nebraska could be organized, Congress would have to repeal part of the Missouri Compromise and allow slavery in the new territory.

At first, Douglas tried to gain Southern support for his bill by saying that any states organized in the new Nebraska territory would be allowed to exercise popular sovereignty, deciding themselves whether to allow slavery. When this did not satisfy Southern

C Critical Thinking

Drawing Conclusions Many abolitionists broke laws designed to uphold the practice of enslavement. Give students five minutes to write their thoughts about the following: Are there some situations in which breaking the law is an acceptable protest? Then have students participate in a class discussion about whether abolitionists should have broken the law to help enslaved persons escape. Extend the discussion to include other situations in which it might be acceptable to break the law as a form of protest. OL

S Skill Practice

Identifying Point of View Organize students into groups to create presentations about the transcontinental railroad. Have half of the groups create presentations that describe the northern route and its benefits. Have the other half of the groups present the southern route and its benefits. Remind students to include information such as major cities, safety, and topology in their presentations. Then have the students vote on a proposal for the railroad based on what they have heard in the presentations. OL CA HR1; HR3

Resources for page 197

Have students read more about debates over the expansion of slavery in the west in: Moments in TIME, Unit 3: The Road to Civil War (1850–1861).

More Skill Practice

Auditory/Musical Some enslaved people learned how to use the Underground Railroad through a folk song entitled "Following the Drinking Gourd." Ask students to read an explanation of the song at http://quest.arc.nasa.gov/ltc/special/mlk/gourd2.html and write one or two paragraphs on how it helped African Americans escape on the Underground Railroad. OL

Chart *Skills*

Answers:
1. the South
2. The South probably achieved slightly more because it kept its basic way of life.

Chart Skills Practice
Ask: What did the Compromise of 1850 not prohibit in the District of Columbia? *(It did not prohibit owning enslaved people.)*

C Critical Thinking

Identifying Central Issues
Have students imagine that they are members of Congress in 1854. Ask students to write speeches addressing President Pierce's opposition to the Kansas-Nebraska Act. Encourage students to create outlines of key points before they begin their drafts. Have students take turns presenting their speeches, and vote on which speeches are most convincing. **AL** **CA** 11WS1.3

S Skill Practice

Historical Interpretation
Organize the class into small groups. Have each group work together on a pamphlet encouraging other antislavery citizens to settle in Kansas. Ask students to include background information on the situation in Kansas and an explanation of why it was important for antislavery settlers to travel there. Collect the pamphlets in a binder and display the binder in your classroom. **OL**
CA CS3; HI1

✓ Reading Check

Answer: Northerners were opposed to the Fugitive Slave Act; also, the opening of the Oregon country and the admission of California into the Union caused further sectional division.

Answers and Additional Support

leaders in the Senate, Douglas proposed to repeal the antislavery provision of the Missouri Compromise and to divide the region into two territories. Nebraska, **adjacent** to the free state of Iowa, appeared to become a free state, while, located west of the slave state of Missouri, Kansas would become a slave state. Warned that the South might secede without such concessions, President Pierce eventually gave his support to the bill. Despite fierce opposition, Congress passed the Kansas-Nebraska Act in May 1854.

Intent on creating an antislavery majority, hordes of Northerners hurried into Kansas. Before the March elections of 1855, however, thousands of armed Missourians—called "border ruffians" in the press—swarmed across the border to vote illegally, helping to elect a pro-slavery legislature. Furious antislavery settlers countered by drafting their own constitution that prohibited slavery. By March 1856, Kansas had two governments, one opposed to slavery and the other supporting it. As more Northern settlers arrived, border ruffians began attacks. "Bleeding Kansas," as newspapers dubbed the territory, had become the scene of a territorial civil war between pro-slavery and antislavery settlers.

✓ Reading Check
Analyzing Why did the Compromise of 1850 not succeed in ending sectional division?

Picturing History

Bleeding Kansas These antislavery settlers in Topeka, Kansas, were among those on both sides who resorted to violence. **What act triggered violence in Kansas?**

198 CHAPTER 2 Growth and Conflict

The Crisis Deepens

Main Idea The slavery controversy shook up political parties and accelerated the crisis between North and South.

Reading Connection Do you know of Supreme Court decisions that have sparked major debates? Read on to learn about Dred Scott, who sued to end his slavery.

The Kansas-Nebraska Act enraged many opponents of slavery because it reopened the territories to slavery and made obsolete the delicate balance previously maintained by the Missouri Compromise. While a few people struck back with violence, others worked for change through the political system.

The Kansas-Nebraska Act shattered the Whig Party. Many Northern Whigs left their party and joined forces with Free-Soilers and a few antislavery Democrats during the congressional elections of 1854 to organize as the **Republican Party.** Their main goal was to stop Southern planters from becoming an aristocracy that controlled the government. Republicans did not agree on whether slavery should be abolished in the Southern states, but they did agree that it had to be kept out of the territories. A large majority of Northern voters shared this view, enabling the Republicans to make great strides in the elections.

At the same time, public anger against the Northern Democrats enabled the American Party—better known as the Know-Nothings because party members were sworn to secrecy—to make gains as well, particularly in the Northeast. The American Party was an anti-Catholic and nativist party. In the 1840s and early 1850s, a large number of immigrants, many of them Irish and German Catholics, had begun to arrive. Prejudice and fears that immigrants would take away jobs enabled the Know-Nothings to win many seats in Congress and the state legislatures in 1854. The party quickly began to founder when Know-Nothings from the Upper South split with Know-Nothings from the North over their support for the Kansas-Nebraska Act. Most Americans considered slavery a far more important issue than immigration. Eventually, the Republican Party absorbed the Northern Know-Nothings.

The 1856 presidential campaign pitted Republican John C. Frémont, Democrat James Buchanan, and former president Millard Fillmore, the Know-Nothing candidate, against

Picturing History

Answer: Kansas-Nebraska Act
Ask: Why did antislavery settlers meet in Topeka? (to draft a constitution prohibiting slavery)

More Skill Practice

Sequencing Information Have students create time lines of the major events in the organization of the Republican Party. Encourage them to use library and Internet resources as well as their textbooks to locate information. Allow students to illustrate their time lines with photographs, drawings, and newspaper headlines. **OL**

each other. Buchanan had not taken a public stand on the Kansas-Nebraska Act and campaigned on the idea that only he could save the Union. When the votes were counted, Buchanan had won easily.

Sectional Divisions Grow Just two days after Buchanan's inauguration, the Supreme Court ruled in a landmark case involving slavery, *Dred Scott v. Sandford*. **Dred Scott** was a Missouri slave who had been taken north to work in free territory for several years. After he returned with his slaveholder to Missouri, Scott sued to end his slavery, arguing that living in free territory had made him a free man. On March 6, 1857, the Supreme Court ruled against Scott. As part of his decision, Chief Justice Roger B. Taney stated that Congress's ban on slavery in the western territories, enacted as part of the Missouri Compromise, was unconstitutional and void.

While Democrats cheered the *Dred Scott* decision, Republicans called it a "willful perversion" of the Constitution. They argued that if Dred Scott could not legally bring suit, then the Supreme Court should have dismissed the case without considering the constitutionality of the Missouri Compromise. 📖 *(For more on Dred Scott v. Sandford, see page 1004.)*

After the *Dred Scott* decision, the conflict in "Bleeding Kansas" intensified. Hoping to end the troubles, Buchanan urged the territory to apply for statehood. The pro-slavery legislature scheduled an election for delegates to a constitutional convention, but antislavery Kansans boycotted it. The resulting constitution, drafted in 1857 in the town of Lecompton, legalized slavery in the territory.

An antislavery majority then voted down the Lecompton constitution in a territory-wide referendum, or popular vote on an issue. Although the Senate approved the vote, Republicans and Northern Democrats in the House blocked the measure, arguing that it ignored the people's will. Finally, in 1858, President Buchanan and Southern leaders in Congress agreed to allow another referendum in Kansas. Again the voters in Kansas overwhelmingly rejected the Lecompton constitution. Not until 1861 did Kansas become a state—a free one.

John Brown's Raid About a year after the second rejection of the Lecompton constitution, national attention shifted to John Brown, a fervent abolitionist who opposed slavery not with words but with violence. After pro-slavery forces sacked the town of Lawrence in the Kansas Territory, Brown took revenge by abducting and murdering five pro-slavery settlers living near Pottawatomie Creek.

Brown developed a plan to incite an **insurrection**, or rebellion, against slaveholders. To obtain weapons, he and about 18 followers seized the federal arsenal at **Harpers Ferry**, Virginia (now West Virginia) on the night of October 16, 1859. A contingent of U.S. Marines, commanded by Colonel Robert E. Lee, rushed from Washington, D.C., to Harpers Ferry. Outnumbered, Brown surrendered, and a Virginia court sentenced him to death.

Many Northerners viewed Brown as a martyr in a noble cause. For most Southerners Brown's raid offered all the proof they needed that Northerners were actively plotting the murder of slaveholders.

✓ **Reading Check** **Evaluating** How did the issue of Kansas statehood reflect the growing division between North and South?

The Union Dissolves

Main Idea The election of Abraham Lincoln led the Southern states to secede from the Union.
⟵TURNING POINT⟶

Reading Connection Think of a time when you were unable to compromise over an issue. Read on to learn why Southern states refused to compromise in 1861 and instead decided to secede from the Union, sparking a bloody civil war.

John Brown's raid on Harpers Ferry became a turning point for the South. Many Southerners were terrified and enraged by the idea that Northerners would deliberately try to arm enslaved people and encourage them to rebel. Although Republican leaders quickly denounced Brown's raid, many Southern newspapers and politicians blamed Republicans for the attack. To many Southerners, the key point was that both the Republicans and John Brown opposed slavery.

In April 1860, with the South still in an uproar, Democrats from across the United States gathered in Charleston, South Carolina, to choose their nominee for president. Southern Democrats wanted their party to uphold the *Dred Scott* decision and defend slaveholders' rights in the territories. Northern Democrats, led by Stephen Douglas, preferred to continue supporting popular sovereignty. When Northerners also rebuffed the idea of a federal slave code in the territories, 50 Southern delegates stormed out of the convention. The walkout meant that neither Douglas nor anyone else could muster the two-thirds majority needed to become the party's nominee.

R **Reading Strategy**

Predicting Place the first two columns on the chart below on the board. **Ask:** Which justices were likely to side with Dred Scott, and which were not? After all students have voted, present the correct information and discuss how sectional opinions affected this Court opinion. *(Curtis and McLean dissented.)*
OL

Justice	Home State at the Time of Appointment to the Court
John Archibald Campbell	Alabama
John Catron	Tennessee
Benjamin R. Curtis	Massachusetts
Peter Vivian Daniel	Virginia
Robert Cooper Grier	Pennsylvania
John McLean	Ohio
Samuel Nelson	New York
Roger Brooke Taney	Maryland
James Moore Wayne	Georgia

S **Skill Practice**

Conducting Research Have students use library and Internet resources to write one-page biographies of John Brown. Remind them to include personal information as well as a description of Brown's raid on Harpers Ferry.
OL **CA** 11WA2.1

✓ **Reading Check**

Answer: Kansas struggled to become a state for four years while the pro-slavery legislature battled the antislavery majority.

⟵TURNING POINT⟶

Why could the raid on Harpers Ferry be seen as a turning point for Southerners? *(Southerners became more convinced that they needed to secede from the Union to keep their way of life.)*

More Skill Practice

Identifying Point of View Have students write two newspaper headlines about the raid on Harpers Ferry, one for a Southern newspaper, and one for a Northern newspaper. Discuss the differences in how each region perceived the raid, and why.
OL **CA** HR2

S Skill Practice

Historical Interpretation Have students use library and Internet resources to research the debates between Lincoln and Douglas and then use that research to write news stories on the debates, detailing the major issues raised. Recommend that students review recent news articles to help them understand the style used in good news reporting. `OL` `CA HI1` `CA 11WS1.1`

U Universal Access

English Learners Provide students with an outline map of the United States with the current state boundaries. Have students create thematic maps by labeling and shading in one color all the states that were part of the Union on February 1, 1861, and labeling and shading in another color all the states that had seceded. Then have students shade the remaining area and label it "Territories." `EL`

Answers and Additional Support

In June 1860, the Democrats reconvened in Baltimore. Again, Southern delegates walked out. The Democrats who remained then chose Stephen Douglas to run for president. The Southerners who had bolted organized their own convention in Richmond and nominated John C. Breckinridge of Kentucky, the sitting vice president.

Meanwhile, many former Whigs and others were alarmed at the **prospect** of Southern secession. They created a new party, the Constitutional Union Party, and chose former Tennessee senator John Bell as their candidate. The party took no position on issues dividing North and South. Their purpose, they said, was to uphold the Constitution and the Union.

The Republicans, realizing they stood no chance in the South, needed a candidate who could sweep most of the North. They turned to Abraham Lincoln, who had gained a national reputation during his debates with Douglas. Although not an abolitionist,

Causes and Effects of the Civil War

Causes

- Disagreement over the legality, morality, and politics of slavery
- Kansas-Nebraska Act sparked violence in Kansas.
- *Dred Scott* ruling voided any limitations on expansion of slavery.
- John Brown's raid on Harpers Ferry polarized North and South.
- Southern states seceded from the Union.
- Confederates attacked Fort Sumter in South Carolina.

Effects

- Slavery was outlawed in the United States.
- Southern states rebuilt their economy.
- African Americans gained citizenship and voting rights.
- The first U.S. civil rights laws were passed.

Graphic Organizer → Skills

Mounting sectional tensions erupted into open warfare in 1861.

Analyzing What do you think was the most important cause of the Civil War? Why?

200 CHAPTER 2 Growth and Conflict

Lincoln believed slavery to be morally wrong, and he opposed its spread into western territories.

During the campaign the Republicans remained true to their free-soil principles, but they reaffirmed the right of the Southern states to preserve slavery within their borders. They also supported higher tariffs to protect manufacturers and workers, a new homestead law for settlers in the West, and federal funds for a transcontinental railroad.

The Republican proposals greatly angered many Southerners. As expected, Lincoln won no Southern states; in fact, his name did not even appear on the ballot in some states. With the Democrats divided, the Republicans won in only their second national campaign. Lincoln won with the electoral votes of all of the free states except New Jersey, whose votes he split with Douglas.

Many Southerners viewed Lincoln's election as a threat to their society and culture, even their lives. They saw no choice but to secede. The dissolution of the Union began with South Carolina, where secessionist sentiment had been burning the hottest for many years. Shortly after Lincoln's election, the state legislature called for a convention. On December 20, 1860, amid marching bands, fireworks, and militia drills, the convention voted unanimously to repeal the state's ratification of the Constitution and dissolve its ties to the Union.

By February 1, 1861, six more states in the Lower South—Mississippi, Florida, Alabama, Georgia, Louisiana, and Texas—had also voted to secede. Although a minority in these states did not want to leave the Union, the majority of Southerners viewed secession as similar to the American Revolution—a necessary course of action to uphold people's rights.

Compromise Fails Although Lincoln was elected president in November 1860, he would not be inaugurated until the following March. The Union's initial response to secession remained the responsibility of President Buchanan. Declaring that the government had no authority to forcibly preserve the Union, Buchanan urged Congress to be conciliatory.

In December, Senator John J. Crittenden of Kentucky proposed a series of amendments to the Constitution. **Crittenden's Compromise,** as the newspapers called it, would guarantee slavery where it already existed. It would also reinstate the Missouri Compromise line and extend it all the way to the California border. Slavery would be prohibited in all territories north of the line and protected in all territories south of the line.

Did You Know?

The Tennessee legislature adopted a "Declaration of Independence" on May 7, 1861, effectively breaking with the Union. Convention delegates did not formally accept secession until passing a referendum on June 8, 1861.

Graphic Organizer → Skills

Answer: Answers will vary but should be supported.

Graphic Organizer Skills Practice
Ask: What type of legislation resulted from the Civil War? (*civil rights laws and legislation abolishing slavery*)

Confederate States of America Jefferson Davis from Mississippi was chosen as the president of the newly formed Confederacy. How did the constitution of the Confederacy differ from the U.S. Constitution?

At Lincoln's request, congressional Republicans voted against Crittenden's Compromise. Accepting slavery in any of the territories, Lincoln argued, "acknowledges that slavery has equal rights with liberty, and surrenders all we have contended for."

On February 8, 1861, delegates from the seceding states met in Montgomery, Alabama, where they declared themselves to be a new nation—the Confederate States of America, also known as the **Confederacy.** They drafted a frame of government based largely on the U.S. Constitution but with some important changes. The Confederate Constitution acknowledged the independence of each state, guaranteed slavery in Confederate territory, banned protective tariffs, and limited the president to a single six-year term.

The convention delegates chose former Mississippi senator **Jefferson Davis** to be president. In his inaugural address, Davis declared, "The time for compromise has now passed. The South is determined to . . . make all who oppose her smell Southern powder and feel Southern steel." He then called on the remaining Southern states to join the Confederacy.

☑ **Reading Check** **Explaining** Why did Southern Democrats walk out of the Democratic Convention?

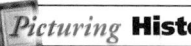
Study Central

For help with the concepts in this section of *American Vision: Modern Times* go to tav.mt.glencoe.com and click on *Study Central.*

SECTION 3 ASSESSMENT

Checking for Understanding

1. **Vocabulary** Define: Manifest Destiny, annexation, popular sovereignty, secession, Underground Railroad, adjacent, transcontinental railroad, insurrection, prospect, Confederacy.
2. **People and Terms** Identify: John C. Frémont, Bear Flag Republic, Wilmot Proviso, Harriet Tubman, Republican Party, Dred Scott, Crittenden's Compromise, Jefferson Davis.
3. **Places** Locate: Harpers Ferry
4. **Explain** why the Gold Rush created a new crisis over slavery.

Reviewing Big Ideas

5. **Comparing and Contrasting** Examine the argument to leave the Union from the perspective of a Secessionist. How does their argument compare with an American colonists' argument for independence from Great Britain. How were the situations similar? How were they different?

Critical Thinking

6. **Historical Analysis** **Synthesizing** How did the ruling in *Dred Scott* v. *Sandford* increase sectional division? **CA HI1; HI2**
7. **Categorizing** Use a graphic organizer similar to the one below to group key events of the 1840s and 1850s according to whether they were executive, legislative, judicial, or nongovernmental.

Executive	
Legislative	
Judicial	
Nongovernmental	

Analyzing Visuals

8. **Examining Photographs** Study the poster on page 196 advertising an antislavery meeting. What was one main reason that the poster designers opposed slavery?

Writing About History

9. **Expository Writing** Write a research report about the Underground Railroad, the California Gold Rush, or the *Dred Scott* decision. In your report, explain what impact the topic had on sectionalism. Make sure you carefully check your report for correct spelling, grammar, and punctuation. **CA 11WS1.1; 11WS1.6; 11WA2.4**

CHAPTER 2 Growth and Conflict **201**

History–Social Science Standards

This feature addresses the following main standard:

11.1 Students analyze the significant events in the founding of the nation and its attempts to realize the philosophy of government described in the Declaration of Independence.

Douglass's Autobiography *Narrative of the Life of Frederick Douglass* was the first of two volumes of Frederick Douglass's autobiography. Douglass felt the need to tell his life story because white abolitionists could never convey a complete picture of slavery.

Read to Discover

Answer: If enslaved people could read, they would think for themselves and question their status.

Understanding Vocabulary

Have students rewrite the sentences in which the vocabulary words appear by using the definitions for those words.

Answers and Additional Support

American LITERATURE

Frederick Douglass was born into slavery in Maryland in 1818. During the course of his incredible life, he escaped from slavery and eventually became renowned for eloquent lectures and writings for the causes of abolition and liberty. One of his most famous works is his autobiography about growing up under the shadow of slavery. In the following excerpt, Douglass is around eight years old, and Mrs. Auld, the wife of his slaveholder, has begun to teach him to read. Mr. Auld discovers what his wife has been doing, and his reaction causes young Frederick to decide to learn to read and write on his own, no matter what.

Read to Discover

Why did some slaveholders not want the enslaved to learn to read?

Reader's Dictionary

revelation: discovery

stratagem: scheme

chattel: property

contemplate: consider

from Narrative of the Life of Frederick Douglass

by Frederick Douglass

▲ *Frederick Douglass welcomes guests to his new office in Washington, D.C.*

Very soon after I went to live with Mr. and Mrs. Auld, she very kindly commenced to teach me the A, B, C. After I had learned this, she assisted me in learning to spell words of three or four letters. Just at this point of my progress, Mr. Auld found out what was going on, and at once forbade Mrs. Auld to instruct me further, telling her, among other things, that it was unlawful, as well as unsafe, to teach a slave to read. . . . ["]Now," said [Mr. Auld], "if you teach that [boy] . . . how to read, there would be no keeping him. It would forever unfit him to be a slave. He would at once become unmanageable, and of no value to his master. As to himself, it could do him no good, but a great deal of harm. It would make him discontented and unhappy." These words sank deep into my heart, stirred up sentiments within that lay slumbering, and called into existence an entirely new train of thought. It was a new and special revelation, explaining dark and mysterious things, with which my youthful understanding had struggled, but struggled in vain. . . . From that moment, I understood the pathway from slavery to freedom. It was just what I wanted, and I got it at a time when I least expected it. Whilst I was saddened by the thought of losing the aid of my kind mistress, I was gladdened by the invaluable instruction which, by the merest accident, I had gained from my master. Though conscious of the difficulty of learning without a teacher, I set out with high hope, and a fixed purpose, at whatever cost of trouble, to learn to read. . . . That which to [Mr. Auld] was a great evil, to be carefully shunned, was to me a great good, to

---

Reading Strategy   ACTIVATING PRIOR KNOWLEDGE

Frederick Douglass struggled to teach himself to read, against very difficult odds. Ask the class to think of other famous Americans throughout history that faced difficult odds but overcame those challenges with determination. *(Students might mention Abraham Lincoln's own efforts to teach himself to read or Rosa Parks' determination to fight discrimination in Montgomery, Alabama.)* **OL** be diligently sought; and the argument which he so warmly urged, against my learning to read, only served to inspire me with a desire and determination to learn. In learning to read, I owe almost as much to the bitter opposition of my master, as to the kindly aid of my mistress. I acknowledge the benefit of both. . . .

I lived in Master Hugh's family about seven years. During this time, I succeeded in learning to read and write. In accomplishing this, I was compelled to resort to various stratagems. I had no regular teacher. My mistress, who had kindly commenced to instruct me, had, in compliance with the advice and direction of her husband, not only ceased to instruct, but had set her face against my being instructed by any one else. It is due, however, to my mistress to say of her, that she

▲ Enslaved African Americans picking cotton.

did not adopt this course of treatment immediately. She at first lacked the depravity indispensable to shutting me up in mental darkness. It was at least necessary for her to have some training in the exercise of irresponsible power, to make her equal to the task of treating me as though I were a brute.

My mistress was, as I have said, a kind and tender-hearted woman; and in the simplicity of her soul she commenced, when I first went to live with her, to treat me as she supposed one human being ought to treat another. In entering upon the duties of a slaveholder, she did not seem to perceive that I sustained to her the relation of a mere chattel, and that for her to treat me as a human being was not only wrong, but dangerously

so. Slavery proved as injurious to her as it did to me. When I went there, she was a pious, warm, and tender-hearted woman. There was no sorrow or suffering for which she had not a tear. She had bread for the hungry, clothes for the naked, and comfort for every mourner that came within her reach. Slavery soon proved its ability to divest her of these heavenly qualities. Under its influence, the tender heart became stone, and the lamblike disposition gave way to one of tiger-like fierceness. The first step in her downward course was in her ceasing to instruct me. She now commenced to practise her husband's precepts. She finally became even more violent in her opposition than her husband himself. . . .

From this time I was most narrowly watched. If I was in a separate room any considerable length of time, I was sure to be suspected of having a book, and was at once called to give an account of myself. All this, however, was too late. . . .

The plan which I adopted, and the one by which I was most successful, was that of making friends of all the little white boys whom I met in the street. As many of these as I could, I converted into teachers. With their kindly aid, obtained at different times and in different places, I finally succeeded in learning to read. When I was sent of errands, I always took my book with me, and by going one part of my errand quickly, I found time to get a lesson before my return. I used also to carry bread with me, enough of which was always in the house, and to which I was always

TEACH

S Skill Practice

Identifying Point of View Have students imagine that they are Mrs. Auld and that their husband has just forbidden them to teach Douglass and the other slaves to read. Ask students to write diary entries in which they must decide whether or not to continue teaching Douglass to read. **Ask: What factors must Mrs. Auld have considered when making her decision to stop the reading lessons?** Invite students to share their completed diary entries with the class. **OL** **CA HI1** **CA 11RC2.5; 11WA2.2**

C Critical Thinking

Analyzing Information Have students copy the following quotation onto a piece of paper: "Slavery proved as injurious to her [Mrs. Auld] as it did to me." **Ask: Do you agree with Douglass's statement? Why or why not?** *(Answers will vary. Students who support the quote should note Mrs. Auld's kind and generous nature; those who oppose the quote should describe the evils of slavery, from which Mrs. Auld was immune.)* **OL**

Block Schedule

Team Teaching This selection from *Narrative of the Life of Frederick Douglass* can be presented in a team teaching context, in conjunction with English or Language Arts.

Resources for pages 202–204

*Have students reads more about Frederick Douglass by assigning "Men of Color, To Arms" in the **Primary Source Reading 2-2**.*

Reading Strategy ❯ EVALUATING

Remind students that *Narrative of the Life of Frederick Douglass* was an autobiography, meaning that it was written by Frederick Douglass about his own experiences. **Ask: Should we assume that Douglass's depictions about his life experiences are accurate because he wrote them himself?** *(Students might say that Douglass was a very politically active individual and may have used his own story to push for the end of slavery in the United States. Therefore, we should not take everything he presents at face value.)* **AL**

▲ *Freed African Americans learn to read in Richmond, Virginia.*

welcome; for I was much better off in this regard than many of the poor white children in our neighborhood. This bread I used to bestow upon the hungry little urchins, who, in return, would give me that more valuable bread of knowledge. . . .

I was now about twelve years old, and the thought of being a *slave for life* began to bear heavily upon my heart. Just about this time, I got hold of a book entitled "The Columbian Orator." Every opportunity I got, I used to read this book. Among much of other interesting matter, I found in it a dialogue between a master and his slave. The slave was represented as having run away from his master three times. The dialogue represented the conversation which took place between them, when the slave was retaken the third time. In this dialogue, the whole argument in behalf of slavery was brought forward by the master, all of which was disposed of by the slave. The slave was made to say some very smart as well as impressive things in reply to his master—things which had the desired though unexpected effect; for the conversation resulted in the voluntary emancipation of the slave on the part of the master.

. . . The more I read, the more I was led to abhor and detest my enslavers. I could regard them in no other light than as a band of successful robbers, who had left their homes, and gone to Africa, and stolen us from our homes, and in a strange land reduced us to slavery. I loathed them as being the meanest as

well as the most wicked of men. As I read and contemplated the subject, behold! that very discontentment which Master Hugh had predicted would follow my learning to read had already come, to torment and sting my soul to unutterable anguish. As I writhed under it, I would at times feel that learning to read had been a curse rather than a blessing. It had given me a view of my wretched condition, without the remedy. It opened my eyes to the horrible pit, but to no ladder upon which to get out. In moments of agony, I envied my fellow-slaves for their stupidity. I have often wished myself a beast. I preferred the condition of the meanest reptile to my own. Any thing, no matter what, to get rid of thinking! It was this everlasting thinking of my condition that tormented me. . . .

R

I often found myself regretting my own existence, and wishing myself dead; and but for the hope of being free, I have no doubt but that I should have killed myself, or done something for which I should have been killed. . . . I looked forward to a time at which it would be safe for me to escape. I was too young to think of doing so immediately; besides, I wished to learn how to write, as I might have occasion to write my own pass. I consoled myself with the hope that I should one day find a good chance. Meanwhile, I would learn to write.

Analyzing Literature

1. **Recall** Why did Mr. Auld oppose the idea of Douglass learning to read?
2. **Interpret** What do you think Douglass means when he speaks of "a revelation, explaining dark and mysterious things"?
   CA 11RC2.4; 11RC2.5; 11RL3.4
3. **Evaluate and Connect** How would you feel if someone had forbidden you to learn to read? What would you do?

Interdisciplinary Activity

Art Design a poster promoting literacy. Include reasons why everyone should learn to read and write and get an education.

Reading on Your Own

For other literature selections that relate to the enslavement of African Americans, you might consider the following book suggestions.

The Fire Next Time (Nonfiction)
by James Baldwin

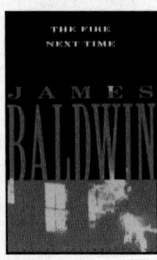

In a powerful letter to his nephew, Baldwin relates his thoughts on racism on the 100th anniversary of the Emancipation Proclamation. Baldwin's essay, which contains his own memories of life in Harlem, powerfully appeals to both African Americans and whites to recognize the perils of racism and to accept that we live in a multicultural society.

Jubilee (Fiction)
by Margaret Walker

This book tells the story of Vyry, the daughter of an enslaved African American woman, and her slaveholder. Readers follow Vyry's life before, during, and after the Civil War as she travels north trying to find her version of the American Dream. Based on the memories of Ms. Walker's maternal grandmother, the story counters the popular images of the Civil War portrayed in the film *Gone With the Wind* by describing life from the point of view of enslaved African Americans.

Beloved (Fiction)
by Toni Morrison

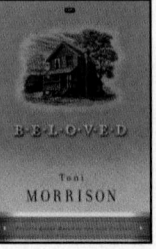

Once an enslaved person on Sweet Home Farm, Seth escapes and travels north with her children. Before being recaptured, she kills a daughter rather than allowing her to suffer the brutal life of slavery. After the Civil War, Beloved, the spirit of Seth's murdered daughter, comes back into her life and complicates her attempts to live a normal family life. Told in a series of flashbacks, Seth's fictional history captures the violence and indignities, as well as the courage and compassion, of thousands of humans who were once enslaved.

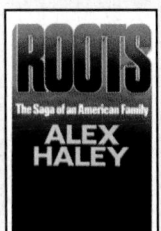

Roots (Biography/Autobiography)
by Alex Haley

This saga of the Haley family begins with Kunta Kinte's capture in Africa and follows his family through seven generations. Made into a popular television mini-series, the book became a symbolic history for many African Americans who also could trace their families back to slavery.

Reading Strategy ⟩ REINFORCING READING SKILLS

To help students practice monitoring, tell them to make adjustments to the rate at which they read. Remind students to slow down when they encounter difficult concepts, connections to previous ideas, new vocabulary, or text that contains large amounts of information. If they do not understand an important idea, they need to reread, review, or read on to clarify what is unclear. **OL**

HISTORY Online

Refer to tav.mt.glencoe.com for additional Glencoe Literature titles, lesson plans, and study guides related to this unit.

TEACH

Cooperative Learning

Multimedia Exhibit Tell students to create a traveling exhibit about the enslavement and freedom of African Americans. Organize students into five groups. Each group will be responsible for one of the following aspects of the exhibit: music, biographies, pamphlets, and primary source documents.

- Music—Have students display religious and folk songs sung by enslaved African Americans that relate to enslavement or the Underground Railroad.

- Biographies—Students should provide brief biographies of a few key figures who helped enslaved African Americans achieve freedom.

- Pamphlets—Pamphlets should identify and summarize literature selections that relate to the enslavement of African Americans and include drawings and photographs.

- Primary documents—Have students locate poems, stories, autobiographies, and essays written by enslaved African Americans or written on the topic of slavery. Students can copy and display relevant pages. **OL**

GLENCOE BOOKLINK

Use **Glencoe BookLink** to create customized reading lists for your students' reading levels, interests, and abilities.

205

FOCUS

SKILLBUILDER ACTIVITY

Project **Daily Focus Skills Transparency 2-4** and have students answer the question.

Guide to Reading

Understanding Vocabulary:
Assign a vocabulary word, person, term, or place to each student. Have each student prepare a 30-second oral presentation related to his or her term.

Answers to Graphic:
First Bull Run: Confederate victory; New Orleans: Union victory; Shiloh: undecisive, high casualties; Seven Days' Battle: undecisive, Union retreats; Second Bull Run: Confederate victory; Antietam: Union victory, Britain remains neutral, Emancipation Proclamation announced; Vicksburg: Union victory; Gettysburg: Union victory, war's turning point; Chattanooga: Union victory; Wilderness/Spotsylvania CH: Union victory; Cold Harbor: Confederate victory; Atlanta: Union victory

Unpacking the Standards

Students will be able to:

- Discuss the events that started the Civil War.
- Analyze the economic and political differences between the North and the South.
- Describe the early battles and events of the war.
- Explain key battles of the Civil War.

SECTION 4 The Civil War

Guide to Reading

Connection
In the previous section, you learned how the division between the North and the South resulted in the secession of the South. In this section, you will discover how the Civil War began and find out about the factors that led to the Union's victory over the Confederate army.

Main Idea
- The plan to resupply Fort Sumter triggered the beginning of the Civil War. (p. 207)
- The North and South each had distinct advantages and disadvantages at the beginning of the Civil War. (p. 208)
- With Union casualties rising, President Lincoln issued the Emancipation Proclamation. (p.210)

- With the help of key victories at Vicksburg and Gettysburg, the North defeated the South after four long years of fighting. (p. 212)

Content Vocabulary
martial law, greenback, conscription, habeas corpus, attrition, siege, mandate

Academic Vocabulary
conceive, subordinate

People and Terms to Identify
Robert E. Lee, Ulysses S. Grant, Emancipation Proclamation, Gettysburg Address, Thirteenth Amendment

Places to Locate
Fort Sumter, Antietam, Vicksburg, Gettysburg, Appomattox Courthouse

Reading Objectives
- **Contrast** the political situations of the Union and Confederacy.
- **Identify** the major battles of the war, and assess their impact.
- **Discuss** Lee's surrender and the events of the war's aftermath.

Reading Strategy
Categorizing As you read about the major battles of the Civil War, complete a chart similar to the one below by filling in the name of each battle and its results.

Battle	Results

Preview of Events

♦ *April 1861*   ♦ *April 1863*   ♦ *April 1865*

April 1861	April 1862	January 1863	July 1863	April 1865
Fort Sumter bombarded	Confederate Congress passes conscription law	Emancipation Proclamation takes effect	Battle of Gettysburg	Lee surrenders at Appomattox Courthouse; Lincoln assassinated.

The following are the main History–Social Science Standards covered in this section.

11.1 Students analyze the significant events in the founding of the nation and its attempts to realize the philosophy of government described in the Declaration of Independence.

11.1.3 Understand the history of the Constitution after 1787 with emphasis on federal versus state authority and growing democratization.

11.1.4 Examine the effects of the Civil War and Reconstruction and of the industrial revolution, including demographic shifts and the emergence in the late nineteenth century of the United States as a world power.

11.10.2 Examine and analyze the key events, policies, and court cases in the evolution of civil rights, including *Dred Scott v. Sandford*, *Plessy v. Ferguson*, *Brown v. Board of Education*, *Regents of the University of California v. Bakke*, and California Proposition 209.

～ *The Big Idea* ～

Differences in economic, political, and social beliefs can lead to division within a nation. Confederate forces took control of Fort Sumter in Charleston, South Carolina, making war with the Union unavoidable. The North maintained several advantages over the South. It had a strong naval tradition, more than twice the population from which to draw an army, a larger treasury to help support the war, and more industries and railroads to manufacture and transport supplies. While the South maintained a stronger military tradition, it could not adequately finance the war and was able to receive only limited overseas supplies due to the North's blockade of Southern ports. After many battles and casualties and much destruction, Confederate forces surrendered. As the country entered the period of Reconstruction, John Wilkes Booth assassinated President Lincoln.

206 CHAPTER 2 Growth and Conflict

SECTION RESOURCES

📂 **Print Material**
- Reproducible Lesson Plan 2-4
- Guided Reading Activity 2-4
- Reading Essentials and Study Guide 2-4
- Active Reading Note-Taking Guide 2-4

🖳 **Transparencies**
- Daily Focus Skills Transparency 2-4
- Section Graphic Organizer Transparency 2-4

Technology
- ⊚ Interactive Tutor Self-Assessment CD-ROM
- ⊚ Exam*View*® Pro Testmaker CD-ROM
- ⊚ Presentation Plus! CD-ROM

The Civil War Begins

Main Idea The plan to resupply Fort Sumter triggered the beginning of the Civil War.

Reading Connection If you believed in a cause, what would you do to convince others to join you? Read on to learn how President Lincoln held on to the border states.

In April Lincoln announced that he intended to send needed supplies to **Fort Sumter** in Charleston Harbor, one of the few federal military bases that Southerners had not already seized. The Confederacy now faced a dilemma.

★ An American Story ★

"I do not pretend to sleep," wrote Mary Chesnut of the night of April 12, 1861. "How can I?" Hours earlier, her husband, former South Carolina senator James Chesnut, had gone by rowboat to Fort Sumter in Charleston Harbor. He was delivering an ultimatum to U.S. Army Major Robert Anderson to surrender the fort by four o'clock in the morning or be fired upon by the South Carolina militia.

Through the long night Mary Chesnut lay awake, until she heard chimes from a local church ring four times. The hour of surrender had arrived, and, she confessed, "I beg[a]n to hope." But her hopes of a peaceful outcome faded when, a half hour later, she heard the cannons begin to boom. "I sprang out of bed. And on my knees . . . I prayed as I never prayed before."

In a nightgown and shawl, Chesnut ran to the roof, where others had gathered to watch the bombardment of Fort Sumter. The sectional conflict that had brewed in debate and broken out in periodic violence had become a war. On her rooftop, Mary Chesnut shivered and felt the first terrifying evidence of the horrors to come. "The regular roar of the cannon—there it was. And who could tell what each volley accomplished of death and destruction."

—adapted from *Mary Chesnut's Civil War*

President Lincoln had tried to avoid war. In his inaugural speech on March 4, 1861, he addressed the seceding states directly, repeating his commitment not to interfere with slavery where it already existed. Still, he insisted that "the Union of these States is perpetual." He did not threaten to attack the seceded states, but he did announce his intention to "hold, occupy, and possess" federal property in those states. Lincoln also made an eloquent plea for reconciliation, stating: "The government will not assail *you*. . . . Though passion may have strained, it must not break our bonds of affection."

When President Lincoln announced his plan to resupply Fort Sumter, Confederate President Jefferson Davis was faced with a problem. To tolerate U.S. troops in the South's most vital Atlantic harbor seemed unacceptable for a sovereign nation. However, firing on the supply ship would undoubtedly provoke war with the United States. Jefferson decided to demand the surrender of Fort Sumter before the supply ship arrived. The fort's commander, U.S. Army Major Robert Anderson, stood fast. Confederate forces then bombarded Fort Sumter for 33 hours on April 12 and 13, until Anderson and his exhausted men gave up. No one had been killed, but the Civil War had begun.

After the fall of Fort Sumter, President Lincoln called for 75,000 volunteers to serve in the military for 90 days. Lincoln's action created a crisis in the Upper South. Many people in those states did not want to secede, but they were not willing to take up arms against fellow Southerners. Between April 17 and June 8, 1861, four more states chose to leave the Union—Virginia, Arkansas, North Carolina, and Tennessee. The Confederate Congress then established Richmond, Virginia, as the capital.

Mary Chesnut ▼

CHAPTER 2 Growth and Conflict **207**

TEACH

C Critical Thinking

Analyzing Information Tell students that in 1790 there were 694,000 enslaved people in the United States. By 1860 there were 3,950,000 enslaved people in the South. **Ask:** Why might political compromise over the slavery questions have been easier after the American Revolution than on the eve of the Civil War? *(Slavery had spread throughout the South by the 1850s, the economy of the South depended on slavery, and a better political climate for compromise may have existed after the Revolution.)* **AL** **CA HI4**

S Skill Practice

Identifying Point of View Write the bracketed quote from Lincoln on the board. Ask students to write short paragraphs or journal entries explaining the quote. **Ask:** What message is Lincoln sending to the seceding states? What is his tone? *(He is reminding the South that despite differences, the United States must remain united; his tone is conciliatory.)* **OL** **CA HI3; HI4**

More Skill Practice

Persuasive Writing Have students imagine that they are advisers to Jefferson Davis. Ask them to write letters to Davis advising him on how to respond to Lincoln's plans to resupply Fort Sumter. Encourage students to share what they have written with the class. **OL** **CA 11WS1.3**

More Skill Practice

Organizing Information Have students create a chart listing the states in one of three categories: *Free States, Slave States that Seceded,* and *Slave States that did not Secede.* For the *States that Seceded,* have students include the date of the state's secession from the Union. **BL**

C₁ Critical Thinking

Identifying Central Issues Tell students that under martial law, anyone supporting secession—or suspected of supporting secession—could be arrested and held without trial. **Ask: What rights do you think people in Maryland referred to in their objections?** *(Students might mention either individual rights guaranteed in the Bill of Rights or the interference of the federal government in states' rights.)* **OL**

C₂ Critical Thinking

Drawing Conclusions As a class, make a list of the issues Robert E. Lee may have weighed as he made his decision about which side to fight for. Have students draw conclusions about what factors weighed most heavily in his decision to turn down Lincoln's offer and volunteer his services to the Confederacy. **OL**

✓ Reading Check

Answer: Many people in these states were not willing to take up arms against fellow Southerners.

Answers and Additional Support

Resources of the Union and of the Confederacy

Population: Union 71%, Confederacy 29%
Manufactured goods: Union 92%, Confederacy 8%
Exports: Union 56%, Confederacy 44%
Merchant ships: Union 90%, Confederacy 10%
Miles of railroad track: Union 72%, Confederacy 28%
Grain production: Union 69%, Confederacy 31%
Number of farms: Union 67%, Confederacy 33%
Iron production: Union 94%, Confederacy 6%
Banking capital: Union 82%, Confederacy 18%

Source: Historical Statistics of the United States

Chart *Skills*

1. **Interpreting Graphs** In which category is the difference between the Union and the Confederacy the greatest?
2. **Making Inferences** What additional factors are not considered when comparing population percentages between the Union and the Confederacy?

With the Upper South gone, Lincoln could not afford to lose the slaveholding border states as well. Delaware seemed safe, but Lincoln worried about Kentucky, Missouri, and particularly Maryland. Virginia's secession had placed a Confederate state across the Potomac River from the nation's capital. If Maryland joined the South, Washington, D.C., would be surrounded by Confederate territory. To prevent Maryland's secession, Lincoln imposed **martial law**—military rule—in Baltimore, where angry mobs had already attacked federal troops. Although many people objected to this suspension of their rights, Maryland stayed in the Union.

Kentucky initially declared neutrality in the conflict, but when Confederate troops occupied part of Kentucky, the state declared war on the Confederacy, and Lincoln sent troops to help. In Missouri, despite strong public support for the Confederacy, the state convention voted to stay in the Union. Federal troops then ended fights between the pro-Union government and secessionists.

The war shattered old loyalties and made enemies of former friends. For the next several years, the bloody war between the states divided Americans and resulted in hundreds of thousands of casualties.

✓ Reading Check
Examining Why did the call for military volunteers lead more states to secede?

208 CHAPTER 2 Growth and Conflict

The Opposing Sides

Main Idea The North and South each had distinct advantages and disadvantages at the beginning of the Civil War.

Reading Connection Do you believe the government is justified limiting civil liberties during wartime? Read on to learn how President Lincoln decided to suspend writs of habeas corpus during the Civil War.

On the same day that he learned his home state of Virginia had voted to secede from the Union, **Robert E. Lee**—one of the best senior officers in the United States Army—received an offer from General Winfield Scott to command Union troops. Although Lee had spoken against secession and considered slavery "a moral and political evil," he refused to fight against the South. Instead, he offered his services to the Confederacy.

Lee was one of hundreds of military officers who resigned to join the Confederacy. In 1860 seven of the nation's eight military colleges were in the South. These colleges provided the region with a large number of trained officers to quickly organize an effective fighting force.

Just as the South had a strong military tradition, the North had a strong naval tradition. More than three-quarters of the Navy's officers came from the North, and the crews of American merchant ships were almost entirely from the North. They provided a large pool of trained sailors for the Union navy as it expanded.

Chart *Skills*

Answers:
1. iron production
2. possible answers: willingness of the people to fight, strength of leadership, demographic makeup of the population

Chart Skills Practice
Ask: In what category are the two sides nearly equal? *(exports)*

The Opposing Economies Although the South had many experienced officers to lead its troops in battle, the North had several economic advantages. In 1860 the population of the North was about 22 million, while the South had about 9 million people. The North's larger population gave it a great advantage in raising an army and in supporting the war effort.

The North's industries also gave the region an important economic advantage over the South. In 1860 almost 90 percent of the nation's factories were located in the Northern states. The North could provide its troops with ammunition and other supplies more easily. In addition, the South had only half as many miles of railroad track as the North and had only one line—from Memphis to Chattanooga—connecting the western states of the Confederacy to the east. This made it much easier for Northern troops to disrupt the Southern rail system and prevent the movement of supplies and troops.

The Union also controlled the national treasury and could expect continued revenue from tariffs. In order to make more money available for emergency use, Congress passed the Legal Tender Act, creating a national currency and allowing the government to issue paper money. The paper money came to be known as **greenbacks,** because of its color.

The Confederacy did not fare as well. Most Southern planters were in debt and unable to buy bonds. Southern banks were small and had few cash reserves; as a result, they could not buy many bonds either. The best hope for the South to raise money was by taxing trade. Then, shortly after the war began, the Union Navy blockaded Southern ports, which reduced trade and revenues. The Confederacy had to resort to direct taxation of its people, but many Southerners refused to pay.

The Confederacy also printed paper money to pay its bills. This caused rapid inflation in the South, and Confederate paper money eventually became almost worthless. By the end of the war, the South had experienced 9,000 percent inflation, compared to only 80 percent in the North.

U₁ **The Political Situation** President Lincoln had to deal with a number of issues. Although many fellow Republicans were abolitionists, Lincoln wanted to preserve the Union, even if it meant allowing slavery to continue. The president also had to contend with the Democrats, who were divided themselves over a possible war.

One major disagreement between Republicans and Democrats concerned the enactment in 1862 of a militia law that allowed states to use **conscription**—or forcing people through a draft into military service —if this was necessary to fill their regiments. Criticism also greeted President Lincoln's decision to suspend writs of **habeas corpus.** A writ of habeas corpus is a court order that requires the government either to charge an imprisoned person with a crime or let the person go free. When writs of habeas corpus are suspended, a person can be imprisoned indefinitely without trial. In this case, President Lincoln suspended the writ for anyone who openly supported the rebels or encouraged others to resist the militia draft. "Must I shoot a simple-minded soldier boy who deserts," the president asked, "while I must not touch a hair of a wily agitator who induces him to desert?"

Although the South had no organized opposition party, Confederate president Jefferson Davis still faced political problems. The Confederate constitution emphasized states' rights and limited the central government's power. This often interfered with Davis's ability to conduct the war with a united commitment from every Confederate state government. Some Southern leaders opposed Davis when he supported conscription and established martial law early in 1862. They also opposed the suspension of writs of habeas corpus, which the South, like the North, had introduced.

The outbreak of the Civil War put the major governments of Europe in a difficult situation. While the United States government did not want the Europeans interfering in the war. Confederate leaders wanted them to recognize the South and provide it with military assistance. Southern leaders knew that European textile factories depended on Southern cotton. To pressure the British and French, many Southern planters agreed to stop selling their cotton in these markets until the Europeans recognized the Confederacy. Despite these efforts, both countries chose not to go to war against the United States.

The First Modern War The North and South were about to embark on what was, in many respects, the first modern war. Unlike earlier European wars, the Civil War involved huge armies that consisted mostly of civilian volunteers and required vast amounts of supplies. By the 1850s, French and American inventors had developed an **U₂** inexpensive conoidal—or cone-shaped—bullet that was accurate at much greater distances. This resulted in much higher casualties. **Attrition**—the wearing down of one side by the other through exhaustion of soldiers and resources—also played a critical role as the war dragged on.

CHAPTER 2 Growth and Conflict **209**

Review the Big Idea

Review the Big Idea for this section, "Differences in economic, political, and social beliefs can lead to division within a nation." Have students compare the political and economic differences between the North and South in 1860. **Ask:** Do the differences reflect the different political viewpoints? *(lack of factories and emphasis on agriculture in the South; Confederate president Davis faced problems getting states to agree to his policies)* **OL**

U₁ Universal Access

English Learners Summarizing information teaches students to reduce information to a simpler form, which may assist English learners. In a class discussion, compare the strengths and weaknesses of the Northern and Southern political situations, and explain how each side's strategies were related to these strengths and weaknesses. Then have each student write a brief summary of the conclusions. **EL**

U₂ Universal Access

Logical/Mathematical Invite a physics teacher or a physicist to explain the science of the conoidal bullet's effectiveness. Ask the speaker to use and define scientific terminology and to demonstrate the applicable laws of physics. **OL**

Did You Know?

In the autumn of 1861, two Confederate diplomats set out from Havana, Cuba, aboard the British vessel *Trent* to meet with European officials. The Union warship *San Jacinto* intercepted the *Trent* and arrested the diplomats. After several tense weeks, the United States freed the men. Although their diplomatic mission ultimately failed, the *Trent* Affair excited interest worldwide.

The Anaconda Plan

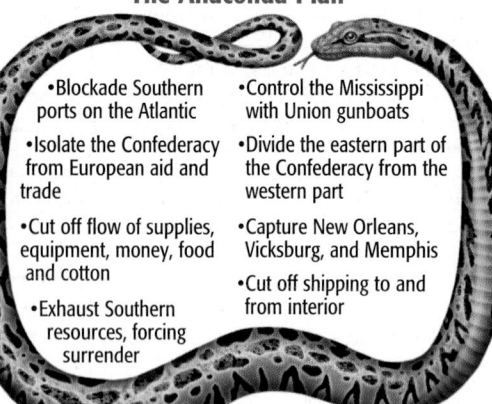

- Blockade Southern ports on the Atlantic
- Isolate the Confederacy from European aid and trade
- Cut off flow of supplies, equipment, money, food and cotton
- Exhaust Southern resources, forcing surrender
- Control the Mississippi with Union gunboats
- Divide the eastern part of the Confederacy from the western part
- Capture New Orleans, Vicksburg, and Memphis
- Cut off shipping to and from interior

Early in the war, Jefferson Davis imagined a struggle similar to the American war for independence against Britain in which Southern generals would pick their battles carefully, attacking and retreating when necessary to avoid heavy losses. By waging a defensive war of attrition, Davis believed the South could force the Union to spend its resources until it became tired of the war and agreed to negotiate. Instead, President Davis felt pressure to strike for a quick victory, especially since many Southerners believed that their military traditions made them superior fighters. In the war, Southern troops went on the offensive in eight battles, suffering 20,000 more casualties than the Union by charging enemy lines. These were heavy losses the South could not afford.

The general in chief of the United States, Winfield Scott, suggested that the Union blockade Confederate ports and send gunboats down the Mississippi River to divide the Confederacy in two. The South, thus separated, would gradually run out of resources and surrender. Many Northerners rejected the strategy, which they called the Anaconda Plan, after a snake that slowly strangles its prey to death. They thought it was too slow and indirect for certain victory. Lincoln eventually agreed to implement Scott's suggestions and imposed a blockade of Southern ports. He and other Union leaders realized that only a long war that focused on destroying the South's armies had any chance of success.

✓ Reading Check **Comparing** In what areas did the opposing sides have advantages and disadvantages?

The Early Stages

Main Idea With Union casualties rising, President Lincoln issued the Emancipation Proclamation.

Reading Connection Do you know someone who lived through the food rationing during World War II? Read on to learn how the war affected daily life.

During the first few months of the war, President Lincoln felt tremendous pressure to strike hard against the South. He approved an assault on Confederate troops gathered near Manassas Junction, Virginia, only 25 miles (40 km) south of Washington, D.C. The First Battle of Bull Run, as it came to be called, started well for the Union as it forced Confederate troops to retreat. Then the tide turned when reinforcements under the command of Thomas J. "Stonewall" Jackson helped the Confederates defeat the Union forces. This outcome made it clear that the North would need a large, well-trained army to prevail against the South.

Lincoln had originally called for 75,000 men to serve for three months. The day after Bull Run, he signed another bill for the enlistment of 500,000 men for three years. The North initially tried to encourage voluntary enlistment by offering a bounty—a sum of money given as a bonus—to individuals who promised three years of military service. Eventually both the Union and the Confederacy instituted the draft.

The Naval War While the Union and Confederacy mobilized their armies, President Lincoln proclaimed a blockade of all Confederate ports in an effort to cut Confederate trade with the world. Although the blockade became increasingly effective as the war dragged on, Union vessels were thinly spread and found it difficult to stop the blockade runners—small, fast vessels the South used to smuggle goods past the blockade, usually at night. By using blockade runners, the South could ship at least some of its cotton to Europe in exchange for shoes, rifles, and other supplies.

As part of its effort to close Southern ports, the Union navy developed a plan to seize New Orleans and gain control of the lower Mississippi River. In February 1862, David G. Farragut took command of a combined Union force consisting of 42 warships and 15,000 soldiers led by General Benjamin Butler. On April 25, 1862, Farragut arrived at New Orleans. Six days later, General Butler's troops took control of the city. The South's largest city, and a center of the cotton trade, was now in Union hands.

Did You Know?

The Civil War saw the rise of new weapons such as the conoidal bullet. The key ingredient in the powerful new weapons was gunpowder. Scholars believe that the Chinese invented this explosive mixture and were using it in fireworks and signals as early as the 900s. In 1304 the Arabs used the powder to develop the first gun. In the centuries that followed, numerous nations would develop and improve on the gun—which made all other weapons before it obsolete.

The War in the West In February 1862, as Farragut prepared for his attack on New Orleans, Union general **Ulysses S. Grant** began a campaign to seize control of the Cumberland and Tennessee Rivers. Control of these rivers would cut Tennessee in two and provide the Union with a river route deep into Confederate territory.

All of Kentucky and most of western Tennessee soon came under Union control. Grant next headed up the Tennessee River to attack Corinth, Mississippi. Seizing Corinth would cut the Confederacy's only rail line connecting Mississippi and western Tennessee to the east. Early on April 6, 1862, Confederate forces launched a surprise attack on Grant's troops, which were camped about 20 miles (32 km) north of Corinth near a small church named Shiloh. The Union won the Battle of Shiloh the following day, but both sides paid an enormous cost. Twenty thousand troops had been killed or wounded, more than in any other battle up to that point. When newspapers demanded Grant be fired because of the high casualties, Lincoln refused, saying, "I can't spare this man; he fights."

The War in the East While Grant fought his battles in the West, another major campaign was being waged in the East to capture Richmond, Virginia, the Confederate capital. In late June 1862, Confederate general Robert E. Lee began a series of attacks on the Union army that became known collectively as the Seven Days' Battle. Although Lee was unable to decisively defeat the Union army, he did force its retreat. Together the two sides suffered over 30,000 casualties.

As Union troops withdrew, Lee decided to attack the Union forces defending Washington. The maneuvers by the two sides led to another battle at Bull Run, near Manassas Junction, the site of the first major battle of the war. The South again forced the North to retreat, leaving the Confederate forces only 20 miles (32 km) from Washington, D.C. Soon after, Lee's forces invaded Maryland.

Both Lee and Jefferson Davis believed that only an invasion would convince the North to accept the South's independence. They also thought that a victory on Northern soil might help the South win recognition from the British and help the Peace Democrats gain control of Congress in the upcoming midterm elections. By heading north, Lee also could feed his troops from Northern farms and draw Union troops out of Virginia during harvest season.

On September 17, 1862, Lee's forces met Union troops under the command of General George B. McClellan at **Antietam** (an·TEE·tuhm) Creek. The Battle of Antietam, the bloodiest one-day battle in American history, ended with over 6,000 men killed and around another 16,000 wounded. Although McClellan did not break Lee's lines, he inflicted so many casualties that Lee decided to retreat to Virginia.

The Battle of Antietam was a crucial victory for the Union. The British government had been ready to intervene in the war as a mediator if Lee's invasion had succeeded. Britain also had begun making plans to recognize the Confederacy in the event the North rejected mediation. Lee's defeat at Antietam changed everything. The British again decided to wait and see how the war progressed. With this decision, the South lost its best chance at gaining international recognition and support. The South's defeat at Antietam had an even more important political impact in the United States. It convinced Lincoln that the time had come to end slavery in the South.

The Emancipation Proclamation Most Democrats opposed any move to end slavery, while Republicans were divided on the issue. With Northern casualties rising to staggering levels, however, more Northerners began to agree that slavery had to end, in part to punish the South and in part to make the soldiers' sacrifices worthwhile.

On September 22, 1862, encouraged by the Union victory at Antietam, Lincoln publicly announced that he would issue the **Emancipation Proclamation**—a decree freeing all enslaved persons in states still in rebellion after January 1, 1863. Because the Proclamation freed enslaved African Americans only in states at war with the Union, it did not address slavery in the border states. Short of a constitutional

▼ *The "Hornet's Nest" at the Battle of Shiloh*

Did You Know?

Many Civil War battles have two names. The Union usually named battles after the nearest body of water, while the Confederacy usually named them after the nearest settlement. Therefore, the battle known as the Battle of Bull Run (a creek) in the North was known as the Battle of Manassas (a town) in the South. Likewise, the Battle of Antietam was remembered in the South as the Battle of Sharpsburg.

amendment, Lincoln could not end slavery in the border states, nor did he want to endanger their loyalty. 📖 *(See page 995 for more on the Emancipation Proclamation.)* The Proclamation, by its very existence, transformed the conflict over preserving the Union into a war of liberation.

Life During the Civil War As the war intensified, the economies of the North and South went in different directions. By the end of 1862, the South's economy had begun to suffer greatly. The collapse of the South's transportation system and the presence of Union troops in several important agricultural regions led to severe food shortages in the winter of 1862. In several communities, food shortages led to riots. Hearing of such hardships, many Confederate soldiers deserted to return home to help their families.

In contrast, the North actually experienced an economic boom because of the war. With its large, well-established banking industry, the North raised money for the war more easily than the South. Its growing industries also supplied Union troops with clothes, munitions, and other necessities.

Innovations in agriculture helped minimize the loss of labor as men left to fight. Greater use of mechanical reapers and mowers made farming possible with fewer workers, many of whom were women. Women also filled labor shortages in various industries, particularly in clothing and shoemaking factories.

Both Union and Confederate soldiers endured a hard life with few comforts. They faced the constant threat of disease and extreme medical procedures if

Picturing **History**

Battlefield Medicine The greatest impact women had on the battlefield was through serving as nurses. In what non-military ways did women contribute to the war effort?

they got injured in battle. Life for prisoners of war was just as difficult, especially in Southern prisons that faced food shortages.

While the war brought hardship to many Americans, it offered new opportunities for African Americans. The Emancipation Proclamation officially permitted African Americans to enlist in the Union army and navy. Almost immediately, thousands of African Americans rushed to join the military.

Women helped in the war effort at home by managing family farms and businesses. Perhaps their most important contribution to the Civil War was in serving as nurses to the wounded. One of the most prominent war nurses was Clara Barton, who left her job in a Washington patent office to aid soldiers on the battlefield. The Civil War was a turning point for the American nursing profession. The courage shown by women helped break down the belief that women were emotionally weaker than men.

✓ Reading Check **Analyzing** Why do you think so many African Americans were willing to volunteer to fight?

The Turning Point

Main Idea With the help of key victories at Vicksburg and Gettysburg, the North defeated the South after four long years of fighting. **-TURNING POINT-**

Reading Connection Recall a time when you faced a situation you had been dreading. Did the outcome surprise you? Read on to learn about Confederate general Robert E. Lee's surrender to Ulysses S. Grant.

In 1863 an end to the war still was not in sight. Two more long years of battle lay ahead for Americans.

Vicksburg and Gettysburg Gaining control of the Mississippi River was a vital element of the Union strategy for winning the Civil War. If the Union could capture **Vicksburg,** Mississippi, the last major Confederate stronghold on the river, then the North could cut the South in two.

On May 19, 1863, Grant launched an all-out assault on Vicksburg, but the city's defenders repulsed the attack and inflicted high casualties. When a second attack also failed, Grant decided to put the city under **siege**—cutting off its food and supplies and bombarding the city until its defenders gave up. On July 4, 1863, with his troops literally on the verge of starvation, the Confederate commander at Vicksburg surrendered.

Emboldened by recent victories against Union troops, Lee decided in June 1863 to invade the North. At the end of June, as Lee's army foraged in the Pennsylvania countryside, some of his troops headed into **Gettysburg,** hoping to seize a supply of shoes. When they arrived near the town, they discovered two brigades of Union cavalry. On July 1, 1863, as Confederates pushed the Union troops out of the town, the main forces of both armies hurried to the scene of the fighting.

On July 2, Lee attacked, but the Union troops held their ground. The following day, Lee ordered nearly 15,000 men under the command of General George E. Pickett and General A.P. Hill to make a massive assault. In the attack, which became known as Pickett's Charge, Union cannons and guns inflicted 7,000 casualties in less than half an hour of fighting.

Pickett's Charge failed to break the Union lines. Fewer than 5,000 men made it up the ridge, and Union troops quickly overwhelmed those who did. "It is all my fault," said Lee. "It is I who have lost this fight." Lee's troops retreated back to Virginia. At Gettysburg, the Union suffered 23,000 casualties, but the South's toll was an estimated 28,000 casualties, more than one-third of Lee's entire force.

The disaster at Gettysburg proved to be the turning point of the war in the East. The Union's victory strengthened the Republicans politically and ensured once again that the British would not recognize the Confederacy. For the remainder of the war, Lee's forces remained on the defensive, slowly giving ground to the advancing Union army.

In November 1863, Lincoln came to Gettysburg to dedicate a part of the battlefield as a cemetery. His speech, the **Gettysburg Address,** became one of the best-known orations in American history. In it, Lincoln reminded his listeners that the nation was "**conceived** in liberty, and dedicated to the proposition that all men are created equal":

> ❝It is . . . for us to be here dedicated to the great task remaining before us—that . . . we here highly resolve that these dead shall not have died in vain; that this, nation, under God, shall have a new birth of freedom; and that the government of the people, by the people, and for the people, shall not perish from the earth.❞
>
> —from the Gettysburg Address

📖 *(See page 996 for the complete text of the Gettysburg Address.)*

Grant Secures Tennessee

After the Union's major victories at Vicksburg and Gettysburg, fierce fighting erupted in Tennessee near Chattanooga, a

Picturing **History**

Vicksburg Besieged Union troops used this house as a headquarters during the siege of Vicksburg. Nearby are Union trenches and the opening to a tunnel being dug under Confederate lines. For how long was the city of Vicksburg under siege by Grant's Union forces?

vital railroad junction. Both the North and South knew that if Union forces captured Chattanooga, they would control a major railroad running south to Atlanta. Following several battles, union forces under the command of General Grant succeeded in scattering the Confederate soldiers who blocked the way to the city.

By the spring of 1864, Grant had accomplished two crucial objectives for the Union. His capture of Vicksburg had given the Union control of the Mississippi River, while his victory at Chattanooga had secured eastern Tennessee and cleared the way for an invasion of Georgia. Lincoln rewarded Grant by appointing him general in chief of the Union forces and promoting him to lieutenant general, a rank no one had held since George Washington. The president had finally found a general he trusted to win the war.

Grant Versus Lee By the spring of 1864, Union leaders knew that the only way to end the long and bloody war was to defeat Lee's army. General Grant put his most trusted **subordinate,** William Tecumseh Sherman, in charge of Union operations in the West. Grant then took command of the Union troops facing Lee. His campaign led to battles in the Wilderness, a densely forested area near Fredericksburg, Virginia, and Spotsylvania Courthouse southeast of the Wilderness. Convinced that his relentless attacks had weakened and demoralized Lee's troops, Grant decided to launch an all-out assault at Cold Harbor, a strategic crossroads northeast of Richmond. The

CHAPTER 2 Growth and Conflict **213**

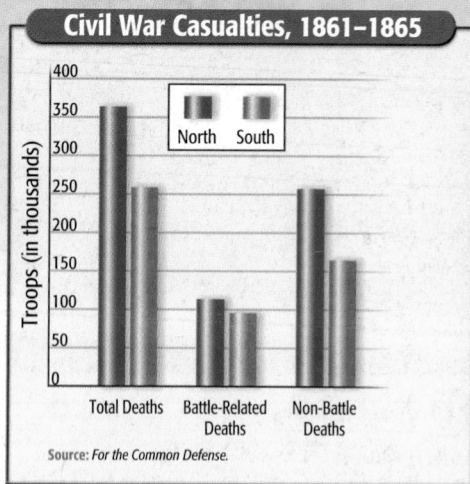

Civil War Casualties, 1861–1865

North South

Source: *For the Common Defense.*

American War Deaths (approximate figures)

Revolutionary War 25,000
War with Mexico 13,000
Korean War 36,500
Other major wars 5,000
Vietnam War 58,000
World War I 107,000
World War II 407,000
Civil War 620,000

Source: *United States Civil War Center; For the Common Defense*

Chart Skills

1. **Interpreting Graphs** How do the battle-related deaths compare to non-battle deaths?
2. **Understanding Cause and Effect** What do these graphs tell you about conditions on and off the battle field in both the North and South?

attack failed miserably, costing the Union 7,000 casualties, compared to only 1,500 for the South.

Grant then tried another plan. He ordered General Philip Sheridan to distract Lee with a cavalry raid outside Richmond. Grant headed south to capture the nearby town of Petersburg and thus cut off the rail line supplying Richmond and Lee's forces. The strength of the city's defenses intimidated the Union troops, who were already exhausted and demoralized. Realizing a full-scale frontal assault would be suicidal, Grant ordered his troops to lay siege to the city.

Union Victories in the South On August 5, 1864, the Union navy under David Farragut tried to secure the last major Confederate port on the Gulf of Mexico east of the Mississippi—Mobile, Alabama. After getting past the Confederate forts, Farragut's ships destroyed a Confederate fleet defending Mobile Bay. Although Farragut did not capture Mobile, he did seal off the bay.

At the same time, General Sherman marched his army from Chattanooga toward Atlanta, Georgia. In late August 1864, his army easily took the city. Sherman's troops set fires to destroy railroads, warehouses, mills, and factories. The fires spread quickly, destroying more than one-third of Atlanta.

On November 15, 1864, Sherman led his troops east across Georgia in what became known as the March to the Sea. The purpose of the march was to make Southern civilians understand the horrors of war and to pressure them into giving up the struggle. Sherman's troops cut a path of destruction through Georgia that was at times 60 miles (97 km)

wide. By December 21, 1864, they had reached the coast and seized Georgia's first settlement, the city of Savannah.

After reaching the Atlantic coast, Sherman turned north and headed into South Carolina, the state that many people believed had started the Civil War. "The whole army," Sherman wrote, "is burning with an insatiable desire to wreak vengeance upon South Carolina." Sherman's troops burned and pillaged nearly everything in front of them. The march greatly demoralized Southerners. As one South Carolinian wrote, "[T]o fight longer seems madness."

The South Surrenders The capture of Atlanta came just in time to revitalize Northern support for the war and for Lincoln himself. On Election Day, voters elected the president to another term. Lincoln interpreted his reelection as an approval of his war policies and as a **mandate,** or clear sign from the voters, to end slavery permanently by amending the Constitution. To get the amendment through Congress, Republicans appealed to Democrats who were against slavery to help them. On January 31, 1865, the **Thirteenth Amendment** to the Constitution, banning slavery in the United States, was narrowly passed by the House of Representatives and was sent to the states for ratification.

Meanwhile, Lee knew that time was running out. On April 1, 1865, Union troops led by Philip Sheridan cut the last rail line into Petersburg at the Battle of Five Forks. The following night, Lee's troops withdrew from their positions near the city and raced west.

Lee's desperate attempt to escape Grant's forces failed when Sheridan's cavalry got ahead of Lee's troops and blocked the road at **Appomattox Courthouse.** When his troops failed to break through, Lee sadly observed, "There is nothing left for me to do but go and see General Grant, and I would rather die a thousand deaths." With his ragged and battered troops surrounded and outnumbered, Lee surrendered to Grant on April 9, 1865.

Grant's generous terms of surrender guaranteed that the United States would not prosecute Confederate soldiers for treason. When Grant agreed to let Confederates take their horses home "to put in a crop to carry themselves and their families through the next winter," Lee thanked him, adding that the kindness would "do much toward conciliating our people." As Lee left he shook hands with Ely Parker, a Senecan who served as Grant's secretary. "I am glad to see a real American here," Lee told the Native American. Parker replied, "We are all Americans."

With the war over, Lincoln delivered a speech describing his plan to restore the Southern states to the Union. In the speech, he mentioned including African Americans in Southern state governments. One listener, actor John Wilkes Booth, sneered to a friend, "That is the last speech he will ever make."

Although his advisers had repeatedly warned him not to appear unescorted in public, Lincoln went to Ford's Theater with his wife to see a play on the evening of April 14, 1865. Just after 10 P.M., Booth slipped quietly behind the president and shot him in the back of the head. Lincoln died the next morning.

The president's death shocked the nation. Once viewed as an unsophisticated man unsuited for the presidency, Lincoln had become the Union's greatest champion. Tens of thousands of men, women, and children lined railroad tracks as Lincoln's body was transported back to Springfield, Illinois.

The North's victory in the Civil War saved the Union and strengthened the power of the federal government over the states. It transformed American society by ending slavery, but it also left the South socially and economically devastated, and many questions unresolved. No one knew how to bring the Southern states back into the Union or what the status of African Americans would be in Southern society. Americans from the North and the South tried to answer these questions in the years following the Civil War—an era known as Reconstruction.

✓ **Reading Check** **Examining** Why did General Sherman march his army to the sea?

HISTORY Online **Study Central**

For help with the concepts in this section of *American Vision: Modern Times* go to tav.mt.glencoe.com and click on *Study Central.*

SECTION 4 ASSESSMENT

Checking for Understanding

1. **Vocabulary** Define: martial law, greenback, conscription, habeas corpus, attrition, siege, conceive, subordinate, mandate.

2. **People and Terms** Identify: Robert E. Lee, Ulysses S. Grant, Emancipation Proclamation, Gettysburg Address, Thirteenth Amendment.

3. **Places** Locate: Fort Sumter, Antietam, Vicksburg, Gettysburg, Appomattox Courthouse.

4. **Explain** why Robert E. Lee refused to command Union troops.

Reviewing Big Ideas

5. **Identifying** What developments prior to the Civil War gave the North an advantage over the South?

Critical Thinking

6. **Historical Analysis** **Analyzing** What effect do you think would the Emancipation Proclamation and the Thirteenth Amendment have on African Americans? Why? **CA HI4**

7. **Organizing** Complete a graphic organizer similar to the one below to explain President Lincoln's reasons for issuing the Emancipation Proclamation and the effects the Proclamation had on the war.

Analyzing Visuals

8. **Examining Graphs** Study the graphs of war deaths on page 214. What would account for the thousands of non-battle deaths listed in one of the graphs?

Writing About History

9. **Descriptive Writing** Imagine that you are living in one of the border states at the beginning of the Civil War. Write a letter to a relative explaining why you plan to join either the Union or Confederate army. Include in your letter specific reasons for your decision. Also discuss any fears you might have about fighting in the war. **CA11WS1.2; 11WA2.1**

CHAPTER 2 Growth and Conflict **215**

SECTION 4 ASSESSMENT ANSWERS

1. Content vocabulary is boldfaced and highlighted in yellow. Academic vocabulary is boldfaced.

2. Robert E. Lee *(p. 208)*, Ulysses S. Grant *(p. 211)*, Emancipation Proclamation *(p. 211)*, Gettysburg Address *(p. 213)*, Thirteenth Amendment *(p. 214)*

3. Fort Sumter *(p. 207)*, Antietam *(p. 211)*, Vicksburg *(p. 212)*, Gettysburg *(p. 213)*, Appomattox Courthouse *(p. 215)*

4. He could not fight against his birthplace.

5. larger population, more industry, controlled the treasury, collected tariffs, had large cash reserves

6. freed African Americans in seceded states, gave hope to all other African Americans

7. reasons: justify sacrifices, punish the South; effects: transformed the war into a war of liberation

8. diseases and unsanitary living conditions

9. Students' letters should offer plausible scenarios.

S Skill Practice

Identifying Point of View Have students imagine how people in the North and the South may have reacted differently to the assassination. Use students' responses to begin a discussion on the status of the Union immediately after Lincoln's death and the end of the Civil War. **OL**

CA HR2

ASSESS

Resources for page 215

Use these resources to assess student mastery.

📁 Section Quiz 2-4

📁 Reading Essentials and Study Guide 2-4

⊙ Interactive Tutor Self-Assessment CD-ROM

📁 California Standards Practice, Grade 11

✓ **Reading Check**

Answer: to make Southern civilians understand the horrors of war and to pressure them into surrendering

HISTORY Online

Study Central provides audio summaries, interactive games, and online graphic organizers to help students review section content.

CLOSE

Expository Writing Have students write editorials on the importance of the battles of either Vicksburg or Gettysburg.

OL **CA HI4** **CA 11WS1.1**

Looking Back...

The Declaration of Independence

Why It Matters

As late as 1860, Jefferson Davis was delivering speeches calling for peace and discouraging Southern secessionists. In 1861, however, delegates from seceding states met in Montgomery and elected Davis president of the Confederacy. Despite his fears about the South's ability to win the war, Davis spoke eloquently in his inaugural address about the justice of the Southern cause. Like many Southerners, Davis believed they were following the principle on which the nation was founded: that people should not have to live under a government that infringes on their basic rights.

The North's point of view was quite different: Southerners were destroying the nation by placing their authority above that of the federal government. The origins of this feud trace back to the Declaration of Independence. In crafting this document, the Founders advocated an entirely new relationship between a government and its citizens. They prompted a continuing debate over how to balance individual and states' rights with the power of a central authority.

Steps to . . . the Declaration of Independence

Over many centuries, there was little development in political theory that addressed the relationship between the individual and the government. The changes that came about after the period known as the Enlightenment culminated in the 1700s with the American Declaration of Independence.

Government by and for the People With very few exceptions, the world knew only monarchies and absolute rulers at the time the Declaration of Independence was written.

Drawing from new political theories, the Declaration put forth a different idea: governments derive "their just powers from the consent of the governed." In other words, governments exist to serve the people.

The main function of a government, the document declared, was to protect the "unalienable rights" of its citizens—the most important of which were the rights to "Life, Liberty and the pursuit of Happiness." When a government failed to live up to this obligation, the people had the right to "throw off such Government, and to provide new Guards for their future security."

In shaping this political philosophy, the Founders looked to the works of many people, including such classical thinkers as Aristotle, who had identified

> "Our present condition . . . illustrates the American idea that governments rest upon the consent of the governed, and that it is the right of the people to alter or abolish governments whenever they become destructive to the ends for which they were established."
>
> —*Jefferson Davis, 1861*

216

EXTENDING THE CONTENT

Secession Most people associate secession with the Civil War, but threats of secession abounded during and after the Revolutionary War. While the fighting raged, Ethan Allen schemed to make Vermont a province of Canada, although he may have been trying to force Congress to recognize Vermont as a separate state rather than a territory of New York. At the same time, James Wilkinson, a Revolutionary officer working secretly for Spain, tried to annex Kentucky to Spain.

Signing of the Declaration of Independence in Philadelphia

three forms of government—democracy, oligarchy, and monarchy. The Founders believed the best government would combine all three forms of government and balance them against each other. The Constitution partly reflects these ideas. The president received powers similar to a monarch; the Senate was intended to protect the elite; and the House of Representatives, elected by the people, was the most democratic. The Founders also looked to the ideas of eighteenth-century Enlightenment thinkers. The greatest influence on American thinking, however, was probably the English philosopher John Locke. Locke's writings promoted the idea that power in society rested ultimately with its citizens.

A List of Grievances In declaring their independence from Britain, colonial leaders argued that the British government had failed to live up to its obligations to the colonists. In a section that has become known as the list of grievances, the Declaration of Independence spells out precisely how the British king had suppressed the rights of the colonists and failed to look out for their interests.

These 27 charges against the king were patterned after several documents, including the English Bill of Rights (1689), which criticized various actions of the king. Ideas for the Declaration's list of grievances also came from several papers of the Stamp Act Congress and the First and Second Continental Congress.

A Debate Over the Constitution The underlying belief of the Declaration of Independence was that government derives its power from the people. This core idea led to a great debate in 1787 over whether to ratify the U.S. Constitution. Those who supported the Constitution, known as Federalists, favored a strong central government in order to create a more organized and unified nation. Antifederalists, those who opposed the Constitution, feared that the creation of a strong central government eventually would lead to

the same kind of tyranny that the colonists had endured under Britain.

In particular, the Antifederalists criticized the fact that the proposed Constitution did not contain a bill of rights to protect the personal liberties of the people. The absence of such protections, argued one Antifederalist leader, "put Civil Liberty and happiness of the people at the Mercy of Rulers who may possess the great unguarded powers given."

Promoting Limited Government In the end, the Federalists agreed to add a bill of rights to the Constitution. The Bill of Rights is the name given to the first ten amendments to the Constitution. These amendments guarantee Americans protection of their basic civil rights, some of which they had demanded in the Declaration of Independence. These included the right to oppose or petition the government for change, the right to a trial by jury, and the right to refuse the quartering of soldiers.

In various other ways, the U.S. Constitution sought to limit the power of government and promote the rights of the people. It created three distinct branches of government: the executive, the legislative, and the judicial. The colonists distrusted concentrated political power, and so the separation of power among the branches was meant to prevent any such concentration.

To reinforce the Founders' goal of limited government, the Constitution also implemented a system of checks and balances among the branches so that no one branch could become too powerful. It also granted members of Congress only a certain number of years in office before they had to run again for election. These limits were meant to prevent any one person or groups of persons from gaining too much political power over the nation.

> **Checking for Understanding**
> 1. According to the Declaration of Independence, what is the main duty of a government?
> 2. How did Aristotle's ideas influence the Founders' approach to the Constitution?
>
> **Critical Thinking**
> 1. How is the U.S. Constitution a compromise between the Federalists and Antifederalists?
> 2. Do you agree or disagree that the secession of the Southern states marked a second American Revolution? Explain.

C₁ Critical Thinking

Identifying Central Issues On the board, write *Basic Rights of Individuals that the Government Should Respect.* Have the class brainstorm ideas they believe belong on the list of individual rights. Use this list as a starting point for a discussion about the Northern and Southern points of view about government and individual rights. **OL**

C₂ Critical Thinking

Drawing Conclusions Tell students that the lines in the Declaration of Independence that read, "... whenever any Form of Government becomes destructive to these ends, it is the Right of the People to alter or to abolish it..." were considered an act of treason by the British government. Conduct a class discussion about the situations in which students think the alteration or abolishment of a government is justified. Then ask if the South had justifiable reasons. Discuss students' points of view on this subject. **AL**

ASSESS/CLOSE

Have students answer the Checking for Understanding and Critical Thinking questions.

Checking for Understanding
1. to protect the rights of citizens
2. Aristotle identified three forms of government: monarchy, oligarchy, and democracy. The Founders created the presidency, Senate, and House of Representatives to combine these three forms into one government.

Critical Thinking
1. By including the Bill of Rights, the Constitution balances the rights of government and the rights of the people.
2. Answers will vary. Students should support their point of view using reasoning related to the Declaration of Independence.

FOCUS

Guide to Reading

Understanding Vocabulary: Have each student write a brief explanation of one word chosen from the academic vocabulary or content vocabulary.

Answers to Graphic: Students should complete the outline by including all headings in the section.

Unpacking the Standards

Students will be able to:

- Explain how the effort to reunite the nation began once the Civil War ended.

- Describe the efforts made during the Congressional Reconstruction period.

- Analyze how the Republican Party drove Reconstruction efforts during this time.

- Discuss the end of Reconstruction.

Answers and Additional Support

SECTION 5 Reconstruction

Guide to Reading

Connection
In the previous section, you learned how war became unavoidable and the North eventually defeated the South. In this section, you will discover the obstacles that Reconstruction presented as the country began to rebuild.

Main Idea
- In the months after the Civil War, the nation began the effort to rebuild and reunite. (p. 219)
- Radical Republicans, angered with President Johnson's actions, designed their own policies. (p. 221)
- As African Americans entered politics, some Southerners began to resist Republican reforms. (p. 223)

- Reconstruction came to an end as Democrats regained power in the South and in Congress. (p. 224)

Content Vocabulary
Reconstruction, amnesty, pocket veto, freedman, black codes, impeach, tenant farmer, sharecropper

Academic Vocabulary
infrastructure, circumstance

People and Terms to Identify
Freedmen's Bureau, Andrew Johnson, Fourteenth Amendment, Military Reconstruction Act, Fifteenth Amendment, Compromise of 1877

Reading Objectives
- **Describe** the major features of congressional Reconstruction and its political impact.

- **Discuss** Republican rule in the South during Reconstruction.
- **Explain** how Reconstruction ended, and contrast the New South and the Old South.

Reading Strategy
Taking Notes As you read about Reconstruction, use the major headings of the section to create an outline similar to the one below.

I. Reconstruction Begins
   A.
   B.
   C.
   D.
II.

Preview of Events

◆1860	◆1865	◆1870	◆1875

| **1864** | **1866** | **1867** | **1870** | **1877** |
| Lincoln vetoes Wade-Davis bill | Congress passes Fourteenth Amendment | Congress passes Military Reconstruction Act | Fifteenth Amendment is ratified | Compromise of 1877 reached |

The following are the main History–Social Science Standards covered in this section.

11.1 Students analyze the significant events in the founding of the nation and its attempts to realize the philosophy of government described in the Declaration of Independence.

11.1.3 Understand the history of the Constitution after 1787 with emphasis on federal versus state authority and growing democratization.

11.1.4 Examine the effects of the Civil War and Reconstruction and of the industrial revolution, including demographic shifts and the emergence in the late nineteenth century of the United States as a world power.

11.10.2 Examine and analyze the key events, policies, and court cases in the evolution of civil rights, including *Dred Scott v. Sandford, Plessy v. Ferguson, Brown v. Board of Education, Regents of the University of California v. Bakke,* and California Proposition 209.

❧ The Big Idea ❧

Social and economic crises lead to new roles for government. The country faced many challenges during Reconstruction, such as securing the rights of African Americans and repairing the South's devastated economy. President Lincoln hoped to initiate plans that would unite the country and help the South recover. Radical Republicans believed his plans were too lenient. After Lincoln's assassination, Andrew Johnson continued his predecessor's moderate policies. Southern states defied the North by continuing to deny rights to African Americans and electing former Confederate officers to Congress. Dissatisfied Radical Republicans gained support and pushed through their Reconstruction plans. Some Southerners formed secret societies to undermine Republican rule. With the country slipping into a deepening economic depression, Democrats were able to win back control of the House of Representatives and gain seats in the Senate. As the political atmosphere shifted, a "New South" began to develop.

218 CHAPTER 2 Growth and Conflict

SECTION RESOURCES

📁 **Print Material**
- Reproducible Lesson Plan 2-5
- Guided Reading Activity 2-5
- Reading Essentials and Study Guide 2-5
- Active Reading Note-Taking Guide 2-5

🎞 **Transparencies**
- Daily Focus Skills Transparency 2-5
- Section Graphic Organizer Transparency 2-5

Technology
- 💿 Interactive Tutor Self-Assessment CD-ROM
- 💿 ExamView® Pro Testmaker CD-ROM
- 💿 Presentation Plus! CD-ROM

Reconstruction Begins

Main Idea In the months after the Civil War, the nation began the effort to rebuild and reunite.

Reading Connection Think of a war you have studied in a history course. What were the terms of achieving peace, and who benefited? Read on to learn about President Lincoln's policies after Union victory in the Civil War.

No one looked forward to a Union victory more than enslaved African Americans in the South. Only a victory could give them the freedom the Emancipation Proclamation had promised.

★ An American Story ★

Houston Holloway was ready for freedom. By 1865 the 20-year-old enslaved man had toiled under three different slaveholders. President Lincoln's Emancipation Proclamation, delivered in 1863, had freed him—but only in theory. The proclamation freed enslaved persons in the Confederacy, but because the Union could not enforce its laws in Confederate territory, many African American men and women in the South remained enslaved. Holloway knew that his only hope of freedom was a Northern victory in the Civil War.

The time of that victory finally arrived. On the spring day in 1865 when Union troops overran his community in Georgia on their way to defeating the Confederacy, Holloway rejoiced upon reaching true freedom:

> ❝I felt like a bird out of a cage. Amen. Amen. Amen. I could hardly ask to feel better than I did that day. . . . The week passed off in a blaze of glory.❞

—quoted in *A Short History of Reconstruction*

Helping Holloway and other freed African Americans find their way as citizens of the United States was only one of a myriad of problems the nation faced. At the end of the Civil War, the South was a defeated region with a devastated economy. While some Southerners were bitter over the Union military victory, for many the more important struggle after the conflict was rebuilding their land and their lives. Meanwhile, the president and Congress grappled with the difficult task of **Reconstruction,** or rebuilding the nation after the war.

Lincoln and the Radical Republicans In December 1863, President Lincoln set forth his moderate plan for reuniting the country in the Proclamation of Amnesty and Reconstruction. Lincoln wanted to reconcile the South with the Union instead of punishing it for treason. He offered a general **amnesty,** or pardon, to all Southerners who took an oath of loyalty to the United States and accepted the Union's proclamations concerning slavery. When 10 percent of a state's voters in the 1860 presidential election had taken this oath, they could organize a new state government. Certain people, such as Confederate government officials and military officers, could not take the oath or be pardoned.

Resistance to Lincoln's plan surfaced at once among a group of Republicans in Congress known as Radical Republicans. Led by Representative Thaddeus Stevens of Pennsylvania and Senator Charles Sumner of Massachusetts, the radicals wanted to prevent the leaders of the Confederacy from returning to power after the war. They also wanted the Republican Party to become a powerful institution in the South. Finally, and perhaps most importantly, they wanted the federal government to help African Americans achieve political equality by guaranteeing their right to vote in the South.

Congressional Republicans knew that the abolition of slavery would give the South more seats in the House of Representatives. Before the Civil War, enslaved people had only counted in Congress as three-fifths of a free person. Now that African Americans were free, the South was entitled to more seats in

▼ *Artist depiction of an emancipated African American*

FREE!

CHAPTER 2 Growth and Conflict **219**

TEACH

C₁ Critical Thinking

Identifying Central Issues Have students read the quote from Houston Holloway on this page. Ask them to make a list of the things a free person can do and that they think freed African Americans may have valued. **Ask:** Which of the freedoms on our list do you think a freed African American would have valued most? Why? Refer to students' responses as you begin a discussion on Reconstruction. **OL**

C₂ Critical Thinking

Predicting Consequences Organize the class into groups of three or four. Have each group make a list of the problems facing newly freed African Americans. Ask one volunteer from each group to share the group's responses, and keep a list of the class's responses on the board. After students have finished reading the section, ask them to return to their lists and revise them as needed. **AL**

Did You Know?

Senator Henry Wilson of Massachusetts summarized the position of Radical Republicans who wanted to give African Americans the right to vote in the South by saying: "[Congress] must see to it that the man made free by the Constitution is a freeman indeed; that he can go where he pleases, work when and for whom he pleases . . . go into schools and educate himself and his children; that the rights and guarantees of the common law are his, and that he walks the earth proud and erect in the conscious dignity of a free man."

R Reading Strategy

Organizing Information Have students complete a two-column chart listing the components of Lincoln's plans for Reconstruction and the Wade-Davis Bill. **Ask: What points make the Wade-Davis Bill harsher than Lincoln's plan?** *(The Wade-Davis Bill forbade all former Confederate government officials and military officers to vote or hold office and required the majority of white males to pledge allegiance to the Union.)* **OL**

S Skill Practice

Sequencing Information Have students use library and Internet resources to research the presidency of Andrew Johnson. Then write the title "Reconstruction During Andrew Johnson's Presidency" on the board and draw a time line that begins with 1865 and ends with 1868. Call on volunteers to come to the board and enter the major events that occurred during these years. Ask students to use information on the time line to write chronological summaries of Reconstruction up to the presidential election of 1868. **OL** **CA CS2**

Answers and Additional Support

Congress. This would endanger Republican control of Congress, unless Republicans could find a way to protect African American voting rights in the South.

Although the radicals knew that giving African Americans in the South the right to vote would help the Republican Party win elections, most were not acting cynically. Many of them had been abolitionists before the Civil War and had pushed Lincoln into making emancipation a goal of the war.

R **The Wade-Davis Bill** Many moderate Republicans thought Lincoln was being too lenient, but they also thought the radicals were going too far in their support for African American equality and voting rights. By the summer of 1864, the moderates and radicals had come up with a plan for Reconstruction that they could both support. This alternative to Lincoln's plan was the Wade-Davis Bill of 1864, which required the majority of the adult white men in a former Confederate state to take an oath of allegiance to the Union. The state could then hold a constitutional convention to create a new state government. The people chosen to attend the constitutional convention had to take an "ironclad" oath asserting that they had never fought against the Union or supported the Confederacy in any way. Each state's convention would then have to abolish slavery, reject all debts the state had acquired as part of the Confederacy, and deprive all former Confederate government officials and military officers of the right to vote or hold office.

Although Congress passed the Wade-Davis Bill, Lincoln blocked it with a **pocket veto,** that is, he let the session of Congress expire without signing the legislation. While Lincoln sympathized with some of the radical goals, he felt that imposing a harsh peace would only alienate many whites in the South.

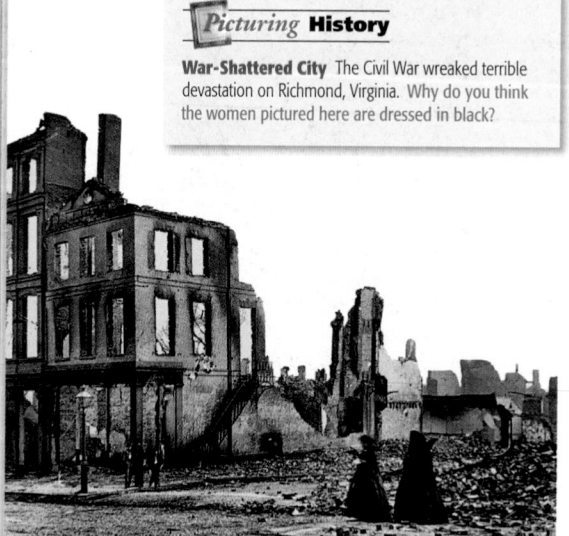

Picturing **History**

War-Shattered City The Civil War wreaked terrible devastation on Richmond, Virginia. Why do you think the women pictured here are dressed in black?

The Freedmen's Bureau Lincoln realized that the South was already in chaos, with thousands unemployed, homeless, and hungry. At the same time, the victorious Union armies had to try to accommodate the large numbers of African Americans who flocked to Union lines as the war progressed. As Sherman marched through Georgia and South Carolina, thousands of freed African Americans—now known as **freedmen**—began following his troops seeking food and shelter.

In March 1865, Congress established the Bureau of Refugees, Freedmen, and Abandoned Lands, better known as the **Freedmen's Bureau.** The Bureau was given the task of feeding and clothing war refugees in the South using surplus army supplies. Beginning in September 1865, it issued nearly 30,000 rations a day for the next year.

The Bureau helped formerly enslaved people find work on plantations and negotiated labor contracts with planters. Many Northerners argued that those who were formerly enslaved should receive land to support themselves now that they were free. To others, however, taking land from plantation owners and giving it to freedmen seemed to violate the nation's cherished commitment to individual property rights. As a result, Congress refused to confirm the right of African Americans to own the lands that had been seized from plantation owners and given to them.

S **Johnson Takes Office** Shortly after Congress established the Freedmen's Bureau, Lincoln was assassinated. Although his successor, Vice President **Andrew Johnson,** was a Democrat from Tennessee, he had remained loyal to the Union. Like Lincoln, he believed in a moderate policy to bring the South back into the Union.

In the summer of 1865, with Congress in recess, Johnson began to implement what he called his restoration program, which closely resembled Lincoln's plan. Johnson offered to pardon all former citizens of the Confederacy who took an oath of loyalty to the Union and to return their property. He excluded from the pardon the same people Lincoln had excluded. Like Lincoln, Johnson also required Southern states to ratify the Thirteenth Amendment abolishing slavery.

The former Confederate states, for the most part, met Johnson's conditions. They then organized new governments and elected people to Congress. By the time Congress gathered for its next session in December 1865, Johnson's plan was well underway. Many members of Congress were astonished and angered when they realized that Southern voters had

Picturing **History**

Answer: They are in mourning, perhaps for relatives who died in the war.
Ask: What do you think these citizens of Richmond may have been feeling? *(possible answers—defeated, angry, determined, hopeless)*

Did You Know?

Although the Freedmen's Bureau could not provide African Americans with land, it made an important contribution in education. The Bureau worked closely with Northern charities to educate formerly enslaved African Americans. It provided housing for schools, paid teachers, and helped train African American teachers.

elected dozens of Confederate leaders to Congress. Moderate Republicans joined with the Radical Republicans and voted to reject the new Southern members of Congress.

Congressional Republicans also were angry that the new Southern state legislatures had passed laws known as **black codes** limiting the rights of African Americans in the South. These codes seemed intended to keep African Americans in a condition similar to slavery. African Americans were generally required to enter into annual labor contracts. Those who did not could be arrested for vagrancy and forced into involuntary servitude. Several codes established specific hours of labor and also required them to get licenses to work in nonagricultural jobs.

✓ Reading Check) **Comparing** How did the reconstruction plans of Lincoln and Congress differ?

Congressional Reconstruction

Main Idea Radical Republicans, angered with President Johnson's actions, designed their own policies.

Reading Connection If you disagree with a political decision, how can you change it? Read on to learn about the Republicans' reaction to Johnson's plan.

With the election of former Confederates to office and the introduction of the black codes, more and more moderate Republicans joined the radicals. Finally, in late 1865, House and Senate leaders created a Joint Committee on Reconstruction to develop their own program for rebuilding the Union.

The Fourteenth Amendment In March 1866, congressional Reconstruction began with the passage of an act intended to override the black codes. The Civil Rights Act of 1866 granted citizenship to all persons born in the United States except for Native Americans. The act guaranteed the rights of African Americans to own property and stated that they were to be treated equally in court. It also gave the federal government the power to sue people who violated those rights. Johnson vetoed the act, arguing that it was unconstitutional and would "[cause] discord among the races." The veto convinced the remaining moderate Republicans to join with the radicals to override Johnson's veto, and the act became law.

Fearing that the Civil Rights Act might later be overturned in court, however, the radicals introduced the **Fourteenth Amendment** to the Constitution. This

Andrew Johnson ▲

amendment granted citizenship to all persons born or naturalized in the United States and declared that no state could deprive any person of life, liberty, or property "without due process of law." It also declared that no state could deny any person "equal protection of the laws." In June 1866, Congress passed the amendment and sent it to the states for ratification. It was ratified in 1868.

President Johnson attacked the Fourteenth Amendment and made it the major issue of the 1866 congressional elections. He hoped Northerners would vote out the Radical Republicans and elect representatives who would support his plan for Reconstruction. Instead, the Republicans achieved an overwhelming victory, winning approximately a three-to-one majority in Congress. They now had the strength of numbers to override any presidential veto and could claim that they had a mandate, or command, from the American people to enact their own Reconstruction program in place of Johnson's plan.

Military Reconstruction Begins In March 1867, Congress passed the **Military Reconstruction Act,** which essentially nullified Johnson's programs. The act divided the former Confederacy, except for Tennessee—which had ratified the Fourteenth Amendment in 1866—into five military districts. A Union general was placed in charge of each district with orders to maintain peace and "protect the rights of persons and property."

In the meantime, each former Confederate state had to hold another constitutional convention to design a constitution acceptable to Congress. The

R **Reading Strategy**

Identifying the Main Idea and Supporting Details As students read this section, remind them that one goal of the Radical Republicans was equal citizenship for African Americans. **Ask:** Why do you think Radical Republicans had difficulty putting equal citizenship into effect during Reconstruction? *(Even some government leaders in the North were not in favor of granting full equality to freed African Americans.)* **AL**

C **Critical Thinking**

Predicting Consequences Write the phrase "Military Reconstruction" on the board. Ask students to predict the response of people living in the former Confederate states to being placed under the charge of a Union general. *(anger or resentment at living under Northern control)* **OL**

✓ Reading Check)

Answer: Congress wanted to make it more difficult for the former Confederate states to reenter the Union.

Did You Know?

In October 1865, Robert E. Lee signed the oath of loyalty to the Union and sought a pardon from the United States government. Officials in Washington, D.C., however, misplaced the oath. Without it, Lee could neither get a pardon nor have his citizenship rights restored. More than 100 years later, the oath was discovered wrapped in a bundle of government documents in the National Archives. Shortly after, Congress issued a resolution restoring Lee's citizenship. President Gerald R. Ford signed it into law in August 1975.

R **Reading Strategy**

R **Reading Strategy**

Monitoring Students may have problems understanding how the new laws restricted the power of the president. Have students describe in their own words how the acts changed the way in which the president usually did business. *(Students should point out that there had never been another person through which presidential orders had to be processed. Until then, the president could remove government officials at will.)* **BL**

S **Skill Practice**

Evaluating Evidence Organize students into several small groups and have them discuss the following question: **If you had been a member of the House of Representatives in 1868, would you have voted for or against the impeachment of President Andrew Johnson? Why?** Call on group representatives to present their decisions and reasons to the rest of the class. **OL** **CA HR3**

✓**Reading Check**

Answer: the Fourteenth Amendment outlawed slavery in the former Confederate states; the Fifteenth Amendment gave voting rights to African Americans, who were more likely to vote Republican and would therefore help the Republicans control Congress.

Answers and Additional Support

NATIONAL GEOGRAPHIC **Military Districts, 1867**

Military District Commander
- General John Schofield
- General Daniel Sickles
- General John Pope
- General Edward Ord
- General Philip Sheridan

1870 Date of readmission to union

MINN., WIS., MICH., IOWA, ILL., IND., OHIO, COLO. TERR., KANS., MO., KY., N. MEX. TERR., UNORG. TERR., CANADA, N.Y., PA., N.J., MD., DEL., W. VA., VA. 1870, TENN. 1866 (not part of a military district), N.C. 1868, ARK. 1868, S.C. 1868, MISS. 1870, ALA. 1868, GA. 1870, TEX. 1870, LA. 1868, FLA. 1868

Gulf of Mexico

MEXICO

0 — 500 miles
0 — 500 kilometers
Lambert Equal-Area projection

ATLANTIC OCEAN 30°N

90°W   TROPIC OF CANCER   80°W

Geography *Skills*

1. **Interpreting Maps** Only one former Confederate state was not part of a military district. What was it?
2. **Applying Geography Skills** How many years after the war was the last Southern state readmitted to the Union?

new state constitutions had to give the right to vote to all adult male citizens, regardless of race. Each also had to ratify the Fourteenth Amendment before it would be allowed to elect people to Congress.

Johnson's Impeachment The Republicans knew that they had the votes to override presidential vetoes, but they also knew that President Johnson could still interfere with their plans by refusing to enforce the laws they passed. To restrict Johnson, Congress passed two new laws: the Command of the Army Act and the Tenure of Office Act. The Command of the Army Act required all orders from the president to go through the headquarters of the general of the army. This was the headquarters of General Grant, whom Congressional Republicans trusted. The Tenure of Office Act required the Senate to approve the president's removal of any government official

whose appointment had required the Senate's consent.

Determined to challenge the Tenure of Office Act, on February 21, 1868, Johnson fired Secretary of War Edwin M. Stanton who supported the Republicans. Three days later, the House of Representatives voted to **impeach** Johnson, meaning that they charged him with "high crimes and misdemeanors" in office. They accused Johnson of breaking the law by refusing to uphold the Tenure of Office Act.

As provided in the Constitution, the Senate then put the president on trial. If two-thirds of the senators found the president guilty of the charges, he would be removed from office. In May 1868, the Senate voted 35 to 19 that Johnson was guilty of high crimes and misdemeanors. This was just one vote short of the votes needed for conviction.

The Election of 1868 Although Johnson remained in office, he finished his term quietly and did not run for election in 1868. That year, the Republicans nominated Ulysses S. Grant. During the campaign, Union troops in the South enabled African Americans to vote in large numbers. As a result, Grant won six Southern states and most of the Northern states. The Republicans also retained large majorities in both houses of Congress.

Congressional Republicans now moved rapidly to expand their Reconstruction program. Recognizing the importance of African American suffrage, the Republican-led Congress passed the **Fifteenth Amendment** to the Constitution. This amendment declared that the right to vote "shall not be denied . . . on account of race, color, or previous condition of servitude." In March 1870, the Fifteenth Amendment was ratified by the states and became part of the Constitution.

✓**Reading Check** **Analyzing** Why did congressional Republicans pass amendments to the Constitution?

222 CHAPTER 2 Growth and Conflict

Geography *Skills*

Answers:
1. Tennessee
2. about 5 years

Geography Skills Practice
Ask: Who was the military district commander for Texas and Louisiana? *(General Philip Sheridan)*

Resources for page 222

Have students read more about the history of African American Voting Rights in the **Linking Past and Present Activity 2.**

Reconstruction and Republican Rule

Main Idea As African Americans entered politics, some Southerners began to resist Republican reforms.

Reading Connection Have you heard of recent activities of the Ku Klux Klan? Read on to find out when and why the KKK was founded.

By the fall of 1870, all of the former Confederate states had rejoined the Union under the congressional Reconstruction plan. With many issues unresolved, Reunification did little to restore harmony between the North and South.

Carpetbaggers and Scalawags During Reconstruction, a large number of Northerners traveled to the South. Many were eventually elected or appointed to positions in the South's new state governments. Southerners, particularly supporters of the Democratic Party, referred to these newcomers as carpetbaggers because some arrived with their belongings in suitcases made of carpet fabric. Local residents saw them as intruders seeking to exploit the South's postwar turmoil for their own gain.

Some white Southerners worked with the Republicans and supported Reconstruction. Other Southerners called these people scalawags—an old Scotch-Irish term for weak, underfed, worthless animals. The scalawags were a diverse group. Some were former Whigs who had grudgingly joined the Democratic Party before the war. Many were owners of small farms who did not want the wealthy planters to regain power. Still others were business people who favored the Republican economic plans for the South.

African Americans Having gained the right to vote, African Americans quickly began organizing politically. Within a few remarkable years, African Americans went from enslaved workers to legislators and administrators on nearly all levels of government. Hundreds of formerly enslaved people served as delegates to the conventions that created the new state constitutions. They also won election to numerous local offices, served in Southern state legislatures, and were elected to the House of Representatives. Two others served in the Senate.

Many African Americans desired an education, something they had been denied under slavery. In the first years of Reconstruction, the Freedmen's Bureau, with the help of Northern charities, had established schools for African Americans across the South. Gradually, the number of both African American students and teachers increased, and by 1876 about 40 percent of all African American children (roughly 600,000 students) attended school in the region.

Formerly enslaved people across the South also worked to establish their own churches. Churches served as the center of many African American communities, as they housed schools and hosted social events and political gatherings.

Republican Politics and Reforms Because of past disloyalty, some Southern whites were barred from participating in the new Southern governments, and many others simply refused to do so. As a result, a coalition of Northerners, Southern-born whites, and African Americans created Republican governments in the Southern states. Republicans had the support of a large number of white Southerners. These were usually poor white farmers, who resented the planters and Democratic Party that had dominated the South before the war.

The newly elected Republican governments in the South quickly instituted a number of reforms. In addition to repealing the black codes, they established state hospitals and institutions for orphans. To improve the **infrastructure,** they rebuilt roads, railways, and bridges damaged during the Civil War and provided funds for the construction of new railroads and industries in the South.

Picturing **History**

Schools for African Americans O.O. Howard, head of the Freedmen's Bureau, is pictured here (far right) with the students of a Freedmen's school. Why do you think these schools were so successful?

S Skill Practice

Conducting Research Have students research and then write short profiles of one of the following African Americans who served in the U.S. House of Representatives between 1870 and 1901: Richard H. Cain, Henry P. Cheatham, Jeremiah Haralson, John A. Hyman, John M. Langston, Jefferson F. Long, John R. Lynch, Alonzo J. Ransier. Encourage students to use library and Internet resources to conduct their research. **OL** **CA HR4**
CA 11WA2.4a; 11WA2.4d

U Universal Access

Advanced Learners Invite interested students to use historical statistical abstracts to find data on African American enrollment in schools from 1860 to 1900. Have students report on what they find and present the information in bar or line graphs. Display the graphs in the classroom. **AL**

Review the Big Idea

Review the Big Idea for this section, "Social and economic crises lead to new roles for government." Tell students that the governments formed in the Southern states involved people not previously part of Southern politics. **Ask:** What might the reaction of white Southerners be to Northerners and African Americans becoming involved in governments in the South? *(Students might predict active resistance to these changes.)* **OL**
CA HI1; HI3

Picturing **History**

Answer: African Americans were eager to learn, and parents were eager for their children to get an education.
Ask: Do you think the school shown in this picture was similar to schools for white children? *(Answers will vary. Remind students that one-room schoolhouses with all ages together were common then.)*

Did You Know?

Radical Reconstruction temporarily changed Southern politics by bringing hundreds of thousands of African Americans into the political process for the first time. This angered many white Southerners, who began to fight back against the federal government's policies.

223

S₁ Skill Practice

Conducting Research Invite interested students to use library and Internet resources to research the militias organized by African Americans and Republicans in response to the actions of the Ku Klux Klan. Have them present their findings in written reports. Remind students to include drawings, photographs, or other visual aids that provide additional information for their reports. **OL**

CA HR4 **CA 11WA2.4**

S₂ Skill Practice

Historical Interpretation
Organize the class into groups of three or four. Have each group work together to create a magazine article describing the events of the Panic of 1873. Encourage students to divide the article into headings such as *Causes*, *Events*, and *Outcomes*, and have each person in the group research and write one section of the article. Then ask one volunteer from each group to share the group's article with the class. **OL**

CA HI1; HI2; HI3 **CA 11WA2.4**

✓ Reading Check

Answer: Poor white farmers and African Americans supported the reforms, but other Southerners did not because they had to pay for the cost of infrastructure and lost money and land.

Answers and Additional Support

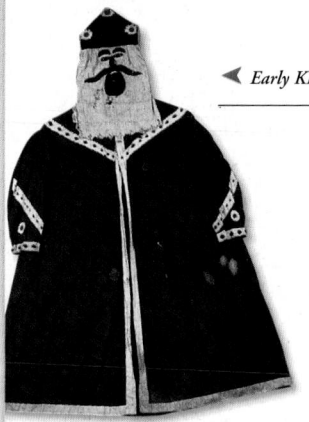

◄ *Early KKK robe and hood*

Most white Southerners scorned these reforms, which did not come without cost. Many state governments were forced to borrow money and to impose high property taxes to pay for the repairs and new programs. Many property owners, unable to pay these new taxes, lost their land.

Southern Resistance Unable to strike openly at the Republicans running their states, some Southern opponents of Reconstruction organized secret societies to undermine Republican rule. The largest of these groups was the Ku Klux Klan. Started in 1866 by former Confederate soldiers in Pulaski, Tennessee, the Klan spread rapidly throughout the South. Hooded, white-robed Klan members rode in bands at night terrorizing African Americans, white Republicans, carpetbaggers, teachers in African American schools, and others who supported the Republican governments. Republicans and African Americans responded to the attacks by organizing their own militias to fight back.

As the violence increased, Congress passed three Enforcement Acts in 1870 and 1871, one of which outlawed the activities of the Klan. Although local authorities and federal agents arrested more than 3,000 Klan members, only a few hundred were convicted and served time in prison.

The Troubled Grant Administration During his first term, Ulysses S. Grant faced a growing number of Republicans who were concerned that interests in making money and selling influence were beginning to dominate the Republican Party. These critics also argued that the economic policies most Republicans supported, such as high tariffs, favored the rich over the poor. Eventually these critics, known as Liberal Republicans, broke with the Republican Party in 1872 and nominated their own

HISTORY Online
Student Web Activity Visit the *American Vision: Modern Times* Web site at tav.mt.glencoe.com and click on *Student Web Activities— Chapter 2* for an activity on Reconstruction.

candidate, the influential newspaper publisher Horace Greeley. Despite this split, Grant easily won reelection.

During Grant's second term, a series of scandals damaged his administration's reputation. In addition, the nation endured a staggering and long-lasting economic crisis that began during Grant's second term. After a powerful banking firm declared bankruptcy, a wave of fear known as the Panic of 1873 quickly spread though the nation's financial community. The panic soon set off a full-fledged depression that lasted until almost the end of the decade.

The scandals in the Grant administration and the nation's deepening economic depression hurt the Republicans politically. In the 1874 midterm elections, the Democrats won back control of the House of Representatives and made gains in the Senate.

✓ **Reading Check** **Explaining** Why did only some Southerners support Republican reforms?

Reconstruction Ends

Main Idea Reconstruction came to an end as Democrats regained power in the South and in Congress.

Reading Connection What values and policies do you associate with today's Republican and Democratic Parties? Read on to learn about the roles these parties played during the Reconstruction period.

The rising power of the Democrats in Congress and Republican concerns over scandals and the economy led to an end of Reconstruction.

Democrats Regain Strength In the 1870s, Democrats began to regain power in the South. They did so in part through intimidation and fraud, and in part by defining the elections as a struggle between whites and African Americans. They also won back support by promising to cut the high taxes the Republicans had imposed and by accusing Republicans of corruption. Southern Democrats viewed their efforts to regain power as a crusade to help save the South from Republican rule. By 1876 the Democrats had taken control of all but three Southern state legislatures.

That year, the nation's presidential election pitted Republican Rutherford B. Hayes, a former governor of Ohio, against Democrat Samuel Tilden, a wealthy corporate lawyer and former governor of New York. On Election Day, twenty electoral votes

224 CHAPTER 2 Growth and Conflict

Did You Know?

Following the Civil War, the railroads in the South had to adopt the Northern gauge for railroad networks to be established. Some 13,000 miles (20,800 km) of track had to be changed.

HISTORY Online

Objectives and answers to the student activity can be found in the **Web Activity Lesson Plan** at tav.mt.glencoe.com.

were disputed. Nineteen of the votes were in the three Southern states controlled by Republicans. As a result, congressional leaders worked out an agreement known as the **Compromise of 1877.**

Historians are not sure if a deal really took place or what its exact terms were. Among the conditions that were reported, the Republicans agreed to withdraw the remaining federal troops from the South. In April 1877, after assuming the presidency, Hayes did pull federal troops out of the South. Without soldiers to support them, the last remaining Republican governments in the South quickly collapsed. Reconstruction had come to an end.

A "New South" Arises During his inaugural speech in March 1877, President Hayes expressed his desire to move the country beyond the quarrelsome years of Reconstruction. Hoping to narrow the divisions of sectionalism that had long plagued the nation, he vowed "to put forth my best efforts in behalf of a civil policy which will forever wipe out . . . the distinction between North and South."

Eventually the South did develop closer ties with the North. Southern leaders realized the South could never return to the pre–Civil War agricultural economy dominated by the planter elite. Instead, these Southerners called for the creation of a "New South" based on a strong industrial economy. An alliance between Southerners and Northern financiers brought great economic changes to some parts of the South. Northern capital helped to build thousands of miles of railroads and dozens of new industries.

The South, in fact, changed very little. Despite its industrial growth, the region remained largely agricultural. As late as 1900, its number of manufacturing establishments equaled only 4 percent of its number of farms. For many African Americans in particular, the end of Reconstruction meant a return to the "old South" and an end to their hopes of owning their own land. Instead many returned to plantations owned by whites, where they, along with many poor white farmers, either worked for wages or became **tenant farmers** paying rent for the land they farmed. Most tenant farmers could not afford to buy their own land and became **sharecroppers.** They paid a share of their crops, often as much as two-thirds, to cover their rent as well as the cost of the seed, fertilizer, tools, and animals they needed.

Although sharecropping allowed African American farmers to control their work schedules and working conditions for the first time in their lives, they rarely had enough crops left over to sell to enable them to buy their own land. The Civil War ended slavery, but Reconstruction's failure left many African Americans, as well as many whites, trapped in economic **circumstances** beyond their control.

✓ **Reading Check** **Explaining** What major issue was settled by the Compromise of 1877?

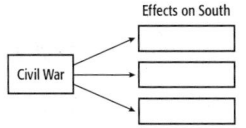 **Study Central**

For help with the concepts in this section of *American Vision: Modern Times* go to tav.mt.glencoe.com and click on *Study Central.*

SECTION 5 ASSESSMENT

Checking for Understanding
1. **Vocabulary** Define: Reconstruction, amnesty, pocket veto, freedman, black codes, impeach, infrastructure, tenant farmer, sharecropper, circumstance.
2. **People and Terms** Identify: Freedmen's Bureau, Andrew Johnson, Fourteenth Amendment, Military Reconstruction Act, Fifteenth Amendment, Compromise of 1877.
3. **Explain** the major goals of the Radical Republicans.

Reviewing Big Ideas
4. **Explaining** What new amendments were added to the Constitution during the Civil War and Reconstruction period?

Critical Thinking
5. **Historical Analysis** **Evaluating** Do you think Presidents Lincoln and Johnson were wise in not seeking harsh treatment of the Southern states? Why or why not? CA HI2
6. **Historical Analysis** **Analyzing** Why did Southerners resent both carpetbaggers and scalawags? CA HI3
7. **Categorizing** Use a graphic organizer similar to the one below to describe the effects of the Civil War.

Effects on South

Civil War →

Analyzing Visuals
8. **Examining Photographs** Study the photograph of O.O. Howard and a Freedmen's school on page 223. How would you describe the children depicted in this photograph?

Writing About History
9. **Expository Writing** Write a short essay explaining what you consider to be the three most important events of the Reconstruction period. Explain why you chose these events. Check your essay for grammar, spelling, and punctuation. CA 11WS1.1; 11WA2.4a

Use these resources to assess student mastery.
📁 Section Quiz 2-5
📁 Reading Essentials and Study Guide 2-5
⦿ Interactive Tutor Self-Assessment CD-ROM
📁 California Standards Practice, Grade 11

✓ **Reading Check**

Answer: It resolved a dispute over electoral votes in the 1877 presidential election between Hayes and Tilden. The Southern states reportedly pledged their electoral votes to Hayes in exchange for the withdrawal of the remaining federal troops from the South.

Study Central provides audio summaries, interactive games, and online graphic organizers to help students review section content.

CLOSE

Organizing Information Have students create two-column charts that list the arguments for and against the success of Reconstruction. OL

SECTION 5 ASSESSMENT ANSWERS

1. Content vocabulary is boldfaced and highlighted in yellow. Academic vocabulary is boldfaced.
2. Freedmen's Bureau (p.220), Andrew Johnson (p. 220), Fourteenth Amendment (p. 221), Military Reconstruction Act (p. 221), Fifteenth Amendment (p. 222), Compromise of 1877 (p. 225)
3. prevent leaders of the Confederacy from returning to power, make the Republican Party more powerful in the South, guarantee African Americans' right to vote
4. Thirteenth, Fourteenth, and Fifteenth Amendments
5. Students might say that this would help heal the wounds of war.
6. felt carpetbaggers were exploiting the South to get rich and that scalawags were betraying the South
7. some effects: ruined economy, destroyed cities, end of slavery
8. serious and nicely dressed
9. Essays should include three events and an explanation for each.

225

FOCUS

History–
Social Science
Standards

This feature addresses the
following standard:

11.10.2 Examine and analyze
the key events, policies, and court
cases in the evolution of civil rights,
including *Dred Scott* v. *Sandford,
Plessy* v. *Ferguson, Brown* v. *Board
of Education, Regents of the
University of California* v. *Bakke,*
and California Proposition 209.

TEACH

R Reading Strategy

Organizing Information Draw
a graphic organizer on the board
similar to the one below. Call
on students to complete the
graphic organizer with the main
provisions of the Fourteenth
Amendment. *(1. Grants citizenship to all persons born or
naturalized in the United States.
2. Forbids states from depriving
any person of life, liberty, or
property without due process of
law. 3. Provides equal protection
of the law.)* **OL**

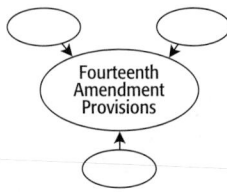

**Answers and
Additional Support**

Why It Matters

The Fourteenth Amendment

R Key provisions of the Fourteenth
Amendment (1868) made all persons born
in the United States citizens of both the
nation and the state where they resided.
States were prohibited from abridging the
rights of citizenship or depriving persons
of due process and equal protection of the
law. The Supreme Court has often cited
the Fourteenth Amendment when reviewing whether state or federal laws and
actions violate the Constitution. The
Court continues to do so today.

1954
In *Brown* v. *Board of Education,* the Court found that segre-
gated education denied minority schoolchildren like Linda
Brown (far left) the equal protection of the laws provided by
the Fourteenth Amendment. This decision partially reversed
Plessy v. *Ferguson.*

Testing the 14th Amendment
♦ *1896*   ♦ *1954*

1896
In *Plessy* v. *Ferguson,* the Supreme
Court decided that Jim Crow laws—
state-mandated segregation of public
facilities such as railroad cars—did not
violate the Fourteenth Amendment.
The Court ruled that separate facilities
could be equal and allowed segregation to continue.

226 CHAPTER 2 Growth and Conflict

EXTENDING THE CONTENT

Ratifying the Fourteenth Amendment The Fourteenth Amendment was proposed on
June 13, 1866. The ratification process finally was completed in July 1868. Even after the
ratification process was completed, states continued to ratify the amendment. On March 18,
1976, Kentucky finally ratified the amendment, 109 years after initially rejecting it.

2000

In the presidential race between George W. Bush and Al Gore (at right), the Supreme Court case of *Bush* v. *Gore* was based on the Fourteenth Amendment. Justices argued that a lack of uniform standards for hand recounts of ballots in Florida violated the equal protection of all the state's voters. The decision allowed Bush to claim a controversial victory.

R

♦ 1963   ♦ 2000

1963

W In *Gideon* v. *Wainright,* the Supreme Court ruled that the state of Florida had violated the due process clause when it refused to appoint a lawyer to represent Clarence Gideon (left). The ruling extended the Bill of Rights to state courts.

ANALYZING THE IMPACT

Check for Understanding
1. **Explaining** What did the Fourteenth Amendment prohibit?

Critical Thinking
2. **Evaluating** What is due process of the law? How was it violated in *Gideon* v. *Wainright*?

R Reading Strategy

Connecting Tell students that in *Bush* v. *Gore,* the Supreme Court ruled that the Florida recount did not treat voters equally because different vote counters used different recount methods and standards. **Ask:** To which part of the amendment does this ruling refer? You might have students read the amendment on page 162 of the textbook. *(last sentence in Section 1: nor deny to any person within its jurisdiction the equal protection of the laws)* **OL**

W Writing Support

Research Report Writing Ask students to conduct library or Internet research to find out about Clarence Gideon's case and the impact of the ruling. Have them write two-page reports to record their research results. **OL** **CA 11WA2.4**

ASSESS/CLOSE

Have students answer the Analyzing the Impact questions.

ANALYZING THE IMPACT

1. States were prohibited from abridging the rights of citizenship or depriving persons of due process and equal protection of the law.

2. Courts must follow proper procedures and rules when trying cases; the state of Florida violated the due process clause when it refused to appoint a lawyer to represent Clarence Gideon.

FOCUS

History–Social Science Standards

This feature addresses the following standard:

11.1.3 Understand the history of the Constitution after 1787 with emphasis on federal versus state authority and growing democratization.

Understanding Vocabulary

Before students begin reading, point out that difficult or unfamiliar words are footnoted throughout the text.

TEACH

R Reading Strategy

Analyzing Text Structure
Mississippi's resolutions claim that the states are separate from one another and only loosely tied together through the Constitution. **Ask:** Do you agree or disagree with Mississippi's interpretation? *(Students' answers will vary, but their answers should be based on an interpretation of the text.)* **OL**

Answers and Additional Support

Primary Sources
Eyewitness to History

Although tensions had been rising between the North and the South, in 1860 no one anticipated a war. After the election of Abraham Lincoln, each side attempted to pressure the other into compromising on the key question of slavery.

SOURCE 1:

In November 1860, Mississippi passed resolutions supporting separation from the United States. These Mississippi Resolves summarized the views of Southern secessionists. They were designed to unite the South and to convince the North that the South was not bluffing.

R Whereas, The Constitutional Union was formed by the several States in their separate **sovereign**[1] capacity for the purpose of mutual advantage and protection;

That the several States are distinct sovereignties, whose supremacy is limited so far only as the same has been delegated by voluntary **compact**[2] to a Federal Government, and when it fails to accomplish the ends for which it was established, the parties to the compact have the right to resume, each State for itself, such delegated powers;

That the institution of slavery existed prior to the formation of the Federal Constitution, and is recognized by its letter, and all efforts to impair its value or lessen its duration by Congress, or any of the free States, is a violation of the compact of Union and is destructive of the ends for which it was ordained, but in defiance of the principles of the Union thus established, the people of the Northern States have assumed a revolutionary position towards the Southern States;

That they have set at defiance that provision of the Constitution which was intended to secure domestic tranquility among the States and promote their general welfare, namely: "No person held to service or labor in one State, under the laws thereof, escaping into another, shall, in consequence of any law or regulation therein, be discharged from such service or labor." . . .

---

[1] **sovereign:** independent
[2] **compact:** agreement

▲ *Francis W. Pickens*

That they declare in every manner in which public opinion is expressed their unalterable determination to exclude from admittance into the Union any new State that tolerates slavery in its Constitution, and thereby force Congress to a condemnation of that species of property; . . .

SOURCE 2:

Francis W. Pickens, the newly elected governor of South Carolina, doubted that it was possible to compromise with the North. In his inauguration speech of December 1860, he urged South Carolina to protect its rights as an independent state.

UNIVERSAL ACCESS

Advanced Learners The first quoted source cites the federal constitution as a justification of slavery. Ask students to review the Constitution on pages 148–167 and make notes on how they think the Constitution did or did not support slavery. *(Answers may vary. Some students will recognize that the Constitution never uses the term* slavery. *Others will note that slavery's existence is reflected in the constitution with the Three-Fifths Clause (Article 1, Section 2).)* **AL**

▲ *President Lincoln delivers his First Inaugural Address.*

This State was one of the original parties to the Federal Compact of the Union. We agreed to it . . . when we were surrounded with great external pressure for purposes of national protection and for the general welfare of all the States equally and alike; and when it ceases to do this it is no longer a perpetual Union. . . .

SOURCE 3:

Abraham Lincoln delivered his Inaugural Address in March 1861 under the growing shadow of war. Supporters of the Union thought that the speech showed Lincoln to be reasonable and generous. Backers of secession heard a threat of force.

One section of our country believes slavery is *right* and ought to be extended, while the other believes it is *wrong* and ought not to be extended. This is the only substantial dispute. . . .

Physically speaking, we can not separate. We can not remove our respective sections from each other nor build an impassable wall between them. A husband and wife may be divorced and go out of the presence and beyond the reach of each other, but the different parts of our country can not do this. . . .

In *your* hands, my dissatisfied fellow-countrymen, and not in *mine,* is the momentous issue of civil war. The Government will not assail *you.* You can have no conflict without being yourselves the aggressors. *You* have no oath registered in heaven to destroy the Government, while I shall have the most solemn one to "preserve, protect, and defend it."

In the Southern States these are two entirely distinct and separate races, and one has been held in **subjugation**[3] to the other by peaceful inheritance from worthy and patriotic ancestors, and all who know the races well know that it is the only form of Government that can preserve both, and administer the blessings of civilization with order and in harmony.

Anything tending to change or weaken this government and the subordination between the races, not only endangers the peace, but the very existence of our security. We have for years warned the Northern people of the dangers they were producing by their wanton and lawless course. We have often appealed to our sister States of the South to act with us in concert upon some firm but moderate system, by which we might be able, if possible, to save the Federal Constitution, and yet feel safe under the general compact of Union. But we could obtain no fair hearing from the North, nor could we see any concerted plan proposed by our co-States of the South, calculated to make us feel safe and secure.

Under all these circumstances, we now have no alternative left but to interpose our sovereign power as an independent State, to Protect the rights and ancient privileges of the people of South Carolina.

[3]**subjugation:** under control

DBQ Document-Based Questions

Historical Analysis   CA HR4; HI2; HI3; HI4

Source 1: Why do you think the Mississippi Resolves describe Northern states as having assumed a revolutionary position?

Source 2: Why does Pickens believe that South Carolina has the right to leave the Union?

Source 3: Why does Lincoln believe that compromise must be reached?

Comparing and Contrasting Sources

How does Lincoln differ from Pickens and the authors of the Mississippi Resolves about the conflict between the North and the South?

W Writing Support

Preparing a Debate Divide the class into two groups. The first group should argue in favor of secession. The other group should argue against secession. Tell each group to use library and Internet resources to develop their debate positions. Give each group time to meet and strategize how to best present their argument. Each group gets 10 minutes to argue their case. Then, ask students to write one-page papers stating which group made a stronger case. AL CA 11WS1.1

C Critical Thinking

Compare and Contrast President Lincoln's Inaugural Address very clearly stated his view of the constitutional union of the states. **Ask:** How is Lincoln's view different from the view stated by the Mississippi resolutions presented in the first document? *(Lincoln believed that the states could not separate themselves legally and peacefully. The Mississippi resolutions claimed that the bonds between states could be separated voluntarily.)* OL

ASSESS/CLOSE

Have students answer the Document-Based Questions.

DBQ   Document-Based Questions

1. Secessionists saw the increasing attacks by Northerners as a radical position, because slavery had been recognized in the Constitution.

2. He feared that Northern opposition to slavery would lead to the freedom of enslaved Africans. This, in turn, would be dangerous to the safety of Southerners.

3. He feared a civil war if the opposing sides could not come to an agreement.

Comparing and Contrasting Sources: Lincoln acknowledges the differences between the regions over slavery, but he names the South as the aggressors in the issue, while Pickens and the Mississippi Resolves indicate a belief that Northerners provoked Southerners into taking their stand on secession.

Reviewing Content Vocabulary

On a sheet of paper, use each of these terms in a sentence.

1. cabinet
2. enumerated powers
3. implied powers
4. judicial review
5. caucus
6. nullification
7. temperance
8. abolition
9. emancipation
10. Manifest Destiny
11. annexation
12. popular sovereignty
13. secession
14. Confederacy
15. martial law
16. conscription
17. habeas corpus
18. attrition
19. mandate
20. Reconstruction
21. amnesty
22. pocket veto
23. freedman
24. black codes
25. impeach

Chapter Summary

Chapter Summary Sectional Tensions

- Fugitive Slave Act passed to help Southerners recover enslaved people who escaped to the North
- Kansas-Nebraska Act passed; angered Northerners by repealing the Missouri Compromise
- *Dred Scott* decision by Southern-dominated Supreme Court upsets Northerners
- Southern States secede, establishing the Confederacy in February 1961

Civil War

- The Battle of Antietam marks the bloodiest one-day battle in U.S. history
- Emancipation Proclamation goes into effect in January 1863
- North wins decisive victories at Gettysburg and Vicksburg
- The Thirteenth Amendment to the Constitution bans slavery in the United States in January 1865

Reconstruction

- Congress passes the Fourteenth and Fifteenth Amendments
- Military Reconstruction Act divides the South into five military districts
- New state constitutions have to guarantee voting rights for citizens
- Compromise of 1877 ends Reconstruction

Reviewing Academic Vocabulary

On a sheet of paper, use each of these terms in a sentence that reflects the term's meaning in the chapter.

26. clause
27. ambiguous
28. item
29. academic
30. adjacent
31. prospect
32. conceive
33. subordinate
34. infrastructure
35. circumstance

Reviewing the Main Ideas

Section 1

36. What were three actions that strengthened the federal government after the War of 1812?

Section 2

37. What issue did the Missouri Compromise temporarily settle?

38. What were the results of the Seneca Falls Convention?

Section 3

39. How did the transcontinental railway contribute to sectional tensions?

Section 4

40. How did the Thirteenth, Fourteenth, and Fifteenth Amendments advance civil rights?

Section 5

41. What were said to be the provisions of the Compromise of 1877?

Critical Thinking

42. **Reading Skill** Questioning Return to the Reading Skill on page 170 and evaluate the questions you formed for the headings under "Apply the Skill." Did the text under each heading provide the answers to your questions?

43. **Civics** President Lincoln suspended writs of habeas corpus to prevent interference with the draft. Do you think suspending civil liberties is justified in some situations? Why or why not?

44. **Analyzing** How did the Fugitive Slave Act and the *Dred Scott* decision affect formerly enslaved African Americans living in the North?

Writing About History

45. **Historical Analysis** Relating Current Events Research in the library and on the Internet and write a report about one group of Native Americans that was forced to move west. Include recent events. **CA** CS4

Reviewing Content Vocabulary

Students' answers will vary. The pages where the words appear in the text are shown in parentheses.

1. cabinet *(p. 173)* 2. enumerated powers *(p. 174)* 3. implied powers *(p. 174)* 4. judicial review *(p. 175)* 5. caucus *(p. 184)* 6. nullification *(p. 185)* 7. temperance *(p. 187)* 8. abolition *(p. 188)* 9. emancipation *(p. 188)* 10. Manifest Destiny *(p. 193)* 11. annexation *(p. 194)* 12. popular sovereignty *(p. 196)* 13. secession *(p. 196)* 14. Confederacy *(p. 201)* 15. martial law *(p. 208)* 16. conscription *(p. 209)* 17. habeas corpus *(p. 209)* 18. attrition *(p. 209)* 19. mandate *(p. 214)* 20. Reconstruction *(p. 219)* 21. amnesty *(p. 219)* 22. pocket veto *(p. 220)* 23. freedmen *(p. 220)* 24. black codes *(p. 221)* 25. impeach *(p. 222)*

Reviewing Academic Vocabulary

Students' answers will vary. The pages where the words appear in the text are shown in parentheses.

26. clause *(p. 174)* 27. ambiguous *(p. 181)* 28. item *(p. 185)* 29. academic *(p. 188)* 30. adjacent *(p. 198)* 31. prospect *(p. 200)* 32. conceive *(p. 213)* 33. subordinate *(p. 213)* 34. infrastructure *(p. 223)* 35. circumstance *(p. 225)*

Reviewing the Main Ideas

36. Answers should include three of the following: creation of new national bank, imposition of protective tariffs, Supreme Court decisions establishing dominance of the nation over states, invasion of Florida, proclamation of the Monroe Doctrine

37. the expansion of slavery into new states

38. beginning of an organized women's movement and Declaration of Sentiments and Resolutions

39. A possible northern starting point raised the issue of whether or not slavery would be allowed in new territories along its route.

Self-Check Quiz

Visit the *American Vision: Modern Times* Web site at tav.mt.glencoe.com and click on *Self-Check Quizzes—Chapter 2* to assess your knowledge of chapter content.

46 . *Big Idea* Imagine that you are a newspaper editor in 1817. You have been asked to write an article on the high and low points of the first four presidential administrations. Use evidence to support your reflections.

47. **Mock Peace Convention** Hold a mock peace convention to try and reverse the secession of the Southern states. As a class, create a convention in which students are delegates from Union or secessionist states. Students should write a position paper for their assigned state proposing an idea that could help the states compromise. Write a summary of the proceedings. CA 11WA2.1a

DBQ **Document-Based Questions**

48. **Interpreting Primary Sources** In *McCulloch* v. *Maryland,* the Supreme Court was asked whether Congress had the power to set up the Bank of the United States. The following excerpt is from Chief Justice John Marshall's ruling. Read the excerpt and answer the questions that follow.

❝The government of the United States . . . though limited in its powers, is supreme; and its laws, when made in pursuance of the constitution, form the supreme law of the land. . . . Among the enumerated powers, we do not find establishing a bank or creating a corporation. But there is no phrase in the instrument which . . . requires that everything granted shall be expressly and minutely described. . . . Among the enumerated powers of government . . . we find the great powers to lay and collect taxes; to borrow money; to regulate commerce; to declare war and conduct a war; and to raise and support armies and navies. . . . A government entrusted with such ample powers . . . must also be entrusted with ample means for their execution. . . . All means which are appropriate, which are plainly adapted to that end, which are not prohibited, but consist with the letter and spirit of the constitution, are constitutional. . . .❞

—from *McCulloch* v. *Maryland*

a. What was Marshall's opinion about the power of the government of the United States? CA 11RC2.5

b. Why do you think the ruling in *McCulloch* v. *Maryland* made American nationalism stronger?

NATIONAL GEOGRAPHIC **Seceding States, 1860–1861**

W. VA. separated from VA. in 1861 and was admitted to the Union in 1863.

On February 8, 1861, delegates from several Southern states created the Confederacy.

S.C. was the first state to secede from the Union.

Union free state
Union slave state
Slave state seceding before Fort Sumter, April 1861
Slave state seceding after Fort Sumter, April 1861
Territory
Union-Confederate border

Geography and History

49. The map above shows seceding states from 1860 to 1861. Study the map and answer the questions below.
   a. **Interpreting Maps** Which slave states remained in the Union after the Fort Sumter attack?
   b. **Applying Geography Skills** Which states did not secede until after the Fort Sumter attack?

Standards Practice

Directions: Choose the best answer to the following question.

50. Which of the following actions reflect President Jefferson's goal of limiting the power of the federal government?

A He increased the size of the army.

B He proposed renewing the Alien and Sedition Acts.

C He dissolved the Republican Party to eliminate political conflict.

D He cut the federal budget.

Standard 11.1.3: Understand the history of the Constitution after 1787 with emphasis on federal versus state authority and growing democratization.

CHAPTER 2 Growth and Conflict **231**

Have students visit the Web site at tav.mt.glencoe.com to review Chapter 2 and take the Self-Check Quiz.

44. Many African Americans were captured and sent back to slavery. Many Northerners defied the act and helped enslaved African Americans escape to freedom. All were probably angered by them.

Writing About History

45. **Historical Analysis** Students' reports will vary but should include information on the Native American group today.

46. *Big Idea* Articles should be written in a news report style. Have students review expository newspaper articles before writing their own articles.

47. Students' position papers should reflect their assigned positions and should include attempts to find a compromise position.

DBQ **Document-Based Questions**

48. **a.** It had both enumerated powers and implied powers and its powers were supreme. **b.** It confirmed the power of the government to act for the nation in areas such as raising funds, declaring wars, and regulating commerce.

Geography and History

49. **a.** Missouri, Kentucky, West Virginia, Maryland, Delaware; **b.** Virginia, North Carolina, Tennessee, Arkansas

Standards Practice

50. D

Bonus Question ?

Ask: Who was the first president to live in the nation's new capital, Washington, D.C.? *(John Adams)*

40. Thirteenth abolished slavery; Fourteenth granted citizenship rights to all persons born or naturalized in the United States and required states to grant due process to all citizens; Fifteenth granted voting rights to citizens of all races

41. granted Hayes the presidency, promised that a Southerner would be postmaster general, promised funds for improvements in the South, and agreed to withdrawal of all remaining troops in the South

Critical Thinking

42. **Reading Skill** Students' responses will vary but should be well reasoned.

43. Answers will vary. Students who support suspending civil rights should be very specific about the conditions under which these rights could be suspended. Students who do not support suspending civil rights should provide adequate reasoning for their points of view.

Chapter 3 Planning Guide

SECTION RESOURCES

MAIN IDEAS	📁 PRINT MATERIALS	TECHNOLOGY RESOURCES
Section 1: Settling the West 1. Miners seeking to strike it rich settled large areas of the West. 2. Ranchers built vast cattle ranches on the Great Plains, while settlers staked out homesteads and began farming the region. 3. The settlement of the West dramatically altered the way of life of the Plains Indians.	• Daily Lecture and Discussion Notes 3-1 • Active Reading Note-Taking Guide 3-1 • Section Quiz 3-1 • Reading Essentials and Study Guide 3-1	Daily Focus Skills Transparency 3-1 Interactive Tutor Self-Assessment CD-ROM ExamView® Pro Testmaker CD-ROM Presentation Plus! CD-ROM California Standards Practice Transparencies
Section 2: Industrialization 1. American industry grew rapidly after the Civil War, bringing revolutionary changes to American society. 2. After the Civil War, the rapid construction of railroads accelerated the nation's industrialization and linked the country together. 3. Big business assumed a more prominent role in American life following the Civil War. 4. In an attempt to improve their working conditions, industrial workers came together to form unions in the late 1800s.	• Daily Lecture and Discussion Notes 3-2 • Active Reading Note-Taking Guide 3-2 • Section Quiz 3-2 • Reading Essentials and Study Guide 3-2	Daily Focus Skills Transparency 3-2 Interactive Tutor Self-Assessment CD-ROM ExamView® Pro Testmaker CD-ROM Presentation Plus! CD-ROM California Standards Practice Transparencies
Section 3: Immigration and Urbanization 1. After the Civil War, millions of immigrants from Europe and Asia settled in the United States. 2. During the three decades following the Civil War, the United States transformed rapidly from a rural nation to a more urban one.	• Daily Lecture and Discussion Notes 3-3 • Active Reading Note-Taking Guide 3-3 • Section Quiz 3-3 • Reading Essentials and Study Guide 3-3	Daily Focus Skills Transparency 3-3 Interactive Tutor Self-Assessment CD-ROM ExamView® Pro Testmaker CD-ROM Presentation Plus! CD-ROM California Standards Practice Transparencies
Section 4: Early Reforms in a Gilded Age 1. Industrialization and urbanization changed American society's ideas and culture in the late 1800s. 2. The pressing problems of the urban poor in the late 1800s and early 1900s stimulated attempts to reform industrial society.	• Daily Lecture and Discussion Notes 3-4 • Active Reading Note-Taking Guide 3-4 • Section Quiz 3-4 • Reading Essentials and Study Guide 3-4	Daily Focus Skills Transparency 3-4 Interactive Tutor Self-Assessment CD-ROM ExamView® Pro Testmaker CD-ROM Presentation Plus! CD-ROM California Standards Practice Transparencies
Section 5: Politics and Reform 1. From 1877 to 1896, Republicans and Democrats were so evenly matched that only a few reforms were possible at the national level. 2. Farmers in economic crisis embraced an independent political movement called populism that emerged in the 1890s to challenge the two major parties. 3. In the late 1800s, Southern states passed laws that denied African Americans the right to vote and imposed segregation.	• Daily Lecture and Discussion Notes 3-5 • Active Reading Note-Taking Guide 3-5 • Section Quiz 3-5 • Reading Essentials and Study Guide 3-5	Daily Focus Skills Transparency 3-5 Interactive Tutor Self-Assessment CD-ROM ExamView® Pro Testmaker CD-ROM Presentation Plus! CD-ROM California Standards Practice Transparencies

🕐 PACING YOUR LESSONS

Chapter Introduction	Section 1	Section 2	Section 3	Section 4	Section 5	Chapter Assessment
½ Day	2 Days	2 Days	2 Days	2 Days	2 Days	½ Day

`0:00` **OUT OF TIME?** 📁 Assign the Chapter 3 *Reading Essentials and Study Guide.*

Chapter 3 Planning Guide

Standards-Based Lesson Plan

 ## History–Social Science Standards Covered in Chapter 3

The standards covered in the chapter are listed below. Use the accompanying activity as you teach the chapter to ensure student mastery of these standards. This activity can be used in combination with the program's print and technology assessment materials.

Standard	Section 1	2	3	4	5
11.1.4 Examine the effects of the Civil War and Reconstruction and of the industrial revolution, including demographic shifts and the emergence in the late nineteenth century of the United States as a world power.	✓	✓	✓		
11.2.1 Know the effects of industrialization on living and working conditions, including the portrayal of working conditions and food safety in Upton Sinclair's *The Jungle*.		✓	✓	✓	✓
11.2.2 Describe the changing landscape, including the growth of cities linked by industry and trade, and the development of cities divided according to race, ethnicity, and class.			✓	✓	✓
11.2.3 Trace the effect of the Americanization movement.			✓		✓
11.2.4 Analyze the effect of urban political machines and responses to them by immigrants and middle-class reformers.			✓	✓	✓
11.6.5 Trace the advances and retreats of organized labor, from the creation of the American Federation of Labor and the Congress of Industrial Organizations to current issues of a postindustrial, multinational economy, including the United Farm Workers in California.		✓		✓	✓

Cumulative Standards-Assessment Activity

The Cumulative Standards-Assessment Activity will help students organize and learn the important information from the chapter. Begin teaching the chapter with this activity, and have students complete it as they read the chapter.

CREATING A CHART FOR ORGANIZING INFORMATION

Purpose Students encounter many dates, names, events, and concepts while studying history. Access to information, however, must also be combined with the ability to make sense of the information. Organizing information in a logical way can help students better understand the facts and their significance. Organizing information incorporates other skills and can require students to practice summarizing, categorizing, sequencing, distinguishing main ideas and supporting details, and recognizing order of importance.

Introduction to Categorizing Information

1. Discuss with students how organizing information can be as important as organizing possessions. In this chapter, students will read about many developments in American industry and society; they will need some way of understanding and retaining all the information they learn. Suggest that they preview the subject matter, pick a few categories that fit the subject, and sketch out an idea for organizing information on the topic. Tell students one way to test if information is organized well is to see if their idea makes sense to someone else.

2. The Industrial Revolution was a time of rapid growth and change. As industry was transformed, so too were people's lives. For this chapter, students can use the chart below in conjunction with any of their own ideas for organizing information. Ask students to copy this chart into their notebooks.

Industrial Revolution in the United States				
Technological Development →	Effect on Industry →	Effect on People	Success ✓	Challenge ✓

3. Encourage students to study the chart and anticipate how it may apply to the reading material. You may want to suggest they take notes while they read. Remind students that their notes should make sense to them later and help jog their memories. They can use their notes to fill in the above chart.

Chapter 3 Planning Guide

READING SUPPORT

- Content Vocabulary Activity 3
- Academic Vocabulary Activity 3
- Reading Skills Activity 3
- Chapter 3 Active Reading Note-Taking Guide
- Chapter 3 Guided Reading Activities
- Chapter 3 Reading Essentials and Study Guide
- American Literature Readings, Unit 1
- *The American Vision: Modern Times* Video Program
- Vocabulary PuzzleMaker CD-ROM
- American History Primary Source Document Library CD-ROM

CRITICAL THINKING

- Critical Thinking Skills Activity 3
- Primary Source Reading 3
- Cause-and-Effect Transparency 3 Strategy and Activity
- Presentation Plus! CD-ROM

UNIVERSAL ACCESS

- Universal Access Activity 3
- English Learner Activity 3
- American Art Prints
- StudentWorks™ Plus CD-ROM
- American Music: Hits Through History
- School-to-Home Connection Activity 3

SKILL PRACTICE

- Map Overlay Transparency 3 Strategy and Activity
- Historical Analysis Skills Activity 3
- Time Line Activity 3
- Reading Skills Activity 3
- Reinforcing Skills Activity 3
- Linking Past and Present Activity 3
- Interpreting Political Cartoons 3
- Geography and History Activity, Unit 1
- MindJogger Videoquiz

WRITING SUPPORT

- Chapter 3 Active Reading Note-Taking Guide
- Writer's Guidebook
- High School Writing Process Transparencies

ASSESSMENT

- Chapter 3 Section Quizzes
- Chapter 3 Tests, Forms A and B
- Authentic Assessment Activity 3
- ExamView® Pro Testmaker CD-ROM
- Interactive Tutor Self-Assessment CD-ROM
- California Standards Practice, Grade 11
- Succeeding on . . .™ the California Standards: Grade 11 History–Social Science CD-ROM

- CD-ROM
- DVD
- Print Material
- Poster

- Transparency
- Music Program
- Videocassette

Chapter 3 Planning Guide

TECHNOLOGY

- StudentWorks™ Plus CD-ROM
- TeacherWorks™ CD-ROM
- ExamView® Pro Testmaker CD-ROM
- Interactive Tutor Self-Assessment CD-ROM
- Presentation Plus! CD-ROM
- Vocabulary PuzzleMaker CD-ROM
- American History Primary Source Document Library CD-ROM
- MindJogger Videoquiz
- *The American Vision: Modern Times* Video Program
- Professional Development in High School Social Studies Video Series
- Teach, Use, and Succeed With *The American Vision: Modern Times*
- American Music: Hits Through History
- Succeeding on . . .™ the California Standards: Grade 11 History–Social Science CD-ROM

SPANISH RESOURCES

- Spanish Activities and Assessment
  - Spanish Vocabulary Activities
  - Spanish Guided Reading Activities
  - Spanish Quizzes and Tests
  - Spanish Reteaching Activities
- Spanish Reading Essentials and Study Guide
- Spanish School-to-Home Connection Activities

TRANSPARENCIES

- Daily Focus Skills Transparencies
- Section Graphic Organizer Transparencies
- Map Overlay Transparencies
- Cause-and-Effect Transparencies
- Unit Time Line Transparencies
- Why It Matters Transparencies
- American Art and Architecture Transparencies
- High School Writing Process Transparencies
- California Standards Practice Transparencies

TEACHER PLANNING

- Daily Lecture and Discussion Notes
- English Learner Handbook
- Building Academic Vocabulary
- *The American Vision: Modern Times* Reading and Study Skills Foldables
- Reading Strategies and Activities for the Social Studies Classroom
- Universal Access for the American History Classroom
- NGS United States Desk Map
- NGS World Atlas
- Chapter 3 Reproducible Lesson Plans on TeacherWorks™ CD-ROM
- California Guide to Daily Intervention

PROFESSIONAL DEVELOPMENT

- Building Academic Vocabulary
- Strategies for Success
- Research-Based Strategies Used to Develop *The American Vision: Modern Times*
- Character Education in the High School Classroom
- Professional Development in High School Social Studies Video Series
- Teach, Use, and Succeed With *The American Vision: Modern Times*

MOMENTS IN TIME

The following resource can help you teach the content of this chapter.

- Unit 4 Division Within (1876–1901)

Chapter 3 Planning Guide

Use our Web site for additional resources. All essential content is covered in the Student Edition.

You and your students can visit tav.mt.glencoe.com, the Web site companion to the **American Vision: Modern Times.** This innovative integration of electronic and print media offers your students a wealth of opportunities. The student text directs students to the Web site for the following options:

- **Chapter Overviews**
- **Self-Check Quizzes**
- **Student Web Activities**
- **Textbook Updates**

Answers to the student Web activities are provided for you in the **Web Activity Lesson Plans.** Additional Web resources and ePuzzles and games are also available.

MASTERING THE STANDARDS

The content and assessment in the Student Edition, Teacher Wraparound Edition, teacher planning materials, and the print and technology products are all standards-based. The use of these products during instruction leads to mastery of the standards.

PRACTICE

- California Standards Practice, Grade 11
- California Standards Practice Transparencies
- School-to-Home Connection

BENCHMARK ASSESSMENT

- Section Quizzes, Chapter Tests, and Authentic Assessment
- Exam*View*® Pro Testmaker CD-ROM
- Succeeding On ... ™ the California Standards; Grade 11 History–Social Science CD-ROM

REMEDIATION

- California Guide to Daily Intervention
- Interactive Tutor Self-Assessment CD-ROM
- Exam*View*® Pro Testmaker CD-ROM
- California Standards Practice, Grade 11
- Reading Essentials and Study Guide

 Dinah Zike's Foldables

Foldables are three-dimensional, interactive graphic organizers that help students practice basic writing skills, review key vocabulary terms, and identify main ideas. Every chapter has a foldable activity in the *Dinah Zike's Reading and Study Skills Foldables* booklet. You can use the foldables as they are presented or modify them to suit the needs of your individual class.

Chapter 3 Planning Guide

 Reading List Generator CD-ROM

 GLENCOE BOOKLINK

The Glencoe BookLink CD-ROM is a database that allows you to search more than 15,000 titles to create a customized reading list for your students.

■ Reading Lists can be organized by students' reading level, author, genre, theme, or area of interest.

■ The database provides Degrees of Reading Power™ (DRP) and Lexile™ readability scores for all selections.

■ A brief summary of each selection is included.

Leveled reading suggestions for this chapter:

For students at a Grade 8 reading level:
■ *The Jungle,* by Upton Sinclair

For students at a Grade 9 reading level:
■ *A Strange and Distant Shore: Indians of the Great Plains in Exile,* by Brent Ashabranner

For students at a Grade 10 reading level:
■ *Industrial Revolution,* by John D. Clare

 READING SUPPORT FROM JAMESTOWN EDUCATION

• *Timed Readings Plus in Social Studies* help students increase their reading rate and fluency while maintaining comprehension. The 400-word passages are similar to those found on state and national assessments.

• *Reading in the Content Area: Social Studies* concentrates on six essential reading skills that help students better comprehend what they read. The book includes 75 high-interest nonfiction passages written at increasing levels of difficulty.

• *Reading Fluency* helps students read smoothly, accurately, and expressively.

• *Jamestown's Reading Improvement,* by renowned reading expert Edward Fry, focuses on helping build your students' comprehension, vocabulary, and skimming and scanning skills.

• *Critical Reading Series* provides high-interest books, each written at three reading levels.

For more information about these products, see the Jamestown Education materials in the Classroom Solutions in the front of this Teacher Wraparound Edition. To order these products, call Glencoe at 1-800-334-7344.

 KEY for Using the Teacher Wraparound Edition

Use this key to help you identify the different types of prompts found in the Teacher Wraparound Edition.

R Reading Strategies activities help you teach reading skills and vocabulary.

C Critical Thinking strategies help students apply and extend what they have learned.

U Universal Access activities provide differentiated instruction for students learning to speak English, along with suggestions for teaching various types of learners.

S Skill Practice strategies help students practice historical analysis and geography skills.

W Writing Support activities provide writing opportunities to help students comprehend the text.

Teaching strategies and activities have been coded for ability level appropriateness.

AL Activities for students working above grade level
OL Activities for students working on grade level
BL Activities for students working below grade level
EL Activities for English learners

FOCUS

History–Social Science Standards

This chapter addresses the following main standards:

11.2 Students analyze the relationship among the rise of industrialization, large-scale rural-to-urban migration, and massive immigration from Southern and Eastern Europe.

11.3 Students analyze the role religion played in the founding of America, its lasting moral, social, and political impacts, and issues regarding religious liberty.

BELLRINGER
SKILLBUILDER ACTIVITY

Write the word *Industry* on the board. Ask students to brainstorm a list of positive and negative words they associate with industry, and save the list. After students have read Chapter 3, ask them to brainstorm another list of the positive and negative effects of industry. Compare the two lists and discuss what has changed.

TEACH

Thinking About the Big Ideas

As you begin teaching each section, use these questions and activities to focus on the Big Idea.

Section 1
Settling the West
Essential Question: How did miners and settlers adjust to their new way of life as they moved West? Inform students that Section 1 will discuss the many hardships miners and settlers had to endure while settling the West. **OL**

CHAPTER 3
1877–1900
The Birth of Modern America

～ *The Big Ideas* ～

SECTION 1: Settling the West
Societies change over time. *Native Americans' way of life came to an end as miners and ranchers found new riches in the West and farmers settled the Great Plains.*

SECTION 2: Industrialization
The Industrial Revolution changed the face of America. *The Industrial Revolution resulted in a nationwide railroad system and a new focus on business and industry.*

SECTION 3: Immigration and Urbanization
The Industrial Revolution changed the face of America. *Immigrants flooded into the United States. Together with rural Americans, they moved into cities that adapted to the increased population.*

SECTION 4: Early Reforms in a Gilded Age
People react to periods of breathtaking social and cultural change in different ways. *While some people espoused individualism and Social Darwinism, others tried to ease the problems that arose from urbanization and industrialization.*

SECTION 5: Politics and Reform
People react to periods of breathtaking social and cultural change in different ways. *Americans disagreed on how to deal with economic and reform issues. African Americans faced increasing discrimination and segregation.*

The *American Vision Modern Times* Video *The Chapter 3 video, "Building America," examines industrial expansion in the United States in the late 1800s.*

United States PRESIDENTS

- **1860** • Transcontinental railroad completed
- **1877** • Farmers' Alliance founded in Texas
- **1879** • Edison perfects lightbulb
- **1882** • Chinese Exclusion Act passed by Congress

Lincoln 1861–1865 | A. Johnson 1865–1869 | Grant 1869–1877 | Hayes 1877–1881 | Garfield 1881 | Arthur 1881–1885

1860   1870   1880

World

- **1867** • British colonies united to form Dominion of Canada
- **1869** • Chemist Dmitri Mendeleyev creates periodic table of elements
- **1876** • Korea forced to trade with Japan
- **1878** • Independent Serbia recognized

232

Section 2
Industrialization
Essential Question: What industry exists in your community? What impact does this industry have on the lives of people in your community? Tell students that in Section 2 they will learn that just as industry affects their daily lives, the industrial growth of the mid-1800s impacted the lives of Americans. **OL**

Section 3
Immigration and Urbanization
Essential Question: What do you think are some of the advantages and disadvantages of city life? Have students imagine what life might have been like in an American city in the mid-1800s. As students read Section 3, remind them that most immigrants could not speak English as they tried to settle in their new country. **OL**

Immigrants arriving at Ellis Island

Section 4
Early Reforms in a Gilded Age
Essential Question: Can you think of current social issues that people want to change? Remind students that people have always been concerned about social issues. Tell them that in Section 4 they will learn about movements that sought to bring changes in the late 1800s. **OL**

Section 5
Politics and Reform
Essential Question: What impact has segregation had on people and on society as a whole? Ask students to trace the problems African Americans faced after the Civil War as they read Section 5. **AL**

Cultural Perspectives

During the late 1800s and early 1900s, many immigrants from Asia—mainly from China—arrived on the West Coast, entering the United States through the Angel Island immigration station in San Francisco Bay. Many immigrants were detained for weeks or even months awaiting approval to enter the United States. To express their hopes and fears, some detainees wrote or carved poetry on the walls of the detention barracks. Have students locate and share examples of Angel Island poetry. What does the poetry reveal about the experiences of immigrants from Asia? **OL**

- **1883**
  - Brooklyn Bridge completed
- **1886**
  - American Federation of Labor founded
- **1890**
  - Sherman Antitrust Act passed
- **1894**
  - Pullman strike begins

- **1896**
  - *Plessy v. Ferguson* creates "separate but equal" doctrine
- **1901**
  - J.P. Morgan forms U.S. Steel

Cleveland 1885–1889

B. Harrison 1889–1893

Cleveland 1893–1897

McKinley 1897–1901

1890   *1900*

- **1885**
  - Indian National Congress organizes for independence from Great Britain
- **1888**
  - Brazil ends slavery
- **1892**
  - Rudolf Diesel patents diesel engine
- **1894**
  - Sino-Japanese War breaks out
- **1896**
  - Modern Olympics begin in Athens, Greece

HISTORY Online
Chapter Overview
Visit the *American Vision: Modern Times* Web site at tav.mt.glencoe.com and click on *Chapter Overviews– Chapter 3* to preview chapter information.

233

FOLDABLES
Study Organizer

Dinah Zike's Foldables are three-dimensional, interactive graphic organizers that help students practice basic writing skills, review key vocabulary terms, and identify main ideas. Have students complete the foldable activity in the *Dinah Zike's Reading and Study Skills Foldables* booklet.

HISTORY Online

Go to tav.mt.glencoe.com for student activities, lesson plans, and links to additional Web resources to help students learn about the Birth of Modern America.

Reading Skill ◄

Why It's Important
Tell students that making comparisons is an important life skill that can be applied to many different situations. Explain that it is particularly helpful when trying to make choices.

1. Introducing the Skill
Hold up a pen and a pencil and ask student volunteers to identify the similarities and differences. **Ask:** How are they alike? How are they different? Use the board to record their answers in a chart like the one below. **BL**

	Similarities	Differences
Pen		
Pencil		

2. Extending the Skill
Have students use the editorial page of your local newspaper to identify two columns that express different viewpoints on the same issue. Ask them to identify the similarities and differences between the two points of view and record the information in a table. Have students present their articles and tables to the class. **OL** **CA 11RC2.5**

Answers and Additional Support

Reading Skill ◄ **Comparing and Contrasting**

Good readers look for similarities and differences in new information they read. This helps them figure out what it means. You do this subconsciously in everyday life. For example, if you meet someone new, you probably compare that person to people you know. Is the person the same or different? If different, what makes that person different?

When you read, comparing and contrasting helps you understand new information. Luckily, authors can use certain signal words to tell you when they are comparing and contrasting information to something you already know. Some signal words for showing similarity are *same, at the same time, like,* and *still.* Signal words for showing differences include *however, rather, but,* or *on the other hand.*

Read the following sentences and notice how signal words describe similarities and differences.

The story of the Comstock Lode is <u>similar</u> to other stories of gold, silver, and copper strikes throughout the West. (page 237)

<u>Like</u> ranching, farming also seemed unsuitable for the Great Plains. (page 239)

<u>At the same time</u>, a new resource, petroleum, began to be exploited. (page 244)

<u>Although</u> the Industrial Revolution began in the United States in the early 1800s, the nation was still largely a farming country when the Civil War erupted. (page 244)

<u>However</u>, employers generally regarded unions as illegitimate conspiracies that interfered with their property rights. (page 250)

In the first three sentences, the authors compare developments in mining and ranching, along with events that occurred at the same time. The last two sentences present contrasts. The fourth sentence contrasts industrialization to the general state of the economy, while the last sentence clarifies the general attitude of employers toward unions.

Apply the Skill

As you read this chapter, take note of the signal words that the authors use to clue you into the causes and effects of different events. Recognizing the signal words will help you better understand the text.

COMPARING
The author uses the words *similar, like,* and *at the same time* to let you know that in these sentences something will be compared.

CONTRASTING
The words *although* and *however* indicate that the author is contrasting something to an event or item that was mentioned earlier.

234

UNIVERSAL ACCESS

English Learners Ask students to draw pictures of two important places in their life, such as home and school, an old neighborhood and a new neighborhood, or two favorite vacation spots. Then have students use their pictures to write paragraphs comparing and contrasting the two places. Encourage students to organize their ideas in tables before they begin writing. Remind them to use signal words to show the similarities and differences between the two places. After students have finished writing, have them work with partners to identify any points they have forgotten to mention or places where their writing seems unclear. **EL**

Historical Analysis Skill — Interpreting Maps

Analysis Skill
Standard CS3

Chronological and Spatial Thinking As you study history, you will use a variety of maps and documents to interpret human movement, including major patterns of domestic and international migration, changing environmental preferences and settlement patterns, the frictions that develop between population groups, and the diffusion of ideas, technological innovations, and goods.

Have you ever traveled somewhere unfamiliar? You, or the people you traveled with, probably used maps or other reference materials to help you find your way. You may have used a small-scale map to plot the general route you would be traveling. Then you may have used a more detailed map or perhaps a map on the Internet for instructions on finding the exact address.

Maps visually represent the physical and political layout of a land. They may describe the shape and elevation of the terrain, such as a contour map, or illustrate the impact of humans on the land, such as the boundaries of nations. Two general types of maps are most commonly used: topographical maps describe physical characteristics, while thematic maps provide specific information, such as roads.

When you look at a map, you need to consider the accuracy of the information presented. For instance, a map created by early explorers will probably not precisely represent the rivers, mountains, and shorelines. Instead, these are approximations of what the explorers knew at the time. You also must take into account when and how, by whom, and for what purpose the map was made. Some maps may be deliberately misleading. For example, it was not uncommon for these same early explorers to exaggerate the size or natural resources of a new land to impress potential investors.

The U.S. National Archives and Records Administration houses many of the nation's most important documents, maps, and other historical artifacts. As with all historical documents, the National Archives suggests that you should read maps with analysis in mind. Whenever you look at maps, consider these questions:

- **Who is the mapmaker?**
- **When was the map made?**
- **What type of map is it?**
- **What is the purpose of the map?**
- **Does the text contain information supported by the map?**

Before you begin studying Chapter 3, take a look at the Geography Handbook on pages 84–91 of your textbook, if you have not done so already. On these pages you can learn more about different types of maps.

Apply the Skill

This chapter contains several maps. For each of the maps, answer the questions above to help you better understand the information.

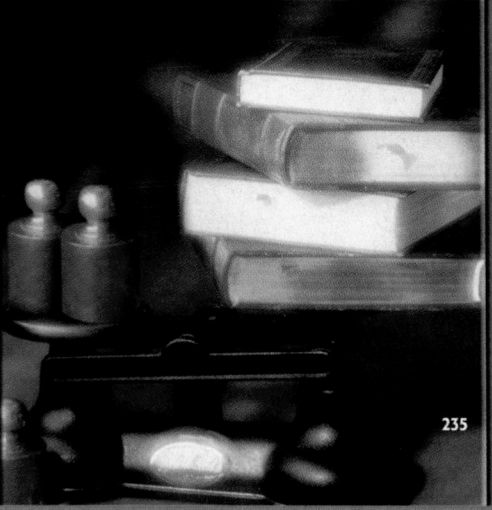

235

Preparing to Read

Historical Analysis

Why It's Important
Explain to students that looking at a map allows the user to see the big picture, including the physical relationship of the various areas depicted. Tell students that to take advantage of seeing the big picture, it is important for them to be able to interpret and understand maps.

1. Introducing the Skill
Ask volunteers to describe the way they get to school each morning. Have students record the steps in a flowchart like the one below. Next, tell students to use their flowcharts to create maps tracing their routes to school. **Ask: Does your map show the physical or political layout of the land, or both? Is it a topographical map or a thematic map, or both? Explain.** Invite students to present their maps to the class. BL

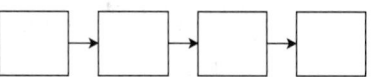

2. Extending the Skill
Have students use magazines to locate two different articles that include maps. Then ask them to write paragraphs comparing and contrasting the two maps according to the following four questions: **(1) When was the map made? (2) What type of map is it? (3) What is the purpose of the map? (4) Does the text contain information supported by the map?** Encourage students to organize their information in a table before writing their paragraphs. **Ask: What information would be lost if the article did not include a map?** OL

UNIVERSAL ACCESS

Visual/Spatial Divide the class into groups of four. Ask each group to look at the maps on pages 239 and 247 and identify where and in what time period railroads were built. Ask groups to briefly discuss and then write a few paragraphs explaining their answers to the following questions: **Are there areas in the country that had more railroads than others? How can you explain the difference?** Invite a representative from each group to share their maps and responses with the class. AL CA CS3

FOCUS

SKILLBUILDER ACTIVITY

Project **Daily Focus Skills Transparency 3-1** and have students answer the question.

Guide to Reading

Understanding Vocabulary:
As students encounter the vocabulary during the reading, have them note each term's usage in context, and write a sentence using the term.

Answers to Graphic:
promoting railroads: improved trade, depleted buffalo; Homestead Act: made land affordable, encroached on hunting grounds and broke treaties; Dawes Act: tried to end conflicts with Native Americans, weakened Native American culture

Unpacking the Standards

Students will be able to:
- Evaluate the importance of mining in the West.
- Analyze the ranching and farming practiced on the Plains.
- Discuss the impact of settlers on Native Americans.

Answers and Additional Support

SECTION 1 Settling the West

Guide to Reading

Connection
In the previous section, you learned about the Reconstruction of the United States after the Civil War. In this section, you will discover how the Gold Rush attracted settlers to the West and how people began to settle the Great Plains.

Main Idea
- Miners seeking to strike it rich settled large areas of the West. (p. 237)
- Ranchers built vast cattle ranches on the Great Plains, while settlers staked out homesteads and began farming the region. (p. 238)
- The settlement of the West dramatically altered the way of life of the Plains Indians. (p. 241)

Content Vocabulary
placer mining, quartz mining, vigilance committee, open range, long drive, homestead, assimilate

Academic Vocabulary
extract, adapt, prior

People and Terms to Identify
Henry Comstock, Homestead Act, Indian Peace Commission, Sitting Bull, Ghost Dance, Dawes Act

Places to Locate
Great Plains, Wheat Belt

Reading Objectives
- **Trace** the growth of the mining industry and big ranches in the West.
- **Explain** how and why people began settling the Great Plains.

- **Summarize** problems caused by attempts to assimilate Native Americans.

Reading Strategy
As you read about the settlement of the West, complete a graphic organizer similar to the one below listing resources and government policies that encouraged settlement, and the effects of these measures on Native Americans.

Resources/ Government Policies	How It Attracted New Settlers	Impact on Native Americans

Preview of Events

◆1860	◆1870	◆1880	◆1890

1859 Comstock Lode discovered in Nevada

1862 Homestead Act

1867 Cattle drives begin on Chisholm Trail

1887 Dawes Act

1890 Wounded Knee Massacre

The following are the main History–Social Science Standards covered in this section.

11.1.4 Examine the effects of the Civil War and Reconstruction and of the Industrial revolution, including demographic shifts and the emergence in the late 19th century of the United States as a world power.

11.2.6 Trace the economic development of the United States and its emergence as a major industrial power, including its gains from trade and the advantage of its physical geography.

⚜ The Big Idea ⚜

Societies change over time. Following Reconstruction, many people moved West in hopes of making fortunes mining newly discovered deposits of gold, silver, and copper needed for industries in the East. As railroads were constructed, settlers also moved to the Great Plains to farm or ranch. This influx of settlers had a profound effect on the lives of the Native Americans who had roamed the Plains for centuries. Hunters and sharpshooters clearing the way for railroads drastically depleted the buffalo herds many Native Americans depended on for survival. Many were forced to relocate or give up their culture by assimilating.

236 CHAPTER 3 The Birth of Modern America

SECTION RESOURCES

📁 **Print Material**
- Reproducible Lesson Plan 3-1
- Guided Reading Activity 3-1
- Reading Essentials and Study Guide 3-1
- Active Reading Note-Taking Guide 3-1

📽 **Transparencies**
- Daily Focus Skills Transparency 3-1
- Section Graphic Organizer Transparency 3-1

Technology
- 💿 Interactive Tutor Self-Assessment CD-ROM
- 💿 Exam*View*® Pro Testmaker CD-ROM
- 💿 Presentation Plus! CD-ROM

Growth of the Mining Industry

 Main Idea Miners seeking to strike it rich settled large areas of the West.

Reading Connection Under what circumstances would you choose to move to another state? Read on to find out what motivated miners to relocate to the western states.

The rich deposits of gold, silver, and copper in the West served the needs of growing industries in the East. They also brought the first wave of settlers that populated the mountain states of the West.

★ An American Story ★

Jacob Waldorf arrived in Virginia City, Nevada, in 1873 to seek his fortune in the fabled silver mines of the Comstock Lode. Like many others, he found work at one of the big mining companies. Seven days a week he toiled in a dangerous mine shaft, earning enough to support his family and buy a little stock in local mining companies. As his son John recalled:

❝The favorite game with our father was stocks. . . . Mother used to say to me, 'Some day we're going back east,' but for years none of the stocks in which Dad invested showed any disposition to furnish us with the price of transportation.❞

In 1877 the stock Waldorf owned skyrocketed in value. "Dad's holdings rose . . . to $10,000 and mother began to talk of buying a farm," John wrote. "The stock kept going upward. Dad was worth $15,000 for at least a minute." He waited for the stock to go even higher before selling, but instead it plummeted: "The bottom fell out of Ophi [a mining stock], and Mother's dream farm fell with it, for Dad was broke."

Jacob Waldorf overcame this financial setback. Earning the respect of his fellow workers, he headed the miners' union in 1880 and later served as a state legislator.

—adapted from *A Kid on the Comstock*

The search for wealth brought many fortune seekers like Jacob Waldorf. News of a mineral discovery in an area would start a stampede of prospectors desperately hoping to strike it rich. Early prospectors would **extract** the shallow deposits of ore largely by hand in a process called **placer mining**, using simple equipment like picks, shovels, and pans. After these surface deposits dwindled, corporations would move in to begin **quartz mining**, which dug deep beneath the surface. As those deposits dried up, commercial mining either disappeared or continued on a restricted basis.

The Big Strike in Nevada The story of the Comstock Lode is similar to other stories of gold, silver, and copper strikes throughout the West. In 1859 a prospector named **Henry Comstock** staked a claim in Six-Mile Canyon, Nevada. The sticky, blue-gray mud found there turned out to be nearly pure silver ore. News of the Comstock strike brought hordes of miners to Virginia City, Nevada. Almost overnight the town went from a frontier outpost to a boomtown of about 30,000, boasting an opera house, shops with furniture and fashions from Europe, several newspapers, and a six-story hotel with the West's first elevator, called a "rising room." When the silver veins were exhausted several years later, the mines closed. Without the mines, the town's economy collapsed, and most of the townspeople moved on in search of new opportunities. This cycle of boom and bust—from boomtown to ghost town—was repeated throughout the mountainous West.

▼ *Miner working the Comstock Lode*

TEACH

R **Reading Strategy**

Scaffolding—Academic Vocabulary The word *circumstances* was introduced in Chapter 2, Section 5. Ask a student to define the word. **BL**

U **Universal Access**

Kinesthetic Have interested students build models to demonstrate the process of panning for gold and silver. Students should demonstrate the process to the class using their models. Tell students to be prepared to answer questions about their models. **OL**

S **Skill Practice**

Conducting Research Ask students to use Internet and library resources to research where and how mining for precious minerals is done in the United States today. **Ask: Is quartz mining still used? What are some of the dangers or drawbacks of today's mining methods?** Have students present their findings on posters and display them in and around the classroom. **OL** **CA HR4**

Did You Know?

Western prospectors used sluices to search riverbeds more quickly than they could with the backbreaking panning method. A sluice diverted the current of a river into earthen or wooden trenches. The water was directed to a box with metal "riffle" bars that disturbed the current, causing heavier minerals to settle to the bottom of the box. A screen at the end of the riffle box prevented the minerals from flowing out.

W Writing Support

Narrative Writing Invite interested students to write a brief autobiographical story from the point of view of an early female inhabitant of a mining town. Remind students to include important information such as their character's name, where she lives, why she came to the mining town, what she does there, and her impressions of the town and its other inhabitants. Encourage students to share their stories with the class. **AL**

CA 11WA2.1a; 11WA2.1c

U Universal Access

Visual/Spatial Have students work together in small groups to create a thematic map showing important mining towns in Colorado, the Dakota Territory, and Montana. Encourage students to use library and Internet resources to locate the information needed to construct their maps. Display the maps throughout your classroom. **OL**

✓ Reading Check

Answer: The discovery of new mines brought hordes of new settlers to the West and created boomtowns overnight.

Answers and Additional Support

During the booms, crime posed a serious problem. Prospectors fought over claims, and thieves haunted the streets and trails. Law enforcers were scarce, and self-appointed volunteers sometimes formed **vigilance committees** to track down and punish wrongdoers. In some cases, they punished the innocent or let the guilty go free, but most people in these communities respected the law and tried to deal firmly but fairly with those accused of crimes.

Mining towns such as Virginia City at first were inhabited mostly by men, but soon they attracted more women. Some women owned property and were influential community leaders. Others worked as cooks or in laundries. Still other women worked at "hurdy-gurdy" houses (named after the mechanical musical instrument), where they danced with men for the price of a drink.

Other Bonanzas Mining also spurred the development of Colorado, the Dakota Territory, and Montana. The discovery of gold near Pikes Peak in 1858 set miners on a frantic rush. Inspired by the phrase "Pikes Peak or Bust," many panned for gold without success and headed home, complaining of a "Pikes Peak hoax."

In truth, there was plenty of gold and silver in the Colorado mountains, but much of it was hidden beneath the surface and hard to extract. One of the richest strikes occurred in the late 1870s in Leadville, named for deep deposits of lead that contained large amounts of silver. By the summer of 1879, as many as 1,000 newcomers per week were pouring into Leadville, creating one of the most famous boomtowns to dot the mining frontier.

Overall, operations at Leadville and other mining towns in Colorado yielded more than $1 billion worth of silver and gold (many billions in today's money). This bonanza spurred the building of railroads through the Rocky Mountains and transformed Denver, the supply point for the mining areas, into the second largest city in the West after San Francisco.

The discovery of gold in the Black Hills of the Dakota Territory and copper in Montana led to rapid development of the northern Great Plains. Miners flooded into the region in the 1870s. After railroads were built in the 1880s, many farmers and ranchers moved to the territory. In 1889, Congress divided the Dakota Territory and admitted North Dakota and South Dakota, as well as Montana, as new states.

✓ Reading Check **Explain** How did the discovery of new mines affect settlement of the West?

238 CHAPTER 3 The Birth of Modern America

Ranching and Farming the Plains

Main Idea Ranchers built vast cattle ranches on the Great Plains, while settlers staked out homesteads and began farming the region.

Reading Connection When you think of cowhands, what images come to mind, and from what sources do these images derive? Read on to learn about the realities of life as a cowboy in the West.

While many Americans headed to the Rocky Mountains to mine gold and silver after the Civil War, others began building vast cattle ranches and farming homesteads on the **Great Plains.** This region extends westward to the Rocky Mountains from around the 100th meridian—an imaginary line running north and south from the central Dakotas through western Texas.

Ranching the Plains In the early 1800s, Americans did not think cattle ranches on the Great Plains were practical. Water was scarce, and cattle from the East could not survive on the tough prairie grasses. Farther south, however, in Texas, there existed a breed of cattle **adapted** to living on the Great Plains.

The Texas longhorn was a breed descended from Spanish cattle that had been brought to Mexico two centuries earlier. Ranchers in Mexico and Texas had allowed their cattle to run wild, and slowly a new breed—the longhorn—had emerged. Lean and rangy, the longhorn could easily survive in the harsh climate of the Plains, and by 1865, as many as 5 million of them roamed the grasslands of Texas.

Mexicans had introduced cattle ranching in California, New Mexico, and Texas before these areas became part of the United States. The industry grew in part because of the **open range**—a vast area of government-owned grassland. The open range covered much of the Great Plains and provided land where ranchers could graze their herds free of charge and unrestricted by the boundaries of private farms.

Mexican cowhands developed the tools and techniques for rounding up and driving cattle. These Hispanic herders taught American cowhands their trade and enriched the English vocabulary with words of Spanish origin, including "lariat," "lasso," and "stampede."

Prior to the Civil War, ranchers had little incentive to round up the longhorns. Beef prices were low, and moving the cattle to eastern markets was not practical. Two developments changed this situation: the

Did You Know?

The residents of Virginia City, Nevada, which was first known as Virginny Town, got some of their news from the *Territorial Enterprise.* The newspaper employed a young reporter named Sam Clemens from Hannibal, Missouri. Most of the readers knew him by his pen name, Mark Twain.

NATIONAL GEOGRAPHIC — Mining Country and Cattle Trails, 1848–1890

Helena, Montana in 1865

Gold | Cattle trails
Silver | Railroads
1890 border

500 miles
500 kilometers
Lambert Equal-Area projection

Cowhands on a cattle drive

Geography *Skills*

1. **Interpreting Maps** What cities were destination points for the Chisholm Trail?
2. **Applying Geography Skills** Why do you think the destination cities at the end of the cattle trails are all located along railroad lines?

Civil War and the construction of the railroads. During the Civil War, eastern cattle were slaughtered in huge numbers to feed the armies of the Union and the Confederacy. After the war, beef prices soared, making it worthwhile to round up the longhorns if a way could be found to move them east.

By the 1860s, railroads had reached the Great Plains. Lines ended at Abilene and Dodge City in Kansas and at Sedalia in Missouri. Ranchers and livestock dealers realized that if the longhorns were rounded up and driven north several hundred miles to the railroad, they could be sold for a huge profit and shipped east to market.

In 1866 ranchers rounded up cattle and drove about 260,000 of them to Sedalia, Missouri. Although only a fraction of the herds survived this first **long drive,** the drive overall was a tremendous success as cattle was

sold for 10 times the price it could get in Texas. As railroads expanded in the West, other trails soon opened from Texas to towns in Kansas, Nebraska, Montana, and Wyoming.

Farming Becomes Big Business Like ranching, farming also seemed unsuitable for the Great Plains. Rainfall averages less than 20 inches per year there, and trees grow naturally only along rivers and streams. During the late 1800s several factors undermined the belief that the Plains was a "Great American Desert." One important factor was the construction of the railroads, which provided easy access to the Great Plains. Railroad companies sold land along the rail lines at low prices and provided credit to prospective settlers. Railroads opened offices throughout the United States and in major cities in

CHAPTER 3   The Birth of Modern America   **239**

Geography *Skills*

Answers:
1. Abilene, Dodge City, and Ellsworth, Kansas
2. Cattle could quickly be transported for slaughter and sold throughout the country.

Geography Skills Practice
Ask: What cities lay on the Western Trail?
(Bandera, Texas; Dodge City, Kansas; and Ogallala, Nebraska)

Did You Know?

When ranchers and farmers settled the Southwest, they displaced many of the Mexican Americans who had lived there for generations. Congressional land acts required these settlers to provide detailed legal proof, but most titles were either not specific, were recorded in Mexico, or were lost.

Europe where land was scarce. Posters and pamphlets proclaimed that booking passage to the Plains was a ticket to prosperity.

The catchy slogan "Rain follows the plow," coined by a Nebraskan to sell the idea that cultivating the Plains would increase rainfall, encouraged settlers. As if to prove the saying correct, the weather cooperated. For more than a decade beginning in the 1870s, rainfall on the Plains was well above average. The lush green of the endless prairies contradicted the popular belief that the region was a desert.

In 1862 the government also supported settlement in the Great Plains region by passing the **Homestead Act.** For a $10 registration fee, an individual could file for a **homestead**—a tract of public land available for settlement. A homesteader could claim up to 160 acres of public land and could receive title to that land after living there for five years. Later government acts increased the size of the tracts available. The Homestead Act provided a legal method for settlers to acquire clear title to property in the West. With their property rights secured, settlers were more willing to move to the Plains.

When settlers arrived on the Plains, they often found life very difficult. The lack of trees and water forced them to build their first homes from sod cut from the ground and to drill wells up to 300 feet deep. Summer temperatures often soared over 100° Fahrenheit. Prairie fires were a constant danger. Sometimes swarms of grasshoppers swept over farms and destroyed the crops. In winter there were terrible blizzards and extreme cold. Despite these challenges, most homesteaders persisted and learned how to live in the harsh environment.

For those who had the financial resources, farming could be highly profitable on the Plains. During the 1880s, many farmers from Minnesota and other Midwestern states moved to the Great Plains to plant wheat, which was more drought-resistant than other crops. They took advantage of the inexpensive land and utilized new farming technology, such as reapers and threshers. This productive new **Wheat Belt** began at the eastern edge of the Great Plains and encompassed much of the Dakotas and the western parts of Nebraska and Kansas.

The bountiful harvests in the Wheat Belt helped the United States become the world's leading exporter of wheat by the 1880s. In fact, wheat became as important to the Great Plains as cotton was to the South. American wheat growers faced rising competition, however, from other wheat-producing nations. In the 1890s, a glut of wheat on the world market caused prices to drop.

✓ **Reading Check** **Analyzing** Why did the Homestead Act motivate settlers to move to the Great Plains?

Picturing **History**

Farming the Great Plains Technology made farming the vast open plains of America feasible. Here horse-drawn binders are being used to gather hay in the late 1800s. What other factors encouraged settlement on the Great Plains?

Profiles IN HISTORY

Sitting Bull
1831–1890

In June 1876, a showdown loomed between Custer's troops and the Lakota Sioux who had left their reservation. Lakota chief Sitting Bull sought help for his people from the supreme power they called *Wakan Tanka,* or the "Great Mystery," by performing the Sun Dance.

Before dancing, an assistant made many small cuts in the chief's arms and shoulders. Then Sitting Bull raised his bleeding arms to heaven and danced around a sacred pole with his eyes on the sun. He continued to dance through the night and into the next day, when he entered a death-like trance. When he revived, he told of a vision in which he saw white soldiers upside down. The Lakota were encouraged by Sitting Bull's dream and the sacrifice he had made for them. Many felt that

his Sun Dance helped bring them victory over Custer.

Sitting Bull remained devoted to the traditional religious practices of his people even after he and his followers reluctantly returned to the reservation under pressure from the army. Federal authorities regarded ceremonies like the Sun Dance—practiced in one form or another by many Plains Indians—as heathen and subversive. In 1883 the federal government outlawed the Sun Dance and many other Native American religious rites.

Native Americans

Main Idea The settlement of the West dramatically altered the way of life of the Plains Indians.

Reading Connection Can you recall a situation in which someone broke a promise or agreement with you? Do you remember your reaction? Read on to find out how Native Americans responded when the government broke treaties during the late 1800s.

For centuries the Great Plains was home to many Native American nations. Some lived in communities as farmers and hunters, but most were nomads who roamed vast distances, following their main source of food—the buffalo.

Despite their differences, the groups of Plains Indians were similar in many ways. They lived in extended family networks and had a close relationship with nature. Plains Indian nations, sometimes numbering several thousand people, were divided into bands consisting of up to 500 people. A governing council headed each band, but most members participated in making decisions. Gender determined the assignment of tasks. Women generally performed domestic tasks: rearing children, cooking, and preparing hides. Men performed tasks such as hunting, trading, and supervising the military life of the band. Most Plains Indians practiced a religion based on a belief in the spiritual power of the natural world.

Cultures Under Pressure As ranchers, miners, and farmers moved onto the Plains, they deprived Native Americans of their hunting grounds, broke treaties guaranteeing certain lands to the Plains Indians, and often forced them to relocate to new territory. Native Americans resisted by attacking wagon trains, stagecoaches, and ranches. Occasionally an entire group would go to war against nearby settlers and troops. Congress became convinced that something had to be done to end the growing conflict with Native Americans on the Great Plains. In 1867 Congress formed an **Indian Peace Commission,** which proposed creating two large reservations on the Plains, one for the Sioux and another for southern Plains Indians. Agents from the federal government's Bureau of Indian Affairs would run the reservations. The army would be given authority to deal with any groups that refused to report or remain there.

This plan was doomed to failure. Pressuring Native American leaders into signing treaties did not ensure that chiefs or their followers would abide by the terms. Those who did move to reservations faced poverty, despair, and the corrupt practices of American traders.

Conflict and Assimilation By the 1870s, many Native Americans on the southern Plains had left the reservations in disgust. They preferred hunting buffalo on the open Plains, so they joined others who had also shunned the reservations. Buffalo, however, were being killed in large numbers by migrants, professional buffalo hunters, and sharpshooters clearing rail

CHAPTER 3   The Birth of Modern America   **241**

S Skill Practice

Evaluating Evidence Organize the class into groups of five. Tell the groups to use Internet and library resources to research the conflict between Native Americans and white settlers. Then ask the groups to list ways that the conflict might have been resolved without violence. Have students work together to write paragraphs explaining one or two of their possible solutions and share their paragraphs with the class. **OL**

CA HR3; HI3; HI4

U Universal Access

Visual/Spatial Have students use their textbooks, library, and Internet resources to create two maps of Native American reservations. One map should show the reservations before the formation of the Indian Peace Commission, and the other should show the reservations after the Commission. Use the maps to discuss how the federal government tried to gain authority over Native Americans in the Great Plains.

AL **CA** CS3

Resources for page 241

Have students read more about Native American assimilation by assigning "The School Days of an Indian Girl (The Cutting of My Long Hair)" in the **American Literature Readings 1.**

Have students read more about Plains Indian Life in **Primary Source Reading 3-1.**

Profiles IN HISTORY

For a time in the mid-1800s, Sitting Bull traveled with Buffalo Bill's Wild West Show.

Ask: Why do you think federal authorities outlawed the Sun Dance and other religious rites? *(Students might answer that federal authorities felt it would be better for everyone if Native Americans abandoned their culture and assimilated into American society as defined by white Christians.)*

Universal Access

Visual/Spatial Tell students to use library and Internet resources to research the Ghost Dance and the music and rituals associated with it. Have students create a display that explains the dance and its elements. **OL**

ASSESS

Resources for page 242

Use these resources to assess student mastery.

📁 Section Quiz 3-1

📁 Reading Essentials and Study Guide 3-1

⊙ Interactive Tutor Self-Assessment CD-ROM

📁 California Standards Practice, Grade 11

✓ Reading Check

Answer: Her book sparked discussions of better treatment for Native Americans.

HISTORY Online

Study Central provides audio summaries, interactive games, and online graphic organizers to help students review section content.

CLOSE

Narrative Writing Have students write journal entries from the view of a person mentioned in this section. **BL**

---

lines for railroad companies. By 1889 very few of the animals remained.

The Lakota Sioux, led by **Sitting Bull,** and the Nez Perce under Chief Joseph tried to resist government efforts to force them back on reservations. Sitting Bull and his followers escaped to Canada, but the remaining Lakota and the Nez Perce had to give up their fight against military forces.

Native American resistance to federal authority finally came to a tragic end on the Lakota Sioux reservation in 1890. Defying the orders of a government agent, the Lakota continued to perform the **Ghost Dance,** a ritual that celebrated a hoped-for day of reckoning. The government agent blamed Sitting Bull, who had returned to the reservation from Canada. The attempt to arrest him ended in an exchange of gunfire and the death of the chief. The participants of the Ghost Dance then fled the reservation. On December 29, 1890, as U.S. troops tried to disarm the Native Americans at Wounded Knee Creek, gunfire broke out. A deadly battle ensued, costing the lives of 25 U.S. soldiers and approximately 200 Lakota men, women, and children.

Even before Wounded Knee, some Americans had long opposed the treatment of Native Americans. Author Helen Hunt Jackson described the years of broken promises and assaults on Native Americans in her book, *A Century of Dishonor,* published in 1881. Jackson's descriptions sparked discussions—even in Congress—of better treatment for Native Americans. Some people believed that the situation would improve only if Native Americans could **assimilate,** or be absorbed, into American society as landowners and citizens. That

meant breaking up reservations into individual allotments, where families could become self-supporting.

This policy became law in 1887 when Congress passed the **Dawes Act.** The act allotted to each head of household 160 acres of reservation land for farming; single adults received 80 acres, and 40 acres were allotted for children. The land that remained after all members had received allotments would be sold to American settlers, with the proceeds going into a trust for Native Americans.

While some Native Americans succeeded as farmers or ranchers, many had little training or enthusiasm for either pursuit. They often found their allotments too small to be profitable, and so they sold them. Some Native American groups had grown attached to their reservations and hated to see them transformed into homesteads for settlers as well as Native Americans.

In the end, the assimilation policy proved a dismal failure. The Plains Indians were doomed because they were dependent on buffalo for food, clothing, fuel, and shelter. When the herds were wiped out, Native Americans on the Plains had no way to sustain their way of life, and few were willing or able to adopt American settlers' lifestyles in place of their traditional cultures.

✓ **Reading Check** **Cause and Effect** What impact did Helen Hunt Jackson's book *A Century of Dishonor* have?

HISTORY *Online* **Study Central**

For help with the concepts in this section of *American Vision: Modern Times* go to tav.mt.glencoe.com and click on **Study Central.**

SECTION 1 ASSESSMENT

Checking for Understanding

1. **Vocabulary** Define: extract, placer mining, vigilance committee, adapt, open range, prior, long drive, homestead, assimilate.
2. **People and Terms** Identify: Henry Comstock, Homestead Act, Indian Peace Commission, Sitting Bull, Ghost Dance, Dawes Act.
3. **Places** Locate: Great Plains, Wheat Belt
4. **Identify** the goals and terms of the Homestead Act.

Reviewing Big Ideas

5. **Explaining** How did the mining industry and the growth of ranching and farming each contribute to the development of the West?

Critical Thinking

6. **Evaluating** What factors contributed to the making of the Wheat Belt in the Great Plains and then to troubled times for wheat farmers in the 1890s?
7. **Analyzing** How would you evaluate the government's policy of assimilation of Native Americans?
8. **Organizing** Use a graphic organizer similar to the one below to demonstrate the cycle of boom and bust in mining.

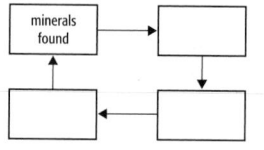

Analyzing Visuals

9. **Analyzing Maps** Examine the map of mining country and cattle trails on page 239. Based on the details of the map, how did railways contribute to the opening and the settling of the West?

Writing About History

10. **Descriptive Writing** Write a summary for the story line of a Hollywood movie. Your summary should realistically portray the lives of a miner, a rancher, or a Native American in the West in the mid- to late 1800s. Be sure to include detailed descriptions of people and places. **CA** 11WS1.2

242 CHAPTER 3 The Birth of Modern America

SECTION 1 ASSESSMENT ANSWERS

1. Content vocabulary is boldfaced and highlighted in yellow. Academic vocabulary is boldfaced.
2. Henry Comstock *(p. 237),* Homestead Act *(p. 240),* Indian Peace Commission *(p. 241),* Sitting Bull *(p. 242),* Ghost Dance *(p. 242),* Dawes Act *(p. 242)*
3. Great Plains *(p. 238),* Wheat Belt

(p. 240)

4. promoted settlement of the Plains
5. encouraged settlement and the creation of towns in the West
6. the Homestead Act, new farming techniques and equipment; good harvests, world competition caused a glut that caused prices to drop

7. unsuccessful because Native Americans were unwilling or unable to live like American settlers
8. settlers arrive→mineral veins are exhausted→local mining economy collapses
9. railroads provided access
10. Students' summaries will vary.

SECTION 2 Industrialization

Guide to Reading

Connection
In the previous section, you learned about the settlement of the West and the Great Plains. In this section, you will discover how the Industrial Revolution changed the United States and created a new focus on business and industry.

Main Idea
- American industry grew rapidly after the Civil War, bringing revolutionary changes to American society. (p. 244)
- After the Civil War, the rapid construction of railroads accelerated the nation's industrialization and linked the country together. (p. 246)
- Big business assumed a more prominent role in American life following the Civil War. (p. 248)

- In an attempt to improve their working conditions, industrial workers came together to form unions in the late 1800s. (p. 249)

Content Vocabulary
gross national product, entrepreneur, laissez-faire, corporation, vertical integration, horizontal integration, monopoly, Marxism, industrial union, closed shop

Academic Vocabulary
practice, distribution, concept

People and Terms to Identify
Alexander Graham Bell, Thomas Alva Edison, Pacific Railway Act, Andrew Carnegie, American Federation of Labor, Samuel Gompers

Reading Objectives
- **Discuss** how the availability of natural resources, new inventions, and the railroads spurred industrial growth.
- **Analyze** how large corporations came to dominate American business and labor.

Reading Strategy
Organizing As you read about the changes brought about by industrialization, complete a graphic organizer similar to the one below listing the causes of industrialization.

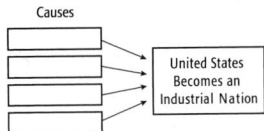

Causes → United States Becomes an Industrial Nation

Preview of Events

◆1860	◆1870	◆1880	◆1890
1862 John D. Rockefeller buys first oil refinery	**1869** First transcontinental railroad completed	**1876** Alexander Graham Bell invents telephone	**1886** American Federation of Labor founded

The following are the main History–Social Science Standards covered in this section.

11.1.4 Examine the effects of the Civil War and Reconstruction and of the Industrial Revolution, including demographic shifts and the emergence in the late 19th century of the United States as a world power.

11.2.1 Know the effects of industrialization on living and working conditions, including the portrayal of working conditions and food safety in Upton Sinclair's *The Jungle*.

11.2.5 Discuss corporate mergers that produced trusts and cartels and the economic and political policies of industrial leaders.

11.2.6 Trace the economic development of the United States and its emergence as a major industrial power, including its gains from trade and the advantage of its physical geography.

❧ The Big Idea ❧

The Industrial Revolution changed the face of America. Industry in the United States flourished following the Civil War. The natural resources industries needed were readily available through mining operations in the West. A large population increase provided a readily available workforce. The increase in industry spurred the expansion of railroads, which further accelerated industrialization as railroads linked the country together. To manage the burgeoning industries, business leaders founded corporations. At the same time, workers began to organize and form unions in an effort to improve their working conditions.

11.6.5 Trace the advances and retreats of organized labor, from the creation of the American Federation of Labor and the Congress of Industrial Organizations to current issues of a postindustrial, multinational economy, including the United Farm Workers in California.

CHAPTER 3 The Birth of Modern America **243**

BELLRINGER
SKILLBUILDER ACTIVITY

Project **Daily Focus Skills Transparency 3-2** and have students answer the question.

Guide to Reading

Understanding Vocabulary: Play vocabulary Bingo by providing students with a blank grid and asking them to write one vocabulary word in each space (remind students to also include a free space). Read off the definitions and have students mark off the corresponding vocabulary words on their grids.

Answers to Graphic: abundance of raw materials, oil production, population increase, free enterprise system, large free trade area, new inventions

Unpacking the Standards

Students will be able to:

- Summarize the growth of American industry after the Civil War.
- Explain the impact of the railroads on the nation's industrialization.
- Describe the rise of big business and the impact of the free enterprise system on industrialization.
- Explain the role of unions in the late 1800s.

SECTION RESOURCES

📖 Print Material
- Reproducible Lesson Plan 3-2
- Guided Reading Activity 3-2
- Reading Essentials and Study Guide 3-2
- Active Reading Note-Taking Guide 3-2

📖 Transparencies
- Daily Focus Skills Transparency 3-2
- Section Graphic Organizer Transparency 3-2

Technology
- 💿 Interactive Tutor Self-Assessment CD-ROM
- 💿 ExamView® Pro Testmaker CD-ROM
- 💿 Presentation Plus! CD-ROM

243

TEACH

W Writing Support

Expository Writing Have students write magazine articles about the invention of the light bulb. Instruct them to write their articles as they might have appeared at the time the light bulb was introduced. **BL**

CA 11WS1.1

U Universal Access

Interpersonal Have each student list the electrical equipment he or she uses during a typical week. Then ask students to identify two adults, one between 40 and 50 years old, and a second between 60 and 70 years old. Have the adults check off the electrical appliances they used as teenagers. Discuss with the class what the lists reflect about the inventions of the twentieth century. **BL**

Answers and Additional Support

The United States Industrializes

Main Idea American industry grew rapidly after the Civil War, bringing revolutionary changes to American society.

Reading Connection If you had to name the invention most valuable in your daily life, what would it be, and why? Read on to learn about the many new inventions that emerged in the late 1800s, and find out how these innovations fueled the nation's industrial growth.

Although the Industrial Revolution began in the United States in the early 1800s, the nation was still largely a farming country when the Civil War erupted. In 1860, out of a population of more than 30 million, only 1.3 million Americans worked in industry. After the Civil War, industry expanded rapidly, and millions of Americans left their farms to work in mines and factories.

★ An American Story ★

On October 21, 1879, Thomas Alva Edison and his team of workers were too excited to sleep. For weeks they had worked to create an electric incandescent lamp, or lightbulb, that would burn for more than a few minutes. For much of the 1800s, inventors had struggled to develop a form of lighting that would be cheaper, safer, and brighter than traditional methods such as candles, whale oil, kerosene, and gas. If Edison and his team could do it, they would change the world. Finally, after weeks of dedicated effort, they turned night into day. Edison later recalled:

W ❝We sat and looked and the lamp continued to burn and the longer it burned the more fascinated we were. None of us could go to bed and there was no sleep for over 40 hours; we sat and just watched it with anxiety growing into elation. It lasted about 45 hours and then I said, 'If it will burn 40 hours now I know I can make it burn a hundred.'❞

—quoted in *Eyewitness to America*

U By the early 1900s, with the help of inventors such as Edison, Americans had transformed the United States into the world's leading industrial nation. By 1914 the nation's **gross national product** (GNP)—the total value of all goods and services produced by a country—was eight times greater than it had been when the Civil War ended.

244 CHAPTER 3 The Birth of Modern America

▲ *Thomas Edison*

Natural Resources An abundance of raw materials was one reason for the nation's industrial success. The United States contained vast natural resources upon which industry in the 1800s depended, including water, timber, coal, iron, and copper. American companies could obtain these resources cheaply and did not have to import them from other countries. Many of the nation's resources were located in the mountains of the American West. The settlement of this region after the Civil War helped to accelerate industrialization, as did the construction of the transcontinental railroad. Railroads brought settlers and miners to the region and carried the resources back to factories in the East.

At the same time, a new resource, petroleum, began to be exploited. Even before the invention of the automobile, petroleum was in high demand because it could be turned into kerosene. Kerosene was used in lanterns and stoves. The American oil industry was built on the demand for kerosene. As oil production rose, it fueled economic expansion.

A Large Workforce The human resources available to American industry were as important as natural resources in enabling the nation to industrialize rapidly. Between 1860 and 1910, the population of the United States almost tripled. This population provided industry with a large workforce and also created greater demand for the consumer goods that factories produced.

Population growth stemmed from two causes: large families and a flood of immigrants. American industry began to grow at a time when social and

More Skill Practice

Research Report Writing Instruct students to write three-page reports on the various uses of petroleum, including kerosene, diesel fuel, and gasoline. Invite students to present their reports to the class. **AL** **CA** 11WA2.4a

Did You Know?

In 1859 Edwin Drake drilled the first oil well in the United States near Titusville, Pennsylvania. By 1900 oil fields from Pennsylvania to Texas had been opened. As oil production rose, it fueled economic expansion.

economic conditions in China and eastern Europe convinced many people to leave their nations and move to the United States in search of a better life. Between 1870 and 1910, roughly 20 million immigrants arrived in the United States. These multitudes added to the growing industrial workforce, helping factories to increase their production and furthering the demand for industrial products.

Free Enterprise Another important factor that enabled the United States to industrialize rapidly was the free enterprise system. At the heart of this system was the profit motive, which attracted **entrepreneurs**—people who risk their capital in organizing and running a business—to manufacturing and transportation.

Another central tenet of free enterprise is the ability of businesses to operate without government control. In the late 1800s, many Americans embraced the idea of **laissez-faire** (leh·say·FAR), literally "let do," a French phrase meaning "let people do as they choose." Supporters of laissez-faire believe the government should not interfere in the economy other than to protect private property rights and maintain peace. These supporters argue that if the government regulates the economy, it increases costs and eventually hurts society more than it helps.

In many respects, the United States **practiced** laissez-faire economics in the late 1800s. State and federal governments kept taxes and spending low and did not impose costly regulations on industry. Nor did they try to control wages and prices. In other ways, the government went beyond laissez-faire and adopted policies intended to help industry, although these policies often had negative results.

By the end of the Civil War, for example, Congress had imposed new tariffs, or duties on imported goods, to protect American industry from foreign competition. While this helped American companies in the United States, it hurt those trying to sell goods overseas, because other countries raised their tariffs against American goods. In particular, it hurt farmers who sold their products to Europe. Ironically, the problems farmers faced may have helped speed up industrialization, as many rural Americans decided to leave their farms and take jobs in the new factories. In addition, by the early 1900s, many American companies were large and highly competitive. Business leaders increasingly began to push for free trade.

New Inventions A flood of inventions helped increase the nation's productive capacity and improved the network of transportation and communications that was vital to the nation's industrial growth.

NATIONAL GEOGRAPHIC Major Industries, c. 1900

Early Pennsylvania oil well ▶

Coal mining
Iron ore
Prairie
Chief manufacturing cities
Iron/Steel mills
Oil field
Railroad
Sawmills

0   200 miles
0   200 kilometers
Lambert Equal-Area projection

 Geography *Skills*

1. **Interpreting Maps** Where were most industrial cities in the Northeast located?
2. **Applying Geography Skills** What natural resources contributed to making Pittsburgh, Pennsylvania, a major steel center?

CHAPTER 3 The Birth of Modern America **245**

U Universal Access

Logical/Mathematical Have students use library and Internet resources to research the numbers and national origins of the immigrants who arrived in the United States between 1870 and 1910. Tell students to create a circle graph illustrating their findings. Remind students to color code the segments of the graph based on nationality. **OL** **CA CS3**

W Writing Support

Persuasive Writing Organize students into pairs and ask them to write speeches either encouraging high tariffs or favoring low tariffs. Make sure topics are evenly split among pairs. Have pairs take turns presenting their speeches before the class, or "Congress." **AL** **CA 11WS1.3**

R Reading Strategy

Sequencing Information Have students research one of the inventions of the late 1800s. Instruct students to create time lines for significant events related to their chosen invention. For example, a time line for the telephone might include the dates for the invention of the telephone keypad, the cordless telephone, and the cell phone. Encourage students to use library and Internet resources for this project. **OL**

Geography *Skills*

Answers:
1. on rail lines
2. iron ore and coal

Geography Skills Practice
Ask: Which states had sawmills? *(Michigan and Wisconsin)*

R₁ Reading Strategy

Connecting Ask students to spend a few minutes using the Internet to research products that General Electric makes today. Keep track of students' answers on the board. For homework, have students look around their house or apartment and keep a list of all the GE products they can find. **BL**

R₂ Reading Strategy

Sequencing Information Have students use the library or Internet to research the year that each of the inventions mentioned on this page was created. Tell students to use the information they discover to create a time line. Ask them to write a paragraph explaining their answer to the following question: **Which of these inventions do you think was the most important? Why?** *(Answers will vary.)* **OL**

✓ Reading Check

Answer: Industry in the 1800s depended on natural resources such as water, timber, coal, iron, and copper. Because these raw materials were abundant in the United States, industry could thrive.

Answers and Additional Support

New inventions led to the founding of new corporations, which produced new wealth and new jobs.

One of the most dramatic inventions in the late 1800s came in the field of communications. In 1874 a young Scottish-American inventor named **Alexander Graham Bell** suggested the idea of a telephone to his assistant, Thomas Watson. Watson recalled, "He had an idea by which he believed it would be possible to talk by telegraph." Bell worked until 1876 before he succeeded in transmitting his voice. The telephone revolutionized both business and personal communication. In 1877 Bell and others organized the Bell Telephone Company, which eventually became the American Telephone and Telegraph Company (AT&T).

Perhaps the most famous inventor of the late 1800s was **Thomas Alva Edison.** A great innovator, Edison worked tirelessly to invent new products and to improve devices created by others. He first achieved international fame in 1877 with the invention of the phonograph. Two years later, Edison perfected the lightbulb and the electric generator. His laboratory then went on to invent or improve several other major devices, including the battery and the motion picture.

R₁ In 1882 the Edison Electric Illuminating Company launched a new industry—and the transformation of American society—when it began to supply electric power to customers in New York City. In 1889 several of Edison's companies merged to form the Edison General Electric Company, which today is known as GE.

As knowledge about technology grew, almost everyone in the United States felt its effects. Shortly after the Civil War, Thaddeus Lowe invented the ice machine, the basis of the refrigerator. In the early 1870s, Gustavus Swift hired an engineer to develop a refrigerated railroad car. New inventions and standardization also improved the clothing and shoe industries. Prices

for food, clothes, shoes, and other products dropped as the United States industrialized.

✓ Reading Check **Analyzing** How much did the availability of resources aid in industrialization? Why?

The Railroads: Linking the Nation

Main Idea After the Civil War, the rapid construction of railroads accelerated the nation's industrialization and linked the country together.

Reading Connection In what ways has technology helped unify the United States in recent years? Read on to learn how railroads helped connect Americans who lived in different sections of the nation.

In 1865 the United States had about 35,000 miles of railroad track, almost all of it east of the Mississippi River. After the Civil War, railroad construction expanded dramatically, linking the distant regions of the nation in a transportation network. By 1900 the United States, now a booming industrial power, boasted more than 200,000 miles of track.

The railroad boom began in 1862 when President Abraham Lincoln signed the **Pacific Railway Act.** This act provided for the construction of a transcontinental railroad by two corporations, the Union Pacific and the Central Pacific railroad companies. To encourage rapid construction, the government offered each company land along its right-of-way. Feverish competition between the two companies developed as each sought to obtain as much public land and money as possible. On May 10, 1869, seven years after the act was signed, hundreds of spectators

Picturing **History**

Inventions of the Late 1800s The incandescent lightbulb, the telephone, the phonograph, and the gasoline-powered car were some of the inventions that changed the lives of Americans. What effect did these and other inventions have on the American economy?

R₂

Did You Know?

Nearly 50 years after Americans completed their transcontinental railroad, the Russians finished the Trans-Siberian Railroad. It ran nearly 5,800 miles (9,330 km) from Moscow in the west to Vladivostok in the east. Construction lasted from 1891 to 1916.

Picturing **History**

Answer: revolutionized business by opening up entirely new markets for inventions and goods to sell
Ask: What happened to Edison's Electric Illuminating Company? *(It eventually became today's GE.)*

NATIONAL GEOGRAPHIC Railroads, 1870 and 1890

Boston
Chicago
New York City
Washington, D.C.
San Francisco
Gulf of Mexico

ATLANTIC OCEAN

PACIFIC OCEAN

0   600 miles
0   600 kilometers
Lambert Equal-Area projection

- ☐ Pacific Time Zone
- ☐ Mountain Time Zone
- ☐ Central Time Zone
- ☐ Eastern Time Zone
- ┼┼ Railroads built by 1870
- ┼┼┼ Railroads built by 1890
- *Time zones and borders shown as of 1890

Miles of Track, 1870–1890

Total Miles of Railroad Operating (in thousands)

175
150
125
100
75
50
25
0

1870 1875 1880 1885 1890

Year

Source: *Historical Statistics of the United States: Colonial Times to 1970.*

Geography *Skills*

1. **Interpreting Maps** What part of the United States saw the greatest expansion in rail lines by 1890?
2. **Applying Geography Skills** In which time zone did the Central Pacific originate?

C Critical Thinking

Analyzing Primary Sources
Give students the following quote describing the Promontory Summit ceremony: "Workmen . . . sought advantageous positions to witness the ceremonies. . . . The officers and invited guests formed on each side of the track. . . . [A] number of spikes were driven in the two adjoining rails . . . and thus the two roads were welded into one . . . line from the Atlantic to the Pacific." Have students use the quote along with information from the text to write a newspaper article reporting the completion of the railroad. **OL**

R Reading Strategy

Inferring Tell students that before railroads stretched across the country, communities determined their own times. Have students discuss why railroads needed to standardize times. Make sure they consider the needs of railroad passengers as well as those of businesses that used the railroads. **OL**

C

gathered at Promontory Summit, Utah, as dignitaries hammered gold and silver spikes into the final rails that joined the rails and completed the first transcontinental railroad.

Railroads Spur Growth The transcontinental railroad was the first of many lines that began to crisscross the nation after the Civil War. This expansion spurred American industrial growth. By linking the nation, railroads helped increase the size of markets for many products. Huge consumers themselves, the railroads also stimulated the economy by spending extraordinary amounts of money on steel, coal, timber, and other necessities.

The railroads, which by 1865 consisted of hundreds of small unconnected lines, began consolidating. Large integrated railroad systems were able to shift cars from one section of the country to another according to seasonal needs and in order to speed long-distance transportation. To improve reliability, in 1883 the American Railway Association divided the country into four time zones, in which the same time would be kept. The new rail systems, along with more powerful locomotives, made railroad operation so efficient that the average rate per mile for a ton of

R

freight dropped from two cents in 1860 to three-fourths of a cent in 1900.

The nationwide rail network helped unite Americans in different regions. The *Omaha Daily Republican* observed in 1883 that railroads had "made the people of the country homogeneous, breaking through the peculiarities and provincialisms which marked separate and unmingling sections." This was a vast overstatement, but it recognized a significant contribution that railroads made to the nation.

The Land Grant System Building and operating railroad lines, especially across the vast unsettled regions of the West, often required more money than most private investors could raise on their own. To encourage railroad construction, the federal government gave land grants to many railroad companies. Railroads would then sell the land to settlers, real estate companies, and other businesses to raise the money they needed to build the railroad.

In the 1850s, the federal government granted individual states more than 28 million acres of public lands to give to the railroads. After the Pacific Railway Acts of 1862 and 1864, the government gave the land directly to the railroad companies.

CHAPTER 3   The Birth of Modern America   **247**

Did You Know?

Opponents of standard time called local time "God's time" because it was based on the laws of nature—the sun's position in the sky. Congress did not successfully pass a law that standardized time zones until 1918.

Geography *Skills*

Answers:
1. Great Plains
2. Pacific

Geography Skills Practice
Ask: What was the only California city that you could reach by train in 1870? *(San Francisco)*

The federal land grant system awarded railroad companies more than 120 million acres of land, an area larger than New England, New York, and Pennsylvania combined. Several railroad companies, including the Union Pacific and the Central Pacific, earned enough money from the government's generous land grants to cover much of the cost of building their lines.

Robber Barons The great wealth many railroad entrepreneurs acquired in the late 1800s led to accusations that they had built their fortunes by swindling investors and taxpayers, bribing government officials, and cheating on their contracts and debts. Bribery occurred frequently in this era, partly because the state and federal governments were so deeply entangled in funding the railroads.

When the existence of corruption in the railroad industry became public, it created the impression that all railroad entrepreneurs were robber barons—people who loot an industry and give nothing back—but the term was not always deserved. One railroad entrepreneur who was clearly not a robber baron was James J. Hill. Hill built and operated the Great Northern Railroad from St. Paul, Minnesota, to Everett, Washington, without any federal land grants or subsidies. The Great Northern became the most successful transcontinental railroad and the only one that was not eventually forced into bankruptcy.

✓ **Reading Check** **Describing** How did the railways help in the industrialization of the United States?

The Rise of Big Business

Main Idea Big business assumed a more prominent role in American life following the Civil War.

Reading Connection In a typical day, what products do you use that have been made by corporations? Read on to learn about the emergence of corporations in the late 1800s.

Before the Civil War, the personal wealth of a few people operating in partnership financed most businesses, including many early factories. Most manufacturing enterprises were very small. By 1900, everything had changed. Big businesses dominated the economy, operating vast complexes of factories, warehouses, offices, and **distribution** facilities.

The Role of Corporations Big business would not have been possible without the corporation. A **corporation** is an organization owned by many people but treated by law as though it were a single person. The people who own the corporation are called stockholders because they own shares of ownership called stock. Issuing stock allows a corporation to raise large amounts of money for big projects while spreading out the financial risk.

Before the 1830s, corporations needed charters by state legislatures. Beginning in the 1830s, states began passing general incorporation laws, allowing companies to become corporations and issue stock without such charters. With the money they raised from the sale of stock, corporations could invest in new technologies, hire a large workforce, and purchase many machines, greatly increasing their efficiency.

Small businesses with high operating costs found it difficult to compete against large corporations. At the time, many people criticized corporations for cutting prices and negotiating rebates, believing that corporations were behaving unethically. Still, many small companies were forced out of business.

The Consolidation of Industry To increase manufacturing efficiency even further, some business owners went one step further in building their business. One example is **Andrew Carnegie,** a Scottish immigrant who rose from bobbin boy in a textile

Analyzing *Political Cartoons*

Big Business Takes Over Large companies, such as Standard Oil, owned by John D. Rockefeller, could negotiate rebates from railroads that wanted his business. How did large business manage to dominate the economy?

Vertical Integration

Purchase of Companies at All Levels of Production

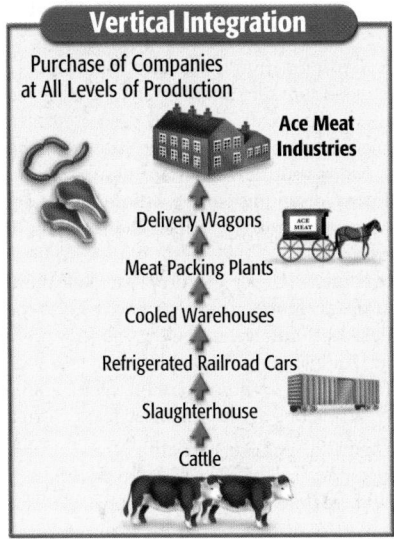

Ace Meat Industries

Delivery Wagons

Meat Packing Plants

Cooled Warehouses

Refrigerated Railroad Cars

Slaughterhouse

Cattle

Horizontal Integration

Purchase of Competing Companies in Same Industry

U.S. Oil Company

Independent Oil Refineries

Chart *Skills*

Horizontal and vertical integration were the two most common business combinations in the late 1800s. **Evaluating** Which combination do you think would yield the most efficient business? Why?

factory to owner of a steel company in Pittsburgh. Carnegie began the **vertical integration** of the steel industry. A company with vertical integration owns all of the different businesses on which it depends for its operation. Instead of paying companies for coal, lime, and iron, Carnegie's company bought coal mines, limestone quarries, and iron ore fields.

Successful business leaders like Carnegie also pushed for **horizontal integration,** or combining many firms engaged in the same type of business into one large corporation. Horizontal integration took place frequently as companies competed. When a company began to lose market share, it would often sell out to competitors to create a larger organization. By 1880, for example, a series of buyouts had enabled Standard Oil, a company owned by John D. Rockefeller and his associates, to gain control of approximately 90 percent of the oil refining industry in the United States. When a single company achieves control of an entire market, it becomes a **monopoly.** Opponents feared monopolies because they believed that a company with a monopoly could charge whatever it wanted for its products. Those who supported monopolies believed that monopolies had to keep prices low because raising prices would encourage competitors to reappear and offer the products for a lower price.

By the late 1800s, many Americans had grown suspicious of large corporations and monopolies. To preserve competition and prevent horizontal integration, many states made it illegal for one company to own stock in another without specific permission from the state legislature. In 1882 Standard Oil formed the first trust, a new way of merging businesses that did not violate the laws against owning other companies. A trust is a legal **concept** that allows one person to manage another person's property. The person who manages another person's property is called a trustee. This arrangement enabled the Standard Oil trustees to control a group of companies as if they were one large merged company.

Many companies also created new organizations called holding companies. A holding company does not produce anything itself. Instead, it owns the stock of companies that produce goods, effectively merging them into one large enterprise.

✓ **Reading Check** **Explaining** What techniques did corporations use to consolidate their industries?

Unions

Main Idea In an attempt to improve their working conditions, industrial workers came together to form unions in the late 1800s.

Reading Connection What do you think would motivate workers to form unions? Read on to learn why government and industry opposed early unions.

While workers saw some improvements in their lives, they also faced many difficulties. Their early attempts at unionization, however, were met with strong opposition.

R Reading Strategy

Connecting Have students think about monopolies that currently exist, such as utility companies. **Ask:** What safeguards are in place to make sure these companies do not overcharge for their products or services? *(Students should mention that government-appointed boards usually have to approve rate schedules and that companies have to justify any rate increases.)* Invite students to discuss how monopolies affect consumers and other businesses. **OL**
CA 11RC2.5

Review the Big Idea

Review the Big Idea for this section, "The Industrial Revolution changed the face of America." Ask students to research the way Andrew Carnegie organized the steel industry. Have them create charts similar to the charts on this page by showing how he integrated individual companies. **Ask:** What potential problems exist if one large business buys all its competitors? *(The resulting monopoly can charge high prices; it has less reason to be highly efficient.)* **AL**

✓ Reading Check

Answer: pools, vertical and horizontal integration, monopolies, trusts, and holding companies

Chart *Skills*

Answer:
Answers may vary. Both could be highly efficient if well managed. Some students may favor vertical integration since they may argue that horizontal integration reduces competition and may lead to less efficient giant businesses.

Did You Know?

In 1898, although Carnegie Steel's output had risen threefold over the previous few years, the number of workers needed to produce the steel had decreased by 400. The use of electricity to drive automatic machinery was largely responsible for the decline in the workforce.

Answers and Additional Support

Working in the United States Industrialization brought about a dramatic rise in the standard of living for all Americans. While only a few entrepreneurs became rich, real wages earned by the average worker rose by about 50 percent between 1860 and 1890. Despite these improvements, the uneven division of income between the working class and the wealthy caused resentment among workers.

In addition, life for workers in industrial America was difficult. As machines replaced skilled labor, work became monotonous. Workers had to perform highly specific, repetitive tasks and could take little pride in their work. Working conditions also often were unhealthy and dangerous. Workers breathed in lint, dust, and toxic fumes. Heavy machines lacking safety devices caused a high number of injuries.

Eventually, many workers decided they needed to organize unions to improve their working conditions. With a union, they could bargain collectively to negotiate higher wages and better working conditions.

Opposition to Unions Workers who wanted to organize a union faced several major problems. There were no laws giving workers the right to organize or requiring owners to negotiate with them. Courts frequently ruled that strikes were "conspiracies in restraint of trade," for which labor leaders might be fined or jailed.

Unions also suffered from the perception that they threatened American institutions. In the late 1800s, the ideas of Karl Marx, called **Marxism,** had become very influential in Europe. Marx argued that the basic force shaping capitalist society was the class struggle between workers and owners. He believed that workers would eventually revolt, seize control of the factories, and overthrow the government. Ultimately, Marx thought, the state would wither away, leaving a Communist society where classes did not exist. Marxism strongly shaped the thinking of European unions.

As Marxist ideas spread in Europe, tens of thousands of European immigrants began arriving in the United States. Anti-immigrant feelings already were strong in the United States. As people began to associate immigrant workers with revolution, they became increasingly suspicious of unions. These fears, as well as the government's duty to maintain law and order, often led officials to use the courts, the police, and even the army to crush strikes and break up unions.

The Struggle to Organize As early as the 1830s, craft workers began forming trade unions limited to people with specific skills. Employers were often forced to recognize and negotiate with these trade unions because they represented workers whose skills they needed. However, employers generally regarded unions as illegitimate conspiracies that interfered with their property rights. Owners of large corporations particularly opposed **industrial unions,** which united all craft workers and common laborers in a particular industry. Although workers attempted on many occasions to create large industrial unions, they rarely succeeded.

Companies used several techniques to prevent unions from forming. They required workers to take oaths or sign contracts promising not to join a union, and they hired detectives to go undercover and identify union organizers. Workers who tried to organize a union or strike were fired and placed on a blacklist—a list of "troublemakers." Once blacklisted, a laborer could get a job only by changing residence, trade, or even his or her name.

If workers formed a union, companies often used a lockout to break it. They locked workers out of the property and refused to pay them. If the union called a strike, employers would hire replacement workers, or strikebreakers, also known as scabs.

In many cases the confrontations with owners and the government led to violence and bloodshed. A riot at Haymarket Square in Chicago led to the eventual discrediting of the Knights of Labor, the first nationwide industrial union. Two strikes, the Great Railroad Strike of 1877 and the Pullman Strike of 1894, involved rail workers who responded to wage cuts. Both times, the army was sent to restore order.

Picturing **History**

Unsafe Working Conditions Workers in the late 1800s often faced unsafe working conditions. Many began to join labor unions in an attempt to improve these conditions. What unsafe conditions does this photograph of a steel mill show?

250 CHAPTER 3 The Birth of Modern America

Picturing **History**

Answer: Workers are dangerously close to molten steel.
Ask: What problems resulted from unsafe working conditions? *(injuries, deaths, and illnesses)*

Did You Know?

On September 6, 1869, 179 coal miners were trapped and died during a fire at the Avondale Coal Mine in Luzerne County, Pennsylvania. Union leader John Siney urged his fellow miners to unionize by saying, "Men, if you must die with your boots on, die for your families, your homes, your country, but do not longer consent to die like rats in a trap."

The American Federation of Labor

Although large-scale industrial unions generally failed in the late 1800s, trade unions continued to prosper. In 1886 delegates from over 20 of the nation's trade unions organized the **American Federation of Labor** (AFL). The AFL's first leader was **Samuel Gompers.** His approach to labor relations, which he called "plain and simple" unionism, helped unions to become accepted in American society.

▲ *Samuel Gompers*

Gompers believed that unions should stay out of politics. He was willing to use the strike but preferred to negotiate. Under Gompers's leadership, the AFL had three main goals. First, it tried to convince companies to recognize unions and to agree to collective bargaining. Second, it pushed for **closed shops,** meaning that companies could only hire union members. Third, it promoted an eight-hour workday.

By 1900 the AFL was the biggest union in the country, with over 500,000 members. Still, at that time, the AFL represented less than 15 percent of all non-farm workers. All unions represented only 18 percent. As the 1900s began, the vast majority of workers remained unorganized, and unions were relatively weak.

Working Women

By 1900 women made up more than 18 percent of the labor force. The type of jobs women did outside the home in the late 1800s and early 1900s reflected society's ideas about what constituted "women's work." Roughly one-third of women worked as domestic servants. Another third worked as teachers, nurses, sales clerks, and secretaries. The remaining third were employed in light industrial jobs that people believed appropriate to their gender. Many worked in the garment industry and food processing plants.

Women received less pay than men even when they performed the same jobs. It was assumed that a woman had a man helping to support her, either her father or her husband, and that a man needed higher wages to support a family. For this reason, most unions, including the AFL, excluded women.

In 1903 two women, Mary Kenney O'Sullivan and Leonora O'Reilly, decided to establish the Women's Trade Union League (WTUL), the first national association dedicated to promoting women's labor issues. The WTUL pushed for an eight-hour work day, the creation of a minimum wage, an end to evening work for women, and the abolition of child labor.

✓ **Reading Check** **Comparing** What specific problems did workers want to remedy by forming unions?

HISTORY Online Study Central

For help with the concepts in this section of *American Vision: Modern Times* go to tav.mt.glencoe.com and click on *Study Central.*

SECTION 2 ASSESSMENT

Checking for Understanding

1. **Vocabulary** Define: gross national product, entrepreneur, laissez-faire, practice, distribution, corporation, horizontal integration, vertical integration, monopoly, concept, Marxism, industrial union, closed shop.

2. **People and Terms** Identify: Alexander Graham Bell, Thomas Alva Edison, Pacific Railway Act, Andrew Carnegie, American Federation of Labor, Samuel Gompers.

3. **Identify** the major inventions that helped spur economic growth.

Reviewing Big Ideas

4. **Explaining** What impact did the development of large businesses have on the economy of the United States?

Critical Thinking

5. **Historical Analysis** **Synthesizing** What role did the federal government play in increasing industrialization in the United States after the Civil War? **CA HI2; HI3**

6. **Analyzing** Why did attempts in the late 1800s to form labor unions fail?

7. **Organizing** Use a graphic organizer similar to the one below to list ways business leaders in the late 1800s tried to eliminate competition.

Attempts to Eliminate Competition

Analyzing Visuals

8. Study the map and graph on railroads and miles of track on page 247. Then make up a quiz of at least five questions based on the information presented.

Writing About History

9. **Persuasive Writing** Imagine that you are an American worker living in one of the nation's large cities. Write a letter to a friend explaining why you support or oppose the work of labor unions. **CA 11WA2.3b**

C Critical Thinking

Making Inferences Have students discuss in class why unions were not more successful in organizing workers. **OL**

ASSESS

Resources for page 251

Use these resources to assess student mastery.

📂 Section Quiz 3-2

📂 Reading Essentials and Study Guide 3-2

⊙ Interactive Tutor Self-Assessment CD-ROM

📂 California Standards Practice, Grade 11

✓ **Reading Check**

Answer: Workers wanted higher wages and better, safer working conditions.

HISTORY Online

Study Central provides audio summaries, interactive games, and online graphic organizers to help students review section content.

CLOSE

Summarizing Ask students to pick the development in this section they think had the most impact on the United States. In a paragraph, have them describe the development and why they chose it. **BL**

SECTION 2 ASSESSMENT ANSWERS

1. Content vocabulary is boldfaced and highlighted in yellow. Academic vocabulary is boldfaced.

2. Alexander Graham Bell *(p. 246)*, Thomas Alva Edison *(p. 246)*, Pacific Railway Act *(p. 246)*, Andrew Carnegie *(p. 248)*, American Federation of Labor *(p. 251)*, Samuel Gompers *(p. 251)*

3. telephone, electric lighting, railroads, refrigerated railroad car

4. Big businesses created cheaper products due to their economies of scale but it put pressure on workers to maintain their rights as laborers.

5. Congress subsidized railroads; sold lands below market value

6. Laws did not give workers the right to unionize. Courts often ruled against unionization efforts.

7. pools, trusts, monopolies, vertical and horizontal integration

8. Students' quizzes will vary. Students should include answers for their quiz questions.

9. Students' letters will vary.

FOCUS

TEACH

R Reading Strategy

Evaluating Understanding people's points of view is vital to interpreting their opinions. **Ask: Have you ever experienced a situation in which two people viewed the same circumstances very differently? What was the outcome?** Explain to students that John D. Rockefeller and George Rice saw the success of the Standard Oil Company from opposite points of view. **BL**

CA 11RC2.4

Answers and Additional Support

You're the Historian

Investigating Standard Oil

By the 1880s, the Standard Oil Company, under the direction of John D. Rockefeller and his associates, had gained control of more than 90 percent of the oil refining business in the United States. Did Standard Oil use unfair tactics? The United States Industrial Commission investigated, calling Rockefeller himself to testify. Rockefeller said his success was due to the efficiency of his company. George Rice, an independent refiner from Marietta, Ohio, told the Industrial Commission that Standard Oil's advantage was criminal collusion with the railroads. Was he right? You're the historian.

Read the following excerpts from the Industrial Commission hearings of 1899. Then complete the questions and activities on the next page.

John D. Rockefeller

Standard Oil stock

From John D. Rockefeller's testimony

Question: To what advantages, or favors, or methods of management do you ascribe chiefly the success of the Standard Oil Company?

Answer [Rockefeller]: I ascribe the success of the Standard to its consistent policy to make the volume of its business large through the merits and cheapness of its products. It has spared no expense in finding, securing, and utilizing the best and cheapest methods of manufacture. It has sought for the best superintendents and workmen and paid the best wages. It has not hesitated to sacrifice old machinery and old plants for new and better ones. It has placed its manufactories at the points where they could supply markets at the least expense. It has not only sought markets for its principal products, but for all possible by-products, sparing no expense in introducing them to the public.

It has not hesitated to invest millions of dollars in methods of cheapening the gathering and distribution of oils by pipe lines, special cars, tank steamers, and tank wagons. . . .

Question: What are, in your judgment, the chief advantages from industrial combinations—(a) financially to stockholders; (b) to the public?

Answer: All the advantages which can be derived from a cooperation of person and aggregation of capital. . . . It is too late to argue about advantages of industrial combinations. They are a necessity. And if Americans are to have the privilege of extending their business in all the States of the Union, and into foreign countries as well, they are a necessity on a large scale, and require the agency of more than one corporation. Their chief advantages are:

1. Command of necessary capital.
2. Extension of limits of business.
3. Increase the number of persons interested in the business.
4. Economy in the business.
5. Improvements and economies which are derived from knowledge of many interested persons of wide experience.
6. Power to give the public improved products at less prices and still make a profit from stockholders.
7. Permanent work and good wages for laborers.

Cartoon criticizing Standard Oil

EXTENDING THE CONTENT

Point of View Historians disagree about some of the issues surrounding the business practices employed by John D. Rockefeller and the Standard Oil Trust. For example, while it was common practice for the railroads to offer rebates to big shippers in a variety of industries, some historical accounts indicate that in addition to rebates, Rockefeller got inside information from the railroads about the business activities of his competitors. Discrepancies can also be found in historical accounts of the business practices of George Rice. Some accounts characterize Rice as a reputable businessman, while others paint him as a charlatan and con man.

Oil derricks

From George Rice's testimony

I am a citizen of the United States. . . . Producer of petroleum for more than 30 years, and a refiner of same for 20 years, but my refinery has been shut down during the past 3 years, owing to the powerful and all-prevailing machinations of the Standard Oil Trust, in criminal collusion and conspiracy with the railroads to destroy my business of 20 years of patient industry, toil, and money in building up, wholly by and through unlawful freight discriminations. I have been driven from pillar to post, from one railway line to another, for 20 years, in the absolutely vain endeavor to get equal and just freight rates with the Standard Oil Trust, so as to be able to run my refinery at anything approaching a profit, but which I have been utterly

unable to do. I have had to consequently shut down, with my business absolutely ruined and my refinery idle. This has been a very sad, bitter, and ruinous experience for me to endure, but I have endeavored to the best of my circumstances and ability to combat it the utmost I could for many a long waiting year, expecting relief through the honest and proper execution of our laws, which have as yet, however, never come. . . .

Outside of rebates or freight discriminations I had no show with the Standard Oil trust, because of their unlawfully acquired monopoly, by which they could temporarily cut only my customers' prices, and below cost, leaving the balance of the town, nine-tenths, uncut. This they can easily do without any appreciable harm to

their general trade, and thus effectually wipe out all competition, as fully set forth. Standard Oil prices generally were so high that I could sell my goods 2 to 3 cents a gallon below their prices and make a nice profit, but these savage attacks and cuts upon my customers' goods, and their consequent loss, plainly showed them their power for evil, and the uselessness to contend against such odds, and they would buy no more of my oil. . . .

Understanding the Issue

1. What potential advantages could companies like Standard Oil offer consumers?
2. What did George Rice believe to be the reason Standard Oil was so successful?
3. How would you assess the credibility of the two accounts?

Activities

1. **Investigate** Today many industries, unions, and special interest groups lobby Congress for favorable legislation. What are the most powerful groups? How do they operate?
2. **Check the News** Are there any companies that recently have been investigated for unfair or monopolistic practices? Collect headlines and news articles and create a bulletin board display.

You're the Historian

R Reading Strategy

Organizing Information Have each student create a two-column chart. In the first column, tell them to list John D. Rockefeller's main arguments. In the second column, have them list George Rice's main arguments. (*Rockefeller: Standard Oil offers the best and cheapest product; industrial combinations are a necessity; industrial combinations offer many advantages, including the power to sell improved products at lower prices and still make a profit. Rice: Standard Oil's collusion with the railroads is illegal; Standard Oil has illegally wiped out all competition; Standard Oil drastically cuts prices to eliminate competition.*) **Ask:** Who do you think made the better arguments: Rockefeller or Rice? Instruct students to write a paragraph or journal entry explaining their answer.
OL **CA** 11RC2.5

W Writing Support

Expository Writing Have students write essays expressing their points of view on the controversy described in this passage. Instruct them to include enough background information in their essays so that someone not familiar with this topic will be able to understand the main ideas. Students may consult one of the popular weekly newsmagazines to see examples of well-written essays. Be sure they express their opinions in the essays. **OL** **CA** 11WS1.3

ASSESS/CLOSE

Have students answer the Understanding the Issue questions and activities.

ANSWERS TO UNDERSTANDING THE ISSUE

1. According to Rockefeller's testimony, consumers would benefit from companies similar to Standard Oil because they would get a better product at a lower price. In addition, these companies claimed to offer permanent work and good wages for laborers.
2. Standard Oil paid little to ship its oil compared to other refiners. Standard Oil also cut its prices drastically to entice competitors' customers so that it could

later eliminate the competition.
3. Students' answers will vary. Students should be able to defend their positions.

Activities Answers
1. Students' answers will vary. You may want students to work in pairs to conduct the necessary research.
2. Students' answers will vary. Recommend that students look in financial newspapers for examples.

FOCUS

Project **Daily Focus Skills Transparency 3-3** and have students answer the question.

Guide to Reading

Understanding Vocabulary: Have students use a dictionary to look up the meanings of the content vocabulary words and the academic vocabulary words. Ask them to write paragraphs using at least three of the vocabulary words from this section.

Answers to Graphic: crime, violence, fire, disease, pollution

Unpacking the Standards

Students will be able to:

- Describe the arrival of thousands of European and Asian immigrants to the United States after the Civil War.
- Explain the impact of immigration and industrialization on the growth of American cities.

Answers and Additional Support

SECTION 3 Immigration and Urbanization

Guide to Reading

Connection
In the previous section, you learned about the growth of industrialization, big business, and labor unions. In this section, you will discover how immigration affected the United States and how the country shifted to a more urban society.

Main Idea
- After the Civil War, millions of immigrants from Europe and Asia settled in the United States. (p. 255)
- During the three decades following the Civil War, the United States transformed rapidly from a rural nation to a more urban one. (p. 258)

Content Vocabulary
nativism, tenement, political machine, graft

Academic Vocabulary
induce, commission

People and Terms to Identify
Chinese Exclusion Act, William M. "Boss" Tweed

Places to Locate
Ellis Island, Angel Island

Reading Objectives
- **Analyze** the effects of immigration on national policy.

- **Evaluate** the changes that cities experienced because of the increased population.

Reading Strategy
As you read about urbanization in the United States in the late 1800s, complete a graphic organizer similar to the one below by filling in the problems people in the nation's urban areas faced.

Problems in Urban Areas

Preview of Events

♦1880	♦1885	♦1890	♦1895
1882 Chinese Exclusion Act passed	**1885** First steel girder construction used in building in Chicago	**1887** American Protective Association founded	**1890** Jacob Riis publishes *How the Other Half Lives*	**1892** Ellis Island immigration center opens

The following are the main History–Social Science Standards covered in this section.

11.1.4 Examine the effects of the Civil War and Reconstruction and of the Industrial Revolution, including demographic shifts and the emergence in the late 19th century of the United States as a world power.

11.2 Students analyze the relationship among the rise of industrialization, large-scale rural-to-urban migration, and massive immigration from Southern and Eastern Europe.

11.2.1 Know the effects of industrialization on living and working conditions, including the portrayal of working conditions and food safety in Upton Sinclair's *The Jungle.*

11.2.2 Describe the changing landscape, including the growth of cities linked by industry and trade, and the development of cities divided according to race, ethnicity, and class.

11.2.3 Trace the effect of the Americanization movement.

⚜ The Big Idea ⚜

The Industrial Revolution changed the face of America. In the three decades following the Civil War, the population of urban areas in the United States approximately tripled. Millions of immigrants came to the United States in search of better lives and jobs created by the Industrial Revolution. Many people in rural areas also migrated to the cities to find better-paying jobs and the modern conveniences city life offered. New materials for buildings and bridges spurred construction and required more workers. The increase in immigrants eventually led to feelings of nativism and bans on immigration. As city populations increased, overcrowding became a problem. People lived in cramped tenements with poor ventilation. Crime was common, and diseases spread quickly in the crowded and unclean streets and buildings. Political machines developed as a way to address some of these problems.

11.2.4 Analyze the effect of urban political machines and responses to them by immigrants and middle-class reformers.

11.3.3 Cite incidences of religious intolerance in the United States (e.g., persecution of Mormons, anti-Catholic sentiment, anti-Semitism).

SECTION RESOURCES

📁 Print Material
- Reproducible Lesson Plan 3-3
- Guided Reading Activity 3-3
- Reading Essentials and Study Guide 3-3
- Active Reading Note-Taking Guide 3-3

📖 Transparencies
- Daily Focus Skills Transparency 3-3
- Section Graphic Organizer Transparency 3-3

Technology
- 💿 Interactive Tutor Self-Assessment CD-ROM
- 💿 ExamView® Pro Testmaker CD-ROM
- 💿 Presentation Plus! CD-ROM

Immigration

Main Idea After the Civil War, millions of immigrants from Europe and Asia settled in the United States.

Reading Connection Think about the ethnic composition of your community. What groups are represented? Read on to learn about the neighborhoods in which immigrants to the United States settled in the late 1800s.

By 1900, more than half of all immigrants in the United States were eastern and southern Europeans, including Italians, Greeks, Poles, Slavs, Slovaks, Russians, and Armenians.

★ An American Story ★

Samuel Goldwyn was born in Warsaw, Poland, in 1879. His family lived in a tiny two-room apartment. As Jews the Goldwyn family feared the pogroms—anti-Jewish riots—that often erupted in the city. At age 16, Goldwyn set out for America, first walking 500 miles to the port of Hamburg, Germany. When he arrived in the United States, Goldwyn worked as a floor sweeper and then as a cutter in a glove factory, putting in 13-hour days. At night, he went to school. Within two years he was a foreman in the factory, and soon after he became a successful glove salesman.

In 1913 Goldwyn visited a nickelodeon, an early movie theater. As he watched the film, he became convinced that this new industry would grow into something big. He used his savings to set up a film company, and in 1914 he released his first movie. The film was an instant success. During his career, Goldwyn helped found three film companies: Paramount Studios, Metro-Goldwyn-Mayer (MGM), and United Artists. All three companies still make movies today. Looking back on his rise from poverty to wealth, Goldwyn commented:

❝When I was a kid . . . the only place I wanted to go was America. I had heard them talking about America, about how free people were in America. . . . Even then America, actually only the name of a faraway country, was a vision of paradise.❞

—adapted from *Goldwyn: A Biography*

Many of the 14 million immigrants who came to the United States between 1860 and 1900 were eastern European Jews. Like Samuel Goldwyn, they came to make a new life for themselves.

Europeans Flood Into the United States

Europeans abandoned their homelands and headed to the United States for many reasons. Many poor rural farmers came simply because the United States had plenty of jobs available and few immigration restrictions. Others moved to avoid forced military service, which in some nations could last for many years. Some, especially Jews living in Poland and Russia, fled to avoid religious persecution.

By the late 1800s, most European governments had made moving to the United States easy. Immigrants were allowed to take their savings with them, and most countries had repealed old laws that had forced peasants to stay in their villages and had banned skilled workers from leaving the country.

Getting to the United States was often very difficult. Most immigrants booked passage in steerage, the most basic and cheapest accommodations on a steamship. In steerage, passengers faced "crowds everywhere, ill smelling bunks, [and] uninviting washrooms," as one observer put it. At the end of a 14-day journey, the passengers usually disembarked at **Ellis Island** in New York Harbor, which served as the processing center for many immigrants arriving on the East Coast after 1892. Most immigrants passed through Ellis Island in about a day. In Ellis Island's

Samuel Goldwyn ▼

TEACH

U Universal Access

Logical/Mathematical Provide the census data below and have students create four circle charts to show the proportion of the U.S. population made up of persons born in the United States and persons born in foreign countries. **OL**

	U.S. Born	Foreign Born
1870	32,676,000	5,480,000
1880	42,869,000	6,499,000
1890	52,919,000	9,198,000
1900	64,344,000	10,263,000

S Skill Practice

Historical Interpretation
Organize students into groups of three to trace the arrival of an immigrant family in the United States. Each group should choose a different nationality and point of entry. Have students discuss the reasons why immigrants left their native countries, where they arrived in the United States, and how they settled into life in their new country. Students should also point out the problems the immigrants faced in their new lives. **OL** **CA** CS3; HI1; HI2; HI3

Resources for page 255

*Have students read more about the immigrant experience by assigning "All Right! Hurry Up!" in the **American Literature Readings 1**.*

*Have students read more about immigrants and the Statue of Liberty in **Linking Past and Present Activity 3**.*

More Skill Practice

Narrative Writing Have students imagine that they are immigrants arriving in the United States from Europe in the late 1800s. Tell them to write letters to their families back home describing the passage across the Atlantic and arrival at Ellis Island. **OL** **CA** 11WA2.1a; 11WA2.1c

ABCNEWS INTERACTIVE™

▣ VIDEOCASSETTE
Historic America Electronic Field Trips
View **Tape 2, Chapter 7:** "Ellis Island."

U Universal Access

Interpersonal Oral histories are a good way to preserve the immigrant experience. Have students interview persons who immigrated to the United States. Their questions might include: reasons for immigrating to the United States; a description of the journey; feelings upon entering the United States; and problems faced, such as finding employment or overcoming the language barrier. **OL**

R Reading Strategy

Visualizing Write the word *Assimilation* in a circle on the board. Have students add spokes out from the circle and label each spoke with a way in which immigrants during this period were asked to assimilate into American culture. Repeat the process by writing *Assimilation Today* in another circle on the board. Discuss how the expectation of immigrants to assimilate has changed and how it is still the same. **OL**

Answers and Additional Support

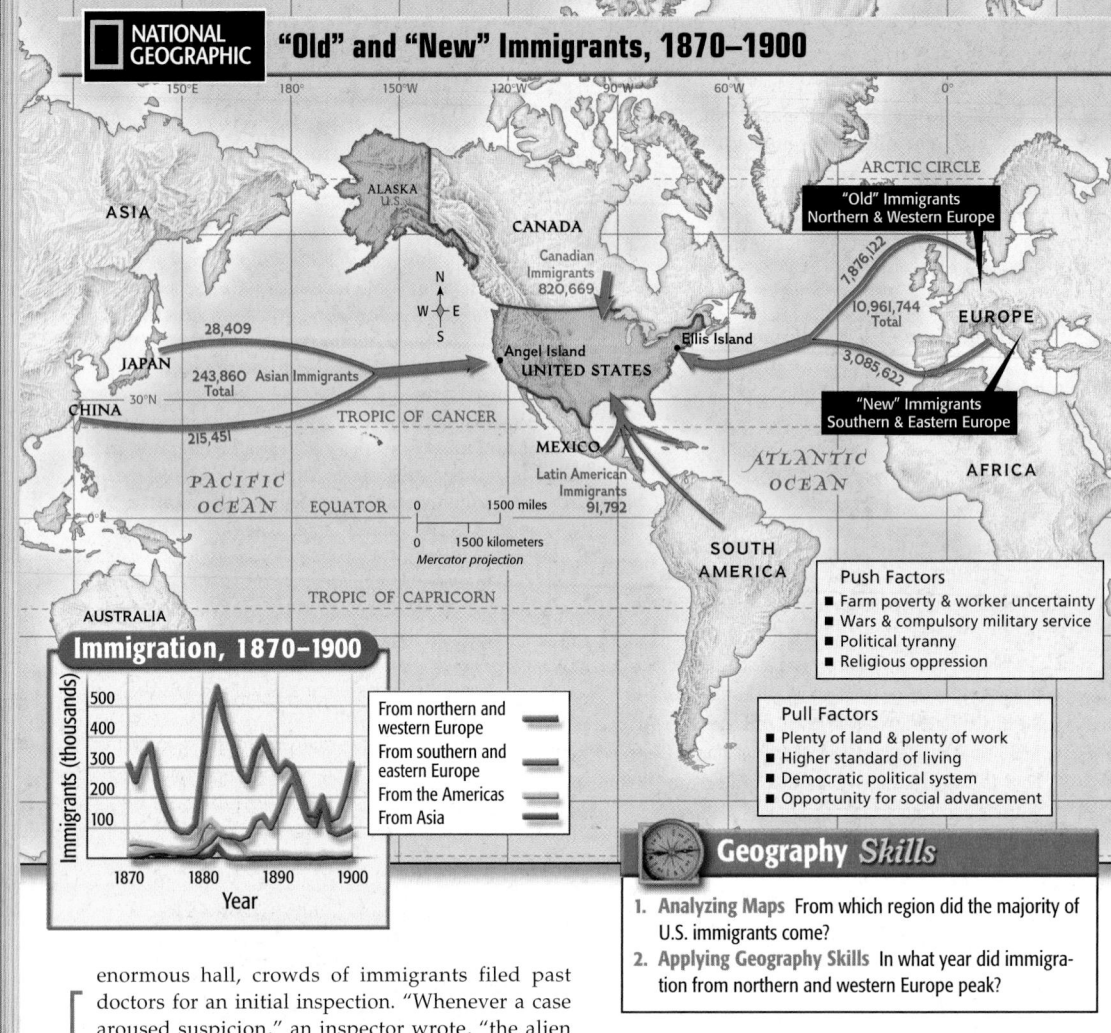

"Old" and "New" Immigrants, 1870–1900

Push Factors
- Farm poverty & worker uncertainty
- Wars & compulsory military service
- Political tyranny
- Religious oppression

Pull Factors
- Plenty of land & plenty of work
- Higher standard of living
- Democratic political system
- Opportunity for social advancement

Immigration, 1870–1900

From northern and western Europe
From southern and eastern Europe
From the Americas
From Asia

Geography Skills

1. **Analyzing Maps** From which region did the majority of U.S. immigrants come?
2. **Applying Geography Skills** In what year did immigration from northern and western Europe peak?

---

enormous hall, crowds of immigrants filed past doctors for an initial inspection. "Whenever a case aroused suspicion," an inspector wrote, "the alien was set aside in a cage apart from the rest . . . and his coat lapel or shirt marked with colored chalk" to indicate the reason for the isolation. Newcomers who failed the inspection might be separated from their families and returned to Europe.

Those immigrants who stayed often settled in larger cities. By the 1890s, they made up significant percentages of some of the country's largest cities, including New York, Chicago, Milwaukee, and Detroit. In the cities, immigrants lived in neighborhoods that were often separated into ethnic groups, such as "Little Italy" or the Jewish "Lower East Side" in New York City. There they spoke their native languages and re-created the churches, synagogues, clubs, and newspapers of their homelands. Jacob Riis, a Danish-born journalist, observed in 1890 that a map

of New York City, "colored to designate nationalities, would show more stripes than on the skin of a zebra."

How well immigrants adjusted depended partly on how quickly they learned English and adapted to American culture. Immigrants also tended to adjust well if they had marketable skills or money, or if they settled among members of their own ethnic group.

As many as one in three immigrants returned to Europe shortly after coming to the United States. Some had never planned to stay and had come simply to make a little money before returning home.

Asian Immigration to America Chinese immigrants began crossing the Pacific to arrive in the United States in the mid-1800s. By that time, China's population had reached about 430 million, and the

---

 Geography *Skills*

Answers:
1. Europe
2. around 1882

Geography Skills Practice
Ask: Where did most Asian immigrants arrive in the United States? *(Angel Island, California)*

Did You Know?

About one out of five newcomers to Ellis Island was marked with an "H" for heart problems, "K" for hernias, "Sc" for scalp problems, or "X" for mental disability.

country was suffering from severe unemployment, poverty, and famine.

The 1848 discovery of gold in California began to lure Chinese immigrants to the United States. Then, in 1850, the Taiping Rebellion erupted in their homeland. This insurrection against the Chinese government took some 20 million lives and caused such suffering that thousands of Chinese left for the United States. In the early 1860s, as the Central Pacific Railroad began construction of its portion of the transcontinental railroad, the demand for railroad workers further increased Chinese immigration.

Chinese immigrants settled mainly in western cities, where they often worked as laborers or servants or in skilled trades. Others worked as merchants. Because native-born Americans kept them out of many businesses, some Chinese immigrants opened their own.

Another group of Asians, the Japanese, also immigrated to the United States. Until 1910, however, their numbers remained small. Between 1900 and 1908, this number increased. Large numbers of Japanese migrated to the United States as Japan began building both an industrial economy and an empire. Both developments disrupted the economy of Japan and caused hardships for its people, thus stimulating emigration.

Until 1910 Asian immigrants arriving in San Francisco first stopped at a two-story shed at the wharf. As many as 500 people at a time were often squeezed into this structure, which Chinese immigrants from Canton called *muk uk*, or "wooden house."

In January 1910, California opened barracks on **Angel Island** to house and process the Asian immigrants. Most of the immigrants were young males in their teens or twenties, who nervously awaited the results of their immigration hearings in dormitories packed with double or triple tiers of bunks. This unpleasant delay could last for months. On the walls of the detention barracks, the immigrants wrote anonymous poems in pencil or ink. Some even carved their verse into the wood.

The Resurgence of Nativism Eventually, the wave of immigration led to increased feelings of nativism on the part of many Americans. **Nativism** is a preference for native-born people and a desire to limit immigration. In the 1840s and 1850s, it had focused primarily on Irish immigrants. Now anti-immigrant feelings focused on Asians, Jews, and eastern Europeans.

Nativists opposed immigration for various reasons. Some feared that the influx of Catholics from Ireland and southern and eastern Europe would swamp the mostly Protestant United States and give the Catholic Church too much power in the American government. Many labor unions also opposed immigration, arguing that immigrants would work for low wages or accept work as strikebreakers, thus undermining American-born workers.

In the Northeast and Midwest, increased feelings of nativism led to the founding of two major anti-immigrant organizations. The American Protective Association was formed in 1887 to stop Catholic immigration. Its membership declined after the economic recession of 1893 ended. In the West, Denis Kearney—himself an Irish immigrant—organized the Workingman's Party of California in the 1870s to fight Chinese immigration. The party won seats in California's legislature and made opposition to Chinese immigration a national issue.

Such concern over unchecked immigration stimulated the passage of a new federal law. Enacted in 1882, the law banned convicts, paupers, and the mentally disabled from immigrating to the United States. The new law also placed a 50¢ head tax on each

Angel Island Over 200,000 immigrants from Japan and China arrived on the West Coast during the late 1800s.

U Universal Access

Visual/Spatial Organize students into groups of three or four. Have each group create a poster encouraging Chinese citizens to move to the United States in the mid-1800s to help with railroad construction. Invite students to explain their posters to the class, and then display the posters around the classroom. **BL**

S Skill Practice

Conducting Research Have students use library and Internet resources to research Angel Island, including photographs of the arrival of immigrants to the island. Have students continue their research to answer the following questions: What is the process for Asian immigrants arriving in the United States today? What about the process has changed or remained the same over the last century? Instruct students to present their findings in a one-page report. **OL**
CA HR4

Review the Big Idea

Review the Big Idea for this section, "The Industrial Revolution changed the face of America." **Ask:** What impact did the immigration of people from Asia have on the United States? *(Many Americans opposed the large influx of immigrants. The Workingman's Party of California was formed to fight Chinese immigration, and the Chinese Exclusion Act severely restricted the Chinese.)* **OL**

COOPERATIVE LEARNING ACTIVITY

Sharing Information Divide the class in half. Tell students in the first group to research the American Protective Association, and those in the second group to research the Workingman's Party of California. Encourage students to use library and Internet resources to conduct their research. Then pair students with partners from the other group to exchange information. **OL**

U **Universal Access**

Logical/Mathematical Have students use library and Internet resources to research the number of Chinese immigrants in 1943. Using this information and their textbooks, have them plot bar graphs that show the numbers of Chinese immigrants to the United States in 1890, 1900, and 1943. **Ask: Why did the number of Chinese immigrants continue to decrease?** *(The Chinese Exclusion Act limited Chinese immigration.)* **OL**

R **Reading Strategy**

Predicting Have students brainstorm what problems they predict might have arisen from rapid urbanization in the United States after the Civil War. Keep track of students' answers on a sheet of paper. After reading this section, have students review the list and revise it to reflect the information in the text. **OL**

✓Reading Check

Answer: Some nativists feared that the influx of Catholics from Ireland and southern and eastern Europe would give the Catholic Church too much power in the American government. Many labor unions also opposed immigration because immigrants would work for low wages or accept work as strikebreakers.

Different Viewpoints

Two Views of Immigration

The history of immigration to the United States has been both celebrated and criticized. Many millions of immigrants arrived in the United States in the late 1800s. The newcomers sought opportunity, enriched American culture, and caused concerns. Here, two political cartoons address the immigration issue.

Pro-Immigration

Uncle Sam plays the role of Noah in this cartoon. As immigrants file two by two into the safety of the ark, they leave behind the dangers of Europe that are darkening the sky. A sign lists some reasons people came to the United States to begin a new life.

Anti-Immigration

"Columbia's Unwelcome Guests" shows another view of immigration. In this 1885 cartoon, the figure of Columbia bars entry to anarchists, Socialists, and Communists who enter from the sewers of Europe's darker society. Some of the inscriptions on the column pedestal beside Columbia read "Anarchy is not liberty," and "When a Man's Rights End, His Neighbor's Begin."

Learning From History

1. **Historical Analysis** According to the cartoon, why were people concerned about immigrants coming to the United States? **CA CS3; HI1; HI3**
2. Which cartoon best expresses your own views on immigration today? Why?

newcomer. That same year, Congress passed the **Chinese Exclusion Act.** This law barred Chinese immigration for 10 years and prevented the Chinese already in the country from becoming citizens. The Chinese in the United States protested that white Americans did not oppose immigration by Italians, Irish, or Germans. Some Chinese organized letter-writing campaigns, petitioned the president, and even filed suit in federal court.

All efforts proved fruitless. Congress renewed the Chinese Exclusion Act in 1892 and then made it permanent in 1902. In 1890 the number of Chinese living in the United States totaled 105,000. By 1900 that number had dropped to just above 74,000. In the 40 years after the passage of the act, the Chinese population in the United States continued to decrease. The act was not repealed until 1943.

✓Reading Check **Explaining** Why did nativists oppose immigration?

258   CHAPTER 3   The Birth of Modern America

Urbanization

R **Main Idea** During the three decades following the Civil War, the United States transformed rapidly from a rural nation to a more urban one.

Reading Connection Do you currently live in an urban, rural, or suburban area? In which of these kinds of areas do you hope to live 10 years from now? Why? Read on to learn what life was like in the late 1800s for residents of urban communities in the United States.

During the three decades after the Civil War, the urban population of the United States—those living in towns with a population of 2,500 or more—grew from around 10 million in 1870 to more than

Answers and Additional Support

Different Viewpoints

Answers:
1. feared anarchy, socialism, and communism
2. Students' answers will vary, but should be defended with reasons.

Resources for page 258

*Have students learn more about immigration to the United States in **Moments in Time, Unit 4: Division Within (1876–1901).***

30 million in 1900. New York City alone, which had over 800,000 inhabitants in 1860, grew to almost 3.5 million by 1900. In 1840 the United States had only 131 cities; by 1900 that number had risen to over 1,700.

The Growth of American Cities Most of the immigrants who poured into the United States in the late 1800s lacked the money to buy farms and the education to obtain higher-paying jobs. They remained in the nation's growing cities, where they toiled long hours for little pay in the rapidly expanding factories. Despite the harshness of their new lives, most immigrants found that the move had still improved their standard of living.

The United States offered immigrants a chance at social mobility, or moving upward in society. Although only a few immigrants rose from poverty to great wealth, many seized the opportunities the American system offered and rose from the working class to the middle class. Although some immigrants faced prejudice, most Americans accepted the idea that people in the lower classes could rise in society.

Many rural Americans also began moving to the cities at this time. Farmers moved to the cities because urban areas offered more and better-paying jobs than did rural areas. Cities had much to offer, too—bright lights, running water, and modern plumbing, plus many things to do and see, including museums, libraries, and theaters.

The New Urban Environment As millions of people flooded into the nation's cities, engineers and architects developed new approaches to housing and transporting such a large number of people. Demand raised the price of land, **inducing** owners to grow upward rather than outward. Soon, tall steel frame buildings called skyscrapers began to appear on American skylines. Chicago's ten-story Home Insurance Building, built in 1885, was the first skyscraper, but other buildings quickly dwarfed it. New York City boasted more skyscrapers than any other city in the world. With limited land, New Yorkers had to build up, not out.

Various kinds of mass transit developed in the late 1800s to move huge numbers of people around cities quickly. In 1890 horsecars—railroad cars pulled by horses—moved about 70 percent of urban traffic in the United States. More than 20 cities, beginning with San Francisco in 1873, installed cable cars, which were pulled along tracks by underground cables. In 1887 engineer Frank J. Sprague developed the electric trolley car.

The Technology of Urbanization

Before the mid-1800s, few buildings exceeded four or five stories. To make wooden and stone structures taller required enormously thick walls in the lower levels.

By the late 1800s, steel companies were making girders capable of bearing a building's weight. Walls no longer had to support the building—a steel frame skeleton was all that was needed. Meanwhile, Elisha Otis invented the safety elevator in 1852, and by the late 1880s, the first electric elevators had been installed, making tall buildings practical.

Steel also changed the way bridges were built. New technology enabled engineers to suspend bridges from steel towers using cables also made of steel. Using this technique, John A. Roebling, a German American engineer, designed New York's Brooklyn Bridge—the largest suspension bridge in the world at the time it was completed in 1883.

Brooklyn Bridge under construction

New York City's Flatiron Building

NATIONAL GEOGRAPHIC
MOMENT in HISTORY

TEEMING TENEMENTS

The swelling tide of immigration to U.S. cities in the late 1800s led to deplorable living conditions and almost unbearable congestion. By 1890, more than two-thirds of New York's 1.5 million residents lived in overcrowded apartment buildings called tenements. On the Lower East Side, one of the most densely populated areas in the world, people frequented vibrant outdoor markets such as this one on Hester Street for goods from eggs to rugs to pots and pans. Gossip, haggling, and cries of street peddlers— mostly in Yiddish in this Jewish neighborhood—echoed down the street from dawn to dusk.

In the largest cities, congestion became so bad that engineers began looking for ways to move mass transit off the streets. Chicago responded by building an elevated railroad, while Boston, followed by New York, built America's first subway systems.

Separation by Class In the growing cities, wealthy people and the working class lived in different parts of town. So too did the middle class. The boundaries between neighborhoods can still be seen in many cities today.

During the last half of the 1800s, the wealthiest families established fashionable districts in the hearts of cities. Americans with enough money could choose to construct a feudal castle, an English manor house, or a Tuscan villa. In New York, Cornelius Vanderbilt's grandson **commissioned** a $3 million French château equipped with a two-story dining room and a marble bathroom.

American industrialization also helped create a growing middle class. The nation's rising middle class included doctors, lawyers, engineers, managers, social workers, architects, and teachers. It was typical for many people in the emerging middle class to move away from the central city. Some took advantage of the new commuter rail lines to move to "streetcar suburbs." During this period, middle-class salaries were about twice that of the average factory worker. In 1905 a college professor earned a middle-class salary of $1,100.

In New York City, three out of four residents squeezed into **tenements,** dark and crowded multi-family apartments. To supplement the average industrial worker's annual income of $490, many families sent their young children to work in factories or rented precious space to a boarder.

Urban Problems and Politics Especially for the working poor, city living posed threats such as crime, violence, fire, disease, and pollution. Native-born Americans often blamed immigrants for the increase in crime and violence. In reality, the crime rate for immigrants was not significantly higher than that for other Americans.

NATIONAL GEOGRAPHIC MOMENT in HISTORY

Many tenement buildings began as tenant houses. These were often large residences of wealthy people who had moved away from the city. Real estate agents subdivided the large rooms into smaller ones for immigrants. Agents, eager to make money, sometimes subdivided the rooms without considering lighting or ventilation.

Did You Know?

In the 1870s, people thought that typing was physically too strenuous and intellectually too complicated for women. As a result, most secretaries were men.

Alcohol contributed to violent crime. Danish immigrant Jacob Riis, who documented slum life in his 1890 book *How the Other Half Lives,* accused saloons of "breeding poverty," corrupting politics, bringing suffering to the wives and children of drunkards, and fostering "the corruption of the child" by selling beer to minors.

Improper sewage disposal contaminated city drinking water and triggered epidemics of typhoid fever and cholera. Though flush toilets and sewer systems existed in the 1870s, pollution remained a severe problem as horse waste was left in the streets, smoke belched from chimneys, and soot and ash accumulated from coal and wood fires.

A new kind of political system, the political machine, developed to meet these urban problems. This system provided essential city services in return for political power. The **political machine,** an informal political group designed to gain and keep power, came about partly because cities had grown much faster than their governments. New city dwellers needed jobs, housing, food, heat, and police protection. In exchange for votes, political machines and the party bosses who ran them eagerly provided these necessities. The payoff for party bosses came on Election Day. Urban immigrant groups, which wielded tremendous voting strength, voted in overwhelming numbers for the political machines.

The party bosses who ran the political machines also controlled the city's finances. Many machine politicians grew rich as the result of fraud or **graft**— getting money through dishonest or questionable means. Outright fraud occurred when party bosses accepted bribes from contractors, who were supposed to compete fairly to win contracts to build streets, sewers, and buildings. Corrupt bosses also

sold permits to their friends to operate public utilities, such as railroads, waterworks, and power systems.

Tammany Hall, the New York Democratic political machine, was the most famous such organization. **William M. "Boss" Tweed** was its corrupt leader during the 1860s and 1870s. Tweed's corruption led him to prison in 1874.

Other cities' machines controlled all the city services, including the police department. For example, St. Louis's boss never feared arrest when he called out to his supporters at the police-supervised voting booth, "Are there any more repeaters out here that want to vote again?" Based in Kansas City, Missouri, the Pendergast brothers, James and Thomas, ran state and city politics from the 1890s until the 1930s.

Opponents of political machines, such as political cartoonist Thomas Nast, blasted bosses for their corruption. Defenders countered that city and state governments were ineffective. Machines provided necessary services and helped to assimilate the masses of new city dwellers.

Reading Check **Evaluating** How did the influx of immigrants affect the cities?

Student Web Activity Visit the *American Vision: Modern Times* Web site at tav.mt.glencoe.com and click on **Student Web Activities– Chapter 3** for an activity on urbanization.

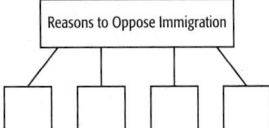 **Study Central**

For help with the concepts in this section of *American Vision: Modern Times* go to tav.mt.glencoe.com and click on **Study Central.**

SECTION 3 ASSESSMENT

Checking for Understanding

1. **Vocabulary** Define: nativism, commission, tenement, political machine, graft.

2. **People and Terms** Identify: Chinese Exclusion Act, William M. "Boss" Tweed.

3. **Places** Locate: Ellis Island, Angel Island.

4. **Describe** where most immigrants to the United States settled in the late 1800s.

Reviewing Big Ideas

5. **Comparing** What impact did industrializaton have on the working class, the middle class, and the wealthy in the late 1800s?

Critical Thinking

6. **Analyzing** What problems could arise in cities in which political machines controlled all services?

7. **Organizing** Complete a graphic organizer similar to the one below by listing reasons nativists opposed immigration to the United States.

Reasons to Oppose Immigration

8. **Examining Photographs** Study the photographs on page 259 of the Brooklyn Bridge and Flatiron Building. Why was it advantageous to construct taller buildings rather than purchase more land?

Writing About History

9. **Persuasive Writing** Imagine that you are a newspaper editor in the late 1800s. Write an editorial in which you support or oppose political machines. Include reasons to support your position. **CA** 11WS1.2; 11WA2.4

CHAPTER 3 The Birth of Modern America **261**

SECTION 3 ASSESSMENT ANSWERS

1. Content vocabulary is boldfaced and highlighted in yellow. Academic vocabulary is boldfaced.

2. Chinese Exclusion Act (p. 258), William M. "Boss" Tweed (p. 261)

3. Ellis Island (p. 255), Angel Island (p. 257)

4. neighborhoods of large cities

5. Each class lived in separate neighborhoods. The middle class grew as a result of industrialization.

6. Leaders of political machines could grow rich off of fraud. City services were run corruptly.

7. influx of Catholics would give Catholic Church too much power, immigrants would weaken unions, would take jobs from Americans

8. land was limited and expensive; allowed more people to work in the cities

9. Students' editorials will vary but should include specific reasons for opinion on political machines.

ASSESS

 Resources for page 261

Use these resources to assess student mastery.

📁 Section Quiz 3-3

📁 Reading Essentials and Study Guide 3-3

⊙ Interactive Tutor Self-Assessment CD-ROM

📁 California Standards Practice, Grade 11

HISTORY Online

Objectives and answers to the student activity can be found in the **Web Activity Lesson Plan** at tav.mt.glencoe.com.

Reading Check

Answer: It led to the development of skyscrapers, mass transit, and tenement housing. Overcrowding in the cities also brought problems such as crime, violence, fire, disease, and pollution.

Study Central provides audio summaries, interactive games, and online graphic organizers to help students review section content.

CLOSE

Evaluating Have students evaluate the services political machines provided for urban settlers. **Ask: Were the benefits provided worth the corruption? Why or why not?** *(Answers will vary; students should use the text to explain their answers.)* **OL**

CA 11RC2.4

Geography&History

FOCUS

History–Social Science Standards

This feature addresses the following standards:

11.2.1 Know the effects of industrialization on living and working conditions, including the portrayal of working conditions and food safety in Upton Sinclair's *The Jungle*.

11.2.2 Describe the changing landscape, including the growth of cities linked by industry and trade, and the development of cities divided according to race, ethnicity, and class.

TEACH

R Reading Strategy

Connecting Tell students to think about a time when they had to move from one home, town, or state to another, or what such a move might be like. **Ask:** **What challenges did you and your family face when you moved, or what challenges might you expect?** *(Answers will vary but may include finding jobs, new school, new people, unfamiliar surroundings, etc.)* Have students write short paragraphs comparing these challenges with the difficulties immigrants saw when they arrived in Chicago at the turn of the century. **OL**

Answers and Additional Support

The Hull House Neighborhood
S. HALSTED STREET

HULL HOUSE

Streets labeled: W. 12TH STREET, BUNKER STREET, DE KOVEN STREET, W. TAYLOR STREET, FORQUER STREET, EWING STREET, W. POLK STREET, S. DES PLAINES STREET, S. JEFFERSON STREET, S. CLINTON STREET

Legend:
- Bohemian
- Chinese
- English speaking
- French Canadian
- French
- German
- Irish
- Italian
- Polish
- Russian
- Scandinavian
- Swiss
- Non-residential

Chicago's apartment buildings, or tenements, were squeezed onto lots that measured 25 by 125 feet (7.6 by 38.1 m). These lots typically held three families and their boarders. Unlike New York City's tenements, most were only two or three stories tall.

262   CHAPTER 3   The Birth of Modern America

EXTENDING THE CONTENT

Urban Problems Urban problems are not new. Many cities in ancient times were large and crowded. Some historians place Rome's population at more than one million by the start of the first century A.D. Within 100 years, overcrowding resulted in many of Rome's citizens living in apartment houses. Some apartments were 5 or 6 stories high and sheltered about 200 people each. Many of the city's residential structures were poorly constructed, and living conditions paralleled those in the impoverished sections of 1800s New York or Chicago.

Immigrants Arrive In Chicago

A major port and a conduit for the nation's east-west rail travel, Chicago was a booming industrial center for the lumber, grain, meatpacking, and mail-order businesses at the end of the 1800s. Since the early 1870s, more ships had been docking in Chicago than in New York, Baltimore, Philadelphia, Charleston, and San Francisco combined. The city's expansion was phenomenal. In 50 years, it grew from a modest frontier town to the second-largest city in the country.

Immigrants swarmed into Chicago seeking jobs. Poles found work slaughtering livestock; Irish laying railroads; Russian and Polish Jews making clothes; Swedes constructing buildings and Italians forging steel. Women established boardinghouses, took in sewing to do at home, and worked in factories. In most factories, the hours were long and the working conditions difficult: noisy, hot, grimy, and overcrowded. By the beginning of the 1900s, three-fourths of the people in this teeming metropolis were European immigrants and their American-born children.

Ethnic neighborhoods dotted the city, as did blocks of tenements thrown up to house the flood of newcomers. The inset map at left—an enlargement of the highlighted rectangle on the lithograph—shows the Hull House neighborhood in Chicago's West Side in 1893. Hull House was established by social reformer Jane Addams to "investigate and improve the conditions in the industrial districts of Chicago." The neighborhood was one of the city's poorest. Its tenement buildings were disease-ridden and dangerous, crowding about 270 residents into each acre. Jane Addams wrote: "The streets are inexpressibly dirty, the number of schools inadequate, sanitary legislation unenforced, the street lighting bad, the paving miserable and altogether lacking in the alleys."

The neighborhood was also one of the most ethnically diverse. As the inset shows, the bewildered new immigrants tended to settle in enclaves that had already been established by others from their homeland. They banded together as they learned about the ways of the new land. Many immigrants found comfort in social life centered on the church or synagogue. Younger immigrants were more eager to abandon their old customs. Many of them quickly adopted American clothes and manners, learned to speak English, and tried to make American friends.

A visiting nurse puts drops in an infant's eyes. Crowded conditions threatened the health of many of the immigrants in Chicago's tenements.

LEARNING FROM GEOGRAPHY

1. How did the location of Chicago influence its development?

2. Pose and answer five questions about the geographic distribution and patterns shown on this model.

263

ANSWERS TO LEARNING FROM GEOGRAPHY

1. Since it developed on the waterfront, Chicago developed both as a port city and a rail city. Ships would transport goods to the city and the goods would be shipped across the country from the rail lines.

2. Students' questions and answers will vary. You may have students trade questions and then have the pairs discuss the answers.

FOCUS

Guide to Reading

Understanding Vocabulary:
Organize students into pairs and have them define the vocabulary words.

Answers to Graphic:
Social Darwinism: theory that human society evolves through competition and natural selection; Laissez-faire: economic doctrine that opposed government programs that interfered with business; Gospel of Wealth: philosophy that wealthy people should give to public charity; Realism: movement in art and literature to portray people realistically

Unpacking the Standards

Students will be able to:

- Explain the impact of industrialization and urbanization on American society.
- Describe attempts to help the urban poor.

Answers and Additional Support

SECTION 4

Early Reforms in a Gilded Age

Guide to Reading

Connection
In the previous section, you learned about the effects of population growth in the cities. In this section, you will discover the effects of industrialization and urbanization on society and efforts for social reform.

Main Idea

- Industrialization and urbanization changed American society's ideas and culture in the late 1800s. (p. 265)
- The pressing problems of the urban poor in the late 1800s and early 1900s stimulated attempts to reform industrial society. (p. 267)

Content Vocabulary
individualism, Social Darwinism, philanthropy, settlement house, Americanization

Academic Vocabulary
evolve, function

People and Terms to Identify
Gilded Age, Herbert Spencer, Social Gospel, Dwight L. Moody, Booker T. Washington

Reading Objectives

- **Evaluate** the influence of Social Darwinism and the Social Gospel movement on American society.

- **Analyze** the efforts of early reformers to help the urban poor.

Reading Strategy
Complete a graphic organizer similar to the one below by filling in the main idea of each of the theories and movements listed.

Theory or Movement	Main Idea
Social Darwinism	
Laissez-Faire	
Gospel of Wealth	
Social Gospel	

Preview of Events

1880	1890	1900
1881 Booker T. Washington founds Tuskegee Institute	**1884** Mark Twain publishes *Huckleberry Finn*	**1889** Jane Addams founds Hull House · **1899** Scott Joplin publishes "The Maple Leaf Rag"

The following are the main History–Social Science Standards covered in this section.

11.1.4 Examine the effects of the Civil War and Reconstruction and of the Industrial Revolution, including demographic shifts and the emergence in the late 19th century of the United States as a world power.

11.2.3 Trace the effect of the Americanization movement.

11.2.4 Analyze the effect of urban political machines and responses to them by immigrants and middle-class reformers.

11.2.7 Analyze the similarities and differences between the ideologies of Social Darwinism and Social Gospel (e.g., using biographies of William Graham Sumner, Billy Sunday, Dwight L. Moody).

11.3.1 Describe the contributions of various religious groups to American civic principles and social reform movements (e.g., civil and human rights, individual responsibility and the work ethic, antimonarchy and self-rule, worker protection, family-centered communities).

✎ The Big Idea ✎

People react to periods of breathtaking social and cultural change in different ways. Historians refer to the late 1800s as the Gilded Age. While everything seemed shiny and golden on the outside, underneath was a society filled with poverty, crime, and a large disparity between the rich and the poor. New philosophies, such as individualism and Social Darwinism, stressed the importance of individual responsibility and hard work to become successful in life. While these ideas were popular, many people became convinced that reform was needed to help end corruption and to assist people in need. Several reform movements began during this time. The Social Gospel movement attempted to reform society based on biblical ideas and beliefs. Other reform efforts included the development of settlement houses, better public education and vocational training, and public libraries.

11.3.2 Analyze the great religious revivals and the leaders involved in them, including the First Great Awakening, the Second Great Awakening, the Civil War revivals, the Social Gospel Movement, the rise of Christian liberal theology in the nineteenth century, the impact of the Second Vatican Council, and the rise of Christian fundamentalism in current times.

SECTION RESOURCES

📂 **Print Material**
- Reproducible Lesson Plan 3-4
- Guided Reading Activity 3-4
- Reading Essentials and Study Guide 3-4
- Active Reading Note-Taking Guide 3-4

🖋 **Transparencies**
- Daily Focus Skills Transparency 3-4
- Section Graphic Organizer Transparency 3-4

Technology
- Interactive Tutor Self-Assessment CD-ROM
- Exam*View*® Pro Testmaker CD-ROM
- Presentation Plus! CD-ROM

The Gilded Age

Main Idea Industrialization and urbanization changed American society's ideas and culture in the late 1800s.

Reading Connection Which scientist came up with the concept of "survival of the fittest" among animal species, and what does this phrase mean? Read on to find out how the notion of "survival of the fittest" was applied to human society.

In 1873 Mark Twain and Charles Warner co-authored a novel about American politics and society entitled *The Gilded Age*. Historians later adopted the term and applied it to the era in American history that begins about 1870 and ends around 1900. This was a time of tremendous change, in which old ideas of society and culture no longer seemed to apply.

★ An American Story ★

In 1872, at the age of 32, William Graham Sumner became a professor of political and social science at Yale College. Sumner's classes were very popular. One of his students, William Lyon Phelps, illustrated Sumner's tough, no-nonsense approach with this example of a class discussion:

Student: "Professor, don't you believe in any government aid to industries?"

Sumner: "No! It's root, hog, or die."

Student: "Yes, but hasn't the hog got a right to root?"

Sumner: "There are no rights. The world owes nobody a living."

Student: "You believe then, Professor, in only one system, the contract-competitive system?"

Sumner: "That's the only sound economic system. All others are fallacies."

Student: "Well, suppose some professor of political economy came along and took your job away from you. Wouldn't you be sore?"

Sumner: "Any other professor is welcome to try. If he gets my job, it is my fault. My business is to teach the subject so well that no one can take the job away from me."

—adapted from *Social Darwinism in American Thought*

Professor Summner was only one of many voices that reflected new ideas about people and how they fit into the new industrial society.

A Changing Culture The decades after the Civil War were in many ways a time of marvels. Amazing new inventions led to rapid industrial growth. Cities expanded to sizes never seen before. Masses of workers thronged the streets. Skyscrapers reached to the sky, and electric lights banished the darkness. Newly wealthy entrepreneurs built spectacular mansions.

By calling this era the **Gilded Age,** however, Twain and Warner were sounding an alarm. Something is gilded if it is covered with gold on the outside but made of cheaper material inside. A gilded age might appear to sparkle, but Twain, Warner, and other writers sought to point out that beneath the surface lay corruption, poverty, crime, and great disparities in wealth between the rich and the poor.

Whether the era was golden or merely gilded, it was certainly a time of great cultural activity. Industrialism and urbanization altered the way Americans looked at themselves and their society, and these changes gave rise to new values, new art, and new forms of entertainment.

"The world owes nobody a living."
—William Graham Sumner

TEACH

U Universal Access

Advanced Learners Ask students to read *The Gilded Age* by Mark Twain and Charles Warner. Have them write three-page reports summarizing the key points of the book. Encourage volunteers to read their reports aloud to the class. **AL**

R Reading Strategy

Predicting Have students use dictionaries to find the definition of the word *gilded.* Before students read Section 4, ask: **Why do you think historians use the word *gilded* instead of *golden* to describe the end of the nineteenth century?** Instruct students to save their responses. After reading Section 4, ask students if their predictions were correct. Have them make a list of events and examples from this era that support their answers. **OL**
CA 11RC2.5

More Skill Practice

Identifying Point of View Have students write two newspaper headlines describing the Gilded Age. The first headline should reflect the point of view of someone who sees problems in the Gilded Age. The second headline should be from the point of view of someone who disagrees with this view of the Gilded Age. **OL**
CA HR2; HR3; HI2

Picturing **History**

Social Darwinism Herbert Spencer's application of the theory of evolution to human society found many followers. How did industrial leaders react to this theory?

One of the strongest beliefs of the era—and one that remains strong today—was the idea of **individualism.** Many Americans firmly believed that no matter how humble their origins, they could rise in society and go as far as their talents and commitment would take them. No one expressed the idea of individualism better than Horatio Alger. Alger, a former minister who eventually left the clergy, wrote more than 100 "rags-to-riches" novels, in which a poor person goes to the big city and becomes successful. Many young people who read these inspiring tales concluded that no matter how many obstacles they faced, success was possible.

Social Darwinism Another powerful idea of the era was Social Darwinism, which strongly reinforced the idea of individualism. English philosopher **Herbert Spencer** first proposed this idea. Historian John Fiske, political scientist William Graham Sumner, and the magazine *Popular Science Monthly* all popularized it in the United States.

Philosopher Herbert Spencer applied Charles Darwin's theory of evolution and natural selection to human society. In his 1859 book, *On the Origin of Species by Means of Natural Selection,* Darwin argued that plant and animal life had **evolved** over the years by a process he called natural selection. In this process, those species that cannot adapt to the environment in which they live gradually die out, while those that do adapt thrive and live on.

Spencer took this biological theory, intended to explain developments over millions of years, and argued that human society also evolved through competition and natural selection. He argued that society progressed and became better because only the fittest people survived.

Spencer and others who shared his views became known as Social Darwinists, and their ideas were known as **Social Darwinism.** "Survival of the fittest" became the catchphrase of their philosophy. By 1902 over 350,000 copies of Spencer's books had been sold in the United States.

Social Darwinism paralleled the economic doctrine of laissez-faire that opposed any government programs that interfered with business. William Graham Sumner, for example, argued in numerous essays that competition would eliminate those who could not adapt. Not surprisingly, industrial leaders like John D. Rockefeller heartily embraced the theory of Social Darwinism. Rockefeller maintained that survival of the fittest, as demonstrated by the growth of huge businesses like his own Standard Oil, was "merely the working out of the law of nature and the law of God."

Rockefeller may have appreciated Spencer's interpretation of evolution, but Darwin's conclusions about the origin of new species frightened and outraged many devout Christians as well as some leading scientists. They rejected the theory of evolution because they believed it contradicted the Bible's account of creation. Some American scholars and ministers, however, concluded that evolution may have been God's way of creating the world. Henry Ward Beecher of Plymouth Church in Brooklyn called himself a "cordial Christian evolutionist." Beecher accepted Spencer's ideas of Social Darwinism and championed the success of American business.

A wealthy and prominent business leader, Andrew Carnegie believed whole-heartedly in Social Darwinism and laissez-faire. At the same time, he thought that those who profited from society owed it something in return. Carnegie attempted to extend and soften the harsh philosophy of Social Darwinism with the Gospel of Wealth. This philosophy held that wealthy Americans bore the responsibility of engaging in **philanthropy**—using their great fortunes to further social progress. Carnegie himself, for example, donated millions of dollars as the "trustee and agent for his poorer brethren." Other industrialists also contributed to social causes. 📖 *(See page 975 for more information on the Gospel of Wealth.)*

Realism Just as Darwin had looked at the natural world scientifically, a new movement in art and literature known as realism attempted to portray people realistically instead of idealizing them as romantic artists had done. Realist painters rejected the idealistic depictions of the world of the earlier 1800s. Thomas Eakins, for example, painted President Hayes working in shirtsleeves instead of in more traditional formal dress.

Writers also attempted to capture the world as they saw it. Mark Twain gave his readers a piercing view of American society in the pre–Civil War era in his 1884 masterpiece, *Adventures of Huckleberry Finn.* Twain was lauded to have written a true American novel, in which the setting, subject matter, characters, and style were unmistakably American. Henry James and Edith Wharton gave their readers stark and realistic portrayals of the upper class.

Popular Culture Industrialization improved the standard of living for many people, enabling them to spend money on entertainment and recreation. Increasingly, urban Americans, unlike rural people, divided their lives into separate units—that of work and home. Saloons played a major role in the life of male workers. Working-class families or single adults who sought excitement and escape could go to amusement parks such as New York's Coney Island.

Spectator sports such as baseball, football, and the new game of basketball gained popularity. With work becoming less physically strenuous, people also looked for leisure activities that involved physical exercise. Lawn tennis, golf, and croquet became popular.

The many people living in cities provided large and eager markets for other types of entertainment. Vaudeville offered a hodgepodge of animal acts, acrobats, gymnasts, and dancers. Like vaudeville, ragtime music, which was based on the patterns of African American music, echoed the hectic pace of city life.

✔ **Reading Check** **Summarizing** What was the main idea of Social Darwinism?

The Rebirth of Reform

Main Idea The pressing problems of the urban poor in the late 1800s and early 1900s stimulated attempts to reform industrial society.

Reading Connection Have you ever participated in a food drive or other community activity to help those in need? Read on to learn how reformers tried to better people's lives.

The tremendous changes brought about by industrialism and urbanization—along with mounting opposition to corrupt political machines—triggered a debate among Americans as to how best to address society's problems. While many Americans embraced the ideas of individualism and Social Darwinism, others argued that society's problems could be fixed only if Americans and their government began to take a more active role in regulating the economy and helping those in need.

 History

Urban Poverty The impoverished lifestyle of many Americans like this mother and child in Chicago was a growing concern among social reformers. **What organizations were created to help the urban poor?**

U₁ Universal Access

Interpersonal Ask students to choose a sport that was played during the Gilded Age and research how the rules are different from those of the modern version. Pair students and ask them to teach one another how to play their chosen sports using the original rules. Instructions should be limited to verbal cues only. As a class, discuss the problems in teaching an activity without visual aids or written directions. **BL**

U₂ Universal Access

Kinesthetic Invite a performing arts teacher or artist to work with your students to produce a vaudeville-style show. Ask the guest to help students understand the kinds of acts performed in vaudeville, and offer suggestions about resources students can use to learn more about vaudeville. Arrange for students to perform for an audience. **AL**

Review the Big Idea

Review the Big Idea for this section, "People react to periods of breathtaking social and cultural change in different ways." As students read the text under the heading "The Rebirth of Reform," have them take notes and then write a summary on the different reform movements that took shape during this time. **OL**

✔ **Reading Check**

Answer: that human society evolves through competition and natural selection—survival of the fittest

Picturing **History**

Answer: Salvation Army and YMCA
Ask: What evidence of poverty can you see in this photograph? *(worn and dirty clothes, used utensils, grime)*

Did You Know?

Thomas Eakins was a painter, sculptor, photographer, and art teacher. Many of his portrait subjects did not appreciate his realistic approach, and his insistence on the use of nude models for teaching also presented problems. Both his realistic style and his teaching techniques achieved great acceptance after his death.

S Skill Practice

Preparing a Debate Assign half the class to debate in favor of Henry George's solution to social inequality. The other half of the class will argue to support Lester Frank Ward's views of Social Darwinism. Make sure that each side uses information from the textbook and accurately reflects this information in their argument. Interested students may also conduct research and provide more information for fellow students before the debate. After debating, discuss with the entire class which social view is more convincing. **AL** **CA** HI1; HI3; HI4

R Reading Strategy

Reading Maps, Graphs, and Charts Have students use the information on the chart entitled "Death Rates for Specific Causes" to create two circle graphs: one showing the causes of death in 1900, and the other showing the causes of death in 1997. Have students use one color per cause of death. Remind students to create a key showing which causes of death the different colors represent. **BL**

Answers and Additional Support

Social Criticism In 1879 journalist Henry George published *Progress and Poverty,* which quickly became a national bestseller. George observed that despite industrial and social progress, "the gulf between the employed and the employer is growing wider. . . . [A]s liveried carriages appear, so do barefoot children." George offered a simple solution of land ownership and a "single tax" to make society more equal and also provide the government with enough money to help the poor. Economists have since rejected George's economic theory. His real importance to American history is that he raised questions about American society and led the way in challenging the ideas of Social Darwinism and laissez-faire economics. Many future reform leaders first became interested in reform because of George's book.

S Lester Frank Ward reached a different conclusion about Social Darwinism than George in his book *Dynamic Sociology.* Ward's ideas, known as Reform Darwinism, stated that people had succeeded in the world not because of their ability to compete but because of their ability to cooperate. Government, he argued, could regulate the economy, cure poverty, and promote education more efficiently than could competition in the marketplace.

Other critics, such as Edward Bellamy, were more extreme in their ideas. Bellamy described an ideal society based on socialism in *Looking Back, 2000–1887.* The ideas of people such as George, Ward, and Bellamy helped shape the thinking of American reformers in the late 1800s.

Criticism of industrial society also appeared in literature in a new style of writing known as naturalism. Writers such as Stephen Crane, Frank Norris, Jack London, and Theodore Dreiser described the power of the natural environment over civilization and told of people whose lives were destroyed through no fault of their own.

Helping the Urban Poor Some critics of industrial society became actively involved in reform movements. From about 1870 until 1920, reformers in the **Social Gospel** movement strove to improve conditions in cities according to the biblical ideals of charity and justice. An early advocate of the Social Gospel, Washington Gladden, a minister from Columbus, Ohio, tried to apply what he called "Christian law" to social problems. During a coal strike in 1884, for example, Gladden preached about the "right and necessity of labor organizations,"

Social Conditions: Past and Present

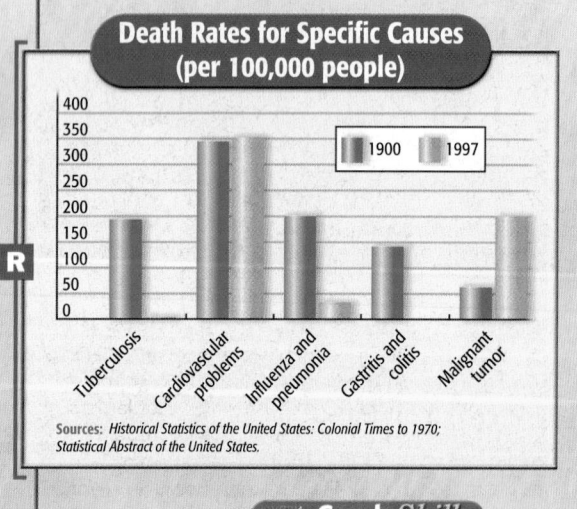

Death Rates for Specific Causes (per 100,000 people)

1900 | 1997

Causes: Tuberculosis, Cardiovascular problems, Influenza and pneumonia, Gastritis and colitis, Malignant tumor

Sources: *Historical Statistics of the United States: Colonial Times to 1970; Statistical Abstract of the United States.*

High School Graduation Rates

1900: 6.4% Graduated, 93.6% Did Not Graduate

1997: 69% Graduated, 31% Did Not Graduate

Sources: *Historical Statistics of the United States, Colonial Times to 1970; Statistical Abstract of the United States.*

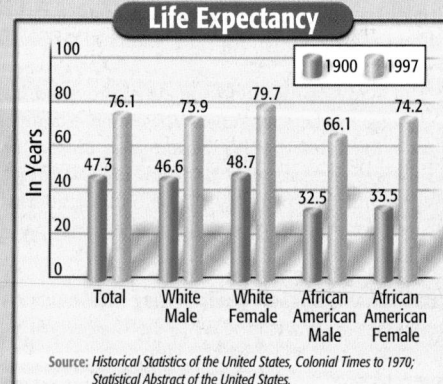

Life Expectancy

1900 | 1997

In Years

Total: 47.3 / 76.1
White Male: 46.6 / 73.9
White Female: 48.7 / 79.7
African American Male: 32.5 / 66.1
African American Female: 33.5 / 74.2

Source: *Historical Statistics of the United States, Colonial Times to 1970; Statistical Abstract of the United States.*

Graph *Skills*

1. **Analyzing Graphs** How many people per 100,000 died of tuberculosis in the year 1900?
2. **Understanding Cause and Effect** Collectively, what do these graphs tell you about social conditions as the twentieth century progressed?

Graph *Skills*

Answers:
1. almost 200 out of every 100,000 people
2. that conditions improved from the start to the end of the 1900s

Graph Skills Practice
Ask: Why do you think a larger percentage of students graduate from high school today than in 1900?
(possible answer: fewer have to go to work full time while in their teens, education is more important for the types of jobs available today)

Profiles IN HISTORY

Booker T. Washington
1856–1915

Born enslaved on a plantation in Virginia, Booker T. Washington spent his childhood working in the coal mines of West Virginia. At age 16 he heard about the Hampton Institute in Virginia, where African Americans could learn farming or a trade. With little money in his pockets, Washington left home and walked nearly 500 miles to the school, where he was able to work as a janitor to pay for his education.

After Washington completed his degree, Hampton hired him as an instructor in 1879. Two years later, Hampton's founder, Samuel Armstrong, asked Washington to organize an agricultural and industrial school for African Americans in Tuskegee, Alabama. The Tuskegee Institute's beginnings were modest. As Washington recalled, it began with 40 students and a "dilapidated shanty." By 1915 the school had over 100 buildings, about 2,000 students, and an endowment of nearly $2 million. Washington himself became a nationally known spokesperson for the African American community.

George Washington Carver
1864–1943

At about 10 years of age, George Washington Carver left his home in Missouri and began traveling on his own. He worked as a servant, hotel clerk, laundry worker, and farmhand in order to get a formal education. In 1894 he graduated from the Iowa State College of Agriculture and Mechanical Arts. Two years later, he became the director of agricultural research at the Tuskegee Institute, where he began experimenting with various crops.

To help Southern sharecroppers overcome their problems of depleted soil, poverty, and poor nutrition, Carver urged them to plant peanuts and soybeans. These plants restored the soil's nitrogen while providing extra protein in the farmers' diets. To make peanut farming profitable, Carver developed over 300 industrial uses for peanuts, including flour, inks, dyes, wood stains, soap, and cosmetics. By 1940 his research had made the peanut the South's second most lucrative crop after cotton.

---

despite the fact that his congregation included top officers of the coal company. Walter Rauschenbusch, a later leader of the movement, believed that competition was the cause of many social problems, causing good people to behave badly. Other ministers opposed certain reform movements. For example, Billy Sunday, a former professional baseball player, in numerous revivals warned people of alcohol. At the same time, he denounced reforms that he thought would threaten traditional society, such as labor unions and women's rights.

The efforts of leaders like Gladden and Rauschenbusch inspired many organized churches to expand their missions. These churches began to take on community **functions** designed to improve society, such as social programs, day care, and helping the poor. The combination of religious faith and interest in reform nourished the growth of the Christian Mission, a social welfare organization that became know as the Salvation Army in 1878. It provided practical aid and religious counseling to the urban poor.

Founded in England, the Young Men's Christian Association (YMCA) tried to help industrial workers and the urban poor by organizing Bible studies, prayer meetings, citizenship training, and fitness activities. One prominent organizer of the American YMCA was **Dwight L. Moody,** the president of the Chicago YMCA in the late 1860s. A gifted preacher and organizer, Moody organized revival meetings in other American cities. In 1870 Moody met Ira Sankey, a hymn writer and singer. Together they introduced the gospel hymn into worship services in the United States and Great Britain. Moody strongly supported charities that helped the poor, but he rejected both the Social Gospel and Social Darwinism. He believed in helping the poor by redeeming their souls and reforming their character.

The settlement house movement, in some ways an offshoot of the Social Gospel movement, attracted idealistic reformers who believed it was their Christian duty to improve living conditions for the poor. During the late 1800s, reformers such as Jane Addams established **settlement houses** in poor neighborhoods. In these establishments, middle-class residents lived with and helped poor residents, mostly immigrants, by providing everything from medical care and English classes to hot lunches for factory workers. Addams, who opened the famous Hull House in Chicago in 1889, inspired many more such settlements across the country. Their efforts helped shape the social work profession, in which women came to play a major role.

CHAPTER 3 The Birth of Modern America **269**

W Writing Support

Research Report Writing Have students contact a social service agency in your community that provides services for the poor. Instruct students to learn about the agency's programs and its clients and write three-page reports on their research. **AL**
CA 11WA2.4d

U Universal Access

English Learners Using visuals to convey information can help students who are learning English. Instruct groups of four students to create logos for the YMCA. Remind students to include words as well as drawings when creating their logos. When they are finished, have students write captions explaining their logos. Display the logos and captions in and around your classroom. **EL**

S Skill Practice

Conducting Research Tell students to research and report on a woman involved in the social work profession in the late 1800s or today. Create a bulletin board entitled "Women and Social Work." Use the bulletin board to post the students' reports along with relevant photographs, information, and newspaper headlines.
OL **CA** HR4

Profiles IN HISTORY

Background: The Tuskegee Institute in Alabama is now known as Tuskegee University.

Ask: Based on the information presented in the profiles on page 269, how were the early lives of Booker T. Washington and George Washington Carver similar? *(They both traveled far from home and worked to put themselves through college.)*

Critical Thinking

Comparing and Contrasting
Ask students to compare public education in the 1800s with that of today. How do the goals and values emphasized compare? **OL**

ASSESS

Resources for page 270

Use these resources to assess student mastery.

📂 Section Quiz 3-4

📂 Reading Essentials and Study Guide 3-4

⊙ Interactive Tutor Self-Assessment CD-ROM

📂 California Standards Practice, Grade 11

Reading Check

Answer: by teaching English and American values

HISTORY
Online

Study Central provides audio summaries, interactive games, and online graphic organizers to help students review section content.

CLOSE

Summarizing Have students summarize reformers' actions during the Gilded Age. **OL**

▲ *Carnegie Library, Shelbyville, Indiana*

Public Education As the United States became increasingly industrialized and urbanized, it needed more workers who were trained and educated. In 1870 around 6,500,000 children attended school. By 1900 that number had risen to over 17,300,000. Public schools were often crucial to the success of immigrant children. It was there the children usually became knowledgeable about American culture, a process known as **Americanization.** To assimilate newcomers into American culture, schools taught immigrant children English, American history, and the responsibilities of citizenship. They also tried to instill discipline and a strong work ethic, values considered important to the nation's progress. Americanization could also pose a problem for immigrant children, however, because sometimes parents worried that it would make the children forget their own cultural traditions.

While grammar schools provided basic education, vocational and technical education in high schools prepared students for specific trades. College attendance also rose during this time, aided by the Morrill Land Grant Act. This Civil War–era law gave federal land grants to states for the purpose of establishing agricultural and mechanical colleges. Private colleges gave access to education for women, whose educational opportunities lagged behind men's.

Not everyone had access to school. In the rush to fund education, cities were way ahead of rural areas. Many African Americans, also, did not have equal educational opportunities. To combat this discrimination, some African Americans started their own schools. The leader of this movement was **Booker T. Washington,** who founded the Tuskegee Institute in Alabama in 1881.

Like public schools, free libraries also made education available to city dwellers. One of the strongest supporters of the public library movement was industrialist Andrew Carnegie, who donated millions of dollars toward the construction of libraries all across the United States. These libraries, as well as the various educational and social reform movements that arose in the late 1800s, helped people cope with the harsher aspects of a newly industrialized society.

☑ **Reading Check** **Explaining** How did the United States try to Americanize immigrants?

 Study Central

For help with the concepts in this section of *American Vision: Modern Times* go to tav.mt.glencoe.com and click on *Study Central.*

SECTION 4 ASSESSMENT

Check for Understanding

1. **Vocabulary** Define: individualism, evolve, Social Darwinism, philanthropy, settlement house, Americanization.
2. **People and Terms** Identify: Gilded Age, Herbert Spencer, Social Gospel, Dwight L. Moody, Booker T. Washington.
3. **Describe** how changes in art and literature reflected the issues and characteristics of the late nineteenth century.

Reviewing Big Ideas

4. **Comparing** How did the Social Darwinists and members of the Social Gospel movement differ in their views of individuals in the industrialized society?

Critical Thinking

5. **Historical Analysis** **Analyzing** Do you think members of the Social Gospel movement and other reformers were successful in helping the urban poor? Explain. **CA HR4; HI3**
6. **Organizing** Complete a graphic organizer similar to the one below to show how Social Darwinism paralleled the economic doctrine of laissez-faire.

Social Darwinism	Laissez-faire

Analyzing Visuals

7. **Examining Photographs** Study the photograph on page 267 of the mother and child. What do you notice in this photograph that reflects the plight of impoverished Americans?

Writing About History

8. **Descriptive Writing** Take on the role of an immigrant in the late 1800s. Write a diary entry in which you describe your feelings about your children becoming Americanized while attending the local public school. **CA 11WS1.2; 11WA2.4**

SECTION 4 ASSESSMENT ANSWERS

1. Content vocabulary is boldfaced and highlighted in yellow. Academic vocabulary is boldfaced.
2. Gilded Age *(p. 265),* Herbert Spencer *(p. 266),* Social Gospel *(p. 268),* Dwight L. Moody *(p. 269),* Booker T. Washington *(p. 270)*
3. Art and literature became more realistic as artists and writers depicted the world realistically.
4. Social Darwinism: survival of the fittest; Social Gospel: some individuals suffer because of competition and should be assisted
5. Answers will vary, but students should provide evidence to support their opinion.
6. Social Darwinism: competition and survival of the fittest; Laissez-faire: business should be free to run based on these "natural laws."
7. Students should use details from the photograph.
8. Students' diary entries should reflect both positive and negative feelings about Americanization.

SECTION 5 Politics and Reform

Guide to Reading

Connection
In the previous section, you learned about efforts to reform society. In this section, you will discover how politics often hindered reform efforts and how African Americans faced increasing discrimination.

Main Idea
- From 1877 to 1896, Republicans and Democrats were so evenly matched that only a few reforms were possible at the national level. (p. 272)
- Farmers in economic crisis embraced an independent political movement called populism that emerged in the 1890s to challenge the two major parties. (p. 275)
- In the late 1800s, Southern states passed laws that denied African Americans the right to vote and imposed segregation. (p. 279)

Content Vocabulary
populism, inflation, deflation, graduated income tax, poll tax, grandfather clause, segregation, Jim Crow laws

Academic Vocabulary
volume, prospective

People and Terms to Identify
Stalwart, Pendleton Act, Interstate Commerce Act, Grange, People's Party, William Jennings Bryan, Ida B. Wells, W.E.B. DuBois

Reading Objectives
- **Explain** why the Republicans and Democrats were so evenly matched during this period and why the People's Party gained support.
- **Discuss** how African Americans in the South were disfranchised and how segregation was legalized.

Reading Strategy
Taking Notes As you read about the stalemate between Republicans and Democrats, the emergence of Populists, and the rise of segregation in the late 1800s, use the major headings of the section to create an outline similar to the one below.

Politics and Reform
I. Stalemate in Washington
   A.
   B.
   C.
   D.

Preview of Events

♦1875	♦1880	♦1885	♦1890	♦1895

1877
Interstate Commerce Act adopted

1877
Florida initiates Jim Crow laws

1890
Sherman Antitrust Act adopted

1892
National People's Party formed

1896
Plessy v. *Ferguson* creates "separate but equal" doctrine

The following are the main History–Social Science Standards covered in this section.

11.1.4 Examine the effects of the Civil War and Reconstruction and of the Industrial Revolution, including demographic shifts and the emergence in the late 19th century of the United States as a world power.

11.2.4 Analyze the effect of urban political machines and responses to them by immigrants and middle-class reformers.

11.2.8 Examine the effects of political programs and activities of Populists.

11.10.2 Examine and analyze the key events, policies, and court cases in the evolution of civil rights, including *Dred Scott v. Sanford, Plessy v. Ferguson, Brown v. Board of Education, Regents of the University of California v. Bakke,* and California Proposition 209.

⚜ The Big Idea ⚜

People react to periods of breathtaking social and cultural change in different ways. In the late 1800s, division between the Democrats and Republicans and corruption in politics prevented lawmakers from addressing many of the nation's problems. Following the election of President Cleveland, economic issues took prominence over the nation's concerns about political corruption. Farmers began to organize to protest high tariffs, which increased the cost of manufactured goods they needed and made it more difficult to sell goods overseas. They embraced a new political movement called populism and created the People's Party in an effort to work for laws to protect their interests. Populism and the People's Party, however, slowly lost momentum. African Americans, particularly in the South, faced increasing discrimination and violence. In the late 1800s, Southern states began denying African Americans the right to vote and enforced segregation. Several African Americans became prominent when they spoke out against discrimination and worked to obtain the right to vote.

CHAPTER 3   The Birth of Modern America   **271**

FOCUS

BELLRINGER
SKILLBUILDER ACTIVITY

Project **Daily Focus Skills Transparency 3-5** and have students answer the question.

Guide to Reading

Understanding Vocabulary: Have students work in pairs to create study cards for each vocabulary word. Instruct students to write the terms on one side of blank note cards. On the other side, have students write definitions or descriptions of the terms, or draw pictures associated with the terms. Have students take turns quizzing each other using their study cards.

Answers to Graphic: Students should complete the outline by including all headings in the section.

Unpacking the Standards

Students will be able to:
- Identify the results of the political stalemate in Washington from 1877 to 1896.
- Explain the rise of populism and its impact on American politics at the turn of the century.
- Describe the segregated society created in the Southern states in the late 1800s.

SECTION RESOURCES

📖 Print Material
- Reproducible Lesson Plan 3-5
- Guided Reading Activity 3-5
- Reading Essentials and Study Guide 3-5
- Active Reading Note-Taking Guide 3-5

📄 Transparencies
- Daily Focus Skills Transparency 3-5
- Section Graphic Organizer Transparency 3-5

Technology
- Interactive Tutor Self-Assessment CD-ROM
- Exam*View*® Pro Testmaker CD-ROM
- Presentation Plus! CD-ROM

TEACH

S Skill Practice

Historical Interpretation Have students write newspaper articles describing the assassination of President Garfield on July 2, 1881. Remind students to include headlines as well as eyewitness accounts describing the shooting. Have students "publish" their articles on poster board and illustrate them with drawings of the event. Display the posters in your classroom. **BL** **CA HI1; HI2; HI3**

W Writing Support

Expository Writing Ask students to conduct research and write brief reports outlining the differences between the Stalwarts and the Halfbreeds. **OL**
CA 11WS1.1; 11WA2.4a

Answers and Additional Support

Stalemate in Washington

Main Idea From 1877 to 1896, Republicans and Democrats were so evenly matched that only a few reforms were possible at the national level.

Reading Connection What U.S. presidents have been assassinated? Read on to learn how the nation and the Congress responded to the killing of President James Garfield.

Many Americans believed that political reforms were necessary to make government more efficient. At the heart of their concerns was the spoils system.

★ An American Story ★

After the election of President James A. Garfield in 1880, many of his supporters tried to claim the "spoils of office"—the government jobs that follow an election victory. One of these job-seekers was Charles Guiteau. In the spring of 1881, Guiteau made daily trips to the White House or State Department, repeatedly asking for a job. Finally, on the night of May 18, he had a crazed inspiration: "[I]f the president was out of the way," he thought, "everything would go better." Unlike Garfield, Guiteau reasoned, Vice President Chester Arthur was comfortable with the old spoils system. Arthur would give him the position he deserved. On July 2, 1881, Guiteau shot President Garfield in a train station near Capitol Hill. In a note left behind, Guiteau stated:

66The President's tragic death was a sad necessity, but it will unite the Republican party and save the Republic. . . . I had no ill-will toward the President. His death was a political necessity. I am a lawyer, theologian, and politician. I am a Stalwart of the Stalwarts. . . .99

—quoted in *Garfield*

For many, the assassination of President Garfield highlighted the need for changes. Although Congress enacted civil service reform, few new policies were introduced in the 1870s and 1880s because Republicans and Democrats were so closely tied in elections.

Cleaning Up Politics Traditionally, under the spoils system, or patronage, government jobs went to supporters of the winning party in an election. Many Americans believed that the spoils system prevented

lawmakers from addressing the nation's issues and corrupted those who worked for the government. By the late 1870s, a movement to reform the civil service began to build support.

Republican President Rutherford B. Hayes attacked the practice of patronage by appointing reformers to his cabinet and replacing officials who owed their jobs to party bosses. His actions infuriated the **"Stalwarts,"** as newspapers called local bosses of Republican political machines. The Stalwarts accused Republican reformers, whom they labeled the "Halfbreeds," of backing reform simply to create openings for their own supporters.

Despite their disagreements, the Republicans nominated a mixed ticket—Halfbreed James Garfield for president and Stalwart Chester A. Arthur for vice president. The ticket managed to win the election, but a few months into his presidency, Garfield was assassinated.

Garfield's assassination further excited public opinion against the spoils system. In 1883 Congress responded by passing the **Pendleton Act,** which set up a civil service system with appointments of candidates based on examinations. Under President Arthur 14,000 jobs (about one-tenth of the total) came under the control of the civil service. The federal government had finally begun to shift away from the spoils system.

Picturing History

National Tragedy A newspaper artist captured the attack on President Garfield. Why was Charles Guiteau obsessed with the idea of killing the president?

Picturing History

Answer: When Guiteau did not get the government job he wanted, he decided to kill Garfield, hoping Arthur would give him a job.
Ask: Do you think this illustration accurately represents the assassination scene? (*Students' answers will vary.*)

More Skill Practice

Visual/Spatial Have students make posters advertising James Garfield for president. Ask students to write captions for each illustration that explain the messages that the ads present. Display the finished products in the classroom. **OL**

NATIONAL GEOGRAPHIC — The Election of 1884

Campaign ribbon

Presidential Election, 1884			
Candidate	Electoral Vote	Popular Vote	Party
Cleveland	219	4,879,507	Democrat
Blaine	182	4,850,293	Republican

Geography *Skills*

1. **Interpreting Maps** What regions did Blaine carry?
2. **Applying Geography Skills** Which three states do you think each candidate most hoped to win? Why?

Two Parties, Neck and Neck Although many people thought corruption prevented lawmakers from addressing the nation's problems, few new policies were introduced in the 1870s and 1880s. During those years, the Republicans and Democrats were evenly divided and had to share power. The Republicans had a voting edge in New England and the Midwest and the support of big business and Great Plains farmers. The Democrats dominated the South and enjoyed strong support in big cities with large Catholic and immigrant populations.

From 1877 to 1896, these voting patterns gave the Democrats an edge in the House of Representatives, where voters in each congressional district elected members directly. The Republicans had the upper hand in the Senate, because state legislatures chose senators and Republicans generally controlled a majority of state governments.

Both parties were well organized to turn out the vote in elections, and narrow margins decided most presidential elections between 1876 and 1896. Twice during this period, in 1876 and 1888, a candidate lost the popular vote but won the election. This happened because even if candidates win several states by slim popular vote margins, they still receive all the electoral votes in those states. These narrow victories then give the candidate an Electoral College majority, regardless of the overall popular vote count.

Although Republicans won four of the six presidential elections between 1876 and 1896, the president often had to contend with a House controlled by Democrats and a Senate dominated by Republicans who did not always agree with him on the issues. Furthermore, this was an era when local political bosses, not the president, controlled the party. The nearly even division of power produced political deadlock at the federal level.

The Election of 1884 As the election of 1884 approached, Democrats saw their best chance to win the White House since before the Civil War. They nominated New York Governor Grover Cleveland, an opponent of Tammany Hall, the corrupt Democratic political machine in New York City. Cleveland's Republican opponent was James G. Blaine, a former speaker of the House of Representatives who was wildly popular among party workers.

The campaign was sensational and frenzied. Because so many voters believed corruption was the main problem in American government, they focused their attention on the personal morals of the candidates. Blaine had been accused during the Crédit Mobilier scandal of profiting financially from

CHAPTER 3 The Birth of Modern America **273**

Geography *Skills*

273

**Answers and
Additional Support**

a political favor he did for the Union Pacific Railroad
while serving as Speaker of the House in the 1870s.
Some Republican reformers were so unhappy with
Blaine that they abandoned their party and supported Cleveland. These renegade reformers became
known as "Mugwumps," from an Algonquian word
meaning "great chiefs."

Cleveland, a bachelor, also faced moral criticism
during the campaign when a newspaper revealed
that he had fathered a child 10 years earlier. Aides
asked Cleveland how they should respond to
reporters seeking to know more about this story, and
he replied, "Tell the truth." By admitting to the
charge, Cleveland preserved his reputation for honesty and retained the support of many Mugwumps.

Blaine hoped that he could make up for the loss of
the Mugwumps by persuading Roman Catholics to
defect from the Democratic Party. His mother was an
Irish Catholic, and there were half a million Irish
Americans in New York state alone at the time.
During the campaign, however, Blaine met with a
Protestant minister who denounced the Democratic
Party for its ties to Catholicism. Because Blaine was
slow to criticize the remark, he lost most of the Irish
American vote. To make matters worse for Blaine,
many pro-temperance Republicans in upstate New
York backed the candidate of the Prohibition Party,
which was dedicated to banning the sale of alcohol.
Cleveland won New York by a margin of about 1,000
votes out of more than 1,000,000 cast, and his victory
in that state decided the election.

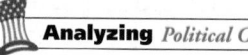 **Analyzing** *Political Cartoons*

Difficult Passage In Greek mythology, Scylla and Charybdis were sea mon-
sters who threatened the hero Odysseus from opposite sides of a narrow strait.
Why do you think the artist chose this image for Grover Cleveland in 1886?

274   CHAPTER 3   The Birth of Modern America

Commerce, Trusts, and Tariffs Economic issues
soon overshadowed the debate about political
reform. With greater industrialization and the
growth of the labor movement, unrest among workers was mounting across the country, and many
strikes occurred in this period. The power of large
corporations also concerned Americans. In particular, small businesses and farmers had become angry
at the railroads. While large corporations such as
Standard Oil were able to negotiate rebates—or partial refunds—and lower rates because of the **volume**
of goods they shipped, others were forced to pay
much higher rates. Although the high fixed costs and
low operating costs of railroads caused much of this
problem, many Americans believed railroads were
gouging customers.

Neither Democrats nor Republicans moved
quickly at the federal level to address these problems.
Both parties believed that government should not
interfere with corporations' property rights, which
courts had held to be the same as those of individuals.
Public pressure finally forced Congress to enact the
Interstate Commerce Act creating the Interstate
Commerce Commission (ICC). This act was the first
federal law designed to regulate interstate commerce.

Congress could not agree on tariffs, though. High
tariffs had helped protect weak domestic manufacturing after the Civil War. Many questioned the
necessity of maintaining high tariffs in the 1880s,
when large American companies were fully capable
of competing internationally. In December 1887,
Democratic President Grover Cleveland, who had
won a highly contested election three years earlier,
proposed lowering tariffs. The House, with a
Democratic majority, passed moderate tariff reductions, but the Republican-controlled Senate rejected
the bill. With Congress deadlocked, tariff reduction
became a major issue in the election of 1888.

Republicans Regain Power In the 1888 presidential campaign, the Republicans and their presidential
candidate, Benjamin Harrison, received large contributions from industrialists who benefited from tariff
protection. Grover Cleveland and the Democrats
campaigned against unnecessarily high tariff rates,
arguing that these taxes effectively raised the prices
of manufactured goods. In one of the closest races in
American history, Harrison lost the popular vote but
won the electoral vote with narrow victories in New
York and Indiana.

The election of 1888 gave the Republicans control
of both houses of Congress as well as the White
House. Using this power, the party passed legislation

to address points of national concern. One major piece of legislation, introduced by Representative William McKinley of Ohio, was a tariff bill that cut tobacco taxes and tariff rates on raw sugar but greatly increased rates on other goods, such as textiles, to discourage people from buying those imports. The McKinley Tariff lowered federal revenue and transformed the nation's budget surplus into a budget deficit.

The Republican-controlled Congress also responded to popular pressure to do something about the power of trusts. Senator John Sherman of Ohio introduced the Sherman Antitrust Act of 1890, which declared illegal any "combination in the form of trust . . . or conspiracy, in restraint of trade or commerce among the several States." The courts were responsible for enforcement, however, and judges saw nothing in this vaguely worded legislation that required them to make big companies change the way they did business. In the years following passage of the act, businesses formed trusts and combinations at a great rate.

✓ **Reading Check** **Explaining** Why were so few new policies introduced at the federal level in the 1870s and 1880s?

Populism

R **Main Idea** Farmers in economic crisis embraced an independent political movement called populism that emerged in the 1890s to challenge the two major parties.

Reading Connection In what ways do today's political parties serve the interests of individual citizens? Read on to learn why a new political party, the Populists, was formed in the late 1800s to address the needs of farmers.

As the midterm congressional election of 1890 approached, some Americans concluded that the two-party system was incapable of solving the nation's problems. That conviction was strongest among farmers, who faced an economic crisis that developed in the years immediately following the Civil War.

C

Unrest in Rural America In those years, farmers were producing more crops, but greater supply tended to lower prices. At the same time, high tariffs increased the cost of the manufactured goods farmers

Picturing **History**

Populist Territory This farm family in Nebraska represents the kind of people who typically supported populism. Why did farmers dislike Eastern bankers?

U **Universal Access**

Advanced Learners Ask students to research the nation's budget surpluses and deficits between 1860 and 1890 and create line graphs showing the changing trends. At each point where the trend shows a change of direction, identify the events that might have brought about these changes. Have students write paragraphs stating how political leaders have contributed to surpluses and deficits. **AL**

R **Reading Strategy**

Scaffolding—Questioning Before students read the text, have them ask themselves questions on what they might learn based on the major heading and subheadings, such as: *I wonder if populism means a movement that was popular, so many people supported it.* This will help students prepare for new information. **BL**

This **Reading Skill** was introduced in Chapter 2.

C **Critical Thinking**

Analyzing Information As students read, ask them to keep notes on the problems farmers faced that turned into an economic crisis for them. Have students list these problems on the board. *(new tools increased yields; more supply meant less profit; high tariffs increased cost of manufactured goods and lowered sales; deflation created financial burden)* **OL** **CA HI6**

✓ **Reading Check**

Answer: Democrats and Republicans were evenly matched and had to share power, which produced a political deadlock at the federal level.

Picturing **History**

Answer: Farmers thought that their problems were due to a shortage of currency and that Eastern bankers had pressured Congress into reducing the money supply.
Ask: What do you think it would be like to spend a winter in this type of dwelling? *(It would be cold and damp.)*

More Skill Practice

Connecting Have students research and report on how the Sherman Antitrust Act was used in the case to try to break up Microsoft in the late 1990s. Encourage students to use the library and Internet to locate information. **AL** **CA CS1**

Answers and Additional Support

needed and made it harder for farmers to sell their goods overseas. Farmers also felt victimized by large and faraway entities: the banks from which they obtained loans and the railroads that set their shipping rates. They doubted that either the Democrats or the Republicans would respond to their concerns. Instead, farmers embraced **populism,** a movement to increase farmers' political power and to work for legislation in their interest.

One problem that greatly concerned farmers was the nation's money supply. To help finance the Union war effort, the United States Treasury had greatly expanded the money supply by issuing millions of dollars in greenbacks—paper currency that could not be exchanged for gold or silver coins. This rapid increase in the money supply without an accompanying increase in goods for sale caused **inflation,** or a decline in the value of money. As the paper money lost value, the prices of goods soared.

After the Civil War, the United States had three types of currency in circulation—greenbacks, gold and silver coins, and national bank notes backed by government bonds. To bring inflation under control, the federal government stopped printing greenbacks and began paying off its bonds. In 1873 Congress also decided to stop making silver into coins. These decisions meant that the United States did not have a large enough money supply to meet the needs of the country's growing economy. As the economy expanded, **deflation**—an increase in the value of money and a decrease in the general level of prices—began. As money increased in value, prices began to fall.

Farmers' Alliance This small band of farmers met in a cabin in Lampasas County, Texas, to form the Farmers' Alliance.

Deflation hit farmers especially hard. Most farmers had to borrow money for seed and other supplies to plant their crops. Because money was in short supply, interest rates began to rise, which increased the amount farmers owed.

Many farmers concluded that Eastern bankers had pressured Congress into reducing the money supply. They began to call for the printing of more greenbacks and the minting of silver coins. Farmers realized that if they were going to convince the government to meet their demands, they needed to organize. In increasing numbers they joined the first national farm organization, the Patrons of Husbandry, better known as the **Grange.** Grangers tried to create cooperatives—marketing organizations that helped farmers by pooling crops and holding them off the market in order to force up prices and by negotiating better shipping rates with the railroads. The Grange's cooperatives ultimately failed, partly because they were too small to have any effect on prices, and partly because Eastern businesses and railroads considered them to be similar to unions— illegitimate conspiracies in restraint of trade—and refused to do business with them.

Meanwhile, several Western states passed "Granger laws" setting maximum rates and prohibiting railroads from charging more for short hauls than for long ones. The railroads fought back by cutting services and refusing to lay new track until the laws were repealed. Then the 1886 Supreme Court ruling in *Wabash* v. *Illinois* greatly limited the states' ability to regulate railroads by ruling that states could not regulate commerce that crossed state lines. *(See page 1007 for more information on* Wabash v. Illinois.)

The Farmers' Alliance By the late 1870s, membership in the Grange had started to fall, and a new organization, the Farmers' Alliance, took its place. Alliance leaders hoped that by establishing very large cooperatives, called exchanges, they could force farm prices up and make loans to farmers at low interest rates. Despite their temporary success, the large cooperatives failed. In many cases, wholesalers, manufacturers, railroads, and bankers discriminated against them, making it difficult for them to stay in business. The exchanges also failed because they were still too small to dramatically affect world prices for farm products.

By 1890 the failure of the Alliance to fix farmers' problems had started a power struggle within the organization. Some Alliance leaders, particularly in the Western states, wanted to form a new party and push for political reforms. Members of the Kansas

Did You Know?

Grange comes from the Middle Latin word *granica*, which is derived from the Latin *granum,* or "grain." At one time the grange was the farm of a monastery, where grain was stored.

Did You Know?

Farmers in 37 states belong to the Grange today. The organization still pursues its original goals of providing educational and social support to farmers and their families.

Alliance formed the **People's Party,** also known as the Populists, and nominated candidates to run for Congress and the state legislature. Most Southern leaders of the Alliance did not want to undermine the Democrats' control of the South. Instead, they endorsed candidates who supported their demands.

The Rise of Populism In 1890 members of the Farmers' Alliance met in Ocala, Florida, and issued what came to be known as the Ocala Demands. These demands called for the free coinage of silver, an end to protective tariffs and national banks, tighter regulation of the railroads, and direct election of senators by voters instead of by state legislatures.

To discourage farmers from voting for Populists, the Republicans in Congress, led by Senator John Sherman, pushed through the Sherman Silver Purchase Act of 1890. This act authorized the United States Treasury to purchase 4.5 million ounces of silver per month. It put more money into circulation and may have reduced the deflation slightly, but it did little to help the farmers.

The midterm elections of 1890 seemed to suggest that farmers' strategies had worked. In the South, several states had pro-Alliance governors and state legislatures, and over 40 Democrats who supported the Alliance program were elected to Congress. The People's Party did equally well in the West.

Despite their promises, few Democrats followed through by supporting the Alliance program, either at the state or the federal level. In May 1891, Western populists met with some labor and reform groups and endorsed the creation of a new national People's Party to run candidates for president. By early 1892 many Southern farmers had also reached the point where they were willing to break with the Democratic Party and join the People's Party.

A Populist for President In July 1892, the newly organized People's Party nominated James B. Weaver to run for president. At their convention in Omaha, Nebraska, party members endorsed a platform, or program, that spelled out the party's positions in strong terms. The platform denounced the government's refusal to coin silver and called for a return to unlimited coinage of silver, federal ownership of railroads, and a **graduated income tax,** one that taxed higher earnings more heavily.

Above all, the Populists wanted government to defend the public against what they saw as greedy and irresponsible private interests. The Omaha platform took positions popular with labor, including calling for an eight-hour workday, restricting immi-

gration, and denouncing strikebreaking. Still, most urban workers preferred to remain within the Democratic Party.

Democratic candidate Grover Cleveland, who wanted to return to the White House after his close defeat in 1888, won with the support of Northern cities and the South. He had 277 votes in the Electoral College, compared to 145 for his Republican opponent Benjamin Harrison. The Populist candidate, James Weaver, did remarkably well, winning four states and splitting two others for a total of 22 electoral votes.

Not long after Cleveland's inauguration in 1893, the nation plunged into the worst economic crisis it had ever experienced. The panic began in March when the Philadelphia and Reading Railroads declared bankruptcy. Many railroads had expanded too rapidly in the period before the panic and now found it hard to repay their loans. The stock market on Wall Street crashed, and banks closed their doors. By 1894 the economy was deep in a depression, with approximately 18 percent of the workforce unemployed.

The Panic of 1893 also created a crisis for the United States Treasury. Many American and European investors who owned U.S. government bonds began cashing in their bonds for gold, leaving the federal government's gold reserves at a dangerously low level. Unlike many Democrats, President Cleveland believed the United States should use gold, not silver or paper money, as the basis for its currency. In an effort to protect the government's reserves, in June 1893 he pushed through the repeal

Picturing **History**

Populist Farmers When attempts to organize support organizations failed, farmers began to turn to populism. Why did farmers and other populists form a new party?

Picturing **History**

Answer: Farmers did not think that either the Democrats or the Republicans would respond to their concerns about lower crop prices, difficulty selling crops overseas, or difficulties with the banks and railroads.

Ask: Who was the first Populist candidate for president? *(James Weaver)*

Did You Know?

The Populist Party had an impact on politics and government far beyond its showing in national elections. Populist proposals that were adopted include the federal income tax (Sixteenth Amendment, 1913), direct election of U.S. senators (Seventeenth Amendment, 1913), the secret ballot (late 1890s), and primary elections (Wisconsin, 1903).

C Critical Thinking

C Critical Thinking

Comparing and Contrasting
Have students work in small groups to brainstorm the characteristics of political candidates that influence voters. *(Answers will vary but may include style, appearance, economic position, trustworthiness, etc.)* **Ask:** In what order of importance would you rate these characteristics for a political candidate? *(Students' ratings will vary.)* **BL**

R Reading Strategy

Summarizing Divide the class into groups of five. **Ask:** What, in your own words, was the dilemma that the Populists faced at their nominating convention? *(They could nominate Bryan and risk losing their own identity or nominate their own candidate and risk losing sufficient support for the silver issue.)* Have groups write their answers in paragraphs and present them to the class. **OL**

Answers and Additional Support

Picturing **History**

C **Campaigns in Contrast** In 1896 Democrat William Jennings Bryan (left) ran an energetic campaign for president, traveling far and wide. Republican William McKinley (right) campaigned from the front porch of his Canton, Ohio, home. How did their campaign styles work out?

of the Sherman Silver Purchase Act, which had allowed the exchange of silver for gold. Cleveland's actions split the Democratic Party into two factions: goldbugs, who believed American currency should be based only on gold, and silverites, who believed coining silver in unlimited quantities would solve the nation's economic crisis.

The Election of 1896 As the election of 1896 approached, leaders of the People's Party decided to make the silver issue the focus of their campaign. They also decided to hold their convention after the Republican and Democratic conventions. They believed the Republicans would endorse a gold standard, which they did. They also expected the Democrats to nominate Cleveland again and hoped that when the People's Party strongly endorsed silver, pro-silver Democrats would abandon their party and vote for the Populists in large numbers.

Unfortunately for the Populists, their political strategy failed. The Democrats did not waver on the silver issue. Instead, they nominated **William Jennings Bryan,** a strong supporter of silver. When the Populists gathered in St. Louis for their own convention, they faced a difficult choice: endorse Bryan and risk undermining their identity as a separate party, or nominate their own candidate and risk splitting the silver vote. They eventually decided to support Bryan.

Bryan waged an unusually energetic campaign for the presidency, traveling thousands of miles and making 600 speeches in 14 weeks. In sharp contrast,

Republican William McKinley, a former governor and member of Congress, conducted what the newspapers called his "Front-Porch Campaign" by meeting with various delegations that came to visit him at his Canton, Ohio, home.

The Republicans campaigned against the Democrats by blaming Cleveland's administration for the depression and promising workers that McKinley would provide a "full dinner pail." This meant a lot more to most urban workers than the issue of silver money. At the same time, most business leaders supported the Republicans, convinced that unlimited silver coinage would ruin the country. Many employers warned their workers that if Bryan won, businesses would fail, unemployment would rise, and wages would be cut.

McKinley's reputation for moderation on labor issues and tolerance toward different ethnic groups helped improve the Republican Party's image with urban workers and immigrants. When the votes were counted, McKinley had won a decisive victory. He captured 51 percent of the popular vote and had a winning margin of 95 electoral votes—hefty numbers in an era of tight elections. By embracing populism and its rural base, Bryan and the Democrats lost the more populous Northern industrial areas where votes were concentrated.

Opposition to the gold-based currency dwindled during McKinley's time in office. The depression was over, and prospectors found gold in Canada in 1896 and in Alaska in 1898. That wealth, combined with new gold strikes in South Africa and other parts of the world, increased the money supply without turning to silver. This meant that credit was easier to obtain and farmers were less distressed. In 1900 the United States officially adopted a gold-based currency.

278 CHAPTER 3 The Birth of Modern America

Picturing **History**

Background: William Jennings Bryan campaigned for the presidency in 1896, 1900, and 1908. He was unsuccessful all three times.
Answer: McKinley won
Ask: Which candidate's style is the closest to the way that modern candidates campaign? *(Bryan's, because of the great distances he traveled seeking to win votes)*

When the silver crusade died out, the Populists lost their momentum. Their efforts to ease the economic hardships of farmers and to regulate big business had not worked. Some of the reforms they favored, however, including the graduated income tax and some governmental regulation of the economy, came about in the next century.

✓ **Reading Check** **Explaining** What were the main goals of the Populist Party?

The Rise of Segregation

Main Idea In the late 1800s, Southern states passed laws that denied African Americans the right to vote and imposed segregation.

Reading Connection What is a "loophole"? Think of a loophole from which you may have benefited or suffered. Then read on to learn how Southern racists used a loophole in the Fifteenth Amendment to prevent African Americans from voting.

After Reconstruction, many African Americans in the rural South lived in conditions that were little better than slavery. They were technically free, but few escaped from grinding poverty. Most were sharecroppers, landless farmers who had to hand over to the landlord a large portion of their crops to cover the cost of rent, seed, tools, and other supplies. They had barely enough income to survive, and they were always in debt.

Resistance and Repression Many African Americans eventually left farming and sought jobs in Southern towns or headed west to claim homesteads. In 1879, 70-year-old Benjamin "Pap" Singleton, himself formerly enslaved, organized a mass migration of thousands of African Americans from the rural South to Kansas. The newspapers called it "an Exodus," like the Hebrews' escape from Egyptian bondage. The migrants themselves came to be known as "Exodusters."

While some African Americans fled the South, others joined with poor white farmers who had created the Farmers' Alliance. In 1886 they created the Colored Farmers' National Alliance. When the Populist Party formed in 1891, many African American farmers became members. They hoped that the new People's Party would unite poor whites and poor blacks to challenge the Democratic Party's power in the South. Populism posed a new challenge to the Democratic Party in the South. If enough poor whites left the party and joined with African American Populists, the new coalition might become unbeatable.

To win back the poor white vote, Democratic leaders began appealing to racism. They warned whites that support for Populists or joint Republican-Populist parties would return the South to "Black Republican" rule similar to Reconstruction. Election officials also began using various methods to make it harder and harder for African Americans to vote.

Disfranchising African Americans The Fifteenth Amendment prohibited states from denying citizens the right to vote on the basis of "race, color, or previous condition of servitude." However, it did not bar the governments from requiring that citizens be literate or own property in order to vote. Using this loophole, Southern states began imposing restrictions that barred nearly all African Americans from voting.

Mississippi took this step first in 1890 by requiring that all citizens registering to vote pay a **poll tax** of $2, a sum beyond the means of most poor African Americans. Mississippi also instituted a literacy test, requiring that **prospective** voters be able to read or understand the state constitution. Few African Americans were able to read, and even those who

Picturing **History**

A Kansas Home Many African Americans left the rural South to find a new life. They usually began with very little. Why were they called Exodusters?

Picturing **History**

Answer: from the term Exodus, referring to the Hebrews' escape from Egypt
Ask: Why did the Exodusters have so little when the arrived in Kansas? *(because they were poor sharecroppers who were in debt)*

R₁ **Reading Strategy**
Previewing Before students read the text under this heading, ask them the following questions: What was the Fifteenth Amendment? *(It prohibited states from denying citizens the right to vote on the basis of "race, color, or previous condition of servitude.")* How could it be used to prevent people from voting? *(Students should brainstorm some answers and make changes to them as they read the text.)* **OL**

R₂ **Reading Strategy**
Organizing Information Organize students into groups of three and assign each group a Southern state. Ask each group to research and identify the specific methods their state used to restrict voting. Have each group prepare a chart that lists the various provisions of its voting law, and the year that the law or state constitutional amendment was passed. Have the groups explain their charts to the class. **OL**

Review the Big Idea
Review the Big Idea for this section, "People react to periods of breathtaking social and cultural change in different ways." Have students use the library and the Internet to research the migration of African Americans to Kansas. They should use their research to write letters describing what life was like once they settled in their new community to family members staying behind. **OL**
CA 11WA2.1a; 11WA2.1b

✓**Reading Check**
Answer: The Populist Party fought for the free coinage of silver, federal ownership of railroads, a graduated income tax, and the direct election of senators.

could often failed the literacy test because local officials deliberately picked complicated passages. Other Southern states adopted similar restrictions. The results were devastating, with the numbers of African Americans registered to vote dropping to a few thousand in several states.

The number of white voters also fell significantly. Local Democratic Party leaders were not sorry to exclude poor whites, because they had helped fuel the Populist revolt. Some states gave whites a special break with the so-called **grandfather clause,** by allowing any man to vote if he had an ancestor who appeared on voting rolls.

Legalizing Segregation In the late 1800s, discrimination was not confined to the South. African Americans in the North had often been barred from many public places used by whites. In the South, **segregation,** or separation of the races, was different because laws enforced and perpetuated the discrimination. The statutes enforcing segregation were known as **Jim Crow laws.**

Picturing **History**

Crusading Journalist Ida B. Wells, seen here with her son, campaigned fiercely against lynching in the 1890s. What two factors did Wells believe to be behind lynchings?

280 CHAPTER 3 The Birth of Modern America

In 1883 the Supreme Court set the stage for legalized segregation by overturning the Civil Rights Act of 1875. That law had prohibited keeping people out of public places on the basis of race, and it also prohibited racial discrimination in selecting jurors. The Supreme Court decision stated that since the Fourteenth Amendment only provided that "no state" could deny citizens equal protection under the law, only state actions were subject to challenge. Private organizations and businesses, such as hotels, theaters, and railroads, were free to practice segregation.

Encouraged by this ruling and by the decline of congressional support for civil rights, Southern states passed a series of laws that enforced segregation in virtually all public places. Southern whites and African Americans could no longer ride together in the same railroad cars, eat in the same dining halls, or even drink from the same water fountains.

In 1892 an African American named Homer Plessy challenged a Louisiana law that forced him to ride in a separate railroad car from whites. He was brought to trial before criminal court judge John H. Ferguson, who rejected Plessy's argument that the law was unconstitutional. In 1896 the Supreme Court, in *Plessy* v. *Ferguson,* upheld the Louisiana law and expressed a new legal doctrine endorsing "separate but equal" facilities for African Americans. *(See page 964 for more information on Plessy v. Ferguson.)* The ruling established the legal basis for discrimination in the South for more than 50 years to come. While public facilities for African Americans in the South were always separate, they were far from equal. In many cases, they were inferior.

African American Response African Americans faced more than legal segregation. In the late 1800s, mob violence increased. Between 1890 and 1899, mobs carried out an average of 187 lynchings—executions without proper court proceedings—each year. Over 80 percent of the lynchings occurred in the South, and nearly 70 percent of the victims were African Americans. **Ida B. Wells,** a fiery young African American woman from Tennessee, launched a fearless crusade against lynching in 1892. She pointed out that greed, not just racial prejudice, was often behind these brutal acts. Although Congress rejected an anti-lynching bill, the number of lynchings decreased significantly in the 1900s due in great part to the efforts of activists such as Wells.

Booker T. Washington, an influential educator, proposed that African Americans concentrate on achieving economic goals rather than legal or political ones. He summed up his views in an 1895 speech known as the Atlanta Compromise. In this address, Washington urged African Americans to postpone the fight for civil rights and instead concentrate on preparing themselves educationally and vocationally for full equality:

> 66 The wisest among my race understand that the agitation of questions of social equality is the extremest folly, and that the enjoyment of all the privileges that will come to us must be the result of severe and constant struggle rather than of artificial forcing. . . . It is important and right that all privileges of the law be ours, but it is vastly more important that we be prepared for the exercise of these privileges. 99
>
> –adapted from *Up From Slavery*

The Atlanta Compromise speech provoked a strong challenge from **W.E.B. Du Bois**, the leader of a new generation of African American activists born after the Civil War. Du Bois pointed out in his 1903 book *The Souls of Black Folk* that white Southerners continued to strip African Americans of their civil rights. African Americans could regain lost ground and achieve full equality only by demanding their rights—especially the right to vote. "[V]oting is necessary to proper manhood," Du Bois wrote, adding that "color discrimination is barbarism." In the years that followed, many African Americans worked to win the vote and end discrimination. The struggle would prove to be a long one.

✓ Reading Check **Identifying** How did Southern states restrict African American voting rights in the 1890s?

"color discrimination is barbarism"

—*W.E.B. Du Bois*

Picturing History

African American Activist W.E.B. Du Bois opposed the Atlanta Compromise. What issue was of particular concern to Du Bois?

HISTORY Online **Study Central**

For help with the concepts in this section of *American Vision: Modern Times* go to tav.mt.glencoe.com and click on *Study Central.*

SECTION 5 ASSESSMENT

Checking for Understanding

1. **Vocabulary Define:** volume, populism, inflation, deflation, graduated income tax, poll tax, prospective, grandfather clause, segregation, Jim Crow laws.

2. **People and Terms:** Identify: Stalwart, Pendleton Act, Interstate Commerce Act, Grange, People's Party, William Jennings Bryan, Ida B. Wells, W.E.B. DuBois.

3. **Describe** the events leading to the Pendleton Act.

Reviewing Big Ideas

4. **Explaining** Why were the Republicans and Democrats not effective, and why did the Populists gain support in the late 1800s?

Critical Thinking

5. **Examining** After Reconstruction, why did many African Americans in the South live in conditions that were little better than slavery?

6. **Organizing** Use a graphic organizer similar to the one below to identify the organizations that formed to help farmers and their goals.

Organization	Goals

7. **Analyzing Photographs** Examine the photograph of an "Exoduster" family on page 279. Pose questions about the photograph to your classmates in a quiz and then have them answer the questions.

Writing About History

8. **Persuasive Writing** Imagine you support the Populist Party and that you have been asked to write copy to be used in a campaign poster for your party's candidates. Include a slogan that provides reasons for people to support the Populists.

CHAPTER 3   The Birth of Modern America   **281**

SECTION 5 ASSESSMENT ANSWERS

1. Content vocabulary is boldfaced and highlighted in yellow. Academic vocabulary is boldfaced.

2. Stalwarts *(p. 272)*, Pendleton Act *(p. 272)*, Interstate Commerce Act *(p. 274)*, Grange *(p. 276)*, People's Party *(p. 277)*, William Jennings Bryan *(p. 278)*, Ida B. Wells *(p. 280)*, W.E.B. Du Bois *(p. 281)*

3. Garfield's assassination exposed the problems of the spoils system.

4. Both main parties held about equal voting strength and would not generate enough support for change; Populists received support from struggling farmers.

5. They owned no property and worked as sharecroppers.

6. Grange: created cooperatives to pool resources; Farmers' Alliance: formed exchanges to raise the price of crops; People's Party: supported free coinage of silver.

7. Students' questions will vary.

8. Slogans should address the issues or the candidates.

ASSESS

Resources for page 281

Use these resources to assess student mastery.

📁 Section Quiz 3-5

📁 Reading Essentials and Study Guide 3-5

💿 Interactive Tutor Self-Assessment CD-ROM

📁 California Standards Practice, Grade 11

Picturing History

Background: W.E.B. Du Bois earned three degrees at Harvard and was one of the founders of the NAACP.

Answer: voting rights

Ask: Who gave the address known as the Atlanta Compromise? *(Booker T. Washington)*

✓ Reading Check

Answer: poll taxes, literacy tests, requiring that voters be property owners, grandfather clause

---

HISTORY Online

Study Central provides audio summaries, interactive games, and online graphic organizers to help students review section content.

CLOSE

Drawing Conclusions Have students describe the major problems of the farmers in the late 1800s. **OL**

TIME NOTEBOOK

FOCUS

History–Social Science Standards

This feature addresses the following standards:

11.2 Students analyze the relationship among the rise of industrialization, large-scale rural-to-urban migration, and massive immigration from Southern and Eastern Europe.

11.2.2 Describe the changing landscape, including the growth of cities linked by industry and trade, and the development of cities divided according to race, ethnicity, and class.

11.10 Students analyze the development of federal civil rights and voting rights.

TEACH

R Reading Strategy

Reading Primary Sources Ask students the following questions after they have read the excerpt of the exposé by Jacob Riis: **What problems does Riis cite in this excerpt?** *(overcrowding, filth, poor water system, and all-night parties)* **How does Riis view the landlords of the building?** *(They are profiting at the expense of the tenants.)* **What problems may children encounter in such crowded conditions?** *(possible answers: sicknesses, lack of attention, a poor night's sleep, poor nutrition)* **OL** **CA** 11RC2.4; 11RL3.8

Answers and Additional Support

Eyewitness

In his exposé of urban poverty, How the Other Half Lives *(1890),* **JACOB RIIS** *documented the living conditions in New York City tenements:*

"The statement once made a sensation that between seventy and eighty children had been found in one tenement. It no longer excites even passing attention, when the sanitary police report counting 101 adults and 91 children in a Crosby Street house, one of twins, built together. The children in the others, if I am not mistaken, numbered 89, a total of 180 for two tenements! Or when midnight inspection in Mulberry Street unearths a hundred and fifty "lodgers" sleeping on filthy floors in two buildings. In spite of brown-stone fittings, plate-glass and mosaic vestibule floors, the water does not rise in summer to the second story, while the beer flows unchecked to the all-night picnics on the roof. The saloon with the side-door and the landlord divide the prosperity of the place between them, and the tenant, in sullen submission, foots the bill."

VERBATIM

❝Tell 'em quick, and tell 'em often.❞

WILLIAM WRIGLEY,
soap salesman and promoter of chewing gum, on his marketing philosophy

❝A pushing, energetic, ingenious person, always awake and trying to get ahead of his neighbors.❞

HENRY ADAMS,
historian, describing the average New Yorker or Chicagoan

❝We cannot all live in cities, yet nearly all seem determined to do so.❞

HORACE GREELEY,
newspaper editor

INDICATORS:
Livin' in the City

Moving off the farm for a factory job? Sharpen your pencil. You'll need to budget carefully to buy all you will need.

Here are the numbers for a Georgia family of four in 1890. The husband is a textile worker, and the wife works at home. There is one child, age 4, and a boarder. They share a two-room, wood-heated, oil-lighted apartment.

INCOME: (annual)

husband's income	$312.00
boarder's rent	10.00
TOTAL INCOME	**$322.00**

EXPENSES: (annual)

medical	$65.00
furniture	46.90
clothing	46.00
rent	21.00
flour/meal	25.00
hog products	17.00
other meat	13.00
vegetables	13.00
lard	6.50
potatoes	6.40
butter	5.00
sugar	4.00
charitable donations	6.10
vacation	3.25
alcohol	3.25
tobacco	3.00
molasses	2.00
other food	27.80
miscellaneous	68.20
TOTAL EXPENSES	**$382.40**

COOPERATIVE LEARNING ACTIVITY

Creating a Magazine Spread Organize the class into four groups. Have each group identify a current social problem and write an exposé-style essay for a magazine. Groups should research the problem and use facts in the essay. Then have groups create magazine spreads for the articles. Students should look at magazines for ideas about page design and photo placement. This activity can be completed using desktop publishing software or the cut-and-paste method. **OL** **CA** 11WS1.5; 11WS1.6

W Milestones

ON THE RUN, 1881. THE JESSE JAMES GANG, after robbing a Chicago, Rock Island, and Pacific train near Winston, Missouri, and killing the conductor and a passenger.

OVERTURNED, 1878. By the Supreme Court, a Louisiana court decision that awarded damages to an African American woman who had been refused admission to a steamship stateroom reserved for whites.

PLAGUED BY GRASSHOPPERS, 1874. THE AMERICAN GREAT PLAINS. Insect swarms a mile wide blot out the midday sun. Two inches deep on the ground, they leave "nothing but the mortgage," as one farmer put it.

CELEBRATED IN EUROPE, 1887. ANNIE OAKLEY, star of Buffalo Bill's Wild West Show. Oakley shot a cigarette from the lips of Crown Prince Wilhelm of Germany. Years later, when the U.S. goes to war against Kaiser Wilhelm, Oakley will quip: "I wish I'd missed that day!"

Susan B. Anthony

Jesse James

REMOVED, 1884. IDA B. WELLS, journalist and former slave, from a ladies coach on a train. Wells refused to move to the smoking car where African Americans were to be seated.

ESTABLISHED, 1883. STANDARD TIME. To accommodate the railroad system, noon will no longer be the moment in a given locality when the sun stands highest in the sky but, instead, will be standard across four time zones. Set your watches!

ARRESTED, 1872. SUSAN B. ANTHONY, for casting a ballot in Rochester, New York. Anthony argued that the Fourteenth and Fifteenth Amendments applied to women.

NUMBERS

1 in 12 Americans living in cities of 100,000 or more in 1865

A crowded New York City street

1 in 5 Americans living in cities in 1896

522 Inhabitants in a one-acre area in the Bowery, New York City

$2 Daily wage for a farm laborer, New York, 1869

$4 Daily wage for a plumber, New York City, 1869

50¢ Price of a pair of boy's knee pants, a parasol, button boots, or a necktie (1870s)

$8 Price of a "Fine All-Wool Suit," 1875

$3 Box seat for four at Gilmore's Concert Garden in New York City

4¢ Price for one pound of fancy white rice, 1896

25¢ Admission to "Barnum's American Museum" (featuring the smallest pair of human beings ever seen!), 1896

EXTENDING THE CONTENT

Urban Pollution In New York City in 1866, a report on sanitary conditions in the city included the following problems: (1) filthy streets; (2) neglected garbage and domestic refuse; (3) obstructed and faulty sewers and drains; (4) neglected privies and stables; (5) cattle pens and large stables in the more populous districts; (6) neglected and filthy markets; (7) slaughterhouses and hide and fat deposits in close proximity to populous streets; (8) droves of cattle and swine in crowded streets; (9) swill-milk stables; (10) bone boiling, fat melting . . . within the city limits; (11) . . . offensive exhalations . . . in gas manufacture; (12) . . . dumping grounds and manure yards in vicinity of populous streets.

W Writing Support

Portfolio Writing Project
Have students use the library or Internet to research one of the people or events listed in the Milestones. Ask them to write descriptive essays about the person or event. Encourage students to read their essays aloud to the class. **OL** **CA** 11WA2.4b

U Universal Access

Logical/Mathematical Have students use library and Internet resources to research the number of Americans living in cities and in rural areas today. Then have them use this number to calculate the percentage of Americans living in cities. **Ask: Has the percentage increased or decreased from 1 in 5 (20%) in 1896? By how much? Why?** Ask students to explain the reasons for the change. **OL** **CA** CS3

S Skill Practice

Conducting Research Tell students to research interesting numbers from life today and organize the information into a database. Then have each student create five questions that can be answered using the database. Students should answer each other's questions. **OL** **CA** CS1; CS3

ASSESS/CLOSE

As a class, discuss whether the quotes in the Verbatim section on page 282 are still valid today.

Visit the **TIME** Web site at **www.time.com** for up-to-date news, weekly magazine articles, editorials, online polls, and an archive of past magazine and Web articles.

FOCUS

Understanding Vocabulary

Before students begin reading, point out that difficult or unfamiliar words are footnoted throughout the text.

TEACH

C Critical Thinking

Predicting Consequences Tell students to find information on the impact of the inventions mentioned in this passage. **Ask: How did these inventions affect American workers?** *(increased speed of production but lessened number of workers needed; workers had to be hired in factories)* **OL**

Answers and Additional Support

284

Primary Sources
Eyewitness to History

Americans struggled to respond to the rapid industrialization of the United States in the years after the Civil War. As business profits grew, many workers were faced with losing their jobs to machines or working in factories under stressful, monotonous, or dangerous conditions.

SOURCE 1

Henry George worked as a journalist in San Francisco. He was puzzled by the existence of extreme wealth and extreme poverty side by side in the United States. George wrote **Progress and Poverty** *in 1879 to argue for economic and social reform.*

At the beginning of this marvelous era it was natural to expect, and it was expected, that labor-saving inventions would lighten the **toil**[1] and improve the condition of the laborer; that the enormous increase in the power of producing wealth would make real poverty a thing of the past. Could a man of the last century . . . have seen, in a vision of the future, the steamship taking the place of the sailing vessel, the railroad train of the wagon, the reaping machine of the **scythe**[2], the threshing machine of the **flail**[3]; . . . could he have conceived of the hundred thousand improvements which these only suggest, what would he have inferred as to the social condition of mankind? . . .

Plainly, in the sight of the imagination, he would have beheld these new forces elevating society from its very foundations, lifting the very poorest above the possibility of want, exempting the very lowest from anxiety for the material needs of life. . . .

Now, however, we are coming into collision with facts which there can be no mistaking. From all parts of the civilized world come complaints of industrial depression; of labor condemned to involuntary idleness. . . . All the dull, deadening pain, all the keen, maddening anguish, that to great masses of men are involved in the words "hard times," afflict the world to-day. . . .

[1] **toil:** work
[2] **scythe:** farm tool with a cutting blade
[3] **flail:** farm tool that pounds

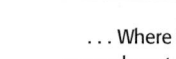

▲ *Henry George*

. . . Where the conditions to which material progress everywhere tends are most fully realized—that is to say, where population is densest, wealth greatest, and the machinery of production and exchange most highly developed—we find the deepest poverty, the sharpest struggle for existence, and the most of enforced idleness.

SOURCE 2

David A. Wells was a scientist and economist. He was one of the first Americans to notice that machines were taking the jobs of workers. In his 1889 book **Recent Economic Changes**, *Wells discussed how advances in technology had begun to change society.*

UNIVERSAL ACCESS

Kinesthetic Divide the class into two groups, one representing factory assembly line workers and the other representing factory supervisors. Give each of the assembly line workers a simple, repetitive task (such as taking a ping pong ball in and out of a cup). Ask each worker to continue doing the assigned task for several minutes. Ask the supervisors to keep an eye on the workers and require them to continually speed up their rate of working. After several minutes of this, tell everyone to stop and write reflections on what they experienced. Have members of each group share their thoughts with the class. **OL**

▲ *Andrew Carnegie*

SOURCE 3:

Andrew Carnegie, the Scottish-born "King of Steel," was the nation's biggest industrialist in the late 1800s. He was also industry's most famous spokesperson, typically celebrating competition and the benefits of life in the United States. Carnegie wrote Triumphant Democracy, *a best-seller, in 1886.*

A community of toilers with an undeveloped continent before them, and destitute of the refinements and elegancies of life—such was the picture presented by the Republic sixty years ago. Contrasted with that of today, we might almost conclude that we were upon another planet and subject to different primary conditions. The development of an unequaled transportation system brings the products of one section to the doors of another, the tropical fruits of Florida and California to Maine, and the ice of New England to the Gulf States. Altogether life has become vastly better worth living than it was a century ago.

Among the rural communities, the change in the conditions is mainly seen in the presence of labor-saving devices, lessening the work in house and field. Mowing and reaping machines, horse rakes, steam plows and threshers, render man's part easy and increase his productive power. Railroads and highways connect him with the rest of the world, and he is no longer isolated or dependent upon his petty village. Markets for his produce are easy of access and transportation swift and cheap. If the roads throughout the country are yet poor compared with those of Europe, the need of good roads has been rendered less imperative by the omnipresent railroad. . . .

[A]s a result of this change in the methods of production . . . the individual no longer works as independently as formerly, but as a private in the ranks, obeying orders, keeping step, as it were, to the tap of the drum, and having nothing to say as to the plan of his work, of its final completion, or of its ultimate use and distribution. In short, the people who work in the modern factory are, as a rule, taught to do one thing—to perform one, and generally a simple, operation; and when there is no more of that kind of work to do, they are in a measure helpless. The result has been that the individualism or independence of the producer in manufacturing has been in a great degree destroyed, and with it has also in a great degree been destroyed the pride which the workman formerly took in his work—that **fertility**[4] of resource which formerly was a special characteristic of American workmen, and that element of skill that comes from long and varied practice and reflection and responsibility. . . .

[4] **fertility:** ability to produce great amounts

DBQ Document-Based Questions

Historical Analysis CA HR2; HR4

Source 1: What did George believe should have happened as the result of technological improvements?

Source 2: According to Wells, how did the life of the individual worker change?

Source 3: According to Carnegie, how has life improved for Americans?

Comparing and Contrasting Sources

Do George, Wells, and Carnegie agree or disagree about the life of the industrial worker? Explain.

W Writing Support

Persuasive Writing Tell students to imagine that they are an industrialist, such as John D. Rockefeller, who employs many unskilled laborers in his factories. Ask each student to write a letter from Rockefeller to David Wells in response to the criticism voiced in source 2. *(Students will likely point out the greatly increased levels of production caused by the factory system and how this system assisted immigrants coming to the United States to find work. It resulted in lowering costs for purchasing goods and generated a great deal of jobs.)* OL

R Reading Strategy

Reading Primary Sources Andrew Carnegie was a great believer in innovation. His factories outproduced those of his rivals because he was constantly upgrading his machinery. **Ask: How does Carnegie believe improved transportation has aided the development of the modern United States?** *(eased transport of goods and products from region to region, increased the sales market for goods, simplified the travel of Americans)* OL

ASSESS/CLOSE

Have students answer the Document-Based Questions.

DBQ Document-Based Questions

1. It should have eased the hardships of work by providing mechanical assistance to labor-intensive jobs.

2. Individual workers had no more independence. They worked as one of many workers, trapped by the rhythm of the machines.

3. Individuals have greater freedom of movement and a wider variety of products available.

Comparing and Contrasting Sources George and Wells agree that mechanization has dehumanized the worker. Workers must work according to the speed and demands of the industrial equipment. Carnegie sees industrialization as providing more benefits than harm. People are more mobile and have access to a wider variety of goods and markets.

Use the following resources to review, assess, and reteach the chapter.

📁 Chapter 3 Tests, Forms A and B

📁 Standardized Tests, Forms A and B

📁 Cumulative Authentic Assessment

🖥 MindJogger Videoquiz

💿 Interactive Tutor Self-Assessment CD-ROM

💿 Exam*View*® Pro Testmaker CD-ROM

💿 Vocabulary PuzzleMaker CD-ROM

💿 Succeeding on . . .™ the California Standards: Grade 11 History–Social Science

📁 California Standards Practice, Grade 11

Reviewing Content Vocabulary

Students' answers will vary. The pages where the words appear in the text are shown in parentheses.

1. homestead *(p. 240)* **2.** gross national product *(p. 244)* **3.** laissez-faire *(p. 245)* **4.** corporation *(p. 248)* **5.** monopoly *(p. 249)* **6.** Marxism *(p. 250)* **7.** industrial union *(p. 250)* **8.** closed shop *(p. 251)* **9.** tenement *(p. 260)* **10.** political machine *(p. 261)* **11.** Social Darwinism *(p. 266)* **12.** populism *(p. 276)* **13.** inflation *(p. 276)* **14.** deflation *(p. 276)* **15.** graduated income tax *(p. 277)* **16.** poll tax *(p. 279)* **17.** grandfather clause *(p. 280)* **18.** Jim Crow laws *(p. 280)*

Reviewing Academic Vocabulary

Students' answers will vary. The pages where the words appear in the text are shown in parentheses.

19. extract *(p. 237)* **20.** adapt *(p. 238)* **21.** distribution *(p. 248)* **22.** concept *(p. 249)* **23.** commission *(p. 261)* **24.** evolve *(p. 266)* **25.** volume *(p. 274)* **26.** prospective *(p. 279)*

Reviewing Content Vocabulary

On a sheet of paper, use each of these terms in a sentence.

1. homestead
2. gross national product
3. laissez-faire
4. corporation
5. monopoly
6. Marxism
7. industrial union
8. closed shop
9. tenement
10. political machine
11. Social Darwinism
12. populism
13. inflation
14. deflation
15. graduated income tax
16. poll tax
17. grandfather clause
18. Jim Crow laws

Chapter Summary

The Birth of Modern America

1860	
	1862 Homestead Act
	John D. Rockefeller buys first oil refinery
	1869 First transcontinental railroad completed
1870	**1876** Alexander Graham Bell invents telephone
	1877 Interstate Commerce Act adopted
	Florida initiates Jim Crow laws
	1882 Chinese Exclusion Act
1880	**1886** American Federation of Labor founded
	1889 Jane Addams founds Hull House
	1890 Wounded Knee Massacre
	Sherman Antitrust Act adopted
1890	
	1892 Ellis Island immigration center opens
	National People's Party formed
	1896 *Plessey v. Ferguson* creates "separate but equal" doctrine
1900	

286

Reviewing Academic Vocabulary

On a sheet of paper, use each of these terms in a sentence that reflects the term's meaning in the chapter.

19. extract	22. concept	25. volume
20. adapt	23. commission	26. prospective
21. distribution	24. evolve	

Reviewing the Main Ideas

Section 1

27. What government act provided an incentive for people to farm the Great Plains?

Section 2

28. Why did workers try to organize labor unions in the United States in the late 1800s?

Section 3

29. What attempts did nativist groups make to decrease immigration to the United States in the late 1800s?

Section 4

30. What movements in the late 1800s addressed urban problems?

Section 5

31. What was the significance of the Supreme Court's ruling in *Plessy v. Ferguson*?

Critical Thinking

32. **Reading Skill** **Comparing and Contrasting** Reread Section 4 of this chapter. Identify the signal words and text that compare information in the text. Then do the same for the signal words and text that contrast information.

33. **Civics** What methods did political machines use to build support in the late 1800s?

34. **Explaining** Why was the type of currency used in the United States an important issue to farmers in the late 1800s?

35. **Organizing** Use a graphic organizer similar to the one below to list the factors that led to making the United States an industrial nation.

Factors Leading to Industrialization

Reviewing the Main Ideas

27. the Homestead Act

28. to change poor working conditions, low pay, and job security

29. set up American Protective Association, set up Working Man's Party of California, worked to get Chinese Exclusion Act passed

30. Social Gospel, revivalism, and settlement house movement

31. Plessy's challenge of a state law forcing him to ride in a separate railroad car led to the Supreme Court decision establishing the "separate but equal" doctrine and continuing social segregation.

Writing About History

36. **Historical Analysis** **Interpreting Maps** Review the map titled "Major Industries" on page 245. Who made this map? What is the purpose of the map? How does the map support the section? **CA CS3**

37. *Big Idea* The United States had an advantage in industrializing due to its resources and large workforce. What resources did the nation have? Why was its workforce large?

38. **Descriptive Writing** Imagine that you are a newspaper editor in the late 1800s. Write an editorial in which you support the philosophy of Social Darwinism or Social Gospel. Identify similarities and differences in the ideologies. Include reasons to support your position. **CA 11WS1.1**

DBQ Document-Based Questions

39. **Interpreting Primary Sources** Americans like Ida Tarbell criticized large corporations such as the Standard Oil Company. In the following excerpt from History of the Standard Oil Company, she warns of the results of Rockefeller's business practices on the nation's morality. Read the excerpt and answer the questions that follow:

> ❝Very often people who admit the facts, who are willing to see that Mr. Rockefeller has employed force and fraud to secure his ends, justify him by declaring, 'It's business.' That is, 'It's business' has come to be a legitimate excuse for hard dealing, sly tricks, special privileges.
>
> As for the ethical side, there is no cure but in an increasing scorn of unfair play. . . . When the businessman who fights to secure special privileges, to crowd his competitor off the track by other than fair competitive methods, receives the same summary disdainful ostracism by his fellows that the doctor or lawyer who is 'unprofessional,' the athlete who abuses the rules, receives, we shall have gone a long way toward making commerce a fit pursuit for our young men.❞
>
> –quoted in *Readings in American History*

a. According to Tarbell, what practices had Rockefeller used to establish the Standard Oil Company?

b. In what way did Tarbell believe the attitudes of the American people contributed to Rockefeller's business practices?

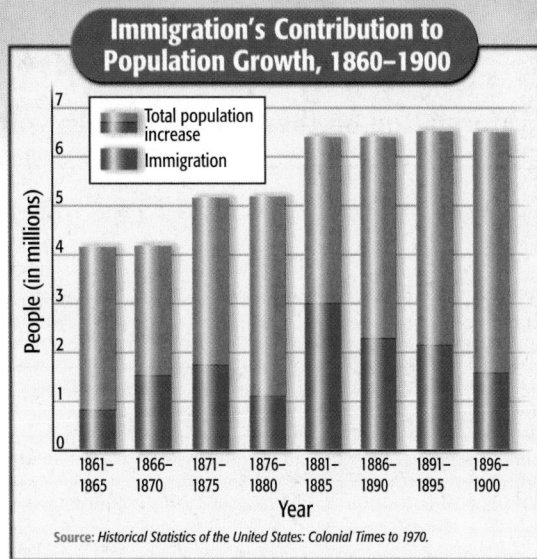

Immigration's Contribution to Population Growth, 1860–1900

Source: *Historical Statistics of the United States: Colonial Times to 1970.*

Geography and History

40. The graph above shows how much immigration contributed to population growth in the United States between 1860 and 1900. Study the graph and answer the questions below.

   a. **Interpreting Graphs** By about how much did the population of the United States increase between 1861 and 1900?

   b. **Understanding Cause and Effect** What is the relationship between immigration and population increase?

Standards Practice

Directions: Choose the best answer to the following question.

41. Labor unions were formed in order to

A protect factory owners and improve workers' wages.

B improve workers' wages and make factories safer.

C make factories safer and prevent lockouts.

D prevent lockouts and fight deflation.

Standard 11.6.5: Trace the advances and retreats of organized labor, from the creation of the American Federation of Labor and the Congress of Industrial Organizations to current issues of a post-industrial multinational economy, including the United Farm Workers in California.

Writing About History

36. **Historical Analysis** National Geographic; shows major industries c. 1900; shows resources, railroads, and industries based on these resources

37. *Big Idea* Students should identify iron ore, water, copper, coal, and timber as resources. The workforce consisted of large families and floods of immigrants.

38. Editorials should choose either Social Darwinism or Social Gospel. Students should clearly identify reasons for their choice.

DBQ Document-Based Questions

39. a. force and fraud; b. the "it's just business" attitude that excused immoral actions

Geography and History

40. a. by about 2.5 million; b. Immigration played a significant role, especially in the period from 1881 to 1885.

Standards Practice

41. B

Bonus Question ?

Ask: What was the only ethnic group to be officially excluded by federal law from immigrating to the United States between 1870 and 1900? *(the Chinese)*

Critical Thinking

32. **Reading Skill** Students should identify all the signal words for comparing and contrasting in Section 4.

33. They provided housing, jobs, food, heat, and police protection to new immigrants unfamiliar with the United States and its culture.

34. Without greenbacks and silver coins, the money supply could not meet the needs of the growing economy. The value of money increased, and crop prices began to fall.

35. large labor force, inventions, abundant natural resources, free enterprise system

Unit 2 Resources

Teaching the Unit

Use the information on these pages to help you teach Unit 2.

History–Social Science Standards Covered in Unit 2

Standard	Chapter 4	5	6
11.2 Students analyze the relationship among the rise of industrialization, large-scale rural-to-urban migration, and massive immigration from Southern and Eastern Europe.	✔	✔	
11.3 Students analyze the role religion played in the founding of America, its lasting moral, social, and political impacts, and issues regarding religious liberty.	✔		
11.4 Students trace the rise of the United States to its role as a world power in the twentieth century.	✔		✔
11.5 Students analyze the major political, social, economic, technological, and cultural developments of the 1920s.		✔	

Pacing Your Lessons

This pacing chart provides time management suggestions for teaching Unit 2.

	Days
Unit 2 Introduction	1
Chapter 4 • **Reading Skill:** Cause and Effect • **Historical Analysis Skill:** Evaluating Past Events • **Sections 1–3** • **You're the Historian:** Who Sank the *Maine?* • **Why It Matters:** The Panama Canal • **Eyewitness to History:** Primary Source Documents	7
Chapter 5 • **Reading Skill:** Making Inferences • **Historical Analysis Skill:** Interpreting Events • **Sections 1–4** • **American Literature:** *The Jungle* by Upton Sinclair • **National Geographic:** Geography & History: The Story of Yosemite • **Eyewitness to History:** Primary Source Documents	8
Chapter 6 • **Reading Skill:** Using Problem/Solution • **Historical Analysis Skill:** Distinguishing Valid and Fallacious Arguments • **Sections 1–4** • **TIME Notebook:** A War to End All Wars: 1914–1918 • **Eyewitness to History:** Primary Source Documents	9

Urban America

Heather Pang
Castilleja School
Palo Alto, California

Select 10 to 15 images from Jacob Riis's *How the Other Half Lives* (available online at http://www.cis.yale.edu/amstud/inforev/riis/title.html and in most libraries). Images of children are particularly effective for this exercise. Show these pictures to the students (slides, scanned images, or photocopies).

Organize the students into small groups and assign each group one of the following roles: city police, local school board, charitable organization, philanthropic guild, schoolchildren, garment district workers, and a merchants' association. Each group should use the pictures as evidence to prepare a report titled "Poverty in the City: What Is to Be Done?" Remind the students that each of these groups will have different reactions to the Riis images depending on their own backgrounds. Each report should list the most significant problems shown in the images and provide suggestions for solutions.

It might be helpful to start the lesson with a short introduction to Riis and the tradition of muckraking journalism.

Previewing the Chapters

Dear American History Teacher:

As you begin to teach this unit, there are themes that recur throughout the chapters that you will want to point out to students.

The expansion of the American economy and its projection beyond the borders of the United States are hallmarks of this period. By the 1890s, with little potential for territorial growth in North America, the United States sought to acquire colonies beyond its borders.

This expansion in turn thrust the nation into the sphere of Great Powers at a time of increasing international tensions that led to World War I. American entry into the war in 1917 created a new era of American power in the world, with its attendant responsibilities.

At home, the growing pains of industrialism spawned many reform movements that came to be called Progressivism. These reforms addressed some of the worst social and economic problems, but did not overcome all of the injustices in American society.

You may want to use the following information at the beginning of each chapter as a lesson launcher to help students begin to focus on what they will be studying.

James M. McPherson

Chapter 4: Becoming a World Power, 1872–1912

(pages 290–321)

During the last decades of the nineteenth century, the United States began involving itself more and more in global affairs. Whether for economic, missionary, or military reasons, Americans balanced the tradition of American isolation versus American imperialism. The Spanish-American War involved the United States for all of these reasons.

Chapter 5: The Progressive Movement, 1890–1919

(pages 322–361)

The Progressive Era defines a period of social change. Progressive reformers began their efforts to improve local and state governments, making them more efficient and equitable. Reforms at state levels, especially the woman suffrage movement, soon became issues for the federal government. Presidents Roosevelt, Taft, and Wilson all supported federal progressive reform,

attempting to use the power of government to regulate private industry and systematize the interaction between public and private organizations.

Chapter 6: World War I and Its Aftermath, 1914–1920

(pages 362–399)

President Woodrow Wilson's opposition to imperialism and belief in democracy guided his foreign policy in the years leading up to World War I. Though initially neutral, the United States eventually entered into the European conflict. Once committed, American politicians used many progressive ideas to organize the wartime economy and mobilize the armed forces. President Wilson's Fourteen Points represented his desire to create a just peace after World War I and to build international organizations to prevent similar wars in the future. The U.S. Senate rejected his peace efforts as the nation turned inward and the economy shifted back to peacetime production. The nation, tired of domestic and international struggles, sought normalcy in the 1920s, signaling an end to the Progressive Era.

FOCUS

History– Social Science Standards

This unit addresses the following main standards:

11.2 Students analyze the relationship among the rise of industrialization, large-scale rural-to-urban migration, and massive immigration from Southern and Eastern Europe.

11.3 Students analyze the role religion played in the founding of America, its lasting moral, social, and political impacts, and issues regarding religious liberty.

11.4 Students trace the rise of the United States to its role as a world power in the twentieth century.

11.5 Students analyze the major political, social, economic, technological, and cultural developments of the 1920s.

Connecting to Past Learning

In Unit 1, students learned about the formation of the United States and its development from the Revolutionary War through the Civil War and Industrialization. In Unit 2, the development of the United States as a world power will be presented.

Unit Launch Activity

Remind students of George Washington's warning to stay away from foreign alliances. Tell them that after the Civil War, the United States developed into a world power. Discuss in class why Americans might have become interested in foreign affairs. **OL**

Why It Matters Activity

Tell students that the Pure Food and Drug Act of 1906 regulated standards on food and drugs. **Ask: How does passage of this act affect us today?** *(Students should mention such things as ingredient lists on food products and quality inspections performed on such food.)* **OL**

288

UNIT 2 Imperialism and Progressivism

1890–1919

World War I pin

Why It Matters

As the United States entered the twentieth century, it grew to become a world power. While the nation was expanding its territory into other parts of the world, conditions at home gave rise to a widespread Progressive movement. This movement worked for various reforms in government, business, and society. While Americans focused on their own country, Europe slid into a devastating world war that eventually involved the United States as well. These crucial years of domestic change and foreign conflict provided important foundations for the world you live in today. The following resources offer more information about this period in American history.

Primary Sources Library

See pages 974–975 for primary source readings to accompany Unit 2.

Use the American History Primary Source Document Library CD-ROM to find additional primary sources about imperialism and progressivism.

American Troops Arriving in Paris July 14, 1918 by J.F. Boucher

288

> "It is hard to fail, but it is worse never to have tried to succeed."

—Theodore Roosevelt, 1899

TEACH

Skill Practice

Recognizing Point of View
Instruct students to read Theodore Roosevelt's quote on the top of this page. **Ask:** What does this quote indicate about Roosevelt's personality? As students read through the unit, instruct them to look for actions Roosevelt took as president that supported this point of view. OL
CA HR4

Skill Practice

Visual Literacy Although the war itself was devastating to Europe, fanfare often accompanied American troops marching into large cities such as Paris. The United States's involvement in the war was brief compared to that of European powers, but the European people often viewed Americans as heroes who had saved Allied countries from complete destruction. **Ask:** What is the mood and tone of this painting? *(Students should use descriptive words to describe what they see in the painting and how they feel about the painting.)* BL

NC LB NO CHILD LEFT BEHIND

Teaching Tip The NCLB Act emphasizes reading. Ask students to write down events and people they will encounter in this unit and keep the list with them as they read. When students find a person or item on the list, they should note the page number and write a brief summary. Students can use this list while studying.

UNIVERSAL ACCESS

Below Grade Level: Have students write the term "world power" on a piece of paper. Underneath the term, ask them to write what they think this term means in their own words. As students study the unit, have them add information and explanations to help them fully understand the term's meaning. BL

Advanced Learners: Ask students to pick one event in Unit 2 they think had a major impact on U.S. history. Have them prepare a two-page paper in which they explain why their chosen event was important. AL

Chapter 4 Planning Guide

SECTION RESOURCES

MAIN IDEAS	PRINT MATERIALS	TECHNOLOGY RESOURCES
Section 1: The Imperialist Vision 1. A desire for world markets and belief in the superiority of white culture led the United States to assert itself as a world power. 2. The desire for new markets led to trade with Japan and the annexation of Hawaii. 3. The United States worked to increase trade with Latin America. 4. The United States began constructing a large navy to protect its international interests.	• Reproducible Lesson Plan 4-1* • Daily Lecture and Discussion Notes 4-1 • Active Reading Note-Taking Guide 4-1 • Guided Reading Activity 4-1 • Section Quiz 4-1 • Reading Essentials and Study Guide 4-1	• Daily Focus Skills Transparency 4-1 • Section Graphic Organizer Transparency 4-1 • Interactive Tutor Self-Assessment CD-ROM • ExamView® Pro Testmaker CD-ROM • Presentation Plus! CD-ROM • California Standards Practice Transparencies
Section 2: The Spanish-American War 1. In support of the Cuban rebellion and in retaliation for the loss of the USS *Maine,* the United States declared war on Spain. 2. The United States fought Spain in both the Pacific and the Caribbean. 3. Victory in the Spanish-American War allowed the United States to expand its holdings in the South Pacific and to control Puerto Rico and Cuba.	• Reproducible Lesson Plan 4-2* • Daily Lecture and Discussion Notes 4-2 • Active Reading Note-Taking Guide 4-2 • Guided Reading Activity 4-2 • Section Quiz 4-2 • Reading Essentials and Study Guide 4-2	• Daily Focus Skills Transparency 4-2 • Section Graphic Organizer Transparency 4-2 • Interactive Tutor Self-Assessment CD-ROM • ExamView® Pro Testmaker CD-ROM • Presentation Plus! CD-ROM • California Standards Practice Transparencies
Section 3: New American Diplomacy 1. Theodore Roosevelt went from governor of New York to president in a few short years and supported the country's rise to a world power. 2. The United States pursued an Open Door policy in China to allow all nations access to China's markets. 3. Theodore Roosevelt pushed for construction of the Panama Canal and declared the intent of the United States to act as a police force in Latin American nations.	• Reproducible Lesson Plan 4-3* • Daily Lecture and Discussion Notes 4-3 • Active Reading Note-Taking Guide 4-3 • Guided Reading Activity 4-3 • Section Quiz 4-3 • Reading Essentials and Study Guide 4-3	• Daily Focus Skills Transparency 4-3 • Section Graphic Organizer Transparency 4-3 • Interactive Tutor Self-Assessment CD-ROM • ExamView® Pro Testmaker CD-ROM • Presentation Plus! CD-ROM • California Standards Practice Transparencies

PACING YOUR LESSONS

Chapter Introduction	Section 1	Section 2	Section 3	Chapter Assessment
½ Day	2 Days	2 Days	2 Days	½ Day

0:00 **OUT OF TIME?** Assign the Chapter 4 *Reading Essentials and Study Guide.*

*Available on TeacherWorks™ CD-ROM

Chapter 4 Planning Guide

Standards-Based Lesson Plan

 History–Social Science Standards Covered in Chapter 4

The standards covered in the chapter are listed below. Use the accompanying activity as you teach the chapter to ensure student mastery of these standards. This activity can be used in combination with the program's print and technology assessment materials.

Standard	Section 1	Section 2	Section 3
11.2.7 Analyze the similarities and differences between the ideologies of Social Darwinism and Social Gospel (e.g., using biographies of William Graham Sumner, Billy Sunday, Dwight L. Moody).	✔		
11.3.2 Analyze the great religious revivals and the leaders involved in them, including the First Great Awakening, the Second Great Awakening, the Civil War revivals, the Social Gospel Movement, the rise of Christian liberal theology in the nineteenth century, the impact of the Second Vatican Council, and the rise of Christian fundamentalism in current times.	✔		
11.4 Students trace the rise of the United States to its role as a world power in the twentieth century.		✔	✔
11.4.1 List the purpose and effects of the Open Door policy.			✔
11.4.2 Describe the Spanish-American War and U.S. expansion in the South Pacific.	✔	✔	✔
11.4.3 Discuss America's role in the Panama Revolution and the building of the Panama Canal.			✔
11.4.4 Explain Theodore Roosevelt's Big Stick diplomacy, William Taft's Dollar Diplomacy, and Woodrow Wilson's Moral Diplomacy, drawing on relevant speeches.			✔

Cumulative Standards-Assessment Activity

The Cumulative Standards-Assessment Activity will help students organize and learn the important information from the chapter. Begin teaching the chapter with this activity, and have students complete it as they read the chapter.

CREATING A MAIN IDEA AND SUPPORTING DETAILS CHART

Purpose Reviewing how to locate main ideas throughout the chapter will help students continue to refine their reading skills. This type of organizer aids students in identifying main ideas and their supporting details. It helps them develop the skill of knowing what is important and what is supportive of the main ideas. Students will need to use information about how the text is structured and combine it with what they know about the topic. Identifying main ideas and details can give students practice in logical and systematic thinking.

Introduction to Modeling

1. Begin the discussion with a brainstorming session. Ask students to list what they know or believe they know about American imperialism. Write the information on an overhead transparency. Have them identify some key main ideas about this period of American expansionism from the list. You might also want to model how certain comments are, in fact, details that support a main idea.

2. Ask students to copy this chart into their notebooks.

As students read each section, ask them to search for a main idea, and have them fill in the chart with as many supporting details as necessary. Encourage them to create more charts as they encounter important concepts during their reading.

3. As part of your chapter review, have students share their charts. Consider asking them to do a final chart with a single main idea for the entire chapter. Encourage them to use their charts as study aids.

Chapter 4 Planning Guide

READING SUPPORT

- 📁 Content Vocabulary Activity 4
- 📁 Academic Vocabulary Activity 4
- 📁 Reading Skills Activity 4
- 📁 Chapter 4 Active Reading Note-Taking Guide
- 📁 Chapter 4 Guided Reading Activities
- 📁 Chapter 4 Reading Essentials and Study Guide
- 🔒📼 *The American Vision: Modern Times* Video Program
- 💿 Vocabulary PuzzleMaker CD-ROM
- 💿 American History Primary Source Document Library CD-ROM

CRITICAL THINKING

- 📁 Critical Thinking Skills Activity 4
- 📁 Primary Source Reading 4
- 📁 Cause-and-Effect Transparency 4 Strategy and Activity
- 💿 Presentation Plus! CD-ROM

UNIVERSAL ACCESS

- 📁 Universal Access Activity 4
- 📁 English Learner Activity 4
- 📙 American Art Prints
- 💿 StudentWorks™ Plus CD-ROM
- 🎵 American Music: Hits Through History
- 📁 School-to-Home Connection Activity 4

SKILL PRACTICE

- 📁 Map Overlay Transparency 4 Strategy and Activity
- 📁 Historical Analysis Skills Activity 4
- 📁 Time Line Activity 4
- 📁 Reading Skills Activity 4
- 📁 Reinforcing Skills Activity 4
- 📁 Linking Past and Present Activity 4
- 📁 Interpreting Political Cartoons 4
- 🔒📼 MindJogger Videoquiz

WRITING SUPPORT

- 📁 Chapter 4 Active Reading Note-Taking Guide
- 📁 Writer's Guidebook
- 📁 High School Writing Process Transparencies

ASSESSMENT

- 📁 Chapter 4 Section Quizzes
- 📁 Chapter 4 Tests, Forms A and B
- 📁 Authentic Assessment Activity 4
- 💿 Exam*View*® Pro Testmaker CD-ROM
- 💿 Interactive Tutor Self-Assessment CD-ROM
- 📁 California Standards Practice, Grade 11
- 💿 Succeeding on . . .™ the California Standards: Grade 11 History–Social Science CD-ROM

💿	CD-ROM	📁	Transparency
📦	DVD	🎵	Music Program
📁	Print Material	📼	Videocassette
📙	Poster		

Chapter 4 Planning Guide

TECHNOLOGY

- StudentWorks™ Plus CD-ROM
- TeacherWorks™ CD-ROM
- ExamView® Pro Testmaker CD-ROM
- Interactive Tutor Self-Assessment CD-ROM
- Presentation Plus! CD-ROM
- Vocabulary PuzzleMaker CD-ROM
- American History Primary Source Document Library CD-ROM
- MindJogger Videoquiz
- *The American Vision: Modern Times* Video Program
- Professional Development in High School Social Studies Video Series
- Teach, Use, and Succeed With *The American Vision: Modern Times*
- American Music: Hits Through History
- Succeeding on . . .™ the California Standards: Grade 11 History–Social Science CD-ROM

SPANISH RESOURCES

- Spanish Activities and Assessment
  - Spanish Vocabulary Activities
  - Spanish Guided Reading Activities
  - Spanish Quizzes and Tests
  - Spanish Reteaching Activities
- Spanish Reading Essentials and Study Guide
- Spanish School-to-Home Connection Activities

TRANSPARENCIES

- Daily Focus Skills Transparencies
- Section Graphic Organizer Transparencies
- Map Overlay Transparencies
- Cause-and-Effect Transparencies
- Unit Time Line Transparencies
- Why It Matters Transparencies
- American Art and Architecture Transparencies
- High School Writing Process Transparencies
- California Standards Practice Transparencies

TEACHER PLANNING

- Daily Lecture and Discussion Notes
- English Learner Handbook
- Building Academic Vocabulary
- *The American Vision: Modern Times* Reading and Study Skills Foldables
- Reading Strategies and Activities for the Social Studies Classroom
- Universal Access for the American History Classroom
- NGS United States Desk Map
- NGS World Atlas
- Chapter 4 Reproducible Lesson Plans on TeacherWorks™ CD-ROM
- California Guide to Daily Intervention

PROFESSIONAL DEVELOPMENT

- Building Academic Vocabulary
- Strategies for Success
- Research-Based Strategies Used to Develop *The American Vision: Modern Times*
- Character Education in the High School Classroom
- Professional Development in High School Social Studies Video Series
- Teach, Use, and Succeed With *The American Vision: Modern Times*

Chapter 4 Planning Guide

TEACHER'S CORNER

Index to National Geographic Magazine:
The following articles relate to this chapter:

- "Alone Across the Arctic Crown," April 1993
- "Remember the *Maine*," February 1998

National Geographic Society Products:
To order the following, call National Geographic at 1–800–368–2728

- *Hawaii: Strangers in Paradise* (Video)
- *Historical Atlas of the United States* (Atlas)

NGS ONLINE

Access National Geographic's new dynamic MapMachine Web site and other geography resources at:

www.nationalgeographic.com

www.nationalgeographic.com/maps

History Online

Use our Web site for additional resources. All essential content is covered in the Student Edition.

You and your students can visit tav.mt.glencoe.com, the Web site companion to the **American Vision: Modern Times.** This innovative integration of electronic and print media offers your students a wealth of opportunities. The student text directs students to the Web site for the following options:

- **Chapter Overviews**
- **Self-Check Quizzes**
- **Student Web Activities**
- **Textbook Updates**

Answers to the student Web activities are provided for you in the **Web Activity Lesson Plans.** Additional Web resources and ePuzzles and games are also available.

MASTERING THE STANDARDS

The content and assessment in the Student Edition, Teacher Wraparound Edition, teacher planning materials, and the print and technology products are all standards-based. The use of these products during instruction leads to mastery of the standards.

PRACTICE
- California Standards Practice, Grade 11
- California Standards Practice Transparencies
- School-to-Home Connection

BENCHMARK ASSESSMENT
- Section Quizzes, Chapter Tests, and Authentic Assessment
- Exam*View*® Pro Testmaker CD-ROM
- Succeeding On . . . ™ the California Standards: Grade 11 History–Social Science CD-ROM

REMEDIATION
- California Guide to Daily Intervention
- Interactive Tutor Self-Assessment CD-ROM
- Exam*View*® Pro Testmaker CD-ROM
- California Standards Practice, Grade 11
- Reading Essentials and Study Guide

FOLDABLES™ Study Organizer
Dinah Zike's Foldables

Foldables are three-dimensional, interactive graphic organizers that help students practice basic writing skills, review key vocabulary terms, and identify main ideas. Every chapter has a foldable activity in the *Dinah Zike's Reading and Study Skills Foldables* booklet. You can use the foldables as they are presented or modify them to suit the needs of your individual class.

A variety of videotape programs are available from A&E Television and The History Channel to provide teaching assistance. To order, call Glencoe at 1-800-334-7344.

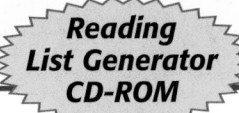

Reading List Generator CD-ROM

GLENCOE BOOKLINK

The Glencoe BookLink CD-ROM is a database that allows you to search more than 15,000 titles to create a customized reading list for your students.

■ Reading Lists can be organized by students' reading level, author, genre, theme, or area of interest.

■ The database provides Degrees of Reading Power™ (DRP) and Lexile™ readability scores for all selections.

■ A brief summary of each selection is included.

Leveled reading suggestions for this chapter:

For students at a Grade 8 reading level:
■ *Theodore Roosevelt: 26th President of the United States,* by Rebecca Stefoff

For students at a Grade 9 reading level:
■ *William McKinley: 25th President of the United States,* by David R. Collins

For students at a Grade 10 reading level:
■ *The Path Between the Seas: The Creation of the Panama Canal 1870–1914,* by David McCullough

READING SUPPORT FROM JAMESTOWN EDUCATION

• *Timed Readings Plus in Social Studies* help students increase their reading rate and fluency while maintaining comprehension. The 400-word passages are similar to those found on state and national assessments.

• *Reading in the Content Area: Social Studies* concentrates on six essential reading skills that help students better comprehend what they read. The book includes 75 high-interest nonfiction passages written at increasing levels of difficulty.

• *Reading Fluency* helps students read smoothly, accurately, and expressively.

• *Jamestown's Reading Improvement,* by renowned reading expert Edward Fry, focuses on helping build your students' comprehension, vocabulary, and skimming and scanning skills.

• *Critical Reading Series* provides high-interest books, each written at three reading levels.

For more information about these products, see the Jamestown Education materials in the Classroom Solutions in the front of this Teacher Wraparound Edition. To order these products, call Glencoe at 1-800-334-7344.

KEY for Using the Teacher Wraparound Edition

Use this key to help you identify the different types of prompts found in the Teacher Wraparound Edition.

R **Reading Strategies** activities help you teach reading skills and vocabulary.

C **Critical Thinking** strategies help students apply and extend what they have learned.

U **Universal Access** activities provide differentiated instruction for students learning to speak English, along with suggestions for teaching various types of learners.

S **Skill Practice** strategies help students practice historical analysis and geography skills.

W **Writing Support** activities provide writing opportunities to help students comprehend the text.

Teaching strategies and activities have been coded for ability level appropriateness.

AL Activities for students working above grade level
OL Activities for students working on grade level
BL Activities for students working below grade level
EL Activities for English learners

FOCUS

History–Social Science Standards

This chapter addresses the following standards:

11.4.2 Describe the Spanish-American War and U.S. expansion in the South Pacific.

11.4.3 Discuss America's role in the Panama Revolution and the building of the Panama Canal.

BELLRINGER
SKILLBUILDER ACTIVITY

Have students list the areas of strength a country would need in order to develop into a world power. After completing Chapter 4, have students write a new list of the economic, industrial, and military advancements that helped the United States become a world power, and compare it against their first list.

TEACH

Thinking About the Big Ideas

As you begin teaching each section, use these questions and activities to focus on the Big Idea.

Section 1
The Imperialist Vision
Essential Question: What is imperialism? *(economic and political dominance of a strong nation over a weak nation)* Can you see evidence of imperial-

---

CHAPTER *1872–1912*

4 Becoming a World Power

~ The Big Ideas ~

SECTION 1: The Imperialist Vision

International competition can lead to conflict and cooperation. *In the late 1800s, the United States began to compete with European countries for overseas markets and power.*

SECTION 2: The Spanish-American War

The fate of nations is forever changed by monumental world events. *After the explosion of the USS* Maine, *the United States defeated Spain in a war and acquired new territories, changing the fate of other nations.*

SECTION 3: New American Diplomacy

America's military and economic strength made it a world power. *Under President Theodore Roosevelt, the United States increased its power and influence on the world stage.*

The *American Vision: Modern Times* **Video** *The Chapter 4 video, "Teddy Roosevelt and Yellow Journalism," chronicles the events leading to the United States becoming a world power.*

1872
• Victoria Claflin Woodhull becomes first female candidate for U.S. president

1881
• President Garfield assassinated by Charles Guiteau

1889
• First Pan-American conference

United States PRESIDENTS

| Grant 1869–1877 | Hayes 1877–1881 | Garfield 1881 | Arthur 1881–1885 | Cleveland 1885–1889 |

1870 *1880* *1890*

World

1874
• Britain annexes Fiji Islands

1876
• Nicholas Otto builds first practical gasoline engine

1880
• John Milne develops the seismograph

1889
• Gustave Eiffel completes tower for Paris World Exhibit

290

---

ism in international situations today? *(Answers will vary according to current events.)* Tell students that in this section they will learn how the United States used imperialism to annex new territories. **AL**

Section 2
The Spanish-American War
Essential Question: What are acceptable reasons for the United States to become involved in a foreign war? *(answers may include: to protect its financial interests; to defend an oppressed country)* As students read this section, instruct them to list the reasons why the United States intervened in Cuba's war with Spain. **OL**

Artist's rendition of Theodore Roosevelt's charge up San Juan Hill

1893
• Americans overthrow Queen Liliuokalani of Hawaii

1898
• U.S. declares war on Spain

1899
• Hay sends Open Door notes

1901
• President McKinley assassinated

SEAL OF THE CANAL ZONE ISTHMUS OF PANAMA

1904
• Panama Canal construction begins
• Roosevelt Corollary to Monroe Doctrine issued

B. Harrison 1889–1893 | Cleveland 1893–1897 | McKinley 1897–1901 | T. Roosevelt 1901–1909 | Taft 1909–1913

1900   *1910*

1895
• Louis and Auguste Lumière introduce motion pictures

1899
• Boer War begins between Great Britain and South African Republic

1900
• Boxer Rebellion begins in China

1904
• Russo-Japanese War begins

HISTORY
Online

Chapter Overview
Visit the *American Vision: Modern Times* Web site at tav.mt.glencoe.com and click on ***Chapter Overviews— Chapter 4*** to preview chapter information.

291

Section 3
New American Diplomacy
Essential Question: What evidence do you see today of the United States being a world power? *(respected military; strong influence in world diplomatic matters; financial strength and strength of U.S. currency)* Tell students that this section will highlight President Roosevelt's actions that helped develop the United States into a world power.
OL

Cultural Perspectives

In the late 1800s, many Americans began to favor expanding their country's power overseas. Many believed that the United States had a duty to spread its civilization to other parts of the world. Have students research the events in the late 1800s in Hawaii, Cuba, and Panama from the points of view of people living in those countries. **Ask:** Did they welcome U.S. intervention? Why or why not? How did their perspectives compare to those of Americans? AL

FOLDABLES™
Study Organizer

Dinah Zike's Foldables are three-dimensional, interactive graphic organizers that help students practice basic writing skills, review key vocabulary terms, and identify main ideas. Have students complete the foldable activity in the *Dinah Zike's Reading and Study Skills Foldables* booklet.

HISTORY
Online

Go to tav.mt.glencoe.com for student activities, lesson plans, and links to additional resources to help students learn about imperialism.

Reading Skill

Why It's Important

Cause and Effect is a text structure used to explain reasons and outcomes of a given event. Developing this skill of identifying cause and effect is important in the study of history because it helps students to interpret the past.

1. Introducing the Skill

Write several hypothetical events on the board, such as "Cancellation of School," or "City-wide Power Outage." Have students brainstorm possible causes and effects of each event. Record their ideas in a graphic organizer similar to the one below. **OL**

City-wide Power Outage	
Possible Causes	*Possible Effects*

2. Extending the Skill

Instruct students to find recent newspaper articles on current international or national events. Have students determine causes and effects of the events and then present their articles in class. **AL**

Answers and Additional Support

Reading Skill Cause and Effect

Authors structure text in different ways to explain information. These structures work like the frame of a house—they hold the information together in a way that helps you understand it. One such structure is cause and effect. Authors use this structure to explain an event or action and its results. Since the job of historians is to explain how and why events occurred, they often use cause and effect.

In some cases there is one reason, or cause, for an event, or effect. However, in real life few events are isolated. Sometimes several causes lead to a single effect, or one cause can have several different results. Often the result of one event can become the cause for another effect. You can recognize this kind of cause-and-effect pattern by asking a focus question based on the main idea of the passage. Then use the focus question to follow the causes and effects of a series of events.

Read the following paragraph and find the causes and effects that followed a U.S. foreign policy decision.

The American decision to force Japan to open trade played an important role in Japanese history. Many Japanese leaders concluded that the time had come to remake their society. In 1868, after a long internal power struggle, Japanese leaders began to Westernize their country. They adopted Western technology and launched their own industrial revolution. By the 1890s, the Japanese had built a powerful modern navy, and they set out to build their own empire in Asia. (page 297)

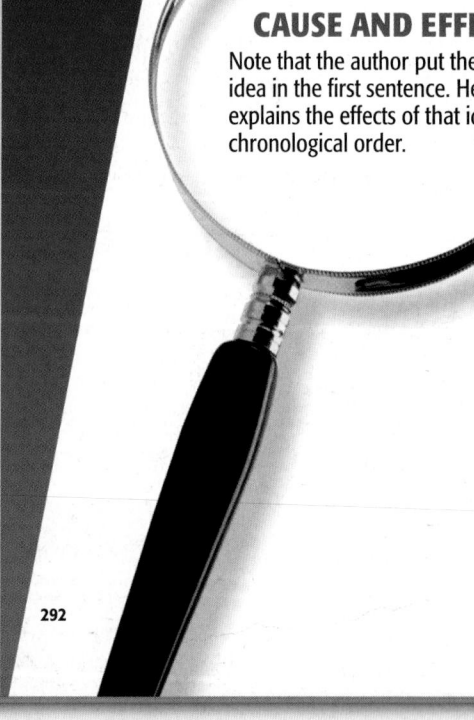

CAUSE AND EFFECT
Note that the author put the main idea in the first sentence. He then explains the effects of that idea in chronological order.

Focus question: What were the results in Japan of the U.S. decision to force open trade?

Effect #1: internal power struggle

Effect #2: decision to adopt Western technology to launch industrial revolution

Effect #3: building of modern navy

Culminating Effect: empire-building

Apply the Skill

As you read this chapter, look for passages that contain causes and effects. For each example, write down the focus question, the effects, and the culminating effect. The more you practice this skill, the easier it will be to recognize the relationship between causes and effects.

292

UNIVERSAL ACCESS

Kinesthetic Learners After students have completed reading Chapter 4, ask them to design a cause-and-effect game. Instruct students to identify specific cause-and-effect relationships in the text. Have them write each cause and effect on a separate note card and place the cards in a stack of cause cards and a stack of effect cards. Students should switch cards with classmates and work to match each cause card with the corresponding effect card. **OL**

Historical Analysis Skill

Analysis Skill Standard CS1

Evaluating Past Events

Chronological and Spatial Thinking As you study history, you should understand that comparing the present with the past will help you understand both past and current events. You should also learn to evaluate past events. Consider events both within their own time and with regard to the consequences they had for today's world. This will help you determine any lessons learned from past events.

Think back to your last year of middle school or junior high. Did you make a decision about extracurricular activities? Maybe you decided to play the trumpet or try out for a sports team. Alternatively, you may have decided to join the debate team, drama club, or start working. How have these actions from your past influenced your life today? Knowing what you know now, what advice would you give your 8th-grade self? In other words, how would you evaluate the decisions you made in 8th grade?

Historians understand that decisions made in the past were based on what people knew and believed at the time. They also realize that, as time goes by, we often change our views on events of the past. By looking at historical events and comparing them to current events, we sometimes can gain insight into our world today.

Read this quote from the well-known writer and historian John Fiske about his views on the duty of English-speaking nations to spread their civilization to other countries. He shared this belief with many other Americans.

The work which the English race began when it colonized North America is destined to go on until every land . . . that is not already the seat of an old civilization shall become English in its language, in its religion, in political habits and traditions, and to a predominant extent in the blood of its people. (page 296)

How did you react to Mr. Fiske's statement? Is this a view Americans share today? Does the issue of English as a superior language relate to arguments that people are making today? How have social norms changed or not changed in the past hundred years?

Apply the Skill

Select one of the countries discussed in this chapter into which the United States extended its influence. Review the events by asking questions similar to the ones above. As you consider the events, keep in mind the circumstances of the time. Then evaluate how the events of the past have shaped the countries involved today.

293

Preparing to Read

Historical Analysis

Why It's Important

Chronological and spatial thinking provides a skill for students to sequentially understand how events unfolded throughout history and to study how past events have shaped and influenced the present.

1. Introducing the Skill

Have students create time lines of significant events in their lifetime thus far. Then instruct students to circle key decisions and events that have impacted who they are today, such as moving to a new state or the death of a close relative. Instruct students to write a paragraph summarizing the effect of the events. **BL** **CA 11WA2.3**

2. Extending the Skill

Have students list on the board current national or international events that are making news headlines. Play a game called "What if?" Discuss how a different action or decision could have affected the outcome of each event. **Ask:** What if the countries involved had agreed to negotiating instead of declaring war? What if the tax levy would have passed instead of failed? Students should use reasoning and logic to support their hypotheses. **AL**

UNIVERSAL ACCESS

English Learners After completing Section 2 of Chapter 4, give English learners practice in verbal communication skills by pairing them with another student to evaluate the impact of the Rough Riders on the Spanish American War. Students should ask each other the following questions: **In what ways did the Rough Riders affect the outcome of the war? What qualities do you see in the Rough Riders that made them good soldiers? Do you think those same qualities are found in men and women currently serving in the armed forces?** **EL**

FOCUS

SKILLBUILDER ACTIVITY

Project **Daily Focus Skills Transparency 4-1** and have students answer the question.

Guide to Reading

Understanding Vocabulary: Have students scan the section for each content vocabulary and academic vocabulary word and write the meaning of each word from the text in their **Active Reading Note-Taking Guide.**

Answers to Graphic: Have students complete the outline based on the headings in this section.

Unpacking the Standards

Students will be able to:

- Explain how the desire for new markets led to support for imperialism.
- Describe U.S. involvement in Japan, Hawaii, and Latin America.
- Discuss the development of the United States Navy.

Answers and Additional Support

SECTION 1 The Imperialist Vision

Guide to Reading

Connection
In the previous chapter, you learned how politics hindered reform efforts and how African Americans faced growing discrimination. In this section, you will discover how Americans began to shift attention from domestic issues to foreign policy and trade.

Main Idea
- A desire for world markets and belief in the superiority of white culture led the United States to assert itself as a world power. (p. 295)
- The desire for new markets led to trade with Japan and the annexation of Hawaii. (p. 296)
- The United States worked to increase trade with Latin America. (p. 298)

- The United States began constructing a large navy to protect its international interests. (p. 299)

Content Vocabulary
imperialism, protectorate

Academic Vocabulary
technology, publish

People and Terms to Identify
Anglo-Saxonism, Matthew C. Perry, Queen Liliuokalani, Pan-Americanism, Alfred T. Mahan, Henry Cabot Lodge

Reading Objectives
- **Analyze** how a desire for more trade and markets led to political change between 1877 and 1898.

- **Cite** the motivations for and methods of American expansion in the Pacific.

Reading Strategy
Organizing As you read about the development of the United States as a world power during the late 1800s, use the major headings of the section to create an outline similar to the one below.

The Imperialist Vision
I. Building Support for Imperialism
   A.
   B.
II.
   A.
   B.

Preview of Events

♦1850		♦1875		♦1900

1853
Commodore Perry arrives in Japan

1888
Samoan Crisis erupts

1890
Alfred T. Mahan's Influence of Sea Power Upon History, 1660–1783 published

1893
American settlers overthrow Queen Liliuokalani of Hawaii

The following are the main History–Social Science Standards covered in this section.

11.2.7 Analyze the similarities and differences between the ideologies of Social Darwinism and Social Gospel (e.g., using biographies of William Graham Sumner, Billy Sunday, Dwight L. Moody).

11.3.2 Analyze the great religious revivals and the leaders involved, including the First Great Awakening, the Second Great Awakening, the Civil War revivals, the Social Gospel Movement, the rise of Christian liberal theology in the 19th century, the impact of the Second Vatican Council, and the rise of Christian fundamentalism in current times.

11.4.2 Describe the Spanish-American War and U.S. expansion in the South Pacific.

≈ The Big Idea ≈

International competition can lead to conflict and cooperation. As the pace of westward expansion slowed, many Americans looked overseas for new opportunities. Some viewed this as a chance to spread American culture and to help those they considered "less civilized." Others believed foreign markets would help the economy. These feelings eventually led to the annexation of Hawaii and to the opening of Japan to trade. The United States also bought many raw materials from Latin America and hoped to increase the sale of manufactured goods to that region. As the United States increased its influence in overseas markets, it developed the need for a strong, modern navy to protect its international interests. By the 1890s, the United States was becoming one of the top naval powers in the world.

294 CHAPTER 4 Becoming a World Power

SECTION RESOURCES

📁 Print Material
- Reproducible Lesson Plan 4-1
- Guided Reading Activity 4-1
- Reading Essentials and Study Guide 4-1
- Active Reading Note-Taking Guide 4-1

🖐 Transparencies
- Daily Focus Skills Transparency 4-1
- Section Graphic Organizer Transparency 4-1

Technology
- 💿 Interactive Tutor Self-Assessment CD-ROM
- 💿 ExamView® Pro Testmaker CD-ROM
- 💿 Presentation Plus! CD-ROM

Building Support for Imperialism

Main Idea A desire for world markets and belief in the superiority of white culture led the United States to assert itself as a world power.

Reading Connection Do you remember what role President George Washington thought the United States should play in world affairs? Read on to find out how Americans' opinions changed in the 1880s.

In the years immediately following the Civil War, most Americans showed little interest in expanding their nation's territory and international influence. Instead, they focused on reconstructing the South, building up the nation's industries, and settling the West. Beginning in the 1880's, however, American opinion began to shift. More and more Americans began to favor expanding American power.

★ *An American Story* ★

On January 16, 1893, 162 United States Marines marched off the warship Boston and onto the shores of Oahu, one of the Hawaiian Islands. John L. Stevens, the American minister to Hawaii, had ordered the troops ashore. He claimed Hawaii's ruler, Queen Liliuokalani, had created widespread turmoil and endangered American lives and property. Stevens had other motives as well. He wanted to make Hawaii, with its profitable sugarcane plantations, part of the United States.

Stevens ordered the American troops to take up positions near Queen Liliuokalani's palace. Although the marines took no action against the Hawaiian government, their presence intimidated the queen's supporters. Within hours, the American settlers in Hawaii abolished the monarchy and set up a provisional—or temporary—government. On February 1, 1893, at the request of the provisional government, Stevens announced that Hawaii was now under American protection, and he hoisted the American flag over Hawaii's government buildings. Several weeks later, Stevens made his support for annexing Hawaii perfectly clear: "The Hawaiian pear is now fully ripe," he wrote, "and this is the golden hour for the United States to pluck it."

—adapted from *A History of the American People*

John Stevens was not alone in his views. Many Americans cheered the events in Hawaii and favored expanding American power. Economic and military competition from other nations, as well as a growing feeling of cultural superiority, led to this shift in opinion.

A Desire for New Markets While the United States focused inward, several European nations were expanding their power overseas. This expansion became known as the New Imperialism. **Imperialism** is the economic and political domination of a strong nation over other weaker nations.

Europeans embarked upon a policy of expansion and imperialism for many reasons. By the late 1800s, high tariffs enacted to protect against foreign competition had reduced trade between industrial countries. Companies had to look overseas for places to sell their products. At the same time, the growth of investment opportunities in western Europe had slowed. Europeans began looking overseas for places to invest their capital.

To protect their investments, the European nations began exerting control over those territories where they invested their capital and sold their products. Some areas became colonies. Many others became protectorates. In a **protectorate,** the imperial power allowed the local rulers to stay in control and protected them against rebellions and invasion. In exchange for this protection, the local rulers usually had to accept advice from the Europeans on how to govern their countries.

As the United States industrialized, many Americans took interest in the new imperialism. With settlers now filling up the western frontier, many Americans concluded that the nation had to develop new overseas markets to keep its economy strong.

"*The Hawaiian pear is now fully ripe...*"

—*John L. Stevens*

TEACH

W **Writing Support**

Research Report Writing Have students conduct library or Internet research to learn more about the reasons for imperialism in Europe. Students should present the results of their research in a three-page report. **OL**

CA 11WA2.4a

R **Reading Strategy**

Analyzing Text Structure If students are unfamiliar with a word in the text, stopping to review its meaning will help them read with confidence. **Ask:** What is the root word for *protectorate*? *(protect)* Have students list as many synonyms as they can for this word. *(shield, defend, save, harbor, shelter)* **OL**

Review the Big Idea

Review the Big Idea for this section, "International competition can lead to conflict and cooperation." As students study this section, have them note how U.S. interest in expanding abroad affected other nations. **Ask:** Do you think the governments of Japan or Hawaii could have done things differently to avoid foreign interference? *(Students may point out that the United States was too powerful to oppose.)* **AL**

Resources for page 295

*Have students read about the debates regarding American imperialism in the **Primary Source Reading 4-1** and **Primary Source Reading 4-2.***

Did You Know?

William Jennings Bryan was nominated for president three times. He lost in 1896, 1900, and 1908. In part his anti-imperialist stand helped to defeat him. Bryan did go on to become secretary of state under President Woodrow Wilson. In that post, he continued to oppose U.S. expansionist policies.

W₁ Writing Support

Letter Writing Have students imagine they live during the late 1800s. Ask them to write a letter to a relative in another country, explaining to them the idea of Anglo-Saxonism and why they think it is popular in the United States. **OL** **CA 11WS1.3**

W₂ Writing Support

Response to Literature Writing Have students use the Internet to locate a copy of *Our Country* by Josiah Strong. Instruct students to read the text and then write a paragraph explaining Strong's connection of Anglo-Saxonism to Christian missionary ideas. **OL** **CA 11RL3.2; 11WA2.2**

R Reading Strategy

Scaffolding—Academic Vocabulary The word *commission* was introduced in Chapter 3, Section 3. Ask a student to define the word. **BL**

✓ Reading Check

Answer: More people believed it was the American destiny to spread its civilization overseas.

Answers and Additional Support

A Feeling of Superiority In addition to economic concerns, other key ideas convinced many Americans to encourage expansion overseas. Many supporters of Social Darwinism argued that nations competed with each other politically, economically, and militarily, and that only the strongest would ultimately survive. They used this idea to justify expanding the power of the United States overseas.

Many Americans, such as the well-known writer and historian John Fiske, took this idea even further. Fiske argued that English-speaking nations had superior character, ideas, and systems of government, and were destined to dominate the planet:

> 66 The work which the English race began when it colonized North America is destined to go on until every land . . . that is not already the seat of an old civilization shall become English in its language, in its religion, in political habits and traditions, and to a predominant extent in the blood of its people. 99
>
> —quoted in *Expansionists of 1898*

W₁ This idea, known as **Anglo-Saxonism,** was popular in Britain and the United States. Many Americans saw it as part of the idea of Manifest Destiny. They believed that after reaching the Pacific Ocean it was the nation's destiny to expand overseas and spread its civilization to other people.

W₂ Another influential advocate of Anglo-Saxonism was Josiah Strong, a popular American minister in the late 1800s. Strong linked Anglo-Saxonism to

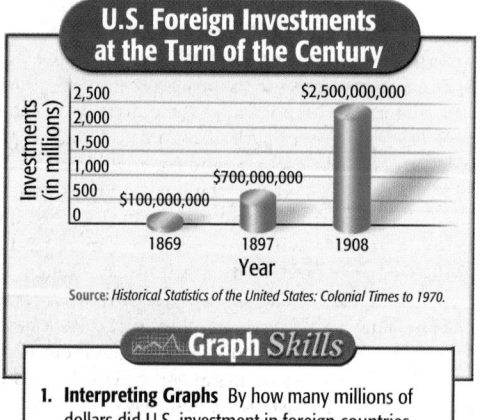

U.S. Foreign Investments at the Turn of the Century

Source: *Historical Statistics of the United States: Colonial Times to 1970.*

📈 Graph *Skills*

1. **Interpreting Graphs** By how many millions of dollars did U.S. investment in foreign countries increase between 1897 and 1908?
2. **Analyzing** How did the expansionist economic policies depicted here affect U.S. diplomacy?

Christian missionary ideas. His ideas influenced many Americans. "The Anglo-Saxon," Strong declared, "[is] divinely commissioned to be, in a peculiar sense, his brother's keeper." By linking missionary work to Anglo-Saxonism, Strong convinced many Americans to support imperialism and an expansion of American power overseas.

R

✓ Reading Check **Summarizing** How did Americans' opinions on overseas expansion begin to change in the 1800s?

Expansion in the Pacific

Main Idea The desire for new markets led to trade with Japan and the annexation of Hawaii.

Reading Connection What products do you use that have been manufactured in Japan? Read on to learn how the United States and Japan became trade partners.

From the earliest days of the Republic, Americans had expanded their nation by moving west. When Americans began looking overseas for new markets in the 1800s, therefore, they naturally tended to look westward. Even before imperialist ideas became popular, Americans had begun expanding across the Pacific Ocean toward East Asia. By the early 1800s, dozens of ships were making the long trip to China every year.

Perry Opens Japan Many American business leaders believed that the United States would benefit from trade with Japan as well as with China. Japan's rulers, however, believed that excessive contact with the West would destroy their culture and only allowed the Chinese and Dutch to trade with their nation.

In 1852, after receiving several petitions from Congress, President Millard Fillmore attempted to persuade Japan to trade with the United States. He ordered Commodore **Matthew C. Perry** to take a naval expedition to Japan to negotiate a trade treaty.

On July 8, 1853, four American warships under Perry's command entered Yedo Bay (today known as Tokyo Bay). The Japanese had never seen steamships before and were impressed by the display of American **technology** and firepower. Perry's arrival in Japan forced the Japanese to make changes internally. Realizing that they could not compete against modern Western technology and weapons, the Japanese signed a treaty opening the ports of Simoda and Hakodadi to American trade on March 31, 1854.

📈 Graph *Skills*

Answers:
1. by $1,800 million
2. caused the U.S. to have greater trade and diplomatic contacts with Asia and Latin America

Graphs Skills Practice
Ask: How would such an increase in foreign investment affect the standing of the United States? *(showed its growing power in the world)*

More Skill Practice

Historical and Social Sciences Analysis Skill Instruct students to use the Internet to expand the information on U.S. foreign investments found in the graph, showing the increases in 1925, 1950, 1975, and 2000. They should analyze the data and determine where the largest period of growth was, and what events contributed to the growth. **OL** **CA HI1**

The American decision to force Japan to open trade played an important role in Japanese history. Many Japanese leaders concluded that the time had come to remake their society. In 1868, after a long internal power struggle, Japanese leaders began to Westernize their country. They adopted Western technology and launched their own industrial revolution. By the 1890s, the Japanese had built a powerful modern navy, and they set out to build their own empire in Asia.

Annexing Hawaii As trade with China and Japan grew in the 1800s, many Americans became interested in Hawaii. Ships traveling between China and the United States regularly stopped in Hawaii to allow their crews to rest and to take on supplies. In 1820 a group of missionaries from New England settled in Hawaii. At about the same time, American whaling ships operating in the North Pacific began using Hawaii as a base.

The American settlers in Hawaii quickly discovered that the climate and soil of the islands were suitable for growing sugarcane. By the mid-1800s, many sugarcane plantations had been established in the islands. In 1872 a severe recession struck Hawaii's economy. Worried that the economic crisis might force the Hawaiians to turn to the British or French for help, the United States Senate ratified a trade treaty in 1875 that exempted Hawaiian sugar from tariffs. Several years later, when the treaty came up for renewal, the Senate insisted that the Hawaiians grant the United States exclusive rights to a naval base at Pearl Harbor.

The trade treaty led to a boom in the Hawaiian sugar industry and wealth for the planters. In 1887 prominent planters pressured Hawaiian King Kalakaua into accepting a new constitution that limited the king's authority and increased the planters' power. These developments angered the Hawaiian people, who feared they were losing control of the country.

Tensions between the planters and the Hawaiians mounted. Congress passed the McKinley Tariff in 1890. Although the tariff eliminated all duties on sugar, it also gave subsidies to sugar producers in the United States. Hawaiian sugar was now more expen-

Picturing **History**

American Imperialism To open Japan to American trade, Commodore Matthew Perry led the U.S. Navy into what is now Tokyo Bay on July 8, 1853. This lithograph shows Perry's forces arriving in Yokohama in March 1854. How did Perry's action affect Japan?

sive than American sugar, despite the lack of tariffs. As sales of Hawaiian sugar declined, the islands' economy went into a tailspin.

In 1891 **Queen Liliuokalani** ascended the Hawaiian throne. Liliuokalani disliked the influence that American settlers had gained in Hawaii. In January 1893, she unsuccessfully attempted to impose a new constitution that would have reasserted her authority as ruler of the Hawaiian people.

Faced with the economic crisis and the queen's actions, the planters backed an attempt to overthrow the monarchy. Supported by the marines from the USS *Boston*, a group of planters forced the queen to give up power and set up a provisional government. They then requested that the United States annex Hawaii. President Cleveland strongly opposed imperialism. He withdrew the annexation treaty from the Senate and tried to restore Liliuokalani to power. Hawaii's new leaders refused to restore Liliuokalani, and they decided to wait until a new president took office who favored annexation. Five years later, the United States annexed Hawaii. *(See page 997 for more text on Hawaiian annexation.)*

✓ **Reading Check** **Explaining** How did the desire to expand into new markets help push the United States to extend its influence into the Pacific?

CHAPTER 4 Becoming a World Power **297**

R₁ Reading Strategy

Summarizing Instruct students to make a list of all the steps the United States took to annex Hawaii. **BL**

R₂ Reading Strategy

Sequencing Information An important aspect of understanding history is understanding how the order of events affect other events. **Ask:** How did the McKinley Tariff affect the economy of Hawaii? *(It provided U.S. sugar producers with subsidies that allowed them to sell sugar at a cheaper rate. Hawaii then sold less sugar to the U.S. and it severely hurt the economy.)* **AL**
CA HI2

R₃ Reading Strategy

Organizing Information Have students look up *monarchy* and *democracy* in the dictionary. Working in pairs, have them list ways the two forms of government are different. **OL**

Resources for page 297

*Have students read more about the transformation of Hawaii in **Linking Past and Present Activity 4**.*

✓ **Reading Check**

Answer: It led them to annex Hawaii and open trade with Japan.

Did You Know?

Queen Liliuokalani was the last reigning monarch of Hawaii before it was annexed to the United States. She possessed musical ability and is better known for writing the song "Aloha Oe" than for her role as queen. After abdicating her throne, she withdrew from public life and died in Honolulu in 1917.

Picturing **History**

Answer: The Japanese could not compete against Western technology and weapons. They adopted Western technology, launched their own industrial revolution, and built a modern navy.
Ask: What objection did the Japanese have in the early 1850s to trading with the United States? *(The Japanese believed contact with the West would destroy their culture.)*

U Universal Access

Visual and Spatial Have students use Internet or library resources to find a diagram of a contemporary battleship. Ask them to compare the two to find out how these ships have developed and changed, as well as which elements have remained the same. **OL**

S Skill Practice

Evaluating Evidence As the United States grew in global power, it attempted to use that power to shape global issues. **Ask:** What were Secretary of State Blaine's goals for the Pan-American conference, and were they met? *(He wanted to create a customs union to reduce tariffs between American nations, as well as a system for these nations to peacefully settle disputes. These ideas were not accepted by the seventeen Latin American nations that attended.)* **AL** **CA HI4**

✓ Reading Check

Answer: He wanted to create a customs union between Latin America and the United States, as well as a system for American nations to work out their disputes peacefully.

Answers and Additional Support

Relations With Latin America

Main Idea The United States worked to increase trade with Latin America.

Reading Connection What products have you used that come from Latin America? Read on to learn how the United States tried to expand its trade relations with Latin America.

Although the United States bought raw materials from Latin America, Latin Americans bought most of their manufactured goods from Europe. American business leaders and government officials wanted to increase the sale of American products to the region. They also wanted the Europeans to recognize the United States as the dominant power in the region.

James G. Blaine, who served as secretary of state in two administrations in the 1880s, led early efforts to expand American influence in Latin America. Blaine proposed that the United States invite the Latin American nations to a conference. The conference would discuss ways in which the American nations could work together to support peace and to increase trade. The idea that the United States and Latin America should work together came to be called **Pan-Americanism.** Blaine's idea became reality in 1889 when the Pan-American conference was held in Washington, D.C. Seventeen Latin American nations attended.

Blaine had two goals for the conference. He wanted to create a customs union between Latin America and the United States. A customs union would require American nations to reduce their tariffs and to treat each other equally in trade. Blaine hoped that a customs union would turn Latin Americans away from European products and toward American products. Blaine also hoped that a common system for settling disputes would keep the Europeans from meddling in American affairs.

Although the warm reception they received in the United States impressed the Latin American delegates to the conference, they rejected both ideas. They did agree, however, to create the Commercial Bureau of the American Republics, an organization that worked to promote cooperation among the nations of the Western Hemisphere. This organization was later known as the Pan-American Union and today is called the Organization of American States (OAS).

✓ Reading Check **Summarizing** How did James Blaine try to increase American influence in Latin America?

TECHNOLOGY & History

Modern Battleships

In the 1880s, the United States Navy modernized its fleet of warships. Moving away from wooden ships powered solely by the wind, the new navy constructed steel-hulled ships with steam-powered engines as well as sails. Probably the most famous ship of this era was the *USS Maine,* one of the U.S. Navy's first armored battleships (depicted at right). It was one of the first U.S. naval vessels with electrical lighting. It had a top speed of 17 knots and a crew of 392 officers and enlisted men. *Which U.S. naval officer argued for the necessity of a modern navy?*

1. The *Maine* was designed for **sail power** as well as steam, but the sails were never fitted on the ship.

2. It had a maximum armor thickness of 12 inches.

3. Eight steam boilers powered two engines.

sail power

cowls

torpedo tubes

galley

steam boilers

magazine

armor

4. Cowls provided fresh air below decks.

5. Food was prepared in the galley.

6. Munitions were stored in the magazine.

TECHNOLOGY & History

Background: The USS *Texas* was the first commissioned battleship in the United States fleet. It was commissioned on August 15, 1895. The battleship carried two 12-inch and six 6-inch guns and was equipped with four 14-inch torpedo tubes. The ship was protected by 12-inch thick steel armor. For its era, it was one of the most powerful ships in the world.

Answer: Captain Alfred T. Mahan, whose *The Influence of Sea Power Upon History, 1660–1783,* persuaded many in government that a modern navy was necessary to protect America's expanding global trade

Building a Modern Navy

Main Idea The United States began constructing a large navy to protect its international interests.

Reading Connection Under what circumstances do you think the United States should go to war? Read on to learn about three instances when the nation nearly went to war.

As imperialism and Anglo-Saxonism gained support in the late 1800s, the United States became increasingly assertive in foreign affairs. In 1888, for example, the country was willing to go to war with Germany over control of the Samoa Islands. Three years later, the United States threatened Chile when a mob attacked American sailors in the port of Valparaíso. All crises eventually ended peacefully.

As both the American people and their government became more willing to risk war in defense of American interests overseas, support for building a large modern navy began to grow. Supporters argued that if the United States did not build up its navy and acquire bases overseas, it would be shut out of foreign markets by the Europeans.

Captain **Alfred T. Mahan,** an officer in the U.S. Navy who taught at the Naval War College, best expressed this argument. In 1890 Mahan **published** his lectures in a book called *The Influence of Sea Power Upon History, 1660–1783.* In this book Mahan pointed out that many prosperous peoples in the past had built large fleets of merchant ships in order to trade with the world. He then suggested that a nation also needed a large navy to protect its merchant ships.

Mahan observed that building a modern navy meant that the United States had to acquire territory for naval bases overseas. In the 1890s, navy warships burned coal to power their engines. To operate a navy far from home, a country needed bases and coaling stations in distant regions to refuel ships.

Mahan's book helped to build public support for a big navy. In Congress two powerful senators, **Henry Cabot Lodge** and Albert J. Beveridge, pushed for the construction of a new navy.

By the 1890s, several different ideas had come together in the United States. Business leaders wanted new markets overseas. Anglo-Saxonism had convinced many Americans that they had a destiny to dominate the world. Growing European imperialism seemed to threaten America's security. Combined with Mahan's influence, these ideas convinced Congress to authorize the construction of a modern American navy.

By the late 1890s, the United States was well on its way to becoming one of the top naval powers in the world. Although it was not yet an imperial power, it had the power to become one if the opportunity arose. In the spring of 1898 the opportunity came when war erupted between Spain and the United States.

✓ **Reading Check** **Explaining** Why did Alfred T. Mahan and Henry Cabot Lodge call for the building of a strong navy?

HISTORY *Online* **Study Central**

For help with the concepts in this section of *American Vision: Modern Times* go to tav.mt.glencoe.com and click on *Study Central.*

SECTION 1 ASSESSMENT

Checking for Understanding

1. **Vocabulary** Define: imperialism, protectorate, technology, publish.

2. **People and Terms** Identify: Anglo-Saxonism, Matthew C. Perry, Queen Liliuokalani, Pan-Americanism, Alfred T. Mahan, Henry Cabot Lodge.

3. **Explain** why Secretary of State James G. Blaine convened the Pan-American conference in 1889.

Reviewing Big Ideas

4. **Identifying** What events in the world convinced Americans to support a large navy?

Critical Thinking

5. **Historical Analysis** **Evaluating** Imagine Hawaii was never annexed and the new Constitution was implemented in 1893. Explain how Hawaii may differ politically, economically, and culturally from what it is today. **CA HI4**

6. **Organizing** Use a graphic organizer to list the factors that led to an imperialist policy in the United States in the 1800s.

Factors Leading to U.S. Imperialist Policy

Analyzing Visuals

7. **Analyzing Art** Study the picture on page 297. How is the U.S. Navy portrayed in relation to the Japanese residents of Yokohama? Do you think the artist shows any bias? Why or why not?

Writing About History

8. **Persuasive Writing** Imagine that you are living in the United States in the 1890s. Write a letter to the president persuading him to support or oppose an imperialist policy. Be sure to use standard grammar, spelling, sentence structure, and punctuation. **CA 11WS1.3**

CHAPTER 4 Becoming a World Power **299**

W **Writing Support**

Persuasive Writing Alfred T. Mahan presented persuasive arguments to support the buildup of the navy in the late 1800s. Have students imagine they are a naval officer today. Ask them to write a letter to Congress to request an increase in the strength of the modern-day navy. **OL** **CA 11WS1.3**

ASSESS

Resources for page 299

Use these resources to assess student mastery.

📁 Section Quiz 4-1

📁 Reading Essentials and Study Guide 4-1

💿 Interactive Tutor Self-Assessment CD-ROM

📁 California Standards Practice, Grade 11

✓ **Reading Check**

Answer: to protect merchant ships and defend the nation's right to trade with other countries

HISTORY *Online*

Study Central provides audio summaries, interactive games, and online graphic organizers to help students review section content.

CLOSE

Connecting Have students write a short summary of the steps outlined in this section that the United States took to become a world power. **OL**

SECTION 1 ASSESSMENT ANSWERS

1. Content vocabulary is boldfaced and highlighted in yellow. Academic vocabulary is boldfaced.

2. Anglo-Saxonism (p. 296), Matthew C. Perry (p. 296), Queen Liliuokalani (p. 297), Pan-Americanism (p. 298), Alfred T. Mahan (p. 299), Henry Cabot Lodge (p. 299)

3. to support peace and increase trade among the Americas

4. Germany tried to control Samoa Islands; Chilean mob attacked American soldiers; U.S. backed Venezuela in border dispute

5. Students' answers will vary. Students should be able to defend their point of view.

6. feeling of superiority, interest in expanding trade, need for strategic military bases, European competition

7. probable bias; U.S. troops more numerous and surround Japanese representatives

8. Letters should express a clear point of view.

299

FOCUS

SKILLBUILDER ACTIVITY

Project **Daily Focus Skills Transparency 4-2** and have students answer the question.

Guide to Reading

Understanding Vocabulary: Have students write all the content vocabulary and academic vocabulary words on index cards, and then write an event or concept on the back of the card that is associated with the name.

Answers to Graphic: Sinking of the *Maine*, sympathy for Cuban revolution, need to protect American investments in Cuba

Unpacking the Standards

Students will be able to:

• List the events that led to the Spanish-American War.

• Understand how Theodore Roosevelt's fame grew due to his actions during the war.

Answers and Additional Support

SECTION 2 — The Spanish-American War

Guide to Reading

Connection
In the previous section, you learned how the United States increased overseas trade and began developing a modern navy. In this section, you will discover how the United States went to war with Spain and how the war expanded American territory.

Main Idea
• In support of the Cuban rebellion and in retaliation for the loss of the USS *Maine*, the United States declared war on Spain. (p. 301)
• The United States fought Spain in both the Pacific and the Caribbean. (p. 303)

• Victory in the Spanish-American War allowed the United States to expand its holdings in the South Pacific and to control Puerto Rico and Cuba. (p. 305)

Content Vocabulary
yellow journalism, jingoism

Academic Vocabulary
resource, violate, virtual

People and Terms to Identify
José Martí, William Randolph Hearst, Joseph Pulitzer, Theodore Roosevelt, Platt Amendment

Reading Objectives
• **Describe** the circumstances that led to war between the United States and Spain in 1898.

• **Explain** how the war made the United States a world power.

Reading Strategy
Organizing As you read about the Spanish-American War, complete a graphic organizer like the one below by listing the circumstances that contributed to war with Spain.

Preview of Events

♦January 1898	♦May 1898	♦September 1898	♦December 1898

February 1898 USS *Maine* explodes

April 1898 U.S. declares war on Spain

May 1898 Dewey destroys Spanish fleet in the Philippines

December 1898 Treaty of Paris ends Spanish-American War

The following are the main History–Social Science Standards covered in this section.

11.4 Students trace the rise of the United States to its role as a world power in the twentieth century.

11.4.2 Describe the Spanish-American War and U.S. expansion in the South Pacific.

～ The Big Idea ～

The fate of nations is forever changed by monumental world events. Many Americans supported the Cuban revolt against Spain. Stories of horrible atrocities committed by the Spanish also fueled support for the Cubans. Fearful of attacks against American citizens, President McKinley sent the battleship USS *Maine* to Havana, Cuba, to prepare for the evacuation of U.S. citizens. For reasons still debated to this day, the *Maine* exploded, killing over half of the sailors and officers on board. Many were quick to blame the Spanish for the explosion. President McKinley, under increasing political pressure, declared war on Spain. The United States fought Spain in both the Philippines and the Caribbean. The larger and more modern U.S. Navy soon defeated the Spanish navy. Victory in the Spanish-American War gave the United States control of territory in the Pacific and the Caribbean.

300 CHAPTER 4 Becoming a World Power

SECTION RESOURCES

Print Material
• Reproducible Lesson Plan 4-2
• Guided Reading Activity 4-2
• Reading Essentials and Study Guide 4-2
• Active Reading Note-Taking Guide 4-2

Transparencies
• Daily Focus Skills Transparency 4-2
• Section Graphic Organizer Transparency 4-2

Technology
• Interactive Tutor Self-Assessment CD-ROM
• ExamView® Pro Testmaker CD-ROM
• Presentation Plus! CD-ROM

The Coming of War

 Main Idea In support of the Cuban rebellion and in retaliation for the loss of the USS *Maine,* the United States declared war on Spain.

Reading Connection Do you remember what led the American colonists to declare their independence? Read on to learn about another colony that rebelled.

In 1898 Cuba was a Spanish colony in the midst of a revolution. The Cuban people were fighting for independence from Spain. Many Americans regarded the Spanish as tyrants and supported the Cubans in their struggle.

★ An American Story ★

Clara Barton, the founder and first president of the American National Red Cross, was working late in her villa overlooking the harbor in Havana, Cuba, on the evening of February 15, 1898. As she and an assistant reviewed some paperwork, an enormous blast lit up the sky. She later recalled:

❝The deafening roar was such a burst of thunder as perhaps one never heard before. And off to the right, out over the bay, the air filled with a blaze of light, and this in turn filled with black specks like huge specters flying in all directions.❞

Barton quickly learned what had happened. The U.S.S. *Maine,* anchored in the Havana harbor, had exploded. Barton rushed to a nearby hospital, where she took a firsthand look at the blast's devastation. The sailors' wounds, she wrote, "were all over them— heads and faces terribly cut, internal wounds, arms, legs, feet and hands burned to the live flesh."

—adapted from *The Spanish War*

Of the 354 officers and sailors aboard the *Maine* that winter night, 266 died. No one is sure why the *Maine* exploded. The size of the explosion indicates that the ship's ammunition supplies blew up. Some experts think that a fire accidentally ignited the ammunition. Others argue that a mine detonated near the ship set off the ammunition.

Americans who supported the Cubans in their revolt quickly jumped to the conclusion that Spain had blown up the *Maine.* Within a matter of weeks, Spain and the United States were at war. Although the fighting only lasted a few months, the outcome dramatically altered the position of the United States on the world stage.

The Cuban Rebellion Begins Cuba was one of Spain's oldest colonies in the Americas. Its sugarcane plantations generated considerable wealth for Spain and produced nearly one-third of the world's sugar in the mid-1800s. Until Spain abolished slavery in 1886, about one-third of the Cuban population was enslaved and forced to work for wealthy landowners on the plantations.

In 1868 Cuban rebels declared independence and launched a guerrilla war against Spanish authorities. Lacking internal support, the rebellion collapsed in 1878. Many Cuban rebels then fled to the United States, where they began planning a new revolution.

One of the exiled leaders was **José Martí,** a writer and poet who was passionately committed to the cause of Cuban independence. While living in New York City in the 1880s, Martí brought together different Cuban exile groups living in the United States. The groups raised funds from sympathetic Americans, purchased weapons, and trained their troops in preparation for an invasion of Cuba.

By the early 1890s, the United States and Cuba had become closely linked economically. Cuba exported much of its sugar to the United States, and Americans had invested approximately $50 million in Cuba's mines, railroads, and sugar plantations.

These economic ties created a crisis in 1894, when the United States imposed new tariffs—including a tariff on sugar—in an effort to protect its troubled economy from foreign competition. The new tariff wrecked the sale of Cuban sugar in the United States and devastated the island's economy.

"[t]he air filled with a blaze of light . . ."
—*Clara Barton*

CHAPTER 4 Becoming a World Power **301**

TEACH

S Skill Practice

Scaffolding—Comparing and Contrasting The American Revolution influenced many other revolutions around the world, but not all these revolutions resulted in similar governments. **Ask:** How was Cuba's struggle for independence similar to and different from the colonies' fight for independence from Great Britain in 1776? *(Both felt they were unfairly treated and deserved independence; the United States had much stronger internal support and better organized armies.)* **OL**
CA HI1; HI2

This **Reading Skill** was introduced in Chapter 3.

C Critical Thinking

Comparing and Contrasting José Martí and Martin Luther King, Jr., were both leaders who spoke about the need for freedom. Have students write an essay comparing Martí's "Thoughts on Liberty" (available online at http://: xld.com/public/cuba/marti.htm) with King's "I Have a Dream" speech. Student essays should address how the ideologies are similar and different. **AL** **CA** 11RC2.5; 11WA2.2

R Reading Strategy

Scaffolding—Academic Vocabulary The word *export* was introduced in Chapter 1, Section 2. Ask a student to define the word. **BL**

Did You Know?

Clara Barton witnessed the actions of the International Red Cross during a stay in Europe in the 1870s. When she returned to the United States, she lobbied the government to create the American Red Cross. She also petitioned the government to join the Geneva Convention, which sets rules of conduct during war.

301

W Writing Support

Persuasive Writing The reference to "yellow journalism" provides an opportunity for students to analyze the impact of the media on the democratic process. Have students select a current national news issue and write a newspaper article utilizing the sensationalist techniques of yellow journalism. Read the articles in class and discuss how these exaggerations can affect public opinion and potential outcomes.
AL **CA** 11WS1.1

S Skill Practice

Visual Literacy Have students examine the picture. **Ask: What details do you see that tell about the relationship between the Cubans and Spanish leaders?** (Cubans are huddling together, looking down and not making eye contact, appearing afraid; Spanish leaders are following closely and watching intently, holding guns and looking intimidating.) **OL**

C Critical Thinking

Making Generalizations
General Valeriano Weyler was criticized as a harsh ruler of Cuba. **Ask: What traits characterize a harsh ruler? What traits define a ruler who is courteous?** (Students' answers will vary.) **OL**

Answers and Additional Support

With Cuba in an economic crisis, Martí's followers launched a new rebellion in February 1895. Although Martí died in battle shortly after returning to Cuba, the revolutionaries seized control of eastern Cuba, declared independence, and formally established the Republic of Cuba in September 1895.

Americans Support the Cubans When the uprising in Cuba began, President Grover Cleveland declared the United States neutral. Outside the White House, however, much of the public openly supported the rebels. Some citizens compared the Cubans' struggle to the American Revolution. A few sympathetic Americans even began smuggling guns from Florida to the Cuban rebels.

What led most Americans to support the rebels were the dramatic stories of Spanish atrocities reported in two of the nation's major newspapers, the *New York Journal* and the *New York World*. The *Journal,* owned by **William Randolph Hearst,** and the *World,* owned by **Joseph Pulitzer,** competed with each other to increase their circulation. The *Journal* reported outrageous stories of the Spanish feeding Cuban prisoners to sharks and dogs. Not to be outdone, the *World* described Cuba as a place with "blood on the roadsides, blood in the fields, blood on the doorsteps, blood, blood, blood!" This kind of sensationalist reporting, in which writers often exaggerated or even made up stories to attract readers, became known as **yellow journalism.**

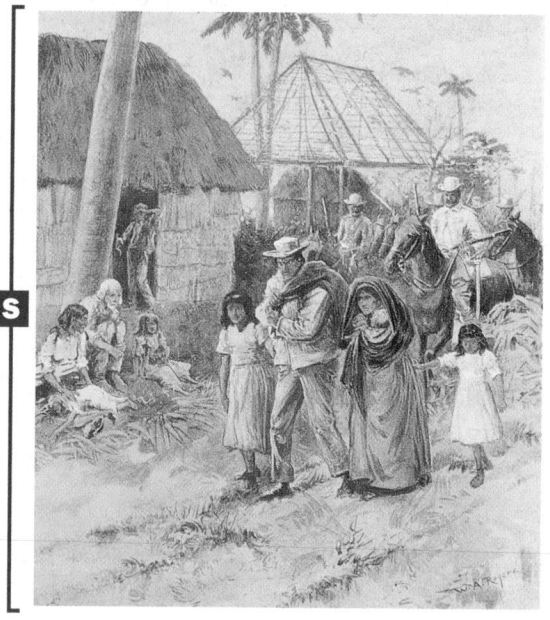

Although the press invented sensational stories to sell more papers, there is no doubt that the Cuban people indeed suffered horribly. The Spanish dispatched nearly 200,000 troops to the island to put down the rebellion and appointed General Valeriano Weyler governor. Weyler's harsh policies quickly earned him the nickname *El Carnicero* ("The Butcher").

The Cuban rebels carried out a guerrilla war. They staged hit-and-run raids, burned plantations and sugar mills, tore up railroad tracks, and attacked supply depots. The rebels knew that many American businesses had invested in Cuba's railroads and plantations. They hoped that the destruction of American property would lead to American intervention in the war.

To prevent Cuban villagers from helping the rebels, Weyler herded hundreds of thousands of rural men, women, and children into "reconcentration camps," where tens of thousands died of starvation and disease. News reports of this brutal treatment of civilians enraged Americans and led to renewed calls for American intervention in the war.

Calling Out for War In 1897 Republican William McKinley became president of the United States. The new president did not want to intervene in the war, believing it would cost too many lives and hurt the economy. In September 1897, he asked the Spanish if the United States could help negotiate an end to the conflict. He made it clear that if the war did not end soon, the United States might have to intervene.

Pressed by McKinley, the Spanish government removed Weyler from power. Spain then offered the Cubans autonomy—the right to their own government—but only if Cuba remained part of the Spanish empire. The Cuban rebels refused to negotiate. They wanted full independence.

Spain's concessions to the rebels enraged many Spanish loyalists in Cuba. In January 1898, the loyalists rioted in Havana. Worried that American citizens in Cuba might be attacked, McKinley made the fateful decision to send the battleship *Maine* to Havana in case the Americans had to be evacuated.

In February 1898, the *New York Journal* printed a private letter written by Enrique Dupuy de Lôme, the Spanish ambassador to the United States. A Cuban agent had intercepted the letter and delivered it to

 History *Through Art*

Cuban Rebellion During the Cuban Revolution in 1895, Spanish general Valeriano Weyler forced much of the Cuban population into guarded camps near military installations. Why were Americans supporting Cuba's fight against Spain?

Did You Know?

William Randolph Hearst sent artist Frederic Remington to Cuba to cover events after the explosion of the *Maine*. When the expected conflict between the United States and Spain did not immediately materialize, the artist asked if he should return home. Hearst cabled back, "You furnish the pictures, I'll furnish the war."

History *Through Art*

Answer: because they regarded the Spanish as tyrants
Ask: What was Cuba's main export product? (sugarcane)

the paper. It described McKinley as "weak and a bidder for the admiration of the crowd." The nation erupted in fury over the insult.

Ambassador de Lôme resigned, but before the furor could die down, the *Maine* exploded in the Havana harbor. The press promptly blamed Spain. Rapidly responding to the hysterical anger of the American public, Congress unanimously authorized the president to spend $50 million for war preparations. Shortly afterward, on March 28, 1898, a naval court of inquiry concluded that a mine had destroyed the *Maine*. Throughout America, people began using the slogan "Remember the *Maine*!" as a rallying cry for war. By early April, President McKinley was under tremendous pressure to go to war. American mobs were demonstrating in the streets against Spain—and against McKinley for refusing to go to war.

Within the Republican Party, **jingoism**, or an attitude of aggressive nationalism, was very strong, especially among younger members of the party. These members were furious at McKinley for not declaring war. Assistant Secretary of the Navy **Theodore Roosevelt**, for one, raged that McKinley had "no more backbone than a chocolate éclair." Many Democrats were also demanding war, and Republicans feared that if McKinley did not go to war, the Democrats would win the presidency in 1900. Finally, on April 11, 1898, McKinley asked Congress to authorize the use of force to end the conflict in Cuba.

On April 19, Congress declared Cuba independent, demanded that Spain withdraw from the island, and authorized the president to use armed force if necessary. In response, on April 24, Spain declared war on the United States. For the first time in 50 years, the United States was at war with another nation.

✓ **Reading Check** **Examining** What conditions led to the Cuban rebellion in 1895?

A War on Two Fronts

Main Idea **The United States fought Spain in both the Pacific and the Caribbean.**

Reading Connection Have you ever had to work on two major tasks at the same time? Read on to learn about a time when the United States had to fight a war in two places.

The Spanish in Cuba were not prepared for war. Tropical diseases and months of hard fighting had weakened their soldiers. Their warships were old and their crews poorly trained. The United States had more battleships, and both sides knew that the war ultimately would be decided at sea. If the United States could defeat Spain's fleet, the Spanish would not be able to get supplies to its troops in Cuba. Eventually, they would have to surrender.

The Philippines The United States Navy was ready for war with Spain. The navy's North Atlantic Squadron blockaded Cuba, and the American fleet based in British Hong Kong was ordered to attack the Spanish fleet in the Philippines. The Philippines was a Spanish colony, and American naval planners were determined to prevent the fleet there from sailing east to attack the United States.

A short time after midnight, on May 1, 1898, Commodore George Dewey led his squadron into Manila Bay in the Philippines. As dawn broke, Dewey's fleet opened fire and rapidly destroyed or captured the severely outgunned Spanish warships.

Dewey's quick victory took McKinley and his advisers by surprise. The army was not yet ready to send troops to help Dewey capture the Philippines. Hastily, the army assembled 20,000 troops to sail from San Francisco to the Philippines. On the way to the Philippines, the American troops also seized the island of Guam, another Spanish possession in the Pacific.

While waiting for the American troops to arrive, Dewey contacted Emilio Aguinaldo, a Filipino revolutionary leader who had staged an unsuccessful uprising against the Spanish in 1896. Aguinaldo quickly launched a new guerrilla war.

At first, Aguinaldo believed the Americans were his allies, but when American troops arrived in the islands he became suspicious. The Americans quickly seized the Philippine capital of Manila from the Spanish but refused to allow Aguinaldo's forces into the city. They also refused to recognize his rebel government. Hostility between the Filipinos and the Americans began to grow as both sides waited for the war with Spain to end.

American Forces Battle in Cuba Unlike the mobilization of the navy, which had been very efficient, the mobilization of the American army was very poorly conducted. Although volunteers flooded into army training camps, the army lacked the **resources** to train and equip them. In many camps, conditions were so unsanitary that epidemics broke out, and hundreds of Americans died. By the end of the war, far more Americans had died in training camps than in actual battle.

CHAPTER 4 Becoming a World Power **303**

Chapter 4 • Section 2

R₁ **Reading Strategy**

Activating Prior Knowledge The slogan "Remember the *Maine*!" is reminiscent of the battle cry "Remember the Alamo!" Ask students to recall facts from this battle. *(In 1836 during the Texas Revolution, Mexican soldiers attacked the Texans in a mission called the Alamo. The Texans lost that battle, but their defeat served as a rallying cry for the rest of the war.)* **OL**

R₂ **Reading Strategy**

Evaluating Have students explain the definition of *jingoism*. *(an attitude of aggressive nationalism)* **Ask:** Do you believe that jingoism exists today? *(Students should give specific examples to support their opinion.)* **AL**

C **Critical Thinking**

Determining Cause and Effect Have students list the factors that show the Spanish were unprepared for conflict with U.S. forces. *(poor training of soldiers, outdated warships, soldiers tired from previous battles, lack of quality leadership)* **OL** **CA HI2**

✓ **Reading Check**

Answer: Spanish oppression, Spanish economic exploitation

More Skill Practice

Narrative Writing Instruct students to write a journal entry on the events of the Battle of Manila Bay. Students can choose to write from the perspective of a naval officer from the American fleet, a Filipino fighting for revolution, or a Spanish soldier watching for the arrival of the U.S. forces. Entries should narrate the sequence of events from the observer's point of view and reflect political and social influences. **OL** **CA 11WS1.2; 11WA2.1c**

303

304

S₁ Skill Practice

Scaffolding—Interpreting Maps Provide students with a world map to compare with the map on p. 304. Using a map scale, have students calculate the distance between the battles in the Caribbean and the Philippines. `OL` `CA CS3`

This `Historical Analysis` skill was introduced in Chapter 3.

U Universal Access

Kinesthetic Using the chalkboard, have the class work together to create a chronological list of the important events of 1898 that were part of the Spanish-American War. Then have students write each event on a separate note card, shuffle the cards, and put them in proper order. This gives English learners a chance to solidify the material and match the cards to what they see on the board. `EL` `CA CS1`

S₂ Skill Practice

Visual Literacy Direct students to the graph of U.S. deaths in the Spanish-American War. Have students calculate the percentage of deaths due to disease and the percentage of deaths in battle. **Ask:** Why was the number of deaths caused by disease so high? *(lack of resources in training camps, unsanitary conditions)* `OL`

Answers and Additional Support

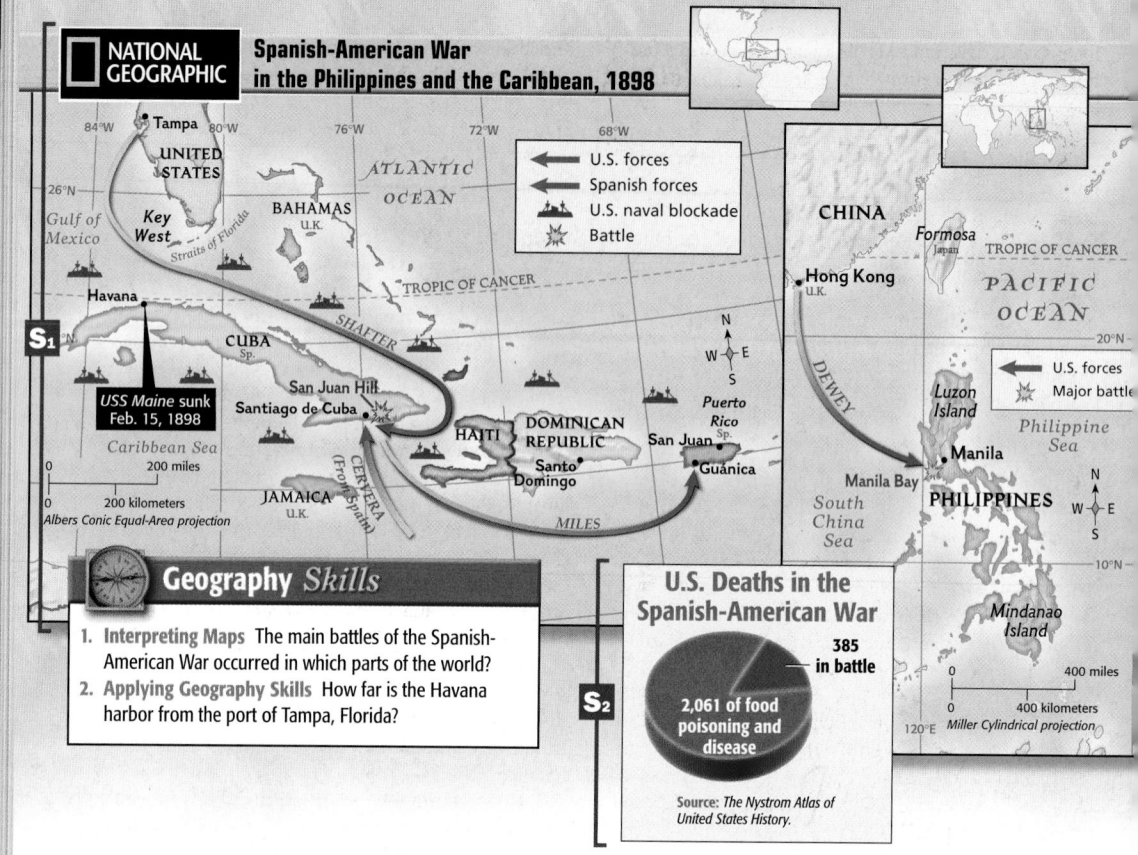

NATIONAL GEOGRAPHIC

Spanish-American War in the Philippines and the Caribbean, 1898

- ← U.S. forces
- → Spanish forces
- ⚓ U.S. naval blockade
- ✶ Battle

USS Maine sunk Feb. 15, 1898

Geography *Skills*

1. **Interpreting Maps** The main battles of the Spanish-American War occurred in which parts of the world?
2. **Applying Geography Skills** How far is the Havana harbor from the port of Tampa, Florida?

U.S. Deaths in the Spanish-American War

- 385 in battle
- 2,061 of food poisoning and disease

Source: *The Nystrom Atlas of United States History.*

Finally, on June 14, 1898, a force of about 17,000 troops landed on the southern coast of Cuba, east of the city of Santiago. A Spanish fleet occupied Santiago Harbor, where it was well protected by powerful shore-based guns. American military planners wanted to capture those guns in order to drive the Spanish fleet out of the harbor and into battle with the American fleet waiting in the waters off the Cuban coast.

Among the American troops advancing toward Santiago was a volunteer cavalry unit from the American West. They were a flamboyant mix of cowboys, miners, and law officers known as the "Rough Riders." The commander of the Rough Riders was Colonel Leonard Wood. Second in command was Theodore Roosevelt, who had resigned from his post as assistant secretary of the navy to join the fight against Spain.

On July 1, American troops attacked the village of El Caney northeast of Santiago. Another force attacked the San Juan Heights, a series of hills overlooking the main road to Santiago. While one group

of soldiers attacked San Juan Hill, the Rough Riders—who were on foot, not horseback—attacked Kettle Hill. After seizing Kettle Hill, Roosevelt and his men assisted in the capture of San Juan Hill.

The Rough Riders did not make their attack alone. Accompanying them up Kettle Hill were the all-black 9th and 10th Cavalry Regiments. Many African Americans had responded to the call for volunteers, and roughly one-fourth of the American troops fighting in Cuba were African American. Four African American soldiers received the Medal of Honor for their bravery during the war.

The Spanish commander in Santiago panicked after the American victories. He immediately ordered the Spanish fleet in the harbor to flee. As the Spanish ships raced out of the harbor on July 3, the American warships guarding the entrance attacked them. In the ensuing battle, the American squadron sank or beached every Spanish vessel.

Spanish resistance in Cuba ended with the surrender of Santiago two weeks later. Soon after, American

---

 ### Geography *Skills*

Answers:
1. in the Caribbean and in the Philippines
2. about 320 miles (515 kilometers)

Geography Skills Practice
Ask: Who was the leader of the Spanish fleet in the Caribbean? *(Cervera)*

More Skill Practice

Visual Literacy Have students re-examine the painting on page 291 after they have read "American Forces Battle in Cuba." **Ask:** What is the discrepancy between the painting and the facts? *(The Rough Riders were on foot, not on horseback.)* `OL`

troops occupied the nearby Spanish colony of Puerto Rico. On August 12, 1898, Spain and the United States agreed to a cease-fire.

✓ **Reading Check** **Describing** How prepared was the U.S. Army to fight a war against Spain?

An American Empire is Born

Main Idea Victory in the Spanish-American War allowed the United States to expand its holdings in the South Pacific and to control Puerto Rico and Cuba.

Reading Connection Do you think that Puerto Rico should become the 51st state? Read on to learn about the beginning of that territory's long association with the United States.

As American and Spanish leaders met to discuss the terms for a peace treaty, Americans debated what to do about their newly acquired lands. Cuba would be given its freedom as promised, and Spain had agreed that the United States would annex Guam and Puerto Rico. The big question was what to do with the Philippines. The United States faced a difficult choice—remain true to its republican ideals or become an imperial power.

The Debate Over Annexation Many supporters of annexing the Philippines emphasized the economic and military benefits of taking the islands. They would provide the United States with a naval base in Asia, a stopover on the way to China, and a large market for American goods.

Other supporters believed America had a duty to teach "less civilized" peoples how to live properly. "Surely this Spanish war has not been a grab for empire," commented a New England minister, "but a heroic effort [to] free the oppressed, and to teach the millions of ignorant, debased human beings thus freed how to live."

Not all Americans supported annexation. Anti-imperialists included industrialist Andrew Carnegie, social worker Jane Addams, writer Samuel Clemens

NATIONAL GEOGRAPHIC

MOMENT in HISTORY

FEISTY LEADER FOR A NEW CENTURY

Theodore Roosevelt (center) embodied the spirit of the United States at the turn of the century: full of vitality, brimming with confidence, and convinced that no job was impossible, no challenge insurmountable. Whether hunting big game in Africa, roping cattle from horseback on a Dakota ranch, or leading his "Rough Riders" cavalry (right) up San Juan Hill during the Spanish-American War, Roosevelt never did anything cautiously or quietly. As president, Roosevelt guided the country into its new, unaccustomed role as a world power.

CHAPTER 4 Becoming a World Power **305**

Chapter 4 • Section 2

S Skill Practice

Visual Literacy Have students examine the "Moment in History" picture on this page. **Ask:** Looking at dress and demeanor, what do you notice that earns the soldiers the title "Rough Riders"? *(boots, guns, cowboy hats, stern countenances; more like cowboy dress than military dress)* **OL**

U Universal Access

Advanced Learners Have high-level students who are interested view the movie *The Rough Riders.* Tell them to write an essay that discusses how the movie mixes fiction with fact, and analyze how closely it depicts historical events. **AL** **CA** 11WA2.4b

Review the Big Idea

Review the Big Idea for this section, "The fate of nations is forever changed by monumental world events." Ask students to write a summary paragraph that describes the territories the United States gained after victory in the Spanish-American War. **OL**

✓ **Reading Check**

Answer: well prepared, with a plan to attack around Santiago to scare the Spanish fleet out of the harbor and into battle with the American Navy

NATIONAL GEOGRAPHIC **MOMENT in HISTORY**

One of Theodore Roosevelt's greatest disappointments was President Woodrow Wilson's refusal to allow him to fight in World War I. Roosevelt was in his late 50s when the United States entered the war.

Did You Know?

When the call went out looking for Rough Riders to join Teddy Roosevelt, the War Office received 23,000 applications. Those accepted consisted of a diverse group that included Princeton football players, Pawnee Indians, cowboys, polo players, and Rhodes Scholars.

S Skill Practice

Identifying Points of View
Divide students into groups of four. Have half of the teams argue for annexation, citing the economic and military benefits of controlling the Philippines. The other half of the teams should argue against annexation, citing how it could hurt the U.S. economy and violate U.S. principles of freedom. Have each team debate its points against a team with the opposing view. **AL** **CA HI4; HI6**

C Critical Thinking

Drawing Conclusions Have students look up the word *treaty* in a dictionary. *(a formal agreement between two or more countries)* **Ask: Why do you think many treaties are signed in a neutral country?** *(promotes fairness and compromise; neither country has an advantage)* **OL**

W Writing Support

Response to Literature Writing
Poems unique to the Filipino-American experience can be found in *Without Names: A Collection of Poems by Bay Area Pilipino American Writers,* by Shirley Ancheta (editor). Have students select one poem and write a paragraph on what they can infer about Filipino culture. **OL** **CA 11RL3.2; 11WA2.2**

Answers and Additional Support

Picturing History

Building an Empire Two Filipino women nervously converse with American troops in the Philippines. Filipino civilians suffered many hardships while Filipino guerrillas fought American troops. Thousands perished from sickness, starvation, and other indirect effects of war. What American policy contributed to civilian hardships in the Philippines?

(Mark Twain), and the leader of the American Federation of Labor, Samuel Gompers. Carnegie argued that the cost of an empire far outweighed the economic benefits it provided. Gompers worried that competition from cheap Filipino labor would drive down American wages. Addams, Clemens, and others believed imperialism **violated** American principles.

President McKinley had to decide what to do with the Philippines. Ultimately, he decided to annex the islands. He later explained his reasoning to a group of ministers:

> ❝And one night late it came to me this way . . .
>
> (1) that we could not give them back to Spain—that would be cowardly and dishonorable; (2) that we could not turn them over to France or Germany . . . that would be bad for business and discreditable; (3) that we could not leave them to themselves—they were unfit for self-government . . . and (4) that there was nothing left for us to do but to take them all, and to educate the Filipinos, and uplift and civilize and Christianize them.❞
>
> —quoted in *A Diplomatic History of the American People*

306   CHAPTER 4   Becoming a World Power

On December 10, 1898, the United States and Spain signed the Treaty of Paris. Under the treaty, Cuba became an independent country, and the United States acquired Puerto Rico and Guam and agreed to pay Spain $20 million for the Philippines. After an intense debate, the Senate ratified the treaty in February 1899. The United States had become an imperial power.

Rebellion in the Philippines The United States quickly learned that controlling its new empire would not be easy. Emilio Aguinaldo called the American decision to annex his homeland a "violent and aggressive seizure." He then ordered his troops to attack the American soldiers in the Philippines.

To fight the Filipino guerrillas, General Arthur MacArthur (the father of the future American general Douglas MacArthur) adopted many of the same policies that America had condemned Spain for using in Cuba. MacArthur set up reconcentration camps to separate guerrillas from civilians. The results were also similar to what had happened in Cuba. Thousands of Filipinos died from disease and starvation.

While MacArthur fought the guerrillas, the first U.S. civilian governor of the islands, William Howard Taft, tried to win over the Filipino people by reforming education, transportation, and health care. New railroads, bridges, and telegraph lines strengthened the economy. A public school system was set up, and new health care policies **virtually** eliminated severe diseases such as cholera and smallpox. These reforms slowly reduced Filipino hostility.

In March 1901, American troops captured Aguinaldo. The following month, Aguinaldo accepted American control of the islands and called on the guerrillas to surrender. By summer 1902, the United States had declared the war over. Eventually the United States allowed the Filipinos a greater role in governing

Emilio Aguinaldo, ➤
revolutionary general and first
president of the Philippines

Picturing History

Answer: Americans set up reconcentration camps in which thousands of Filipinos died from disease and starvation.
Ask: How did President McKinley justify annexation? *(American duty to "civilize" and Christianize Filipinos)*

their own country. By the mid-1930s, they were permitted to elect their own congress and president. Finally, in 1946, the United States granted independence to the Philippines.

Governing Puerto Rico Another pressing question facing the United States government was how to govern Puerto Rico. In 1900 Congress passed the Foraker Act, making Puerto Rico an unincorporated territory. This meant that Puerto Ricans were not U.S. citizens and had no constitutional rights. The act also stated that Congress could pass whatever laws it wanted for the island.

Congress gradually allowed the inhabitants of Puerto Rico a certain degree of self-government. In 1917 the United States made Puerto Ricans citizens of the United States. In 1947 the island was given the right to elect its own governor. At this time a debate began over whether to grant Puerto Rico statehood, allow it to become an independent country, or continue it as a commonwealth of the United States. This debate over Puerto Rico's status continues as Puerto Rico is still a commonwealth today.

Cuba and the Platt Amendment After the war, the United States established a military government in Cuba. Although the United States had promised to secure Cuban independence, President McKinley took steps to ensure that Cuba would remain tied to the United States. He allowed the Cubans to prepare a new constitution for their country, but he attached conditions. A special amendment that Senator Orville Platt attached to the 1901 army appropriations bill described those conditions.

The **Platt Amendment** specified the following: (1) Cuba could not make any treaty with another nation that would weaken its independence or allow another foreign power to gain territory in Cuba; (2) Cuba had to allow the United States to buy or lease naval stations in Cuba; (3) Cuba's debts had to be kept low to prevent foreign countries from landing troops to enforce payment; and (4) the United States would have the right to intervene to protect Cuban independence and keep order.

Although the Cubans rejected the Platt Amendment at first, they quickly realized that unless they accepted it, the United States would maintain its military government of the island. Reluctantly, they added the amendment to their constitution. The Platt Amendment governed relations between the United States and Cuba until its repeal in 1934. It effectively made Cuba an American protectorate.

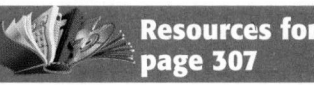

HISTORY Online

Student Web Activity Visit the *American Vision: Modern Times* Web site at tav.mt.glencoe.com and click on *Student Web Activities–Chapter 4* for an activity on American imperialism.

✓ Reading Check **Explaining** What were the arguments for and against establishing an American empire?

HISTORY Online **Study Central**

For help with the concepts in this section of *American Vision: Modern Times* go to tav.mt.glencoe.com and click on *Study Central.*

SECTION 2 ASSESSMENT

Checking for Understanding

1. **Vocabulary** Define: yellow journalism, jingoism, resources, violated, virtually.
2. **People and Terms** Identify: José Martí, William Randolph Hearst, Joseph Pulitzer, Theodore Roosevelt, Platt Amendment.
3. **Explain** why many Americans blamed Spain for the explosion of the USS *Maine*.

Reviewing Big Ideas

4. **Understanding** Why did many Filipinos feel betrayed by the U.S. government after the Spanish-American War?

Critical Thinking

5. **Interpreting** Do you think President McKinley could have taken a different course of action with Spain over Cuba? If so, what kind? If not, why not?
6. **Categorizing** Complete a graphic organizer similar to the one below by summarizing the effects of the United States annexing lands obtained after the Spanish-American War.

Lands Annexed	Effects

Analyzing Visuals

7. **Analyzing Art** Examine the painting on page 291. Considering what you have learned about the Rough Riders and this battle, what is inaccurate about the painting? What kind of artistic bias is evident in this painting?

Writing About History

8. **Descriptive Writing** Imagine that you are a Filipino living during the time of the U.S. annexation of the Philippine Islands. Write a journal entry in which you describe your feelings about U.S. control of the islands. **CA** 11WS1.2; 11WA2.1b

CHAPTER 4 Becoming a World Power **307**

SECTION 2 ASSESSMENT ANSWERS

1. Content vocabulary is boldfaced and highlighted in yellow. Academic vocabulary is boldfaced.
2. José Martí *(p. 301)*, William Randolph Hearst *(p. 302)*, Joseph Pulitzer *(p. 302)*, Theodore Roosevelt *(p. 303)*, Platt Amendment *(p. 307)*
3. Cuba was fighting for its independence, and many Americans saw the Spanish as tyrants.
4. The Filipinos did not want their homeland annexed.
5. Students' answers will vary.
6. Puerto Rico: U.S. control of its government; Puerto Ricans: are U.S. citizens from 1917; Philippines: provide a naval base to guard U.S. trade; some improvements in Filipino schools, roads, and healthcare
7. They are on horseback in the painting; they were actually on foot. It glorifies the Rough Riders.
8. Journal entries will vary. Entries should be written from the point of view of a Filipino.

307

You're *the* Historian

Who Sank the *Maine?*

D uring Cuba's revolt against Spain, the American battleship *Maine* dropped anchor in the Havana harbor to protect American interests in Cuba. On the night of February 15, 1898, the ship exploded and 266 Americans lost their lives. The United States sent a court of inquiry to Havana on February 21. Despite the lack of evidence concerning the source of the explosion, American newspapers and many public officials claimed that Spain was responsible. Pressured on all sides, President McKinley sent Spain an ultimatum that led to war. Who—or what—really sank the *Maine?*

Read the following excerpts from testimony and evidence. Then answer the questions and complete the activities that follow.

Captain Charles Sigsbee

From the commander and an early interview

Telegraph from the commander of the *Maine* to the secretary of the navy, February 15:

"Maine blown up in Havana harbor at nine forty to-night and destroyed. Many wounded and doubtless more killed or drowned. . . . Public opinion should be suspended until further report. . . . Many Spanish officers, including representatives of General Blanco, now with us to express sympathy."

–Captain Charles D. Sigsbee

The court of inquiry was interested in discovering whether the explosion had come from inside or outside the ship. If it came from inside, was it sabotage or an accident? If it came from outside, who or what caused it? Before the court met, the *Washington Evening Star* published a February 18 interview with the U.S. Navy's leading ordnance expert:

"We know of no instances where the explosion of a torpedo or mine under the ship's bottom has exploded the magazine [powder and explosives] within. It has simply torn a great hole in the side or bottom, through which water entered, and in consequence of which the ship sunk. Magazine explosions, on the contrary, produce effects exactly similar to the effects of the explosion on the *Maine.* When it

Newspaper headline

> **WHO DESTROYED THE MAINE $50,000 REWARD**
> **NEW YORK JOURNAL**
> **AND ADVERTISER**
> **DESTRUCTION OF THE WAR SHIP MAINE WAS THE WORK OF AN ENEMY**
> **$50,000!** **$50,000!**
> **$50,000 REWARD!** Assistant Secretary Roosevelt **$50,000 REWARD!**
> For the Detection of the Convinced the Explosion of For the Detection of the
> Perpetrator of the the War Ship Was Not Perpetrator of
> Maine Outrage! an Accident. the Maine Outrage!

comes to seeking the cause of the explosion of the *Maine's* magazine, we should naturally look not for the improbable or unusual causes. . . . The most common of these is through fires in the bunkers."

–Philip R. Alger

USS Maine

EXTENDING THE CONTENT

Artifacts From the *Maine* When the USS *Maine* was raised from Havana Harbor in 1911, some members of Congress wanted a piece. Frank B. Willis, a representative from Ohio, claimed Captain Sigbee's enameled-steel bathtub. After his hometown of Urbana turned down the gift of the bathtub, the people of Findlay, Ohio, took possession of it. When the bathtub arrived in Findlay in 1913, disappointed citizens saw that the artifact was not quite the treasure they had hoped for. After being underwater for 14 years, the tub was rusted and ugly. Displayed in various places in Findlay over the years, it now resides in the Hancock Historical Museum.

Engraving of the explosion

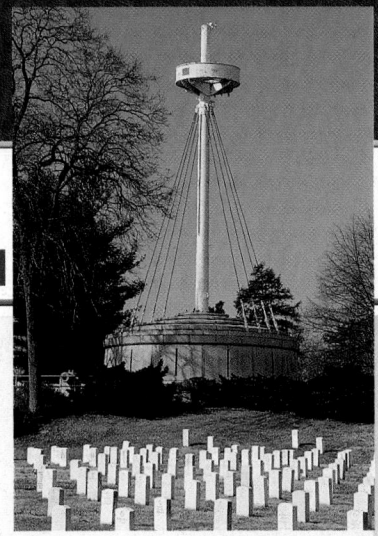

Mast of the Maine at Arlington National Cemetery

From the inquiry and later reports

As the court of inquiry concluded its investigation, it considered reports of the divers who examined the *Maine* and evidence that suggested there had been two explosions. On March 11, 1898, Lieutenant Commander Adolph Marix, judge advocate of the court of inquiry, questioned Commander George A. Converse, who was brought in as a technical expert.

Marix: Looking at the plan of the *Maine*'s forward 10-inch and 6-inch magazines, would it be possible for them to have exploded, torn out the ship's side on both sides, and leave that part of the ship forward of frame 18 so water borne as to raise the after portion of that part of the ship, drag it aft, and bring the vertical keel into the condition you see in the sketch?

Converse: It is difficult for me to realize that that effect could have been produced by an explosion of the kind supposed.

Marix: Do you think, then, necessarily, there must have been an underwater mine to produce these explosions?

Converse: Indications are that an underwater explosion produced the conditions there.

In 1911 the U.S. Navy raised the *Maine* from Havana's harbor. The navy's board of inspection reexamined the ship, and its findings were similar to those of 1898. Then, in 1976, Admiral H.G. Rickover and other naval historians gathered a team of experts to examine the official court records of 1898 and 1911. This team's conclusions were very different.

1911 board conclusion:

The board finds that the injuries to the bottom of the *Maine* above described were caused by the explosion of a charge of a low form of explosive exterior to the ship between frames 28 and 31.

H.G. Rickover team conclusion:

The general character of the overall wrecked structure of the *Maine*, with hull sides and whole deck structures peeled back, leaves no doubt that a large internal explosion occurred. . . .

The mines available in 1898 are believed to have been incapable of igniting the *Maine* magazine if they exploded on the harbor bottom or against the ship side. . . . It is most unlikely that the *Maine* explosion was indeed initiated by a mine. . . .

The available evidence is consistent with an internal explosion alone. . . . The most likely source was heat from a fire in the coal bunker adjacent to the 6-inch reserve magazine.

Understanding the Issue

1. Why did the original investigation's conclusion that there was an underwater explosion lead to war with Spain?
2. If there had been an underwater explosion, was it logical to conclude that a Spanish person planted the mine? Why or why not? Is this an example of a biased opinion?
3. Why did the 1976 review conclude that the explosion came from inside the *Maine*?

Activities

1. **Rewriting History** Suppose that the initial court of inquiry had concluded that an internal explosion sank the *Maine*. Write a paragraph describing an alternate course history could have taken in the following year.
2. **Oral Report** Read a biography of one of these key players in the decision of the United States to go to war: Hearst, Roosevelt, or McKinley. Write a short oral presentation on this person's perspective and influence on the war.

FOCUS

Guide to Reading

Understanding Vocabulary: Have students study the content vocabulary and the academic vocabulary in this section. Then give students a definition and instruct them to give you the correct word.

Answers to Graphic: Save time, save money, help the United States remain a world power

Unpacking the Standards

Students will be able to:

• Discuss the Open Door policy and the countries involved.

• Explain the reasons why the construction of the Panama Canal was important to the United States.

• Show how President Roosevelt's Big Stick diplomacy applied to United States foreign relations.

Answers and Additional Support

SECTION 3 New American Diplomacy

Guide to Reading

Connection
In the previous section, you learned how the United States expanded its territory by defeating Spain in the Spanish-American War. In this section, you will discover how President Theodore Roosevelt helped the United States increase its power and influence around the world.

Main Idea
• Theodore Roosevelt went from governor of New York to president in a few short years and supported the country's rise to a world power. (p. 311)
• The United States pursued an Open Door policy in China to allow all nations access to China's markets. (p. 312)

Preview of Events

♦1898	♦1900	♦1902	♦1904
1899 Secretary of State Hay sends first Open Door note	**1900** Boxer Rebellion erupts in China	**1901** McKinley assassinated; Theodore Roosevelt becomes president	**1904** Construction of Panama Canal begins

• Theodore Roosevelt pushed for construction of the Panama Canal and declared the intent of the United States to act as a police force in Latin American nations. (p. 313)

Content Vocabulary
sphere of influence, Open Door policy, dollar diplomacy

Academic Vocabulary
exploit, tension, intervene

Events to Identify
Boxer Rebellion, "Great White Fleet," Hay-Pauncefote Treaty, Roosevelt Corollary

Reading Objectives
• **Critique** Theodore Roosevelt's foreign policy as president.

• **Explain** the Open Door policy and its effects on relations between the United States and Asia.

Reading Strategy
Organizing As you read about the increasing presence of the United States in the world, complete a graphic organizer like the one below by listing the reasons President Roosevelt gave for wanting a canal in Central America.

Reasons to Build Canal

❧ The Big Idea ❧

America's military and economic strength made it a world power. Following the death of President McKinley, Theodore Roosevelt became president. Roosevelt was an energetic and enthusiastic man who believed the United States should increase its power in the world. President Roosevelt established the Open Door policy with China to guarantee the United States would have the ability to trade with that nation. He also pushed for the construction of a canal through Central America and backed Panama in a revolt against Cuba. After Panama declared independence, the United States signed a treaty with Panama guaranteeing the construction of the canal. President Roosevelt declared that, if necessary, the United States would intervene in any Latin American country to ensure stability in the Western Hemisphere.

SECTION RESOURCES

📖 **Print Material**
• Reproducible Lesson Plan 4-3
• Guided Reading Activity 4-3
• Reading Essentials and Study Guide 4-3
• Active Reading Note-Taking Guide 4-3

💡 **Transparencies**
• Daily Focus Skills Transparency 4-3
• Section Graphic Organizer Transparency 4-3

Technology
💿 Interactive Tutor Self-Assessment CD-ROM
💿 ExamView® Pro Testmaker CD-ROM
💿 Presentation Plus! CD-ROM

Theodore Roosevelt's Rise to Power

Main Idea Theodore Roosevelt went from governor of New York to president in a few short years and supported the country's rise to a world power.

Reading Connection Whom do you consider a person likely to succeed in anything he or she does? Read on to find out about one such charismatic person.

Theodore Roosevelt's **exploits** during the Spanish-American War made him famous and enabled him to win the election for governor of New York in November 1898. In 1900 President McKinley asked Roosevelt to run as his vice president. Less than a year later, a tragic turn of events thrust Roosevelt into the White House and international politics.

★ An American Story ★

Upon arriving in Panama in 1904, Dr. William Crawford Gorgas, a U.S. Army doctor and chief sanitary officer to the Panama Canal project, quickly realized that death awaited American workers. The United States was about to begin constructing the Panama Canal to connect the Atlantic and Pacific Oceans. The task would be daunting because the dense jungles of Panama were home to swarms of mosquitoes that spread the deadly disease of yellow fever.

Gorgas set out to lessen the threat of disease by keeping mosquitoes from breeding. He and his crew drained swamps, gullies, and other sources of stagnant water, a main breeding ground for mosquitoes. On those areas of water they could not drain, they spread kerosene and oil, which killed the mosquito eggs before they hatched. They also fumigated nearly every home in the region and destroyed buckets, pots, and other outdoor containers that local residents let fill up with rainwater. In two years Gorgas and his crew had wiped out yellow fever in the area.

—adapted from *The Strength to Move a Mountain*

The construction of the Panama Canal might never have taken place had Theodore Roosevelt not become president. "Teddy," as the press called him, gained the presidency largely by accident.

The Election of 1900 The election of 1900 once again pitted President McKinley against William Jennings Bryan. Bryan, an anti-imperialist, attacked the Republicans for their support of imperialism in Asia. McKinley focused on the country's increased prosperity. Employing the slogan "Four Years More of the Full Dinner Pail," the Republicans promised good times ahead if McKinley was reelected. He did indeed win the election by a wide margin, and Theodore Roosevelt became vice president.

On September 6, 1901, as President McKinley greeted the public during an appearance in Buffalo, New York, a gunman stepped from the crowd. The man was Leon Czolgosz, an avowed anarchist, who opposed all forms of government. Czolgosz fired two shots and hit the president. A few days later, McKinley died from his wounds. Czolgosz was executed on October 29, 1901.

Theodore Roosevelt, just 42 years old at the time, became the youngest person ever to become president. Roosevelt had been chosen as McKinley's running mate because Republican leaders knew his powerful charisma and heroic war record would be a great asset. They also hoped the relatively powerless position of vice president would quiet his reform-minded spirit. Now they cringed at the thought of Roosevelt in the White House. Republican senator Mark Hanna exclaimed, "Now look, that . . . cowboy is president of the United States!"

Roosevelt Becomes President Roosevelt brought to the presidency an energy and enthusiasm rarely seen before in the office. Such vigor stemmed in part from his childhood. Born into a wealthy New York family, Roosevelt was a sickly child who endured a host of ailments, including poor eyesight and asthma.

Dr. William Gorgas ➤

TEACH

S Skill Practice

Conducting Research Using the Internet as a resource, have students research how many other U.S. presidents were assassinated while in office. Students should list their names in chronological order, and the names of the vice presidents who succeeded them. **BL** **CA HR4**

R Reading Strategy

Predicting Have students identify the differences between the leadership styles of Presidents McKinley and Roosevelt and predict how they think other countries would have responded to the change in leadership. *(Students may note that McKinley was not a strong decision maker, and that Roosevelt was strong and decisive; other countries might respect the new leadership more or might fear it.)* **AL**

Review the Big Idea

Review the Big Idea for this section, "America's military and economic strength made it a world power." Have students create T-charts with the headings *Asia* and *Caribbean.* As they read the section, have students write down ways in which the United States increased its power under the appropriate headings. **OL**

Did You Know?

Theodore Roosevelt's final words are reported to have been, "Put out the light." He is buried in Young Memorial Cemetery, Oyster Bay, New York.

Roosevelt pushed himself to overcome his frailties. He mastered marksmanship and horseback riding and could row up to 20 miles a day. He took up boxing and wrestling in college and continued with both throughout his life, practicing the belief that competition and conflict keep one healthy.

Roosevelt became a strong proponent of increasing American power on the world stage. Just as he refused to sit around idly in life, the president warned Americans not to "sit huddled" and become "an assemblage of well-to-do hucksters who care nothing for what happens beyond." Roosevelt also accepted some of the ideas of Anglo-Saxonism. He believed that the United States had a duty to shape the "less civilized" corners of the earth. The new president intended to make the country a world power.

✓ **Reading Check** **Summarizing** What was President Roosevelt's opinion on the role of the United States as a world power?

American Diplomacy in Asia

Main Idea The United States pursued an Open Door policy in China to allow all nations access to China's markets.

Reading Connection Why would the ability to sell goods to China be considered important? Read on to find out about trade with China in the late 1800s.

In 1899 the United States was a major power in Asia, with naval bases all across the Pacific. Operating from those bases, the United States Navy—now the third largest in the world—was capable of exerting American power anywhere in East Asia.

The nation's primary interest in Asia, however, was not conquest but commerce. Between 1895 and 1900, American exports to China increased by four times. Although China bought only about two percent of all the goods exported by the United States, the vast Chinese markets excited American business leaders, especially those in the textile, oil, and steel industries.

The Open Door Policy In 1894 war erupted between China and Japan over Korea, which at that time was part of the Chinese empire. European and American leaders expected China, with its massive armed forces, to defeat Japan easily. These Western observers were astonished when Japan, with a more modern army and a powerful navy, easily defeated China. In the peace treaty, China granted Korea independence. China also gave Japan territory in Manchuria that included the important city of Port Arthur. The war showed that Japan had successfully adopted Western technology and industry. It also demonstrated that China was far weaker than anyone had thought.

Japan's rising power greatly worried the Russians. They did not want Japan to acquire the territory in Manchuria, because it bordered Russia. Backed by France and Germany, Russia forced Japan to give the part of Manchuria it had acquired back to China. Then, in 1898, Russia demanded that China lease the territory to Russia instead.

Leasing a territory meant that it would still belong to China, even though a foreign government would maintain overall control. Germany and France demanded leaseholds in China, and Britain insisted on several as well. Each "leasehold" became the center of a country's **sphere of influence,** an area where a foreign nation controlled economic development such as railroad construction, mining, and other key industries.

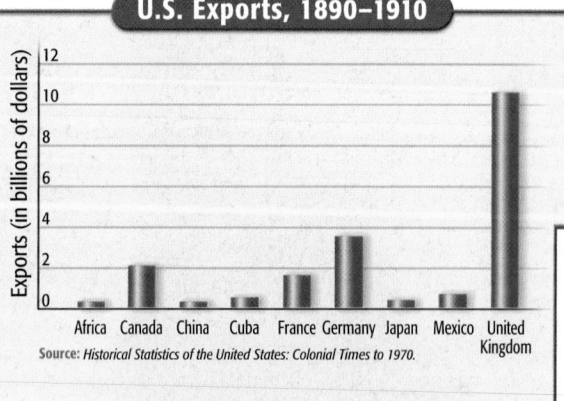

U.S. Exports, 1890–1910

Exports (in billions of dollars)

Africa · Canada · China · Cuba · France · Germany · Japan · Mexico · United Kingdom

Source: *Historical Statistics of the United States: Colonial Times to 1970.*

Graph Skills

1. **Interpreting Graphs** Which country ranked third in total U.S. exports from 1890 to 1910?
2. **Making Generalizations** Why do you think that the vast majority of U.S. exports were going to the United Kingdom?

These events in northern China greatly worried the United States. President McKinley and Secretary of State John Hay both supported what they called an **Open Door policy**, in which all countries should be allowed to trade with China. In 1899 Hay sent notes to countries with leaseholds in China asking them not to discriminate against other nations that wanted to do business with the Chinese inside each leasehold. The Europeans and Japanese received the Open Door proposals coolly. Each power claimed to accept them in principle but refused to act on them unless all of the others agreed to do so as well. Hay refused to consider this a rebuff. Once he had received assurances from all of the great powers, he declared that the United States expected the other powers to abide by the plan.

The Boxer Rebellion While foreign countries debated who should control China, secret Chinese societies were organizing to get rid of foreign control. Westerners referred to one such group as the Boxers, because when translated their name meant "righteous, harmonious fists." In 1900 the group rose up to wipe out "foreign devils" and their Christian converts, whom they believed were corrupting Chinese society. In what became known as the **Boxer Rebellion,** group members besieged foreign embassies in Beijing, killing more than 200 foreigners and taking others prisoner. In August 1900, an international force that included U.S. troops stepped in and quashed the rebellion.

During the crisis, Secretary of State Hay and British leaders worked to persuade European nations not to use the Boxer Rebellion as an excuse to partition China. In a second set of Open Door notes, Hay convinced the participating powers to back away from a full-scale retaliation against China. He urged them instead to accept compensation from China for any damage that the rebellion caused. After some discussion, China was never broken up into colonies. As a result, the United States retained access to China's lucrative trade in tea, spices, and silk and maintained an increasingly larger market for its own goods.

Balancing Power in East Asia As president, Theodore Roosevelt supported the Open Door policy in China and worked to prevent any single nation from monopolizing trade there. This concern prompted Roosevelt to step in to help negotiate peace in a war between Japan and Russia in 1905. At a peace conference in Portsmouth, New Hampshire, Roosevelt convinced the Russians to recognize Japan's territorial gains and persuaded the Japanese

▲ *Imprisoned members of the Boxer society*

to stop fighting and to seek no further territory. For his efforts in ending the war, Roosevelt won the Nobel Peace Prize in 1906.

In the years after the peace treaty, relations between the United States and Japan steadily grew worse. As the two nations vied for greater influence in Asia, they held each other in check through a series of agreements. They agreed to respect each other's territorial possessions, to uphold the Open Door policy, and to support China's independence.

In 1907 President Roosevelt sent 16 battleships of the new United States Navy, known as the **"Great White Fleet,"** on a voyage around the world to showcase the nation's military might. The tour made a stop in Japan to demonstrate that the United States could and would uphold its interests in Asia. This visit did not help ease the growing tensions between the two countries throughout the early 1900s.

✓**Reading Check** **Explaining** What was the purpose of the Open Door policy?

A Growing Presence in the Caribbean

Main Idea Theodore Roosevelt pushed for construction of the Panama Canal and declared the intent of the United States to act as a police force in Latin American nations.

Reading Connection Have you ever tried to find a shortcut to save time when traveling from one place to another? Read on to learn about a canal that dramatically reduced travel and shipping time.

Theodore Roosevelt believed in a strong global military presence. He insisted that displaying American power to the world would make nations

CHAPTER 4 Becoming a World Power **313**

C **Critical Thinking**

Drawing Conclusions John Hay served as secretary of state under President McKinley and was involved in implementing the Open Door policy. **Ask:** What is the role of the secretary of state in the presidential administration? What characteristics would make a good secretary of state? *(Students' answers may include: a firm negotiator, diplomacy, persuasiveness, persistence, a respected character, trustworthiness)* **OL**

R₁ **Reading Strategy**

Inferring Secretary of State Hay was successful in persuading European powers not to retaliate against China after the Boxer Rebellion. **Ask:** How did Hay convince the European nations to leave China alone? *(Hay convinced the European nations to receive compensation from China for all the damages caused by the rebellion.)* **OL**

R₂ **Reading Strategy**

Connecting Alfred Nobel, Swedish chemist and inventor of dynamite, left $9 million to found the Nobel Prizes. Ask students to research the five fields to which prizes are awarded. *(physics, chemistry, physiology, literature, and peace)* Then have students identify one other recipient of the Nobel Prize and write a paragraph about his or her achievements. **AL** **CA** 11WA2.4d

✓**Reading Check**

Answer: to ensure that all nations had access to China's market

More Skill Practice

Drawing Conclusions Theodore Roosevelt is often portrayed as a very belligerent figure, but he was also a skilled political negotiator. **Ask:** What factors may have made Russia and Japan willing to agree to the negotiations laid out by President Roosevelt? *(financial costs of the war; destruction to their country; ending the loss of life)* **OL**

Did You Know?

The Boxers, also known as the Righteous and Harmonious Fists, were members of a secret society opposed to foreign influence in China. As the Boxers laid siege to the foreign legations in Beijing, diplomats, foreign civilians, and Chinese Christians were trapped behind barricades for nearly 60 days before an international rescue team ended the uprising.

S Skill Practice

Interpreting Quotations Direct students to Roosevelt's quote, "Speak softly, and carry a big stick." Ask students to interpret this quotation and discuss how they saw this philosophy demonstrated in Roosevelt's foreign policies. *(Students' answers will vary but should be based on information found in the textbook.)* **OL**

CA 11RC2.5; 11RL3.2

W Writing Support

Persuasive Writing Have students imagine they are President Roosevelt. Ask them to write a speech to persuade the American people that his actions in sending ships to Panama were justified. Divide the students into groups of four or five in which they will listen to each other's speeches. Have them critique the reasoning used in each speech and its overall effectiveness. **AL**

CA 11WS1.1; 11WS1.5

R Reading Strategy

Scaffolding—Academic Vocabulary The word *define* was introduced in the Constitution Handbook on p. 141. Ask a student to define the word. **BL**

Answers and Additional Support

S think twice about fighting, thus promoting global peace. He often expressed this belief with a West African saying, "Speak softly and carry a big stick." Roosevelt's "big stick" policy was perhaps most evident in the Caribbean.

The Panama Canal One of Roosevelt's most dramatic actions in the Caribbean was the acquisition of the Panama Canal Zone in 1903. Roosevelt and others viewed the construction of a canal through Central America as vital to American power in the world. A canal would save time and money for both commercial and military shipping.

As early as 1850, the United States and Great Britain had signed a treaty in which each nation had agreed not to build a canal without the other's participation. Because of its strong interest in a canal, however, the United States negotiated a new treaty. In 1901, the United States and Great Britain signed the **Hay-Pauncefote Treaty,** which gave the United States the exclusive right to build and control any proposed canal through Central America.

A French company had begun digging a canal through Panama in 1881. By 1889, however, it abandoned its efforts because of bankruptcy and terrible losses from disease among the workers. The company was reorganized in 1894, but its operations practically ceased and its only hope was to sell its rights to digging the canal.

The United States had long considered two possible canal sites, one through Nicaragua and one through Panama. The French company eased this

Analyzing *Political Cartoons*

American Imperialism This cartoon displays Roosevelt's belief that the United States should "speak softly and carry a big stick" in foreign affairs. In what part of the world did Roosevelt's quote originate?

314 CHAPTER 4 Becoming a World Power

---

choice by offering to sell its rights and property in Panama to the United States.

In 1903 Panama was still part of Colombia. Secretary of State Hay offered Colombia $10 million and a yearly rent of $250,000 for the right to construct the canal and to control a narrow strip of land on either side of it. The Colombian government refused the offer.

Revolt in Panama Some Panamanians feared losing the commercial benefits of the canal. Panama had opposed Colombian rule since the mid-1800s, and the canal issue added to the **tensions.** In addition, the French company was still concerned that the United States would build the canal in Nicaragua instead. The French company's agent, Philippe Bunau-Varilla, and Panamanian officials decided that the only way to ensure the canal would be built was to declare independence and make their own deal with the United States. Bunau-Varilla arranged for a small army to stage an uprising in Panama.

On November 3, 1903, Bunau-Varilla's forces revolted. President Roosevelt sent ships to Panama to prevent Colombian interference. Within a few days, the United States recognized Panama's independence. Less than two weeks later, the two nations signed a treaty allowing the canal to be built.

W Protesters condemned Roosevelt's actions as unjustifiable aggression. The president countered that he had advanced "the needs of collective civilization" by building a canal that shortened the distance between the Atlantic and the Pacific by about 8,000 nautical miles (14,816 km).

R **The Roosevelt Corollary** The growing American involvement in foreign affairs caused Roosevelt to expand his "big stick" diplomacy. In an address to Congress in 1904, the president defined what came to be known as the **Roosevelt Corollary** to the Monroe Doctrine. To prevent European nations from sending troops to the Caribbean or Central America, he announced that the United States would **intervene** in Latin American affairs when necessary to maintain stability in the Western Hemisphere:

> 66 Chronic wrongdoing . . . may, in America, as elsewhere, ultimately require intervention by some civilized nation, and in the Western Hemisphere the adherence of the United States to the Monroe Doctrine may force the United States, however reluctantly . . . to the exercise of an international police power. 99

> —quoted in *The Growth of the United States*

Did You Know?

Many U.S. legislators opposed the Roosevelt Corollary, claiming that his actions were unconstitutional because it was the Senate's right to make such decisions. Most Americans approved of the corollary, however, so the Senate agreed in 1907 to a treaty that maintained U.S. control of Dominican customs.

Analyzing *Political Cartoons*

Answer: It was a West African saying.
Ask: How did a "big stick" promote peace?
(According to Roosevelt, it would discourage nations from fighting.)

The United States first applied the Roosevelt Corollary in the Dominican Republic, which had fallen behind on its debt payments to European nations. In 1905, worried that the Europeans were getting ready to send troops, Roosevelt sent American marines to the Dominican Republic to collect customs tariffs to make the debt payments. Roosevelt feared that European troops would hinder American trade with the Dominican Republic.

Latin American nations resented the growing American influence in the region. Roosevelt's successor, William Howard Taft, continued Roosevelt's policies, however, with an emphasis on helping Latin American industry. He believed that if American business leaders supported Latin American development, everyone would benefit. The United States would increase its trade, American businesses would increase their profits, and countries in Latin America would rise out of poverty and social disorder, and European nations would have no reason to intervene in the region. Taft's policy came to be called **dollar diplomacy.**

Although Taft described his brand of diplomacy as "substituting dollars for bullets," in Nicaragua he used both. In 1911 American bankers began making loans to Nicaragua to support its shaky government. The following year, civil unrest forced the Nicaraguan president to appeal for greater assistance. American marines entered the country, replaced the collector of customs with an American agent, and formed a committee of two Americans and one Nicaraguan to control the customs commissions. American troops stayed to support both the government and customs until 1925.

✓ **Reading Check** **Describing** What did the Roosevelt Corollary state?

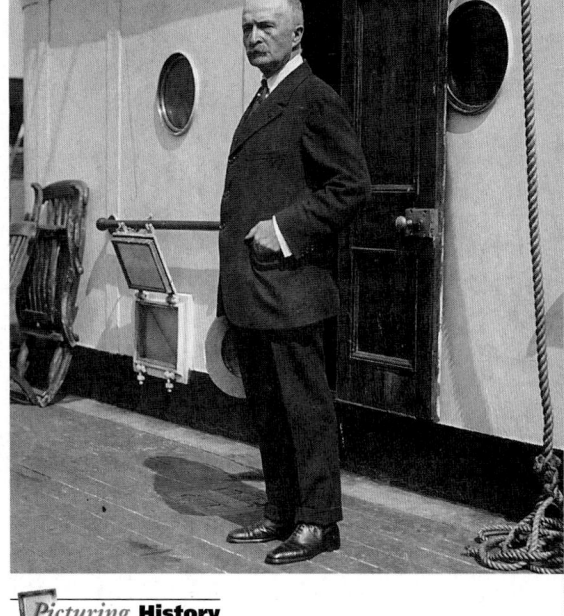

Picturing History

Bunau-Varilla Philippe Bunau-Varilla was instrumental in convincing President Roosevelt to build the canal through Panama instead of Nicaragua. As a representative of Panama to the United States, he also negotiated the Hay–Pauncefote Treaty, which gave the United States control of the Panama Canal. Many people viewed Roosevelt's actions in Panama as unjustifiable aggression. Roosevelt later defended his actions in the Roosevelt Corollary. Why did Roosevelt believe that U.S. involvement in Latin American affairs was so important?

HISTORY Online **Study Central**

For help with the concepts in this section of *American Vision: Modern Times* go to tav.mt.glencoe.com and click on *Study Central.*

SECTION 3 ASSESSMENT

Checking for Understanding

1. **Vocabulary** Define: exploits, sphere of influence, Open Door policy, tensions, intervene, dollar diplomacy.

2. **People and Terms** Identify: Boxer Rebellion, "Great White Fleet," Hay-Pauncefote Treaty, Roosevelt Corollary.

Reviewing Big Ideas

3. **Interpreting** Why do you think Latin American nations resented American influence in the region?

Critical Thinking

4. **Analyzing** How did the Open Door policy and dollar diplomacy affect U.S. relations with other countries?

5. **Organizing** Use a graphic organizer to summarize the results of the Open Door policy in China.

Analyzing Visuals

6. **Analyzing Graphs** Examine the graph on page 312. Why do you think such a small number of U.S. exports went to China and Japan?

Writing About History

7. **Persuasive Writing** Imagine you are Theodore Roosevelt, and write a speech justifying the actions that led to the building of the Panama Canal. Be specific in your reasons.
   CA 11WS1.2; 11WS1.3

CHAPTER 4 Becoming a World Power **315**

SECTION 3 ASSESSMENT ANSWERS

1. Content vocabulary is boldfaced and highlighted in yellow. Academic vocabulary is boldfaced.

2. Boxer Rebellion (p. 313), "Great White Fleet" (p. 313), Hay Pauncefote Treaty (p. 314), Roosevelt Corollary (p. 314)

3. Possible answers: They wanted the right to self-determination.

They knew that America would act in its own interests, not the interests of Latin America.

4. The Open Door policy kept China open to U.S. trade; dollar diplomacy generally created Latin American resentment.

5. all countries could trade with China; prevented warfare

between competing nations

6. Possible answers: American products were in low demand; Chinese and Japanese could not afford them.

7. Students' speeches will vary. Speeches should include benefits to the United States and to other countries.

ASSESS

Resources for page 315

Use these resources to assess student mastery.

📂 Section Quiz 4-3

📂 Reading Essentials and Study Guide 4-3

⊚ Interactive Tutor Self-Assessment CD-ROM

📂 California Standards Practice, Grade 11

Picturing History

Answer: Roosevelt wanted to keep out European nations.
Ask: What did President Taft think about the corollary? (He built on Roosevelt's policies by supporting Latin American industry.)

✓ **Reading Check**

Answer: The United States would intervene in Latin America to prevent European intervention and to maintain stability in the Western Hemisphere.

HISTORY Online

Study Central provides audio summaries, interactive games, and online graphic organizers to help students review section content.

CLOSE

Drawing Conclusions Ask students to recall the Monroe Doctrine. **Ask:** Was the Roosevelt Corollary a logical extension of its principles? Ask students to write a paragraph to defend their arguments. **AL**
CA 11WA2.3b

315

FOCUS

TEACH

R Reading Strategy

Determining Importance
Working as a class, create a list of
reasons why construction of the
Panama Canal was important to
the United States. *(Students may
answer: increase trade opportunities; help the U.S. defend its
assets; save time; save money)*
OL

C Critical Thinking

Analyzing Information Have
students use information from
the Internet to chart the growth
in volume of cargo passing
through the Panama Canal in the
past 100 years. Using the data
gathered, instruct students to
write a two-page report listing
reasons for the significant growth.
AL **CA 11WA2.4**

S Skill Practice

Visual Literacy Tell students to
examine the cartoon and ask
what details they observe. Then
have students write a caption for
the cartoon. **OL**

The Panama Canal

R One of the most impressive feats of
engineering in the world, the Panama
Canal was built under a 1903 U.S. treaty
with Panama. It took 10 years to build,
required more than 40,000 laborers, and
cost almost $390 million. The canal
stretches 50 miles (80 km) across the
mountainous regions of Panama.
In 1977 a new treaty took effect that gave
Panama control of the canal as of
December 31, 1999.

▲ Trade
C Nearly 13,000 oceangoing vessels pass through the canal
annually. Roughly 60 percent of the cargo is coming from or
going to U.S. ports. The canal's relative share of world cargo
has declined somewhat, but its absolute volume has grown
with the continued expansion of global trade.

▲ Military Impact
Huge quantities of war materials and
thousands of troops passed through the
canal during World War II, the Korean
War, and the Vietnam War. The strategic
location of the canal makes its neutrality
critical in times of war.

A Cartoonist's View ➤
Many people criticized
Roosevelt's role in building the
Panama Canal. They believed
that he was trying to dominate
S Latin America. The canal was
also costly in terms of human
life. Accidents and disease
claimed the lives of 5,609
people, including about
4,500 Caribbean laborers.

THE MAN WHO CAN MAKE THE DIRT FLY.

EXTENDING THE CONTENT

Building the Panama Canal The construction of the Panama Canal involved three main
engineering projects. First, the workers had to excavate the Galliard Cut, which was 300 feet
(91 meters) wide across the isthmus. Next, they had to build a dam across the Chagres River
to create an artificial lake. Finally, they had to construct the canal's locks. The hardest job
was digging the Galliard Cut, because the hill through which the cut runs consists of soft,
volcanic material. When workers dug a hole, more rock and earth would slide into the space
or push up from below.

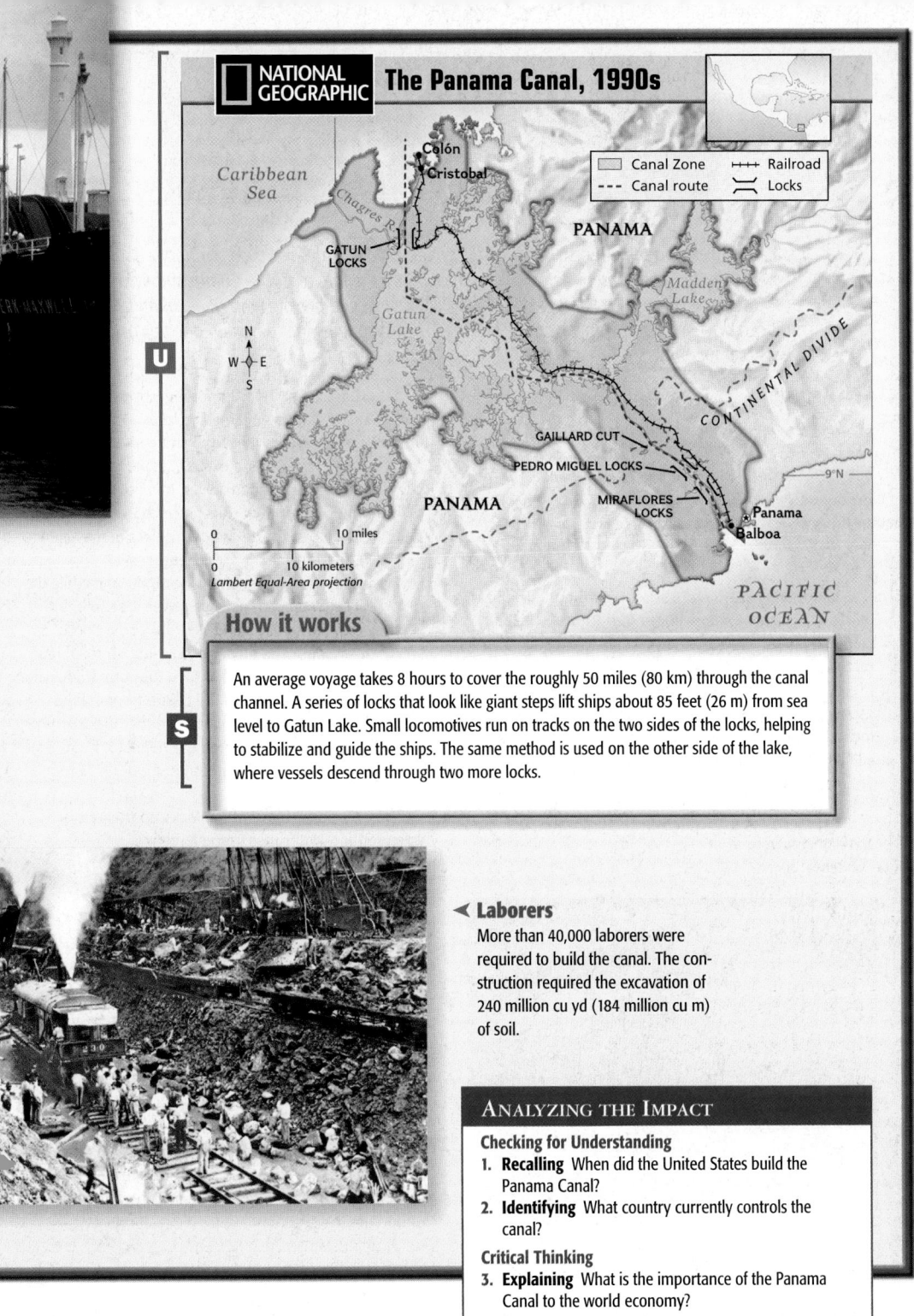

NATIONAL GEOGRAPHIC — The Panama Canal, 1990s

Legend:
- Canal Zone
- Canal route
- Railroad
- Locks

Caribbean Sea

Colón
Cristobal

PANAMA

Chagres R.

GATUN LOCKS

Gatun Lake

Madden Lake

CONTINENTAL DIVIDE

9°N

PANAMA

GAILLARD CUT

PEDRO MIGUEL LOCKS

MIRAFLORES LOCKS

Panama
Balboa

PACIFIC OCEAN

N W E S

0   10 miles
0   10 kilometers
Lambert Equal-Area projection

How it works

An average voyage takes 8 hours to cover the roughly 50 miles (80 km) through the canal channel. A series of locks that look like giant steps lift ships about 85 feet (26 m) from sea level to Gatun Lake. Small locomotives run on tracks on the two sides of the locks, helping to stabilize and guide the ships. The same method is used on the other side of the lake, where vessels descend through two more locks.

◄ Laborers

More than 40,000 laborers were required to build the canal. The construction required the excavation of 240 million cu yd (184 million cu m) of soil.

ANALYZING THE IMPACT

Checking for Understanding
1. **Recalling** When did the United States build the Panama Canal?
2. **Identifying** What country currently controls the canal?

Critical Thinking
3. **Explaining** What is the importance of the Panama Canal to the world economy?

CHAPTER 4 Becoming a World Power **317**

ANALYZING THE IMPACT

1. A treaty to build the canal was signed in 1903. Construction took 10 years.

2. Panama took control of the canal on December 31, 1999.

3. The canal significantly cuts travel time for ships that before had to go around the southern tip of South America.

317

FOCUS

History–Social Science Standards

This feature addresses the following standard:

11.4.2 Describe the Spanish-American War and U.S. expansion in the South Pacific.

Understanding Vocabulary

Before students begin reading, point out that difficult or unfamiliar words are footnoted throughout the text.

TEACH

R **Reading Strategy**

Summarizing Tell students to read Bryan's assessment of the Filipino people carefully. **Ask:** **How does Bryan view the Filipinos?** *(less equal than Americans but able to learn and govern if given the freedom to do so)* **OL**

Answers and Additional Support

318

Primary Sources
Eyewitness to History

In the treaty ending the Spanish-American War, the United States received a number of former Spanish colonies. The United States quickly decided on the fate of Cuba, Guam, and Puerto Rico. One issue remained—what to do with the Philippines. Before the war, annexation had not been discussed. Now, however, the future of the Philippines led to heated debates over the merits of imperialism.

SOURCE 1:

William Jennings Bryan, the Democratic candidate, opposed President William McKinley in the election of 1900. If elected, Bryan promised to grant immediate independence to the Philippines. In a speech he delivered in Chicago in 1899, Bryan attacked the major arguments of the imperialists.

The Imperialists do not desire to clothe the Filipinos with all the rights and privileges of American citizenship; they want to exercise **sovereignty**[1] over an alien race and they expect to rule the new subjects upon a theory entirely at **variance**[2] with constitutional government. Victoria is Queen of Great Britain and Empress of India; shall we change the title of our executive and call him the President of the United States and Emperor of the Philippines? . . .

---

[1]**sovereignty:** control
[2]**variance:** against

▲ *William Jennings Bryan, seen here in a campaign speech in his 1896 bid for the presidency*

R We are told that the Filipinos are not capable of self-government; that has a familiar ring. . . . The Filipinos are not far enough advanced to share in the government of the people of the United States, but they are competent to govern themselves. It is not fair to compare them with our own citizens, because the American people have been educating themselves in the science of government for nearly three centuries. . . .

Give the Filipinos time and opportunity and while they never will catch up with us, unless we cease to improve, yet they may some day stand where we stand now. . . .

When the desire to steal become uncontrollable in an individual he is declared to be a **kleptomaniac**[3] and is sent to an asylum; when the desire to grab land becomes uncontrollable we are told that the "currents of destiny are flowing through the hearts of men" and that the American people are entering upon "a manifest mission."

Shame upon a logic which locks up the petty offender and enthrones grand larceny. . . .

SOURCE 2:

Theodore Roosevelt fought against the Spanish in Cuba during the Spanish-American War. His heroism had made him famous, and the Republicans chose him as President McKinley's vice-presidential running mate in the election of 1900. In a speech delivered in Chicago in 1899, Roosevelt responded to Bryan's earlier remarks.

In the . . . [Philippines] . . . we are confronted by most difficult problems. It is cowardly to shrink from solving them in the proper way; for solved they must be, if not by us, then by some stronger and more manful race; if we are too weak, too selfish, or too foolish to solve them some bolder and abler people must undertake the solution. . . .

---

[3]**kleptomaniac:** thief

UNIVERSAL ACCESS

Advanced Learners Ask students to use library and Internet resources to find out how newspapers covered the Spanish-American War and the Philippine annexation. Each student should make a time line that tracks when the first headline story covering the Spanish-American War appeared in the newspaper and count how many days this was the main story of the paper. Tell students to also note what story became the main story that replaced the war. Students should also note how many newspaper articles, editorials, and letters to the editor focused on the war. **AL** **CA HI3**

▲ *Senator Orville H. Platt*

Many of their people are utterly unfit for self-government and show no signs of becoming fit. Others may in time become fit, but at present can only take part in self-government under a wise supervision at once firm and beneficent. We have driven Spanish tyranny from the islands. If we now let it be replaced by savage **anarchy**[4], our work has been for harm and not for good. I have scant patience with those who fear to undertake the task of governing the Philippines. . . . I have even scanter patience with those who . . . rant about "liberty" and the "consent of the governed" in order to excuse themselves for their unwillingness to play the part of men. . . .

I preach to you, then, my countrymen, that our country calls not for the life of ease, but for the life of strenuous endeavor. The twentieth century looms before us big with the fate of many nations. . . . [I]f we shrink from the hard contests where men must win at hazard of their lives and at the risk of all they hold dear, then the bolder and stronger peoples will pass us by and will win for themselves the domination of the world.

SOURCE 3:

After the Spanish-American War, the United States granted Cuba its independence, but President McKinley and others doubted that the Cubans had the ability to govern themselves. In 1901 Senator Orville H. Platt of Connecticut made a list of conditions that Cuba had to meet. These conditions were known as the Platt Amendment.

➤ [4]**anarchy:** no government

The President of the U.S. is hereby authorized to "leave the government and control of the island of Cuba to its people" so soon as a government shall have been established in said island under a constitution which shall . . . define the future relations of the United States with Cuba, substantially as follows:

I. That the government of Cuba shall never enter into any treaty or other compact with any foreign power or powers which will impair or tend to impair the independence of Cuba, nor in any manner authorize or permit any foreign power or powers to obtain . . . control over any portion of said island. . . .

III. That the government of Cuba consents that the United States may exercise the right to intervene for the preservation of Cuban independence, the maintenance of a government adequate for the protection of life, property, and individual liberty. . . .

V. That the government of Cuba will execute, and, as far as necessary, extend, the plans already devised or other plans to be mutually agreed upon, for the sanitation of the cities of the island, to the end that a recurrence of epidemic and infectious diseases may be prevented, thereby assuring protection to the people and commerce of Cuba, as well as to the commerce of the southern ports of the United States and the people residing therein. . . .

VII. That to enable the United States to maintain the independence of Cuba, and to protect the people thereof, as well as for its defense, the government of Cuba will sell or lease to the United States lands necessary for coaling or naval stations. . . .

DBQ Document-Based Questions

Historical Analysis CA HR4, HI1, HI2

Source 1: Why did Bryan believe that taking the Philippines was wrong?

Source 2: Why did Roosevelt believe the United States should hold on to the Philippines?

Source 3: What restrictions did the Platt Amendment impose on Cuba?

Comparing and Contrasting Sources

How did Bryan, Roosevelt, and Platt differ in their views about the role of the United States in international politics and about the competence of people in other countries to govern themselves?

S Skill Practice

Preparing a Debate Divide the class into three groups: one that supports Roosevelt's point of view, one that is opposed to his beliefs, and one that consists of undecided observers. Tell the first two groups to use the sources and arguments of Bryan and Theodore Roosevelt as a starting point for their research on their positions. Ask each group to prepare a ten-minute presentation that supports their position and criticizes the other group. Ask the observer group to evaluate which argument was the most persuasive. **OL** **CA HR1; HR3**

C Critical Thinking

Analyzing Primary Sources The Spanish-American War was fought, in part, to grant Cuba its independence. Ask students to define the word *independence* and then consider if the Platt Amendment reflects their definition of the word. *(Students should realize that the amendment put such restrictions on Cuba's freedom of governance and choice that it was not supportive of actual independence.)* **OL**

ASSESS/CLOSE

Have students answer the Document-Based Questions.

DBQ Document-Based Questions

1. Annexing and ruling over the Philippines without offering Filipinos American citizenship was at odds with constitutional government.
2. The country may fall into anarchy since many people were not capable of self-government without initial supervision.
3. Cuba could not sign treaties with another government that would threaten its independence or permit another government to gain control over the island.

Comparing and Contrasting: Bryan: Filipinos are inferior to Americans, but they can educate themselves to achieve self-governance; Roosevelt: Filipinos are not ready to govern themselves, the U.S. must supervise; Platt: Cubans were incapable of self-government

Resources for pages 320–321

Use the following resources to review, assess, and reteach the chapter.

📁 Chapter 4 Tests, Forms A and B

📁 Standardized Tests, Forms A and B

📁 Cumulative Authentic Assessment

🔒 MindJogger Videoquiz

💿 Interactive Tutor Self-Assessment CD-ROM

💿 ExamView® Pro Testmaker CD-ROM

💿 Vocabulary PuzzleMaker CD-ROM

💿 Succeeding on . . .™ the California Standards: Grade 11 History–Social Science

📁 California Standards Practice, Grade 11

Reviewing Content Vocabulary

Students' answers will vary. The pages where the words appear in the text are shown in parentheses.

1. imperialism *(p. 295)* **2.** protectorate *(p. 295)* **3.** Anglo-Saxonism *(p. 296)* **4.** Pan-Americanism *(p. 298)* **5.** yellow journalism *(p. 302)* **6.** jingoism *(p. 303)* **7.** sphere of influence *(p. 312)* **8.** Open Door policy *(p. 313)* **9.** dollar diplomacy *(p. 315)*

Reviewing Academic Vocabulary

Students' answers will vary. The pages where the words appear in the text are shown in parentheses.

10. technology *(p. 296)* **11.** publish *(p. 299)* **12.** resource *(p. 303)* **13.** violate *(p. 306)* **14.** virtual *(p. 306)* **15.** exploit *(p. 311)* **16.** tension *(p. 314)* **17.** intervene *(p. 314)*

Standards 11.2.7, 11.3.2, 11.4, 11.4.1, 11.4.2, 11.4.3, 11.4.4

Reviewing Content Vocabulary

On a sheet of paper, use each of these terms in a sentence.

1. imperialism
2. protectorate
3. Anglo-Saxonism
4. Pan-Americanism
5. yellow journalism
6. jingoism
7. sphere of influence
8. Open Door policy
9. dollar diplomacy

Reviewing Academic Vocabulary

On a sheet of paper, use each of these terms in a sentence that reflects the term's meaning in the chapter.

10. technology
11. publish
12. resource
13. violate
14. virtual
15. exploit
16. tension
17. intervene

Reviewing the Main Idea

Section 1

18. Why did the United States seek to become a world power?

Section 2

19. What were the provisions of the Treaty of Paris of 1898?

Section 3

20. What was dollar diplomacy?

Critical Thinking

21. **Explaining** What was the significance of the year 1898 as a turning point for the United States?

22. **Civics** Explain how and why the United States acquired Hawaii. Include the reasons the acquisition of Hawaii was considered essential to U.S. national interests.

23. **Organizing** Using a graphic organizer similar to the one below, list ways that American imperialism affected Hawaii, Cuba, and the Philippines.

```
            U.S. Imperialism
        ┌────────┼────────┐
        ↓        ↓        ↓
    Hawaii     Cuba   the Philippines
```

24. **Reading Skill** **Cause and Effect** Reread the information about the Panama Canal on page 314. Then create a cause-and-effect list similar to the one on page 292.

Writing About History

25. **Historical Analysis** **Evaluating Past Events** Research the Panama Canal today. How did the canal change Panama? Did the construction of the canal benefit or hurt Panama? Cite evidence to support your decision. **CA CS1**

26. **Big Idea** Write a newspaper editorial supporting imperialism. Give specific examples of how the United States became an imperial power under the McKinley administration. **CA 11WA2.1b; 11WA2.4a**

Chapter Summary

U.S. Actions

In the Pacific
- Expanded Chinese and Japanese markets
- Annexed the Midway Islands as refueling depots for expanded navy
- Built coaling stations on Samoan Islands
- American business leaders led successful campaign for Hawaiian annexation
- Victory over Spain gave U.S. control over Guam and the Philippines

In Latin America
- At Pan-American Conference, invited Latin American countries to trade with U.S.
- Supported Cuba's rebellion against Spain, leading to Spanish-American War; victory over Spain gave U.S. control over Cuba, Puerto Rico
- Built the Panama Canal
- Issued the Roosevelt Corollary stating that the U.S. would intervene in Latin America to maintain stability

320 CHAPTER 4 Becoming a World Power

Reviewing the Main Ideas

18. It wanted to compete economically and militarily with other countries, and there was a growing feeling of superiority.

19. Cuba became an independent country, the United States acquired Puerto Rico and Guam, and the United States agreed to pay Spain $20 million for the Philippines.

20. It was the policy that placed less emphasis on military force and more on investing American dollars in Latin America.

Critical Thinking

21. The United States declared war on Spain. After the war the U.S. gained territory outside the continental United States and established itself as a world power. The United States also annexed Hawaii in 1898.

Self-Check Quiz
Visit the *American Vision: Modern Times* Web site at
tav.mt.glencoe.com and click on *Self-Check Quizzes—
Chapter 4* to assess your knowledge of chapter content.

DBQ Document-Based Questions

27. **Interpreting Primary Sources** After the Spanish-American War, Carl Schurz, the leader of the liberal wing of the Republican Party, opposed American expansion abroad. In the following excerpt, Schurz attacks the arguments for taking over the Philippine Islands.

❝Taking a general view of the Philippines as a commercial market for us, I need not again argue against the barbarous notion that in order to have a profitable trade with a country we must own it. . . . It is equally needless to show to any well-informed person that the profits of the trade with the islands themselves can never amount to the cost of making and maintaining the conquest of the Philippines.

But there is another point of real importance. Many imperialists admit that our trade with the Philippines themselves will not nearly be worth its cost; but they say that we must have the Philippines as a foothold, a sort of power station, for the expansion of our trade on the Asiatic continent, especially in China. Admitting this, for argument's sake, I ask what kind of a foothold we should really need. Coaling stations and docks for our fleet, and facilities for the establishment of commercial houses and depots. That is all. And now I ask further, whether we could not easily have had these things if we had, instead of making war upon the Filipinos, favored the independence of the islands. Everybody knows that we could. We might have those things now for the mere asking if we stopped the war and came to a friendly understanding with the Filipinos tomorrow. . . .❞

—quoted in *The Policy of Imperialism*

a. How does Schurz counter the argument that annexation of the Philippines was necessary to make the nation a commercial market for the United States?
CA 11RC2.4; 11RC2.5

b. What action other than annexation does Schurz suggest the United States could have taken to obtain the coaling stations, docks, and depots it needed for trade with Asia?
CA 11RC2.4; 11RC2.5

NATIONAL GEOGRAPHIC

U.S. Possessions in the Pacific, 1899

U.S. possessions with date acquired

Mercator projection

Geography and History

28. The map on this page shows the expansion of the United States in 1900. Study the map and answer the following questions.
   a. **Interpreting Maps** Approximately how far west is the island of Guam from the west coast of the United States?
   b. **Applying Geography Skills** According to the map, what U.S.-acquired territory is farthest west?

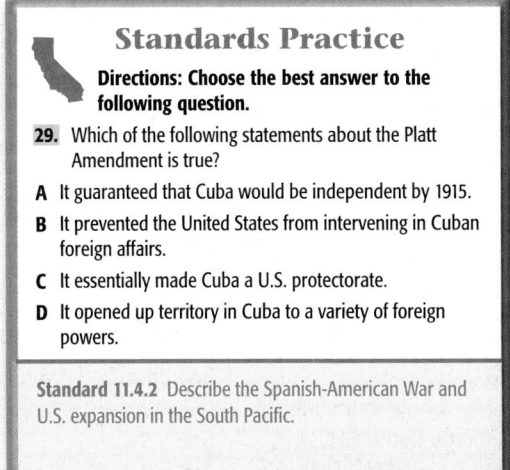

Standards Practice

Directions: Choose the best answer to the following question.

29. Which of the following statements about the Platt Amendment is true?

A It guaranteed that Cuba would be independent by 1915.

B It prevented the United States from intervening in Cuban foreign affairs.

C It essentially made Cuba a U.S. protectorate.

D It opened up territory in Cuba to a variety of foreign powers.

Standard 11.4.2 Describe the Spanish-American War and U.S. expansion in the South Pacific.

HISTORY Online

Have students visit the Web site at tav.mt.glencoe.com to review Chapter 4 and take the Self-Check Quiz.

Writing About History

25. **Historical Analysis** Students' answers will vary but should include support for their arguments.

26. *Big Idea* Article should be concise and include facts of the McKinley administration's policy concerning imperialism.

DBQ Document-Based Questions

27. **a.** The cost of conquest and maintaining control is more than the potential profit. **b.** We could have favored and supported their independence and kept open communication.

Geography and History

28. **a.** approximately 6,500 miles (10,500 kilometers); **b.** the Philippines

Standards Practice

29. C

Bonus Question ?

Ask: What was the cause of the Boxer Rebellion in China? *(The fear of foreign control of China caused several secret societies to band together and attack foreign embassies.)*

22. Students' answers may vary but trade and a strategic location in the Pacific were main reasons for the acquisition of Hawaii. Students should recall that the planters forced Queen Liliuokalani to give up power and then created a government. The United States eventually annexed Hawaii.

23. Hawaii: eventually became a state. Cuba: U.S. set up a military government and forced them to add the Platt Amendment to their constitution, effectively making them a protectorate until 1934. Philippines: U.S. controlled the Filipino government until, by the mid-1930s, Filipinos were granted some self-government. They were granted independence in 1946.

24. **Reading Skill** Students' lists will vary but should include a focus question, causes, and a culminating event.

Chapter 5 Planning Guide

SECTION RESOURCES

MAIN IDEAS	📁 PRINT MATERIALS	TECHNOLOGY RESOURCES
Section 1: The Roots of Progressivism 1. The Progressive movement was an attempt to use scientific principles to improve society. 2. One form of progressivism focused on ways to use business practices to make government more efficient. 3. Progressive policies in Wisconsin led to election reforms. 4. Many progressives joined the national suffrage movement. 5. Many progressives focused on social welfare problems, such as child labor, public health, and prohibition. 6. Progressives also focused on regulating big business.	• Reproducible Lesson Plan 5-1* • Daily Lecture and Discussion Notes 5-1 • Active Reading Note-Taking Guide 5-1 • Guided Reading Activity 5-1 • Section Quiz 5-1 • Reading Essentials and Study Guide 5-1	📖 Daily Focus Skills Transparency 5-1 📖 Section Graphic Organizer Transparency 5-1 💿 Interactive Tutor Self-Assessment CD-ROM 💿 Exam*View*® Pro Testmaker CD-ROM 💿 Presentation Plus! CD-ROM 📖 California Standards Practice Transparencies
Section 2: Roosevelt in Office 1. Theodore Roosevelt, who believed in progressive ideals for the nation, took on big business. 2. Theodore Roosevelt and Congress expanded the power of government by passing several acts regulating meat inspection, food and drugs, and conservation of the environment.	• Reproducible Lesson Plan 5-2* • Daily Lecture and Discussion Notes 5-2 • Active Reading Note-Taking Guide 5-2 • Guided Reading Activity 5-2 • Section Quiz 5-2 • Reading Essentials and Study Guide 5-2	📖 Daily Focus Skills Transparency 5-2 📖 Section Graphic Organizer Transparency 5-2 💿 Interactive Tutor Self-Assessment CD-ROM 💿 Exam*View*® Pro Testmaker CD-ROM 💿 Presentation Plus! CD-ROM 📖 California Standards Practice Transparencies
Section 3: The Taft Administration 1. William Howard Taft, elected to continue Theodore Roosevelt's policies, had difficulties with tariff and conservation issues. 2. Taft worked to pass progressive reforms.	• Reproducible Lesson Plan 5-3* • Daily Lecture and Discussion Notes 5-3 • Active Reading Note-Taking Guide 5-3 • Guided Reading Activity 5-3 • Section Quiz 5-3 • Reading Essentials and Study Guide 5-3	📖 Daily Focus Skills Transparency 5-3 📖 Section Graphic Organizer Transparency 5-3 💿 Interactive Tutor Self-Assessment CD-ROM 💿 Exam*View*® Pro Testmaker CD-ROM 💿 Presentation Plus! CD-ROM 📖 California Standards Practice Transparencies
Section 4: The Wilson Years 1. Woodrow Wilson's "New Freedom" campaign won him the White House after Republican voters split over Taft and Roosevelt. 2. President Wilson reformed tariffs and banks and oversaw the creation of the Federal Trade Commission. 3. Wilson continued to support progressive reforms as he faced reelection in 1916. 4. Progressivism changed the view many people had about the government's role in social issues.	• Reproducible Lesson Plan 5-4* • Daily Lecture and Discussion Notes 5-4 • Active Reading Note-Taking Guide 5-4 • Guided Reading Activity 5-4 • Section Quiz 5-4 • Reading Essentials and Study Guide 5-4	📖 Daily Focus Skills Transparency 5-4 📖 Section Graphic Organizer Transparency 5-4 💿 Interactive Tutor Self-Assessment CD-ROM 💿 Exam*View*® Pro Testmaker CD-ROM 💿 Presentation Plus! CD-ROM 📖 California Standards Practice Transparencies

🕐 PACING YOUR LESSONS

Chapter Introduction	Section 1	Section 2	Section 3	Section 4	Chapter Assessment
½ Day	2 Days	2 Days	1 Day	2 Days	½ Day

0:00 **OUT OF TIME?** 📁 Assign the Chapter 5 *Reading Essentials and Study Guide.*

*Available on TeacherWorks™ CD-ROM

Chapter 5 Planning Guide

Standards-Based Lesson Plan

History–Social Science Standards Covered in Chapter 5

The standards covered in the chapter are listed below. Use the accompanying activity as you teach the chapter to ensure student mastery of these standards. This activity can be used in combination with the program's print and technology assessment materials.

Standard	Section 1	2	3	4
11.2 Students analyze the relationship among the rise of industrialization, large-scale rural-to-urban migration, and massive immigration from Southern and Eastern Europe.		✔	✔	✔
11.2.1 Know the effects of industrialization on living and working conditions, including the portrayal of working conditions and food safety in Upton Sinclair's *The Jungle*.		✔		✔
11.2.5 Discuss corporate mergers that produced trusts and cartels and the economic and political policies of industrial leaders.		✔		
11.2.9 Understand the effect of political programs and activities of the Progressives (e.g., federal regulation of railroad transport, Children's Bureau, the Sixteenth Amendment, Theodore Roosevelt, Hiram Johnson).	✔		✔	✔
11.5.3 Examine the passage of the Eighteenth Amendment to the Constitution and the Volstead Act (Prohibition).	✔			
11.5.4 Analyze the passage of the Nineteenth Amendment and the changing role of women in society.	✔			

Cumulative Standards-Assessment Activity

The Cumulative Standards-Assessment Activity will help students organize and learn the important information from the chapter. Begin teaching the chapter with this activity, and have students complete it as they read the chapter.

CREATING A CHART FOR QUESTIONING

Purpose Questioning is a skill that can be used to monitor comprehension as students read. By asking themselves questions on a particular section, answering the questions, and checking the answers, they can make sure that they are absorbing the material and ready to move on to the next segment of text. Asking questions can also help ensure students are seeking out the deeper meanings of what they are reading.

Introduction to Questioning

1. Discuss how learning occurs not only when we learn names and dates of events, but also when we seek out the meaning and significance of the events.
2. Ask students to read a selection from the previous chapter. While they do so, write a question on the board aimed at a key concept. After students are finished reading, ask volunteers to answer the question and have the class check these answers against the text.
3. Ask students to copy this chart into their notebooks:

Question: _____

Answer: _____

Correct ☐   Incorrect ☐

Correction/Other
Interpretation: _____

_____

As students read each section, have them use this chart to ask questions and answer them. Remind them to check the questions and answers against the text to ensure that they are correct. If they find an answer that is not correct, they should use the *Correction* line to fix the problem. Questions that interpret meaning may not be easily identified as correct or incorrect, so you may want students to think of and write down an alternate interpretation. Remind students that their questions should focus on key concepts in the text, not less important material. As you review the chapter, ask volunteers to share their questions and discuss which ones successfully identified key concepts. Encourage them to use their questions as study aids.

Chapter 5 Planning Guide

READING SUPPORT

- Content Vocabulary Activity 5
- Academic Vocabulary Activity 5
- Reading Skills Activity 5
- Chapter 5 Active Reading Note-Taking Guide
- Chapter 5 Guided Reading Activities
- Chapter 5 Reading Essentials and Study Guide
- American Literature Readings, Unit 2
- *The American Vision: Modern Times* Video Program
- Vocabulary PuzzleMaker CD-ROM
- American History Primary Source Document Library CD-ROM

CRITICAL THINKING

- Critical Thinking Skills Activity 5
- Primary Source Reading 5
- Cause-and-Effect Transparency 5 Strategy and Activity
- Presentation Plus! CD-ROM

UNIVERSAL ACCESS

- Universal Access Activity 5
- English Learner Activity 5
- American Art Prints
- StudentWorks™ Plus CD-ROM
- American Music: Hits Through History
- School-to-Home Connection Activity 5

SKILL PRACTICE

- Map Overlay Transparency 5 Strategy and Activity
- Historical Analysis Skills Activity 5
- Time Line Activity 5
- Reading Skills Activity 5
- Reinforcing Skills Activity 5
- Linking Past and Present Activity 5
- Interpreting Political Cartoons 5
- Geography and History Activity, Unit 2
- Economics and History Activity, Unit 2
- History Simulations and Problem Solving, Unit 2
- MindJogger Videoquiz

WRITING SUPPORT

- Chapter 5 Active Reading Note-Taking Guide
- Writer's Guidebook
- High School Writing Process Transparencies

ASSESSMENT

- Chapter 5 Section Quizzes
- Chapter 5 Tests, Forms A and B
- Authentic Assessment Activity 5
- Exam*View*® Pro Testmaker CD-ROM
- Interactive Tutor Self-Assessment CD-ROM
- California Standards Practice, Grade 11
- Succeeding on . . .™ the California Standards: Grade 11 History–Social Science CD-ROM

- CD-ROM
- DVD
- Print Material
- Poster

- Transparency
- Music Program
- Videocassette

Chapter 5 Planning Guide

TECHNOLOGY

- StudentWorks™ Plus CD-ROM
- TeacherWorks™ CD-ROM
- ExamView® Pro Testmaker CD-ROM
- Interactive Tutor Self-Assessment CD-ROM
- Presentation Plus! CD-ROM
- Vocabulary PuzzleMaker CD-ROM
- American History Primary Source Document Library CD-ROM
- MindJogger Videoquiz
- *The American Vision: Modern Times* Video Program
- Professional Development in High School Social Studies Video Series
- Teach, Use, and Succeed With *The American Vision: Modern Times*
- American Music: Hits Through History
- Succeeding on . . .™ the California Standards: Grade 11 History–Social Science CD-ROM

SPANISH RESOURCES

- Spanish Activities and Assessment
  - Spanish Vocabulary Activities
  - Spanish Guided Reading Activities
  - Spanish Quizzes and Tests
  - Spanish Reteaching Activities
- Spanish Reading Essentials and Study Guide
- Spanish School-to-Home Connection Activities

TRANSPARENCIES

- Daily Focus Skills Transparencies
- Section Graphic Organizer Transparencies
- Map Overlay Transparencies
- Cause-and-Effect Transparencies
- Unit Time Line Transparencies
- Why It Matters Transparencies
- American Art and Architecture Transparencies
- High School Writing Process Transparencies
- California Standards Practice Transparencies

TEACHER PLANNING

- Daily Lecture and Discussion Notes
- English Learner Handbook
- Building Academic Vocabulary
- *The American Vision: Modern Times* Reading and Study Skills Foldables
- Reading Strategies and Activities for the Social Studies Classroom
- Universal Access for the American History Classroom
- NGS United States Desk Map
- NGS World Atlas
- Chapter 5 Reproducible Lesson Plans on TeacherWorks™ CD-ROM
- California Guide to Daily Intervention

PROFESSIONAL DEVELOPMENT

- Building Academic Vocabulary
- Strategies for Success
- Research-Based Strategies Used to Develop *The American Vision: Modern Times*
- Character Education in the High School Classroom
- Professional Development in High School Social Studies Video Series
- Teach, Use, and Succeed With *The American Vision: Modern Times*

MOMENTS IN TIME

The following resource can help you teach the content of this chapter.

- Unit 5 The Progressive Era (1890–1919)

Chapter 5 Planning Guide

NATIONAL GEOGRAPHIC TEACHER'S CORNER

Index to National Geographic Magazine:
The following articles relate to this chapter:

- "Kodiak, Alaska's Island Refuge," November 1993
- "Wrangell-St. Elias: Alaska's Sky-High Wilderness," May 1994

National Geographic Society Products:
To order the following, call National Geographic at 1–800–368–2728

- *Eyewitness to the 20th Century* (Book)
- *Historical Atlas of the United States* (Atlas)

NGS ONLINE

Access National Geographic's new dynamic MapMachine Web site and other geography resources at:

www.nationalgeographic.com

www.nationalgeographic.com/maps

MASTERING THE STANDARDS

The content and assessment in the Student Edition, Teacher Wraparound Edition, teacher planning materials, and the print and technology products are all standards-based. The use of these products during instruction leads to mastery of the standards.

PRACTICE
- California Standards Practice, Grade 11
- California Standards Practice Transparencies
- School-to-Home Connection

BENCHMARK ASSESSMENT
- Section Quizzes, Chapter Tests, and Authentic Assessment
- ExamView® Pro Testmaker CD-ROM
- Succeeding On . . . ™ the California Standards: Grade 11 History–Social Science CD-ROM

REMEDIATION
- California Guide to Daily Intervention
- Interactive Tutor Self-Assessment CD-ROM
- ExamView® Pro Testmaker CD-ROM
- California Standards Practice, Grade 11
- Reading Essentials and Study Guide

History Online

Use our Web site for additional resources. All essential content is covered in the Student Edition.

You and your students can visit tav.mt.glencoe.com, the Web site companion to the **American Vision: Modern Times.** This innovative integration of electronic and print media offers your students a wealth of opportunities. The student text directs students to the Web site for the following options:

- **Chapter Overviews**
- **Self-Check Quizzes**
- **Student Web Activities**
- **Textbook Updates**

Answers to the student Web activities are provided for you in the **Web Activity Lesson Plans.** Additional Web resources and ePuzzles and games are also available.

FOLDABLES™
Study Organizer
Dinah Zike's Foldables

Foldables are three-dimensional, interactive graphic organizers that help students practice basic writing skills, review key vocabulary terms, and identify main ideas. Every chapter has a foldable activity in the *Dinah Zike's Reading and Study Skills Foldables* booklet. You can use the foldables as they are presented or modify them to suit the needs of your individual class.

A variety of videotape programs are available from A&E Television and The History Channel to provide teaching assistance. To order, call Glencoe at 1-800-334-7344.

Chapter 5 Planning Guide

Reading List Generator CD-ROM

GLENCOE BOOKLINK

The Glencoe BookLink CD-ROM is a database that allows you to search more than 15,000 titles to create a customized reading list for your students.

- Reading Lists can be organized by students' reading level, author, genre, theme, or area of interest.
- The database provides Degrees of Reading Power™ (DRP) and Lexile™ readability scores for all selections.
- A brief summary of each selection is included.

Leveled reading suggestions for this chapter:

For students at a Grade 8 reading level:
- *William H. Taft: 27th President of the United States,* by Lucille Falkof

For students at a Grade 9 reading level:
- *The Jungle,* by Upton Sinclair

For students at a Grade 10 reading level:
- *Not for Ourselves Alone,* by Geoffrey Ward and Ken Burns

READING SUPPORT FROM JAMESTOWN EDUCATION

- *Timed Readings Plus in Social Studies* help students increase their reading rate and fluency while maintaining comprehension. The 400-word passages are similar to those found on state and national assessments.
- *Reading in the Content Area: Social Studies* concentrates on six essential reading skills that help students better comprehend what they read. The book includes 75 high-interest nonfiction passages written at increasing levels of difficulty.
- *Reading Fluency* helps students read smoothly, accurately, and expressively.
- *Jamestown's Reading Improvement,* by renowned reading expert Edward Fry, focuses on helping build your students' comprehension, vocabulary, and skimming and scanning skills.
- *Critical Reading Series* provides high-interest books, each written at three reading levels.

For more information about these products, see the Jamestown Education materials in the Classroom Solutions in the front of this Teacher Wraparound Edition. To order these products, call Glencoe at 1-800-334-7344.

KEY for Using the Teacher Wraparound Edition

Use this key to help you identify the different types of prompts found in the Teacher Wraparound Edition.

R **Reading Strategies** activities help you teach reading skills and vocabulary.

C **Critical Thinking** strategies help students apply and extend what they have learned.

U **Universal Access** activities provide differentiated instruction for students learning to speak English, along with suggestions for teaching various types of learners.

S **Skill Practice** strategies help students practice historical analysis and geography skills.

W **Writing Support** activities provide writing opportunities to help students comprehend the text.

Teaching strategies and activities have been coded for ability level appropriateness.

AL Activities for students working above grade level
OL Activities for students working on grade level
BL Activities for students working below grade level
EL Activities for English learners

FOCUS

BELLRINGER
SKILLBUILDER ACTIVITY

Have students discuss the meaning of the word *progressive.* Tell students that Chapter 5 will focus on progressivism, which was a movement of reforms and ideas to fix the problems in American society. **Ask: Do you see any problems in today's society that are in need of reform?** After reading the chapter, have students identify different areas of reform that they read about and did not include in their original answer.

CHAPTER 5

1890–1919
The Progressive Movement

⋰ The Big Ideas ⋱

SECTION 1: The Roots of Progressivism

Social and economic crises lead to new roles for government. *As Americans became more aware of the social problems affecting the United States, progressives began to look to the government to help solve these problems and regulate big business.*

SECTION 2: Roosevelt in Office

Social and economic crises lead to new roles for government. *When Theodore Roosevelt, a progressive, won the presidency in 1901, progressivism entered national politics.*

SECTION 3: The Taft Administration

Social and economic crises lead to new roles for government. *William Howard Taft was a more moderate progressive than Theodore Roosevelt, but he still continued several progressive reforms.*

SECTION 4: The Wilson Years

Social and economic crises lead to new roles for government. *When the Progressive era ended, the role of the federal government had changed, and people expected the government to take action in regulating the economy and solving social issues.*

 The *American Vision: Modern Times* Video *The Chapter 5 video, "The Stockyard Jungle," portrays the horrors of the meatpacking industry first investigated by Upton Sinclair.*

1889
• Hull House opens in Chicago

1890
• Jacob Riis's *How the Other Half Lives* published

1902
• Maryland workers' compensation laws passed

1904
• Ida Tarbell's *History of the Standard Oil Company* published

United States PRESIDENTS

B. Harrison 1889–1893 | *Cleveland* 1893–1897 | *McKinley* 1897–1901 | *T. Roosevelt* 1901–1909

1890   1900

World

1884
• Toynbee Hall, first settlement house, established in London

1900
• Freud's *Interpretation of Dreams* published

1902
• Anglo-Japanese alliance formed

1903
• Russian Bolshevik Party established by Lenin

322

TEACH

Thinking About the Big Ideas

As you begin teaching each section, use these questions and activities to focus on the Big Idea.

Section 1
The Roots of Progressivism
Essential Question: What are jobs in the United States that women have not held? *(U.S. president, NFL football player, etc.)* **What kinds of jobs do women hold now that would not have been available to them in the early 1900s?** *(women can hold jobs as CEOs, astronauts, serve at West Point, etc.)* BL

Section 2
Roosevelt in Office
Essential Question: What are the main accomplishments of the current U.S. president? *(Students' answers will vary.)* Tell students that in this section they will learn about many of the accomplishments of Theodore Roosevelt during his presidency. After reading the section, lead students in a discussion comparing the strengths and weaknesses of both presidents. OL

Women marching for the vote in New York City, 1912

1905
• Industrial Workers of the World founded

1906
• Pure Food and Drug Act passed

1910
• Mann-Elkins Act passed

1913
• Seventeenth Amendment ratified

1920
• Nineteenth Amendment ratified, guaranteeing women's voting rights

VOTE **YES** Nov. 2

VOTE FOR WOMAN SUFFRAGE NOVEMBER 2ND

WOMAN SUFFRAGE VOTE YES OCTOBER 19

Taft 1909–1913

Wilson 1913–1921

1910

1920

1910
• Mexican Revolution

1914
• World War I begins in Europe

1905
• Einstein's theory of relativity formulated

HISTORY
Online

Chapter Overview
Visit the *American Vision: Modern Times* Web site at tav.mt.glencoe.com and click on *Chapter Overviews— Chapter 5* to preview chapter information.

323

Section 3
The Taft Administration
Essential Question: What are the positive and negative connotations of being considered a moderate? *(positive: being trusted not to be extreme or rash; negative: being thought of as indecisive or weak)* Tell students that this section will focus on President William Howard Taft's moderate approach to progressive reforms. **AL**

Section 4
The Wilson Years
Essential Question: In what ways do big business monopolies hurt the consumer? *(There is little competition so consumers are forced to pay higher prices for services; there is less motivation for the company to provide a high level of service.)* Tell students that this section will highlight some of the reforms in big business that continue to benefit us today. **OL**

Cultural Perspectives

Present or read to students the following quotation from Susan B. Anthony: "Resolved, that the women of this nation in 1876, have greater cause for discontent, rebellion and revolution than the men of 1776." Have students write a short response to this quote, describing their reactions to Anthony's words. In small groups or as a class, discuss Anthony's comparison of the two time periods. Ask students to consider what it reveals about women's changing roles and perspectives in American society at the time. **OL**

FOLDABLES™
Study Organizer

Dinah Zike's Foldables are three-dimensional, interactive graphic organizers that help students practice basic writing skills, review key vocabulary terms, and identify main ideas. Have students complete the foldable activity in the *Dinah Zike's Reading and Study Skills Foldables* booklet.

HISTORY
Online

Go to tav.mt.glencoe.com for student activities, lesson plans, and links to additional Web resources to help students learn about the Progressive movement.

Reading Skill

Why It's Important
This feature will aid students in developing the skill of making inferences, which will enable students to better comprehend the materials they read. Students will also be able to apply the principles they have learned to other situations.

1. Introducing the Skill
Have students list as many synonyms for *infer* as they can: *(conclude, deduct, speculate, interpret, etc.)* **Ask: What skills would help you make good inferences?** Organize student answers in a graphic organizer similar to the one shown below. **OL**

Skills Needed for Making Inferences

Analyzing | Asking Questions | Thoroughness

2. Extending the Skill
Have students select an editorial from a local newspaper. After reading the editorial, they should consider what conclusions they can draw about the writer's biases and political beliefs. Have students write a summary of their findings and share them with the class. **OL**

Answers and Additional Support

Reading Skill ❯ Making Inferences

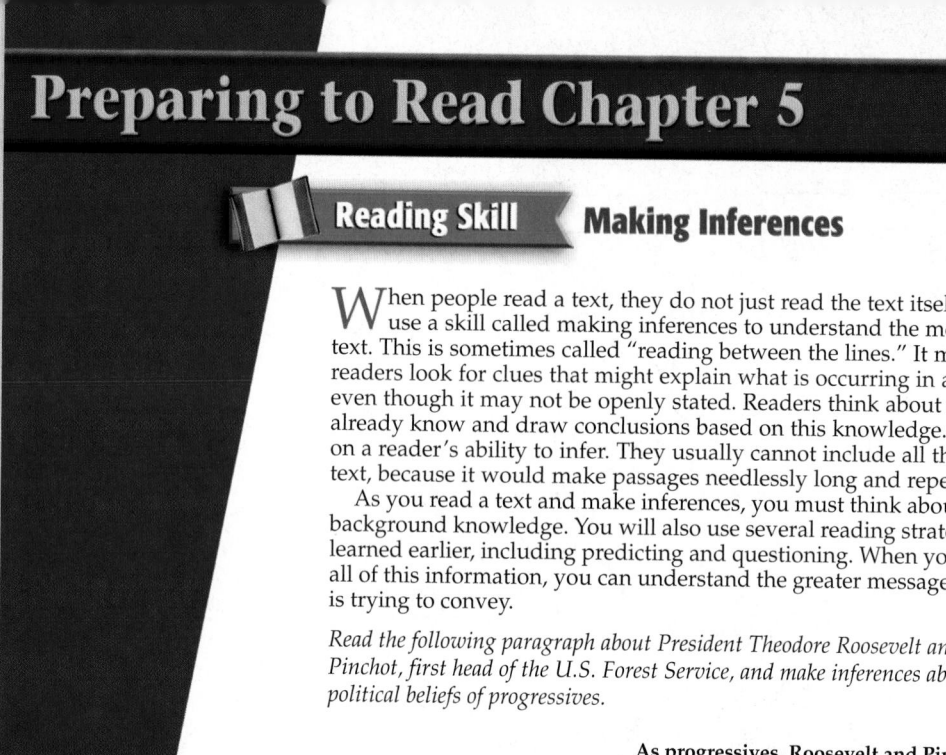

When people read a text, they do not just read the text itself. They also use a skill called making inferences to understand the meaning of the text. This is sometimes called "reading between the lines." It means that readers look for clues that might explain what is occurring in a passage even though it may not be openly stated. Readers think about what they already know and draw conclusions based on this knowledge. Authors rely on a reader's ability to infer. They usually cannot include all the details in a text, because it would make passages needlessly long and repetitive.

As you read a text and make inferences, you must think about your own background knowledge. You will also use several reading strategies you learned earlier, including predicting and questioning. When you combine all of this information, you can understand the greater message the author is trying to convey.

Read the following paragraph about President Theodore Roosevelt and Gifford Pinchot, first head of the U.S. Forest Service, and make inferences about the political beliefs of progressives.

> As progressives, Roosevelt and Pinchot both believed trained experts in forestry and resource management should apply the same scientific standards to the landscape that others were applying to the management of cities and industry. They rejected the laissez-faire argument that the best way to preserve public land was to sell it to lumber companies, who would then carefully conserve it because it was a source of their profits. With President Roosevelt's support, Pinchot's department drew up regulations to control lumbering on federal lands. (pages 344–345)

MAKING INFERENCES
Use your background knowledge to understand the passage. What do you remember reading about Roosevelt taking on big businesses and trusts?

As you read, you can identify which policies Roosevelt and Pinchot supported and which they opposed. Both believed in scientific standards of forestry management and regulation of the lumber industry. They opposed a laissez-faire approach to managing and selling public land. You also can infer that the president did not trust the lumber industry to operate in the public interest and therefore government regulations were necessary.

Apply the Skill
Read the text under the heading "Beginnings of Progressivism" on pages 327–328. As you read, identify the information you gather from the text. Then think about the background knowledge from earlier chapters you have used to understand the passage.

324

UNIVERSAL ACCESS

Verbal/Linguistic Upon finishing the chapter, have students write a short speech from the point of view of one of the people listed under People and Terms to Identify in one of the sections of this chapter. Without identifying whom they chose, have students read their speeches aloud. The class should then make inferences about whose perspective is being presented, drawing conclusions based on the person's opinions and experiences. **AL**

Historical Analysis Skill — Interpreting Events

Historical Interpretation When you learn to interpret events, it helps you understand their meaning, implication, and impact. One way to interpret is by recognizing and examining how events could have taken other directions.

As you complete your high school education, you might be thinking about what you will do after graduation. Perhaps you will go to college, or you are considering a job in a specific industry. Consider how your life will be affected by your final decision. Will you stay close to your hometown, or will you move to another state? Will you work for a small company or a multinational corporation? Imagine the people that you won't meet and the experiences you may not have by choosing one direction over another, and the impact this choice could have on the direction of your life.

When historians interpret past events, they too consider how different choices might have affected the course of history. Using this skill helps them analyze past events. It also helps them understand the impact of decisions that were made based on the events of the time.

Read this passage from your textbook about the suffrage movement at the end of the Civil War.

The debate over the Fourteenth and Fifteenth Amendments split the suffrage movement into two groups: the National Woman Suffrage Association, . . . and the American Woman Suffrage Association. . . .
This split reduced the movement's effectiveness. In 1878 a constitutional amendment granting woman suffrage was introduced in Congress, but it failed to pass. Few state governments granted women the right to vote either. . . . By 1900 only Wyoming, Idaho, Utah, and Colorado had granted women full voting rights. (page 331)

Consider how long it took for women to gain the right to vote. Why would each group focus on their own strategy for gaining voting rights? How might the outcome have been different had the two groups agreed on a unified strategy? How do you think the split affected history?

Apply the Skill

Choose one of the major areas on which progressives focused, such as child labor, temperance, or trusts. Review the various events regarding the topic. Then consider how events might have unfolded differently if muckrakers and reformers had not turned their attention to your chosen issue.

325

Historical Analysis

Why It's Important
Learning how to interpret historical events will help students to grasp the importance of these events and to understand their impact on our lives today.

1. Introducing the Skill
Ask students to consider the financial, social, and professional effects a doctor might experience while setting up a practice in a rural community. Then have students consider the same effects on the doctor if the practice was built in an urban or a suburban setting. How would the different settings change the doctor's professional and personal life and his finances? Record students' answers in a chart similar to the one below, listing the advantages and disadvantages of each decision. **OL** **CA H14**

	Rural	City
Economic		
Social		
Professional		

2. Extending the Skill
Have students bring a newspaper article of a recent sporting event to class. Instruct students to review the highlights of the game. Then have students consider what the losing coach and players might have done differently to change the outcome of the game. **OL**

UNIVERSAL ACCESS

English Learners This exercise will give English learners an opportunity to connect the subject matter to their daily life experience. Tell students that women's roles and influence changed dramatically after women received the right to vote. **Ask:** How would life be different today if women had never gained the right to vote? Do you think women would still have made as much progress as they have in other areas, such as employment opportunities and equal pay? Encourage English learners to verbalize their opinions. **EL**

FOCUS

Guide to Reading

Understanding Vocabulary: As students read the section, have them write the definition of each content vocabulary word to show their understanding of the word.

Answers to Graphic: people could improve society with a strong faith in science; government should help solve society's problems; government needed to be more efficient; senators should be directly elected; women should vote

Unpacking the Standards

Students will be able to:

- Understand the goals of progressivism.

- Describe the changes made in local, state, and federal government.

- Outline the events that brought on the woman suffrage movement.

- Identify the reasons progressives supported prohibition.

SECTION 1

The Roots of Progressivism

Guide to Reading

Connection
In the previous chapter, you learned how the United States increased its power and influence around the world. In this section, you will discover the beginning of the Progressive movement and a focus on domestic reform.

Main Idea
- The Progressive movement was an attempt to use scientific principles to improve society. (p. 327)
- One form of progressivism focused on ways to use business practices to make government more efficient. (p. 328)
- Progressive policies in Wisconsin became widespread, leading to election reforms. (p. 330)
- Many progressives joined the suffrage movement to gain women the right to vote in national elections. (p. 330)

- Many progressives focused on social welfare problems, such as child labor, public health, and prohibition. (p. 333)
- Another form of progressivism focused on federal regulation of big business. (p. 335)

Content Vocabulary
progressivism, muckraker, commission plan, direct primary, initiative, referendum, recall, suffrage, temperance, prohibition, socialism

Academic Vocabulary
legislation, strategy, funds, advocate

People and Terms to Identify
Jacob Riis, Robert La Follette, Alice Paul

Reading Objectives
- **Discuss** the rise of the Progressive movement.

- **Evaluate** the impact of initiative, referendum, and recall, and of the Seventeenth Amendment.

Reading Strategy
Organizing As you read about the beginnings of progressivism, complete a graphic organizer similar to the one below by filling in the beliefs of progressives.

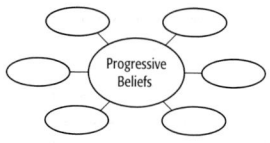

Progressive Beliefs

Preview of Events

♦1890	♦1900	♦1910	♦1920
1890 Jacob Riis's *How the Other Half Lives* published	**1901** Galveston, Texas, adopts commission system	**1913** Seventeenth Amendment provides for direct election of senators	**1920** Nineteenth Amendment gives women the right to vote

⁓ The Big Idea ⁓

Social and economic crises lead to new roles for government. During the late 1800s, Americans again became concerned with social problems in the United States. Progressives focused on a variety of issues and how to address them. Some believed that government should solve social problems, while others thought that science or business held the answers. Many progressives focused on improving government by making it either more efficient or more democratic. Others joined in the suffrage movement and worked to gain women the right to vote in national elections. Still other progressives focused on child labor, public welfare, prohibition, and regulation of big business.

SECTION RESOURCES

📁 **Print Material**
- Reproducible Lesson Plan 5-1
- Guided Reading Activity 5-1
- Reading Essentials and Study Guide 5-1
- Active Reading Note-Taking Guide 5-1

🖥 **Transparencies**
- Daily Focus Skills Transparency 5-1
- Section Graphic Organizer Transparency 5-1

Technology
- 💿 Interactive Tutor Self-Assessment CD-ROM
- 💿 Exam*View*® Pro Testmaker CD-ROM
- 💿 Presentation Plus! CD-ROM

The Rise of Progressivism

Main Idea The Progressive movement was an attempt to use scientific principles to improve society.

Reading Connection What areas of public life do you believe still need to be reformed? Read on to learn about a movement in the late 1800s that tried to reform many of the ills of society at the time.

In the early 1900s, as the effects of industrialization and urbanization became apparent, a series of reform efforts transformed American society. These reforms ranged from government reform to social welfare and woman suffrage. Historians refer to this era in American history—from about 1890 to 1920—as the Progressive Era.

★ An American Story ★

In 1917 suffragist Rose Winslow and several other women, including Alice Paul, founder of the National Woman's Party, were arrested for obstructing traffic and blocking sidewalks. The women had been picketing the White House to draw attention to the fact that women did not yet have the right to vote in federal elections. After being sentenced to seven months in jail, Paul, Winslow, and other women prisoners went on a hunger strike. Prison authorities forced the prisoners to eat. Winslow smuggled details of their plight out to the public:

66 We have been in solitary for five weeks. . . . I have felt quite feeble the last few days—faint, so that I could hardly get my hair brushed, my arms ached so. But today I am well again. . . . [Alice Paul] dreaded forcible feeding frightfully, and I hate to think how she must be feeling. . . . I am really all right. If this continues very long I perhaps won't be. All the officers here know we are making this hunger strike [so] that women fighting for liberty may be considered political prisoners. . . . [W]e don't want women ever to have to do this over again. 99

—quoted in *Jailed for Freedom*

Progressive reform efforts were not limited to women's voting rights. Progressives came from different backgrounds, focused on a variety of issues, and did not always agree on solutions to solve the nation's problems.

Who Were the Progressives? Progressivism was not a tightly organized political movement with a specific set of reforms. Instead, it was a collection of different ideas and activities. Progressives had many different views about how to fix the problems they believed existed in American society.

Progressives generally believed that industrialism and urbanization had created many social problems. Most agreed that the government should take a more active role in solving society's problems. Progressives belonged to both major political parties and usually were urban, educated middle-class Americans. Many leaders of the Progressive movement worked as journalists, social workers, educators, politicians, and members of the clergy.

Beginnings of Progressivism Progressivism was partly a reaction against laissez-faire economics and its emphasis on an unregulated market. After seeing the poverty of the working class and the filth and crime of urban society, these reformers began to doubt the free market's ability to address those problems. At the same time, they doubted that the government in its present form could fix those problems. First, they believed the government required reform. They concluded that before the government could be used to fix the problems of society, the government itself must be fixed.

▼ *A police officer arresting two suffragists in Washington, D.C.*

TEACH

U Universal Access

English Learners Students who are learning English as a second language are often hesitant to voice their questions in class. Instruct students to write down words and concepts that they don't understand as they read about the development of progressivism. Collect the lists, and take time to address their questions. **EL**

R₁ Reading Strategy

Using Word Parts Ask students to find the definition of laissez-faire in the dictionary. *(A doctrine opposing governmental interference in businesses beyond what is necessary to maintain peace.)* **Ask:** From where does the term originate? *(It is a French term meaning "to let alone.")* **OL**

R₂ Reading Strategy

Scaffolding—Predicting Ask students to think of a current social problem. *(poverty, inner-city crime, drugs, etc.)* **Ask:** How might a modern day progressive respond to this issue? *(Students' answers will vary but should reflect information presented in the section.)* **OL**

This **Reading Skill** was introduced in Chapter 1.

Did You Know?

The hunger strike technique employed by American suffragists was also used by women struggling for equal rights in Great Britain in the previous decade.

One reason progressives believed people could improve society was because they had a strong faith in science and technology. The application of scientific knowledge had produced the lightbulb, the telephone, the automobile, and the airplane. It had built skyscrapers and railroads. Science and technology had benefited people; thus progressives believed using scientific principles could also produce solutions for society.

The Muckrakers Among the first people to articulate Progressive ideas was a group of crusading journalists who investigated social conditions and political corruption. These writers became known as **muckrakers** after a speech by President Theodore Roosevelt:

❝Now, it is very necessary that we should not flinch from seeing what is vile and debasing. There is filth on the floor and it must be scraped up with the muckrake; and there are times and places where this service is the most needed of all the services that can be performed....❞

—Washington, D.C., April 14, 1906

Picturing History

Muckrakers *McClure's* published Ida Tarbell's exposé on Standard Oil. What issues particularly concerned the muckrakers?

By the early 1900s, American publishers were competing to expose the most corruption and scandal. A group of aggressive 10¢ and 15¢ magazines grew in popularity at this time, including *McClure's*, *Collier's*, and *Munsey's*.

Muckrakers uncovered corruption in many areas. Some concentrated on what they considered the unfair practices of large American corporations. In *McClure's*, for example, Ida Tarbell published a series of articles critical of the Standard Oil Company. In *Everybody's Magazine*, Charles Edward Russell attacked the beef industry.

Other muckrakers targeted government. David Graham Philips described how money influenced the Senate, while Lincoln Steffens, another *McClure's* reporter, reported on vote stealing and other corrupt practices of urban political machines. These were later collected into a book, *The Shame of the Cities*.

Still other muckrakers concentrated on social problems. In his influential book *How the Other Half Lives*, published in 1890, **Jacob Riis** described the poverty, disease, and crime that afflicted many immigrant neighborhoods in New York City. The muckrakers' articles led to a general public debate on social and economic problems and put pressure on politicians to introduce reforms.

✓ Reading Check **Describing** How did the muckrakers help spark the Progressive movement?

Making Government Efficient

Main Idea One form of progressivism focused on ways to use business practices to make government more efficient.

Reading Connection In what ways do you try to use your time and resources wisely and efficiently? Read on to find out about political programs the progressives designed to make the government more efficient.

There were many different types of progressivism. Different causes led to different approaches, and progressives even took opposing positions on how to solve some problems.

One group of progressives focused on making government more efficient. They believed that many problems in society could be solved if government worked properly. Efficiency progressives took their ideas from business. These progressives believed business had become more efficient by applying the principles of scientific management.

The ideas of scientific management had been developed in the late 1800s and were popularized by Frederick W. Taylor in his book *The Principles of Scientific Management,* published in 1911. Taylor described how a company could become more efficient by managing time, breaking tasks down into small parts, and using standardized tools.

Efficiency progressives argued that managing a modern city required experts, not politicians. They did not want more democracy in government, for they believed that the democratic process led to compromise and corruption. In most American cities, the mayor or city council chose the heads of city departments. Traditionally, these jobs went to political supporters and friends, who often knew little about city services.

Efficiency progressives wanted either a commission plan or a council-manager system. Under the **commission plan,** a city's government would be divided into several departments, which would each be placed under the control of an expert

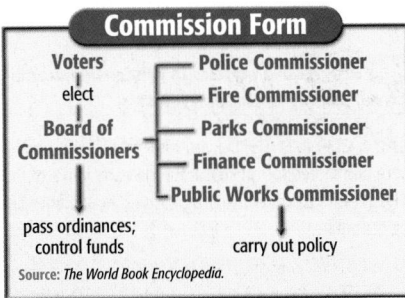

Mayor-Council Form

Voters
↓ elect

Mayor ——— City Council
actions approved by
↓ appoints

Heads of City Departments → carry out policy

Source: *The World Book Encyclopedia.*

Commission Form

Voters
↓ elect
Board of Commissioners
├ Police Commissioner
├ Fire Commissioner
├ Parks Commissioner
├ Finance Commissioner
└ Public Works Commissioner

pass ordinances; control funds   carry out policy

Source: *The World Book Encyclopedia.*

Council-Manager Form

Voters
↓ elect
City Council (makes policy)
↓ elects
Mayor

hires → City Manager (Chief Administrator)
↓ appoints
Heads of City Departments
↓ carry out policy

Source: *The World Book Encyclopedia.*

A City and a Storm

On September 8, 1900, a massive hurricane devastated the city of Galveston, Texas. About 6,000 people died. When the political machine that controlled the city government proved incapable of responding to the disaster, local business leaders convinced the state to let them take control. In April 1901, Galveston introduced the commission system of government. Under this system, Galveston chose five commissioners to replace the mayor and city council.

Four commissioners were local business leaders. When the city quickly recovered, reformers in other cities were impressed. Galveston's experience seemed to prove the benefits of running a city like a business by dividing its government into departments and placing each under an expert commissioner. Many other cities soon followed, adopting either the commission plan or the council-manager system.

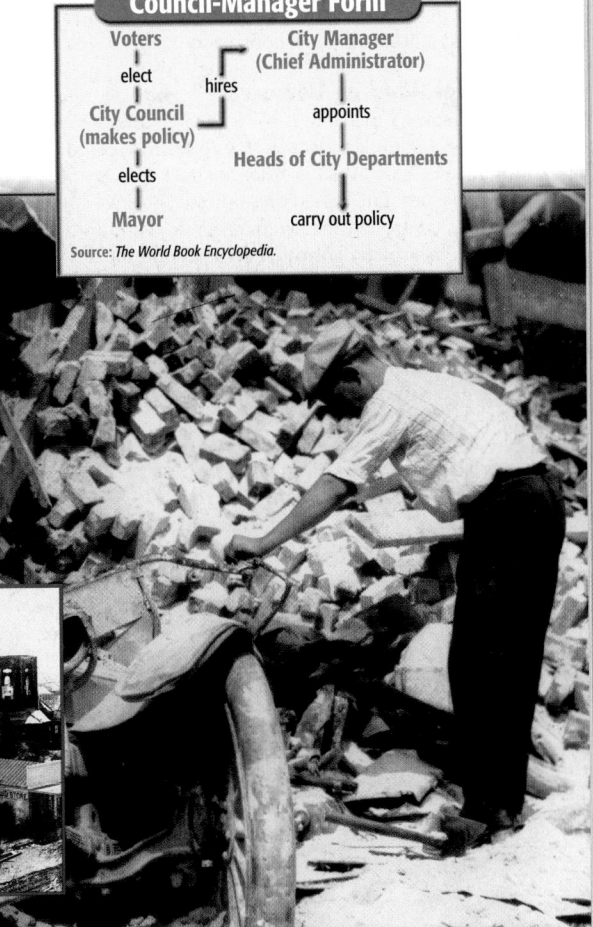

C Critical Thinking

Identifying Central Issues
In addition to Galveston, two Midwestern cities saw notable reforms during this time. In Toledo, Ohio, Mayor Samuel "Golden Rule" Jones established municipal ownership of public utilities and tackled police corruption. In Detroit, Michigan, Mayor Hazen Pingree set up new schools, parks, and work programs. **Ask:** What form of local government do we have? *(Students' answers will vary depending on where they live.)* OL

R₁ Reading Strategy

Determining the Main Idea
Invite a local government official to speak to the class about how your local government is structured. Have students take notes on all elected officials and the duties of each. OL

R₂ Reading Strategy

Visual Literacy Instruct students to examine the picture. **Ask:** What do you observe that could present potential challenges to people removing the rubble? *(Answers may include: lack of modern equipment; small pieces of rock requiring tedious work; very time intensive; large piles of debris.)* BL

More Skill Practice

Analyzing Information Have students compare the charts of the three types of local government. **Ask:** Which type of government do you think provides the best balance of power? Which gives voters the strongest voice in selecting officials? Which type do you think would be most effective? *(Students' answers should reflect an understanding of the charts' information.)* AL

Chapter 5 • Section 1

S Skill Practice

Historical Interpretation
Instruct students to list the reforms that were directly or indirectly a result of Robert La Follette's democratic philosophies. *(direct primary, initiative, referendum, and recall)* Have students write an essay explaining the importance of these reforms to our democratic process today.
AL **CA CS1**

R Reading Strategy

Using Context Clues Unfamiliar phrases can prevent students from understanding the deeper meaning of a statement. **Ask:** What did Charles Edward Russell mean when he said that the Senate had become "only a chamber of butlers for industrialists and financiers"? *(Senators served wealthy businessmen rather than the people of their state.)* **OL** **CA 11RC2.5**

✓Reading Check
Answer: because government could not carry out reforms unless it was reformed first

✓Reading Check
Answer: Allowing the public to elect senators made the Senate more democratic. It was intended to end corruption but instead removed one of the state government's checks on federal power.

Answers and Additional Support

330

commissioner. These progressives argued that a board of commissioners or a city manager with expertise in city services should hire the specialists to run city departments. Galveston, Texas, adopted the commission system in 1901. Other cities soon followed.

✓**Reading Check** **Explaining** Why did progressives want to reorganize city government?

Democracy and Progressivism

Main Idea Progressive policies in Wisconsin became widespread, leading to election reforms.

Reading Connection Do you remember how candidates were nominated for office during the early years of the nation? Read on to discover the progressives' new method for choosing candidates.

Not all progressives agreed with the efficiency progressives. Many believed that society needed more democracy, not less. They wanted to make elected officials more responsive to voters.

"Laboratory of Democracy" Political reform first came to the state level when Wisconsin voters elected Republican **Robert La Follette** to be governor. La Follette used his office to attack the way political parties ran their conventions. Because party bosses controlled the selection of convention delegates, they also controlled which candidates were chosen to run for office. La Follette pressured the state legislature to require each party to hold a **direct primary,** in which all party members could vote for a candidate to run in the general election.

La Follette's great reform success gave Wisconsin a reputation as the "laboratory of democracy." La Follette claimed, "Democracy is based upon knowledge.... The only way to beat the boss ... is to keep the people thoroughly informed."

Inspired by La Follette, progressives in other states pushed for similar electoral changes. To force state legislators to respond to voters, three new reforms were introduced in many states. The **initiative** allowed a group of citizens to introduce **legislation** and required the legislature to vote on it. The **referendum** allowed proposed legislation to be submitted to the voters for approval. The **recall** allowed voters to demand a special election to remove an elected official from office before his or her term had expired.

330 CHAPTER 5 The Progressive Movement

Direct Election of Senators Another reform the progressives favored affected the federal government—the direct election of senators. As originally written, the United States Constitution directed each state legislature to elect two senators from that state. Political machines or large trusts often influenced the election of senators, who then repaid their supporters with federal contracts and jobs. By the early 1900s, muckraker Charles Edward Russell charged that the Senate had become "only a chamber of butlers for industrialists and financiers."

To counter Senate corruption, progressives called for the direct election of senators by all state voters. In 1912 Congress passed a direct-election amendment. Although the direct election of senators was intended to end corruption, it also removed one of the state legislatures' checks on federal power. In 1913 the amendment was ratified, becoming the Seventeenth Amendment to the Constitution.

✓**Reading Check** **Evaluating** What was the impact of the Seventeenth Amendment? What was it intended to solve?

The Suffrage Movement

Main Idea Many progressives joined the suffrage movement to gain women the right to vote in national elections. ⌐TURNING POINT¬

Reading Connection How would you feel if you were unable to vote for your country's leaders because of your gender? Read on to find out how women defeated that bias in 1920.

In July 1848, Elizabeth Cady Stanton and Lucretia Mott organized the first women's rights convention in Seneca Falls, New York. Stanton proposed to the delegates that their first priority should be getting women the right to vote. The movement for women's voting rights became known as the suffrage movement. **Suffrage** is the right to vote.

Woman suffrage was an important issue for progressives. Although the suffrage movement began well before progressivism emerged, many progressives joined the movement in the late 1800s and early 1900s.

Early Problems The suffrage movement got off to a slow start. Women suffragists were accused of being unfeminine and immoral. Several were physically attacked. The movement also remained weak because many of its supporters were abolitionists as

More Skill Practice

Determining the Main Idea One goal of progressives was to make government more responsive to the voters. **Ask:** What is a political initiative? *(the right of a group of citizens to introduce a matter for legislation)* What does it mean to take initiative in a situation? *(to take the first step; originating a new idea)* **OL**

⌐TURNING POINT¬

In addition to being allowed to own and run their own ranches and farms, Western women were the first to win the right to vote. Based on the information from the map on page 332, where did women first receive the right to vote? *(territory of Wyoming in 1869)* **BL** well. In the years before the Civil War, they preferred to concentrate on abolishing slavery and spent less time working for woman suffrage.

After the Civil War, the Republicans in Congress introduced the Fourteenth and Fifteenth Amendments to the Constitution to protect the voting rights of African Americans. Several leaders of the woman suffrage movement had wanted these amendments worded to give women the right to vote as well. They were bitterly disappointed when Republicans refused.

The debate over the Fourteenth and Fifteenth Amendments split the suffrage movement into two groups: the National Woman Suffrage Association, led by Elizabeth Cady Stanton and Susan B. Anthony, and the American Woman Suffrage Association, led by Lucy Stone and Julia Ward Howe. The National Woman Suffrage Association wanted to focus on passing a constitutional amendment allowing woman suffrage. The American Woman Suffrage Association believed that the best **strategy** was to convince state governments to give women the right to vote before trying to amend the Constitution.

This split reduced the movement's effectiveness. In 1878 a constitutional amendment granting woman suffrage was introduced in Congress, but it failed to pass. Few state governments granted women the right to vote either. With the woman suffrage movement divided between goals, it was difficult for the movement to be successful. By 1900 only Wyoming, Idaho, Utah, and Colorado had granted women full voting rights.

The Movement Builds Support In 1890 the two groups united to form the National American Woman Suffrage Association (NAWSA). The movement still did not make significant gains, however, until about 1910. Part of the problem was convincing women to become politically active. As the Progressive movement began, however, many middle-class women concluded that they needed the vote to promote the social reforms they favored. Many working-class women also wanted the vote to ensure passage of labor laws protecting women.

As the suffrage movement grew, members began lobbying lawmakers, organizing marches, and delivering speeches on street corners. By the end of 1912, Washington, Oregon, California, Arizona, and Kansas had granted women full voting rights. On March 3, 1913, the day before President Wilson's inauguration, suffragists marched in Washington, D.C., to draw attention to their cause.

Profiles IN HISTORY

Susan B. Anthony
1820–1906

Susan B. Anthony was born in Adams, Massachusetts, to Quaker parents. Quakers were generally more supportive of women's rights than some other groups, and so Anthony was able to receive a good education. She finished her schooling at the age of 17. Anthony then worked as a teacher in New York, but she was fired after protesting that her pay was one-fifth the amount of her male colleagues. She found another job, however, as a principal at New York's Canajoharie Academy. Between 1848 and 1863, Anthony was involved in both the temperance and abolitionist movements.

Her involvement in the drive for women's equality began in 1851 after she met Elizabeth Cady Stanton. Between 1854 and 1860, the duo

attempted to change discriminatory laws in New York. In 1869 Anthony and Stanton organized the National Woman Suffrage Association and began promoting an amendment to grant woman suffrage. Anthony and 12 other women illegally cast votes in the presidential election of 1872. They were arrested and convicted, but the judge feared that the jury would rule in Anthony's favor. He dismissed the jury and fined Anthony instead. She refused to pay the $100 fine, but the judge decided to let her go, afraid that appealing the case might generate sympathy for the suffrage movement.

In 1883 Anthony traveled to Europe, and she helped form the International Council of Women in 1888. This organization represented the rights of women in 48 countries. She died in Rochester, New York, in 1906. Though Anthony did not live to see her dream of woman

suffrage become reality, the United States government honored her by placing her portrait on a new dollar coin in 1979.

Profiles IN HISTORY

Background: Susan B. Anthony was the first woman depicted on a U.S. coin. Unfortunately, the Susan B. Anthony dollar was not well received by the general public, who felt it was too similar in size to the quarter. The coin is no longer minted. **Ask:** Many women get paid less than their male counterparts. Why do you think employers pay different wages? *(Students' answers will vary.)*

Chapter 5 • Section 1

C Critical Thinking

Comparing and Contrasting Protests by citizens for or against government policies continue to be part of American life. Ask students to conduct research on the protest efforts of Alice Paul. Then have them research recent protests of the World Trade Organization. Have students compare and contrast these protests. **OL**

R Reading Strategy

Scaffolding—Academic Vocabulary The word *resource* was introduced in Chapter 4, Section 2. Ask a student to define the word. **BL**

S Skill Practice

Conducting Research The Nineteenth Amendment expanded the rights of American citizens. Have students select one of the amendments to the Constitution on pages 159–167 and then conduct further research on the amendment. Then have students write an essay defending its importance to our rights as American citizens. **AL** **CA HR4**

✓ Reading Check

Answer: Women lobbied effectively at the state level. Their defeat of local candidates helped convince Congress to pass the Nineteenth Amendment.

Answers and Additional Support

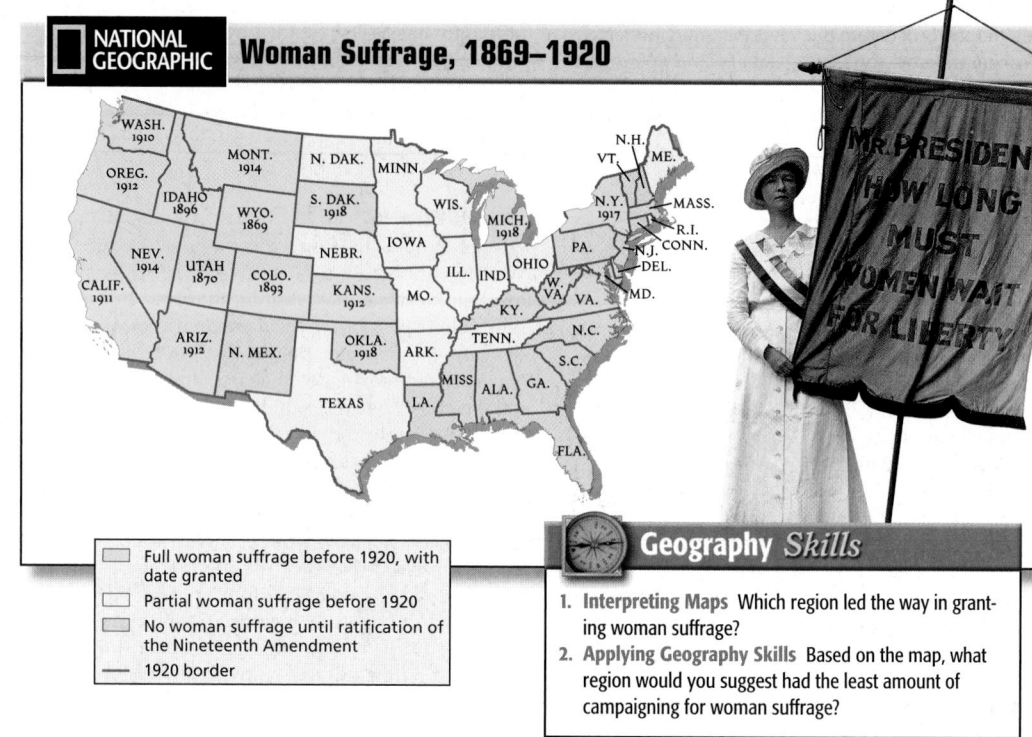

NATIONAL GEOGRAPHIC

Woman Suffrage, 1869–1920

WASH. 1910
OREG. 1912
MONT. 1914
IDAHO 1896
NEV. 1914
CALIF. 1911
UTAH 1870
ARIZ. 1912
WYO. 1869
COLO. 1893
N. MEX.
N. DAK.
S. DAK. 1918
NEBR.
KANS. 1912
OKLA. 1918
TEXAS
MINN.
IOWA
MO.
ARK.
LA.
WIS.
ILL.
IND.
KY.
TENN.
MISS.
ALA.
MICH. 1918
OHIO
W. VA.
VA.
N.C.
S.C.
GA.
FLA.
PA.
N.Y. 1917
N.H.
VT.
ME.
MASS.
R.I.
CONN.
N.J.
DEL.
MD.

☐ Full woman suffrage before 1920, with date granted
☐ Partial woman suffrage before 1920
☐ No woman suffrage until ratification of the Nineteenth Amendment
— 1920 border

Geography *Skills*

1. **Interpreting Maps** Which region led the way in granting woman suffrage?
2. **Applying Geography Skills** Based on the map, what region would you suggest had the least amount of campaigning for woman suffrage?

Alice Paul, a Quaker social worker who headed NAWSA's congressional committee, had organized the Washington march. Paul, a graduate of Swarthmore College who also received a Ph.D. from the University of Pennsylvania, was jailed three times for demonstrating for woman suffrage. Paul wanted to use protests to force President Wilson to take action on suffrage. Her activities alarmed other members of NAWSA who wanted to negotiate with Wilson. Paul decided to leave NAWSA and formed the National Woman's Party. Her supporters picketed the White House, blocked sidewalks, chained themselves to lampposts, and went on hunger strikes if arrested.

In 1915 Carrie Chapman Catt, a graduate of Iowa State College (now Iowa State University) and a peace advocate, became NAWSA's leader. Catt developed what she called her "Winning Plan" to mobilize the suffrage movement nationwide in one final push to gain voting rights. She also threw NAWSA's support behind Wilson in the 1916 election. Although Wilson did not endorse a woman suffrage amendment, he supported the Democratic Party's call for states to give women the vote.

The Nineteenth Amendment In 1869, long before NAWSA was formed, Wyoming became the first state or territory to grant women the right to vote within its borders. Other states soon began to follow Wyoming's lead. As the suffrage movement gained momentum, more states granted women the right to vote, and Congress began to favor a constitutional amendment. In 1918 the House of Representatives passed a woman suffrage amendment. Wilson then addressed the Senate, asking it to vote for the amendment. Despite his efforts, the amendment failed to pass by two votes.

During the midterm elections of 1918, Catt used NAWSA's resources to defeat two anti-suffrage senators. The following year, in June 1919, the Senate finally passed the Nineteenth Amendment by just more than the two-thirds vote needed. On August 26, 1920, after three-fourths of the states had voted to ratify it, the Nineteenth Amendment guaranteeing women the right to vote went into effect.

✓ Reading Check **Evaluating** How successful were women in lobbying to achieve passage of the Nineteenth Amendment?

332 CHAPTER 5 The Progressive Movement

 ### Geography *Skills*

Answers:
1. the West
2. the South

Geography Skills Practice
Ask: In which states did women have full voting rights in 1900? *(Wyoming, Idaho, Utah, and Colorado)*

Did You Know?

In 1872 Victoria Woodhull became the first woman to run for president of the United States. Susan B. Anthony was arrested during the election for casting an illegal vote.

Social Welfare Progressivism

Main Idea Many progressives focused on social welfare problems, such as child labor, public health, and prohibition.

Reading Connection In what ways could you try to make the world a better place for others? Read to learn how progressives worked to eliminate the problems caused by child labor, unsafe workplace conditions, and alcohol consumption.

While many progressives focused on reforming the political system, others focused on social problems, such as crime, illiteracy, alcohol abuse, child labor, and the health and safety of Americans. These social welfare progressives created charities to help the poor and the disadvantaged. They also pushed for new laws they hoped would fix social problems.

The Campaign Against Child Labor Probably the most emotional Progressive issue was the campaign against child labor. Children had always worked on family farms, but the factory work that many children performed was monotonous, and the conditions were often unhealthy. In 1900 over 1.7 million children under the age of 16 worked outside the home. Reformers established a National Child Labor Committee in 1904 to work to abolish child labor.

Muckraker John Spargo's 1906 book *The Bitter Cry of the Children* presented detailed evidence on child labor conditions. He told of coal mines where thousands of "breaker boys" were hired at age 9 or 10 to pick slag out of coal and were paid 60¢ for a 10-hour day. He described how the work bent their backs permanently and often crippled their hands. Reports like these convinced states to pass laws that set a minimum age for employment and established other limits on child labor, such as maximum hours children could work. At the same time, many states began passing compulsory education laws, requiring young children to be in school instead of at work.

By the early 1900s, the number of child laborers had begun to decline. For many families, the new wealth generated by industry enabled them to survive

NATIONAL GEOGRAPHIC
MOMENT in HISTORY

YOUTHFUL PROTEST
Two young immigrants march in a New York City demonstration against child labor practices in 1907. Both young women wear banners proclaiming the same message—one in English, the other in Yiddish. Such protests helped publicize the exploitation of children in dingy, dangerous "sweatshops" in American cities. At the dawn of the twentieth century, more than a million children—some as young as eight—labored long hours in factories. The weight of popular opinion finally forced state governments to pass laws protecting young workers.

CHAPTER 5 The Progressive Movement **333**

NATIONAL GEOGRAPHIC **MOMENT in HISTORY**

The term sweatshop comes from the "sweating system" of subcontracting. A garment manufacturer, for instance, gave material to a go-between, who then subcontracted the work to tailors and seamstresses who worked at home or in small shops. Workers were paid by the piece, not by the hour. They therefore "sweated" because they had to work very fast.

without having their children work. For others, the child labor and compulsory education laws meant that wives had to work instead.

Health and Safety Codes Many adult workers also labored in difficult conditions. Factories, coal mines, and railroads were particularly dangerous. For example, in 1911 a terrible fire swept through Triangle Shirtwaist Company in New York City. Nearly 150 women workers died, trapped by doors locked from the outside. Outrage at the deaths caused New York City to pass strict building codes dealing with fire hazards, unsafe machinery, and working conditions.

During the early 1900s, thousands of people died or were injured on the job, but they and their families received little compensation. Progressives joined union leaders to pressure states for workers' compensation laws. These laws established insurance **funds** financed by employers. Workers injured in industrial accidents received payments from the funds.

Some progressives also favored zoning laws as a method of protecting the public. These laws divided a town or city into zones for commercial, residential, or other development, thereby regulating how land and buildings could be used. Building codes set minimum standards for light, air, room size, and sanitation, and required buildings to have fire escapes. Health codes required restaurants and other facilities to maintain clean environments for their patrons.

The Prohibition Movement Many progressives believed alcohol was responsible for many problems in American life. Settlement house workers hated the effects of drinking on families. Scarce wages were spent on alcohol, and drinking sometimes led to physical abuse and sickness. Many Christians also opposed alcohol.

Some employers believed drinking hurt workers' efficiency, while political reformers viewed the saloon as the informal headquarters of the machine politics they opposed. The **temperance** movement, which **advocated** the moderation or elimination of alcohol, emerged from these concerns.

For the most part, women led the temperance movement. In 1874 a group of women formed the Women's Christian Temperance Union (WCTU). By 1911 the WCTU had nearly 250,000 members. In 1893 another organization—the Anti-Saloon League—was formed. At first the temperance movement worked to reduce alcohol consumption. Later it pressed for **prohibition**—laws banning the manufacture, sale, and consumption of alcohol.

✓ **Reading Check** **Examining** What actions did progressives take to deal with the issue of child labor?

Picturing **History**

Triangle Shirtwaist Factory Fire Children were not the only ones who faced difficult and even hazardous working conditions. This fire in New York City in 1911 killed nearly 150 women. What safety measures and technology do people have today to help prevent deaths during a fire that people might not have had in 1911?

Progressives Versus Big Business

Main Idea Another form of progressivism focused on federal regulation of big business.

Reading Connection Do you remember how the federal government supported big business, such as the railroads, during the rise of industry after the Civil War? Read on to find out how the progressives now tried to limit the power of big business.

A fourth group of progressives focused their efforts on regulating big business. Many progressives believed that wealth was concentrated in the hands of too few people. In particular, many became concerned about trusts and holding companies—giant corporations that dominated many industries.

Progressives disagreed, however, over how to regulate big business. Some believed government should break up big companies to restore competition. This idea led to the Sherman Antitrust Act in 1890. Others argued that big business was the most efficient way to organize the economy. They pushed for the creation of government agencies to regulate big companies. The Interstate Commerce Commission (ICC), created in 1887, was an early example of this kind of Progressive thinking.

Some progressives went even further and advocated **socialism**—the idea that the government should own and operate industry for the community as a whole. They wanted the government to buy up large companies, especially industries that affected everyone, such as railroads and utilities.

At its peak, socialism had some national support. Eugene Debs, the former American Railway Union

▲ *Eugene Debs (right) with running mate Emil Seidel (left)*

leader, won nearly a million votes as the American Socialist Party candidate for president in 1912. Most progressives and Americans, however, believed in the American system of free enterprise.

Efforts to regulate business were focused at the national level. Congress passed a number of proposals to regulate the economy under presidents Theodore Roosevelt, William Taft, and Woodrow Wilson.

 Reading Check **Evaluating** What was the impact of Eugene Debs and the Socialist Party on the 1912 election?

HISTORY Online **Study Central**

For help with the concepts in this section of *American Vision: Modern Times* go to tav.mt.glencoe.com and click on **Study Central**.

SECTION 1 ASSESSMENT

Checking for Understanding

1. **Vocabulary** Define: progressivism, muckraker, commission plan, direct primary, initiative, legislation, referendum, recall, suffrage, strategy, funds, temperance, advocated, prohibition, socialism.
2. **People and Terms** Identify: Jacob Riis, Robert La Follette, Alice Paul.
3. **Identify** what was provided for by the Nineteenth Amendment to the Constitution.

Reviewing Big Ideas

4. **Explaining** How did initiative, referendum, and recall change democracy in the United States?

Critical Thinking

5. **Historical Analysis** **Evaluating** Identify the different issues associated with social welfare progressivism. How do these ideals influence society today? **CA CS1; HI1**
6. **Organizing** Use a graphic organizer similar to the one below to list the kinds of problems that muckrakers exposed.

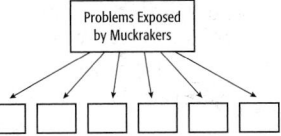

Analyzing Visuals

7. **Examining Charts** Study the charts on page 329. Under which system do voters seem to have the most control over department heads? Why do you think so?

Writing About History

8. **Persuasive Writing** Some women in the early 1900s suggested that the Constitution needed an equal rights amendment. Imagine you are living then. Write a letter to the editor of your local paper supporting or opposing such an amendment. **CA 11WS1.1; 11WS1.2**

CHAPTER 5 The Progressive Movement **335**

SECTION 1 ASSESSMENT ANSWERS

1. Content vocabulary is boldfaced and highlighted in yellow. Academic vocabulary is boldfaced.
2. Jacob Riis *(p. 328)*, Robert LaFollette *(p. 330)*, Alice Paul *(p. 332)*
3. The Nineteenth Amendment granted women the right to vote.
4. They gave voters more power to

introduce legislation, to approve legislation, and to remove elected officials.

5. Social problems such as crime, illiteracy, alcohol abuse, child labor, and health and safety; Students' answers will vary.
6. unfair business practices, corrupt political practices, social problems

7. mayor-council form or the commission form–voters elect the person to whom the department heads report
8. Students' letters will vary. Letters should clearly express a point of view.

U **Universal Access**

Below Grade Level To help students understand this passage, provide a quick review of trusts, monopolies, and holding companies. Have students provide their own descriptions to show their understanding of these terms. **BL**

ASSESS

 Resources for page 335

Use these resources to assess student mastery.

📁 Section Quiz 5-1

📁 Reading Essentials and Study Guide 5-1

🔘 Interactive Tutor Self-Assessment CD-ROM

📁 California Standards Practice, Grade 11

✓ **Reading Check**

Answer: election showed socialism unlikely to succeed in the United States

HISTORY Online

Study Central provides audio summaries, interactive games, and online graphic organizers to help students review section content.

CLOSE

Advanced Learners Invite interested students to write a two- to three-page biographical profile of one of the persons mentioned in this section or a description of a progressive group or governmental agency that was developed during this time. **AL**

FOCUS

History–Social Science Standards

This feature addresses the following standards:

11.2 Students analyze the relationship among the rise of industrialization, large-scale rural-to-urban migration, and massive immigration from Southern and Eastern Europe.

11.2.1 Know the effects of industrialization on living and working conditions, including the portrayal of working conditions and food safety in Upton Sinclair's *The Jungle.*

Summary

The Jungle is the story of Lithuanian immigrant Jurgis Rudkus, whose family works in a Chicago meatpacking plant. They experience poor wages, dangerous working conditions, and unfair labor practices. After Jurgis's family suffers a tragedy, he is introduced to socialism.

Read to Discover

Answer: greed, jealousy, and hatred

Understanding Vocabulary

Before students begin reading, remind them to read **The Reader's Dictionary** to better understand the literature excerpt.

Answers and Additional Support

American LITERATURE

from The Jungle
by Upton Sinclair

Born in Maryland in 1878, **Upton Sinclair** spent his life writing about and trying to change what he saw as wrong in the United States. One of his most famous novels, *The Jungle,* deals with working conditions and the rights of immigrants. The novel tells the story of Jurgis Rudkus, a Lithuanian immigrant who comes to the United States with his family in the early 1900s, dreaming of wealth and freedom. What he finds is "Packingtown," the bustling, filthy stockyards of Chicago. In the following excerpt, Sinclair describes the system Jurgis comes to know after gaining his first job in a meatpacking plant.

Read to Discover
What qualities did Sinclair believe a person must have to succeed in Packingtown?

Reader's Dictionary
killing-beds: areas where cattle were slaughtered

dismayed: alarmed, disheartened

universality: the state of including all

pitted: set against each other

caldron: a large kettle or pot for boiling

knave: a tricky, deceitful person

trice: short period of time

This was the first time in his life that he had ever really worked, it seemed to Jurgis; it was the first time that he had ever had anything to do which took all he had in him. Jurgis had stood with the rest up in the gallery and watched the men on the killing-beds, marveling at their speed and power as if they had been wonderful machines; it somehow never occurred to one to think of the flesh-and-blood side of it— that is, not until he actually got down into the pit and took off his coat. Then he saw things in a different light, he got at the inside of them. The pace they set here, it was one that called for every faculty of a man—from the instant the first steer fell till the sounding of the noon whistle, and again from half-past twelve till heaven only knew what hour in the late afternoon or evening, there was never one instant's rest for a man, for his hand or his eye or his brain. Jurgis saw how they managed it; there were portions of the work which deter- mined the pace of the rest, and for these they had picked men whom they paid high wages, and whom they changed frequently. You might easily pick out these pace-makers, for they worked under the eye of the bosses, and they worked like men possessed. This was called "speeding up the gang," and if any man could not keep up with the pace, there were hundreds outside begging to try.

Yet Jurgis did not mind it; he rather enjoyed it. It saved him the necessity of flinging his arms about and fidgeting as he did in most work. He would laugh to himself as he ran down the line, darting a glance now and then at the man ahead of him. It was not the pleasantest work one could think of, but it was necessary work; and what more had a man the right to ask than a chance to do something useful, and to get good pay for doing it?

So Jurgis thought, and so he spoke, in his bold, free way; very much to his surprise, he found that it had a

---

Reading Strategy — IDENTIFYING THE MAIN IDEA

Have students create a graphic organizer of Sinclair's main idea in this excerpt. Instruct students to write "Corruption of Managers and Supervisors" in the center of a piece of paper and draw a circle around it. Have students draw lines leading from the circle to smaller circles. Students should fill in the smaller circles with the details Sinclair used to reveal manager corruption. **OL** tendency to get him into trouble. For most of the men here took a fearfully different view of the thing. He was quite dismayed when he first began to find it out—that most of the men hated their work. It seemed strange, it was even terrible, when you came to find out the universality of the sentiment; but it was certainly the fact—they hated their work. They hated the bosses and they hated the owners; they hated the whole place, the whole neighborhood—even the whole city, with an all-inclusive hatred, bitter and fierce. Women and little children would fall to cursing about it; it was rotten, rotten as hell—everything was rotten. When Jurgis would ask them what they meant, they would begin to get suspicious, and content themselves with saying, "Never mind, you stay here and see for yourself."

▲ A supervisor watches as slaughterhouse workers push hogs through a scalding trough.

. . . Jurgis had made some friends by this time, and he sought one of them and asked what this meant. The friend, who was named Tamoszius Kuszleika, was a sharp little man who folded hides on the killing-beds, and he listened to what Jurgis had to say without seeming at all surprised. They were common enough, he said, such cases of petty graft. It was simply some boss who proposed to add a little to his income. After Jurgis had been there awhile he would know that the plants were simply honeycombed with rottenness of that sort—the bosses grafted off the men, and they grafted off each other; and some day the superintendent would find out about the boss,

and then he would graft off the boss. Warming to the subject, Tamoszius went on to explain the situation. Here was Durham's, for instance, owned by a man who was trying to make as much money out of it as he could, and did not care in the least how he did it; and underneath him, ranged in ranks and grades like an army, were managers and superintendents and foremen, each one driving the man next below him and trying to squeeze out of him as much work as possible. And all the men of the same rank were pitted against each other; the accounts of each were kept separately, and every man lived in terror of losing his job, if another made a better record than he. So from top to bottom the place was simply a seething caldron of jealousies and hatreds; there was no loyalty or decency anywhere about it, there was no place in it where a man counted for anything against a dollar. And worse than there being no decency, there was not even any honesty. The reason for that? Who could say? It must have been old Durham in the beginning; it was a heritage which the self-made merchant had left to his son, along with his millions.

Jurgis would find out these things for himself, if he stayed there long enough; it was the men [like him] who had to do all the dirty jobs, and so there was no deceiving them; and they caught the spirit of the place, and did like all the rest. Jurgis had come there, and thought he was going to make himself

American LITERATURE

TEACH

W Writing Support

Persuasive Writing Instruct students to take notes as they read this literature selection and then write a letter to President Roosevelt from the perspective of a 1906 United States citizen who has just read *The Jungle.* The letter should urge the president to take action in reforming the meatpacking industry, citing specific problems or deficiencies that were exposed in the book. OL
CA 11WS1.3

R Reading Strategy

Using Context Clues Have students look up words that might have a different meaning in this context, such as *honeycombed.* BL

S Skill Practice

Identifying Point of View Have students write a short narrative from the perspective of a plant supervisor. Students should include the supervisor's motivation and his attitude toward the plant workers. AL

U Universal Access

English Learners Pair up English learners with classmates proficient in English. Have the partners take turns retelling Sinclair's excerpt orally. The English learners can model the skills they observe in their classmate. EL

Resources for page 337

*Have students learn more about the Progressive Era in **Moments in Time, Unit 5: the Progressive Era (1890–1919).***

Did You Know?

Upton Sinclair set out to expose the poor working conditions of immigrants, but readers focused on how the meatpacking industry affected *them.*

 Block Schedule

Team Teaching This selection from *The Jungle* can be presented with English or Language Arts.

American LITERATURE

R₁ Reading Strategy

Visual Literacy Have students examine the picture. **Ask:** Which man appears to be the supervisor? *(the one in the suit taking notes)* What differences do you notice between the supervisor and the workers? *(His work seems to require less exertion; his clothes are neat and business-like, while the workers' clothes are old and stained.)* **BL**

C Critical Thinking

Making Inferences Tell students to write a paragraph describing the qualities of a person who could successfully work at the meatpacking plant. **OL**

R₂ Reading Strategy

Evaluating Tell students to find instances in the text where corners were cut when processing meat. *("Downers" were processed just like other cattle.)* **OL**

ASSESS/CLOSE

Have students answer the Analyzing Literature questions and complete the Interdisciplinary Activity.

Answers and Additional Support

R₁

▲ *Workers in a meatpacking plant*

C useful, and rise and become a skilled man; but he would soon find out his error—for nobody rose in Packingtown by doing good work. You could lay that down for a rule—if you met a man who was rising in Packingtown, you met a knave. That man who had been sent to Jurgis's father by the boss, *he* would rise; the man who told tales and spied upon his fellows would rise; but the man who minded his own business and did his work— why, they would "speed him up" till they had worn him out, and then they would throw him into the gutter.

. . . One curious thing he had noticed, the very first day, in his profession of shoveller of guts; which was the sharp trick of the floor-bosses whenever there chanced to come a "slunk" calf. Any man who knows anything about butchering knows that the flesh of a cow that is about to calve, or has just calved, is not fit for food. A good many of these came every day to the packing houses—and, of course, if they had chosen, it would have been an easy matter for the packers to keep them till they were fit for food. But for the saving of time and fodder, it was the law that cows of **R₂** that sort came along with the others, and whoever noticed it would tell the boss, and the boss would start up a conversation with the government inspector, and the two would stroll away. So in a trice the carcass of the cow would be cleaned out, and entrails would have vanished; it was Jurgis's task to slide them into the trap, calves and all, and on the floor below they took out these "slunk" calves, and butchered them for meat, and used even the skins of them.

One day a man slipped and hurt his leg; and that afternoon, when the last of the cattle had been disposed of, and the men were leaving, Jurgis was ordered to remain and do some special work which this injured man had usually done. It was late, almost dark, and the government inspectors had all gone, and there were only a dozen or two of men on the floor. That day they had killed about four thousand cattle, and these cattle had come in freight trains from far states, and some of them had got hurt. There were some with broken legs, and some with gored sides; there were some that had died, from what cause no one could say; and they were all to be disposed of, here in darkness and silence. "Downers," the men called them; and the packing house had a special elevator upon which they were raised to the killing-beds, where the gang proceeded to handle them, with an air of businesslike nonchalance which said plainer than any words that it was a matter of everyday routine. It took a couple of hours to get them out of the way, and in the end Jurgis saw them go into the chilling rooms with the rest of the meat, being carefully scattered here and there so that they could not be identified. When he came home that night he was in a very somber mood, having begun to see at last how those might be right who had laughed at him for his faith in America.

Analyzing Literature

1. According to the passage, what is the plant owner's main goal?
2. What does Sinclair mean when he says, ". . . there was no place in it where a man counted for anything against a dollar. . . ."?
   CA 11RC2.5

Interdisciplinary Activity

Government When it was published, *The Jungle* was so shocking that it launched a government investigation of the meatpacking industry. The investigation eventually led to the establishment of laws regulating the industry. Using the Internet, research these laws and read about how they are enforced today. Write a short report on your findings.

Answers to Analyzing Literature

1. His main goal is to make money.
2. He means that making money was more important than human life.

Interdisciplinary Activity
Students' reports will vary. Remind students to include bibliographic information about the sources they use.

Reading on Your Own

For other literature selections that relate to social problems and reform movements, you might consider the following book suggestions.

Twenty Years at Hull-House (Autobiography)
by Jane Addams

Jane Addams was one of the reformers of the late 1800s and early 1900s who sought to help immigrants in crowded Chicago. She founded Hull House, a settlement house, where she lived until she died at age 75. Her autobiography describes her experiences during the first 20 years of Hull House.

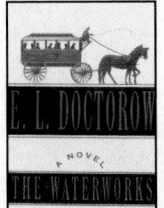

The Waterworks (Fiction)
by E.L. Doctorov

This book tells the story of newspaper editor McIlvaine who looks into the disappearance of one of his freelancers, Martin Pemberton. In the process, the city of New York becomes a central character in the novel as Doctorov describes the impact of industrialization, the political machine, corrupt police, and greedy tycoons.

Voices from the Fields: Children of Migrant Farm Workers Tell Their Stories (Nonfiction)
by S. Beth Atkin

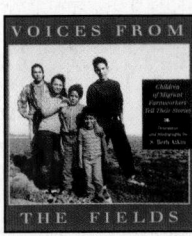

S. Beth Atkin is a writer and photographer who focuses her work on children. This 1993 title relates in pictures and words the difficult lives of nine children of migrant workers in California today. In their stories, written in both English and Spanish, the children talk about long work hours, problems with gangs, and the difficulties that come with changing schools frequently.

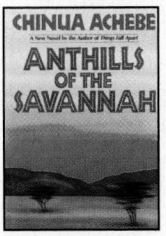

Anthills of the Savannah (Fiction)
by Chinua Achebe

Nigerian-born Achebe set this novel in the fictional African country of Kangan, which has just received independence. The fictional lives of an elected official, a statesman, and a journalist show how governmental power and corruption soon erode society and end the great hopes of the new nation.

Cooperative Learning

Free-Form Mapping Divide students into groups and assign each group one of the books listed in the bibliography. After the groups have completed reading their selection, instruct them to create a free-form map to illustrate the content. Give each group a large sheet of paper and some colored markers. Each group should discuss the main ideas and concepts presented in the book they read. Students should then use words, pictures, and diagrams to illustrate their ideas. Have each group present their maps to the class.

Sequence Mapping Students can extend their free-form mapping activity by placing their main ideas in the order in which they occurred.

Preparing for Assessment Free-form mapping and sequence mapping can also be used to review the material covered in the American Literature spread. Have student groups create a free-form map to illustrate the main points Upton Sinclair made in this excerpt from *The Jungle.*
OL

Reading Strategy   REINFORCING READING SKILLS

As students read this excerpt from Upton Sinclair's *The Jungle,* have them practice the skill of making inferences. Ask students to consider the purpose of Sinclair's writing and what they have learned about the political history of the Progressive Era. From this knowledge, have them make inferences about Sinclair's own political ideology.

FOCUS

BELLRINGER
SKILLBUILDER ACTIVITY

Project **Daily Focus Skills Transparency 5-2** and have students answer the question.

Guide to Reading

Understanding Vocabulary: Have students create a database of the content vocabulary and academic vocabulary while reading this section.

Answers to Graphic: Have students complete the outline based on the headings in this section.

Unpacking the Standards

Students will be able to:

- Identify how President Roosevelt used arbitration to settle the coal strike of 1902.
- Analyze how Roosevelt's lawsuits against trusts affected the establishment of future trusts.
- Identify how Upton Sinclair's *The Jungle* contributed to the passage of the Meat Inspection Act.

Answers and Additional Support

SECTION 2 Roosevelt in Office

Guide to Reading

Connection
In the previous section, you learned about the Progressive movement. In this section, you will discover how progressive ideals became prominent in national politics.

Main Idea
- Theodore Roosevelt, who believed in progressive ideals for the nation, took on big business. (p. 341)
- Theodore Roosevelt and Congress expanded the power of government by passing several acts regulating meat inspection, food and drugs, and conservation of the environment. (p. 344)

Content Vocabulary
arbitration

Academic Vocabulary
trigger, issue, environmental

People and Terms to Identify
Square Deal, Northern Securities, United Mine Workers, Hepburn Act, Upton Sinclair

Reading Objectives
- **Describe** various efforts to regulate concentrated corporate power.
- **Discuss** Theodore Roosevelt's interest in environmental conservation.

Reading Strategy
Taking Notes As you read about the administration of President Theodore Roosevelt, use the major headings of the section to create an outline similar to the one below.

> Roosevelt in Office
> I. Roosevelt Revives the Presidency
>   A.
>   B.
>   C.
>   D.
> II.

Preview of Events

♦1900	♦1902	♦1904	♦1906
1901 Theodore Roosevelt becomes president after William McKinley's death	**1902** United Mine Workers go on strike	**1903** Roosevelt sets up Bureau of Corporations	**1906** Upton Sinclair's *The Jungle* published **1906** Meat Inspection Act passed

The following are the main History–Social Science Standards covered in this section.

11.2 Students analyze the relationship among the rise of industrialization, large-scale rural-to-urban migration, and massive immigration from Southern and Eastern Europe.

11.2.1 Know the effects of industrialization on living and working conditions, including the portrayal of working conditions and food safety in Upton Sinclair's *The Jungle*.

11.2.5 Discuss corporate mergers that produced trusts and cartels and the economic and political policies of industrial leaders.

11.2.9 Understand the effect of political programs and activities of the Progressives (e.g., federal regulation of railroad transport, Children's Bureau, the Sixteenth Amendment, Theodore Roosevelt, Hiram Johnson).

The Big Idea

Social and economic crises lead to new roles for government. Following the election of Theodore Roosevelt, progressive reforms and ideas became more prominent in national politics. Although Roosevelt recognized and appreciated the efficiency of large corporations, he also felt they had a responsibility to consider the public welfare. Therefore, he worked to supervise big business without destroying it. The Bureau of Corporations monitored big business, and the attorney general was able to bring antitrust lawsuits against companies if necessary. As public concern regarding medicine and food handling increased, President Roosevelt and Congress passed several acts to help protect the public. Perhaps the area in which President Roosevelt made the greatest impact, however, was environmental conservation.

SECTION RESOURCES

Print Material
- Reproducible Lesson Plan 5-2
- Guided Reading Activity 5-2
- Reading Essentials and Study Guide 5-2
- Active Reading Note-Taking Guide 5-2

Transparencies
- Daily Focus Skills Transparency 5-2
- Section Graphic Organizer Transparency 5-2

Technology
- Interactive Tutor Self-Assessment CD-ROM
- ExamView® Pro Testmaker CD-ROM
- Presentation Plus! CD-ROM

Roosevelt Revives the Presidency

Main Idea Theodore Roosevelt, who believed in progressive ideals for the nation, took on big business.

Reading Connection How much do you think a president's personal beliefs should shape national policy? Read on to learn how Theodore Roosevelt, with the help of Congress, used his ideas to change trusts and big business.

Theodore Roosevelt, better known as "Teddy," took office at age 42—the youngest person ever to serve as president. Roosevelt was intensely competitive, strong-willed, and extremely energetic.

★ An American Story ★

William McKinley's assassination brought Teddy Roosevelt to the presidency. Despite the tragic circumstances, he took to the office with great joy. A man who loved the outdoors and physical activity, Roosevelt impressed many people as a new kind of president. One visitor wrote that after spending time with Roosevelt, "you go home and wring the personality out of your clothes."

The famous muckraker, Lincoln Steffens, already knew Roosevelt as a fellow reformer. Steffens went to Washington to see his friend, and this is what he saw:

66His offices were crowded with people, mostly reformers, all day long. . . .He strode triumphant around among us, talking and shaking hands, dictating and signing letters, and laughing. Washington, the whole country, was in mourning, and no doubt the President felt he should hold himself down; he didn't; he tried to but his joy showed in every word and movement. . . .With his feet, his fists, his face and his free words, he laughed at his luck. . . .And he laughed with glee at the power and place that had come to him.99

—quoted in *Theodore Roosevelt, A Life*

In international affairs, Roosevelt was a Social Darwinist. He believed the United States was in competition with the other nations of the world and that only the fittest would survive. Domestically, however, Roosevelt was a committed progressive, who firmly believed that government should actively balance the needs of competing groups in American society.

"I shall see to it," Roosevelt declared in 1904, "that every man has a square deal, no less and no more." During his second term, his reform programs became known as the **Square Deal.** To Roosevelt, it was not inconsistent to believe in Social Darwinism and Progressivism at the same time. He believed the United States needed to adopt progressive reforms in order to maintain an efficient society that could compete successfully against other nations.

Roosevelt Takes on the Trusts Although he admired competition, Roosevelt was also concerned with efficiency. He believed that trusts and other large business organizations were very efficient and part of the reason for America's prosperity. Yet Roosevelt remained concerned that in the pursuit of their private interests, some trusts were hurting the public interest. He wanted to find a way to supervise big business without destroying its economic efficiency. When the *New York Sun* declared that Roosevelt was "bringing wealth to its knees," the president disagreed. "We draw the line against misconduct," he declared, "not against wealth."

During Roosevelt's first year in office, a fight for control of the Burlington Railroad erupted on the New York Stock Exchange. On one side was E.H. Harriman of the Union Pacific Railroad. On the other side were James J. Hill and J.P. Morgan of the Great Northern and Northern Pacific Railroads. The stock battle almost **triggered** a financial panic that

▼ *Theodore Roosevelt*

CHAPTER 5   The Progressive Movement   **341**

Did You Know?

On December 3, 1901, Roosevelt made his first annual address to Congress. His speech focused on the need for the federal government to restrain large corporations and trusts. During his presidency, he initiated 44 lawsuits against trusts.

TEACH

U Universal Access

Visual/Spatial Have students read the description and then draw a political cartoon focusing on Roosevelt. Suggest that they use characters from contemporary culture or traditional stories such as fairy tales. **AL**

S Skill Practice

Evaluating Evidence Ask students to recall what they learned about progressivism in the previous section. As they read through the section, have them write down any of Roosevelt's decisions or policies that reflected his belief in progressivism. **OL** **CA HI1**

R Reading Strategy

Evaluating President Roosevelt wanted to find a balance between business and public interest. **Ask:** Why did the president think big business was efficient? *(Students might say that big businesses could produce many goods fast at low prices.)* **OL**

Review the Big Idea

Review the Big Idea for this section, "Social and economic crises lead to new roles for government." As students read this section, have them select one of the actions President Roosevelt took to regulate business. Students should write a one-page report about the action, showing how it demonstrated increased government involvement. **OL**

Answers and Additional Support

C Critical Thinking

Determining Cause and Effect
President Roosevelt was not afraid to use the power of the government to shape the operations of the economy. **Ask: How do you think President Roosevelt's victory over Northern Securities would affect the attempts of other businesses to create trusts?** *(Businesses would be less likely to form trusts after witnessing Roosevelt's aggressive approach toward violators of the Sherman Antitrust Act.)* **AL**

R Reading Strategy

Scaffolding—Academic Vocabulary The word *violate* was introduced in Chapter 4, Section 2. Ask a student to define the word. **BL**

W Writing Support

Research Report Writing
Using library or Internet resources, instruct students to research the types of health problems that were common to coal workers. Have students write a summary of their findings. **OL**

CA 11WA2.4a; 11WA2.4b

Answers and Additional Support

could have plunged the nation into a recession. The three men ultimately compromised by creating a giant new holding company called **Northern Securities.**

The formation of the Northern Securities Company alarmed many Americans, including Roosevelt. The stock battle that led to its creation seemed a classic example of private interests acting in a way that threatened the nation as a whole. Roosevelt decided that the company was in violation of the Sherman Antitrust Act. In early 1902, he ordered his attorney general to file a lawsuit against Northern Securities.

In 1904 in *Northern Securities* v. *the United States,* the Supreme Court ruled five to four that Northern Securities had violated the Sherman Antitrust Act. The dissenting justices argued that the Sherman Antitrust Act did not ban companies from buying or selling stock to each other. They observed that Northern Securities had not hurt commerce. It had

Analyzing *Political Cartoons*

Corporate Giants This 1904 cartoon portrays Roosevelt as "Jack the Giant-Killer," but he actually restrained very few trusts. Why do you think the scene is set on Wall Street?

342 CHAPTER 5 The Progressive Movement

not tried to keep other companies from competing, and it had not tried to raise railroad rates. In fact, rates had fallen on railroads owned by Northern Securities. Although the court was sharply divided, Roosevelt declared the decision a great victory. Newspapers hailed Roosevelt as a "trustbuster," and his popularity soared. *(See page 1006 for more information on* Northern Securities v. the United States.)

The Coal Strike of 1902 As president, Roosevelt regarded himself as the nation's head manager. He believed it was his job to keep society operating efficiently by preventing conflict between the nation's different groups and their interests. In the fall of 1902, he put these beliefs into practice.

The previous spring, the **United Mine Workers** (UMW) union had called a strike of the miners who dug anthracite, or hard coal. Nearly 150,000 workers walked out of eastern Pennsylvania's anthracite mines demanding a pay increase, a reduction in work hours, and recognition for their union.

As the months passed and the strike continued, coal prices began to rise. To Roosevelt it was another example of groups pursuing their private interests at the expense of the nation. If the strike dragged on too long, the country would face a coal shortage that could shut down factories and leave many people's homes cold with winter fast approaching.

Roosevelt urged the union and the owners to accept **arbitration**—a settlement imposed by an outside party. The union agreed. The mine owners, determined to destroy the UMW, did not. One owner, George Baer, declared, "The rights and interests of the laboring man will be protected and cared for not by the labor agitators, but by the Christian men to

John D. Rockefeller

J.P. Morgan

James J. Hill

T. Roosevelt

Analyzing *Political Cartoons*

Answer: Wall Street was the major financial center of the nation.
Ask: How did the artist make his point of view known? *(by choosing a familiar story and by the relative size of the components of the drawing)*

More Skill Practice

Connecting Have students look up the meaning of *arbitration* in the dictionary. *(the settlement of a dispute by an appointed person)* **Ask: How might a teacher arbitrate a disagreement between two students who are accusing each other of copying test answers?** *(Students' answers will vary.)* **BL**

whom God in His infinite wisdom has given the control of the property interests of the country."

The mine owners' stubbornness infuriated Roosevelt, as it did much of the public. Roosevelt threatened to order the army to run the mines. Fearful of this, the mine owners finally accepted arbitration. By intervening in the dispute, Roosevelt had taken the first step toward establishing the federal government as an honest broker between powerful groups in society.

The Bureau of Corporations Despite his lawsuit against Northern Securities and his role in the coal strike, Roosevelt was not opposed to big business. He believed most trusts benefited the economy and that breaking them up would do more harm than good. Instead, Roosevelt proposed the creation of a new federal agency to investigate corporations and publicize the results. He believed the most effective way to keep big business from abusing its power was through knowledge and providing the public with the facts.

In 1903 Roosevelt convinced Congress to create the Department of Commerce and Labor. G.B. Cortelyou was appointed the first secretary of the new department. Within this department would be a division called the Bureau of Corporations, with the authority to investigate corporations and issue reports on their activities.

The following year, the Bureau of Corporations began investigating U.S. Steel. Created in 1901, U.S. Steel was a gigantic holding company. Worried about a possible antitrust lawsuit, the company's leaders met privately with Roosevelt and offered a deal. They would open their account books and records to the Bureau of Corporations. In exchange, if the Bureau found anything wrong, the company would be advised privately and allowed to correct the problem without having to go to court.

Roosevelt accepted this "gentlemen's agreement," as he called it. Shortly afterward he made similar deals with other companies. These arrangements gave Roosevelt the ability to regulate big business and continue the economic benefit of big business without having to sacrifice economic efficiency by breaking up the trusts.

Congress Follows In addition to creating the Department of Commerce and Labor, Congress passed the Expedition Act, which gave federal antitrust suits precedence on the dockets of circuit courts. Then, in 1906, Roosevelt pushed the **Hepburn Act** through Congress. This act was intended to strengthen

Picturing **History**

Miner's Lot In the early 1900s, miners worked long hours under dangerous conditions for little pay. In an effort to obtain better compensation, reduction in work hours, and recognition of their union, many workers went on strike. How did Roosevelt respond when they went on strike?

the Interstate Commerce Commission (ICC). An early effort to regulate the railroad industry, the ICC had been ineffective because it lacked sufficient authority.

The Hepburn Act tried to strengthen the ICC by giving it the power to set railroad rates. The agency originally was intended to regulate rates to ensure that companies did not compete unfairly. At first, railroad companies were suspicious of the ICC and tied up its decisions by challenging them in court. Eventually, the railroads realized that they could work with the ICC to set rates and regulations that limited competition and prevented new competitors from entering the industry. Over time the ICC became a supporter of the railroads' interests, and by 1920 it had begun setting rates at levels intended to ensure the industry's profits.

✓ Reading Check **Comparing** What was the purpose of the Interstate Commerce Commission, and how successful was it?

CHAPTER 5 The Progressive Movement **343**

C **Critical Thinking**

Drawing Conclusions Have students create a table showing the advantages and disadvantages of a gentlemen's agreement. **Ask:** Do you think this is the best way to resolve conflicts between the government and industry? (*Supportive students may point out that this type of agreement helps achieve quick resolutions to problems by eliminating formal legal action. Critical students might state that these private deals do not educate the public to the problems existing in society.*) **OL**

U **Universal Access**

Verbal/Linguistic Individually ask each student in the class to verbally restate his or her understanding of the Hepburn Act. Help students to state clearly the act's purpose, and then have them transfer their answers into sentences. **OL**

✓ Reading Check

Answer: regulated railroad rates so that companies did not compete unfairly; not very—lacked authority

Picturing **History**

Answer: He worked to get the labor union and mine owners to accept arbitration as a way to settle the strike.
Ask: Why did mine owners finally accept arbitration as a way to settle the strike? (*Roosevelt threatened to bring in the military to run the mines.*)

Consumer Protection and Conservation

Main Idea Theodore Roosevelt and Congress expanded the power of government by passing several acts regulating meat inspection, food and drugs, and conservation of the environment. **⌐TURNING POINT⌐**

Reading Connection Have you ever visited a national park or forest and enjoyed the outdoors? Read on to discover how Theodore Roosevelt helped make some of these national parks and forests possible.

When Roosevelt took office, he was not greatly concerned about consumer issues, but by 1905 consumer protection had become a national issue. That year, a journalist named Samuel Hopkins Adams published a series of articles in *Collier's* magazine describing the patent medicine business.

Many companies were patenting and marketing potions they claimed would cure a variety of ills. Many patent medicines were little more than alcohol, colored water, and sugar. Others contained caffeine, opium, cocaine, and other dangerous compounds. Consumers had no way to know what they were taking, nor did they receive any assurance that the medicines worked as claimed.

Many Americans were equally concerned about the food they ate. Dr. W.H. Wiley, chief chemist at the United States Department of Agriculture, had issued reports documenting the dangerous preservatives being used in what he called "embalmed meat." Then, in 1906, **Upton Sinclair** published *The Jungle*. Based on Sinclair's close observations of the slaughterhouses of Chicago, the powerful book featured appalling descriptions of conditions in the meatpacking industry:

R

> ❝There would come all the way back from Europe old sausage that had been rejected, and that was moldy and white—it would be dosed with borax and glycerine, and dumped into the hoppers, and made over again for home consumption. . . . There would be meat stored in great piles in rooms; and the water from leaky roofs would drip over it, and thousands of rats would race about upon it.❞
>
> —from *The Jungle*

Sinclair's book was a best-seller. It made consumers ill—and angry. Roosevelt and Congress responded with the Meat Inspection Act. It required

federal inspection of meat sold through interstate commerce and required the Agriculture Department to set standards of cleanliness in meatpacking plants. The Pure Food and Drug Act, passed on the same day in 1906, prohibited the manufacture, sale, or shipment of impure or falsely labeled food and drugs.

C₁

Conservation Roosevelt put his stamp on the presidency most clearly in the area of **environmental** conservation. Realizing that the nation's bountiful natural resources were being used up at an alarming rate, Roosevelt urged Americans to conserve these resources.

An enthusiastic outdoorsman, Roosevelt valued the country's minerals, animals, and rugged terrain. Roosevelt urged Americans to conserve these resources. He cautioned against unregulated exploitation of public lands and believed in conservation to manage the nation's resources. As president, Roosevelt eagerly assumed the role of manager. He argued that the government must distinguish "between the man who skins the land and the man who develops the country. I am going to work with, and only with, the man who develops the country."

Land Development in the West Roosevelt quickly applied his philosophy in the dry Western states, where farmers and city dwellers competed for scarce water. In 1902 Roosevelt supported passage of the Newlands Reclamation Act, authorizing the use of Federal funds from public land sales to apply for irrigation and land development projects. Thus, it was the federal government that began the large-scale transformation of the West's landscape and economy.

C₂

Timber Resources Roosevelt also backed efforts to save the nation's forests through careful management of the timber resources of the West. He appointed his close friend Gifford Pinchot to head the United States Forest Service. "The natural resources," Pinchot said, "must be developed and preserved for the benefit of the many and not merely for the profit of a few." With the president's support, Pinchot's department drew up regulations controlling lumbering on federal lands.

As progressives, Roosevelt and Pinchot both believed that trained experts in forestry and resource management should apply the same scientific standards to the landscape that others were applying to the management of cities and industry. They rejected the laissez-faire argument that the best way to preserve public land was to sell it to lumber companies, who would then carefully conserve it because it was the source of their profits. With President Roosevelt's support, Pinchot's department drew up regulations to control lumbering on federal lands.

Roosevelt took other steps as well to conserve the nation's natural resources. He added over 100 million acres to the protected national forests, thus quadrupling their area. In addition, he established 5 new national parks and 51 federal wildlife reservations.

Roosevelt's Legacy President Roosevelt changed the role of the federal government and the nature of the presidency. Increasingly, Americans began to look to the federal government to solve the nation's economic and social problems. Under Roosevelt, the executive branch of government had dramatically increased its power. The ICC could set rates and regulations for the railroad industry to support fair competition. The Agriculture Department could inspect food to help protect public health and safety. The Bureau of Corporations could monitor business, and the attorney general could rapidly bring antitrust lawsuits under the Expedition Act.

 Reading Check **Examining** How did Roosevelt's policies help protect the health of consumers and the conservation of natural resources?

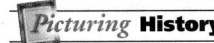 **Picturing History**

Crowd Pleaser Teddy Roosevelt's energetic speaking style captivated audiences across the nation. What impact did he have on the office of the presidency?

 HISTORY Online Study Central

For help with the concepts in this section of *American Vision: Modern Times* go to tav.mt.glencoe.com and click on **Study Central**.

SECTION 2 ASSESSMENT

Checking for Understanding

1. **Vocabulary** Define: trigger, arbitration, issue, environmental.
2. **People and Terms** Identify: Square Deal, Northern Securities, United Mine Workers, Hepburn Act, Upton Sinclair.
3. **Explain** the intent of the Hepburn Act.

Reviewing Big Ideas

4. **Analyzing** How did Upton Sinclair contribute to involving the federal government in protecting consumers?

Critical Thinking

5. **Evaluating** Do you agree with Roosevelt's use of the Sherman Antitrust Act against Northern Securities? Give specific reasons for your opinion.
6. **Organizing** Use a graphic organizer similar to the one below to list the results of the Coal Strike of 1902.

Results of 1902 Coal Strike

Analyzing Visuals

7. **Analyzing Photographs** Look at the photograph on this page. What do you think President Roosevelt's speech is concerning? Choose an issue and create brief remarks for a speech by President Roosevelt.

Writing About History

8. **Descriptive Writing** Imagine that you are living in the early 1900s and that you have just read Upton Sinclair's *The Jungle*. Write a letter to a friend explaining what the novel is about and how it characterizes the Progressive era. **CA** 11WA2.2a

---

SECTION 2 ASSESSMENT ANSWERS

1. Content vocabulary is boldfaced and highlighted in yellow. Academic vocabulary is boldfaced.
2. Square Deal *(p. 341)*, Northern Securities *(p. 342)*, United Mine Workers *(p. 342)*, Hepburn Act *(p. 343)*, Upton Sinclair *(p. 344)*
3. The Hepburn Act attempted to strengthen the ICC by giving it the power to set railroad rates.
4. His book, *The Jungle*, raised awareness of conditions in the meatpacking industry.
5. Students' answers will vary but should be specific, citing examples for their opinions.
6. Coal prices rose, use of arbitration, established precedent for future strikes
7. Students' answers will vary. Speeches should be about issues important to Roosevelt.
8. Students' letters will vary. Letters should include as much detail as possible based on information presented in this section.

 Resources for page 345

Use these resources to assess student mastery.

▭ Section Quiz 5-2

▭ Reading Essentials and Study Guide 5-2

◉ Interactive Tutor Self-Assessment CD-ROM

▭ California Standards Practice, Grade 11

Picturing **History**

Answer: increased power of the president
Ask: Why do you think people listened and responded to Roosevelt? *(He was both a charismatic speaker and an energetic leader who got things done.)*

✔ **Reading Check**

Answer: The policies controlled lumbering on federal land and created national forests and wildlife reservations to protect timber and wildlife.

 HISTORY Online

Study Central provides audio summaries, interactive games, and online graphic organizers to help students review section content.

CLOSE

Expository Writing Have students write an essay on what they feel were the main contributions of Theodore Roosevelt during his presidency. **OL**
CA 11WS1.3

345

Geography & History

FOCUS

History– Social Science Standards

This feature addresses the following standards:

11.2.9 Understand the effect of political programs and activities of the Progressives (e.g., federal regulation of the railroad transport, Children's Bureau, the Sixteenth Amendment, Theodore Roosevelt, Hiram Johnson).

11.11.5 Trace the impact of, need for, and controversies associated with environmental conservation, expansion of the national park system, and the development of environmental protection laws, with particular attention to the interaction between environmental protection advocates and property rights advocates.

TEACH

U Universal Access

Interpersonal Organize students into nine groups and assign each group one of the national parks shown on the map on p. 346. Have the groups create a display about the park and its natural beauty. **BL**

Answers and Additional Support

CATHEDRAL RANGE

Clou
9,926 f

Yosemite Point

Eagle Peak

Upper Yosemite Falls
1,430 ft. (436 m)

El Capitan
7,569 ft. (2,307 m)

Yosemite Falls
total drop
2,425 ft. (739 m)

Royal Arches

Cath
Spi

Yosemite Valley
4,000 ft. (1,219 m)

Cathedral Rocks

Bridalveil Fall
620 ft. (189 m)

Merced River

Early National Parks

- Mount Rainier, 1899
- Sullys Hill, 1904
- Crater Lake, 1902
- Yellowstone, 1872
- Wind Cave, 1903
- Yosemite, 1890
- General Grant (Kings Canyon), 1890
- Sequoia, 1890
- Mesa Verde, 1906

Pacific Ocean

Atlantic Ocean

Gulf of Mexico

OUR GROWING HERITAGE

This map of the United States shows 9 of the national parks that existed by the end of President Theodore Roosevelt's administration. Roosevelt established 5 national parks, 4 of which still exist today. He also established 51 wildlife preserves and 150 national forests.

U

346   CHAPTER 5   The Progressive Movement

EXTENDING THE CONTENT

Conservationist Theodore Roosevelt first visited the Badlands in 1883. As an avid hunter, he came to hunt bison but soon learned that the animals were virtually extinct as a result of hide hunters and disease. As he spent more time in the West, Roosevelt became alarmed at the environmental damage being done to the land and the wildlife. He translated his concerns into action when he became president, creating national parks, bird and game reserves, and national forests.

The Story of Yosemite

T he breathtaking beauty of the Yosemite Valley has always astounded visitors to California's High Sierra. In 1851 volunteer soldiers came upon the valley. One officer felt a "peculiar exalted sensation" as he marveled at his surroundings.

The officer's reaction was a natural one. Carved by glaciers and rivers, the seven-mile-long valley into which he and his men rode lies at an elevation of 4,000 feet (1219 m). Above them rose the near-vertical cliffs and great granite monoliths of El Capitan, Half Dome, and Cathedral Rocks. Down onto the valley floor poured the waters of Bridalveil Fall. A dozen other waterfalls spilled over sheer cliffs elsewhere in the valley, some of them— like Yosemite Falls at 2,425 feet (739 m)—among the highest on Earth. Within five years, horseback parties were coming to gaze at Bridalveil Fall and the face of El Capitan. The tourists had found Yosemite.

To guarantee that the public could continue to enjoy the beauty, in 1864 President Abraham Lincoln granted the valley to California as a wilderness preserve. In so doing, Lincoln laid the foundation for the national park system. (The first official national park, Yellowstone, was not created until eight years later.) By the late 1880s Yosemite was attracting about 5,000 visitors a year. John Muir and other conservationists were anxious to preserve the area. Muir had spent years tramping through the woods and up and down the

President Theodore Roosevelt and John Muir stand atop Glacier Point.

mountains and glaciers of the park. His compelling descriptions swayed many influential people. In 1890 Congress expanded the protected area and made Yosemite an official national park.

In many ways Yosemite established a pattern for our national park system. It started programs to teach visitors about native plants and wildlife and was the first park to build a museum to help visitors understand and enjoy the region.

In 1903 President Theodore Roosevelt visited the park with Muir. The natural beauty of the valley captivated the environmentalist president and stimulated his desire to protect vast areas of the country. "We are not building this country of ours for a day," declared Roosevelt. "It is to last through the ages." During his presidency Roosevelt enlarged Yosemite, established the U.S. Forest Service, and put millions of acres of land under federal protection. In 1916 the National Park Service was established, and today it manages more than 380 areas, including 57 national parks.

C (margin marker)

Sightseers admire Yosemite Falls as they ride along Glacier Point Trail in 1901. Today some 3.5 million tourists visit the park each year.

W (margin marker)

(map labels, left side)
ome ,693 m)
Nevada Falls 594 ft. (181 m)
Glacier Point 7,214 ft. (2,199 m)
Sentinel Rock
dalveil Creek

LEARNING FROM GEOGRAPHY

1. How was the Yosemite Valley formed?

2. How did the establishment of the national park system help to conserve natural resources?

347

ANSWERS TO LEARNING FROM GEOGRAPHY

1. Yosemite Valley was created by glaciers and rivers.

2. It protected the land by establishing ways in which the land could be used, and it established programs to teach people about the rich plant and animal life.

BELLRINGER
SKILLBUILDER ACTIVITY

Project **Daily Focus Skills Transparency 5-3** and have students answer the question.

Guide to Reading

Understanding Vocabulary: Have students write down all the content vocabulary and the academic vocabulary in this section, followed by the correct definition.

Answers to Graphic: progressives' campaign to unseat Cannon as Speaker of the House, Payne-Aldrich Tarriff, Ballinger-Pinchot controversy

Unpacking the Standards

Students will be able to:

- Explain how Taft experienced difficulties as president but continued the Progressive reform movement.

- List reasons the Progressives were unhappy with President Taft's handling of progressive reforms.

Answers and Additional Support

SECTION 3
The Taft Administration

Guide to Reading

Connection
In the previous section, you learned how President Roosevelt's progressive reforms affected the United States. In this section, you will discover how President Taft, a more moderate progressive, continued progressive reforms.

Main Idea
- William Howard Taft, elected to continue Theodore Roosevelt's policies, had difficulties with tariff and conservation issues. (p. 349)
- Taft worked to pass progressive reforms. (p. 351)

Content Vocabulary
syndicate, insubordination

Academic Vocabulary
dynamic, scheme, establish

People and Terms to Identify
Joseph G. Cannon, Payne-Aldrich Tariff, Richard A. Ballinger

Reading Objectives
- **Explain** how Theodore Roosevelt helped Taft get elected.
- **Discuss** why progressives were disappointed with Taft as president.

Reading Strategy
Organizing As you read about progressivism in this section, complete a graphic organizer similar to the one below listing Taft's conflicts with the progressives.

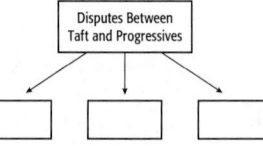

Disputes Between Taft and Progressives

Preview of Events

♦1908	♦1909	♦1910	♦1911	♦1912
1908 Taft elected president	**1909** Ballinger-Pinchot controversy	**1910** Mann-Elkins Act passed	**1911** Antitrust lawsuit filed against U.S. Steel	**1912** Roosevelt challenges Taft for Republican nomination

The following are the main History–Social Science Standards covered in this section.

11.2 Students analyze the relationship among the rise of industrialization, large-scale rural-to-urban migration, and massive immigration from Southern and Eastern Europe.

11.2.9 Understand the effect of political programs and activities of the Progressives (e.g., federal regulation of railroad transport, Children's Bureau, the Sixteenth Amendment, Theodore Roosevelt, Hiram Johnson).

❧ The Big Idea ❧

Social and economic crises lead to new roles for government. President Taft worked to lower tariffs in order to help consumers and increase competition. His actions, however, angered many progressives. The Ballinger-Pinchot controversy that followed destroyed Taft's reputation with progressive reformers. Despite the controversies and division with reformers, Taft managed several successes while in office. He established the Children's Bureau to investigate child labor, increased the regulatory powers of the ICC, set up the Bureau of Mines, protected national forests, and brought an antitrust lawsuit against U.S. Steel.

348 CHAPTER 5 The Progressive Movement

SECTION RESOURCES

📂 Print Material
- Reproducible Lesson Plan 5-3
- Guided Reading Activity 5-3
- Reading Essentials and Study Guide 5-3
- Active Reading Note-Taking Guide 5-3

🖌 Transparencies
- Daily Focus Skills Transparency 5-3
- Section Graphic Organizer Transparency 5-3

Technology
- ⊕ Interactive Tutor Self-Assessment CD-ROM
- ⊕ Exam*View*® Pro Testmaker CD-ROM
- ⊕ Presentation Plus! CD-ROM

Taft Becomes President

Main Idea William Howard Taft, elected to continue Theodore Roosevelt's policies, had difficulties with tariff and conservation issues.

Reading Connection What national leaders have tried to carry on the policies of the person they succeeded in office? Read on to learn of such an attempt that appeared to fail in the early 1900s.

William Howard Taft had been Theodore Roosevelt's most trusted lieutenant. He had served as a judge, as governor of the Philippines, and as Roosevelt's secretary of war. In fact, he seemed an acceptable successor to almost everyone.

★ An American Story ★

One evening in January 1908, President Theodore Roosevelt sat chatting with Secretary of War William Howard Taft and his wife, Nellie, in the second-floor White House library. The mood was relaxed. Seated comfortably in his easy chair, Roosevelt was talking about a subject he had often discussed with his guests: the future role of Taft. Roosevelt toyed with a couple of options. "At one time it looks like the presidency," he mused, considering a future role for his trusted lieutenant, "then again it looks like the chief justiceship."

The Tafts knew that Roosevelt had the power to bring about either of these options. "Make it the presidency," interrupted Nellie Taft, always ambitious about her husband's career. Taft himself was less convinced that he would make a good chief executive. "Make it the chief justiceship," he uttered.

In the end, Taft bowed to the wishes of his wife and boss. Following George Washington's example and honoring his own promise of 1904, Roosevelt decided not to seek reelection in 1908. Instead, he endorsed an experienced administrator and moderate progressive to run for president on the Republican ticket: William Howard Taft.

—adapted from *The American Heritage Pictorial History of the Presidents of the United States*

Thanks to Roosevelt's efforts, Taft easily received his party's nomination for the 1908 election. The Democratic candidate, twice-defeated William Jennings Bryan, lost once more.

Taft's Approach to Government "My dear Theodore," Taft wrote to his old friend a couple of weeks after assuming office. "When I am addressed as 'Mr. President,' I turn to see whether you are at my elbow." The comment was telling.

In that same letter, Taft admitted some of his early fears about his presidency:

> ❝I have no doubt that when you return you will find me very much under suspicion. . . . I have not the prestige which you had. . . . I am not attempting quite as much as you did . . . and so I fear that a large part of the public will feel as if I had fallen away from your ideals; but you know me better and will understand that I am still working away on the same old plan.❞
>
> —quoted in *The American Heritage Pictorial History of the Presidents of the United States*

Roosevelt and Taft were very different people. Roosevelt was a **dynamic** person who loved the spotlight and the rough-and-tumble world of politics. He had grand ideas and **schemes** but left the details of administering them to others. Taft was the opposite in many ways. He was a skillful administrator and judge. He disliked political maneuvering and preferred to avoid conflict with others. Unlike Roosevelt, who acted quickly and decisively on issues, Taft responded slowly, approaching problems from a legalistic point of view. "I don't like politics," he wrote, "I don't like the limelight." Although committed to many progressive ideas, Taft's personality and approach to politics quickly brought him into conflict with progressives.

William Howard Taft ▼

CHAPTER 5 The Progressive Movement **349**

More Skill Practice

Visual/Spatial Instruct students to take two sheets of paper and write "President Roosevelt" in the center of one and "President Taft" in the center of the other. Around each name have students write words that describe each president's leadership style or personality. Circle any traits that both men have in common. [OL]

TEACH

R₁ Reading Strategy

Using Context Clues Roosevelt called Taft a leader who possessed "a hearty sympathy for the oppressed." **Ask: What does it mean to be oppressed?** *(kept down by cruel or unjust use of power; burdened)* **Are there any oppressed people in our society?** *(Students' answers will vary.)* [OL] [CA 11RC2.5]

R₂ Reading Strategy

Organizing Information Provide the data below and ask students to make a pair of circle graphs showing the results of the presidential election of 1908.

Candidate	Popular Vote	Electoral Vote
Taft, Rep.	7,675,320	321
Bryan, Dem.	6,412,294	162

[BL]

W Writing Support

Narrative Writing Have students imagine they are President Taft's speech writer and then write his Inaugural Address. The speech should contain the goals of Taft's presidency. *(Students' papers will vary but should reflect Taft's progressive ideals.)* [OL] [CA 11WS1.1]

Review the Big Idea

Review the Big Idea for this section, "Social and economic crises lead to new roles for government." Have students identify the policies that President Taft followed during his presidency. **Ask: How did his policies show that Taft was a progressive?** *(Students should mention antitrust suits, the Children's Bureau, and conservation.)* [OL]

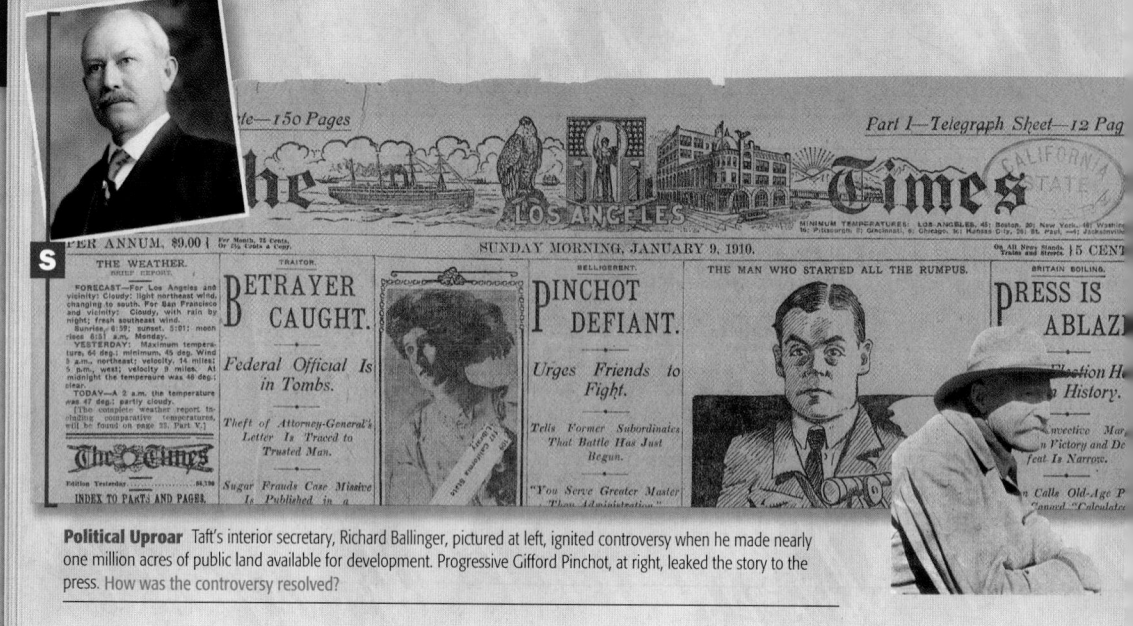

Political Uproar Taft's interior secretary, Richard Ballinger, pictured at left, ignited controversy when he made nearly one million acres of public land available for development. Progressive Gifford Pinchot, at right, leaked the story to the press. How was the controversy resolved?

The Payne-Aldrich Tariff Act Like many progressives, Taft believed high tariffs limited competition, hurt consumers, and protected trusts. Roosevelt had warned him to stay away from tariff reform because it would divide the Republican Party. Taft, however, went ahead and called Congress into special session to lower tariff rates.

To pass a new tariff, Taft needed the help of Speaker of the House **Joseph G. Cannon.** As Speaker, Cannon appointed all committees and decided which bills they handled. By exercising almost total control over debate, Cannon could push some bills through without discussion and see that others never came to a vote. Progressives wanted to unseat Cannon because he often blocked their legislation.

Taft disagreed with the effort to unseat Cannon. He pressured progressive Republicans into stopping their campaign against Cannon. In exchange, Cannon quickly pushed the tariff bill through the House of Representatives. Taft's compromise angered many progressives. The following year, they defied the president by joining with House Democrats and removing Cannon from power.

Taft further alienated progressives when the tariff bill went to the Senate. The powerful head of the Senate Finance Committee, Republican Nelson Aldrich from Rhode Island, wanted to protect high tariffs, as did many other conservative senators. The result was the **Payne-Aldrich Tariff,** which cut tariffs hardly at all and actually raised them on some goods. After discussions with Aldrich and other senators,

however, Taft decided to accept the new tariff. Progressives felt betrayed and outraged by Taft's decision: "I knew the fire had gone out of [the Progressive movement]," recalled chief forester Gifford Pinchot after Roosevelt left office. "Washington was a dead town. Its leader was gone, and in his place [was] a man whose fundamental desire was to keep out of trouble."

The Ballinger-Pinchot Controversy With Taft's standing among Republican progressives deteriorating, a sensational controversy broke in 1909 helping destroy Taft's popularity with reformers for good. Many progressives had been unhappy when Taft replaced Roosevelt's secretary of the interior, James R. Garfield, an aggressive conservationist, with **Richard A. Ballinger,** a more conservative corporate lawyer. Suspicion of Ballinger grew when he tried to make nearly a million acres of public forests and mineral reserves available for private development.

During this mounting concern, Gifford Pinchot charged the new secretary with having once plotted to turn over valuable public lands in Alaska to a private **syndicate,** or business group, for personal profit. Pinchot took the charges to the president. Taft's attorney general found the charges were groundless.

Still not satisfied, Pinchot leaked the story to the press and asked Congress to investigate. Taft fired Pinchot for **insubordination,** or disobedience. The congressional committee appointed to study the controversy cleared Ballinger.

350 CHAPTER 5 The Progressive Movement

By signing the Payne-Aldrich Tariff Act, supporting Ballinger against Pinchot, and backing Cannon, Taft gave the impression that he had "sold the Square Deal down the river." Popular indignation was so great that the congressional elections of 1910 resulted in a sweeping Democratic victory, with Democrats taking the majority in the House and Democrats and Progressive Republicans grabbing control of the Senate from the conservatives.

✓ **Reading Check** **Summarizing** What problems did President Taft have with progressives on tariff issues?

Taft's Progressive Reforms

 Main Idea **Taft worked to pass progressive reforms.**

Reading Connection Do you know people who let others take credit and recognition for their work? Read on to learn about William Howard Taft's record as a progressive.

Despite his political problems, Taft also had several successes. Although Roosevelt was nicknamed the "trustbuster," Taft was a strong supporter of competition and actually brought twice as many antitrust cases in four years as his predecessor had in seven.

In other areas, too, Taft was at least as strong a progressive as Roosevelt. Taft **established** the Children's Bureau, a federal agency similar to Roosevelt's Bureau of Corporations. The Children's Bureau investigated and publicized problems with child labor. Taft also supported the Mann-Elkins Act of 1910, which increased the regulatory powers of the ICC.

The Ballinger-Pinchot controversy aside, Taft was also a dedicated conservationist. His contributions in this area actually equaled or surpassed those of Roosevelt. Taft set up the Bureau of Mines to monitor the activities of mining companies, expanded the national forests, and protected waterpower sites from private development.

Although disturbed by stories of Taft's "betrayal" of progressivism, Roosevelt at first refused to criticize the president. Then, in October 1911, Taft announced an antitrust lawsuit against U.S. Steel, claiming that the company's decision to buy the Tennessee Coal and Iron Company in 1907 had violated the Sherman Antitrust Act.

The lawsuit was the final straw for Roosevelt. As president, he had approved U.S. Steel's plan to buy the company. Roosevelt believed Taft's focus on breaking up trusts was destroying the carefully crafted system of cooperation and regulation that Roosevelt had established. In November 1911, Roosevelt publicly criticized Taft's decision. Roosevelt argued that the best way to deal with the trusts was to allow them to exist while at the same time increasing government's ability to regulate them.

Having broken with Taft, it was only a matter of time before progressives convinced Roosevelt to reenter politics. In late February 1912, Roosevelt announced that he would attempt to replace Taft as the 1912 Republican nominee for president.

✓ **Reading Check** **Evaluating** How did President Taft's accomplishments regarding conservation and trustbusting compare to President Roosevelt's?

 HISTORY Online **Study Central**
For help with the concepts in this section of *American Vision: Modern Times* go to tav.mt.glencoe.com and click on *Study Central.*

SECTION 3 ASSESSMENT

Checking for Understanding

1. **Vocabulary** Define: dynamic, schemes, syndicate, insubordination, established.
2. **People and Terms** Identify: Joseph G. Cannon, Payne-Aldrich Tariff, Richard Ballinger.
3. **Describe** how Taft helped conservation efforts, alleviated child labor problems, and strengthened the ICC.

Reviewing Big Ideas

4. **Examining** How did replacing Roosevelt's secretary of the interior cause a dispute between Taft and the progressives?

Critical Thinking

5. **Comparing** What was the difference between Roosevelt and Taft regarding the relationship between the president and Congress?
6. **Organizing** Use a graphic organizer like the one below to list Taft's Progressive reforms.

Taft's Progressive Reforms

Analyzing Visuals

7. **Examining Photographs** Study the photograph on page 350. Note the structure of the newspaper. How would you compare the layout of the newspaper in the photograph with the style of today's newspapers?

Writing About History

8. **Descriptive Writing** Write a magazine article in which you defend or criticize President Taft's administration in terms of its support of progressivism.
   CA 11WS1.1

CHAPTER 5 The Progressive Movement **351**

SECTION 3 ASSESSMENT ANSWERS

1. Content vocabulary is boldfaced and highlighted in yellow. Academic vocabulary is boldfaced.
2. Joseph G. Cannon (p. 350), Payne-Aldrich Tariff (p. 350), Richard Ballinger (p. 350)
3. expanded national forests, protected water sites, set up a commission to investigate child labor,

supported the Mann-Elkins Act
4. Garfield, an aggressive conservationist, was replaced by Ballinger, a conservative corporate lawyer.
5. Roosevelt came up with great ideas and left administration up to others while Taft preferred administration.
6. Children's Bureau, Mann-Elkins

Act, Bureau of Mines
7. The newspapers of today have color photos and print and focus on one major cover story. This newspaper has several stories on the cover to grab the readers' attention.
8. Students' articles should back up their defense or criticism with fact.

Visualizing Have students create posters that progressives might have carried to protest President Taft's policies and actions in office. **BL**

ASSESS

 Resources for page 351

Use these resources to assess student mastery.

📂 Section Quiz 5-3

📂 Reading Essentials and Study Guide 5-3

⊙ Interactive Tutor Self-Assessment CD-ROM

📂 California Standards Practice, Grade 11

✓ **Reading Check**

Answer: Taft alienated them when he did not veto the Payne-Aldrich Tariff, which hardly cut tariffs and actually raised a few.

✓ **Reading Check**

Answer: Taft equaled or surpassed Roosevelt's actions.

HISTORY Online

Study Central provides audio summaries, interactive games, and online graphic organizers to help students review section content.

CLOSE

Evaluating Discuss in class why progressives were unhappy with President Taft's support of progressive reforms. **OL**

351

FOCUS

SKILLBUILDER ACTIVITY

Project **Daily Focus Skills Transparency 5-4** and have students answer the question.

Guide to Reading

Understanding Vocabulary:
Have students write the content vocabulary and academic vocabulary words on index cards. On the back of each card have students write words or concepts that define the word.

Answers to Graphic:
Economic: Federal Reserve Act, Antitrust Act, Underwood Tariff, Federal Trade Commission; Social: Keating-Owen Child Labor Act, Adamson Act

Unpacking the Standards

Students will be able to:

- Explain how President Wilson continued progressive reform efforts in the areas of tariffs and antitrust legislation.
- Research the establishment of the Federal Reserve System.
- Discuss the limits of progressive reforms.

Answers and Additional Support

SECTION 4 The Wilson Years

Guide to Reading

Connection
In the previous section, you learned about President Taft's reforms and the growing conflict within the Progressive movement. In this section, you will discover how Woodrow Wilson won the presidency and learn about the reforms he continued.

Main Idea
- Woodrow Wilson's "New Freedom" campaign won him the White House after Republican voters split over Taft and Roosevelt. (p. 353)
- President Wilson reformed tariffs and banks and oversaw the creation of the Federal Trade Commission. (p. 354)

- Wilson continued to support progressive reforms as he faced reelection in 1916. (p. 356)
- Progressivism changed the view many people had about the government's role in social issues. (p. 357)

Content Vocabulary
income tax, unfair trade practices

Academic Vocabulary
capacity, levying, labor, foundation

People and Terms to Identify
Progressive Party, New Nationalism, New Freedom, Federal Trade Commission, National Association for the Advancement of Colored People

Reading Objectives
- **Describe** Wilson's economic and social reforms.
- **Evaluate** the legacy of the Progressive movement.

Reading Strategy
Categorizing As you read about progressivism during the Wilson administration, complete a chart similar to the one below by listing Wilson's Progressive economic and social reforms.

Economic Reforms	Social Reforms

Preview of Events

♦1912		♦1914		♦1916

1912
Woodrow Wilson elected president

1913
Federal Reserve Act passed

1914
Federal Trade Commission Act passed

1916
Keating-Owen Child Labor Act passed

The following are the main History–Social Science Standards covered in this section.

11.2 Students analyze the relationship among the rise of industrialization, large-scale rural-to-urban migration, and massive immigration from Southern and Eastern Europe.

11.2.1 Know the effects of industrialization on living and working conditions, including the portrayal of working conditions and food safety in Upton Sinclair's *The Jungle.*

11.2.9 Understand the effect of political programs and activities of the Progressives (e.g., federal regulation of railroad transport, Children's Bureau, the Sixteenth Amendment, Theodore Roosevelt, Hiram Johnson).

❧ The Big Idea ❧

Social and economic crises lead to new roles for government. President Wilson supported progressivism and successfully worked to lower tariffs, reform banks, establish the eight-hour workday, and pass the Federal Farm Loan Act. He was less successful, however, with child labor regulation. Progressives in Congress demanded antitrust action and established the Federal Trade Commission and the Clayton Antitrust Act. While the Progressive movement addressed many social problems, it did not focus on religious and racial issues. Still, those who were not native-born white males now had the hope and desire to take action. The public now expected the government to take an active role in regulating the economy and addressing social issues.

352 CHAPTER 5 The Progressive Movement

SECTION RESOURCES

📂 **Print Material**
- Reproducible Lesson Plan 5-4
- Guided Reading Activity 5-4
- Reading Essentials and Study Guide 5-4
- Active Reading Note-Taking Guide 5-4

🖵 **Transparencies**
- Daily Focus Skills Transparency 5-4
- Section Graphic Organizer Transparency 5-4

Technology
- ⊚ Interactive Tutor Self-Assessment CD-ROM
- ⊚ ExamView® Pro Testmaker CD-ROM
- ⊚ Presentation Plus! CD-ROM

The Election of 1912

Main Idea Woodrow Wilson's "New Freedom" campaign won him the White House after Republican voters split over Taft and Roosevelt.

Reading Connection What political slogans have you heard during campaigns for office or school elections? Read on to learn about the "New Freedom" and "New Nationalism" of the 1912 election.

The 1912 presidential campaign featured a current president, a former president, and an academic who had entered politics only two years earlier.

★ *An American Story* ★

On September 15, 1910, in the Taylor Opera House in Trenton, New Jersey, a young progressive named Joseph Patrick Tumulty watched as a lean man with iron-gray hair made his way toward the stage. The man was Thomas Woodrow Wilson, the Democratic Party's nominee for governor.

Wilson was the choice of the party bosses. As Tumulty recalled, progressives were "feeling sullen, beaten, and hopelessly impotent." To Tumulty's astonishment, Wilson announced: "I shall enter upon the duties of the office of governor, if elected, with absolutely no pledge of any kind to prevent me from serving the people of the state with singleness of purpose."

Tumulty knew that Wilson was declaring his independence from the New Jersey political machine. It brought the progressives at the convention roaring to their feet. From one came the cry, "Thank God, at last, a leader has come!"

Two years later, Woodrow Wilson was the Democrats' nominee for the presidency, an office they had won only twice since the Civil War. This time they were confident of victory, for Wilson, a committed progressive, faced a Republican Party wracked by division.

—adapted from *Wilson: The Road to the White House*

The election's outcome determined the path of the Progressive movement and helped shape the nation's path in the 1900s.

The Republican Party Splits Believing that President Taft had failed to live up to Progressive ideals, Theodore Roosevelt informed seven state governors that he was willing to accept the Republican nomination. "My hat is in the ring!" he declared. "The fight is on."

The struggle for control of the Republican Party reached its climax at the national convention in Chicago in June. Conservatives rallied behind Taft. Most of the progressives lined up for Roosevelt. When it became clear that Taft's delegates controlled the nomination, Roosevelt decided to leave the party and campaign as an independent. "We stand at Armageddon," he told his supporters, "and we battle for the Lord."

Declaring himself "fit as a bull moose," Roosevelt became the presidential candidate for the newly formed **Progressive Party,** nicknamed the Bull Moose Party. Because Taft had alienated so many groups, the election of 1912 became a contest between two progressives: the Bull Moose Roosevelt and the Democrat Wilson.

Wilson's Character and Background Woodrow Wilson entered politics as a firm progressive. As governor of New Jersey, he pushed one Progressive reform after another through the statehouse. He revamped election laws, established utility regulatory boards, and allowed cities to change to the commissioner form of government. In less than two years, New Jersey became a model of Progressive reform.

A Woodrow Wilson election poster ▼

FOR GOVERNOR

WOODROW WILSON

CHAPTER 5 The Progressive Movement **353**

TEACH

R **Reading Strategy**

Scaffolding—Academic Vocabulary The word *academic* was introduced in Chapter 2, Section 2. Ask a student to define the word. **BL**

C **Critical Thinking**

Making Inferences Remind students that Theodore Roosevelt's Bull Moose Party competed with President Taft's support in the Republican Party. **Ask:** Without a split in the Republican Party, do you think Woodrow Wilson still would have won the presidency? *(Students should give reasons to support their opinions. These opinions should be based upon information provided in the text.)* **AL**

S **Skill Practice**

Visual Literacy Instruct students to examine the portrait of Woodrow Wilson. **Ask:** What descriptive words come to mind about Wilson as you observe his dress and demeanor? *(Answers may include: formal, stern, intellectual, precise, purposeful, or determined.)* **BL**

Review the Big Idea

Review the Big Idea for this section, "Social and economic crises lead to new roles for government." As students read this section, have them note the policies President Wilson put into place in a graphic organizer similar to the one below. **BL**

Economy	
Welfare	

Did You Know?

Prior to the 1912 election, the last time either the Republican or Democratic party split because it was unable to decide on a single candidate was in the 1860 election that preceded the Civil War. The Democrats nominated a Northern and a Southern candidate. Abraham Lincoln won the election with less than forty percent of the total popular vote.

W Writing Support

Persuasive Writing Have students select either Roosevelt's "New Nationalism" or Taft's "New Freedom" and write a one-page paper defending the superiority and merits of the program. Then select the best-written paper on each program and have those students read their papers in class. Have the rest of the class vote on which paper gave the best argument for its program.
OL **CA** 11WA2.4a

R Reading Strategy

Skimming Have students glance at the text under the heading "Regulating the Economy." **Ask: About what key issues do you expect to learn?** (tariff reform, bank reform, and antitrust action) **BL**

✓ Reading Check

Answer: Theodore Roosevelt, William Howard Taft, and Woodrow Wilson

Answers and Additional Support

"New Freedom" Versus "New Nationalism"

The election of 1912 was a contest between two men who supported progressivism, although they had different approaches to reform. Roosevelt accepted the economic power of the trusts as a fact of life and proposed a more powerful federal government and a strong executive to regulate them. Roosevelt also outlined a complete program of reforms. He favored legislation to protect women and children in the labor force and supported workers' compensation for those injured on the job. He also wanted a federal trade commission to regulate industry in a manner similar to the ICC's authority over railroads. Roosevelt called his program the **New Nationalism.**

Wilson countered with what he called the **New Freedom.** He criticized Roosevelt's program as one that supported "regulated monopoly." Monopolies, he believed, were evils to be destroyed, not regulated. Wilson argued that Roosevelt's approach gave the federal government too much power in the economy. "The history of liberty," Wilson declared, "is the history of the limitation of governmental power. . . . If America is not to have free enterprise, then she can have freedom of no sort whatever."

Wilson Is Elected As expected, Roosevelt and Taft split the Republican voters, enabling Wilson to win

Picturing **History**

The New Freedom Woodrow Wilson initially believed that government should break up trusts. Why did Wilson favor economic competition?

the Electoral College and the election with 435 votes, even though he received less than 42 percent of the popular vote—less than Roosevelt and Taft combined. For the first time since Grover Cleveland's election in 1892, a Democrat became president of the United States.

✓ Reading Check **Summarizing** Who were the three major candidates in the presidential election of 1912?

Regulating the Economy

Main Idea President Wilson reformed tariffs and banks and oversaw the creation of the Federal Trade Commission.

Reading Connection Are you aware of recent economic concerns and presidential responses to them? Read on to learn the ways that Woodrow Wilson took economic action after his election.

The new chief executive lost no time in embarking on his program of reform. He immediately took charge of the government. "The president is at liberty, both in law and conscience, to be as big a man as he can," Wilson had once written. "His **capacity** will set the limit." During his eight years as president, Wilson demonstrated his power as he crafted reforms affecting tariffs, the banking system, trusts, and workers' rights.

Reforming Tariffs Five weeks after taking office, Wilson appeared before Congress, the first president to do so since John Adams. He had come to present his bill to reduce tariffs.

He personally lobbied members of Congress to support the tariff reduction bill. Not even Roosevelt had taken such an active role in promoting special legislation. In Wilson's message to Congress, he declared that high tariffs had "built up a set of privileges and exemptions from competition behind which it was easy . . . to organize monopoly until . . . nothing is obliged to stand the tests of efficiency and economy."

Wilson believed that the pressure of foreign competition would lead American manufacturers to improve their products and lower their prices. Lower tariff rates, he claimed, would help businesses by putting them under the "constant necessity to be efficient, economical, and enterprising."

In 1913 the Democrat-controlled Congress passed the Underwood Tariff and Wilson signed it into law. This piece of legislation reduced the average tariff on

Picturing **History**

Answer: He believed economic freedom was more important than efficiency.
Ask: Of what state was Wilson governor?
(New Jersey)

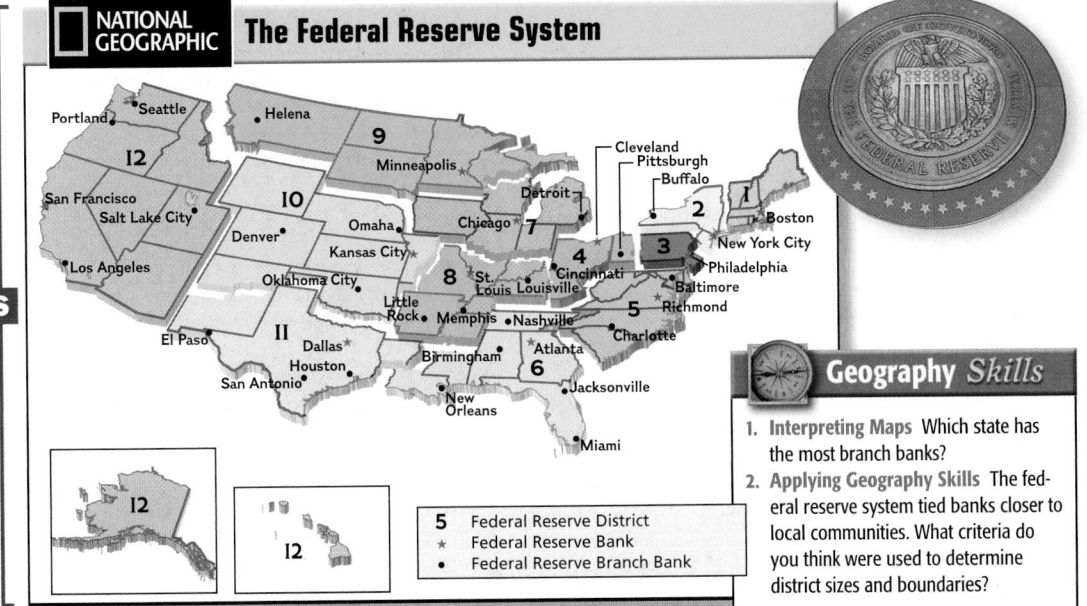

NATIONAL GEOGRAPHIC — The Federal Reserve System

Geography Skills

1. **Interpreting Maps** Which state has the most branch banks?
2. **Applying Geography Skills** The federal reserve system tied banks closer to local communities. What criteria do you think were used to determine district sizes and boundaries?

Legend:
- **5** Federal Reserve District
- ★ Federal Reserve Bank
- • Federal Reserve Branch Bank

S Skill Practice

Visual Literacy Instruct students to study the map and then to identify in which cities the Federal Reserve banks are located. **Ask: What do these cities have in common?** (*larger metropolitan areas with greater populations*)
OL   CA CS3

C Critical Thinking

Making Inferences The introduction of an individualized income tax created an important source of revenue for the federal government. **Ask: In what ways could the federal government utilize funds raised by an income tax on individual earnings?** (*Answers could include salaries of government officials, funding of government programs, maintenance of federal buildings, or federal litigation.*) OL

W Writing Support

Research Report Writing Have students write a report on the establishment of the Federal Reserve System and its role in our banking system. Students may use the library or the Internet to gather resources. OL
CA 11WA2.4

U Universal Access

English Learners Bring a property trading game to class. Display the board and explain the basic rules if necessary. Then assign each student a partner, making sure that English learners are paired with someone who is strong in subject matter. Have each pair present a lesson based on the game. For example, students might purchase all the railroads to explain what trusts were, how they operated in this era, and how the president tried to prevent them. EL

imported goods to about 30 percent of the value of the goods, or about half the tariff rate of the 1890s.

An important section of the Underwood Tariff Act was the provision for **levying** an **income tax,** or a direct tax on the earnings of individuals and corporations. The Constitution originally prohibited direct taxes unless they were apportioned among the states on the basis of population. In other words, the states would pay the income tax, not individuals, and states with more people would pay more tax. Passage of the Sixteenth Amendment in 1913, however, made it legal for the federal government to tax the income of individuals directly. This system remains in place today.

Reforming the Banks The United States had not had a central bank since the 1830s. During the economic depressions that hit the country periodically after that time, hundreds of small banks collapsed, wiping out the life savings of many of their customers. The most recent of these crises had been in 1907.

To restore public confidence in the banking system, Wilson supported the establishment of a Federal Reserve system. Banks would have to keep a portion of their deposits in a regional reserve bank, which would provide a financial cushion against unanticipated losses.

At the center of the Federal Reserve system would be a Board of Governors, appointed by the president. The Board could set the interest rates the reserve banks charged other banks, thereby indirectly con-

trolling the interest rates of the entire nation and the amount of money in circulation. This gave the Board the ability to fight inflation by raising interest rates and to stimulate the economy during a recession by lowering interest rates. Congress approved the new system at the end of 1913. The Federal Reserve Act became one of the most significant pieces of legislation in American history.

Antitrust Action During his campaign, Wilson had promised to restore competition to the economy by breaking up big business monopolies. Roosevelt argued that Wilson's ideas were unrealistic because big business was more efficient and unlikely to be replaced by smaller, more competitive firms. Once in office, Wilson's opinion shifted, and he came to agree with Roosevelt—but progressives in Congress continued to demand action against big business.

In the summer of 1914, at Wilson's request, Congress created the **Federal Trade Commission** (FTC) to monitor American business. The FTC had the power to investigate companies and issue "cease and desist" orders against companies engaging in **unfair trade practices,** or those which hurt competition. The FTC could be taken to court if a business disagreed with its rulings.

Wilson did not want the FTC to break up big business. Instead, it was to work with business to limit activities that unfairly limited competition. He deliberately appointed conservative business leaders to serve as the FTC's first commissioners.

CHAPTER 5 The Progressive Movement **355**

Geography Skills

Answers:
1. Texas
2. Students' answers will vary but may include population density and size of a region's economy.

Geography Skills Practice
Ask: What is the role of the Board of Governors? (*This body sets the branch interest rates, thereby adjusting the amount of money that is circulating nationally.*)

Progressives in Congress responded by passing the Clayton Antitrust Act. The act banned tying agreements, which required retailers who bought from one company to stop selling a competitor's products. It also banned price discrimination, and manufacturers could no longer give wholesale discounts to chain stores and other retailers.

Before the act passed, labor unions lobbied Congress to exempt unions from the antitrust laws. The Clayton Antitrust Act specifically declared that unions were not unlawful combinations in restraint of trade. When the bill became law, Samuel Gompers, head of the American Federation of Labor, called the Clayton Antitrust Act the worker's "Magna Carta," because it gave unions the right to exist.

Reading Check **Evaluating** What was the impact of the passage of the Sixteenth Amendment?

Federal Aid and Social Welfare

Main Idea Wilson continued to support progressive reforms as he faced reelection in 1916.

Reading Connection What strategies did previous presidents use to secure their reelection? Read on to discover President Wilson's actions as he tried to win voters.

By the fall of 1914, Wilson believed that his New Freedom program was essentially complete. As a result, he began to retreat from activism.

The congressional elections of 1914, however, shattered the president's complacency. Democrats suffered major losses in the House of Representatives, and voters who had supported the Bull Moose Party in 1912 began returning to the Republicans. Realizing that he would not be able to rely on a divided opposition when he ran for reelection in 1916, Wilson began to support further reforms.

In 1916, for example, Wilson signed the first federal law regulating child **labor.** The Keating-Owen Child Labor Act prohibited the employment of children under the age of 14 in factories producing goods for interstate commerce. The Supreme Court declared the law unconstitutional on the grounds that child labor was not interstate commerce and therefore only states could regulate it. Wilson's effort, however, helped his reputation with progressive voters.

Two other acts Wilson supported were the Adamson Act and the Federal Farm Loan Act. The Adamson Act established the eight-hour workday for railroad workers and provided for additional compensation for any time worked over eight hours. The Federal Farm Loan Act created 12 Federal Land Banks to provide farmers with long-term loans at low interest rates. Farmers were able to borrow up to 50 percent of the value of their land. The act enabled small farmers to be more competitive with larger farms and businesses. Both acts were passed by Congress in 1916.

Reading Check **Examining** How did the Adamson Act improve labor conditions in the United States?

Picturing **History**

Factory Girls
The young girls pictured in this photo are knitters in a hosiery factory. The young girl in front must stand on a stool to see what she is knitting. Factory jobs were often dangerous and required long, tiring hours. Why did the Supreme Court find the Keating-Owens law unconstitutional?

The Legacy of Progressivism

Main Idea Progressivism changed the view many people had about the government's role in social issues.

Reading Connection Do you believe that groups of people have been left out of "the American dream"? Read on to find out about the failures and successes of progressivism.

During his presidency, Wilson had built upon Roosevelt's **foundation**. He expanded the role of the federal government and of the president.

A New Kind of Government Progressivism made important political changes in the United States. Most Americans did not expect the government to pass laws protecting workers or regulating big business. In fact, many courts had previously ruled that it was unconstitutional for the government to do so.

By the end of the Progressive era, however, both legal and public opinion had shifted. Increasingly, Americans expected the government, particularly the federal government, to play a more active role in regulating the economy and solving social problems.

The Limits of Progressivism The most conspicuous limit to progressivism was its failure to address African American and religious issues. African Americans themselves were absorbing the reform spirit, fueling their desire for advancement.

In 1905 W.E.B. Du Bois and 28 other African American leaders met at Niagara Falls to demand full political rights for African Americans. They met on the Canadian side because no hotel on the American side would accept them. There they launched the Niagara Movement. This meeting was one of many steps leading to the founding of the **National Association for the Advancement of Colored People** (NAACP) in 1909. Du Bois and other NAACP founders believed that the vote was essential to bring about an end to lynching and racial discrimination. "The power of the ballot we need in sheer self-defense," Du Bois said, "else what shall save us from a second slavery?"

Progressivism also did not address anti-Semitism. Lawyer Sigmund Livingston founded the Anti-Defamation League (ADL) in 1913 to fight for civil liberties for Jews and to protect Jews against discrimination in housing, employment, education.

Despite the failure of most progressives to focus on racial and religious issues, Progressive reform helped change American society. Although many groups were excluded, the progressives expanded democracy and improved the quality of life for millions. As the country entered World War I, however, Americans soon turned from reforming their own society to a crusade to "make the world safe for democracy."

✓ **Reading Check** **Evaluating** How did progressivism change American beliefs about the federal government?

HISTORY Online **Study Central**
For help with the concepts in this section of *American Vision: Modern Times* go to tav.mt.glencoe.com and click on *Study Central*.

SECTION 4 ASSESSMENT

Checking for Understanding
1. **Vocabulary** Define: capacity, levying, income tax, unfair trade practices, labor, foundation.
2. **People and Terms** Identify: Progressive Party, New Nationalism, New Freedom, Federal Trade Commission, National Association for the Advancement of Colored People.
3. **Explain** why President Wilson proposed the establishment of the Federal Reserve System.

Reviewing Big Ideas
4. **Identifying** What new federal agencies increased the government's power to regulate the economy?

Critical Thinking
5. **Analyzing** Which of Wilson's reforms do you consider most important? Why?
6. **Organizing** Use a graphic organizer similar to the one below to list the effects progressivism had on American society.

Effects of Progressivism

Analyzing Visuals
7. **Analyzing Photographs** Study the photograph on page 356. What details do you see in the image that might have contributed to the Keating-Owen Child Labor Act?

Writing About History
8. **Expository Writing** Imagine that you are a newspaper editor during the Wilson administration. Write an article on the shortcomings of the Progressive movement in terms of racial issues. Provide ideas about how the movement might have addressed discrimination and segregation. **CA 11WS1.1**

SECTION 4 ASSESSMENT ANSWERS

1. Content vocabulary is boldfaced and highlighted in yellow. Academic vocabulary is boldfaced.
2. Progressive Party (p. 353), New Nationalism (p. 354), New Freedom (p. 354), Federal Trade Commission (p. 355), National Association for the Advancement of Colored People (p. 357)
3. to restore public confidence in the banking system
4. the Federal Reserve System and the Federal Trade Commission
5. Students' answers will vary but should include a reasonable argument.
6. expanded democracy, improved quality of life, expanded government role
7. Small children are operating dangerous equipment.
8. Students' editorials will vary. Students should point out specific shortcomings and suggest ways that the progressives could have addressed the social problem.

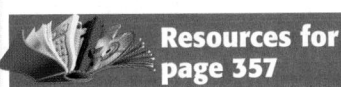

S Skill Practice
Historical Interpretation
Instruct students to create a database of Presidents Roosevelt, Taft, and Wilson. Have them list the progressive policies each president initiated while in office. Then have students write a paragraph identifying which president they feel made the greatest contribution to progressivism and why.
OL **CA HI1**

ASSESS

Resources for page 357

Use these resources to assess student mastery.
- Section Quiz 5-4
- Reading Essentials and Study Guide 5-4
- Interactive Tutor Self-Assessment CD-ROM
- California Standards Practice, Grade 11

✓ **Reading Check**

Answer: expanded democracy and raised expectations of the federal government's role in the economy and society

HISTORY Online

Study Central provides audio summaries, interactive games, and online graphic organizers to help students review section content.

CLOSE

Drawing Conclusions Ask students to reread the paragraph on Wilson's character and background on page 353. Then have them write a one-page report that describes how Wilson carried his progressive ideas into the White House. **OL** **CA 11WA2.4**

357

FOCUS

Understanding Vocabulary

Before students begin reading,
point out that difficult or unfamiliar words are footnoted throughout the text.

TEACH

R Reading Strategy

**Identifying the Main Idea and
Supporting Details** Women
were able to organize into groups
that protested and fought for the
right to vote. **Ask: According to
Duniway, what was the basic
obstacle that made it difficult
for women to gain the right to
vote?** *(Women had to rely on
male legislators to change the
Constitution.)* **OL** **CA 11RC2.5**

Answers and Additional Support

Primary Sources
Eyewitness to History

*For most of the history of the United States, women did not have the right to vote. A man served
as the head of his household, and he voted as the representative of his family. As women
became more involved outside the home, they started to demand a voice in their government.
The battle became increasingly heated until women finally won the vote in 1920.*

Source 1:

*Abigail Scott Duniway became the
sole supporter of her six children after
her husband was disabled in an accident. She earned a living as a writer
and led the fight for woman suffrage
in Oregon. In 1899 she gave a speech
promoting women's right to vote
before the annual meeting of the
National American Woman Suffrage
Association in Michigan.*

▲ *Abigail Scott Duniway*

The first fact to be considered,
when working to win the ballot, is
that there is but one way by which
we may hope to obtain it, and that is
by and through the affirmative votes of men. We may
theorize, organize, appeal, argue, coax, **cajole**[1] and
threaten men till doomsday; we may secure their pettings, praises, flattery, and every appearance of **acquiescence**[2] in our demands; we may believe with all our
hearts in the sincerity of their promises to vote as we
dictate, but all of this will avail us nothing unless they
deposit their affirmative votes in the ballot box.

Every man who stops to argue the case, as an
opponent, tells us that he "loves women," and, while
wondering much that he should consider such a declaration necessary, I have always admired the loyal
spirit that prompts his utterance. But, gentlemen, . . .
there is another side to this expression of loyalty.
Not only is our movement not instigated in a spirit
of warfare between the sexes, but it is engendered,
altogether in the spirit of harmony, and interdependence between men and women. . . . In order

to gain the votes of men, so we
can win the ballot, we must show
them that we are inspired by the
same patriotic motives that induce
them to prize it. A home without a
man in it, is only half a home. A
government without women in it,
is only half a government. . . .

. . . Your next step must be to
impress upon all men the fact that
we are not intending to interfere,
in any way, with their rights; and all
we ask is to be allowed to decide,
for ourselves, also as to what our
rights should be.

Source 2:

*Mrs. Arthur M. Dodge, a widow and the mother of six sons,
led the National Association Opposed to Woman Suffrage.
She believed that allowing women to vote would threaten
the family. In 1913 she explained her views to a reporter for
the New York Times.*

That is a sad state of things, isn't it? Home has been
the woman's business and her love and life for centuries. It is the foundation of society, the basis of all
morals. Without the home we should become unmoral
and without morals society, in turn, must perish. . . .

To offset the suspicion in the public mind that suffrage means destruction to the home, the leaders of
the movement are now bending every effort to prove
otherwise. Watch the newspapers and periodicals of
recent days and those of days immediately to come
and you will find a flood of pictures showing suffrage
leaders with their progressive cheeks pressed tight
against the velvet faces of their babies. They doubtless
have decided that this variation of the plan of their

[1]**cajole:** persuade
[2]**acquiescence:** passive acceptance

UNIVERSAL ACCESS

Visual/Spatial Suffragists often carried signs supporting their cause during protests. Have
students create slogans that could be used on a sign for woman suffrage. The class should
use library and Internet resources to find pictures of actual suffrage slogans and use them
as examples to design slogans of their own. Tell each student to create two slogans and ask
students to discuss their slogans with the class. **BL**

publicity is necessary as a means of proving to the public that a suffragist can be a mother. . . .

I don't want to seem discourteous toward my sisters in the suffrage movement. I believe the greater portion of them are not really aware of what they do. I am certain the majority of them do not desire to bring about destruction of the home, with all that must imply—of loose or no domestic life; . . .

I am no advocate of **retrogression**[3] among women. I believe in education, culture, full development. In these days woman, to do the best which in her lies for her own home, must get much for it from outside. My point is that she must get these outside things for the benefit of her home and not neglect her home so that she may go adventuring for them for her benefit, amusement, and dissipation.

Source 3:

After women's contributions helped the United States gain victory in World War I, President Woodrow Wilson became a supporter of woman suffrage. On September 30, 1918, he presented his views to the U.S. Senate.

I regard the concurrence of the Senate in the constitutional amendment proposing the extension of the suffrage to women as vitally essential to the successful **prosecution**[4] of the great war of humanity in which we are engaged. . . .

. . . If we be indeed democrats and wish to lead the world to democracy, we can ask other peoples to accept in proof of our sincerity and our ability to lead them whither they wish to be led, nothing less persuasive and convincing than our actions. . . .

If we reject measures like this, in ignorant defiance of what a new age has brought forth, of what they have seen but we have not, they will cease to believe in us; they will cease to follow or to trust us. They have seen their own governments . . . like that of Great Britain, which did not profess to be democratic, promise readily and as of course this justice to women, though they had before refused it; the strange revelations of this war having made many things new and plain to governments as well as to peoples.

Are we alone to refuse to learn the lesson? Are we alone to ask and take the utmost that our women can give—service and sacrifice of every kind—and still say we do not see what title that gives them to stand by our

[3]**retrogression:** regression, returning to a less complex level of development
[4]**prosecution:** pursuit

▲ *President Wilson addresses Congress*

side in the guidance of the affairs of their nation and ours? We have made partners of the women in this war. Shall we admit them only to a partnership of suffering and sacrifice and toil and not to a partnership of privilege and right? This war could not have been fought, either by the other nations engaged or by America, if it had not been for the services of the women—services rendered in every sphere—not merely in the fields of effort in which we have been accustomed to see them work, but wherever men have worked and upon the very skirts and edges of the battle itself. . . .

. . . The tasks of the women lie at the very heart of the war and I know how much stronger that heart will beat if you do this just thing and show our women that you trust them as much as you in fact and of necessity depend upon them. . . .

DBQ Document-Based Questions

Historical Analysis CA HR4; HI1; HI3

Source 1: Why does Duniway believe that women should be allowed to vote?

Source 2: What does Dodge believe will happen if women are allowed to vote?

Source 3: Why does Wilson believe that it is important for the United States to extend the right to vote to women?

Comparing and Contrasting Sources

How do Duniway, Dodge, and Wilson differ in their beliefs about the place of women in government?

R Reading Strategy

Summarizing Point out to students that not all women were in favor of gaining the right to vote in the early twentieth century, as the document from Mrs. Arthur M. Dodge illustrates. **Ask: How would you describe Mrs. Dodge's view about the proper role of women?** *(A woman's primary responsibility is to take care of the home. Women should be educated and involve themselves in society, but these things should not detract from their responsibilities at home.)* BL
CA 11RC2.5

W Writing Support

Persuasive Writing Ask students to read President Wilson's speech to Congress. Imagine that you are trying to convince someone to support woman suffrage in 1918. Write a paragraph detailing the points you would make to persuade the other person to your point of view. OL
CA 11WS1.3

ASSESS/CLOSE

Have students answer the Document-Based Questions.

DBQ Document-Based Questions

1. Women want to vote because they are inspired by patriotism. They love the country just as men do.
2. Woman suffrage will threaten the care of the home and family.
3. The United States must grant women the right to vote in order to solidify its position as a leader in the world. Women served the country during the war and are entitled to vote.

Comparing and Contrasting Sources: Duniway thinks that women should be allowed to participate equally in government and define their own rights. Dodge believes that motherhood is the highest honor for women, not participation in government. Wilson argues that women have earned the right to vote and participate in politics due to their war service.

Resources for pages 360–361

Use the following resources to review, assess, and reteach the chapter.

📁 Chapter 5 Tests, Forms A and B

📁 Standardized Tests, Forms A and B

📁 Cumulative Authentic Assessment

📱 MindJogger Videoquiz

💿 Interactive Tutor Self-Assessment CD-ROM

💿 Exam*View*® Pro Testmaker CD-ROM

💿 Vocabulary PuzzleMaker CD-ROM

💿 Succeeding on . . .™ the California Standards: Grade 11 History–Social Science

📁 California Standards Practice, Grade 11

Reviewing Content Vocabulary

Students' answers will vary. The pages where the words appear in the text are shown in parentheses.

1. progressivism *(p. 327)* **2.** commission plan *(p. 329)* **3.** direct primary *(p. 330)* **4.** initiative *(p. 330)* **5.** referendum *(p. 330)* **6.** suffrage *(p. 330)* **7.** temperance *(p. 334)* **8.** prohibition *(p. 334)* **9.** socialism *(p. 335)* **10.** arbitration *(p. 342)* **11.** syndicate *(p. 350)* **12.** unfair trade practices *(p. 355)*

Reviewing Academic Vocabulary

Students' answers will vary. The pages where the words appear in the text are shown in parentheses.

13. legislation *(p. 330)* **14.** strategy *(p. 331)* **15.** funds *(p. 334)* **16.** advocate *(p. 334)* **17.** trigger *(p. 341)* **18.** issues *(p. 344)* **19.** environmental *(p. 344)* **20.** dynamic *(p. 349)* **21.** schemes *(p. 349)* **22.** establish *(p. 351)* **23.** capacity *(p. 354)* **24.** levying *(p. 355)* **25.** labor *(p. 356)* **26.** foundation *(p. 357)*

360

Reviewing Content Vocabulary

On a sheet of paper, use each of these terms in a sentence.

1. progressivism
2. commission plan
3. direct primary
4. initiative
5. referendum
6. suffrage
7. temperance
8. prohibition
9. socialism
10. arbitration
11. syndicate
12. unfair trade practices

Reviewing Academic Vocabulary

On a sheet of paper, use each of these terms in a sentence that reflects the term's meaning in the chapter.

13. legislation
14. strategy
15. funds
16. advocate
17. trigger
18. issues
19. environmental
20. dynamic
21. schemes
22. establish
23. capacity
24. levying
25. labor
26. foundation

Reviewing the Main Ideas

Section 1

27. What were the characteristics of the Progressive era?

Section 2

28. What was the goal of the Hepburn Act? Do you think the act was successful?

Section 3

29. List three ways President Taft alienated progressives.

Section 4

30. How did President Wilson attempt to reform the banking industry?

Critical Thinking

31. **Reading Skill** **Making Inferences** Review the text under the heading "Taft's Approach to Government" on page 349. What inference can you make concerning the political relationship between Presidents Taft and Roosevelt?

32. **Civics** How did Wisconsin governor Robert La Follette help to expand democracy in the United States?

33. **Organizing** Use a graphic organizer similar to the one below to list the economic, political, and social welfare reforms brought about during the Progressive era.

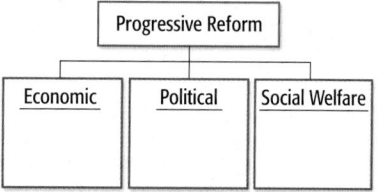

Chapter Summary

Basic Beliefs of Progressives

- People could improve society by relying on science and knowledge.
- Industrialism and urbanization caused problems.
- Government should fix problems.
- To achieve reform, government itself had to be reformed.

Government Reforms

- Commission and city-manager forms of government were adopted.
- Direct primary system let citizens choose office candidates.
- Initiative, referendum, and recall were adopted.
- Seventeenth Amendment gave voters right to elect senators directly.
- Nineteenth Amendment gave women the right to vote.

Business Regulation

- Interstate Commerce Commission was strengthened.
- Consumer protection laws were passed.
- Federal Trade Commission was set up to regulate business.
- Federal Reserve System was set up to control money supply.

Social Reforms

- Zoning laws and building codes improved urban housing.
- Child labor laws were passed.
- Workers' compensation laws were passed.
- Temperance movement worked to ban alcohol.

360 CHAPTER 5 The Progressive Movement

Reviewing the Main Ideas

27. belief that people could improve society, that government should play an active role in reform

28. The goal of the Hepburn Act was to strengthen the Interstate Commerce Commission (ICC). Students' answers will vary.

29. the Ballinger-Pinchot Controversy, the Payne-Aldrich Tariff Act, and by supporting Cannon

30. He set up the Federal Reserve System to control the circulation of money in the United States.

Critical Thinking

31. **Reading Skill** Students' answers will vary.

32. pressured the state legislature to require each party to hold a direct primary, weakening the party caucus system

33. Economic: Federal Reserve Act, Sherman Antitrust Act, Underwood Tariff, Hepburn Act, Mann-Elkins Act, Newlands Reclamation Act; Political: city government structure, Nineteenth Amendment, direct primaries, direct election of senators, initiative, referendum, and

Visit the *American Vision: Modern Times* Web site at tav.mt.glencoe.com and click on *Self-Check Quizzes—Chapter 5* to assess your knowledge of chapter content.

Writing About History

34. **Historical Analysis** **Interpreting Events** Reread the text under the heading "The Election of 1912" on pages 353–354. How was this contest different from previous presidential elections? Explain how the outcome might have been different if Roosevelt had not participated in the election. **CA HI4**

35. *Big Idea* Worker safety was an important issue for progressives. Research three worker safety laws in your state, and describe how they benefit workers.

DBQ **Document-Based Questions**

36. **Interpreting Primary Sources** Ida Husted Harper was a newspaper reporter, and a strong supporter of suffrage for women. In the following excerpt, she examines the attitudes toward the kinds of work women should do.

66 The moment we accept the theory that women must enter wage-earning occupations only when compelled to do so by poverty, that moment we degrade labor and lower the status of all women who are engaged in it. . . .

There is not, there never has been, an effort 'to create a sentiment that home is no place for a girl.' A good home is the one place above all others for a girl, as it is for a boy. It is her rest, her haven, her protection, but this does not necessarily imply that she must not engage in any work outside its limits. . . .

It is wholly impracticable to draw a dividing line between the employments which are suitable and those which are unsuitable for women. They have just as much right as men to decide this question for themselves. . . .

It is not intended to argue that every woman should leave the home and go into business, but only that those who wish to do so shall have the opportunity, and that men shall no longer monopolize the gainful occupations. 99

—quoted in *The Independent,* 1901

a. What views does Ida Harper have on the kinds of work women should do?

b. What kinds of work-related issues do women face today?

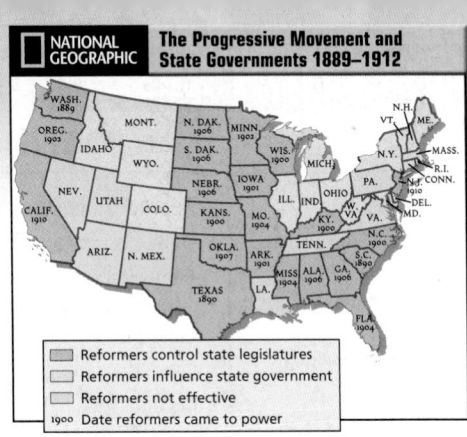

NATIONAL GEOGRAPHIC
The Progressive Movement and State Governments 1889–1912

Reformers control state legislatures
Reformers influence state government
Reformers not effective
1900 Date reformers came to power

Geography and History

37. The map above shows the relationship between the Progressive movement and state governments. Study the map and answer the questions below.
  a. **Interpreting Maps** Which three states came under the control of reformers before Wisconsin did?
  b. **Applying Geography Skills** What generalization can you make about progressives in state governments?

Standards Practice

Directions: Choose the best answer to the following question.

38. In 1920 women won an important victory when the Nineteenth Amendment was ratified. What did this amendment accomplish?

A It required colleges to accept women.

B It guaranteed child care for workers' children.

C It granted women the right to vote.

D It guaranteed equal wages for equal work.

Standard 11.5.4 Analyze the passage of the Nineteenth Amendment and the changing role of women in society.

Online

Have students visit the Web site at tav.mt.glencoe.com to review Chapter 5 and take the Self-Check Quiz.

DBQ **Document-Based Questions**

36. a. She believed women could work at the same jobs as men. **b.** Possible answers: lower wages, sexual harassment, discrimination, difficulty finding child care

Geography and History

37. a. Texas, Washington, and South Carolina **b.** Reformers were most active in the South, Great Plains, and Far West.

Standards Practice

38. C

Bonus Question?

Ask: What does the term *suffrage* mean? *(the right to vote)*

---

recall; Social Welfare: Keating-Owen Child Labor Act, Adamson Act, Meat Inspection Act, Pure Food and Drug Act

Writing About History

34. **Historical Analysis** The Republican Party split when Theodore Roosevelt formed the Progressive Party, and the election pitted two candidates with the same goals against one another. Without Roosevelt, Taft may have been reelected.

35. *Big Idea* Students should highlight the benefits of worker safety laws.

Chapter 6 Planning Guide

SECTION RESOURCES

MAIN IDEAS	📁 PRINT MATERIALS	TECHNOLOGY RESOURCES
Section 1: The United States Enters World War I 1. President Wilson promoted a moral approach to diplomacy in his attempts to bring democracy to Mexico. 2. Old alliances and nationalist sentiments among European nations set the stage for World War I. 3. British propaganda and business interests led most Americans to a pro-British stance on the war. 4. Despite efforts to stay officially neutral, the United States entered the war after German submarines destroyed American ships.	• Reproducible Lesson Plan 6-1* • Daily Lecture and Discussion Notes 6-1 • Active Reading Note-Taking Guide 6-1 • Guided Reading Activity 6-1 • Section Quiz 6-1 • Reading Essentials and Study Guide 6-1	📖 Daily Focus Skills Transparency 6-1 📖 Section Graphic Organizer Transparency 6-1 💿 Interactive Tutor Self-Assessment CD-ROM 💿 ExamView® Pro Testmaker CD-ROM 💿 Presentation Plus! CD-ROM 📖 California Standards Practice Transparencies
Section 2: The Home Front 1. The United States instituted a draft for military service, and African Americans and women took on new roles. 2. The government used Progressive ideas to manage the economy and pay for the war. 3. Women, African Americans, and Mexican Americans all helped to fill labor shortages created by the draft. 4. Propaganda and limits on civil liberties were part of domestic life during World War I.	• Reproducible Lesson Plan 6-2* • Daily Lecture and Discussion Notes 6-2 • Active Reading Note-Taking Guide 6-2 • Guided Reading Activity 6-2 • Section Quiz 6-2 • Reading Essentials and Study Guide 6-2	📖 Daily Focus Skills Transparency 6-2 📖 Section Graphic Organizer Transparency 6-2 💿 Interactive Tutor Self-Assessment CD-ROM 💿 ExamView® Pro Testmaker CD-ROM 💿 Presentation Plus! CD-ROM 📖 California Standards Practice Transparencies
Section 3: A Bloody Conflict 1. New technologies made World War I the first modern war. 2. American soldiers entered the war, boosting morale and fighting courageously. 3. The United States rejected Wilson's generous peace plan and the League of Nations.	• Reproducible Lesson Plan 6-3* • Daily Lecture and Discussion Notes 6-3 • Active Reading Note-Taking Guide 6-3 • Guided Reading Activity 6-3 • Section Quiz 6-3 • Reading Essentials and Study Guide 6-3	📖 Daily Focus Skills Transparency 6-3 📖 Section Graphic Organizer Transparency 6-3 💿 Interactive Tutor Self-Assessment CD-ROM 💿 ExamView® Pro Testmaker CD-ROM 💿 Presentation Plus! CD-ROM 📖 California Standards Practice Transparencies
Section 4: The War's Impact 1. After the war, when business tried to decrease wages and inflation lowered buying power, workers went on strike across the nation. 2. Race riots swept the nation as returning soldiers competed against African Americans for jobs and housing. 3. Fear of a Communist revolution caused a nationwide panic. 4. Warren G. Harding won the 1920 presidential election with the promise of a return to "normalcy."	• Reproducible Lesson Plan 6-4* • Daily Lecture and Discussion Notes 6-4 • Active Reading Note-Taking Guide 6-4 • Guided Reading Activity 6-4 • Section Quiz 6-4 • Reading Essentials and Study Guide 6-4	📖 Daily Focus Skills Transparency 6-4 📖 Section Graphic Organizer Transparency 6-4 💿 Interactive Tutor Self-Assessment CD-ROM 💿 ExamView® Pro Testmaker CD-ROM 💿 Presentation Plus! CD-ROM 📖 California Standards Practice Transparencies

PACING YOUR LESSONS

Chapter Introduction	Section 1	Section 2	Section 3	Section 4	Chapter Assessment
½ Day	2 Days	2 Days	2 Days	2 Days	½ Day

0:00 OUT OF TIME? 📁 Assign the Chapter 6 *Reading Essentials and Study Guide.*

*Available on TeacherWorks™ CD-ROM

Chapter 6 Planning Guide

Standards-Based Lesson Plan

 History–Social Science Standards Covered in Chapter 6

e standards covered in the chapter are listed below. Use the accompanying activity as you teach the chapter to ensure student astery of these standards. This activity can be used in combination with the program's print and technology assessment materials.

Standard	Section			
	1	2	3	4
1.4 Students trace the rise of the United States to its role as a world power in the twentieth century.	✔	✔	✔	✔
1.4.4 Explain Theodore Roosevelt's Big Stick diplomacy, William Taft's Dollar Diplomacy, and Woodrow Wilson's Moral Diplomacy, drawing on relevant speeches.	✔		✔	
1.4.5 Analyze the political, economic, and social ramifications of World War I on the home front.	✔	✔		✔

Cumulative Standards-Assessment Activity

e Cumulative Standards-Assessment Activity will help students organize and learn the important information from the chapter. gin teaching the chapter with this activity, and have students complete it as they read the chapter.

CREATING A CHART FOR ACTIVATING PRIOR KNOWLEDGE

Purpose By activating prior knowledge, students relate new content o information they already know. This process helps them set a urpose for their reading and exercises their ability to see connec-ions. Most students will benefit from this activity, but because it tarts with what is familiar, it may be of particular help to students who struggle with frustration, a feeling of being overwhelmed, or a ack of concentration.

ntroduction to Activating Prior Knowledge

1. Write on the board the topic of this chapter—World War I. Have the class brainstorm facts that they already know about this topic. Ask: How will the information you already know help you understand the new information? Then ask: What questions do you have about this topic?

2. Ask students to copy the chart to the right into their notebooks:

What I Know	What Questions I Have	What I Learned	How I Can Learn More

First, have students scan each section's headings and subhead-ings and develop a list of topics covered in the chapter. Ask them to create a chart for each of those topics. Before reading each section, they should complete the first two columns of the chart, identifying what they already know and what they would like to learn. As students read, they can complete the third column. Caution students to read carefully for any statements in the "What I Know" column that are not accurate. They should correct these statements.

3. As you review the chapter, ask volunteers to name some of the new information they acquired. Encourage the class to list resources in the fourth column of their charts that they might use to do further research on a topic.

Chapter 6 Planning Guide

READING SUPPORT

- Content Vocabulary Activity 6
- Academic Vocabulary Activity 6
- Reading Skills Activity 6
- Chapter 6 Active Reading Note-Taking Guide
- Chapter 6 Guided Reading Activities
- Chapter 6 Reading Essentials and Study Guide
- American Literature Readings, Unit 2
- *The American Vision: Modern Times* Video Program
- Vocabulary PuzzleMaker CD-ROM
- American History Primary Source Document Library CD-ROM

CRITICAL THINKING

- Critical Thinking Skills Activity 6
- Primary Source Reading 6
- Cause-and-Effect Transparency 6 Strategy and Activity
- Presentation Plus! CD-ROM

UNIVERSAL ACCESS

- Universal Access Activity 6
- English Learner Activity 6
- American Art Prints
- StudentWorks™ Plus CD-ROM
- American Music: Hits Through History
- School-to-Home Connection Activity 6

SKILL PRACTICE

- Map Overlay Transparency 6 Strategy and Activity
- Historical Analysis Skills Activity 6
- Time Line Activity 6
- Reading Skills Activity 6
- Reinforcing Skills Activity 6
- Linking Past and Present Activity 6
- Interpreting Political Cartoons 6
- MindJogger Videoquiz

WRITING SUPPORT

- Chapter 6 Active Reading Note-Taking Guide
- Writer's Guidebook
- High School Writing Process Transparencies

ASSESSMENT

- Chapter 6 Section Quizzes
- Chapter 6 Tests, Forms A and B
- Authentic Assessment Activity 6
- ExamView® Pro Testmaker CD-ROM
- Interactive Tutor Self-Assessment CD-ROM
- California Standards Practice, Grade 11
- Succeeding on . . .™ the California Standards: Grade 11 History–Social Science CD-ROM

- CD-ROM
- DVD
- Print Material
- Poster

- Transparency
- Music Program
- Videocassette

Chapter 6 Planning Guide

TECHNOLOGY

- StudentWorks™ Plus CD-ROM
- TeacherWorks™ CD-ROM
- ExamView® Pro Testmaker CD-ROM
- Interactive Tutor Self-Assessment CD-ROM
- Presentation Plus! CD-ROM
- Vocabulary PuzzleMaker CD-ROM
- American History Primary Source Document Library CD-ROM
- MindJogger Videoquiz
- *The American Vision: Modern Times* Video Program
- Professional Development in High School Social Studies Video Series
- Teach, Use, and Succeed With *The American Vision: Modern Times*
- American Music: Hits Through History
- Succeeding on . . .™ the California Standards: Grade 11 History–Social Science CD-ROM

SPANISH RESOURCES

- Spanish Activities and Assessment
  - Spanish Vocabulary Activities
  - Spanish Guided Reading Activities
  - Spanish Quizzes and Tests
  - Spanish Reteaching Activities
- Spanish Reading Essentials and Study Guide
- Spanish School-to-Home Connection Activities

TRANSPARENCIES

- Daily Focus Skills Transparencies
- Section Graphic Organizer Transparencies
- Map Overlay Transparencies
- Cause-and-Effect Transparencies
- Unit Time Line Transparencies
- Why It Matters Transparencies
- American Art and Architecture Transparencies
- High School Writing Process Transparencies
- California Standards Practice Transparencies

TEACHER PLANNING

- Daily Lecture and Discussion Notes
- English Learner Handbook
- Building Academic Vocabulary
- *The American Vision: Modern Times* Reading and Study Skills Foldables
- Reading Strategies and Activities for the Social Studies Classroom
- Universal Access for the American History Classroom
- NGS United States Desk Map
- NGS World Atlas
- Chapter 6 Reproducible Lesson Plans on TeacherWorks™ CD-ROM
- California Guide to Daily Intervention

PROFESSIONAL DEVELOPMENT

- Building Academic Vocabulary
- Strategies for Success
- Research-Based Strategies Used to Develop *The American Vision: Modern Times*
- Character Education in the High School Classroom
- Professional Development in High School Social Studies Video Series
- Teach, Use, and Succeed With *The American Vision: Modern Times*

MOMENTS IN TIME

The following resource can help you teach the content of this chapter.

- Unit 6 World War I (1914–1919)

Chapter 6 Planning Guide

TEACHER'S CORNER

Index to National Geographic Magazine:
The following articles relate to this chapter:

- "The Bolshevik Revolution," October 1992
- "Riddle of the *Lusitania*," April 1994
- "St. Petersburg, Capital of the Tsars," December 1993
- "The Wings of War," March 1994

National Geographic Society Products:
To order the following, call National Geographic at 1–800–368–2728

- *Historical Atlas of the United States* (Atlas)
- *1917: Revolution in Russia* (Video)
- *1914–1918: World War I* (Video)

NGS ONLINE

Access National Geographic's new dynamic MapMachine Web site and other geography resources at:

www.nationalgeographic.com

www.nationalgeographic.com/maps

History Online

Use our Web site for additional resources. All essential content is covered in the Student Edition.

You and your students can visit tav.mt.glencoe.com, the Web site companion to the **American Vision: Modern Times.** This innovative integration of electronic and print media offers your students a wealth of opportunities. The student text directs students to the Web site for the following options:

- **Chapter Overviews**
- **Self-Check Quizzes**
- **Student Web Activities**
- **Textbook Updates**

Answers to the student Web activities are provided for you in the **Web Activity Lesson Plans.** Additional Web resources and ePuzzles and games are also available.

MASTERING THE STANDARDS

The content and assessment in the Student Edition, Teacher Wraparound Edition, teacher planning materials, and the print and technology products are all standards-based. The use of these products during instruction leads to mastery of the standards.

PRACTICE
- California Standards Practice, Grade 11
- California Standards Practice Transparencies
- School-to-Home Connection

BENCHMARK ASSESSMENT
- Section Quizzes, Chapter Tests, and Authentic Assessment
- ExamView® Pro Testmaker CD-ROM
- Succeeding On ... ™ the California Standards: Grade 11 History–Social Science CD-ROM

REMEDIATION
- California Guide to Daily Intervention
- Interactive Tutor Self-Assessment CD-ROM
- ExamView® Pro Testmaker CD-ROM
- California Standards Practice, Grade 11
- Reading Essentials and Study Guide

FOLDABLES™ Study Organizer

Dinah Zike's Foldables

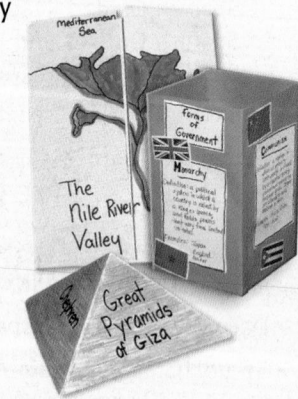

Foldables are three-dimensional, interactive graphic organizers that help students practice basic writing skills, review key vocabulary terms, and identify main ideas. Every chapter has a foldable activity in the *Dinah Zike's Reading and Study Skills Foldables* booklet. You can use the foldables as they are presented or modify them to suit the needs of your individual class.

A variety of videotape programs are available from A&E Television and The History Channel to provide teaching assistance. To order, call Glencoe at 1-800-334-7344.

Chapter 6 Planning Guide

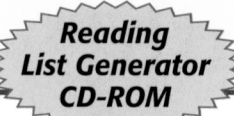
KEY for Using the Teacher Wraparound Edition

Use this key to help you identify the different types of prompts found in the Teacher Wraparound Edition.

R Reading Strategies activities help you teach reading skills and vocabulary.

C Critical Thinking strategies help students apply and extend what they have learned.

U Universal Access activities provide differentiated instruction for students learning to speak English, along with suggestions for teaching various types of learners.

S Skill Practice strategies help students practice historical analysis and geography skills.

W Writing Support activities provide writing opportunities to help students comprehend the text.

Teaching strategies and activities have been coded for ability level appropriateness.

AL Activities for students working above grade level
OL Activities for students working on grade level
BL Activities for students working below grade level
EL Activities for English learners

History–Social Science Standards

This chapter addresses the following standards:

11.4 Students trace the rise of the United States to its role as a world power in the twentieth century.

11.4.5 Analyze the political, economic, and social ramifications of World War I on the home front.

11.5 Students analyze the major political, social, economic, technological, and cultural developments of the 1920s.

11.5.2 Analyze the international and domestic events, interests, and philosophies that prompted attacks on civil liberties, including the Palmer Raids, Marcus Garvey's "back-to-Africa" movement, the Ku Klux Klan, and immigration quotas and the responses of organizations such as the American Civil Liberties Union, the National Association for the Advancement of Colored People, and the Anti-Defamation League to those attacks.

SKILLBUILDER ACTIVITY

Have students write down and save their responses. **Ask: How has the United States's involvement in World War I impacted our lives today?** After completing Chapter 6, have students evaluate their answers and add any additional information that they learned from the chapter.

TEACH

Thinking About the Big Ideas

As you begin teaching each section, use these questions and activities to focus on the Big Idea.

CHAPTER
6

1914–1920
World War I and Its Aftermath

❧ *The Big Ideas* ❧

SECTION 1: The United States Enters World War I

The fate of nations is forever changed by monumental world events. *Although the United States tried to remain neutral, events soon pushed the nation into World War I.*

SECTION 2: The Home Front

The fate of nations is forever changed by monumental world events. *To successfully fight the war, the United States had to mobilize the entire nation and citizens had to assume new roles and responsibilities.*

SECTION 3: A Bloody Conflict

The fate of nations is forever changed by monumental world events. *After four years of fighting, World War I ended in November of 1918.*

SECTION 4: The War's Impact

The fate of nations is forever changed by monumental world events. *As American society moved from war to peace, turmoil in the economy and fear of communism caused a series of domestic upheavals.*

The *American Vision: Modern Times* Video *The Chapter 6 video, "Cousins: Royalty and World War I," explains how royal marriages and complex political alliances contributed to the outbreak of war in Europe.*

United States PRESIDENTS

1913
• Woodrow Wilson begins his first presidential term

Wilson 1913–1921

1913

1915
• The *Lusitania* is sunk

1915

1917
• U.S. enters war

"The world must be made safe for Democracy!"
—*Woodrow Wilson*

1917

World

1914
• Archduke Franz Ferdinand assassinated; war begins in Europe

1915
• Italy joins Allies in war
• Japan gains rights in Chinese territory

1916
• British suppress Easter Rebellion in Ireland
• Battle of the Somme begins in July

1917
• Bolshevik Revolution begins in October
• Balfour Declaration favors setting up a Jewish homeland in Palestine

362

Section 1
The United States Enters World War I
Essential Question: What is neutrality? *(supporting neither side in a quarrel or war)* **When would you remain neutral in a conflict with friends, and what would cause you to intervene?** Tell students that in this section they will learn how the United States attempted to remain neutral in World War I and what finally led to U.S. involvement. **OL**

Section 2
The Home Front
Essential Question: If the United States was currently preparing for war, what needs would be different than those of preparing for World War I? What needs would be the same? Have students discuss what a country would need in order to be prepared for war. Tell them that this section will focus on how the United States mobilized for World War I. **OL**

American soldiers in the 23rd Infantry fire on German positions in the Argonne Forest.

Section 3
A Bloody Conflict
Essential Question: What are some synonyms for reparations? *(compensation, restitution, amends)* **In what situations are people required to make reparations?** *(replacing a damaged item; paying for repairs when causing a car accident; court cases)* Tell students that this section will discuss the reparations Germany was forced to make after World War I. `OL`

Section 4
The War's Impact
Essential Question: How does a strike affect consumers? *(services become unavailable, costs rise)* Have students discuss reasons that workers go on strike. *(poor working conditions, lack of benefits, low wages)* Tell students that this section will cover some of the strikes that resulted from the economic upheaval following World War I. `OL`

Cultural Perspectives

Remind students that the United States entered World War I with the pledge to "make the world safe for democracy." At the same time, however, many Americans continued to face discrimination and prejudice at home. Have students research the roles and contributions of African Americans during World War I. Encourage them to search for primary source materials to analyze the experiences of African Americans. How did they feel about their treatment at home and abroad? How did their wartime experiences affect their outlook and actions after the war?

1918
- Congress passes Sedition Act
- Battle of Argonne Forest begins in September
- Armistice ends fighting on November 11

I WANT YOU *for the* **U.S. ARMY ENLIST NOW**

1919
- Race riots and strikes take place in Northern cities
- Red Scare and Palmer raids target Communists in the U.S.

Harding 1921–1923

1919   *1921*

1918
- Treaty of Brest-Litovsk ends Russian-German war

1919
- Treaty of Versailles conference begins

1920
- British government creates the Northern Ireland province

1921
- Irish Free State established by signed treaty

HISTORY Online

Chapter Overview
Visit the *American Vision: Modern Times* Web site at tav.mt.glencoe.com and click on *Chapter Overviews– Chapter 6* to preview chapter information.

363

FOLDABLES™
Study Organizer

Dinah Zike's Foldables are three-dimensional, interactive graphic organizers that help students practice basic writing skills, review key vocabulary terms, and identify main ideas. Have students complete the foldable activity in the *Dinah Zike's Reading and Study Skills Foldables* booklet.

HISTORY Online

Go to tav.mt.glencoe.com for student activities, lesson plans, and links to additional resources to help students learn about the United States's involvement in World War I.

Why It's Important
This feature will provide students with the skills to identify and analyze problems and solutions in the text.

1. Introducing the Skill
Make a copy on the board of the graphic organizer shown below. Ask students to recall what they learned in Chapter 5 about the Boxer Rebellion. (see p. 313) Have students analyze the conflict by answering the questions in the graphic organizer. **OL**

PROBLEM	SOLUTION
Who had the problem?	
Who solved the problem?	Solution to problem
Cause of problem	Outcomes of solution
Effects of problem	

2. Extending the Skill
Have students find a newspaper article that features a situation which shows a problem and solution. Instruct students to use the model of the graphic organizer above to analyze the problem and solution presented in their article and then share their analysis in class. **OL**

Answers and Additional Support

Preparing to Read Chapter 6

Using Problem/Solution

When authors structure a text, they sometimes use problem and solution to explain a situation and to give reasons for an outcome. This structure is similar to the cause and effect text structure. In cause and effect, authors usually address broader issues. In a problem solution text, authors present a specific problem and specific outcomes. Some of these outcomes, or solutions, are positive ones, while others can be more negative. It is important that you learn to understand how a person, government, or society arrived at a decision. Often in history, there are several competing problems that require complex solutions.

Problems and solutions are often presented over the course of one or more paragraphs. You can recognize a problem/solution structure by asking who had the problem, what may have caused the problem, and what its effects were. You can find the solution by identifying who solved the problem, what the solution was, and what the outcomes of this solution were.

Read the excerpts below and notice how the author has used problem/solution to explain how the government addressed the problem of funding the war effort.

USING PROBLEM/SOLUTION
Problem/solution can sometimes be identified by signal words. Look for words like *problem, difficulty, challenge, solution, improve,* and *response.*

By the end of World War I, the United States was spending about $44 million a day—leading to a total expenditure of about $32 billion for the entire conflict. To fund the war effort, Congress raised income tax rates. Congress also placed new taxes on corporate profits and an extra tax on the profits of arms factories.

Taxes, however, could not pay for the war. To raise money, the government borrowed over $20 billion from the American people by selling Liberty Bonds and Victory Bonds. (p. 378)

In the excerpt, the U.S. government had the problem of high expenses caused by World War I. The solution was for Congress to raise taxes and sell war bonds. The outcome is not directly stated in these paragraphs. Since no other solutions are listed, though, you can imply that the solution was enough to solve the problem.

Apply the Skill

As you read through pages 366–395, find other paragraphs that reflect a problem/solution structure. On a separate sheet of paper, write down the problem, the people who faced the problem, the cause, and the effects. Then note the people who solved the problem, the solution, and the eventual outcome of the solution.

364

UNIVERSAL ACCESS

English Learners The United States faced many problems after World War I, such as fear of communism, changes in the workforce, and turmoil in the economy. After reading Section 4, have students select one of the problems and draw a picture of both the problem and the solution to the problem. This provides English learners with a non-verbal means of expressing what they have learned. **EL**

Historical Analysis Skill

Distinguishing Valid and Fallacious Arguments

Historical Research, Evidence, and Point of View Learning to distinguish valid and fallacious arguments will help you become a critical reader who is able to separate acceptable from misleading information.

Do you remember hearing an advertisement for or listening to the campaign speech of someone running for political office? As you know, hopeful politicians make campaign promises. You probably also know that some of the campaign advertisements contain fallacious, or misleading, arguments about a candidate's position or qualifications. As a voter, you should learn to distinguish between valid and misleading arguments.

Historians also need to determine which arguments are valid and which are fallacious. They apply this skill when they research information, interpret history, and explain varying points of view.

Read the following quote from President Woodrow Wilson, asking Congress for a declaration of war against Germany.

"It is a fearful thing to lead this great peaceful people into war.... But the right is more precious than peace, and we shall fight for the things which we have always carried nearest to our hearts—for democracy, for the right of those who submit to authority to have a voice in their own governments, for the rights and liberties of small nations...." (page 374)

President Wilson faced national forces that opposed his "moral diplomacy" approach to foreign policy. Look for the arguments he uses in this quote to convince Congress to vote for the declaration of war. Do these arguments mention concrete reasons to go to war? What other reasons do you think should be mentioned?

Apply the Skill

As you read the text under "American Neutrality" and "Moving Toward War" on pages 371–374, determine which information politicians could have used to voice their opinions for and against the war and consider whether they would be valid or fallacious arguments.

365

UNIVERSAL ACCESS

FOCUS

BELLRINGER
SKILLBUILDER ACTIVITY

Project **Daily Focus Skills Transparency 6-1** and have students answer the question.

Guide to Reading

Understanding Vocabulary: Have students create a matching quiz by listing the key words for this section in a single column on the left side of a piece of paper and the words' definitions out of order in a column on the right side. Have students take one another's quizzes.

Answers to Graphic: Balkan crisis, alliance system, naval race, assassination of Franz Ferdinand

Unpacking the Standards

Students will be able to:

• Compare President Wilson's moral diplomacy decisions to President Roosevelt's "Big Stick" diplomacy.

• Identify how the U.S. was economically tied to the Allies before World War I.

Answers and Additional Support

SECTION 1

The United States Enters World War I

Guide to Reading

Connection
In the previous chapter, you learned about President Wilson's reforms and the effects of the Progressive Era. In this section, you will discover what events led to the United States entering World War I.

Main Idea
• President Wilson promoted a moral approach to diplomacy in his attempts to bring democracy to Mexico. (p. 367)
• Old alliances and nationalist sentiments among European nations set the stage for World War I. (p. 368)
• British propaganda and business interests led most Americans to a pro-British stance on the war. (p. 371)

• Despite efforts to stay officially neutral, the United States entered the war after German submarines destroyed American ships. (p. 372)

Content Vocabulary
guerrilla, nationalism, self-determination, propaganda, contraband, U-boat

Academic Vocabulary
stability, emphasis, erode

People and Terms to Identify
Pancho Villa, Franz Ferdinand, Allies, Central Powers, Sussex Pledge, Zimmermann telegram

Reading Objectives
• Describe the principles that guided President Wilson's foreign policy.

• Discuss the causes and results of American intervention in Mexico and the Caribbean.
• Explain the causes of World War I and why the United States entered the war in 1917.

Reading Strategy
Organizing As you read about the start of World War I, complete a graphic organizer similar to the one below by identifying the factors that contributed to the conflict.

Factors Contributing to World War I

Preview of Events

♦1914	♦1915	♦1916	♦1917
April 1914 U.S. Marines occupy Veracruz, Mexico	**June 1914** Assassination of Archduke Franz Ferdinand	**July 1914** World War I begins	**May 1915** Sinking of the *Lusitania*	**April 1917** United States enters the war

The following are the main History–Social Science Standards covered in this section.

11.4 Students trace the rise of the United States to its role as a world power in the twentieth century.

11.4.4 Explain Theodore Roosevelt's Big Stick diplomacy, William Taft's Dollar Diplomacy, and Woodrow Wilson's Moral Diplomacy, drawing on relevant speeches.

11.4.5 Analyze the political, economic and social ramifications of World War I on the home front.

~ The Big Idea ~

The fate of nations is forever changed by monumental world events. President Wilson believed that promoting democracy around the world would make the United States more stable and prosperous. These ideals led to U.S. involvement in the Mexican Revolution. In Europe, tensions following the unification of German states resulted in alliances between nations. Austria-Hungary and Serbia went to war after Serbian nationalists assassinated the heir to the Austria-Hungary throne. The system of alliances guaranteed that other nations would join the conflict. World War I had begun. Although the United States tried to remain neutral, it entered the war on the side of the Allies in 1917.

366 CHAPTER 6 World War I and Its Aftermath

SECTION RESOURCES

📁 **Print Material**
• Reproducible Lesson Plan 6-1
• Guided Reading Activity 6-1
• Reading Essentials and Study Guide 6-1
• Active Reading Note-Taking Guide 6-1

📽 **Transparencies**
• Daily Focus Skills Transparency 6-1
• Section Graphic Organizer Transparency 6-1

Technology
🔘 Interactive Tutor Self-Assessment CD-ROM
🔘 ExamView® Pro Testmaker CD-ROM
🔘 Presentation Plus! CD-ROM

Woodrow Wilson's Diplomacy

 President Wilson promoted a moral approach to diplomacy in his attempts to bring democracy to Mexico.

Reading Connection Do you know someone who attempted to lead others by setting a good example? Read on to learn how President Wilson tried to use moral ideas in dealing with Mexico.

As president, Wilson resolved to "strike a new note in international affairs" and to see that "sheer honesty and even unselfishness . . . should prevail over nationalistic self-seeking in American foreign policy." Wilson believed that democracy was essential to a nation's **stability** and prosperity, and that the United States should promote democracy in order to ensure a peaceful world free of revolution and war. Other forces at work, at home, and abroad frustrated his hope to lead the world by moral example.

★ An American Story ★

Edith O'Shaughnessy could not sleep on the rainy night of April 20, 1914. Living at the American embassy in Mexico City, the wife of diplomat Nelson O'Shaughnessy was well aware of the growing crisis between Mexico and the United States. Earlier that day, President Wilson had asked Congress to authorize the use of force against Mexico. In her diary, O'Shaughnessy described the tensions in the Mexican capital:

❝I can't sleep. National and personal potentialities [possibilities] are surging through my brain. Three stalwart railroad men came to the Embassy this evening. They brought reports of a plan for the massacre of Americans in the street to-night, but, strange and wonderful thing, a heavy rain is falling. . . . Rain is as potent as shell-fire in clearing the streets, and I don't think there will be any trouble.❞

The next day, O'Shaughnessy reported that the conflict had begun: "We are in Mexico, in full intervention! . . . Marines are due to-day in Vera Cruz. . . ."

—adapted from *A Diplomat's Wife in Mexico*

Wilson strongly opposed imperialism. His policy of Moral Diplomacy forced him to become involved in the Mexican revolution.

The Mexican Revolution From 1884 to 1911, a dictator, Porfirio Díaz, ruled Mexico. Díaz encouraged foreign investment in Mexico to help develop the nation's industry. A few wealthy landowners dominated Mexican society. The majority of the people were poor and landless, and they were increasingly frustrated by their circumstances. In 1911 a revolution erupted, forcing Díaz to flee the country.

Francisco Madero, a reformer who appeared to support democracy, constitutional government, and land reform, replaced Díaz. Madero, however, proved to be an unskilled administrator. Frustrated with Mexico's continued decline, army officers plotted against Madero. Shortly before Wilson took office, General Victoriano Huerta seized power in Mexico, and Madero was murdered—presumably on Huerta's orders.

Huerta's brutality repulsed Wilson, who refused to recognize the new government. Wilson believed the United States had the moral obligation to discriminate between good and bad governments and intervene to put good people in power. Wilson was convinced that without the support of the United States, Huerta soon would be overthrown. Wilson, therefore, tried to prevent weapons from reaching Huerta, and he permitted Americans to arm other political factions within Mexico. In a message Wilson sent to authorities in Mexico he stated:

"Mexico is starving and without a government . . . the people and Government of the United States cannot stand indifferently by and do nothing. . . ."

Wilson's desire to lead by moral example and promote Moral Diplomacy found him deeply involved in Mexico's political affairs.

Raising the flag at Veracruz ▶

CHAPTER 6 World War I and Its Aftermath **367**

TEACH

R₁ Reading Strategy

Evaluating As students read the section, have them list evidences they see of President Wilson's strong opposition to imperialism in his decision making and his actions toward European nations at war. **OL**

R₂ Reading Strategy

Organizing Information Have students create a graphic organizer like the one displayed below. Tell students to fill in the graphic organizer with information about Mexico's changing leadership as they read the text. **OL**

Name of Mexico's Leader	Reason for Removal From Power

C Critical Thinking

Analyzing Information Have students name the three Mexican leaders who were in power during the time of the Mexican Revolution. **Ask: What negative aspects do you see in their leadership styles?** *(Diaz: favored the rich and ignored the rights of the poor; Madero: poor administrator who caused Mexico's problems to worsen; Huerta: forceful and brutal)* **AL**

Did You Know?

In addition to *A Diplomat's Wife in Mexico*, Edith O'Shaughnessy also wrote *Diplomatic Days* and *Intimate Pages of Mexican History*. All of these works were based on her experiences while living in Mexico.

Wilson Sends Troops Into Mexico In April 1914, American sailors visiting the city of Tampico were arrested after entering a restricted area. Though they were quickly released, their American commander demanded an apology. The Mexicans refused. Wilson used the refusal as an opportunity to overthrow Huerta. He sent marines to seize the Mexican port of Veracruz.

Although the president expected the Mexican people to welcome his action, anti-American riots broke out in Mexico. Wilson then accepted international mediation to settle the dispute. Venustiano Carranza, whose forces had acquired arms from the United States, became Mexico's president.

Mexican forces opposed to Carranza were not appeased, and they conducted raids into the United States hoping to force Wilson to intervene. **Pancho Villa** (VEE·yah) led a group of **guerrillas**—an armed band that uses surprise attacks and sabotage rather than open warfare—that burned the town of Columbus, New Mexico, and killed a number of Americans. Wilson responded by sending more than 6,000 U.S. troops under General John J. Pershing across the border to find and capture Villa. The expedition dragged on as Pershing failed to capture the guerrillas. Wilson's growing concern over the war raging in Europe finally caused him to recall Pershing's troops in 1917.

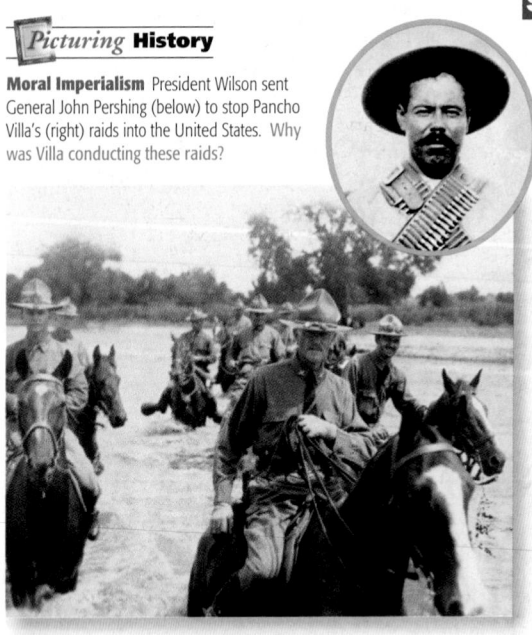

Picturing **History**

Moral Imperialism President Wilson sent General John Pershing (below) to stop Pancho Villa's (right) raids into the United States. Why was Villa conducting these raids?

368 CHAPTER 6 World War I and Its Aftermath

Wilson's Mexican policy damaged U.S. foreign relations abroad. The British ridiculed the president's actions, calling it an attempt to "shoot the Mexicans into self-government." Latin Americans regarded his "moral imperialism" as no improvement on Theodore Roosevelt's "big stick" diplomacy. In fact, Wilson followed Roosevelt's example with his actions in the Caribbean. During his first term, Wilson sent marines into Nicaragua, Haiti, and the Dominican Republic to preserve order and to set up governments that he hoped would be more stable and democratic than the current regimes.

✓ Reading Check **Examining** Why did President Wilson intervene in Mexico?

The Outbreak of World War I

Main Idea Old alliances and nationalist sentiments among European nations set the stage for World War I.

Reading Connection What stories are you familiar with that are based on old feuds or alliances? Read on to discover how European nations formed political alliances that brought most of the continent into war.

Despite more than 40 years of general peace, tensions among European nations were building in 1914. Throughout the late 1800s and early 1900s, complex alliances, a naval race, and concern over nationalism created problems among the powers of Europe and set the stage for a monumental war.

The Alliance System The roots of World War I date back to the 1860s. In 1864, while Americans fought the Civil War, the German kingdom of Prussia launched the first of a series of wars to unite the various German states into one nation. By 1871 Prussia had united Germany and proclaimed the birth of the German Empire. The new German nation rapidly industrialized and quickly became one of the most powerful nations in the world.

The creation of Germany transformed European politics. In 1870, as part of their plan to unify Germany, the Prussians had attacked and defeated France. They then forced the French to give up territory along the German border. From that point forward, France and Germany were enemies. To protect itself, Germany signed alliances with Italy and with Austria-Hungary, a huge empire that controlled much of southeastern Europe. This became known as the Triple Alliance.

The new alliance alarmed Russian leaders, who feared that Germany intended to expand eastward into Russia. Russia and Austria-Hungary were also competing for influence in southeastern Europe. Many of the people of southeastern Europe were Slavs—the same ethnic group as the Russians—and the Russians wanted to support them against Austria-Hungary. As a result, Russia and France had a common interest in opposing Germany and Austria-Hungary. In 1894 they signed the Franco-Russian Alliance.

The Naval Race While the other major powers of Europe divided into competing alliances, Great Britain remained neutral. Then, in 1898, the Germans began to build a navy challenging Great Britain's historical dominance at sea. By the early 1900s, an arms race had begun between Great Britain and Germany, as both sides raced to build warships. The naval race greatly increased tensions between Germany and Britain and convinced the British to establish closer relations with France and Russia. The British refused to sign a formal alliance, so their new relationship with the French and Russians became known as an "entente cordiale"—a friendly understanding. Britain, France, and Russia became known as the Triple Entente.

The Balkan Crisis By the late 1800s, **nationalism**, or a feeling of intense pride of one's homeland, had become a powerful idea in Europe. Nationalists place primary **emphasis** on promoting their homeland's culture and interests above those of other countries. Nationalism was one of the reasons for the tensions among the European powers. Each nation viewed the others as competitors, and many people were willing to go to war to expand their nation at the expense of others.

One of the basic ideas of nationalism is the right to **self-determination**—the idea that people who belong to a nation should have their own country and government. In the 1800s, nationalism led to a crisis in southeastern Europe in the region known as the Balkans. Historically, the Ottoman Empire and the Austro-Hungarian Empire had ruled the Balkans. Both of these empires were made up of many different nations. As nationalism became a powerful force in the 1800s, the different national groups within these empires began to press for independence.

Among the groups pushing for independence were the Serbs, Bosnians, Croats, and Slovenes. These people all spoke similar languages and had come to see themselves as one people. They called themselves South Slavs, or Yugoslavs. The first of these people to obtain independence were the Serbs, who formed a nation called Serbia between the Ottoman and Austro-Hungarian empires. Serbs believed their nation's mission was to unite the South Slavs.

Russia supported the Serbs, while Austria-Hungary did what it could to limit Serbia's growth. In 1908 Austria-Hungary annexed Bosnia, which at the time belonged to the Ottoman Empire. The Serbs were furious. They wanted Bosnia to be part of their nation. The annexation demonstrated to the Serbs that Austria-Hungary had no intention of letting the Slavic people in its empire become independent.

A Continent Goes to War In late June 1914, the heir to the Austro-Hungarian throne, the Archduke **Franz Ferdinand,** visited the Bosnian capital of Sarajevo. As he and his wife rode through the city, a Bosnian revolutionary named Gavrilo Princip rushed their open car and shot the couple to death. The assassin was a member of a Serbian nationalist group nicknamed the "Black Hand." The assassination took place with the knowledge of Serbian officials who hoped to start a war that would bring down the Austro-Hungarian Empire.

The Austro-Hungarian government blamed Serbia for the attack and decided the time had come to crush Serbia in order to prevent Slavic nationalism from undermining its empire. Knowing an attack on Serbia might trigger a war with Russia, the Austrians asked their German allies for support. Germany promised to support Austria-Hungary if war erupted.

Austria-Hungary then issued an ultimatum to the Serbian government. The Serbs counted on Russia to

Fateful Couple Archduke Franz Ferdinand and wife Sophia visit Sarajevo the day of the assassination.

R₁ Reading Strategy

Categorizing Information Have students list the members of the Triple Alliance and the Triple Entente. Below each name have students list the factors that caused these countries to become allies. **OL**

R₂ Reading Strategy

Scaffolding—Academic Vocabulary The word *tension* was introduced in Chapter 4, Section 3. Ask a student to define the word. **BL**

W Writing Support

Narrative Writing Have students write a newspaper article from the point of view of a reporter who witnessed the assassination of Archduke Franz Ferdinand. Instruct students to use narrative and descriptive techniques in their article. **BL**
CA 11WA2.1a

S Skill Practice

Visual Literacy Ask students to study the picture. **Ask: What do you observe that would make an assassination attempt easy?** *(riders in the car were exposed due to no top on car; large hats provided big targets; archduke in full view)* **OL CA HI1**

More Skill Practice

Questioning Instruct students to review the definition of *jingoism*. (p. 303) **Ask: How does jingoism differ from nationalism?** *(Nationalism is a feeling of pride in one's country, while jingoism is a form of nationalism that promotes aggressive action.)* **OL**

Visual Literacy Have students study the map on this page. Ask them to list the countries involved at the beginning of World War I. Based on the location of each country, have students list the advantages and disadvantages each country might have faced.
AL **CA CS3**

U **Universal Access**

Kinesthetic Instruct students to write on index cards the main events listed on the time line of 1914. Then have students shuffle the cards and put them in chronological order without referring to the text. **BL**

R **Reading Strategy**

Sequencing Information Have students create a map of Europe at the beginning of World War I. Ask them to label the countries and indicate the order in which the countries involved in the conflict declared war. **BL**

Answers and Additional Support

370

back them up, and the Russians, in turn, counted on France. French leaders were worried that they might someday be caught alone in a war with Germany, so they were determined to keep Russia as an ally. They promised to support Russia if war began.

R On July 28, Austria declared war on Serbia. Russia immediately mobilized its army, including troops stationed on the German border. On August 1, Germany declared war on Russia. Two days later, it declared war on France. World War I had begun.

NATIONAL GEOGRAPHIC **European Alliances, 1914**

June 28, 1914 Archduke Franz Ferdinand assassinated by Serb nationalist.

Bulgaria joined the Central Powers in 1915. Romania joined the Allies in 1916.

Italy refused to honor Central Powers alliance and joined Allied Powers on May 23, 1915.

Greece did not enter the war until 1917.

Allied Powers
Central Powers
Neutral nations
Initial troop movements of Central Powers

Geography *Skills*

1. **Interpreting Maps** Which nations comprised the Central Powers in 1914?
2. **Applying Geography Skills** What was the name of the southeastern European region that sparked the beginning of the war?

June 28 Assassination of Archduke Franz Ferdinand

July 28 Austria-Hungary declares war on Serbia

August 3 Germany declares war on France, begins invasion of Belgium

August 6 Austria-Hungary declares war on Russia

July 1914

August 1914

July 30 Russia begins mobilizing troops in defense of Serbia

August 1 Germany declares war on Russia

August 4 Britain declares war on Germany

August 12 France and Great Britain declare war on Austria-Hungary

370   CHAPTER 6   World War I and Its Aftermath

More Skill Practice

Visual/Spatial Have students use the map on p. 370 to measure the distances between the capitals of the countries within the Triple Alliance and Triple Entente. **Ask: Why might it be beneficial for Allied nations to be located near each other?** *(Possible answer: It might speed each nation's ability to send troops, supplies, and aid to each other quickly.)* **OL**

Geography *Skills*

Answers:
1. Germany, Austria-Hungary, Bulgaria, Ottoman Empire, Italy joined Allies in 1915
2. Balkans

Geography Skills Practice
Ask: Into what country did the Central Powers send troops? *(France)*

Germany's Plan Fails Germany had long been prepared for war against France and Russia. It immediately launched a massive invasion of France, hoping to knock the French out of the war. It would then be able to send its troops east to deal with the Russians.

The German plan had one major problem. It required the German forces to advance through neutral Belgium in order to encircle the French troops. The British had guaranteed Belgium's neutrality. When German troops crossed the Belgian frontier, Britain declared war on Germany.

With Britain's declaration of war, all members of the Triple Entente were now involved in the war. Those fighting for the Triple Entente were called the **Allies.** France, Russia, and Great Britain formed the backbone of the Allies. Italy joined them in 1915 after the other Allies promised to cede Austro-Hungarian territory to Italy after the war.

Italy's decision to join the Allies broke up the Triple Alliance. What remained of that former alliance—Germany and Austria-Hungary—joined with the Ottoman Empire and Bulgaria to form the **Central Powers.**

The German plan seemed to work at first. German troops swept through Belgium and headed into France, driving back the French and British forces. Then, to the great surprise of the Germans, Russian troops invaded Germany. The Germans had not expected Russia to mobilize so quickly and had not prepared for an immediate war in the east. They were forced to pull some of their troops away from the attack on France and send them to the eastern front to stop the Russians. This weakened the German forces just enough to give the Allies a chance to stop them. The Germans drove to within 30 miles (48 km) of Paris, but stubborn resistance by British and French troops at the Battle of the Marne finally stopped the German advance. Because the swift German attack had failed to defeat the French, both sides became locked in a bloody stalemate along hundreds of miles of trenches that would barely change position for the next three years.

The Central Powers had greater success on the Eastern Front. German and Austrian forces stopped the Russian attack and then went on the offensive. They swept across hundreds of miles of territory and took hundreds of thousands of prisoners. Russia suffered 2 million killed, wounded, or captured in 1915 alone, but it kept fighting.

✓ **Reading Check** **Explaining** What incident triggered the beginning of World War I?

American Neutrality

Main Idea British propaganda and business interests led most Americans to a pro-British stance on the war.

Reading Connection Have you ever decided to buy a product based on the advertising? Read on to learn about the effects of propaganda and U.S. efforts to stay neutral.

When the fighting began, President Wilson declared the United States to be neutral in an attempt to keep the country from being drawn into a foreign war. "We must be impartial in thought as well as in action," Wilson stated. For many Americans, however, that proved difficult to do.

Americans Take Sides Despite the president's plea, many Americans showed support for one side or the other. This was especially true for recent immigrants from Europe. Many of the 8 million German Americans, for example, supported their homeland. The nation's 4.5 million Irish Americans, whose endured centuries of British rule, also sympathized with the Central Powers.

In general, though, American public opinion favored the Allied cause. Many Americans valued the heritage, language, and political ideals they shared with Britain. Others treasured America's historic links with France, a great friend to America during the Revolutionary War.

Pro-British Sentiment One select group of Americans was decidedly pro-British: President Wilson's cabinet. Only Secretary of State William Jennings Bryan favored neutrality. The other cabinet members, as well as Bryan's chief adviser, Robert Lansing, and Walter Hines Page, the American ambassador to Britain, argued forcefully on behalf of Britain. American military leaders also backed the British. They believed that an Allied victory was the only way to preserve the international balance of power.

British officials worked diligently to win American support. One method they used was **propaganda,** or information designed to influence opinion. Both the Allies and the Central Powers used propaganda, but German propaganda was mostly anti-Russian and did not appeal to most Americans. British propaganda, on the other hand, was extremely skillful. Furthermore, Britain cut the transatlantic telegraph cable from Europe to the United States, limiting news about the war mainly to British reports. Stories

CHAPTER 6   World War I and Its Aftermath   **371**

Review the Big Idea
Review the Big Idea for this section, "The fate of nations is forever changed by monumental world events." Ask the class to create a cause-and-effect chart that tracks how Germany's invasion of France affected the course of World War I. **BL**

S Skill Practice
Using Geography Skills
Provide students with a topographical map of Europe. Instruct them to research the path Germany hoped to take through Belgium and eventually to Paris. Have students trace the path and then mark the location where French resistance stopped the German advance. **OL** **CA CS3**

R₁ Reading Strategy
Predicting While war enveloped Europe, American politicians attempted to remain uninvolved in the global conflict. **Ask: As foreign tensions escalate, do you think it will be possible for President Wilson to maintain his neutral stance? Why or why not?** *(Students may state that it will not be possible as the United States becomes more directly affected by events overseas.)* **OL**

R₂ Reading Strategy
Setting a Purpose Have students discuss the differences between news reporting, propaganda, and advertising. Ask students to identify the purpose and value of each. **AL**

✓ **Reading Check**
Answer: assassination of Archduke Franz Ferdinand and his wife

More Skill Practice

Making Inferences When presented with complex situations, it is human nature to search out the root cause of the problem. **Ask: Do you think any one nation or group of nations was primarily responsible for World War I?** *(Students may argue that there was a single group or nation responsible, or they may argue that several nations or groups were equally responsible. Students should give specific evidence to support their opinions.)* **AL**

C Critical Thinking

Analyzing Information
The United States experienced economic difficulties as the war raged on in Europe. **Ask:** In what ways was the United States tied economically to the war? *(trade with Allied countries suffered during the war; prices could rise as goods were harder to get; loans to Allies were costly and risky)* **OL**

R Reading Strategy

Activating Prior Knowledge
Point out to students the desire of many Americans to remain neutral. **Ask:** Why did many Americans want to avoid involvement? *(history of neutrality and avoiding entangling alliances)* **OL**

✓ Reading Check

Answer: Many American banks invested in an Allied victory and made loans to the Allies.

Answers and Additional Support

arrived depicting numerous German war atrocities, including the charge that Germans used corpses from the battlefield to make fertilizer and soap. Although many such reports were questionable, enough Americans believed them to help sway American support in favor of the Allies.

Business Links American business interests also leaned toward the Allies. Companies in the United States, particularly on the East Coast, had strong ties with businesses in the Allied countries. As business leader, Thomas W. Lamont stated, "Our firm had never for one moment been neutral: we did not know how to be. From the very start we did everything that we could to contribute to the cause of the Allies."

Many American banks began to invest heavily in an Allied victory. American loans to the cash-hungry Allies skyrocketed. By 1917 such loans would total over $2 billion. Other American banks, particularly in the Midwest, where pro-German feelings were strongest, also lent some $27 million to Germany. Even more might have been lent, but most foreign loans required the approval of William McAdoo, the secretary of the Treasury. McAdoo was strongly pro-British and did what he could to limit loans to Germany. As a result, the country's pros-perity was intertwined with the military fortunes of Britain, France, and Russia. If the Allies won, the money would be paid back; if not, the money might be lost forever.

✓ Reading Check **Evaluating** How was American prosperity intertwined with the military fortunes of the Allies?

Moving Toward War

Main Idea Despite efforts to stay officially neutral, the United States entered the war after German submarines destroyed American ships.

Reading Connection Describe a time when you tried to remain neutral during a disagreement between friends. What steps did you take? Read on to discover how Germany's actions at sea led America to war.

Although most Americans supported the Allies and hoped for their victory, they did not want to join the conflict. They still remembered the events of the Civil War. However, a series of events gradually eroded American neutrality and drew the nation into the war firmly on the side of the Allies.

Profiles IN HISTORY

Jeannette Rankin *1880–1973*

As he addressed the "Gentlemen of the Congress" on April 2, 1917, President Woodrow Wilson actually misspoke. Sitting in the chamber listening to the president's request for a declaration of war against Germany was Representative Jeannette Rankin–the first woman ever elected to Congress.

Rankin was born in Missoula, Montana, in 1880. She became a social worker and participated in the woman suffrage movement. In 1916 she was elected to the U.S. House of Representatives from Montana–one of the few states at that time that allowed women to vote. As a representative, Rankin sponsored legislation to grant federal voting rights for women and to provide health services for them.

Apart from her title as the first woman in Congress, Rankin is remembered most for her strong pacifism. She was one of 56 legislators who voted against the nation's entry into World War I. "I want to stand by my country," she said, "but I cannot vote for war."

In 1940 Rankin ran again for Congress as a representative from Montana. She ran on an isolationist policy and won. In 1941 she was the only member of Congress to vote against declaring war on Japan and entering World War II.

After leaving Congress in 1943, Rankin continued working for peace. In 1968, at 87 years of age, she led thousands of women in the March on Washington to oppose the Vietnam War.

Profiles IN HISTORY

Background: Although she represented all that suffragists were striving for, Rankin alienated herself from many suffragists when she voted against entering World War I. After her vote, several suffragist groups in New York canceled her speaking engagements.
Ask: How did Jeannette Rankin demonstrate her commitment to pacifism? *(voting against entry into World War I, voting against entry into World War II, protesting against the Vietnam War)*

The British Blockade Shortly after the war began, the British deployed their navy to blockade Germany and keep it from obtaining supplies. The British planted mines in the North Sea and forced neutral ships into port for inspections in case they were trying to transport valuable materials to Germany or its neutral neighbors. British officials also expanded their definition of **contraband,** or prohibited materials, to prevent neutral countries from shipping food to Germany.

The Germans knew that the Allies depended on food, equipment, and other supplies from both the United States and their overseas empires. If Germany could strangle that trade, it could starve the British and French into surrendering. To get around Britain's blockade, the Germans deployed submarines known as **U-boats**—from the German word *Unterseeboot* (meaning "underwater boat"). In February 1915, the Germans announced that they would attempt to sink without warning any ship they found in the waters around Britain.

Germany's announcement triggered outrage in the United States and elsewhere. Attacking civilian vessels without warning violated an international treaty stipulating that military vessels must reveal their intentions to merchant ships and make provisions for the safety of the targeted ship's crew and passengers before sinking it. The Germans claimed that many merchant ships were actually warships in disguise and that their U-boats would be placed at great risk if they revealed themselves before firing.

The issue reached a crisis on May 7, 1915. Despite warnings from Germany, the British passenger liner *Lusitania* entered the war zone. A submerged German submarine fired on the ship, killing nearly 1,200 passengers—including 128 Americans. Many Americans were outraged and regarded the attack as an act of terrorism, not war. Others argued that the passengers traveling on ships of foreign nations did so at their own risk.

Wilson steered a middle course on the issue of the U-boats. He refused to take extreme measures against Germany, saying that the United States was "too proud to fight." Nevertheless, he sent several diplomatic notes to Germany insisting that its government safeguard the lives of noncombatants in the war zones.

Late in March 1916, Wilson's policy was tested when a U-boat torpedoed the French passenger ship *Sussex,* injuring several Americans on board. Although Wilson's closest advisers favored breaking off diplomatic relations with Germany immediately, the president, busy with the crisis in Mexico, chose to issue one last warning. He demanded that the

German government abandon its methods of submarine warfare or risk war with the United States.

Germany did not want to strengthen the Allies by drawing the United States into the war. It promised with certain conditions to no longer sink merchant ships without warning. The Sussex Pledge, as it was called, met the foreign-policy goals of both Germany and President Wilson by keeping the United States out of the war a little longer.

Wilson's efforts to keep American soldiers at home played an important part in his reelection bid in 1916. Campaigning as the "peace" candidate, his campaign slogan, "He kept us out of the war," helped lead Wilson to a narrow victory over the Republican nominee, Charles Evans Hughes.

The United States Declares War Following Wilson's reelection, events quickly brought the country to the brink of war. In January 1917, a German official named Arthur Zimmermann cabled the German ambassador in Mexico, instructing him to make an offer to the Mexican government. Zimmermann proposed that Mexico ally itself with Germany in the event of war between Germany and the United States. In return, Mexico would regain its "lost territory in Texas, New Mexico, and Arizona" after the war. Germany hoped Mexico would tie down the American forces and prevent them from being sent to Europe. British intelligence intercepted the **Zimmermann telegram.** Shortly afterward, it was leaked to American newspapers. Furious, many Americans now concluded war with Germany was necessary.

Then, on February 1, 1917, Germany resumed unrestricted submarine warfare. German military leaders believed that they could starve Britain into submission in four to six months if their U-boats could return to a more aggressive approach of sinking all ships on sight. Although they recognized that their actions might draw the United States into the war, the Germans did not believe that the Americans could raise an army and transport it to Europe in time to prevent the Allies from collapsing.

Between February 3 and March 21, German U-boats sank six American merchant ships without warning. Finally roused to action,

Student Web Activity Visit the *American Vision: Modern Times* Web site at tav.mt.glencoe.com and click on *Student Web Activities—Chapter 6* for an activity on World War I.

R₁ Reading Strategy

Using Word Parts Sometimes an unfamiliar word can be separated into its different parts to help students understand its meaning. **Ask: What does the prefix *contra* mean?** *(against)* **What are some other words that use this prefix, and what are their meanings?** *(contrary: opposed to; contradict: to deny a statement)* **OL**

U Universal Access

Visual/Spatial Instruct students to find a picture of a German U-boat through library or Internet resources. Have students write a description of the features of the submarine. **BL**

R₂ Reading Strategy

Sequencing Information Have students create a time line which highlights the events that led the United States to enter World War I. **OL**

Did You Know?

The presidential election of 1916 was the closest in three decades, with Wilson winning 49 percent of the vote to Hughes's 46 percent. Wilson had benefited from many public endorsements by movie actors and baseball players such as Ty Cobb.

Objectives and answers to the student activity can be found in the **Web Activity Lesson Plan** at tav.mt.glencoe.com.

ASSESS

Picturing **History**

Answer: British blockade, sinking of passenger liners, Germany's attempt to ally with Mexico

✓**Reading Check**

Answer: Germany's sinking of passenger and merchant ships led outraged Americans to side with Britain.

HISTORY Online

Study Central provides audio summaries, interactive games, and online graphic organizers to help students review section content.

CLOSE

Summarizing Have students discuss why the U.S. entered the war.

BL

374

"The world must be made safe for democracy."

—*Woodrow Wilson, April 1917*

Picturing **History**

Americans Go to War Congress voted heavily in favor of entering the European war. Here, excited Americans wave from an Army recruitment truck. What events pushed the United States to finally declare war?

President Wilson appeared before a special session of Congress on April 2, 1917, to ask for a declaration of war against Germany.

❝It is a fearful thing to lead this great peaceful people into war. . . . But the right is more precious than peace, and we shall fight for the things which we have always carried nearest to our hearts—for democracy, for the right of those who submit to authority to have a voice in their own governments, for the rights and liberties of small nations. . . .❞

—quoted in the Congressional Record, 1917

After a spirited debate, the Senate passed the resolution on April 4 by a vote of 82 to 6. The House concurred 373 to 50 on April 6, and Wilson signed the resolution. America was now at war.

✓**Reading Check** **Summarizing** How did Germany's use of unrestricted submarine warfare lead to American entry into World War I?

HISTORY Online Study Central

For help with the concepts in this section of *American Vision: Modern Times* go to tav.mt.glencoe.com and click on *Study Central.*

SECTION 1 ASSESSMENT

Checking for Understanding

1. **Vocabulary** Define: stability, guerrilla, nationalism, emphasis, self-determination, propaganda, erode, contraband, U-boat.
2. **People and Terms** Identify: Pancho Villa, Franz Ferdinand, Allies, Central Powers, Sussex Pledge, Zimmermann telegram.
3. **Name** the two alliances that Europe was divided into at the start of World War I.

Reviewing Big Ideas

4. **Concluding** Why did most of President Wilson's cabinet members support the British?

Critical Thinking

5. **Historical Analysis** **Synthesizing** How did European nationalism contribute to the outbreak of World War I? **CA HI1**
6. **Organizing** Use a graphic organizer similar to the one below to identify the events that led the United States to enter World War I.

Events
□ → U.S. Enters World War I
□ →

Analyzing Visuals

7. **Analyzing Time Lines** Examine the time line on page 370. How does the order in which countries declared war reflect the European alliance system?

Writing About History

8. **Expository Writing** Imagine that you are a Mexican citizen living in Mexico between 1914 and 1917. Write a script for a radio newscast in which you discuss American actions in Mexico. Include specific events and information. **CA 11WA2.4a**

SECTION 1 ASSESSMENT ANSWERS

1. Content vocabulary is boldfaced and highlighted in yellow. Academic vocabulary is boldfaced.
2. Pancho Villa (*p. 368*), Franz Ferdinand (*p. 369*), Allies (*p. 371*), Central Powers (*p. 371*), Sussex Pledge (*p. 373*), Zimmermann telegram (*p. 373*)
3. Triple Alliance and Triple Entente
4. They believed that Allied victory was the only way to preserve the international balance of power, and they cited the close historical ties with Great Britain and France.
5. Each major ethnic group in European empires wanted its own country.
6. Unrestricted submarine warfare; Germany's attempt to ally with Mexico
7. When one country declared war, its allies declared war.
8. Students' scripts will vary. Encourage students to act out their scripts as if they were actually on the radio.

SECTION 2 The Home Front

Guide to Reading

Connection
In the previous section, you learned about the events that led to U.S. involvement in World War I. In this section, you will discover how the United States prepared for war at home.

Main Idea
- The United States instituted a draft for military service, and African Americans and women took on new roles. (p. 376)
- The government used Progressive ideas to manage the economy and pay for the war. (p. 377)
- Women, African Americans, and Mexican Americans all helped to fill labor shortages created by the draft. (p. 378)

- Propaganda and limits on civil liberties were part of domestic life during World War I. (p. 379)

Content Vocabulary
conscription, victory garden, espionage

Academic Vocabulary
draft, migrate, constitute

People and Terms to Identify
War Industries Board, Bernard Baruch, Liberty Bond, Victory Bond, Committee on Public Information

Reading Objectives
- **Analyze** how the United States raised an army and won support for World War I.

- **Explain** how the economy was controlled to support the war.

Reading Strategy
Taking Notes As you read about how the United States mobilized for war, use the major headings of the section to create an outline similar to the one below.

The Home Front
I. Building Up the Military
  A.
  B.
  C.
II.
  A.
  B.

Preview of Events

1917	1918		1919

1917
Selective Service Act and Espionage Act passed

May 1918
Sedition Act passed

September 1918
Eugene Debs imprisoned

1919
Schenck v. *United States*

The following are the main History–Social Science Standards covered in this section.

11.4 Students trace the rise of the United States to its role as a world power in the twentieth century.

11.4.5 Analyze the political, economic, and social ramifications of World War I on the home front.

⚜ The Big Idea ⚜

The fate of nations is forever changed by monumental world events. World War I brought far-reaching changes to the United States. Although many people enlisted in the army, the government instituted a draft to increase the number of combat troops. This created job vacancies and new opportunities for women and minorities. Many African Americans and Mexican Americans migrated north to work in factories, and women also took industrial jobs. Mexicans migrated to the United States to fill agricultural jobs in the Southwest. Government agencies facilitated cooperation between government and big business, rationed food and fuel, and sold bonds to raise money for the war. To ensure support for the war, Congress passed—and the Supreme Court upheld—laws restricting antiwar activities and certain civil liberties. The Supreme Court upheld limitations on free speech that threatened the safety of citizens or hindered the war effort.

CHAPTER 6 World War I and Its Aftermath **375**

SECTION RESOURCES

📁 Print Material
- Reproducible Lesson Plan 6-2
- Guided Reading Activity 6-2
- Reading Essentials and Study Guide 6-2
- Active Reading Note-Taking Guide 6-2

📽 Transparencies
- Daily Focus Skills Transparency 6-2
- Section Graphic Organizer Transparency 6-2

Technology
- ⊕ Interactive Tutor Self-Assessment CD-ROM
- ⊕ Exam*View*® Pro Testmaker CD-ROM
- ⊕ Presentation Plus! CD-ROM

BELLRINGER
SKILLBUILDER ACTIVITY

Project **Daily Focus Skills Transparency 6-2** and have students answer the question.

Guide to Reading

Understanding Vocabulary: Write a content vocabulary word or an academic vocabulary word on the board. Have students race to see who can find the definition in the text the fastest. Continue until all the words are covered.

Answers to Graphic:
I. Building Up the Military
  A. Selective Service
  B. African Americans in the War
  C. Women in the Military
II. Organizing Industry

Students should complete the outline by using all the heads in this section.

🏴 Unpacking the Standards

Students will be able to:

- Identify the impact women, African Americans, and Mexican Americans had upon the workforce during World War I and changes in their roles once the soldiers returned from war to their jobs.

- Describe how the United States created new agencies to mobilize the economy, draft soldiers, and build public support for the war.

TEACH

R₁ Reading Strategy

Previewing Students can quickly gain an understanding of what the text will be about by looking over features, such as headings and subheadings, charted information, illustrations, graphics, and captions. Have students preview this section by looking over these elements before they begin to read. **OL**

R₂ Reading Strategy

Understanding Vocabulary Have students paraphrase their understanding of *conscription*. **Ask: Do you believe it is the duty of all able-bodied individuals to serve in the military, or should they have a choice to abstain?** *(Students' answers will vary. They should also remember that during World War I only men were allowed to serve in combat.)* **OL**

U Universal Access

Verbal/Linguistic Instruct students to write a three-minute speech persuading young men to enlist in the army in 1917. Students can use background patriotic music, posters, emotionally charged rhetoric, and symbolism to make their speeches more convincing. Have students present their speeches in class. **OL**

Answers and Additional Support

R₁ Building Up the Military

Main Idea The United States instituted a draft for military service, and African Americans and women took on new roles.

Reading Connection Describe a time you were required to do something that you might not have done otherwise. Read on to learn about the selective service system.

After Congress declared war on Germany in April 1917, young men from across the nation swamped recruiting offices eager to volunteer for the war. Historian William Langer, who served in World War I, recalled the enthusiasm of the young recruits:

★ An American Story ★

66What strikes me most, I think, is the eagerness of the men to get to France and above all to reach the front. One would think that, after almost four years of war, after the most detailed and realistic accounts of the murderous fighting . . . to say nothing of the day-to-day agony of trench warfare, it would have been all but impossible to get anyone to serve without duress. But it was not so. We and many thousands of others volunteered. Perhaps we were offended by the arrogance of the German U-boat campaign, and convinced Kaiserism must be smashed, once and for all. Possibly we already felt that, in the American interest, Western democracy must not be allowed to go under. But . . . most of us, young, were simply fascinated by the prospect of adventure and heroism. . . . Here was our one great chance for excitement and risk.99

—quoted in *Doughboy War*

◀ *World War I recruiting poster.*

When the United States declared war against Germany in April 1917, progressives controlled the federal government. They did not abandon their ideas simply because a war had begun. Instead, they applied progressive ideas to fighting the war.

Selective Service When the United States entered the war in 1917, the army and National Guard together had slightly more than 370,000 troops. Although many men volunteered after war was declared, many felt more soldiers needed to be **drafted.**

R₂

Many progressives believed that **conscription**—forced military service—was a violation of democratic and republican principles. Realizing a draft was necessary, however, Congress, with Wilson's support, created a new system called selective service. Instead of having the military run the draft, the Selective Service Act of 1917 required all men between 21 and 30 to register for the draft. A lottery randomly determined the order they were called before a local draft board in charge of selecting or exempting people from military service.

U

The thousands of local boards were the heart of the system. The members of the draft boards were civilians from local communities. Progressives believed local people, understanding community needs, would know which men to draft. Eventually about 2.8 million Americans were drafted.

Volunteers for War Not all American soldiers were drafted. Of the approximately 2 million men who volunteered, there were many reasons for deciding to enlist. Some had grown up listening to stories of the Civil War and the Spanish-American War. They saw this war as a great adventure and wanted to fight for their country's cause. To soldiers such as Justin Klingenberger, "War consisted of following the flag over a shell-torn field, with fixed bayonet . . . pushing the Hun back from trench to trench. . . ." Although the horrors of the war soon became clear to the American troops, their morale remained high, helping to ensure an Allied victory.

African Americans in the War Of the nearly 400,000 African Americans who were drafted, about 42,000 served overseas as combat troops. African American soldiers encountered discrimination and prejudice in the army. They served in racially segregated units almost always under white officers.

Despite these challenges, many African American soldiers fought with distinction in the war. For example, the African American 92nd and 93rd Infantry

Did You Know?

At least three army nurses were awarded the Distinguished Service Cross, the nation's second-highest military honor. Several received the Distinguished Service Medal, our highest noncombat award.

More Skill Practice

Identifying Central Issues Instruct students to list as many reasons as they can why Americans volunteered for military service in World War I. **Ask: What causes would make you willing to volunteer for military service?** *(Students' answers will vary.)* **OL**

Divisions fought in bitter battles along the Western Front. Many of them won praise from both the French commander, Marshal Henri Pétain, and the United States commander, General John Pershing. The entire 369th Infantry Regiment won the highly prized French decoration, the Croix de Guerre ("war cross"), for gallantry in combat.

Women in the Military World War I was the first war in which women officially served in the armed forces, although only in noncombat positions. Women nurses had served in both the army and navy since the early 1900s, but as auxiliaries. Before World War I, nurses were not assigned ranks, and the women were not technically enlisted in the army or navy.

As the military prepared for war in 1917, it faced a severe shortage of clerical workers because so many men were assigned to active duty. Early in 1917, the navy authorized the enlistment of women to meet its clerical needs. By the end of the war, over 11,000 women had served in the navy. Although most performed clerical duties, others served as radio operators, electricians, pharmacists, and photographers.

The army still did not enlist women. Instead, it hired them as temporary clerical workers. The only women to actually serve in the army were in the Army Nursing Corps. Army nurses were the only women in the military sent overseas during the war. Over 20,000 nurses served in the army during the war, including more than 10,000 overseas.

✓ **Reading Check** **Describing** How did Congress ensure that the military had enough troops to fight the war?

Organizing Industry

Main Idea The government used Progressive ideas to manage the economy and pay for the war.

Reading Connection In what ways do you help conserve food or fuel resources? Read on to learn about America's response to the needs of the military in World War I.

The progressive emphasis on careful planning and scientific management shaped the federal government's approach to mobilizing the American war economy. To efficiently manage the relationship

Picturing **History**

Women and War Although not allowed in combat, many women served in auxiliary positions, such as nursing. Here, Birmingham, Alabama, women collect money during a Red Cross parade in 1918. In what other capacities did women serve during the war?

between the federal government and private companies, Congress created special boards. These boards emphasized cooperation between big business and government. Business executives, professional managers, and government representatives staffed the boards. Their goal was to ensure the most efficient use of national resources to further the war effort.

The War Industries Board One of the first agencies established was the **War Industries Board** (WIB). Created in July 1917, the WIB's job was to coordinate the production of war materials. At first, President Wilson was reluctant to give the WIB much authority over the economy, but by March 1918, he decided industrial production needed better coordination. The WIB was reorganized and **Bernard Baruch** was appointed to run it. Under this Wall Street stockbroker's supervision, the WIB told manufacturers what to produce. It controlled the flow of raw materials, ordered the construction of new factories, and occasionally, with the president's approval, set prices.

Food and Fuel Perhaps the most successful government agency was the Food Administration, run by Herbert Hoover. This agency was responsible for increasing food production while reducing civilian consumption. Instead of using rationing, Hoover encouraged Americans to save food on their own. Using the slogan "Food Will Win the War—Don't Waste It," the Food Administration encouraged families to "Hooverize" by "serving just enough" and by having Wheatless Mondays, Meatless Tuesdays, and

CHAPTER 6 World War I and Its Aftermath **377**

Picturing **History**

Answer: secretaries, radio operators, electricians, and pharmacists, among others
Ask: Why did the Navy finally enlist women? (to meet its clerical needs)

Did You Know?

During World War I there were five Liberty and Victory Bond campaigns that raised $23 billion. This money came from a nation with a total annual income of $70 billion and reflected Americans' wholehearted support of the war.

W **Writing Strategy**

Expository Writing Ask students to write a one-page paper that describes gains for women due to World War I and limitations that remained imposed on them. **AL** **CA** 11WA2.4a

C **Critical Thinking**

Making Inferences Discuss in class the steps the government took to keep the economy strong during the war. **Ask:** What other ways can you think of that citizens could sacrifice financially to help the country during war time? (Answers might include: volunteering their time; sending blankets to soldiers; recycling; conserving fuel by walking instead of driving when possible.) **BL**

Review the Big Idea

Review the Big Idea for this section, "The fate of nations is forever changed by monumental world events." Ask students to write a one-page paper explaining U.S. attempts to organize the nation's war-time industry. **OL** **CA** 11WA2.4b

R **Reading Strategy**

Cooperative Learning Divide students into small groups. Instruct the groups to design a poster that the Food and Drug Administration could have used to encourage food rationing. Display the posters in the classroom. **OL**

✓ **Reading Check**

Answer: The Selective Service Act of 1917 required all men ages 21 to 30 to register for the draft.

377

Porkless Thursdays. Hoover also encouraged citizens to plant **victory gardens** to raise their own vegetables, leaving more for the troops.

While Hoover managed food production, the Fuel Administration, run by Harry Garfield, tried to manage the nation's use of coal and oil. To conserve energy, Garfield introduced daylight savings time and shortened workweeks for factories that did not make war materials.

Paying for the War By the end of World War I, the United States was spending about $44 million a day—leading to a total expenditure of about $32 billion for the entire conflict. To fund the war effort, Congress raised income tax rates. Congress also placed new taxes on corporate profits and an extra tax on the profits of arms factories.

Taxes, however, could not pay for the war. To raise money, the government borrowed over $20 billion from the American people by selling **Liberty Bonds** and **Victory Bonds.** By buying the bonds, Americans were loaning the government money. The government agreed to repay the money with interest in a specified number of years. Posters, rallies, and "Liberty Loan sermons" encouraged people to buy the bonds as an act of patriotism.

✓ **Reading Check** **Summarizing** What federal agencies helped control American industries during the war?

Mobilizing the Workforce

Main Idea Women, African Americans, and Mexican Americans all helped to fill labor shortages created by the draft.

Reading Connection How did women and African Americans assist on the home front and the military during the Civil War? Read on to learn of their contributions to World War I.

Officials knew they needed workers to cooperate if mobilization was to succeed. To prevent strikes from disrupting the war effort, the government established the National War Labor Board (NWLB) in March 1918. Chaired by William Howard Taft and Frank Walsh, a labor attorney, the NWLB tried to mediate labor disputes that might otherwise lead to strikes.

The NWLB frequently pressured industry to grant important concessions to workers, including wage increases, an eight-hour workday, and the right of unions to organize and bargain collectively. In exchange, labor leaders agreed not to disrupt war production with strikes or other disturbances. As a result, membership in unions increased by just over one million between 1917 and 1919.

Women Support Industry The war increased work opportunities for women, who filled industrial

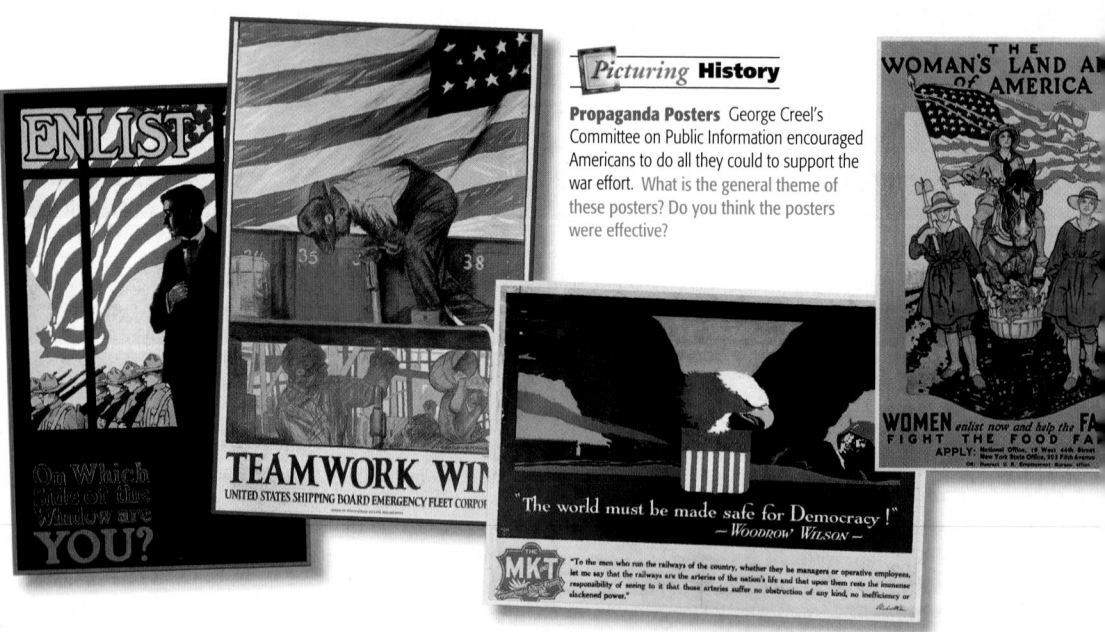

Picturing History

Propaganda Posters George Creel's Committee on Public Information encouraged Americans to do all they could to support the war effort. What is the general theme of these posters? Do you think the posters were effective?

Picturing History

Answer: The general theme is supporting the war effort. The posters were effective in reminding people of their patriotic duty.

Ask: What was the main message of each of these posters? *(Students' answers will vary. Some ideas might include encouraging men to enlist in the armed forces, coming together at work for the war effort, patriotic messages about democracy, and encouraging victory gardens.)*

jobs vacated by men serving in the military. These included positions in the shipping, manufacturing, and railroad industries. These new jobs for women, however, were not permanent. After the war, when the servicemen returned home, most women returned to their previous jobs or stopped working.

The Great Migration Begins With fewer immigrants and white workers being drafted, the war also opened new doors for African Americans. Wartime job openings and high wages drew thousands of African Americans to factories producing war materials. Encouraged by recruiting agents promising high wages and plentiful work, between 300,000 and 500,000 African Americans left the South to settle in Northern cities. This massive population movement became known as the "Great Migration." It greatly altered the racial makeup of such cities as Chicago, New York, Cleveland, and Detroit.

Mexican Americans Head North African Americans were not the only group to migrate north. Continued political turmoil in Mexico and the wartime labor shortage in the United States convinced many Mexicans to head north. Between 1917 and 1920, over 100,000 Mexicans **migrated** into Texas, Arizona, California, and New Mexico, providing labor for the farms and ranches of the Southwest.

Meanwhile, tens of thousands of Mexican Americans headed north to Chicago, St. Louis, Omaha, and other cities to take wartime factory jobs. Many Mexican Americans faced hostility and discrimination when they arrived in American cities. Like other immigrants before them, they tended to settle in their own separate neighborhoods, called barrios, where they could support each other.

✔ **Reading Check** **Evaluating** How permanent were women's advances in the wartime workplace?

Ensuring Public Support

Main Idea Propaganda and limits on civil liberties were part of domestic life during World War I.

Reading Connection Under what circumstances do you believe the government has a right to limit civil liberties? Read on to learn about the limitations imposed during World War I.

Progressives in the government did not think coordinating business and labor was enough to ensure the success of the war effort. They also believed that the government should take steps to shape public opinion and build support for the war.

Selling the War A new government agency, the **Committee on Public Information,** had the task of "selling" the war to the American people. The head of the CPI was journalist George Creel, who recruited advertising executives, commercial artists, authors, songwriters, entertainers, public speakers, and motion picture companies to help sway public opinion in favor of the war.

The CPI distributed pamphlets and posters, issued press releases, and arranged for thousands of short patriotic talks, called "four-minute speeches," to be delivered at movie theaters and public halls and gathering places. The Four-Minute Men urged audiences to support the war in various ways, from buying war bonds to reporting draft dodgers to the proper authorities.

CHAPTER 6   World War I and Its Aftermath   **379**

Federal Mobilization Agencies

Agency	Purpose
War Industries Board	Organized industry to increase efficiency, maximizing production
Railroad Administration	Assumed temporary control of rail lines to modernize equipment and increase operating efficiency
Food Administration	Supervised agricultural production, promoted food conservation and rationing
Fuel Administration	Increased production of coal and oil; maintained conservation of fuel with such innovations as daylight savings time
National War Labor Board	Maintained cooperation between industry management and labor unions; acted as mediator to prevent and quickly settle disputes
Committee on Public Information	Provided propaganda to rally citizen support for all aspects of the war effort

Chart Skills

1. **Interpreting Charts** Which agency worked with manufacturers and labor unions?
2. **Analyzing** How did the Fuel Administration's daylight savings time plan achieve its goal?

R Reading Strategy

Predicting Many actions taken by the government during the war were viewed as emergency measures and were not intended to be permanent social changes. **Ask:** When the war is over and servicemen return to their jobs, how do you think women, African Americans, and Mexican Americans, who have taken on these jobs, will be affected? *(Students may predict such things as more unemployment; poverty; racial tensions; minorities forced to lower paying jobs.)* **AL**

S Skill Practice

Using Geography Skills Provide students with a map of the United States and have them locate the major cities affected by the Great Migration. **Ask:** Why do you think these cities attracted so many African Americans? *(large cities with vast opportunities; centers of business and industry)* **OL** **CA CS3**

U Universal Access

Special Education Listening in class to several World War I songs, such as "Over There," "Pack Up Your Troubles in Your Old Kit Bag," and "Keep the Home Fires Burning," may provide an opportunity to engage students who have difficulty relating to the content in more traditional ways. Have students listen to the songs and prompt them to discuss their understanding of the lyrics. **Ask:** Do you think these songs were effective in swaying public opinion in favor of the war? *(Students' answers will vary.)* **BL**

✔ **Reading Check**

Answer: The gains were mostly temporary.

Chart Skills

Answer:
1. National War Labor Board
2. Because Daylight Savings Time moved sunset one hour later, people used less fuel.

Chart Skills Practice
Ask: Which of the federal mobilization agencies do you think had the greatest impact on ordinary citizens? *(Many students will note that the Committee on Public Information had the broadest impact.)*

R Reading Strategy

Scaffolding—Academic Vocabulary The word *legislation* was introduced in Chapter 5, Section 1. Ask a student to define the word. **BL**

S Skill Practice

Historical Interpretation
During times of war, the government often tries to expand its powers in order to take emergency measures. **Ask:** Why would it be easy for someone to be falsely accused of spying under the Espionage Act of 1917? *(The actions considered espionage were subjective. It is hard to define interfering with the war effort or showing disloyalty.)* **AL** **CA HI4**

C Critical Thinking

Drawing Conclusions Remind students that a sedition act was also passed during John Adams's presidential administration. **Ask:** Do you believe the Sedition Act violated citizens' right to free speech? *(Students should defend their answers.)* **OL**

Answers and Additional Support

Different Viewpoints

Abrams v. United States, 1919

The Espionage Act of 1917 made it a crime to "willfully utter, print, write, or publish any disloyal, profane, scurrilous or abusive language about the government." Although the act limited First Amendment freedoms, many Americans believed winning World War I was more important. *(See page 962 for more information on* Abrams v. the United States.*)*

Justice John H. Clarke delivered the majority opinion:

It is argued, somewhat faintly, that the acts charged against the defendants were not unlawful because within the protection of that freedom . . . of speech and of the press . . . and that the entire Espionage Act is unconstitutional. . . .

. . . the plain purpose of their propaganda was to excite, at the supreme crisis of the war, disaffection, sedition, riots, and, as they hoped, revolution, in this country for the purpose of embarrassing, and, if possible, defeating the military plans of the Government in Europe. . . . [T]he language of these circulars was obviously intended to provoke and to encourage resistance to the United States in the war, as the third count runs, and the defendants, in terms, plainly urged and advocated a resort to a general strike of workers in ammunition factories for the purpose of curtailing the production of ordnance and munitions necessary and essential to the prosecution of the war. . . . Thus, it is clear not only that some evidence, but that much persuasive evidence, was before the jury tending to prove that the defendants were guilty as charged. . . .

Justice Oliver Wendell Holmes, Jr., dissenting:

It is only the present danger of immediate evil or an intent to bring it about that warrants Congress in setting a limit to the expression of opinion where private rights are not concerned. Congress certainly cannot forbid all effort to change the mind of the country. Now nobody can suppose that the surreptitious publishing of a silly leaflet by an unknown man, without more, would present any immediate danger that its opinions would hinder the success of the government arms or have any appreciable tendency to do so.

In this case, sentences of twenty years' imprisonment have been imposed for the publishing of two leaflets that I believe the defendants had as much right to publish as the Government has to publish the Constitution of the United States now vainly invoked by them. . . . I regret that I cannot put into more impressive words my belief that, in their conviction upon this indictment, the defendants were deprived of their rights under the Constitution of the United States.

Amendment I

—Congress shall make no law respecting an establishment of religion, or prohibiting the free exercise thereof; or abridging the freedom of speech, or of the press; or the right of the people peaceably to assemble, and to petition the Government for a redress of grievances.

Learning From History

1. What were the charges against the defendants?
2. On what key point did Holmes and Clarke disagree?

Despite these efforts to build support for the war, several groups supported draft dodgers and their right to object to serving in the war. Over the years, these groups developed into the American Civil Liberties Union (ACLU). Founded in 1920, the ACLU works to protect people's rights. It focuses on three major areas of civil liberties: freedom of inquiry and expression, equality for all before the law, and due process.

R **Civil Liberties Curtailed** In addition to using propaganda and persuasion, the government also restricted some civil liberties by passing legislation to fight antiwar activities or enemies at home. **Espionage,** or spying to acquire secret government information, was addressed in the Espionage Act of 1917, which established penalties and prison terms for anyone who gave aid to the enemy. This act also penalized disloyalty, giving false reports, or otherwise interfering with the war effort. The Post Office even hired college professors to translate foreign periodicals to find out if they contained antiwar messages.

S

The Sedition Act of 1918 expanded the meaning of the Espionage Act to make illegal any public expression of opposition to the war. In practice, it allowed officials to prosecute anyone who criticized the president or the government. Combined, these laws generated over 1,500 prosecutions and 1,000 convictions.

C

Different Viewpoints

Answers:
1. inciting revolution
2. freedom of the press and freedom of speech
Ask: Why did Justice Holmes dissent from the majority opinion? *(He believed that the writers had constitutional protection in writing and publishing their leaflets.)*

Resources for page 380

Have students learn more about World War I by assigning the following:

📁 *Primary Source Reading 6-1*

📁 *Moments in Time, Unit 6: World War I (1914–1919)*

A Climate of Suspicion The fear of spies and emphasis on patriotism quickly led to the mistreatment and persecution of German Americans. To avoid German-sounding names, advertisers began to call sauerkraut "Liberty cabbage" and hamburger "Salisbury steak." Many schools dropped German language classes from their curricula, and orchestras stopped performing the music of Beethoven, Schubert, Wagner, and other German composers. Anti-German feelings sometimes led to violence against innocent citizens.

German Americans were not the only ones under suspicion. Mobs attacked labor activists, socialists, and pacifists. Newspapers ads urged Americans to monitor the activities of their fellow citizens. Americans even formed private organizations, such as the American Protective League and the Boy Spies of America, to spy on neighbors and coworkers. Secretary of War Newton Baker expressed concern about the growing intolerance:

66 There is a growing frenzy of suspicion and hostility toward disloyalty. I am afraid we are going to have a good many instances of people roughly treated on very slight evidence of disloyalty. Already a number of men and some women have been tarred and feathered, and a portion of the press is urging with great vehemence more strenuous efforts at detection and punishment. 99

–quoted in *Echoes of Distant Thunder*

▲ *George Creel*

The Supreme Court Limits Free Speech Despite protests against the government's tactics, however, the courts generally upheld the principle behind them. Although the First Amendment specifically states that "Congress shall make no law . . . abridging the freedom of speech, or of the press," the Supreme Court decided otherwise, departing from a strict literal interpretation of the Constitution.

In the landmark case of *Schenck v. the United States* (1919), the Supreme Court ruled that an individual's freedom of speech could be curbed when the words uttered **constitute** a "clear and present danger." The Court used as an example someone yelling "Fire!" in a crowded theater. It described such an event as a situation in which freedom of speech would be superseded by the theatergoers' right to safety. The Court's majority opinion stated, "When a nation is at war, many things that might be said in times of peace are such a hindrance to its effort that their utterance will not be endured so long as [soldiers] fight. . . ." 📖 *(See page 1007 for more information on Schenck v. the* United States*.)*

✓ **Reading Check** **Explaining** Why did Congress pass the Espionage Act in 1917?

HISTORY Online **Study Central**

For help with the concepts in this section of *American Vision: Modern Times* go to tav.mt.glencoe.com and click on **Study Central**.

SECTION 2 ASSESSMENT

Checking for Understanding

1. **Vocabulary** Define: draft, conscription, victory garden, migrate, espionage, constitute.

2. **People and Terms** Identify: War Industries Board, Bernard Baruch, Liberty Bond, Victory Bond, Committee on Public Information.

3. **Describe** the contributions of African Americans during the war.

Reviewing Big Ideas

4. **Summarizing** How did government efforts to ensure support for the war conflict with democratic ideals?

Critical Thinking

5. **Analyzing** How did World War I cause the federal government to change its relationship with the business world?

6. **Organizing** Use a graphic organizer similar to the one below to identify the effects of the war on the American workforce.

Effects of War on U.S. Workforce

Analyzing Visuals

7. **Analyzing Posters** Examine the posters on page 378. How do these images encourage support for the war? How effective do you think they would be today?

Writing About History

8. **Persuasive Writing** Imagine that you are working for the Committee on Public Information. Write text for an advertisement or lyrics to a song in which you attempt to sway public opinion in favor of the war. CA 11WS1.5

CHAPTER 6 World War I and Its Aftermath **381**

S Skill Practice

Identifying Points of View On the board list the headings *Labor Activists, Socialists,* and *Pacifists.* Under each heading have students cite reasons why American citizens might have viewed these groups with suspicion, and then analyze what is faulty or unfair about these suspicions. *(Students' answers will vary but should reflect information from the text.)*
OL CA HR1

ASSESS

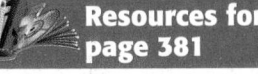

Resources for page 381

Use these resources to assess student mastery.

📁 Section Quiz 6-2

📁 Reading Essentials and Study Guide 6-2

⊙ Interactive Tutor Self-Assessment CD-ROM

📁 California Standards Practice, Grade 11

✓ **Reading Check**

Answer: to control public opinion and stop antiwar supporters

HISTORY Online

Study Central provides audio summaries, interactive games, and online graphic organizers to help students review section content.

CLOSE

Below Grade Level Instruct students to go back through the section and locate the main idea in each paragraph. If needed, team up classmates so that struggling students will have assistance with this activity. BL

381

SECTION 2 ASSESSMENT ANSWERS

1. Content vocabulary is boldfaced and highlighted in yellow. Academic vocabulary is boldfaced.

2. War Industries Board (p. 377), Bernard Baruch (p. 377), Liberty Bond (p. 378), Victory Bond (p. 378), Committee on Public Information (p. 379)

3. About 400,000 African Americans were drafted to serve in the war; many received high praise for their courage from French generals.

4. limited free speech and freedom of the press

5. Special boards were created that encouraged cooperation between business and government.

6. Effects should include increased job opportunities for women and African Americans.

7. Supporting the war is portrayed as admirable; other answers will vary.

8. Answers will vary. Invite students to display or perform their work.

TIME NOTEBOOK

FOCUS

History–Social Science Standards

This feature addresses the following standards:

11.4 Students trace the rise of the United States to its role as a world power in the twentieth century.

11.4.5 Analyze the political, economic, and social ramifications of World War I on the home front.

TEACH

W Writing Support

Research Report Writing Have interested students research non-military inventions that occurred between 1914 and 1918. Have students write a report on their findings. While reports are being presented, have the class create a time line of the various inventions. **AL** **CA 11WS1.6**

Answers and Additional Support

American soldiers set sail for Europe.

World War Firsts

Human ingenuity goes to work in the service of war:

AERIAL COMBAT, 1914. War takes to the air. Two Allied aircraft chase two German planes across Britain.

GAS ATTACKS, 1915. The German High Command admits to using chlorine gas bombs and shells on the field of combat. Deadly mustard gas is used in 1917.

GAS MASKS. Issued to Allied soldiers in 1915.

DONKEY'S EARS. A new trench periscope enables soldiers to observe the battleground from the relative safety of a trench without risking sniper fire.

BIG BERTHA. Enormous howitzer gun bombards Paris. "Big Bertha," named after the wife of its manufacturer, is thought to be located nearly 63 miles behind German lines. Moving at night on railroad tracks, the gun is difficult for the Allies to locate.

Color My World

Some bright spots in a dark decade:

- Color newspaper supplements (1914)
- 3-D films (1915)
- Nail polish (1916)
- Three-color traffic lights (1918)
- Color photography introduced by Eastman Kodak (1914)

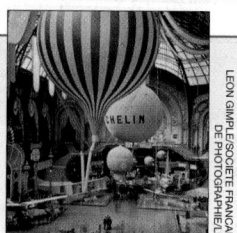

One of the first color photographs

VERBATIM

❝My message was one of death for young men. How odd to applaud that.❞
> **WOODROW WILSON,** *on returning to the White House after asking Congress for a declaration of war, 1917*

❝Food is Ammunition—Don't Waste It❞
> **POSTER FROM U.S. FOOD ADMINISTRATION,** *administered by Herbert Hoover*

❝I have had a hard time getting over this war. My old world died.❞
> **RAY STANNARD BAKER,** *journalist*

❝Let us, while this war lasts, forget our special grievances and close our ranks shoulder to shoulder with our own white fellow citizens and the allied nations that are fighting for democracy.❞
> **W.E.B. DU BOIS,** *African American scholar and leader, 1918*

❝America has at one bound become a world power in a sense she never was before.❞
> **BRITISH PRIME MINISTER DAVID LLOYD GEORGE,** *on the U.S. entry into World War I, 1917*

❝In the camps I saw barrels mounted on sticks on which zealous captains were endeavoring to teach their men how to ride a horse.❞
> **THEODORE ROOSEVELT,** *on touring U.S. military training facilities, 1917*

❝The war was over, and it seemed as if everything in the world were possible, and everything was new, and that peace was going to be all we dreamed about.❞
> **FLORENCE HARRIMAN,** *Red Cross volunteer, in Paris on Armistice Day, 1918*

COOPERATIVE LEARNING ACTIVITY

Creating a Magazine Spread Organize the class into groups of four or five. Have students create a magazine spread about America's war on terrorism. Although students may use ideas from recent news magazines, encourage the groups to look for their own unique angle for the spread. Students should look at current magazines and books for ideas about page design. This activity can be completed using desktop publishing software or the more traditional cut-and-paste method. **OL**

How to Make a Doughboy

Take one American infantryman.

BROWN BROTHERS

1. Arm with 107 pieces of fighting equipment, including:
   - rifle
   - rifle cartridges
   - cartridge belt
   - steel helmet
   - clubs
   - knives
   - gas mask
   - wire cutters
   - trench tool
   - bayonet and scabbard
   - grenades

2. Add 50 articles of clothing, including 3 wool blankets and a bedsack.

3. Equip with eating utensils and 11 cooking implements.

4. Train well.

TOTAL COST: $156.30

(not including training and transportation to Europe)

Milestones

REPATRIATED, APRIL 10, 1917. VLADIMIR ILYICH LENIN, to Russia, after an 11-year absence. The leader of the leftist Bolshevik party hopes to reorganize his revolutionary group.

CULVER PICTURES

Vladimir Lenin

SHOT DOWN AND KILLED, APRIL 22, 1918. "THE RED BARON," Manfred von Richthofen, Germany's ace pilot. Von Richthofen destroyed more than 80 Allied aircraft. On hearing of the Red Baron's death, English fighter pilot Edward Mannock said, "I hope he roasted all the way down."

BROWN BROTHERS

Jeannette Rankin

ELECTED, NOVEMBER 7, 1916. JEANNETTE RANKIN of Montana, to the U.S. Congress. The first woman congressional representative explained her victory by saying that women "got the vote in Montana because the spirit of pioneer days was still alive."

EXECUTED, OCTOBER 15, 1917. MATA HARI, in France, for espionage. The famous Dutch dancer was sentenced to death for spying for the Germans.

NUMBERS 1915

$1,040 Average annual income for workers in finance, insurance, and real estate

$687 Average income for industrial workers (higher for union workers, lower for nonunion workers)

$510 Average income for retail trade workers

$355 Average income for farm laborers

$342 Average income for domestic servants

$328 Average income for public school teachers

$11.95 Cost of a bicycle

BROWN BROTHERS

$1.15 Cost of a baseball

$1 Average cost of a hotel room

39¢ Cost of one dozen eggs

5¢ Cost of a glass of cola

7¢ Cost of a large roll of toilet paper

W Writing Support

Research Report Writing

Have students research information about the doughboys, such as why they were given their name, what they did between battles, and what their life in the trenches was like. Based on their research, have students write a profile of the average World War I soldier. **OL** **CA** 11WA2.1e; 11WA2.4a

C₁ Critical Thinking

Analyzing Information

Have students select one of the famous people mentioned in the Milestones. Ask each student to learn one new thing about the person selected. Have volunteers share their findings with the class. **BL**

C₂ Critical Thinking

Comparing and Contrasting

Ask students to construct a chart that shows the cost of these listed items today and the increase in their prices. **OL**

ASSESS/CLOSE

Visit the **TIME** Web site at www.time.com for up-to-date news, weekly editorials, online polls, and an archive of past magazine and Web articles.

EXTENDING THE CONTENT

Stars and Stripes *Stars and Stripes,* the armed forces newspaper staffed entirely by soldiers, was first published in 1918. In addition to being a source of information and morale for soldiers, it provided many young journalists and cartoonists with their first jobs. Two well-known cartoonists whose work appeared in *Stars and Stripes* were Milt Caniff ("Terry and the Pirates") and Bill Mauldin, who won the Pulitzer Prize in 1945 for his "Willie" and "GI Joe" cartoons.

FOCUS

BELLRINGER
SKILLBUILDER ACTIVITY

Project **Daily Focus Skills Transparency 6-3** and have students answer the question.

Guide to Reading

Understanding Vocabulary: Have students look through the section to identify the content vocabulary and academic vocabulary words and use each in a sentence.

Answers to Graphic: airplanes, poison gas, machine guns, trenches, tanks

Unpacking the Standards

Students will be able to:

- Explain how changes in technology affected the course of the war.

- Analyze President Wilson's peace plan following World War I and reasons it was rejected by Congress.

Answers and Additional Support

SECTION 3 A Bloody Conflict

Guide to Reading

Connection
In the previous section, you learned about the home front. In this section, you will find out about World War I and its end.

Main Idea
- New technologies made World War I the first modern war. (p. 385)
- American soldiers entered the war, boosting morale and fighting courageously. (p. 386)
- The United States rejected Wilson's generous peace plan and the League of Nations. (p. 388)

Content Vocabulary
convoy, armistice, reparations

Academic Vocabulary
network, adequately, resolve

People and Terms to Identify
Vladimir Lenin, Treaty of Brest-Litovsk, Fourteen Points, League of Nations, Treaty of Versailles

Reading Objectives
- **Discuss** the fighting techniques used in World War I.
- **Characterize** the American response to the Treaty of Versailles.

Reading Strategy
Organizing As you read about the battles of World War I, complete a graphic organizer similar to the one below by listing the kinds of warfare and technology used in the fighting.

Warfare and Technology Used in World War I

Preview of Events

♦1915   ♦1917   ♦1919

July 1916 Battle of the Somme begins

November 1917 Communists seize power in Russia

March 1918 Treaty of Brest-Litovsk ends war between Russia and Germany

September 1918 Beginning of Battle of the Argonne Forest

November 1918 Armistice ends war

The following are the main History–Social Science Standards covered in this section.

11.4 Students trace the rise of the United States to its role as a world power in the twentieth century.

11.4.4 Explain Theodore Roosevelt's Big Stick diplomacy, William Taft's Dollar Diplomacy, and Woodrow Wilson's Moral Diplomacy, drawing on relevant speeches.

≈ The Big Idea ≈

The fate of nations is forever changed by monumental world events. World War I changed the nature of combat. Soldiers faced trench warfare, poison gas, and tanks and airplanes in battle. Even before the end of the war, President Wilson had proposed a plan known as the Fourteen Points. The leaders of the victorious countries considered this plan too lenient toward Germany and instead approved the Treaty of Versailles. The treaty stripped Germany of its armed forces and required the country to pay heavy reparations. The treaty also dissolved four empires—Russia, the Ottoman Empire, the German Empire, and Austria-Hungary—and created nine new countries. While the Treaty of Versailles did call for the creation of the League of Nations, the United States never joined, because Congress refused to approve the treaty.

384 CHAPTER 6   World War I and Its Aftermath

SECTION RESOURCES

📂 Print Material
- Reproducible Lesson Plan 6-3
- Guided Reading Activity 6-3
- Reading Essentials and Study Guide 6-3
- Active Reading Note-Taking Guide 6-3

🔦 Transparencies
- Daily Focus Skills Transparency 6-3
- Section Graphic Organizer Transparency 6-3

Technology
- 💿 Interactive Tutor Self-Assessment CD-ROM
- 💿 ExamView® Pro Testmaker CD-ROM
- 💿 Presentation Plus! CD-ROM

Combat in World War I

Main Idea New technologies made World War I the first modern war.

Reading Connection What new technologies have been developed or proposed in your lifetime? Read on to learn about the weapons that World War I personnel faced.

By the spring of 1917, World War I had devastated Europe. Old-fashioned strategies and new technologies resulted in terrible destruction. Many Americans and Europeans, however, believed American troops would quickly bring the war to an end.

★ An American Story ★

General John J. Pershing, commander of the American forces in World War I, could not help but feel a sense of pride and excitement as he watched the Second Battalion of the First Division's 16th Infantry march through the streets of Paris on July 4, 1917:

❝ . . . The battalion was joined by a great crowd, many women forcing their way into the ranks and swinging along arm in arm with the men. With wreaths about their necks and bouquets in their hats and rifles, the column looked like a moving flower garden. With only a semblance of military formation, the animated throng pushed its way through avenues of people to the martial strains of the French band and the still more thrilling music of cheering voices.❞

—quoted in
The Yanks Are Coming

While his men marched through Paris, Pershing raced to Picpus Cemetery, the burial place of the Marquis de Lafayette, a French noble who had fought in the American Revolution. One of Pershing's officers, Colonel Charles E. Stanton, raised his hand in salute and acknowledged the continuing American-French relationship by proclaiming, "Lafayette, we are here!"

▲ *John J. Pershing*

Trench Warfare The American soldiers who went to Europe knew they would face a war different from any war they had seen before. Trench warfare and technological innovations had changed the battlefield. The early offensives of 1914 quickly demonstrated that the nature of warfare had changed. Troops that dug themselves in and relied upon modern rifles and a new weapon—the rapidfire machine gun—could easily hold off the attacking forces. On the Western Front, troops dug a **network** of trenches that stretched from the English Channel to the Swiss border. The space between the opposing trenches was known as "no man's land," a rough, barren landscape pockmarked with craters from artillery fire. Many soldiers would lose their lives in this no man's land as they attempted to attack enemy trenches.

To break through enemy lines, both sides began with massive artillery barrages. Then bayonet wielding soldiers would scramble out of their trenches, race across no man's land, and hurl grenades into the enemy's trenches. The results were often disastrous. The artillery barrages rarely destroyed the enemy defenses, leaving the enemy with ample artillery to fire at attacking troops. The troops crossing no man's land were easily stopped by enemy machine guns and rifle fire. This kind of assault caused staggeringly high casualties. In major battles, both sides often lost several hundred thousand men.

These battles produced horrific scenes of death and destruction, as one American soldier noted in his diary:

❝ Many dead Germans along the road. One heap on a manure pile . . . Devastation everywhere. Our barrage has rooted up the entire territory like a ploughed field. Dead horses galore, many of them have a hind quarter cut off—the Huns [Germans] need food. Dead men here and there.❞

—quoted in
The American Spirit

New Technology As it became clear that charging enemy trenches could bring only limited success at great cost, both sides began to develop new technologies to help them break through enemy lines. In April 1915, the Germans first used poison gas in the

CHAPTER 6 World War I and Its Aftermath **385**

TEACH

W Writing Support

Narrative Writing Have students take on the role of a young soldier leaving for war. Instruct them to write a letter to a family member or close friend. The letter should explain why the person is going to war, what he or she fears, and what the relative or friend can do to help. **BL** **CA** 11WA2.4a

R Reading Strategy

Analyzing Tell students to read the description of trench warfare. **Ask:** Why were casualty rates so high in World War I? (*Troops crossing the open spaces between trenches known as "no man's land" were easily gunned down by enemy fire.*) **BL**

C Critical Thinking

Drawing Conclusions Have students list the types of technological developments used in World War I. **Ask:** Which new technology do you think had the greatest impact on the war? (*Students' answers are likely to vary, but all students should defend their answers with a reasoned argument, based on textbook information.*) **OL**

Did You Know?

Corpses left in trenches, as well as food scraps, attracted many rats. Since rats propagate rapidly (one pair of rats can produce 880 offspring in a year), the trenches soon became infested. The rats became large and bold and would even eat a wounded man if he could not defend himself.

Skill Practice

Using Geography Skills

Instruct students to analyze the maps on pages 386 and 387. Have students divide a piece of paper into three columns entitled "Allied Victory," "Central Powers Victory," and "Indecisive Battle," and then list each battle fought during the war under the correct heading. **OL** **CA CS3**

Writing Skill

Research Report Writing

Have students select one battle from World War I and write a short research report. The paper should include each side's strategy, advantages or disadvantages, the types of warfare used, and the outcome of the battle. **AL**
CA 11WA2.1a

Reading Strategy

Determining Importance

As students read the text under the heading "The Americans and Victory," have them note the turning points in the war that led to an Allied victory. **OL**

✓ Reading Check

Answer: machine guns, tanks, airplanes, poison gas

Answers and Additional Support

NATIONAL GEOGRAPHIC **Battles of World War I, 1914–1918**

Allied Powers
Central Powers
Neutral nations
German unrestricted submarine warfare zone
Allied offensives
Central Powers' offensives
Farthest advance of Central Powers
Line of trench warfare, 1915–1917
Allied victory
Central Powers' victory
Indecisive battle

❻ Lusitania sunk May 7, 1915
Battles of Ypres ❸ Oct.–Nov. 1914 ❹ Apr.–May 1915
❶ Tannenberg Aug. 1914
❽ Battle of the Somme July–Nov. 1916
❼ Battle of Verdun Feb.–Dec. 1916
❷ First Battle of the Marne Sept. 1914
❾ Caporetto Oct.–Dec. 1917
❺ Gallipoli Apr. 1915–Jan. 1916

Petrograd (St. Petersburg)

0 500 miles
0 500 kilometers
Lambert Azimuthal Equal-Area projection

Second Battle of Ypres. The fumes caused vomiting, blindness, and suffocation. Soon afterward the Allies also began using poison gas, and gas masks became a necessary part of a soldier's equipment.

In 1916 the British introduced the tank into battle. The first tanks were very slow and cumbersome, mechanically unreliable, and fairly easy to destroy. They could roll over barbed wire and trenches, but there were usually not enough of them to make a difference. While tanks did help troops, they did not revolutionize warfare in World War I.

World War I also saw the first use of airplanes in combat. At first, planes were used mainly to observe enemy activities. Soon, the Allies and Central Powers used them to drop small bombs. As technology advanced, they also attached machine guns to aircraft to engage in deadly air battles known as dogfights.

✓ Reading Check **Describing** What new technologies were introduced in World War I?

The Americans and Victory

Main Idea American soldiers entered the war, boosting morale and fighting courageously.

Personal Connection Do you recall a time in your life when you had to boost someone's morale or be courageous? Read on to learn about Americans who helped the Allies win World War I.

Wave upon wave of American troops marched into this bloody stalemate—nearly 2 million before the war's end. These "doughboys," a nickname for American soldiers, were largely inexperienced, but they were fresh, so their presence immediately boosted the morale of Allied forces.

Winning the War at Sea No American troopships were sunk on their way to Europe—an accomplishment due largely to the efforts of American

Did You Know?

Three pilots who flew bombers in World War I were among the best known fighters of the war. American Eddie Rickenbacker shot down 22 planes during the war. Flying aces from other countries also became famous. Manfred von Richthofen of Germany, known as the "Red Baron," was credited with 80 victories, and Rene Fonck of France with 75.

Resources for page 386

*Have students read about the new technologies used in World War I in the **Linking Past and Present Activity 6**.*

Western Front, 1914–1918

0 50 miles
0 50 kilometers
Albers Conic Equal-Area projection

NETHERLANDS

English Channel

Ypres
Oct.–Nov. 1914
Apr.–May 1915
July 1917

Antwerp
Sept. 1914

Neuve
Chapelle
Mar. 1915

Mons
Aug. 1914

BELGIUM

GERMANY

Le Cateau
Aug. 1914

Somme
July–Nov. 1916

Guise
Aug. 1914

LUX.

Verdun
Feb.–Dec. 1916

Somme Offensive
1918

Aisne Offensive
1918

St. Mihiel
Sept. 1918

Belleau Wood
June 1918

Argonne Forest
Sept.–Nov. 1918

Morhange
Aug. 1914

Paris

FRANCE

Château–Thierry
May–June 1918

First Battle
of the Marne
Sept. 1914

Allied Powers — **Allied offensives**
Central Powers — **Central Powers' offensives**
Neutral nations — **Farthest advance of Central Powers**
☆ **Allied victory** --- **Line of trench warfare, 1915–1917**
☆ **Central Powers' victory** — **Armistice Line, 1918**
☆ **Indecisive battle**

World War I Military Deaths*

British Empire 908,400
France 1,385,000
Italy 650,000
Russia 1,700,000
Romania 335,700
United States 107,000
Others 74,200
Bulgaria 87,500
Ottoman Empire 325,000
Austria-Hungary 1,200,000
Germany 1,773,000

Allies

Central Powers

* Figures are approximate

Geography *Skills*

1. **Interpreting Maps** Where did the majority of World War I battles occur?
2. **Interpreting Charts** Which nation suffered the largest number of military deaths during World War I?

Admiral William S. Sims. For most of the war, the British preferred to fight German submarines by sending warships to find them. Meanwhile, merchant ships would race across the Atlantic individually. The British approach had not worked well, and submarines had inflicted heavy losses on British shipping.

Sims proposed that merchant ships and troop transports be gathered into groups, called **convoys,** and escorted across the Atlantic by warships. If submarines wanted to attack a convoy, they would have to get past the warships protecting it. The convoy system greatly reduced shipping losses and ensured that American troops arrived safely in Europe. They arrived during a pivotal time in late 1917.

Russia Leaves the War In March 1917, riots broke out in Russia over the government's handling of the war and over the scarcity of food and fuel. On March 15, Czar Nicholas II, the leader of the Russian Empire, abdicated his throne. Political leadership in

Russia passed into the hands of a provisional, or temporary, government, consisting largely of moderate representatives who supported Russia's continued participation in World War I. The government, however, was unable to **adequately** deal with the major problems, such as food shortages, that were afflicting the nation.

The Bolsheviks, a group of Communists, soon competed for power in Russia. In November 1917, **Vladimir Lenin,** the leader of the Bolshevik Party, overthrew the Russian government and established a Communist government.

Germany's military fortunes improved with the Bolshevik takeover of Russia. Lenin's first act after seizing power was to pull Russia out of the war and concentrate on establishing a Communist state. He accomplished this by agreeing to the **Treaty of Brest-Litovsk** with Germany on March 3, 1918. Under this treaty, Russia lost substantial territory, giving up Ukraine, its Polish and Baltic territories, and Finland. However, the treaty also removed the German army

CHAPTER 6 World War I and Its Aftermath **387**

Review the Big Idea

Review the Big Idea for this section, "The fate of nations is forever changed by monumental world events." Ask students to review the circle graph of World War I military deaths. **Ask: How did the number of Russian deaths affect the nation?** *(Russia pulled out of the war early and the government was overthrown.)* **OL**

R Reading Strategy

Connecting Ask students to define the word *convoy* as both a noun and a verb. *(noun: a group of cars, trucks, or ships traveling together; verb: to escort or guide)* **Ask: Where do you typically see convoys today?** *(trucks traveling together on the highway)* **BL**

S Skill Practice

Chronological Thinking Have students create a time line of the events that led to Russia leaving the war. **OL** **CA CS1**

W Writing Support

Research Report Writing Using library or Internet resources, have students write a biographical report on Vladimir Lenin, focusing on his Communist beliefs and his leadership philosophies. **AL**
CA 11WA2.4a

Geography *Skills*

Answers:
1. along the Western Front in France
2. Germany—1,773,000

Geography Skills Practice
Ask: Approximately how many military deaths did the United States suffer in World War I?
(107,000)

387

Visual Literacy Have students refer back to the photo of the Argonne Forest on p. 363. **Ask: What conditions do you observe that would make fighting difficult?** *(Answers might include: fog, mud, lack of leaves to provide cover.)* **EL** **CA HI4**

C Critical Thinking

Identifying Central Issues Write the following statement on the board: "The peace treaty in Europe did not establish a lasting peace." Have students work in pairs to find reasons that support this statement, and discuss their findings. **OL**

W Writing Support

Summary Writing Have students create a database of the four leaders of the Allied nations. Instruct students to include the number of years each served as leader and any information on other international conflicts in which they were involved. From the facts students gather, have them write a paragraph on which leader they feel was the most experienced. **OL** **CA 11WA2.3a**

✓ Reading Check

Answer: to pull Russia out of the war and establish a Communist state

Answers and Additional Support

---

from the remaining Russian lands. With the Eastern Front settled, Germany was now free to concentrate its forces in the west.

The German Offensive Falters On March 21, 1918, the Germans launched a massive attack along the Western Front. German forces, reinforced with troops from the Russian front, pushed deeply into Allied lines. By early June, they were less than 40 miles (64 km) from Paris.

American troops played an important role in containing the German offensive. In late May, as the German offensive continued, the Americans launched their first major attack, quickly capturing the village of Cantigny. On June 1, American and French troops blocked the German drive on Paris at the town of Château-Thierry. On July 15, the Germans launched one last massive attack in a determined attempt to take Paris, but American and French troops held their ground.

S **The Battle of the Argonne Forest** With the German drive stalled, French Marshal Ferdinand Foch, supreme commander of the Allied forces, ordered massive counterattacks all along the front. In mid-September, American troops drove back German forces at the battle of Saint-Mihiel. The attack was a prelude to a massive American offensive in the region between the Meuse River and the Argonne Forest. General Pershing assembled over 600,000 American troops, some 40,000 tons of supplies, and roughly 4,000 artillery pieces for the most massive attack in American history.

The attack began on September 26, 1918. Slowly, the German positions fell to the advancing American troops. The Germans inflicted heavy casualties on the American forces, but by early November, the Americans had shattered the German defenses and opened a hole in the German lines.

Alvin York After taking command of his patrol in the Battle of Argonne Forest, York received the Medal of Honor and French Croix de Guerre. Upon returning home, the war hero founded a school for underprivileged children.

388 CHAPTER 6 World War I and Its Aftermath

The War Ends While fighting raged along the Western Front, a revolution engulfed Austria-Hungary, and the Ottoman Turks surrendered. Faced with the surrender of their allies and a naval mutiny at Kiel in early November, the people of Berlin rose in rebellion on November 9 and forced the German emperor to step down. At the 11th hour on the 11th day of the 11th month, 1918, the fighting stopped. Germany had finally signed an **armistice,** or cease-fire, that ended the war.

✓ Reading Check **Explaining** What was Vladimir Lenin's first goal after controlling Russia in 1917?

C A Flawed Peace

Main Idea The United States rejected Wilson's generous peace plan and the League of Nations.

Reading Connection How might your feelings toward a peace plan differ if you were a citizen of a defeated country compared to a victorious country? Read on to learn why the U.S. Senate would not ratify the Treaty of Versailles.

In January 1919, a peace conference began in Paris to try to **resolve** the complicated issues arising from World War I. The principal figures in the negotiations were the "Big Four," the leaders of the victorious **W** Allied nations: President Wilson of the United States, British prime minister David Lloyd George, French premier Georges Clemenceau, and Italian prime minister Vittorio Orlando. Germany was not invited to participate.

Wilson had presented his plan, known as the **Fourteen Points,** to Congress in January 1918. The Fourteen Points were based on "the principle of justice to all peoples and nationalities." In the first five points, the president proposed to eliminate the general causes of the war through free trade, disarmament, freedom of the seas, impartial adjustment of colonial claims, and open diplomacy instead of secret agreements. The next eight points addressed the right of self-determination. They also required the Central Powers to evacuate all of the countries invaded during the war, including France, Belgium, and Russia. The fourteenth point, perhaps the most important one to Wilson, called for the creation of a "general association of nations" known as the **League of Nations.** The League's member nations would help preserve peace and prevent future wars by pledging to respect and protect each other's territory and political independence. *(See page 998 for the text of the Fourteen Points.)*

More Skill Practice

Determining Importance Instruct students to use the Internet to research information on the League of Nations. **Ask: In what year was it dissolved, and why?** *(1946; it was ineffective in stopping the military aggression that led to World War II)* **What organization took its place?** *(the United Nations)* **OL**

The Treaty of Versailles As the peace talks progressed in the Palace of Versailles (vehr·SY), it became clear that Wilson's ideas did not coincide with the interests of the other Allied governments. They criticized his plan as too lenient toward Germany.

The **Treaty of Versailles,** signed by Germany on June 28, 1919, had weakened or discarded many of Wilson's proposals. Under the treaty, Germany was stripped of its armed forces. It also had to pay **reparations,** or war damages, to the Allies in the amount of $33 billion, a sum far beyond its financial means. Perhaps most humiliating, Germany had to acknowledge guilt for the outbreak and devastation of World War I.

The war itself resulted in the dissolution of four empires: the Russian Empire, the Ottoman Empire, which lost territory in the war and fell to revolution in 1922, the German Empire after the abdication of the emperor and loss of territory in the treaty, and Austria-Hungary, which was split into separate countries. Furthermore, nine new countries were established in Europe, including Yugoslavia, Poland, and Czechoslovakia.

While Wilson expressed disappointment in the treaty, he found consolation in its call for the creation of his cherished League of Nations. He returned home to win approval for the treaty.

The U.S. Senate Rejects the Treaty The Treaty of Versailles, especially the League of Nations, faced immediate opposition from numerous U.S. lawmakers. A key group of senators, nicknamed "the Irreconcilables" in the press because they were unwilling to compromise, assailed the League as the kind of "entangling alliance" that Washington, Jefferson, and Monroe had warned against. These critics feared that the League might supersede the power of Congress to declare war and thus force the United States to fight in numerous foreign conflicts.

A larger group of senators, known as the "Reservationists," was led by the powerful chairman of the Foreign Relations committee, Henry Cabot Lodge. This group supported the League but would ratify the treaty only with amendments that would preserve the nation's freedom to act independently.

Convinced that he could defeat his opposition by winning public support, Wilson took his case directly to the American people. Starting in Ohio in September 1919, he traveled 8,000 miles and made over 30 major speeches in three weeks. The physical strain of his tour, however, proved too great. Wilson collapsed in Colorado on September 25 and returned to the White House. There, he suffered a stroke and was bedridden for months, isolated from even his closest advisers but determined not to compromise with the Senate.

The Senate voted in November 1919 and again in March 1920, but it refused to ratify the treaty. After Wilson left office in 1921, the United States negotiated separate peace treaties with each of the Central Powers. The League of Nations, the foundation of President Wilson's plan for lasting world peace, took shape without the United States.

✓ **Reading Check** **Examining** What major issues did Wilson's Fourteen Points address?

HISTORY Online **Study Central**

For help with the concepts in this section of *American Vision: Modern Times* go to tav.mt.glencoe.com and click on *Study Central.*

SECTION 3 ASSESSMENT

Checking for Understanding

1. **Vocabulary** Define: network, convoy, adequately, armistice, resolve, reparations.
2. **People and Terms** Identify: Vladimir Lenin, Treaty of Brest-Litovsk, Fourteen Points, League of Nations, Treaty of Versailles.
3. **List** the four nations that dominated the Paris peace conference in 1919.

Reviewing Big Ideas

4. **Recalling** Why did President Wilson propose his Fourteen Points?

Critical Thinking

5. **Analyzing** What impact did John J. Pershing and the Battle of the Argonne Forest have on World War I?
6. **Organizing** Use a graphic organizer to list the results of World War I.

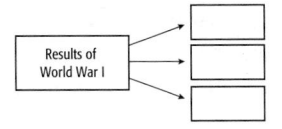

Analyzing Visuals

7. **Analyzing Maps and Charts** Examine the map and chart on page 387. Prepare a quiz with questions based on information from both. Give the quiz to some of your classmates.

Writing About History

8. **Descriptive Writing** Imagine that you are an American soldier fighting in Europe during World War I. Write a letter home describing your situation, and explain why you are there. **CA** 11WS1.2; 11WA2.1c

CHAPTER 6 World War I and Its Aftermath **389**

SECTION 3 ASSESSMENT ANSWERS

1. Content vocabulary is boldfaced and highlighted in yellow. Academic vocabulary is boldfaced.
2. Vladimir Lenin *(p. 387),* Treaty of Brest-Litovsk *(p. 387),* Fourteen Points *(p. 388),* League of Nations *(p. 388),* Treaty of Versailles *(p. 389)*
3. Italy, Britain, France, and the U. S.
4. Wilson wanted his plan to provide justice for all people and nationalities.
5. Pershing and the Allied attack at the Argonne Forest shattered German defenses and opened a hole in the German line.
6. League of Nations, dissolution of four empires, nine new European countries, Germany pays reparations
7. Instruct students to provide answers for all questions posed.
8. Letters should focus on the soldier's reaction to his situation.

S Skill Practice
Identifying Point of View
Ask students to summarize the opinions of the "Irreconcilables" and "Reservationists" toward the treaty of Versailles. **OL** **CA HI3**

ASSESS

Resources for page 389

Use these resources to assess student mastery.
📂 Section Quiz 6-3
📂 Reading Essentials and Study Guide 6-3
💿 Interactive Tutor Self-Assessment CD-ROM
📂 California Standards Practice, Grade 11

✓ **Reading Check**

Answer: free trade, disarmament, freedom of the seas, impartial adjustment of colonial claims, open diplomacy, self-determination, creation of the League of Nations

HISTORY Online

Study Central provides audio summaries, interactive games, and online graphic organizers to help students review section content.

CLOSE

Summarizing Ask the class to discuss fighting strategies of World War I. **OL**

FOCUS

SKILLBUILDER ACTIVITY

Project **Daily Focus Skills Transparency 6-4** and have students answer the question.

Guide to Reading

Understanding Vocabulary: Have students scan the section and write a sentence using each of the content vocabulary and academic vocabulary words in context.

Answers to Graphic: Rapid inflation, mass demand for goods, strikes

Unpacking the Standards

Students will be able to:

• Analyze how economic problems led to labor strikes and racial unrest.

• Explain how the Red Scare led to a violation of the rights of many Americans.

Answers and Additional Support

SECTION 4 The War's Impact

Guide to Reading

Connection
In the previous section, you learned how the war changed Europe. In this section, you will discover how the United States reacted to the change from war to peace.

Main Idea
• After the war, when businesses tried to decrease wages and inflation lowered buying power, workers went on strike across the nation. (p. 391)
• Race riots swept the nation as returning soldiers competed against African Americans for jobs and housing. (p. 392)
• Fear of a Communist revolution caused a nationwide panic. (p. 393)
• Warren G. Harding won the 1920 presidential election with the promise of a return to "normalcy." (p. 395)

Content Vocabulary
cost of living, general strike, deport

Academic Vocabulary
widespread, authorities, restoration

People and Terms to Identify
Red Scare, A. Mitchell Palmer, J. Edgar Hoover

Reading Objectives
• **Describe** the effects of the postwar recession on the United States.
• **Explain** the causes of increased racial tensions after the war.
• **Discuss** the causes of and reaction to the Red Scare.

• **List** the major issues of the 1920 presidential campaign and describe the election's results.

Reading Strategy
Organizing As you read about the war's aftermath, complete a graphic organizer similar to the one below to list the effects of the end of World War I on the American economy.

Preview of Events

♦1917	♦1918	♦1919	♦1920
1917 Riots erupt in East St. Louis, Illinois	**1918** House approves Nineteenth Amendment giving women the right to vote	**1919** Race riots and strikes erupt in numerous northern cities	**1920** Red Scare and Palmer raids

The following are the main History–Social Science Standards covered in this section.

11.4 Students trace the rise of the United States to its role as a world power in the twentieth century.

11.4.5 Analyze the political, economic and social ramifications of World War I on the home front.

⚜ The Big Idea ⚜

The fate of nations is forever changed by monumental world events. The end of rationing brought a rush to buy goods that had been limited. The demand for products brought higher prices and inflation. Despite the cost-of-living increases, companies kept wages low because higher wages raised their operating costs. The number of unionized workers had increased during the war, and many workers now organized strikes to protest rising costs and low wages. The tension increased as soldiers returned home and began looking for jobs. Race riots erupted as minorities and returning soldiers competed for jobs and housing. A fear of communism also gripped the country during what was known as the Red Scare. Warren G. Harding was able to win the 1920 presidential election by assuring Americans that he would return the country to "normalcy."

390   CHAPTER 6   World War I and Its Aftermath

SECTION RESOURCES

📂 Print Material
• Reproducible Lesson Plan 6-4
• Guided Reading Activity 6-4
• Reading Essentials and Study Guide 6-4
• Active Reading Note-Taking Guide 6-4

📇 Transparencies
• Daily Focus Skills Transparency 6-4
• Section Graphic Organizer Transparency 6-4

Technology
• Interactive Tutor Self-Assessment CD-ROM
• ExamView® Pro Testmaker CD-ROM
• Presentation Plus! CD-ROM

An Economy in Turmoil

1 *Main Idea* After the war, when businesses tried to decrease wages and inflation lowered buying power, workers went on strike across the nation.

Reading Connection How might inflation affect you or your family's spending habits? Read on to learn about the effects of postwar inflation and loss of wages.

The end of World War I brought great upheaval to American society. When the war ended, government agencies removed their controls from the American economy. This released pent-up demand in the economy. People raced to buy goods that had been rationed, while businesses rapidly raised prices they had been forced to keep low during the war. The result was rapid inflation.

★ An American Story ★

On August 20, 1919, Mary Harris Jones, also known as "Mother" Jones, was thrown in jail in Homestead, Pennsylvania. The 89-year-old had just finished delivering a fiery, impassioned speech in an attempt to gain support for steel unions. Referring to the owners of the big steel companies, she said:

❝Our Kaisers sit up and smoke seventy-five cent cigars and have lackeys with knee pants bring them champagne while you starve, while you grow old at forty, stoking their furnaces. You pull in your belts while they banquet. They have stomachs two miles long and two miles wide and you fill them. . . . If Gary [chair of U.S. Steel] wants to work twelve hours a day, let him go in the blooming mill and work. What we want is a little leisure, time for music, playgrounds, a decent home, books, and the things that make life worthwhile.❞

—quoted in *Labor in Crisis*

2 Inflation rates seemed to support Mother Jones's appeal. In 1919 prices rose at an average of more than 15 percent. Inflation greatly increased the **cost of living**—the cost of food, clothing, shelter, and other essentials that people need to survive.

Inflation Leads to Strikes Many companies had been forced to raise wages during the war, but inflation now threatened to wipe out all the gains workers had made. While workers wanted higher wages to keep up with inflation, companies wanted to hold down wages because inflation was also driving up their operating costs.

During the war, the number of workers in unions had increased dramatically. By the time the war ended, workers were better organized and much more capable of organizing strikes than they had been before. Many business leaders, on the other hand, were determined to break the power of the unions and roll back the gains labor had made. These circumstances led to an enormous wave of strikes in 1919. By the end of the year, more than 3,600 strikes involving more than 4 million workers had taken place.

The Seattle General Strike The first major strike took place in Seattle, when some 35,000 shipyard workers demanded higher wages and shorter hours. Soon other unions in Seattle joined the shipyard workers and organized a general strike. A **general strike** involves all workers living in a certain location, not just workers in a particular industry. The Seattle general strike involved more than 60,000 people and paralyzed the city for five days. Although the strikers returned to work without making any gains, their actions worried many Americans because the general strike was a common tactic used in Europe by Communists and other radical groups.

The Boston Police Strike Perhaps the most famous strike of 1919 took place in Boston, when roughly 75 percent of the police force walked off the job. Riots and looting soon erupted in the city, forcing the governor of Massachusetts, Calvin Coolidge, to send in the National Guard. When the strikers tried to return to work, the police commissioner refused to accept them. He hired a new police force instead.

Despite protests, Coolidge agreed the men should be fired. He declared, "There is no right to strike

▼ *"Mother" Jones*

More Skill Practice

Predicting Consequences Students should realize that our economy is made up of many different elements that interact with one another. **Ask:** What would be some of the results if our community's police force were to go on strike? *(Answers may include: increased traffic accidents due to speeding and breaking traffic laws; increased robberies; rise in injuries; social unrest)* **OL**

TEACH

R₁ Reading Strategy

Categorizing Information Have students create a graphic organizer with five columns labeled "Who," "Where," "When," "How Many," and "Results." Label the rows with the three major strikes discussed in this section. As students read, have them use this graphic organizer to compare the strikes. **OL**

R₂ Reading Strategy

Scaffolding—Questioning Students are often unfamiliar with economic concepts and need the meaning of these terms reinforced. **Ask:** What is inflation? *(a decrease in money value and a rise in prices)* What are some results of inflation? *(consumer uncertainty causes people to buy less; businesses fail; international trade decreases; interest rates go up; fewer people can afford to purchase houses or cars; more unemployment)* **OL**

This **Reading Skill** was introduced in Chapter 2.

C Critical Thinking

Determining Cause and Effect Have students list all the businesses and services they can think of that might be involved if their city or community were to hold a general strike. *(Answers may include: medical personnel, phone company, electric and gas company, truckers, teachers, factory workers, etc.)* **Ask:** How would your daily life be affected by such a strike? *(Students' answers will vary.)* **BL**

against the public safety by anybody, anywhere, anytime." Coolidge's response brought him to national attention and earned him **widespread** public support. It also convinced the Republicans to make Coolidge their vice presidential candidate in the 1920 election.

The Steel Strike Shortly after the police strike ended, one of the largest strikes in American history began when an estimated 350,000 steelworkers went on strike for higher pay, shorter hours, and recognition of their union. Elbert H. Gary, the head of U.S. Steel, refused even to talk to union leaders. Instead, the company set out to break the union by using anti-immigrant feelings to divide the workers.

Many steelworkers were immigrants. The company blamed the strike on foreign radicals and called for loyal Americans to return to work. Meanwhile, the company hired African Americans and Mexicans as replacement workers and managed to keep its steel mills operating despite the strike. Clashes between company guards and strikers were frequent, and in Gary, Indiana, a riot left 18 strikers dead. In early

January of 1920, the strike collapsed. The failure of the strike set back the union cause in the steel industry. Steelworkers remained unorganized until 1937.

✓ **Reading Check** **Explaining** What caused the wave of strikes in 1919?

Racial Unrest

Main Idea Race riots swept the nation as returning soldiers competed against African Americans for jobs and housing.

Reading Connection Describe your feelings during a time when you competed against someone in a game or academic competition. Read on to learn how the returning soldiers caused racial unrest when they looked for jobs.

Adding to the nation's economic turmoil was the return of hundreds of thousands of American soldiers from Europe who needed to find employment.

NATIONAL GEOGRAPHIC
MOMENT in HISTORY

HERO'S HOMECOMING
A wounded soldier of the 369th Regiment, the Harlem "Hell-Fighters," accepts congratulations during a victory parade through New York City in 1919. Facing discrimination within their own army, African American soldiers at the front received a warm reception from their French allies. "I have never before experienced what it meant really to be free, to taste real liberty," one soldier wrote home, "in a phrase, 'to be a man.'" Two African American infantry divisions suffered some 6,000 casualties, but at war's end, they still came home to a segregated American society.

NATIONAL GEOGRAPHIC MOMENT in HISTORY

Historians believe that the bands that accompanied African American regiments introduced jazz and ragtime to Europeans.

Effects of World War I on the United States

Developments in the War

- War-torn economies of Europe
- Russian Revolution
- Industrial demand of wartime
- Sacrifices of wartime; disappointment with Versailles Peace Treaty

Effects on U.S.

- Boom in U.S. economy; emergence of U.S. as world industrial leader
- "Red Scare" in postwar U.S.; suspicion of immigrants
- Internal migration in U.S., especially African American migration to Northern cities
- Failure to join League of Nations

Graphic Organizer → Skills

World War I had profound effects on the United States.

Interpreting Why did the destruction of European economies cause an industrial boom in the United States?

Many African Americans who had moved north during the war were also competing for jobs and housing. Frustration and racism combined to produce violence. In the summer of 1919, over 20 race riots broke out across the nation.

The worst violence occurred in Chicago. On a hot July day, African Americans went to a whites-only beach. Both sides began throwing stones at each other. Whites also threw stones at an African American teenager swimming near the beach to prevent him from coming ashore, and he drowned. A full-scale riot then erupted in the city. Angry African Americans attacked white neighborhoods while whites attacked African American neighborhoods. The riot lasted for several days. In the end, 38 people died—15 white and 23 black—and over 500 were injured.

✓ **Reading Check** **Analyzing** Why did the end of the war lead to race riots?

The Red Scare

Main Idea Fear of a Communist revolution caused a nationwide panic.

Reading Connection Why do you think people might fear a Communist revolution? Read on to find out about the U.S. response to the Russian Revolution.

The wave of strikes in 1919 helped to fuel fears that Communists were conspiring to start a revolution in the United States. Americans had been stunned when Lenin and the Bolsheviks seized power and

withdrew Russia from the war. Americans had become very anti-German as the war progressed, and when the Communists withdrew Russia from the war they seemed to be helping Germany. American anger at Germany quickly expanded into anger at Communists as well. Americans began to associate communism with being unpatriotic and disloyal.

Americans had long been suspicious of Communist ideas. Throughout the late 1800s, many Americans had accused immigrants of importing radical socialist and Communist ideas into the United States and blamed them for labor unrest and violence. Now Communists had seized control of an entire nation, and fears surged that they would try to incite revolutions elsewhere. These fears seemed to be confirmed in 1919, when the Soviet Union formed the Communist International—an organization for coordinating the activities of Communist parties in other countries.

The Red Scare Begins As strikes erupted across the United States in 1919, the fear that Communists, or "reds," as they were called, might seize power led to a nationwide panic known as the **Red Scare.** Seattle's mayor, Ole Hanson, spoke for others when he condemned the leaders of the Seattle general strike as revolutionaries who wanted to "take possession of our American government and try to duplicate the anarchy of Russia."

In April the postal service intercepted more than 30 parcels addressed to leading businesspeople and politicians that were triggered to explode when opened. In June eight bombs in eight cities exploded within minutes of one another, suggesting a nationwide conspiracy. One of them damaged the home of

CHAPTER 6 World War I and Its Aftermath **393**

W Writing Support

Narrative Writing Have half of the class write an eyewitness account of an African American viewing the Chicago riot, while the other half of the students write the account from the point of view of a newspaper reporter describing the event. Read the narratives aloud in class. **OL**

CA 11WS1.2

R₁ Reading Strategy

Activating Prior Knowledge Discuss with students any existing understanding they have of communism. Reinforce their understanding by having students use an encyclopedia or other resource to help write a summary of the basic ideologies of communism. **BL**

C Critical Thinking

Drawing Conclusions Remind students that the Red Scare targeted Communists. **Ask:** Why did Americans fear the Communists and blame them for violence in America? *(They had long associated communism with unionization efforts and so blamed the recent violence on these ties.)* **OL**

R₂ Reading Strategy

Scaffolding—Academic Vocabulary The word *trigger* was introduced in Chapter 5, Section 2. Have a student define the word. **BL**

✓ **Reading Check**

Answer: Returning soldiers and African Americans competed for jobs.

Graphic Organizer → Skills

Answer:
American industry was undamaged by the war and was needed to help rebuild Europe.

Graphic Organizer Skills Practice
Ask: What development during the war most contributed to the Red Scare? *(Russian Revolution)*

Did You Know?

J. Edgar Hoover went on to become Director of the Federal Bureau of Investigation from 1924 to 1972 where he served under a record eight presidents.

Picturing **History**

Terror in the Streets After the House of Morgan—a bank in New York City—was damaged by a bomb in 1920, Attorney General A. Mitchell Palmer instituted raids on antigovernment activists and many immigrants, often violating their civil liberties in the process. Whom did Palmer appoint to coordinate these investigations?

United States Attorney General **A. Mitchell Palmer** in Washington, D.C. Most people believed the bombings were the work of Communists or other revolutionaries trying to destroy the American way of life.

The Palmer Raids Declaring that a "blaze of revolution" was "burning up the foundations of society," Palmer took action. He established a special division within the Justice Department, the General Intelligence Division, headed by **J. Edgar Hoover.** This division eventually became the Federal Bureau of Investigation (FBI). From late 1919 to the spring of 1920, Palmer organized a series of raids on the headquarters of various radical organizations. Although evidence pointed to no single group as the bombers, Palmer's agents focused on foreign residents and immigrants. The **authorities** detained thousands of suspects and **deported,** or expelled from the country, approximately 500 of them.

Palmer's agents often disregarded the civil liberties of the suspects. Officers entered homes and offices without search warrants. People were mistreated and jailed for indefinite periods of time and were not allowed to talk to their attorneys.

For a while, Palmer was regarded as a national hero. His raids, however, failed to turn up any hard evidence of revolutionary conspiracy. When his dire prediction that violence would rock the nation on May Day 1920—a popular European celebration of workers—proved wrong, Palmer lost much of his credibility and soon faded from prominence.

The Red Scare greatly influenced people's attitudes during the 1920s. Americans often linked radicalism with immigrants, and that attitude led to a call for Congress to limit immigration.

✓ Reading Check **Examining** After World War I, why were Americans suspicious of some union leaders?

394 CHAPTER 6 World War I and Its Aftermath

An End to Progressivism

Main Idea Warren G. Harding won the 1920 presidential election with the promise of a return to "normalcy."

Reading Connection Compared to now, does the period of time before September 11, 2001, seem more "normal" to you? Read on to discover how a hope for a more normal time gave a presidential candidate an election victory.

Economic problems, labor unrest, and racial tensions, as well as the fresh memories of World War I, all combined to create a general sense of disillusionment in the United States. By 1920 Americans wanted an end to the upheaval. During the 1920 campaign, Ohio Governor James M. Cox and his running mate, Assistant Secretary of the Navy Franklin D. Roosevelt, ran on a platform of keeping alive Woodrow Wilson's progressive ideals. The Republican candidate, Warren G. Harding, called for a return to "normalcy." He urged that what the United States needed was a return to the simpler days before the Progressive Era reforms:

R

> ❝[Our] present need is not heroics, but healing; not nostrums, but normalcy; not revolution, but **restoration;** not agitation, but adjustment; not surgery, but serenity; not the dramatic, but the dispassionate; . . . not submergence in internationality, but sustainment in triumphant nationality.❞
>
> —quoted in *Portrait of a Nation*

Harding's sentiments struck a chord with voters, and he won the election by a landslide margin of

▲ *A. Mitchell Palmer and J. Edgar Hoover* ▶

over 7 million votes. Americans were weary of more crusades to reform society and the world. They hoped to put the country's racial and labor unrest and economic troubles behind them and build a more prosperous and stable society.

 Reading Check **Explaining** How was Harding able to win the presidential election of 1920?

HISTORY Online **Study Central**

For help with the concepts in this section of *American Vision: Modern Times* go to tav.mt.glencoe.com and click on *Study Central.*

SECTION 4 ASSESSMENT

Checking for Understanding

1. **Vocabulary** Define: cost of living, general strike, widespread, authorities, deport, restoration.
2. **People and Terms** Identify: Red Scare, A. Mitchell Palmer, J. Edgar Hoover.
3. **Describe** the conditions that African Americans faced after the end of World War I.

Reviewing Big Ideas

4. **Summarizing** Why did Republican Warren G. Harding win the election of 1920?

Critical Thinking

5. **Analyzing** Provide evidence to explain how the Palmer raids deprived some citizens of their civil and political rights?
6. **Organizing** Use a graphic organizer similar to the one below to list the causes of the Red Scare in the United States.

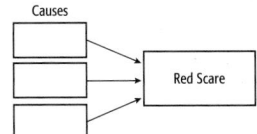

Causes → Red Scare

Analyzing Visuals

7. **Analyzing Photographs** Study the photograph on page 392. How might parades such as this one mobilize African Americans to work for an end to discrimination?

Writing About History

8. **Descriptive Writing** Imagine that you are a European immigrant working in a factory in the United States in 1919. Write a letter to a relative in Europe explaining economic conditions in America and why workers are striking.
   CA 11WS1.2; 11WA2.1c

CHAPTER 6   World War I and Its Aftermath   **395**

SECTION 4 ASSESSMENT ANSWERS

1. Content vocabulary is boldfaced and highlighted in yellow. Academic vocabulary is boldfaced.
2. Red Scare (p. 393), A. Mitchell Palmer (p. 394), J. Edgar Hoover (p. 394)
3. They faced racism and intense competition for housing and jobs.

4. He campaigned on a return to "normalcy," which many wanted.
5. They abused civil liberties by searching without a warrant, jailing subjects indefinitely, and limiting lawyer-client communication.
6. strikes, bombings, and Palmer Raids, fear of Communists seizing power

7. African Americans would note that they had fought for their country and deserved to be treated equally.
8. Students' letters will vary, but should describe inflation, the cost of living, and business opposition to unions.

R **Reading Strategy**

Interpreting Quotations
Harding's quotation presents many contrasts. Divide students into groups and assign to each group one of the phrases containing a contrast, such as "not heroics, but healing," or "not nostrums, but normalcy." Have each group discuss the phrase and explain its meaning. **OL**

ASSESS

Resources for page 395

Use these resources to assess student mastery.

🗁 Section Quiz 6-4

🗁 Reading Essentials and Study Guide 6-4

💿 Interactive Tutor Self-Assessment CD-ROM

🗁 California Standards Practice, Grade 11

✓ **Reading Check**

Answer: by campaigning for a return to a simpler time before racial and labor unrest and economic troubles

HISTORY Online

Study Central provides audio summaries, interactive games, and online graphic organizers to help students review section content.

CLOSE

Categorizing Information
Tell the class to create a graphic organizer showing the causes of and reactions to the Red Scare. **OL**

FOCUS

Understanding Vocabulary

Before students begin reading, point out that difficult or unfamiliar words are footnoted throughout the text.

TEACH

W Writing Support

Expository Writing Newton Baker's letter describes an incident that occurred when a man appeared to be disloyal. **Ask:** Could such an incident happen in today's society? *(Students' answers will vary.)* Tell students to write a two-page paper that considers how such a story might be told in a modern context. *(Student papers might change the nationality of the suspect. The item that angers the foreigner could be different.)* **OL**

CA 11WA2.1c

Answers and Additional Support

Primary Sources
Eyewitness to History

During World War I, government leaders feared that ethnic Americans were not loyal to the United States. In addition, officials sought to stifle dissent in order to help the war effort. With official encouragement, Americans began to lash out at all things German and to target opponents of the war. The legal system supported these actions.

Source 1:

Newton Baker served as secretary of war during World War I. He believed that the government had the right to prosecute people opposed to the war. He also believed, however, that the government needed to be very careful about how it handled opposition, since anti-German feelings were running dangerously high. In 1917 he expressed his concerns in a letter to Major General Tasker Bliss, chief of staff of the U.S. Army.

The spirit of the country seems unusually good, but there is a growing frenzy of suspicion and hostility toward disloyalty. I am afraid we are going to have a good many instances of people roughly treated on very slight evidence of disloyalty. Already a number of men and some women have been 'tarred and feathered,' and a portion of the press is urging . . . more strenuous efforts at detection and punishment.

In Cleveland a few days ago a foreign-looking man got into a street car and taking a seat noticed pasted in the window next to him a Liberty Loan poster, which he immediately tore down, tore into small bits, and stamped under his feet. The people in the car surged around him with the demand that he be lynched, when a secret service man showed his badge and placed him under arrest, taking him in a car to the police station, where he was searched and found to have two Liberty Bonds in his pocket and to be a non-English-speaking Pole. When an interpreter was procured it was discovered that the circular which he had destroyed had had on it a picture of the German Emperor, which had so infuriated the fellow that he destroyed the circular to show his vehement hatred of the common enemy. As he was unable to speak a single word of English, he would undoubtedly have been hanged but for the intervention and entirely accidental presence of the secret service agent.

▲ *Henry L. Stimson*

Source 2:

Henry Stimson had been secretary of war under President William Howard Taft. He spent World War I as a colonel in the U.S. Army in France. In a 1917 pamphlet, he expressed his concern about recent immigrants and their children who did not face up to their responsibility to serve in the military.

We are a composite nation. We have been inspired by the noble hope of making this land a home of freedom and equal opportunity for all races. And into our land there has been pouring a great stream of immigration composed largely of men who never had the lesson in loyalty to American institutions which was instilled into our fathers by the wars, the **privations**[1] and the common experiences of our national growth. Many of these men have come here, not to assume, but to escape a national duty. Many of them have very imperfect notions

> ───────────────────────
[1] **privation:** sacrifice

---

of responsibility towards the state, let alone the duty of sleepless vigilance required for the preservation of liberty. We have taken them on faith; we have given them everything we have, in the way of freedom and political power and we have given them very little in the way of care or education in the duties which went with that freedom and power. We have apparently expected that they would learn the difficult art of self-government by merely breathing our free air without effort on our own part and we are beginning to learn our mistake. We have had some ugly **revelations**[2] of the imperfect way in which our existing institutions have performed the duty of assimilating such immigrants. . . . Could there be a better way found to bring home to our foreign born citizens and their children the duty of loyalty to this country and the fact that free government has responsibilities, as well as privileges, than to have their children learn that lesson, shoulder to shoulder with our native born youth?

▲ *Oliver Wendell Holmes*

Source 3:

The 1917 Espionage Act made it a crime to cause or attempt to cause refusal of duty in the military forces of the United States. Charles Schenck sent antiwar pamphlets to two men drafted for military service. In these pamphlets he argued that no one should be forced into the military. Schenck was arrested and charged with conspiring to violate the Espionage Act. In 1919 Chief Justice Oliver Wendell Holmes wrote the U.S. Supreme Court ruling against Schenck.

The document in question, upon its first printed side, recited the 1st section of the 13th Amendment, said that the idea **embodied**[3] in it was violated by the Conscription Act, and that a conscript is little better than a convict. . . . It said: "Do not submit to intimidation;" but in form at least confined itself to peaceful measures, such as a petition for the repeal of the act. The other and later printed side of the sheet was headed, "Assert Your Rights." It stated reasons for alleging that anyone violated the Constitution when he refused to recognize "your right to assert your opposition to the draft," and

[2] **revelation:** discovery
[3] **embody:** contain

went on: "If you do not assert and support your rights, you are helping to deny or **disparage**[4] rights which it is the solemn duty of all citizens and residents of the United States to retain.". . . Of course the document would not have been sent unless it had been intended to have some effect, and we do not see what effect it could be expected to have upon persons subject to the draft except to influence them to obstruct the carrying of it out. . . .

. . . We admit that in many places and in ordinary times the defendants, in saying all that was said in the circular, would have been within their constitutional rights. But the character of every act depends upon the circumstances in which it is done. The most stringent protection of free speech would not protect a man in falsely shouting fire in a theatre, and causing a panic. . . . The question in every case is whether the words used are used in such circumstances and are of such a nature as to create clear and present danger that they will bring about the substantive evils that Congress has a right to prevent. It is a question of proximity and degree. When a nation is at war many things that might be said in time of peace are such a hindrance to its effort that their utterance will not be endured so long as men fight, and that no court could regard them as protected by any constitutional right. . . .

[4] **disparage:** degrade

DBQ   Document-Based Questions

Historical Analysis   ◄ CA HR4; HI1; HI2; HI3

Source 1: What did Baker fear would happen with growing intolerance toward dissent?

Source 2: What was Stimson's concern about the perceived attitude of immigrants toward military service?

Source 3: Why did the Supreme Court decide against Schenck?

Comparing and Contrasting Sources
According to Baker, Stimson, and the Supreme Court, what are the responsibilities of citizens in wartime?

U Universal Access

English Learners Henry Stimson argued that immigrants to the United States were not effectively integrated into American society. **Ask: Has the United States improved its efforts to assimilate immigrants? Is this a priority in modern society?** *(Students will likely state that modern culture places less emphasis on assimilation and encourages a mixture of cultures.)* If there are recent immigrants or English learners in the class, ask them to provide their own unique perspective to the issue of assimilation. EL

R Reading Strategy

Summarizing Tell students to carefully read Chief Justice Holmes's explanation for why Charles Schenck's antiwar pamphlet was not protected by the First Amendment. **Ask: What is the basis of the chief justice's interpretation?** *(times of war are emergency situations that justify a restriction on freedoms granted in times of peace)* OL

ASSESS/CLOSE

Have students answer the Document-Based Questions.

DBQ   Document-Based Questions

1. He feared that people might harm or kill those suspected of disloyalty.
2. Immigrants had no respect for the responsibilities of citizenship such as the sacrifice involved with military service.
3. His pamphlets could not be protected as free speech because these statements could obstruct the war effort.

Comparing and Contrasting
Baker believed that citizens should continue to respect laws and not harm someone even if that person was suspected of being disloyal. Stimson believed that children of foreign-born parents should enlist in the military to show their loyalty to the United States. The Supreme Court's decision indicates that citizens should support the war effort.

Resources for pages 398–399

Use the following resources to review, assess, and reteach the chapter.

📁 Chapter 6 Tests, Forms A and B

📁 Standardized Tests, Forms A and B

📁 Cumulative Authentic Assessment

🔒 MindJogger Videoquiz

💿 Interactive Tutor Self-Assessment CD-ROM

💿 Exam*View*® Pro Testmaker CD-ROM

💿 Vocabulary PuzzleMaker CD-ROM

⬤ Succeeding on . . .™ the California Standards: Grade 11 History–Social Science

📁 California Standards Practice, Grade 11

Reviewing Content Vocabulary
Students' answers will vary. The pages where the words appear in the text are shown in parentheses.

1. guerrilla *(p. 368)* **2.** nationalism *(p. 369)* **3.** self-determination *(p. 369)* **4.** propaganda *(p. 371)* **5.** contraband *(p. 373)* **6.** U-boat *(p. 373)* **7.** conscription *(p. 376)* **8.** victory garden *(p. 378)* **9.** espionage *(p. 380)* **10.** convoy *(p. 387)* **11.** armistice *(p. 388)* **12.** reparations *(p. 389)* **13.** cost of living *(p. 391)* **14.** general strike *(p. 391)* **15.** deport *(p. 394)*

Reviewing Academic Vocabulary
Students' answers will vary. The pages where the words appear in the text are shown in parentheses.

16. stability *(p. 367)* **17.** emphasis *(p. 369)* **18.** eroded *(p. 372)* **19.** draft *(p. 376)* **20.** migrate *(p. 379)* **21.** constitute *(p. 381)* **22.** network *(p. 385)* **23.** adequately *(p. 387)* **24.** resolve

Reviewing Key Terms
On a sheet of paper, use each of these terms in a sentence.

1. guerrilla
2. nationalism
3. self-determination
4. propaganda
5. contraband
6. U-boat
7. conscription
8. victory garden
9. espionage
10. convoy
11. armistice
12. reparations
13. cost of living
14. general strike
15. deport

Reviewing Academic Vocabulary
On a sheet of paper, use each of these terms in a sentence that reflects the term's meaning in the chapter.

16. stability
17. emphasis
18. erode
19. draft
20. migrate
21. constitute
22. network
23. adequately
24. resolve
25. widespread
26. authorities
27. restoration

Reviewing the Main Ideas

Section 1
28. What factors contributed to the start of World War I in Europe?

Section 2
29. What role did American women play in the war effort during World War I?

Section 3
30. What were the provisions of the Treaty of Versailles?

Section 4
31. What were the Palmer raids?

Critical Thinking

32. **Reading Skill** **Problem/Solution** Reread the text under the headings "Trench Warfare" and "New Technology" on pages 385–386. Create your own table identifying the problem, the solution, and the outcome of the solution.

33. **Civics** Do you think government action to suppress opposition to World War I was justified? Why or why not?

34. **Organizing** Use a table like the one below to list the significant events of each year from 1914 to 1918.

Year	Event	Significance
1914		
1915		
1916		
1917		
1918		

Chapter Summary

Mobilizing for War

Armed Forces
- Congress passed Selective Service Act which required young men ages 21–30 to register for the draft
- Employed women in non-combat roles

Domestic Front
- War Industries Board controlled war materials and production
- Committee on Public Information created war propaganda
- Government worked with employers and labor to ensure production
- Congress passed Espionage and Sedition Acts to limit opposition to the war
- Congress increased taxes and sold Liberty Bonds to pay for war

Postwar Problems
- Cost of living greatly increased
- Economic problems led to racial violence and widespread strikes
- Fear of communism led to Red Scare and Palmer raids

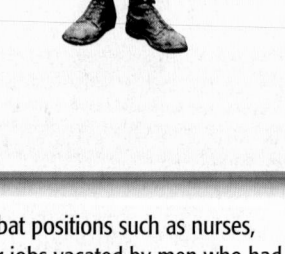

(p. 388) **25.** widespread *(p. 392)* **26.** authorities *(p. 394)* **27.** restoration *(p. 395)*

Reviewing the Main Ideas

28. the alliance system, the naval buildup, nationalism in the Balkans, and the assassination of Archduke Franz Ferdinand

29. Women filled noncombat positions such as nurses, clerical help, and other jobs vacated by men who had become soldiers.

30. Germany was stripped of its armed forces, forced to accept guilt for the war, and made to pay reparations to the Allies.

31. raids of various radical organizations to round up suspects to deport or imprison

HISTORY Online

Self-Check Quiz
Visit the *American Vision: Modern Times* Web site at
tav.mt.glencoe.com and click on *Self-Check Quizzes—Chapter 6* to assess your knowledge of chapter content.

Writing About History

35. **Historical Analysis** Distinguishing Valid and Fallacious Arguments Write a newspaper editorial identifying various arguments about the Palmer Raids as valid or fallacious. **CA HR1**

36. *Big Idea* Both the British and the American governments used propaganda to garner support for the war. Use the library and other resources to find examples of these propaganda techniques. Compile your research in an illustrated and captioned poster, and display it in the classroom. **CA 11WS1.1; 11WS1.6**

37. **Persuasive Writing** Take on the role of a newspaper editor in 1919. Write an editorial favoring or opposing ratification of the Treaty of Versailles. **CA 11WS1.1**

DBQ Document-Based Questions

38. **Interpreting Primary Sources** On September 12, 1918, Socialist leader Eugene V. Debs was convicted of violating the Espionage Act. Debs later spoke to the court at his sentencing. Read his speech and answer the questions that follow.

❝I look upon the Espionage laws as a despotic enactment in flagrant conflict with democratic principles and with the spirit of free institutions. . . . I am opposed to the social system in which we live. . . . I believe in fundamental change, but if possible by peaceful and orderly means. . . .

I am thinking this morning of the men in the mills and factories, . . . of the women who for a paltry wage are compelled to work out their barren lives; of the little children who in this system are robbed of their childhood and . . . forced into industrial dungeons. . . . In this high noon of our twentieth century Christian civilization, money is still so much more important than the flesh and blood of childhood. In very truth, gold is god. . . .❞

—quoted in *Echoes of Distant Thunder*

a. According to Debs, what were some problems in American society at this time? How did he believe change should be brought about? **CA 11RC2.5**

b. How did Debs seem to feel about the Espionage Act? Do you agree with him? Why or why not? **CA 11RC2.5**

NATIONAL GEOGRAPHIC — Europe After World War I, 1920

Former Austria-Hungary boundary
Former German boundary
Former Russian boundary
National boundary
⊛ Capital city

Geography and History

39. The map on this page shows the geographical changes in Europe after World War I. Study the map and answer the questions below.

a. **Interpreting Maps** After World War I, what new countries were formed using territory that had belonged to Austria-Hungary?

b. **Applying Geography Skills** What countries acquired territory from the former Russian Empire?

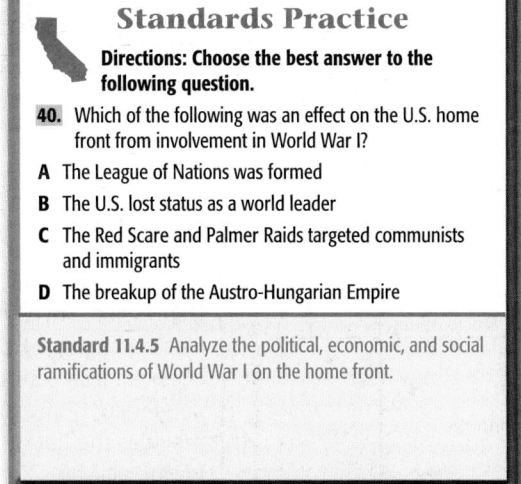

Standards Practice

Directions: Choose the best answer to the following question.

40. Which of the following was an effect on the U.S. home front from involvement in World War I?

A The League of Nations was formed

B The U.S. lost status as a world leader

C The Red Scare and Palmer Raids targeted communists and immigrants

D The breakup of the Austro-Hungarian Empire

Standard 11.4.5 Analyze the political, economic, and social ramifications of World War I on the home front.

HISTORY Online

Have students visit the Web site at tav.mt.glencoe.com to review Chapter 6 and take the Self-Check Quiz.

36. *Big Idea* Posters should reflect the types of propaganda used during World War I.

37. Editorials will vary. Students should clearly express an opinion about ratification of the treaty.

DBQ Document-Based Questions

38. a. Problems: low wages, child labor, love of money; change should be peaceful and orderly **b.** He calls it despotic and states that it violates the principles of democracy. Students' responses should consider the need to balance liberty and safety.

Geography and History

39. a. Czechoslovakia, Austria, Hungary, Romania, and parts of Yugoslavia, Italy, and Poland; **b.** Poland, Lithuania, Latvia, Estonia, Finland, and part of Romania

Standards Practice

40. C

Bonus Question ?

Ask: What was the name of the Austrian archduke whose assassination started World War I? *(Franz Ferdinand)*

Critical Thinking

32. **Reading Skill** problem: trench warfare; solutions: machine guns, poisonous gas, tanks, and airplanes; overall solution: the side with the best technology wins the war

33. A possible answer is that it protected American people from Communist propaganda. A possible negative answer is that it violated civil rights and liberties.

34. 1914: beginning of World War I; 1915: *Lusitania* sunk, Americans side with British; 1916: fighting in trenches worsens; 1917: United States commits resources and soldiers to help Allies; 1918: Americans break through German lines, leading to Germany's defeat

Writing About History

35. **Historical Analysis** Students' answers will vary.

Unit 3 Resources

Teaching the Unit

Use the information on these pages to help you teach Unit 3.

History–Social Science Standards Covered in Unit 3

Standard	Chapter 7	8	9	10
11.2 Students analyze the relationship among the rise of industrialization, large-scale rural-to-urban migration, and massive immigration from Southern and Eastern Europe.	✔	✔		
11.3 Students analyze the role religion played in the founding of America, its lasting moral, social, and political impacts, and issues regarding religious liberty.	✔			
11.4 Students trace the rise of the United States to its role as a world power in the twentieth century.		✔		
11.5 Students analyze the major political, social, economic, technological, and cultural developments of the 1920s.	✔	✔	✔	
11.6 Students analyze the different explanations for the Great Depression and how the New Deal fundamentally changed the role of the federal government.			✔	✔

Pacing Your Lessons

This pacing chart provides time management suggestions for teaching Unit 3.

	Days
Unit 3 Introduction	1
Chapter 7 • **Reading Skill:** Connecting • **Historical Analysis Skill:** Interpreting Events • **Sections 1–3** • **What Life Was Like:** Flappers • **American Literature:** Selected Poems by Langston Hughes • **Eyewitness to History:** Primary Source Documents	6
Chapter 8 • **Reading Skill:** Summarizing • **Historical Analysis Skill:** Analyzing Economic Behavior • **Sections 1–3** • **Eyewitness to History:** Primary Source Documents	6
Chapter 9 • **Reading Skill:** Visualizing • **Historical Analysis Skill:** Developing a Hypothesis • **Sections 1–3** • **What Life Was Like:** 1930s Entertainment • **Eyewitness to History:** Primary Source Documents	7
Chapter 10 • **Reading Skill:** Recognizing Time and Sequence • **Historical Analysis Skill:** Analyzing Environmental Issues • **Sections 1–3** • **Why It Matters:** The TVA • **Eyewitness to History:** Primary Source Documents	6

 Teacher to Teacher

Beginning of the Great Depression: 1929–1932

As a class, read from the text or other source about life in the early part of the Depression. Focus on the lifestyle changes that occurred as a result of the deepening Depression. This provides the background for the activity.

Once the students show an understanding of the changes in life during the Depression, have the students visit the American Memory Web site, located at memory.loc.gov, and find three different pictures of the time period from three different regions. Once the students have found their pictures, have them write a short story describing the background of that picture based on the life changes in America.

John Lever
Green River High School
Green River, Wyoming

Unit 3 Resources

Previewing the Chapters

Dear American History Teacher:

As you begin to teach this unit, themes recur throughout the chapters that you will want to point out to students. The material in this unit covers one of the most turbulent periods in modern history. Although the two decades discussed are very different—one a period of great economic growth and cultural innovation, the other a period of economic catastrophe and political transformation—there are also many themes that link these decades to one another.

The Great Depression of the 1930s was the product of some of the weaknesses of the economy in the 1920s, and the New Deal itself drew heavily, particularly in its early years, on some of the political innovations of the 1920s and of the Hoover years. The growth of mass culture as a defining element of American life continued through both the 1920s and the 1930s. Throughout this period, the United States was dealing with an unstable world.

When you teach this period, try to introduce students both to the contrasts between the 1920s and 1930s and to the continuities that link them to one another. Also make sure students remain aware of the tremendous influence of the legacy of World War I and the coming of World War II on the internal life of the nation.

Chapter 7: The Jazz Age, 1921–1929
(pages 402–439)

The 1920s saw a resurgence in racial and cultural tensions. People also began to explore new avenues for entertainment, including sports, movies and radio shows, and a more relaxed moral attitude prevailed. The Harlem Renaissance brought new trends in music, literature, and art. Organizations such as the NAACP worked against segregation and discrimination.

Chapter 8: Normalcy and Good Times, 1921–1929
(pages 440–463)

Warren Harding's administration was plagued by scandal. After Harding died, Calvin Coolidge assumed the presidency and regained the public's trust. Mass production—made possible by the invention of the assembly line—and consumers eager to buy goods fueled the economy. Increases in productivity and decreases in foreign markets after the war ended led to lower prices for farmers and caused an agricultural depression.

Chapter 9: The Great Depression Begins, 1929–1932
(pages 464–493)

Herbert Hoover won the presidential election with promises of triumph over poverty. Rising stock prices during the late 1920s encouraged people to make risky investments. When the stock market crashed in 1929, banks failed across the nation. The stock market crash, uneven distribution of income, and the Federal Reserve's mistakes contributed to the Great Depression. People lost their jobs and their homes. President Hoover's efforts to help the economy did not succeed.

Chapter 10: Roosevelt and the New Deal, 1933–1939
(pages 494–529)

Franklin D. Roosevelt was elected president in 1932 over Herbert Hoover. During his first 100 days in office, President Roosevelt sent 15 major acts aimed at financial recovery to Congress; his policies became known as the New Deal. After winning reelection in 1936, Roosevelt continued to push reforms to improve the economy.

FOCUS

History–Social Science Standards

This unit addresses the following main standards:

11.5 Students analyze the major political, social, economic, technological, and cultural developments of the 1920s.

11.6 Students analyze the different explanations for the Great Depression and how the New Deal fundamentally changed the role of the federal government.

Connecting to Past Learning

Unit 2 taught students about the development of the modern United States after the Civil War era. Unit 3 describes the Boom and Bust cycles the United States experienced from 1920 to 1941.

Unit Launch Activity

Point out to the class that the early part of this unit's time span was a carefree time, seen by some as a decadent period prior to the hardships of economic depression and war. Ask students to discuss why they believe the 1920s was a decade of great cultural change. **OL**

*W*hy It Matters Activity

Ask students to define an economic cycle. Tell them that the economic problems that triggered the Great Depression brought a new awareness of economic cycles. Have each student bring in an article from a newspaper or an Internet news source to share with the class about the current state of the economy. **Ask: How important do you think economic news is to your daily life? OL**

400

UNIT 3 Boom and Bust 1920–1941

*W*hy It Matters

After World War I, the United States enjoyed a time of prosperity and confidence. The decade of the 1920s saw rising stock prices and increased consumer spending. It also witnessed cultural innovations such as jazz music and motion pictures. At the end of the 1920s, however, several economic problems combined to trigger the Great Depression that began in 1929. Understanding the events of these decades will help you understand American society today. The following resources offer more information about this period in American history.

Hatbox depicting a New York street scene

Primary Sources Library

See pages 976–977 for primary source readings to accompany Unit 3.

Use the American History Primary Source Document Library CD-ROM to find additional primary sources about the Roaring Twenties and the Great Depression.

Sixth Avenue Elevated at Third St. by John Sloan, 1928

400

TEAM TEACHING ACTIVITY

ART Invite the art teacher to your class to explain the Art Deco style and show classic examples of the style. Then have students research your local community for examples of Art Deco architecture, art, and design. If possible, have students take photos of the examples to present to the class. Have students point out why the samples they have chosen illustrate Art Deco style. **AL**

"I have no fears for the future of our country. It is bright with hope."

—Herbert Hoover, 1929

TEACH

Skill Practice

Identifying Point of View From what point of view was Hoover speaking in 1929? *(Possible answer: He had just been elected president and was trying to keep panic down after the stock market crash in October.)* **Ask:** What had been the experience of the country during most of the 1920s? *(postwar prosperity for most)* Were there any people who would have disagreed with Hoover's assessment during the 1920s? *(Possible answer: family farmers, African Americans, Native Americans, some immigrants)* OL CA HR3

Skill Practice

Visual Literacy Flappers such as the ones pictured in the art are iconic depictions of the 1920s. Despite the carefree attitude many had during that decadent decade, the Great Depression soon followed, bringing with it hardship. Have students discuss why they think the 1920s was a decade of great cultural change. **Ask:** What symbols of the modern era are depicted in this painting? *(cars, the elevated train, tall buildings, street lamps)* OL CA HI4

NO CHILD LEFT BEHIND

Teaching Tip The NCLB Act emphasizes reading. Ask students to write down events and people they will encounter in this unit and keep the list with them as they read. When students find a person or item on the list, they should note the page number and write a brief summary. Students can use this list while studying.

UNIVERSAL ACCESS

Interpersonal Tell students that no matter what the country's economic circumstances, there are always people who do not have adequate food, clothing, or shelter. Have students learn about the needs of a local food or clothing pantry. Then ask students to plan a food or clothing drive for the benefit of the pantry. BL

Chapter 7 Planning Guide

SECTION RESOURCES

Main Ideas	📁 Print Materials	Technology Resources
Section 1: A Clash of Values 1. During the 1920s, anti-immigrant and racist feelings increased. 2. Fearing new immigrants, the federal government enacted several laws to limit immigration. 3. An emphasis on youth and personal freedom led to a more relaxed moral attitude. 4. Fundamentalists promoted the authority of the Bible and defended the Protestant faith. 5. Congress passed the Eighteenth Amendment and the Volstead Act to prohibit alcohol, but the laws largely failed to create positive social change.	• Reproducible Lesson Plan 7-1* • Daily Lecture and Discussion Notes 7-1 • Active Reading Note-Taking Guide 7-1 • Guided Reading Activity 7-1 • Section Quiz 7-1 • Reading Essentials and Study Guide 7-1	📙 Daily Focus Skills Transparency 7-1 📙 Section Graphic Organizer Transparency 7-1 💿 Interactive Tutor Self-Assessment CD-ROM 💿 ExamView® Pro Testmaker CD-ROM 💿 Presentation Plus! CD-ROM 📙 California Standards Practice Transparencies
Section 2: Cultural Innovations 1. New York City's Greeenwich Village and Chicago's South Side became known as centers for new artistic work. 2. Many people in the 1920s enjoyed new forms of entertainment.	• Reproducible Lesson Plan 7-2* • Daily Lecture and Discussion Notes 7-2 • Active Reading Note-Taking Guide 7-2 • Guided Reading Activity 7-2 • Section Quiz 7-2 • Reading Essentials and Study Guide 7-2	📙 Daily Focus Skills Transparency 7-2 📙 Section Graphic Organizer Transparency 7-2 💿 Interactive Tutor Self-Assessment CD-ROM 💿 ExamView® Pro Testmaker CD-ROM 💿 Presentation Plus! CD-ROM 📙 California Standards Practice Transparencies
Section 3: African American Culture 1. The Harlem Renaissance sparked new trends in literature, music, and art and featured the work of writers such as Langston Hughes and Zora Neale Hurston. 2. African Americans steadily worked to win more rights.	• Reproducible Lesson Plan 7-3* • Daily Lecture and Discussion Notes 7-3 • Active Reading Note-Taking Guide 7-3 • Guided Reading Activity 7-3 • Section Quiz 7-3 • Reading Essentials and Study Guide 7-3	📙 Daily Focus Skills Transparency 7-3 📙 Section Graphic Organizer Transparency 7-3 💿 Interactive Tutor Self-Assessment CD-ROM 💿 ExamView® Pro Testmaker CD-ROM 💿 Presentation Plus! CD-ROM 📙 California Standards Practice Transparencies

PACING YOUR LESSONS

Chapter Introduction	Section 1	Section 2	Section 3	Chapter Assessment
½ Day	2 Days	1 Day	2 Days	½ Day

`0:00` **OUT OF TIME?** 📁 Assign the Chapter 7 *Reading Essentials and Study Guide.*

*Available on TeacherWorks™ CD-ROM

Chapter 7 Planning Guide

Standards-Based Lesson Plan

 History–Social Science Standards Covered in Chapter 7

The standards covered in the chapter are listed below. Use the accompanying activity as you teach the chapter to ensure student mastery of these standards. This activity can be used in combination with the program's print and technology assessment materials.

Standard	Section 1	2	3
11.2.3 Trace the effect of the Americanization movement.	✔		
11.3.3 Cite incidences of religious intolerance in the United States (e.g., persecution of Mormons, anti-Catholic sentiment, anti-Semitism).	✔		
11.5.2 Analyze the international and domestic events, interests, and philosophies that prompted attacks on civil liberties, including the Palmer Raids, Marcus Garvey's "back-to-Africa" movement, the Ku Klux Klan, and immigration quotas and the responses of organizations such as the American Civil Liberties Union, the National Association for the Advancement of Colored People, and the Anti-Defamation League to those attacks.	✔		✔
11.5.3 Examine the passage of the Eighteenth Amendment to the Constitution and the Volstead Act (Prohibition).	✔		
11.5.4 Analyze the passage of the Nineteenth Amendment and the changing role of women in society.	✔		
11.5.5 Describe the Harlem Renaissance and new trends in literature, music, and art, with special attention to the work of writers (e.g., Zora Neale Hurston, Langston Hughes).		✔	
11.5.6 Trace the growth and effects of radio and movies and their role in the worldwide diffusion of popular culture.		✔	✔

Cumulative Standards-Assessment Activity

The Cumulative Standards-Assessment Activity will help students organize and learn the important information from the chapter. Begin teaching the chapter with this activity, and have students complete it as they read the chapter.

CREATING A SUMMARY

Purpose By writing effective summaries, students identify the key points in a text and the most important information related to those points. Summarizing is also useful for committing important historical information to memory and gauging what students have learned and what they still need to learn.

Introduction to Summarizing

1. Review the steps in summarizing:
   - Distinguish main ideas from supporting details.
   - Describe the main ideas in your own words.
   - Keep summaries short and focused.
2. Model how to summarize the text under the first subheading of Section 1 by helping students reduce the information in a few sentences.

3. Ask students to copy this diagram into their notebooks:

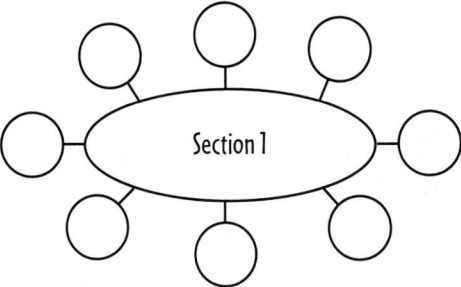

Tell students to write key phrases in the web diagram as they read the section and then use their notes to summarize the section. They can do this exercise for each section in the chapter and use these summaries as study aids.

Chapter 7 Planning Guide

READING SUPPORT

- Content Vocabulary Activity 7
- Academic Vocabulary Activity 7
- Reading Skills Activity 7
- Chapter 7 Active Reading Note-Taking Guide
- Chapter 7 Guided Reading Activities
- Chapter 7 Reading Essentials and Study Guide
- American Literature Readings, Unit 3
- *The American Vision: Modern Times* Video Program
- Vocabulary PuzzleMaker CD-ROM
- American History Primary Source Document Library CD-ROM

CRITICAL THINKING

- Critical Thinking Skills Activity 7
- Primary Source Reading 7
- Cause-and-Effect Transparency 7 Strategy and Activity
- Presentation Plus! CD-ROM

UNIVERSAL ACCESS

- Universal Access Activity 7
- English Learner Activity 7
- American Art Prints
- StudentWorks™ Plus CD-ROM
- American Music: Hits Through History
- School-to-Home Connection Activity 7

SKILL PRACTICE

- Map Overlay Transparency 7 Strategy and Activity
- Historical Analysis Skills Activity 7
- Time Line Activity 7
- Reading Skills Activity 7
- Reinforcing Skills Activity 7
- Linking Past and Present Activity 7
- Interpreting Political Cartoons 7
- History Simulations and Problem Solving, Unit 3
- MindJogger Videoquiz

WRITING SUPPORT

- Chapter 7 Active Reading Note-Taking Guide
- Writer's Guidebook
- High School Writing Process Transparencies

ASSESSMENT

- Chapter 7 Section Quizzes
- Chapter 7 Tests, Forms A and B
- Authentic Assessment Activity 4
- ExamView® Pro Testmaker CD-ROM
- Interactive Tutor Self-Assessment CD-ROM
- California Standards Practice, Grade 11
- Succeeding on . . .™ the California Standards: Grade 11 History–Social Science CD-ROM

CD-ROM		Transparency	
DVD		Music Program	
Print Material		Videocassette	
Poster			

Chapter 7 Planning Guide

TECHNOLOGY

- StudentWorks™ Plus CD-ROM
- TeacherWorks™ CD-ROM
- ExamView® Pro Testmaker CD-ROM
- Interactive Tutor Self-Assessment CD-ROM
- Presentation Plus! CD-ROM
- Vocabulary PuzzleMaker CD-ROM
- American History Primary Source Document Library CD-ROM
- MindJogger Videoquiz
- *The American Vision: Modern Times* Video Program
- Professional Development in High School Social Studies Video Series
- Teach, Use, and Succeed With *The American Vision: Modern Times*
- American Music: Hits Through History
- Succeeding on . . .™ the California Standards: Grade 11 History–Social Science CD-ROM

SPANISH RESOURCES

- Spanish Activities and Assessment
  - Spanish Vocabulary Activities
  - Spanish Guided Reading Activities
  - Spanish Quizzes and Tests
  - Spanish Reteaching Activities
- Spanish Reading Essentials and Study Guide
- Spanish School-to-Home Connection Activities

TRANSPARENCIES

- Daily Focus Skills Transparencies
- Section Graphic Organizer Transparencies
- Map Overlay Transparencies
- Cause-and-Effect Transparencies
- Unit Time Line Transparencies
- Why It Matters Transparencies
- American Art and Architecture Transparencies
- High School Writing Process Transparencies
- California Standards Practice Transparencies

TEACHER PLANNING

- Daily Lecture and Discussion Notes
- English Learner Handbook
- Building Academic Vocabulary
- *The American Vision: Modern Times* Reading and Study Skills Foldables
- Reading Strategies and Activities for the Social Studies Classroom
- Universal Access for the American History Classroom
- NGS United States Desk Map
- NGS World Atlas
- Chapter 7 Reproducible Lesson Plans on TeacherWorks™ CD-ROM
- California Guide to Daily Intervention

PROFESSIONAL DEVELOPMENT

- Building Academic Vocabulary
- Strategies for Success
- Research-Based Strategies Used to Develop *The American Vision: Modern Times*
- Character Education in the High School Classroom
- Professional Development in High School Social Studies Video Series
- Teach, Use, and Succeed With *The American Vision: Modern Times*

Chapter 7 Planning Guide

NATIONAL GEOGRAPHIC — TEACHER'S CORNER

Index to National Geographic Magazine:
The following articles relate to this chapter:

- "Chicago: Welcome to the Neighborhood," May 1991
- "Growing up in East Harlem," May 1990
- "Offbeat New Orleans," January 1995
- "Traveling the Blue Highway," April 1999

National Geographic Society Products:
To order the following, call National Geographic at 1–800–368–2728

- *Eyewitness to the 20th Century* (Book)
- *Historical Atlas of the United States* (Atlas)
- *Immigration: The Triumph of Hope* (Video)

NGS ONLINE

Access National Geographic's new dynamic MapMachine Web site and other geography resources at:

www.nationalgeographic.com
www.nationalgeographic.com/maps

MASTERING THE STANDARDS

The content and assessment in the Student Edition, Teacher Wraparound Edition, teacher planning materials, and the print and technology products are all standards-based. The use of these products during instruction leads to mastery of the standards.

PRACTICE
- California Standards Practice, Grade 11
- California Standards Practice Transparencies
- School-to-Home Connection

BENCHMARK ASSESSMENT
- Section Quizzes, Chapter Tests, and Authentic Assessment
- Exam*View*® Pro Testmaker CD-ROM
- Succeeding On ... ™ the California Standards: Grade 11 History–Social Science CD-ROM

REMEDIATION
- California Guide to Daily Intervention
- Interactive Tutor Self-Assessment CD-ROM
- Exam*View*® Pro Testmaker CD-ROM
- California Standards Practice, Grade 11
- Reading Essentials and Study Guide

History Online

Use our Web site for additional resources. All essential content is covered in the Student Edition.

You and your students can visit tav.mt.glencoe.com, the Web site companion to the **American Vision: Modern Times.** This innovative integration of electronic and print media offers your students a wealth of opportunities. The student text directs students to the Web site for the following options:

- **Chapter Overviews**
- **Self-Check Quizzes**
- **Student Web Activities**
- **Textbook Updates**

Answers to the student Web activities are provided for you in the **Web Activity Lesson Plans.** Additional Web resources and ePuzzles and games are also available.

FOLDABLES™ Study Organizer — Dinah Zike's Foldables

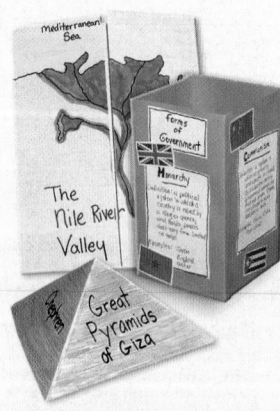

Foldables are three-dimensional, interactive graphic organizers that help students practice basic writing skills, review key vocabulary terms, and identify main ideas. Every chapter has a foldable activity in the *Dinah Zike's Reading and Study Skills Foldables* booklet. You can use the foldables as they are presented or modify them to suit the needs of your individual class.

A variety of videotape programs are available from A&E Television and The History Channel to provide teaching assistance. To order, call Glencoe at 1-800-334-7344.

Chapter 7 Planning Guide

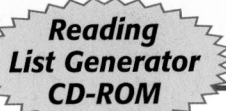

The Glencoe BookLink CD-ROM is a database that allows you to search more than 15,000 titles to create a customized reading list for your students.

- Reading Lists can be organized by students' reading level, author, genre, theme, or area of interest.
- The database provides Degrees of Reading Power™ (DRP) and Lexile™ readability scores for all selections.
- A brief summary of each selection is included.

Leveled reading suggestions for this chapter:

For students at a Grade 8 reading level:
- *Afro-American Fragment,* by Langston Hughes

For students at a Grade 9 reading level:
- *Jazz: The Great American Art,* by Gene Seymour

For students at a Grade 10 reading level:
- *Pride and Promise: The Harlem Renaissance,* by Kathryn Cryan-Hicks

- *Timed Readings Plus in Social Studies* help students increase their reading rate and fluency while maintaining comprehension. The 400-word passages are similar to those found on state and national assessments.
- *Reading in the Content Area: Social Studies* concentrates on six essential reading skills that help students better comprehend what they read. The book includes 75 high-interest nonfiction passages written at increasing levels of difficulty.
- *Reading Fluency* helps students read smoothly, accurately, and expressively.
- *Jamestown's Reading Improvement,* by renowned reading expert Edward Fry, focuses on helping build your students' comprehension, vocabulary, and skimming and scanning skills.
- *Critical Reading Series* provides high-interest books, each written at three reading levels.

For more information about these products, see the Jamestown Education materials in the Classroom Solutions in the front of this Teacher Wraparound Edition. To order these products, call Glencoe at 1-800-334-7344.

KEY for Using the Teacher Wraparound Edition

Use this key to help you identify the different types of prompts found in the Teacher Wraparound Edition.

R   **Reading Strategies** activities help you teach reading skills and vocabulary.

C   **Critical Thinking** strategies help students apply and extend what they have learned.

U   **Universal Access** activities provide differentiated instruction for students learning to speak English, along with suggestions for teaching various types of learners.

S   **Skill Practice** strategies help students practice historical analysis and geography skills.

W   **Writing Support** activities provide writing opportunities to help students comprehend the text.

Teaching strategies and activities have been coded for ability level appropriateness.

AL   Activities for students working above grade level
OL   Activities for students working on grade level
BL   Activities for students working below grade level
EL   Activities for English learners

History–Social Science Standards

This chapter addresses the following standards:

11.2 Students analyze the relationship among the rise of industrialization, large-scale rural-to-urban migration, and massive immigration from Southern and Eastern Europe.

11.2.3 Trace the effect of the Americanization movement.

11.3 Students analyze the role religion played in the founding of America, its lasting moral, social, and political impacts, and issues regarding religious liberty.

11.5 Students analyze the major political, social, economic, technological, and cultural developments of the 1920s.

BELLRINGER
SKILLBUILDER ACTIVITY

Ask students what they know about jazz music. Ask them if the name "The Jazz Age" accurately describes the 1920s. Give students 10 minutes to write a brief response to this question, and ask them to save their responses. At the end of the chapter, have students revisit their responses and share with the class what they learned that confirmed their predictions or surprised them.

TEACH

Thinking About the Big Ideas

As you begin teaching each section, use these questions and activities to focus on the Big Idea.

CHAPTER 7

1921–1929

The Jazz Age

❧ The Big Ideas ❧

SECTION 1: A Clash of Values

People react to periods of breathtaking social and cultural change in different ways. *During the 1920s, clashes between traditional and modern values shook the United States.*

SECTION 2: Cultural Innovations

People react to periods of breathtaking social and cultural change in different ways. *The 1920s, an era of exciting and innovative cultural trends, witnessed changes in art, literature, and popular culture.*

SECTION 3: African American Culture

People react to periods of breathtaking social and cultural change in different ways. *The large population of African Americans in northern cities after the "Great Migration" helped spur the Harlem Renaissance.*

The *American Vision: Modern Times* Video *The Chapter 7 video, "The Harlem Renaissance," focuses on Harlem's lively arts and music scene and the movement's contributions to American culture.*

1915
- New Ku Klux Klan founded

1921
- Emergency Quota Act passed, limiting immigration

1922
- Antilynching bill passes in House

1920
- Marcus Garvey leads march through Harlem

United States PRESIDENTS

Wilson 1913–1921

Harding 1921–1923

1915   *1920*

World

1917
- British government's Balfour Declaration supports national home for Jewish people in Palestine

1921
- Ireland becomes an independent country

1922
- Mussolini and Fascists take power in Italy

402

Section 1
A Clash of Values

Essential Question: Are there any areas of culture in which you disagree with your parents or other adults? For example, do you enjoy the same or different music, movies, dances, or games? Why do you think this is so? After the discussion, tell students that in Section 1, they will learn about some social and cultural changes that caused clashes during the 1920s. **OL**

Section 2
Cultural Innovations

Essential Question: Do you like change? Are there changes, such as moving or going to a new school, that bother you? How do you react to changes you cannot control? Ask students to freewrite on these questions. When they have finished, invite volunteers to share their ideas. Then tell students that in Section 2, they will learn about the changes that occurred in the arts during the 1920s. **BL**

This photograph of jazz musicians captures the boisterous spirit of the 1920s.

Section 3
African American Culture
Essential Question: What factors do you think inspire artists? Do you know of any places or events that have inspired artists? After discussing the questions, tell students that in Section 3, they will learn about a great artistic flowering in New York's Harlem during the 1920s. **OL**

Cultural Perspectives

Gather several examples of jazz music composed by popular African American artists of the 1920s and poetry by writers of the Harlem Renaissance. Analyze and interpret the selections as a class or in small groups. Have students discuss common themes that emerge and what these pieces reveal about the lives of African Americans in the 1920s. **AL**

1925
• Scopes trial begins
• F. Scott Fitzgerald's *The Great Gatsby* published

1924
• National Origins Act passed

1926
• Langston Hughes's *The Weary Blues* published

1927
• First feature film with sound debuts
• Lindbergh completes first solo transatlantic flight

Coolidge 1923–1929

Hoover 1929–1933

1925   *1930*

1924
• Britain recognizes the USSR

1926
• Pavlov's *Conditioned Reflexes* published

1928
• Chiang Kai-shek elected president of China

1923
• Turkish Republic founded

HISTORY Online
Chapter Overview
Visit the *American Vision: Modern Times* Web site at tav.mt.glencoe.com and click on **Chapter Overviews–Chapter 7** to preview chapter information.

403

Dinah Zike's Foldables are three-dimensional, interactive graphic organizers that help students practice basic writing skills, review key vocabulary terms, and identify main ideas. Have students complete the foldable activity in the *Dinah Zike's Reading and Study Skills Foldables* booklet.

HISTORY Online
Go to tav.mt.glencoe.com for student activities, lesson plans, and links to additional resources to help students learn about the Jazz Age.

Reading Skill

Why It's Important

The skill of connecting asks students to make a connection to the text. Students are more likely to continue reading and trying to understand a text to which they feel connected in some way.

1. Introducing the Skill

Have students work in pairs to analyze a modern teen star in music, movies, or television. Have each pair fill out a graphic organizer similar to the one below. **Ask: Why do you think that teens appreciate and support these teen stars?** *(They feel a connection to the teens that they do not generally feel toward older entertainers.)* Point out that students can also connect to a text through finding ways in which they are linked to the content. **BL**

Who	What Entertainment Medium	Why Teens Like Him or Her

2. Extending the Skill

Ask students to observe an event geared toward teens, such as an athletic contest or a school play or concert. Have them take notes on ways in which they connected to the event. As students share their responses, look for strategies that students can transfer from "live" events to reading text. **OL**

Answers and Additional Support

Reading Skill ▸ Connecting

Effective readers make connections between what they read and what they know. Some connections are based on personal experiences (text-to-self). Readers can also make connections to things they have read in other books (text-to-text) and to things that happen in other places (text-to-world). Making these connections allows you, the reader, to add new knowledge to what you already know. It helps you understand the relationship between events of the past and present. Finally, when you make good connections, you are more likely to remember the information you have read.

After reading a paragraph or passage, stop and ask yourself a connecting question. Does the text remind you of something that has happened in your life? Does it make you think of something you have read? Does it make you think of a person or event in another place or time?

Read the following paragraph and ask a connecting question of a partner.

> **Thanks to radio and motion pictures, sports such as baseball and boxing reached new heights of popularity in the 1920s. Baseball star Babe Ruth became a national hero, famous for hitting hundreds of home runs. As one broadcaster later remarked, "He wasn't a baseball player. He was a worldwide celebrity, an international star, the likes of which baseball has never seen since."** (pages 420–421)

CONNECTING

Authors sometimes use quotes to evoke connections in the mind of the reader. This technique gives voice to the text and reminds the reader that history is a story well told.

While reading the passage, you might have made the following connections:

Text-to-self: Do you recall the first time you saw a major sports celebrity, such as Tiger Woods or Michael Jordan? Do you remember how it feels to win a game?

Text-to-text: Have you read about or seen film footage of Babe Ruth?

Text-to-world: Has mass media made celebrity commonplace in today's society?

Apply the Skill

As you read this chapter, pause periodically and make a connection based on something you have just read. Try to make such connections with important ideas, times, and topics in your life. Remember that the better the connection, the more likely you are to remember the new information.

404

UNIVERSAL ACCESS

Auditory/Musical Play for students pieces of popular music from different decades. As they listen, challenge them to find at least one way in which they can connect to the piece. *(For example, the crooners of the 1950s sang about love, which is still a popular theme. The music of the 1920s used syncopated rhythms that continue to be used.)* **OL**

Historical Analysis Skill — Interpreting Events

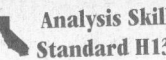

Analysis Skill
Standard H13

Historical Interpretation Learning about the context of past events and interpreting events within that context will help you better understand the events and their impact.

As you learned earlier, there was a time in United States history in which many citizens could not vote. Similarly, voting rights have been restricted in other parts of the world across time. For example, in Ancient Greece only men who owned property could vote. Today it would be unthinkable to exclude people from voting based on their wealth, gender, or ethnicity. It is important for you to understand these events within the context of the time. Applying today's standard to past events could lead to a misrepresentation of history.

One of the critical responsibilities of historians is to interpret historical events within their social, political, and economic contexts. As you learned in chapter 4, historians also compare past events with present-day realities. Limiting the analysis to one or the other, however, results in understanding only parts of past events.

Read this passage from your textbook about the Scopes Trial in Tennessee.

In 1925 Tennessee passed the Butler Act, which outlawed any teaching that denied "the story of the Divine Creation of man as taught in the Bible. . . ." The American Civil Liberties Union (ACLU) advertised for a teacher who would be willing to be arrested for teaching evolution. John T. Scopes . . . volunteered to be the test case. . . .
. . . After eight days of trial, Scopes was found guilty and fined $100. . . . (pages 411–412)

Reading about the case by itself probably would leave you confused about the reasons for the trial. Similarly, if you were to interpret this landmark case by today's standards, you would not understand the context surrounding the trial. Once you learn about the cultural clashes in the 1920s, such as those between science and religion, you will understand the growing division between traditional and modern views during that time. You will also better understand the circumstances surrounding the trial and its impact.

Apply the Skill

As you read the text under "African American Politics" on pages 429–431, consider the segregation and discrimination African Americans faced at the time. This will help you understand their efforts to gain a political voice and to fight for legal rights.

405

Historical Analysis

Why It's Important

Interpreting events within their context involves looking at historical events as they were understood at the time they occurred. Many people are unable to place the events of the past in proper perspective because they cannot appreciate the cultural context of the time. Using contemporary standards to interpret or view the past can lead to misunderstanding or a false sense of superiority, which can make it hard to see one's own biases and cultural assumptions.

1. Introducing the Skill

Divide the class into three groups. Assign each group one of the following topics: lowering the age for teenagers to purchase alcohol or tobacco, to purchase tickets to R-rated films, or to drive a car. Ask students in each group to complete a chart similar to the one below. After students have had a chance to develop their arguments, have them share their ideas. Point out that adults have a different cultural and historical context than adolescents, having grown up in a different time period. Tell them that different perspectives may extend across age, culture, and nationality. **OL**

	Reasons For	Reasons Against
What I Think		
What Adults I Know Think		

2. Extending the Skill

Have students interview at least one adult on his or her viewpoint about a current event topic in the news. Lead a discussion based on the responses the students gather, looking for contexts that shape ideas. **OL**

UNIVERSAL ACCESS

English Learners Ask students who are from non-Anglo cultures to brainstorm a list of attitudes that they find odd or about which adults they know have complained. *(For example, Asian and Latino cultures typically place great value on not shaming the family and on hard work.)* Allow volunteers time to share some of the cultural differences they have had to confront, giving the class opportunity to understand another perspective. **EL**

FOCUS

BELLRINGER
SKILLBUILDER ACTIVITY

Project **Daily Focus Skills Transparency 7-1** and have students answer the question.

Guide to Reading

Understanding Vocabulary: Have students look at the vocabulary lists for the section as you pronounce each word. Invite students to share the meanings of any terms that are already familiar to them.

Answers to Graphic:
Causes: job competition, immigrant influx, eugenics, recession; Effects: KKK, Sacco-Vanzetti case, immigration restrictions

Unpacking the Standards

Students will be able to:
- Identify the results of nativism during the 1920s.
- Discuss the role of religion in anti-immigrant sentiment of the 1920s.
- Explain the influence of Fundamentalism on state and national laws.

Answers and Additional Support

SECTION 1 A Clash of Values

Guide to Reading

Connection
In the previous chapter, you learned how World War I affected the United States. In this section, you will discover how modern and traditional values clashed and changed society.

Main Idea
- During the 1920s, anti-immigrant and racist feelings increased. (p. 407)
- Fearing new immigrants, the federal government enacted several laws to limit immigration. (p. 408)
- An emphasis on youth and personal freedom led to a more relaxed moral attitude. p. (p. 410)

- Fundamentalists promoted the authority of the Bible and defended the Protestant faith. (p. 411)
- Congress passed the Eighteenth Amendment and the Volstead Act to prohibit alcohol, but the laws largely failed to create positive social change. (p. 412)

Content Vocabulary
anarchist, eugenics, flapper, evolution, creationism, police powers, speakeasy

Academic Vocabulary
source, aspect, ethic

People and Terms to Identify
Ku Klux Klan, Emergency Quota Act, Fundamentalism

Reading Objectives
- **Explain** the rise of racism and nativism in the 1920s.
- **Describe** the clash of values in the 1920s and the changing status of women.

Reading Strategy
Organizing As you read about Americans' reactions to immigrants in the 1920s, complete a graphic organizer similar to the one below by filling in the causes and effects of anti-immigrant prejudices.

Causes   Effects

Anti-Immigrant
Prejudices

Preview of Events

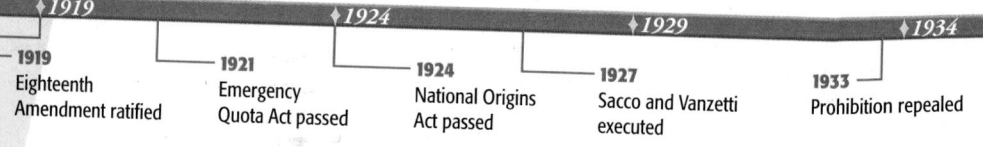

◆1919	◆1924	◆1929	◆1934

1919
Eighteenth Amendment ratified

1921
Emergency Quota Act passed

1924
National Origins Act passed

1927
Sacco and Vanzetti executed

1933
Prohibition repealed

The following are the main History–Social Science Standards covered in this section.

11.2.3 Trace the effect of the Americanization movement.

11.3.3 Cite incidences of religious intolerance in the United States (e.g., persecution of Mormons, anti-Catholic sentiment, anti-Semitism).

11.5.2 Analyze the international and domestic events, interests, and philosophies that prompted attacks on civil liberties, including the Palmer Raids, Marcus Garvey's "back-to-Africa" movement, the Ku Klux Klan, immigration quotas and the responses of organizations such as the American Civil Liberties Union, the National Association for the Advancement of Colored People, and the Anti-Defamation League to those attacks.

11.5.3 Examine the passage of the Eighteenth Amendment to the Constitution and the Volstead Act (Prohibition).

11.5.4 Analyze the passage of the Nineteenth Amendment and the changing role of women in society.

～ The Big Idea ～

People react to periods of breathtaking social and cultural change in different ways. The 1920s began with an increase in anti-immigrant and racist feelings, fueled by an economic recession and the influx of immigrants. In response, Congress passed several laws limiting immigration. Many women and young people adopted a more relaxed moral attitude that conflicted with traditional roles, values, and morals. Fundamentalists tried to combat these new attitudes by promoting a literal interpretation of the Bible and by defending the Protestant faith. The Eighteenth Amendment and the Volstead Act prohibited alcohol but did not stop the new moral attitude as many had hoped.

406 CHAPTER 7   The Jazz Age

SECTION RESOURCES

📁 **Print Material**
- Reproducible Lesson Plan 7-1
- Guided Reading Activity 7-1
- Reading Essentials and Study Guide 7-1
- Active Reading Note-Taking Guide 7-1

🖥 **Transparencies**
- Daily Focus Skills Transparency 7-1
- Section Graphic Organizer Transparency 7-1

Technology
- Interactive Tutor Self-Assessment CD-ROM
- ExamView® Pro Testmaker CD-ROM
- Presentation Plus! CD-ROM

Nativism Resurges

Main Idea During the 1920s, anti-immigrant and racist feelings increased.

Reading Connection Describe a time when you traveled to another school, state, or country. How were people and their way of life different? Read on to learn about the tensions that caused a resurgence of nativism in the United States.

As the 1920s opened, an economic recession, an influx of immigrants, and racial and cultural tensions combined to create an atmosphere of disillusionment and intolerance. The fear and prejudice many felt toward Germans and Communists expanded to include all immigrants. This triggered a general rise in racism and in nativism, the desire to protect the interests of native-born Americans against those of immigrants.

During World War I, immigration to the United States dropped sharply. By 1921, however, it had returned to prewar levels, with the majority of immigrants at this time coming from southern and eastern Europe. Many Americans saw immigrants as a threat to stability and order. The arrival of millions of immigrants also seemed to pose a threat to the four million recently demobilized military men and women searching for work in an economy with soaring unemployment and rising prices.

★ An American Story ★

In 1911 Alfred Levitt left a small town in Russia to immigrate to New York City. Like many immigrants before and since, he had big ambitions, despite his poor English and lack of education. He wanted to forget his Russian heritage and become a successful American:

66My conscious drive when I got here was to escape the rigors of poverty, to become somebody of importance. This I don't mean economically, but someone who can justify his presence on the planet. I wonder: Who am I? What am I here for? At seventeen years, the first question for me, though, was: What was I going to do? What will I become? . . . I made up my mind, as young as I was, that I'm going to amount to something in the world, and I'm not going to continue being one of those who starve.99

—quoted in *Centenarians: The Story of the Twentieth Century by the Americans Who Lived It*

Levitt did indeed "amount to something." A successful artist, he lived the rest of his life in New York City. Twenty of his paintings are part of the permanent collection of the city's Metropolitan Museum of Art.

Not all immigrants, many of whom were unskilled workers, fared so well. As they sought to enter the workforce and establish a foothold in American life, many of them encountered ethnic and religious prejudices. The experience of two Italian immigrants, Nicola Sacco and Bartolomeo Vanzetti, exemplified the prejudices and fears of the period.

The Sacco-Vanzetti Case Shortly after 3:00 P.M. on April 15, 1920, two men shot and killed two employees of the Slater & Morrill Shoe Company in South Braintree, Massachusetts, and robbed the company of its $15,000 payroll. Police subsequently arrested Nicola Sacco, a shoemaker, and Bartolomeo Vanzetti, a fish peddler.

The Sacco and Vanzetti case created a furor, as newspapers around the country revealed that the two immigrants were **anarchists,** or people who oppose all forms of government. They also discovered that Sacco owned a gun similar to the murder weapon and that the bullets used in the murders matched those in Sacco's gun. Although no one at the time knew if Sacco and Vanzetti were guilty, many people leaped to that conclusion because the two men were Italian immigrants and anarchists. Others viewed the case as an example of prejudice against people based on their ethnic origin and political beliefs.

On July 14, 1921, a jury found Sacco and Vanzetti guilty, and the judge sentenced them to death. Many Americans, caught up in the antiforeign fever of the

▲ *Alfred Levitt (standing)*

TEACH

U Universal Access

English Learners To address the needs of students who have difficulty reading, have students create an outline using the subheadings of the section. Once they have completed the outline, encourage them to listen to the Audio Program and highlight or circle the topics in their outline as they are discussed. **EL**

R₁ Reading Strategy

Scaffolding—Comparing and Contrasting Some cultural issues in America have recurred from one generation to the next. **Ask: Recall an earlier time in American history when nativism first emerged.** *(the 1850s)* Have students work in small groups to create Venn diagrams showing similarities and differences in the events of the 1850s and those of the 1920s. Ask them to draw conclusions about the recurring causes of nativism based on their diagrams. **OL**
CA CS1

This **Reading Skill** was introduced in Chapter 3.

R₂ Reading Strategy

Scaffolding—Academic Vocabulary The word *immigrate* was introduced in Chapter 1, Section 1. Ask a student to define the word. **BL**

Review the Big Idea

Review the Big Idea for this section, "People react to periods of breathtaking social and cultural change in different ways." Ask the class to explain why the Sacco-Vanzetti trial caused such turmoil in the U.S. at this time. *(general distrust of immigrants and antigovernment activists concerned people after World War I.)* **AL CA HI1**

More Skill Practice

Determining Cause and Effect The cause-and-effect structure explores the reasons for an occurrence and the results of previous events. Write the following headings on the board: CAUSES→EVENT→EFFECTS. Under *Event,* write "Nativism." As students read through the section, have them complete the chain by adding the causes and effects related to the rise of nativism during the 1920s. *(Causes: influx of immigrants; rise in racism; economic recession; Effects: eugenics movement; return of the Ku Klux Klan; Emergency Quota and National Origins Acts)* **OL CA HI1**

408

R₁ Reading Strategy

Using Word Parts *Eugenics* begins with the Greek prefix *eu-*, meaning "good." Invite students to share other words with this prefix. Have them use dictionaries to find the meanings of these terms. **OL**

R₂ Reading Strategy

Scaffolding—Academic Vocabulary The word *strategy* was introduced in Chapter 5, Section 1. Ask a student to define the word. **BL**

S Skill Practice

Conducting Research Ask students to locate U.S. immigration statistics from 1890–1930, and compare two countries from western and eastern Europe. **Ask: What differences are observed from this data?** *(Students should correctly interpret the data they have gathered.)* Use the data to construct a chart showing the effects of the immigration laws of 1920 and 1924. Ask students to write a brief paragraph explaining their findings. **OL** **CA HR4**

✓ Reading Check

Answer: fear of Communists, nativism, economic competition, eugenics

Answers and Additional Support

---

time, applauded the verdict and the penalty. Over the next six years, lawyers filed numerous appeals for a new trial, but all were denied. In April 1927, a special Massachusetts commission studied the case and upheld the verdict. Four months later, on August 23, 1927, Sacco and Vanzetti were executed, proclaiming their innocence all the while. 📖 *(See You're the Historian on pages 416–417 for more information on Sacco and Vanzetti.)*

Pseudo-Scientific Racism Nativist and racist feelings in the 1920s were reinforced by the beliefs of the eugenics movement. **Eugenics** is a pseudo-science (or false science) that deals with improving hereditary traits. Developed in Europe in the early 1900s, eugenics emphasized that human inequalities were inherited and warned against breeding the "unfit" or "inferior." Eugenics fueled the nativists' argument for the superiority of the "original" American stock—white Protestants of northern European descent. Political, intellectual, and cultural figures like Woodrow Wilson and Henry Cabot Lodge embraced eugenics. By doing so, they lent authority to racist theories, which reinvigorated the nativist argument for strict immigration control.

Return of the Ku Klux Klan At the forefront of the movement to restrict immigration was the **Ku Klux Klan,** or KKK. The old KKK had flourished in the South after the Civil War and used threats

and violence to intimidate newly freed African Americans. The new Klan had other targets as well—Catholics, Jews, immigrants, and other groups believed to represent "un-American" values.

William J. Simmons founded the new Ku Klux Klan in Atlanta, Georgia, in 1915. A former circuit riding Methodist preacher, Simmons pledged to preserve America's white, Protestant civilization. In the 1920s, Klan publicity claimed that the organization was fighting for "Americanism."

The Klan attracted few members until 1920, when Simmons hired public relations entrepreneurs Edward Young Clarke and Elizabeth Tyler, paying them a commission of $8 of every $10 initiation fee for a new Klan recruit. Clarke and Tyler divided the nation into regions and paid more than 1,000 "salespeople" to promote the Klan. As a result of their strategy, membership in the Ku Klux Klan exploded, reaching nearly 4 million by 1924 as it spread beyond the South and into Northern cities.

Following the membership boom, the Klan began to decline largely as a result of scandals and power struggles involving its leaders. Membership shrank, and politicians whom the Klan supported were voted out of office. The sharp reduction in immigrants due to new immigration laws further disabled the Klan, depriving it of a major issue. The Klan never again had a major impact on national politics.

✓ **Reading Check** **Explaining** How did eugenics reinforce nativist ideals?

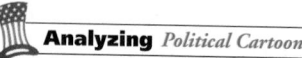

Analyzing *Political Cartoons*

New Immigrants This cartoon portrays the feelings of many Americans who were opposed to immigration. What comment does the cartoon make about immigrants?

S Controlling Immigration

Main Idea **Fearing new immigrants, the federal government enacted several laws to limit immigration.**

Reading Connection Discuss quotas you are aware of, such as class size or the number of students allowed on a team, and compare them to the immigration quotas set by the government. Read on to discover how the United States limited immigration during the 1920s.

After World War I, American immigration policies changed in response to the postwar recession and nativist pleas to "Keep America American." Even big business, which previously favored unrestricted immigration as a **source** of cheap labor, now feared the new immigrants as radicals.

Analyzing *Political Cartoons*

Answer: It implies that other countries were sending their unwanted citizens to the United States.

Ask: Why did some people have such a strong opposition to the new wave of immigrants? *(competition for scarce jobs, fear that immigrants were anarchists and revolutionaries)*

In 1921 President Harding signed the **Emergency Quota Act,** which established a temporary quota system, limiting immigration. According to this act, only three percent of the total number of foreign-born people of a nationality already living in the United States, as indicated in the 1910 census, could be admitted in a single year. This theoretically restricted the number of immigrants from all countries, but in practice it discriminated heavily against people from southern and eastern Europe. Ethnic identity and national origin thus determined admission to the United States.

Henry Curran, the commissioner of Ellis Island from 1922 to 1926, commented on the heartbreak caused by the Emergency Quota Act:

66 The hardest quota cases were those that separated families. When part of the family had been born in a country with a quota still open, while the other part had been born in a country whose quota was exhausted, the law let in the first part and deported the other part. Mothers were torn from children, husbands from wives. The law came down like a sword between them. 99

—quoted in *Ellis Island: Echoes from a Nation's Past*

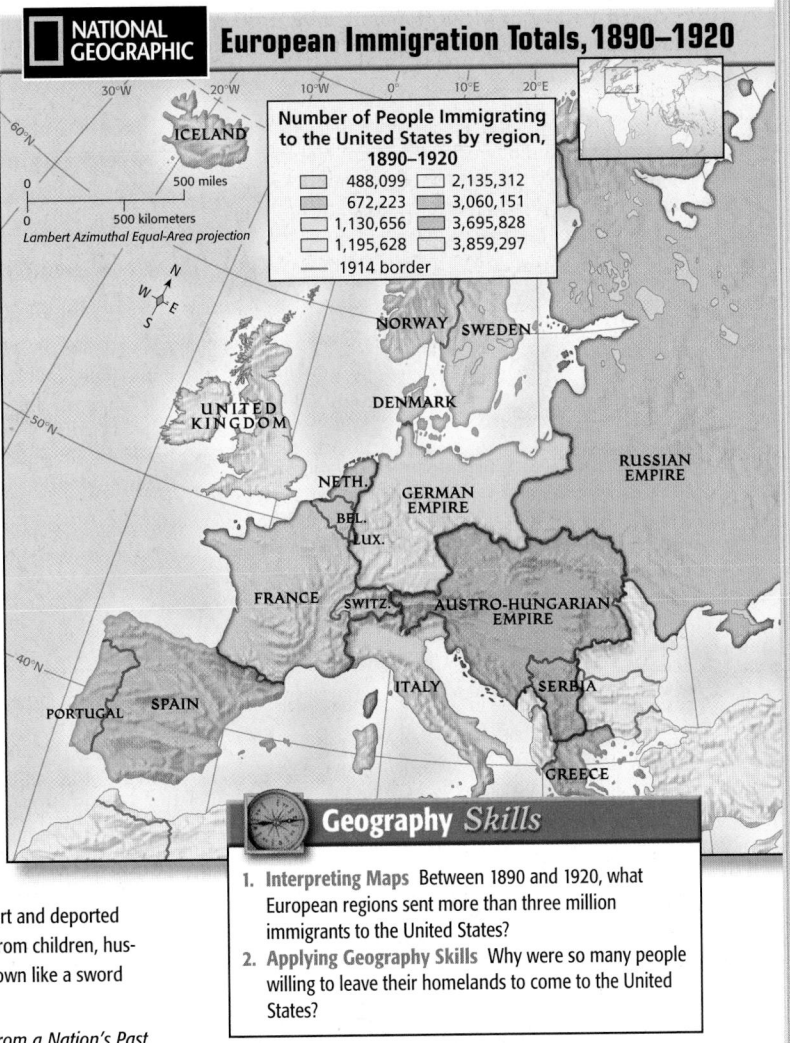

NATIONAL GEOGRAPHIC European Immigration Totals, 1890–1920

Number of People Immigrating to the United States by region, 1890–1920

488,099	2,135,312
672,223	3,060,151
1,130,656	3,695,828
1,195,628	3,859,297
— 1914 border	

0 ——— 500 miles
0 ——— 500 kilometers
Lambert Azimuthal Equal-Area projection

Geography Skills

1. **Interpreting Maps** Between 1890 and 1920, what European regions sent more than three million immigrants to the United States?
2. **Applying Geography Skills** Why were so many people willing to leave their homelands to come to the United States?

The National Origins Act of 1924 In 1924 the National Origins Act made immigrant restriction a permanent policy. The law also tightened the quota system, setting quotas at two percent of each national group residing in the country in 1890. By moving back the year to 1890, an even larger proportion of the quotas were allotted to immigrants from northwestern Europe.

A second part of the act, which took effect in 1929, replaced the 1924 quotas with a limit of 150,000 immigrants admitted per year. In addition, the percentage allotted to each nationality would now be based on the total percentage of each nationality within the entire American population according to the 1920 census. This resulted in an unequal balance of immigrants from northwestern European countries, which accounted for 87 percent of the total immigration quota.

Hispanic Immigration to the United States
The immigration acts of 1921 and 1924 reduced the available labor pool in the United States. While workers and unions rejoiced at the reduction in competition for jobs, employers desperately needed laborers for agriculture, mining, and railroad work. Mexican immigrants helped to fill this need.

CHAPTER 7 The Jazz Age **409**

R₁ Reading Strategy

Scaffolding—Academic Vocabulary The word *practice* was introduced in Chapter 3, Section 2. Ask a student to define the word. **BL**

R₂ Reading Strategy

Activating Prior Knowledge Ask students to read the quote from Henry Curran on this page. **Ask:** In what other time of American history were families separated in a manner described in this quote? *(Students should mention that in the antebellum South enslaved families were sometimes separated in a similar manner.)* **OL** **CA 11RL3.2**

S Skill Practice

Visual Literacy Ask students to create a political cartoon that depicts the impact of the National Origins Act of 1924 on the balance of nationalities coming to the United States. **AL** **CA HI1**

Chapter 7 • Section 1

Geography Skills

Answers:
1. Italy, Austro-Hungarian/Russian Empires, Serbia
2. They hoped to find greater opportunities.

Geography Skills Practice
Ask: From what countries did the fewest number of people emigrate? *(France, the Netherlands, Belgium, Luxembourg, and Switzerland)*

Did You Know?

The number of women college undergraduates doubled from 1910 to 1920. During the 1920s, several schools for women that are still highly regarded were founded, including Sarah Lawrence College in New York and Bennington College in Vermont.

Answers and Additional Support

W Writing Support

Narrative Writing Ask students to imagine themselves as young people during the 1920s. Have them write a narrative in the form of a letter or diary entry about the effect that the new morality, automobiles, women in the workplace, or education have on their lives. **OL** **CA 11WS1.2**

R Reading Strategy

Visual Literacy Many people were shocked by the new fashions of the 1920s, especially by the shorter skirts that women started wearing. Some women even put rouge on their knees to emphasize their visibility. In Utah, legislators proposed a law that would have involved fines and prison sentences for women whose skirts reached more than three inches above their ankles. **Ask:** What kind of dress code does your school enforce? Do you think the rules are necessary? *(Students' answers will vary depending on their opinions of dress codes.)* **BL**

✓ Reading Check

Answer: severely limited immigration from all countries except Mexico and those in northwestern Europe

---

The first wave of Mexican immigration to the United States followed the passage of the Newlands Reclamation Act of 1902, which provided funds for irrigation projects in the arid Southwest. Factory farms soon dominated the landscape, and they needed large numbers of agricultural laborers. By 1914 more than 70,000 Mexican immigrants had poured into the United States, many of them fleeing the aftermath of the Mexican Revolution of 1910.

More than 600,000 Mexicans arrived in the United States between 1914 and the end of the 1920s. The National Origins Act of 1924 exempted natives of the Western Hemisphere from the quota system. As the demand for cheap farm labor in California and the Southwest steadily increased, Mexican immigrants crossed the border in record numbers.

✓ **Reading Check** **Explaining** What was the result of the National Origins Act exemption on Western Hemisphere nations?

The New Morality

W

Main Idea An emphasis on youth and personal freedom led to a more relaxed moral attitude.

Reading Connection How do you think older generations view your generation? Read on to find out about the changes in morality in the United States during the 1920s.

Many groups that wanted to restrict immigration also wanted to preserve what they considered to be traditional values. They feared that a "new morality"

▼ *Dr. Florence Sabin*

was taking over the nation. Challenging traditional ways of seeing and thinking, the new morality glorified youth and personal freedom and influenced various **aspects** of American society.

The New Morality Ideals of the loving family and personal satisfaction—views popularized in magazines and other media—influenced popular views on relationships. As the loving and emotional aspects of marriage grew in importance, the ideas of romance, pleasure, and friendship became linked to successful marriages. Advice books in the 1920s dispensed such hints as, "Have lots of pleasure that both husband and wife enjoy . . . and above all, be good friends."

Women in the workforce also began to define the new morality. Many single, working-class women held jobs simply because they needed the wages for themselves or for their families. For some young, single women, work was a way to break away from parental authority and establish a personal identity. Work also provided the wages that allowed women to participate in the consumer culture.

Women who attended college in the 1920s often found support for their emerging sense of independence. Women's colleges, in particular, encouraged their students to pursue careers and to challenge traditional ideas about the nature of women and their role in society.

The automobile also played a role in encouraging the new morality. The nation's youth loved cars because cars made them more independent and allowed them to escape the careful watch of their parents. Instead of socializing at home with the family, many youths could now use cars to seek new forms of entertainment with their friends and to find privacy.

Women in the 1920s Fashion took on a modern look during the 1920s, as women "bobbed," or shortened, their hair and wore flesh-colored silk stockings. It also emphasized the youthful appearance of glamorous stage and screen stars. In this new culture, the carefree, chic "flapper" played a prominent role.

R Though hardly typical of American women at the time, the **flapper**—a young, dramatic, stylish, and unconventional woman—personified women's changing behavior in the 1920s. The flapper smoked cigarettes, drank prohibited liquor, and dressed in attire considered too revealing by previous generations.

While flappers pursued social freedoms, other women sought financial independence by entering the workforce, many of them as salesclerks,

---

More Skill Practice

Connecting Have students work in small groups to compare the content of modern women's magazines with women's magazines from the 1920s that you borrowed from the library. **Ask:** Has the information in these magazines changed over time? The groups should list similarities and differences they notice and then present their findings to the class. **OL**

Resources for page 410

*Have students read more about increased social freedom for women in the **Linking Past and Present Activity 7.***

secretaries, or telephone operators. There were a few women who made contributions in science, medicine, law, or literature. In science, Florence Sabin's medical research led to a dramatic drop in death rates from tuberculosis. In literature, Edith Wharton received the Pulitzer Prize for her novel *The Age of Innocence*. Public health nurse Margaret Sanger, believing that the standard of living could be improved if families limited the number of children they had, founded the American Birth Control League in 1921. This organization became Planned Parenthood in the 1940s. In 1928 Margaret Mead, one of the first female anthropologists, published the highly regarded study, *Coming of Age in Samoa*, which described life in a Pacific island culture.

✓ **Reading Check** **Identifying** What political, social, and economic contributions did women make to American society in the 1920s?

The Fundamentalist Movement

Main Idea Fundamentalists promoted the authority of the Bible and defended the Protestant faith.

Reading Connection What are some issues that you feel strongly about? Read on to learn how people who followed the beliefs of Fundamentalism tried to prevent what they saw as moral decline.

While many Americans embraced the new morality, millions more feared that the country was losing its traditional values. To these Americans, the modern consumer culture, relaxed **ethics,** and growing urbanism symbolized the nation's moral decline. Many of these people, especially those in small rural towns, responded by joining a religious movement known as **Fundamentalism**—a name derived from a series of pamphlets titled *The Fundamentals*, published by oil millionaire Lyman Stewart.

Fundamentalist Beliefs Fundamentalists believed that the Bible was literally true and without error. They defended the Protestant faith against ideas that implied that human beings derived their moral behavior from society and nature, not God. In particular, Fundamentalists rejected Charles Darwin's theory of **evolution,** which said that human beings had developed from lower forms of life over the course of millions of years. Instead, they believed in **creationism**—the belief that God created the world as described in the Bible.

▲ *View of Scopes Trial*

Two popular evangelical preachers, Billy Sunday and Aimee Semple McPherson, stirred Fundamentalists' passions by preaching traditional religious and moral values in very nontraditional ways. A former professional baseball player, Sunday drew huge crowds with his rapid-fire sermons and on-stage showmanship. McPherson conducted her revivals and faith healings in Los Angeles in a flamboyant theatrical style, using stage sets and costumes that expressed the themes of her highly emotional sermons.

The Scopes Trial Evolutionists and creationists eventually clashed in a historic trial. In 1925 Tennessee passed the Butler Act, which outlawed any teaching that denied "the story of the Divine Creation of man as taught in the Bible," and taught instead that "man descended from a lower order of animals." The American Civil Liberties Union (ACLU) advertised for a teacher who would be willing to be arrested for teaching evolution. John T. Scopes, a high school biology teacher in Dayton, Tennessee, volunteered to be the test case. He taught evolution and was subsequently arrested and put on trial.

CHAPTER 7 The Jazz Age **411**

Did You Know?

The charismatic preacher Aimee Semple McPherson gained notoriety for a five-week disappearance she claimed was a kidnapping. In the following years, many lawsuits were also filed against her, often for libel or slander.

S₁ Skill Practice

Conducting Research Ask students to find out the number of women in the workforce in 1900, 1910, 1920, and 1930. In addition, have them locate the average annual wage for women during those years. Students should then create graphs showing the economic gains that women achieved during those decades. **AL**
CA CS2

R Reading Strategy

Using Word Parts Ask students to call out common suffixes and list them on the board. (*-ed, -ing, -al, -er, -ly, -ment, ism, -ist, -ior, -tion,* etc.) Then have students skim the text under the heading "The Fundamentalist Movement," writing down the words that include suffixes. Review the meanings of these suffixes. Challenge students to work in teams to build other words using suffixes you select. **OL**

S₂ Skill Practice

Scaffolding—Interpreting Events Have students work in groups to analyze reasons for the growth of Fundamentalism. Ask students to suggest ideas and events. Advanced students may be encouraged to look at contemporary events that have triggered a rise in Islamic fundamentalism and to compare these events with the 1920s and Protestant fundamentalism. **AL** **CA HI1**

This **Historical Analysis** skill was introduced in Chapter 5.

✓ **Reading Check**

Answer: Some pursued social freedoms, entered the workforce, and contributed to medicine, literature, and science. Many others focused on enhancing traditional marriage relationships.

C Critical Thinking

C Critical Thinking

Making Generalizations Ask the following question to start a class discussion: **What attempts to limit alcohol consumption have been made in recent years?** *(restrictions on advertisements for hard liquor on television, warning labels on alcohol products, high taxes on alcohol, education programs, MADD, SADD)* Ask whether students think these attempts have been successful and whether other alternatives should be considered. **OL**

R Reading Strategy

Evaluating Have students evaluate the wisdom of the Prohibition movement. **Ask: How could this effort have been better enforced? Why did the movement fail? What were the economic effects of Prohibition?** *(Students' answers will vary but should demonstrate an effort to understand and analyze the information presented in this section.)* **OL**

✓ Reading Check

Answer: They believed in the authority of the Bible and creationism.

Answers and Additional Support

The trial took place in the summer of 1925. William Jennings Bryan, a three-time Democratic presidential candidate, was the prosecutor and represented the creationists. Clarence Darrow, one of the country's most celebrated trial lawyers, defended Scopes. After eight days of trial, Scopes was found guilty and the judged fined him $100, although the conviction was later overturned by the Tennessee Supreme Court on a technicality. In Tennessee at the time of the trial, judges could not issue fines, only juries could issue fines. Parts of the trial had been broadcast over the radio, and Darrow's blistering cross-examination of Bryan did little for the Fundamentalist cause. Increasingly, Fundamentalists found themselves isolated from mainstream Protestantism, and their commitment to political activism declined.

✓ **Reading Check** **Explaining** What were the major beliefs of Fundamentalists?

Prohibition

R **Main Idea** Congress passed the Eighteenth Amendment and the Volstead Act to prohibit alcohol, but the laws largely failed to create positive social change.

Reading Connection Do you think the government should try to regulate the moral behavior of its citizens? Read on to learn about efforts during the 1920s to eliminate social problems brought on by drinking alcohol.

The movement to ban alcohol had been building throughout the late 1800s. By the early 1900s, many progressives and traditionalists supported prohibition. Many people believed the prohibition of alcohol would help reduce unemployment, domestic violence, and poverty. Their support helped pass the Eighteenth Amendment, which took effect in January 1920.

▼ A group of men destroy bottles of alcohol by throwing them against the side of a building. Onlookers cheer the destruction as empty crates litter the street.

C ▲ **Prohibition in Action** Federal revenue agents carried out the laws of Prohibition by destroying barrels of alcohol. Here an agent uses an axe to bust open barrels and drain alcohol down the storm sewer. **How successful were their enforcement efforts?**

Did You Know?

Tennessee's law against teaching evolution remained in effect until 1967. Kansas attempted to pass a similar law at the beginning of the twenty-first century.

Picturing **History**

Answer: not very successful
Ask: How did the American public respond to Prohibition? Give some examples to support your answer. *(many blatantly ignored the law; speakeasies, organized crime supplied alcohol, bootlegging, smuggling)*

In an effort to enforce the amendment, Congress passed the National Prohibition Act, also known as the Volstead Act. Enforcing Prohibition now became the responsibility of the U.S. Treasury Department. While treasury agents had enforced federal tax laws for many years, **police powers**—a government's power to control people and property in the interest of public safety, health, welfare, and morals—had generally been reserved for the state governments. The Eighteenth Amendment granted federal and state governments the power to enforce Prohibition, marking a dramatic increase in federal police powers.

The Treasury Department's new Prohibition Unit struggled to enforce Prohibition. During the 1920s, treasury agents made more than 540,000 arrests, but Americans were not deterred by the arrests and persisted in blatantly ignoring the law. People flocked to secret bars called **speakeasies**, where they could purchase illegal alcohol. In New York City alone, an estimated 32,000 such bars sold liquor illegally. Liquor also was readily available in rural America, where bootlegging—the illegal production and distribution of liquor—was common.

Organized crime specialized in supplying and often running these speakeasies, which popped up all over the country. The huge profits that could be made supplying liquor encouraged some people to become smugglers, bringing liquor into the United States from Canada and the Caribbean. Smuggling and the consumption of liquor by millions helped create an illegal billion-dollar industry for gangsters. More than 70 federal agents were killed while enforcing Prohibition in the 1920s.

Crime became big business, and some gangsters had enough money to corrupt local politicians. Al Capone, one of the most successful and violent gangsters of the era, had many police officers, judges, and other officials on his payroll. Capone dominated organized crime in Chicago, where he ran bootlegging and other criminal rackets. Eliot Ness, the leader of a special Treasury Department task force, and nine agents he selected, were assigned the task of bringing Capone to justice. To achieve this goal, Ness and his group worked to shut down breweries where Capone illegally manufactured liquor. The press called Ness and his men "The Untouchables" because they would not take bribes. Capone was finally convicted of tax evasion and sentenced to 11 years in prison.

The battle to repeal Prohibition began almost as soon as the Eighteenth Amendment was ratified. Supporters of repeal believed Prohibition was excessive and prudish and associated it with "priggish fanaticism." The ratification of the Twenty-first Amendment in 1933 repealed the Eighteenth Amendment and ended federally-mandated Prohibition. It was a defeat for the supporters of traditional values and those who favored the use of federal police powers to achieve moral reform.

☑ **Reading Check** **Analyzing** Analyze the reasons for the adoption of the Eighteenth Amendment.

HISTORY Online **Study Central**

For help with the concepts in this section of *American Vision: Modern Times* go to tav.mt.glencoe.com and click on *Study Central.*

SECTION 1 ASSESSMENT

Checking for Understanding

1. **Vocabulary** Define: anarchist, eugenics, source, aspect, flapper, ethic, evolution, creationism, police powers, speakeasy.
2. **People and Terms** Identify: Ku Klux Klan, Emergency Quota Act, Fundamentalism.
3. **Explain** why the Eighteenth Amendment was repealed.

Reviewing Big Ideas

4. **Examining** How did the passage of the Eighteenth Amendment and the Volstead Act change the federal government's role?

Critical Thinking

5. **Historical Analysis** **Synthesizing** Why were immigrants from Mexico not included in the quota system set by the immigration acts? **CA HI4**
6. **Categorizing** Use a graphic organizer similar to the one below to list the provisions of the immigration acts passed in the 1920s.

Act	Provisions

Analyzing Visuals

7. **Analyzing Photographs** Study the image on page 412 of the federal agent destroying barrels of alcohol. Why do you think the barrels were destroyed in public with a crowd watching?

Writing About History

8. **Persuasive Writing** Imagine it is the 1920s. Write a letter to your senator to persuade him or her to either continue to support Prohibition or to work for its repeal. **CA 11WA2.4a**

CHAPTER 7   The Jazz Age   **413**

SECTION 1 ASSESSMENT ANSWERS

1. Content vocabulary is boldfaced and highlighted in yellow. Academic vocabulary is boldfaced.
2. Ku Klux Klan *(p. 408)*, Emergency Quota Act *(p.409)*, Fundamentalism, *(p. 411)*
3. People recognized that Prohibition was not successful.
4. The federal government obtained police powers to enforce the law.
5. They provided cheap labor.
6. 1921 Emergency Quota Act limited the number of immigrants to 3 percent of the existing immigrant population based on the 1910 census; 1924 National Origins Act limited the number of immigrants to 2 percent of the existing immigrant population based on the 1890 census
7. to intimidate people, hoping to make them fearful and submissive in the face of federal authority
8. Letters should clearly express a point of view.

R Reading Strategy

Using Word Parts Compound words are common in English. Remind students that these words are sometimes written as two words (*police powers and high jump*), hyphenated (*ex-president and merry-go-round*), or as two words put together (*speakeasy and pinecone*). If students are uncertain about which form to use for a particular compound word, encourage them to use a dictionary. **EL**

ASSESS

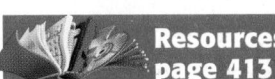
Resources for page 413

Use these resources to assess student mastery.

📁 Section Quiz 7-1

📁 Reading Essentials and Study Guide 7-1

💿 Interactive Tutor Self-Assessment CD-ROM

📁 California Standards Practice, Grade 11

☑ **Reading Check**

Answer: Many people believed Prohibition would help reduce unemployment, domestic violence, and poverty.

HISTORY Online

Study Central provides audio summaries, interactive games, and online graphic organizers to help students review section content.

CLOSE

Summarizing Ask students to explain the resurgence, impact, and decline of the Ku Klux Klan. **OL**

413

What Life Was Like...

FOCUS

History– Social Science Standards

This feature addresses the following standards:

11.5 Students analyze the major political, social, economic, technological, and cultural developments of the 1920s.

11.5.4 Analyze the passage of the Nineteenth Amendment and the changing role of women in society.

11.5.6 Trace the growth and effects of radio and movies and their role in the worldwide diffusion of popular culture.

TEACH

C Critical Thinking

Analyzing Primary Sources
Ask a volunteer to read aloud the quotation by G. Stanley Hall. Ask students to identify the tone of the paragraph. Have them make predictions about Hall's age and status. *(Students may say that Hall appears to be a good observer, but somewhat amused or appalled by the flapper's outfit. He may be an older man who doesn't understand the new styles.)* **AL**

Answers and Additional Support

What Life Was Like...

Flappers

Perhaps no other symbol of the 1920s captured the spirit of the time like the flapper. Psychologist G. Stanley Hall wrote his observation of a typical flapper:

C ❝She wore a knitted hat, with hardly any brim, of a flame or bonfire hue; a henna scarf; two strings of Betty beads, of different colors, twisted together; an open short coat, with ample pockets; a skirt with vertical stripes. . . . Her stockings were woolen and of brilliant hue. But most noticeable of all were her high overshoes, or galoshes. One seemed to be turned down at the top and entirely unbuckled, while the other was fastened below and flapped about her trim ankle in a way that compelled attention.❞

—quoted in *We, the American Women*

Flapper Hairstyle
Actress Colleen Moore wears a pageboy haircut that was popular in the 1920s.

New Forms of Expression
Rebelling against older, more formal dancing styles, these Charleston dancers perform steps that one observer described as "knock-kneed and pigeon-toed."

414 CHAPTER 7 The Jazz Age

Did You Know?

A law drafted in Ohio would have required skirts to touch the instep of the foot. Had this law been passed, it is unclear how the police would have tried to enforce the regulation.

More Skill Practice

Organizing Information Have each student create a graphic organizer similar to the one below to fill out as they read the feature.

New Ideas of the 1920s

(Possible Answers to graphic: clothing styles, dances, hair styles, entertainment forms) **BL**

Charleston

The Charleston, named after the city of Charleston, South Carolina, was the dance craze of the 1920s. Women who did the Charleston were called flappers, perhaps because of the way they flapped their arms while doing the dance.

R₂

R₁

Modern Clothing

Women's clothing changed significantly in the 1920s. Hemlines were much shorter and showed more of the body. Stylish new hats also emphasized bold colors and a freer design.

UNDERSTANDING THE TIME

Checking for Understanding
1. **Identifying** How did women's clothing change in the 1920s?

Critical Thinking
2. **Evaluating** How would you describe the connection of flappers to the roles of women in society during the 1920s?

R₁ Reading Strategy

Making Connections Clothing styles is one quick way to differentiate one time period from another. **Ask: How does modern clothing compare to clothing of the 1920s?** *(Possible answers: clothing today is less formal, more synthetic fabrics; in both eras, boldly colored hats were popular and clothing expressed a person's identity with a group)* **OL**

R₂ Reading Strategy

Reading Support Draw students' attention to the women's clothing in the photos and drawing. What generalizations can they make about fashion and the probable consequences of the styles? *(All of the dresses were sleeveless and straight with a dropped waist. Women who followed fashion were probably more conscious of their weight and shape because there was less fabric to hide beneath.)* **OL**

ASSESS/CLOSE

Have students answer the Checking for Understanding and Critical Thinking questions.

ANSWERS TO ANAYLYZING THE TIME

1. Hemlines were much shorter, and hats featured bold colors and freer designs.
2. Flappers personified the changing roles of women in society in the 1920s. Flappers sought social freedoms, while other women pursued political and economic freedoms.

415

FOCUS

TEACH

R **Reading Strategy**

Taking Notes Have students create a two-column chart that lists the speakers and the main ideas of each speaker. Tell students to form pairs and compare their charts. **BL**

Answers and Additional Support

You're the Historian

Painting supporting the accused

The Sacco-Vanzetti Case

On April 15, 1920, in South Braintree, Massachusetts, armed robbers murdered two factory employees during a payroll holdup. Police arrested two Italian immigrants and anarchists—Nicola Sacco and Bartolomeo Vanzetti—as suspects. After a court found the two men guilty, defense attorneys fought for six years for a new trial. The attorneys believed the trial had shown signs of prejudice, intimidation, and dishonesty. Did Sacco and Vanzetti receive a fair trial, or were they victims of the troubled atmosphere in the United States at the time? You're the historian.

Read the following excerpts from testimony and evidence. Then complete the questions and activities that follow.

R **From trial testimony**

The defense produced several people who supported the defendants' alibis. When arrested, Nicola Sacco had been carrying a pistol. The prosecuting attorney questioned Captain Proctor, a Massachusetts State Police ballistics expert, about the gun.

Q. Captain Proctor, have you an opinion as to whether bullet three was fired from the Colt automatic which is in evidence [Sacco's pistol]?

A. I have.

Q. And what is your opinion?

A. My opinion is that it is consistent with being fired by that pistol.

Defense experts, however, testified that in their judgment, bullet three had not been fired from Sacco's gun. The defense called on Sacco to testify, which gave the prosecution an opportunity to ask Sacco about his political beliefs.

Q. Did you say yesterday you love a free country?

A. Yes, sir.

Q. Did you love this country in the month of May 1917? [At this time, Sacco had gone to Mexico to escape military service.]

A. If you can, Mr. Katzman, if you give me that, —I could explain.

Q. There are two words you can use, Mr. Sacco, yes or no.

A. Yes.

[later]

Q. What did you mean when you said yesterday you loved a free country?

A. . . .When I came to this country I saw there was not what I was thinking before. . . . I could see the best men, intelligent, education, they been arrested and sent to prison and died in prison . . . and Debs, one of the great men in his country, he is in prison . . . because he is a socialist. He wanted the laboring class

to have better conditions . . . but they put him in prison. . . . They want the working class to be low all the times.

The jury returned a verdict of guilty. In the sentencing phase, Bartolomeo Vanzetti was asked to explain why he should not be sentenced to death.

I am suffering because I am a radical, and indeed I am a radical. I have suffered because I am an Italian, and indeed I am an Italian. I have suffered more for my family and for my beloved than for myself, but I am so convinced to be right that if you could execute me two times, and if I could be reborn two other times, I would live again to do what I have done already. . . . You know I am innocent. That is the same words I pronounced seven years ago. You condemn two innocent men.

416 CHAPTER 7 The Jazz Age

EXTENDING THE CONTENT

Due Process The Sacco-Vanzetti case influenced the Supreme Court's actions in the 1950s and 1960s under the leadership of Chief Justice Earl Warren. In more than one case, the Court ruled that the due process clause of the Bill of Rights extended to the states. This, in effect, altered the legal system in many states. Massachusetts had already changed its laws in 1939 to allow a new trial not only if the verdict violated the law, but also if it went against the evidence presented at the trial.

The Boston Daily Globe

MADEIROS, SACCO, VANZETTI DIED IN CHAIR THIS MORNING

Electrocuted in That Order Soon After Midnight—All Reject Religious Consolation to the Last—Two Make Statements

Headline announcing the execution

Comments on the case

The Sacco-Vanzetti case aroused indignation among intellectuals from the 1920s on. They generally agreed that the two were found guilty because they were Italian radicals, not because there was clear evidence against them. However, two students of the case, Robert Hanson, a local historian, and Francis Russell, who wrote two books on the case, believe Sacco and Vanzetti received a fair trial. Russell cites James Graham, an attorney for Sacco:

We spent considerable time with him [Vanzetti] at the Plymouth County Jail as the case was drawing to a close. . . . Toward the end of the discussion Mr. Vahey said to Vanzetti, in substance, "I can advise you as to what the District Attorney may inquire about the effect of your failure to take the stand, but you are the one who has to make the decision as to whether you will testify or not."

Workers showing support for Sacco (right) and Vanzetti (left)

Vanzetti replied,

I don't think I can improve on the alibi which has been established. I had better not take the stand.

Russell also reports that Carlo Tresca, an anarchist who had supported the two Italians, told friends that Sacco was guilty, Vanzetti innocent. Then Russell quotes a letter from labor writer Paul Jacobs:

. . . I had a close friend, Anthony Ramuglia. . . . One day he came to me and said he had a story he wanted me to write. . . . The story was that when he was a young man around the anarchist movement in Boston, he had been approached by one of Sacco's witnesses for his alibi in the restaurant at lunch. My friend Tony agreed, and evidently, was carefully coached in what he was to say, when suddenly he remembered that on the day in question

he had actually been in jail in St. Louis and so might obviously be found out as a perjurer. He told someone about this and was relieved of his responsibilities. . . . I asked Tony whether he thought Sacco and Vanzetti were really guilty, and he replied in much the same way as you quote Tresca. "Sacco could have done it but Vanzetti was never capable of such a thing."

Understanding the Issue

1. Why did the defense attorneys believe that the defendants were not given a fair trial?
2. Why do you think the prosecution questioned Sacco on his political beliefs?
3. After studying the historical context of the case and the frame of reference of the jury, how might a modern historian argue that Sacco and Vanzetti did not receive a fair trial?

Activities

1. **Investigate** Check your local library or the Internet and prepare a report on the latest information on the case. **CA 11WS1.6**
2. **Create a Simulation** Recreate the trial. Research the testimony and the people involved in the case. Assign roles to class members, including witnesses, jury members, a prosecutor, a defense attorney, and a judge.

CHAPTER 7   The Jazz Age   **417**

C **Critical Thinking**

Analyzing Primary Sources
After students read the trial testimony excerpt, remind them that the defendants were Italian and gave some of their testimony in Italian, which had to be translated for the judge and jury. **Ask: How do you think the witnesses' inability to speak English well affected their credibility?** *(Students should recognize that this inability should not have affected their credibility, but that bias toward immigrants—especially from southern and eastern Europe—might have unfairly influenced the jury.)* **Do you think that people who do not speak English well face similar bias in the United States today?** *(Answers will vary. Students may note that they do not face the same degree of bias, but that bias still exists.)* **AL**

S **Skill Practice**

Conducting Research Invite students to use newspapers, library resources, or the Internet to find current legal cases, at national, state, or local levels, in which they see parallels to the Sacco-Vanzetti case in some way. Perhaps the defendants are foreign-born or the jury seems to have a foregone conclusion in the case. Have students follow the cases and then report to the class on the outcome. **OL**

ASSESS/CLOSE

Have students answer the Understanding the Issue questions. The activities may be assigned as a wrap-up or extension project.

ANSWERS TO UNDERSTANDING THE ISSUE

1. They argued that the defendants were found guilty because of their political views, not because of the evidence against them.
2. They wanted to establish that his radical views made him dangerous, regardless of whether he actually committed the crime.
3. A historian might argue that since the evidence was inconclusive, the verdict was unfounded.

Activities

1. Reports should consider the quality of the arguments presented.
2. Encourage students to prepare for their assigned roles. At the end of the trial, have the jury read its verdict, then discuss as a class the various opinions and thoughts about the event.

FOCUS

BELLRINGER
SKILLBUILDER ACTIVITY

Project **Daily Focus Skills Transparency 7-2** and have students answer the question.

Guide to Reading

Understanding Vocabulary: Invite volunteers to share what they know about any of the people named in the list of People and Terms to Identify.

Answers to Graphic:
Art: diverse, individual expression influence by European art movement; Literature: various styles and subject matter, themes of disillusionment and emptiness; Popular Culture: sports heroes, Hollywood allure, radio shows, jazz, and blues.

Unpacking the Standards

Students will be able to:

- Discuss the new developments in art and literature during this decade.
- Summarize the growth of popular culture, including interest in sports and entertainment in the 1920s.

Answers and Additional Support

SECTION 2 Cultural Innovations

Guide to Reading

Connection
In the previous section, you learned about the social and cultural changes that occurred during the 1920s. In this section, you will discover cultural trends in art, literature, and entertainment during that time.

Main Idea
- New York City's Greenwich Village and Chicago's South Side became known as centers for new artistic work. (p. 419)
- Many people in the 1920s enjoyed new forms of entertainment. (p. 420)

Content Vocabulary
mass media

Academic Vocabulary
emerge, diverse, unify

People and Terms to Identify
Bohemian, Carl Sandburg, Eugene O'Neill, Ernest Hemingway, F. Scott Fitzgerald

Reading Objectives
- **Describe** the explosion of art and literature and the disillusionment of 1920s artists.
- **Summarize** the effects of sports, movies, radio, and music on popular culture.

Reading Strategy
Organizing As you read about the 1920s, complete a graphic organizer like the one below by filling in the main characteristics or art, literature, and popular culture that reflect the era.

Cultural Movement	Main Characteristics
Art	
Literature	
Popular Culture	

Preview of Events

♦1922	♦1924	♦1926	♦1928

1923 Coca-Cola creates the six-pack

1925 F. Scott Fitzgerald's *The Great Gatsby* published

1927 Babe Ruth hits 60 home runs

1927 First feature-length sound motion picture, *The Jazz Singer*

1927 Charles Lindbergh makes solo transatlantic flight

The following are the main History–Social Science Standards covered in this section.

11.5 Students analyze the major political, social, economic, technological, and cultural developments of the 1920s.

11.5.5 Describe the Harlem Renaissance and new trends in literature, music, and art, with special attention to the work of writers (e.g., Zora Neale Hurston, Langston Hughes).

11.5.6 Trace the growth and effects of radio and movies and their role in the worldwide diffusion of popular culture.

❧ The Big Idea ❧

People react to periods of breathtaking social and cultural change in different ways. New York City's Greenwich Village and Chicago's South Side developed into new artistic centers. There artists, writers, and intellectuals led new and unconventional lifestyles. A broad variety of artistic styles expressed the individual's role in the modern world. People also enjoyed new forms of popular culture and entertainment such as sporting events, motion pictures, radio shows, and music. Mass media spread new ideas and attitudes across the nation and helped instill a feeling of unity.

418 CHAPTER 7 The Jazz Age

SECTION RESOURCES

📁 Print Material
- Reproducible Lesson Plan 7-2
- Guided Reading Activity 7-2
- Reading Essentials and Study Guide 7-2
- Active Reading Note-Taking Guide 7-2

🎞 Transparencies
- Daily Focus Skills Transparency 7-2
- Section Graphic Organizer Transparency 7-2

Technology
- 🖥 Interactive Tutor Self-Assessment CD-ROM
- 🖥 ExamView® Pro Testmaker CD-ROM
- 🖥 Presentation Plus! CD-ROM

Art and Literature

Main Idea New York City's Greenwich Village and Chicago's South Side became known as centers for new artistic work.

Reading Connection What museums or art centers are you aware of in your community? Read on to find out about the flowering of the arts during the 1920s in the United States.

During this time, American artists and writers challenged traditional ideas. These artists explored what it meant to be "modern," and they searched for meaning in the **emerging** challenges of the modern world.

★ An American Story ★

On May 20, 1927, a lanky, sandy-haired young man named Charles Lindbergh took off from an airfield on Long Island, New York, in a small, single-engine plane called the *Spirit of St. Louis* and headed east across the Atlantic Ocean. The next evening—more than 33 hours after Lindbergh left New York—thousands of people waited anxiously at the small Le Bourget airfield outside Paris, France. Attention was riveted on the sky, and the spectators strained their eyes as they watched Lindbergh's small airplane softly slip out of the darkness. When the plane landed, the crowd ecstatically greeted the pilot, who had just completed a historic event—the first solo nonstop flight across the Atlantic Ocean.

In an era when people questioned ideals and heroes, Lindbergh's historic flight symbolized American progress in the modern age, and his solo triumph restored Americans' belief in the courageous, pioneering individual. American writer F. Scott Fitzgerald said of Lindbergh:

❝A young Minnesotan who seemed to have nothing to do with his generation did a heroic thing, and for the moment people set down their glasses in country clubs and speakeasies and thought of their old dreams.❞

—quoted in *Echoes of the Jazz Age*

The modern age symbolized by Lindbergh's historic transatlantic flight was reflected strongly in American art, literature, and popular culture.

Greenwich Village and the South Side Many artists, writers, and intellectuals of the era flocked to Manhattan's Greenwich Village and Chicago's South Side. As writer Brooks Atkinson noted in a memoir,

❝The Village was no prude . . . no matter what you did you could hardly be conspicuous. On my street the middle-aged lady in knickers who aired her cat on a pink ribbon twice a day and the rosy-cheeked damsel in overalls who split kindling wood on the side walk . . . were hardly more conspicuous than the formal citizenry. To become conspicuous you would probably have to shoot someone in the street.❞

—from *New York's Greenwich Village*

The artistic and unconventional, or **Bohemian,** lifestyle of these neighborhoods offered young artists and writers new lifestyles.

Modern American Art European art movements greatly influenced the modernists of American art. Perhaps most striking was the **diverse** range of artistic styles, each attempting to express the individual, modern experience.

Taking his cue from the bold and colorful Impressionism of French artist Paul Cézanne, American painter John Marin drew on nature as well as the urban dynamics of New York for inspiration, explaining, "the whole city is alive; buildings, people, all are alive; and the more they move me the more I feel them to be alive." Painter Charles Scheeler applied the influences of photography and the geometric forms of Cubism to

▼ *Charles Lindbergh and his* Spirit of St. Louis

R₁ **Reading Strategy**

Activating Prior Knowledge Review with students the characteristics of Realism in art. Ask students when Realism first became a major movement in the arts in the United States and why. *(during the Gilded Age, as a reaction against the Romantics and Transcendentalists)* **Ask:** Do you recall other visual artists and writers that we have dicussed who were Realists? *(Thomas Eakins, William Dean Howells, Henry James, Edith Wharton)* **OL**

R₂ **Reading Strategy**

Organizing Information Have students each create a thematic table similar to the one below. The first column should be labeled *Writer,* the second column labeled *Genre,* and the third should be labeled *Description or Characteristic.* Students should fill in their tables as they read this portion of the text. **BL**

Writer	Genre	Description or Characteristic

Review the Big Idea

Review the Big Idea for this section, "People react to periods of breathtaking social and cultural change in different ways." Ask the class to study a piece of art from this period and write a two-page paper about the style or characteristics of this art. Request that students share their research with their classmates. **AL** **CA** 11WS1.1

Did You Know?

Orteig Prize By completing his transatlantic flight, Lindbergh won the Orteig prize, a $25,000 award put up by New York City hotel owner Raymond Orteig in 1919. Several pilots before Lindbergh failed to make the solo flight. Lindbergh asked nine St. Louis businessmen to help him finance the manufacturing of a special plane, which he helped design. As a test, in May 1927, Lindbergh flew the plane from San Diego to New York City, with an overnight stop in St. Louis. The flight took 20 hours 21 minutes, a transcontinental record.

Answers and Additional Support

urban and rural American landscapes. Edward Hopper revived the visual accuracy of Realism in his haunting scenes. His paintings conveyed a modern sense of disenchantment and isolation.

Poets and Writers Poets and writers of the 1920s varied greatly in their styles and subject matter. Chicago poet **Carl Sandburg** used common speech to glorify the Midwest. In Greenwich Village, Edna St. Vincent Millay, in her poem "First Fig," expressed women's freedom and equality and praised a life intensely lived:

> ❝My candle burns at both ends;
> It will not last the night;
> But ah, my foes, and oh, my friends—
> It gives a lovely light.❞

Several poets of this time had an important impact on the literary culture. Poets such as Ezra Pound, Amy Lowell, and William Carlos Williams used clear, concise images to express moments in time. Some poets concentrated on what they considered the negative effects of modernism. In his poem "The Hollow Men," for example, T.S. Eliot described a world filled with empty dreams and "hollow men," and he foresaw a world that would end "not with a bang but a whimper."

Among playwrights, one of the most innovative was **Eugene O'Neill.** His plays portrayed realistic characters and situations, offering a vision of life that sometimes touched on the tragic.

Many novelists, affected by the experiences of World War I, wrote about disillusionment and reevaluated the myths of American heroes. They often created characters who were "heroic antiheroes"— flawed individuals who still had heroic qualities of mind and spirit. **Ernest Hemingway,** who served as an ambulance driver in Italy during World War I, was one such writer. His fiction presented a new literary style characterized by direct, simple, and concise prose, as when he wrote about war in such works as *For Whom the Bell Tolls* and *A Farewell to Arms.*

John Dos Passos, a critic of America's capitalist culture, experimented with the form of the novel in his innovative trilogy *U.S.A.*, which combined fiction, biography, news headlines, and prose poems. Sinclair Lewis wrote about the absurdities of traditional life in small-town America in his novels *Main Street* and *Babbitt.* **F. Scott Fitzgerald,** perhaps the most famous writer of the era, created colorful, glamorous characters who chased futile dreams in *The Great Gatsby,* a novel that poignantly exposed the superficiality of much of modern society.

✓ **Reading Check** **Examining** Why did many artists, writers, and intellectuals flock to New York City's Greenwich Village and Chicago's South Side during the 1920s?

Popular Culture

Main Idea Many people in the 1920s enjoyed new forms of entertainment.

Reading Connection What new forms of entertainment make up today's popular culture? Read on to learn about the ways that Americans spent their leisure time during the 1920s.

The economic prosperity of the 1920s provided many Americans with more leisure time and more spending money, which they devoted to making their lives more enjoyable. Millions of Americans eagerly watched and participated in sports and enjoyed music, theater, and other forms of popular entertainment. They also fell in love with radio shows and motion pictures.

Baseball, Boxing, and Other Sports Thanks to radio and motion pictures, sports such as baseball and boxing reached new heights of popularity in the 1920s. Baseball star Babe Ruth became a national hero, famous for hitting hundreds of home runs. As one broadcaster later remarked, "He wasn't a baseball player. He was a worldwide celebrity, an international star, the likes of which base-

🎨 History *Through Art*

Lonely People Like many of his works, Edward Hopper's *Nighthawks* depicts isolated people. This piece is an example of an artistic style of the time that expresses the new modern environment. How do you think this painting reflects the experience of small-town people who moved to the cities?

ball has never seen since." Sports fans also idolized boxer Jack Dempsey. Dempsey held the title of world heavyweight champion from 1919 until 1926, when he lost it to Gene Tunney.

Americans eagerly followed other sports and sports figures, too. Newspaper coverage helped generate enthusiasm for college football. One of the most famous players of the 1920s was Red Grange of the University of Illinois. Grange was known as the "Galloping Ghost" because of his speed and ability to evade members of opposing teams.

Millions of sports fans also were thrilled by the achievements of Bobby Jones, the best golfer of the decade, and tennis players Bill Tilden and Helen Wills, who dominated world tennis. In 1927 swimmer Gertrude Ederle enchanted Americans when she shattered records by swimming the English Channel in a little over 14 hours.

The Rise of Hollywood Although sports became increasingly popular in the 1920s, nothing quite matched the allure of motion pictures. Technology had not yet made sound possible in films, so theaters hired piano players to provide music during the feature, while subtitles revealed the plot. Audiences thronged to see such stars as Mary Pickford, Charlie Chaplin, Tom Mix, Douglas Fairbanks, Gloria Swanson, Rudolph Valentino, and Clara Bow. In 1927 the first "talking" picture—*The Jazz Singer*—was produced, and the golden age of Hollywood began.

Popular Radio Shows and Music Radio also enjoyed a large following during the Jazz Age. In 1920, in one of the first commercial radio broadcasts in history, listeners of station KDKA in Pittsburgh learned the news of Warren G. Harding's landslide victory in the presidential election. Within two years, Americans could turn the dial to more than 400 different radio stations around the country.

Most stations in the 1920s played the popular music of the day, such as "Yes! We Have No Bananas" and "Lover Come Back Again." Broadcasts such as *The Eveready Hour* offered everything from classical music to comedy. In one of the most popular radio shows, *Amos 'n' Andy,* the trials and tribulations of two African American characters (portrayed by white actors) captured the nation's attention every evening, but unfortunately reinforced African American stereotypes.

The **mass media**—radio, movies, newspapers, and magazines aimed at a broad audience—did more than just entertain. They fostered a sense of shared national experience that helped **unify** the nation and spread the new ideas and attitudes of the time.

▲ *Babe Ruth*

Reading Check

Summarizing How did the American economy of the 1920s affect popular culture?

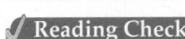
HISTORY Online
Study Central

For help with the concepts in this section of *American Vision: Modern Times* go to tav.mt.glencoe.com and click on *Study Central.*

SECTION 2 ASSESSMENT

Checking for Understanding

1. **Vocabulary** Define: emerge, diverse, mass media, unify.
2. **People and Terms** Identify: Bohemian, Carl Sandburg, Eugene O'Neill, Ernest Hemingway, F. Scott Fitzgerald.
3. **Describe** the main themes of artists and writers during the 1920s.

Reviewing Big Ideas

4. **Summarizing** How did writers, artists, and popular culture of the 1920s affect traditional ideas in the United States?

Critical Thinking

5. **Synthesizing** How did World War I influence the literature written during the 1920s?
6. **Organizing** Use a graphic organizer similar to the one below to list the effects of mass media on American culture.

Effects

Mass Media of 1920s

Analyzing Visuals

7. **Interpreting Art** Study the Edward Hopper painting, *Nighthawks,* on page 420. How do different elements of this piece work to convey a sense of isolation?

Writing About History

8. **Descriptive Writing** Imagine that you have moved to New York's Greenwich Village in the 1920s. Write a letter to a friend describing the atmosphere in your neighborhood. **CA** 11WS1.2

SECTION 2 ASSESSMENT ANSWERS

1. Content vocabulary is boldfaced and highlighted in yellow. Academic vocabulary is boldfaced.
2. Bohemian *(p. 419),* Carl Sandburg *(p. 420),* Eugene O'Neill *(p. 420),* Ernest Hemingway *(p. 420),* F. Scott Fitzgerald *(p. 420)*
3. disenchantment, isolation, disillusionment, and emptiness
4. They broke down patterns of narrow focus on local interest.
5. It led many writers to portray disillusionment and to reevaluate the myths of American heroes.
6. broke down patterns of provincialism, unified Americans, spread new ideas and attitudes
7. One man eats by himself, there

are only three customers in the diner, there is only one person working at the diner, and there are no people on the sidewalk or in the street.
8. Letters should include words and phrases popular at the time.

C Critical Thinking

Drawing Conclusions Have students read the material on mass entertainment. **Ask: Can you find any links between the early forms of film, radio, and print material and today's examples of these formats?** Encourage students to discuss how entertainment today is similar to and different from the 1920s. OL

ASSESS

Resources for page 421

Use these resources to assess student mastery.

📁 Section Quiz 7-2

📁 Reading Essentials and Study Guide 7-2

⊙ Interactive Tutor Self-Assessment CD-ROM

📁 California Standards Practice, Grade 11

Reading Check

Answer: Economic prosperity gave Americans more leisure time and spending money.

HISTORY Online

Study Central provides audio summaries, interactive games, and online graphic organizers to help students review section content.

CLOSE

Summarizing Have students describe the reasons for the disillusionment among 1920s artists. OL

421

FOCUS

TIME NOTEBOOK

History– Social Science Standards

This feature addresses the following standards:

11.2 Students analyze the relationship among the rise of industrialization, large-scale rural-to-urban migration, and massive immigration from Southern and Eastern Europe.

11.2.3 Trace the effect of the Americanization movement.

11.3 Students analyze the role religion played in the founding of America, its lasting moral, social, and political impacts, and issues regarding religious liberty.

11.5 Students analyze the major political, social, economic, technological, and cultural developments of the 1920s.

TEACH

U Universal Access

Auditory/Musical Have students work in groups to select one Louis Armstrong recording and find photos to illustrate the mood and tone of the piece. Have the groups combine the music and photos into a multimedia tribute to the jazz legend. Have the groups share their representations with the class and, if possible, select several of the presentations to be made to a wider audience.

OL **CA** 11WS1.6

Answers and Additional Support

BETTMANN/CORBIS

Appreciation

LOUIS DANIEL ARMSTRONG *Writer Stanley Crouch remembers Louis Armstrong, a Jazz Age great.*

Pops. Sweet Papa Dip. Satchmo. He had perfect pitch and perfect rhythm. His improvised melodies and singing could be as lofty as a moon flight or as low-down as the blood drops of a street thug dying in the gutter. The extent of his influence across jazz and across American music continues to this day.

Not only do we hear Armstrong in trumpet players who represent the present renaissance in jazz, we can also detect his influence in certain rhythms that sweep from country-and-western music to rap.

Louis Daniel Armstrong was born in New Orleans on August 4, 1901. It was at a home for troubled kids that young Louis first put his lips to the mouthpiece of a cornet and later, a trumpet.

In 1922 Armstrong went to Chicago, where he joined King Oliver and his Creole Jazz Band. The band brought out the people and all the musicians, black and white, who wanted to know how it was truly done.

When he first played in New York City in 1924, his improvisations set the city on its head. The stiff rhythms of the time were slashed away by his combination of the percussive and the soaring. He soon returned to Chicago, perfected what he was doing, and made one record after another.

Louis Armstrong was so much, in fact, that every school of jazz since has had to address how he interpreted the basics of the idiom—swing, blues, ballads, and Afro-Hispanic rhythms. His freedom, his wit, and his discipline give his music a perpetual position in the wave of the future that is the station of all great art.

VERBATIM

❝The great creators of the government . . . thought of America as a light to the world, as created to lead the world in the assertion of the right of peoples and the rights of free nations.❞

WOODROW WILSON,
in defense of the League of Nations, 1920

❝We seek no part in directing the destinies of the Old World.❞
WARREN G. HARDING,
Inaugural Address, 1921

❝Here was a new generation, . . . dedicated more than the last to the fear of poverty and the worship of success; grown up to find . . . all wars fought, all faiths in man shaken.❞

CULVER PICTURES

F. Scott Fitzgerald

F. SCOTT FITZGERALD,
author, This Side of Paradise

❝There has been a change for the worse during the past year in feminine dress, dancing, manners and general moral standards. [One should] realize the serious ethical consequences of immodesty in girls' dress.❞
from the **PITTSBURGH OBSERVER**

❝[In New York] I saw 7,000,000 two-legged animals penned in an evil smelling cage, . . . streets as unkempt as a Russian steppe, . . . rubbish, waste paper, cigar butts. . . . One glance and you know no master hand directs.❞
article in Soviet newspaper **PRAVDA**
describing New York City in 1925

COOPERATIVE LEARNING ACTIVITY

Creating a Magazine Spread Organize the class into small groups. Tell them that they are to create a magazine spread that includes articles or items about each section of Chapter 7. Students should look at current magazines and books for ideas about page design. This activity can be completed using desktop publishing software or the more traditional cut-and-paste method. **OL**

Hide the Hooch

BROWN BROTHERS

Ingenious Americans are finding unusual places to store their liquor under Prohibition:

- canes
- hot water bottles
- shoe heels
- rolled newspaper
- folds of coats
- perfume bottles

Milestones

EMBARRASSED, 1920. TEXAS SENATOR MORRIS SHEPPARD, a leading proponent of the Eighteenth Amendment, when a large whiskey still is found on his farm.

ERASED, 1922. THE WORD "OBEY," from the Episcopal marriage ceremony, by a vote of American Episcopal bishops.

DIED, 1923. HOMER MOREHOUSE, 27, in the 87th hour of a record-setting 90-hour, 10-minute dance marathon.

EXONERATED, 1921. EIGHT CHICAGO WHITE SOX PLAYERS charged with taking bribes to throw the 1919 World Series. The players were found "not guilty" when grand jury testimony disappeared. Newly appointed commissioner of baseball Kenesaw Mountain Landis banned the "Black Sox" from baseball.

CULVER PICTURES

MAKING A COMEBACK. SANTA CLAUS, after falling into low favor in the last decade. Aiming at children, advertisers are marketing St. Nick heavily.

WHAT'S NEW
Invented This Decade

How did we live without . . .

- push-button elevators
- neon signs
- oven thermostats
- electric razors
- tissues
- spiral-bound notebooks
- motels
- dry ice
- zippers

- pop-up toasters
- flavored yogurt
- car radios
- adhesive tape
- food disposals
- water skiing
- automatic potato peeler
- self-winding wristwatch

Beautiful Goodrich ZIPPERS

BROWN BROTHERS

NUMBERS

60,000
Families with radios in 1922

9,000,000
Motor vehicles registered in U.S. in 1920

$2,467,946
Income tax paid by Henry Ford in 1924

500,000
People who wrote to Henry Ford in 1924 begging for money

33.5 Number of hours Charles Lindbergh spent in his nonstop flight from New York to Paris on May 20, 1927

1,800 Tons of ticker tape and shredded paper dropped on Charles Lindbergh in his parade in New York City

$16,000 Cost of cleaning up after the parade

7,000 Job offers received by Lindbergh

3.5 million
Number of letters received by Lindbergh

BROWN BROTHERS

Charles Lindbergh

CHAPTER 7   The Jazz Age   **423**

C Critical Thinking

Comparing and Contrasting
Have students create two political cartoons, one expressing the popular sentiment about Prohibition and one expressing the concerns over alcohol consumption today. **AL**

W Writing Support

Portfolio Writing Project
Have students research one of the inventions mentioned. Students should discover what preceded the invention, who invented it, and what improvements were made to the product. Students should also decide if the invention is still relevant today or has become obsolete. Based on their research, students should write a two-page report about their chosen invention. **OL**
CA 11WA2.4a

ASSESS/CLOSE

Have students select an item listed under *Numbers* and find a correlating statistic for today.

TIME Visit the Time Web site at www.time.com for up-to-date news, weekly magazine articles, editorials, online polls, and an archive of past magazine and Web articles.

EXTENDING THE CONTENT

Banned From the Game Commissioner Landis banned all White Sox players from professional baseball, saying that "regardless of the verdict of the juries, no player who throws a ball game, no player who undertakes or promises to throw a ball game, no player who sits in confidence with a bunch of crooked players and does not promptly tell his club about it, will ever play professional baseball." The ban remained in effect, and none of the players were ever allowed to participate in professional baseball again.

Looking Back...

Religious Freedom in the United States

Why It Matters During the summer of 1925, a young teacher, John Scopes, was put on trial for teaching evolution in defiance of Tennessee law. The Scopes trial involved more than a debate between science and religion. It also involved the constitutional principle of the separation of church and state. This principle is based on the First Amendment, which states that the federal government cannot establish an official religion or interfere with a person's right to practice a religion. In 1926 an appeals court upheld Tennessee's law. In 1968, however, the United States Supreme Court ruled that laws banning the teaching of evolution were unconstitutional because they indirectly helped to establish an official religion. From early colonial times, Americans have struggled to preserve their right to worship as they choose and to define the proper relationship between the church and the government.

Steps to . . . Religious Freedom

R The American tradition of religious freedom began in the 1600s. England's government persecuted people who did not worship in the manner required by the Church of England. Among the persecuted were Puritans, Catholics, and Quakers, many of whom moved to America in search of religious freedom.

Colonial Beginnings In 1620 the Pilgrims established the Plymouth colony so that they could practice their faith freely. Ten years later, thousands of Puritans, led by John Winthrop, established the colony of Massachusetts. In 1634 Lord Baltimore established Maryland as a refuge for Catholics fleeing persecution, and in 1681 William Penn, a Quaker, founded Pennsylvania, promising religious tolerance to all who settled there.

Church and State At first the Massachusetts Puritans did not practice separation of church and state. Instead they enacted policies that promoted the Puritan faith. For example, taxes supported the Puritan churches; laws required citizens to attend church; and only church members were allowed to vote. People who expressed ideas contrary to Puritan beliefs could be banished.

In the 1630s, Massachusetts banished many people for their religious beliefs, including Roger Williams and Anne Hutchinson. Williams, Hutchinson, and others joined together to create the colony of Rhode

> *"The Civil rights of none shall be abridged on account of religious belief or worship, nor shall any national religion be established. . . ."*
>
> —James Madison

424

EXTENDING THE CONTENT

The Final Word After the Bill of Rights was debated and passed in each house of Congress, a committee met to agree to the final wording. The House version of the First Amendment read: "Congress shall make no law establishing religion, or to prevent the free exercise thereof, or to infringe the rights of conscience." The Senate version read: "Congress shall make no law establishing articles of faith or a mode of worship, or prohibiting the free exercise of religion." The final wording was accepted by the House on September 24, 1789, and by the Senate on September 25, 1789.

Virginia colonists attending Old Bruton Church

Island, where church and state were kept separate and the government did not try to coerce religious belief. Meanwhile, in 1639, settlers in Connecticut adopted the Fundamental Orders of Connecticut. These Orders allowed non-church members to vote.

The Great Awakening

During the early 1700s, a period of religious revivalism known as the Great Awakening strengthened the idea of religious freedom. Ministers began preaching the importance of each individual's commitment to faith. The Great Awakening divided many congregations and led to the rise of the Baptists and Presbyterians. It also led to greater religious tolerance. By the time of the American Revolution, the idea of freedom of religion was widely accepted in the American colonies.

The Virginia Statute for Religious Freedom

In 1786, shortly after the American Revolution, Virginia passed the Statute for Religious Freedom. Its author, Thomas Jefferson, believed religious toleration to be one of the most important aspects of a free society. The Virginia statute stated that "all men shall be free to profess... their opinion in matters of religions, and that the same shall in no wise...affect their civil capacities."

A Constitutional Guarantee

American leaders guaranteed religious freedom in the new U.S. Constitution. The First Amendment states that "Congress shall make no law respecting an establishment of religion, or prohibiting the free exercise thereof." This sentence consists of two parts. The establishment clause forbids the federal government from creating an official religion or supporting religious activities. The free exercise clause forbids the government from suppressing freedom of religious worship.

Continuing Issues

Like many other ideas in the Constitution, the idea of religious freedom has been reinterpreted over time. In the 1879 case *Reynolds* v. *United States,* the U.S. Supreme Court ruled that freedom of religion is not absolute. Religious practices that violate the law or undermine the public interest, the Court declared, were not protected by the First Amendment.

One of the most controversial issues has been the role of religion in the public schools. In 1962, in *Engel* v. *Vitale,* the Court ruled that states could not require official prayers to be recited in schools. In 1963, in *Abingdon School District* v. *Schempp,* the Court also ruled out daily Bible readings in schools. In 1990, however, the Court ruled that student groups could study the Bible and pray together because they were private individuals, not school officials. With religion an integral part of many Americans' lives, the nation continues to grapple with the problem of balancing freedom of religion with the need to avoid federal support of a particular church.

Checking for Understanding

1. How did the Great Awakening promote greater religious tolerance?
2. What did the Supreme Court rule in *Reynolds* v. *United States?*

Critical Thinking

1. How has the establishment clause of the First Amendment been applied to public schools?
2. Why do you think freedom of religion is such an important and controversial right?

Checking for Understanding

1. The Great Awakening fostered the founding of many new churches. These new churches increased religious tolerance.
2. According to *Reynolds* v. *United States,* religious practices that violated the law or undermined the public interest were not protected by the First Amendment.

Critical Thinking

1. Two Supreme Court decisions, *Engel* v. *Vitale* and *Abingdon School District* v. *Schempp* ruled that school-sponsored prayers are unconstitutional. The issue continues to be debated.
2. Answers will vary. Encourage students to use specific examples in their responses.

FOCUS

SKILLBUILDER ACTIVITY

Project **Daily Focus Skills Transparency 7-3** and have students answer the question.

Guide to Reading

Understanding Vocabulary: Suggest to students the idea of a notebook section they can use as a word bank. Whenever they come to an unfamiliar term, they should copy it into the word section of their notebook, along with the definition.

Answers to Graphic:
Causes: Great Migration and racial pride; Effects: important African American writers, jazz, blues, theater; also sparked political change

Unpacking the Standards

Students will be able to:

- Describe the growth of African American culture during the Harlem Renaissance.
- Identify the attacks on civil liberties for African Americans and their political response.

Answers and Additional Support

426

SECTION 3 African American Culture

Guide to Reading

Connection
In the previous section, you learned about the changes in cultural trends and entertainment that occurred during the 1920s. In this section, you will discover the Harlem Renaissance and find out how African Americans worked to gain more rights.

Main Idea
- The Harlem Renaissance sparked new trends in literature, music, and art and featured the work of writers such as Langston Hughes and Zora Neale Hurston. (p. 427)
- African Americans steadily worked to win more rights. (p. 429)

Content Vocabulary
jazz, blues

Academic Vocabulary
sought, author, impact

People and Terms to Identify
Great Migration, Harlem Renaissance, Claude McKay, Langston Hughes, Cotton Club, Marcus Garvey

Reading Objectives
- **Describe** the Harlem Renaissance and the rediscovery of African American cultural roots.

- **Explain** the increase in African American political activism.

Reading Strategy
Organizing As you read about the African American experience in the 1920s, complete a graphic organizer similar to the one below by filling in the causes and effects of the Harlem Renaissance.

Causes   Effects

Harlem
Renaissance

Preview of Events

◆1922	◆1924	◆1926	◆1928
1922	1924	1926	1928
Antilynching bill passes in the House but not in the Senate	The Negro League holds its first world series	Langston Hughes's *The Weary Blues* published	Claude McKay's *Home to Harlem* published

The following are the main History–Social Science Standards covered in this section.

11.5 Students analyze the major political, social, economic, technological, and cultural developments of the 1920s.

11.5.2 Analyze the international and domestic events, interests, and philosophies that prompted attacks on civil liberties, including the Palmer Raids, Marcus Garvey's "back-to-Africa" movement, the Ku Klux Klan, immigration quotas and the responses of organizations such as the American Civil Liberties Union, the National Association for the Advancement of Colored People, and the Anti-Defamation League to those attacks.

11.5.6 Trace the growth and effects of radio and movies and their role in the worldwide diffusion of popular culture.

⁓ The Big Idea ⁓

People react to periods of breathtaking social and cultural change in different ways. The New York City neighborhood of Harlem became the epicenter for a flowering of African American literature, music, and art—a development known as the Harlem Renaissance. New forms of music such as jazz, blues, and ragtime developed. African American authors began writing about defiance and contempt for racism. The large population of African Americans in northern cities following the Great Migration led to large voting blocs and political gains. The NAACP worked to end segregation and discrimination. Black Nationalism, a new movement promoted by Marcus Garvey, instilled pride in black culture and hope for the future in many African Americans.

426 CHAPTER 7 The Jazz Age

SECTION RESOURCES

📁 **Print Material**
- Reproducible Lesson Plan 7-3
- Guided Reading Activity 7-3
- Reading Essentials and Study Guide 7-3
- Active Reading Note-Taking Guide 7-3

🖥 **Transparencies**
- Daily Focus Skills Transparency 7-3
- Section Graphic Organizer Transparency 7-3

Technology
- Interactive Tutor Self-Assessment CD-ROM
- ExamView® Pro Testmaker CD-ROM
- Presentation Plus! CD-ROM

The Harlem Renaissance

Main Idea The Harlem Renaissance sparked new trends in literature, music, and art and featured the work of writers such as Langston Hughes and Zora Neale Hurston.

Reading Connection What examples of integrating different cultures do you see in today's music and visual arts? Read on to learn about the contributions of African Americans to the arts during the 1920s.

After World War I, hundreds of thousands of African Americans joined in what was called the **Great Migration** from the rural South to industrial cities in the North. By moving north, African Americans **sought** to escape the segregated society of the South, to find economic opportunities, and to build better lives. After World War I, black populations swelled in large northern cities. The cities were full of nightclubs and music, particularly in the New York City neighborhood of Harlem—the heart and soul of the African American renaissance.

★ An American Story ★

On August 8, 1922, a young cornet player named Louis Armstrong took the train from New Orleans to Chicago. His hero, the bandleader Joe "King" Oliver, had sent a telegram to Armstrong offering him a job. Here, Armstrong recalls his trip:

❝When I got to the station in Chicago, I couldn't see Joe Oliver anywhere . . . I'd never seen a city that big. All those tall buildings, I thought they were universities. I said, no, this is the wrong city. I was just fixing to take the next train back home . . . when a red cap [train porter] Joe had left word with came up to me. He took me to the Lincoln Gardens and when I got to the door there and heard Joe and his band wailing so good, I said to myself, 'No, I ain't supposed to be in this band. They're too good.'❞

The next night, near the end of the show, Oliver let Armstrong perform a solo. Armstrong later recalled his feelings: "I had hit the big time. I was up North with the greats. I was playing with my idol, the King, Joe Oliver. My boyhood dream had come true at last."

—quoted in *The African American Family Album*

Louis Armstrong's first impressions of Chicago and his desire to fulfill a dream were probably similar to the first impressions and desires of the hundreds of thousands of other African Americans who migrated north. It was in Harlem that African Americans created an environment that stimulated artistic development, racial pride, a sense of community, and political organization. The result was a flowering of African American arts that became known as the **Harlem Renaissance**.

The Writers Considered the first important writer of the Harlem Renaissance, **Claude McKay** emigrated from Sunny Ville, Jamaica to New York in 1912. There, he translated the shock of American racism into *Harlem Shadows*, a collection of poetry published in 1922. In such poems as "The Lynching" and "If We Must Die," McKay's eloquent verse expressed a proud defiance and bitter contempt of racism—two striking characteristics of Harlem Renaissance writing.

One of the most prolific, original, and versatile writers of the Harlem Renaissance was **Langston Hughes.** Born in Joplin, Missouri, Hughes became a leading voice of the African American experience in the United States. 📖 (See *American Literature* on page 432 for more information on Langston Hughes.)

▼ *Louis Armstrong*

TEACH

R₁ Reading Strategy

Activating Prior Knowledge Remind students that many African Americans have moved to the North from the rural South. **Ask:** When and why did the Great Migration begin? *(during World War I, when African Americans left the South for jobs in Northern cities)* Challenge students to recall an earlier time when African Americans moved from the South. *(the Exodusters, who left the rural South in 1879 for Kansas in search of land and freedom from share-cropping and poverty)* **OL**

R₂ Reading Strategy

Scaffolding—Academic Vocabulary The word *migrate* was introduced in Chapter 6, Section 2. Ask a student to define the word. **BL**

R₃ Reading Strategy

Reading Primary/Secondary Sources Have students select a poem by an African American poet of the Harlem Renaissance and prepare to read it aloud for the class. Suggest that students work in pairs as they practice reading the poetry with the proper rhythm and intonation. **OL**

Did You Know?

African American musicians were not recorded in the early twentieth century. White record companies would buy songs written by African Americans for white singers to record. In 1921 Harry Herbert Pace formed Black Swan Records. During its brief existence, the company, which Pace first ran from his basement in Harlem, recorded for and marketed to the African American consumer. At its height, Black Swan produced and sold 7,000 recordings daily.

C Critical Thinking

Comparing and Contrasting
Have students choose any two artists of the Harlem Renaissance who worked in two different mediums. Have them create graphic organizers, such as Venn diagrams that graphically summarize their similarities and differences. Allow time for students to share their findings with the class. **OL**

R Reading Strategy

Multiple Meanings Ask students to identify different parts of speech or different meanings of the words *jazz* and *blues*. (For example, the verb *jazz up* means "enliven"; *blue* is also an adjective.) **EL**

**Answers and
Additional Support**

C Harlem Renaissance **authors** continue to influence writers today. Zora Neale Hurston published her first novels, *Jonah's Gourd Vine* and *Their Eyes Were Watching God,* in the 1930s. These works influenced such contemporary authors as Ralph Ellison and Toni Morrison. Hurston's personal and spirited portrayals of rural African American culture, often set in Florida where she grew up, were also the first major stories featuring African American females as central characters. Other notable writers of the Harlem Renaissance include Countee Cullen, Alain Locke, Dorothy West, and Nella Larsen.

Jazz, Blues, and the Theater Shortly after Louis Armstrong arrived in Chicago from New Orleans, he introduced an improvisational, early form of **jazz**, a style of music influenced by Dixieland music and ragtime, with its ragged rhythms and syncopated melodies.

In 1925, three years after joining Joe "King" Oliver's band, Armstrong awed fellow musicians with a series of recordings made with his group, the "Hot Five." In these recordings, especially in the song "Cornet Chop Suey," Armstrong broke away from the New Orleans tradition of ensemble or group playing by performing highly imaginative solos. He became the first great cornet and trumpet soloist in jazz music.

Picturing **History**

Renaissance Writers Claude McKay wrote about his Jamaican homeland, while Zora Neale Hurston celebrated the courage of African Americans in the rural South. How did these writers contribute to African Americans' cultural identity?

428   CHAPTER 7   The Jazz Age

Ragtime also influenced the composer, pianist, and bandleader Duke Ellington, who listened as a teenager to ragtime piano players in Washington, D.C. In 1923 Ellington formed a small band, moved to New York, and began playing in speakeasies and clubs. He soon created his own sound, a blend of improvisation and orchestration using different combinations of instruments. The Ellington style appeared in such hits as "Mood Indigo" and "Sophisticated Lady."

R Like many other African American entertainers, Ellington got his start at the **Cotton Club**, one of the most famous Harlem nightspots. Years later, reflecting on the music of this era, Ellington said, "Everything, and I repeat, *everything* had to swing. And that was just it, those cats really had it; they had that soul. And you know you can't just play some of this music without soul. Soul is very important."

Bessie Smith seemed to symbolize soul. Her emotional singing style and commanding voice earned her the title "the Empress of the Blues." Smith sang of unfulfilled love, poverty, and oppression—the classic themes of the **blues,** a soulful style of music that evolved from African American spirituals. Born in Tennessee, Smith started performing in tent shows, saloons, and small theaters in the South. Discovered by Ma Rainey, one of the first great blues singers, Smith later performed with many of the greatest jazz bands of the era, including those of Louis Armstrong and Benny Goodman. Her first recorded song, "Down Hearted Blues," became a major hit in 1923.

While jazz and blues filled the air during the Harlem Renaissance, the theater arts were also flourishing. *Shuffle Along,* the first musical written, produced, and performed by African Americans, made its debut on Broadway in 1921. The show's success helped launch a number of careers, including those of Florence Mills and Paul Robeson.

Paul Robeson, a celebrated singer and actor, received wide acclaim in the title role of a 1924 New York production of *Emperor Jones,* a play by Eugene O'Neill. In 1928 Robeson gained fame for his work in the musical *Show Boat.* He also often appeared at the Apollo Theater, another famous entertainment club in Harlem. Robeson's fame ultimately spread to Europe, where he became well known as a singer and actor.

HISTORY *Online*

Student Web Activity Visit the *American Vision: Modern Times* Web site at tav.mt.glencoe.com and click on *Student Web Activities—Chapter 7* for an activity on the Jazz Age.

HISTORY *Online*

Objectives and answers to the student activity can be found in the **Web Activity Lesson Plan** at tav.mt.glencoe.com.

Picturing **History**

Answer: by writing proudly about their own experience
Ask: What two striking characteristics of Harlem Renaissance writing are evident in some of McKay's poetry? *(proud defiance and bitter contempt of racism)*

Perhaps the most daring performer of the era, Josephine Baker transformed a childhood knack for flamboyance into a career as a well-known singer and dancer. Baker performed on Broadway but went to Paris to dance in 1925. Baker took Paris by storm, launching an international career.

The Harlem Renaissance brought international fame to African American arts. It also sparked a political transformation in the United States.

✓ **Reading Check** **Analyzing** Analyze how African Americans helped shape the national identity through the use of music and literature.

African American Politics

Main Idea **African Americans steadily worked to win more rights.**

Reading Connection How does a sense of positive self-esteem help you perform better? Read on to discover ways that African Americans formed a new sense of pride.

The racial pride that sparked the artistic achievements of the Harlem Renaissance also fueled the political and economic aspirations of many African

Americans. The postwar years saw the development of new attitudes among African Americans, who forged new roles in life and in politics. For many, the sight of the 1,300 African American men of the Fifteenth Regiment of New York's National Guard, returning from the war and marching through Manhattan and home to Harlem, symbolized these aspirations. W.E.B. Du Bois, editor of *The Crisis*, captured the new sense of dignity and defiance of African Americans:

> ❝We return.
> We return from fighting.
> We return fighting.
> Make way for democracy! We saved it in France, and by the Great Jehovah, we will save it in the United States of America, or know the reason why.❞
>
> –from *When Harlem Was in Vogue*

Picturing **History**

Harlem Renaissance The growing fame of African American artists, who often performed (but could not be patrons) at Harlem's "Cotton Club," encouraged a flamboyant lifestyle. What conditions encouraged the growth of African American art?

Ⓤ **Universal Access**

Auditory/Musical Have students listen to recordings of jazz and blues performances by popular musicians of the 1920s, such as Duke Ellington, Josephine Baker, and Bessie Smith. Instruct students to use the library or Internet resources to find out more about the performer they have selected. Then have students create a profile of that person's life and music. Students may wish to place the information in a time line or other visual format. **OL**

Review the Big Idea

Review the Big Idea for this section, "People react to periods of breathtaking social and cultural change in different ways." Ask students to research the history of W.E.B. DuBois's magazine *The Crisis*. Tell them to write a three-page paper on the importance of the publication, especially during this growth period of African American political power. Students should present their papers to the class. **AL**
CA 11WA2.4d

✓ **Reading Check**

Answer: They developed the rhythms and sound of jazz and the blues; their literature reflected the African American as part of American life.

Picturing **History**

Answer: After World War I, many African Americans moved to large cities where they found many nightclubs that welcomed them as performers. The African American community in these cities stimulated artistic development, racial pride, a sense of community, and political organization.
Ask: Although they made economic gains, what persistent problems still existed for African Americans? *(segregation and racial prejudice)*

The Black Vote in the North The Great Migration had a significant **impact** on the political power of African Americans in the North. As their numbers grew in certain city neighborhoods, African Americans became a powerful voting bloc that could sometimes sway the outcome of elections.

At election time, most African American voters in the North cast their votes for Republicans, the party of Abraham Lincoln. In 1928 African American voters in Chicago achieved a significant political breakthrough. Voting as a bloc, they helped elect Oscar DePriest, the first African American representative in Congress from a Northern state. During his three terms in Congress, DePriest introduced laws to provide pensions to formerly enslaved African Americans over 75 years old, to declare Lincoln's birthday a public holiday, and to fine and imprison officials who allowed lynchings of prisoners.

The NAACP Battles Lynching On the legal front, the National Association for the Advancement of Colored People (NAACP) battled valiantly but often unsuccessfully against segregation and discrimination against African Americans. Its efforts focused primarily on lobbying public officials and working through the court system.

From its beginning in 1909, the NAACP lobbied and protested against the horrors of lynching. The NAACP's persistent efforts led to the passage of anti-lynching legislation in the House of Representatives in 1922. The Senate defeated the bill, but the NAACP continued to lobby against lynching throughout the 1920s and 1930s. Its ongoing efforts kept the issue in the news and probably helped to reduce the number of lynchings that took place.

One of the NAACP's greatest political triumphs occurred in 1930 with the defeat of Judge John J. Parker's nomination to the U.S. Supreme Court. The NAACP joined with labor unions to launch a highly organized national campaign against the North Carolina judge, who allegedly was racist and antilabor. By a narrow margin, the Senate refused to confirm Parker's nomination. His defeat demonstrated that African American voters and lobby groups had finally begun to achieve enough influence to affect national politics and change decisions in Congress.

While some people were fighting for integration and improvement in the economic and political position of African Americans, other groups began to emphasize black nationalism and black pride. Eventually, some began to call for black separation from white society.

Black Nationalism and Marcus Garvey A dynamic black leader from Jamaica, **Marcus Garvey**, captured the imagination of millions of African Americans with his call for "Negro Nationalism," which glorified the black culture and traditions of the past.

Inspired by Booker T. Washington's call for self-reliance, Garvey founded the Universal Negro Improvement Association (UNIA), an organization aimed at promoting black pride and unity. The central message of Garvey's Harlem-based movement was that African Americans could gain economic and political power by educating themselves. Garvey also advocated separation and independence from whites.

In 1920, at the height of his power, Garvey presided over an international conference in the UNIA Liberty Hall in Harlem. After the convention,

▼ *The NAACP pickets Crime Conference in Washington, D.C.*

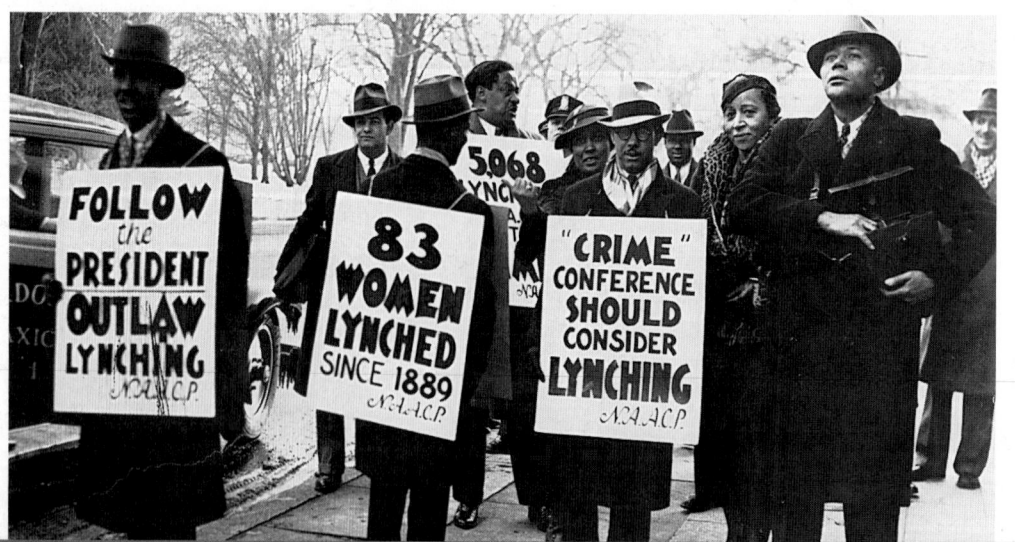

Did You Know?

Marcus Garvey founded the Universal Negro Improvement Association in 1914 while living in Jamaica. He arrived in the United States in March 1916. Having no money, he moved in with a Jamaican family in Harlem, New York City. He found work as a printer and earned money to fund the UNIA by speaking as a soapbox orator on a Harlem street corner.

Picturing History

Black Nationalism Marcus Garvey's Universal Negro Improvement Association advocated African American self-reliance and separation from whites and white society. **What eventually happened to Garvey and his movement?**

about 50,000 people, led by Garvey, marched through the streets of Harlem in a show of support. Garvey told his followers they would never find justice or freedom in America, and he proposed to lead them to Africa.

Garvey's plan to create a settlement in the African country of Liberia alarmed France and Great Britain, which governed surrounding territories. In the United States, the emerging African American middle class and intellectuals distanced themselves from Garvey and his push for racial purity and separation. FBI officials saw UNIA as a dangerous catalyst for black uprisings in urban areas.

Garvey also alienated key figures in the Harlem Renaissance by characterizing them as "weak-kneed and cringing . . . [flatterers of] the white man." Garvey was convicted of mail fraud in 1923 and served time in prison. In 1927 President Coolidge commuted Garvey's sentence and used Garvey's immigrant status to have him deported to Jamaica. Garvey's subsequent attempts to revitalize his movement from abroad failed.

Despite Garvey's failure to keep his movement alive, he inspired millions of African Americans with a sense of pride in their heritage and hope for the future. That sense of pride and hope survived long after Garvey and his "back to Africa" movement was gone. This pride and hope reemerged strongly during the 1950s and played a vital role in the civil rights movement of the 1960s.

Reading Check **Summarizing** How did World War I change attitudes among African Americans toward themselves and their country?

HISTORY Online **Study Central**

For help with the concepts in this section of *American Vision: Modern Times* go to tav.mt.glencoe.com and click on *Study Central*.

SECTION 3 ASSESSMENT

Checking for Understanding

1. **Vocabulary** Define: sought, author, jazz, blues, impact.
2. **People and Terms** Identify: Great Migration, Harlem Renaissance, Claude McKay, Langston Hughes, Cotton Club, Marcus Garvey.
3. **Explain** the importance of the defeat of Judge John Parker's nomination to the U.S. Supreme Court.
4. **Describe** the goals of Marcus Garvey's Universal Negro Improvement Association.

Reviewing Big Ideas

5. **Identifying** What actions did the NAACP take to expand political rights for African Americans?

Critical Thinking

6. **Historical Analysis** **Synthesizing** How did the Great Migration affect the political power of African Americans in the North? **CA HI1**
7. **Analyzing** How did Duke Ellington create a new musical style that grew out of the ragtime tradition?
8. **Organizing** Use a graphic organizer similar to the one below to describe the impact of the Harlem Renaissance on U.S. society.

Impact of Harlem Renaissance

Analyzing Visuals

9. **Examining Photographs** Study the images on page 429 of the Cotton Club and African Americans posing by their car. Describe an element featured in these photographs that reveal how African Americans helped shape the social culture of the 1920s.

Writing About History

10. **Descriptive Writing** Imagine that you witnessed the African American men of the Fifteenth Regiment of New York's National Guard, who came back from the war, marched through Manhattan and home to Harlem. Write a newspaper article describing the scene of the men's return. **CA 11WS1.1**

CHAPTER 7 The Jazz Age **431**

SECTION 3 ASSESSMENT ANSWERS

1. Content vocabulary is boldfaced and highlighted in yellow. Academic vocabulary is boldfaced.
2. Great Migration *(p. 427)*, Harlem Renaissance *(p. 427)*, Claude McKay *(p. 427)*, Langston Hughes *(p. 427)*, Cotton Club *(p. 428)*, Marcus Garvey *(p. 430)*
3. showed political strength of African Americans
4. emphasized black pride and separate African American society
5. lobbied and worked through the courts
6. created a strong voting bloc
7. distinctive orchestration and improvisation
8. literature; new styles of music; theater; political influence
9. style of clothing
10. Students' paragraphs should focus on emotional responses.

Chapter 7 • Section 3

ASSESS

 Resources for page 431

Use these resources to assess student mastery.

📁 Section Quiz 7-3

📁 Reading Essentials and Study Guide 7-3

💿 Interactive Tutor Self-Assessment CD-ROM

📁 California Standards Practice, Grade 11

Picturing **History**

Answer: He was convicted of mail fraud and deported. His attempts to revive his movement worldwide failed.

Reading Check

Answer: African Americans saw themselves as defenders of democracy and thus entitled to all the rights of citizens.

 HISTORY Online

Study Central provides audio summaries, interactive games, and online graphic organizers to help students review section content.

CLOSE

Summarizing Ask students to identify examples of how African Americans celebrate their African heritage today. *(Answers will vary, but students might mention the growth of Kwanzaa celebrations in the United States or the observance of Black History Month every February.)* **BL**

FOCUS

History–Social Science Standards

This feature addresses the following standard:

11.5.5 Describe the Harlem Renaissance and new trends in literature, music, and art, with special attention to the work of writers (e.g. Zora Neale Hurston, Langston Hughes).

Langston Hughes in the following poems expresses both the pride and the frustration of the African Americans during the early part of the twentieth century.

Read to Discover

Answer: The poem indicates that African Americans are not currently accepted in American society but they will be in the future.

Understanding Vocabulary

Before students begin reading have them review the **Reader's Dictionary.** Point out that difficult words are footnoted throughout the text.

TEACH

R Reading Strategy

Using Maps, Charts, and Graphs Have students work in small groups to locate and label on a world map the rivers mentioned in this poem. **Ask: What does Hughes want readers to understand by mentioning these rivers?** *(African Americans have a connection to their historical African heritage.)* **BL**

432

American LITERATURE

Selected Poems
by Langston Hughes

Langston Hughes was born in Joplin, Missouri, in 1902. After high school Hughes went on to Columbia University to study engineering, but he soon dropped out to pursue his first love—poetry. Hughes published his first poem, "The Negro Speaks of Rivers," in 1921 at the age of 19. He eventually became known as the "Poet Laureate of Harlem" and wrote over 850 poems during his lifetime. The poems on the following pages are a sampling of Hughes's work during the 1920s.

Read to Discover

What is Hughes's perception of the place of African Americans in society at the time he wrote these poems?

Reader's Dictionary

Euphrates: River in the Middle East

Congo and **Nile:** Rivers in Africa

lulled: calmed; soothed

syncopated: marked by rhythm stressing a weak beat

pallor: paleness

The Negro Speaks of Rivers

I've known rivers:
I've known rivers ancient as the
    world and older than the
flow of human blood in human
    veins.

My soul has grown deep like the
    rivers.

R
I bathed in the Euphrates when
    dawns were young.
I built my hut near the Congo and it
    lulled me to sleep.
I looked upon the Nile and raised
    the pyramids above it.
I heard the singing of the Mississippi
    when Abe Lincoln went down to
    New Orleans, and I've seen its
    muddy bosom turn all golden in
    the sunset.

I've known rivers:
Ancient, dusky rivers
My soul has grown deep like the
    rivers.

I, Too

I, too, sing America.

I am the darker brother.
They send me to eat in the kitchen
When company comes,
But I laugh,
And eat well,
And grow strong.

Tomorrow,
I'll be at the table
When company comes.
Nobody'll dare
Say to me,
"Eat in the kitchen,"
Then.

Besides,
They'll see how beautiful I am
And be ashamed—

I, too, am America.

Reading Strategy | CONNECTING

Imitating other writers is a useful technique to improve writing skills. Remind the class that imitation is not plagiarism, which is literary theft. After reading "The Negro Speaks of Rivers," point out some of the features of the poem, such as the repetition and the stanzas beginning with *I* plus an action verb. Ask students to focus on one aspect of themselves and one common natural or manufactured item, such as "The High School Student Speaks of Trees" or "The Musician Speaks of Drums." Encourage them to write free verse poems in the style of Langston Hughes.

OL **CA** 11RL3.2; 11RL3.4

The Weary Blues

Droning a drowsy syncopated tune,
Rocking back and forth to a mellow croon,
    I heard a Negro play.
Down on Lenox Avenue the other night
By the pale dull pallor of an old gas light
    He did a lazy sway. . . .
    He did a lazy sway. . . .
To the tune o' those Weary Blues.
With his ebony hands on each ivory key
He made that poor piano moan with melody.
    O Blues!
Swaying to and fro on his rickety stool
He played that sad raggy tune like a musical fool.
    Sweet Blues!
Coming from a black man's soul.
    O Blues!
In a deep song voice with a melancholy tone
I heard that Negro sing, that old piano moan—
    "Ain't got nobody in all this world,
    Ain't got nobody but ma self.
    I's gwine to quit ma frownin'
    And put ma troubles on the shelf."

Thump, thump, thump, went his foot on the floor.
He played a few chords then he sang some more—
    "I got the Weary Blues
    And I can't be satisfied.
    Got the Weary Blues
    And can't be satisfied—
    I ain't happy no mo'
    And I wish that I had died."
And far into the night he crooned that tune.
The stars went out and so did the moon.
The singer stopped playing and went to bed
While the Weary Blues echoed through his head.
He slept like a rock or a man that's dead.

Lenox Avenue: Midnight

The rhythm of life
Is a jazz rhythm,
Honey.
The gods are laughing at us.

The broken heart of love
The weary, weary heart of pain,—

    Overtones,
    Undertones,
To the rumble of street cars,
To the swish of rain.

Lenox Avenue,
Honey.
Midnight,
And the gods are laughing at us.

▲ *African American jazz band*

Block Schedule

Team Teaching This selection of poems by Langston Hughes can be presented in conjunction with English or Language Arts.

R Reading Strategy

Analyzing Text Structure Call on a volunteer to read aloud the poem "The Weary Blues." Ask students what they observe and hear as they follow along in the text. Lead students to discover that the lines of the poem and the flow of it are intended to mimic the feeling of the blues song being referred to in the poem. After students think about this, ask them to try reading the poem again, imagining the tempo of the slow, weary song in their minds. **OL**
CA 11RL3.2; 11RL3.4

W Writing Support

Research Report Writing Ask students to research the history of the poem "Lenox Avenue: Midnight" and identify the Lenox Avenue that the poem refers to. Tell students to write a one-page paper explaining the importance of this street. **AL**
CA 11RL3.2; 11WA2.2

Resources for page 433

*Have students read more about the poetry of Langston Hughes in the **American Literature Readings 3**.*

EXTENDING THE CONTENT

Family Connections James Mercer Langston Hughes spent most of his childhood with his maternal grandmother, Mary Langston, in Lawrence, Kansas. Mrs. Langston's first husband had been a member of John Brown's raiding party on Harpers Ferry. Mrs. Langston introduced Hughes to *Crisis* magazine, the official magazine of the NAACP, published by W.E.B. Du Bois. Hughes wrote "The Negro Speaks of Rivers" after observing a sunset on the Mississippi River on a trip to visit his father in Mexico. The poem was dedicated to DuBois and published in *Crisis*.

▲ *Street scene in Harlem in the 1920s*

Mother to Son

Well, son, I'll tell you:
Life for me ain't been no crystal stair.
It's had tacks in it,
And splinters,
And boards torn up,
And places with no carpet on the floor—
Bare.
But all the time
I'se been a-climbin' on,
And reachin' landin's,
And turnin' corners,
And sometimes goin' in the dark
Where there ain't been no light.
So, boy, don't you turn back.
Don't you set down on the steps
'Cause you finds it's kinder hard.
Don't you fall now—
For I'se still goin', honey,
I'se still climbin',
And life for me ain't been no crystal stair.

Aunt Sue's Stories

Aunt Sue has a head full of stories.
Aunt Sue has a whole heart full of stories.
Summer nights on the front porch
Aunt Sue cuddles a brown-faced child to her bosom
And tells him stories.

Black slaves
Working in the hot sun,
And black slaves
Walking in the dewy night,
And black slaves
Singing sorrow songs on the banks of a mighty river
Mingle themselves softly
In the flow of old Aunt Sue's voice,
Mingle themselves softly
In the dark shadows that cross and recross
Aunt Sue's stories.

And the dark-faced child, listening,
Knows that Aunt Sue's stories are real stories,
He knows that Aunt Sue never got her stories
Out of any book at all,
But that they came
Right out of her own life.

The dark-faced child is quiet
Of a summer night
Listening to Aunt Sue's stories.

Analyzing Literature

1. **Recall and Interpret** How do you think Hughes's use of punctuation and line breaks helps convey his point in the poems? **CA 11RL3.4**

2. **Evaluate and Connect** Do you think these poems convey a positive message or a negative one? Why? **CA 11RL3.2**

Interdisciplinary Activity

Response Writing The poem "I, Too" is a response to Walt Whitman's poem, "I Hear America Singing." Using the Internet or other resources, find and read Whitman's poem. In small groups, try to figure out how Hughes's poem ties in to Whitman's. Then write your own response poem to "I Hear America Singing."

Reading on Your Own

*For other literature selections that relate to the Harlem Renaissance,
you might consider the following book suggestions.*

Black Boy (Autobiography)
by Richard Wright

A prominent author of the Harlem Renaissance, Wright details his struggles growing up black in extreme poverty in the early 1900s. Although he did not attend school regularly until high school, he found different jobs to earn money for books and eventually graduated as the valedictorian of his school.

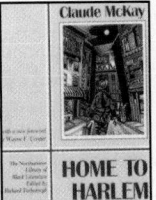

Home to Harlem (Fiction)
by Claude McKay

This was the first novel by an African American to hit the best-seller list and established Claude McKay as an important contributor to the Harlem Renaissance. We learn about the back alleys where drinking and gambling take place in Harlem during the Jazz Age. Jake Brown rises above those who give in to the depression of poverty and enjoys the blessings of life he finds.

God's Trombones (Poetry)
by James Weldon Johnson

Johnson, a lawyer, author, and diplomat, was an important literary figure during the 1920s. Believing that black preachers' voices were like trombones, he wrote a series of sermons in poetic form in this collection.

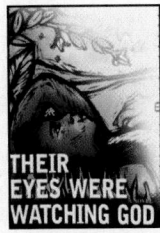

Their Eyes Were Watching God (Fiction)
by Zora Neale Hurston

The most important female African American writer of the Harlem Renaissance, Hurston uses local dialect to tell the story of Janie Crawford, who suffers through two loveless marriages before finding a fulfilling match with Tea Cake, a laborer and gambler.

CHAPTER 7   The Jazz Age   **435**

HISTORY Online

Refer to tav.mt.glencoe.com for additional Glencoe Literature titles, lesson plans, and study guides related to this unit.

Cooperative Learning

Investigating Authors Divide the class into four groups. Assign each group one of the books suggested for reading. Have each group read their book and find out more information about the author of their book. Invite them to design a way to share what they have learned, such as a radio play or visual display. Allow time for students to present their findings to the class.

Author Time Line Have students use the author information that they have gathered to design a time line. One side of the time line should be based on the writer's life; the other should contain information about the Harlem Renaissance.

Author Comparisons Re-divide the groups so that each has a member from every author group. Have students work together to identify similarities and differences among the four writers. Challenge the groups to design a graphic organizer that incorporates and displays the comparisons and contrasts. **OL**

GLENCOE BOOKLINK

Use **Glencoe BookLink** to create customized reading lists for your students' reading levels, interests, and abilities.

Reading Strategy   REINFORCING READING SKILLS

To help students practice their understanding of making connections—which is one of the reading skills presented in this unit—remind students to pay attention to how words and phrases used in the poetry of Langston Hughes help connect the reader to an emotion or described experience. Students may write down possible connections as they read, making it easier for them to remember these details after they have finished reviewing the selection.

FOCUS

History–Social Science Standards

This feature addresses the following standard:

11.5.3 Examine the passage of the Eighteenth Amendment to the Constitution and the Volstead Act (Prohibition).

Understanding Vocabulary

Before students begin reading, point out that difficult or unfamiliar words are footnoted throughout the text.

TEACH

R Reading Strategy

Inferring Jack London's letter shows that he had a very strong opinion about Prohibition. He seemed comfortable in allowing the government to set severe restrictions on this aspect of private life. **Ask:** Why is London so opposed to legislation that is not absolute, something he calls "half-measures"? *(Vaguely constructed laws are unfair because they target some members of society and not others.)* **OL**

Answers and Additional Support

Primary Sources
Eyewitness to History

The use of alcohol has led to heated arguments over private behavior and public policy for much of American history. In the early 1900s, many people saw drinking not only as sinful but also as a significant threat to the well-being of the family. Others objected to government involvement in private life. As the debate became more intense in the years leading to the 1919 passage of Prohibition, both sides argued about the best way to protect the United States.

SOURCE 1:

Jack London, a famous author from Oakland, California, usually wrote about the struggle of man against nature. Despite being a heavy drinker, he supported Prohibition. In a letter to a friend in 1916, London explained his willingness to make a personal sacrifice and give up alcohol.

SOURCE 2:

Richard Bartholdt, a German-born Republican congressman from Missouri, was one of the main opponents of Prohibition. He did not believe that the majority had the right to take away the freedom to drink alcohol from the minority. In 1914 Bartholdt listed his reasons against Prohibition.

NEVER HAD MUCH EXPERIENCE WITH WINE-GRAPE GROWING. THE VINEYARDS I BOUGHT WERE OLD WORKED OUT WORTHLESS SO I PULLED OUT THE VINES AND PLANTED OTHER CROPS. I STILL WORK ON A FEW ACRES OF PROFITABLE WINE GRAPES. MY POSITION ON ALCHOHOL IS ABSOLUTE NATION-WIDE PROHIBITION. I MEAN ABSOLUTE. I HAVE NO PATIENCE IN HALF-WAY MEASURES. HALF-WAY MEASURES ARE UNFAIR ARE TANTAMOUT TO CONFISCATION AND ARE PROVOCATIVE OF UNDERHAND CHEATING LYING AND LAW-BREAKING. WHEN THE NATION GOES IN FOR NATIONWIDE PROHIBITION THAT WILL BE THE END OF ALCOHOL AND THERE WILL BE NO CHEATING LYING NOR LAW-BREAKING. PERSONALLY I SHALL CONTINUE TO DRINK ALCOHOL FOR AS LONG AS IT IS ACCESSIBLE. WHEN ABSOLUTE PROHIBITION MAKES ALCOHOL INACCESSIBLE I SHALL STOP DRINKING AND IT WON'T BE ANY HARDSHIP ON ME AND ON MEN LIKE ME WHOSE NAME IS LEGION. AND THE GENERATION OF BOYS AFTER US WILL NOT KNOW ANYTHING ABOUT ALCOHOL SAVE THAT IT WAS A STUPID VICE OF THEIR SAVAGE ANCESTORS.

▲ *Jack London*

Prohibition is a deathblow to the liberty of the individual because it prohibits what is not wrong in itself. . . . The exercise of rights which concern persons individually, and whose exercise does not injure the neighbor, is a basic condition of freedom which prohibition violates. The right to eat and drink what we please is an **inalienable**[1] human right of which even a majority can not deprive us without at the same time robbing us of our liberty. . . . The prohibition movement teaches us, however, that such tyranny after all is possible under self-government by the majority misusing its political liberty or its right to govern for the purpose of restricting personal liberty. In other words, we are dealing in this case with . . . "the tyranny of the majority," an evil against which the Nation must protect itself if it desires to remain free; for individual lib-

---

[1] **inalienable:** unremovable

UNIVERSAL ACCESS

Advanced Learners Have students use library and Internet resources to learn about the history of alcohol restrictions in their community. Ask them to investigate what kinds of current restrictions there are on alcohol consumption and try to determine the purpose of these laws. For example, some places do not allow beer and wine sales on Sundays. Tell students to present their research in a three-page report. **AL** **CA 11WA2.4**

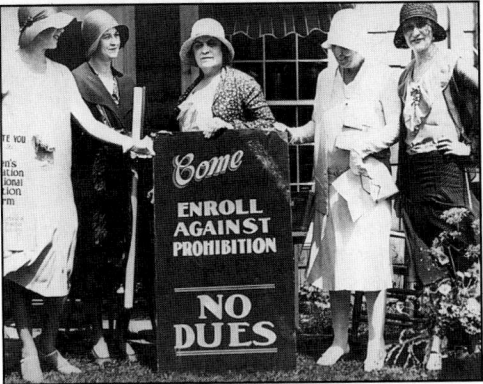

▲ *Women soliciting members for their anti-Prohibition club*

erty, the right of personal conduct, is an inalienable human right which should never be taken away either by majorities or by law or constitution. From this we can see how much larger than the mere drink problem this question really is, for if it were right in one respect to take away from the individual the privilege of self-control it would be right in all other respects, and the final outcome could be nothing less than a condition of complete slavery.

Our opponents say, "We do not propose to prohibit drinking, but merely the manufacture and sale of beverages," but remember that this hypocritical and **insidious**[2] **subterfuge**[3] is the very means by which despots always robbed the people of their liberties.

SOURCE 3:

The Anti-Saloon League, one of the main organizations supporting Prohibition, appealed to patriotism in its literature. During World War I, German Americans were suspected of being disloyal to the United States. Since most brewers had German backgrounds, the League took advantage of anger toward Germans on a 1918 Ohio election poster.

REMEMBER

The liquor traffic fought for permission to sell **intoxicants**[4] to soldiers, knowing full well that drinking would make our boys less fit to win the war.

[2]**insidious:** sly
[3]**subterfuge:** deception
[4]**intoxicant:** beverage containing alcohol

Breweries went on burning coal to make a harmful product when factories, stores, churches, and schools had to close down.

Millions of bushels of grain were consumed to manufacture intoxicants while patriotic people of America limited their food.

Millions of pounds of sugar were used in making intoxicants, while people were doing without sugar.

Thousands and thousands of cars were used for shipments to and from breweries when absolutely essential war-work was seriously delayed by car shortage.

The brewers financed the traitorous German-American Alliance, whose president received a medal from the Hun **kaiser**[5].

The Liquor Traffic has put its selfish interests above America's winning the war. It has resisted the measures to even partially eliminate its evils.

The Liquor Traffic has curtailed only when compelled to—only when Uncle Sam "put the screws to it."

The Liquor Traffic is a menace—from every viewpoint—and ought to be abolished now and forever.

Vote "Yes" for Prohibition Nov. 5th.

Take away the "camouflage" with which the Liquor Traffic tries to disguise itself and the sinister figure pictured here stands revealed.

Take away the smooth phrases and cunning twists of the liquor Traffic's appeal For Permission to continue its career; get right down to naked truth and you will see that the liquor traffic is asking fathers of Ohio to "give me your boys." . . .

Are you with them? Are YOU for the Booze Huns or for the boys?

[5]**kaiser:** German king

DBQ Document-Based Questions

Historical Analysis `CA HR4; HI3`

Source 1: Why does London plan to stop drinking?

Source 2: What is Bartholdt's main argument against Prohibition?

Source 3: How does the Anti-Saloon League tie together the makers of alcoholic beverages and anti-German sentiments?

Comparing and Contrasting Sources

How do London, Bartholdt, and the Anti-Saloon League believe that the United States will be changed by Prohibition?

DBQ Document-Based Questions

1. Prohibition will make alcohol inaccessible.
2. Prohibition takes away one of the basic liberties—to eat and drink what one pleases.
3. Alcohol manufacture and transport does not support troops. The Anti-Saloon League associates brewers with Germany.

Comparing and Contrasting Sources
London argues that society will be better off because people will not have the vice. Bartholdt thinks that society will suffer because of the restriction of people's liberties and the tyranny of the majority. The Anti-Saloon League poster suggests that removing the alcohol and its harmful effects will improve society. Resources devoted to this industry can be used to support the war effort.

Reviewing Content Vocabulary

Students' answers will vary. The pages where the words appear in the text are shown in parentheses.

1. anarchist *(p. 407)* **2.** eugenics *(p. 408)* **3.** flapper *(p. 410)* **4.** evolution *(p. 411)* **5.** creationism *(p. 411)* **6.** police powers *(p. 413)* **7.** speakeasy *(p. 413)* **8.** mass media *(p. 421)* **9.** jazz *(p. 428)* **10.** blues *(p. 428)*

Reviewing Academic Vocabulary

Students' answers will vary. The pages where the words appear in the text are shown in parentheses.

11. source *(p. 408)* **12.** aspect *(p. 410)* **13.** ethic *(p. 411)* **14.** emerging *(p. 419)* **15.** diverse *(p. 419)* **16.** unify *(p. 421)* **17.** sought *(p. 427)* **18.** authors *(p. 428)* **19.** impact *(p. 430)*

Reviewing Content Vocabulary

On a sheet of paper, use each of these terms in a sentence.

1. anarchist
2. eugenics
3. flapper
4. evolution
5. creationism
6. police powers
7. speakeasy
8. mass media
9. jazz
10. blues

Chapter Summary

Cultural Changes

- The "new morality" emphasized youth and beauty
- Young people and women gained more independence
- The working class enjoyed more leisure time
- The mass media expanded

African American Renaissance

Harlem Renaissance
- Breakthrough period for African American arts
- Literature revealed racial pride and contempt of racism
- Jazz and blues popularized

Political Renaissance
- Great Migration created strong African American voting blocs in Northern cities
- First African American elected to Congress from a Northern state
- NAACP battled segregation and discrimination

Revitalized Traditional Values

- Fundamentalists preached traditional religious values
- Emphasis on family and moral values
- Traditionalists supported Prohibition

Nativism

- Nativists used eugenics as a pseudo-scientific basis for ethnic and religious prejudice
- The new Ku Klux Klan targeted African Americans, Jews, Catholics, immigrants, and other groups they considered to be "un-American"
- Congress established immigration quotas

438 CHAPTER 7 The Jazz Age

Reviewing Academic Vocabulary

On a sheet of paper, use each of these terms in a sentence that reflects the term's meaning in the chapter.

11. source
12. aspect
13. ethic
14. emerging
15. diverse
16. unify
17. sought
18. author
19. impact

Reviewing the Main Ideas

Section 1

20. Why was there a rise in racism and nativism in the 1920s?

21. What was the Fundamentalist movement?

Section 2

22. Why did artists and writers move to Greenwich Village and Chicago's South Side in the 1920s?

Section 3

23. Why was Harlem the center of the African American renaissance?

24. What were two reasons for the rise in African American political activism?

Critical Thinking

25. **Reading Skill** **Connecting** Review the reading skill on page 427. Then reread "Jazz, Blues, and the Theater" on pages 428–429. Write and answer your own questions for text-to-self, text-to-text, and text-to-world connections.

26. **Civics** In what ways did the new morality change American family life?

27. **Analyzing** Analyze the causes and effects of the changing role of women in the 1920s.

28. **Identifying** List three works of American art or literature that convey universal themes.

29. **Evaluating** Assess the value or importance of the Scopes trial to the Fundamentalist Movement in terms of the trial's causes and results.

30. **Categorizing** Use a graphic organizer similar to the one below to list the major organizations and movements of the 1920s and their goals or purposes.

Organizations/Movements	Goals/Purposes

Reviewing the Main Ideas

20. influx of immigrants and a recession

21. It was a religious movement to reassert the Bible's authority in life.

22. The communities offered freedom from conformity and traditional ideas.

23. because of its large, concentrated African American population

24. Harlem Renaissance and African American experience in World War I

Critical Thinking

25. **Reading Skill** Students' statements will vary but should create three connections for text-to-self, text-to-text, text-to-world reading connections.

438

Visit the *American Vision: Modern Times* Web site at tav.mt.glencoe.com and click on *Self-Check Quizzes—Chapter 7* to assess your knowledge of chapter content.

Writing About History

31. **Historical Analysis** **Interpreting Events Within the Context** Reread the text under the "The New Morality" on pages 410–411. Explain why people might have interpreted the changing roles of women in society in the 1920s differently than they would today. **CA HI3**

32. *Big Idea* Write a journal entry from the perspective of a young adult in the late 1920s. Describe an aspect of popular culture which you enjoy. **CA 11WS1.2**

33. **Persuasive Writing** Imagine that you are living during the early 1920s. Marcus Garvey is campaigning to lead African Americans to a new settlement to be founded in Liberia. Write a letter to a newspaper editor in which you take a position on the merits of Garvey's plan. In your letter, describe how you think this plan will affect the nation and your own community. **CA 11WA2.4a**

DBQ **Document-Based Questions**

34. **Interpreting Primary Sources** Arna Bontemps was a poet who started his writing career during the Harlem Renaissance. Read the poem and answer the questions that follow.

A Black Man Talks of Reaping

I have sown beside all waters in my day.
I planted deep, within my heart the fear
That wind or fowl would take the grain away.
I planted safe against this stark, lean year.

I scattered seed enough to plant the land
In rows from Canada to Mexico
But for my reaping only what the hand
Can hold at once is all that I can show.

Yet what I sowed and what the orchard yields
My brother's sons are gathering stalk and root,
Small wonder then my children glean in fields
They have not sown, and feed on bitter fruit.

a. What does Bontemps mean by "what the hand can hold at once is all that I can show" and "bitter fruit"? **CA 11RL3.4**

b. What major theme of Harlem Renaissance writing is evident in this poem? **CA 11RC2.5**

U.S. Immigration, 1921 and 1925

1921
- Canada and Latin America 15%
- Central Europe 22%
- Asia 3%
- Other countries 2%
- Northern and Western Europe 16%
- Eastern and Southern Europe 42%

1925
- Canada and Latin America 48%
- Asia 1%
- Other countries 1%
- Northern and Western Europe 27%
- Central Europe 19%
- Eastern and Southern Europe 4%

Source: *Historical Statistics of the United States*

Geography and History

35. The circle graphs above show immigration numbers in the United States in 1921 and 1925. Study the graphs and answer the questions below.

   a. **Interpreting Graphs** What significant changes in immigration do the circle graphs show?

   b. **Applying Geography Skills** Why did these changes in immigration occur between 1921 and 1925?

Standards Practice

Directions: Choose the best answer to the following question.

36. Which of the following events of the 1920s contributed to a renewed nativist movement?

A Economic recession

B Harlem Renaissance

C Scopes trial

D Prohibition

Standard 11.5.2: Analyze the international and domestic events, interests, and philosophies that prompted attacks on civil liberties, including the Palmer Raids, Marcus Garvey's "back-to-Africa" movement, the Ku Klux Klan, and immigration quotas and the responses of organizations such as the American Civil Liberties Union, the National Association for the Advancement of Colored People, and the Anti-Defamation League to those attacks.

Online

Have students visit the Web site at tav.mt.glencoe.com to review Chapter 7 and take the Self-Check Quiz.

Writing About History

31. **Historical Analysis** Students' answers will vary. Responses should focus on how the perspective of women's changing roles differs from the 1920s to today.

32. *Big Idea* Students' answers will vary.

33. Letters to the editor will vary but should express a point of view.

DBQ **Document-Based Questions**

34. **a.** he has worked hard all his life but has little to show for it; **b.** disillusionment

Geography and History

35. **a.** They show a dramatic increase in the percentage of immigrants from Latin America and a dramatic decrease in the percentage of immigrants from Eastern and Southern Europe. **b.** changes in immigration laws

Standards Practice

36. A

Bonus Question ?

Ask: Billy Sunday and Aimee Semple McPherson are both regarded as examples of what religious movement of the 1920? *(Fundamentalism)*

---

26. The new morality emphasized personal freedom over parental authority and led women to pursue an identity outside the home.

27. Causes: new morality, more education, and job experience; Effects: greater public freedom, women's contributions in new fields

28. Students' answers will vary but should include reasonable examples from the text.

29. The trial was set in motion from the fundamentalist belief in creationism. The trial created a debate over science and religion. In the end the trial created a critical view of Fundamentalism.

30. the new morality aimed to expand individual freedom; Fundamentalism aimed to restore the Bible's authority; Prohibition aimed to ban alcohol

Chapter 8 Planning Guide

SECTION RESOURCES

MAIN IDEAS	📁 PRINT MATERIALS	TECHNOLOGY RESOURCES
Section 1: Presidential Politics 1. After appointing several friends to positions in the government, President Harding endured a presidency plagued by scandal. 2. Calvin Coolidge steered the country toward an emphasis on business and personal virtue.	• Reproducible Lesson Plan 8-1* • Daily Lecture and Discussion Notes 8-1 • Active Reading Note-Taking Guide 8-1 • Guided Reading Activity 8-1 • Section Quiz 8-1 • Reading Essentials and Study Guide 8-1	Daily Focus Skills Transparency 8-1 Section Graphic Organizer Transparency 8-1 Interactive Tutor Self-Assessment CD-ROM ExamView® Pro Testmaker CD-ROM Presentation Plus! CD-ROM California Standards Practice Transparencies
Section 2: A Growing Economy 1. Mass production and the assembly line allowed new industries, such as automobile and airplane manufacturing, to grow. 2. Easily available credit and advertising combined to create a nation of consumers eager for new goods. 3. Increases in productivity and decreases in foreign markets led to lower prices for farmers.	• Reproducible Lesson Plan 8-2* • Daily Lecture and Discussion Notes 8-2 • Active Reading Note-Taking Guide 8-2 • Guided Reading Activity 8-2 • Section Quiz 8-2 • Reading Essentials and Study Guide 8-2	Daily Focus Skills Transparency 8-2 Section Graphic Organizer Transparency 8-2 Interactive Tutor Self-Assessment CD-ROM ExamView® Pro Testmaker CD-ROM Presentation Plus! CD-ROM California Standards Practice Transparencies
Section 3: The Policies of Prosperity 1. During the 1920s, Andrew Mellon and Herbert Hoover worked to improve business efficiency and promote economic growth. 2. Although the United States returned to a policy of isolationism after World War I, various treaties attempted to limit the arms trade and the possibility of a future war.	• Reproducible Lesson Plan 8-3* • Daily Lecture and Discussion Notes 8-3 • Active Reading Note-Taking Guide 8-3 • Guided Reading Activity 8-3 • Section Quiz 8-3 • Reading Essentials and Study Guide 8-3	Daily Focus Skills Transparency 8-3 Section Graphic Organizer Transparency 8-3 Interactive Tutor Self-Assessment CD-ROM ExamView® Pro Testmaker CD-ROM Presentation Plus! CD-ROM California Standards Practice Transparencies

PACING YOUR LESSONS

Chapter Introduction	Section 1	Section 2	Section 3	Chapter Assessment
½ Day	1 Day	2 Days	2 Days	½ Day

0:00 OUT OF TIME? 📁 Assign the Chapter 8 *Reading Essentials and Study Guide.*

*Available on TeacherWorks™ CD-ROM

Chapter 8 Planning Guide

Standards-Based Lesson Plan

 History–Social Science Standards Covered in Chapter 8

The standards covered in the chapter are listed below. Use the accompanying activity as you teach the chapter to ensure student mastery of these standards. This activity can be used in combination with the program's print and technology assessment materials.

Standard	Section 1	2	3
11.2 Students analyze the relationship among the rise of industrialization, large-scale rural-to-urban migration, and massive immigration from Southern and Eastern Europe.	✔		
11.4.5 Analyze the political, economic and social ramifications of World War I on the home front.		✔	✔
11.5 Students analyze the major political, social, economic, technological, and cultural developments of the 1920s.	✔		✔
11.5.1 Discuss the policies of Presidents Warren Harding, Calvin Coolidge, and Herbert Hoover.	✔	✔	✔
11.5.6 Trace the growth and effects of radio and movies and their role in the worldwide diffusion of popular culture.		✔	
11.5.7 Discuss the rise of mass production techniques, the growth of cities, the impact of new technologies (e.g., the automobile, electricity), and the resulting prosperity and effect on the American landscape.		✔	

Cumulative Standards-Assessment Activity

The Cumulative Standards-Assessment Activity will help students organize and learn the important information from the chapter. Begin teaching the chapter with this activity, and have students complete it as they read the chapter.

CREATING AN OUTLINE

Purpose Outlining is a useful skill for taking notes and writing papers. When studying written material, outlining can help students understand the structure of the text and the relationship among the ideas, which, in turn, enables them to evaluate the material. Outlining requires students to place information in a logical order and is a good starting point when writing a paper.

Introduction to Outlining

1. Review with the class the steps in creating an outline:
   • Write only words and phrases needed, not complete sentences.
   • Note related but less important details under the main ideas.
   • For formal outlines, label the main heads with Roman numerals (I, II), subheads with capital letters (A, B), and details with Arabic numerals (1, 2).
   • Include at least two entries for each level of heading.
   • Indent each level.
   • Be grammatically consistent.

2. Ask students to copy this outline form in their notebooks:

I. _____
  A. _____
    1. _____
    2. _____
  B. _____
    1. _____
    2. _____
II. _____
  A. _____
    1. _____
    2. _____

Have students outline the content of each section as they read. Remind them that at least two points for each level is suggested, but some topics may require more points and some may require fewer.

3. Urge students to use their outlines to help them review the chapter.

Chapter 8 Planning Guide

READING SUPPORT

- Content Vocabulary Activity 8
- Academic Vocabulary Activity 8
- Reading Skills Activity 8
- Chapter 8 Active Reading Note-Taking Guide
- Chapter 8 Guided Reading Activities
- Chapter 8 Reading Essentials and Study Guide
- *The American Vision: Modern Times* Video Program
- Vocabulary PuzzleMaker CD-ROM
- American History Primary Source Document Library CD-ROM

CRITICAL THINKING

- Critical Thinking Skills Activity 8
- Primary Source Reading 8
- Cause-and-Effect Transparency 8 Strategy and Activity
- Presentation Plus! CD-ROM

UNIVERSAL ACCESS

- Universal Access Activity 8
- English Learner Activity 8
- American Art Prints
- StudentWorks™ Plus CD-ROM
- American Music: Hits Through History
- School-to-Home Connection Activity 8

SKILL PRACTICE

- Map Overlay Transparency 8 Strategy and Activity
- Historical Analysis Skills Activity 8
- Time Line Activity 8
- Reading Skills Activity 8
- Reinforcing Skills Activity 8
- Linking Past and Present Activity 8
- Interpreting Political Cartoons 8
- MindJogger Videoquiz

WRITING SUPPORT

- Chapter 8 Active Reading Note-Taking Guide
- Writer's Guidebook
- High School Writing Process Transparencies

ASSESSMENT

- Chapter 8 Section Quizzes
- Chapter 8 Tests, Forms A and B
- Authentic Assessment Activity 8
- Exam*View*® Pro Testmaker CD-ROM
- Interactive Tutor Self-Assessment CD-ROM
- California Standards Practice, Grade 11
- Succeeding on . . .™ the California Standards: Grade 11 History–Social Science CD-ROM

- CD-ROM
- DVD
- Print Material
- Poster

- Transparency
- Music Program
- Videocassette

Chapter 8 Planning Guide

TECHNOLOGY

- StudentWorks™ Plus CD-ROM
- TeacherWorks™ CD-ROM
- ExamView® Pro Testmaker CD-ROM
- Interactive Tutor Self-Assessment CD-ROM
- Presentation Plus! CD-ROM
- Vocabulary PuzzleMaker CD-ROM
- American History Primary Source Document Library CD-ROM
- MindJogger Videoquiz
- *The American Vision: Modern Times* Video Program
- Professional Development in High School Social Studies Video Series
- Teach, Use, and Succeed With *The American Vision: Modern Times*
- American Music: Hits Through History
- Succeeding on . . .™ the California Standards: Grade 11 History–Social Science CD-ROM

SPANISH RESOURCES

- Spanish Activities and Assessment
  - Spanish Vocabulary Activities
  - Spanish Guided Reading Activities
  - Spanish Quizzes and Tests
  - Spanish Reteaching Activities
- Spanish Reading Essentials and Study Guide
- Spanish School-to-Home Connection Activities

TRANSPARENCIES

- Daily Focus Skills Transparencies
- Section Graphic Organizer Transparencies
- Map Overlay Transparencies
- Cause-and-Effect Transparencies
- Unit Time Line Transparencies
- Why It Matters Transparencies
- American Art and Architecture Transparencies
- High School Writing Process Transparencies
- California Standards Practice Transparencies

TEACHER PLANNING

- Daily Lecture and Discussion Notes
- English Learner Handbook
- Building Academic Vocabulary
- *The American Vision: Modern Times* Reading and Study Skills Foldables
- Reading Strategies and Activities for the Social Studies Classroom
- Universal Access for the American History Classroom
- NGS United States Desk Map
- NGS World Atlas
- Chapter 8 Reproducible Lesson Plans on TeacherWorks™ CD-ROM
- California Guide to Daily Intervention

PROFESSIONAL DEVELOPMENT

- Building Academic Vocabulary
- Strategies for Success
- Research-Based Strategies Used to Develop *The American Vision: Modern Times*
- Character Education in the High School Classroom
- Professional Development in High School Social Studies Video Series
- Teach, Use, and Succeed With *The American Vision: Modern Times*

Chapter 8 Planning Guide

TEACHER'S CORNER

Index to National Geographic Magazine:
The following article relates to this chapter:

• "The Okies—Beyond the Great Depression," September 1984

National Geographic Society Products:
To order the following, call National Geographic at 1–800–368–2728

• *Eyewitness to the 20th Century* (Book)
• *Historical Atlas of the United States* (Atlas)

NGS ONLINE

Access National Geographic's new dynamic MapMachine Web site and other geography resources at:

www.nationalgeographic.com

www.nationalgeographic.com/maps

Use our Web site for additional resources. All essential content is covered in the Student Edition.

You and your students can visit tav.mt.glencoe.com, the Web site companion to the **American Vision: Modern Times.** This innovative integration of electronic and print media offers your students a wealth of opportunities. The student text directs students to the Web site for the following options:

• **Chapter Overviews**
• **Self-Check Quizzes**
• **Student Web Activities**
• **Textbook Updates**

Answers to the student Web activities are provided for you in the **Web Activity Lesson Plans.** Additional Web resources and ePuzzles and games are also available.

MASTERING THE STANDARDS

The content and assessment in the Student Edition, Teacher Wraparound Edition, teacher planning materials, and the print and technology products are all standards-based. The use of these products during instruction leads to mastery of the standards.

PRACTICE
• California Standards Practice, Grade 11
• California Standards Practice Transparencies
• School-to-Home Connection

BENCHMARK ASSESSMENT
• Section Quizzes, Chapter Tests, and Authentic Assessment
• *ExamView*® Pro Testmaker CD-ROM
• Succeeding On ... ™ the California Standards: Grade 11 History–Social Science CD-ROM

REMEDIATION
• California Guide to Daily Intervention
• Interactive Tutor Self-Assessment CD-ROM
• *ExamView*® Pro Testmaker CD-ROM
• California Standards Practice, Grade 11
• Reading Essentials and Study Guide

FOLDABLES Study Organizer

Dinah Zike's Foldables

Foldables are three-dimensional, interactive graphic organizers that help students practice basic writing skills, review key vocabulary terms, and identify main ideas. Every chapter has a foldable activity in the *Dinah Zike's Reading and Study Skills Foldables* booklet. You can use the foldables as they are presented or modify them to suit the needs of your individual class.

A variety of videotape programs are available from A&E Television and The History Channel to provide teaching assistance. To order, call Glencoe at 1-800-334-7344.

Chapter 8 Planning Guide

KEY for Using the Teacher Wraparound Edition

Use this key to help you identify the different types of prompts found in the Teacher Wraparound Edition.

R **Reading Strategies** activities help you teach reading skills and vocabulary.

C **Critical Thinking** strategies help students apply and extend what they have learned.

U **Universal Access** activities provide differentiated instruction for students learning to speak English, along with suggestions for teaching various types of learners.

S **Skill Practice** strategies help students practice historical analysis and geography skills.

W **Writing Support** activities provide writing opportunities to help students comprehend the text.

Teaching strategies and activities have been coded for ability level appropriateness.

AL Activities for students working above grade level
OL Activities for students working on grade level
BL Activities for students working below grade level
EL Activities for English learners

FOCUS

History–Social Science Standards

This chapter addresses the following standards:

11.5.1 Discuss the policies of Presidents Warren Harding, Calvin Coolidge, and Herbert Hoover.

11.5.7 Discuss the rise of mass production techniques, the growth of cities, the impact of new technologies (e.g., the automobile, electricity), and the resulting prosperity and effect on the American landscape.

11.6.1 Describe the monetary issues of the late nineteenth and early twentieth centuries that gave rise to the establishment of the Federal Reserve and the weaknesses in key sectors of the economy in the late 1920s.

BELLRINGER
SKILLBUILDER ACTIVITY

Have each student create a word web for the word *normal*. Then have students share their responses, writing their ideas in a word web on the board. Tell students that a presidential campaign after the end of World War I focused on returning to what the candidate called normalcy. Discuss with the class why such a campaign would be effective. Ask students to keep their word webs. After students complete Chapter 8, revisit the exercise to see what additional terms they can add to the webs that pertain to the 1920s.

CHAPTER 8

1921–1929

Normalcy and Good Times

~ *The Big Ideas* ~

SECTION 1: Presidential Politics
Societies change over time. *President Calvin Coolidge tried to get the country back on track after the scandals of the Harding administration.*

SECTION 2: A Growing Economy
Societies change over time. *The United States experienced stunning economic growth during the 1920s.*

SECTION 3: The Policies of Prosperity
Societies change over time. *While the economic policies of the U.S. government led to prosperity for many during the 1920s, these policies were not without consequences.*

The *American Vision: Modern Times* **Video** *The Chapter 8 video "Tuning in to Radio in the 1920s," describes the growth of a mass media culture in the United States and the importance of the radio.*

1920
- Women vote in national election for the first time

1921
- Washington Conference convenes
- Farm Bloc organized in U.S. Congress

1923
- Teapot Dome scandal erupts
- Ford Motor Company gains 50 percent of the new car market
- President Harding dies

1924
- Dawes Plan negotiated with France, Britain, and Germany
- Calvin Coolidge elected president

United States PRESIDENTS
Harding 1921–1923 | Coolidge 1923–1929
1921 | 1923 | 1925

World

1923
- Hitler's Munich coup fails

1924
- Leader of Soviet Union, Vladimir Lenin, dies

1925
- Soldier-leader Reza Khan pronounced shah of Iran

440

TEACH

Thinking About the Big Ideas

As you begin teaching each section, use these questions and activities to focus on the Big Idea.

Section 1
Presidential Politics
Essential Question: What are some ways that people try to return to everyday life after a natural disaster, such as an earthquake or forest fire? After students have discussed this question, tell them that in Section 1 they will learn about how the United States tried to return to normal life after World War I ended. **OL**

Opening Night, Ziegfeld Follies by Howard A. Thain captures the excitement surrounding the opening of a new musical revue in New York City.

1926
- British General Strike paralyzes the British economy

1927
- 15 millionth Model T built

1927

1928
- Kellogg-Briand Pact proposes an end to war

1929
- U.S. radio sales exceed $800 million

Hoover 1929–1933

1929

1929
- Lateran Treaties with Italy make the Vatican sovereign territory

HISTORY Online

Chapter Overview
Visit the *American Vision: Modern Times* Web site at tav.mt.glencoe.com and click on *Chapter Overviews–Chapter 8* to preview chapter information.

441

Section 2
A Growing Economy
Essential Question: What motivates people to invest in the stock market? Do you believe the risks are worth it? Provide students with examples of stock market report graphs from the newspaper or Internet. Have them work in pairs to note the trend of the market. Then tell students that during the 1920s, the United States experienced huge economic growth, which they will learn about in Section 2. **OL**

Section 3
The Policies of Prosperity
Essential Question: If a government wants to encourage business, what policies could it follow? Tell students that as they read Section 3, they will discover how the United States government supported business's growth during the 1920s. **OL**

Cultural Perspectives

The assembly line greatly reduced the manufacturing costs for automobiles. Ford was hailed as an innovator who made the automobile affordable to average Americans. However, the assembly line placed a non-stop demand on the workers for the Ford Motor Company. Ask students to research the changes that the assembly line brought to the work environment, looking especially for primary source materials from the men who worked on the assembly line. **Ask:** Did the workers see the benefits of the assembly line, or were they most concerned with how it impacted their daily work environment? **OL**
CA HR2

FOLDABLES
Study Organizer

Dinah Zike's Foldables are three-dimensional, interactive graphic organizers that help students practice basic writing skills, review key vocabulary terms, and identify main ideas. Have students complete the foldable activity in the *Dinah Zike's Reading and Study Skills Foldables* booklet.

HISTORY Online

Go to tav.mt.glencoe.com for student activities, lesson plans, and links to additional resources to help students learn about the 1920s.

Reading Skill

Why It's Important

Summarizing involves restating key facts in a brief manner. It is an effective tool for studying United States history, which conveys a great deal of information in a chapter.

1. Introducing the Skill

Distribute photocopied book jacket summaries of young adult novels. Using the summaries, have students work in small groups to complete charts similar to the one below. Then ask students to practice the skill of summarizing as they read their textbooks. OL

Name of Book	
Number of Pages	
Key Words	
Summary Word Count	

2. Extending the Skill

Ask students to write book jacket copy for children's books. If your school is connected to an elementary school, you may wish to work with one of its teachers to pair your students and discuss the summaries. BL

Answers and Additional Support

Preparing to Read Chapter 8

Reading Skill — Summarizing

Did you know that summarizing happens while you are reading, not just after you have finished reading? Good readers stop periodically to summarize information in their minds or on paper. This means they restate important ideas using only a few words. Summarizing helps the readers make sure they understand what they have read. It also helps good readers predict what might come next in the text.

Use the natural breaks in the text, such as just before a new heading, as a good point to stop and summarize. This break is the author's way of telling you the information is complete for the heading you just finished reading. Another good place to summarize is at the end of a paragraph that contains a lot of information. As you summarize, consider the facts you learned, the questions you posed, and the connections and inferences you made as you read. These facts and thoughts should lead you to a summary statement.

Read the passage below. While you are reading, note the facts and your thinking about those facts on a sheet of paper.

SUMMARIZING

Summarizing is critical to effective note taking. Use a Cornell note-taking system to capture important facts and summarize information.

Cars revolutionized American life. Although many small businesses declined during the 1920s, the automobile created new small-business opportunities for such enterprises as garages and gas stations.

The automobile eased the isolation of rural life, putting towns within reach of many farmers and the countryside a mere ride away for city dwellers. Cars also enabled more people to live farther from work. An entirely new kind of consumer and worker, the auto commuter, appeared. Commuters lived in growing suburban communities and drove to work in the city. (page 451)

Your summary might be similar to this: *The growth of the car industry created new businesses and changed people's lifestyles, especially with regard to where they lived and worked.*

Apply the Skill

As you read, stop periodically to summarize the information the text has provided. Try summarizing on paper and in your mind. As you summarize information, with your teacher's permission, talk to other students to find out how they summarized a specific section.

UNIVERSAL ACCESS

Below Grade Level Ask students to summarize a section that they recently studied in a textbook from another course. Suggest that they photocopy the text that explains the process and use a highlighter to emphasize key information. Remind students never to write in books, such as library books and textbooks that do not belong to them. BL

Historical Analysis Skill   Analysis Skill Standard H16
Analyzing Economic Behavior

Historical Interpretation As you study history, you should learn to show the connections, casual and otherwise, between particular historical events and the larger social, economic, and political trends and developments.

Conducting cost-benefit analyses and applying basic economic indicators will help you analyze and understand the economic behavior of the U.S. economy.

When you were younger, you probably received an allowance that was the same amount every week. As you get older, you're likely to be paid by the job. In other words, you can make more money by taking on more jobs, such as babysitting, mowing lawns, and washing cars. When you charge $5 to wash a car and you wash 1 car in 2 hours, your hourly earnings are fairly low. When you wash 4 cars in 2 hours, your pay rate increases. Of course, you still have to do a good job. If the quality of your work suffers as you get faster, you will lose customers and your earnings will decrease.

Historians and economists recognize that economic growth is based on economic performance indicators, such as the rate of production, distribution, and use of goods and services. Through their analysis of the use of goods and services, historians and economists determine whether production and distribution are operating with little waste or at a savings.

Read this passage from your textbook on the impact of the assembly line on the production and the price of Model Ts.

In 1908, the Model Ts first year, it sold for $850. In 1914 mass production reduced the price to $490. Three years later, improved assembly-line methods and a high volume of sales brought the price down to $360. By 1924 Model Ts were selling for $295, and Ford sold millions of them. (pages 450–451)

Why do you think the Model T got cheaper as time went on? Do you think that the amount of cars sold increased or decreased over this period of time? What do you think the impact of mass production is on an industry? What new industries or products needed to be created as a result of the availability of cars for the average American? How has mass production influenced the economy of the United States?

Apply the Skill

As you read the text under "The Rise of New Industries" and "The Consumer Society" on pages 450–454, ask yourself questions similar to the ones above about new industries. Consider the impact new industries and technological changes had on other industries and the U.S. economy.

443

Historical Analysis

Why It's Important
Historians use a variety of economic indicators, such as the rate of production, distribution, and the use of goods and services to detect patterns of economic behavior.

1. Introducing the Skill
Have students read the text under the heading "The Airline Industry" on pages 452–453. Have them list the milestone events discussed. Ask the class to analyze the economic impact of each event in a chart similar to the one below. **AL** **CA HI1; HI6**

Event	economic impact
1919: Transcontinental mail service	
1925: Kelly Act	
1926: Air Commerce Act	
1928: Airlines offer business flights	

2. Extending the Skill
Have students investigate mass production factories in their community or within the state. Using the Internet or library resources, have them determine the productivity of a factory and its impact on the local economy. **OL** **CA HI1; HI6**

UNIVERSAL ACCESS

Visual/Spatial Invite students to create charts or graphs that present the information and data they acquired while conducting the research for the Extending the Skill activity. These charts or graphs should be shared with the rest of the class. Allow time for students to explain their materials and for the other students to ask questions. Display the finished visual aids in the classroom while studying this chapter. **OL**

FOCUS

SKILLBUILDER ACTIVITY

 Project **Daily Focus Skills Transparency 8-1** and have students answer the question.

Guide to Reading

Understanding Vocabulary:
Have students list the academic vocabulary terms on a note-taking page. As they read, ask students to write the term's definition as they encounter it.

Answers to Graphic:
Presidential Politics
I. The Harding Administration
   A. A Self-Doubter in the White House
   B. The Ohio Gang
Students should complete the outline by including all heads in the section.

Unpacking the Standards

Students will be able to:

• Explain the domestic political scandals that occurred during the Harding administration.

• Discuss how Calvin Coolidge worked to restore integrity in the White House.

Answers and Additional Support

SECTION 1 Presidential Politics

Guide to Reading

Connection
In the previous chapter, you learned about the social and cultural changes that occurred during the 1920s. In this section, you will discover how President Coolidge focused the country on business and personal virtue after the scandals of the Harding Administration.

Main Idea
• After appointing several friends to positions in the government, President Harding endured a presidency plagued by scandal. (p. 445)
• Calvin Coolidge steered the country toward an emphasis on business and personal virtue. (p. 447)

Content Vocabulary
normalcy, immunity

Academic Vocabulary
presume, integrity, percent

People and Terms to Identify
Ohio Gang, Albert B. Fall, Teapot Dome scandal, Progressive Party, Robert M. La Follette

Reading Objectives
• **Describe** the corruption that tainted the Harding administration.
• **Explain** how Calvin Coolidge restored public confidence after assuming the presidency.

Reading Strategy
Taking Notes As you read about Presidents Harding and Coolidge, use the major headings of the section to create an outline similar to the one below.

Presidential Politics
I. The Harding Administration
   A.
   B.
II.
   A.
   B.

Preview of Events

◆1920	◆1922	◆1924	◆1926

1920 — Women vote in national election for the first time; Warren G. Harding elected president

1923 — Teapot Dome scandal; Harding dies; Calvin Coolidge becomes president

1924 — Coolidge elected president in his own right

The following are the main History–Social Science Standards covered in this section.

11.2 Students analyze the relationship among the rise of industrialization, large-scale rural-to-urban migration, and massive immigration from Southern and Eastern Europe.

11.2.9 Understand the effect of political programs and activities of the Progressives (e.g., federal regulation of railroad transport, Children's Bureau, the Sixteenth Amendment, Theodore Roosevelt, Hiram Johnson).

11.5 Students analyze the major political, social, economic, technological, and cultural developments of the 1920s.

11.5.1 Discuss the policies of Presidents Warren Harding, Calvin Coolidge, and Herbert Hoover.

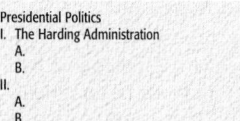

❧ The Big Idea ❧

Societies change over time. While in office, President Harding appointed many friends to government positions. This led to several scandals and accusations of corruption. Following Harding's death, Calvin Coolidge became president and worked to restore integrity to the presidency. Coolidge continued the nation's expanding prosperity and put a strong focus on business. With Democrats divided over a candidate, President Coolidge easily won the 1924 election.

SECTION RESOURCES

📂 **Print Material**
• Reproducible Lesson Plan 8-1
• Guided Reading Activity 8-1
• Reading Essentials and Study Guide 8-1
• Active Reading Note-Taking Guide 8-1

📄 **Transparencies**
• Daily Focus Skills Transparency 8-1
• Section Graphic Organizer Transparency 8-1

Technology
🖲 Interactive Tutor Self-Assessment CD-ROM
🖲 Exam*View*® Pro Testmaker CD-ROM
🖲 Presentation Plus! CD-ROM

The Harding Administration

Main Idea After appointing several friends to positions in the government, President Harding endured a presidency plagued by scandal.

Reading Connection If you were captain of a team and had to choose between your friend or a better player for a teammate, whom would you choose? Read on to learn about the difficulties Warren G. Harding faced as a result of poor choices for his government appointments.

The oldest of eight children, Warren G. Harding was born in 1865 in Corsica, Ohio. As an adult, he was active in civic and fraternal organizations, and he also published the *Marion Daily Star*. In 1898 Harding was elected to the Ohio legislature. He fit in comfortably with the powerful Ohio Republican political machine and won election as lieutenant governor in 1903. He failed in his bid for governor in 1910 but was elected to the United States Senate four years later. After serving one term in the Senate, Harding ran for and won the presidency with Calvin Coolidge as vice president in 1920.

★ An American Story ★

In August 1923, Vice President Calvin Coolidge was taking a short vacation at his family's homestead in Plymouth Notch, Vermont. The straitlaced Coolidge went to bed at 9:00 as usual on August 2, but at 2:30 A.M., his father woke him. "I noticed that his voice trembled," Coolidge said later. "I knew that something of the gravest nature had occurred." After learning that President Warren G. Harding was dead, Coolidge dressed hurriedly and went downstairs. Shortly afterward, in a small, sparsely furnished room lit by a flickering kerosene lamp, the elder Coolidge, a farmer and justice of the peace, got out the family Bible and administered the presidential oath of office to his son. Later, while painting a portrait of the new president, artist Charles Hopkinson asked, "Mr. Coolidge, what was the first thought that came into your mind when you were told that Mr. Harding was dead and the presidency was yours?" Coolidge replied, "I thought I could swing it."

—adapted from *Flappers, Bootleggers, "Typhoid Mary" and the Bomb*

Calvin Coolidge assumed the presidency during a time when Americans yearned to go back to simpler and steadier times after the carnage of World War I. Coolidge's predecessor, Warren G. Harding, had tailored his presidency to this goal.

A Self-Doubter in the White House With his silver hair and impressive bearing, Harding looked like a president, but he thought he lacked the intellectual qualifications for the job. "I have such a sure understanding of my own inefficiency," he once said, "that I should really be ashamed to **presume** myself fitted to reach out for a place of such responsibility."

Despite such doubts, Harding's political philosophy fit in well with the times. He ran on the campaign slogan to return to **normalcy,** or a return to "normal" life after the war. Harding's charm and genial manner endeared him to the nation. The quiet gloom of President Wilson's last years was replaced by the open, easygoing atmosphere of the first days of the Harding administration. On the day of his election, he went out to play a round of golf—a confident, relaxed gesture.

The Ohio Gang Harding made several distinguished appointments to the cabinet, including former Supreme Court justice Charles Evans Hughes as secretary of state, former Food Administrator Herbert Hoover as secretary of commerce, and business tycoon Andrew Mellon as secretary of the treasury.

Many of Harding's other appointments, however, were disastrous. He gave many cabinet posts and other high-level jobs to friends and political allies from Ohio. Harding named Charles "Doc" Sawyer from Marion, Ohio, as White House physician, a post that came with the rank of brigadier general.

▼ *Calvin Coolidge (right) being sworn in as president after his 1924 election*

CHAPTER 8 Normalcy and Good Times **445**

TEACH

S Skill Practice

Chronological Thinking
As students read the first paragraph of the section, have them create a time line or flowchart showing Harding's path to the White House. **OL** **CA CS2**

R Reading Strategy

Scaffolding—Connecting Ask students to read the text entitled "A Self-Doubter in the White House." Tell students to think about a time when they faced a challenge or responsibility that they were not sure they were ready for, such as the time they took a driver's test or tried out for a team. **Ask:** What helped you move forward? (*Students' answers will vary.*) **BL**

This **Reading Skill** was introduced in Chapter 7.

C Critical Thinking

Making Generalizations After students read the lesson on the Ohio Gang, challenge them to make generalizations about Harding's judgments. Then have them work together in small groups to list qualities that appointees to political office should have. **OL**

Did You Know?

Florence Harding had been the circulation manager of the Ohio newspaper her husband owned, making it profitable enough to finance her husband's political career. She was the first president's wife to hold press conferences for women reporters and to fly in an airplane. Harding spoke out for the rights of women in employment, politics, schools, and sports.

S Skill Practice

**Scaffolding—Evaluating Past
Events** At the time of Harding's
death, some people believed that
Mrs. Harding poisoned her husband to spare him the humiliation of the breaking scandals and
possible impeachment. Some
thought that her refusal to allow
an autopsy proved she was guilty.
Encourage interested students to
investigate the events surrounding Harding's death and to evaluate the evidence they find. Allow
time for students to share their
findings with the class. **AL**
CA HR4

This **Historical Analysis** skill was
introduced in Chapter 4.

R Reading Strategy

Connecting The Harding administration has been remembered
by historians for its several political scandals. **Ask: In what other
presidential administrations
have there been presidential
scandals?** *(Students may mention the Nixon administration or
the Clinton administration.)* **What
were the scandals surrounding
these examples?** *(Nixon:
Watergate; Clinton: Monica
Lewinsky)* **OL** **CA HI1**

✓ Reading Check

Answer: Americans yearned
for simpler times after World
War I.

© N. Y. "Tribune."

🎩 Analyzing *Political Cartoons*

Teapot Dome Scandal In this cartoon, Democrats are enjoying the
troubles the Teapot Dome scandal has caused for the GOP elephant.
Who is shown being dragged along by the scandal? Why?

Harding made his boyhood friend Daniel Crissinger
chairman of the Federal Reserve Board and selected
Colonel Charles R. Forbes—another Ohio acquain-
tance—to head the Veterans Bureau. Harding felt
more comfortable among his old poker-playing
friends, known as the **Ohio Gang,** than he did
around such sober and serious people as Herbert
Hoover. Alice Roosevelt Longworth, the daughter of
Theodore Roosevelt, was a keen observer of
Washington society. She wrote that it was common to
find the Ohio Gang in the White House study, and
here she describes a typical scene:

    ❝The air [would be] heavy with tobacco smoke,
trays with bottles containing every imaginable brand
of whiskey . . . cards and poker chips at hand—a
general atmosphere of waistcoat unbuttoned, feet
on desk, and spittoons alongside.❞

    —quoted in *The Perils of Prosperity, 1914–1932*

446 CHAPTER 8 Normalcy and Good Times

The Ohio Gang did more than drink, smoke, and
play poker with the president. Some members used
their positions to sell government jobs, pardons from
criminal convictions, and protection from prosecution. Forbes sold scarce medical supplies from veterans hospitals and kept the money for himself, costing
the taxpayers over $200 million. When Harding
learned what was going on, he complained privately
that he had been betrayed. He said that he had no
troubles with his enemies, but his friends were a different story: "They're the ones that keep me walking
the floor nights!"

In June 1923, amid the scandal in the Veterans
Bureau and rumors of other unethical behavior,
Harding and the First Lady left to tour the West. En
route from Alaska to California, he became ill with
what was probably a heart attack. He died in San
Francisco on August 2, shortly before the news of the
Forbes scandal broke.

The Teapot Dome Scandal Other scandals also
came to light. Harding's secretary of the interior,
Albert B. Fall, secretly allowed private interests to
lease lands containing U.S. Navy oil reserves at
Teapot Dome, Wyoming, and Elk Hills, California. In
return, Fall received bribes from these private interests totaling more than $300,000. Eventually the
Senate investigated what the newspapers named the
Teapot Dome scandal, and Secretary Fall became the
first cabinet officer in history to go to prison.

The last Harding administration scandal involved
Attorney General Harry Daugherty, Harding's former campaign manager. It concerned a German
owned American company that the American government had seized during World War I as enemy
property. To acquire the company and its valuable
chemical patents, a German agent bribed a
"go-between" politician, and a portion of the
bribe ended up in an Ohio bank account that
Daugherty controlled.

Under investigation by his own Justice
Department, Daugherty refused to turn over
requested files and bank records. He also refused to
testify under oath, claiming **immunity,** or freedom
from prosecution, on the grounds that he had had
confidential dealings with the president. Daugherty's
actions disgusted the new president, Calvin
Coolidge, who demanded his resignation. The tattered reputation of Harding's presidency dissolved
in scandal and corruption.

✓ Reading Check **Describing** Why was Harding's
emphasis on "normalcy" an effective campaign strategy?

🎩 Analyzing *Political Cartoons*

Answer: Secretary of the Interior Albert Fall;
because he was involved in the Teapot Dome
scandal
**Ask: What do you think might have happened
to Harding had he not died in 1923?** *(Students
might mention that he probably would not have
been reelected.)*

The Coolidge Administration

Main Idea Calvin Coolidge steered the country toward an emphasis on business and personal virtue.

Reading Connection Do you think Coolidge's motto, "The chief business of the American people is business," is appropriate for today? Why or why not? Read on to discover how Coolidge's administration handled the issues of the time.

Just as Harding's promise of "normalcy" had appealed to war-weary voters in 1920, the virtue of his successor came as a welcome change from the turmoil of the Harding administration's corruption. Born on July 4, 1872, John Calvin Coolidge grew up on the Vermont farm that his family had worked for five generations. While governor of Massachusetts, Coolidge rose to national prominence for his handling of the Boston police strike in 1919. Shortly afterward, he was asked to run as Harding's vice president.

"Silent Cal" Takes Over Coolidge was very different from Harding. Harding had enjoyed the easy conversation and company of old friends. Coolidge, joked a critic, could be "silent in five languages." With his simple and frugal manner, he contrasted not only with Harding but also with the spirit of the time, the booming, materialistic era of the Roaring Twenties.

Coolidge quickly distanced himself from the Harding administration. He named Harlan Fiske Stone, dean of the Columbia Law School, to replace Daugherty as attorney general. He also asked the most capable cabinet members—Hughes, Mellon, and Hoover—to stay on.

Coolidge's philosophy of government was simple. He believed that prosperity rested on business leadership and that part of his job as president was to make sure that government interfered with business and industry as little as possible. He once said, "Four-fifths of all our troubles in this life would disappear if we would only sit down and keep still."

Calmly and cautiously, Coolidge worked to restore **integrity** to the presidency. Coolidge's presidency avoided crises and continued the nation's expanding prosperity. Coolidge easily won the Republican Party's nomination for president in 1924.

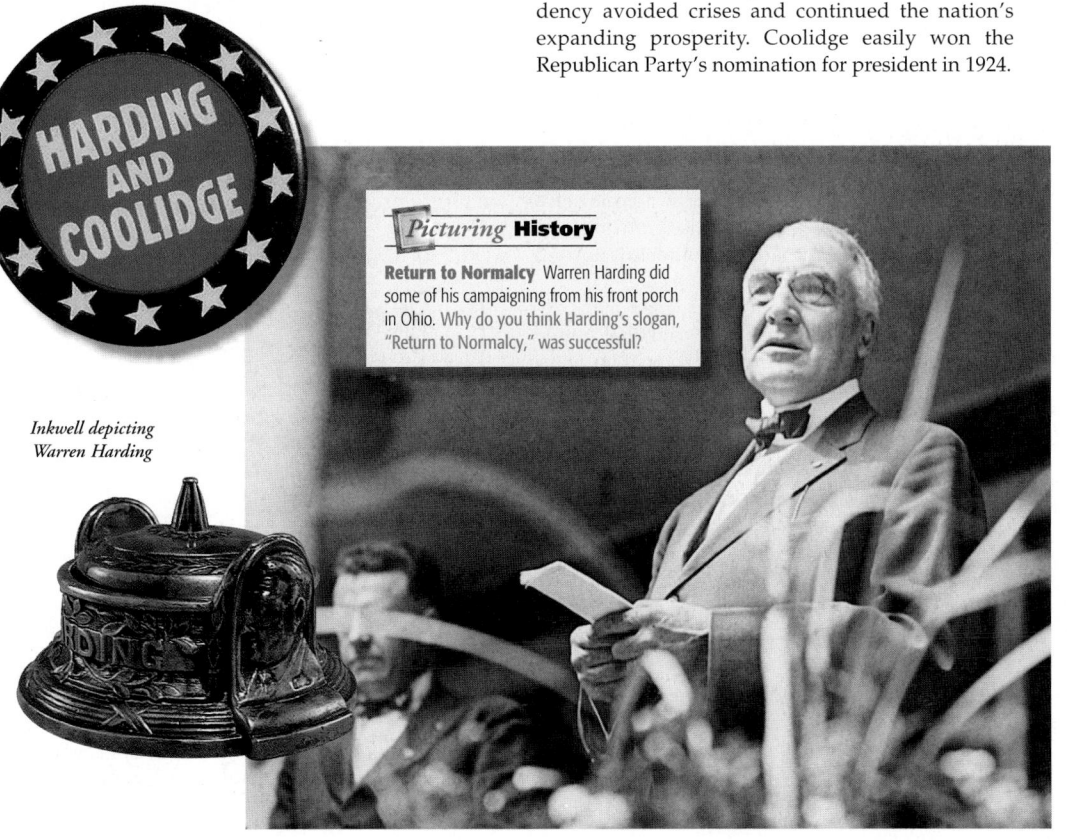

Inkwell depicting Warren Harding

Picturing History

Return to Normalcy Warren Harding did some of his campaigning from his front porch in Ohio. Why do you think Harding's slogan, "Return to Normalcy," was successful?

CHAPTER 8 Normalcy and Good Times **447**

Picturing History

Answer: Many people wanted a less activist government after the war.
Ask: What characteristics made Harding look presidential? *(handsome, silver hair, impressive bearing)*

C Critical Thinking

Comparing and Contrasting Ask students to make a brief table that lists the characteristics of both Warren Harding and Calvin Coolidge. Suggest that students consider the following categories, but encourage them to add more of their own: *home state, personality, age, political style,* and *presidential goals.* **Ask:** Are there more similarities or more differences between these two men? If students can find only similarities or only differences, encourage them to consider different categories to add to their table. **OL**

W Writing Support

Letter Writing Tell students to imagine that a presidential candidate living today used these words from Calvin Coolidge to describe his views of proper presidential actions: "Four-fifths of all our troubles in this life would disappear if we would only sit down and keep still." **Ask:** Do you think this political philosophy can work in our times? Tell students to write a letter to the editor of a national news publication in support of, or against, this philosophy. *(Students' letters should clearly state their reaction toward this quote and why they support or disagree with this political philosophy.)* **AL** **CA 11WS1.3**

Review the Big Idea

Review the Big Idea for this section, "Societies change over time." Tell the class to discuss the differences between Presidents Harding and Coolidge. **Ask:** Which president do you think would be best suited to lead the country today? *(Answers will vary. Some students may believe neither man is suitable.)* **BL**

ASSESS

Resources for page 448

Use these resources to assess student mastery.

📁 Section Quiz 8-1

📁 Reading Essentials and Study Guide 8-1

💿 Interactive Tutor Self-Assessment CD-ROM

📁 California Standards Practice, Grade 11

Picturing History

Answer: positively; awarded him more than half of the popular vote

---

Reading Check

Answer: He distanced himself from the Harding administration.

HISTORY Online

Study Central provides audio summaries, interactive games, and online graphic organizers to help students review section content.

CLOSE

Summarizing Have students explain how Calvin Coolidge restored public confidence after assuming the presidency. **OL**

Picturing History

Cool Coolidge President Coolidge believed the nation would run more smoothly if the government was less involved. How did the public react to Coolidge's message on Election Day?

The Election of 1924 Even though the scandals of the Harding administration presented the Democrats with a ready-made issue, they lost the chance for victory. Deeply divided between their urban Eastern constituency and their rural following in the South and West, the Democrats had difficulty agreeing on a nominee. They finally compromised on John W. Davis of West Virginia after 103 attempts to find someone acceptable to a majority of the delegates.

The Republicans effectively campaigned on the slogan "Keep Cool with Coolidge," and they urged Americans to retain the party that favored business.

In his economic policies, Coolidge aligned himself—and the government—with prosperity and big business. Not everyone was content to choose between the Republicans and Democrats. Defectors from both parties joined farm, labor, and religious activists to form the new **Progressive Party,** nominating Wisconsin senator **Robert M. La Follette** as their candidate. Although La Follette captured 16.6 **percent** of the popular vote, or a total of almost 5 million, he and Davis combined could not keep the Republicans from winning the election. Coolidge won easily with more than half the popular vote and 382 electoral votes.

In a speech to the American Society of Newspaper Editors in 1925, Coolidge said, "The chief business of the American people is business. The man who builds a factory builds a temple. The man who works there worships there." The *Wall Street Journal* joyously exclaimed, "Never before, here or anywhere else, has a government been so completely fused with business." By avoiding war, reform, and scandal, Coolidge promised to give the United States the normalcy Harding had failed to deliver.

✓ **Reading Check** **Summarizing** How did Calvin Coolidge restore public confidence after becoming president?

HISTORY Online — Study Central

For help with the concepts in this section of *American Vision: Modern Times* go to tav.mt.glencoe.com and click on *Study Central.*

SECTION 1 ASSESSMENT

Checking for Understanding

1. **Vocabulary** Define: presume, normalcy, immunity, integrity, percent.
2. **People and Terms** Identify: Ohio Gang, Albert B. Fall, Teapot Dome scandal, Robert M. La Follette.
3. **Evaluate** the effects of the Teapot Dome scandal on citizens' views of the federal government.

Reviewing Big Ideas

4. **Explaining** How did the Ohio Gang tarnish the Harding Administration?

Critical Thinking

5. **Interpreting** How did the Democrats lose the chance for victory in the election of 1924?
6. **Categorizing** Use a graphic organizer similar to the one below to compare and contrast the politics and presidencies of Harding and Coolidge.

	Politics	Presidency
Harding		
Coolidge		

Analyzing Visuals

7. **Analyzing Photographs** Examine the photograph of Calvin Coolidge on this page. How did Coolidge's actions demonstrate effective leadership following the Harding administration?

Writing About History

8. **Expository Writing** Imagine you are a newspaper reporter during President Harding's term. Write an article breaking the news of the Teapot Dome scandal. **CA** 11WA2.4a

448 CHAPTER 8 Normalcy and Good Times

SECTION 1 ASSESSMENT ANSWERS

1. Content vocabulary is boldfaced and highlighted in yellow. Academic vocabulary is boldfaced.
2. Ohio Gang (*p. 446*), Albert B. Fall (*p. 446*), Teapot Dome scandal (*p. 446*), Robert M. La Follette (*p. 448*)
3. Citizens began to view the government as corrupt.

4. used their positions for personal advantage
5. could not agree on a nominee
6. Harding: open politics, scandal-ridden presidency; Coolidge: simple politics, business-oriented presidency
7. avoided scandal, supported business prosperity

8. Students' articles will vary. Articles' style should be similar to a news story with an attention-grabbing lead.

SECTION 2 A Growing Economy

Guide to Reading

Connection
In the previous section, you learned about the Harding and Coolidge administrations. In this section, you will read about the economic growth and prosperity the country experienced during the 1920s.

Main Idea
- Mass production and the assembly line allowed new industries, such as automobile and airplane manufacturing, to grow. (p. 450)
- Easily available credit and advertising combined to create a nation of consumers eager for new goods. (p. 453)
- Increases in productivity and decreases in foreign markets led to lower prices for farmers. (p. 455)

Content Vocabulary
mass production, assembly line, welfare capitalism, open shop

Academic Vocabulary
innovation, consumer, structure

People and Terms to Identify
Model T, Charles Lindbergh, National Broadcasting Company, Columbia Broadcasting System

Reading Objectives
- **Analyze** how the growing importance of the automobile and other new industries improved the U.S. standard of living.
- **Analyze** the growing economic crisis in farming in the 1920s.

Reading Strategy
Organizing As you read about the booming era of the 1920s, complete a graphic organizer to analyze the causes of economic growth and prosperity in the 1920s.

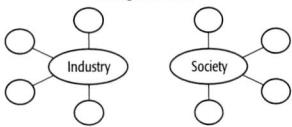

Changes in 1920s

Industry   Society

Preview of Events

◆1920	◆1923	◆1926	◆1929

1920
First commercial radio broadcast

1922
Congress passes Fordney-McCumber Act

1923
Ford gains 50 percent of the new car market

1927
The 15 millionth Ford Model T rolls off the assembly line

1929
U.S. radio sales exceed $800 million

The following are the main History–Social Science Standards covered in this section.

11.2.1 Know the effects of industrialization on living and working conditions, including the portrayal of working conditions and food safety in Upton Sinclair's The Jungle.

11.4.5 Analyze the political, economic and social ramifications of World War I on the home front.

11.5.1 Discuss the policies of Presidents Warren Harding, Calvin Coolidge, and Herbert Hoover.

11.5.4 Analyze the passage of the Nineteenth Amendment and the changing role of women in society.

11.5.6 Trace the growth and effects of radio and movies and their role in the worldwide diffusion of popular culture.

11.5.7 Discuss the rise of mass production techniques, the growth of cities, the impact of new technologies (e.g., the automobile, electricity), and

∾ The Big Idea ∾

Societies change over time. During the 1920s, mass production and the assembly line revolutionized industry and society. Wages increased and work hours decreased, providing people with more time and more money to spend on new consumer goods. The growing automobile industry gave rise to new businesses and eased the isolation of rural populations. The airline and radio industries also expanded. Advertising became an important tool for selling goods, and more people began to purchase items on credit. While many people benefited from the prosperous economy, farmers suffered from falling agricultural prices when technological advances increased yields.

the resulting prosperity and effect on the American landscape.

CHAPTER 8   Normalcy and Good Times   **449**

SECTION RESOURCES

📁 Print Material
- Reproducible Lesson Plan 8-2
- Guided Reading Activity 8-2
- Reading Essentials and Study Guide 8-2
- Active Reading Note-Taking Guide 8-2

📊 Transparencies
- Daily Focus Skills Transparency 8-2
- Section Graphic Organizer Transparency 8-2

Technology
- ⓘ Interactive Tutor Self-Assessment CD-ROM
- ⓘ ExamView® Pro Testmaker CD-ROM
- ⓘ Presentation Plus! CD-ROM

FOCUS

BELLRINGER
SKILLBUILDER ACTIVITY

Project **Daily Focus Skills Transparency 8-2** and have students answer the question.

Guide to Reading

Understanding Vocabulary: Have students look through the section to identify the content vocabulary and academic vocabulary words and use each in a sentence.

Answers to Graphic: Industry: air travel, automobiles, consumer goods, radio; Society: consumer-oriented, consumer credit, workers shifting from farming to industry, labor-saving devices, growing mobility

Unpacking the Standards

Students will be able to:
- Analyze the effects of mass production on living and working conditions.
- Describe the growth and effects of radio and movies and their role in the worldwide diffusion of popular culture and the growth of a consumer society in this country.
- Discuss how the weak agricultural market contrasted with the otherwise prosperous appearance of the 1920s.

TEACH

C Critical Thinking

Making Generalizations Write the following sentence on the board: "The business technology of the 1920s created an era of prosperity." Have students find three facts in the section to support the generalization. Write their answers on the board as students state them. Then have students make a generalization about new industries and find three facts that support their generalization. **OL**

U Universal Access

English Learners Students who are beginning to learn English may have difficulty with multiple meanings and parts of speech for new words. For example, *mass, production, assembly,* and *line* can all be used as either verbs or nouns, depending on the context. Encourage students to make vocabulary index cards that include all possible meanings. Or, have students divide an index card into fourths. In one section of the card, students should write the word. In another section, students should write the definition of the word. In a third section, students should write an antonym for the word. In the final section, students can draw simple illustrations that will help them remember the word. **EL**

Answers and Additional Support

The Rise of New Industries

Main Idea Mass production and the assembly line allowed new industries, such as automobile and airplane manufacturing, to grow.

C Reading Connection How would businesses, governments, and your family be affected if airline travel did not exist? Read on to learn how the transportation industry changed during the 1920s and 1930s.

The technological innovations of the late 1800s continued to show their effects into the next century. None of them, though, had a greater impact than the automobile.

★ An American Story ★

At around 2:00 A.M. on June 4, 1896, Henry Ford and his friend Jim Bishop readied Ford's "horseless carriage" for a test. The shop doors were too small for the contraption to pass through, so Ford immediately seized a sledgehammer and began knocking out an opening in the brick. Ford later recalled the scene that followed:

❝Mr. Bishop had his bicycle ready to ride ahead and warn drivers of horse-drawn vehicles—if indeed any were to be met with at such an hour. . . . I set the choke and spun the flywheel. As the motor roared and sputtered to life, I climbed aboard and started off. . . .❞

There were many such trips in the following days. Bishop would bicycle ahead, stopping at saloons and stores to warn people that they should come out and hold their horses. Many of the onlookers responded by calling out, "Crazy Henry!" As he climbed out of the car, Ford invariably responded, "Yes, crazy. Crazy like a fox."

—adapted from *The Fords: An American Epic*

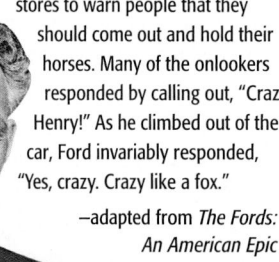

◀ *Henry Ford*

Although neither Henry Ford nor Jim Bishop realized it at the time, "Crazy Henry's" horseless carriage would revolutionize American transportation and with it American society. By the 1920s, the automobile had become an accepted part of American life. In a 1925 survey conducted in Muncie, Indiana, 21 out of 26 families who owned cars did not have bathtubs with running water. Explaining why her family decided a car was more important than indoor plumbing, a farm wife said, "You can't ride to town in a bathtub."

The automobile was just one part of a rising standard of living that Americans experienced in the 1920s. Real per capita earnings, essentially unchanged during the previous 30 years, soared 22 percent. Meanwhile, as Americans' wages increased, their work hours decreased. In 1923 U.S. Steel cut its daily work shift from 12 hours to 8 hours. In 1926 Henry Ford cut the workweek for his employees from six days to five, and International Harvester, a maker of trucks, tractors, and other farm machinery, instituted an annual two-week paid vacation for employees.

U At the same time, the rise of **mass production,** or large-scale product manufacturing usually done by machinery, created more supply and reduced consumer costs. This formula reshaped the American economy. Within this prosperous and productive atmosphere, **innovation** thrived and new industries emerged.

The Assembly Line Another major industrial development enormously increased manufacturing efficiency. First adopted by carmaker Henry Ford, the **assembly line** divided operations into simple tasks that unskilled workers could do and cut unnecessary motion to a minimum. In 1913 Ford installed the first moving assembly line at his plant in Highland Park, Michigan. By the following year, workers were building automobiles every 93 minutes. Previously, the task had taken 12 hours. By 1925 a Ford car was rolling off the line every 10 seconds. "The way to make automobiles," Ford said, "is to make one automobile like another . . . to make them come through the factory all alike, just as one pin is like another pin when it comes from the pin factory."

Ford's assembly-line product was the **Model T**—affectionately called the "Tin Lizzie" or "Flivver." In 1908, the Model T's first year, it sold for $850. In 1914 mass production reduced the price to $490. Three years later, improved assembly-line methods and a high volume of sales brought the price down to $360. By 1924 Model Ts were selling for $295, and Ford sold

---

Did You Know?

Henry Ford adapted ideas and relied on the encouragement of others. His assembly line was possible because of Eli Whitney's concept of interchangeable parts. As a young man, Ford worked for Thomas Edison's company. Edison told Ford to persist in his idea for a car that ran on liquid fuel, rather than by electric or steam power.

millions of them. His business philosophy was simple: lower the cost per car and thereby increase the volume of sales. "Every time I reduce the charge for our car by one dollar," he boasted, "I get a thousand new buyers." In this way, Ford made the automobile available to millions of American **consumers.**

Ford also increased his workers' wages in 1914 to an unprecedented $5 a day and reduced the workday to eight-hour shifts. Ford took these dramatic steps to build up workers' loyalty and to undercut union organizers.

There were strings attached, however, to the wage increase. Ford created a "Sociological Department," which set requirements workers had to meet. For instance, the common practice of renting living space to nonfamily members was strictly forbidden. Investigators visited employees' homes to verify their eligibility and to see that they spent their wages in approved ways. Workers who transgressed could be disqualified from extra pay, suspended, or even fired.

The low prices made possible by Ford's mass-production methods not only created an immense market for his cars but also spawned imitators. By the mid-1920s, other car manufacturers, notably General Motors and Chrysler, competed successfully with Ford.

The auto industry spurred growth in other industries, such as rubber, plate glass, nickel, and lead. Automaking alone consumed 15 percent of the nation's steel, and the flood of cars stimulated a tremendous expansion of the petroleum industry.

The Social Impact of the Automobile Henry Ford was the force behind a social revolution related to the automobile. He almost single-handedly changed the auto from a toy of the wealthy to an affordable necessity for the middle class.

Cars revolutionized American life. Although many small businesses declined during the 1920s, the automobile created new small-business opportunities for such enterprises as garages and gas stations.

The automobile eased the isolation of rural life, putting towns within reach of many farmers and the countryside a mere ride away for city dwellers. Cars also enabled more people to live farther from work. An entirely new kind of consumer and worker, the auto commuter, appeared. Commuters lived in growing suburban communities and drove to work in the city.

TECHNOLOGY & History

The Assembly Line

The idea of an assembly line had existed before Henry Ford, but he helped popularize its use in manufacturing. Ford combined sub-assembly lines into one continuously moving line, which was positioned at waist level to reduce back strain. Ford's Highland Park factory featured a multistoried assembly line that reduced the construction time of a single Model T from 12 hours, 8 minutes to 1 hour, 33 minutes. *How did Ford's assembly technique affect the price of his product?*

1 Tires were assembled and delivered downstairs using chutes.

2 Engines and gas tanks were assembled at other ends of the factory floor and delivered to the chassis sub-assembly.

3 Automobile were assembled and dropped onto the separately-assembled chassis with a pully.

In 1914 Ford Motor Company produced 308,162 automobiles—more than all other auto manufacturers combined.

CHAPTER 8 Normalcy and Good Times **451**

451

Profiles IN HISTORY

Bessie Coleman
c. 1892–1926

Bessie Coleman was the first African American woman to receive a pilot's license and the first to become a stunt pilot. She performed in her first air show in September 1922 in Garden City, Long Island.

Coleman was born in Atlanta, Texas, to an African American mother and a Choctaw father. Too poor to attend college for more than one term, she moved to Chicago to become a pilot. No flight school she applied to, however, was willing to admit an African American. With the help of a Chicago publisher, Coleman then went to France to train. Back home, she championed the African American cause through her public statements and impressive flying feats.

Coleman's achievements inspired the founding of Chicago's Coffey School of Aeronautics. Its graduates helped train the U.S. military's first African American pilots, the Tuskegee Airmen, who served with distinction in World War II.

Amelia Earhart
1897–1937

Amelia Earhart, perhaps the world's most celebrated woman pilot, saw her first airplane at the Iowa State Fair when she was 10 years old. She was unimpressed: "It was a thing of rusty wire and wood and not at all interesting. . . ." In her early 20s, however, she attended a California "aerial meet," a fateful decision.

Known for promoting women's flying, Earhart seemed destined for celebrity from early on. By 1932 she was flying solo across the Atlantic.

Earhart's most daring flight was her last. In 1937 she set out to fly around the world with her navigator. Two-thirds of the trip was covered when their plane disappeared. On the trip, she had written her husband, "Please know I am quite aware of the hazards. . . . I want to do it because I want to do it. Women must try to do things as men have tried."

The Consumer Goods Industry

Many other new goods came on the market to take advantage of rising disposable income. Americans bought such innovations as electric razors, disposable facial tissues, frozen foods, and home hair dye.

Many of the new products were created for the home. As indoor plumbing became more common, Americans' concern for hygiene spawned the development of numerous household cleaning products. By appealing to people's health concerns, advertisers were able to convince homemakers to buy cleansers to protect their families from disease.

New appliances advertised as labor-savers changed the home. Electric irons, vacuum cleaners, washing machines, refrigerators, gas stoves, and improved glass cookware changed the way people cleaned their homes and prepared meals.

Another lucrative category of consumer products focused on Americans' concerns with fashion, youthful appearance, and success in personal and business endeavors. Mouthwash, deodorants, cosmetics, and perfumes became popular products in the 1920s.

The Airline Industry

After the successful flight of the Wright brothers at Kitty Hawk in 1903, the aviation industry began to develop rapidly. Leading the way was American inventor Glenn Curtiss. Curtiss owned a motorcycle company in Hammondsport, New York. Fascinated by airplanes, he agreed in 1907 to become director of experiments at the Aerial Experiment Association, an organization founded by Alexander Graham Bell.

Within a year, Curtiss had invented ailerons—surfaces attached to wings that can be tilted to steer the plane. Ailerons made it possible to build rigid wings and much larger aircraft. They are still used on aircraft today. In 1912 Curtiss designed the first flying boat. In 1919 one of his flying boats became the first aircraft to cross the Atlantic.

Curtiss's company began building aircraft, and it made the first airplane sales in the United States. The company grew from a single factory to a huge industrial enterprise during World War I, as orders flooded in from allied governments for his biplanes and engines. Although Curtiss retired in 1920, his inventions made possible the airline industry that emerged in the 1920s.

After entrepreneurs such as Curtiss started building practical aircraft, the federal government began to support the airline industry. President Wilson's postmaster general had introduced the world's first regular airmail service in 1918 by hiring pilots to fly

Profiles IN HISTORY

mail between Washington, D.C., and New York. In 1919 the Post Office expanded airmail service across the continent. The aviation industry received an economic boost in 1925 with the passage of the Kelly Act, which authorized postal officials to contract with private airplane operators to carry mail.

In 1926 the aviation industry received another boost with the passage of the Air Commerce Act, which provided federal aid for building airports. It was the extraordinary transatlantic solo flight of former airmail pilot **Charles Lindbergh** in 1927, however, that demonstrated the possibilities of aviation and won popular support for commercial flight. By the end of 1928, 48 commercial airlines were serving 355 American cities.

To increase flying, advertisers praised the benefits of commercial flying for business executives, as in this 1928 ad for the Ford Motor Company's "Trimotor" plane: "When the occasion comes for your first time up, it will not be to 'joy-ride' in an antiquated and hazardous machine; but far more probably it will be to reach some distant meeting-place in advance of business competition!"

The Radio Industry In 1912 Edwin Armstrong, an American engineer, invented a special circuit that made long-range radio transmission of voice and music practical. The radio industry began a few years later. In November 1920, the Westinghouse Company broadcast the news of Harding's landslide election victory from station KDKA in Pittsburgh—one of the first public broadcasts in history. That success persuaded Westinghouse to open other stations. In 1926 the **National Broadcasting Company** (NBC) established a permanent network of stations to distribute daily programs. By 1927 almost 700 stations dotted the country, and the Federal Radio Commission was established to regulate them. Sales of radio equipment skyrocketed from $12.2 million in 1921 to $842.5 million in 1929, by which time 10 million radio sets were in use in the United States.

In 1928 the **Columbia Broadcasting System (CBS)** assembled a coast-to-coast network of stations to rival NBC. The two networks sold advertising time and hired popular musicians, actors, and comedians from vaudeville, movies, and the nightclub circuit to appear on their shows. In 1928 Americans experienced complete coverage of the first presidential election campaign conducted over the airwaves, when the radio networks sold more than $1 million in advertising time to the Republican and Democratic Parties.

✓ **Reading Check** **Analyzing** How did technological innovations such as the assembly line impact the nature of work?

The Consumer Society

Main Idea Easily available credit and advertising combined to create a nation of consumers eager for new goods.

Reading Connection Have you ever purchased something with credit or bought an item because of advertising? Read on to discover the beginnings of the widespread consumer culture in America.

Higher wages and shorter workdays resulted in a decade-long buying spree that kept the economy booming. Shifting from traditional attitudes of thrift and prudence, Americans in the 1920s enthusiastically accepted their new role as consumers.

Easy Credit A major aspect of the economic boom was the growth of individual borrowing. The prosperity of the 1920s gave many Americans the confidence to go into debt to buy new consumer goods.

Credit had been available before the boom, but most Americans had considered debt to be shameful. Now, however, American attitudes toward debt started changing as people began believing in their ability to pay their debts over time. Many listened to the sales pitch, "Buy now and pay in easy installments," and racked up debts for the family car, radio, furniture, washing machine, and vacuum cleaner. Americans bought 75 percent of their radios and

▲ *Washing machine advertisement*

CHAPTER 8 Normalcy and Good Times **453**

Did You Know?

Born in 1902, Charles Lindbergh grew up in Minnesota. After two years at the University of Wisconsin, he started flying as a stunt pilot. Lindbergh completed flight training to become an Army Air Service Reserve pilot. Later he flew mail between Chicago and St. Louis. An offer of $25,000 to become the first pilot to fly nonstop from New York to Paris inspired Lindbergh's famous flight over the Atlantic Ocean.

60 percent of their automobiles on the installment plan. Some started buying on credit at a faster rate than their incomes increased.

Mass Advertising When inventor Otto Rohwedder developed a commercial bread slicer in 1928, he faced a problem common to new inventions: the bread slicer was a device that made a product—sliced bread—that no one knew they needed. To create consumers for their new products, manufacturers turned to advertising, another booming industry in the 1920s.

Advertisers created appealing, persuasive messages that linked their clients' products with qualities associated with the modern era, such as progress, convenience, leisure, success, fashion, and style. In a 1924 magazine advertisement for deodorant, the headline read, "Flappers they may be—but they know the art of feminine appeal!" An advertisement for a prepared spaghetti product told the busy homemaker that heating is the same as cooking: "Just one thing to do and it's ready to serve." Advertisers also preyed on consumers' fears and anxieties, whether they be jarred nerves due to the hectic pace of modern life or insecurities about one's status or weight.

The Managerial Revolution By the early 1920s, many industries had begun to create modern organizational **structures.** Companies were divided into divisions with different functions, such as sales, marketing, accounting, and operations. To run these divisions, businesses needed to hire managers. Managers freed executives and owners from the day-to-day business of running their companies and allowed them to develop long-range plans and goals.

The managerial revolution in companies created a new career—the professional manager—and companies began to hire large numbers of people with managerial training from business schools. The large numbers of managers helped to expand the size of the middle class, which in turn added to the nation's prosperity. Similarly, so many companies relied on new technology to drive their business that engineers were also in very high demand. They too joined the ranks of the rapidly growing middle class.

Welfare Capitalism Middle-class Americans were not the only members of the new consumer society. Industrial workers also prospered in the 1920s, partly due to rising wages and partly because many corporations introduced what came to be called **welfare capitalism.** Companies allowed workers to buy stock, participate in profit sharing, and receive benefits such as medical care and pensions.

Benefits programs also made unions seem unnecessary to many workers. During the 1920s, unions lost both influence and membership. Employers promoted the **open shop**—a workplace where employees were not required to join a union. With benefits covering some of their basic needs, workers were able to spend more of their income. Many eagerly purchased consumer goods they previously could not afford.

✓**Reading Check** **Analyzing Bias** How did advertisers try to convince Americans to buy their products?

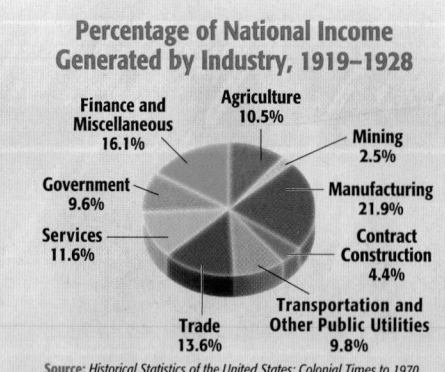

Percentage of National Income Generated by Industry, 1919–1928

Finance and Miscellaneous 16.1%
Agriculture 10.5%
Mining 2.5%
Government 9.6%
Manufacturing 21.9%
Services 11.6%
Contract Construction 4.4%
Trade 13.6%
Transportation and Other Public Utilities 9.8%

Source: *Historical Statistics of the United States: Colonial Times to 1970.*

Farm Wages

Monthly Wages (including room and board)

$55 $50 $45 $40 $35 $30

1920 1922 1924 1926 1928 1930
Year

Source: *Historical Statistics of the United States: Colonial Times to 1970.*

Graph Skills

1. **Interpreting Graphs** How far did farm wages fall between 1920 and 1930?
2. **Understanding Cause and Effect** What caused the decline in wages? Do you think farmers could have done anything to prevent this?

Graph Skills

Answers:
1. about $13 per month
2. higher production rates, increased debt, and a drop in foreign sales

Graph Skills Practice
Ask: **From 1920 to 1930, when were farm wages lowest and highest?** (*lowest in 1922, highest in 1920*)

The Farm Crisis Returns

Main Idea Increases in productivity and decreases in foreign markets led to lower prices for farmers.

Reading Connection How often do you eat fresh vegetables and fruit grown by local farmers or your own family? Read on to find out what President Coolidge thought about subsidizing industries such as farming and manufacturing.

American farmers did not share in the prosperity of the 1920s. As a group, they earned less than one-third of the average income for workers in the rest of the economy. Technological advances in fertilizers, pesticides, seed varieties, and farm machinery allowed them to produce more, but higher yields without a corresponding increase in demand meant that they received lower prices. Between 1920 and 1921, corn prices dropped almost 19 percent, and wheat went from $1.83 a bushel to $1.03. The cost to farmers of the improved technology, meanwhile, continued to increase.

Changing Market Conditions Many factors contributed to this "quiet depression" in American agriculture. During the war, the government had urged farmers to produce more to meet the great need for food supplies in Europe. Many farmers borrowed heavily to buy new land (at inflated prices) and new machinery in order to raise more crops. Sales were strong, prices were high, and farmers prospered. After the war, however, European farm output rose, and the debt-ridden countries of Europe had little to spend on American farm products. Congress had unintention-

ally made matters worse when it passed the Fordney-McCumber Act in 1922. This act raised tariffs dramatically in an effort to protect American industry from foreign competition. By dampening the American market for foreign goods, it provoked a reaction in foreign markets against American agricultural products. Farmers in the United States could no longer sell as much of their output overseas, and prices tumbled.

Helping Farmers Some members of Congress tried to help the farmers. Every year from 1924 to 1928, Senator Charles McNary of Oregon and Representative Gilbert Haugen of Iowa proposed the McNary-Haugen Bill, which called for the federal government to purchase surplus crops and sell them abroad while protecting the American market with a high tariff. They believed their plan would immediately raise the domestic price of crops, aiding farmers as the Fordney-McCumber tariffs helped manufacturers.

Congress passed the bill twice, but President Coolidge vetoed it both times. He argued that with money flowing to farmers under this law, the farmers would be encouraged to produce even greater surplus volumes, which the government would be unable to sell. American farmers remained mired in recession. Their problems would only grow worse when the Great Depression began in 1929.

Reading Check **Synthesizing** What factors led to the growing economic crisis in farming in the 1920s?

Study Central

For help with the concepts in this section of *American Vision: Modern Times* go to tav.mt.glencoe.com and click on *Study Central.*

SECTION 2 ASSESSMENT

Checking for Understanding

1. **Vocabulary** Define: mass production, innovation, assembly line, consumer, structure, welfare capitalism, open shop.

2. **People and Terms** Identify: Model T, Charles Lindbergh, National Broadcasting Company, Columbia Broadcasting System.

3. **Summarize** the factors that led to the new consumer society in the United States during the 1920s.

Reviewing Big Ideas

4. **Describing** How did the automobile impact American society?

Critical Thinking

5. **Analyzing** How did the United States government help spur the growth of the airline industry?

6. **Organizing** Use a graphic organizer similar to the one below to list some of the new industries that grew in importance during the 1920s.

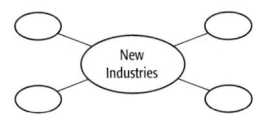
New Industries

Analyzing Visuals

7. **Analyzing Advertisements** Examine the advertisement on page 453. How did the growing consumer culture impact the nation's economy?

Writing About History

8. **Expository Writing** Write an article for a contemporary newspaper analyzing the impact of Charles Lindbergh's transatlantic flight on the development of aviation in the United States and the world. **CA 11WA2.3c**

CHAPTER 8 Normalcy and Good Times **455**

SECTION 2 ASSESSMENT ANSWERS

1. Content vocabulary is boldfaced and highlighted in yellow. Academic vocabulary is boldfaced.

2. Model T *(p. 450)*, Charles Lindbergh *(p. 453)*, National Broadcasting Company *(p. 453)*, Columbia Broadcasting System *(p. 453)*

3. mass production, easy credit, mass advertisement, and economic prosperity

4. eased rural isolation, allowed workers to live farther away from work

5. governmental airmail service and funds for airports

6. airline, automobile, consumer goods, radio

7. raised standard of living, encouraged Americans to buy new goods

8. Students' articles will vary but should contain factual information.

S **Skill Practice**

Chronological Thinking Ask students to create a time line that shows the various economic difficulties and solutions that farmers faced before the 1920s. *(Possible answers include Shays's Rebellion, falling prices after the Civil War ended, or the work of the Grange in the late 1800s.)* **OL**
CA CS1

ASSESS

Resources for page 455

Use these resources to assess student mastery.

📁 Section Quiz 8-2

📁 Reading Essentials and Study Guide 8-2

💿 Interactive Tutor Self-Assessment CD-ROM

📁 California Standards Practice, Grade 11

Reading Check

Answer: a decline in foreign markets and increased productivity

HISTORY Online

Study Central provides audio summaries, interactive games, and online graphic organizers to help students review section content.

CLOSE

Evaluating Divide the class into groups to discuss people's changing attitude toward big business in the 1920s. **OL**

FOCUS

BELLRINGER
SKILLBUILDER ACTIVITY

Project **Daily Focus Skills Transparency 8-3** and have students answer the question.

Guide to Reading

Understanding Vocabulary: Knowing the meaning of suffixes can help students understand unfamiliar terms. Have students look at the vocabulary words to find the suffixes (*-ic, -ive, -ism, -ium*). Encourage them to use a dictionary to find the meaning of these suffixes.

Answers to Graphic: less government regulation of business, tax cuts, refinancing of national debt, reduced government spending

Unpacking the Standards

Students will be able to:
- Explain efforts made to shape the postwar economy.
- Describe the attempts to create diplomatic agreements that would prevent another world-wide war.

Answers and Additional Support

SECTION 3 # The Policies of Prosperity

Guide to Reading

Connection
In the previous section, you learned how industry changed society. In this section, you will discover how the government encouraged the economic growth of the 1920s.

Main Idea
- During the 1920s, Andrew Mellon and Herbert Hoover worked to improve business efficiency and promote economic growth. (p. 457)
- Although the United States returned to a policy of isolationism after World War I, various treaties attempted to limit the arms trade and the possibility of a future war. (p. 458)

Content Vocabulary
supply-side economics, cooperative individualism, isolationism, moratorium

Academic Vocabulary
principle, philosophy, reverse

People and Terms to Identify
Charles G. Dawes, Charles Evans Hughes, Kellogg-Briand Pact

Reading Objectives
- **Explain** Andrew Mellon's economic strategies for maintaining prosperity.
- **Describe** how the United States remained involved in world affairs without joining the League of Nations.

Reading Strategy
Organizing As you read about government policies in the 1920s, complete a graphic organizer similar to the one below by filling in ways the government attempted to stimulate economic growth and prosperity.

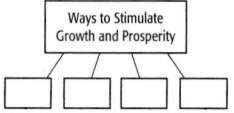

Ways to Stimulate Growth and Prosperity

Preview of Events

◆1920	◆1923	◆1926	◆1929
1921 Washington Conference begins discussing naval disarmament	**1922** Fordney-McCumber Act passed	**1924** Dawes Plan negotiated with France, Britain, and Germany	**1928** Kellogg-Briand Pact signed by 15 nations

The following are the main History–Social Science Standards covered in this section.

11.4 Students trace the rise of the United States to its role as a world power in the twentieth century.

11.4.5 Analyze the political, economic and social ramifications of World War I on the home front.

11.4.6 Trace the declining role of Great Britain and the expanding role of the United States in world affairs after World War II.

11.5 Students analyze the major political, social, economic, technological, and cultural developments of the 1920s.

11.5.1 Discuss the policies of Presidents Warren Harding, Calvin Coolidge, and Herbert Hoover.

❧ The Big Idea ❧

Societies change over time. Under the guidance of Secretary of the Treasury Andrew Mellon, the government created policies that encouraged economic growth and contributed to the stock market boom. Mellon focused on reducing the federal debt and lowering taxes. President Hoover also created agencies to help American businesses prosper. Although many Americans favored isolationism, the country had grown too powerful to remain completey isolated. The United States tried unsuccessfully to help European countries repay war debts. During the Washington Conference, the United States and eight other nations took steps to avoid future wars and end the naval arms race.

456   CHAPTER 8   Normalcy and Good Times

SECTION RESOURCES

📂 Print Material
- Reproducible Lesson Plan 8-3
- Guided Reading Activity 8-3
- Reading Essentials and Study Guide 8-3
- Active Reading Note-Taking Guide 8-3

🖌 Transparencies
- Daily Focus Skills Transparency 8-3
- Section Graphic Organizer Transparency 8-3

Technology
- Interactive Tutor Self-Assessment CD-ROM
- *ExamView*® Pro Testmaker CD-ROM
- Presentation Plus! CD-ROM

Promoting Prosperity

 Main Idea During the 1920s, Andrew Mellon and Herbert Hoover worked to improve business efficiency and promote economic growth.

Reading Connection Have you ever used a credit card or purchased something on credit? Read on to learn how Andrew Mellon, the Secretary of the Treasury, tried to reduce the nation's debt.

Andrew Mellon became the chief architect of economic policy in the United States in the 1920s, and he served as secretary of the treasury in three successive Republican administrations.

★ An American Story ★

After Election Day 1920, President-elect Harding began searching for a qualified American to serve as secretary of the treasury. The leading candidate was Andrew W. Mellon, a successful banker and industrialist, but Harding worried about Mellon's ties to industry and his relative anonymity. Harding's campaign manager, Harry Daugherty, reassured the president with a ringing endorsement of Mellon:

66 A man who can quietly make the millions this modest-looking man has gathered in is little short of a magician. If there is one thing he knows it's money. He will make for you the greatest Secretary of the Treasury since Alexander Hamilton. . . . 99

—adapted from *Mellon's Millions*

Harry Daugherty's confidence in Andrew Mellon proved to be well founded. Mellon's policies encouraged growth and led to a stock market boom.

The Mellon Program Mellon firmly believed that the government should apply business **principles** to its operations. In 1921 he convinced Congress to create both the Bureau of the Budget to prepare a unified federal budget and the General Accounting Office to track government spending.

When Mellon took office, he had three major goals—to balance the budget, to reduce the government's debt, and to cut taxes. He was convinced that these policies would ensure prosperity.

Mellon began by cutting government spending. The federal budget fell from $6.4 billion to less than $3 billion in seven years. One major expense was the interest on the national debt. World War I costs had raised the debt from $5.7 billion in 1917 to almost $26 billion by 1920. Mellon refinanced the debt to lower the interest on it and persuaded the Federal Reserve to lower its interest rates as well. These steps, combined with increased tax revenue from the nation's economic boom, reduced the debt by $7 billion between 1921 and 1929.

Mellon also focused on reducing tax rates. He believed that high taxes reduced the money available for private investment and prevented business expansion. Mellon further argued that high tax rates actually reduced the amount of tax money the government collected. If taxes were lower, businesses and consumers would spend and invest their extra money, causing the economy to grow. As the economy grew, Americans would earn more money, and the government would actually collect more taxes at a lower rate than it would if it kept tax rates high. This idea is known today as **supply-side economics.**

At Mellon's urging, Congress dramatically reduced tax rates. When Mellon took office, most taxpayers paid 4 percent federal income tax, while wealthy Americans in the highest bracket paid 73 percent. By 1928 most Americans paid .5 percent while the wealthiest Americans paid 25 percent. While many of Mellon's economic policies were beneficial in the short-term, they would contribute to the stock market crash in 1929 and the Great Depression.

Hoover's Cooperative Individualism Mellon's program was only part of the government's effort to promote economic growth. Secretary of Commerce Herbert Hoover tried to promote economic stability in various industries by balancing government

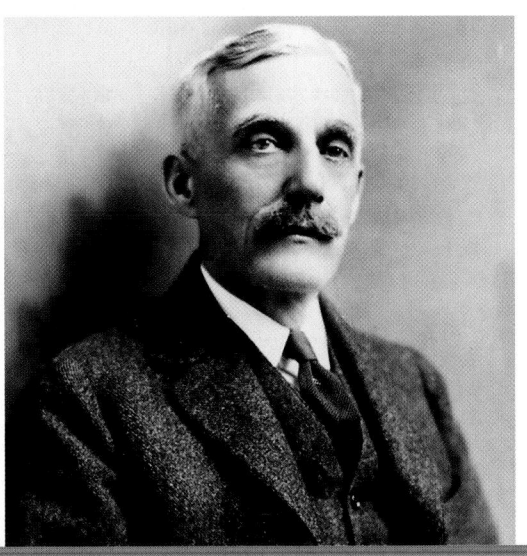

▼ *Andrew W. Mellon*

TEACH

R₁ **Reading Strategy**

Identifying the Main Idea and Supporting Details As students read the material on the Mellon program, have them create graphic organizers depicting Mellon's three goals and the ways he attempted to meet them.
BL **CA** 11RL2.5

Review the Big Idea

Review the Big Idea for this section, "Societies change over time." Have students review the three points of the Mellon program.
Ask: Could federal spending be cut in a similar way today? *(Answers will vary. Students should note that the government spends a great deal more today on benefits that Americans have come to rely upon.)* **OL**
CA 11RL3.2

U **Universal Access**

Advanced Learners Have interested students find out about Secretary of Commerce Herbert Hoover's initiatives and programs that are still in existence, such as the Federal Radio Commission. Tell students that names may have changed. Ask them to research the history of one program or agency along with its current focus. Have them present their findings to the class in a brief oral report accompanied by visuals. **AL** **CA** 11WS1.6

R₂ **Reading Strategy**

Scaffolding—Academic Vocabulary The word *stability* was introduced in Chapter 6, Section 1. Ask a student to define the word. **BL**

More Skill Practice

Analyzing Text Structure Encourage students to use dictionaries to learn about the histories of words. **Ask:** Why is it helpful to understand the history of a word and how it was used at different times? *(Students may point out that by adding this information to a word's definition, they are better able to retain the word's meaning.)* For example, the word *economics* comes from a Greek word that combined the words for house, *oikos,* and to manage, *nemein.* **OL**

Picturing History

Harding's Cabinet Some members of Harding's cabinet (posing here with the president, seated center, in 1921) were effective administrators. What agencies did President Hoover create during his administration?

regulation with his own **philosophy** of **cooperative individualism.** This idea encouraged manufacturers and distributors to form their own trade associations, which would voluntarily share information with the government. Hoover believed this system would promote economic efficiency.

To assist American businesses, Hoover also created several other agencies. He expanded the Bureau of Foreign and Domestic Commerce to find new markets and business opportunities for American companies. He also established the Bureau of Aviation to regulate and support the airline industry and the Federal Radio Commission, which set rules regarding radio frequencies and radio transmitters.

✓ **Reading Check** **Evaluating** What government policies were intended to promote economic growth and improve business efficiency in the 1920s?

Trade and Arms Control

Main Idea Although the United States returned to a policy of isolationism after World War I, various treaties attempted to limit the arms trade and the possibility of a future war.

Reading Connection Do you think it is possible to have a world without war? Read on to discover attempts to ensure peace after World War I ended.

Before World War I the United States had owed billions of dollars more to foreign investors than foreigners owed to Americans. By the end of the war,

the situation was **reversed.** Former wartime allies owed the United States more than $10 billion in war debts incurred for food and armaments. By the 1920s the United States was the dominant economic power in the world—its national income far greater than that of Britain, Germany, France, and Japan combined. This new power presented the United States with a unique diplomatic challenge.

Isolationism In his victory speech after the 1920 election, President Harding declared the issue of American involvement in the League of Nations "deceased." The majority of Americans, tired of being entangled in the baffling, mutually hostile, and dangerous politics of Europe, favored **isolationism.** They simply wanted to be left alone to pursue prosperity.

The United States, however, was too powerful, too economically interconnected with other countries, and too widely involved in international affairs to retreat into isolationism. American delegations participated in many League conferences. It was United States policy to promote peace through agreements with individual countries rather than doing so through the collective efforts of the League. Total isolationism became difficult, if not impossible.

The Dawes Plan The United States's former wartime allies had difficulty making the payments on their immense war debts. They claimed that high American tariffs had closed the American market to their products and hampered their economic recovery. If they could not sell their products in the United States, they could not acquire the money they needed to pay off their war debts. They also argued that the United States should be willing to bear more of the financial burden because it had suffered far fewer wartime casualties than its allies.

The United States government took the stance that American taxpayers should not be asked to assume the debts of others. American officials argued further that America's allies had gained new territory as a result of the victory over Germany, while the United States had gained nothing. These countries also were receiving reparations—huge cash payments Germany was required to make as punishment for starting the war and causing so much destruction. These payments, however, were completely crippling the German economy.

It was vital for the United States that European economies be healthy so that the Europeans could buy American exports and repay their war debts. Thus, in 1924, **Charles G. Dawes,** an American

Picturing History

Answer: He advocated cooperative individualism under which manufacturers and distributors formed trade associations that shared information with the government.

banker and diplomat, negotiated an agreement with France, Britain, and Germany by which American banks would make loans to the Germans that would enable them to meet their reparations payments. At the same time, Britain and France would accept less in reparations and pay more on their war debts.

Although well intended, the Dawes Plan did little to ease Europe's economic problems. Britain, France, and Germany went through the motions of paying what they owed while in fact going deeper into debt to American banks and corporations.

The Washington Conference Despite severe economic hardship, the major powers were involved in a costly postwar naval arms race. To help halt this arms race, the United States invited representatives from eight major countries—Great Britain, France, Italy, China, Japan, Belgium, the Netherlands, and Portugal—to Washington to discuss disarmament. The Washington Conference opened on November 12, 1921.

In his address to the delegates, Secretary of State **Charles Evans Hughes** proposed a 10-year **moratorium**—or pause—on the construction of major new warships. He also proposed a list of warships in each country's navy to be destroyed, beginning with some American battleships. The delegates cheered Hughes's speech and then entered into lengthy negotiations.

Their efforts produced three agreements. In the Five-Power Naval Limitation Treaty, Britain, France, Italy, Japan, and the United States essentially formalized Hughes's proposal. The Four-Power Treaty between the United States, Japan, France, and Britain

recognized each country's island possessions in the Pacific. Finally, all the participating countries signed the Nine-Power Treaty, which guaranteed China's independence.

As a long-term effort to prevent war, the conference had some serious shortcomings. It did nothing to limit land forces. It also angered the Japanese because it required Japan to maintain a smaller navy than either the United States or Great Britain. It did, however, give Americans cause to look forward to a period of peace, recovery, and prosperity.

Abolishing War The apparent success of the Washington Conference boosted the belief that written agreements could end war altogether. Perhaps the highest expression of that idea occurred when U.S. Secretary of State Frank Kellogg and French Foreign Minister Aristide Briand proposed a treaty to outlaw war. On August 27, 1928, the United States and 14 other nations signed the **Kellogg-Briand Pact.** Eventually 62 nations ratified it.

Though it had no binding force, the pact was hailed as a victory for peace. It stated that all signing nations agreed to abandon war and to settle all disputes by peaceful means. The Kellogg-Briand Pact and the Dawes Plan were perhaps the most notable foreign policy achievements of the Coolidge administration.

✓ **Reading Check** **Identifying** Why did the Dawes Plan fail to ease Europe's economic problems?

HISTORY Online **Study Central**

For help with the concepts in this section of *American Vision: Modern Times* go to **tav.mt.glencoe.com** and click on **Study Central.**

SECTION 3 ASSESSMENT

Checking for Understanding

1. **Vocabulary** Define: principle, supply-side economics, philosophy, cooperative individualism, reverse, isolationism, moratorium.

2. **People and Terms** Identify: Charles G. Dawes, Charles Evans Hughes, Kellogg-Briand Pact.

Reviewing Big Ideas

3. **Determining** Why did Andrew Mellon work to reduce federal tax rates?

Critical Thinking

4. **Evaluating** What efforts did the United States make to promote permanent peace and worldwide economic recovery? Were these efforts successful? Explain your answer.

5. **Categorizing** Use a graphic organizer like the one below to list the major terms of the treaties resulting from the Washington Conference.

Major Terms of Treaties	

Analyzing Visuals

6. **Analyzing Photographs** Study the photograph on page 458 of President Harding's cabinet of advisers. What differences do you see between politics and the media then and now?

Writing About History

7. **Persuasive Writing** Imagine you are an American business owner or farmer in the 1920s. Write a letter to your representatives in Congress explaining why you think cutting tax rates is a good or bad idea. **CA** 11WA2.3a

CHAPTER 8 Normalcy and Good Times **459**

C Critical Thinking

Drawing Conclusions Have students work in small groups to craft some ideas for bringing peace to the world. They should consider either a regional or global approach. Ask each group to develop an advertising campaign based on their discussions. **OL**

ASSESS

Resources for page 459

Use these resources to assess student mastery.

📁 Section Quiz 8-3

📁 Reading Essentials and Study Guide 8-3

💿 Interactive Tutor Self-Assessment CD-ROM

📁 California Standards Practice, Grade 11

✓ **Reading Check**

Answer: It caused Britain, France, and Germany to go further into debt.

HISTORY Online

Study Central provides audio summaries, interactive games, and online graphic organizers to help students review section content.

CLOSE

Inferring Have students explain how the U.S. remained involved in world affairs without being a League of Nations member. **BL**

Primary Sources
Eyewitness to History

In the 1920s, new technologies transformed the lives of Americans. The automobile and the radio reduced the distance between people and communities. New household appliances altered people's lives. In often-heated debates, Americans argued about the value of these new machines and gadgets.

SOURCE 1:

Stephanie Kosior married a Connecticut farmer with three children. She was responsible for handling all of the household work. In the 1920s, the Kosior farm was not equipped with modern appliances. In a radio broadcast aired in 1981, she talked about those days.

[W]e had one of those cast iron stoves. Well, I had to have that wood stove going in the summer to cook and bake. You know, I used to say this, thinking out loud, I said, "I've got to get out of this kitchen or I'm gonna go crazy." This, you know, the heat. You look at today, now, do you realize how I appreciate that hot water? You know, so many years, and I still don't take it for granted. Having all the hot water I want. Or having an automatic machine. You know what means to me? Today, the modern women, they take all that for granted.

When I got my automatic washing machine, I couldn't believe it. You know what I was doing? I was looking for any kind of laundry, just so I could use that. I couldn't *believe* that I could put my clothes in there, and that they got washed and rinsed automatically. Because what I used to do, the blankets I used to wash by hand, and rinse them. Can you like think about all that now? A lot of the, you know, those farm women that worked so hard, and got oh so many different problems later, physical, as a result. . . .

▲ *First meal cooked using an electric range*

. . . Do you realize I had to keep putting fuel wood in that stove, in that heat, and. . . . Can you imagine the heat in that kitchen? . . . That's one thing I don't think I ever want to do again.

Oh no, it's easy now. They have conveniences now, canners, electricity, electric stoves, fans. It was a tough life. . . .

SOURCE 2:

In the mid-1920s, the General Federation of Women's Clubs conducted a survey that indicated most women preferred to own automobiles, telephones, and radios rather than vacuum cleaners and sewing machines. The organization concluded that women wanted to escape boredom more than avoid hard work. In a letter to the March 1926 Women's Home Companion, *Mrs. C.S. of Washington challenged this idea.*

[T]he radio, the piano, and so on, elbowing the washboard and tubs, are viewed with amazement. Here is where you lost the meaning of it all.

The Mother doesn't have time, in her inefficient kitchen routine, to enjoy these things, as you suggest. Her life is a perpetual round of recurring tasks. Why, then, did she consent to the purchase of these things?

Her job is to make a happy home. She must establish good conditions for the family, to secure normal lives for the children, and hold them in a charmed circle until they are strong enough for the world's temptations, despite the poverty. . . .

▲ *A farm family listens to the radio in 1925.*

If to-morrow some great fortune would grant me three hundred dollars would I cast away my tubs and **washboard**[1], with which I weekly grind out the family washings? Or equip my ancient kitchen with the loveliness of **linoleum**[2], gas range, kitchen cabinet? Or indulge in refrigerator, washer, and electric iron?

Alas, no, though my heart yearns for them. I would buy a piano that these children might learn right now, as they should, the love of music. I would buy good books and some better furniture to make the home brighter for them. For now is the time they need such things so badly, not a few years later, say after Mother has had her kitchen modernized.

That is what the statistics you gathered say to me, a humble but ambitious mother.

SOURCE 3:

M.J. Caveney, writing in the April 1920 Collier's *magazine, described the effects of the new medium of radio on life in the northern wilderness.*

---

[1] **washboard:** a metallic board on which clothes were rubbed during washing
[2] **linoleum:** a smooth-surfaced floor covering

I am in a log shack in Canada's northland. . . . Three bosom friends are here in the shack with me— my ax, my dog, and my **wireless**[3] receiving set. These are vital possessions. If I lose my ax, a frozen death awaits me when the wood fire dies. If I lose my dog—well, you who love your dogs in places where human friends abound just remember where I am. If I lose my wireless set, then I am again cut off from the great outside world which I have so recently regained. . . .

I reach over and touch a switch and the music of an orchestra playing at Newark, N.J., fills the room. . . . A slight turn of the magic knob and I am at Pittsburgh, Pa., listening to a man telling stories to thousands of America's listening children. With that magic knob I can command the musical programs and press news sent out from a dozen radio broadcasting stations. At will I amuse myself or garner the details of a busy world where things are happening. . . .

. . . I may be at "the back of beyond," but the whole world has marched right up to the edge of the little copper switch at my elbow.

[3] **wireless:** radio

DBQ   Document-Based Questions

Historical Analysis — CA CS3; HR4; HI3

Source 1: How did new household appliances improve Kosior's life?

Source 2: How did Mrs. C.S. disagree with the survey on modern technology?

Source 3: What was the effect of radio upon Caveney?

Comparing and contrasting sources:
How do Kosior, Mrs. C.S., and Caveney agree in their views about the impact of new technologies and the value of these technologies?

R Reading Strategy

Connecting Ask students to carefully read the second source and explain why the author would not spend her money on the latest modern appliances. *(She is more concerned about providing culture for her family.)* Tell the class to ask ten people— family or friends outside the classroom—this question: **If you were given $300, what would you spend it on?** Ask each student to keep lists of the answers they receive and report back to the class. Use this data to begin a discussion on the relative importance of material goods in modern society. OL CA 11WA2.3b

C Critical Thinking

Comparing and Contrasting Have students compare the impact of the radio in the 1920s with impact of the Internet on contemporary society. **Ask: What are the similarities and differences in these two popular mediums?** *(similarities: both spread information and entertainment to anyone with a connection, even in distant places; differences: radio restricted the ability to broadcast, Internet may be changed by user)* OL CA HI1

DBQ   Document-Based Questions

1. They reduced the amount of physical labor that she had to do, especially for cooking meals and washing clothes.
2. People should adopt modern technology, not to enjoy it, but to use it to create a happy home.
3. The radio allowed Caveney to have access to daily news and entertainment programs. These things kept him in contact with the outside world.

Comparing and Contrasting Sources: They indicate that the new technologies have had a great positive impact on their lives and are quite valuable. Kosier's household appliances reduced the work required for cooking meals and washing clothes. Mrs. C.S.'s letter states that they help provide a happy home. Finally, Caveney is grateful that the radio keeps him from being isolated.

Reviewing Content Vocabulary

Students' answers will vary. The pages where the words appear in the text are shown in parentheses.

1. normalcy *(p. 445)* **2.** immunity *(p. 446)* **3.** mass production *(p. 450)* **4.** assembly line *(p. 450)* **5.** welfare capitalism *(p. 454)* **6.** open shop *(p. 454)* **7.** supply-side economics *(p. 457)* **8.** cooperative individualism *(p. 458)* **9.** isolationism *(p. 458)* **10.** moratorium *(p. 459)*

Reviewing Academic Vocabulary

Students' answers will vary. The pages where the words appear in the text are shown in parentheses.

11. presume *(p. 445)* **12.** integrity *(p. 447)* **13.** percent *(p. 448)* **14.** innovation *(p. 450)* **15.** consumer *(p. 451)* **16.** structure *(p. 454)* **17.** principle *(p. 457)* **18.** philosophy *(p. 458)* **19.** reverse *(p. 458)*

CHAPTER 8 ASSESSMENT and ACTIVITIES

Standards 11.2, 11.2.1, 11.2.9, 11.4, 11.4.5, 11.4.6, 11.5, 11.5.1, 11.5.4, 11.5.6, 11.5.7

Reviewing Content Vocabulary

On a sheet of paper, use each of these terms in a sentence.

1. normalcy
2. immunity
3. mass production
4. assembly line
5. welfare capitalism
6. open shop
7. supply-side economics
8. cooperative individualism
9. isolationism
10. moratorium

Reviewing Academic Vocabulary

On a sheet of paper, use each of these terms in a sentence that reflects the term's meaning in the chapter.

11. presume
12. integrity
13. percent
14. innovation
15. consumer
16. structure
17. principle
18. philosophy
19. reverse

Reviewing the Main Ideas

Section 1

20. How did President Coolidge restore public confidence?

Section 2

21. What were four new industries, besides the automobile industry, that grew in importance during the 1920s?

22. How did Henry Ford increase worker loyalty and impact the labor movement?

Section 3

23. What were Andrew Mellon's strategies for maintaining post-war American prosperity?

24. What was the goal of the Kellogg-Briand Pact?

Critical Thinking

25. **Reading Skill** **Summarizing** Summarize the United States's attempts at trade and arms control during the 1920s. Do you think these attempts were effective?

26. **Civics** Based on what you know, why did people support Robert La Follette in the election of 1924? Explain what role a third-party candidate may play in presidential elections.

27. **Organizing** Use a graphic organizer like the one below to list the factors that helped create a new consumer society in the United States during the 1920s.

New Consumer Society

Chapter Summary

Government's Role
- Minimal interference with business
- Cut government spending and debt
- Eliminated or reduced taxes
- High tariffs

Business Innovation
- Mass production reduced prices
- Technology such as autos, airplanes, and radios led to new industries
- New consumer goods fueled manufacturing boom

New Consumer Society
- More disposable income
- More leisure time
- Easily available credit
- Mass advertising

Prosperity

462

Reviewing the Main Ideas

20. Coolidge distanced himself from the Harding administration and named the most capable individuals to his cabinet.

21. automobile-related industries such as garage and gas stations, the consumer good, airlines, and radio industries

22. He increased workers' wages and reduced the workday, weakening the power of unions.

23. reduce taxes, reduce federal debt, balance the budget

24. a written pact between countries to outlaw war and settle all disputes by peaceful means

Self-Check Quiz
Visit the *American Vision: Modern Times* Web site at
tav.mt.glencoe.com and click on *Self-Check Quizzes–
Chapter 8* to assess your knowledge of chapter content.

Writing About History

28. **Historical Analysis** | Analyzing Economic Behavior
Research the production of the personal computer during
the last 30 years. Explain how computers have impacted the
U.S. economy. Has their use increased or decreased? How
has the price of computers changed? Have new industries
been created?

29. *Big Idea* Describe how automobiles changed the standard of living during the 1920s. Explain their cultural and
economic effects on society.

DBQ | Document-Based Questions

30. **Interpreting Primary Sources** In December 1928, President
Coolidge delivered his annual State of the Union message to
Congress. Read the excerpt and answer the questions that
follow.

❝The great wealth created by our enterprise and industry, and saved by our economy, has had the widest distribution among our own people, and has gone out in a
steady stream to serve the charity and the business of the
world. The requirements of existence have passed beyond
the standard of necessity into the region of luxury.

. . . The country can regard the present with satisfaction
and anticipate the future with optimism. The main
source of these unexplained blessings lies in the
integrity and character of the American people. They
have had great faith, which they have supplemented
with mighty works. . . . Yet these remarkable powers
would have been exerted almost in vain without the
constant cooperation and careful administration of the
Federal Government. . . . ❞

–from President Coolidge's Annual Message to Congress,
December 4, 1928

a. According to Coolidge, how should Americans feel about
the present economy and the future economy?

b. Whom does Coolidge credit for U.S. prosperity?

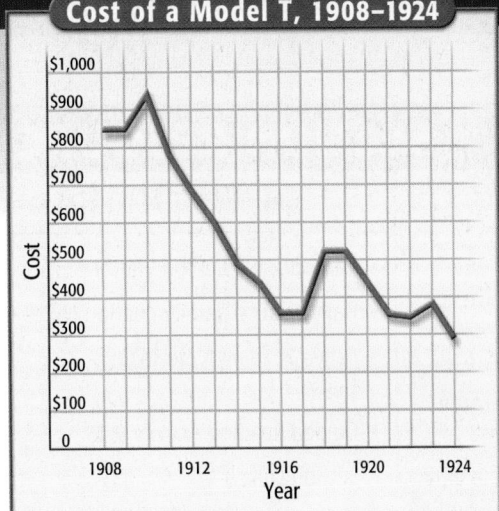

Cost of a Model T, 1908–1924

Year (x-axis): 1908, 1912, 1916, 1920, 1924
Cost (y-axis): $0 to $1,000

Economics and History

31. The graph above shows the cost of a new Model T automobile between 1908 and 1924. Study the graph and answer the
questions below.

a. **Interpreting Graphs** By how much did the cost of the
Model T drop from 1908 to 1920?

b. **Evaluating** How was Henry Ford able to lower the price
of the Model T?

Standards Practice

**Directions: Choose the phrase that best
completes the following sentence.**

32. One of the effects of World War I on the American
economy was

A a sharp rise in unemployment.

B stronger government control over industry.

C a sharp decrease in taxes.

D the abolition of labor unions, which were seen as
unpatriotic.

Standard 11.4.5: Analyze the political, economic, and social
ramifications of World War I on the home front.

Have students visit the Web site at
tav.mt.glencoe.com to review Chapter
8 and take the Self-Check Quiz.

Writing About History

28. **Historical Analysis** | Students'
answers will vary.

29. *Big Idea* Automobiles allowed people to travel much greater distances
more quickly and allowed workers
to live outside cities. Rural
Americans' sense of isolation also
decreased. Successful mass production resulted in new and cheaper
consumer goods.

DBQ | Document-Based Questions

30. **a.** Coolidge says they should be satisfied and optimistic. **b.** He credits
the American people.

Economics and History

31. **a.** about $400; **b.** decreased produc-
tivity costs, increased productivity
level and sales volume

Standards Practice

32. B

Bonus Question ?

**Ask: What was the Teapot Dome
scandal?** *(During the Harding
administration, government lands
containing large reserves of oil in
Teapot Dome, Wyoming, were
leased to private interest.)*

Critical Thinking

25. **Reading Skill** | Students' answers will vary. The stu-
dents should identify the role of the Dawes Plan, the
Washington Conference, and the Kellogg-Briand Pact
in U.S. foreign policy.

26. Sample Answer: The Harding administration was full of
scandal and the Democrats were divided in choosing a
candidate. Robert La Follette provided an alternative in
the Progressive movement. Third-party candidates
allow people to vote for individuals not in line with the
two major parties.

27. shorter workday, higher wages, mass production techniques, easy consumer credit, mass advertising, managerial revolution

463

Chapter 9 Planning Guide

SECTION RESOURCES

MAIN IDEAS	📁 PRINT MATERIALS	TECHNOLOGY RESOURCES
Section 1: Causes of the Depression 1. In an election marked by religious prejudice and the issue of Prohibition, Herbert Hoover won the presidency in a landslide. 2. The long period of rising stock prices led many people to risky investment practices. 3. The October 1929 stock market crash led to bank failures across the nation. 4. An uneven distribution of income, the lack of foreign markets for exports, and the Federal Reserve's mistakes contributed to the Great Depression.	• Reproducible Lesson Plan 9-1* • Daily Lecture and Discussion Notes 9-1 • Active Reading Note-Taking Guide 9-1 • Guided Reading Activity 9-1 • Section Quiz 9-1 • Reading Essentials and Study Guide 9-1	Daily Focus Skills Transparency 9-1 Section Graphic Organizer Transparency 9-1 Interactive Tutor Self-Assessment CD-ROM Exam*View*® Pro Testmaker CD-ROM Presentation Plus! CD-ROM California Standards Practice Transparencies
Section 2: Life During the Depression 1. As banks continued to fail and people lost jobs and homes, soup kitchens and shantytowns sprang up throughout the United States. Droughts during the 1930s made the Depression even worse for farmers. 2. Movies and radio shows allowed people to forget temporarily the miseries of the Depression. 3. Painters, photographers, and writers all captured the experiences of people during the Great Depression.	• Reproducible Lesson Plan 9-2* • Daily Lecture and Discussion Notes 9-2 • Active Reading Note-Taking Guide 9-2 • Guided Reading Activity 9-2 • Section Quiz 9-2 • Reading Essentials and Study Guide 9-2	Daily Focus Skills Transparency 9-2 Section Graphic Organizer Transparency 9-2 Interactive Tutor Self-Assessment CD-ROM Exam*View*® Pro Testmaker CD-ROM Presentation Plus! CD-ROM California Standards Practice Transparencies
Section 3: Hoover Responds 1. President Hoover's cautious efforts to help the economy did not succeed; Republicans lost many seats in Congress during the midterm elections. 2. President Hoover tried to help banks recover and offer limited help to citizens directly, but it was too late. 3. Farmers, veterans, and others who were suffering grew frustrated and protested against the government's inability to help them.	• Reproducible Lesson Plan 9-3* • Daily Lecture and Discussion Notes 9-3 • Active Reading Note-Taking Guide 9-3 • Guided Reading Activity 9-3 • Section Quiz 9-3 • Reading Essentials and Study Guide 9-3	Daily Focus Skills Transparency 9-3 Section Graphic Organizer Transparency 9-3 Interactive Tutor Self-Assessment CD-ROM Exam*View*® Pro Testmaker CD-ROM Presentation Plus! CD-ROM California Standards Practice Transparencies

PACING YOUR LESSONS

Chapter Introduction	Section 1	Section 2	Section 3	Chapter Assessment
½ Day	2 Days	2 Days	2 Days	½ Day

0:00 OUT OF TIME? 📁 Assign the Chapter 9 *Reading Essentials and Study Guide.*

*Available on TeacherWorks™ CD-ROM

Chapter 9 Planning Guide

Standards-Based Lesson Plan

History–Social Science Standards Covered in Chapter 9

The standards covered in the chapter are listed below. Use the accompanying activity as you teach the chapter to ensure student mastery of these standards. This activity can be used in combination with the program's print and technology assessment materials.

Standard	Section 1	2	3
11.5.1 Discuss the policies of Presidents Warren Harding, Calvin Coolidge, and Herbert Hoover.	✔		
11.6 Students analyze the different explanations for the Great Depression and how the New Deal fundamentally changed the role of the federal government.		✔	✔
11.6.1 Describe the monetary issues of the late nineteenth and early twentieth centuries that gave rise to the establishment of the Federal Reserve and the weaknesses in key sectors of the economy in the late 1920s.	✔		
11.6.2 Understand the explanations of the principal causes of the Great Depression and the steps taken by the Federal Reserve, Congress, and Presidents Herbert Hoover and Franklin Delano Roosevelt to combat the economic crisis.	✔		
11.6.3 Discuss the human toll of the Depression, natural disasters, and unwise agricultural practices and their effects on the depopulation of rural regions and on political movements of the left and right, with particular attention to the Dust Bowl refugees and their social and economic impacts in California.		✔	✔

Cumulative Standards-Assessment Activity

The Cumulative Standards-Assessment Activity will help students organize and learn the important information from the chapter. Begin teaching the chapter with this activity, and have students complete it as they read the chapter.

CREATING A SEQUENCING CHART

Purpose Sequencing events is a vital skill when studying history. Understanding the proper sequence of events helps students when they carry out critical thinking tasks, such as identifying cause-and-effect relationships and making generalizations about trends or developments. Using graphic organizers like time lines to record events also helps students see how concepts from different parts of a chapter are related in time, preventing the misconception that content presented later necessarily occurred later in time.

Introduction to Sequencing

1. Discuss how chronological thinking will help students understand history in a linear way, but it also will help them see the intersections of events and make the connections that are crucial to comprehending the deeper meanings of historical events.

2. Model how to construct a time line by asking students to identify key dates in the previous chapter and briefly state what happened and why it was important. Explain how signal words like *first, next, then, later,* and *finally* can help them identify

sequence. Write students' suggestions on the board. After you have four or five dates, sequence them properly in a time line.

3. Ask students to copy this chart into their notebooks:

Date	Event and Significance

Explain that students should collect all the dates and events from the chapter before constructing their sequencing charts. If not, the result could become messy if they have to add dates encountered in a later section between two dates identified earlier and there is not sufficient room. After they have finished taking notes, they should make their sequencing charts.

4. As you review the chapter, ask volunteers to name some of the key dates they identified. Encourage them to use their sequencing charts as study aids.

Chapter 9 Planning Guide

READING SUPPORT

- Content Vocabulary Activity 9
- Academic Vocabulary Activity 9
- Reading Skills Activity 9
- Chapter 9 Active Reading Note-Taking Guide
- Chapter 9 Guided Reading Activities
- Chapter 9 Reading Essentials and Study Guide
- American Literature Readings, Unit 3
- *The American Vision: Modern Times* Video Program
- Vocabulary PuzzleMaker CD-ROM
- American History Primary Source Document Library CD-ROM

SKILL PRACTICE

- Map Overlay Transparency 9 Strategy and Activity
- Historical Analysis Skills Activity 9
- Time Line Activity 9
- Reading Skills Activity 9
- Reinforcing Skills Activity 9
- Linking Past and Present Activity 9
- Interpreting Political Cartoons 9
- Economics and History Activity, Unit 3
- MindJogger Videoquiz

WRITING SUPPORT

- Chapter 9 Active Reading Note-Taking Guide
- Writer's Guidebook
- High School Writing Process Transparencies

CRITICAL THINKING

- Critical Thinking Skills Activity 9
- Primary Source Reading 9
- Cause-and-Effect Transparency 9 Strategy and Activity
- Presentation Plus! CD-ROM

ASSESSMENT

- Chapter 9 Section Quizzes
- Chapter 9 Tests, Forms A and B
- Authentic Assessment Activity 9
- *ExamView*® Pro Testmaker CD-ROM
- Interactive Tutor Self-Assessment CD-ROM
- California Standards Practice, Grade 11
- Succeeding on . . .™ the California Standards: Grade 11 History–Social Science CD-ROM

UNIVERSAL ACCESS

- Universal Access Activity 9
- English Learner Activity 9
- American Art Prints
- StudentWorks™ Plus CD-ROM
- American Music: Hits Through History
- School-to-Home Connection Activity 9

CD-ROM	Transparency
DVD	Music Program
Print Material	Videocassette
Poster	

Chapter 9 Planning Guide

TECHNOLOGY

- StudentWorks™ Plus CD-ROM
- TeacherWorks™ CD-ROM
- ExamView® Pro Testmaker CD-ROM
- Interactive Tutor Self-Assessment CD-ROM
- Presentation Plus! CD-ROM
- Vocabulary PuzzleMaker CD-ROM
- American History Primary Source Document Library CD-ROM
- MindJogger Videoquiz
- *The American Vision: Modern Times* Video Program
- Professional Development in High School Social Studies Video Series
- Teach, Use, and Succeed With *The American Vision: Modern Times*
- American Music: Hits Through History
- Succeeding on . . .™ the California Standards: Grade 11 History–Social Science CD-ROM

SPANISH RESOURCES

- Spanish Activities and Assessment
  - Spanish Vocabulary Activities
  - Spanish Guided Reading Activities
  - Spanish Quizzes and Tests
  - Spanish Reteaching Activities
- Spanish Reading Essentials and Study Guide
- Spanish School-to-Home Connection Activities

TRANSPARENCIES

- Daily Focus Skills Transparencies
- Section Graphic Organizer Transparencies
- Map Overlay Transparencies
- Cause-and-Effect Transparencies
- Unit Time Line Transparencies
- Why It Matters Transparencies
- American Art and Architecture Transparencies
- High School Writing Process Transparencies
- California Standards Practice Transparencies

TEACHER PLANNING

- Daily Lecture and Discussion Notes
- English Learner Handbook
- Building Academic Vocabulary
- *The American Vision: Modern Times* Reading and Study Skills Foldables
- Reading Strategies and Activities for the Social Studies Classroom
- Universal Access for the American History Classroom
- NGS United States Desk Map
- NGS World Atlas
- Chapter 9 Reproducible Lesson Plans on TeacherWorks™ CD-ROM
- California Guide to Daily Intervention

PROFESSIONAL DEVELOPMENT

- Building Academic Vocabulary
- Strategies for Success
- Research-Based Strategies Used to Develop *The American Vision: Modern Times*
- Character Education in the High School Classroom
- Professional Development in High School Social Studies Video Series
- Teach, Use, and Succeed With *The American Vision: Modern Times*

Chapter 9 Planning Guide

TEACHER'S CORNER

Index to National Geographic Magazine:
The following article relates to this chapter:

- "The Okies–Beyond the Great Depression," September 1984

National Geographic Society Products:
To order the following, call National Geographic at 1–800–368–2728

- *1929–1941: The Great Depression* (Video)
- *Eyewitness to the 20th Century* (Book)
- *Historical Atlas of the United States* (Atlas)

NGS ONLINE

Access National Geographic's new dynamic MapMachine Web site and other geography resources at:

www.nationalgeographic.com

www.nationalgeographic.com/maps

Use our Web site for additional resources. All essential content is covered in the Student Edition.

You and your students can visit tav.mt.glencoe.com, the Web site companion to the **American Vision: Modern Times.** This innovative integration of electronic and print media offers your students a wealth of opportunities. The student text directs students to the Web site for the following options:

- **Chapter Overviews**
- **Self-Check Quizzes**
- **Student Web Activities**
- **Textbook Updates**

Answers to the student Web activities are provided for you in the **Web Activity Lesson Plans.** Additional Web resources and ePuzzles and games are also available.

MASTERING THE STANDARDS

The content and assessment in the Student Edition, Teacher Wraparound Edition, teacher planning materials, and the print and technology products are all standards-based. The use of these products during instruction leads to mastery of the standards.

PRACTICE
- California Standards Practice, Grade 11
- California Standards Practice Transparencies
- School-to-Home Connection

BENCHMARK ASSESSMENT
- Section Quizzes, Chapter Tests, and Authentic Assessment
- Exam*View*® Pro Testmaker CD-ROM
- Succeeding On . . . ™ the California Standards: Grade 11 History–Social Science CD-ROM

REMEDIATION
- California Guide to Daily Intervention
- Interactive Tutor Self-Assessment CD-ROM
- Exam*View*® Pro Testmaker CD-ROM
- California Standards Practice, Grade 11
- Reading Essentials and Study Guide

FOLDABLES™
Study Organizer
Dinah Zike's Foldables

Foldables are three-dimensional, interactive graphic organizers that help students practice basic writing skills, review key vocabulary terms, and identify main ideas. Every chapter has a foldable activity in the *Dinah Zike's Reading and Study Skills Foldables* booklet. You can use the foldables as they are presented or modify them to suit the needs of your individual class.

A variety of videotape programs are available from A&E Television and The History Channel to provide teaching assistance. To order, call Glencoe at 1-800-334-7344.

Chapter 9 Planning Guide

KEY for Using the Teacher Wraparound Edition

Use this key to help you identify the different types of prompts found in the Teacher Wraparound Edition.

R **Reading Strategies** activities help you teach reading skills and vocabulary.

C **Critical Thinking** strategies help students apply and extend what they have learned.

U **Universal Access** activities provide differentiated instruction for students learning to speak English, along with suggestions for teaching various types of learners.

S **Skill Practice** strategies help students practice historical analysis and geography skills.

W **Writing Support** activities provide writing opportunities to help students comprehend the text.

Teaching strategies and activities have been coded for ability level appropriateness.

AL Activities for students working above grade level
OL Activities for students working on grade level
BL Activities for students working below grade level
EL Activities for English learners

FOCUS

History–Social Science Standards

This chapter addresses the following standards:

11.5.1 Discuss the policies of Presidents Warren Harding, Calvin Coolidge, and Herbert Hoover.

11.6.2 Understand the explanations of the principal causes of the Great Depression and the steps taken by the Federal Reserve, Congress, and Presidents Herbert Hoover and Franklin Delano Roosevelt to combat the economic crisis.

11.6.3 Discuss the human toll of the Depression, natural disasters, and unwise agricultural practices and their effects on the depopulation of rural regions and on political movements of the left and right, with particular attention to the Dust Bowl refugees and their social and economic impacts in California.

BELLRINGER
SKILLBUILDER ACTIVITY

Discuss with students the question, **How do business and government cooperate today?** Have each student keep a list of the class responses. After studying the chapter, invite students to return to their lists and work in small groups to draw comparisons and contrasts between the relationship of government and business during the 1920s and today.

TEACH

Thinking About the Big Ideas

As you begin teaching each section, use these questions and activities to focus on the Big Idea.

464

CHAPTER
9

1929–1932

The Great Depression Begins

⇜ Big Ideas ⇝

SECTION 1: Causes of the Depression

Societies change over time. *Inflated stock prices, overproduction, high tariffs, uneven distribution of wealth, and mistakes by the Federal Reserve led to the Great Depression.*

SECTION 2: Life During the Depression

Societies change over time. *Many people were impoverished during the Great Depression, but some found ways to cope with the hard times.*

SECTION 3: Hoover Responds

Social and economic crises lead to new roles for government. *President Hoover's philosophy of government guided his response to the Depression.*

 The *American Vision: Modern Times* **Video** *The Chapter 9 video, "Brother, Can You Spare a Dime?" chronicles Depression-era life in the United States.*

October 29, 1929
• Stock market crashes on Black Tuesday

1930
• Grant Wood paints *American Gothic*

June 1930
• Hawley-Smoot Tariff passed

Hoover
1929–1933

United States
PRESIDENTS

1929   *1930*   *1931*

World

1929
• Remarque's *All Quiet on the Western Front* published

1930
• Ras Tafari becomes Emperor Haile Selassie of Ethiopia

1931
• Gandhi released from prison in India, ending second passive resistance campaign against British rule

464

Section 1
Causes of the Depression

Essential Question: What is one thing that has changed in society since a parent or another adult you know was your age? Ask students to talk with an adult at home, at school, or at church and bring their interviewee's responses to class to form the basis of a class discussion. Then tell students that during the close of the 1920s, society began to change once again, which they will learn about in Section 1. **OL**

Section 2
Life During the Depression

Essential Question: How do you handle the tough times in your life? Have students write a response to this topic and then invite volunteers

Girls pump for water during a dust storm in Springfield, Colorado.

October 1931
• National Credit Corporation created

1932
• Drought sweeps Great Plains

July 1932
• Bonus Marchers forced out of Washington, D.C.

January 1932
• Reconstruction Finance Corporation created

F. Roosevelt 1933–1945

1932　　*1933*

September 21, 1931
• Britain abandons gold standard

1932
• Salazar becomes premier of Portugal

February 1932
• Japan sets up puppet government in Manchukuo in northern China

HISTORY Online

Chapter Overview
Visit the *American Vision: Modern Times* Web site at tav.mt.glencoe.com and click on *Chapter Overviews– Chapter 9* to preview chapter information.

to share their responses. Tell students that in Section 2 they will learn about how several people coped with difficult circumstances during the Great Depression. **OL**

Section 3
Hoover Responds
Essential Question: Why do government policies change over time? Ask students to consider ways that the government's role has changed during their lifetimes, such as in its policies toward welfare and terrorism. Tell students that in Section 3 they will read about ways the government changed to try to meet the challenges of the Great Depression. **OL**

Cultural Perspectives

During the Great Depression, many Americans lost their jobs and homes. Many of these newly homeless people lined up at soup kitchens and erected shacks on unused or public lands. Have students think about the similarities and differences between the plight of homeless Americans in the 1930s and today. How do the demographics, the response of the government and the community, and the response of the homeless people themselves compare? **OL**

FOLDABLES™
Study Organizer

Dinah Zike's Foldables are three-dimensional, interactive graphic organizers that help students practice basic writing skills, review key vocabulary terms, and identify main ideas. Have students complete the foldable activity in the *Dinah Zike's Reading and Study Skills Foldables* booklet.

HISTORY Online

Go to tav.mt.glencoe.com for student activities, lesson plans, and links to additional resources to help students learn about the Great Depression.

Reading Skill

Why It's Important

Visualizing helps prevent history from being a list of facts and dates. At key points in the text, you may wish to read aloud the scene and ask students to visualize it. Then have volunteers share their images.

1. Introducing the Skill

Have students create tables like the one below, listing five descriptive words for each of the five senses. Students can use their lists to help them create mental pictures of what they read. **BL**

Sense	Descriptive Words
Sight	
Touch	
Smell	
Taste	
Sound	

2. Extending the Skill

Challenge the class to visualize a local site as it might have been in the 1920s. Ask them to use a table similar to the one above to record descriptors for each sense. If possible, invite a member of the local historical society to bring copies of historical photographs of the community. Have students evaluate their ideas against the historical reality. **OL**

Answers and Additional Support

Reading Skill — Visualizing

Authors use descriptive language to create a picture of a person, location, time, or event. These words appeal to the senses and may include sights, sounds, or smells. Authors also use quotes to describe feelings and emotions in order to make the text come alive to the reader. Effective readers take the time to visualize people, places, and events. They also use pictures and diagrams on the page to understand what they are reading.

You can recognize opportunities to visualize by the number of details an author includes. Quotes will also help you identify text passages that may help you create an image in your mind. Look for descriptive language to help you understand the passage. Photographs, maps, diagrams, and charts will also assist you in visualizing text by giving you additional information.

VISUALIZING

Note the highlighted phrases and the vivid images they create. Then look at the photograph on page 475 of the unemployed man. Does this help you create a mental image of Dynamite's father?

Read the following paragraph about the impact of the Great Depression on one family and notice the number of details. Make a picture in your mind as you read.

A young girl with the **unusual name of Dynamite Garland** was living with her family in **Cleveland, Ohio, in the 1930s** when her father, a **railroad worker**, lost his job. Unable to afford rent, they gave up their home and moved into a **two-car garage.**

The hardest aspect of living in a garage was getting through the **frigid winters.** "We would **sleep with rugs and blankets over the top of us,**" Garland later recalled. "In the morning we'd . . . **get some snow and put it on the stove and melt it and wash 'round our faces.**" When Garland's father found a **part-time** job in a Chinese restaurant, the family "**lived on those fried noodles.**" (page 475)

As you try to visualize the life of Dynamite—not the exact description the authors have provided—imagine the size of a two-car garage. How might you and your family fit in such a space, and how would you arrange for living and sleeping areas? Also note how the author mentions the "frigid" winters. What might you do to heat this area?

Apply the Skill

After you have visualized what life was like for Dynamite, with your teacher's permission discuss these images with a partner. How closely does your partner's image match your mental picture? Now reread the passage. Did your ideas change?

UNIVERSAL ACCESS

Visual/Spatial Encourage students to sketch or in some other way visually represent a scene from the chapter. Use student artwork as part of a classroom display on the Depression era. **OL**

Historical Analysis Skill

Developing a Hypothesis

Historical Research, Evidence, and Point of View When you prepare research on a topic in history, you should construct a hypothesis. You can test it by collecting, evaluating, and employing information from multiple primary and secondary sources. Finally, you can apply your hypothesis by preparing oral and written presentations.

Why is the sky blue? Have you ever asked that question? Do you have an explanation? If you do, you could test your explanation. We call your un-tested explanation a hypothesis. You can collect information and data to test your hypothesis and either prove or disprove it. We all construct hypotheses to explain events and actions.

Historians construct hypotheses to test their ideas and explanations. Since historians were not present for the events they study, they use many different primary and secondary sources to test their hypotheses. For example, historians might make a prediction about a possible solution to a problem based on what they know about a topic. If their hypothesis is still valid after their research, then they can be reasonably sure that they were correct in their initial prediction.

Read this paragraph about the roots of the Great Depression.

The stock market crash helped put the economy into a recession. Yet the crash would not have led to a long-lasting depression if other forces had not been at work. The roots of the Great Depression were deeply entangled in the economy of the 1920s. (page 472)

You learn in this paragraph that the author believes there were multiple causes for the Great Depression. The author has made a hypothesis. How could the economy of the 1920s have led to the Great Depression? You will find the author's explanations for this statement in the following pages.

Apply the Skill

Construct a hypothesis about the collapse of the U.S. economy. Also hypothesize the role that business, banking, and consumer spending played in our economy. As you study the next two chapters, collect information that will allow you to test your hypotheses. Remember that in the previous chapter you learned that technological and managerial innovations allowed American companies to increase their production dramatically. However, also consider the law of supply and demand which suggests that when a product is plentiful, its value will decrease.

467

FOCUS

SKILLBUILDER ACTIVITY

Project **Daily Focus Skills Transparency 9-1** and have students answer the question.

Guide to Reading

Understanding Vocabulary: Have students create vocabulary cards for each term, with the terms on the front and the definitions on the back of the cards. Encourage them to review the cards before tests.

Answers to Graphic: Hoover: Republican, Quaker, engineer, eight years as Secretary of Commerce, favored Prohibition; Smith: Democrat, Catholic, four-time governor of New York, opposed Prohibition.

Unpacking the Standards

Students will be able to:

- Discuss the events of the 1928 presidential election.
- Explain the principal causes of the Great Depression.
- Identify the steps taken by the federal government to combat the economic crisis.

Answers and Additional Support

SECTION 1

Causes of the Depression

Guide to Reading

Connection
In the previous chapter, you learned about the prosperity of the 1920s. In this section, you will discover the factors that contributed to the Great Depression.

Main Idea
- In an election marked by religious prejudice and the issue of Prohibition, Herbert Hoover won the presidency in a landslide. (p. 469)
- The long period of rising stock prices led many people to risky investment practices. (p. 470)
- The October 1929 stock market crash led to bank failures across the nation. (p. 471)

- An uneven distribution of income, the lack of foreign markets for exports, and the Federal Reserve's mistakes contributed to the Great Depression. (p. 472)

Content Vocabulary
stock market, bull market, margin, margin call, speculation, installment

Academic Vocabulary
invest, sum, reaction

People and Terms to Identify
Alfred E. Smith, Black Tuesday, Hawley-Smoot Tariff

Reading Objectives
- **Describe** the characteristics of the 1920s stock market.
- **Identify** the causes of the Great Depression.

Reading Strategy
Categorizing As you read about the election of 1928, complete a graphic organizer similar to the one below comparing the backgrounds and issues of the presidential candidates.

1928 Presidential Campaign

Candidate	Background	Issues

Preview of Events

◆November 1928	◆September 1929	◆July 1930

November 1928
Herbert Hoover elected president

October 24, 1929
Stocks fall during Black Thursday

October 29, 1929
Black Tuesday stock market crash

June 1930
Congress passes Hawley-Smoot Tariff

The following are the main History–Social Science Standards covered in this section.

11.5.1 Discuss the policies of Presidents Warren Harding, Calvin Coolidge, and Herbert Hoover.

11.6.1 Describe the monetary issues of the late nineteenth and early twentieth centuries that gave rise to the establishment of the Federal Reserve and the weaknesses in key sectors of the economy in the late 1920s.

11.6.2 Understand the explanations of the principal causes of the Great Depression and the steps taken by the Federal Reserve, Congress and Presidents Herbert Hoover and Franklin Delano Roosevelt to combat the economic crisis.

❧ The Big Idea ❧

Societies change over time. Following the presidential election of Herbert Hoover, most Americans were optimistic about the future of the country. Stock prices were soaring, and many people invested in the stock market. As the number of new investors began to dwindle, the market first slowed and then crashed. The stock market crash resulted in the collapse of many banks. At the same time, overproduction brought an excess of products that many people could not afford to buy. This led factories to lower production and lay off workers. Due to a low number of exports, companies were not able to make up for the reduction in consumer spending. All of these factors, combined with the Federal Reserve's decision to keep interest rates low, led to an economic depression.

468 CHAPTER 9 The Great Depression Begins

SECTION RESOURCES

📂 Print Material
- Reproducible Lesson Plan 9-1
- Guided Reading Activity 9-1
- Reading Essentials and Study Guide 9-1
- Active Reading Note-Taking Guide 9-1

📑 Transparencies
- Daily Focus Skills Transparency 9-1
- Section Graphic Organizer Transparency 9-1

Technology
- ⦿ Interactive Tutor Self-Assessment CD-ROM
- ⦿ ExamView® Pro Testmaker CD-ROM
- ⦿ Presentation Plus! CD-ROM

The Election of 1928

 Main Idea In an election marked by religious prejudice and the issue of Prohibition, Herbert Hoover won the presidency in a landslide.

Reading Connection What issues in school elections or local elections have been important to you? Read on to learn about important campaign issues in the 1928 election.

The economic collapse that began in 1929 had seemed unimaginable only a year earlier. Many people found themselves without work as jobs became scarce.

★ An American Story ★

In the years just after the 1929 stock market crash, Annetta Gibson taught English in a Rockford, Illinois, grade school. As a teacher, Gibson was lucky because she was at least able to keep her job, unlike many other American workers.

66Everyone knew that the teachers' salaries were being held up. . . . The stores charged anything we wanted, and we'd pay them when we got paid, so it wasn't too bad.

The one thing that was bad was that we had worked hard at school to get the children to save. . . . The children would bring, oh, maybe just a few pennies that they would put in their banks. Some of them had nice little bank accounts when the Depression hit, and some of them never got their money back. It wasn't too good a lesson . . . because they thought they might as well spend their money as save it and then have it gone.99

–quoted in *Centenarians: The Story of the Twentieth Century by the Americans Who Lived It*

In the election of 1928, the presidential candidates vied with each other to paint a rosy picture of the future. Republican Herbert Hoover declared, "We are nearer to the final triumph over poverty than ever before in the history of any land."

The Candidates When Calvin Coolidge decided not to run for president in 1928, he cleared the way for Herbert Hoover to head the Republican ticket. A successful engineer and former head of the Food Administration during World War I, Hoover had also spent over seven years as secretary of commerce in the Harding and Coolidge administrations. The Democrats chose **Alfred E. Smith,** four-time governor of New York. Smith was an Irish American from New York's Lower East Side and the first Roman Catholic ever nominated to run for president.

Campaign Issues By 1928 Prohibition had become a major issue among voters. Because he favored the ban on liquor sales, Hoover was considered a "dry" in the popular language of the day. Smith, who disliked the ban, was a "wet."

The candidates' religious differences sparked a smear campaign against Smith. Many Protestants were willing to believe that the Catholic Church financed the Democratic Party and would rule the United States if Smith got into the White House. These slurs embarrassed Hoover, a Quaker, and he tried to quash them, but the charges seriously damaged Smith's candidacy.

Smith's biggest problem, however, was the prosperity of the 1920s, for which the Republicans took full credit. Republican candidates promised to continue the trend with such slogans as "two cars in every garage." Hoover received over 6 million more votes than Smith and won the Electoral College in a landslide, 444 to 87.

On March 4, 1929, an audience of 50,000 stood in the rain to hear Hoover's inaugural speech. Sound movie cameras covered the inauguration for the first time and radios broadcast the address worldwide. "I have no fears for the future of our country," Hoover said. "It is bright with hope."

☑ **Reading Check** **Examining** What campaign issues led to Herbert Hoover's election to the presidency?

▼ *Bank run at a Newark, New Jersey bank*

More Skill Practice

Using Context Clues Review with students the political meanings of the slang terms *wet* and *dry.* **Ask:** Can you think of any slang terms that are common to current politics? *(red state, blue state, neocon)* OL

TEACH

 Reading Strategy

Monitoring One of the most important reading strategies students can learn is that of monitoring comprehension as they read. Students should recognize when they have missed some of the content. Tell students to monitor their comprehension by asking themselves questions as they read through the text under the heading "The Election of 1928." If they do not understand an important concept, they should reread, review, or read on to clarify what is unclear. OL CA 11RL2.4

C Critical Thinking

Comparing and Contrasting Write on the board the following three issues that helped determine the outcome of the 1928 presidential election: *prosperity, Prohibition,* and *Protestantism.* Ask students to write down one example for each issue, showing how it worked against Smith and for Hoover. Allow students to work in pairs to check their answers. Then ask for volunteers to share their answers with the class. OL

Resources for page 469

*Have students read more about the election of 1928 in the **Primary Source Reading 9-1.***

☑ **Reading Check**

Answer: Prohibition, religious values, economic prosperity

469

The Long Bull Market

Main Idea The long period of rising stock prices led many people to risky investment practices.

Reading Connection What are your strategies for saving money? Read on to find out about people's efforts to make money in the stock market during the 1920s.

 The wave of optimism that swept Hoover into the White House also drove stock prices to new highs. The **stock market** was established as a system for buying and selling shares of companies. Sometimes circumstances in the stock market lead to a long period of rising stock prices, which is known as a **bull market.** In the late 1920s a prolonged bull market convinced many Americans to **invest** heavily in stocks. By 1929 about 3 million Americans, or roughly 10 percent of households, owned stocks.

As the market continued to soar, many investors began buying stocks on **margin,** meaning they made only a small cash down payment—as low as 10 percent of the price. With $1,000 an investor could buy $10,000 worth of stock. The other $9,000 would come as a loan from a stockbroker, who earned both a commission on the sale and interest on the loan. The broker held the stock as collateral.

As long as stock prices kept rising, buying on margin was safe. For example, an investor who borrowed money to buy $10,000 worth of stocks had to wait only a short time for them to rise to $11,000 in value. The investor could then sell the stock, repay the loan, and make $1,000 in profit. The problem came if the stock price began to fall. To protect the loan, a broker could issue a **margin call,** demanding the investor repay the loan at once. As a result, many investors were very sensitive to any fall in stock prices. If prices fell, they had to sell quickly, or they might not be able to repay their loans.

The Great Depression

Causes

- Overproduction and low demand leads to employee layoffs
- Low wages reduce consumer buying power
- High tariffs restrict foreign demand for American goods
- Unemployment reduces buying power further

HOOVER POOR FARM
FLWD
HARD TIMES ARE STILL HOOVER AND OVER US

Cyclical Effect

Automobile sales declined. This loss of demand meant less demand for:

Which helped contribute further to...

Textiles Oil
Steel Rubber

$ Unemployment
Lower wages

Industry slowed, which caused:

Stock Prices, 1920–1932

Price per Share

— Annual high
— Annual low

$350
$300
$250
$200
$150
$100
$50
0

1920 1922 1924 1926 1928 1930 1932
Dow-Jones Industrial Averages
Source: Standard and Poor's *Security Price Index Record.*

📈 Graph *Skills*

1. **Interpreting Graphs** Stock prices peaked in 1929. Before this peak, when did they begin to rise sharply?
2. **Making Generalizations** How did the decline in auto sales affect many other industries?

470 CHAPTER 9 The Great Depression Begins

Before the late 1920s, the prices investors paid for stocks generally reflected the stocks' true value. If a company made a profit or had good future sales prospects, its stock price rose, while a drop in earnings or an aging product line could send the price down. In the late 1920s, however, hordes of new investors bid prices up without regard to a company's earnings and profits. Buyers, hoping to make a fortune overnight, engaged in **speculation.** Instead of investing in the future of the companies, speculators took risks, betting that the market would continue to climb, thus enabling them to make money quickly.

✓ **Reading Check** **Summarizing** What was the stock market like in the 1920s?

The Great Crash

Main Idea The October 1929 stock market crash led to bank failures across the nation.

Reading Connection If a stock market crash were to occur today, how would your family be affected? Read on to learn about the stock market collapse in 1929.

The bull market lasted only as long as investors continued putting new money into it. By the latter half of 1929, the market was running out of new customers. In September professional investors sensed danger and began to sell off their holdings. Prices slipped. Other investors sold shares to pay the interest on their brokerage loans. Prices fell further.

Crash! On Monday, October 21, Groucho Marx, the comic star of stage and screen, was awakened by a telephone call from his broker. "You'd better get down here with some cash to cover your margin," the broker said. The stock market had plunged. The dazed comedian had to pay back the money he had borrowed to buy stocks, which were now selling for far less than he had paid.

Other brokers made similar margin calls. Frightened customers put their stocks up for sale at a frenzied pace, driving the market into a tailspin. When Marx arrived at the brokerage, he found ticker tape "knee deep on the floor." He further recalled, "People were shouting orders to sell and others were frantically scribbling checks in vain efforts to save their original investments."

On October 24, a day that came to be called Black Thursday, the market plummeted further. Marx was wiped out. He had earned a small fortune from plays

Picturing History

Herbert Hoover The nation and its new president felt confident about the future in early 1929. **Why were Americans so optimistic?**

and films, and now it was gone in the blink of an eye. Like many other investors, he was deeply in debt. Arthur Marx recalled his father's final visit to the brokerage, as Groucho looked around and spotted his broker:

> ❝He was sitting in front of the now-stilled ticker-tape machine, with his head buried in his hands. Ticker tape was strewn around him on the floor, and the place . . . looked as if it hadn't been swept out in a week. Groucho tapped [him] on the shoulder and said, 'Aren't you the fellow who said nothing could go wrong?' 'I guess I made a mistake,' the broker wearily replied. 'No, I'm the one who made a mistake,' snapped Groucho. 'I listened to you.'❞

–quoted in *1929: The Year of the Great Crash*

The following week, on October 29, a day later dubbed **Black Tuesday,** prices took the steepest dive yet. That day stocks lost $10 to $15 billion in value.

By mid-November stock prices had dropped by over one-third. Some $30 billion was lost, a **sum** roughly equal to the total wages earned by Americans in 1929. The stock market crash was not the major cause of the Great Depression, but it undermined the economy's ability to hold out against its other weaknesses.

CHAPTER 9 The Great Depression Begins **471**

R₁ **Reading Strategy**

Scaffolding—Academic Vocabulary The word *prospect* was introduced in Chapter 2, Section 4. Ask a student to define the word. **BL**

R₂ **Reading Strategy**

Identifying the Main Idea and Supporting Details Have students create outlines of the material under this heading to show the main ideas and supporting details. Tell students that the outlines can later be used for review of the section prior to a quiz or test. **OL**

W **Writing Support**

Expository Writing Highlight the quote by Groucho Marx on this page. Ask students to write a journal entry that either defends or criticizes stock brokers during this time. Should they have been more cautious, or did the economic conditions of the period only become clear after the Depression began? **AL** **CA HR3**

✓ **Reading Check**

Answer: bull market, a long period of rising stock prices

Picturing History

Background: Herbert Hoover was born in Iowa, grew up in Oregon, and graduated from Stanford University.
Answer: The economy and stock market were growing.
Ask: What campaign slogan did Hoover use to assure Americans of continuing prosperity? *(two cars in every garage)*

C Critical Thinking

Analyzing Information Have students create graphic organizers that demonstrate the cause-and-effect relationships presented under the heading "Banks in a Tailspin." **BL** **CA 11RC2.4**

W Writing Support

Persuasive Writing Invite students to write letters to the editor of a major newspaper in their community as if they were adults during the 1920s. Challenge them to take a position on something they have learned under this heading and write a persuasive letter stating their opinion. **OL**
CA 11WS1.3

R Reading Strategy

Scaffolding—Academic Vocabulary The word *capacity* was introduced in Chapter 5, Section 4. Ask a student to define the word. **BL**

Review the Big Idea

Review the Big Idea for this section, "Societies change over time." Ask students to use the library and Internet resources to identify how the banking system changed as a result of the stock market crash. **OL**

✓ Reading Check

Answer: The bank failures triggered a crisis of confidence in the banking system. Many people made runs on the banks, causing them to collapse.

C **Banks in a Tailspin** The market crash severely weakened the nation's banks in two ways. First, many banks had lent money to stock speculators. Second, many banks had invested depositors' money in the stock market, hoping for higher returns than they could get by using the money for conventional loans.

When stock values collapsed, the banks lost money on their investments, and the speculators defaulted on their loans. Having suffered serious losses, many banks cut back drastically on the loans they made. With less credit available, consumers and businesses were unable to borrow as much money as they had previously. This helped to put the economy into a recession.

For some banks, the losses they suffered in the crash were more than they could absorb, and they were forced to close. At that time, the government did not insure bank deposits; therefore, if a bank collapsed, customers lost their savings. The bank failures in 1929 and early 1930 triggered a crisis of confidence in the banking system.

News of bank failures worried many Americans. They began to make runs on the nation's banks, causing the banks to collapse. A bank run takes place when many depositors decide to withdraw their money at one time, usually for fear the bank is going to collapse. During this time, there were no guarantees to protect people's money in case of a bank collapse.

Most banks make a profit by lending money received from depositors and collecting interest on the loans. The bank holds on to only a fraction of the depositors' money to cover everyday business, such as occasional withdrawals. Ordinarily that reserve is enough to meet the bank's needs, but if too many people withdraw their money, the bank will eventually collapse. During the first two years of the Depression, more than 3,000 banks—over 10 percent of the nation's total—were forced to close.

✓ **Reading Check** **Evaluating** How did bank failures contribute to the Great Depression?

History *Through Art*

Wall Street Panic This painting shows the confusion and chaos surrounding the financial industry in October 1929. How does the artist depict a sense of disorder?

472   CHAPTER 9   The Great Depression Begins

The Roots of the Great Depression

Main Idea An uneven distribution of income, the lack of foreign markets for exports, and the Federal Reserve's mistakes contributed to the Great Depression.

Reading Connection What do you believe is the current distribution of income in America? Read on to learn about the distribution of income just prior to the Great Depression.

The stock market crash helped put the economy into a recession. Yet the crash would not have led to a long-lasting depression if other forces had not been at work. The roots of the Great Depression were deeply entangled in the economy of the 1920s.

The Uneven Distribution of Income Most economists agree that overproduction was a key cause of the Depression. More efficient machinery increased the production capacity of both factories and farms.

Most Americans did not earn enough to buy up the flood of goods they helped produce. While manufacturing output per person-hour rose 32 percent, the average worker's wage increased only 8 percent. In 1929 the top 5 percent of all American households earned 30 percent of the nation's income. By contrast, about two-thirds of families earned less than $2,500 a year, leaving them little expendable income.

Did You Know?

Some of the country's leading financiers tried to avert the crash by pumping money into the market, but others wanted to profit from the panic. The president of Chase National Bank sold 42,506 shares of his own bank's stock, bought them back later in the year at a lower price, and made a profit of $4 million.

History *Through Art*

Answer: the urgent sense of movement; the paper littered on the floor; the shocked looks of several figures
Ask: What occurred on Black Tuesday?
(Stocks lost $10 to $15 billion in value in their steepest drop.)

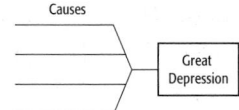
▲ *Newspaper headline the day after Black Tuesday*

During the 1920s many Americans bought high-cost items on the **installment** plan, under which they would make a small down payment and pay the rest in monthly installments. Some buyers could not pay off their debts without reducing other purchases. This low consumption then led manufacturers to cut production and lay off employees.

The slowdown in retail manufacturing had repercussions throughout the economy. When radio sales slumped, for example, makers cut back on their orders for copper wire, wood cabinets, and glass radio tubes. Montana copper miners, Minnesota lumberjacks, and Ohio glassworkers, in turn, lost their jobs. Jobless workers had to cut back purchases, further reducing sales. This kind of chain **reaction** put more and more Americans out of work.

The Loss of Export Sales Many jobs might have been saved if American manufacturers had sold more goods abroad. As the bull market of the 1920s accelerated, U.S. banks made high-interest loans to stock speculators instead of lending money to foreign companies. Without these loans from U.S. banks, foreign companies purchased fewer American products.

Matters grew worse after June 1930, when Congress passed the **Hawley-Smoot Tariff** raising the average tariff rate to the highest level in American history. The Hawley-Smoot Tariff aimed to protect American manufacturers from foreign competition, but it damaged American sales abroad. Because imports now cost much more, Americans bought fewer of them. Foreign countries responded by raising their own tariffs against American products, and this caused fewer American products to be sold overseas. In 1932 U.S. exports fell to about one-fifth of what they had been in 1929, which hurt both American companies and farmers.

Mistakes by the Federal Reserve Just as consumers were able to buy more goods on credit, access to easy money propelled the stock market. Instead of raising interest rates to curb excessive speculation, the Federal Reserve Board kept its rates very low.

The Board's failure to raise interest rates contributed to the Depression in two ways. First, by keeping rates low, it encouraged member banks to make risky loans. Second, low interest rates led business leaders to think the economy was still expanding. As a result, they borrowed more money to expand production, which led to overproduction when sales were falling. When the Depression hit, companies had to lay off workers to cut costs. Then the Fed made another mistake. It raised interest rates, tightening credit. The economy continued to spiral downward.

☑ **Reading Check** **Examining** How did the decline in worldwide trade contribute to the Depression?

HISTORY Online **Study Central**

For help with the concepts in this section of *American Vision: Modern Times* go to tav.mt.glencoe.com and click on **Study Central.**

SECTION 1 ASSESSMENT

Checking for Understanding

1. **Vocabulary** Define: stock market, bull market, invest, margin, margin call, speculation, sum installment, reaction.
2. **People and Terms** Identify: Alfred E. Smith, Black Tuesday, Hawley-Smoot Tariff.
3. **Explain** the significance of the stock market crash, including Black Tuesday.

Reviewing Big Ideas

4. **Interpreting** How did the practices of buying on margin and speculation cause the stock market to rise?

Critical Thinking

5. **Evaluating** Why did the stock market crash cause banks to fail?
6. **Organizing** Use a graphic organizer similar to the one below to list the causes of the Great Depression.

Causes → Great Depression

Analyzing Visuals

7. **Analyzing Graphs** Study the graphs on page 470. Note that decreased demand for automobiles ultimately led to layoffs. These layoffs further decreased the demand for automobiles. What do you think might have ended this cycle?

Writing About History

8. **Expository Writing** Write an article for a financial magazine explaining the rapid decline of the stock market in 1929 and the reasons for the Black Tuesday crash. CA 11WA2.1a

CHAPTER 9   The Great Depression Begins   **473**

SECTION 1 ASSESSMENT ANSWERS

1. Content vocabulary is boldfaced and highlighted in yellow. Academic vocabulary is boldfaced.
2. Alfred E. Smith *(p. 469)*, Black Tuesday *(p. 471)*, Hawley-Smoot Tariff *(p. 473)*
3. The Great Depression began.
4. Speculation drove up market prices beyond the stocks' value.
5. Banks had lent money to speculators and had invested depositors' money in stocks.
6. uneven distribution of wealth, decline in sales, mistakes by the Federal Reserve
7. Answers will vary. Students may suggest that businesses could have avoided layoffs or that the government could have intervened.
8. Students' articles will vary but should include appropriate vocabulary.

R Reading Strategy

Scaffolding—Connecting Ask students to give examples of some current merchandise that is often purchased using installment plans. *(cars, furniture, major appliances, computer or sound systems)* You may wish to provide some advertising circulars for the class to peruse. Have students explain how best to use this technique and how to avoid being caught in a downward financial spiral. OL CA 11RL2.4

This [Reading Skill] was introduced in Chapter 7.

ASSESS

Resources for page 473

Use these resources to assess student mastery.

📁 Section Quiz 9-1

📁 Reading Essentials and Study Guide 9-1

⊙ Interactive Tutor Self-Assessment CD-ROM

📁 California Standards Practice, Grade 11

☑ **Reading Check**

Answer: Tariffs damaged American sales abroad and discouraged imports.

HISTORY Online

Study Central provides audio summaries, interactive games, and online graphic organizers to help students review section content.

CLOSE

Summarizing Ask the class to list the causes of the Great Depression. OL

473

FOCUS

SKILLBUILDER ACTIVITY

Project **Daily Focus Skills Transparency 9-2** and have students answer the question.

Guide to Reading

Understanding Vocabulary:
Ask: What are words like *shantytown* and *soap opera* called? *(compound words)* Remind students that compound words can be written as one word, two words, or hyphenated.

Answers to Graphic: Students should complete the outline using the headings in the section.

Unpacking the Standards

Students will be able to:

• Discuss the human toll of the Depression, natural disasters, and unwise agricultural practices.

• Determine the effects of the Depression on internal migration and political movements of the left and right.

Answers and Additional Support

SECTION 2 — Life During the Depression

Guide to Reading

Connection
In the previous section, you learned about the causes of the Great Depression. In this section, you will discover how the Depression worsened and people sought escape from the hardships.

Main Idea
• As banks continued to fail and people lost jobs and homes, soup kitchens and shantytowns sprang up throughout the United States. Droughts during the 1930s made the Depression even worse for farmers. (p. 475)
• Movies and radio shows allowed people to forget temporarily the miseries of the Depression. (p. 477)

• Painters, photographers, and writers all captured the experiences of people during the Great Depression. (p. 479)

Content Vocabulary
bailiff, shantytown, Hooverville, hobo, Dust Bowl, soap opera

Academic Vocabulary
suspend, colleague, technique

People and Terms to Identify
Walt Disney, Grant Wood, John Steinbeck, William Faulkner

Reading Objectives
• **Describe** how the Great Depression affected American families.

• **Discuss** how artists portrayed the effects of the Depression.

Reading Strategy
Taking Notes As you read about life in the United States during the Great Depression, use the major headings of the section to create an outline similar to the one below.

Life During the Depression
I. The Depression Worsens
   A.
   B.
   C.
II.

Preview of Events

♦1930	♦1935	♦1940

1930	**1932**	**1934**	**1937**	**1939**
Grant Wood paints *American Gothic*	Drought sweeps Great Plains	Dust storms destroy 300 million acres	Walt Disney releases *Snow White and the Seven Dwarfs*	Popular musical *The Wizard of Oz* released

The following are the main History–Social Science Standards covered in this section.

11.6 Students analyze the different explanations for the Great Depression and how the New Deal fundamentally changed the role of the federal government.

11.6.3 Discuss the human toll of the Depression, natural disasters, and unwise agricultural practices and their effects on the depopulation of rural regions and on political movements of the left and right, with particular attention to the Dust Bowl refugees and their social and economic impacts in California.

～ *The Big Idea* ～

Societies change over time. As the Depression worsened, many people could not afford housing. They lived in makeshift villages and traveled from town to town in search of work. When the Dust Bowl hit in the Great Plains, many more found themselves without jobs or places to live. People found escape from their troubles in movies or radio programs, which allowed them brief visits into a more exciting and happier world. At the same time, Depression hardships inspired painters, photographers, and writers to depict their views of life under such difficult circumstances.

474 CHAPTER 9 The Great Depression Begins

SECTION RESOURCES

📂 **Print Material**
• Reproducible Lesson Plan 9-2
• Guided Reading Activity 9-2
• Reading Essentials and Study Guide 9-2
• Active Reading Note-Taking Guide 9-2

🕯 **Transparencies**
• Daily Focus Skills Transparency 9-2
• Section Graphic Organizer Transparency 9-2

Technology
🔘 Interactive Tutor Self-Assessment CD-ROM
🔘 Exam*View*® Pro Testmaker CD-ROM
🔘 Presentation Plus! CD-ROM

The Depression Worsens

Main Idea As banks continued to fail and people lost jobs and homes, soup kitchens and shantytowns sprang up throughout the United States. Droughts during the 1930s made the Depression worse for farmers.

Reading Connection Have you or someone you know ever helped serve in a local soup kitchen or food pantry? Read on to discover how people relied on private charities for their meals during the Great Depression.

In 1930, 1,352 banks **suspended** operations across the nation, more than twice the number of bank failures in 1929. As the Depression grew steadily worse during Hoover's administration, many people found themselves unable to afford housing.

★ An American Story ★

A young girl with the unusual name of Dynamite Garland was living with her family in Cleveland, Ohio, in the 1930s when her father, a railroad worker, lost his job. Unable to afford rent, they gave up their home and moved into a two-car garage.

The hardest aspect of living in a garage was getting through the frigid winters. "We would sleep with rugs and blankets over the top of us," Garland later recalled. "In the morning we'd . . . get some snow and put it on the stove and melt it and wash 'round our faces." When Garland's father found a part-time job in a Chinese restaurant, the family "lived on those fried noodles."

On Sundays the family looked at houses for sale. "That was a recreation during the Depression," said Garland. "You'd go and see where you'd put this and where you could put that, and this is gonna be my room." In this way, the family tried to focus on better times. Movies and radio programs also provided a brief escape from their troubles, but the struggle to survive left little room for pleasure.

—adapted from *Hard Times*

By 1933 more than 9,000 banks had failed. In 1932 alone some 30,000 companies went out of business. By 1933 more than 12 million workers were unemployed—about one fourth of the workforce. Average family income dropped from $2,300 in 1929 to $1,600 a few years later.

Lining Up at Soup Kitchens People without jobs often went hungry. Whenever possible they joined bread lines to receive a free handout of food or lined up outside soup kitchens, which private charities set up to give poor people a meal.

Peggy Terry, a young girl in Oklahoma City during the Depression, later told an interviewer how each day after school, her mother sent her to the soup kitchen:

> ❝If you happened to be one of the first ones in line, you didn't get anything but water that was on top. So we'd ask the guy that was ladling out soup into the buckets—everybody had to bring their own bucket to get the soup—he'd dip the greasy, watery stuff off the top. So we'd ask him to please dip down to get some meat and potatoes from the bottom of the kettle. But he wouldn't do it.❞

—quoted in *Hard Times*

Living in Makeshift Villages Families or individuals who could not pay their rent or mortgage lost their homes. Some of them, paralyzed by fear and humiliation over their sudden misfortune, simply would not or could not move. Their landlord would then ask the court for an eviction notice. Court officers called **bailiffs** then ejected the nonpaying tenants, piling their belongings in the street.

Throughout the country, newly homeless people put up shacks on unused or public lands, forming communities called **shantytowns.** Blaming the president for their plight, people referred to such places as **Hoovervilles.**

An unemployed man advertising his skills ▶

CHAPTER 9 The Great Depression Begins **475**

TEACH

R₁ Reading Strategy

Connecting Remind students of the more recent difficult circumstances that America has faced, such as the attacks on the World Trade Center and the Pentagon on September 11, 2001. Ask them what positive and negative emotions and activities came about because of the tragedies. Then ask students to apply those ideas to the Great Depression. What do they think might have happened to the people who lived during that time? **BL**

R₂ Reading Strategy

Questioning Have students work in pairs to ask each other interview questions that a journalist might have asked during the Great Depression. The questions should concern the government's response to the Depression and the interviewee's opinions about that response. Students should include as much of the information they have gathered while reading this section as possible. **OL** **CA** 11RL2.4

Resources for page 475

Have students learn more about the effects of unemployment in the United States by reading "#38" from The People, Yes *in the **American Literature Readings 3.***

More Skill Practice

Analyzing Word Choice Remind students of the importance of word choice in creating the proper tone in writing. Have students use a thesaurus to find synonyms for the word *hobo*. (*homeless, vagrant, tramp, vagabond, bum*) Then have them work in pairs to vary the tone of a sentence by changing the word. Discuss the difference in tone for the words *shantytown, Hooverville, slum, ghetto,* and *barrio*. Ask students when and how each word might be used for the greatest effect. **OL**

S Skill Practice

Visual Literacy Draw students' attention to the photograph. **Ask:**
How does the photo convey the despair of migrant workers?
(the worry lines in the woman's face, the children hiding from a stranger with a camera, the worn clothing) Have students imagine the woman's story after this photograph was taken. **BL** **CA HI1**

U Universal Access

English Learners The text under the heading "The Dust Bowl" contains descriptive words that may not be familiar to English learners. *(blanketed, scant, whipped, withered, makeshift)* Encourage these students to keep a notebook of unfamiliar terms and to check dictionaries for their meanings. Students can list the new words in one column, and then write definitions or synonyms in the second column. **EL**

Answers and Additional Support

HISTORY Online
Student Web Activity Visit the *American Vision: Modern Times* Web site at tav.mt.glencoe.com and click on **Student Web Activities– Chapter 9** for an activity on the Great Depression.

In search of work or a better life, many homeless and unemployed Americans began to wander around the country, walking, hitchhiking, or, most often, "riding the rails." These wanderers, called **hobos,** would sneak past railroad police to slip into open boxcars on freight trains for a ride to somewhere else. They camped in "hobo jungles," usually situated near rail yards. Hundreds of thousands of people, mostly boys and young men, wandered from place to place in this fashion, sleeping and eating where they could.

The Dust Bowl Farmers soon faced a new disaster. Since the beginnings of homesteading on the Great Plains, farmers had gambled with nature. Their plows had uprooted the wild grasses that held the soil's moisture. The new settlers then blanketed the region with wheat fields.

When crop prices dropped in the 1920s, however, Midwestern farmers left many of their fields uncultivated. Then, beginning in 1932, a terrible drought struck the Great Plains. With neither grass nor wheat to hold the scant rainfall, the soil dried to dust. From the Dakotas to Texas, America's pastures and wheat fields became a vast **"Dust Bowl."**

Winds whipped the arid earth, blowing it aloft and blackening the sky. When the dust settled, it buried crops and livestock and piled up against farmhouses like snow. No matter how carefully farm families sealed their homes, dust covered everything. As the drought persisted, the number of yearly dust storms grew, from 22 in 1934 to 72 in 1937.

Only some Midwestern and Great Plains farmers managed to hold on to their land. If their withered fields were mortgaged, they had to turn them over to the banks. Then, nearly penniless, many families packed their belongings and headed west. Since many migrants were from Oklahoma, they became

NATIONAL GEOGRAPHIC
MOMENT in HISTORY

IMAGE OF AN ERA
Lasting a decade, the Great Depression deprived many Americans of jobs, land, and livelihoods. Plummeting crop prices and farms withering under drought, and dust clouds forced many families to take to the road in search of work, often with little success. Dismayed by scenes of destitution and homelessness, photographer Dorothea Lange joined the Resettlement Administration in 1935. In 1936 in rural Nipomo, California, Lange photographed this "Migrant Mother," a 32-year-old woman with seven children. She had just sold her car tires to buy food.

476 CHAPTER 9 The Great Depression Begins

NATIONAL GEOGRAPHIC **MOMENT in HISTORY**

During the 1930s, the Resettlement Administration trained recreational leaders by having them gather the folk music of many immigrant groups. Today the Library of Congress has the song sheets from this project.

HISTORY Online

Objectives and answers to the student activity can be found in the **Web Activity Lesson Plan** at tav.mt.glencoe.com.

NATIONAL GEOGRAPHIC — Dust Bowl, 1930s

Legend:
- State with population loss, 1930–1940
- Area with severe loss of topsoil
- Area with moderate loss of topsoil
- Movement of people
- Destination of Dust Bowl emigrants

Okies escaping the Dust Bowl

500 miles
500 kilometers
Lambert Azimuthal Equal-Area projection

Geography *Skills*

1. **Interpreting Maps** Which states lost population in the 1930s?
2. **Applying Geography Skills** Why did most of the routes shown on the map lead to cities?

W known as "Okies." Many migrants believed they would find a better life in California, which was thought to have a perfect climate for agriculture and plenty of work available. California soon became overwhelmed with the number of migrant workers. Many migrants were met with hostility from those already living in California because of competition for jobs. Most remained homeless and impoverished.

✓ **Reading Check** **Explaining** What chain of events turned the once-fertile Great Plains into the Dust Bowl?

Escaping the Depression

Main Idea Movies and radio shows allowed people to forget the miseries of the Depression.

Reading Connection How do movies and other forms of media help you get through difficult times? Read on to learn ways that people coped with the Great Depression.

Despite the devastatingly hard times, Americans could escape—if only for an hour or two—through entertainment. Most people could scrape together

the money to go to the movies, or they could sit with their families and listen to one of the many radio programs broadcast across the country. Entertainment provided an escape from the difficult times.

The Hollywood Fantasy Factory Ordinary citizens often went to the movies to see people who were rich, happy, and successful. The 60 to 90 million weekly viewers walked into a fantasy world of thrills and romance. Comical screenplays offered a welcome release from daily worries. Groucho Marx wisecracked while his brothers' antics provoked hilarity in such films as *Animal Crackers*.

R Many European actors, writers, and directors, fleeing economic hardship and the threat of dictatorships, went to Hollywood in the 1920s and 1930s. Two European women emerged as superstars. Germany's Marlene Dietrich portrayed a range of roles with subtlety in movies such as *Morocco* and *Shanghai Express*. Swedish actress Greta Garbo often played a doomed beauty, direct and unhesitating in her speech and actions, and was the highest paid female in the United States during the mid-1930s.

Moviegoers also loved cartoons. **Walt Disney** produced the first feature-length animated film, *Snow*

Writing Support

Narrative Writing Invite students to imagine that they are "Okies." Have each student write a letter to a family member telling of their experiences in the Dust Bowl, either at the time it happened or as a recollection after it was over. Encourage students to use sensory detail and specific language. **OL** **CA** 11WA2.1c

Reading Strategy

Scaffolding—Academic Vocabulary The word *emerge* was introduced in Chapter 7, Section 2. Ask a student to define the word. **BL**

Review the Big Idea

Review the Big Idea for this section, "Societies change over time." Tell students that in 1938, 80 million movie tickets were sold weekly. If each ticket represented one person—which it did not since some people saw movies twice a week— that would have been 65 percent of the total population. Ask students to research the number of tickets sold for the current year and calculate a population percentage. **AL**

✓ **Reading Check**

Answer: uprooting the wild grasses, a drop in crop prices, and terrible drought

---

Geography *Skills*

Answers:
1. South Dakota, Nebraska, Kansas, Oklahoma
2. Cities had more job possibilities.

Geography Skills Practice
Ask: To what city did North Dakota farmers migrate? *(Fargo)*

More Skill Practice

Logical/Mathematical Have students use library or Internet resources, such as the *Statistical Abstract of the United States,* to locate and graph unemployment rates for the 1930s. Then ask them to compare unemployment figures for the past 10 years and write a brief paragraph contrasting the data. **AL**

477

White and the Seven Dwarfs, in 1937. Its box office appeal may have spurred MGM two years later to produce *The Wizard of Oz,* a colorful musical that lifted viewers' spirits.

Even when films focused on serious subjects, they usually contained a note of optimism. In *Mr. Smith Goes to Washington,* James Stewart plays a naïve youth leader who becomes a senator. He dramatically exposes the corruption of some of his **colleagues** and calls upon his fellow senators to see the American political system as the peak of "what man's carved out for himself after centuries of fighting for something better than just jungle law."

Gone with the Wind, an elaborately costumed film nearly four hours long, topped the Depression-era epics. Its heroine, Scarlett O'Hara, played by British actress Vivien Leigh, struggles to maintain her life on a Georgia plantation during and after the Civil War. Romance enters as Clark Gable, playing the masterful Rhett Butler, woos Scarlett. Audiences found inspiration in Scarlett's unassailable will to survive.

S **On the Air** While movie drama captured the imagination, radio offered entertainment on a more personal level. People listened to the radio every day, gathering around the big wooden box in the living room. It could have been the voice of the president or a newscaster that held their attention. More often it was the comedy of Jack Benny or George Burns and Gracie Allen, or the adventures of a hero like the Green Hornet.

One of the most popular heroes was the Lone Ranger, who fought injustice in the Old West with the help of his "faithful Indian companion," Tonto. The listener needed only to picture the hero with a black mask hiding his identity, as he fired a silver bullet to knock a gun from an outlaw's hand.

Daytime radio dramas carried their stories over from day to day. Programs such as *The Guiding Light* depicted middle-class families confronting illness, conflict, and other problems. These short dramas allowed listeners to escape into a world more exciting than their own. The shows' sponsors were often makers of laundry soaps, so the shows were nicknamed **soap operas.**

While the Depression tore at the fabric of many towns, radio created a new type of community. Even strangers found common ground in discussing the lives of radio characters.

✓ **Reading Check** **Evaluating** What movies and radio shows entertained Americans during the Depression?

Profiles IN HISTORY

Dorothea Lange
1895–1965

Before she had ever used a camera, Dorothea Lange knew she wanted to be a photographer. After finishing high school, she took a photography course in New York, then traveled around the world. Lange earned her keep by taking and selling photos. Her trip ended in San Francisco.

In San Francisco, Lange photographed homeless people and uncovered the desperation of her subjects. One day, while driving through California's Central Valley, Lange noticed a sign: "Pea-Pickers Camp." On impulse, she stopped. She approached a woman and her children gazing listlessly out of a tattered tent. Lange took five pictures while the mother "sat in that lean-to tent with her children huddled around her, and seemed to know that my pictures might help her, and so she helped me."

In the mid-1930s, Lange traveled through the Dust Bowl states, capturing the ravages of dust storms. When the images were reproduced in a best-selling book, *American Exodus,* the state of California created camps to shelter migrant workers.

Profiles IN HISTORY

Background: Lange started her career as a portrait photographer, often taking pictures of wealthy individuals and families. Lange worked for several government agencies documenting American life.

Ask: How do you think Lange's photographs helped officials in California decide to create camps to shelter migrant workers? *(Her work brought the problem to officials' attention and made it seem more real.)*

The Depression in Art

Main Idea Painters, photographers, and writers all captured the experiences of people during the Great Depression.

Reading Connection Have you ever written a poem, story, or diary entry or drawn a picture to express how you were feeling at a particular time? Read on to find out about the artists of the 1930s and their portrayals of the nation.

Art and literature also flourished in the harsh and emotional 1930s. The homeless and unemployed became the subject of pictures and stories as artists and writers tried to portray life around them.

Thomas Hart Benton and **Grant Wood** led the regionalist school, which emphasized traditional American values, especially those of the rural Midwest and South. Wood's most famous painting, *American Gothic,* portrays a stern farmer and his daughter in front of their humble farmhouse. The portrait pays tribute to no-nonsense Midwesterners while at the same time gently making fun of their severity.

Novelists such as **John Steinbeck** added flesh and blood to journalists' reports of poverty and misfortune. Their writing evoked both sympathy for their characters and indignation at social injustice. In *The Grapes of Wrath,* published in 1939, Steinbeck tells the story of an Oklahoma family fleeing the Dust Bowl to find a new life in California. Steinbeck had seen firsthand the plight of migrant farm families uprooted by the Dust Bowl. After visiting camps of these families he had a better understanding of their fears. He described "people in flight" along Route 66. Inside one old jalopy sat the members of a family, worrying:

❝There goes a gasket. Got to go on. Find a nice place to camp. . . . The food's getting low, the money's getting low. When we can't buy no more gas—what then? Danny in the back seat wants a cup a water. Little fella's thirsty.❞

–from *The Grapes of Wrath*

Other novelists of this time influenced literary style itself. In *The Sound and the Fury,* for example, author **William Faulkner** shows what his characters are thinking and feeling before they speak. Using this stream of consciousness **technique,** he exposes hidden attitudes of Southern whites and African Americans in a fictional Mississippi county. Another Southern writer, Thomas Wolfe, used the facts of his own life to examine the theme of artistic creation in such powerful novels as *Look Homeward Angel.*

While the written word remained powerful, the printed image was growing in influence. Magazine photographers roamed the nation armed with the new 35-millimeter cameras, seeking new subjects. Photojournalist Margaret Bourke-White's striking pictures, displayed in *Fortune* magazine, showed the ravages of drought. In 1936 *Time* magazine publisher Henry Luce introduced *Life,* a weekly photojournalism magazine that enjoyed instant success.

Reading Check **Examining** How did artists, photographers, and writers, such as John Steinbeck, reflect the characteristics of the 1930s?

HISTORY *Online* **Study Central**

For help with the concepts in this section of *American Vision: Modern Times* go to tav.mt.glencoe.com and click on *Study Central.*

SECTION 2 ASSESSMENT

Checking for Understanding

1. **Vocabulary** Define: suspend, bailiff, shantytown, Hooverville, hobo, Dust Bowl, colleague, soap opera, technique.
2. **People and Terms** Identify: Walt Disney, Grant Wood, John Steinbeck, William Faulkner.
3. **Explain** what caused the Dust Bowl conditions on the Great Plains.

Reviewing Big Ideas

4. **Describing** In what ways did people seek to forget about the Depression?

Critical Thinking

5. **Historical Analysis** **Making Inferences** Why do you think *Life* magazine was so popular during the 1930s? **CA HI1; HI3**
6. **Organizing** Use a graphic organizer to list the effects of the Great Depression.

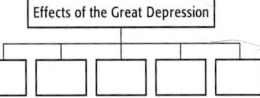

Effects of the Great Depression

Analyzing Visuals

7. **Analyzing Photos** Study the photograph on page 476. Think of three adjectives that you would use to describe the people in the photograph. Using these adjectives, write a paragraph describing the family pictured.

Writing About History

8. **Descriptive Writing** Imagine that you are living during the Great Depression. Write a journal entry describing a day in your life. **CA 11WA2.1c; 11WA2.1e**

CHAPTER 9 The Great Depression Begins **479**

SECTION 2 ASSESSMENT ANSWERS

1. Content vocabulary is boldfaced and highlighted in yellow. Academic vocabulary is boldfaced.
2. Walt Disney (p. 477), Grant Wood (p. 479), John Steinbeck (p. 479), William Faulkner (p. 479)
3. uncultivated fields, depletion of grasslands protecting soil, and drought

4. Americans looked to radio and motion pictures as an escape.
5. Its photos provided a powerful commentary on American life.
6. bank failures, unemployment, hunger, homelessness, and hardship
7. Students' paragraphs will vary. Possible adjectives are *desperate,*

defeated, and *discouraged.*
8. Students' journal entries will vary. Encourage students to take on the role of someone living during the Depression.

R **Reading Strategy**

Scaffolding—Academic Vocabulary The word *publish* was introduced in Chapter 4, Section 1. Ask a student to define the word. **BL**

ASSESS

Resources for page 479

Use these resources to assess student mastery.

📁 Section Quiz 9-2

📁 Reading Essentials and Study Guide 9-2

⊙ Interactive Tutor Self-Assessment CD-ROM

📁 California Standards Practice, Grade 11

Resources for page 479

Have students read more about literature of the 1930s in the **Primary Source Reading 9-2.**

✓ **Reading Check**

Answer: by depicting the homeless and unemployed in their works

HISTORY *Online*

Study Central provides audio summaries, interactive games, and online graphic organizers to help students review section content.

CLOSE

Evaluating Have students discuss how artists captured the effects of the Depression. **OL**

479

FOCUS

History– Social Science Standards

This feature addresses the following standard:

11.5.6 Trace the growth and effects of radio and movies and their role in the worldwide diffusion of popular culture.

Reading Connection

Ask students what forms of popular entertainment they have enjoyed during the past week. Did they attend a movie, musical concert, or play a board game? Tell students that this feature highlights the recreational activities of the 1930s.

TEACH

R Reading Strategy

Predicting Ask students to discuss current entertainment fads. **Ask:** Are there forms of entertainment now that you think will not be around in 50 years? *(Answers will vary.)* BL

Answers and Additional Support

1930s Entertainment

During the Depression, people needed entertainment more than ever. Movies topped the list of ways to escape everyday hardship, but music and dance were popular as well. For really cheap entertainment, one could stay at home and play cards or board games.

Dance Craze •

R Dance marathons got their start in the manic 1920s, but they gained wide popularity in the 1930s. Couples might dance hundreds of hours, until they were exhausted. The last couple standing could win substantial prize money.

• **Movie Escapism**

Movies cost less than 25¢ in many places, so children could afford to go, too. These children display door prizes handed out during a matinee in California.

480 CHAPTER 9 The Great Depression Begins

EXTENDING THE CONTENT

George Gershwin After publishing his first song when he was 14, George Gershwin went on to compose pieces, such as *Rhapsody in Blue* and *An American in Paris,* that blended classical, jazz, and blues music. Gershwin wrote one of his most famous pieces after reading DuBose Hayward's novel *Porgy,* about African Americans living on coastal islands near Charleston, South Carolina. He lived for a summer on the islands, taking in the sounds and rhythms of the place before writing his masterpiece, *Porgy and Bess.* His brother Ira was the lyricist for many of the songs Gershwin wrote. When Gershwin died in 1937 at age 39, America lost one of the great composers of the twentieth century.

Monopoly
Monopoly was a major 1930s fad. Players of this board game moved pieces around, buying and developing "property" in a race to amass a fortune in fake money.

Music
The legendary Jimmie Lunceford Orchestra was one of many big band orchestras of the 1930s. Whether touring the country in one-night gigs or playing on the radio, they drew a huge following.

UNDERSTANDING THE TIME

Checking for Understanding
1. **Identifying** What entertainment was cheap and could be played at home?

Critical Thinking
2. **Making Connections** How would you compare the ideas of entertainment today with the 1930s?

R **Reading Strategy**

Analyzing Tell students to review the game of Monopoly. **Ask: How does the game reflect the 1930s?** *(Answers will vary, but students may point out the low rents as one time indicator.)* **BL**

U **Universal Access**

Auditory/Musical Have interested students find out more about the Big Band Era of the 1930s and 1940s. Suggest they answer the following questions: Who were the major conductors? What were some of the most famous orchestra pieces? What impact did the recording industry have on the big bands? **OL**

ASSESS

Have students answer the Checking for Understanding and Critical Thinking questions.

CLOSE

Have students imagine that they are living during the 1930s. Ask them to write a series of journal entries about their summer activities. Students should use information from the feature. **BL**
CA 11WA2.1a

ANSWERS TO ANAYLYZING THE TIME

1. Card and board games could be played at home with little expense.

2. Students' answers will vary. Each must focus on the similarities or differences in entertainment.

481

FOCUS

Guide to Reading

Understanding Vocabulary: Have students identify the prefixes in the vocabulary words. *(fore-, com-, con-)* Ask students what the prefixes mean. Have them check dictionaries for the meanings of the terms they do not understand.

Answers to Graphic: keep factories open and stop slashing wages—business leaders did not comply; increase public works—little effect; pump money into the economy—too limited to reverse the collapse

Unpacking the Standards

Students will be able to:

• Identify President Hoover's strategies for improving the economy.

• Discuss the protests of groups within the nation.

Answers and Additional Support

Guide to Reading

Connection
In the previous section, you learned how the Depression worsened and people sought escape. In this section, you will discover how President Hoover tried unsuccessfully to help the economy.

Main Idea

• President Hoover's cautious efforts to help the economy did not succeed; Republicans lost many seats in Congress during the midterm elections. (p. 483)

• President Hoover tried to help banks recover and offer limited help to citizens directly, but it was too late. (p. 484)

• Farmers, veterans, and others who were suffering grew frustrated and protested against the government's inability to help them. (p. 485)

Content Vocabulary
public works, relief, foreclose

Academic Vocabulary
series, community, contribute

People and Terms to Identify
Reconstruction Finance Corporation, Bonus Army

Reading Objectives

• **Evaluate** President Hoover's attempts to revive the economy.

• **Analyze** the limitations of Hoover's recovery plans.

Reading Strategy
Categorizing As you read about Hoover's response to the Depression, complete a graphic organizer by listing his major initiatives and their results.

Preview of Events

♦1931 ♦1932 ♦1933

October 1931
National Credit Corporation created

January 1932
Congress approves Reconstruction Finance Corporation

July 1932
Congress passes Emergency Relief and Construction Act; soldiers rout the Bonus Marchers

---

The following are the main History–Social Science Standards covered in this section.

11.6 Students analyze the different explanations for the Great Depression and how the New Deal fundamentally changed the role of the federal government.

11.6.3 Discuss the human toll of the Depression, natural disasters, and unwise agricultural practices and their effects on the depopulation of rural regions and on political movements of the left and right, with particular attention to the Dust Bowl refugees and their social and economic impacts in California.

⁓ The Big Idea ⁓

Social and economic crises lead to new roles for government. President Hoover was cautious in his efforts to improve the economy. He also tried to present an optimistic outlook of the country's economic situation. Voters responded to worsening unemployment by not reelecting many Republicans to office. Hoover then asked Congress for laws to fund banks and to provide relief, but these efforts came too late and were too limited to help. Farmers, veterans, and others who were suffering began to protest the government and its inability to assist people.

SECTION RESOURCES

📁 Print Material
• Reproducible Lesson Plan 9-3
• Guided Reading Activity 9-3
• Reading Essentials and Study Guide 9-3
• Active Reading Note-Taking Guide 9-3

Transparencies
• Daily Focus Skills Transparency 9-3
• Section Graphic Organizer Transparency 9-3

Technology
• Interactive Tutor Self-Assessment CD-ROM
• Exam*View*® Pro Testmaker CD-ROM
• Presentation Plus! CD-ROM

Promoting Recovery

Main Idea President Hoover's cautious efforts to help the economy did not succeed; Republicans lost many seats in Congress during the midterm elections.

Reading Connection What efforts would you have taken to help the economy if you had been president? Read on to learn about the public works efforts of the early 1930s.

President Hoover hoped to downplay the public's fears over the economy. He wanted to avoid more bank runs and layoffs by urging consumers and business leaders to become more rational in their decision-making. Critics of Hoover's approach believed the government should be more truthful with the public.

★ An American Story ★

In December 1929, Mayor Joseph Heffernan of Youngstown, Ohio, listened impatiently to fellow public officials assembled in the Cleveland Chamber of Commerce hall. He had been called to one of a series of conferences on unemployment that President Hoover had arranged. At the conference, Heffernan grew restless as he listened to the other speakers. He felt that it would take too long to pass their confident proposals for ending unemployment, and by that time, it would be too late to prevent a depression. He asked the other conference members, "Why not tell people the truth?"

Youngstown business leaders criticized Heffernan for trying to tell his constituents how bad the economic outlook was. Heffernan later recalled that one of them said to him, "Don't emphasize hard times and everything will be all right."

The man who rebuked Mayor Heffernan expressed what many, including President Hoover himself, believed in late 1929: The country merely needed to regain its confidence. As the crisis worsened, Hoover took steps to help the economy recover, but only within the limits of his philosophy of government.

—adapted from *The Great Depression*

On Friday, October 25, the day after Black Thursday, President Hoover issued a statement assuring the nation that industry was "on a sound and prosperous basis." In March 1930 he told the public that "the worst effects of the crash . . . will have passed during the next 60 days." Critics derided his optimism as conditions worsened.

Voluntary Efforts and Public Works Despite his soothing words, Hoover was seriously worried about the economy. He organized a **series** of conferences, bringing together the heads of banks, railroads, and other big businesses, as well as labor and government officials.

He won a pledge from industry to keep factories open and to stop slashing wages. By 1931, however, business leaders had abandoned those pledges. Hoover's next step was to increase **public works**—government-financed building projects. The resulting construction jobs could replace some of those lost in the private sector. He urged governors and mayors throughout the nation to increase public works spending.

Hoover's actions did spur construction increases, but the effort made up for only a small fraction of the jobs lost in the private sector. The only way the government could create enough new jobs would be to massively increase government spending, which Hoover refused to do.

The problem was that someone had to pay for public works projects. If the government raised taxes to pay for them, it would take money away from consumers and hurt businesses that were already struggling. If the government decided to keep taxes low and run a budget deficit instead—spending

"Why not tell people the truth?"

—*Mayor Joseph Heffernan*

TEACH

R Reading Strategy

Identifying the Main Idea and Supporting Details Students should identify the main ideas as they read the section. Remind them that text features, such as headings, subheadings, boldfaced terms, and graphics, are good indicators of main ideas. As students read, have them use outlines or graphic organizers to make lists. **BL**

C Critical Thinking

Identifying Central Issues President Hoover did not want to use the government to end the economic crisis, but critics disagreed. **Ask:** What responsibility does the government have to keep the economy healthy? Ask students to provide examples from current news at the state or national level to illustrate their points. **AL**

U Universal Access

Interpersonal Have students work in small groups to locate public works projects in the community or state. Each group should find a current project and if possible one from the 1930s. Have them create charts or other visuals comparing and contrasting the projects in areas such as cost, number of laborers, time required, and intended outcomes. Ask each group to report its findings to the class. **OL**

Did You Know?

White House physician Admiral Joel T. Boone invented the game Hoover Ball to keep the president physically fit. It was a combination of tennis, volleyball, and medicine ball. Two teams of 2 to 4 players served a six-pound medicine ball over an eight-foot net on a court similar to one used for tennis. The opponent had to catch it on the fly and immediately return it, attempting to put it where it could not be returned. The game was scored exactly like tennis. The side that missed the ball or threw it out of bounds lost the point. The game was played every morning on the south lawn of the White House.

Different Viewpoints

more money than it collected in taxes—it would have to borrow the money from banks. If the government did this, less money would be available for businesses that wanted to expand and for consumers who wanted mortgages or other loans. Hoover feared that deficit spending would actually delay an economic recovery.

The Midterm Election As the congressional elections of 1930 approached, most Americans felt that worsening unemployment posed a grave threat to their well-being. Citizens blamed the party in power for the stumbling economy. The Republicans lost 49 seats and their majority in the House of Representatives; they held on to the Senate by a single vote.

✓ **Reading Check** **Examining** Why did Hoover oppose deficit spending?

Pumping Money Into the Economy

R **Main Idea** President Hoover tried to help banks recover and offer limited help to citizens directly, but it was too late.

Reading Connection Do you know anyone who has been unemployed? What government programs were available to help them? Read on to find out about the "too little, too late" attempts to help the economy in the 1930s.

Hoover soon turned his attention to the problem of money. There was very little in the economy now that so many banks had collapsed. The government, he believed, had to make sure that banks could make loans to corporations so they could expand production and rehire workers.

R Reading Strategy

Connecting President Hoover took a cautious approach to the growing economic problems in the United States. His efforts did not result in dramatic improvement for the nation's economic troubles. Consequently, Hoover has been viewed negatively by many Americans and some historians. **Ask:** Is history's assessment of Hoover fair? *(Students' answers will vary, but should be based on an assessment of the information presented. If anyone argues that Hoover deserved a better historical evaluation, make sure they have solid arguments for their statement.)* **OL**

CA HR2; HR3

Review the Big Idea

Review the Big Idea for this section, "Social and economic crises lead to new roles for government." Ask the class to read the primary sources in Differing Viewpoints. Then tell them to summarize the differences in the ways Hoover and Roosevelt were willing to use the government to fix the economy. **OL**

✓ Reading Check

Answer: He believed it would delay an economic recovery.

Different Viewpoints

What Should the Government's Role in the Economy Be?

The government's role in the economy was an important issue in the 1932 presidential election, when the country was in the throes of the Depression. President Herbert Hoover explained in a 1928 speech why a limited government role was best, while President Franklin Roosevelt argued in his inaugural address in 1933 that an expanded government role was necessary.

from Hoover's Madison Square Garden Address, 1928

"During one hundred and fifty years we have built up a form of self-government and a social system which is peculiarly our own. . . . It is founded upon a particular conception of self-government in which decentralized local responsibility is the very base. . . .

During the war we necessarily turned to the government to solve every difficult economic problem. . . . However justified in time of war, if continued in peacetime it would destroy . . . our progress and freedom. . . . The acceptance of these ideas would have meant the destruction of self-government through centralization of government. It would have meant the undermining of the individual initiative and enterprise through which our people have grown to unparalleled greatness."

from Roosevelt's Inaugural Address, 1933

"Our greatest primary task is to put people to work. This is no unsolvable problem if we face it wisely and courageously. It can be accomplished in part by direct recruiting by the Government itself, treating the task as we would treat the emergency of a war, but at the same time, through this employment, accomplishing greatly needed projects to stimulate and reorganize the use of our natural resources.

. . . The task can be helped . . . by national planning for and supervision of all forms of transportation and of communications and other utilities which have a definitely public character. There are many ways in which it can be helped, but it can never be helped merely by talking about it. We must act and act quickly.

. . . We now realize as we have never realized before our interdependence on each other; . . . that if we are to go forward, we must move as a trained and loyal army willing to sacrifice for the good of a common discipline."

Learning From History

1. **Analyzing Arguments** What did Hoover fear would happen if government programs started during World War I were continued after the war?
2. **Making Inferences** How do you think Roosevelt views the relationship of government and the economy? What policies did he want to implement with transportation and communication companies?

Answers and Additional Support

Different Viewpoints

Answers:
1. It would destroy freedom and initiative.
2. Roosevelt viewed the economy and the government as mutually dependent. He wanted the transportation and communications companies to be supervised by the government.

Ask: Do you think that Hoover might have changed his mind by the time Roosevelt was inaugurated? *(Students' answers will vary.)*

Trying to Rescue the Banks The president asked the Federal Reserve Board to put more currency into circulation, but the Board refused. In an attempt to ease the money shortage, Hoover set up the National Credit Corporation (NCC) in October 1931. The NCC created a pool of money to enable troubled banks to continue lending money in their **communities.** Hoover then persuaded a number of New York bankers to **contribute** to the NCC. Their contributions, however, did not meet the nation's needs.

By 1932 Hoover concluded that the only way to provide funding for borrowers was for the government to do the lending. He requested that Congress set up the **Reconstruction Finance Corporation** (RFC) to make loans to banks, railroads, and agricultural institutions. By early 1932, the RFC had lent about $238 million to approximately 160 banks, 60 railroads, and 18 building-and-loan organizations. The RFC was overly cautious, however. It failed to increase its loans in sufficient amounts to meet the need, and the economy continued its decline.

Direct Help for Citizens From the start, Hoover strongly opposed the federal government's participation in **relief**—money that went directly to impoverished families. He believed that only state and city governments should dispense relief. By the spring of 1932, however, they were running out of money.

In 1932 political support was building for a relief measure, and Congress passed the Emergency Relief and Construction Act. Although reluctant, Hoover signed the bill on July 21. The new act called for $1.5 billion for public works and $300 million in loans to the states for direct relief. By this time, however, the new program could not reverse the accelerating collapse.

✓ **Reading Check** **Summarizing** Why did Hoover oppose the federal government's participation in relief programs?

Picturing **History**

White Angel Breadline In the absence of federally funded relief programs, some charities and individuals set up breadlines to distribute food to those in need. In 1932 a wealthy woman nicknamed the "White Angel" set up a breadline in San Francisco. Dorothea Lange captured the hopelessness of the Depression in this famous photograph of the breadline. **How does this photograph express the hardships of the Depression?**

In an Angry Mood

W **Main Idea** Farmers, veterans, and others who were suffering grew frustrated and protested against the government's inability to help them.

Reading Connection Have you ever felt strongly enough about an issue to consider protesting government policies? Read on to discover what happened when veterans marched to Washington, D.C., in 1932.

In the months after the Wall Street crash, Americans had seemed resigned to bad economic news. By 1931, however, they were growing increasingly discontented, and open acts of revolt began to occur.

Hunger Marches In January 1931, around 500 men and women in Oklahoma City, shouting angrily about hunger and joblessness, broke into a grocery store and looted it. Crowds began showing up at rallies and "hunger marches" held by the American Communist Party, which was eager to take advantage

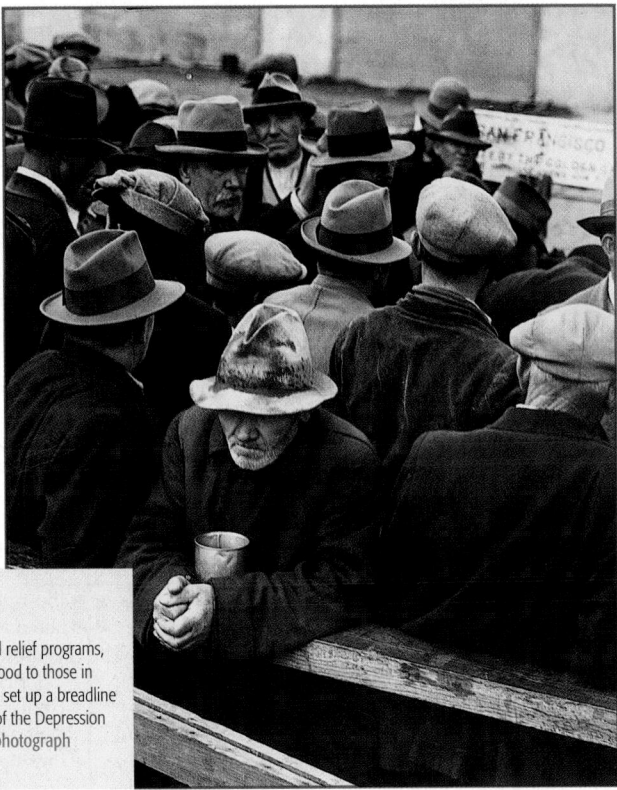

CHAPTER 9   The Great Depression Begins   **485**

R **Reading Strategy**

Organizing Information
Tell students that the history of the 1930s contains references to many acronyms, such as the NCC and RFC. Encourage students to keep Cornell notes on all of the acronyms, listing acronyms in the first column and the full title with a line or two about the role that the organization filled in the second column. Tell students that the notes will be useful later as they study for an exam or quiz. They can also use them as reference, preventing the need to go back to the text for a reminder of the organization's work. **OL**

W **Writing Support**

Narrative Writing Ask students to select one of the protests discussed under the heading, "In an Angry Mood." Have them assume the role of one of the participants and write a description of the protest. Remind students to use sensory details in their writing.
OL **CA** 11WS1.2; 11WA2.1c

Resources for page 485

📂 Have students learn more about strikes during the Great Depression by reading from "The Strike" in the **American Literature Readings 3.**

✓ **Reading Check**

Answer: He felt that only state and city governments should give out relief.

Picturing **History**

Answer: It shows the grim, tired faces of men forced to stand in a long line to receive bread.
Ask: Why did this photograph become a symbol of the Depression? (It humanized the suffering of people during the Depression.)

Did You Know?

The board game Monopoly was invented during the Depression. Charles Darrow was an unemployed Pennsylvania engineer when he designed the famous game in the early 1930s.

S Skill Practice

Visual Literacy Point out the signs that the children in the smaller picture are carrying. Ask students to deduce who had written the signs. *(Probably the parents or other adults; the writing does not look like a small child's writing.)* **Ask:** What do the expressions on the children's faces suggest? *(They are serious, as if they realize the importance of what they are doing.)* OL

CA HI1

R Reading Strategy

Activating Prior Knowledge
Point out to students the protest marches that were occurring near Washington, D.C., in the early years of the Depression. **Ask:** What other protest actions have occurred in the United States that you can recall? Were they successful? *(Students might mention early historical actions such as Shays's Rebellion, which was not successful in changing the distribution of land in the Virginia colonies; the Whiskey Rebellion, which was successful in alerting officials to the economic problems inherent in the Articles of Confederation; the woman suffrage movement was eventually successful in granting women the right to vote; the progressive movement helped generate government reforms in local, state, and the federal government.)* OL

Answers and Additional Support

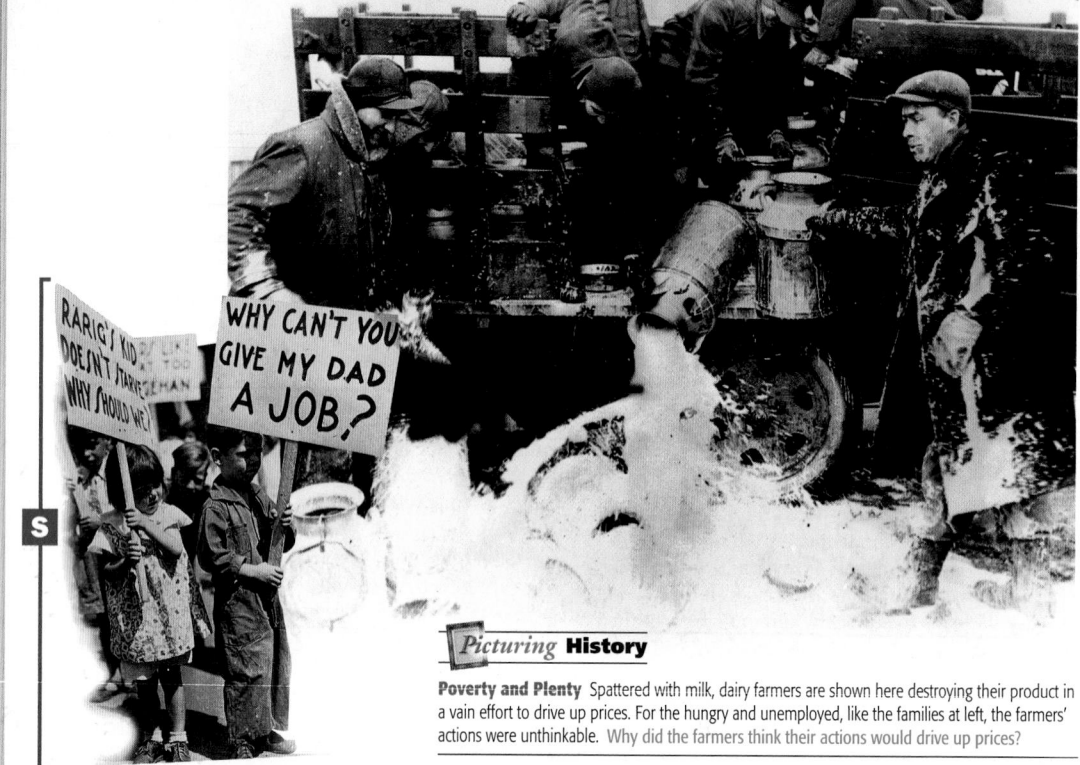

Picturing **History**

Poverty and Plenty Spattered with milk, dairy farmers are shown here destroying their product in a vain effort to drive up prices. For the hungry and unemployed, like the families at left, the farmers' actions were unthinkable. *Why did the farmers think their actions would drive up prices?*

of national problems to change the American form of government. On December 5, 1932, a freezing day in the nation's capital, around 1,200 hunger marchers assembled and chanted, "Feed the hungry, tax the rich." Police herded them into a blocked-off area, where they had to spend the night sleeping on the sidewalk or in trucks. The police denied them food, water, and medical treatment until some members of Congress insisted on the marchers' right to petition their government. They were then released and permitted to march to Capitol Hill.

Farmers Revolt In the summer of 1932, farmers also took matters into their own hands. Beginning in the boom days of World War I, many farmers had heavily mortgaged their land to pay for seed, feed, and equipment. After the war, prices sank so low that farmers could not even earn back their costs, let alone make a profit. Between 1930 and 1934 creditors **foreclosed** on nearly one million farms, taking possession of them and evicting the families.

Some farmers began destroying their crops in a desperate attempt to raise crop prices by reducing the supply. In Nebraska grain growers burned corn to heat their homes in the winter. In Iowa food growers forcibly prevented the delivery of vegetables to distributors. Georgia dairy farmers blocked high-

ways and stopped milk trucks, emptying the milk cans into ditches.

The Bonus Marchers In appreciation of the World War I service of American soldiers and sailors, Congress in 1924 had enacted a $1,000 bonus for each veteran, to be distributed in 1945. The economic crisis, however, made the wait more difficult. In 1931 Texas congressman Wright Patman introduced a bill in the House of Representatives that authorized early payment of the veterans' bonuses. The bill later passed the House and moved to the Senate for debate.

In May 1932 several hundred Portland, Oregon, veterans set off on a month-long march to Washington to lobby Congress to pass the legislation. As they moved east, other veterans joined them until they numbered about 1,000. Wearing ragged military uniforms, they trudged along the highways or rode the rails, singing old war songs and reminiscing about army days. The press termed the marchers the **"Bonus Army."**

Once in Washington, the marchers camped in Hoovervilles. As weeks went by, additional veterans joined them, until the Bonus Army swelled to 15,000. President Hoover acknowledged the veterans' petition rights but refused to meet with them.

Did You Know?

In 1931 a Christmas tree was placed amid the rubble from some demolished buildings. Workers who still had jobs decorated the tree with tin cans and paper. A few years later at the same site, the official Rockefeller Center tree tradition was inaugurated.

Picturing **History**

Answer: By lowering supply, they hoped to raise prices.
Ask: Why is the image of a child carrying this sign especially powerful? *(It plays on the emotions and highlights the innocent victims.)*

Clearing Out the Bonus Marchers Fierce battles resulted when President Hoover ordered the Washington, D.C., police to evict the Bonus Army from public buildings and land they had been occupying. How did the public feel when they saw or heard about this event?

When the Senate voted the new bonus bill down, veterans waiting outside the Capitol began to grumble, until one of their leaders started them singing "America." Gradually their anger cooled, and many returned home. A significant number of the marchers, however, stayed on since they had no job prospects, homes, or families to return to. Some moved from the camps to unoccupied buildings downtown.

In late July, Hoover ordered the buildings cleared. The police made the first try, but one of them panicked and fired into a crowd, killing two veterans. The Washington, D.C., government then called in the army. Army chief of staff Douglas MacArthur ignored Hoover's orders to clear the buildings but to leave the camps alone. He sent cavalry, infantry, and tanks to clear the veterans from the city.

A Federal Trade Commission member, A. Everette McIntyre, watched as the infantry "fixed their bayonets and also fixed their gas masks over their faces. At orders they brought their bayonets at thrust and moved in. The bayonets were used to jab people to make them move." Soon unarmed veterans were on the run with 700 soldiers at their heels. The soldiers tear-gassed stragglers and burned the shacks. Tear gas killed a baby boy.

The nationwide press coverage and newsreel images of veterans under assault by troops presented an ugly picture to the public. Many did not agree with the action taken against the veterans. The routing of the veterans hounded the president throughout his 1932 reelection campaign.

Hoover failed to resolve the crisis of the Depression, but he did more to expand the economic role of the federal government than any previous president. The Reconstruction Finance Corporation marked the first time the federal government had established a federal agency to stimulate the economy during peacetime. These successes, however, did not change the public's view. It was the image of the routed Bonus Marchers and the lingering Depression that shaped the public's perception of President Hoover.

 Reading Check **Evaluating** How did Americans react as the Depression continued?

HISTORY Online **Study Central**

For help with the concepts in this section of *American Vision: Modern Times* go to tav.mt.glencoe.com and click on *Study Central.*

SECTION 3 ASSESSMENT

Checking for Understanding

1. **Vocabulary** Define: series, public works, community, contribute, relief, foreclose.
2. **People and Terms** Identify: Reconstruction Finance Corporation, Bonus Army.
3. **Summarize** three major initiatives taken by Hoover to improve the economy and the results of each.

Reviewing Big Ideas

4. **Describing** What did business leaders promise Hoover they would do to help the economy? Did they keep their promises?

Critical Thinking

5. **Historical Analysis** **Interpreting** How did President Hoover's philosophy of government guide his response to the Depression? **CA HI2; HI3**
6. **Organizing** Use a graphic organizer similar to the one below to list American reactions to the Depression.

American Reactions

Analyzing Visuals

7. **Picturing History** Study the photographs on page 486. The farmers shown would rather dump their milk than sell it. What did they hope to achieve by their actions? How do you think hungry Americans viewed this photo?

Writing About History

8. **Persuasive Writing** Imagine that you are a veteran of World War I. Write a letter to members of Congress explaining your circumstances and asking them to give you your bonus early. **CA 11WS1.2; 11 WA2.1c**

CHAPTER 9 The Great Depression Begins **487**

 ASSESS

Resources for page 487

Use these resources to assess student mastery.

📁 Section Quiz 9-3

📁 Reading Essentials and Study Guide 9-3

🔘 Interactive Tutor Self-Assessment CD-ROM

📁 California Standards Practice, Grade 11

Picturing **History**

Answer: They had a negative reaction toward Hoover.
Ask: What alternatives do you think the government had? *(Students' answers will vary.)*

 Reading Check

Answer: Reactions included hunger marches, farmers' revolts, and the Bonus Army march.

 HISTORY Online

Study Central provides audio summaries, interactive games, and online graphic organizers to help students review section content.

CLOSE

Analyzing Information Have students analyze the limitations of Hoover's recovery plans. **OL**

SECTION 3 ASSESSMENT ANSWERS

1. Content vocabulary is boldfaced and highlighted in yellow. Academic vocabulary is boldfaced.
2. Reconstruction Finance Corporation (p. 485), Bonus Army (p. 486)
3. Conferences with industry leaders did not secure cooperation; funding from the National Credit Corporation and Reconstruction Finance Corporation could not rescue banks; relief programs too late to stop the collapse
4. They promised to keep factories open and stop slashing wages; no.
5. Belief in volunteerism and loans, rather than direct relief, restricted his actions.
6. bonus marchers, discontent, farmers' revolts, hunger strikes, squatting
7. They hoped to drive up prices by limiting supply.
8. Students' letters will vary. Letters should be written from the perspective of a World War I veteran.

NATIONAL GEOGRAPHIC

Geography&History

FOCUS

History–Social Science Standards

This feature addresses the following standards:

11.6 Students analyze the different explanations for the Great Depression and how the New Deal fundamentally changed the role of the federal government.

11.6.4 Analyze the effects of and the controversies arising from New Deal economic policies and the expanded role of the federal government in society and the economy since the 1930s (e.g., Works Progress Administration, Social Security, National Labor Relations Board, farm programs, regional development policies, and energy development projects such as the Tennessee Valley Authority, California Central Valley Project, and Bonneville Dam).

TEACH

C Critical Thinking

Analyzing Information Have students study the map and read the feature. Then have them create questions for a trivia game based on the information in the text. Divide the class into teams and have students pose their questions and see who can answer the questions most quickly. If you choose, you can keep score and provide a small prize to the winners. **OL**

Answers and Additional Support

488

25%
NEVADA

56%
•Los Angeles

19%
ARIZONA

Lake Powell

Lake Mead

Las Vegas **Hoover Dam**

Colorado River

THE FLOW OF ELECTRICITY

Today Hoover Dam generates more than 4 billion kilowatt-hours of electricity per year—enough to keep machines humming and lights burning for over a million people. More than half of that electricity is sent to California; the remainder goes to Nevada and Arizona (see inset map).

(Map labels: Lake Mohave, EL DORADO MOUNTAINS, 95, to Flagstaff, NEVADA ARIZONA, Power line, Black Canyon, HOOVER DAM, 93, Boulder Islands, Fortification Hill 3718 ft. (1133 m), Sentinel Island, BLACK MOUNTAINS, ARIZONA NEVADA, LA)

EXTENDING THE CONTENT

Protecting the Dam During World War II, Hoover Dam was considered a prime target because it supplied water and electricity to so many people. Pillbox guns emplacements were scattered in the hills surrounding the dam. These emplacements were crewed 24 hours a day during the war. One of the emplacements on the Arizona side of the dam remains. The dam is still protected around the clock. Security measures vary, but no vehicle is allowed to stop on the dam, and no pedestrian traffic is allowed around or on the dam at night. At times of heightened alert, the authorities restrict the types of vehicles that can drive on the road over the dam.

Hoover Dam

American farmers and settlers in the low-lying valleys of southern California and southwestern Arizona have been tapping the waters of the Colorado River for more than a century. Thanks to irrigation canals, the parched desert valleys became year-round gardens that provided fruit and vegetables for the nation. At times, however, the unpredictable river would decrease to a trickle. Other times, it became a raging torrent, destroying all in its path. The federal government decided to dam the Colorado to control it. In 1931 construction began in Black Canyon, whose high rock walls made it an ideal site. Here, on the border between Arizona and Nevada, would rise one of the most ambitious engineering projects the world had ever seen: the Hoover Dam.

Named after President Herbert Hoover, the dam was built in the middle of a forbidding desert. Everything had to be imported, including labor. There was no shortage of candidates. The country was in the grips of the Great Depression; thousands of unemployed workers flocked to the remote canyon. To accommodate them, an entire town was built— Boulder City, Nevada.

The new arrivals faced brutal conditions. Men worked in three shifts around the clock. Summer temperatures climbed higher than 120 degrees in the canyon, and even those who worked at night had to endure temperatures of more than 85 degrees. Still, the project was completed in less than five years. Lake Mead, the 115-mile-long reservoir created by the dam, is large enough to hold two years' worth of the average flow of the Colorado River—enough to cover the entire state of New York with one foot of water. The benefits to the Southwest were immense. Hoover Dam created much-needed employment. It also provided a regular supply of water, irrigating over a million acres of rich agricultural land and producing hydroelectric power, which has allowed Southwestern cities to grow.

Suspended on ropes, "high scalers" armed with dynamite and jackhammers prepare the walls of Black Canyon to take the concrete of Hoover Dam. Such work was hazardous. Twenty-four workers fell to their deaths during construction of the dam.

Hoover Dam and Environs
- ········ State boundary
- – – – Aqueduct
- —— Road
- ✶—✶ Power line
- Urban area

Scale varies in this perspective

McCullough Range

Henderson 515

River Mountains 582

Aqueduct   to Las Vegas

Las Vegas Bay

wallow Bay

S Hoover Dam, a major supplier of hydroelectric power, is more than 700 feet (213 m) tall and contains about 4,360,000 cubic yards of concrete—enough for a two-lane highway from Los Angeles to Boston.

LEARNING FROM GEOGRAPHY

1. Why did the federal government decide to dam the Colorado River?

2. Why did engineers choose the Black Canyon site?

489

ANSWERS TO LEARNING FROM GEOGRAPHY

1. The river was dammed to control its unpredictable flow.
2. The high rock walls made Black Canyon the preferred site for the dam.

FOCUS

History–Social Science Standards

This feature addresses the following standard:

11.6.3 Discuss the human toll of the Depression, natural disasters, and unwise agricultural practices and their effects on the depopulation of rural regions and on political movements of the left and right, with particular attention to the Dust Bowl refugees and their social and economic impacts in California.

Understanding Vocabulary

Before students begin reading, point out that difficult or unfamiliar words are footnoted throughout the text.

TEACH

U Universal Access

Visual/Spatial Ask students to find pictures in magazines or on the Internet that depict the Dust Bowl. Tell them to display the pictures in a photo collage and then ask the class to describe what they see and what feeling the pictures convey about this time period. **OL**

Answers and Additional Support

Primary Sources
Eyewitness to History

During the early years of the Great Depression, Americans were scared and desperate. No previous economic downturn had been as deep or as long lasting. With no end to the disaster in sight, many people lost hope of a better future.

SOURCE 1

Caroline A. Henderson and her husband had been farming wheat and raising cattle in Eva, Oklahoma, for 28 years. The Dust Bowl made life difficult for her and her family. In a letter published in the Atlantic Monthly *in May 1936, Henderson described conditions in the Dust Bowl in June 1935 to a friend in Maryland.*

Our recent transition from rain-soaked eastern Kansas with its green pastures, **luxuriant**[1] foliage, abundance of flowers, and promise of a generous harvest, to the dust-covered desolation of No Man's Land was a difficult change. . . . Wearing our shade hats, with handkerchiefs tied over our faces and vaseline in our nostrils, we have been trying to rescue our home from the accumulations of wind-blown dust which penetrates wherever air can go. It is an almost hopeless task, for there is rarely a day when at some time the dust clouds do not roll over. 'Visibility' approaches zero and everything is covered again with a **silt-like**[2] deposit which may vary in depth from a film to actual ripples on the kitchen floor. . . .

. . . In May a friend in the southwestern county of Kansas voluntarily sent me a list of the people who had already left their immediate neighborhood or were packed up and ready to go. The list included

▲ *Students use new "radio ears" at a school for the deaf.*

109 persons in 26 families, substantial people, most of whom had been in that **locality**[3] over ten years, and some as long as forty years. In these families there had been two deaths from dust pneumonia. Others in the neighborhood were ill at the time. Fewer actual residents have left our neighborhood, but on a sixty-mile trip yesterday to procure tractor repairs we saw many pitiful reminders of broken hopes and apparently wasted effort. Little abandoned homes where people had drilled deep wells for the precious water, had set trees and vines, built reservoirs, and fenced in gardens, —with everything now walled in or half buried by banks of drifted soil, —told a painful story of loss and disappointment. . . .

SOURCE 2

In 1934 Ann Marie Low was a 22-year-old living with her parents and two siblings on a farm in southeastern North Dakota. She took teaching jobs to help support her family. In her diary, Low described the daily struggle with dust storms and the bleak prospects for the future.

April 25, 1934, Wednesday

Last weekend was the worst dust storm we ever had. We've been having quite a bit of blowing dirt every year since the drouth [drought] started, not only

[1]**luxuriant:** much growth
[2]**silt-like:** soil

[3]**locality:** neighborhood

UNIVERSAL ACCESS

Interpersonal Divide the class into three groups and ask each group to discuss the following question: **Was the Depression more difficult for people in the cities or in rural areas?** *(Students' answers may vary. Some students may argue that it was more difficult in rural areas because there were fewer private charities or social services available to farm families. Others may say that life in the city was more difficult because there were more people gathered there who were hungry and out of work. In addition, city dwellers could not grow their own food.)* **OL**

SOURCE 3

Ed Smalley grew up on a cotton farm near Fort Worth, Texas. He lost the farm after his father's death but found work as a waiter in the city. In 1939 he looked back at the early years of the Great Depression in an interview with a writer from the Federal Writers' Project of the Works Progress Administration.

[I]n January, 1930, the café where I worked went busted. I was out of a job and I couldn't find a single thing to work at. I was young and had no training, and lots of people were out of work. I had nothing to do all the balance of that winter, and when spring came I was down to $30. . . .

I bummed around in Georgia and South Carolina for three or four weeks. Everywhere I went it was the same old story—'No help wanted.' My clothes got pretty dirty and soiled from sleeping out. I could wash my shirt and underwear, but I had no money to have my suit cleaned and pressed.

But there were lots of people on the road worse off than me. I was young, in good health, and had only myself to look out for. That summer I met whole families wandering around homeless and broke, even women with babies in their arms.

Between Augusta and Charlotte I met a man, his wife, and seven children. The oldest child was only eleven and the youngest was a nursing baby. I guess the baby was the luckiest in the lot because he had something to eat. The other children were all hungry. Some of the little ones were crying for food.

▲ *A man reads in front of his Chicago shantytown shack.*

here but all over the Great Plains. Many days this spring the air is just full of dirt coming, literally, for hundreds of miles. It sifts into everything. After we wash the dishes and put them away, so much dust sifts into the cupboards we must wash them again before the next meal. Clothes in the closets are covered with dust.

Last weekend no one was taking an automobile out for fear of ruining the motor. I rode Roany to Frank's place to return a gear. To find my way I had to ride right beside the fence, scarcely able to see from one fence post to the next.

Newspapers say the deaths of many babies and old people are attributed to breathing in so much dirt. . . .

May 7, 1934, Monday
. . . Miss Eston, the practice teaching supervisor, told me her salary has been cut to $75.00 after all the years she has been teaching in Jamestown. She wants to get married. School boards will not hire married women teachers in these hard times because they have husbands to support them. Her fiancé is the sole support of his widowed mother and can't support a wife, too. So she is just stuck in her job, hoping she won't get another salary cut because she can scarcely live on what she makes and dress the way she is expected to.

DBQ Document-Based Questions

Historical Analysis CA CS3; HI1

Source 1: According to Henderson, why were people leaving their neighborhoods during the Dust Bowl?

Source 2: How did the Great Depression affect Miss Eston?

Source 3: What problems did Smalley experience while looking for work?

Comparing and Contrasting Sources
How would you compare the accounts of Henderson, Low, and Smalley concerning the impact of the Great Depression?

W Writing Support

Narrative Writing Ask students to write a journal entry as a person from the city or rural area during the Depression, describing their families, what life is like, and what they do to survive. Remind students to use the most descriptive language possible and provide important details so it seems believable that they experienced these events. Students may conduct research to make their passages more believable; however, emphasize that they must not plagiarize the works of others. **OL CA** 11WA2.1c

C Critical Thinking

Comparing and Contrasting Have students use library and Internet resources to research what kind of social services where available for unemployed people or farmers during the Depression. What kind of social services are available for people now? Ask students to write a two-page report that presents their findings. **OL CA** 11WS1.3; 11WA2.4d

ASSESS/CLOSE

Have students answer the Document-Based Questions.

DBQ Document-Based Questions

1. They were leaving because the dust had made life unbearable.
2. Her salary had been reduced. She also wanted to get married, but during the Depression the school board would not allow married women to teach. Since her fiancé could not support her, she could not get married.
3. He could not find work and had to sleep outside.

Comparing and Contrasting Sources: Their experiences all illustrate the difficulties that people had surviving the Depression. Henderson states that people had to give up their farms because of the weather. Low discusses how dust made it difficult to drive and how jobs were affected. Smalley lost his farm during the Depression and traveled around looking for a job.

Reviewing Content Vocabulary

Students' answers will vary. The pages where the words appear in the text are shown in parentheses.

1. stock market *(p. 470)* **2.** bull market *(p. 470)* **3.** margin *(p. 470)* **4.** margin call *(p. 470)* **5.** speculation *(p. 471)* **6.** installment *(p. 473)* **7.** bailiff *(p. 475)* **8.** shantytown *(p. 475)* **9.** Hooverville *(p. 475)* **10.** hobo *(p. 476)* **11.** Dust Bowl *(p. 476)* **12.** soap opera *(p. 478)* **13.** public works *(p. 483)* **14.** relief *(p. 485)* **15.** foreclose *(p. 486)*

Reviewing Academic Vocabulary

Students' answers will vary. The pages where the words appear in the text are shown in parentheses.

16. invest *(p. 470)* **17.** sum *(p. 471)* **18.** reaction *(p. 473)* **19.** suspend *(p. 475)* **20.** colleague *(p. 478)* **21.** technique *(p. 479)* **22.** series *(p. 483)* **23.** community *(p. 485)* **24.** contribute *(p. 485)*

Reviewing Content Vocabulary

On a sheet of paper, use each of these terms in a sentence.

1. stock market	**6.** installment	**11.** Dust Bowl
2. bull market	**7.** bailiff	**12.** soap opera
3. margin	**8.** shantytown	**13.** public works
4. margin call	**9.** Hooverville	**14.** relief
5. speculation	**10.** hobo	**15.** foreclose

Reviewing Academic Vocabulary

On a sheet of paper, use each of these terms in a sentence that reflects the term's meaning in the chapter.

16. invest	**19.** suspend	**22.** series
17. sum	**20.** colleague	**23.** community
18. reaction	**21.** technique	**24.** contribute

Reviewing the Main Ideas

Section 1

25. What was the character of the stock market in the late 1920s, and what caused it to crash?

Section 2

26. How did artists and writers capture the effects of the Great Depression?

27. Why did "Okies" migrate to California during the Great Depression, and what happened to them once they got there?

Section 3

28. What three major initiatives did President Hoover take to try to help the economy of the United States?

Critical Thinking

29. **Reading Skill** Visualizing Reread the text under "The Dust Bowl" on pages 476–477. Identify descriptive words and passages from the text on a sheet of paper. Trade lists with a partner and compare notes. Did their list create a different visual image? Explain.

30. **Analyzing** Many people in the United States were impoverished during the Depression, yet 60 to 90 million weekly viewers paid to see movies. Why do you think movies were so popular?

31. **Civics** Explain the purpose of the Reconstruction Finance Corporation (RFC) created by President Hoover. Who benefited from this program?

32. **Evaluating** Do you think President Hoover could have done more to relieve the hardship caused by the Great Depression? Why or why not?

33. **Identifying** What approaches were used in literature and photography to highlight social problems during the Depression?

34. **Categorizing** Use a graphic organizer similar to the one below to list the causes and effects of the Great Depression.

Causes	Effects

Chapter Summary

Stock Market Helps Trigger Depression
- Bull market encouraged widespread speculation.
- Many investors bought stocks on margin.
- Sharp drop in market prices left investors in debt.
- Bank closings left many in debt.

Underlying Causes of Great Depression
- Overproduction and low interest rates
- Uneven distribution of income, which led to low demand
- Depressed farm sector
- Weak international market with high tariffs

Downward Momentum of the Great Depression

Low Sales → Job Layoffs → Less Income → Fewer Purchases → Lower Sales → More Job Layoffs

---

Reviewing the Main Ideas

25. It was a bull market that crashed because stocks were overvalued and many people had purchased stocks on margin.

26. They focused on pictures and stories of the homeless and unemployed.

27. They migrated searching for work. Many ended up working as homeless migrant laborers.

28. voluntary conferences with industry leaders, National Credit Corporation, Reconstruction Finance Corporation

Critical Thinking

29. **Reading Skill** Lists should reflect the descriptive words from the text.

30. Movies gave people an escape from their own lives.

Visit the *American Vision: Modern Times* Web site at
tav.mt.glencoe.com and click on *Self-Check Quizzes—
Chapter 9* to assess your knowledge of chapter content.

Writing About History

35. **Historical Analysis** **Developing a Hypothesis**
Construct a hypothesis about life during the Depression.
How did individuals escape the Depression? Collect additional information from primary and secondary sources to
provide evidence for your hypothesis. Write a one- to two-
page report on your findings. **CA HR4** **CA 11WA2.4a**

36. *Big Idea* Write an editorial evaluating President Hoover's
actions during the Great Depression. Could he have done
more to relieve the country's hardships? Why or why not?
CA 11WS1.1

DBQ **Document-Based Questions**

37. **Interpreting Primary Sources** E.Y. Harburg lived during the
Great Depression. After he lost his business, he became a
poet and lyricist. He wrote the lyrics to one of the most
famous songs of the time, "Brother, Can You Spare a Dime?"
Read an excerpt of the lyrics to this song and answer the
questions that follow.

> ❝They used to tell me I was building a dream
> With peace and glory ahead—
> Why should I be standing on line
> Just waiting for bread?
>
> Once I built a railroad, made it run,
> Made it run against time.
> Once I built a railroad,
> Now it's done—
> Brother, can you spare a dime?
>
> Once I built a tower to the sun.
> Brick and rivet and lime,
> Once I built a tower,
> Now it's done—
> Brother, can you spare a dime?❞

a. How was the narrator's life different before the Great
Depression than it was during it?

b. During the 1932 presidential campaign, the Republicans
tried to discourage the radio networks from playing this
song. Why do you think they did that?

Crop Prices, 1910–1935

Wheat (price per bushel)
Corn (price per bushel)
Cotton (price per pound)

Price of Crops: $2.60, $2.20, $1.80, $1.40, $1.00, $0.60, $0.20

Year: 1910, 1915, 1920, 1925, 1930, 1935

Source: Historical Statistics of the United States: Colonial Times to 1970.

Economics and History

38. The graph above shows fluctuations in crop prices between
the years 1910 and 1935. Study the graph and answer the
questions below.
a. **Interpreting Graphs** What trend does this graph show
about wheat and corn prices in the 1930s?
b. **Analyzing** Between which 10-year span did the greatest
increase in farm prices occur? Which 10-year span saw
the greatest decrease?

Standards Practice

**Directions: Choose the best answer to the
following question.**

39. A major reason for the collapse of the American
economy after 1929 was

A high interest rates.

B decreased farm production.

C low tariffs at home and abroad.

D overproduction of consumer goods.

Standard 11.6.2: Understand the explanations of the principal causes of the Great Depression and the steps taken by
the Federal Reserve, Congress, and Presidents Herbert
Hoover and Franklin Delano Roosevelt to combat the economic crisis.

Online

Have students visit the Web site at
tav.mt.glencoe.com to review Chapter
9 and take the Self-Check Quiz.

Writing About History

35. **Historical Analysis** Students should
identify escapism techniques for
society during the Depression.
Reports will vary.

36. *Big Idea* Students' editorials will
vary. Possible explanations: Yes, the
government should have gotten
more involved in relief efforts. No,
the problems were so great that
there was nothing more the government could do.

DBQ **Document-Based Questions**

37. a. He was a productive worker, now
is unemployed. **b.** Students might
say that hearing the song suggested
criticism of society and discouraged
the unemployed.

Economics and History

38. a. They declined sharply in the early
1930s, then rose steadily. **b.** For the
most *volatile* ten-year period, students will choose 1915 to 1925 when
graph lines rise and plummet dramatically; for the ten-year period in
which there was the *greatest overall
difference* in farm prices, students
should add the price points of all
three crops and figure the difference, yielding the answer *between
1910 and 1920.*

Standards Practice

39. D

---

31. The RFC made loans to banks, railroads, building-and-
loan organizations and agricultural institutions.

32. Students' answers may vary but should be supported
by evidence and examples.

33. Writing and visual styles evoked sympathy for the
homeless and unemployed. Stream-of-consciousness
writing illuminated peoples' thoughts and emotions.

34. Causes: overproduction, uneven distribution of wealth,
decline in exports and sales, mistakes by the Federal
Reserve, stock market crash; Effects: unemployment,
poverty, migration, government programs to influence
the economy

Bonus Question ?

Ask: What does the phrase "Dust
Bowl" refer to? (*Starting in 1932,
a prolonged drought caused great
clouds of dust to blanket the region
from Texas to the Dakotas.*)

493

Chapter 10 Planning Guide

SECTION RESOURCES

MAIN IDEAS	🗀 PRINT MATERIALS	TECHNOLOGY RESOURCES
Section 1: The First New Deal 1. After serving as governor of New York, Franklin D. Roosevelt was elected president in 1932. 2. During his first 100 days in office, President Roosevelt sent 15 major acts aimed at financial recovery to Congress. 3. President Roosevelt took steps to strengthen the banks and the stock market. 4. New legislation tried to address the economic problems of farms and industry. 5. Congress created two new programs to help homeowners and farmers who had difficulty paying their mortgages. 6. Unemployed people found work through several government programs, such as the Public Works Administration and the Civil Works Administration.	• Reproducible Lesson Plan 10–1* • Daily Lecture and Discussion Notes 10–1 • Active Reading Note-Taking Guide 10–1 • Guided Reading Activity 10–1 • Section Quiz 10–1 • Reading Essentials and Study Guide 10–1	📖 Daily Focus Skills Transparency 10–1 📖 Section Graphic Organizer Transparency 10–1 💿 Interactive Tutor Self-Assessment CD-ROM 💿 ExamView® Pro Testmaker CD-ROM 💿 Presentation Plus! CD-ROM 📖 California Standards Practice Transparencies
Section 2: The Second New Deal 1. With improvement in the economy slower than expected, Roosevelt faced opposition from several different people and groups. 2. In 1935 Roosevelt began the Second New Deal, which included the Works Progress Administration and several other programs. 3. Aided by the Wagner Act, workers used sit-down strikes to protect their right to organize, and union membership increased rapidly. 4. The Social Security Act guaranteed benefits for the elderly and the unemployed.	• Reproducible Lesson Plan 10–2* • Daily Lecture and Discussion Notes 10–2 • Active Reading Note-Taking Guide 10–2 • Guided Reading Activity 10–2 • Section Quiz 10–2 • Reading Essentials and Study Guide 10–2	📖 Daily Focus Skills Transparency 10–2 📖 Section Graphic Organizer Transparency 10–2 💿 Interactive Tutor Self-Assessment CD-ROM 💿 ExamView® Pro Testmaker CD-ROM 💿 Presentation Plus! CD-ROM 📖 California Standards Practice Transparencies
Section 3: The New Deal Coalition 1. After winning reelection in 1936, Roosevelt faced controversies over the plan to increase the size of the Supreme Court and over a recession caused by his desire to stop deficit spending. 2. Roosevelt and his colleagues continued to push for reforms in housing, farming, and labor. 3. The New Deal expanded the role of the federal government in society and the economy by providing a safety net for many people.	• Reproducible Lesson Plan 10–3* • Daily Lecture and Discussion Notes 10–3 • Active Reading Note-Taking Guide 10–3 • Guided Reading Activity 10–3 • Section Quiz 10–3 • Reading Essentials and Study Guide 10–3	📖 Daily Focus Skills Transparency 10–3 📖 Section Graphic Organizer Transparency 10–3 💿 Interactive Tutor Self-Assessment CD-ROM 💿 ExamView® Pro Testmaker CD-ROM 💿 Presentation Plus! CD-ROM 📖 California Standards Practice Transparencies

PACING YOUR LESSONS

Chapter Introduction	Section 1	Section 2	Section 3	Chapter Assessment
½ Day	1 Day	2 Days	2 Days	½ Day

`0:00` OUT OF TIME? 🗀 Assign the Chapter 10 *Reading Essentials and Study Guide.*

*Available on TeacherWorks™ CD-ROM

Chapter 10 Planning Guide

Standards-Based Lesson Plan

 ## History–Social Science Standards Covered in Chapter 10

e standards covered in the chapter are listed below. Use the accompanying activity as you teach the chapter to ensure student astery of these standards. This activity can be used in combination with the program's print and technology assessment materials.

Standard	Section		
	1	2	3
11.6.2 Understand the explanations of the principal causes of the Great Depression and the steps taken by the Federal Reserve, Congress, and Presidents Herbert Hoover and Franklin Delano Roosevelt to combat the economic crisis.	✓		
11.6.4 Analyze the effects of and the controversies arising from New Deal economic policies and the expanded role of the federal government in society and the economy since the 1930s (e.g., Works Progress Administration, Social Security, National Labor Relations Board, farm programs, regional development policies, and energy development projects such as the Tennessee Valley Authority, California Central Valley Project, and Bonneville Dam).	✓	✓	✓
11.6.5 Trace the advances and retreats of organized labor, from the creation of the American Federation of Labor and the Congress of Industrial Organizations to current issues of a postindustrial, multinational economy, including the United Farm Workers in California.		✓	✓

Cumulative Standards-Assessment Activity

e Cumulative Standards-Assessment Activity will help students organize and learn the important information from the chapter. gin teaching the chapter with this activity, and have students complete it as they read the chapter.

CREATING A DIAGRAM FOR COMPARING AND CONTRASTING

Purpose Comparing and contrasting is a technique useful for finding the similarities and differences between people, movements, or ideas. This tool is particularly useful when studying two sides in a conflict or two regions of a country.

Introduction to Comparing and Contrasting

1. Remind the class that comparing and contrasting is used when two subjects are similar enough that they share some characteristics.

2. Demonstrate the technique by guiding students in comparing and contrasting the impact World War I had on the United States with the impact it had on Britain.

3. Ask students to copy the diagram on the right into their notebooks. As students read this chapter, have them use a Venn diagram to compare and contrast the First New Deal with the

Second New Deal. Tell students to compare both the programs' characteristics and their effects.

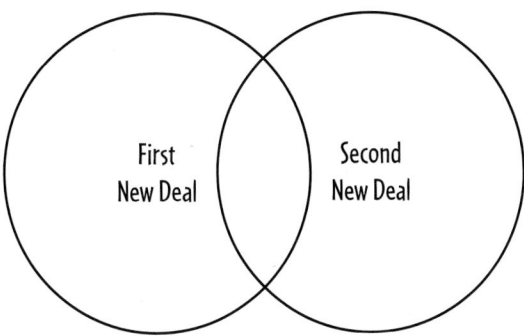

4. As you review the chapter, divide the class into groups and have students share their diagrams. Encourage them to use their diagrams as study aids.

Chapter 10 Planning Guide

READING SUPPORT

- Content Vocabulary Activity 10
- Academic Vocabulary Activity 10
- Reading Skills Activity 10
- Chapter 10 Active Reading Note-Taking Guide
- Chapter 10 Guided Reading Activities
- Chapter 10 Reading Essentials and Study Guide
- American Literature Readings, Unit 3
- *The American Vision: Modern Times* Video Program
- Vocabulary PuzzleMaker CD-ROM
- American History Primary Source Document Library CD-ROM

CRITICAL THINKING

- Critical Thinking Skills Activity 10
- Primary Source Reading 10
- Cause-and-Effect Transparency 10 Strategy and Activity
- Presentation Plus! CD-ROM

UNIVERSAL ACCESS

- Universal Access Activity 10
- English Learner Activity 10
- American Art Prints
- StudentWorks™ Plus CD-ROM
- American Music: Hits Through History
- School-to-Home Connection Activity 10

SKILL PRACTICE

- Map Overlay Transparency 10 Strategy and Activity
- Historical Analysis Skills Activity 10
- Time Line Activity 10
- Reading Skills Activity 10
- Reinforcing Skills Activity 10
- Linking Past and Present Activity 10
- Interpreting Political Cartoons 10
- Geography and History Activity, Unit 3
- MindJogger Videoquiz

WRITING SUPPORT

- Chapter 10 Active Reading Note-Taking Guide
- Writer's Guidebook
- High School Writing Process Transparencies

ASSESSMENT

- Chapter 10 Section Quizzes
- Chapter 10 Tests, Forms A and B
- Authentic Assessment Activity 10
- Exam*View*® Pro Testmaker CD-ROM
- Interactive Tutor Self-Assessment CD-ROM
- California Standards Practice, Grade 11
- Succeeding on . . .™ the California Standards: Grade 11 History–Social Science CD-ROM

CD-ROM	Transparency
DVD	Music Program
Print Material	Videocassette
Poster	

Chapter 10 Planning Guide

TECHNOLOGY

- StudentWorks™ Plus CD-ROM
- TeacherWorks™ CD-ROM
- ExamView® Pro Testmaker CD-ROM
- Interactive Tutor Self-Assessment CD-ROM
- Presentation Plus! CD-ROM
- Vocabulary PuzzleMaker CD-ROM
- American History Primary Source Document Library CD-ROM
- MindJogger Videoquiz
- *The American Vision: Modern Times* Video Program
- Professional Development in High School Social Studies Video Series
- Teach, Use, and Succeed With *The American Vision: Modern Times*
- American Music: Hits Through History
- Succeeding on . . .™ the California Standards: Grade 11 History–Social Science CD-ROM

SPANISH RESOURCES

- Spanish Activities and Assessment
  - Spanish Vocabulary Activities
  - Spanish Guided Reading Activities
  - Spanish Quizzes and Tests
  - Spanish Reteaching Activities
- Spanish Reading Essentials and Study Guide
- Spanish School-to-Home Connection Activities

TRANSPARENCIES

- Daily Focus Skills Transparencies
- Section Graphic Organizer Transparencies
- Map Overlay Transparencies
- Cause-and-Effect Transparencies
- Unit Time Line Transparencies
- Why It Matters Transparencies
- American Art and Architecture Transparencies
- High School Writing Process Transparencies
- California Standards Practice Transparencies

TEACHER PLANNING

- Daily Lecture and Discussion Notes
- English Learner Handbook
- Building Academic Vocabulary
- *The American Vision: Modern Times* Reading and Study Skills Foldables
- Reading Strategies and Activities for the Social Studies Classroom
- Universal Access for the American History Classroom
- NGS United States Desk Map
- NGS World Atlas
- Chapter 10 Reproducible Lesson Plans on TeacherWorks™ CD-ROM
- California Guide to Daily Intervention

PROFESSIONAL DEVELOPMENT

- Building Academic Vocabulary
- Strategies for Success
- Research-Based Strategies Used to Develop *The American Vision: Modern Times*
- Character Education in the High School Classroom
- Professional Development in High School Social Studies Video Series
- Teach, Use, and Succeed With *The American Vision: Modern Times*

MOMENTS IN TIME

The following resource can help you teach the content of this chapter.

- Unit 7 Exuberance and Despair (1917–1939)

Chapter 10 Planning Guide

 History Online

Use our Web site for additional resources. All essential content is covered in the Student Edition.

You and your students can visit tav.mt.glencoe.com, the Web site companion to the **American Vision: Modern Times.** This innovative integration of electronic and print media offers your students a wealth of opportunities. The student text directs students to the Web site for the following options:

• **Chapter Overviews**
• **Self-Check Quizzes**
• **Student Web Activities**
• **Textbook Updates**

Answers to the student Web activities are provided for you in the **Web Activity Lesson Plans.** Additional Web resources and ePuzzles and games are also available.

MASTERING THE STANDARDS

The content and assessment in the Student Edition, Teacher Wraparound Edition, teacher planning materials, and the print and technology products are all standards-based. The use of these products during instruction leads to mastery of the standards.

PRACTICE
• California Standards Practice, Grade 11
• California Standards Practice Transparencies
• School-to-Home Connection

BENCHMARK ASSESSMENT
• Section Quizzes, Chapter Tests, and Authentic Assessment
• Exam*View* ® Pro Testmaker CD-ROM
• Succeeding On . . . ™ the California Standards: Grade 11 History–Social Science CD-ROM

REMEDIATION
• California Guide to Daily Intervention
• Interactive Tutor Self-Assessment CD-ROM
• Exam*View* ® Pro Testmaker CD-ROM
• California Standards Practice, Grade 11
• Reading Essentials and Study Guide

 FOLDABLES™ Study Organizer

Dinah Zike's Foldables

Foldables are three-dimensional, interactive graphic organizers that help students practice basic writing skills, review key vocabulary terms, and identify main ideas. Every chapter has a foldable activity in the *Dinah Zike's Reading and Study Skills Foldables* booklet. You can use the foldables as they are presented or modify them to suit the needs of your individual class.

  THE HISTORY CHANNEL.

A variety of videotape programs are available from A&E Television and The History Channel to provide teaching assistance. To order, call Glencoe at 1-800-334-7344.

Chapter 10 Planning Guide

KEY for Using the Teacher Wraparound Edition

Use this key to help you identify the different types of prompts found in the Teacher Wraparound Edition.

R Reading Strategies activities help you teach reading skills and vocabulary.

C Critical Thinking strategies help students apply and extend what they have learned.

U Universal Access activities provide differentiated instruction for students learning to speak English, along with suggestions for teaching various types of learners.

S Skill Practice strategies help students practice historical analysis and geography skills.

W Writing Support activities provide writing opportunities to help students comprehend the text.

Teaching strategies and activities have been coded for ability level appropriateness.

AL Activities for students working above grade level
OL Activities for students working on grade level
BL Activities for students working below grade level
EL Activities for English learners

History–Social Science Standards

This chapter addresses the following main standard:

11.6 Students analyze the different explanations for the Great Depression and how the New Deal fundamentally changed the role of the federal government.

SKILLBUILDER ACTIVITY

Have students think about how Social Security benefits people today. **Ask:** Is Social Security used in the ways in which it was originally intended? After students have read the chapter, return to this question for a more complete discussion.

TEACH

Thinking About the Big Ideas

As you begin teaching each section, use these questions and activities to focus on the Big Idea.

Section 1
The First New Deal
Essential Question: How do banks assure that your money is safe in a savings account? *(Students might mention FDIC.)* Tell students that one of the first New Deal laws created federal safeguards for bank deposits. In Section 1, students will learn more about this and other New Deal programs. **OL**

CHAPTER
10

1933–1939

Roosevelt and the New Deal

❧ *The Big Ideas* ❧

SECTION 1: The First New Deal

Social and economic crises lead to new roles for government. *In the first 100 days of Roosevelt's presidency, his team initiated a series of laws that transformed the United States.*

SECTION 2: The Second New Deal

Social and economic crises lead to new roles for government. *In 1935 Roosevelt introduced new programs to help unions, the elderly, and the unemployed.*

SECTION 3: The New Deal Coalition

Social and economic crises lead to new roles for government. *Backed by a new coalition of voters, Roosevelt easily won a second term, but the opposition of conservatives weakened his ability to achieve additional reforms.*

The *American Vision: Modern Times* Video *The Chapter 10 video, "Franklin D. Roosevelt and the New Deal," describes the personal and political challenges Franklin Roosevelt faced as president.*

United States PRESIDENTS

1928
• Franklin Delano Roosevelt elected governor of New York

1929
• Great Depression begins

Hoover 1929–1933

1931
• The Empire State Building opens for business

1933
• Gold standard abandoned
• Federal Emergency Relief Act and Agricultural Adjustment Act passed

F. Roosevelt 1933–1945

1928　　　*1931*　　　*1934*

World

1928
• Alexander Fleming discovers penicillin

1930
• Germany's Nazi Party wins 107 seats in Reichstag

1931
• German unemployment reaches 5.6 million
• Surrealist artist Salvador Dali paints *Persistence of Memory*

1933
• Adolf Hitler appointed German chancellor
• Japan withdraws from League of Nations

494

Section 2
The Second New Deal
Essential Question: Identify ways today's government assists the elderly and those who are unemployed. *(Students should point out government programs such as the Social Security Administration, Medicare, or Medicaid.)*

The Second New Deal focused on helping lessen the social impacts of the Great Depression. Tell students that in Section 2 they will read about New Deal programs created for these groups of people. **OL**

In this Ben Shahn mural detail, New Deal planners (at right) design the town of Jersey Homesteads as a home for impoverished immigrants.

— **1935**
• Supreme Court strikes down NIRA
• Social Security Act passed

1937
• Court-packing bill defeated
• "Roosevelt recession" begins

1938
• Fair Labor Standards Act passed

1937

1940

1936
• Civil War erupts in Spain

1938
• Hitler annexes Austria

1939
• World War II begins

HISTORY Online

Chapter Overview
Visit the *American Vision: Modern Times* Web site at tav.mt.glencoe.com and click on ***Chapter Overviews—Chapter 10*** to preview chapter information.

495

Section 3
The New Deal Coalition
Essential Question: What are some factors that can be an obstacle to success and achievement? Following the discussion, tell students that they will read about ways that FDR's success was limited in his second term. **OL**

Cultural Perspectives

In the decades after the Civil War, African Americans had tended to support the Republican Party, while the white South was the strength of the Democratic Party. By the 1930s, however, during President Franklin Roosevelt's second term in office, a new coalition of farmers, laborers, African Americans, new immigrants, ethnic minorities, women, and others came to form the core of the Democratic Party in the South. Have students find out what led to this reorganization of the party. **Ask:** What specific things did Roosevelt do to gain the support of these groups? Which groups of Americans form the core of the Republican and Democratic Parties today? **OL**

FOLDABLES™
Study Organizer

Dinah Zike's Foldables are three-dimensional, interactive graphic organizers that help students practice basic writing skills, review key vocabulary terms, and identify main ideas. Have students complete the foldable activity in the *Dinah Zike's Reading and Study Skills Foldables* booklet.

HISTORY Online

Go to tav.mt.glencoe.com for student activities, lesson plans, and links to additional resources to help students learn about Roosevelt and the New Deal.

Reading Skill ◄

Why It's Important
Recognizing time and sequence requires the ability to place events in the correct order. This skill is particularly necessary in the study of history, when so many events are linked by themes that extend across centuries.

1. Introducing the Skill
Have students look at the Section 1 subheading, "The CCC," on page 505. Have them list the words that indicate sequence as they read, using the chart below. **BL**

Sequence of Events	Words or Phrases from the Text
First	*Beginning in March, 1933*
Then	*by midsummer*
How Long	*six months to a year*
Finally	*By the time it closed down*

2. Extending the Skill
Have students create time lines or graphic organizers for the following month, showing when major assignments are due for all of their classes. Encourage them to create these regularly if they do not already have calendars for this purpose, so they can see the correct order of assigned projects. **BL**

Answers and Additional Support

Preparing to Read Chapter 10

Reading Skill ◄ Recognizing Time and Sequence

Time is the basis for studying history. Since historians describe and explain change over time, they must first know the order of events or developments. They cannot talk about cause and effect or problems and solutions if they don't know what happened first. This means that historians describe a series of actions from beginning to end. Such an order is called chronological order. Chronological order helps readers understand a process over time. Graphs and time lines also help convey the time and sequence of events in history.

Authors often use signal words to let their reader know that they will discuss information in the order of occurrence. You know an author is calling attention to time and sequence when you see words and phrases such as *first, second, last, finally, next, then, since, soon, previously, before, after, meanwhile, at the same time,* and *at last.* The most obvious signals, of course, are days, dates, and times.

Read the following paragraph and notice how signal words help you anticipate a time-ordered explanation.

RECOGNIZING TIME AND SEQUENCE
Make a time connection— imagine how much time elapses during the event described. Hours? A day? Months or years?

On his very first night in office, Roosevelt told Secretary of the Treasury William H. Woodin he wanted an emergency banking bill ready for Congress in less than five days. The following afternoon, Roosevelt declared a national bank holiday, temporarily closing all banks....
On the day Congress convened, the House of Representatives unanimously passed the Emergency Banking Relief Act after only 38 minutes of debate....
On March 12, President Roosevelt addressed the nation by radio.... When banks opened the day after the speech, deposits far outweighed withdrawals. The banking crisis was over. (page 502)

Apply the Skill

Read through the text under the headings "FDR's Early Political Career" and "Governor of New York." As you read, look for words that signal chronological order to help you understand the sequence of events and the time that elapsed. This will help when you take notes because you will learn to place events in the correct order.

496

UNIVERSAL ACCESS

Kinesthetic Have interested students act out a section of the chapter using narration, emphasizing the words that signal time. Suggest that they do two versions, one with the events in scrambled order, and the other with the events in the correct order. Follow the performance with a discussion of how the second performance made more sense. **OL**

Historical Analysis Skill

Analysis Skill Standard H15

Analyzing Environmental Issues

Historical Interpretation As you study history, you should analyze human modifications of landscapes and examine the resulting environmental policy issues.

It is important for us to realize that our actions impact Earth and the landscape the planet provides. Humans have modified the environment in which they live for millennia with various results. How has the landscape in your community been altered by construction of roads, bridges, or buildings? In order to ensure that the environment continues to sustain life on this planet, we must continually assess the impact of our actions.

Read these passages about two New Deal programs—the Civilian Conservation Corps (CCC) and the Tennessee Valley Authority (TVA)—that had a great impact on the environment.

Beginning in March 1933, the CCC offered unemployed young men 18 to 25 years old the opportunity to work under the direction of the national forestry service planting trees, fighting forest fires, and building reservoirs. (page 505)

The TVA erected 20 dams, employing up to 40,000 workers at a time. The agency also reforested millions of acres, built fertilizer factories and power plants, and strung thousands of miles of wire to bring electricity to rural families for the first time. (page 508)

While the CCC and the TVA did much to help unemployed workers and boost the economy, they also made changes in the nation's landscape. How would the building of reservoirs change the environment? What impact did planting thousands of trees have on the landscape? What effects do you think the damming of major rivers had on the environment? What sort of changes in the environment do you think happened when these dams slowed the movement of billions of gallons of water in the rivers?

Apply the Skill

As you read the chapter, make a list of the programs created under the New Deal that changed the landscape. Write down the individual projects, and note your ideas on how these projects changed the environment.

497

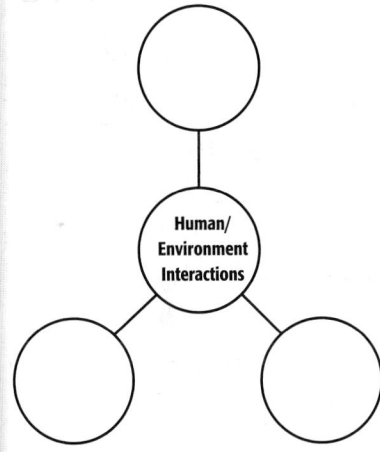

Historical Analysis

Why It's Important
Each new generation becomes responsible for creating public policy and voting on environmental issues and must be accustomed to taking into account the effect of policy on the natural environment. Being able to project consequences of actions is a key skill for all citizens.

1. Introducing the Skill
On the board, create a graphic organizer similar to the one below. Have students indicate ways in which humans have interacted with the natural landscape in your community or county, or the state. **OL** **CA HI5**

Human/ Environment Interactions

2. Extending the Skill
Ask students to investigate one aspect of how humans and nature interact. For example, how might the construction of a new mall affect the wildlife in the area? Students should write brief news articles detailing their findings. **OL** **CA HI5**

UNIVERSAL ACCESS

Verbal/Linguistic Have students present a radio play based on their findings from one of the assignments above. They should have at least three different characters/voices represented in the play. Encourage students to dramatize a situation so that it is both informative and entertaining. **AL** **CA HI5** **CA 11WS1.2**

FOCUS

BELLRINGER
SKILLBUILDER ACTIVITY

Project **Daily Focus Skills Transparency 10-1** and have students answer the question.

Guide to Reading

Understanding Vocabulary: Have students write a vocabulary term and its definition on one side of an index card and draw a picture of the word on the other side. Have students guess a partner's word by looking at the drawing.

Answers to Graphic: bank runs, unprotected bank deposits, stock fraud, and the plight of farmers

Unpacking the Standards

Students will be able to:

• Describe how Franklin Roosevelt's election impacted the mood of the nation.

• Explain specific attempts to repair the nation's economy.

• Analyze ways the New Deal provided debt relief and work for the unemployed.

Answers and Additional Support

SECTION 1 The First New Deal

Guide to Reading

Connection
In the previous chapter, you learned how President Hoover tried to ease the difficulties of the early years of the Great Depression. In this section, you will discover how President Roosevelt introduced the First New Deal.

Main Idea
• After serving as governor of New York, Franklin D. Roosevelt was elected president in 1932. (p. 499)
• During his first 100 days in office, President Roosevelt sent 15 major acts aimed at financial recovery to Congress. (p. 501)
• President Roosevelt took steps to strengthen the banks and the stock market. (p. 502)
• New legislation tried to address the economic problems of farms and industry. (p. 503)

• Congress created two new programs to help homeowners and farmers who had difficulty paying their mortgages. (p. 504)
• Unemployed people found work through several government programs, such as the Public Works Administration and the Civil Works Administration. (p. 505)

Content Vocabulary
fireside chat

Academic Vocabulary
apparent, ideology, fundamental

People and Terms to Identify
New Deal, gold standard, bank holiday, Hundred Days, Securities and Exchange Commission, Federal Deposit Insurance Corporation, Agricultural Adjustment Administration, Civilian Conservation Corps

Reading Objectives
• **Discuss** Franklin Roosevelt's early political career.
• **Explain** the worsening situation in the U.S. banking system in the early 1930s.
• **List** three programs of the First New Deal that provided jobs for the unemployed.

Reading Strategy
Sequencing As you read about President Roosevelt's first three months in office, complete a time line similar to the one below to record the major problems he addressed during this time.

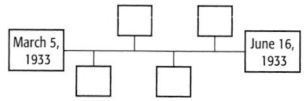

Preview of Events

| ◆1905 | ◆1915 | ◆1925 | ◆1935 |

1905
Franklin Roosevelt and Eleanor Roosevelt marry

1910
Roosevelt elected to New York State Senate

1921
Roosevelt stricken with polio

1928
Roosevelt elected governor of New York

The following are the main History–Social Science Standards covered in this section.

11.6.2 Understand the explanations of the principal causes of the Great Depression and the steps taken by the Federal Reserve, Congress and Presidents Herbert Hoover and Franklin Delano Roosevelt to combat the economic crisis.

11.6.4 Analyze the effects of and the controversies arising from New Deal economic policies and the expanded role of the federal government in society and the economy since the 1930s (e.g., Works Progress Administration, Social Security, National Labor Relations Board, farm programs, regional development policies, and energy development projects such as the Tennessee Valley Authority, California Central Valley Project, and Bonneville Dam).

∞ The Big Idea ∞

Social and economic crises lead to new roles for government. After winning the 1932 election, President Roosevelt surrounded himself with a diverse group of advisers who helped him create programs to pull the country out of the Depression. Based on these ideas, during the Hundred Days, Congress passed 15 major acts that later became known as the First New Deal. These acts focused on banking and stock market regulation and plans for managing farms and industry. For the first time, the government also implemented relief programs that directly helped the unemployed. While the programs did not end the Depression, they gave many people hope for the future.

498 CHAPTER 10 Roosevelt and the New Deal

SECTION RESOURCES

📁 **Print Material**
• Reproducible Lesson Plan 10-1
• Guided Reading Activity 10-1
• Reading Essentials and Study Guide 10-1
• Active Reading Note-Taking Guide 10-1

🖥 **Transparencies**
• Daily Focus Skills Transparency 10-1
• Section Graphic Organizer Transparency 10-1

Technology
🖥 Interactive Tutor Self-Assessment CD-ROM
🖥 ExamView® Pro Testmaker CD-ROM
🖥 Presentation Plus! CD-ROM

Roosevelt Takes Office

Main Idea After serving as governor of New York, Franklin D. Roosevelt was elected president in 1932.

Reading Connection Do you believe family connections are helpful or necessary to participate in politics? Read on to learn about one man whose family connections may have helped him become president.

When Franklin Delano Roosevelt came into office, he was bursting with ideas to help the United States recover from the Depression. The president, however, had no clear agenda. The previous spring, during his campaign for the presidential nomination, Roosevelt revealed the approach he would take as president. "The country needs," Roosevelt explained, "bold, persistent experimentation. . . . Above all, try something."

★ *An American Story* ★

In the 1920s, cowboy and comedian Will Rogers said that his life's work was "to rescue the country from the hands of the politicians." He used his sharp wit to go after these public figures. A friend of presidents and politicians of both parties, Rogers nevertheless satirized them mercilessly in public appearances and on the radio.

With FDR, however, Rogers changed his tune: "President Roosevelt closed the banks before lunch and called Congress into session while he was having dessert. . . .The whole country is with him. . . .Even if he does what is wrong they are with him, just so he does something. . . .If he burned down the Capitol, we would cheer and say, 'Well, we at least got a fire started anyhow.'"

As Roosevelt's New Deal gained momentum, Rogers praised the resulting flurry of legislation: "Mr. Roosevelt just makes out a little list of things every morning that he wants [Congress] to do . . .and the whole country is better off."

—adapted from *Will Rogers: A Biography*

In mid-June 1932, with the country deep in the Depression, Republicans had nominated Herbert Hoover to run for a second term as president. Later that month, the Democrats, after four ballots and a great deal of negotiating, chose Roosevelt, the popular governor of New York. When he won the nomina-tion, Roosevelt broke with tradition by flying to Chicago to deliver the first acceptance speech ever made to a nominating convention. Roosevelt's speech set the tone for his campaign:

> ❝The appearance before a National Convention of its nominee for President . . . is unprecedented and unusual, but these are unprecedented and unusual times. . . . Let it also be symbolic that in so doing I broke traditions. Let it be from now on the task of our Party to break foolish traditions. . . . It is inevitable that the main issue of this campaign should revolve about . . . a depression so deep that it is without precedent. . . . Republican leaders not only have failed in material things, they have failed in national vision, because in disaster they have held out no hope. . . . I pledge you, I pledge myself, to a new deal for the American people.❞
>
> —quoted in *The Public Papers and Addresses of Franklin D. Roosevelt*

The next day, a cartoonist used the words "new deal" to stand for Roosevelt's program. From that point forward, Roosevelt's policies for ending the Depression became known as the **New Deal.** Roosevelt's confidence that he could make things better contrasted sharply with Hoover's **apparent** failure to do anything effective. On Election Day, Roosevelt won the Electoral College in a landslide, 472 votes to 59, and he received nearly 23 million votes to slightly less than 16 million for Hoover in the general election.

▼ *Franklin Delano Roosevelt and Will Rogers*

CHAPTER 10   Roosevelt and the New Deal   **499**

TEACH

W Writing Support

Narrative Writing Ask students to imagine that they have just been nominated to run for president or another high government office. Challenge them to craft an acceptance speech that reflects current concerns. **OL**
CA 11WS1.1; 11WS1.5

R Reading Strategy

Analyzing Text Structure Have a volunteer read aloud Roosevelt's words. Have students look through the text for examples of Roosevelt's use of repetition as a rhetorical device. *(unprecedented/precedent, unusual, broke/break, failed, pledge)* Discuss with students effective use of repetition in writing or speaking to emphasize a point and to maintain coherence. **OL**
CA 11RC2.4

S Skill Practice

Visual Literacy Direct students' attention to the photograph of Franklin Roosevelt and Will Rogers. **Ask:** What do you observe about the body language of the group and the mood of the rally? How does this contrast with the mood of the nation in 1932? *(The men in the photograph seem relaxed and at ease. Roosevelt is laughing heartily and others around him are laughing, smiling, and enjoying themselves. The atmosphere at the rally is happy and upbeat, which sharply contrasts with a nation in the midst of a depression.)* **BL** **CA** HI1

More Skill Practice

English Learners Roosevelt's vocabulary, which clearly reveals his excellent education and background, may be challenging for English learners. Help them identify the prefixes, suffixes, and roots of terms such as *appearance, unprecedented,* and *symbolic.* Remind students that even the longest words are often merely a combination of word parts that can be taken apart and understood. **EL**

S Skill Practice

Scaffolding—Developing a Hypothesis Have students imagine the various reactions that voters might have had to FDR's polio and why they might have held those views. **Ask: How do you think voters would respond today to a presidential candidate who could not walk?** OL

CA HR3; HI1; HI3

This Historical Analysis skill was introduced in Chapter 9.

C Critical Thinking

Making Inferences Offer students an alternative vision of the 1932 presidential election. **Ask: What do you infer might have happened to Franklin Roosevelt's political career if the stock market had not crashed in 1929?** *(Students' inferences will vary but might include the likelihood of Roosevelt not winning the presidential election or possibly not being nominated as a presidential candidate by the Democratic Party. Perhaps the presidency would have remained Republican with Herbert Hoover being reelected.)* AL CA 11RC2.4

Answers and Additional Support

Roosevelt's Early Political Career Franklin Roosevelt, born in 1882 to a wealthy New York family, married Eleanor Roosevelt in 1905. They were distantly related through former president Theodore Roosevelt—her uncle and his cousin. Likable, optimistic, and intensely competitive, FDR seemed made for a life in politics. Shortly after graduating from Columbia Law School, Roosevelt won a seat in the New York State Senate, where he earned a reputation as a progressive reformer willing to stand up to the party bosses. Under Woodrow Wilson, he became assistant secretary of the navy, a position he held through World War I.

In 1920 Roosevelt temporarily withdrew from politics. The next year he caught the paralyzing disease known as polio. Undaunted, Roosevelt began a vigorous exercise program, while Eleanor kept his name prominent in the New York Democratic Party. In 1928 he was rewarded by being elected governor New York. His policies as governor made him very popular. He cut taxes for farmers, worked to reduce the rates charged by public utilities, and in 1931 pushed through the New York legislature a new state agency to help unemployed New Yorkers.

Roosevelt's popularity in New York paved the way for his presidential nomination in 1932. Many Americans applauded his use of the government's power to help people in economic distress. Others believed that his struggle against polio had given him a better understanding of their hardships. Perhaps most important, Americans saw in Roosevelt an energy and optimism that gave them hope despite the tough economic times. After Roosevelt became president, his serenity and confidence amazed many people. When one aide commented on his attitude, Roosevelt replied, "If you had spent two years in bed, trying to wiggle your big toe, after that anything else would seem easy."

Roosevelt Is Inaugurated Although Roosevelt won the presidency in November 1932, the country's unemployed and homeless had to endure one more winter as they waited for his inauguration on March 4, 1933. All through the winter, unemployment continued to rise. Meanwhile, bank runs greatly increased, further threatening the nation's banking system. Some of the bank runs occurred because people feared Roosevelt would abandon the **gold standard**

" . . . the only thing we have to fear is fear itself . . . "

—*Franklin D. Roosevelt*

Picturing **History**

Inspiring Words President Roosevelt used his first Inaugural Address of March 1933 to rally the nation's spirits. What problems had made the nation anxious and fearful?

Picturing **History**

Answer: high unemployment, massive bank failures, and the weak economy

Did You Know?

After FDR's election, Eleanor Roosevelt served as not only his legs, but also his eyes and ears, traveling around the nation to see factories and check on federal projects. When the Second Bonus Army arrived in Washington, D.C., FDR welcomed them and sent his wife to visit them.

and reduce the value of the dollar in order to fight the Depression. Under the gold standard, one ounce of gold equaled a set number of dollars. To reduce the value of the dollar, the United States would have to stop exchanging dollars for gold. Many Americans, and foreign investors, decided to take their money out of the banks and convert it to gold before it lost its value.

Across the nation, people stood in long lines with paper bags and suitcases, waiting to withdraw their money from banks. By March 1933, over 4,000 banks had collapsed, wiping out 9 million savings accounts. In 38 states, governors declared **bank holidays**—closing the remaining banks before bank runs could put them out of business.

By the day of Roosevelt's inauguration, most of the nation's banks were closed. One in four workers was unemployed. The economy seemed paralyzed. Roosevelt knew he had to restore the nation's confidence. "First of all," the president declared in his Inaugural Address, "let me assert my firm belief that the only thing we have to fear is fear itself. . . . This nation asks for action, and action now!"

✓ **Reading Check** **Interpreting** What events in Roosevelt's life shaped his ideas and character?

The Hundred Days Begins

Main Idea During his first 100 days in office, President Roosevelt sent 15 major acts aimed at financial recovery to Congress.

Reading Connection Do you think it is wise for a national leader to be surrounded with people who agree with all of the leader's ideas? Why do you think as you do? Read on to learn about Roosevelt's choices for advisers.

Roosevelt assembled a team of advisers, which sometimes was called the Brain Trust. With the help of this team, the new president began to send bill after bill to Congress. Between March 9 and June 16, 1933—which came to be called the **Hundred Days**—Congress passed 15 major acts to meet the economic crisis, setting a pace for new legislation that has never been equaled. Together, these programs made up what would later be called the First New Deal.

▲ *People rush to California bank to withdraw their money*

Origins of the New Deal The New Deal was not based on a clear strategy shaped by a single philosophy. Roosevelt was not an intellectual, nor did he have a strong political **ideology.** He was a practical politician. FDR was willing to try a variety of approaches both to see whether they worked and whether they were helping or hurting him politically.

To generate new ideas and programs, Roosevelt sought advice from a wide range of advisers with experience in academia, business, agriculture, government, law, and social work. The president deliberately chose advisers who disagreed with each other. He wanted to hear many different points of view, and by setting his advisers against one another, Roosevelt ensured that he alone made the final decision on what policies to pursue.

A Divided Administration Roosevelt's advisers were divided roughly into three main groups. Despite their disagreements, most of the advisers had grown up in the Progressive Era, and their approaches reflected progressive ideas. They generally favored some form of government intervention in the economy—although they disagreed over what the government's role should be.

One group that was very influential during the early years of Roosevelt's administration supported

CHAPTER 10 Roosevelt and the New Deal **501**

R₁ Reading Strategy

Scaffolding—Academic Vocabulary The word *restore* was introduced in Chapter 6, Section 4. Ask a student to define the word. **BL**

S Skill Practice

Conducting Research Divide students into groups, and ask them to use library resources or the Internet to trace the history of a bill that was recently passed in Congress. Ask each group to report on the sponsors of the bill, its basic content, and any debates about the bill in Congress. **AL**
CA HR4

R₂ Reading Strategy

Using Context Clues Point out the term "fireside chats" to students. **Ask: What do you think is the emotional impact created by using the two words Roosevelt chose?** *(cozy, casual talking among friends)* Remind students in their own writing to consider the emotional weight of the words they choose. **OL**
CA 11WS1.5

✓ Reading Check

Answer: One group wanted joint government-business cooperation; another, government control of business; a third, more competition.

Answers and Additional Support

the "New Nationalism" of Theodore Roosevelt. These advisers believed that business and government should work together to manage the economy. They had been very impressed by business–government cooperation on the War Industries Board during World War I. They believed that if government agencies worked with businesses to regulate wages, prices, and production, they could lift the economy out of the Depression.

A second group of advisers in the Roosevelt administration went even further. They distrusted big business and blamed business leaders for causing the Depression. These advisers wanted government planners to run key parts of the economy.

A third group in Roosevelt's administration supported the "New Freedom" of Woodrow Wilson. They too blamed large trusts for the Depression, but they believed the government had to restore competition to the economy. These advisers wanted Roosevelt to support "trust busting" by breaking up big companies and allowing competition to set wages, prices, and production levels. They also thought the government should impose regulations on the economy to keep competition fair.

✓ Reading Check
Summarizing What ideas did Roosevelt's advisers support?

Picturing History

Presidential Assurances President Roosevelt often used radio addresses to calm the public's fears during the Great Depression. At the beginning of his first term, he encouraged Americans to put their money back in federally inspected banks. Why do you think the president declared a bank holiday?

502 CHAPTER 10 Roosevelt and the New Deal

Fixing the Banks and the Stock Market

Main Idea President Roosevelt took steps to strengthen the banks and the stock market.

Reading Connection Describe a time you listened to or watched a presidential address. Read on to discover how President Roosevelt and his cabinet restored confidence in America's financial institutions.

As the debate over policies and programs swirled around him, President Roosevelt took office with one thing clear in his mind. Very few of the proposed solutions would work as long as the nation's banks remained closed. President Roosevelt knew the first thing he had to do was restore the American people's confidence in the banking system. He immediately began to work on his plan.

The Emergency Banking Relief Act On his very first night in office, Roosevelt told Secretary of the Treasury William H. Woodin he wanted an emergency banking bill ready for Congress in less than five days. The following afternoon, Roosevelt declared a national bank holiday, temporarily closing all banks, and called Congress into a special session scheduled to begin on March 9, 1933.

On the day Congress convened, the House of Representatives unanimously passed the Emergency Banking Relief Act after only 38 minutes of debate. The Senate approved the bill that evening, and Roosevelt signed it into law shortly afterward. The new law required federal examiners to survey the nation's banks and issue Treasury Department licenses to those that were financially sound.

On March 12, President Roosevelt addressed the nation by radio. Sixty million people listened to this first of many **"fireside chats,"** direct talks FDR held with the American people to let them know what he was trying to accomplish. He told the people that their money would now be secure if they put it back into the banks. "I assure you that it is safer to keep your money in a reopened bank than under the mattress." When banks opened the day after the speech, deposits far outweighed withdrawals. The banking crisis was over.

Picturing History

Answer: It would provide a brief interval during which depositors could not withdraw money. Roosevelt hoped to restore confidence in the banking system.
Ask: How many people listened to Roosevelt's fireside chat on March 12, 1933? *(60 million)*

More Skill Practice

Analyzing Primary Sources Have students listen to a recording of one of FDR's fireside chats. Then have them view a live broadcast of the current president speaking. Have students discuss how the two speeches compare. Ask students how the speaking styles reflect both the individuals and current events. **AL**

Regulating Banks and Brokers Although President Roosevelt had restored confidence in the banking system, many of his advisers who favored trust-busting and fair competition urged him to go further. They pushed for new regulations for both banks and the stock market. Roosevelt agreed with their ideas and threw his support behind the Securities Act of 1933 and the Glass-Steagall Banking Act.

The Securities Act required companies that sold stocks and bonds to provide complete and truthful information to investors. The following year Congress created an independent agency, the **Securities and Exchange Commission** (SEC), to regulate the stock market and prevent fraud.

The Glass-Steagall Act separated commercial banking from investment banking. Commercial banks handle everyday transactions. They take deposits, pay interest, cash checks, and loan money for mortgages and other business activities. Under the Glass-Steagall Act, these banks were no longer permitted to risk depositors' money by using it to speculate on the stock market. To further protect depositors, the Glass-Steagall Act also created the **Federal Deposit Insurance Corporation** (FDIC) to provide government insurance for bank deposits up to a certain amount. By protecting depositors in this way, the FDIC greatly increased public confidence in the banking system.

✓ **Reading Check** **Explaining** How did the government restore confidence in the banking system?

Managing Farms and Industry

Main Idea New legislation tried to address the economic problems of farms and industry.

Reading Connection Do you believe federal agencies should help manage the economy? Read on to learn about the farm programs created during the First New Deal.

Many of Roosevelt's advisers believed that both farmers and businesses were suffering because prices were too low and production too high. Several advisers believed competition was inefficient and bad for the economy. They wanted business and government to work together and favored the creation of federal agencies to manage the economy.

The Agricultural Adjustment Administration

The nation's farmers had been hit hard by the Depression. One week after calling Congress into special session, Roosevelt announced plans for a new farm program. Working closely with the leaders of the nation's farm organizations, Secretary of Agriculture Henry Wallace raced to complete a new farm bill before planting season began.

The Agricultural Adjustment Act that Roosevelt asked Congress to pass was based on a simple idea—that prices for farm goods were low because farmers grew too much food. Under Roosevelt's program, the government would pay farmers not to raise certain livestock, such as hogs, and not to grow certain crops, such as cotton, corn, wheat, and tobacco. The farm program was administered by the **Agricultural Adjustment Administration** (AAA).

By the time the AAA was organized, however, farmers had already planted their crops for the year and begun raising the season's livestock. To prevent cotton—which was already at a very low price—from reaching the market, the AAA paid cotton farmers about $100 million to plow under about 25 percent of their crop. Similarly, hog producers slaughtered 6 million piglets instead of fattening them for market.

Over the next two years, farmers withdrew millions of acres from production and received more than $1 billion in support payments. The program accomplished its goal: The farm surplus fell greatly by 1936. Food prices then rose, as did total farm income, which quickly increased by more than 50 percent.

In a nation caught in a Depression, however, raising food prices drew harsh criticism. Furthermore, not all farmers benefited. Large commercial farmers, who concentrated on one crop, profited more than smaller farmers who raised several products. Worse, thousands of poor tenant farmers—many of them African Americans—became homeless and jobless when landlords chose their fields to be taken out of production.

A Blueprint for Industrial Recovery The government turned its attention from farming to manufacturing in June 1933, when Roosevelt and Congress enacted the National Industrial Recovery Act (NIRA). The NIRA suspended the antitrust laws and allowed business, labor, and government to cooperate in setting up voluntary rules for each industry.

These rules were known as codes of fair competition. Some codes set prices, established minimum wages, and limited factories to two shifts per day so production could be spread to as many firms as possible. Other codes shortened workers' hours with the goal of creating additional jobs. Another provision in the law guaranteed workers the right to form unions.

CHAPTER 10 Roosevelt and the New Deal **503**

Review the Big Idea

Review the Big Idea for this section, "Social and economic crises lead to new roles for government." Have students work in pairs to create diagrams showing how the banking system worked before and after the Glass-Steagall Act and the creation of the Federal Deposit Insurance Corporation. Suggest that students add visuals, such as play money, to make their diagrams more visually appealing. **OL**
CA HI1

S Skill Practice

Identifying Point of View
Divide the class into groups of four. Assign the students in each group one of the following roles: large commercial farmer, tenant farmer, official of the Agricultural Adjustment Administration, or person living in the city facing rising food prices. Within their groups, have students role-play their responses to the Agricultural Adjustment Administration's program for raising farm income. When the groups have finished, moderate a class discussion on the pros and cons of the AAA's program. **OL** **CA** HR2; HI1; HI3

✓ Reading Check

Answer: Roosevelt ordered a bank holiday, signed the Emergency Banking Relief Act into law, and addressed the nation in a "fireside chat." He also supported the Glass-Steagall Act, which created the FDIC to provide government insurance for bank deposits.

Did You Know?

Since 1933 the Federal Deposit Insurance Corporation (FDIC) has insured bank deposits. Originally the FDIC insured each bank account for up to $5,000. Today accounts are insured up to $100,000.

Did You Know?

Franklin Roosevelt averaged two press conferences a week throughout his presidency. These were informal affairs with as many as 200 reporters crammed into the Oval Office to hear the president's pronouncements. Roosevelt answered questions off the cuff and seemed to know each reporter by name.

S Skill Practice

Visual Literacy Have students identify the bird used in the graphic for the NRA. *(eagle)* **Ask: What is the bird holding in its talons?** *(lightning bolts, a piece of machinery)* Invite students to share their ideas on the significance of the symbols chosen for this sign. *(Possible ideas: The eagle is the national bird; the machinery part indicated hard work by those in factories; the lightning bolts indicated power.)*

OL **CA HI3**

U Universal Access

Visual/ Spatial Invite students with artistic interest and ability to design posters for one of the programs mentioned in this section. Encourage them to investigate the graphic arts designs of the 1930s to use as models for authenticity. Allow students time to explain their choice of symbols and slogans to the class. Display the posters in the classroom. **OL**

✓ Reading Check

Answer: The AAA paid farmers to limit production. The NIRA set prices, established minimum wages, limited shifts, shortened work hours, and guaranteed workers the right to form unions.

Under the leadership of Hugh Johnson, the National Recovery Administration (NRA) ran the entire program. Business owners who signed code agreements received signs displaying the NRA's symbol—a blue eagle—and the slogan, "We do our part." Since the NRA had limited power to enforce the codes, it used public opinion to pressure companies into going along. It urged consumers to buy goods only from companies that displayed the blue eagle.

The NRA did produce a revival of a few industries, but the gains proved short-lived. Small companies complained, justifiably, that large corporations wrote the codes to favor themselves. More efficient companies disliked price fixing, which limited competition and made it hard for them to increase their market share by cutting prices. Employers disliked codes that gave workers the right to form unions and bargain collectively over wages and hours. They also argued that paying high minimum wages forced them to charge higher prices to cover their costs.

The codes were also very difficult to administer, and business leaders often ignored them. It became obvious that the NRA was failing when industrial production actually fell after the organization was established. By the time the Supreme Court declared the NRA to be unconstitutional in 1935, it had already lost much of its political support.

✓ Reading Check

Examining What were the provisions of the Agricultural Adjustment Act and the National Industrial Recovery Act?

S

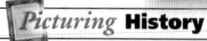

Picturing History

The NRA Eagle As a symbol of the National Recovery Administration, this eagle informed consumers about industries that were meeting the standards of the National Industrial Recovery Act. How successful was the NRA?

504 CHAPTER 10 Roosevelt and the New Deal

U Providing Debt Relief

Main Idea Congress created two new programs to help homeowners and farmers who had difficulty paying their mortgages.

Reading Connection Do you think governments should help people keep their own homes or farms? Why or why not? Read on to find out about the help offered during Roosevelt's first term in office.

While some of Roosevelt's advisers believed low prices had caused the Depression, others believed that debt was the main obstacle to economic recovery. With incomes falling, people had to use most of their money to pay their debts and had little left over to buy goods or pay for services. Many Americans, terrified of losing their homes and farms, deliberately cut back on their spending to make sure they could pay their mortgages. President Roosevelt responded to the crisis by introducing several policies intended to assist Americans with their debts.

The Home Owners' Loan Corporation To help homeowners pay their mortgages, Roosevelt asked Congress to establish the Home Owners' Loan Corporation (HOLC). The HOLC bought the mortgages of many homeowners who were behind in their payments. It then restructured them with longer terms of repayment and lower interest rates. Roughly 10 percent of the nation's homeowners received a HOLC loan.

The HOLC did not help everyone. It only made loans to homeowners who were still employed. When people lost their jobs and could no longer pay their mortgages, the HOLC foreclosed on their property, just as a bank would have done. By 1938 the HOLC had foreclosed on more than 100,000 mortgages. Despite these failures, the HOLC helped refinance one out of every five mortgages on private homes in the United States.

The Farm Credit Administration Three days after Congress authorized the creation of the HOLC, it authorized the Farm Credit Administration (FCA) to begin helping farmers refinance their mortgages. Over the next seven months, the FCA lent four times as much money to farmers as the entire banking system had done the year before. It was also able to push interest rates substantially lower. "I would be without a roof over my head if it hadn't been for the government loan," wrote one of the millions of farmers who were saved by FCA loans.

Picturing History

Background: Even though the Supreme Court declared the NRA unconstitutional, many of its labor provisions were reenacted in later legislation.
Answer: The NRA failed to accomplish many of its goals.
Ask: What was the slogan of the NRA? *(We do our part.)*

Although FCA loans helped many farmers in the short term, their long-term value can be questioned. FCA loans helped less efficient farmers keep their land, but giving loans to poor farmers meant that the money was not available to loan to more efficient businesses in the economy. Although FCA loans may have slowed the overall economic recovery, they did help many desperate and impoverished people hold onto their land.

✓ **Reading Check** **Identifying** What New Deal programs helped farmers and homeowners?

Spending and Relief Programs

Main Idea Unemployed people found work through several government programs, such as the Public Works Administration and the Civil Works Administration.

Reading Connection Are there projects in your community that could be completed with the help of federal programs? Read on to learn about new programs that Roosevelt and Congress created for people in need of jobs.

While many of Roosevelt's advisers emphasized tinkering with prices and providing debt relief in order to cure the Depression, others maintained that the **fundamental** cause of the Depression was low consumption. People were simply not buying enough products to keep the economy going. The fastest way out of the Depression, these advisers asserted, was to get money directly into the hands of needy individuals.

Neither President Roosevelt nor his advisers wanted simply to give money to the unemployed. They argued that recipients were more likely to maintain work skills and self-respect if they earned their money. As a result, Roosevelt urged Congress to establish a series of government agencies that would organize work programs for the unemployed.

The CCC The most highly praised New Deal work relief program was the **Civilian Conservation Corps (CCC),** which combined Roosevelt's love of nature and commitment to conservation with the need to help the unemployed. Beginning in March 1933, the CCC offered unemployed young men 18 to 25 years old the opportunity to work under the direction of the national forestry service planting trees, fighting forest fires, and building reservoirs.

The young men lived in camps near their work areas and earned $30 a month. By midsummer the CCC had created some 1,500 camps. The average

Picturing **History**

The Civilian Conservation Corps FDR satisfied both the nation's need for employment and his love of nature with the CCC. Workers planted forests, built reservoirs, and received a monthly salary. In what year did the CCC halt operations?

CCC worker returned home after six months to a year of service better nourished than before and with greater self-respect. "I weighed about 160 pounds when I went there, and when I left, I was 190," said one. "It made a man of me, all right." By the time it closed down in 1942, the CCC had put 3 million young men to work outdoors.

Public Works and Emergency Relief A few weeks after authorizing the CCC, Congress established the Federal Emergency Relief Administration (FERA). FERA did not initially create projects for the unemployed. Instead, it channeled money—a half-billion dollars in all—to state and local agencies to fund their relief projects. The leader of FERA was Harry Hopkins, whose nervous energy and sarcastic manner put off many people. Despite his personality, Hopkins became one of the most influential people in Roosevelt's administration.

Half an hour after meeting with Roosevelt to discuss his new job, Hopkins set up a desk in the hallway of his new office. In the next two hours, he spent $5 million on relief projects. When critics charged that some of the projects did not make sense in the long run, Hopkins replied, "People don't eat in the long run—they eat every day."

CHAPTER 10 Roosevelt and the New Deal **505**

R₁ Reading Strategy

Scaffolding—Academic Vocabulary The word *emphasis* was introduced in Chapter 6, Section 1. Ask a student to define the word. **BL**

R₂ Reading Strategy

Predicting The Civilian Conservation Corps gave the unemployed temporary work and improved the environment at the same time. **Ask:** Do you think that young people today would be interested in joining a group modeled on the Civilian Conservation Corps? *(Students' answers will vary. Students might say that some young people are interested in volunteering. They might also note that many young peoples' lives are too secure to get involved in a service group of this kind.)* Challenge interested students to find any local programs that are designed for adolescent volunteers, particularly dealing with the environment. **OL**

S Skill Practice

Conducting Research Have students find out more information on one of the people who designed or oversaw one of Roosevelt's New Deal programs, such as Frances Perkins or Harry Hopkins. Challenge students to present their information to the class in character as the person they have chosen to study. **AL**
CA HR4

✓ **Reading Check**

Answer: Home Owners' Loan Corporation and Farm Credit Administration

Picturing **History**

Answer: 1942
Ask: Why do you think the CCC was closed down in 1942? *(The United States entered World War II.)*

More Skill Practice

Visual Literacy Have students examine the photograph and deduce what equipment might have been issued to CCC workers. *(boots, work gloves, tools)* **Ask:** How might these things have compared to what the person had before entering the program? *(Volunteers may not have owned such items before.)* **OL**

R Reading Strategy

Reading Maps, Graphs, and Charts Ask students to consider the economic and social situation of the years during which these agencies were created. **Ask:** Which of the listed agencies do you think was most important? Why? *(Answers will vary, but they should be based on sound reasoning.)* **OL**

U Universal Access

Advanced Learners Ask interested students to investigate the actions of the Civil Works Administration and determine if any public facilities were built or improved in their community or in a nearby area. Tell participating students to write a three- to five-page report that summarizes the impact of their chosen CWA project on the community then and possibly today. **AL**

In June 1933, Congress authorized the creation of another federal relief agency—the Public Works Administration (PWA). Roosevelt knew that nearly one-third of the nation's unemployed were in the construction industry. To put them back to work, the PWA began a series of construction projects.

Unlike other relief efforts, these projects focused on economic investment. Workers built and improved highways, dams, sewer systems, water-works, schools, and other government facilities. Among others, the PWA authorized dams in the West to provide needed water and electricity for economic development. The largest project was the Grand Coulee Dam in Washington, which brought cheap electricity to the Pacific Northwest. Other major dams included the Bonneville and Boulder (now the Hoover Dam).

In most cases, the PWA did not hire workers directly, but instead awarded contracts to construction companies. By insisting that contractors hire African Americans, the agency broke down some of the longstanding racial barriers in the construction trades.

The Central Valley Project (CVP), funded in 1935 by the Emergency Relief Construction Act, provided for the construction of the Contra Costa Canal, Shasta Dam, and Folsom Dam. These components of the CVP help prevent water shortages, flooding, and generate electrical power for California's Central Valley and much of the San Francisco Bay area.

The CWA By the fall of 1933, neither FERA nor the PWA had reduced unemployment significantly. Hopkins realized that unless the federal government acted quickly, a huge number of unemployed would be in severe distress once winter began. After Hopkins explained the situation, President Roosevelt authorized him to set up the Civil Works Administration (CWA).

Unlike the PWA, the CWA hired workers directly and put them on the federal government's payroll. That winter the CWA employed 4 million people, 300,000 of them women. Under Hopkins's direction, the agency built or improved 1,000 airports, 500,000 miles of roads, 40,000 school buildings, and 3,500 playgrounds, parks, and playing fields.

The First New Deal, 1933–1935

Agency	Established	Function
Civilian Conservation Corps (CCC)	March 1933	Employed single men, ages 18–25, for natural resource conservation
Tennessee Valley Authority (TVA)	May 1933	Built hydroelectric plants and dams aimed at improving seven Southern states and attracting industry to the South
Agricultural Adjustment Act (AAA)	May 1933	Reduced agricultural surplus and raised prices for struggling farmers
Federal Emergency Relief Agency (FERA)	May 1933	Granted federal money to state and local governments to be used to help the unemployed
National Recovery Administration (NRA)	June 1933	Controlled industrial production and prices with industry-created codes of fair competition
Federal Deposit Insurance Corporation (FDIC)	June 1933	Guaranteed bank deposits up to $2,500
Public Works Administration (PWA)	June 1933	Provided employment in construction of airports, parks, schools, and roads
Civil Works Administration (CWA)	November 1933 (cancelled 1934)	Provided employment in construction of airports, parks, schools, and roads
Securities and Exchange Commission (SEC)	June 1934	Regulated the stock market to avoid dishonest practices

Chart *Skills*

1. **Interpreting Charts** Which of the programs listed was cancelled the year after it was established?
2. **Examining** What steps did the AAA take to ensure its listed function?

Answers and Additional Support

Chart *Skills*

Answer:
1. Civil Works Administration
2. AAA paid farmers not to raise certain livestock, not to raise certain crops, to plow under cotton, and to slaughter piglets.

Chart Skills Practice
Ask: How many programs were established to directly help the unemployed? *(four—CCC, FERA, PWA, CWA)*

The cost of the CWA was huge—the program spent nearly $1 billion in just five months. A former colleague remembered Hopkins as "the kind of guy that seldom wrote a letter. He'd just call and say, 'Send a million dollars to Arkansas, and five million to New York. People are in need.'"

Although the CWA helped many people get through the winter, the program would not last much longer. President Roosevelt was alarmed at how quickly the agency was spending money. He did not want Americans to get used to the federal government providing them with jobs. Warning that the CWA would "become a habit with the country," Roosevelt insisted that it be shut down. "We must not take the position," the president explained, "that we are going to have a permanent depression in this country." By early April 1934, just over 5 months after it was created, Hopkins had shut down the CWA and fired the 4 million workers the agency had hired.

By the end of his first year in office, President Roosevelt had convinced Congress to pass an astonishing array of programs and policies. The programs passed during the First New Deal did not restore prosperity, but they all reflected Roosevelt's zeal for action, his willingness to experiment, and his openness to new ideas. Perhaps the most important result of the First New Deal was a noticeable change in the spirit of the American people. Roosevelt's actions had inspired hope and optimism when it was needed most, and Americans' faith in their nation had been restored.

CWA Man works on a building as part of the CWA program

Reading Check **Identifying** What three New Deal programs provided work relief to the unemployed?

For help with the concepts in this section of *American Vision: Modern Times* go to tav.mt.glencoe.com and click on *Study Central.*

SECTION 1 ASSESSMENT

Checking for Understanding

1. **Vocabulary** Define: apparent, ideology, fireside chat, fundamental.
2. **People and Terms** Identify: New Deal, gold standard, bank holiday, Hundred Days, Securities and Exchange Commission, Federal Deposit Insurance Corporation, Agricultural Adjustment Administration, Civilian Conservation Corps.
3. **Summarize** the different viewpoints of Roosevelt's advisers.

Reviewing Big Ideas

4. **Reviewing** How did the Glass-Steagall Act and the FDIC help make the banking industry safer?

Critical Thinking

5. **Interpreting** Did the CCC, CWA, and PWA achieve their goals? Explain your answer.
6. **Organizing** Use a graphic organizer like the one below to list the major agencies of the First New Deal.

Roosevelt's New Agencies

Analyzing Visuals

7. **Analyzing Charts** Examine the chart on page 506. How did the various agencies listed change the historical role of the federal government?

Writing About History

8. **Expository Writing** Research the Agricultural Adjustment Act by rereading the text on page 503. Use library resources and the Internet to complete your research. Then write an article explaining the benefits and drawbacks of this piece of legislation. **CA** 11WA2.2c

CHAPTER 10 Roosevelt and the New Deal **507**

SECTION 1 ASSESSMENT ANSWERS

1. Content vocabulary is boldfaced and highlighted in yellow. Academic vocabulary is boldfaced.
2. New Deal *(p. 499),* gold standard *(p. 500),* bank holiday *(p. 501),* Hundred Days *(p. 501),* SEC *(p. 503),* FDIC *(p. 503),* AAA *(p. 503),* CCC *(p. 505)*
3. One group wanted joint government-business cooperation; another wanted greater government control; another wanted to increase competition.
4. protected depositors' money; insured bank deposits
5. They temporarily employed workers, but did not reduce unemployment significantly.
6. Answers should match text information.
7. Answers should explain the various ways the government increased its role.
8. Articles should cover both sides of the issue.

TEACH

C Critical Thinking

Drawing Conclusions
Encourage students to think beyond the local circumstances of the TVA project and consider the region's greater good. **Ask:** *Why would the government pay people to build dams? (Students should brainstorm the benefits brought by the TVA.)* **OL**

Why It Matters

The TVA

Perhaps no New Deal program produced as many visible benefits as the Tennessee Valley Authority (TVA). This dam-building project was a bold venture to control floods, conserve forestlands, and bring electricity to rural America. The TVA created a comprehensive plan for developing a vast seven-state region drained by the Tennessee and Cumberland Rivers and populated mainly by poor farmers working worn-out land. The TVA erected 20 dams, employing up to 40,000 workers at a time. The agency also reforested millions of acres, built fertilizer factories and power plants, and strung thousands of miles of wire to bring electricity to rural families for the first time.

▲ Recreation
Millions of people each year fish, swim, ski, white-water raft, or go boating on the reservoirs. Sometimes the reservoir system is referred to as the "Great Lakes of the South."

◄ Flood Control
In spring 1984, torrential rains would have brought the Tennessee River crest to almost 20 feet (6 m) above flood level. However, by storing water in reservoirs behind dams such as Dawson Dam and releasing it slowly, the TVA prevented most potential flooding.

C

Answers and Additional Support

508 CHAPTER 10 Roosevelt and the New Deal

EXTENDING THE CONTENT

A Changing Mission The TVA's original mission focused on making the Tennessee River navigable and on controlling floods. In addition, reforestation and land reclamation were part of the mission. The agency was also charged with the responsibility of generating electrical power and assisting with industrial and agricultural development. Today the TVA's mission focuses on the sustained, integrated development of the region. Supplying reliable and economical power, supporting the river system, and stimulating economic growth are key to the mission. **Ask:** Which seven states are directly affected by the TVA? *(Alabama, Georgia, Kentucky, Mississippi, North Carolina, Tennessee, and Virginia)*

NATIONAL GEOGRAPHIC

The TVA, 1940

Legend:
- Area supplied with power from the TVA
- — Dam
- ■ Steam power plant

Albers Conic Equal-Area projection

0 — 100 miles
0 — 100 kilometers

The TVA Today

The TVA's power facilities include 29 hydroelectric dams, 11 fossil-fuel plants, 3 nuclear power plants, 4 combustion-turbine plants, a pumped-storage facility, and 17,000 miles of transmission lines. These facilities provide power to nearly 8 million people in the seven-state region.

ANALYZING THE IMPACT

Checking for Understanding
1. **Identify** In addition to creating jobs, what was the purpose of the TVA?

Critical Thinking
2. **Evaluate** Explain the importance of the TVA projects to people living in the region drained by the Tennessee and Cumberland Rivers.

BELLRINGER
SKILLBUILDER ACTIVITY

Project **Daily Focus Skills Transparency 10-2** and have students answer the question.

Guide to Reading

Understanding Vocabulary:
Divide the class into three groups and assign each group an equal number of terms to define. Then have students use the words in an appropriate historical context.

Answers to Graphic:
See the chart on page 516.

Unpacking the Standards

Students will be able to:

- Identify individuals who criticized the New Deal and discuss their reasoning.
- Explain the programs and goals that defined the Second New Deal.
- Describe the circumstances surrounding the growth of industrial unions.
- Discuss the impact of the Social Security Act.

Answers and Additional Support

SECTION 2   The Second New Deal

Guide to Reading

Connection
In the previous section, you learned about President Roosevelt's early efforts to end the Great Depression. In this section, you will discover how the president initiated a new series of laws as an answer to critics and to help the economy.

Main Idea
- With improvement in the economy slower than expected, Roosevelt faced opposition from several different people and groups. (p. 511)
- In 1935 Roosevelt began the Second New Deal, which included the Works Progress Administration and several other programs. (p. 513)

- Aided by the Wagner Act, workers used sit-down strikes to protect their right to organize, and union membership increased rapidly. (p. 514)
- The Social Security Act guaranteed benefits for the elderly and the unemployed. (p. 516)

Content Vocabulary
deficit spending, binding arbitration, sit-down strike

Academic Vocabulary
finance, thereby, crucial

People and Terms to Identify
American Liberty League, Works Progress Administration, National Labor Relations Board, Social Security Act

Reading Objectives
Describe the political challenges Roosevelt faced in the mid-1930s.
Explain why the Social Security Act is still regarded as an important piece of legislation.

Reading Strategy
Organizing As you read about President Roosevelt's Second New Deal, complete a graphic organizer like the one below by filling in his main legislative successes during this period.

Legislation	Provisions

Preview of Events

◆April 1935	◆June 1935	◆August 1935	◆October 1935

April 1935
Works Progress Administration founded

May 1935
Supreme Court strikes down NIRA

July 1935
National Labor Relations Act becomes law

August 1935
Social Security Act adopted

November 1935
John L. Lewis forms Committee for Industrial Organization

The following are the main History–Social Science Standards covered in this section.

11.6.4 Analyze the effects of and the controversies arising from New Deal economic policies and the expanded role of the federal government in society and the economy since the 1930s (e.g., Works Progress Administration, Social Security, National Labor Relations Board, farm programs, regional development policies, and energy development projects such as the Tennessee Valley Authority, California Central Valley Project, and Bonneville Dam).

11.6.5 Trace the advances and retreats of organized labor, from the creation of the American Federation of Labor and the Congress of Industrial Organizations to current issues of a postindustrial multinational economy, including the United Farm Workers in California.

◦≈ The Big Idea ≈◦

Social and economic crises lead to new roles for government. Both the right and the left criticized the First New Deal. The right disliked Roosevelt's deficit spending. The left thought the president did not go far enough in helping Americans and suggested higher taxes for the wealthy, nationalization of banks, and a national pension plan. At the same time, the Supreme Court struck down parts of the First New Deal as unconstitutional. The president responded with a new set of legislative acts called the Second New Deal. The Works Progress Administration had already begun employing millions of Americans. Now workers gained more rights, including the right to form unions. The Social Security Act also provided the nation's first old-age and unemployment benefits.

510   CHAPTER 10   Roosevelt and the New Deal

SECTION RESOURCES

📖 Print Material
- Reproducible Lesson Plan 10-2
- Guided Reading Activity 10-2
- Reading Essentials and Study Guide 10-2
- Active Reading Note-Taking Guide 10-2

🖥 Transparencies
- Daily Focus Skills Transparency 10-2
- Section Graphic Organizer Transparency 10-2

Technology
- Interactive Tutor Self-Assessment CD-ROM
- ExamView® Pro Testmaker CD-ROM
- Presentation Plus! CD-ROM

Challenges to the New Deal

Main Idea With improvement in the economy slower than expected, Roosevelt faced opposition from several different people and groups.

Reading Connection Do you know anyone who is easily able to convince others to follow his or her ideas? Read on to learn about several people who used this power against Roosevelt and his New Deal policies.

The New Deal had been in effect for two years, yet the economy had shown only a slight improvement. Although more than 2 million new jobs had been created, more than 10 million workers remained unemployed, and the nation's total income remained about half of what it had been in 1929. As one of Harry Hopkins's aides reported on a visit to Houston, Texas, "Nobody seems to think any more that the thing [the New Deal] is going to work."

★ An American Story ★

Harry Hopkins, head of the Federal Emergency Relief Administration, worked long hours in his Washington office, a bare, dingy room with exposed water pipes. He preferred this space to the grandeur of the more conventional offices of high-ranking officials. Here he often defended the New Deal's work relief programs when reporters dropped by, and he lashed out at New Deal critics with headline-making phrases. "Some people just can't stand to see others make a decent living," he said, or, "Hunger is not debatable."

Sometimes Hopkins went on the road to talk about his job. Once, on a trip to his home state of Iowa, Hopkins was extolling New Deal policies to a sympathetic audience when a voice from the crowd shouted, "Who's going to pay for it?" Without a word Hopkins peeled off his jacket, loosened his tie, and rolled up his sleeves. Then his voice ripped through the utter stillness, "You are!"

—adapted from *The Politics of Upheaval*

President Roosevelt appreciated Harry Hopkins's feistiness. He needed effective speakers who were willing to contend with his adversaries. Although Roosevelt had been tremendously popular during his first two years in office, opposition to his policies had begun to grow.

Criticism From Left and Right Hostility toward Roosevelt came from both the right wing and the left wing of the political spectrum. People on the right generally believed the New Deal had imposed too many regulations on business.

The right wing also included many Southern Democrats who believed the New Deal had expanded the federal government's power at the expense of states' rights.

The right wing had opposed the New Deal from the beginning, but by late 1934, the opposition began to increase. To pay for his programs, Roosevelt had begun **deficit spending.** He had abandoned a balanced budget and begun borrowing money to pay for his programs. Many business leaders became greatly alarmed at the government's growing deficit.

In August 1934, business leaders and anti-New Deal politicians from both parties joined together to create the **American Liberty League.** Its purpose was to organize opposition to the New Deal and "teach the necessity of respect for the rights of person and property."

While criticisms from the right threatened to split the Democratic Party and reduce business support for Roosevelt, another serious challenge to the New Deal came from the left. People on the left believed Roosevelt had not gone far enough. They wanted the government to intervene even more dramatically in the economy to shift wealth from the rich to middle-income and poor Americans.

Harry Hopkins ▼

CHAPTER 10   Roosevelt and the New Deal   **511**

TEACH

U Universal Access

Interpersonal Organize the class into discussion groups of six people. One group member should play Franklin Roosevelt, while the other group members each should play one of the following roles: a farm laborer, a factory worker, an unemployed person, a business leader, or a retired person. Have the groups read Section 2 to find out what each person's criticism of Roosevelt would be and how Roosevelt would have responded to that criticism. Then have each group role-play a meeting between the citizens and Roosevelt. **OL**
CA 11WS1.2

Review the Big Idea

Review the Big Idea for this section, "Social and economic crises lead to new roles for government." Ask students to read the concerns of the right-wing opposition to the New Deal. Tell students to write a two-page report describing these concerns. Students may use library and Internet resources to assist them.
OL **CA** 11WA2.4a

R Reading Strategy

Scaffolding—Academic Vocabulary The word *intervene* was introduced in Chapter 4, Section 3. Ask a student to define the word. **BL**

Did You Know?

The American Liberty League had two objectives: to teach respect for the rights of person and property, and to teach that it was the duty of government to encourage private enterprise and protect property.

Critics From the Left Huey Long and Father Charles Coughlin claimed the New Deal did not do enough to help the poor.

Huey Long Perhaps the most serious threat from the left came from Democratic senator Huey Long of Louisiana. Long captivated audiences with folksy humor and fiery oratory. As governor of Louisiana, Long had championed the downtrodden. He had improved schools, colleges; and hospitals, and had built roads and bridges. These benefits made Long very popular and enabled him to build a powerful and corrupt political machine.

Long's attacks on the rich gave him a national following, too. His supporters organized some 27,000 "Share Our Wealth" clubs across the country. Pollsters estimated that if he ran against Roosevelt as a third-party candidate in 1936, Long would win several million votes—enough, they believed, to ensure a Republican victory.

Father Coughlin Huey Long's challenge to Roosevelt became even more credible when his supporters were combined with those of Father Charles Coughlin, a Catholic priest in Detroit. Coughlin had a popular radio show that attracted a weekly audience of about 30 to 45 million Americans.

Originally a New Deal supporter, Coughlin had become impatient with its moderate reforms. He called instead for heavy taxes on the wealthy and nationalization of the banking system. In the spring of 1935, Coughlin organized the National Union for Social Justice, which some Democrats feared was the first step to creating a new political party. By the late 1930s, Coughlin began to lose influence by praising fascism and making comments many considered anti-Semitic.

The Townsend Plan A third left-wing challenge to Roosevelt came from Dr. Francis Townsend, a former public health official. Townsend proposed that the federal government pay citizens over age 60 a pension of $200 a month. Recipients would have to retire and spend their entire pension check each month. He believed the plan would increase spending and remove people from the labor force, freeing up jobs for the unemployed.

Townsend's proposal attracted millions of supporters, especially among the elderly, who mobilized as a political force for the first time in American history. Townsend's program was particularly popular in the West. When combined with Long's support in the Midwest and South and Coughlin's support among urban Catholics in the Northeast, there was a real possibility of a coalition that would draw enough votes away from Roosevelt to prevent his reelection in 1936.

✓ **Reading Check** **Examining** What groups of people challenged Roosevelt and the New Deal? What concerns did they have?

Launching the Second New Deal

Main Idea In 1935 Roosevelt began the Second New Deal, which included the Works Progress Administration and several other programs.

Reading Connection What role do you think art and literature should play in public life? Read on to find out about a federal program designed to employ artists, actors, and musicians.

Although he remained tremendously popular with the American people, Roosevelt realized that his political support could be undermined by the attacks from his opponents on the left and right. He was also disturbed by the failure of the New Deal to generate a rapid economic recovery. In 1935 he launched what came to be called the Second New Deal—another series of programs and reforms that he hoped would speed up the nation's recovery, provide economic security to every American, and ensure his reelection in 1936.

The WPA In January 1935, Roosevelt began by asking Congress for nearly $5 billion "for work relief and to increase employment by providing useful projects." Much of the money would be given to the **Works Progress Administration** (WPA), a new federal agency headed by Harry Hopkins. "The big boss is ready to go places in a big way," Hopkins told a colleague.

Over the next several years, the WPA spent $11 billion. Its 8.5 million workers constructed about 650,000 miles of highways, roads, and streets, 125,000 public buildings, and more than 8,000 parks. It built or improved more than 124,000 bridges and 853 airports.

The WPA's most controversial program was "Federal Number One," a section of the Professional Projects Division that offered work to artists, musicians, theater people, and writers. "They've got to eat just like other people," Hopkins commented to critics of the program. The artists created thousands of murals and sculptural works to beautify the walls and halls of public buildings. Musicians established 30 city symphony orchestras, as well as hundreds of smaller musical groups. The Federal Theater Project **financed** playwrights, actors, and directors. The program also funded historians who interviewed former slaves to document American history. The program helped record important information about the history of the United States, as well as improve the aesthetic quality of many public buildings.

The Supreme Court's Role When Roosevelt asked Congress to fund the WPA in January 1935, he had expected quick action on the bill. He quickly discovered that opposition to his programs was growing in Congress. The bill creating the WPA did not pass until April 1935. By late May, Congress was preparing to adjourn for the summer, leaving Roosevelt with very few accomplishments.

Suddenly, the political situation shifted. On May 27, 1935, the Supreme Court unanimously struck down the National Industrial Recovery Act in *Schechter* v. *United States*. The Schechter brothers, who had a poultry business in Brooklyn, New York, had been convicted in 1933 of violating the NIRA's Live Poultry Code. They had sold diseased chickens and violated the code's wage-and-hour provisions. 📖 *(See page 1006 for more about Schechter v. United States.)*

In what became known as the "sick chicken case," the Court ruled that employees of a slaughterhouse were only involved in the slaughtering and sale of chickens in a local area. Because employees were not involved in interstate commerce, their wages and hours could not be regulated by the NIRA's code for wage-and-hour provisions. More importantly, however, the court ruled that the Constitution did not allow Congress to delegate its powers to the executive branch. Thus it considered the NIRA codes unconstitutional. The decision worried Roosevelt. The ruling suggested that the Court could soon strike down the rest of the New Deal as well.

Shortly after the Schechter decision, Roosevelt sprang into action. With the Court threatening to strike down the New Deal and with growing challenges from the left and right, the president knew he needed a new series of programs to keep voters' support. He called congressional leaders to a White House conference. Pounding his desk, he thundered that Congress could not go home until it passed his new bills. That summer, Congress began what the press nicknamed the "second hundred days" and worked feverishly to pass Roosevelt's programs.

✓ **Reading Check** **Examining** How did the Supreme Court's ruling affect the New Deal?

HISTORY Online

Student Web Activity Visit the *American Vision: Modern Times* Web site at tav.mt.glencoe.com and click on **Student Web Activities— Chapter 10** for an activity on the New Deal.

C **Critical Thinking**

Determining Cause and Effect Have students skim through the text under this heading, looking for instances of cause and effect between President Roosevelt and his critics. Ask them to look for and to list how Roosevelt modified government programs and his overall goals to maintain voter support and still fight the economic hardships present in the nation. **OL** **CA HI2** **CA 11RC2.4**

R **Reading Strategy**

Connecting Ask students to use library or Internet resources to find out about contemporary controversies over National Endowment for the Arts funding. Students should also discover how the NEA is funded and what kinds of programs it in turn funds. Have students compare the public reaction to the NEA grants and to "Federal Number One," as well as speculate on the reasons for the reaction. **AL**

✓ **Reading Check**

Answer: By threatening to derail the New Deal, the ruling caused Roosevelt and the Congress to pass much legislation very quickly.

CHAPTER 10 Roosevelt and the New Deal **513**

HISTORY Online

Objectives and answers to the student activity can be found in the **Web Activity Lesson Plan** at tav.mt.glencoe.com.

Did You Know?

The Federal Theater was among the most exciting and innovating projects of the WPA. Orson Welles staged Shakespeare's *Macbeth*, using an all African American cast. Many Federal Theater productions used the "living newspaper" technique, often taking on the style and method of radio and documentary cinema to build morality plays about current events.

NATIONAL GEOGRAPHIC

MOMENT in HISTORY

BRIEF RESPITE FOR FDR
Enjoying a short break from the pressures of dealing with the country's economic woes, President Franklin D. Roosevelt holds his beloved dog Fala while chatting with the granddaughter of the family gardener at his Hyde Park, New York, estate. The president and his staff, with the help of the press, took great pains to conceal his polio-induced paralysis. He was never filmed or photographed being wheeled or carried from place to place. This rare snapshot is one of the few known to exist that shows Roosevelt seated in his wheelchair.

R The Rise of Industrial Unions

Main Idea Aided by the Wagner Act, workers used sit-down strikes to protect their right to organize, and union membership increased rapidly.

Reading Connection How did leaders respond to major railroad strikes in the late 1800s? How would you respond to a strike if you were in a leadership position? Read on to learn about a new, effective method of striking and its results.

When the Supreme Court ruled against the NIRA, it also struck down the section of the law that established labor's right to organize. President Roosevelt and the Democrats in Congress knew that the working-class vote was very important in winning reelection in 1936. They also believed that unions could help end the Depression. They thought that high union wages would let workers spend more money, **thereby** boosting the economy. Opponents

disagreed, arguing that high wages forced companies to charge higher prices and to hire fewer people. Despite these concerns, Congress pushed ahead with new labor legislation.

The National Labor Relations Act In July 1935, Congress passed the National Labor Relations Act, also called the Wagner Act after its author, Democratic senator Robert Wagner of New York. The act guaranteed workers the right to organize unions without interference from employers and to bargain collectively. The law set up the **National Labor Relations Board** (NLRB), which consists of five members appointed by the United States President and approved by the Senate. Members serve five-year terms and receive assistance from 33 regional directors. The NLRB organized factory elections by secret ballot to determine whether workers wanted a union. The NLRB then certified the successful unions.

The new law also set up a process whereby dissatisfied union members could take their complaints to

---

NATIONAL GEOGRAPHIC MOMENT in HISTORY

This is one of only two photographs that show Roosevelt seated in a wheelchair. In January 2001 a new portion of the Roosevelt Memorial in Washington, D.C., was unveiled. The statue shows Roosevelt seated in a wheelchair. After initial resistance, his family now supports the addition of the statue. His grandson David Roosevelt said, "I hope that when young people—a young person who goes to visit the FDR Memorial who perhaps is in a wheelchair herself or himself—when they first see the entrance and when they see FDR in a wheelchair, they will say, 'I can do that, too.'"

binding arbitration, in which a neutral party would listen to both sides and decide the issues. The NLRB was authorized to investigate the actions of employers and had the power to issue "cease and desist" orders against unfair practices.

The CIO The Wagner Act stimulated a burst of labor activity. In the mid-1930s, the United Mine Workers union, led by John L. Lewis, began working with several other unions to organize workers in industries where unions did not yet exist. They formed the Committee for Industrial Organization (CIO) in 1935.

The CIO set out to organize industrial unions, or unions that included all workers in a particular industry, skilled and unskilled. The CIO began by focusing on the automobile and steel industries—two of the largest industries in America where workers were not yet organized into unions.

Sit-Down Strikes In late December 1936, officials at the General Motors auto-body plant in Cleveland, Ohio, demoted two union men. In an unplanned protest, a shift of 135 workers sat down and launched an unprecedented kind of strike. They stopped working but refused to leave the factory. This stopped the work flow and also prevented the factories from bringing in replacement workers. A few days later, the workers at the company's plant in Flint, Michigan, launched their own **sit-down strike,** as the press quickly dubbed it. Workers at other plants followed suit or carried out traditional strikes. Bruce Bliven, editor of *The New Republic* magazine, was among the few journalists allowed into the plant. Regarding the condition of the strike, he reported:

> 66 The place was remarkably neat and tidy, at least as clean as it is under normal conditions. Beds were made up on the floor of each car, the seats being removed if necessary. . . . I could not see—and I looked for it carefully—the slightest damage done anywhere to the General Motors Corporation. The nearly completed car bodies, for example, were as clean as they would be in the salesroom, their glass and metal shining. 99
>
> –quoted in *The Great Depression*

Violence broke out in Flint when police launched a tear gas assault on one of the smaller plants. The

Trying to Improve Working Conditions

Autoworkers stage a sit-down strike in 1937 in Flint, Michigan.

Union Membership, 1933–1943

Source: *Historical Statistics of the United States: Colonial Times to 1970.*

Graph *Skills*

1. **Interpreting Graphs** Approximately how many people were union members in 1936?
2. **Understanding Cause and Effect** Why did union membership increase steadily after 1936?

515

S Skill Practice

Visual Literacy Draw students' attention to the photograph of the men on strike in Flint, Michigan. **Ask:** What do you observe that may be different from a working strike today? *(The men are not wearing uniforms or work clothes; some are in white shirts and ties. Many of the men are wearing hats. Each man is reading a newspaper or magazine. Strikes today are more commonly walk-out strikes, with striking workers marching outside a factory and holding up posters and banners.)* **BL** **CA HI3**

R Reading Strategy

Inferring What does Bruce Bliven's comment say about the expectations of striking workers? *(They will damage equipment.)* **OL**

Resources for page 515

Have students read more about efforts to increase the power of unions in the **Primary Source Reading 10-1.**

Graph *Skills*

Answer:
1. approximately 4 million
2. Union membership increased as a result of passage of the Wagner Act.

Graph Skills Practice
Ask: What was the approximate increase in labor membership between 1933 and 1943? *(approximately 10 million)*

515

Skill Practice

Conducting Research The financial security of the Social Security Administration has been a growing political issue for several years now. Divide the class into four or five groups. **Ask: Are you concerned that the promise of Social Security benefits will not be met when you reach retirement age? Is it fair for you to fund programs that might not benefit you directly? Ask** students to discuss these questions within their groups and devise ways to visually display each group's consensus opinions. When the activity is finished, compare each group's findings. **Ask: Is there a common pattern to the information that you are uncovering here? Explain your observations.** *(Students should note if there is a pattern present in the data, and they should offer opinions on what they have learned and observed.)* **OL**

CA HI4

R **Reading Strategy**

Scaffolding—Academic Vocabulary The word *funds* was introduced in Chapter 5, Section 1. Ask a student to define the word. **BL**

✓**Reading Check**

Answer: the right to organize unions without interference; collective bargaining

Answers and Additional Support

strikers turned back the attack with whatever was at hand—door hinges, bottles, stones, and balls of ice. The police wounded more than a dozen strikers with gunfire, but the strike held. On February 11, 1937, the company gave in and recognized the CIO's United Auto Workers (UAW) as its employees' sole bargaining agent. The UAW quickly became one of the most powerful unions in the United States.

The United States Steel Corporation, the nation's largest steel producer, decided it did not want to repeat the General Motors experience with striking workers. The company recognized the CIO's United Steelworkers of America, which won a 40-hour workweek and a 10-percent pay raise. Smaller steel producers did not initially recognize unions, and strikes broke out around the country. By 1941, however, the steelworkers' union had contracts with the entire industry.

In the late 1930s, workers in other industries also sat down at their jobs to gain union recognition. In only six years, total union membership tripled from roughly 3 million in 1933 to about 9 million in 1939. In 1938 the CIO changed its name to the Congress of Industrial Organizations and became a federation of industrial unions.

✓**Reading Check** *Examining* What provisions did the National Labor Relations Act establish?

The Second New Deal, 1935

Agency/Legislation	Function
Works Progress Administration (WPA)	Combated unemployment; created jobs throughout economy
Rural Electrification Administration (REA)	Brought electricity to isolated agricultural areas
Social Security Act	Created unemployment system, disability insurance, old-age pension, and child welfare benefits
Public Utility Holding Company Act	Eliminated unfair practices and abuses of utility companies
Banking Act	Strengthened the Federal Reserve
Resettlement Act	Assisted poor families and sharecroppers in beginning new farms or purchasing land

Chart *Skills*

1. **Interpreting Charts** What did the Resettlement Act try to accomplish?
2. **Understanding Cause and Effect** How did these acts create a safety net for American citizens?

The Social Security Act

S *Main Idea* **The Social Security Act guaranteed benefits for the elderly and the unemployed.**

Reading Connection Do you think that the elderly and others in need receive enough government assistance? Read on to find out about a program to help the elderly and people with disabilities.

After passing the Wagner Act, Congress began work on a bill that ranks as one of the most important pieces of legislation in American history. This was the **Social Security Act,** which became law in August 1935. Its major goal was to provide some security for the elderly and for unemployed workers.

With the support of Secretary of Labor Frances Perkins, Roosevelt and his team spent months preparing the bill. The framers viewed it primarily as an insurance bill. Workers earned the right to receive benefits because they paid premiums. The Social Security Act provided two social insurance programs. A federal program provided retirement insurance. The individual states administered a program **R** for unemployment compensation that used federal funds. The legislation also provided modest welfare payments to other needy people, including those with disabilities and poor families with young dependent children.

The core of Social Security was the monthly retirement benefit, which people could collect when they stopped working at age 65. Another important benefit—unemployment insurance—supplied a temporary income to unemployed workers looking for new jobs. Some critics did not like the fact that the money came from payroll taxes imposed on workers and employers, but to Roosevelt these taxes were **crucial:** "We put those payroll contributions there so as to give the contributors a legal, moral, and political right to collect their pensions and the unemployment benefits."

Chart *Skills*

Answer:
1. The act assisted poor families and sharecroppers in beginning new farms or purchasing land.
2. They protected laborers, created insurance for the unemployed and the elderly, and strengthened the economy.

Chart Skills Practice
Ask: What problem did the Rural Electrification Administration address? *(the lack of electricity in isolated rural areas)*

Picturing History

Social Security President Roosevelt signs the Social Security Act of 1935 among supporters of the act. While critics did not like that contributions were payroll deducted, Roosevelt argued that this was vital to the social security program. *Why did Roosevelt believe it was so important for contributions to be payroll deducted?*

Since the people receiving benefits had already paid for them, he explained, "no politician can ever scrap my social security program." What Roosevelt did not anticipate was that in the future, Congress would borrow money from the Social Security fund to pay for other programs while failing to raise payroll deductions enough to pay for the benefits.

The Social Security Act created a Social Security Board (SSB) to oversee the administration of the new program. In 1939 the SSB became part of the new Federal Security Agency. Six years later, in 1946, the SSB was reorganized and renamed the Social Security Administration, a designation it has kept until today.

Social Security helped many people, but initially it left out many of the neediest members of society—farm and domestic workers. Some 65 percent of all African American workers in the 1930s fell into these two categories. In 1939 the act was expanded to also include dependents and survivors of workers. It was not until 1950 that the coverage was again expanded, this time to include full-time farm and domestic workers. Nevertheless, Social Security established the principle that the federal government should be responsible for those who, through no fault of their own, are unable to work.

Reading Check **Explaining** How did the Social Security Act protect workers?

HISTORY Online **Study Central**

For help with the concepts in this section of *American Vision: Modern Times* go to tav.mt.glencoe.com and click on *Study Central.*

SECTION 2 ASSESSMENT

Checking for Understanding

1. **Vocabulary** Define: deficit spending, financed, thereby, binding arbitration, sit-down strike, Social Security Act, crucial.

2. **People and Terms** Identify: American Liberty League, Works Progress Administration, National Labor Relations Board.

3. **Contrast** the ideas of Father Charles Coughlin, Senator Huey Long, and Dr. Francis Townsend.

Reviewing Big Ideas

4. **Explaining** How did the New Deal contribute to the growth of industrial unions?

Critical Thinking

5. **Historical Analysis** **Analyzing** Why is the Social Security Act an important piece of legislation? **CA CS1; HI1**

6. **Organizing** Use a graphic organizer similar to the one below to list the political challenges Roosevelt faced in his first term.

Political Challenges

Analyzing Visuals

7. **Analyzing Graphs** Examine the photo and graph on page 515. How did successful strikes such as the sit-down strike shown in the photograph lead to a rise in union membership?

Writing About History

8. **Descriptive Writing** Imagine you are either a General Motors worker or a member of management during the sit-down strike in Flint, Michigan. Write a letter to your local newspaper describing the strike and explaining your actions during it. **CA 11WA2.1c**

CHAPTER 10 Roosevelt and the New Deal **517**

SECTION 2 ASSESSMENT ANSWERS

1. Content vocabulary is boldfaced and highlighted in yellow. Academic vocabulary is boldfaced.

2. American Liberty League (p. 511), Works Progress Administration (p. 513), National Labor Relations Board (p. 514)

3. Coughlin: tax the rich and nationalize the banking system; Long: share the wealth; Townsend: pensions for the elderly

4. Legislation such as the Wagner Act encouraged workers to organize unions where none existed and set up a process to protect unions as they developed.

5. It forced the government to protect the unemployed.

6. American Liberty League, left-wing Democrats, urban Catholics

7. As workers saw that unions helped them, more workers supported and joined unions.

8. Letters should clearly express a point of view.

Looking Back...

The Role of the Federal Government

Why It Matters The New Deal dramatically expanded the federal government's role. To address the Depression, federal programs were directed at everything from the economy to caring for the country's unemployed, aged, and sick. Many critics opposed this new federal activity, and the Supreme Court struck down several New Deal programs as unconstitutional. At the same time, the Court also issued decisions that dramatically increased the federal government's role. The debate over the power and role of the federal government echoed debates from earlier times in the nation's history.

Steps To ... a Strong Federal Government

The growth of federal power began with the writing of the Constitution itself. When the American Revolution began, the individual state governments were very suspicious of centralized power. They did not want to create a strong national government that might endanger their liberties.

Federalism In drafting the new Constitution in 1787, the Founders adopted the idea of federalism. Federalism refers to a system under which power is shared between the national or federal government and the state governments. The Constitution divides government authority. It gives the national government specific powers but reserves all other powers to the states or to the people.

The Founders saw federalism as a way to forge a strong union while preserving the states as a check on federal power.

Necessary and Proper Clause The Constitution also gives the federal government implied powers. These are powers that the government has, even though they are not written down, because without them the government could not carry out the powers it has been expressly given.

The basis for implied powers is the Constitution's necessary and proper clause (art. 1, sec. 8). This clause gives Congress the power to make laws that are "necessary and proper" for it to execute its powers under the Constitution. The necessary and proper clause has been used many times to expand the federal government's power.

The debate over implied powers began in George Washington's administration in a dispute about the

> *"The government of the United States, then, though limited in its powers is supreme; and its laws, when made in pursuance of the Constitution, form the supreme law of the land ... "*
>
> —U.S. Supreme Court Chief Justice John Marshall, 1819

518

EXTENDING THE CONTENT

Fighting Poverty Fighting poverty has been at the root of most of the efforts to move powers from either private organizations or state governments to the federal government. Before the Great Depression, most people in need looked to charities and churches for relief. The massive unemployment and poverty created by the Great Depression was beyond the means of existing charities. Government programs such as the New Deal under Roosevelt and the Great Society under Johnson greatly increased the role of the federal government in providing relief. More recent presidents have reduced the federal government's role in fighting poverty because of the fear that existing programs fostered dependency.

The Federal System

Powers of the National Government	Powers Shared by National and State Governments	Powers Reserved for State Governments
• Regulate interstate and foreign trade	• Collect taxes	• Regulate trade within the state
• Raise/support armed forces	• Borrow money	• Write business/corporate laws
• Declare war/make peace	• Make and enforce laws	• Establish and maintain public schools
• Coin and print money	• Establish and maintain courts	• Set up local governments
• Grant patents/copyrights	• Charter banks	• Pass marriage/divorce laws
• Establish federal courts	• Provide for public welfare	• Conduct elections
• Govern territories and admit new states		• Ratify constitutional amendments
• Set weights/measures		
• Establish a postal system		
• Regulate immigration		

creation of a national bank. Alexander Hamilton believed a bank was convenient and not prohibited in carrying out the government's treasury functions, while Thomas Jefferson believed the federal government could not create a bank since it was not absolutely necessary. Washington sided with Hamilton, and the bank was created.

The Supreme Court, under the leadership of Chief Justice John Marshall, strongly defended the idea that the necessary and proper clause gave the federal government wide-ranging powers. In 1819, in *McCulloch* v. *Maryland,* the Court ruled that the necessary and proper clause allowed the federal government to use any method that was convenient for carrying out its express powers, as long as it was not specifically forbidden in the Constitution.

The Commerce Clause Another clause in the Constitution that has been used to expand the federal government's power is the commerce clause. The Constitution gives the federal government the power to regulate commerce with foreign nations and between the states. Over time, the definition of the word *commerce* has played an important role in determining the powers of the federal government.

In 1824 the Supreme Court ruled in *Gibbons* v. *Ogden* that the commerce clause meant that anything crossing state lines could be regulated by the federal government. In the late 1800s and early 1900s, however, the Court ruled that federal laws regulating industry, agriculture, child labor, and

unions were unconstitutional because such activities took place within states, not across state lines. During the New Deal, however, the Supreme Court's opinion shifted. In 1937 it ruled in *NLRB* v. *Jones and Laughlin Steel* that the commerce clause allowed the federal government to regulate industry within states.

The Fourteenth Amendment Perhaps the most dramatic increase in federal power took place following the Civil War. The new Fourteenth Amendment banned states from depriving people of their life, liberty, or property "without due process of law" and prohibited states from denying people the "equal protection of the laws." Both the due process clause and the equal protection clause have been used repeatedly by the Supreme Court to extend the Bill of Rights to the states and to end segregation of African Americans. As a result, by the late twentieth century, the federal government had acquired powers far beyond those envisioned in 1787.

Checking for Understanding
1. What is the necessary and proper clause in the Constitution?
2. In what ways did the Supreme Court use the commerce clause?

Critical Thinking
1. Do you agree with Jefferson's or Hamilton's view of implied powers? Explain.
2. How did the Fourteenth Amendment increase federal power?

Looking Back...

W Writing Support
Summary Writing Have students examine the chart on this page, and then choose one item from each column—a federal power, a shared power, and a power reserved for state governments. Students should then write a paragraph suggesting reasons why each power has been designated for the federal or state government, or why it is shared. (*For example, only the federal government coins money because separate state monetary systems would inhibit interstate commerce.*) OL CA 11WS1.3

C Critical Thinking
Analyzing Primary Sources Ask students to research the Supreme Court ruling in the 2000 presidential election. Ask them to find out if either side in the case cited the *Martin* v. *Hunter's Lessee* ruling. Then have students write paragraphs stating how the 2000 presidential election case revisited the issue of states' rights versus federal authority. AL

ASSESS/CLOSE

Have students answer the Checking for Understanding and Critical Thinking questions.

Checking for Understanding
1. Article 1, Section 8 creates implied powers: Congress may pass laws necessary and proper to carrying out the federal government's constitutional powers.
2. The Court has often used the clause to expand federal power by interpreting *commerce* broadly. In the late 1800s, it used the clause to limit federal regulatory power by interpreting it narrowly.

Critical Thinking
1. Some students will say the government should only be allowed to do what is absolutely necessary; others may say that anything that is convenient and not prohibited should be allowed.
2. Due process and equal protection clauses allowed the Supreme Court to expand federal power and to apply the Bill of Rights to the states.

FOCUS

SKILLBUILDER ACTIVITY

Project **Daily Focus Skills Transparency 10-3** and have students answer the question.

Guide to Reading

Understanding Vocabulary:
Have students look at the vocabulary lists for the section as you pronounce each word. Remind them that proper names always begin with capital letters. Invite students to share the meanings of any terms that are already familiar to them.

Answers to Graphic:
Students should complete the outline by including all headings in the section.

Unpacking the Standards

Students will be able to:

- Describe the events of FDR's second term.
- Identify the final reforms that made up the New Deal.
- Discuss the lasting impact of the New Deal on the United States.

Answers and Additional Support

SECTION 3 — The New Deal Coalition

Guide to Reading

Connection
In the previous section, you learned about the Second New Deal. In this section, you will discover how President Roosevelt faced the problems brought by Supreme Court decisions and a new recession.

Main Idea
- After winning reelection in 1936, Roosevelt faced controversies over the plan to increase the size of the Supreme Court and over a recession caused by his desire to stop deficit spending. (p. 521)
- Roosevelt and his colleagues continued to push for reforms in housing, farming, and labor. (p. 523)

- The New Deal expanded the role of the federal government in society and the economy by providing a safety net for many people. (p. 525)

Content Vocabulary
broker state, safety net

Academic Vocabulary
demonstrate, enhance, mediate

Names and Terms
Frances Perkins, court-packing, Henry Morgenthau, John Maynard Keynes

Reading Objectives
- **Explain** the achievements and the defeats of Roosevelt's second term.

- **Analyze** how the New Deal affected Americans' sense of security and their attitude toward the role of government. (p. 525)

Reading Strategy
Taking Notes As you read about the New Deal Coalition, use the major headings of the section to create an outline similar to the one below.

The New Deal Coalition
I. Roosevelt's Second Term
  A.
  B.
  C.
II.
  A.
  B.

Preview of Events

♦1936	♦1937	♦1938
1936 FDR reelected	**1937** Court-packing bill defeated; Farm Tenant Act; National Housing Act	**1937** Roosevelt Recession begins **1938** Fair Labor Standards Act passed

The following are the main History–Social Science Standards covered in this section.

11.6.4 Analyze the effects of and the controversies arising from New Deal economic policies and the expanded role of the federal government in society and the economy since the 1930s (e.g., Works Progress Administration, Social Security, National Labor Relations Board, farm programs, regional development policies, and energy development projects such as the Tennessee Valley Authority, California Central Valley Project, and Bonneville Dam).

11.6.5 Trace the advances and retreats of organized labor, from the creation of the American Federation of Labor and the Congress of Industrial Organizations to current issues of a postindustrial multinational economy, including the United Farm Workers in California.

～ The Big Idea ～

Social and economic crises lead to new roles for government. President Roosevelt won overwhelmingly in the 1936 election, but he lost support with his court-packing plan and a recession that hit the following year. Conservative Democrats now began to work with Republicans to oppose new legislation. The president tried to push ahead with more New Deal programs to strengthen the economy and aid Americans. He was able to get a housing bill, a loan program for farmers, and a revised labor law approved, but Congress balked at most of his bills. Still, the role of the federal government had increased considerably, and the nation began to expect the government to provide a safety net for average Americans.

520 CHAPTER 10 Roosevelt and the New Deal

SECTION RESOURCES

📁 Print Material
- Reproducible Lesson Plan 10-3
- Guided Reading Activity 10-3
- Reading Essentials and Study Guide 10-3
- Active Reading Note-Taking Guide 10-3

🖥 Transparencies
- Daily Focus Skills Transparency 10-3
- Section Graphic Organizer Transparency 10-3

Technology
- Interactive Tutor Self-Assessment CD-ROM
- ExamView® Pro Testmaker CD-ROM
- Presentation Plus! CD-ROM

Roosevelt's Second Term

Main Idea After winning reelection in 1936, Roosevelt faced controversies over the plan to increase the size of the Supreme Court and over a recession caused by his desire to stop deficit spending.

Reading Connection Describe a time you had to reach a consensus within a group. Read on to learn how Roosevelt tried to gain Supreme Court approval for his programs.

A dramatic shift in party allegiance by African Americans was part of a historic political realignment triggered by FDR's New Deal. As the election of 1936 approached, millions of voters believed they owed their jobs, mortgages, or salvaged bank accounts to the New Deal.

★ An American Story ★

One day in 1932, Emma Guffey Miller, the sister of Democratic senator Joseph Guffey, was having her nails done at a salon in Pittsburgh. Her manicurist mentioned that Robert Vann, publisher of the *Pittsburgh Courier,* a leading African American newspaper, wanted to see the senator. When Senator Guffey met Vann, Vann told him that the Democrats could win most of the 280,000 African American votes in Pennsylvania if they made the effort.

Since the Civil War, most African Americans had voted for the Republicans. Now times had changed. The Depression had hit the African American community very hard, and Republicans had done little to help. In talks to African American voters, Vann often said, "My friends, go home and turn Lincoln's picture to the wall. That debt has been paid in full."

Guffey was impressed. He persuaded party leaders to appoint Vann to lead "the first really effective Negro division a Democratic campaign committee ever had." By 1936 the majority of African American voters had switched their support to the Democratic Party.

—adapted from *The Politics of Upheaval*

The white South, which had been the core of the Democratic Party, now became just one part of a new coalition that included farmers, laborers, African Americans, new immigrants, ethnic minorities, women, progressives, and intellectuals. First Lady Eleanor Roosevelt helped bring about the change in the African American and women's vote. She had demonstrated strong sympathies toward these groups, with whom she spoke in her many tours of the country. She recounted her experiences to her husband and persuaded him to address at least some of their problems in his New Deal programs.

African Americans and women made some modest gains during the New Deal. For example, the president appointed a number of African Americans to positions in his administration; informally, they became known as the Black Cabinet. Roosevelt also tried to ensure that New Deal relief programs did not exclude African Americans.

A similar approach guided New Deal policies toward women. Roosevelt appointed the first woman to a cabinet post, Secretary of Labor **Frances Perkins,** and assigned many women to lower-level jobs in the federal bureaucracy. Even so, the general view was that women did not need federal government action to ensure equal treatment, but rather to provide certain protections for them.

The Election of 1936 To oppose Roosevelt, the Republicans nominated Kansas Governor Alfred Landon. Although Landon favored some New Deal policies, he declared it was time "to unshackle initiative and free the spirit of American enterprise." As the election neared, Landon became more aggressive. The New Deal "violates the basic ideals of the American system," he declared. "If we are to preserve our American form of government, this administration must be defeated."

Despite Landon's attacks, Roosevelt and the New Deal remained overwhelmingly popular with the American people. The challenge from left-wing radicals also proved much weaker than expected—primarily because Huey Long had been assassinated in Louisiana in September of 1935. Long's supporters

"... go home and turn Lincoln's picture to the wall."

—*Robert Vann*

CHAPTER 10   Roosevelt and the New Deal   **521**

TEACH

W Writing Support

Research Report Writing Have students investigate the current involvement of African Americans and women in politics. Encourage them to set up charts that compare information for the New Deal era and the present on matters such as the number of women in Congress and the percentage of total Congresspersons they represent. Also ask them to select one person to focus on and to report on his or her career. **OL**
CA 11WA2.1a

R Reading Strategy

Categorizing Information Have students create graphic organizers to summarize the content of the segment "The Election of 1936." Tell them to place the phrase *Why Roosevelt Won the Election* in a central box or circle. Then have them draw other boxes or circles stating the factors that led to FDR's reelection. Remind them that these graphic organizers make good review devices. **BL** **CA** HI2

Did You Know?

Both Franklin and Eleanor Roosevelt were in favor of equal rights for African Americans. When FDR was a student at Harvard, he wrote to segregated colleges in the South, encouraging them to accept African American students, as Harvard did. When the Daughters of the American Revolution refused in 1939 to allow African American singer Marian Anderson to perform in Washington's Constitution Hall, Eleanor resigned from the organization and set up a concert on the steps of the Lincoln Memorial. On the Easter Sunday Anderson performed, 75,000 people heard her sing.

S₁ Skill Practice

Conducting Research Have interested students conduct research about the current Supreme Court justices. Encourage them to consider their background, ages, race, and gender. **Ask: How do these justices differ from the Supreme Court justices in Roosevelt's era?** *(Students will likely focus on the presence of women and African Americans on the modern Supreme Court. Guide them to also consider the mix of liberals versus conservatives in the two eras.)* **AL** **CA CS1; HR4**

S₂ Skill Practice

Visual Literacy Point out to students the campaign sign on this page. **Ask: Why do you think FDR used a rose on his campaign materials?** *(Students may suggest that it is memorable and also indicated the preferred pronunciation of his name.)* **EL** **CA HR4**

R Reading Strategy

Scaffolding—Academic Vocabulary The word *scheme* was introduced in Chapter 5, Section 3. Ask a student to define the word. **BL**

Answers and Additional Support

joined with those of Father Coughlin and Francis Townsend in the summer of 1936 to form a new political movement called the Union Party, but without a strong leader, the party had no chance.

On Election Day, Roosevelt swept to victory in one of the largest landslides in American history. He won more than 60 percent of the popular vote and carried every state except Maine and Vermont.

The Court-Packing Plan Although popular opinion supported most of the president's programs, the Supreme Court saw things differently. In January 1936, the Court declared the Agricultural Adjustment Act to be unconstitutional. With cases pending on Social Security and the Wagner Act, it seemed likely the Court would strike down nearly all of the major New Deal programs.

Roosevelt was furious that a handful of jurists, "nine old men" as he called them, were blocking the wishes of a majority of the people. After winning reelection, he decided to try to change the political balance on the Supreme Court. Claiming that the Court was overburdened with work, Roosevelt sent Congress a bill to increase the number of justices: If any justice had served for 10 years and did not retire within six months after reaching the age of 70, the president could appoint an additional justice to the Court. Since four justices were in their 70s and two more were in their late 60s, the bill, if passed, would

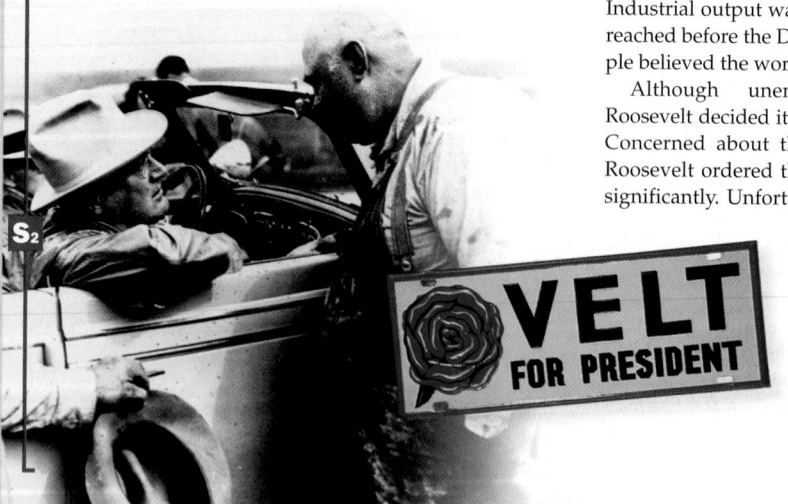

Picturing **History**

Campaigning in 1936 During the 1936 election, FDR's Democratic Party brought together farmers, like this North Dakotan, and many other groups of Americans to form a new coalition of political supporters. This coalition helped give Roosevelt a strong re-election victory. *What different groups made up this coalition?*

allow Roosevelt to quickly appoint as many as six new justices.

The **court-packing** plan, as the press called it, was Roosevelt's first serious political mistake as president. Although Congress had the power to change the size of the Court, the scheme created the impression that the president was trying to interfere with the Constitution's separation of powers and undermine the Court's independence.

The issue split the Democratic Party. Many Southern Democrats feared Roosevelt's plan would put justices on the Court who would overturn segregation. At the same time, African American leaders worried that once Roosevelt set the precedent of changing the Court's makeup, a future president might pack the Court with justices opposed to civil rights. Many Americans believed the plan would give the president too much power.

Despite the uproar over the scheme, Roosevelt's actions appeared to force the Supreme Court to back down. In April 1937, the Court upheld the Wagner Act, and in May it declared the Social Security Act to be constitutional. Shortly afterward, one of the more conservative judges resigned, enabling Roosevelt to appoint a supporter of the New Deal to the Court.

In mid-July, the Senate quietly killed the court-packing bill without bringing it to a vote. Although Roosevelt had achieved his goal of changing the Court's view of the New Deal, the fight over the plan had hurt his reputation with the American people and encouraged conservative Democrats in Congress to work with Republicans to oppose further New Deal proposals.

The Roosevelt Recession In late 1937, Roosevelt's reputation suffered another blow when unemployment suddenly surged. Earlier in the year, the economy had seemed to be on the verge of full recovery. Industrial output was almost back to the level it had reached before the Depression began, and many people believed the worst was over.

Although unemployment remained high, Roosevelt decided it was time to balance the budget. Concerned about the dangers of too much debt, Roosevelt ordered the WPA and the PWA to be cut significantly. Unfortunately, Roosevelt cut spending just as the first Social Security payroll taxes removed $2 billion from the economy. Almost immediately the economy plummeted. By the end of 1937, about two million people had been thrown out of work.

Picturing **History**

Answer: farmers, union members, African Americans, new immigrants, ethnic minorities, intellectuals, progressives
Ask: Why do you think so many different groups supported Roosevelt's bid for reelection? *(Many people were benefiting from the initiatives of his first term in office.)*

Resources for page 522

*Have students read more about Roosevelt's efforts to "pack" the Supreme Court in the **Primary Source Reading 10-2.***

Profiles IN HISTORY

Mary McLeod Bethune
1875–1955

Mary McLeod Bethune was born into a poor South Carolina family, the 15th of 17 children. Although she worked from a young age picking cotton and washing clothes, Bethune was determined to get an education. She won a scholarship to a seminary in North Carolina and later graduated from the Moody Bible Institute in Chicago. Bethune then began teaching at the Haines Institute. In 1904 she founded a school in Florida for the children of African American railroad workers. "I rang doorbells," she later recalled. "I wrote articles . . . distributed leaflets, [and] invaded churches, clubs, lodges, [and] chambers of commerce." Gradually she raised enough money to found the Daytona Normal and Industrial School, later known as Bethune College.

Bethune's efforts gained her a national reputation. In the 1920s, she visited the White House to discuss African American affairs. She also became a good friend of Eleanor Roosevelt. In 1936 FDR appointed her director of the Negro Division of the National Youth Administration (NYA), which provided job training for young people. Bethune also founded the National Council of Negro Women to support civil rights. In later years, she advised Presidents Truman and Eisenhower.

Frances Perkins
1882–1965

From the moment she became FDR's secretary of labor at the age of 50, Frances Perkins confronted the challenge of being the first female cabinet member in the nation's history.

Perkins studied social work at Columbia University. Early in her career, she assisted Jane Addams at Hull House and worked with Florence Kelley of the Consumers' League. From her lobbying efforts there, Perkins learned how to deal with politicians.

Perkins first met Roosevelt when she worked for the New York Committee on Safety, lobbying state legislators to limit the workweek for women to 54 hours. When Roosevelt became governor in 1928, he appointed Perkins state industrial commissioner.

After Roosevelt won the presidency in 1932, he asked Perkins to head the Department of Labor. Upon taking the job, Perkins found many areas that needed improvement: offices that were run down, disorganized files, and lax work schedules, conditions she quickly remedied.

Given her background, it was fitting that one of Perkins's major tasks was to head the team that designed the Social Security program. She also supervised implementation of the Fair Labor Standards Act and built up the Bureau of Labor Statistics.

The recession of 1937 led to a debate inside Roosevelt's administration over what to do. Treasury Secretary **Henry Morgenthau** favored balancing the budget and cutting spending. This would reassure business leaders and encourage them to invest in the economy. Harry Hopkins, head of the WPA, and Harold Ickes, head of the PWA, both disagreed with Morgenthau and pushed for more government spending. They pointed to a new theory called "Keynesianism" to support their arguments.

Keynesianism was based on the theories of an influential British economist named **John Maynard Keynes.** In 1936 Keynes published a book that discussed the causes of recessions. He argued that the government should spend heavily during a recession, even if it had to run a deficit, in order to jump-start the economy.

According to Keynesian economics, Roosevelt had done exactly the wrong thing when he reduced government spending on programs in 1937. At first Roosevelt was reluctant to begin deficit spending again. Many critics of his policies had argued that the recession proved the American people were becoming too dependent on government spending, and

Roosevelt worried they might be right. Finally, in the spring of 1938, with no recovery in sight, President Roosevelt gave in. He asked Congress to approve $3.75 billion for the PWA, the WPA, and other programs with hope that government spending would stimulate the economy.

✓ **Reading Check** **Summarizing** What events weakened Roosevelt's reputation in 1937?

The Last New Deal Reforms

Main Idea Roosevelt and his colleagues continued to push for reforms in housing, farming, and labor.

Reading Connection Should the government make loans to people who want to buy houses or farms? Read on to find out about the final programs of the New Deal.

In his second inaugural speech, Roosevelt had pointed out that despite the nation's progress in climbing out of the Depression, many Americans still endured crippling poverty:

CHAPTER 10 Roosevelt and the New Deal **523**

Profiles IN HISTORY

"Come along. We're going to the Trans-Lux to hiss Roosevelt."

Analyzing *Political Cartoons*

Traitor to His Class By 1936 many wealthy Americans believed that FDR had turned his back on his own upbringing, and they actively worked to prevent his re-election. How did the New Deal change the way many people view government?

> ❝In this nation I see tens of millions of its citizens—a substantial part of its whole population—who at this very moment are denied the greater part of what the very lowest standards of today call the necessities of life.... I see one-third of a nation ill-housed, ill-clad, ill-nourished.... The test of our progress is not whether we add more to the abundance of those who have much; it is whether we provide enough for those who have too little.❞
>
> —quoted in *Public Papers and Addresses of Franklin D. Roosevelt*

Despite the president's idealistic goals, the fight over the court-packing scheme and the recession of 1937 had weakened Roosevelt politically. Although he pushed ahead with a new series of New Deal programs, his successes were limited.

The National Housing Act One of the president's goals for his second term was to provide better hous-

ing for the nation's poor. The Home Owners Loan Corporation had helped many middle-class citizens, but it had not provided housing for those who could not afford a mortgage. Eleanor Roosevelt, who had toured poverty-stricken regions of Appalachia and the Deep South, was among those urging the president to do something.

Senator Wagner, who shared the First Lady's concerns, prepared a new housing bill with Roosevelt's full support. The 1937 National Housing Act established the United States Housing Authority, which received $500 million to subsidize loans for builders willing to buy blocks of slums and build low-cost housing.

The Farm Security Administration Before the Supreme Court struck it down, the Agricultural Adjustment Administration had paid many farmers to take land out of production to force food prices to rise. The price-support program raised farm income, but it badly hurt tenant farmers. Landowners often expelled tenants from the land in order to take it out of production. About 150,000 white and 195,000 African American tenants left farming during the 1930s for this reason.

To stop this trend, the Farm Security Administration was created in 1937 to give loans to tenants so they could purchase farms. Over the next four years it extended loans of about $1 billion. Members of Congress, many of whom believed the program made agricultural problems worse by increasing farm production and driving down prices, kept its appropriations at a low level.

The Fair Labor Standards Act In 1938 New Dealers were still trying to reinstate important pro-labor regulations to make up for the Supreme Court's dismantling of the NIRA in 1935. The Fair Labor Standards Act of 1938 provided more protection for workers, abolished child labor, and established a 40-hour workweek for many workers to come into effect within three years.

Congress, however, was beginning to turn against the New Deal. The recession of 1937 enabled the Republicans to win many seats in Congress in the midterm elections of 1938. Together with conservative Southern Democrats, they began blocking further New Deal legislation. Roosevelt, meanwhile, became increasingly preoccupied with the growing international threat posed by Germany and Japan. By 1939 the New Deal era had come to an end.

✓**Reading Check** **Examining** What groups did Roosevelt's last New Deal programs try to help?

The Legacy of the New Deal

R *Main Idea* The New Deal expanded the role of the federal government in society and the economy by providing a safety net for many people.

Reading Connection Do you think it is the government's responsibility to provide help for those in need? Read on to learn how people felt about the government as the New Deal came to an end.

In terms of its main goal of ending the Depression, the New Deal was only a limited success. Unemployment remained high, and economic recovery was not complete until after World War II. Even so, the New Deal gave many Americans a stronger sense of security and stability.

The Broker State As a whole, the New Deal tended to operate so that it balanced competing economic interests. Business leaders, farmers, workers, consumers, homeowners, and others now looked to government to protect their interests.

The federal government's ability to take on this new role was **enhanced** by two important Supreme Court decisions. In 1937, in *NLRB* v. *Jones and Laughlin Steel,* the Court ruled that the federal government had the constitutional authority, under the interstate commerce clause, to regulate production within a state. In 1942, in *Wickard* v. *Filburn* the Court used a similar argument to allow the federal government to regulate consumption in the states. These decisions increased federal power over the economy and allowed it to **mediate** between competing groups. 📖 *(See pages 1006 and 1007 for more information on these Supreme Court cases.)*

In taking on this mediating role, the New Deal established what some have called the **broker state,** working out conflicts among different interests. This broker role has continued under the administrations of both parties ever since.

Government's New Role Probably the biggest change the New Deal brought about was the new public attitude toward government. Roosevelt's programs had succeeded in creating something of a **safety net** for average Americans—safeguards and relief programs that protected them against economic disaster. By the time the Roosevelt years were over, the American people felt that the government had a duty to maintain this safety net even though it required a larger, more expensive federal government than at any time in American history.

Critics continued to argue that the New Deal made the government too powerful. Another legacy of the New Deal, therefore, is a debate that has continued to the present over how much the government should intervene in the economy or support the disadvantaged.

Throughout the hard times of the Depression, most Americans maintained a surprising degree of confidence in the American system. Journalist Dorothy Thompson expressed this feeling in 1940:

> 66We have behind us eight terrible years of a crisis.... Here we are, and our basic institutions are still intact, our people relatively prosperous and most important of all, our society relatively affectionate.... No country is so well off.99

✓ **Reading Check** **Summarizing** What was the legacy of Roosevelt's New Deal?

 Study Central

For help with the concepts in this section of *American Vision: Modern Times* go to **tav.mt.glencoe.com** and click on *Study Central.*

SECTION 3 ASSESSMENT

Checking for Understanding

1. **Vocabulary** Define: demonstrate, enhance, mediate, broker state, safety net.
2. **People and Terms** Identify: Frances Perkins, court-packing, Henry Morgenthau, John Maynard Keynes.
3. **Explain** Roosevelt's court-packing plan and how it was received.

Reviewing Big Ideas

4. **Identifying** What groups made up the New Deal coalition?

Critical Thinking

5. **Interpreting** How did the New Deal change attitudes toward government?
6. **Categorizing** Use a chart like the one below to list the achievements and defeats of Roosevelt's second term.

Achievements	Defeats

Analyzing Visuals

7. **Analyzing Photographs** Study the photograph on page 522. What does it suggest about Roosevelt's method of campaigning?

Writing About History

8. **Persuasive Writing** Write an essay evaluating the effectiveness of New Deal measures in ending the Depression. **CA** 11WS1.3

CHAPTER 10 Roosevelt and the New Deal **525**

SECTION 3 ASSESSMENT ANSWERS

1. Content vocabulary is boldfaced and highlighted in yellow. Academic vocabulary is boldfaced.
2. Frances Perkins *(p. 521)*, court-packing *(p. 522)*, Henry Morgenthau *(p. 523)*, John Maynard Keyes *(p. 523)*
3. wanted to change the political balance of the Supreme Court; seen as interfering with separation of powers
4. African Americans, farmers, labor, minorities, new immigrants, women, intellectuals, and progressives
5. Americans felt government had a duty to maintain a safety net.
6. Achievements: Court upholds reforms, National Housing Act, Fair Labor Standards Act; Defeats: Depression continues, WPA/PWA, court-packing plan
7. It shows he went directly to the people.
8. Essays should reflect that the New Deal was a mixed success.

FOCUS

Primary Sources
Eyewitness to History

History–Social Science Standards

This feature addresses the following standard:

11.6.2 Understand the explanations of the principal causes of the Great Depression and the steps taken by the Federal Reserve, Congress, and Presidents Herbert Hoover and Franklin Delano Roosevelt to combat the economic crisis.

Understanding Vocabulary

Before students begin reading, point out that difficult or unfamiliar words are footnoted throughout the text.

TEACH

S Skill Practice

Historical Interpretation Ask students to imagine themselves living in 1933, listening to Roosevelt's Inaugural Address on the radio. Invite volunteers to describe their responses to the speech and what effect they think his words had on Americans during this economic crisis. Ask students to identify words and phrases in the Address that offer hope or reassurance. **OL** **CA HI3**

Answers and Additional Support

In 1933 Americans were desperate for change. President Franklin D. Roosevelt promised to experiment, to act decisively, and to use the government as a weapon against the Great Depression. While Roosevelt faced criticism for his New Deal programs, many people were grateful for the help they received.

SOURCE 1:

In his Inaugural Address on March 4, 1933, President Roosevelt outlined in broad terms his plans to pull the nation out of the Depression. Roosevelt compared the Great Depression to a war he needed to fight by all possible means.

I am certain that my fellow Americans expect that on my induction into the Presidency I will address them with a **candor**[1] and a decision which the present situation of our Nation impels. This is preeminently the time to speak the whole truth, frankly and boldly. Nor need we shrink from honestly facing conditions in our country today. This great Nation will endure as it has endured, will revive and will prosper. So, first of all, let me assert my firm belief that the only thing we have to fear is fear itself—nameless, unreasoning, unjustified terror which paralyzes needed efforts to convert retreat into advance. . . .

In such a spirit on my part and on yours we face our common difficulties. They concern, thank God, only material things. Values have shrunken to fantastic levels; taxes have risen; our ability to pay has fallen; government of all kinds is faced by serious **curtailment**[2] of income; the means of exchange are frozen in the currents of trade; the withered leaves of industrial enterprise lie on every side; farmers find no markets for their produce; the savings of many years in thousands of families are gone.

More important, a host of unemployed citizens face the grim problems of existence, and an equally great number **toil**[3] with little return. Only a foolish optimist can deny the dark realities of the moment. . . .

[1] **candor:** honesty
[2] **curtailment:** reduction
[3] **toil:** work

▲ *President Roosevelt delivers his First Inaugural Address.*

. . . This Nation asks for action, and action now. . . .

But in the event that the Congress shall fail to take one of these two courses [I outlined], and in the event that the national emergency is still critical, I shall not evade the clear course of duty that will then confront me. I shall ask the Congress for the one remaining instrument to meet the crisis—broad Executive power to wage a war against the emergency, as great as the power that would be given to me if we were in fact invaded by a foreign foe.

UNIVERSAL ACCESS

Interpersonal In his Inaugural Address, President Roosevelt compared the Great Depression to a war. Have students work in groups of five to create time lines of specific economic and social events and facts that bring to life the "common difficulties" and "national emergency" that Americans faced in the 1930s. As students conduct research for their time lines, tell them to locate sources to support each of Roosevelt's points. Encourage them to use a variety of primary and secondary sources, including printed publications, personal records, and artifacts. Ask students to analyze the completed and displayed time lines, making inferences and generalizations about the effect of the Great Depression on the lives of Americans. **OL**

▲ *Artist Lucille Lloyd paints a new mural in the California State Building in Los Angeles as part of the WPA Federal Art Project.*

SOURCE 2:

As part of Roosevelt's New Deal, the staff of the Federal Writer's Project of the Works Progress Administration collected life histories. Nineteen-year-old Millard Ketchum, one of the men interviewed in 1938, talked about his experience with the Civilian Conservation Corps (CCC).

Millard Ketchum had just come in from his day's work in the field. He was still in his blue CCC work uniform. "This is better clothes than I ever had at home," he said, "before I got to the CCC. You see, at home they was so many of us, we couldn't have much clothes to wear and in summer time we jist [just] didn't wear no shoes, and no shirts much, nor nothing else much. . . ."

I asked if he wanted to stay with the CCC.

"Yes'm, as long as I kin [can], because I git [get] plenty to eat here. I didn't always at home, not the same kind of stuff, anyhow. Guess we had plenty, such as it was, at home, but it jist wasn't good like this, nor enough of it for the kind it was. I git to go more, git to see more. I'm learning too. I watch the others, and then, I have more clothes and can keep cleaner too. . . .

. . . I git thirty dollars a month and send twenty-two of it home to them. They need it! My papa he don't make enough to do for all, jist renting and farming like he does."

SOURCE 3:

In 1939 an interviewer from the Federal Writer's Project spoke with Eugenia Martin. The granddaughter of enslaved persons and the widow of a church minister, she worked for the Works Progress Administration as a housekeeping aide in Atlanta.

Of course husband left me a little money, very little however, at his death and this was soon exhausted. I then tried to get work to maintain myself. I made every attempt to get work in private industry and being unsuccessful, I was compelled to get work on WPA. I was reluctant at first to go to WPA, for . . . it had seemingly been the consensus of many that only the shiftless, lazy and lower types resorted to relief agencies. . . . but I was growing more and more in need and this caused me to keep on trying. I finally succeeded in being certified and then was later assigned to work. . . .

. . . I had worked in the church, coming in contact with the poor and needy, the sick and suffering but it was nothing compared with that which I found or experienced on this project. I never realized before just what was out there in those alleys, in the slums, the poverty and illiteracy that existed there. I am glad that I have had the opportunity to work on WPA, first because it has provided me a livelihood and second for the experience I've gotten, which I wouldn't have gotten otherwise. It enabled me to keep up . . . my home. I haven't been able to save anything since working on WPA but it enabled me to carry on. I simply could not have held out this long had it not been for WPA. . . .

DBQ — Document-Based Questions

Historical Analysis CA HR4; HI1; HI3

Source 1: What steps is Roosevelt willing to take to solve the nation's problems?

Source 2: Why did Ketchum enjoy being in the CCC?

Source 3: What were Martin's views of the WPA?

Comparing and Contrasting Sources:
Do you think the accounts of Ketchum and Martin justify Roosevelt's strong approach to government programs? Explain.

R Reading Strategy

Monitoring After students read Millard Ketchum's account, ask them to think about the kinds of things that Ketchum talks about and why they are important to him. Then have students summarize how the Civilian Conservation Corps affected the nineteen-year-old man's life during the Great Depression. **BL**

S Skill Practice

Conducting Research Tell students that during the Great Depression, the Federal Writers' Project employed professional and non-professional writers to collect the life histories of thousands of Americans. Have students conduct online research at the Library of Congress American Memory Web site (www.memory.loc.gov/ammem) and locate at least two other first-person narratives that describe how people coped with life during the Depression. Invite volunteers to read the primary sources aloud. As a class, discuss the topics that were of most concern to people and what these topics reveal about life at that time. **OL**

W Writing Support

Expository Writing Ask students to write paragraphs that explain why the experiences of Eugenia Martin could be used to support Roosevelt's New Deal economic policies and programs and to refute critics of the expanded role of the federal government. **OL** **CA 11WA2.2**

ASSESS/CLOSE

Have students answer the Document-Based Questions.

DBQ — Document-Based Questions

1. Roosevelt is willing to speak truthfully and frankly with the American people and take decisive action, including asking Congress for "broad Executive power," as if the country were at war.
2. The CCC provided him with clothing, food, and income—far better provisions than he had at home.
3. She was wary at first of the WPA, thinking that it provided relief for lazy people. Her views changed as she struggled harder and harder to make a living and keep her home and as she saw the dire needs of others. In the end, she was grateful for the WPA.

Comparing and Contrasting Sources: Students should support their views with details and examples from the sources.

527

Reviewing Content Vocabulary

Students' answers will vary. The pages where the words appear in the text are shown in parentheses.

1. gold standard *(p. 500)* **2.** fireside chat *(p. 502)* **3.** deficit spending *(p. 511)* **4.** binding arbitration *(p. 515)* **5.** sit-down strike *(p. 515)* **6.** Social Security Act *(p. 516)* **7.** broker state *(p. 525)* **8.** safety net *(p. 525)*

Reviewing Academic Vocabulary

Students' answers will vary. The pages where the words appear in the text are shown in parentheses.

9. apparent *(p. 499)* **10.** ideology *(p. 501)* **11.** fundamental *(p. 505)* **12.** finance *(p. 513)* **13.** thereby *(p. 514)* **14.** crucial *(p. 516)* **15.** demonstrate *(p. 521)* **16.** enhance *(p. 525)* **17.** mediate *(p. 525)*

CHAPTER 10 ASSESSMENT and ACTIVITIES

Standards 11.6.2, 11.6.4, 11.6.5

Reviewing Key Terms

On a sheet of paper, use each of these terms in a sentence.

1. gold standard
2. fireside chat
3. deficit spending
4. binding arbitration
5. sit-down strike
6. Social Security Act
7. broker state
8. safety net

Reviewing Academic Vocabulary

On a sheet of paper, use each of these terms in a sentence that reflects the term's meaning in the chapter.

9. apparent
10. ideology
11. fundamental
12. finance
13. thereby
14. crucial
15. demonstrate
16. enhance
17. mediate

Reviewing the Main Ideas

Section 1

18. Why did the federal government create work programs during the Depression?

Section 2

19. How did the Wagner Act contribute to the growth of unions?

Section 3

20. Why did President Roosevelt devise the court-packing plan?

Critical Thinking

21. **Reading Skill** Recognizing Time and Sequence
Create a time line identifying key events from the New Deal. Then write a brief letter identifying the sequence of events. Be sure to include signal words and phrases.

22. **Civics** Identify the political opposition to the New Deal. Why did these individuals and groups disagree with President Roosevelt's programs?

23. **Categorizing** Use a graphic organizer like the one below to list groups of people helped by each program.

New Deal Agencies		Whom It Helped
NRA	→	
AAA	→	
FDIC	→	
HOLC	→	
CCC	→	

Chapter Summary

Major New Deal Programs

Financial and Debt
- Emergency Banking Relief Act regulated banks.
- Federal Deposit Insurance Corporation insured bank deposits.
- Farm Credit Administration refinanced farm mortgages.
- Home Owners' Loan Corporation financed homeowners' mortgages.

Work and Relief
- Civilian Conservation Corps created forestry jobs for young men.
- Federal Emergency Relief Administration funded city and state relief programs.
- Public Works Administration created work programs to build public projects, such as roads, bridges, and schools.

Agriculture and Industry
- Agricultural Adjustment Administration paid farmers to limit surplus production.
- National Industrial Recovery Act limited industrial production and set prices.
- National Labor Relations Act gave workers the right to organize unions and bargain collectively.
- Tennessee Valley Authority financed rural electrification and helped develop the economy of a seven-state region.

Social "Safety Net"
- Social Security Act provided:
  – income for elderly, handicapped, and unemployed.
  – monthly retirement benefit for people over 65

528 CHAPTER 10 Roosevelt and the New Deal

Reviewing the Main Ideas

18. The programs were designed to speed up economic recovery by providing income to American workers.

19. The Wagner Act gave workers the right to organize without interference and forced companies to recognize unions as bargaining agents.

20. He was frustrated with the defeats he had suffered and wanted to change the makeup of the Supreme Court.

Critical Thinking

21. **Reading Skill** Students' time lines should include key events from the New Deal. Letters will vary.

22. The American Liberty League thought the New Deal expanded the federal government's power at the expense of states' rights; Senator Huey Long, Father Coughlin, and Dr. Francis Townsend wanted the government to intervene more.

HISTORY Online

Self-Check Quiz
Visit the *American Vision: Modern Times* Web site at tav.mt.glencoe.com and click on **Self-Check Quizzes— Chapter 10** to assess your knowledge of chapter content.

Writing About History

24. **Historical Analysis** **Analyzing Environmental Issues**
Choose a federal, state, or local government building project such as new roads, airports, or reservoirs. Write an editorial to the local newspaper explaining how this project will impact the environment. **CA HI5**

25. *Big Idea* Choose one of the New Deal programs. Describe its goals and evaluate its success or failure.

26. **Expository Writing** Under Economic Crisis and the New Deal on the American History Primary Source Document Library CD-ROM, read Roosevelt's First Inaugural Address. Work with another student to write a commentary on the address and then present it as a radio broadcast to the class. Your commentary should include opinions about Roosevelt's economic ideas.

DBQ Document-Based Questions

27. **Interpreting Primary Sources** In her autobiography, Eleanor Roosevelt wrote about discussions she had with people across the country. Read the excerpt and answer the questions that follow.

66This trip to the mining areas was my first contact with the work being done by the Quakers. I liked the idea of trying to put people to work to help themselves. The men were started on projects and taught to use their abilities to develop new skills. The women were encouraged to revive any household arts they might once have known but which they had neglected in the drab life of the mining village. This was only the first of many trips into the mining districts but it was the one that started the homestead idea [placing people in planned communities with homes, farms, and jobs]. . . . It was all experimental work, but it was designed to get people off relief, to put them to work building their own homes and to give them enough land to start growing food.99

a. Why did Eleanor Roosevelt like the Quaker project?

b. Based on this excerpt, do you think that Eleanor Roosevelt supported her husband's New Deal programs? Explain your answer.

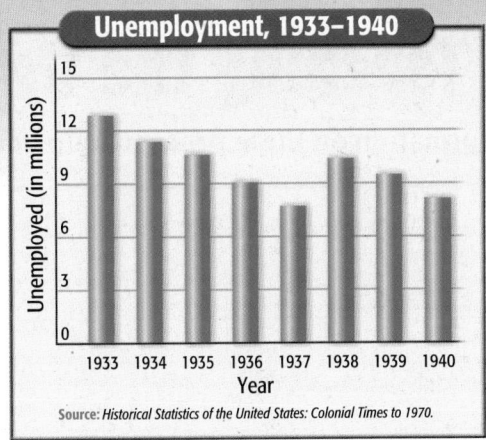

Unemployment, 1933–1940

Source: Historical Statistics of the United States: Colonial Times to 1970.

Economics and History

28. Examine the graph above showing unemployment figures, and then answer the questions below.

a. **Interpreting Graphs** What was the difference in unemployment between 1937 and 1938?

b. **Analyzing** Why did unemployment decline between 1933 and 1937? Why did it increase in 1938?

Standards Practice

Directions: Choose the best answer to the following question.

29. Which of the following is true of the bills passed during the first Hundred Days of FDR's presidency?

A They were intended to provide long-term relief to American citizens.

B They were known as the Second New Deal.

C They were designed as temporary measures to restart the economy.

D They were the subjects of divisive and protracted debate in Congress.

Standard 11.6.2: Understand the explanations of the principal causes of the Great Depression and the steps taken by the Federal Reserve, Congress, and Presidents Herbert Hoover and Franklin Delano Roosevelt to combat the economic crisis.

CHAPTER 10   Roosevelt and the New Deal   **529**

CHAPTER 10
Assessment and Activities

HISTORY Online

Have students visit the Web site at tav.mt.glencoe.com to review Chapter 10 and take the Self-Check Quiz.

DBQ Document-Based Questions

27. **a.** It emphasized individual initiative in improving the lives of miners. **b.** She did support his New Deal programs and often advised him on people's needs.

Economics and History

28. **a.** It increases from approximately 8 million to 10.5 million. **b.** It declined due to the New Deal programs and an improving economy. It increased in 1938 as a result of recession and reduced funding for some New Deal programs.

Standards Practice

29. C

Bonus Question?

Ask: What board game became a national fad during the 1930s?
(Monopoly)

---

23. NRA: industrial workers; AAA: farmers; FDIC: bank depositors; HOLC: middle-class homeowners; CCC: single men ages 18–25

Writing About History

24. **Historical Analysis** Students' editorials will vary.

25. *Big Idea* Students' choice of New Deal programs will vary. Each program should be clearly evaluated on its goals and successes.

26. Allow time for students to present their radio broadcasts. Students could place the scripts or recordings in their portfolios.

Unit 4 Resources

Teaching the Unit

Use the information on these pages to help you teach Unit 4.

History–Social Science Standards Covered in Unit 4

Standard	Chapter 11	12	13	14
11.7 Students analyze America's participation in World War II.	✔	✔		
11.8 Students analyze the economic boom and social transformation of post–World War II America.			✔	✔
11.9 Students analyze U.S. foreign policy since World War II.		✔	✔	

Pacing Your Lessons

This pacing chart provides time management suggestions for teaching Unit 4.

	Days
Unit 4 Introduction	1
Chapter 11 • **Reading Skill:** Making Inferences • **Historical Analysis Skill:** Understanding Change • **Sections 1–4** • **Eyewitness to History:** Primary Source Documents	9
Chapter 12 • **Reading Skill:** Cause and Effect • **Historical Analysis Skill:** Evaluating Interpretation • **Sections 1–5** • **American Literature:** *Farewell to Manzanar* by Jeanne Wakatsuki Houston and James D. Houston • **National Geographic:** A Day for Heroes • **Eyewitness to History:** Primary Source Documents	11
Chapter 13 • **Reading Skill:** Question-Answer Relationships • **Historical Analysis Skill:** Bias and Prejudice • **Sections 1–4** • **Eyewitness to History:** Primary Source Documents	9
Chapter 14 • **Reading Skill:** Question-Answer Relationships • **Historical Analysis Skill:** Analyzing and Understanding Change • **Sections 1–4** • **Why It Matters:** Interstate Highways • **TIME Notebook:** An Age of Prosperity • **Eyewitness to History:** Primary Source Documents	9

Teacher to Teacher

American History Journal

Dr. Jerry A. Micelle
Calcasieu Career Center
Lake Charles, LA

Ask students to find and analyze five pictures that span the time period from 1945 to 1960. Consider the following questions and others that come to mind.

- Where is the photograph taken?
- What is occurring? What are the expressions on the subjects' faces, and why might that be important?
- What types of objects are being held or used?
- What might that tell you?
- What does the photograph tell you about the level of science and technology during the era?
- What does the photograph tell you about clothing styles and fashion?

Next, have students find quotations they can relate to each picture. Finally, have them write reports on their five pictures.

Unit 4 Resources

Previewing the Chapters

Dear American History Teacher:

As you begin to teach this unit, there are themes that recur throughout the chapters that you will want to point out to students.

In this unit, students will monitor a debate between those Americans who wanted the U.S. to stay out of another war, and those who felt that the U.S. had a responsibility to resist the spread of tyranny. That debate ended when Japan attacked Pearl Harbor.

World War II became a total war that affected every citizen. Vast numbers of American volunteers and conscripts fought in Africa, Europe, and across the Pacific, while civilians mobilized on the home front. New opportunities opened for women and minorities in the defense industries. Yet Japanese Americans suffered grievous restrictions of their civil liberties.

Victory in World War II was followed closely by a prolonged Cold War in which the United States and its allies confronted the Communist bloc nations. International tensions, especially the anxiety over the threat of nuclear war, spurred investigations of Communist subversion within the United States.

By studying these events, your students will be able to consider the links between U.S. foreign policy and its domestic politics.

Donald A. Ritchie

Chapter 11: A World in Flames, 1931–1941

(pages 532–567)

Germany invaded Poland in 1939, thus beginning World War II. In addition to invading neighboring countries, Adolf Hitler was persecuting European Jews. While Europe fought this war, the United States adopted a policy of neutrality, hoping to keep the country out of war. In 1941 Japan attacked the American naval base in Pearl Harbor, Hawaii, and the United States entered the war.

Chapter 12: America and World War II, 1941–1945

(pages 568–621)

The United States moved into a wartime economy, manufacturing for the war and instating a draft. With so many men in the military, jobs opened up for women and most minorities on the home front. The Allies gained victory in Europe after the D-Day invasion. When the United States dropped atomic bombs on Hiroshima and Nagasaki, Japan surrendered. The war was finally over.

Chapter 13: The Cold War Begins, 1945–1960

(pages 622–661)

After World War II, a different kind of conflict developed between the superpowers of the United States and the Soviet Union. The Cold War was characterized by tense relations between the two countries and an increasing build-up of arms on both sides. While the Soviet Union worked to maintain control over Eastern Europe, the United States gave attention to stopping communism at home and abroad.

Chapter 14: Postwar America, 1945–1960

(pages 662–697)

After World War II, the United States transitioned to a peacetime economy. The average income of American workers increased, and many had more leisure time and more money to spend on entertainment. Despite this prosperity, many minorities and rural whites struggled with poverty. Minorities also faced discrimination.

FOCUS

History–Social Science Standards

This unit addresses the following main standards:

11.7 Students analyze America's participation in World War II.

11.8 Students analyze the economic boom and social transformation of post-World War II America.

11.9 Students analyze U.S. foreign policy since World War II.

Connecting to Past Learning

In Unit 3 students learned about the economic ups-and-downs the United States experienced from 1920 to 1941. In Unit 4 students will explore the domestic and global struggles faced by the United States between 1931 and 1960, from World War II through the early years of the Cold War.

Unit Launch Activity

Divide the class into groups of five. Activate prior knowledge by asking each group to make a list of events they believe helped cause World War II and the main ideas they can recall about life in the 1950s. Ask each student to write down these ideas and to refer to and amend the list as they read the chapters in this unit. **OL**

Why It Matters Activity

Ask the class to brainstorm the reasons that countries become involved in wars. Divide the class into groups of four and tell each group to research a place currently involved in warfare. The groups should focus on the origins of the conflict and possible resolutions. Have each group present their findings in a five-minute oral report. After the groups have shared their information, ask students if they think another world war is possible.
OL **CA HI2** **CA 11WS1.6**

530

UNIT
4 Global Struggles

1931–1960

Why It Matters

The rise of dictatorships in the 1930s led to World War II, the most destructive war in the history of the world. After the war, the fragile alliance between the United States and the Soviet Union collapsed into the Cold War—a period of intense political, economic, and military competition. Learning about the events of this crucial period in our nation's history will help you understand the events occurring in the nation and around the world today. The following resources offer more information about this period in American history.

Primary Sources Library

See pages 976–977 for primary source readings to accompany Unit 4.

Use the American History Primary Source Document Library CD-ROM to find additional primary sources about global struggles.

530

Dog tags

American soldier in World War II

TEAM TEACHING ACTIVITY

ECONOMICS Tell students that war and its aftermath usually have a dramatic impact on a nation's economy. The booming economy following World War II affected millions of Americans and can still be felt today. Cold War military spending, new home construction, and demand for consumer goods all played a role in the healthy economy. Work with an economics teacher to coordinate the study of the economic trends of the postwar years and how the U.S. economy has been affected by international disputes since World War II. **OL**

"*More than an end to war, we want an end to the beginning of all wars.*"

—Franklin D. Roosevelt, 1945

TEACH

Skill Practice

Identifying Point of View
Ask students to write short paragraphs interpreting President Roosevelt's quote on this page. Invite volunteers to read what they have written aloud to the class. *(Answers will vary, but students may note that Roosevelt meant that it is most important to find diplomatic solutions to disputes rather than resort to war.)* OL

Universal Access

Visual/Spatial Have students describe what they see in the photograph and ask them what sacrifices were made by American soldiers. *(Students' answers will vary. They might mention the physical surroundings of the soldier shown in the photograph, time away from family, and the threat of injury or death.)* BL

NC LB — NO CHILD LEFT BEHIND

Teaching Tip The goals of the NCLB Act include mastering computer technologies. To help students become proficient users of technology, include assignments that use different technologies to expand students' awareness of history concepts and sharpen technology skills. Here are some suggestions:

- Ask students to search the Internet for topics using search engines.
- Have students use graphing, note-taking, or outlining software as they read the chapters.
- Encourage students to use computer-presentation programs when reporting to the class.

UNIVERSAL ACCESS

Auditory/Musical Organize students into small groups. Have each group use music from the 1940s and 1950s to prepare an "Evening of Musical Entertainment." Arrange for each group to share its program at a local assisted living or nursing home facility. Encourage students to be creative in their presentation. Have each group member write a few paragraphs about his or her experience. BL CA 11WA2.3a

531

Chapter 11 Planning Guide

SECTION RESOURCES

Main Ideas	Print Materials	Technology Resources
Section 1: America and the World 1. Strong dictatorial rulers took control of the governments of Italy, the USSR, Japan, and Germany. 2. Despite Roosevelt's emphasis on internationalism, most Americans felt that they did not want to be involved in another war in Europe.	• Reproducible Lesson Plan 11-1* • Daily Lecture and Discussion Notes 11-1 • Active Reading Note-Taking Guide 11-1 • Guided Reading Activity 11-1 • Section Quiz 11-1 • Reading Essentials and Study Guide 11-1	Daily Focus Skills Transparency 11-1 Section Graphic Organizer Transparency 11-1 Interactive Tutor Self-Assessment CD-ROM ExamView® Pro Testmaker CD-ROM Presentation Plus! CD-ROM California Standards Practice Transparencies
Section 2: World War II Begins 1. European nations tried to prevent war by giving in to Hitler's demands. 2. Although Poland and France fell to the Nazis, the British were able to evacuate thousands of trapped British and French troops from Dunkirk in France. 3. Disregarding the bombing of London and other major cities, Britain's Winston Churchill stood firm against the threat of Nazi invasion.	• Reproducible Lesson Plan 11-2* • Daily Lecture and Discussion Notes 11-2 • Active Reading Note-Taking Guide 11-2 • Guided Reading Activity 11-2 • Section Quiz 11-2 • Reading Essentials and Study Guide 11-2	Daily Focus Skills Transparency 11-2 Section Graphic Organizer Transparency 11-2 Interactive Tutor Self-Assessment CD-ROM ExamView® Pro Testmaker CD-ROM Presentation Plus! CD-ROM California Standards Practice Transparencies
Section 3: The Holocaust 1. The Nazis blamed the Jews for everything and required them to resign their jobs and wear special clothing or live in specially designated sections of town. 2. Hitler's atrocities included sending millions of Jews to concentration camps and extermination camps.	• Reproducible Lesson Plan 11-3* • Daily Lecture and Discussion Notes 11-3 • Active Reading Note-Taking Guide 11-3 • Guided Reading Activity 11-3 • Section Quiz 11-3 • Reading Essentials and Study Guide 11-3	Daily Focus Skills Transparency 11-3 Section Graphic Organizer Transparency 11-3 Interactive Tutor Self-Assessment CD-ROM ExamView® Pro Testmaker CD-ROM Presentation Plus! CD-ROM California Standards Practice Transparencies
Section 4: America Enters the War 1. Despite the Neutrality Act of 1939, FDR supported the British with a destroyer-for-bases deal. 2. In the midst of a debate about whether America should remain neutral, Roosevelt was elected for a third term. 3. Roosevelt and Congress continued to support the British through the Lend-Lease Act and the idea of a hemispheric defense zone. 4. Angered by American policies that aided the British and an embargo on Japanese goods, the Japanese attacked the naval base at Pearl Harbor, forcing the United States to declare war.	• Reproducible Lesson Plan 11-4* • Daily Lecture and Discussion Notes 11-4 • Active Reading Note-Taking Guide 11-4 • Guided Reading Activity 11-4 • Section Quiz 11-4 • Reading Essentials and Study Guide 11-4	Daily Focus Skills Transparency 11-4 Section Graphic Organizer Transparency 11-4 Interactive Tutor Self-Assessment CD-ROM ExamView® Pro Testmaker CD-ROM Presentation Plus! CD-ROM California Standards Practice Transparencies

PACING YOUR LESSONS

Chapter Introduction	Section 1	Section 2	Section 3	Section 4	Chapter Assessment
½ Day	2 Days	2 Days	2 Days	2 Days	½ Day

0:00 OUT OF TIME? Assign the Chapter 11 *Reading Essentials and Study Guide.*

*Available on TeacherWorks™ CD-ROM

532A

Chapter 11 Planning Guide

Standards-Based Lesson Plan

 History–Social Science Standards Covered in Chapter 11

e standards covered in the chapter are listed below. Use the accompanying activity as you teach the chapter to ensure student astery of these standards. This activity can be used in combination with the program's print and technology assessment materials.

Standard	Section 1	2	3	4
11.7.1 Examine the origins of American involvement in the war, with an emphasis on the events that precipitated the attack on Pearl Harbor.	✔	✔		✔
11.7.4 Analyze Roosevelt's foreign policy during World War II (e.g., Four Freedoms speech).	✔	✔		✔
11.7.5 Discuss the constitutional issues and impact of events on the U.S. home front, including the internment of Japanese Americans (e.g., *Fred Korematsu v. United States of America*) and the restrictions on German and Italian resident aliens; the response of the administration to Hitler's atrocities against Jews and other groups; the roles of women in military production; and the roles and growing political demands of African Americans.			✔	
11.7.6 Describe major developments in aviation, weaponry, communication, and medicine and the war's impact on the location of American industry and use of resources.		✔	✔	

Cumulative Standards-Assessment Activity

e Cumulative Standards-Assessment Activity will help students organize and learn the important information from the chapter. gin teaching the chapter with this activity, and have students complete it as they read the chapter.

CREATING A CAUSE-AND-EFFECT CHART

Purpose Using cause and effect as a study tool will enable students to see how prevailing attitudes and ideas are related to political and social events and how historical events are related to each other. Making cause-and-effect connections will also help students understand the importance of studying history and can lead to lessons on individual responsibility, comprehending interconnectedness, and applying lessons of the past to the present and future.

Introduction to Making Connections

1. Begin by choosing a cause and effect from current events. Ask students to explain how the effect resulted from the cause. In addition, see if they can list other effects of the cause. Then encourage students to relate this current event to their own lives. What effect might it have on them, their families, friends, or neighbors?

2. Explain to students how they can use the same skill to understand the significance of historical events.

3. Ask students to copy this chart into their notebooks:

Causes	Effects

Ask the class to chart causes and effects from the chapter as they read. Remind them that one cause may have many effects.

4. As part of the chapter review, have students share their charts of causes and effects. Allow discussion to develop around items about which the students disagree. Encourage the class to use their charts as study aids.

Chapter 11 Planning Guide

READING SUPPORT

- 📁 Content Vocabulary Activity 11
- 📁 Academic Vocabulary Activity 11
- 📁 Reading Skills Activity 11
- 📁 Chapter 11 Active Reading Note-Taking Guide
- 📁 Chapter 11 Guided Reading Activities
- 📁 Chapter 11 Reading Essentials and Study Guide
- 💿📼 *The American Vision: Modern Times* Video Program
- 💿 Vocabulary PuzzleMaker CD-ROM
- 💿 American History Primary Source Document Library CD-ROM

CRITICAL THINKING

- 📁 Critical Thinking Skills Activity 11
- 📁 Primary Source Reading 11
- 📁 Cause-and-Effect Transparency 11 Strategy and Activity
- 💿 Presentation Plus! CD-ROM

UNIVERSAL ACCESS

- 📁 Universal Access Activity 11
- 📁 English Learner Activity 11
- 📗 American Art Prints
- 💿 StudentWorks™ Plus CD-ROM
- 🎵 American Music: Hits Through History
- 📁 School-to-Home Connection Activity 11

SKILL PRACTICE

- 📁 Map Overlay Transparency 11 Strategy and Activity
- 📁 Historical Analysis Skills Activity 11
- 📁 Time Line Activity 11
- 📁 Reading Skills Activity 11
- 📁 Reinforcing Skills Activity 11
- 📁 Linking Past and Present Activity 11
- 📁 Interpreting Political Cartoons 11
- 💿📼 MindJogger Videoquiz

WRITING SUPPORT

- 📁 Chapter 11 Active Reading Note-Taking Guide
- 📁 Writer's Guidebook
- 📁 High School Writing Process Transparencies

ASSESSMENT

- 📁 Chapter 11 Section Quizzes
- 📁 Chapter 11 Tests, Forms A and B
- 📁 Authentic Assessment Activity 11
- 💿 Exam*View*® Pro Testmaker CD-ROM
- 💿 Interactive Tutor Self-Assessment CD-ROM
- 📁 California Standards Practice, Grade 11
- 💿 Succeeding on . . .™ the California Standards: Grade 11 History–Social Science CD-ROM

💿	CD-ROM	💧	Transparency
🔒	DVD	🎵	Music Program
📁	Print Material	📼	Videocassette
📗	Poster		

Chapter 11 Planning Guide

TECHNOLOGY

- StudentWorks™ Plus CD-ROM
- TeacherWorks™ CD-ROM
- *ExamView®* Pro Testmaker CD-ROM
- Interactive Tutor Self-Assessment CD-ROM
- Presentation Plus! CD-ROM
- Vocabulary PuzzleMaker CD-ROM
- American History Primary Source Document Library CD-ROM
- MindJogger Videoquiz
- *The American Vision: Modern Times* Video Program
- Professional Development in High School Social Studies Video Series
- Teach, Use, and Succeed With *The American Vision: Modern Times*
- American Music: Hits Through History
- Succeeding on . . .™ the California Standards: Grade 11 History–Social Science CD-ROM

SPANISH RESOURCES

- Spanish Activities and Assessment
  - Spanish Vocabulary Activities
  - Spanish Guided Reading Activities
  - Spanish Quizzes and Tests
  - Spanish Reteaching Activities
- Spanish Reading Essentials and Study Guide
- Spanish School-to-Home Connection Activities

TRANSPARENCIES

- Daily Focus Skills Transparencies
- Section Graphic Organizer Transparencies
- Map Overlay Transparencies
- Cause-and-Effect Transparencies
- Unit Time Line Transparencies
- Why It Matters Transparencies
- American Art and Architecture Transparencies
- High School Writing Process Transparencies
- California Standards Practice Transparencies

TEACHER PLANNING

- Daily Lecture and Discussion Notes
- English Learner Handbook
- Building Academic Vocabulary
- *The American Vision: Modern Times* Reading and Study Skills Foldables
- Reading Strategies and Activities for the Social Studies Classroom
- Universal Access for the American History Classroom
- NGS United States Desk Map
- NGS World Atlas
- Chapter 11 Reproducible Lesson Plans on TeacherWorks™ CD-ROM
- California Guide to Daily Intervention

PROFESSIONAL DEVELOPMENT

- Building Academic Vocabulary
- Strategies for Success
- Research-Based Strategies Used to Develop *The American Vision: Modern Times*
- Character Education in the High School Classroom
- Professional Development in High School Social Studies Video Series
- Teach, Use, and Succeed With *The American Vision: Modern Times*

MOMENTS IN TIME

The following resource can help you teach the content of this chapter.
- Unit 8 World War II (1939–1945)

Chapter 11 Planning Guide

TEACHER'S CORNER

Index to National Geographic Magazine:
The following articles relate to this chapter:

- "The *Bismarck* Found," November 1989
- "Blueprints for Victory," May 1995
- "Pearl Harbor: A Return to the Day of Infamy," December 1991
- "Remembering the Blitz," July 1991

National Geographic Society Products:
To order the following, call National Geographic at 1–800–368–2728

- *Eyewitness to the 20th Century* (Book)
- *Historical Atlas of the United States* (Atlas)
- *PicturePack: World War II Era* (Transparencies)
- *PictureShow: World War II Era* (CD-ROM)

NGS ONLINE

Access National Geographic's new dynamic MapMachine Web site and other geography resources at:

www.nationalgeographic.com

www.nationalgeographic.com/maps

MASTERING THE STANDARDS

The content and assessment in the Student Edition, Teacher Wraparound Edition, teacher planning materials, and the print and technology products are all standards-based. The use of these products during instruction leads to mastery of the standards.

PRACTICE
- California Standards Practice, Grade 11
- California Standards Practice Transparencies
- School-to-Home Connection

BENCHMARK ASSESSMENT
- Section Quizzes, Chapter Tests, and Authentic Assessment
- Exam*View*® Pro Testmaker CD-ROM
- Succeeding On . . . ™ the California Standards: Grade 11 History–Social Science CD-ROM

REMEDIATION
- California Guide to Daily Intervention
- Interactive Tutor Self-Assessment CD-ROM
- Exam*View*® Pro Testmaker CD-ROM
- California Standards Practice, Grade 11
- Reading Essentials and Study Guide

History Online

Use our Web site for additional resources. All essential content is covered in the Student Edition.

You and your students can visit tav.mt.glencoe.com, the Web site companion to the **American Vision: Modern Times.** This innovative integration of electronic and print media offers your students a wealth of opportunities. The student text directs students to the Web site for the following options:

- **Chapter Overviews**
- **Self-Check Quizzes**
- **Student Web Activities**
- **Textbook Updates**

Answers to the student Web activities are provided for you in the **Web Activity Lesson Plans.** Additional Web resources and ePuzzles and games are also available.

FOLDABLES™ Study Organizer

Dinah Zike's Foldables

Foldables are three-dimensional, interactive graphic organizers that help students practice basic writing skills, review key vocabulary terms, and identify main ideas. Every chapter has a foldable activity in the *Dinah Zike's Reading and Study Skills Foldables* booklet. You can use the foldables as they are presented or modify them to suit the needs of your individual class.

THE HISTORY CHANNEL®

A variety of videotape programs are available from A&E Television and The History Channel to provide teaching assistance. To order, call Glencoe at 1-800-334-7344.

Reading List Generator CD-ROM

GLENCOE BOOKLINK

The Glencoe BookLink CD-ROM is a database that allows you to search more than 15,000 titles to create a customized reading list for your students.

- Reading Lists can be organized by students' reading level, author, genre, theme, or area of interest.
- The database provides Degrees of Reading Power™ (DRP) and Lexile™ readability scores for all selections.
- A brief summary of each selection is included.

Leveled reading suggestions for this chapter:

For students at a Grade 8 reading level:
- *Desert Exile: The Uprooting of a Japanese American Family,* by Yoshiko Uchida

For students at a Grade 9 reading level:
- *Those Incredible Women of World War II,* by Karen Zeinert

For students at a Grade 10 reading level:
- *Tell Them We Remember: The Story of the Holocaust,* by Susan D. Bachrach

READING SUPPORT FROM JAMESTOWN EDUCATION

- *Timed Readings Plus in Social Studies* help students increase their reading rate and fluency while maintaining comprehension. The 400-word passages are similar to those found on state and national assessments.
- *Reading in the Content Area: Social Studies* concentrates on six essential reading skills that help students better comprehend what they read. The book includes 75 high-interest nonfiction passages written at increasing levels of difficulty.
- *Reading Fluency* helps students read smoothly, accurately, and expressively.
- *Jamestown's Reading Improvement,* by renowned reading expert Edward Fry, focuses on helping build your students' comprehension, vocabulary, and skimming and scanning skills.
- *Critical Reading Series* provides high-interest books, each written at three reading levels.

For more information about these products, see the Jamestown Education materials in the Classroom Solutions in the front of this Teacher Wraparound Edition. To order these products, call Glencoe at 1-800-334-7344.

KEY for Using the Teacher Wraparound Edition

Use this key to help you identify the different types of prompts found in the Teacher Wraparound Edition.

R — Reading Strategies activities help you teach reading skills and vocabulary.

C — Critical Thinking strategies help students apply and extend what they have learned.

U — Universal Access activities provide differentiated instruction for students learning to speak English, along with suggestions for teaching various types of learners.

S — Skill Practice strategies help students practice historical analysis and geography skills.

W — Writing Support activities provide writing opportunities to help students comprehend the text.

Teaching strategies and activities have been coded for ability level appropriateness.

AL Activities for students working above grade level
OL Activities for students working on grade level
BL Activities for students working below grade level
EL Activities for English learners

FOCUS

**History–
Social Science
Standards**

This chapter addresses the
following standards:

11.7 Students analyze America's
participation in World War II.

11.7.1 Examine the origins of
American involvement in the war,
with an emphasis on the events
that precipitated the attack on
Pearl Harbor.

BELLRINGER
SKILLBUILDER ACTIVITY

Ask students if they
would support or
oppose U.S. involvement in a
conflict between other countries if it might result in a
world war. *(Students should
give reasons for their positions.)* After students have
read Chapter 11, tell them to
list the costs of U.S. involvement in World War II and ask
if they still would have supported involvement in the
war.

TEACH

Thinking About
the Big Ideas

*As you begin teaching each sec-
tion, use these questions and
activities to focus on the Big Idea.*

Section 1
America and the World
**Essential Question: How
did the conditions of some
European nations, particularly
Germany, at the end of World
War I, affect the rise of dicta-
torships before World War II?**

CHAPTER 11

1931–1941

A World
in Flames

～ *The Big Ideas* ～

SECTION 1: America and the World

Societies change over time. *In the years following World War I, aggressive and expansionist governments took power in both Europe and Asia.*

SECTION 2: World War II Begins

The fate of nations is forever changed by monumental world events. *World War II officially
began with the Nazi invasion of Poland and the French and British declaration of war on Germany in
September 1939.*

SECTION 3: The Holocaust

The fate of nations is forever changed by monumental world events. *Nazis steadily increased
their persecution of Jews and eventually set up death camps and tried to kill all the Jews in Europe.*

SECTION 4: America Enters the War

The fate of nations is forever changed by monumental world events. *When World War II first
began, the United States attempted to continue its prewar policy of neutrality.*

The *American Vision: Modern Times* **Video** *The Chapter 11 video,
"Holocaust Stories," presents firsthand accounts from survivors of the Holocaust.*

1932
• Bonus Army arrives
in Washington, D.C.

1931
• Jane Addams awarded
Nobel Peace Prize

1933
• Franklin Delano
Roosevelt inaugurated

1935
• First Neutrality
Act passed

*NATIONAL DEFENSE at
any EXPENSE
But
KEEP OUR BOYS AT HOME
America First Committee*

*F. Roosevelt
1933–1945*

**United
States**
PRESIDENTS

1930   *1933*   *1936*

World

1931
• Japan invades
Manchuria

1933
• Hitler appointed
chancellor of Germany

1936
• Hitler reoccupies
Rhineland
• Spanish Civil War begins

532

---

*(Students may note that poverty, economic
depression, and rising resentment of the Allied
nations all contributed to the growth of new
aggressive governments between the world
wars.)* Tell students that they will learn in
Section 1 how Germany, Italy, the Soviet Union,
and Japan all developed dictatorships during
the 1930s. **OL**

Section 2
World War II Begins
**Essential Question: How did some European
nations try to avoid another continental war
prior to 1939?** *(Students should discuss the
appeasement policies that Britain and France
adopted to keep Nazi Germany in check.)* Have
students write brief paragraphs explaining
whether or not appeasement is an effective
foreign policy for current conflicts. **OL**

German chancellor Adolf Hitler reviews a parade of Nazi troops.

Section 3
The Holocaust
Essential Question: **Have you or anyone you know been discriminated against based on appearance, nationality, religious beliefs, or some other factor?** Have the class discuss what life must have been like for Jewish Europeans as Hitler's campaign against the Jews intensified. Tell students they will learn more about the Holocaust in Section 3. **OL** **CA** 11WA2.1a

Section 4
America Enters the War
Essential Question: **Is an attack on American soil automatic grounds for war, or are there other possible responses?** Tell students that Section 4 will discuss how most Americans were committed to neutrality in World War II until the Japanese attack on Pearl Harbor on December 7, 1941. **BL**

Cultural Perspectives

During the Holocaust, the Jews were devastated when Nazis killed millions of Jews as part of the "final solution." Many Jews, including survivors of the Holocaust, believe in the importance of bearing witness to those who suffered and died during the Holocaust, of "never forgetting" the tragedy that changed the fate of Jews worldwide. Have students find out how Jewish people today remember the Holocaust. What traditions have emerged to remember those who were killed? Why is it so important to Jewish people to "never forget" what happened during the Holocaust? **OL**

1937
• Neutrality Act limits trade with all warring nations

1938
• Munich Conference appeases Hitler

1939
• SS *St. Louis* denied permission to dock in United States

1940
• Roosevelt makes "destroyers-for-bases" deal with Britain

1939
• World War II begins with Hitler's attack on Poland

1940
• France falls to the Nazis

1941
• Roosevelt and Churchill coauthor Atlantic Charter

December 7, 1941
• Japan attacks Pearl Harbor

1939 *1942*

HISTORY Online

Chapter Overview
Visit the *American Vision: Modern Times* Web site at tav.mt.glencoe.com and click on ***Chapter Overviews–Chapter 11*** to preview chapter information.

533

FOLDABLES
Study Organizer

Dinah Zike's Foldables are three-dimensional, interactive graphic organizers that help students practice basic writing skills, review key vocabulary terms, and identify main ideas. Have students complete the foldable activity in the *Dinah Zike's Reading and Study Skills Foldables* booklet.

HISTORY Online

Go to tav.mt.glencoe.com for student activities, lesson plans, and links to additional resources to help students learn about the start of World War II in Europe.

Reading Skill

Why It's Important

Remind the class that you first studied this Reading Skill in Chapter 5. A successful reader must be able to make inferences because writers cannot put every single bit of information into all text. Some information must be understood through context.

1. Introducing the Skill

Ask students to write short paragraphs describing how they get ready for school each morning. Have them trade paragraphs with a classmate. As students read each others' paragraphs, have them write down questions and their inferred answers in a chart like the one below. **BL**

Questions	Inferred Answers

2. Extending the Skill

Students may make inferences to visuals as well as text. Ask the class to study the political cartoon on page 558 and write short paragraphs that explain the purpose of the cartoon. **Ask: What is the main point? How do you know?** *(While the United States is friendly with its European allies, it is not willing to send weapons and other war materials to their aid.)* **OL**

Answers and Additional Support

Reading Skill Making Inferences

You learned in Chapter 5 that effective readers use a skill called making inferences to understand the deeper, and sometimes hidden, meanings of the text. While some may call it "reading between the lines," it is really a process of questioning, predicting, and connecting in order to understand what is not directly said.

An excellent way to improve your skills of making inferences is to talk with a partner about the material you just read. You will often discover that different people understand the same text in slightly different ways. When you talk with someone else about your predictions, questions, and connections, both of you benefit from the ideas you gather from the information in the text. You can also learn from one another how to develop and refine the skills necessary to make inferences.

Read the following paragraph about the beginning days of World War II and use inferences to draw conclusions about how each of the countries mentioned felt about the war in western Eurove.

> In contrast to the war in Poland, western Europe remained eerily quiet. The Germans referred to this situation as the *sitzkrieg,* or sitting war. The British called it the "Bore War," while American newspapers nicknamed it the "Phony War." The British sent troops to assist France, but because both countries remained on the defensive, waiting for the Germans to attack, there were no battles or warfare. (page 545)

MAKING INFERENCES

Use your background knowledge to help you understand the passage. What do you already know about World War II?

Apply the Skill

After you have read the passage, think about the various names the Germans, British, and Americans used to describe the war in western Europe. Then discuss these questions with a partner:

- **Based on this passage, how did Germany feel about the war?**

- **Is this similar to, or different from, the British and American outlooks?**

- **What do you believe the public wanted in these countries?**

- **What do you expect will happen next?**

534

UNIVERSAL ACCESS

English Learners Students who are learning English as a second language might face special difficulties in the skill of making inferences. To help English learners overcome this problem, pair them with an English speaker when they practice this reading skill. As the pairs answer the questions, have them pause to review each other's work. Encourage English-speaking students to explain their reasoning to the English learner. In this way, both students can practice the skill and learn to view the textbook information from a new perspective. **EL**

Historical Analysis Skill

Understanding Change

Analysis Skill Standard HI2

Historical Interpretation When you study historical events, you will learn to recognize the complexity of historical causes and effects, including the limitations on determining cause and effect.

You learned in Chapter 1 that events can cause changes. At times these changes occur quickly, while other times they spread over many years. To understand cause and effect is to know why and how an event occurred. A *cause* is an action or situation that produces an event. What happens as a result of a cause is an *effect*. Sometimes the effect of one event can be the cause of future events.

Historians use cause-and-effect relationships to explain why events occurred. As they analyze events, they know that there are limitations to their cause-and-effect analyses. In some cases the causes are not clear, while in other cases the effects may not be known for decades.

Read the following passages about the increasing involvement of the United States into World War II.

Worried that growing German and Italian aggression might lead to war, Congress passed the Neutrality Act of 1935. (page 540)

President Roosevelt officially proclaimed the United States neutral two days after Britain and France declared war on Germany. Despite this declaration, he was determined to do all he could to help the two countries in their struggle against Hitler. (page 557)

Widespread public acceptance of the destroyers-for-bases deal demonstrated a marked change in American public opinion. The shift began after the German invasion of France and the rescue of Allied forces at Dunkirk. (page 558)

By December 1940, Great Britain had run out of funds. . . . Roosevelt came up with a way to remove the cash requirement of the Neutrality Act. . . . Congress passed the Lend-Lease Act by a wide margin. (pages 559–560)

In the mid-1930s, Americans did not want to get involved in another war in Europe. They took steps with the Neutrality Act of 1935 to avoid such an involvement. With increasing German aggression, the United States began to aid the Allies in Europe, first with the destroyers-for-bases deal and then with the Lend-Lease Act.

Apply the Skill

Read the text under the heading "Japan Attacks the United States" on pages 561–563 of your textbook. Explain how President Roosevelt's efforts to help Britain led to Japan's decision to attack the United States.

535

Preparing to Read

Historical Analysis

Why It's Important
Remind students that they experience changes every day. They may think about why the change happened (cause) as well as what impact the change might have on their lives (effect). Similarly, students should examine the causes and effects of historical events in order to understand their significance.

1. Introducing the Skill
Have students imagine a car accident, and then ask them to brainstorm possible causes and effects of the crash. Record students' answers in a graphic like the one below. **BL**

Causes	Event	Effects
	CRASH	

(Possible causes: slippery roads, speeding, careless driver; Possible effects: injury, damage to vehicles, driver receives a ticket)

2. Extending the Skill
Have students read a newspaper account of a recent criminal or civil trial. They should determine at least one cause and one effect of that trial and show the cause-and-effect relationship in a chart. Remind students to consider far-reaching as well as immediate effects of the event. **OL** **CA HI2**

UNIVERSAL ACCESS

Advanced Learners Ask students to identify one of the major events discussed in this chapter. Tell the class to brainstorm what the effects might have been if the opposite outcome had occurred. *(Responses will vary. For example, what if there had never been a Holocaust?)* **Ask: How would your life be different today under these different circumstances? What important things would change? What would remain the same?** Have students write stories or poems that illustrate what life would be like if this historical event had turned out differently.
AL

FOCUS

BELLRINGER
SKILLBUILDER ACTIVITY

Project **Daily Focus Skills Transparency** 11-1 and have students answer the question.

Guide to Reading

Understanding Vocabulary: Have students write paragraphs using at least three of the content vocabulary and academic vocabulary words.

Answers to Graphic: Students should complete the outline using the headings in the section.

Unpacking the Standards

Students will be able to:

• Explain how dictators came to power in Europe.

• Analyze why the United States chose to remain neutral during the start of the European conflict.

Answers and Additional Support

SECTION 1

America and the World

Guide to Reading

Connection
In the previous chapter, you learned about President Roosevelt's efforts to end the Great Depression. In this section, you will discover how events in Europe and Asia pushed the nation to adopt a policy of neutrality.

Main Idea
• Strong dictatorial rulers took control of the governments of Italy, the USSR, Japan, and Germany. (p. 537)
• Despite Roosevelt's emphasis on internationalism, most Americans felt that they did not want to be involved in another war in Europe. (p. 539)

Content Vocabulary
fascism, internationalism

Academic Vocabulary
impose, investigate, civil

People and Terms to Identify
Benito Mussolini, Vladimir Lenin, Joseph Stalin, Adolf Hitler, Manchuria, Neutrality Act of 1935

Reading Objectives
• **Describe** how postwar conditions contributed to the rise of antidemocratic governments in Europe.

• **Explain** why many Americans supported a policy of isolationism in the 1930s.

Reading Strategy
Taking Notes As you read about the events in Europe and Asia after World War I, use the major headings of the section to create an outline similar to the one below.

America and the World
I. The Rise of Dictators
  A.
  B.
  C.
  D.
II.

Preview of Events

◆1922	◆1927	◆1932	◆1937

1922
Fascist Party takes power in Italy; USSR established

1931
Japan takes control of Manchuria

1933
Hitler takes power in Germany

1935
Congress passes first Neutrality Act

1937
Japan attacks China

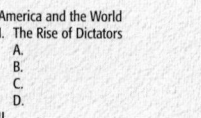

The following are the main History–Social Science Standards covered in this section.

11.7.1 Examine the origins of American involvement in the war, with an emphasis on the events that precipitated the attack on Pearl Harbor.

11.7.4 Analyze Roosevelt's foreign policy during World War II (e.g., Four Freedoms speech).

❧ The Big Idea ❧

Societies change over time. While the United States was battling the Great Depression, European nations saw the rise of dictatorships. Italy's Benito Mussolini based his leadership on the ideas of fascism and anti-communism; Joseph Stalin cemented Communist rule in Russia; and in Germany, Adolf Hitler and the Nazi Party based their rule on nationalism. In Japan, militarists gained control of the government and pursued a policy of expansion in Asia. Discouraged Americans responded to these developments by supporting isolationism. Congress began to legislate neutrality, hoping to keep the United States out of any future wars.

536 CHAPTER 11 A World in Flames

SECTION RESOURCES

📂 Print Material
• Reproducible Lesson Plan 11-1
• Guided Reading Activity 11-1
• Reading Essentials and Study Guide 11-1
• Active Reading Note-Taking Guide 11-1

🖾 Transparencies
• Daily Focus Skills Transparency 11-1
• Section Graphic Organizer Transparency 11-1

Technology
🖲 Interactive Tutor Self-Assessment CD-ROM
🖲 *ExamView®* Pro Testmaker CD-ROM
🖲 Presentation Plus! CD-ROM

The Rise of Dictators

Main Idea Strong dictatorial rulers took control of the governments of Italy, the USSR, Japan, and Germany.

Reading Connection How do you think your life would change if you lived in a country ruled by a dictator? Read on to learn about repressive governments that arose during the 1920s and 1930s.

When World War I ended in 1918, the future of democracy in Europe seemed bright. President Woodrow Wilson announced, "Everything for which America fought has been accomplished." Wilson hoped that the United States could "aid in the establishment of just democracy throughout the world." Instead, the treaty that ended the war, along with the economic depression that followed, contributed to the rise of antidemocratic governments in both Europe and Asia.

★ An American Story ★

In August 1934, American journalist Dorothy Thompson received an urgent call from the porter at her Berlin hotel. A member of Germany's secret state police wanted to talk to her. Thompson had been reporting on Adolf Hitler's rise to power, and she had written various anti-Nazi articles for the American press. In one she described the beautiful singing she had heard at a Hitler youth camp, where thousands of boys ages 10 to 16 marched and sang. The boys' lovely voices echoing across the hills stirred Thompson, but the words on an enormous banner hanging across one hillside chilled her:

❝It was so prominent that every child could see it many times a day. It was white, and there was a swastika painted on it, and besides that only seven words, seven immense black words: YOU WERE BORN TO DIE FOR GERMANY.❞

When Thompson met with the police, they ordered her to leave Germany immediately. "I, fortunately, am an American," Thompson observed, "so I was merely sent to Paris. Worse things can happen to one."

–quoted in *The Women Who Wrote the War*

It was less than 20 years since Woodrow Wilson expressed his optimism about the world that the dictatorial German government expelled Dorothy Thompson. The antidemocratic governments of Europe and Asia were already strong.

S **Mussolini and Fascism in Italy** One of Europe's first major dictatorships arose in Italy. There, a former schoolmaster and journalist named **Benito Mussolini** returned from World War I convinced that his country needed a strong leader.

In 1919 Mussolini founded Italy's Fascist Party. **Fascism** was a kind of aggressive nationalism. Fascists believed that the nation was more important than the individual. They argued that individualism made countries weak and that a strong government led by a dictator was needed to **impose** order on society. Fascists believed a nation became great by expanding its territory and building up its military.

R₁ Fascism was also strongly anticommunist. After the Communist revolution in Russia, many Europeans feared that Communists, allied with labor unions, were trying to bring down their governments. Mussolini exploited these fears by portraying fascism as a barrier to Communism. Fascism began to stand for the protection of private property and of the middle class. Mussolini also offered the working class full employment and social security. He stressed national prestige, pledging to return Italy to the glories of the Roman Empire.

R₂ Backed by the Fascist militia known as the Blackshirts, Mussolini threatened to march on Rome in 1922, claiming he was coming to defend Italy against a Communist revolution. Liberal members of the Italian parliament insisted that the king declare martial law. When he refused, the cabinet resigned. Conservative advisers then persuaded the king to appoint Mussolini as the premier.

"I, fortunately, am an American . . ."
—*Dorothy Thompson*

CHAPTER 11 A World in Flames **537**

TEACH

S **Skill Practice**

Evaluating Evidence Organize students into groups. Tell each group to create a propaganda poster describing the benefits of fascism to the Italian people. *(Answers will vary but should include the protection of private property and the middle class, full employment and social security for the middle class, and a return to national glory)* Hang posters on the board and compare them. **Ask:** Are any of the posters misleading? Do they oversimplify the issue? Ask students to write paragraphs describing which posters are most convincing, and why. **OL**
CA HR1; HI1

R₁ **Reading Strategy**

Scaffolding—Academic Vocabulary The word *exploit* was introduced in Chapter 4, Section 3. Ask a student to define the word. **BL**

R₂ **Reading Strategy**

Scaffolding—Summarizing Have students list reasons why the Italian people supported Mussolini's rising dictatorship. **Ask:** Why did the rest of Italy not unite against him? *(fear of communism, desire to protect private property and the middle class, employment and social security, desire for national prestige and glory)* **OL**

This **Reading Skill** was introduced in Chapter 8.

Did You Know?

The word *fascist* comes from the Latin word *fasces,* or the rods and axes that Roman officials carried in ancient times to represent their authority.

Review the Big Idea

Review the Big Idea for this section, "Societies change over time." Have students create a time line showing the major events in the rise of dictatorship in the Soviet Union, beginning with the Russian Revolution in 1917 and ending with Stalin's industrialization effort in 1927. **Ask: How much did the political structure of Russia change over the span of a single decade?** `BL` `CA CS2`

U Universal Access

English Learners Have students create thematic maps of Europe that show the territorial changes included in the Treaty of Versailles. Include new countries created; land gained by Italy, France, Belgium, and Denmark; and demilitarized areas. Have students use their maps to explain why Germany felt slighted by the treaty and how that affected later events. `EL`

R Reading Strategy

Connecting Have students use a dictionary to define the term "scapegoat." Then ask students to identify how Jews were used as scapegoats by Hitler. **Ask: Do you see incidents of groups of people being used as scapegoats today? What happens when people are made scapegoats?** (*Answers will vary.*) `OL`

Answers and Additional Support

Once in office, Mussolini worked quickly to destroy democracy and set up a dictatorship. Weary of strikes and riots, many Italians welcomed Mussolini's leadership. With the support of industrialists, landowners, and the Roman Catholic Church, Mussolini—who took the title of *Il Duce,* or "The Leader"—embarked on an ambitious program of bringing order to Italy.

Stalin Takes Over the USSR The Communists were a much larger force in Russia than in Italy. After the Russian Revolution began in 1917, the Bolshevik Party, led by **Vladimir Lenin,** established Communist governments throughout the Russian empire. In 1922 they renamed these territories the Union of Soviet Socialist Republics (USSR). They then proceeded to establish control over these territories. To do this, the Communists instituted one-party rule, suppressed individual liberties, and punished opponents. After Lenin died in 1924, a power struggle began. By 1926, **Joseph Stalin** had become the new Soviet dictator. In 1927 Stalin began a massive effort to industrialize his country. Tolerating no opposition to his rule, the effort brought about the deaths of 8 to 10 million peasants who resisted the Communist policies.

Picturing History

Supreme Soviets Joseph Stalin (right) took over control of the Soviet Union after Lenin's death in 1924. He was determined to modernize and industrialize his nation. How many people died while opposing Stalin's leadership?

Hitler and Nazism in Germany Adolf Hitler was a fervent anticommunist and an admirer of Mussolini. Hitler had fought for Germany in World War I. Germany's surrender and the subsequent Versailles Treaty left him and many other Germans with a smoldering hatred for the victorious Allies and for the German government that had accepted the peace terms.

The political and economic chaos in postwar Germany led to the rise of new political parties. One of these was the National Socialist German Workers' Party, or the Nazi Party. The party did not represent the working class, as its name suggested, but was nationalistic and anticommunist. Adolf Hitler was one of the party's first recruits.

In November 1923, the Nazis tried to seize power by marching on city hall in Munich, Germany. Hitler intended to seize power locally and then march on Berlin, the German capital, but the plan failed and Hitler was arrested.

While in prison, Hitler wrote his autobiography, titled *Mein Kampf* ("My Struggle"). In the book, Hitler called for the unification of all Germans under one government. He claimed that Germans, particularly blond, blue-eyed Germans, belonged to a "master race" called Aryans. He argued that Germans needed more lebensraum, or living space, and called for Germany to expand east into Poland and Russia. According to Hitler, the Slavic people of Eastern Europe belonged to an inferior race, which Germans should enslave. Hitler's prejudice was strongest, however, toward Jews. He believed that Jews were responsible for many of the world's problems, especially for Germany's defeat in World War I.

After his release from prison, Hitler changed his tactics. Instead of trying to seize power violently, he focused on getting Nazis elected to the Reichstag, the lower house of the German parliament. When the Great Depression struck Germany, many desperate Germans began to vote for radical parties, including the Nazis and Communists. By 1932 the Nazis were the largest party in the Reichstag.

Many traditional German leaders supported Hitler's nationalism. They believed that if they helped Hitler become leader of Germany legally, they could control him. In 1933 the German president appointed Hitler as chancellor, or prime minister.

After taking office, Hitler called for new elections. He then ordered the police to crack down on the Socialist and Communist Parties. Storm Troopers, as the Nazi paramilitary units were called, began intimidating voters. After the election, the Reichstag, dominated by the Nazis and other right-wing

---

Picturing History

Answer: 8 to 10 million people
Ask: How did the Bolsheviks establish control over the territories of the former Russian Empire? (*They established Communist governments, instituted one-party rule, suppressed individual liberties, and punished opponents.*)

Resources for page 538

*Have students read more about the thoughts of Adolf Hitler in the **Primary Source Reading 11-1**.*

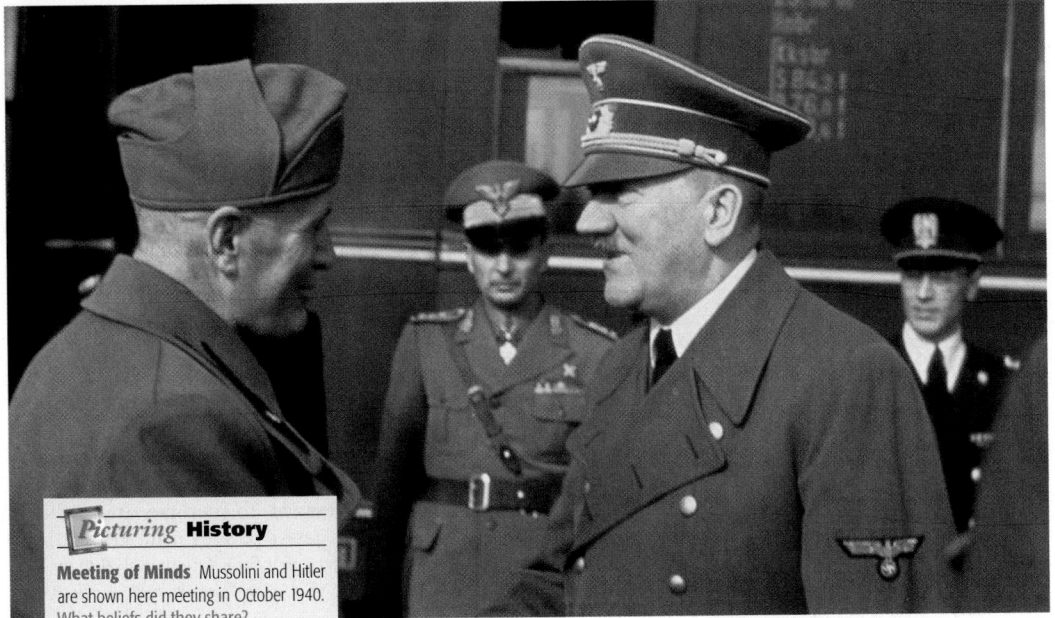

Picturing **History**

Meeting of Minds Mussolini and Hitler are shown here meeting in October 1940. What beliefs did they share?

parties, voted to give Hitler dictatorial powers. In 1934 Hitler became president, which gave him control of the army. He then gave himself the new title of führer, or "leader." The following year, he began to rebuild Germany's military, in violation of the Treaty of Versailles.

Militarists Gain Control of Japan In Japan, as in Germany, difficult economic times helped undermine the political system. Japanese industries had to import nearly all of the resources they needed to produce goods. During the 1920s, Japan did not earn enough money from its exports to pay for its imports, which limited economic growth and increased unemployment. When the Depression struck, other countries raised their tariffs. This made the situation even worse.

Many Japanese military officers blamed the country's problems on corrupt politicians. Most officers believed that Japan was destined to dominate East Asia. Many also believed that democracy was "un-Japanese" and bad for the country.

Japanese military leaders and the civilians who supported them argued that the only way for Japan to get needed resources was to seize territory. They targeted the resource-rich province of **Manchuria** in northern China as the perfect place to conquer.

A group of Japanese officers decided to act without the government's permission. In September 1931, the Japanese army invaded Manchuria. After the invasion began, the Japanese government tried to

end the war, but when the Japanese prime minister began negotiations, officers assassinated him. From that point forward, the military was effectively in control. Although Japan still had a civilian government, it now supported the nationalist policy of expanding the empire, and it appointed several military officers to serve as prime minister.

✓ **Reading Check** **Examining** How did postwar conditions contribute to the rise of dictatorships in Europe?

America Turns to Neutrality

Main Idea Despite Roosevelt's emphasis on internationalism, most Americans felt that they did not want to be involved in another war in Europe.

Reading Connection Do you think that the United States should become involved in the wars of other nations even when it is not under attack? Read on to discover the attitude of Americans during the 1930s.

The rise of dictatorships and militarism after World War I discouraged many Americans. The sacrifices they had made during the war seemed pointless. Once again, Americans began to support isolationism, or the belief that the United States should avoid international commitments that might drag the nation into another war.

CHAPTER 11 A World in Flames **539**

Did You Know?

A section of Amy Tan's popular novel *The Joy Luck Club* was set during the troubled times between China and Japan during the 1930s.

Picturing **History**

Answer: Both were extreme nationalists who wanted to expand their territories and build up the military.
Ask: What political objectives did the two leaders have in common? *(desire for a totalitarian state, building up the military, and territorial expansion)*

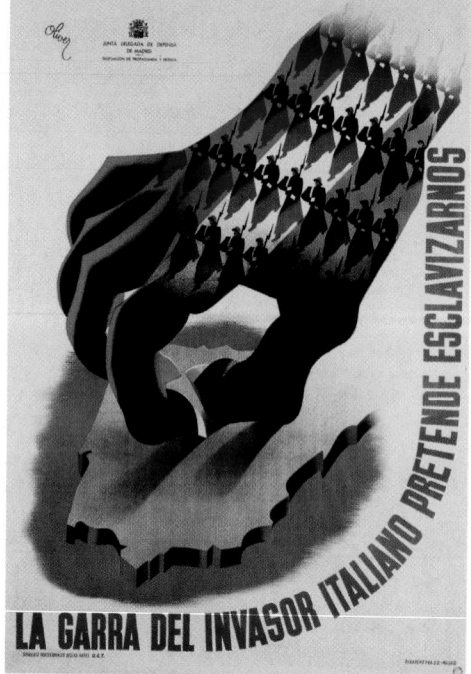

LA GARRA DEL INVASOR ITALIANO PRETENDE ESCLAVIZARNOS

Picturing **History**

Anti-Fascist Propaganda Spanish general Francisco Franco led the Fascist rebellion that received support from Hitler and Mussolini. This poster translates to "The claw of the Italian invader intends to make slaves of us." How did the United States respond to these events?

The Nye Committee Isolationist ideas became even stronger in the early 1930s for two reasons. When the Depression began, many European nations found it difficult to repay money they had borrowed during World War I. In June 1934, all of the debtor nations except Finland announced they would no longer repay their war debts.

At about the same time, dozens of books and articles appeared arguing that arms manufacturers had tricked the United States into entering World War I. In 1934 Senator Gerald P. Nye of North Dakota held hearings to **investigate** the country's involvement in World War I. The Nye Committee documented the huge profits that arms factories had made during the war. The report created the impression that these businesses influenced the U.S. decision to go to war. The European refusal to repay their loans and the Nye Committee's findings turned even more Americans toward isolationism.

540 CHAPTER 11 A World in Flames

Legislating Neutrality Worried that growing German and Italian aggression might lead to war, Congress passed the **Neutrality Act of 1935.** Based on the belief that arms sales had helped bring the United States into World War I, the act made it illegal for Americans to sell arms to any country at war.

In 1936 a rebellion erupted in Spain after a coalition of Republicans, Socialists, and Communists was elected. General Francisco Franco led the rebellion. Franco was backed by the Falangists, or Spanish Fascists, army officers, landowners, and Catholic Church leaders.

The revolt quickly became a **civil** war and attracted worldwide attention. The Soviet Union provided arms and advisers to the government forces, while Germany and Italy sent tanks, airplanes, and soldiers to help Franco. To keep the United States neutral, Congress passed another neutrality act, banning the sale of arms to either side in a civil war.

Shortly after the Spanish Civil War began in 1936, Hitler and Mussolini signed an agreement pledging to cooperate on several international issues. Mussolini referred to this new relationship with Germany as the Rome-Berlin Axis. The following month, Japan aligned itself with Germany and Italy when it signed the Anti-Comintern Pact with Germany. The pact required the two countries to exchange information about Communist groups. Together Germany, Italy, and Japan became known as the Axis Powers, although they did not formally become allies until September 1940.

With the situation in Europe getting worse, Congress passed the Neutrality Act of 1937. This act continued the ban on selling arms to nations at war, but it also required warring countries to buy nonmilitary supplies from the United States on a "cash-and-carry" basis. If a country at war wanted goods from the United States, it had to send its own ships to pick up the goods, and it had to pay cash. Loans were not allowed. Isolationists knew that attacks on neutral American ships carrying supplies to Europe had helped bring the country into World War I. They were determined to prevent it from happening again.

Roosevelt and Internationalism When he took office in 1933, President Roosevelt declared that "our international relations, though vastly important, are in point of time and necessity secondary to the establishment of a sound national economy." Roosevelt knew that ending the Depression was his first priority, but he was not an isolationist. He supported **internationalism,** the idea that trade between nations creates prosperity and helps to prevent war.

Internationalists also believed the United States should try to preserve peace in the world.

Roosevelt supported internationalism but knew that the public wanted neutrality. He warned that the neutrality acts "might drag us into war instead of keeping us out," but he did not veto the bills. Isolationism was too strong to resist.

In July 1937, Japanese forces in Manchuria launched a full-scale attack on China. Roosevelt decided to help the Chinese. Since neither China nor Japan had actually declared war, Roosevelt claimed the Neutrality Act of 1937 did not apply, and he authorized the sale of weapons from the United States to China. He warned that the nation should not stand by and let an "epidemic of lawlessness" infect the world:

❝When an epidemic of physical disease starts to spread, the community . . . joins in a quarantine of the patients in order to protect the health of the community against the spread of the disease. . . . War is a contagion, whether it be declared or undeclared. . . . There is no escape through mere isolation or neutrality. . . .❞

–quoted in *Freedom from Fear*

Despite Roosevelt's words, Americans were still not willing to risk another war to stop aggression overseas. "It is a terrible thing," the president said, "to look over your shoulder when you are trying to lead—and find no one there."

✓ **Reading Check** **Evaluating** Why did many Americans support isolationism?

Picturing **History**

Imperial Expansion In 1931 Japan occupied the northeast Chinese province of Manchuria. In 1937 the Japanese invaded all of China, prompting FDR to authorize the sale of arms to the Chinese Army. **How did Roosevelt justify his actions in light of the Neutrality Act?**

HISTORY *Online* **Study Central**

For help with the concepts in this section of *American Vision: Modern Times* go to tav.mt.glencoe.com and click on *Study Central*.

SECTION 1 ASSESSMENT

Checking for Understanding

1. **Vocabulary** Define: fascism, impose, investigate, civil, internationalism.
2. **People and Terms** Identify: Benito Mussolini, Vladimir Lenin, Joseph Stalin, Adolf Hitler, Manchuria, Neutrality Act of 1935.
3. **Explain** why isolationism was strong in the United States in the early 1930s.

Reviewing Big Ideas

4. **Examining** What events caused President Roosevelt to become more of an internationalist?

Critical Thinking

5. **Historical Analysis** **Interpreting** Why did antidemocratic governments rise to power in postwar Europe and Asia? Could the United States have slowed or prevented their rise? Explain. **CA HI1**
6. **Categorizing** Use a graphic organizer similar to the one below to compare the antidemocratic governments that arose in Europe and Asia.

Country	Dictator	Ideology

Analyzing Visuals

7. **Analyzing Art** Study the Spanish Civil War era propaganda poster reproduced on page 540. Without being told the phrase, how would you be able to discover the poster's meaning?

Writing About History

8. **Persuasive Writing** Write a newspaper editorial urging fellow citizens to embrace either isolationism or internationalism after World War I. Be certain to include reasons your readers should back a specific position. **CA** 11WS1.1; 11WA2.3a

CHAPTER 11 A World in Flames **541**

ASSESS

Resources for page 541

Use these resources to assess student mastery.

📁 Section Quiz 11-1

📁 Reading Essentials and Study Guide 11-1

⊙ Interactive Tutor Self-Assessment CD-ROM

📁 California Standards Practice, Grade 11

Picturing **History**

Answer: He argued that arms sales could be made since war had not been officially declared.
Ask: What did internationalists believe about the economy? *(They believed trade between nations created prosperity and helped prevent war.)*

✓ **Reading Check**

Answer: They felt remaining apart from European conflicts would avoid another war.

HISTORY *Online*

Study Central provides audio summaries, interactive games, and online graphic organizers to help students review section content.

CLOSE

Summarizing Have students list the U.S. actions taken to remain neutral in the 1930s. **BL**

SECTION 1 ASSESSMENT ANSWERS

1. Content vocabulary is boldfaced and highlighted in yellow. Academic vocabulary is boldfaced.
2. Benito Mussolini *(p. 537)*, Vladimir Lenin *(p. 538)*, Joseph Stalin *(p. 538)*, Adolf Hitler *(p. 538)*, Manchuria *(p. 539)*, Neutrality Act of 1935 *(p. 539)*
3. unpaid European war debts; belief that arms manufacturers influenced U.S. to enter World War I
4. Japanese invasion of China
5. unhappiness with Treaty of Versailles terms; worldwide economic depression; answers will vary.
6. Italy: Mussolini, Fascism; USSR: Stalin, Communism; Germany: Hitler, Nazism; Japan: Japanese military, militarism
7. a cruel claw-like hand is trying to grasp the country; colors of Italian flag superimposed on hand
8. Editorials will vary.

FOCUS

BELLRINGER
SKILLBUILDER ACTIVITY

Project **Daily Focus Skills Transparency 11-2** and have students answer the question.

Guide to Reading

Understanding Vocabulary:
Assign one of the vocabulary words to each student. Ask students to prepare 30-second oral presentations on their assigned words.

Answers to Graphic:
Hitler calls for German unity; Hitler threatens to invade Austria; the *Anschluss;* Germany claims Sudetenland; Germany demands return of Danzig; Germany annexes Czechoslovakia; Nazi-Soviet Nonaggression Pact; Germany invades Poland

Unpacking the Standards

Students will be able to:

- Describe how European leaders attempted to appease Adolf Hitler and avoid war.
- Explain the onset of another continental war in Europe.
- Discuss Britain's resolve in the early years of the war.

Answers and Additional Support

SECTION 2 — World War II Begins

Guide to Reading

Connection
In the previous section, you learned how the United States tried to stay neutral as militarism gained strength in the world. In this section, you will read about the circumstances surrounding the beginning of World War II.

Main Idea
- European nations tried to prevent war by giving in to Hitler's demands. (p. 543)
- Although Poland and France fell to the Nazis, the British were able to evacuate thousands of trapped British and French troops from Dunkirk in France. (p. 544)

Content Vocabulary
appeasement, blitzkrieg

Academic Vocabulary
regime, furthermore, anticipate

People and Terms to Identify
Anschluss, Maginot Line, Winston Churchill, Battle of Britain

Reading Objectives
- **Explain** why Hitler was able to take over Austria and Czechoslovakia.

- Disregarding the bombing of London and other major cities, Britain's Winston Churchill stood firm against the threat of Nazi invasion. (p. 547)

- **Describe** the early events of the war and why Britain was able to resist the Nazis.

Reading Strategy
Sequencing As you read about the events leading up to the beginning of World War II, record them by completing a time line similar to the one below.

| 1937 | March 1938 | Oct. 1938 | Aug. 1939 | Sept. 1939 |
| Feb. 1938 | Sept. 1938 | March 1939 | | |

Preview of Events

◆1938	◆1939	◆1940	◆1941
March 1938 Hitler announces German-Austrian unification	**August 1939** Hitler and Stalin sign Nazi-Soviet pact / **September 1939** World War II begins	**June 1940** France surrenders to Germany	**August 1940** Battle of Britain begins

The following are the main History–Social Science Standards covered in this section.

11.7.1 Examine the origins of American involvement in the war, with an emphasis on the events that precipitated the attack on Pearl Harbor.

11.7.4 Analyze Roosevelt's foreign policies during World War II (e.g., Four Freedoms speech).

11.7.6 Describe major developments in aviation, weaponry, communication, and medicine and the war's impact on the location of American industry and use of resources.

⚜ The Big Idea ⚜

The fate of nations is forever changed by monumental world events.
After establishing his rule in Germany, Adolf Hitler began his conquest of Europe by seizing Austria. His claims to the Sudetenland in Czechoslovakia prompted Great Britain and France to pursue a policy of appeasement to avoid war. Despite an agreement, Hitler sent troops into Czechoslovakia and demanded the return of Danzig, a Polish seaport with German roots. When Germany invaded Poland and began the war, Britain and France fulfilled their promise to come to the aid of Poland. Hitler's tactics led to a quick victory in Poland and the fall of France. Britain remained defiant despite constant bombing raids by the Germans.

542 CHAPTER 11 A World in Flames

SECTION RESOURCES

🗁 Print Material
- Reproducible Lesson Plan 11-2
- Guided Reading Activity 11-2
- Reading Essentials and Study Guide 11-2
- Active Reading Note-Taking Guide 11-2

🖋 Transparencies
- Daily Focus Skills Transparency 11-2
- Section Graphic Organizer Transparency 11-2

Technology
- Interactive Tutor Self-Assessment CD-ROM
- ExamView® Pro Testmaker CD-ROM
- Presentation Plus! CD-ROM

"Peace in Our Time"

Main Idea European nations tried to prevent war by giving in to Hitler's demands.

Reading Connection Do you think giving in to Hitler's demands was a good idea? Read on to learn about the events leading to another world war.

Prior to 1940, when the Nazi **regime** was much weaker, European leaders did not try to stop Hitler. Instead, they vainly tried to buy peace by giving in to his demands. By 1940, however, the German army had been rebuilt, and Hitler was bent on conquest.

★ An American Story ★

In February 1940, President Franklin Roosevelt sent Undersecretary of State Sumner Welles to Europe to report on the political situation. A few months earlier, Germany had invaded Poland, and Roosevelt hoped to negotiate peace before wider hostilities erupted.

In Italy Welles found Mussolini intent on war and judged that "there was not the slightest chance of any successful negotiation." In Paris Welles glumly noted the "sullen apathy" in people's faces and concluded that France had little will to resist a German onslaught. After speaking to Hitler, Welles concluded that a negotiated peace settlement was impossible: "It was only too tragically plain that all decisions had already been made." In London, Welles did not feel the sense of doom he had in Paris. The British, he reported, would "fight to the very last ditch." Welles later reflected on his mission:

> 66 Only one thing could have deflected Hitler from his purpose: the sure knowledge that the power of the United States would be directed against him if he attempted to carry out his intention of conquering the world by force. . . . At that time no representative of this government could have been authorized to intimate any such thing. . . . My mission, therefore, was a forlorn hope. 99
>
> —quoted in *Roosevelt and Churchill*

Whether or not the United States could have forced Hitler to negotiate is uncertain. Europe's leaders had several reasons for hoping that Hitler could

be satisfied and war avoided. First, the memory of World War I made many leaders fearful of another bloody conflict. Second, some thought Hitler's demand that all German-speaking regions of Europe be united with Germany was reasonable. Third, many people assumed that the Nazis would be more interested in peace once they gained more territory.

The Austrian *Anschluss* In late 1937, Hitler stepped up his call for the unification of all German-speaking people, including those in Austria and Czechoslovakia. Seizing Austria and Czechoslovakia would also gain food supplies, defensible frontiers, and soldiers for Germany. Hitler believed that Germany could only expand its territory by "resort[ing] to force with its attendant risks."

In February 1938, Hitler threatened to invade German-speaking Austria, his native land, unless Austrian Nazis were given important government posts. Austria's chancellor quickly gave in to this demand. Several weeks later, the chancellor tried to put the matter of unification with Germany to a democratic vote. Fearing the outcome, Hitler sent troops into Austria in March and announced the *Anschluss*, or unification, of Austria and Germany.

The Munich Crisis and Appeasement Shortly after Germany annexed Austria, Hitler announced German claims to the Sudetenland, an area of Czechoslovakia with a large German-speaking population. Since Austrians shared a common culture and language with Germany, many people had accepted the *Anschluss*. In Czechoslovakia, however, people spoke several different languages. In addition, while Austria had an authoritarian government, Czechoslovakia was a democracy. **Furthermore**, Austria had no allies to help it defend itself, but Czechoslovakia was allied with France and the Soviet Union.

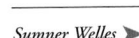
Sumner Welles ▶

TEACH

R Reading Strategy

Scaffolding—Academic Vocabulary The word *authority* was introduced in Chapter 6, Section 4. Ask a student to define the word. **BL**

S Skill Practice

Scaffolding—Interpreting Events Tell students to pretend that they are the leader of a European country. Ask them to write speeches reassuring their citizens that war can be avoided by giving in to Hitler's demands. *(Note: Remind students to remember their audience and to use strong persuasive language and evidence to support their argument.)* **OL** **CA** CS1; HI2; HI3; HI4

This **Historical Analysis** skill was introduced in Chapter 7.

C Critical Thinking

Predicting Consequences Have students use a historical atlas to locate a map of Eastern Europe in the mid-1930s. Tell them to predict the nations most vulnerable to German annexation or invasion. Ask students about some of the motivations Germany had for expanding its territory. *(Answers will vary but should include the unification of German-speaking peoples, access to more natural resources, and defensible frontiers.)* **AL**

More Skill Practice

Summarizing Ask students to list reasons why many Austrians accepted the *Anschluss*. **Ask:** Why did Austrians not unite to keep Hitler out of their country? *(Austrians shared a common culture and language with Germany, had an authoritarian government, and had no allies to help them defend themselves.)* **OL**

Appeasement in Action At Munich in September 1938, Mussolini (third from left), Britain's Neville Chamberlain (second from left), and Hitler (second from right) were among those deciding Czechoslovakia's fate.

The Czechs strongly resisted Germany's demands for the Sudetenland. France threatened to fight if Germany attacked, and the Soviet Union also promised assistance. British Prime Minister Neville Chamberlain publicly promised to support France.

Representatives of Britain, France, Italy, and Germany agreed to meet in Munich to decide Czechoslovakia's fate. At the Munich Conference on September 29, 1938, Britain and France agreed to Hitler's demands, a policy that came to be known as **appeasement.** Appeasement is the policy of giving concessions in exchange for peace. Supporters of appeasement mistakenly believed that Hitler had a few limited demands. They felt that if they gave Hitler what he wanted, he would be satisfied and war would be avoided. Czechoslovakia was informed that it must give up the Sudetenland or fight Germany on its own.

Chamberlain had gambled that sacrificing part of Czechoslovakia would satisfy Hitler. He also knew that Britain's military was not ready for war. When Chamberlain returned home he promised "a peace with honor . . . peace in our time," but he also began to speed up British rearmament.

The following March, in brazen violation of the Munich agreement, Germany sent troops into Czechoslovakia and broke up the country. Slovakia became independent in name, but it was actually a satellite state under German control. The Czech lands became a German protectorate.

Danzig and the Polish Corridor After the Munich conference, Hitler turned his sights on Poland. In October 1938, he demanded the return of Danzig, a Baltic Sea port with strong German roots. Although Danzig was more than 90 percent German, it had been separated from Germany at the end of

World War I to give Poland access to the sea. Hitler also requested a highway and railroad across the Polish Corridor, which separated western Germany from the German state of East Prussia.

Hitler's demands on Poland convinced the British and French that appeasement had failed. On March 31, 1939, the British announced that if Poland went to war to defend its territory, Britain and France would come to its aid. This encouraged the Polish government to refuse Hitler's demands.

In May 1939, Hitler ordered the German army to prepare to invade Poland. He also ordered his foreign minister to begin negotiations with the USSR. If Germany was going to fight Britain and France, Hitler wantd to avoid the strain on his army of having to fight the Soviets too.

The Nazi-Soviet Nonaggression Pact When German officials proposed a nonaggression treaty to the Soviets, Stalin agreed. He believed the best way to protect the USSR was to turn the capitalist nations against each other. If the treaty worked, Germany would go to war against Britain and France, and the USSR would be safe.

On August 23, 1939, Germany and the USSR signed the nonaggression pact. The Nazi-Soviet pact shocked the world. Communism and Nazism were supposed to be totally opposed to each other. Leaders in Britain and France knew that Hitler made the deal to free himself for war against their countries and Poland. They did not know that the treaty also contained a secret deal between Germany and the Soviet Union to divide Poland between them.

✓ **Reading Check** **Explaining** What were three reasons European leaders agreed to a policy of appeasement?

The War Begins

Main Idea Although Poland and France fell to the Nazis, the British were able to evacuate thousands of trapped British and French troops from Dunkirk in France.

Reading Connection Can you think of a historical or contemporary situation in which people acted heroically to save those in danger? Read on to learn of the heroism of civilians and armed forces in World War II.

On September 1, 1939, Germany invaded Poland from the west, and soon after the Soviets invaded from the east. On September 3, Britain and France declared war on Germany, marking the start of World War II.

544   CHAPTER 11   A World in Flames

Did You Know?

The Baltic city of Gdansk (Danzig in German) has alternated through its history between being a politically free city or part of Poland or German-speaking Prussia. It was a part of Prussia until the Treaty of Versailles, when it became a free city again. Identification with Germany has been strong, however. In the 1930s, Nazi officials were voted into the majority of the city assembly. Gunter Grass writes of this era in his book *The Tin Drum.*

Blitzkrieg in Poland Poland bravely resisted Germany's onslaught but was unable to stop the attack. The Germans used a new type of warfare called **blitzkrieg**, or lightning war. Blitzkrieg used large numbers of massed tanks to break through and rapidly encircle enemy positions. Supporting the tanks were waves of aircraft that bombed enemy positions and dropped paratroopers to cut their supply lines. Blitzkrieg depended on radios to coordinate the tanks and aircraft. The attack left the German enemy completely surrounded, cut off from supplies, and with heavy losses. The Polish army was unable to cope with the German attack. On September 27, the Polish capital of Warsaw fell to the Germans. By October 5, 1939, the Polish army had been defeated.

The Fall of France In contrast to the war in Poland, western Europe remained eerily quiet. The Germans referred to this situation as the *sitzkrieg,* or sitting war. The British called it the "Bore War," while American newspapers nicknamed it the "Phony War." The British sent troops to assist France, but because both countries remained on the defensive, waiting for the Germans to attack, there were no battles or warfare.

After World War I, the French had built a line of concrete bunkers and fortifications called the **Maginot Line** along the German border. Rather than risk their troops by attacking, the French preferred to wait behind the Maginot Line for the Germans to approach. Unfortunately, this decision allowed Germany to concentrate on Poland first, without the need to simultaneously fight the French, before turning west to face the British and French.

After conquering Poland, Hitler and his generals decided to attack Norway and Denmark before invading France. France continued to wait for attack. Germany's industry depended on iron ore from Sweden that had to be shipped down Norway's coast part of the year. If the British sent troops to Norway, they could block the iron shipments. On April 9, 1940, the attack began, and within a month, Germany controlled both countries.

Review the Big Idea

Review the Big Idea for this section, "The fate of nations is forever changed by monumental world events." Have students organize the text on the map into a time line that shows in chronological order when German invasions and occupations occurred. Students should use the numbers on the map to help them organize the information. **Ask: Why do you think Germany invaded the European nations in this order?** *(Answers may vary but should include geographic location, unification of German-speaking peoples, and/or access to natural resources.)* **OL** **CA** CS2

S Skill Practice

Conducting Research Have students research and map the Maginot Line and the Siegfried Line. During World War II the Siegfried Line was a defensive line in western Germany along the border between Germany and France. Ask students to discover when the plan was put forward and by whom, what was proposed, why more of the planned fortifications were not built, and why, ultimately, the line did not achieve its purpose. **OL** **CA** HR3; HI2

NATIONAL GEOGRAPHIC
Axis Expansion, 1935–1941

② Germany occupies Rhineland, March 1936
⑦ Battle of Britain, Aug. 1940–Oct. 1940
⑤ Invasion of Poland, Sept. 1, 1939
⑧ Invasion of USSR, June 1941
⑥ Fall of France, June 1940
④ Annexation of Sudetenland, Sept. 1938
③ Austrian *Anschluss*, 1938
① Italy invades Ethiopia, Oct. 1935

Legend:
- Axis nations
- Axis satellite states
- Axis conquests
- Allied control
- Neutral countries
- Axis advance
- International boundary, Jan. 1938
- Maginot Line

500 miles / 500 kilometers
Lambert Azimuthal Equal-Area projection

Geography *Skills*

1. **Interpreting Maps** Satellite states were independent in name, but they were under German control. What was the French satellite state called?
2. **Applying Geography Skills** Why was Czechoslovakia physically in danger once the *Anschluss* took place?

Did You Know?

In 1939, the Polish military consisted of outdated infantry and horse cavalry. They were ineffectual against the 1,500 planes, including *Stuka* dive bombers, and the panzers, or German tanks. Also, they were not prepared for their invaders, whom Hitler had instructed to "close their hearts to pity."

Geography *Skills*

Answers:
1. Vichy
2. It was nearly surrounded by Germany and German-controlled Austria.

Geography Skills Practice
Ask: Why did Hitler sign a pact with the USSR before invading Poland? *(He did not want to fight a war on two fronts simultaneously.)*

W Writing Support

Narrative Writing Have students pretend that they are Allied soldiers awaiting rescue in Belgium during the German invasion. Assign them to work together in small groups to write letters describing their experiences to a loved one at home.
OL **CA** 11WS1.1

U Universal Access

Advanced Learners Invite interested students to create a model depicting the evacuation of Dunkirk. Encourage students to use library and Internet resources for this project. **AL**

C Critical Thinking

Predicting Consequences Review with students Britain's historical and political ties with the United States. **Ask: What effect do you think the Battle of Dunkirk had on the U.S. policy of isolationism? Why?** *(American sympathy with Britain in the Battle of Dunkirk helped to lift the United States out of its policy of isolationism.)* **OL**

✓ Reading Check

Answer: Germans used a new type of warfare, the *blitzkrieg*, that used large numbers of tanks, infantry, and air power in a coordinated attack.

Answers and Additional Support

Dunkirk Allied troops wade out to ships waiting to evacuate them from Dunkirk

With his northern flank secure, Hitler turned his attention to France. Hitler planned to go around the Maginot Line, which protected France's border with Germany but not France's border with Belgium and Luxembourg. To get around the Maginot Line, the Germans would have to invade the Netherlands, Belgium, and Luxembourg first—which is exactly what they did. On May 10, Hitler launched a new blitzkrieg in the west. While German troops parachuted into the Netherlands, an army of tanks rolled into Belgium and Luxembourg.

The British and French had expected the German attack. As soon as it began, British and French forces raced north into Belgium. This was a mistake. Instead of sending their tanks through the open countryside of central Belgium, the Germans sent their main force through the Ardennes Mountains of Luxembourg and eastern Belgium. The French did not think that large numbers of tanks could move through the mountains, and they had left only a few troops to defend that part of the border. The Germans easily smashed through the French lines, then raced west

across northern France to the English Channel. The British and French armies were still in Belgium and could not move back into France quickly enough. They were now trapped in Belgium.

The Miracle at Dunkirk After trapping the Allied forces in Belgium, the Germans began to drive them toward the English Channel. The only hope for Britain and France was to evacuate their surviving troops by sea, but the Germans had captured all but one port, Dunkirk, a small town in northern France near the Belgian border.

As German forces closed in on Dunkirk, Hitler suddenly ordered them to stop. No one is sure why he gave this order. Historians know that Hitler was nervous about risking his tank forces, and he wanted to wait until more infantry arrived. Hermann Goering, the head of the German air force, was also assuring Hitler that aircraft alone could destroy the trapped soldiers. There is also some evidence that Hitler thought that the British would be more willing to accept peace if the Germans did not humiliate them by destroying their forces at Dunkirk.

Whatever Hitler's reasons, his order provided a three-day delay. This gave the British time to strengthen their lines and begin the evacuation. Some 850 ships of all sizes, from navy warships to small sailboats operated by civilian volunteers, headed to Dunkirk from England. The British had hoped to rescue about 45,000 troops. Instead, when the evacuation ended on June 4, an estimated 338,000 British and French troops had been saved. This stunning success led British newspapers to refer to the evacuation as the "Miracle at Dunkirk."

The evacuation had its price, however. Almost all of the British army's equipment remained at Dunkirk—90,000 rifles, 7,000 tons of ammunition, and 120,000 vehicles. If Hitler invaded Britain, it would be almost impossible to stop him from conquering the country.

Three weeks later, on June 22, 1940, Hitler accepted the French surrender in the same railway car in which the Germans had surrendered at the end of World War I. Germany now occupied much of northern France and its Atlantic coastline. To govern the rest of the country, Germany installed a puppet government at the town of Vichy and made Marshal Philippe Pétain the new government's figurehead leader. Pétain predicted that Britain "will have her neck wrung like a chicken."

✓ Reading Check **Summarizing** Why was Germany able to overtake Poland?

546 CHAPTER 11 A World in Flames

More Skill Practice

Spatial Thinking Give each student a copy of a map of wartime Europe. Ask students to draw lines tracing Hitler's path of invasion ending with France *(Poland, Norway, Denmark, the Netherlands, Belgium, and Luxembourg)*. Have them write a few paragraphs explaining why it was necessary for Germany to conquer each of these countries before invading France. *(Norway and Denmark were necessary to protect iron shipments from Sweden and to secure Germany's northern flank; the Netherlands, Belgium, and Luxembourg provided a route around the Maginot Line.)* **OL** **CA** CS3; HI3

Britain Remains Defiant

Main Idea Disregarding the bombing of London and other major cities, Britain's Winston Churchill stood firm against the threat of Nazi invasion.

Reading Connection Describe a time when you felt the odds were against you. How did you react? Read on to find out about the resolve of the British when faced with Nazi air attack.

Neither Pétain nor Adolf Hitler **anticipated** the bravery of the British people or the spirit of their leader, **Winston Churchill,** who had replaced Neville Chamberlain as prime minister. Hitler fully expected the British to negotiate peace after France surrendered. For Winston Churchill, however, peace was not an option. The war was a fight to defend civilization. On June 4, 1940, Churchill delivered a defiant speech in Parliament, intended not only to rally the British people but to alert the isolationist United States to Britain's plight:

66Even though large tracts of Europe have fallen . . . we shall not flag or fail. . . . We shall defend our island, whatever the cost may be, we shall fight on the beaches, we shall fight on the landing grounds, we shall fight in the fields and in the streets, we shall fight in the hills; we shall never surrender.99

—quoted in *Freedom from Fear*

When Hitler realized that Britain would not surrender, he ordered his commanders to prepare to invade. Only the choppy waters of the narrow English Channel separated Britain from Germany's powerful army, but getting across the Channel posed a major challenge. Germany had few transport ships, and the British air force would sink them if they tried to land troops in England. To invade, therefore, Germany first had to defeat the British air force.

In June 1940, the German air force, called the *Luftwaffe,* began to attack British shipping in the English Channel. Then, in mid-August, the *Luftwaffe* launched an all-out air battle to destroy the British

NATIONAL GEOGRAPHIC
MOMENT in HISTORY

NEVER GIVE IN

Few photographs capture the British resolve to keep a stiff upper lip better than this one. Night after night between September 1940 and May 1941, German warplanes rained bombs on London, Coventry, and other British cities. The attacks were intended to destroy British morale and war production, but Royal Air Force pilots shot down bombers faster than Germany could replace them. Plucky British civilians, like this milkman making his rounds through a debris-strewn London street, remained determined to carry on as usual each morning.

CHAPTER 11 A World in Flames **547**

Chapter 11 • Section 2

R **Reading Strategy**

Scaffolding—Academic Vocabulary The word *resolve* was introduced in Chapter 6, Section 3. Ask a student to define the word. **BL**

C **Critical Thinking**

Drawing Conclusions Have students reexamine the photo on this page. **Ask:** Why did the German air force bomb civilian targets? *(to demoralize resistance)* Then ask students to explain why they think British resolve was actually strengthened as a result of the bombings. Have students suggest other factors that might influence a population's response to aerial attacks on civilians. **OL**

W **Writing Support**

Research Report Writing Tell students that after the evacuation of Dunkirk, Winston Churchill warned Parliament that "Wars are not won by evacuations." Have students research and write two-page reports on how Churchill's and Britain's resolve not to surrender affected both isolationists and internationalists in the United States. **AL** **CA HI2**

Did You Know?

Henri Philippe Omer Petain, leader of France after the German takeover, defended his truce with Germany by arguing that it was necessary to prevent France from being overwhelmed by Germany. He lost most of his supporters when he allowed thousands of French citizens to be sent to Germany as laborers.

NATIONAL GEOGRAPHIC MOMENT in HISTORY

Ask: What does this picture symbolize? *(determination of the British to live their usual lives despite the war)*

ASSESS

Resources for page 548

Use these resources to assess student mastery.

📁 Section Quiz 11-2

📁 Reading Essentials and Study Guide 11-2

💿 Interactive Tutor Self-Assessment CD-ROM

📁 California Standards Practice, Grade 11

Picturing **History**

Answer: radar

Ask: Where did British citizens in London go to find safety from the bombings? *(London's subways)*

✓ **Reading Check**

Answer: Germany had too few transport ships to invade Britain; the British had developed radar

Study Central provides audio summaries, interactive games, and online graphic organizers to help students review section content.

CLOSE

Summarizing Summarize with the class the content of the section by creating a time line of the major events. **BL**

Picturing **History**

Never Surrender Hitler ordered Nazi aircraft to bomb British cities, intending to weaken the people's will. Though shaken, the British, like the dome of St. Paul's Cathedral (right), stood firm. What technology allowed the outnumbered Royal Air Force to resist the German *Luftwaffe*?

Royal Air Force. This air battle, which lasted into the fall of 1940, became known as the **Battle of Britain.**

On August 23, German bombers accidentally bombed London, the British capital. This attack on civilians enraged the British, who responded by bombing Berlin the following night. For the first time in the war, bombs fell on the German capital. Infuriated, Hitler ordered the *Luftwaffe* to stop its attacks on British military targets and to concentrate on bombing London.

Hitler's goal now was to terrorize the British people into surrendering. The British people endured, however, hiding out in the city's subway tunnels whenever German bombers appeared. Hitler's attempt to destroy the morale of the British people failed.

Although the Royal Air Force was greatly outnumbered, the British had one major advantage. They had developed a new technology called radar. Using radar stations placed along their coast, the British were able to detect incoming German aircraft and direct British fighters to intercept them.

Day after day, with the ability to detect German aircraft, the British fighters inflicted more losses on the Germans than they suffered. The skill of a few hundred pilots saved Britain from invasion. Praising the pilots, Churchill told Parliament, "Never in the field of human conflict was so much owed by so many to so few." On October 12, 1940, Hitler cancelled the invasion of Britain.

✓ **Reading Check** **Evaluating** Why was Britain able to resist Hitler and the Nazis?

HISTORY *Online* **Study Central**

For help with the concepts in this section of *American Vision: Modern Times* go to tav.mt.glencoe.com and click on *Study Central.*

SECTION 2 ASSESSMENT

Checking for Understanding

1. **Vocabulary** Define: regime, furthermore, appeasement, blitzkrieg, anticipate.
2. **People and Terms** Identify: *Anschluss,* Maginot Line, Winston Churchill, Battle of Britain.
3. **Explain** why Hitler was able to take over Austria and Czechoslovakia.

Reviewing Big Ideas

4. **Describing** How did the policy of appeasement affect France and Great Britain?

Critical Thinking

5. **Historical Analysis** **Evaluating** Why do you think the British were able to prevent the Germans from invading their country? Do you think Hitler was wise in canceling the attempted invasion? **CA HI4**

6. **Organizing** Use a graphic organizer similar to the one below to list the early events of the war in Poland and western Europe.

Events	

Analyzing Visuals

7. **Analyzing Photographs** Study the photographs on pages 547 and 548. How do they reflect the British resolve to "never surrender"?

Writing About History

8. **Expository Writing** Using library or Internet resources, find more information on the German annexation of Czechoslovakia. Use the information to write a report detailing the events leading up to and including the annexation. Share your report with the class. **CA 11WS1.6; 11WA2.4b; 11WA2.4d**

548 CHAPTER 11 A World in Flames

SECTION 2 ASSESSMENT ANSWERS

1. Content vocabulary is boldfaced and highlighted in yellow. Academic vocabulary is boldfaced.
2. *Anschluss (p. 543),* Maginot Line *(p. 545),* Winston Churchill *(p. 547),* Battle of Britain *(p. 548)*
3. Britain and France gave in to Hitler's demands.
4. France was not prepared for German attack; Britain left to fight alone
5. Britain was an island, with a strong air force, navy, and radar stations.
6. Germany and Soviets invade Poland; Britain and France enter the war; Germany invades Norway, Denmark, Belgium, the Netherlands, Luxembourg, and France
7. shows British desire to continue with their daily routines and activities in spite of devastation
8. Reports should include details about the political and social structure of Czechoslovakia before the annexation.

SECTION 3 The Holocaust

Guide to Reading

Connection
In the previous section, you learned how Hitler's aggressive actions led to World War II. In this section, you will discover the Nazi ideology about Jews and the "final solution."

Main Idea
- The Nazis blamed the Jews for everything and required them to resign their jobs and wear special clothing or live in specially designated sections of town. (p. 550)
- Hitler's atrocities included sending millions of Jews to concentration camps and extermination camps. (p. 553)

Content Vocabulary
Holocaust, concentration camp, extermination camp

Academic Vocabulary
implement, prohibit, method

People and Terms to Identify
Shoah, Nuremberg Laws, Wannsee Conference

Reading Objectives
- **Describe** Nazi prejudices against Jews and early persecution of German Jews.
- **Explain** the methods Hitler used to try to exterminate Europe's Jewish population.

Reading Strategy
Organizing As you read about the Holocaust, complete a graphic organizer similar to the one below by listing examples of Nazi persecution of German Jews.

```
Examples
of        ├──────
Persecution ├──────
          ├──────
          ├──────
          ├──────
```

Preview of Events

◆1933	◆1936	◆1939	◆1942

Autumn 1935
Nuremberg Laws deprive German Jews of citizenship

November 1938
Anti-Jewish violence erupts during *Kristallnacht*

June 1939
SS *St. Louis* denied permission to dock in the United States

January 1942
Nazis' Wannsee Conference determines "final solution" for Jews

---

The following are the main History–Social Science Standards covered in this section.

11.7.5 Discuss the constitutional issues and impact of events on the U.S. home front, including the internment of Japanese Americans (e.g., *Fred Korematsu v. United States of America*) and the restrictions on German and Italian resident aliens; the response of the administration to Hitler's atrocities against Jews and other groups; the roles of women in military production; and the roles and growing political demands of African Americans.

11.7.6 Describe major developments in aviation, weaponry, communication, and medicine and the war's impact on the location of American industry and use of resources.

❧ The Big Idea ❧

The fate of nations is forever changed by monumental world events. Once the Nazis had taken power in Germany, they quickly acted on Hitler's racial policies. They enacted laws denying citizenship to Jews and taking away their rights. Soon Jews faced severe unemployment and violence. Many Jews tried to flee the country, and some managed to escape to the United States or other European countries. Immigration was made difficult because many countries, including the United States, imposed restrictions. Jews who remained in Germany faced the concentration camps and extermination camps that marked the Nazis' pursuit of the "final solution."

CHAPTER 11   A World in Flames   **549**

FOCUS

BELLRINGER
SKILLBUILDER ACTIVITY

Project **Daily Focus Skills Transparency 11-3** and have students answer the question.

Guide to Reading

Understanding Vocabulary: Have students look up the proper pronunciations of the content vocabulary words.

Answers to Graphic: segregated from the rest of the population, lost their jobs, stripped of citizenship, prohibited from voting or holding office, had identifying mark put in passport, confined to concentration camps, killed at extermination camps

Unpacking the Standards

Students will be able to:
- Describe how the Nazis systematically targeted Jews in Germany and throughout Europe.
- Discuss the impact of the Holocaust.

SECTION RESOURCES

📖 Print Material
- Reproducible Lesson Plan 11-3
- Guided Reading Activity 11-3
- Reading Essentials and Study Guide 11-3
- Active Reading Note-Taking Guide 11-3

📽 Transparencies
- Daily Focus Skills Transparency 11-3
- Section Graphic Organizer Transparency 11-3

Technology
- 💿 Interactive Tutor Self-Assessment CD-ROM
- 💿 Exam*View®* Pro Testmaker CD-ROM
- 💿 Presentation Plus! CD-ROM

TEACH

R Reading Strategy

Organizing Information Tell students to imagine they are German Jews living in the 1930s. Have them make two lists, one showing the reasons to stay in Germany, and one showing the reasons to leave. *(reasons to stay: established lives, friends, family, jobs, national pride, belief that conditions would improve; reasons to leave: religious persecution, Nuremberg Laws, worsening conditions)* **Ask:** If you were a Jew living in Germany in the 1930s, would you have stayed? Why or why not? Remind students that they should make their decisions based on the information available to Jews at the time. Have each student write a paragraph explaining their decision.
OL **CA HI3**

C Critical Thinking

Comparing and Contrasting Have students work in pairs to prepare charts that compare the U.S. Bill of Rights and the rights that the Nuremberg Laws denied the Jews. Use the charts as a basis for a class discussion about the effects of Nazi rule on the Jews.
OL

Answers and Additional Support

Nazi Persecution of the Jews

Main Idea The Nazis blamed the Jews for everything and required them to resign their jobs and wear special clothing or live in specially designated sections of town.

Reading Connection Describe how you would feel and react if you were a Jewish person living under these restrictions in Nazi Germany. Read on to learn about the prejudice against Jewish people in Nazi Germany.

During the **Holocaust,** the catastrophe that ravaged Europe's Jews, the Nazis killed nearly 6 million Jews. The Nazis also killed millions of people from other groups they considered inferior. The Hebrew term for the Holocaust is **Shoah,** meaning "catastrophe," but it is often used specifically to refer to the Nazi campaign to exterminate the Jews during World War II.

★ An American Story ★

Mira Ryczke was born in 1923 to a middle-class Jewish family in Danzig, Poland, a port on the Baltic Sea. After World War II broke out in September 1939, the Nazis expelled Danzig's Jews to Warsaw, where they were forced to live in deplorable conditions in a special area known as the Warsaw ghetto. In 1943 the Nazis emptied the Warsaw ghetto. The Ryczkes had to ride for three days in a suffocating cattle car headed for Auschwitz, the infamous Nazi death camp, and its neighboring camp of Birkenau.

After arriving at the camps, the terrified newcomers learned that a selection was to take place. When 20-year-old Mira asked what the selection was for, an old-time prisoner pointed to chimneys on top of a building and replied, "Selected for the gas chambers to go up in smoke." Mira later wrote:

66[W]e were told by the old-timers to try to look strong, healthy, and to walk in an upright position when our turn came. . . . Because the women I was with were young, only a few were taken out. Their numbers, tattooed on their left arms, were written down by the SS, and after a few days during roll call, their tattoo numbers were called out and these women were marched to the gas chamber.99

—quoted in *Echoes from the Holocaust*

Mira Ryczke and her family were only a few of the millions of Jews who suffered terrible persecution before and during World War II.

Nazi Ideology Once the Nazis took power in Germany, they acted swiftly to **implement** the political racial policies Hitler had outlined in *Mein Kampf.* Although the Nazis persecuted anyone who dared oppose them, as well as people with disabilities, Gypsies, homosexuals, and Slavic peoples, they reserved their strongest hatred for the Jews. This loathing went far beyond the European anti-Semitism common at the time. Over the centuries, people who were prejudiced against Jews had put down Jewish religious practices and discriminated against Jews in many ways. For example, Jews were sometimes segregated in ghettos or **prohibited** from owning land. For the Nazis, however, all Jewish people were evil no matter what their religion, occupation, or education.

The Nuremberg Laws After the Nazis took power, they quickly moved to deprive German Jews of many rights that all citizens had long taken for granted. In September 1935, the **Nuremberg Laws** took citizenship away from Jewish Germans and banned marriage between Jews and other Germans. Two months later, another decree defined a Jew as a person with at least one Jewish grandparent and prohibited Jews from holding public office or voting. Other laws forbade Jews from employing female German servants under age 35 and compelled Jews with German sounding names to adopt "Jewish" names. Soon the passports of Jews were marked with a red "J" to clearly identify them as Jewish.

◀ *Mira Ryczke*

Did You Know?

Holocaust means a sacrifice consumed by fire, especially a complete or thorough sacrifice or destruction.

ABCNEWS INTERACTIVE™

VIDEOCASSETTE
Historic America Electronic Field Trips
View **Tape 2, Chapter 9:** "The Holocaust Museum."

By the summer of 1936, at least half of Germany's Jews were jobless, having lost the right to work as civil servants, journalists, farmers, teachers, and actors. In 1938 the Nazis also banned Jews from practicing law and medicine and from operating businesses. With no source of income, life became very difficult.

Despite worsening conditions, many Jews chose to remain in Germany during the early years of Nazi rule. Well integrated into German society before this time, they were reluctant to leave and give up the lives they had built there. Many also thought that conditions would surely improve after a time. In fact, they soon became worse.

Kristallnacht On November 7, 1938, a young Jewish refugee named Herschel Grynszpan shot and killed a German diplomat in Paris. Grynszpan's father and 10,000 other Jews had been deported from Germany to Poland, and the distraught young man was seeking revenge for this act and for the persecution of the Jews in general.

In retaliation for the killing, an infuriated Hitler ordered his minister of propaganda, Joseph Goebbels, to stage attacks against the Jews that would appear to be a spontaneous popular reaction to news of the murder. On the night of November 9, this plan played out in a spree of destruction.

In Vienna a Jewish child named Frederick Morton watched in terror that night as 10 young Nazi Storm Troopers broke into his family's apartment:

66They yanked out every drawer in every one of our chests and cupboards, and tossed each in the air. They let the cutlery jangle across the floor, the clothes scatter, and stepped over the mess to fling the next drawer.... 'We might be back,' the leader said. On the way out he threw our mother-of-pearl ashtray over his shoulder, like confetti. We did not speak or move or breathe until we heard their boots against the pavement.99

—quoted in *Facing History and Ourselves*

The anti-Jewish violence that erupted throughout Germany and Austria that night came to be called *Kristallnacht*, or "night of broken glass," because broken glass littered the streets afterward. When daylight came, more than 90 Jews lay dead, hundreds were badly injured, and thousands more were terrorized. The Nazis had forbidden police to interfere while roving bands of thugs destroyed 7,500 Jewish businesses and wrecked over 180 synagogues.

The lawlessness of *Kristallnacht* did not end with the dawn. Following that night of violence, the Gestapo, the government's secret police, arrested at least 20,000 wealthy Jews, releasing them only if they

The Final Solution

Before the war, a Jewish family in Germany poses for a photograph during a family outing. Few members of this family would survive the war.

On *Kristallnacht*, roaming bands of thugs destroyed Jewish property and menaced Jewish families throughout Germany.

agreed to emigrate and surrender all their possessions. The state also confiscated insurance payments owed to Jewish owners of ruined businesses.

The week after *Kristallnacht,* Nazi interior minister Hermann Goering added insult to injury by fining the Jewish community to pay for the damage. "German Jewry," he proclaimed "shall, as punishment for their abominable crimes . . . have to make a contribution for one billion marks. . . . I would like to say that I would not like to be a Jew in Germany."

Jewish Refugees Try to Flee *Kristallnacht* and its aftermath marked a significant escalation in the Nazi policy of persecution against the Jews. Many Jews, including Frederick Morton's family, decided that it was time to leave and fled to the United States. Between 1933, when Hitler took power, and the start of World War II in 1939, some 350,000 Jews escaped Nazi-controlled Germany. These emigrants included prominent scientists such as Albert Einstein and businesspeople like Otto Frank, who resettled his family in Amsterdam in 1933. Otto's daughter Anne Frank would later keep a diary of her family's life in hiding after the Nazis overran the Netherlands.

By 1938 the American consulate in Stuttgart, Germany, had a backlog of over 100,000 visa applications from Jews trying to leave Germany and come to the United States. Following the Nazi *Anschluss,* 3,000 Austrian Jews each day applied for American visas.

Many never received visas to the United States or to the other countries where they applied. As a result, millions of Jews remained trapped in Nazi-dominated Europe.

Several factors limited Jewish immigration to the United States. First, Nazi orders prohibited Jews from taking more than about four dollars out of Germany. Second, many countries refused to accept Jewish immigrants. In the United States, laws restricted granting a visa to anyone "likely to become a public charge." American customs officials tended to assume that this applied to Jews since Germany had forced them to leave any wealth behind. High unemployment rates in the 1930s also made immigration politically unpopular. Few Americans wanted to raise immigration quotas, even to accommodate European refugees. The existing immigration policy allowed only a total of 150,000 immigrants annually, with a fixed quota from each country. The law permitted no exceptions for refugees or victims of persecution.

At an international conference on refugees in 1938, several European countries, the United States, and Latin America stated their regret that they could not take in more of Germany's Jews without raising their immigration quotas. Meanwhile, Nazi propaganda chief Joseph Goebbels announced that "if there is any country that believes it has not enough Jews, I shall gladly turn over to it all our Jews." Hitler also declared himself "ready to put all these criminals at the disposal of these countries . . . even on luxury ships."

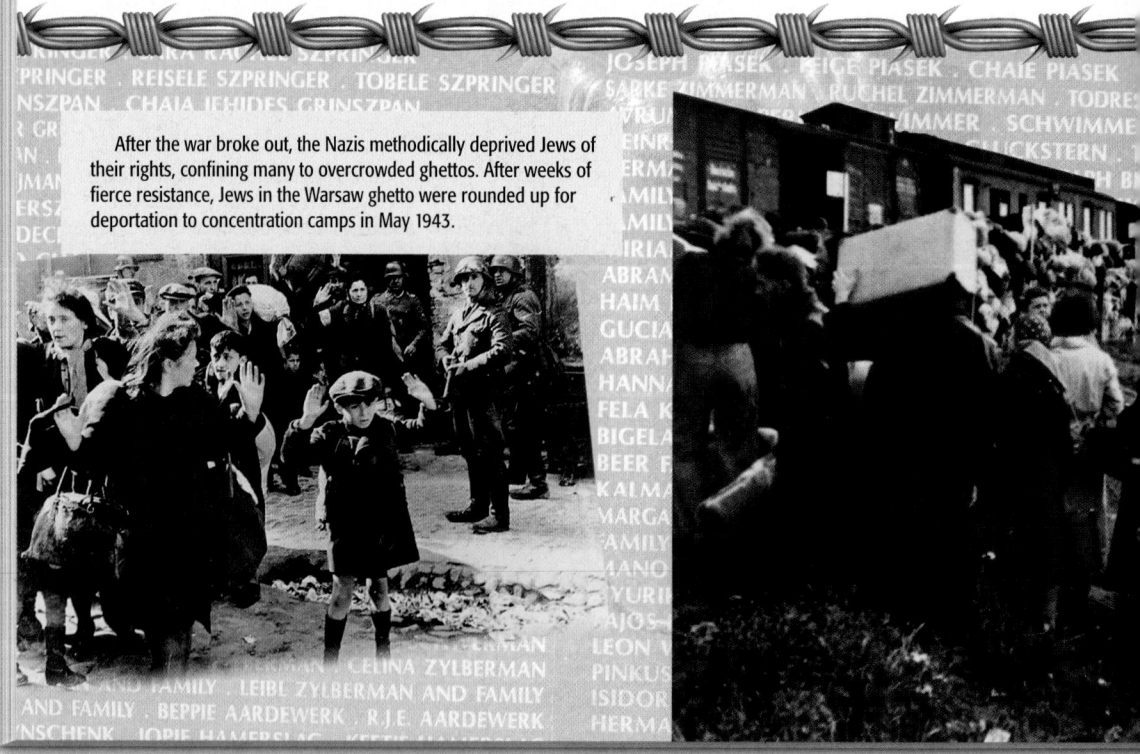

After the war broke out, the Nazis methodically deprived Jews of their rights, confining many to overcrowded ghettos. After weeks of fierce resistance, Jews in the Warsaw ghetto were rounded up for deportation to concentration camps in May 1943.

Did You Know?

From 1933 to 1938, the United States accepted over 100,000 German Jewish refugees, more than any other single nation. Among them was fifteen-year-old Henry Kissinger, who later became Secretary of State and a winner of the Nobel Peace Prize.

As war loomed in 1939, many ships departed from Germany crammed with Jews desperate to escape. Some of their visas, however, had been forged or sold illegally, and Mexico, Paraguay, Argentina, and Costa Rica all denied access to Jews with such documents. So too did the United States.

On May 27, 1939, the SS *St. Louis* entered the harbor in Havana, Cuba, with 930 Jewish refugees on board. Most of these passengers hoped to go to the United States eventually, but they had certificates improperly issued by Cuba's director of immigration giving them permission to land in Cuba. When the ships arrived in Havana, the Cuban government, partly in response to anti-Semitic sentiment stirred up by Nazi propaganda, revoked the certificates and refused to let the refugees come ashore. For several days, the ship's captain steered his ship in circles off the coast of Florida, awaiting official permission to dock at a United States port. Denied such permission, the ship turned back toward Europe on June 6. The forlorn passengers finally disembarked in France, Holland, Belgium, and Great Britain. Within two years, the first three of these countries fell under Nazi domination. Many of the refugees brought to these countries aboard the SS *St. Louis* perished in the Nazis' "final solution."

✓ **Reading Check** **Analyzing** Why did many Jews remain in Germany even though they were persecuted?

The Final Solution

Main Idea Hitler's atrocities included sending millions of Jews to concentration camps and extermination camps.

Reading Connection Explain your opinion on forcing political prisoners to work hard labor. Read on to discover more about the work camps the Nazis built.

On January 20, 1942, 15 Nazi leaders met at the **Wannsee Conference,** held in a Berlin suburb, to determine the "final solution of the Jewish question." Previous "solutions" had included rounding up Jews, Gypsies, and Slavs from conquered areas, shooting them, and piling them into mass graves. Another **method** required forcing Jews and other "undesirables" into trucks and then piping in exhaust fumes to kill them. These methods, however, had proven too slow and inefficient for the Nazis. The T4 Project, set up by Hitler, used various methods to kill people with disabilities that were in the government's care in an effort to find the method Nazis would use at extermination camps.

At Wannsee, the Nazis made plans to round up Jews from the vast areas of Nazi-controlled Europe and take them to detention centers known as **concentration camps.** There, healthy individuals would work as slave

W **Writing Support**

Narrative Writing Ask students to imagine that they are Jewish refugees on board the SS *St. Louis.* Tell them to write letters home to a loved one describing their ordeal. OL CA 11WS1.1; 11WS1.2

U **Universal Access**

English Learners Have students locate the major concentration and extermination camps and calculate the distance of each from the nearest large city. Then ask students to discuss how residents of the cities must have reacted, what they must have known, and why they did not act to rescue the people in the camps. EL

✓ **Reading Check**

Answer: Jews remained because of restrictions on immigration to other countries, because they thought conditions would improve, because Germany was their home, or because they either had no money or their savings would be lost if they emigrated.

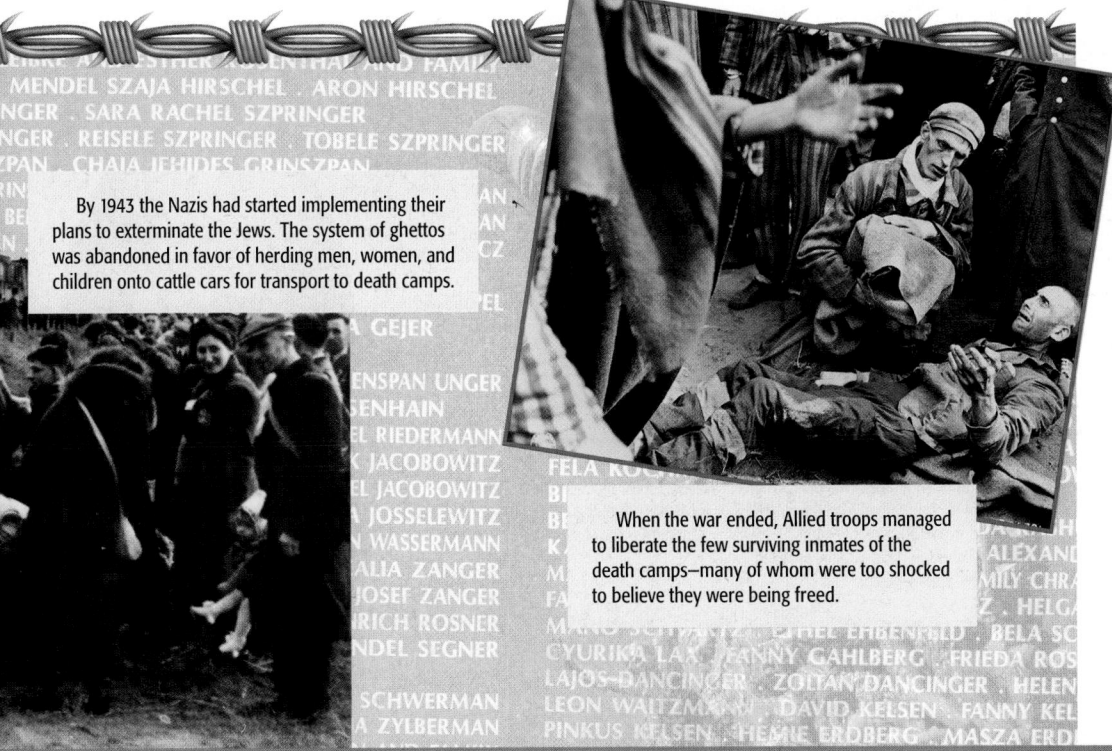

By 1943 the Nazis had started implementing their plans to exterminate the Jews. The system of ghettos was abandoned in favor of herding men, women, and children onto cattle cars for transport to death camps.

When the war ended, Allied troops managed to liberate the few surviving inmates of the death camps—many of whom were too shocked to believe they were being freed.

Did You Know?

When trains heading for concentration camps stopped at railway stations, citizens who tried to give water to the Jews on board were prevented from doing so by armed guards.

Review the Big Idea

Review the Big Idea for this section, "The fate of nations is forever changed by monumental world events." Tell students that wars have always involved the killing of innocent civilians. Ask students to explain what made the killing of the Jewish people by the Nazis in World War II different. Based on the class discussion, have students write essays that compare and contrast the collateral killing of civilians during a war with the intentional killing of people in concentration and execution camps. **OL**

CA 11WA2.3b

R Reading Strategy

Identifying Central Issues
Journalist C.L. Sulzberger reported that after General Eisenhower first visited a concentration camp, "He cabled Washington and London to send journalists and members of Congress and Parliament to Germany as soon as possible." Eisenhower wanted no one to doubt the extent of the atrocities that had been committed. His fears have been partly justified, for today some individuals insist that the Holocaust did not take place. Have students research who has tried to deny the Holocaust and how their denials have been received. Discuss their findings in class. **OL**

Answers and Additional Support

554

---

laborers until they dropped dead of exhaustion, disease, or malnutrition. Most others, including the elderly, the infirm, and young children, would be sent to **extermination camps,** attached to many of the concentration camps, to be executed in massive gas chambers.

Concentration Camps The Nazis had established their first concentration camps in 1933 to jail political opponents. After the war began, the Nazis built concentration camps throughout Europe.

Buchenwald, one of the first and largest concentration camps, was built near the town of Weimar in Germany in 1937. During its operation, over 200,000 prisoners worked 12-hour shifts as slave laborers in nearby factories. Though Buchenwald had no gas chambers, hundreds of prisoners died there every month as a result of exhaustion and the horrible living conditions.

Leon Bass, a young American soldier, described viewing a barracks in Buchenwald at the end of the war. Built to hold 50 people, the room had housed more than 150, with bunks built almost to the ceiling. Bass recalled:

> ❝I looked at a bottom bunk and there I saw one man. He was too weak to get up; he could just barely turn his head. He was skin and bones. He looked like a skeleton; and his eyes were deep set. He didn't utter a sound; he just looked at me with those eyes, and they still haunt me today.❞
>
> –quoted in *Facing History and Ourselves*

Extermination Camps After the Wannsee Conference, the Nazis built extermination facilities in a number of the concentration camps, mostly in Poland, to kill Jews more efficiently. At these camps, including the infamous Treblinka and Auschwitz, Jews were the Nazis' main victims. Auschwitz alone housed about 100,000 people in 300 prison barracks. Its gas chambers, built to kill 2,000 people at a time, sometimes gassed 12,000 people in a day. Of the estimated 1,600,000 people who died at Auschwitz, about 1,300,000 were Jews. The other 300,000 were Poles, Soviet prisoners-of-war, and Gypsies.

R Upon arrival at Auschwitz, healthy prisoners such as Mira Ryczke were selected for slave labor. Elderly or people with disabilities, the sick, and mothers and children went immediately to the gas chambers, after which their bodies were burned in giant crematoriums. In her memoirs, Ryczke described "columns of people marching slowly toward the gas chambers" and "the horrible stench in the air—the smell of burning human flesh. I have never forgotten that smell."

Profiles IN HISTORY

Albert Einstein
1879–1955

Among the Jews who left Nazi Germany in the early 1930s was Albert Einstein, whose brilliant scientific theories revolutionized physics. Einstein gained international fame in 1919 when the Royal Society of London announced that calculations had supported his general theory of relativity. Einstein's fame increased after he won the Nobel Prize for Physics in 1921. Lecture invitations poured in from around the world.

Einstein never actively practiced Judaism, but he did proudly identify himself as a Jew. As anti-Semitism took hold in Germany, Einstein's worldwide fame contrasted with the insults he faced in Berlin for practicing "Bolshevism [Communism] in physics." His public support for Zionism, the right of Jews to settle in Palestine (later Israel), aroused further anger among Nazis.

Soon after Hitler became Germany's chancellor in 1933, Einstein renounced his citizenship and left Germany for Belgium. Fears for his life prompted friends to take him secretly by private yacht to England. He later settled in Princeton, New Jersey.

A pacifist who had opposed World War I, Einstein ironically saw his scientific ideas applied to the creation of a powerful and destructive weapon, the atomic bomb. After the United States detonated the first atomic bomb in combat over Hiroshima, Japan, in 1945, Einstein devoted his final years to promoting pacifism. The scientist's greatest legacy, however, would be the revolutionary scientific discoveries he had made in the early 1900s. As Einstein himself had observed, "Politics are for the moment. An equation is for eternity."

Profiles IN HISTORY

Background: Because they were persecuted in Germany, a number of brilliant Jewish German scientists immigrated to the United States in the 1930s.

Ask: When and why did Einstein leave Germany? *(in 1933 when Hitler became chancellor; Hitler's policies were anti-Semitic)*

NATIONAL GEOGRAPHIC **Jewish Losses, 1939–1945**

Geography Skills

1. **Interpreting Maps** What country had the highest number of Jews in its population killed?
2. **Applying Geography Skills** A relatively low percentage of Italy's Jewish population died in the Holocaust. From this information, how would you compare Fascists and Nazis in terms of their Jewish policies?

DENMARK 500
North Sea
Baltic Sea
BALTIC STATES 228,000
RUSSIAN S.S.R. 107,000
NETHERLANDS 105,000
BYELORUSSIAN S.S.R. 245,000
BELGIUM 40,000
GERMANY AND AUSTRIA 210,000
POLAND 3,000,000
CZECHOSLOVAKIA 155,000
UKRAINIAN S.S.R. 900,000
FRANCE 90,000
HUNGARY 450,000
ITALY 8,000
ROMANIA 300,000
YUGOSLAVIA 26,000
Black Sea
Adriatic Sea
BULGARIA 14,000
GREECE 54,000

Percentage of Jewish Population Annihilated
83–90
50–60
65–77
11–26

FRANCE 90,000 **Number of Jews killed under Nazi racial policies**

0 — 200 miles
0 — 200 kilometers
Lambert Azimuthal Equal-Area projection

In only a few years, Jewish culture, which had existed in Europe for over 1,000 years, had been virtually obliterated by the Nazis in the lands they conquered. Despite exhaustive debate, there is still great controversy about why and how an event so horrifying as the Holocaust could have occurred. No consensus has been reached, but most historians point to a number of factors: the German people's sense of injury after World War I; severe economic problems; Hitler's control over the German nation; the lack of a strong tradition of representative government in Germany; German fear of Hitler's secret police; and a long history of anti-Jewish prejudice and discrimination in Europe.

Reading Check **Summarizing** What methods did Hitler use to try to exterminate Europe's Jewish population?

HISTORY Online **Study Central**

For help with the concepts in this section of *American Vision: Modern Times* go to **tav.mt.glencoe.com** and click on **Study Central.**

SECTION 3 ASSESSMENT

Checking for Understanding

1. **Vocabulary** Define: Holocaust, implement, prohibit, method, concentration camp, extermination camp.
2. **People and Terms** Identify: Shoah, Nuremberg Laws, Wannsee Conference.
3. **List** the groups of people who were persecuted by the Nazis.

Reviewing Big Ideas

4. **Examining** What are some factors that attempt to explain the Holocaust?

Critical Thinking

5. **Historical Analysis** **Analyzing** What responsibilities did you think other nations had to stop the persecution of Jews in Germany and German held territories of Europe? **CA HI4**
6. **Organizing** Use a graphic organizer similar to the one below to list the methods used to try to exterminate Europe's Jewish population.

Extermination Methods

Analyzing Visuals

7. **Analyzing Photographs** Study the photographs of the Final Solution on pages 551–553. How do the photographs show the systematic destruction of Jewish life?

Writing About History

8. **Descriptive Writing** Take on the role of a person living in Germany during *Kristallnacht.* Write a diary entry describing the events of that night. Include a description of events during the days following *Kristallnacht* as well. **CA 11WA2.1a; 11WA2.1c; 11WA2.3a**

CHAPTER 11 A World in Flames **555**

SECTION 3 ASSESSMENT ANSWERS

1. Content vocabulary is boldfaced and highlighted in yellow. Academic vocabulary is boldfaced.
2. Shoah (p. 550), Nuremberg Laws (p. 550), Wannsee Conference (p. 554)
3. Jews, disabled, Gypsies, homosexuals, Slavic peoples
4. Hitler's dictatorship; European anti-Semitism, propaganda, fear
5. Answers will vary. Students should clearly identify and support their opinions.
6. gas chambers, malnutrition, untreated disease, worked to death
7. shows stages of Hitler's campaign, from civil discrimination and violence to deportation to camps
8. Students' diary entries should focus on events surrounding *Kristallnacht,* as told from a Jewish perspective.

ASSESS

Resources for page 555

Use these resources to assess student mastery.

Section Quiz 11-3

Reading Essentials and Study Guide 11-3

Interactive Tutor Self-Assessment CD-ROM

California Standards Practice, Grade 11

Geography Skills

Answers:
1. Poland (3 million)
2. Fascists were not as anti-Semitic as the Nazis.

Geography Skills Practice Ask: Which of the Soviet Socialist Republics had the smallest percentage of their Jewish population killed under the Nazis? *(Russian S.S.R.)*

Reading Check

Answer: Some died of exhaustion, disease, or malnutrition in concentration camps. Others were executed in gas chambers at extermination camps.

HISTORY Online

Study Central provides audio summaries, interactive games, and online graphic organizers to help students review section content.

CLOSE

Summarizing Have students summarize the gradually intensifying steps of Hitler's campaign against the Jews. **OL**

FOCUS

SKILLBUILDER ACTIVITY

Project **Daily Focus Skills Transparency 11-4** and have students answer the question.

Guide to Reading

Understanding Vocabulary: Have students write sentences that contain each of the content and academic vocabulary words.

Answers to Graphic: Britain's struggle with Germany, Japan's attack on Pearl Harbor

Unpacking the Standards

Students will be able to:

- Explain how President Roosevelt aided Great Britain despite neutrality.
- Analyze the desire of isolationists to keep the United States out of the war.
- Discuss how the United States grew more involved in the fringes of World War II.
- Describe how Japan's attack on Pearl Harbor brought the United States into the war.

Answers and Additional Support

556

SECTION 4 America Enters the War

Guide to Reading

Connection
In the previous section, you learned about the Holocaust the Jews faced in Germany. In this section, you will discover how the United States was drawn into the war.

Main Idea
- Despite the Neutrality Act of 1939, FDR supported the British with a destroyer-for-bases deal. (p. 557)
- In the midst of a debate about whether America should remain neutral, Roosevelt was elected for a third term. (p. 558)
- Roosevelt and Congress continued to support the British through the Lend-Lease Act and the idea of a hemispheric defense zone. (p. 559)

- Angered by American policies that aided the British and an embargo on Japanese goods, the Japanese attacked the naval base at Pearl Harbor, forcing the United States to declare war. (p. 561)

Content Vocabulary
hemispheric defense zone, strategic materials

Academic Vocabulary
eliminate, policy, primary

People and Terms to Identify
America First Committee, Lend-Lease Act, Atlantic Charter

Reading Objectives
- **Explain** how Roosevelt helped Britain while maintaining official neutrality.
- **Trace** the events that led to increasing tensions, and ultimately war, between the United States and Japan.

Reading Strategy
Organizing As you read about the efforts of the United States to stay neutral in the war, complete a graphic organizer similar to the one below by naming two events that shifted American opinion toward helping the Allies.

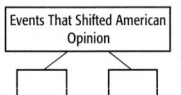
Events That Shifted American Opinion

Preview of Events

♦September 1940	♦March 1941	♦August 1941	♦December 1941

September 1940
FDR makes destroyers-for-bases deal with Britain

March 1941
Congress passes Lend-Lease Act

August 1941
Roosevelt and Churchill sign Atlantic Charter

October 1941
Germans sink *Reuben James*

December 7, 1941
Japan attacks Pearl Harbor

The following are the main History–Social Science Standards covered in this section.

11.7.1 Examine the origins of American involvement in the war, with an emphasis on the events that precipitated the attack on Pearl Harbor.

11.7.4 Analyze Roosevelt's foreign policies during World War II (e.g., Four Freedoms speech).

❦ The Big Idea ❦

The fate of nations is forever changed by monumental world events. While Jews faced the Holocaust in Germany, Americans continued to debate isolationist policy. President Roosevelt declared the United States officially neutral at the beginning of the war, but he supported laws that allowed him to help Great Britain. He was able to make a destroyers-for-bases deal with Britain and pushed through the Lend-Lease Act. To establish safe shipping in the Atlantic, he developed the idea of a hemispheric defense zone. At the same time, Roosevelt began policies to discourage Japan from attacking the British Empire in the Pacific, restricting exports to Japan and extending aid to China. When Japan sent troops to Indochina, the president added further restrictions. Japan responded by attacking the U.S. naval base in Pearl Harbor, Hawaii.

SECTION RESOURCES

📁 Print Material
- Reproducible Lesson Plan 11-4
- Guided Reading Activity 11-4
- Reading Essentials and Study Guide 11-4
- Active Reading Note-Taking Guide 11-4

🔖 Transparencies
- Daily Focus Skills Transparency 11-4
- Section Graphic Organizer Transparency 11-4

Technology
- 🔘 Interactive Tutor Self-Assessment CD-ROM
- 🔘 Exam*View*® Pro Testmaker CD-ROM
- 🔘 Presentation Plus! CD-ROM

FDR Supports England

 Main Idea Despite the Neutrality Act of 1939, FDR supported the British with a destroyer-for-bases deal.

Reading Connection Should presidents be able to work around the decisions of Congress? Read on to learn how Roosevelt followed his own instincts to help Britain.

On December 7, 1941, the Japanese attacked the Pearl Harbor naval base in Hawaii. The attack surprised many Americans. Most people had believed that Germany posed the greatest danger.

★ An American Story ★

December 7, 1941, dawned like any other Sunday in Hawaii, where teenager Daniel Inouye lived with his family. Like other Americans who lived through the experience, Inouye would never forget what he was doing the moment American isolationism ended:

❝As soon as I finished brushing my teeth and pulled on my trousers, I automatically clicked on the little radio that stood on the shelf above my bed. I remember that I was buttoning my shirt and looking out the window . . . when the hum of the warming set gave way to a frenzied voice. 'This is no test,' the voice cried out. 'Pearl Harbor is being bombed by the Japanese!'❞

The Inouye family ran outside and gazed toward the naval base at Pearl Harbor:

"And then we saw the planes. They came zooming up out of that sea of gray smoke, flying north toward where we stood and climbing into the bluest part of the sky, and they came in twos and threes, in neat formations, and if it hadn't been for that red ball on their wings, the rising sun of the Japanese Empire, you could easily believe that they were Americans, flying over in precise military salute.❞

–quoted in *Eyewitness to America*

What Americans did not realize was that the causes of the Japanese attack could be traced back more than 40 years to the tension between the United States and Japan over the Open Door Policy. This tension escalated two years earlier with President Roosevelt's policies for helping Britain against Germany.

The Neutrality Act of 1939 President Roosevelt officially proclaimed the United States neutral two days after Britain and France declared war on Germany. Despite this declaration, he was determined to do all he could to help the two countries in their struggle against Hitler. Soon after the war began, Roosevelt called Congress into a special session to revise the neutrality laws.

He asked Congress to **eliminate** the ban on arms sales to nations at war. Public opinion strongly supported the president. Congress passed the new law, but isolationists demanded a price for the revision. Under the Neutrality Act of 1939, warring nations could buy weapons from the United States only if they paid cash and carried the arms on their own ships.

Destroyers-for-Bases Deal In the spring of 1940, the United States faced its first test in remaining neutral. In May British Prime Minister Winston Churchill began asking Roosevelt to transfer old American destroyers to Britain. Britain had lost nearly half its destroyers and needed more to protect its cargo ships from German submarines and to block any German attempt to invade Britain.

Determined to give Churchill the destroyers, Roosevelt used a loophole in the provision of the Neutrality Act that required cash for purchases. In exchange for the right to build American bases on British-controlled Newfoundland, Bermuda, and islands in the Caribbean, Roosevelt sent 50 old American destroyers to Britain. Since the deal did not involve an actual sale, the Neutrality Act did not apply. On September 3, 1940, he announced his action to an astonished press.

✔ **Reading Check** **Examining** How were the Neutrality Acts revised?

Daniel Inouye after joining the U.S. Army's 442nd Infantry ➤

CHAPTER 11 A World in Flames **557**

Did You Know?

Isolationist sentiment in the United States arose in part from the fact that the nation was an ocean away from the conflicts in both Europe and Asia.

TEACH

R₁ **Reading Strategy**

Activating Prior Knowledge Remind students how President Wilson tried to maintain neutrality during World War I. **Ask: Which president was more successful in maintaining a neutral stance?** *(Students may say that neither president was successful, since neutrality was violated in both cases. Some students may say that Wilson was more careful in his neutral actions than Roosevelt was.)* OL

R₂ **Reading Strategy**

Scaffolding—Academic Vocabulary The word *revise* was introduced in Chapter 1, Section 3. Ask a student to define the word. BL

W **Writing Support**

Persuasive Writing Tell students to imagine that they are living during the time the destroyers-for-bases deal was announced in the United States. Have students choose to be either a supporter of American neutrality or someone who wishes the United States to help its European allies. Students should write letters to their newspaper that reflect their selected opinions and explain their stance to the newspaper editor. *(Students' letters will vary but should be based on reasonable arguments.)* OL

CA 11WA2.3b

✔ **Reading Check**

Answer: They were adjusted to allow the United States to sell arms to warring countries as long as they paid cash and carried the goods away on their own ships.

Answers and Additional Support

S Skill Practice

Identifying Point of View
Organize the class into three groups representing the views in the isolationist debate. Assign one group to be the Fight for Freedom Committee, one to be the Committee to Defend America by Aiding the Allies, and one to be the America First Committee. Have each group develop a one-paragraph position statement and present it to the class. Discuss the reasons for the varying opinions as a class. **OL** **CA HR3; HR4; HI1**

R Reading Strategy

Using Context Clues Ask students to define the word *unprecedented.* Provide them with the following tips to use context to determine meaning: look before, at, and after the unfamiliar word for context clues; connect what you already know with what the author has written; predict a possible meaning; apply the meaning in the sentence; decide if the meaning makes sense; if the meaning does not make sense, try again. After the students have gone through this process, ask them to write an improved definition. **BL**

✓ Reading Check

Answer: Americans wanted to stay with a president they knew during this period of unrest.

Analyzing *Political Cartoons*

Peace Above All Many Americans were willing to help European democracies but did not want to sell them arms. In what ways did the United States assist these nations?

S The Isolationist Debate

Main Idea In the midst of a debate about whether America should remain neutral, Roosevelt was elected for a third term.

Reading Connection Do you believe that holders of public office should be limited in the number of terms they serve? Read on to find out about Roosevelt's decision to break with the traditional two terms of office.

Widespread public acceptance of the destroyers-for-bases deal demonstrated a marked change in American public opinion. Americans were now more open to the idea of assisting the Allies. The shift began after the German invasion of France and the rescue of Allied forces at Dunkirk. By July 1940 most Americans favored offering limited aid to the Allies.

The Range of Opinion American opinion was hardly unanimous. While most people were open to aiding the Allies, there were those who believed the United States should not offer even limited assistance. In fact, beginning in the spring of 1940, a spirited

debate took place between people who wanted greater American involvement in World War II and those who felt that the United States should remain neutral.

At one extreme was the Fight for Freedom Committee, a group which urged the repeal of all neutrality laws and wanted stronger action against Germany. Closer to the center, the Committee to Defend America by Aiding the Allies, headed by journalist William Allen White, pressed for increased American aid to the Allies but opposed armed intervention.

Roosevelt's destroyers-for-bases deal led to the founding of the **America First Committee** in September of 1940. The America First Committee was a staunchly isolationist group that firmly opposed any American intervention or aid to the Allies. The group had many famous members, including aviator Charles Lindbergh, former governor Philip LaFollette, and Senator Gerald Nye. The committee attempted to influence elections and public opinion in support of isolationism with speeches and publications.

The Election of 1940 The heated debate over neutrality took place in the midst of the 1940 presidential election campaign. For several months Americans had wondered whether President Roosevelt would follow long-standing tradition by retiring at the end of his second term. With the United States in a precarious position, many people feared that a change of leaders might not be in the country's best interest. Roosevelt decided to run for an unprecedented third term.

During the campaign, FDR steered a careful course between neutrality and intervention. The Republican nominee, Wendell Willkie, did the same, promising that he too would stay out of the war but assist the Allies. The voters re-elected Roosevelt by a wide margin, preferring to stick with a president they knew during this crisis period.

✓ Reading Check **Analyzing** Why did Roosevelt win an unprecedented third term in office?

Analyzing *Political Cartoons*

Answer: instituted a cash-and-carry policy for arms sales to France and Britain; Roosevelt's destroyers-for-bases deal

Edging Toward War

Main Idea Roosevelt and Congress continued to support the British through the Lend-Lease Act and the idea of a hemispheric defense zone.

Reading Connection How far from its shores should a nation defend its borders? Read on to discover how Roosevelt expanded the area of American defense.

With the election safely over, President Roosevelt was able to expand the nation's role in the war. Britain was fighting for democracy, he said, and the United States had to help Britain in this endeavor. Speaking to Congress, the president listed the "Four Freedoms" for which both the United States and Great Britain stood: freedom of speech, freedom of worship, freedom from want, and freedom from fear. *(See page 999 for an excerpt from this speech.)*

The Lend-Lease Act By December 1940, Great Britain had run out of funds to wage its war against Germany. Since Britain was unable to provide the cash needed to purchase weapons, President Roosevelt came up with a way to remove the cash requirement of the Neutrality Act.

With the **Lend-Lease Act,** the United States would be able to lend or lease arms to any country considered "vital to the defense of the United States." This act meant that the United States could send much needed weapons to Britain without cash payment if Britain promised to return or pay rent for them after the war.

The president warned that if Britain fell, an "unholy alliance" of Germany, Japan, and Italy would keep trying to conquer the world, and then "all of us in all the Americas would be living at the point of a gun." The president argued that the United States should become the "great arsenal of democracy" to keep the British fighting and make it unnecessary for Americans to go to war.

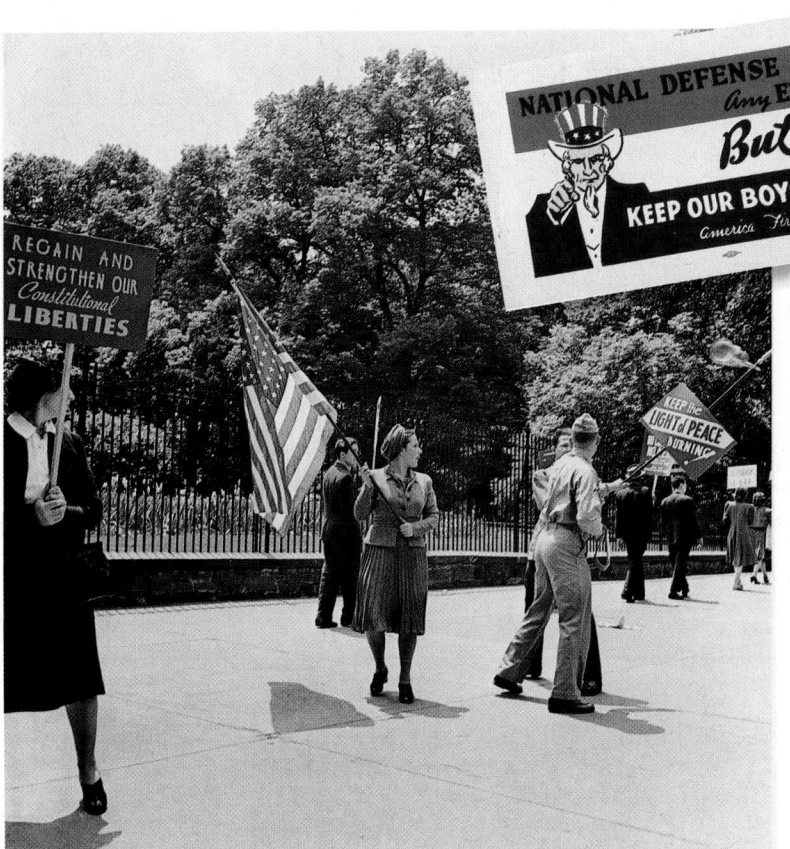

Picturing **History**

Neutrality Debate The America First Committee strongly opposed the increasingly weak neutrality of the United States. Here an American soldier confronts an isolationist marching outside the White House. How did the Lend-Lease Act further weaken the nation's official neutrality?

U Universal Access

Visual/Spatial Have students work in pairs to create charts listing Roosevelt's "Four Freedoms" and their basis in the U.S. Bill of Rights. Students should then describe in brief sentences how Germany and Japan limited these freedoms. **OL**

R Reading Strategy

Determining the Main Idea Ask students to read about the Lend-Lease Act discussed on this page. **Ask: After reading the terms of this agreement between Great Britain and the United States, do you think that the United States was truly remaining neutral?** *(Students' answers will vary.)* **OL**
CA 11RC2.5

Review the Big Idea

Review the Big Idea for this section, "The fate of nations is forever changed by monumental world events." As students read the text under the heading "Edging Toward War," ask them to list events and decisions that pushed the U.S. closer to involvement in the war. **OL**

 Resources for page 559

*Have students read more about President Roosevelt's "Four Freedoms" speech in the **Primary Source Reading 11-2.***

Picturing **History**

Answer: It involved the United States in the war by lending or leasing arms to any country fighting Hitler.
Ask: What messages were protesters trying to convey? *(support for the country but not for the war)*

S Skill Practice

Conducting Research Ask students to research how much aid under the Lend-Lease program went to Great Britain and how much aid the Soviet Union received. Tell students to graph the data they discover. Their data graphs can be displayed in the classroom. **OL** **CA HR4**

U Universal Access

English Learners Supply students with maps of the Atlantic Ocean and tell them to use markers or colored pencils to shade in where they think the hemispheric defense zone might have been. **Ask:** Does this division seem fair to you? Do you agree with Roosevelt's decision to establish this zone? Why or why not? (Students' answers will vary.) **EL**

Answers and Additional Support

The America First Committee disagreed, but Congress passed the Lend-Lease Act by a wide margin. By the time the program ended, the United States had contributed more than $40 billion in weapons, vehicles, and other supplies to the Allied war effort.

S While shipments of supplies to Britain began at once, lend-lease aid eventually went to the Soviet Union as well. After calling off the invasion of Britain, Hitler returned to his original goal of carving out lebensraum for Germany in eastern Europe. In June 1941, in violation of the Nazi-Soviet pact, Hitler launched a massive invasion of the Soviet Union. Although Churchill detested communism and considered Stalin a harsh dictator, he vowed that any person or state "who fights against Nazism will have our aid." Roosevelt, too, supported this **policy.**

The Hemispheric Defense Zone Congressional approval of the Lend-Lease Act did not solve the problem of how to get American arms and supplies to Britain. German submarines patrolling the Atlantic Ocean were sinking hundreds of thousands of tons of shipping each month, and the British navy simply did not have enough ships in the Atlantic to stop them.

U Roosevelt could not simply order the U.S. Navy to protect British cargo ships, since the United States was still technically neutral. Instead, he developed the idea of a **hemispheric defense zone.** Roosevelt declared that the entire western half of the Atlantic was part of the Western Hemisphere and, therefore, neutral. He then ordered the U.S. Navy to patrol the western Atlantic and reveal the locations of German submarines to the British.

The Atlantic Charter In August 1941, Roosevelt and Churchill met face-to-face onboard American and British warships anchored near Newfoundland. During these meetings, the two men agreed on the text of the **Atlantic Charter.** It committed the two leaders to a postwar world of democracy, nonaggression, free

NATIONAL GEOGRAPHIC **Pearl Harbor, Hawaii, December 7, 1941**

PACIFIC OCEAN

Kaena Point

FIRST WAVE

Kahuku Point

Opana radar station

Kahuku

Waialua

Haleiwa Field

Laie

SECOND WAVE

Waianae

Wahiawa

Wheeler Field
7:51, 9:10 A.M.

Ford Island
Naval Air Station
7:55, 9:02 A.M.

Nanakuli

Waipahu

Kaneohe
Naval Air Station
7:53, 8:55 A.M.

Ewa Marine Corps
Air Station
7:53, 9:05 A.M.

Pearl
City

Ewa Beach

Hickam Field
7:55, 9:05 A.M.

Honolulu

Battleship Row

Kaneohe

O   A   H   U

Kailua

Bellows Field
8:30, 9:00 A.M.

Diamond Head

First wave of Japanese aircraft
Second wave of Japanese aircraft
7:51 A.M. Time of initial attack (First wave)
8:55 A.M. Time of initial attack (Second wave)
Airfield
Airfield attacked
Radar site
Town

Did You Know?

After Hitler's invasion, nearly 40 percent of the Soviet Union's 170 million citizens were caught behind enemy lines.

Did You Know?

Though it was unofficial and nonbinding, the Atlantic Charter brought a much-needed morale boost to the Allies and later became the foundation for the formation of the United Nations.

trade, economic advancement, and freedom of the seas. Churchill later said that FDR pledged to "force an 'incident' . . . which would justify him in opening hostilities" with Germany.

An incident quickly presented itself. In early September a German U-boat fired on the American destroyer *Greer*, which had been radioing the U-boat's position to the British. Roosevelt promptly responded by ordering American ships to follow a "shoot-on-sight" policy toward German submarines.

The Germans escalated hostilities with the United States the following month when they targeted two American destroyers. One of them, the *Reuben James*, broke in two after being torpedoed. It sank into the frigid waters of the North Atlantic, where 115 sailors died. As the end of 1941 grew near, Germany and the United States continued a tense standoff in the North Atlantic.

✓ Reading Check **Evaluating** How did the Lend-Lease Act help the Allied war effort?

Japan Attacks the United States

Main Idea Angered by American policies that aided the British and an embargo on Japanese goods, the Japanese attacked the naval base at Pearl Harbor, forcing the United States to declare war.

Reading Connection Do you know of a situation in which a person became involved in a dispute because a friend or family member was involved? Read on to learn how Japan and its allies were able to draw the United States into a world conflict.

Despite the growing tensions in the Atlantic, the Japanese attack on Pearl Harbor was what finally brought the United States into World War II. Ironically, Japan's decision to attack the United States was a direct result of Roosevelt's efforts to help Britain in its war against Germany.

"above and beyond the call of duty"

DORIE MILLER
Received the Navy Cross at Pearl Harbor, May 27, 1942

❶ 6:45 A.M.: The destroyer *Ward* sinks a Japanese midget submarine near the entrance to Pearl Harbor.

❷ 7:02 to 7:39 A.M.: Army radar at Opana tracks a cloud of aircraft approaching from the north. An officer at Fort Shafter concludes it is a flight of B-17s due in from California.

❸ 7:49 A.M.: The first wave of 183 Japanese planes is ordered to attack. The force includes 40 torpedo bombers and 49 high-altitude bombers—each armed with a single projectile—bound for Battleship Row. Other bombers and Zero fighters attack airfields.

❹ 8:55 A.M.: The second wave of 167 planes renews the attack on airfields and ships. Oil tanks and most ship-repair facilities are ignored, an omission the Japanese later regret.

Americans responded heroically to Japan's attack on Pearl Harbor: 16 men received the Medal of Honor, the nation's highest award; 5 were awarded the Distinguished Service Cross; and 69 received the Silver Star. The Navy Cross was awarded to another 51, including Dorie Miller, World War II's first recognized African American hero, who bravely operated an antiaircraft gun on his ship during the Japanese attack.

W **Writing Support**

Persuasive Writing Ask students to imagine that they are President Roosevelt preparing to write a message to Congress explaining why the United States should stop insisting on neutrality and respond to German hostilities with more force. Have students write and present messages to the classroom "Congress." **AL**
CA 11WS1.3

R **Reading Strategy**

Sequencing Information Use the information included on the map to list all of the presented events in chronological order. Have students look for patterns in the path of the Japanese aircraft. **Ask:** How does the path of the second wave of attacks compare with the first wave? Why do you think the Japanese chose to use these particular routes to attack? *(Students' answers will vary.)* **OL** **CA** CS2

✓ Reading Check

Answer: by getting arms to the Allies

ABCNEWS
INTERACTIVE™

VIDEOCASSETTE
Historic America Electronic Field Trips

View **Tape 2, Chapter 8:** "The U.S.S. *Arizona* Memorial."

R₁ Reading Strategy

Organizing Information Have students outline the ways Roosevelt discouraged Japan from attacking the British Empire. *(Answers may vary but should include the Export Control Act, lend-lease aid to China, the freezing of Japanese assets in the United States, and the oil embargo on Japan.)* **OL**

C Critical Thinking

Comparing and Contrasting Remind students of the embargo of scrap metal to Japan ordered by Roosevelt in 1940. The embargo was later extended to other products with military uses. Discuss the embargoes imposed against Iraq in 1990 and Haiti in 1993. Ask students to write their opinions on whether embargoes are successful in preventing war or accomplishing the goals established by the nations that impose them. **OL** **CA 11WS1.3**

R₂ Reading Strategy

Analyzing Maps Provide students with a map of Southeast Asia in 1941. Have them identify the Strait of Malacca. **Ask:** *Why do you think the Strait of Malacca was so important? (Since much of East-West trade went through the strait, its control would allow the Japanese to keep other powers out of the region.)* **OL**

America Embargoes Japan Between August 1939 and December 1941, Roosevelt's **primary** goal was to help Britain and its allies defeat Germany. He knew that one of the problems Britain faced was the need to keep much of its navy in Asia to protect British territories there from Japanese attack. As German submarines began sinking British shipping, the British began moving warships from Southeast Asia to the Atlantic, leaving their empire vulnerable. In response, Roosevelt introduced policies to discourage the Japanese from attacking the British Empire.

Roosevelt began by putting economic pressure on Japan. Japan depended on the United States for many key materials, including scrap iron, steel, and especially oil. Approximately 80 percent of Japan's oil came from the United States. In July 1940, Congress passed the Export Control Act, giving Roosevelt the power to restrict the sale of **strategic materials** (materials important for fighting a war) to other nations. Roosevelt immediately blocked the sale of airplane fuel and scrap iron to Japan. Furious, the Japanese signed an alliance with Germany and Italy, formally becoming a member of the Axis.

In 1941 Roosevelt began sending lend-lease aid to China. Japan had invaded China in 1937, and by 1941, it controlled much of the Chinese coast. Roosevelt hoped that lend-lease aid would enable the Chinese to tie down the Japanese and prevent them from attacking elsewhere. Despite assistance with weapons from the United States, the strategy failed. By July 1941, the Japanese had sent troops into southern Indochina, posing a direct threat to the British Empire. Japanese aircraft were now in position to strike British shipping in the Strait of Malacca and bomb Hong Kong and Singapore.

Roosevelt responded very quickly to the Japanese threat against the British Empire. He froze all Japanese assets in the United States, reduced the amount of oil being shipped to Japan, and sent General Douglas MacArthur to the Philippines to build up American defenses there.

Roosevelt made it clear that he would lift the oil embargo against Japan only if Japan withdrew from Indochina and made peace with China. With the war against China now in jeopardy because of a lack of oil and other resources, the Japanese military began making plans to attack the resource-rich British and Dutch colonies in Southeast Asia. The Japanese also decided to seize the Philippines and to attack the American fleet at Pearl Harbor. They could not risk leaving the United States with a navy in the Pacific to oppose their plans. While the Japanese prepared for war, negotiations with the United States continued, but neither side would back down. On November 26, 1941, six Japanese aircraft carriers, two battleships, and several other warships set sail for Hawaii.

Japan Attacks Pearl Harbor The Japanese government appeared to be continuing negotiations with the United States in good faith. This was part of Japan's strategy to surprise the United States. American intelligence had decoded Japanese communications that made it clear that Japan had no intention of reaching an agreement and, instead, was preparing to go to war against the United States.

◀ *Attack on Pearl Harbor*

562 CHAPTER 11 A World in Flames

Did You Know?

To gain direct access to natural resources, Japanese military leaders aimed to build an empire in the Pacific. The U.S. Pacific Fleet was headquartered at Oahu island in Hawaii—approximately 70 warships, including 8 battleships and 24 auxiliary vessels, were stationed at Pearl Harbor on the island. Thus, Japanese military leaders saw the fleet as an obstacle that had to be destroyed if they were to achieve their goals.

On November 27, American commanders at the Pearl Harbor naval base received a war warning from Washington, but Hawaii was not mentioned as a possible target. It was a great distance from Japan to Hawaii, and Washington officials doubted Japan would try to launch such a long-range attack. This would prove to be a fatal error.

The failure to collect sufficient information and the failure of the branches of the U.S. military to share the available information left Pearl Harbor an open target. The result was devastating. Japan's surprise attack on December 7, 1941, sank or damaged 21 ships of the U.S. Pacific Fleet, including 8 battleships, 3 cruisers, 4 destroyers, and 6 other vessels. The attack also destroyed 188 airplanes and killed 2,403 Americans. Another 1,178 were injured.

On the night of the attack, a gray-faced Roosevelt met with his cabinet to tell them the country now faced the most serious crisis since the outbreak of the Civil War. The next day, the president asked Congress to declare war:

66Yesterday, December 7, 1941—a date which will live in infamy—the United States of America was suddenly and deliberately attacked by the naval and air forces of Japan. . . . I believe I interpret the will of the Congress and of the people when I assert that we will not only defend ourselves to the uttermost, but we will make very certain that this form of treachery shall never endanger us again. . . . No matter how long it may take us . . . the American people in their righteous might will win through to absolute victory.99

—quoted in *Franklin D. Roosevelt: A Rendezvous with Destiny*

Following the president's speech, the Senate voted, unanimously, 82 to 0, and the House 388 to 1 to declare war on Japan.

Germany Declares War

Although Japan was now at war with the United States, Hitler did not have to declare war on the Americans. The terms of the alliance with Japan specified that Germany only had to come to Japan's aid if Japan was attacked, not if Japan attacked another country. Hitler, however, had grown frustrated with the American navy's attacks on German submarines, and he believed the time had come to declare war on the United States.

Hitler greatly underestimated the strength of the United States, and he expected the Japanese to easily defeat the Americans in the Pacific. He hoped that by helping Japan against the United States, he could count on Japanese support against the Soviet Union once the Americans had been beaten. On December 11, Germany and Italy both declared war on the United States.

HISTORY Online

Student Web Activity Visit the *American Vision: Modern Times* Web site at tav.mt.glencoe.com and click on *Student Web Activities—Chapter 11* for an activity on Pearl Harbor.

✓ **Reading Check** **Examining** What finally caused the United States to become involved in World War II?

HISTORY Online **Study Central**

For help with the concepts in this section of *American Vision: Modern Times* go to tav.mt.glencoe.com and click on *Study Central*.

SECTION 4 ASSESSMENT

Checking for Understanding

1. **Vocabulary** Define: eliminate, policy, hemispheric defense zone, primary, strategic materials.

2. **People and Terms** Identify: America First Committee, Lend-Lease Act, Atlantic Charter.

Reviewing Big Ideas

3. **Justifying** After Roosevelt made the destroyers-for-bases deal with Britain, some Americans called him a dictator. Do you think Roosevelt was right or wrong in his actions? Explain your answer.

Critical Thinking

4. **Interpreting** Why was the United States unprepared for Japan's attack on Pearl Harbor?

5. **Organizing** Use a graphic organizer to list how Roosevelt helped Britain while maintaining official neutrality.

Help to Britain

Analyzing Visuals

6. **Analyzing Maps** Study the map on pages 560–561. Based on the geography of Oahu, why was the location of Pearl Harbor selected for a naval base?

Writing About History

7. **Persuasive Writing** Take on the role of an American in 1940. Write a letter to the editor of your newspaper explaining why you think the United States should either remain neutral or become involved in World War II. CA 11WS1.2

ASSESS

Resources for page 563

Use these resources to assess student mastery.

📁 Section Quiz 11-4

📁 Reading Essentials and Study Guide 11-4

💿 Interactive Tutor Self-Assessment CD-ROM

📁 California Standards Practice, Grade 11

HISTORY Online

Objectives and answers to the student activity can be found in the **Web Activity Lesson Plan** at tav.mt.glencoe.com.

✓ **Reading Check**

Answer: attack on Pearl Harbor

HISTORY Online

Study Central provides audio summaries, interactive games, and online graphic organizers to help students review section content.

CLOSE

Organizing Information Have students create chronological summaries explaining the events that eventually led to war between the United States and Japan. BL

SECTION 4 ASSESSMENT ANSWERS

1. Content vocabulary is boldfaced and highlighted in yellow. Academic vocabulary is boldfaced.

2. America First Committee *(p. 558),* Lend-Lease Act *(p. 559),* Atlantic Charter *(p. 560)*

3. Some may say it was important to stop Germany, others that Roosevelt violated the Neutrality Act.

4. The United States was still negotiating with Japan and had failed to collect sufficient information. The U.S. military had not shared information among the various branches.

5. destroyers for bases, Lend-Lease Act, hemispheric defense zone

6. It was sheltered and provided easy access to the ocean.

7. Students' letters will vary but should express clear and reasoned opinions.

563

FOCUS

Understanding Vocabulary

Before students begin reading, point out that difficult or unfamiliar words are footnoted throughout the text.

TEACH

C Critical Thinking

Analyzing Information Have students explain in their own words James Bryant Conant's point of view toward Nazi Germany. Then ask them why Conant comes to the conclusion that "Action is the only answer" in the fight against Germany. Students should identify specific details in the primary source that Conant uses to support his point of view, as well as the conclusion he draws. **OL** **CA** 11RC2.4; 11RC2.5

Answers and Additional Support

Primary Sources
Eyewitness to History

With the onset of World War II in Europe, Americans began to debate whether or not to join the fight against Germany. President Franklin D. Roosevelt argued that the United States had an obligation to aid democracies. Many other Americans disagreed. They wanted nothing to do with international affairs and opposed any actions that would lead to war.

SOURCE 1:

James Bryant Conant, the president of Harvard University, strongly supported Roosevelt. From 1939 on, Conant was involved in the Office of Scientific Research and Development, where he chaired the National Defense Research Council and was central in the development of the atomic bomb. In 1940 he was asked to give his opinion about the world crisis confronting the United States.

Let me ask you to visualize our future as a democratic free people in a world dominated by ruthless **totalitarian**[1] states. There are those who argue that Hitler's war machine, when its task is done in Europe, will be converted to an instrument of peaceful industrial activity. I do not think so. There are those who imagine that a government which has broken promise after promise, which has scorned the Democratic countries and all they stand for, which mocks and laughs at free institutions as a basis for civilization – that such a government can live in a peaceful relationship with the United States. I do not think so.

To my mind a complete Nazi victory over France and England would be, by necessity, but a prelude to Hitler's attempt to dominate the world. If Germany were triumphant, at best there would result an armed truce. . . . Our way of life would be endangered for years to come. . . .

At this moment, today, the war is in effect veering towards our shores. The issue before the United States is, I repeat, can we live as a free, peaceful, relatively unarmed people in a world dominated by the totalitarian states? . . .

. . . Action is the only answer, action which may help immediately, action which will be to the Allies an earnest and encouragement of help to come. . . .

▲ *James Bryant Conant*

SOURCE 2:

The America First Committee opposed the entrance of the United States into World War II. It was frequently asked about the national interests of the American people. In 1941 the Committee gave the following response.

It is difficult, of course, to define our national interests, but it is always safe to assume that our chief national interest is the maintenance of our democracy and the well-being of our own American people. It is true that we have a stake in the maintenance of democracy throughout the world. It is also true that many Americans have commercial interests abroad which they are naturally interested in protecting. It is far from certain, however, that this war or our involvement in it will protect any of those interests.

---

[1] **totalitarian:** a form of government in which the political leader has full control and opposition is outlawed

---

UNIVERSAL ACCESS

Interpersonal Point out to students that the contrasting opinions expressed in the primary sources illustrate the disagreement about whether or not Americans should join World War II. Have students work in pairs and identify in each document the author's main idea or argument. Have each pair organize the information in a three-column chart with the headings *James Bryant Conant, America First Committee,* and *Charles A. Lindbergh.* Then ask student pairs to add the supporting details that each author uses to support the main argument. Finally, students should write one-sentence summaries of each author's point of view about U.S. involvement in World War II. **OL** **CA** 11RC2.4

Our part should be first of all to protect our own democracy. Since experience has taught us that democracy vanishes in wartime, it would seem that the surest way to keep our form of government is to avoid involvement. We should also seek an adequate national defense to make sure that we can maintain our territorial integrity in the event we are attacked by a foreign power.

If, after announcing their intention to stay out of the war, as they have repeatedly done, the American people wish to aid Great Britain, they should do so. But they should make certain to keep aid and direct participation separate.

SOURCE 3:

Charles A. Lindbergh became an international hero in 1927 with the first transatlantic flight. When World War II broke out, he became an outspoken opponent of U.S. involvement. Lindbergh joined the America First Committee and toured the country, giving speeches such as this one reported in the April 24, 1941 New York Times.

It is not only our right, but it is our obligation as American citizens to look at this war objectively and to weigh our chances for success if we should enter it. I have attempted to do this, especially from the standpoint of aviation; and I have been forced to the conclusion that we cannot win this war for England, regardless of how much assistance we send.

I ask you to look at the map of Europe today and see if you can suggest any way in which we could win this war if we entered it. Suppose we had a large army in America, trained and equipped. Where would we send it to fight? The campaigns of the war show only too clearly how difficult it is to force a landing, or to maintain an army, on a hostile coast. . . .

The United States is better situated from a military standpoint than any other nation in the world. Even in our present condition of unpreparedness no foreign power is in a position to invade us today. If we concentrate on our own defenses and build the strength that

▲ *Charles Lindbergh at an America First Committee rally*

this nation should maintain, no foreign army will ever attempt to land on American shores.

War is not inevitable for this country. Such a claim is defeatism in the true sense. No one can make us fight abroad unless we ourselves are willing to do so. No one will attempt to fight us here if we arm ourselves as a great nation should be armed. . . .

The time has come when those of us who believe in an independent American destiny must band together and organize for strength. We have been led toward war by a minority of our people. This minority has power. It has influence. It has a loud voice. But it does not represent the American people.

DBQ Document-Based Questions

Historical Analysis CA HR4; HI3

Source 1: Why does Conant believe that the United States should join the war?

Source 2: According to America First, what are the obligations of the United States?

Source 3: Why does Lindbergh believe that the United States can avoid the war?

Comparing and Contrasting Sources

How do Conant, Lindbergh, and America First Committee differ in their views about the best way to protect the United States?

DBQ Document-Based Questions

1. because a world dominated by totalitarian states would endanger our democracy
2. the maintenance of our democracy and the well-being of the American people
3. He believes that no foreign power can invade the country, and no one can make Americans fight if they are unwilling to do so.

Comparing and Contrasting Sources: Conant thinks the best way to protect the United States and its democratic way of life is to stop the Nazis and the spread of totalitarianism; the America First Committee states that U.S. national interests should come first; and Lindbergh believes U.S. involvement in the war can be avoided because no foreign power can attack the United States on its own soil.

Resources for pages 566–567

Use the following resources to review, assess, and reteach the chapter.

📁 Chapter 11 Tests, Forms A and B

📁 Standardized Tests, Forms A and B

📁 Cumulative Authentic Assessment

💾 MindJogger Videoquiz

⊙ Interactive Tutor Self-Assessment CD-ROM

⊙ Exam*View*® Pro Testmaker CD-ROM

⊙ Vocabulary PuzzleMaker CD-ROM

⊙ Succeeding on . . .™ the California Standards: Grade 11 History–Social Science

📁 California Standards Practice, Grade 11

Reviewing Content Vocabulary

Students' answers will vary. The pages where the words appear in the text are shown in parentheses.

1. fascism *(p. 537)* **2.** internationalism *(p. 540)* **3.** appeasement *(p. 544)* **4.** blitzkrieg *(p. 545)* **5.** Holocaust *(p. 550)* **6.** concentration camp *(p. 553)* **7.** extermination camp *(p. 554)* **8.** hemispheric defense zone *(p. 560)* **9.** strategic materials *(p. 562)*

Reviewing Academic Vocabulary

Students' answers will vary. The pages where the words appear in the text are shown in parentheses.

10. impose *(p. 537)* **11.** civil *(p. 540)* **12.** regime *(p. 543)* **13.** furthermore *(p. 543)* **14.** anticipate *(p. 547)* **15.** implement *(p. 550)* **16.** prohibit *(p. 550)* **17.** policy *(p. 560)* **18.** primary *(p. 562)*

Reviewing Content Vocabulary

On a sheet of paper, use each of these terms in a sentence.

1. fascism
2. internationalism
3. appeasement
4. blitzkrieg
5. Holocaust
6. concentration camp
7. extermination camp
8. hemispheric defense zone
9. strategic materials

Reviewing Academic Vocabulary

On a sheet of paper, use each of these terms in a sentence that reflects the term's meaning in the chapter.

10. impose
11. civil
12. regime
13. furthermore
14. anticipate
15. implement
16. prohibit
17. policy
18. primary

Reviewing the Main Ideas

Section 1

19. Who was the leader of Fascist Italy?

Section 2

20. Why was Austria easier for Hitler to annex than Czechoslovakia?

Standards 11.7.1, 11.7.4, 11.7.5, 11.7.6

Section 3

21. What were four ways that Nazis persecuted Jews?

Section 4

22. In what three ways did Roosevelt help Britain during the early years of World War II while maintaining an American policy of neutrality?

Critical Thinking

23. **Reading Skill** Making Inferences Review the text "Jewish Refugees Try to Flee" on pages 552–553. Explain what factors limited Jewish immigration to the United States. Why did other countries not allow entrance for the refugees? Discuss your answers with a partner. How do your answers differ from those of your partner?

24. **Analyze** How did the rise of dictatorships and the attack on Pearl Harbor cause the United States to become involved in World War II?

25. **Civics** How did President Roosevelt use the power of the executive office to support the British and circumvent the Neutrality Acts?

Chapter Summary

Axis

Italy
- Mussolini's Fascist Party believed in supreme power of the state
- Cooperated with Germany from 1936 onward

Germany
- Hitler's Nazi Party believed in all-powerful state, territorial expansion, and ethnic purity
- Invaded Poland in 1939, France in 1940, and the USSR in 1941

Japan
- Military leaders pushed for territorial expansion
- Attacked Manchuria in 1931
- Invaded China in 1937
- Attacked Pearl Harbor in 1941

USSR
- Communists, led by harsh dictator Joseph Stalin, created industrial power
- Signed non-aggression pact with Germany in 1939
- Received U.S. aid; eventually fought with Allies to defeat Germany

Allies

United States
- Passed Neutrality Acts in 1935, 1937, and 1939
- Gave lend-lease aid to Britain, China, and the USSR
- Declared war on Japan in 1941

Great Britain
- Tried to appease Hitler by allowing territorial growth
- Declared war on Germany in 1939
- Resisted German attack in 1940
- Received U.S. aid through lend-lease program and cash-and-carry provision

France
- Along with Great Britain, tried to appease Hitler
- Declared war on Germany in 1939 after Poland was invaded
- Occupied by Nazis in 1940

Reviewing the Main Ideas

19. Benito Mussolini

20. Austrians spoke German and had an authoritarian government. Czechoslovakians spoke several languages and had a democratic government and allies.

21. Nazis took away their civil liberties, seized their property, imprisoned them, and killed them.

22. Roosevelt made a destroyers-for-bases deal, got Congress to pass the Lend-Lease Act, and developed the hemispheric defense zone strategy.

Critical Thinking

23. **Reading Skill** Students' answers will vary. Possible explanation: During the 1930s unemployment was high in the United States. The U.S. restricted visas to anyone who might become a public charge. Other countries turned Jewish immigrants away for forged or illegally sold documents.

24. The United States sided with democratically-based governments, particularly after Nazi Germany attacked

26. Organizing Use a graphic organizer similar to the one below to list countries that Hitler and the Nazis seized between 1936 and 1940.

Countries Seized by Hitler and the Nazis

Writing About History

27. **Historical Analysis** **Understanding Change** Explain why some individuals believe the policy of appeasement was a cause for World War II. Do you think the war may have causes other than appeasement? Explain your answer. **CA HI2**

28. *Big Idea* Research and write a report explaining at least three possible reasons why the Japanese attacked the United States at Pearl Harbor.

DBQ **Document-Based Questions**

29. Interpreting Primary Sources The America First Committee organized to prevent American involvement in the war. On April 24, 1941, aviator Charles Lindbergh, a leading spokesperson for this committee, delivered a speech in New York. Read the excerpt from his speech and answer the questions that follow.

❝War is not inevitable for this country. Such a claim is defeatism in the true sense. No one can make us fight abroad unless we ourselves are willing to do so. No one will attempt to fight us here if we arm ourselves as a great nation should be armed. Over a hundred million people in this nation are opposed to entering the war. If the principles of democracy mean anything at all, that is reason enough for us to stay out. If we are forced into war against the wishes of an overwhelming majority of our people, we will have proved democracy such a failure at home that there will be little use fighting for it abroad.❞

a. Why did Lindbergh favor isolationism?
b. How do you think Lindbergh might have felt about isolationism after the attack on Pearl Harbor? **CA 11RL3.8**

NATIONAL GEOGRAPHIC

Nazi Concentration and Extermination Camps, 1933–1945

⊛ Capital city
■ Nazi concentration camp/ death camp

0   200 miles
0   200 kilometers
Lambert Azimuthal Equal-Area projection

Geography and History

30. The map above shows Nazi concentration and extermination camps. Study it and answer these questions.
   a. Interpreting Maps In which two countries were most of the concentration and extermination camps located? Why were they located there?
   b. Applying Geography Skills What can you conclude about the extent of the Nazis' "final solution"?

HISTORY
Online

Have students visit the Web site at tav.mt.glencoe.com to review Chapter 11 and take the Self-Check Quiz.

DBQ **Document-Based Questions**

29. a. Lindbergh believed that many Americans were against entering the war and that in a democratic nation, their wishes should be listened to. **b.** Students' answers will vary. It might not have changed his mind; he believed we needed to protect ourselves.

Geography and History

30. a. Germany and Poland; **b.** The Nazis applied the "Final Solution" in Germany and in all the countries they conquered.

Standards Practice

31. D

Bonus Question ❓

Ask: What is the name of the German-born Nobel prize-winning physicist whose scientific theories revolutionized modern physics? *(Albert Einstein)*

France and Britain; Pearl Harbor was an outright attack on the United States.

25. FDR asked Congress to revise the Neutrality Acts. The revision allowed sales of arms to warring countries as long as they paid cash and carried the arms on their ships. This policy of cash and carry and the destroyers-for-bases deal allowed Roosevelt to support the British while circumventing the Neutrality Acts.

26. Austria, Czechoslovakia, Poland, Denmark, Belgium, France, Luxembourg, the Netherlands, Norway

Writing About History

27. **Historical Analysis** Students' answers will vary but should include well-reasoned arguments.

28. *Big Idea* Students' answers will vary. Students should discuss the policies Roosevelt used to help the British defend their territories in Southeast Asia.

Chapter 12 Planning Guide

SECTION RESOURCES

MAIN IDEAS	🗂 PRINT MATERIALS	TECHNOLOGY RESOURCES
Section 1: Mobilizing for War 1. The U.S. government encouraged and assisted industry in improving manufacturing for a wartime economy. 2. Automobile manufacturers and shipyards produced vehicles and other equipment for the war. 3. Despite continued barriers to full equality in the armed forces, African Americans and women made unique contributions to the war effort.	• Daily Lecture and Discussion Notes 12-1 • Active Reading Note-Taking Guide 12-1 • Section Quiz 12-1 • Reading Essentials and Study Guide 12-1	📑 Daily Focus Skills Transparency 12-1 💿 Interactive Tutor Self-Assessment CD-ROM 💿 ExamView® Pro Testmaker CD-ROM 💿 Presentation Plus! CD-ROM 📑 California Standards Practice Transparencies
Section 2: The Early Battles 1. Japanese and American naval forces battled for control of the Pacific. 2. American and British forces defeated the Germans in North Africa and in the Atlantic, while Soviet forces defeated Germany at Stalingrad.	• Daily Lecture and Discussion Notes 12-2 • Active Reading Note-Taking Guide 12-2 • Section Quiz 12-2 • Reading Essentials and Study Guide 12-2	📑 Daily Focus Skills Transparency 12-2 💿 Interactive Tutor Self-Assessment CD-ROM 💿 ExamView® Pro Testmaker CD-ROM 💿 Presentation Plus! CD-ROM 📑 California Standards Practice Transparencies
Section 3: Life on the Home Front 1. The changing roles in the workplace and growing political demands opened doors to new work for women and minorities. 2. During the war, many people moved in search of jobs, while many Americans were forced from their homes into internment camps. 3. Civilians made many sacrifices during the war to help ensure victory for the Allies.	• Daily Lecture and Discussion Notes 12-3 • Active Reading Note-Taking Guide 12-3 • Section Quiz 12-3 • Reading Essentials and Study Guide 12-3	📑 Daily Focus Skills Transparency 12-3 💿 Interactive Tutor Self-Assessment CD-ROM 💿 ExamView® Pro Testmaker CD-ROM 💿 Presentation Plus! CD-ROM 📑 California Standards Practice Transparencies
Section 4: Pushing the Axis Back 1. At the Casablanca Conference, Roosevelt and Churchill planned a wartime strategy that included increased bombing of Germany and an attack on Sicily. 2. The Allied invasion of France took place on June 6, 1944, which was known as D-Day. 3. General MacArthur's strategy involved taking back islands in the Pacific, one island at a time, to push back the Japanese.	• Daily Lecture and Discussion Notes 12-4 • Active Reading Note-Taking Guide 12-4 • Section Quiz 12-4 • Reading Essentials and Study Guide 12-4	📑 Daily Focus Skills Transparency 12-4 💿 Interactive Tutor Self-Assessment CD-ROM 💿 ExamView® Pro Testmaker CD-ROM 💿 Presentation Plus! CD-ROM 📑 California Standards Practice Transparencies
Section 5: The War Ends 1. After the Battle of the Bulge, Germany had few military resources to continue fighting the war. 2. Hoping to shorten the war, President Truman decided to drop atomic bombs on the Japanese cities of Hiroshima and Nagasaki. 3. The Allied nations attempted to prevent future wars by creating the United Nations and by bringing war criminals to trial.	• Daily Lecture and Discussion Notes 12-5 • Active Reading Note-Taking Guide 12-5 • Section Quiz 12-5 • Reading Essentials and Study Guide 12-5	📑 Daily Focus Skills Transparency 12-5 💿 Interactive Tutor Self-Assessment CD-ROM 💿 ExamView® Pro Testmaker CD-ROM 💿 Presentation Plus! CD-ROM 📑 California Standards Practice Transparencies

🕛 PACING YOUR LESSONS

Chapter Introduction	Section 1	Section 2	Section 3	Section 4	Section 5	Chapter Assessment
½ Day	2 Days	2 Days	2 Days	2 Days	2 Days	½ Day

`0:00` **OUT OF TIME?** 🗂 Assign the Chapter 12 *Reading Essentials and Study Guide.*

Chapter 12 Planning Guide

Standards-Based Lesson Plan

 History–Social Science Standards Covered in Chapter 12

The standards covered in the chapter are listed below. Use the accompanying activity as you teach the chapter to ensure student mastery of these standards. This activity can be used in combination with the program's print and technology assessment materials.

Standard	Section				
	1	2	3	4	5
11.7 Students analyze America's participation in World War II.	✔	✔	✔	✔	✔
11.9.1 Discuss the establishment of the United Nations and International Declaration of Human Rights, International Monetary Fund, World Bank, and General Agreement on Tariffs and Trade (GATT) and their importance in shaping modern Europe and maintaining peace and international order.					✔
11.10.1 Explain how demands of African Americans helped produce a stimulus for civil rights, including President Roosevelt's ban on racial discrimination in defense industries in 1941, and how African Americans' service in World War II produced a stimulus for President Truman's decision to end segregation in the armed forces in 1948.	✔		✔		

Cumulative Standards-Assessment Activity

The Cumulative Standards-Assessment Activity will help students organize and learn the important information from the chapter. Begin teaching the chapter with this activity, and have students complete it as they read the chapter.

CREATING A CHART FOR ORGANIZING INFORMATION

Purpose Students encounter many dates, names, events, and concepts in studying Social Studies. Students need to make sense of this information in a logical way to understand the facts and their significance. Organizing information incorporates other skills and can require students to practice summarizing, categorizing, sequencing, distinguishing main ideas and supporting details, and recognizing the order of importance of information.

Introduction to Categorizing Information

1. In this chapter, students will read about many developments in World War II. They will need some way of understanding and retaining all the information they learn. Ask: With so many ways to organize information, how do you choose? Suggest to students that they preview the subject matter, pick a few categories that fit the subject, and sketch out an idea for organizing information on the topic. Tell students one way to test if information is well organized is to see if their idea makes sense to someone else.

2. For this chapter, students can use the chart below in conjunction with any of their own ideas for organizing information. Ask students to copy this chart into their notebooks.

United States in World War II		
Pacific Front	Atlantic Front	Home Front

3. Encourage them to study the chart and anticipate how it may apply to the reading material. You may want to suggest they take notes while they read. Remind students that their notes should make sense to them later and help jog their memories. They can use their notes to fill in the above chart.

Chapter 12 Planning Guide

READING SUPPORT

- Content Vocabulary Activity 12
- Academic Vocabulary Activity 12
- Reading Skills Activity 12
- Chapter 12 Active Reading Note-Taking Guide
- Chapter 12 Guided Reading Activities
- Chapter 12 Reading Essentials and Study Guide
- American Literature Readings, Unit 4
- *The American Vision: Modern Times* Video Program
- Vocabulary PuzzleMaker CD-ROM
- American History Primary Source Document Library CD-ROM

CRITICAL THINKING

- Critical Thinking Skills Activity 12
- Primary Source Reading 12
- Cause-and-Effect Transparency 12 Strategy and Activity
- Presentation Plus! CD-ROM

UNIVERSAL ACCESS

- Universal Access Activity 12
- English Learner Activity 12
- American Art Prints
- StudentWorks™ Plus CD-ROM
- American Music: Hits Through History
- School-to-Home Connection Activity 12

SKILL PRACTICE

- Map Overlay Transparency 12 Strategy and Activity
- Historical Analysis Skills Activity 12
- Time Line Activity 12
- Reading Skills Activity 12
- Reinforcing Skills Activity 12
- Linking Past and Present Activity 12
- Interpreting Political Cartoons 12
- Geography and History Activity, Unit 4
- MindJogger Videoquiz

WRITING SUPPORT

- Chapter 12 Active Reading Note-Taking Guide
- Writer's Guidebook
- High School Writing Process Transparencies

ASSESSMENT

- Chapter 12 Section Quizzes
- Chapter 12 Tests, Forms A and B
- Authentic Assessment Activity 12
- Exam*View*® Pro Testmaker CD-ROM
- Interactive Tutor Self-Assessment CD-ROM
- California Standards Practice, Grade 11
- Succeeding on . . .™ the California Standards: Grade 11 History–Social Science CD-ROM

- CD-ROM
- DVD
- Print Material
- Poster

- Transparency
- Music Program
- Videocassette

Chapter 12 Planning Guide

TECHNOLOGY

- StudentWorks™ Plus CD-ROM
- TeacherWorks™ CD-ROM
- ExamView® Pro Testmaker CD-ROM
- Interactive Tutor Self-Assessment CD-ROM
- Presentation Plus! CD-ROM
- Vocabulary PuzzleMaker CD-ROM
- American History Primary Source Document Library CD-ROM
- MindJogger Videoquiz
- *The American Vision: Modern Times* Video Program
- Professional Development in High School Social Studies Video Series
- Teach, Use, and Succeed With *The American Vision: Modern Times*
- American Music: Hits Through History
- Succeeding on . . .™ the California Standards: Grade 11 History–Social Science CD-ROM

SPANISH RESOURCES

- Spanish Activities and Assessment
  - Spanish Vocabulary Activities
  - Spanish Guided Reading Activities
  - Spanish Quizzes and Tests
  - Spanish Reteaching Activities
- Spanish Reading Essentials and Study Guide
- Spanish School-to-Home Connection Activities

TRANSPARENCIES

- Daily Focus Skills Transparencies
- Section Graphic Organizer Transparencies
- Map Overlay Transparencies
- Cause-and-Effect Transparencies
- Unit Time Line Transparencies
- Why It Matters Transparencies
- American Art and Architecture Transparencies
- High School Writing Process Transparencies
- California Standards Practice Transparencies

TEACHER PLANNING

- Daily Lecture and Discussion Notes
- English Learner Handbook
- Building Academic Vocabulary
- *The American Vision: Modern Times* Reading and Study Skills Foldables
- Reading Strategies and Activities for the Social Studies Classroom
- Universal Access for the American History Classroom
- NGS United States Desk Map
- NGS World Atlas
- Chapter 12 Reproducible Lesson Plans on TeacherWorks™ CD-ROM
- California Guide to Daily Intervention

PROFESSIONAL DEVELOPMENT

- Building Academic Vocabulary
- Strategies for Success
- Research-Based Strategies Used to Develop *The American Vision: Modern Times*
- Character Education in the High School Classroom
- Professional Development in High School Social Studies Video Series
- Teach, Use, and Succeed With *The American Vision: Modern Times*

Chapter 12 Planning Guide

TEACHER'S CORNER

Index to National Geographic Magazine:

The following articles relate to this chapter:

- "Douglas MacArthur: An American Soldier," March 1992
- "Hiroshima," August 1995
- "Living with Radiation," April 1989

National Geographic Society Products:

To order the following, call National Geographic at 1–800–368–2728

- *Eyewitness to the 20th Century* (Book)
- *Historical Atlas of the United States* (Atlas)
- *PicturePack: World War II Era* (Transparencies)
- *PictureShow: World War II Era* (CD-ROM)

NGS ONLINE

Access National Geographic's new dynamic MapMachine Web site and other geography resources at:

www.nationalgeographic.com

www.nationalgeographic.com/maps

MASTERING THE STANDARDS

The content and assessment in the Student Edition, Teacher Wraparound Edition, teacher planning materials, and the print and technology products are all standards-based. The use of these products during instruction leads to mastery of the standards.

PRACTICE
- California Standards Practice, Grade 11
- California Standards Practice Transparencies
- School-to-Home Connection

BENCHMARK ASSESSMENT
- Section Quizzes, Chapter Tests, and Authentic Assessment
- Exam*View* ® Pro Testmaker CD-ROM
- Succeeding On . . . ™ the California Standards: Grade 11 History–Social Science CD-ROM

REMEDIATION
- California Guide to Daily Intervention
- Interactive Tutor Self-Assessment CD-ROM
- Exam*View* ® Pro Testmaker CD-ROM
- California Standards Practice, Grade 11
- Reading Essentials and Study Guide

History Online

Use our Web site for additional resources. All essential content is covered in the Student Edition.

You and your students can visit tav.mt.glencoe.com, the Web site companion to the **American Vision: Modern Times.** This innovative integration of electronic and print media offers your students a wealth of opportunities. The student text directs students to the Web site for the following options:

- **Chapter Overviews**
- **Self-Check Quizzes**
- **Student Web Activities**
- **Textbook Updates**

Answers to the student Web activities are provided for you in the **Web Activity Lesson Plans.** Additional Web resources and ePuzzles and games are also available.

FOLDABLES™ Study Organizer

Dinah Zike's Foldables

Foldables are three-dimensional, interactive graphic organizers that help students practice basic writing skills, review key vocabulary terms, and identify main ideas. Every chapter has a foldable activity in the *Dinah Zike's Reading and Study Skills Foldables* booklet. You can use the foldables as they are presented or modify them to suit the needs of your individual class.

A variety of videotape programs are available from A&E Television and The History Channel to provide teaching assistance. To order, call Glencoe at 1-800-334-7344.

Chapter 12 Planning Guide

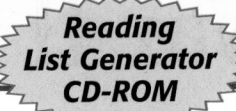
KEY for Using the Teacher Wraparound Edition

Use this key to help you identify the different types of prompts found in the Teacher Wraparound Edition.

R **Reading Strategies** activities help you teach reading skills and vocabulary.

C **Critical Thinking** strategies help students apply and extend what they have learned.

U **Universal Access** activities provide differentiated instruction for students learning to speak English, along with suggestions for teaching various types of learners.

S **Skill Practice** strategies help students practice historical analysis and geography skills.

W **Writing Support** activities provide writing opportunities to help students comprehend the text.

Teaching strategies and activities have been coded for ability level appropriateness.

AL Activities for students working above grade level
OL Activities for students working on grade level
BL Activities for students working below grade level
EL Activities for English learners

FOCUS

History–Social Science Standards

This chapter addresses the following standards:

11.7 Students analyze America's participation in World War II.

11.7.2 Explain U.S. and Allied wartime strategy, including the major battles of Midway, Normandy, Iwo Jima, Okinawa, and the Battle of the Bulge.

BELLRINGER
SKILLBUILDER ACTIVITY

Ask students to write one-page papers analyzing the decision to inter Japanese Americans in detention camps and to drop atomic bombs on two Japanese cities. After students have read Chapter 12, have them consider the historical justifications of these actions and see if they still hold the same views from the beginning of the chapter.

TEACH

Thinking About the Big Ideas

As you begin teaching each section, use these questions and activities to focus on the Big Idea.

Section 1
Mobilizing for War
Essential Question: How might you have responded to the need to prepare the nation for the war effort? *(Answers will vary but may include enlisting in the armed forces, applying for a job in a munitions factory, or carpooling to school to save fuel.)* Explain to students that Section 1 will describe how the United

---

CHAPTER 12
1941–1945
America and World War II

～ The Big Ideas ～

SECTION 1: Mobilizing for War

People react to periods of breathtaking social and cultural change in different ways. *As the United States quickly mobilized its economy and armed forces to fight World War II, African Americans and women assumed new roles in society.*

SECTION 2: The Early Battles

The fate of nations is forever changed by monumental world events. *By late 1942, the Allies had stopped the German and Japanese advance.*

SECTION 3: Life on the Home Front

People react to periods of breathtaking social and cultural change in different ways. *The new challenges of World War II brought many changes to the lives of women and minorities.*

SECTION 4: Pushing the Axis Back

The fate of nations is forever changed by monumental world events. *The Allies slowly pushed back the German and Japanese forces in 1943 and 1944.*

SECTION 5: The War Ends

The fate of nations is forever changed by monumental world events. *The ferocious military campaigns of 1945 finally convinced the Axis Powers to surrender and the Allies to set up organizations to prevent another global war.*

The American Vision: Modern Times Video *The Chapter 12 video, "Japanese American Internment Camps," chronicles the treatment of Japanese Americans during World War II.*

United States PRESIDENTS

F. Roosevelt 1933–1945

1941
- President Roosevelt forbids racial discrimination in defense industries
- United States enters World War II

1942
- Women's Army Auxiliary Corps established
- Japanese American relocation ordered

1943
- Detroit race riots
- Zoot suit riots in Los Angeles

1941   *1942*   *1943*

World

1941
- Japan attacks Pearl Harbor and the Philippines

1942
- Japan takes Philippines; MacArthur vows: "I shall return."
- Americans turn the tide in the Pacific at the Battle of Midway

1943
- Battle of Tarawa
- Germans defeated at Stalingrad
- Allied forces land in Italy

568

States went to war suddenly and thus had to prepare very quickly. **OL**

Section 2
The Early Battles
Essential Question: What unique decisions did the United States face as a result of fighting a war on two fronts? *(whether to fight both wars with equal strength or whether to emphasize one front and one enemy over the other)*

Tell students that the United States had to balance the operations against the Japanese in the Pacific with the war against Germany and Italy in North Africa and Europe. **AL**

Section 3
Life on the Home Front
Essential Question: How do you think populations in the United States, such as women, African Americans, and Japanese Americans,

responded to the war? Organize the class into three groups each representing one of the population groups mentioned above and ask each group to discuss how they should respond to the war. Invite volunteers to share their thoughts with the entire class. **OL**

Section 4
Pushing the Axis Back
Essential Question: Why were Americans willing to keep fighting a war with such a high number of American casualties? *(Answers will vary. Students may note a desire to protect American freedom, to stop German expansion and the Holocaust, and revenge for Pearl Harbor.)* Tell students that in Section 4 they will learn about the large number of casualties in World War II. **OL**

Section 5
The War Ends
Essential Question: Why do you think the United States used nuclear weapons against Japan? Tell students that the American decision to drop atomic bombs on Japanese cities continues to be a focus of discussion. They will find out more about the debate in Section 5. **OL**

Allied soldiers landing at Omaha Beach in Normandy on D-Day—June 6, 1944

1945
• Franklin Roosevelt dies in office; Harry S Truman becomes president

1944
• Supreme Court rules in *Korematsu v. the United States* that Japanese American relocation is constitutional

Truman 1945–1953

1944

1945

1944
• Eisenhower leads D-Day invasion
• Battle of Leyte Gulf

1945
• United States drops atomic bomb on Japan
• World War II ends

HISTORY
Online
Chapter Overview
Visit the *American Vision: Modern Times* Web site at tav.mt.glencoe.com and click on *Chapter Overviews— Chapter 12* to preview chapter information.

569

Cultural Perspectives

Remind students that many Americans faced discrimination in their own society during World War II. Divide students into groups and have each group select one of the following peoples: women, African Americans, Native Americans, or Asian Americans. Students should research the wartime roles or contributions of their assigned people and then create short presentations that address these questions: What challenges did this group face during *and* after the war? How did they feel about this? **OL**

FOLDABLES™
Study Organizer

Dinah Zike's Foldables are three-dimensional, interactive graphic organizers that help students practice basic writing skills, review key vocabulary terms, and identify main ideas. Have students complete the foldable activity in the *Dinah Zike's Reading and Study Skills Foldables* booklet.

HISTORY
Online

Go to tav.mt.glencoe.com for student activities, lesson plans, and links to additional resources to help students learn about the United States and World War II.

Preparing to Read Chapter 12

Why It's Important
Remind students that it is important to understand how or why an event occurred. What action or situation caused a particular event? What were the effects or consequences of that particular action or situation?

1. Introducing the Skill
Ask students to remember a time when they were sick with a cold. Tell them to recall events that caused them to get sick, as well as the effects of their illness. Have students record their answers in a flow chart like the one below. *(Answers will vary. For example, students may list not getting enough sleep or poor nutrition as causes and missing school as an effect.)* **BL**

Causes	Event	Effects
	COLD	

2. Extending the Skill
Have students read an account of a current event in your community newspaper. Students should underline any signal words in the article and then determine at least one cause and one effect of that event. Have students show the cause-and-effect relationship in a chart. **OL**

Answers and Additional Support

Reading Skill — **Cause and Effect**

In Chapter 4 you learned how authors structure text to talk about cause and effect. Authors use cause and effect to show how one event can lead to another event. Often there are several causes, just as there can be several different effects.

When you first read a text, you may find it difficult to determine individual causes and effects. Sometimes authors use signal words to let you know that they are describing a cause or an effect. Signal words for causes include *because, when, if, cause,* and *reason.* Words like *then, so, which, effect, response,* and *result* signal an effect.

Read the following sentences and notice how the signal words help you locate the cause and effect in each statement.

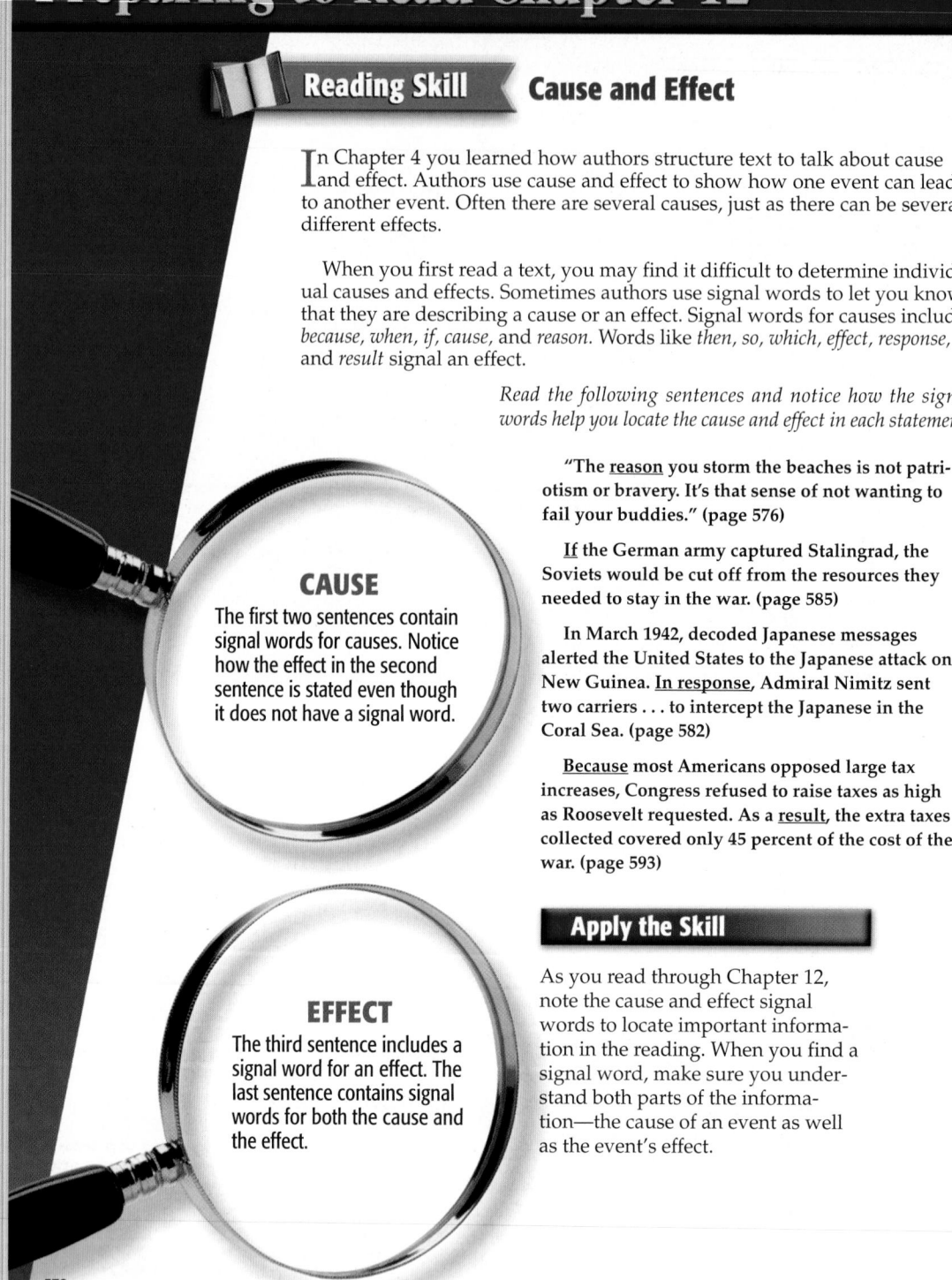

CAUSE
The first two sentences contain signal words for causes. Notice how the effect in the second sentence is stated even though it does not have a signal word.

EFFECT
The third sentence includes a signal word for an effect. The last sentence contains signal words for both the cause and the effect.

"The <u>reason</u> you storm the beaches is not patriotism or bravery. It's that sense of not wanting to fail your buddies." (page 576)

<u>If</u> the German army captured Stalingrad, the Soviets would be cut off from the resources they needed to stay in the war. (page 585)

In March 1942, decoded Japanese messages alerted the United States to the Japanese attack on New Guinea. <u>In response</u>, Admiral Nimitz sent two carriers . . . to intercept the Japanese in the Coral Sea. (page 582)

<u>Because</u> most Americans opposed large tax increases, Congress refused to raise taxes as high as Roosevelt requested. As a <u>result</u>, the extra taxes collected covered only 45 percent of the cost of the war. (page 593)

Apply the Skill

As you read through Chapter 12, note the cause and effect signal words to locate important information in the reading. When you find a signal word, make sure you understand both parts of the information—the cause of an event as well as the event's effect.

570

UNIVERSAL ACCESS

Naturalist To demonstrate cause and effect, use examples from nature and biology. For example, have students explain how or why malaria occurs in human beings *(bite of infected mosquito)* or why some animals hibernate during the winter *(lack of food).* Emphasize that cause-and-effect relationships in history may be less certain or obvious than those in science and nature. **OL**

Historical Analysis Skill — Evaluating Interpretations

Analysis Skill Standard HR3

Historical Research, Evidence, and Point of View When studying history, you should learn to evaluate major debates among historians concerning alternative interpretations of the past, including an analysis of the author's use of evidence and the distinctions between sound generalizations and misleading oversimplifications.

When you discuss an issue with your friends or in class, do you simply state your opinions, or do you support your viewpoints with evidence? You may find that if you can find information that confirms what you believe, others are more likely to agree with you. Similarly, historians try to find evidence that supports their views when they write about events.

As historians analyze information, they realize that there are different interpretations of the past. Although historians look at the same body of sources and information, they often arrive at different conclusions for historical events. These differences in interpretation may result if historians select only some sources in their research because they do not have the time to look at all pieces of evidence. Other times, differences may occur because historians begin with different presumptions, or hypotheses (see Chapter 9) based on their general approach to history. In either case, historians may differ in their analyses of historical events.

Read the following passages about the debate among historians about dropping the atomic bomb in World War II.

Historian Gar Alperovitz maintains that Truman possessed alternatives to the atomic bomb but chose to use the weapon in order to force Japan's surrender before the Soviet Union could mount an invasion and subsequently occupy Japanese territory. (page 614)

Historian Herbert Feis argues that Truman's desire to avoid an invasion of Japan, thus saving thousands of lives on both sides, motivated his decision to drop the bomb. (page 615)

The historians in the passages above both had access to the same sources, yet they have reached very different conclusions about the reasons why President Truman ordered to drop the atomic bomb. Gar Alperovitz believes that the president had ulterior motives beyond saving lives to use the new weapon. Herbert Feis, on the other hand, presents the desire to keep casualties to a minimum as the main reason for Truman's decision.

Apply the Skill

Think about the debate among historians about the atomic bomb as you read through the information on the bomb in Section 5 of this chapter. How does the account in your textbook compare to the passages above? Do the textbook authors agree with Alperovitz or Feis? Explain your answer.

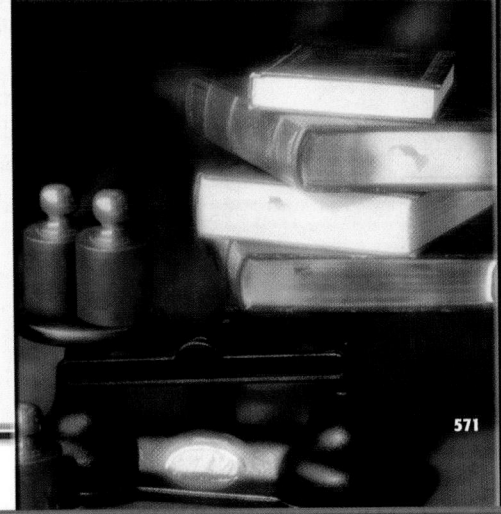

571

Historical Analysis

Why It's Important
Tell students that people often have different opinions about the same events or issues because they interpret them from different points of view. A person's point of view can be shaped by age, gender, racial or ethnic background, economic class, religion, and life experiences. Remind students that historians also differ in their historical analyses.

1. Introducing the Skill
Have students brainstorm a list of possible reasons why two people may experience the same movie and reach different conclusions about it. **Ask:** What factors might have influenced different points of view? **OL**

2. Extending the Skill
Have students look in a newspaper or magazine to find an editorial or letter to the editor that expresses a point of view on an issue. Ask the class to write paragraphs analyzing the author's point of view. Remind everyone to consider the following questions: What factors might influence the author's interpretation of events? What evidence does the author use to support his or her position? Have students compare the editorial's point of view with their own and explain why they agree or disagree with the author. **OL** **CA HR3**
CA 11RC2.5

UNIVERSAL ACCESS

English Learners Ask students to use library and Internet resources to locate two political cartoons that illustrate opposing sides of an issue. Have them write brief paragraphs explaining each of the cartoons. Remind students to discuss how the two authors have visually interpreted the same event or issue differently. **EL** **CA HR2; HR3**

FOCUS

BELLRINGER
SKILLBUILDER ACTIVITY

Project **Daily Focus Skills Transparency 12-1** and have students answer the question.

Guide to Reading

Understanding Vocabulary: Have students write two questions that can be answered using the content vocabulary.

Answers to Graphic: A restructured Reconstruction Finance Corporation, War Production Board, Office of War Mobilization, draft board (under Selective Service and Training Act)

Unpacking the Standards

Students will be able to:

- Examine how the United States successfully adjusted to a wartime economy.

- Describe how the economy, spurred by military needs, roared back to life following the Great Depression.

- Analyze the recruitment efforts for the armed forces.

Answers and Additional Support

SECTION 1 Mobilizing for War

Guide to Reading

Connection
In the previous chapter, you learned about the events that surrounded the onset of World War II. In this section, you will discover how the United States mobilized for the war.

Main Idea
- The U.S. government encouraged and assisted industry in improving manufacturing for a wartime economy. (p. 573)
- Automobile manufacturers and shipyards produced vehicles and other equipment for the war. (p. 574)
- Despite continued barriers to full equality in the armed forces, African Americans and women made unique contributions to the war effort. (p. 576)

Content Vocabulary
cost-plus, disfranchise

Academic Vocabulary
incentive, priority, consult

People and Terms to Identify
Reconstruction Finance Corporation, Liberty ship, War Production Board, Selective Service and Training Act

Reading Objectives
- **Explain** how the United States mobilized its economy.
- **Describe** the issues involved in raising an American army.

Reading Strategy
Organizing As you read about American mobilization for World War II, complete a graphic organizer like the one below by filling in the agencies the U.S. government created to mobilize the nation's economy for war.

Government Agencies Created to Mobilize the Economy

Preview of Events

♦1940	♦1941	♦1942	♦1943
1940 Fall of France; Selective Service Act	**December 7, 1941** Japan attacks Pearl Harbor	**1942** Women's Army Auxiliary Corps (WAAC) established	**1943** Office of War Mobilization (OWM) established

The following are the main History–Social Science Standards covered in this section.

11.7.3 Identify the roles and sacrifices of individual American soldiers, as well as the unique contributions of the special fighting forces (e.g., the Tuskegee Airmen, the 442nd Regimental Combat team, the Navajo Code Talkers).

11.7.5 Discuss the constitutional issues and impact of events on the U.S. home front, including the internment of Japanese Americans (e.g., *Fred Korematsu v. United States of America*) and the restrictions on German and Italian resident aliens; the response of the administration to Hitler's atrocities against Jews and other groups; the roles of women in military production; and the roles and growing political demands of African Americans.

11.7.6 Describe major developments in aviation, weaponry, communication, and medicine and the war's impact on the location of American industry and use of resources.

✎ The Big Idea ✎

People react to periods of breathtaking social and cultural change in different ways. Even before the United States officially entered the war, President Roosevelt had begun to prepare the American economy by building up the country's defenses. Now the conversion to a wartime economy went at a rapid pace, with a new agency to control the production of jeeps, tanks, airplanes, and ships. Americans, who before had been to a large degree isolationists, approved a draft. Enlistees served in segregated units, but African Americans began to push for more rights, and World War II saw the first African American combat units. Women also advanced during the war, serving for the first time in the military itself rather than in auxiliary units.

11.10.1 Explain how demands of African Americans helped produce a stimulus for civil rights, including President Roosevelt's ban on racial discrimination in defense industries in 1941, and how African Americans' service in World War II produced a stimulus for President Truman's decision to end segregation in the armed forces in 1948.

11.11.3 Describe the changing roles of women in society as reflected in the entry of more women into the labor force and the changing family structure.

572 CHAPTER 12 America and World War II

SECTION RESOURCES

📁 **Print Material**
- Reproducible Lesson Plan 12-1
- Guided Reading Activity 12-1
- Reading Essentials and Study Guide 12-1
- Active Reading Note-Taking Guide 12-1

📊 **Transparencies**
- Daily Focus Skills Transparency 12-1
- Section Graphic Organizer Transparency 12-1

Technology
- 💿 Interactive Tutor Self-Assessment CD-ROM
- 💿 ExamView® Pro Testmaker CD-ROM
- 💿 Presentation Plus! CD-ROM

Converting the Economy

Main Idea The U.S. government encouraged and assisted industry in improving manufacturing for a wartime economy.

Reading Connection What motivates you to work better or faster? Read on to learn how the U.S. government motivated industry during World War II.

President Roosevelt was concerned with the difficulty of fighting a global war. The attack on Pearl Harbor, however, convinced him that the United States must take action.

★ An American Story ★

Shortly after 1:30 P.M. on December 7, 1941, Secretary of the Navy Frank Knox phoned President Roosevelt at the White House. "Mr. President," Knox said, "it looks like the Japanese have attacked Pearl Harbor." A few minutes later, Admiral Harold Stark, chief of naval operations, phoned and confirmed the attack.

As Eleanor Roosevelt passed by the president's study, she knew immediately something very bad had happened:

"All the secretaries were there, two telephones were in use, the senior military aides were on their way with messages." Eleanor also noticed that President Roosevelt remained calm: "His reaction to any event was always to be calm. If it was something that was bad, he just became almost like an iceberg, and there was never the slightest emotion that was allowed to show."

Turning to his wife, President Roosevelt expressed anger at the Japanese: "I never wanted to have to fight this war on two fronts. We haven't got the Navy to fight in both the Atlantic and Pacific.... We will have to build up the Navy and the Air Force and that will mean we will have to take a good many defeats before we can have a victory."

—adapted from *No Ordinary Time*

Unlike the president, British Prime Minister Winston Churchill was not worried. Churchill knew that victory in modern war depended on a nation's industrial power. He compared the American economy to a gigantic boiler: "Once the fire is lighted under it there is no limit to the power it can generate."

Churchill was right. The industrial output of the United States during the war astounded the rest of the world. American workers were twice as productive as German workers and five times more productive than Japanese workers. American war production turned the tide in favor of the Allies. In less than four years, the United States achieved what no other nation had ever done—it fought and won a two-front war against two powerful military empires, forcing each to surrender unconditionally.

R The United States was able to expand its war production so rapidly after the attack on Pearl Harbor in part because the government had begun to mobilize the economy before the country entered the war. When the German blitzkrieg swept into France in May 1940, President Roosevelt declared a national emergency and announced a plan to build 50,000 warplanes a year. Shocked by the success of the German attack, many Americans were willing to build up the country's defenses.

W Roosevelt and his advisers believed that the best way to rapidly mobilize the economy was to give industry an **incentive** to move quickly. As Henry Stimson, the new secretary of war, wrote in his diary: "If you are going to try and go to war, or to prepare for war, in a capitalist country, you have got to let business make money out of the process or business won't work."

▼ *Franklin D. Roosevelt*

TEACH

R Reading Strategy

Evaluating Point out to students that Germany's successful invasion of France pushed the United States further and further from its formal neutral stance. **Ask:** Do you think it was acceptable for President Roosevelt to react to the fall of France as he did? Do you think events might have unfolded differently if the United States had not begun to prepare for war when it did, prior to the Pearl Harbor attack? *(Students' answers will vary. A possible answer might be that the overall outcome of the war would have remained the same, but the eventual end of the war would have occurred later.)* **OL** **CA HI2; HI4**

W Writing Support

Expository Writing Ask students to reread the statement made by Henry Stimson. Divide the class into four groups and ask the groups to discuss whether their group agrees, disagrees, or has a mixed reaction to Stimson's opinion. Each group should then write a summary of their group's reaction. Have a representative of each group present their summary to the class. **OL**
CA 11WA2.2c

Did You Know?

Before the attack on Pearl Harbor, eight out of ten Americans opposed entering World War II.

R **Reading Strategy**

Setting a Purpose Ask students to imagine that they are working in the government agency responsible for mobilizing the American economy for wartime production. **Ask:** What are the top three industrial priorities for a country shifting from domestic to war production? *(Answers will vary.)* **AL**

U **Universal Access**

Visual/Spatial Have students create a bulletin board about U.S. industry as the nation prepared for war. The board should include such information as level of unemployment, production figures for several industries, and other important economic indicators. Each category should compare data before and after mobilization began. **OL**

✓**Reading Check**

Answer: The cost-plus program encouraged companies to produce many products quickly and in quantity. The RFC made loans to help companies convert to war production.

Answers and Additional Support

Normally when the government needed military equipment, it would ask companies to bid for the contract, but that system was too slow in wartime. Instead of asking for bids, the government signed **cost-plus** contracts. The government agreed to pay a company whatever it cost to make a product plus a guaranteed percentage of the costs as profit. Under the cost-plus system, the more a company produced and the faster it did the work, the more money it would make. The system was not cheap, but it did get war materials produced quickly and in quantity.

Although cost-plus convinced many companies to convert to war production, others could not afford to reequip their factories to make military goods. To convince more companies to convert, Congress gave new authority to the **Reconstruction Finance Corporation** (RFC). The RFC, a government agency set up during the Depression, was now permitted to make loans to companies to help them cover the cost of converting to war production.

✓**Reading Check** **Analyzing** What government policies helped American industry to produce large quantities of war materials?

American Industry Gets the Job Done

Main Idea Automobile manufacturers and shipyards produced vehicles and other equipment for the war.

Reading Connection Name products you use that would be in high demand during a war. Read on to discover the role of shipyards in World War II.

By the fall of 1941, much had already been done to prepare the economy for war, but it was still only partially mobilized. Although many companies were producing military equipment, most still preferred to make consumer goods. The Depression was ending and sales were rising. The Japanese attack on Pearl Harbor, however, changed everything. By the summer of 1942, almost all major industries and some 200,000 companies had converted to war production. Together they made the nation's wartime "miracle" possible.

Tanks Replace Cars The automobile industry was uniquely suited to the mass production of military

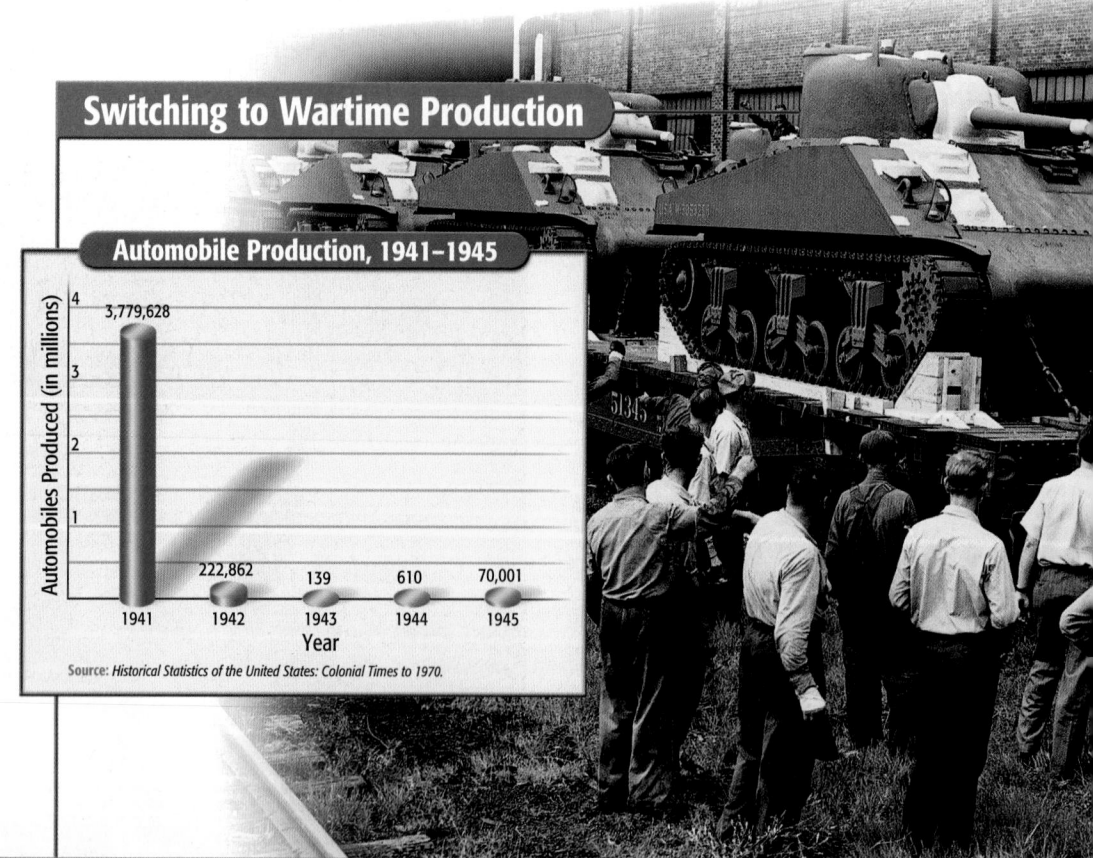

Switching to Wartime Production

Automobile Production, 1941–1945

Automobiles Produced (in millions)

Year	Automobiles Produced
1941	3,779,628
1942	222,862
1943	139
1944	610
1945	70,001

Source: *Historical Statistics of the United States: Colonial Times to 1970.*

Did You Know?

In September 1941, an internal report within the Roosevelt administration concluded that the earliest that U.S. armed forces could be mobilized, trained, and equipped for extensive military operations would be July 1, 1943. However, American troops were fighting the Japanese in the Pacific and fighting the Axis in Europe in 1942.

equipment. Automobile factories began to produce trucks, jeeps, and tanks. This was critical in modern warfare because the country that could move troops and supplies most quickly usually won the battle. As General George C. Marshall, chief of staff for the United States Army, observed:

❝The greatest advantage the United States enjoyed on the ground in the fighting was . . . the jeep and the two-and-a-half ton truck. These are the instruments that moved and supplied United States troops in battle, while the German army . . . depended on animal transport. . . . The United States, profiting from the mass production achievements of its automotive industry . . . had mobility that completely outclassed the enemy.❞

–quoted in *Miracle of World War II*

Automobile factories did not just produce vehicles. They also built artillery, rifles, mines, helmets, pontoon bridges, cooking pots, and dozens of other pieces of military equipment. Henry Ford launched one of the most ambitious projects when he created an assembly line for the enormous B-24 bomber known as "the Liberator" at Willow Run Airport near Detroit. By the end of the war, the factory had built over 8,600 aircraft. Overall, the automobile industry produced nearly one-third of the military equipment manufactured during the war.

Building the Liberty Ships Henry Kaiser's shipyards more than matched Ford's achievement in aircraft production. Kaiser's shipyards built many ships, but they were best known for their production of Liberty ships. The **Liberty ship** was the basic cargo ship used during the war. Most Liberty ships were welded instead of riveted. Welded ships were cheap, easy to build, and very hard to sink compared to riveted ships.

When a riveted ship was hit, the rivets often came loose, causing the ship to fall apart and sink. A welded ship's hull was fused into one solid piece of steel. A torpedo might blow a hole in it, but the hull would not come apart. A damaged Liberty ship could often get back to port, make repairs, and return to service. Welded ships saved cargo as well as lives.

The War Production Board As American companies converted to wartime production, many business leaders became frustrated with the mobilization process. Government agencies argued constantly about supplies and contracts and whose orders had the highest priority. The process was not only frustrating, but the disorder also hindered production.

After Pearl Harbor, President Roosevelt tried to improve the system by creating the **War Production Board** (WPB) in January 1942. The chairman, Donald M. Nelson, and the WPB received authority to set **priorities** and production goals and to control the distribution of raw materials and supplies. Almost immediately, the WPB clashed with the military. Military agencies continued to sign contracts without **consulting** with the WPB. Over a period of three years, the WPB supervised the production of $185 billion in military weapons and supplies. Finally, in 1943, Roosevelt established the Office of War Mobilization (OWM) to settle arguments between the different agencies.

✓ **Reading Check** **Explaining** What military need led to the production of Liberty ships?

Tank Production, 1941–1945

Year	Tanks Produced (in thousands)
1941	4,203
1942	23,884
1943	29,497
1944	17,565
1945	11,184

Source: *Historical Statistics of the United States: Colonial Times to 1970.*

Graph Skills

1. **Interpreting Graphs** How does the number of tanks produced relate to the number of automobiles produced in the previous graph?
2. **Making Generalizations** How do these two graphs illustrate the commitment of the United States to winning the war?

CHAPTER 12 America and World War II **575**

S Skill Practice

Conducting Research Assign students to pairs to write interviews of Henry Ford. One student, the reporter, will ask the questions, and the other student will answer them. Encourage students to use the library and the Internet to research their questions and answers. **BL**

U Universal Access

Visual/Spatial Tell students to imagine that they are nominating a historical figure for a new stamp commemorating the World War II mobilization effort. They may nominate either Henry Ford or Henry Kaiser. Ask the following questions: Whom would you choose, and why? What would your stamp look like? Have each student draw a picture of their stamp, and then write a letter persuading the U.S. Postal Service to consider their choice. **BL**

W Writing Support

Research Report Writing Assign students to groups to research Liberty ships. Encourage them to use the Internet and library to find pictures as well as information about the ships. **Ask:** How important were Liberty ships to the Allied victory in World War II? Tell each group to create a one-page report, and then have groups share their reports with the class. **OL**
CA 11WS1.3

✓ **Reading Check**

Answer: the need to have ships that were cheap, easy to build, and hard to sink

Graph Skills

Answers:
1. As the production of cars decreases, the production of tanks increases. When tank production is at its highest, auto production is at its lowest. When the production of tanks decreases, the production of automobiles increases.
2. The graphs show that producing tanks to help win the war took precedence over producing automobiles.

Graph Skills Practice
Ask: Why does the production of tanks jump so sharply between 1941 and 1942? (*U.S. entered the war at the end of 1941.*)

Building an Army

Main Idea Despite continued barriers to full equality in the armed forces, African Americans and women made unique contributions to the war effort.

Reading Connection Have you ever been in a situation where you had to get along with people you did not know and who were different from you? Read on to discover how basic training helped new soldiers form bonds with strangers.

Converting factories to war production was only part of the mobilization process. If the United States was actually going to fight and win the war, the country also needed to build up its armed forces.

Creating an Army Within days of Germany's attack on Poland, President Roosevelt expanded the army to 227,000 soldiers. After France surrendered to Germany in June 1940, two members of Congress introduced the **Selective Service and Training Act,** a plan for the first peacetime draft in American history. Before the spring of 1940, college students, labor unions, isolationists, and most members of Congress had opposed a peacetime draft. Many people's opinions changed, however, after Germany defeated France. In September Congress approved the draft by a wide margin.

You're in the Army Now At first the flood of draftees overwhelmed the army's training facilities. Many recruits had to live in tents and use temporary facilities. The army also endured equipment shortages. Troops carried sticks representing guns, threw stones simulating grenades, and practiced maneuvers with trucks carrying signs that read "TANK."

New draftees were initially sent to a reception center, where they were given physical exams and injections against smallpox and typhoid. The draftees were then issued uniforms, boots, and whatever equipment was available. The clothing bore the label "G.I.," meaning "Government Issue," which is why American soldiers were called "GIs."

After taking aptitude tests, recruits were sent to basic training for eight weeks. They learned how to handle weapons, load backpacks, read maps, pitch tents, and dig trenches. Trainees drilled and exercised constantly and learned how to work as a team.

After the war, many veterans complained that basic training had been useless. Soldiers were rushed through too quickly, and the physical training left them too tired to learn the skills they needed. A sergeant in Italy told a reporter for *Yank* magazine that during a recent battle, a new soldier had held up his rifle and yelled, "How do I load this thing?"

Despite its problems, basic training helped to break down barriers between soldiers. Recruits came from all over the country, and training together made them into a unit. Training created a "special sense of kinship," one soldier noted. "The reason you storm the beaches is not patriotism or bravery. It's that sense of not wanting to fail your buddies."

A Segregated Army Although basic training promoted unity, most recruits did not encounter Americans from every part of society. At the start of the war, the U.S. military was completely segregated. White recruits did not train alongside African Americans. African Americans had separate barracks, latrines, mess halls, and recreational facilities.

Once trained, African Americans were organized into their own military units, but white officers were generally in command of them. Most military leaders also wanted to keep African American soldiers out of combat and assigned them to construction and supply units.

History *Through Art*

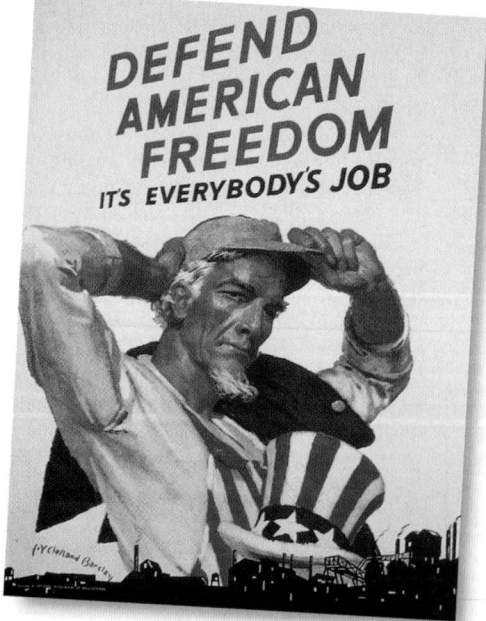

WW II Posters War posters were designed to help encourage and inform the American public. How would you have felt to see a poster such as this one?

DEFEND AMERICAN FREEDOM IT'S EVERYBODY'S JOB

Pushing for "Double V" Some African Americans did not want to support the war. As one student at a black college noted: "The Army Jim Crows us. . . . Employers and labor unions shut us out. Lynchings continue. We are disenfranchised . . . and spat upon. What more could Hitler do to us than that?" By **disfranchised,** the student meant that African Americans were often denied their right to vote. Despite the bitterness, most African Americans agreed with African American writer Saunders Redding that they should support their country:

> 66There are many things about this war I do not like . . . yet I believe in the war. . . . We know that whatever the mad logic of [Hitler's] New Order there is no hope for us under it. The ethnic theories of the Hitler 'master folk' admit of no chance of freedom. . . .This is a war to keep [people] free. The struggle to broaden and lengthen the road of freedom—our own private and important war to enlarge freedom here in America—will come later. . . . I believe in this War because I believe in America. I believe in what America professes to stand for. . . .99
>
> —quoted in *America at War*

Many African American leaders combined patriotism with protest. In 1941 the National Urban League set two goals for its members: "(1) To promote effective participation of [African Americans] in all phases of the war effort. . . . (2) To formulate plans for building the kind of United States in which we wish to live after the war is over. . . ."

The *Pittsburgh Courier,* a leading African American newspaper, embraced these ideas and launched what it called the "Double V" campaign. African Americans, the paper argued, should join the War effort in order to achieve a double victory—a victory over Hitler's racism abroad and a victory over racism at home. If the United States wanted to portray itself as a defender of democracy, Americans might be willing to end discrimination in their own country.

President Roosevelt knew that African American voters had played an important role in his election victories. Under pressure from African American leaders, he ordered the army air force, navy, and marines to begin recruiting African Americans, and he directed the army to put African Americans into combat. He also appointed Colonel Benjamin O. Davis, the highest-ranking African American officer in the U.S. Army, to the rank of brigadier general.

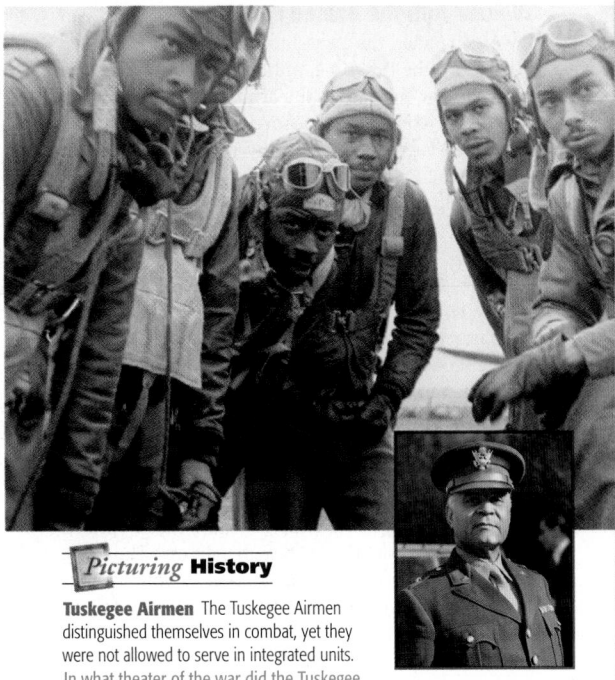

Picturing **History**

Tuskegee Airmen The Tuskegee Airmen distinguished themselves in combat, yet they were not allowed to serve in integrated units. In what theater of the war did the Tuskegee Airmen serve?

▲ *Benjamin O. Davis*

African Americans in Combat Many African Americans made brave contributions during the war in the armed forces. In response to the president's order, the army air force created the 99th Pursuit Squadron, an African American unit that trained in Tuskegee, Alabama. These African American fighter pilots became known as the Tuskegee Airmen. After General Davis urged the military to put African Americans into combat, the 99th Pursuit Squadron was sent to the Mediterranean in April 1943. The squadron played an important role during the Battle of Anzio in Italy.

African Americans also performed well in the army. The all-African American 761st Tank Battalion was commended for its service during the Battle of the Bulge. Fighting in northwest Europe, African Americans in the 614th Tank Destroyer Battalion won 8 Silver Stars for distinguished service, 28 Bronze Stars, and 79 Purple Hearts.

Although the military did not end all segregation during the war, it did integrate military bases in 1943 and steadily expanded the role of African Americans within the armed forces. These successes paved the way for President Truman's decision to fully integrate the military in 1948.

CHAPTER 12 America and World War II **577**

Using Word Parts Have students use prefixes to unlock the meanings of unknown words. A *prefix* is a word part that comes before a base word or a root and changes the meaning of the word. For example, *dis-* means "the opposite of" and is found in words such as disobey, displease, or disown. Have students use prefixes to help them identify the meaning of the word *disfranchised.* **BL**

Review the Big Idea

Review the Big Idea for this section, "People react to periods of breathtaking social and cultural change in different ways." Tell students to review the quote from Saunders Redding. **Ask:** Do you agree with Redding that African Americans had a duty to support their country despite the discrimination they faced at home? Why or why not? Have students write paragraphs supporting their positions. **OL**

CA HI3

C **Critical Thinking**

Predicting Consequences Partly in response to the efforts of the Double V campaign, President Roosevelt worked to integrate the armed forces. **Ask:** How do you think both white and African American servicemen reacted to Roosevelt's initial order to desegregate the armed forces? *(Answers will vary but should make note of the atmosphere of racial discrimination in the U.S. in the 1940s.)* **OL**

W **Writing Support**

Persuasive Writing Tell students to write letters to the editor stating that African Americans should be integrated into the armed forces. Have students share their letters with the class. **OL** **CA 11WS1.1**

Picturing **History**

Background: By the war's end, the Tuskegee Airmen had shot down 111 enemy aircraft, destroyed 150 enemy aircraft on the ground, and, in a rare feat, used machine gun fire from the air to sink a German destroyer.

Answer: European

Ask: Why did the military begin to recruit African Americans? *(President Roosevelt ordered them to recruit African Americans.)*

ASSESS

Resources for page 578

Use these resources to assess student mastery.

📂 Section Quiz 12-1

📂 Reading Essentials and Study Guide 12-1

💿 Interactive Tutor Self-Assessment CD-ROM

📂 California Standards Practice, Grade 11

Picturing **History**

Answer: Before the war women's education and career choices were limited. It is likely that army officials thought that women were not mentally or physically capable of combat.

Ask: Which service was the first to allow women's units? *(the army)*

✓ Reading Check

Answer: African Americans had several units that gave distinguished service. Women were allowed to serve in non-combat units.

HISTORY Online

Study Central provides audio summaries, interactive games, and online graphic organizers to help students review section content.

CLOSE

Visual/Spatial Assign students to groups of three or four. Tell them to design monuments commemorating women in World War II. Have each group write a paragraph describing their design and share their monuments with the class. **OL**

578

Women Join the Armed Forces As in World War I, women joined the armed forces. The army enlisted women for the first time, although they were barred from combat. Instead, as the army's recruiting slogan suggested, women were needed to "release a man for combat." Many jobs in the army were administrative and clerical. By assigning women to these jobs, more men would be available for combat.

Congress first allowed women in the military in May 1942, when it established the Women's Army Auxiliary Corps (WAAC) and appointed Oveta Culp Hobby, an official with the War Department, to serve as its first director. Although pleased about the establishment of the WAAC, many women were unhappy that it was an auxiliary corps and not part of the regular army. A little over a year later, the army replaced the WAAC with the Women's Army Corps (WAC). Director Hobby was assigned the rank of colonel. "You have a debt and a date," Hobby explained to those training to be the nation's first women officers. "A debt to democracy, a date with destiny." The Coast Guard, the navy, and the marines quickly followed the army and set up their own women's units. In addition to serving in these new organizations, another 68,000 women served as nurses in the army and navy.

Americans Go to War The Americans who went to war in 1941 were not well trained. Most of the troops had no previous military experience. Most of the officers had never led men in combat. The armed forces mirrored many of the tensions and prejudices of American society. Despite these challenges, the United States armed forces performed well in battle. Of all the major powers involved in the war, the United States suffered the fewest casualties in combat.

Picturing **History**

Women Pilots General Barney M. Giles inspects the guard of honor of the Women Airforce Service Pilots (WASPS) at Avenger Field in Sweetwater, Texas. Many pilots wore Filfinella patches (right) for good luck. **Why do you think the army refused to allow women to fly in combat?**

American troops never adopted the spit-and-polish style of the Europeans. When they arrived at the front, Americans' uniforms were usually a mess, and they rarely marched in step. When one Czechoslovakian was asked what he thought of the sloppy, unprofessional American soldiers, he commented, "They walk like free men."

✓ Reading Check **Summarizing** How did the status of women and African Americans in the armed forces change during the war?

HISTORY Online Study Central

For help with the concepts in this section of *American Vision: Modern Times* go to **tav.mt.glencoe.com** and click on *Study Central.*

SECTION 1 ASSESSMENT

Checking for Understanding

1. **Vocabulary** Define: incentive, cost-plus, Liberty ship, priority, consult, disfranchise.
2. **People and Terms** Identify: Reconstruction Finance Corporation, War Production Board, Selective Service and Training Act.
3. **Describe** the role of the OWM in the war production effort.

Reviewing Big Ideas

4. **Making Inferences** Why do you think African Americans were willing to fight in the war even though they suffered discrimination in American society?

Critical Thinking

5. **Evaluating** How effectively did American industry rally behind the war effort? Give examples to support your opinion.
6. **Categorizing** Use a graphic organizer like the one below to list the challenges facing the United States as it mobilized for war.

Challenges to Mobilization

Analyzing Visuals

7. **Analyzing Graphs** Study the graphs of automobile and tank production on pages 574 and 575. Why did automobile production decrease while tank production increased?

Writing About History

8. **Descriptive Writing** Take on the role of a draftee who has just completed the first week of basic training. Write a letter to your parents telling them about basic training and what you hope to accomplish once the training is over. **CA** 11WS1.1; 11WS1.2

SECTION 1 ASSESSMENT ANSWERS

1. Content vocabulary is boldfaced and highlighted in yellow. Academic vocabulary is boldfaced.
2. Reconstruction Finance Corporation *(p. 574)*, War Production Board *(p. 575)*, Selective Service and Training Act *(p. 576)*
3. The OWM resolved conflicts among mobilization agencies.

4. They opposed Hitler's ethnic theories, believed America should wage this war, and demonstrated their support for democracy and equality at home and overseas.
5. By 1942, almost all major industries were producing trucks, jeeps, and tanks.
6. converting to wartime economy,

building an army, training troops
7. Auto manufacturers were producing tanks rather than cars.
8. Answers should be in the form of a letter.

SECTION 2 — The Early Battles

Guide to Reading

Connection
In the previous section, you learned how the United States mobilized for war. In this section, you will discover the course of the early battles in the Atlantic and the Pacific.

Main Idea
- Japanese and American naval forces battled for control of the Pacific. (p. 580)
- American and British forces defeated the Germans in North Africa and in the Atlantic, while Soviet forces defeated Germany at Stalingrad. (p. 583)

Content Vocabulary
periphery, convoy system

Academic Vocabulary
assign, transmit, intensify

People and Terms to Identify
Chester Nimitz, Douglas MacArthur, James Doolittle, George Patton

Reading Objectives
- **Analyze** how the Allies were able to fight a war on two fronts and turn the war against the Axis in the Pacific, Russia, and the North Atlantic.

- **Explain** why Stalingrad is considered a major turning point of the war.

Reading Strategy
Sequencing As you read about the military campaigns of 1942, complete a time line similar to the one below to record the major battles discussed and the victor in each.

Preview of Events

◆1942   ◆1943   ◆1944

May 1942
Fall of the Philippines; Battle of the Coral Sea

June 1942
Battle of Midway

February 1943
Germans defeated at Stalingrad

May 1943
Germans driven out of North Africa

The following are the main History–Social Science Standards covered in this section.

11.7.2 Explain U.S. and Allied wartime strategy, including the major battles of Midway, Normandy, Iwo Jima, Okinawa, and the Battle of the Bulge.

11.7.3 Identify the roles and sacrifices of individual American soldiers, as well as the unique contributions of the special fighting forces (e.g., the Tuskegee Airmen, the 442nd Regimental Combat team, the Navajo Code Talkers).

∿ The Big Idea ∿

The fate of nations is forever changed by monumental world events. At first, the United States suffered setbacks in the Pacific with the fall of the Philippines. In order to boost Americans' morale, President Roosevelt ordered a mission to begin bombing attacks on Japan. The Japanese now set out to destroy the U.S. fleet. Americans were able to break the Japanese secret code and defeat the Japanese in two battles. At the same time, the United States and Great Britain began their campaign to attack Germany from the periphery by taking control of North Africa. The Allies also devised new ways to combat German submarines in the Atlantic. When Germany was defeated at the Battle of Stalingrad, the tide of war had changed both in Europe and Asia.

FOCUS

BELLRINGER
SKILLBUILDER ACTIVITY

Project **Daily Focus Skills Transparency 12-2** and have students answer the question.

Guide to Reading

Understanding Vocabulary:
Have students write paragraphs containing at least two of the academic vocabulary words and two of the content vocabulary words introduced in this section.

Answers to Graphic:
April 1942, Doolittle Raid, Allies; May 1942, Philippines, Axis; May 1942, Coral Sea, Allies; June 1942, Midway, Allies; November 1942, Stalingrad, Allies; May 1943, North Africa, Allies

Unpacking the Standards

Students will be able to:

- Describe how the United States struck back at the Japanese Empire following Pearl Harbor.

- Analyze how the United States began to assist the Allies in the fight against Nazi Germany.

SECTION RESOURCES

🗁 Print Material
- Reproducible Lesson Plan 12-2
- Guided Reading Activity 12-2
- Reading Essentials and Study Guide 12-2
- Active Reading Note-Taking Guide 12-2

🖳 Transparencies
- Daily Focus Skills Transparency 12-2
- Section Graphic Organizer Transparency 12-2

Technology
- 🖭 Interactive Tutor Self-Assessment CD-ROM
- 🖭 Exam*View*® Pro Testmaker CD-ROM
- 🖭 Presentation Plus! CD-ROM

TEACH

Review the Big Idea

Review the Big Idea for this section, "The fate of nations is forever changed by monumental world events." List the events from this section on the board. As students read the section, have them identify which Axis power was involved in each incident and determine the outcome of the event. **OL**

W Writing Support

Summary Writing Ask students to use library and Internet resources to find out more about General Douglas MacArthur. Have them write two-page papers that discuss the importance of General MacArthur to the war effort and evaluate President Roosevelt's decision to evacuate MacArthur's forces. **OL** **CA** 11WS1.6

Answers and Additional Support

Holding the Line Against Japan

Main Idea Japanese and American naval forces battled for control of the Pacific.

Reading Connection Have you ever had to change your plans to accomplish a goal? Read on to learn how the Japanese modified their battle plans against U.S. naval forces in the Pacific.

The United States suffered losses to its fleet at Pearl Harbor and faced superior fighter planes in combat. These two obstacles challenged the United States to develop new strategies to fight the war.

★ An American Story ★

On June 4, 1942, Lieutenant Commander James Thach climbed into his F4F Wildcat fighter plane. Thach knew that the Japanese Zero fighter planes were better than his Wildcat. To improve his chances against them, he had developed a new tactic he called the "Thach weave." At the Battle of Midway, he had his first chance to try it:

❝So we boarded our planes. All of us were highly excited and admittedly nervous. . . . A very short time after, Zero fighters came down on us—I figured there were twenty. . . . The air was just like a beehive, and I wasn't sure that anything would work. And then my weave began to work! I got a good shot at two Zeros and burned them . . . then Ram, my wingman, radioed: 'There's a Zero on my tail.' . . . I was really angry then. I was mad because my poor little wingman had never been in combat before [and] this Zero was about to chew him to pieces. I probably should have ducked under the Zero, but I lost my temper and decided to keep my fire going into him so he'd pull out. He did, and I just missed him by a few feet. I saw flames coming out of his airplane. This was like playing chicken on the highway with two automobiles headed for each other, except we were shooting at each other as well.❞

—quoted in *The Pacific War Remembered*

While officers like James Thach developed new tactics to fight the Japanese, the commander of the United States Navy in the Pacific, Admiral **Chester Nimitz**, began planning operations against the Japanese navy. Although the Japanese had badly damaged the American fleet at Pearl Harbor, they

James S. Thach ▲

had missed the American aircraft carriers, which were at sea on a mission. The United States had several carriers in the Pacific, and Nimitz was determined to use them. In the days just after Pearl Harbor, however, he could do little to stop Japan's advance into Southeast Asia.

The Fall of the Philippines A few hours after they bombed Pearl Harbor, the Japanese attacked American airfields located in the Philippines. Two days later, Japanese troops landed in the islands. The American and Filipino forces defending the Philippines were badly outnumbered. Their commander, General **Douglas MacArthur**, decided to retreat to the Bataan Peninsula. Using the peninsula's rugged terrain, MacArthur's troops were able to hold out for more than three months. Gradually, the lack of supplies along with diseases such as malaria, scurvy, and dysentery took their toll. Realizing MacArthur's capture would demoralize the American people, President Roosevelt ordered the general to evacuate to Australia. In Australia MacArthur made a promise: "I came through, and I shall return."

On April 9, 1942, the weary defenders of Bataan finally surrendered. Nearly 78,000 prisoners of war were forced to march—sick, exhausted, and starving—65 miles (105 km) to a Japanese prison camp. Thousands died on this march, which came to be known as the Bataan Death March. Here one captured American, Leon Beck, recalls the nightmare:

Did You Know?

Of the 78,000 Allied prisoners of war who began the six-day march from Bataan, only 54,000 survived.

66They'd halt us in front of these big artesian wells . . . so we could see the water and they wouldn't let us have any. Anyone who would make a break for water would be shot or bayoneted. Then they were left there. Finally, it got so bad further along the road that you never got away from the stench of death. There were bodies laying all along the road in various degrees of decomposition—swollen, burst open, maggots crawling by the thousands. . . .99

—quoted in *Death March: The Survivors of Bataan*

Although the troops in the Bataan Peninsula surrendered, a small force held out on the island of Corregidor in Manila Bay. Finally, in May 1942, Corregidor surrendered. The Philippines had fallen.

The Doolittle Raid Even before the fall of the Philippines, President Roosevelt was searching for a way to raise the morale of the American people. He wanted to bomb Tokyo, but American planes could reach Tokyo only if an aircraft carrier brought them close enough. Unfortunately, Japanese ships in the North Pacific prevented carriers from getting close enough to Japan to launch their short-range bombers.

In early 1942, a military planner suggested replacing the carrier's usual short-range bombers with long-range B-25 bombers that could attack from farther away. Although B-25s could take off from a carrier, they could not land on its short deck. After attacking Japan, they would have to land in China.

President Roosevelt put Lieutenant Colonel **James Doolittle** in command of the mission. At the end of March, a crane loaded sixteen B-25s onto the aircraft carrier *Hornet*. The next day the *Hornet* headed west across the Pacific. On April 18, American bombs fell on Japan for the first time.

A Change in Japanese Strategy While Americans were overjoyed that the air force had finally struck back, Japanese leaders were aghast. Doolittle's bombs could have killed the emperor. The Doolittle raid convinced Japanese leaders to change their strategy.

Before the raid, the Japanese Navy had been arguing about what to do next. The officers in charge of the navy's planning wanted to cut American supply lines to Australia by capturing the south coast of New Guinea. The commander of the fleet, Admiral Yamamoto, wanted to attack Midway Island—the last American base in the North Pacific west of Hawaii. Yamamoto believed that attacking Midway would lure the American fleet into battle and enable his fleet to destroy it.

After Doolittle's raid, the planners dropped their opposition to Yamamoto's plan. The American fleet had to be destroyed in order to protect Tokyo from bombing. The attack on New Guinea would still go ahead, but only three aircraft carriers were **assigned** to the mission. All of the other carriers were ordered to prepare for an assault on Midway.

The Battle of the Coral Sea The Japanese believed that they could proceed with two different attacks. They thought the United States was unaware of Japan's activity and would not be able to respond in time. Japan did not know that an American team of code breakers, based in Hawaii, had already broken the Japanese Navy's secret code for conducting operations.

Striking Back: The Doolittle Raid, April 18, 1942

The plan for the Doolittle raid was to launch B-25 bombers from aircraft carriers between 450 and 650 miles from Japan. The planes would bomb selected targets, and fly another 1,200 miles to airfields in China.

All went well until the Japanese discovered the carriers more than 150 miles from the proposed launch site. Instead of canceling the mission, the bombers took off early. The planes reached Japan and dropped their bombs, but they did not have enough fuel to reach the friendly airfields in China. The crews were forced to bail out or crash-land, and only 71 of the 80 crew members survived. Nevertheless, the raid provided an instant boost to sagging American morale.

Planes arrive in China
Carriers launch B-25s
Tokyo is bombed

More Skill Practice

Making Inferences The U.S. used B-24 and B-29 bombers during World War II, along with the B-25s used for the Doolittle raid. Ask students why they think American leaders decided not to cancel the mission. *(Because the Japanese had bombed American soil and captured U.S. forces, American leaders felt that bombing Japan would raise American morale.)* OL

Did You Know?

Coral Sea was the first battle in history to be fought entirely from aircraft carriers.

W₁ Writing Support

Journal Writing Following the devastation of the Pearl Harbor attack, it took the U.S. military some time to organize and accomplish significant gains against Japanese aggression in the Pacific. **Ask:** Do you remember a time in your life when a small victory provided an important boost in morale? Tell students to write short paragraphs or journal entries recounting the experiences and their importance. *(Possible answers could include winning a sports game, scoring well on a test, etc.)* OL CA 11WA2.1b

W₂ Writing Support

Research Report Writing Ask students to prepare one-page reports on the military career of Lieutenant Colonel James Doolittle. The reports should address how Doolittle contributed to the war effort and what he did earlier or later in his career. Have students share their reports with the class. OL CA 11WA2.1a

U₁ Universal Access

English Learners Have students review the text under the heading "A Change in Japanese Strategy" and then teach it to a partner. Have the student doing the teaching ask questions about what has been taught. Direct the teaching students to review any concepts that the learners did not understand. EL CA 11RC2.4; 11RC2.5

U₂ Universal Access

Below Grade Level Have interested students create a model depicting the Battle of the Coral Sea. Encourage them to use library and Internet resources to make their model as accurate as possible. BL

581

S₁ Skill Practice

Visual Literacy Have students organize the information from the map into a time line. Based on the time line they have created, ask students to identify the point when the battle seemed to shift toward a decisive Allied victory. *(Answers will vary, but students should note the sinking of three Japanese carriers as a significant event.)* `OL` `CA HI2; HI4`

S₂ Skill Practice

Conducting Research Have students work in groups to research and report on the military vessels and planes used in the Battle of Midway. Ask them to illustrate their work with photos, drawings, and models. Create a display area to showcase students' work. `OL` `CA HR4`

Answers and Additional Support

NATIONAL GEOGRAPHIC Battle of Midway, 1942

① June 4, 4:30 A.M. Japanese carriers launch 108 warplanes to strike U.S. base at Midway.

② June 4, 6:16 A.M. U.S. fighters clash with attackers.

③ June 4, 6:30 A.M. Japanese begin bombing Midway.

④ June 4, 7:08 A.M. U.S. fliers from Midway begin attacking Japanese fleet.

⑤ June 4, 9:17 A.M. Japanese planes return. Fleet turns to engage U.S. carriers.

⑥ June 4, 10:22-10:28 A.M. U.S. Dive-bombers score direct hits on *Kaga*, *Akagi*, and *Soryu*.

⑦ June 4, noon. Planes from the *Hiryu* attack U.S. carriers. *Yorktown* hit. The ship is abandoned but remains afloat.

⑧ June 4, 5:01 P.M. *Yorktown* fliers join *Enterprise* attack on the *Hiryu*, setting it ablaze.

⑨ June 6, 1:31 P.M. Japanese submarine *I-168* torpedoes the *Yorktown*, which sinks the next morning.

Course of *Enterprise* and *Hornet*

Course of *Yorktown*

Course of Japanese fleet

Hiryu sinks ✕
Akagi sinks ✕ *Soryu* sinks ✕
Kaga sinks ✕
Yorktown sinks

Line of U.S. submarines stationed 170 miles from Midway.

Kure Atoll (U.S.)

Midway Islands (U.S.)

PACIFIC OCEAN

U.S. Dauntless dive-bomber

N S E W

● U.S. actions
● Japanese actions

Geography *Skills*

1. **Interpreting Maps** When did Japan launch the attack on Midway?
2. **Applying Geography Skills** Why were aircraft carriers so vital to the war in the Pacific?

In March 1942, decoded Japanese messages alerted the United States to the Japanese attack on New Guinea. In response, Admiral Nimitz sent two carriers, the *Yorktown* and the *Lexington,* to intercept the Japanese in the Coral Sea. There, in early May, carriers from both sides launched all-out airstrikes against each other. Although the Japanese sank the *Lexington* and badly damaged the *Yorktown,* the American attacks forced the Japanese to call off their landing on the south coast of New Guinea. The American supply lines to Australia stayed open.

The Battle of Midway Back at Pearl Harbor, the code-breaking team that had alerted Nimitz to the attack on New Guinea now learned of the plan to attack Midway. With so many ships at sea, Admiral Yamamoto **transmitted** the plans for the Midway attack by radio, using the same code the Americans had already cracked.

Admiral Nimitz had been waiting for the opportunity to ambush the Japanese fleet. He immediately ordered carriers to take up positions near Midway. Unaware they were heading into an ambush, the Japanese launched their aircraft against Midway on

June 4, 1942. The island was ready. The Japanese planes ran into a blizzard of antiaircraft fire, and 38 of them were shot down.

As the Japanese prepared a second wave to attack Midway, aircraft from the American carriers *Hornet, Yorktown,* and *Enterprise* launched a counterattack. The American planes caught the Japanese carriers with fuel, bombs, and aircraft exposed on their flight decks. Within minutes three Japanese carriers were reduced to burning wrecks. A fourth was sunk a few hours later. By nightfall Admiral Yamamoto ordered his remaining ships to retreat.

The Battle of Midway was a turning point in the war. The Japanese Navy lost four of its largest carriers—the heart of its fleet. Just six months after Pearl Harbor, the United States had stopped the Japanese advance in the Pacific. As Admiral Ernest King, the commander in chief of the U.S. Navy, later observed, Midway "put an end to the long period of Japanese

582 CHAPTER 12 America and World War II

Geography *Skills*

Background: Before World War II, few of the indigenous peoples of the islands of the South Pacific had encountered people from other parts of the world.

Answers:
1. June 4, 1942, 4:30 A.M.
2. Aircraft carriers reduced the distance planes had to fly and the amount of fuel they consumed.

Geography Skills Practice
Ask: What general direction did the *Enterprise* and *Hornet* take? *(southwest)*

JAPANESE FORCES To destroy the U.S. Pacific Fleet, crippled by the 1941 attack on Pearl Harbor, Japan plots an occupation of two Aleutian islands and an invasion of Midway. Strategists believe that the twin actions will lure U.S. carriers to their doom. Two Japanese carriers and 58 other ships sail for the Aleutians. For Midway, Japan commits 4 large carriers, 2 light carriers, 280 planes, 7 battleships, 14 cruisers, 15 submarines, 42 destroyers, and more than 30 supporting ships. These include transports carrying 5,000 troops to take Midway.

U.S. FORCES No battleships guard U.S. carriers sent to Midway to engage the enemy fleet. Into combat go 3 carriers, including battle-damaged Yorktown. Protecting them are 8 cruisers and 16 destroyers. The U.S. has a total of 360 aircraft, including 234 carrier-based fighters and small bombers. Based on Midway are 28 fighters, 46 small bombers, 31 PBY Catalina scout planes, 4 Marauder medium bombers, and 17 Flying Fortresses. Most pilots on Midway have never flown in combat.

offensive action." The victory was not without devastating costs, however. The battle killed 362 Americans and 3,057 Japanese. Afterward, one naval officer wrote to his wife: "Let no one tell you or let you believe that this war is anything other than a grim, terrible business."

✓ Reading Check **Explaining** Why was the Battle of Midway considered a turning point?

Turning Back the German Army

Main Idea American and British forces defeated the Germans in North Africa and in the Atlantic, while Soviet forces defeated Germany at Stalingrad.

Reading Connection Have you ever been rewarded for being persistent or brave? Read on to discover how persistence and bravery won battles against German forces.

In 1942 Allied forces began to win victories in Europe as well. Almost from the moment the United States entered the war, Joseph Stalin, the leader of the

Soviet Union, urged President Roosevelt to open a second front in Europe. Stalin appreciated the Lend-Lease supplies that the United States had sent, but the Soviets needed more than supplies. The Soviet people were still doing most of the fighting. If British and American troops opened a second front by attacking Germany from the west, it would take pressure off the Soviet Union.

Roosevelt wanted to get American troops into battle in Europe, but Prime Minister Churchill urged caution. He did not believe the United States and Great Britain were ready to launch a full-scale invasion of Europe. Instead Churchill wanted to attack the **periphery**, or edges, of the German empire. Roosevelt agreed with Churchill's plan, and in July 1942 he ordered the invasion of Morocco and Algeria—two French territories indirectly under German control.

The Struggle for North Africa Roosevelt decided to invade Morocco and Algeria for two reasons. First, the invasion would give the army some experience without requiring a lot of troops. More importantly, once American troops were in North Africa, they would be able to help British troops fighting the Germans in Egypt.

Egypt was very important to Britain because of the Suez Canal. Most of Britain's empire, including India, Hong Kong, Singapore, Malaya, and Australia, used the canal to send supplies to Britain. Britain would be devastated if it lost the canal. The German forces in the area, known as the "Afrika Korps," were commanded by General Erwin Rommel—a brilliant leader whose success earned him the nickname "Desert Fox."

The British forced Rommel to retreat at the battle of El Alamein, but his forces remained a serious threat. On November 8, 1942, the American invasion of North Africa began under the command of General Dwight D. Eisenhower. The American forces in Morocco, led by General **George Patton**, quickly captured the city of Casablanca, while those in Algeria seized the cities of Oran and Algiers. The Americans then headed east into Tunisia, while British forces headed west into Libya. The plan was to trap Rommel between the two Allied forces.

HISTORY Online

Student Web Activity Visit the *American Vision: Modern Times* Web site at tav.mt.glencoe.com and click on *Student Web Activities— Chapter 12* for an activity on America and World War II.

U Universal Access

Logical/Mathematical Have students read the passage describing Churchill's and Roosevelt's opposing plans. Ask students to brainstorm arguments that both men might use to support their decisions. After the initial brainstorming sessions, ask students to pick the two or three best arguments and discuss those as a class. **OL** **CA HI3**

C Critical Thinking

Identifying Central Issues Have students work in groups to write a press release from President Roosevelt to the American people explaining the necessity of invading North Africa. Make sure that as president, they explain the importance of undertaking this campaign rather than focusing on defeating the Japanese first before targeting the German army. **OL** **CA HI4**

Resources for page 583

Have students read more about Americans in the North African campaign in the ***Primary Source Readings 12-1.***

✓ Reading Check

Answer: The Japanese lost four large carriers and their initiative.

Did You Know?

The Japanese flag shown on this page is the regimental flag for the Japanese cavalry and infantry. The national flag of Japan since 1870 has consisted of a white background with a red circle in the middle. The red circle is said to symbolize the rising sun.

HISTORY Online

Objectives and answers to the student activity can be found in the **Web Activity Lesson Plan** at tav.mt.glencoe.com.

U Universal Access

Visual/Spatial Ask students to research the system of convoys that the United States and its allies developed to protect ships crossing the Atlantic Ocean. Tell students to draw diagrams that show the placement of the various ships used in a convoy formation. Display the diagrams in the classroom. **OL**

W Writing Support

Research Report Writing
Germany used submarines very effectively in World War I. Ask students to use library and Internet resources to write three-page papers on how submarine technology improved between 1914 and 1942. **AL** **CA** 11WS1.6

Answers and Additional Support

Profiles IN HISTORY

Fleet Admiral Chester W. Nimitz
1885–1966

Taking command of the Pacific Fleet after the bombing of Pearl Harbor, Admiral Chester Nimitz did not view the Japanese attack as a complete disaster. The United States still had its aircraft carriers, and base facilities were in good repair. Even though the battle fleet was at the bottom of the harbor, most of the ships could be retrieved and repaired. If the Japanese had attacked the fleet at sea, nothing would have been salvageable.

Nimitz believed that the only way to win the war was to keep constant pressure on the Japanese. He ordered attacks in early 1942 and firmly backed the Doolittle raid. Nimitz planned the American campaigns that turned the tide of war at Midway and Guadalcanal. Nimitz kept the pressure on the Japanese throughout the war, and he signed the Japanese surrender document as the official representative of the United States government in 1945. In less than four years, he had taken a badly damaged fleet and made it victorious throughout the Pacific.

Admiral Isoroku Yamamoto *1884–1943*

The son of a schoolmaster, Isoroku Yamamoto spent his entire adult life in the military. In the 1930s he was one of the few Japanese leaders who opposed war with the United States. Yamamoto did so not because he was a pacifist, but because he feared Japan would lose.

When he realized that Japan's leaders were intent on war, Yamamoto became convinced that Japan's only hope lay in launching a surprise attack that would destroy the American Pacific Fleet. Although some officers opposed his plan, Yamamoto won out, and he planned and implemented the attack on Pearl Harbor. During the first years of the war, he enjoyed tremendous prestige because of Japanese victories he helped engineer.

In April 1943 the admiral took an inspection flight of several islands. Having already broken the Japanese codes, the Americans knew of the flight. On April 18, American fighters shot down Yamamoto's plane in the South Pacific, and the admiral was killed in the attack.

When the American troops advanced into the mountains of western Tunisia, they had to fight the German army for the first time. They did not do well. At the Battle of Kasserine Pass, the Americans were outmaneuvered and outfought. They suffered roughly 7,000 casualties and lost nearly 200 tanks. Eisenhower fired the general who led the attack and put Patton in command. Together, the American and British forces finally pushed the Germans back. On May 13, 1943, the last German forces in North Africa surrendered.

The Battle of the Atlantic As American and British troops fought the German army in North Africa, the war against German submarines in the Atlantic Ocean continued to **intensify.** After Germany declared war on the United States, German submarines entered American coastal waters. They found American cargo ships to be easy targets, especially at night when the glow from the cities in the night sky silhouetted the vessels. To protect the ships, cities on the East Coast dimmed their lights every evening. People also put up special "blackout curtains" and drove with their headlights off.

By August 1942, German submarines had sunk about 360 American ships along the American coast. So many oil tankers were sunk that gasoline and fuel oil had to be rationed. To keep oil flowing, the government built the first long-distance oil pipeline, stretching some 1,250 miles (2,010 km) from the Texas oil fields to Pennsylvania.

The loss of so many ships convinced the U.S. Navy to set up a **convoy system.** Under this system, cargo ships traveled in groups and were escorted by navy warships. The convoy system improved the situation dramatically. It made it much harder for a submarine to torpedo a cargo ship and escape without being attacked.

The spring of 1942 marked the high point of the German submarine campaign. In May and June alone, over 1.2 million tons of shipping were sunk. Yet in those same two months, American and British shipyards built over 1.1 million tons of new shipping. From July 1942 onward, American shipyards produced more ships than German submarines managed to sink. At the same time, American airplanes and warships began to use new technology, including radar, sonar, and depth charges, to locate and attack

---

Profiles IN HISTORY

Use a Venn diagram to compare and contrast the lives and military careers of Nimitz and Yamamoto.

submarines. As the new technology began to take its toll on German submarines, the Battle of the Atlantic slowly turned in favor of the Allies.

Stalingrad In the spring of 1942, before the Battle of the Atlantic turned against Germany, Adolf Hitler was very confident he would win the war. Rommel's troops were pushing the British back in Egypt. German submarines were sinking American ships rapidly, and the German army was ready to launch a new offensive to knock the Soviets out of the war.

Hitler was convinced that the only way to defeat the Soviet Union was to destroy its economy. In May 1942, he ordered his army to capture strategic oil fields, industries, and farmlands in southern Russia and Ukraine. The key to the attack was the city of Stalingrad. The city controlled the Volga River and was a major railroad junction. If the German army captured Stalingrad, the Soviets would be cut off from the resources they needed to stay in the war.

When German troops entered Stalingrad in mid-September, Stalin ordered his troops to hold the city at all cost. Retreat was forbidden. The Germans were forced to fight from house to house, losing thousands of soldiers in the process.

On November 23, Soviet reinforcements arrived and surrounded Stalingrad, trapping almost 250,000 German troops. When the battle ended, 91,000 Germans had surrendered, although only 5,000 of them survived the Soviet prison camps and returned home after the war. The Battle of Stalingrad was

 Picturing **History**

Halting the German Advance Soviet troops assault German positions in Stalingrad in November 1942. Why did the Soviet army need to hold on to the city of Stalingrad?

a major turning point in the war. Just as the Battle of Midway put the Japanese on the defensive for the rest of the war, the Battle of Stalingrad put the Germans on the defensive as well.

 Reading Check **Evaluating** What did the Allies do to win the Battle of the Atlantic?

HISTORY *Online* **Study Central**

For help with the concepts in this section of *American Vision: Modern Times* go to tav.mt.glencoe.com and click on **Study Central.**

SECTION 2 ASSESSMENT

Checking for Understanding

1. **Vocabulary** Define: assign, transmit, periphery, intensify, convoy system.
2. **People and Terms** Identify: Chester Nimitz, Douglas MacArthur, James Doolittle, George Patton.
3. **Explain** the American strategy in North Africa.

Reviewing Big Ideas

4. **Identifying** How did the Battle at Stalingrad change the fate of the Allies and the momentum of the war?

Critical Thinking

5. **Analyzing** How did code breakers help stop Japanese advances?
6. **Evaluating** How were the Americans able to win the Battle of the Atlantic?
7. **Organizing** Use a graphic organizer like the one below to list the reasons the Battle of Midway was a major turning point in the war.

Battle of Midway

Analyzing Visuals

8. **Examining Maps** Study the map of Midway on page 582. Why do you think the Japanese forces attacked when they did?

Writing About History

9. **Descriptive Writing** Take on the role of an American soldier fighting in the Pacific in World War II. Write a letter to your family explaining what conditions are like for you and what you hope to accomplish during the war.
   CA 11WA2.1e

CHAPTER 12 America and World War II **585**

SECTION 2 ASSESSMENT ANSWERS

1. Content vocabulary is boldfaced and highlighted in yellow. Academic vocabulary is boldfaced.
2. Chester Nimitz *(p. 580)*, Douglas MacArthur *(p. 580)*, James Doolittle *(p. 581)*, George Patton *(p. 583)*
3. The army gained experience and helped the British in Egypt.
4. gave the Allies an important win and improved morale
5. They alerted the U.S. to the imminent attacks on New Guinea and Midway.
6. the convoy system protected cargo ships; radar, sonar, and depth charges located and damaged German submarines
7. Japanese navy lost four carriers; stopped the Japanese advance in the Pacific; ended Japanese offensive
8. Answers may note that early morning attacks held an element of surprise.
9. Letters should focus on soldiers' emotions and activities.

FOCUS

BELLRINGER
SKILLBUILDER ACTIVITY

Project **Daily Focus Skills Transparency 12-3** and have students answer the question.

Guide to Reading

Understanding Vocabulary: Have students create posters that visualize two of the content vocabulary words.

Answers to Graphic: Women—Before: few job opportunities, low pay; After: better selection. African Americans—Before: few opportunities; After: Fair Employment Practices oversight. Still needed: Answers will vary for both groups.

Unpacking the Standards

Students will be able to:

- Describe increased job opportunities for minorities and women.
- Analyze how the population in the United States shifted.
- Discuss how the war impacted the home front.

Answers and Additional Support

SECTION 3 Life on the Home Front

Guide to Reading

Connection
In the previous section, you learned about the early battles of the war. In this section, you will discover how the war impacted the daily lives of Americans.

Main Idea
- The changing roles in the workplace and growing political demands opened doors to new work for women and minorities. (p. 587)
- During the war, many people moved in search of jobs, while many Japanese Americans were forced from their homes into internment camps. (p. 589)

Preview of Events

- Civilians made many sacrifices during the war to help ensure victory for the Allies. (p. 591)

Content Vocabulary
Sunbelt, rationing, victory garden

Academic Vocabulary
perspective, allocate, integrate

People and Terms to Identify
Rosie the Riveter, A. Philip Randolph, zoot suit, E bond

Reading Objectives
- **Describe** how the wartime economy created opportunities for women and minorities.

- **Discuss** how Americans coped with shortages and rapidly rising prices.

Reading Strategy
Categorizing As you read about the challenges facing Americans on the home front, complete a graphic organizer listing opportunities for women and African Americans before and after the war. Also evaluate what progress still needed to be made after the war.

Opportunities	Before War	After War	Still Needed
Women			
African Americans			

Preview of Events

◆1941	◆1942	◆1943	◆1944

June 1941
Executive Order 8802 forbids race discrimination in industries with government contracts

August 1941
Roosevelt creates the Office of Price Administration

February 1942
Japanese American relocation ordered

June 1943
Race riots in Detroit; zoot suit riots in Los Angeles

The following are the main History–Social Science Standards covered in this section.

11.7.3 Identify the roles and sacrifices of individual American soldiers, as well as the unique contributions of the special fighting forces (e.g., the Tuskegee Airmen, the 442nd Regimental Combat team, the Navajo Code Talkers).

11.7.5 Discuss the constitutional issues and impact of events on the U.S. home front, including the internment of Japanese Americans (e.g., *Fred Korematsu* v. *United States of America*) and the restrictions on German and Italian resident aliens; the response of the administration to Hitler's atrocities against Jews and other groups; the roles of women in military production; the roles and growing political demands of African Americans.

11.7.6 Describe major developments in aviation, weaponry, communication, and medicine and the war's impact on the location of American industry and use of resources.

11.10.1 Explain how demands of African Americans helped produce a stimulus for civil rights, including President Roosevelt's ban on racial discrimination in defense industries in 1941, and how African

~ The Big Idea ~

People react to periods of breathtaking social and cultural change in different ways. With so many white men in the military, job opportunities opened for women and minorities. Most women took clerical jobs, but those in factories helped change attitudes about women in the workplace. African Americans gained new civil rights and access to new jobs. Mexicans came into the United States to fill farm jobs. Many people moved to find jobs in the new factories, creating a housing crisis and new problems with racism. While most minorities were able to gain some rights, Japanese Americans along the West Coast had to endure relocation and internment. Throughout the war, American life included wage and price regulations, rationing, victory gardens, and war bond drives.

Americans' service in World War II produced a stimulus for President Truman's decision to end segregation in the armed forces in 1948.

11.10.4 Examine the roles of civil rights advocates (e.g., A. Philip Randolph, Martin Luther King, Jr., Malcom X, Thurgood Marshall, James Farmer, Rosa Parks), including the significance of Martin Luther

King, Jr.'s "Letter from Birmingham Jail" and "I Have a Dream" speech.

11.11.3 Describe the changing roles of women in society as reflected in the entry of more women into the labor force and the changing family structure.

586 CHAPTER 12 America and World War II

SECTION RESOURCES

📂 Print Material
- Reproducible Lesson Plan 12-3
- Guided Reading Activity 12-3
- Reading Essentials and Study Guide 12-3
- Active Reading Note-Taking Guide 12-3

📝 Transparencies
- Daily Focus Skills Transparency 12-3
- Section Graphic Organizer Transparency 12-3

Technology
- 💿 Interactive Tutor Self-Assessment CD-ROM
- 💿 ExamView® Pro Testmaker CD-ROM
- 💿 Presentation Plus! CD-ROM

Women and Minorities Gain Ground

Main Idea The changing roles in the workplace and growing political demands opened doors to new work for women and minorities.

Reading Connection Discuss the benefits that wartime production provided women and minorities and how these effects would be different today. Read on to find out about advances that women and minorities achieved during World War II.

As American troops fought their first battles against the Germans and Japanese, the war began to dramatically change American society at home. In contrast to the devastation the war brought to large parts of Europe and Asia, World War II had a positive effect on American society. The war finally put an end to the Great Depression. Mobilizing the economy created almost 19 million new jobs and nearly doubled the average family's income. Many Americans now enjoyed living in a more prosperous time.

★ An American Story ★

Laura Briggs was a young woman living on a farm in Idaho when World War II began. As with many other Americans, the war completely changed her outlook on life:

66When I was growing up, it was very much depression times. . . . As farm prices [during the war] began to get better and better, farm times became good times. . . . We and most other farmers went from a tarpaper shack to a new frame house with indoor plumbing. Now we had an electric stove instead of a wood-burning one, and running water at the sink. . . . The war made many changes in our town. I think the most important is that aspirations changed. People suddenly had the idea, 'Hey I can reach that. I can have that. I can do that. I could even send my kid to college if I wanted to.'99

—quoted in *Wartime America: The World War II Home Front*

When the war began, American defense factories wanted to hire white men. With so many men in the military, though, there simply were not enough white men to fill all of the jobs. Under pressure to produce, employers began to recruit women and minorities.

Women in the Defense Plants During the Depression, many people believed married women should not work outside the home, especially if it meant taking jobs away from men trying to support their families. Most women who did work were young, single, and employed in traditional female jobs. The wartime labor shortage, however, forced factories to recruit married women to do industrial jobs that traditionally had been reserved for men.

Although the government hired nearly 4 million women for mostly clerical jobs, it was the women in the factories who captured the public's imagination. The great symbol of the campaign to hire women was **"Rosie the Riveter,"** a character from a popular song by the Four Vagabonds. The lyrics told of Rosie, who worked in a factory while her boyfriend served in the marines. Images of Rosie appeared on posters, in newspapers, and in magazines. Eventually 2.5 million women went to work in shipyards, aircraft factories, and other manufacturing plants. For many older middle-class women like Inez Sauer, working in a factory changed their **perspective:**

66I learned that just because you're a woman and have never worked is no reason you can't learn. The job really broadened me. . . . I had always been in a shell; I'd always been protected. But at Boeing I found a freedom and an independence I had never known. After the war I could never go back to playing bridge again, being a clubwoman. . . . when I knew there were things you could use your mind for. The war changed my life completely.99

—quoted in *Eyewitness to World War II*

▼ *"Rosie the Riveter" symbolized new roles for women*

CHAPTER 12   America and World War II   **587**

TEACH

W Writing Support

Narrative Writing Have students take on the role of a young woman who just took a job working in a defense factory during the war and is writing to her grandmother about her first few days on the job. Letters should describe the feelings this young woman has about her job, whether they are positive or negative. **BL** **CA** 11WA2.1a; 11WA2.1b

C Critical Thinking

Predicting Consequences Have students review the quote from factory worker Inez Sauer on this page. **Ask:** How do you think women reacted to leaving their jobs and returning home at the end of World War II? Why? *Tell students to write short paragraphs supporting their answers.* **OL**

Resources for page 587

*Have students read more about increased work opportunities for women at home during the war in **Primary Source Readings 12-2.***

Did You Know?

"Rosie the Riveter" was a response to "Tokyo Rose" and "Axis Sally," enemy characters who broadcast anti-Allied propaganda over the radio in the Pacific and in Europe.

Did You Know?

While President Roosevelt's Fair Employment Practices Commission gave African Americans equal pay in war industries and government jobs and improved their wages in general, most African Americans still faced "last-hired, first-fired" policies and severe housing discrimination.

R₁ Reading Strategy

Activating Prior Knowledge
Ask students to read the text under the heading "African Americans Demand War Work." Remind them that in other times of crisis, minorities have used circumstances to gain social and economic opportunities. Ask students to identify when in the past this has occurred and who benefited. *(Students might point to the slight gains that African Americans and women made during World War I and the gains that industrial workers experienced during the Great Depression.)*

OL **CA HI1**

R₂ Reading Strategy

Monitoring Work with students to brainstorm a list of stereotypes people had about Mexican Americans in the 1940s. **Ask: Are Hispanic Americans today harmed by stereotyping?** Create a second list of present-day negative stereotypes of Hispanic Americans. Tell students to note in journals negative media stereotypes for one week. Have students share their findings with the class. **OL** **CA HI1**

✓ Reading Check

Answer: Mobilizing the economy for war production created nearly 19 million new jobs and nearly doubled the average family's income.

Although most women left the factories after the war, their success permanently changed American attitudes about women in the workplace.

African Americans Demand War Work

Although factories were hiring women, they resisted hiring African Americans. Frustrated by the situation, **A. Philip Randolph,** the head of the Brotherhood of Sleeping Car Porters—a major union for African American railroad workers—decided to take action. He informed President Roosevelt that he was organizing "from ten to fifty thousand [African Americans] to march on Washington in the interest of securing jobs . . . in national defense and . . . integration into the military and naval forces."

In response, Roosevelt issued Executive Order 8802, on June 25, 1941. The order declared, "there shall be no discrimination in the employment of workers in defense industries or government because of race, creed, color or national origin." To enforce the order, the president created the Fair Employment Practices Commission—the first civil rights agency established by the federal government since the Reconstruction era.

Mexicans Become Farmworkers The wartime economy needed workers in many different areas. To help farmers in the Southwest overcome the labor shortage, the government introduced the Bracero Program in 1942. *Bracero* is Spanish for worker. The federal government arranged for Mexican farmworkers to help in the harvest. Over 200,000 Mexicans came to the United States to help harvest fruit and vegetables in the Southwest. Many also helped to build and maintain railroads. The Bracero Program continued until 1964. Migrant farmworkers became an important part of the Southwest's agricultural system.

✓ **Reading Check** **Describing** How did mobilizing the economy help end the Depression?

Profiles IN HISTORY

The Navajo Code Talkers
1942–1945

When American marines stormed an enemy beach, they used radios to communicate. Using radios, however, meant that the Japanese could intercept and translate the messages. In the midst of the battle, however, there was no time to use a code machine. Acting upon the suggestion of Philip Johnston, an engineer who had lived on a Navajo reservation as a child, the marines recruited Navajos to serve as "code talkers."

The Navajo language was a "hidden language"–it had no written alphabet and was known only to the Navajo and a few missionaries and anthropologists. The Navajo recruits developed a code using words from their own language to represent military terms. For example, the Navajo word *jay-sho,* or "buzzard," was code for bomber; *lotso,* or "whale," meant battleship; and *na-ma-si,* or "potatoes," stood for grenades.

Code talkers proved invaluable in combat. They could relay a message in minutes that would have taken a code machine operator hours to encipher and transmit. At the battle of Iwo Jima, code talkers transmitted more than 800 messages during the first 48 hours as the marines struggled to get ashore under intense bombardment.

Over 400 Navajo served in the marine corps as code talkers. Sworn to secrecy, their mission was not revealed until many years after the war. In 2001 Congress awarded the code talkers the Congressional Gold Medal to recognize their unique contribution to the war effort.

Profiles IN HISTORY

One of the advantages of using Navajo code talkers was that a three-line English message could be encoded, transmitted, and decoded in about 20 seconds. Code machines in use at the time took at least 30 minutes to perform the same task.

Ask: What is the significance of the Navajo language being a "hidden language"? *(Because the language has no written alphabet and was known only to a few people, it was a very secure code.)*

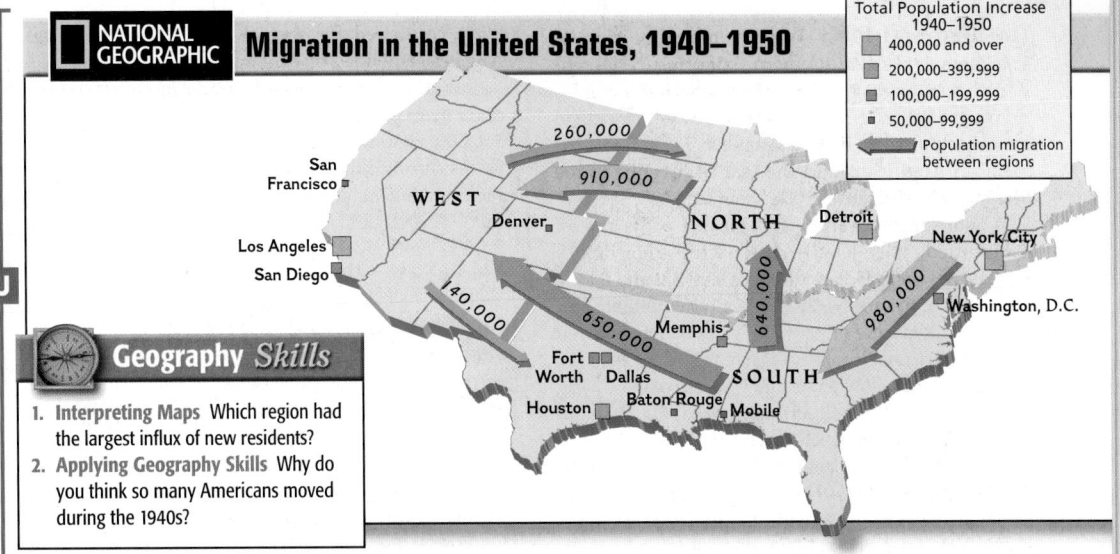

NATIONAL GEOGRAPHIC **Migration in the United States, 1940–1950**

Total Population Increase
1940–1950
- 400,000 and over
- 200,000–399,999
- 100,000–199,999
- 50,000–99,999

← Population migration between regions

WEST
San Francisco
Los Angeles
San Diego
Denver

260,000
910,000
140,000
650,000

NORTH
Detroit
New York City
Washington, D.C.

640,000
980,000

SOUTH
Memphis
Fort Worth   Dallas
Houston   Baton Rouge   Mobile

Geography Skills

1. **Interpreting Maps** Which region had the largest influx of new residents?
2. **Applying Geography Skills** Why do you think so many Americans moved during the 1940s?

A Nation on the Move

Main Idea During the war, many people moved in search of jobs, while many Japanese Americans were forced from their homes into internment camps.

Reading Connection Do you know of anyone who has moved to get a better job or go to a better school? Read on to learn about the many people who went where the jobs were during World War II.

The wartime economy created millions of new jobs, but the Americans who wanted these jobs did not always live nearby. To get to the jobs, 15 million Americans moved during the war. Although the assembly plants of the Midwest and the shipyards of the Northeast attracted many workers, most Americans headed west and south in search of the new jobs.

Taken together, the growth of southern California and the expansion of cities in the Deep South created a new industrial region—the **Sunbelt.** For the first time since the Industrial Revolution began in the United States, the South and West led the way in manufacturing and urbanization.

The Housing Crisis Perhaps the most difficult task facing cities with war industries was deciding where to put the thousands of new workers. Many people had to live in tents and tiny trailers. To help solve the

housing crisis, the federal government **allocated** over $1.2 billion to build public housing, schools, and community centers during the war.

Although prefabricated government housing had tiny rooms, thin walls, poor heating, and almost no privacy, it was better than no housing at all. Nearly two million people lived in government built housing during the war.

Racism Explodes Into Violence African Americans began to leave the South in great numbers during World War I, but this "Great Migration," as historians usually refer to it, slowed during the Depression. When jobs in war factories opened up for African Americans during World War II, the Great Migration resumed. When African Americans arrived in the crowded cities of the North and West, however, the local residents often greeted them with suspicion and intolerance. Sometimes these attitudes led to violence.

The worst racial violence of the war erupted in Detroit on Sunday, June 20, 1943. The weather that day was sweltering. To cool off, nearly 100,000 people crowded into Belle Isle, a park on the Detroit River. Fights erupted between gangs of white and African American teenage girls. These fights triggered others, and a full-scale riot erupted across the city. By the time the violence ended, 25 African Americans and 9 whites had been killed. Despite the appalling violence in Detroit, African American leaders remained committed to their Double V campaign.

Geography Skills

Background: Remind students that during World War II the United States consisted of only 48 states. Alaska and Hawaii had not yet become states.

Answers:
1. the West, with 1,560,000 (650,000 from the South and 910,000 from the North)
2. job opportunities

Geography Skills Practice
Give students a list of the 48 states and ask them to use the map to classify the states by region.

U Universal Access

English Learners Have students use the data from the map on this page to create a three-column chart listing the regions of the United States *(North, South, West)*, how many people left each region in the 1940s, and how many people came to each region in the 1940s. Then tell students to create two circle graphs. The first graph should show the total number of people departing, broken down by region; the second graph should show the total number of people arriving, broken down by region. Tell students to use different colored slices for each region and to prepare legends to correlate the colors with the regions. **EL** **CA CS3**

R Reading Strategy

Activating Prior Knowledge Wartime crises can sometimes create unrest at home. **Ask:** Do you recall racial unrest and other moments of social turmoil that occurred during World War I? *(Students should recall the prejudice and suspicion directed toward German-Americans during World War I and the anti-Communist Red Scare that occurred following World War I.)* **OL** **CA H1**

U **Universal Access**

Visual/Spatial Tell students to use library or Internet resources to find pictures of World War II era fashions, including the zoot suit and the victory suit. **Ask:** Why was the victory suit considered patriotic? *(Victory suits saved fabric for the war.)* Have students use the pictures they found to make posters to hang up in the classroom. **OL**

S **Skill Practice**

Conducting Research Have students give two-minute oral presentations on Hispanic Americans in the armed forces during World War II. Reports should include information such as the number of Hispanic Americans that served, and the opportunities and restrictions that they faced during this period. Encourage students to use library and Internet resources to locate information. **OL**
CA HR4

Answers and Additional Support

The Zoot Suit Riots Wartime prejudice erupted elsewhere as well. In southern California, racial tensions became entangled with juvenile delinquency. Across the nation, crimes committed by young people rose dramatically. In Los Angeles, racism against Mexican Americans and the fear of juvenile crime became linked because of the "zoot suit."

A **zoot suit** had very baggy, pleated pants and an overstuffed, knee-length jacket with wide lapels. Accessories included a wide-brimmed hat and a long key chain. Zoot-suit wearers usually wore their hair long, gathered into a ducktail. The zoot suit angered many Americans. In order to save fabric for the war, most men wore a "victory suit"—a suit with no vest, no cuffs, a short jacket, and narrow lapels. By comparison, the zoot suit seemed unpatriotic.

In California, Mexican American teenagers adopted the zoot suit. In June 1943, after hearing rumors that zoot suiters had attacked several sailors, 2,500 soldiers and sailors stormed into Mexican American neighborhoods in Los Angeles. They attacked Mexican American teenagers, cut their hair, and tore off their zoot suits. The police did not intervene, and the vio-

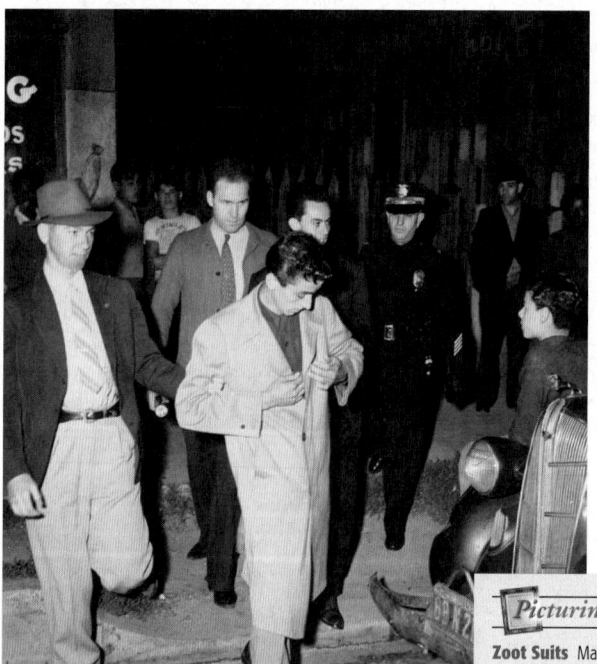

lence continued for several days. The city of Los Angeles responded by banning the zoot suit.

Racial hostility against Mexican Americans did not deter them from joining the war effort. Approximately 500,000 Hispanic Americans served in the armed forces during the war. Most—about 400,000—were Mexican American. Another 65,000 were from Puerto Rico. They fought in Europe, North Africa, and the Pacific, and by the end of the war, 17 Mexican Americans had received the Medal of Honor.

Japanese American Relocation When Japan attacked Pearl Harbor, many West Coast Americans turned their anger against Japanese Americans. Mobs attacked Japanese American businesses and homes. Banks would not cash their checks, and grocers refused to sell them food.

Newspapers printed rumors about Japanese spies in the Japanese American community. Members of Congress, mayors, and many business and labor leaders demanded that all people of Japanese ancestry be removed from the West Coast. They did not believe that Japanese Americans would remain loyal to the United States in the face of war with Japan.

On February 19, 1942, President Roosevelt gave in to pressure and signed an order allowing the War Department to declare any part of the United States to be a military zone and to remove anybody they wanted from that zone. Secretary of War Henry Stimson declared most of the West Coast a military zone and ordered all people of Japanese ancestry to evacuate to 10 internment camps.

Not all Japanese Americans accepted the relocation without protest. Fred Korematsu argued that his rights had been violated and took his case to the Supreme Court. In December 1944, in *Korematsu* v. *the United States,* the Supreme Court ruled that the relocation was constitutional because it was based not on race, but on "military urgency." Shortly afterward, the Court did rule in *Ex Parte Endo* that loyal American

Picturing **History**

Zoot Suits Many Americans considered the long, baggy zoot suit worn by some Mexican American teenagers unpatriotic. Riots erupted in Los Angeles in June of 1943 after it was rumored that "zoot suiters" had attacked several sailors. The riots lasted several days and left more than a hundred people injured. Why did many Americans consider the zoot suit unpatriotic?

590 CHAPTER 12 America and World War II

Picturing **History**

Answer: The excessive use of fabric was viewed as an unpatriotic waste of resources best devoted to the war effort.

Resources for page 590

Have students read more about the treatment of Japanese Americans during the war by assigning The Invisible Thread *in the **American Literature Readings 3.***

NATIONAL GEOGRAPHIC
MOMENT in HISTORY

BEHIND BARBED WIRE

As wartime hysteria mounted, the U.S. government rounded up 120,000 people of Japanese ancestry—77,000 of whom were American citizens—and forced them into internment camps in early 1942. Given just days to sell their homes, businesses, and personal property, whole families were marched under military guard to rail depots, then sent to remote, inhospitable sites where they lived in cramped barracks surrounded by barbed wire and watchtowers. By 1945, with the tide of war turned, most had been released, but they did not get an official apology or financial compensation until 1988.

citizens could not be held against their will. In early 1945, the government began to release the Japanese Americans from the camps. 📖 *(See page 1005 for more information on* Korematsu v. the United States.)

Despite the fears and rumors, no Japanese American was ever tried for espionage or sabotage. Japanese Americans served as translators for the army during the war in the Pacific. The all-Japanese 100th Battalion, later **integrated** into the 442nd Regimental Combat Team, was the most highly decorated unit in World War II.

After the war, the Japanese American Citizens League (JACL) tried to help Japanese Americans who had lost property during the relocation. In 1988 President Reagan apologized to Japanese Americans on behalf of the U.S. government and signed legislation granting $20,000 to each surviving Japanese American who had been interned.

Japanese Americans were not the only ones who faced discrimination. Because the United States was also at war with Italy and Germany, many Italian and German immigrants were subject to harassment. Many lost jobs because of curfews, were subject to

police searches, confiscation of fishing boats used to provide a source of income, forced relocations, and even internment. The lack of available housing and controls on wages and prices made life even more difficult for some immigrants.

 Reading Check **Comparing** Why did racism lead to violence in Detroit and Los Angeles in 1943?

Daily Life in Wartime America

Main Idea Civilians made many sacrifices during the war to help ensure victory for the Allies.

Reading Connection How would you respond to government rationing of food? Read on to find out more about rationing of food and other supplies during World War II.

Housing problems and racial tensions were serious difficulties during the war, but mobilization strained society in many other ways as well. Prices

CHAPTER 12 America and World War II **591**

U Universal Access

Interpersonal Have students work in small groups to create short plays about daily life in the Japanese internment camps during the war. Have the groups present their plays to the rest of the class. As a class, discuss what students have learned about life in internment camps. **AL**

Review the Big Idea

Review the Big Idea for this section, "People react to periods of breathtaking social and cultural change in different ways." In 1942 the U.S. government removed more than 100,000 people of Japanese birth and ancestry from their homes on the Pacific Coast to relocation centers. There was also a desire to relocate Americans of German and Italian descent from the West Coast, but only 10,000 were moved. **Ask: Do you think the government ever has the right to relocate or keep a group in detention? Why or why not?** *(Some students who oppose the relocation policy might suggest that it was a violation of civil rights; others might say that sometimes the country's security takes precedence over civil rights.)* **AL** **CA HR1**

Resources for page 591

Have students read more about daily life during the war years by assigning the reading selection from The Good War *in the* **American Literature Readings 3.**

NATIONAL GEOGRAPHIC MOMENT in HISTORY

Have students look at the map of internment camps on page 595. Ask them what they think the conditions were like in these locations. Have students look at the picture on this page and describe the emotions that these young boys are probably feeling.

More Skill Practice

Activating Prior Knowledge Review the Bill of Rights on pages 159–160 with students. Then ask them to make a list of which of these rights were violated when Japanese Americans were placed in relocation centers and internment camps during the war. **OL**

✓**Reading Check**

Answer: African Americans who migrated to Detroit were often met with suspicion and intolerance. In Los Angeles, racism against Mexican Americans and fear of juvenile crime became linked because of zoot suits. These attitudes sometimes led to violence.

rose, materials were in short supply, and the question of how to pay for it all loomed ominously over the entire war effort.

Wage and Price Controls As the economy mobilized, the president became concerned with the possibility of inflation. Both wages and prices began to rise quickly during the war because of the high demand for workers and raw materials. To stabilize both wages and prices, Roosevelt created the Office of Price Administration (OPA) and the Office of Economic Stabilization (OES). The OES regulated wages and the price of farm products. The OPA regulated all other prices. Despite some problems with labor unions, the OPA and OES were able to keep inflation under control.

While the OPA and OES worked to control inflation, the War Labor Board (WLB) tried to prevent strikes that might endanger the war effort. In support, most American unions issued a "no strike pledge" and, instead of striking, asked the WLB to serve as a mediator in wage disputes. By the end of the war, the WLB had helped to settle over 17,000 disputes involving more than 12 million workers.

Blue Points, Red Points The demand for raw materials and supplies created shortages. The OPA began **rationing**, or limiting the availability of, many products to make sure enough were available for military use. Meat and sugar were rationed to provide enough for the army. To save gasoline and rubber, gasoline was rationed, driving was restricted, and the speed limit was set at 35 miles per hour.

Every month each household would pick up a book of ration coupons. Blue coupons, called blue points, controlled processed foods. Red coupons, or red points, controlled meats, fats, and oils. Other coupons controlled items such as coffee and sugar. When people bought food, they had to give enough coupon points to cover their purchases.

Victory Gardens and Scrap Drives Americans also planted gardens to produce more food for the war effort. Any area of land might become a garden—backyards, schoolyards, city parks, and empty lots. The government encouraged **victory gardens** by praising them in film reels, pamphlets, and official statements.

Certain raw materials were so vital to the war effort that the government organized scrap drives.

Picturing **History**

Rationing Products War rationing affected everyone. Women painted seams on their legs to make it appear they were wearing stockings, because silk was needed to make parachutes instead of stockings. Why was rationing so vital to the war effort?

592 CHAPTER 12 America and World War II

Picturing **History**

Answer: It allowed enough goods to be available for the war effort.
Ask: What types of goods were rationed? *(silk, meat, sugar, gasoline, processed foods, fats, and oils)*

Analyzing *Political Cartoons*

Turning Off the Lights Early in the war, lights from eastern cities silhouetted ships along the east coast, making them easy targets for German submarines. Americans were asked to turn out lights or put up dark curtains. What point is the cartoon making to Americans?

Illumination for the Shooting Gallery

THESE ARE **YOUR LIGHTS**, MISTER!

 N.Y. CITY

Dr. Seuss

Americans collected spare rubber, tin, aluminum, and steel. They donated pots, tires, tin cans, car bumpers, broken radiators, and rusting bicycles. Oils and fats were so important to the production of explosives that the WPB set up fat-collecting stations. Americans would exchange bacon grease and meat drippings for extra ration coupons. The scrap drives were very successful and one more reason for the success of American industry during the war.

Paying for the War The United States had to pay for all of the equipment and supplies it needed. The federal government spent more than $300 billion during World War II—more money than it had spent from Washington's administration to the end of Franklin Roosevelt's second term.

To raise money, the government raised taxes. Because most Americans opposed large tax increases, Congress refused to raise taxes as high as Roosevelt requested. As a result, the extra taxes collected covered only 45 percent of the cost of the war.

To raise the rest of the money, the government issued war bonds. When Americans bought bonds, they were loaning money to the government. In exchange for the money, the government promised that the bonds could be cashed in at some future date for the purchase price plus interest. The most common bonds were **E bonds,** which sold for $18.75 and could be redeemed for $25.00 after 10 years.

Individual Americans bought nearly $50 billion worth of war bonds. Banks, insurance companies, and other financial institutions bought the rest—over $100 billion worth of bonds.

"V" for Victory Despite the hardships, the overwhelming majority of Americans believed the war had to be fought. Although the war brought many changes to the United States, most Americans remained united behind one goal—winning the war.

 Reading Check **Evaluating** How did rationing affect daily life in the United States? How did it affect the economy?

HISTORY Online **Study Central**

For help with the concepts in this section of *American Vision: Modern Times* go to tav.mt.glencoe.com and click on *Study Central.*

SECTION 3 ASSESSMENT

Checking for Understanding

1. **Vocabulary** Define: perspective, sunbelt, allocate, integrate, rationing, victory garden.
2. **People and Terms** Identify: Rosie the Riveter, A. Philip Randolph, zoot suit, E bond.
3. **Explain** how the federal government expanded during the war.

Reviewing Big Ideas

4. **Analyzing** What changes did American citizens and industry have to make to adapt to the war?

Critical Thinking

5. **Evaluating** If you had been a government official during the war, how would you have proposed paying for the war?
6. **Categorizing** Use a graphic organizer like the one below to list the results of increased racial tensions during the war.

Racial Tensions

Result   Result   Result

Analyzing Visuals

7. **Examining Maps** Study the map on page 589. Which cities had populations over 400,000?
8. **Analyzing Photographs** Study the photograph on page 591. Why were Japanese Americans interned?

Writing About History

9. **Persuasive Writing** Write a newspaper editorial urging fellow citizens to conserve resources so that these resources can be diverted to the war effort.
CA 11WS1.1; 11WS1.5

SECTION 3 ASSESSMENT ANSWERS

1. Content vocabulary is boldfaced and highlighted in yellow. Academic vocabulary is boldfaced.
2. Rosie the Riveter *(p. 587),* A. Philip Randolph *(p. 588),* zoot suit *(p. 590),* E bond *(p. 593)*
3. New government agencies controlled the economy, raised taxes, and issued war bonds.
4. Industry and workers accepted wage and price controls and agreed to settle wage disputes by using WLB mediators. Citizens accepted rationing, planted victory gardens, recycled, and purchased war bonds.
5. Students' answers should include a rationale for their plan.
6. racial violence in Detroit, juvenile delinquency, Japanese internment
7. Los Angeles, Houston, New York
8. Many believed that they would not remain loyal to the United States.
9. Students' editorials should follow the style of a newspaper editorial.

ASSESS

 Resources for page 593

Use these resources to assess student mastery.

📂 Section Quiz 12-3

📂 Reading Essentials and Study Guide 12-3

💿 Interactive Tutor Self-Assessment CD-ROM

📂 California Standards Practice, Grade 11

Analyzing *Political Cartoons*

Answer: to be conscious of the dangers their city lights pose to American sailors
Have students evaluate the cartoon.
Ask: Would the picture convince you to participate in blackouts? Why or why not? *(Answers will vary.)*

Reading Check

Answer: Rationing limited access to common products, but allowed people to purchase necessities.

HISTORY Online

Study Central provides audio summaries, interactive games, and online graphic organizers to help students review section content.

CLOSE

Connecting As a class, discuss the effects of prejudice in society by focusing on groups discriminated against in the 1940s and today. **OL**

FOCUS

History–Social Science Standards

This feature addresses the following standard:

11.7.5 Discuss the constitutional issues and impact of events on the U.S. home front, including the internment of Japanese Americans (e.g., *Fred Korematsu v. United States of America*) and the restrictions on German and Italian resident aliens; the response of the administration to Hitler's atrocities against Jews and other groups; the roles of women in military production; and the roles and growing political demands of African Americans.

This passage from *Farewell to Manzanar* describes the experiences of Jeanne Wakatsuki and her family as they arrive at a Japanese internment camp.

Read to Discover

Answer: The barracks are crudely built and unfinished.

Understanding Vocabulary

Before students begin reading, ask them to review the **Reader's Dictionary** to better understand the literature excerpt.

Answers and Additional Support

Jeanne Wakatsuki Houston was born in Inglewood, California. In 1942, when she was seven years old, her family was uprooted from their home and sent to live at the Manzanar internment camp in California. The detainees had committed no crimes. They were detained simply because of their heritage.

Farewell to Manzanar is the story of the Wakatsuki family's attempt to survive the indignities of forced detention and living behind barbed wire in the United States.

Read to Discover

How does Jeanne Wakatsuki Houston describe the internment camp that is to be her new home? What does her description remind you of?

Reader's Dictionary

barracks: plain and barren lodgings usually used to house soldiers

milling: wandering

savory: seasoned with spices

from Farewell to Manzanar

by Jeanne Wakatsuki Houston and James D. Houston

The following excerpt describes Jeanne Wakatsuki's first impressions as she and her family arrived at the internment camp.

Kiyo and my sister May and I enrolled in the local school, and what sticks in my memory from those few weeks is the teacher—not her looks, her remoteness. In Ocean Park my teacher had been a kind, grandmotherly women who used to sail with us in Papa's boat from time to time and who wept the day we had to leave. In Boyle Heights the teacher felt cold and distant. I was confused by all the moving and was having trouble with the classwork, but she would never help me out. She would have nothing to do with me.

This was the first time I had felt outright hostility from a Caucasian. Looking back, it is easy enough to explain. Public attitudes toward the Japanese in California were shifting rapidly. In the first few months of the Pacific war, America was on the run. Tolerance had turned to distrust and irrational fear. The hundred-year-old tradition of anti-Orientalism on the west coast soon resurfaced, more vicious than ever. Its result became clear about a month later, when we were told to make our third and final move.

The name Manzanar meant nothing to us when we left Boyle Heights. We didn't know where it was or what it was. We went because the government ordered us to. And, in the case of my older brothers and sisters, we went with a certain sense of relief. They had all heard stories of Japanese homes being attacked, of beatings in the streets of California towns. They were as frightened of the Caucasians as Caucasians were of us. Moving, under what appeared to be government protection, to an area less directly threatened by the war seemed not such a bad idea at all. For some it actually sounded like a fine adventure.

Our pickup point was a Buddhist church in Los Angeles. It was very early, and misty, when we got there with our luggage. Mama had bought heavy coats for all of us. She grew up in eastern Washington and knew that anywhere inland in early April would be cold. I was proud of my new coat, and I remember sitting on a duffel bag trying to be friendly with the

---

Reading Strategy | SEQUENCING INFORMATION

Point out that authors do not always describe events in the exact order in which they occurred in real life; sometimes authors use techniques such as flashback to move back and forth in time. In order to help students understand the order of events in the excerpt, have them create time lines entitled "Jeanne Wakatsuki Arrives at Manzanar." Instead of dates, have students list the key events mentioned in the excerpt. Students should begin the time lines with the departure from Boyle Heights and end when her sister leaves for Idaho. Encourage students to use photographs and drawings to illustrate their time lines. Display the time lines in your classroom while you discuss the excerpt. **EL**

Greyhound driver. I smiled at him. He didn't smile back. He was befriending no one. Someone tied a numbered tag to my collar and to the duffel bag (each family was given a number and that became our official designation until the camps were closed), some one else passed out box lunches for the trip, and we climbed aboard.

I had never been outside Los Angeles County, never traveled more than ten miles from the coast, had never even ridden on a bus. I was full of excitement, the way any kid would be, and wanted to look out the window. But for the first few hours the shades were drawn. Around me other people played cards, read magazines, dozed, waiting. I settled back, waiting too, and finally fell asleep. The bus felt very secure to me. Almost half its passengers were immediate relatives. Mama and my older brothers had succeeded in keeping most of us together, on the same bus, headed for the same camp. I didn't realize until much later what a job that was. The strategy had been, first to have everyone living in the same district when the evacuation began, and then to get all of us included under the same family number, even though names had been changed by marriage. Many families weren't as lucky as ours and suffered months of anguish while trying to arrange transfers from one camp to another.

We rode all day. By the time we reached our destination, the shades were up. It was late afternoon. The first thing I saw was a yellow swirl across a blurred, reddish setting sun. The bus was being pelted by what sounded like splattering rain. It wasn't rain. This was my first look at something I would soon know very well, a billowing flurry of dust and sand churned up by the wind through Owens Valley.

We drove past a barbed-wire fence, through a gate, and into an open space where trunks and sacks and packages had been dumped from the baggage trucks that drove out ahead of us. I could see a few tents set up, the first rows of black barracks, and beyond them, blurred by sand, rows of barracks that seemed to spread for miles across this plain. People were sitting on cartons or milling around, with their backs to the wind, waiting to see which friends or relatives might be on this bus. As we approached, they turned or stood up, and some moved toward us expectantly.

But inside the bus no one stirred. No one waved or spoke. They just stared out the windows, ominously silent. I didn't understand this. Hadn't we finally arrived, our whole family intact? I opened a window, leaned out and yelled happily. "Hey! This whole bus is full of Wakatsukis!"

Outside the greeters smiled. Inside there was an explosion of laughter, hysterical, tension-breaking laughter that left my brothers choking and whacking each other across the shoulders.

We had pulled up just in time for dinner. The mess halls weren't completed yet. An outdoor chow line snaked around a half-finished building that broke a good part of the wind. They issued us army mess kits, the round metal kind that fold over, and plopped in scoops of canned Vienna sausage, canned string beans, steamed rice that had been cooked too long, and on top of the rice a serving of canned apricots. The Caucasian servers were thinking that the fruit poured over rice would make a good dessert. Among the Japanese, of course, rice is never eaten with sweet foods, only with salty or savory foods. Few of us could eat such a mixture. But at this point no one dared protest. It would have been impolite. I was horrified when I saw the apricot syrup seeping through my little mound of rice. I opened my mouth to complain. My mother jabbed me in the back to keep quiet. We moved on through the line and joined the others squatting in the lee of half-raised walls, dabbing courteously at what was, for almost everyone there, an inedible concoction.

After dinner we were taken to Block 16, a cluster of fifteen barracks that had just been finished a day or

TEACH

U Universal Access

Auditory/Musical Divide the classroom into groups of three. Have each group work together to write lyrics to a song describing Jeanne Wakatsuki's experience of the bus ride to Manzanar. Invite volunteers to read their lyrics aloud to the class. **OL**
CA 11WA2.1.c

R Reading Strategy

Using Context Clues Help students to better understand new vocabulary words by having them use each vocabulary word, such as *milling,* in a sentence. Ask students to write each of their sentences on a sheet of paper. Below their sentences, have them write the sentences from the excerpt that includes the new vocabulary word. Students should rewrite the sentences, substituting the definitions for the vocabulary words. **BL**

W Writing Support

Research Report Writing Ask students to use library and Internet resources to research the history of one of the other Japanese internment camps shown on the map on this page. Ask each student to write a three-page report that gives an overview of how long the camp operated, how many people were housed there, and how it compared to Wakatsuki's description of Manzanar. **AL** **CA 11WS1.6**

 Block Schedule

Team Teaching This selection from *Farewell to Manzanar* can be presented in a team teaching context, in conjunction with English or Language Arts.

Reading Strategy   EVALUATING

Explain to students that *Farewell to Manzanar* is based on real events, but remind the class that Houston was only seven years old when she experienced these events. **Ask:** How accurate are the events described here? Do you think Houston was keeping a careful diary of her daily experiences? Does this change the overall impact of what you are reading? *(Students may point out that even if Houston did not keep a daily diary of experiences, it does not detract from the main point of her book—the disruption and difficulties experienced by Japanese Americans during their internment.)* **OL** **CA 11RC2.4**

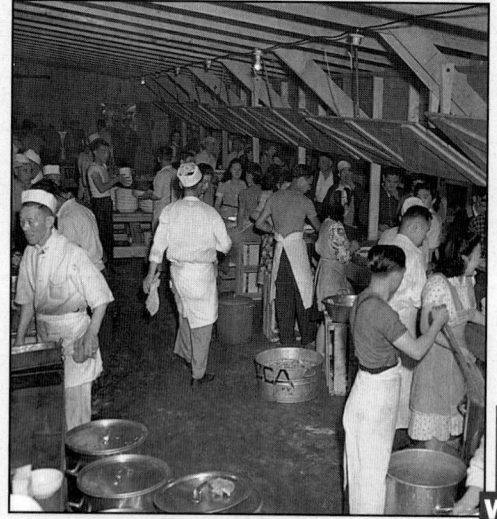

▲ *Food line at internment camp*

so earlier—although finished was hardly the word for it. The shacks were built of one thickness of pine planking covered with tarpaper. They sat on concrete footings, with about two feet of open space between the floorboards and the ground. Gaps showed between the planks, and as the weeks passed and the green wood dried out, the gaps widened. Knotholes gaped in the uncovered floor.

Each barracks was divided into six units, sixteen by twenty feet, about the size of a living room, with one bare bulb hanging from the ceiling and an oil stove for heat. We were assigned two of these for the twelve people in our family group; and our official family "number" was enlarged by three digits—16 plus the number of this barracks. We were issued steel army cots, two brown army blankets each, and some mattress covers, which my brothers stuffed with straw.

The first task was to divide up what space we had for sleeping. Bill and Woody contributed a blanket each and partitioned off the first room: one side for Bill and Tomi, one side for Woody and Chizu and their baby girl. Woody also got the stove, for heating formulas.

The people who had it hardest during the first few months were young couples like these, many of whom had married before the evacuation began, in order not to be separated and sent to different camps. Our two rooms were crowded, but at least it was all in the family. My oldest sister and her husband were shoved into one of those sixteen-by-twenty-foot compartments with six people they had never seen before—two other couples, one recently married like themselves, the other with two teenage boys. Partitioning off a room like that wasn't easy. It was bitter cold when we arrived, and the wind did not abate. All they had to use for room dividers were those army blankets, two of which were barely enough to keep one person warm. They argued over whose blanket should be sacrificed and later argued about noise at night—the parents wanted their boys asleep by 9:00 p.m.—and they continued arguing over matters like that for six months, until my sister and her husband left to harvest sugar beets in Idaho. It was grueling work up there, and wages were pitiful, but when the call came through camp for workers to alleviate the wartime labor shortage, it sounded better than their life at Manzanar. They knew they'd have, if nothing else, a room, perhaps a cabin of their own. . . .

We woke early, shivering and coated with dust that had blown up through the knotholes and in through the slits around the doorway. During the night Mama had unpacked all our clothes and heaped them on our beds for warmth. Now our cubicle looked as if a great laundry bag had exploded and then been sprayed with fine dust. . . .

Analyzing Literature

1. **Recall and Interpret** How did the food served at the camp show a lack of understanding of Japanese culture? **CA 11RC2.4**

2. **Evaluate and Connect** Why do you think the families in the camps were assigned numbers?

Interdisciplinary Activity

Art and Architecture Draw plans for a community memorial for remembering Japanese Americans who were treated unfairly during World War II.

Answers to Analyzing Literature

1. Students' answers will vary depending on their understanding of Japanese culture. Answers should mention that rice is never eaten with sweet foods.
2. Students' answers will vary. Camp officials likely chose to use numbers because they found Japanese names difficult to spell and pronounce.

Interdisciplinary Activity
The plans for the memorial should show details including the size and shape of the memorial. The plans should emphasize how community members might interact with the memorial.

Reading on Your Own

For other literature selections that relate to Japanese culture, Japanese Americans, and World War II, you might consider the following book suggestions.

Citizen 13660 (Nonfiction)
by Miné Okubo

Born in 1912, Okubo received her master's degree in fine arts from the University of California at Berkeley. Using her artistic skills, she recounts with ink drawings and words her experiences in a Japanese internment camp during World War II.

One Sunny Day (Autobiography)
by Hideko Tamura Snider

When Hideko Tamura was 10 years old, the atomic bomb devastated her home in Hiroshima. In this powerful narrative, Hideko describes her life before the bombing, the explosion itself, and the influence of that trauma upon her life in Japan and later the United States. Her years in the States provided her with unusual insight into the relationship between Japanese and American cultures and the lasting impact of the bombing of Hiroshima.

Desert Exile: The Uprooting of a Japanese-American Family (Autobiography)
by Yoshiko Uchida

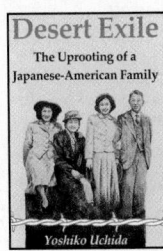

Uchida had to move to an internment camp during her senior year at the University of California at Berkeley. Her autobiography provides another view of life at an internment camp experienced by Japanese American citizens during the Second World War.

Snow Falling on Cedars (Fiction)
by David Guterson

With palpable, anti-Japanese sentiment in the background, a Japanese American fisherman fights for his reputation and his life in a murder trial set in Puget Sound during the 1950s.

American LITERATURE

HISTORY Online

Refer to <u>tav.mt.glencoe.com</u> for additional Glencoe Literature titles, lesson plans, and study guides related to this unit.

TEACH

Cooperative Learning

Sequencing Information When students read a new book, especially on a historical topic they may know little about, it is helpful to organize the main events and ideas of the book in an outline form. Assign each student one of the books listed on this page. After students have read their books, organize them into groups based on the book they have read. Tell each group to work together to create an outline of the book they have read. Groups can use the table of contents as the main headings of the outline. **OL**

GLENCOE BOOKLINK

Use **Glencoe BookLink** to create customized reading lists for your students' reading levels, interests, and abilities.

📖 **Reading Strategy**   **REINFORCING READING SKILLS**

You can use reading assignments to help students practice their understanding of cause-and-effect relationships—the reading skill introduced in this unit on page 570. Remind students to pay attention to how decisions and events discussed in their reading affect later events. Students may keep notes to track cause-and-effect relationships as they read, making it easier for them to remember these details after they have finished reading. **OL**

FOCUS

Guide to Reading

Understanding Vocabulary: Have students write three questions that can be answered using the academic vocabulary.

Answers to Graphic:
Pacific—Tarawa Atoll, Gilbert Islands, 1943, Allies; Guam, August 1944, Allies; Europe—Sicily, July–August 1943, Allies; D-Day, June 1944, Allies

Unpacking the Standards

Students will be able to:

- Explain how the U.S. strategy in Europe began to shift the tide of the war.
- Discuss the Allied plan for the final invasion of Europe.
- Evaluate the efforts to go on the offensive in the Pacific.

Answers and Additional Support

SECTION 4 Pushing the Axis Back

Guide to Reading

Connection

In the previous section, you learned about life on the home front. In this section, you will discover how the Allies began to achieve victories on all fronts.

Main Idea

- At the Casablanca Conference, Roosevelt and Churchill planned a wartime strategy that included increased bombing of Germany and an attack on Sicily. (p. 599)
- The Allied invasion of France took place on June 6, 1944, which was known as D-Day. (p. 601)

- General MacArthur's strategy involved taking back islands in the Pacific, one island at a time, to push back the Japanese. (p. 603)

Content Vocabulary
amphtrac, kamikaze

Academic Vocabulary
approximately, code, pose

People and Terms to Identify
Casablanca Conference, Operation Overlord, D-Day, Omar Bradley, Guadalcanal

Reading Objectives
- **Describe** the goals of the two major offensives the Allies launched in Europe in 1943.
- **Explain** the American strategy for pushing the Japanese back in the Pacific.

Reading Strategy
Organizing As you read about the major battles of 1943 and 1944, complete a graphic organizer similar to the one below by filling in the names of the battles fought. Indicate whether each battle was an Allied or an Axis victory.

Preview of Events

◆1943	◆1944	◆1945

January 1943
Casablanca Conference

July 1943
The Allies invade Italy

November 1943
Roosevelt, Churchill, and Stalin meet at Tehran

June 6, 1944
D-Day invasion begins

October 20, 1944
MacArthur returns to the Philippines

The following are the main History–Social Science Standards covered in this section.

11.7.2 Explain U.S. and Allied wartime strategy, including the major battles of Midway, Normandy, Iwo Jima, Okinawa, and the Battle of the Bulge.

11.7.3 Identify the roles and sacrifices of individual American soldiers, as well as the unique contributions of the special fighting forces (e.g., the Tuskegee Airmen, the 442nd Regimental Combat team, the Navajo Code Talkers).

11.7.4 Analyze Roosevelt's foreign policy during World War II (e.g., Four Freedoms speech).

11.7.6 Describe major developments in aviation, weaponry, communication, and medicine and the war's impact on the location of American industry and use of resources.

⁓ The Big Idea ⁓

The fate of nations is forever changed by monumental world events. The United States fought a two-front war. In Europe, the Allies decided to bomb Germany, which led to severe oil shortages, a wrecked railroad system, and significant damage to aircraft factories in that country. At the same time, Allied troops took Italy in a campaign lasting almost a year. The leaders of the United States, Great Britain, and the Soviet Union met to discuss further war plans and a future international peacekeeping organization. The plans led to Operation Overlord, the Allied invasion of France. In the Pacific, the United States adopted a two-pronged attack, retaking the Philippines and advancing toward Japan by island-hopping in the central Pacific.

SECTION RESOURCES

📁 **Print Material**
- Reproducible Lesson Plan 12-4
- Guided Reading Activity 12-4
- Reading Essentials and Study Guide 12-4
- Active Reading Note-Taking Guide 12-4

🖥 **Transparencies**
- Daily Focus Skills Transparency 12-4
- Section Graphic Organizer Transparency 12-4

Technology
- 🖱 Interactive Tutor Self-Assessment CD-ROM
- 🖱 ExamView® Pro Testmaker CD-ROM
- 🖱 Presentation Plus! CD-ROM

Striking Back at the Third Reich

Main Idea At the Casablanca Conference, Roosevelt and Churchill planned a wartime strategy that included increased bombing of Germany and an attack on Sicily.

Reading Connection Have you ever created a strategy to win a game or to tackle a tough assignment? Read on to learn about Roosevelt's meetings in Casablanca and Tehran.

The first large Allied invasion of the war—the attack on North Africa in November 1942—had shown that the Allies could mount a large-scale invasion from the sea. Storming a beach under enemy control, however, can be a terrifying ordeal. There is no cover on a beach, no place to hide, and no way to turn back. Launching an invasion from the sea is very risky. Unfortunately, the Allies had no choice. If they were going to win the war, they had to land their troops in Europe and on islands in the Pacific.

★ An American Story ★

On the morning of June 6, 1944, Lieutenant John Bentz Carroll of the 16th Infantry Regiment scrambled down a net ladder from his troop ship to a small landing craft tossing in the waves 30 feet (9 m) below. The invasion of France had begun. Carroll's platoon would be among the first Americans to land in Normandy. Their objective was a beach, code-named "Omaha":

❝Two hundred yards out, we took a direct hit. . . . [A machine gun] was shooting a rat-tattat on the front of the boat. Somehow or other, the ramp door opened up . . . and the men in front were being struck by machine gun fire. Everyone started to jump off into the water. They were being hit as they jumped, the machine gun fire was so heavy. . . . The tide was moving us so rapidly. . . . We would grab out on some of those underwater obstructions and mines built on telephone poles and girders, and hang on. We'd take cover, then make a dash through the surf to the next one, fifty feet beyond. The men would line up behind those poles. They'd say, 'You go—you go—you go,' and then it got so bad everyone just had to go anyway, because the waves were hitting with such intensity on these things.❞

—quoted in *D-Day: Piercing the Atlantic Wall*

The success of the landings convinced Roosevelt that it was time to meet with Churchill to plan the next step. In January 1943, the president headed to Casablanca, Morocco, to meet the prime minister.

At the **Casablanca Conference,** Roosevelt and Churchill agreed to step up the bombing of Germany. The goal of this new campaign was "the progressive destruction of the German military, industrial, and economic system, and the undermining of the morale of the German people." The Allies also agreed to attack the Axis on the island of Sicily. Churchill called Italy the "soft underbelly" of Europe and was convinced that the Italians would quit the war if the Allies invaded their homeland.

Strategic Bombing The Allies had been bombing Germany even before the Casablanca Conference. Britain's Royal Air Force had dropped an average of 2,300 tons (2,093 t) of explosives on Germany every month for over three years. The United States Eighth Army Air Force had joined the campaign in the summer of 1942, and they had dropped an additional 1,500 tons (1,365 t) of bombs by the end of the year.

These numbers were tiny, however, compared to the massive new campaign. Between January 1943 and May 1945, the Royal Air Force and the United States Eighth Army Air Force dropped **approximately** 53,000 tons (48,230 t) of explosives on Germany every month.

The bombing campaign did not destroy Germany's economy or undermine German morale, but it did cause a severe oil shortage and wrecked the railroad system. It also destroyed so many aircraft factories that Germany's air force could not replace its combat losses. By the time the Allies landed in France, they had total control of the air, ensuring that their troops would not be bombed.

▼ *Men boarding landing craft on D-Day*

Did You Know?

Roosevelt and Churchill agreed at the Casablanca Conference that the Allies would not end the war with Germany until the Axis states agreed to an unconditional surrender.

TEACH

Review the Big Idea

Review the Big Idea for this section, "The fate of nations is forever changed by monumental world events." Divide the class into four groups. Ask each group to read Lt. John Carroll's description of the D-Day invasion. Tell the groups to identify three other important days in U.S. history and write paragraphs explaining each day's significance. Ask each group to present their choices and discuss them. **OL** **CA HI1; HI4**

R Reading Strategy

Summarizing Have students imagine that they are reporters covering the Casablanca Conference. Ask them to write one-page articles describing the conference, including who was there and what was decided. **BL**
CA 11WA2.1b

U Universal Access

Logical/Mathematical Have students calculate the total amount of Allied explosives dropped on Germany by multiplying the amount dropped per month by the number of months of bombing. Share the results of the students' calculations. **Ask:** *Why was it so important to destroy Germany's air force before landing in France?* (Destroying the German air force meant that the Allies would have total control of the air so that their troops would not be bombed when landing in France.) **OL**

U Universal Access

Interpersonal Organize the class into groups of four to report on the Italian campaign. Assign each group a special responsibility, such as research, graphic presentation, or the Italian perspective. Encourage students to use library and Internet resources to find information. Work together as a class to synthesize each group's research into an in-depth report of the American invasion of Italy. **OL** **CA HR4** **CA 11WA2.4**

R₁ Reading Strategy

Scaffolding—Academic Vocabulary The word *series* was introduced in Chapter 9, Section 3. Ask a student to define the word. **BL**

R₂ Reading Strategy

Visualizing Ask students to create a political cartoon based on Italy's surrender to the Allies on September 8, 1943. Students may use library and Internet resources to evaluate existing political cartoons for styles ideas. Have students explain their cartoons to the class. **OL**

Answers and Additional Support

Striking at the Soft Underbelly As the bombing campaign against Germany intensified, the plan for the invasion of Sicily moved ahead as well. General Dwight D. Eisenhower was placed in overall command of the invasion. General Patton and the British General Bernard Montgomery were put in charge of the actual forces on the ground. The invasion began before dawn on July 10, 1943. Despite bad weather, the Allied troops made it ashore with few casualties. A new vehicle, the DUKW—an amphibious truck—proved very effective in bringing supplies and artillery to the soldiers on the beach.

Eight days after the troops came ashore, American tanks led by General Patton smashed through enemy lines and captured the western half of the island. After capturing western Sicily, Patton's troops headed east, staging a series of daring end-runs around the German positions, while the British, under Montgomery, attacked from the south. By August 18, the Germans had evacuated the island.

The attack on Sicily created a crisis within the Italian government. The king of Italy, Victor Emmanuel, and a group of Italian generals decided that it was time to get rid of Mussolini. On July 25, 1943, the king invited the dictator to his palace. "My dear Duce," the king began, "it's no longer any good. Italy has gone to bits. The soldiers don't want to fight anymore. At this moment, you are the most hated man in Italy." The king then placed Mussolini under arrest, and the new Italian government began secretly negotiating with the Allies for Italy's surrender.

On September 8, 1943, the Italian government publicly announced Italy's surrender. The following day, American troops landed at Salerno. Although stunned by the surrender, Hitler was not about to lose Italy to the Allies. German troops went into action at once. They seized control of northern Italy, including Rome, attacked the Americans at Salerno, and put Mussolini back in power.

To stop the Allied advance, the German army took up positions near the heavily fortified town of Cassino. The terrain near Cassino was steep, barren, and rocky. Instead of attacking such difficult terrain, the Allies chose to land at Anzio, behind German lines. They hoped the maneuver would force the Germans to retreat. Instead of retreating, however, the Germans surrounded the Allied troops near Anzio.

It took the Allies five months to break through the German lines at Cassino and Anzio. Finally, in late May 1944, the Germans were forced to retreat. Less than two weeks later, the Allies captured Rome.

Fighting in Italy continued, however, until May 2, 1945. The Italian campaign was one of the bloodiest in the war. It cost the Allies more than 300,000 casualties.

Picturing History

Softening the Gustav Line Infantrymen fire an 81-millimeter mortar to soften the German Gustav Line near the Rapido River. Why do you think the Allies decided to attack first in Italy rather than in France?

Did You Know?

Leaflets signed by Roosevelt and Churchill and dropped onto Rome from Allied planes on July 17, 1943, read, "The time has come for you, the Italian people, to decide whether Italians shall die for Mussolini and Hitler—or live for Italy and civilization."

Picturing History

Background: Being in the infantry meant working as a team. Each soldier had a specific role, and the team counted on each member to perform that role efficiently.

Answer: The Allies thought that the Italians would quit the war if their territory was invaded.

The Big Three Stalin, Roosevelt, and Churchill meet at Tehran.

Roosevelt Meets Stalin at Tehran Roosevelt wanted to meet with Stalin before the Allies launched the invasion of France. In late 1943 Stalin agreed, and he proposed that Roosevelt and Churchill meet him in Tehran, Iran.

The leaders reached several agreements. Stalin promised to launch a full-scale offensive against the Germans when the Allies invaded France in 1944. Roosevelt and Stalin then agreed to break up Germany after the war so that it would never again threaten world peace. Stalin also promised that once Germany was beaten, the Soviet Union would help the United States defeat Japan. He also accepted Roosevelt's proposal to create an international organization to help keep the peace after the war.

✓ **Reading Check** **Explaining** What two major decisions did the Allies make at Casablanca?

Landing in France

Main Idea The Allied invasion of France took place on June 6, 1944, which was known as D-Day.

Reading Connection Do you know anyone who has served in the armed forces? Read on to find out how General Eisenhower determined the time to invade France.

After the conference in Tehran, Roosevelt headed to Cairo, Egypt, where he and Churchill continued planning the invasion of France. One major decision still had to be made. The president had to choose the commander for **Operation Overlord**—the **code** name for the planned invasion.

Roosevelt wanted to appoint General George C. Marshall, Chief of Staff for the United States Army, but he depended on Marshall for military advice and did not want to send him to Europe. Instead, the president selected General Eisenhower to command the invasion.

Planning Operation Overlord Knowing that the Allies would eventually invade France, Hitler had fortified the coast. Although these defenses were formidable, the Allies did have one advantage—the element of surprise. The Germans did not know when or where the Allies would land. They believed that the Allies would land in Pas-de-Calais—the area of France closest to Britain. To convince the Germans they were right, the Allies placed inflated rubber tanks, empty tents, and dummy landing craft along the coast across from Calais. To German spy planes, the decoys looked real, and they succeeded in fooling the Germans. The real target was not Pas-de-Calais, but Normandy.

By the spring of 1944, everything was ready. Over 1.5 million American soldiers, 12,000 airplanes, and more than 5 million tons (4.6 million t) of equipment had been sent to England. Only one thing was left to do—pick the date and give the command to go. The invasion had to begin at night to hide the ships crossing the English Channel. The ships had to arrive at low tide so that they could see the beach obstacles. The low tide had to come at dawn so that gunners bombarding the coast could see their targets. Before the main landing on the beaches, paratroopers would

---

More Skill Practice

Connecting As a class, discuss how each of the following influenced Operation Overlord: the weather, the decoys placed along the coast opposite Calais, and the choice of five beaches for landing the troops. **OL**

C **Critical Thinking**

Predicting Consequences Remind students that the United States and the Soviet Union have different political and economic structures. Ask students what difficulties may have arisen after the war when these two nations had to decide on how to divide and govern Germany. *(Answers will vary but should note the difficulty of democracy and communism coming together in a single country.)* **OL** **CA HI1; HI2**

R **Reading Strategy**

Determining Importance Have students explain the significance of the promises that Stalin made at the Tehran Conference. *(By agreeing to launch a full-scale offensive against the Germans when the Allies invaded France, Stalin guaranteed that Germany would be defending itself on two fronts. Stalin also promised to declare war on Japan after Germany was defeated, and he agreed to support an international organization aimed at postwar peacekeeping.)* **OL** **CA HI4**

U **Universal Access**

Visual/Spatial Have students identify the coast of Normandy on a map. **Ask:** Why did the Allies choose to land at Normandy, rather than at Pas-de-Calais as the Germans had predicted? Tell students to use library and Internet resources to research their answers. *(Students should note issues such as the element of surprise; geography and location of the beaches; access to crucial ports; etc.)* **OL**

✓ **Reading Check**

Answer: to step up the bombing of Germany and attack the Axis at Sicily

601

R Reading Strategy

Organizing Information
Remind students of the difficulty Eisenhower had in deciding whether or not to launch the D-Day invasion on June 6, 1944. Have students work in pairs to create two-column charts. In one column, they should list the reasons in favor of launching the invasion. *(small window of opportunity, break in the weather, fit the requirements of low tide at dawn and moonlight)* In the other column, they should list the reasons against it. *(heavy cloud cover, strong winds, high waves)* **Ask:** If you were one of Eisenhower's advisers, would you have advised him to go ahead with the invasion on June 6? Why or why not? *(Students' answers will vary.)*
OL **CA HI2; HI4**

U Universal Access

Visual/Spatial Ask interested students to sketch the typical battle gear of Allied soldiers during the D-Day invasion. Have students write paragraphs to accompany each sketch that describe the items and how they were used during the invasion. **BL**

Answers and Additional Support

be dropped behind enemy lines. They required a moonlit night in order to see where to land. Perhaps most important of all, the weather had to be good. A storm would ground the airplanes, and high waves would swamp the landing craft.

Given all these conditions, there were only a few days each month when the invasion could begin. The first opportunity would last from June 5 to 7, 1944. Eisenhower's planning staff referred to the day any operation began by the letter D. The date for the invasion, therefore, came to be known as **D-Day.** Heavy cloud cover, strong winds, and high waves made it impossible to land on June 5. A day later the weather briefly improved. The Channel was still rough, but the landing ships and aircraft could operate. It was a difficult decision. Eisenhower's advisers were split on what to do. After looking at weather forecasts one last time, shortly after midnight on June 6, 1944, Eisenhower gave the final order: "OK, we'll go."

The Longest Day Nearly 7,000 ships carrying more than 100,000 soldiers set sail for the coast of Normandy on June 6, 1944. At the same time, 23,000 paratroopers were dropped inland, east and west of the beaches. Allied fighter-bombers raced up and down the coast, hitting bridges, bunkers, and radar sites. As dawn broke, the warships in the Allied fleet let loose with a tremendous barrage of fire. Thousands of shells rained down on the beaches, code-named "Utah," "Omaha," "Gold," "Sword," and "Juno."

The American landing at Utah Beach went very well. The German defenses were weak, and in less than three hours American troops had captured the beach and moved inland, suffering less than 200 casualties in the process. On the eastern flank, the British and Canadian landings also went well. By the end of the day, British and Canadian forces were several miles inland.

Omaha Beach, however, was a different story. Under intense German fire, the American assault almost disintegrated. As General **Omar Bradley,** the commander of the American forces landing at Omaha and Utah, grimly watched the carnage, he began making plans to evacuate Omaha. Slowly, however, the American troops began to knock out the German defenses. More landing craft arrived, ramming their way through the obstacles to get to the beach. Nearly 2,500 Americans were either killed or wounded on Omaha, but by early afternoon Bradley received this message: "Troops formerly pinned

What If...

Operation Overlord Had Failed?

In what some historians believe was the most important weather prediction in military history, Group Captain James Stagg, chief meteorologist for the Royal Air Force, predicted gradual clearing for Normandy, France, on June 6, 1944. The prediction was critical for General Dwight D. Eisenhower, Supreme Commander of the Allied Expeditionary Forces. He had already delayed Operation Overlord once. The invasion forces of Operation Overlord were assembled and ready to go at a moment's notice. Everything depended upon a break in the bad weather so that the assault would take the Germans by surprise. Eisenhower trusted the weather prediction and believed in the battle plan. The day before the invasion, however, he wrote the following note on a small piece of paper—a message he would deliver in the event the invasion failed. He mistakenly jotted "July 5" on the bottom and stuck the note in his wallet.

❝Our landings in the Cherbourg-Havre area have failed to gain a satisfactory foothold and I have withdrawn the troops. My decision to attack at this time and place was based upon the best information available. The troops, the air and the Navy did all that Bravery and devotion to duty could do. If any blame or fault attaches to the attempt it is mine alone.❞

Did You Know?

In addition to naval craft, the Allies sent nearly 13,000 aircraft and dropped 11,912 tons of explosives during the invasion. The Germans, on the other hand, had 319 aircraft in the area, and only a hundred of them were fighters.

down on beaches . . . [are] advancing up heights behind beaches." By the end of the day, nearly 35,000 American troops had landed at Omaha, and another 23,000 had landed at Utah. Over 75,000 British and Canadian troops were on shore as well. The invasion had succeeded.

✓ **Reading Check** **Summarizing** What conditions had to be met before Eisenhower could order D-Day to begin?

Driving the Japanese Back

Main Idea General MacArthur's strategy involved taking back islands in the Pacific, one island at a time, to push back the Japanese.

Reading Connection Have you ever found it useful to formulate a strategy? Read on to discover how the Allies took back the islands that the Japanese had held.

While the buildup for the invasion of France was taking place in Britain, American military leaders were also developing a strategy to defeat Japan. The American plan called for a two-pronged attack. The Pacific Fleet, commanded by Admiral Nimitz, would advance through the central Pacific by hopping from

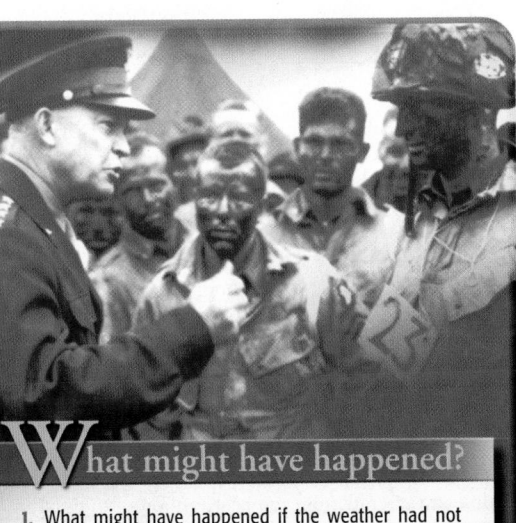

What might have happened?

1. What might have happened if the weather had not changed and the troops had landed amidst fog and rain?

2. What if the invasion had been delayed and the element of surprise lost?

one island to the next, closer and closer to Japan. Meanwhile, General MacArthur's troops would advance through the Solomon Islands, capture the north coast of New Guinea, and then launch an invasion to retake the Philippines.

Island-Hopping in the Pacific By the fall of 1943, the navy was ready to launch its island-hopping campaign, but the geography of the central Pacific **posed** a problem. Many of the islands were coral reef atolls. The water over the coral reef was not always deep enough to allow landing craft to get to the shore. If the landing craft ran aground on the reef, the troops would have to wade to the beach. As the approximately 5,000 United States Marines who landed at Tarawa Atoll learned, wading ashore could cause very high casualties.

Tarawa, part of the Gilbert Islands, was the Navy's first objective in the Pacific. When the landing craft hit the reef, at least 20 ships ran aground. The marines had to plunge into shoulder-high water and wade several hundred yards to the beach. Raked by Japanese fire, only one marine in three made it ashore. Once the marines reached the beach the battle was still far from over. As reporter Robert Sherrod wrote, the marines faced savage hand-to-hand fighting:

> ❝A Marine jumped over the seawall and began throwing blocks of fused TNT into a coconut-log pillbox. . . . Two more Marines scaled the seawall, one of them carrying a twin-cylindered tank strapped to their shoulders, the other holding the nozzle of the flame thrower. As another charge of TNT boomed inside the pillbox, causing smoke and dust to billow out, a khaki-clad figure ran out the side entrance. The flame thrower, waiting for him, caught him in its withering stream of intense fire. As soon as it touched him, the [Japanese soldier] flared up like a piece of celluloid. He was dead instantly . . . charred almost to nothingness.❞
> —from *Tarawa: The Story of a Battle*

Over 1,000 marines died on Tarawa. Photos of bodies lying crumpled next to burning landing craft shocked Americans back home. Many people began to wonder how many lives it would cost to defeat Japan.

Although many troops died wading ashore, one vehicle had been able to cross the reef and deliver its troops onto the beaches. The vehicle was the LVT—a boat with tank tracks. Nicknamed the "Alligator," the amphibious tractor, or **amphtrac,** had been invented in the late 1930s to rescue people in Florida swamps.

CHAPTER 12 America and World War II **603**

603

Island-Hopping in the Pacific, 1942–1945

Geography *Skills*

1. **Interpreting Maps** Where did the first major battle between the American and Japanese forces in the South Pacific take place?
2. **Applying Geography Skills** Why do you think Americans adopted the policy of island-hopping?

It had never been used in combat, and not until 1941 did the navy decide to buy 200 of them. Had more been available at Tarawa, the number of American casualties probably would have been much lower.

The assault on the next major objective—Kwajalein Atoll in the Marshall Islands—went much more smoothly. This time all of the troops went ashore in amphtracs. Although the Japanese resisted fiercely, the marines captured Kwajalein and nearby Eniwetok with far fewer casualties.

After the Marshall Islands, the navy targeted the Mariana Islands. American military planners wanted to use the Marianas as a base for a new heavy bomber, the B-29 Superfortress. The B-29 could fly farther than any other plane in the world. From airfields in the Marianas, B-29s could bomb Japan. Admiral Nimitz decided to invade three of the Mariana Islands: Saipan, Tinian, and Guam. Despite strong Japanese resistance, American troops captured all three by August 1944. A few months later, B-29 bombers began bombing Japan.

MacArthur Returns to the Philippines As the forces under Admiral Nimitz hopped across the central Pacific, General MacArthur's troops began their own campaign in the southwest Pacific. The campaign began with the invasion of **Guadalcanal** in August 1942. It continued until early 1944, when MacArthur's troops finally captured enough islands to surround Rabaul, the main Japanese base in the region. In response the Japanese withdrew their ships and aircraft from the base, although they left 100,000 troops behind to hold the island.

Worried that the navy's advance across the central Pacific was leaving him behind, MacArthur ordered his forces to leap nearly 600 miles (966 km) past Rabaul to capture the Japanese base at Hollandia on the north coast of New Guinea. Shortly after securing

604 CHAPTER 12 America and World War II

 Geography *Skills*

Answers:
1. Leyte Gulf: October 23–26, 1944
2. to acquire bases to move supplies and troops closer and closer to Japan

Geography Skills Practice
Ask: What are the approximate distances between Hawaii and the Gilbert Islands *(appx. 2,500 miles [4,000 km])*, Hawaii and Guam *(appx. 4,300 miles [7,000 km])*, and Hawaii and Midway *(appx. 1,600 miles [2,600 km])*?

New Guinea, MacArthur's troops seized the island of Morotai—the last stop before the Philippines.

In order to take back the Philippines, the United States assembled an enormous invasion force. In October 1944, more than 700 ships carrying over 160,000 troops sailed for Leyte Gulf in the Philippines. On October 20, the troops began to land on Leyte, an island located on the eastern side of the Philippines. A few hours after the invasion began, MacArthur headed to the beach. Upon reaching the shore, he strode to a radio and spoke into the microphone: "People of the Philippines, I have returned. By the grace of Almighty God, our forces stand again on Philippine soil."

To stop the American invasion, the Japanese sent four aircraft carriers toward the Philippines from the north and secretly dispatched another fleet to the west. Believing the Japanese carriers were leading the main attack, most of the American carriers protecting the invasion left Leyte Gulf and headed north to stop them. Seizing their chance, the Japanese warships to the west raced through the Philippine Islands into Leyte Gulf and ambushed the remaining American ships.

The Battle of Leyte Gulf was the largest naval battle in history. It was also the first time that the Japanese used **kamikaze** attacks. *Kamikaze* means "divine wind" in Japanese. It refers to the great storm that destroyed the Mongol fleet during its invasion of Japan in the thirteenth century.

Kamikaze pilots would deliberately crash their planes into American ships, killing themselves but also inflicting severe damage. Luckily for the Americans, just as their situation was becoming desperate, the Japanese commander, believing more American ships were on the way, ordered a retreat.

A Triumphant Return In October 1944, Douglas MacArthur fulfilled his promise and returned to the Philippines.

Although the Japanese retreated, recapturing the Philippines was a long and grueling process. Over 80,000 Japanese were killed; less than 1,000 surrendered. MacArthur's troops did not capture Manila until March 1945. The battle destroyed the city and killed many civilians. The remaining Japanese retreated into the rugged terrain north of Manila, and they were still fighting when word came in August 1945 that Japan had surrendered.

 Describing What strategy did the United States Navy use to advance across the Pacific?

 Study Central

For help with the concepts in this section of *American Vision: Modern Times* go to tav.mt.glencoe.com and click on *Study Central.*

SECTION 4 ASSESSMENT

Checking for Understanding

1. **Vocabulary** Define: approximately, code, pose, amphtrac, kamikaze.
2. **People and Terms** Identify: Casablanca Conference, Operation Overlord, D-Day, Omar Bradley, Guadalcanal.
3. **Explain** why D-Day's success was so vital to an Allied victory.

Reviewing Big Ideas

4. **Identifying** How did the geography of the Pacific affect American strategy?

Critical Thinking

5. **Historical Analysis** **Analyzing** What made the invasion of Normandy so important? **CA HI4**
6. **Organizing** Use a graphic organizer to explain the significance of each leader listed below.

Leader	Significance
Dwight Eisenhower	
George Patton	
George Marshall	
Omar Bradley	
Douglas MacArthur	

Analyzing Visuals

7. **Examining Photographs** Study the photograph on this page. What effect do you think MacArthur's return had on Philippine morale?

Writing About History

8. **Expository Writing** Using library or Internet resources, find more information on one of the battles discussed in this section. Use the information to write a report detailing the importance of the battle. Share your report with the class. **CA** 11WS1.6; 11WA2.4b

CHAPTER 12   America and World War II   **605**

SECTION 4 ASSESSMENT ANSWERS

1. Content vocabulary is boldfaced and highlighted in yellow. Academic vocabulary is boldfaced.
2. Casablanca Conference (p. 599), Operation Overlord (p. 601), D-Day (p. 602), Omar Bradley (p. 602), Guadalcanal (p. 604)
3. It would force the Germans to fight on two fronts.

4. Coral reefs around some of the atolls made landing craft hard to maneuver. They began using amphtracs to land the soldiers.
5. The Germans now had to fight a two-front war, which stretched their resources even further. The Soviet Union had promised help in defeating the Japanese once

the Germans were defeated.
6. Answers should match chapter content.
7. Answers may vary. They welcomed him because they had been treated harshly by the Japanese.
8. Reports should include details that do not appear in the student text.

C **Critical Thinking**

Drawing Conclusions General MacArthur returned to the Philippines about two years after he left in 1942. **Ask: Why was it so important for the Allies to recapture the Philippines?** *(Students' answers will vary but should indicate a lift in morale.)* **OL**

ASSESS

Resources for page 605

Use these resources to assess student mastery.

📂 Section Quiz 12-4

📂 Reading Essentials and Study Guide 12-4

💿 Interactive Tutor Self-Assessment CD-ROM

📂 California Standards Practice, Grade 11

✓ Reading Check

Answer: They moved from island to island, advancing slowly toward Japan.

Study Central provides audio summaries, interactive games, and online graphic organizers to help students review section content.

CLOSE

Summarizing Ask students to list five important events that occurred between 1941–1945 and explain how they affected U.S. foreign and domestic policy. **OL**

FOCUS

History–Social Science Standards

This feature addresses the following standard:

11.7.2 Explain U.S. and Allied wartime strategy, including the major battles of Midway, Normandy, Iwo Jima, Okinawa, and the Battle of the Bulge.

TEACH

R Reading Strategy

Reading Maps, Graphs, and Charts Ask the class to examine the map of the Normandy invasion on D-Day, paying careful attention to the legend that identifies the symbols and markings used on the map. **Ask: What are the three most important pieces of information displayed on this map?** *(Answers may vary, but students should primarily identify the time of the first wave's departure, the location of Allied troops at the end of D-Day, and the location of the Allies on the second day.)* **OL**

Answers and Additional Support

SLOW GOING

Allied planners had hoped that American forces landing at Omaha early on June 6, 1944, would advance 5 to 10 miles after 24 hours of fighting. Stiff German resistance, however, stopped the invaders cold on the beach. Progress inland was excruciatingly slow and painful. The Americans reached their first-day objective (dotted blue line on map) only after more than two days of bloody fighting. Despite terrible losses, American forces successfully carried out one of the most crucial missions of the war.

606 CHAPTER 12 America and World War II

EXTENDING THE CONTENT

Mulberrys After the D-Day invasion, artificial harbors known as mulberrys were constructed off the coast of Normandy. Once built, they were capable of moving 7,000 tons of vehicles and goods each day, greatly assisting the expanding invasion of Western Europe that began at Normandy. Each mulberry utilized miles of flexible steel roadways that floated on steel or concrete pontoons. The roadways stopped at piers that reached down to the bottom of the English Channel. Ships were sunk alongside the roadways to protect the structures from the waves. Each mulberry consisted of over 140,000 tons of concrete and 105,000 tons of steel.

A Day for Heroes

The selection of a site for the largest amphibious landing in history was one of the biggest decisions of World War II. Allied planners needed a sheltered location with flat, firm beaches and within range of friendly fighter planes based in England.

There had to be enough roads and paths to move jeeps and trucks off the beaches and to accommodate the hundreds of thousands of American, Canadian, and British troops set to stream ashore following the invasion. An airfield and a seaport that the Allies could use were also needed. Most important was a reasonable expectation of achieving the element of surprise.

Five beaches on the northern coast of Normandy, France, met all the criteria and were chosen as invasion sites. On D-Day the attack on four beaches—Utah in the west and Gold, Juno, and Sword in the east (inset, opposite page)—went according to plan. But at Omaha Beach (map), between Utah and Gold, the bravery and determination of the U.S. 1st Infantry Division was tested in one of the fiercest battles of the war.

Surrounded at both ends by cliffs that rose wall-like from the sea, Omaha was only four miles long. It was the only sand beach in the area, however, and thus the only place for a landing. Unless the Allies were to leave a 20-mile gap between Utah and Gold, they would have to come ashore at Omaha Beach.

Troops crowd into a landing craft to head across the English Channel to Omaha Beach.

To repel the Allies at the water's edge, the Germans built a fortress atop the cliffs at Pointe du Hoc overlooking Omaha from the west. They dug trenches and guns into the 150-foot bluffs lining the beach and along five ravines leading off it (see map).

Wading into the surf, the Americans advanced toward Omaha Beach. Many men were cut down as the doors of their landing craft opened. The survivors had to cross more than 300 yards across a tidal flat strewn with man-made obstacles. Winds and a current pushed landing craft into clumps as the men moved ashore. As a result, soldiers ran onto the beach in groups and became easy targets. Of the more than 9,000 Allied casualties on D-Day, Omaha accounted for about one-third.

Although many died, the Americans took control of the beach and fought their way inland. As General Omar Bradley later wrote, **"Every man who set foot on Omaha Beach that day was a hero."**

C

R

D-Day Forces

A-L	U.S. Company — 200 men
116th	U.S. Battalion — 900 men
Rn.	U.S. Rangers
916th	German infantry — forces associated with German battalion

German resistance point

German coastal defense

U.S. stronghold

Landing craft

Landing craft — sunk

Battleship

Cruiser

Transport

Hedgerows

Town

Scale varies in this perspective

Bandaged and shell-shocked, infantrymen from the American 1st Division wait to be evacuated after landing on Omaha Beach.

LEARNING FROM GEOGRAPHY

1. Why did the Allies choose Normandy as the site of the invasion?

2. Why was the landing at Omaha Beach so much more difficult than U.S. leaders expected?

C Critical Thinking

Comparing and Contrasting
The invasion of Omaha Beach was one of the fiercest battle fronts of World War II. Many movies about D-Day have been made since the battle occurred. Ask students to use the library and Internet resources to select two movies that are about or depict the D-Day invasion. Each student should watch the movies, keeping notes on how each movie depicts the battle of Omaha Beach. Ask students to write a one-page report that compares and contrasts how each movie portrays the battle. **OL**
CA 11WA2.4b

R Reading Strategy

Connecting Ask students to read the quote by General Omar Bradley that ends this feature. Tell students to find other quotes regarding D-Day and write brief biographies on the individuals who stated the quotes. Ask volunteers to read their quotes aloud and discuss the history of the persons quoted. **OL**

ASSESS/CLOSE

Have students answer the Learning from Geography questions.

NGS ONLINE

Access National Geographic's Web site for current events, atlas updates, activities, links, interactive features, and archives at www.nationalgeographic.com.

ANSWERS TO LEARNING FROM GEOGRAPHY

1. Normandy provided the necessary criteria to support such a massive invasion plan—roads, an airfield, a seaport, and the element of surprise.

2. The open beach exposed the invading soldiers to protected enemy fire; obstacles on the beach slowed the soldiers' advance; wind and current grouped soldiers together in easily targeted clumps.

FOCUS

SKILLBUILDER ACTIVITY

Project **Daily Focus Skills Transparency 12-5** and have students answer the question.

Guide to Reading

Understanding Vocabulary: Divide the class into three groups and ask each group to prepare a brief presentation on one of the content vocabulary words.

Answers to Graphic: Students should complete the outline by including all headings in the section.

Unpacking the Standards

Students will be able to:

- Describe the defeat of the Nazi government in Germany.
- Explain the turn of events that led to the defeat of the Japanese Empire.
- Discuss the problems that the Allied nations faced in rebuilding the world torn apart by World War II.

Answers and Additional Support

SECTION 5 The War Ends

Guide to Reading

Connection
In the previous section, you learned how the Allies turned the tide both in Europe and the Pacific. In this section, you will learn about the road to victory against Germany and Japan and the creation of the United Nations.

Main Idea
- After the Battle of the Bulge, Germany had few military resources to continue fighting the war. (p. 609)
- Hoping to shorten the war, President Truman decided to drop atomic bombs on the Japanese cities of Hiroshima and Nagasaki. (p. 612)

- The Allied nations attempted to prevent future wars by creating the United Nations and by bringing war criminals to trial. (p. 616)

Content Vocabulary
hedgerow, napalm, charter

Academic Vocabulary
successor, error, reluctant

People and Terms to Identify
Battle of the Bulge, V-E Day, Harry S. Truman, Curtis LeMay, Manhattan Project, V-J Day, United Nations

Reading Objectives
- **Explain** the tactics the Allies used to invade Germany and to defeat Japan.

- **Outline** the reasons the Allies created the United Nations and held war crimes trials.

Reading Strategy
Taking Notes As you read about the end of World War II and the organizations set up to maintain global peace, use the major headings of the section to create an outline similar to the one below.

The War Ends
I. The Third Reich Collapses
  A.
  B.
II.
  A.
  B.

Preview of Events

♦1944	♦1945	♦1946

December 16, 1944	**February 19, 1945**	**April 12, 1945**	**May 7, 1945**	**August 15, 1945**
Battle of the Bulge begins	American troops invade Iwo Jima	Franklin Roosevelt dies; Harry Truman becomes president	Germany surrenders	V-J Day, Japan surrenders

The following are the main History–Social Science Standards covered in this section.

11.7.2 Explain U.S. and Allied wartime strategy, including the major battles of Midway, Normandy, Iwo Jima, Okinawa, and the Battle of the Bulge.

11.7.3 Identify the roles and sacrifices of individual American soldiers, as well as the unique contributions of the special fighting forces (e.g., the Tuskegee Airmen, the 442nd Regimental Combat team, the Navajo Code Talkers).

11.7.5 Discuss the constitutional issues and impact of events on the U.S. home front, including the internment of Japanese Americans (e.g., *Fred Korematsu v. United States of America*) and the restrictions on German and Italian resident aliens; the response of the administration to Hitler's atrocities against Jews and other groups; the roles of women in military production; and the roles and growing political demands of African Americans.

11.7.6 Describe major developments in aviation, weaponry, communication, and medicine and the

❧ The Big Idea ❧

The fate of nations is forever changed by monumental world events. After the D-Day invasion, the Allies fought one last German offensive before defeating the Nazis. In the meantime, the war in the Pacific intensified, despite the firebombing of Japan and slow Allied gains. With the Japanese refusing to surrender unconditionally, commanders became convinced that only an invasion of Japan would end the war. Truman, who became president after Roosevelt's death, decided to use a new weapon—the atomic bomb. After the military dropped atomic bombs on Hiroshima and Nagasaki, Japan surrendered. The Allies formed a military tribunal to try German and Japanese leaders for war crimes. At the same time, delegates from 39 countries created the United Nations.

war's impact on the location of American industry and use of resources.

11.7.7 Discuss the decision to drop atomic bombs and the consequences of the decision (Hiroshima and Nagasaki).

11.9.1 Discuss the establishment of the United Nations and International Declaration of Human Rights, International Monetary Fund, World Bank, and General Agreement on Tariffs and Trade (GATT) and their importance in shaping modern Europe and maintaining peace and international order.

608 CHAPTER 12 America and World War II

SECTION RESOURCES

📁 Print Material
- Reproducible Lesson Plan 12-5
- Guided Reading Activity 12-5
- Reading Essentials and Study Guide 12-5
- Active Reading Note-Taking Guide 12-5

📖 Transparencies
- Daily Focus Skills Transparency 12-5
- Section Graphic Organizer Transparency 12-5

Technology
- 💿 Interactive Tutor Self-Assessment CD-ROM
- 💿 Exam*View*® Pro Testmaker CD-ROM
- 💿 Presentation Plus! CD-ROM

The Third Reich Collapses

Main Idea After the Battle of the Bulge, Germany had few military resources to continue fighting the war.

Reading Connection What needed resources did the Germans lose at the Battle of the Bulge? Read on to learn how Germany surrendered unconditionally.

Well before the war ended, President Roosevelt and other Allied leaders were aware that the Nazis were committing atrocities. When Allied soldiers arrived in Germany, they witnessed the extent of the Nazis' horrible acts.

★ An American Story ★

In 1945 Captain Luther Fletcher entered the German concentration camp at Buchenwald with a group of Germans who were being forced to see what their country had done. In his diary Fletcher described what they witnessed:

❝They saw blackened skeletons and skulls in the ovens of the crematorium. In the yard outside, they saw a heap of white human ashes and bones. . . . [The] dead were stripped of their clothing and lay naked, many stacked like cordwood waiting to be burned at the crematory. At one time 5,000 had been stacked on the vacant lot next to the crematory. . . . At headquarters of the SS troops who ran the place were lamp shades made from human skin. . . . Often, the guide said, the SS wished to make an example of someone in killing him. . . . They used what I call hay hooks, catching him under the chin and the other in the back of the neck. He hung in this manner until he died.❞

–quoted in *World War II: From the Battle Front to the Home Front*

In 1943 the Allies officially declared that they would punish the Nazis for their crimes after the war. Meanwhile, Roosevelt was convinced that the best way to put an end to the concentration camps was to destroy the Nazi regime. To do that, he believed the Allies had to dedicate their resources to breaking out of Normandy, liberating France, and conquering Germany.

Although D-Day had been a success, it was only the beginning. Surrounding many fields in Normandy were **hedgerows**—dirt walls, several feet thick, covered in shrubbery. The hedgerows had been built to fence in cattle and crops, but they also enabled the Germans to take cover from the enemy and fiercely defend their positions. The battle of the hedgerows ended on July 25, 1944, when 2,500 American bombers managed to blow a hole in the German lines, enabling American tanks to race through the gap.

As the Allies broke out of Normandy, the French Resistance—a group of French civilians who had secretly organized to resist the German occupation of their country—staged a rebellion in Paris. When the Allied forces liberated Paris on August 25, they found the streets filled with French citizens celebrating their victory. Three weeks later, American troops were within 20 miles (32 km) of the German border.

The Battle of the Bulge As the Allies closed in on Germany, Hitler decided to stage one last desperate offensive. His goal was to cut off the Allied supplies coming through the port of Antwerp, Belgium. The attack began just before dawn on December 16, 1944. Six inches (15 cm) of snow covered the ground, and the weather was bitterly cold. Moving rapidly, the Germans were able to catch the American defenders by surprise.

As the German troops raced west, their lines bulged outward, and the attack became known as the **Battle of the Bulge.**

▼ *Jewish prisoners at a German concentration camp*

CHAPTER 12 America and World War II **609**

TEACH

U Universal Access

Sharing Information Group students into teams of four and assign each member of the teams a number from one to four. Divide the text under the heading "The Battle of the Bulge" into four parts and number the parts. Have everyone with the number one meet to study and discuss the first part of the section. Do the same for each of the other parts. Reunite the home teams and have each member of the team share his or her knowledge about the battle. OL

R Reading Strategy

Identifying the Main Idea Have students imagine that they are the editor of a prominent American newspaper. Tell them to write newspaper headlines for the date of December 16, 1944. BL

More Skill Practice

Evaluating Evidence As a class, discuss the troop movements of the Axis and the Allies during the Battle of the Bulge. Have students identify good and poor strategic moves related to the battle. Then ask students how the strategy used by each side affected the outcome of the battle. OL CA HR4; HI2

S Skill Practice

Conducting Research Remind students that World War II involved many smaller nations as well as the great Allied and Axis powers like Germany and the United States. Countries such as Romania, Bulgaria, Turkey, and Denmark also had an effect on the outcome of the war. Tell the class to examine the map on page 610 and identify all of the Allied and Axis countries in a two-column chart. Divide students into groups of four to study one of these smaller countries, identify their position as an Allied, Axis, or neutral nation, and determine their role in World War II.

OL **CA** HI1; HI4

U Universal Access

Interpersonal Have students locate someone in the community who remembers V-E Day, and ask them to relate their memories of the celebration. If no one can be found, ask students to conduct newspaper research to gather reports of the time period using primary sources. Tell students to share their findings with the class.

OL

Answers and Additional Support

NATIONAL GEOGRAPHIC

World War II in Europe and Africa, 1939–1945

Major Axis powers
Greatest extent of Axis control
Allied or Allied-controlled
Neutral powers
← Allied advance
← Supply line
— International boundary, Jan. 1938

Part of the German plan called for the capture of the town of Bastogne, where several important roads converged. If the Allies held Bastogne, it would greatly delay the German advance. American reinforcements raced to the town, arriving just ahead of the Germans. The Germans then surrounded the town and demanded that the Americans surrender. The American commander sent back a one-word reply: "Nuts!"

Shortly after the Germans surrounded the Americans, Eisenhower ordered General Patton to rescue them. Three days later, faster than anyone expected in the midst of a snowstorm, Patton's troops slammed into the German lines. As the weather cleared, Allied aircraft began hitting German fuel depots. On Christmas Eve, out of fuel and weakened by heavy losses, the German troops driving toward Antwerp were forced to halt. Two days later, Patton's troops broke through to Bastogne.

Although fighting continued for three weeks, the United States had won the Battle of the Bulge. On January 8, the Germans began to withdraw. They had suffered more than 100,000 casualties and lost many tanks and aircraft. They now had very little left to prevent the Allies from entering Germany.

U V-E Day: The War Ends in Europe While American and British forces fought to liberate France, the Soviet Union began a massive attack on German troops in Russia. By the time the Battle of the Bulge ended, the Soviets had driven Hitler's forces out of Russia and back across Poland. By February 1945, Soviet troops had reached the Oder River. They were only 35 miles (56 km) from Berlin.

610 CHAPTER 12 America and World War II

Did You Know?

Germany accepted unconditional surrender on May 7, 1945, in a small schoolhouse in France. The armistice took effect the next day—V-E Day. In Moscow, gigantic rays of light were projected into the air to celebrate. In the United States the Washington Monument, the Capitol Dome, and the Statue of Liberty were lit at night for the very first time since the attack on Pearl Harbor. After less than a month in office, President Truman reflected on this triumph when he addressed the nation by saying, "This is a solemn, but glorious hour. I only wish FDR had lived to witness this day."

Rise and Fall of Axis Powers

1939

1942

1945

Axis-controlled territory
Bi-Polar Oblique projection

Axis Expansion The Axis powers included Germany, Italy, Austria, and the Sudetenland.

Axis Control At their height, the Axis controlled almost all of Europe and North Africa.

Axis Collapse The Allies invaded Germany from the east and the west.

Military and Civilian Deaths in World War II

Country	Military Deaths	Civilian Deaths
USSR	11,000,000	6,700,000
Germany	3,250,000	2,350,000
Japan	1,740,000	393,000
China	1,400,000	8,000,000
Poland	110,000	5,300,000
United States	405,000	2,000
Great Britain	306,000	61,000
Italy	227,000	60,000
France	122,000	470,000

Source: *World War II: A Statistical Survey.* (Figures are approximate.)

WW I

Military 86%

Civilian 14%

WW II

Civilian 54%

Military 46%

War Casualties World War II took more lives than any other war in history. More civilians than soldiers died in the war.

Geography *Skills*

1. **Interpreting Maps** Which European countries remained neutral during the war?
2. **Applying Geography Skills** How did the Soviet Union receive supplies during the war?

R₁

R₂

S

As the Soviets crossed Germany's eastern border, American forces attacked Germany's western border. By the first week of March, 1945, American troops had fought their way to the Rhine River, Germany's last major line of defense in the west. Then on March 7, American soldiers captured the heights above the town of Remagen. Gazing down at the town, platoon leader Emmet J. Burrows was amazed at what he saw. The Ludendorf Bridge across the Rhine was still intact. The Germans had not blown it up. The American troops raced across the bridge, driving back the German defenders. By the end of the day, American tanks were across the Rhine. Hearing the news, General Bradley yelled, "Hot dog . . . this will bust them wide open."

As German defenses crumbled, American troops raced east, closing to within 70 miles (113 km) of Berlin. On April 16, Soviet troops finally smashed through the German defenses on the Oder River. Five days later, they reached the outskirts of Berlin.

Deep in his Berlin bunker, Adolf Hitler knew the end was near. On April 30, 1945, he put a pistol in his mouth and pulled the trigger. His secretary, Martin Bormann, carried Hitler's body outside, doused it in gasoline, and set it on fire. Before killing himself, Hitler chose Grand Admiral Karl Doenitz to be his **successor.** Doenitz tried to surrender to the Americans and British while continuing to fight the

CHAPTER 12   America and World War II   **611**

Geography *Skills*

Background: Stalin had originally cooperated with Hitler. Churchill and Roosevelt delayed an attack in Europe, forcing the Soviets to face the Germans alone. This increased the Soviets' losses and weakened them as a postwar power.

Answers:
1. Ireland, Portugal, Spain, Sweden, Switzerland, and Turkey

2. They received supplies across the Atlantic, around the Scandinavian Peninsula, and across the Arctic Circle, through Iran and across the Caspian Sea.

Geography Skills Practice
Ask: Which countries had the highest number of military and civilian deaths during World War II? *(military: USSR; civilian: China)*

R₁ Reading Strategy

Reading Maps, Graphs, and Charts Have students add the total number of military and civilian deaths displayed in the chart on this page. Ask them to determine the percentages of military and civilian deaths for each country. Next, have students create a third column for the table, adding the number of civilian and military deaths for each country. Students should total the new column and again find the percentages. They can refer to the percentages as you ask several questions about them. For example, what percentage of total civilian deaths did Poland experience? *(21.3%)* **OL**

R₂ Reading Strategy

Predicting Tell students that the American troops arrived at the Ludendorf Bridge forty-five minutes before it was scheduled to be destroyed by Nazi engineers. **Ask: Would it have significantly affected the outcome of these events if the American troops had arrived too late?** *(Students will likely answer that the overall outcome would not have changed and that the Allied troops simply would have found another way to continue their advance.)* **OL** **CA HI2; HI4**

S Skill Practice

Graphing Data Organize students into groups of three or four. Have each group research the number of military deaths that occurred during World War II. Ask each group to prepare two circle graphs, one showing the Allied losses and one showing the Axis losses. Each piece of the circles should represent the losses suffered by each of the major countries on the two sides. Encourage groups to label the graphs clearly. **OL**

Soviets, but Eisenhower insisted on unconditional surrender. On May 7, 1945, Germany surrendered unconditionally. The next day—May 8, 1945—was proclaimed **V-E Day,** for "Victory in Europe."

✓ Reading Check **Explaining** Why was the Battle of the Bulge such a disastrous defeat for Germany?

Japan Is Defeated

Main Idea **Hoping to shorten the war, President Truman decided to drop atomic bombs on the Japanese cities of Hiroshima and Nagasaki.**

Reading Connection Do you believe President Truman was justified in dropping atomic bombs on Japan? Read on to discover the events that led to Truman's decision.

Unfortunately, President Roosevelt did not live to see the defeat of Germany. On April 12, 1945, while vacationing in Warm Springs, Georgia, he suffered a stroke and died. His vice president, **Harry S. Truman,** became president during this difficult time.

The next day, Truman told reporters: "Boys, if you ever pray, pray for me now. . . . When they told me yesterday what had happened, I felt like the moon, the stars, and all the planets had fallen on me." Despite feeling overwhelmed, Truman began at once to make decisions about the war. Although Germany surrendered a few weeks later, the war with Japan continued to intensify, and Truman was forced to make some of the most difficult decisions of the war during his first six months in office.

Uncommon Valor on Iwo Jima On November 24, 1944, bombs fell on Tokyo for the first time since the 1942 Doolittle raid. Above the city flew 80 B-29 Superfortress bombers that had traveled over 1,500 miles (2,414 km) from new American bases in the Mariana Islands.

At first the B-29s did little damage because they kept missing their targets. Japan was simply too far away: By the time the B-29s reached Japan, they did not have enough fuel left to fix their navigational **errors** or to adjust for high winds. The solution was to capture an island closer to Japan, where the B-29s could refuel. After studying the problem, American military planners decided to invade Iwo Jima.

Iwo Jima was perfectly located, roughly halfway between the Marianas and Japan, but its geography

"uncommon valor was a common virtue"

—*Admiral Chester W. Nimitz*

Picturing History

Planting the Flag Photographer Joe Rosenthal won the Pulitzer Prize for this photo of five marines and a navy medical corpsman raising the flag on Iwo Jima. How do you think photographs such as this one affected American morale? Why?

Picturing History

Background: The monument based on this famous photo pays tribute to the nearly 7,000 Americans who gave their lives in the battle of Iwo Jima. The monument was sculpted by Felix W. de Weldon. The sculptor made plaster casts of the faces of the three members of the flag raisers who survived World War II. The other three figures were created from photos. The monument stands in Arlington National Cemetery.

Answer: They boosted American morale because they saw the American forces gaining ground and winning victories.

Ask: What do you think Nimitz meant by his quote? (*He meant that doing the heroic was commonplace among the soldiers who landed on Iwo Jima.*)

was formidable. At its southern tip was Mount Suribachi, a dormant volcano. The terrain was rugged, with rocky cliffs, jagged ravines, and dozens of caves. Volcanic ash covered the ground. Even worse, the Japanese had built a vast network of caves and concrete bunkers connected by miles of tunnels.

On February 19, 1945, 60,000 U.S. Marines landed on Iwo Jima. As the troops leapt from the amphtracs, they sank up to their ankles in the soft ash. Meanwhile, Japanese artillery began to pound the invaders. Robert Sherrod, who had been on Tarawa, was shocked: "[The marines] died with the greatest possible violence. Nowhere in the Pacific have I seen such badly mangled bodies. Many were cut squarely in half. Legs and arms lay 50 feet (15 m) away from any body."

Inch by inch, the marines crawled inland, using flamethrowers and explosives to attack the Japanese bunkers. More than 6,800 marines were killed before the island was captured. Admiral Nimitz later wrote that on Iwo Jima, "uncommon valor was a common virtue."

Firebombing Devastates Japan While American engineers prepared airfields on Iwo Jima, General **Curtis LeMay,** commander of the B-29s based in the Marianas, decided to change strategy. To help the B-29s hit their targets, he ordered them to drop bombs filled with **napalm**—a kind of a jellied gasoline. The bombs were designed not only to explode but also to start fires. Even if the B-29s missed their targets, the fires they started would spread to the intended targets.

The use of firebombs was very controversial because the fires would also kill civilians; however, LeMay could think of no other way to destroy Japan's war production quickly. Loaded with firebombs, B-29s attacked Tokyo on March 9, 1945. As strong winds fanned the flames, the firestorm grew so intense that it sucked the oxygen out of the air, asphyxiating thousands. As one survivor later recalled:

❝The fires were incredible . . . with flames leaping hundreds of feet into the air. . . . Many people were gasping for breath. With every passing moment the air became more foul . . . the noise was a continuing crashing roar. . . . Firewinds filled with burning particles rushed up and down the streets. I watched people . . . running for their lives. . . . The flames raced after them like living things, striking them down. . . . Wherever I turned my eyes, I saw people . . . seeking air to breathe.❞

—quoted in *New History of World War II*

The Tokyo firebombing killed over 80,000 people and destroyed more than 250,000 buildings. By the

Picturing **History**

Ship Attacks Kamikaze attacks intensified in 1945, hitting the USS *Bunker Hill* and many other American ships. Why do you think these Japanese kamikaze pilots were willing to fly suicide missions?

end of June 1945, Japan's six most important industrial cities had been firebombed, destroying almost half of their total urban area. By the end of the war, the B-29s had firebombed 67 Japanese cities.

The Invasion of Okinawa Despite the massive damage the firebombing caused, there were few signs in the spring of 1945 that Japan was ready to quit. Many American officials believed the Japanese would not surrender until Japan had been invaded. To prepare for the invasion, the United States needed a base near Japan to stockpile supplies and build up troops. Iwo Jima was small and still too far away. After much discussion, military planners chose Okinawa—only 350 miles (563 km) from Japan.

American troops landed on Okinawa on April 1, 1945. Instead of defending the beaches, the Japanese troops took up positions in the island's rugged mountains. To dig the Japanese out of their caves and bunkers, the Americans had to fight their way up steep slopes against constant machine gun and artillery fire. More than 12,000 American soldiers, sailors, and marines died during the fighting, but by June 22, 1945, Okinawa had finally been captured.

CHAPTER 12 America and World War II **613**

R **Reading Strategy**

Scaffolding—Academic Vocabulary The word *network* was introduced in Chapter 6, Section 3. Ask a student to define the word. **BL**

W₁ **Writing Support**

Descriptive Writing Tell students to imagine that they are journalists witnessing the American landing on Iwo Jima. Have them work in small groups to create news articles describing what they have seen. Remind them that newspaper articles begin with a brief summary of the most relevant facts and then add more descriptive elements of the story in later paragraphs. **OL**
CA 11WA2.1a; 11WA2.1c

W₂ **Writing Support**

Response to Film Writing Have students rent or borrow *Grave of the Fireflies*, a Japanese movie about the devastation caused by the firebombing of Japan. Ask students to prepare two- to three-minute critiques of the movie after watching it. **AL**

Review the Big Idea

Review the Big Idea for this section, "The fate of nations is forever changed by monumental world events." Have students discuss their views about the use of firebombs on Japan and the death of Japanese civilians. Encourage students to explain the reasoning behind their opinions.
OL **CA** HR3; HI3

Picturing **History**

Background: The inset photo shows a kamikaze attack. U.S. naval vessels were hit hundreds of times by kamikazes while invading Okinawa.
Answer: They would die for the emperor; the empire would see them as heroes.
Ask: What were the terms that Japan wanted before agreeing to surrender? *(They wanted the emperor to stay in power.)*

Did You Know?

Okinawa was not initially considered a possible landing site for American forces because of its size (65 miles long and 18 miles wide at its widest point) and its civilian population, the largest yet encountered by the Allies in the Pacific campaign.

The Terms for Surrender Shortly after the United States captured Okinawa, the Japanese emperor urged his government to find a way to end the war. The biggest problem was the American demand for unconditional surrender. Many Japanese leaders were willing to surrender but on one condition—the emperor had to stay in power.

American officials knew that the fate of the emperor was the most important issue for the Japanese. Most Americans, however, blamed the emperor for the war and wanted him removed from power. President Truman was **reluctant** to go against public opinion. Furthermore, he knew the United States was almost ready to test a new weapon that might force Japan to surrender without any conditions. The new weapon was the atomic bomb.

The Manhattan Project In 1939 Leo Szilard, one of the world's top physicists, learned that German scientists had split the uranium atom. Szilard had been the first scientist to suggest that splitting the atom might release enormous energy. Worried that the Nazis were working on an atomic bomb, Szilard convinced the world's best-known physicist, Albert Einstein, to sign a letter Szilard had drafted and send it to President Roosevelt. In the letter Einstein warned that by using uranium, "extremely powerful bombs of a new type may . . . be constructed."

Roosevelt responded by setting up a scientific committee to study the issue. The committee remained skeptical until 1941, when they met with British scientists who were already working on an atomic bomb. The British research so impressed the Americans that they convinced Roosevelt to begin a program to build an atomic bomb.

The American program to build an atomic bomb was code-named the **Manhattan Project** and was headed by General Leslie R. Groves. The project's first breakthrough came in 1942, when Szilard and Enrico Fermi, another physicist, built the world's first nuclear reactor at the University of Chicago. Groves organized a team of engineers and scientists

Different Viewpoints

Dropping the Atomic Bomb: Was It the Right Decision?

More than half a century later, people continue to debate what some historians have called the most important event of the twentieth century—President Truman's order to drop the atomic bomb on Japan. Did his momentous decision shorten the war and save lives on both sides, or was it prompted by Truman's fear that the Soviet Union, poised to invade, would gain control of Japan after the war?

A historian opposes Truman's decision:

Historian Gar Alperovitz maintains that Truman possessed alternatives to the atomic bomb but chose to use the weapon in order to force Japan's surrender before the Soviet Union could mount an invasion and subsequently occupy Japanese territory.

"Quite simply, it is not true that the atomic bomb was used because it was the only way to save the 'hundreds of thousands' or 'millions' of lives as was subsequently claimed. The readily available options were to modify the surrender terms and/or await the shock of the Russian attack.

Perhaps it is here, most poignantly, that we confront our own reluctance to ask the difficult questions—for even if one were to accept the most inflated estimates of lives saved by the atomic bomb, the fact remains that it was an act of violent destruction aimed at large concentrations of noncombatants."

—quoted in *The Decision to Use the Atomic Bomb, and the Architecture of an American Myth*

Hiroshima in the aftermath of the atomic bomb

to build an atomic bomb at a secret laboratory in Los Alamos, New Mexico. J. Robert Oppenheimer led the team. On July 16, 1945, they detonated the world's first atomic bomb near Alamogordo, New Mexico.

The Decision to Drop the Bomb Even before the bomb was tested, American officials began to debate how to use it. Admiral William Leahy, chairman of the Joint Chiefs of Staff, opposed using the bomb because it killed civilians indiscriminately. He believed that an economic blockade and conventional bombing would convince Japan to surrender.

Secretary of War Henry Stimson wanted to warn the Japanese about the bomb while at the same time telling them that they could keep the emperor if they surrendered. Secretary of State James Byrnes, however, wanted to drop the bomb without any warning to shock Japan into surrendering.

President Truman later wrote that he "regarded the bomb as a military weapon and never had any doubts that it should be used." His advisers had warned him to expect massive casualties if the United States invaded Japan. Truman believed it was his duty as president to use every weapon available to save American lives.

The Allies threatened Japan with "prompt and utter destruction" if the nation did not surrender unconditionally, but the Japanese did not reply. Truman then ordered the military to drop the bomb. On August 6, 1945, a B-29 bomber named the *Enola Gay* dropped an atomic bomb, code-named "Little Boy," on Hiroshima, an important industrial city. The bomb was dropped at 8:15 A.M. Forty-three seconds later, it exploded. Heat, radiation, and an enormous shock wave slammed into Hiroshima.

The bomb destroyed 76,000 buildings—about 63 percent of the city. Somewhere between 80,000 and 120,000 people died instantly, and thousands more died later from burns and radiation sickness. Everywhere, as witness Nozaki Kiyoshi recalled, were "horrific scenes":

> **❝**The center of the city was still burning bright red, like live charcoal. Roof tiles were popping. We passed numerous war dead who had been carbonized. . . . We found five or six half-burned roofless streetcars. Inside were piles of corpses smoldering under white smoke. . . . A young mother lay face down, her baby tucked under her breast. They looked more like pink wax dolls than human beings.**❞**
>
> —quoted in *Senso: The Japanese Remember the Pacific War*

The bombing stunned Japan. Three days later, on August 9, the Soviet Union declared war on Japan. Later that day, the United States dropped another atomic bomb, code-named "Fat Man," on the city of Nagasaki, killing between 35,000 and 74,000 people.

Faced with such massive destruction and the shock of the Soviets joining the war, the Japanese emperor ordered his government to surrender. On August 15, 1945—**V-J Day**—Japan surrendered. On the other side of the world, Americans celebrated. For American soldiers the news was especially good. As one veteran recalled: "We would not be obliged to run up the beaches near Tokyo assault firing while being mortared and shelled. . . . We were going to live. We were going to grow up to adulthood after all." The long war was finally over. The United States and its allies, after a tremendous effort, had freed Europe from Nazi tyranny and put an end to Japanese aggression in Asia.

✓**Reading Check** **Analyzing** What issues did Truman consider before using the atomic bomb?

A historian defends Truman's decision:

Historian Herbert Feis argues that Truman's desire to avoid an invasion of Japan, thus saving thousands of lives on both sides, motivated his decision to drop the bomb.

"Our right, legal and historical, to use the bomb may thus well be defended; but those who made the decision to use it were not much concerned over these considerations, taking them for granted. Their thoughts about its employment were governed by one reason which was deemed imperative: that by using the bomb, the agony of war might be ended more quickly.

The primary and sustaining aim from the start of the great exertion to make the bomb was military, and the impelling reason for the decision to use it was military—to end the war victoriously as soon as possible."

—quoted in *Japan Subdued: The Atomic Bomb and the End of the War in the Pacific*

Learning From History

1. Which of the above interpretations do you think is the most valid? Why?
2. Using the Internet or other resources, find an account of the bombing from the point of a Japanese citizen. How does it differ from the accounts above, and why?

CHAPTER 12 America and World War II **615**

R **Reading Strategy**

Organizing Information Have students create two-column charts listing the reasons for and against using the atomic bomb against Japan. *(pro: end the war, save American lives; con: massive civilian casualties, other methods exist to ensure Japanese surrender)* Tell students to imagine that they are one of Truman's advisers. Ask students to write one-page papers convincing Truman of their position on whether or not to drop the bomb.
OL **CA** 11WS1.3

C **Critical Thinking**

Predicting Consequences Read students the following quotation by President Truman announcing the use of the atomic bomb: "[The Japanese] may expect a rain from the air, the like of which has never been seen on this earth." Ask them to discuss the ways in which the atomic bomb altered international politics. **OL**

S **Skill Practice**

Evaluating Evidence Have students work in small groups to write an answer to the following question: Armed with all of the knowledge that Truman and his advisers had, how would you have ended the war in the Pacific? Invite the groups to share their solutions with the class. **OL** **CA** HR3; HI3

✓**Reading Check**

Answer: the potentially massive casualties involved in a ground invasion of Japan and his duty to save American lives

---

Different Viewpoints

Organize the students into small groups to debate the following: Truman's decision to drop the atomic bomb was or was not morally and ethically justified.
Answers:
1. Answers will vary but should focus on the use of evidence and potential bias.
2. Answers will vary but should include details from the selected narrative.

Did You Know?

The effects of a nuclear explosion depend on the size of the bomb, weather conditions, terrain, and the point of the explosion in relationship to the earth's surface. The bomb dropped on Hiroshima was smaller than the Nagasaki bomb, but more people were killed in Hiroshima due to the city's flat terrain.

Building a New World

Main Idea The Allied nations attempted to prevent future wars by creating the United Nations and by bringing war criminals to trial.

Reading Connection How effective was the League of Nations that was founded after World War I? Read on to learn about another group, the United Nations, founded at the end of World War II.

Well before the war ended, President Roosevelt had begun to think about what the world would be like after the war. The president had wanted to ensure that war would never again engulf the world.

Creating the United Nations President Roosevelt believed that a new international political organization could prevent another world war. In 1944, at the Dumbarton Oaks Estate in Washington, D.C., delegates from 39 countries met to discuss the new organization, which was to be called the **United Nations** (UN).

The delegates at the conference agreed that the UN would have a General Assembly, where every member nation in the world would have one vote.

The UN would also have a Security Council with 11 members. Five countries would be permanent members of the Security Council: Britain, France, China, the Soviet Union, and the United States—the five big powers that had led the fight against the Axis. These five permanent members would each have veto power.

On April 25, 1945, representatives from 50 countries came to San Francisco to officially organize the United Nations and design its **charter**, or constitution. The General Assembly was given the power to vote on resolutions, to choose the non-permanent members of the Security Council, and to vote on the UN budget. The Security Council was responsible for international peace and security. It could investigate any international problem and propose settlements to countries that had disputes with each other. It could also take action to preserve the peace, including asking its members to use military force to uphold a UN resolution.

Putting the Enemy on Trial Although the Allies had declared their intention to punish German and Japanese leaders for their war crimes, they did not work out the details until the summer of 1945. In early August, the United States, Britain, France, and

▼ *Dumbarton Oaks Conference, 1944*

More Skill Practice

Analyzing Primary Sources In his opening statement at the Nuremberg Trials, Robert Jackson, chief counsel for the United States, said, "The wrongs we seek to condemn and punish have been so calculated, so malignant and so devastating, that civilization cannot tolerate their being ignored because it cannot survive their being repeated." **Ask: Do you agree with Jackson's statement that civilization could not survive another Holocaust? Why or why not?** Have students write short paragraphs or journal entries explaining their positions. `OL`

Nuremberg Trials Hermann Wilhelm Goering, the highest-ranking Nazi official to testify at the Nuremberg Trials, defends himself while seated in the witness stand.

the Soviet Union created the International Military Tribunal (IMT). At the Nuremberg trials in Nuremberg, Germany, the IMT tried German leaders suspected of committing war crimes.

Twenty-two leaders of Nazi Germany were prosecuted at Nuremberg. Three were acquitted and another seven were given prison sentences. The remaining 12 were sentenced to death by hanging. Trials of lower-ranking government officials and military officers continued until April 1949. Those trials led to the execution of 24 more German leaders. Another 107 were given prison sentences.

Similar trials were held in Tokyo for the leaders of wartime Japan. The IMT for the Far East charged 25 Japanese leaders with a variety of war crimes. Significantly, the Allies did not indict the Japanese emperor. They feared that any attempt to put him on trial would lead to an uprising by the Japanese people. Eighteen Japanese defendants were sentenced to prison. The rest were sentenced to death by hanging.

The war crimes trials punished many of the people responsible for World War II and the Holocaust, but they were also part of the American plan for building a better world. As Robert Jackson, chief counsel for the United States at Nuremberg, observed in his opening statement to the court: "The wrongs we seek to condemn and punish have been so calculated, so malignant and so devastating, that civilization cannot tolerate their being ignored because it cannot survive their being repeated."

 Reading Check **Describing** How is the United Nations organized?

HISTORY Online **Study Central**

For help with the concepts in this section of *American Vision: Modern Times* go to tav.mt.glencoe.com and click on *Study Central*.

SECTION 5 ASSESSMENT

Checking for Understanding

1. **Vocabulary** Define: hedgerow, successor, error, napalm, reluctant, charter.
2. **People and Terms** Identify: Battle of the Bulge, V-E Day, Harry S. Truman, Curtis LeMay, Manhattan Project, V-J Day, United Nations.
3. **List** the major campaigns on the European and Pacific fronts in 1945.
4. **Explain** how the United States developed the atomic bomb.
5. **Describe** the war crimes trials.

Reviewing Big Ideas

6. **Making Assumptions** Why do you think the goal of world peace has yet to be achieved?

Critical Thinking

7. **Analyzing** If you had been an adviser to President Truman, what advice would you have given him about dropping the atomic bomb? Give reasons why you would have given this advice. **CA HR1; HR2**
8. **Categorizing** Using a graphic organizer like the one below, fill in the structure of the United Nations.

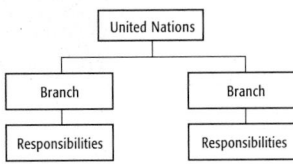

Analyzing Visuals

9. **Examining Photographs** Study the photograph on page 614 of Hiroshima after the atomic bomb was dropped. What effect do you think this photograph may have had on the American public? Why?

Writing About History

10. **Descriptive Writing** Imagine you are a war correspondent who has seen the D-Day beaches and Nazi concentration camps. Write an editorial explaining why the American sacrifices were necessary and whether or not Americans have a civic duty to fight for their country. **CA 11WS1.1; 11WS 2.1a; 11WA2.1e**

CHAPTER 12 America and World War II **617**

SECTION 5 ASSESSMENT ANSWERS

1. Content vocabulary is boldfaced and highlighted in yellow. Academic vocabulary is boldfaced.
2. Battle of the Bulge *(p. 609)*, V-E Day *(p. 612)*, Harry S. Truman *(p. 612)*, Curtis LeMay *(p. 613)*, Manhattan Project *(p. 614)*, V-J Day *(p. 615)*, United Nations *(p. 616)*
3. Battle of the Bulge, Iwo Jima, Okinawa
4. secretly in New Mexico
5. 3 Nazis acquitted, 7 imprisoned, 12 executed; 18 Japanese imprisoned, 7 executed
6. Answers will vary.
7. Answers will vary but should be defensible.
8. General Assembly: voting body; Security Council: international security.
9. Students may say that many would have been shocked.
10. Student editorials will vary but may mention the need to preserve freedom, to protect civilians, and to defend rights.

FOCUS

History–Social Science Standards

This feature addresses the following standard:

11.7.3 Identify the roles and sacrifices of individual American soldiers, as well as the unique contributions of the special fighting forces (e.g., the Tuskegee Airmen, the 442nd Regimental Combat team, the Navajo Code Talkers).

Understanding Vocabulary

Before students begin reading, point out that difficult or unfamiliar words are footnoted throughout the text.

TEACH

W Writing Support

Connecting Ask students to think about a time when they have experienced extreme stress. Have them write a short paragraph or journal entry describing the stressful situation as well as their physical *and* emotional reactions to it. Use students' responses to discuss the difficulties faced by American soldiers in World War II. **BL**

CA 11WA2.1c; 11WA2.3a

Answers and Additional Support

Primary Sources
Eyewitness to History

World War II has been called a "good war" because Americans were united and soldiers were proud to be serving. Although many of the wartime experiences on the homefront were positive, the war itself was devastating. Combat was brutal and demanding, with men in action suffering terribly. To the soldiers who fought, the war was not "good."

SOURCE 1:

Private Justin Gray served with the army's Third Ranger Battalion in Sicily and Italy. He was involved in a routine mission guarding a piece of artillery along the front lines. The guard mission suddenly turned into combat. In 1945 Gray reported to Yank, *the U.S. Army's weekly magazine, about the incident.*

I opened up my dinner unit and began to eat. Everybody was just as relaxed. We called back and forth to each other. We might as well have been out of combat. It was a beautiful clear day. . . .

Suddenly I saw something moving in the brush about 12 yards away. My jaw froze. I felt like vomiting. It was a **Jerry**.[1] Only one I hoped. . . . He came out in the open, looked around and turned to signal the others to come through. Another came in sight. . . . Instinctively I must have dropped my food and picked up my rifle. . . .

Without looking around I knew that Gerhardt had seen them, too. I knew I should have held my fire, but my finger squeezed the trigger. Almost immediately Gerhardt fired at the second one. Both of the Jerries went down. And then we knew there were many more Germans behind them. You could hear them moving in the bushes maybe 20 yards away, fanning out to see if we were an isolated unit or the main line. . . .

I heard a scream on my left. Nemo was standing up, his **tommy gun**[2] in his hands. He was hit in the chest. He ran at the Germans. . . .

It was time to leave the position. More Jerries were coming up. We all knew now that it was a full-fledged German assault on the main American lines. We could do no more good there. Bills gave the order and we started to retreat in pairs. Gerhardt covered me. I covered Gerhardt. We had to leave Nemo behind.

[1] **Jerry:** German soldier
[2] **tommy gun:** machine gun

SOURCE 2:

Sergeant Marion M. (Mack) Morriss was a member of the staff of Yank. *In 1943 he participated in the invasion of New Georgia in the Solomon Islands in the Pacific. He reported on how the Americans were slowly pushing back Japanese troops in his article, "The Five-Day Attack on Hastings Ridge."*

The American outfit, wise in jungle combat, makes a habit of remaining silent and stationary at night; then, if anything moves or makes a noise, it must be the enemy. This is a measure taken in self-defense, but apparently one man forgot it.

Lying in his foxhole, he looked up to see a dark figure approaching, walking straight upright. The infantryman, curious, demanded: "Who . . . are you?" The figure moved boldly up to him, dropped a grenade and moved on. . . .

▲ *Marines in the Solomon Islands*

UNIVERSAL ACCESS

English Learners Help students to visualize the battle described by Private Gray by asking them to draw a picture of the scene. Remind them to include Gerhardt, Nemo, Gray, and the other soldiers in their illustration. Finally, have students use their pictures to write short paragraphs describing the battle. Encourage them to share their illustrations and paragraphs with the class. **EL**

▲ *Allied bomber attacking plant in Ludwigshaven, Germany*

Sgt. George Ray of Walla Walla, Wash., occupied a hole with Bonow and Dolecheck. Three [Japanese] moved toward them. When the first [Japanese] reached the hole Ray quietly spitted him on a **bayonet.**[3] The second went down under a hand grenade. The third came on. Ray picked up his helmet and hurled it into the [Japanese's] face. For a while no more [Japanese] appeared. Then a grenade landed in the hole. Bonow was lying with his helmet between his legs and the grenade hit in the helmet, tearing his calf muscles almost completely away. Bonow kept silent. Dolecheck, next to him, knew he was hit but it was not until two hours later that Ray was aware of it. Bonow made no sound until he was evacuated next morning. Even a whispered word might have meant the death of all three.

In another foxhole a mortar shell tore off a man's arm below the elbow. His buddies were all around him, silent in the dark. Next morning they found he had bled to death, in silence.

SOURCE 3:

Private Joseph Dever enlisted in the Army Signal Corps after graduating from Boston College in 1942. He later transferred to the Army-Air Force. In a 1945 article in Yank, *Dever describes how disoriented he was when he returned to Boston after flying combat missions in Europe.*

[3]**bayonet:** spear attached to the tip of a rifle

Fifty missions always seemed incredible to me. How could anyone ever come back to the States after 50 missions? How could anyone step off a DC-4 in East Boston and quietly take a taxicab to the Hotel Statler after having been over Europe 50 times? . . .

I'm just like them now; I mean the gunners I knew at armament school—the exotic GIs with 50 missions, with their wings, their rainbow service ribbons, their medals and the quiet, easy way they had about them. They'd say: "You'll get your chance, kid." "Yeah, it's kinda rough up there." I wanted some day to be wordless, humble and friendly with the other eager kids the way the gunners were with me. How far away it all seemed then: 50 missions, the ribbons and the quiet, easy manner.

And now I'm riding through East Boston; I'm just like they were. I know a . . . of a lot of things, but I would rather turn my face away and ask about your brother John. . . . I know what **flak**[4] is now. I know how a gunner can make a chapel out of the **Sperry lower ball**;[5] . . . I know what the enemy looks like. There is also, of course, the blood fleck, the mother-mercy-calling and the blubbering, steel-given death of the nice guys who were hilariously drunk with you just a few nights before.

And now I'm looking at Boston. My taxi driver is a maniac at the wheel, as all taxi drivers are. He is doing 47 miles an hour through this big-city street. On a street in Berlin he would listen for the menacing wail of the air-raid sirens.

[4]**flak:** bursting shells fired from antiaircraft artillery
[5]**Sperry lower ball:** small area at the bottom of a plane that houses a machine gun.

DBQ Document-Based Questions

Historical Analysis   CA HR4; HI3

Source 1: Why did Gray leave Nemo behind?

Source 2: What would happen to his friends if a wounded American in the jungle made a noise?

Source 3: Why do men like Dever, who have flown many missions, often refuse to go into detail about combat?

Comparing and Contrasting Sources: How do Gray, Morriss, and Devers agree in their descriptions of World War II?

DBQ Document-Based Questions

1. Nemo had been shot in the chest and could not be evacuated with the others.
2. American soldiers who moved or made noise could accidentally be shot by other American soldiers.
3. Experienced soldiers often do not like to describe the horrors of combat.

Comparing and Contrasting Sources: Answers may vary, but students should note that all three writers describe the brutality of combat and the suffering of soldiers.

619

Reviewing Content Vocabulary

On a sheet of paper, use each of these terms in a sentence.

1. cost-plus
2. Liberty ship
3. disfranchise
4. periphery
5. convoy system
6. Sunbelt
7. rationing
8. victory garden
9. amphtrac
10. kamikaze
11. hedgerow
12. napalm

Reviewing Academic Vocabulary

On a sheet of paper, use each of these terms in a sentence that reflects the term's meaning in the chapter.

13. incentive
14. priority
15. consult
16. assign
17. transmit
18. intensify
19. perspective
20. allocate
21. integrate
22. approximately
23. code
24. pose
25. successor
26. error
27. reluctant

Reviewing Main Ideas

Section 1
28. How did the American government ensure that there were enough necessities to supply the war effort?

Section 2
29. Why was the Battle of Stalingrad considered a turning point in the war?

Section 3
30. How did the war effort change employment opportunities for women and African Americans?

Section 4
31. What four agreements did "The Big Three" make at Tehran?

Section 5
32. Why were the victories on Iwo Jima and Okinawa so vital to the Allies?

Critical Thinking

33. **Reading Skill** **Cause and Effect** Review the text under the heading "Japan Is Defeated" on pages 612–615. Write a statement for each paragraph, identifying cause and effect by using signal words.

34. **Analyzing** Do you think the opportunities that opened up for women during World War II would have developed if the United States had stayed out of the war? Explain your answer.

35. **Synthesizing** Why do you think the United States was able to successfully fight a war on multiple fronts?

36. **Civics** Explain the Selective Service and Training Act. What was the purpose of the act? Why did opinions about it change?

37. **Categorizing** Use a concept web similar to the one below to list the major campaigns the United States fought in the Pacific and in Europe.

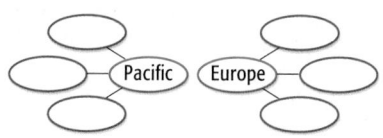

Chapter Summary

	1941	1942	1943	1944	1945
The Pacific	Japan attacks Pearl Harbor on December 7.	The United States defeats Japan in the Battles of the Coral Sea and Midway.	The United States launches its island-hopping campaign.	The United States retakes the Philippines.	The United States drops atomic bombs; Japan surrenders on August 15.
Europe and North Africa		The Allies turn the tide in the Battle of the Atlantic.	The Allies invade Italy; Germans surrender at Stalingrad.	The Allies invade Normandy on June 6.	Germany surrenders unconditionally on May 7.
The Home Front	President Roosevelt forbids race discrimination in defense industries.	WAAC is established; Japanese American relocation is ordered.	OWM is established; Detroit and Zoot Suit Riots occur.	The case of *Korematsu* v. *United States* is decided.	The UN charter is signed.

HISTORY Online

Self-Check Quiz

Visit the *American Vision: Modern Times* Web site at tav.mt.glencoe.com and click on *Self-Check Quizzes–Chapter 12* to assess your knowledge of chapter content.

Writing About History

38. **Historical Analysis** **Evaluating Interpretations** Use library or Internet sources to find other discussions on the use of the atomic bomb. How do these viewpoints differ from those of the authors on pages 614–615? **CA HR3**

39. *Big Idea* Imagine you are an American soldier in World War II. Choose either Europe or the Pacific for the location of your service. Write a letter home discussing the major turning points in each campaign. **CA 11WA2.1a**

40. **Persuasive Writing** Assume the role of an immigrant who fled Fascist Europe in 1933 and has become a U.S. citizen. You have just read about the proposed United Nations, and you want to write your senator to urge that the United States join the organization or boycott it. Choose which position you support, and write a letter trying to convince the senator to support your position. **CA 11WS1.1; 11WS1.2**

DBQ Document-Based Questions

41. **Interpreting Primary Sources** Many historians believe that the civil rights movement of the 1950s and 1960s had its roots in the Double V campaign and the March on Washington. Alexander Allen, a member of the Urban League during the war, believed that World War II was a turning point for African Americans. Read the excerpt and answer the questions that follow.

    ❝Up to that point the doors to industrial and economic opportunity were largely closed. Under the pressure of war, the pressures of government policy, the pressures of world opinion, the pressures of blacks themselves and their allies, all this began to change. . . . The war forced the federal government to take a stronger position with reference to discrimination, and things began to change as a result. There was a tremendous attitudinal change that grew out of the war. There had been a new experience for blacks, and many weren't willing to go back to the way it was before.❞

             —quoted in *Wartime America*

a. How did the war change the status of African Americans in American society? **CA 11RC2.4**

b. Why do you think the war forced the government to take a stronger position on discrimination in the workplace?

NATIONAL GEOGRAPHIC

Battle of the Bulge, December 1944–January 1945

- ← U.S. forces
- ← British forces
- ← German forces

▲▲▲▲ Front line at date shown.

0   15 miles
0   15 kilometers
Albers Conic Equal-Area projection

American units at Bastogne were encircled on Dec. 19, and relieved on Dec. 26.

Geography and History

42. The map above shows troop movements at the Battle of the Bulge. Study the map and answer the questions below.

  a. **Interpreting Maps** At what location did the Germans surround American forces on December 25?

  b. **Applying Geography Skills** What geographic features did the Germans encounter as they attacked? What information on the map shows you this?

Standards Practice

Directions: Choose the best answer to the following question.

43. Why did Germany declare war on the United States in 1941?

A Because Germany annexed part of Czechoslovakia

B Because Germany invaded Poland

C Because Germany was frustrated with the U.S. Navy attacks on German submarines

D Because of the non-aggression pact between Russia and Germany

Standard 11.7.1: Examine the origins of American involvement in the war, with an emphasis on the events that precipitated the attack on Pearl Harbor.

HISTORY Online

Have students visit the Web site at tav.mt.glencoe.com to review Chapter 12 and take the Self-Check Quiz.

Writing About History

38. **Historical Analysis** Students should discuss their research.

39. *Big Idea* Students' letters and details will vary with the choice of fronts.

40. Letters should express a clear and reasoned opinion using standard grammar, spelling, sentence structure, and punctuation.

DBQ Document-Based Questions

41. **a.** It allowed many to work in industry and benefit from such work for the first time. Most were not willing to return to the way things had been. **b.** Possible answers: the war effort demanded a large domestic workforce; wished to avoid work stoppages

Geography and History

42. **a.** Bastogne; **b.** rivers and mountainous terrain; the dark shading in the south, as opposed to flatter northern areas

Standards Practice

43. C

Bonus Question ?

Ask: Why was the Battle of Midway so crucial to the war in the Pacific? *(Losing four carriers gutted the heart of the Japanese fleet and stopped Japan's ability to advance in the Pacific.)*

Critical Thinking

33. **Reading Skill** Students' statements will vary. Students should use signal words to identify cause and effect.

34. Answers may vary. Students should use knowledge of women's past experiences as part of their answer.

35. Answers will vary. Students should note that most industrial production was geared to supporting both fronts and that the United States had personnel available to wage both fronts of the war.

36. The act created the first peacetime draft. It was opposed by college students, labor unions, and isolationists. It passed in 1940 after Germany defeated France and opinions changed.

37. Pacific: Coral Sea, Midway, Guadalcanal, Iwo Jima, Okinawa; Europe: African campaign, Battle of the Atlantic, Stalingrad, D-Day, Battle of the Bulge

Chapter 13 Planning Guide

SECTION RESOURCES

Main Ideas	Print Materials	Technology Resources
Section 1: Origins of the Cold War 1. While the Soviets were concerned with protecting their territory, Americans were focusing on the economic causes of war. 2. At the Yalta Conference, the Allies determined the postwar plan for the world. 3. Differences between American and Soviet goals flared at the Potsdam Conference, where President Truman decided to take a hard line against the Soviets.	• Reproducible Lesson Plan 13-1* • Daily Lecture and Discussion Notes 13-1 • Active Reading Note-Taking Guide 13-1 • Guided Reading Activity 13-1 • Section Quiz 13-1 • Reading Essentials and Study Guide 13-1	• Daily Focus Skills Transparency 13-1 • Section Graphic Organizer Transparency 13-1 • Interactive Tutor Self-Assessment CD-ROM • ExamView® Pro Testmaker CD-ROM • Presentation Plus! CD-ROM • California Standards Practice Transparencies
Section 2: The Early Cold War Years 1. As the Cold War continued, President Truman issued the Truman Doctrine and authorized the Marshall Plan. 2. For nearly a year, the United States airlifted supplies to West Berlin after the Soviets set up a land blockade. 3. China became a Communist nation in 1949 after the United States increased aid to Japan to deter communist expansion in other Asian countries. 4. The United Nations sent armed forces to South Korea to prevent a Communist takeover.	• Reproducible Lesson Plan 13-2* • Daily Lecture and Discussion Notes 13-2 • Active Reading Note-Taking Guide 13-2 • Guided Reading Activity 13-2 • Section Quiz 13-2 • Reading Essentials and Study Guide 13-2	• Daily Focus Skills Transparency 13-2 • Section Graphic Organizer Transparency 13-2 • Interactive Tutor Self-Assessment CD-ROM • ExamView® Pro Testmaker CD-ROM • Presentation Plus! CD-ROM • California Standards Practice Transparencies
Section 3: The Cold War and American Society 1. As Cold War tensions rose, Americans worked to combat communist influence at home. 2. The Red Scare intensified as Senator Joseph McCarthy presided over a Senate committee charged with exposing Communists in government. 3. Fear of nuclear attack and of communism dominated American popular culture during the early Cold War years.	• Reproducible Lesson Plan 13-3* • Daily Lecture and Discussion Notes 13-3 • Active Reading Note-Taking Guide 13-3 • Guided Reading Activity 13-3 • Section Quiz 13-3 • Reading Essentials and Study Guide 13-3	• Daily Focus Skills Transparency 13-3 • Section Graphic Organizer Transparency 13-3 • Interactive Tutor Self-Assessment CD-ROM • ExamView® Pro Testmaker CD-ROM • Presentation Plus! CD-ROM • California Standards Practice Transparencies
Section 4: Eisenhower's Policies 1. Eisenhower advocated a policy of massive strength to combat communist influence. 2. Although he ended the Korean War as he had promised, President Eisenhower faced new foreign policy challenges as Cold War tensions rose. 3. President Eisenhower used the Central Intelligence Agency to remove anti-American leaders and to fight Communist takeovers. 4. Despite attempts to cooperate, tension remained high between the Soviet and American heads of state.	• Reproducible Lesson Plan 13-4* • Daily Lecture and Discussion Notes 13-4 • Active Reading Note-Taking Guide 13-4 • Guided Reading Activity 13-4 • Section Quiz 13-4 • Reading Essentials and Study Guide 13-4	• Daily Focus Skills Transparency 13-4 • Section Graphic Organizer Transparency 13-4 • Interactive Tutor Self-Assessment CD-ROM • ExamView® Pro Testmaker CD-ROM • Presentation Plus! CD-ROM • California Standards Practice Transparencies

PACING YOUR LESSONS

Chapter Introduction	Section 1	Section 2	Section 3	Section 4	Chapter Assessment
½ Day	2 Days	2 Days	2 Days	2 Days	½ Day

0:00 **OUT OF TIME?** Assign the Chapter 13 *Reading Essentials and Study Guide.*

*Available on TeacherWorks™ CD-ROM

Chapter 13 Planning Guide

Standards-Based Lesson Plan

 History–Social Science Standards Covered in Chapter 13

The standards covered in the chapter are listed below. Use the accompanying activity as you teach the chapter to ensure student mastery of these standards. This activity can be used in combination with the program's print and technology assessment materials.

Standard	Section 1	2	3	4
11.4.6 Trace the declining role of Great Britain and the expanding role of the United States in world affairs after World War II.	✔	✔		
11.7.8 Analyze the effect of massive aid given to Western Europe under the Marshall Plan to rebuild itself after the war and the importance of a rebuilt Europe to the U.S. economy.		✔		
11.8.4 Analyze new federal government spending on defense, welfare, interest on the national debt, and federal and state spending on education, including the California Master Plan.				✔
11.8.7 Describe the effects on society and the economy of technological developments since 1945, including the computer revolution, changes in communication, advances in medicine, and improvements in agricultural technology.			✔	✔
11.9.2 Understand the role of military alliances, including NATO and SEATO, in deterring communist aggression and maintaining security during the Cold War.	✔	✔		✔
11.9.3 Trace the origins and geopolitical consequences (foreign and domestic) of the Cold War and containment policy.	✔	✔	✔	✔

Cumulative Standards-Assessment Activity

The Cumulative Standards-Assessment Activity will help students organize and learn the important information from the chapter. Begin teaching the chapter with this activity, and have students complete it as they read the chapter.

Creating a Chart for Making Generalizations

Purpose Explain that generalizations—broad statements that should be based on observable or accurate information—are useful when you want to summarize large amounts of information. Studying the facts in order to support a broader generalization can focus students as they read and help them retain information.

Introduction to Reading with Purpose

1. Review with the class the steps in making valid generalizations:
   - Collect related facts about the subject matter.
   - Identify similarities among these facts.
   - Make a generalization that is consistent with most of the facts gathered.

2. Ask students to list what they know about the Cold War. Have them make generalizations about this period of American history.

3. Have students copy this chart into their notebooks:

   Supporting Facts
   _____
   _____   (Generalization)
   _____
   _____

   As they read, students should identify facts that support their generalizations.

4. As part of the chapter review, have students share their generalization charts. Guide the class in constructively critiquing the generalizations until students are satisfied that the generalizations are supported by the facts.

Chapter 13 Planning Guide

READING SUPPORT

- Content Vocabulary Activity 13
- Academic Vocabulary Activity 13
- Reading Skills Activity 13
- Chapter 13 Active Reading Note-Taking Guide
- Chapter 13 Guided Reading Activities
- Chapter 13 Reading Essentials and Study Guide
- *The American Vision: Modern Times* Video Program
- Vocabulary PuzzleMaker CD-ROM
- American History Primary Source Document Library CD-ROM

CRITICAL THINKING

- Critical Thinking Skills Activity 13
- Primary Source Reading 13
- Cause-and-Effect Transparency 13 Strategy and Activity
- Presentation Plus! CD-ROM

UNIVERSAL ACCESS

- Universal Access Activity 13
- English Learner Activity 13
- American Art Prints
- StudentWorks™ Plus CD-ROM
- American Music: Hits Through History
- School-to-Home Connection Activity 13

SKILL PRACTICE

- Map Overlay Transparency 13 Strategy and Activity
- Historical Analysis Skills Activity 13
- Time Line Activity 13
- Reading Skills Activity 13
- Reinforcing Skills Activity 13
- Linking Past and Present Activity 13
- Interpreting Political Cartoons 13
- History Simulations and Problem Solving, Unit 4
- MindJogger Videoquiz

WRITING SUPPORT

- Chapter 13 Active Reading Note-Taking Guide
- Writer's Guidebook
- High School Writing Process Transparencies

ASSESSMENT

- Chapter 13 Section Quizzes
- Chapter 13 Tests, Forms A and B
- Authentic Assessment Activity 13
- ExamView® Pro Testmaker CD-ROM
- Interactive Tutor Self-Assessment CD-ROM
- California Standards Practice, Grade 11
- Succeeding on . . .™ the California Standards: Grade 11 History–Social Science CD-ROM

- CD-ROM
- DVD
- Print Material
- Poster

- Transparency
- Music Program
- Videocassette

622C

Chapter 13 Planning Guide

TECHNOLOGY

- StudentWorks™ Plus CD-ROM
- TeacherWorks™ CD-ROM
- Exam*View*® Pro Testmaker CD-ROM
- Interactive Tutor Self-Assessment CD-ROM
- Presentation Plus! CD-ROM
- Vocabulary PuzzleMaker CD-ROM
- American History Primary Source Document Library CD-ROM
- MindJogger Videoquiz
- *The American Vision: Modern Times* Video Program
- Professional Development in High School Social Studies Video Series
- Teach, Use, and Succeed With *The American Vision: Modern Times*
- American Music: Hits Through History
- Succeeding on . . .™ the California Standards: Grade 11 History–Social Science CD-ROM

SPANISH RESOURCES

- Spanish Activities and Assessment
  - Spanish Vocabulary Activities
  - Spanish Guided Reading Activities
  - Spanish Quizzes and Tests
  - Spanish Reteaching Activities
- Spanish Reading Essentials and Study Guide
- Spanish School-to-Home Connection Activities

TRANSPARENCIES

- Daily Focus Skills Transparencies
- Section Graphic Organizer Transparencies
- Map Overlay Transparencies
- Cause-and-Effect Transparencies
- Unit Time Line Transparencies
- Why It Matters Transparencies
- American Art and Architecture Transparencies
- High School Writing Process Transparencies
- California Standards Practice Transparencies

TEACHER PLANNING

- Daily Lecture and Discussion Notes
- English Learner Handbook
- Building Academic Vocabulary
- *The American Vision: Modern Times* Reading and Study Skills Foldables
- Reading Strategies and Activities for the Social Studies Classroom
- Universal Access for the American History Classroom
- NGS United States Desk Map
- NGS World Atlas
- Chapter 13 Reproducible Lesson Plans on TeacherWorks™ CD-ROM
- California Guide to Daily Intervention

PROFESSIONAL DEVELOPMENT

- Building Academic Vocabulary
- Strategies for Success
- Research-Based Strategies Used to Develop *The American Vision: Modern Times*
- Character Education in the High School Classroom
- Professional Development in High School Social Studies Video Series
- Teach, Use, and Succeed With *The American Vision: Modern Times*

MOMENTS IN TIME

The following resource can help you teach the content of this chapter.
- Unit 9 The Cold War (1947–1962)

Chapter 13 Planning Guide

 TEACHER'S CORNER

Index to National Geographic Magazine:
The following article relates to this chapter:

• "Bikini's Nuclear Graveyard," June 1992

National Geographic Society Products:
To order the following, call National Geographic at 1–800–368–2728

• *1945–1989: The Cold War* (Video)
• *Europe: The Road to Unity* (Video)

NGS ONLINE

Access National Geographic's new dynamic MapMachine Web site and other geography resources at:

www.nationalgeographic.com

www.nationalgeographic.com/maps

Use our Web site for additional resources. All essential content is covered in the Student Edition.

You and your students can visit tav.mt.glencoe.com, the Web site companion to the **American Vision: Modern Times.** This innovative integration of electronic and print media offers your students a wealth of opportunities. The student text directs students to the Web site for the following options:

• **Chapter Overviews**   • **Student Web Activities**
• **Self-Check Quizzes**   • **Textbook Updates**

Answers to the student Web activities are provided for you in the **Web Activity Lesson Plans.** Additional Web resources and ePuzzles and games are also available.

 Dinah Zike's Foldables

Foldables are three-dimensional, interactive graphic organizers that help students practice basic writing skills, review key vocabulary terms, and identify main ideas. Every chapter has a foldable activity in the *Dinah Zike's Reading and Study Skills Foldables* booklet. You can use the foldables as they are presented or modify them to suit the needs of your individual class.

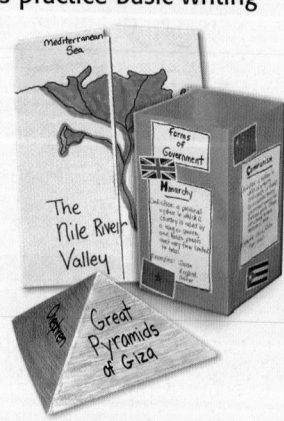

MASTERING THE STANDARDS

The content and assessment in the Student Edition, Teacher Wraparound Edition, teacher planning materials, and the print and technology products are all standards-based. The use of these products during instruction leads to mastery of the standards.

PRACTICE
• California Standards Practice, Grade 11
• California Standards Practice Transparencies
• School-to-Home Connection

BENCHMARK ASSESSMENT
• Section Quizzes, Chapter Tests, and Authentic Assessment
• ExamView® Pro Testmaker CD-ROM
• Succeeding On . . . ™ the California Standards: Grade 11 History–Social Science CD-ROM

REMEDIATION
• California Guide to Daily Intervention
• Interactive Tutor Self-Assessment CD-ROM
• ExamView® Pro Testmaker CD-ROM
• California Standards Practice, Grade 11
• Reading Essentials and Study Guide

A variety of videotape programs are available from A&E Television and The History Channel to provide teaching assistance. To order, call Glencoe at 1-800-334-7344.

Chapter 13 Planning Guide

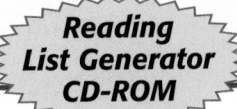

Reading List Generator CD-ROM

GLENCOE BOOKLINK

The Glencoe BookLink CD-ROM is a database that allows you to search more than 15,000 titles to create a customized reading list for your students.

■ Reading Lists can be organized by students' reading level, author, genre, theme, or area of interest.

■ The database provides Degrees of Reading Power™ (DRP) and Lexile™ readability scores for all selections.

■ A brief summary of each selection is included.

Leveled reading suggestions for this chapter:

For students at a Grade 8 reading level:
■ *Naming Names,* by Victor S. Navasky

For students at a Grade 9 reading level:
■ *The Opening of the Suez Canal,* by Carol Zeman Rothkopf

For students at a Grade 10 reading level:
■ *South Korea: A Study of an Economically Developing Country,* by Sung-Hoon Jung

READING SUPPORT FROM JAMESTOWN EDUCATION

- *Timed Readings Plus in Social Studies* help students increase their reading rate and fluency while maintaining comprehension. The 400-word passages are similar to those found on state and national assessments.

- *Reading in the Content Area: Social Studies* concentrates on six essential reading skills that help students better comprehend what they read. The book includes 75 high-interest nonfiction passages written at increasing levels of difficulty.

- *Reading Fluency* helps students read smoothly, accurately, and expressively.

- *Jamestown's Reading Improvement,* by renowned reading expert Edward Fry, focuses on helping build your students' comprehension, vocabulary, and skimming and scanning skills.

- *Critical Reading Series* provides high-interest books, each written at three reading levels.

For more information about these products, see the Jamestown Education materials in the Classroom Solutions in the front of this Teacher Wraparound Edition. To order these products, call Glencoe at 1-800-334-7344.

KEY for Using the Teacher Wraparound Edition

Use this key to help you identify the different types of prompts found in the Teacher Wraparound Edition.

R **Reading Strategies** activities help you teach reading skills and vocabulary.

C **Critical Thinking** strategies help students apply and extend what they have learned.

U **Universal Access** activities provide differentiated instruction for students learning to speak English, along with suggestions for teaching various types of learners.

S **Skill Practice** strategies help students practice historical analysis and geography skills.

W **Writing Support** activities provide writing opportunities to help students comprehend the text.

Teaching strategies and activities have been coded for ability level appropriateness.

AL Activities for students working above grade level
OL Activities for students working on grade level
BL Activities for students working below grade level
EL Activities for English learners

FOCUS

History–Social Science Standards

This chapter addresses the following standards:

11.9.2 Understand the role of military alliances, including NATO and SEATO, in deterring communist aggression and maintaining security during the Cold War.

11.9.3 Trace the origins and geopolitical consequences (foreign and domestic) of the Cold War and containment policy, including the following: the era of McCarthyism, instances of domestic Communism (e.g., Alger Hiss) and blacklisting; the Truman Doctrine; the Berlin Blockade; the Bay of Pigs Invasion and the Cuban Missle Crisis; atomic testing in the American West, the "mutual assured destruction" doctrine, and disarmament policies; the Vietnam War; Latin American policy.

BELLRINGER
SKILLBUILDER ACTIVITY

Have students work in small groups to create their own definitions for the terms *communism* and *democracy*. Ask them to write paragraphs describing why they think communism and democracy could not peacefully coexist in the decades immediately following World War II. After students have finished reading Chapter 13, have them return to their definitions and revise them as needed.

CHAPTER **13**

1945–1960

The Cold War Begins

✤ The Big Ideas ✤

SECTION 1: Origins of the Cold War

International competition can lead to conflict and cooperation. *The detonation of the atomic bomb and the end of World War II led to disagreements among the "Big Three" wartime Allies and a shift in American attitudes toward the Soviet Union.*

SECTION 2: The Early Cold War Years

The fate of nations is forever changed by monumental world events. *As the Cold War began, the United States struggled to oppose Communist aggression in Europe and Asia through political, economic, and military measures.*

SECTION 3: The Cold War and American Society

Social and economic crises lead to new roles for government. *The Cold War heightened Americans' fear of Communist infiltration and atomic attack.*

SECTION 4: Eisenhower's Policies

The fate of nations is forever changed by monumental world events. *As president, Eisenhower developed new policies to contain and compete with communism.*

The *American Vision: Modern Times* Video *The Chapter 13 video, "Symbols of the Cold War," examines the era by focusing on the crisis of the Berlin airlift.*

1945
• Yalta conference
• Franklin Roosevelt dies

1947
• Truman Doctrine declared

1948
• Berlin airlift begins

1949
• NATO established

1950
• McCarthy charges that Communists staff the U.S. State Department
• Korean War begins

United States
PRESIDENTS

Truman
1945–1953

1945   *1950*

World

1945
• Italian women gain right to vote

1946
• Orwell's *Animal Farm* published

1948
• State of Israel created

1949
• People's Republic of China established

1952
• Britain produces an atomic bomb

622

TEACH

Thinking About the Big Ideas

As you begin teaching each section, use these questions and activities to focus on the Big Idea.

Section 1
Origins of the Cold War
Essential Question: **Why were the Soviet Union and the United States unable to find common ground after World War II?** *(The Soviets were concerned with preventing another western invasion; the U.S. wanted to promote democracy and avoid more totalitarian governments.)* Tell students that they will learn more

about the issues surrounding the future of Eastern Europe in Section 1. **OL**

Section 2
The Early Cold War Years
Essential Question: **Why do you think the United States was so determined to stop communism from spreading?** *(The differences in the two systems of government and the recent experience of stopping Nazi aggression helped*

During Nixon's 1959 visit to Moscow, the vice president exchanged angry words with Soviet leader Nikita Khrushchev during the "kitchen" debate at an exhibit at the U.S. Trade and Cultural Fair.

1953
- Rosenbergs executed for treason
- Armistice reached in Korean War

Eisenhower 1953–1961

1959
- Khrushchev and Eisenhower hold summit

1960
- U-2 incident

1955

1960

1953
- Stalin dies

1956
- Suez Canal crisis
- Hungarians rise up against their Communist government

1957
- Soviet Union launches *Sputnik*

HISTORY Online

Chapter Overview
Visit the *American Vision: Modern Times* Web site at tav.mt.glencoe.com and click on **Chapter Overviews– Chapter 13** to preview chapter information.

623

convince U.S. leaders that communism should not spread further.) Tell the class that the evaluations about communism during these early Cold War years affected U.S. foreign policy for several decades thereafter. **AL**

Section 3
The Cold War and American Society
Essential Question: How did the Cold War and the fear of communism influence American life and government in the 1950s? Remind students that Americans in the 1950s lived under the constant threat of war with the Soviet Union. **OL**

Section 4
Eisenhower's Policies
Essential Question: What positive events do you think resulted from U.S.-Soviet competition? *(Answers may include greater productivity, new technology, and national pride.)* Have students identify positive and negative effects of a competition in their own lives. Explain that in Section 4 they will learn that the Cold War was a time of intense competition between the U.S. and the Soviet Union. **BL**

Cultural Perspectives

After World War II and amid rising tensions between the Western democracies and the Soviet Union, Germany was officially divided into eastern and western parts. Assign half of the students to find out how this division impacted the lives of ordinary Germans. How did the people react? How did it affect their families and communities? Ask the other group to research the reunification of Germany in 1990. How did the people react? How did it change their lives yet again? **OL**

FOLDABLES™
Study Organizer

Dinah Zike's Foldables are three-dimensional, interactive graphic organizers that help students practice basic writing skills, review key vocabulary terms, and identify main ideas. Have students complete the foldable activity in the *Dinah Zike's Reading and Study Skills Foldables* booklet.

HISTORY Online

Go to tav.mt.glencoe.com for student activities, lesson plans, and links to additional resources to help students learn about the early years of the Cold War.

Reading Skill

Why It's Important
Tell students that understanding the different types of questions allows them to gain a better sense of how and where to locate answers.

1. Introducing the Skill
Write the following questions on the board: (1) Who was the fourth president of the United States? (2) Why did the United States enter World War II? (3) Why did the United States declare independence from Britain? (4) What is the population of California? Have students assign each question to a type in a chart like the one below. **BL**

"Right There"	"Think and Search"

2. Extending the Skill
Instruct students to look at a newspaper photograph and caption, and have them develop five questions about it. Then ask them to read the article to answer their questions. **Ask: Which questions had "right there" answers, and which ones required readers to "think and search"?** Encourage students to use their work to make generalizations about question-and-answer relationships. **OL**

Answers and Additional Support

Reading Skill | Question-Answer Relationship

Effective readers recognize the different types of questions that they find in reviews and tests. They understand that they can find answers to some questions in the book, while they have to use their experiences and background knowledge to answer other questions.

Sometimes you can find the answer to a question in a single sentence—the answer is "right there." Other questions require you to "think and search." This means that you will find parts of the answer in more than one sentence. Some people call these types of questions text-explicit. They mean that the text provides an explicit, or clear, answer to the question.

Read the passage about the formation of NATO. Then use the highlighted and underlined words to discuss the questions below with a partner.

NATO initially included 12 countries: the **United States, Canada, Britain, France, Italy, Belgium, Denmark, Portugal, the Netherlands, Norway, Luxembourg,** and **Iceland**. NATO members agreed to <u>come to the aid of any member who was attacked</u>. For the first time in its history, the United States had committed itself to maintaining peace in Europe. Six years later, the United States and its allies decided to allow **West Germany** to rearm and join NATO. (page 636)

Questions: What did NATO members agree to do?

Answer: Use the underlined words to help you answer the question.

This is a "right there" question because the question uses words and phrases directly from the text.

Question: What nations were members of NATO?

Answer: Use the highlighted words to help you answer the question.

This is a "think and search" question because the answer comes from more than one sentence.

QUESTION-ANSWER RELATIONSHIP

Read questions on tests carefully. Even if a question features words from the text, this does not guarantee that it is a text-explicit question.

Apply the Skill

Look closely at the Reading Check questions throughout the chapter. Most of these questions are examples of either "right there" or "think and search" questions. You should use the text to find the answer to these kinds of questions. As you read through the chapter, determine for each Reading Check question whether it is a "right there" question, a "think and search" question, or a different type of question.

624

UNIVERSAL ACCESS

Visual/Spatial Have students locate a graph, chart, map, or other visual aid in Chapter 13. Remind students that visuals and graphics also ask two types of questions—those with "right there" answers that can be found by simply looking at the visual aid, and those that require a reader to "think and search" to find the answer. Have each student practice this skill by writing one type of each question from the graphic or visual that they located. Invite students to share their visuals and questions with the class. **OL**

Historical Analysis Skill   Bias and Prejudice

Analysis Skill
Standard HR2

Historical Research, Evidence, and Point of View As you read about history, you need to learn to identify bias and prejudice in historical interpretations.

By the time you are a junior in high school, you may have heard someone being called a name that is derogatory. What do you think motivated the person who used offensive terms to belittle someone else? What was that person trying to accomplish?

Historians recognize that some people are motivated by bias and prejudice. Throughout history there have been people who have used their hate to oppress others. They also interpret events and the actions of others through their biased perspective. When people who are motivated by bias and prejudice hold positions of power, they can make life difficult for individuals or even whole groups of people.

Read the following excerpt from a speech by Senator Joseph McCarthy.

While I cannot take the time to name all the men in the State Department who have been named as members of the Communist Party and members of a spy ring, I have here in my hand a list of 205 that were known to the Secretary of State as being members of the Communist Party and who nevertheless are still working and shaping the policy of the State Department. (page 646)

You will read in this chapter that McCarthy made his accusations during a time when fear of communism pervaded the United States. Although the list never appeared, McCarthy continued to accuse people, based on his prejudice about communism. Later research of this time in American history revealed that McCarthy's prejudices and biases were so great that many innocent people were falsely accused.

Apply the Skill

You will learn in this chapter about the beginnings of the Cold War between the United States and the Soviet Union. As you read Section 3, note how the fear of communism pervaded the United States and influenced not only politics but also the personal lives of Americans. Write down in your notebook each major event or development caused or influenced by that fear.

625

Historical Analysis

Why It's Important
Point out that everyone is biased. Remind students that without using reason, people rely on gut emotional reactions, favoring some things and disapproving of others. It is important to recognize bias and prejudice when interpreting historical events.

1. Introducing the Skill
Have students list anonymously on a piece of paper two of their own biases, either positive or negative. After collecting the papers, read some of the biases aloud for class discussion. **Ask:** Which biases are positive, and which are negative? How might they be helpful or harmful? Record some of the responses in a chart like the one below. `OL`

Positive Bias	Negative Bias

2. Extending the Skill
Have students review television programs, newspaper editorials, or pamphlets from political candidates and interest groups in your community. Ask them to write short reports analyzing the material for evidence of bias or prejudice. `OL` `CA HR2`

UNIVERSAL ACCESS

English Learners Help English learners understand this skill by identifying the following steps in detecting biases: (1) Identify the writer's or speaker's purpose; (2) Watch for emotionally charged language such as *exploit, terrorize,* and *cheat;* (3) Look for visual images that provoke a strong emotional response; (4) Look for overgeneralizations such as *unique, honest,* and *everybody;* (5) Notice italics, underlining, and punctuation that highlight particular ideas; (6) Examine the material to determine whether it presents equal coverage of differing views.
`EL`

FOCUS

SKILLBUILDER ACTIVITY

Project **Daily Focus Skills Transparency 13-1** and have students answer the question.

Guide to Reading

Understanding Vocabulary: Have students use each content vocabulary word in a sentence.

Answers to Graphic: Yalta: Poland's government recognized, free elections for Poland, Declaration of Liberated Europe, Germany divided, German reparations set; Potsdam: German-Polish border established, German reparations to the Soviet Union restructured

Unpacking the Standards

Students will be able to:

- Explain why cooperation between the United States and the Soviet Union ended.

- Analyze the discussions during the Yalta Conference.

- Discuss President Truman's hard line of negotiations with the Soviet Union.

Answers and Additional Support

SECTION 1 Origins of the Cold War

Guide to Reading

Connection
In the previous chapter, you learned how the Allies defeated Germany and Japan in World War II. In this section, you will examine the beginnings of the Cold War.

Main Idea
- While the Soviets were concerned with protecting their territory, Americans were focusing on the economic causes of war. (p. 627)
- At the Yalta Conference, the Allies determined the postwar plan for the world. (p. 628)

- Differences between American and Soviet goals flared at the Potsdam Conference, where President Truman decided to take a hard line against the Soviets. (p. 629)

Content Vocabulary
Cold War, iron curtain

Academic Vocabulary
route, temporary, element

People and Terms to Identify
Potsdam, satellite nation

Reading Objectives
- **Explain** the growing tensions between the United States and the Soviet Union at the end of World War II.

- **Identify** the goals of Stalin's foreign policy immediately after the war.

Reading Strategy
Categorizing As you read about the origins of the Cold War, complete a graphic organizer similar to the one below by filling in the names of the conferences held among the "Big Three" Allies and the outcomes of each.

Conferences	Outcomes

Preview of Events

◆ February 1945	◆ July 1945	◆ December 1945	◆ May 1946

February 1945 — Yalta conference held in the USSR

April 1945 — President Roosevelt dies

July 1945 — Potsdam conference convenes in Germany

March 1946 — Churchill delivers "iron curtain" speech

The following are the main History–Social Science Standards covered in this section.

11.4.6 Trace the declining role of Great Britain and the expanding role of the United States in world affairs after World War II.

11.7.4 Analyze Roosevelt's foreign policy during World War II (e.g., Four Freedoms speech).

11.9.1 Discuss the establishment of the United Nations and International Declaration of Human Rights, International Monetary Fund, World Bank, and General Agreement on Tariffs and Trade (GATT) and their importance in shaping modern Europe and maintaining peace and international order.

11.9.2 Understand the role of military alliances, including NATO and SEATO, in deterring communist aggression and maintaining security during the Cold War.

11.9.3 Trace the origins and geopolitical consequences (foreign and domestic) of the Cold War and containment policy, including the following: the era of McCarthyism, instances of domestic

❧ The Big Idea ❧

International competition can lead to conflict and cooperation. Even before the end of World War II, the alliance between the Soviet Union and the United States had become strained. The Soviets voiced concerns about security issues, and the Americans focused on economic concerns and democracy. At two conferences, the two nations, along with Great Britain, decided the fates of Germany and Poland. Tensions increased when the Soviet Union refused to uphold an agreement to grant European nations the right to establish democratic governments. With the Soviet army in control of Eastern Europe, communism spread, and the countries had to follow Soviet-approved policies.

Communism (e.g., Alger Hiss) and blacklisting; the Truman Doctrine; the Berlin Blockade; the Korean War; the Bay of Pigs invasion and the Cuban Missile Crisis; atomic testing in the American West, the "mutual assured destruction" doctrine, and disarmament policies; the Vietnam War; Latin American policy.

11.9.4 List the effects of foreign policy on domestic policies and vice versa (e.g., protests during the war in Vietnam, the "nuclear freeze" movement).

626   CHAPTER 13   The Cold War Begins

SECTION RESOURCES

📂 Print Material
- Reproducible Lesson Plan 13-1
- Guided Reading Activity 13-1
- Reading Essentials and Study Guide 13-1
- Active Reading Note-Taking Guide 13-1

📖 Transparencies
- Daily Focus Skills Transparency 13-1
- Section Graphic Organizer Transparency 13-1

Technology
- 💿 Interactive Tutor Self-Assessment CD-ROM
- 💿 ExamView® Pro Testmaker CD-ROM
- 💿 Presentation Plus! CD-ROM

A Clash of Interests

 Main Idea While the Soviets were concerned with protecting their territory, Americans were focusing on the economic causes of war.

Reading Connection Have you ever had a different perspective on an issue than a friend or family member? Read on to learn about the different perspectives of the Soviets and Americans after World War II.

Even before World War II ended, the wartime alliance between the United States and the Soviet Union had begun to show signs of strain. President Roosevelt had hoped that a victory over the Axis and the creation of the United Nations would lead to a more peaceful world. Instead, the United States and the Soviet Union became increasingly hostile toward each other after the war.

★ An American Story ★

On April 23, 1945, President Harry S. Truman welcomed Soviet Foreign Minister Vyacheslav Molotov into the Oval Office of the White House. Truman had been president for less than two weeks, but he was determined to get tough with Molotov.

Truman told the Soviet diplomat how disgusted he was with Moscow's refusal to permit free elections in Poland, expressing his "deep disappointment" that the Soviet Union was not carrying out its agreements. Bluntly, he warned Molotov that Soviet defiance would seriously shake the confidence of the United States and Great Britain in their wartime ally.

Molotov began to explain the Soviet position, but Truman interrupted again and again, repeating his demand that Stalin "carry out that agreement in accordance with his word." Astonished, Molotov blurted out, "I have never been talked to like that in my life!" "Carry out your agreements," the president snapped back, "and you won't get talked to like that!"

—adapted from *The Cold War: A History*

The hostilities between the United States and the Soviet Union led to an era of confrontation and competition between the two countries that lasted from about 1946 to 1990. This era became known as the **Cold War.**

Soviet Security Concerns Tensions between the United States and the Soviet Union began to increase because the two sides had different goals. As the war ended, Soviet leaders became concerned about security. Germany had invaded Russia twice in less than 30 years. The Soviets wanted to keep Germany weak and make sure that the countries between Germany and the Soviet Union were under Soviet control.

Although security concerns influenced their thinking, Soviet leaders were also Communists. They believed that communism was a superior economic system that would eventually replace capitalism and that the Soviet Union should encourage communism in other nations. Soviet leaders also accepted Lenin's theory that capitalist countries eventually would try to destroy communism. This made Soviet leaders suspicious of capitalist nations.

American Economic Concerns While Soviet leaders focused on securing their borders, American leaders focused on economic problems. Many American officials believed that the Depression had caused World War II. Without it, Hitler would never have come to power, and Japan would not have wanted to expand its empire.

American advisers also thought the Depression had been overly severe because countries cut back on trade. They believed that when nations seal themselves off economically, it forces them to go to war to get the resources they need. By 1945 President Roosevelt and his advisers were convinced that economic growth was the key to world peace. They wanted to promote economic growth by increasing world trade.

▼ *Harry S. Truman*

TEACH

R₁ Reading Strategy

Sequencing Information As students read this chapter, ask them to create a time line that traces the growing strain between the United States and the Soviet Union. The time line may be used as a study aid for later review. **BL**

R₂ Reading Strategy

Scaffolding—Summarizing Have students identify the goals of Stalin's foreign policy immediately after World War II. **OL**

This **Reading Skill** was introduced in Chapter 8.

R₃ Reading Strategy

Organizing Information Have each student make a two-column list showing the postwar concerns of the Soviet Union and the United States. Use these lists to guide a class discussion on mounting tensions between these two nations at the start of the Cold War. **OL**

Did You Know?

The only two superpowers left after World War II were the United States and the Soviet Union; they had as much productive capacity between them as the rest of the world combined.

Universal Access

Visual/Spatial Have students create a thematic map that shows the countries affected by the Yalta decisions. Instruct students to indicate where the Soviets did not abide by the Yalta agreement. **OL**

Writing Support

Narrative Writing Ask students to study the photograph on this page. **Ask: What do you imagine was going through this boy's mind when this photo was taken? What thoughts and emotions was he experiencing?** Instruct students to write short stories about the war from the perspective of the little boy in the picture. **OL** **CA 11WS1.2**

Review the Big Idea

Review the Big Idea for this section, "International competition can lead to conflict and cooperation." Ask students to review the information on the Yalta Conference and discuss how each nation made compromises to achieve its goals. **OL**

Reading Check

Answer: in hopes that trade and free enterprise would increase prosperity and peace

Answers and Additional Support

American leaders believed that democratic government with protections for people's rights made countries more stable and peaceful. They also thought that the free enterprise system was the best **route** to prosperity.

Reading Check **Describing** Why did U.S. leaders promote both international trade and free enterprise?

The Yalta Conference

Main Idea At the Yalta Conference, the Allies determined the postwar plan for the world.

Reading Connection Have you ever had to work with a team or group to make an important decision? Read on to find out how the Allies determined to deal with Germany after the war.

In February 1945 the Allied leaders, President Roosevelt, Britain's Winston Churchill, and Soviet leader Joseph Stalin, met at the Soviet resort of Yalta

NATIONAL GEOGRAPHIC
MOMENT in HISTORY

AID FOR WAR'S YOUNGEST VICTIMS
The gift of a new pair of shoes from the American Red Cross lights up the face of a young Austrian refugee. Millions of people across Europe were uprooted by almost six years of fighting that seldom distinguished between combatants and civilians. Millions more fled as victorious Soviet troops advanced through Eastern Europe into Germany at the end of World War II. The fate of the refugees became enmeshed in the growing power struggle between the United States and the Soviet Union, which turned the former allies into Cold War enemies.

to plan the postwar world. There, Stalin reaffirmed the Soviet pledge to enter the war against Japan after Germany was defeated. Several agreements reached at Yalta, however, later played an important role in causing the Cold War.

Poland The first issue the leaders discussed at Yalta was what to do about Poland. Shortly after the Germans invaded Poland, the Polish government leaders had fled to Britain. In 1944, however, Soviet troops drove back the Germans and entered Poland. As the Soviets liberated Poland from German control, the Soviets encouraged Polish Communists to set up a new government. This meant there were now two governments claiming the right to govern Poland, one Communist and one non-Communist. President Roosevelt and Prime Minister Churchill both argued that the Poles should be free to choose their own government and not have one forced on them. "This is what we went to war against Germany for," Churchill explained, "that Poland should be free and sovereign."

628 CHAPTER 13 The Cold War Begins

Did You Know?

Stalin demanded that Germany pay 20 billion dollars in war reparations, half of which would go directly to the Soviet Union.

NATIONAL GEOGRAPHIC MOMENT in HISTORY

As a neutral country, Switzerland accepted refugees from the war, although it did close its borders during part of the war. Those who were able to support themselves were allowed to live and work freely in Switzerland. Those who could not support themselves lived in work camps run by the Swiss police.

Stalin quickly responded to Churchill's comments. According to Stalin, the Polish government had to be friendly to the Soviet Union. It was a matter of "life and death." Eventually, the three leaders compromised. Roosevelt and Churchill agreed to recognize the Polish government set up by the Soviets. Stalin agreed that the government would include members of the prewar Polish government and that free elections would be held as soon as possible.

Declaration of Liberated Europe After reaching a compromise on Poland, Roosevelt, Churchill, and Stalin agreed to issue the Declaration of Liberated Europe. The declaration asserted "the right of all people to choose the form of government under which they will live."

The Allies promised that the people of Europe would be allowed "to create democratic institutions of their own choice." They also promised to create **temporary** governments that represented "all democratic **elements**" and pledged "the earliest possible establishment through free elections of governments responsive to the will of the people."

Dividing Germany After agreeing to a set of principles for liberating Europe, the conference focused on Germany. Roosevelt, Churchill, and Stalin agreed to divide Germany into four zones. Great Britain, the United States, the Soviet Union, and France would each control one zone. The same four countries would also divide the city of Berlin, even though it was in the Soviet zone.

Although pleased with the decision to divide Germany, Stalin also wanted to weaken the country economically. He demanded that Germany pay heavy reparations for the war damage it caused. Roosevelt agreed, but he insisted reparations be based on Germany's ability to pay. He also suggested, and Stalin agreed, that Germany pay reparations with trade goods and products instead of cash. The Allies would also be allowed to remove industrial machinery, railroad cars, and other equipment from Germany as reparations.

This decision did not resolve the issue. Over the next few years, arguments about reparations and economic policy in Germany increased tension between the United States and the Soviet Union. These arguments became one of the major causes of the Cold War.

Tensions Begin to Rise The Yalta decisions shaped the expectations of the United States. Two weeks after Yalta, the Soviets pressured the King of Romania into appointing a Communist government.

Germany in Ruins World War II devastated many German cities. Here a woman sits among the ruins of Cologne, a northern city on the Rhine River.

The United States accused the Soviets of violating the Declaration of Liberated Europe.

Soon afterward, the Soviets refused to allow more than three non-Communist Poles to serve in the 18-member Polish government. There was also no indication that they intended to hold free elections in Poland as promised. On April 1, President Roosevelt informed the Soviets that their actions in Poland were not acceptable. Eleven days later, with Soviet-American relations deteriorating, President Roosevelt died, and Vice President Harry Truman took office.

✓ **Reading Check** **Identifying** What did the Allies decide at Yalta?

Truman Takes Control

Main Idea Differences between American and Soviet goals flared at the Potsdam Conference, where President Truman decided to take a hard line against the Soviets.

Reading Connection Describe a time when you had to work with someone who had different ideas than you. Read on to discover the different opinions that Stalin and Truman held about postwar Germany.

Although inexperienced in diplomacy, Truman already had his own views about how to deal with the Soviets. Truman was strongly anticommunist and suspicious of Stalin. He believed World War II had begun

CHAPTER 13   The Cold War Begins   **629**

R₁ **Reading Strategy**

Scaffolding—Academic Vocabulary The word *principles* was introduced in Chapter 8, Section 3. Ask a student to define the word. **BL**

R₂ **Reading Strategy**

Activating Prior Knowledge The United States and the Soviet Union compromised on the issue of German reparations. **Ask:** How do terms of this compromise reflect lessons learned from World War I? *(Roosevelt wanted Germany to pay only what the country could afford to pay rather than impose reparation payments beyond Germany's means, as in World War I.)* **AL**

S **Skill Practice**

Analyzing Photographs Review the photograph on this page. Instruct students to pay particular attention to the woman's expression as she gazes back at the photographer. **Ask:** What is her attitude toward the photographer? Have students write paragraphs explaining their impressions. **OL** **CA HR4; HI3** **CA 11WS1.5**

✓ **Reading Check**

Answer: They decided Poland's government and border, Europeans' right to choose their own government, and the division of Germany into four zones.

Did You Know?

Over 750 years old, Berlin has been a major European center since the 1700s. Following the reunification of Germany in 1990, Berlin was reestablished as the capital in 1991.

because Britain had tried to appease Hitler. He was determined not to make the same mistake with Stalin. "We must stand up to the Russians," he told Secretary of State Edward Stettinius, the day after taking office.

Ten days later, Truman did exactly that during his meeting with Soviet Foreign Minister Molotov. Truman immediately brought up the issue of Poland and demanded that Stalin hold free elections as he promised at Yalta. Molotov took the unexpectedly strong message back to Stalin. The meeting marked an important shift in Soviet-American relations and set the stage for further confrontations.

The Potsdam Conference In July 1945, with the war against Japan still raging, Truman finally met Stalin at **Potsdam,** near Berlin. Both men had come to Potsdam primarily to work out a deal on Germany.

Truman was now convinced that German industry was critical. Unless Germany's economy was allowed to revive, the rest of Europe would never recover, and the German people might turn to communism out of desperation.

Stalin and his advisers were equally convinced that they needed reparations from Germany. The war had devastated their economy. Soviet troops had begun stripping their zone in Germany of its machinery and industrial equipment for use back home, but Stalin wanted Germany to pay much more.

At the conference, Truman took a firm stand against heavy reparations. He insisted that Germany's industry had to be allowed to recover. Truman suggested that the Soviets take reparations from their zone, while the Allies allowed industry to revive in the other zones. Stalin opposed this idea since the Soviet zone was mostly agricultural. It could not provide all of the reparations the Soviets wanted.

In order to get the Soviets to accept the deal, Truman offered Stalin a small amount of German industrial equipment from the other zones but required the Soviets to pay for part of the equipment with food shipments from their zone. He also offered to accept the new German-Polish border the Soviets had established.

Stalin did not like Truman's proposal. At Potsdam, Truman learned that the atomic bomb had been successfully tested, and he told Stalin about the test. Stalin suspected Truman was trying to bully him into a deal and that the Americans were trying to limit reparations to keep the Soviets weak. Despite his suspicions, Stalin had to accept the deal. American and British troops controlled Germany's industrial heartland, and there was no way for the Soviets to get any reparations except by cooperating. Nevertheless, the Potsdam conference marked yet another increase in tensions between the Soviets and the Americans, further paving the way for the Cold War.

Picturing **History**

Potsdam Trio Issues about Germany dominated the Potsdam meeting, which was attended by (from left to right) Britain's Clement Attlee, President Truman, and Soviet leader Joseph Stalin. What agreement did they reach regarding reparations?

NATIONAL GEOGRAPHIC   **Divided Europe, 1948**

Communist nations
Non-Communist nations

Geography *Skills*

1. **Interpreting Maps** What nation was divided into Communist and non-Communist zones?
2. **Applying Geography Skills** Why did so many Eastern European nations have Communist governments?

The Iron Curtain Descends Although Truman had won the argument over reparations, he had less success on other issues at Potsdam. The Soviets refused to make any stronger commitments to uphold the Declaration of Liberated Europe. The presence of the Soviet army in Eastern Europe ensured that eventually, pro-Soviet Communist governments would be established in Poland, Romania, Bulgaria, Hungary, and Czechoslovakia. "This war is not as in the past," Stalin commented. "Whoever occupies a territory also imposes his own social system. . . . It cannot be otherwise."

The Communist countries of Eastern Europe came to be called **satellite nations.** Although not under direct Soviet control, they had to remain Communist and friendly to the Soviet Union. They also had to follow policies that the Soviets approved.

As he watched the Communist takeover in Eastern Europe, Winston Churchill coined a phrase to describe what had happened. On March 5, 1946, in a speech delivered in Fulton, Missouri, Churchill said:

> ❝From Stettin in the Baltic to Trieste in the Adriatic, an iron curtain has descended across the continent. Behind that line lie all the capitals of the ancient states of central and Eastern Europe. . . . All these famous cities and the populations around them lie in what I must call the Soviet sphere, and all are subject, in one form or another, not only to Soviet influence, but to a very high and in some cases increasing measure of control from Moscow.❞
>
> –quoted in *The United States and the Origins of the Cold War, 1941–1947*

With the **iron curtain** separating the Communist nations of Eastern Europe from the West, the World War II era had come to an end. The Cold War was about to begin.

✓ **Reading Check** **Explaining** How did the Potsdam conference hurt Soviet-American relations?

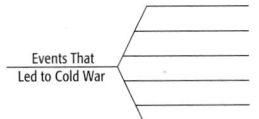

HISTORY *Online* Study Central

For help with the concepts in this section of *American Vision: Modern Times* go to tav.mt.glencoe.com and click on *Study Central.*

SECTION 1 ASSESSMENT

Checking for Understanding

1. **Vocabulary** Define: Cold War, route, temporary, element, iron curtain.
2. **People and Terms** Identify: Potsdam, satellite nation.
3. **Describe** Why did tensions grow between the United States and the Soviet Union after World War II?

Reviewing Big Ideas

4. **Explaining** At Yalta, what agreement did the "Big Three" come to about Germany's future after World War II?

Critical Thinking

5. **Historical Analysis** **Synthesizing** Do you think Roosevelt could have prevented the Cold War? Why or why not? **CA HI4**

6. **Organizing** Use a graphic organizer similar to the one below to list events that led to the Cold War.

Events That Led to Cold War

Analyzing Visuals

7. **Analyzing Maps** Study the map on this page. Why did the Soviet Union want the countries on its western border to have strong Communist governments? **CA CS3**

Writing About History

8. **Expository Writing** Imagine you are an adviser to President Truman. Write a report explaining your interpretation of Churchill's iron curtain speech. **CA 11RC2.4; 11RL3.8**

CHAPTER 13   The Cold War Begins   **631**

SECTION 1 ASSESSMENT ANSWERS

1. Content vocabulary is boldfaced and highlighted in yellow. Academic vocabulary is boldfaced.
2. Potsdam (*p. 630*), satellite nation (*p. 631*)
3. had different goals for Germany and Eastern Europe
4. Germany was divided into four zones controlled by Great Britain, France, the Soviet Union, and the United States.
5. Students who think it could have been prevented might say that Soviet needs might have been accommodated. Students who think it was inevitable may say that the Soviets had already broken several promises.
6. disagreement over Germany, Soviets' refusal to honor Declaration of Liberated Europe, Soviet actions in Poland, Potsdam Conference
7. to protect itself from invasion by Germany
8. Reports should include specific references to Churchill's speech.

Resources for page 631

Use these resources to assess student mastery.

📁 Section Quiz 13-1

📁 Reading Essentials and Study Guide 13-1

💿 Interactive Tutor Self-Assessment CD-ROM

📁 California Standards Practice, Grade 11

Geography *Skills*

Answers:
1. Germany
2. They were occupied by Soviet troops and forced to seat Communist governments.

Geography Skills Practice
Ask: With which Communist countries did Austria share a border? *(Yugoslavia, Hungary, and Czechoslovakia)*

✓ **Reading Check**

Answer: It increased tension because Stalin suspected that Truman wanted to limit reparations to keep the Soviet Union weak.

HISTORY *Online*

Study Central provides audio summaries, interactive games, and online graphic organizers to help students review section content.

CLOSE

Analyzing Primary Sources
Ask students to read and analyze Winston Churchill's "iron curtain" speech. **AL**

631

FOCUS

SKILLBUILDER ACTIVITY

Project **Daily Focus Skills Transparency 13-2** and have students answer the question.

Guide to Reading

Understanding Vocabulary:
Have students explain the vocabulary terms to partners in their own words.

Answers to Graphic:
Answers might include: 1945: Soviet-U.S. division of Korea; June 1950: North Korea invades South Korea; November 1950: China intervenes; April 1951: MacArthur fired

Unpacking the Standards

Students will be able to:

- Define the containment policy of the United States during the Cold War era.
- Discuss how the United States supported its allies during the Berlin Crisis.
- Describe how the Cold War guided policies in Asia.
- Analyze the events of the Korean War.

Answers and Additional Support

SECTION 2 The Early Cold War Years

Guide to Reading

Connection
In the previous section, you learned about the origins of the Cold War. In this section, you will discover how the Cold War led to crises and conflict.

Main Idea
- As the Cold War continued, President Truman issued the Truman Doctrine and authorized the Marshall Plan. (p. 633)
- For nearly a year, the United States airlifted supplies to West Berlin after the Soviets set up a land blockade. (p. 634)

- China became a Communist nation in 1949 after the United States increased aid to Japan to deter Communist expansion in other Asian countries. (p. 636)
- The United Nations sent armed forces to South Korea to prevent a Communist takeover. (p. 637)

Content Vocabulary
containment, limited war

Academic Vocabulary
mutual, retain, parallel

People and Terms to Identify
George Kennan, Marshall Plan, NATO

Reading Objectives
- **Describe** the American view of the Soviet Union and the policy of containment.
- **Explain** the causes of the Korean War.

Reading Strategy
Sequencing As you read about the Cold War, complete a time line similar to the one below by recording the major events involving the Korean War.

```
1945 ─┐         ┌─ 1951
      └─  ┌──┐ ─┘
          └──┘
```

Preview of Events

♦1947	♦1948	♦1949	♦1950
March 1947 Truman Doctrine declared	**June 1948** Berlin airlift begins	**April 1949** NATO forms	**October 1949** People's Republic of China established	**June 1950** Korean War begins

The following are the main History–Social Science Standards covered in this section.

11.4.6 Trace the declining role of Great Britain and the expanding role of the United States in world affairs after World War II.

11.7.8 Analyze the effect of massive aid given to Western Europe under the Marshall Plan to rebuild itself after the war and the importance of a rebuilt Europe to the U.S. economy.

11.8.5 Describe the increased powers of the presidency in response to the Great Depression, World War II, and the Cold War.

11.9.1 Discuss the establishment of the United Nations and International Declaration of Human Rights, International Monetary Fund, World Bank, and General Agreement on Tariffs and Trade (GATT) and their importance in shaping modern Europe and maintaining peace and international order.

11.9.2 Understand the role of military alliances, including NATO and SEATO, in deterring communist aggression and maintaining security during the Cold War.

The Big Idea

The fate of nations is forever changed by monumental world events. As the Soviets showed themselves increasingly unwilling to cooperate with the West, the United States developed a new policy of containment. President Truman declared that the United States was willing to aid any nation threatened by Communist aggression and to help with the recovery of Western Europe. A crisis in Iran and the Soviet blockade of West Berlin seemed to prove the Soviets' intent to spread communism. This prompted the creation of several defensive alliances. The Cold War spread to Asia with the fall of China to communism. The Korean War prompted the United States to begin a military buildup.

11.9.3 Trace the origins and geopolitical consequences (foreign and domestic) of the Cold War and containment policy, including the following: the era of McCarthyism, instances of domestic Communism (e.g., Alger Hiss) and blacklisting; the Truman Doctrine; the Berlin Blockade; the Korean War; the Bay of Pigs invasion and the Cuban Missile Crisis; atomic testing in the American West, the "mutual assured destruction" doctrine, and disarmament policies; the Vietnam War; Latin American policy.

632 CHAPTER 13   The Cold War Begins

 SECTION RESOURCES

📂 Print Material
- Reproducible Lesson Plan 13-2
- Guided Reading Activity 13-2
- Reading Essentials and Study Guide 13-2
- Active Reading Note-Taking Guide 13-2

🖐 Transparencies
- Daily Focus Skills Transparency 13-2
- Section Graphic Organizer Transparency 13-2

Technology
- 💿 Interactive Tutor Self-Assessment CD-ROM
- 💿 ExamView® Pro Testmaker CD-ROM
- 💿 Presentation Plus! CD-ROM

Containing Communism

Main Idea As the Cold War continued, President Truman issued the Truman Doctrine and authorized the Marshall Plan.

Reading Connection Do you believe that the United States should help independent nations move toward more democratic forms of government? Read on to learn about President Truman's commitment to helping other nations remain free.

The early Cold War shaped the politics and economics of many parts of the world. Americans showed a special commitment to Europe when the Soviet Union cut off the newly formed West Berlin from supply routes.

★ An American Story ★

Air Force lieutenant Gail Halvorsen was one of the pilots who airlifted supplies into Berlin in 1948. On one of his days off, he was shooting a home movie outside Berlin's Tempelhof Airport and soon drew a crowd of curious boys and girls. As a wartime pilot, Halvorsen had met children in other cities. They would playfully confront American soldiers, asking, "Any gum, chum?" While digging into his pockets for gum, Halvorsen had an idea. He said that if the children would wait at the end of the runway the next day, he would drop candy from his airplane.

The next day, eager children gathered at the airport. As Halvorsen's plane flew overhead, three small white parachutes floated down with a payload of candy. Halvorsen's "chocolate bombs" became a routine, earning him the nickname *Schokoladenflieger* ("chocolate-flyer"). Other pilots joined in, and by the end of the airlift, American pilots had dropped 250,000 candy parachutes for the children of Berlin.

—adapted from *Berlin in the Balance*

The airlift of supplies to West Berlin reassured Europeans that the United States would help them rebuild their lives, even in the shadow of growing Soviet hostility. It also signaled the end of earlier efforts to cooperate with the Soviets. These efforts, which began during the war, continued after Germany's defeat. In late 1945, the foreign ministers of the former wartime Allies met first in London, then in Moscow, to discuss the future of Europe and Asia.

W Although Ernest Bevin, the British foreign minister, and James Byrnes, the American secretary of state, pushed the Soviets to hold free elections in Eastern Europe, the Soviets refused to budge. "Our relations with the Russians," Bevin bleakly concluded, "are drifting into the same condition as that in which we had found ourselves with Hitler."

The Long Telegram Increasingly exasperated by the Soviets' refusal to cooperate, officials at the State Department asked the American Embassy in Moscow to explain Soviet behavior. On February 22, 1946, diplomat **George Kennan** responded with what came to be known as the Long Telegram, a 5,540-word cable message explaining his views of Soviet goals.

According to Kennan, the Soviets' view of the world came from a traditional "Russian sense of insecurity" and fear of the West, intensified by the Communist ideas of Lenin and Stalin. Because Communists believed that they were in a long-term historical struggle against capitalism, Kennan argued, it was impossible to reach any permanent settlement with them.

S Kennan, therefore, proposed what became the basic American policy throughout the Cold War: "a long term, patient but firm and vigilant containment of Russian expansive tendencies." Kennan explained that, in his opinion, the Soviet system had several major economic and political weaknesses. If the United States could keep the Soviets from expanding their power, it was only a matter of time until the Soviet system would fall apart. Kennan believed that communism could be beaten without going to war. The Long Telegram gave rise to the policy of **containment**—keeping communism within its present territory through the use of diplomatic, economic, and military actions.

▼ *The Berlin airlift became a symbol of American determination.*

TEACH

W Writing Support

Persuasive Writing Tell students to imagine that they are a representative of the United States or Great Britain. Have students work alone or in pairs to write letters to the Soviet government encouraging them to hold free elections in Eastern Europe. **OL** **CA** 11WS1.1

S Skill Practice

Identifying Point of View Divide the class into two groups. Have one group of students develop a list of reasons why the Truman administration should support the policy of containment. The other group should develop a list of reasons why the administration should oppose the policy. Have each group present their lists. Ask the class to vote to select the position that makes the most sense to them. **OL**
CA HR2; HR3; HI3

More Skill Practice

Interpreting Primary Sources Have interested students find copies of the Long Telegram either in the library or on the Internet. Ask them to select one part of the telegram and analyze it. Students should then write summaries of the part they selected and an explanation of how it explains Soviet and U.S. foreign policy during this time period. You may want to assign different parts of the telegram to students so that the entire telegram is summarized. **AL** **CA** HR2; HI1 **CA** 11RC2.4; 11RC2.5

Universal Access

Logical/Mathematical Instruct students to create flowcharts showing the key events of the crisis in Iran, beginning with the U.S. placement of troops in southern Iran during World War II and ending with Iran's rejection of a Soviet-Iranian oil company. *(Flowcharts should include key events from the text.)* **OL**

U₁ Universal Access

Logical/Mathematical Instruct students to create flowcharts showing the key events of the crisis in Iran, beginning with the U.S. placement of troops in southern Iran during World War II and ending with Iran's rejection of a Soviet-Iranian oil company. *(Flowcharts should include key events from the text.)* **OL**

U₂ Universal Access

Visual/Spatial Provide students with a map of Eastern Europe and the Middle East. Ask them to identify the following places on the map: Turkey, the straits of the Dardanelles, the Black Sea, and the Mediterranean Sea. **Ask:** **Why was it so important for the Soviet Union to gain control of Turkey?** *(The straits of the Dardanelles were a vital route from Soviet Black Sea ports to the Mediterranean.)* **BL**

✓ Reading Check

Answer: fight Soviet aggression in Greece and Turkey, stabilize Europe's economy to defeat communism

Answers and Additional Support

634

Crisis in Iran While Truman's administration discussed Kennan's ideas, a series of crises erupted in the spring and summer of 1946. These crises seemed to prove that Kennan was right about the Soviets. The first crisis began in Iran in March 1946.

During World War II, the United States had put troops in southern Iran while Soviet troops occupied northern Iran to secure a supply line from the Persian Gulf. After the war, instead of withdrawing as promised, the Soviet troops remained. Stalin then began demanding access to Iran's oil supplies. To increase the pressure, Soviet troops helped local Communists in northern Iran establish a separate government.

To American officials, these actions signaled a Soviet push into the Middle East. Secretary of State James Byrnes sent Moscow a strong message demanding that they withdraw. At the same time, the battleship USS *Missouri* sailed into the eastern Mediterranean. The pressure seemed to work. Soviet forces withdrew, having been promised a joint Soviet-Iranian oil company. The Iranian parliament later rejected the plan.

The Truman Doctrine Frustrated in Iran, Stalin turned to Turkey. There the straits of the Dardanelles were a vital route from Soviet Black Sea ports to the Mediterranean. For centuries Russia had wanted to control this strategic route. In August 1946, Stalin demanded joint control of the Dardanelles with Turkey. Presidential adviser Dean Acheson saw this move as the first step in a Soviet plan to control the Mideast, and he advised Truman to make a show of force. The president ordered the new aircraft carrier *Franklin D. Roosevelt* to join the *Missouri* in protecting Turkey and the eastern Mediterranean.

While the United States supported Turkey, Britain tried to help Greece. In August 1946, Greek Communists launched a guerrilla war against the Greek government. For about six months, British troops helped the Greeks fight the guerrillas. The effort strained Britain's economy, which was still weak from World War II. In February 1947, Britain informed the United States that it could no longer afford to help Greece.

On March 12, 1947, Truman went before Congress to ask for $400 million to fight Communist aggression in Greece and Turkey. His speech outlined a policy which became known as the Truman Doctrine. Its goal was to aid "free peoples who are resisting attempted subjugation by armed minorities or by outside pressures." Its immediate effects were to stabilize the Greek government and ease Soviet demands in Turkey. In the long run, it pledged the United States to fight communism worldwide.

The Marshall Plan Meanwhile, postwar Western Europe faced grave problems. Economies were in ruin, people were near starvation, and political chaos was at hand. The terrible winter of 1946 made things worse.

In June 1947, Secretary of State George C. Marshall proposed the European Recovery Program, or **Marshall Plan,** which would give European nations American aid to rebuild their economies. Truman saw the Marshall Plan and the Truman Doctrine as "two halves of the same walnut," both essential for containment. Marshall offered help to all nations planning a recovery program:

❝Our policy is not directed against any country or doctrine, but against hunger, poverty, desperation and chaos. Its purpose should be the revival of a working economy in the world so as to permit the emergence of political and social conditions in which free institutions can exist. . . .❞

—quoted in *Marshall: A Hero for Our Times*

The Soviet Union and its satellite nations in Eastern Europe rejected the offer. Instead, the Soviets developed their own economic program. This action further separated Europe into competing regions. The Marshall Plan pumped billions of dollars worth of supplies, machinery, and food into Western Europe. Western Europe's recovery weakened the appeal of communism and opened new markets for trade.

✓ Reading Check **Summarizing** What were the goals of the Truman Doctrine and the Marshall Plan?

The Berlin Crisis

Main Idea **For nearly a year, the United States airlifted supplies to West Berlin after the Soviets set up a land blockade.**

Reading Connection What is the difference between being stubborn and being determined? Read on to find out about a lengthy effort to keep West Germany free.

The Marshall Plan was only one part of the American strategy to rebuild Europe. President Truman and his advisers believed that Western Europe's prosperity depended on Germany's recovery. The Soviets, however, still wanted Germany to pay reparations to the Soviet Union. Eventually, the dispute over Germany brought the United States and the Soviet Union to the brink of war.

More Skill Practice

English Learners It is often difficult for English learners to understand how words shape our feelings about events. Have students examine the quote on page 634 and make a list of words they believe have an emotional impact. Then ask what emotions these words held for people in the United States and in postwar Europe. **EL**

Did You Know?

Senator Robert A. Taft opposed the Marshall Plan, calling it a "global giveaway program." He was concerned that the plan would bankrupt the United States.

West Germany Is Founded By early 1948, U.S. officials had concluded that the Soviets were deliberately trying to undermine Germany's economy. In response, the United States, Great Britain, and France announced that they were merging their zones in Germany and allowing the Germans to have their own government. They also agreed to merge their zones in Berlin and to make West Berlin part of the new German republic.

The new nation was officially called the Federal Republic of Germany, but it became known as West Germany. West Germany's economy was completely separate from the Soviet zone, which eventually became known as East Germany. West Germany was not allowed to have a military, but in most respects, it was independent.

The Berlin Airlift The decision to create West Germany convinced the Soviets that they would never get the reparations they wanted. In late June 1948, Soviet troops cut all road and rail traffic to West Berlin. The blockade provoked a crisis. President Truman sent long-range bombers with atomic weapons to bases in Britain. General Lucius Clay, the American commander in Germany, warned that if Berlin fell, West Germany would be next.

The challenge was to keep West Berlin alive without provoking war with the Soviets. In June 1948, Truman ordered the Berlin airlift to begin. For 11 months, cargo planes brought in over 2 million tons of supplies, providing Berliners with food, medicine, and coal. Stalin finally lifted the blockade on May 12. The Berlin airlift became a symbol of American determination to stand by the divided city.

NATO The Berlin blockade convinced many Americans that the Soviets were bent on conquest. Both the public and Congress began to support a military alliance with Western Europe. By April 1949, an agreement had been reached to create the North Atlantic Treaty Organization (NATO)—a **mutual** defense alliance.

NATIONAL GEOGRAPHIC — NATO and the Warsaw Pact, 1955

Legend:
- "Iron Curtain"
- Communist nations not in Warsaw Pact
- Warsaw Pact countries
- Non-Communist nations not in NATO
- NATO countries
- ⊛ Capital

500 miles
500 kilometers
Lambert Azimuthal Equal-Area projection

Geography *Skills*

By the mid-1950s, two powerful military alliances, NATO and the Warsaw Pact, were facing each other in Europe. **Applying Geography Skills** How many European nations had Communist governments in 1955?

636

NATO initially included 12 countries: the United States, Canada, Britain, France, Italy, Belgium, Denmark, Portugal, the Netherlands, Norway, Luxembourg, and Iceland. NATO members agreed to come to the aid of any member who was attacked. Six years later, the United States and its allies decided to allow West Germany to rearm and join NATO. This decision alarmed Soviet leaders, who responded by organizing a military alliance in Eastern Europe, known as the Warsaw Pact. The United States also joined other alliances. The Organization of American States (OAS) started in 1948, and the Southeast Asia Treaty Organization (SEATO) formed in 1954.

✓ Reading Check **Evaluating** What triggered the beginning of the Berlin airlift?

The Cold War Spreads to East Asia

Main Idea China became a Communist nation in 1949 after the United States increased aid to Japan to deter Communist expansion in other Asian countries.

Reading Connection Why do you think increasing trade with Japan would help deter communism? Read on to discover how Americans helped Japan rebuild after the war.

The Cold War eventually spread beyond Europe. Conflicts also emerged in Asia, where events in China and Korea brought about a new attitude toward Japan.

Civil War and Revolution in China In China, Communist forces led by Mao Zedong had been struggling against the Nationalist government led by Chiang Kai-shek since the late 1920s. During World War II, the two sides suspended their war to resist Japanese occupation. With the end of World War II, however, civil war broke out again. Although Mao made great gains, neither side could win, and neither would accept a compromise.

To prevent a Communist revolution in Asia, the United States sent the Nationalist government $2 billion in aid beginning in the mid-1940s, but it squandered this advantage with poor military planning and corruption. By 1949 the Communists had captured the Chinese capital of Beijing and moved southward, while support for the Nationalists declined.

In August 1949, the State Department discontinued aid to the Chinese Nationalists. The defeated Nationalists then fled the Chinese mainland for the small island of Taiwan (Formosa). The victorious Communists established the People's Republic of China in October 1949.

After the Fall China's fall to communism shocked Americans. To make matters worse, in September 1949 the Soviet Union announced that it had successfully tested its first atomic weapon. Then, early in 1950, the People's Republic of China and the Soviet Union signed a treaty of friendship and alliance. Many Western leaders feared that China and the Soviet Union would support Communist revolutions in other nations.

The United States kept formal diplomatic relations with only the Nationalists in Taiwan. It used its veto

Causes and Effects of the Cold War

Causes
- Soviet Union controls Eastern Europe after World War II.
- Chinese Communists win control of mainland China.
- United States and Soviet Union explode atomic bombs.

Effects
- Marshall Plan provides aid to Western Europe.
- Western nations form NATO; Communist nations respond with Warsaw Pact.
- Korean War erupts.
- American and Soviet arms race begins.
- Red Scare leads to hunt for Communists in the United States.

Graphic Organizer → Skills

The Cold War between the United States and the Soviet Union dominated postwar politics.

Evaluating What do you think was the most important cause of the Cold War? Why?

636 CHAPTER 13   The Cold War Begins

Different Viewpoints

Should the War in Korea Be Expanded?

A controversy between President Harry S Truman and General Douglas MacArthur began shortly after the outbreak of the Korean War. It reached a climax when the president relieved MacArthur of his command. Truman believed in a limited war in Korea, while MacArthur wanted total victory.

President Harry S. Truman defends limited war:

The Kremlin [Soviet Union] is trying, and has been trying for a long time, to drive a wedge between us and the other nations. It wants to see us isolated. It wants to see us distrusted. It wants to see us feared and hated by our allies. Our allies agree with us in the course we are following. They do not believe that we should take the initiative to widen the conflict in the Far East. If the United States were to widen the conflict, we might well have to go it alone.

If we go it alone in Asia, we may destroy the unity of the free nations against aggression. Our European allies are nearer to Russia than we are. They are in far greater danger. . . . Going it alone brought the world to the disaster of World War II. . . .

I do not propose to strip this country of its allies in the face of Soviet danger. The path of collective security is our only sure defense against the dangers that threaten us.

General Douglas MacArthur addresses Congress, April 19, 1951:

History teaches with unmistakable emphasis that appeasement but begets new and bloodier war. . . . Like blackmail, it lays the basis for new and successively greater demands, until, as in blackmail, violence becomes the only other alternative. Why, my soldiers asked of me, surrender military advantage to an enemy in the field? I could not answer.

It was my constant effort to preserve them and end this savage conflict honorably and with the least loss of time and minimum sacrifice of life.

I am closing 52 years of military service. . . . But I still remember the refrain of one of the most popular barrack ballads of that day which proclaimed most proudly that—

"Old soldiers never die, they just fade away." And like the old soldier of that ballad, I now close my military career and just fade away—an old soldier who tried to do his duty as God gave him the light to see that duty. Good-by.

Learning From History

1. **Identifying Central Issues** How did MacArthur view Truman's decision to fight a limited war in Korea? How did Truman see it?
2. **Making Inferences** On the basis of what authority did Truman fire MacArthur?

power in the UN Security Council to keep representatives of the new Communist China out of the UN, allowing the Nationalists to **retain** their seat.

The Chinese revolution brought about a significant change in American policy toward Japan. At the end of World War II, General Douglas MacArthur had taken charge of occupied Japan. His mission was to introduce democracy and keep Japan from threatening war again. Once the United States lost China as its chief ally in Asia, it adopted policies to encourage the rapid recovery of Japan's industrial economy. Just as the United States viewed West Germany as the key to defending all of Europe against communism, it saw Japan as the key to defending Asia.

✓ **Reading Check** **Analyzing** How did the revolution in China affect American foreign policy with Japan?

The Korean War

Main Idea The United Nations sent armed forces to South Korea to prevent a Communist takeover.

Reading Connection Have you ever had to make tough decisions as a group leader or team captain? Read on to discover why President Truman fired General MacArthur during the Korean War.

At the end of World War II, American and Soviet forces entered Korea to disarm the Japanese troops stationed there. The Allies divided Korea at the 38th

CHAPTER 13 The Cold War Begins **637**

C Critical Thinking

Drawing Conclusions The Truman administration's policy of limited war was met with criticism by groups in the United States that wanted a more aggressive challenge toward Communist actions. **Ask:** Do you think that it was correct to be cautious about involving the United States in a war against Communist countries and to involve the United Nations? Explain. *(Students' answers will vary. Some might suggest that the United States should have used its military strength to defeat communism quickly. Other students might suggest that this was a potentially dangerous maneuver, especially considering the concerns over nuclear war.)* **AL**

W Writing Support

Persuasive Writing Ask students to use library and Internet resources to research MacArthur's actions in Korea after the Inchon landing. Students should then write letters to Truman as if they were MacArthur, trying to convince Truman to expand the war against China. **OL** **CA 11WS1.3**

Answers and Additional Support

parallel of latitude. Soviet troops controlled the north, while American troops controlled the south.

As the Cold War began, talks to reunify Korea broke down. A Communist Korean government was organized in the north, while an American-backed government controlled the south. Both governments claimed authority over all of Korea, and border clashes were common. The Soviet Union provided extensive military aid to the North Koreans, who quickly built up a large, well-equipped army. On June 25, 1950, North Korean troops invaded into the south, rapidly driving back the poorly equipped South Korean forces.

The UN Intervenes Truman saw the Communist invasion of South Korea as a test of the containment policy and ordered United States naval and airpower into action. He then called on the United Nations to act. Truman succeeded because the Soviet delegate was boycotting the Security Council over its China policy and was not present to veto the American proposal. With the pledge of UN troops, Truman ordered General MacArthur to send American troops from Japan to the Korean peninsula.

The American and South Korean troops were driven back into a small pocket of territory near the port of Pusan. Inside the "Pusan perimeter," as it came to be called, the troops stubbornly resisted the North Korean onslaught, buying time for MacArthur to organize reinforcements.

On September 15, MacArthur ordered a daring invasion behind enemy lines at the port of Inchon. The Inchon landing took the North Koreans by surprise. Within weeks they were in full retreat back across the 38th parallel. Truman then gave the order

NATIONAL GEOGRAPHIC — **Korean War, 1950–1953**

June 25, 1950–November 24, 1950
- UN-held territory, Sept. 15, 1950
- North Korean advance
- UN counteroffensive
- UN front line, Nov. 24, 1950

① MacArthur lands, Sept. 15, 1950
② Liberated by UN, Sept. 28, 1950
③ Taken by UN, Oct. 19, 1950
④ Chinese counteroffensive, Nov. 26, 1950
⑤ Armistice line, July 27, 1953

November 24, 1950–July 27, 1953
- UN front line, Nov. 24, 1950
- Chinese counteroffensive, Nov. 25, 1950
- Farthest Chinese advance, Jan. 24, 1951
- UN advance, Jan. 25, 1951

Lambert Conformal Conic projection

Geography Skills

1. **Interpreting Maps** Along what latitude was Korea divided into two nations after World War II?
2. **Applying Geography Skills** In debates over expanding the Korean War, why do you think Truman opposed MacArthur's request to bomb bridges on the Yalu River?

Geography Skills

Answers:
1. 38 degrees North
2. Truman did not want to risk bringing the Chinese into the war, or to use the atomic bomb.

Geography Skills Practice
Ask: What was the importance of the Yalu River in the Korean War? (*It was the boundary between China and North Korea.*)

to pursue the North Koreans beyond the 38th parallel. MacArthur pushed the North Koreans north to the Yalu River, the border with China.

China Enters the War The Communist Chinese government saw the advancing UN troops as a threat and warned the forces to halt their advance. When those warnings were ignored, China launched a massive attack across the Yalu River in November. Hundreds of thousands of Chinese troops flooded across the border, driving the UN forces back across the 38th parallel.

As his troops fell back, an angry MacArthur demanded approval to expand the war against China. He asked for a blockade of Chinese ports, the use of Chiang Kai-shek's Nationalist forces, and the bombing of Chinese cities with atomic weapons.

Truman Fires MacArthur President Truman refused MacArthur's demands because he did not want to expand the war into China or to use the atomic bomb. MacArthur persisted. He publicly criticized the president, saying, "There is no substitute for victory."

Determined to maintain control of policy and show that the president commanded the military, an exasperated Truman fired MacArthur for insubordination in April 1951. MacArthur, who remained popular despite being fired, returned home to parades and a hero's welcome. Despite criticism, Truman remained committed to **limited war**—a war fought to achieve a limited objective, such as containing communism.

Changes in Policy Truman chose General Matthew Ridgway to replace MacArthur. By mid-1951, the UN forces had pushed the Chinese and North Korean forces back across the 38th parallel. The war then settled down into a series of relatively small battles over hills and other local objectives. In November 1951, peace negotiations began, but an armistice would not be signed until July 1953. More than 33,600 American soldiers died in action in the Korean War, and more than 2,800 died from accidents or from disease.

The Korean War marked an important turning point in the Cold War. Until 1950 the United States had preferred to use political pressure and economic aid to contain communism. After the Korean War began, the United States embarked on a major military buildup.

The Korean War also helped expand the Cold War to Asia. Before 1950 the United States had focused on Europe as the most important area in which to contain communism. After the Korean War began, the United States became more militarily involved in Asia. Defense agreements were signed with Japan, South Korea, Taiwan, the Philippines, and Australia. American aid also began to flow to the French forces fighting Communist guerrillas in Vietnam.

☑ **Reading Check** **Analyzing** How did President Truman view the Communist invasion of South Korea?

HISTORY Online **Student Web Activity** Visit the *American Vision: Modern Times* Web site at tav.mt.glencoe.com and click on *Student Web Activities— Chapter 13* for an activity on the Cold War.

HISTORY Online **Study Central**
For help with the concepts in this section of *American Vision: Modern Times* go to tav.mt.glencoe.com and click on *Study Central.*

SECTION 2 ASSESSMENT

Checking for Understanding

1. **Vocabulary** Define: containment, mutual, retain, parallel, limited war.
2. **People and Terms** Identify: George Kennan, Marshall Plan, NATO.
3. **Examine** How did the Truman Doctrine and the Marshall Plan address the spread of communism?

Reviewing Big Ideas

4. **Explaining** What long-term Cold War strategy did the United States follow?

Critical Thinking

5. **Evaluating** How did the Long Telegram influence American policy?
6. **Categorizing** Use a graphic organizer similar to the one below to list early conflicts between the USSR and the U.S.

Conflicts Between the USSR and the U.S.

Analyzing Visuals

7. **Analyzing Maps** Study the maps of the Korean War on page 638. When did the United Nations control the most territory in Korea? When did both sides finally agree upon an armistice line?

Writing About History

8. **Persuasive Writing** Write a letter to the editor of a newspaper explaining whether you agree or disagree with President Truman's firing of General MacArthur. **CA** 11WS1.1; 11WS1.5

SECTION 2 ASSESSMENT ANSWERS

1. Content vocabulary is boldfaced and highlighted in yellow. Academic vocabulary is boldfaced.
2. George Kennan *(p. 633)*, Marshall Plan *(p. 634)*, NATO *(p. 636)*
3. They would help any country fight against communism and they would help rebuild economies to strengthen the resistance to communism.
4. the policy of containing communism through international aid, diplomacy, and a strong military
5. It recommended patient but firm and vigilant containment of Russian expansion.
6. crisis in Iran, Berlin crisis, Korean War
7. November 1950; July 27, 1953
8. Students' letters will vary. Letters should express a point of view based on facts.

Chapter 13 • Section 2

ASSESS

Resources for page 639

Use these resources to assess student mastery.

📂 Section Quiz 13-2

📂 Reading Essentials and Study Guide 13-2

🔵 Interactive Tutor Self-Assessment CD-ROM

📂 California Standards Practice, Grade 11

HISTORY Online
Objectives and answers to the student activity can be found in the **Web Activity Lesson Plan** at tav.mt.glencoe.com.

☑ **Reading Check**
Answer: Truman viewed it as a test of the United States containment policy.

HISTORY Online
Study Central provides audio summaries, interactive games, and online graphic organizers to help students review section content.

CLOSE

Determining Cause and Effect Have students create cause-and-effect organizers for the Korean War. **BL**

Looking Back...

FOCUS

History–Social Science Standards

This feature addresses the following standards:

11.1 Students analyze the significant events in the founding of the nation and its attempts to realize the philosophy of government described in the Declaration of Independence.

11.1.1 Describe the Enlightenment and the rise of democratic ideas as the context in which the nation was founded.

TEACH

R **Reading Strategy**

Scaffolding–Cause and Effect
The textbook states that "the colonists had a right to rebel because the British were suppressing their basic rights." **Ask:** **What do you believe were the most critical actions taken by the British in the colonial period that led to rebellion?** *(Answers will vary but should include events and laws that were discussed in Chapter 1.)*
OL

This **Reading Skill** was introduced in Chapters 4 and 12.

Answers and Additional Support

640

The American Revolution

Why It Matters The Cold War between the United States and the Soviet Union stemmed from a number of factors, from mutual fear and mistrust to a desire by both superpowers to spread their influence around the world. On another level, however, the effort to contain communism reflected a basic tradition of Americans first seen in the American Revolution: standing up to tyranny and fighting for freedom.

The United States was founded on the principles of individual liberty and democratic rule. Since then, Americans have felt a special duty to promote these ideals and challenge any attempt to undermine them abroad as well as at home. In confronting the Soviet Union, Americans believed they were carrying on a long tradition of battling oppression and despotism.

Steps to . . . the American Revolution

R A central idea behind the American Revolution was that the colonists had a right to rebel because the British were suppressing their basic rights. Americans have remained committed to this political principle. By contrast, many of these rights—for example, the right to free speech or to own property—were not recognized in the Soviet Union.

Samuel Adams Few colonists were as unyielding in their opposition to British rule as Samuel Adams. Adams was one the most outspoken of the patriots and the founder of the prominent resistance group, the Sons of Liberty. He admired the ideas of English philosopher John Locke, agreeing with Locke that every citizen enjoyed the natural rights of life, liberty, and property.

A government, Adams declared, "has no right to absolute, arbitrary power over the lives of and fortunes of the people. . . . "

Thomas Jefferson Perhaps no colonist did more to advance freedom than Thomas Jefferson, one of the main authors of the Declaration of Independence. When the debate over whether to fight Great Britain began, Jefferson was one of many who argued that personal liberty and self-determination were worth fighting for.

"We have counted the cost of this contest and find nothing so dreadful as voluntary slavery," Jefferson stated in a 1775 declaration cowritten with

"If we wish to be free; if we mean to preserve inviolate those inestimable privileges for which we have been so long contending; if we mean not basely to abandon the noble struggle in which we have been so long engaged, . . . we must fight!"

—*Patrick Henry, 1775*

640

EXTENDING THE CONTENT

Stalin's Response The impact of the Soviets' lack of a free press—one of the keystones of the American constitutional system—is demonstrated by some of Stalin's statements. For example, after Winston Churchill's "iron curtain" speech, Stalin came up with his own characterization of geopolitical changes. Stalin claimed that the West was racist. He compared the West to "Hitler and his friends," and said Churchill was arguing that "only nations speaking the English language are fully valuable nations. . . ." Under the Soviet system, no journalist or scholar could challenge the accuracy of Stalin's statement.

American vs. Soviet Government Systems

U.S. Constitutional System	Soviet System
Bill of Rights to protect individual rights with access to independent judiciary	Soviet constitution states protections, but they are not enforced; no independent judiciary
Free elections	Government-controlled elections
Representative government at federal, state, and local levels	Central Committee of Communist Party in control of central, state, and local government
Police under civilian control	Police under party control; active secret police unit to control dissent
Free press	State-controlled press
Military under control of elected civilian government bodies	Military under control of central leadership of Communist Party
Extensive private property ownership	State ownership of major industries; very limited private ownership

John Dickinson. "Honor, justice, and humanity forbid us tamely to surrender that freedom which we received from our gallant ancestors, and which our [descendants] have a right to receive from us."

George Washington During the Revolution, George Washington's duties were mostly military, but he believed strongly in civilian government. He showed his political beliefs at the end of the Revolutionary War, when he learned that a group of military officers who had not been paid were considering seizing control of the government. He criticized the plotters and expressed his disgust with the idea of military rule. Such an action, Washington declared, "has something so shocking in it that humanity revolts at the idea. . . ." Washington's position reflected his commitment to a government by the people.

Benjamin Franklin Benjamin Franklin, the American philosopher, diplomat, and inventor, also supported independence. For a long time, Franklin was friendly to Great Britain, but he eventually came to see British rule as oppressive. In a satirical 1773 piece entitled *Rules by Which a Great Empire May Be Reduced to a Small One,* Benjamin Franklin explained that Britain was following all the necessary steps to create a colonial rebellion:

"If you are told of discontents in your colonies, never believe that they are general, or that you have given occasion for them; therefore, do not think of applying any remedy, or of changing any offensive measure. . . ."

Free Speech and Free Press Free speech and freedom of the press were important freedoms for which the colonists fought. Before the American Revolution, colonists could be charged with sedition for criticizing the government. After the Revolution, many state constitutions guaranteed the right to free speech and a free press.

The Virginia Declaration of Rights of 1776 stated that "the freedom of the press is one of the greatest bulwarks of liberty and can never be restrained but by despotic governments." These ideas led to the lines in the First Amendment of the Constitution guaranteeing free speech and freedom of the press. These freedoms are rarely found in Communist societies or in military dictatorships. Protecting these freedoms was one more reason the United States opposed the spread of communism.

Check for Understanding
1. What doctrine of John Locke did Samuel Adams promote?
2. What principle did George Washington believe was important in the relationship between government and the military?

Critical Thinking
1. Why do you think that dictatorships and other tyrannical forms of governments oppose freedom of the press?
2. In what ways were the revolutionary leaders mentioned here similar to American leaders during the Cold War?

FOCUS

SKILLBUILDER ACTIVITY

Project **Daily Focus Skills Transparency 13-3** and have students answer the question.

Guide to Reading

Understanding Vocabulary:
Ask students to write a half-page paragraph about one of the content vocabulary words.

Answers to Graphic:
Students should complete the outline by including all headings in the section.

Unpacking the Standards

Students will be able to:

• Explain the occurrence of the second Red Scare following World War II.

• Analyze the reasons for and circumstances surrounding McCarthyism.

• Describe social life and social concerns during the early years of the Cold War.

Answers and Additional Support

The Cold War and American Society

Guide to Reading

Connection
In the previous section, you learned about the first crises of the Cold War. In this section, you will discover how the Cold War changed American society.

Main Idea
• As Cold War tensions rose, Americans worked to combat Communist influence at home. (p. 643)
• The Red Scare intensified as Senator Joseph McCarthy presided over a Senate committee charged with exposing Communists in government. (p. 646)

• Fear of nuclear attack and of communism dominated American popular culture during the early Cold War years. (p. 648)

Content Vocabulary
subversion, perjury, censure, fallout, fallout shelter

Academic Vocabulary
confirm, sole, nuclear

People and Terms to Identify
loyalty review program, Alger Hiss, McCarran Act, McCarthyism

Reading Objectives
• **Describe** the new Red Scare.
• **Discuss** how American society reflected fears of the nuclear age.

Reading Strategy
Taking Notes As you read about American reaction to the Cold War, use the major headings of the section to create an outline similar to the one below.

The Cold War and American Society
I. A New Red Scare
   A. The Loyalty Review Program
   B.
   C.
   D.

Preview of Events

◆1947   ◆1950   ◆1953

March 1947
Loyalty Review Board established

February 1950
McCarthy claims to have a list of Communists in the State Department

September 1950
McCarran Act passed

June 1953
Rosenbergs executed

The following are the main History–Social Science Standards covered in this section.

11.8.7 Describe the effects on society and the economy of technological developments since 1945, including the computer revolution, changes in communication, advances in medicine, and improvements in agricultural technology.

11.8.8 Discuss forms of popular culture, with emphasis on their origins and geographic diffusion (e.g., jazz and other forms of popular music, professional sports, architectural and artistic styles).

11.9.3 Trace the origins and geopolitical consequences (foreign and domestic) of the Cold War and containment policy, including the following: the era of McCarthyism, instances of domestic Communism (e.g., Alger Hiss) and blacklisting; the Truman Doctrine; the Berlin Blockade; the Korean War; the Bay of Pigs invasion and the Cuban Missile Crisis; atomic testing in the American West, the "mutual assured destruction" doctrine, and disarmament policies; the Vietnam War; Latin American policy.

11.9.4 List the effects of foreign policy on domestic policies and vice versa (e.g., protests during the war in Vietnam, the "nuclear freeze" movement).

⚞ *The Big Idea* ⚟

Social and economic crises lead to new roles for government. Americans grew concerned about Communists not only overseas but also in the United States. Such concerns led to a new Red Scare, the establishment of a loyalty review program, an anti-Communist law, and a congressional committee to investigate Communist activities. Several spy convictions provided fuel for Senator McCarthy's allegations. At the same time, Americans grew concerned about and prepared for a possible Soviet nuclear attack on the United States.

642 CHAPTER 13 The Cold War Begins

SECTION RESOURCES

📁 Print Material
• Reproducible Lesson Plan 13-3
• Guided Reading Activity 13-3
• Reading Essentials and Study Guide 13-3
• Active Reading Note-Taking Guide 13-3

Transparencies
• Daily Focus Skills Transparency 13-3
• Section Graphic Organizer Transparency 13-3

Technology
🅢 Interactive Tutor Self-Assessment CD-ROM
🅢 Exam*View*® Pro Testmaker CD-ROM
🅢 Presentation Plus! CD-ROM

A New Red Scare

Main Idea As Cold War tensions rose, Americans worked to combat Communist influence at home.

Reading Connection Describe a time in American history when rumors and fears created a distrustful environment. Read on to learn about the new Red Scare.

During the 1950s, many ordinary people had their lives disrupted. Accusations of Communists in the United States and of Communist infiltration of the government tapped into fears that the Communists were trying to take over the world.

★ An American Story ★

In the 1940s, Ruth Goldberg belonged to the Parent-Teacher Association in Queens, New York. In 1947 she agreed to run for PTA president, but the campaign turned nasty. Because Goldberg had associated with people with left-wing interests, a rumor spread through the neighborhood that she was a Communist. Suddenly Goldberg's quiet life became terrifying. Callers threatened her, and the local priest denounced her in his sermons. One afternoon, Goldberg's eight-year-old son came home in tears. A playmate had told him, "You know, your mother's a Red. She should be put up against a wall and shot."

Looking back much later, Goldberg saw the PTA campaign as part of a bigger and more complex pattern of distrust and hatred. "It was a small thing, but it was an indication of what had happened with the Cold War, with this Red specter—that somebody like me could be a danger to a community."

—adapted from *Red Scare*

The Red Scare began in September 1945, when a clerk named Igor Gouzenko walked out of the Soviet Embassy in Ottawa, Canada, and defected. Gouzenko carried documents revealing a massive effort by the Soviet Union to infiltrate organizations and government agencies in Canada and the United States in order to obtain information on the atomic bomb.

The Gouzenko case stunned Americans. It implied that spies had infiltrated the American government. Soon, however, the search for spies escalated into a general fear of Communist subversion. **Subversion** is the effort to secretly weaken a society and overthrow its government. As the Cold War intensified in 1946 and early 1947, Americans began to fear that Communists were secretly working to subvert the American government.

The Loyalty Review Program In early 1947, just nine days after his powerful speech announcing the Truman Doctrine, the president established a **loyalty review program** to screen all federal employees. Rather than calm public suspicion, Truman's action seemed to **confirm** fears that Communists had infiltrated the government and helped increase the fear of communism sweeping the nation.

Between 1947 and 1951, over 6 million federal employees were screened for their loyalty—a term difficult to define. A person might become a suspect for reading certain books, belonging to various groups, traveling overseas, or even seeing certain foreign films. About 14,000 employees were subject to intensive scrutiny from the Federal Bureau of Investigation (FBI). Some 2,000 employees quit their jobs during the check, many under pressure. Another 212 were fired for "questionable loyalty," though no actual evidence against them was uncovered.

HUAC Although the FBI helped screen federal employees, FBI Director J. Edgar Hoover was not satisfied. In 1947 Hoover went before the House Un-American Activities Committee (HUAC). Formed in 1938 to investigate both Communist and Fascist activities in the United States, HUAC was a relatively minor committee until Hoover catapulted it to prominence.

Hoover urged HUAC to hold public hearings on Communist subversion. The committee, Hoover said, could reveal "the diabolic machinations of sinister

Book produced during the ▶ Red Scare of the 1950s

AMERICA BETRAYED

... the tragic consequences of REDS on the Government payroll

TEACH

C Critical Thinking

Drawing Conclusions Assign students to small groups. Have each group work together to come up with a definition of the word *loyalty*. Have them share their definitions with the class. **Ask:** What is difficult about defining *loyalty* in absolute terms? At what point might the right to question one's government be considered "disloyalty"? (*Students' answers will vary but should show an attempt to evaluate the textbook materials.*) Have students record their responses in short paragraphs or journal entries. **OL**

U Universal Access

Verbal/Linguistic To help demonstrate the impact of the second Red Scare, invite two volunteers to portray a HUAC member and someone called to testify before the committee. Have the HUAC member question the witness for several minutes about Communist influence in his or her workplace and among his or her friends and family. Afterward, ask participants and listeners to share their reactions. **OL**

More Skill Practice

Historical Interpretation To better understand the Cold War fears, have students take the role of a person during that time and write a journal entry. They should take one of the following roles: a history teacher finding out that the FBI is investigating her; a blacklisted actor having just returned from an audition; an office worker who has discussed the Hiss or Rosenberg case with coworkers; or someone whose family is discussing building a fallout shelter. **OL** • **CA HR4; HI3**

Picturing **History**

Convicted of Conspiracy Ethel and Julius Rosenberg were convicted of transmitting atomic secrets to Soviet Russia. *What sentence did they receive?*

figures engaged in un-American activities." Once Communists were identified, he explained, the public would isolate them and end their influence. Hoover's aim was to expose not just Communists but also "Communist sympathizers" and "fellow travelers." Under Hoover's leadership, the FBI sent agents to infiltrate groups suspected of subversion and wiretapped thousands of telephones.

Alger Hiss In 1948 Whittaker Chambers, a *Time* magazine editor and former Communist Party member, testified to HUAC that several government officials were also former Communists or spies.

The most prominent government official named by Chambers was **Alger Hiss,** a lawyer and diplomat who had served in Roosevelt's administration, attended the Yalta conference, and taken part in organizing the United Nations. After Hiss sued him for libel, Chambers testified before a grand jury that in 1937 and 1938 Hiss gave him secret documents from the State Department. Hiss denied being either a spy or a member of the Communist Party, and he also denied ever having known Chambers.

The committee was ready to drop the investigation until Representative Richard Nixon of California convinced his colleagues to continue the hearings to determine whether Hiss or Chambers had lied. As the committee continued to question Hiss, he admitted that he had indeed met Chambers in the 1930s. When Chambers continued to claim that Hiss was a Communist, Hiss sued him, claiming that his accusations were unfounded and malicious.

To defend himself, Chambers produced copies of secret documents along with microfilm that he had hidden in a hollow pumpkin on his farm. These "pumpkin papers," Chambers claimed, proved that he was telling the truth. A jury agreed and convicted Hiss of **perjury,** or lying under oath.

The Rosenbergs Another sensational spy case centered around accusations that American Communists had sold the secrets of the atomic bomb. Many people did not believe that the Soviet Union could

Hollywood on Trial

One of HUAC's first hearings focused on the film industry as a powerful cultural force that Communists might use and manipulate. Its interviews routinely began, "Are you now, or have you ever been, a member of the Communist Party?" As fear of Communists in Hollywood spread, producers then drew up a blacklist and agreed not to hire anyone in the film industry who was believed to be a Communist or who refused to cooperate with the committee. The blacklist created an atmosphere of distrust and fear. People could be blacklisted for making chance remarks, criticizing HUAC, or knowing a suspected Communist.

Ronald Reagan, head of the Screen Actors Guild at the time, testified that there were Communists in Hollywood.

Ten screenwriters, known as the "Hollywood Ten" (shown here with their lawyers) used their Fifth Amendment right to protect themselves from self-incrimination and refused to testify before HUAC.

Did You Know?

Of the film industry people investigated by HUAC, ten went to prison. This group, often referred to as "The Hollywood Ten," consisted of Alvah Bessie, Herbert J. Biberman, Lester Cole, Edward Dmytryk, Ring Lardner, Jr., John Howard Lawson, Albert Maltz, Samuel Ornitz, Adrian Scott, and Dalton Trumbo.

Picturing **History**

Answer: condemned to death for espionage
Ask: Do you think the Soviet Union could have produced an atomic bomb without help? Why or why not? *(Most students will likely note that it probably would have taken the Soviet Union longer without help.)*

have produced an atomic bomb in 1949 without help. This belief intensified the hunt for spies.

In 1950 the hunt led to Klaus Fuchs, a British scientist who admitted sending information to the Soviet Union. His testimony led the FBI to arrest Julius and Ethel Rosenberg, a New York couple who were members of the Communist Party. The government charged them with heading a Soviet spy ring.

The Rosenbergs denied the charges but were condemned to death for espionage. Many people believed that they were not leaders or spies, but victims caught up in the wave of anti-Communist frenzy. Appeals, public expressions of support, and pleas for clemency failed, however, and the couple was executed in June 1953.

Project Venona The American public hotly debated the guilt or innocence of individuals like the Rosenbergs who were accused as spies. There was, however, solid evidence of Soviet espionage, although very few Americans knew it at the time. In 1946 American cryptographers working for a project code-named "Venona" cracked the Soviet spy code of the time, enabling them to read approximately 3,000 messages between Moscow and the United States collected during the Cold War. The messages confirmed extensive Soviet spying and sent federal investigators on a massive hunt. To keep the Soviets

from learning how thoroughly the United States had penetrated their codes, authorities chose not to make the intercepted messages public. Not until 1995 did the government reveal Project Venona's existence. The Venona documents provided strong evidence that the Rosenbergs were guilty.

The Red Scare Spreads Following the federal government's example, many state and local governments, universities, businesses, unions, and churches began their own efforts to find Communists. The University of California required its 11,000 faculty members to take loyalty oaths and fired 157 who refused to do so. Many Catholic groups became strongly anti-Communist and urged their members to identify Communists within the church.

The Taft-Hartley Act required union leaders to take oaths that they were not Communists, but many union leaders did not object. Instead they launched their own efforts to purge Communists from their organizations. The president of the CIO called Communist sympathizers "skulking cowards" and "apostles of hate." The CIO eventually expelled 11 unions that refused to remove Communist leaders from their organization.

✔ **Reading Check** **Explaining** What was the purpose of the loyalty review boards and HUAC?

Red Channels, published in 1950, was prepared by three ex-FBI agents. The booklet claimed to identify 151 subversive entertainers in radio and television.

A number of well-known Hollywood celebrities, including actors Humphrey Bogart and Lauren Bacall (front row), went to Washington to protest HUAC's investigation of alleged Communists.

CHAPTER 13 The Cold War Begins **645**

S **Skill Practice**

Scaffolding—Evaluating Past Events Have students write two newspaper headlines about the execution of the Rosenbergs. Tell them that one headline should be from the point of view of someone who believes that the Rosenbergs were innocent of the charges, and the other should be from the point of view of someone who believes that the couple was guilty of espionage. **OL**
CA HR2; HI3

This **Historical Analysis** skill was introduced in Chapter 4.

R **Reading Strategy**

Summarizing Have students write a description of the growing Red Scare. Instruct them to include key issues, such as the efforts of government, universities, churches, and unions to find and punish suspected Communists. Each summary should be a page in length and students should be prepared to discuss their summary with the class. **OL**

Review the Big Idea

Review the Big Idea for this section, "Social and economic crises lead to new roles for government." Tell students to conduct library and Internet research on Project Venona. Each student should write a two-page paper on the use of spies to uncover traitors. **Ask:** Is this a good function for the government? *(Answers will vary.)* **AL**

✔ **Reading Check**

Answer: to check for Communists who might have infiltrated the government of the United States

Did You Know?

Many people, including Albert Einstein and Pope Pius XII, urged clemency for the Rosenbergs. Files released after the fall of the Soviet Union seem to indicate that the Rosenbergs were guilty. However, information based on a 1996 interview with David Greenglass, Ethel Rosenberg's brother, puts Ethel's guilt in doubt.

Answers and Additional Support

"A Conspiracy So Immense"

Main Idea The Red Scare intensified as Senator Joseph McCarthy presided over a Senate committee charged with exposing Communists in government.

Reading Connection Do you believe a person is innocent until proven guilty? Read on to discover how accusations alone could ruin a person's career during the era of McCarthyism.

In 1949 the Red Scare intensified even further. That year, the Soviet Union successfully tested an atomic bomb, and China fell to communism. To many Americans these events seemed to prove that the United States was losing the Cold War. Deeply concerned, they wanted an explanation as to why their government was failing. As a result, many continued to believe that Communists had infiltrated the government and remained undetected.

In February 1950, soon after Alger Hiss's perjury conviction, a little-known Wisconsin senator gave a political speech to a Republican women's group in West Virginia. Halfway through his speech, Senator Joseph R. McCarthy made a surprising statement:

▼ *George C. Marshall*

646   CHAPTER 13   The Cold War Begins

❝While I cannot take the time to name all the men in the State Department who have been named as members of the Communist Party and members of a spy ring, I have here in my hand a list of 205 that were known to the Secretary of State as being members of the Communist Party and who nevertheless are still working and shaping the policy of the State Department.❞

—quoted in *The Fifties*

By the next day, the Associated Press had picked up the statement and sent it to papers all over the country. When McCarthy arrived at the Denver airport, reporters crowded around him and asked to see his list of Communists in the state department. McCarthy replied that he would be happy to show them the list, but unfortunately, it was packed in his bag on the plane. In fact, the list never appeared. McCarthy, however, continued to make charges and draw attention.

McCarthy's Charges Born in 1908 near Appleton, Wisconsin, Joseph R. McCarthy studied law and served in World War II before his first run for the Senate. McCarthy's 1946 political campaign sounded the keynote of his career. Without making any specific charges or offering any proof, McCarthy accused his opponent, Robert M. La Follette, Jr., of being "communistically inclined." Fear of communism, plus McCarthy's intense speeches, won him the election.

After becoming a senator, McCarthy continued to proclaim that Communists were a danger both at home and abroad. To some of his audiences, he distributed a booklet called "The Party of Betrayal," which accused Democratic Party leaders of corruption and of protecting Communists. Secretary of State Dean Acheson was a frequent target. According to McCarthy, Acheson was incompetent and a tool of Stalin. He wildly accused George C. Marshall, the former army chief of staff and secretary of state, of disloyalty as a member of "a conspiracy so immense as to dwarf any previous such ventures in the history of man."

McCarthy was not alone in making such charges. In the prevailing mood of anxiety about communism, many Americans were ready to believe them.

The McCarran Internal Security Act In 1950, with the Korean War underway and McCarthy and others arousing fears of Communist spies, Congress passed the Internal Security Act, usually called the **McCarran Act.** Declaring that "world Communism has as its **sole** purpose the establishment of a totalitarian dictatorship in America," Senator Pat McCarran

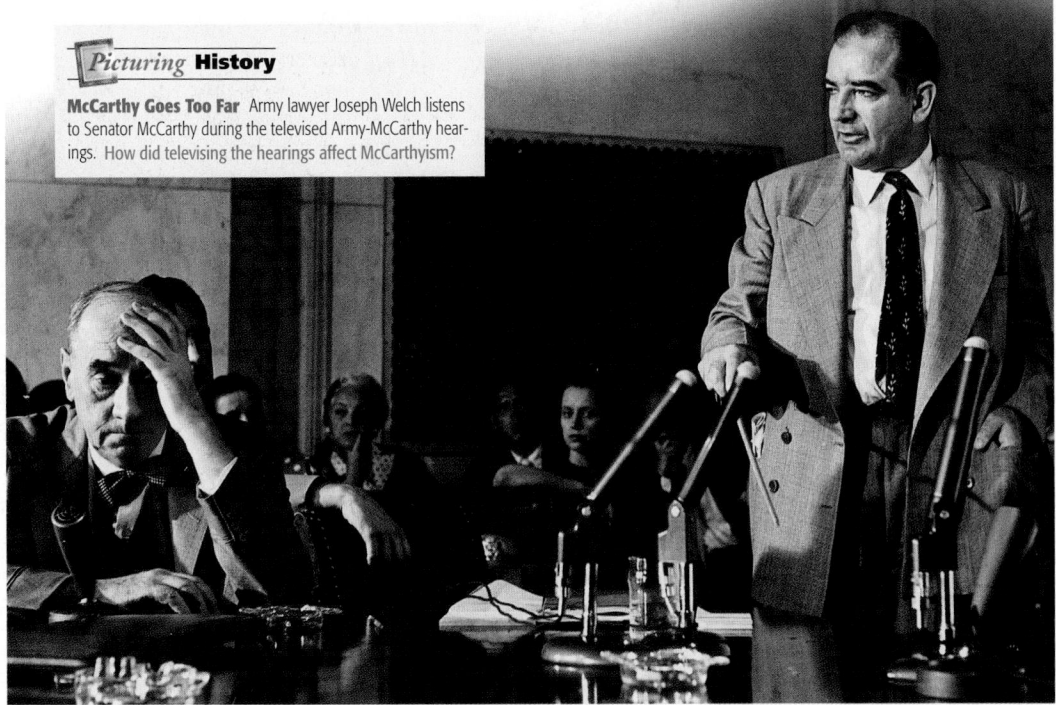

Picturing History

McCarthy Goes Too Far Army lawyer Joseph Welch listens to Senator McCarthy during the televised Army-McCarthy hearings. How did televising the hearings affect McCarthyism?

C **Critical Thinking**

Making Inferences The McCarthy era officially ended with McCarthy's death in 1957. In the end few spies were purged from the United States government. Yet for many people, the impact of McCarthy was felt for a lifetime. During the 1950s, many workers in a variety of industries lost their jobs because they were accused of having Communist sympathies. Although some of those accused probably were Communists, many others were not. **Ask: Why do you think that fellow workers might have been afraid to stand up for their friends?** *(for fear of being accused themselves)* **OL**

of Nevada offered a way to fight "treachery, infiltration, sabotage, and terrorism." The act made it illegal to "combine, conspire, or agree with any other person to perform any act which would substantially contribute to . . . the establishment of a totalitarian government." The law required all Communist Party and "Communist-front" organizations to register with the United States attorney general and publish their records. The act also created other restrictions for Communists. For example, they could not get passports to travel abroad.

The McCarran Act did not stop there. In case of a national emergency, it allowed the arrest and detention of Communists and Communist sympathizers. Unwilling to punish people for their opinions, Truman vetoed the bill, but Congress easily passed it over his veto in 1950. Later Supreme Court cases, however, ensured that the McCarran Act would never be very effective.

McCarthy's Tactics After the 1952 election gave the Republicans control of Congress, McCarthy became chairman of the Senate subcommittee on investigations. Using the power of his committee to force government officials to testify about alleged Communist influences, McCarthy turned the investigation into a witch hunt—a search for disloyalty

based on flimsy evidence and irrational fears. His tactic of damaging reputations with vague and unfounded charges became known as **McCarthyism**.

McCarthy's theatrics and sensational accusations drew the attention of the press, which put him in the headlines and quoted him widely. When he questioned witnesses, McCarthy would badger them and then refuse to accept their answers. His tactics left a cloud of suspicion that McCarthy and others interpreted as guilt. Furthermore, people were afraid to challenge him for fear of becoming targets themselves.

McCarthy's Downfall In 1954 McCarthy began to look for Soviet spies in the United States Army. Alerted to his intentions, the army conducted its own internal investigation and found no spies or any suspicion of espionage. Furious at the denial, McCarthy took his investigation onto television. He questioned and challenged officers in a harsh voice, harassing them about trivial details and accusing them of misconduct.

During weeks of televised Army McCarthy hearings in the spring of 1954, millions of Americans watched McCarthy bully witnesses. His popular support started to fade. Finally, to strike back at the army lawyer, Joseph Welch, McCarthy brought up

U₁ **Universal Access**

Special Education Have students draw political cartoons on the effect Senator Joseph McCarthy had on the American people. The cartoons should express a clear opinion about McCarthy's tactics. **BL**

U₂ **Universal Access**

Interpersonal Have interested students use library and Internet sources to find information on the Army-McCarthy hearings. Divide the class into pairs and ask each group to make a poster using headlines and sayings based on their research of the hearings. **OL**

CHAPTER 13 The Cold War Begins **647**

Did You Know?

Many Americans were afraid to challenge McCarthy. Even Dwight D. Eisenhower, running for president in 1952, did not speak out against him, though Eisenhower disliked McCarthy's tactics. Once he was elected president, he worked with congressional leaders to undermine McCarthy's authority.

Picturing History

Answer: Television drew national attention to the hearings. When people saw McCarthy's bullying tactics, the support for his accusations waned.
Ask: Who finally stood up to McCarthy?
(an army lawyer named Joseph Welch)

Visual Literacy Ask students to examine the Cold War era images on this page. **Ask: What fears help define the era we now live in?** *(Answers will vary.)* Tell students to create a photo collage illustrating their answer. **OL**

CA CS1

R **Reading Strategy**

Organizing Information In 1945 the United States exploded the first atomic bomb in New Mexico. The Soviet Union tested its first atomic bomb in 1949. Ask students to make a chart that includes all the countries that have developed nuclear weapons since 1945. The chart should include the name of each country and the year that each nation conducted its first successful nuclear test. **OL**

✓ **Reading Check**

Answer: It ruined many careers, colored political life, and influenced popular culture.

Answers and Additional Support

Picturing **History**

Signs of the Times During the Cold War, the media often gave survival tips for the nuclear holocaust many saw just around the corner. At right, a California resident works on his fallout shelter. How did such fears affect American politics?

the past of a young lawyer in Welch's firm who had been a member of a Communist-front organization during his law school years. Welch, who was fully aware of the young man's past, now exploded at McCarthy for possibly ruining the young man's career: "Until this moment, I think I never really gauged your cruelty or your recklessness. . . .You have done enough. Have you no sense of decency, sir, at long last? Have you left no sense of decency?"

Spectators cheered. Welch had said aloud what many Americans had been thinking. One senator on the committee, Stuart Symington of Missouri, was also repelled: "The American people have had a look at you for six weeks. You are not fooling anyone." McCarthy had lost the power to arouse fear. Newspaper headlines repeated, "Have you no sense of decency?"

Later that year, the Senate passed a vote of **censure,** or formal disapproval, against McCarthy—one of the most serious criticisms it can level against a member. His influence gone, McCarthy faded from public view. Although he remained in the Senate, he had little influence. He died in 1957, a broken and embittered man.

✓ **Reading Check** **Evaluating** What were the effects of McCarthyism?

Life During the Early Cold War

Main Idea Fear of nuclear attack and of communism dominated American popular culture during the early Cold War years.

Reading Connection How was popular culture and life in the 1950s different from today? Read on to find out what people were watching and reading during the Cold War.

The Red Scare and the spread of **nuclear** weapons had a profound impact on life in the 1950s. Fear of communism and of nuclear war dominated life for ordinary Americans as well as for government leaders throughout the era.

R

Facing the Bomb Already upset by the first Soviet atomic test in 1949, Americans were shocked when the USSR again successfully tested the much more powerful hydrogen bomb, or H-bomb, in 1953. This was less than a year after the United States had tested its own H-bomb.

Americans prepared for a surprise Soviet attack. Schools set aside special areas as bomb shelters. In bomb drills, students learned to duck under their

Resources for page 648

Have students learn more about 1950s society by assigning

📂 **Primary Source Readings 13-3**

📂 **Moments in Time, Unit 9: The Cold War (1947–1962)**

Picturing **History**

Answer: led to HUAC, the McCarran Act, and increased concern with national defense
Ask: What kinds of things were in the "survival kit" that is displayed in this illustration? *(bottled water, first aid kit, flashlights, canned food)*

desks, turn away from the windows, and cover their heads with their hands. These "duck-and-cover" actions were supposed to protect them from a nuclear bomb blast.

"Duck-and-cover" might have made people feel safe, but it would not have protected them from deadly nuclear radiation. According to experts, for every person killed outright by a nuclear blast, four more would die later from **fallout,** the radiation left over after a blast. To protect themselves, some families built backyard **fallout shelters** and stocked them with canned food.

Popular Culture in the Cold War Worries about nuclear war and Communist infiltration filled people's imaginations. Cold War nightmares soon appeared in films and popular fiction.

Matt Cvetic was an FBI undercover informant who secretly infiltrated the Communist Party in Pittsburgh. His story captivated magazine readers in the *Saturday Evening Post* in 1950 and came to the screen the next year as *I Was a Communist for the FBI*. Another suspense film, *Walk East on Beacon* (1951), features the FBI's activities in an espionage case. In 1953 television took up the theme with a series about an undercover FBI counterspy who was also a Communist Party official. Each week, *I Led Three Lives* kept television viewers on edge.

In 1954 author Philip Wylie published *Tomorrow!* This novel describes the horrific effects of nuclear war on an unprepared American city. As an adviser on civil defense, Wylie had failed to convince the federal government to play a strong role in building bomb shelters. Frustrated, he wrote this novel to educate the public about the horrors of atomic war.

▲ *Students practice a "duck and cover" bomb drill.*

At the same time these fears were haunting Americans, the country was enjoying postwar prosperity and optimism. That spirit, combined with McCarthyism, witch hunts, fears of Communist infiltration, and the threat of atomic attack, made the early 1950s a time of contrasts. As the 1952 election approached, Americans were looking for someone or something that would make them feel secure.

 Reading Check **Describing** How did the Cold War affect life in the 1950s?

HISTORY Online **Study Central**

For help with the concepts in this section of *American Vision: Modern Times* go to tav.mt.glencoe.com and click on *Study Central.*

SECTION 3 ASSESSMENT

Checking for Understanding

1. **Vocabulary** Define: subversion, confirm, perjury, sole, censure, nuclear, fallout, fallout shelter.
2. **People and Terms** Identify: loyalty review program, Alger Hiss, McCarran Act, McCarthyism.
3. **Explain** the goals of Project Venona.
4. **Review Facts** What did the McCarran Act propose to do?

Reviewing Big Ideas

5. **Describing** How did McCarthyism and the Red Scare change American society and government?

Critical Thinking

6. **Historical Analysis** **Interpreting** Why did McCarthy initially receive a lot of support for his efforts to expose Communists? **CA HI3**
7. **Organizing** Use a graphic organizer to list the causes and effects of the new Red Scare.

Causes   Effects

Red Scare

Analyzing Visuals

8. **Analyzing Photographs** Study the photograph on page 647 of the Army-McCarthy hearings. From their postures, how would you describe the attitude of army lawyer Joseph Welch toward Senator Joseph McCarthy? Do you think Welch respects McCarthy's presentation?

Writing About History

9. **Persuasive Writing** Imagine you are a newspaper editor during the McCarthy hearings. Write an editorial supporting or condemning Senator McCarthy. Defend your position. **CA 11WS1.1; 11WS2.3a**

CHAPTER 13 The Cold War Begins **649**

SECTION 3 ASSESSMENT ANSWERS

1. Content vocabulary is boldfaced and highlighted in yellow. Academic vocabulary is boldfaced.
2. loyalty review program *(p. 643),* Alger Hiss *(p. 644),* McCarran Act *(p. 646),* McCarthyism *(p. 647)*
3. to crack the Soviet spy code, and confirm Soviet spying
4. to make it illegal to associate with or be a Communist
5. While people were enjoying postwar prosperity and optimism, they feared communism and an atomic attack.
6. People feared communism.
7. Causes: Gouzenko case, Alger Hiss trial, Rosenbergs, Russia's successful test of an atomic bomb; Effects: Loyalty Review Program, HUAC, McCarran Act, McCarthyism, fallout shelters, etc.
8. Students might suggest disgust or annoyance.
9. Students' editorials will vary. Editorials should address the tactics McCarthy used and express a clear point of view.

FOCUS

BELLRINGER
SKILLBUILDER ACTIVITY

Project **Daily Focus Skills Transparency 13-4** and have students answer the question.

Guide to Reading

Understanding Vocabulary:
Have students choose two of the content vocabulary terms and use them in a sentence.

Answers to Graphic:
brinksmanship, covert action, massive retaliation

Unpacking the Standards

Students will be able to:

- Describe President Eisenhower's plans to revamp the U.S. military.

- Explain Eisenhower's diplomatic strategy of brinksmanship.

- Evaluate the American efforts to continue containing Communist growth around the world.

- Analyze the tensions that remained between the Soviet Union and the United States.

Answers and Additional Support

SECTION 4 Eisenhower's Policies

Guide to Reading

Connection
In the previous section, you learned how the Cold War led to a new Red Scare in the United States. In this section, you will read about President Eisenhower's response to the Cold War.

Main Idea

- Eisenhower advocated a policy of massive strength to combat Communist influence. (p. 651)
- Although he ended the Korean War as he had promised, President Eisenhower faced new foreign policy challenges as Cold War tensions rose. (p. 652)
- President Eisenhower used the Central Intelligence Agency to remove anti-American leaders and to fight Communist takeovers. (p. 654)

- Despite attempts to cooperate, tensions remained high between the Soviet and American heads of state. (p. 656)

Content Vocabulary
massive retaliation, brinkmanship, covert, developing nation, military-industrial complex

Academic Vocabulary
dominant, estate, imply

People and Terms to Identify
Sputnik, Central Intelligence Agency

Reading Objectives
- **Evaluate** Eisenhower's military policy known as the "New Look."

- **Debate** the effectiveness of Eisenhower's foreign policy.

Reading Strategy
Organizing As you read about Eisenhower's presidency, complete a graphic organizer similar to the one below by filling in aspects of Eisenhower's "New Look."

Eisenhower's "New Look"

Preview of Events

◆1952	◆1955	◆1958	◆1961

July 1953
Armistice in Korean War

October 1956
Hungarian revolution

October 1956
Suez Canal crisis

October 4, 1957
Soviet Union launches Sputnik

May 1960
U-2 incident

The following are the main History–Social Science Standards covered in this section.

11.8.4 Analyze new federal government spending on defense, welfare, interest on the national debt, and federal and state spending on education, including the California Master Plan.

11.8.5 Describe the increased powers of the presidency in response to the Great Depression, World War II, and the Cold War.

11.8.7 Describe the effects on society and the economy of technological developments since 1945, including the computer revolution, changes in communication, advances in medicine, and improvements in agricultural technology.

11.9.2 Understand the role of military alliances, including NATO and SEATO, in deterring communist aggression and maintaining security during the Cold War.

11.9.3 Trace the origins and geopolitical consequences (foreign and domestic) of the Cold War and containment policy, including the following: the era of McCarthyism, instances of domestic

Communism (e.g., Alger Hiss) and blacklisting; the Truman Doctrine; the Berlin Blockade; the Korean War; the Bay of Pigs invasion and the Cuban Missile Crisis; atomic testing in the American West, the "mutual assured destruction" doctrine, and disarmament policies; the Vietnam War; Latin American policy.

✦ The Big Idea ✦

The fate of nations is forever changed by monumental world events. Upon taking office, President Eisenhower focused on strengthening the nation's economy. He cut millions in defense spending by developing a new defense policy called massive retaliation, which threatened the use of nuclear weapons to fight communism. Congress reacted to the Soviet development of a space satellite with the creation of a space agency and increased funding for education. In the meantime, Eisenhower put his new foreign policy approach of brinkmanship into action to end the war in Korea and to deal with crises in Taiwan and the Suez Canal. He also approved covert operations to contain and fight communism in developing nations. A failed uprising in Hungary further increased tensions.

11.9.4 List the effects of foreign policy on domestic policies and vice versa (e.g., protests during the war in Vietnam, the "nuclear freeze" movement).

11.9.6 Describe U.S. Middle East policy and its strategic, political, and economic interests, including those related to the Gulf War.

650 CHAPTER 13 The Cold War Begins

📖 SECTION RESOURCES

📂 Print Material
- Reproducible Lesson Plan 13-4
- Guided Reading Activity 13-4
- Reading Essentials and Study Guide 13-4
- Active Reading Note-Taking Guide 13-4

📋 Transparencies
- Daily Focus Skills Transparency 13-4
- Section Graphic Organizer Transparency 13-4

Technology
- 🖲 Interactive Tutor Self-Assessment CD-ROM
- 🖲 Exam*View*® Pro Testmaker CD-ROM
- 🖲 Presentation Plus! CD-ROM

Eisenhower's "New Look"

Main Idea Eisenhower advocated a policy of massive strength to combat Communist influence.

Reading Connection What are your school's requirements in math and sciences? Read on to discover how Americans came to emphasize education in the sciences.

By late 1959, the United States and the Soviet Union were in the beginning stages of decreasing tension between the two countries. This progress halted, however, when the Soviet Union shot down a U.S. spy plane flying over Russian territory.

★ An American Story ★

On May 1, 1960, CIA pilot Francis Gary Powers sat in the cockpit of his U-2 spy plane, flying at more than 60,000 feet over Afghanistan. His mission was to fly over suspected Soviet missile bases and photograph them.

As Powers passed over the forbidden border into the Soviet Union, he felt a familiar thrill. "There was no abrupt change in topography," he remembered, "yet the moment you crossed the border, you sensed the difference.... Knowing there were people who would shoot you down if they could created a strange tension.... I wondered how the Russians felt, knowing I was up here, unable to do anything about it.... I could imagine their frustration and rage."

Suddenly, Powers heard a dull thump. A surface-to-air missile exploded nearby in a flash of orange. The plane's wings snapped off, leaving the spinning aircraft plummeting down towards the earth. Powers screamed, "I've had it now!"

The downing of Powers's plane set off one of the major confrontations of the Cold War during the presidency of Dwight D. Eisenhower.

—adapted from *May-Day: The U-2 Affair*

At the end of 1952, eight years prior to the downing of Francis Gary Powers's plane, many Americans were ready for a change in leadership. The Cold War had much to do with that attitude. Many Americans believed that Truman's foreign policy was not working. The Soviet Union had acquired the atomic bomb and consolidated its hold on Eastern Europe. China

had fallen to communism, and American troops had been sent across the Pacific to fight in the Korean War.

Tired of the criticism and uncertain he could win, Truman decided not to run again. The Democrats nominated Adlai Stevenson, governor of Illinois. The Republicans chose Dwight D. Eisenhower, the general who had organized the D-Day invasion.

Despite Stevenson's charming personality and skilled speech making, he had no chance against a national hero who had helped win World War II. Americans were looking for someone they could trust to lead the nation in its Cold War struggle against communism. Eisenhower won in a landslide.

"More Bang for the Buck" The Cold War shaped Eisenhower's thinking from the moment he took office. Eisenhower was convinced that the key to victory in the Cold War was not simply military might but also a strong economy. The United States had to show the world that free enterprise could produce the most prosperous society. At the same time, economic prosperity would prevent Communists from gaining support in the United States.

As a professional soldier, Eisenhower knew the costs associated with large-scale conventional war. Preparing for that kind of warfare, he believed, would cost far too much money. "We cannot defend the nation in a way which will exhaust our economy," Eisenhower declared. A "New Look" in defense policy was needed. Instead of maintaining a

▼ *Francis Gary Powers*

651

Did You Know?

Francis Gary Powers was held in a Russian prison until he was exchanged for a Russian spy. Afterward he flew a helicopter for a Los Angeles TV station. He died in August 1977 in a helicopter crash and is buried in Arlington National Cemetery.

TEACH

Review the Big Idea

Review the Big Idea for this section, "The fate of nations is forever changed by monumental world events." Divide the class into groups of five and ask each group to agree or disagree with the text's assertion that the U-2 spy plane incident reversed a period of U.S. and Soviet cooperation. Ask a member of each group to explain the group's opinion. **OL** **CA** 11RC2.4; 11RL3.2

R₁ Reading Strategy

Scaffolding–Academic Vocabulary The word *prior* was introduced in Chapter 3, Section 1. Ask a student to define the word. **BL**

R₂ Reading Strategy

Outlining Have students create outlines illustrating Eisenhower's role in World War II. **Ask:** How did Eisenhower's participation in World War II help him win the presidency? (*The American people trusted Eisenhower because of his successful leadership role during the war.*) **OL**

U Universal Access

English Learners Help students understand the meaning of the phrase "landslide victory" by having them use a dictionary to find the definition of *landslide*. Discuss landslides as a geographical phenomenon. Ask students to theorize how this information can be applied to describing the outcome of an election. **EL**

Drawing Conclusions Have each student make a two-column chart. One column should list the advantages of Eisenhower's policy of massive retaliation. The other column should list the disadvantages. *(advantages: avoids traditional wars, decreases military spending; disadvantages: massive civilian loss of life)* Ask students to use their charts to write a paragraph explaining whether or not they agree with the policy of massive retaliation. **OL**

CA 11WS1.3

U **Universal Access**

Visual/Spatial Organize the class into groups of three or four. Have each group plan and prepare a poster explaining Eisenhower's approach to the Sputnik crisis. Have the groups display their posters and then discuss the ways in which Eisenhower changed military priorities. **OL**

R **Reading Strategy**

Scaffolding–Academic Vocabulary The word *apparent* was introduced in Chapter 10, Section 1. Ask a student to define the word. **BL**

✓**Reading Check**

Answer: He cut military spending while increasing America's nuclear arsenal.

Answers and Additional Support

"So Russia Launched a Satellite, but Has It Made Cars With Fins Yet?"

Analyzing *Political Cartoons*

Cold War Worries The speaker here is comparing American prosperity with the Soviets' launching of *Sputnik.* What is the cartoonist's intent?

large and expensive army, the nation "must be prepared to use atomic weapons in all forms." Nuclear weapons, he said, gave "more bang for the buck."

Massive Retaliation The Korean War had convinced Eisenhower that the United States could not contain communism by fighting a series of small wars. Such wars were unpopular and too expensive. Instead, they had to be prevented from happening in the first place. The best way to do that seemed to be to threaten to use nuclear weapons if a Communist state tried to seize territory by force. This policy came to be called **massive retaliation.**

The new policy enabled Eisenhower to cut military spending from $50 billion to $34 billion. He did this by cutting back the army, which required a lot of money to maintain. At the same time, he increased America's nuclear arsenal from about 1,000 bombs in 1953 to about 18,000 bombs in 1961.

The *Sputnik* **Crisis** The New Look's emphasis on nuclear weapons required new technology to deliver them. In 1955 the air force unveiled the huge B-52 bomber, which was designed to fly across continents and drop nuclear bombs anywhere in the world.

Because bombers could be shot down, Eisenhower also began development of intercontinental ballistic missiles (ICBMs) that could deliver bombs anywhere in the world. He also began a program to build submarines capable of launching nuclear missiles.

As the United States began to develop long-range nuclear missiles, Americans were stunned to discover the Soviet Union had already developed their own. On October 4, 1957, the Soviets launched *Sputnik,* the first artificial satellite to orbit the earth. This technological triumph alarmed Americans, who took it as a sign that the United States was falling behind the Soviet Union in missile technology.

Eisenhower insisted he was not worried just because the Soviets "put one small ball into the air." Members of Congress, on the other hand, feared the nation was falling behind in scientific research. The following year, Congress created the National Aeronautics and Space Administration (NASA) to coordinate research in rocket science and space exploration. It also passed the National Defense Education Act (NDEA), which provided funds for education and training in science, math, and foreign languages.

✓**Reading Check** **Summarizing** How did Eisenhower alter the nature of defense spending?

Brinkmanship In Action

Main Idea **Although he ended the Korean War as he had promised, President Eisenhower faced new foreign policy challenges as Cold War tensions rose.**

Reading Connection Do you think the United States should ever use nuclear weapons to carry out foreign policy? Read on to learn how President Eisenhower used the threat of nuclear force during his first term.

President Eisenhower's apparent willingness to threaten nuclear war to maintain the peace worried some people. Secretary of State John Foster Dulles, however, the **dominant** figure in the nation's foreign policy in the 1950s, strongly defended the policy:

❝You have to take chances for peace, just as you must take chances in war. Some say that we were brought to the verge of war. Of course we were brought to the verge of war. The ability to get to the verge without getting into the war is the necessary art. . . . If you try to run away from it, if you are scared to go to the brink, you are lost. We've had to look it square in the face. . . . We walked to the brink and we looked it in the face. We took strong action.❞

—quoted in *Rise to Globalism*

Did You Know?

Sputnik, the name of the Soviet satellite, started its own language trend, as words gained a *-nik* ending for a foreign-sounding effect. For example, *beatnik* described a young person influenced by the style of Beat writers such as Jack Kerouac and Allen Ginsberg, and *peacenik* was used to describe a peace activist.

Analyzing *Political Cartoons*

Answer: The cartoonist is conveying anxiety in an ironic manner—the United States has built fancy consumer goods, but it is behind in space technology.

Ask: Do you think the cartoonist would have supported Eisenhower's defense plans? *(The cartoonist likely would have supported his plans.)*

Critics called this **brinkmanship**—the willingness to go to the brink of war to force the other side to back down—and argued that it was too dangerous. Several times, however, President Eisenhower felt compelled to threaten nuclear war during a crisis.

The Korean War Ends

During his campaign for the presidency, Eisenhower had said, "I shall go to Korea," promising to end the costly and increasingly unpopular war. On December 4, 1952, just weeks after his election, he kept his promise. Bundled against the freezing Korean winter, the president-elect talked with frontline commanders and their troops.

Eisenhower became convinced that the ongoing battle was costing too many lives and bringing too few victories. "Small attacks on small hills," the former general declared, "[will] not end this war." The president then quietly let the Chinese know that the United States might continue the Korean War "under circumstances of our own choosing"—a hint at nuclear attack.

The threat to go to the brink of nuclear war seemed to work. In July 1953, negotiators signed an armistice. The battle line between the two sides, which was very near the prewar boundary, became the border between North Korea and South Korea. A "demilitarized zone" (DMZ) separated them. There was no victory, but the war had at least stopped the spread of communism in Korea—the goal of containment. American troops are still based in Korea, helping South Korea defend its border.

The Taiwan Crisis

Shortly after the war ended, a new crisis erupted in Asia. Although the Chinese Communists had taken power in mainland China, the Chinese Nationalists still controlled Taiwan and several small islands along China's coast.

In the fall of 1954, China threatened to seize two of the islands from the Nationalists. Eisenhower saw Taiwan as part of the "anticommunist barrier" in Asia. When China began shelling the islands and announced that Taiwan would soon be liberated, Eisenhower asked Congress to authorize the use of force to defend Taiwan.

Eisenhower then warned the Chinese that any attempt to invade Taiwan would be resisted by American naval forces stationed nearby. He and Dulles hinted that they would use nuclear weapons to stop an invasion. Soon afterward, China backed down.

TECHNOLOGY & History

The Hydrogen Bomb

The atomic bomb dropped on Hiroshima in 1945 had an explosive force of 20,000 tons of TNT. As devastating as that bomb was, the hydrogen bomb was exponentially more powerful. Designed by Edward Teller and Stanislaw Ulam, the hydrogen test bomb, nicknamed "Mike," was first detonated on November 1, 1952. Its explosive force was equal to 10 million tons of TNT. **How did the two explosive devices combine to create an explosion?**

1 The **plutonium core** provides the radiation from plutonium essential for a fusion reaction.

High explosive charges

uranium shield

Plutonium 239

2 The **primary device** sets off a smaller atomic explosion that creates x-ray radiation pressure.

3 In the **secondary device**, the fusion process begins when pressure builds inside the bomb casing from the release of radiation.

CHAPTER 13 The Cold War Begins **653**

Universal Access

Advanced Learners Have students write and present a verse that either supports or opposes the concept of brinkmanship. Encourage students to examine different styles of poetry before writing their verse. Have volunteers present their verses to the class and have the class identify whether they express support or opposition for brinkmanship. **AL**
CA 11RL3.4

Universal Access

Logical/Mathematical The estimated number of civilian casualties caused by the Hiroshima atomic bomb was 80,000 to 120,000. Tell students to use this information and the data in the Technology & History feature to calculate the potential loss of life from the hydrogen bomb "Mike." *("Mike" had an explosive force 500 times greater than the bomb dropped on Hiroshima. Thus, 500 times more people would have been killed. Answer: 40 million to 60 million casualties)* **OL**

Critical Thinking

Identifying Central Issues Have students work in teams to prepare 30-minute special news reports about the 1954 Taiwan Crisis. Divide them into groups of five students, and tell each group to organize itself into a team, including a segment producer, researchers, and writers. Ask for volunteers from each group to present their report. **AL**

Resources for page 653

*Have students read more about the history of nuclear weapons in the **Linking Past and Present Activity 13**.*

TECHNOLOGY & History

Background: The Soviets also had a highly secret program to create a hydrogen bomb. A famous Orthodox monastery housed the design team, which successfully tested the Soviet hydrogen bomb on August 12, 1953.
Answer: The primary device sets off a smaller atomic explosion, creating x-ray radiation pressure. The secondary device creates the fusion process when pressure from the first device builds inside the bomb casing.
Ask: Why did Eisenhower favor nuclear weapons? *(He believed the cost to fight a conventional war was too great; having nuclear weapons would create sufficient threat to deter war and be more cost efficient.)*

Picturing History

Distinguished Brothers John Foster Dulles (right) became secretary of state under Eisenhower; his brother Allen Dulles (center) was director of the CIA in the 1950s. With what policy is John Foster Dulles associated?

R **The Suez Crisis** The year after Eisenhower went to the brink of war with China, a serious crisis erupted in the Middle East. Eisenhower's goal in the Middle East was to prevent Arab nations from aligning with the Soviet Union. To build support among Arabs, Dulles offered to help Egypt finance the construction of a dam on the Nile River. The Egyptians eagerly accepted the American offer.

The deal ran into trouble in Congress, however, because Egypt had bought weapons from Communist Czechoslovakia. Dulles was forced to withdraw the offer. A week later, Egyptian troops seized control of the Suez Canal from the Anglo-French company that had controlled it. The Egyptians intended to use the canal's profits to pay for the dam.

The British and French responded quickly to the Suez Crisis. In October 1956, British and French troops invaded Egypt. Eisenhower was furious with Britain and France. He declared they had made a "complete mess and botch of things." The situation

654   CHAPTER 13   The Cold War Begins

became even more tense when the Soviet Union threatened rocket attacks on Britain and France and offered to send troops to help Egypt. Eisenhower immediately put American nuclear forces on alert, noting, "If those fellows start something, we may have to hit them— and if necessary, with everything in the bucket."

Under strong American pressure, the British and French called off their invasion. The Soviet Union had won a major diplomatic victory, however, by supporting Egypt. Soon afterward, other Arab nations began accepting Soviet aid as well.

✓**Reading Check** **Identifying** What was brinkmanship?

Fighting Communism Covertly

Main Idea President Eisenhower used the Central Intelligence Agency to remove anti-American leaders and to fight Communist takeovers.

Reading Connection Do you know anyone who has worked for a government agency? Read on to learn about the CIA's beginnings.

President Eisenhower relied on brinkmanship on several occasions, but he knew it could not work in all situations. It could prevent war, but it could not, for example, prevent Communists from staging revolutions within countries. To prevent Communist uprisings in other countries, Eisenhower decided to use **covert,** or hidden, operations conducted by the **Central Intelligence Agency** (CIA).

Containment in Developing Nations Many of the CIA's operations took place in **developing nations**—nations with primarily agricultural economies. Many of these countries blamed European imperialism and American capitalism for their problems. Their leaders looked to the Soviet Union as a model of how to industrialize their countries. They often threatened to nationalize, or put under government control, foreign businesses operating in their countries.

American officials feared that these leaders might align their nations with the Soviet Union or even stage a Communist revolution. One way to stop developing nations from moving into the Communist camp was to provide them with financial aid, as Eisenhower had tried to do in Egypt. In some cases, however, where the threat of communism seemed stronger, the CIA staged covert operations to overthrow anti-American leaders and replace them with pro-American leaders.

Iran and Guatemala Two examples of covert operations that achieved American objectives took place in Iran and Guatemala. By 1953 Iranian Prime Minister Mohammed Mossadegh had already nationalized the Anglo-Iranian Oil Company. He seemed ready to make an oil deal with the Soviet Union. In 1953 Mossadegh moved against the pro-American Shah of Iran, who was temporarily forced into exile. Dulles quickly sent agents to organize street riots and arrange a coup that ousted Mossadegh, and the Shah returned to power.

The following year, the CIA acted to protect American-owned property in Guatemala. In 1951 Jacobo Arbenz Guzmán won election as president of Guatemala with Communist support. His land reform program took over large **estates,** including those of the American-owned United Fruit Company. In May 1954, Communist Czechoslovakia delivered arms to Guatemala. The CIA responded by arming the Guatemalan opposition and training them at secret camps in Nicaragua and Honduras. Shortly after these CIA-trained forces invaded Guatemala, Arbenz Guzmán left office.

Uprising in Hungary Covert operations did not always work as Eisenhower hoped. In 1953 Stalin died, and a power struggle began in the Soviet Union. Immediately following Stalin's death, several high-ranking officials worked together to serve as Stalin's replacement. This joint leadership, however, lasted for only a brief period before a struggle for sole leadership of the Soviet Union ensued. By 1956 Nikita Khrushchev had emerged as the leader of the Soviet Union. That year, Khrushchev delivered a secret speech to Soviet leaders. He attacked Stalin's policies and insisted there were many ways to build a Communist society. Although the speech was secret, the CIA obtained a copy. With Eisenhower's permission, the CIA arranged for it to be broadcast to Eastern Europe in an effort to undermine Communist rule.

Many Eastern Europeans had long been frustrated with Communist rule. Hearing Khrushchev's speech further discredited communism and increased the frustrations of many people. In June 1956, riots erupted in Eastern Europe. By late October, a full scale uprising had begun in Hungary. Although Khrushchev was willing to tolerate greater freedom in Eastern Europe, he had never meant to **imply** that the Soviets would tolerate an end to communism in

▼ *Russian tanks patrol a street in Budapest, Hungary, following an attemped revolt*

C **Critical Thinking**

Evaluating Action The overthrow of the leftist Guatemalan government was made possible by the activities of the Central Intelligence Agency. **Ask: Is secret aggression, such as that performed here by the CIA, justifiable? Why or why not? What events in your lifetime have helped shape your opinion?** *(Students' answers and examples will vary.)* **AL**

S **Skill Practice**

Conducting Research Invite interested students to research the leadership struggle that took place in the Soviet Union immediately after the death of Stalin in 1953. Have students create a two-column chart listing the main players in the power struggle (including Nikita Khrushchev) and their roles. Invite students to share their charts with the class. **OL** **CA** HI2; HI4

U **Universal Access**

Advanced Learners Have interested students research the social, cultural, and historical factors that affected the Hungarians' reaction to Communist control. Encourage students to use library and Internet resources to gather their research information, and tell them to write a two-page paper presenting their findings. **AL**

Did You Know?

Many people in Iran resented the Shah's close ties with the West. Their anger at the Shah's attachment to Western ideas and customs helped fuel the 1979 revolt against him. Mohammed Reza Shah Pahlavi died in exile in 1980.

Eastern Europe. Soon after the uprising began, Soviet tanks rolled into Budapest, the capital of Hungary, and crushed the rebellion.

✓ **Reading Check** **Explaining** Why did Eisenhower use covert operations?

Continuing Tensions

Main Idea Despite attempts to cooperate, tensions remained high between the Soviet and American heads of state.

Reading Connection Have you ever been involved in successful conflict resolution? Read on to discover efforts at peaceful resolution of differences between capitalist and Communist countries.

W The uprising in Hungary forced Khrushchev to reassert Soviet power and the superiority of communism. Previously, he had supported "peaceful coexistence" with capitalism. Now he accused the "capitalist countries" of starting a "feverish arms **W** race." In 1957, after the launch of Sputnik, Khrushchev boasted, "We will bury capitalism. . . . Your grandchildren will live under communism."

In late 1958 Khrushchev demanded that the United States, Great Britain, and France withdraw their troops from West Berlin. United States Secretary of State John Dulles rejected Khrushchev's demands. If the Soviets threatened Berlin, Dulles announced, NATO would respond, "if need be by military force." Brinkmanship worked again, and Khrushchev backed down.

In an effort to improve relations between the United States and the Soviet Union, Eisenhower **R** invited Khrushchev to visit the United States in late 1959. The visit went well, and the two leaders agreed to hold a summit in Paris in 1960. A summit is a formal face-to-face meeting of leaders from different countries to discuss important issues.

Shortly before the summit was to begin, the Soviet Union shot down the American U-2 spy plane piloted by Francis Gary Powers. At first, Eisenhower

Breakdown in Relations

In 1959 Premier Khrushchev visited several cities in the United States and met with President Eisenhower. The two leaders agreed to a summit in Paris the following year. About two weeks before the summit, the Soviets shot down an American U-2 spy plane over their territory. Eisenhower, believing that pilot Francis Gary Powers was dead, at first denied the allegations but then took responsibility for this and other flights. Khrushchev was not satisfied with the apology and left Paris before the summit started. He also withdrew an invitation to Eisenhower to visit the Soviet Union.

656 CHAPTER 13 The Cold War Begins

> "I confess I lay down my official responsibility in this field with a definite sense of disappointment. . . . I wish I could say that a lasting peace is in sight."
>
> —*President Dwight D. Eisenhower*

claimed that the aircraft was a weather plane that had strayed off course. Then Khrushchev dramatically produced the pilot. Eisenhower refused to apologize, saying the flights had protected American security. In response, Khrushchev broke up the summit.

In this climate of heightened tension, President Eisenhower prepared to leave office. In January 1961, he delivered a farewell address to the nation. In the address, he pointed out that a new relationship had developed between the military establishment and the defense industry. He warned Americans to be on guard against the immense influence of this **military-industrial complex** in a democracy. Although he had avoided war and kept communism contained, Eisenhower admitted to some frustration that a lasting peace had not been obtained.

☑ Reading Check **Evaluating** Why did Eisenhower warn Americans about the military-industrial complex?

Picturing History

President Eisenhower Leaves Office Eisenhower left the White House amid heightened tensions and failed peace efforts with the Soviet Union. Why do you think Eisenhower was frustrated that a lasting peace with the Soviet Union had not been obtained?

HISTORY Online — Study Central

For help with the concepts in this section of *American Vision: Modern Times* go to tav.mt.glencoe.com and click on *Study Central.*

SECTION 4 ASSESSMENT

Checking for Understanding

1. **Vocabulary** Define: massive retaliation, dominant, brinkmanship, covert, developing nation, estate, imply, military-industrial complex.

2. **People and Terms** Identify: *Sputnik,* Central Intelligence Agency.

3. **Summarize** What was the significance of the Soviet Union's launching of *Sputnik* in 1957?

Reviewing Big Ideas

4. **Explaining** How did technology shape Eisenhower's military policy?

Critical Thinking

5. **Interpreting** Do you think Eisenhower's foreign policy was successful? Why or why not?

6. **Organizing** Use a graphic organizer similar to the one below to list Eisenhower's strategies for containing communism.

Strategies for Containing Communism

Analyzing Visuals

7. **Analyzing Photographs** Study the photograph on page 655. Do you think the streets of Budapest are usually this empty? What effect might the tanks have had on the residents?

Writing About History

8. **Persuasive Writing** Imagine you are a member of Eisenhower's cabinet. Defend or attack brinkmanship as a foreign policy tactic. Be sure to provide specific reasons for your point of view. **CA 11WA2.2c**

CHAPTER 13   The Cold War Begins   **657**

ASSESS

Resources for page 657

Use these resources to assess student mastery.

📁 Section Quiz 13-4

📁 Reading Essentials and Study Guide 13-4

💿 Interactive Tutor Self-Assessment CD-ROM

📁 California Standards Practice, Grade 11

Picturing History

Answer: He wanted to leave U.S. relations with the Soviet Union better than when he began his presidential term.

☑ Reading Check

Answer: He thought that a military-industrial complex could threaten democracy.

HISTORY Online

Study Central provides audio summaries, interactive games, and online graphic organizers to help students review section content.

CLOSE

Evaluating Have students debate the effectiveness of Eisenhower's foreign policy. **OL**

657

FOCUS

History–Social Science Standards

This feature addresses the following standard:

11.9.3 Trace the origins and geopolitical consequences (foreign and domestic) of the Cold War and containment policy, including the following: the era of McCarthyism, instances of domestic Communism (e.g., Alger Hiss) and blacklisting; the Truman Doctrine; the Berlin Blockade; the Korean War; the Bay of Pigs Invasion and the Cuban Missile Crisis; atomic testing in the American West, the "mutual assured destruction" doctrine, and disarmament policies; the Vietnam War; Latin American policy.

Understanding Vocabulary

Before students begin reading, point out that difficult or unfamiliar words are footnoted throughout the text.

TEACH

C Critical Thinking

Identifying Central Issues Ask students to consider the following question: **Why would Republicans use the issue of communism in the upcoming election?** *(Truman believed they were using fear to gain voter loyalty.)* Ask the class to discuss how fear was used for political gain in the postwar years. **OL**

Primary Sources
Eyewitness to History

In the years after World War II, fear of communism took deep root in the United States. The idea that Communists had planted spies in powerful places terrified many Americans. Some people believed that Communists did not deserve the same protections granted to other Americans, and they approved of measures that might otherwise have been considered violations of individual rights.

SOURCE 1:

During the 1948 election campaign, Republicans charged that President Harry S. Truman was soft on communism. Truman believed that protecting basic rights was the best way to combat communism. He responded to the Republicans' attacks in a speech on September 28.

Here in Oklahoma City, in the heart of the nation, I consider it appropriate to discuss a subject of great importance to all Americans—the relationship of communism to our national security.

I should like the American people to consider the damage that is being done to our national security by irresponsible persons who place their own political interests above the security of the Nation.

I regret to say that there are some people in the Republican Party who are trying to create the false impression that communism is a powerful force in American life. These Republicans know that this is not true.

The time has come when we should take a frank and earnest look at the record about communism and our national security.

First, let me remind you of a few basic facts which are often overlooked.

Our country is strong enough to resist and overcome all the forces of communism—and it will remain so.

Our Government is not endangered by Communist **infiltration.**[1] It has preserved its integrity—and it will continue to do so.

The FBI and our other security forces are capable, informed, and alert—and will remain so. . . .

I am forced to the conclusion that Republican leaders are thinking more about the November election than about the welfare of this great country.

[1] **infiltration:** people having secretly established themselves

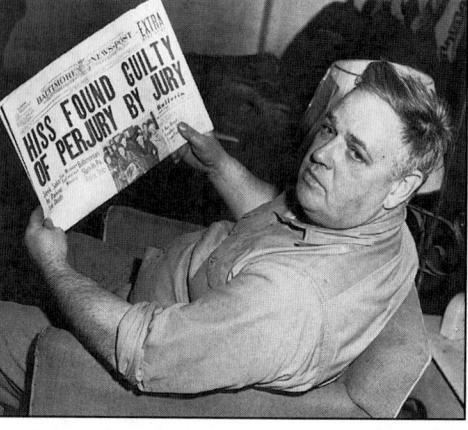

▲ *Whittaker Chambers*

SOURCE 2:

Whittaker Chambers, a journalist, became a spy for the Soviet Union in the 1930s. Upon leaving the Communist Party, he tried to expose the Communist underground. In testimony before the House Un-American Activities Committee (HUAC) on August 3, 1948, Chambers accused Alger Hiss of being a Communist.

CHAMBERS: I joined the Communist Party in 1924. . . . The purpose of this group at this time was not primarily **espionage.**[2] Its original purpose was the Communist infiltration of the American Government. But espionage was certainly one of its eventual objectives. Let no one be surprised at this statement. Disloyalty is a matter of principle with every member of the Communist Party. . . .

[2] **espionage:** spying

UNIVERSAL ACCESS

Logical/Mathematical Have students summarize the main reasons why President Truman did not view communism as a major threat to the United States. *(The country was strong enough to resist communism; the government had not been infiltrated by Communists; security forces such as the FBI were strong.)* Then ask students to pretend that they are living in the United States during the McCarthy era, and tell them to write a short newspaper editorial explaining their answers to the following questions: **In your opinion, are the reasons given by Truman sufficient to assure you that communism is not a threat to the United States? Why or why not?** Provide students with examples of editorials to use as models. **OL** **CA 11WS1.3**

▲ *Alger Hiss testifying before the House Un-American Activities Committee*

[Representative Karl E.] MUNDT: Miss Bentley testified before our committee and said that in her capacity as courier between Communist headquarters in New York and Washington, I think chronologically she followed you as courier and did that work, she mentioned that she also brought Communist literature and instructions from New York to Washington. Did you also do that?

CHAMBERS: I did. . . .

STRIPLING: When you left the Communist Party in 1937 did you approach any of these seven to break with you?

CHAMBERS: No. The only one of those people whom I approached was Alger Hiss. I went to the Hiss home one evening at what I considered considerable risk to myself and found Mrs. Hiss at home.

. . . Mrs. Hiss attempted while I was there to make a call, which I can only presume was to other Communists, but I quickly went to the telephone and she hung up, and Mr. Hiss came in shortly afterward, and we talked and I tried to break him away from the party.

As a matter of fact, he cried when we separated[,] when I left him, but he absolutely refused to break.

. . . I was very fond of Mr. Hiss.

SOURCE 3:

Alger Hiss had worked as a high-ranking State Department official under President Franklin D. Roosevelt. In 1948 he headed the Carnegie Endowment for International Peace. Two days after Chambers's testimony, Hiss strongly denied the charges brought against him.

I am here at my own request to deny unqualifiedly various statements about me which were made before this committee by one Whittaker Chambers the day before yesterday. I appreciate the committee's having promptly granted my request. I welcome the opportunity to answer to the best of my ability any inquiries the members of this committee may wish to ask me.

I am not and never have been a member of the Communist Party. I do not and never have adhered to the **tenets**[3] of the Communist Party. I am not and never have been a member of any Communist-front organization. I have never followed the Communist Party line, directly or indirectly. To the best of my knowledge, none of my friends is a Communist. . . .

To the best of my knowledge, I never heard of Whittaker Chambers until in 1947, when two representatives of the Federal Bureau of Investigation asked me if I knew him and various other people, some of whom I knew and some of whom I did not know. I said I did not know Chambers. So far as I know, I have never laid eyes on him, and I should like to have the opportunity to do so. . . .

[3]**tenets:** beliefs

DBQ Document-Based Questions

Historical Analysis   CA HR4; HI2

Source 1: Why does Truman believe that communism is not a danger to the United States?

Source 2: Why does Chambers believe that Communists are dangerous?

Source 3: How does Hiss deny that he is a Communist?

Comparing and Contrasting Sources:
How does the accusation that Alger Hiss was a Communist reflect the views of Truman and Chambers?

Primary Sources
Eyewitness to History

U Universal Access

Advanced Learners Divide the class into groups of three or four. Encourage each group to use Whittaker Chambers' testimony to write a short skit, or one-act play, illustrating the night that Chambers visited Alger Hiss's home to convince Hiss to break with the Communist Party. Each student should play one of the following roles: Whittaker Chambers, Mrs. Hiss, Alger Hiss, and the person whom Mrs. Hiss calls on the phone. Instruct students that their skit should make it clear whether or not Mr. and Mrs. Hiss are members of the Communist Party. After all the groups have performed their skits, lead the class in a discussion of which skits were the most convincing, and why. AL

W Writing Support

Persuasive Writing Have students work in pairs to write two letters to the House Un-American Activities Committee (HUAC). The first letter should argue that Hiss is a Communist; the second letter should argue that he is not a Communist. Encourage students to use library and Internet resources, as well as their textbook, to provide evidence for their claims. Then invite volunteers to read their letters aloud to the class as if they are reading them before the HUAC. OL

ASSESS/CLOSE

Have students answer the Document-Based Questions.

DBQ Document-Based Questions

Historical Analysis

1. According to Truman, the United States is strong enough to resist communism; the government has not been infiltrated; and security forces are strong.

2. Communist Party objectives include espionage and infiltration of the U.S. government.

3. Hiss denies membership in the Communist Party and denies holding any Communist beliefs or knowing any Communists.

Comparing and Contrasting Sources

Answers will vary; students may note that the accusation of Hiss proves Truman's view that the hunt for Communists has gone too far, or Chambers' view that Communists have infiltrated the U.S. government.

Reviewing Content Vocabulary

Students' answers will vary. The pages where the words appear in the text are shown in parentheses.

1. Cold War (p. 627) **2.** iron curtain (p. 631) **3.** containment (p. 633) **4.** limited war (p. 639) **5.** subversion (p. 643) **6.** perjury (p. 644) **7.** censure (p. 648) **8.** fallout (p. 649) **9.** fallout shelter (p. 649) **10.** massive retaliation (p. 652) **11.** brinkmanship (p. 653) **12.** covert (p. 654) **13.** developing nation (p. 654) **14.** military-industrial complex (p. 657)

Reviewing Academic Vocabulary

Students' answers will vary. The pages where the words appear in the text are shown in parentheses.

15. element (p. 629) **16.** retain (p. 637) **17.** mutual (p. 635) **18.** parallel (p. 638) **19.** sole (p. 646) **20.** nuclear (p. 648) **21.** dominant (p. 652) **22.** estate (p. 658) **23.** imply (p. 655)

Standards 11.4.6, 11.7.4, 11.7.8, 11.8.4, 11.8.5, 11.8.7, 11.8.8, 11.9.1 11.9.2, 11.9.3, 11.9.4, 11.9.6

Reviewing Content Vocabulary

On a sheet of paper, use each of these terms in a sentence.

1. Cold War
2. iron curtain
3. containment
4. limited war
5. subversion
6. perjury
7. censure
8. fallout
9. fallout shelter
10. massive retaliation
11. brinkmanship
12. covert
13. developing nation
14. military-industrial complex

Reviewing Academic Vocabulary

On a sheet of paper, use each of these terms in a sentence that reflects the term's meaning in the chapter.

15. element
16. retain
17. mutual
18. parallel
19. sole
20. nuclear
21. dominant
22. estate
23. imply

Reviewing the Main Ideas

Section 1

24. How did Stalin's postwar foreign policy goals add to the growing tensions between the United States and the USSR?

Section 2

25. Why were NATO and the Warsaw Pact formed?

Section 3

26. What were the effects of the new Red Scare on federal employees?

Section 4

27. What was President Eisenhower's "new look" for the military?

Critical Thinking

28. 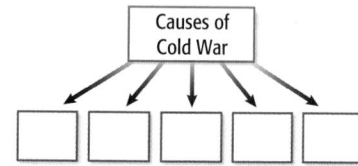 **Reading Skill** **Question-Answer Relationship**
Review page 624 and answer the following question: How did the Korean War achieve its goal even though the war was lost?

29. **Civics** In what possible ways did the Red Scare of the 1950s limit free speech and the right to dissent?

30. **Organizing** Use a graphic organizer similar to the one below to list the causes of the Cold War.

```
        Causes of
        Cold War
   ┌───┬───┼───┬───┐
   │   │   │   │   │
  [ ] [ ] [ ] [ ] [ ]
```

Chapter Summary

The Cold War

	Soviet Union		Western Allies
General Goals	• To create a protective sphere of Communist countries along European border • To promote the spread of communism		• To contain the spread of communism by supporting capitalist democratic governments
In Europe	• Occupied Eastern European nations and saw that Communist governments were established		• Expected free elections to occur in Soviet-controlled Eastern Europe
In the Middle East	• Sought access to oil in Iran • Aided Communists in Greece and pressured Turkey for access to the Mediterranean		• Forced Soviet withdrawal from Iran • Pledged aid to halt Soviet threats to Turkey and Greece
In Asia	• Communists seize power in China in 1949 • China and Soviet Union signed treaty of friendship and alliance • Communist North Korea invaded South Korea to start Korean War • Chinese troops fought for North Korea		• Aided China's Nationalist government • Dedicated money and troops to establish democratic stronghold in Japan • United Nations troops sent to fight for South Korea in Korean War
At Home	• Promoted development of high-technology weapons and surveillance		• Focused on the development of advanced technology weapons

---

Reviewing the Main Ideas

24. Stalin's push for German reparations and for a Communist government in Poland conflicted with United States's desire for democracy in Poland and economic recovery for Germany.

25. NATO was formed to maintain peace and freedom for European nations, and the Warsaw Pact was formed to achieve Soviet foreign policy goals.

26. Federal employees faced stricter screening and termination if they were suspected of being disloyal.

27. Eisenhower favored the use of atomic weapons, instead of maintaining a large and expensive army.

Self-Check Quiz

Visit the *American Vision: Modern Times* Web site at tav.mt.glencoe.com and click on *Self-Check Quizzes—Chapter 13* to assess your knowledge of chapter content.

Writing About History

31. **Historical Analysis** **Bias and Prejudice** Reread the speeches in Different Viewpoints on page 637. What might have influenced the points of views of President Truman and General Douglas MacArthur? Create a cause-and-effect chart showing possible reasons for their biases and the effects their experiences have had on their opinions. **CA HR2**

32. *Big Idea* Use the Internet and other resources to find out more about American life during the Cold War. Then create a report about society at this time, and present your report to the class. Your report could discuss politics, the fear of communism, and events in popular culture. **CA 11WS1.1; 11WS1.6**

33. **Persuasive Writing** Imagine that you have witnessed the crowds giving General MacArthur a hero's welcome. Write an opinion piece for a magazine justifying his reception or criticizing it because of his disagreement with Truman. **CA 11WA2.1a**

DBQ Document-Based Questions

34. **Interpreting Primary Sources** Margaret Chase Smith, a Republican from Maine, was elected to the Senate in 1948. Smith was upset by Joseph McCarthy's accusations and hoped her senior colleagues would reprimand him. When they failed to do so, Smith made her "Declaration of Conscience" speech. Read the excerpt and answer the questions that follow.

❝As a United States Senator, I am not proud of the way in which the Senate has been made a publicity platform for irresponsible sensationalism. I am not proud of the reckless abandon in which unproved charges have been hurled from this side of the aisle. I am not proud of the obviously staged, undignified countercharges that have been attempted in retaliation from the other side of the aisle. . . . I am not proud of the way we smear outsiders from the Floor of the Senate and hide behind the cloak of congressional immunity. . . .

As an American, I am shocked at the way Republicans and Democrats alike are playing directly into the Communist design of 'confuse, divide, and conquer'. . . . I want to see our nation recapture the strength and unity it once had when we fought the enemy instead of ourselves.❞

a. With whom is Smith angry, and why?

b. According to Smith, who is really dividing the nation?

NATIONAL GEOGRAPHIC
The Occupation of Berlin After World War II, 1945

Tegel
EAST GERMANY
West Berlin
Brandenburg Gate
Gatow
East Berlin
Tempelhof

✈ Airports
☐ American sector
☐ British sector
☐ French sector
☐ Soviet sector

0   5 miles
0   5 kilometers
Albers Conic Equal-Area projection

Geography and History

35. The map above shows the occupation of Berlin after World War II. Study the map and answer the questions below.

a. **Interpreting Maps** How was West Berlin's location a disadvantage?

b. **Applying Geography Skills** What transportation advantage did West Berlin have over East Berlin?

Standards Practice

Directions: Choose the phrase that best completes the following sentence.

36. One historical lesson of McCarthy's approach is the realization that

A loyalty oaths prevent spying.

B communism is influential in prosperous times.

C Communist agents had infiltrated all levels of the U.S. government.

D public fear of traitors can lead to false accusations and unfair consequences.

Standard 11.9.3: Trace the origins and geopolitical consequences (foreign and domestic) of the Cold War and containment policy, including the following: the era of McCarthyism, instances of domestic Communism (e.g., Alger Hiss) and blacklisting; the Truman Doctrine; the Berlin Blockade; the Korean War; the Bay of Pigs invasion and the Cuban Missile Crisis; atomic testing in the American West, the "mutual assured destruction" doctrine, and disarmament policies; the Vietnam War; Latin American policy.

Self-Check Quiz

Have students visit the Web site at tav.mt.glencoe.com to review Chapter 13 and take the Self-Check Quiz.

Writing About History

31. **Historical Analysis** Students' cause-and-effect charts will vary.

32. *Big Idea* Reports will vary but should reflect elements of American life during the 1950s.

33. Students' opinion pieces will vary but should clearly express a reasoned opinion supporting or opposing MacArthur's reception.

DBQ Document-Based Questions

34. **a.** with the Senate because of its behavior in pursuing suspected Communists; **b.** believed the Republicans and Democrats were driving the nation

Geography and History

35. **a.** It was completely surround by East Germany; blockaded it; **b.** It had three airports that were used to shuttle food and supplies to the Berliners.

Standards Practice

36. D

Bonus Question ?

Ask: How long did the era called the Cold War last? *(from 1946 to 1991)*

Critical Thinking

28. **Reading Skill** The U.S. became more militarily involved in containing communism in Asia, not just in Europe.

29. The Loyalty Review Program, the McCarran Act, the Taft-Hartley Act, and McCarthyism were ways to limit free speech and dissent.

30. Soviet-U.S. conflict over Soviet control of Eastern Europe and Soviet reparations demands from Germany; U.S. fear of Communist influence or control in the Middle East and Asia

Chapter 14 Planning Guide

SECTION RESOURCES

MAIN IDEAS	📁 PRINT MATERIALS	TECHNOLOGY RESOURCES
Section 1: Truman and Eisenhower 1. Despite inflation and labor strikes, the United States successfully transitioned to a peacetime economy. 2. Throughout his administration, President Truman had an uneasy working relationship with Congress. 3. Eisenhower considered his political beliefs middle of the road and tried to balance activism and economic conservatism.	• Reproducible Lesson Plan 14-1* • Daily Lecture and Discussion Notes 14-1 • Active Reading Note-Taking Guide 14-1 • Guided Reading Activity 14-1 • Section Quiz 14-1 • Reading Essentials and Study Guide 14-1	• Daily Focus Skills Transparency 14-1 • Section Graphic Organizer Transparency 14-1 • Interactive Tutor Self-Assessment CD-ROM • ExamView® Pro Testmaker CD-ROM • Presentation Plus! CD-ROM • California Standards Practice Transparencies
Section 2: The Affluent Society 1. An increase in service sector and professional jobs led to a great increase in American income from 1940 to 1955. 2. Despite a baby boom and cultural pressure, the number of women in the workforce increased. 3. Technological developments included the computer revolution, advances in medicine, and new conquests of outer space.	• Reproducible Lesson Plan 14-2* • Daily Lecture and Discussion Notes 14-2 • Active Reading Note-Taking Guide 14-2 • Guided Reading Activity 14-2 • Section Quiz 14-2 • Reading Essentials and Study Guide 14-2	• Daily Focus Skills Transparency 14-2 • Section Graphic Organizer Transparency 14-2 • Interactive Tutor Self-Assessment CD-ROM • ExamView® Pro Testmaker CD-ROM • Presentation Plus! CD-ROM • California Standards Practice Transparencies
Section 3: Popular Culture of the 1950s 1. Technological enhancements increased the popularity of television and movies. 2. Rock 'n' roll music and the literature of the beat movement defined youth culture. 3. Although few African Americans performed on television, many had a profound impact on early rock 'n' roll.	• Reproducible Lesson Plan 14-3* • Daily Lecture and Discussion Notes 14-3 • Active Reading Note-Taking Guide 14-3 • Guided Reading Activity 14-3 • Section Quiz 14-3 • Reading Essentials and Study Guide 14-3	• Daily Focus Skills Transparency 14-3 • Section Graphic Organizer Transparency 14-3 • Interactive Tutor Self-Assessment CD-ROM • ExamView® Pro Testmaker CD-ROM • Presentation Plus! CD-ROM • California Standards Practice Transparencies
Section 4: The Other Side of American Life 1. Despite the growing affluence of much of the nation, many groups still lived in poverty. 2. Concerns about rising juvenile delinquency and failing educational systems surfaced during the late 1950s.	• Reproducible Lesson Plan 14-4* • Daily Lecture and Discussion Notes 14-4 • Active Reading Note-Taking Guide 14-4 • Guided Reading Activity 14-4 • Section Quiz 14-4 • Reading Essentials and Study Guide 14-4	• Daily Focus Skills Transparency 14-4 • Section Graphic Organizer Transparency 14-4 • Interactive Tutor Self-Assessment CD-ROM • ExamView® Pro Testmaker CD-ROM • Presentation Plus! CD-ROM • California Standards Practice Transparencies

PACING YOUR LESSONS

Chapter Introduction	Section 1	Section 2	Section 3	Section 4	Chapter Assessment
½ Day	2 Days	2 Days	2 Days	2 Days	½ Day

0:00 OUT OF TIME? 📁 Assign the Chapter 14 *Reading Essentials and Study Guide.*

*Available on TeacherWorks™ CD-ROM

Chapter 14 Planning Guide

Standards-Based Lesson Plan

 History–Social Science Standards Covered in Chapter 14

The standards covered in the chapter are listed below. Use the accompanying activity as you teach the chapter to ensure student mastery of these standards. This activity can be used in combination with the program's print and technology assessment materials.

Standard	Section 1	Section 2	Section 3	Section 4
11.8.1 Trace the growth of service sector, white collar, and professional sector jobs in business and government.		✔		
11.8.2 Describe the significance of Mexican immigration and its relationship to the agricultural economy, especially in California.				✔
11.8.3 Examine Truman's labor policy and congressional reaction to it.	✔			
11.8.7 Describe the effects on society and the economy of technological developments since 1945, including the computer revolution, changes in communication, advances in medicine, and improvements in agricultural technology.		✔		
11.10.1 Explain how demands of African Americans helped produce a stimulus for civil rights, including President Roosevelt's ban on racial discrimination in defense industries in 1941, and how African Americans' service in World War II produced a stimulus for President Truman's decision to end segregation in the armed forces in 1948.	✔			✔
11.11.2 Discuss the significant domestic policy speeches of Truman, Eisenhower, Kennedy, Johnson, Nixon, Carter, Reagan, Bush, and Clinton (e.g., with regard to education, civil rights, economic policy, environmental policy).	✔			

Cumulative Standards-Assessment Activity

The Cumulative Standards-Assessment Activity will help students organize and learn the important information from the chapter. Begin teaching the chapter with this activity, and have students complete it as they read the chapter.

CREATING A MAIN IDEA AND SUPPORTING DETAILS CHART

Purpose Reviewing how to locate main ideas throughout the chapter will help students continue to refine their reading skills. This type of organizer aids students in identifying main ideas and their supporting details. It helps them develop the skill of knowing what is important and what is supportive of the main ideas. Students will need to use information about how the text is structured and combine it with what they know about the topic. Identifying main ideas and details can give students practice in logical and systematic thinking.

Introduction to Modeling

1. Begin the discussion with a brainstorming session. Ask students to list what they know or believe they know about this period of American history. Write the information on an overhead transparency. Have them identify some key main ideas that emerge in their comments. You might also want to model how certain comments are, in fact, details that support a main idea.

2. Ask students to copy this chart into their notebooks.

Supporting Details

Main Ideas

As students read each section, ask them to search for a main idea and have them fill in the chart with as many supporting details as necessary. Encourage them to create more charts as they encounter important concepts during their reading.

3. As part of your chapter review, have students share their charts. Consider asking them to do a final chart with a single main idea for the entire chapter. Encourage them to use their charts as study aids.

Chapter 14 Planning Guide

READING SUPPORT

- 📁 Content Vocabulary Activity 14
- 📁 Academic Vocabulary Activity 14
- 📁 Reading Skills Activity 14
- 📁 Chapter 14 Active Reading Note-Taking Guide
- 📁 Chapter 14 Guided Reading Activities
- 📁 Chapter 14 Reading Essentials and Study Guide
- 📁 American Literature Readings, Unit 4
- 📼 *The American Vision: Modern Times* Video Program
- 💿 Vocabulary PuzzleMaker CD-ROM
- 💿 American History Primary Source Document Library CD-ROM

CRITICAL THINKING

- 📁 Critical Thinking Skills Activity 14
- 📁 Primary Source Reading 14
- 📁 Cause-and-Effect Transparency 14 Strategy and Activity
- 💿 Presentation Plus! CD-ROM

UNIVERSAL ACCESS

- 📁 Universal Access Activity 14
- 📁 English Learner Activity 14
- 📕 American Art Prints
- 💿 StudentWorks™ Plus CD-ROM
- 🎵 American Music: Hits Through History
- 📁 School-to-Home Connection Activity 14

SKILL PRACTICE

- 📁 Map Overlay Transparency 14 Strategy and Activity
- 📁 Historical Analysis Skills Activity 14
- 📁 Time Line Activity 14
- 📁 Reading Skills Activity 14
- 📁 Reinforcing Skills Activity 14
- 📁 Linking Past and Present Activity 14
- 📁 Interpreting Political Cartoons 14
- 📁 Economics and History Activity, Unit 4
- 📼 MindJogger Videoquiz

WRITING SUPPORT

- 📁 Chapter 14 Active Reading Note-Taking Guide
- 📁 Writer's Guidebook
- 📁 High School Writing Process Transparencies

ASSESSMENT

- 📁 Chapter 14 Section Quizzes
- 📁 Chapter 14 Tests, Forms A and B
- 📁 Authentic Assessment Activity 14
- 💿 Exam*View*® Pro Testmaker CD-ROM
- 💿 Interactive Tutor Self-Assessment CD-ROM
- 📁 California Standards Practice, Grade 11
- 💿 Succeeding on . . .™ the California Standards: Grade 11 History–Social Science CD-ROM

💿 CD-ROM	🖨 Transparency
📀 DVD	🎵 Music Program
📁 Print Material	📼 Videocassette
📕 Poster	

Chapter 14 Planning Guide

TECHNOLOGY

- StudentWorks™ Plus CD-ROM
- TeacherWorks™ CD-ROM
- ExamView® Pro Testmaker CD-ROM
- Interactive Tutor Self-Assessment CD-ROM
- Presentation Plus! CD-ROM
- Vocabulary PuzzleMaker CD-ROM
- American History Primary Source Document Library CD-ROM
- MindJogger Videoquiz
- *The American Vision: Modern Times* Video Program
- Professional Development in High School Social Studies Video Series
- Teach, Use, and Succeed With *The American Vision: Modern Times*
- American Music: Hits Through History
- Succeeding on . . .™ the California Standards: Grade 11 History–Social Science CD-ROM

SPANISH RESOURCES

- Spanish Activities and Assessment
  - Spanish Vocabulary Activities
  - Spanish Guided Reading Activities
  - Spanish Quizzes and Tests
  - Spanish Reteaching Activities
- Spanish Reading Essentials and Study Guide
- Spanish School-to-Home Connection Activities

TRANSPARENCIES

- Daily Focus Skills Transparencies
- Section Graphic Organizer Transparencies
- Map Overlay Transparencies
- Cause-and-Effect Transparencies
- Unit Time Line Transparencies
- Why It Matters Transparencies
- American Art and Architecture Transparencies
- High School Writing Process Transparencies
- California Standards Practice Transparencies

TEACHER PLANNING

- Daily Lecture and Discussion Notes
- English Learner Handbook
- Building Academic Vocabulary
- *The American Vision: Modern Times* Reading and Study Skills Foldables
- Reading Strategies and Activities for the Social Studies Classroom
- Universal Access for the American History Classroom
- NGS United States Desk Map
- NGS World Atlas
- Chapter 14 Reproducible Lesson Plans on TeacherWorks™ CD-ROM
- California Guide to Daily Intervention

PROFESSIONAL DEVELOPMENT

- Building Academic Vocabulary
- Strategies for Success
- Research-Based Strategies Used to Develop *The American Vision: Modern Times*
- Character Education in the High School Classroom
- Professional Development in High School Social Studies Video Series
- Teach, Use, and Succeed With *The American Vision: Modern Times*

Chapter 14 Planning Guide

 TEACHER'S CORNER

Index to National Geographic Magazine:
The following articles relate to this chapter:

- "Alone Across the Arctic Crown," April 1993
- "Kodiak, Alaska's Island Refuge," November 1993
- "Bikini's Nuclear Graveyard," June 1992

National Geographic Society Products:
To order the following, call National Geographic at 1–800–368–2728

- *1945–1989: The Cold War* (Video)
- *Eyewitness to the 20th Century* (Book)

NGS ONLINE

Access National Geographic's new dynamic MapMachine Web site and other geography resources at:

www.nationalgeographic.com
www.nationalgeographic.com/maps

Use our Web site for additional resources. All essential content is covered in the Student Edition.

You and your students can visit tav.mt.glencoe.com, the Web site companion to the **American Vision: Modern Times.** This innovative integration of electronic and print media offers your students a wealth of opportunities. The student text directs students to the Web site for the following options:

- **Chapter Overviews**
- **Self-Check Quizzes**
- **Student Web Activities**
- **Textbook Updates**

Answers to the student Web activities are provided for you in the **Web Activity Lesson Plans.** Additional Web resources and ePuzzles and games are also available.

MASTERING THE STANDARDS

The content and assessment in the Student Edition, Teacher Wraparound Edition, teacher planning materials, and the print and technology products are all standards-based. The use of these products during instruction leads to mastery of the standards.

PRACTICE
- California Standards Practice, Grade 11
- California Standards Practice Transparencies
- School-to-Home Connection

BENCHMARK ASSESSMENT
- Section Quizzes, Chapter Tests, and Authentic Assessment
- Exam*View* Pro Testmaker CD-ROM
- Succeeding On . . . ™ the California Standards: Grade 11 History–Social Science CD-ROM

REMEDIATION
- California Guide to Daily Intervention
- Interactive Tutor Self-Assessment CD-ROM
- Exam*View* Pro Testmaker CD-ROM
- California Standards Practice, Grade 11
- Reading Essentials and Study Guide

 Dinah Zike's Foldables

Foldables are three-dimensional, interactive graphic organizers that help students practice basic writing skills, review key vocabulary terms, and identify main ideas. Every chapter has a foldable activity in the *Dinah Zike's Reading and Study Skills Foldables* booklet. You can use the foldables as they are presented or modify them to suit the needs of your individual class.

 Biography THE HISTORY CHANNEL.

A variety of videotape programs are available from A&E Television and The History Channel to provide teaching assistance. To order, call Glencoe at 1-800-334-7344.

Chapter 14 Planning Guide

Reading List Generator CD-ROM

The Glencoe BookLink CD-ROM is a database that allows you to search more than 15,000 titles to create a customized reading list for your students.

■ Reading Lists can be organized by students' reading level, author, genre, theme, or area of interest.

■ The database provides Degrees of Reading Power™ (DRP) and Lexile™ readability scores for all selections.

■ A brief summary of each selection is included.

Leveled reading suggestions for this chapter:

For students at a Grade 8 reading level:
■ *Young, Black, and Determined: A Biography of Lorraine Hansberry,* by Patricia C. McKissack & Fredrick L. McKissack

For students at a Grade 9 reading level:
■ *Zap!: A Brief History of Television,* by Marian Calabro

For students at a Grade 10 reading level:
■ *Spiders in the House and Workers in the Field,* by Ernesto Galarza

READING SUPPORT FROM JAMESTOWN EDUCATION

• *Timed Readings Plus in Social Studies* help students increase their reading rate and fluency while maintaining comprehension. The 400-word passages are similar to those found on state and national assessments.

• *Reading in the Content Area: Social Studies* concentrates on six essential reading skills that help students better comprehend what they read. The book includes 75 high-interest nonfiction passages written at increasing levels of difficulty.

• *Reading Fluency* helps students read smoothly, accurately, and expressively.

• *Jamestown's Reading Improvement,* by renowned reading expert Edward Fry, focuses on helping build your students' comprehension, vocabulary, and skimming and scanning skills.

• *Critical Reading Series* provides high-interest books, each written at three reading levels.

For more information about these products, see the Jamestown Education materials in the Classroom Solutions in the front of this Teacher Wraparound Edition. To order these products, call Glencoe at 1-800-334-7344.

KEY for Using the Teacher Wraparound Edition

Use this key to help you identify the different types of prompts found in the Teacher Wraparound Edition.

R **Reading Strategies** activities help you teach reading skills and vocabulary.

C **Critical Thinking** strategies help students apply and extend what they have learned.

U **Universal Access** activities provide differentiated instruction for students learning to speak English, along with suggestions for teaching various types of learners.

S **Skill Practice** strategies help students practice historical analysis and geography skills.

W **Writing Support** activities provide writing opportunities to help students comprehend the text.

Teaching strategies and activities have been coded for ability level appropriateness.

AL Activities for students working above grade level
OL Activities for students working on grade level
BL Activities for students working below grade level
EL Activities for English learners

FOCUS

History–Social Science Standards

This chapter addresses the following main standard:

11.8 Students analyze the economic boom and social transformation of post–World War II America.

BELLRINGER
SKILLBUILDER ACTIVITY

Ask students to brainstorm a list of ways that economic prosperity affected Americans in the 1950s. *(Students may note greater purchasing power, the development of improved technologies, or increased leisure time.)* After reading Chapter 14, have students write paragraphs comparing and contrasting the advantages enjoyed by prosperous Americans with the experiences of many minority, rural, and/or poor Americans in the 1950s.

TEACH

Thinking About the Big Ideas

As you begin teaching each section, use these questions and activities to focus on the Big Idea.

Section 1
Truman and Eisenhower

Essential Question: What social and economic changes might a country face immediately after a war? *(Students may note the influx of returning veterans into the work force or the loss of jobs as a result of a lack of need for war production.)* One of the important issues facing the

---

CHAPTER
14
1945–1960
Postwar America

~ *The Big Ideas* ~

SECTION 1: Truman and Eisenhower

The fate of nations is forever changed by monumental world events. *After World War II, the Truman and Eisenhower administrations set out to help the nation adjust to peacetime.*

SECTION 2: The Affluent Society

Societies change over time. *The postwar economic boom brought great changes to society, including the ways many Americans worked and lived.*

SECTION 3: Popular Culture of the 1950s

Societies change over time. *During the carefree and prosperous 1950s, Americans turned to television, new forms of music, cinema, and literature for entertainment.*

SECTION 4: The Other Side of American Life

Societies change over time. *Not everyone in the United States prospered during the nation's postwar boom, as millions of minorities and rural whites struggled daily with poverty.*

The *American Vision: Modern Times* Video *The Chapter 14 video, "America Takes to the Roads," describes the cultural impact of the automobile and its importance to the growing baby boom generation.*

United States PRESIDENTS

- **1944**
  - GI Bill enacted
- *Truman 1945–1953*
- **1946**
  - Series of work strikes plagues country
- **1947**
  - Levittown construction begins
- **1948**
  - Truman elected president

1944   *1948*   *1952*

World

- **1946**
  - Juan Perón elected president of Argentina
- **1948**
  - South Africa introduces apartheid
- **1952**
  - Scientists led by Edward Teller develop hydrogen bomb

662

Truman and Eisenhower administrations was how to help the nation make the transition to peacetime. Tell students that they will learn more about these issues in Section 1. **OL**

Section 2
The Affluent Society

Essential Question: Why do you think suburbs were so popular during this period?

What advantages did they offer middle-class families over city living? *(Housing was newly built and affordable, accommodating the need for new housing following the increase in families because of the baby boom.)* Explain to students that in Section 2 they will learn how along with the economic boom of the postwar period came a mass migration from cities to suburbs and the development of new technologies. **AL**

These confident newlyweds capture the prosperous attitude of postwar America.

1953
• Lucille Ball gives birth in real life and on her television show

1955
• Salk polio vaccine becomes widely available

Eisenhower 1953–1961

1956
• Elvis Presley appears on *The Ed Sullivan Show*
• Federal Highway Act passed

1957
• Estimated 40 million television sets in use in United States

1958
• Galbraith's *The Affluent Society* published

1956   *1960*

1954
• Gamal Abdel Nasser takes power in Egypt

1956
• Suez Canal crisis erupts

1957
• USSR launches *Sputnik I* and *Sputnik II* satellites

HISTORY Online
Chapter Overview
Visit the *American Vision: Modern Times* Web site at tav.mt.glencoe.com and click on *Chapter Overviews– Chapter 14* to preview chapter information.

663

FOLDABLES™ Study Organizer

Dinah Zike's Foldables are three-dimensional, interactive graphic organizers that help students practice basic writing skills, review key vocabulary terms, and identify main ideas. Have students complete the foldable activity in the *Dinah Zike's Reading and Study Skills Foldables* booklet.

HISTORY Online

Go to tav.mt.glencoe.com for student activities, lesson plans, and links to additional Web resources to help students learn about postwar America.

Section 3
Popular Culture of the 1950s
Essential Question: Does the mass media have a positive or a negative impact on society? Have students write a short paragraph answering the essential question. Explain that in Section 3 they will find out about the tremendous effect of the sudden rise in popularity of television on American society in the 1950s. **BL**

Section 4
The Other Side of American Life
Essential Question: Is it possible to eliminate all poverty in our society? *(Students may say that while it is essential, it may be an impossible goal.)* Remind students that not every American enjoyed prosperity in the booming postwar economy. Ask them to predict which groups of Americans remained poor during this period. *(minorities, Native Americans, Appalachians, farmers, single mothers)* Have students speculate about the reasons why these groups were left out of the postwar boom while others were not. **OL**

Cultural Perspectives

Visit the library or search online to find images representative of 1950s America. Examples could include advertisements, pictures depicting stereotypical images of minorities, and photographs showing the poverty in inner cities or Appalachia. Have students work in small groups to make observations and discuss what they have seen.
Ask: What do these images tell you about 1950s America? What did society value? Did all Americans take part in the postwar prosperity?

663

Reading Skill

Why It's Important

Tell students that learning to analyze the information in books by using their own experiences and opinions will help them gain a better understanding of what they read.

1. Introducing the Skill

Ask students to brainstorm a list of questions to ask when purchasing a new car. Keep track of their responses in a table like the one below. *(Examples include: How much does the car cost? How safe is the car?)* Remind students that questions for which they can easily find answers are similar to text-explicit questions, while those that require more information or analysis are similar to text-implicit questions. **BL**

Text-explicit	Text-implicit

2. Extending the Skill

Provide students with a magazine article and ask them to turn its title into a question. **Ask: Do you think this is a text-implicit or text-explicit question? How do you know?** Have students use the article to practice writing and answering both types of questions. **OL**

Answers and Additional Support

Reading Skill   Question-Answer Relationships

In the last chapter, we looked at questions that require answers directly from the book. There are other questions that ask you to use information based on your experiences and opinions. These questions ask you to analyze and interpret information in your textbook. It is important to recognize the difference between the different types of questions so that you know where to find the answers—in the book or in your head.

One type of question is called "author and you" because you need to use information from the book and from your own experiences to supply the answer. Another type is called "on your own" because it comes from your prior knowledge and experiences. In both cases, the information in the book may influence your answer, but it is not the primary source. Some people call these types of questions text-implicit. This means that the answer is somewhat hidden and may require that you use information from other sources, such as your own experiences.

QUESTION–ANSWER RELATIONSHIPS

Remember to use evidence from the text as well as your opinions and experiences to answer text-implicit questions.

Read the following paragraph about the role of women during the 1950s. Then read the questions below and discuss the answers with a partner.

Many women focused on their traditional role of homemaker during the 1950s. . . . Many Americans assumed that a good mother should stay home to take care of her children.

"Let's face it, girls," declared one female writer in *Better Homes and Gardens* in April 1955, "that wonderful guy in your house—and in mine—is building your house, your happiness and the opportunities that will come to your children." The magazine advised stay-at-home wives to "set their sights on a happy home, a host of friends and a bright future through success in HIS job." **(page 677)**

Question: How did society view women during the 1950s?

This is an "author and you" question because you need to use information from the text as well as your own knowledge to provide the answer.

Question: How would readers interpret this article today?

This is an "on your own" question because it requires you to think about your own knowledge, opinions, and experiences.

Apply the Skill

Look closely at the questions in each section assessment and in the chapter assessment. Many of those are examples of either "author and you" or "on your own" questions. As you answer these questions, determine for each what type of question it is.

UNIVERSAL ACCESS

Visual/Spatial Have students work in pairs to create posters illustrating the roles of women in the 1950s. Encourage them to use the information on pages 677–678 to create text-implicit questions. Students should then practice answering these questions by allowing their posters to reflect their own views and opinions as well as what they read about women during this time period. **OL**

Historical Analysis Skill

Analyzing and Understanding Change

Analysis Skill Standard CS2

Chronological and Spatial Thinking You should learn to analyze how change happens at different rates at different times. You should also understand that some aspects can change while others remain the same, and that change is complicated and affects not only technology and politics but also values and beliefs.

Do you remember a time when everyone in your family was sick? Maybe it was a cold that was passed around your house. Did you notice that everyone who became sick recovered from their illnesses at different rates? The economies of countries are similar in that they expand and contract at different rates at different times. In fact, the same language used in the health field is often used to describe the economy of a country.

Historians understand that change in a nation's history is complex and can occur at different rates at different times. Like your families, economies may be quick or slow to recover from a recession, depression, or war.

Read the following passage about the concerns of Americans about the postwar economy of the United States.

After the war many Americans feared the return to a peacetime economy. They worried that after military production halted and millions of former soldiers glutted the labor market, unemployment and recession might sweep the country. (page 667)

You learned in the previous chapter that when World War II ended, the economies of Germany, Japan, and Great Britain were in ruins. As the nations of Europe and Asia set out to rebuild, they relied upon the United States to provide the manufactured goods necessary for reconstruction.

What effects do you think the reconstruction efforts had upon the U.S. economy? Do you think these effects would have an impact on the lives of Americans? Can you think of other events that would affect the economy of the United States?

Apply the Skill

Before you read, make a prediction about the economy of the United States in the 1950s. As you read the chapter, write down the individual events and issues that played a role in the postwar economy, and how they brought about change. Make sure you outline the impact of politics, technology, and values and beliefs each had on the economy. After reading the chapter, review your prediction. Identify and analyze the differences between your prediction and actual events.

665

Historical Analysis

Why It's Important
Ask students what would happen if they decided to start studying for five hours every night. How would their performance in school change? Inform students that in order to gain a better understanding of historical events, they should start by making a prediction about what changes might result from the event. Then, as they read, they can note the outcome of events and compare the actual results with their predictions.

1. Introducing the Skill
Remind the class that change does not happen at an even rate. Ask students to think about what kinds of people they were when they first started high school. **Ask: What did you look like? Who were your friends? What were your interests? Opinions?** Then have them think about the answers to these same questions now. **Ask: How have you changed from the beginning of high school to today? What aspects of your personality have changed? What has remained the same?** **BL** **CA** CS2

2. Extending the Skill
Have students use library and Internet resources to locate articles about major historical events. Ask them to write a short paragraph responding to the following questions: **What changes have occurred as a result of this event? How has the event affected technology, politics, and values and beliefs?** Invite students to share their articles and paragraphs with the class. **OL** **CA** CS2 **CA** 11WA2.3c

UNIVERSAL ACCESS

Logical/Mathematical Have students use library or Internet resources to research the costs of post–World War II reconstruction. Then have students make circle graphs showing the proportion of U.S. aid to each of the following nations: France, Germany, Japan, and Great Britain. Finally, ask students to write short paragraphs explaining their answers to the following question: **Do you think the United States had a responsibility to aid devastated European and Asian nations after World War II, including its former enemies? Why or why not?** Encourage students to share their circle graphs and paragraphs with the class. **AL** **CA** 11WA2.4a

FOCUS

SKILLBUILDER ACTIVITY

Project **Daily Focus Skills Transparency 14-1** and have students answer the question.

Guide to Reading

Understanding Vocabulary: Have students correctly assign the content vocabulary to the Truman or Eisenhower administration.

Answers to Graphic: increased consumer spending, higher prices, rising inflation, labor unrest

Unpacking the Standards

Students will be able to:

- Explain how the American economy returned to a peacetime footing following the turmoil of Depression and wartime mobilization.
- Describe the main goals of Harry Truman's domestic policies.
- Analyze the presidency of Dwight Eisenhower.

Answers and Additional Support

SECTION 1

Truman and Eisenhower

Guide to Reading

Connection
In the previous chapter, you learned about the beginning of the Cold War. In this section, you will discover how transitioning to a peacetime economy after World War II changed the nation.

Main Idea
- Despite inflation and labor strikes, the United States successfully transitioned to a peacetime economy. (p. 667)
- Throughout his administration, President Truman had an uneasy working relationship with Congress. (p. 668)
- Eisenhower considered his political beliefs middle of the road and tried to balance activism and economic conservatism. (p. 670)

Content Vocabulary
closed shop, right-to-work law, union shop, featherbedding, dynamic conservatism

Academic Vocabulary
restrain, subsidy, transition

Terms to Identify
GI Bill, "Do-Nothing Congress," Fair Deal, Federal Highway Act

Reading Objectives
- **Explain** the Truman administration's efforts on the domestic front.
- **Describe** President Eisenhower's domestic agenda.

Reading Strategy
Categorizing As you read about the Truman and Eisenhower administrations, complete a graphic organizer similar to the one below by listing the characteristics of the postwar economy of the United States.

Characteristics of a Postwar Economy

Preview of Events

♦1944	♦1947	♦1950	♦1953

1944
Congress passes GI Bill

1946
Strikes take place across the country

1948
Harry S. Truman wins presidential election

1952
Dwight D. Eisenhower wins presidential election

The following are the main History–Social Science Standards covered in this section.

11.8.3 Examine Truman's labor policy and congressional reaction to it.

11.8.4 Analyze new federal government spending on defense, welfare, interest on the national debt, and federal and state spending on education, including the California Master Plan.

11.10.1 Explain how demands of African Americans helped produce a stimulus for civil rights, including President Roosevelt's ban on racial discrimination in defense industries in 1941, and how African Americans' service in World War II produced a stimulus for President Truman's decision to end segregation in the armed forces in 1948.

11.11.2 Discuss the significant domestic policy speeches of Truman, Eisenhower, Kennedy, Johnson, Nixon, Carter, Reagan, Bush, and Clinton (e.g., with regard to education, civil rights, economic policy, environmental policy).

❧ The Big Idea ❧

The fate of nations is forever changed by monumental world events. Labor strikes for better wages led the new conservative Congress to pass legislation limiting the power of unions. Many of Truman's legislative proposals were defeated in Congress. With backing from laborers, African Americans, and farmers, Truman was able to win reelection in 1948. Congress eventually passed several of Truman's Fair Deal proposals. After winning the election of 1952, President Dwight Eisenhower worked to balance activism and economic conservatism.

666 CHAPTER 14 Postwar America

SECTION RESOURCES

📁 Print Material
- Reproducible Lesson Plan 14-1
- Guided Reading Activity 14-1
- Reading Essentials and Study Guide 14-1
- Active Reading Note-Taking Guide 14-1

🖎 Transparencies
- Daily Focus Skills Transparency 14-1
- Section Graphic Organizer Transparency 14-1

Technology
- 🖳 Interactive Tutor Self-Assessment CD-ROM
- 🖳 ExamView® Pro Testmaker CD-ROM
- 🖳 Presentation Plus! CD-ROM

Return to a Peacetime Economy

Main Idea Despite inflation and labor strikes, the United States successfully transitioned to a peacetime economy.

Reading Connection Would you consider going on strike to obtain certain rights and privileges? Read on to learn how Truman dealt with mining and railroad strikers.

After the war, many Americans feared the return to a peacetime economy. They worried that after military production halted and millions of former soldiers glutted the labor market, unemployment and recession might sweep the country. Despite such worries, the economy continued to grow. Consumer spending, which had been limited during the war, helped ward off a recession.

★ An American Story ★

As World War II ended, Robert Eubanks was worried as he prepared for his discharge from the army. He had joined the army because, as an African American, it was hard for him to find a job that paid well. Then he heard about something known as the GI Bill, a government program that paid veterans' tuition for college and provided a living allowance. Eubanks took advantage of the program and enrolled at the Illinois Institute of Technology. He earned three degrees on the GI Bill and eventually became a professor at the University of Illinois.

Years later Eubanks recalled how his life was changed by the bill. "It's very hard to explain how things were during the 1940s," he said. "The restrictions on blacks then were rough. The GI Bill gave me my start on being a professional instead of a stock clerk."

—adapted from *When Dreams Came True*

The Servicemen's Readjustment Act, popularly called the **GI Bill,** further boosted the economy. The act provided generous loans to veterans to help them establish businesses, buy homes, and attend college.

Inflation and Strikes The postwar economy was not without its problems. A greater demand for goods led to higher prices, and this rising inflation soon triggered labor unrest. As the cost of living rose, workers across the country went on strike for better pay. Work stoppages soon affected the automobile, electrical, steel, and mining industries.

Afraid that the nation's energy supply would be drastically reduced, President Truman forced striking miners to return to work. Truman ordered government seizure of the mines while pressuring mine owners to grant the union most of its demands. The president also halted a strike that shut down the nation's railroads by threatening to draft the striking workers into the army.

Republican Victory Labor unrest and high prices prompted many Americans to call for a change. The Republicans seized upon these sentiments during the 1946 congressional elections, winning control of both houses of Congress for the first time since 1930.

The new conservative Congress quickly set out to curb the power of organized labor. Legislators proposed a measure known as the Taft-Hartley Act, which outlawed the **closed shop,** or the practice of forcing business owners to hire only union members. Under the law, states could pass **right-to-work laws,** which outlawed **union shops** (shops in which new workers were required to join the union). The measure also prohibited **featherbedding,** the practice of limiting work output in order to create more jobs. When the bill reached Truman he vetoed it, arguing:

> ❝ . . . [It would] reverse the basic direction of our national labor policy, inject the government into private economic affairs on an unprecedented scale, and conflict with important principles of our democratic society. Its provisions would cause more strikes, not fewer. ❞
>
> —quoted in *The Growth of the American Republic*

The GI Bill African American soldiers review the benefits of the GI Bill, which included loans to attend college and to buy homes.

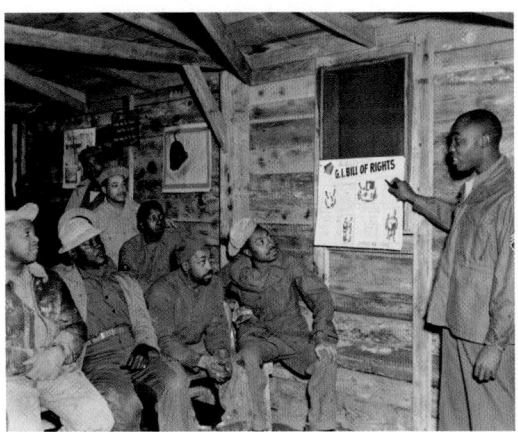

U Universal Access

Below Grade Level Have students imagine that they are labor union organizers in the years immediately following World War II. Assign students to work in pairs to create posters encouraging other laborers to strike. *(Posters will vary but should note that workers wanted better pay to keep up with growing inflation.)* **BL**

C Critical Thinking

Determining a Point of View The Taft-Hartley Act created controversy for the Truman administration. Have students determine their positions on the following statement: *The president should have the right to halt economically damaging strikes for a "cooling off" period. (Students' answers will vary, but their positions need to be substantiated with specific reasons.)* **OL**

Review the Big Idea

Review the Big Idea for this section, "The fate of nations is forever changed by monumental world events." As students read through Section 1, have them list on a piece of paper how World War II affected events and policies during the post-war years. **OL**

Did You Know?

In addition to providing low interest loans to help veterans buy homes and farms, the GI Bill provided unemployment benefits for veterans who could not find jobs.

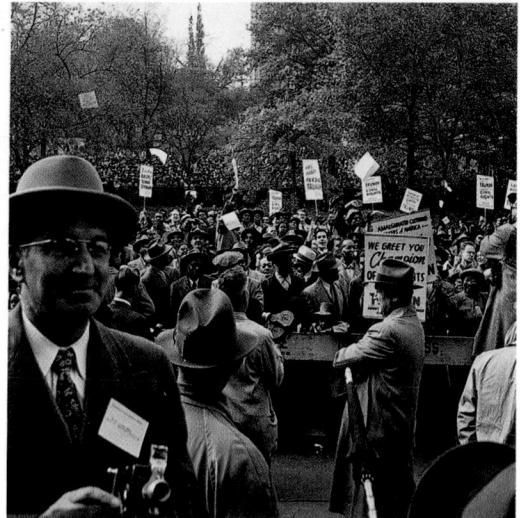

Picturing **History**

African Americans Rally for Truman During the 1948 election, President Truman spoke at many rallies similar to this one in New York City. What legislative proposals by President Truman built African American political support?

The president's concerns, however, did little to sway Congress, which passed the Taft-Hartley Act in 1947 despite President Truman's veto. Its supporters claimed the law held irresponsible unions in check just as the Wagner Act of 1935 had **restrained** antiunion activities and employers. Labor leaders called the act a "slave labor" law and insisted that it erased many of the gains that unions had made since 1933.

✓ **Reading Check** **Explaining** Why did Truman veto the Taft-Hartley Act?

R Truman's Domestic Program

Main Idea Throughout his administration, President Truman had an uneasy working relationship with Congress.

Reading Connection Why is it important that Congress and the president work together in crafting legislation? Read on to discover the relationship between Truman and federal legislators.

The Democratic Party's loss of members in the 1946 elections did not dampen President Truman's spirits or his plans. Shortly after taking office, Truman had proposed a series of domestic measures that sought to continue the work done as part of

Franklin Roosevelt's New Deal. During his tenure in office, Truman worked to push this agenda through Congress.

Truman's Legislative Agenda To continue the efforts of the New Deal, Truman proposed several legislative measures. The president's proposals included the expansion of Social Security benefits; the raising of the legal minimum wage from 40¢ to 75¢ an hour; a program to ensure full employment through aggressive use of federal spending and investment; public housing and slum clearance; long-range environmental and public works planning; and a system of national health insurance.

Truman also boldly asked Congress in February 1948 to pass a broad civil rights bill that would protect African Americans' right to vote, abolish poll taxes, and make lynching a federal crime. He also issued an executive order barring discrimination in federal employment, and he ended segregation in the armed forces.

Most of Truman's legislative efforts, however, met with little success in Congress. A coalition of Republicans and conservative Southern Democrats defeated many of his proposals. While these defeats angered Truman, with the upcoming election of 1948 the president soon had to worry about other matters.

The Election of 1948 As the presidential election of 1948 approached, most observers gave Truman little chance of winning. Some Americans still believed that he lacked the stature for the job, and they viewed his administration as weak and inept.

Divisions within the Democratic Party also seemed to spell disaster for Truman. At the Democratic Convention that summer, two factions abandoned the party altogether. Reacting angrily to Truman's support of civil rights, a group of Southern Democrats walked out of the Democratic Convention. They formed the States' Rights, or Dixiecrat, Party and nominated South Carolina governor Strom Thurmond as their presidential candidate. At the same time, the party's more liberal members were frustrated by Truman's ineffective domestic policies and critical of his anti-Soviet foreign policy. They formed a new Progressive Party, with Henry A. Wallace as their presidential candidate.

The president's Republican opponent was New York governor Thomas Dewey, a dignified and popular candidate who seemed unbeatable. After polling 50 political writers, *Newsweek* magazine declared three weeks before the election, "The landslide for Dewey will sweep the country."

Perhaps the only one who gave Truman a chance to win was Truman himself. "I know every one of those 50 fellows," he declared about the writers polled in *Newsweek.* "There isn't one of them has enough sense to pound sand in a rat hole." Ignoring the polls, the feisty president poured his efforts into an energetic campaign. He traveled more than 20,000 miles by train and made more than 350 speeches. Along the way, Truman attacked the majority Republican Congress as "do-nothing, good-for-nothing" for refusing to enact his legislative agenda.

Truman's attacks on the **"Do-Nothing Congress"** did not mention that both he and Congress had been very busy dealing with foreign policy matters. Congress had passed the Truman Doctrine's aid program to Greece and Turkey, as well as the Marshall Plan. It had also created the Department of Defense and the CIA and established the Joint Chiefs of Staff as a permanent organization. The 80th Congress, therefore, did not "do nothing" as Truman charged, but its accomplishments were in areas that did not affect most Americans directly. As a result, Truman's charges began to stick, and to the surprise of almost everyone, his efforts paid off.

With a great deal of support from laborers, African Americans, and farmers, Truman won a narrow but stunning victory over Dewey. Perhaps just as remarkable as the president's victory was the resurgence of the Democratic Party. When the dust had cleared after Election Day, Democrats had regained control of both houses of Congress.

The Fair Deal Truman's State of the Union message to the new Congress repeated the domestic agenda he had put forth previously. "Every segment of our population and every individual," he declared, "has a right to expect from . . . government a fair deal." Whether intentional or not, the president had coined a name—the **Fair Deal**—to set his program apart from the New Deal.

The 81st Congress did not completely embrace Truman's Fair Deal. Legislators did raise the legal minimum wage to 75¢ an hour. They also approved an important expansion of the Social Security system, increasing benefits by 77 percent and extending them to 10 million additional people. Congress also

HISTORY Online

Student Web Activity Visit the *American Vision: Modern Times* Web site at tav.mt.glencoe.com and click on **Student Web Activities– Chapter 14** for an activity on postwar America.

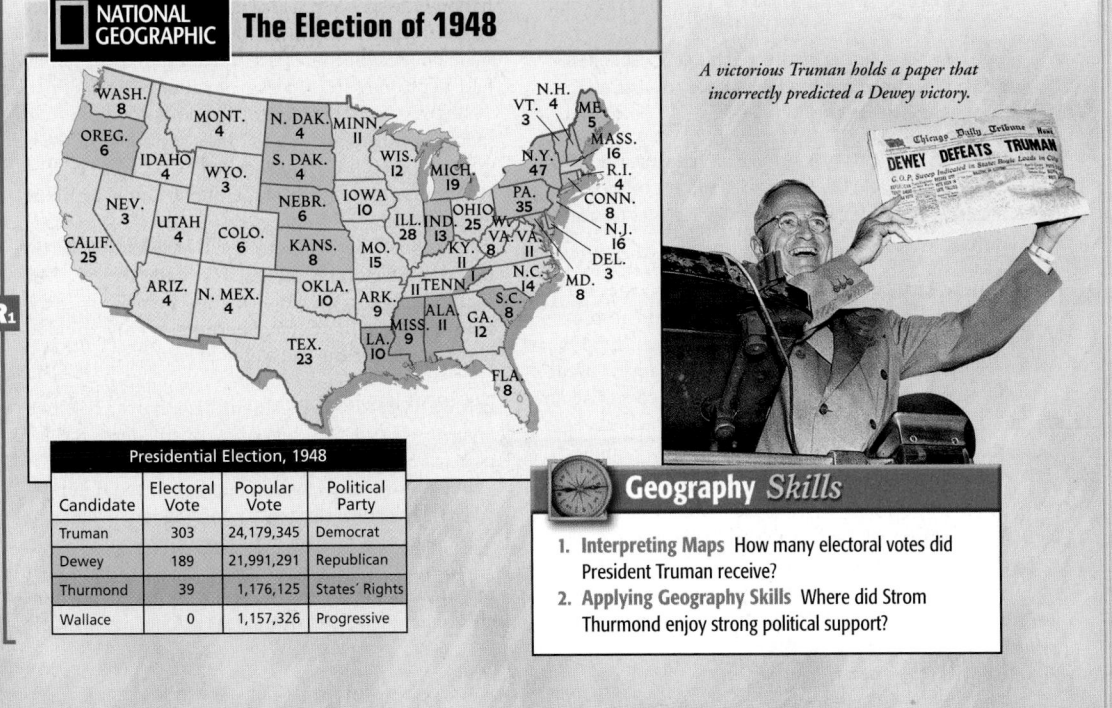

NATIONAL GEOGRAPHIC **The Election of 1948**

A victorious Truman holds a paper that incorrectly predicted a Dewey victory.

Presidential Election, 1948			
Candidate	Electoral Vote	Popular Vote	Political Party
Truman	303	24,179,345	Democrat
Dewey	189	21,991,291	Republican
Thurmond	39	1,176,125	States' Rights
Wallace	0	1,157,326	Progressive

Geography *Skills*

1. **Interpreting Maps** How many electoral votes did President Truman receive?
2. **Applying Geography Skills** Where did Strom Thurmond enjoy strong political support?

HISTORY Online

Objectives and answers to the student activity can be found in the **Web Activity Lesson Plan** at tav.mt.glencoe.com.

Geography *Skills*

Answers:
1. 303
2. Alabama, Louisiana, Mississippi, South Carolina, and eastern Tennessee

Geography Skills Practice
Ask: In which Western state did the voters turn out for Dewey? *(Oregon)*

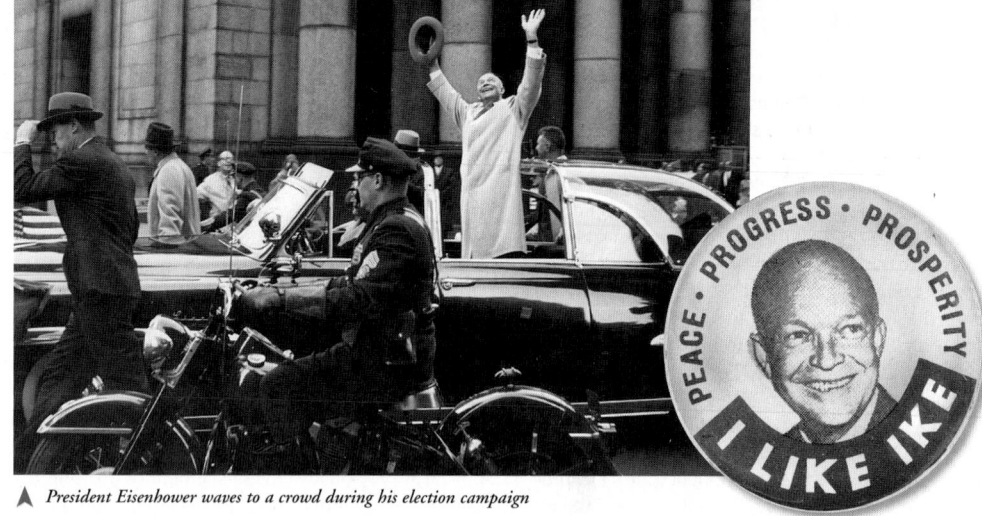

▲ *President Eisenhower waves to a crowd during his election campaign*

Universal Access

Visual/Spatial Organize the class into groups of four. Have each group create two campaign posters for the election of 1952, one in favor of Eisenhower and the other in favor of Adlai Stevenson. Ask volunteers to share their posters with the class. Use the posters as a starting point to discuss the key issues of the 1952 presidential election. **OL**

Skill Practice

Evaluating Evidence President Eisenhower used the phrase "middle of the road" to describe his political beliefs. Assign students to work in groups of three or four to create tables listing Eisenhower's conservative policies in one column, and his liberal policies in the other. When the groups have completed their tables, **ask: Do you agree that Eisenhower's political beliefs could be described as "middle of the road"? Why or why not?** *(Answers will vary.)* **OL** **CA HR1**

Reading Check

Answer: The victory of Truman and the Democrats paved the way for the Fair Deal legislation, some of which was approved by Congress.

Answers and Additional Support

passed the National Housing Act of 1949, which provided for the construction of over 800,000 units of low-income housing and long-term rent **subsidies.**

Congress refused, however, to pass national health insurance or to provide subsidies for farmers or federal aid for schools. In addition, legislators opposed Truman's efforts to enact civil rights legislation.

Reading Check **Describing** What was the impact of the election of 1948?

The Eisenhower Years

Main Idea Eisenhower considered his political beliefs middle of the road and tried to balance activism and economic conservatism.

Reading Connection Would a candidate running on a "middle of the road" platform appeal to you as a voter? Read on to learn about Eisenhower's accomplishments as president.

In 1950 the United States went to war in Korea. The war consumed the nation's attention and resources and basically ended Truman's Fair Deal. By 1952, with the war a bloody stalemate and his approval rating dropping quickly, Truman declined to run again for the presidency. With no Democratic incumbent to face, Republicans pinned their hopes of regaining the White House on a popular World War II hero.

The Election of 1952 Dwight Eisenhower decided to run as the Republican nominee for president in 1952. His running mate was a young California senator, Richard Nixon. The Democrats nominated Illinois governor Adlai Stevenson, a witty and eloquent speaker who had the support of leading liberals and organized labor.

The Republicans adopted the slogan: "It's time for a change!" The warm and friendly Eisenhower, known as "Ike," promised to end the war in Korea. "I like Ike" became the Republican rallying cry.

Eisenhower's campaign soon came under fire as reports surfaced that Richard Nixon had received gifts from California business leaders totaling $18,000 while he was a senator. For a while, it looked as if Nixon might be dropped from the ticket. In a nationwide speech broadcast on radio and television, Nixon insisted the funds had been used for legitimate political purposes. He did admit that his family had kept one gift, a cocker spaniel puppy named "Checkers." He declared, "The kids love the dog, [and] regardless about what they say about it, we're going to keep it." This so-called "Checkers speech" won praise from much of the public and kept Nixon on the ticket.

Eisenhower won the election by a landslide, carrying the Electoral College 442 votes to 89. The Republicans also gained an eight-seat majority in the House, while the Senate became evenly divided between Democrats and Republicans.

Ike as President President Eisenhower had two favorite phrases. "Middle of the road" described his political beliefs, which fell midway between conservative and liberal. He also referred to the notion of **"dynamic conservatism,"** which meant balancing economic conservatism with some activism.

Eisenhower wasted little time in showing his conservative side. The new president's cabinet appointments included several business leaders. Under their

Did You Know?

By the time a cease-fire was concluded in Korea, the total death toll for both sides had reached 600,000 soldiers and as many as two million civilians. The border between North and South Korea was re-established in roughly the same place as before the war. In the early 2000s, it remained the most heavily fortified border in the world.

guidance, Eisenhower ended government price and rent controls, which many conservatives had viewed as unnecessary federal control over the business community. The Eisenhower administration viewed business growth as vital to the nation. The president's secretary of defense, formerly the president of General Motors, declared to the Senate that "what is good for our country is good for General Motors, and vice versa."

Eisenhower's conservatism showed itself in other ways as well. In an attempt to curb the federal budget, the president vetoed a school construction bill and agreed to slash government aid to public housing. Along with these cuts, he supported some modest tax reductions.

Eisenhower also targeted the federal government's continuing aid to businesses, or what he termed "creeping socialism." Shortly after taking office, the president abolished the Reconstruction Finance Corporation (RFC), which since 1932 had lent money to banks, railroads, and other large institutions in financial trouble. Another Depression-era agency, the Tennessee Valley Authority (TVA), also came under Eisenhower's economic scrutiny. During his presidency, appropriations for the TVA fell from $185 million to $12 million.

In some areas, President Eisenhower took an activist role. For example, he advocated the passage of two large government projects. During the 1950s, as the number of Americans who owned cars increased, so too did the need for greater and more efficient travel routes. In 1956 Congress responded to this growing need by passing the **Federal Highway Act,** the largest public works program in American history. The act appropriated $25 billion for a 10-year effort to construct more than 40,000 miles (64,400 km)

of interstate highways. Congress also authorized construction of the Great Lakes-St. Lawrence Seaway to connect the Great Lakes with the Atlantic Ocean through a series of locks on the St. Lawrence River. Three previous presidents had been unable to reach agreements with Canada to build this waterway to aid international shipping. Through Eisenhower's efforts, the two nations finally agreed on a plan to complete the project.

Extending the New Deal Although President Eisenhower cut federal spending and worked to limit the federal government's role in the nation's economy, he also agreed to extend the Social Security system to an additional 10 million people. He also extended unemployment compensation to an additional 4 million citizens and agreed to increase the minimum hourly wage from 75¢ to $1 and to continue to provide some government aid to farmers.

By the time Eisenhower ran for a second term in 1956—a race he won easily—the nation had successfully completed the **transition** from a wartime to a peacetime economy. The battles between liberals and conservatives over whether to continue New Deal policies would continue. In the meantime, however, most Americans focused their energy on enjoying what had become a decade of tremendous prosperity.

✓ **Reading Check** **Evaluating** What conservative and activist measures did Eisenhower take during his administration?

HISTORY *Online* **Study Central**

For help with the concepts in this section of *American Vision: Modern Times* go to tav.mt.glencoe.com and click on *Study Central.*

SECTION 1 ASSESSMENT

Checking for Understanding

1. **Vocabulary** Define: closed shop, right-to-work law, union shop, featherbedding, restrain, subsidy, dynamic conservatism, transition.

2. **People and Terms** Identify: GI Bill, "Do-Nothing Congress," Fair Deal, Federal Highway Act.

Reviewing Big Ideas

3. **Examining** What programs did Congress pass from Truman's Fair Deal? What programs did Congress refuse?

Critical Thinking

4. **Historical Analysis** **Interpreting** In what ways did the Taft-Hartley Act hurt labor unions? **CA HI1; HI2**

5. **Categorizing** Use a graphic organizer to compare the agendas of the Truman and Eisenhower administrations.

Analyzing Visuals

6. **Analyzing Maps** Study the map on page 669. Which parts of the country did Dewey win? Why do you think he did so well in these areas?

Writing About History

7. **Persuasive Writing** Take on the role of a member of Congress during the Truman administration. Write a speech in which you try to persuade the 81st Congress to either pass or defeat Truman's Fair Deal measures.
CA 11WS1.1; 11WA2.3b

CHAPTER 14 Postwar America **671**

SECTION 1 ASSESSMENT ANSWERS

1. Content vocabulary is boldfaced and highlighted in yellow. Academic vocabulary is boldfaced.

2. GI Bill (p. 667), "Do-Nothing Congress" (p. 669), Fair Deal (p. 669), Federal Highway Act (p. 671)

3. Passed: minimum wage, Social Security, low-income housing and long-term rent subsidies; Refused: national health insurance, subsidies for farmers, federal aid for schools, civil rights legislation.

4. It outlawed closed shops, allowed states to outlaw union shops, and prohibited featherbedding.

5. Truman: increase government involvement in business, expand federal spending; Eisenhower: limit government involvement in business, curb federal spending

6. Northeast, Great Plains; governor of New York, strong in traditional Republican areas

7. Students' speeches will vary. Speeches should focus on several components of the Fair Deal.

U **Universal Access**

English Learners Before reading this paragraph, have students write a short paragraph or journal entry describing what they think Eisenhower meant by the phrase "creeping socialism." **EL**

ASSESS

 Resources for page 671

Use these resources to assess student mastery.

📂 Section Quiz 14-1

📂 Reading Essentials and Study Guide 14-1

⊙ Interactive Tutor Self-Assessment CD-ROM

📂 California Standards Practice, Grade 11

✓ **Reading Check**

Answer: reduced government control over business, cut spending on public housing; passed the Federal Highway Act, extended the Social Security system, and increased the minimum wage

HISTORY *Online*

Study Central provides audio summaries, interactive games, and online graphic organizers to help students review section content.

CLOSE

Persuasive Writing Have students imagine that they are advisers to the president. Tell them to write letters to Eisenhower convincing him to support the Federal Highway Act. (*Answers will vary but should note increasing car ownership as well as the need for greater and more efficient travel routes.*) **BL**
CA 11WS1.3

671

FOCUS

History–Social Science Standards

This feature addresses the following standards:

11.8 Students analyze the economic boom and social transformation of post-World War II America.

11.8.7 Describe the effects on society and the economy of technological developments since 1945, including the computer revolution, changes in communication, advances in medicine, and improvements in agricultural technology.

Reading Connection

Ask students to write a paragraph describing a trip they took using the interstate highway system. Remind them when writing their descriptions to include common features of interstates, such as road signs, fast food restaurants, billboards, rest stops, and other landmarks. **Ask: How would your journey have been different fifty years ago?** Invite students to share their responses with the class. **OL**

TEACH

C Critical Thinking

Making Inferences Organize students into groups of three or four to brainstorm some of the negative effects of the national interstate system. *(Answers may include loss of farmland or other natural resources; financial cost of construction and upkeep; loss of regional differences, etc.)*
Ask: Are the advantages of a national highway system worth the costs? Have students explain their reasons. **OL**

Why It Matters

Interstate Highways

As Cold War tensions rose, American officials realized that the ability to move troops and military equipment across the country quickly and efficiently could very well determine whether the nation could survive attack. Since the haphazard system of two-lane highways that crisscrossed America could not handle such a task, the Eisenhower administration proposed a 41,000-mile network of multi-lane interstate highways. The interstate system changed American life in several significant ways.

NATIONAL GEOGRAPHIC **The Interstate System, 2000**

— Interstate highways (free)
— Interstate highways (toll)

More Efficient Distribution of Goods ➤
The interstates made the distribution of goods faster and more efficient. In the 1990s, trucks moved more than 6 billion tons of goods each year, nearly half of all commercial transports in the United States. Most of these trucks used interstates.

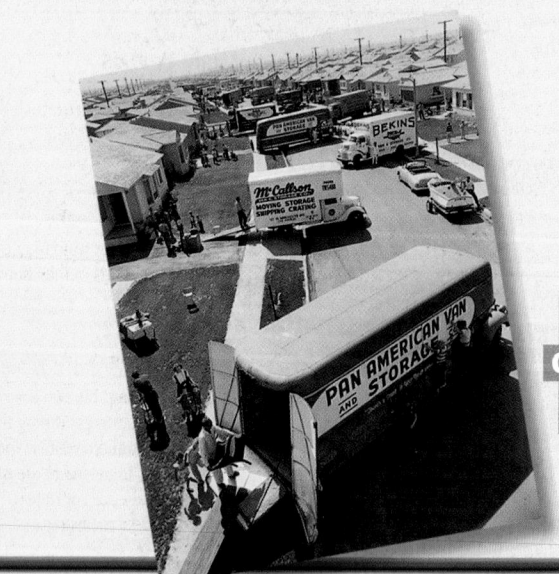

◀ **Suburbanization and Urban Sprawl**
C The interstate system contributed to the growth of suburban communities and the eventual geographic spread of centerless cities. Using the interstates, suburbanites could commute to their jobs miles away.

672 CHAPTER 14 Postwar America

EXTENDING THE CONTENT

Interstate Highways The numbering system for interstate highways is a good example of effective planning. One- and two-digit numbers designate all major routes. The north-south routes use odd numbers while the east-west routes use even numbers. East-west routes begin with the lowest numbers along the southern border of the United States, and north-south routes begin with the lowest numbers along the West Coast.

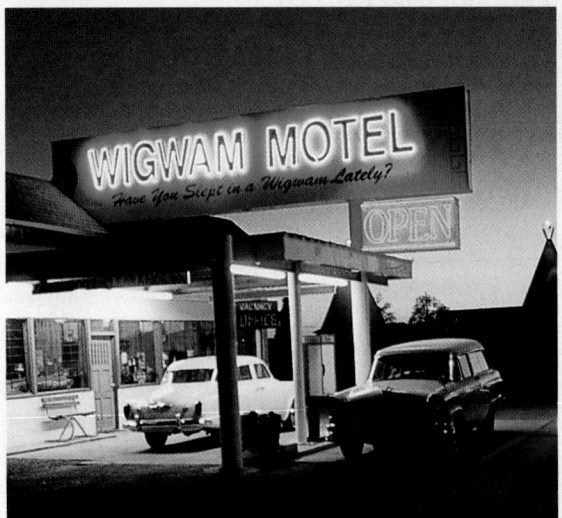

A New Road Culture ➤
The interstates created an automobile society. In 1997 $687 billion were spent on private automobiles compared to $22.8 billion for public transit. Additionally, chains of fast food restaurants and motels replaced independent operators across the country.

Speed of Travel

The interstate highways drastically decreased the time it took to travel across the continent. In 1919 a young Dwight D. Eisenhower joined 294 other members of the army to travel the 2,800 miles from Washington, D.C., to San Francisco. They made the trip in 62 days, averaging 5 miles per hour. During World War II, General Eisenhower was impressed with the modern design of Germany's freeway system, the Autobahn. "The old convoy," he said, "had started me thinking about good, two-lane highways, but Germany had made me see the wisdom of broader ribbons across the land." Wide lanes and controlled entrance and exit points allowed cars to travel at much higher speeds. Using the interstate highways, Eisenhower's trip would now take 4½ days.

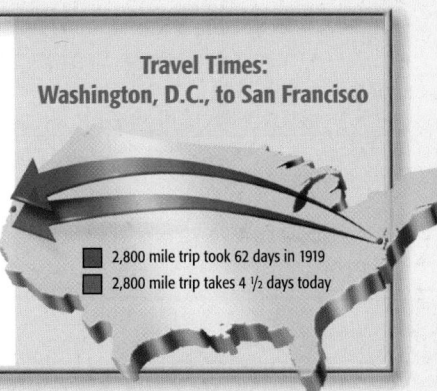

**Travel Times:
Washington, D.C., to San Francisco**

▮ 2,800 mile trip took 62 days in 1919
▮ 2,800 mile trip takes 4 ½ days today

ANALYZING THE IMPACT

Check for Understanding

1. **Identify** How was the initial purpose of the interstate highway system related to the Cold War?

Critical Thinking

2. **Evaluate** Explain the value of the interstate highway system in your area. Is the system an important part or your area's economy and culture?

ANALYZING THE IMPACT

1. The initial purpose was to facilitate the movement of troops and military equipment across the country in the event of an attack.

2. Students' answers will vary. Answers must focus on the economic and cultural value to the area. Possible Answers: more shipping and business, ability to travel to museums or go on vacations.

673

FOCUS

BELLRINGER
SKILLBUILDER ACTIVITY

Project **Daily Focus Skills Transparency 14-2** and have students answer the question.

Guide to Reading

Understanding Vocabulary: Have students write a word or phrase next to each vocabulary word to clarify its meaning.

Answers to Graphic: 1946, earliest computer; 1947, transistor developed; 1955, injection polio vaccine developed; 1958, satellite launched

Unpacking the Standards

Students will be able to:

- Describe the state of the post-war American economy.
- Explain the rising birth rate following World War II and its impact on the post-war family.
- Analyze advances in science and technology during this era.

Answers and Additional Support

SECTION 2 The Affluent Society

Guide to Reading

Connection
In the previous section, you learned about the transition of the United States to a peacetime economy. In this section, you will discover the great changes a postwar economic boom brought to American society.

Main Idea
- An increase in service sector and professional jobs led to a great increase in American income from 1940 to 1955. (p. 675)
- Despite a baby boom and cultural pressure, the number of women in the workforce increased. (p. 677)

- Technological changes included the development of early computers, advances in medicine, and new conquests of outer space. (p. 678)

Content Vocabulary
white-collar, blue-collar, multinational corporation, franchise, baby boom

Academic Vocabulary
accompany, benefit, generate

People and Terms to Identify
John Kenneth Galbraith, David Riesman, Levittown, Jonas Salk

Reading Objectives
- **Explain** the reasons for and the effects of the nation's economic boom.

- **Describe** changes to the American family that took place during the 1950s.
- **Discuss** the technological and medical discoveries of the 1950s.

Reading Strategy
Sequencing As you read about American society in the 1950s, complete a time line similar to the one below by recording the scientific and technological breakthroughs of the time.

Preview of Events

◆1946	◆1950	◆1954	◆1958
1947 Construction of Levittown begins	**1950** David Riesman's *The Lonely Crowd* published	**1955** Salk polio vaccine becomes widely available	**1958** John Kenneth Galbraith's *The Affluent Society* published

---

The following are the main History–Social Science Standards covered in this section.

11.8.1 Trace the growth of service sector, white collar, and professional sector jobs in business and government.

11.8.7 Describe the effects on society and the economy of technological developments since 1945, including the computer revolution, changes in communication, advances in medicine, and improvements in agricultural technology.

11.10.7 Analyze the women's rights movement from the era of Elizabeth Stanton and Susan Anthony and the passage of the Nineteenth Amendment to the movement launched in the 1960s, including differing perspectives on the roles of women.

11.11.3 Describe the changing roles of women in society as reflected in the entry of more women into the labor force and the changing family structure.

11.11.7 Explain how the federal, state, and local governments have responded to demographic and social changes such as population shifts to the suburbs, racial concentrations in the cities, Frostbelt-to-Sunbelt migration, international migration, decline of family farms, increases in out-of-wedlock births, and drug abuse.

⟨≈ *The Big Idea* ≈⟩

Societies change over time. Between 1940 and 1955, the income of American workers increased as the number of white-collar jobs grew. People began to purchase more luxury items and buy homes in the suburbs. During this time, the country also experienced a baby boom. Despite an emphasis on women's roles as homemakers, the number of women in the workplace increased. Advances in technology and medicine brought about the development of early computers, new medicines, and the world's first space satellite.

674 CHAPTER 14 Postwar America

SECTION RESOURCES

📁 Print Material
- Reproducible Lesson Plan 14-2
- Guided Reading Activity 14-2
- Reading Essentials and Study Guide 14-2
- Active Reading Note-Taking Guide 14-2

🖌 Transparencies
- Daily Focus Skills Transparency 14-2
- Section Graphic Organizer Transparency 14-2

Technology
- Interactive Tutor Self-Assessment CD-ROM
- Exam*View*® Pro Testmaker CD-ROM
- Presentation Plus! CD-ROM

American Abundance

 An increase in service sector and professional jobs led to a great increase in American income from 1940 to 1955.

Reading Connection Did you shop or eat at a franchise this week? Read on to find out about the growth of franchises and multinational corporations during the 1950s.

In 1958 economist **John Kenneth Galbraith** published *The Affluent Society*, in which he claimed that the nation's postwar prosperity was a new phenomenon. In the past, Galbraith said, all societies had an "economy of scarcity," meaning that a lack of resources and overpopulation had limited economic productivity. Now, the United States and a few other industrialized nations had created what Galbraith called an "economy of abundance." An abundance of goods and services allowed many people to enjoy a standard of living they never before thought possible. Kemmons Wilson was one example of how the standard of living was changing.

★ An American Story ★

In the summer of 1951, Kemmons Wilson traveled with his family from Memphis, Tennessee, to Washington, D.C. He noticed that some of the motels they stayed in were terrible. Each added a $2 charge per child to the standard room price, and many were located far from restaurants, forcing travelers back into their cars to search for meals.

Frustrated, Wilson decided to build a motel chain that would provide interstate travelers with comfortable lodgings. They would be located near good family restaurants and allow kids to stay free. Together with a group of investors, Wilson began building the Holiday Inn motel chain. Families loved his motels, and soon Holiday Inns were sprouting up all over the country.

Wilson said he never doubted the success of his endeavor. "I like to think that I'm so . . . normal that anything I like, everybody else is going to like too," he said. "The idea that my instincts are out of line just doesn't occur to me." His prosperity mirrored a growing affluence in the nation. This time of prosperity made the shortages of the Great Depression and World War II a distant memory.

—adapted from *Watching TV: Four Decades of American Television*

Kemmons Wilson's motel chain proved successful largely because the 1950s was a decade of incredible prosperity.

The Spread of Wealth Some critics accused Galbraith of overstating the situation, but the facts and figures seemed to support his theory. Between 1940 and 1960, the average income of American families roughly tripled. Americans in all income brackets—poor, middle-class, and wealthy—experienced this rapid rise in income. The dramatic rise in home ownership also showed that the income of average families had risen significantly. Between 1940 and 1960, the number of Americans owning their own homes rose from about 43 to about 62 percent.

Accompanying the country's economic growth were dramatic changes in work environments. Mechanization in farms and factories meant that fewer farmers and laborers were needed to provide the public with food and goods. As a result, more Americans began working in what are called **white-collar** jobs, such as those in sales and management. In 1956, for the first time, white-collar workers outnumbered **blue-collar** workers, or people who perform physical labor in industry.

Multinationals and Franchises Many white-collar employees worked for large corporations. As these businesses competed with each other, some expanded overseas. These **multinational corporations** located themselves closer to important raw materials and **benefited** from a cheaper labor pool, which made them more competitive.

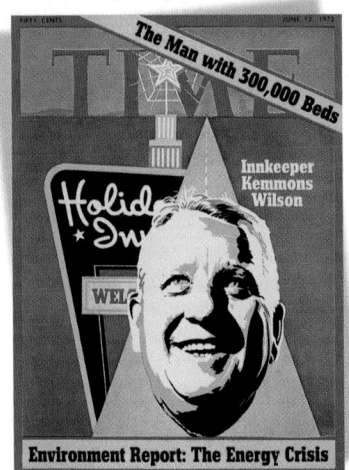

Kemmons Wilson on magazine cover ▼

C **Critical Thinking**

Determining Cause and Effect To balance high levels of production with consumer demand, business and government often encouraged built-in obsolescence, generated new demand with advertising, and shipped excess food and technology to less-advantaged nations. Ask students to discuss what would happen if an oversupply of goods vanished. **Ask: How would these policies change in an economy of scarcity?** *(Students' answers will vary.)* **AL**

R **Reading Strategy**

Summarizing Have students read the paragraphs under "The Spread of Wealth" and then summarize what they have just read. When the summaries are complete, have students share their summaries with a classmate to determine if all the main ideas are included. **BL**

Review the Big Idea

Review the Big Idea for this section, "Societies change over time." Have students research the cost of a modest suburban home built in their community during the 1950s and the cost of the same home today. Instruct students to include an exterior sketch or photograph, a floor plan, and a description of special features such as a patio or garage. Encourage students to use library and Internet resources to locate real estate records. Use the reports as a starting point for a discussion about the affordability of housing in the 1950s and today. **AL**

More Skill Practice

Logical/Mathematical Provide the data below and ask students to chart the U.S. home ownership rate from 1900 to 2000. Ask students to offer explanations for noticeable trends.

2000	67.4%	1960	61.9%	1920	45.6%
1990	64.2%	1950	55.0%	1910	45.9%
1980	64.4%	1940	43.6%	1900	46.7%
1970	62.9%	1930	47.8%	**OL**	

"He never wastes a minute, J.P.—that's his lunch."

Analyzing *Political Cartoons*

The Organization Man In the 1950s, more and more people worked in white-collar corporate jobs. Some social critics worried that this development emphasized conformity. In what other ways did society encourage people to conform?

The 1950s also witnessed the rise of **franchises,** in which a person owns and runs one or several stores of a chain operation. Because many business leaders believed that consumers valued dependability and familiarity, the owners of chain operations often demanded that their franchises present a uniform look and style.

The Organization Man Like franchise owners, many corporate leaders also expected their employees to conform to company standards. In general, corporations did not desire free-thinking individuals or people who might speak out or criticize the company. Some social observers recognized this phenomenon and disapproved of it. In his 1950 book, *The Lonely Crowd*, sociologist **David Riesman** argued that this conformity was changing people. Formerly, he claimed, people were "inner-directed," judging themselves on the basis of their own values and the esteem of their families. Now, however, people were becoming "other-directed," concerning themselves with winning the approval of the corporation or community.

In his 1956 book *The Organization Man*, writer William H. Whyte, Jr., criticized the similarity many business organizations in the United States cultivated in order to keep any individual from dominating. "In group doctrine," Whyte wrote, "the strong

personality is viewed with overwhelming suspicion," and the person with ideas is considered "a threat."

In the 1950s, more and more people worked in white-collar corporate jobs. Some social critics worried that this development emphasized conformity. In what other ways did society encourage people to conform?

The New Consumerism The conformity of the 1950s included people's desires to own the same new products as their neighbors. With more disposable income, Americans bought more luxury items, such as refrigerators, washing machines, vacuum cleaners, and air conditioners. Americans also bought a variety of labor-saving machines. As *House and Garden* magazine boasted in a 1954 article, coffeemakers, blenders, and lawn trimmers "[replaced] the talents of caretaker, gardener, cook, [and] maid."

Accompanying the nation's spending spree was the growth of more sophisticated advertising. Advertising became the fastest-growing industry in the United States, as manufacturers employed new marketing techniques to sell their products. These techniques were carefully planned to whet the consumer's appetite. The purpose of these advertisers was to influence choices among brands of goods that were essentially the same. According to the elaborate advertising campaigns of the time, a freezer became a promise of plenty, a second car became a symbol of status, and a mouthwash became the key to immediate success.

The Growth of Suburbia Advertisers targeted their ads to consumers who had money to spend. Many of these consumers lived in the nation's growing suburbs that grew up around cities.

Levittown, New York, was one of the earliest of the new suburbs. The driving force behind this planned residential community was Bill Levitt, who mass-produced hundreds of simple and similar looking homes in a potato field 10 miles east of New York City. Between 1947 and 1951, thousands of families rushed to buy the inexpensive homes, and soon other communities similar to Levittown sprang up throughout the United States.

Suburbs became increasingly popular throughout the 1950s, accounting for about 85 percent of new home construction. The number of suburban dwellers doubled, while the population of cities themselves rose only 10 percent. Reasons for the rapid growth of suburbia varied. Some people wanted to escape the crime and congestion of city neighborhoods. Others viewed life in the suburbs as a move up to a better life for themselves and their children. In contrast to city life, suburbia offered a more

Did You Know?

Three Levittowns were built, the first on Long Island, the second in Bucks County, Pennsylvania, and the third in Willingboro, New Jersey. These planned communities allowed people to live in smaller communities but commute to larger cities.

picturesque environment. As developers in earlier periods had done, the developers of the 1950s attracted home buyers with promises of fresh air, green lawns, and trees.

Affordability became a key factor in attracting home buyers to the suburbs. Because the GI Bill offered low-interest loans, new housing was more affordable during the postwar period than at any other time in American history. Equally attractive was the government's offer of income tax deductions for home mortgage interest payments and property taxes. For millions of Americans, the suburbs came to symbolize the American dream. They owned their homes, sent their children to good schools, lived in safe communities, and enjoyed economic security.

Nevertheless, some social commentators, such as architect Lewis Mumford and writer John Keats, viewed such plain and identical-looking communities as another sign of conformity. "You too can find a box of your own," wrote Keats, "inhabited by people whose age, income, number of children, problems, habits, conversations, dress, possessions, perhaps even blood types are almost precisely like yours."

✓ **Reading Check** **Interpreting** What were two causes and effects of the economic boom of the 1950s?

The 1950s Family

Main Idea Despite a baby boom and cultural pressure, the number of women in the workforce increased.

Reading Connection Do most of the women you know work outside the home? Read on to learn about the number of women who held jobs and raised families in the 1950s.

In addition to all the other transformations taking place in the nation during the 1950s, the American family also was changing. Across the country, many families grew larger, and more married women entered the workforce.

The Baby Boom The American birthrate exploded after World War II. From 1945 to 1961, a period known as the **baby boom,** more than 65 million children were born in the United States. At the height of the baby boom, a child was born every seven seconds.

Several factors contributed to the baby boom. First, young couples who had delayed marriage during World War II and the Korean War could now marry, buy homes, and begin their families. In addition, the government encouraged the growth of fami-

lies by offering generous GI benefits for home purchases. Finally, on television and in magazines, popular culture celebrated pregnancy, parenthood, and large families.

Women in the Fifties Many women focused on their traditional role of homemaker during the 1950s. Even though 8 million American women had gone to work during the war, the new postwar emphasis on having babies and establishing families now discouraged women from seeking employment. Many Americans assumed that a good mother should stay home to take care of her children.

"Let's face it, girls," declared one female writer in *Better Homes and Gardens* in April 1955, "that wonderful guy in your house—and in mine—is building your house, your happiness and the opportunities that will come to your children." The magazine advised stay-at-home wives to "set their sights on a happy home, a host of friends and a bright future through success in HIS job."

Despite the popular emphasis on homemaking, however, the number of women who held jobs

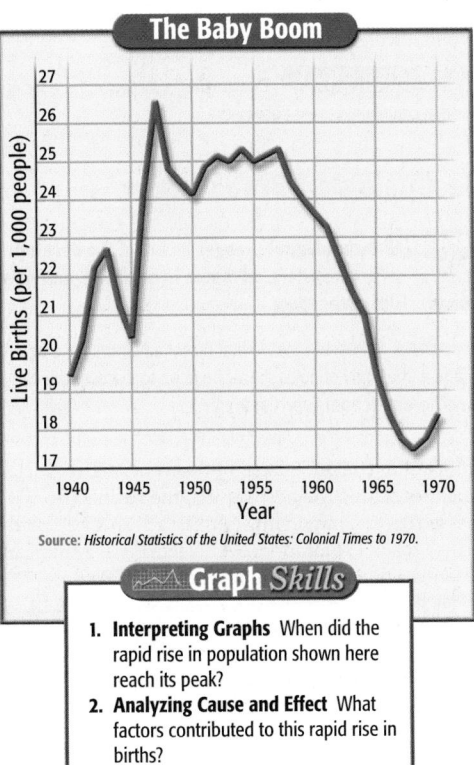

The Baby Boom

Live Births (per 1,000 people) vs. Year (1940–1970)

Source: *Historical Statistics of the United States: Colonial Times to 1970.*

Graph Skills

1. **Interpreting Graphs** When did the rapid rise in population shown here reach its peak?
2. **Analyzing Cause and Effect** What factors contributed to this rapid rise in births?

CHAPTER 14 Postwar America **677**

R₁ Reading Strategy

Scaffolding—Academic Vocabulary The word *contribute* was introduced in Chapter 9, Section 3. Ask a student to define the word. **BL**

C Critical Thinking

Comparing and Contrasting Have students write a few paragraphs or a journal entry comparing and contrasting women's roles in the 1950s and women's roles today. Remind them to include such issues as jobs outside the home, housekeeping and children, and the importance of marriage. Ask students to read what they have written aloud to the class, and discuss the important ways that American women's roles have shifted in the last 50 years. **BL**

R₂ Reading Strategy

Scaffolding—Inferring During the 1950s, the number of women who held jobs outside the home increased even though traditional homemaking was quite popular at the time. Have students work in pairs to decide why this was so. *(Answers may vary but students should note the desire to maintain a comfortable lifestyle, "keep up with the Joneses," and gain personal satisfaction and fulfillment.)* **OL**

This **Reading Skill** was introduced in Chapter 5.

✓ **Reading Check**

Answer: causes: new business techniques and improved technology; effects: answers may include consumerism and growth of suburbs.

Graph Skills

Answers:
1. about 1947
2. Couples had delayed marriage until after the war and could now afford a family, and popular culture celebrated pregnancy, parenthood, and large families.

Graph Skills Practice
Ask: What do you suppose caused the birthrate to rise again in the late 1960s? *(The first baby boomers were having children of their own.)*

Profiles IN HISTORY

Dr. Jonas Salk
1914–1995

The man who developed the vaccine for one of the nation's most feared diseases almost did not go into medicine. Jonas Salk enrolled in college as a pre-law student but soon changed his mind. "My mother didn't think I would make a very good lawyer," Salk said, "probably because I could never win an argument with her." Salk switched his major to pre-med and went on to become a research scientist.

Salk initially directed the search for a cure to the dreaded ailment of polio at the University of Pittsburgh's Virus Research Laboratory. Every so often, Salk would make rounds in the over-

crowded polio wards of nearby Municipal Hospital, where nurses described their feelings of pity and helpless rage as paralyzed children cried for water. As one nurse said, "I can remember how the staff used to kid Dr. Salk—kidding in earnest—telling him to hurry up and do something."

Salk became famous for his breakthrough vaccine. The shy doctor, however, did not desire fame. About his becoming a celebrity, Salk observed that it was "a transitory thing and you wait till it blows over. Eventually people will start thinking, 'That poor guy,' and leave me alone. Then I'll be able to get back to my laboratory."

outside the home actually increased during the 1950s. Most women who went to work did so in order to help their families maintain their comfortable lifestyles. By 1960 nearly one-third of all married women were part of the paid workforce.

✓ **Reading Check** **Evaluating** What were three factors that contributed to the baby boom?

R₁ Technological Breakthroughs

Main Idea Technological changes included the development of early computers, advances in medicine, and new conquests of outer space.

Reading Connection What recent advances have been made in the study of outer space? Read on to discover the early satellite launch from Cape Canaveral.

As the United States underwent many social changes during the postwar era, the nation also witnessed several important scientific advances. In medicine, space exploration, and electronics, American scientists broke new ground during the 1950s.

Advances in Electronics The electronics industry made rapid advances after World War II. In 1947 three American physicists—John Bardeen, Walter H. Brattain, and William Shockley—developed the transistor, a tiny device that **generated** electric signals and made it possible to miniaturize radios and calculators.

The age of computers also dawned in the postwar era. In 1946 scientists working under a U.S. Army contract developed one of the nation's earliest computers—known as ENIAC (Electronic Numerical Integrator and Computer)—to make military calculations. Several years later, a newer model called UNIVAC (Universal Automatic Computer) would handle business data and launch the computer revolution. The computer, along with changes and improvements in communication and transportation systems, allowed many Americans to work more quickly and efficiently. As a result, families in the 1950s had more free time, and new forms of leisure activity became popular.

R₂ Medical Miracles The medical breakthroughs of the 1950s included the development of powerful antibiotics to fight infection; the introduction of new drugs to combat arthritis, diabetes, cancer, and heart disease; and groundbreaking advances in surgical techniques. Polio, however, continued to baffle the medical profession.

Periodic polio epidemics had been occurring in the United States since 1916. Franklin Roosevelt contracted the disease as a young man and used a wheelchair for the remainder of his life. In the 1940s and 1950s, however, polio struck the nation in epidemic proportions. Officially known as infantile paralysis because it generally targeted the young, the disease brought a wave of terror to the country. No one knew where or when polio would strike, but an epidemic broke out in some area of the country each summer, sometimes paralyzing or killing its victims. People

Profiles IN HISTORY

watched helplessly while neighbors fell sick. Some died or needed an iron lung as part of their treatment. Iron lungs were large metal tanks with pumps that helped patients breathe.

Because no one knew what caused the disease, parents searched for ways to safeguard their families each summer. Some sent their children to the country to avoid excessive contact with others. Public swimming pools and beaches were closed. Parks and playgrounds across the country stood deserted. Nevertheless, the disease continued to strike. In 1952 a record 58,000 new cases were reported.

Finally, a research scientist named **Jonas Salk** developed an injectable vaccine that prevented polio. Salk first tested the vaccine on himself, his wife, and his three sons. It was then tested on 2 million schoolchildren. In 1955 the vaccine was declared safe and effective and became available to the general public. The results were spectacular. New cases of polio fell to 5,700 in 1958 and then to 3,277 in 1960. American scientist Albert Sabin then developed an oral vaccine for polio. Because it was safer and more convenient than Salk's injection vaccine, the Sabin vaccine became the most common form of treatment against the disease. In the years to come, the threat of polio in the United States would almost completely disappear.

Conquering Space After the Soviet Union launched *Sputnik,* the world's first space satellite, in October 1957, the United States hastened to catch up with its Cold War rival. Less than four months later, on January 31, 1958, the United States launched its own satellite from Cape Canaveral, Florida. Reporter Milton Bracker described the jubilant scene:

66As the firing command neared, a deadly silence fell on those who were watching. In the glare of the searchlights, a stream of liquid oxygen could be seen venting like a lavender cloud from the side of the seventy-foot rocket. . . . At fourteen and one-half seconds after time zero, after the priming fuel had ignited almost invisibly, the main stage engine came to life with an immeasurable thrust of flame in all directions. . . . With thousands of eyes following it, the rocket dug into the night and accelerated as its sound loudened. Spectators on near-by beaches pointed and craned their necks and cried, 'There it is!' and began to cheer.99

—quoted in *Voices from America's Past*

Meanwhile, engineers were building smoother and faster commercial planes. Poet Carl Sandburg wrote about taking the first American jet flight from New York to Los Angeles. The trip took only five and a half hours. "You search for words to describe the speed of this flight," wrote an amazed Sandburg. "You are whisked . . . from an ocean on one side of the continent to an ocean on the opposite side in less time than it takes the sun to trace a 90-degree arc across the sky."

☑ **Reading Check** **Examining** What medical and technological advances met specific needs in the late 1940s and 1950s?

HISTORY Online Study Central

For help with the concepts in this section of *American Vision: Modern Times* go to tav.mt.glencoe.com and click on **Study Central.**

SECTION 2 ASSESSMENT

Checking for Understanding

1. **Vocabulary** Define: accompany, white-collar, blue-collar, multinational corporation, benefit, franchise, baby boom, generate.

2. **People and Terms** Identify: John Kenneth Galbraith, David Riesman, Levittown, Jonas Salk.

3. **Describe** how and why the suburbs became popular places to live.

Reviewing Big Ideas

4. **Explaining** How was the affluent society of the United States in the 1950s different from previous decades?

Critical Thinking

5. **Historical Analysis** **Interpreting** What caused the advertising industry boom in the 1950s? CA H11

6. **Organizing** Use a graphic organizer similar to the one below to list the causes and effects of the economic boom of the 1950s.

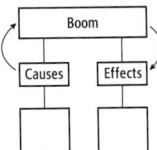

Analyzing Visuals

7. **Analyzing Photographs** Study the photograph of Kemmons Wilson on the cover of TIME magazine on page 675. Using the information in this section, who or what would you put on the cover of a magazine if you were the editor? Sketch your cover on a sheet of paper.

Writing About History

8. **Descriptive Writing** Write an article for a magazine such as *Better Homes and Gardens* describing changes the American family underwent during the 1950s. CA 11WA2.3c

---

SECTION 2 ASSESSMENT ANSWERS

1. Content vocabulary is boldfaced and highlighted in yellow. Academic vocabulary is boldfaced.

2. John Kenneth Galbraith (p. 675), David Riesman (p. 676), Levittown (p. 676), Jonas Salk (p. 679)

3. some wanted to escape urban problems; more people were able to afford homes and automobiles

4. The lives of many Americans improved significantly.

5. Advertisers competed for Americans' disposable income.

6. Causes: new business techniques, improved technology; Effects: answers may include consumerism and suburban growth

7. Students' magazine covers will vary.

8. Articles should use realistic examples and offer explanations for the changes.

Drawing Conclusions Inform students that some parents today choose not to have their children vaccinated against polio due to religious or personal beliefs, or the fear of medical complications. Invite students to research the health and safety risks associated with common vaccines, such as the polio vaccine. Have students record their findings in a one-page report. OL

ASSESS

Resources for page 679

Use these resources to assess student mastery.

📁 Section Quiz 14-2

📁 Reading Essentials and Study Guide 14-2

💿 Interactive Tutor Self-Assessment CD-ROM

📁 California Standards Practice, Grade 11

☑ **Reading Check**

Answer: antibiotics; drugs for arthritis, diabetes, cancer, and heart disease; new surgical techniques; polio vaccine

HISTORY Online

Study Central provides audio summaries, interactive games, and online graphic organizers to help students review section content.

CLOSE

Evaluating Have students describe changes in the American family that took place during the 1950s. OL

679

FOCUS

BELLRINGER
SKILLBUILDER ACTIVITY

Project **Daily Focus Skills Transparency 14-3** and have students answer the question.

Guide to Reading

Understanding Vocabulary: Have students create a database of the vocabulary words, adding facts as they learn about each word.

Answers to Graphic:
Television: action shows, game shows, situation comedies, variety shows; radio: recorded music, news, weather, talk shows; cinema: cinemascope, 3-D movies; music: rock 'n' roll; literature: the beat movement

Unpacking the Standards

Students will be able to:

• Describe the growth of American mass media during the 1950s.

• Discuss the elements that helped define the youth culture of this decade.

Answers and Additional Support

SECTION 3
Popular Culture of the 1950s

Guide to Reading

Connection
In the previous section, you learned about the changes an economic boom brought to American society. In this section, you will discover how Americans entertained themselves in the 1950s.

Main Idea
• Technological enhancements increased the popularity of television and movies. (p. 681)
• Rock 'n' roll music and the literature of the beat movement defined youth culture. (p. 683)

• Although few African Americans performed on television, many had a profound impact on early rock 'n' roll. (p. 685)

Content Vocabulary
generation gap

Academic Vocabulary
device, controversial

People to Identify
Ed Sullivan, Alan Freed, Elvis Presley, Jack Kerouac, Nat King Cole

Reading Objectives
• **Explain** the characteristics of the new youth culture.

• **Discuss** the contributions of African Americans to 1950s culture.

Reading Strategy
Categorizing As you read about the popular culture of the 1950s, complete a graphic organizer similar to the one below comparing new forms of mass media during the 1950s.

New Forms of Mass Media	Description

Preview of Events

♦1955   ♦1956   ♦1957   ♦1958

1955
The quiz show *The $64,000 Question* debuts

1956
Elvis Presley appears on the *Ed Sullivan Show;* Allen Ginsberg's "Howl" published

1957
40 million television sets in use in the United States

1958
TV quiz show scandals begin to surface

The following are the main History–Social Science Standards covered in this section.

11.8.8 Discuss forms of popular culture, with emphasis on their origins and geographic diffusion (e.g., jazz and other forms of popular music, professional sports, architectural and artistic styles).

~ *The Big Idea* ~

Societies change over time. With more money and time available, Americans bought more televisions. Comedies, action and adventure shows, variety programs, and game shows captivated viewers. Hollywood tried to regain audiences with 3-D films and new panoramic screens. A new youth culture that developed during this time embraced rock 'n' roll and the literature of the beat movement. While few African Americans were able to perform on television, many still had a profound impact on rock 'n' roll.

SECTION RESOURCES

Print Material
• Reproducible Lesson Plan 14-3
• Guided Reading Activity 14-3
• Reading Essentials and Study Guide 14-3
• Active Reading Note-Taking Guide 14-3

Transparencies
• Daily Focus Skills Transparency 14-3
• Section Graphic Organizer Transparency 14-3

Technology
• Interactive Tutor Self-Assessment CD-ROM
• Exam*View*® Pro Testmaker CD-ROM
• Presentation Plus! CD-ROM

The New Mass Media

Main Idea Technological enhancements increased the popularity of television and movies.

Reading Connection What television shows do you like to watch? Read on to learn about the early television shows and stars.

Although regular television broadcasts had begun in the early 1940s, there were few stations, and sets were expensive. By the end of the 1950s, however, the small, black-and-white-screened sets sat in living rooms across the country. One of the shows of the time that captivated audiences was *I Love Lucy.*

★ An American Story ★

In 1953 Lucille Ball and her real-life husband, Desi Arnaz, were starring in one of the most popular shows on American television, *I Love Lucy.* In January, Ball had a baby—both in real life and on her show. Her pregnancy and the birth of her baby became a national event that captivated her audience. A pre-filmed segment of the show showed Lucy and her husband going to the hospital to have the baby, and the show was broadcast only a few hours after the real birth. More than two-thirds of the nation's television sets tuned in, an audience of around 44 million viewers. Far fewer people watched the next day when television broadcast a presidential inauguration.

I Love Lucy was so popular that some people actually set up their work schedules around the show. Marshall Field's, which had previously held sales on the same night the show was on, eventually switched its sales to a different night. A sign on its shop window explained, "We love Lucy too, so we're closing on Monday nights." A relatively new medium, television had swept the nation by the mid-1950s.

—adapted from *Watching TV: Four Decades of American Television*¹

Television's popularity forced the other forms of mass media—namely motion pictures and radio—to innovate in order to keep their audiences.

The Rise of Television Popularity During World War II, televisions became more affordable for consumers. In 1946 it is estimated there were between 7,000 and 8,000 sets in the entire United States. By 1957 there were 40 million television sets in use. Over 80 percent of households had televisions.

By the late 1950s, television news had become an important vehicle for information. Television advertising spawned a growing market for many new products. Advertising, after all, provided television with the money that allowed it to flourish. As one critic concluded, "Programs on television are simply a **device** to keep the advertisements and commercials from bumping loudly together." Televised athletic events gradually made professional and college sports one of the most prominent sources of entertainment.

Comedy, Action, and Games Early television programs fell into several main categories including comedy, action and adventure, and variety-style entertainment. Laughter proved popular in other formats besides the half-hour situation comedy. Many of the early television comedy shows, such as those starring Bob Hope and Jack Benny, were adapted from popular old radio shows. Benny enjoyed considerable television success with his routines of bad violin playing and stingy behavior.

Television watchers in the 1950s also relished action shows. Westerns such as *Hopalong Cassidy, The Lone Ranger,* and *Gunsmoke* grew quickly in popularity. Viewers also enjoyed police programs such as *Dragnet,* a hugely successful show featuring Joe Friday and his partner hunting down a new criminal each week.

▼ *Lucille Ball and Desi Arnaz*

S **Skill Practice**

Evaluating Evidence Have students watch a rerun of a television program that was popular during the 1950s, such as *I Love Lucy* or *The Many Loves of Dobie Gillis.* Tell them to make a list of the styles, slang expressions, attitudes, and behaviors that are different from those of today. Discuss the lists and then compile them into a 1950s culture dictionary. **OL**

R **Reading Strategy**

Organizing Information Have students develop a list of the various types of television shows such as situation comedies, dramas, reality shows, and game shows. Tell them to pick their three favorite types. Tally the student responses and indicate the top five vote-getters. **Ask: Why have different types of shows been popular in different periods of television history?** *(Students may point out that television shows usually reflect the culture and specific concerns of their time.)* **BL**

Did You Know?

Invented in the 1930s, television became popular in the late 1940s. By 1960 nearly 90 percent of American families owned at least one set—mostly black and white. Although the Columbia Broadcasting System presented the first commercial color telecast in 1953, color television remained too expensive during the 1950s for widespread use.

Did You Know?

The Swanson Company created frozen individual meals in 1952 and called these meals TV dinners in 1954. Swanson sold 10 million TV dinners the first year they were distributed nationally. By the time the TV dinner celebrated its 45th birthday, Americans were buying 3 million a week.

Variety shows such as **Ed Sullivan's** *Toast of the Town* provided a mix of comedy, opera, popular song, dance, acrobatics, and juggling. Quiz shows attracted large audiences, too, after the 1955 debut of *The $64,000 Question*. In this show and its many imitators, two contestants tried to answer questions from separate glass-encased booths. The questions, stored between shows in a bank vault, arrived at the studio at airtime in the hands of a stern faced bank executive flanked by two armed guards. The contestants competed head-to-head, with the winner returning the following week to face a new challenger.

In 1956 the quiz show *Twenty-One* caused an uproar across the nation after Charles Van Doren, a young assistant professor with a modest income, won $129,000 during his weeks on the program. The viewing public soon learned, however, that Van Doren and many of the other contestants had received the answers to the questions in advance. Before a congressional committee in 1959, Van Doren admitted his role in the scandal and apologized to his many fans, saying, "I was involved, deeply involved, in a deception." In the wake of the *Twenty-One* fraud, many quiz shows went off the air.

U Hollywood Adapts to the Times

As the popularity of television grew, movies lost viewers. "Hollywood's like Egypt," lamented producer David Selznick in 1951. "Full of crumbling pyramids." While the film business may not have been collapsing, it certainly did suffer after the war. Attendance dropped from 82 million in 1946 to 36 million by 1950. By 1960, when some 50 million Americans owned a television, one-fifth of the nation's movie theaters had closed.

▼ *Charles Van Doren with quiz show host Jack Berry*

MR. VAN DOREN

Throughout the decade, Hollywood struggled mightily to recapture its audience. "Don't be a 'Living Room Captive,'" one industry ad pleaded. "Step out and see a great movie!" When contests, door prizes, and an advertising campaign announcing that "Movies Are Better Than Ever" failed to lure people out of their homes, Hollywood began to try to make films more exciting. Between 1952 and 1954, audiences of 3-D films received special glasses that gave the impression that a monster or a knife was lunging directly at them from off the screen. Viewers, however, soon tired of both the glasses and the often ridiculous plots of 3-D movies.

Cinemascope, movies shown on large, panoramic screens, finally gave Hollywood a reliable lure. Widescreen spectacles like *The Robe, The Ten Commandments,* and *Around the World in 80 Days* cost a great deal of money to produce. These blockbusters, however, made up for their cost by attracting huge audiences and netting large profits. The movie industry also made progress by taking the "if you can't beat 'em, join 'em" approach. Hollywood eventually began to film programs especially for television and also sold old movies, which could be rebroadcast cheaply, to the networks.

Like television, the films of the fifties for the most part adhered to the conformity of the times. Roles for single women who did not want families were few and far between. For example, each of Marilyn Monroe's film roles featured the blond movie star as married, soon to be married, or unhappy that she was not married.

Movies routinely portrayed African Americans in stereotypical roles, such as maids, servants, or sidekicks for white heroes. Even when African Americans took leading roles, they were often one-dimensional characters who rarely showed human emotions or characteristics. African American actor Sidney Poitier resented having to play such parts:

> ❝The black characters usually come out on the screen as saints, as the other-cheek-turners, as people who are not really people: who are so nice and good. . . . As a matter of fact, I'm just dying to play villains.❞
>
> —quoted in *The Fifties: The Way We Really Were*

Radio Draws Them In Television also lured away radio listeners and forced the radio industry, like Hollywood, to develop new ways to win back audiences. After television took over many of radio's concepts, radio stations began to specialize in

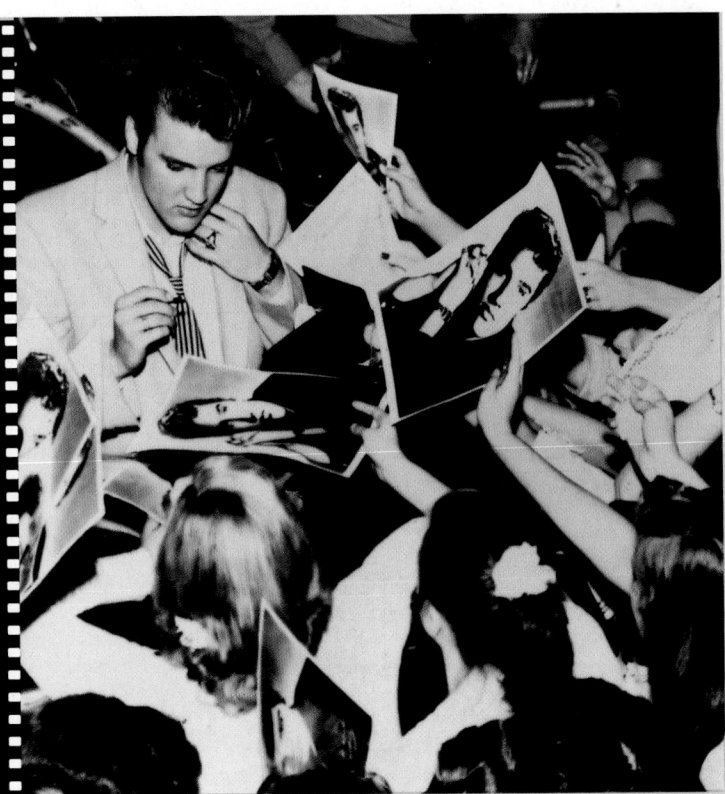

NATIONAL GEOGRAPHIC
MOMENT in HISTORY

THE KING OF ROCK

Elvis Presley, shown here signing autographs after a performance in Houston, took American youth in the 1950s by storm. Parents, on the other hand, were less than thrilled with his music—a blend of African American-inspired rhythm and blues and early rock 'n' roll—and his hip-swiveling gyrations on stage. For Presley's first appearance on *The Ed Sullivan Show*, the host insisted that cameras show him only from the waist up. Elvis added to his fame by starring in a string of films that audiences loved but critics panned.

presenting recorded music, news, public-service programming, and shows for specific audiences.

As a result of this targeted programming, radio stations survived and even flourished. Their numbers more than doubled between 1948, when 1,680 stations were broadcasting to the nation, and 1957, when more than 3,600 stations filled the airwaves.

✓ **Reading Check** **Identifying** How did the television industry affect the U.S. economy?

The New Youth Culture

Main Idea Rock 'n' roll music and the literature of the beat movement defined youth culture.

Reading Connection How does the music and literature of your generation differ from that of the 1950s? Read on to find out about the beginnings of a unique youth culture.

While Americans of all ages embraced the new mass media, some of the nation's youth rebelled against such a message. During the 1950s, a number of young Americans turned their backs on the conformist ideals adult society promoted. Although these youths were a small minority, their actions brought them widespread attention. In general, these young people longed for greater excitement and freedom, and they found an outlet for such feelings of restlessness in new and **controversial** styles of music and literature.

Rock 'n' Roll In the early 1950s, rock 'n' roll emerged as the distinctive music of the new generation. In 1951 at a record store in downtown Cleveland, Ohio, radio disc jockey **Alan Freed** noticed white teenagers buying African American rhythm and blues records and dancing to the music in the store. Freed later recalled, "I wondered for about a week. Then I went to the station manager talked him into permitting me to follow my classical program with a rock 'n' roll party." Calling himself "Moondog," Freed aired his first program on July 11, 1951. Just as the disc jockey had suspected, the listeners went crazy for it. Soon, white artists began making music that stemmed from these African American rhythms and sounds, and a new form of music, rock 'n' roll, had been born.

CHAPTER 14 Postwar America **683**

Review the Big Idea

Review the Big Idea for this section, "Societies change over time." Illustrate the importance of the development of rock 'n' roll to students by having them compare its impact to new forms of music during the late 1990s and early 2000s. **Ask:** How does the role of this new form of music compare to the role rock 'n' roll played in the past? What elements are the same? What elements are different? **OL**

C Critical Thinking

Analyzing Primary Sources Have students use the Internet or the library to locate the lyrics to a popular rock 'n' roll song of the 1950s. Ask students to write one paragraph summarizing some of the key images, ideas, or themes in the song. Then have them write a second paragraph describing how these lyrics represented the concerns of American teenagers of the time period. **AL**

Resources for page 683

*Have students learn more about music of the new youth culture by reading the **Linking Past and Present Activity 14.***

✓ **Reading Check**

Answer: Television spawned a growing market for many new products through advertising and damaged the movie industry until movies adapted to the changing times.

Did You Know?

The Rock and Roll Hall of Fame and Museum opened in Cleveland, Ohio, on September 2, 1995. Artists and musical groups become eligible for induction into the Hall of Fame 25 years after the release of their first record. Early inductees included Chuck Berry, Elvis Presley, and Little Richard.

NATIONAL GEOGRAPHIC
MOMENT in HISTORY

Dancing became extremely popular among teenagers in the 1950s. Teenagers continued to dance the jitterbug that their parents had originated, in addition to their own creations such as line dances, the twist, the bop, the Watusi, the stroll, the slide, the pony, and the monkey.

C Critical Thinking

Comparing and Contrasting In class, play a song by Frank Sinatra. Have students give a brief description of the lyrics to the song as well as the music itself. Then repeat the activity with a song by Elvis Presley. Tell students to write paragraphs that address the following questions: **What elements of the music seem similar? What elements seem different?** Use the comparisons as a starting point to discuss the generation gap in 1950s America. **OL**

U Universal Access

Auditory/Musical One way to trace the beginnings of the generation gap is to review the top-selling records during the 1950s. In 1952, for example, such hits as "Blue Tango" dominated the pop charts. By 1956 Doris Day's "Whatever Will Be, Will Be (Que Sera Sera)" competed with Elvis Presley's "Hound Dog." By 1959 rock 'n' roll was pushing for ever-greater dominance on the charts. Ask students to discuss how the music reflected a changing American society. **OL**

✓ Reading Check

Answer: It provided an outlet for feelings of restlessness, separated children and parents, and created a bond among the young.

With a loud and heavy beat that made it ideal for dancing along with lyrics about romance, cars, and other themes that spoke to young people, rock 'n' roll grew wildly popular among the nation's teens. Before long boys and girls around the country were rushing out to buy the latest hits from such artists as Buddy Holly, Chuck Berry, and Bill Haley and the Comets. In 1956 teenagers found their first rock 'n' roll hero in **Elvis Presley.** Presley, who had been born in rural Mississippi and grown up poor in Memphis, Tennessee, eventually claimed the title of "King of Rock 'n' Roll."

While in high school, Presley had learned to play guitar and sing by imitating the rhythm and blues music he heard on the radio. By 1956 Elvis had a record deal with RCA Victor, a movie contract, and public appearances on several television shows. At first the popular television variety show host Ed Sullivan refused to invite Presley on, insisting that the rock 'n' roll music was not fit for a family oriented show. When a competing show featuring Presley upset his own high ratings, however, Sullivan relented. He ended up paying Presley $50,000 per performance for three appearances, more than triple the amount he had paid any other performer.

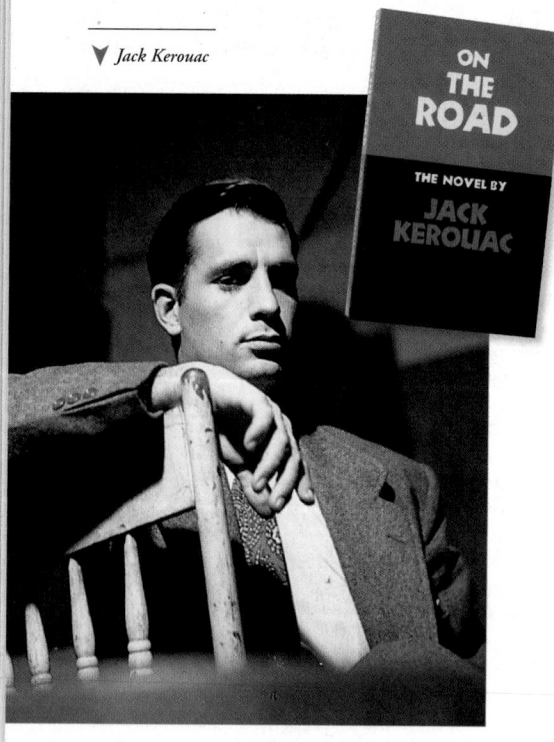

▼ *Jack Kerouac*

684   CHAPTER 14   Postwar America

The dark-haired and handsome Presley owed his wild popularity as much to his moves as to his music. During his performances he would gyrate his hips and dance in other suggestive ways that shocked many in the audience. Presley himself admitted the importance of this part of his act:

❝I'm not kidding myself. My voice alone is just an ordinary voice. What people come to see is how I use it. If I stand still while I'm singing, I'm dead, man. I might as well go back to driving a truck.❞

—quoted in *God's Country: America in the Fifties*

Not surprisingly, parents—many of whom listened to Frank Sinatra and other more mellow and mainstream artists—condemned rock 'n' roll as loud, mindless, and dangerous. The city council of San Antonio, Texas, actually banned rock 'n' roll from the jukeboxes at public swimming pools. The music, the council declared, "attracted undesirable elements given to practicing their gyrations in abbreviated bathing suits." A minister in Boston complained that "rock and roll inflames and excites youth."

The rock 'n' roll hits that teens bought in record numbers united them in a world their parents did not share. Thus in the 1950s rock 'n' roll helped to create what became known as the **generation gap,** or the cultural separation between children and their parents.

The Beat Movement If rock 'n' roll helped to create a generation gap, a group of mostly white artists who called themselves the beats highlighted a values gap in the 1950s United States. The term *beat* may have come from the feeling among group members of being "beaten down" by American culture, or from jazz musicians who would say, "I'm beat right down to my socks."

The beats sought to live unconventional lives as fugitives from a culture they despised. Beat poets, writers, and artists harshly criticized what they considered the sterility and conformity of American life, the meaninglessness of American politics, and the emptiness of popular culture.

In 1956, 29-year-old beat poet Allen Ginsberg published a long poem called "Howl," which blasted modern American life. Another beat member, **Jack Kerouac,** published *On the Road* in 1957. Although Kerouac's book about his freewheeling adventures with a car thief and con artist shocked some readers, the book went on to become a classic in modern American literature.

✓ Reading Check **Summarizing** How did rock 'n' roll help create the generation gap?

More Skill Practice

Conducting Research Encourage interested students to interview someone who was a teenager or young adult during the 1950s. Have them use the interviews to write magazine-style articles about what life was like during that era. Keep present-day magazines on hand to give students a sense of the style of magazine articles. **AL**

Resources for page 684

Have students learn more about the literature of the beat generation by reading the **Primary Source Reading 14-2.**

African American Entertainers

Main Idea Although few African Americans performed on television, many had a profound impact on early rock 'n' roll.

Reading Connection What African American entertainers currently have shows on television? Read on to discover the discrimination nonwhite performers faced during the 1950s.

While artists such as Jack Kerouac rejected American culture, African American entertainers struggled to find acceptance in a country that often treated them as second-class citizens. With a few notable exceptions, television tended to shut out African Americans. In 1956, NBC gave a popular African American singer named **Nat King Cole** his own 15-minute musical variety show. In 1958, after 64 episodes, NBC canceled the show after failing to secure a national sponsor for a show hosted by an African American.

African American rock 'n' roll singers had more luck gaining acceptance. The talented African American singers and groups who recorded hit songs in the fifties included Chuck Berry, Ray Charles, Little Richard, and the Drifters. The latter years of the 1950s also saw the rise of several African American women's groups, including the Crystals, the Chiffons, the Shirelles, and the Ronettes. With their catchy, popular sound, these groups became the musical ancestors of the famous late 1960s groups Martha and the Vandellas and the Supremes.

Over time, the music of the early rock 'n' roll artists had a profound influence on music through-

 History

African American Entertainers Rhythm and blues music provided the roots of the 1950s rock 'n' roll sound. Did African American rock 'n' roll artists experience the same acceptance as artists like Elvis Presley? Why or why not?

out the world. Little Richard and Chuck Berry, for example, provided inspiration for the Beatles, whose music swept Britain and the world in the 1960s. Elvis's music transformed generations of rock 'n' roll bands that were to follow him and other pioneers of rock. Despite the innovations in music and the economic boom of the 1950s, not all Americans were part of the affluent society. For much of the country's minorities and rural poor, the American dream remained well out of reach.

Reading Check **Evaluating** What impact did American rock 'n' roll artists have on the rest of the world?

HISTORY Online **Study Central**

For help with the concepts in this section of *American Vision: Modern Times* go to tav.mt.glencoe.com and click on **Study Central**.

SECTION 3 ASSESSMENT

Checking for Understanding

1. **Vocabulary** Define: device, controversial, generation gap.
2. **People and Terms** Identify: Ed Sullivan, Alan Freed, Elvis Presley, Jack Kerouac, Nat King Cole.
3. **Explain** what happened to motion pictures and radio when television became popular.

Reviewing Big Ideas

4. **Describing** What roles did African Americans play in television and rock 'n' roll?

Critical Thinking

5. **Comparing** How did the themes of television shows of the 1950s differ from the themes of the literature of the beat movement?
6. **Organizing** Use a graphic organizer similar to the one below to list the styles of music and literature that made up the new youth culture of the 1950s.

New Youth Culture

Analyzing Visuals

7. **Analyzing Photographs** Study the photograph on page 682. In the 1950s television game shows were a trend in programming. What new trends exist in television programming today? Do you think television is as popular today as it was in the 1950s? Explain your answer.

Writing About History

8. **Expository Writing** Imagine you are a beat writer in the 1950s. Explain to your readers how the themes you write about are universal themes that could apply to everyone. **CA** 11WA2.4a

SECTION 3 ASSESSMENT ANSWERS

1. Content vocabulary is boldfaced and highlighted in yellow. Academic vocabulary is boldfaced.
2. Ed Sullivan (p. 682), Alan Freed (p. 683), Elvis Presley (p. 684), Jack Kerouac (p. 684), Nat King Cole (p. 685)
3. Motion picture attendance and radio listenership dropped for

a while.
4. They had limited opportunities on television but more success in the music industry.
5. Television shows depicted middle-class values endorsing American society; beat literature depicted it as meaningless and sterile.
6. rock 'n' roll and beat literature

7. Students' answers will vary. Possible answers include reality television and sporting events such as the Super Bowl.
8. Students' papers will vary. Papers should describe beat themes as being applicable to more than just American culture.

Resources for page 685

Use these resources to assess student mastery.

- Section Quiz 14-3
- Reading Essentials and Study Guide 14-3
- Interactive Tutor Self-Assessment CD-ROM
- California Standards Practice, Grade 11

 History

Answer: No, television tended to shut them out, and they often were treated as second-class citizens. **Ask:** Why was Nat King Cole's television show canceled before it aired? (*The network was unable to find a sponsor willing to back an African American performer.*)

Reading Check

Answer: They influenced music throughout the world and inspired such bands as the Beatles.

HISTORY Online

Study Central provides audio summaries, interactive games, and online graphic organizers to help students review section content.

CLOSE

Kinesthetic Have students present a skit, complete with costumes and props, to highlight the characteristics of the new youth culture. **OL**

TIME NOTEBOOK

FOCUS

History–Social Science Standards

This feature addresses the following standards:

11.8 Students analyze the economic boom and social transformation of post-World War II America.

11.8.8 Discuss forms of popular culture, with emphasis on their origins and geographic diffusion (e.g., jazz and other forms of popular music, professional sports, architectural and artisitic styles).

Reading Connection

Film Connection Invite students to rent or borrow the film *Rebel Without a Cause.* After viewing the film, have students write a short paragraph or journal entry explaining why they think James Dean's character was symbolic for the American youth of the 1950s. **OL**

TEACH

C Critical Thinking

Identifying Central Issues Have students review the quotes in the Verbatim section and discuss each item as it relates to the people and themes found in the textbook. **OL**

Answers and Additional Support

BETTMANN/CORBIS

Profile

JAMES DEAN *had a brief but spectacular career as a film star. His role in* Rebel Without a Cause *made him an icon for American youth in the mid-50s. In 1955 Dean was killed in a car crash. He was 24.*

"I guess I have as good an insight into this rising generation as any other young man my age. Therefore, when I do play a youth, I try to imitate life. *Rebel Without a Cause* deals with the problems of modern youth. . . . If you want the kids to come and see the picture, you've got to try to reach them on their own grounds. If a picture is psychologically motivated, if there is truth in the relationships in it, then I think that picture will do good."

—*from an interview for* Rebel Without a Cause

VERBATIM

"It will make a wonderful place for the children to play in, and it will be a good storehouse, too."

> **MRS. RUTH CALHOUN,**
> *mother of three, on her backyard fallout shelter, 1951*

"Riddle: What's college? That's where girls who are above cooking and sewing go to meet a man they can spend their lives cooking and sewing for."

> *ad for Gimbel's department store campus clothes, 1952*

"Radioactive poisoning of the atmosphere and hence annihilation of any life on Earth has been brought within the range of technical possibilities."

> **ALBERT EINSTEIN,**
> *physicist, 1950*

"If the television craze continues with the present level of programs, we are destined to have a nation of morons."

> **DANIEL MARSH,**
> *President of Boston University, 1950*

"Every time the Russians throw an American in jail, the House Un-American Activities Committee throws an American in jail to get even."

> **MORT SAHL,**
> *comedian, 1950s*

WINNERS & LOSERS

ARCHIVE PHOTOS

Poodle Cut

POODLE CUTS
Short, curly hairstyle gains wide popularity and acceptance

TV GUIDE
New weekly magazine achieves circulation of 6.5 million by 1959

PALMER PAINT COMPANY OF DETROIT
Sells 12 million paint-by-number kits ranging from simple landscapes and portraits to Leonardo da Vinci's *The Last Supper*

THE DUCKTAIL
Banned in several Massachusetts schools in 1957

COLLIER'S
The respected magazine loses circulation, publishes its final edition on January 4, 1957

LEONARDO DA VINCI'S *THE LAST SUPPER*
Now everyone can paint their own copy to hang in their homes

The Ducktail

SUPER STOCK

COOPERATIVE LEARNING ACTIVITY

Creating a Magazine Spread Organize the class into small groups and ask them to create their own two-page magazine spreads of one year between 1950 and 1960. Encourage students to use elements similar to those that appear in the text but to be creative as they select information. Students should look at current magazines and books for ideas about page design. This activity can be completed using desktop publishing software or the more traditional cut-and-paste method. **OL**

1950s WORD PLAY
Translation, Please!

Match the word to its meaning.

Teen-Age Lingo

1. cool
2. hang loose
3. hairy
4. yo-yo

a. a dull person, an outsider
b. worthy of approval
c. formidable
d. don't worry

answers: 1. b; 2. d; 3. c; 4. a

Bomb Shelter

BETTMANN/CORBIS

Be Prepared

"Know the Bomb's True Dangers. Know the Steps You Can Take to Escape Them!—You Can Survive."
Government pamphlet, 1950

DIGGING YOUR OWN BOMB SHELTER? Better go shopping. Below is a list of items included with the $3,000 Mark I Kidde Kokoon, designed to accommodate a family of five for a three- to five-day underground stay.

- air blower
- radiation detector
- protective apparel suit
- face respirator
- radiation charts (4)
- hand shovel combination (for digging out after the blast)
- gasoline driven generator
- gasoline (10 gallons)

- chemical toilet
- toilet chemicals (2 gallons)
- bunks (5)
- mattresses and blankets (5)
- air pump (for blowing up mattresses)
- incandescent bulbs (2) 40 watts
- fuses (2) 5 amperes
- clock—non-electric

- first aid kit
- waterless hand cleaner
- sterno stove
- canned water (10 gallons)
- canned food (meat, powdered milk, cereal, sugar, etc.)
- paper products

NUMBERS 1957

3¢ Cost of first-class postage stamp

19¢ Cost of loaf of bread

25¢ Cost of issue of *Sports Illustrated*

35¢ Cost of movie ticket

50¢ Cost of gallon of milk (delivered)

$2.05 Average hourly wage

$2,845 Cost of new car

POPPERFOTO/ARCHIVE PHOTO

$5,234 Median income for a family of four

$19,500 Median price to buy a home

American Scene, 1950–1960
(MILLIONS)

24.3	35.5
1950	1960

Children 5–14

1.8	4.0
1950	1960

Girl Scouts & Brownies

2.0	3.8
1950	1960

Bicycle Production

1.5	6.6
1950	1960

National Forest Campers

2.8	5.8
1950	1960

Outboard Motors in Use

U Universal Access

Interpersonal Have students interview friends and relatives who lived during the 1950s to learn more about teenage lingo. Make a list of all the words and definitions that students bring in. **BL**

R₁ Reading Strategy

Connecting Have students review the information about bomb shelters. **Ask:** Have you experienced or heard about any similar kind of preparedness effort? *(Answers will vary, but many students will have had personal experience with preparing for a terrorist attack, Y2K, or for natural disasters such as tornadoes.)* **BL**

R₂ Reading Strategy

Reading Maps, Graphs, and Charts Have students look at the graphs on page 687 and explain the differences between 1950 and 1960. **Ask:** Why is there an increase in each category? *(As the number of children grew, so did the number participating in sports and recreation.)* **OL**

ASSESS/CLOSE

Visit the **TIME** Web site at **www.time.com** for up-to-date news, weekly magazine articles, editorials, online polls, and an archive of past magazine and Web articles.

Did You Know?

The race to build bombs even more powerful than the atomic bombs dropped on Hiroshima and Nagasaki marked the 1950s. President Dwight D. Eisenhower was a strong supporter of the effort to stockpile large numbers of hydrogen bombs. He believed that the bombs would provide U.S. security at an affordable price. However, by 1960 he had realized the potential horrors of a war of hydrogen bombs and reported to the National Security Council that "war no longer has any logic whatsoever."

FOCUS

SKILLBUILDER ACTIVITY

Project **Daily Focus Skills Transparency 14-4** and have students answer the question.

Guide to Reading

Understanding Vocabulary:
Have students write short paragraphs using at least three of the content and academic vocabulary words.

Answers to Graphic:
Have students complete the outline using the headings in the section.

Unpacking the Standards

Students will be able to:

• Describe the existence of poverty amidst the general prosperity of the post-war period.

• Analyze the concerns over what was viewed as juvenile delinquency during this period.

Answers and Additional Support

SECTION 4

The Other Side of American Life

Guide to Reading

Connection
In the previous section, you learned about new forms of entertainment. In this section, you will discover how some Americans were left out of the new prosperity.

Main Idea
• Despite the growing affluence of much of the nation, many groups still lived in poverty. (p. 689)
• Concerns about rising juvenile delinquency and failing educational systems surfaced during the late 1950s. (p. 692)

Content Vocabulary
poverty line, urban renewal, termination policy, juvenile delinquency

Academic Vocabulary
abstraction, conformity, technical

People and Terms to Identify
Michael Harrington, Bracero program

Reading Objectives
• **Identify** those groups that found themselves left out of the American economic boom following World War II.
• **Explain** the factors that contributed to the poverty among various groups.

Reading Strategy
Taking Notes As you read about social problems in the United States in the 1950s, use the major headings of the section to create an outline similar to the one below.

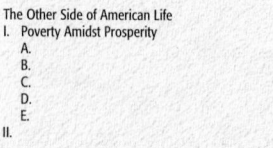

The Other Side of American Life
I. Poverty Amidst Prosperity
   A.
   B.
   C.
   D.
   E.
II.

Preview of Events

♦1953	♦1956	♦1959	♦1962
1953 Federal government institutes termination policy directed at Native Americans	**1955** Rudolf Flesch's *Why Johnny Can't Read* published	**1959** *A Raisin in the Sun* opens on Broadway	**1962** Michael Harrington's *The Other America* published

The following are the main History–Social Science Standards covered in this section.

11.8.2 Describe the significance of Mexican immigration and its relationship to the agricultural economy, especially in California.

11.8.4 Analyze new federal government spending on defense, welfare, interest on the national debt, and federal and state spending on education, including the California Master Plan.

11.10.1 Explain how demands of African Americans helped produce a stimulus for civil rights, including President Roosevelt's ban on racial discrimination in defense industries in 1941, and how African Americans' service in World War II produced a stimulus for President Truman's decision to end segregation in the armed forces in 1948.

⁓ The Big Idea ⁓

Societies change over time. Despite the increasing prosperity in the United States, many minorities and rural whites continued to struggle with poverty. When people and businesses moved from the cities to the suburbs, the inner cities began to decline. Many of the people left behind were African Americans who faced racial discrimination when searching for employment. Hispanics and Native Americans often faced similar problems. During the 1950s, as people left Appalachia to search for better lives in the cities, they left behind the elderly and those who could not travel. The result was extreme poverty, along with poor nutrition and insufficient healthcare, for those who remained. Americans paid more attention to a rise in juvenile delinquency and inadequate educational systems.

688 CHAPTER 14 Postwar America

SECTION RESOURCES

📂 Print Material
• Reproducible Lesson Plan 14-4
• Guided Reading Activity 14-4
• Reading Essentials and Study Guide 14-4
• Active Reading Note-Taking Guide 14-4

🖌 Transparencies
• Daily Focus Skills Transparency 14-4
• Section Graphic Organizer Transparency 14-4

Technology
🔘 Interactive Tutor Self-Assessment CD-ROM
🔘 Exam*View*® Pro Testmaker CD-ROM
🔘 Presentation Plus! CD-ROM

Poverty Amidst Prosperity

 Main Idea Despite the growing affluence of much of the nation, many groups still lived in poverty.

Reading Connection Are the pockets of poverty in America today the same as they were in the 1950s? Read on to discover groups who were left out of the general economic boom of the 1950s.

The booming 1950s saw a tremendous expansion of the middle class. In 1950, about 1 in 3 Americans were poor. By 1959, only 1 in 5 were poor. Despite these dramatic gains, about 30 million people still lived below the **poverty line,** a figure set by the government to reflect the minimum income required to support a family. Such poverty remained invisible to most Americans, who assumed that the country's general prosperity had provided everyone with a comfortable existence.

★ An American Story ★

In 1959 Lorraine Hansberry's play, *A Raisin in the Sun,* opened on Broadway. The play told the story of a working-class African American family struggling against poverty and racism. The title referred to a Langston Hughes poem that wonders what happens to an unrealized dream: "Does it dry up like a raisin in the sun?" Hansberry's play won the New York Drama **W** Critics Circle Award for the best play of the year. Reflecting later upon the play's theme, she wrote:

66Vulgarity, blind conformity, and mass lethargy need not triumph in the land of Lincoln and Frederick Douglass.... There is simply no reason why dreams should dry up like raisins or prunes or anything else in the United States.... I believe that we can impose beauty on our future.99

—adapted from *To Be Young, Gifted, and Black*

Michael Harrington was another writer concerned with poverty in the United States. In his book, *The Other America,* published in 1962, he alerted those in the mainstream to what he saw in the run-down and hidden communities of the country:

66Tens of millions of Americans are, at this very moment, maimed in body and spirit, existing at levels beneath those necessary for human decency. If these people are not starving, they are hungry, and sometimes fat with hunger, for that is what cheap foods **R** do. They are without adequate housing and education and medical care.99

—from *The Other America*

The poor included single mothers and the elderly; minority immigrants such as Puerto Ricans and Mexicans; rural Americans, black and white; people with disabilities; and inner city residents, who remained stuck in crowded slums as wealthier citizens fled to the suburbs. Poverty also gripped many Americans in the nation's Appalachian region, which stretches from Pennsylvania to Georgia, as well as Native Americans, many of whom endured grinding poverty whether they stayed on reservations or migrated to cities.

The Decline of the Inner City The poverty in the 1950s was most apparent in the nation's urban centers. As white families moved to the suburbs, many inner cities became home to poorer, less educated minority groups. The centers of many cities deteriorated, because as the middle class moved out, their tax money went with them. This deprived inner cities of the tax dollars necessary to provide adequate public transportation, housing, and other services.

S When government tried to help inner city residents, it often made matters worse. During the 1950s, for example, **urban renewal** programs tried to

▼ *Lorraine Hansberry*

CHAPTER 14   Postwar America   **689**

TEACH

W **Writing Support**

Response to Literature Writing Have students use the library or Internet to locate Langston Hughes's poem "A Dream Deferred," from which Lorraine Hansberry's play *A Raisin in the Sun* drew its name. Instruct students to read the poem and to write one-page responses. Remind them to address the following questions in their responses: What elements of the poem did you find successful? Less successful? What key images do you remember from the poem? What does Hughes seem to be saying about dreams that remain unrealized? Why do you think that Lorraine Hansberry chose the phrase "a raisin in the sun" as the title for her play? Invite students to share their responses with the class. **OL**

CA 11RL3.4; 11WA2.2a; 11WA2.2c

R **Reading Strategy**

Scaffolding—Academic Vocabulary The word *adequate* was introduced in Chapter 6, Section 3. Ask a student to define the word. **BL**

S **Skill Practice**

Scaffolding—Understanding Change Have students conduct additional research on one urban renewal project of the 1950s and the changes this project has undergone from the 1950s to today. They should determine the problems the project created, the steps government took to remedy the problems, and any new problems that developed. Have students present their findings in three-page reports. **OL** **CA** CS2

This Historical Analysis skill was introduced in Chapter 11.

Resources for page 689

Have students learn more about the decline of the inner city by reading an excerpt from The Living is Easy *in the* **American Literature Readings 4.**

Did You Know?

Lorraine Hansberry achieved another first on April 7, 1959, when she became the first African American, and only the fifth woman, to win the prestigious New York Drama Critics Circle Award for her first play, *A Raisin in the Sun.*

Review the Big Idea

Review the Big Idea for this section, "Societies change over time." Explain that between 1941 and 1945, one out of every five Americans moved from one area of the country to another. During that time, more than 700,000 African Americans left the South to move to the North and the West. Ask students to consider what kinds of challenges such migration presented for individuals and communities. **OL**

S Skill Practice

Visual Literacy Have students re-examine the photo of the young girl on this page. Invite interested students to write a story or poem from the perspective of the girl, describing her life in inner-city Chicago. Encourage students to add photos or drawings and to share their stories and poems with the class. **AL**
CA HI3; HI4 **CA** 11WS1.5

U Universal Access

Advanced Learners Tell students that music has long been a way for people to express their emotions. Challenge interested students to take the impressions they have gained while reading the chapter to compose and perform a song expressing the plight of Hispanic laborers in the Bracero program during the 1950s. **AL**

Answers and Additional Support

eliminate poverty by tearing down slums and erecting new high-rise buildings for poor residents. The crowded, anonymous conditions of these high-rise projects, however, often created an atmosphere of violence. The government also unwittingly encouraged the residents of public housing to remain poor by evicting them as soon as they began to earn any money. In the end, urban renewal programs actually destroyed more housing space than they created. Too often in the name of urban improvement, the wrecking ball destroyed poor people's homes to make way for roadways, parks, universities, tree lined boulevards, or shopping centers.

African Americans Many of the citizens left behind in the cities as families fled to the suburbs were African American. The large number of African American inner city residents resulted largely from the migration of more than 3 million African Americans from the South to the North between 1940 and 1960.

Picturing **History**

Inner-City Poverty This young African American girl in Chicago's inner city struggles to fill a bowl with water that has frozen due to lack of heat. Why did the numbers of poor in the country's inner cities grow in the 1950s?

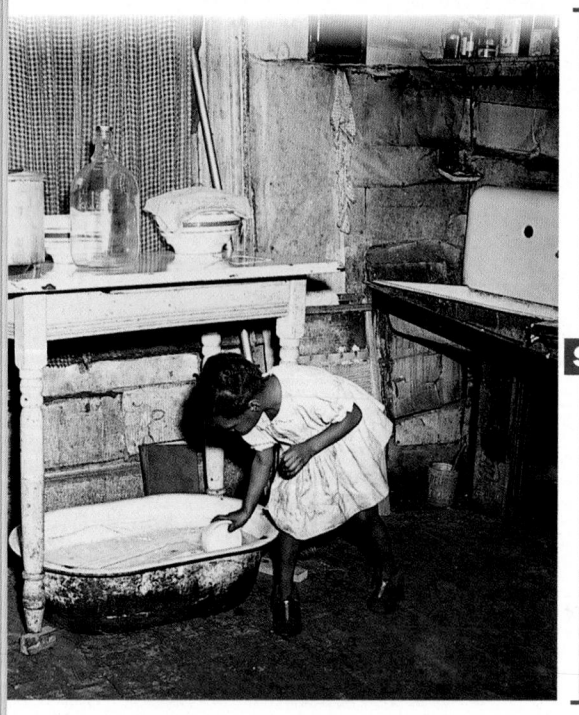

690 CHAPTER 14 Postwar America

Many African Americans had migrated in hopes of finding greater economic opportunity and escaping violence and racial intimidation. For many of these migrants, however, life proved to be little better in Northern cities. Fewer and fewer jobs were available as numerous factories and mills left the cities for suburbs and smaller towns in order to cut their costs. Long-standing patterns of racial discrimination in schools, housing, hiring, and salaries in the North kept inner-city African Americans poor. The last hired and the first fired for good jobs, they often remained stuck in the worst-paying occupations. In 1958 African American salaries, on average, equaled only 51 percent of what whites earned.

Poverty and racial discrimination also deprived many African Americans of other benefits, such as decent medical care. Responding to a correspondent who had seen *A Raisin in the Sun,* Lorraine Hansberry wrote, "The ghettos are killing us; not only our dreams . . . but our very bodies. It is not an **abstraction** to us that the average [African American] has a life expectancy of five to ten years less than the average white." Several African American groups, such as the NAACP and the Congress of Racial Equality (CORE), pressed for greater economic opportunity for African Americans. In general, however, these organizations met with little success.

Hispanics African Americans were not the only minority group that struggled with poverty. Much of the nation's Hispanic population faced the same problems. During the 1950s and early 1960s, the **Bracero program** brought nearly 5 million Mexicans to the United States to work on farms and ranches in the Southwest. The Braceros were temporary contract workers, and many later returned home. Some came with their families, however, and about 350,000 settled permanently in the United States.

These laborers, who worked on large farms throughout the country, lived a life of extreme poverty and hardship. They toiled long hours for little pay in conditions that were often unbearable. As Michael Harrington noted, "[The nation's migrant laborers] work ten-eleven-twelve hour days in temperatures over one hundred degrees. Sometimes there is no drinking water. . . . Women and children work on ladders and with hazardous machinery. Babies are brought to the field and are placed in 'cradles' of wood boxes."

Away from the fields, many Mexican families lived in small, crudely built shacks, while some did not even have a roof over their heads. "They sleep

Picturing **History**

Answer: Poor immigrants as well as African Americans from the South moved to the cities.
Ask: How did government programs make things worse for the urban poor? *(Urban renewal replaced slums with high-rise buildings that were plagued by violence. The poor were evicted from government housing when they earned too much money.)*

More Skill Practice

Predicting Remind students that the life of minorities in the 1950s was very different from the life that middle-class Americans were enjoying. Have students discuss the differences that existed among the classes in the United States. Then ask them to predict the problems that were likely to result from these differences. **OL**

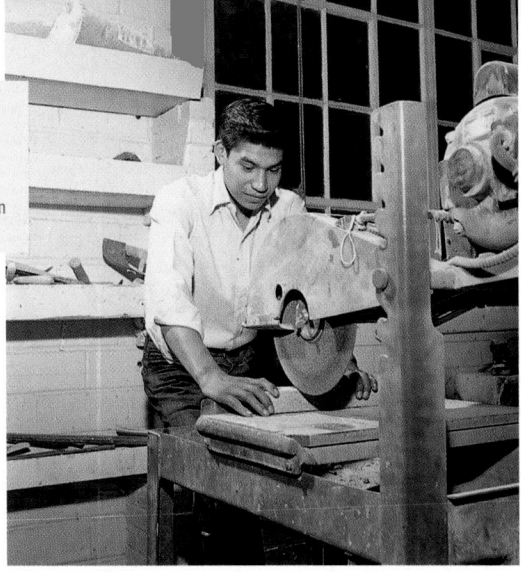

Picturing **History**

Vocational Training Native American Franklin Beaver learns to become a stone mason at this vocational school sponsored by the U.S. Indian Bureau. Why was the government trying to bring Native Americans into mainstream society?

where they can, some in the open," Harrington noted about one group of migrant workers. "They eat when they can (and sometimes what they can)." The nation would pay little attention to the plight of Mexican farm laborers until the 1960s, when the workers began to organize for greater rights.

Native Americans Native Americans also faced challenges throughout the postwar era of prosperity. By the middle of the 1900s, Native Americans—who made up less than one percent of the population—were the poorest group in the nation. Average annual family income for Native American families, for example, was $1,000 less than that for African Americans.

After World War II, during which many Native American soldiers had served with distinction, the U.S. government launched a program to bring Native Americans into mainstream society—whether they wanted to assimilate or not. Under the plan, which became known as the **termination policy,** the federal government withdrew all official recognition of the Native American groups as legal entities and made them subject to the same laws as white citizens. At the same time, the government encouraged Native Americans to blend in to larger society by helping them move off the reservations to cities such as Minneapolis, Minnesota.

Although the idea of integrating Native Americans into mainstream society began with good intentions, some of its supporters had more selfish goals. Speculators and developers sometimes gained rich farmland at the expense of destitute Native American groups.

Most Native Americans found termination a disastrous policy that only deepened their poverty. In the mid-1950s, for example, the Welfare Council of Minneapolis described Native American living conditions in that city as miserable. "One Indian family of five or six, living in two rooms, will take in relatives and friends who come from the reservations seeking jobs until perhaps fifteen people will be crowded into the space," the council reported. During the 1950s, Native Americans in Minneapolis could expect to live only 37 years, compared to 46 years for all Minnesota Native Americans and

68 years for other Minneapolis residents. Benjamin Reifel, a Sioux, described the widespread despair that the termination policy produced:

❝The Indians believed that when the dark clouds of war passed from the skies overhead, their rising tide of expectations, though temporarily stalled, would again reappear. Instead they were threatened by termination . . . Soaring expectations began to plunge. Termination took on the connotation of extermination for many.❞

—quoted in *The Earth Shall Weep*

Appalachia The nation's minorities were not the only people dealing with poverty. The picturesque streams and mountains of Appalachia hid the ruined mines, scarred hills, and abandoned farms of impoverished families who had dwelled in these hills for generations.

During the 1950s, 1.5 million people abandoned Appalachia to seek a better life in the nation's cities. They left behind elderly and other less mobile residents. "Whole counties," wrote one reporter who visited the region, "are precariously held together by a flour-and-dried-milk paste of surplus foods. . . . The men who are no longer needed in the mines and the farmers who cannot compete . . . have themselves become surplus commodities in the mountains."

A host of statistics spoke to Appalachia's misery. Studies revealed high rates of nutritional deficiency and infant mortality. Appalachia had fewer doctors per thousand people than the rest of the country,

CHAPTER 14 Postwar America **691**

S Skill Practice

Conducting Research Ask students to use library or Internet resources to research teenage crime. They should use their research to write two-page reports on the actual amount of juvenile crime during the 1950s and to compare it to juvenile crime levels today. Have students share their findings with the class and indicate whether this data supports the fear that authorities had about juvenile delinquency during the 1950s. **AL**

CA HR1; HR3; HR4; HI2

C Critical Thinking

Comparing and Contrasting Have students discuss the possible causes for the rise in juvenile delinquency in the 1950s. Ask if they think the same conditions exist today. Explore the similarities and differences that they note. **OL**

✓ Reading Check

Answer: African Americans, Hispanics, Native Americans, people in Appalachia

Answers and Additional Support

and the doctors it did have were older than those in other areas. In addition, schooling in the region was considered even worse than in inner city slums.

✓ **Reading Check** **Identifying** Which groups of people were left out of the country's economic boom of the 1950s?

Juvenile Delinquency

 Main Idea Concerns about rising juvenile delinquency and failing educational systems surfaced during the late 1950s.

Reading Connection Describe the differences and similarities between juveniles in the 1950s and juveniles today. Read on to discover the growing rate of juvenile delinquency during the 1950s.

During the 1950s, many middle-class white Americans found it easy to ignore the poverty and racism that afflicted many of the nation's minorities, since they themselves were removed from it. Some social problems, however, became impossible to ignore.

One problem at this time was a rise in, or at least a rise in the reporting of, **juvenile delinquency**—antisocial or criminal behavior of young people. Between 1948 and 1953, the United States saw a 45 percent rise in juvenile crime rates. A popular 1954 book titled *1,000,000 Delinquents* correctly calculated that in the following year, about 1 million young people would get into some kind of criminal trouble. Car thefts topped the list of juvenile crimes, but people were also alarmed at the behavior of young people who belonged to gangs and committed muggings, rape, and even murder.

Americans could not agree on what had triggered the rise in delinquency. Experts blamed it on a host of reasons, including poverty, lack of religion, television, movies, comic books, racism, busy parents, a rising divorce rate, and anxiety over the military draft. Some cultural critics claimed that young people were rebelling against the hypocrisy and **conformity** of their parents. Conservative commentators pinned the

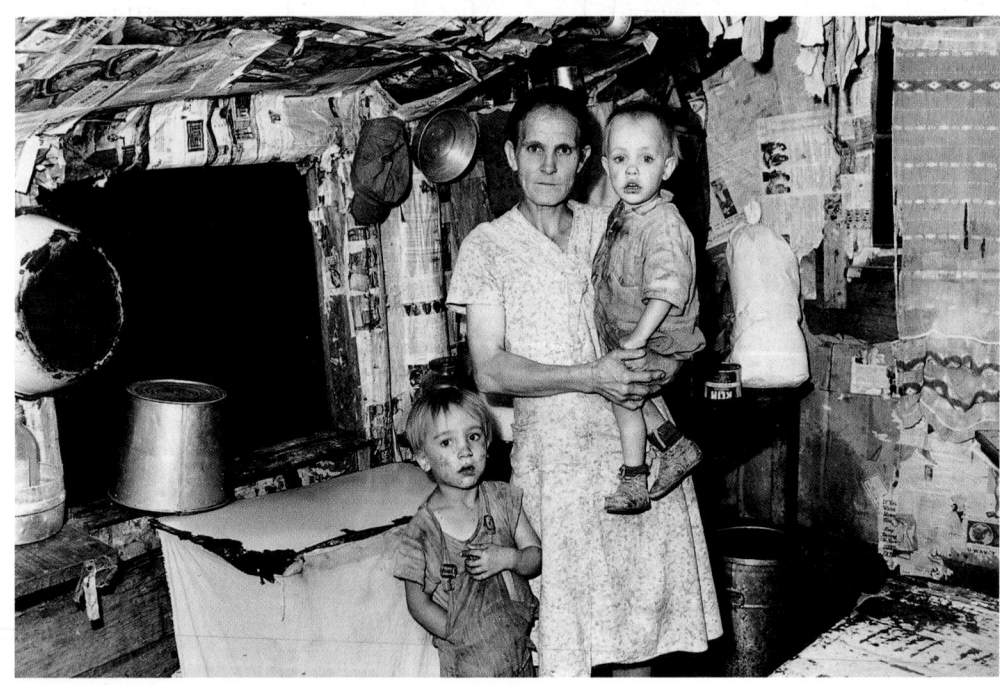

🖼 *Picturing* **History**

Poverty in Appalachia This mining family lived in the kind of extreme poverty that was often overlooked in the 1950s. Eight people lived in this three-room house lined with newspaper. Why was infant mortality so high in Appalachia?

692 CHAPTER 14 Postwar America

🖼 *Picturing* **History**

Answer: nutritional deficiencies, few doctors, and poor living conditions
Ask: Why do you think newspapers cover the walls in this house? *(to provide some insulation, to keep out cold drafts and insects)*

blame on a lack of discipline. Doting parents, complained Bishop Fulton J. Sheen, had raised bored children who sought new thrills, such as "alcohol, marijuana, even murder." Liberal observers preferred to pinpoint social causes, blaming teen violence on poverty and feelings of hopelessness among underprivileged youths. Delinquency in the 1950s, however, cut across class and racial lines—the majority of car thieves, for example, had grown up in middle-class homes.

Most teens, of course, steered clear of gangs, drugs, and crime. Nonetheless, the public tended to stereotype young people as juvenile delinquents, especially those teens who favored unconventional clothing, long hair, or street slang.

Many parents were also growing concerned over the nation's educational system. As baby boomers began entering the school system, they ignited a spurt in school construction. During the 1950s, school enrollments increased by 13 million. School districts struggled to erect new buildings and hire new teachers. Nevertheless, shortages sprang up in both buildings and the people to staff them.

Americans' education worries only intensified in 1957 after the Soviet Union launched the world's first space satellites, *Sputnik I* and *Sputnik II.* Many Americans felt they had fallen behind their Cold War enemy and blamed what they felt was a lack of **technical** education in the nation's schools. *Life* magazine proclaimed a "Crisis in Education," and

Rebelling Against Conformity This biker, one of the Louisville "Outlaws," fits the stereotype of the 1950s juvenile delinquent.

offered a grim warning: "What has long been an ignored national problem, *Sputnik* has made a recognized crisis." In the wake of the *Sputnik* launches, efforts began to improve math and science education in the schools. Profound fears about the country's young people, it seemed, dominated the end of a decade that had brought great progress for many Americans.

 Reading Check **Evaluating** How did many Americans feel about the education system of the 1950s?

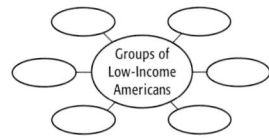 **Study Central**
For help with the concepts in this section of *American Vision: Modern Times* go to tav.mt.glencoe.com and click on *Study Central.*

SECTION 4 ASSESSMENT

Checking for Understanding
1. **Vocabulary** Define: poverty line, urban renewal, abstraction, termination policy, juvenile delinquency, conformity, technical.
2. **People and Terms** Identify: Michael Harrington, Bracero program.
3. **Evaluate** how the federal government's termination policy affected Native Americans.

Reviewing Big Ideas
4. **Explaining** Why did urban renewal fail the poor of the inner cities?

Critical Thinking
5. **Interpreting** What were some possible reasons for a dramatic rise in juvenile delinquency in the 1950s?
6. **Organizing** Use a graphic organizer similar to the one below to list the groups of Americans who were left out of the country's postwar economic boom.

Groups of Low-Income Americans

Analyzing Visuals
7. **Analyzing Photographs** Study the photograph on this page. What in the photograph might attract young people to this type of life? Why would others oppose such a life?

Writing About History
8. **Expository Writing** Using library or Internet resources, find information about juvenile delinquency in the United States today to write a report. Compare today's problems with those of the 1950s. Share your report with the class. **CA** 11WS1.6

CHAPTER 14   Postwar America   **693**

Primary Sources
Eyewitness to History

FOCUS

History–Social Science Standards

This feature addresses the following main standard:

11.8 Students analyze the economic boom and social transformation of post-World War II America.

Understanding Vocabulary

Before students begin reading, point out that difficult or unfamiliar words are footnoted throughout the text.

TEACH

R Reading Strategy

Connecting Before reading this selection, ask students if they would use the word *benevolent* to describe modern U.S. society. Then have them write brief descriptions of our society. After reading, students should compare 1950s society with their own descriptions of modern society.
OL

Answers and Additional Support

694

The 1950s has been depicted as a period of prosperity and conformity. Retreating from the turmoil of World War II and the threat of the Cold War, Americans tried to cling to the security of home and family.

SOURCE 1:

R *Sociologist William H. Whyte, Jr., studied the lives and beliefs of men who worked in large businesses. In* The Organization Man, *published in 1956, he reported that rugged individualism had disappeared in favor of conformity.*

Not in the materialism of heroes but in their attitude toward society is where the change has taken place. In older fiction there was some element of conflict between the individual and his environment; no matter how much assisted by coincidence, the hero had to do something—or at least seem to do something—before he got his reward. Rarely now. Society is so **benevolent**[1] that there is no conflict left in it for anyone to be rebellious about. The hero only thinks there is.

Stories must have at least the appearance of a conflict if they are to be stories, but contemporary writers get around this by taking a chunk of environment and then in some fashion disguising its true goodness from the hero. Since this means that the hero's troubles stem from a false image of life, the climax is easily resolved. The author simply tears the veil away. It was really okay all along only the hero didn't know it. Relieved, the hero learns the wisdom of accepting what probably would have happened anyway. . . .

But the general run of current self-improvement books shows a rather steep divergence from the old tradition. On the surface they do not seem to, and

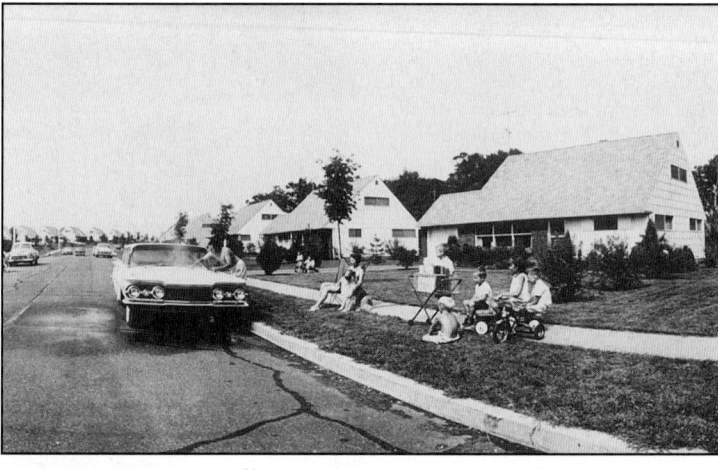

▲ *A typical street in Levittown, Pennsylvania*

their titles promise the old fare. Essentially, however, what they tell you to do is to adjust to the situation rather than change it. . . . [T]he picture they present is one of an essentially benevolent society, and the peace of mind or the positive thinking **extolled**[2] is a kind of resignation to it.

SOURCE 2:

William Levitt responded to the enormous demand for housing after World War II by constructing entirely new neighborhoods in several states. A Time *article from July 3, 1950, describes one of these neighborhoods.*

Like its counterparts across the land, Levittown is an entirely new kind of community. Despite its size, it is not incorporated, thus has no mayor, no police force, nor any of the other traditional city officers of its own.

[1]**benevolent:** kind

[2]**extolled:** highly praised

UNIVERSAL ACCESS

Advanced Learners Point out to students that William H. Whyte, Jr., draws upon the literary tradition of the "hero" and literary elements—such as conflict and climax—to illustrate his point about changes in society. Ask students to create two-column charts with the labels "Rugged Individualism" and "Conformity." Then have them list in the appropriate columns the characteristics of the hero within each context and describe the hero's relationship with society and how the hero responds to conflict. Ask students to use the information in their comparison-contrast charts to make predictions about consequences that might result from the disappearance of rugged individualism and the emergence of conformity. Invite volunteers to share their predictions. **AL**

▲ *Elvis Presley on* The Steve Allen Show

SOURCE 3:

Elvis Presley's swiveling hips upset many people. He became the target of those who believed that rock 'n' roll was too dangerous for American youth. In the July 16, 1956, issue of Newsweek, *John Lardner reviewed Presley's appearance on* The Steve Allen Show.

There is nothing to be said against Elvis—and many people have said it—except that when placed in front of a microphone, he behaves like an outboard motor. . . .

Nonetheless, we all watched with interest last week when one of our number, Steve Allen, made a public attempt to neutralize, calm, or de-twitch Elvis Presley, the lively singer.

Allen did this, one assumes, in what he personally considers the best interests of civilization. . . . Civilization today is sharply divided into two schools which cannot stand the sight of each other. One school, Allen's . . . believes in underplaying, or underbidding, or waiting 'em out. The other, Presley's, is committed to the strategy of open defiance, of confusing 'em, of yelling 'em down. The hips and the Adam's apple . . . must be quicker than the eye. . . .

When Allen made his move last week to mute and frustrate Presley . . . [he] was nervous, like a man trying to embalm a firecracker. Presley was distraught, like Huckleberry Finn, when the widow put him in a store suit and told him not to gap or scratch.

Allen's ethics were questionable from the start. He fouled Presley . . . by dressing him like a corpse, in white tie and **tails**.[3] This is a costume often seen on star performers at funerals, but only when the deceased has specifically requested it in his will. Elvis made no such request—or for that matter, no will. . . .

[3]**tails:** man's tuxedo coat with long tapering ends

It has no movies, no nightclubs and only three bars (all in the community shopping centers).

And Levittown has very few old people. Few of its more than 40,000 residents are past 35; of some 8,000 children, scarcely 900 are more than seven years old. In front of almost every house along Levittown's 100 miles of winding streets sits a tricycle or a baby carriage. In Levittown, all activity stops from 12 to 2 in the afternoon; that is nap time. Said one Levittowner last week, "Everyone is so young that sometimes it's hard to remember how to get along with older people."

The community has an almost antiseptic air. Levittown streets, which have such fanciful names as Satellite, Horizon, Haymaker, are bare and flat as hospital corridors. Like a hospital, Levittown has rules all its own. Fences are not allowed (though here and there a home-owner has broken the rule). The plot of grass around each home must be cut at least once a week; if not, Bill Levitt's men mow the grass and send the bill. Wash cannot be hung out to dry on an ordinary clothesline; it must be arranged on rotary, removable drying racks, and then not on weekends or holidays. . . .

DBQ Document-Based Questions

Historical Analysis CA HR4; HI2

Source 1: Why does Whyte believe that conflict has disappeared?

Source 2: How were the people in Levittown similar?

Source 3: According to Lardner, why did some people dislike Elvis?

Comparing and Contrasting Sources
How is conformity addressed in each of the accounts?

Reading Strategy
Monitoring Ask students to explain why the author of the *Time* article describes Levittown as having an "antiseptic air." *(The community is clean and well-ordered like a hospital.)* OL

Universal Access
Verbal/Linguistic After students read about Levittown, have them write brief essays in which they explain whether they would like to live in a planned community. As a class, discuss the positive and negative aspects of growing up in a planned community. OL

Writing Support
Summary Writing Remind students that a good summary communicates the main ideas of a selection in a logical order. Have students write summaries that explain in their own words what Steve Allen tried to do to Elvis Presley, and why. BL

ASSESS/CLOSE
Have students answer the Document-Based Questions.

DBQ Document-Based Questions

1. He believes conflict has disappeared because society has become benevolent, or kind.
2. Most were under the age of 35 with young children. Their homes and yards had to conform to the rules of Levittown.
3. Some people disliked how he performed in front of an audience—"like an outboard motor."

Comparing and Contrasting Sources: Source 1 discusses the replacement of rugged individualism with conformity; Source 2 describes the planned conformity of life in Levittown; Source 3 addresses the attempts to make people conform to what is considered acceptable behavior.

Reviewing Content Vocabulary

Students' answers will vary. The pages where the words appear in the text are shown in parentheses.

1. closed shop *(p. 667)* **2.** right-to-work law *(p. 667)* **3.** union shop *(p. 667)* **4.** featherbedding *(p. 667)* **5.** dynamic conservatism *(p. 670)* **6.** white-collar *(p. 675)* **7.** blue-collar *(p. 675)* **8.** multinational corporation *(p. 675)* **9.** franchise *(p. 676)* **10.** baby boom *(p. 677)* **11.** generation gap *(p. 684)* **12.** poverty line *(p. 689)* **13.** urban renewal *(p. 689)* **14.** termination policy *(p. 691)* **15.** juvenile delinquency *(p. 692)*

Reviewing Academic Vocabulary

Students' answers will vary. The pages where the words appear in the text are shown in parentheses.

16. restrain *(p. 668)* **17.** subsidy *(p. 670)* **18.** transition *(p. 671)* **19.** accompany *(p. 675)* **20.** benefit *(p. 675)* **21.** generate *(p. 678)* **22.** device *(p. 681)* **23.** controversial *(p. 683)* **24.** abstraction *(p. 690)* **25.** conformity *(p. 692)* **26.** technical *(p. 693)*

CHAPTER 14 ASSESSMENT and ACTIVITIES

Standards 11.8, 11.8.1, 11.8.2, 11.8.3, 11.8.4, 11.8.7, 11.8.8, 11.10, 11.10.1, 11.10.7, 11.11.2, 11.11.3, 11.11.7

Reviewing Content Vocabulary

On a sheet of paper, use each of these terms in a sentence.

1. closed shop
2. right-to-work law
3. union shop
4. featherbedding
5. dynamic conservatism
6. white-collar
7. blue-collar
8. multinational corporation
9. franchise
10. baby boom
11. generation gap
12. poverty line
13. urban renewal
14. termination policy
15. juvenile delinquency

Reviewing Academic Vocabulary

On a sheet of paper, use each of these terms in a sentence that reflects the term's meaning in the chapter.

16. restrain
17. subsidy
18. transition
19. accompany
20. benefit
21. generate
22. device
23. controversial
24. abstraction
25. conformity
26. technical

Reviewing the Main Ideas

Section 1

27. How did the GI Bill boost the economy after World War II?

Section 2

28. What caused many Americans to move to the suburbs in the 1950s?

Section 3

29. How did the radio industry win back audiences after television developed?

Section 4

30. Which groups of Americans found themselves left out of the postwar economic boom?

Critical Thinking

31. **Reading Skill** **Question-Answer Relationships** Review pages 678–679. Write and answer two questions on technological breakthroughs during the 1950s. Identify questions as "author and you" or "on your own" relationships.

32. **Civics** Give examples of the expansion of executive powers during the Truman and Eisenhower administrations in response to the Cold War.

33. **Explaining** How has mass media changed since the 1950s?

Chapter Summary

	Signs of Prosperity	Signs of Inequality
Economy	• The GI Bill provided loans to millions of war veterans. • Consumer spending increased rapidly. • More Americans owned homes than ever before.	• Workers went on strike for higher wages. • Truman's civil rights bill did not pass. • Eisenhower cut back New Deal programs.
Population Patterns	• The U.S. population grew dramatically. • The number of working women increased.	• Financially able people moved from crowded cities to new suburbs. • Many poor people remained in cities that now faced major economic and social problems.
Science, Technology, and Medicine	• Medical breakthroughs included the polio vaccine, antibiotics, and treatments for heart disease, arthritis, cancer, and diabetes. • Improvements in communication, transportation, and electronics allowed Americans to work more efficiently.	• Many poor people in inner cities and rural areas had limited access to health care.
Popular Culture	• Popular culture included new forms of music, radio, cinema, and literature. • Television replaced radio as the nation's newest form of mass media.	• African Americans and other minorities were, for the most part, not depicted on television. • Many television programs promoted stereotypical gender roles.

Reviewing the Main Ideas

27. The GI Bill provided loans to veterans to establish businesses, buy homes, and attend college.

28. They wanted to escape urban crime and make a better life for their families. They had automobiles to transport them to and from work.

29. Radio specialized in presenting recorded music, news, talk shows, weather, and public-service programming rather than competing with television for comedies, dramas, and soap operas.

30. Single mothers, the elderly, minority immigrants, rural Americans, inner-city residents, African Americans, Hispanics, Native Americans, and people in Appalachia were left out of the postwar economic boom.

34. Evaluating What factors led to a rise in juvenile delinquency in the United States during the 1950s? `CA HI1`

35. Organizing Use a graphic organizer similar to the one below to list the changes to the American family during the 1950s.

Changes to American Family

Writing About History

36. `Historical Analysis` **Analyzing and Understanding Change** How did Truman aid the civil rights movement? Explain what changed for African Americans in the 1950s and why other aspects of society remained the same. `CA CS2`

37. *Big Idea* Write a letter to a friend describing how the American economy changed following World War II. Your letter should describe the changes that impacted society both economically and culturally.

DBQ ▶ Document-Based Questions

38. Interpreting Primary Sources George Gallup, one of the nation's first pollsters, spoke at the University of Iowa in 1953 about the importance of mass media in the United States. Read the excerpt and answer the questions that follow.

❝One of the real threats to America's future place in the world is a citizenry which duly elects to be entertained and not informed. From the time the typical citizen arises and looks at his morning newspaper until he turns off his radio or television set before going to bed, he has unwittingly cast his vote a hundred times for entertainment or for education. Without his knowing it, he has helped to determine the very character of our three most important media of communication—the press, radio, and television. . . .❞

—quoted in *Vital Speeches of the Day*

a. According to Gallup, what is a threat to the future of the United States in the world?

b. How do American citizens determine what is read, seen, and heard in the mass media?

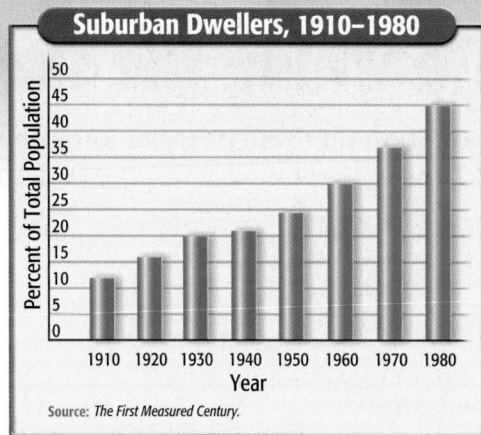

Suburban Dwellers, 1910–1980

Percent of Total Population (y-axis: 0 to 50)
Year (x-axis: 1910, 1920, 1930, 1940, 1950, 1960, 1970, 1980)

Source: *The First Measured Century.*

Geography and History

39. The graph above shows the number of suburban dwellers in the United States as a percentage of the total population. Study the data displayed in the graph and answer the questions below.

a. Interpreting Graphs What trend in the percentage of suburban dwellers does this graph show?

b. Understanding Cause and Effect How might the trend of suburban dwellers shown on this graph have affected life in suburbs and cities?

Standards Practice

Directions: Choose the best answer to the following question.

40. Which of the following was a technological breakthrough in the 1950s?

A the introduction of new vaccines to fight diabetes and cancer

B the invention of the radio

C the first vaccine that prevented polio

D the development of personal computers

Standard 11.8.7: Describe the effects on society and the economy of technological developments since 1945, including the computer revolution, changes in communication, advances in medicine, and improvements in agricultural technology.

CHAPTER 14 Postwar America **697**

Writing About History

36. `Historical Analysis` Students should mention the end of segregation in the armed forces, the executive order barring discrimination in federal employment, and his attempt for a broad civil rights bill.

37. *Big Idea* Students' letters will vary but should explain how the economy leaned towards prosperity. Students should mention some aspect of popular culture emerging more prominently such as television, movies, and radio.

DBQ ▶ Document-Based Questions

38. a. He feared a citizenry that chose to be entertained and not informed. **b.** They do it by the choices they make in forms of entertainment.

Geography and History

39. a. rising; **b.** caused urban life to decline and suburban life to become the ideal

Standards Practice

40. C

Bonus Question ?

Ask: What does the term *Baby Boom* refer to? *(a 16-year period from 1945 to 1961 when 65 million children were born in the United States)*

Critical Thinking

31. `Reading Skill` Students' questions should be clearly identified as either "author and you" or "on your own."

32. Truman with Congress created the Department of Defense, the CIA, and established the Joint Chiefs of Staff. Eisenhower advocated the passing of the Federal Highway Act.

33. Mass media has become more pervasive. Hundreds of radio and television stations, as well as the Internet, are available 24 hours a day, 7 days a week.

34. Different reasons were suggested, including poverty, lack of supervision, media influences, racism, lack of discipline or of religion.

35. the move to suburbs, travel by automobile, growing gap between generations

Unit 5 Resources

Teaching the Unit

Use the information on these pages to help you teach Unit 5.

History–Social Science Standards Covered in Unit 5

Standard	Chapter 15	16	17	18
11.8 Students analyze the economic boom and social transformation of post–World War II America.	✔		✔	✔
11.9 Students analyze U.S. foreign policy since World War II.	✔		✔	✔
11.10 Students analyze the development of federal civil rights and voting rights.	✔	✔	✔	✔
11.11 Students analyze the major social problems and domestic policy issues in contemporary American society.	✔	✔		✔

Pacing Your Lessons

This pacing chart provides time management suggestions for teaching Unit 5.

	Days
Unit 5 Introduction	1
Chapter 15 • **Reading Skill:** Synthesizing • **Historical Analysis Skill:** Identifying Bias • **Sections 1–3** • **TIME Notebook:** New Frontiers: 1961–1968 • **Why It Matters:** The Space Program • **Eyewitness to History:** Primary Source Documents	7
Chapter 16 • **Reading Skill:** Determining Importance • **Historical Analysis Skill:** Showing Connections • **Sections 1–3** • **Eyewitness to History:** Primary Source Documents	7
Chapter 17 • **Reading Skill:** Questioning the Author • **Historical Analysis Skill:** Comparing Present and Past • **Sections 1–4** • **Eyewitness to History:** Primary Source Documents	9
Chapter 18 • **Reading Skill:** Evaluating • **Historical Analysis Skill:** Historical Connections • **Sections 1–4** • **American Literature:** *The Yellow Wallpaper* by Charlotte Perkins Gilman • **National Geographic:** Global Cars • **Eyewitness to History:** Primary Source Documents	9

Teacher to Teacher

Birmingham's 16th Street Baptist Church Bombing Lesson Plan

This activity helps students understand how the civil rights movement in the United States affected students their own age.

First, read and discuss literature that focuses on the tensions in Birmingham in 1963. Present Associated Press file photos of the era and discuss the Robert Chambliss trial. Then watch, discuss, and take notes on Spike Lee's documentary *4 Little Girls.* To end this section, have students read the latest news surrounding this event.

**Jason Follett
Malcolm Price
Laboratory School
Cedar Falls, Iowa**

Students should build story maps with the climax and resolution clearly identified. Using the story maps, students can create hand-drawn or computer-drawn graphic novels of the bombing as well as student guides to drawing a graphic novel. Examples of non-humor graphic novels can be obtained through the Federal Reserve System. The best way to evaluate these graphic novels is to use a rubric.

Unit 5 Resources

Previewing the Chapters

Dear American History Teacher:

As you begin to teach this unit, there are themes that recur throughout the chapters that you will want to point out to students.

These two and a half decades represented an era of dramatic change in American history. The Cold War, following World War II, served as the backdrop to many of these events and should be reemphasized as you discuss the social and political upheavals of the 1960s and 1970s. The decades of the 1950s and 1960s witnessed some of the greatest social movements of the twentieth century—the civil rights movement, the student movement, the women's rights movement, and the counterculture movement.

These were years of relative prosperity, rising expectations, and the desire to end poverty and suffering among all Americans, as illustrated in Lyndon Johnson's Great Society. Students should also get a sense of how the nation divided over American foreign policy, especially U.S. involvement in the Vietnam War. The struggle for civil rights was also central to this era, and discussing the role of leaders such as Martin Luther King, Jr., Thurgood Marshall, and Rosa Parks is an effective way to engage students in this subject matter.

Albert S. Broussard

Chapter 15: The New Frontier and the Great Society, 1961–1968
(pages 700–735)

John F. Kennedy became president in 1960 and worked to oppose the spread of communism. This period of the Cold War saw the Bay of Pigs invasion, the Cuban missile crisis, and the space race. President Kennedy was assassinated in 1963. Lyndon B. Johnson, his successor, created programs to provide assistance to disadvantaged Americans.

Chapter 16: The Civil Rights Movement, 1954–1968
(pages 736–767)

The civil rights movement involved widespread action to increase the voting power of African Americans, end racial segregation, and change other inequalities that African Americans faced. Peaceful protests and boycotts were organized by leaders such as Martin Luther King, Jr., and significant court victories were gained. Violence and unrest grew, however, particularly in the South, where many resisted the changes in society.

Chapter 17: The Vietnam War, 1954–1975
(pages 768–801)

Cold War politics led the United States to enter the Vietnam War in 1965. As more American soldiers died, an antiwar movement grew. Johnson, with his popularity waning, decided not to seek reelection. Richard Nixon became president in 1969 and gradually reduced the number of troops in the war. American involvement in the war ended after a cease-fire was signed, but North Vietnamese troops invaded South Vietnam and united the country under Communist rule.

Chapter 18: The Politics of Protest, 1960–1980
(pages 802–843)

In the 1960s, a counterculture grew away from the traditional mainstream society. Young people became active in new spiritual movements and social causes. Despite fragmentation, the women's movement affected profound changes in American society. Minorities continued to organize and fight for civil rights.

FOCUS

History–Social Science Standards

This unit addresses the following main standards:

11.10 Students analyze the development of federal civil rights and voting rights.

11.11 Students analyze the major social problems and domestic policy issues in contemporary American society.

Connecting to Past Learning

In Unit 4 students learned about the global struggles of World War II and the Cold War, events that shaped the history of many countries and influenced the path of global events for many decades. In Unit 5 students will analyze the tumultuous period between 1954 and 1980 when many attempts were made to shape American society at home and American actions abroad.

Unit Launch Activity

Have students interview someone who was growing up or an adult in the late 1960s and the 1970s. Interviews should focus on how this era influences the United States today. Students should prepare transcripts, audios, or videos of their interviews for presentation. Ask for volunteers to share insightful portions of their interviews as you discuss the importance of this era to life in America today. **OL**

Why It Matters Activity

Ask students to create time lines that include events they consider important during the years 1954–1980. Once the time lines are complete, ask students to explain why they selected these events. **BL**

698

UNIT 5 A Time of Upheaval

1954–1980

Why It Matters

From a presidential assassination to massive governmental programs, from the Vietnam War to the civil rights movement, the post–World War II decades immensely affected the lives of Americans. The nation struggled to put its social and political ideals into practice while fighting military wars overseas and social wars at home. Understanding how these events unfolded provides a window to the world you live in today. The following resources offer more information about this period in American history.

Primary Sources Library

See pages 978–979 for primary source readings to accompany Unit 5.

Use the American History Primary Source Document Library CD-ROM to find additional primary sources about imperialism and progressivism.

698

Poster from the March on Washington

Mural on building in Davenport, Iowa

TEAM TEACHING ACTIVITY

MUSIC Ask the music teacher to share classic examples of the protest music that was popular in the 1960s and 1970s. Have students examine the lyrics and pose questions to the teacher about what particular phrases mean. Ask students to compile a database of the new words they learn, along with their meanings. Encourage students to add to this database as they study this unit. **OL**

"What we won when all of our people united . . . must not now be lost in suspicion, distrust, selfishness, and politics. . . ."

—*Lyndon Johnson, 1968*

We must learn to live together as brothers or perish together as fools.

True Peace is not merely the absence of tension, it is the Presence of Justice.

A sound mind has no spe color in which to be heard carries out an em message of every race. Sherwin Q. R

STOP LOOK
LISTEN AND
HEAR THE PEACE

NELSON MANDELA

VIDENCE FROM ANDELA'S TRIAL

TEACH

Skill Practice

Identifying Point of View Have students read the quote from Lyndon Johnson shown at the top of this page. **Ask: What two periods of time do you think President Johnson is referring to in this statement?** *(Students should realize that the time "when all of our people united" refers to the World War II era and that the current period of "suspicion, distrust, selfishness, and politics" refers to the Vietnam and civil rights era.)* **AL**

Universal Access

Visual/Spatial The social movements of the late 1960s and the 1970s encouraged many artists to paint murals on buildings, usually in inner-city neighborhoods and near freeways. African Americans and Hispanics created many of the murals that can be seen in cities across the nation. **Ask: Describe what you see. What symbols do you recognize? How does this mural reflect history, culture, or events?** *(Students should recognize Martin Luther King, Jr. The central figure in the middle of the mural is identified as Nelson Mandela. Students can provide their own interpretation of the other images and statements shown.)* **OL**

NC LB No Child Left Behind

Teaching Tip The NCLB Act emphasizes reading. Ask students to write down events and people they will encounter in this unit and keep the list with them as they read. When students find a person or item on the list, they should note the page number and write a brief summary. Students can use this list while studying.

UNIVERSAL ACCESS

English Learners: Have students write down any unfamiliar words that they find on these unit opener pages. Then have pairs of students look up these terms in a dictionary. **EL**

Visual/Spatial: Ask students to name a significant event that occurred during the decades of this unit. The class should locate in an atlas where the chosen event took place. **OL**

Advanced Learners: Have students research and prepare reports called "Turning Points." Reports should focus on at least one event that changed the course of history between the years 1954 and 1980. **AL**

699

Chapter 15 Planning Guide

SECTION RESOURCES

Main Ideas	📁 Print Materials	Technology Resources
Section 1: The New Frontier 1. John F. Kennedy won the first media-dominated presidential election. 2. With Kennedy's election, a youthful and enthusiastic First Family entered the White House. 3. Despite an uneasy relationship with Congress, Kennedy managed to get several parts of his domestic agenda passed. 4. Under Chief Justice Earl Warren, the Supreme Court took a more activist role.	• Reproducible Lesson Plan 15-1* • Daily Lecture and Discussion Notes 15-1 • Active Reading Note-Taking Guide 15-1 • Guided Reading Activity 15-1 • Section Quiz 15-1 • Reading Essentials and Study Guide 15-1	🖳 Daily Focus Skills Transparency 15-1 🖳 Section Graphic Organizer Transparency 15-1 💿 Interactive Tutor Self-Assessment CD-ROM 💿 ExamView® Pro Testmaker CD-ROM 💿 Presentation Plus! CD-ROM 🖳 California Standards Practice Transparencies
Section 2: JFK and the Cold War 1. President Kennedy developed new programs to combat the spread of communism. 2. President Kennedy faced foreign policy crises in Cuba and Berlin. 3. President Kennedy was assassinated in Dallas, Texas, on November 22, 1963.	• Reproducible Lesson Plan 15-2* • Daily Lecture and Discussion Notes 15-2 • Active Reading Note-Taking Guide 15-2 • Guided Reading Activity 15-2 • Section Quiz 15-2 • Reading Essentials and Study Guide 15-2	🖳 Daily Focus Skills Transparency 15-2 🖳 Section Graphic Organizer Transparency 15-2 💿 Interactive Tutor Self-Assessment CD-ROM 💿 ExamView® Pro Testmaker CD-ROM 💿 Presentation Plus! CD-ROM 🖳 California Standards Practice Transparencies
Section 3: The Great Society 1. President Johnson's longtime experience in Congress helped him push through several of President Kennedy's antipoverty bills. 2. Johnson's Great Society programs provided assistance to disadvantaged Americans. 3. Although controversial, the Great Society programs improved the lives of thousands of people.	• Reproducible Lesson Plan 15-3* • Daily Lecture and Discussion Notes 15-3 • Active Reading Note-Taking Guide 15-3 • Guided Reading Activity 15-3 • Section Quiz 15-3 • Reading Essentials and Study Guide 15-3	🖳 Daily Focus Skills Transparency 15-3 🖳 Section Graphic Organizer Transparency 15-3 💿 Interactive Tutor Self-Assessment CD-ROM 💿 ExamView® Pro Testmaker CD-ROM 💿 Presentation Plus! CD-ROM 🖳 California Standards Practice Transparencies

PACING YOUR LESSONS

Chapter Introduction	Section 1	Section 2	Section 3	Chapter Assessment
½ Day	2 Days	2 Days	2 Days	½ Day

0:00 OUT OF TIME? 📁 Assign the Chapter 15 *Reading Essentials and Study Guide.*

*Available on TeacherWorks™ CD-ROM

Chapter 15 Planning Guide

Standards-Based Lesson Plan

 History–Social Science Standards Covered in Chapter 15

The standards covered in the chapter are listed below. Use the accompanying activity as you teach the chapter to ensure student mastery of these standards. This activity can be used in combination with the program's print and technology assessment materials.

Standard	Section 1	Section 2	Section 3
11.8.4 Analyze new federal government spending on defense, welfare, interest on the national debt, and federal and state spending on education, including the California Master Plan.	✔		✔
11.9.3 Trace the origins and geopolitical consequences (foreign and domestic) of the Cold War and containment policy, including the following: the era of McCarthyism, instances of domestic Communism (e.g., Alger Hiss) and blacklisting; the Truman Doctrine; the Berlin Blockade; the Korean War; the Bay of Pigs invasion and the Cuban Missile Crisis; atomic testing in the American West, the "mutual assured destruction" doctrine, and disarmament policies; the Vietnam War; Latin American policy.		✔	
11.11.2 Discuss the significant domestic policy speeches of Truman, Eisenhower, Kennedy, Johnson, Nixon, Carter, Reagan, Bush, and Clinton (e.g., with regard to education, civil rights, economic policy, environmental policy).	✔		✔
11.11.6 Analyze the persistence of poverty and how different analyses of this issue influence welfare reform, health insurance reform, and other social policies.			✔

Cumulative Standards-Assessment Activity

The Cumulative Standards-Assessment Activity will help students organize and learn the important information from the chapter. Begin teaching the chapter with this activity, and have students complete it as they read the chapter.

CREATING A CHART FOR QUESTIONING

Purpose Questioning is a skill that can be used to monitor comprehension as students read. By asking themselves questions on a particular section, answering the questions, and checking the answers, they can make sure that they are absorbing the material and are ready to move on to the next segment of text. Asking questions can also help ensure students are seeking out the deeper meanings of what they are reading.

Introduction to Questioning

1. Discuss how learning occurs not only when we learn names and dates of events, but also when we seek out the meaning and significance of the events.

2. Model the skill by directing students to any page of text from the previous chapter. Have the students read the section and, while they do so, write a question on the board aimed at a key concept. After students have completed their reading, ask volunteers to answer the question. Then have students check the answers against the text to see if they are correct.

3. Ask students to copy this chart into their notebooks:

Question: _____
Answer: _____
Correct ☐
Incorrect ☐
Correction/Other Interpretation: _____

As students read each section, have them use this format to ask questions and answer them. Their questions should not only ask who, what, where, and when, but also why and how. Remind them to check the questions and answers against the text to ensure that they are correct. Instruct them that if they find an answer that is not correct they should use the *Correction* line to fix the problem. Questions interpreting meaning may not be easily identified as correct or incorrect, so you may want students to think of and write down an alternate interpretation. Remind students that their questions should focus on key concepts in the text, not less important material.

4. As you review the chapter, ask volunteers to share their questions. Encourage them to use their questions as study aids.

Chapter 15 Planning Guide

READING SUPPORT

- Content Vocabulary Activity 15
- Academic Vocabulary Activity 15
- Reading Skills Activity 15
- Chapter 15 Active Reading Note-Taking Guide
- Chapter 15 Guided Reading Activities
- Chapter 15 Reading Essentials and Study Guide
- *The American Vision: Modern Times* Video Program
- Vocabulary PuzzleMaker CD-ROM
- American History Primary Source Document Library CD-ROM

CRITICAL THINKING

- Critical Thinking Skills Activity 15
- Primary Source Reading 15
- Cause-and-Effect Transparency 15 Strategy and Activity
- Presentation Plus! CD-ROM

UNIVERSAL ACCESS

- Universal Access Activity 15
- English Learner Activity 15
- American Art Prints
- StudentWorks™ Plus CD-ROM
- American Music: Hits Through History
- School-to-Home Connection Activity 15

SKILL PRACTICE

- Map Overlay Transparency 15 Strategy and Activity
- Historical Analysis Skills Activity 15
- Time Line Activity 15
- Reading Skills Activity 15
- Reinforcing Skills Activity 15
- Linking Past and Present Activity 15
- Interpreting Political Cartoons 15
- MindJogger Videoquiz

WRITING SUPPORT

- Chapter 15 Active Reading Note-Taking Guide
- Writer's Guidebook
- High School Writing Process Transparencies

ASSESSMENT

- Chapter 15 Section Quizzes
- Chapter 15 Tests, Forms A and B
- Authentic Assessment Activity 15
- ExamView® Pro Testmaker CD-ROM
- Interactive Tutor Self-Assessment CD-ROM
- California Standards Practice, Grade 11
- Succeeding on . . .™ the California Standards: Grade 11 History–Social Science CD-ROM

CD-ROM	Transparency
DVD	Music Program
Print Material	Videocassette
Poster	

Chapter 15 Planning Guide

TECHNOLOGY

- StudentWorks™ Plus CD-ROM
- TeacherWorks™ CD-ROM
- ExamView® Pro Testmaker CD-ROM
- Interactive Tutor Self-Assessment CD-ROM
- Presentation Plus! CD-ROM
- Vocabulary PuzzleMaker CD-ROM
- American History Primary Source Document Library CD-ROM
- MindJogger Videoquiz
- *The American Vision: Modern Times* Video Program
- Professional Development in High School Social Studies Video Series
- Teach, Use, and Succeed With *The American Vision: Modern Times*
- American Music: Hits Through History
- Succeeding on . . .™ the California Standards: Grade 11 History–Social Science CD-ROM

SPANISH RESOURCES

- Spanish Activities and Assessment
  - Spanish Vocabulary Activities
  - Spanish Guided Reading Activities
  - Spanish Quizzes and Tests
  - Spanish Reteaching Activities
- Spanish Reading Essentials and Study Guide
- Spanish School-to-Home Connection Activities

TRANSPARENCIES

- Daily Focus Skills Transparencies
- Section Graphic Organizer Transparencies
- Map Overlay Transparencies
- Cause-and-Effect Transparencies
- Unit Time Line Transparencies
- Why It Matters Transparencies
- American Art and Architecture Transparencies
- High School Writing Process Transparencies
- California Standards Practice Transparencies

TEACHER PLANNING

- Daily Lecture and Discussion Notes
- English Learner Handbook
- Building Academic Vocabulary
- *The American Vision: Modern Times* Reading and Study Skills Foldables
- Reading Strategies and Activities for the Social Studies Classroom
- Universal Access for the American History Classroom
- NGS United States Desk Map
- NGS World Atlas
- Chapter 15 Reproducible Lesson Plans on TeacherWorks™ CD-ROM
- California Guide to Daily Intervention

PROFESSIONAL DEVELOPMENT

- Building Academic Vocabulary
- Strategies for Success
- Research-Based Strategies Used to Develop *The American Vision: Modern Times*
- Character Education in the High School Classroom
- Professional Development in High School Social Studies Video Series
- Teach, Use, and Succeed With *The American Vision: Modern Times*

Chapter 15 Planning Guide

Index to National Geographic Magazine:

The following articles relate to this chapter:

- "Alone Across the Arctic Crown," April 1993
- "Bikini's Nuclear Graveyard," June 1992
- "Kodiak, Alaska's Island Refuge," November 1993
- "Wrangell-St. Elias: Alaska's Sky-High Wilderness," May 1994

National Geographic Society Products:

To order the following, call National Geographic at 1–800–368–2728

- *1945–1989: The Cold War* (Video)
- *Eyewitness to the 20th Century* (Book)
- *Historical Atlas of the United States* (Atlas)

NGS ONLINE

Access National Geographic's new dynamic MapMachine Web site and other geography resources at:

www.nationalgeographic.com

www.nationalgeographic.com/maps

MASTERING THE STANDARDS

The content and assessment in the Student Edition, Teacher Wraparound Edition, teacher planning materials, and the print and technology products are all standards-based. The use of these products during instruction leads to mastery of the standards.

PRACTICE
- California Standards Practice, Grade 11
- California Standards Practice Transparencies
- School-to-Home Connection

BENCHMARK ASSESSMENT
- Section Quizzes, Chapter Tests, and Authentic Assessment
- Exam*View*® Pro Testmaker CD-ROM
- Succeeding On . . . ™ the California Standards: Grade 11 History–Social Science CD-ROM

REMEDIATION
- California Guide to Daily Intervention
- Interactive Tutor Self-Assessment CD-ROM
- Exam*View*® Pro Testmaker CD-ROM
- California Standards Practice, Grade 11
- Reading Essentials and Study Guide

Use our Web site for additional resources. All essential content is covered in the Student Edition.

You and your students can visit tav.mt.glencoe.com, the Web site companion to the **American Vision: Modern Times.** This innovative integration of electronic and print media offers your students a wealth of opportunities. The student text directs students to the Web site for the following options:

- **Chapter Overviews**
- **Self-Check Quizzes**
- **Student Web Activities**
- **Textbook Updates**

Answers to the student Web activities are provided for you in the **Web Activity Lesson Plans.** Additional Web resources and ePuzzles and games are also available.

Dinah Zike's Foldables

Foldables are three-dimensional, interactive graphic organizers that help students practice basic writing skills, review key vocabulary terms, and identify main ideas. Every chapter has a foldable activity in the *Dinah Zike's Reading and Study Skills Foldables* booklet. You can use the foldables as they are presented or modify them to suit the needs of your individual class.

A variety of videotape programs are available from A&E Television and The History Channel to provide teaching assistance. To order, call Glencoe at 1-800-334-7344.

700E

Chapter 15 Planning Guide

Reading List Generator CD-ROM

GLENCOE BOOKLINK

The Glencoe BookLink CD-ROM is a database that allows you to search more than 15,000 titles to create a customized reading list for your students.

- Reading Lists can be organized by students' reading level, author, genre, theme, or area of interest.
- The database provides Degrees of Reading Power™ (DRP) and Lexile™ readability scores for all selections.
- A brief summary of each selection is included.

Leveled reading suggestions for this chapter:

For students at a Grade 8 reading level:
- *How Did We Find Out About Computers?,* by Isaac Asimov

For students at a Grade 9 reading level:
- *A Thousand Days: John F. Kennedy in the White House,* by Arthur M. Schlesinger, Jr.

For students at a Grade 10 reading level:
- *The First Men in Space,* by Gregory P. Kennedy

READING SUPPORT FROM JAMESTOWN EDUCATION

- *Timed Readings Plus in Social Studies* help students increase their reading rate and fluency while maintaining comprehension. The 400-word passages are similar to those found on state and national assessments.
- *Reading in the Content Area: Social Studies* concentrates on six essential reading skills that help students better comprehend what they read. The book includes 75 high-interest nonfiction passages written at increasing levels of difficulty.
- *Reading Fluency* helps students read smoothly, accurately, and expressively.
- *Jamestown's Reading Improvement,* by renowned reading expert Edward Fry, focuses on helping build your students' comprehension, vocabulary, and skimming and scanning skills.
- *Critical Reading Series* provides high-interest books, each written at three reading levels.

For more information about these products, see the Jamestown Education materials in the Classroom Solutions in the front of this Teacher Wraparound Edition. To order these products, call Glencoe at 1-800-334-7344.

KEY for Using the Teacher Wraparound Edition

Use this key to help you identify the different types of prompts found in the Teacher Wraparound Edition.

R **Reading Strategies** activities help you teach reading skills and vocabulary.

C **Critical Thinking** strategies help students apply and extend what they have learned.

U **Universal Access** activities provide differentiated instruction for students learning to speak English, along with suggestions for teaching various types of learners.

S **Skill Practice** strategies help students practice historical analysis and geography skills.

W **Writing Support** activities provide writing opportunities to help students comprehend the text.

Teaching strategies and activities have been coded for ability level appropriateness.

AL Activities for students working above grade level
OL Activities for students working on grade level
BL Activities for students working below grade level
EL Activities for English learners

History–Social Science Standards

This chapter addresses the following main standards:

11.9 Students analyze U.S. foreign policy since World War II.

11.11 Students analyze the major social problems and domestic policy issues in contemporary American society.

SKILLBUILDER ACTIVITY

Have students brainstorm words that they think of or associate with the term *frontier,* and place them on a chart for reference later. *(Answers will vary but may include: boundary, edge, limit, early American, pre-revolutionary, horizon)*

TEACH

Thinking About the Big Ideas

As you begin teaching each section, use these questions and activities to focus on the Big Idea.

Section 1
The New Frontier

Essential Question: What types of changes can occur as a result of success? What types of setbacks can occur when trying to achieve success? *(Students' answers will vary based on prior knowledge and personal experiences.)* Tell students that as they read Section 1, they will learn

---

CHAPTER

15

1961–1968

The New Frontier and the Great Society

≈ *Big Ideas* ≈

SECTION 1: The New Frontier

Societies change over time. *John F. Kennedy encountered both success and setbacks on the domestic front.*

SECTION 2: JFK and the Cold War

The fate of nations is forever changed by monumental world events. *As president, John F. Kennedy had to confront the challenges and fears of the Cold War.*

SECTION 3: The Great Society

Societies change over time. *Lyndon Johnson greatly expanded Kennedy's agenda with far-reaching social and economic programs.*

The *American Vision: Modern Times* **Video** *The Chapter 15 video, "A New Frontier: The Space Race," explores the dramatic history of the American space program.*

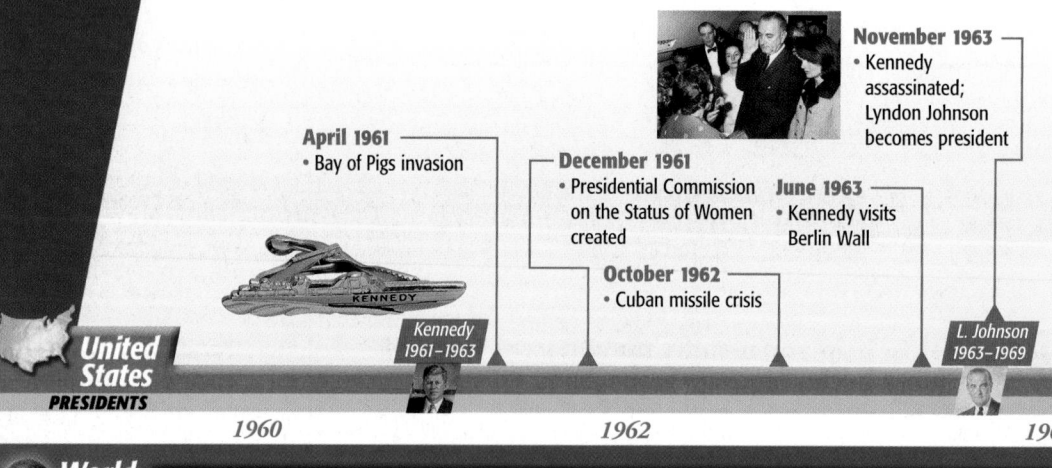

April 1961
• Bay of Pigs invasion

December 1961
• Presidential Commission on the Status of Women created

June 1963
• Kennedy visits Berlin Wall

October 1962
• Cuban missile crisis

November 1963
• Kennedy assassinated; Lyndon Johnson becomes president

United States
PRESIDENTS

Kennedy 1961–1963

L. Johnson 1963–1969

1960　　　*1962*　　　*1964*

World

1959
• Cuban revolution brings Castro to power

April 1961
• Eichmann goes on trial for crimes against Jews

August 1961
• Construction of Berlin Wall begins

1964
• South Africa's Nelson Mandela sentenced to life in prison

700

---

how John F. Kennedy encountered both success and setbacks on the domestic front. **OL**

Section 2
JFK and the Cold War

Essential Question: What factors can influence people's concerns about their own community, national government, or a foreign government? Discuss the answers as a class.

(Answers may include education, communication, family/peer influence.) **Ask: Is it possible to live without a fear of conflicts with other nations?** As students read Section 2, remind them to think about the fears that U.S citizens, as well as President John F. Kennedy, may have felt during the confrontations and challenges of the Cold War. **OL**

Essential Question: How important is it for the government to provide adequate health care, education, and consumer and environmental protection? *(Students' answers will vary.)* **Ask:** How would the elderly and low-income families receive care? How would education be affected? How would the environment as well as consumers be protected? As students read Section 3, remind them to think about how far-reaching Lyndon Johnson's programs and agenda were. OL

Cultural Perspectives

The 1950s and 1960s were decades of rapid social change in the United States. Have students work in small groups to find out about advances made by women, minorities, and the disadvantaged under the Kennedy and Johnson administrations. **Ask: Which program, reform, or action that occurred during this period has had the most enduring legacy?** Students will need to investigate what reforms took place, evaluate them, and decide which they believe was the most important. Remind students that they should be able to defend their choices with logical, specific reasoning. OL

President John F. Kennedy at his inaugural ball in 1961

July 1965
• Congress establishes Medicare and Medicaid programs

October 1966
• Fair Packaging and Labeling Act passed

March 1968
• Lyndon Johnson announces that he will not run for re-election

1966

1968

1966
• Indira Gandhi becomes prime minister of India

1968
• Student riots paralyze France

HISTORY Online

Chapter Overview
Visit the *American Vision: Modern Times* Web site at tav.mt.glencoe.com and click on ***Chapter Overviews— Chapter 15*** to preview chapter information.

701

FOLDABLES™ Study Organizer

Dinah Zike's Foldables are three-dimensional, interactive graphic organizers that help students practice basic writing skills, review key vocabulary terms, and identify main ideas. Have students complete the foldable activity in the *Dinah Zike's Reading and Study Skills Foldables* booklet.

HISTORY Online

Go to tav.mt.glencoe.com for student activities, lesson plans, and links to additional Web resources to help students learn about the New Frontier and Great Society.

Why It's Important

When students synthesize information, they must identify the important points of what they read and then combine those points to develop a broader awareness of events and actions outside the specific information studied.

1. Introducing the Skill

Divide the class into pairs. Ask one student of each pair to write three clues about an important historical individual in a chart like the one below. Have the other student read the clues and guess the correct person. **OL**

Clues	Person
Clue #1	
Clue #2	
Clue #3	

2. Extending the Skill

Ask students to individually select a heading and accompanying text from a previous section of the textbook. Tell them to read their selected texts and write summary paragraphs that synthesize the main information presented. **OL**

Answers and Additional Support

Preparing to Read Chapter 15

Reading Skill — **Synthesizing**

Good readers look for patterns of information to understand relationships between and among ideas. This information often emerges over the course of many pages of text. When you locate information from more than one place in a text and then use it together to understand and interpret the text, you are synthesizing.

One step in synthesizing is to organize the information in order to make comparisons and draw conclusions. You should look for patterns that help you identify major themes and draw conclusions about the material. You should also look for summary paragraphs that explain relationships between events, ideas, and concepts. These summary paragraphs help you to synthesize the information that was discussed in previous paragraphs or pages.

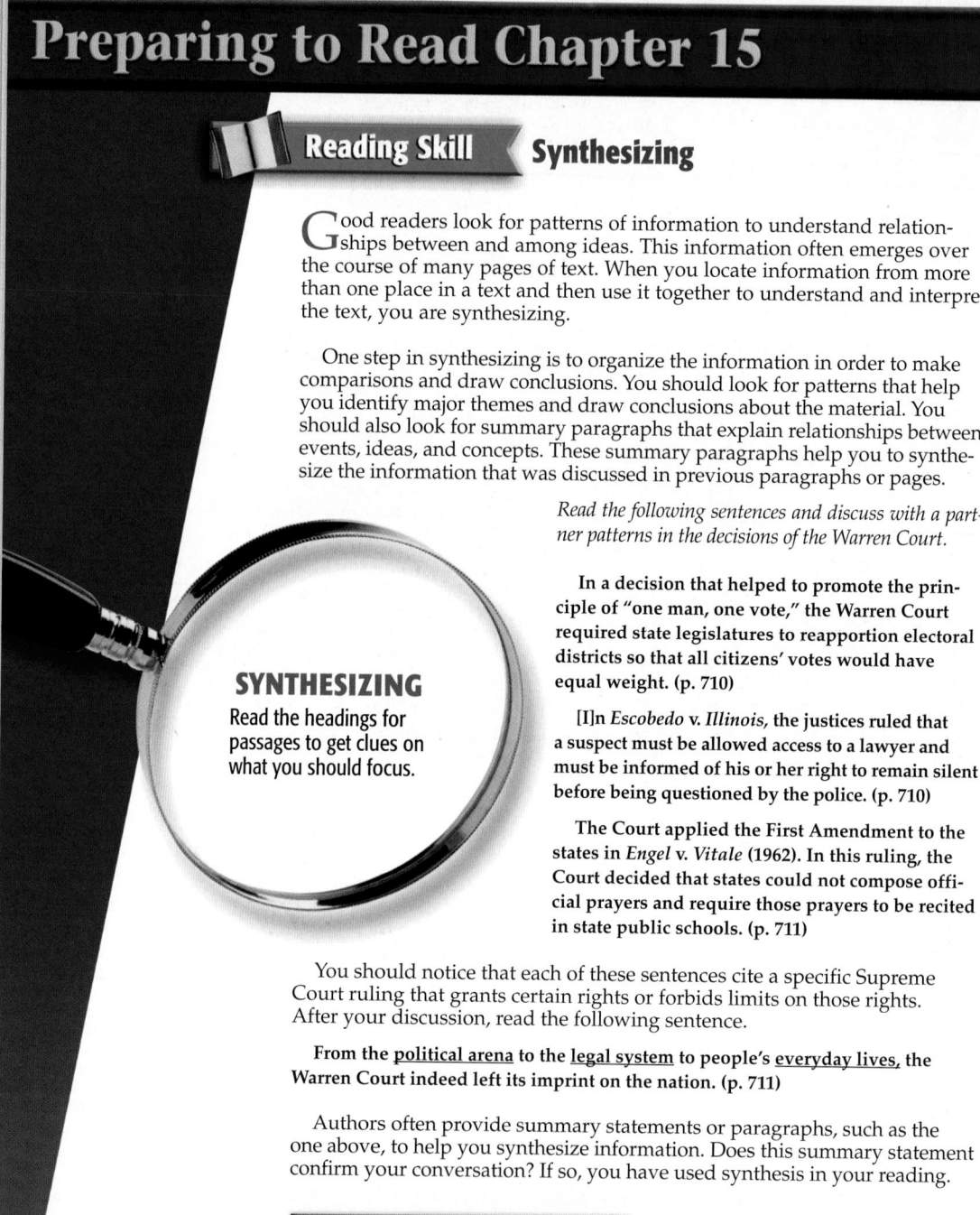

SYNTHESIZING
Read the headings for passages to get clues on what you should focus.

Read the following sentences and discuss with a partner patterns in the decisions of the Warren Court.

In a decision that helped to promote the principle of "one man, one vote," the Warren Court required state legislatures to reapportion electoral districts so that all citizens' votes would have equal weight. (p. 710)

[I]n *Escobedo* v. *Illinois,* the justices ruled that a suspect must be allowed access to a lawyer and must be informed of his or her right to remain silent before being questioned by the police. (p. 710)

The Court applied the First Amendment to the states in *Engel* v. *Vitale* (1962). In this ruling, the Court decided that states could not compose official prayers and require those prayers to be recited in state public schools. (p. 711)

You should notice that each of these sentences cite a specific Supreme Court ruling that grants certain rights or forbids limits on those rights. After your discussion, read the following sentence.

From the <u>political arena</u> to the <u>legal system</u> to people's <u>everyday lives,</u> the Warren Court indeed left its imprint on the nation. (p. 711)

Authors often provide summary statements or paragraphs, such as the one above, to help you synthesize information. Does this summary statement confirm your conversation? If so, you have used synthesis in your reading.

Apply the Skill

As you read Section 2 of this chapter, note the main themes mentioned. Then write a brief summary statement. Review the section to see if you can find sentences similar to your summary statement.

UNIVERSAL ACCESS

Logical/Mathematical Some students may find it easier to synthesize their reading by first organizing the information in a chart. Ask each student to practice this organizational method by creating a chart that lists *Main Idea, Themes, Connections,* and *Summaries.* As they read, they should take notes, filling in the columns under these headings. When they are finished with their reading, this chart will help them synthesize the information more effectively. **OL**

Historical Analysis Skill — Identifying Bias

Historical Research, Evidence, and Point of View As you read history texts, you should learn how to identify bias and prejudice in historical interpretations.

What do you think when you hear the word *bias*? The term is sometimes used to express strong negative opinions. It is often paired with the words *prejudice* or *racism*. The word *bias* can also be used to describe a strong positive opinion. Imagine a friend setting you up on a date with his or her cousin. While there might be some things about the cousin your friend may not like, your friend is likely biased and will focus on the positive aspects of your date.

Historians are concerned about bias and prejudice because they want to prevent a one-sided account of an issue or event. To avoid personal bias, historians research information from many sources to broaden their point of view. Then, they support their point of view with evidence, such as references to facts, examples, and historical parallels. This allows historians to keep their biases in check.

At the same time, you as the reader should be aware that historians, like all other people, hold specific views. You should learn to identify any bias and prejudice that may be present in any interpretation of historical events these authors present. You should also realize that when you read quotes, the people who are cited have a specific background and reason for the words they have said. When you interpret their words, you need to keep this background information in mind.

Read the following quote by Pierre Salinger, President John F. Kennedy's press secretary, describing Kennedy's charisma.

> "None of us will ever have a better job as long as we live. . . . The big *plus*—the fringe benefit that made it all worthwhile—was JFK himself. . . ." (p. 707)

As you read this quote, consider the source. Why might Mr. Salinger describe his work the way he did? What biases could Mr. Salinger posses? What might have created these biases?

Apply the Skill

As you read this chapter, you'll find several quotes from people who lived during this time. Consider the source of each. What biases might these people hold? How are these biases expressed in the quote?

703

Historical Analysis

Why It's Important
A good reader and careful observer of history must be able to identify bias. Understanding bias is the best way to evaluate the unstated or implied opinions of a text students are reading.

1. Introducing the Skill
Divide the class into pairs. Ask each student pair to separately write down characteristics of a famous person in a chart like the one below. Then have students identify any differences in their views of the person. Discuss as a class why differences in characterization occur. **OL**

	Famous Person
Student A	
Student B	

2. Extending the Skill
Ask the class to read about George Kennan's Long Telegram on page 633 or read the excerpts of the telegram on page 1021. Have students identify instances of bias in his evaluation of the Soviet Union. Discuss students' observations as a class. **OL**
CA HR2

UNIVERSAL ACCESS

English Learners Students from a different country or culture might be more able to recognize biases in the statements or phrases that people make every day but do not think are offensive. Ask students to read through the local newspaper for a week, searching for and collecting articles that show instances of cultural bias in statements that people make. Discuss as a class why some students may think certain statements show a bias, while other students do not. Try to brainstorm ways that these types of biased statements can be prevented. **EL**
CA HR2

FOCUS

SKILLBUILDER ACTIVITY

Project **Daily Focus Skills Transparency 15-1** and have students answer the question.

Guide to Reading

Understanding Vocabulary:
Have students define the following terms in their own words: missile gap, New Frontier, arbitrary, reapportionment, due process.

Answers to Graphic:
Successes: more funds in defense and space exploration, some advances in women's rights, economic improvement; Setbacks: health insurance for the elderly, a Department of Urban Affairs, federal aid to education, aid to migrant workers.

Unpacking the Standards

Students will be able to:

• Explain the events surrounding the election of 1960.

• Describe the image portrayed by John F. Kennedy.

• Analyze the achievements and failures of the Kennedy administration's domestic policies.

• Evaluate the importance of the Supreme Court during the tenure of Chief Justice Earl Warren.

SECTION 1 The New Frontier

Guide to Reading

Connection
In the previous chapter, you learned about the economic and social changes that occurred during the 1950s. In this section, you will discover how the country viewed President Kennedy's domestic agenda and the Warren Court.

Main Idea
• John F. Kennedy won the first media-dominated presidential election. (p. 705)
• With Kennedy's election, a youthful and enthusiastic First Family entered the White House. (p. 706)

• Despite an uneasy relationship with Congress, Kennedy managed to get several parts of his domestic agenda passed. (p. 707)
• Under Chief Justice Earl Warren, the Supreme Court took a more activist role. (p. 709)

Content Vocabulary
missile gap, reapportionment, due process

Academic Vocabulary
medium, reside, arbitrary

People and Terms to Identify
New Frontier, Earl Warren

Reading Objectives
• **Summarize** Kennedy's economic policies.
• **Explain** why Congress often did not support Kennedy's proposals.

Reading Strategy
Categorizing As you read about the presidency of John F. Kennedy, complete a graphic organizer similar to the one below by filling in the domestic successes and setbacks of Kennedy's administration.

Successes	Setbacks

Preview of Events

◆1960	◆1961	◆1962	◆1963
1960 — John Kennedy defeats Richard Nixon for the presidency	**1961** — Kennedy creates Presidential Commission on the Status of Women	**1962** — Supreme Court issues *Baker* v. *Carr* ruling	**1963** — Kennedy signs Equal Pay Act for women

The following are the main History–Social Science Standards covered in this section.

11.8.4 Analyze new federal government spending on defense, welfare, interest on the national debt, and federal and state spending on education, including the California Master Plan.

11.10.2 Examine and analyze the key events, policies, and court cases in the evolution of civil rights, including *Dred Scott v. Sanford, Plessy v. Ferguson, Brown v. Board of Education, Regents of the University of California v. Bakke,* and California Proposition 209.

11.10.7 Analyze the women's rights movement from the era of Elizabeth Stanton and Susan Anthony and the passage of the Nineteenth Amendment to the movement launched in the 1960s, including differing perspectives on the roles of women.

11.11.2 Discuss the significant domestic policy speeches of Truman, Eisenhower, Kennedy, Johnson, Nixon, Carter, Reagan, Bush, and Clinton (e.g., with regard to education, civil rights, economic policy, environmental policy).

11.11.3 Describe the changing roles of women in society as reflected in the entry of more women into the labor force and the changing family structure.

∼ *The Big Idea* ∼

Societies change over time. President Kennedy won the first media-dominated presidential campaign, which focused on issues such as the economy and the Cold War. The new First Family captivated the country. Many were taken with the president's youth and optimism. Despite Kennedy's charm, however, Congress did not approve many of his domestic programs. The president was able to improve the nation's economy and advance women's rights. The Warren Court, however, had an even more powerful impact on the United States.

704 CHAPTER 15 The New Frontier and the Great Society

SECTION RESOURCES

📁 Print Material
• Reproducible Lesson Plan 15-1
• Guided Reading Activity 15-1
• Reading Essentials and Study Guide 15-1
• Active Reading Note-Taking Guide 15-1

🎞 Transparencies
• Daily Focus Skills Transparency 15-1
• Section Graphic Organizer Transparency 15-1

Technology
🅢 Interactive Tutor Self-Assessment CD-ROM
🅢 ExamView® Pro Testmaker CD-ROM
🅢 Presentation Plus! CD-ROM

The Election of 1960

Main Idea John F. Kennedy won the first media-dominated presidential election.

Reading Connection Have you ever watched a televised debate or debated a topic? Read on to learn about the first major election influenced by the media.

The television debates of the 1960 presidential election had an enormous impact. Following the first debate, the media focused more strongly on the appearance of the candidates. Suddenly the whole country seemed to have become experts on makeup and television lighting. One Republican leader even wondered if the Democrats had supplied Nixon's makeup.

★ An American Story ★

On September 26, 1960, at 9:30 P.M. eastern standard time, streets all across the United States grew strangely still. An estimated 75 million people sat indoors, focused on their television sets, where they saw two men standing behind lecterns. One was John F. Kennedy, and the other was Richard M. Nixon.

For the first time, thanks to the wonders of television, two presidential candidates were coming right into the nation's living rooms to debate. Americans were enthralled: "You hear each man directly," observed one. "There's nothing between you and what he says," added another. "You can see which man gets rattled easily."

The man who seemed to get rattled easily was Nixon. Kennedy, the Democratic nominee, looked healthy, strong, and confident. Nixon, the Republicans' choice, came across as tired and frazzled. "He appeared ill," one viewer commented. In fact, Nixon had been ill recently. Kennedy had a glowing tan, while Nixon's face was pale and drawn, shadowed by the stubble of a beard. As one observer noted, "Nixon's eyes darted around, perspiration was clearly noticeable on his chin, and with the tight shots . . . these things were more obvious."

—adapted from *The Great Debate*

With that debate, the era of television politics had begun. Though television had been used in campaigns as early as 1948, it was not until the 1960

election that a large majority of voters used the **medium** as a voting tool. The nation itself seemed on the brink of a new age. Having lived through a decade of unprecedented prosperity and the onset of the Cold War and the atomic age, Americans looked to the future with excitement and anxiety.

Both candidates shared the desire to lead the nation through the challenges of a new decade, but they differed in many ways. Kennedy, a Catholic, came from a wealthy and influential Massachusetts family. Nixon, a Quaker, was a Californian from a financially struggling family. Kennedy seemed outgoing and relaxed, while Nixon struck many as formal and even stiff in manner.

A New Kind of Campaign Compared to earlier campaigns, the 1960 presidential race made new use of television, with both major parties spending substantial amounts of money on television advertisements. The Democrats spent over $6 million in television and radio spots, while the Republicans spent more than $7.5 million.

Not everyone was happy with this new emphasis on image. Television news commentator Eric Sevareid complained that the candidates had become "packaged products," and he stated that "the Processed Politician has finally arrived."

The Main Issues The campaign centered on the economy and the Cold War. Although the candidates presented different styles, they differed little on these two issues. Both promised to boost the economy, and both portrayed themselves as "Cold Warriors" determined to stop the forces of communism.

John F. Kennedy (right) and Richard Nixon (below) in the 1960 debate

CHAPTER 15   The New Frontier and the Great Society   **705**

TEACH

U₁ Universal Access

Kinesthetic Arrange to videotape students as you conduct mock debates on topics of interest to students. As a class, watch the videotapes and have students select which debaters look comfortable and which look uncomfortable. Have students note particular mannerisms or actions that make people look comfortable in front of the camera. **OL**

R Reading Strategy

Connecting The election of 1960 was viewed as the first presidential campaign that operated under a new set of rules. **Ask: What was the main complaint about the new use of technology in elections?** *(Too much money was spent to create a "packaged candidate.")* **How is this similar to today's campaign technologies?** *(candidates utilize TV, radio, and Internet—even targeting specific voter groups; concerns about limitations on campaign spending)* **OL**

U₂ Universal Access

Visual/Spatial Tell students that first impressions often weigh heavily on a person's assessment of an individual. Have students look at the photos of the presidential candidates and describe what they believe the personalities, beliefs, and character would be. *(Kennedy: youthful, fun, honest, energetic, kind; Nixon: older, tired)* **OL**

Resources for page 705

*Have students read more about the influence of the media and presidential campaigns in the **Linking Past and Present Activity 15**.*

More Skill Practice

Analyzing Visuals Have students create election posters for either candidate for the presidential election. Ask them to consider world and national issues during the time of the election. Have students discuss these topics on their posters. Hang their finished posters in the classroom or hall. **OL**

S **Skill Practice**

Scaffolding—Interpreting Maps Point out to students that the 1960 presidential election had one of the closest outcomes in U.S. history. Ask students to read the information on the election results in the textbook and conduct further research using the library and Internet resources. Tell them to use blank outline maps of the United States to color and create maps that show the results of the popular vote and the Electoral College vote. Display the maps around the classroom. **OL** **CA CS3**

This **Historical Analysis** skill was introduced in Chapter 3.

U **Universal Access**

Advanced Learners Organize the class into three groups. Assign each group one of the following topics: Kennedy's childhood and family background, Kennedy's college years and military service, Kennedy's political background. Have the groups research their topic. Then have the groups work together to prepare a display providing a portrait of John F. Kennedy. **AL**

✓Reading Check

Answer: The issues were the economy and the Cold War.

Answers and Additional Support

Picturing **History**

Presidential Billboard A billboard in Manhattan displays the presidential candidates, including a "dark horse" and "scratch." Presidential campaign slogans from the past elections are also listed. A Kennedy tie clasp and Nixon pendant are also featured. What is the artist's purpose for including a "dark horse" and "scratch" among the candidates?

Kennedy argued that the nation faced serious threats from the Soviets. In Cuba, Fidel Castro was allying himself with the Soviet Union. At home, many people lived in fear of a Soviet nuclear attack.

Kennedy voiced his concern about a suspected **"missile gap,"** in which the United States lagged behind the Soviets in weaponry. (Decades later, Americans learned that, in fact, the only area where the Soviet Union was briefly ahead was in rocketry.) The nation, Kennedy argued, had grown complacent and aimless. "It is time to get this country moving again."

Nixon countered that the United States was on the right track under the current administration. "I'm tired of hearing our opponents downgrade the United States," the vice president said. Nixon also warned that the Democrats' fiscal policies would boost inflation, and that only he had the necessary foreign policy experience to guide the nation.

Kennedy came under scrutiny about his religion. The United States had never had a Catholic president, and many Protestants had concerns about Kennedy. Kennedy decided to confront this issue openly in a speech. "I believe in an America where the separation of the church and state is absolute," he said, "where no Catholic prelate would tell the president, should he be a Catholic, how to act."

S The four televised debates strongly influenced the outcome of the election, one of the closest in American history. Kennedy won the popular vote by 119,000 out of 68 million votes cast and the Electoral College by 303 votes to 219. In several states only a few thousand votes could have swung the Electoral College numbers the other way.

✓Reading Check **Identifying** What were two main issues of the 1960 presidential election?

U **The Kennedy Mystique**

Main Idea With Kennedy's election, a youthful and enthusiastic First Family entered the White House.

Reading Connection Do you think a person's charm and charisma can help them get elected? Read on to discover how JFK's charisma resembled that of another president.

Despite his narrow victory, John F. Kennedy, commonly referred to as JFK, captured the imagination of the American public as few presidents before him had. During the campaign, many had been taken with Kennedy's youth and optimism. The new president strongly reinforced this impression when he gave his Inaugural Address.

Inauguration Day, January 20, 1961, was crisp and cold in Washington, D.C. At the site of the ceremony, a crowd gathered, wrapped in coats and blankets. As Kennedy rose to take the oath of office, he wore neither a coat nor a hat. During his speech, the new president declared, "The torch has been passed to a new generation," and he called on his fellow citizens to take a more active role in making the United States a better place. "My fellow Americans," he exclaimed,

706 CHAPTER 15 The New Frontier and the Great Society

Picturing **History**

Answer: The artist wanted to show that Americans had many candidates from which to choose.

Ask: What do you think is the main message of the poster? *(Americans should vote.)*

Did You Know?

The 1960 vote was so close that Nixon considered demanding a recount, but then decided against it. He explained that if there was a recount, "the organization of the new administration and the orderly transfer of responsibility from the old to the new might be delayed for months. The situation within the entire federal government would be chaotic."

"ask not what your country can do for you—ask what you can do for your country."

Kennedy, his wife Jacqueline, their children Caroline and John, and their extended family seemed to have been created for media coverage. Reporters followed the family everywhere. Kennedy himself was a master of the media. He was the first to broadcast his press conferences live on television.

The Kennedy charisma inspired many of his staff members. His press secretary, Pierre Salinger, put this feeling into words:

> 66None of us will ever have a better job as long as we live. . . . The big *plus*—the fringe benefit that made it all worthwhile—was JFK himself. . . . Our faith in him and in what he was trying to do was absolute, and he could impart to our work together a sense of challenge and adventure—a feeling that he was moving, and the world with him, toward a better time.99
>
> —quoted in *With Kennedy*

✓**Reading Check** **Summarizing** In what ways did John F. Kennedy inspire the nation?

Success and Setback on the Domestic Front

Main Idea Despite an uneasy relationship with Congress, Kennedy managed to get several parts of his domestic agenda passed.

Reading Connection Do you think Kennedy's efforts to help expand women's rights were enough? Read on to find out how Kennedy's programs were designed to help women.

Not everyone in the nation fell for the Kennedy mystique. His high culture, elite Northeast upbringing, and Catholicism irritated some Americans. Congress also was less than taken with the new president. Upon entering office, President Kennedy set out to implement a legislative agenda, which became known as the **New Frontier.** He hoped to increase aid to education, provide health insurance to the elderly, create a Department of Urban Affairs, and help migrant workers. He would soon find that transforming lofty ideals into real legislation was no easy task on Capitol Hill.

Kennedy Struggles With Congress Although the Democratic Party enjoyed large majorities in both houses of Congress, Kennedy was unable to push through many of his domestic programs. Kennedy had trailed Nixon in many Democratic districts and had not helped many Democrats get elected. Those who did win, therefore, did not feel they owed him anything. As one Democrat in Congress told *U.S. News & World Report*, "A good many [congressional representatives] were elected in 1960 in spite of his presence on the ticket rather than because his name was there." As a result, legislators found it easy to follow their own interests rather than those of the president.

In addition, Republicans as well as conservative Southern Democrats—who were responsible for holding the Democratic majority in Congress—viewed the New Frontier as too big and too costly. Senator Everett Dirksen, Republican minority leader from Illinois, claimed that Kennedy's efforts to increase the power and reach of the federal government would push the nation down an ominous path.

In the end, Congress defeated a number of JFK's proposals, including health insurance for the elderly, a Department of Urban Affairs, and federal aid to education. The president often resisted calls to push harder for his agenda. He decided not to fight every battle on Capitol Hill and preferred to reserve his bargaining power for issues that were both truly important and obtainable.

Picturing **History**

The Kennedy White House Jacqueline Kennedy (center right) brought youthful elegance and style to the White House. Why do you think the media scrutinized the First Family so much?

CHAPTER 15 The New Frontier and the Great Society **707**

R₁ **Reading Strategy**

Predicting Have students identify the major heading on this page. *(Success and Setback on the Domestic Front)* **Ask: What does that heading signal to you as a reader?** *(The achievements and defeats of America will be discussed.)* **OL**

U **Universal Access**

Verbal/Linguistic Ask students about the meaning of the word *frontier.* As a class, discuss both the *denotation* of the word *(what the word means)* and the *connotation (what the word suggests beyond the literal meaning).* **Ask: Why do you think Kennedy named his new program the New Frontier?** *(It signaled a new area of American exploration, much like the American West had once been the area to explore.)* **OL**

R₂ **Reading Strategy**

Scaffolding—Academic Vocabulary The word *implement* was introduced in Chapter 11, Section 3. Ask a student to define the word. **BL**

✓**Reading Check**

Answer: Kennedy inspired the nation with his optimism, his youth, and his ability to handle the media.

Picturing **History**

Answer: Students' answers will vary. Students might suggest that the young family provided good stories for the media, and the family encouraged the attention.
Ask: What technology helped make scrutiny of the Kennedy's possible? *(television)*

Did You Know?

John Kennedy, his wife and their two small children were the youngest family to live in the White House since Theodore Roosevelt's days.

C₁ Critical Thinking

Predicting Consequences
Have students read only the bracketed paragraph. **Ask:** How do you think Congress, businesses, and labor leaders might have reacted to these suggestions? *(Students should note that this would require close cooperation among all parties.)* **AL**

C₂ Critical Thinking

Determining Cause and Effect
Ask students to create cause-and-effect charts that display the events surrounding the conflict described on this page between the unions and the steel industry. Students can use the cause-and-effect charts found in the textbook for one suggestion on how to design their charts. **OL**

R Reading Strategy

Scaffolding—Academic Vocabulary The word *invest* was introduced in Chapter 9, Section 1. Ask a student to define the word. **BL**

Strengthening the Economy Kennedy did achieve some victories in Congress, particularly in his efforts to improve the nation's economy. The American economy, which had soared through much of the 1950s, had slowed by the end of the decade. From 1960 to 1961, the growth rate of the gross national product was only 2 percent, while the unemployment rate hovered near 7 percent of the workforce, the second-highest figure since World War II.

C₁ In an effort to increase growth and create more jobs, Kennedy advocated the New Deal strategy of deficit spending, first implemented during Franklin Roosevelt's presidency. The new president convinced Congress to invest more funds in defense and in space exploration. Such spending did indeed create more jobs and stimulate economic growth. Reluctant to rely too heavily on deficit spending, which tends to cause inflation, Kennedy also sought to boost the economy by increasing business production and efficiency. In addition, his administration asked businesses to hold down prices and labor leaders to hold down pay increases.

C₂ Prodded by Secretary of Labor Arthur Goldberg, labor unions in the steel industry agreed to reduce their demands for higher wages. In 1962, however, several steel companies raised prices sharply.

The president threatened to have the Department of Defense buy cheaper steel from foreign companies and instructed the Justice Department to investigate whether the steel industry was guilty of price-fixing. In response to Kennedy's tactics, the steel companies backed down and cut their prices. To achieve this victory, however, the president had strained his relations with the nation's business community.

In an effort to get the economy moving, Kennedy also adopted supply-side ideas and pushed for a cut in tax rates. When opponents argued that a tax cut would only help the wealthy, Kennedy asserted that lower taxes meant businesses would have more money to expand, which would create new jobs and benefit everybody. "A rising tide lifts all boats," Kennedy explained, as a way to illustrate how tax cuts would stimulate the economy and help all Americans.

Congress refused to pass the tax cut because many members feared it would cause inflation. However, they did support Kennedy's request to raise the minimum wage and his proposal for an Area Redevelopment Act and a Housing Act. These two programs provided funds to poor areas. They helped to clear slums, create jobs, and build low-income housing.

Women's Rights Kennedy also helped women make strides during the 1960s. Although Kennedy never appointed a woman to his cabinet, a number of women worked in prominent positions in his

Strengthening the Economy New housing projects were developed as part of the Area Redevelopment Act and Housing Act.

Did You Know?

The President's Commission on the Status of Women was first chaired by the wife of former president Franklin Delano Roosevelt, Eleanor Roosevelt, until her death in 1962.

Major Decisions of the Warren Court, 1954–1967

Civil Rights	
Brown v. *Board of Education* (1954)	Segregation in public schools unconstitutional
Baker v. *Carr* (1962)	Established that federal courts can hear lawsuits seeking to force state authorities to redraw electoral districts
Reynolds v. *Sims* (1964)	State legislative districts should be equal in population
Heart of Atlanta Motel v. *United States* (1964)	Desegregation of public accommodations established in the Civil Rights Act of 1964 is legal
Loving v. *Virginia* (1967)	States may not ban interracial marriage
Due Process	
Mapp v. *Ohio* (1961)	Unlawfully seized evidence is inadmissible at trial
Gideon v. *Wainwright* (1963)	Suspects are entitled to court-appointed attorney if unable to afford one on their own
Escobedo v. *Illinois* (1964)	Accused has the right to an attorney during police questioning
Miranda v. *Arizona* (1966)	Police must inform suspects of their rights during the arrest process
Freedom of Religion and Freedom of Speech	
Engel v. *Vitale* (1962)	State-mandated prayer in school banned
Abington School District v. *Schempp* (1963)	State-mandated Bible readings in school banned
New York Times v. *Sullivan* (1964)	Celebrities may sue the media for libel only in certain circumstances

Chart *Skills*

1. **Interpreting Charts** Analyze the effects *Brown* v. *Board of Education* and *Reynolds* v. *Sims* had on the nation.
2. **Summarizing** What three major areas of policy did the Warren Court's decisions affect?

administration, including Esther Peterson, assistant secretary of labor and director of the Women's Bureau of the Department of Labor.

Kennedy advanced women's rights in other ways as well. In 1961 he created the Presidential Commission on the Status of Women. The commission called for federal action against gender discrimination and affirmed the right of women to equally paid employment. Kennedy responded by issuing an executive order ending gender discrimination in the federal civil service, and in 1963 he signed the Equal Pay Act for women. The commission also sparked the creation of similar groups on the state level and inspired many women to work together to further their interests.

R₁

Reading Check **Evaluating** Why did Kennedy have difficulty getting his New Frontier legislation passed?

Warren Court Reforms

Main Idea Under Chief Justice Earl Warren, the Supreme Court took a more activist role.

Reading Connection Have you ever watched a television show where a police officer read someone their rights? Read on to learn about the origin of this process.

During the Kennedy years, the Supreme Court also took an active role in social issues. In 1953 President Eisenhower had nominated **Earl Warren**, the popular Republican governor of California, to become Chief Justice of the United States. More so than previous courts, the Warren Court took an activist stance, helping to shape national policy by taking a forceful stand on a number of key issues of the day.

"One Man, One Vote" One of the Warren Court's more notable decisions had a powerful impact on who would hold political power in the United States.

CHAPTER 15 The New Frontier and the Great Society **709**

Review the Big Idea

Review the Big Idea for this section, "Societies change over time." Ask students to write a two-page paper that reflects how the Supreme Court cases listed in the chart have changed American society. In their papers, students should evaluate whether or not these changes have been beneficial. **AL** **CA** 11WS1.1

R₁ Reading Strategy

Scaffolding—Connecting
President Kennedy played a role in increasing the political power of women. **Ask:** Who are the women past or present with prominent positions in our state and national governments? (Some answers may include: Hillary Rodham Clinton—former First Lady and only president's wife elected to the U.S. Senate; Elizabeth Dole—president of the American Red Cross and senator; Geraldine Ferraro—female candidate for vice president of the United States; Zelma Watson George—delegate to the U.N., opera singer; Sandra Day O'Connor—first female associate justice of the Supreme Court.) **OL**

This **Reading Skill** was introduced in Chapter 7.

R₂ Reading Strategy

Identifying the Main Idea and Supporting Details The Warren-led Supreme Court made many decisions that have shaped everyday life in the modern United States. **Ask:** List on a piece of paper your understanding of the cases that are reserved for the United States Supreme Court. (Students should know that most cases reach the Supreme Court on appeal and that only a few cases originate there.) **OL**

Chart *Skills*

Answers:
1. Students should discuss school integration and reapportionment.
2. It affected civil rights, due process, and freedom of religion and speech.

Chart Skills Practice
Ask: Which cases are related to the separation of church and state? (*Engel v. Vitale* and *Abington School District v. Schempp*)

✓ Reading Check

Answer: The legislation was perceived as too expensive and too broad in scope.

709

This decision concerned **reapportionment,** or the way in which states draw up political districts based on changes in population. By 1960 many more Americans **resided** in cities and suburbs than in rural areas. Yet many states had failed to restructure their electoral districts to reflect that change.

In Tennessee, for example, a rural county with only 2,340 voters had 1 representative in the state assembly, while an urban county with 133 times more voters had only 7. The vote of a city dweller counted for less than the vote of a rural resident. Some Tennessee voters took the matter to court.

The *Baker* v. *Carr* case reached the Supreme Court after a federal court ruled that the issue should be solved by legislation. The Fourteenth Amendment specifically gives Congress authority to enforce voting rights. In 1962 the Supreme Court ruled that the federal courts did have jurisdiction and sent the matter back to the lower courts. *(See page 1004 for more information on* Baker *v.* Carr.)

Two years later, in June 1964, the Supreme Court ruled in *Reynolds* v. *Sims* that the current apportionment system in most states was indeed unconstitutional. In a decision that helped to promote the principle of "one man, one vote," the Warren Court required state legislatures to reapportion electoral districts so that all citizens' votes would have equal weight. The Court's decision was a momentous one, for it shifted political power throughout the country from rural and often conservative areas to urban areas, where more liberal voters resided. The Court's decision also boosted the political power of African Americans and Hispanics, who typically lived in cities. *(See page 1006 for more information on* Reynolds *v.* Sims.)

Extending Due Process In a series of historic rulings in the 1960s, the U.S. Supreme Court began to use the Fourteenth Amendment to apply the Bill of Rights to the states. Originally, the Bill of Rights applied only to the federal government. Many states had their own bill of rights, but some federal rights did not exist at the state level. The Fourteenth Amendment stated that "no state shall . . . deprive any person of life, liberty, or property without due process of law." **Due process** means that the law may not treat individuals unfairly, **arbitrarily,** or unreasonably, and that courts must follow proper procedures and rules when trying cases. Due process ensures that all people are treated the same by the court system. In the 1960s, the Supreme Court ruled in several cases that upholding due process meant applying the federal bill of rights to the states.

In 1961 the Supreme Court ruled in *Mapp* v. *Ohio* that state courts could not consider evidence obtained in violation of the federal Constitution. In *Gideon* v. *Wainwright* (1963), the Court ruled that a defendant in a state court had the right to a lawyer, regardless of his or her ability to pay. The following year, in *Escobedo* v. *Illinois,* the justices ruled that a suspect must be allowed access to a lawyer and must be informed of his or her right to remain silent before being questioned by the police. *Miranda* v. *Arizona* (1966) went even further, requiring that authorities immediately give suspects a fourfold warning. The warning consisted of informing suspects that they have the right to remain silent, that anything they say can and will be used against them in court, that they have a right to a lawyer while being questioned, and that if they cannot afford a lawyer, the court will appoint one for them. Today these warnings are known as the Miranda rights. *(See pages 1005–1006 for more information on* Mapp *v.* Ohio, Gideon *v.* Wainwright, Escobedo *v.* Illinois, *and* Miranda *v.* Arizona.)

Many citizens and police departments and even some of the

◄ *Ernesto Miranda (right) and his attorney*

710 CHAPTER 15 The New Frontier and the Great Society

More Skill Practice

Supreme Court justices accused the Warren Court of favoring criminals. There were others, however, who cheered the decisions, seeing them as promoting the rights of all citizens, even the less privileged.

Prayer and Privacy The Supreme Court also handed down decisions affecting the relationship between church and state. The Court applied the First Amendment to the states in *Engel v. Vitale* (1962). In this ruling, the Court decided that states could not compose official prayers and require those prayers to be recited in state public schools. The ruling upheld the separation of church and state. The following year, in *Abington School District v. Schempp*, it followed up with a similar decision by ruling against state-mandated Bible readings in public schools. Weighing in on another controversial issue, the Court ruled in *Griswold v. Connecticut* (1965) that prohibiting the sale and use of birth control devices violated citizens' constitutional right to privacy. 📖 *(See pages 1005–1006 for more information on these Supreme Court cases.)*

As with most controversial rulings of the Warren Court, these decisions delighted some and deeply disturbed others. What most people did agree upon, however, was the Court's pivotal role in shaping the country's national policy. The Warren Court, wrote *New York Times* columnist Anthony Lewis, "has brought about more social change than most Congresses and most Presidents."

Activist Court The Warren Court poses for its official portrait in 1962, with Chief Justice Earl Warren front and center.

From the political arena to the legal system to people's everyday lives, the Warren Court indeed left its imprint on the nation. Meanwhile, away from the domestic arena, President Kennedy worked to make his mark on the country's foreign affairs during a time of rising Cold War tensions.

 Reading Check **Examining** What was the significance of the Warren Court's "One Man, One Vote" ruling in the *Reynolds* v. *Simms* case?

HISTORY Online **Study Central**

For help with the concepts in this section of *American Vision: Modern Times* go to tav.mt.glencoe.com and click on *Study Central*.

SECTION 1 ASSESSMENT

Checking for Understanding

1. **Vocabulary** Define: medium, missile gap, reapportionment, reside, due process, arbitrary.
2. **People and Terms** Identify: New Frontier, Earl Warren.
3. **Summarize** the progress made for women's rights during Kennedy's administration.

Reviewing Big Ideas

4. **Explaining** How did President Kennedy advance women's rights?

Critical Thinking

5. **Historical Analysis** **Interpreting** In what way was the 1960 presidential election a turning point in campaign history? **CA HI3**
6. **Organizing** Use a graphic organizer similar to the one below to list the economic policies of the Kennedy administration.

Economic Policies

Analyzing Visuals

7. **Analyzing Charts** Study the chart of Warren Court decisions on page 709. How did the Court expand the rights of the accused? Were these sound decisions? Why or why not?

Writing About History

8. **Expository Writing** In his Inaugural Address, President Kennedy asked his fellow Americans to "Ask what you can do for your country." Respond to this statement in an essay. **CA 11WA2.4a**

CHAPTER 15   The New Frontier and the Great Society   **711**

SECTION 1 ASSESSMENT ANSWERS

1. Content vocabulary is boldfaced and highlighted in yellow. Academic vocabulary is boldfaced.
2. New Frontier *(p. 707)*, Earl Warren *(p. 709)*
3. Presidential Commission on the Status of Women, ending gender discrimination in federal civil service, and the Equal Pay Act

4. He placed a number of women in his administration, created the Presidential Commission on the Status of Women, issued an executive order ending gender discrimination in the federal civil service, and signed the Equal Pay Act.
5. Television played a key role.
6. a cut in tax rates, an increase in

funds for defense and space exploration, an increase in the minimum wage, housing and redevelopment
7. Students should summarize the decisions and weigh individual rights against police concerns.
8. Students' essays should interpret Kennedy's statement.

R **Reading Strategy**

Reading Primary Sources Have students read the text of the First Amendment on page 159 of the textbook. **Ask: What sort of difficulties does this amendment create in American social and political activities?** *(Students should discuss the continuing disagreements over separation of church and state.)* **AL**

ASSESS

 Resources for page 711

Use these resources to assess student mastery.

📁 Section Quiz 15-1

📁 Reading Essentials and Study Guide 15-1

💿 Interactive Tutor Self-Assessment CD-ROM

📁 California Standards Practice, Grade 11

Reading Check

Answer: All citizens' votes would have equal weight regardless of where they lived.

 HISTORY Online

Study Central provides audio summaries, interactive games, and online graphic organizers to help students review section content.

CLOSE

Advanced Learners Ask students to learn more about the life and career of one of the justices who served on the Warren Court and present their findings in a two-page report. **AL**

711

TIME NOTEBOOK

FOCUS

History– Social Science Standards

This feature addresses the following standards:

11.8 Students analyze the economic boom and social transformation of post-World War II America.

11.8.8 Discuss forms of popular culture, with emphasis on their origins and geographic diffusion (e.g., jazz and other forms of popular music, professional sports, architectural and artistic styles).

TEACH

W Writing Support

Narrative Writing Tell students to write responses to President Lyndon Johnson's speech as if they were speechwriter and policy adviser Richard Goodwin. Remind them to explain both emotional and intellectual reactions and thoughts in their responses. **OL** **CA 11WS1.2**

Answers and Additional Support

BETTMANN/CORBIS

Eyewitness

On May 22, 1964, **PRESIDENT LYNDON JOHNSON** *delivered a speech in Ann Arbor, Michigan, outlining his domestic agenda that would become known as "The Great Society." Speechwriter and policy adviser Richard Goodwin watched the speech on videotape the next morning back in Washington. He recalls his reaction:*

Then, with the cheers, at first muted as if the audience were surprised at their own response, then mounting toward unrestrained, accepting delight, Johnson concluded: "There are those timid souls who say . . . we are condemned to a soulless wealth. I do not agree. We have the power to shape civilization. . . . But we need your will, your labor, your hearts. . . . So let us from this moment begin our work, so that in the future men will look back and say: It was then, after a long and weary way, that man turned the exploits of his genius to the full enrichment of his life."

Watching the film in the White House basement, almost involuntarily I added my applause to the tumultuous acclaim coming from the sound track. . . . I clapped for the President, and for our country.

WHAT IS A PIP, ANYWAY?

Match these rock 'n' roll headliners with their supporting acts.

1. Paul Revere and   a. the Union Gap
2. Martha and   b. the Supremes
3. Gary Puckett and   c. the Miracles
4. Gladys Knight and   d. the Vandellas
5. Smokey Robinson and   e. the Raiders
6. Diana Ross and   f. the Pips

answers: 1. e; 2. d; 3. a; 4. f; 5. c; 6. b

VERBATIM

"Is there any place we can catch them? What can we do? Are we working 24 hours a day? Can we go around the moon before them?"
PRESIDENT JOHN F. KENNEDY,
to Lyndon B. Johnson, after hearing that Soviet cosmonaut Yuri Gagarin had orbited the earth, 1961

"It was quite a day. I don't know what you can say about a day when you see four beautiful sunsets. . . . This is a little unusual, I think."
COLONEL JOHN GLENN,
in orbit, 1962

"There are tens of millions of Americans who are beyond the welfare state. Taken as a whole there is a culture of poverty . . . bad health, poor housing, low levels of aspiration and high levels of mental distress. Twenty percent of a nation, some 32,000,000."
MICHAEL HARRINGTON,
The Culture of Poverty, *1962*

"I have a dream."
MARTIN LUTHER KING, JR.
1963

"I don't see an American dream; . . . I see an American nightmare . . . Three hundred and ten years we worked in this country without a dime in return."
MALCOLM X,
1964

"The Great Society rests on abundance and liberty for all. It demands an end to poverty and racial injustice."
LYNDON B. JOHNSON,
1964

"In 1962, the starving residents of an isolated Indian village received 1 plow and 1,700 pounds of seeds. They ate the seeds."
PEACE CORPS AD,
1965

UNIVERSAL ACCESS

Visual/Spatial Organize the class into ten groups, assigning each group one of the years in the 1960s. Have students create their own two-page magazine spreads for their assigned years. Encourage the groups to use elements similar to those that appear in the Time Notebook, but to be creative as they select information that is of particular interest. Students should look at current magazines and books for ideas about page design. This activity can be completed using desktop publishing software or the more traditional cut-and-paste method. **AL**

TIME
NOTEBOOK

Space Race

Want to capture some of the glamour and excitement of space exploration? Create a new nickname for your city. You won't be the first.

CITY	NICKNAME
Danbury, CT	Space Age City
Muscle Shoals, AL	Space Age City
Houston, TX	Space City, USA
Galveston, TX	Space Port, USA
Cape Kennedy, FL	Spaceport, USA
Blacksburg, VA	Space Age Community
Huntsville, AL	~~Rocket City, USA~~
	~~Space City, USA~~
	~~Space Capital of the Nation~~
	Space Capital of the World

RALPH MORSE/TIMEPIX

John Glenn, first American to orbit Earth

Milestones

PERFORMED IN ENGLISH, 1962. THE CATHOLIC MASS, following Pope John XXIII's Second Vatican Council. "Vatican II" allows the Latin mass to be translated into local languages around the world.

ENROLLED, 1962. JAMES MEREDITH, at the University of Mississippi, following a Supreme Court ruling that ordered his admission to the previously segregated school. Rioting and a showdown with state officials who wished to bar his enrollment preceded Meredith's entrance to classes.

BROKEN, 1965. 25-DAY FAST BY CÉSAR CHÁVEZ, labor organizer. His protest convinced others to join his nonviolent strike against the grape growers; shoppers boycotted table grapes in sympathy.

STRIPPED, 1967. MUHAMMAD ALI, of his heavyweight champion title, after refusing induction into the army following a rejection of his application for conscientious objector status. The boxer was arrested, given a five-year sentence, and fined $10,000.

PICKETED, 1968. The Miss America Pageant in Atlantic City, by protesters who believe the contest's emphasis on women's physical beauty is degrading and minimizes the importance of women's intellect.

AP

REMOVED, 1968. TOY GUNS, from the Sears, Roebuck Christmas catalog after the assassinations of Martin Luther King, Jr., and Robert Kennedy.

NUMBERS

7% of African American adults registered to vote in Mississippi in 1964 before passage of the Voting Rights Act of 1965

67% of African American adults in Mississippi registered to vote in 1969

70% of white adults registered to vote in 1964, nationwide

90% of white adults registered to vote nationwide in 1969

57 Number of days senators filibustered to hold up passage of the Civil Rights Bill in 1964

14 1/2 Hours duration of all-night speech delivered by Senator Robert Byrd before a cloture vote stopped the filibuster

72% of elementary and high school teachers approve of corporal punishment as a disciplinary measure in 1961

HULTON-DEUTSCH COLLECTION/CORBIS

$80-90 Weekly pay for a clerk/typist in New York in 1965

$200 Rent for a two-bedroom apartment at Broadway and 72nd Street on New York City's Upper West Side in 1965

R Reading Strategy

Sequencing Information Tell students to make time lines using the dates from the Milestones. They should then add six additional dates and events to their time lines. Ask volunteers to display their time lines and explain why they chose the additional events. **BL**

C Critical Thinking

Comparing and Contrasting Ask students to examine the numbers presented on this page. Tell students to use library and Internet resources to find the current numbers for the data on registered voters. Students should then expand their research to find out how many registered voters in each category actually went to the polls. They may also include relevant dates for their community or state. **OL**

EXTENDING THE CONTENT

Popular Culture In 1963 the top 10 television programs were: 1. *The Beverly Hillbillies*, 2. *Bonanza*, 3. *The Dick Van Dyke Show*, 4. *Petticoat Junction*, 5. *The Andy Griffith Show*, 6. *I Love Lucy*, 7. *Candid Camera*, 8. *The Ed Sullian Show*, 9. *The Danny Thomas Show*, and 10. *My Favorite Martian*. The Limbo Rock, introduced by Chubby Checker, was the popular dance craze. The Beach Boys, with their melodic songs about hot rods and surfing, had five hit songs in 1963. *Cleopatra*, a film starring Elizabeth Taylor and Richard Burton, opened and was the most expensive film ever made to that date.

FOCUS

Project **Daily Focus Skills Transparency 15-2** and have students answer the question.

Guide to Reading

Understanding Vocabulary: Have students pair up to write and answer several questions about one of the words or terms.

Answers to Graphic:
January 1959, Castro's overthrow of Batista; April 17, 1961, Bay of Pigs; June 1961, Kennedy and Khrushchev meet in Vienna; October 1962, Cuban missile crisis; October 1962, Soviets agree to remove missiles from Cuba

Unpacking the Standards

Students will be able to:

• Explain how President Kennedy dealt with Cold War challenges.

• Analyze the events surrounding the Bay of Pigs Invasion and the Cuban Missile Crisis.

• Describe the impact of John F. Kennedy's assassination.

Answers and Additional Support

SECTION 2 · JFK and the Cold War

Guide to Reading

Connection
In the previous section, you learned about the Kennedy administration and the Warren Court. In this section, you will discover how President Kennedy worked to end the spread of communism.

Main Idea
• President Kennedy developed new programs to combat the spread of communism. (p. 715)
• President Kennedy faced foreign policy crises in Cuba and Berlin. (p. 717)
• President Kennedy was assassinated in Dallas, Texas, on November 22, 1963. (p. 718)

Content Vocabulary
flexible response, space race

Academic Vocabulary
institute, symbol, theory

People and Terms to Identify
Peace Corps, Berlin Wall, Warren Commission

Reading Objectives
• **Describe** Kennedy's plan for the armed forces.
• **Explain** how the Cold War influenced foreign aid and the space program.

Reading Strategy
Sequencing As you read about the crises of the Cold War, complete a time line similar to the one below to record the major events of the Cold War in the late 1950s and early 1960s.

Jan. 1959 — Aug. 1963

Preview of Events

♦1961	♦1962	♦1963	♦1964

April 1961 — Bay of Pigs invasion
May 1961 — Kennedy informs Congress of moon expedition goal
October 1962 — Cuban missile crisis
September 1963 — Senate ratifies Limited Test Ban Treaty
November 22, 1963 — Kennedy assassinated

The following are the main History–Social Science Standards covered in this section.

11.8.5 Describe the increased powers of the presidency in response to the Great Depression, World War II, and the Cold War.

11.8.7 Describe the effects on society and the economy of technological developments since 1945, including the computer revolution, changes in communication, advances in medicine, and improvements in agricultural technology.

11.9.3 Trace the origins and geopolitical consequences (foreign and domestic) of the Cold War and containment policy, including the following: the era of McCarthyism, instances of domestic Communism (e.g., Alger Hiss) and blacklisting; the Truman Doctrine; the Berlin Blockade; the Korean War; the Bay of Pigs invasion and the Cuban Missile Crisis; atomic testing in the American West, the "mutual assured destruction" doctrine, and disarmament policies; the Vietnam War; Latin American policy.

⁓ *The Big Idea* ⁓

The fate of nations is forever changed by monumental world events. President Kennedy believed the United States should prepare to fight Communist aggression by increasing troops and weapons and depending less on nuclear arms. He also hoped to improve relations with Latin America. Adding to the tensions of the Cold War, the United States and the Soviet Union began a space race. Cold War tensions heightened with the Bay of Pigs invasion, the construction of the Berlin Wall, and the Cuban missile crisis. Kennedy's presidency came to a shocking end when he was assassinated on November 22, 1963.

714 CHAPTER 15 The New Frontier and the Great Society

SECTION RESOURCES

📂 Print Material
• Reproducible Lesson Plan 15-2
• Guided Reading Activity 15-2
• Reading Essentials and Study Guide 15-2
• Active Reading Note-Taking Guide 15-2

🔖 Transparencies
• Daily Focus Skills Transparency 15-2
• Section Graphic Organizer Transparency 15-2

Technology
🔘 Interactive Tutor Self-Assessment CD-ROM
🔘 Exam*View*® Pro Testmaker CD-ROM
🔘 Presentation Plus! CD-ROM

Kennedy Confronts Global Challenges

Main Idea President Kennedy developed new programs to combat the spread of communism.

Reading Connection Would you consider joining the Peace Corps and working in Latin America and other parts of the world? Read on to find out about diplomatic efforts in Latin America during Kennedy's presidency.

As President Kennedy entered the White House, the nation's dangerous rivalry with the Soviet Union continued to intensify. In the fall of 1962, the tension between the United States and the Soviet Union reached a boiling point.

★ An American Story ★

Like millions of other Americans in late October 1962, Tami Gold was having trouble concentrating on anything. For several tension-filled days that fall, the world seemed headed for nuclear destruction. U.S. officials had discovered that the Soviet Union had placed missiles in Cuba—a mere 90 miles (145 km) from the shores of the United States. When the Soviets refused to remove the weapons, a bitter weeklong standoff ensued in which the two superpowers hurled threats and warnings at each other and moved to the brink of nuclear war. Gold, then a seventh-grade student in Long Island, New York, recalled the events of one particular day:

❝I remember I was in the bathroom of the school . . . when they had said over the loud speaker . . . that everyone had to return to their homerooms immediately and get instruction from their homeroom teacher. And it was probably one of the scariest moments of my life, it was like the sensation that our country could go to war and I didn't understand at all what it was about, but the fact that the country could go to war at any moment was really really present. . . . It was chilling, it was scary, it was really nauseating. . . .❞

—quoted in *Collective Memories of the Cuban Missile Crisis*

The Cuban missile crisis, as the standoff came to be called, may have been the most dramatic foreign policy episode Kennedy faced. It was not the only one, however, the president had to deal with.

From the start, Kennedy appeared ready to stand up to the Soviets. Upon taking the oath of office, the new president devoted much of his Inaugural Address to the role of the United States in a divided world:

R₁ ❝Let the word go forth from this time and place . . . that the torch has been passed to a new generation of Americans—born in this century, tempered by war, disciplined by a hard and bitter peace, proud of our ancient heritage—and unwilling to witness or permit the slow undoing of those human rights to which this nation has always been committed. . . . Let every nation know, whether it wishes us well or ill, that we shall pay any price, bear any burden, meet any hardship, support any friend, oppose any foe, to assure the survival and the success of liberty.❞

—quoted in *Let the Word Go Forth*

A More Flexible Response Kennedy took office at a time of growing global instability. Nationalism was exploding throughout the developing world, and the Soviet Union actively supported "wars of national liberation." *Newsweek* magazine wrote that the "greatest single problem that faces John Kennedy is how to meet the aggressive power of the Communist bloc."

R₂ Kennedy felt that Eisenhower had relied too heavily on nuclear weapons, which could only be used in extreme situations. To allow for a **"flexible response"** if nations needed help against Communist movements, the president pushed for a buildup of conventional troops and weapons.

" . . . it was probably one of the scariest moments of my life, . . ."

—Tami Gold

▲ *Emergency water supplied by Department of Defense*

TEACH

Review the Big Idea

Review the Big Idea for this section, "The fate of nations is forever changed by monumental world events." Ask the class to rank the events mentioned in this section in order of historical importance and to write short paragraphs explaining their rankings. Use these rankings to discuss the events of this section as a class. **OL**

R₁ Reading Strategy

Evaluating Evaluating requires making a judgment or forming an opinion. To help students learn how to evaluate information, ask them to read the quotation. **Ask:** Is the author qualified to write on this subject? Is the point of view biased? Is there another point of view not expressed here? Are opinions backed with facts, statistics, and examples? **OL**

R₂ Reading Strategy

Using Context Clues Have students explain what they think "flexible response" means. *(the policy of allowing conventional troops and weapons to be used against Communist movements)* **Ask:** Why do you think Kennedy would choose this method? *(Kennedy felt that Eisenhower had relied too heavily on nuclear weapons and not enough on conventional troops and weapons.)* **OL**

Did You Know?

The Army Special Forces are known as the Green Berets. In the Navy, these Special Forces troops are called the Navy Seals.

The Peace Corps A Peace Corps volunteer describes the construction of a new school for villagers in Dadar, India.

In adopting this plan, Kennedy supported the Special Forces, a small army unit created in the 1950s to wage guerrilla warfare in limited conflicts. Kennedy expanded it and allowed the soldiers to wear their distinctive "Green Beret" headgear.

Aid to Other Countries One area of the world where Kennedy wanted to renew diplomatic focus was Latin America. Conditions in much of Latin American society were not good: Governments were often in the hands of the wealthy few and many of their citizens lived in extreme poverty. In some Latin American countries, these conditions spurred the growth of leftwing movements aimed at overthrowing their governments. When the United States was involved in Latin America, it was usually to help existing governments stay in power in order to prevent Communist movements from flourishing. Poor Latin Americans resented this intrusion, just as they resented American corporations that had business operations in their countries, a presence that was seen as a kind of imperialism.

To improve relations between the United States and Latin America, President Kennedy proposed an Alliance for Progress, a series of cooperative aid projects with Latin American governments. The alliance was designed to create a "free and prosperous Latin America" that would be less likely to support Communist-inspired revolutions.

Over a 10-year period, the United States pledged $20 billion to help Latin American countries establish better schools, housing, health care, and fairer land distribution. The results were mixed. In some countries—notably Chile, Colombia, Venezuela, and the Central American republics—the alliance did promote real reform. In others, governing rulers used the money to keep themselves in power.

The Peace Corps Another program aimed at helping less developed nations fight poverty was the **Peace Corps,** an organization that sent young Americans to perform humanitarian services in these countries.

After rigorous training, volunteers spent two years in countries that requested assistance. They laid out sewage systems in Bolivia and trained medical technicians in Chad. Others taught English or helped to build roads and construct new schools. By late 1963 thousands of Peace Corps volunteers were serving in over 30 countries. Today, the Peace Corps is still active and remains one of Kennedy's most enduring legacies.

The Cold War Moves Into Space In 1961 Yuri Gagarin, a Soviet astronaut, became the first person to orbit the earth. Again, as in 1957 when they launched *Sputnik,* the first satellite, the Soviets had beaten the United States in the **space race.** President Kennedy worried about the impact of the flight on the Cold War. Soviet successes in space might convince the world that communism was better than capitalism. "Is there any place we can catch them?" Kennedy asked Vice President Johnson.

After consulting experts, Johnson gave Kennedy an idea. Less than six weeks after the Soviet flight, the president appeared before Congress. "Whatever mankind must undertake, free men must fully share," Kennedy announced. "I believe that this nation should commit itself to achieving the goal, before this decade is out, of landing a man on the moon."

Kennedy's speech set in motion a massive effort by NASA and American industry to produce the necessary technology. In early 1962 John Glenn became the first American to orbit the earth. By 1965 American spacecraft had begun carrying two men at a time into orbit. Three years later the United States launched three men into orbit in a capsule called *Apollo. Apollo* was launched using the Saturn V, the largest and most powerful rocket ever built. Standing 363 feet (111 m) tall, the Saturn V was capable of giving both *Apollo* and the lunar module—which astronauts would use to land on the moon—enough velocity to escape Earth's gravitational pull and reach the moon.

On July 16, 1969, a Saturn V lifted off a launch pad in Florida carrying three American astronauts: Neil Armstrong, Edwin "Buzz" Aldrin, and Michael Collins. On July 20, Armstrong and Aldrin boarded their lunar module, named *Eagle,* and headed to the moon. After a few tense minutes, Armstrong radioed the NASA flight center in Texas: "Houston . . . the *Eagle* has landed."

Did You Know?

Since the Peace Corps was established in 1961, over 171,000 volunteers have served in 137 countries. Volunteer sectors include education, environment, health, business, and agriculture. In 2004 there were 7,533 Peace Corps volunteers serving in 72 countries.

Armstrong opened the hatch and climbed down to the surface, becoming the first human being to walk on the moon. As he set foot on the lunar soil, Armstrong announced: "That's one small step for man, one giant leap for mankind." American technology and determination had reached out across 238,000 miles to put men on the moon. America had won the space race and decisively demonstrated its technological superiority over the Soviet Union.

Reading Check **Examining** What global challenges did Kennedy face during his presidency?

Crises of the Cold War

Main Idea President Kennedy faced foreign policy crises in Cuba and Berlin.

Reading Connection Do you believe that the embargo against Cuba should be lifted? Read on to learn about the difficulties President Kennedy faced from that country.

President Kennedy's efforts to combat Communist influence in other countries led to some of the most intense crises of the Cold War. At times these crises left Americans and people in many other nations wondering whether the world would survive.

The Bay of Pigs The first crisis occurred in Cuba, only 90 miles (145 km) from American shores. There, Fidel Castro had overthrown the corrupt Cuban dictator Fulgencio Batista in 1959. Almost immediately, Castro established ties with the Soviet Union, **instituted** drastic land reforms, and seized foreign-owned businesses, many of them American. Cuba's alliance with the Soviets worried many Americans. The Communists were now too close for comfort, and Soviet Premier Nikita Khrushchev had indicated he would strengthen Cuba's military.

Fearing that the Soviets would use Cuba as a base to spread revolution throughout the Western Hemisphere, President Eisenhower authorized the Central Intelligence Agency (CIA) to secretly train and arm Cuban exiles, known as La Brigada, to invade the island. The invasion was intended to ignite a popular uprising against Castro.

When Kennedy became president, his advisers approved the plan. In office fewer than three months and trusting his experts, Kennedy agreed to the operation

HISTORY Online
Student Web Activity Visit the *American Vision: Modern Times* Web site at tav.mt.glencoe.com and click on **Student Web Activities— Chapter 15** for an activity on the New Frontier.

MISSILE ERECTOR

5 TRUCKS UNDER CAMOUFLAGE NETTING

CABLE

THEODOLITE STATION

5 TRUCKS UNDER CAMOUFLAGE NETTING

MISSILE SHELTER TENTS

Picturing History

Cold War Peak Fears of communism peaked during the Cuban missile crisis. Routine reconnaissance flights over Cuba revealed the construction of missile sites, fueling facilities, and launch pads. *What steps did Kennedy take to deal with the crisis?*

Picturing History

Answer: He announced the existence of the missiles, ordered a naval blockade, demanded the dismantling of the sites, warned that the U.S. was ready to respond with force to any attack, and negotiated a settlement with the Soviet Union.

HISTORY Online

Objectives and answers to the student activity can be found in the **Web Activity Lesson Plan** at tav.mt.glencoe.com.

U **Universal Access**

Below Grade Level Tell students to read about the landing of American astronauts on the moon. **Ask:** *Was it necessary or simply symbolic that Americans were able to land successfully on the moon? (Answers will vary, but some students might state that the moon landing had more to do with a symbolic defeat of the Soviet Union during the Cold War than with achieving a scientific goal. Other students might disagree, claiming that many useful scientific and technological improvements came out of the early space program.)* **BL**

R **Reading Strategy**

Scaffolding—Academic Vocabulary The word *demonstrate* was introduced in Chapter 10, Section 4. Ask a student to define the word. **BL**

W **Writing Support**

Research Report Writing Divide the class into three equal groups. Ask students to research the Bay of Pigs invasion and assign each group a different aspect of the event. One group should focus on plans for the invasion developed by the Eisenhower administration, and the second group should focus on the Kennedy administration's involvement in the Bay of Pigs invasion. Ask the third group to investigate the invasion from Cuba's point of view. Each group should write a three- to five-page report presenting its findings. **AL**
CA HR2; HR3

Reading Check

Answer: the spread of communism, the Cuban missile crisis, Latin American relations, and reducing the threat of nuclear war

W Writing Support

Writing a Speech Have each student create a speech that President Kennedy might have given during the Cuban missile crisis. Students should relate the crisis to broader themes of the Kennedy administration. Ask volunteers to present their speeches to the class. **OL** **CA** 11WA2.1a

S Skill Practice

Evaluating Evidence Divided into two teams, have students research the assassination of President Kennedy and develop historical investigations. One team should investigate the argument that Lee Harvey Oswald was a lone assassin, while the second team should look into the conspiracy theory. Students should use historical records and primary and secondary sources to support or enhance their presentations. Allow time to debate students' findings. **AL** **CA** HR3

✓ Reading Check

Answer: The Soviet Union agreed to remove the missiles and Kennedy publicly agreed not to invade Cuba. Privately, Kennedy agreed to remove missiles from Turkey.

---

with some changes. On April 17, 1961, 1,400 armed Cuban exiles landed at the Bay of Pigs on the south coast of Cuba. The invasion was a disaster. La Brigada's boats ran aground on coral reefs, Kennedy cancelled their air support to keep United States involvement a secret, and the expected popular uprising never happened. Within two days, Castro's forces killed or captured almost all the members of La Brigada. The outcome alarmed Kennedy. The action exposed an American plot to overthrow a neighbor's government and made the United States look weak and disorganized.

The Berlin Wall Goes Up Still reeling from the Bay of Pigs fiasco, Kennedy faced another foreign policy challenge in June 1961 when he met with Khrushchev in Vienna, Austria. Khrushchev wanted to stop the flood of Germans pouring out of Communist East Germany into West Berlin. He demanded that the Western powers recognize East Germany and that the United States, Great Britain, and France withdraw from Berlin, a city lying completely within East Germany. Kennedy refused and reaffirmed the West's commitment to West Berlin.

Khrushchev retaliated by building a wall through Berlin, sealing off the Soviet sector. Guards posted along the wall shot at anyone trying to escape from the East. For nearly 30 years afterward, the **Berlin Wall** stood as a visible **symbol** of the Cold War division between East and West.

The Cuban Missile Crisis By far the most terrifying crisis of the Kennedy era occurred the next year. Once again, the crisis dealt with Cuba. Over the summer of 1962, American intelligence agencies learned that Soviet technicians and equipment had arrived in Cuba. On October 22, President Kennedy announced on television that American spy planes had taken aerial photographs showing that the Soviet Union had placed long-range missiles in Cuba. Enemy missiles stationed so close to the United States posed a dangerous threat.

Kennedy ordered a naval blockade to stop the Soviets from delivering more missiles, and he demanded that they dismantle existing missile sites. As Soviet ships headed toward the blockade, Americans braced themselves for war.

After a flurry of secret negotiations, the Soviet Union offered a deal. It would remove the missiles if the United States promised not to invade Cuba and to remove its missiles from Turkey near the Soviet border.

Neither Kennedy nor Khrushchev wanted nuclear war. "Only lunatics . . . who themselves want to perish and before they die destroy the world, could do

this," wrote the Soviet leader. On October 28, the leaders reached an agreement. Kennedy publicly agreed not to invade Cuba and privately agreed to remove the Turkish missiles; the Soviets agreed to remove their missiles from Cuba. The world could breathe again.

The Impact of the Cuban Missile Crisis The Cuban missile crisis brought the world closer to nuclear war than at any time since World War II. Both the United States and the Soviet Union had been forced to consider the consequences of such a war. In the following months, each country seemed ready to work to lessen world tensions. In August 1963, the United States and the Soviet Union concluded years of negotiation by agreeing to a treaty to ban the testing of nuclear weapons in the atmosphere—the first step toward mutual arms reduction since the beginning of the Cold War.

In the long run, however, the missile crisis had ominous consequences. The humiliating retreat the United States forced upon the Soviet leadership contributed to Nikita Khrushchev's fall from power in October 1964. Perhaps more importantly, the crisis gave the Soviets evidence of their military inferiority and helped produce a dramatic Soviet arms buildup over the next two decades. This buildup contributed to a comparable military increase in the United States in the early 1980s.

✓ **Reading Check** **Summarizing** How was the Cuban missile crisis resolved?

The Death of a President

Main Idea President Kennedy was assassinated in Dallas, Texas, on November 22, 1963.

Reading Connection Do you know someone who can recall the day Kennedy was assassinated? What do they recall about that day? Read on to discover the details of Kennedy's assassination.

Soon after the Senate ratified the test ban treaty, John F. Kennedy's presidency came to a shocking and tragic end. On November 22, 1963, Kennedy and his wife traveled to Texas with Vice President Lyndon Johnson for a series of political appearances. As the presidential motorcade drove slowly through the crowded streets of Dallas, gunfire rang out. Someone had shot the president twice—once in the throat and

718 CHAPTER 15 The New Frontier and the Great Society

Did You Know?

Although the city of Berlin had been divided into East Berlin and West Berlin since the end of World War II, in August 1961 an actual wall of concrete, barbed wire, and stone 12 feet high and 103 miles long was erected. Where a wall could not be built, buildings were closed or bricked up.

Resources for page 718

*Have students read more about the Cuban missile crisis in the **Primary Source Reading 15-1**.*

once in the head. The country watched in horror as shocked government officials sped Kennedy to a nearby hospital, where he was pronounced dead moments later.

Lee Harvey Oswald, the man accused of killing Kennedy, appeared to be a confused and embittered Marxist who had spent time in the Soviet Union. He himself was shot to death while in police custody two days after the assassination. The bizarre situation led some to speculate that the second gunman, local nightclub owner Jack Ruby, killed Oswald to protect others involved in the crime. In 1964 a national commission headed by Chief Justice Warren concluded that Oswald was the lone assassin. The report of the **Warren Commission** left some questions unanswered, and **theories** about a conspiracy to kill the president have persisted, though none has gained wide acceptance.

In the wake of the assassination, the United States and the world went into mourning. Americans across the land sobbed in public. Thousands traveled to Washington, D.C., and waited in a line that stretched for several miles outside the Capitol in order to walk silently past the president's flag-draped casket. Millions of others spent hours in front of their televisions mourning the loss of the president by simply watching people file past the casket.

John F. Kennedy served as president for little more than 1,000 days. Yet his powerful personality and active approach to the presidency made a profound impression on most Americans. Aided by the tidal wave of emotion that followed the president's death, his successor, Lyndon Johnson, set out to implement the programs Kennedy had left behind.

 Reading Check **Evaluating** How did Kennedy's presidency end?

 Picturing History

A Final Salute John F. Kennedy, Jr. (right) bravely salutes his father's coffin during the state funeral. How did people around the world react to JFK's assassination?

HISTORY Online **Study Central**

For help with the concepts in this section of *American Vision: Modern Times* go to tav.mt.glencoe.com and click on *Study Central.*

SECTION 2 ASSESSMENT

Checking for Understanding

1. **Vocabulary** Define: flexible response, space race, institute, symbol, theory.
2. **People and Terms** Identify: Peace Corps, Berlin Wall, Warren Commission.
3. **Explain** the goals of the Alliance for Progress.

Reviewing Big Ideas

4. **Describing** What was Kennedy's goal for the United States in the space race?

Critical Thinking

5. **Interpreting** What was the role of foreign aid in the relations between the United States and Latin America?
6. **Organizing** Use a graphic organizer similar to the one below to list the programs that Kennedy used to reduce the threat of nuclear war and to try to stem communism.

Analyzing Visuals

7. **Analyzing Photographs** Study the photograph on pages 717. Explain how aerial photos were important for information during the Cold War.

Writing About History

8. **Descriptive Writing** Take on the role of an American citizen during the Cuban missile crisis. Write a journal entry describing the mood of the country during that time.
CA 11WA2.1a; 11WA2.1e

CHAPTER 15   The New Frontier and the Great Society   **719**

SECTION 2 ASSESSMENT ANSWERS

1. Content vocabulary is boldfaced and highlighted in yellow. Academic vocabulary is boldfaced.
2. Peace Corps (p. 716), Berlin Wall (p. 718), Warren Commission (p. 719)
3. The goals were to create cooperative aid projects that helped estab-

lish better schools, improve housing, distribute land more equitably, and improve health care.
4. to beat the Soviets to the moon
5. to help governments stay in power and prevent Communist revolutions

6. conventional weaponry program, aid to foreign governments, the Peace Corps
7. Aerial photos allowed the U.S. to assess the situation during the Cuban missile crisis.
8. Journal entries will vary but should focus on emotions.

 Picturing **History**

Answer: People brought flowers to American embassies or wept.
Ask: When was President Kennedy assassinated? *(November 22, 1963)*

✔ **Reading Check**

Answer: He was assassinated.

 HISTORY Online

Study Central provides audio summaries, interactive games, and online graphic organizers to help students review section content.

CLOSE

Visual/Spatial Many Americans found inspiration in Kennedy's idealism, grieved at his death, and recaptured some hope for their country in President Johnson's determination. Ask students to create posters that they feel capture the essence of the Kennedy presidency. **OL**

FOCUS

History–Social Science Standards

This feature addresses the following standard:

11.8.7 Describe the effects on society and the economy of technological developments since 1945, including the computer revolution, changes in communication, advances in medicine, and improvements in agricultural technology.

TEACH

W Writing Support

Persuasive Writing President Kennedy stated that sending men to the moon was "hard" and would "measure the best of our energies and skills." Since then the space program has had many triumphs and a few tragedies. **Ask: Should the space program continue sending manned missions into space, or are there better alternatives?** Have students write two-page papers answering this question. Tell them to use the library to gather information that supports their positions. **OL** **CA** 11WA2.4b; 11WA2.4d

Answers and Additional Support

Why It Matters

The Space Program

In 1962 President Kennedy responded to those who questioned the nation's effort to reach the moon: "But why, some say, the moon? Why choose this as our goal? And they may well ask, why climb the highest mountain? Why, 35 years ago, fly the Atlantic? . . . We choose to go to the moon. We choose to go to the moon in this decade and do the other things, not because they are easy, but because they are hard, because that goal will serve to organize and measure the best of our energies and skills, because that challenge is one that we are willing to accept, one we are unwilling to postpone, and one which we intend to win. . . ."

The Saturn V moon rocket is the most powerful rocket ever built.

◄ Assistance for People With Disabilities

The NASA tele-operator and robot technology was used to develop a voice-controlled wheelchair and manipulator. Using a minicomputer, the wheelchair responds to 35 single-word voice commands, helping people with physical disabilities perform tasks like picking up packages, opening doors, and turning on appliances.

New Products

By the time Neil Armstrong and Buzz Aldrin walked on the moon, NASA had spent over $33 billion. Since then, the space program has greatly benefited Americans. Space research has led to many new products, technologies, and manufacturing processes.

EXTENDING THE CONTENT

Sputnik When the Soviets launched *Sputnik I* on October 4, 1957, American scientists were concerned about the military implications. The launching of *Sputnik II* a month later caused even more concern. Much larger than its predecessor and carrying a passenger—a dog named Laika—*Sputnik II* was propelled into space by an incredibly powerful rocket, which might, it seemed, be modified to carry missiles against the United States.

Buzz Aldrin on the moon, July 1969

Increased Safety ➤
Remote-controlled robots reduce human injury levels because they can perform hazardous tasks men and women used to carry out. Robots can also perform operations no human being ever could, such as volcano research on the Puna Ridge of Kilauea, Hawaii.

Communication Advances ⋀
A communications satellite now in development will provide better telephone, television, and data service between western Europe, the Americas, and Africa. Another communications satellite has improved ship-to-shore communications, which used to be interrupted frequently by bad weather.

ANALYZING THE IMPACT

Checking for Understanding

1. **Explaining** What new products or innovations were results of the space research?

Critical Thinking

2. **Analyzing** Do you think the United States still participates in the "space race"? Explain your answer.

CHAPTER 15   The New Frontier and the Great Society   **721**

FOCUS

SKILLBUILDER ACTIVITY

Project **Daily Focus Skills Transparency 15-3** and have students answer the question.

Guide to Reading

Understanding Vocabulary: Have students create word search puzzles using the vocabulary words and their definitions. Allow students time to trade and complete the puzzles.

Answers to Graphic: Programs include HUD, Job Corps, Medicaid, Medicare, Project Head Start. *(See chart, page 727 for summary.)*

Unpacking the Standards

Students will be able to:

- Describe the circumstances leading to Lyndon Johnson's presidency.
- Discuss the goals of President Johnson's Great Society programs.
- Evaluate the legacy of the Great Society effort.

Answers and Additional Support

SECTION 3 The Great Society

Guide to Reading

Connection
In the previous section, you learned how Cold War tensions escalated under President Kennedy. In this section, you will discover how President Johnson expanded on Kennedy's domestic agenda.

Main Idea
- President Johnson's longtime experience in Congress helped him push through several of President Kennedy's antipoverty bills. (p. 723)
- Johnson's Great Society programs provided assistance to disadvantaged Americans. (p. 726)

- Although controversial, the Great Society programs improved the lives of thousands of people. (p. 728)

Content Vocabulary
consensus, war on poverty

Academic Vocabulary
analogy, confine, sector

People and Terms to Identify
VISTA, Great Society, Medicare, Medicaid, Head Start, Robert Weaver

Reading Objectives
- **Explain** what inspired Johnson's Great Society programs.

- **Identify** several specific health and employment programs of the Johnson administration.

Reading Strategy
Organizing As you read about Lyndon Johnson's presidency, complete a graphic organizer similar to the one below to list the social and economic programs started during his administration.

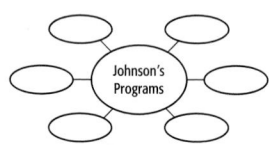

Johnson's Programs

Preview of Events

◆November 1963	◆June 1964	◆January 1965	◆August 1965

November 1963
Johnson becomes president upon Kennedy's death

August 1964
Congress enacts Economic Opportunity Act

November 1964
Johnson wins election as president

July 1965
Congress passes Medical Care Act, establishing Medicare and Medicaid

---

The following are the main History–Social Science Standards covered in this section.

11.8.4 Analyze new federal government spending on defense, welfare, interest on the national debt, and federal and state spending on education, including the California Master Plan.

11.11.1 Discuss the reasons for the nation's changing immigration policy, with emphasis on how the Immigration Act of 1965 and successor acts have transformed American society.

11.11.2 Discuss the significant domestic policy speeches of Truman, Eisenhower, Kennedy, Johnson, Nixon, Carter, Reagan, Bush, and Clinton (e.g., with regard to education, civil rights, economic policy, environmental policy).

11.11.6 Analyze the persistence of poverty and how different analyses of this issue influence welfare reform, health insurance reform, and other social policies.

11.11.7 Explain how the federal, state, and local governments have responded to demographic and social changes such as population shifts to the suburbs, racial concentrations in the cities,

Frostbelt-to-Sunbelt migration, international migration, decline of family farms, increases in out-of-wedlock births, and drug abuse.

❧ The Big Idea ❧

Societies change over time. President Johnson had more experience than Kennedy in dealing with Congress and was able to get several of Kennedy's programs approved. After he was elected president, Johnson worked to get his Great Society initiatives, focusing on health and welfare, education, and poverty, approved. The effectiveness of these programs is often debated. They did, however, improve the lives of many Americans.

722 CHAPTER 15 The New Frontier and the Great Society

SECTION RESOURCES

📂 Print Material
- Reproducible Lesson Plan 15-3
- Guided Reading Activity 15-3
- Reading Essentials and Study Guide 15-3
- Active Reading Note-Taking Guide 15-3

🖥 Transparencies
- Daily Focus Skills Transparency 15-3
- Section Graphic Organizer Transparency 15-3

Technology
- Interactive Tutor Self-Assessment CD-ROM
- ExamView® Pro Testmaker CD-ROM
- Presentation Plus! CD-ROM

Johnson Takes the Reins

Main Idea President Johnson's longtime experience in Congress helped him push through several of President Kennedy's antipoverty bills.

Reading Connection How do you think someone's early life affects their career choices? Read on to learn how Lyndon Johnson's early life prepared him for the presidency.

The United States that President Lyndon Johnson inherited from John F. Kennedy appeared to be a booming, bustling place. From new shopping malls to new roads with new cars to fill them, everything in the country seemed to shout prosperity. Away from the nation's affluent suburbs, however, was another country, one inhabited by the poor, the ill-fed, the ill-housed, and the ill-educated.

★ *An American Story* ★

In 1961, 61-year-old John Rath lived in a sparsely furnished room in Chicago. In the room sat a stove, a sink, a package of cereal, and a tiny icebox. The plaster on the wall was crumbling, the ceiling was cracked, and the window shades were smudged. Telling his story to an interviewer, Rath said:

66I come home to an empty room. I don't even have a dog. No, this is not the kind of life I would choose. If a man had a little piece of land or something, a farm, or well . . . anyway, you've got to have something. You sit down in a place like this, you grit your teeth, you follow me? So many of them are doing that, they sit down, they don't know what to do, they go out. I see 'em in the middle of the night, they take a walk. Don't know what to do. Have no home environment, don't have a dog, don't having nothing . . . just a big zero.99

—quoted in *Division Street: America*

John Rath's life was not the image that many Americans had of their country in the mid-1960s. Writer Michael Harrington examined the nation's impoverished areas in his 1962 book, *The Other America.* Harrington claimed that while the truly poor numbered almost 50 million, they remained largely hidden in city slums, in rural areas, in the Deep South, and on Native American reservations.

Harrington's book moved many Americans and inspired both President Kennedy and his successor, Lyndon Johnson, to make the elimination of poverty a major policy goal. The nation was prosperous, and many leaders had come to believe that the economy could be managed so that prosperity would be permanent. They believed the federal government could afford to fund a new antipoverty program.

Lyndon Johnson decided to continue with Kennedy's plan soon after taking office. Immediately after President Kennedy was pronounced dead, officials whisked Johnson to the airport. At 2:38 P.M. on November 22, 1963, he stood in the cabin of Air Force One, the president's plane, with Jacqueline Kennedy on one side of him and his wife, Lady Bird, on the other. Johnson raised his right hand, placed his left hand on a Bible, and took the oath of office.

Johnson knew that he had to assure a stunned public that he could hold the nation together, that he was a leader. He later recalled the urgency with which he had to act:

66A nation stunned, shaken to its very heart, had to be reassured that the government was not in a state of paralysis . . . that the business of the United States would proceed. I knew that not only the nation but the whole world would be anxiously following every move I made—watching, judging, weighing, balancing. . . . It was imperative that I grasp the reins of power and do so without delay. Any hesitation or wavering, any false step, any sign of self-doubt, could have been disastrous.99

—quoted in *Lyndon Johnson and the American Dream*

▼ *Urban poverty in Chicago*

CHAPTER 15 The New Frontier and the Great Society **723**

TEACH

C Critical Thinking

Identifying Central Issues Ask students to read the statement made by John Rath on this page. **Ask:** What are your impressions of Mr. Rath's statement? Who do you think is responsible for solving Mr. Rath's problem? *(Students will have different reactions to the circumstances Mr. Rath describes. Some may believe that the government is responsible for providing ways for Rath to improve his life, while others may argue that he is responsible for solving his own problems.)* **OL**

W Writing Support

Response to Literature Writing Ask students to think of other books that helped change people's opinions about society and possibly influenced the goals and actions of the national government. Students should write two-page reports discussing the books they chose. Ask the class to discuss the reports. *(Students might think of* Uncle Tom's Cabin, The Jungle, *or* How the Other Half Lives.*)* **AL** **CA** 11WA2.2c

Did You Know?

Lyndon Baines Johnson was the second man named Johnson to assume the mantle of the presidency after an assassination. Andrew Johnson became president after President Lincoln was killed.

Days after the assassination, Johnson appeared before Congress and urged the nation to move on. "The ideas and ideals which [Kennedy] so nobly represented must and will be translated into effective action," he stated. "John Kennedy's death commands what his life conveyed—that America must move forward."

Johnson's Leadership Style Lyndon Baines Johnson was born and raised in the "hill country" of central Texas, near the banks of the Pedernales River. He remained a Texan in his heart and in his life.

Johnson's style posed a striking contrast with Kennedy's. He was a man of impressive stature who spoke directly, convincingly, and even roughly at times. His style was more that of a persuasive and personable politician than of the elegant society man. Finding it difficult to gain acceptance from the Eastern establishment in the nation's capital, he often reveled in his rough image.

Johnson had honed his style in long years of public service. By the time he became president at age 55, he already had 26 years of congressional experience

Picturing **History**

Home on the Range Born and raised in Texas, President Johnson loved to get back to his ranch in the Texas hill country. How does this image contrast with those of his predecessors?

behind him. He had been a congressional staffer, a member of the U.S. House of Representatives, a U.S. senator, Senate majority leader, and vice president.

As he moved up the political ladder, Johnson developed a reputation as a man who got things done. He did favors, twisted arms, bargained, flattered, and threatened. The tactics he used to persuade others became known throughout Washington as the "Johnson treatment." Several writers described this often overpowering and intimidating style:

> ❝The Treatment could last ten minutes or four hours. . . . Its tone could be supplication, accusation, cajolery, exuberance, scorn, tears, complaint, the hint of threat. It was all these together. . . . Interjections from the target were rare. Johnson anticipated them before they could be spoken. He moved in close, his face a scant millimeter from his target, his eyes widening and narrowing, his eyebrows rising and falling. From his pocket poured clippings, memos, statistics. Mimicry, humor, and the genius of **analogy** made The Treatment an almost hypnotic experience and rendered the target stunned and helpless.❞
>
> –from *Lyndon Johnson: The Exercise of Power*

With every technique he could think of, Johnson sought to find **consensus**, or general agreement. His ability to build coalitions had made him one of the most effective and powerful leaders in the Senate's history.

A War on Poverty As president, Johnson used his considerable talents to push through a number of Kennedy's initiatives. Before the end of 1964, he won passage of a tax cut, a major civil rights bill, and a significant anti-poverty program.

Why was this powerful man so concerned about poor people? Johnson liked to exaggerate the poor conditions of his childhood for dramatic effect, but he had in fact known hard times. He had also seen extreme poverty firsthand in a brief career as a teacher in a low-income area. Johnson understood suffering, and he believed deeply in social action. He felt that a wealthy, powerful government could and should try to improve the lives of its citizens. Kennedy himself had said of Johnson, "He really cares about this nation." Finally, there was Johnson's ambition. He wanted to achieve great things so that history would record him as a great president. Attacking poverty was a good place to begin.

Plans for an anti-poverty program were already in place when Johnson took office, and he knew that he

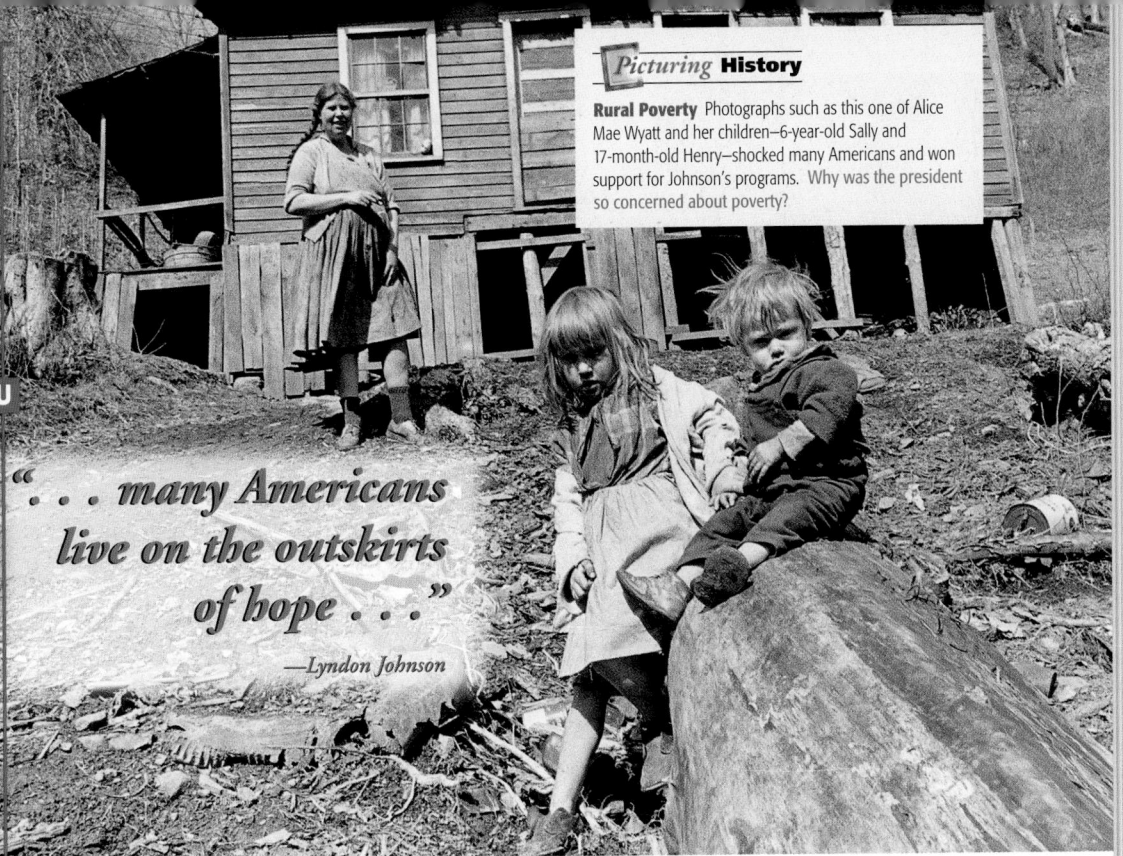

" *. . . many Americans live on the outskirts of hope . . .* "

—*Lyndon Johnson*

would be able to command strong support for any program that could be linked to Kennedy. In his State of the Union address to Congress in 1964, barely seven weeks after taking office, President Johnson told his audience: "Unfortunately, many Americans live on the outskirts of hope, some because of their poverty and some because of their color and all too many because of both." Johnson concluded his speech by announcing that his administration was declaring an "unconditional **war on poverty** in America."

By the summer of 1964, Johnson had convinced Congress to pass the Economic Opportunity Act. The act established a wide range of programs aimed at creating jobs and fighting poverty. It also created a new government agency, the Office of Economic Opportunity (OEO) to coordinate the new programs. Many of the new programs were directed at young Americans living in the inner city. The Neighborhood Youth Corps provided work-study programs to help underprivileged young men and women earn a high school diploma or college degree. The Job Corps tried to help young unemployed people find jobs. One of the more dramatic programs introduced was VISTA

(Volunteers in Service to America), which was essentially a domestic Peace Corps. **VISTA** put young people with skills and community-minded ideals to work in poor neighborhoods and rural areas to help people overcome poverty.

The Election of 1964 As early as April 1964, *Fortune* magazine declared, "Lyndon Johnson has achieved a breadth of public approval few observers would have believed possible when he took office." Johnson had little time to enjoy such praise, for he was soon to run for the office he had first gained through a tragic event.

Johnson's Republican opponent in the 1964 presidential election was Barry Goldwater of Arizona, a senator known for his outspoken conservatism. He set the tone for his campaign when he accepted his party's nomination, declaring, "Extremism in the defense of liberty is no vice! And let me remind you also that moderation in the pursuit of justice is no virtue!"

Few Americans were ready to embrace Goldwater's message, which was too aggressive for a nation nervous about nuclear war. On Election Day,

C Critical Thinking

Drawing Conclusions Remind students that Lyndon Johnson's election was considered a landslide. Discuss with students local, state, or other federal elections that may also fit this category.
Ask: What were the reasons for the results? What effect did personality, campaigning style, issues, and national events outside the candidates' control have on the election? *(Students' answers will vary but should point out the probable popularity of the winning candidate.)* Based on the discussion, have students draw conclusions about what is needed for a landslide victory. **OL**

R Reading Strategy

Predicting Have students describe what they think President Johnson meant by "Great Society." Students should then make predictions about the success of Johnson's plan and guess if any of Johnson's programs are still in place today. *(Students should predict that some of the programs were successful due to government consensus. Answers may include: Medicare, Medicaid, and Head Start.)* **OL**

✔ Reading Check

Answer: the existence of pockets of extreme poverty in a generally prosperous society

Answers and Additional Support

Picturing History

Conservative Stance Senator Barry Goldwater's conservative ideas were not very popular in 1964, and they posed little challenge to President Johnson. *How many states did Goldwater win?*

C Johnson won in a landslide, winning all but five southern states and Arizona. "For the first time in my life," he said later, "I truly felt loved by the American people."

✔ **Reading Check** **Examining** What inspired the war on poverty?

The Great Society

Main Idea Johnson's Great Society programs provided assistance to disadvantaged Americans.

Reading Connection What reforms do you think are most needed today? Read on to find out about the programs Lyndon Johnson initiated.

R After his election, President Johnson began working with Congress to create the "Great Society" he had promised the American people. Major goals of the civil rights movement were achieved with the passage of the Civil Rights Act of 1964, which barred discrimination of many kinds, and the Voting Rights Act of 1965, which ensured African Americans' right to vote.

The **Great Society** was Johnson's vision of the more perfect and equitable society the United States could and should become. According to Bill Moyers, who served as Johnson's press secretary, Johnson admired Franklin Roosevelt and wanted to fulfill FDR's mission. To do that would require a program that would be on the same large scale as the New Deal.

Johnson's goals were consistent with the times for several reasons. The civil rights movement had brought the grievances of African Americans to the forefront, reminding many that greater equality of opportunity had yet to be realized. Economics also supported Johnson's goal. The economy was strong, and many believed it would remain so indefinitely. There was no reason, therefore, that poverty could not be significantly reduced—especially when some had so much and others had so little.

Johnson first elaborated on the goals of the Great Society during a speech at the University of Michigan. It was clear that the president did not intend only to expand relief to the poor or to **confine** government efforts to material things. The president wanted, he said, to build a better society for all, a society "where leisure is a welcome chance to build and reflect, . . .where the city of man serves not only the needs of the body and the demands of commerce but the desire for beauty and the hunger for community. . . ."

This ambitious vision encompassed a multitude of programs. In the three years between 1965 and 1968, more than 60 programs were passed. Among the most significant programs were **Medicare** and **Medicaid.** Health care reform had been a major issue since the days of Harry Truman. By the 1960s, public support for better health care benefits had solidified. Medicare had especially strong support since it was directed at the entire elderly population—in 1965, around half of those over the age of 65 had no health insurance.

Johnson convinced Congress to set up Medicare as a health insurance program funded through the Social Security system. Medicare's twin program, Medicaid, financed health care for welfare recipients, those who were living below the poverty line. Like the New Deal's Social Security program, both programs created what have been called "entitlements," that is, they entitle certain categories of Americans to benefits. Today, the cost of these programs has become a permanent part of the U.S. budget.

Great Society programs also strongly supported education. For Johnson, who had taught school when he was a young man, education was a personal passion. Vice President Hubert Humphrey once said that

Picturing History

Answer: Goldwater carried six states—five Southern states and his home state of Arizona.
Ask: How did people react to Goldwater's aggressive message? *(They were nervous about nuclear war and did not respond positively to Goldwater's aggressiveness.)*

Johnson "was a nut on education. . . . [He] believed in it, just like some people believe in miracle cures."

The Elementary and Secondary Education Act of 1965 granted millions of dollars to public and private schools for classroom materials and special education programs. Efforts to improve education also extended to preschoolers, where Project **Head Start,** administered by the Office of Economic Opportunity, was directed at children from disadvantaged circumstances. Another program, Upward Bound, was designed to provide college preparation for low-income teenagers. Some states added their own educational legislation. California, for example, passed laws to improve higher education facilities in 1960 with the California Master Plan. The plan established a network of public higher education facilities and helped ensure that all California residents who graduate in the top percentages of their high school class would be able to attend a California university.

Improvements in health and education were only the beginning of the Great Society programs. Johnson believed conditions in the cities—poor schools, crime,

slum housing, poverty, and pollution—blighted the lives of those who lived there. He urged Congress to act on legislation addressing this issue. One created a new cabinet agency, the Department of Housing and Urban Development, in 1965. Its first secretary, **Robert Weaver,** was the first African American to serve in a cabinet. A broad-based program informally called "Model Cities" authorized federal subsidies to many cities nationwide. The funds, matched by local and state contributions, supported an array of programs, including transportation, health care, housing, and policing. Legislation also authorized about $8 billion to build houses for people with low- and middle-incomes.

One notable Great Society measure changed the composition of the American population: the Immigration Reform Act of 1965. For a brief time, this act maintained a strict limit on the number of immigrants admitted to the United States each year: 170,000 from the Eastern Hemisphere and 120,000 from the Western Hemisphere. It did, however, eliminate the national origins system established in the 1920s, which had given preference to northern

C Critical Thinking

Drawing Conclusions Tell students that Franklin Roosevelt appointed 27-year-old Lyndon Baines Johnson to serve as the national youth administrator for the state of Texas. Under Johnson's leadership, thousands of young people returned to high school, and thousands found work on government or private projects. Ask students how Johnson's early experience under Franklin Roosevelt's New Deal influenced his Great Society legislation in the 1960s. OL

Review the Big Idea

Review the Big Idea for this section, "Societies change over time." Ask students to play the role of a person living in poverty. Have them write letters explaining to President Johnson what life was like in poverty and how a specific Great Society program has improved their lives. OL
CA 11WA2.1a; 11WA2.1c

U Universal Access

Below Grade Level Tell students that Head Start began as a summer program, but by 1970 most programs were year-round. In 2003 Head Start enrollment was over 900,000 which included 104,683 children from California enrolled at an average cost of $7,092 per child. Ask students to discuss the costs and benefits of this program and list responses on the board. BL

Major Great Society Programs

Health and Welfare	Education	The "War on Poverty"	Consumer and Environmental Protection
Medicare (1965) established a comprehensive health insurance program for all elderly people; financed through the Social Security system.	**The Elementary and Secondary Education Act** (1965) targeted aid to students and funded related activities such as adult education and education counseling.	**The Office of Economic Opportunity** (1964) oversaw many programs to improve life in inner cities, including Job Corps, an education and job training program for at-risk youth.	**The Water Quality Act and Clean Air Acts** (1965) supported development of standards and goals for water and air quality.
Medicaid (1965) funded by federal and state governments, provided health and medical assistance to families with low incomes.	**Higher Education Act** (1965) supported college tuition scholarships, student loans, and work-study programs for students with low- and middle-incomes.	**Housing and Urban Development Act** (1965) established new housing subsidy programs and made federal loans and public housing grants easier to obtain.	**The Highway Safety Act** (1966) supported highway safety by improving federal, state, and local coordination and by creating training standards for emergency medical technicians.
Child Nutrition Act (1966) established a school breakfast program and expanded the school lunch program and milk program to improve nutrition for children from families with low incomes.	**Project Head Start** (1965) funded a preschool program for the disadvantaged.	**Demonstration Cities and Metropolitan Development Act** (1966) helped revitalize urban areas through a variety of social and economic programs.	**The Fair Packaging and Labeling Act** (1966) required all consumer products to have true and informative labels.

Chart *Skills*

1. **Interpreting Charts** What was the purpose of the Office of Economic Opportunity?
2. **Evaluating** Which Great Society program do you think had the most impact on American society? Why?

Chart *Skills*

Answers:
1. The Office of Economic Opportunity oversaw many inner city programs.
2. Students' answers will vary but they should be able to explain how their chosen programs changed society.

Chart Skills Practice

Ask: How did health and welfare programs promote education? *(Child nutrition made students better able to learn from the educational programs offered.)*

Answers and Additional Support

R Reading Strategy

Recalling Information Have students recall from page 726 their predictions of what Johnson meant by "Great Society." Based on what they have learned, ask students to redefine "Great Society." Students should also recall their predictions of Johnson's programs and discuss their failure or success. **OL**

C Critical Thinking

Comparing and Contrasting Tell students to read the description of VISTA in the National Geographic Moments in History box found on this page. **Ask:** **What other government programs do you know that emphasize(d) community volunteering?** *(Students may suggest Americorps, President George H.W. Bush's "Thousand Points of Light" campaign, or George W. Bush's faith-based initiative.)* **OL**

✓ Reading Check

Answer: They included health, housing, job, and educational programs.

Answers and Additional Support

European immigrants. The new measure opened wider the door of the United States to newcomers from all parts of Europe, Asia, and Africa.

✓ **Reading Check** **Summarizing** What were the Great Society programs?

Legacy of the Great Society

Main Idea Although controversial, the Great Society programs improved the lives of thousands of people.

Reading Connection What Great Society programs do you think were the most helpful? Read on to learn of the lasting impact of Johnson's Great Society.

R The Great Society programs touched nearly every aspect of American life and improved thousands, if not millions, of lives. In the years since President Johnson left office, however, debate has continued over whether or not the Great Society was truly a success. In many ways, the impact of the Great Society

was limited. In his rush to get as much done as he could, Johnson did not calculate exactly how his programs might work. As a result, some of them did not work as well as people had hoped. Furthermore, the programs grew so quickly they were often unmanageable and difficult to evaluate. Cities, states, and groups eligible for aid began to expect immediate and life-changing benefits. These expectations often left many feeling frustrated and angry. Other Americans opposed the massive growth of federal programs and criticized the Great Society for intruding too much into their lives.

A lack of funds also hurt the effectiveness of Great Society programs. The programs themselves were expensive enough. When Johnson attempted to fund both his grand domestic agenda and the increasingly costly war in Vietnam, the Great Society eventually suffered. Some Great Society initiatives have survived to the present, however. These include Medicare and Medicaid, two cabinet agencies—the Department of Transportation and the Department of Housing and Urban Development (HUD)—and Project Head Start. Overall, the programs provided

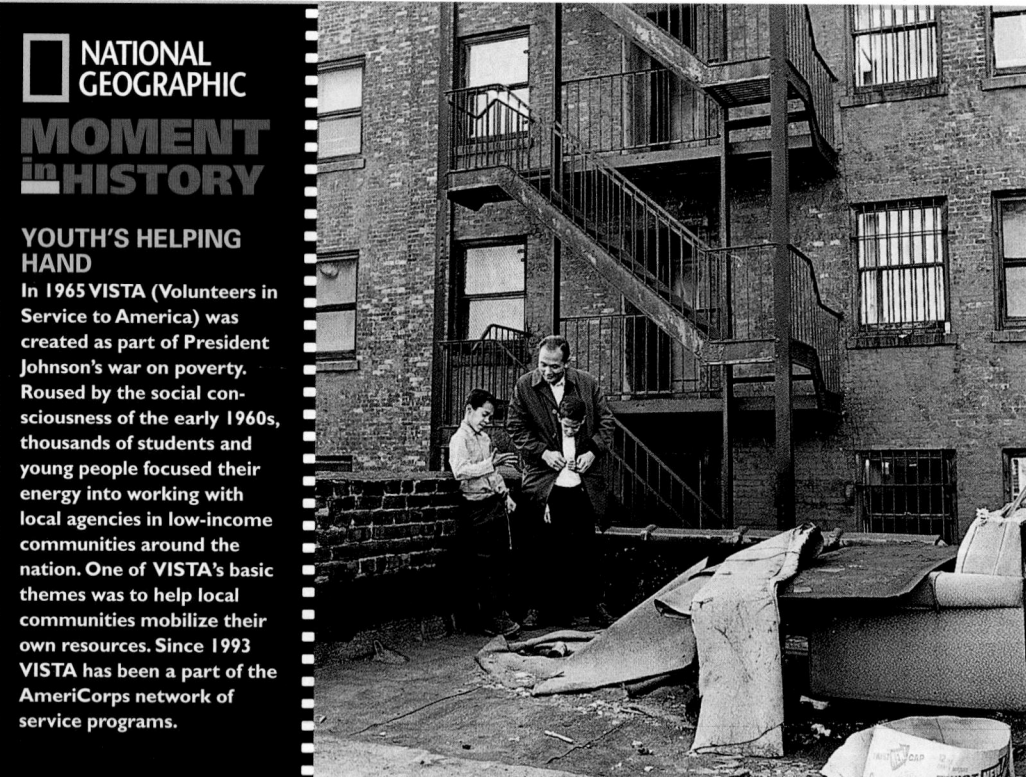

NATIONAL GEOGRAPHIC
MOMENT in HISTORY

C

YOUTH'S HELPING HAND
In 1965 VISTA (Volunteers in Service to America) was created as part of President Johnson's war on poverty. Roused by the social consciousness of the early 1960s, thousands of students and young people focused their energy into working with local agencies in low-income communities around the nation. One of VISTA's basic themes was to help local communities mobilize their own resources. Since 1993 VISTA has been a part of the AmeriCorps network of service programs.

NATIONAL GEOGRAPHIC **MOMENT in HISTORY**

Ask: How do you think programs such as VISTA brought out the positive, giving side of Americans? *(It allowed them to help people who were less fortunate.)*

Profiles IN HISTORY

Esther Peterson
1906–1997

In the 1930s, Boston employers asked women who sewed aprons for them to switch from square pockets to a more difficult heart-shaped pocket, but they did not offer any increase in pay. Esther Peterson, a local teacher and outspoken advocate for women's rights, led the workers in a strike for more money. The women won their pay raise. For 60 years, Esther Peterson continued to use her tact and will to fight for women's rights, trade unions, and consumers.

Born in Provo, Utah, as Esther Eggertsen, Peterson became a teacher in the 1930s. She taught milliners, telephone operators, and garment workers at the innovative Bryn Mawr Summer School for Women Workers in Industry. In 1961 President Kennedy selected her to serve as Assistant Secretary of Labor and Director of the Women's Bureau. Peterson then encouraged Kennedy to create a Presidential Commission on the Status of Women to focus attention on working women.

Under President Johnson, Peterson served as Special Assistant for Consumer Affairs, where she worked on consumer concerns. Lynda Johnson Robb, daughter of President Johnson, described Peterson this way: "She had

a velvet hammer and talked people into doing what was right, even if we didn't know it at the time." Peterson continued to use her "velvet hammer" for the public good throughout her long life. At the time of her death at the age of 91, she was actively promoting senior citizens' health issues.

---

some important benefits to poorer communities and gave political and administrative experience to minority groups.

An important legacy of the Great Society was the questions it produced, questions Americans continue to consider. How can the federal government help its citizens who are economically disadvantaged? How much government help can a society have without weakening the private **sector?** How much help can its people receive without losing motivation to fight against hardships on their own?

Lyndon Johnson came into office determined to change the United States in a way few other presidents had attempted. If he fell short, it was perhaps that the goals he set were so high. In evaluating the administration's efforts, the *New York Times* wrote, "The walls of the ghettos are not going to topple overnight, nor is it possible to wipe out the heritage of generations of social, economic, and educational deprivation by the stroke of a Presidential pen."

 Reading Check **Evaluating** What was the impact of the Great Society?

 HISTORY Online **Study Central**

For help with the concepts in this section of *American Vision: Modern Times* go to tav.mt.glencoe.com and click on *Study Central.*

SECTION 3 ASSESSMENT

Checking for Understanding
1. **Vocabulary** Define: analogy, consensus, war on poverty, confine, sector.
2. **People and Terms** Identify: VISTA, Great Society, Medicare, Medicaid, Head Start, Robert Weaver.
3. **Describe** how the Great Society programs were inspired.

Reviewing Big Ideas
4. **Analyzing** How did Johnson's war on poverty strive to ensure greater fairness in American society?

Critical Thinking
5. **Historical Analysis** **Interpreting** What were three legacies of the Great Society? **CA CS1**
6. **Organizing** Use a graphic organizer similar to the one below to list five Great Society initiatives that have survived to the present.

Great Society Initiatives

Analyzing Visuals
7. **Photographs** Study the photograph on page 725. Why do you think pictures such as this one would help build support for the war on poverty?

Writing About History
8. **Descriptive Writing** Take on the role of a biographer. Write a chapter in a biography of Lyndon Johnson in which you compare and contrast his leadership style to that of John Kennedy. **CA 11WS1.1**

CHAPTER 15   The New Frontier and the Great Society   **729**

SECTION 3 ASSESSMENT ANSWERS

1. Content vocabulary is boldfaced and highlighted in yellow. Academic vocabulary is boldfaced.
2. VISTA *(p. 725)*, Great Society *(p. 726)*, Medicare *(p. 726)*, Medicaid *(p. 726)*, Head Start *(p. 727)*, Robert Weaver *(p. 727)*
3. Johnson wanted to fulfill FDR's mission for a nation of equal opportunity.
4. by offering the less fortunate education, training, and access to jobs
5. Answers should reflect text, for example, Medicare and Medicaid, political experience for minorities, and Head Start.
6. Medicare, Medicaid, Department of Transportation, Department of Housing and Urban Development, Project Head Start
7. Answers will vary. Students should describe the emotions evoked by such photographs.
8. Chapters should include specific information about the leadership styles of the two men.

ASSESS

 Resources for page 729

Use these resources to assess student mastery.

📁 Section Quiz 15-3

📁 Reading Essentials and Study Guide 15-3

🌐 Interactive Tutor Self-Assessment CD-ROM

📁 California Standards Practice, Grade 11

Profiles IN HISTORY

In 1981 Esther Peterson was awarded the nation's highest civilian award—the Presidential Medal of Freedom.
Ask: For what causes did Esther Peterson fight? *(women's rights, trade unions, and consumer rights)*

Reading Check

Answer: It improved millions of lives and reshaped government.

HISTORY Online

Study Central provides audio summaries, interactive games, and online graphic organizers to help students review section content.

CLOSE

Persuasive Writing Tell students to list three characteristics of a good leader on a sheet of paper. Using this list, have students evaluate the accomplishments of either Kennedy or Johnson in brief paragraphs. **OL**
CA 11WS1.3

Looking Back...

The Bill of Rights

FOCUS

History– Social Science Standards

This feature addresses the following standards:

11.1.1 Describe the Enlightenment and the rise of democratic ideas as the context in which the nation was founded.

11.1.2 Analyze the ideological origins of the American Revolution, the Founding Fathers' philosophy of divinely bestowed unalienable natural rights, the debates on the drafting and ratification of the Constitution, and the addition of the Bill of Rights.

TEACH

W Writing Support

Summary Writing List each of the basic rights on the board. Have students think of specific examples from the colonial period in which the British denied these rights to the colonists. Have students write their examples on the board to create a chart that they can use for later reference. Students should then write brief paragraphs summarizing how British actions affected the creation of the Bill of Rights. **OL**

CA 11WA2.1a

Answers and Additional Support

Why It Matters In 1962 Clarence Earl Gideon was arrested for breaking into a Florida pool hall. When he asked for a lawyer, the judge refused. Defendants in Florida were not entitled to a court-appointed lawyer except in death penalty cases. Gideon then appealed to the Supreme Court, arguing that the Constitution's Sixth Amendment guaranteed the right to a lawyer. In 1963, in *Gideon* v. *Wainright,* the Supreme Court decided that the Sixth Amendment applied to both state and federal courts. The court ruled that having a lawyer in a criminal case is a fundamental right.

W For over 200 years, the first ten amendments to the Constitution, known as the Bill of Rights, have protected the rights of Americans. Five of the amendments specify rights Americans have in federal court. In the 1960s, the Supreme Court extended many of these rights to the state and local levels.

Steps To . . . the Bill of Rights

During the Middle Ages, kings had great power, but to pass a new law they usually obtained the consent of a council of important nobles. This custom of ruling with "noble consent" was not written into law until 1215.

From Liberties to Rights In 1215 King John of England faced a rebellion of many of the English nobles. Under pressure, he signed the **Magna Carta.** In this document the king promised "to all freemen of our kingdom . . . all the underwritten liberties, to be had and held by them and their heirs, of us and our heirs forever." After 1215 the English king was expected to rule in accordance with the Magna Carta.

When the Enlightenment began in the 1600s, a new idea of rights emerged. Several writers argued that kings could not give rights to people. Instead, every person was born with rights that the government could not violate. **John Locke** was an advocate of this new idea. His book, *Two Treatises of Government,* became very influential in the American colonies.

In 1688 the English Parliament helped remove King James II from the throne in what was known as the Glorious Revolution. Before the new king and queen took the throne, Parliament demanded they accept the **English Bill of Rights.** The English Bill of Rights strongly influenced American ideas. When the American Revolution began, revolutionaries accused the British of violating many of these rights.

The Magna Carta

> *"We hold these truths to be self-evident, that all men are created equal, that they are endowed by their Creator with certain unalienable rights, that among these are Life, Liberty, and the pursuit of Happiness."*
>
> —*Thomas Jefferson, The Declaration of Independence*

730

EXTENDING THE CONTENT

Magna Carta Although the Magna Carta placed some legal restraints on the king, it extended rights only to nobles (who were the freemen) and did nothing for the common people. Throughout Europe's kingdoms, the rights of individuals were very limited. In France, dukes who determined the rights of common people on the lands they controlled held most of the power. Even when a French legislature was created, the townspeople were given only one collective vote as the third estate.

Origins of the Bill of Rights

Basic Rights	Magna Carta (1215)	English Bill of Rights (1689)	Virginia Declaration of Rights (1776)	Virginia Statute for Religious Freedom (1786)	American Bill of Rights (1791)
No state religion				●	●
Freedom of worship		● limited	●	●	●
Freedom of speech		●	●		●
Right to petition		● limited			●
Right to bear arms					●
No quartering troops in private homes without permission				●	●
No searches and seizures without a specific search warrant	●		●		●
Government cannot take away life, liberty, or property unless it follows proper court procedures (due process)	●	●	●		●
Right to a speedy public trial by jury and to a lawyer	●	●	●	●	●
No excessive bail, fines, or cruel and unusual punishment	●	●	●		●

The American Revolution In the 1760s, in order to stop smuggling in the American colonies, the British began sending accused smugglers to vice admiralty courts. These courts had no juries. In the Declaration of Independence, Americans accused the British of "depriving us . . . of the benefits of trial by jury" as guaranteed in the Magna Carta and the English Bill of Rights. Americans later wrote the Fifth and Sixth Amendments of the Bill of Rights to prevent similar abuses by the American federal government.

Also to stop smuggling, the British issued "writs of assistance" authorizing officials to search private property as they saw fit. Americans later wrote the Fourth Amendment to prevent officials from conducting searches without specific search warrants.

Free Speech In England, free speech was limited by laws against sedition. Sedition is the encouraging of opposition to the government. The only exception applied to Parliament. The English Bill of Rights stated that "freedom of speech . . . in parliament, ought not to be . . . questioned."

The Founders of the United States knew that the American Revolution could not have happened had they been unable to make speeches or print their ideas in newspapers. When the Bill of Rights was submitted, a ban on any federal law restricting free speech or freedom of the press was prominent in the First Amendment.

Putting Rights Into the Constitution When the Constitution was drafted, it did not include a list of rights because supporters believed the new federal government's checks and balances would protect people's rights. When the Constitution was submitted to the states for ratification, however, opponents argued that without a list of rights, the Constitution would lead to a tyrannical federal government.

George Mason, who drafted Virginia's Declaration of Rights, was a leader of the opposition. To get the Constitution ratified, supporters promised a Bill of Rights. In September 1789, James Madison prepared 12 amendments to the Constitution. In wording these amendments, Madison relied heavily on Virginia's Declaration of Rights. Ten of the amendments were ratified. Together, they make up the Bill of Rights.

Checking for Understanding
1. How many rights are in the Bill of Rights?
2. Which amendments in the Bill of Rights protect rights the British violated in the 1760s?

Critical Thinking
1. Which right do you think is the most important? Why?
2. Do Americans have any other rights other than those listed in the Bill of Rights? What are they?

Checking for Understanding
1. The Bill of Rights contains 10 basic rights.
2. In the 1760s, the British violated the right to proper court procedures (Fifth Amendment), the right to a speedy public trial (Sixth Amendment), and the right to be protected from searches and seizures without a warrant (Fourth Amendment).

Critical Thinking
1. Students should state specific reasons for their choices.
2. Students should recognize that Americans have other rights under the Constitution, the other amendments to the Constitution, and, to a certain extent, under individual state constitutions.

FOCUS

History–Social Science Standards

This feature addresses the following standard:

11.9.3 Trace the origins and geopolitical consequences (foreign and domestic) of the Cold War and containment policy, including the following: the era of McCarthyism, instances of domestic Communism (e.g., Alger Hiss) and blacklisting; the Truman Doctrine; the Berlin Blockade; the Korean War; the Bay of Pigs Invasion and the Cuban Missile Crisis; atomic testing in the American West, the "mutual assured destruction" doctrine, and disarmament policies; the Vietnam War; Latin American policy.

Understanding Vocabulary

Before students begin reading, point out that difficult or unfamiliar words are footnoted throughout the text.

TEACH

R Reading Strategy

Identifying the Main Idea and Supporting Details President Kennedy states that the Soviet decision to place missiles on Cuban soil is a "deliberately provocative" act. Have students identify examples and details in the source that support this assertion. **OL**

On October 14, 1962, American spy planes photographed missile sites that the Soviets had installed in Cuba. After days of deliberations, exchanges of diplomatic letters, rallying of allies, exhausting meetings, and military preparation, President Kennedy informed the nation of the development. The fear of nuclear war gripped many Americans.

SOURCE 1:

In a televised address on October 22, 1962, President John F. Kennedy told Americans about the Soviet missile sites in Cuba. He demanded the Soviets withdraw the missiles and imposed a blockade of Cuba.

The urgent transformation of Cuba into an important strategic base—by the presence of these large, long-range, and clearly offensive weapons of sudden mass destruction—**constitutes**[1] an explicit threat to the peace and security of all the Americas. . . .

The size of this undertaking makes clear that it has been planned for some months. Yet only last month, after I had made clear the distinction between any introduction of ground-to-ground missiles and the existence of defensive antiaircraft missiles, the Soviet Government publicly stated on September 11 that, and I quote, "The armaments and military equipment sent to Cuba are designed exclusively for defensive purposes." . . .

Neither the United States of America nor the world community of nations can tolerate deliberate deception and offensive threats on the part of any nation, large or small. We no longer live in a world where only the actual firing of weapons represents a sufficient challenge to a nation's security to constitute maximum peril. Nuclear weapons are so destructive and **ballistic**[2] missiles are so swift that any substantially increased possibility of their use or any sudden change in their deployment may well be regarded as a definite threat to peace. . . .

[T]his secret, swift, and extraordinary buildup of Communist missiles—in an area well known to have a special and historical relationship to the United States

▲ *President Kennedy and White House officials discuss Cuba.*

and the nations of the Western Hemisphere, in violation of Soviet assurances, and in defiance of American and hemispheric policy—this sudden, clandestine decision to station strategic weapons for the first time outside of Soviet soil—is a deliberately provocative and unjustified change in the *status quo* which cannot be accepted by this country if our courage and our commitments are ever to be trusted again by either friend or foe.

SOURCE 2:

Kennedy surrounded himself with a small group of talented advisers, the Executive Committee of National Security Council. On October 27, five days after Kennedy's address to the nation, this committee received a message from Soviet premier Nikita Khrushchev.

You wish to ensure the security of your country, and this is understandable. But Cuba, too, wants the same thing; all countries want to maintain their security. But how are we, the Soviet Union, our government, to

---

[1]**constitutes:** forms
[2]**ballistic missile:** a weapon that flies to its target

UNIVERSAL ACCESS

Verbal/Linguistic Ask students to identify adjectives the president used in his address to describe the Soviet buildup of missiles in Cuba. *(Examples include deliberate, offensive, secret, swift, extraordinary, sudden, clandestine.)* Then ask students to use library and Internet resources to locate headlines from newspapers on the day following President Kennedy's television address. Display the headlines for all students to review. As a class, discuss the implication and impact that the president's words had on the American people and what the headlines reveal about the event within the context in which it unfolded. **AL**

▲ *Nikita Khrushchev and Raul Castro meet in Moscow, USSR in 1962*

SOURCE 3:

The United States believed that it won the crisis because of superior military might and a willingness to use force. Raymond Garthoff, an intelligence analyst in the State Department, summarized this belief in a memo for the undersecretary of state on October 29, 1962.

The short-run effects should be very favorable to the US. Unquestionably the US will emerge from this confrontation with increased prestige world-wide. . . . [T]he Soviets are not prepared to risk a decisive military showdown with the US over issues involving the extension of Soviet power. . . .

Soviet ability to penetrate Latin America should suffer a reversal, though a base for future penetration may remain in Cuba for some time. Soviet intentions have been unmasked, and Soviet inability to force its will clearly demonstrated. . . .

. . . Unquestionably the Soviet defeat will have its impact on Soviet thinking and policymaking. Over the long run, one effect may be to make the Soviets far more responsive to our efforts at finding peaceful solutions to the whole range of world problems. However, and this is an important qualification, this effect is certain to take a considerable period of time. . . .

If we have learned anything from this experience, it is that weakness, even only apparent weakness, invited Soviet **transgression**.[3] At the same time, firmness in the last analysis will force the Soviets to back away from rash initiatives. . . .

[3]**transgression:** violation

assess your actions which are expressed in the fact that you have surrounded the Soviet Union with military bases; placed military bases literally around our country; and stationed your missile armaments there? This is no secret. Responsible Americans openly declare that it is so. Your missiles are located in Britain, are located in Italy, and are aimed at us. Your missiles are located in Turkey.

You are disturbed over Cuba. You say that this disturbs you because it is 90 miles by sea from the coast of the United States of America. But Turkey adjoins us; our sentries patrol back and forth and see each other. Do you consider, then, that you have the right to demand security for your own country and the removal of the weapons you call offensive, but do not accord the same right to us? You have placed destructive missile weapons, which you call offensive, in Turkey, literally next to us. . . .

I therefore make this proposal: We are willing to remove from Cuba the [missiles] which you regard as offensive. We are willing to carry this out. . . . Your representatives will make a declaration to the effect that the United States, for its part, considering the uneasiness and anxiety of the Soviet government, will remove its comparable [missiles] from Turkey. . . .

DBQ — Document-Based Questions

Historical Analysis CA HI2; HI3

Source 1: Why does Kennedy want missiles removed from Cuba?

Source 2: How does Khrushchev justify placing Soviet missiles in Cuba?

Source 3: According to Garthoff, how has the United States benefited from the crisis?

Comparing and Contrasting Sources

How does Khruschchev differ in his views from Kennedy and Garthoff about the causes of the Cuban missile crisis?

CHAPTER 15 The New Frontier and the Great Society **733**

R₁ Reading Strategy

Evaluating Ask students to explain whether or not they think Khrushchev's response to Kennedy, comparing Turkey and Cuba, is valid. Have students use details from the primary source to support or illustrate their responses. OL

R₂ Reading Strategy

Monitoring Ask students to explain the proposal Khrushchev made to Kennedy. *(He proposed that the Soviets remove the missiles from Cuba if the United States removes its missiles from Turkey.)* BL

W Writing Support

Summary Writing After students read Raymond Garthoff's memo, ask them to write summaries of the short-term and long-term effects of the Cuban missile crisis. OL CA 11WS1.6

ASSESS/CLOSE

Have students answer the Document-Based Questions.

DBQ — Document-Based Questions

1. The missiles pose an explicit threat to the security of the United States.
2. He cites the location of U.S. missiles in Turkey aimed at the Soviet Union.
3. Benefits to the United States include increased prestige around the world because of the nation's strong stance against the Soviets.

Comparing and Contrasting Sources
Khrushchev believes that the placement of U.S. missiles in Turkey, which adjoins the Soviet Union, is the reason for the placement of Soviet missiles in Cuba and the cause of the crisis. Kennedy and Garthoff believe that the Soviet Union acted offensively.

Resources for pages 734–735

Use the following resources to review, assess, and reteach the chapter.

📂 Chapter 15 Tests, Forms A and B

📂 Standardized Tests, Forms A and B

📂 Cumulative Authentic Assessment

🔒 MindJogger Videoquiz

◉ Interactive Tutor Self-Assessment CD-ROM

◉ Exam*View*® Pro Testmaker CD-ROM

◉ Vocabulary PuzzleMaker CD-ROM

◉ Succeeding on . . .™ the California Standards: Grade 11 History–Social Science

📂 California Standards Practice, Grade 11

Reviewing Content Vocabulary

Students' answers will vary. The pages where the words appear in the text are shown in parentheses.

1. missile gap *(p. 706)* **2.** reapportionment *(p. 710)* **3.** due process *(p. 710)* **4.** flexible response *(p. 715)* **5.** space race *(p. 716)* **6.** consensus *(p. 724)* **7.** war on poverty *(p. 725)*

Reviewing Academic Vocabulary

Students' answers will vary. The pages where the words appear in the text are shown in parentheses.

8. medium *(p. 705)* **9.** reside *(p. 710)* **10.** arbitrary *(p. 710)* **11.** institute *(p. 717)* **12.** symbol *(p. 718)* **13.** theory *(p. 719)* **14.** analogy *(p. 724)* **15.** confine *(p. 726)* **16.** sector *(p. 729)*

Reviewing Content Vocabulary

On a sheet of paper, use each of these terms in a sentence.

1. missile gap
2. reapportionment
3. due process
4. flexible response
5. space race
6. consensus
7. war on poverty

Reviewing Academic Vocabulary

On a sheet of paper, use each of these terms in a sentence that reflects the term's meaning in the chapter.

8. medium
9. reside
10. arbitrary
11. institute
12. symbol
13. theory
14. analogy
15. confine
16. sector

Reviewing the Main Ideas

Section 1

17. How was the 1960 presidential election a new kind of campaign?

18. What was Kennedy's response to the steel industry's decision to raise prices sharply?

Section 2

19. What were three programs set up by Kennedy to reduce the threat of nuclear war and to try to stem communism?

🐻 Standards 11.8.4, 11.8.5, 11.8.7, 11.9.3, 11.10.2, 11.10.7, 11.11.1, 11.11.2, 11.11.3, 11.11.6, 11.11.7

Section 3

20. What inspired President Johnson's war on poverty?

21. Which Great Society initiatives are still in effect today?

Critical Thinking

22. **Reading Skill** **Synthesizing** Identify the summary ideas under the heading "The Great Society" from pages 726–728. Would you agree with this summary? Write your own summary of one or two paragraphs about Johnson's Great Society.

23. **Civics** Why were Medicare and Medicaid landmark pieces of legislation in American history?

24. **Evaluating** In the 1960 presidential debate, most radio listeners thought Nixon had won, while most television viewers thought Kennedy had. Why do you think this was so?

25. **Drawing Conclusions** How did Kennedy help prevent Communist movements from flourishing in Latin America?

26. **Analyzing** President Kennedy was unable to pass civil rights legislation. What were some of the factors that allowed President Johnson to push civil rights forward after Kennedy's assassination?

27. **Evaluating** How did the Warren Court decisions in *Baker* v. *Carr* and *Reynolds* v. *Sims* affect voting power in the nation?

Chapter Summary

The New Frontier and the Great Society

Domestic Programs

- Office of Economic Opportunity fights illiteracy, unemployment, and disease.
- Civil Rights Act of 1964 prohibits race discrimination and social segregation.
- Voting Rights Act protects the right to vote.
- Medicare and Medicaid Acts provide federal medical aid to the elderly and poor.
- Elementary and Secondary Education Act increases aid for public schools.

Foreign Policy

- "Flexible response" policy maintains opposition to communism.
- U.S. pledges aid to struggling Latin American nations.
- Peace Corps offers humanitarian aid in poor countries.
- Nuclear Test Ban Treaty with the Soviet Union eases Cold War tensions.

Supreme Court Cases

- *Reynolds* v. *Sims* boosts voting power of urban dwellers, including many minorities.
- Extension of due process gives more protection to people accused of crimes.
- Court rules that states could not require prayer and Bible readings in public schools.

734 CHAPTER 15 The New Frontier and the Great Society

Reviewing the Main Ideas

17. The campaign marked the first time that television played a major role, including the televised debate between Kennedy and Nixon.

18. He threatened to buy steel from foreign companies and investigated price fixing.

19. conventional weaponry program, foreign aid, the Peace Corps

20. Johnson's personal experiences and the nation's ability to finance programs

21. Among programs or agencies still in effect are Medicare, Medicaid, Head Start, Department of Transportation, and Department of Housing and Urban Development.

28. **Organizing** Use a graphic organizer similar to the one below to list the crises of the Cold War during the Kennedy administration.

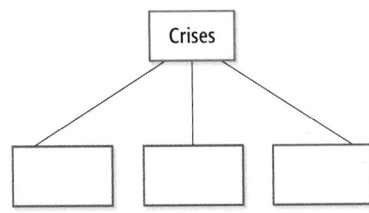

Writing About History

29. [**Historical Analysis**] **Identifying Bias** Review President Kennedy's quote under "The Space Program" on page 720. What biases might President Kennedy have held for competing in the space race? How did he express this in his quote? [CA HR2]

30. *Big Idea* Search the Internet to check the status of a specific Great Society program today. Find out how the program has changed since it was initiated. Write a report on your findings. [CA 11WS1.6]

31. **Expository Writing** Assume the role of a historian. Evaluate the effectiveness of Kennedy's New Frontier and Johnson's Great Society programs. Write an article for a historical journal explaining the successes and setbacks of each president's policy agendas. [CA 11WA2.4a]

[DBQ] Document-Based Questions

32. **Interpreting Primary Sources** Although the standard of living for most Americans rose dramatically throughout the 1960s, some Americans remained mired in poverty. Reread the excerpt on page 723 in which John Rath discusses his personal experiences with coping with poverty in his sparsely furnished room in Chicago. Then answer the following questions.

 a. What does Rath think might help him to have some purpose in his life? [CA 11RC2.4]

 b. What does Rath mean when he says: "You sit down in a place like this, you grit your teeth. . . ."? [CA 11RC2.5]

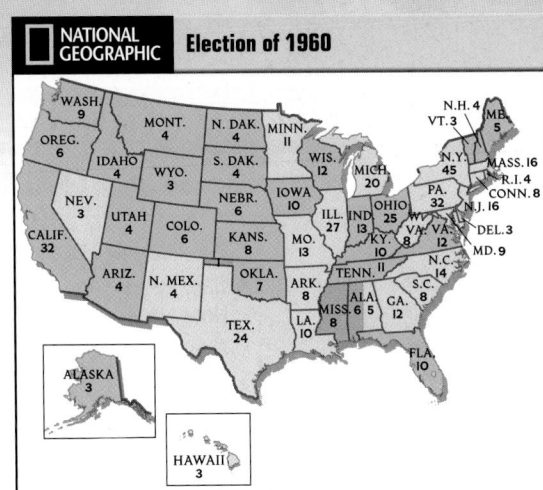

NATIONAL GEOGRAPHIC Election of 1960

Geography and History

33. The map on this page shows the results of the presidential election of 1960. Study the map and answer the questions below.

 a. **Interpreting Maps** Which regions of the country supported Kennedy? Which regions supported Nixon?

 b. **Applying Geography Skills** What would have happened if Kennedy had lost New York to Nixon?

Standards Practice

Directions: Choose the best answer to the following question.

34. Which of the following was a measure President Kennedy took to strengthen the economy?

A He utilized deficit spending.

B He discouraged space exploration.

C He asked labor leaders to request pay increases.

D He increased state authority at the expense of federal authority.

Standard 11.8.4: Analyze new federal government spending on defense, welfare, interest on the national debt, and federal and state spending on education, including the California Master Plan.

CHAPTER 15 The New Frontier and the Great Society **735**

Online

Have students visit the Web site at tav.mt.glencoe.com to review Chapter 15 and take the Self-Check Quiz.

27. In *Baker* v. *Carr,* the court ruled that the federal government has the right to enforce voting rights in the states. In *Reynolds* v. *Sims,* the court ruled that many states' apportionment plans were unconstitutional.

28. Bay of Pigs, Berlin Wall, Cuban missile crisis

Writing About History

29. [**Historical Analysis**] Students' answers will vary. Possible answer: President Kennedy could be swayed in his desire to win the space race because of the Cold War.

30. *Big Idea* Students' reports will vary. You may want to have students work in pairs on this activity.

31. Students' articles will vary but should use the perspective of history to evaluate the successes and failures of the program.

[DBQ] Document-Based Questions

32. **a.** owning his home; **b.** The statement shows helplessness, desperation, and frustration.

Geography and History

33. **a.** Nixon: Midwest, West; Kennedy: Northeast, some Southern and Midwestern states; **b.** Nixon would have won the election by six electoral votes.

Standards Practice

34. A

Bonus Question ?

Ask: Which president started the Peace Corps? *(Kennedy)*

Critical Thinking

22. [**Reading Skill**] Students' summary paragraphs will vary but should focus on Johnson's Great Society programs.

23. They represented the first time that the U.S. government had funded health care on a large scale.

24. Kennedy's physical appearance and demeanor made a positive impact on the television audience. Their reaction to Nixon's appearance and demeanor was negative. Because they could only hear the candidates, radio listeners had a different reaction.

25. He provided aid to Latin America so that countries would be less likely to support communist-inspired revolutions.

26. the civil rights movement, Kennedy's death, Johnson's style of leadership

Chapter 16 Planning Guide

SECTION RESOURCES

MAIN IDEAS	📁 PRINT MATERIALS	TECHNOLOGY RESOURCES
Section 1: The Movement Begins 1. African Americans won court victories, increased their voting power, and began using sit-ins to desegregate public places. 2. The *Brown* v. *Board of Education* ruling ignited protest and encouraged African Americans to challenge other forms of segregation. 3. African American churches in the South provided leadership and meeting places for the civil rights movement. 4. President Eisenhower sent the U.S. Army to enforce the authority of the federal government.	• Reproducible Lesson Plan 16-1* • Daily Lecture and Discussion Notes 16-1 • Active Reading Note-Taking Guide 16-1 • Guided Reading Activity 16-1 • Section Quiz 16-1 • Reading Essentials and Study Guide 16-1	✎ Daily Focus Skills Transparency 16-1 ✎ Section Graphic Organizer Transparency 16-1 💿 Interactive Tutor Self-Assessment CD-ROM 💿 Exam*View*® Pro Testmaker CD-ROM 💿 Presentation Plus! CD-ROM ✎ California Standards Practice Transparencies
Section 2: Challenging Segregation 1. Students staged sit-ins at restaurants to end segregation. 2. Students formed the Student Nonviolent Coordinating Committee (SNCC) to organize efforts for desegregation and voter registration throughout the South. 3. Teams of African Americans and whites rode buses into the South to protest the continued, illegal segregation. 4. Reluctant to offend Southern members of Congress and preoccupied with foreign affairs, President Kennedy responded slowly to the growing violence in the South. 5. President Kennedy used the violent events in the South as a platform to announce his civil rights bill. 6. President Johnson called for a new voting rights law after hostile crowds severely beat civil rights demonstrators.	• Reproducible Lesson Plan 16-2* • Daily Lecture and Discussion Notes 16-2 • Active Reading Note-Taking Guide 16-2 • Guided Reading Activity 16-2 • Section Quiz 16-2 • Reading Essentials and Study Guide 16-2	✎ Daily Focus Skills Transparency 16-2 ✎ Section Graphic Organizer Transparency 16-2 💿 Interactive Tutor Self-Assessment CD-ROM 💿 Exam*View*® Pro Testmaker CD-ROM 💿 Presentation Plus! CD-ROM ✎ California Standards Practice Transparencies
Section 3: New Issues 1. The civil rights struggle turned violent in the nation's cities in 1965. 2. Martin Luther King, Jr., began to focus more on economic inequalities in 1965. 3. Impatient with the slower gains of the nonviolent movement, young African Americans called for black power. 4. After Dr. King was assassinated in Memphis, Tennessee, Congress passed the Civil Rights Act of 1968.	• Reproducible Lesson Plan 16-3* • Daily Lecture and Discussion Notes 16-3 • Active Reading Note-Taking Guide 16-3 • Guided Reading Activity 16-3 • Section Quiz 16-3 • Reading Essentials and Study Guide 16-3	✎ Daily Focus Skills Transparency 16-3 ✎ Section Graphic Organizer Transparency 16-3 💿 Interactive Tutor Self-Assessment CD-ROM 💿 Exam*View*® Pro Testmaker CD-ROM 💿 Presentation Plus! CD-ROM ✎ California Standards Practice Transparencies

PACING YOUR LESSONS

Chapter Introduction	Section 1	Section 2	Section 3	Chapter Assessment
½ Day	2 Days	2 Days	2 Days	½ Day

`0:00` OUT OF TIME? 📁 Assign the Chapter 16 *Reading Essentials and Study Guide.*

*Available on TeacherWorks™ CD-ROM

Chapter 16 Planning Guide

Standards-Based Lesson Plan

 History–Social Science Standards Covered in Chapter 16

The standards covered in the chapter are listed below. Use the accompanying activity as you teach the chapter to ensure student mastery of these standards. This activity can be used in combination with the program's print and technology assessment materials.

Standard	Section 1	2	3
11.10.2 Examine and analyze the key events, policies, and court cases in the evolution of civil rights, including *Dred Scott* v. *Sandford, Plessy* v. *Ferguson, Brown* v. *Board of Education, Regents of the University of California* v. *Bakke,* and California Proposition 209.	✔		
11.10.3 Describe the collaboration on legal strategy between African American and white civil rights lawyers to end racial segregation in higher education.	✔		
11.10.4 Examine the roles of civil rights advocates (e.g., A. Philip Randolph, Martin Luther King, Jr., Malcolm X, Thurgood Marshall, James Farmer, Rosa Parks), including the significance of Martin Luther King, Jr.'s "Letter from Birmingham Jail" and "I Have a Dream" speech.	✔	✔	✔
11.10.5 Discuss the diffusion of the civil rights movement of African Americans from the churches of the rural South and the urban North, including the resistance to racial desegregation in Little Rock and Birmingham, and how the advances influenced the agendas, strategies, and effectiveness of the quests of American Indians, Asian Americans, and Hispanic Americans for civil rights and equal opportunities.	✔	✔	
11.10.6 Analyze the passage and effects of civil rights and voting rights legislation (e.g., 1964 Civil Rights Act, Voting Rights Act of 1965) and the Twenty-Fourth Amendment, with an emphasis on equality of access to education and to the political process.	✔	✔	

Cumulative Standards-Assessment Activity

The Cumulative Standards-Assessment Activity will help students organize and learn the important information from the chapter. Begin teaching the chapter with this activity, and have students complete it as they read the chapter.

CREATING A CHART FOR ACTIVATING PRIOR KNOWLEDGE

Purpose By activating prior knowledge, students relate new content to information they already know. This process helps them set a purpose for their reading and exercises their ability to see connections.

Introduction to Activating Prior Knowledge

1. Have students brainstorm facts that they already know about the civil rights movement. Ask students to consider how the information they already know helps them understand the new information.

2. Ask students to copy this chart into their notebooks:

What I Know	What Questions I Have	What I Learned	How I Can Learn More

First, have students scan each section's headings and subheadings and develop a list of topics covered in the chapter. Ask them to create a chart for each of those topics. Before reading each section, they should complete the first two columns of the chart, identifying what they already know and would like to learn. As they read, they can complete the third column.

3. As you review the chapter, ask volunteers to name some of the new information they acquired. Encourage them to list resources in the fourth column of their charts that they might use to do further research on a topic.

Chapter 16 Planning Guide

READING SUPPORT

- Content Vocabulary Activity 16
- Academic Vocabulary Activity 16
- Reading Skills Activity 16
- Chapter 16 Active Reading Note-Taking Guide
- Chapter 16 Guided Reading Activities
- Chapter 16 Reading Essentials and Study Guide
- American Literature Readings, Unit 5
- *The American Vision: Modern Times* Video Program
- Vocabulary PuzzleMaker CD-ROM
- American History Primary Source Document Library CD-ROM

CRITICAL THINKING

- Critical Thinking Skills Activity 16
- Primary Source Reading 16
- Cause-and-Effect Transparency 16 Strategy and Activity
- Presentation Plus! CD-ROM

UNIVERSAL ACCESS

- Universal Access Activity 16
- English Learner Activity 16
- American Art Prints
- StudentWorks™ Plus CD-ROM
- American Music: Hits Through History
- School-to-Home Connection Activity 16

SKILL PRACTICE

- Map Overlay Transparency 16 Strategy and Activity
- Historical Analysis Skills Activity 16
- Time Line Activity 16
- Reading Skills Activity 16
- Reinforcing Skills Activity 16
- Linking Past and Present Activity 16
- Interpreting Political Cartoons 16
- History Simulations and Problem Solving, Unit 5
- MindJogger Videoquiz

WRITING SUPPORT

- Chapter 16 Active Reading Note-Taking Guide
- Writer's Guidebook
- High School Writing Process Transparencies

ASSESSMENT

- Chapter 16 Section Quizzes
- Chapter 16 Tests, Forms A and B
- Authentic Assessment Activity 16
- Exam*View*® Pro Testmaker CD-ROM
- Interactive Tutor Self-Assessment CD-ROM
- California Standards Practice, Grade 11
- Succeeding on . . .™ the California Standards: Grade 11 History–Social Science CD-ROM

CD-ROM		Transparency	
DVD		Music Program	
Print Material		Videocassette	
Poster			

Chapter 16 Planning Guide

TECHNOLOGY

- StudentWorks™ Plus CD-ROM
- TeacherWorks™ CD-ROM
- Exam*View*® Pro Testmaker CD-ROM
- Interactive Tutor Self-Assessment CD-ROM
- Presentation Plus! CD-ROM
- Vocabulary PuzzleMaker CD-ROM
- American History Primary Source Document Library CD-ROM
- MindJogger Videoquiz
- *The American Vision: Modern Times* Video Program
- Professional Development in High School Social Studies Video Series
- Teach, Use, and Succeed With *The American Vision: Modern Times*
- American Music: Hits Through History
- Succeeding on . . .™ the California Standards: Grade 11 History–Social Science CD-ROM

SPANISH RESOURCES

- Spanish Activities and Assessment
  - Spanish Vocabulary Activities
  - Spanish Guided Reading Activities
  - Spanish Quizzes and Tests
  - Spanish Reteaching Activities
- Spanish Reading Essentials and Study Guide
- Spanish School-to-Home Connection Activities

TRANSPARENCIES

- Daily Focus Skills Transparencies
- Section Graphic Organizer Transparencies
- Map Overlay Transparencies
- Cause-and-Effect Transparencies
- Unit Time Line Transparencies
- Why It Matters Transparencies
- American Art and Architecture Transparencies
- High School Writing Process Transparencies
- California Standards Practice Transparencies

TEACHER PLANNING

- Daily Lecture and Discussion Notes
- English Learner Handbook
- Building Academic Vocabulary
- *The American Vision: Modern Times* Reading and Study Skills Foldables
- Reading Strategies and Activities for the Social Studies Classroom
- Universal Access for the American History Classroom
- NGS United States Desk Map
- NGS World Atlas
- Chapter 16 Reproducible Lesson Plans on TeacherWorks™ CD-ROM
- California Guide to Daily Intervention

PROFESSIONAL DEVELOPMENT

- Building Academic Vocabulary
- Strategies for Success
- Research-Based Strategies Used to Develop *The American Vision: Modern Times*
- Character Education in the High School Classroom
- Professional Development in High School Social Studies Video Series
- Teach, Use, and Succeed With *The American Vision: Modern Times*

MOMENTS IN TIME

The following resource can help you teach the content of this chapter.
- Unit 10 The Civil Rights Era (1954–1963)

Chapter 16 Planning Guide

TEACHER'S CORNER

Index to National Geographic Magazine:
The following articles relate to this chapter:

- "I Dream a World: America's Black Women," August 1989
- "National Trail to Recall Civil Rights Marches," March 1994
- "Philadelphia's African Americans," August 1990
- "Selma to Montgomery: The Road to Equality," February 2000

National Geographic Society Products:
To order the following, call National Geographic at 1–800–368–2728

- *Historical Atlas of the United States* (Atlas)
- *NGS Picture Show: Civil Rights* (CD-ROM, Transparencies)

NGS ONLINE

Access National Geographic's new dynamic MapMachine Web site and other geography resources at:

www.nationalgeographic.com

www.nationalgeographic.com/maps

MASTERING THE STANDARDS

The content and assessment in the Student Edition, Teacher Wraparound Edition, teacher planning materials, and the print and technology products are all standards-based. The use of these products during instruction leads to mastery of the standards.

PRACTICE
- California Standards Practice, Grade 11
- California Standards Practice Transparencies
- School-to-Home Connection

BENCHMARK ASSESSMENT
- Section Quizzes, Chapter Tests, and Authentic Assessment
- ExamView® Pro Testmaker CD-ROM
- Succeeding On...™ the California Standards: Grade 11 History–Social Science CD-ROM

REMEDIATION
- California Guide to Daily Intervention
- Interactive Tutor Self-Assessment CD-ROM
- ExamView® Pro Testmaker CD-ROM
- California Standards Practice, Grade 11
- Reading Essentials and Study Guide

History Online

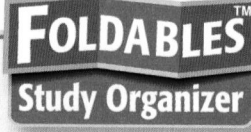

Use our Web site for additional resources. All essential content is covered in the Student Edition.

You and your students can visit tav.mt.glencoe.com, the Web site companion to the **American Vision: Modern Times.** This innovative integration of electronic and print media offers your students a wealth of opportunities. The student text directs students to the Web site for the following options:

- **Chapter Overviews**
- **Self-Check Quizzes**
- **Student Web Activities**
- **Textbook Updates**

Answers to the student Web activities are provided for you in the **Web Activity Lesson Plans.** Additional Web resources and ePuzzles and games are also available.

FOLDABLES™ Study Organizer
Dinah Zike's Foldables

Foldables are three-dimensional, interactive graphic organizers that help students practice basic writing skills, review key vocabulary terms, and identify main ideas. Every chapter has a foldable activity in the *Dinah Zike's Reading and Study Skills Foldables* booklet. You can use the foldables as they are presented or modify them to suit the needs of your individual class.

A variety of videotape programs are available from A&E Television and The History Channel to provide teaching assistance. To order, call Glencoe at 1-800-334-7344.

Chapter 16 Planning Guide

Reading List Generator CD-ROM

GLENCOE BOOKLINK

The Glencoe BookLink CD-ROM is a database that allows you to search more than 15,000 titles to create a customized reading list for your students.

■ Reading Lists can be organized by students' reading level, author, genre, theme, or area of interest.

■ The database provides Degrees of Reading Power™ (DRP) and Lexile™ readability scores for all selections.

■ A brief summary of each selection is included.

Leveled reading suggestions for this chapter:

For students at a Grade 8 reading level:
■ *Mississippi Challenge,* by Mildred Pitts Walter

For students at a Grade 9 reading level:
■ *Thurgood Marshall: Champion of Justice,* by G. S. Prentzas

For students at a Grade 10 reading level:
■ *Why We Can't Wait,* by Martin Luther King, Jr.

READING SUPPORT FROM JAMESTOWN EDUCATION

• *Timed Readings Plus in Social Studies* help students increase their reading rate and fluency while maintaining comprehension. The 400-word passages are similar to those found on state and national assessments.

• *Reading in the Content Area: Social Studies* concentrates on six essential reading skills that help students better comprehend what they read. The book includes 75 high-interest nonfiction passages written at increasing levels of difficulty.

• *Reading Fluency* helps students read smoothly, accurately, and expressively.

• *Jamestown's Reading Improvement,* by renowned reading expert Edward Fry, focuses on helping build your students' comprehension, vocabulary, and skimming and scanning skills.

• *Critical Reading Series* provides high-interest books, each written at three reading levels.

For more information about these products, see the Jamestown Education materials in the Classroom Solutions in the front of this Teacher Wraparound Edition. To order these products, call Glencoe at 1-800-334-7344.

KEY for Using the Teacher Wraparound Edition

Use this key to help you identify the different types of prompts found in the Teacher Wraparound Edition.

R **Reading Strategies** activities help you teach reading skills and vocabulary.

C **Critical Thinking** strategies help students apply and extend what they have learned.

U **Universal Access** activities provide differentiated instruction for students learning to speak English, along with suggestions for teaching various types of learners.

S **Skill Practice** strategies help students practice historical analysis and geography skills.

W **Writing Support** activities provide writing opportunities to help students comprehend the text.

Teaching strategies and activities have been coded for ability level appropriateness.

AL Activities for students working above grade level
OL Activities for students working on grade level
BL Activities for students working below grade level
EL Activities for English learners

FOCUS

History–Social Science Standards

This chapter addresses the following standards:

11.10 Students analyze the development of federal civil rights and voting rights.

11.10.2 Examine and analyze the key events, policies and court cases in the evolution of civil rights, including *Dred Scott* v. *Sandford*, *Plessy* v. *Ferguson*, *Brown* v. *Board of Education*, *Regents of the University of California* v. *Bakke*, and California Proposition 209.

11.10.4 Examine the role of civil rights advocates (e.g., A. Philip Randolph, Martin Luther King, Jr., Malcolm X, Thurgood Marshall, James Farmer, Rosa Parks), including the significance of Martin Luther King, Jr.'s "Letter from Birmingham Jail" and "I Have a Dream" speech.

11.10.6 Analyze the passage and effects of civil rights and voting rights legislation (e.g., 1964 Civil Rights Act, Voting Rights Act of 1965) and the Twenty-Fourth Amendment, with an emphasis on equality of access to education and to the political process.

SKILLBUILDER ACTIVITY

 Ask students what impact they think the civil rights movement had on their communities. Students should evaluate their answers after completing the chapter.

TEACH

Thinking About the Big Ideas

As you begin teaching each section, use these questions and activities to focus on the Big Idea.

CHAPTER 16 *1954–1968*

The Civil Rights Movement

⚜ *The Big Ideas* ⚜

SECTION 1: The Movement Begins

People react to periods of breathtaking social and cultural change in different ways. *After World War II, supporters of civil rights began challenging segregation in the United States.*

SECTION 2: Challenging Segregation

Social and economic crises lead to new roles for government. *African American citizens and white supporters created organizations that directed protests, targeted specific inequalities, and attracted the attention of the mass media and the government.*

SECTION 3: New Issues

People react to periods of breathtaking social and cultural change in different ways. *In the mid-1960s, civil rights leaders began to understand that merely winning political rights for African Americans would not address the economic problems of African Americans.*

The *American Vision: Modern Times* **Video** *The Chapter 16 video, "The Civil Rights Movement," chronicles the milestones of the movement to win rights for African Americans.*

1954
• *Brown* v. *Board of Education* ruling issued by Supreme Court

1955
• Rosa Parks refuses to give up bus seat; Montgomery bus boycott begins in Alabama

1957
• Eisenhower sends troops to a Little Rock, Arkansas, high school to ensure integration

1960
• Sit-in protests begin

United States PRESIDENTS
Eisenhower 1953–1961

Kennedy 1961–1963

1953　　　　　*1957*　　　　　*1961*

World

1955
• West Germany admitted to NATO

1958
• Pasternak's *Dr. Zhivago* awarded Nobel Prize for Literature

1959
• Mary Leakey discovers 1.7 million-year-old hominid skull fragment in Tanzania

1960
• France successfully tests nuclear weapons

736

Section 1
The Movement Begins
Essential Question: What makes someone a hero? *(Students' answers will vary.)* Tell students that in Section 1, they will learn about some African Americans who began to challenge segregation in the United States after World War II, initiating the birth of the modern civil rights movement. `OL`

Section 2
Challenging Segregation
Essential Question: Have you ever been the victim of racism or discrimination? Have students discuss the circumstances under which they found themselves in that situation. Then tell them that in Section 2 they will find out how African Americans and their white supporters organized despite the tremendous problems they faced. `OL`

Americans march from Selma, Alabama, to Montgomery in support of the civil rights movement.

1963
• Over 200,000 civil rights supporters march on Washington, D.C.

Johnson 1963–1969

1965
• Malcolm X assassinated
• Race riots erupt in Los Angeles neighborhood of Watts

I HAVE A DREAM
Dr. Martin Luther King, Jr.

1968
• Civil Rights Act of 1968 passed
• Martin Luther King, Jr., assassinated

1965   *1969*

1963
• Organization of African Unity formed
• Kenya becomes an independent nation

1965
• China's Cultural Revolution begins

1967
• Arab-Israeli War brings many Palestinians under Israeli rule

HISTORY Online

Chapter Overview
Visit the *American Vision: Modern Times* Web site at tav.mt.glencoe.com and click on *Chapter Overviews–Chapter 16* to preview chapter information.

737

Section 3
New Issues
Essential Question: Do individuals still fight for civil rights today? Have students list the areas where they believe more progress needs to be made. As students read Section 3, ask them to think about how civil rights leaders in the mid-1960s began to understand that merely winning political rights for African Americans would not address the problem of African Americans' economic status. **OL**

Cultural Perspectives

The civil rights movement gathered steam during the 1950s, as various individuals and groups organized efforts to obtain equal rights and desegregate society. Activate students' prior knowledge by having them discuss in small groups what they already know about important people, organizations, or legislation from the civil rights era. Then ask students to consider what long-term effect those efforts have had on society. **Ask:** Do discrimination and segregation continue to exist today? What gains toward equality have been achieved? What obstacles remain to be overcome? **OL**

FOLDABLES
Study Organizer

Dinah Zike's Foldables are three-dimensional, interactive graphic organizers that help students practice basic writing skills, review key vocabulary terms, and identify main ideas. Have students complete the foldable activity in the *Dinah Zike's Reading and Study Skills Foldables* booklet.

HISTORY Online

Go to tav.mt.glencoe.com for student activities, lesson plans, and links to additional Web resources to help students learn about the civil rights movement.

Reading Skill

Why It's Important

Determining importance is a reading skill that helps students differentiate between key information and supporting information. Students need to practice this skill in order to help them read their textbook effectively.

1. Introducing the Skill

Select a paragraph from this chapter and tell the class to read it carefully, asking the questions described on this page. Ask each student to write the answers to the following questions in a chart similar to the one below. **OL**

Questions	Evidence
What is the topic sentence?	
What is the paragraph's main idea?	
What are the paragraph's supporting details?	

2. Extending the Skill

Inform students that practicing this skill is the best way to become proficient. Have students select an article from a news magazine, identify the important information, and explain their findings to the class. **OL**

Answers and Additional Support

Reading Skill ▷ **Determining Importance**

When you start reading a textbook, the amount of information in it can seem overwhelming. As a reader, you should learn to recognize what is important in each paragraph, section, and chapter. This allows you to focus your study on key elements of the text.

The chapter and section introductions alert you to the big ideas in the chapter. The headings in the sections can provide clues that point you in the right direction for locating important information. They help you form predictions about the content and identify more specific concepts related to the big ideas. Finally, as you read individual paragraphs, identify the topic sentences and separate these from the interesting, but less important, details. Also, the last sentence in a paragraph can be a summary or list an end result.

Read the following paragraph about the continuing bus boycott in Montgomery, Alabama.

DETERMINING IMPORTANCE

Notice how the author elaborates on the topic sentence with interesting details. These details remind us that history is a story well told.

Stirred by King's powerful words, African Americans in Montgomery continued their boycott of the bus system for over a year. Instead of riding the bus, they organized car pools or walked to work. They refused to be intimidated, yet they remained peaceful and avoided violence. Meanwhile Rosa Parks's legal challenge to bus segregation worked its way through the courts. **Finally, in December 1956, the Supreme Court affirmed the decision of a special three-judge panel declaring Alabama's laws requiring segregation on buses to be unconstitutional.** (page 745)

The chapter introduction on page 736 and the headings in Section 1 help you focus on the main idea in the paragraph, the Montgomery bus boycott and one of its leaders, Martin Luther King, Jr. The highlighted sentences in the paragraph tell you the most important facts about the boycott.

Apply the Skill

Before you read Section 1 of this chapter, note the clues you gather from the chapter and section introductions, the headings, and the highlighted terms. Then, as you read, identify the topic sentences of each paragraph. After you have read the section, write a summary of the section based on the clues and the topic sentences.

738 CHAPTER 16 The Civil Rights Movement

UNIVERSAL ACCESS

English Learners Students who struggle to read a second language have special difficulty identifying the most important details in what they read. Pair English learners with English-speaking students to provide assistance overcoming the language barrier. Having the English speakers work through the reading with other students will help them as well, by forcing them to reevaluate the information from another perspective. **EL**

Historical Analysis Skill Showing Connections

Analysis Skill
Standard H11

Historical Interpretation You will better understand historical events if you learn to show the connections, causal and otherwise, between particular historical events and larger social, economic, and political trends and developments.

Throughout history, major events have had a lasting effect on the social, economic, and political trends of a nation. Older members of your family probably remember the assassinations of John F. Kennedy and Martin Luther King, Jr. You probably remember the terrorist attacks on the World Trade Center in New York City and the Pentagon in Washington, D.C., on September 11, 2001.

When historians study events in history, they consider not only the events themselves, but also the social, economic, and political outcomes of these events. Historians are interested in the connections between such events and the impact they have on society.

Read the following excerpts and assess the impact of the civil rights movement.

African Americans enjoyed increased political power. Before World War I, most African Americans lived in the South, where they were largely excluded from voting. During the Great Migration, many moved to Northern cities, where they were allowed to vote. Increasingly, Northern politicians sought their votes and listened to their concerns. (page 742)

The Brown decision marked a dramatic reversal of the ideas expressed in the *Plessy* v. *Ferguson* case. *Brown* v. *Board of Education* applied only to public schools, but the ruling threatened the entire system of segregation. (page 743)

In the wake of Dr. King's death, Congress passed the Civil Rights Act of 1968. The act contained a fair housing provision outlawing discrimination in housing sales and rentals and gave the Justice Department authority to bring suits against such discrimination. (page 763)

You learn in the first excerpt that African Americans were gaining political power and a political voice. The second excerpt describes how one court case began to shake up the social system of segregation in the South. In the final excerpt you learn about some economic gains African Americans made.

Apply the Skill

Create a chart with the headings "Society," "Economy," and "Politics." As you read this chapter, write down information on the impact of the civil rights movement in each of the areas below the appropriate heading. This information will help you better understand the impact of the civil rights movement on the nation.

Historical Analysis

Why It's Important
Every historian needs to be able to identify and show the connections between events and the society or circumstances that caused the events. Understanding connections helps students see why events happened.

1. Introducing the Skill
Ask students to create time lines, similar to the one below, of important events in their lives. As they construct their time lines, ask them to identify the connections they see between the experiences they list. **BL**

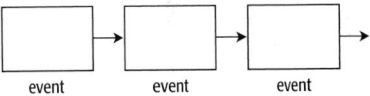

event   event   event

2. Extending the Skill
Divide the class into five groups and provide each group a topic from an earlier chapter they have studied. Instruct the groups to review the textbook and their notes to identify political, social, and/or economic trends that arose because of a connection to the event they are assigned. Ask each group to draw a flowchart demonstrating the connections that they have identified and present their graphic to the rest of the class. **OL** **CA HI1**

UNIVERSAL ACCESS

Kinesthetic If students have trouble identifying the connections between historical events, suggest that they write down significant events on note cards as they read. For each new event listed on a note card, students can experiment with organizing the note cards' placement and location in a pattern that visually depicts connections between events. If students rethink the connections between events, they can move their note cards into a new pattern that shows their new understanding. **OL**

FOCUS

SKILLBUILDER ACTIVITY

 Project **Daily Focus Skills Transparency 16-1** and have students answer the question.

Guide to Reading

Understanding Vocabulary: Have students create databases using the vocabulary words, adding facts as they learn more about each word or term.

Answers to Graphic: segregation, lack of voting rights, African American experiences in World War II

Unpacking the Standards

Students will be able to:

- Discuss the origins of the civil rights movement in the post–World War II years.
- Describe the events that began the civil rights movement.
- Evaluate the important role of African American churches during this time.
- Analyze the role that President Eisenhower played in the civil rights movement.

Answers and Additional Support

SECTION **1** The Movement Begins

Guide to Reading

Connection
In the previous chapter, you learned how the domestic agendas of Presidents Kennedy and Johnson affected the United States. In this section, you will learn about the early years of the civil rights movement.

Main Idea
- African Americans won court victories, increased their voting power, and began using sit-ins to desegregate public places. (p. 741)
- The *Brown* v. *Board of Education* ruling ignited protest and encouraged African Americans to challenge other forms of segregation. (p. 742)

- African American churches in the South provided leadership and meeting places for the civil rights movement. (p. 745)
- President Eisenhower sent the U.S. Army to enforce the authority of the federal government. (p. 746)

Content Vocabulary
separate-but-equal, de facto segregation, sit-in

Academic Vocabulary
inherent, specific, register

People and Terms to Identify
NAACP, Thurgood Marshall, Linda Brown, Martin Luther King, Jr., Southern Christian Leadership Conference

Reading Objectives
- **Explain** the origin of the Southern Christian Leadership Conference.
- **Discuss** the changing role of the federal government in civil rights enforcement.

Reading Strategy
Organizing As you read about the birth of the civil rights movement, complete a graphic organizer similar to the one below by filling in the causes of the civil rights movement.

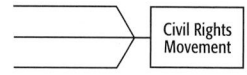
Civil Rights Movement

Preview of Events

1954	1955	1956	1957

1954 — *Brown* v. *Board of Education of Topeka, Kansas,* decision

1955 — Rosa Parks refuses to give up bus seat in Montgomery, Alabama

1956 — Group of 101 Southern members of Congress sign Southern Manifesto

1957 — Southern Christian Leadership Conference formed

The following are the main History–Social Science Standards covered in this section.

11.10.2 Examine and analyze the key events, policies, and court cases in the evolution of civil rights, including *Dred Scott v. Sanford, Plessy v. Ferguson, Brown v. Board of Education, Regents of the University of California v. Bakke,* and California Proposition 209.

11.10.3 Describe the collaboration on legal strategy between African American and white civil rights lawyers to end racial segregation in higher education.

11.10.4 Examine the roles of civil rights advocates (e.g., A. Philip Randolph, Martin Luther King, Jr., Malcolm X, Thurgood Marshall, James Farmer, Rosa Parks), including the significance of Martin Luther King, Jr.'s "Letter from Birmingham Jail" and "I Have a Dream" speech.

11.10.5 Discuss the diffusion of the civil rights movement of African Americans from the churches of the rural South and the urban North, including the resistance to racial desegregation

~ The Big Idea ~

People react to periods of breathtaking social and cultural change in different ways. Over the years, the NAACP had won several court victories against segregation. African Americans also began to gain political power. Realizing their growing political strength, more African Americans began to challenge segregation through court cases and protests. African American churches were instrumental in encouraging the civil rights movement, with ministers taking on leadership roles. While President Eisenhower favored gradual desegregation, he did not support the protests or court challenges, and he sent federal troops to Arkansas to uphold court rulings. The ensuing violence convinced Eisenhower and many members of Congress to pass the Civil Rights Act of 1957.

in Little Rock and Birmingham, and how the advances influenced the agendas, strategies, and effectiveness of the quests of American Indians, Asian Americans, and Hispanic Americans for civil rights and equal opportunities.

11.10.6 Analyze the passage and effects of civil rights and voting rights legislation (e.g., 1964 Civil Rights Act, Voting Rights Act of 1965) and the Twenty-Fourth Amendment, with an emphasis on equality of access to education and to the political process.

SECTION RESOURCES

📁 Print Material
- Reproducible Lesson Plan 16-1
- Guided Reading Activity 16-1
- Reading Essentials and Study Guide 16-1
- Active Reading Note-Taking Guide 16-1

🔖 Transparencies
- Daily Focus Skills Transparency 16-1
- Section Graphic Organizer Transparency 16-1

Technology
- 💿 Interactive Tutor Self-Assessment CD-ROM
- 💿 Exam*View*® Pro Testmaker CD-ROM
- 💿 Presentation Plus! CD-ROM

The Origins of the Movement

 Main Idea African Americans won court victories, increased their voting power, and began using sit-ins to desegregate public places.

Reading Connection Are you registered to vote or do you plan to register when you are 18? Read on to learn how African Americans increased their voting power and worked to desegregate public places.

In 1896, the Supreme Court declared segregation constitutional in the *Plessy* v. *Ferguson* case when it established the **"separate-but-equal"** doctrine. Laws segregating African Americans were permitted as long as equal facilities were provided for them. It was not until 1955 that the first major challenge to this ruling occurred.

★ An American Story ★

On December 1, 1955, Rosa Parks left her job as a seamstress in Montgomery, Alabama, and boarded a bus to go home. In 1955 buses in Montgomery reserved seats in the front for whites and seats in the rear for African Americans. Seats in the middle were open to African Americans, but only if there were few whites on the bus.

Rosa Parks took a seat just behind the white section. Soon all of the seats on the bus were filled. When the bus driver noticed a white man standing at the front of the bus, he told Parks and three other African Americans in her row to get up and let the white man sit down. Nobody moved. The driver cautioned, "You better make it light on yourselves and let me have those seats." The other three African Americans rose, but Rosa Parks did not. The driver then called the Montgomery police, who took Parks into custody.

News of the arrest soon reached E.D. Nixon, a former president of the local chapter of the National Association for the Advancement of Colored People (NAACP). Nixon wanted to challenge bus segregation in court, and he told Parks, "With your permission we can break down segregation on the bus with your case." Parks told Nixon, "If you think it will mean something to Montgomery and do some good, I'll be happy to go along with it."

—adapted from Parting the Waters: America in the King Years

When Rosa Parks agreed to challenge segregation in court, she did not know that her decision would launch the modern civil rights movement. Within days of her arrest, African Americans in Montgomery had organized a boycott of the bus system. Mass protests began across the nation. After decades of segregation and inequality, many African Americans had decided the time had come to demand equal rights. The struggle, however, would not be easy.

In some states, particularly in the South, "Jim Crow" laws segregated buses and trains, schools, restaurants, swimming pools, parks, and other public facilities. Segregation was not confined to states that had passed "Jim Crow" laws. In other states, each community could decide whether to pass segregation laws. Areas without laws requiring segregation often had **de facto segregation**—segregation by custom and tradition. Challenging both laws and tradition would not be easy.

Court Challenges Begin The civil rights movement had been building for a long time. Since 1909, the **National Association for the Advancement of Colored People** (NAACP) had supported court cases intended to overturn segregation. Over the years, the NAACP achieved some victories. In 1935, for example, the Supreme Court ruled in *Norris* v. *Alabama* that Alabama's exclusion of African Americans from juries violated their right to equal protection under the law. In 1946 the Court ruled in *Morgan* v. *Virginia* that segregation on interstate buses was unconstitutional. In 1950 it ruled in *Sweatt* v. *Painter* that state law schools had to admit qualified African American

Rosa Parks ▼

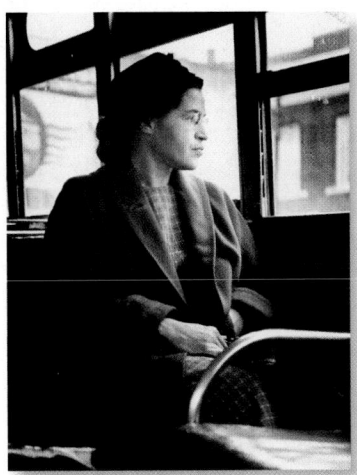

CHAPTER 16   The Civil Rights Movement   **741**

TEACH

W **Writing Support**

Narrative Writing Ask students to play the part of reporter and write brief news articles describing the events that took place the day Rosa Parks refused to give up her seat on an Alabama bus. **OL**
CA 11WA2.1a

R **Reading Strategy**

Using Word Parts Ask students to look up the words *de facto* and *de jure* in the dictionary. *(de facto: existing or being such in actual fact though not by legal establishment, official recognition; de jure: by right or legal establishment)* **Ask:** Compare these formal dictionary definitions with the more narrative-style definitions found in the textbook and discuss which definition works best in conveying the meanings of these words. *(Most students will probably prefer the less formal definition that sets the word meaning in a readable context, but some may understand the more formal definitions better.)* **OL**

More Skill Practice

Expository Writing In 1942, *An American Dilemma,* by author Gunnar Myrdal was published. The Swedish sociologist argued that the American ideas of equality and human rights conflicted with that time period's social belief that African Americans were inferior. Ask students to use library and Internet resources to research *An American Dilemma.* They should write a three-page report judging how this book accurately viewed the coming civil rights movement. **AL** **CA** 11RC2.4; 11WA2.2a; 11WA2.2c

R₁ Reading Strategy

Connecting Have students think about a time when their family or someone they know moved. **Ask: Did the move provide different or better opportunities?** *(Students' answers will vary.)* Have students consider how their answers apply to the movement of African American families during the Great Migration. **OL**

R₂ Reading Strategy

Scaffolding—Questioning Tell students that a *sit-in* is a non-violent protest. **Ask: If you were given the chance to participate in this type of demonstration, would you, and why?** *(Students should provide sound reasons for their answers.)* **OL**

This **Reading Skill** was introduced in Chapter 2.

W Writing Support

Expository Writing To help students identify with Linda Brown, ask them to write paragraphs or journal entries about how it might have felt to attend a school where they were not wanted. **OL**
CA 11WA2.1c

✓ Reading Check

Answer: The ruling said the segregation was constitutional as long as equal facilities were provided for African Americans.

Answers and Additional Support

Student Web Activity Visit the *American Vision: Modern Times* Web site at tav.mt.glencoe.com and click on *Student Web Activities– Chapter 16* for an activity on the civil rights movement.

applicants, even if parallel black law schools existed. 📖 *(See pages 1006–1007 for more information on these cases.)*

New Political Power In addition to a string of court victories, African Americans enjoyed increased political power. Before World War I, most African Americans lived in the South, where they were **R₁** largely excluded from voting. During the Great Migration, many moved to Northern cities, where they were allowed to vote. Increasingly, Northern politicians sought their votes and listened to their concerns.

During the 1930s, many African Americans benefited from FDR's New Deal programs. Thus they began supporting the Democratic Party, giving it new strength in the North. This wing of the party was now able to counter Southern Democrats, who often supported segregation.

The Push for Desegregation During World War II, African American leaders began to use their new political power to demand more rights. Their efforts helped end discrimination in factories that held government contracts and increased opportunities for African Americans in the military.

R₂ In Chicago in 1942, James Farmer and George Houser founded the Congress of Racial Equality (CORE). CORE began using **sit-ins,** a form of protest first used by union workers in the 1930s. In 1943 CORE attempted to desegregate restaurants that refused to serve African Americans. Using the sit-in strategy, members of CORE went to segregated restaurants. If they were denied service, they sat down and refused to leave. The sit-ins were intended to shame restaurant managers into integrating their restaurants. Using these protests, CORE successfully integrated many restaurants, theaters, and other public facilities in Chicago, Detroit, Denver, and Syracuse.

✓ Reading Check **Examining** How had the ruling in *Plessy* v. *Ferguson* contributed to segregation?

The Civil Rights Movement Begins

Main Idea The *Brown v. Board of Education* ruling ignited protest and encouraged African Americans to challenge other forms of segregation.

Reading Connection Do you think that one person has the power to change things for the better? Read on to learn how the courage and hard work of individuals helped reform society.

When World War II ended, many African American soldiers returned home optimistic that their country would appreciate their loyalty and sacrifice. In the 1950s, when change did not come as quickly as hoped, their determination to change prejudices led to protests—and to the emergence of the civil rights movement.

Brown v. Board of Education After World War II, the NAACP continued to challenge segregation with the help of Charles Houston, a law professor and mentor to many African American lawyers.

From 1939 to 1961, the NAACP's chief counsel and director of its Legal Defense and Education Fund was the brilliant African American attorney **Thurgood Marshall.** After World War II, Marshall turned his attention to public schools, seeking out cases that might result in overturning *Plessy* v. *Ferguson.* Marshall worked with local lawyers, both African American and white. He also relied on the advice of many experts, including law professors, lawyers, sociologists, and psychologists.

In 1954 the Supreme Court decided to combine several different cases and issue a general ruling on segregation in schools. One of the cases involved a young African American girl named **Linda Brown,** who was denied admission to her neighborhood school in Topeka, Kansas, because of her race. She was told to attend an all-black school across town. With the help of the NAACP, her parents then sued the Topeka school board.

On May 17, 1954, the Supreme Court ruled unanimously in the case of *Brown v. Board of Education of Topeka, Kansas*, that segregation in public schools was unconstitutional and

W

Separate but Unequal Linda Brown's court case ended decades of official segregation in the South.

Objectives and answers to the student activity can be found in the **Web Activity Lesson Plan** at tav.mt.glencoe.com.

Resources for page 742

Have students read more about the social discrimination faced by African Americans in the South by assigning "Down at the Cross—Letter From a Region in My Mind" in the **American Literature Readings 5.**

NATIONAL GEOGRAPHIC
MOMENT in HISTORY

AMERICAN SEGREGATION

In an Oklahoma City streetcar station in 1939, a man takes a drink from a water cooler labeled "COLORED." Racially segregated facilities—waiting rooms, railroad cars, lavatories, and drinking fountains—were prevalent all across the South. Under the so-called Jim Crow system, African Americans were legally entitled to "separate-but-equal" education, housing, and social services. In practice, however, only a small percentage of public funds earmarked for schools, streets, police, and other expenses found its way to African American neighborhoods.

R₁ Reading Strategy

Activating Prior Knowledge
Ask students to name other times in U.S. history in which Southerners protested a rule with a written document. *(Answers may include The South Carolina Exposition and Protest.)* **AL**

Review the Big Idea

Review the Big Idea for this section, "People react to periods of breathtaking social and cultural change in different ways." Remind students that many people in the South reacted strongly to the *Brown* decision. **Ask: Why do you think so many Southerners opposed the Supreme Court decision?** Use the question as a basis for a class discussion on desegregation in the South. Also have students discuss what may have happened if Southerners had been more supportive of the ruling. **AL** **CA HI3; HI4**

R₂ Reading Strategy

Scaffolding—Academic Vocabulary The word *reaction* was introduced in Chapter 9, Section 1. Ask a student to define the word. **BL**

violated the equal protection clause of the Fourteenth Amendment. Chief Justice Earl Warren summed up the Court's decision when he wrote: "In the field of public education, the doctrine of separate but equal has no place. Separate educational facilities are **inherently** unequal."

The Southern Manifesto The Brown decision marked a dramatic reversal of the ideas expressed in the *Plessy* v. *Ferguson* case. *Brown* v. *Board of Education* applied only to public schools, but the ruling threatened the entire system of segregation. Although it convinced many African Americans that the time had come to challenge other forms of segregation, it also angered many white Southerners, who became even more determined to defend segregation.

Although some school districts in border states integrated their schools in compliance with the Court's ruling, anger and opposition were far more common reactions. In Washington, D.C., Senator Harry F. Byrd of Virginia called on Southerners to adopt "massive resistance" against the ruling. Across

the South, hundreds of thousands of white Americans joined citizens' councils to pressure their local governments and school boards into defying the Supreme Court. Many states adopted pupil assignment laws that created requirements other than race that schools could use to prevent African Americans from attending white schools.

The Supreme Court inadvertently encouraged white resistance when it followed up its decision in *Brown* v. *Board* a year later. The Court ordered school districts to proceed "with all deliberate speed" to end school segregation. The wording was vague enough that many districts were able to keep their schools segregated for many more years.

Massive resistance also appeared in the halls of Congress. In 1956 a group of 101 Southern members of Congress signed the Southern Manifesto, which denounced the Supreme Court's ruling as "a clear abuse of judicial power" and pledged to use "all lawful means" to reverse the decision. Although the Southern Manifesto had no legal standing, it encouraged white Southerners to defy the Supreme Court.

CHAPTER 16   The Civil Rights Movement   **743**

 Resources for page 743

*Students can learn more about school desegregation by reading **Moments in Time, Unit 10: The Civil Rights Era (1954–1963).***

 NATIONAL GEOGRAPHIC **MOMENT in HISTORY**

Ask: How did the disparity between white and "colored" facilities indicate that America had not changed its views on race? *(It showed that African Americans were still being treated as second-class citizens.)*

743

The Montgomery Bus Boycott In the midst of the uproar over the *Brown v. Board of Education* case, Rosa Parks made her decision to challenge segregation of public transportation. Outraged by Parks's arrest, Jo Ann Robinson, head of a local organization called the Women's Political Council, called on African Americans to boycott Montgomery's buses on the day Rosa Parks appeared in court.

The boycott was a dramatic success. That afternoon, several African American leaders formed the Montgomery Improvement Association to run the boycott and to negotiate with city leaders for an end to segregation. They elected a 26-year-old pastor named **Martin Luther King, Jr.,** to lead them.

On the evening of December 5, 1955, a meeting was held at Dexter Avenue Baptist Church, where Dr. King was pastor. In the deep, resonant tones and powerful phrases that characterized his speaking style, King encouraged the people to continue their protest. "There comes a time, my friends," he said, "when people get tired of being thrown into the abyss of humiliation, where they experience the bleakness of nagging despair." He explained, however, that the protest had to be peaceful:

> **❝**Now let us say that we are not advocating violence. . . . The only weapon we have in our hands this evening is the weapon of protest. If we were incarcerated behind the iron curtains of a communistic nation—we couldn't do this. If we were trapped in the dungeon of a totalitarian regime—we couldn't do this. But the great glory of American democracy is the right to protest for right!**❞**
>
> —quoted in *Parting the Waters: America in the King Years*

King had earned a Ph.D. in theology from Boston University. He believed that the only moral way to end segregation and racism was through nonviolent passive resistance. He told his followers, "We must use the weapon of love. We must realize that so many people are taught to hate us that they are not totally

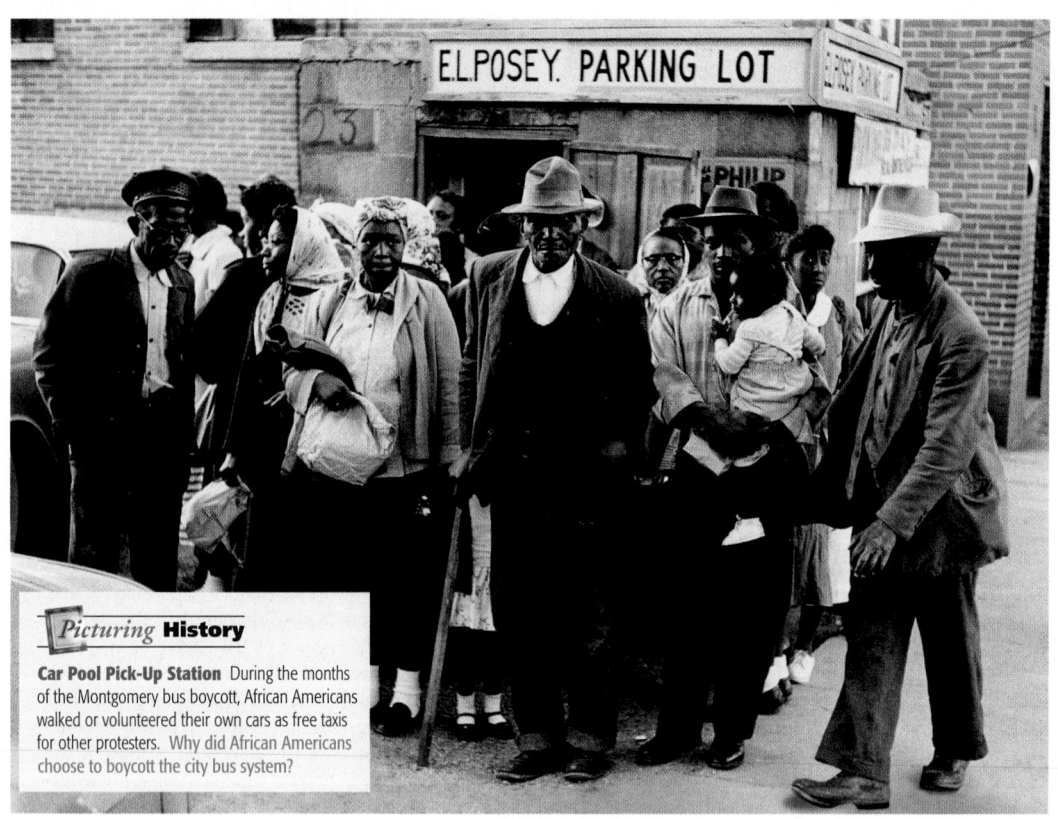

Picturing **History**

Car Pool Pick-Up Station During the months of the Montgomery bus boycott, African Americans walked or volunteered their own cars as free taxis for other protesters. Why did African Americans choose to boycott the city bus system?

Picturing **History**

Answer: They were protesting Rosa Parks's arrest and segregation.
Ask: How much of a sacrifice do you think African Americans made by boycotting public buses? *(Students' answers will vary. Students should recognize that buses were the only means of transportation that many African Americans could afford.)*

Profiles IN HISTORY

Thurgood Marshall
1908–1993

Over his long lifetime, Thurgood Marshall made many contributions to the civil rights movement. Perhaps his most famous accomplishment was representing the NAACP in the *Brown* v. *Board of Education* case.

Marshall's speaking style was both simple and direct. During the *Brown* case, Justice Frankfurter asked Marshall for a definition of equal. "Equal means getting the same thing, at the same time and in the same place," Marshall answered.

Born into a middle-class Baltimore family in 1908, Marshall earned a law degree from Howard University Law

School. The school's dean, Charles Hamilton Houston, enlisted Marshall to work for the NAACP. Together the two laid out the legal strategy for challenging discrimination in many arenas of American life.

Marshall became the first African American on the Supreme Court when President Lyndon Johnson appointed him in 1967. On the Court, he remained a voice for civil rights. In his view, the Constitution was not perfect because it had accepted slavery. Its ideas of liberty, justice, and equality had to be refined. "The true miracle of the Constitution," he once wrote, "was not the birth of the Constitution, but its life."

responsible for their hate." African Americans, he urged, must say to racists and segregationists: "We will soon wear you down by our capacity to suffer, and in winning our freedom we will so appeal to your heart and conscience that we will win you in the process."

King drew upon the philosophy and techniques of Indian leader Mohandas Gandhi, who had used non-violent resistance effectively against British rule in India. Like Gandhi, King encouraged his followers to disobey unjust laws. Believing in people's ability to transform themselves, King was certain that public opinion would eventually force the government to end segregation.

Stirred by King's powerful words, African Americans in Montgomery continued their boycott of the bus system for over a year. Instead of riding the bus, they organized car pools or walked to work. They refused to be intimidated, yet they remained peaceful and avoided violence. Meanwhile Rosa Parks's legal challenge to bus segregation worked its way through the courts. Finally, in December 1956, the Supreme Court affirmed the decision of a special three-judge panel declaring Alabama's laws requiring segregation on buses to be unconstitutional.

✓ **Reading Check** **Describing** What was the ruling in *Brown* v. *Board of Education*?

African American Churches

Main Idea African American churches in the South provided leadership and meeting places for the civil rights movement.

Reading Connection Can you name any organizations that help with social issues? Read on to discover the political impact of African American churches and their ministers in the civil rights movement.

Martin Luther King, Jr., was not the only prominent minister involved in the bus boycott. Many of the other leaders were African American ministers. The boycott could not have succeeded without the support of the African American churches and ministers in the city. As the civil rights movement gained momentum, African American churches continued to play a critical role. They served as forums for many of the protests and planning meetings, and they also mobilized many of the volunteers for **specific** civil rights campaigns.

After the Montgomery bus boycott demonstrated that nonviolent protest could be successful, African American ministers led by King established the **Southern Christian Leadership Conference** (SCLC) in 1957. The SCLC set out to eliminate segregation from American society and to encourage African

CHAPTER 16 The Civil Rights Movement **745**

R Reading Strategy

Skimming Ask students to skim the text to find information on President Eisenhower's personal beliefs and his public stance on segregation. *(Personally he felt segregation and racism would change as U.S. values would change. Publicly he upheld the federal court's decisions to desegregate.)* **OL**
CA 11RC2.4; 11RC2.5

W Writing Support

Narrative Writing Tell students to imagine that they are newspaper reporters assigned to cover the day that the nine African American students integrated Central High School in Little Rock, Arkansas. Ask them to write news articles describing the scene on that day, making sure to use descriptive language to illustrate the actions and emotions of the students, protesters, and any other people involved in the event. **OL**
CA 11WA2.1b; 11WA2.1c; 11WA2.4c

✓ Reading Check

Answer: They supported boycotts, nonviolent demonstrations, and voter registration.

Answers and Additional Support

Americans to **register** to vote. Dr. King served as the SCLC's first president. Under his leadership, the organization challenged segregation at the voting booths and in public transportation, housing, and public accommodations.

✓ Reading Check **Summarizing** What role did African American churches play in the civil rights movement?

Eisenhower and Civil Rights

Main Idea President Eisenhower sent the U.S. Army to enforce the authority of the federal government.

Reading Connection Do you believe the president has the responsibility to uphold the rulings of the Supreme Court? Read on to learn what President Eisenhower did when events in Little Rock, Arkansas, challenged the federal government.

President Eisenhower sympathized with the goals of the civil rights movement, and he personally disagreed with segregation. Following the precedent set by President Truman, he ordered navy shipyards and veterans' hospitals to be desegregated.

At the same time, however, Eisenhower disagreed with those who wanted to roll back segregation through protests and court rulings. He believed that people had to allow segregation and racism to end gradually as values changed. With the nation in the midst of the Cold War, he worried that challenging

white Southerners on segregation might divide the nation and lead to violence at a time when the country had to pull together. Publicly, he refused to endorse the *Brown* v. *Board of Education* decision. Privately, he remarked, "I don't believe you can change the hearts of men with laws or decisions."

Despite his belief that the *Brown* v. *Board of Education* decision was wrong, Eisenhower felt he had to uphold the authority of the federal government, including its court system. As a result, he became the first president since Reconstruction to send federal troops into the South to protect the constitutional rights of African Americans.

Crisis in Little Rock In September 1957, the school board in Little Rock, Arkansas, won a court order to admit nine African American students to Central High, a school with 2,000 white students. Little Rock was a racially moderate Southern city, as was most of the state of Arkansas. A number of Arkansas communities, as well as the state university, had already begun to desegregate their schools.

The governor of Arkansas, Orval Faubus, was believed to be a moderate on racial issues, unlike many other Southern politicians. Faubus was determined to win reelection, however, and so he began to campaign as a defender of white supremacy. He ordered troops from the Arkansas National Guard to prevent the nine African American students from entering the school. The next day, as National Guard troops surrounded the school, an angry white mob

Picturing **History**

Crisis in Little Rock Fifteen-year-old Elizabeth Eckford (in sunglasses at right) braves an angry crowd of Central High School students in Arkansas. How did Governor Orval Faubus react to attempts to integrate the high school?

Picturing **History**

Answer: He ordered National Guard troops to prevent the African American students from entering the school.
Ask: How do you think Elizabeth Eckford felt on the day this picture was taken? *(Students' answers will vary. Students might indicate that she was frightened, lonely, sad, or angry.)*

Did You Know?

In 1947 Jackie Robinson integrated major-league baseball. African American prizefighters and jockeys had been successful even before 1904 when Charles W. Follis became the first African American professional football player. It was not until 1950 that the NBA Boston Celtics signed its first African American basketball player, Charles Cooper.

joined the troops to protest the integration plan and to intimidate the African American students trying to register.

Television coverage of this episode placed Little Rock at the center of national attention. Faubus had used the armed forces of a state to oppose the authority of the federal government—the first such challenge to the Constitution since the Civil War. Eisenhower knew that he could not allow Faubus to defy the federal government. After a conference between Eisenhower and Faubus proved fruitless, the district court ordered the governor to remove the troops. Instead of ending the crisis, however, Faubus simply left the school to the mob. After the African American students entered the school, angry whites beat at least two African American reporters and broke many of the school's windows. The mob came so close to capturing the terrified African American students that the police had to take them to safety.

The mob violence finally pushed President Eisenhower's patience to the breaking point. Federal authority had to be upheld. He immediately ordered the U.S. Army to send troops to Little Rock. By nightfall 1,000 soldiers of the elite 101st Airborne Division had arrived. By 5:00 A.M. the troops had encircled the school, bayonets ready. A few hours later, the nine African American students arrived in an army station wagon, and they walked into the high school. The law had been upheld, but the troops were forced to remain in Little Rock for the rest of the school year.

New Civil Rights Legislation The same year that the Little Rock crisis began, Congress passed the first civil rights law since Reconstruction. The Civil Rights

Act of 1957 was intended to protect the right of African Americans to vote. Eisenhower believed firmly in the right to vote, and he viewed it as his responsibility to protect voting rights. He also knew that if he sent a civil rights bill to Congress, conservative Southern Democrats would try to block the legislation. In 1956 he did send the bill to Congress, hoping not only to split the Democratic Party but also to convince more African Americans to vote Republican.

As Eisenhower had expected, several Southern senators did try to stop the Civil Rights Act of 1957. Despite these difficulties, the Senate majority leader, Democrat Lyndon Johnson, put together a compromise that enabled the act to pass. Although its final form was much weaker than originally intended, the act still brought the power of the federal government into the civil rights debate. The act created a civil rights division within the Department of Justice and gave it the authority to seek court injunctions against anyone interfering with the right to vote. It also created the United States Commission on Civil Rights to investigate allegations of denial of voting rights. After the bill passed, the SCLC announced a campaign to register 2 million new African American voters.

Reading Check **Explaining** Why did President Eisenhower intervene in the civil rights controversy?

HISTORY Online — Study Central

For help with the concepts in this section of *American Vision: Modern Times* go to tav.mt.glencoe.com and click on *Study Central.*

SECTION 1 ASSESSMENT

Checking for Understanding

1. **Vocabulary** Define: separate-but-equal, de facto segregation, sit-in, inherent, specific, register.
2. **People and Terms** Identify: NAACP, Thurgood Marshall, Linda Brown, Martin Luther King, Jr., Southern Christian Leadership Conference.
3. **State** the outcome of the *Brown* v. *Board of Education* case.

Reviewing Big Ideas

4. **Explaining** Why did the role of the federal government in civil rights enforcement change?

Critical Thinking

5. **Interpreting** Do you think the civil rights movement would have been successful in gaining civil rights for African Americans without the help of the NAACP and the SCLC? Explain.
6. **Organizing** Use a graphic organizer similar to the one below to list the efforts made to end segregation.

Efforts to End Segregation

Analyzing Visuals

7. **Examining Photographs** Study the photograph of Central High School students on page 746. How would you describe Elizabeth Eckford's demeanor compared to those around her? What might this tell you about her character?

Writing About History

8. **Expository Writing** Take on the role of an African American soldier returning to the United States after fighting in World War II. Write a letter to the editor of your local newspaper describing your expectations of civil rights as an American citizen. **CA** 11WA2.3a

CHAPTER 16 The Civil Rights Movement **747**

SECTION 1 ASSESSMENT ANSWERS

1. Content vocabulary is boldfaced and highlighted in yellow. Academic vocabulary is boldfaced.
2. NAACP *(p. 741)*, Thurgood Marshall *(p. 742)*, Linda Brown *(p. 742)*, Martin Luther King, Jr. *(p. 744)*, Southern Christian Leadership Conference *(p. 745)*
3. Segregation in public schools is

unconstitutional.
4. because its authority and decisions were challenged by individual states
5. Students should recognize that the NAACP and SCLC provided financial support, leadership, and organization to the civil rights movement.

6. founding of CORE, NAACP court challenges, bus boycott, voter registration movement
7. Students' answers will vary but should recognize her courage.
8. Letters should include specific expectations.

FOCUS

BELLRINGER
SKILLBUILDER ACTIVITY

Project **Daily Focus Skills Transparency 16-2** and have students answer the question.

Guide to Reading

Understanding Vocabulary: Have students look up the words *filibuster* and *cloture* in the glossary. Then have them write the definitions in their own words.

Answers to Graphic:
Cause: sit-in movement, *Effect:* brought attention to the civil rights movement; *Cause:* Freedom Riders, *Effect:* Kennedy's decision to control violence; *Cause:* King's release from jail, *Effect:* African American support for Kennedy; *Cause:* Selma march, *Effect:* African American voter registration

Unpacking the Standards

Students will be able to:

- Describe the tactics and efforts used during the sit-in movement.

- Analyze the leadership provided by the Student Nonviolent Coordinating Committee.

- Discuss the efforts of the Freedom Riders.

- Explain John F. Kennedy's civil rights efforts.

- Evaluate the importance of the Civil Rights Act of 1964.

- Describe the efforts to secure African American voting rights.

SECTION 2 Challenging Segregation

Guide to Reading

Connection
In the previous section, you learned about the beginnings of the civil rights movement. In this section, you will discover how African American students and white supporters joined the movement to protest civil inequalities.

Main Idea
- Students staged sit-ins at restaurants to end segregation. (p. 749)
- Students formed the Student Nonviolent Coordinating Committee (SNCC) to organize efforts for desegregation and voter registration throughout the South. (p. 750)
- Teams of African Americans and whites rode buses into the South to protest the continued, illegal segregation. (p. 750)

- Reluctant to offend Southern members of Congress and preoccupied with foreign affairs, President Kennedy responded slowly to the growing violence in the South. (p. 751)
- President Kennedy used the violent events in the South as a platform to announce his civil rights bill. (p. 753)
- President Johnson called for a new voting rights law after hostile crowds severely beat civil rights demonstrators. (p. 755)

Content Vocabulary
Freedom Riders, filibuster, cloture, poll tax

Academic Vocabulary
legality, attain, comprehensive

People and Terms to Identify
Jesse Jackson, Ella Baker, Civil Rights Act of 1964

Reading Objectives
- **Evaluate** the Civil Rights Act of 1964.
- **Summarize** the efforts to establish voting rights for African Americans.

Reading Strategy
Organizing As you read about challenges to segregation in the South, complete a cause-and-effect chart like the one below.

Cause	Effect
Sit-In Movement	
Freedom Riders	
	African American support of Kennedy
	African American voter registration

Preview of Events

1960	1962	1964	1966

May 1961
Freedom Riders attempt to desegregate interstate buses in the South

Spring 1963
Martin Luther King, Jr., jailed in Birmingham

August 28, 1963
March on Washington

July 1964
President Johnson signs Civil Rights Act of 1964

1965
Voting Rights Act passed

The following are the main History–Social Science Standards covered in this section.

11.10.4 Examine the roles of civil rights advocates (e.g., A. Philip Randolph, Martin Luther King, Jr., Malcolm X, Thurgood Marshall, James Farmer, Rosa Parks), including the significance of Martin Luther King, Jr.'s "Letter from Birmingham Jail" and "I Have a Dream" speech.

11.10.5 Discuss the diffusion of the civil rights movement of African Americans from the churches of the rural South and the urban North, including the resistance to racial desegregation in Little Rock and Birmingham, and how the advances influenced the agendas, strategies, and effectiveness of the quests of American Indians, Asian Americans, and Hispanic Americans for civil rights and equal opportunities.

11.10.6 Analyze the passage and effects of civil rights and voting rights legislation (e.g., 1964 Civil Rights Act, Voting Rights Act of 1965) and the

Twenty-Fourth Amendment, with an emphasis on equality of access to education and to the political process.

11.11.2 Discuss the significant domestic policy speeches of Truman, Eisenhower, Kennedy, Johnson, Nixon, Carter, Reagan, Bush, and Clinton (e.g., with regard to education, civil rights, economic policy, environmental policy).

◈ The Big Idea ◈

Social and economic crises lead to new roles for government. Students staged sit-ins and joined organizations as a way to peacefully protest segregation. These groups often faced violence from angry mobs. Many Americans were shocked by the violence they saw on television as peaceful protestors were attacked. President Kennedy at first was slow to respond to the violence, but he later took legal action and sent federal troops to enforce desegregation rulings. After violence in Birmingham, Alabama, continued to escalate, Kennedy began to push for a civil rights bill. After Kennedy's assassination, Congress passed the Civil Rights Act of 1964. African Americans, however, continued to face violence and struggled to vote.

SECTION RESOURCES

📁 Print Material
- Reproducible Lesson Plan 16-2
- Guided Reading Activity 16-2
- Reading Essentials and Study Guide 16-2
- Active Reading Note-Taking Guide 16-2

Transparencies
- Daily Focus Skills Transparency 16-2
- Section Graphic Organizer Transparency 16-2

Technology
- Interactive Tutor Self-Assessment CD-ROM
- ExamView® Pro Testmaker CD-ROM
- Presentation Plus! CD-ROM

The Sit-In Movement

Main Idea Students staged sit-ins at restaurants to end segregation.

Reading Connection Would you risk your personal safety to participate in a sit-in? Read on to learn of the response of young people to the sit-in movement of the early 1960s.

A new mass movement for civil rights began in North Carolina with just four students. Disgusted with segregation and discrimination against African Americans, the four students decided to take action in a new way. Called a sit-in, this type of protest soon spread to more than 100 cities.

★ An American Story ★

The sit-in movement began in Greensboro, North Carolina. There, in the fall of 1959, four young African Americans—Joseph McNeil, Ezell Blair, Jr., David Richmond, and Franklin McCain—enrolled at North Carolina Agricultural and Technical College in Greensboro. The four freshmen became close friends and spent evenings talking about the civil rights movement. In January 1960, McNeil told his friends that he thought the time had come to take action, and he suggested a sit-in at the whites-only lunch counter in the nearby Woolworth's department store.

"All of us were afraid," Richmond later recalled, "but we went and did it." On February 1, 1960, the four friends entered the Woolworth's. They purchased school supplies and then sat at the lunch counter and ordered coffee. When they were refused service, Blair said, "I beg your pardon, but you just served us at [the checkout] counter. Why can't we be served at the counter here?" The students stayed at the counter until it closed, then announced that they would sit at the counter every day until they were given the same service as white customers.

As they left the store, the four were excited. McNeil recalled, "I just felt I had powers within me, a superhuman strength that would come forward." McCain was also energized, saying, "I probably felt better that day than I've ever felt in my life."

—adapted from *Civilities and Civil Rights*

News of the daring sit-in at the Woolworth's store spread quickly across Greensboro, North Carolina.

The following day, 29 African American students arrived at Woolworth's determined to sit at the counter until they were served. By the end of the week, over 300 students were taking part.

The sit-in movement brought large numbers of idealistic and energized college students into the civil rights struggle. Many African American students had become discouraged by the slow pace of desegregation. Students like **Jesse Jackson**, a student leader at North Carolina Agricultural and Technical College, wanted to see things change. The sit-in offered them a way to take matters into their own hands in a peaceful but powerful way.

At first, the leaders of the NAACP and the SCLC were nervous about the sit-in movement. They feared that students did not have the discipline to remain nonviolent if they were provoked enough. For the most part, the students proved them wrong. Those conducting sit-ins were heckled by bystanders, punched, kicked, beaten with clubs, and burned with cigarettes, hot coffee, and acid—but most did not fight back. They remained peaceful, and their heroic behavior, contrasted with the violence and anger they faced, grabbed the nation's attention.

Reading Check **Examining** What were the effects of the sit-in movement?

Picturing **History**

Sit-Ins Fight Segregation African American students challenged Southern segregation laws by demanding equal service at lunch counters. How did the NAACP initially feel about the sit-in movement?

U Universal Access

Auditory/Musical Have students work in pairs to write song lyrics to be performed at a civil rights protest event. The lyrics should be based on the events mentioned in this section. Recommend that students research some of the traditional songs used during the era for examples and style. Encourage them to set the lyrics to music. Invite volunteers to perform their songs for the class. **OL**

R Reading Strategy

Using Maps, Graphs, and Charts Have students create a chart similar to the one shown below to illustrate the activities of the persons mentioned in this section. **OL**

Working for Civil Rights	
Name	Involvement
Working to Maintain Segregation	
Name	Involvement

Reading Check

Answer: It got the nation's attention and gave people a way to get involved in the civil rights movement.

Did You Know?

In 1984 and 1988 Jesse Jackson made runs for the Democratic Party's presidential nomination. Although he failed both times, in 1988 Jackson won six state primaries in the South as well as the Michigan caucus.

Picturing **History**

Answer: NAACP leaders were nervous because they feared students may become violent if provoked.
Ask: How did young people staging sit-ins generally behave? *(They were nonviolent.)*

Universal Access

Below Grade Level Have students create brochures encouraging people to register to vote. Remind students that their brochures should reference some of the dangers that African Americans faced when attempting to register. **BL**

Skill Practice

Conducting Research Organize the class into two groups to research the ease or difficulty of registering to vote in the 1960s versus today. One group can research the registration procedures used before 1965. The other group should focus on registering and voting today. Students can study either their own community and state or choose another state. Have students make displays showing the process, including options such as registering in person, by mail, or online. **OL** **CA CS1; HI1**

Reading Check

Answer: She urged students to create SNCC.

Answers and Additional Support

SNCC

Main Idea Students formed the Student Nonviolent Coordinating Committee (SNCC) to organize efforts for desegregation and voter registration throughout the South.

Reading Connection What organizations for young people exist in your school or community? Read on to learn about a unique group of young Americans.

As the sit-ins spread, student leaders in different states realized that they needed to coordinate their efforts. The person who brought them together was **Ella Baker,** the 55-year-old executive director of the SCLC. In April 1960, Baker invited student leaders to attend a convention at Shaw University in Raleigh, North Carolina. At the convention, Baker urged students to create their own organization instead of joining the NAACP or the SCLC. Students, she said, had "the right to direct their own affairs and even make their own mistakes."

The students agreed with Baker and established the Student Nonviolent Coordinating Committee (SNCC). Among SNCC's early leaders were Marion Barry, who later served as mayor of Washington, D.C., and John Lewis, who later became a member of Congress. African American college students from all across the South made up the majority of SNCC's members, although many whites also joined.

▼ *SNCC and CORE members protest peacefully before the opening of the Democratic Convention.*

750 CHAPTER 16 The Civil Rights Movement

Between 1960 and 1965, SNCC played a key role in desegregating public facilities in dozens of Southern communities. SNCC also began sending volunteers into rural areas of the Deep South to register African Americans to vote. The idea for what came to be called the Voter Education Project began with Robert Moses, an SNCC volunteer from New York. Moses pointed out that the civil rights movement tended to focus on urban areas. He urged SNCC to fill in the gap by helping rural African Americans. Moses himself went to rural Mississippi, where African Americans who tried to register to vote frequently met with violence.

Despite the danger, many SNCC volunteers headed to Mississippi and other parts of the Deep South. Several had their lives threatened, and others were beaten. In 1964 local officials in Mississippi brutally murdered three SNCC workers.

One SNCC organizer, a former sharecropper named Fannie Lou Hamer, had been evicted from her farm after registering to vote. She was then arrested in Mississippi for urging other African Americans to register, and she was severely beaten by the police while in jail. She then helped organize the Mississippi Freedom Democratic Party, and she challenged the **legality** of the segregated Democratic Party at the 1964 Democratic National Convention.

✓ **Reading Check** **Explaining** What role did Ella Baker play in forming SNCC?

The Freedom Riders

Main Idea Teams of African Americans and whites rode buses into the South to protest the continued, illegal segregation.

Reading Connection Would you become active for something you believe is right? Read on to learn how attempts to integrate bus travel in the South were received.

Despite rulings that outlawed segregation in interstate bus service, bus travel remained segregated in much of the South. In 1961 CORE leader James Farmer asked teams of African Americans and whites to travel into the South to draw attention to the South's refusal to integrate bus terminals. The teams became known as the **Freedom Riders.**

In early May 1961, the first Freedom Riders boarded several southbound interstate buses. When the buses carrying them arrived in Anniston, Birmingham, and Montgomery, Alabama, angry white mobs attacked them. The mobs slit the bus tires and

More Skill Practice

Research Report Writing Using library and Internet resources, have students research one of the following organizations: SNCC, CORE, NAACP, or SCLC. Ask students to write two-page reports describing the organization's leaders, actions, and contributions to the civil rights movement. **OL** **CA HI1** **CA 11WA2.4**

threw rocks at the windows. In Anniston, someone threw a firebomb into one bus, although fortunately no one was killed.

In Birmingham the riders emerged from a bus to face a gang of young men armed with baseball bats, chains, and lead pipes. They beat the riders viciously. One witness later reported, "You couldn't see their faces through the blood." The head of the police in Birmingham, Theophilus Eugene ("Bull") Connor, explained that there had been no police at the bus station because it was Mother's Day, and he had given many of his officers the day off. FBI evidence later showed that Connor had contacted the local Ku Klux Klan and told them he wanted the Freedom Riders beaten until "it looked like a bulldog got a hold of them."

The violence in Alabama made national news, shocking many Americans. The attack on the Freedom Riders came less than four months after President John F. Kennedy took office. The new president felt compelled to do something to get the violence under control.

Picturing **History**

Riding Into Danger On May 14, 1961, Freedom Riders were driven from their bus outside of Anniston, Alabama, when angry townspeople set the bus on fire. Which civil rights protest organization coordinated the Freedom Riders?

✓ **Reading Check** **Summarizing** What was the goal of the Freedom Riders?

John F. Kennedy and Civil Rights

Main Idea Reluctant to offend Southern members of Congress and preoccupied with foreign affairs, President Kennedy responded slowly to the growing violence in the South.

Reading Connection Have you ever witnessed a nonviolent protest, either in person or on television? Read on to discover what happened to nonviolent protesters in Alabama.

While campaigning for the presidency in 1960, John F. Kennedy promised to actively support the civil rights movement if elected. His brother, Robert F. Kennedy, had used his influence to get Dr. King released from jail after a demonstration in Georgia.

African Americans responded by voting overwhelmingly for Kennedy. Their votes helped him narrowly win several key states, including Illinois, which Kennedy won by less than 9,000 votes. Once in office, however, Kennedy at first seemed as cautious as Eisenhower on civil rights, which disappointed many African Americans. Kennedy knew

that he needed the support of many Southern senators to get other programs he wanted through Congress, and that any attempt to push through new civil rights legislation would anger them.

Kennedy did, however, name approximately 40 African Americans to high-level positions in the federal government. He also appointed Thurgood Marshall to a judgeship on the Second Circuit Appeals Court in New York—one level below the Supreme Court and the highest judicial position an African American had **attained** to that point. Kennedy also created the Committee on Equal Employment Opportunity (CEEO) to stop the federal bureaucracy from discriminating against African Americans when hiring and promoting people.

The Justice Department Takes Action Although President Kennedy was unwilling to challenge Southern Democrats in Congress, he allowed the Justice Department, run by his brother Robert, to actively support the civil rights movement. Robert Kennedy tried to help African Americans register to vote by having the civil rights division of the Justice Department file lawsuits throughout the South.

When violence erupted against the Freedom Riders, the Kennedys came to their aid as well, although not at first. At the time the Freedom Riders took action, President Kennedy was preparing for a meeting with Nikita Khrushchev, the leader of the Soviet Union. Kennedy did not want violence in the South to disrupt the meeting by giving the impression that his country was weak and divided.

CHAPTER 16 The Civil Rights Movement **751**

S **Skill Practice**

Scaffolding—Visualizing Presidential aide John Siegenthaler was a witness at the bus terminal. Read his account to the class: "The Freedom Riders emerging from the bus were being mauled. It looked like two hundred, three hundred people all over them. There were screams and shouts. . . ." Ask students to close their eyes and imagine this scene. Then students should write or draw what they see and justify how the text supports their image. **OL** **CA HI3** **CA 11RC2.4**

This **Reading Skill** was introduced in Chapter 9.

R **Reading Strategy**

Activating Prior Knowledge The Ku Klux Klan was originally organized in the Southern states during the Reconstruction era after the Civil War. **Ask:** Based on information you have previously learned, what was the KKK's position on integration? *(The Klan was opposed to ending social segregation. Klan members believed that African Americans were inferior and did not deserve civil equality.)* **OL**

✓ **Reading Check**

Answer: CORE wanted to draw attention to segregation in Southern bus terminals.

Picturing **History**

Answer: CORE (Congress of Racial Equality)
Ask: Who was responsible for the violence against the Freedom Riders in Birmingham, Alabama? *(Ku Klux Klan)*

After the Freedom Riders were attacked in Montgomery, the Kennedys publicly urged them to stop the rides and give everybody a "cooling off" period. James Farmer replied that African Americans "have been cooling off now for 350 years. If we cool off anymore, we'll be in a deep freeze." Instead he announced that the Freedom Riders planned to head into Mississippi on their next trip.

To stop the violence, President Kennedy made a deal with Senator James Eastland of Mississippi, a strong supporter of segregation. If Eastland would use his influence in Mississippi to prevent violence, Kennedy would not object if the Mississippi police arrested the Freedom Riders. Eastland kept the deal. No violence occurred when the buses arrived in Jackson, Mississippi, but the riders were arrested.

The cost of bailing the Freedom Riders out of jail used up most of CORE's funds, which meant that the rides would have to end unless more money could be found. When Thurgood Marshall learned of the situation, he offered James Farmer the use of the NAACP's Legal Defense Fund's huge bail bond account to keep the rides going.

When President Kennedy returned from his meeting with Khrushchev and found that the Freedom Riders were still active, he changed his position and ordered the Interstate Commerce Commission to tighten its regulations against segregated bus terminals. In the meantime, Robert Kennedy ordered the Justice Department to take legal action against Southern cities that were maintaining segregated bus terminals. The continuing pressure of CORE and the actions of the ICC and the Justice Department finally produced results. By late 1962, segregation in interstate travel had come to an end.

James Meredith As the Freedom Riders were trying to desegregate bus terminals, efforts continued to integrate Southern schools. On the very day John F. Kennedy was inaugurated, an African American air force veteran named James Meredith applied for a transfer to the University of Mississippi. Up to that point, the university had avoided complying with the Supreme Court ruling ending segregated education.

In September 1962, Meredith tried to register at the university's admissions office, only to find Ross Barnett, the governor of Mississippi, blocking his path. Although Meredith had a court order directing the university to register him, Governor Barnett stated emphatically, "Never! We will never surrender to the evil and illegal forces of tyranny."

Frustrated, President Kennedy dispatched 500 federal marshals to escort Meredith to the campus. Shortly after Meredith and the marshals arrived, an angry white mob attacked the campus, and a full-scale riot erupted. The mob hurled rocks, bottles, bricks, and acid at the marshals. Some people fired shotguns at them. The marshals responded with tear gas, but they were under orders not to fire.

The fighting continued all night. By morning, 160 marshals had been wounded. Reluctantly Kennedy ordered the army to send several thousand troops to the campus. For the rest of the year, Meredith attended classes at the University of Mississippi under federal guard. He graduated the following August.

Violence in Birmingham The events in Mississippi frustrated Martin Luther King, Jr., and other civil rights leaders. Although they were pleased that Kennedy had intervened to protect Meredith's rights, they were disappointed that the president had not seized the moment to push for a new civil rights law. When the Cuban missile crisis began the following month, civil rights issues dropped out of the news, and for the next several months, foreign policy became the main priority at the White House.

Reflecting on the problem, Dr. King came to a difficult decision. It seemed to him that only when violence and disorder got out of hand would the federal government intervene. "We've got to have a crisis to bargain with," one of his advisers observed. King agreed. In the spring of 1963, he decided to launch demonstrations in Birmingham, Alabama, knowing they would probably provoke a violent response. He believed it was the only way to get President Kennedy to actively support civil rights.

The situation in Birmingham was volatile. Public Safety Commissioner Bull Connor, who had arranged for the attack on the Freedom Riders, was now running for mayor. Eight days after the protests began, King was arrested and held for a time in solitary confinement. While in prison, King began writing on scraps of paper that had been smuggled into his cell. The "Letter From a Birmingham Jail" that he produced is one of the most eloquent defenses of nonviolent protest ever written.

In his letter, King explained that although the protesters were breaking the law, they were following a higher moral law based on divine justice. To the charge that the protests created racial tensions, King argued that the protests "merely bring to the surface the hidden tension that is already alive." Injustice, he insisted, had to be exposed "to the light of human conscience and the air of national opinion before it can be cured."

After King was released, the protests began to grow again. Bull Connor responded with force, ordering the police to use clubs, police dogs, and high-pressure fire hoses on the demonstrators, including women and children. Millions of people across the nation watched the graphic violence on television. Outraged by the brutality and worried that the government was losing control, Kennedy ordered his aides to prepare a new civil rights bill.

✓ **Reading Check** **Evaluating** How did President Kennedy help the civil rights movement?

The Civil Rights Act of 1964

Main Idea President Kennedy used the violent events in the South as a platform to announce his civil rights bill.

Reading Connection What provisions to protect the civil rights of African Americans were added to the Constitution after the Civil War? Read on to learn about new legal steps taken during the 1960s.

Determined to introduce a civil rights bill, Kennedy now waited for a dramatic opportunity to address the nation on the issue. Shortly after the violence in Birmingham had shocked the nation, Alabama's governor, George Wallace, gave the president his chance. Wallace was committed to segregation. At his inauguration, he had stated, "I draw a line in the dust . . . and I say, Segregation now! Segregation tomorrow! Segregation forever!" On June 11, 1963, Wallace personally stood in front of the University of Alabama's admissions office to block the enrollment of two African Americans. He stayed until federal marshals ordered him to stand aside.

President Kennedy seized the moment to announce his civil rights bill. That evening, he went on television to speak to the American people about a "moral issue . . . as old as the scriptures and as clear as the American Constitution":

❝The heart of the question is whether . . . we are going to treat our fellow Americans as we want to be treated. If an American, because his skin is dark, cannot eat lunch in a restaurant open to the public, if he cannot send his children to the best public school available, if he cannot vote for the public officials who will represent him . . . then who among us would be content to have the color of his skin changed and stand in his place?❞

One hundred years of delay have passed since President Lincoln freed the slaves, yet their heirs, their grandsons, are not fully free. . . . And this nation, for all its hopes and all its boasts, will not be fully free until all its citizens are free. . . . Now the time has come for this nation to fulfill its promise.❞

—from Kennedy's White House Address, June 11, 1963

The March on Washington Dr. King realized that Kennedy would have a very difficult time pushing his civil rights bill through Congress. Therefore, he searched for a way to lobby Congress and to build more public support for the civil rights movement. When A. Philip Randolph suggested a march on Washington, King agreed.

On August 28, 1963, more than 200,000 demonstrators of all races flocked to the nation's capital. The audience heard speeches and sang hymns and songs as they gathered peacefully near the Lincoln Memorial. Dr. King then delivered a powerful speech outlining his dream of freedom and equality for all Americans:

Picturing **History**

Forcing Change Birmingham police used high-pressure hoses to force civil rights protesters to stop their marches. Why did King's followers offer no resistance?

S

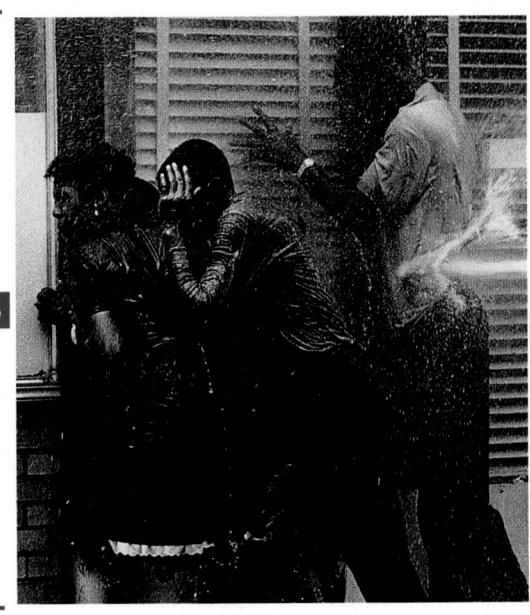

CHAPTER 16 The Civil Rights Movement **753**

Universal Access

Interpersonal This speech, given at the foot of the Lincoln Memorial, became one of the most significant speeches in American history. In 1986 President Reagan announced that the third Monday of January would be a federal legal holiday to honor Dr. Martin Luther King, Jr. Currently this is the only U.S. holiday honoring an African American. **Ask:** *What other ways might exist to honor the efforts of Martin Luther King, Jr., and the other leaders of the civil rights movement? (Students' suggestions will vary, but the discussion should be focused on efforts that could actually be organized and performed.)* **BL**

Critical Thinking

Predicting Consequences
Although African Americans had gained much by 1964, much remained to be done. Ask students to identify areas they think should be improved to ensure that all Americans have equal rights. Have them write their ideas in the form of letters to their representative in Congress. Invite volunteers to read their letters aloud to the class. **OL** **CA 11WS1.3**

Answers and Additional Support

"I have a dream"
—*Martin Luther King, Jr.*

Picturing **History**

A Dream Deferred The 1963 March on Washington was the emotional high point of the civil rights movement. Its nonviolent atmosphere and Dr. King's eloquent speech made it one of the most momentous American events of the twentieth century. **What significant legislation resulted from the March on Washington?**

> ❝I have a dream that one day this nation will rise up and live out the true meaning of its creed . . . that all men are created equal. . . . I have a dream that one day . . . the sons of former slaves and the sons of former slave owners will be able to sit together at the table of brotherhood. . . . I have a dream that my four little children will one day live in a nation where they will not be judged by the color of their skin but by the content of their character. I have a dream . . . when all of God's children, black men and white men, Jews and Gentiles, Protestants and Catholics, will be able to join hands and sing . . . 'Free at last, Free at last, Thank God Almighty, we are free at last.'❞
>
> –quoted in *Freedom Bound: A History of America's Civil Rights Movement*

King's speech and the peacefulness and dignity of the March on Washington had built strong momentum for the civil rights bill. Despite the growing support, however, opponents in Congress continued to do what they could to slow the bill down. These opponents used tactics such as dragging out their committee investigations and using procedural rules to delay votes.

The Civil Rights Bill Becomes Law Although the civil rights bill was likely to pass the House of Representatives, where a majority of Republicans and Northern Democrats supported the measure, it faced a much more difficult time in the Senate. There, a small group of determined senators would try to block the bill indefinitely. Because of procedural rules, it would be possible for senators to delay a vote.

In the U.S. Senate, senators are allowed to speak for as long as they like when a bill is being debated. The Senate cannot vote on a bill until all senators have finished speaking. A **filibuster** occurs when a small group of senators take turns speaking and refuse to stop the debate and allow a bill to come to a vote. Today a filibuster can be stopped if at least 60 senators vote for **cloture,** a motion which cuts off debate and forces a vote. In the 1960s, however, 67 senators had to vote for cloture to stop a filibuster.

754 CHAPTER 16 The Civil Rights Movement

Picturing **History**

Answer: Civil Rights Act of 1964
Ask: How long did it take after the March on Washington for the Civil Rights Act of 1964 to be passed? *(a little over ten months)*

Resources for page 754

*Students can learn more about the March on Washington by reading **Moments in Time, Unit 10: The Civil Rights Era (1954–1963).***

This meant that a minority of senators opposed to civil rights could easily prevent the majority from enacting new civil rights laws.

Worried the bill would never pass, many African Americans became even more disheartened. Then President Kennedy was assassinated in Dallas, Texas, on November 22, 1963, and his vice president, Lyndon Johnson, became president. Johnson was from Texas and had been the leader of the Senate Democrats before becoming vice president. Although he had helped push the Civil Rights Acts of 1957 and 1960 through the Senate, he had done so by weakening their provisions and by compromising with other Southern senators. Many were skeptical that Johnson would support the civil rights bill.

To the surprise of the civil rights movement, Johnson committed himself wholeheartedly to getting Kennedy's program, including the civil rights bill, through Congress. Unlike Kennedy, Johnson was very familiar with how Congress operated, having served there for many years. He knew how to build public support, how to put pressure on members of Congress, and how to use the rules and procedures to get what he wanted.

In February 1964, President Johnson's leadership began to produce results. The civil rights bill passed the House of Representatives by a majority of 290 to 130. The debate then moved to the Senate. In June, after 87 days of filibuster, the Senate finally voted to end debate by a margin of 71 to 29—four votes over the two-thirds needed for cloture. On July 2, 1964, President Johnson signed the **Civil Rights Act of 1964** into law.

The Civil Rights Act of 1964 was the most **comprehensive** civil rights law Congress had ever enacted. It gave the federal government broad power to prevent racial discrimination in a number of areas. The law made segregation illegal in most places of public accommodation, and it gave citizens of all races and nationalities equal access to such facilities as restaurants, parks, libraries, and theaters. The law gave the attorney general more power to bring lawsuits to force school desegregation, and it required private employers to end discrimination in the workplace. It also established the Equal Employment Opportunity Commission (EEOC) as a permanent agency in the federal government. This commission monitors the ban on job discrimination by race, religion, gender, and national origin.

✔ **Reading Check** **Examining** How did Dr. King lobby Congress to expand the right to participate in the democratic process?

The Struggle for Voting Rights

Main Idea President Johnson called for a new voting rights law after hostile crowds severely beat civil rights demonstrators.

Reading Connection How had Southern states historically kept African Americans from voting? Read on to learn about the Voting Rights Act of 1965.

Even after the Civil Rights Act of 1964 was passed, voting rights were far from secure. The act had focused on segregation and job discrimination but did little to address voting issues. The Twenty-fourth Amendment, ratified in 1964, helped by eliminating **poll taxes,** or fees paid in order to vote, in federal (but not state) elections. African Americans still faced hurdles, however, when they tried to vote. Despite violent attacks, the SCLC and SNCC stepped up their voter registration efforts in the South.

Across the South, bombs exploded in African American businesses and churches. Between June and October 1964, 24 African American churches in Mississippi alone were destroyed. Convinced that a new law was needed, Dr. King decided to stage another dramatic protest.

The Selma March In January 1965, the SCLC and Dr. King selected Selma, Alabama, as the focal point for their campaign. Although African Americans

Voting Rights In the early 1960s, African Americans focused on increasing their political power.

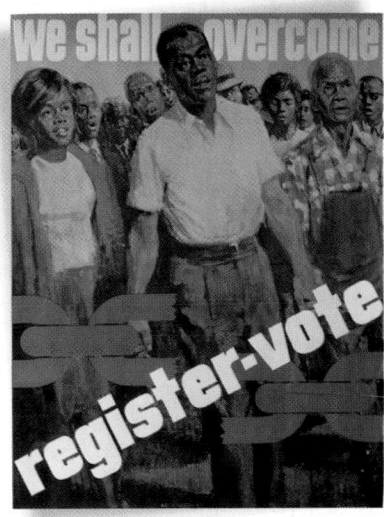

CHAPTER 16 The Civil Rights Movement **755**

ASSESS

Resources for page 756

Use these resources to assess student mastery.

📂 Section Quiz 16-2

📂 Reading Essentials and Study Guide 16-2

💿 Interactive Tutor Self-Assessment CD-ROM

📂 California Standards Practice, Grade 11

✓ Reading Check

Answer: It eliminated poll taxes in federal elections.

Study Central provides audio summaries, interactive games, and online graphic organizers to help students review section content.

CLOSE

Evaluating Students should understand that laws and society often progress at different speeds. Have students evaluate the Civil Rights Act of 1965 and explain why more African Americans are not in Congress today. **OL**

Answers and Additional Support

---

made up a majority of Selma's population, they comprised only 3 percent of registered voters. To prevent African Americans from registering to vote, Sheriff Jim Clark had deputized and armed dozens of white citizens. His posse terrorized African Americans and frequently attacked demonstrators with clubs and electric cattle prods.

Just weeks after receiving the Nobel Peace Prize in Oslo, Norway, for his work in the civil rights movement, Dr. King stated, "We are not asking, we are demanding the ballot." King's demonstrations in Selma led to approximately 2,000 African Americans, including schoolchildren, being arrested by Sheriff Clark. Clark's men attacked and beat many of the demonstrators.

To keep pressure on the president and Congress, Dr. King joined with SNCC activists and organized a "march for freedom" from Selma to the state capitol in Montgomery. On Sunday, March 7, 1965, the march began with the SCLC's Hosea Williams and SNCC's John Lewis leading 500 protesters.

As the protesters approached the Edmund Pettus Bridge, which led out of Selma, Sheriff Clark ordered them to disperse. While the marchers kneeled in prayer, more than 200 state troopers and deputized citizens rushed the demonstrators. Many were beaten in full view of television cameras. This brutal attack, known later as "Bloody Sunday," left 70 African Americans hospitalized and many more injured.

The nation was stunned as it viewed the shocking footage. Watching the events from the White House, President Johnson became furious and decided to take action. Eight days later, he appeared before a nationally televised joint session of the legislature to propose a new voting rights law.

The Voting Rights Act of 1965 On August 3, 1965, the House of Representatives passed the voting rights bill by a wide margin. The following day, the Senate also passed the bill. The Voting Rights Act of 1965 authorized the attorney general to send federal examiners to register qualified voters, bypassing local officials who often refused to register African Americans. The law also suspended discriminatory devices such as literacy tests in counties where less than half of all adults had been allowed to vote.

The results were dramatic. By the end of the year, almost 250,000 African Americans had registered as new voters. The number of African American elected officials in the South also increased, from about 100 in 1965 to more than 5,000 in 1990.

The passage of the Voting Rights Act of 1965 marked a turning point in the civil rights movement. The movement had now achieved its two major legislative goals. Segregation had been outlawed, and new federal laws were in place to protect voting rights.

After 1965 the movement began to shift its focus. It began to pay more attention to achieving full social and economic equality for African Americans. As part of that effort, the movement turned its attention to the problems of African Americans trapped in poverty and living in ghettos.

✓ Reading Check **Summarizing** How did the Twenty-fourth Amendment affect African American voting rights?

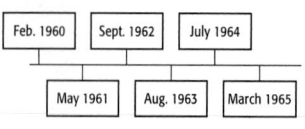 **Study Central**

For help with the concepts in this section of *American Vision: Modern Times* go to tav.mt.glencoe.com and click on *Study Central.*

SECTION 2 ASSESSMENT

Checking for Understanding

1. **Vocabulary** Define: legality, Freedom Riders, attain, filibuster, cloture, comprehensive, poll tax.
2. **People and Terms** Identify: Jesse Jackson, Ella Baker, Civil Rights Act of 1964.
3. **Describe** the provisions of the Civil Rights Act of 1964 aimed at ending segregation and racial discrimination.

Reviewing Big Ideas

4. **Examining** How did television help the civil rights movement?

Critical Thinking

5. **Historical Analysis** **Evaluating** How did protesting and lobbying lead to the passage of the Voting Rights Act of 1965? **CA HI2**
6. **Sequencing** Use a time line like the one below to show relative chronology of events in the civil rights movement.

Feb. 1960	Sept. 1962	July 1964

May 1961	Aug. 1963	March 1965

Analyzing Visuals

7. **Examining Photographs** Study the photographs in this section. What elements of the photographs show the sacrifices African Americans made in the civil rights movement?

Writing About History

8. **Descriptive Writing** Take on the role of a journalist for the student newspaper of a college in 1960. Write an article for the newspaper describing the sit-in movement taking place across the country.
CA 11WA2.1c

SECTION 2 ASSESSMENT ANSWERS

1. Content vocabulary is boldfaced and highlighted in yellow. Academic vocabulary is boldfaced.
2. Jesse Jackson (*p. 749*), Ella Baker (*p. 750*), Civil Rights Act of 1964 (*p. 753*)
3. The act gave the federal government broad powers to prevent

racial discrimination in a number of areas.
4. Television brought national attention to the civil rights movement.
5. Police resistance to peaceful protests, seen on TV, raised sympathy for the civil rights cause.
6. 1960: sit-ins in Greensboro; 1961: Freedom Riders; 1962: James

Meredith enters the University of Mississippi; 1963: March on Washington; 1964: Civil Rights Act; 1965: Selma march
7. Photographs show the humiliations African Americans endured.
8. Students' articles will vary but must be historically accurate.

SECTION 3 New Issues

Guide to Reading

Connection
In the previous section, you learned how African Americans worked to gain civil rights and voting rights. In this section, you will discover why civil rights leaders turned their attention to economic problems facing African Americans.

Main Idea
• The civil rights struggle turned violent in the nation's cities in 1965. (p. 758)
• Martin Luther King, Jr., began to focus more on economic inequalities in 1965. (p. 759)
• Impatient with the slower gains of the nonviolent movement, young African Americans called for black power. (p. 760)

• After Dr. King was assassinated in Memphis, Tennessee, Congress passed the Civil Rights Act of 1968. (p. 762)

Content Vocabulary
racism, black power

Academic Vocabulary
channel, status, psychological

People and Terms to Identify
Chicago Movement, Richard Daley, Stokely Carmichael, Malcolm X, Black Panthers

Reading Objectives
• **Describe** the division between Dr. Martin Luther King, Jr., and the black power movement.

• **Discuss** the direction and progress of the civil rights movement after 1968.

Reading Strategy
Organizing As you read about the changing focus of the civil rights movement, complete a chart similar to the one below. Fill in five major violent events and their results.

Event	Result

Preview of Events

◆1965	◆1966	◆1967	◆1968

1965
Watts riots break out in Los Angeles; Malcolm X assassinated

1966
Chicago Movement fails

1967
Kerner Commission studies problems of inner cities

1968
Dr. Martin Luther King, Jr., assassinated

The following are the main History–Social Science Standards covered in this section.

11.10.4 Examine the roles of civil rights advocates (e.g., A. Philip Randolph, Martin Luther King, Jr., Malcolm X, Thurgood Marshall, James Farmer, Rosa Parks), including the significance of Martin Luther King, Jr.'s "Letter from Birmingham Jail" and "I Have a Dream" speech.

11.11.7 Explain how the federal, state, and local governments have responded to demographic and social changes such as population shifts to the suburbs, racial concentrations in the cities, Frostbelt-to-Sunbelt migration, international migration, decline of family farms, increases in out-of-wedlock births, and drug abuse.

❧ *The Big Idea* ☙

People react to periods of breathtaking social and cultural change in different ways. Violence over the civil rights struggle continued to escalate. More activists, concerned that increasing political rights would not address all the problems African Americans faced, began to focus on improving economic conditions. Increasing numbers of young African Americans became frustrated with nonviolent protests and the slow progress. These people began to call for black power and stronger actions to gain equality. Following the assassination of Martin Luther King, Jr., Congress passed the Civil Rights Act of 1968.

CHAPTER 16   The Civil Rights Movement   **757**

SECTION RESOURCES

📂 Print Material
• Reproducible Lesson Plan 16-3
• Guided Reading Activity 16-3
• Reading Essentials and Study Guide 16-3
• Active Reading Note-Taking Guide 16-3

🖥 Transparencies
• Daily Focus Skills Transparency 16-3
• Section Graphic Organizer Transparency 16-3

Technology
🖲 Interactive Tutor Self-Assessment CD-ROM
🖲 ExamView® Pro Testmaker CD-ROM
🖲 Presentation Plus! CD-ROM

FOCUS

BELLRINGER SKILLBUILDER ACTIVITY

📖 Project **Daily Focus Skills Transparency 16-3** and have students answer the question.

Guide to Reading

Understanding Vocabulary: Have students scan the section to preview the content vocabulary, the academic vocabulary, and the people and terms to identify.

Answers to Graphic:
Event: Dessie Mae Williams is killed, *Result:* riots; *Event:* Watts Riot, *Result:* Kerner Commission report on urban riots; *Event:* Malcolm X breaks with the Nation of Islam, *Result:* Malcolm X assassinated; *Event:* King supports strike by African American sanitation workers in Memphis, *Result:* King assassinated

⬤ Unpacking the Standards

Students will be able to:

• Discuss the problems that urban African Americans faced during this decade.

• Describe how the civil rights movement attempted to shift some of its emphasis on the problem of economic inequality.

• Explain the development of the Black Power movement.

• Discuss the events surrounding the assassination of Dr. Martin Luther King, Jr.

757

TEACH

R₁ Reading Strategy

Scaffolding—Academic Vocabulary The word *approximately* was introduced in Chapter 12, Section 4. Ask a student to define the word. **BL**

R₂ Reading Strategy

Evaluating Point out to students that prejudice toward and discrimination of African Americans was not limited to the South. **Ask: How were African Americans treated in the North and West? How did treatment there differ from the legal segregation of the South?** *(Possible answers may include: informal segregation of neighborhoods, economic discrimination that limited the ability of African Americans to function in society on a truly equal basis.)* **OL**

R₃ Reading Strategy

Identifying the Main Idea and Supporting Details Remind the class that a majority of African Americans lived in urban areas of the United States. **Ask: What were the main issues facing the urban poor?** *(low-paying jobs, unemployment, illness and infant death, crime, and single-parent households)* **OL**

Answers and Additional Support

Problems Facing Urban African Americans

Main Idea The civil rights struggle turned violent in the nation's cities in 1965.

Reading Connection When did the Great Migration of African Americans to northern cities occur? Read on to learn more about the racism that they continued to face in the 1960s.

Despite the passage of several civil rights laws in the 1950s and 1960s, **racism**—prejudice or discrimination toward someone because of his or her race—was still common in American society. In 1965, tensions over this discrimination erupted in violence.

★ An American Story ★

Thursday, July 12, 1965, was hot and humid in Chicago. That evening Dessie Mae Williams, a 23-year-old African American woman, stood on the corner near the firehouse at 4000 West Wilcox Street. A firetruck sped out of the firehouse, and the driver lost control. The truck smashed into a stop sign near Williams, and the sign struck and killed her.

African Americans had already picketed this firehouse because it was not integrated. Hearing of Williams's death, 200 neighborhood young people streamed into the street, surrounding the firehouse. For two nights, rioting and disorder reigned. Angry youths threw bricks and bottles at the firehouse and nearby windows. Shouting gangs pelted police with rocks and accosted whites and beat them. **R₁** Approximately 75 people were injured.

African American detectives, clergy, and National Guard members eventually restored order. Mayor Richard Daley then summoned both white and black leaders to discuss the area's problems. An 18-year-old man who had been in the riot admitted that he had lost his head. "We're sorry about the bricks and bottles," he said, "but when you get pushed, you shove back. Man, you don't like to stand on a corner and be told to get off it when you got nowhere else to go."

—adapted from *Anyplace But Here*

Changing the law could not change people's attitudes immediately, nor could it help those African Americans trapped in poverty in the nation's big cities. In 1965, nearly 70 percent of African Americans

lived in large cities. Many had moved from the South to the big cities of the North and West during the Great Migration of the 1920s and 1940s. There, they often found the same prejudice and discrimination that had plagued them in the South. Many whites refused to live with African Americans in the same neighborhood. When African Americans moved into **R₂** a neighborhood, whites often moved out. Real estate agents and landlords in white neighborhoods refused to rent or sell to African Americans, who often found it difficult to arrange for mortgages at local banks.

Even if African Americans had been allowed to move into white neighborhoods, poverty trapped many of them in inner cities while whites moved to the suburbs. Many African Americans found themselves **channeled** into low-paying jobs. They served as custodians and maids, porters and dock workers, with little chance of advancement. Those who did better typically found employment as blue-collar **R₃** workers in factories, but very few advanced beyond that. In 1965 only 15 percent of African Americans held professional, managerial, or clerical jobs, compared to 44 percent of whites. Almost half of all African American families lived in poverty, and the median income of an African American family was only 55 percent of that of the average white family. African American unemployment was typically twice that of whites.

Poor neighborhoods in the nation's major cities were overcrowded and dirty, leading to higher rates of illness and infant mortality. At the same time, the crime rate increased in the 1960s, particularly in low-income neighborhoods. Incidents of juvenile delinquency rose, as did the rate of young people dropping out of school. Complicating matters even more was a rise in the number of single-parent

▼ *Dr. Martin Luther King, Jr., marching with protesters in Chicago*

Did You Know?

Many African American artists used African motifs in their creations, which often expressed outrage with society or portrayed scenes from African American history. An example is *Wall of Love* by William Walker.

Analyzing *Political Cartoons*

"Perilous Going" This political cartoon highlights the problems that American cities were experiencing in the mid-1960s. Why did riots break out in the Los Angeles neighborhood of Watts?

households. All poor neighborhoods suffered from these problems, but because more African Americans lived in poverty, their communities were disproportionately affected.

Many African Americans living in urban poverty knew the civil rights movement had made enormous gains, but when they looked at their own circumstances, nothing seemed to be changing. The movement had raised their hopes, but their everyday problems were economic and social, and therefore harder to address. As a result, their anger and frustration began to rise—until it finally erupted.

The Watts Riot Just five days after President Johnson signed the Voting Rights Act, a race riot broke out in Watts, an African American neighborhood in Los Angeles. Allegations of police brutality had served as the catalyst of this uprising, which lasted for six days and required over 14,000 members of the National Guard and 1,500 law officers to restore order. Rioters burned and looted entire neighborhoods and destroyed about $45 million in property. They killed 34 people, and about 900 suffered injuries.

More rioting was yet to come. Race riots broke out in dozens of American cities between 1965 and 1968. It seemed that they could explode at any place and at any time. The worst riot took place in Detroit in 1967. Burning, looting, and skirmishes with police and National Guard members resulted in 43 deaths and over 1,000 wounded. Eventually the U.S. Army sent in tanks and soldiers armed with machine guns to get control of the situation. Nearly 4,000 fires destroyed 1,300 buildings, and the damage in property loss was estimated at $250 million. The governor of Michigan, who viewed the smoldering city from a helicopter, remarked that Detroit looked like "a city that had been bombed."

The Kerner Commission In 1967 President Johnson appointed the National Advisory Commission on Civil Disorders, headed by Governor Otto Kerner of Illinois, to study the causes of the urban riots and to make recommendations to prevent them from happening again in the future. The Kerner Commission, as it became known, conducted a detailed study of the problem. The commission blamed white society and white

racism for the majority of the problems in the inner city. "Our nation is moving toward two societies, one black, one white—separate and unequal," it concluded.

The commission recommended the creation of 2 million new jobs in inner cities, the construction of 6 million new units of public housing, and a renewed federal commitment to fight de facto segregation. President Johnson's war on poverty, which addressed some of the same concerns for inner-city jobs and housing, was already underway. Saddled with massive spending for the Vietnam War, however, President Johnson never endorsed the recommendations of the commission.

✓ **Reading Check** **Explaining** What was the federal government's response to race riots?

The Shift to Economic Rights

Main Idea Martin Luther King, Jr., began to focus more on economic inequalities in 1965.

Reading Connection What do you think causes mobs to form and to act violently? Read on to learn about the Chicago mobs that Dr. King faced.

By the mid-1960s, a number of African American leaders were becoming increasingly critical of Martin Luther King's nonviolent strategy. They felt it had

CHAPTER 16   The Civil Rights Movement   **759**

Review the Big Idea

Review the Big Idea for this section, "People react to periods of breathtaking social and cultural change in different ways." By the mid-1960s, significant advances had been made to improve African American civil rights, but full equality had not been achieved. **Ask:** What changes do you think remained to be made? *(economic equality and social desegregation)* As students read the text under the heading "The Shift to Economic Rights," have them take notes on the efforts made to improve economic conditions for African Americans and summarize what they learned in brief paragraphs. **BL**

R Reading Strategy

Evaluating The urban riots in the mid-1960s concerned President Johnson. He requested a study to determine their causes. **Ask:** What did the Kerner Commission mean by "separate and unequal?" *(Discrimination, poverty, high unemployment, poor schools, deficient housing, inability to attain health care, as well as intolerance and brutality led to a feeling that the American society was being divided down racial lines.)* **OL**

✓ Reading Check

Answer: United States Army troops were deployed, and the Kerner Commission recommended reforms to prevent further riots.

Analyzing *Political Cartoons*

Answer: Allegations of police brutality sparked the riots.

Ask: What symbol does the cartoon use to highlight the problems of riots, tension, and racial violence in cities? *(mines)*

R Reading Strategy

Inferring Why did the Chicago Movement make little headway toward equality? *(Some whites opposed King's efforts. Rental businesses and banks agreed to open up housing but did not follow through.)* **OL**

S Skill Practice

Scaffolding—Distinguishing Valid and Fallacious Arguments Form volunteers into two groups to debate the topic of black power. Ask one group to present arguments supporting the idea that African Americans should take a more aggressive stance on gaining their civil rights. The other group should argue that turning away from King's emphasis on nonviolence harmed the civil rights movement. Have each side present their views to the class and provide supporting evidence. As students debate, encourage the class to evaluate the arguments based on their validity. **AL** **CA** HR1; HR4

This **Historical Analysis** skill was introduced in Chapter 6.

✓ Reading Check

Answer: by meeting with local leaders to discuss housing and economic reforms

Answers and Additional Support

failed to improve the economic position of African Americans. What good was the right to dine at restaurants or stay at hotels if most African Americans could not afford these services anyway? Dr. King became sensitive to this criticism, and in 1965 he began to focus on economic issues.

In 1965 Albert Raby, president of a council of community organizations that worked to improve conditions for Chicago's poor, invited Dr. King to visit the city. Dr. King and his staff had never conducted a civil rights campaign in the North. By focusing on the problems that African Americans faced in Chicago, Dr. King believed he could call greater attention to poverty and other racial problems that lay beneath the urban race riots.

To call attention to the deplorable housing conditions that many African American families faced, Dr. King and his wife Coretta moved into a slum apartment in an African American neighborhood in Chicago. Dr. King and the SCLC hoped to work with local leaders to improve the economic **status** of African Americans in Chicago's poor neighborhoods.

The **Chicago Movement**, however, made little headway. When Dr. King led a march through the all-white suburb of Marquette Park to demonstrate the need for open housing, he was met by angry white mobs similar to those in Birmingham and Selma. Mayor **Richard Daley** ordered the Chicago police to protect the marchers, but he wanted to avoid any repeat of the violence. He met with Dr. King and proposed a new program to clean up the slums. Associations of realtors and bankers also agreed to promote open housing. In theory, mortgages and rental property would be available to everyone, regardless of race. In practice, very little changed.

✓ Reading Check **Describing** How did Dr. King and SCLC leaders hope to address economic concerns?

Black Power

S **Main Idea** Impatient with the slower gains of the nonviolent movement, young African Americans called for black power.

Reading Connection How did Dr. King work to avoid violence? Read on to find out how some African Americans broke with Dr. King's approach.

Dr. King's failure in Chicago seemed to show that nonviolent protests could do little to change economic problems. After 1965 many African Americans, especially young people living in cities, began to turn away from King. The ongoing race riots in Los Angeles, Detroit, and other cities in the United States added to their frustration. Some leaders called for more aggressive forms of protest. Their new strategies ranged from armed self-defense to the suggestion that the government set aside a number of states where African Americans could live free from the presence of whites.

As African Americans became more assertive, they placed less emphasis on cooperation with sympathetic whites. Some African American organizations, including CORE and SNCC, voted to expel all whites from leadership positions within their organizations, believing that African Americans alone should determine the course and direction of their struggle.

Many young African Americans called for **black power**, a term that had many different meanings. A few interpreted black power to mean that physical self-defense and even violence were acceptable in defense of one's freedom—a clear rejection of Dr. King's philosophy. To most, including **Stokely Carmichael**, the leader of SNCC in 1966, the term meant that African

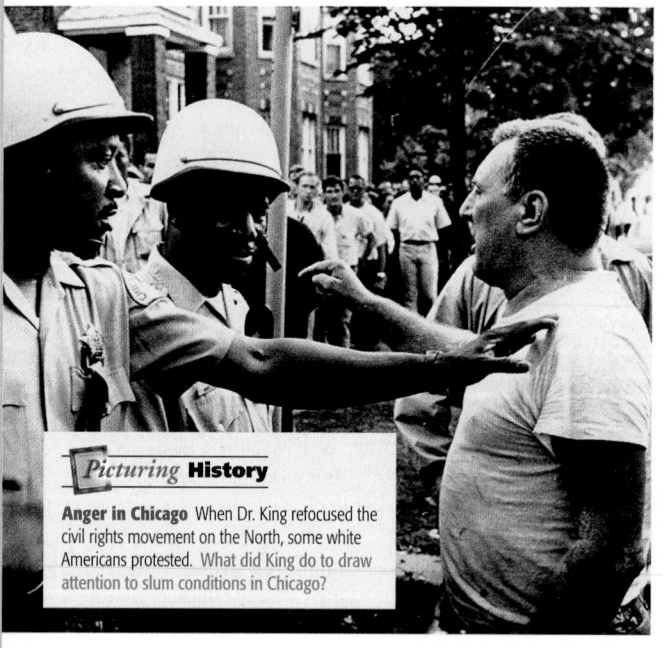

Picturing History

Anger in Chicago When Dr. King refocused the civil rights movement on the North, some white Americans protested. What did King do to draw attention to slum conditions in Chicago?

760 CHAPTER 16 The Civil Rights Movement

Picturing History

Answer: King and his wife moved into a slum apartment in Chicago.
Ask: Why did whites protest when the civil right movement moved to the North? *(There was prejudice and racism in the North.)*

Americans should control the social, political, and economic direction of their struggle:

> 66This is the significance of black power as a slogan. For once, black people are going to use the words they want to use—not just the words whites want to hear. . . . The need for **psychological** equality is the reason why SNCC today believes that blacks must organize in the black community. Only black people can . . . create in the community an aroused and continuing black consciousness. . . . Black people must do things for themselves; they must get . . . money they will control and spend themselves; they must conduct tutorial programs themselves so that black children can identify with black people.99

—from the *New York Review of Books,*
September 1966

Picturing **History**

Malcolm X Makes His Point
Once the most visible spokesperson for the Nation of Islam, Malcolm X originally disagreed with Dr. King's passive protest tactics. What did the "X" in his name symbolize?

Black power also stressed pride in the African American cultural group. It emphasized racial distinctiveness rather than cultural assimilation—the process by which minority groups adapt to the dominant culture in a society. African Americans showed pride in their racial heritage by adopting new Afro hairstyles and African-style clothing. Many also took on African names. In universities, students demanded that African and African American Studies courses be adopted as part of the standard school curriculum. Dr. King and some other leaders criticized black power as a philosophy of hopelessness and despair. The idea was very popular, however, in the poor urban neighborhoods where many African Americans resided.

Malcolm X and the Nation of Islam By the early 1960s, a man named **Malcolm X** had become a symbol of the black power movement that was sweeping the nation. Born Malcolm Little in Omaha, Nebraska, he experienced a difficult childhood and adolescence. He drifted into a life of crime, and in 1946, he was sentenced to six years in prison for burglary.

Prison transformed Malcolm. He began to educate himself, and he played an active role in the prison debate society. Eventually he joined the Nation of Islam, commonly known as the Black Muslims, who were led by Elijah Muhammad. Despite their name, the Black Muslims do not hold the same beliefs as mainstream Muslims. The Nation of Islam preached black nationalism. Like Marcus Garvey in the 1920s, Black Muslims believed that African Americans

should separate themselves from whites and form their own self-governing communities.

Shortly after joining the Nation of Islam, Malcolm Little changed his name to Malcolm X. The "X" stood as a symbol for the family name of his African ancestors who had been enslaved. Malcolm argued that his true family name had been stolen from him by slavery, and he did not intend to use the name white society had given him.

The Black Muslims viewed themselves as their own nation and attempted to make themselves as economically self-sufficient as possible. They ran their own businesses, organized their own schools, established their own weekly newspaper *(Muhammad Speaks)*, and encouraged their members to respect each other and to strengthen their families. Although the Black Muslims did not advocate violence, they did advocate self-defense. Malcolm X was a powerful and charismatic speaker, and his criticisms of white society and the mainstream civil rights movement gained national attention for the Nation of Islam.

By 1964 Malcolm X had broken with the Black Muslims. Discouraged by scandals involving the Nation of Islam's leader, he went to the Muslim holy city of Makkah (also called Mecca) in Saudi Arabia. After seeing Muslims from many different races worshipping together, he concluded that an integrated society was possible. In a revealing letter describing his pilgrimage to Makkah, he stated that many whites that he met during the pilgrimage displayed a

CHAPTER 16   The Civil Rights Movement   **761**

R₁ Reading Strategy

Summarizing Tell students to write their definition of black power on note cards. After reading the chapter, ask students to reflect on their previous definitions. **Ask: Does your definition need to be adjusted based on what you have learned?** OL

R₂ Reading Strategy

Organizing Information Tell students to make time lines of the important events impacting the life of Malcolm X. If students are unsure about how to construct their time lines, suggest that they use a style similar to that found in the textbook. BL

U Universal Access

Visual/Spatial Have students work in pairs to read about and find images of one of the radical African American groups such as the Nation of Islam or the Black Panthers. Have each pair create a photo essay of their chosen group. Tell students that the essays should involve photos and descriptive captions that give readers insight into the goals of the organization and motives for specific actions. OL

Resources for page 761

Have students read more about Malcolm X in the **Primary Source Reading 16-2.**

Picturing **History**

Background: Because they were treated as property, very few enslaved people had last names. If they did have a last name, it was often the name of the slaveholder. Members of the Nation of Islam adopted the "X" to eliminate the historical ties to their enslaved past.

Answer: The X was a symbol for the family name of the African ancestors.

Ask: What belief did Malcolm X share with Marcus Garvey? *(Both believed that African Americans should form their own self-governing communities; Malcolm X later abandoned separatism.)*

W Writing Support

Summary Writing Ask students to explain in a three-paragraph paper why the Black Panthers considered themselves heirs to Malcolm X. *(Both wanted to stand up and fight to bring about social, economic, and political equality. In 1964 Malcolm X divorced himself from the more militant views of the Nation of Islam and began arguing that social integration of the races was possible.)* **OL** **CA** 11WS1.6

C Critical Thinking

Identifying Central Issues Ask students to consider the following questions and write their thoughts and responses on a sheet of paper. Is violence in self-defense, or in response to violence, justifiable? Is nonviolent civil disobedience an effective strategy for attaining full equality? After students have had a chance to write down their thoughts, conduct a class discussion about the differences between violent and nonviolent protests. Encourage students to share differing views as they explore these complex concepts. **AL**

✓ Reading Check

Answer: King was nonviolent; the black power movement advocated aggressive self-defense, even violence.

Answers and Additional Support

---

spirit of brotherhood that gave him a new, positive insight into race relations.

After Malcolm X broke with the Nation of Islam, he continued to criticize the organization and its leader, Elijah Muhammad. Because of this, three organization members shot and killed him in February 1965 while he was giving a speech in New York. Although Malcolm X left the Nation of Islam before his death, his speeches and ideas from those years with the Black Muslims are those for which he is most remembered. In Malcolm's view, African Americans may have been victims in the past, but they did not have to allow racism to victimize them in the present. His ideas have influenced African Americans to take pride in their own culture and to believe in their ability to make their way in the world.

W **The Black Panthers** Malcolm X's ideas influenced a new generation of militant African American leaders who also preached black power, black nationalism, and economic self-sufficiency. In 1966 in

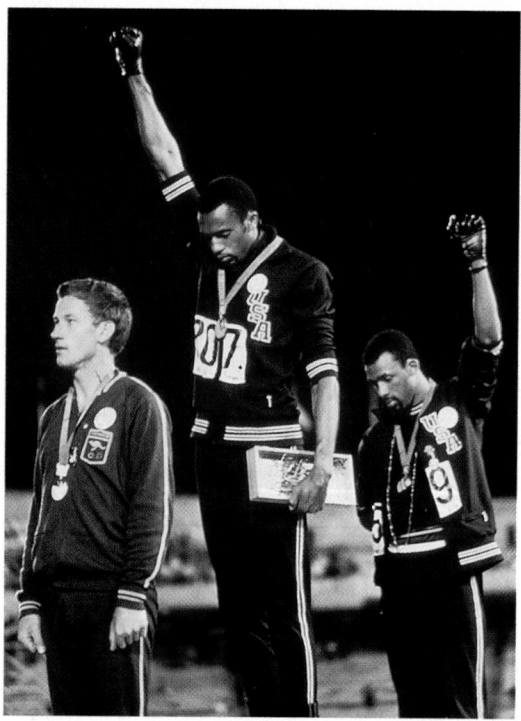

Picturing History

Black Power U.S. athletes Tommie Smith and John Carlos give the black power salute during the medal ceremony at the 1968 Olympic Games in Mexico City. How did black power supporters demonstrate their belief in the movement?

762 CHAPTER 16 The Civil Rights Movement

Oakland, California, Huey Newton, Bobby Seale, and Eldridge Cleaver organized the Black Panther Party for Self-Defense, or the **Black Panthers,** as they were known. They considered themselves the heirs of Malcolm X, and they recruited most of their members from poor urban communities across the nation.

C The Black Panthers believed that a revolution was necessary in the United States, and they urged African Americans to arm themselves and confront white society in order to force whites to grant them equal rights. Black Panther leaders adopted a "Ten-Point Program," which called for black empowerment, an end to racial oppression, and control of major institutions and services in the African American community, such as schools, law enforcement, housing, and medical facilities. Eldridge Cleaver, who served as the minister of culture, articulated many of the organization's objectives in his 1967 best-selling book, *Soul on Ice.*

✓ Reading Check **Describing** What caused a division between Dr. Martin Luther King, Jr., and the black power movement?

The Assassination of Martin Luther King, Jr.

Main Idea After Dr. King was assassinated in Memphis, Tennessee, Congress passed the Civil Rights Act of 1968.

Reading Connection Do you know someone who remembers the assassination of Dr. King? Read on to discover the events surrounding King's early death.

By the late 1960s, the civil rights movement had fragmented into dozens of competing organizations with philosophies for reaching equality. At the same time, the emergence of black power and the call by some African Americans for violent action angered many white civil rights supporters. This made further legislation to help blacks economically less likely.

In this atmosphere, Dr. King went to Memphis, Tennessee, to support a strike of African American sanitation workers in March 1968. At the time, the SCLC had been planning a national "Poor People's Campaign" to promote economic advancement for all impoverished Americans. The purpose of this campaign, the most ambitious one that Dr. King would ever lead, was to lobby the federal government to commit billions of dollars to end poverty and unemployment in the United States. People of all

---

Picturing History

Answer: They gave this black power salute by raising a clenched fist.
Ask: Where did the Black Panthers recruit most of their members? *(in poor, urban communities)*

Did You Know?

Eldridge Cleaver was shot in an altercation with police in 1968 and then fled to Algeria and Paris to live in exile. Cleaver returned to the United States in 1975. Later he abandoned his previous views and ran for political office.

Picturing History

Atlanta Mourns Martin Luther King, Jr. The nation joined Coretta Scott King (left) in sorrow following the assassination of her husband in 1968. Why was King in Memphis at the time of his death?

races and nationalities were to converge on the nation's capital, as they had in 1963 during the March on Washington, where they would camp out until both Congress and President Johnson agreed to pass the requested legislation to fund the proposal.

On the evening of April 4, 1968, as he stood on his hotel balcony in Memphis, Dr. King was assassinated by a sniper. Ironically, he had told a gathering at a local African American church just the previous night, "I've been to the mountaintop. . . .I've looked over and I've seen the Promised Land. I may not get there with you, but I want you to know tonight that we as a people will get to the Promised Land."

Dr. King's assassination touched off both national mourning and riots in more than 100 cities, including Washington, D.C. The Reverend Ralph Abernathy, who had served as a trusted assistant to Dr. King for many years, led the Poor People's Campaign in King's absence. The demonstration, however, did not achieve any of the major objectives that either King or the SCLC had hoped it would.

In the wake of Dr. King's death, Congress passed the Civil Rights Act of 1968. The act contained a fair housing provision outlawing discrimination in housing sales and rentals and gave the Justice Department authority to bring suits against such discrimination.

Dr. King's death marked the end of an era in American history. Although the civil rights movement continued, it lacked the unity of purpose and vision that Dr. King had given it. Under his leadership, and with the help of tens of thousands of dedicated African Americans, many of whom were students, the civil rights movement transformed American society. Although many problems remain to be resolved, the achievements of the civil rights movement in the 1950s and 1960s dramatically improved life for African Americans, creating new opportunities where none had existed before.

 Reading Check **Summarizing** What were the goals of the Poor People's Campaign?

HISTORY Online **Study Central**

For help with the concepts in this section of *American Vision: Modern Times* go to tav.mt.glencoe.com and click on *Study Central.*

SECTION 3 ASSESSMENT

Checking for Understanding

1. **Vocabulary** Define: racism, channel, status, black power, psychological.
2. **People and Terms** Identify: Chicago Movement, Richard Daley, Stokely Carmichael, Malcolm X, Black Panthers.
3. **Explain** the goals of the Nation of Islam in the 1960s.
4. **Summarize** the findings of the Kerner Commission.

Reviewing Big Ideas

5. **Justifying** How was the Civil Rights Act of 1968 designed to help end discrimination?

Critical Thinking

6. **Identifying Cause and Effect** What were the effects of the assassination of Dr. Martin Luther King, Jr.?
7. **Categorizing** Using a graphic organizer like the one below, list the main views of the three leaders listed.

Leader	Views
Dr. Martin Luther King, Jr.	
Malcolm X	
Eldridge Cleaver	

Analyzing Visuals

8. **Analyzing Political Cartoons** The cartoon on page 759 suggests that the violence of the mid-1960s was as bad as the violence of the Vietnam War going on at the same time. What images does the cartoonist use to compare violence at home with the violence of the war?

Writing About History

9. **Expository Writing** Take on the role of a reporter in the late 1960s. Imagine you have interviewed a follower of Dr. King and a Black Panther member. Write out a transcript of each interview.

CHAPTER 16   The Civil Rights Movement   **763**

ASSESS

 Resources for page 763

Use these resources to assess student mastery.

📁 Section Quiz 16-3

📁 Reading Essentials and Study Guide 16-3

💿 Interactive Tutor Self-Assessment CD-ROM

📁 California Standards Practice, Grade 11

Picturing History

Answer: to support a strike by African American sanitation workers

Reading Check

Answer: The Poor People's Campaign promoted economic advancement for all impoverished Americans.

HISTORY Online

Study Central provides audio summaries, interactive games, and online graphic organizers to help students review section content.

CLOSE

Evaluating Have students discuss the direction and progress of the civil rights movement after 1968. **OL**

SECTION 3 ASSESSMENT ANSWERS

1. Content vocabulary is boldfaced and highlighted in yellow. Academic vocabulary is boldfaced.
2. Chicago Movement *(p. 760)*, Richard Daley *(p. 760)*, Stokely Carmichael *(p. 760)*, Malcolm X *(p. 761)*, Black Panthers *(p. 762)*
3. It wanted separate self-governing communities for African Americans.
4. It blamed racism for inner-city problems and urged job and housing programs.
5. by outlawing housing discrimination
6. It touched off both national mourning and riots; the Civil Rights Act of 1968 was passed.
7. King: nonviolent protest; Malcolm X: self-defense and separatism; Cleaver: revolution
8. the ocean ships, floating mines
9. Students' articles will vary but should be written as if a reporter were describing an interview.

FOCUS

History–Social Science Standards

This feature addresses the following standard:

11.10.4 Examine the roles of civil rights advocates (e.g., A. Philip Randolph, Martin Luther King, Jr., Malcolm X, Thurgood Marshall, James Farmer, Rosa Parks), including the significance of Martin Luther King, Jr.'s "Letter from a Birmingham Jail" and "I Have a Dream" speech.

Understanding Vocabulary

Before students begin reading, point out that difficult or unfamiliar words are footnoted throughout the text.

TEACH

C Critical Thinking

Identifying Central Issues
Ask students to write journal entries describing what it might have been like to witness Rosa Parks's refusal to give up her bus seat. Invite volunteers to read what they have written aloud to the class. **OL**
CA 11WA2.1a; 11WA2.1b

Answers and Additional Support

Primary Sources
Eyewitness to History

Since the Civil War, African Americans had fought for civil rights. They supported court cases that challenged segregation and formed organizations to better accomplish their goals. Little did they know that one woman's challenge of segregation in Montgomery, Alabama, would begin an organized civil rights movement.

SOURCE 1:

On December 1, 1955, Rosa Parks had just completed a long day of work as a seamstress in a department store in downtown Montgomery. In her autobiography, Rosa Parks: My Story, *she described what happened when she got on a city bus to go home.*

I knew they [the National Association for the Advancement of Colored People] needed a plaintiff who was beyond reproach. . . . But that is not why I refused to give up my bus seat to a white man. . . . I did not intend to get arrested. If I had been paying attention, I wouldn't even have gotten on that bus. . . .

When I got off from work that evening. . . . I didn't look to see who was driving. . . . It was the same driver who had put me off the bus back in 1943, twelve years earlier. . . . And he was still mean-looking. . . . Most of the time if I saw him on a bus, I wouldn't get on it.

I saw a vacant seat in the middle of the bus and took it. . . . The next stop was the Empire Theater, and some whites got on. They filled up the white seats, and one man was left standing. The driver . . . looked back at us. He said, "Let me have those front seats." . . . Didn't anybody move. We just sat there, the four of us. . . .

The man in the window seat next to me stood up . . . and then I looked across the aisle and saw that the two women were also standing. . . .

I thought back to the time when I used to sit up all night and didn't sleep, and my grandfather would have his gun right by the fireplace, or if he had his one-horse wagon going anywhere, he always had his gun in the back of the wagon. People always say that I didn't give up my seat because I was tired, but his isn't true. I was not tired physically. . . . No, the only tired I was, was tired of giving in. . . . I chose to remain.

▲ *Rosa Parks in an interview before a bus boycott court trial on March 29, 1956*

SOURCE 2:

In response to Parks's arrest, the Women's Political Council (WPC) called for a boycott of Montgomery city buses. Jo Ann Gibson Robinson, a professor of English at Alabama State College, chaired this organization of black women.

In Montgomery in 1955, no one was **brazen**[1] enough to announce publicly that black people might boycott city buses for the specific purpose of *integrating* those buses. Just to say that minorities wanted "better seating arrangements" was bad enough. That was the term the two sides, white and black, always used later in discussing the boycott. The word "integration" never came up. Certainly all blacks knew not to use that word while riding the bus. To admit that black Americans were

[1] **brazen:** bold

UNIVERSAL ACCESS

Visual/Spatial Divide the class into groups of four. Have each group work together to create a poster illustrating key events in the civil rights movement. Students may use photographs or original drawings, as well as poems, song lyrics, newspaper headlines, or other media to complete the assignment. Encourage the groups to use library and Internet resources, as well as their textbook, to locate elements for their posters. Display the completed posters around your classroom while discussing the civil rights movement. **OL**

seeking to integrate would have been too much; there probably would have been much bloodshed and arrests of those who dared to disclose such an idea! That is why, during the boycott negotiations to come, the Men of Montgomery and other organizations always said that blacks would sit from the back toward front, and whites would sit from the front of the bus toward the back, until all seats were taken.

The WPC, however, knew all the time that black Americans were working for integration, pure and simple. No front toward back, or vice versa! We knew we were human beings; that neither whites nor blacks were responsible for their color; that someday those buses, of necessity, had to be integrated; and that after integration neither would be worse off. . . . We were, then, bent on integration. There were those afraid to admit it. But, we knew that deep down in the secret minds of all—teachers, students, and community—black Americans wanted integration. That way we would achieve equality. The only way.

SOURCE 3:

On December 5, 1955, male African American leaders formed the Montgomery Improvement Association. They elected Dr. Martin Luther King, Jr., to head the group. King addressed a mass meeting later that day.

We are here this evening to say to those who have mistreated us so long that we are tired—tired of being segregated and humiliated, tired of being kicked around by the brutal feet of oppression. We have no alternative but protest. For many years, we have shown amazing patience. We have sometimes given our white brothers the feeling that we liked the way we were being treated. But we come here tonight to be saved from that patience that makes us patient with anything less than freedom and justice. . . .

One of the greatest glories of democracy is the right to protest for right. . . . These organizations [the Ku Klux Klan and the White Citizens Councils] are protesting for the **perpetuation**[2] of injustice in the community, we are protesting for the birth of justice in the community. Their methods lead to violence and lawlessness. But in our protest there will be no cross burnings. No white person will be taken from his home by a hooded Negro mob and brutally murdered. . . . We will be guided by the highest principles of law and order. . . .

[2]**perpetuation:** permanence

▲ *Martin Luther King, Jr., surrounded by followers after his court trial on March 23, 1956*

Our method will be that of persuasion, not coercion. We will only say to people, "Let your conscience be your guide. . . . [O]ur actions must be guided by the deepest principles of our Christian faith. Love must be our regulating ideal. Once again we must hear the words of Jesus echoing across the centuries, 'Love your enemies, bless them that curse you, and pray for them that despitefully use you'.". . .

DBQ   Document-Based Questions

Historical Analysis   CA HR4; HI1

Source 1: Why did Parks refuse to give up her seat to a white man?

Source 2: According to Robinson, why did people in Montgomery not use the word *integration*?

Source 3: How does King compare the efforts planned for his organization to those of organizations that opposed African Americans?

Comparing and Contrasting Sources

What is the common strand that connects the ideas of Parks, King, and Robinson?

W **Writing Support**

Essay Writing Have students consider the statement that the boycotters avoided discussing the larger goal of integrating. **Ask:** If you had been a civil rights organizer, what intermediate goals would you have aimed to achieve first? Have students write two-page essays explaining their short-term goals and how these would have helped achieve full social equality. AL CA 11WA2.3b

U **Universal Access**

Verbal/Linguistic Ask students to consider the following question: If Martin Luther King, Jr., came to your school today, what might he say about the state of race relations in your town? Why? After allowing some time for discussion, have students work alone or in pairs to write a speech by Dr. King addressing your school. Encourage them to research several speeches by Dr. King to gain a sense of his style and technique. Finally, invite volunteers to read their speeches aloud to the class. Write some of the major points students are making on the board and use them to continue discussion of the civil rights movement and the status of civil rights in the United States today. AL

ASSESS/CLOSE

Have students answer the Document-Based Questions.

DBQ   Document-Based Questions

1. Parks was tired of giving in to white people.
2. People were afraid of being arrested or killed.
3. King's organization was fighting for justice rather than injustice and would rely on persuasion rather than coercion.

Comparing and Contrasting Sources
Answers will vary; students should note that all three authors believe in promoting change and civil rights for African Americans.

CHAPTER
16 ASSESSMENT and ACTIVITIES

Resources for pages 766–767

Use the following resources to review, assess, and reteach the chapter.

📂 Chapter 16 Tests, Forms A and B

📂 Standardized Tests, Forms A and B

📂 Cumulative Authentic Assessment

🔒 MindJogger Videoquiz

⊙ Interactive Tutor Self-Assessment CD-ROM

⊙ ExamView® Pro Testmaker CD-ROM

⊙ Vocabulary PuzzleMaker CD-ROM

⊛ Succeeding on . . .™ the California Standards: Grade 11 History–Social Science

📂 California Standards Practice, Grade 11

Reviewing Content Vocabulary

Students' answers will vary. The pages where the words appear in the text are shown in parentheses.

1. separate-but-equal (p. 741) **2.** de facto segregation (p. 741) **3.** sit-in (p. 742) **4.** Freedom Riders (p. 750) **5.** filibuster (p. 754) **6.** cloture (p. 754) **7.** poll tax (p. 755) **8.** racism (p. 758) **9.** black power (p. 760)

Reviewing Academic Vocabulary

Students' answers will vary. The pages where the words appear in the text are shown in parentheses.

10. inherent (p. 742) **11.** specific (p. 745) **12.** register (p. 746) **13.** legality (p. 750) **14.** attain (p. 751) **15.** comprehensive (p. 755) **16.** channel (p. 758) **17.** status (p. 760) **18.** psychological (p. 761)

Reviewing Content Vocabulary

On a sheet of paper, use each of these terms in a sentence.

1. separate-but-equal
2. de facto segregation
3. sit-in
4. Freedom Riders
5. filibuster
6. cloture
7. poll tax
8. racism
9. black power

Reviewing Academic Vocabulary

On a sheet of paper, use each of these terms in a sentence that reflects the term's meaning in the chapter.

10. inherent
11. specific
12. register
13. legality
14. attain
15. comprehensive
16. channel
17. status
18. psychological

Reviewing the Main Ideas

Section 1

19. What event led to the bus boycott in Montgomery, Alabama?

Standards 11.10.2, 11.10.3, 11.10.4, 11.10.5, 11.10.6, 11.11.2, 11.11.7

20. Why was the decision in *Brown* v. *Board of Education* a significant step toward ending segregation?

Section 2

21. Why was SNCC formed, and what was its role in the civil rights movement?

Section 3

22. What were two changes in the focus of the civil rights movement in the mid-1960s?

Critical Thinking

23. **Reading Skill** **Determining Importance** After the Civil Rights Act of 1964 was passed, what steps did Dr. King take to protect African American voting rights? What were the results of his actions?

24. **Civics** Explain the Voting Rights Act of 1965. How did it increase voter registration?

25. **Evaluating** Why did the civil rights movement make fewer gains after 1968?

Chapter Summary

Major Events in the Civil Rights Movement

1954
- *Brown* v. *Board of Education* attacks school segregation.
- Separate-but-equal doctrine in education is ruled unconstitutional.

1957
- SCLC is formed to fight segregation and encourage African Americans to vote.
- Eisenhower sends army troops to Little Rock, Arkansas.

1963
- Birmingham demonstrations and the March on Washington help build support for the civil rights movement.

1965
- Voting Rights Act ensures African Americans of the right to vote.
- Watts riot sparks several years of urban racial violence.
- Splinter groups within the civil rights movement advocate more aggressive means of gaining racial equality.

◆*1954* ◆*1961* ◆*1968*

1955
- Rosa Parks inspires Montgomery bus boycott.

1960
- Sit-ins begin and spread to over 100 cities.
- SNCC is formed and leads fight against segregated public facilities.

1961
- Freedom Rides begin.

1964
- Twenty-fourth Amendment abolishes poll tax.
- Civil Rights Act of 1964 outlaws discrimination based on race, gender, religion, or national origin, and gives equal access to public facilities.

1968
- Dr. Martin Luther King, Jr. assassinated.
- Civil Rights Act of 1968 outlaws discrimination in the sale and rental of housing.

Reviewing the Main Ideas

19. Rosa Parks's arrest led to the bus boycott.

20. It was the first case in which the Court found segregation to be unconstitutional.

21. It worked for desegregation of public facilities and voter registration.

22. It moved from focusing on ending segregation to focusing on full social and economic equality. It also moved from nonviolent resistance to militancy.

Critical Thinking

23. **Reading Skill** He organized the March on Washington to garner support for the bill. His effort helped build momentum, but Congress balked until after Kennedy's assassination.

24. The act authorized the attorney general to send federal examiners to register qualified voters, bypassing local officials. The act resulted in over 250,000 African Americans registering as new voters from August to the end of the year.

Self-Check Quiz

Visit the *American Vision: Modern Times* Web site at tav.mt.glencoe.com and click on *Self-Check Quizzes—Chapter 16* to access your knowledge of the chapter content.

26. Organizing Use a graphic organizer similar to the one below to compare examples of civil rights legislation.

Civil Rights Legislation	Provisions
Civil Rights Act 1957	
Twenty-Fourth Amendment	
Voting Rights Act	
Civil Rights Act of 1964	
Civil Rights Act of 1968	

Writing About History

27. **Historical Analysis** **Showing Connections** Research the social, economic, and political effects of the Watts Riot in 1965 and the Detroit Riot in 1967. Then write a two-page paper outlining the impact these events had on the nation. **CA HI1**

28. *Big Idea* Research interviews with Martin Luther King, Jr., and Malcolm X. Take notes on their different points of view, and then prepare a chart illustrating similarities, differences, and any bias which shaped their beliefs.

DBQ **Document-Based Questions**

29. Interpreting Primary Sources In Birmingham, Alabama in the spring of 1963, Martin Luther King, Jr., was jailed and held in solitary confinement. While in prison, he wrote "Letter from a Birmingham Jail," a defense of his nonviolent protests.

❝You may well ask: . . . Why sit-ins, marches and so forth? Isn't negotiation a better path?" . . . Indeed, this is the very purpose of direct action. Nonviolent direct action seeks to create such a crisis . . . that a community . . . is forced to confront the issue. . . .

. . . You express a great deal of anxiety over our willingness to break laws. . . . One may . . . ask: "How can you advocate breaking some laws and obeying others?" The answer lies in the fact that there are two types of laws: just and unjust. . . . One has not only a legal but a moral responsibility to obey just laws. Conversely, one has a moral responsibility to disobey unjust laws. . . .❞

a. Why did the author feel direct action was necessary?

b. Can you identify just and unjust laws throughout history? Would you disobey an unjust law?

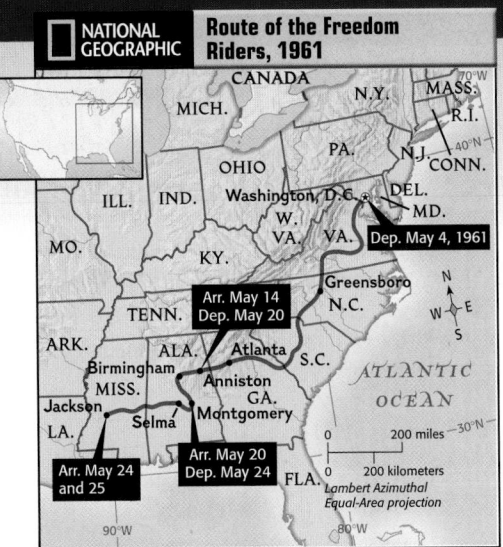

NATIONAL GEOGRAPHIC | **Route of the Freedom Riders, 1961**

Dep. May 4, 1961
Arr. May 14 / Dep. May 20
Greensboro N.C.
Atlanta
Birmingham
Anniston
Montgomery
Selma
Jackson
Arr. May 24 and 25
Arr. May 20 / Dep. May 24
ATLANTIC OCEAN
0 200 miles
0 200 kilometers
Lambert Azimuthal Equal-Area projection

Geography and History

30. The map on this page shows routes of Freedom Riders. Study the map and answer the questions below.

a. Interpreting Maps Which states did the Freedom Riders travel through? What was their final destination?

b. Applying Geography Skills Why do you think the Freedom Riders faced protests during this trip?

Standards Practice

Directions: Choose the phrase that best completes the following statement.

31. One difference between the strategies of Dr. Martin Luther King, Jr., and some later civil rights groups was that King was committed to

A ending discrimination in housing and unemployment.

B using only nonviolent forms of protest.

C demanding equal rights for African Americans.

D gaining improvements in living conditions for African Americans.

Standard 11.10.4: Examine the roles of civil rights advocates (e.g., A. Philip Randolph, Martin Luther King, Jr., Malcolm X, Thurgood Marshall, James Farmer, Rosa Parks), including the significance of Martin Luther King, Jr.'s "Letter from Birmingham Jail" and "I Have a Dream" speech.

CHAPTER 16   The Civil Rights Movement   **767**

CHAPTER 16
Assessment and Activities

Have students visit the Web site at tav.mt.glencoe.com to review Chapter 16 and take the Self-Check Quiz.

Writing About History

27. **Historical Analysis** Students' papers should clearly outline the effects of the riots on all parts of the country.

28. *Big Idea* Charts should show the similarities and differences between the two leaders.

DBQ **Document-Based Questions**

29. a. to force the community to confront the issue **b.** Students' answers will vary. They should focus on laws considered unjust.

Geography and History

30. a. Maryland, Viginia, North Carolina, South Carolina, Georgia, Alabama; final destination: Jackson, Mississippi; **b.** because they wanted to desegregate society

Standards Practice

31. B

Bonus Question ?

Ask: What was the purpose of the March on Washington? *(to build public support for passage of the Civil Rights Act of 1964)*

---

25. After Martin Luther King, Jr., was assassinated, the movement fragmented; also, economic gains were harder to win.

26. Civil Rights Act of 1957: created the civil rights division of the Department of Justice to support the right to vote, created the United States Commission of Civil Rights; Twenty-fourth Amendment: ended poll taxes; Voting Rights Act: authorized the attorney general to send federal examiners to register qualified voters;

Civil Rights Act of 1964: gave the federal government broad powers to prevent racial discrimination, required equal access to public facilities for citizens of all races, established the EEOC, required private employers to end workplace discrimination, gave the attorney general power to bring lawsuits to force school desegregation; Civil Rights Act of 1968: outlawed discrimination in housing.

767

Chapter 17 Planning Guide

SECTION RESOURCES

MAIN IDEAS	📁 PRINT MATERIALS	TECHNOLOGY RESOURCES
Section 1: The United States Focuses on Vietnam 1. The United States supported the French in an effort to prevent the further spread of communism. 2. A newly independent Vietnam was divided in two, the communist North and the pro-Western South.	• Reproducible Lesson Plan 17-1* • Daily Lecture and Discussion Notes 17-1 • Active Reading Note-Taking Guide 17-1 • Guided Reading Activity 17-1 • Section Quiz 17-1 • Reading Essentials and Study Guide 17-1	• Daily Focus Skills Transparency 17-1 • Section Graphic Organizer Transparency 17-1 • Interactive Tutor Self-Assessment CD-ROM • ExamView® Pro Testmaker CD-ROM • Presentation Plus! CD-ROM • California Standards Practice Transparencies
Section 2: Going to War in Vietnam 1. American assistance to South Vietnam increased. 2. President Johnson sent troops to aid South Vietnam against communism. 3. American troops faced guerrilla warfare and a war of attrition.	• Reproducible Lesson Plan 17-2* • Daily Lecture and Discussion Notes 17-2 • Active Reading Note-Taking Guide 17-2 • Guided Reading Activity 17-2 • Section Quiz 17-2 • Reading Essentials and Study Guide 17-2	• Daily Focus Skills Transparency 17-2 • Section Graphic Organizer Transparency 17-2 • Interactive Tutor Self-Assessment CD-ROM • ExamView® Pro Testmaker CD-ROM • Presentation Plus! CD-ROM • California Standards Practice Transparencies
Section 3: Vietnam Divides the Nation 1. Americans grew discouraged as the death toll increased and official reports contradicted the reality of the war. 2. Protests during the war focused on the draft policy. 3. With violence escalating and his popularity dwindling, Johnson decided not to seek another term of office.	• Reproducible Lesson Plan 17-3* • Daily Lecture and Discussion Notes 17-3 • Active Reading Note-Taking Guide 17-3 • Guided Reading Activity 17-3 • Section Quiz 17-3 • Reading Essentials and Study Guide 17-3	• Daily Focus Skills Transparency 17-3 • Section Graphic Organizer Transparency 17-3 • Interactive Tutor Self-Assessment CD-ROM • ExamView® Pro Testmaker CD-ROM • Presentation Plus! CD-ROM • California Standards Practice Transparencies
Section 4: The War Winds Down 1. President Nixon reduced the number of troops in Vietnam and relied on Henry Kissinger to negotiate peace. 2. Protests in the United States continued after the invasion of Cambodia and the killing of South Vietnamese citizens. 3. South Vietnam fell to North Vietnam shortly after the removal of United States troops. 4. Vietnam veterans had a difficult time returning to civilian life.	• Reproducible Lesson Plan 17-4* • Daily Lecture and Discussion Notes 17-4 • Active Reading Note-Taking Guide 17-4 • Guided Reading Activity 17-4 • Section Quiz 17-4 • Reading Essentials and Study Guide 17-4	• Daily Focus Skills Transparency 17-4 • Section Graphic Organizer Transparency 17-4 • Interactive Tutor Self-Assessment CD-ROM • ExamView® Pro Testmaker CD-ROM • Presentation Plus! CD-ROM • California Standards Practice Transparencies

⏱ PACING YOUR LESSONS

Chapter Introduction	Section 1	Section 2	Section 3	Section 4	Chapter Assessment
½ Day	2 Days	2 Days	2 Days	2 Days	½ Day

0:00 OUT OF TIME? 📁 Assign the Chapter 17 *Reading Essentials and Study Guide.*

*Available on TeacherWorks™ CD-ROM

Chapter 17 Planning Guide

Standards-Based Lesson Plan

 History–Social Science Standards Covered in Chapter 17

The standards covered in the chapter are listed below. Use the accompanying activity as you teach the chapter to ensure student mastery of these standards. This activity can be used in combination with the program's print and technology assessment materials.

Standard	Section 1	2	3	4
11.8.5 Describe the increased powers of the presidency in response to the Great Depression, World War II, and the Cold War.		✔		
11.9.2 Understand the role of military alliances, including NATO and SEATO, in deterring communist aggression and maintaining security during the Cold War.	✔			
11.9.3 Trace the origins and geopolitical consequences (foreign and domestic) of the Cold War and containment policy, including the following: the era of McCarthyism, instances of domestic Communism (e.g., Alger Hiss) and blacklisting; the Truman Doctrine; the Berlin Blockade; the Korean War; the Bay of Pigs invasion and the Cuban Missile Crisis; atomic testing in the American West, the "mutual assured destruction" doctrine, and disarmament policies; the Vietnam War; Latin American policy.	✔	✔	✔	✔
11.9.4 List the effects of foreign policy on domestic policies and vice versa (e.g., protests during the war in Vietnam, the "nuclear freeze" movement).			✔	✔

Cumulative Standards-Assessment Activity

The Cumulative Standards-Assessment Activity will help students organize and learn the important information from the chapter. Begin teaching the chapter with this activity, and have students complete it as they read the chapter.

CREATING A SEQUENCING CHART

Purpose Sequencing events is a vital skill when studying history. Understanding the proper sequence of events helps students when they carry out critical thinking tasks, such as identifying cause-and-effect relationships and generalizing about trends or developments. Using graphic organizers like time lines to record events also helps students see how material from different parts of a chapter are related in time, preventing the misconception that content presented later necessarily occurred later in time.

Introduction to Sequencing

1. Discuss how chronological thinking will help students understand history in a linear way, but also will help them see the intersections of events and make the connections that are crucial to comprehending the deeper meanings of historical events.

2. Model how to construct a time line by asking students to identify key dates in the previous chapter and briefly state what happened and why it was important. Explain how signal words like *first, next, then, later,* and *finally* can help them identify

sequence. Write students' suggestions on the board. After you have four or five dates, sequence them properly in a time line.

3. Ask students to copy this chart into their notebooks:

Date	Event and Significance

Explain that students should collect all the dates and events from the chapter before constructing their time charts. If not, the result could become messy if they have to add dates encountered in a later section between two dates identified earlier. Students should make their time lines after they have finished taking notes.

4. As you review the chapter, ask volunteers to name some of the key dates they identified. Encourage all students to use their time lines as study aids.

Chapter 17 Planning Guide

READING SUPPORT

- Content Vocabulary Activity 17
- Academic Vocabulary Activity 17
- Reading Skills Activity 17
- Chapter 17 Active Reading Note-Taking Guide
- Chapter 17 Guided Reading Activities
- Chapter 17 Reading Essentials and Study Guide
- American Literature Readings, Unit 5
- *The American Vision: Modern Times* Video Program
- Vocabulary PuzzleMaker CD-ROM
- American History Primary Source Document Library CD-ROM

CRITICAL THINKING

- Critical Thinking Skills Activity 17
- Primary Source Reading 17
- Cause-and-Effect Transparency 17 Strategy and Activity
- Presentation Plus! CD-ROM

UNIVERSAL ACCESS

- Universal Access Activity 17
- English Learner Activity 17
- American Art Prints
- StudentWorks™ Plus CD-ROM
- American Music: Hits Through History
- School-to-Home Connection Activity 17

SKILL PRACTICE

- Map Overlay Transparency 17 Strategy and Activity
- Historical Analysis Skills Activity 17
- Time Line Activity 17
- Reading Skills Activity 17
- Reinforcing Skills Activity 17
- Linking Past and Present Activity 17
- Interpreting Political Cartoons 17
- MindJogger Videoquiz

WRITING SUPPORT

- Chapter 17 Active Reading Note-Taking Guide
- Writer's Guidebook
- High School Writing Process Transparencies

ASSESSMENT

- Chapter 17 Section Quizzes
- Chapter 17 Tests, Forms A and B
- Authentic Assessment Activity 17
- ExamView® Pro Testmaker CD-ROM
- Interactive Tutor Self-Assessment CD-ROM
- California Standards Practice, Grade 11
- Succeeding on . . .™ the California Standards: Grade 11 History–Social Science CD-ROM

- CD-ROM
- DVD
- Print Material
- Poster

- Transparency
- Music Program
- Videocassette

Chapter 17 Planning Guide

TECHNOLOGY

- StudentWorks™ Plus CD-ROM
- TeacherWorks™ CD-ROM
- ExamView® Pro Testmaker CD-ROM
- Interactive Tutor Self-Assessment CD-ROM
- Presentation Plus! CD-ROM
- Vocabulary PuzzleMaker CD-ROM
- American History Primary Source Document Library CD-ROM
- MindJogger Videoquiz
- *The American Vision: Modern Times* Video Program
- Professional Development in High School Social Studies Video Series
- Teach, Use, and Succeed With *The American Vision: Modern Times*
- American Music: Hits Through History
- Succeeding on . . .™ the California Standards: Grade 11 History–Social Science CD-ROM

SPANISH RESOURCES

- Spanish Activities and Assessment
  - Spanish Vocabulary Activities
  - Spanish Guided Reading Activities
  - Spanish Quizzes and Tests
  - Spanish Reteaching Activities
- Spanish Reading Essentials and Study Guide
- Spanish School-to-Home Connection Activities

TRANSPARENCIES

- Daily Focus Skills Transparencies
- Section Graphic Organizer Transparencies
- Map Overlay Transparencies
- Cause-and-Effect Transparencies
- Unit Time Line Transparencies
- Why It Matters Transparencies
- American Art and Architecture Transparencies
- High School Writing Process Transparencies
- California Standards Practice Transparencies

TEACHER PLANNING

- Daily Lecture and Discussion Notes
- English Learner Handbook
- Building Academic Vocabulary
- *The American Vision: Modern Times* Reading and Study Skills Foldables
- Reading Strategies and Activities for the Social Studies Classroom
- Universal Access for the American History Classroom
- NGS United States Desk Map
- NGS World Atlas
- Chapter 17 Reproducible Lesson Plans on TeacherWorks™ CD-ROM
- California Guide to Daily Intervention

PROFESSIONAL DEVELOPMENT

- Building Academic Vocabulary
- Strategies for Success
- Research-Based Strategies Used to Develop *The American Vision: Modern Times*
- Character Education in the High School Classroom
- Professional Development in High School Social Studies Video Series
- Teach, Use, and Succeed With *The American Vision: Modern Times*

MOMENTS IN TIME

The following resource can help you teach the content of this chapter.

- Unit 12 The Vietnam War (1968–1970)

Chapter 17 Planning Guide

TEACHER'S CORNER

Index to National Geographic Magazine:
The following articles relate to this chapter:

- "Hong Kong—Plight of the Boat People," February 1991
- "The Mekong," February 1993
- "The New Saigon," April 1995
- "Vietnam Memorial: To Heal a Nation," May 1985
- "Vietnam: The Hard Road to Peace," November 1989

National Geographic Society Products:
To order the following, call National Geographic at 1–800–368–2728

- *Historical Atlas of the United States* (Atlas)
- *Historical Atlas of the World* (Atlas)

NGS ONLINE

Access National Geographic's new dynamic MapMachine Web site and other geography resources at:

www.nationalgeographic.com

www.nationalgeographic.com/maps

MASTERING THE STANDARDS

The content and assessment in the Student Edition, Teacher Wraparound Edition, teacher planning materials, and the print and technology products are all standards-based. The use of these products during instruction leads to mastery of the standards.

PRACTICE
- California Standards Practice, Grade 11
- California Standards Practice Transparencies
- School-to-Home Connection

BENCHMARK ASSESSMENT
- Section Quizzes, Chapter Tests, and Authentic Assessment
- ExamView® Pro Testmaker CD-ROM
- Succeeding On . . . ™ the California Standards: Grade 11 History–Social Science CD-ROM

REMEDIATION
- California Guide to Daily Intervention
- Interactive Tutor Self-Assessment CD-ROM
- ExamView® Pro Testmaker CD-ROM
- California Standards Practice, Grade 11
- Reading Essentials and Study Guide

Use our Web site for additional resources. All essential content is covered in the Student Edition.

You and your students can visit tav.mt.glencoe.com, the Web site companion to the **American Vision: Modern Times.** This innovative integration of electronic and print media offers your students a wealth of opportunities. The student text directs students to the Web site for the following options:

- **Chapter Overviews**
- **Self-Check Quizzes**
- **Student Web Activities**
- **Textbook Updates**

Answers to the student Web activities are provided for you in the **Web Activity Lesson Plans.** Additional Web resources and ePuzzles and games are also available.

 Dinah Zike's Foldables

Foldables are three-dimensional, interactive graphic organizers that help students practice basic writing skills, review key vocabulary terms, and identify main ideas. Every chapter has a foldable activity in the *Dinah Zike's Reading and Study Skills Foldables* booklet. You can use the foldables as they are presented or modify them to suit the needs of your individual class.

A variety of videotape programs are available from A&E Television and The History Channel to provide teaching assistance. To order, call Glencoe at 1-800-334-7344.

Chapter 17 Planning Guide

Reading List Generator CD-ROM

The Glencoe BookLink CD-ROM is a database that allows you to search more than 15,000 titles to create a customized reading list for your students.

- Reading Lists can be organized by students' reading level, author, genre, theme, or area of interest.
- The database provides Degrees of Reading Power™ (DRP) and Lexile™ readability scores for all selections.
- A brief summary of each selection is included.

Leveled reading suggestions for this chapter:

For students at a Grade 8 reading level:
- ***Scholastic Encyclopedia of the United States at War,*** by June A. English & Thomas D. Jones

For students at a Grade 9 reading level:
- ***Ain't Gonna Study War No More,*** by Milton Meltzer

For students at a Grade 10 reading level:
- from the ***Prison Diary: Autumn Night,*** by Ho Chi Minh

READING SUPPORT FROM JAMESTOWN EDUCATION

- ***Timed Readings Plus in Social Studies*** help students increase their reading rate and fluency while maintaining comprehension. The 400-word passages are similar to those found on state and national assessments.
- ***Reading in the Content Area: Social Studies*** concentrates on six essential reading skills that help students better comprehend what they read. The book includes 75 high-interest nonfiction passages written at increasing levels of difficulty.
- ***Reading Fluency*** helps students read smoothly, accurately, and expressively.
- ***Jamestown's Reading Improvement,*** by renowned reading expert Edward Fry, focuses on helping build your students' comprehension, vocabulary, and skimming and scanning skills.
- ***Critical Reading Series*** provides high-interest books, each written at three reading levels.

For more information about these products, see the Jamestown Education materials in the Classroom Solutions in the front of this Teacher Wraparound Edition. To order these products, call Glencoe at 17-800-334-7344.

KEY for Using the Teacher Wraparound Edition

Use this key to help you identify the different types of prompts found in the Teacher Wraparound Edition.

R **Reading Strategies** activities help you teach reading skills and vocabulary.

C **Critical Thinking** strategies help students apply and extend what they have learned.

U **Universal Access** activities provide differentiated instruction for students learning to speak English, along with suggestions for teaching various types of learners.

S **Skill Practice** strategies help students practice historical analysis and geography skills.

W **Writing Support** activities provide writing opportunities to help students comprehend the text.

Teaching strategies and activities have been coded for ability level appropriateness.

AL Activities for students working above grade level
OL Activities for students working on grade level
BL Activities for students working below grade level
EL Activities for English learners

FOCUS

History–Social Science Standards

This chapter addresses the following standards:

11.9.3 Trace the origins and geopolitical consequences (foreign and domestic) of the Cold War and containment policy, including the following: the era of McCarthyism, instances of domestic Communism (e.g., Alger Hiss) and blacklisting; the Truman Doctrine; the Berlin Blockade; the Korean War; the Bay of Pigs Invasion and the Cuban Missile Crisis; atomic testing in the American West, the "mutual assured destruction" doctrine, and disarmament policies; the Vietnam War; Latin American policy.

11.9.4 List the effects of foreign policy on domestic policies and vice versa (e.g., protests during the war in Vietnam, the "nuclear freeze" movement).

BELLRINGER
SKILLBUILDER ACTIVITY

Have students create a three-column chart titled *The Vietnam War.* Explain that they will fill out the chart by writing what they **K**now about this topic in the first column, what they **W**ant or need to know in the second, and what they **L**earned in the third. Model how to fill out the chart by eliciting responses such as "the Tet Offensive" to write in the first column.

TEACH

Thinking About the Big Ideas

As you begin teaching each section, use these questions and activities to focus on the Big Idea.

CHAPTER **17** **1954–1975**

The Vietnam War

~ *The Big Ideas* ~

SECTION 1: The United States Focuses on Vietnam

The fate of nations is forever changed by monumental world events. *American efforts to stop the spread of communism led to U.S. involvement in the affairs of Vietnam.*

SECTION 2: Going to War in Vietnam

The fate of nations is forever changed by monumental world events. *After providing South Vietnam with much aid and support, the United States finally sent in troops to fight as well.*

SECTION 3: Vietnam Divides the Nation

People react to periods of breathtaking social and cultural change in different ways. *The experience of Vietnam produced sharp divisions between Americans who supported the war and those who did not.*

SECTION 4: The War Winds Down

The fate of nations is forever changed by monumental world events. *After nearly eight years of fighting in Vietnam, the United States withdrew its forces.*

The *American Vision: Modern Times* **Video** *The Chapter 17 video, "Vietnam: A Different War," explores the causes and the impact of this longest war in American history.*

1954
- Vietminh defeat French
- Geneva Accords signed

1964
- Congress passes Gulf of Tonkin Resolution

1965
- U.S. combat troops arrive in Vietnam

United States
PRESIDENTS

Eisenhower 1953–1961

Kennedy 1961–1963

L. Johnson 1963–1969

1955   *1960*   *1965*

World

1955
- Khrushchev is dominant leader in USSR

1958
- De Gaulle heads France's Fifth Republic

1964
- Japan introduces first high-speed passenger train

768

Section 1
The United States Focuses on Vietnam

Essential Question: How do events in other countries impact the United States? Discuss students' responses, making sure to incorporate the concepts of global interdependence and the global balance of power. Tell students that as they read Section 1, they will learn how American efforts to stop the spread of communism led to U.S. involvement in the affairs of Vietnam.
OL

Section 2
Going to War in Vietnam

Essential Question: Have you ever helped a person in need? How? Why? Tell students that in Section 2, they will find out that after providing South Vietnam with much aid and support, the United States finally sent troops to fight as well. **BL**

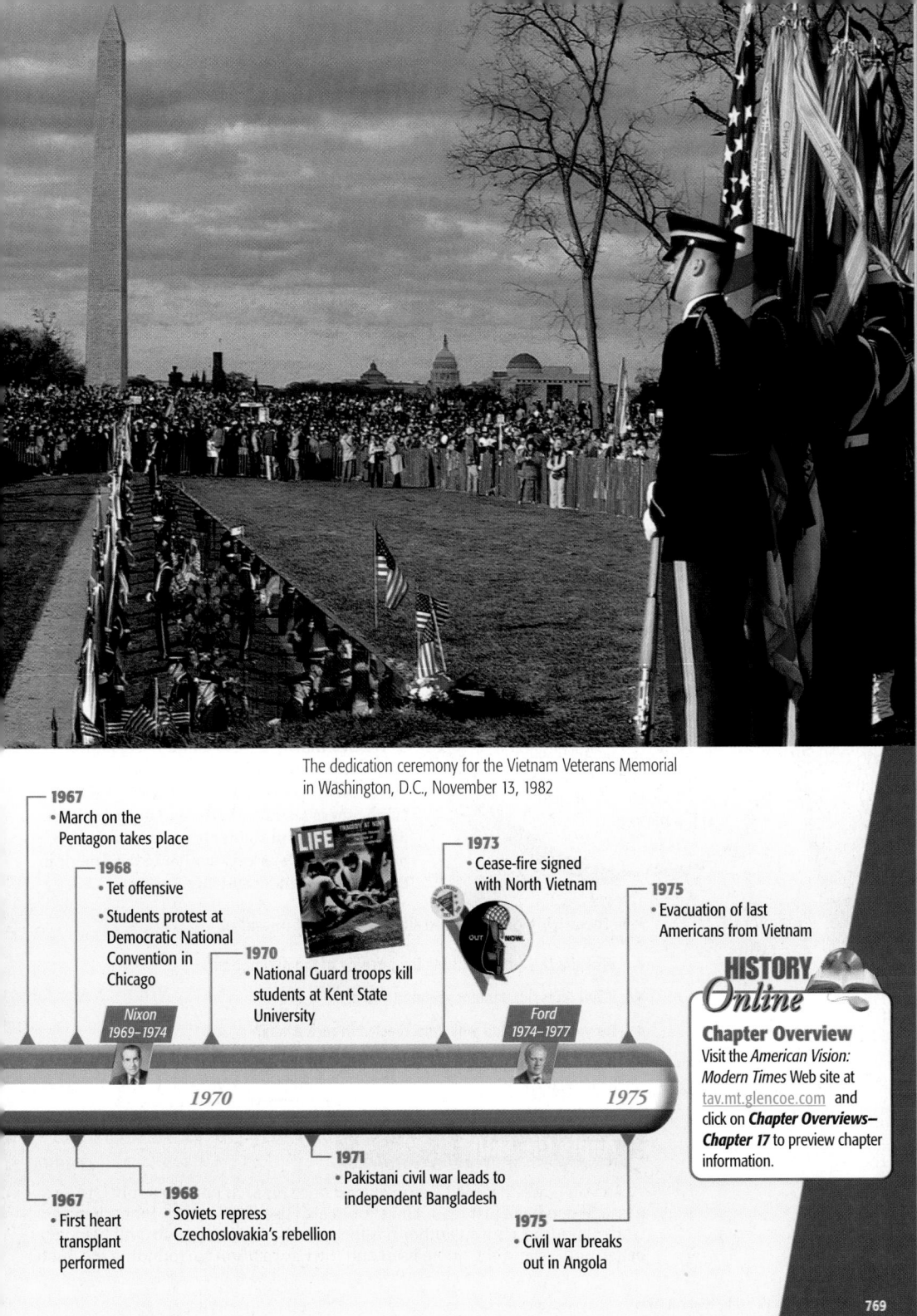

The dedication ceremony for the Vietnam Veterans Memorial in Washington, D.C., November 13, 1982

1967
• March on the Pentagon takes place

1968
• Tet offensive
• Students protest at Democratic National Convention in Chicago

1970
• National Guard troops kill students at Kent State University

1973
• Cease-fire signed with North Vietnam

1975
• Evacuation of last Americans from Vietnam

Nixon 1969–1974

Ford 1974–1977

LIFE

1970   1975

1967
• First heart transplant performed

1968
• Soviets repress Czechoslovakia's rebellion

1971
• Pakistani civil war leads to independent Bangladesh

1975
• Civil war breaks out in Angola

HISTORY Online

Chapter Overview
Visit the *American Vision: Modern Times* Web site at tav.mt.glencoe.com and click on *Chapter Overviews—Chapter 17* to preview chapter information.

769

Section 3
Vietnam Divides the Nation
Essential Question: Have you ever fought with a friend or sibling? Why did fights occur, and what were the results? Tell students that Section 3 will show them how the experience of Vietnam produced sharp divisions between Americans who supported the war and those who did not. **BL**

Section 4
The War Winds Down
Essential Question: What do Americans usually think of when they remember the Vietnam War? As students read Section 4, remind them to consider how, after nearly eight years of fighting in Vietnam, the United States withdrew its forces. **OL**

Cultural Perspectives

The Vietnam War was the first major conflict broadcast to the American people by the mass media. As Secretary of State Dean Rusk said, "This was the first struggle fought on television in everybody's living room every day." **Ask:** What effect might this coverage have had on American society at home as well as American troops fighting abroad? Have students write brief responses to this question, and then discuss the responses as a class. Focus on issues such as the influence of the mass media, or the conflict between the public's right to information and the government's need to protect information. **OL**

FOLDABLES™
Study Organizer

Dinah Zike's Foldables are three-dimensional, interactive graphic organizers that help students practice basic writing skills, review key vocabulary terms, and identify main ideas. Have students complete the foldable activity in the *Dinah Zike's Reading and Study Skills Foldables* booklet.

HISTORY Online

Go to tav.mt.glencoe.com for student activities, lesson plans, and links to additional Web resources to help students learn about U.S. involvement in Vietnam.

Preparing to Read

Reading Skill

Why It's Important

Good readers should not take what they read at face value. Instead they should question the information in a reading passage, trying to understand why the author wrote the material in that specific way. Questioning the author helps students understand what they read more effectively.

1. Introducing the Skill

Divide the class into groups of four. Ask each group to select a primary source document in the back of the textbook. Then tell the groups to read the document and write down three questions they would ask the author if they could. Tell them to record their questions in a chart similar to the one below. **OL**

Document	Author	Questions
		1.
		2.
		3.

2. Extending the Skill

Present the class with a recent newspaper or magazine article on a current national event. Tell each student to read the article, then have the class collaborate to find ways to question the text and information presented in the article. **OL**

Answers and Additional Support

Reading Skill — Questioning the Author

While reading this textbook, do you ever wonder what the author was thinking when he wrote a passage? If so, you have questioned the author in your mind. Effective readers understand that every author writes for an audience. When you create questions for the author, you help yourself get to the deeper meaning of the text. You will find answers to some of your questions in the text, but some questions will remain open-ended. The reading strategy called Questioning the Author (QtA) helps you to make connections and read beyond the text.

You can use QtA at any time, whether you are reading the main text or the American Story near the beginning of each section. Stop occasionally during the reading to ask yourself about the author's purpose for a passage, the clarity of the passage, or about experiences that link this information to something else. You will also notice that this textbook contains extended quotes from the people of the time. When you see these quotes, ask yourself why the author has included them.

QUESTIONING THE AUTHOR

Always ask yourself if what you are reading makes sense. If it doesn't, you can reread a passage or discuss it with your teacher or, with your teacher's permission, with a partner.

Read the passage below about American officer Archimedes Patti, who helped Vietminh leader Ho Chi Minh write the Vietnam Declaration of Independence in 1945.

> When a translator read aloud the opening— "All men are created equal; they are endowed by their Creator with certain unalienable rights; among these are life, liberty, and the pursuit of happiness"—Patti suddenly sat up, startled, recognizing the words as very similar to the American Declaration of Independence. (p. 774)

Use these QtA questions to discuss the text passage.

- **Why did the author include the opening of the declaration?**
- **What does this sentence remind you of?**
- **Do you understand why Patti reacted in such a way?**
- **Based on what you know about the origin of the quote, what do you think will happen next?**

Apply the Skill

As you read Chapter 17, stop at least once on each page to apply QtA to a passage you have just read. You should also use this strategy for each quote. Understanding why an author has included a particular quote will help you better understand the quote itself and the information surrounding the quote.

UNIVERSAL ACCESS

Interpersonal Ask students to share the magazine or newspaper article with a parent, grandparent, or older sibling. Each student should ask this person what questions he or she might ask the author of the article, and why. Have students report their discussion to the class, making sure to identify the age of the person they spoke with. Have students discuss how their interviewee's questions might be different from those the students formulated, and how age may have influenced the types of questions asked. **OL**

Historical Analysis Skill — Comparing Present and Past

Analysis Skill Standard CS1

Chronological and Spatial Thinking You will understand history better if you learn to compare the present with the past, evaluate the consequences of past events and decisions, and determine the lessons that were learned.

Imagine that you have walked into class and face a test for which you did not prepare. How do you react? When people are faced with a problem, some might ignore it, hoping it will go away. Others may run away from the problem. Still others might face the problem, trying to influence the potential outcome. You may find that the most effective way to address a problem is to review past solutions to similar problems that you or others have tried.

When historians try to understand events, they often use a similar strategy. Historians review information to see if they recognize any patterns. They then use their prior knowledge of similar historical events to compare these events. The events may have occurred before or after the event they are studying. Historians also may compare present events with those that occurred in the past, evaluating the consequences of past events in order to determine lessons learned.

Read the following passage to see how President Dwight Eisenhower used the consequences of the past in his policy decisions on Vietnam.

You have a row of dominoes set up, you knock over the first one, and what will happen to the last one is the certainty that it will go over very quickly. . . . Asia, after all, has already lost 450 million of its peoples to the Communist dictatorship, and we simply can't afford greater losses. . . . (page 775)

As you learned in previous chapters, after World War II the United States was concerned about the spread of communism around the world. When President Eisenhower took office, China had become a communist country and the United States was negotiating an armistice with communist North Korea. Eisenhower feared that if Vietnam, too, fell to communism, other nations in Southeast Asia would follow. This concern influenced Eisenhower's decision to support the French against the Vietminh.

Apply the Skill

As you read the chapter, note how the domino theory influenced United States policy in Vietnam through 1975. At the same time, determine what lessons were learned, or not learned, from this policy.

771

Preparing to Read

Historical Analysis

Why It's Important

History is about the past, but it is studied and written about in the present. A useful skill for readers is to compare past and present. This way students can learn how past events have affected later events.

1. Introducing the Skill

Have students ask their parents about experiences they had as teenagers in the following areas: school, dating, and after-school activities. After students have gathered this information, ask them to compare their parents' responses to their own experiences at the same age. Students can identify the similarities and differences by placing the information in Venn diagrams similar to the one below. **BL**

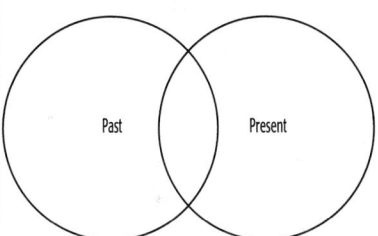

Past — Present

2. Extending the Skill

Divide the class into groups of five and tell each group to identify the differences in how Americans viewed the Vietnam War at the time and how it is viewed today. Each group should write a one-page paper explaining the war's interpretation. **OL CA CS1**

UNIVERSAL ACCESS

English Learners Americans view the Vietnam War from a particular perspective. Students from other countries most likely view the war differently. Ask foreign-born students in your class to describe what opinions, if any, they have regarding the Vietnam War. Have students compare these views with those of students born in the United States. Ask the class to consider possible reasons for any differences they identified. **EL**

FOCUS

Guide to Reading

Understanding Vocabulary: Have students use a standard dictionary or online resource to learn the correct pronunciation of the content vocabulary and academic vocabulary. For example, some dictionary sites have an audio feature where the user can hear words pronounced correctly.

Answers to Graphic: fall of China to communism and the outbreak of the Korean War

Unpacking the Standards

Students will be able to:

• Explain how the United States initially became involved in the Vietnam War.

• Describe how the Vietnamese nationalists drove the French out of the country in 1954.

Answers and Additional Support

SECTION 1

The United States Focuses on Vietnam

Guide to Reading

Connection
In the previous chapter, you learned about the civil rights movement. In this section, you will discover how the United States became involved in a war in Vietnam.

Main Idea
• The United States supported the French in an effort to prevent the further spread of communism. (p. 773)
• A newly independent Vietnam was divided in two, the communist North and the pro-Western South. (p. 775)

Content Vocabulary
domino theory, guerrilla

Academic Vocabulary
region, occupy, principal

People and Terms to Identify
Ho Chi Minh, Dien Bien Phu, Ngo Dinh Diem

Reading Objectives
• **Describe** the nationalist motives of Vietnamese leader Ho Chi Minh.
• **Explain** the origins of American involvement in Vietnam during the 1950s.

Reading Strategy
Organizing As you read about the increasing involvement of the United States in Vietnam, complete a graphic organizer similar to the one below by providing reasons that the United States aided France in Vietnam.

Reasons for U.S. Support of France

Preview of Events

◆1946   ◆1950   ◆1954

1946 — French-Vietminh War begins

1950 — The United States supplies military aid to France

1954 — Vietminh defeat French at Dien Bien Phu; Geneva Accords signed in Paris

1956 — Ngo Dinh Diem refuses to participate in nationwide elections in Vietnam

---

The following are the main History–Social Science Standards covered in this section.

11.9.2 Understand the role of military alliances, including NATO and SEATO, in deterring communist aggression and maintaining security during the Cold War.

11.9.3 Trace the origins and geopolitical consequences (foreign and domestic) of the Cold War and containment policy, including the following: the era of McCarthyism, instances of domestic Communism (e.g., Alger Hiss) and blacklisting; the Truman Doctrine; the Berlin Blockade; the Korean War; the Bay of Pigs invasion and the Cuban Missile Crisis; atomic testing in the American West, the "mutual assured destruction" doctrine, and disarmament policies; the Vietnam War; Latin American policy.

⁓ The Big Idea ⁓

The fate of nations is forever changed by monumental world events. In a continuing effort to stop the spread of communism, the United States began to support France's efforts to control Vietnam after World War II. Despite the help of the United States, the French eventually were defeated by the Vietminh. During negotiations to end the war, the Geneva Accords divided Vietnam into two sections—the pro-Communist North and the pro-Western South. When France pulled out, the United States stepped in to aid South Vietnam as tensions between the North and South escalated.

SECTION RESOURCES

📖 Print Material
• Reproducible Lesson Plan 17-1
• Guided Reading Activity 17-1
• Reading Essentials and Study Guide 17-1
• Active Reading Note-Taking Guide 17-1

📽 Transparencies
• Daily Focus Skills Transparency 17-1
• Section Graphic Organizer Transparency 17-1

Technology
🖥 Interactive Tutor Self-Assessment CD-ROM
🖥 Exam*View*® Pro Testmaker CD-ROM
🖥 Presentation Plus! CD-ROM

Early American Involvement in Vietnam

Main Idea The United States supported the French in an effort to prevent the further spread of communism.

Reading Connection Have you ever played dominoes? Read on to learn how the concept of a popular game shaped U.S. foreign policy.

In the late 1940s and early 1950s, most Americans knew little about Vietnam. During this time, however, American officials came to view the nation as increasingly important in the campaign to halt the spread of communism. American military forces were eventually sent to Vietnam to help combat communism.

★ An American Story ★

In 1965 the first major battle between American and North Vietnamese soldiers took place in the Ia Drang Valley in South Vietnam. During the battle, a platoon of American soldiers was cut off and surrounded. Lieutenant Joe Marm's platoon was among those sent to rescue the trapped Americans. When his men came under heavy fire, Marm acted quickly: "I told the men to hold their fire.... Then I ran forward.... That's the principle we use in the infantry, 'Lead by your own example.'" Marm raced across open ground and hurled grenades at the enemy, and although he was shot in the jaw, he managed to kill the troops firing at his men. For his extraordinary bravery, Lieutenant Marm received the Medal of Honor:

❝I feel I'm the recipient of the medal for the many, many brave soldiers whose deeds go unsung . . . [T]he medal is as much theirs as it is mine. It's always tough to get men to go into battle, but we were a tight unit, and there were Americans out there that we were trying to get to. We're all in it together, and we were fighting for each other and for our guys. . . . I had the best soldiers. . . . They were fearless, and they were just great Americans and they're going to go down in history.❞

–quoted in *The Soldiers' Story*

Troop involvement in Vietnam happened slowly, though. Despite its concern about communism, the United States at first was reluctant to get directly involved in the country or to support the French who had been the colonial power in Vietnam before World War II.

The Growth of Vietnamese Nationalism When the Japanese seized power in Vietnam during World War II, it was one more example of foreigners ruling the Vietnamese people. China had controlled the **region** off and on for hundreds of years. From the late 1800s until World War II, France ruled Vietnam and neighboring Laos and Cambodia—a region known collectively as French Indochina.

By the early 1900s, nationalism had become a powerful force in Vietnam. The Vietnamese formed several political parties to push for independence or reform of the French colonial government. One of the leaders of the nationalist movement was Nguyen Tat Thanh—better known by his alias, **Ho Chi Minh,** or "Bringer of Light." He was born in 1890 in central Vietnam. As a young man, Ho Chi Minh taught at a village school. At the age of 21, he sailed for Europe on a French freighter, paying his passage by working in the galley. During his travels abroad, including a stay in the Soviet Union, Ho Chi Minh became an advocate of communism. In 1930 he returned to Southeast Asia, where he helped found the Indochinese Communist Party and worked to overthrow French rule.

Ho Chi Minh's activities made him a wanted man. He fled Indochina and spent several years in exile in the Soviet Union and China. In 1941 he returned to

"We're all in it together . . ."

—Lieutenant Joe Marm

Chapter 17 • Section 1

TEACH

C Critical Thinking

Analyzing Primary Sources
Ask students to use the library to read some soldiers' memoirs of their service in Vietnam. Ask students to focus specifically on any remembrances of what the soldiers knew or did not know about the country as they trained for their missions. Discuss the findings in class and look for common themes. **OL** **CA 11RC2.5**

R₁ Reading Strategy

Using Context Clues Ask students to look up the word *nationalism* in the dictionary and define the term in their own words. *(Students' definitions will vary but should indicate a desire for independence rather than domination by a foreign country.)* **BL**

R₂ Reading Strategy

Activating Prior Knowledge Ask students to give examples of Communist governments that are discussed in previous chapters. *(the Soviet Union, China, Cuba)* **OL**

Did You Know?

Situated on the western bank of the Saigon River, Saigon is now called Ho Chi Minh City. It is the largest city in Vietnam with a population of almost 6 million.

W Writing Support

Research Report Writing
Ask students to read the passage about Ho Chi Minh receiving inspiration from the Declaration of Independence and reread the preamble to the Declaration of Independence (page 120). Have students research and write two-page reports that identify other nations that were inspired by the success of the American Revolution and describe the documents that helped define the United States. *(Reports might identify France, Poland, or some countries in Latin America.)* **AL**

CA 11WA2.4

U Universal Access

English Learners Have students examine each of the photographs in this section. Then ask them to write a sentence explaining what they learned about Vietnam and its people from observing the photographs. Encourage students to pay particular attention to peoples' activities and their facial expressions. **EL**

Vietnam. By then Japan had seized control of the country. Ho Chi Minh organized a nationalist group called the Vietminh. The group united both Communists and non-Communists in the struggle to expel the Japanese forces. Soon afterward, the United States began sending military aid to the Vietminh.

The United States Supports the French With the Allies' victory over Japan in August 1945, the Japanese surrendered control of Indochina. Ho Chi Minh and his forces quickly announced that Vietnam was an independent nation. He even crafted a Vietnam Declaration of Independence. Archimedes Patti, an American officer stationed in Vietnam at the time, helped the rebel leader write the document. When a translator read aloud the opening—"All men are created equal; they are endowed by their Creator with certain inalienable rights; among these are liberty, life, and the pursuit of happiness"—Patti suddenly sat up, startled, recognizing the words as very similar to the American Declaration of Independence.

> ❝I stopped him and turned to Ho in amazement and asked if he really intended to use it in his declaration . . . Ho sat back in his chair, his palms together with fingertips touching his lips ever so lightly, as though meditating. Then, with a gentle smile he asked softly, 'Should I not use it?' I felt sheepish and embarrassed. Of course, I answered, why should he not?❞
>
> —quoted in *The Perfect War*

France, however, had no intention of seeing Vietnam become independent. Seeking to regain their colonial empire in Southeast Asia, French troops returned to Vietnam in 1946 and drove the Vietminh forces into hiding in the countryside. By 1949 French officials had set up a new government in Vietnam.

Picturing **History**

Rural Economy Most of Vietnam's people live in the country's low-lying fertile lands near the Red River delta in the north and the Mekong River delta in the south. What does the image below sug about the use of human labor in the country's agricultural econ

NATIONAL GEOGRAPHIC **Indochina, 1959**

CHINA
BURMA 1948
NORTH VIETNAM 1954 — Hanoi
LAOS 1954
Vientiane
Gulf of Tonkin
Rangoon
THAILAND Never a European colony
Bangkok
CAMBODIA 1954
Phnom Penh
SOUTH VIETNAM 1954
Saigon
Gulf of Thailand
South China Sea

200 miles / 200 kilometers / Miller Cylindrical projection

1954 Date of independence

Geography *Skills*

1. **Interpreting Maps** What three countries border North and South Vietnam?
2. **Applying Geography Skills** A mountain chain extends nearly 800 miles (1,290 km) from North to South Vietnam. How do you think this terrain aided the Vietnamese guerrillas who were fighting U.S. troops?

Answers and Additional Support

Geography *Skills*

Answers:
1. Cambodia, China, and Laos
2. They used it to their advantage to launch hit-and-run and ambush attacks.

Geography Skills Practice
Ask: What forms the east coast of Vietnam? *(Gulf of Tonkin and the South China Sea)*

Picturing **History**

Answer: that it is labor intensive
Ask: What can you assume about the standard of living in Vietnam? *(low standard of living, probably at subsistence level)*

Nationalist Leader Ho Chi Minh was already involved in fighting for Vietnam's independence when this photograph was taken in 1946. What foreign country was he opposing at that time?

The Vietminh fought back against the French-dominated regime and slowly increased their control over large areas of the countryside. As fighting between the two sides escalated, France appealed to the United States for help.

France's request for assistance put American officials in a difficult position. The United States opposed colonialism. It had pressured the Dutch to give up their empire in Indonesia, and it supported the British decision to give India independence in 1947. In Vietnam, however, the independence movement had become entangled with the Communist movement. American officials did not think France should control Vietnam, but they did not want Vietnam to be Communist either.

Two events convinced the Truman administration to help France—the fall of China to communism, and the outbreak of the Korean War. Korea, in particular, convinced American officials that the Soviet Union had begun a major push to impose communism on East Asia. Shortly after the Korean War began, Truman authorized a massive program of military aid to French forces fighting in Vietnam.

On taking office in 1953, President Eisenhower continued to support the French military campaign against the Vietminh. By 1954 the United States was paying roughly three-fourths of France's war costs. During a news conference that year, Eisenhower defended United States policy in Vietnam by stressing what became known as the **domino theory**—the belief that if Vietnam fell to communism, so too would the other nations of Southeast Asia:

❝You have a row of dominoes set up, you knock over the first one, and what will happen to the last one is the certainty that it will go over very quickly. . . . Asia, after all, has already lost 450 million of its peoples to the Communist dictatorship, and we simply can't afford greater losses. . . .❞

—quoted in *America in Vietnam*

✓**Reading Check** **Summarizing** Why did Ho Chi Minh lead a resistance movement against France?

The Vietminh Drive Out the French

Main Idea A newly independent Vietnam was divided in two, the communist North and the pro-Western South.

Reading Connection When was the United States divided between a "north" and "south"? Read on to discover how the United States became involved in a pending civil war.

Despite significant amounts of aid from the United States, the French struggled against the Vietminh, who consistently frustrated the French with hit-and-run and ambush tactics. These are the tactics of **guerrillas,** irregular troops who usually blend into the civilian population and are often difficult for regular armies to fight. The mounting casualties and the inability of the French to defeat the Vietminh made the war very unpopular in France. Finally, in 1954, the struggle reached a turning point.

Defeat at Dien Bien Phu In 1954 the French commander ordered his forces to **occupy** the mountain town of **Dien Bien Phu.** Seizing the town would interfere with the Vietminh's supply lines and force them into open battle.

Soon afterward, a huge Vietminh force surrounded Dien Bien Phu and began bombarding the town. "Shells rained down on us without stopping

CHAPTER 17 The Vietnam War **775**

Review the Big Idea
Review the Big Idea for this section, "The fate of nations is forever changed by monumental world events." Ask the class to consider why the United States struggled with the decision to help France. *(U.S. foreign policy typically rejected colonial governments. However, communism was seen as a larger danger than supporting France's colonial control of Vietnam.)* Ask the class to brainstorm reasons U.S. foreign policy advisers might have used to convince the president to get involved in Vietnam. **OL**

R₁ **Reading Strategy**
Scaffolding—Academic Vocabulary The word *impose* was introduced in Chapter 11, Section 1. Ask a student to define the word. **BL**

R₂ **Reading Strategy**
Activating Prior Knowledge Ask students to discover the origin of the word *guerrilla*. *(a Spanish word meaning "little war")* **Ask:** Can you think of another country that utilized guerrilla tactics to wear down and frustrate a superior military opponent? *(Students should realize that American minutemen used similar tactics during the American Revolution.)* **BL**

✓**Reading Check**
Answer: He sought independence for Vietnam.

ASSESS

Resources for page 776

Use these resources to assess student mastery.

📂 Section Quiz 17-1

📂 Reading Essentials and Study Guide 17-1

⦿ Interactive Tutor Self-Assessment CD-ROM

📂 California Standards Practice, Grade 11

Picturing **History**

Answer: It convinced the French to make peace and withdraw from Indochina.

✓ **Reading Check**

Answer: caused the French to withdraw and led to the Geneva Accords

HISTORY Online

Study Central provides audio summaries, interactive games, and online graphic organizers to help students review section content.

CLOSE

Connecting Have students explain the origins of American involvement in Vietnam during the 1950s. OL

Picturing **History**

Last Stand French troops assemble a tank near the Dien Bien Phu airfield shortly before their defeat by the Vietminh. How did this defeat influence French policy in Indochina?

led by a nationalist leader named **Ngo Dinh Diem** (NOH DIHN deh·EHM). Like Ho Chi Minh, Diem had been educated abroad, but unlike the North Vietnamese leader, Diem was pro-Western and fiercely anti-Communist. A Catholic, he welcomed the roughly one million North Vietnamese Catholics who migrated south to escape Ho Chi Minh's rule.

When the time came in 1956 to hold countrywide elections, as called for by the Geneva Accords, Diem refused. He knew that the Communist-controlled north would not allow genuinely free elections, and that Ho Chi Minh would almost certainly have won as a result. Eisenhower supported Diem and increased American military and economic aid to South Vietnam. In the wake of Diem's actions, tensions between the North and South intensified. The nation seemed headed toward civil war, with the United States caught in the middle of it.

like a hailstorm on a fall evening," recalled one French soldier. "Bunker after bunker, trench after trench collapsed, burying under them men and weapons." On May 7, 1954, the French force at Dien Bien Phu fell to the Vietminh. The defeat convinced the French to make peace and withdraw from Indochina.

Geneva Accords Negotiations to end the conflict were held in Geneva, Switzerland. The Geneva Accords temporarily divided Vietnam along the 17th parallel, with Ho Chi Minh and the Vietminh in control of North Vietnam and a pro-Western regime in control of the South. In 1956 elections were to be held to reunite the country under a single government. The Geneva Conference also recognized Cambodia's independence. (Laos had gained independence the previous year.)

Shortly after the Geneva Accords partitioned Vietnam, the French finally left. The United States almost immediately stepped in and became the **principal** protector of the new government in the South,

✓ **Reading Check** **Examining** What was the effect of the French defeat at Dien Bien Phu?

HISTORY Online **Study Central**

For help with the concepts in this section of *American Vision: Modern Times* go to tav.mt.glencoe.com and click on *Study Central.*

SECTION 1 ASSESSMENT

Checking for Understanding

1. **Vocabulary** Define: region, domino theory, guerrilla, occupy, principal.
2. **People and Terms** Identify: Ho Chi Minh, Dien Bien Phu, Ngo Dinh Diem.
3. **Explain** the goals of the Vietminh.

Reviewing Big Ideas

4. **Analyzing** Why did Ngo Dinh Diem refuse to hold country-wide elections in Vietnam in 1956?

Critical Thinking

5. **Historical Analysis** **Interpreting** Why do you think the United States supported the government of Ngo Dinh Diem? CA HI2; HI3
6. **Organizing** Use a graphic organizer like the one below to list provisions of the Geneva Accords.

Geneva Accords Provisions

Analyzing Visuals

7. **Analyzing** Photographs Study the Vietnam scene on page 774. How would you describe the contrast between American and Vietnamese societies? How do you think this contrast influenced American thinking toward the war?

Writing About History

8. **Descriptive Writing** Take on the role of a Vietnamese peasant in the 1940s. Write a journal entry on your thoughts toward the French. CA 11WS1.2

SECTION 1 ASSESSMENT ANSWERS

1. Content vocabulary is boldfaced and highlighted in yellow. Academic vocabulary is boldfaced.
2. Ho Chi Minh (p. 773), Dien Bien Phu (p. 775), Ngo Dinh Diem (p. 776)
3. The Vietminh fought for independence first from Japan, then from France.
4. He feared he would lose to the Vietnamese Communist Party.
5. because he was pro-Western and anti-Communist
6. temporarily divided Vietnam at 17th parallel; attempted to reunite nation with countrywide elections planned for 1956
7. Vietnam appeared to be less prosperous than the United States, so it was easy to believe the United States could defeat the Vietnamese.
8. Students' journal entries should be written from a peasant's perspective.

SECTION 2 Going to War in Vietnam

Guide to Reading

Connection
In the previous section, you learned how the United States became involved in Vietnam. In this section, you will discover how the United States eventually sent troops into Vietnam.

Main Idea
• American assistance to South Vietnam increased. (p. 778)
• President Johnson sent troops to aid South Vietnam against communism. (p. 779)
• American troops faced guerrilla warfare and a war of attrition. (p. 781)

Content Vocabulary
napalm, Agent Orange

Academic Vocabulary
administration, coincidental, sustain

People and Terms to Identify
Vietcong, Gulf of Tonkin Resolution, Ho Chi Minh trail

Reading Objectives
• **Describe** how President Johnson deepened American involvement in Vietnam.

• **Discuss** how the Vietcong and the North Vietnamese were able to frustrate the American military.

Reading Strategy
Taking Notes As you read about the beginnings of the Vietnam War, use the major headings of the section to create an outline similar to the one below.

Going to War in Vietnam
I. American Involvement Deepens
   A.
   B.
II.
   A.
   B.

Preview of Events

| 1963 | 1964 | 1965 | 1966 |

1963
Number of American military advisers in South Vietnam reaches around 15,000

1964
Congress passes Gulf of Tonkin Resolution

1965
The United States begins bombing North Vietnam; first American combat troops arrive in Vietnam

---

The following are the main History–Social Science Standards covered in this section.

11.8.5 Describe the increased powers of the presidency in response to the Great Depression, World War II, and the Cold War.

11.9.3 Trace the origins and geopolitical consequences (foreign and domestic) of the Cold War and containment policy, including the following: the era of McCarthyism, instances of domestic Communism (e.g., Alger Hiss) and blacklisting; the Truman Doctrine; the Berlin Blockade; the Korean War; the Bay of Pigs invasion and the Cuban Missile Crisis; atomic testing in the American West, the "mutual assured destruction" doctrine, and disarmament policies; the Vietnam War; Latin American policy.

❧ The Big Idea ❧

The fate of nations is forever changed by monumental world events. The events in Vietnam eventually led to an armed struggle between North and South. The United States continued its support because it believed the success of South Vietnam was vital in the battle against communism. Following the assassination of Ngo Dinh Diem, the United States became more involved in the conflict. Military aid, earlier restricted to military advisers, now included a bombing campaign and combat troops. The Vietcong used ambushes and guerrilla warfare against American soldiers. As the war raged on, the number of killed and injured Americans continued to grow. Many Americans began to question the nation's involvement in the war.

CHAPTER 17   The Vietnam War   **777**

SECTION RESOURCES

📂 **Print Material**
• Reproducible Lesson Plan 17-2
• Guided Reading Activity 17-2
• Reading Essentials and Study Guide 17-2
• Active Reading Note-Taking Guide 17-2

🖼 **Transparencies**
• Daily Focus Skills Transparency 17-2
• Section Graphic Organizer Transparency 17-2

Technology
⊙ Interactive Tutor Self-Assessment CD-ROM
⊙ Exam*View*® Pro Testmaker CD-ROM
⊙ Presentation Plus! CD-ROM

FOCUS

BELLRINGER
SKILLBUILDER ACTIVITY

Project **Daily Focus Skills Transparency 17-2** and have students answer the question.

Guide to Reading

Understanding Vocabulary:
Have students look up the content vocabulary words and academic vocabulary words in the glossary. Then have them write a description or definition of each using their own words.

Answers to Graphic:
Going to War in Vietnam
I. American Involvement Deepens
   A. Kennedy Takes Over
   B. The Overthrow of Diem
II. Johnson and Vietnam
   A. The Gulf of Tonkin Resolution
   B. The United States Sends in Troops
III. A Bloody Stalemate Emerges
   A. Frustrating Warfare
   B. Determined Enemy

Unpacking the Standards

Students will be able to:
• Describe how U.S. involvement in Vietnam deepened.
• Explain how President Johnson conducted the war in Vietnam.
• Analyze how the war evolved into a stalemate.

TEACH

W Writing Support

Summary Writing Ask students to review the text that describes the growth of Vietcong support. Have them write short paragraphs explaining why the Vietcong received support from the Vietnamese. *(Many Vietnamese rejected the Diem government and were afraid of retaliation by the Vietcong if they opposed them.)* **OL** **CA 11WS1.1**

R Reading Strategy

Summarizing American involvement in Vietnam deepened throughout the terms of several different presidential administrations. **Ask: Why did Kennedy commit more troops and support to the Vietnam conflict?** *(Kennedy acted within the mindset of the Cold War containment theory that Communist expansion should be resisted around the world. He also did not wish to appear "soft" on communism and open himself to political criticism from the growing number of congressional Republicans.)* **OL**

Answers and Additional Support

American Involvement Deepens

 American assistance to South Vietnam increased.

Reading Connection Do you think the American government should encourage the spread of democracy? Read on to learn about American efforts to support a free South Vietnam.

In the mid-1950s, American officials decided to support the government of South Vietnam in its struggle against North Vietnam. Both President Eisenhower and President Kennedy sent military aid and hundreds of advisers. Over time, though, sending advisers did not seem to be enough. By the time President Johnson took office, American involvement had increased significantly, and within two years, the president committed ground troops.

★ An American Story ★

Marlene Kramel joined the Army Nurse Corps in 1965 when she was 21, and she went to Vietnam the following year. She was working in a makeshift hospital on what was a particularly quiet night. Most of the patients who filled the beds that evening were suffering from malaria.

Suddenly, a row of helicopters roared in from over the horizon, carrying wounded from a nearby battle. As the casualties came in on stretchers, the hospital turned chaotic. Doctors ran about the facility screaming orders and frantically trying to treat patients.

The only nurse on duty at the time, Kramel felt overwhelmed by the confusion. "Every one of the doctors is yelling for me," she recalled. "I didn't know what to do next. 'Start this. Do that.' Everybody's yelling at me. I couldn't do enough." Things happened so quickly that night, she insisted, that she could not remember most of it. "I can't remember blood, even. I can only remember, 'What am I going to do?' And the doctors moving at tremendous speed. And I'm there. And I'm not able to move fast enough.... That's all I remember."

—adapted from *The Living and the Dead*

During Eisenhower's term in office, troop involvement did not seem imminent, and U.S. aid was limited. Ngo Dinh Diem's refusal to hold national

elections brought a quick response by Ho Chi Minh and his followers. They began an armed struggle to reunify the nation. Their first step consisted of organizing a new guerrilla army, which became known as the **Vietcong.** As fighting began between the Vietcong and South Vietnam's forces, President Eisenhower increased American aid and sent hundreds of military advisers to train South Vietnam's army.

Despite American assistance, the Vietcong continued to grow more powerful, in part because many Vietnamese opposed Diem's government, and in part because of the Vietcong's use of terror. By 1961, the Vietcong had assassinated thousands of government officials and established control over much of the countryside. In response, Diem looked increasingly to the United States to keep South Vietnam from collapsing.

Kennedy Takes Over On taking office in 1961, President Kennedy continued the nation's policy of support for South Vietnam. Like presidents Truman and Eisenhower before him, Kennedy saw the Southeast Asian country as vitally important in the battle against communism.

In political terms, Kennedy needed to appear tough on communism, since Republicans often accused Democrats of having lost China to communism during the Truman **administration.** Kennedy's administration sharply increased military aid and sent more advisers to Vietnam. From 1961 to late 1963, the number of American military personnel in South Vietnam jumped from about 2,000 to around 15,000.

"Everybody's yelling at me. I couldn't do enough."

—*Marlene Kramel*

More Skill Practice

Research Report Writing Concerned about the spread of communism beyond North Vietnam, in 1961 the U.S. government authorized CIA operatives to recruit and train the Hmong of Laos. Ask students to research how these guerrilla fighters operated against Pathet Lao Communist groups and North Vietnamese soldiers traveling from North Vietnam to South Vietnam through Laos. Students should present their research in three-page reports that evaluate the contributions made by the Hmong fighters and that discuss the secret U.S. support of these soldiers between 1961 and the end of the Vietnam War. **AL**
CA 11WA2.4b; 11WA2.4d

American officials believed the Vietcong continued to grow because Diem's government was unpopular and corrupt. They urged him to create a more democratic government and to introduce reforms to help Vietnam's peasants. Diem introduced some limited reforms, but they had little effect.

One program Diem introduced, at the urging of American advisers, made the situation worse. The South Vietnamese created special fortified villages, known as strategic hamlets. These villages were protected by machine guns, bunkers, trenches, and barbed wire. Vietnamese officials then moved villagers to the strategic hamlets, partly to protect them from the Vietcong, and partly to prevent them from giving aid to the Vietcong. The program proved to be extremely unpopular. Many peasants resented being uprooted from their villages, where they had worked to build farms and where many of their ancestors lay buried.

The Overthrow of Diem Diem made himself even more unpopular by discriminating against Buddhism, one of the country's most widely practiced religions. In the spring of 1963, Diem, a Catholic, banned the traditional religious flags for Buddha's birthday. When Buddhists took to the streets in protest, Diem's police killed 9 people and injured 14 others. In the demonstrations that followed, a Buddhist monk set himself on fire, the first of several to do so. The photograph of his self-destruction appeared on television and on the front pages of newspapers around the world. It was a stark symbol of the opposition to Diem.

In August 1963, American ambassador Henry Cabot Lodge arrived in Vietnam. He quickly learned that Diem's unpopularity had so alarmed several Vietnamese generals that they were plotting to overthrow him. When Lodge expressed American sympathy for their cause, the generals launched a military coup. They seized power on November 1, 1963, and executed Diem shortly afterward.

Diem's overthrow only made matters worse. Despite his unpopularity with some Vietnamese, Diem had been a respected nationalist and a capable administrator. After his death, South Vietnam's government grew increasingly weak and unstable. The United States became even more deeply involved in order to prop up the weak South Vietnamese government. **Coincidentally,** three weeks after Diem's death, President Kennedy was also assassinated. The presidency, as well as the growing problem of Vietnam, now belonged to Kennedy's vice president, Lyndon Johnson.

✓ **Reading Check** **Examining** What was the main goal of the Vietcong?

Johnson and Vietnam

Main Idea President Johnson sent troops to aid South Vietnam against communism.

Reading Connection In what other nations had the United States become involved in an effort to promote the ideals of freedom? Read on to find out how President Johnson gained war powers from Congress to assist South Vietnam.

Initially President Johnson exercised caution and restraint regarding the conflict in Vietnam. "We seek no wider war," he repeatedly promised. At the same time, Johnson was determined to prevent South Vietnam from becoming Communist. "The battle against communism," he declared shortly before becoming president, "must be joined . . . with strength and determination."

Picturing **History**

Self-Immolation On June 11, 1963, flames erupted around a Buddhist monk as he set himself on fire to protest government religious policies. What policies did Ngo Dinh Diem take toward Buddhism?

CHAPTER 17 The Vietnam War **779**

C **Critical Thinking**

Determining Cause and Effect Tell students to read about the strategic hamlet policy. **Ask:** Why did this effort backfire on the Diem government? *(Students should point out that the forced uprooting of people made them resent the Diem government more. It also made them more susceptible to the arguments of the Vietcong, namely that the Diem government was simply following American orders and the Vietnamese people should set up a new government that was responsive to the peoples' concerns.)* **OL**

R **Reading Strategy**

Scaffolding—Academic Vocabulary The word *symbol* was introduced in Chapter 15, Section 2. Ask a student to define the word. **BL**

W₁ **Writing Support**

Letter Writing Have students write letters to the editor about U.S. support for the Diem regime. Remind them that their editorials should support or oppose the actions of the United States and use clear arguments to bolster their positions. **AL** **CA** 11WS1.1; 11WS1.3

W₂ **Writing Support**

Persuasive Writing Ask students to imagine they are White House advisers, and have them write a letter advising President Johnson on the course of action he should take regarding the Vietnam War. Students should refer to previous chapter information to make their letters persuasive. **AL** **CA** 11WS1.1; 11WS1.3

✓ **Reading Check**

Answer: The Vietcong wanted to reunify Vietnam.

Picturing **History**

Answer: Diem discriminated against Buddhism by doing such things as banning the traditional religious flags used to celebrate the birthday of Buddha.
Ask: What message was the monk trying to send when he set himself on fire? *(He wanted to draw attention to the opposition to Diem.)*

Did You Know?

Buddhism is a major world religion, founded in northeastern India. It is based on the teachings of Siddhartha Gautama, who is known as the Buddha, or Enlightened One. Buddhism is the fourth largest religion in the world with an estimated 360 million followers.

R₁ Reading Strategy

Questioning Ask students what the phrase "soft on communism" implies. *(It implies that someone is not aggressive enough in fighting against the growth of communism.)* **Ask:** Why would Johnson be sensitive to accusations of being soft on communism? *(Johnson was worried about the negative perception it would have during the election and that Americans might choose to replace him as president.)* **BL**

R₂ Reading Strategy

Evaluating Tell students that a more in-depth analysis on the Gulf of Tonkin incident is found on pages 784–785. **Ask:** Why did the Gulf of Tonkin Resolution have little opposition in Congress? *(Congress was reluctant to deny the funding and resources needed to support the U.S. effort.)* **OL**

Politics also played a role in Johnson's Vietnam policy. Like Kennedy, Johnson remembered that many Republicans blamed the Truman administration for the fall of China to communism in 1949. Johnson hoped to prevent another country from becoming Communist. Should the Democrats also "lose" Vietnam, Johnson feared, it might cause a "mean and destructive debate that would shatter my Presidency, kill my administration, and damage our democracy."

The Gulf of Tonkin Resolution On August 2, 1964, President Johnson announced that North Vietnamese torpedo boats had fired on two American destroyers in the Gulf of Tonkin. Two days later, the president reported that another similar attack against American ships had taken place. Johnson was campaigning for the presidency and was very sensitive to accusations of being soft on communism. He insisted that North Vietnam's attacks were unprovoked and

immediately ordered American aircraft to attack North Vietnamese ships and naval facilities. Johnson did not reveal that the American warships had been helping the South Vietnamese conduct electronic spying and commando raids against North Vietnam.

Johnson then asked Congress to authorize the use of force to defend American forces. Congress agreed to Johnson's request with little debate. Most members of Congress agreed with Republican Representative Ross Adair of Indiana, who defiantly declared, "The American flag has been fired upon. We will not and cannot tolerate such things."

On August 7, 1964, the Senate and House passed the **Gulf of Tonkin Resolution**, authorizing the president to "take all necessary measures to repel any armed attack against the forces of the United States and to prevent further aggression." With only two dissenting votes, Congress had, in effect, handed its war powers over to the president. 📖 *(See page 1003 for more on the Gulf of Tonkin Resolution.)*

Different Viewpoints

The Vietnam War

As the war in Vietnam dragged on, a clear division of American opinion emerged. In January 1966, George W. Ball, undersecretary of state to President Johnson, delivered an address to indicate "how we got [to Vietnam] and why we must stay." George F. Kennan, former ambassador to Russia, testified before the Senate Foreign Relations Committee that same year, arguing that American involvement in Vietnam was "something we would not choose deliberately if the choice were ours to make all over again today."

George W. Ball:

"[T]he conflict in Vietnam is a product of the great shifts and changes triggered by the Second World War. Out of the war, two continent-wide powers emerged—the United States and the Soviet Union. The colonial systems through which the nations of Western Europe had governed more than a third of the people of the world were, one by one, dismantled.

. . . [E]ven while the new national boundaries were still being marked on the map, the Soviet Union under Stalin exploited the confusion to push out the perimeter of its power and influence in an effort to extend the outer limits of Communist domination by force or the threat of force.

The bloody encounters in [Vietnam] are thus in a real sense battles and skirmishes in a continuing war to prevent one Communist power after another from violating internationally recognized boundary lines fixing the outer limits of Communist dominion.

. . . The evidence shows clearly enough that, at the time of French withdrawal . . . the Communist regime in Hanoi never intended that South Vietnam should develop in freedom.

. . . In the long run our hopes for the people of South Vietnam reflect our hopes for people everywhere. What we seek is a world living in peace and freedom."

Answers and Additional Support

Did You Know?

GI slang referred to helicopters as TWA—teenie-weenie-airline. Helicopters were used on a massive scale during the Vietnam War. With gas turbines replacing piston engines, the helicopters had remarkable range and maneuverability.

The United States Sends in Troops Shortly after Congress passed the Gulf of Tonkin Resolution, the Vietcong began to attack bases where American advisers were stationed in South Vietnam. The attacks began in the fall of 1964 and continued to escalate. After a Vietcong attack on a base at Pleiku in February 1965 left 7 Americans dead and more than 100 wounded, President Johnson decided to respond. Less than 14 hours after the attack, American aircraft assaulted North Vietnam.

After the airstrikes, one poll showed that Johnson's approval rating on his handling of Vietnam jumped from 41 percent to 60 percent. The president's actions also met with strong approval from his closest advisers, including Secretary of Defense Robert McNamara and National Security Adviser McGeorge Bundy.

There were some dissenters in the White House, chief among them Undersecretary of State George Ball, a long-time critic of U.S. policy in Vietnam. He warned that if the United States got too deeply involved in Vietnam, it might become difficult to get out. "Once on the tiger's back," he warned, "we cannot be sure of picking the place to dismount."

The majority of the advisers who surrounded Johnson, however, firmly believed the nation had a duty to halt communism in Vietnam. They thought it was necessary to maintain stability in Southeast Asia and to ensure the United States's continuing power and prestige in the world. In a memo to the president, Bundy argued:

> 66 The stakes in Vietnam are extremely high. The American investment is very large, and American responsibility is a fact of life which is palpable in the atmosphere of Asia, and even elsewhere. The international prestige of the U.S. and a substantial part of our influence are directly at risk in Vietnam. 99
>
> —quoted in *The Best and the Brightest*

In March 1965, Johnson expanded American involvement by shifting his policy to a **sustained** bombing campaign against North Vietnam. The campaign was named Operation Rolling Thunder. That month the president also ordered the first combat troops into Vietnam. American soldiers were now fighting alongside South Vietnamese troops against the Vietcong.

✓ **Reading Check** **Describing** How did politics play a role in President Johnson's Vietnam policy?

A Bloody Stalemate Emerges

Main Idea American troops faced guerrilla warfare and a war of attrition.

Reading Connection When had guerrilla warfare been used in the United States? Read on to discover the effects of guerrilla warfare in Vietnam.

By the end of 1965, more than 180,000 American combat troops were fighting in Vietnam. In 1966 that number doubled. Since the American military was extremely strong, it marched into Vietnam with great confidence. "America seemed omnipotent then," said Philip Caputo, one of the first marines to arrive. "We saw ourselves as the champions of a 'cause that was destined to triumph.'"

Frustrating Warfare Lacking the firepower of the Americans, the Vietcong used ambushes, booby traps, and guerrilla tactics. Ronald J. Glasser, an

CHAPTER 17 The Vietnam War **781**

George F. Kennan:

"Vietnam is not a region of major military and industrial importance. It is difficult to believe that any decisive developments of the world situation would be determined in normal circumstances by what happens on that territory. . . . Even a situation in which South Vietnam was controlled exclusively by the Vietcong, while regrettable . . . would not, in my opinion, present dangers great enough to justify our direct military intervention.

. . . To attempt to crush North Vietnamese strength to a point where [it] could no longer give any support for Vietcong political activity in the South, would . . . have the effect of bringing in Chinese forces at some point.

. . . Our motives are widely misinterpreted, and the spectacle emphasized and reproduced in thousands of press photographs and stories . . . produces reactions among millions of people throughout the world profoundly detrimental to the image we would like them to hold of this country."

Learning From History

1. **Recognizing Ideologies** How do the two speakers assess the value of Vietnam and its people to the United States? CA 11RC2.5
2. **Making Inferences** Why does George Kennan believe that the United States government got involved in Vietnam when it did? How does he feel about this involvement? CA 11RC2.4

Different Viewpoints

Learning from History
Answers:

1. Ball argues that the United States is committed to the people of Vietnam and wants to protect them from communism. Kennan argues that Vietnam has no particular significance to the United States, and while it would be unfortunate if the Vietcong took over, it would not present a danger great enough for the United States to take military action.

2. He believes that the United States was misguided in entering the war and that it has hurt the national image.

C **Critical Thinking**

Identifying Assumptions The United States mistakenly assumed that it could fight the Vietcong in the rice fields and jungles of Vietnam with troops trained to fight on the battlefields of Western Europe. Discuss with students other assumptions of American leaders that proved to be incorrect. *(that better and more equipment would result in American victory; that the South Vietnamese would welcome the American soldiers)* **OL**

S **Skill Practice**

Scaffolding—Analyzing Environmental Issues Have students locate maps and photographs of Vietnam. Students should describe the topography and vegetation of Vietnam. **Ask: What effect would defoliating trees and removing vegetation have on the Vietnam War?** *(denied enemy cover or places to conceal)* **EL** **CA HI5**

This **Historical Analysis** skill was introduced in Chapter 10.

Answers and Additional Support

NATIONAL GEOGRAPHIC
MOMENT in HISTORY

AMERICA'S LONGEST WAR

Clinging to his M-16 rifle, a wounded American Marine is shown after being pulled to safety by a fellow soldier. In the late 1950s, American military advisers were sent to help the South Vietnamese army fight guerrillas known as the Vietcong, who were receiving weapons, supplies, and training from Communist North Vietnam. The dense jungles of Vietnam made fighting the guerrillas very difficult. By 1968 about 500,000 U.S. troops were fighting in the increasingly unpopular war. American forces finally withdrew in March 1973.

American army doctor, described the devastating effects of one of these booby traps:

> 66 Three quarters of the way through the tangle, a trooper brushed against a two-inch vine, and a grenade slung at chest high went off, shattering the right side of his head and body. . . . Nearby troopers took hold of the unconscious soldier and, half carrying, half dragging him, pulled him the rest of the way through the jungle. 99

—quoted in *Vietnam, A History*

The Vietcong also frustrated American troops by blending in with the general population and then quickly vanishing. "It was a sheer physical impossibility to keep the enemy from slipping away whenever he wished," one American general said. Journalist Linda Martin noted, "It's a war where nothing is ever quite certain and nowhere is ever quite safe."

C To counter the Vietcong's tactics, American troops went on "search and destroy" missions. They tried to find enemy troops, bomb their positions, destroy their supply lines, and force them into the open.

American forces also sought to take away the Vietcong's ability to hide in the thick jungles by literally destroying the landscape. American planes **C** dropped **napalm,** a jellied gasoline that explodes on contact. They also used **Agent Orange,** a chemical that strips leaves from trees and shrubs, turning farmland and forest into wasteland.

A Determined Enemy United States military leaders underestimated the Vietcong's strength. They also misjudged the enemy's stamina. American generals believed that continuously bombing and killing large numbers of Vietcong would destroy the enemy's morale and force them to give up. The guerrillas, however, had no intention of surrendering, and they were willing to accept huge losses in human lives.

In the Vietcong's war effort, North Vietnamese support was a major factor. Although the Vietcong forces were made up of many South Vietnamese, North Vietnam provided arms, advisers, and significant leadership. Later in the war, as Vietcong casualties mounted, North Vietnam began sending regular North Vietnamese Army units to fight in South Vietnam.

NATIONAL GEOGRAPHIC MOMENT in HISTORY

Lucy, Andy Griffith, and Gomer Pyle were mainstays on American television in 1968. The images of the Vietnam War were a sharp contrast.

Did You Know?

The name Agent Orange came from the orange-striped 55 gallon barrels the herbicide was shipped in from 1965 to 1970. After the war, veterans were worried about their exposure to the herbicide. Chemicals contained in Agent Orange have since been found to cause cancer and other health problems.

North Vietnam sent arms and supplies south by way of a network of jungle paths known as the **Ho Chi Minh trail.** The trail wound through the countries of Cambodia and Laos, bypassing the border between North and South Vietnam. Because the trail passed through countries not directly involved in the war, President Johnson refused to allow a full-scale attack on the trail to shut it down.

North Vietnam itself received military weapons and other support from the Soviet Union and China. One of the main reasons President Johnson refused to order a full-scale invasion of North Vietnam was his fear that such an attack would bring China into the war, as had happened in Korea. By placing limits on the war, however, Johnson made it very difficult to win. Instead of conquering enemy territory, American troops were forced to fight a war of attrition—a strategy of defeating the enemy forces by slowly wearing them down. This strategy led troops to conduct grisly body counts after battles to determine how many enemy soldiers had been killed.

Bombing from American planes killed as many as 220,000 Vietnamese between 1965 and 1967. Nevertheless, the Vietcong and North Vietnamese troops showed no sign of surrendering. Meanwhile, American casualties continued to mount. By the end of 1966, more than 6,700 American soldiers had been killed.

As the number of Americans killed and wounded continued to grow, the notion of a quick and decisive victory grew increasingly remote. As a result, many citizens back home began to question the nation's involvement in the war.

Reading Check **Describing** What tactics did the United States adopt to fight the Vietcong?

Vietnam War Deaths, 1965–1972

Number of Deaths (in thousands)

Legend:
- Total
- Killed in action
- Died of wounds
- Missing, presumed dead

Years: 1965 1966 1967 1968 1969 1970 1971 1972

Source: *Statistical Abstract of the United States.*

Graph Skills

1. **Interpreting Graphs** How many American soldiers were killed in action in 1968, and how many died of wounds?
2. **Generalizing** The number of wounded and killed rose rapidly from 1965 to 1968 and then fell quickly over the next few years. By 1970, how much had the total number killed dropped from the peak number of deaths in 1968?

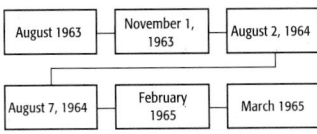

HISTORY Online **Study Central**

For help with the concepts in this section of *American Vision: Modern Times* go to tav.mt.glencoe.com and click on *Study Central.*

SECTION 2 ASSESSMENT

Checking for Understanding

1. **Vocabulary** Define: administration, coincidental, sustain, napalm, Agent Orange.
2. **People and Terms** Identify: Vietcong, Gulf of Tonkin Resolution, Ho Chi Minh trail.
3. **Explain** how the Gulf of Tonkin Resolution affected the powers of Congress and the presidency.

Reviewing Big Ideas

4. **Examining** Why did the United States use napalm and Agent Orange in its fight against the Vietcong?

Critical Thinking

5. **Analyzing** Why did fighting in Vietnam turn into a stalemate by the mid-1960s?
6. **Sequencing** Complete a time line similar to the one below to fill in events leading to American involvement in Vietnam.

August 1963 → November 1, 1963 → August 2, 1964

August 7, 1964 → February 1965 → March 1965

Analyzing Visuals

7. **Analyzing Photographs** Look closely at the photograph on page 779 of Buddhist monk Reverend Quang Duc. What in the photograph suggests that this event was planned by Buddhists to protest their treatment in South Vietnam?

Writing About History

8. **Persuasive Writing** Imagine that you are a member of Congress in August 1964. Based on the Constitution, write a statement supporting or opposing the Gulf of Tonkin Resolution. **CA 11WS1.1**

SECTION 2 ASSESSMENT ANSWERS

1. Content vocabulary is boldfaced and highlighted in yellow. Academic vocabulary is boldfaced.
2. Vietcong (p. 778), Gulf of Tonkin Resolution (p. 780), Ho Chi Minh trail (p. 783)
3. It gave congressional war powers to the president.
4. to destroy the landscape so the Vietcong could not hide in the jungle
5. The Vietcong showed no signs of surrendering and Johnson refused to order a full-scale invasion.
6. August 1963, Henry Cabot Lodge arrives in Vietnam; November 1, 1963, Diem is overthrown; August 2, 1964, Gulf of Tonkin incident; August 7, 1964, Gulf of Tonkin Resolution; February 1965, attack on Pleiku base; March 1965, Johnson expands bombing campaign
7. The presence of the Buddhist onlookers suggests a planned event.
8. Students' statements should express a point of view.

ASSESS

Resources for page 783

Use these resources to assess student mastery.

📁 Section Quiz 17-2

📁 Reading Essentials and Study Guide 17-2

💿 Interactive Tutor Self-Assessment CD-ROM

📁 California Standards Practice, Grade 11

Graph Skills

Answers:
1. about 12,000
2. by about 10,000

Graph Skills Practice
Ask: How many American military personnel were killed in action in 1967? *(about 7,000)*

Reading Check

Answer: search and destroy missions, bombing, the use of napalm and Agent Orange

HISTORY Online

Study Central provides audio summaries, interactive games, and online graphic organizers to help students review section content.

CLOSE

Summary Writing Ask students to write one-page papers describing Vietcong tactics. **OL**

783

FOCUS

History–Social Science Standards

This feature addresses the following standard:

11.9.3 Trace the origins and geopolitical consequences (foreign and domestic) of the Cold War and containment policy, including the following: the era of McCarthyism, instances of domestic Communism (e.g., Alger Hiss) and blacklisting; the Truman Doctrine; the Berlin Blockade; the Korean War; the Bay of Pigs Invasion and the Cuban Missile Crisis; atomic testing in the American West, the "mutual assured destruction" doctrine, and disarmament policies; the Vietnam War; Latin American policy.

TEACH

S Skill Practice

Preparing Oral Presentations
To help students better understand the Gulf of Tonkin incident, divide the class into four groups to research the following topics: foreign involvement in Indochina, rise of communism in Indochina, events that led to U.S. involvement in Vietnam, and public opinion in the United States. Have students conduct research and make oral presentations about their topics.

OL | **CA** HR3; HR4; HI1; HI2; HI3; HI4
CA 11WS1.6

Answers and Additional Support

You're the Historian

President Lyndon Johnson

Incident in the Gulf of Tonkin

In 1964 the Vietcong in South Vietnam were trying to topple the government and unite the country under communism. To prevent this, the United States had already committed money, supplies, and advisers. President Johnson asked Congress to authorize using force after reports that North Vietnam had made unprovoked attacks on U.S. warships in the Gulf of Tonkin. Congress responded with the Gulf of Tonkin Resolution. Had the warship USS *Maddox* provoked the attack? Was Johnson fully informed of events in the Gulf? You're the historian.

Read the following excerpts, then answer the questions and complete the activities that follow.

From accounts of an unprovoked attack

The sources advising President Johnson on the Gulf of Tonkin incident included the navy and the Defense Department. These excerpts suggest how difficult it was to know what had happened—and also how tension influenced the American interpretation.

U.S. Navy Commander John Herrick of the USS *Maddox*:
I am being approached by high-speed craft with apparent intention of torpedo attack. I intend to open fire in self-defense if necessary.

—**from a cable of August 2, 1964**

U.S. Defense Department:
While on routine patrol in international waters . . . the U.S. destroyer *Maddox* underwent an unprovoked attack by three PT-type boats in . . . the Tonkin Gulf.

The attacking boats launched three torpedoes and used 37-millimeter gunfire. The *Maddox* answered with 5-inch gunfire. . . . The PT boats were driven off, with one seen to be badly damaged and not moving. . . .

No casualties or damage were sustained by the *Maddox* or the aircraft.

—**from a press release of August 2, 1964**

National Security Council Meeting:
Secretary McNamara: The North Vietnamese PT boats have continued their attacks on the two U.S. destroyers in international waters in the Gulf of Tonkin. . . .

Secretary Rusk: An immediate and direct action by us is necessary. The unprovoked attack on the high seas is an act of war for all practical purposes. . . .

CIA Director McCone: The proposed U.S. reprisals will result in sharp North Vietnamese military action, but such actions would not represent a deliberate decision to provoke or accept a major escalation of the Vietnamese war.

President Johnson: Do they want a war by attacking our ships in the middle of the Gulf of Tonkin?

U.S. Intelligence Agency Director Rowan: Do we know for a fact that the North Vietnamese provocation took place?

Secretary McNamara: We will know definitely in the morning.

—**August 2, 1964**

Secretary Rusk:
We believe that present OPLAN 34-A activities are beginning to rattle Hanoi [capital of North Vietnam], and the *Maddox* incident is directly related to their effort to resist these activities. We have no intention of yielding to pressure.

—**from a top secret telegram to Ambassador Maxwell Taylor (South Vietnam), August 3, 1964**

EXTENDING THE CONTENT

Boat People Tell students that many Vietnamese fled by boat to escape political tensions. Unfortunately, some "boat people" found themselves caught in racial tensions. For example, in 1979 Vietnamese "boat people" who were mostly ethnic Chinese arrived in Malaysia, already an ethnically diverse country. So intense was the fear that the arrival of the Vietnamese would upset the country's ethnic balance that, instead of welcoming the newcomers, the Malaysian government issued orders to shoot any "boat person" found landing on Malaysian shores.

Secretary McNamara

From accounts of a possible mistake

Two days after the alleged attack, the Turner Joy joined the Maddox in the Gulf. On the night of August 4, 1964, the two destroyers experienced a series of events they interpreted as a second attack. However, Commander Herrick later revised this report. President Johnson referred to the "repeated" attacks later when he asked Congress for war powers.

Commander Herrick:
Review of action makes many contacts and torpedoes fired appear doubtful. Freak weather effects on radar and overeager sonarmen may have accounted for many reports. No actual visual sightings by *Maddox*. Suggest complete evaluation before any further action. . . .

Turner Joy also reports no actual visual sightings or wake. . . . Entire action leaves many doubts except for apparent attempt to ambush at beginning.

—from two cables of August 4, 1964

President Johnson:
The initial attack on the destroyer *Maddox*, on August 2, was repeated today by a number of hostile vessels attacking two U.S. destroyers with torpedoes. The destroyers and supporting aircraft acted at once on the orders I gave after the initial act of aggression. . . . Repeated acts of violence against the Armed Forces of the United States must be met not only with alert defense, but with positive reply.

—in a television and radio address, August 4, 1964

In 1968 Senator William Fulbright opened an investigation into the 1964 Gulf of Tonkin incident. The following exchange took place between Senator Fulbright and Secretary McNamara.

Secretary McNamara: I don't believe Commander Herrick in his cable stated that he had doubt that the attack took place. He questioned certain details of the attack. . . . Secondly, his doubts were resolved that afternoon before the retaliatory action was taken.

Senator Fulbright: I think he went further than that. He advised you not to do anything until it had been reevaluated. . . . It is a very strong statement.

Vietcong guerrillas

Secretary McNamara: Nothing was done until it was reevaluated.

Senator Fulbright: He says "Suggest complete reevaluation before any further action." Now that is a very strong recommendation from a man on the scene in charge of the operation. . . . Both committees, except for the Senator from Oregon [Morse], unanimously accepted your testimony then as the whole story, and I must say this raises very serious questions about how you make decisions to go to war.

Understanding the Issue

1. What statement by Rusk suggests the United States may have provoked the attack on the *Maddox?*
2. Do you think President Johnson was misled by his advisers? Explain.
3. How soon after the alleged attacks did the president address the American people? Did the United States rush to judgment in this case? Explain.

Activities

1. **Investigate** What were the conclusions of the Fulbright investigations into the Gulf of Tonkin incident? Check sources, including the Internet.
2. **Discuss** Research and review American decisions to go to war in 1898, 1917, and 1941. What were the concerns? Do you think the nation made the right decisions?

You're *the* Historian

S Skill Practice

Conducting an Interview Have students conduct a brief interview with someone who was a teenager or adult at the time of the Gulf of Tonkin incident. Encourage them to learn what the interviewee remembers about the event and what impact the event had on his or her life. Ask students to ascertain if the person being interviewed remembers any controversy regarding the interpretation of the Gulf of Tonkin events or if everyone simply accepted the facts of the incident as they were presented at the time. Invite students to share what they learned with the class. **OL**

C Critical Thinking

Analyzing Primary Sources Have students review the exchange between McNamara and Fulbright. **Ask:** What is the source of their disagreement? *(Fulbright questioned McNamara's interpretation of the cable by Herrick and the need to begin the retaliation for the event in the Gulf.)* **AL**

ASSESS/CLOSE

Have students answer the Understanding the Issue questions and complete the activities.

ANSWERS TO UNDERSTANDING THE ISSUE

1. He named a plan of activity, the OPLAN 34-A, which implies that the United States had some type of operation underway.
2. Students' answers will vary. Students should support their points of view with facts and clear observations.
3. Two days. Students may say that the cable Commander Herrick sent on August 4 suggests more time was needed to verify the facts.

Activities Answers
1. Answers may vary depending on the research undertaken. Students should learn that although Fulbright originally supported the administration, he came to believe that Congress had been deceived.
2. You may elect to assign this activity to be done in groups with each group member researching one of the wars. Students' conclusions will vary.

785

FOCUS

BELLRINGER
SKILLBUILDER ACTIVITY

Project **Daily Focus Skills Transparency 17-3** and have students answer the question.

Guide to Reading

Understanding Vocabulary: Have students scan the section to learn the meanings of the content and academic vocabulary words.

Answers to Graphic: Reasons for opposition to Vietnam War: credibility gap, unfair draft system, immorality of defending a corrupt dictatorship in South Vietnam, and belief that it was a civil war in which the United States had no business

Unpacking the Standards

Students will be able to:

- Analyze the concern that the American people had over what the government said versus what it did.
- Explain the development of the antiwar protests.
- Discuss the importance of the events of 1968.

Answers and Additional Support

SECTION 3 Vietnam Divides the Nation

Guide to Reading

Connection
In the previous section, you learned how U.S. troops became involved in the Vietnam War. In this section, you will find out how the war divided the nation.

Main Idea
- Americans grew discouraged as the death toll increased and official reports contradicted the reality of the war. (p. 787)
- Protests during the war focused on the draft policy. (p. 788)
- With violence escalating and his popularity dwindling, Johnson decided not to seek another term of office. (p. 789)

Content Vocabulary
credibility gap, teach-in, dove, hawk

Academic Vocabulary
contradict, proportion, alternative

People and Terms to Identify
William Westmoreland, Tet offensive

Reading Objective
- **Analyze** why support for the war began to weaken.
- **Describe** the motives of those in the antiwar movement.

Reading Strategy
Organizing As you read about Americans' reactions to the Vietnam War, complete a graphic organizer like the one below to list the reasons for opposition to the war.

Reasons for Opposition to Vietnam War

Preview of Events

◆1965	◆1966	◆1967	◆1968
1965 Teach-ins on college campuses begin	**1966** Senate Foreign Relations Committee begins Vietnam hearings	**1967** March on the Pentagon	**January 1968** Tet offensive

The following are the main History–Social Science Standards covered in this section.

11.9.3 Trace the origins and geo-political consequences (foreign and domestic) of the Cold War and containment policy, including the following: the era of McCarthyism, instances of domestic Communism (e.g., Alger Hiss) and blacklisting; the Truman Doctrine; the Berlin Blockade; the Korean War; the Bay of Pigs invasion and the Cuban Missile Crisis; atomic testing in the American West, the "mutual assured destruction" doctrine, and disarmament policies; the Vietnam War; Latin American policy.

11.9.4 List the effects of foreign policy on domestic policies and vice versa (e.g., protests during the war in Vietnam, the "nuclear freeze" movement).

11.10.4 Examine the roles of civil rights advocates (e.g., A. Philip Randolph, Martin Luther King, Jr., Malcolm X, Thurgood Marshall, James Farmer, Rosa Parks), including the significance of Martin Luther King, Jr.'s "Letter from Birmingham Jail" and "I Have a Dream" speech.

～ The Big Idea ～

People react to periods of breathtaking social and cultural change in different ways. As the war raged on and the death toll of American soldiers grew, an antiwar movement began, with protesters holding teach-ins and antiwar rallies to speak out against the war and the draft. Not all Americans opposed the war. Supporters accused protesters of being unpatriotic. Following the Tet offensive, political support for President Johnson began to decline. Faced with steadily decreasing approval ratings, Johnson decided not to seek reelection. The division within the Democratic Party and voter dissatisfaction with the war led to the election of Republican nominee Richard Nixon.

786 CHAPTER 17 The Vietnam War

SECTION RESOURCES

📂 Print Material
- Reproducible Lesson Plan 17-3
- Guided Reading Activity 17-3
- Reading Essentials and Study Guide 17-3
- Active Reading Note-Taking Guide 17-3

🖨 Transparencies
- Daily Focus Skills Transparency 17-3
- Section Graphic Organizer Transparency 17-3

Technology
- 💿 Interactive Tutor Self-Assessment CD-ROM
- 💿 ExamView® Pro Testmaker CD-ROM
- 💿 Presentation Plus! CD-ROM

A Growing Credibility Gap

Main Idea Americans grew discouraged as the death toll increased and official reports contradicted the reality of the war.

Reading Connection What role does the media play in covering the events of a war? Read on to learn about the effect of television on the Vietnam War.

When American troops first entered the Vietnam War in the spring of 1965, many Americans had supported the military effort. A Gallup poll published around that time showed that 66 percent of Americans approved of the policy in Vietnam. As the war dragged on, however, public support began to drop.

★ An American Story ★

Martin Jezer, a 27-year-old copywriter living in New York City, had never considered himself a radical. "I campaigned for Lyndon Johnson in 1964," he recalled. As his opposition to the war in Vietnam grew, however, Jezer decided to stage a public protest.

On April 15, 1967, he and dozens of other young men gathered with their military draft cards in New York's Central Park. Before an audience of reporters, photographers, FBI officials, and citizens, the men pulled out matches and lighters and burned the cards.

❝We began singing freedom songs and chanting, 'Resist! Resist!' and 'Burn Draft Cards, Not People'.... People in the audience were applauding us, shouting encouragement. Then some guys began to come out of the audience with draft cards in hand. They burned them. Alone, in pairs, by threes they came. Each flaming draft card brought renewed cheering and more people out of the crowd.... Some of the draft card burners were girls, wives, or girlfriends of male card burners.... It lasted this way for about half an hour.❞

—quoted in *The Vietnam War: Opposing Viewpoints*

Jezer's protest was just one of many as American opposition to the Vietnam War grew. Suspicion of the government's truthfulness about the war was a significant reason. Throughout the early years of the war, the American commander in South Vietnam, General **William Westmoreland,** reported that the enemy was on the brink of defeat. In 1967 he confi-

dently declared that the "enemy's hopes are bankrupt" and added, "we have reached an important point where the end begins to come into view."

Contradicting such reports were less optimistic media accounts, especially on television. Vietnam was the first "television war," with footage of combat appearing nightly on the evening news. Day after day, millions of people saw images of wounded and dead Americans and began to doubt government reports. In the view of many, a **credibility gap** had developed, meaning it was hard to believe what the Johnson administration said about the war.

Congress, which had given the president a nearly free hand in Vietnam, soon grew uncertain about the war. Beginning in February 1966, the Senate Foreign Relations Committee held "educational" hearings on Vietnam, calling in Secretary of State Dean Rusk and other policy makers to explain the administration's war program. The committee also listened to critics

Analyzing *Political Cartoons*

Dark Passage One particular phrase came to represent the government's claims that it was on the verge of ending the Vietnam War: "the light at the end of the tunnel." Why did many people become skeptical about such government claims?

TEACH

W Writing Support

Persuasive Writing Ask students to imagine they are organizing a group to protest the Vietnam War. Have them discuss their opinions on the war, using the information in the textbook as a starting point. Tell students that based on the discussion, they should write concise mission statements that explain the group, its mission, its goals, and its methods. **OL** **CA 11WS1.3**

R Reading Strategy

Scaffolding—Inferring Ask students to consider how the broadcast of war footage on television helped influence the "credibility gap" that is discussed in this section. *(The American people were able to see and evaluate the progress of the war themselves and what they saw and understood did not seem to match the statements of government officials.)* **Ask:** Do you think such a difference between government reports and news media coverage is possible today? *(Students should note that with the use of satellite television and the Internet, news coverage is even more immediate today, so reports would have to be more accurate.)* **OL**

This **Reading Skill** was introduced in Chapter 11.

Analyzing *Political Cartoons*

Answer: Television news reports were different from what military leaders were reporting.
Ask: What are the people in the cartoon doing? *(They are feeling their way along a dark tunnel because there is no "light at the end of the tunnel.")*

Comparing and Contrasting
Divide the class into four equal groups. Within each group, have students discuss what similarities and differences they see between the civil rights protests and the antiwar protests. Tell each group to create a chart to show the results of their discussion. **OL**

R Reading Strategy

Connecting Ask students to consider how they would have reacted to receiving their draft card during the time of the Vietnam War. Call on students to share their feelings. Remind students to support their pro-war or antiwar sentiment with information from the text. **BL** **CA HI3; HI4**

✓ Reading Check

Answer: Combat footage appeared nightly on the evening news.

Answers and Additional Support

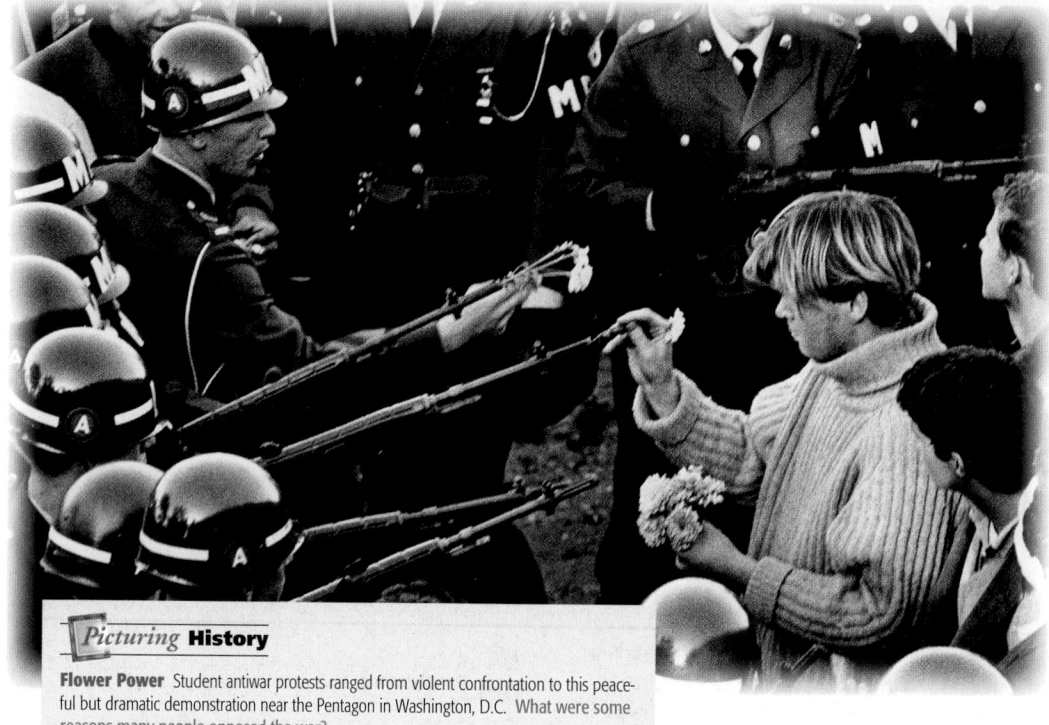

Picturing **History**

Flower Power Student antiwar protests ranged from violent confrontation to this peaceful but dramatic demonstration near the Pentagon in Washington, D.C. What were some reasons many people opposed the war?

such as American diplomat George Kennan. Although Kennan had helped create the policy of containment, he argued that Vietnam was not strategically important to the United States.

✓ Reading Check **Explaining** Why was the Vietnam War the first "television war"?

An Antiwar Movement Emerges

Main Idea Protests during the war focused on the draft policy.

Reading Connection Have you ever been chosen to compete on a team or participate in a task you did not like? Read on to discover the controversies of and responses to the draft during the Vietnam War.

C As casualties mounted in Vietnam, many people began to protest publicly against the war and to demand that the United States pull out. Although many other Americans supported the war, opponents of the conflict received the most attention.

Teach-Ins Begin In March 1965, a group of faculty members and students at the University of Michigan abandoned their classes and joined together in a

teach-in. Here, they informally discussed the issues surrounding the war and reaffirmed their reasons for opposing it. The gathering inspired teach-ins at many campuses. In May 1965, 122 colleges held a "National Teach-In" by radio for more than 100,000 antiwar demonstrators.

People who opposed the war did so for different reasons. Some saw the conflict as a civil war in which the United States had no business. Others viewed South Vietnam as a corrupt dictatorship and insisted that defending that country was immoral and unjust.

R **Anger at the Draft** Young protesters especially focused on what they saw as an unfair draft system. At the beginning of the war, a college student was often able to defer military service until after graduation. By contrast, young people from low-income families were more likely to be sent to Vietnam because they were unable to afford college. This meant minorities, particularly African Americans, made up a disproportionately large number of the soldiers in Vietnam. By 1967, for example, African Americans accounted for about 20 percent of American combat deaths—about twice their **proportion** of the population within the United States. That number would decline to roughly match their population proportion by the war's end.

Picturing **History**

Answer: People opposed the war because of the credibility gap, the unfair draft system, the corrupt government of South Vietnam, and the belief that it was a civil war in which the United States had no business.
Ask: Why do you think the young man in the photograph is putting flowers in the barrels of the weapons? *(Students will recognize the symbolism—flowers for the peace movement.)*

The high number of African Americans and poor Americans dying in Vietnam angered African American leaders, including Dr. Martin Luther King, Jr. Early on, King had refrained from speaking out against the war for fear that it would draw attention from the civil rights movement. In April 1967, however, he broke his silence and publicly condemned the conflict:

> 66Somehow this madness must cease. I speak as a child of God and brother to the suffering poor of Vietnam and the poor of America who are paying the double price of smashed hopes at home and death and corruption in Vietnam. I speak as a citizen of the world, for the world as it stands aghast at the path we have taken. I speak as an American to the leader of my own nation. The great initiative in this war is ours. The initiative to stop must be ours.99
>
> —quoted in *A Testament of Hope*

As the war escalated, American officials increased the draft call, putting many college students at risk. An estimated 500,000 draftees refused to go. Many publicly burned their draft cards or simply did not report when called for induction. Some fled the country, moving to Canada, Sweden, or other nations. Others stayed and went to prison rather than fight in a war they opposed.

Between 1965 and 1968, officials prosecuted more than 3,300 Americans for refusing to serve. The draft became less of an issue in 1969 when the government introduced a lottery system, in which only those with low lottery numbers were subject to the draft.

Protests against the war were not confined to college campuses. Demonstrators held public rallies and marches in towns across the country. In April 1965, Students for a Democratic Society (SDS), a left-wing student organization, organized a march on Washington, D.C., that drew more than 20,000 participants. Two years later, in October 1967, a rally at Washington's Lincoln Memorial drew tens of thousands of protesters as well.

Anger over the draft also fueled discussions of voting age. Many draftees argued that if they were old enough to fight, they were old enough to vote. In 1971 the Twenty-sixth Amendment to the Constitution was ratified, giving all citizens age 18 and older the right to vote.

Hawks and Doves In the face of growing opposition to the war, President Johnson remained determined to continue fighting. The president was not alone in his views. Although the antiwar protesters

became a vocal group, they did not represent majority opinion on Vietnam. In a poll taken in mid-1967, about 68 percent of the respondents favored continuing the war, compared to about 32 percent who wanted to end it. Of those Americans who supported the policy in Vietnam, many openly criticized the protesters for a lack of patriotism.

By 1968 the nation seemed to be divided into two camps. Those who wanted the United States to withdraw from Vietnam were known as **doves.** Those who insisted that the United States stay and fight came to be known as **hawks.** As the two groups debated, the war took a dramatic turn for the worse, and the nation endured a year of shock and crisis.

✓ **Reading Check** **Explaining** What led to the passage of the Twenty-sixth Amendment?

1968: The Pivotal Year

Main Idea With violence escalating and his popularity dwindling, Johnson decided not to seek another term of office.

Reading Connection Have you ever decided not to continue participating in a group or extra-curricular activity? Read on to find out about the events that caused President Johnson not to run for reelection.

The most turbulent year of the chaotic 1960s was 1968. The year saw a shocking political announcement, a pair of traumatic assassinations, and a violent political convention. First, however, the nation endured a surprise attack in Vietnam.

The Tet Offensive On January 30, 1968, during Tet, the Vietnamese New Year, the Vietcong and North Vietnamese launched a massive surprise attack. In this **Tet offensive,** the guerrilla fighters attacked virtually all American airbases in South Vietnam and most of the South's major cities and provincial capitals. The bloodiest battle took place in Hué, South Vietnam's third largest city. The Communist forces seized much of the city, and it took American and South Vietnamese troops almost four weeks to drive them out. Afterward, American troops found mass graves. The Communist forces had massacred the city's political and religious leaders as well as many foreigners, intellectuals, and others associated with South Vietnam's government. Nearly 3,000 bodies were found. Thousands more remained missing.

CHAPTER 17   The Vietnam War   **789**

Did You Know?

The Tet offensive caught the United States military completely off guard. In the words of a West Point textbook published after the war, Tet was an "intelligence failure ranking with Pearl Harbor."

U **Universal Access**

Advanced Learners Have students read the quote by Martin Luther King, Jr. **Ask:** What concern does Dr. King voice in this statement? (*African Americans and poor Americans represent too high a percentage of the soldiers serving in Vietnam.*) Ask students to research and write three-page reports that investigate the percentage of African Americans that served in the military during the Vietnam War. Papers should explain and analyze the data presented. **AL**
CA HR4

R **Reading Strategy**

Scaffolding—Academic Vocabulary The word *confine* was introduced in Chapter 15, Section 3. Ask a student to define the word. **BL**

Review the Big Idea

Review the Big Idea for this section, "People react to periods of breathtaking social and cultural change in different ways." Divide the class into two equal groups, one representing "hawks" and the other representing "doves." Allow each group a few days to research their group's stance on the Vietnam War and to prepare for a debate on this topic: "The Proper Action for the United States, regarding Vietnam, is _____." You may present students with a completed statement or ask students to offer suggestions for a topic. **OL**
CA HR4; HI3

✓ **Reading Check**

Answer: Protests over the draft led to discussion about the right of draft-age citizens to vote and the passage of the Twenty-sixth Amendment.

W Writing Support

Expository Writing Have students imagine they are President Johnson's press secretary. Tell them that they must write a short press release that explains the administration's view of the Tet offensive and its results. Students should realize that a press release by the administration most likely would emphasize the lack of military success by the North Vietnamese. **AL** **CA** 11WA2.4a

S Skill Practice

Visual Literacy To illustrate the differences between the presidential candidates in 1968, organize students into five groups. Assign one of the following people to each group: Eugene McCarthy, Robert F. Kennedy, Hubert H. Humphrey, George Wallace, and Richard Nixon. Have members of each group write three words that describe their candidate and one sentence about their candidate's political views. They should then work together to create a campaign button, banner, or logo for their candidate. Have groups share and discuss their ideas. **OL** **CA HR4**

R Reading Strategy

Scaffolding—Academic Vocabulary The word *primary* was introduced in Chapter 11, Section 4. Ask a student to define the word. **BL**

Answers and Additional Support

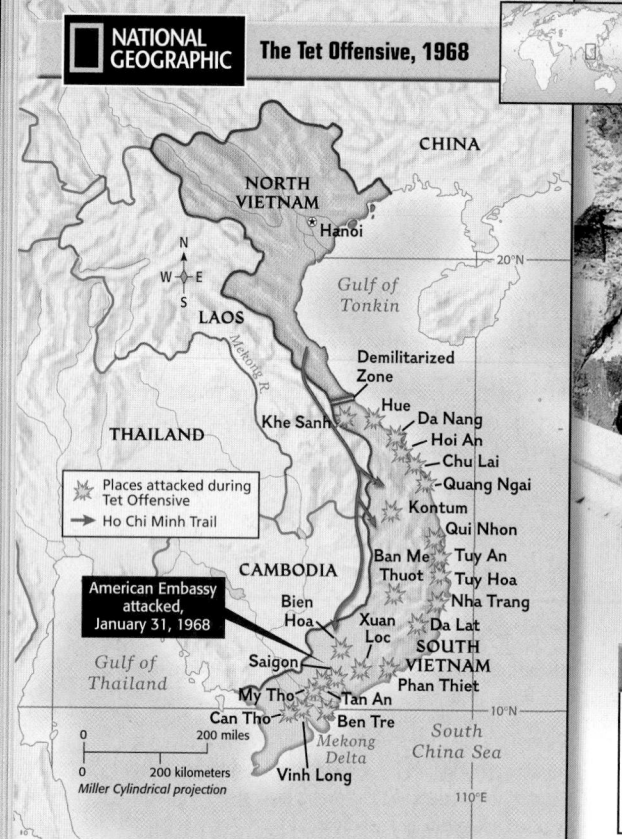

The Tet Offensive, 1968 — NATIONAL GEOGRAPHIC

- Places attacked during Tet Offensive
- Ho Chi Minh Trail

American Embassy attacked, January 31, 1968

A view of the U.S. embassy in Saigon after it was bombed during the Tet offensive.

Geography *Skills*

1. **Interpreting Maps** Most of the Ho Chi Minh Trail lies within which countries?
2. **Applying Geography Skills** How broad was the Tet offensive, and why did this shock Americans?

Militarily, Tet turned out to be a disaster for the Communist forces. After about a month of fighting, the American and South Vietnamese soldiers repelled the enemy troops, inflicting heavy losses on them. General Westmoreland boasted that the Communists' "well-laid plans went afoul," while President Johnson triumphantly added that the enemy's effort had ended in "complete failure."

In fact, the North Vietnamese had scored a major political victory. The American people were shocked that an enemy supposedly on the verge of defeat could launch such a large-scale attack. When General Westmoreland requested 206,000 troops in addition to the 500,000 already in Vietnam, it seemed to be an admission that the United States could not win the war.

To make matters worse, the media, which had tried to remain balanced in their war coverage, now openly criticized the effort. Walter Cronkite, then the nation's most respected newscaster, announced after Tet that it seemed "more certain than ever that the bloody experience in Vietnam is to end in a stalemate."

790 CHAPTER 17 The Vietnam War

Public opinion no longer favored the president. In the weeks following the Tet offensive, the president's approval rating plummeted to a dismal 35 percent, while support for his handling of the war fell even lower, to 26 percent.

Johnson Leaves the Presidential Race With the war growing increasingly unpopular and Johnson's credibility all but gone, some Democrats began looking for an **alternative** candidate to nominate for president in 1968. In November 1967, even before the Tet disaster, a little-known liberal senator from Minnesota, Eugene McCarthy, became the first dove to announce his candidacy against Johnson. In March 1968, McCarthy stunned the nation by winning more than 40 percent of the votes in the New Hampshire primary and almost defeating the president. Realizing that Johnson was vulnerable, Senator Robert Kennedy, who also opposed the war, quickly entered the race for the Democratic nomination.

With the division in the country and within his own party growing, Johnson addressed the public on

Geography *Skills*

Answers:
1. Laos and Cambodia
2. Attacks were on almost all U.S. bases and major South Vietnamese cities. It showed that the United States did not have the level of control its generals were portraying.

Geography Skills Practice
Ask: Why was the Ho Chi Minh trail located outside Vietnam? *(because the U.S. was not at war with Laos or Cambodia)*

television on March 31, 1968. He stunned viewers by stating, "I have concluded that I should not permit the presidency to become involved in the partisan divisions that are developing in this political year. Accordingly, I shall not seek, and I will not accept, the nomination of my party for another term as your President."

A Season of Violence Following Johnson's announcement, the nation endured even more shocking events. In April James Earl Ray was arrested for killing Dr. Martin Luther King, Jr., an event which led to riots in several major cities. Just two months later, another assassination rocked the country—that of Robert Kennedy. Kennedy, who appeared to be on his way to winning the Democratic nomination, was gunned down on June 5 in a California hotel just after winning the state's Democratic primary.

The violence seemed to culminate with a chaotic and well-publicized clash between protesters and police at the Democratic National Convention in Chicago. Thousands of protesters descended on the August convention, demanding that the Democrats adopt an antiwar platform. On the third day of the convention, the delegates chose Hubert Humphrey, President Johnson's vice president, as their presidential nominee.

Nixon Wins the Presidency The violence and chaos now associated with the Democratic Party benefited the 1968 Republican presidential candidate, Richard Nixon. Although defeated in the 1960 election, Nixon had remained active in national politics. A third candidate, Governor George Wallace of Alabama, also decided to run in 1968 as an independent. Wallace, an outspoken segregationist, sought to attract those Americans who felt threatened by the civil rights movement and urban social unrest.

Public opinion polls gave Nixon a wide lead over Humphrey and Wallace. Nixon's campaign promise to unify the nation and restore law and order appealed to many Americans. Nixon also declared that he had a plan for ending the war in Vietnam.

At first Humphrey's support of President Johnson's Vietnam policies hurt his campaign. After Humphrey broke with the president and called for a complete end to the bombing of North Vietnam, he began to move up in the polls. A week before the election, President Johnson announced that the bombing of North Vietnam had halted and that a cease-fire would follow.

Johnson's announcement had come too late. In the end, Nixon's promises to end the war and restore order at home were enough to sway the American people. On Election Day, Nixon defeated Humphrey by more than 100 electoral votes, although he won the popular vote by a slim margin of just over 43 percent to Humphrey's 42.7. Wallace helped account for the razor-thin margin by winning 46 electoral votes and more than 13 percent of the popular vote.

Speaking to reporters after his election, Nixon recalled seeing a young girl carrying a sign at one of his rallies that said: "Bring Us Together." This, he promised, would be his chief goal as president.

Reading Check **Explaining** Why did President Johnson decide not to run for reelection in 1968?

HISTORY Online **Study Central**
For help with the concepts in this section of *American Vision: Modern Times* go to tav.mt.glencoe.com and click on *Study Central.*

SECTION 3 ASSESSMENT

Checking for Understanding

1. **Vocabulary** Define: contradict, credibility gap, teach-in, proportion, dove, hawk, alternative.

2. **People and Terms** Identify: William Westmoreland, Tet offensive.

3. **Summarize** three important events that occurred in 1968.

Reviewing Big Ideas

4. **Explaining** Why did many people believe that the Vietnam War reflected racial and economic injustices in the United States?

Critical Thinking

5. **Synthesizing** Why did support of the Vietnam War begin to dwindle by the late 1960s?

6. **Organizing** Use a graphic organizer similar to the one below to list the effects of the Tet offensive.

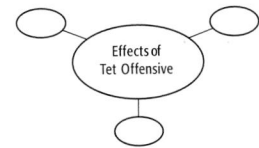

Effects of Tet Offensive

Analyzing Visuals

7. **Analyzing Photographs** Study the photograph on page 788. The phrase "flower power" was a slogan of the hippie movement. Explain what you think the phrase meant and how it was used to express opposition to the war.

Writing About History

8. **Expository Writing** Imagine that you are living in 1968. Write an editorial for the local newspaper in which you explain your reasons for either supporting or opposing the Vietnam War.
CA 11WA2.4a

CHAPTER 17 The Vietnam War **791**

C Critical Thinking

Making Inferences Remind students that Robert Kennedy was the brother of assassinated President John F. Kennedy. **Ask: What effect did the murders of Robert Kennedy and Dr. Martin Luther King, Jr., as well as the rising totals of war casualties have on the American public?** *(Answers may include: increased cynicism towards the government, a fear of losing control, a loss of hope.)* **OL**

ASSESS

Resources for page 791

Use these resources to assess student mastery.

📁 Section Quiz 17-3

📁 Reading Essentials and Study Guide 17-3

💿 Interactive Tutor Self-Assessment CD-ROM

📁 California Standards Practice, Grade 11

Reading Check

Answer: He did not want the presidency to become involved in partisan divisions.

HISTORY Online

Study Central provides audio summaries, interactive games, and online graphic organizers to help students review section content.

CLOSE

Analyzing Information
After students have read the section, have them analyze how the Gulf of Tonkin incident and Johnson's campaign pledges to not commit American troops to the conflict became crucial issues by 1967 and 1968. **OL**

SECTION 3 ASSESSMENT ANSWERS

1. Content vocabulary is boldfaced and highlighted in yellow. Academic vocabulary is boldfaced.

2. William Westmoreland (p. 787), Tet offensive (p. 789)

3. any three of the following: Tet offensive, Johnson's not running, Democratic National Convention, King and Kennedy assassinations

4. Low-income and minority men were more likely to be drafted.

5. mounting casualties, the draft, credibility gap, media coverage

6. war appeared unwinnable, support for war dropped, Johnson lost credibility

7. Flowers represented the growing peace movement.

8. Students' paragraphs should express a clear point of view.

FOCUS

SKILLBUILDER ACTIVITY

Project **Daily Focus Skills Transparency 17-4** and have students answer the question.

Guide to Reading

Understanding Vocabulary: Have students look up the vocabulary words in the glossary and use two of them in a sentence.

Answers to Graphic: Kissinger appointment, linkage policy, Vietnamization, bombing campaign, Cambodian invasion

Unpacking the Standards

Students will be able to:

- Describe how Richard Nixon tried to end U.S. involvement in the Vietnam War.
- Discuss how the United States withdrew its military forces from Vietnam.
- Analyze the lasting impact of the Vietnam War.

Answers and Additional Support

792

SECTION 4 The War Winds Down

Guide to Reading

Connection
In the previous section, you learned how the war divided the United States. In this section, you will learn about President Nixon's decision to pull out of Vietnam.

Main Idea
- President Nixon reduced the number of troops in Vietnam and relied on Henry Kissinger to negotiate peace. (p. 793)
- Protests in the United States continued after the invasion of Cambodia and the killing of South Vietnamese citizens. (p. 793)
- South Vietnam fell to North Vietnam shortly after the removal of United States troops. (p. 795)

- Vietnam veterans had a difficult time returning to civilian life. (p. 796)

Content Vocabulary
linkage

Academic Vocabulary
ultimate, generation, explicit

People and Terms to Identify
Henry Kissinger, Vietnamization, Pentagon Papers, War Powers Act

Reading Objectives
- **Explain** the events of Nixon's first administration that inspired more antiwar protests.

- **Summarize** the major lessons the United States learned from the Vietnam War experience.

Reading Strategy
Organizing As you read about the end of the Vietnam War, complete a graphic organizer similar to the one below by listing the steps that President Nixon took to end American involvement in Vietnam.

Steps Nixon Took

Preview of Events

◆1969   ◆1971   ◆1973   ◆1975

1969 Secret peace negotiations between the U.S. and North Vietnam begin

1972 Nixon initiates Christmas bombing

1973 Cease-fire signed

1975 Evacuation of the last Americans from Vietnam

The following are the main History–Social Science Standards covered in this section.

11.9.3 Trace the origins and geopolitical consequences (foreign and domestic) of the Cold War and containment policy, including the following: the era of McCarthyism, instances of domestic Communism (e.g., Alger Hiss) and blacklisting; the Truman Doctrine; the Berlin Blockade; the Korean War; the Bay of Pigs invasion and the Cuban Missile Crisis; atomic testing in the American West, the "mutual assured destruction" doctrine, and disarmament policies; the Vietnam War; Latin American policy.

11.9.4 List the effects of foreign policy on domestic policies and vice versa (e.g., protests during the war in Vietnam, the "nuclear freeze" movement).

⁓ The Big Idea ⁓

The fate of nations is forever changed by monumental world events. President Nixon reduced the number of troops in Vietnam and worked to end U.S. involvement in the war. He appointed Henry Kissinger to negotiate peace with North Vietnam. The nation remained divided, however, as the war continued. Nixon's decision to invade Cambodia and the revelations of the Pentagon Papers led to increased protests. After continued peace negotiations, the United States finally ended its involvement in Vietnam. The peace agreement did not last long. Soon after the withdrawal of American troops, the North Vietnamese invaded the South and united Vietnam under Communist rule.

792 CHAPTER 17 The Vietnam War

SECTION RESOURCES

📁 Print Material
- Reproducible Lesson Plan 17-4
- Guided Reading Activity 17-4
- Reading Essentials and Study Guide 17-4
- Active Reading Note-Taking Guide 17-4

🖹 Transparencies
- Daily Focus Skills Transparency 17-4
- Section Graphic Organizer Transparency 17-4

Technology
- 💿 Interactive Tutor Self-Assessment CD-ROM
- 💿 ExamView® Pro Testmaker CD-ROM
- 💿 Presentation Plus! CD-ROM

Nixon Moves to End the War

 Main Idea President Nixon reduced the number of troops in Vietnam and relied on Henry Kissinger to negotiate peace.

Reading Connection Have you ever tried to resolve a disagreement between friends? Read on to learn about the process of attempting to negotiate peace.

Shortly after taking office, President Nixon began taking steps to end the nation's involvement in the war. It was not until 1975 that Frank Snepp became one of the last Americans to leave Vietnam.

★ An American Story ★

On the evening of April 29, 1975, Frank Snepp, a young CIA officer, scrambled up to the American embassy rooftop to catch one of the last helicopters out of Saigon. Throughout that day, Snepp had witnessed the desperation of the South Vietnamese people as they besieged the embassy grounds in an effort to escape the approaching Communist army. Now he was leaving. Later, he recalled the scene:

❝The roof of the Embassy was a vision out of a nightmare. In the center of the dimly lit helo-pad a CH-47 was already waiting for us, its engines setting up a roar like a primeval scream. The crew and controllers all wore what looked like oversized football helmets, and in the blinking under-light of the landing signals they reminded me of grotesque insects rearing on their hindquarters. Out beyond the edge of the building a Phantom jet streaked across the horizon as tracers darted up here and there into the night sky.❞

—quoted in *Decent Interval*

More than five years before Frank Snepp left Vietnam, President Nixon began working toward ending the war. As a first step, he appointed Harvard professor **Henry Kissinger** as special assistant for national security affairs and gave him wide authority to use diplomacy to end the conflict. Kissinger embarked upon a policy he called **linkage,** which meant improving relations with the Soviet Union and China—suppliers of aid to North Vietnam—so he could persuade them to cut back on their aid.

Kissinger also rekindled peace talks with the North Vietnamese. In August 1969, Kissinger entered into secret negotiations with North Vietnam's negotiator, Le Duc Tho. In their talks, which dragged on for four years, Kissinger and Le Duc Tho argued over a possible cease-fire, the return of American prisoners of war, and the **ultimate** fate of South Vietnam.

Meanwhile, Nixon cut back the number of American troops in Vietnam. Known as **Vietnamization,** this process involved the gradual withdrawal of U.S. troops while South Vietnam assumed more of the fighting. On June 8, 1969, Nixon announced the withdrawal of 25,000 soldiers. Nixon refused to view this troop withdrawal as a form of surrender. He was determined to maintain a strong American presence in Vietnam to ensure bargaining power during peace negotiations. In support of that goal, the president increased airstrikes against North Vietnam and began bombing Vietcong sanctuaries in neighboring Cambodia.

✓ **Reading Check** **Identifying** When did secret negotiations with the North Vietnamese begin?

Turmoil at Home Continues

Main Idea Protests in the United States continued after the invasion of Cambodia and the killing of South Vietnamese citizens.

Reading Connection What do you think are the most effective ways to bring about a change in government policy? Read on to find out about the demonstrations in the United States as the war continued.

Even though the United States had begun scaling back its involvement in Vietnam, the American home front remained divided and volatile as Nixon's war policies stirred up new waves of protest.

"The roof of the Embassy was a vision out of a nightmare."

—*Frank Snepp*

CHAPTER 17   The Vietnam War   **793**

Chapter 17 • Section 4

TEACH

R Reading Strategy

Using Context Clues Ask students to look up the definition of *link. (an association or a relationship)* Then have students find the word *linkage* in the dictionary. Ask students to consider how the definition of the term *linkage* connected directly with Kissinger's policy of linkage. *(A parallel or reciprocal relationship was developed with the Soviet Union and China to aid North Vietnam.)* **BL**

C Critical Thinking

Predicting Consequences Remind students that President Nixon wished to turn more of the war strategy and troop deployment to the South Vietnamese. **Ask:** What immediate results might Nixon expect to have as a result of Vietnamization? *(Answers may include: reduce antiwar protests and gain more political support at home, fewer American casualties)* **OL**

Resources for page 793

Have student read more about President Nixon's plans to change American involvement in the Vietnam War in the Primary Source Reading 17-2.

✓ **Reading Check**
Answer: August 1969

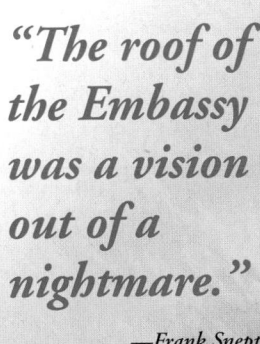

ABCNEWS INTERACTIVE™

▦ **VIDEOCASSETTE**
Historic America Electronic Field Trips
View **Tape 2, Chapter 10:** "The Vietnam Veterans Memorial."

Answers and Additional Support

Massacre at My Lai In November 1969, Americans learned of a horrifying event. That month, the media reported that in the spring of 1968, an American platoon under the command of Lieutenant William Calley had massacred possibly more than 200 unarmed South Vietnamese civilians in the hamlet of My Lai. Most of the victims were old men, women, and children. Calley eventually went to prison for his role in the killings.

Most American soldiers acted responsibly and honorably throughout the war. The actions of one soldier, however, increased the feeling among many citizens that this was a brutal and senseless conflict. Jan Barry, a founder of the Vietnam Veterans Against the War, viewed the massacre at My Lai as a symbol of the dilemma his **generation** faced in the conflict:

> ❝To kill on military orders and be a criminal, or to refuse to kill and be a criminal is the moral agony of America's Vietnam war generation. It is what has forced upward of sixty thousand young Americans, draft resisters and deserters to Canada, and created one hundred thousand military deserters a year in this country and abroad.❞
>
> –quoted in *Who Spoke Up?*

The Invasion of Cambodia Sparks Protest
Americans heard more startling news when Nixon announced in April 1970 that American troops had invaded Cambodia. The troops wanted to destroy Vietcong military bases there.

Many viewed the Cambodian invasion as a widening of the war, and it set off many protests. At Kent State University on May 4, 1970, Ohio National Guard soldiers, armed with tear gas and rifles, fired on demonstrators without an order to do so. The soldiers killed four students and wounded at least nine others. Ten days later, police killed two African American students during a demonstration at Jackson State College in Mississippi.

The Pentagon Papers
In addition to sparking violence on campuses, the invasion of Cambodia cost Nixon significant congressional support. Numerous legislators expressed outrage over the president's failure to notify them of the action. In December 1970, an angry Congress repealed the Gulf of Tonkin Resolution, which had given the president near complete power in directing the war in Vietnam.

Support for the war weakened further in 1971 when Daniel Ellsberg, a disillusioned former Defense Department worker, leaked what became known as the **Pentagon Papers** to the *New York Times.* The documents revealed that many government officials during the Johnson administration privately questioned the war while publicly defending it.

The documents contained details of decisions that were made by the presidents and their advisers without the consent of Congress. They also showed how the various administrations acted to deceive Congress, the press, and the public about the situation in Vietnam. The Pentagon Papers confirmed what many Americans had long believed: The government had not been honest with them.

✓ Reading Check **Evaluating**
What did the Pentagon Papers confirm for many Americans?

Picturing History

National Trauma When members of the Ohio National Guard fired on Kent State University demonstrators, the event triggered a nationwide student strike that forced hundreds of colleges and universities to close. How does this image connect with the phrase "the war at home"?

794

Profiles IN HISTORY

Roy P. Benavidez
1935–1998

Roy P. Benavidez received the Medal of Honor, the nation's highest award for heroism, for his actions in the Vietnam War. Growing up, Benavidez worked on the streets selling empty soda bottles and cleaning a local stockyard. His father's family had been *vaqueros* (cowboys from Mexico), immigrating in the 1830s during the Texas War for Independence. His mother, a Yaqui Native American, was born in northern Mexico. Both parents died by the time Benavidez was seven, and he was raised by his uncle.

A tough life made Benavidez a fighter. In May 1968 while fighting in Vietnam, Benavidez rescued members of his Special Forces group who were surrounded by the enemy. Wounded three times while getting to the men by helicopter, he stayed with them some eight hours, preparing an evacuation. Then while carrying the men to the rescue helicopters, he was attacked from behind but managed to kill his attacker. Only after loading all the dead and wounded did Benavidez himself board a helicopter.

The United States Pulls Out of Vietnam

Main Idea South Vietnam fell to North Vietnam shortly after the removal of United States troops.

Reading Connection What effect can Congress have on a war? Read on to learn how in 1975 Congress refused to support continued assistance to South Vietnam.

By 1971 polls showed that nearly two-thirds of Americans wanted to end the Vietnam War as quickly as possible. In April 1972, President Nixon dropped his longtime insistence that North Vietnamese troops had to withdraw from South Vietnam before any peace treaty could be signed. In October, less than a month before the 1972 presidential election, Henry Kissinger emerged from his secret talks with Le Duc Tho to announce that "peace is at hand."

A month later, Americans went to the polls to decide on a president. Senator George McGovern, the Democratic candidate, was an outspoken critic of the war. He did not appeal to many middle-class Americans, however, who were tired of antiwar protesters. When the votes were cast, Nixon won re-election in a landslide.

The Two Sides Reach Peace Just weeks after the presidential election, the peace negotiations broke down. South Vietnam's president, Nguyen Van Thieu, refused to agree to any plan that left North Vietnamese troops in the South. Kissinger tried to win additional concessions from the Communists, but talks broke off in mid-December.

The next day, to force North Vietnam to resume negotiations, the Nixon administration began the most destructive air raids of the entire war. In what became known as the "Christmas bombings," American B-52s dropped thousands of tons of bombs on North Vietnamese targets for 12 straight days, pausing only on Christmas day.

In the wake of the bombing campaign, the United States and North Vietnam returned to the bargaining table. Thieu finally gave in to American pressure and allowed North Vietnamese troops to remain in the South. On January 27, 1973, the warring sides signed an agreement "ending the war and restoring the peace in Vietnam."

The United States promised to withdraw the rest of its troops, and both sides agreed to an exchange of prisoners of war. The parties did not resolve the issue of South Vietnam's future, however. After almost eight years of war—the longest war in American history—the nation ended its direct involvement in Vietnam.

CHAPTER 17   The Vietnam War   **795**

U Universal Access

Auditory/Musical Bring to class a recording of Bob Dylan's song "Blowin' in the Wind." Have students summarize what the lyrics are saying and why the music helps convey the message of the lyrics. Then ask students to research other protest songs of the Vietnam War era. Discuss in class how these songs reflect the turmoil this war brought on the United States. **AL**

R Reading Strategy

Evaluating Even though Nixon eventually wanted to reduce the role of the U.S. military in Vietnam, he authorized intense bombing raids on North Vietnam. **Ask:** What were the objectives of the Christmas attacks? *(to apply additional pressure to force parties to the peace table)* **OL**

Profiles IN HISTORY

Roy Benavidez originally received the Distinguished Service Cross from General William C. Westmoreland for his brave actions. After the general heard more details about Benavidez's heroism years later, the medal was upgraded. President Reagan presented the Medal of Honor to Benavidez in a White House ceremony in 1981, making the master sergeant one of 41 Hispanic Americans to have received the nation's highest award for heroism. Since then, a U.S. Navy ship and a non-commissioned officer academy have been named after Benavidez.

Review the Big Idea

Review the Big Idea for this section, "The fate of nations is forever changed by monumental world events." Tell students that the South Vietnamese government collapsed about a month after the North Vietnamese army began its March 1975 invasion. **Ask: Why did the South Vietnamese government collapse so quickly?** *(Students may say that the South Vietnamese government had always relied on the United States in order to function. Nixon's resignation and Congress's refusal of more funds prevented more help when the invasion began.)* **OL**
CA HI1; HI4

R Reading Strategy

Summarizing Organize the class into groups of five to seven students. After students have read the section, ask each group to answer this statement: **The war in Vietnam was tragic because** _____. You can either provide a key word or ask the groups to write their own. Everyone in the group should provide at least one original answer. Have one student in each group present the responses to the class. As a class, look for common elements in the responses. **OL**

✓ Reading Check

Answer: Kissinger tried to win additional concessions.

Answers and Additional Support

Picturing **History**

Desperate Pleas When President Ford ordered all Americans to leave Vietnam immediately in April 1975, many Saigon residents stormed the U.S. embassy pleading for rescue. When did the North Vietnamese take control of Saigon?

South Vietnam Falls The United States had barely pulled out its last troops from Vietnam when the peace agreement collapsed. In March 1975, the North Vietnamese army launched a full-scale invasion of the South. Thieu desperately appealed to Washington, D.C., for help.

President Nixon had assured Thieu during the peace negotiations that the United States "[would] respond with full force should the settlement be violated by North Vietnam." Nixon, however, had resigned under pressure following the Watergate scandal. The new president, Gerald Ford, asked for funds to aid the South Vietnamese, but Congress refused.

On April 30, the North Vietnamese captured Saigon, South Vietnam's capital, and united Vietnam under Communist rule. They then renamed Saigon Ho Chi Minh City.

✓ Reading Check **Explaining** Why did the peace talks break down in December 1972?

796   CHAPTER 17   The Vietnam War

The Legacy of Vietnam

Main Idea Vietnam veterans had a difficult time returning to civilian life.

Reading Connection Have you ever visited a war memorial? Read on to discover how a war memorial helped heal some of the divisions that the Vietnam War created.

R "The lessons of the past in Vietnam," President Ford declared in 1975, "have already been learned—learned by Presidents, learned by Congress, learned by the American people—and we should have our focus on the future." Although Americans tried to put the war behind them, Vietnam left a deep and lasting impact on American society.

The War's Human Toll The United States paid a heavy price for its involvement in Vietnam, in both lives lost and monetary expenses. The war had cost the nation over $170 billion in direct costs and much more in indirect economic expenses. More significantly, it had resulted in the deaths of approximately 58,000 young Americans and the injury of more than 300,000. In Vietnam, around one million North and South Vietnamese soldiers died in the conflict, as did countless civilians.

Even after they returned home from fighting, some American veterans, as in other wars, found it hard to escape the war's impact. Many soldiers faced a variety of psychological problems. Army Specialist Doug Johnson recalled the concerns he faced on returning home:

❝It took a while for me to recognize that I did suffer some psychological problems in trying to deal with my experience in Vietnam. The first recollection I have of the effect took place shortly after I arrived back in the States. One evening . . . I went to see a movie on post. I don't recall the name of the movie or what it was about, but I remember there was a sad part, and that I started crying uncontrollably. It hadn't dawned on me before this episode that I had . . . succeeded in burying my emotions.❞

—quoted in *Touched by the Dragon*

Picturing **History**

Answer: April 30, 1975
Ask: Why did Saigon residents want to be rescued? *(They feared retribution from the North Vietnamese for their support of the United States.)*

Resources for page 796

Have students read more about the struggle of the Vietnam veterans to come to grips with their experiences during the war by assigning "Second Lieutenant Parvin Zelmer, U.S.M.C." in the **American Literature Readings 5.**

One reason it may have been harder for some Vietnam veterans to readjust to civilian life was that many considered the war a defeat. Many Americans wanted to forget the war. Thus, the sacrifices of many veterans often went unrecognized. There were relatively few welcome-home parades and celebrations after the war. To some soldiers, this diminished their sacrifices.

The war also lingered for the American families whose relatives and friends were classified as prisoners of war (POWs) or missing in action (MIA). Despite many official investigations, these families were not convinced that the government had told the truth about POW/MIA policies during the last years of the war. Many were left not knowing if their loved ones were dead or alive or if they would ever return home.

The nation finally began to come to terms with the war almost a decade later. In 1982 the nation dedicated the Vietnam Veterans Memorial in Washington, D.C., a large black stone wall inscribed with the names of those killed and missing in action in the war. "It's a first step to remind America of what we did," veteran Larry Cox of Virginia said at the dedication of the monument.

The War's Impact on the Nation The long Vietnam War also left its mark on the nation as a whole. In 1973 Congress passed the **War Powers Act** as a way to reestablish some limits on executive power. The act required the president to inform Congress of any commitment of troops abroad within 48 hours and to withdraw them in 60 to 90 days unless Congress **explicitly** approved the troop commitment.

The legislation addresses the struggle between the executive and legislative branches over what checks and balances are proper in matters of war and foreign policy. No president has recognized this limitation, and the courts have tended to avoid the issue as a strictly political question. In general, the war shook the nation's confidence and led some to embrace a new kind of isolationism. In the years after the war, many Americans became more reluctant to intervene in the affairs of other nations and to commit United States troops in conflicts overseas.

On the domestic front, the Vietnam War increased Americans' cynicism about their government. Many felt the nation's leaders had misled them. Americans were still not convinced they had been told the whole truth. Together with Watergate, a scandal that broke as the war was winding down, Vietnam made Americans more wary of their leaders.

Student Web Activity Visit the *American Vision: Modern Times* Web site at tav.mt.glencoe.com and click on *Student Web Activities— Chapter 17* for an activity on the Vietnam War.

✓ **Reading Check** **Describing** How did the Vietnam War affect Americans' attitudes toward international conflicts and the use of United States troops overseas?

 Study Central

For help with the concepts in this section of *American Vision: Modern Times* go to tav.mt.glencoe.com and click on *Study Central.*

SECTION 4 ASSESSMENT

Checking for Understanding

1. **Vocabulary** Define: linkage, ultimate, generation, explicit.

2. **People and Terms** Identify: Henry Kissinger, Vietnamization, Pentagon Papers, War Powers Act.

3. **Describe** what happened in Vietnam in 1975 after the United States withdrew.

Reviewing Big Ideas

4. **Explaining** Why did Congress pass the War Powers Act? How did this act reflect a struggle between the legislative and executive branches?

Critical Thinking

5. **Historical Analysis** **Analyzing** Why did the invasion of Cambodia cost President Nixon congressional support? **CA** H11

6. **Organizing** Use a graphic organizer similar to the one below to list the effects of the Vietnam War on the nation.

Effects of Vietnam War

Analyzing Visuals

7. **Analyzing Photographs** Study the photograph on page 796 of South Vietnamese citizens attempting to enter the U.S. embassy. How do you think this image affected American attitudes toward the war? Why do you think so?

Writing About History

8. **Descriptive Writing** Imagine that you are a college student in 1970. Write a journal entry expressing your feelings about the events at Kent State University and Jackson State College. **CA** 11WA2.1a; 11WA2.1b

CHAPTER 17   The Vietnam War   **797**

ASSESS

Resources for page 797

Use these resources to assess student mastery.

📁 Section Quiz 17-4

📁 Reading Essentials and Study Guide 17-4

💿 Interactive Tutor Self-Assessment CD-ROM

📁 California Standards Practice, Grade 11

HISTORY Online

Objectives and answers to the student activity can be found in the **Web Activity Lesson Plan** at tav.mt.glencoe.com.

Resources for page 797

Have students read more about Vietnam War prisoners of war in the Linking Past and Present Activity 17.

✓ **Reading Check**

Answer: became more reluctant to intervene in other countries' affairs

HISTORY Online

Study Central provides audio summaries, interactive games, and online graphic organizers to help students review section content.

CLOSE

Summarizing Have students summarize the lessons of the Vietnam War. OL

SECTION 4 ASSESSMENT ANSWERS

1. Content vocabulary is boldfaced and highlighted in yellow. Academic vocabulary is boldfaced.

2. Henry Kissinger *(p. 793)*, Vietnamization *(p. 793)*, Pentagon Papers *(p. 794)*, War Powers Act *(p. 797)*

3. North Vietnam took control of South Vietnam, uniting the two countries under Communist rule.

4. to limit executive power; reflected the struggle over checks and balances in war and foreign policy between the executive and legislative branches

5. Nixon failed to notify Congress of this action in advance, costing him congressional support.

6. American cynicism toward government, war dead and casualties, cost, and War Powers Act

7. Answers will vary. Responses could include relief at getting out of the war or guilt for leaving allies behind.

8. Journal entries should focus on feelings.

FOCUS

History–Social Science Standards

This feature addresses the following standard:

11.9.3 Trace the origins and geopolitical consequences (foreign and domestic) of the Cold War and containment policy, including the following: the era of McCarthyism, instances of domestic Communism (e.g., Alger Hiss) and blacklisting; the Truman Doctrine; the Berlin Blockade; the Korean War; the Bay of Pigs Invasion and the Cuban Missile Crisis; atomic testing in the American West, the "mutual assured destruction" doctrine, and disarmament policies; the Vietnam War; Latin American policy.

Understanding Vocabulary

Before students begin reading, point out that difficult or unfamiliar words are footnoted throughout the text.

TEACH

R Reading Strategy

Connecting Read the bracketed sentence to the class. **Ask:** Are there situations today in which these concerns might be voiced? *(Students' answers will vary.)* **OL** **CA CS1**

Answers and Additional Support

Primary Sources
Eyewitness to History

The United States steadily increased its involvement in Vietnam following World War II. During the 1960s, as the United States began sending ground troops to Vietnam and protests started at home, Vietnam became a subject of sharp debate.

SOURCE 1:

Senator J. William Fulbright, a Democrat from Arkansas, chaired the Senate Foreign Relations Committee. One of the earliest and most vocal congressional opponents of the Vietnam War, he spoke before the Senate on May 5, 1966.

The attitude above all others which I feel sure is no longer valid is the arrogance of power, the tendency of great nations to equate power with virtue and major responsibilities with a universal mission. The dilemmas involved are preeminently American dilemmas, not because America has weaknesses that others do not have but because America is powerful as no nation has ever been before and the discrepancy between its power and the power of others appears to be increasing. . . .

▼ *Senator William Fulbright (right) talks with Defense Secretary Robert McNamara (left)*

We are now engaged in a war to "defend freedom" in South Vietnam. . . . The official war aims of the United States Government, as I understand them, are to defeat what is regarded as North Vietnamese aggression, to demonstrate the **futility**[1] of what the communists call "wars of national liberation," and to create conditions under which the South Vietnamese people will be able freely to determine their own future. . . . What I do doubt—and doubt very much—is the ability of the United States to achieve these aims by the means being used. I do not question the power of our weapons and the efficiency of our **logistics**[2]. . . . What I do question is the ability of the United States, or France or any other Western nation, to go into a small, alien, undeveloped Asian nation and create stability where there is chaos, the will to fight where there is defeatism, democracy where there is no tradition of it and honest government where corruption is almost a way of life. . . .

SOURCE 2:

Edwin Willis, a Democrat who had represented Louisiana since 1949, chaired the House Un-American Activities Committee. In the spring of 1968, he reported to the full House about what he believed to be Communist infiltration of the student and antiwar movements.

At the culmination of Vietnam Week last year, the American citizen was left stunned. Indelibly stamped on his mind were the front page photos of his country's beloved flag being burned in New York City. Other photographs of the demonstrations showed an unruly mob waving flags of the Vietcong and raising large portraits of Ho Chi Minh. . . .

➤ ────────────────────
[1]**futility:** uselessness
[2]**logistics:** detailed handling of military operations

UNIVERSAL ACCESS

English Learners Students learning English might have problems expressing their thoughts about the war in words. Organize the class into groups of three and have each group create a poster board with images that show the debate over the war. One side should provide material supporting U.S. involvement in Vietnam, while the other side should show material opposing it. Encourage students to use library and Internet resources, along with their textbooks, to locate photographs, original drawings, newspaper headlines, poems, and any other artifacts to complete their posters. Then ask a volunteer from each group to present the group's poster to the class. **EL** **CA 11WS1.6**

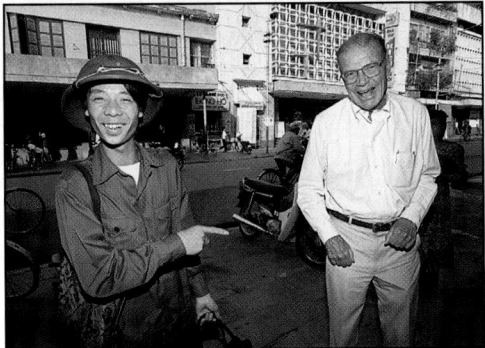

▲ *Robert McNamara in Hanoi in 1995*

. . . On April 15, 1967, demonstrations were clearly staged in defiance of the determination of our people to help resist Communist aggression in Southeast Asia. . . .

What began as a "Massive protest demonstration against U.S. Government policy" in Vietnam, was skillfully maneuvered into a carnival of unmistakable support for a Communist victory in Vietnam. . . .

W The student strike and mass actions day April 27, 1968—will be the Communist run vehicle of irresponsible dissent and internal disruption within the United States. This dissent and disruption is designed to benefit the North Vietnamese enemy and the world Communist movement in general by undermining public support of the present U.S. policy of resisting Communist aggression in South Vietnam. . . .

If the Communists are successful in inducing a significant number of college and high school students to strike . . . the international Communist propaganda network will use this incident to attempt to: First, create widespread demand for reversal of present U.S. foreign policy; second, propagandistically give aid and comfort to Communists everywhere in the world Communist movement, but particularly in Vietnam; and third, further dampen the resolve of America's allies who presently support U.S. policy in Vietnam, and make the war effort appear solely "America's problem."

SOURCE 3:

Robert S. McNamara served as secretary of defense under President Lyndon B. Johnson. In his 1995 memoir, McNamara concluded that he and the Johnson administration made a mistake in July 1965 when they escalated U.S. military involvement in Vietnam.

We of the Kennedy and Johnson administrations who participated in the decision on Vietnam acted according to what we thought were the principles and traditions of this nation. We made our decisions in light of those values. . . .

On July 21 [1965], I returned to Washington and presented the report I had prepared along the way to the president. It began with a frank but disturbing assessment:

> The situation in South Vietnam is worse than a year ago. . . . There are no signs that we have throttled the inflow of supplies for the VC [Vietcong]. . . . Nor have our air attacks in North Vietnam produced tangible evidence of the willingness on the part of Hanoi to come to the conference table in a reasonable mood. . . .

R I then reviewed the three alternatives we had examined so many times before: (1) withdraw under the best conditions obtainable—almost certainly meaning something close to unconditional surrender; (2) continue at the present level—almost certainly forcing us into Option 1 later; or (3) expand our forces. . . .

I was driven to Option 3, which I considered "**prerequisite**[3] to the achievement of any acceptable settlement." I ended by expressing my judgment that "the course of action recommended . . . stands a good chance of achieving an acceptable outcome within a reasonable time." Subsequent events proved my judgment wrong.

> ➤ [3]**prerequisite:** something required to meet an end

DBQ Document-Based Questions

Historical Analysis   CA HR3; HI3

Source 1: Why does Fulbright believe that the United States will fail in Vietnam?

Source 2: Why does Willis believe that protests aid the enemy?

Source 3: According to McNamara, why did the United States increase its troop strength in Vietnam?

Comparing and Contrasting Sources
How do Fulbright, Willis, and McNamara differ on the reasons for American involvement in Vietnam?

DBQ Document-Based Questions

Historical Analysis
1. The U.S. cannot institute stability and democracy in an undeveloped, unstable Asian nation.
2. He believes that protests will aid the Communist enemy by undermining public support of America's role in the Vietnam War and discouraging America's allies.
3. Increasing troop strength in Vietnam was the only way to achieve an acceptable outcome within a reasonable period of time.

Comparing and Contrasting Sources
Fulbright believes the goal of the war is to liberate the South Vietnamese, while Willis thinks that the goal of the war is to fight communism. McNamara states that entering the war represents the principles and traditions of the United States.

799

Reviewing Content Vocabulary

Students' answers will vary. The pages where the words appear in the text are shown in parentheses.

1. domino theory *(p. 775)* **2.** guerrilla *(p. 775)* **3.** Vietcong *(p. 778)* **4.** napalm *(p. 782)* **5.** credibility gap *(p. 787)* **6.** teach-in *(p. 788)* **7.** dove *(p. 789)* **8.** hawk *(p. 789)* **9.** linkage *(p. 793)* **10.** Vietnamization *(p. 793)*

Reviewing Academic Vocabulary

Students' answers will vary. The pages where the words appear in the text are shown in parentheses.

11. region *(p. 773)* **12.** occupy *(p. 775)* **13.** principal *(p. 776)* **14.** administration *(p. 778)* **15.** coincidental *(p. 779)* **16.** sustain *(p. 781)* **17.** contradict *(p. 787)* **18.** proportion *(p. 788)* **19.** alternative *(p. 790)* **20.** ultimate *(p. 793)* **21.** generation *(p. 794)* **22.** explicit *(p. 797)*

CHAPTER 17 ASSESSMENT and ACTIVITIES

Reviewing Key Terms

On a sheet of paper, use each of these terms in a sentence.

1. domino theory
2. guerrilla
3. Vietcong
4. napalm
5. credibility gap
6. teach-in
7. dove
8. hawk
9. linkage
10. Vietnamization

Chapter Summary

American Involvement in Vietnam

Roots of the Conflict

- Eisenhower financially supported French war against Vietnam
- Geneva Accords established North and South Vietnam
- U.S.-backed leader of South Vietnam refused national elections, fearing defeat by Communist opponent
- Kennedy sharply increased military aid and presence in South Vietnam
- Johnson escalated U.S. involvement and gained war powers after the incident in the Gulf of Tonkin

Full-Scale War

- President Johnson responded to a Vietcong attack with aggressive airstrikes; American people applauded his actions
- U.S. committed over 380,000 ground troops to fighting in Vietnam by the end of 1966

Opposition to the War

- American people questioned the government's honesty about the war, creating the so-called "credibility gap"
- Wartime economy hurt domestic spending efforts
- President Nixon was elected largely on promises to end the war and unite the divided country

The End of the War

- Nixon withdrew troops but increased airstrikes
- American troops pulled out after a 1973 peace agreement
- Congress passed the War Powers Act to limit the power of the president during times of war

---

Reviewing Academic Vocabulary

On a sheet of paper, use each of these terms in a sentence that reflects the term's meaning in the chapter.

11. region	**15.** coincidental	**19.** alternative
12. occupy	**16.** sustain	**20.** ultimate
13. principal	**17.** contradict	**21.** generation
14. administration	**18.** proportion	**22.** explicit

Reviewing the Main Ideas

Section 1

23. How did President Eisenhower defend American policy in Vietnam?

Section 2

24. What actions made Ngo Dinh Diem an unpopular leader in South Vietnam?

Section 3

25. What was the effect of the Tet offensive on Americans?

Section 4

26. What did the Pentagon Papers reveal?

Critical Thinking

27. **Reading Skill** Questioning the Author Reread the text under the heading "The Invasion of Cambodia Sparks Protest" on page 794. In your opinion, what is the author's purpose for this passage? What personal connection can you make with this passage?

28. **Civics** How did Americans show their frustration with the direction the country was taking in 1968?

29. **Organizing** Use a graphic organizer to list the reasons the United States became involved in Vietnam and the effects the war had on the nation.

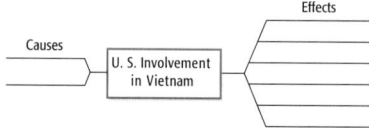

Writing About History

30. **Historical Analysis** Comparing Present and Past Explain in a letter to your congressional representative why the War Powers Act was passed and its consequences for the U.S. government today. Provide evidence for your claims. **CA CS1**

Reviewing the Main Ideas

23. President Eisenhower defended involvement in Vietnam by stressing the domino theory and the need to stop the spread of communism.

24. Ngo Dinh Diem was unpopular due to the strategic hamlet policy and his discrimination against Buddhism.

25. The Tet offensive began to turn American public opinion against the war. Mainstream media began to criticize the war and Johnson decided not to run for another term as president.

26. The Pentagon Papers revealed that U.S. government officials had not been honest about the war's progress.

HISTORY Online

Self-Check Quiz

Visit the *American Vision: Modern Times* Web site at **tav.mt.glencoe.com** and click on *Self-Check Quizzes– Chapter 17* to assess your knowledge of chapter content.

31. *Big Idea* Write an editorial to your local newspaper supporting or opposing the Twenty-sixth Amendment to the Constitution. Explain the amendment and discuss its importance to the antiwar movement. **CA** 11WA2.4a

DBQ Document-Based Questions

32. Interpreting Primary Sources In the 1960s many young Americans enlisted or were drafted for military service. Some believed they had a duty to serve their country. Many had no clear idea of what they were doing or why. In the following excerpt, a young man interviewed for Mark Baker's book *Nam* presents his thoughts about going to war.

❝I read a lot of pacifist literature to determine whether or not I was a conscientious objector. I finally concluded that I wasn't. . . . The one clear decision I made in 1968 about me and the war was that if I was going to get out of it, I was going to get out in a legal way. I was not going to defraud the system in order to beat the system. I wasn't going to leave the country, because the odds of coming back looked real slim. . . .

With all my terror of going into the Army . . . there was something seductive about it, too. I was seduced by World War II and John Wayne movies. . . . I had been, as we all were, victimized by a romantic, truly uninformed view of war.❞

—quoted in *Nam*

a. What options did the young man have regarding going to war?

b. Do you think World War II movies gave him a realistic view of what fighting in Vietnam would be like?

Geography and History

33. The map on this page shows supply routes and troop movements during the Vietnam War. Study the map and answer the questions below.

a. Interpreting Maps What nations besides North and South Vietnam were the sites of battles or invasions?

b. Analyzing Why did the Ho Chi Minh Trail pass through Laos and Cambodia instead of South Vietnam?

NATIONAL GEOGRAPHIC — The Vietnam War

Map labels: CHINA, Dien Bien Phu, Hanoi, Haiphong, LAOS, NORTH VIETNAM, Gulf of Tonkin, 20°N, Khe Sanh, Demilitarized Zone, 17th Parallel, THAILAND, Quang Tri, Hue, Da Nang, Tam Ky, Chu Lai, My Lai Massacre March 16, 1968, Invasion of Laos Feb. 8–March, 1971, Pleiku, Qui Nhon, CAMBODIA, SOUTH VIETNAM, Ban Me Thuot, Nha Trang, Invasion of Cambodia May 1–June 29, 1970, Phnom Penh, Phoc Binh, Gulf of Thailand, Saigon, Long Binh, Can Tho, Mekong Delta, South China Sea, 10°N, Khanh Hung, Quan Long, 110°E, Ho Chi Minh Trail

Map legend: Major U.S. and South Vietnamese troop movements; Major North Vietnamese supply lines; U.S. bases

0 — 150 miles
0 — 150 kilometers
Miller Cylindrical projection

Standards Practice

Directions: Choose the phrase that best completes the following statement.

34. The purpose of the War Powers Act was to ensure that the president would

A have greater authority over the military.

B consult Congress before committing troops to extended conflicts.

C have the authority to sign treaties without Senate approval.

D have a freer hand in fighting the spread of communism.

Standard 11.8.5: Describe the increased powers of the presidency in response to the Great Depression, World War II, and the Cold War.

CHAPTER 17   The Vietnam War   **801**

HISTORY Online

Have students visit the Web site at **tav.mt.glencoe.com** to review Chapter 17 and take the Self-Check Quiz.

Writing About History

30. **Historical Analysis** Students' answers will vary on determining how the act impacts government today. Students should explain the War Powers Act as being created to curb executive power. It required the president to inform Congress within 48 hours of sending troops abroad and withdraw them in 60 to 90 days unless Congress approves the troop commitment.

31. *Big Idea* Editorials will vary. Students should explain the Twenty-sixth Amendment as allowing all citizens age 18 or older the right to vote in all state and federal elections.

DBQ Document-Based Questions

32. a. He could declare he was a conscientious objector, he could avoid service in a legal way, he could leave the country, or he could fight. **b.** No, he realized that the view of war presented in movies had been romanticized.

Geography and History

33. a. Laos and Cambodia were also invaded. **b.** The Ho Chi Minh trail passed through Laos and Cambodia to avoid discovery and capture of troops and supplies passing along the trail.

Standards Practice

34. B

Bonus Question?

Ask: What is the name of the university in Ohio where four students were killed by National Guard troops? *(Kent State University)*

Critical Thinking

27. **Reading Skill** Students' opinions on the purpose of the passage and the personal connection will vary. Possible answer: The author wanted to establish the violent turn of events in protesting the Vietnam War. Protests are visible in the United States and not all turn violent.

28. They elected Nixon, participated in violence, and protested.

29. causes: fall of China to communism and the outbreak of the Korean War; effects: cynicism toward government, casualties and war dead, cost, protests, War Powers Act

801

Chapter 18 Planning Guide

SECTION RESOURCES

MAIN IDEAS	📁 PRINT MATERIALS	TECHNOLOGY RESOURCES
Section 1: The Student Movement and the Counterculture 1. The youth protest movement of the 1960s included Students for a Democratic Society (SDS) and the Free Speech Movement. 2. During the 1960s some young people rebelled against the values of the older generation. 3. Mainstream culture gradually accepted some of the ideas and styles of the youth movement.	• Reproducible Lesson Plan 18-1* • Daily Lecture and Discussion Notes 18-1 • Active Reading Note-Taking Guide 18-1 • Guided Reading Activity 18-1 • Section Quiz 18-1 • Reading Essentials and Study Guide 18-1	• Daily Focus Skills Transparency 18-1 • Section Graphic Organizer Transparency 18-1 • Interactive Tutor Self-Assessment CD-ROM • ExamView® Pro Testmaker CD-ROM • Presentation Plus! CD-ROM • California Standards Practice Transparencies
Section 2: The Feminist Movement 1. The women's movement became fragmented after women won the right to vote. 2. Women began to seek changes in society through legislative action and organizations. 3. The women's movement experienced success and failures in the fight for equality.	• Reproducible Lesson Plan 18-2* • Daily Lecture and Discussion Notes 18-2 • Active Reading Note-Taking Guide 18-2 • Guided Reading Activity 18-2 • Section Quiz 18-2 • Reading Essentials and Study Guide 18-2	• Daily Focus Skills Transparency 18-2 • Section Graphic Organizer Transparency 18-2 • Interactive Tutor Self-Assessment CD-ROM • ExamView® Pro Testmaker CD-ROM • Presentation Plus! CD-ROM • California Standards Practice Transparencies
Section 3: New Approaches to Civil Rights 1. Minorities in America continued fighting for reform and increased civil rights. 2. Hispanic Americans worked to improve their rights by organizing a farm workers' union and calling for bilingual education. 3. The American Indian Movement (AIM) used protests and legal battles to win victories in the quest for civil rights and equal opportunities.	• Reproducible Lesson Plan 18-3* • Daily Lecture and Discussion Notes 18-3 • Active Reading Note-Taking Guide 18-3 • Guided Reading Activity 18-3 • Section Quiz 18-3 • Reading Essentials and Study Guide 18-3	• Daily Focus Skills Transparency 18-3 • Section Graphic Organizer Transparency 18-3 • Interactive Tutor Self-Assessment CD-ROM • ExamView® Pro Testmaker CD-ROM • Presentation Plus! CD-ROM • California Standards Practice Transparencies
Section 4: Saving the Earth 1. Rachel Carson's book *Silent Spring* warned the public of the dangers of pollution and pesticides. 2. In the early 1970s, Congress passed legislation to protect the nation's air, water, and endangered species. 3. Concerns about the quality and safety of many products, including automobiles, led to new legislation protecting consumers.	• Reproducible Lesson Plan 18-4* • Daily Lecture and Discussion Notes 18-4 • Active Reading Note-Taking Guide 18-4 • Guided Reading Activity 18-4 • Section Quiz 18-4 • Reading Essentials and Study Guide 18-4	• Daily Focus Skills Transparency 18-4 • Section Graphic Organizer Transparency 18-4 • Interactive Tutor Self-Assessment CD-ROM • ExamView® Pro Testmaker CD-ROM • Presentation Plus! CD-ROM • California Standards Practice Transparencies

PACING YOUR LESSONS

Chapter Introduction	Section 1	Section 2	Section 3	Section 4	Chapter Assessment
½ Day	2 Days	2 Days	2 Days	2 Days	½ Day

0:00 OUT OF TIME? 📁 Assign the Chapter 18 *Reading Essentials and Study Guide.*

*Available on TeacherWorks™ CD-ROM

Chapter 18 Planning Guide

Standards-Based Lesson Plan

 ## History–Social Science Standards Covered in Chapter 18

The standards covered in the chapter are listed below. Use the accompanying activity as you teach the chapter to ensure student mastery of these standards. This activity can be used in combination with the program's print and technology assessment materials.

Standard	Section 1	2	3	4
11.3.4 Discuss the expanding religious pluralism in the United States and California that resulted from large-scale immigration in the twentieth century.	✔			
11.6.5 Trace the advances and retreats of organized labor, from the creation of the American Federation of Labor and the Congress of Industrial Organizations to current issues of a postindustrial, multinational economy, including the United Farm Workers in California.			✔	
11.8.6 Discuss the diverse environmental regions of North America, their relationship to local economies, and the origins and prospects of environmental problems in those regions.				✔
11.10 Students analyze the development of federal civil rights and voting rights.	✔	✔	✔	
11.11.1 Discuss the reasons for the nation's changing immigration policy, with emphasis on how the Immigration Act of 1965 and successor acts have transformed American society.			✔	
11.11.3 Describe the changing roles of women in society as reflected in the entry of more women into the labor force and the changing family structure.		✔		
11.11.5 Trace the impact of, need for, and controversies associated with environmental conservation, expansion of the national park system, and the development of environmental protection laws, with particular attention to the interaction between environmental protection advocates and property rights advocates.				✔

Cumulative Standards-Assessment Activity

The Cumulative Standards-Assessment Activity will help students organize and learn the important information from the chapter. Begin teaching the chapter with this activity, and have students complete it as they read the chapter.

CREATING A DIAGRAM FOR COMPARING AND CONTRASTING

Purpose Comparing and contrasting is a technique useful for finding the similarities and differences between people, movements, or ideas. This tool is particularly useful when studying two sides in a conflict or two regions of a country.

Introduction to Comparing and Contrasting

1. Remind the class that comparing and contrasting is used when two subjects are similar enough that they share some characteristics.

2. Review the technique that students used in Chapter 10 to make the diagram about the First New Deal and the Second New Deal.

3. Ask students to copy the Venn diagram to the right into their notebooks:

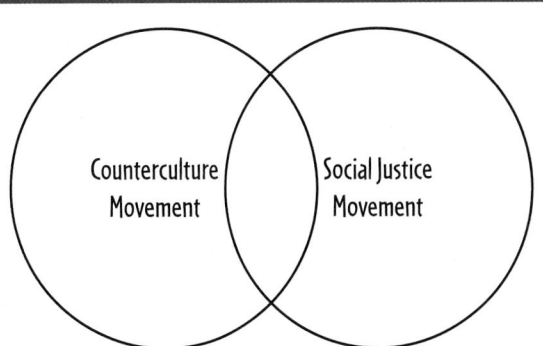

As students read this chapter, have them use a Venn diagram to compare and contrast the counterculture movement with social justice movements such as the feminist movement, civil rights movement, or environmental movement.

4. As you review the chapter, divide the class into groups and have students share their diagrams. Encourage them to use their charts as study aids.

Chapter 18 Planning Guide

READING SUPPORT

- Content Vocabulary Activity 18
- Academic Vocabulary Activity 18
- Reading Skills Activity 18
- Chapter 18 Active Reading Note-Taking Guide
- Chapter 18 Guided Reading Activities
- Chapter 18 Reading Essentials and Study Guide
- American Literature Readings, Unit 5
- *The American Vision: Modern Times* Video Program
- Vocabulary PuzzleMaker CD-ROM
- American History Primary Source Document Library CD-ROM

CRITICAL THINKING

- Critical Thinking Skills Activity 18
- Primary Source Reading 18
- Cause-and-Effect Transparency 18 Strategy and Activity
- Presentation Plus! CD-ROM

UNIVERSAL ACCESS

- Universal Access Activity 18
- English Learner Activity 18
- American Art Prints
- StudentWorks™ Plus CD-ROM
- American Music: Hits Through History
- School-to-Home Connection Activity 18

SKILL PRACTICE

- Map Overlay Transparency 18 Strategy and Activity
- Historical Analysis Skills Activity 18
- Time Line Activity 18
- Reading Skills Activity 18
- Reinforcing Skills Activity 18
- Linking Past and Present Activity 18
- Interpreting Political Cartoons 18
- Geography and History Activity, Unit 5
- Economics and History Activity, Unit 5
- MindJogger Videoquiz

WRITING SUPPORT

- Chapter 18 Active Reading Note-Taking Guide
- Writer's Guidebook
- High School Writing Process Transparencies

ASSESSMENT

- Chapter 18 Section Quizzes
- Chapter 18 Tests, Forms A and B
- Authentic Assessment Activity 18
- ExamView® Pro Testmaker CD-ROM
- Interactive Tutor Self-Assessment CD-ROM
- California Standards Practice, Grade 11
- Succeeding on . . .™ the California Standards: Grade 11 History–Social Science CD-ROM

- CD-ROM
- DVD
- Print Material
- Poster

- Transparency
- Music Program
- Videocassette

Chapter 18 Planning Guide

TECHNOLOGY

- StudentWorks™ Plus CD-ROM
- TeacherWorks™ CD-ROM
- ExamView® Pro Testmaker CD-ROM
- Interactive Tutor Self-Assessment CD-ROM
- Presentation Plus! CD-ROM
- Vocabulary PuzzleMaker CD-ROM
- American History Primary Source Document Library CD-ROM
- MindJogger Videoquiz
- *The American Vision: Modern Times* Video Program
- Professional Development in High School Social Studies Video Series
- Teach, Use, and Succeed With *The American Vision: Modern Times*
- American Music: Hits Through History
- Succeeding on . . .™ the California Standards: Grade 11 History–Social Science CD-ROM

SPANISH RESOURCES

- Spanish Activities and Assessment
  - Spanish Vocabulary Activities
  - Spanish Guided Reading Activities
  - Spanish Quizzes and Tests
  - Spanish Reteaching Activities
- Spanish Reading Essentials and Study Guide
- Spanish School-to-Home Connection Activities

TRANSPARENCIES

- Daily Focus Skills Transparencies
- Section Graphic Organizer Transparencies
- Map Overlay Transparencies
- Cause-and-Effect Transparencies
- Unit Time Line Transparencies
- Why It Matters Transparencies
- American Art and Architecture Transparencies
- High School Writing Process Transparencies
- California Standards Practice Transparencies

TEACHER PLANNING

- Daily Lecture and Discussion Notes
- English Learner Handbook
- Building Academic Vocabulary
- *The American Vision: Modern Times* Reading and Study Skills Foldables
- Reading Strategies and Activities for the Social Studies Classroom
- Universal Access for the American History Classroom
- NGS United States Desk Map
- NGS World Atlas
- Chapter 18 Reproducible Lesson Plans on TeacherWorks™ CD-ROM
- California Guide to Daily Intervention

PROFESSIONAL DEVELOPMENT

- Building Academic Vocabulary
- Strategies for Success
- Research-Based Strategies Used to Develop *The American Vision: Modern Times*
- Character Education in the High School Classroom
- Professional Development in High School Social Studies Video Series
- Teach, Use, and Succeed With *The American Vision: Modern Times*

MOMENTS IN TIME

The following resource can help you teach the content of this chapter.

- Unit 11 Equality for Women (1966–1978)

Chapter 18 Planning Guide

TEACHER'S CORNER

Index to National Geographic Magazine:
The following articles relate to this chapter:

- "Great Lakes: Troubled Water," July 1987
- "I Dream a World: America's Black Women," August 1989
- "Our Polluted Runoff," February 1996

National Geographic Society Products:
To order the following, call National Geographic at 1–800–368–2728

- *Branches of Government Series* (Video)
- *Democratic Government Series: The United States* (Video)
- *Historical Atlas of the United States* (Atlas)

NGS ONLINE

Access National Geographic's new dynamic MapMachine Web site and other geography resources at:

www.nationalgeographic.com
www.nationalgeographic.com/maps

MASTERING THE STANDARDS

The content and assessment in the Student Edition, Teacher Wraparound Edition, teacher planning materials, and the print and technology products are all standards-based. The use of these products during instruction leads to mastery of the standards.

PRACTICE
- California Standards Practice, Grade 11
- California Standards Practice Transparencies
- School-to-Home Connection

BENCHMARK ASSESSMENT
- Section Quizzes, Chapter Tests, and Authentic Assessment
- ExamView® Pro Testmaker CD-ROM
- Succeeding On . . . ™ the California Standards: Grade 11 History–Social Science CD-ROM

REMEDIATION
- California Guide to Daily Intervention
- Interactive Tutor Self-Assessment CD-ROM
- ExamView® Pro Testmaker CD-ROM
- California Standards Practice, Grade 11
- Reading Essentials and Study Guide

Use our Web site for additional resources. All essential content is covered in the Student Edition.

You and your students can visit tav.mt.glencoe.com, the Web site companion to the **American Vision: Modern Times.** This innovative integration of electronic and print media offers your students a wealth of opportunities. The student text directs students to the Web site for the following options:

- **Chapter Overviews**
- **Self-Check Quizzes**
- **Student Web Activities**
- **Textbook Updates**

Answers to the student Web activities are provided for you in the **Web Activity Lesson Plans.** Additional Web resources and ePuzzles and games are also available.

Dinah Zike's Foldables

Foldables are three-dimensional, interactive graphic organizers that help students practice basic writing skills, review key vocabulary terms, and identify main ideas. Every chapter has a foldable activity in the *Dinah Zike's Reading and Study Skills Foldables* booklet. You can use the foldables as they are presented or modify them to suit the needs of your individual class.

A variety of videotape programs are available from A&E Television and The History Channel to provide teaching assistance. To order, call Glencoe at 1-800-334-7344.

Chapter 18 Planning Guide

KEY for Using the Teacher Wraparound Edition

Use this key to help you identify the different types of prompts found in the Teacher Wraparound Edition.

R **Reading Strategies** activities help you teach reading skills and vocabulary.

C **Critical Thinking** strategies help students apply and extend what they have learned.

U **Universal Access** activities provide differentiated instruction for students learning to speak English, along with suggestions for teaching various types of learners.

S **Skill Practice** strategies help students practice historical analysis and geography skills.

W **Writing Support** activities provide writing opportunities to help students comprehend the text.

Teaching strategies and activities have been coded for ability level appropriateness.

AL Activities for students working above grade level
OL Activities for students working on grade level
BL Activities for students working below grade level
EL Activities for English learners

FOCUS

History–Social Science Standards

This chapter addresses the following standards:

11.10.5 Discuss the diffusion of the civil rights movement of African Americans from the churches of the rural South and the urban North, including the resistance to racial desegregation in Little Rock and Birmingham, and how the advances influenced the agendas, strategies, and effectiveness of the quests of American Indians, Asian Americans, and Hispanic Americans for civil rights and equal opportunities.

11.10.7 Analyze the women's rights movement from the era of Elizabeth Cady Stanton and Susan B. Anthony and the passage of the Nineteenth Amendment to the movement launched in the 1960s, including differing perspectives on the roles of women.

11.11.5 Trace the impact of, need for, and controversies associated with environmental conservation, expansion of the national park system, and the development of environmental protection laws, with particular attention to the interaction between environmental protection advocates and property rights advocates.

SKILLBUILDER ACTIVITY

Have students make a prediction about how the efforts of the protesters in the 1960s and 1970s continue to influence the workplace and economic opportunities of women and ethnic groups today. Students should evaluate their answers after they have completed the chapter.

CHAPTER
18
1960–1980
The Politics of Protest

⚜ *The Big Ideas* ⚜

SECTION 1: The Student Movement and the Counterculture
Societies change over time. *During the 1960s, many of the country's young people raised their voices in protest against numerous aspects of American society.*

SECTION 2: The Feminist Movement
Social and economic crises lead to new roles for government. *During the 1960s and 1970s, a large number of American women organized to push for greater rights and opportunities in society.*

SECTION 3: New Approaches to Civil Rights
The quest for equality is eternal. *Throughout the 1960s and 1970s, minority groups developed new ways to improve their status in the United States.*

SECTION 4: Saving the Earth
Societies change over time. *During the 1960s and 1970s, environmental issues became a significant concern for many Americans.*

The *American Vision: Modern Times* Video *The Chapter 18 video, "Behind the Scenes with César," profiles the role that César Chávez played in the United Farm Workers organization.*

1966
• National Organization for Women (NOW) organized

1962
• Rachel Carson's *Silent Spring* published

1963
• Betty Friedan's *The Feminine Mystique* published

1969
• Woodstock music festival held in New York

1970
• First Earth Day observed

LOVE IT OR LEAVE

United States PRESIDENTS

| Eisenhower 1953–1961 | Kennedy 1961–1963 | L. Johnson 1963–1969 | | Nixon 1969–1974 |

1960   *1965*   *1970*

World

1962
• China and Soviet Union have diplomatic disagreements

1964
• China becomes world's fifth nuclear power

1966
• Indira Gandhi becomes prime minister of India

1968
• Soviet Union halts democratic uprising in Czechoslovakia

802

TEACH

Thinking About the Big Ideas

As you begin teaching each section, use these questions and activities to focus on the Big Idea.

Section 1
The Student Movement and the Counterculture
Essential Question: What issues are most relevant to you as an American citizen? Ask students what they have done or can do to express their concern about this issue. Tell students that in Section 1 they will learn how young people worked against numerous aspects of American society. **BL**

Section 2
The Feminist Movement

Essential Question: What is a feminist? Does feminism affect boys and men? Discuss why or why not. Tell students that they will learn in Section 2 how women organized to gain greater rights and opportunities. **OL**

Section 3
New Approaches to Civil Rights

Essential Question: How can a minority group bring about changes that affect an entire society? As students read Section 3, remind them to think about how minority groups developed new ways to improve their status in the United States. **OL**

Section 4
Saving the Earth

Essential Question: What issues face our local government? National? Global? As students read Section 4, remind them to think about what environmental issues are significant concerns that may be affecting their personal environment. **AL**

Cultural Perspectives

During the 1960s and 1970s, several groups of Americans began to demand greater rights. Organize students into teams, with each team choosing one of the following groups: women, African Americans, Hispanic Americans, or Native Americans. Each team should find at least four important dates or events in their chosen group's efforts to gain civil rights and equal opportunities. Have the teams combine their findings on one large time line, then work as a class to identify and explain similarities and differences in the actions and outcomes. **OL**

Labor leader César Chávez meeting with farmworkers

1972
• Use of pesticide DDT banned

1973
• Supreme Court issues *Roe* v. *Wade* ruling
• AIM and government clash at Wounded Knee, South Dakota

1979
• Nuclear accident at Three Mile Island

Ford
1974–1977

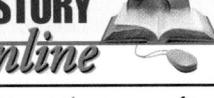
Carter
1977–1981

1975

1980

1972
• Britain imposes direct rule on Northern Ireland

1975
• End of the Portuguese empires in Africa

1979
• Ayatollah Khomeini leads Islamic overthrow of Iran

HISTORY *Online*

Chapter Overview
Visit the *American Vision: Modern Times* Web site at tav.mt.glencoe.com and click on *Chapter Overviews– Chapter 18* to preview chapter information.

803

FOLDABLES™
Study Organizer

Dinah Zike's Foldables are three-dimensional, interactive graphic organizers that help students practice basic writing skills, review key vocabulary terms, and identify main ideas. Have students complete the foldable activity in the *Dinah Zike's Reading and Study Skills Foldables* booklet.

HISTORY *Online*

Go to tav.mt.glencoe.com for student activities, lesson plans, and links to additional Web resources to help students learn about the protest movements of the 1960s and 1970s.

Why It's Important

Evaluating is a key to successful, critical reading. Students should question the historical information they read and try to understand why the material is presented to them in this way.

1. Introducing the Skill

Ask students to evaluate the school's dress code policy. As they read the policy text, remind them to ask questions about the way and reasons the regulation is written. Students should keep notes of their interpretation in a table similar to the one below. **OL**

Who?	*students*
What?	*guidelines for student dress code*
When?	
Where?	
Why?	
How?	

2. Extending the Skill

Ask the class to read the text under the heading *"The Feminine Mystique"* on pages 815–816. Then have them work together to evaluate the information presented. **Ask: What is your reaction to the text? Why did you react in that way? OL**

Answers and Additional Support

Preparing to Read Chapter 18

Effective readers evaluate information as they read. They draw conclusions and form opinions about events, ideas, and people in history. For example, at times readers may disagree with the decision made by a historical figure or approve of the actions of a group of people. It is important for you to form opinions about what you read. It is also important that you are able to support your opinions. This will help you understand the text better.

As you read, imagine what might make a person or group of people behave in a particular way. Ask yourself questions about their motives, as well as whether you need more information. Notice when you react strongly to something you read, whether it is positive or negative. Why do you feel that way?

Read the following passage about a girl joining her school's swim team in 1971 and write a sentence or two about your reaction to the reading.

EVALUATING

Consider your own background knowledge and experiences when evaluating—what do you already know about this topic?

In 1971, [Kathy] Striebel, a high school junior in St. Paul, Minnesota, wanted to compete for her school's swim team, but the school did not allow girls to join. Kathy's mother, Charlotte, . . . filed a grievance with the city's human rights department, and officials required the school to allow Kathy to swim.

Shortly after joining the team, Kathy beat out one of the boys and earned a spot at a meet. As she stood on the block waiting to swim, the opposing coach declared that she was ineligible to compete because the meet was outside St. Paul. . . . "They pulled that little girl right off the block," Charlotte Striebel recalled angrily. (page 817)

How did you react to this story? What do you believe is the author's opinion, and why do you think so? Do you think your evaluation of the passage influenced the way you feel about what the passage says?

Apply the Skill

While you read the text under "Fighting for Greater Opportunity" on pages 825–827 of your textbook, write down your opinions on the issues you learn about. Make sure you include reasons for your opinions.

UNIVERSAL ACCESS

Intrapersonal As students read the first two sections of this chapter, ask them to write down their questions about and reactions to the text. Students should review this list at the midpoint of the chapter to see if they are consistently asking the same questions or having the same reaction to the text. **Ask: What patterns do you see in your evaluations of the text? Are you consistent in your interpretation of the material?** Encourage students to reflect on their own reactions and see if they can broaden their evaluations as they read the last two sections of the chapter. **OL**

Historical Analysis Skill

Historical Connections

Analysis Skill Standard HI1

Historical Interpretation You should recognize that there can be causal and other connections between particular historical events and larger social, economic, and political trends and developments.

When two events are related and connected in time, we often think that one event caused the other. Of course there can be other relationships between events. Have you ever flipped a light switch and had all of the power in your house shut off? If you tripped a breaker and caused the power to shut off, your action caused the power outage. You would call the relationship between these two events causal. Perhaps, though, a power line worker stopped the flow of power in your neighborhood to repair a transformer just as you turned the switch. In this case, it was a coincidence that the events occurred at the same time. Such a relationship is considered a correlation, and the events are called correlational.

Read the following passages about protest movements.

College life empowered young people with a newfound sense of freedom and independence. It also allowed them to meet and bond with others who shared their feelings about society and fears about the future. It was on college campuses across the nation where the protest movements would rage the loudest. **(page 808)**

Women had also gained a better understanding of their inequalities in society from their experiences in the civil rights and antiwar movements. Often they were restricted to menial tasks and rarely had a say in any policy decisions. From the broader perspective, the women's movement was part of the 1960s quest for rights. **(page 815)**

Based on these passages, do you think the protests during the Vietnam War caused the women's movement? Did they only share a correlation because they occurred at the same time? Did these protests show a historical trend towards greater civic involvement by ordinary people?

Apply the Skill

As you read through the chapter, identify the protest movements that developed and the shape they took. Then try to determine whether the movements were correlational or causal. If causal, state which movements caused other movements to develop.

805

Historical Analysis

Why It's Important
Historians need to be able to make connections between a specific event and larger trends in the world. Otherwise, events may not make sense.

1. Introducing the Skill
Ask students to list three events in their lives and try to relate these events to trends or events in recent history. Students should organize their reflections in a chart similar to the one below. *(Students might, for example, connect their moving into a larger house to an upswing in the nation's economy.)* **OL**

Event	Trend

2. Extending the Skill
Divide the class into groups of four and ask each group to review local newspapers and national news magazines to find a major event being discussed in the media. Ask the groups to continue practicing the connecting skill by listing all of the economic, political, and social trends that are relevant to this news event. They should write one-page reports explaining the connections they made and the reasoning behind their choices. You may want to approve the events selected before the groups write their reports. **OL** **CA HI1**

UNIVERSAL ACCESS

Visual/Spatial Some students are better at expressing themselves visually rather than in writing. Ask the groups to illustrate the reports they wrote in the Extending the Skill activity using their own art or images from newspapers, the Internet, and other media sources. Students should organize the imagery on large pieces of poster board so that the connections they explained in writing are clear in their visual presentations. Ask the groups to use their reports and visual displays to explain their reasoning. **OL**

FOCUS

BELLRINGER
SKILLBUILDER ACTIVITY

Project **Daily Focus Skills Transparency 18-1** and have students answer the question.

Guide to Reading

Understanding Vocabulary: Have students write short sentences to describe each of the content vocabulary words and the academic vocabulary words.

Answers to Graphic: Students should complete the outline using the headings in the section.

Unpacking the Standards

Students will be able to:

- Discuss the development of the 1960s youth movement.
- Analyze the composition and goals of the counterculture.
- Explain the impact of the counterculture.

Answers and Additional Support

SECTION 1

The Student Movement and the Counterculture

Guide to Reading

Connection
In the previous chapter, you learned about the Vietnam War. In this section, you will learn how the student movement and the counterculture developed and influenced American society.

Main Idea
- The youth protest movement of the 1960s included Students for a Democratic Society (SDS) and the Free Speech Movement. (p. 807)
- During the 1960s some young people rebelled against the values of the older generation. (p. 809)
- Mainstream culture gradually accepted some of the ideas and styles of the youth movement. (p. 811)

Content Vocabulary
counterculture, commune

Academic Vocabulary
validate, rational, derive

People and Terms to Identify
Port Huron Statement, Tom Hayden, Haight-Ashbury district, Jimi Hendrix

Reading Objectives
- **Explain** the origins of the nation's youth movement.
- **Define** the goals of serious members of the counterculture.

Reading Strategy
Taking Notes As you read about the student movement and culture of the 1960s, use the major headings of the section to create an outline similar to the one below.

The Student Movement and the Counterculture
I. The Growth of the Youth Movement
  A.
  B.
  C.
II.
  A.
  B.

Preview of Events

◆1961	◆1964	◆1967	◆1970
1962 — Students for a Democratic Society deliver Port Huron Statement	**1964** — Free Speech Movement begins; the Beatles embark on their first U.S. tour	**August, 1969** — 400,000 young people gather at Woodstock music festival	

The following are the main History–Social Science Standards covered in this section:

11.3 Students analyze the role religion played in the founding of America, its lasting moral, social and political impacts, and issues regarding religious liberty.

11.3.4 Discuss the expanding religious pluralism in the United States and California that resulted from large-scale immigration in the twentieth century.

11.9.4 List the effects of foreign policy on domestic policies and vice versa (e.g., protests during the war in Vietnam, the "nuclear freeze" movement).

⟶ The Big Idea ⟵

Societies change over time. During the 1960s, many young people grew concerned about the nation's future and became active in social causes. More young people enrolled in colleges, and on college campuses several groups formed that aimed at bringing attention to what they saw as political and social injustices. The counterculture movement attempted to break away from traditional society. Some people embraced new spiritual movements and religions. While the counterculture movement did not last long, it did have a lasting impact on society. Mainstream society gradually accepted some aspects of the counterculture, such as its fashion, art, music, and dance.

806 CHAPTER 18 The Politics of Protest

SECTION RESOURCES

📂 Print Material
- Reproducible Lesson Plan 18-1
- Guided Reading Activity 18-1
- Reading Essentials and Study Guide 18-1
- Active Reading Note-Taking Guide 18-1

Transparencies
- Daily Focus Skills Transparency 18-1
- Section Graphic Organizer Transparency 18-1

Technology
- Interactive Tutor Self-Assessment CD-ROM
- ExamView® Pro Testmaker CD-ROM
- Presentation Plus! CD-ROM

The Growth of the Youth Movement

Main Idea The youth protest movement of the 1960s included Students for a Democratic Society (SDS) and the Free Speech Movement.

Reading Connection Do you belong to or know of any groups that work to improve society? Read on to learn how the youth of the 1960s protested the social injustices of their time.

The 1960s was one of the most tumultuous and chaotic decades in United States history. The decade also gave birth to a conspicuous youth movement, which challenged the American political and social system and conventional middle-class values. Perhaps no other time in the nation's history witnessed such protest.

★ An American Story ★

On December 2, 1964, Mario Savio, a 20-year-old philosophy student at the University of California at Berkeley, stood before a supportive crowd at the school's administration building. The massive "sit in" demonstration was the climax of a month long battle between school officials and students over unpopular campus policies. Facing the crowd, Savio urged them to continue pressuring school officials. In his speech he called the university a cold and heartless "machine" that deserved to be shut down.

66There's a time when the operation of the machine becomes so odious, makes you so sick at heart, that you . . . can't even tacitly take part," he declared. "And you've got to put your bodies upon the gears and upon the wheels . . . you've got to make it stop. And you've got to indicate to the people who run it, to the people who own it, that unless you're free the machine will be prevented from working at all.99

—quoted in *Decade of Shocks*

The 1960s was a decade of protests and movements to change society. It was the 1950s, however, that gave rise to this time of change.

The Roots of the Movement The roots of the 1960s youth movement stretched back to the 1950s. In the decade after World War II, the nation's economy boomed, and much of the country enjoyed a time of peace and prosperity. Prosperity did not extend to all, however, and some, especially the artists and writers of the "beat" movement, had openly criticized American society. They believed it valued conformity over independence and financial gain over spiritual and social advancement. Meanwhile, such events as the growing nuclear arms race between the United States and the Soviet Union made many more of the nation's youth uneasy about their future. Writer Todd Gitlin, who was a senior at the Bronx High School of Science in 1959, recalls the warning that the editors of his student yearbook delivered.

66In today's atomic age . . . the flames of war would write *finis* not only to our civilization, but to our very existence. Mankind may find itself unable to rise again should it be consumed in a nuclear pyre of its own making. In the years to come, members of this class will bear an ever-increasing responsibility for the preservation of the heritage given us.99

—from *The Sixties*

Concern about the future led many young people to become more active in social causes, from the civil rights movement to President Kennedy's Peace Corps. The emergence of the youth movement grew out of the huge numbers of people of the postwar "baby boom" generation. By 1970, 58.4 percent of the American population was 34 years old or younger. (By comparison, those 34 or younger in 2000 represented an estimated 48.9 percent.)

◄ *Mario Savio*

CHAPTER 18 The Politics of Protest **807**

R₁ Reading Strategy

Questioning Students might not be familiar with literary figures from the "beat" movement, but they may know the term *beatnik*. **Ask:** What is meant by the term "beat" movement? *(artists, poets, and musicians who adopted a bohemian lifestyle while rejecting traditional American values and material possessions)* OL

R₂ Reading Strategy

Connecting Ask students to raise their hand if they are involved in a civic group, and have them identify that group. **Ask:** How does this work affect the way you view issues? Have students recall the information learned in earlier chapters about the Peace Corps. BL

R₃ Reading Strategy

Using Context Clues Ask students what is meant by the term *baby boom*. *(1946–1964 saw a large increase in the American birth rate.)* **Ask:** What contributed to the baby boom? *(Answers should include: men returning from World War II, combined with the material affluence of the postwar period.)* BL

Did You Know?

The term "Beat Generation" is a label Jack Kerouac invented during a conversation with fellow novelist John Clellon Holmes. A later writing by Holmes titled "This Is the Beat Generation" made the term a mainstream phrase.

The early 1960s saw another phenomenon that fueled the youth movement—the rapid increase in enrollment at colleges throughout the nation. The economic boom of the 1950s led to a boom in higher education, since more families could afford to send their children to college. Between 1960 and 1966, enrollment in 4-year institutions rose from 3.1 million to almost 5 million students. College life empowered young people with a newfound sense of freedom and independence. It also allowed them to meet and bond with others who shared their feelings about society and fears about the future. It was on college campuses across the nation where the protest movements would rage the loudest.

Students for a Democratic Society Some youths were concerned most about the injustices they saw in the country's political and social system. In their view, a few wealthy elites controlled politics, and wealth itself was unfairly divided. These young people formed what came to be known as the New Left. (The "new" left differed from the "old" left of the 1930s, which had advocated socialism and communism.) A prominent organization of this group was the Students for a Democratic Society (SDS). It defined its views in a 1962 declaration known as the

Port Huron Statement. Written largely by **Tom Hayden,** editor of the University of Michigan's student newspaper, the declaration called for an end to apathy and urged citizens to stop accepting a country run by big corporations and big government.

SDS groups focused on protesting the Vietnam War, but they also addressed such issues as poverty, campus regulations, nuclear power, and racism. In 1968, for example, SDS leaders assisted in an eight-day occupation of several buildings at Columbia University in New York City to protest the administration's plan to build a new gym in an area that served as a neighborhood park near Harlem.

The Free Speech Movement Another group of protesters who captured the nation's attention were members of the Free Speech Movement, led by Mario Savio and others at the University of California at Berkeley. The issue that sparked the movement was the university's decision in the fall of 1964 to restrict students' rights to distribute literature and to recruit volunteers for political causes on campus. The protesters, however, quickly targeted more general campus matters and drew in more and more supporters.

Like many college students, those at Berkeley were disgruntled with the practices at their university. Officials divided huge classes into sections taught by graduate students, while many professors claimed they were too busy with research to meet with students. Faceless administrators made rules that were not always easy to obey and imposed punishments for violations. Isolated in this impersonal environment, many Berkeley students found a purpose in the Free Speech Movement.

The struggle between school administrators and students peaked on December 2, 1964, with the sit-in and Savio's famous speech at the administration building. Early the next morning, California Governor Pat Brown sent in 600 police officers to break up the demonstration. Police arrested more than 700 protesters.

DON'T TRUST ANYONE OVER 30

Picturing **History**

Youth Movement The Students for a Democratic Society (SDS) worked to address many of the problems they saw in the 1960s. Made up primarily of college students, the group was suspicious of the motives of adults. Where did the SDS begin its reform crusade?

The arrests set off a new and even larger protest movement. Within a few days, thousands of Berkeley students participated in a campus-wide strike, stopping classes for two days. Much of the faculty also voiced its support for the Free Speech Movement. In the face of this growing opposition, the administration gave in to the students' demands shortly before the Christmas recess.

The following week, the Supreme Court **validated** the students' First Amendment rights to freedom of speech and assembly on campus. In a unanimous vote, the Court upheld the section of the Civil Rights Act assuring these rights in places offering public accommodations, which, by definition, included college campuses. The Berkeley revolt was one of the earliest outbursts in a decade of campus turmoil. The tactics the protesters used there—abandoning classes and occupying buildings—would serve as a model for college demonstrators across the country.

✓ **Reading Check** **Synthesizing** What were three reasons for the growth of the youth movement of the 1960s?

The Counterculture

Main Idea During the 1960s some young people rebelled against the values of the older generation.

Reading Connection Do you know of any groups that rebel against the older generation today? Read on to learn about the utopias of the 1960s.

While a number of young Americans in the 1960s sought to challenge the system, others wanted to leave it and build their own society. Throughout the decade, thousands of mostly white youths turned away from their middle- and upper-class existence and created a new lifestyle—one that promoted the virtues of flamboyant dress, rock music, drug use, and free and independent living. With their alternative ways of life, these young men and women formed what became known as the **counterculture** and were commonly called "hippies."

Hippie Culture Originally, hippie culture represented a rebellion against the dominant culture in the United States. This included a rejection of Western civilization, of **rationality**, order, and the traditional val-

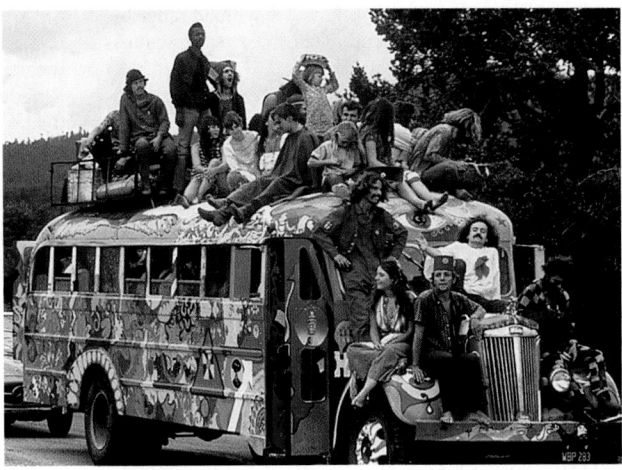

Picturing **History**

The Counterculture Commonly known as "hippies," members of the counterculture separated themselves from society in the 1960s by trying to create their own culture of love and tolerance. What western city was a focal point of the hippie culture?

ues of the middle class. At its core, the counterculture held up a utopian ideal: the ideal of a society that was freer, closer to nature, and full of love, empathy, tolerance, and cooperation. Much of this was in reaction to the 1950s American stereotype of the man in the gray flannel suit who led a constricted and colorless life.

When the movement grew larger, many of the newcomers did not always understand these original ideas of the counterculture. For them, what mattered were the outward signs that defined the movement—long hair, Native American headbands, cowboy boots, long dresses, shabby jeans, and the use of drugs such as marijuana and LSD. Drug use, especially, came to be associated with the hippie culture.

Many hippies desired to literally drop out of society by leaving home and living together with other youths in **communes**—group living arrangements in which members shared everything and worked together. A number of hippies established communes in small and rural communities, while others lived together in parks or crowded apartments in the nation's large cities. One of the most popular hippie destinations became San Francisco's **Haight-Ashbury district.** By the mid 1960s, thousands of hippies had flocked there.

New Religious Movements In their rejection of materialism, many members of the counterculture

R **Reading Strategy**

Activating Prior Knowledge Have students recall the words of the First Amendment. *(Point students to page 159 of the textbook for the text of this amendment.)* **Ask:** **What are some other laws that preserve and protect the civil liberties of individuals?** *(the Bill of Rights; the Thirteenth, Fourteenth, and Fifteenth Amendments; the 1964 Civil Rights Act; the Voting Rights Act of 1965)* **OL**

W **Writing Support**

Letter Writing Ask students to imagine that they are the parent of a child who is participating in the counterculture of the 1960s. Have them write a letter to their child discussing their thoughts about the counterculture. The letters should mention the lifestyle issues referred to in the text, such as communal living, religion, or drug usage. Students should explain in the letters why they think youths at the time may have considered these lifestyles attractive. *(Students' letters will vary.)* **OL** **CA** 11WA2.3c

U **Universal Access**

Visual/Spatial Ask students to examine the image of the counterculture lifestyle on this page. Divide the class into pairs so that students can discuss what the visual tells them about the counterculture. **EL**

✓**Reading Check**

Answer: concern about the future, increased college enrollment, injustices in the political and social system

Picturing **History**

Answer: San Francisco, California
Ask: **What were some of the outward signs that defined the hippie movement?** *(Students' answers will vary. They might mention long hair, headbands, cowboy boots, long dresses, shabby jeans, and drug use.)*

Did You Know?

In addition to the language of the counterculture, there was a look. Counterculture youth liked to borrow clothing styles from other cultures, especially from cultures that were less involved with mass industry than the United States. Popular styles included colorful patterned pullover shirts, dashikis from Africa, and paisley designs from India and Persia.

W Writing Support

Research Report Writing After students read the text on this page about the impact of religious sects, tell them to use library and Internet resources to write a three-page report. This report should explain the basic beliefs of a 1960s sect and provide a brief history of the group and its impact (if any) on 1960s culture. AL CA 11WA2.4a

R Reading Strategy

Summarizing Have students summarize the issues that led to the decline of the counterculture. *(criminal activity, drug related deaths, personal maturing)*

embraced spirituality. This included a broad range of beliefs, from astrology and magic to Eastern religions and new forms of Christianity.

Many of the religious groups centered around authoritarian leaders. In these groups, the leader dominated others and controlled their lives, sometimes to the point of arranging marriages between members. Religion became the central experience in the believer's life. The authoritarian figure was a sort of parent figure, and believers formed an extended family that took the place of the family into which a member had been born. This could lead to painful conflicts. Some parents accused religious sects of using mind-control methods; some attempted to recapture and "deprogram" their children.

Two new religious groups that attracted considerable attention beginning in the 1960s were the Unification Church and the Hare Krishna movement. Both were offshoots of established religions, and both came from abroad. Members of the Unification Church were popularly known as "Moonies," after their Korean-born founder, the Reverend Sun Myung Moon. He claimed to have had a vision in which Jesus told Moon that he was the next messiah and was charged with restoring the Kingdom of God on Earth. The Hare Krishnas traced their spiritual lineage to a Hindu sect that began in India in the 1400s and worshiped the god Krishna. In dress, diet, worship, and general style of living, Hare Krishnas tried to emulate these Hindu practitioners of another time and place.

R The Counterculture Declines After a few years, the counterculture movement began to deteriorate. Some hippie communities in the cities soon turned into seedy and dangerous places where muggings and other criminal activity became all too frequent. The glamour and excitement of drug use soon waned, especially as more and more young people became addicted or died from overdoses. In addition, a number of the people involved in the movement had gotten older and moved on in life. Upon witnessing the decline of Haight-Ashbury, one writer dismissed the one-time booming urban

NATIONAL GEOGRAPHIC

MOMENT in HISTORY

WOODSTOCK NATION
In August 1969, more than 400,000 young people descended on a 600-acre farm in upstate New York for what was billed as "three days of peace and music." Organizers of the Woodstock Music and Art Fair were overwhelmed by the turnout. Massive traffic jams, supply shortages, inadequate first aid and sanitation facilities, and torrential rainfall did not dampen the joyous spirit of the crowd. People shared their food and blankets, bathed in the rain, and listened to an amazing collection of some of the greatest musicians of the 1960s.

810 CHAPTER 18 The Politics of Protest

Answers and Additional Support

Did You Know?

Moonies were married in mass wedding ceremonies known as "Blessings." Reverend Moon and his wife presided over the ceremonies. Moonies believed that blessed couples would have sinless children.

NATIONAL GEOGRAPHIC MOMENT in HISTORY

Most Woodstock festival-goers were white, middle- or upper-class, and between 16 and 30 years of age.

commune as "the desperate attempt of a handful of pathetically unequipped children to create a community out of a social vacuum." In the end, most of the young men and women of the counterculture, unable to establish an ideal community and support themselves, returned to mainstream society.

✓ **Reading Check**

Summarizing What were the core ideals of members of the counterculture?

History *Through Art*

Pop Art Artists like Roy Lichtenstein mocked certain aspects of American life by using common examples of commercial art, such as comics and advertisements. What statement is this piece of art making?

Impact of the Counterculture

Main Idea Mainstream culture gradually accepted some of the ideas and styles of the youth movement.

Reading Connection Do young people today try to make a political statement by the way they dress or by the art forms they enjoy? Read on to learn how the 1960s youth culture affected the wider culture.

In the long run, the counterculture did change American life in some ways. Over time, mainstream America accepted many of these changes.

Fashion The counterculture generation, as one observer of the 1960s noted, dressed in costumes rather than in occupational or class uniforms. The colorful, beaded, braided, patched, and fringed garments that both men and women wore turned the fashion industry upside down. The international fashion world took its cues from young men and women on the street. As a result, men's clothing became more colorful, and women's clothing became more comfortable.

Protesters often expressed themselves with their clothing. The counterculture adopted military surplus attire not only because it was inexpensive, but also because it expressed rejection of materialist values and blurred the lines of social class. For the same reasons, clothing of another age was recycled, and worn-out clothing was repaired with patches. Ethnic clothing was popular for similar reasons. Beads and fringes imitated Native American costumes, while tie-dyed shirts borrowed techniques from India and Africa.

Perhaps the most potent symbol of the era was hair. A popular 1967 musical about the period was titled, fittingly, *Hair*. Long hair on a young man was the ultimate symbol of defiance. Slogans appeared, such as "Make America beautiful—give a hippie a haircut." School officials debated the acceptable length of a student's hair—could it curl over the collar or not? Once the initial shock wore off, however, longer hair on men and more individual clothing for both genders became generally accepted. What was once clothing of defiance was now mainstream.

Art During the 1960s, one art critic observed, the distinctions between traditional art and popular art, or pop art, dissolved. Pop art **derived** its subject matter from elements of popular culture, such as photographs, comic books, advertisements, and brand name products. Artist Andy Warhol, for example, used images of famous people, such as Marilyn Monroe and Elizabeth Taylor, and repeated them over and over. Warhol also reproduced items such as cans of soup, making the pictures as realistic as possible. Roy Lichtenstein used frames from comic strips as his inspirations. He employed the bold primary colors of red, yellow, and black, and put words like *blam* and *pow* into his paintings in comic book fashion.

Pop artists expected these symbols of popular culture to carry some of the same meaning as they did in their original form. The artists sometimes referred to themselves as only the "agents" of the art and said it was up to the observer to give meaning to the work and thus become part of it.

Music and Dance Counterculture musicians hoped that their music, rock 'n' roll, would be the means of toppling the establishment and reforming

CHAPTER 18 The Politics of Protest **811**

811

Review the Big Idea

Review the Big Idea for this section, "Societies change over time." Discuss with students how the clothing of the counterculture generation was an expression of protest and how it affected the fashion of the time. **Ask:** Do young people today use fashion as a way of separating themselves from the dominant culture, or is fashion used in a different manner today? *(Some will state that fashion is used to separate them from adult society, but others may say that fashion is used in a very conformist manner today—segmenting groups into different social strata.)* OL
CA 11WA2.3b

S Skill Practice

Visual Literacy Discuss items from current popular culture that could be transformed into pop art. Have each student create a drawing that focuses on one image from everyday life. **Ask:** How is your picture similar to the ones by Andy Warhol or other pop artists? *(Students' pictures will vary; however, they should be made up of ordinary objects from everyday life. The objects should be distorted, enlarged, simplified, and colored differently.)* OL **CA** CS3

✓ **Reading Check**

Answer: a society that was freer, closer to nature, and full of love, empathy, tolerance, and cooperation

Did You Know?

Hair remained on Broadway from September 1968 until July 1972. It closed after 1,742 performances.

History *Through Art*

Answer: that war is not a game—it is destructive and dangerous
Ask: What characterized pop art? *(It used popular culture for its subject matter, and it expected the symbols of popular culture to carry the same meaning as they did in their original form. They encouraged observers to become part of the art through their interpretation of it.)*

ASSESS

Resources for page 812

Use these resources to assess student mastery.

☞ Section Quiz 18-1

☞ Reading Essentials and Study Guide 18-1

◉ Interactive Tutor Self-Assessment CD-ROM

☞ California Standards Practice, Grade 11

✓Reading Check

Answer: changes in fashion, music, dance, and the idea that alternatives to mainstream culture were possible

HISTORY Online

Study Central provides audio summaries, interactive games, and online graphic organizers to help students review section content.

CLOSE

Summarizing Have students define the goals of the members of the counterculture. **OL**

Answers and Additional Support

▲ *Jimi Hendrix performing at Woodstock*

society. This did not happen because rock music was absorbed into the mainstream, where it brought material success worth billions of dollars to performers, promoters, and record companies.

One of the most famous rock groups, the Beatles, took the country by storm in 1964. "Beatlemania" swept the country, inspiring hundreds of other rock 'n' roll groups both in Great Britain and the United States.

Many of the new groups combined rock 'n' roll rhythms with lyrics that expressed the fears and hopes of the new generation and the widening rift between them and their parents. Bob Dylan provided

these lyrics, as did the Beatles and many other musicians, while spirited performers like Janis Joplin made the songs come alive.

The use of electrically amplified instruments also drastically changed the sound and feel of the new music. One master of this new sound was **Jimi Hendrix,** a guitarist from Seattle. Hendrix lived overseas and achieved stardom only after returning to the United States with the influx of musicians from Great Britain. His innovative guitar playing continues to influence musicians today.

At festivals such as Woodstock, in upstate New York in August 1969, and Altamont, California, later that year, hundreds of thousands of people got together to celebrate the new music. Though the fast-paced, energetic beat of rock 'n' roll was made for dancing, the style of dancing had changed dramatically. Each person danced without a partner, surrounded by others who also danced alone—a perfect metaphor for the counterculture, which stressed individuality within the group.

Headline-grabbing events such as Woodstock made it difficult for the nation to ignore the youth movement. By this time, however, other groups in society were also raising their voices in protest. For example, many women began renewing their generations-old efforts for equality, hoping to expand upon the successes gained during the early 1900s.

✓Reading Check Evaluating What lasting impact did the counterculture have on the nation?

HISTORY Online Study Central

For help with the concepts in this section of *American Vision: Modern Times* go to tav.mt.glencoe.com and click on *Study Central.*

SECTION 1 ASSESSMENT

Checking for Understanding

1. **Vocabulary** Define: validate, counterculture, rational, commune, derive.
2. **People and Terms** Identify: Port Huron Statement, Tom Hayden, Haight-Ashbury district, Jimi Hendrix.
3. **Summarize** two legacies of the counterculture movement.

Reviewing Big Ideas

4. **Explaining** How did the U.S. Supreme Court validate the actions of the members of the Free Speech Movement?

Critical Thinking

5. **Contrasting** How were hippies different from members of the New Left?
6. **Analyzing** Why did the counterculture movement decline?
7. **Organizing** Use a graphic organizer similar to the one below to list the causes of the youth movement.

Causes → Youth Movement

Analyzing Visuals

8. **Analyzing Photographs** Look closely at the photograph of a group of hippies and their bus on page 809. How does the bus itself represent values of the counterculture?

Writing About History

9. **Descriptive Writing** Imagine you are a journalist in the 1960s. Write an article in which you visit an art gallery and describe the popular art you see. **CA** 11WA2.1e

SECTION 1 ASSESSMENT ANSWERS

1. Content vocabulary is boldfaced and highlighted in yellow. Academic vocabulary is boldfaced.
2. Port Huron Statement (p. 808), Tom Hayden (p. 808), Haight-Ashbury district (p. 809), Jimi Hendrix (p. 812)
3. It contributed new styles of popular culture and encouraged greater self-expression.
4. It upheld the right to freedom of speech and assembly on campus.
5. Hippies were more interested in creating a utopian lifestyle than in politics.
6. Many participants were unable to establish an ideal community or support themselves.
7. concern about the future; "baby boom"; social injustice
8. colorful, individualized appearance, communal transport
9. Students' articles will vary. Articles should include descriptions of what a journalist might have seen.

Guide to Reading

Connection
In the previous section, you learned about the effects of the student and counterculture movements on society. In this section, you will discover how many women organized for greater rights during the 1960s and 1970s.

Main Idea
- The women's movement became fragmented after women won the right to vote. (p. 814)
- Women began to seek changes in society through legislative action and organizations. (p. 815)
- The women's movement experienced success and failures in the fight for equality. (p. 816)

Content Vocabulary
feminism, Title IX

Academic Vocabulary
gender, integral, bias

People and Terms to Identify
Equal Pay Act, Equal Employment Opportunity Commission, Betty Friedan, National Organization for Women, Phyllis Schlafly

Reading Objectives
- **Describe** the workplace concerns that fueled the growth of the women's movement.

- **Identify** major achievements of the women's movement.

Reading Strategy
Categorizing As you read about the women's movement, use a graphic organizer similar to the one below to compare the ideas of the two organizations that formed when the women's movement split.

Organization	Ideas

Preview of Events

◆1963   ◆1970   ◆1977   ◆1984

1963
Betty Friedan's *The Feminine Mystique* published

1966
Women activists form NOW

1973
Roe v. *Wade* decision ensures abortion rights

1982
Equal Rights Amendment fails

The following are the main History–Social Science Standards covered in this section.

11.10.7 Analyze the women's rights movement from the era of Elizabeth Stanton and Susan Anthony and the passage of the Nineteenth Amendment to the movement launched in the 1960s, including differing perspectives on the roles of women.

11.11.3 Describe the changing roles of women in society as reflected in the entry of more women into the labor force and the changing family structure.

11.11.7 Explain how the federal, state, and local governments have responded to demographic and social changes such as population shifts to the suburbs, racial concentrations in the cities, Frostbelt-to-Sunbelt migration, international migration, decline of family farms, increases in out-of-wedlock births, and drug abuse.

✎ *The Big Idea* ✎

Social and economic crises lead to new roles for government. By the 1960s, many women had become increasingly dissatisfied with society's perception of women in the workplace. Some began to join organizations aimed at improving their role in society. Many of these organizations sought change through new legislation. The women's movement forced the government to take action on issues such as education, but it was divided over the Equal Rights Amendment. While the amendment eventually failed, the women's movement did bring about profound changes in American society.

FOCUS

BELLRINGER
SKILLBUILDER ACTIVITY

Project **Daily Focus Skills Transparency 18-2** and have students answer the question.

Guide to Reading

Understanding Vocabulary: Have students write three questions that can be answered using the content vocabulary words and the academic vocabulary words.

Answers to Graphic: League of Women Voters: promoted laws to protect women and children; National Woman's Party: opposed protective legislation.

Unpacking the Standards

Students will be able to:
- Analyze the state of the women's movement at the start of the 1960s.
- Explain how the effort to secure equality for women was reinvigorated.
- Discuss the successes and failures of the movement during this period.

SECTION RESOURCES

📂 Print Material
- Reproducible Lesson Plan 18-2
- Guided Reading Activity 18-2
- Reading Essentials and Study Guide 18-2
- Active Reading Note-Taking Guide 18-2

📽 Transparencies
- Daily Focus Skills Transparency 18-2
- Section Graphic Organizer Transparency 18-2

Technology
- 💿 Interactive Tutor Self-Assessment CD-ROM
- 💿 Exam*View*® Pro Testmaker CD-ROM
- 💿 Presentation Plus! CD-ROM

813

TEACH

R₁ Reading Strategy

Scaffolding—Using Question-Answer Relationships Prior to reading the text, have students answer these questions: What is the material about? What do I already know about this topic? *(the strengthening of the women's movement; to identify major achievements of the women's movement)* As they read the text under this heading, have students continue to ask questions about the text to make sure they understand what they are reading. **OL**

This **Reading Skill** was introduced in Chapters 13 and 14.

R₂ Reading Strategy

Connecting Have students discuss women's career choices today. **Ask: Do you think that parents, teachers, counselors, and others today steer women toward some careers and away from others?** *(Students' answers will vary, but most students should agree that the social limitations placed upon women today are far fewer than those in the 1960s.)* **OL**

✔ Reading Check

Answer: Many took jobs outside the home.

Answers and Additional Support

R₁ A Weakened Women's Movement

Main Idea The women's movement became fragmented after women won the right to vote.

Reading Connection Where are women still fighting for political rights? Read on to discover how the American women's movement divided after women won the right to vote.

★ *An American Story* ★

In 1960 the housewife-oriented magazine *Redbook* asked readers to send examples of "Why Young Mothers Feel Trapped." Some 24,000 women responded. One of them was Herma Snider, a housewife and mother of three in Nevada. Snider wrote that as a high school and college student, she had dreamed of a career in journalism. After getting married and having three children, that dream died.

"Cemented to my house by three young children," she wrote, "there were days in which I saw no adult human being except the milkman as he made his deliveries and spoke to no one from the time my husband left in the morning until he returned at night." She added, "Each night as I tucked my sons into bed, I thanked God that they would grow up to be *men,* that they would able to teach, write, heal, advise, travel, or do anything else they chose."

Desperate for greater fulfillment in her life, Snider eventually took a job as a part-time hotel clerk. About this decision, she said:

❝My cashier's job is not the glamorous career I once dreamed of. And I know that it can be said that my solution is not a solution at all, merely an escape. But it seems to me that when the demands of children and household threaten to suffocate you, an escape *is* a solution.❞

—quoted in *The Female Experience: An American Documentary*

Feminism, the belief that men and women should be equal politically, economically, and socially, had been a weak and often embattled force since the adoption of the Nineteenth Amendment guaranteeing women's voting rights in 1920. Soon after the amendment's passage, the women's movement split into two camps. One group, the League of Women Voters, tended to promote laws to protect women

and children, such as limiting the hours they could work. The National Woman's Party (NWP), on the other hand, opposed protective legislation for women. The NWP believed it reinforced workplace discrimination. In 1923 the NWP persuaded members of Congress to introduce the first Equal Rights Amendment aimed at forbidding federal, state, and local laws from discriminating on the basis of **gender.** Since the women's movement was divided, however, Congress could afford to ignore the amendment.

The onset of World War II provided women with greater opportunity, at least temporarily. With many men enlisted in the army, women became an **integral** part of the nation's workforce. When the war ended, however, many women lost their jobs to the returning men.

R₂

Despite having to return to their domestic work, many women gradually reentered the labor market. By 1960 they made up almost 40 percent of the nation's workforce. Yet many people continued to believe that women, even college-educated women, could better serve society by remaining in the home to influence the next generation of men.

✔ Reading Check

Examining How did World War II affect women?

▼ *A 1960s-era women's magazine*

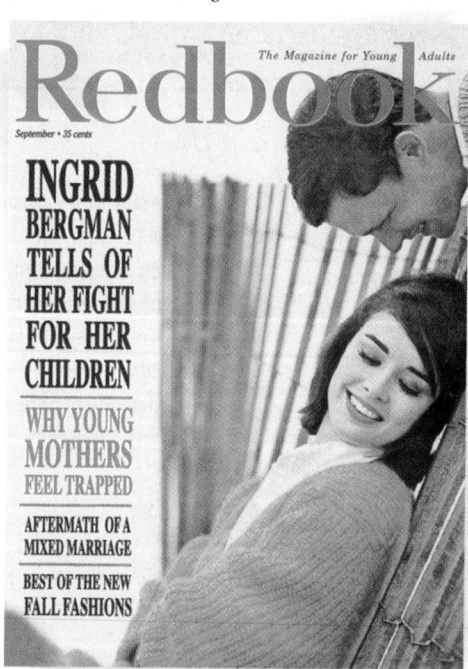

The Women's Movement Reawakens

Main Idea Women began to seek changes in society through legislative action and organizations.

Reading Connection Are there organizations today that continue to fight for equal rights? Read on to learn about a book that helped define the reawakened women's movement.

By the early 1960s, many women were increasingly resentful of a world where newspaper ads separated jobs by gender, clubs refused them memberships, banks denied them credit, and, worst of all, they often were paid less for the same work. Generally, women found themselves shut out of higher-paying and prestigious professions such as law, medicine, and finance. Although about 40 percent of American women were in the workforce in the 1960s, three-fourths of them worked in lower paying and routine clerical, sales, or factory jobs, or as cleaning women and hospital attendants. As more women entered the workforce, the protest against inequities grew louder.

Women had also gained a better understanding of their inequality in society from their experiences in the civil rights and antiwar movements. Often they were restricted to menial tasks and rarely had a say in any policy decisions. From the broader perspective, the women's movement was part of the 1960s quest for rights.

Fighting for Workplace Rights Two forces helped bring the women's movement to life again. One was the mass protest of ordinary women. The second was a government initiative: the President's Commission on the Status of Women, established by President Kennedy and headed by Eleanor Roosevelt. The commission's report highlighted the problems of women in the workplace and helped create networks of feminist activists, who lobbied Congress for women's legislation. In 1963, with the support of labor, they won passage of the **Equal Pay Act,** which in most cases outlawed paying men more than women for the same job.

Congress gave women another boost by including them in the 1964 Civil Rights Act, a measure originally designed to fight racial **bias.** Title VII of the act outlawed job discrimination by private employers not only on the basis of race, color, religion, and national origin, but also of gender. This measure became decisive legal basis for advances made by the women's movement.

Picturing **History**

Perfect Home, Perfect Wife This image of a proud wife in her spotless kitchen reflects some of the traditional ideas of the 1950s and 1960s. What did the women's movement criticize about these ideas?

The Civil Rights Act created a new federal agency charged with administering the new law. The **Equal Employment Opportunity Commission** (EEOC) was officially operating in July 1965. Government administrators projected that in its first year, the EEOC would receive approximately 2,000 charges of unlawful employment practices. Instead, the Commission actually received almost 9,000 separate charges in its first year of operation.

The Feminine Mystique Many date the women's movement from the publication of **Betty Friedan's** *The Feminine Mystique* in 1963. Friedan had traveled around the country interviewing the women who had graduated with her from Smith College in 1942. She found that while most of these women reported having everything they could want in life, they still felt unfulfilled. Friedan described these feelings in her book:

> ❝The problem lay buried, unspoken, for many years in the minds of American women. . . . Each suburban wife struggled with it alone. As she made the beds, shopped for groceries . . . chauffeured Cub Scouts and Brownies . . . she was afraid to ask even of herself the silent question—'Is this all?'❞
>
> —from *The Feminine Mystique*

CHAPTER 18   The Politics of Protest   **815**

S Skill Practice

Visual Literacy Divide students into groups of three or four. Have each group create their own magazine cover as if they were editor Gloria Steinem. Students should draw upon the information learned in the chapter pertaining to the women's movement for cover articles and photos. **OL**

U Universal Access

English Learners Pick out the most important points of the text under this heading, and then have students use the subheads to create a study outline. As they complete each subhead, have them write notes about the important points. Then encourage students to discuss their outlines with a partner and make any modifications that would improve the outline. **EL**

Resources for page 816

Have students read more about The Feminine Mystique *in the* **American Literature Readings 5.**

✓ Reading Check

Answer: the mass protest of ordinary women, and the President's Commission on the Status of Women

Answers and Additional Support

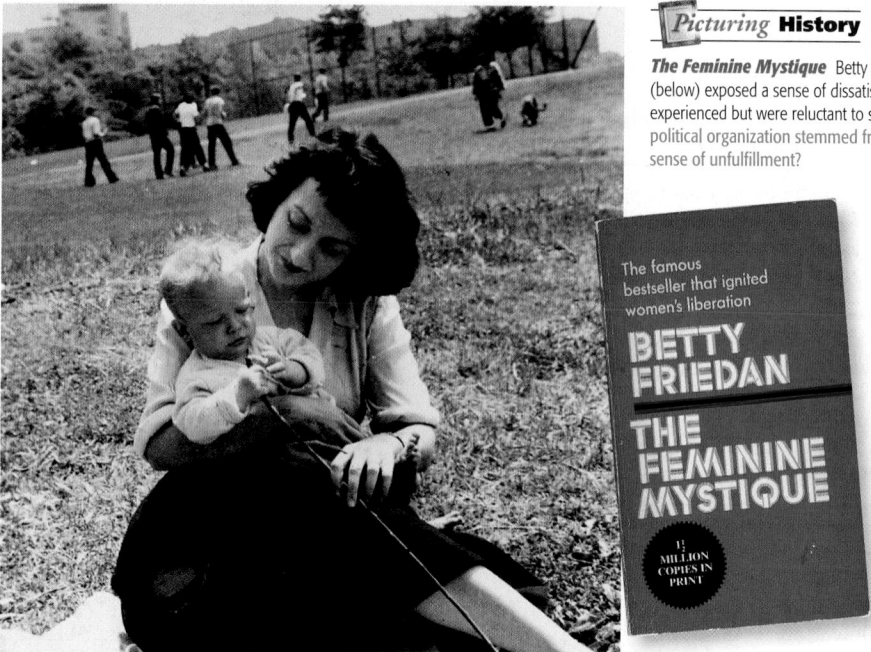

Picturing **History**

The Feminine Mystique Betty Friedan's best-selling book (below) exposed a sense of dissatisfaction that many women experienced but were reluctant to speak about openly. What political organization stemmed from women's growing sense of unfulfillment?

The famous bestseller that ignited women's liberation

BETTY FRIEDAN

THE FEMININE MYSTIQUE

1½ MILLION COPIES IN PRINT

Friedan's book became a best-seller. Many women soon began reaching out to one another, pouring out their anger and sadness in what came to be known as consciousness-raising sessions. While they talked informally about their unhappiness, they were building the base for a nationwide movement.

The Time Is NOW In June 1966, Friedan returned to a thought that she and others had been considering, the need for women to form a national organization. On the back of a napkin, she scribbled down her intentions "to take the actions needed to bring women into the mainstream of American society, now . . . in fully equal partnership with men." Friedan and others then set out to form the **National Organization for Women** (NOW).

NOW soon leapt off the napkin and into the headlines. In October 1966, a group of about 300 women and men held the founding conference of NOW. "The time has come," its founders declared, "to confront with concrete action the conditions which now prevent women from enjoying the equality of opportunity and freedom of choice which is their right as individual Americans and as human beings."

The new organization began by demanding greater educational opportunities for women. The group also focused much of its energy on aiding women in the workplace. NOW leaders denounced

the exclusion of women from certain professions and from politics. They lashed out against the practice of paying women less than men for equal work, a practice they claimed the Equal Pay Act had not eliminated.

The efforts to pass the Equal Rights Amendment pushed the organization's membership over 200,000. By July 1972, the movement even had a magazine of its own, *Ms.*, which kept readers informed on women's issues. The editor of the new magazine was Gloria Steinem, an author and public figure who was one of the movement's leading figures.

✓ Reading Check **Identifying** What two forces helped bring the women's movement to life again?

Successes and Failures

Main Idea The women's movement experienced success and failures in the fight for equality.

Reading Connection What one issue would you work to improve for women? Read on to find out about the improvements made in the 1960s and 1970s.

During the late 1960s and early 1970s, the women's movement fought to enforce Title VII of the Civil Rights Act, lobbied to repeal laws against abortion,

Picturing **History**

Answer: NOW (National Organization for Women)
Ask: Some people wrongly assumed that Friedan and other feminists were antifamily. How does this photo portray Friedan? *(as a caring mother)*

Did You Know?

Ms. magazine is now located in the offices of the Feminist Majority Foundation in Los Angeles, California, and Arlington, Virginia. The magazine continues to receive national and international awards as a magazine focused on issues relating to women's status, women's rights, and women's point of view.

and worked for legislation against gender discrimination in employment, housing, and education. Along the way, the movement experienced success as well as failure.

Striving for Equality in Education One of the movement's notable achievements was in education. Kathy Striebel's story highlighted the discrimination female students often faced in the early 1970s. In 1971, Striebel, a high school junior in St. Paul, Minnesota, wanted to compete for her school's swim team, but the school did not allow girls to join. Kathy's mother, Charlotte, was a member of the local NOW chapter. Through it, she learned that St. Paul had recently passed an ordinance prohibiting gender discrimination in education. She filed a grievance with the city's human rights department, and officials required the school to allow Kathy to swim.

Shortly after joining the team, Kathy beat out one of the boys and earned a spot at a meet. As she stood on the block waiting to swim, the opposing coach declared that she was ineligible to compete because the meet was outside St. Paul and thus beyond the jurisdiction of its laws. "They pulled that little girl right off the block," Charlotte Striebel recalled angrily.

Recognizing the problem, leaders of the movement pushed lawmakers to enact federal legislation banning gender discrimination in education. In 1972 Congress responded by passing a law known collectively as the Educational Amendments. One section, **Title IX,** prohibited federally funded schools from discriminating against girls and young women in nearly all aspects of its operations, from admissions to athletics. Many schools implemented this new law slowly or not at all, but women now had federal law on their side.

Roe v. Wade One of the most important goals for many women activists was the repeal of laws against abortion. Until 1973, the right to regulate abortion was reserved to the states. This was in keeping with the original plan of the Constitution, which reserved all police power—the power to control people and property in the interest of safety, health, welfare, and morals—to the state. Early in the country's history, some abortion was permitted in the early stages of pregnancy, but after the middle of the 1800s, when states adopted statutory law, abortion was prohibited except to save the life of the mother. Women who chose to have an abortion faced criminal prosecution.

In the late 1960s, some states began adopting more liberal abortion laws. For example, several states allowed abortion if carrying a baby to term might endanger the woman's mental health or if she was a victim of rape or incest. The big change came with the 1973 Supreme Court decision in *Roe* v. *Wade*. The

Profiles IN HISTORY

Shirley Chisholm
1924–2005

Shirley Chisholm once remarked, "Of my two 'handicaps,' being female put more obstacles in my path than being black." Her attempts to overcome these obstacles propelled the Brooklyn, New York, native into the national spotlight and provided encouragement for other women and African Americans attempting to overcome discrimination.

Chisholm first gained national prominence when she defeated two other candidates for Congress from New York's 12th District in 1968. Upon her swearing in, she became the first African American woman to serve in the United States Congress.

In Congress Chisholm became an ardent defender of several causes. An opponent of the seniority system, she protested the

ways that party leaders assigned House members to committees and was instrumental in changing them. Chisholm was an early opponent of arms sales to South Africa's racist regime. She also worked on education issues and to increase day care programs, and she cosponsored a bill to guarantee an annual income to families.

In 1972 Chisholm ran for the Democratic nomination for president. She campaigned extensively and entered primaries in 12 states, winning 28 delegates and receiving 152 first ballot votes at the convention.

She returned to Congress after the convention and continued her crusade to help women and minorities for several more terms. She declined to run for re-election in 1982, citing the difficulties of campaigning for liberal issues in an increasingly conservative political atmosphere.

CHAPTER 18 The Politics of Protest **817**

Review the Big Idea
Review the Big Idea for this section, "Social and economic crises lead to new roles for government." Have students consider the athletic programs at your school. **Ask: How did Title IX affect the programs? What might the sports programs look like if the law had not passed in 1972?** *(possible answers: fewer sports available at school, different schools allowed different levels of female participation because there was no overarching federal regulation)* `OL`

W Writing Support

Research Report Writing Ask students to write a three-page report that focuses on the life of Shirley Chisholm. Tell students to fill in details about the important events in her life that are not fully developed in the Profiles in History feature on this page. Have students be ready to present their reports to the class.
`AL` `CA 11WA2.4d`

Profiles IN HISTORY

Ask: What were the two handicaps Shirley Chisholm faced, and which did she find more difficult to overcome? *(She thought that being a woman put more obstacles in her way than being African American.)*

W Writing Support

Summary Writing Ask students to look up in the library or on the Internet the Supreme Court ruling on *Roe v. Wade* and summarize the majority decision and any concurrent or dissenting opinions. Students may use abstracts of the opinions. **AL**

R Reading Strategy

Evaluating The Equal Rights Amendment never gathered enough support to become a constitutional amendment. **Ask: Why were people opposed to giving gender equality a constitutional protection?** *(Some feared that making this a constitutional right would eliminate some laws that were designed to give special protections to women or subject women to the draft.)* **OL**

Answers and Additional Support

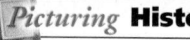 *Picturing* **History**

Opposing Viewpoints The Equal Rights Amendment had strong support, but it also had strong opposition, led by Phyllis Schlafly. How many states ratified the ERA?

Supreme Court ruled that state governments could not regulate abortion during the first three months of pregnancy, a time that was interpreted as being within a woman's constitutional right to privacy. During the second three months of pregnancy, states could regulate abortions on the basis of the health of the mother. States could ban abortion in the final three months except in cases of a medical emergency.

Those in favor of protecting abortion rights cheered *Roe* v. *Wade* as a victory, but the issue was far from settled. The decision gave rise to the right-to-life movement, whose members consider abortion morally wrong and advocate its total ban. After the *Roe* v. *Wade* ruling, the two sides began an impassioned battle that continues today. (*For more information on* Roe v. Wade, *see page 1006.*)

The Equal Rights Amendment In 1972 Congress passed the Equal Rights Amendment (ERA). To become part of the Constitution, this amendment to protect women against discrimination had to be ratified by 38 states. Many states did so—35 by 1979—but there was significant opposition to the amendment as well. Some people feared the ERA would take away some traditional rights, such as the right to alimony in divorce cases or the right to have single-gender colleges. Another fear was that women would be subjected to the military draft. One outspoken opponent was **Phyllis Schlafly,** who organized the Stop-ERA campaign. She became active in politics after earning a master's degree from Harvard in 1945 and later a law degree. Schlafly testified before 30 state legislatures against the ERA, which finally failed in 1982.

 Picturing **History**

Answer: 35
Ask: Why did the Equal Rights Amendment fail? *(Only 35 states ratified the amendment. It needed 38 states, 75 percent, to be officially ratified.)*

Resources for page 818

Have students learn more about the women's movement by assigning:

📂 *Linking Past and Present Activity 18*

📂 *Moments in Time, Unit 11: Equality for Women (1966–1978).*

The Impact of the Women's Movement Despite the failure of the ERA, the women's movement would ultimately bring about profound changes in society. Since the 1970s, many more women have pursued college degrees and careers outside of the home than did so in previous decades. Since the women's movement began, two-career families are much more common than they were in the 1950s and 1960s, although a need for greater family income due to the increased cost of living may also be a factor. Mothers working outside the home are more accepted and more common than they were in the 1950s and 1960s. Employers began to offer employees options to help make work more compatible with family life, including flexible hours, on-site child care, and job-sharing.

Even though the women's movement helped change social attitudes toward women, an income gap between men and women still exists. A major reason for the income gap is that most working women still hold lower-paying jobs such as bank tellers, administrative assistants, cashiers, school-teachers, and nurses. Also, many women choose to leave or reduce their hours at work to bear and care for their children. This choice to combine careers and more traditional roles is one that fewer men make. It is in professional jobs that women have made the most dramatic gains since the 1970s. By the end of the 1900s, women made up roughly one-fourth of the nation's doctors and lawyers. By 2000 they comprised over 40 percent of the nation's graduates receiving degrees in these fields.

 Picturing **History**

Women in the Workplace Since the 1970s, the number of women working outside the home has increased. Here, a woman and man work side-by-side. Why might an income gap exist between men and women?

 Reading Check **Summarizing** What successes and failures did the women's movement experience during the late 1960s and early 1970s?

HISTORY *Online* **Study Central**

For help with the concepts in this section of *American Vision: Modern Times* go to tav.mt.glencoe.com and click on *Study Central.*

SECTION 2 ASSESSMENT

Checking for Understanding

1. **Vocabulary** Define: feminism, gender, integral, bias, Title IX.
2. **People and Terms** Identify: Equal Pay Act, Equal Employment Opportunity Commission, Betty Friedan, National Organization for Women, Phyllis Schlafly.
3. **Summarize** Shirley Chisholm's political contributions.

Reviewing Big Ideas

4. **Describing** How have women's rights improved since the 1960s?

Critical Thinking

5. **Synthesizing** What two events weakened the women's movement?
6. **Organizing** Use a graphic organizer similar to the one below to list the major achievements of the women's movement.

Achievements

Analyzing Visuals

7. **Analyzing Photographs** Study the photo on page 815 of a housewife in her kitchen. Think about depictions of housewives in modern television or magazine advertisements you have seen. How would you compare the photo on page 815 with today's images?

Writing About History

8. **Persuasive Writing** Take on the role of a supporter or opponent of the ERA. Write a letter to the editor of your local newspaper to persuade people to support your position. **CA** 11WA2.3a

CHAPTER 18 The Politics of Protest **819**

SECTION 2 ASSESSMENT ANSWERS

1. Content vocabulary is boldfaced and highlighted in yellow. Academic vocabulary is boldfaced.
2. Equal Pay Act (p. 815), Equal Employment Opportunity Commission (p. 815), National Organization for Women (p. 816), Betty Friedan (p. 818), Phyllis Schlafly (p. 818)

3. The first African American woman in Congress, she helped reform the House committee appointment system and worked on education and day care.
4. More women have achieved equal pay for the same job, more career choices, and more political power.
5. division with the women's

movement and World War II
6. Equal Pay Act; inclusion in Title VII of the 1964 Civil Rights Act; Title IX; *Roe* v. *Wade;* more career possibilities
7. Answers will vary. Answers could mention that current depictions are realistic.
8. Students' letters will vary.

819

FOCUS

Charlotte Perkins Gilman drew on her own experience after the birth of her first child in writing *The Yellow Wallpaper.*

Read to Discover

Answer: The narrator feels that doing something other than resting would improve her health. Her family does not believe she is sick.

Understanding Vocabulary

Before students begin reading, ask them to review the **Reader's Dictionary** in preparation for best understanding the literature excerpt.

Answers and Additional Support

American LITERATURE

Charlotte Perkins Gilman was a prominent American social critic and feminist writer in the late 1800s and early 1900s. In her most famous work, *The Yellow Wallpaper* (1899), she presents the story of a woman diagnosed with hysteria, for which a doctor has prescribed total rest. Cut off from any intellectual activity, the woman is slowly driven mad by her "cure."

In this work, Gilman speaks out against a common belief of the time–that women were generally unfit for scholarship. The story, obscure for almost 50 years, has become a staple of many college literary courses.

Read to Discover

How does the narrator feel about her "illness"? How does her opinion differ from that of her physician and her family?

Reader's Dictionary

scoff: make fun of

phosphates: a carbonated drink, often used as medicine in the 1800s and early 1900s

congenial: agreeable; pleasant

flamboyant: elaborately colorful

from The Yellow Wallpaper
by Charlotte Perkins Gilman

In the following excerpt, the narrator of the story, writing in a secret journal, is describing her "illness" and how her husband John and others feel about it.

John is practical in the extreme. He has no patience with faith, an intense horror of superstition, and he scoffs openly at any talk of things not to be felt and seen and put down in figures.

John is a physician, and *perhaps*—(I would not say it to a living soul, of course, but this is dead paper and a great relief to my mind)—*perhaps* that is one reason I do not get well faster.

You see he does not believe I am sick!

And what can one do?

If a physician of high standing, and one's own husband, assures friends and relatives that there is really nothing the matter with one but temporary nervous depression—a slight hysterical tendency—what is one to do?

My brother is also a physician, and also of high standing, and he says the same thing.

So I take phosphates or phospites—whichever it is, and tonics, and journeys, and air, and exercise, and am absolutely forbidden to "work" until I am well again.

Personally, I disagree with their ideas.

Personally, I believe that congenial work, with excitement and change, would do me good.

But what is one to do?

▲ *Narrator from the film version of* The Yellow Wallpaper

I did write for a while in spite of them; but it *does* exhaust me a good deal—having to be so sly about it, or else meet with heavy opposition.

I sometimes fancy that my condition if I had less opposition and more society and stimulus—but John says the very worst thing I can do is to think about my condition, and I confess it always makes me feel bad. . . .

I get unreasonably angry with John sometimes. I'm sure I never used to be so sensitive. I think it is due to this nervous condition.

But John says if I feel so, I shall neglect proper self-control; so I take pains to control myself—before him, at least, and that makes me very tired.

I don't like our room a bit.

Reading Strategy — CONNECTING

Ask students to think about a time in their lives when they were trying to make people understand something they experienced but were not believed. Tell them to think about the details of that dilemma and have them share what they remember about the incident with the rest of the class. Encourage students to describe the circumstances and explore how the incident made them feel. **OL**

I wanted one downstairs that opened on the piazza and had roses all over the window, and such pretty old-fashioned chintz hangings! but John would not hear of it.

He said there was only one window and no room for two beds, and no near room for him if he took another.

He is very careful and loving, and hardly lets me stir without special direction.

I have a schedule prescription for each hour in the day; he takes all care from me, and so I feel basely ungrateful not to value it more.

He said we came here solely on my account, that I was to have perfect rest and all the air I could get. "Your exercise depends on your strength, my dear," said he, "and your food somewhat on your appetite; but air you can absorb all the time." So we took the nursery at the top of the house.

▲ Refuge, by Isidro Nonell

It is a big, airy room, the whole floor nearly, with windows that look all ways, and air and sunshine galore. It was nursery first and then playroom and gymnasium, I should judge; for the windows are barred for little children, and there are rings and things in the walls.

The paint and paper look as if a boys' school had used it. It is stripped off—the paper—in great patches all around the head of my bed, about as far as I can reach, and in a great place on the other side of the room low down. I never saw a worse paper in my life.

One of those sprawling flamboyant patterns committing every artistic sin.

It is dull enough to confuse the eye in following, pronounced enough to constantly irritate and provoke study, and when you follow the lame uncertain curves for a little distance they suddenly commit suicide—plunge off at outrageous angles, destroy themselves in unheard of contradictions.

The color is repellent, almost revolting; a smouldering unclean yellow, strangely faded by the slow-turning sunlight.

It is a dull yet lurid orange in some places, a sickly sulphur tint in others.

No wonder the children hated it! I should hate it myself if I had to live in this room long.

There comes John, and I must put this away,—he hates to have me write a word.

We have been here two weeks, and I haven't felt like writing before, since that first day.

I am sitting by the window now, up in this atrocious nursery, and there is nothing to hinder my writing as much as I please, save lack of strength.

John is away all day, and even some nights when his cases are serious.

I am glad my case is not serious!

But these nervous troubles are dreadfully depressing.

John does not know how much I really suffer. He knows there is no *reason* to suffer, and that satisfies him.

Of course it is only nervousness. It does weigh on me so not to do my duty in any way!

I meant to be such a help to John, such a real rest

Block Schedule

Team Teaching This selection from *The Yellow Wallpaper* can be presented in a team teaching context, in conjunction with English or Language Arts.

R **Reading Strategy**

Understanding the Main Idea and Supporting Details Have students consider John's reason not to repaper the room. **Ask:** *What does his reasoning say about John?* (He feels she is imagining her dislike of the paper. Also, he believes that if the wallpaper is changed, then she will find something else to dislike. This shows that he does not value her opinions very highly.) **AL**

W **Writing Support**

Letter Writing Ask students to imagine themselves as the narrator. Have them write letters to a close friend from this point-of-view, describing their feelings and fears as they are confined to this room. **OL** **CA** 11WA2.1b; 11WA2.1e

ASSESS

Have students answer the Analyzing Literature questions and complete the Interdisciplinary Activity.

CLOSE

Monitoring Ask students to identify how the narrator occupies her mind during her confinement in the room. Tell them to list all instances they can find and discuss these instances as a class. **OL**

822

▲ *Woman in a psychiatric hospital*

and comfort, and here I am a comparative burden already! . . .

I suppose John never was nervous in his life. He laughs at me so about this wall-paper!

At first he meant to repaper the room, but afterwards he said that I was letting it get the better of me, and that nothing was worse for a nervous patient than to give way to such fancies.

He said that after the wall-paper was changed it would be the heavy bedstead, and then the barred windows, and then that gate at the head of the stairs, and so on.

"You know the place is doing you good," he said, "and really, dear, I don't care to renovate the house just for a three months' rental."

"Then do let us go downstairs," I said, "there are such pretty rooms there."

Then he took me in his arms and called me a blessed little goose, and said he would go down to the cellar, if I wished, and have it whitewashed into the bargain.

But he is right enough about the beds and windows and things.

It is an airy and comfortable room as any one need wish, and, of course, I would not be so silly as to make him uncomfortable just for a whim.

I'm really getting quite fond of the big room, all but that horrid paper. . . .

Well, the Fourth of July is over! The people are gone and I am tired out. John thought it might do me good to see a little company, so we just had mother and Nellie and the children down for a week.

Of course I didn't do a thing. Jennie sees to everything now.

But it tired me all the same.

John says if I don't pick up faster he shall send me to Weir Mitchell in the fall.

But I don't want to go there at all. I had a friend who was in his hands once, and she says he is just like John and my brother, only more so!

Besides, it is such an undertaking to go so far.

I don't feel as if it was worth while to turn my hand over for anything, and I'm getting dreadfully fretful and querulous.

I cry at nothing, and cry most of the time.

Of course I don't when John is here, or anybody else, but when I am alone.

And I am alone a good deal just now. . . .

I'm getting really fond of the room in spite of the wall-paper. Perhaps *because* of the wall-paper.

It dwells in my mind so!

Analyzing Literature

1. What is the main idea in this passage? How does it support the author's point? **CA** 11RC2.4

2. Does the narrator think this remedy will help her? Why or why not? What clues can you find about how the narrator feels about her illness?

Interdisciplinary Activity
Science Using the Internet and other resources, research some ways that diseases and illnesses were treated in the 1800s and 1900s. Do we still use these treatments today? Create a chart showing the progression of treatment for some of the illnesses you researched.

Answers to Analyzing Literature

1. The passage shows how women were treated more like children than adults. The female narrator is ignored and forced to follow the orders of her physician husband. The author is making the point that women were more capable of scholarship and educated activity than they were given credit for.

2. The narrator tries to believe that the remedy will help, but she doesn't believe she is sick in the first place.

Interdisciplinary Activity
Students' answers and charts will vary, based upon their research.

Reading on Your Own

For other literature selections that relate to the growing awareness of women's issues, you might consider the following book suggestions.

The Awakening (Fiction)
by Kate Chopin

First published in 1899, this novel marks the beginning of feminist literature. Unhappy with her own marriage, Edna Pontellier discovers her desire for more fulfillment than her comfortable but unchallenging role as mother and wife can provide.

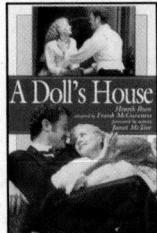

A Doll's House (Drama)
by Henrik Ibsen

Nora Hellmer slowly awakens to the realization that she has been ruled by either her father or her husband her whole life. When she tries to finance a vacation for her husband, she finds her independence.

Reading Lolita in Tehran (Autobiography)
by Azar Nafisi

After the revolution in Iran limits the freedom of women, a group of intellectual college students secretly meet with a former professor to discuss great literature of the twentieth century. Living in the oppressive world of the Ayatollah Khomeini's regime where women are considered insignificant, the literature discussions become essential for this group in maintaining their value as women and individuals.

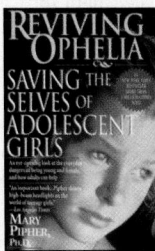

Reviving Ophelia: Saving the Selves of Adolescent Girls (Nonfiction)
by Mary Pipher, Ph.D.

After treating adolescent girls for 20 years, Dr. Pipher explains how the media and culture contribute to the serious problems of depression, eating disorders, and other mental disorders that plague young women at this time of life.

HISTORY Online

Refer to tav.mt.glencoe.com for additional Glencoe Literature titles, lesson plans, and study guides related to this unit.

TEACH

Cooperative Learning

Summarizing Organize the class into groups and ask each group to choose another book written about the struggles of women facing social inequality and a growing emphasis on women's issues. Students may wish to select from the books listed here or identify another book through their own research. After the groups have read their chosen book, tell each group to divide the chapters evenly among the group members. Each person should write a summary paragraph explaining the content of the assigned chapter. Have groups share their book summaries with another group. See if groups can properly understand the other books based on the summaries. **OL** **CA** 11WA2.2

GLENCOE BOOKLINK

Use **Glencoe BookLink** to create customized reading lists for your students' reading levels, interests, and abilities.

Reading Strategy ⟩ REINFORCING READING SKILLS

To help students practice questioning the author, ask them to keep a list of questions they think of as they read. Students may wish to get clarification on why a particular event happened as it did, why a character acted in a certain circumstance, or why the author used particular words and phrases. Once all questions are finished, use these questions to generate class discussion on the craft of authorship and why the author made certain decisions. **AL**

Guide to Reading

Understanding Vocabulary: Have students define the vocabulary in their own words.

Answers to Graphic:
1966: UFW pushed for better wages and working conditions; 1968: AIM protested Native American conditions; 1969: *La Raza Unida* organized Mexican Americans; 1971: PUSH and CBC focused on African American concerns

Unpacking the Standards

Students will be able to:

- Investigate how other minority groups and disadvantaged populations worked to achieve equality.
- Discuss how Hispanic Americans, especially César Chávez, strove for equality.
- Describe how Native Americans worked to improve their civil rights.

Answers and Additional Support

SECTION 3 New Approaches to Civil Rights

Guide to Reading

Connection
In the previous section, you learned about the women's movement. In this section, you will discover how minority groups worked to improve their status.

Main Idea
- Minorities in America continued fighting for reform and increased civil rights. (p. 825)
- Hispanic Americans worked to improve their rights by organizing a farm workers' union and calling for bilingual education. (p. 828)

- The American Indian Movement (AIM) used protests and legal battles to win victories in the quest for civil rights and equal opportunities. (p. 829)

Content Vocabulary
affirmative action, busing, bilingualism

Academic Vocabulary
federal, contract, guarantee

People and Terms to Identify
Allan Bakke, Jesse Jackson, Congressional Black Caucus, César Chávez, *La Raza Unida,* American Indian Movement

Reading Objectives
- **Describe** the goal of affirmative action policies.
- **Analyze** the rise of Hispanic and Native American protests.

Reading Strategy
Sequencing As you read about the civil rights movement's new approaches, complete a time line similar to the one below to record new groups and their actions.

```
              ┌──────┐
              │ 1968 │
              └──────┘
 ┌──────┐                    ┌──────┐
 │ 1966 │                    │ 1971 │
 └──────┘                    └──────┘
              ┌──────┐
              │ 1969 │
              └──────┘
```

Preview of Events

◆1965 ————————————————— ◆1969 ————————————————————— ◆1973

1966
Hispanic Americans form United Farm Workers of America

1968
Kerner Commission reports on racism in the United States

1969
Hispanic leaders form *La Raza Unida*

1973
Native Americans and government clash in South Dakota

The following are the main History–Social Science Standards covered in this section.

11.6.5 Trace the advances and retreats of organized labor, from the creation of the American Federation of Labor and the Congress of Industrial Organizations to current issues of a post-industrial multinational economy, including the United Farm Workers in California.

11.9.7 Examine relations between the United States and Mexico in the twentieth century, including key economic, political, immigration, and environmental issues.

11.10.2 Examine and analyze the key events, policies, and court cases in the evolution of civil rights, including *Dred Scott v. Sanford, Plessy v. Ferguson, Brown v. Board of Education, Regents of the University of California v. Bakke,* and California Proposition 209.

11.10.4 Examine the roles of civil rights advocates (e.g., A. Philip Randolph, Martin Luther King, Jr., Malcom X, Thurgood Marshall, James Farmer, Rosa Parks), including the significance of Martin Luther King, Jr.'s "Letter from Birmingham Jail" and "I Have a Dream" speech.

11.10.5 Discuss the diffusion of the civil rights movement of African Americans from the churches of the rural South and the urban North, including the resistance to racial desegregation in Little Rock and Birmingham, and how the advances influenced the agendas, strategies, and effectiveness of the quests

of American Indians, Asian Americans, and Hispanic Americans for civil rights and equal opportunities.

11.11.1 Discuss the reasons for the nation's changing immigration policy, with emphasis on how the Immigration Act of 1965 and successor acts have transformed American society.

The Big Idea

The quest for equality is eternal. During this time of protest, many minority groups began fighting for increased civil rights. Some of these groups, such as Hispanic Americans and Native Americans, began to organize on a large scale for the first time. African Americans also continued their fight for civil equality by focusing on jobs and educational improvements. New African American, Asian American, and Pacific Islander political leaders emerged. These leaders helped push for greater awareness and legislation to improve civil equality.

824 CHAPTER 18 The Politics of Protest

Fighting for Greater Opportunity

Main Idea Minorities in America continued fighting for reform and increased civil rights.

Reading Connection Have you ever taken the bus to school? Read on to learn about busing and the efforts to achieve educational improvements for minorities.

During this time of heightened protest in the United States, Native Americans began raising their voices for reform and change.

★ *An American Story* ★

In 1968 Vernon and Clyde Bellecourt, along with other Native Americans in Minneapolis, were struggling to earn a living. The Bellecourts decided to take a stand against their conditions. Spurred by the 1960s protest movements and by reawakened pride in their culture, the brothers helped organize the American Indian Movement (AIM). AIM's goal was to combat discrimination and brutality by the local police. Vernon recalled how AIM worked:

66They got a small grant from the Urban League of Minneapolis to put two-way radios in their cars and to get tape recorders and cameras. They would listen to the police calls, and when they heard . . . that police were being dispatched to a certain community or bar, they'd show up with cameras and take pictures of the police using more than normal restraint on people. . . . AIM would show up and have attorneys ready. Often they would beat the police back to the station. They would have a bondsman there, and they'd start filing lawsuits against the police department.99

—quoted in *Native American Testimony*

Other groups also began protesting for reform and improved living conditions. During the 1960s and early 1970s, Hispanic Americans organized to improve their status in society. In the wake of the assassination of Dr. Martin Luther King, Jr., African Americans continued their fight for greater civil rights, now focusing more on access to jobs.

Affirmative Action By the end of the 1960s, many African American leaders expressed a growing sense of frustration. Although most legal forms of racial discrimination had been dismantled, many African Americans felt there had been little improvement in their daily lives. In the eyes of leading civil rights activists, the problems facing most African Americans lay in their lack of access to good jobs and adequate schooling. As a result, leaders of the civil rights movement began to focus their energies on these problems.

As part of their effort, civil rights leaders looked to an initiative known as affirmative action. Enforced through executive orders and **federal** policies, **affirmative action** called for companies and institutions doing business with the federal government to actively recruit African American employees with the hope that this would lead to improved social and economic status. Officials later expanded affirmative action to include other minority groups and women.

Supporters of the policy argued that because so few companies hired from these groups in the past, they had had little chance to develop necessary job skills. If businesses opened their doors wider to minorities, more of them could begin building better lives.

In one example of affirmative action's impact, Atlanta witnessed a significant increase in minority job opportunities shortly after Maynard Jackson became its first African American mayor in 1973. When Jackson took office, less than one percent of all city **contracts** went to African Americans, even though they made up about half of Atlanta's population. Jackson used the expansion of the city's airport to redress this imbalance by opening the bidding process for airport contracts more widely to minority firms. Through his efforts, small companies and minority firms took on 25 percent of all airport construction work, earning them some $125 million in contracts.

Vernon Bellecourt ▼

TEACH

R Reading Strategy

Using Context Clues Ask students to give their own definition of *affirmative action.* Have them locate the definition in the dictionary. Discuss any differences between those two definitions. **BL**

S Skill Practice

Scaffolding—Identifying Bias The use of affirmative action as a way of improving the economic status of minority groups has been controversial ever since its inception in the 1960s. Divide the class into two groups and ask one group to research and prepare debating points that support the use of affirmative action methods. Ask the other group to research and prepare debating points that challenge the use of these methods. As each group presents its argument, have the other group identify any bias present in their opponents' point of view. **OL** **CA HR1; HR3; HR4; HI1**

This **Historical Analysis** skill was introduced in Chapter 15.

Review the Big Idea

Review the Big Idea for this section, "The quest for equality is eternal." Ask students to make a list of how social equality for minorities has improved since the 1960s and what remains to be accomplished. **OL**

Did You Know?

The phrase "affirmative action" was first used in 1961 by President John F. Kennedy when he issued an executive order proclaiming that federal contractors should "take affirmative action" to ensure fair treatment of employees and job applicants, regardless of their race, religion, color, or national origin.

825

Challenges to Affirmative Action Affirmative action programs did not go unchallenged. Critics viewed them as a form of "reverse discrimination." They claimed that qualified white workers were kept from jobs, promotions, and a place in schools because a certain number of such positions had been set aside for minorities or women.

One of the more notable challenges to affirmative action came in 1974, after officials at the University of California Medical School at Davis turned down the admission of a white applicant named **Allan Bakke** for a second time. When Bakke learned that slots had been set aside for minorities, he sued the school. Bakke argued that by admitting minority applicants, some of whom had scored lower than Bakke on their exams, the school had discriminated against him due to his race.

In 1978, in *University of California Regents v. Bakke,* the Supreme Court, in a 5 to 4 ruling, declared that the university had indeed violated Bakke's rights. On the other hand, it ruled that schools could use racial criteria as part of their admissions process so long as they did not use "fixed quotas." While *Bakke* was not a strong and definitive ruling, the Court had nevertheless supported affirmative action programs as constitutional. *(See page 1006 for more information on* University of California Regents v. Bakke.*)*

The debate over affirmative action continued through the 1980s, and by the mid-1990s, opponents had begun organizing politically to end affirmative action programs. In 1995 the University of California's Board of Regents voted to end the use of race in its admissions policy. The push to end the university's affirmative action program was led by Ward Connerly, an African American board member and business owner. Connerly strongly believed that affirmative action treated people unequally.

Connerly went on to lead the campaign for Proposition 209, an amendment to California's constitution that banned the state from giving preferential treatment on the basis of race, gender, ethnicity, or national origin. After Californians voted in favor of Proposition 209 in 1996, citizens in other states increased their efforts to ban affirmative action programs. The debate continues to the present.

Equal Access to Education By the early 1970s, African American leaders also had begun to push harder for educational improvements. In the 1954 case of *Brown v. Board of Education of Topeka, Kansas,* the Supreme Court had ordered an end to segregated public schools. In the 1960s, however, many schools remained segregated as local communities moved slowly to comply with the Court. Since children normally went to neighborhood public schools, segregation in schooling reflected the race segregation of neighborhoods. White schools were usually far superior to African American schools, as Ruth Baston of the NAACP noted in 1965 after visiting Boston schools:

> ❝When we would go to white schools, we'd see these lovely classrooms with a small number of children in each class. The teachers were permanent. We'd see wonderful materials. When we'd go to our schools, we'd see overcrowded classrooms, children sitting out in the corridors. And so then we decided that where there were a large number of white students, that's where the care went. That's where the books went. That's where the money went.❞
>
> —quoted in *Freedom Bound*

To ensure desegregated schools, local governments resorted to a policy known as **busing,** transporting children to schools outside their neighborhoods to achieve greater racial balance. The Supreme Court upheld the constitutionality of busing in the 1971 case, *Swann v. Charlotte-Mecklenburg Board of Education.* *(See page 1007 for more information on* Swann v. Charlotte-Mecklenburg Board of Education.*)*

Picturing **History**

Equal Opportunity Allan Bakke graduated from medical school after the Supreme Court overturned the University of California's use of specific racial quotas. How did the *Bakke* case affect affirmative action?

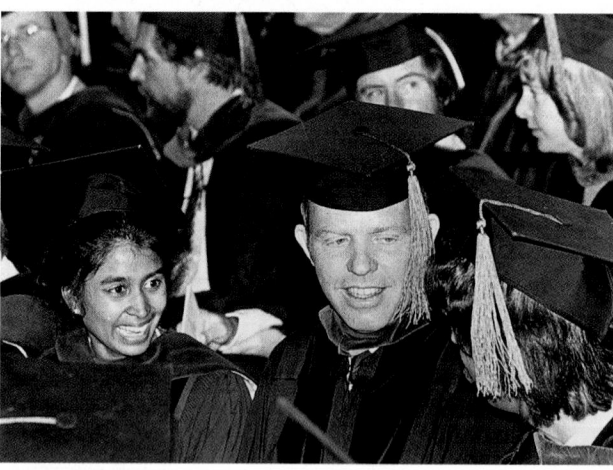

Picturing **History**
Answer: supported affirmative action but ruled against fixed quotas
Ask: What changed about affirmative action in the 1990s? *(Opponents organized to end such programs.)*

Did You Know?
Stokely Carmichael turned down scholarships to other colleges in order to attend Howard University, a historically African American university. Following graduation from Howard, he again turned down scholarships, this time for graduate studies, and went to work for SNCC.

Picturing **History**

New African American Leadership Andrew Young and Jesse Jackson both worked with Dr. Martin Luther King, Jr., in the civil rights movement. Young went on to become the first African American ambassador to the United Nations, while Jackson has become a prominent member of the Democratic Party. *What group of African American members of Congress became influential in the 1970s?*

R₁ Many whites responded to busing by taking their children out of public schools. Nearly 20,000 white students left Boston's public system for parochial and private schools. By late 1976, African Americans, Hispanics, and other minorities made up the majority of Boston's public school students. This "white flight" also occurred in other cities.

New Political Leaders In their struggle for equal opportunity, African Americans found new political leaders in people such as **Jesse Jackson.** In 1971 Jackson founded People United to Save Humanity, or PUSH, a group aimed at registering voters, developing African American businesses, and broadening educational opportunities. In 1984 and 1988, Jackson sought the Democratic presidential nomination. Although both attempts were unsuccessful, Jackson did win over millions of voters.

African Americans and Asian Americans and Pacific Islanders also became more influential in Congress. In 1957, Dalip Singh from California was elected to Congress. Both Daniel K. Inouye and Spark Matsunaga were elected to Congress in 1962 to represent Hawaii. Two years later, in 1964, Patsy Takemoto Mink of Hawaii became the first Asian-American woman elected to Congress. In 1971,

R₂ African American members of Congress reorganized an existing organization into the **Congressional Black Caucus** in order to more clearly represent the concerns of African Americans.

Another leader who emerged was Louis Farrakhan of the Nation of Islam. In 1994, he helped organize the Million Man March, a gathering of African American men in Washington, D.C. to promote self-reliance and community responsibility.

With increasing political influence, Asian and Pacific Americans also began to organize to achieve racial equality and social justice. The first notable action of the Asian American Movement occurred in 1968 at the Third World Strike at San Francisco State College. This month long strike became the longest student-led strike in United States history. Many minority groups and organizations gathered to protest for racial equality. In 1977, Asian Pacific Americans received recognition from the government when congress passed a resolution declaring the first 10 days of May as Asian/Pacific Heritage Week. President Jimmy Carter approved this resolution in 1978, designating this week as an annual celebration.

✓ **Reading Check** **Examining** What were the goals of affirmative action policies?

CHAPTER 18 The Politics of Protest **827**

R₁ **Reading Strategy**

Questioning Have students consider what is meant by the phrase "white flight." **Ask: How do you think this affected the success of inner-city schools?** *(Over time it caused a loss of taxable revenue for inner-city schools.)* **OL**

R₂ **Reading Strategy**

Inferring Ask students to list some of the concerns of African Americans they think might be addressed by the Congressional Black Caucus. *(Answers could include: employment and welfare reform, affirmative action progress, minority business, and education.)* **AL**

✓ **Reading Check**

Answer: improve educational and social and economic opportunities for African Americans, and actively recruit minorities, including women, for jobs

Picturing **History**

Answer: Congressional Black Caucus
Ask: What organization did Jesse Jackson found? *(People United to Save Humanity)*

Did You Know?

Reverend Jesse Jackson did not make a bid for president in 1992 or 1996. Jackson's previous campaigns met many of his goals, such as higher voter registration and black voter turnout. His goals also included recognition that African Americans could be viable national candidates.

U Universal Access

Logical/ Mathematical As immigration diversifies the U.S. population, the pressure to ensure equal rights for all also increases. Have students review immigration data, such as those from the U.S. Citizenship and Immigration Services Web site (http://uscis.gov/graphics/). Students should create a graph showing the current top three regions chosen by immigrants and the top five nations of origin of immigrants. **AL** **CA** CS3

W Writing Support

Research Report Writing Ask students to write a three-page biographical report on César Chávez's efforts to organize Hispanic farm workers and improve their working conditions. Have them consider Chávez's impact by determining how successful he was in accomplishing his goals and whether any changes he caused had a lasting impact. **AL** **CA** 11WA2.3b; 11WA2.4d

Answers and Additional Support

Profiles IN HISTORY

Dolores Huerta
1930–

Dolores Huerta began her career as an elementary school teacher, but she soon left, believing that she could do more good for Mexican Americans outside the classroom. "I couldn't stand seeing kids come to class hungry and needing shoes," she said. "I thought I could do more by organizing farmworkers than by trying to teach their hungry children."

In the early 1950s, Huerta helped found the Stockton, California, chapter of the Community Service Organization (CSO). This grassroots group led voter registration drives, pushed for improved public services, and fought for legislation on behalf of low-income workers.

It was through her work with the CSO that Huerta met César Chávez. Together, they organized farmworkers into a union and fought for better wages and working conditions.

José Angel Gutiérrez
1944–

As a young social activist, José Angel Gutiérrez set out to organize Mexican Americans from Crystal City, Texas, into a political force. In 1970 his newly founded political party, *La Raza Unida,* participated in local elections. Over the next few years, Mexican Americans gained control of Crystal City's school system and government.

As *La Raza Unida* gained a more national following, Gutiérrez became a prominent figure. He eventually stepped away from the political scene, serving first as a judge and then as a college professor. Gutiérrez found it difficult to stay away from politics, however, and in 1993, he ran unsuccessfully for a U.S. Senate seat. After that, he established his own legal center. Looking upon Gutiérrez's career, one historian said, "He represents the new breed of Chicano professionals produced by the colleges and universities, but he is still a Chicano with the old dream of revolution."

Hispanic Americans Organize

Main Idea Hispanic Americans worked to improve their rights by organizing a farm workers' union and calling for bilingual education.

Reading Connection Have you studied a foreign language? What was the experience like? Read on to discover how Hispanic Americans fought for education in Spanish as well as English.

Hispanic Americans also worked for greater rights in this period. In 1960 about 3 million Hispanics lived in the United States. This number increased rapidly after the passage of the Immigration Act of 1965.

Hispanics came to the United States from countries such as Cuba and Mexico to flee repressive political regimes or to find jobs and better lives. The largest group was Mexican Americans, many of whom arrived during and after World War II to work on huge farms in the South and West.

Many Hispanics arrived illegally, sometimes crossing the U.S.-Mexican border with the help of "coyotes," often unscrupulous guides who charged huge sums of money for their services. Because they lacked legal protection, they were often exploited by employers, working under poor conditions for little pay.

César Chávez and the UFW One notable Hispanic American campaign was the effort to win rights for farmworkers. Most Mexican American farm laborers earned little pay, received few benefits, and had no job security. In the early 1960s, **César Chávez** and Dolores Huerta organized two groups that fought for farmworkers. In 1965 the groups cooperated in a strike against California growers to demand union recognition, increased wages, and better benefits.

When employers resisted, Chávez enlisted college students, churches, and civil rights groups to organize a national boycott of table grapes, one of California's largest agricultural products. An estimated 17 million citizens stopped buying them, and industry profits tumbled.

Under the sponsorship of the American Federation of Labor and Congress of Industrial Organization (AFL-CIO), in 1966 Chávez and Huerta merged their two organizations into one—the United Farm Workers (UFW). The union's combined strength ensured that the boycott would continue. The boycott ended in 1970, when the grape growers finally agreed to a contract to raise wages and improve working conditions.

Profiles IN HISTORY

Ask: What motivated Dolores Huerta to become an activist? *(After seeing children come to school hungry and needing shoes, she decided she could do more by organizing farm workers than by teaching school.)*

Growing Political Activism The League of United Latin American Citizens, or LULAC, founded in Corpus Christi, Texas, in 1929, had long worked for Mexican American rights in the court system, in hiring, and in education. In 1954 LULAC brought the landmark case of *Hernandez* v. *the State of Texas* to the Supreme Court, winning the right of Mexican Americans to serve on juries.

Hispanic Americans became more politically active during the 1960s and 1970s. In 1969 José Angel Gutiérrez organized a new political party in Texas called *La Raza Unida,* or "the United People." The group mobilized Mexican American voters to push for job training programs and greater access to financial institutions.

One issue both Hispanic students and political leaders promoted was **bilingualism,** the practice of teaching immigrant students in their own language while they also learned English. Many Hispanics argued they would be at a competitive disadvantage with native English speakers unless they had schooling in their native language. Congress supported their arguments, passing the Bilingual Education Act in 1968. This directed school districts to set up classes for immigrants in their own language.

In recent years there has been some movement away from bilingualism in states with large Hispanic populations. Some educators argue that total immersion in English is the soundest road to educational success. Some American voters opposed bilingual education, believing it makes it more difficult for a child to adjust to American culture and that it was costly besides. The U.S. Supreme Court, however, upheld bilingualism in 1974.

✓ **Reading Check** **Explaining** How did Hispanic Americans increase their economic opportunities in the 1960s?

Native Americans Raise Their Voices

Main Idea The American Indian Movement (AIM) used protests and legal battles to win victories in the quest for civil rights and equal opportunities.

Reading Connection Do you remember earlier efforts to assist Native Americans? Read on to learn about events in the 1960s that brought some political gains to Native Americans.

Native Americans in 1970 were one of the nation's smallest minority groups, constituting less than one percent of the U.S. population. Few minority groups,

however, had more justifiable grievances than the descendants of America's original inhabitants. Native Americans were at a disadvantage in income, education, and healthcare. The average annual family income of Native Americans was $1,000 less than that of African Americans. The Native American unemployment rate was 10 times the national rate. Joblessness was particularly high on reservation lands, where nearly half of all Native Americans lived. Most urban Native Americans suffered from discrimination and from limited education and training. The bleakest statistic of all showed that life expectancy among Native Americans was almost seven years below the national average. To improve conditions, many Native Americans began organizing in the late 1960s and 1970s.

A Protest Movement Emerges In 1961 more than 400 members of 67 Native American groups gathered in Chicago to discuss ways to address their numerous problems. They issued a manifesto, known as the Declaration of Indian Purpose, calling for policies to create greater economic opportunities on reservations.

HISTORY Online

Student Web Activity Visit the *American Vision: Modern Times* Web site at tav.mt.glencoe.com and click on *Student Web Activities— Chapter 18* for an activity on protest movements.

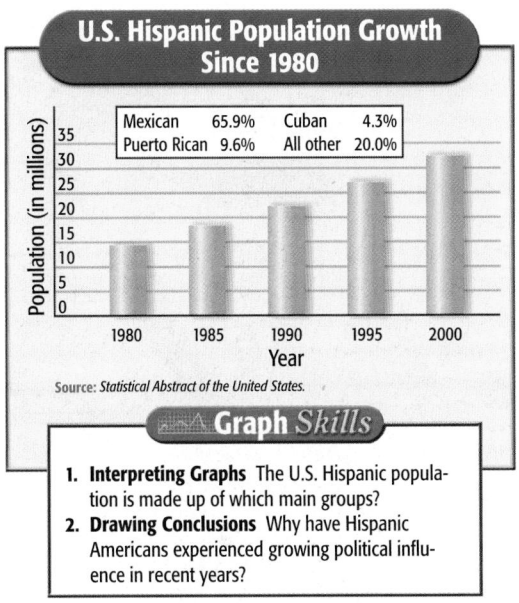

U.S. Hispanic Population Growth Since 1980

Mexican 65.9%	Cuban 4.3%
Puerto Rican 9.6%	All other 20.0%

Population (in millions) — Year: 1980, 1985, 1990, 1995, 2000

Source: *Statistical Abstract of the United States.*

 Graph Skills

1. **Interpreting Graphs** The U.S. Hispanic population is made up of which main groups?
2. **Drawing Conclusions** Why have Hispanic Americans experienced growing political influence in recent years?

R₁ **Reading Strategy**

Questioning Hispanic Americans found new ways to improve their social standing in the 1960s. **Ask:** How are interest groups like the United Farm Workers and political parties such as *La Raza Unida* similar? *(They work toward an effort or a cause.)* **BL**

S **Skill Practice**

Conducting a Debate Organize the class into two groups. Tell the groups that they are to prepare for a debate about bilingual education. Have one group concentrate on the advantages of bilingual education and the other group concentrate on the disadvantages. Tell the groups to research facts and theories to support their assigned point of view. Conduct an informal debate in which each side presents its case and rebuts the point of view of the other side. Encourage all students to participate. **OL**

CA HR1; HR2; HR3; HR4

R₂ **Reading Strategy**

Scaffolding—Academic Vocabulary The word *constitute* was introduced in Chapter 6, Section 2. Ask a student to define the word. **BL**

Resources for page 829

Have students read more about Native American efforts to improve their civil rights in the Primary Source Reading 18-2.

HISTORY Online

Objectives and answers to the student activity can be found in the **Web Activity Lesson Plan** at tav.mt.glencoe.com.

Graph Skills

Answers:
1. Mexican, Puerto Rican, and Cuban
2. growing numbers and political and labor organizations

Graph Skills Practice
Ask: What other national origins might be represented in the Hispanic population? *(any country in Central or South America)*

✓**Reading Check**

Answer: By forming the UFW and *La Raza Unida* and staging boycotts, they increased their wages, won contracts, improved working conditions, and lobbied successfully to achieve the Bilingual Education Act.

829

R Reading Strategy

Evaluating Evaluate how the American Indian Movement helped the nation understand the issues facing Native Americans. **Ask:** What concerns did the Native American protesters want to address? *(less cultural integration, better educational funding, more local control on reservations)* BL

U Universal Access

Interpersonal To help students understand the attitudes behind the act, have them analyze the following question: How do increased powers for Native American government help on a reservation? *(They help Native Americans to preserve their customs and culture, which were previously threatened by a policy of assimilation. They also allow Native Americans self-determination, where before they had to follow rules set up by the Bureau of Indian Affairs.)* OL

Resources for page 830

*Have students read more about the Native American protest movement by assigning "Proclamation to the Great White Father and All His People" in the **American Literature Readings 5.***

Answers and Additional Support

Unlike other groups demanding more assimilation into mainstream society, many Native Americans wanted greater independence from it. They hoped to preserve their culture and heritage by not assimilating completely with American culture. Native Americans took a step toward this goal in 1968 when Congress passed the Indian Civil Rights Act. It **guaranteed** reservation residents the protections of the Bill of Rights, but it also recognized the legitimacy of local reservation law.

Some Native Americans thought the reforms the government had introduced were too modest. In their view, the many years of effort to gain more rights did not provide enough gains. As a response, they formed more militant groups. Typically, such groups employed a more combative style. One of these groups, the **American Indian Movement** (AIM), was organized in 1968 to fight high unemployment, inadequate housing, and racial discrimination. The group also focused on treaty rights and worked to regain tribal lands. In 1969, as a symbolic protest, AIM occupied the abandoned federal prison on Alcatraz Island in San Francisco Bay for 19 months, claiming ownership "by right of discovery."

A more famous and violent protest occurred almost two years later at Wounded Knee, South Dakota, where federal troops had killed around 150 Sioux in 1890. In February 1973, AIM members seized and occupied the town of Wounded Knee for 70 days. They demanded radical changes in the administration of reservations and that the government honor its long-forgotten treaty obligations to Native Americans. A brief clash between the occupiers and the FBI killed two Native Americans and wounded several on both sides. Shortly thereafter, the siege came to an end.

Native Americans Make Notable Gains The Native American movement fell short of achieving all its goals, but it did win some notable victories. In 1975 Congress passed the Indian Self-Determination and Educational Assistance Act, which increased funds for

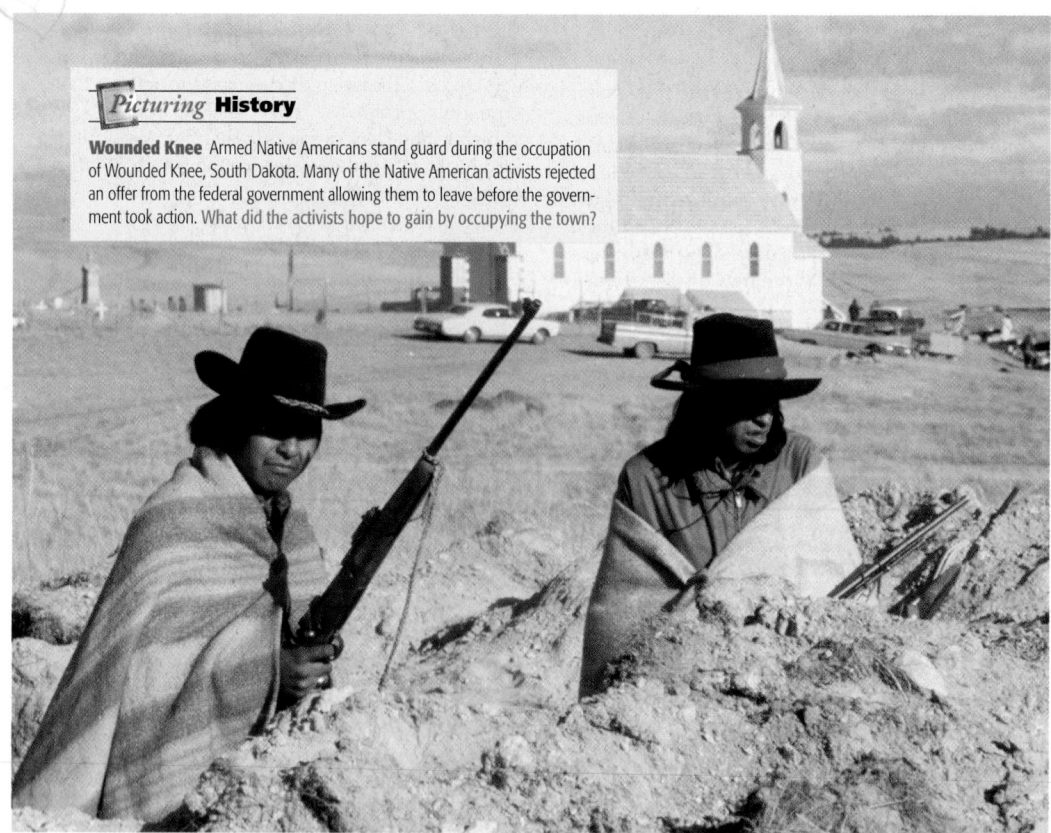

Picturing History

Wounded Knee Armed Native Americans stand guard during the occupation of Wounded Knee, South Dakota. Many of the Native American activists rejected an offer from the federal government allowing them to leave before the government took action. What did the activists hope to gain by occupying the town?

More Skill Practice

Using Geography Skills Using a map, have students locate and label Native American land and reservations. EL

CA CS3

Picturing History

Answer: The activists hoped to get the government to improve reservation administration and honor some treaty promises broken throughout history.

Native American education and expanded control in administering federal programs. More Native Americans also moved into policy-making positions at the Bureau of Indian Affairs, and the agency pushed for more Native American self determination.

Through the federal court system, Native Americans also won a number of the land and water rights they sought. The Pueblo of Taos, New Mexico, regained property rights to Blue Lake, a place sacred to their religion. In 1980, a federal court settled a claim of the Passamaquoddy and the Penobscot groups. The government paid the groups $81.5 million to relinquish their claim on land in the state of Maine. The two groups purchased 300,000 acres with the money and invested much of the remainder. Other court decisions gave Native American groups authority to impose taxes on businesses on their reservations and to perform other sovereign functions.

Since Native Americans first began to organize, many reservations have dramatically improved their economic conditions by actively developing businesses, such as electric plants, resorts, cattle ranches, and oil and gas wells. More recently, gambling casinos have become a successful enterprise. Because of rulings on sovereignty, Native Americans in some areas are allowed to operate gaming establishments under their own laws even though state laws prevent others from doing so. In these ways, Native Americans have tried to regain control of their economic future, just as other American minorities did in the 1960s and 1970s.

 Picturing **History**

Native American Rights Many Native Americans, like this high school student, worked to gain more freedom and improve their lives. The increase in Native American organizations has led to improved quality of life and economic conditions. How have reservations been able to improve their economic conditions?

✓ **Reading Check** **Analyzing** What conditions led Native Americans to organize in the 1960s?

 HISTORY
Online **Study Central**

For help with the concepts in this section of *American Vision: Modern Times* go to tav.mt.glencoe.com and click on *Study Central.*

SECTION 3 ASSESSMENT

Checking for Understanding
1. **Vocabulary** Define: federal, affirmative action, contract, busing, bilingualism, guarantee.
2. **People and Terms** Identify: Allan Bakke, Jesse Jackson, Congressional Black Caucus, César Chávez, *La Raza Unida,* American Indian Movement.
3. **Analyze** how the *Bakke* case, along with other cases, affected affirmative action.

Reviewing Big Ideas
4. **Explaining** How did the Supreme Court support civil rights during the 1970s? Cite two court cases and their decisions.

Critical Thinking
5. **Historical Analysis** **Synthesizing** Why have African Americans become significantly more influential in the U.S. Congress since the early 1970s? **CA HI1**
6. **Categorizing** Use a graphic organizer similar to the one below to identify civil rights leaders and their causes during the 1960s and 1970s.

Civil Rights Leaders	Causes

Analyzing Visuals
7. **Analyzing Graphs** Study the graph on page 829 of U.S. Hispanic population growth since 1980. The largest percentage of Hispanics is represented by Mexican Americans. What was the approximate percentage growth for Hispanic Americans from 1980 to 2000?

Writing About History
8. **Expository Writing** Write a magazine article about the conditions that gave rise to the Native American protest movement of the 1960s and 1970s. In your article, discuss the movement's goals and activities. **CA 11WA2.1a**

CHAPTER 18 The Politics of Protest **831**

SECTION 3 ASSESSMENT ANSWERS

1. Content vocabulary is boldfaced and highlighted in yellow. Academic vocabulary is boldfaced.
2. Allan Bakke *(p. 826),* Jesse Jackson *(p. 827),* Congressional Black Caucus *(p. 827),* César Chávez *(p. 828),* La Raza Unida *(p. 829),* American Indian Movement *(p. 830)*
3. It challenged affirmative action as reverse discrimination.
4. *Swann* v. *Charlotte-Mecklenburg Board of Education:* constitutionality of busing; *University of California Regents* v. *Bakke:* constitutionality of affirmative action
5. CBC was organized in Congress.
6. Jackson: political power of African Americans; Chávez: rights of farm workers; Gutiérrez: Mexican American vote; Bellecourt brothers: Native American interests
7. about 100%
8. Students' articles will vary. Articles should focus on the reasons for the protest movement.

Resources for page 831

Use these resources to assess student mastery.

📁 Section Quiz 18-3

📁 Reading Essentials and Study Guide 18-3

💿 Interactive Tutor Self-Assessment CD-ROM

📁 California Standards Practice, Grade 11

 Picturing **History**

Answer: by developing businesses such as electric plants, resorts, and oil wells, as well as by operating gaming establishments

✓ **Reading Check**

Answer: low average family income, unemployment 10 times the national rate, discrimination, limited education, and decreased life expectancy

 HISTORY
Online

Study Central provides audio summaries, interactive games, and online graphic organizers to help students review section content.

CLOSE

Organizing Information Have students create a two-columned chart, listing Native American issues in one column and the outcome in the second column. **OL**

FOCUS

BELLRINGER
SKILLBUILDER ACTIVITY

Project **Daily Focus Skills Transparency 18-4** and have students answer the question.

Guide to Reading

Understanding Vocabulary:
Have students scan the section to become familiar with the content vocabulary words and the academic vocabulary words.

Answers to Graphic:
Clean Air Act, Clean Water Act, Earth Day celebration, Endangered Species Act, creation of the Environmental Protection Agency (EPA)

Unpacking the Standards

Students will be able to:

• Explain the growth of the environmental movement.

• Discuss the goals of the environmental movement.

• Analyze the efforts of the consumer movement.

Answers and Additional Support

Guide to Reading

Connection
In the previous section, you learned how minority groups gained greater civil equality. In this section, you will discover how Americans grew concerned about environmental issues.

Main Idea

• Rachel Carson's book *Silent Spring* warned the public of the dangers of pollution and pesticides. (p. 833)

• In the early 1970s, Congress passed legislation to protect the nation's air, water, and endangered species. (p.834)

• Concerns about the quality and safety of many products, including automobiles, led to new legislation protecting consumers. (p. 836)

Content Vocabulary
smog, fossil fuel

Academic Vocabulary
publication, nonetheless, consequence

People and Terms to Identify
Rachel Carson, Environmental Protection Agency, Three Mile Island, Ralph Nader

Reading Objectives
• **Explain** the origins of the environmental movement.
• **Identify** the significant measures taken to combat environmental problems.

Reading Strategy
Organizing As you read about the nation's environmental problems in the 1960s and 1970s, complete a graphic organizer by including actions taken to combat these problems.

Actions Taken

Preview of Events

♦1962	♦1968	♦1974	♦1980

1962
Rachel Carson's *Silent Spring* published

1965
Ralph Nader's *Unsafe at Any Speed* published

1970
First Earth Day celebrated; EPA established

1972
U.S. bans use of pesticide DDT

1979
Nuclear accident at Three Mile Island

The following are the main History–Social Science Standards covered in this section.

11.8.6 Discuss the diverse environmental regions of North America, their relationship to local economies, and the origins and prospects of environmental problems in those regions.

11.11.5 Trace the impact of, need for, and controversies associated with environmental conservation, expansion of the national park system, and the development of environmental protection laws, with particular attention to the interaction between environmental protection advocates and property right advocates.

11.11.7 Explain how the federal, state, and local governments have responded to demographic and social changes such as population shifts to the suburbs, racial concentrations in the cities, Frostbelt-to-Sunbelt migration, international migration, decline of family farms, increases in out-of-wedlock births, and drug abuse.

~≪ The Big Idea ≫~

Societies change over time. During the 1960s and 1970s, Americans became aware of environmental problems. As the dangers of pesticides such as DDT became known, individuals and groups began efforts to halt their use. The environmental movement gained public support, and the government began to take action by establishing the Environmental Protection Agency. Congress passed several acts aimed at protecting the nation's air, water, and endangered species. Many citizens were also concerned with nuclear energy and its effects on the environment and people's health. People also began to question the safety of consumer goods. The consumer movement led to new legislation to protect consumers from defective and unsafe products, including automobiles.

832 CHAPTER 18 The Politics of Protest

SECTION RESOURCES

📁 Print Material
• Reproducible Lesson Plan 18-4
• Guided Reading Activity 18-4
• Reading Essentials and Study Guide 18-4
• Active Reading Note-Taking Guide 18-4

⚡ Transparencies
• Daily Focus Skills Transparency 18-4
• Section Graphic Organizer Transparency 18-4

Technology
🔵 Interactive Tutor Self-Assessment CD-ROM
🔵 Exam*View*® Pro Testmaker CD-ROM
🔵 Presentation Plus! CD-ROM

The Beginnings of Environmentalism

 Rachel Carson's book *Silent Spring* warned the public of the dangers of pollution and pesticides.

Reading Connection Do you recycle or take other steps to protect the environment? Read on to learn of the controversies associated with environmental conservation and the development of environmental protection laws.

During the 1960s and 1970s, a growing number of Americans began to focus on environmental issues. They argued that pesticides had damaged wildlife and that pollution had fouled the nation's air and water.

★ An American Story ★

In 1966 Carol Yannacone of Patchogue, a small community on Long Island, New York, learned that officials were using a powerful pesticide, DDT, as part of a mosquito control operation in a local lake. Alarmed that the pesticide would poison lakes and streams, Yannacone and her husband, Victor, an attorney, contacted several local scientists, who confirmed their suspicions. The Yannacones then successfully sued to halt the use of the pesticide.

The Yannacones had discovered a new strategy for addressing environmental concerns. The legal system, Victor Yannacone insisted, was the one place where facts and evidence, not politics and emotions, would decide the outcome:

❝A court . . . is the only forum in which a full inquiry into questions of environmental significance can be carried on. . . . Only on the witness stand, protected by the rules of evidence though subject to cross-examination, can a scientist be free of the harassment of legislators seeking re-election of higher political office; free from the glare of the controversy-seeking media; free from unsubstantiated attacks of self-styled experts representing vested economic interests and yet who are not subject to cross examination.❞

—quoted in *Since Silent Spring*

Shortly after the Yannacones' court victory, the scientists involved in the case established the Environmental Defense Fund and used its contributions for a series of legal actions across the country to halt DDT spraying. Their efforts led to a nationwide ban on the use of the pesticide in 1972.

The effort to ban DDT was only one aspect of a larger environmental movement that took shape in the 1960s and 1970s. The person who sounded the loudest alarm bell was not a political leader or prominent academic, but a soft-spoken marine biologist, **Rachel Carson.** Carson's 1962 book *Silent Spring* assailed the increasing use of pesticides, particularly DDT. She contended that while pesticides curbed insect populations, they also killed birds, fish, and other creatures that might ingest them. Carson warned Americans of a "silent spring," in which there would be few birds left to usher spring in with their songs. In her book, she imagined such a scene from a fictitious town:

❝There was a strange stillness. The birds, for example—where had they gone? Many people spoke of them, puzzled and disturbed. . . . On the mornings that had once throbbed with the dawn chorus of robins, catbirds, doves, jays, wrens, and scores of other bird voices there was now no sound; only silence lay over the fields and woods and marsh.❞

—from *Silent Spring*

Picturing **History**

The Power of One Rachel Carson, a marine biologist, sounded a warning note for the environment. Her concern over how humans affect the environment helped start a new reform movement. What pesticide in particular worried Carson?

TEACH

C Critical Thinking

Determining Cause and Effect Ask students to answer the following questions: **What elements in the air are pollutants?** *(smog, smoke, chemical fumes)* **What can cause air pollution?** *(automobiles, factories)* **Does air pollution affect people, and if so, how?** *(People with asthma or other respiratory illnesses can be easily affected in highly polluted areas.)* **OL** **CA HI5**

S Skill Practice

Visual Literacy Have students draw a picture of what they believe marine biologist Rachel Carson meant by the phrase "silent spring." *(Students' pictures will differ but should depict a lack of birds, insects, and fish. Students might also find ways to illustrate how larger animals in the food chain might be affected.)* **OL** **CA HI1**

Picturing **History**

Answer: DDT
Ask: What was the name of the book Carson wrote assailing the use of pesticides? *(Silent Spring)*

R Reading Strategy

Categorizing Information
Have students brainstorm ideas to improve the environment. Divide issues into categories labeled land, air, or water. Try to get down as many different ideas as possible. After all ideas are exhausted, refine the list into ideas that are feasible and ideas that are less useful. **OL** **CA HI5**

U Universal Access

Kinesthetic Ask students to collect samples of all the items that can be recycled in your community. After cleaning or sanitizing the items, have them create a work of art with these items that could be used as a reminder to recycle. Have students display their creations in class and select the ones that best encourage recycling to display in a prominent place in your school. **OL**

✓ Reading Check

Answer: wildlife, air, and water resources

Picturing **History**

Environmental Awareness Numerous oil spills and events such as Earth Day have brought environmental concerns to the attention of Americans. What issues does the Sierra Club address?

Silent Spring became one of the most controversial and powerful books of the 1960s. It sold nearly half a million copies within six months of its **publication** and was widely discussed. The chemical industry was outraged and began an intense campaign to discredit Carson and her arguments. **Nonetheless,** many Americans took Carson's warnings to heart and began to focus on environmental issues.

Reading Check **Identifying** What natural resources did environmental groups want to protect?

The Environmental Movement

R **Main Idea** In the early 1970s, Congress passed legislation to protect the nation's air, water, and endangered species.

Reading Connection Who do you think should be responsible for protecting the public against environmental disasters? Read on to discover ways that the federal government became involved in the environmental movement.

During the 1960s, Americans began to feel that environmental problems plagued every region of the nation. In the Northwest, timber companies were cutting down acres of forestland. **Smog,** or fog made

heavier and darker by smoke and chemical fumes, was smothering major cities. In 1969 a major oil spill off Santa Barbara, California, ruined miles of beach and killed scores of birds and aquatic animals. A dike project in the Florida Everglades indirectly killed millions of birds and animals. Meanwhile, pollution and garbage had caused nearly all the fish to disappear from Lake Erie. By 1970 a growing number of citizens were convinced that the time had come to do something about protecting the environment.

A Grassroots Effort Begins Many observers point to April 1970 as the unofficial beginning of the environmental movement. That month, the nation held its first Earth Day celebration, a day devoted to addressing the country's environmental concerns. The national response was overwhelming. In thousands of colleges and secondary schools and in hundreds of communities, millions of Americans participated in activities to show their environmental awareness, from picking up litter to demonstrating against air pollution.

Senator Gaylord Nelson of Wisconsin, who had put forth the idea of an Earth Day celebration, commented on the event: "The people cared and Earth Day became the first opportunity they ever had to join in a nationwide demonstration to send a message to the politicians—a message to tell them to wake up and do something."

After Earth Day, the grassroots effort intensified. Citizens formed local environmental groups, while nonprofit organizations such as the Sierra Club, the Audubon Society, and the Wilderness Society gained prominence. These organizations worked to protect the environment and promote the conservation of natural resources. In 1970 activists started the Natural Resources Defense Council to coordinate a nationwide network of scientists, lawyers, and activists working on environmental problems.

The Government Steps In With the environmental movement gaining public support, the federal government took action. In 1970 President Nixon signed the National Environmental Policy Act, which created the **Environmental Protection Agency** (EPA). The EPA took on the job of setting and enforcing pollution standards, promoting research, and

Answers and Additional Support

Picturing **History**

Answer: preservation of the environment and conservation of natural resources

Did You Know?

By the early 1970s, 70 percent of Americans ranked the environment as the nation's most pressing problem. That same year, an estimated 20 million people participated in Earth Day—a rally to improve the environment. Across the country more than 14,000 schools and communities held events to raise awareness of environmental issues.

coordinating antipollution activities with state and local governments. The agency also monitored the impact of other federal agencies on the environment.

The Clean Air Act also became law in 1970. This act established emissions standards for factories and automobiles. It also ordered that all industries comply with such standards within five years.

In following years, Congress passed two more pieces of significant environmental legislation. The Clean Water Act (1972) restricted the discharge of pollutants into the nation's lakes and rivers, and the Endangered Species Act (1973) established measures for saving threatened animal species. Over time these laws reduced smog and cut pollution levels.

In 1984 the World Court settled a boundary dispute between the United States and Canada over commercial fishing in the Georges Bank. The bank was divided between the countries by a border known as the Hague Line. This reduced the number of U.S. fishing boats and briefly replenished the number of fish in the bank.

Love Canal Despite the flurry of federal environmental legislation, Americans continued to mobilize on the community level throughout the 1970s. One of the most powerful displays of community activism occurred in a housing development near Niagara Falls, New York, known as Love Canal.

In the 1970s, residents of Love Canal noticed a rising number of health problems in their community, including nerve damage, blood diseases, cancer, miscarriages, and birth defects. They soon learned that their community sat atop a decades-old toxic waste dump. Over time its hazardous contents had leaked into the ground.

Led by a local woman, Lois Gibbs, the residents joined together and demanded that the government take steps to address these health threats. Hindered at first by local and state officials, the residents refused to back down, and by 1978 they had made their struggle known to the entire nation. That year, in the face of mounting public pressure and evidence of the dangers posed by the dump, the state permanently relocated more than 200 families.

In 1980, after hearing protests from the families who still lived near the landfill, President Carter declared Love Canal a federal disaster area and moved over 600 remaining families to new locations. In 1983 Love Canal residents sued the company that had created the dump site and settled the case for $20 million. The site was cleaned up by sealing the waste within an underground bunker and burning homes located above the dumping ground.

Concerns Over Nuclear Energy During the 1970s, an increasing number of citizens expressed concern over the growth of nuclear power. Supporters of nuclear energy hailed it as a cleaner and less expensive alternative to **fossil fuels,** such as coal, oil, and natural gas, which are in limited supply. Opponents warned of the risks, particularly the devastating **consequences** of an accidental radiation release into the air.

The debate moved to the nation's forefront in 1979. In the early hours of March 28, one of the reactors at the **Three Mile Island** nuclear facility outside Harrisburg, Pennsylvania, overheated after its cooling system failed. While plant officials scrambled to fix the problem, low levels of radiation escaped from the reactor.

Officials evacuated many nearby residents, while others fled on their own. Citizens and community groups expressed outrage in protest rallies. Officials closed down the reactor and sealed the leak. The Nuclear Regulatory Commission, the federal agency that regulates the nuclear power industry, eventually declared the plant safe.

The accident at Three Mile Island had a powerful impact and left much of the public in great doubt about the safety of nuclear energy. Such doubts have continued. Since Three Mile Island, 60 nuclear power plants have been shut down or abandoned, and no new facilities have been built since 1973.

Spraying pesticides ▼

CHAPTER 18   The Politics of Protest   **835**

C Critical Thinking

Drawing Conclusions Inform students that politicians must consider if progress or preservation is more important when they make laws that affect nature. **Ask: Should the timber industry be allowed to cut down a forest area?** *(Some might suggest that its cultivation would provide jobs and land to live on, but others might say the forest should be preserved, keeping creatures and plants alive.)* **OL** **CA HI5**

R₁ Reading Strategy

Connecting Remind students that Lois Gibbs, a citizen of Love Canal, brought her community together to fight local environmental issues. Students should realize that just one person can make a difference. Have them discuss ways that they can make a difference by becoming involved in a community activity or social group. **BL**

R₂ Reading Strategy

Scaffolding—Academic Vocabulary The word *pose* was introduced in Chapter 12, Section 4. Ask a student to define the word. **BL**

Review the Big Idea

Review the Big Idea for this section, "Societies change over time." Ask students to consider what life would be like if fossil fuels were totally depleted. *(Without alternative energy sources, electrical appliances would not function and automobiles would be useless.)* **Ask: How would the lack of fossil fuels affect the economy?** *(Alternative energy sources might be more expensive, raising the price of goods and slowing the economy down because people might not be able to afford many things.)*

Did You Know?

When the environmental movement began in the early 1960s, Americans generated approximately 2.7 pounds of trash per person per day. In 2003 the figure had risen to 4.39 pounds of trash per day and up to 56 tons of trash per year created by the average person.

Did You Know?

Since cleaning and revitalizing efforts began at Love Canal, new homeowners have moved into the habitable areas. More than 260 previously abandoned homes have been sold to new residents, regenerating the neighborhood.

TECHNOLOGY & History

Solar Energy

Concerns in the 1970s about the environment and safe energy led to a strong interest in solar energy. Sunlight is composed of photons, particles of solar energy. The use of photovoltaic (PV) cells allows solar energy to be used for a wide range of energy needs, from powering generators to running agricultural water pumps or simple calculators. *Why was solar power seen as an environmentally friendly power source?*

1 Solar arrays or panels are made up of thousands of PV cells and capture the sun's rays.

2 This magnification shows the composition of a PV cell.

3 This schematic shows a cross-section of a cell and how its electrons respond to sunlight to create a flow of electricity.

W The Debate Over Environmentalism The environmentalist movement that emerged in the 1970s led to a new political debate in American society. As environmentalists began proposing regulations they believed would help the environment, opponents began arguing that the regulations had hidden costs.

One controversial issue involved DDT. The World Health Organization has estimated that DDT saved 25 million lives worldwide by killing disease-spreading pests such as mosquitoes and lice. Despite DDT's value in reducing disease, however, most nations followed the U.S. example and banned the pesticide. Soon afterward, cases of malaria and typhus began to rise again worldwide.

The debate over DDT demonstrated the difficulty in balancing the costs and benefits of environmental regulations. Supporters of nuclear power have pointed out that coal-fired power plants also put people at risk. Miners regularly develop black lung disease and die in mining accidents while mining coal for power plants. Coal-fired plants also pollute the air. Yet requiring power plants, cars, and factories to reduce their air pollution may drive up the cost of goods. This can lead to fewer jobs and more poverty, and make more products unaffordable to people of modest means. Environmental regulations can also clash with people's property rights. As a result, the environmentalist movement became increasingly controversial in the 1980s and 1990s, as interest groups, business leaders, and politicians took sides in the debate over the costs and benefits of environmentalist policies. The debate has continued to shape politics to the present day.

✓Reading Check **Summarizing** What is the environmental movement's main goal?

The Consumer Movement

R *Main Idea* Concerns about the quality and safety of many products, including automobiles, led to new legislation protecting consumers.

Reading Connection What are some of the safety features that are now standard in vehicles? Read on to find out about the beginnings of a consumer safety movement.

During the 1960s and 1970s, a number of citizens also questioned the quality and safety of the many new "technologically advanced" products flooding the market. In an atmosphere of protest and overall distrust of authority, more and more buyers

TECHNOLOGY & History

Answer: It is renewable, easily obtained, thought to be relatively inexpensive, and can be used in many ways.
Ask: What are other renewable forms of energy in use today? *(possible answers: wind power, hydroelectric power)*

demanded product safety, accurate information, and a voice in government formulation of consumer policy.

Perhaps the most notable figure of this new consumer protection movement was **Ralph Nader,** a young lawyer from Connecticut. In the early 1960s, Nader noted what he considered an alarmingly high number of automobile fatalities. He presented his findings in a 1965 book, *Unsafe at Any Speed.* Nader charged car manufacturers with putting style, cost, and speed ahead of safety. He also challenged one of the auto industry's long-held claims that drivers were to blame for most auto accidents:

66 The American automobile is produced exclusively to the standards which the manufacturer decides to establish. It comes into the marketplace unchecked. When a car becomes involved in an accident, the entire investigatory, enforcement and claims apparatus that makes up the post-accident response looks almost invariably to driver failure as the cause.... Accommodated by superficial standards of accident investigation, the car manufacturers exude presumptions of engineering excellence and reliability, and this reputation is accepted by many unknowing motorists. 99

—from Unsafe at Any Speed

Nader's efforts received an accidental boost from an unlikely source: the auto industry. Shortly after his book came out, a car company hired private detectives to follow Nader in an attempt to uncover information that might discredit him. The detectives found nothing, and when this corporate spying incident came to light, the publicity pushed *Unsafe at Any Speed* up the bestseller list. As a result, the public became much more aware of auto safety issues. Nader sued the car company for invasion of privacy and used the settlement money to fund several consumer organizations.

Nader's efforts helped spur Congress to pass the National Traffic and Motor Vehicle Safety Act in 1966. The act set mandatory safety standards and established a procedure for notifying car owners about defects. For the first time, the automobile industry was subject to federal safety regulations. Carmakers had to incorporate safety standards into their car designs so that auto crashes would be less devastating. Requirements that called for the installation of seat belts, door locks, safer fuel tanks, and other improvements have since saved hundreds of thousands of lives and prevented millions of injuries.

Nader's success led to calls for a closer examination of numerous other consumer goods during the 1960s and 1970s. Organizations lobbied Congress and state legislatures to pass laws regulating such products as dangerous toys, flammable fabrics, and potentially unsafe meat and poultry.

☑ **Reading Check** **Describing** What was the impact of the consumer protection movement?

HISTORY *Online* 📖 **Study Central**

For help with the concepts in this section of *American Vision: Modern Times* go to tav.mt.glencoe.com and click on *Study Central.*

SECTION 4 ASSESSMENT

Checking for Understanding

1. **Vocabulary** Define: publication, nonetheless, smog, fossil fuel, consequence.
2. **People and Terms** Identify: Rachel Carson, Environmental Protection Agency, Three Mile Island, Ralph Nader.
3. **List** three measures taken to combat environmental problems in the 1960s and 1970s.

Reviewing Big Ideas

4. **Identifying** What groups lobbied for government legislation to protect the environment in the 1960s and 1970s?

Critical Thinking

5. **Evaluating** Which environmental issue do you think is the most pressing problem the environment faces today? Explain your response. **CA HI5**
6. **Categorizing** Use a graphic organizer similar to the one below to list the environmental laws passed in the 1970s and explain their purposes.

Environmental Legislation	Purpose

Analyzing Visuals

7. **Analyzing Posters** Examine the "Love It or Leave It" poster on page 834. This phrase was first used by Vietnam War supporters, directed toward critics of the war and referring to the United States instead of the earth. How has the phrase been adapted here?

Writing About History

8. **Descriptive Writing** Take on the role of an investigative reporter and describe the environmental disaster at either Love Canal or Three Mile Island. Explain how community activism brought the issue to the nation's attention. **CA 11WA2.1a**

CHAPTER 18 The Politics of Protest **837**

S **Skill Practice**

Scaffolding—Comparing Past and Present Students should create and label two automobile renderings. The first should have the absence of all safety features. The second drawing should contain safety information learned from the text relating to the National Traffic and Motor Vehicle Safety Act. Students may include any further safety additions they feel necessary in the second drawing. **OL** **CA** CS1; HI1; HI4

This skill was introduced in Chapter 17.

ASSESS

☑ **Reading Check**

Answer: It raised awareness about the quality and safety of products.

HISTORY *Online*

Study Central provides audio summaries, interactive games, and online graphic organizers to help students review section content.

CLOSE

Summarizing Have students explain the origins of the environmental movement. **OL**

NATIONAL GEOGRAPHIC
Geography&History

FOCUS

History–Social Science Standards

This feature addresses the following standard:

11.8.7 Describe the effects on society and the economy of technological developments since 1945, including the computer revolution, changes in communication, advances in medicine, and improvements in agricultural technology.

Have students identify the continents that contribute the parts and labor needed to assemble the Chevrolet Corvette. *(North America, South America, Europe, Asia, and Australia)*

TEACH

C Critical Thinking

Making Generalizations Have students study the map and read the feature. Ask them to write a sentence that makes a generalization about how economic interdependence fosters communication and affects countries' willingness to resolve differences without resorting to war. **OL**

Answers and Additional Support

Engines are made in **Canada** close to the automotive assembly centers of the United States.

CANADA

GERMANY

Transmissions are manufactured in **Mexico**, where labor costs are relatively low.

UNITED STATES
Bowling Green, KY.

MEXICO

ECUADOR

Light and durable balsa wood **floor plates** are produced in **Ecuador**, because the wood is abundant there.

The production of a GM Chevrolet Corvette in Bowling Green, Kentucky, requires the assembly of components from around the world: an engine from Canada, a transmission from Mexico, balsa wood floor plates from Ecuador, switches from Germany, circuit boards from several Asian nations, and brakes from Australia.

838 CHAPTER 18 The Politics of Protest

EXTENDING THE CONTENT

Museum Delivery Corvette owners can take delivery of their new vehicle at The National Corvette Museum in Bowling Green, Kentucky. Their cars are placed in the museum, on exhibit with the classic Corvettes displayed in the museum. New owners can take pictures of their cars in the museum display before the cars are removed from the museum and presented to them. Owners who select this option for delivery are also treated to a VIP tour of the museum, receive a specially designed Corvette Museum Delivery decal, and get a one-year membership to the museum.

Global Cars

A **German** factory produces very high quality **switches** that can easily be shipped to the United States.

JAPAN

Circuit boards are assembled with parts from **Japan, Thailand,** and **Singapore.**

AND

APORE

AUSTRALIA

An **Australian** company with manufacturing facilities in the United States provides the premier **brake pads** needed in high-performance vehicles.

The globalization of the world economy since the end of World War II has revolutionized the way in which industries and corporations operate. Tremendous advances in technology, communications, and the transport of goods have enabled corporations to turn more and more often to manufacturing facilities and resources around the world. The car industry is a good example of this trend.

For decades American automakers have operated assembly plants in foreign countries, including Brazil, Poland, India, and China. Car companies have also established plants abroad that manufacture particular components, which are then assembled in an American factory. As shown on the world map on the left, foreign manufacturers build major components of the Chevrolet Corvette and ship them to Bowling Green, Kentucky. There, workers assemble the parts—along with some 1,900 others manufactured by about 400 suppliers—into the finished car. The process of finding part suppliers outside of the company, known as "outsourcing," is one way multinational corporations try to gain a competitive advantage over their rivals. Companies contract with foreign suppliers that meet a combination of criteria, including cost, quality, and ease of delivery.

Computers and the Internet have made worldwide communication dramatically easier, faster, and cheaper.

A worker assembles a Corvette at a plant in Bowling Green, Kentucky.

Technological advances have also made manufacturing more efficient. For example, automakers can keep track of parts and suppliers so that the essential components can be delivered to factories from anywhere in the world "just in time" to assemble the finished product.

Multinational corporations now account for about two-thirds of the world's trade in products. Global corporations have become enormous, and the largest ones are wealthier than entire countries. The income of General Motors, for instance, rivals gross national products of the mid-sized economies of nations such as South Africa, Turkey, and Saudi Arabia.

The auto industry has come a long way since Henry Ford perfected assembly line production techniques that made cars affordable for the mass market. Today's automakers have adopted global assembly lines, applying Ford's innovations—standardized job tasks and division of labor—across international boundaries.

Cars are shipped all over the world. Here, Japanese cars are unloaded from a large container ship in Baltimore, Maryland.

LEARNING FROM GEOGRAPHY

1. What three criteria are considered in decisions about suppliers?

2. Why might geography no longer be as big a factor as it once was in the location of a production plant?

CHAPTER 18   The Politics of Protest   **839**

ANSWERS TO LEARNING FROM GEOGRAPHY

1. The criteria are cost, quality, and ease of delivery.

2. Answers may vary. Students should note that improved communication and transport allow parts to be delivered to the assembly line just when they are needed.

FOCUS

Understanding Vocabulary

Before students begin reading, point out that difficult or unfamiliar words are footnoted throughout the text.

TEACH

C Critical Thinking

Making Inferences Ask students to identify why, according to Betty Friedan, many women considered *The Feminine Mystique* to be a threat. *(The book challenged women's accepted ways of life and removed a level of comfort they had.)* **OL**

Answers and Additional Support

840

Primary Sources
Eyewitness to History

In the 1960s, feminism became a major issue on the national agenda. Many women had become disenchanted with their lives and turned their anger into a political movement. By the 1970s, the movement began to stall as conservative activists working against feminists rose to power.

SOURCE 1:

Betty Friedan helped start the women's movement of the 1960s by publishing The Feminine Mystique *in 1963. She argued that society had pressured women to ignore their intellect and to sacrifice themselves entirely to the needs of the family. In her 1976 memoir, Friedan recalled the reaction to her book.*

The emotions that book stirred up in women were not simple. In addition to the dozens, then hundreds, by now thousands of letters of relief, I received many angry letters from women. In fact, I would hear of cocktail parties being broken up by women arguing over my book. . . .

A woman called in to a television program in Detroit where I was publicizing the book. "Tell her to go back and take care of her own children and stop putting ideas into my daughter's head," the woman sputtered angrily. "Being a mother is all women were meant to be; I would never leave any child of mine with a babysitter." Thinking to suggest she might feel different a little later, I said, "How old is your youngest child?" "Twenty-three," said the lifelong mother. . . .

I got very few angry letters from men. From the very beginning, there was much less hostility from men than one might have expected. Many women told me their husbands had bought *The Feminine*

▲ *Founders of NOW, Chairman of the Board Dr. Kathryn F. Clarenbach and President Betty Friedan*

Mystique for them to read. It was much more of a threat to women—the challenge, the possibility, the risk and test of moving in society as a person on one's own—than to their husbands. From the beginning, many men seemed to sense that women's liberation would liberate them. It was women who felt the fear—and the relief.

SOURCE 2:

The National Organization for Women (NOW), co-founded by Friedan in 1966, formed chiefly to fight gender discrimination in the workplace. Its statement of purpose asked for women's full involvement in American society and an equal partnership with men.

We, men and women who hereby constitute ourselves as the National Organization for Women, believe that the time has come for a new movement toward true equality for all women in America, and toward a fully equal partnership of the sexes, as part of the world-wide revolution of human rights now taking place within and beyond our national borders.

The purpose of NOW is to take action to bring women into full participation in the mainstream of American society now, exercising all the privileges and responsibilities thereof in truly equal partnership with men. . . .

UNIVERSAL ACCESS

Interpersonal Have students work in small groups to create time lines of key events and people in the women's rights movement, beginning with the era of Elizabeth Cady Stanton until today. As students conduct research for their time lines, challenge them to locate sources that illustrate differing and changing perspectives on the roles of women in society, the family, and the workplace. Encourage them to include a variety of primary and secondary sources, including printed publications, personal records, artifacts, quotations, and photographs. Display the time lines and have students analyze them to make inferences and generalizations about the effect of the women's movement on the role of women in society, the family, and the labor force. **OL**

NOW is dedicated to the proposition that women first and foremost are human beings, who, like all other people in our society, must have the chance to develop their fullest human potential. We believe that women can achieve such equality only by accepting to the full the challenges and responsibilities they share with all other people in our society, as part of the decision-making mainstream of American political, economic and social life. . . .

WE BELIEVE THAT women will do most to create a new image of women by *acting* now, and by speaking out in behalf of their own equality, freedom, and human dignity—not in pleas for special privilege, nor in **enmity**[1] toward men, who are also victims of the current half-equality between the sexes—but in an active, self-respecting partnership with men. By so doing, women will develop confidence in their own ability to determine actively, in partnership with men, the conditions of their life, their choices, their future and their society.

SOURCE 3:

Phyllis Schlafly a conservative attorney from Illinois, led the antifeminist movement. In her 1977 book, The Power of the Positive Woman, *Schlafly stressed that women's liberation posed a threat to women.*

The Positive Woman starts with the assumption that the world is her oyster. She rejoices in the creative capability within her body and the power potential of her mind and spirit. She understands that men and women are different, and that those very differences provide the key to her success as a person and fulfillment as a woman.

The women's liberationist, on the other hand, is imprisoned by her own negative view of herself and of her place in the world around her. . . .

This is the self-articulated dog-in-the-manger, chip-on-the-shoulder, fundamental **dogma**[2] of the

[1]**enmity:** anger
[2]**dogma:** something presented as authoritative without proof

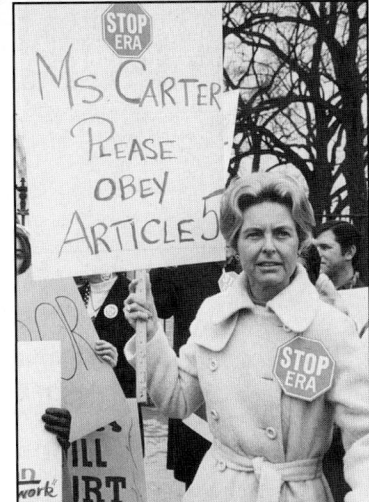
▲ *Phyllis Schlafly*

women's liberation movement. Someone—it is not clear who, perhaps God, perhaps the "Establishment," perhaps a conspiracy of male chauvinist pigs—dealt women a foul blow by making them female. It becomes necessary, therefore, for women to agitate and demonstrate and hurl demands on society in order to wrest from an oppressive male-dominated social structure the status that has been wrongfully denied to women through the centuries.

By its very nature, therefore, the women's liberation movement precipitates a series of conflict situations—in the legislatures, in the courts, in the schools, in industry—with man targeted as the enemy. Confrontation replaces cooperation as the watchword of all relationships. Women and men become adversaries instead of partners. . . .

. . . A Positive Woman cannot defeat a man in a wrestling or boxing match, but she can motivate him, inspire him, encourage him, teach him, restrain him, reward him, and have power over him that he can never achieve over her with all his muscle. How or whether a Positive Woman uses her power is determined solely by the way she alone defines her goals and develops her skills.

DBQ   Document-Based Questions

Historical Analysis   CA HI2; HI3

Source 1: How does Friedan describe the response of women and men to her book?

Source 2: What is the main goal of NOW?

Source 3: Why does Schlafly believe that women's liberation is a threat to women?

Comparing and Contrasting Sources
How do Friedan, Schlafly, and NOW differ in their descriptions on how women and men viewed each other?

C Critical Thinking

Analyzing Information Ask students to explain how NOW believes that women can achieve equality. *(by accepting the challenges and responsibilities of full membership in society and by participating in political, economic, and social decisions of American life)* OL

W Writing Support

Expository Writing Ask students to write a brief essay in which they compare and contrast "the Positive Woman" and "the women's liberationist," as Phyllis Schlafly describes them. Invite students to explain why they do or do not agree with Schlafly's perspective. OL CA 11RC2.5

U Universal Access

Visual/Spatial Have students draw upon Schlafly's description of the Positive Woman to create a poster or cartoon that illustrates the Positive Woman's characteristics and powers. Point out to students that their cartoons may either satirize or support Schlafly's description. EL

ASSESS/CLOSE

Have students answer the Document-Based Questions.

DBQ   Document-Based Questions

1. Many women responded in anger; in contrast, men encouraged their wives to read the book.
2. The organization's goal is "to bring women into full participation in the mainstream of American society."
3. Schlafly says that women's liberation imprisons women in negative self-views and places women in a series of conflicts, namely against men, thus making men and women enemies instead of partners.

Comparing and Contrasting Sources: Friedan sees women in isolated roles as mothers and wives; NOW describes the goal of women and men in an equal partnership; Schlafly views women and men as very different from each other—a difference that should be used to women's advantage.

Reviewing Content Vocabulary

Students' answers will vary. The pages where the words appear in the text are shown in parentheses.

1. counterculture *(p. 809)* 2. commune *(p. 809)* 3. feminism *(p. 814)* 4. Title IX *(p. 817)* 5. affirmative action *(p. 825)* 6. busing *(p. 826)* 7. bilingualism *(p. 829)* 8. smog *(p. 834)* 9. fossil fuel *(p. 835)*

Reviewing Academic Vocabulary

Students' answers will vary. The pages where the words appear in the text are shown in parentheses.

10. validate *(p. 809)* 11. rational *(p. 809)* 12. derive *(p. 811)* 13. gender *(p. 814)* 14. integral *(p. 814)* 15. bias *(p. 815)* 16. federal *(p. 825)* 17. contract *(p. 825)* 18. guarantee *(p. 830)* 19. publication *(p. 834)* 20. nonetheless *(p. 834)* 21. consequence *(p. 835)*

Standards 11.3, 11.3.4, 11.6.5, 11.8.6, 11.9.4, 11.9.7, 11.10.2, 11.10.4, 11.10.5, 11.10.7, 11.11.1, 11.11.3, 11.11.5, 11.11.7

Reviewing Content Vocabulary

On a sheet of paper, use each of these terms in a sentence.

1. counterculture
2. commune
3. feminism
4. Title IX
5. affirmative action
6. busing
7. bilingualism
8. smog
9. fossil fuel

Reviewing Academic Vocabulary

On a sheet of paper, use each of these terms in a sentence that reflects the term's meaning in the chapter.

10. validate
11. rational
12. derive
13. gender
14. integral
15. bias
16. federal
17. contract
18. guarantee
19. publication
20. nonetheless
21. consequence

Reviewing the Main Ideas

Section 1

22. What was the Free Speech Movement?

Section 2

23. How did Title VII of the Civil Rights Act of 1964 promote women's equality?

Section 3

24. How did Native Americans expand their political rights and economic opportunities in the 1960s and 1970s?

Section 4

25. How did the environmental movement begin?

Critical Thinking

26. **Reading Skill** **Evaluating** Reread "A Protest Movement Emerges" on pages 829–830. How did you react to this passage? Did your opinion of Native American protests change?

27. **Civics** Examine the 1978 Supreme Court's decision on preferential college admissions in *Regents of the University of California v. Bakke*. Do you agree or disagree with the Court's decision? Explain your position.

28. **Analyzing** In what ways did the counterculture movement change American society?

29. **Drawing Conclusions** Why do you think so many protest movements emerged in the United States during the 1960s and 1970s?

Chapter Summary

Speaking Out for Equality

Youth Movement	Women's Movement	Minority Groups	Environmental and Consumer Groups
Protests Status Quo	**Regains Momentum**	**Continue the Fight**	**New Concerns Emerge**
• Grows out of earlier "beat" movement	• Fights for equal economic rights in workplace and society	• Expand on earlier success and speed up access to previous gains	• First Earth Day sparks widespread awareness of environmental issues
• Becomes increasingly influential as "baby boom" generation matures	• Demands equal opportunities in education	• Affirmative Action advocates equality in work environment for minority and disadvantaged groups	• Federal government establishes pollution standards and begins monitoring environmental problems
• Protests injustices facing African Americans, the poor, and the disadvantaged	• *Roe* v. *Wade* expands access to abortion	• Native Americans gain more power on reservations and fight discrimination, unemployment, police brutality, and poverty	• State and federal legislatures pass laws regulating the safety standards for a wide variety of consumer products
• Free Speech Movement establishes tactics of boycotting college classes and occupying buildings		• Hispanic Americans lobby for better working conditions and job training	
• Hippie counterculture rebels against system, visualizes utopian ideals			

842 CHAPTER 18 The Politics of Protest

Reviewing the Main Ideas

22. Student protesters from the University of California at Berkeley opposed university restrictions of freedom of speech and the right to assemble. They protested with a campus-wide strike and by occupying buildings.

23. Title VII outlawed job discrimination on the basis of gender as well as of race, color, religion, and national origin.

24. By protesting, Native Americans helped get legislation passed that provided education assistance, land and water rights, the right to tax reservations, and other sovereign functions.

25. The environmental movement began with the Earth Day celebration.

HISTORY Online

Self-Check Quiz

Visit the *American Vision: Modern Times* Web site at tav.mt.glencoe.com and click on *Self-Check Quizzes—Chapter 18* to assess your knowledge of chapter content.

30. Organizing Use a graphic organizer to list the protest movements of the 1960s and 1970s and their goals.

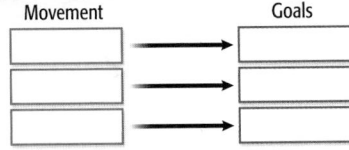

Writing About History

31. **Historical Analysis** **Historical Connections** Research Rachel Carson's *Silent Spring*. What connections can you make between its publication and the environmental laws of the 1970s? CA HI1

32. Big Idea Write an article for your local newspaper about student protests in the 1960s and 1970s. Explain the reasons for the protests.

DBQ **Document-Based Questions**

33. Interpreting Primary Sources In 1965 the National Farm Workers Association founded by César Chávez staged a strike against grape growers from Delano. Read the excerpt from *The Plan of Delano* and answer the following questions.

❝ . . . We seek our basic, God-given rights as human beings. . . . We are ready to give up everything, even our lives in our fight for social justice. We shall do it without violence because that is our destiny. . . .

. . . We will strike. . . . We are poor, we are humble, and our only choice is to strike in those ranches where we are not treated with the respect we deserve as working men, where our rights as free and sovereign men are not recognized. . . . We want to be equal with all the working men in the nation; we want a just wage, better working conditions, a decent future for our children. To those who oppose us . . . we say that we are going to continue fighting until we die, or we win. We Shall Overcome. ❞

a. What groups would oppose the strike?

b. Can you make a connection between this strike and the civil rights movement? What is similar or different?

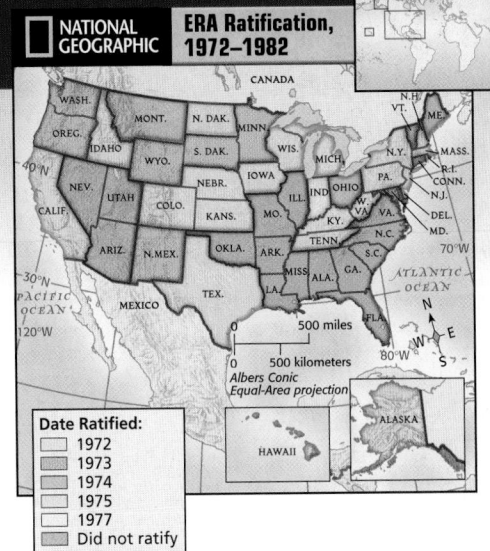

NATIONAL GEOGRAPHIC **ERA Ratification, 1972–1982**

Date Ratified:
- 1972
- 1973
- 1974
- 1975
- 1977
- Did not ratify

Geography and History

34. The map above shows the states that ratified the ERA. Study the map and answer the questions below.

a. Interpreting Maps How many states had ratified the Equal Rights Amendment by 1977?

b. Applying Geography Skills What conclusion can you draw about the distribution of states that did not approve the ERA?

Standards Practice

Directions: Choose the phrase that best completes the following sentence.

35. Congress did not act on the first proposed Equal Rights Amendment because

A the amendment did not do enough to protect women and children.

B the National Woman's Party opposed the amendment.

C the amendment lacked support due to a divided women's movement.

D the amendment did not address discrimination by gender.

Standard 11.10.7: Analyze the women's rights movement from the era of Elizabeth Stanton and Susan Anthony and the passage of the Nineteenth Amendment to the movement launched in the 1960s, including differing perspectives on the roles of women.

HISTORY Online

Have students visit the Web site at tav.mt.glencoe.com to review Chapter 18 and take the Self-Check Quiz.

Writing About History

31. **Historical Analysis** Students will make the connection that Rachel Carson's *Silent Spring* was written in 1962 before the environmental laws of the 1970s. Students should describe the connection between the book and the environmental movement.

32. Big Idea Students' articles will vary but should identify students' protests.

DBQ **Document-Based Questions**

33. a. the grape growers **b.** Both movements operated with nonviolent resistance and wanted equality.

Geography and History

34. a. 35 states had ratified the ERA by 1977. **b.** States that did not ratify the ERA tended to be in the more socially conservative and rural areas of the country.

Standards Practice

35. C

Bonus Question ?

Ask: Who was the first African American woman to serve in Congress? *(Shirley Chisholm)*

Critical Thinking

26. **Reading Skill** Students' opinions will vary.

27. Students need to support their argument for or against *Regents of the University of California v. Bakke,* providing valid arguments.

28. Over time, mainstream America accepted many of the ideas of the counterculture. Individuality and self-expression became more accepted. Counterculture styles of clothing, art, music, and dance came to be considered normal.

29. Answers will vary. Students should note the relative prosperity of many Americans and the growing sense of disillusionment on the part of groups left out of social, economic, and political life.

30. Youth: improve the political and social system; Women: women's rights; Hispanics: voting and economic rights; Native Americans: economic opportunities and independence; Environment: protect the environment

Unit 6 Resources

Teaching the Unit

Use the information on these pages to help you teach Unit 6.

History–Social Science Standards Covered in Unit 6

Standard	Chapter 19	20	21
11.3 Students analyze the role religion played in the founding of America, its lasting moral, social, and political impacts, and issues regarding religious liberty.	✔	✔	
11.8 Students analyze the economic boom and social transformation of post–World War II America.	✔	✔	✔
11.9 Students analyze U.S. foreign policy since World War II.	✔	✔	✔
11.11 Students analyze the major social problems and domestic policy issues in contemporary American society.	✔	✔	✔

Pacing Your Lessons

This pacing chart provides time management suggestions for teaching Unit 6.

	Days
Unit 6 Introduction	1
Chapter 19 • **Reading Skill:** Using Problem/Solution • **Historical Analysis Skill:** Interpreting Events • **Sections 1–4** • **What Life Was Like:** Disco • **Eyewitness to History:** Primary Source Documents	9
Chapter 20 • **Reading Skill:** Comparing and Contrasting • **Historical Analysis Skill:** Analyzing Migration • **Sections 1–4** • **National Geographic:** Geography & History: Urban America on the Move • **American Literature:** *Hunger of Memory* by Richard Rodriguez • **Why It Matters:** Strait of Hormuz • **Eyewitness to History:** Primary Source Documents	9
Chapter 21 • **Reading Skill:** Monitoring and Clarifying • **Historical Analysis Skill:** Relating Current Events • **Sections 1–5** • **Looking Back:** Representative Government • **Eyewitness to History:** Primary Source Documents	9

Teacher to Teacher

Honing Research Skills

This activity helps students understand some of the significant events that happened at the end of the twentieth century, as well as learn how to find relevant information using library and Internet resources.

List 10 to 15 significant events discussed in this unit. Students, working alone or in pairs, will choose one event and create either a Web page or a PowerPoint® presentation. Before beginning research, walk students through the library's reference materials. The reference librarian can help students learn how to research on the Internet and to use other online resources.

The final PowerPoint® presentation or Web page should be turned in as a computer file to the teacher. The teacher can then use the presentation with other classes or allow the students to make the presentation.

Linda Kelley
Connally High School
Waco, Texas

Previewing the Chapters

Dear American History Teacher:

As you begin to teach this unit, there are themes that recur throughout the chapters that you will want to point out to students.

The last unit in this textbook offers some unique opportunities for connecting students to the major themes of American history. The trends and events that this unit covers occurred during their lifetimes and may have directly affected them. This unit deals with sweeping changes, both nationally and globally, at the end of the twentieth century. It follows political and demographic shifts within the United States, as well as the collapse of the Soviet Union and the end of the Cold War.

In studying this unit, most students can readily relate to the development of personal computers and the rise of the Internet. They can recall a recent election that was in the news. Most students will have memories of the tragic events on September 11, 2001. Such personal links should enable them to better understand the impact of earlier forms of science and technology, of previous elections, and of other traumatic national events. You might consider teaching the material from the last chapter first to frame the past through students' present experiences.

Donald A. Ritchie

Chapter 19: Politics and Economics, 1971–1980

(pages 846–881)

President Nixon, elected in 1968, worked to ease international tensions caused by the Cold War. The Watergate scandal led Nixon to resign in 1974 and damaged Americans' trust in the government. The 1970s were also marked by recession and an energy crisis resulting from an oil embargo. Both Presidents Ford and Carter had little success in repairing the economy.

Chapter 20: Resurgence of Conservatism, 1980–1992

(pages 882–925)

President Ronald Reagan was elected in 1980. Reagan, believing in a smaller government, cut social service programs, deregulated industry, and issued tax cuts. During Reagan's two-term presidency, the country had the largest military buildup ever seen in peacetime. Meanwhile, economic recovery, new technology, and new social problems brought a change in American culture. The Cold War finally ended in the early 1990s when the Communist Soviet Union collapsed.

Chapter 21: Into a New Century, 1992–present

(pages 926–965)

The 1990s were a time of prosperity. Democrat Bill Clinton won the 1992 election against incumbent President George Bush. Clinton passed reforms for health care and welfare, but his second term was tainted by personal problems. A technological revolution increased communication across the globe. The United States benefited from major developments in medicine and agriculture. New trade agreements were made between nations, and a new global economy emerged. George W. Bush won the presidency in the controversial race of 2000. In September 2001, the United States was attacked by terrorists, which led to a war in Afghanistan. In 2003 President Bush began a controversial war in Iraq that exhibited the political divisions in the United States. However, these decades have also shown that the nations of the world are interdependent, and that international conflicts and the use of natural resources are of concern to all of us.

FOCUS

History– Social Science Standards

This unit addresses the following main standards:

11.9 Students analyze U.S. foreign policy since World War II.

11.11 Students analyze the major social problems and domestic policy issues in contemporary American society.

Connecting to Past Learning

In Unit 5 students learned about the turmoil of protests and reforms in the United States between 1954 and 1980. In Unit 6 students will learn about the political and economic changes in the modern United States and the differing global role of the country in the twenty-first century.

Unit Launch Activity

Ask students to pick a major event that occurred between 1968 and the present. Each student should conduct research on that event and write a three-page report detailing the significance of the event in this period of American history. Students also should explain why they chose this event. **OL**

Why It Matters Activity

Have students write down one fact they know or opinion they have about each of the following presidents: Ronald Reagan, George H.W. Bush, Bill Clinton, and George W. Bush. Have volunteers share their statements with the class, and ask the class to identify each statement as fact or opinion. **BL**

844

UNIT 6
A Changing Society

1968–Present

Why It Matters

A reassessment of postwar developments marked the last three decades of the twentieth century. The Cold War ended and political boundaries were redrawn. The United States remained a global force, but the role of the federal government was diminished in the wake of scandal and a renewed conservatism. As the United States entered a new century, the nation continued to redefine itself. The country's social diversity posed new challenges and provided new strength to the nation. Understanding the shifts of this period will help prepare you for your future. The following resources offer more information about this time in American history.

Primary Sources Library

See pages 978–981 for primary source readings to accompany Unit 6.

Use the **American History Primary Source Document Library CD-ROM** to find additional primary sources about imperialism and progressivism.

844

Handheld computer and stylus

New Yorkers celebrate the millennium, January 1, 2000

TEAM TEACHING ACTIVITY

MICROCHIPS Invite the science or technology teacher to share with students the basic makeup of a microchip and explain how we use microchips in a variety of products daily. As part of the discussion, have the class create a list of all the products they use that include microchip technology. Encourage class members to add to the list as they study this unit. **BL**

> "I was not elected to serve one party, but to serve one nation."
>
> —George W. Bush, 2001

TEACH

Reading Strategy

Questioning Tell students to read the quote by George W. Bush on this page. **Ask: What were the circumstances surrounding this statement?** *(Students should remember that this statement refers to the contested presidential election in 2000. George W. Bush made it after Al Gore conceded the election, following several weeks of vote counting.)* **OL**

Skill Practice

Visual Literacy The celebration in New York's Times Square at the beginning of the year 2000 was a significant milestone for many people. **Ask: What made the arrival of 2000 a significant celebration, more important than other years?** *(Students should note that people celebrated the start of a new millennium, even though the next millennium actually would not begin until the following New Year's Eve.)* **OL**

NC LB — NO CHILD LEFT BEHIND

Teaching Tip The NCLB Act emphasizes reading. Ask students to write down events and people they will encounter in this unit and keep the list with them as they read. When students find a person or item on the list, they should note the page number and write a brief summary. Students can use this list while studying.

UNIVERSAL ACCESS

English Learners If you have students who recently moved to the United States from other countries, ask them to describe how the country of their birth celebrates the coming of a new year. Discuss the similarities and differences between this celebration and the one shown in New York City. **EL**

Auditory/Musical Play the song "Auld Lang Syne" for the class and have student write down the lyrics as they listen. Discuss what the song lyrics mean. Ask students why they believe this song has become a traditional song for New Year's Eve. **BL**

Chapter 19 Planning Guide

SECTION RESOURCES

Main Ideas	📁 Print Materials	Technology Resources
Section 1: The Nixon Administration 1. Nixon won the 1968 election by appealing to a "silent majority" of conservatives. 2. With the support of national security adviser Henry Kissinger, Nixon forged better relationships with China and the Soviet Union.	• Reproducible Lesson Plan 19-1* • Daily Lecture and Discussion Notes 19-1 • Active Reading Note-Taking Guide 19-1 • Guided Reading Activity 19-1 • Section Quiz 19-1 • Reading Essentials and Study Guide 19-1	🖐 Daily Focus Skills Transparency 19-1 🖐 Section Graphic Organizer Transparency 19-1 💿 Interactive Tutor Self-Assessment CD-ROM 💿 ExamView® Pro Testmaker CD-ROM 💿 Presentation Plus! CD-ROM 🖐 California Standards Practice Transparencies
Section 2: The Watergate Scandal 1. President Nixon sought reelection amid a scandal over the Watergate break-in. 2. After the televised 1973 Watergate hearings in the Senate, President Nixon resigned from office. 3. The Watergate scandal eroded public confidence in the federal government.	• Reproducible Lesson Plan 19-2* • Daily Lecture and Discussion Notes 19-2 • Active Reading Note-Taking Guide 19-2 • Guided Reading Activity 19-2 • Section Quiz 19-2 • Reading Essentials and Study Guide 19-2	🖐 Daily Focus Skills Transparency 19-2 🖐 Section Graphic Organizer Transparency 19-2 💿 Interactive Tutor Self-Assessment CD-ROM 💿 ExamView® Pro Testmaker CD-ROM 💿 Presentation Plus! CD-ROM 🖐 California Standards Practice Transparencies
Section 3: Ford and Carter 1. Inflation, a stagnant economy, and an oil embargo created an economic crisis during the 1970s. 2. Gerald Ford attempted to fight inflation at home and sought détente abroad. 3. Despite trying several strategies, Carter could not solve the problem of inflation. 4. Carter attempted to craft a moral foreign policy in the Middle East and Latin America.	• Reproducible Lesson Plan 19-3* • Daily Lecture and Discussion Notes 19-3 • Active Reading Note-Taking Guide 19-3 • Guided Reading Activity 19-3 • Section Quiz 19-3 • Reading Essentials and Study Guide 19-3	🖐 Daily Focus Skills Transparency 19-3 🖐 Section Graphic Organizer Transparency 19-3 💿 Interactive Tutor Self-Assessment CD-ROM 💿 ExamView® Pro Testmaker CD-ROM 💿 Presentation Plus! CD-ROM 🖐 California Standards Practice Transparencies
Section 4: The "Me" Decade: Life in the 1970s 1. During the 1970s, Americans turned to new spiritual movements to find meaning in their lives. 2. Television sitcoms began dealing with more difficult aspects of American life, and disco swept the country.	• Reproducible Lesson Plan 19-4* • Daily Lecture and Discussion Notes 19-4 • Active Reading Note-Taking Guide 19-4 • Guided Reading Activity 19-4 • Section Quiz 19-4 • Reading Essentials and Study Guide 19-4	🖐 Daily Focus Skills Transparency 19-4 🖐 Section Graphic Organizer Transparency 19-4 💿 Interactive Tutor Self-Assessment CD-ROM 💿 ExamView® Pro Testmaker CD-ROM 💿 Presentation Plus! CD-ROM 🖐 California Standards Practice Transparencies

PACING YOUR LESSONS

Chapter Introduction	Section 1	Section 2	Section 3	Section 4	Chapter Assessment
½ Day	2 Days	2 Days	2 Days	2 Days	½ Day

`0:00` **OUT OF TIME?** 📁 Assign the Chapter 19 *Reading Essentials and Study Guide.*

*Available on TeacherWorks™ CD-ROM

Chapter 19 Planning Guide

Standards-Based Lesson Plan

 History–Social Science Standards Covered in Chapter 19

The standards covered in the chapter are listed below. Use the accompanying activity as you teach the chapter to ensure student mastery of these standards. This activity can be used in combination with the program's print and technology assessment materials.

Standard	Section 1	Section 2	Section 3	Section 4
11.8.4 Analyze new federal government spending on defense, welfare, interest on the national debt, and federal and state spending on education, including the California Master Plan.	✔			
11.8.8 Discuss forms of popular culture, with emphasis on their origins and geographic diffusion (e.g., jazz and other forms of popular music, professional sports, architectural and artistic styles).				✔
11.9.3 Trace the origins and geopolitical consequences (foreign and domestic) of the Cold War and containment policy, including the following: the era of McCarthyism, instances of domestic Communism (e.g., Alger Hiss) and blacklisting; the Truman Doctrine; the Berlin Blockade; the Korean War; the Bay of Pigs invasion and the Cuban Missile Crisis; atomic testing in the American West, the "mutual assured destruction" doctrine, and disarmament policies; the Vietnam War; Latin American policy.	✔		✔	
11.11.2 Discuss the significant domestic policy speeches of Truman, Eisenhower, Kennedy, Johnson, Nixon, Carter, Reagan, Bush, and Clinton (e.g., with regard to education, civil rights, economic policy, environmental policy).	✔		✔	
11.11.4 Explain the constitutional crisis originating from the Watergate scandal.		✔	✔	

Cumulative Standards-Assessment Activity

The Cumulative Standards-Assessment Activity will help students organize and learn the important information from the chapter. Begin teaching the chapter with this activity, and have students complete it as they read the chapter.

CREATING AN OUTLINE

Purpose Outlining is a useful skill for both taking notes and writing papers. When studying written material, outlining can help students understand the structure of the writing and the relationship among the ideas, which, in turn, enables them to absorb the material. Outlining requires students to place information in a logical order and is a good starting point when writing a paper.

Introduction to Outlining

1. Review with the class the steps in creating an outline:
   - Write only words and phrases needed, not complete sentences.
   - Note related but less important details under the main ideas.
   - For formal outlines, label the main heads with Roman numerals (I, II), subheads with capital letters (A, B), and details with Arabic numerals (1, 2).
   - Include at least two entries for each level of heading.
   - Indent each level.
   - Be grammatically consistent.

2. Ask students to copy this structure in their notebooks:

I. _____
  A. _____
    1. _____
    2. _____
  B. _____
    1. _____
    2. _____
II. _____
  A. _____
    1. _____
    2. _____

Have students outline the content of each section as they read. Remind them that at least two points for each level is suggested, but some topics may require more points.

3. Urge students to use their outlines to help them review the chapter.

Chapter 19 Planning Guide

READING SUPPORT

- Content Vocabulary Activity 19
- Academic Vocabulary Activity 19
- Reading Skills Activity 19
- Chapter 19 Active Reading Note-Taking Guide
- Chapter 19 Guided Reading Activities
- Chapter 19 Reading Essentials and Study Guide
- *The American Vision: Modern Times* Video Program
- Vocabulary PuzzleMaker CD-ROM
- American History Primary Source Document Library CD-ROM

CRITICAL THINKING

- Critical Thinking Skills Activity 19
- Primary Source Reading 19
- Cause-and-Effect Transparency 19 Strategy and Activity
- Presentation Plus! CD-ROM

UNIVERSAL ACCESS

- Universal Access Activity 19
- English Learner Activity 19
- American Art Prints
- StudentWorks™ Plus CD-ROM
- American Music: Hits Through History
- School-to-Home Connection Activity 19

SKILL PRACTICE

- Map Overlay Transparency 19 Strategy and Activity
- Historical Analysis Skills Activity 19
- Time Line Activity 19
- Reading Skills Activity 19
- Reinforcing Skills Activity 19
- Linking Past and Present Activity 19
- Interpreting Political Cartoons 19
- History Simulations and Problem Solving, Unit 6
- MindJogger Videoquiz

WRITING SUPPORT

- Chapter 19 Active Reading Note-Taking Guide
- Writer's Guidebook
- High School Writing Process Transparencies

ASSESSMENT

- Chapter 19 Section Quizzes
- Chapter 19 Tests, Forms A and B
- Authentic Assessment Activity 19
- ExamView® Pro Testmaker CD-ROM
- Interactive Tutor Self-Assessment CD-ROM
- California Standards Practice, Grade 11
- Succeeding on . . .™ the California Standards: Grade 11 History–Social Science CD-ROM

- CD-ROM
- DVD
- Print Material
- Poster
- Transparency
- Music Program
- Videocassette

Chapter 19 Planning Guide

TECHNOLOGY

- StudentWorks™ Plus CD-ROM
- TeacherWorks™ CD-ROM
- ExamView® Pro Testmaker CD-ROM
- Interactive Tutor Self-Assessment CD-ROM
- Presentation Plus! CD-ROM
- Vocabulary PuzzleMaker CD-ROM
- American History Primary Source Document Library CD-ROM
- MindJogger Videoquiz
- *The American Vision: Modern Times* Video Program
- Professional Development in High School Social Studies Video Series
- Teach, Use, and Succeed With *The American Vision: Modern Times*
- American Music: Hits Through History
- Succeeding on . . .™ the California Standards: Grade 11 History–Social Science CD-ROM

SPANISH RESOURCES

- Spanish Activities and Assessment
  - Spanish Vocabulary Activities
  - Spanish Guided Reading Activities
  - Spanish Quizzes and Tests
  - Spanish Reteaching Activities
- Spanish Reading Essentials and Study Guide
- Spanish School-to-Home Connection Activities

TRANSPARENCIES

- Daily Focus Skills Transparencies
- Section Graphic Organizer Transparencies
- Map Overlay Transparencies
- Cause-and-Effect Transparencies
- Unit Time Line Transparencies
- Why It Matters Transparencies
- American Art and Architecture Transparencies
- High School Writing Process Transparencies
- California Standards Practice Transparencies

TEACHER PLANNING

- Daily Lecture and Discussion Notes
- English Learner Handbook
- Building Academic Vocabulary
- *The American Vision: Modern Times* Reading and Study Skills Foldables
- Reading Strategies and Activities for the Social Studies Classroom
- Universal Access for the American History Classroom
- NGS United States Desk Map
- NGS World Atlas
- Chapter 19 Reproducible Lesson Plans on TeacherWorks™ CD-ROM
- California Guide to Daily Intervention

PROFESSIONAL DEVELOPMENT

- Building Academic Vocabulary
- Strategies for Success
- Research-Based Strategies Used to Develop *The American Vision: Modern Times*
- Character Education in the High School Classroom
- Professional Development in High School Social Studies Video Series
- Teach, Use, and Succeed With *The American Vision: Modern Times*

MOMENTS IN TIME

The following resource can help you teach the content of this chapter.

- Unit 13 The Watergate Crisis (1971–1974)

Chapter 19 Planning Guide

TEACHER'S CORNER

Index to National Geographic Magazine:
The following articles relate to this chapter:

- "Great Lakes: Troubled Water," July 1987
- "Our Polluted Runoff," February 1996

National Geographic Society Products:
To order the following, call National Geographic at 1–800–368–2728

- *Branches of Government Series* (Video)
- *Democratic Government Series: The United States* (Video)
- *Historical Atlas of the United States* (Atlas)

NGS ONLINE

Access National Geographic's new dynamic MapMachine Web site and other geography resources at:

www.nationalgeographic.com

www.nationalgeographic.com/maps

MASTERING THE STANDARDS

The content and assessment in the Student Edition, Teacher Wraparound Edition, teacher planning materials, and the print and technology products are all standards-based. The use of these products during instruction leads to mastery of the standards.

PRACTICE
- California Standards Practice, Grade 11
- California Standards Practice Transparencies
- School-to-Home Connection

BENCHMARK ASSESSMENT
- Section Quizzes, Chapter Tests, and Authentic Assessment
- Exam*View*® Pro Testmaker CD-ROM
- Succeeding On . . . ™ the California Standards: Grade 11 History–Social Science CD-ROM

REMEDIATION
- California Guide to Daily Intervention
- Interactive Tutor Self-Assessment CD-ROM
- Exam*View*® Pro Testmaker CD-ROM
- California Standards Practice, Grade 11
- Reading Essentials and Study Guide

Use our Web site for additional resources. All essential content is covered in the Student Edition.

You and your students can visit tav.mt.glencoe.com, the Web site companion to the **American Vision: Modern Times.** This innovative integration of electronic and print media offers your students a wealth of opportunities. The student text directs students to the Web site for the following options:

- **Chapter Overviews**
- **Self-Check Quizzes**
- **Student Web Activities**
- **Textbook Updates**

Answers to the student Web activities are provided for you in the **Web Activity Lesson Plans.** Additional Web resources and ePuzzles and games are also available.

Dinah Zike's Foldables

Foldables are three-dimensional, interactive graphic organizers that help students practice basic writing skills, review key vocabulary terms, and identify main ideas. Every chapter has a foldable activity in the *Dinah Zike's Reading and Study Skills Foldables* booklet. You can use the foldables as they are presented or modify them to suit the needs of your individual class.

A variety of videotape programs are available from A&E Television and The History Channel to provide teaching assistance. To order, call Glencoe at 1-800-334-7344.

Chapter 19 Planning Guide

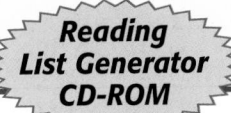
KEY for Using the Teacher Wraparound Edition

Use this key to help you identify the different types of prompts found in the Teacher Wraparound Edition.

R **Reading Strategies** activities help you teach reading skills and vocabulary.

C **Critical Thinking** strategies help students apply and extend what they have learned.

U **Universal Access** activities provide differentiated instruction for students learning to speak English, along with suggestions for teaching various types of learners.

S **Skill Practice** strategies help students practice historical analysis and geography skills.

W **Writing Support** activities provide writing opportunities to help students comprehend the text.

Teaching strategies and activities have been coded for ability level appropriateness.

AL Activities for students working above grade level
OL Activities for students working on grade level
BL Activities for students working below grade level
EL Activities for English learners

FOCUS

History–Social Science Standards

This chapter addresses the following main standards:

11.8 Students analyze the economic boom and social transformation of post–World War II America.

11.9 Students analyze U.S. foreign policy since World War II.

11.11 Students analyze the major social problems and domestic policy issues in contemporary American society.

BELLRINGER
SKILLBUILDER ACTIVITY

Tell students that President Nixon was a polarizing figure in American history. **Ask: What is your opinion of Richard Nixon, based on what you know of him before reading this chapter?** Have students write down their opinions and save them. After studying the Nixon presidency, have students compare their initial opinions with those they now hold.

TEACH

Thinking About the Big Ideas

As you begin teaching each section, use these questions and activities to focus on the Big Idea.

Section 1
The Nixon Administration

Essential Question: What are traditional values? Have student share their responses and write

---

CHAPTER 19

1971–1980

Politics and Economics

❧ *The Big Ideas* ❧

SECTION 1: The Nixon Administration

International competition can lead to conflict and cooperation. *President Nixon sought to restore law and order and traditional values at home and to ease Cold War tensions abroad.*

SECTION 2: The Watergate Scandal

Societies change over time. *During his second term, President Nixon became embroiled in a scandal that ultimately forced him to resign.*

SECTION 3: Ford and Carter

Social and economic crises lead to new roles for government. *During the 1970s, Presidents Gerald Ford and Jimmy Carter attempted to lead the United States through both domestic and foreign crises.*

SECTION 4: The "Me" Decade: Life in the 1970s

Societies change over time. *In the midst of widespread cynicism about their leaders and concerns about the economy, Americans sought fulfillment and escape during the 1970s.*

The *American Vision: Modern Times* **Video** *The Chapter 19 video, "The Watergate Break-In," examines the circumstances surrounding this scandal.*

1972
• Nixon visits China and the Soviet Union
• Watergate burglars arrested at Democratic National Committee headquarters

1973
• *Roe v. Wade* Supreme Court decision legalizes abortion
• Senate Watergate investigations begin
• OPEC price increases cause inflation

1974
• Nixon resigns
• Gerald Ford becomes president

United States PRESIDENTS
Nixon 1969–1974
Ford 1974–1977

1971   *1974*

World

1971
• People's Republic of China admitted to UN

1973
• Britain, Ireland, and Denmark join Common Market

1974
• India becomes world's sixth nuclear power

846

---

them below the question. **Then ask: How does the phrase "law and order" relate to these values?** *(Answers may include the idea that if people are taught to respect one another's rights and property as they are growing up, then they will be more likely to become law-abiding citizens as they get older.)* **OL**

Section 2
The Watergate Scandal

Essential Question: Is character shaped by life experiences or is it inalienable? *(Some students may conclude that it is a mixture of both of these factors.)* Tell students that Section 2 will focus on how President Nixon's political scandal reflected his character. **OL**

President Nixon with Chinese premier Zhou Enlai (on Nixon's right) during Nixon's historic visit to China in 1972

1975
• President Ford signs Helsinki Accords

1976
• Jimmy Carter elected president

Carter
1977–1981

1977

1979
• Iranian revolutionaries seize U.S. embassy in Tehran

plant a
WIN
garden

NO
GAS

1980

1976
• Mao Zedong dies

1977
• Human rights manifesto signed by 241 Czech activists and intellectuals

1979
• Sandinista guerrillas overthrow dictatorship of Somoza

• Margaret Thatcher becomes prime minister of Great Britain

HISTORY
Online

Chapter Overview
Visit the *American Vision: Modern Times* Web site at tav.mt.glencoe.com and click on *Chapter Overviews–Chapter 19* to preview chapter information.

847

Section 3
Ford and Carter
Essential Question: If leaders face a crisis, should they respond quickly or consider all of the options? *(Students may conclude that it will depend on the nature of the crisis.)* Tell students that in Section 3 they will read about two presidents who faced many difficult choices and crises. OL

Section 4
The "Me" Decade: Life in the 1970s
Essential Question: What is individualism, and is it good or bad for society? *(It is a personal search for fulfillment. It could allow individuals to reach their full potential or make people selfish.)* This section will focus on the "Me" decade of the 1970s and will examine how cynicism about leaders and the economy fed this trend. OL

Cultural Perspectives

People respond in various ways to events and challenges facing their country and their society. The 1970s was dubbed the "me" decade in reference to many Americans' quest for greater individual satisfaction. Have students think about the issues or values that are foremost in the minds of many Americans today. **Ask: What do people value or view as important today? Why? What name might an observer use to characterize American society in the first decade of the twenty-first century?** OL

FOLDABLES™
Study Organizer

Dinah Zike's Foldables are three-dimensional, interactive graphic organizers that help students practice basic writing skills, review key vocabulary terms, and identify main ideas. Have students complete the foldable activity in the *Dinah Zike's Reading and Study Skills Foldables* booklet.

HISTORY
Online

Go to tav.mt.glencoe.com for student activities, lesson plans, and links to additional Web resources to help students learn about the politics and economics of the 1970s.

Why It's Important

The problem/solution strategy is an effective way to explain the decisions and the dilemmas of the historical time period surrounding those decisions. It is an important way to ensure that students understand that historical events are not inevitable and could have turned out differently had a different solution to a problem been attempted.

1. Introducing the Skill

Have students identify the problem, solution, and results of President Carter's energy policy and complete a chain-of-events chart similar to the one below. Discuss how the plan conflicted with the idea of energy deregulation. **Ask:** What about it was contradictory? OL

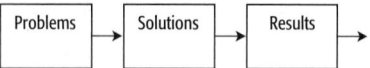

2. Extending the Skill

After discussing the reading selection and some of the reasons why Carter's energy plan did not work, have students complete a chain-of-events chart similar to the one above identifying other solutions Carter might have taken and possible results from a different energy plan. Discuss our nation's approach to energy issues today. AL

Answers and Additional Support

Preparing to Read Chapter 19

Reading Skill ◀ **Using Problem/Solution**

We first looked at problem/solution text structures in Chapter 6. You learned that solutions to problems are not always good ones. Still, it is important to understand how a person, government, or society arrived at a decision. Authors use the text structure of problem/solution to explain such decisions and the dilemmas of the time surrounding those decisions.

Effective readers look for signal words to recognize a problem/solution text structure. Signal words for a problem include *trouble, challenge, puzzle, difficulty, problem, question, crisis,* or *doubt.* Words such as *answer, solve, idea, agree, discovery, improve, propose, solution, overcome, resolve, response, decision,* or *reply* signal a solution.

Read the excerpt below and notice how the author has used problem/solution to explain how the government addressed the economic crisis in the 1970s.

USING PROBLEM/ SOLUTION

In this excerpt, signal words are underlined. The highlighted words provide clues about the outcome of the solution. Note that the phrase "did not solve" shows you the negative outcome of the problem.

[President] Carter felt that the nation's most serious <u>problem</u> was its dependence on foreign oil. . . . "Our <u>decision</u> about energy will test the character of the American people and the ability of the President and Congress to govern this nation," Carter stated.

Carter <u>proposed</u> a national energy program to conserve oil. . . .

Carter <u>agreed</u> to support deregulation but insisted on a "windfall profits tax" to <u>prevent</u> oil companies from overcharging consumers. The tax, however, **conflicted** with the basic <u>idea</u> of deregulation. . . . In the end, Carter's **contradictory** plan <u>did not solve</u> the country's energy crisis. (pages 867–868)

In the first sentence of the excerpt, you find a clear statement of the main problem—the nation's dependence on foreign oil. The proposed solution consists of a national energy program, deregulation, and a windfall profits tax. Finally, you read about the results, or outcome, of the solution. The author clearly states that the policies worked against each other and thus could not solve the crisis.

Apply the Skill

As you read about Nixon's foreign policy on pages 854–856 of your textbook, write down the problems and solutions Nixon wanted to address with his foreign policy. Note any signal words or other words that help define the problem and possible solutions. Also describe any outcome of his policy.

UNIVERSAL ACCESS

Below Level Have students use a dictionary to explain the relationship between the words *conflicted* and *contradictory.* (conflicted—beliefs that are very different and cannot easily exist together; contradictory—two ideas that are unable to be true at the same time) Ask students to write a paragraph describing a problem and a solution discussed in this chapter. Students should try to use the words *conflicted* and *contradictory* in the paragraph. BL

Historical Analysis Skill — Interpreting Events

Analysis Skill
Standard HI4

Historical Interpretation In order to understand the impact of historical events, you need to comprehend the meaning, implication, and impact of these events and recognize that events could have taken other directions.

In Chapter 5 you learned that historians consider how historical events could have unfolded differently if the participants in those events had made different choices. To understand the meaning, implication, and impact of historical events, historians examine the motives and actions of individuals or groups involved in those events. In the analysis of motives and actions, historians consider the participants' prior experiences and goals. Then historians determine the significance of the events. Based on what they have learned, they consider alternative directions the event could have taken. Thinking about alternatives helps historians gain a clearer understanding of events and people.

Read the following passages from your textbook about the events surrounding the Watergate investigation in 1973 and the choices President Nixon made as the events unfolded.

All the while, the White House strongly denied any involvement in the break-in. Nixon's press secretary dismissed the incident as a "third-rate burglary attempt," while the president himself told the American public, "The White House has had no involvement whatever in this particular incident." (page 859)

As the nation held its collective breath in anticipation, investigators finally found indisputable evidence against the president. One of the unedited tapes revealed that on June 23, 1972, just six days after the Watergate burglary, Nixon had ordered the CIA to stop the FBI's investigation of the break-in. With this news, even the president's strongest supporters conceded that impeachment and conviction in the Senate now seemed inevitable. (page 861)

Examine the actions of President Nixon, his press secretary, and the investigators. Based on the passage, what do you think were the motives of each? How might their motives have influenced their actions? What do you think might have happened had Nixon immediately admitted to, and apologized for, the Watergate break-in?

Apply the Skill

As you read about the Watergate scandal in Section 3, stop after each major heading and subheading. Consider the information you have read about the people involved in the scandal. Think about the choices each made and the circumstances surrounding the choices. Then consider how a different choice may have changed the events and the investigation.

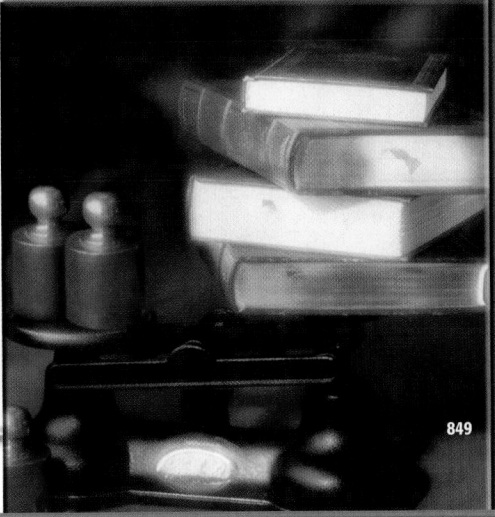
849

UNIVERSAL ACCESS

Advanced Learners As students read through this chapter, have them note events that can be interpreted in different, possibly opposite ways. Divide the class into groups of six. Ask each group to pick one of these events and create a short dramatic skit that demonstrates the possible different interpretations of this event. Students may wish to retell the historical event, or they might choose to display the choices surrounding that event from someone who witnessed the event. **AL**

Historical Analysis

Why It's Important
Students should understand that humans have free will to make the right decision and that those decisions shape the course of events. The Watergate scandal provides a perfect example of how individual action can make a great difference in the course of history.

1. Introducing the Skill
Ask students to recall any individuals in history who chose to make decisions based on their moral beliefs, despite the difficult obstacles they faced. *(possible answers include Martin Luther King, Jr., Oskar Schindler, Mohandas Gandhi)* **Ask: What does this reveal about the person's character? What does it tell us about the ability of one person to affect history?** Tell students to place their thoughts about these people in a chart similar to the one below. **OL**
CA HI4

Person	Thoughts

2. Extending the Skill
Have students discuss the pros and cons of telling the truth. **Ask: Is it always better to tell the truth, or is it sometimes better to keep something a secret?** *(Some may see the choice as situational, while others will view it in absolute terms.)* Divide the class into groups of three and ask them to find three moments in U.S. history where the group believes it was best to keep a secret. Ask each group to explain why they chose these moments and to describe how not keeping a secret might have changed events. **OL**

FOCUS

BELLRINGER
SKILLBUILDER ACTIVITY

Project **Daily Focus Skills Transparency 19-1** and have students answer the question.

Guide to Reading

Understanding Vocabulary:
Have students look up the meanings of the content vocabulary words and the academic vocabulary words in the glossary and use each word in a sentence.

Answers to Graphic:
Nixon Administration
Domestic   Foreign
  policy   policy
New Federalism   Détente

Unpacking the Standards

Students will be able to:

• Explain the factors that led to Nixon's victory in 1968 and his domestic agenda.

• Discuss Nixon's foreign policy achievements.

Answers and Additional Support

SECTION 1 | The Nixon Administration

Guide to Reading

Connection
In the previous chapter, you learned about the social, political, and environmental movements of the 1960s and 1970s. In this section, you will discover how President Nixon worked to restore traditional values at home and ease Cold War tensions abroad.

Main Idea
• Nixon won the 1968 election by appealing to a "silent majority" of conservatives. (p. 851)
• With the support of national security adviser Henry Kissinger, Nixon forged better relationships with China and the Soviet Union. (p. 854)

Content Vocabulary
revenue sharing, impound, détente, summit

Academic Vocabulary
supplement, notion, potential

People and Terms to Identify
Southern strategy, Henry Kissinger

Reading Objectives
• **Describe** Nixon's domestic agenda.
• **Discuss** Nixon's foreign policy achievements.

Reading Strategy
Organizing As you read about President Nixon's administration, complete a graphic organizer by listing his domestic and foreign policies.

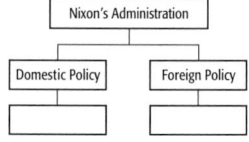

Preview of Events

◆1968	◆1970	◆1972	◆1974

1968
Nixon wins presidential election

1969
Nixon proposes Family Assistance Plan

February 1972
Nixon visits China

May 1972
Moscow hosts American-Soviet summit

The following are the main History–Social Science Standards covered in this section.

11.8.4 Analyze new federal government spending on defense, welfare, interest on the national debt, and federal and state spending on education, including the California Master Plan.

11.9.3 Trace the origins and geopolitical consequences (foreign and domestic) of the Cold War and containment policy, including the following: the era of McCarthyism, instances of domestic Communism (e.g., Alger Hiss) and blacklisting; the Truman Doctrine; the Berlin Blockade; the Korean War; the Bay of Pigs invasion and the Cuban Missile Crisis; atomic testing in the American West, the "mutual assured destruction" doctrine, and disarmament policies; the Vietnam War; Latin American policy.

⟡ The Big Idea ⟡

International competition can lead to conflict and cooperation. Richard Nixon won the 1968 presidential election by appealing to Southern states and a large number of conservative voters. As president, Nixon instituted his policy of New Federalism, finding ways to give state and local governments more control. The president also set out to improve relations with China and the Soviet Union. The U.S. policy of détente enabled the countries to cooperate with one another and led to the signing of a treaty limiting nuclear arms between the Soviet Union and the United States.

11.11.2 Discuss the significant domestic policy speeches of Truman, Eisenhower, Kennedy, Johnson, Nixon, Carter, Reagan, Bush, and Clinton (e.g., with regard to education, civil rights, economic policy, environmental policy).

11.11.6 Analyze the persistence of poverty and how different analyses of this issue influence welfare reform, health insurance reform, and other social policies.

11.11.7 Explain how the federal, state, and local governments have responded to demographic and social changes such as population shifts to the suburbs, racial concentrations in the cities, Frostbelt-to-Sunbelt migration, international migration, decline of family farms, increases in out-of-wedlock births, and drug abuse.

850 CHAPTER 19 Politics and Economics

SECTION RESOURCES

📁 Print Material
• Reproducible Lesson Plan 19-1
• Guided Reading Activity 19-1
• Reading Essentials and Study Guide 19-1
• Active Reading Note-Taking Guide 19-1

📊 Transparencies
• Daily Focus Skills Transparency 19-1
• Section Graphic Organizer Transparency 19-1

Technology
◎ Interactive Tutor Self-Assessment CD-ROM
◎ Exam*View*® Pro Testmaker CD-ROM
◎ Presentation Plus! CD-ROM

Appealing to Middle America

Main Idea Nixon won the 1968 election by appealing to a "silent majority" of conservatives.

Reading Connection Do you view your community as politically and socially liberal or conservative? Read on to find out about the strategies Nixon used to convince conservative Southerners to vote for him.

Many Americans longed for an end to the violence and turmoil that seemed to plague the nation in the 1960s.

★ An American Story ★

Millions of Americans saw police and demonstrators clash on the streets of Chicago at the Democratic National Convention in late August 1968. Many television viewers were outraged at the police tactics they saw. G.L. Halbert, however, was not one of them. To make his support of police efforts public, Halbert wrote a letter to *Newsweek* magazine:

66 Congratulations to Mayor Daley and the Chicago police on their tough handling of the yippies, Vietniks, and newsmen. If more mayors and police departments had the courage to crack down on those who carry only the flags of our enemies and newsmen who consistently slant their coverage of events in favor of those who would undermine and disrupt our country, there would be greater freedom for the majority of Americans rather than greater lawlessness for the few. It is a tragedy that such individuals are allowed to cringe behind our constitutional guarantees after they have wreaked destruction by their agitation. 99

—quoted in *Newsweek*, September 16, 1968

R₁ The views expressed by G.L. Halbert were not unusual. While they did not shout as loudly as the protesters, many Americans supported the government and desired change. The presidential candidate in 1968 who appealed to many of these frustrated citizens was Richard Nixon, a Republican. Nixon aimed many of his campaign messages at these Americans, whom he referred to as "Middle America" and the "silent majority." He promised them "peace with honor" in Vietnam, law and order, a streamlined government, and a return to more traditional values at home.

The Election of 1968 Nixon's principal opponent in the 1968 presidential election was Democrat Hubert Humphrey, who had served as vice president under Lyndon Johnson. Nixon also had to wage his campaign against a strong third-party candidate, George Wallace, an experienced Southern politician and avowed supporter of segregation. In a 1964 bid for the Democratic presidential nomination, the former Alabama governor had attracted considerable support.

On Election Day, Wallace captured an impressive 13.5 percent of the popular vote, the best showing of a third-party candidate since 1924. Nixon managed a victory, however, receiving 43.4 percent of the popular vote to Humphrey's 42.7 and 301 electoral votes to Humphrey's 191.

R₂ The Southern Strategy One of the keys to Nixon's victory was his surprisingly strong showing in the South. Even though the South had long been a Democratic stronghold, Nixon had refused to concede the region. To gain Southern support, Nixon had met with powerful South Carolina senator Strom Thurmond and won his backing by promising several things: to appoint only conservatives to the federal courts, to name a Southerner to the Supreme Court, to oppose court-ordered busing, and to choose a vice presidential candidate acceptable to the South. (Nixon ultimately chose Spiro Agnew, governor of the border state of Maryland.)

Nixon's efforts paid off on Election Day. Large numbers of white Southerners deserted the Democratic Party, granting Humphrey only one victory in that region—in Lyndon Johnson's home state of Texas. While Wallace claimed most of the states in the Deep South, Nixon captured Virginia, Tennessee, Kentucky, and North Carolina. Senator Strom Thurmond's support delivered his state of South Carolina for the Republicans as well.

▼ *Students and police clash at the 1968 Democratic National Convention*

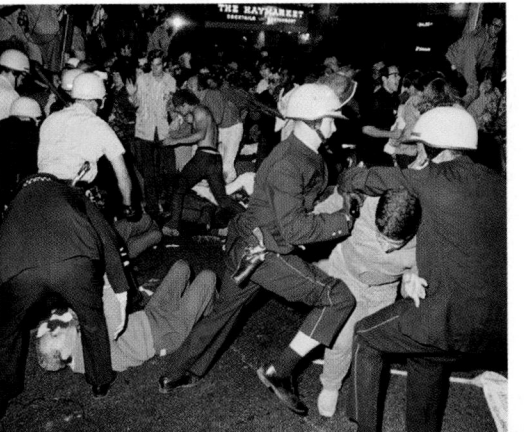

R₁ Reading Strategy

Making Inferences Have students speculate what they think Nixon meant when he referred to "Middle America" and the "silent majority." *(The large number of politically moderate Americans frustrated with radical dissent.)* **Ask:** Why did Nixon feel this was an important audience for him in his presidential campaign? *(They were likely to vote for him as a moderate candidate.)* **OL** **CA** 11RC2.4

R₂ Reading Strategy

Activating Prior Knowledge Analyze the background of Nixon's "Southern strategy" by having students recall from the post-Civil War Reconstruction period the reason the Democratic Party became strong in the South. *(During Reconstruction, Republicans sought to radically change Southern society. White Southerners joined the Democratic Party, which promised to uphold Southern traditional values.)* **OL**

More Skill Practice

English Learners Have students draw pictures or icons to represent the content vocabulary for this section. Then have them use at least one of their drawings in a political cartoon to illustrate an event, concept, or issue discussed in this section. Tell students to write an explanation or caption under the cartoon. **EL**

Geography *Skills*

Answers:
1. Midwest and West
2. If a candidate has only a plurality in a state's popular vote, he or she still receives all of its electoral votes.

Geography Skills Practice
Which New England states voted for Nixon? (*New Hampshire and Vermont*) Which Western state voted for Humphrey? (*Washington*)

R Reading Strategy

Scaffolding—Evaluating Nixon worked hard during the election to appeal to the South, a region that had voted for the Democratic Party for the last several elections. **Ask: How did Nixon strive to fulfill his promises to powerful Southern supporters after the election?** *(He tried to slow desegregation efforts started by previous presidential administrations and the Supreme Court.)*

OL

This **Reading Skill** was introduced in Chapter 18.

S Skill Practice

Scaffolding—Showing Connections Working in pairs, ask students to explain why the Burger Court may have disappointed some conservatives. **Ask: What did the conservatives expect? Were their expectations unrealistic? Why or why not?** *(The court did not reverse decisions about defendants' rights. Conservatives may have considered the court's decisions to be too liberal.)* **AL** **CA CS1**

This **Historical Analysis** skill was introduced in Chapter 16.

Answers and Additional Support

Following his victory, Nixon set out to attract even more Southerners to the Republican Party, an effort that became known as the **Southern strategy.** Toward this end, the president fulfilled his agreements with Thurmond and took steps to slow desegregation. During his tenure, Nixon worked to overturn several civil rights policies. He reversed a Johnson administration policy, for example, that had cut off federal funds for racially segregated schools.

A Law-and-Order President Having also won the presidency with a promise of law and order, Nixon immediately set out to battle crime in America. His administration specifically targeted the nation's antiwar protesters. Attorney General John Mitchell declared that he stood ready to prosecute "hard-line militants" who crossed state lines to stir up riots. Mitchell's deputy, Richard Kleindienst, went even further with the boast, "We're going to enforce the law against draft evaders, against radical students, against deserters, against civil disorders, against organized crime, and against street crime."

President Nixon also went on the attack against the recent Supreme Court rulings that expanded the rights of accused criminals. Nixon opposed these rulings and openly criticized the Court and its chief justice, Earl Warren. The president promised to fill vacancies on the Supreme Court with judges who would support the rights of law enforcement over the rights of suspected criminals.

When Chief Justice Warren retired shortly after Nixon took office, the president replaced him with Warren Burger, a respected conservative judge. The president also placed three other conservative justices on the Court, including one justice from the South. The Burger Court did not reverse Warren Court rulings pertaining to the rights of criminal suspects. It did, however, refuse to expand those rights further. For example, in *Stone v. Powell* (1976), it agreed to limits on the rights of defendants to appeal state convictions to the federal judiciary. The Court also continued to uphold capital punishment as constitutional. 📖 *(See page 1007 for more information on Stone v. Powell.)*

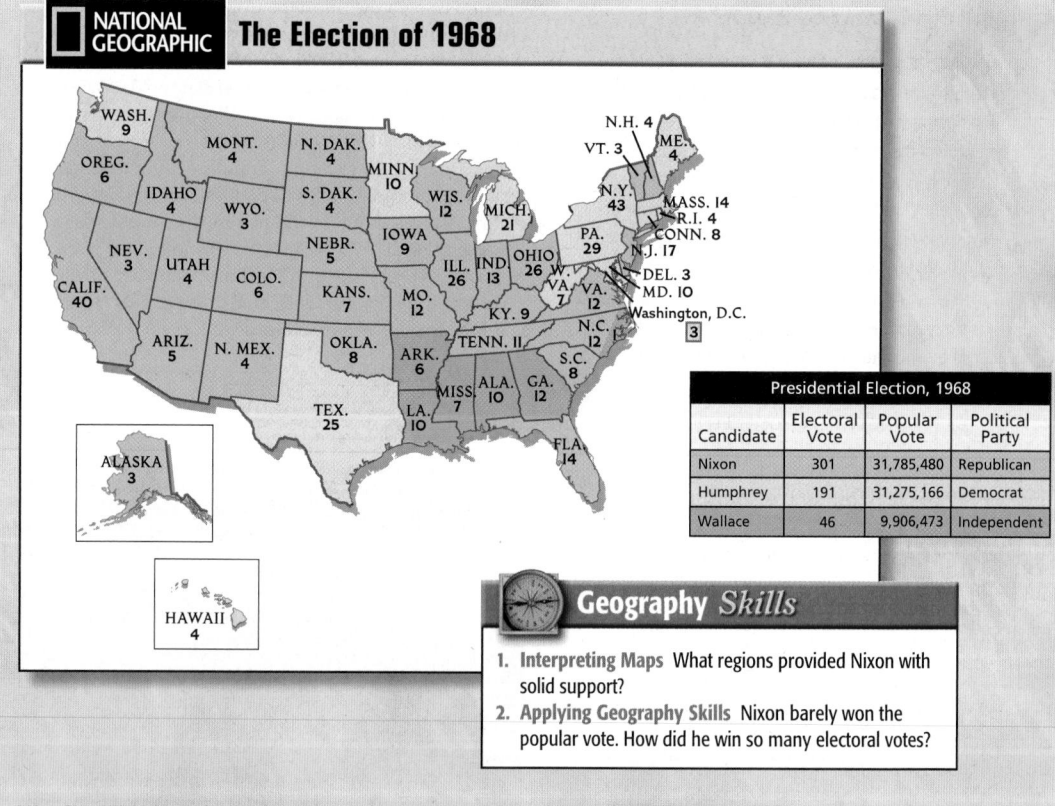

NATIONAL GEOGRAPHIC **The Election of 1968**

Presidential Election, 1968			
Candidate	Electoral Vote	Popular Vote	Political Party
Nixon	301	31,785,480	Republican
Humphrey	191	31,275,166	Democrat
Wallace	46	9,906,473	Independent

Geography *Skills*

1. **Interpreting Maps** What regions provided Nixon with solid support?
2. **Applying Geography Skills** Nixon barely won the popular vote. How did he win so many electoral votes?

Geography *Skills*

Answers:
1. Midwest and West
2. If a candidate has only a plurality in a state's popular vote, he or she still receives all of its electoral votes.

Geography Skills Practice
Which New England states voted for Nixon? (*New Hampshire and Vermont*) **Which Western state voted for Humphrey?** (*Washington*)

Profiles IN HISTORY

Romana Acosta Bañuelos 1925–

On her first day of business in downtown Los Angeles, California, Romana Acosta Bañuelos made $36 selling tortillas. That was in 1949. She made great strides after that, becoming a successful businessperson and serving as U.S. treasurer in the 1970s.

Born in 1925 in a small town in Arizona to Mexican American immigrants, Bañuelos spent part of her childhood on a relative's small ranch in Mexico. Rising early, she tended the crops and helped her mother make empanadas (Mexican turnovers) to sell to local restaurants. "My mother was the type of woman that taught us how to live in any place and work with what we have."

That lesson inspired Bañuelos to start her own business when she returned to the United States at the age of 19. Gradually her business grew, and by the mid-1960s, it was thriving. In 1979 Romana's Mexican Food Products employed about 400 people and had sales of some $12 million annually.

Bañuelos worked at more than accumulating wealth. She contributed to scholarships for Mexican American students, especially those interested in business, which Bañuelos believes is an important path to political influence. With a number of partners, she also founded the Pan-American National Bank. It too was successful.

Bañuelos' success and community leadership led to President Nixon's appointing her as U.S. Treasurer in 1971.

The New Federalism President Nixon's Republican constituency also favored dismantling a number of federal programs and giving more control to state and local governments. Nixon called this New Federalism. He argued that it would provide the government agencies that were closest to the citizens the opportunity to address more of their issues.

"I reject the patronizing idea that government in Washington, D.C., is inevitably more wise and more efficient than government at the state or local level," Nixon declared. "The idea that a bureaucratic elite in Washington knows what's best for people . . . is really a contention that people cannot govern themselves." Under the New Federalism program, Congress passed a series of revenue-sharing bills that granted federal funds to state and local agencies.

Although **revenue sharing** was intended to give state and local agencies more power, over time it gave the federal government new power. As states came to depend on federal funds, the federal government could impose conditions on the states. Unless they met those conditions, their funds would be cut off.

While he worked to limit federal government responsibilities, Nixon also sought to increase the power of the executive branch. Nixon did not build many strong relationships in Congress. His lack of camaraderie with lawmakers and the fact that the Republican Party controlled neither house led to struggles with the legislative branch. Nixon often responded by trying to work around Congress and use greater executive authority. For instance, when Congress appropriated money for programs he opposed, Nixon **impounded,** or refused to release, the funds. The Supreme Court eventually declared the practice of impoundment unconstitutional.

The Family Assistance Plan One federal program Nixon sought to reform was the nation's welfare system—Aid to Families with Dependent Children (AFDC). The program had many critics, Republican and Democratic alike. They argued that AFDC was structured so that it was actually better for poor people to apply for benefits than to take a low-paying job. A mother who had such a job, for example, would then have to pay for child care, sometimes leaving her with less income than she had on welfare. There was also great inequity among states since each was allowed to develop its own guidelines.

In 1969 Nixon proposed replacing the AFDC with the Family Assistance Plan. The plan called for providing needy families a guaranteed yearly grant of $1,600, which could be **supplemented** by outside earnings. Many liberals applauded the plan as a significant step toward expanding federal responsibility for the poor. Nixon, however, presented the program in a conservative light, arguing it would reduce federal supervision and encourage welfare recipients to become more responsible.

CHAPTER 19 Politics and Economics **853**

Profiles IN HISTORY

Although the program won approval in the House in 1970, it soon came under harsh attack from the public and politicians. Welfare recipients complained that the federal grant was too low, while conservatives, who disapproved of guaranteed income, also criticized the plan. Such opposition led to the program's defeat in the Senate.

✓ Reading Check **Evaluating** What impact did third-party candidate George Wallace have on the 1968 election?

Nixon's Foreign Policy

Main Idea With the support of national security adviser Henry Kissinger, Nixon forged better relationships with China and the Soviet Union.

Reading Connection How do you think a president should balance his efforts between domestic and foreign affairs? Read on to learn about Nixon's strategies for dealing with communist countries.

Despite Nixon's domestic initiatives, a State Department official later recalled that the president had a "monumental disinterest in domestic policies."

▼ *Henry Kissinger*

Nixon once expressed his hope that a "competent cabinet" of advisers could run the country. This would allow him to focus his energies on the subject that truly fascinated him, foreign affairs. Embarking on an ambitious foreign policy agenda that included historic encounters with both China and the Soviet Union, Nixon set out to leave his mark on the world stage.

Nixon and Kissinger In a move that would greatly influence his foreign policy, Nixon chose as his national security adviser **Henry Kissinger,** a former Harvard professor. As a teenager Kissinger had fled to the United States from Germany with his family in 1938 to escape Nazi persecution of Jews. He had served as a foreign policy consultant for Presidents Kennedy and Johnson. Though Secretary of State William Rogers technically outranked him, Kissinger soon took the lead in helping shape Nixon's foreign policy.

Nixon and Kissinger shared views on many issues. Both believed simply abandoning the war in Vietnam would damage the United States's position in the world. Thus they worked toward a gradual withdrawal. Nixon and Kissinger also believed in shaping a foreign policy rooted in practical approaches rather than ideologies. They felt the nation's decades-long anticommunist crusade had created a foreign policy that was too rigid and often worked against the nation's interests. While both leaders wanted to continue to contain communism, they believed that engagement and negotiation with Communists offered a better way for the United States to achieve its international goals. As a surprised nation watched, Nixon and Kissinger put their philosophy into practice by forging friendlier relations with the Soviet Union and China.

The Establishment of Détente The Soviet Union was not initially pleased when Nixon, a man with a history of outspoken anticommunist actions, became president. The Washington correspondent for the Soviet newspaper *Izvestia,* Yuri Barsukov, had called the election "unwelcome news for Moscow" and predicted that Soviet leaders "would have to deal with a very stubborn president."

Things did not turn out that way, however. Nixon was still a staunch anticommunist, but he came to reject the **notion** of a bipolar world in which the superpowers of the United States and the Soviet Union confronted one another. He believed the United States needed to understand the growing role that China, Japan, and Western Europe would soon play. This "multipolar" world of the future demanded a different approach to American foreign policy.

With Kissinger's help, Nixon fashioned an approach called **détente,** or relaxation of tensions, between the United States and its two major Communist rivals, the Soviet Union and China. In explaining détente to the American people, Nixon said that the United States had to build a better relationship with its main rivals in the interests of world peace:

❝We must understand that détente is not a love fest. It is an understanding between nations that have opposite purposes, but which share common interests, including the avoidance of a nuclear war. Such an understanding can work—that is, restrain aggression and deter war—only as long as the **potential** aggressor is made to recognize that neither aggression nor war will be profitable.❞

—quoted in *The Limits of Power*

 Nixon Visits China Détente began with an effort to improve American-Chinese relations. Since 1949, when a Communist government came to power in China, the United States had refused to recognize the Communists as the legitimate rulers. Instead, the American government recognized the exiled regime on the island of Taiwan as the Chinese government. Having long supported this policy, Nixon now set out to reverse it. He began by lifting trade and travel restrictions and withdrawing the Seventh Fleet from defending Taiwan.

After a series of highly secret negotiations between Kissinger and Chinese leaders, Nixon announced that he would visit China in February 1972. During the historic trip, the leaders of both nations agreed to establish "more normal" relations between their countries. In a statement that epitomized the notion of détente, Nixon told his Chinese hosts during a banquet toast, "Let us start a long march together, not in lockstep, but on different roads leading to the same goal, the goal of building a world structure of peace and justice."

In taking this trip, Nixon hoped not only to strengthen ties with the Chinese, but also to encourage the Soviets to more actively pursue diplomacy. Since the 1960s, a rift had developed between the Communist governments of the Soviet Union and China. Troops of the two nations occasionally clashed along their borders. Nixon believed détente with China would encourage Soviet premier Leonid Brezhnev to be more accommodating with the United States.

U.S.-Soviet Tensions Ease Nixon's feelings about the Soviets proved correct. Shortly after the public

 Analyzing *Political Cartoons*

Arms Buildup Anxiety The urgent need to negotiate a reduction in nuclear arms is demonstrated in this 1970 cartoon. When was the SALT I agreement finally signed?

R learned of U.S. negotiations with China, the Soviets proposed an American-Soviet **summit,** or high-level diplomatic meeting, to be held in May 1972. On May 22, President Nixon flew to Moscow for a weeklong summit. Thus, he became the first American president since World War II to visit the Soviet Union.

Before Nixon's visit, Secretary of Commerce Maurice Stans spent 11 days in the Soviet Union. In his visits to a tractor plant, a steel mill, and an oil field, Stans recalled, "It was as friendly a meeting as if I were representing California and negotiating with the state of Arizona." Before leaving, however, Stans requested a favor from his Soviet host, Alexei Kosygin:

CHAPTER 19   Politics and Economics   **855**

Review the Big Idea

Review the Big Idea for this section, "International competition can lead to conflict and cooperation." Tell students to analyze the quote from Nixon's *The Limits of Power.* **Ask:** Which audience did this statement address? What was the purpose of this statement, and was it successful? Why or why not? *(audience: the American public; purpose and success: to convince public of the benefits of détente, which it successfully achieved; responses for the success will vary)* **OL**
CA 11RC2.5; 11RL3.8

W Writing Support

Summary Writing Have students write a press release detailing the strategic goals of Nixon's visit to China. Remind them to focus on the main ideas or key points. Tell students that a good press release uses an inverted pyramid format with the most important information in the first sentence of the release. **OL**
CA 11WA2.4a; 11WA2.4d

R Reading Strategy

Using Context Clues Ask students to explain why they think a high-level diplomatic meeting is called a "summit." *(The meeting attendees usually represent the highest level—or summit—of government officials.)* **OL**

Analyzing *Political Cartoons*

Answer: 1972
Ask: Why do you think the cartoonist drew the bombs perilously perched on top of one another like a shaky tower? *(Students' answers will vary. A possible answer is that the cartoonist wanted to incorporate the concept of escalation and the shaky nature of the negotiations.)*

Universal Access

English Learners While initially confusing for English learners, acronyms can be a helpful tool for remembering complicated items. **Ask: What are some acronyms you are familiar with? (possible answers may include CIA, FBI, TGIF)** EL

ASSESS

Resources for page 856

Use these resources to assess student mastery.

📂 Section Quiz 19-1

📂 Reading Essentials and Study Guide 19-1

💿 Interactive Tutor Self-Assessment CD-ROM

📂 California Standards Practice, Grade 11

 Picturing **History**

Answer: relaxation of tensions

✓ **Reading Check**

Answer: signed SALT I, agreed to increase trade and exchange scientific information

Study Central provides audio summaries, interactive games, and online graphic organizers to help students review section content.

CLOSE

Evaluating Evidence Ask students to review the section to construct a T-chart comparing Nixon's domestic and foreign achievements. OL CA HR1; HR3

856

Picturing **History**

Détente Discussion Soviet premier Leonid Brezhnev listens to President Nixon during Brezhnev's June 1973 visit to Washington, D.C. On June 22 the two signed an agreement on the prevention of nuclear war. **What does the word détente mean?**

> **❝**'There is one thing I hope you will take care of: on the highway into Moscow there is a great big billboard with the United States pictured as a vicious killer, with a sword in one hand and a gun in the other, killing people all over the world. I don't think that will be a good entrance for President Nixon, and the sign ought to come down.' He said, 'It will.'**❞**
>
> —quoted in *Nixon: An Oral History of His Presidency*

During the historic Moscow summit, the two superpowers, the United States and Soviet Union, signed the first Strategic Arms Limitation Treaty, or SALT I, a plan to limit nuclear arms. The two nations had been working on this plan for over two years. Nixon and Brezhnev also agreed to increase trade and the exchange of scientific information.

Détente profoundly eased tensions between the Soviet Union and the United States. By the end of Nixon's presidency, one Soviet official admitted that "the United States and the Soviet Union had their best relationship of the whole Cold War period."

President Nixon indeed had made his mark on the world stage. For the first time in over two decades, the world breathed a sigh of relief because nuclear war seemed less likely. As he basked in the glow of his 1972 foreign policy triumphs, however, trouble was brewing on the home front. A scandal was about to engulf his presidency and plunge the nation into one of its greatest constitutional crises.

✓ **Reading Check** **Summarizing** What were the results of the 1972 American-Soviet summit?

 Study Central

For help with the concepts in this section of *American Vision: Modern Times* go to tav.mt.glencoe.com and click on *Study Central.*

SECTION 1 ASSESSMENT

Checking for Understanding

1. **Vocabulary** Define: revenue sharing, impound, supplement, notion, détente, potential, summit.
2. **People and Terms** Identify: Southern strategy, Henry Kissinger.
3. **Describe** Nixon's New Federalism policy.

Reviewing Big Ideas

4. **Explaining** What were the results of Nixon's policy of détente?

Critical Thinking

5. **Historical Analysis** **Evaluating** How did Nixon's China visit affect Soviet relations? CA HI1
6. **Categorizing** Use a graphic organizer similar to the one below to describe how President Nixon established détente in the countries listed.

China	
Soviet Union	

Analyzing Visuals

7. **Analyzing Political Cartoons** Study the cartoon on page 855. What is the artist's message about the impact of the arms buildup on the average citizen in both the Soviet Union and the United States?

Writing About History

8. **Expository Writing** Take on the role of a member of President Nixon's staff. Write a press release explaining Nixon's domestic and foreign policies. CA 11WS1.2

SECTION 1 ASSESSMENT ANSWERS

1. Content vocabulary is boldfaced and highlighted in yellow. Academic vocabulary is boldfaced.
2. Southern strategy *(p. 852)*, Henry Kissinger *(p. 854)*
3. He granted federal funds to state and local agencies.
4. Détente eased tensions between the United States and the Soviet Union and led to more normal relations between the U.S. and China.
5. The Soviet Union became more accommodating to the United States.
6. China: lifted trade and travel restrictions, withdrew Seventh Fleet from Taiwan; Soviet Union: increased trade, signed SALT I, exchanged scientific information
7. The arms race burdened citizens.
8. Students' press releases will vary. Students should be instructed on the proper format for a news release.

SECTION 2 The Watergate Scandal

Guide to Reading

Connection

In the previous section, you learned about the 1968 election of President Nixon and détente. In this section, you will discover how a scandal forced President Nixon to resign during his second term.

Main Idea

- President Nixon sought reelection amid a scandal over the Watergate break-in. (p. 858)
- After the televised 1973 Watergate hearings in the Senate, President Nixon resigned from office. (p. 859)
- The Watergate scandal eroded public confidence in the federal government. (p. 861)

Content Vocabulary

executive privilege, impeach

Academic Vocabulary

attribute, obtain, inevitable

People and Terms to Identify

Sam J. Ervin, John Dean, Federal Campaign Act Amendments

Reading Objectives

- **Describe** the character of Richard Nixon and the attitude of his White House.
- **Explain** the Watergate scandal and discuss its effects.

Reading Strategy

Taking Notes As you read about the Watergate scandal, use the major headings of the section to create an outline similar to the one below.

The Watergate Scandal
I. The Roots of Watergate
   A.
   B.
   C.
II.
   A.
   B.

Preview of Events

June 1972   ♦March 1973   ♦December 1973   ♦September 1974

June 1972
Burglars arrested in Democratic National Committee headquarters at Watergate complex

May 1973
Senate begins Watergate investigation

October 1973
Battle over White House tapes leads to "Saturday Night Massacre"

August 1974
Nixon resigns

The following are the main History–Social Science Standards covered in this section.

11.11.4 Explain the constitutional crisis originating from the Watergate scandal.

❧ The Big Idea ❧

Societies change over time. Scandals consumed President Nixon's second term as president. The revelation that Vice President Spiro Agnew had accepted bribes when he was a governor forced him to resign. Then a burglary trial revealed that the Nixon administration had orchestrated a break-in at the Democratic headquarters. The Watergate cover-up began to crumble with testimony of White House and campaign officials and news of recordings. Faced with impeachment, Nixon resigned from office. In the wake of the scandals, Congress enacted a series of new laws to limit the power of the executive branch. Still, Watergate left the American people with weakened trust in the government.

CHAPTER 19   Politics and Economics   **857**

FOCUS

Guide to Reading

Understanding Vocabulary: Tell students to write a short summary of the Watergate scandal using all of the content vocabulary words and the people and terms to identify.

Answers to Graphic:
I. The Roots of Watergate
   A. Nixon and His "Enemies"
   B. Mounting a Reelection Fight
   C. The Cover-Up Begins
II. The Cover-Up Unravels
   A. The First Cracks Show
   B. A Summer of Shocking Testimony
   C. The Case of the Tapes
   D. Nixon Resigns
III. The Impact of Watergate

Unpacking the Standards

Students will be able to:

- Describe the character of Richard Nixon and the attitude of his White House.
- Explain the events surrounding the Watergate investigation.
- Discuss the long-term impact of the Watergate scandal.

SECTION RESOURCES

📁 Print Material
- Reproducible Lesson Plan 19-2
- Guided Reading Activity 19-2
- Reading Essentials and Study Guide 19-2
- Active Reading Note-Taking Guide 19-2

🖨 Transparencies
- Daily Focus Skills Transparency 19-2
- Section Graphic Organizer Transparency 19-2

Technology
- 💿 Interactive Tutor Self-Assessment CD-ROM
- 💿 ExamView® Pro Testmaker CD-ROM
- 💿 Presentation Plus! CD-ROM

TEACH

R Reading Strategy

Inferring Tell students that Nixon's fear of people trying to weaken his administration helped set the stage for the Watergate scandal. **Ask:** Who might Nixon have considered a radical and counted as an enemy? *(Answers could include peace protesters, student activists, and political opponents.)* OL

C Critical Thinking

Making Inferences The text offers two views of Nixon's position entering into the 1972 election. **Ask:** Do you think President Nixon would have been reelected without the the Watergate break-in and other illegal activities? *(Students' answers will vary.)* OL

Resources for page 858

*Have students read more about the Watergate scandal in the **Primary Source Reading 19-1** and in **Moments in TIME Unit 13: The Watergate Crisis (1972–1974).***

Answers and Additional Support

The Roots of Watergate

Main Idea President Nixon sought reelection amid a scandal over the Watergate break-in.

Reading Connection What actions would you consider acceptable in a political campaign? Read on to learn about the efforts of Nixon's campaign team.

A seemingly simple burglary at the Watergate complex soon developed into a major political scandal.

★ An American Story ★

As Bob Woodward, a young reporter for the *Washington Post,* sat in a Washington, D.C., courtroom on the morning of June 17, 1972, he was in a rather foul mood. His editor had ruined his Saturday by calling him in to cover a seemingly insignificant but bizarre incident. In the early hours of that morning, five men had broken into the Democratic National Committee (DNC) headquarters in the city's Watergate apartment-office complex.

Woodward sat toward the back of the courtroom listening to the bail proceedings for the five defendants. At one point, the judge asked each man his occupation. One of the men, James McCord, answered that he was retired from government service. "Where in government?" asked the judge. "CIA," McCord whispered. Woodward sprang to attention. Why was a former member of the Central Intelligence Agency involved in what seemed to be nothing more than a burglary?

Over the next two years, Woodward and another reporter, Carl Bernstein, would investigate this question. In so doing, they uncovered a scandal that helped bring about a grave constitutional crisis and eventually forced the president to resign.

—adapted from *All the President's Men*

The scandal known as Watergate originated from the Nixon administration's attempts to cover up its involvement in the break-in at the Democratic National Committee (DNC) headquarters, along with other illegal actions committed during Nixon's reelection campaign. A number of scholars **attribute** the scandal in large part to the character of Richard Nixon and the atmosphere that he and his advisers created in the White House.

Nixon and His "Enemies" Richard Nixon had fought hard to become president. He had battled back from numerous political defeats, including a loss to John Kennedy in the 1960 presidential election, to win the presidency in 1968. Along the way, however, Nixon had grown defensive, secretive, and often resentful of his critics.

In addition, Nixon had become president during a time when the United States was still very much at war with itself. Race riots and protests over the Vietnam War continued to consume the country. In Nixon's view, these protesters and other "radicals" were out to bring down his administration. Nixon was so consumed with his opponents that he compiled an "enemies list" filled with people—from politicians to members of the media—whom he considered a threat to his presidency.

Mounting a Reelection Fight As Nixon's reelection campaign got under way in 1972, many in his administration expressed optimism about winning a second term. The president had just finished triumphant trips to China and the Soviet Union. In May, former Alabama governor George Wallace, who had mounted a strong third-party campaign in 1968, had dropped his bid for another run at the White House after an assassin's bullet paralyzed him. Meanwhile, Nixon's Democratic opponent, South Dakota senator George McGovern, was viewed as too liberal on many issues.

At the same time, Nixon's hold on the presidency was uncertain. Despite the high approval ratings for the president's summit meetings in Beijing and Moscow, the unpopular Vietnam War still raged. Nixon staffers also remembered how close the margin of Nixon's 1968 victory had been. Seeking to gain an

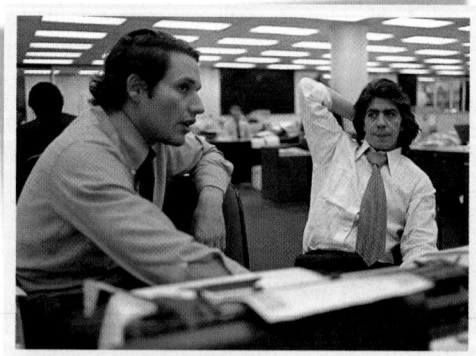

▼ *Reporters Bob Woodward and Carl Bernstein*

Did You Know?

Bob Woodward describes how he became involved in the Watergate story this way: "It was a beautiful Saturday morning. June 17, 1972. The editors essentially said, 'Who would be dumb enough to come in [to the office]?' And they called me. Of course I came in. Eight people worked on that story the first day. The next morning was Sunday. Again, a beautiful day. Who came into the office to follow the story? Carl and myself."

edge in every way they could, Nixon's team engaged in a host of subversive tactics, from spying on opposition rallies to spreading rumors and false reports.

These tactics included an effort to steal information from the Democratic Party's headquarters. In the early hours of June 17, 1972, five Nixon supporters broke into the party's office at the Watergate complex in Washington, D.C. They had intended to **obtain** any sensitive campaign information and to place wiretaps on the office telephones. While the burglars were at work, a security guard making his rounds spotted a piece of tape holding a door lock. The guard ripped off the tape, but when he passed the door later, he noticed that it had been replaced. He quickly called police, who arrived shortly and arrested the men.

The Cover-Up Begins In the wake of the Watergate break-in, the media discovered that one of the burglars, James McCord, was not only an ex-CIA official but also a member of the Committee for the Reelection of the President (CRP). Reports soon surfaced that the burglars had been paid to execute the break-in from a secret CRP fund controlled by the White House.

As questions swirled about a possible White House connection to the burglary, the cover-up began. Administration officials destroyed incriminating documents and provided false testimony to investigators. Meanwhile, President Nixon stepped in. While the president may not have ordered the break-in, he did order a cover-up. With Nixon's consent, administration officials asked the CIA to intervene and stop the FBI from inquiring into the source of the money paid to the burglars. Their justification was that such an investigation would threaten national security.

All the while, the White House strongly denied any involvement in the break-in. Nixon's press secretary dismissed the incident as a "third-rate burglary attempt," while the president himself told the American public, "The White House has had no involvement whatever in this particular incident."

The strategy worked. Most Americans believed President Nixon. Despite efforts by the media, in particular the *Washington Post*, to keep the story alive, few people paid much attention to the Watergate affair during the 1972 presidential campaign. On Election Day, Nixon won reelection by one of the largest margins in history with nearly 61 percent of the popular vote compared to 37.5 percent for George McGovern. The electoral vote was 520 votes for Nixon and 17 for McGovern.

✓ **Reading Check** **Examining** Why did members of the CRP break into the Democratic National Committee headquarters?

The Cover-Up Unravels

Main Idea After the televised 1973 Watergate hearings in the Senate, President Nixon resigned from office.

Reading Connection Who takes over the presidency if both the president and vice president resign or are otherwise incapacitated? Read on to learn why both the president and vice president resigned in 1973.

Shortly after his triumphant reelection, an exuberant and confident Nixon told his cabinet and staff that 1973 "can be and should be the best year ever."

HISTORY Online

Student Web Activity Visit the *American Vision: Modern Times* Web site at tav.mt.glencoe.com and click on **Student Web Activities—Chapter 19** for an activity on the 1970s.

Picturing History

Watergate Hotel The hotel gave its name to the scandal that brought down President Nixon. Hotel guard Frank Willis, pictured here, reported to police the evidence of a break-in at the Democratic National Committee headquarters there. What was Nixon's response to the break-in?

CHAPTER 19 Politics and Economics **859**

In a matter of months, however, the Watergate affair would erupt, and the coming year would be one of the president's worst.

The First Cracks Show In 1973 the Watergate burglars went on trial. Under relentless prodding from federal judge John J. Sirica, McCord agreed to cooperate with both a grand jury investigation and with the Senate's Select Committee on Presidential Campaign Activities, which had been recently established under Senator **Sam J. Ervin** of North Carolina. McCord's testimony opened a floodgate of confessions, and a parade of White House and campaign officials exposed one illegality after another over the next several months. Foremost among the officials was counsel to the president **John Dean,** a member of the inner circle of the White House who leveled allegations against Nixon himself.

A Summer of Shocking Testimony In June 1973, John Dean testified before Senator Ervin's committee that former Attorney General John Mitchell had ordered the Watergate break-in and that Nixon had played an active role in attempting to cover up any

Picturing **History**

Sitting in Judgment Representative Barbara Jordan from Texas was an outspoken member of the House Judiciary Committee. What was this committee's role in the impeachment process?

White House involvement. As a shocked nation absorbed Dean's testimony, the Nixon administration strongly denied the charges.

A standoff ensued for the next month, as the Senate committee attempted to determine who was telling the truth. Then, on July 16, the answer appeared unexpectedly. On that day, White House aide Alexander Butterfield testified that Nixon had ordered a taping system installed in the White House to record all conversations. The president had done so, Butterfield said, to help him write his memoirs after he left office. For members of the committee, however, the tapes would tell them exactly what the president knew and when he knew it.

The Case of the Tapes All the groups investigating the scandal sought access to the tapes. Nixon refused, pleading **executive privilege**—the principle that White House conversations should remain confidential to protect national security. A special prosecutor appointed by the president to handle the Watergate cases, Archibald Cox, took Nixon to court in October 1973 to force him to give up the recordings. Nixon, clearly growing desperate, ordered Attorney General Elliot Richardson, and then Richardson's deputy, to fire Cox. Both men refused to follow the order and resigned in protest. Solicitor General Robert Bork finally fired Cox, but the incident, nicknamed the "Saturday Night Massacre" in the press, badly damaged Nixon's reputation with the public.

The fall of 1973 proved to be a disastrous time for Nixon for other reasons as well. His vice president, Spiro Agnew, was forced to resign in disgrace. Investigators had discovered that Agnew had taken bribes from state contractors while he was governor of Maryland and that he had continued to accept bribes while serving in Washington. Gerald Ford, the Republican leader of the House of Representatives, became the new vice president. Nixon then had to defend himself against allegations about his own past financial dealings.

Nixon Resigns In an effort to quiet the growing outrage over his actions, President Nixon appointed a new special prosecutor, Texas lawyer Leon Jaworski, who proved no less determined than Cox to obtain the president's tapes. In April 1974, Nixon released edited transcripts of the tapes, claiming that they proved his innocence. Investigators felt otherwise and went to court again to force Nixon to turn over the unedited tapes. In July the Supreme Court ruled that the president had to turn over the tapes

High Political Drama After resigning his office on August 9, 1974, President Nixon and his family say goodbye to aides and friends on the White House lawn. On the capital's streets, a reader takes in the news in the *Washington Post,* the newspaper that started the Watergate investigation. Who replaced Nixon as president?

themselves, not just the transcripts. With nowhere else to appeal, Nixon handed over the tapes.

Several days later, the House Judiciary Committee voted to **impeach** Nixon, or officially charge him of presidential misconduct. The committee charged that Nixon had obstructed justice in the Watergate cover-up; misused federal agencies to violate the rights of citizens; and defied the authority of Congress by refusing to deliver tapes and other materials that the committee had requested. The next step was for the entire House of Representatives to vote whether or not to impeach the president.

As the nation held its collective breath in anticipation, investigators finally found indisputable evidence against the president. One of the unedited tapes revealed that on June 23, 1972, just six days after the Watergate burglary, Nixon had ordered the CIA to stop the FBI's investigation of the break-in. With this news, even the president's strongest supporters conceded that impeachment and conviction in the Senate now seemed **inevitable.** On August 9, 1974, Nixon resigned his office in disgrace. Gerald Ford took the oath of office and became the nation's 38th president.

Reading Check **Explaining** What was the significance of John Dean's testimony before the Senate committee?

The Impact of Watergate

Main Idea The Watergate scandal eroded public confidence in the federal government.

Reading Connection Do you believe in limiting the amount of money that a politician can spend on an election? Read on to learn about Congress's attempts in the 1970s to limit campaign spending and to enforce election laws.

Upon taking office, President Ford urged Americans to put the Watergate affair behind them and move on. "Our long national nightmare is over," he declared. The effects of the scandal, however, endured long after Richard Nixon's resignation.

The Watergate crisis prompted a series of new laws intended to limit the power of the executive branch. In the 1970s Congress passed a number of laws aimed at reestablishing a greater balance of power in government. **The Federal Campaign Act Amendments** limited campaign contributions and established an independent agency to administer stricter election laws. The Ethics in Government Act required financial disclosure by high government officials in all three branches of government. The FBI Domestic Security Investigation Guidelines restricted

CHAPTER 19 Politics and Economics **861**

ASSESS

Resources for page 862

Use these resources to assess student mastery.

📂 Section Quiz 19-2

📂 Reading Essentials and Study Guide 19-2

⊙ Interactive Tutor Self-Assessment CD-ROM

📂 California Standards Practice, Grade 11

Analyzing
Political Cartoons

Answer: Many Americans became distrustful of politicians.

✓ Reading Check

Answer: Congress wanted to reestablish the balance of power between the branches of government.

HISTORY Online

Study Central provides audio summaries, interactive games, and online graphic organizers to help students review section content.

CLOSE

Evaluating Watergate raised skepticism about the federal government. Have students discuss whether people are still skeptical about politics today. **OL**

Analyzing *Political Cartoons*

Watergate Scandal In this cartoon, the top of the White House is represented by a tape recorder. What effect did the Watergate affair have on the nation?

the bureau's political intelligence-gathering activities. After Watergate, Congress also established a means for appointing an independent counsel to investigate and prosecute wrongdoing by high government officials.

Despite these efforts, Watergate left many Americans with a deep distrust of their public officials. Speaking some 20 years after the Watergate affair, Alexander Haig, a former high-level Nixon aide, said the scandal had produced, "a fundamental discrediting of respect for the presidency . . . [and] a new skepticism about politics, in general,

which every American feels to this day." On the other hand, some Americans saw the Watergate affair as proof that in the United States, no person is above the law. As Bob Woodward observed:

❝Watergate was probably a good thing for the country; it was a good, sobering lesson. Accountability to the law applies to everyone. The problem with kings and prime ministers and presidents is that they think that they are above it, and there is no accountability, and that they have some special rights, and privileges, and status. And a process that says: No. We have our laws and believe them, and they apply to everyone, is a very good thing.❞

—quoted in *Nixon: An Oral History of His Presidency*

After the ordeal of Watergate, most Americans attempted to put the affair behind them. In the years ahead, however, the nation encountered a host of new troubles.

✓ Reading Check **Evaluating** Why did Congress pass new laws after the Watergate scandal?

HISTORY Online Study Central

For help with the concepts in this section of *American Vision: Modern Times* go to tav.mt.glencoe.com and click on *Study Central.*

SECTION 2 ASSESSMENT

Checking for Understanding

1. **Vocabulary** Define: attribute, obtain, executive privilege, impeach, inevitable.
2. **People and Places** Identify: Sam J. Ervin, John Dean, Federal Campaign Act Amendments.
3. **Evaluate** the effects of the Watergate scandal on the way American citizens viewed the federal government.

Reviewing Big Ideas

4. **Explaining** How did the Watergate scandal alter the balance of power between the executive and legislative branches of government?

Critical Thinking

5. **Historical Analysis** **Evaluating** How did the discovery of the White House tapes change the Watergate cover-up investigation? **CA HI1; HI4**
6. **Organizing** Using a graphic organizer similar to the one below, fill in the effects of the Watergate scandal.

Effects of Watergate Scandal

Analyzing Visuals

7. **Analyzing Photographs** Study the photograph on page 861. How would you describe the scene of Nixon's leave taking? What in the photo suggests that this is a formal occasion? Why do you think this ceremony might be important for the nation?

Writing About History

8. **Descriptive Writing** Take on the role of a television news analyst. Write a script in which you explain the Watergate scandal and analyze the factors that led to the scandal. **CA 11WS1.2**

862 CHAPTER 19 Politics and Economics

SECTION 2 ASSESSMENT ANSWERS

1. Content vocabulary is boldfaced and highlighted in yellow. Academic vocabulary is boldfaced.
2. Sam J. Ervin *(p. 860)*, John Dean *(p. 860)*, Federal Campaign Act Amendments *(p. 861)*
3. Many citizens distrusted the government, especially the presidency, while some saw the events

as proof that no one is above the law.
4. It led to laws that limit the power of the executive branch.
5. It led to an abuse of executive privilege, but resulted in proof of Nixon's guilt.
6. Nixon's resignation, Federal Campaign Acts Amendments,

Ethics in Government Act, FBI Domestic Security Investigation Guidelines
7. Students answer should thoughtfully consider the photograph.
8. Students' scripts will vary. Scripts should include suggested visuals.

SECTION 3 Ford and Carter

Guide to Reading

Connection
In the previous section, you learned about the Watergate scandal. In this section, you will discover how Presidents Ford and Carter led the nation through both domestic and foreign crises.

Main Idea
- Inflation, a stagnant economy, and an oil embargo created an economic crisis during the 1970s. (p. 864)
- Gerald Ford attempted to fight inflation at home and sought détente abroad. (p. 866)
- Despite trying several strategies, Carter could not solve the problem of inflation. (p. 867)

- Carter attempted to craft a moral foreign policy in the Middle East and Latin America. (p. 868)

Content Vocabulary
inflation, embargo, stagflation

Academic Vocabulary
norm, acknowledge, devote

Terms to Identify
Helsinki Accords, Department of Energy

Reading Objectives
- **Explain** the reasons for economic troubles in the United States during the 1970s.

- **Discuss** Jimmy Carter's domestic and foreign policies.

Reading Strategy
Organizing As you read about the administrations of Presidents Ford and Carter, complete a graphic organizer listing the causes of economic problems in the 1970s.

Causes

[Causes boxes] → Economic Problems in the 1970s

Preview of Events

◆1973   ◆1975   ◆1977   ◆1979

1973
OPEC price increases cause inflation in the United States

1974
President Ford pardons Richard Nixon

1976
Jimmy Carter wins presidential election

1979
Iranian revolutionaries seize U.S. embassy in Iran

The following are the main History–Social Science Standards covered in this section.

11.9.3 Trace the origins and geopolitical consequences (foreign and domestic) of the Cold War and containment policy, including the following: the era of McCarthyism, instances of domestic Communism (e.g., Alger Hiss) and blacklisting; the Truman Doctrine; the Berlin Blockade; the Korean War; the Bay of Pigs invasion and the Cuban Missile Crisis; atomic testing in the American West, the "mutual assured destruction" doctrine, and disarmament policies; the Vietnam War; Latin American policy.

11.9.6 Describe U.S. Middle East policy and its strategic, political, and economic interests, including those related to the Gulf War.

11.11.2 Discuss the significant domestic policy speeches of Truman, Eisenhower, Kennedy, Johnson, Nixon, Carter, Reagan, Bush, and Clinton (e.g., with regard to education, civil rights, economic policy, environmental policy).

11.11.4 Explain the constitutional crisis originating from the Watergate scandal.

❧ The Big Idea ❧

Social and economic crises lead to new roles for government. During the 1970s, the postwar prosperity of the 1950s and 1960s ended. Inflation, a stagnant economy, and an oil embargo combined to create an economic crisis. Faced with the worst recession since the Great Depression, President Ford instituted several plans to improve the economy, to no avail. He also continued efforts to improve relations with China and the Soviet Union. With the economy continuing to decline, Jimmy Carter defeated President Ford in the 1976 presidential election. President Carter's efforts to improve the economy and end the energy crisis were equally unsuccessful. His attempts to base foreign policy on morality met with both success and failure. Carter was able to help negotiate a peace treaty between Israel and Egypt but could not negotiate the release of 52 Americans taken hostage in Iran.

CHAPTER 19   Politics and Economics   **863**

FOCUS

BELLRINGER
SKILLBUILDER ACTIVITY

Project **Daily Focus Skills Transparency 19-3** and have students answer the question.

Guide to Reading

Understanding Vocabulary: Ask students to read the information on the Helsinki Accords on page 866. Have them provide a definition of the word *accord*. (*It is an agreement.*) **Ask:** Is an accord the same thing as a treaty? (*Yes. Both terms refer to a formal agreement on discussed issues.*)

Answers to Graphic: rising costs of raw materials and rising costs of fossil fuel, increased international competition, insufficient training for new jobs

Unpacking the Standards

Students will be able to:
- Explain the reasons for economic troubles in the United States during the 1970s.
- Describe President Gerald Ford's efforts to fix the economy.
- Analyze President Jimmy Carter's economic and foreign policy.

SECTION RESOURCES

📂 Print Material
- Reproducible Lesson Plan 19-3
- Guided Reading Activity 19-3
- Reading Essentials and Study Guide 19-3
- Active Reading Note-Taking Guide 19-3

Transparencies
- Daily Focus Skills Transparency 19-3
- Section Graphic Organizer Transparency 19-3

Technology

- Interactive Tutor Self-Assessment CD-ROM
- ExamView® Pro Testmaker CD-ROM
- Presentation Plus! CD-ROM

TEACH

R Reading Strategy

Setting a Purpose Have students create comprehension questions for the headings and subheadings in Section 3, before they begin reading. These questions should help students focus their attention while reading. For example, the following questions work well for the next two subheadings: Why did the American economy slow down? and What made the economy stagnate? The answers to these questions also serve as notes for this section. **OL**

S Skill Practice

Using Geography Skills Have students research to identify the member countries of OPEC and mark those countries on a world map. Have them use the map to identify the regions of the world in which a large percentage of the world's oil reserves are found. **Ask:** Why is it important for the United States to pay close attention to the oil-producing nations of the world? *(The U.S. economy is heavily based on the availability of imported fossil fuels such as petroleum.)* **OL**
CA CS4

Answers and Additional Support

R The Economic Crisis of the 1970s

Main Idea Inflation, a stagnant economy, and an oil embargo created an economic crisis during the 1970s.

Reading Connection How much do you depend on gasoline and other fossil fuels? Read on to learn how President Nixon tried to solve the nation's economic problems.

Since the end of World War II, the American economy had been the envy of the world. During the 1950s and 1960s, many Americans enjoyed remarkable prosperity and had come to assume it was the **norm**. During the 1970s, however, many Americans began to realize that this prosperity could not last.

★ An American Story ★

On a sunny February day in 1977, Ellen Griffith and her fiancé, Roger Everson, both of Nashville, Tennessee, sat together in a place where neither of them dreamed they would be—the state unemployment office. Just a month before, Griffith, a 20-year-old salesclerk in a shopping center, and Everson, 21, had been excitedly making wedding plans. Now, with Everson laid off and Griffith on a reduced work schedule, the young couple had decided to put their future plans on hold. "It cost something to get married, you know," said Everson.

What had landed the two in this predicament was a one-two punch of a particularly bitter winter and an energy shortage that had gone on for much of the decade. The brutally cold weather in the Midwest and East had increased the demand for oil and fuel, already in short supply throughout the country. In response, the government had asked numerous companies and shops to conserve energy by cutting back on their business hours. As a result, Griffith saw her work schedule slashed from 40 hours per week to 20 hours.

As the couple sat stoically in the unemployment office waiting for their names to be called, Griffith wondered how she would pay her bills on her reduced salary and whatever she might be able to get from the state. "I just feel like we've been rained on," she said glumly.

—adapted from the *New York Times,* February 3, 1977

The prosperity enjoyed by many Americans rested in large part on easy access to raw materials around the world and a strong manufacturing industry at home. By the 1970s, however, both access to raw materials and domestic manufacturing began to disappear, creating economic problems for many.

A Mighty Economic Machine Slows The nation's economic troubles began in the mid-1960s, when President Johnson significantly increased federal deficit spending in an attempt to fund both the Vietnam War and his Great Society program without raising taxes. This pumped large amounts of money into the economy, which spurred **inflation,** or a rise in the cost of goods.

Rising costs of raw materials due to greater competition for them was another cause of inflation. In particular, the rising cost of oil dealt a strong blow to the nation's economy. More than any other nation, the United States based its economy on the easy availability of cheap and plentiful fossil fuels and had become heavily dependent on imports from the Middle East and Africa.

For years, the Organization of Petroleum Exporting Countries (OPEC) sold oil for its member countries. Prices remained low until the early 1970s, when OPEC decided to use oil as a political and economic weapon. In 1973 the Yom Kippur War was raging between Israel and its Arab neighbors. Tension had existed between Israel and the Arab world ever since the founding of modern Israel in 1948. Since most Arab states did not recognize Israel's right to exist, U.S. support of Israel made American relations with Arab states uneasy.

▼ *Lines of jobseekers at an unemployment office*

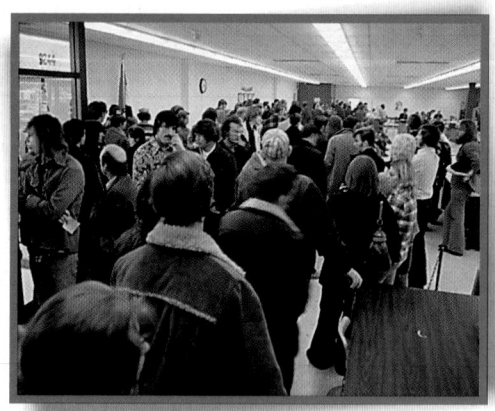

Did You Know?

OPEC is responsible for approximately 40 percent of the world's oil production and controls 75 percent of the world's proven oil reserves.

Now OPEC announced that its members would **embargo**, or stop shipping, petroleum to countries that supported Israel, namely the United States and some Western European nations. OPEC also raised the price of crude oil by 70 percent, and then by another 130 percent a few months later.

Even before the oil embargo, President Nixon and Congress had tried to protect the American people from rising world oil prices by imposing a complex system of price controls. These controls forced oil companies to charge consumers low prices for gasoline and heating oil, even though the price of imported crude oil was rising. Oil companies could afford to do this because some of the oil they bought came from low-priced domestic sources. After OPEC

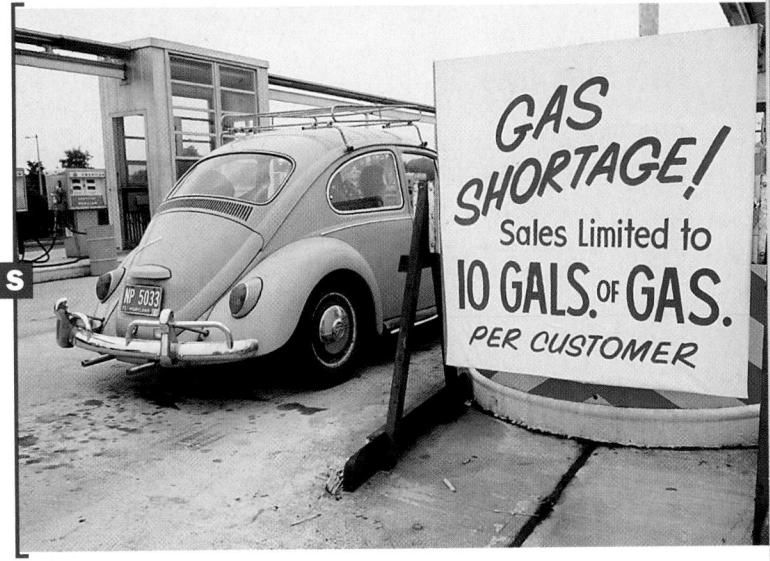

Picturing **History**

A Scarce Commodity Americans had to schedule their lives around the availability of gasoline during the OPEC oil embargo. Why did OPEC institute the embargo?

raised its prices, however, the price controls created an oil shortage. There was not enough cheap oil available domestically to supply demand, and oil companies could no longer afford to pay world oil prices and still make a profit. If there had been no price controls, gasoline prices would have risen—but there would not have been an oil shortage.

Although the embargo ended a few months after it began, oil prices continued to rise. OPEC raised prices three more times in the 1970s and again in 1980. By that time, the price of a barrel of crude oil had risen from $3 in 1973 to $30 in 1980. The dramatic increase helped accelerate inflation throughout the American economy.

A Stagnant Economy Another economic problem was the decline of the manufacturing sector. In the years following World War II, the United States had dominated international trade, but by the 1970s, it faced increased international competition. Many manufacturing plants were now decades old and less efficient than the newer plants that Japan and European industrial nations built after the war.

These factors forced many factories to close, and millions of workers lost their jobs. The result was a growing pool of unemployed and underemployed workers.

Thus in the early 1970s President Nixon faced a new and puzzling economic dilemma that came to be

known as **"stagflation,"** a combination of rising prices and economic stagnation. Economists who emphasized the demand side of economic theory, including supporters of Keynesianism, did not think that inflation and recession could occur at the same time. They believed that demand drives prices and that inflation would only occur in a booming economy when demand for goods was high. As a result, they did not know what fiscal policy the government should pursue. Increased spending might help end the recession, but it would increase inflation. Raising taxes might slow inflation but would prolong the recession.

Nixon decided to focus on controlling inflation. The government moved first to cut spending and raise taxes. The president hoped that higher taxes would prompt Americans to spend less, which would ease the demand on goods and drive down prices. Congress and much of the public, however, protested the idea of a tax hike. Nixon then tried to reduce consumer spending by getting the Federal Reserve Board to raise interest rates. When this failed, the president tried to stop inflation by imposing a 90-day freeze on wages and prices and then issuing federal regulations limiting future wage and price increases. This had little success.

✓ **Reading Check** **Explaining** How did President Nixon attempt to stop stagflation?

CHAPTER 19 Politics and Economics **865**

C **Critical Thinking**

Determining Cause and Effect Have students look up the words *embargo* and *stagflation* and discuss the definitions of these words in class. **Ask: How did the petroleum embargo contribute to the stagflation in the U.S. economy?** *(The embargo helped cause oil prices to rise. The rising prices combined with a decline in manufacturing. These two circumstances caused "stagflation.")* **OL**

S **Skill Practice**

Visual Literacy Tell students to examine the picture of the gas station on this page. **Ask: Why did the station owner limit the number of gallons sold per customer?** *(to allow more people to buy gas and to stretch limited supplies)* **How would this shortage affect other consumer decisions?** *(There was more interest in purchasing cars with increased fuel efficiency.)* **OL**
CA HI1; HI3; HI6

R **Reading Strategy**

Scaffolding—Academic Vocabulary The word *theory* was introduced in Chapter 15, Section 2. Ask a student to define the word. **BL**

✓ **Reading Check**

Answer: The government cut spending and raised taxes, the Federal Reserve raised interest rates, and the president imposed a 90-day freeze on wages and prices and issued regulations to limit future wage and price increases.

Resources for page 865

Have students read more about the energy crisis in the **Linking Past and Present Activity 19.**

Picturing **History**

Answer: because the United States supported Israel in the Yom Kippur War
Ask: Before the 1973 OPEC embargo, what was the price of a barrel of crude oil? *($3)*

R Reading Strategy

Making Inferences Students might need some help understanding some of the references of this time period. **Ask:** When President Ford said, "I'm a Ford, not a Lincoln" what double meaning did his remark have? *(He was humorously referring to the dependable if somewhat dull Ford automobile. In contrast, the Lincoln automobile—a prestigious, high-quality car—was a reference to President Lincoln.)* **OL** **CA** 11RC2.4

W Writing Support

Persuasive Writing Ask students to write an editorial defending President Ford's pardon of Nixon. Before they write, have pairs of students brainstorm the reasons for pardoning Nixon. Remind students to support their opinions with facts, to avoid first person, and to use transitional words to link paragraphs together. **OL** **CA** 11WA2.4a; 11WA2.4d

Ford Takes Over

Main Idea Gerald Ford attempted to fight inflation at home and sought détente abroad.

Reading Connection Do you think national leaders should be tried in federal court when they break the law? Read on to find out why Gerald Ford chose not to bring Nixon to trial.

When Nixon resigned in 1974, the nation's inflation rate was still high, despite many efforts to reduce prices. Meanwhile, the unemployment rate was over five percent. It would now be up to Gerald Ford to confront stagflation.

Most Americans considered Gerald Ford a decent and honest if not particularly dynamic leader. When he became vice president, Ford had readily **acknowledged** his bland personality. "I'm a Ford, not a Lincoln," he said. Still, the new president boasted excellent credentials, including a degree from Yale Law School, naval service during World War II, and service in the House of Representatives since 1949. His fellow Republicans had elected him as minority leader in 1965. Ford would need to draw on all his experience during his time in office.

Ford Pardons Nixon On September 8, 1974, Ford announced that he would grant a "full, free, and absolute pardon" to Richard Nixon for any crimes he "committed or may have committed or taken part in" while president. "This is an American tragedy in which we all have played a part," he told the nation. "It could go on and on and on, or someone must write the end to it."

Ford insisted he was acting not out of sympathy for Nixon, but in the public interest. Ford's position was that he wanted to avoid the division that charges against Nixon and a public trial would create. Nonetheless, the pardon aroused fierce criticism. Ford's approval ratings soon plunged from 71 percent to 50 percent.

Ford Tries to "Whip" Inflation By 1975 the American economy was in its worst recession since the Great Depression, with unemployment at nearly nine percent. Rejecting the notion of mandatory wage and price controls to reduce inflation, Ford requested voluntary controls. Under a plan known as WIN—Whip Inflation Now—he urged Americans to cut back on their oil and gas consumption. The plan stirred up little enthusiasm and eventually failed. The president then turned to cutting government spending and advocating higher interest rates to curb inflation. This too failed.

As Ford attempted to revive the economy, he also attempted to limit federal authority, balance the budget, and keep taxes low. Ford vetoed more than 50 bills that the Democratic-led Congress passed during the first two years of his administration.

Ford's Foreign Policy In foreign policy, Ford continued Nixon's general strategy. Ford kept Kissinger on as secretary of state and continued to pursue détente with the Soviets and the Chinese. In August 1975 he met with leaders of NATO and the Warsaw Pact to sign the **Helsinki Accords.** Under the accords, the parties recognized the borders of Eastern Europe established at the end of World War II. The Soviets in return promised to uphold certain basic human rights, including the right to move across national borders. The subsequent Soviet failure to uphold these basic rights turned many Americans against détente.

Ford also encountered problems in Southeast Asia. In May 1975, Cambodia seized the *Mayaguez,* an American cargo ship traveling near its shores,

Picturing **History**

Reassuring Presence After the turmoil of Watergate, President Gerald Ford, shown here with First Lady Betty Ford, was a comforting leader, but he was unable to solve the problem of inflation. Through what methods did Ford try to "whip inflation now"?

Picturing **History**

Answer: He suggested voluntary measures to cut back on energy use and government solutions, such as cutting back on spending and advocating higher interest rates.
Ask: What kind of garden was the predecessor of the WIN garden? *(the victory gardens of World War II)*

claiming that it had been on an intelligence-gathering mission. Calling the ship's seizure an "act of piracy," Ford dispatched U.S. Marines to retrieve it. Cambodia released the crew before the marines arrived.

The Election of 1976 As the 1976 presidential election approached, Americans were pessimistic and unsure of the future. With rising inflation and unemployment, many citizens were undergoing an adverse change of lifestyle. There were equally serious problems in foreign affairs. Political turmoil in developing nations threatened world stability, while the Soviet Union was pursuing an aggressive foreign policy. Americans, therefore, looked to elect a man who could meet these challenges.

The presidential race pitted Gerald Ford against James Earl Carter, Jr., or Jimmy Carter, as he liked to be called. Carter was somewhat of a political outsider. A former governor of Georgia, Carter had no national political experience. Nonetheless, he had won the Democratic primary with an inspiring and well–organized campaign. Carter sought to take advantage of his outsider image, promising to restore morality and honesty to the federal government. He also promised new programs for energy development, tax reform, welfare reform, and national medical care.

It was Carter's image as a moral and upstanding individual that attracted most supporters. Ford meanwhile characterized Carter as a liberal whose social program spending would produce higher rates of inflation and require tax increases.

In the end, Carter edged Ford with 50.1 percent of the popular vote to Ford's 47.9 percent, while capturing 297 electoral votes to Ford's 240. On Inauguration Day, to demonstrate his man-of-the-people style, Carter declined the traditional limousine ride and walked from the Capitol to the White House.

✓ **Reading Check** **Examining** What steps did President Ford take to try to control inflation?

Carter Battles the Economic Crisis

Main Idea **Despite trying several strategies, Carter could not solve the problem of inflation.**

Reading Connection Why do you think calls for Americans to use less energy generally fail? Read on to discover President Carter's difficulties with the economy and leadership.

Carter **devoted** much of his domestic agenda to trying to fix the economy. At first he tried to end the recession and reduce unemployment by increasing

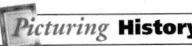 *Picturing* **History**

Change of Pace Jimmy Carter underscored his campaign image of being a new kind of politician by walking to the White House after his inauguration. What about Carter's image in 1976 might have been appealing to the public?

government spending and cutting taxes. When inflation surged in 1978, he changed his mind. He delayed the tax cuts and vetoed the spending programs he had himself proposed to Congress. He then tried to ease inflation by reducing the money supply and raising interest rates. His main focus, however, was on the energy crisis. In the end, none of his efforts succeeded.

A "War" Against Consumption Carter felt that the nation's most serious problem was its dependence on foreign oil. In one of his first national addresses, he tried to rally Americans to support what he termed a "war" against rising energy consumption. "Our decision about energy will test the character of the American people and the ability of the President and Congress to govern this nation," Carter stated.

Carter proposed a national energy program to conserve oil and to promote the use of coal and

CHAPTER 19 Politics and Economics **867**

Review the Big Idea
Review the Big Idea for this section, "Social and economic crises lead to new roles for government." As students read about the election of 1976, ask them to identify why Jimmy Carter gained supporters. *(Carter's image as a moral and upstanding individual)* **Ask:** Why did this image appeal to voters at this time? *(Some of the public felt misled by the government during the Vietnam War, which was confirmed somewhat by the Watergate scandal. People hoped Carter could restore order and credibility.)* OL

C Critical Thinking
Making Inferences Gerald Ford lost the popular vote for president by a very thin margin in 1976. **Ask:** If you were President Ford, what might you have done differently to win the public trust? *(Possible answers: not pardoning Nixon and working more closely with the Democrats in Congress to pass legislation)* OL

✓ **Reading Check**
Answer: Ford urged Americans to cut back on gas and oil consumption and undertake other energy conserving measures; he cut government spending and advocated higher interest rates; he attempted to limit federal authority, balance the budget, and keep taxes low.

Did You Know?
The position of vice president has often been satirized and seen as less than desirable. When asked to consider being Jimmy Carter's vice presidential nominee, Congressman Morris Udall said, "I am against vice in all forms, including the vice presidency."

Picturing **History**
Answer: He had a down-to-earth image that appealed to people after the less accessible personalities of Nixon and Ford.

Analyzing *Political Cartoons*

Coping With Shortages Cartoonist Brant Parker reflected the public's frustration over the oil shortages of the 1970s. What message does the cartoonist convey with the statement "the figs are next"?

renewable energy sources such as solar power. He persuaded Congress to create a **Department of Energy** and also asked Americans to make personal sacrifices to reduce their energy consumption. Most of the public complied as best they could, although many ignored the president's suggestion.

At the same time, many business leaders and economists urged the president and Congress to deregulate the oil industry. The regulations, first imposed as part of President Nixon's price control plan, limited the ability of oil companies to pass on OPEC price increases to American consumers. As a result, oil companies found it difficult to make a profit, and they lacked the capital to invest in new domestic oil wells. These regulations, combined with OPEC price increases, helped create the energy crisis of the 1970s. Carter agreed to support deregulation but insisted on a "windfall profits tax" to prevent oil companies from overcharging consumers. The tax, however, conflicted with the basic idea of deregulation, which was to free up corporate capital for use in searching for new sources of oil. In the end, Carter's contradictory plan did not solve the country's energy crisis.

In the summer of 1979, instability in the Middle East produced a second major fuel shortage and deepened the nation's economic problems. Under increasing pressure to act, Carter made several proposals in a television address. The speech was notable for Carter's bleak assessment of the national condition. He complained about a "crisis of confidence" that had struck "at the very heart and soul of our national will." The address became known as the "malaise" speech, although Carter had not specifically used that word. Many Americans interpreted the speech not as a timely warning but as Carter blaming the people for his failures.

Carter's Leadership Problems In retrospect, President Carter's difficulties in solving the nation's economic problems lay in his inexperience and inability to work with Congress. Carter, who was proud of his outsider status, made little effort to reach out to Washington's legislative leaders. As a result, Congress blocked many of his energy proposals.

Carter also failed to translate his ideas into a concrete set of goals to inspire the nation. He offered no unifying theme for his administration, but instead followed a cautious middle course that left people confused. By 1979 public opinion polls showed that Carter's popularity had dropped lower than President Nixon's during Watergate.

✔ Reading Check **Summarizing** To what did President Carter devote much of his domestic agenda?

R Carter's Foreign Policy

Main Idea Carter attempted to craft a moral foreign policy in the Middle East and Latin America.

Reading Connection How do you think the United States should deal with terrorism? Read on to learn about the nation's response to the Iran hostage crisis in 1979.

In contrast to his uncertain leadership at home, Carter's foreign policy was more clearly defined. A man of strong religious beliefs, Carter argued that the United States must try to be "right and honest and truthful and decent" in dealing with other nations. Yet it was on the international front that President Carter suffered one of his most devastating defeats.

Analyzing *Political Cartoons*

Answer: Because of American dependence on foreign oil, the cartoonist implies that OPEC countries could dictate to the U.S. government.

Resources for page 868

*Have students read more about President Carter's "crisis of confidence" speech in the **Primary Source Reading 19-2**.*

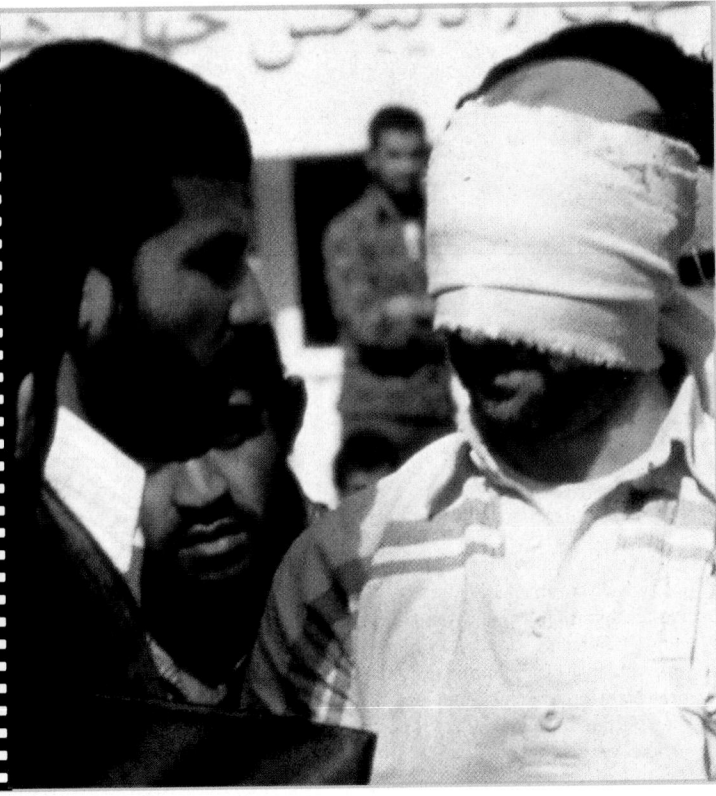

NATIONAL GEOGRAPHIC
MOMENT in HISTORY

HOSTAGE TO TERROR

Bound and blindfolded, American diplomat Jerry Miele is led out of the U.S. embassy in Tehran, Iran, after militants stormed the building on November 4, 1979. Ten months earlier, an Islamic fundamentalist revolution had overthrown the Shah of Iran, a staunch American ally. President Carter's decision to allow the ailing Shah to seek medical treatment in the United States led to the embassy takeover. Of the Americans taken captive, 52 were held for more than a year. The crisis contributed to Carter's defeat in the presidential election in 1980.

R Reading Strategy

Activating Prior Knowledge Have students recall who built the Panama Canal and when. *(The United States began the canal in 1903 and finished it in 1914.)* **Ask:** Was it a good decision to give control of the canal to Panama? *(Answers will vary, but supporters of Carter will point out that this action was an attempt by Carter to improve the relationship between the United States and Latin America.)* OL

S Skill Practice

Conducting Research The signing of the Camp David Accords was a high point of U.S. involvement in the Middle East. Have students research the Camp David Accords and tell them to plan a presentation on their research. Students could give oral reports, perform skits depicting individuals at the signing ceremony, or present multimedia presentations. They should also provide brief written reports that feature analysis, solid documentation, and historical accuracy. OL
CA HR4

Morality in Foreign Policy Carter had set the tone for his foreign policy in his inaugural speech, when he announced, "Our commitment to human rights must be absolute.... The powerful must not persecute the weak, and human dignity must be enhanced." With the help of his foreign policy team—including Andrew Young, the first African American ambassador to the United Nations—Carter strove to achieve these goals.

The president put his principles into practice in Latin America. To remove a major symbol of U.S. interventionism in the region, he moved to give the Panamanians control of the Panama Canal. The United States had built and run the canal since 1903. In 1978 the president won Senate ratification of two Panama Canal treaties, which transferred control of the canal to Panama on December 31, 1999.

Most dramatically, Carter singled out the Soviet Union as a violator of human rights. He strongly condemned, for example, the Soviet practice of imprisoning people who protested against the government. Relations between the two superpowers suf-

fered a further setback when Soviet troops invaded the Central Asian nation of Afghanistan in December 1979. Carter responded by imposing an embargo on the sale of grain to the Soviet Union and boycotting the 1980 Summer Olympic Games in Moscow. Under the Carter administration, détente virtually collapsed.

Triumph and Failure in the Middle East It was in the volatile Middle East that President Carter met his greatest foreign policy triumph and his greatest failure. In 1978 Carter helped broker a historic peace treaty, known as the Camp David Accords, between Israel and Egypt, two nations that had been bitter enemies for decades. The treaty was formally signed in 1979. Most other Arab nations in the region opposed the treaty, but it marked a first step to achieving peace in the Middle East.

Just months after the Camp David Accords, Carter encountered a crisis in Iran. The United States had long supported Iran's monarch, the Shah, because Iran was a major oil supplier and a buffer against Soviet expansion in the Middle East. The Shah,

NATIONAL GEOGRAPHIC MOMENT in HISTORY

For over 14 months, the hostage crisis dominated the news. Some television stations opened or closed their newscasts with statements such as, "Good evening on day 334 of the Iranian hostage crisis." Thus, the crisis stayed at the forefront of public attention. Many people hung yellow ribbons around trees as a constant reminder of the hostages' plight.

More Skill Practice

Visual Literacy The images of the hostages stayed in the public mind throughout the crisis. Have students look at the picture on page 869. **Ask:** How do you think Americans reacted to Carter's leadership and the actions of the Iranian radicals during this time? *(People were frustrated with Carter's inability to resolve the crisis and angry at the actions of the Iranians.)* OL

ASSESS

Resources for page 870

Use these resources to assess student mastery.

📁 Section Quiz 19-3

📁 Reading Essentials and Study Guide 19-3

💿 Interactive Tutor Self-Assessment CD-ROM

📁 California Standards Practice, Grade 11

Picturing **History**

Answer: Carter tried negotiations and a rescue attempt. The rescue mission failed and negotiations were only successful the day Carter left office.

☑ **Reading Check**

Answer: the need to be honest, truthful, and decent in foreign relations

Online

Study Central provides audio summaries, interactive games, and online graphic organizers to help students review section content.

CLOSE

Evaluating Have students discuss Jimmy Carter's domestic and foreign policies. **OL**

Picturing **History**

Hostages Released David Roeder, one of the 52 American hostages held in Iran for 444 days, waves to a crowd in Frankfurt, West Germany, after being released. How did the Carter administration attempt to free the hostages? Were the attempts successful?

however, had grown increasingly unpopular in Iran. He was a repressive ruler and had introduced Westernizing reforms to Iranian society. The Islamic clergy fiercely opposed the Shah's reforms. Opposition to the Shah grew, and in January 1979 protesters forced him to flee. An Islamic republic was then declared.

The new regime, headed by religious leader Ayatollah Khomeini, distrusted the United States because of its ties to the Shah. In November 1979, revolutionaries stormed the American embassy in Tehran and held 52 Americans hostage. The militants threatened to kill the hostages or try them as spies.

The Carter administration tried unsuccessfully to negotiate for the hostages' release. In April 1980, as pressure mounted, Carter approved a daring rescue

attempt. To the nation's dismay, the rescue mission failed when several helicopters malfunctioned and one crashed in the desert. Eight servicemen died in the accident. Hamilton Jordan, President Carter's chief of staff, described the gloomy atmosphere in the White House the day after the crash:

❝I arrived at the White House a few minutes before the President went on television to tell the nation about the catastrophe. He looked exhausted and careworn. . . . The mood at the senior staff meeting was somber and awkward. I sensed that we were all uncomfortable, like when a loved one dies and friends don't quite know what to say. . . . After the meeting, I wandered around the White House. . . . My thoughts kept returning to the bodies [of the servicemen] in the desert.❞

—quoted in *Crisis: The Last Year of the Carter Presidency*

The crisis continued into the fall of 1980. Every night, news programs reminded viewers how many days the hostages had been held. The president's inability to free the hostages cost him support in the 1980 presidential election. Negotiations with Iran continued right up to Carter's last day in office. Ironically, on January 20, 1981, the day Carter left office, Iran released the Americans, ending their 444 days in captivity.

☑ **Reading Check** **Summarizing** What was President Carter's main foreign policy theme?

Online **Study Central**

For help with the concepts in this section of *American Vision: Modern Times* go to tav.mt.glencoe.com and click on *Study Central.*

SECTION 3 ASSESSMENT

Checking for Understanding

1. **Vocabulary** Define: norm, inflation, embargo, stagflation, acknowledge, devote.
2. **People and Terms** Identify: Helsinki Accords, Department of Energy.
3. **Identify** the achievement and failure President Carter experienced in the Middle East during his administration.

Reviewing Big Ideas

4. **Describing** How did President Carter attempt to deal with the nation's energy crisis?

Critical Thinking

5. **Evaluating** Do you think President Ford should have pardoned Richard Nixon? Why or why not?
6. **Organizing** Complete a graphic organizer similar to the one below by listing the ways that President Carter applied his human rights ideas to his foreign policy.

Carter's Human Rights Foreign Policy

Analyzing Visuals

7. **Analyzing Photographs** Study the photograph on page 869. What effect do you think images such as this one had on Americans who were living or traveling in other countries?

Writing About History

8. **Expository Writing** Write an essay identifying what you believe to be President Carter's most important foreign policy achievement. Explain your choice. **CA 11WA2.1b**

870 CHAPTER 19 Politics and Economics

SECTION 3 ASSESSMENT ANSWERS

1. Content vocabulary is boldfaced and highlighted in yellow. Academic vocabulary is boldfaced.
2. Helsinki Accords *(p. 866),* Department of Energy *(p. 868)*
3. the Camp David Accords and the hostage crisis in Iran
4. Carter proposed a national energy program to conserve oil and pro-

mote the use of renewable energy sources, created the Department of Energy, and deregulated the oil industry.
5. Students' answers will vary. Some students may say the pardon saved the nation from witnessing a divisive trial. Others may say that Nixon escaped punishment.

6. Answers should reflect text information, particularly about the Soviet Union and Panama on page 869.
7. They would fear attacks on themselves.
8. Students' essays will vary. Essays should include facts to support the position taken.

SECTION 4 The "Me" Decade: Life in the 1970s

Guide to Reading

Connection
In the previous section, you learned about the economic and foreign policy issues facing the United States during the 1970s. In this section, you will discover how Americans sought fulfillment and escape during that decade.

Main Idea
- During the 1970s, Americans turned to new spiritual movements to find meaning in their lives. (p. 872)
- Television sitcoms began dealing with more difficult aspects of American life, and disco swept the country. (p. 873)

Content Vocabulary
guru, transcendental meditation, disco

Academic Vocabulary
mental, denote, interact

Terms to Identify
New Age movement, *All in the Family*

Reading Objectives
- **Explain** the emergence of new spiritual movements and religions.
- **Discuss** social changes of the 1970s.

Reading Strategy
Categorizing As you read about life in the United States in the 1970s, complete a graphic organizer similar to the one below by listing the changes that occurred in family life during that time.

Changes in Family Life

Preview of Events

◆1970	◆1973	◆1976	◆1979

1971
All in the Family debuts

1974
Good Times debuts

1977
Disco mania peaks with release of *Saturday Night Fever*; *The Complete Book of Running* published.

The following are the main History–Social Science Standards covered in this section.

11.3.4 Discuss the expanding religious pluralism in the United States and California that resulted from large-scale immigration in the twentieth century.

11.8.8 Discuss forms of popular culture, with emphasis on their origins and geographic diffusion (e.g., jazz and other forms of popular music, professional sports, architectural and artistic styles).

11.10.7 Analyze the women's rights movement from the era of Elizabeth Stanton and Susan Anthony and the passage of the Nineteenth Amendment to the movement launched in the 1960s, including differing perspectives on the roles of women.

11.11.3 Describe the changing roles of women in society as reflected in the entry of more women into the labor force and the changing family structure.

❧ The Big Idea ❧

Societies change over time. As a means of overcoming the country's problems, many Americans sought escape in new fads, forms of entertainment, and spiritual movements. Many Americans turned inward and looked for new ways to find fulfillment. Some embraced the New Age movement, while others turned to new religions. Television shows began to discuss subjects that were once taboo and to address the harsh situations some Americans faced. Music took on new forms, and disco became popular. Americans also embraced new fashions, and fitness activities became popular ways to socialize and stay fit.

CHAPTER 19 Politics and Economics **871**

TEACH

W **Writing Support**

Narrative Writing Have groups of five students write a scene set in the 1970s that is a conversation between a homemaker, an automobile factory manager, an unemployed worker, a college student, and a newspaper reporter. Each person should express positive or negative views of the country's future. *(negative issues: energy crisis, foreign competition, rising inflation, unemployment rates, social and economic inequality, changing values; positive issues: Vietnam War and 1960s protests largely over, improving society for women and African Americans)* Have each group present their scripts in dramatic fashion. **OL**
CA 11WA2.1a; 11WA2.1b

R **Reading Strategy**

Using Context Clues Ask students to explain the "New Age movement." *(social movement that used a variety of philosophies and belief systems to find spirituality in areas outside of traditional religions)* Remind students that the New Age movement consisted of several movements—separate groups that tend to be grouped together because of their differences from mainstream religions and practices. **OL**

Answers and Additional Support

The Search for Fulfillment

Main Idea During the 1970s, Americans turned to new spiritual movements to find meaning in their lives.

Reading Connection Do you know of any spiritual movements followed today? Read on to learn about the new religions that became popular during the 1970s.

W Many Americans during the 1970s remained optimistic that the United States would eventually move beyond the Watergate scandal, the Vietnam War, and the country's nagging economic problems.

★ An American Story ★

As the United States prepared to celebrate its bicentennial on July 4, 1976, a reporter asked Stoyan Christowe for his views on the state of the nation on the eve of its 200th birthday. The 77-year-old Vermont resident acknowledged that the United States was "in pretty bad shape," but added that the country would turn around—as it always had.

❝I believe in this country. I've always believed in it. There is a quotation by Benjamin Franklin, in a letter to George Washington during the Revolutionary War. Franklin talked of a cornfield during a drought, and how the cornstalks have shriveled and curled, and it was a sad sight. And then, he said a thunderstorm came along, spilling rain, and a day or two after, the sun came out, and the corn came to life, and it was a delight. . . . I know we're going through a kind of turmoil now, but the country is okay. . . . My faith in this country was never shaken. Like that cornfield—the sun will shine again, and the rains will come, and brother, those cornstalks will revive, and it will be a beautiful sight.❞

—quoted in *Newsweek,* July 4, 1976

Some Americans sought new ways to get on with their daily lives while overcoming the country's problems. As a way of coping with anxious times, they sought escape, laughter, and fulfillment in a wide range of fads, entertainment, and spiritual movements.

Writer Tom Wolfe labeled the 1970s the "me" decade, referring to the idea that many Americans grew more self-obsessed in this decade as they strove for greater individual satisfaction. Indeed, the most popular books of the period included such titles as *I'm OK, You're OK; How to Be Your Own Best Friend;*

and *Looking Out for Number One.* Journalist Richard Michael Levine argued that in light of the growing feelings of despair and cynicism about American society, it was little wonder that many people turned inward. In their quest for self-improvement, many Americans were willing to embrace new movements.

R **The New Age Movement** Disenchanted with conventional religions, some young men and women sought fulfillment through secular movements and activities that made up the **New Age movement.** New Age enthusiasts believed that people were responsible for everything from self-healing to creating the world. They believed spiritual enlightenment could be found in common practices, not just in traditional churchgoing. They tried activities such as yoga, martial arts, and chanting to achieve fuller spiritual awareness. Kathy Smith, a college student during the 1970s, recalled how she and others claimed to find "Zen," or enlightenment, in running and other physical activities:

❝They were beginning to understand how exercise affects your soul, how it affects your being. People started getting in the 'Zen' of things: the Zen of tennis, the Zen of working out, the Zen of motorcycle repair, the Zen of running. I, like many others, started connecting physical activity to the spiritual side. People also started looking at yoga and tai chi, and not only the stretching aspects of these disciplines but the **mental** aspects. Now they were working the body, the mind, and the spirit.❞

—quoted in *The Century*

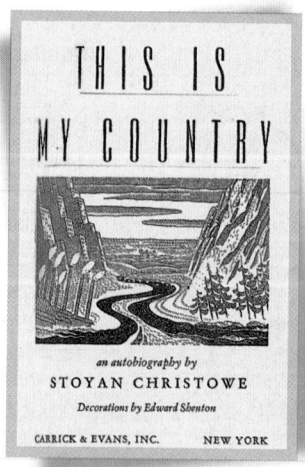

THIS IS MY COUNTRY

an autobiography by
STOYAN CHRISTOWE
Decorations by Edward Shenton

CARRICK & EVANS, INC.   NEW YORK

▲ *Cover of Stoyan Christowe's book*

More Skill Practice

Sequencing Information The fitness craze of the 1970s has continued through today. How has it changed from the 1970s? *(Student responses may include more emphasis on body building and looking good rather than just fitness or the growth of extreme sports. Also, there is less emphasis on fitness as a path to spirituality.)* **OL**

The New Age movement took many different paths to transform individuals and society. Some New Agers extolled the power of crystals and gemstones to improve life; others touted astrology. Some were inspired by the Eastern belief in reincarnation, which taught that people could be reborn many times until reaching perfection. Awareness of former lives was supposed to bring knowledge of the true inner self.

Transcendental Meditation Many Americans who were dissatisfied with established religions sought new religions. A number of these new religions originated in Asia and centered on the teachings of **gurus,** or mystical leaders. One of the more well-known gurus was Maharishi Mahesh Yogi. A native of India, Maharishi moved to the United States in 1959, where he led a spiritual movement known as **transcendental meditation.** Maharishi worked in relative obscurity until 1967, when the wildly popular rock group The Beatles began to explore his teachings. Their attention brought an American following to Maharishi and his spiritual movement. Transcendental meditation suggested daily meditation and the silent repetition of spiritual mantras as a way of achieving peak intelligence, harmony, and health. If all the people on Earth practiced transcendental meditation, its advocates believed, the world would enjoy peace.

Changing Families The search for fulfillment had an impact on many women and American families. The different campaigns of the era, especially the women's movement, began to change how many women viewed their roles as wives and mothers. By 1970, 60 percent of women between the ages of 16 and 24 had joined the labor force. Between 1970 and 1980, women aged 25 to 34 had the largest annual percentage growth in the workforce.

These changes, in turn, led to changes in family life. With women increasingly active outside the home, smaller families became the norm. Many women began to pursue careers, educational opportunities, and other interests instead of focusing solely on the traditional roles of wife and mother. The birthrate fell to an all-time low in 1976, and parents and their children began spending less time together. A greater number of families also split apart, as the divorce rate doubled from 2.5 divorces per thousand people in 1966 to 5 per thousand 10 years later.

Reading Check **Summarizing** What were the basic beliefs of the New Age movement?

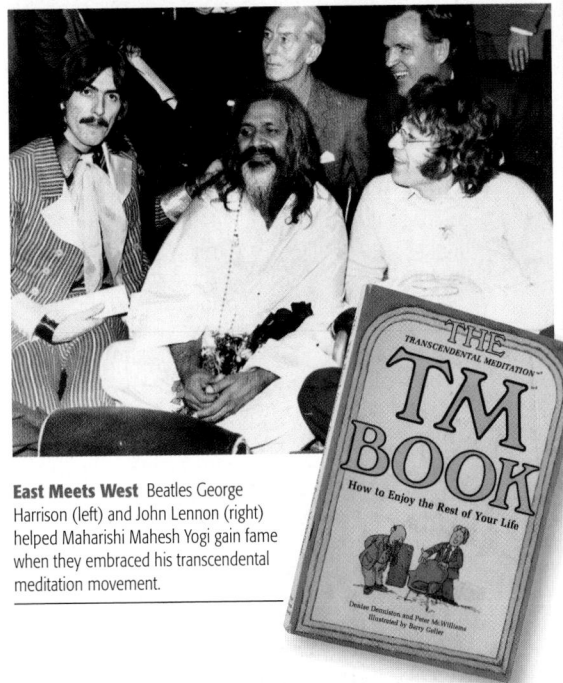

East Meets West Beatles George Harrison (left) and John Lennon (right) helped Maharishi Mahesh Yogi gain fame when they embraced his transcendental meditation movement.

Cultural Trends in the 1970s

Main Idea Television sitcoms began dealing with more difficult aspects of American life, and disco swept the country.

Reading Connection What type of television programming do you watch? Read on to find out about the impact of the 1970s television shows. -TURNING POINT-

Popular culture in the 1970s reflected many of the changes taking place in society. Television now sometimes portrayed women in independent roles or took on formerly taboo subjects such as racism, poverty, and abortion. Meanwhile, Americans listened and danced to new forms of music and sought fun and escape in a variety of new fads.

Television in the 1970s The decade opened with a revolutionary new situation comedy on Saturday nights. Unlike earlier sitcoms, *The Mary Tyler Moore Show* featured an unmarried woman with a meaningful career at its center. Actress Mary Tyler Moore played the main character, Mary Richards, who had left a small town for a big-city job as a television news producer. Mary sparred with her gruff but caring boss, despaired over the shallowness of the blow-dried news announcer, and had adventures with friends. Mary also went on dates but never got around to marrying.

Review the Big Idea

Review the Big Idea for this section, "Societies change over time." Tell students that during the 1970s many New Age movements grew in popularity. **Ask:** Who might be drawn to transcendental meditation after seeing The Beatles photo on this page and hearing about the support of the movement from two of The Beatles? *(young people, music fans)* OL

R Reading Strategy

Connecting Have students reflect on television shows that are popular today. **Ask:** Do reality shows and other shows popular today seem realistic in their depictions of everyday life? *(Students might point out that while the shows are not scripted, and therefore are more "real" than fictional sitcoms, the situations the contestants are placed in are very artificial.)* OL

✓ Reading Check

Answer: New Age enthusiasts embraced the idea that people were responsible for and capable of almost anything. They believed spiritual enlightenment could be found in many different ways, not just traditional churchgoing.

-TURNING POINT-

The 1970s was a time of social change. Popular culture, especially television, reflected these changes. **Ask:** What television programs reflected changing social trends? (*The Mary Tyler Moore Show, All in the Family, and* The Jeffersons *reflected a nation that was growing more accepting of women's empowerment and racial equality.*) OL

Did You Know?

In January 1977, ABC broadcast the *Roots* miniseries and received huge ratings. Based on Alex Haley's 1976 novel, *Roots* traced the history of an African family's enslaved experience through several generations. Media coverage at the time indicated that restaurants and shops noticed a decline in business during the broadcast.

The debut of the sitcom *All in the Family* in January 1971 marked an even bigger turning point in television programming. The show took risks by confronting potentially volatile social issues and by featuring a controversial hero, the blue-collar and bigoted Archie Bunker. Archie called his wife Edith "Dingbat" and his liberal son-in-law "Meathead." He also mocked his feminist daughter and various ethnic groups. Though Archie prided himself on being the man of the house, he never won any arguments with his liberal family or his African American neighbors.

By carefully mixing humor and sensitive issues and by not preaching to its audience, *All in the Family* provided viewers with a way to examine their own feelings about issues such as racism. Producer Norman Lear claimed that the show "holds a mirror up to our prejudices. . . . We laugh now, swallowing just the littlest bit of truth about ourselves. . . ."

Several years later, Archie Bunker's African American neighbors became the stars of another television series, *The Jeffersons*. George Jefferson, like Archie, was opinionated and prejudiced but ultimately likable. *The Jeffersons* portrayed African Americans in a new light: as successful and respected. *Maude,* another spin-off from *All in the Family,* featured Edith Bunker's feminist cousin, who had recently remarried after her third divorce. The strong-willed Maude did not need to depend on her new husband, Walter. This popular

All in the Family Many Americans saw a little of themselves in the characters of this popular sitcom.

program drew intense controversy in 1972 when Maude made the difficult decision to have an abortion.

Maude's African American maid, Florida, generated another series in 1974. Starring Esther Rolle as Florida, *Good Times* portrayed an African American family struggling to raise three children in a low-income housing development in Chicago.

Music of the 1970s The music of this period reflected the end of the 1960s youth and protest movements. The hard-driving rock of the tumultuous 1960s gave way to softer sounds. "The fading out of ear numbing, mind-blowing acid rock," *Time* commented in 1971, "is related to the softening of the youth revolution." The music became more reflective and less political, reflecting a desire to seek fulfillment from within. "These days, nobody wants to hear songs that have a message," said a member of the rock group Chicago. Popular entertainers in tune with the new meditative atmosphere included singers Barry Manilow and John Denver and the bands ABBA and the Eagles.

The 1970s also saw the rise of **disco** music. The disco craze of the later 1970s began in African American and Latin nightclubs. There, disc jockeys played recorded dance music with a loud and persistent beat. The fast pace and easy rhythm attracted fans, but disco also seemed well suited for the "me generation." Unlike rock 'n' roll, disco allowed the people dancing to it to assume greater prominence than the music. As the co-owner of a popular discotheque in New York described the phenomena, "Everybody secretly likes to be on center stage and here we give them a huge space to do it all on."

Gus Rodriguez, who had moved with his family from Puerto Rico to Brooklyn 20 years earlier, recalled going to discos with his friends in the mid-1970s:

❝We would go to the discos several times a week, but the weekends were always the best. Getting ready to go out was sort of a ritual, especially on Saturdays. During the day you would go buy that shirt, or that belt, or those platform shoes, all of which seemed incredibly important at the time. You had to have a particular type of look. And we all dressed the same way. We would call each other up to coordinate what color suits everybody was wearing—who's wearing the powder-blue suit, who's wearing the white suit, who's wearing this, who's wearing that. And then we would carefully iron everything so it was just so.❞

—quoted in *The Century*

Disco mania reached its peak after the 1977 movie, *Saturday Night Fever*. In the film, a middle-class Italian American teenager played by John Travolta transformed himself into a white-suited disco king each Saturday night. The movie's soundtrack sold millions of copies and spurred a wave of disco openings across the country and around the world.

Fads and Fashions In addition to disco, the nation embraced many other fads during the 1970s. Americans by the millions bought T-shirts that bore personalized messages, while teenagers flew down suburban and city streets on skateboards. Obsessed with self-discovery, a number of Americans slipped mood rings on their fingers to get in touch with their innermost feelings. Supposedly, the ring's color changed to match the wearer's ever-changing mood. Blue, for example, signaled happiness and bliss, while gray **denoted** nervousness and anxiety.

Meanwhile, millions of drivers bought citizens band ("CB") radios for their vehicles. This radio system allowed drivers to talk to each other over a two-way frequency within a range of a few miles. Many truck drivers installed the radios in an effort to warn each other of police and speed traps. Soon, however, average drivers had purchased them, mostly for entertainment purposes. Drivers adopted their own CB name, or "handle," and talked to each other using CB jargon and code words.

Fitness was another trend during the "me" decade, as many Americans turned to exercise to improve the way they felt and looked. One popular type of exercise in the 1970s was aerobics. Physician Kenneth H. Cooper popularized the exercise concept in his 1968 book *Aerobics*. It was a way to achieve cardiovascular fitness without the drudgery and isolation that often accompanies physical exercise. This new way to stay

▲ *Children enjoy skateboarding during the 1970s*

fit while having fun and **interacting** socially with others quickly gained popularity. By the mid-1970s, men and women were dancing in gyms across the country. Running also attracted a wide following, as scores of Americans began pounding the pavement to stay fit and trim. In a testament to the popularity of running, athlete Jim Fixx's work *The Complete Book of Running* was a bestseller following its publication in 1977.

By the end of the 1970s, a number of these fads and trends began to fade. A decade in which Americans came to recognize their country's vulnerability and its limits had ended. As the new decade dawned, Americans looked forward to regaining confidence in their country and optimism in their own futures.

 Reading Check **Examining** What was the impact of disco music on American society?

 Study Central

For help with the concepts in this section of *American Vision: Modern Times* go to tav.mt.glencoe.com and click on *Study Central*.

SECTION 4 ASSESSMENT

Checking for Understanding
1. **Vocabulary** Define: mental, guru, transcendental meditation, disco, denote, interact.
2. **People and Terms** Identify: New Age movement, *All in the Family*.
3. **Summarize** the basic beliefs of followers of transcendental meditation.

Reviewing Big Ideas
4. **Describing** What new cultural trends affected American society in the 1970s?

Critical Thinking
5. **Analyzing** How did television in the 1970s reflect society at that time?
6. **Organizing** Complete a graphic organizer similar to the one below by listing the cultural trends of the 1970s.

Cultural Trends of the 1970s

Analyzing Visuals
7. **Analyzing Photographs** Study the photographs in the "What Life Was Like" feature on pages 876–877. How has popular music and fashion changed since the 1970s?

Writing About History
8. **Descriptive Writing** View a television program that was popular in the 1970s. Write a description of the program and explain how it reflected society at that time. CA 11WA2.1e

CHAPTER 19 Politics and Economics **875**

SECTION 4 ASSESSMENT ANSWERS

1. Content vocabulary is boldfaced and highlighted in yellow. Academic vocabulary is boldfaced.
2. New Age movement *(p. 872)*, *All in the Family (p. 874)*
3. daily meditation and mantras as a way of achieving peak intelligence, harmony, and health
4. television dealt with controversial issues; transcendental meditation; disco and new fashion developed; fitness became a craze
5. Television portrayed characters in situations similar to what viewers were experiencing.
6. disco music, CBs, fitness, social issues on television, T-shirts with messages, mood rings
7. Dance music has become more varied; fashions less tailored and more casual
8. Students' descriptions will vary. Encourage students to comment on the content, music, wardrobe, language, and settings used in the television program.

875

What *Life* Was Like...

FOCUS

History– Social Science Standards

This feature addresses the following standards:

11.8 Students analyze the economic boom and social transformation of post–World War II America.

11.8.8 Discuss forms of popular culture, with emphasis on their origins and geographic diffusion (e.g., jazz and other forms of popular music, professional sports, architectural and artistic styles).

TEACH

U Universal Access

Cultural Perspectives U.S. culture often has an impact on the cultures of other countries. People in other nations watch translated versions of American television and movies and buy American-style clothing. Divide the class into groups of three and ask each group to research ways that 1970s popular culture impacted other nations around the world. Each group should write a three-page report of their findings. Encourage the groups to use visual images that demonstrate the presence of American culture around the world. **AL**

Answers and Additional Support

Disco

The counterculture of the 1960s provided music designed to raise people's consciousness of social issues. The disco music of the 1970s, with its simple lyrics and intense beats, was designed simply to entertain. By the end of the decade, millions of people throughout the nation and the world were dancing under flashing disco lights.

Bee Gees
Disco fans around the country and the world danced to the sounds of the Australian group the Bee Gees. The movie *Saturday Night Fever* featured their music and catapulted them into the limelight.

Fashion
New styles of clothing, first associated with disco patrons, became common for everyone. Men wore brightly patterned synthetic shirts, bell-bottom pants, and platform shoes or boots. Women wore wildly patterned dresses or jumpsuits with high heels or boots.

876 CHAPTER 19 Politics and Economics

EXTENDING THE CONTENT

Rise and Fall of Disco Deejays in underground clubs were the first to give exposure to disco music in the 1960s. As it gained more popularity, it reached the airwaves. In addition to the Bee Gees, Tina Turner, and The Jackson 5, other artists made a name for themselves. Among them were Donna Summer, Gloria Gaynor, Kool and the Gang, and the Village People. European disco also became popular in the United States, with the Swedish group ABBA as its main representative. By the early 1980s disco faded in popularity, but it remained alive in clubs, and some artists, such as the Bee Gees and Donna Summer, continued to tour the country giving concerts.

Saturday Night Fever
John Travolta played the role of Tony Manero in this 1977 film. By day Tony worked as a clerk in a Brooklyn store. At night, however, he transformed himself into a disco star. A popular success, the film showed Tony as a young working-class kid with a dream to escape his ordinary existence. Life at the disco provided a road to that escape.

R • **Music** •
Music icons of the early 1970s included Tina Turner and The Jackson 5. The music of The Jackson 5 was an upbeat pop-soul mix that differed from the typical Motown sound of previous years.

UNDERSTANDING THE TIME

Checking for Understanding
1. **Identifying** What were the new styles in fashion for men and women?

Critical Thinking
2. **Explaining** How would you compare the pop culture of the 1970s to the pop culture of today? Explain what ideas are similar and what ideas are different.

S **Skill Practice**
Scaffolding—Identifying Connections Have students think about the connections between the disco culture and particular historical and larger social and economic trends and developments. **Ask: In what ways did disco reflect American society in the 1970s?** *(Students should consider the differences between the youth culture of the 1960s, which stressed a rejection of material values and a search for spiritual enlightenment, and the Disco culture of the late 1970s, which reflected an increasing interest in flashiness, pure entertainment, and consumerism.)* **AL** **CA** HI1, HI3
This **Historical Analysis** skill was introduced in Chapter 12.

R **Reading Strategy**
Organizing Information Ask students to review the imagery and text on this spread, identifying what separated the fashion, music, and culture of the 1970s from current culture. Students should list differences in graphic organizers similar to the one shown below. *(Answers could include: 70s collars tended to be wider, fabrics were more "metallic" and colorful, pant legs flared more dramatically. Other differences will depend upon the styles and entertainment of today.)* **BL** **CA** CS4; HI1

Differences by decade	
1970s	today

ASSESS/CLOSE

Have students answer the Checking for Understanding and Critical Thinking Questions.

ANSWERS TO UNDERSTANDING THE TIME

Checking for Understanding
1. men: brightly patterned synthetic shirts, bell-bottom pants, and platform shoes or boots; women: wild patterned dresses or jumpsuits, high heels or boots

Critical Thinking
2. Students' answers will vary but should compare styles from the 1970s to the present.

FOCUS

Understanding Vocabulary

Before students begin reading, point out that difficult or unfamiliar words are footnoted throughout the text.

TEACH

R Reading Strategy

Connecting Tell students to think about a time when they had to quit something. Invite volunteers to share their memories with the class. Then discuss the Watergate scandal by asking: **Do you think putting the interest of the country first was the main reason for Nixon's resignation?** *(Answers will vary.)* **OL**

Answers and Additional Support

Primary Sources
Eyewitness to History

The Watergate scandal deeply shocked and divided the country. When congressional investigations showed evidence that President Nixon was far more involved than he first admitted, he resigned from the presidency.

SOURCE 1:

On August 9, 1974, as he faced certain impeachment for the Watergate scandal, President Nixon became the first person to resign from the presidency. Nixon announced his impending resignation in a nationwide television address on the evening of August 8.

In all the decisions I have made in my public life, I have always tried to do what was best for the Nation. Throughout the long and difficult period of Watergate, I have felt it was my duty to persevere, to make every possible effort to complete the term of office to which you elected me. . . .

I have never been a quitter. To leave office before my time is completed is **abhorrent**[1] to every instinct in my body. But as President, I must put the interest of America first. America needs a full-time President and a full-time Congress, particularly at this time with problems we face at home and abroad. . . .

I regret deeply any injuries that may have been done in the course of the events that led to this decision. I would say only that if some of my judgments were wrong, and some were wrong, they were made in what I believed at the time to be the best interest of the Nation.

To those who have stood with me during these past difficult months, to my family, my friends, to many others who joined in supporting my cause because they believed it was right, I will be eternally grateful for your support.

And to those who have not felt able to give me your support, let me say I leave with no bitterness toward those who have opposed me, because all of us, in the final analysis, have been concerned with the good of the country, however our judgments might differ.

[1] **abhorrent:** detestable

▲ *The House Judiciary Committee moves to recommend the impeachment of President Nixon on July 30, 1974.*

SOURCE 2:

The House of Representatives accepted the report of the House Judiciary Committee on August 20, 1974, ending the impeachment process. Committee members were aware that they were writing for the historical record. One member, California Democrat Don Edwards, added his supplemental views to the report.

In his attempts to **subvert**[2] the processes of representative government and the guarantees of the Bill of Rights, Mr. Nixon and his associates used repeatedly the justification he described as "national security."

It was a familiar theme, referred to by James Madison in a letter to Jefferson in 1786. "Perhaps it is a universal truth," wrote the author of the Bill of Rights, "that the loss of liberty at home is to be

[2] **subvert:** undermine

UNIVERSAL ACCESS

Interpersonal Have students interview a relative or friend who remembers the Watergate scandal. First, have them prepare a list of interview questions such as: **How did you feel when you learned that President Nixon was resigning from office? Did the scandal change your opinions about democracy?** Remind students to take notes or tape-record the answers they receive. Then have them write a two-page report detailing what they learned in the interview. Encourage students to illustrate their report with original drawings, headlines, or historical photographs. **OL**

SOURCE 3:

On September 8, 1974, President Gerald Ford granted former president Richard Nixon a full pardon for all offenses. The pardon was extremely controversial and ended Ford's brief honeymoon with Congress and the American people.

There are no historic or legal precedents to which I can turn in this matter, none that precisely fit the circumstances of a private citizen who has resigned the presidency of the United States. But it is common knowledge that serious allegations and accusations hang like a sword over our former President's head, threatening his health, as he tries to reshape his life, a great part of which was spent in the service of this country and by the mandate of its people.

After years of bitter controversy and divisive national debate, I have been advised and I am compelled to conclude that many months and perhaps more years will have to pass before Richard Nixon could obtain a fair trial by jury in any jurisdiction of the United States. . . .

I deeply believe in equal justice for all Americans, whatever their station or former station. The law, whether human or divine, is no respecter of persons but the law is a respecter of reality. The facts as I see them are that a former President of the United States, instead of enjoying equal treatment with any other citizen accused of violating the law, would be cruelly and excessively penalized either in preserving the presumption of his innocence or in obtaining a speedy determination of his guilt in order to repay a legal debt to society.

During this long period of delay and potential litigation, ugly passions would again be aroused, and our people would again be polarized in their opinions, and the credibility of our free institutions of government would again be challenged at home and abroad. . . .

▲ *President Ford announces Nixon's pardon.*

charged to the provisions against dangers, real or pretended, from abroad." . . .

I found it immensely disturbing that the talented and distinguished counsel for Mr. Nixon in the impeachment inquiry supported the view that the mere invocation of the catch phrase "national security" justified illegal wiretaps and personal surveillances. Indeed, he told the Judiciary Committee that in his view a President should be impeached for *not* proceeding as Mr. Nixon did.

So, I am writing these supplementary views to emphasize the urgency of Madison's two hundred year old warning. Congress, the press, and indeed all of the American people must be vigilant to the perils of the subversive notion that any public official, the President or a policeman, possesses a kind of inherent power to set aside the Constitution whenever he thinks the public interest, or "national security" warrants it. That notion is the essential **postulate**[3] of tyranny.

³**postulate:** claim or theory

DBQ — Document-Based Questions

Historical Analysis CA CSI; HR2; HR4; HI2

Source 1: Why is Nixon resigning?

Source 2: According to Edwards, why were Nixon's actions wrong?

Source 3: Why is Ford granting a pardon to Nixon?

Comparing and Contrasting Sources
Based on Nixon, Edwards, and Ford, how should democratic government be protected? Explain.

W Writing Support

Persuasive Writing Divide the class into groups of four. Tell the groups to read about Don Edwards's fears about the abuse of "national security." Tell each group to write a one-page response to this question: **Which do you think should dominate: personal rights and liberties or the safety of the majority? Why?** Invite a volunteer from each group to read the group's statement. Then allow time for the groups to pose questions to one another. Finally, have students work independently to write a paragraph or journal entry that explains their answer to the following question: **In your opinion, which group wrote the most persuasive argument? Why?** Remind students to provide evidence or quotations to support their claims. OL CA 11WA2.2a

R Reading Strategy

Reading Primary Sources After the class has read the pardon, ask if Ford's effort improved Americans' attitudes toward former President Nixon. *(Answers will vary.)* Have students use library and Internet resources to locate newspaper or magazine articles or editorials written in response to the pardon. Then ask students to write a short essay explaining their answers to the following questions: **Do you think the author of the article agrees or disagrees with Ford's pardon of Nixon? How do you know?** Remind students to quote words or phrases from the article that reveal the author's tone. OL
CA 11RC2.5

DBQ   Document-Based Questions

Historical Analysis
1. Nixon is facing impeachment and wants the nation to re-focus on other problems at home and abroad.
2. He believed that Nixon acted tyrannically by setting aside rights guaranteed under the Constitution in the name of "national security."

3. Ford feels that Nixon is being overly penalized for his crimes and is not able to receive equal justice.

Comparing and Contrasting Sources
Answers will vary. Students may note that Nixon, Edwards, and Ford all believed that Americans should be united in the protection of democratic ideals.

ASSESS/CLOSE

Have students answer the Document-Based Questions.

Standards 11.3, 11.3.4, 11.8.4, 11.8.8, 11.9.3, 11.9.6, 11.10.7, 11.11, 11.11.2, 11.11.3, 11.11.4, 11.11.6, 11.11.7

Resources for pages 880–881

Use the following resources to review, assess, and reteach the chapter.

- Chapter 19 Tests, Forms A and B
- Standardized Tests, Forms A and B
- Cumulative Authentic Assessment
- MindJogger Videoquiz
- Interactive Tutor Self-Assessment CD-ROM
- ExamView® Pro Testmaker CD-ROM
- Vocabulary PuzzleMaker CD-ROM
- Succeeding on . . .™ the California Standards: Grade 11 History–Social Science
- California Standards Practice, Grade 11

Reviewing Content Vocabulary

Students' answers will vary. The pages where the words appear in the text are shown in parentheses.

1. impound *(p. 853)* **2.** détente *(p. 855)* **3.** summit *(p. 855)* **4.** executive privilege *(p. 860)* **5.** impeach *(p. 861)* **6.** inflation *(p. 864)* **7.** embargo *(p. 865)* **8.** stagflation *(p. 865)* **9.** guru *(p. 873)* **10.** transcendental meditation *(p. 873)* **11.** disco *(p. 874)*

Reviewing Academic Vocabulary

Students' answers will vary. The pages where the words appear in the text are shown in parentheses.

12. supplement *(p. 853)* **13.** notion *(p. 854)* **14.** potential *(p. 855)* **15.** attribute *(p. 858)* **16.** obtain *(p. 859)* **17.** inevitable *(p. 861)* **18.** norm *(p. 864)* **19.** acknowledge *(p. 866)* **20.** devote *(p. 867)* **21.** mental *(p. 872)* **22.** denote *(p. 875)* **23.** interact *(p. 875)*

Reviewing Content Vocabulary

On a sheet of paper, use each of these terms in a sentence.

1. impound
2. détente
3. summit
4. executive privilege
5. impeach
6. inflation
7. embargo
8. stagflation
9. guru
10. transcendental meditation
11. disco

Reviewing Academic Vocabulary

On a sheet of paper, use each of these terms in a sentence that reflects the term's meaning in the chapter.

12. supplement
13. notion
14. potential
15. attribute
16. obtain
17. inevitable
18. norm
19. acknowledge
20. devote
21. mental
22. denote
23. interact

Reviewing the Main Ideas

Section 1
24. What were the main aspects of President Nixon's domestic and foreign policies?

Section 2
25. What was the impact of the Watergate scandal on the American people?

Section 3
26. Why did President Nixon freeze wages and prices in the early 1970s?

27. What factors caused economic problems in the United States in the 1970s?

Section 4
28. What changes in family life occurred in the United States in the 1970s?

Critical Thinking

29. **Reading Skill** Using Problem/Solution Reread the text "Triumph and Failure in the Middle East" on pages 869–870. Write down the foreign policy problems and solutions Jimmy Carter faced while president. What were the results of the problems?

30. **Civics** Identify the new laws intended to limit the power of the executive branch following the Watergate scandal.

31. **Evaluating** What impact did cultural phenomena such as disco music and exercise trends have on the U.S. economy?

32. **Categorizing** Complete a chart similar to the one below by listing the attempts each president made to strengthen the nation's economy.

President	Attempts to Strengthen Economy
Nixon	
Ford	
Carter	

Writing About History

33. **Historical Analysis** Interpreting Events What might have happened differently in the Middle East if President Carter had not allowed the Shah to seek medical treatment in the U.S.? **CA HI4**

Chapter Summary

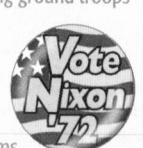

Uniting a Divided Country
- Nixon's conservative politics appeal to "Middle America."
- Nixon begins pulling ground troops out of Vietnam.
- Tensions with Soviet Union and China ease.
- Nixon signs treaty limiting nuclear arms.

Scandal and Economic Turmoil
- Watergate scandal brings down Nixon.
- Congress enacts new laws to limit presidential power.
- Inflation, energy crisis, and foreign competition cause economic slowdown.
- Ford and Carter fail to revive economy.

Challenging Traditional Values
- New Age movement advocates self-fulfillment.
- More women join the workforce.
- Television shows prominently feature African Americans and independent women; address sensitive issues such as racism and abortion.

880 CHAPTER 19 Politics and Economics

Reviewing the Main Ideas

24. Nixon's domestic policy focused on the New Federalism, and his foreign policy focused on détente.

25. Most Americans lost trust in public officials.

26. President Nixon believed wage and price freezes would stop stagflation, a combination of rising prices and economic stagnation.

27. rising oil prices, increased international competition, low job training for new jobs, and a decline in manufacturing

28. Changes in family life included smaller families, more divorces, parents and children spending less time together, and women becoming more active in the workplace and outside the home.

HISTORY Online

Self-Check Quiz

Visit the *American Vision–Modern Times* Web site at tav.mt.glencoe.com and click on **Self-Check Quizzes– Chapter 19** to access your knowledge of the chapter content.

---

34. *Big Idea* Examine an artifact from this era. You can find artifacts in museums, art galleries, and even in your own home. What sorts of artifacts could you find about the 1970s? Create a chart listing possible artifacts and how they represent the 1970s.

DBQ Document-Based Questions

35. **Interpreting Primary Sources** When the Arab-Israeli War of 1973 developed into a stalemate, the Arab nations imposed an oil embargo on the United States, the chief supporter of Israel. Because Arab countries supplied much of the oil used in the United States, the embargo created an energy crisis. The excerpt below is taken from an article in the December 3, 1973, issue of *U.S. News & World Report.* It details the growing energy problems that the United States was facing at that time. Read the excerpt and answer the questions that follow.

❝Evidence of the full dimensions of the energy crisis in this country is becoming more clear each day.

• Electric-power brownouts, even blackouts, are predicted for many parts of the U.S. before the end of the year.

• Voltage reduction of 5 percent from 4 P.M. to 8 P.M. each day was ordered starting November 26 in all six New England States, where fuel shortages threaten homes, schools, factories. . . .

• As a first step to cut gasoline use, President Nixon was reportedly ready to order closing of service stations nationwide from 9 P.M. Saturday to midnight Sunday on weekends. . . .

• Immediate rationing of gasoline and fuel oil is being urged on the President by top oil-industry executives. . . .

   One major piece of legislation . . . directs the President to take measures necessary to reduce the nation's energy demands by 25 percent within four weeks.

   Speed limits would be cut nationally; lighting and heating of public and commercial buildings would be curtailed; homeowners would be given tax deductions to winterize their homes. . . .

   Other pending measures would impose year round daylight saving time and would open naval oil reserves for intensive exploration. . . .❞

a. What proposals did the U.S. government make to deal with the energy crisis?

b. What lessons do you think the United States might have learned from the crisis?

Inflation, 1960–1992

Economics and History

36. The graph above shows inflation rates in the United States from 1960 to 1992. Study the graph and answer the questions below.

   a. **Interpreting Graphs** How did the nation's inflation rate change between 1965 and 1980?

   b. **Determining Cause and Effect** What factor was most important in causing this change?

Standards Practice

Directions: Choose the phrase that best completes the following sentence.

37. As a political conservative, President Nixon wanted to

A increase federal spending on welfare programs.

B take more aggressive federal action to speed desegregation.

C return power to state governments.

D appoint activist-minded justices to the Supreme Court.

Standard 11.11: Students analyze the major social problems and domestic policy issues in contemporary American society.

CHAPTER 19   Politics and Economics   881

Critical Thinking

29. **Reading Skill** **Problems:** turmoil in the Middle East between Israel and Egypt; Revolutionaries in Iran held 52 Americans hostage; **Solutions:** Carter brokered Camp David Accords; negotiating the release of hostages failed and rescue mission failed when helicopters malfunctioned and crashed

30. Federal Campaign Act Amendments, Ethics in Government Act, and the FBI Domestic Security Investigation Guidelines

31. Disco music led to the opening of dance clubs; exercise clubs opened throughout the country. Each helped the economy expand.

32. Nixon: cut spending, raised taxes, raised interest rates, and froze wages and prices; Ford: urged Americans to cut back on gas and oil consumption and undertake other energy-conserving measures; cut government spending and advocated higher interest rates, attempted to limit federal authority, balance the budget, and keep taxes low; Carter: increased

---

CHAPTER 19
Assessment and Activities

HISTORY Online

Have students visit the Web site at tav.mt.glencoe.com to review Chapter 19 and take the Self-Check Quiz.

government spending, cut taxes, reduced the money supply, and raised interest rates

Writing About History

33. **Historical Analysis** Students' answers will vary. Answers should be logical and concise.

34. *Big Idea* Students' charts will vary but should include analysis of 1970s artifacts.

DBQ Document-Based Questions

35. **a.** Proposals included cutting speed limits, curtailing heat and lighting in public buildings, giving tax deductions for homeowners to winterize their homes, imposing year-round daylight savings time, and opening the naval oil reserves for exploration. **b.** Students' answers will vary.

Economics and History

36. **a.** The inflation rate increased from under 2 percent in 1965 to over 12 percent in 1980. **b.** The rise in the price of crude oil was the biggest factor for the ballooning rate of inflation.

Standards Practice

37. C

Bonus Question?

Ask: What did the impeachment process test? *(the system of checks and balances)*

881

Chapter 20 Planning Guide

SECTION RESOURCES

MAIN IDEAS	🗀 PRINT MATERIALS	TECHNOLOGY RESOURCES
Section 1: The New Conservatism 1. Conservatives and liberals disagree on the role of government. 2. Americans turned to conservatism in a reaction against the government's influence on the economy. 3. Geographical regions tend to support either liberal or conservative ideas.	• Reproducible Lesson Plan 20-1* • Daily Lecture and Discussion Notes 20-1 • Active Reading Note-Taking Guide 20-1 • Guided Reading Activity 20-1 • Section Quiz 20-1 • Reading Essentials and Study Guide 20-1	Daily Focus Skills Transparency 20-1 Section Graphic Organizer Transparency 20-1 Interactive Tutor Self-Assessment CD-ROM Exam*View*® Pro Testmaker CD-ROM Presentation Plus! CD-ROM California Standards Practice Transparencies
Section 2: The Reagan Years 1. President Reagan's experiences in Hollywood and as governor of California led to his successful campaign for presidency. 2. Believing that government was part of the problem, President Reagan cut social service programs, sponsored tax cuts, and deregulated industry. 3. President Reagan oversaw the largest peacetime buildup of the military in American history. 4. President Reagan supported governments fighting communism, a policy known as the Reagan Doctrine. 5. President Reagan's decision to place nuclear missiles in Western Europe triggered calls for a "nuclear freeze."	• Reproducible Lesson Plan 20-2* • Daily Lecture and Discussion Notes 20-2 • Active Reading Note-Taking Guide 20-2 • Guided Reading Activity 20-2 • Section Quiz 20-2 • Reading Essentials and Study Guide 20-2	Daily Focus Skills Transparency 20-2 Section Graphic Organizer Transparency 20-2 Interactive Tutor Self-Assessment CD-ROM Exam*View*® Pro Testmaker CD-ROM Presentation Plus! CD-ROM California Standards Practice Transparencies
Section 3: Life in the 1980s 1. The economic recovery and spending habits of young urban professionals brought on a boom. 2. New technologies expanded music, video, and television capabilities. 3. Social problems such as drug and alcohol abuse, crime, and the AIDS epidemic affected many people during the 1980s. 4. Many groups became more politically active during the 1980s. 5. As the nation sent out space shuttles and prepared for space stations, it experienced gains and losses.	• Reproducible Lesson Plan 20-3* • Daily Lecture and Discussion Notes 20-3 • Active Reading Note-Taking Guide 20-3 • Guided Reading Activity 20-3 • Section Quiz 20-3 • Reading Essentials and Study Guide 20-3	Daily Focus Skills Transparency 20-3 Section Graphic Organizer Transparency 20-3 Interactive Tutor Self-Assessment CD-ROM Exam*View*® Pro Testmaker CD-ROM Presentation Plus! CD-ROM California Standards Practice Transparencies
Section 4: The End of the Cold War 1. Since many Americans had benefited from the economic boom of the 1980s, they elected Republican George Bush as president in 1988. 2. Reforms in the Soviet Union and the collapse of the Communist regime led to the end of the Cold War. 3. Bush used his foreign policy expertise to deal with crises in China, Panama, and the Persian Gulf. 4. To stimulate the economy, President Bush raised taxes, but lost the election to Bill Clinton.	• Reproducible Lesson Plan 20-4* • Daily Lecture and Discussion Notes 20-4 • Active Reading Note-Taking Guide 20-4 • Guided Reading Activity 20-4 • Section Quiz 20-4 • Reading Essentials and Study Guide 20-4	Daily Focus Skills Transparency 20-4 Section Graphic Organizer Transparency 20-4 Interactive Tutor Self-Assessment CD-ROM Exam*View*® Pro Testmaker CD-ROM Presentation Plus! CD-ROM California Standards Practice Transparencies

PACING YOUR LESSONS

Chapter Introduction	Section 1	Section 2	Section 3	Section 4	Chapter Assessment
½ Day	2 Days	2 Days	2 Days	2 Days	½ Day

0:00 OUT OF TIME? 🗀 Assign the Chapter 20 *Reading Essentials and Study Guide.*

*Available on TeacherWorks™ CD-ROM

Chapter 20 Planning Guide

Standards-Based Lesson Plan

 History–Social Science Standards Covered in Chapter 20

The standards covered in the chapter are listed below. Use the accompanying activity as you teach the chapter to ensure student mastery of these standards. This activity can be used in combination with the program's print and technology assessment materials.

Standard	Section 1	2	3	4
11.3.2 Analyze the great religious revivals and the leaders involved in them, including the First Great Awakening, the Second Great Awakening, the Civil War revivals, the Social Gospel Movement, the rise of Christian liberal theology in the nineteenth century, the impact of the Second Vatican Council, and the rise of Christian fundamentalism in current times.	✔			
11.8.4 Analyze new federal government spending on defense, welfare, interest on the national debt, and federal and state spending on education, including the California Master Plan.		✔		✔
11.9.5 Analyze the role of the Reagan administration and other factors in the victory of the West in the Cold War.		✔		✔
11.9.6 Describe U.S. Middle East policy and its strategic, political, and economic interests, including those related to the Gulf War.		✔		✔
11.11.2 Discuss the significant domestic policy speeches of Truman, Eisenhower, Kennedy, Johnson, Nixon, Carter, Reagan, Bush, and Clinton (e.g., with regard to education, civil rights, economic policy, environmental policy).		✔		
11.11.7 Explain how the federal, state, and local governments have responded to demographic and social changes such as population shifts to the suburbs, racial concentrations in the cities, Frostbelt-to-Sunbelt migration, international migration, decline of family farms, increases in out-of-wedlock births, and drug abuse.	✔		✔	✔

Cumulative Standards-Assessment Activity

The Cumulative Standards-Assessment Activity will help students organize and learn the important information from the chapter. Begin teaching the chapter with this activity, and have students complete it as they read the chapter.

CREATING A CAUSE-AND-EFFECT CHART

Purpose Using cause and effect as a study tool will enable students to see how prevailing attitudes and ideas are related to political and social events, and how historical events are related to each other. Making cause-and-effect connections will also help students understand the importance of studying history and can lead to lessons on individual responsibility, comprehending interconnectedness, and applying lessons of the past to the present and future.

Introduction to Making Connections

1. Begin by choosing a cause and effect from current events. Ask students to explain how the effect resulted from the cause. In addition, see if they can list other effects of the cause. Then encourage students to relate this current event to their own lives. What effect might it have on them, their families, friends, or neighbors?

2. Explain to students how they can use the same skill to understand the significance of historical events.

3. Ask students to copy this chart into their notebooks.

Causes	Effects

Ask the class to chart causes and effects from the chapter as they read. Remind them that one cause may have many effects.

4. As part of the chapter review, have students share their charts of causes and effects. Allow discussion to develop around items about which the students disagree. Encourage the class to use their charts as study aids.

Chapter 20 Planning Guide

READING SUPPORT

- Content Vocabulary Activity 20
- Academic Vocabulary Activity 20
- Reading Skills Activity 20
- Chapter 20 Active Reading Note-Taking Guide
- Chapter 20 Guided Reading Activities
- Chapter 20 Reading Essentials and Study Guide
- American Literature Readings, Unit 6
- *The American Vision: Modern Times* Video Program
- Vocabulary PuzzleMaker CD-ROM
- American History Primary Source Document Library CD-ROM

CRITICAL THINKING

- Critical Thinking Skills Activity 20
- Primary Source Reading 20
- Cause-and-Effect Transparency 20 Strategy and Activity
- Presentation Plus! CD-ROM

UNIVERSAL ACCESS

- Universal Access Activity 20
- English Learner Activity 20
- American Art Prints
- StudentWorks™ Plus CD-ROM
- American Music: Hits Through History
- School-to-Home Connection Activity 20

SKILL PRACTICE

- Map Overlay Transparency 20 Strategy and Activity
- Historical Analysis Skills Activity 20
- Time Line Activity 20
- Reading Skills Activity 20
- Reinforcing Skills Activity 20
- Linking Past and Present Activity 20
- Interpreting Political Cartoons 20
- MindJogger Videoquiz

WRITING SUPPORT

- Chapter 20 Active Reading Note-Taking Guide
- Writer's Guidebook
- High School Writing Process Transparencies

ASSESSMENT

- Chapter 20 Section Quizzes
- Chapter 20 Tests, Forms A and B
- Authentic Assessment Activity 20
- Exam*View*® Pro Testmaker CD-ROM
- Interactive Tutor Self-Assessment CD-ROM
- California Standards Practice, Grade 11
- Succeeding on . . .™ the California Standards: Grade 11 History–Social Science CD-ROM

- CD-ROM
- DVD
- Print Material
- Poster
- Transparency
- Music Program
- Videocassette

Chapter 20 Planning Guide

TECHNOLOGY

- StudentWorks™ Plus CD-ROM
- TeacherWorks™ CD-ROM
- ExamView® Pro Testmaker CD-ROM
- Interactive Tutor Self-Assessment CD-ROM
- Presentation Plus! CD-ROM
- Vocabulary PuzzleMaker CD-ROM
- American History Primary Source Document Library CD-ROM
- MindJogger Videoquiz
- *The American Vision: Modern Times* Video Program
- Professional Development in High School Social Studies Video Series
- Teach, Use, and Succeed With *The American Vision: Modern Times*
- American Music: Hits Through History
- Succeeding on . . .™ the California Standards: Grade 11 History–Social Science CD-ROM

SPANISH RESOURCES

- Spanish Activities and Assessment
  - Spanish Vocabulary Activities
  - Spanish Guided Reading Activities
  - Spanish Quizzes and Tests
  - Spanish Reteaching Activities
- Spanish Reading Essentials and Study Guide
- Spanish School-to-Home Connection Activities

TRANSPARENCIES

- Daily Focus Skills Transparencies
- Section Graphic Organizer Transparencies
- Map Overlay Transparencies
- Cause-and-Effect Transparencies
- Unit Time Line Transparencies
- Why It Matters Transparencies
- American Art and Architecture Transparencies
- High School Writing Process Transparencies
- California Standards Practice Transparencies

TEACHER PLANNING

- Daily Lecture and Discussion Notes
- English Learner Handbook
- Building Academic Vocabulary
- *The American Vision: Modern Times* Reading and Study Skills Foldables
- Reading Strategies and Activities for the Social Studies Classroom
- Universal Access for the American History Classroom
- NGS United States Desk Map
- NGS World Atlas
- Chapter 20 Reproducible Lesson Plans on TeacherWorks™ CD-ROM
- California Guide to Daily Intervention

PROFESSIONAL DEVELOPMENT

- Building Academic Vocabulary
- Strategies for Success
- Research-Based Strategies Used to Develop *The American Vision: Modern Times*
- Character Education in the High School Classroom
- Professional Development in High School Social Studies Video Series
- Teach, Use, and Succeed With *The American Vision: Modern Times*

TEACHER'S CORNER

Index to National Geographic Magazine:

The following articles relate to this chapter:

- "Alcohol, the Legal Drug," February 1992
- "A Broken Empire," March 1993
- "Persian Gulf Pollution," February 1992

National Geographic Society Products:

To order the following, call National Geographic at 1–800–368–2728

- *Branches of Government Series* (Video)
- *Democratic Government Series: The United States* (Video)
- *Historical Atlas of the United States* (Atlas)
- *National Geographic Atlas for Young Explorers–Classroom Library Edition* (Guide, Transparencies, Resource Masters)

NGS ONLINE

Access National Geographic's new dynamic MapMachine Web site and other geography resources at:

www.nationalgeographic.com

www.nationalgeographic.com/maps

MASTERING THE STANDARDS

The content and assessment in the Student Edition, Teacher Wraparound Edition, teacher planning materials, and the print and technology products are all standards-based. The use of these products during instruction leads to mastery of the standards.

PRACTICE
- California Standards Practice, Grade 11
- California Standards Practice Transparencies
- School-to-Home Connection

BENCHMARK ASSESSMENT
- Section Quizzes, Chapter Tests, and Authentic Assessment
- ExamView® Pro Testmaker CD-ROM
- Succeeding On ... ™ the California Standards: Grade 11 History–Social Science CD-ROM

REMEDIATION
- California Guide to Daily Intervention
- Interactive Tutor Self-Assessment CD-ROM
- ExamView® Pro Testmaker CD-ROM
- California Standards Practice, Grade 11
- Reading Essentials and Study Guide

 History Online

Use our Web site for additional resources. All essential content is covered in the Student Edition.

You and your students can visit tav.mt.glencoe.com, the Web site companion to the **American Vision: Modern Times.** This innovative integration of electronic and print media offers your students a wealth of opportunities. The student text directs students to the Web site for the following options:

- **Chapter Overviews**
- **Self-Check Quizzes**
- **Student Web Activities**
- **Textbook Updates**

Answers to the student Web activities are provided for you in the **Web Activity Lesson Plans.** Additional Web resources and ePuzzles and games are also available.

 FOLDABLES™ Study Organizer — Dinah Zike's Foldables

Foldables are three-dimensional, interactive graphic organizers that help students practice basic writing skills, review key vocabulary terms, and identify main ideas. Every chapter has a foldable activity in the *Dinah Zike's Reading and Study Skills Foldables* booklet. You can use the foldables as they are presented or modify them to suit the needs of your individual class.

A variety of videotape programs are available from A&E Television and The History Channel to provide teaching assistance. To order, call Glencoe at 1-800-334-7344.

Chapter 20 Planning Guide

KEY for Using the Teacher Wraparound Edition

Use this key to help you identify the different types of prompts found in the Teacher Wraparound Edition.

R **Reading Strategies** activities help you teach reading skills and vocabulary.

C **Critical Thinking** strategies help students apply and extend what they have learned.

U **Universal Access** activities provide differentiated instruction for students learning to speak English, along with suggestions for teaching various types of learners.

S **Skill Practice** strategies help students practice historical analysis and geography skills.

W **Writing Support** activities provide writing opportunities to help students comprehend the text.

Teaching strategies and activities have been coded for ability level appropriateness.

AL Activities for students working above grade level
OL Activities for students working on grade level
BL Activities for students working below grade level
EL Activities for English learners

FOCUS

History–Social Science Standards

This chapter addresses the following main standards:

11.8 Students analyze the economic boom and social transformation of post–World War II America.

11.9 Students analyze U.S. foreign policy since World War II.

BELLRINGER
SKILLBUILDER ACTIVITY

Read the following quotes to the class: "The role of government is to do for people what people cannot do at all for themselves"; and "Government is not the solution to our problem. Government is the problem." Ask students to form two groups based on the quote with which they agree. Each group should prepare arguments supporting their quote to present to the class.

TEACH

Thinking About the Big Ideas

As you begin teaching each section, use these questions and activities to focus on the Big Idea.

Section 1
The New Conservatism
Essential Question: What political changes following World War II supported the growth of political conservatism? *(The focus on defeating the Soviet Union renewed the debate about the role and power of the federal government. Some saw the Cold War as a religious fight between good and evil, which increased*

CHAPTER
1980–1992
20 Resurgence of Conservatism

❧ *The Big Ideas* ❧

SECTION 1: The New Conservatism
Societies change over time. *In the 1980s, discontent with government and changes in society resulted in the rise of a new conservative coalition.*

SECTION 2: The Reagan Years
International competition can lead to conflict and cooperation. *The presidency of Ronald Reagan brought a new conservative attitude to government.*

SECTION 3: Life in the 1980s
Societies change over time. *The 1980s was a decade characterized by wealth, but it was also a time of renewed activism.*

SECTION 4: The End of the Cold War
International competition can lead to conflict and cooperation. *President George Bush's foreign policy commanded broad support, but his domestic agenda did not.*

The *American Vision: Modern Times* Video *The Chapter 20 video, "Tear Down This Wall!" describes the history of the Berlin Wall, one of the Cold War's most powerful symbols.*

United States PRESIDENTS

Carter 1977–1981
Reagan 1981–1989

1979
• Jerry Falwell's "Moral Majority" movement begins

1981
• American hostages released in Iran
• Launch of *Columbia*, first space shuttle

1983
• U.S. Marine barracks bombed in Lebanon

1979   *1982*   *1985*

World

1979
• Iranian revolution establishes Islamic republic
• Soviets invade Afghanistan

1980
• War begins between Iran and Iraq

1985
• Mikhail Gorbachev becomes leader of Soviet Union

882

---

the influence of conservatives in politics.) Tell students that Section 1 will discuss the rise of the new conservative coalition during the early 1980s. **OL**

Section 2
The Reagan Years
Essential Question: Is American politics characterized by conflict or cooperation? *(Govern-*

ment is actually designed for both, but excessive conflict makes it run less effectively.) After students have discussed the questions, tell them that many citizens in the early 1980s were ready to combat a government they believed was increasingly controlling their lives. Section 2 tells how the Reagan presidency brought a different attitude and approach to this issue. **BL**

President Reagan at the Berlin Wall in 1987

1986
- Iran-Contra scandal enters the news

1987
- INF Treaty between U.S. and USSR reduces land-based intermediate-range nuclear missiles

1988
- More than 35,000 cases of AIDS diagnosed for the year

G. Bush 1989–1993

1988

1986
- Dictatorship of Ferdinand Marcos overthrown in the Philippines

1989
- Tiananmen Square protests for democracy break out in China
- Several Communist governments in Eastern Europe collapse

1990
- Germany reunified into one nation

1991
- Persian Gulf War occurs between Iraq and UN coalition

1991

1991
- Soviet Union dissolves

HISTORY Online

Chapter Overview
Visit the *American Vision: Modern Times* Web site at tav.mt.glencoe.com and click on *Chapter Overviews— Chapter 20* to preview chapter information.

883

Section 3
Life in the 1980s
Essential Question: What are the greatest social problems in the United States today? Have students quickly list the problems they see as the most important facing society today. (*drugs, AIDS, homelessness, alcoholism, crime*) Tell students that Section 3 will examine how activists in the 1980s addressed the social issues of the decade. OL

Section 4
The End of the Cold War
Essential Question: What areas of problems do presidents face? Make a T-chart on the board with the headings *Foreign Policy* and *Domestic Policy*. Have students brainstorm presidential responsibilities in these areas. (*foreign policy: diplomacy, foreign treaties, trade policies, military; domestic agenda: homeland security, education, health care, taxes, transportation*) Tell students that as they read Section 4, they will learn how the first President Bush's foreign policy was popular, while his domestic agenda was not. OL

Cultural Perspectives

The 1980s experienced a resurgence of conservatism, largely the result of concerns over the economy and communism. Remind students that when domestic or foreign affairs become turbulent, people tend to avoid challenging traditions. Have students ask several adults whether they would describe themselves as liberal or conservative. Tell students to keep track of the age of each respondent. As a class, tally the results of the poll. **Ask:** What patterns can you identify in the results? What issues or events might have affected people's responses? OL

FOLDABLES™
Study Organizer

Dinah Zike's Foldables are three-dimensional, interactive graphic organizers that help students practice basic writing skills, review key vocabulary terms, and identify main ideas. Have students complete the foldable activity in the *Dinah Zike's Reading and Study Skills Foldables* booklet.

HISTORY Online

Go to tav.mt.glencoe.com for student activities, lesson plans, and links to additional Web resources to help students learn about the Reagan presidency and the end of the Cold War.

Preparing to Read

Reading Skill

Why It's Important

Comparing and contrasting helps students to understand similarities and differences as they acquire new information. This categorization is an essential tool for all readers, especially in the area of social studies.

1. Introducing the Skill

Have students place the headings *Liberal* and *Conservative* at the top of each circle of a Venn diagram similar to the one below. As they read Section 1, ask them to list information under the appropriate headings. **Ask: How are both sets of political beliefs alike?** *(Both are political philosophies.)* Have students record their answers in the intersecting part of the circles. **OL**

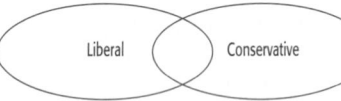

2. Extending the Skill

Have students find a magazine or newspaper article that compares and contrasts people, places, things, events, or ideas. They should underline any signal words and then organize the information in a Venn diagram. Have students present their articles and Venn diagrams to the class. **BL**

Answers and Additional Support

Preparing to Read Chapter 20

Reading Skill   Comparing and Contrasting

In Chapter 3 you learned that good readers look for similarities and differences in new information they read. This helps them figure out what the information means. You use comparing and contrasting subconsciously in everyday life. If you meet someone new, you probably compare that person to people you know. Is the person the same or different? If different, what makes that person different?

When you read, comparing and contrasting helps you understand new information. Luckily, certain signal words tell you when the author is comparing and contrasting information. Some signal words for showing similarity are *same, at the same time, on one side, like,* and *still.* Words that signal differences include *although, however, rather, but, unlike, on the other side.*

Read the following paragraph on the differences between two political beliefs.

> <u>On one side</u> of the debate are people who call themselves liberals; <u>on the other side</u> are those who identify themselves as conservatives. . . . <u>Although</u> liberals favor government intervention in the economy, they are suspicious of any attempt by the government to regulate social behavior. . . . <u>Unlike</u> liberals, conservatives have a fundamental distrust of the power of government, particularly the federal government. . . . For this reason, conservatives generally oppose high taxes and government programs that transfer wealth from the rich to those who are less wealthy. (pages 887–888)

COMPARING AND CONTRASTING

Headings can provide a clue for text structures. The title of this heading is "Conservatism and Liberalism." This title tells you that two different items will be described or explained, which likely means that they will be compared and contrasted.

Notice how signal words focus your attention. The first sentence points out the two groups that will be compared (*liberals and conservatives*) by using signal words (*on one side; on the other side*). The next sentence describes one group, the liberals, in more detail. Note the use of the word *although.* You can see here that even though one group is compared to another, this sentence points out differences in views within just one group. The last two sentences explain how the views of conservatives differ from those of liberals.

Apply the Skill

As you read Section 4, compare and contrast the events described under the headings "The Cold War Ends" and "The 'New World Order'" on pages 916–918 of your textbook. Note any signal words you recognize. These signal words will help you identify key points in the text and allow you to review information quickly.

884

UNIVERSAL ACCESS

Logical/Mathematical Ask the class to compare and contrast people, places, things, events, or ideas by creating a T-chart with the headings *How They Are Alike* and *How They Are Different.* Have them list the similarities on one side of the chart and the differences on the other side. Students can further divide the lists by creating subcategories such as size, shape, behavior, beliefs, and so on, depending upon the two things being compared or contrasted. **BL**

Historical Analysis Skill — Analyzing Migration

Analysis Skill
Standard CS3

Chronological and Spatial Thinking As you study history, you will use a variety of maps and documents to interpret human movement, including major patterns of domestic and international migration, changing environmental preferences and settlement patterns, the frictions that develop between population groups, and the diffusion of ideas, technological innovations, and goods.

Do you live in the same house in which you were born? If so, you're a rare American. Most people change residences during their lifetime, some even several times. Historians track such moves. They study human migration both between countries and within countries as they attempt to explain human behavior and history. Analyzing migration patterns allows them to examine how ideas, technology, and goods have spread within local areas, regions, and the world.

Read the following excerpt to learn more about the effects of this migration to the Sunbelt.

This pattern began to change during World War II, when large numbers of Americans moved south and west to take jobs in the war factories. The movement to the South and West—together known as the Sunbelt—continued after the war. . . . As the Sunbelt's economy expanded, Americans living in those regions began to view the federal government differently from people living in the Northeast. . . .

. . . [P]roblems prompted people in the Northeast to look to the federal government for programs and regulations that would help them solve their problems.

. . . Americans in the Sunbelt opposed high taxes and federal regulations that threatened to interfere with their region's growth. . . .

Americans living in the West also responded to conservative attacks on the size and power of the federal government. Westerners were proud of their frontier heritage and spirit of "rugged individualism." (pages 889–890)

The passage explains that the political interests of people in the United States varied depending on which region they lived in. The Northwest experienced problems, and so the people there tended to look for the federal government for help. Those Americans living in the South and West experienced an economic boom and preferred less government influence.

Apply the Skill

As you read this chapter, consider the ways in which information and ideas were spread throughout the Sunbelt. How did the beliefs of people in the Sunbelt influence the politics in the 1980s? What changes in the economy and tax structure did people living in the Sunbelt advocate?

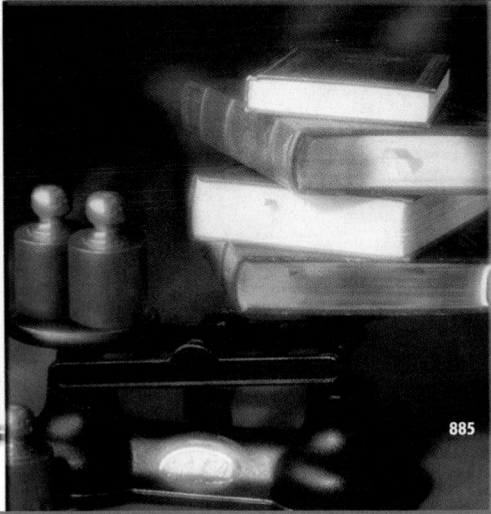

885

Historical Analysis

Why It's Important
Change over time is an important concept for students to consider in their understanding of migration in U.S. history. In particular, the regional population shift to the Sunbelt came to have important political repercussions.

1. Introducing the Skill
Working in pairs with atlases, have students complete blank outline maps of California. They should identify geographical features within the state, such as deserts, mountains, valleys, hills, coastal areas, and the Pacific Ocean. Point out to students that California's varied geography and pleasant climate have made it a favorite for travelers and settlers throughout colonial and American history. **Ask: Do you believe that geographic setting has any influence on the political beliefs of the inhabitants?** *(Students might agree that geography plays a strong role in local political issues, such as water usage and energy consumption, but they may not agree that geography alone affects national politics.)*
OL **CA** CS3

2. Extending the Skill
Ask students to visit the Census Bureau's American FactFinder Web site and research population growth in the Sunbelt states. Have them compare population levels from the 1960 census with figures from the 2000 census and create bar graphs showing population growth in the various states. Students should add the national population figures as a base. They may also research the numbers for several Midwest and Northeast states and add them to their bar graphs to compare against the Sunbelt states. **OL**
CA CS3

UNIVERSAL ACCESS

Visual/Spatial Tell students that the U.S. Census Bureau has kept population records of the United States since 1790. While this was initially done to provide data needed to assign the proper numbers of members in the House of Representatives, the Census Bureau now supplies a wide variety of information about growth and change in the United States. Ask the class to use library and Internet resources to locate the most recent edition of the Census Bureau publication *Statistical Abstract.* Ask the class to work together to create a map of the United States that shows the shifting center of population. **EL**

FOCUS

SKILLBUILDER ACTIVITY

📖 Project **Daily Focus Skills Transparency 20-1** and have students answer the question.

Guide to Reading

Understanding Vocabulary: Ask students to make a list of the content vocabulary and the academic vocabulary words in this section and then add a symbol, name, or phrase for each to help them remember the word's meaning.

Answers to Graphic: Students should complete the outline by including all headings in the section.

Unpacking the Standards

Students will be able to:

• Explain how discontent with government led to a rise in Americans' conservative political views.

• Describe how the nation's population shifts led to a change in voting patterns.

Answers and Additional Support

SECTION 1 The New Conservatism

Guide to Reading

Connection
In the previous chapter, you learned about the Nixon, Ford, and Carter administrations. In this section, you will discover what caused the rise of a new conservative coalition.

Main Idea
• Conservatives and liberals disagree on the role of government. (p. 887)
• Americans turned to conservatism as a reaction against the government's influence on the economy. (p. 888)
• Geographical regions tend to support either liberal or conservative ideas. (p. 888)

Content Vocabulary
liberal, conservative, televangelist

Academic Vocabulary
instance

People and Terms to Identify
William F. Buckley, Sunbelt, Billy Graham, Moral Majority

Reading Objectives
• **Explain** how discontent with government led to a conservative shift in Americans' political convictions.
• **Describe** how the nation's population shifts led to a change in voting patterns.

Reading Strategy
Taking Notes As you read about the rise of a new conservative coalition in the United States, use the major headings of the section to create an outline similar to the one below.

The New Conservatism
I. Conservatism and Liberalism
   A.
   B.
II.
   A.

Preview of Events

♦1965	♦1970	♦1975	♦1980

1964
Conservative Barry Goldwater is defeated for presidency

1972
Nixon wins reelection

1976
Reagan challenges Ford for nomination

1979
Jerry Falwell's "Moral Majority" movement begins

1980
Reagan wins presidential election

The following are the main History–Social Science Standards covered in this section.

11.3.2 Analyze the great religious revivals and the leaders involved in them, including the First Great Awakening, the Second Great Awakening, the Civil War revivals, the Social Gospel Movement, the rise of Christian liberal theology in the nineteenth century, the impact of the Second Vatican Council, and the rise of Christian fundamentalism in current times.

11.8.6 Discuss the diverse environmental regions of North America, their relationship to local economies, and the origins and prospects of environmental problems in those regions.

11.9.4 List the effects of foreign policy on domestic policies and vice versa (e.g., protests during the war in Vietnam, the "nuclear freeze" movement).

11.11.7 Explain how the federal, state, and local governments have responded to demographic and social changes such as population shifts to the suburbs, racial concentrations in the cities, Frostbelt-to-Sunbelt migration, international migration, decline of family farms, increases in out-of-wedlock births, and drug abuse.

The Big Idea

Societies change over time. Many Americans began to turn to conservative ideals in response to the Cold War. Some believed liberal economic policies did not reflect American values. Others thought liberals were to blame for the spread of Soviet power. Many people with deep religious faith viewed the war against communism as a battle between good and evil and supported conservative politicians. Conservative ideals appealed to many Americans who were tired of the protests, riots, and economic problems that had plagued the nation. These factors combined to create a resurgence of conservatism.

886 CHAPTER 20 Resurgence of Conservatism

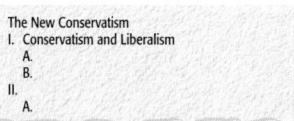

SECTION RESOURCES

📖 Print Material
• Reproducible Lesson Plan 20-1
• Guided Reading Activity 20-1
• Reading Essentials and Study Guide 20-1
• Active Reading Note-Taking Guide 20-1

🖥 Transparencies
• Daily Focus Skills Transparency 20-1
• Section Graphic Organizer Transparency 20-1

Technology
🔘 Interactive Tutor Self-Assessment CD-ROM
🔘 Exam*View*® Pro Testmaker CD-ROM
🔘 Presentation Plus! CD-ROM

Conservatism and Liberalism

Main Idea Conservatives and liberals disagree on the role of government.

Reading Connection In what other categories are voters sometimes grouped? Read on to learn more about conservative and liberal ideas of government.

Liberal ideas generally dominated American politics for much of the 1900s, but conservative ideas gained significant support among Americans in the 1970s.

★ An American Story ★

Midge Decter, a New Yorker and a writer for the conservative publication *Commentary*, was appalled at the terror that hit her city on a hot July night in 1977. On the night of July 13, the power failed in New York City. Street lights went dark. Elevators, subways, and air conditioners stopped running. The blackout left millions of people in darkness, and looting and arson rocked the city.

City officials and the media blamed the lawlessness on the anger and despair of youth in neglected areas. "They were just waiting for something like this so they could go berserk," said Lydia Rivers, a Brooklyn resident. Decter, however, had other ideas about who was to blame for the terror in her city:

❝The answer is that all those young men went on their spree of looting because they had been given permission to do so. They had been given permission to do so by all the papers and magazines, movies and documentaries—all the outlets for the purveying of enlightened liberal attitude and progressive liberal policy—which had for years and years been proclaiming that race and poverty were sufficient excuses for lawlessness. . . .❞

—quoted in *Commentary*, September 1977

Midge Decter's article blaming liberalism for the riots in New York during the 1977 blackout exemplifies a debate in American politics that continues to the present day. On one side of the debate are people who call themselves liberals; on the other side are those who identify themselves as conservatives. In 1980 Ronald Reagan, a strong conservative, was elected president.

Liberalism In American politics today, people who call themselves **liberals** believe several basic ideas. In general, liberals believe that the government should regulate the economy to protect people from the power of large corporations and wealthy elites. Liberals also believe that the government, particularly the federal government, should play an active role in helping disadvantaged Americans, partly through social programs and partly by putting more of society's tax burden on wealthier people.

Although liberals favor government intervention in the economy, they are suspicious of any attempt by the government to regulate social behavior. They are strong supporters of free speech and privacy, and they are opposed to the government supporting or endorsing religious beliefs, no matter how indirectly. They believe that a diverse society made up of many different races, cultures, and ethnic groups tends to be more creative and energetic. Liberals often support high taxes on the wealthy. They believe that most social problems have their roots in economic inequality.

Conservatism Unlike liberals, **conservatives** generally have a fundamental distrust of the power of government, particularly the federal government. They support the original intent of the Constitution and believe that governmental power should be divided into different branches and split between the state and federal levels to limit its ability to intrude into people's lives.

Conservatives believe that if the government regulates the economy, it makes the economy less efficient, resulting in less wealth and more poverty. They believe that the free enterprise system is the best way to organize society. They often argue that if people and businesses are free to make their own economic choices, there will be more wealth and a higher standard of living for everyone.

Midge Decter ▶

CHAPTER 20   Resurgence of Conservatism   **887**

TEACH

R Reading Strategy

Scaffolding—Synthesizing As students read about the differences between liberalism and conservatism, have them take notes on the reasons why conservatism increased beginning in the 1970s. After they have completed the section, ask them to synthesize the information by writing summaries about the emergence of conservatism. **OL** **CA HI1**

This **Reading Skill** was introduced in Chapter 15.

S Skill Practice

Creating a Time Line The text states that liberal ideas dominated American politics for much of the 1900s. Ask each student to create a time line that displays what each student believes are the important liberal government actions of the twentieth century. Compare the time lines to create a class time line. Add any important events that the students failed to list. **AL** **CA CS1; HI4**

Did You Know?

According to some reports of the blackout, 50 cars were stolen from a car dealership in the Bronx, the police made over 3,000 arrests, and the fire department responded to more than 1,500 false alarms.

For this reason, conservatives generally oppose high taxes and government programs that transfer wealth from the rich to those who are less wealthy. They believe that taxes and government programs discourage investment, take away people's incentive to work hard, and reduce the amount of freedom in society.

The more the government regulates the economy, conservatives argue, the more it will have to regulate every aspect of people's behavior. Ultimately, conservatives fear, the government will so restrict people's economic freedom that Americans will no longer be able to improve their standard of living.

Many conservatives believe that religious faith is vitally important in sustaining society. They believe most social problems result from issues of morality and character—issues, they argue, that are best addressed through commitment to a religious faith and through the private efforts of individuals and communities helping those in need. Despite this general belief, conservatives do support the use of the governmental police powers to regulate social behavior in some **instances.**

✔ Reading Check **Contrasting** How do liberal and conservative opinions about government differ?

Conservatism Revives

Main Idea Americans turned to conservatism as a reaction against the government's influence on the economy.

Reading Connection What trends in voting do you notice today? Read on to discover more about the end of the dominance of liberalism and the swing toward conservatism.

During the New Deal era of the 1930s, conservative ideas had lost much of their influence in national politics. In the years following World War II, however, conservatism began to revive.

Conservatism and the Cold War Support for conservative ideas began to revive for two major reasons, both related to the Cold War. First, the struggle against communism revived the debate about the role of the government in the economy. Some Americans believed that liberal economic ideas were slowly leading the United States toward communism and became determined to stop this trend. They also thought the United States had failed to stop the spread of Soviet power because liberals did not fully understand the need for a strong anticommunist foreign policy.

At the same time, many Americans viewed the Cold War in religious terms. Communism rejected religion and emphasized the material side of life. To Americans with a deep religious faith, the struggle against communism was a struggle between good and evil. Liberalism, which emphasizes economic welfare, gradually lost the support of many religious Americans to conservatism.

Conservatives Organize In 1955 a young conservative named **William F. Buckley** founded a new conservative magazine called *National Review.* Buckley's magazine helped to revive conservative ideas in the United States. Buckley debated in front of college students and appeared on radio and television shows, spreading conservative ideas to an even wider audience.

Within the Republican Party, conservatives, particularly young conservatives, began to push their ideas and demand a greater role in party decision-making. In 1960 some 90 young conservative leaders met at Buckley's family estate and founded Young Americans for Freedom (YAF), an independent conservative group, to push their ideas and to support conservative candidates.

By 1964 the new conservative movement had achieved enough influence within the Republican Party to enable the conservative Barry Goldwater to win the nomination for president. To the dismay of the conservatives, however, President Johnson easily defeated Goldwater and won the election in a landslide.

✔ Reading Check **Explaining** Why did conservatism revive in the 1950s?

R₂ Conservatism Gains Support

Main Idea Geographical regions tend to support either liberal or conservative ideas.

Reading Connection Politically, how would you define yourself or the region in which you live? Read on to learn about the growing political power of voters in the Southwest.

Conservatism could not have become a mass movement if Americans had not responded to conservative ideas. The events of the late 1960s and 1970s played an important role in convincing Americans to support conservatism. After Goldwater's huge loss in 1964, American society moved decisively in a conservative direction.

Did You Know?

In 1965 William F. Buckley unsuccessfully ran for mayor of New York City. He hosted the television show "Firing Line" between 1966 and 1969, and is the author of five books.

Rise of the Sunbelt, 1950–1980

NATIONAL GEOGRAPHIC

WASH.
2,378,963
4,132,000

OREG.
1,521,341
2,633,000

IDAHO
588,637
944,000

MONT.

N. DAK.

MINN.

NEV.
106,083
800,000

WYO.
290,529
470,000

S. DAK.

WIS.

ME.

VT.
N.H.
N.Y. MASS.
R.I.
CONN.

UTAH
688,862
1,461,000

COLO.
1,325,089
2,890,000

NEBR.

IOWA

MICH.

PA.

N.J.

CALIF.
10,586,223
23,668,000

KANS.

ILL. IND.

OHIO

W. VA.

DEL.
MD.

VA.

ARIZ.
749,587
2,718,000

N. MEX.
681,187
1,303,000

OKLA.

MO.

KY.

TENN.

N.C.

S.C.

ARK.

MISS. ALA.

GA.
3,444,578
5,463,000

PACIFIC
OCEAN

TEX.
7,711,194
14,229,000

LA.

FLA.
2,771,305
9,746,000

ATLANTIC
OCEAN

MEXICO

Gulf of
Mexico

CANADA

TROPIC OF CANCER

Key:
- Sunbelt states
- 749,587 Population (1950)
- 944,000 Population (1980)
- Percent growth (1 bar equals 50% growth)
- Population shown only for states having 50% or more population growth between 1950 and 1980

0   500 miles
0   500 kilometers
Lambert Azimuthal Equal-area projection

N
W—E
S

40°N
30°N
120°W
110°W
20°N

Geography *Skills*

1. **Interpreting Maps** Which Sunbelt states have more than 8 million residents?
2. **Applying Geography Skills** Nevada has the highest percentage growth in population for the time period shown. Looking at its 1950 population, how would you explain this large percentage increase?

The Rise of the Sunbelt One of the problems facing conservatives in the 1950s and early 1960s was that they generally split their votes between the Republicans and the Democrats. Two regions of the country, the South and the West, were more conservative than other areas. Southern conservatives, however, generally voted for the Democrats, while conservatives in the West voted Republican. This meant that the party that won the heavily populated Northeast would win the election. Since the Northeast strongly supported liberal ideas, both parties were pulled toward liberal policies.

This pattern began to change during World War II, when large numbers of Americans moved south and west to take jobs in the war factories. The movement to the South and West—together known as the **Sunbelt**—continued after the war. Adding to the growth of the Sunbelt during the 1980s and 1990s was a surge in immigrants, mostly from Asia and Mexico. As the Sunbelt's economy expanded, Americans living in those regions began to view the federal government differently from people living in

the Northeast. Federal, state, and local governments had to change to respond to new and unique needs.

Sunbelt Conservatism Industry in the Northeast was in decline, leading to the region's nickname—the Rust Belt. This region had more unemployed people than any other, and its cities were often congested and polluted. These problems prompted Americans in the Northeast to look to the federal government for programs and regulations that would help them solve their problems.

In contrast, Americans in the Sunbelt opposed high taxes and federal regulations that threatened to interfere with their region's growth. Many white Southerners were also angry with the Democrats for supporting civil rights, which they interpreted as an effort by the federal government to impose its policies on the South.

CHAPTER 20   Resurgence of Conservatism   **889**

Geography *Skills*

Answers:
1. California, Texas, and Florida
2. Nevada had the smallest state population in 1950. Since the percentage growth is based on the population in 1950, a state with a small population will likely have a large percentage growth.

When Barry Goldwater argued in 1964 that the federal government was becoming too strong, many Southerners agreed. For the first time since Reconstruction, they began voting Republican in large numbers. Although Goldwater lost the election, his candidacy showed Republicans that the best way to attract Southern votes was to support conservative policies.

Americans living in the West also responded to conservative attacks on the size and power of the federal government. Westerners were proud of their frontier heritage and spirit of "rugged individualism." They resented federal environmental regulations that limited ranching, controlled water use, and restricted the development of the region's natural resources. Western anger over such policies inspired the "Sagebrush Rebellion" of the early 1970s—a widespread protest led by conservatives against federal laws hindering the region's development.

By 1980 the population of the Sunbelt had surpassed the Northeast. This gave the conservative regions of the country more electoral votes and, therefore, more influence in shaping party policies. With Southerners shifting their votes to the Republican Party, conservatives could now build a coalition to elect a president.

▼ *Supporters of Proposition 13 celebrate after it is passed*

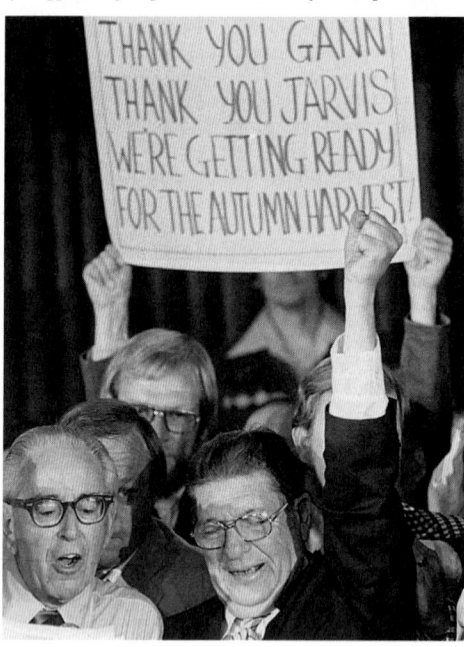

Suburban Conservatism As crime soared during the 1960s and 1970s, many Americans moved to suburbs. Even there, however, they found the quiet middle-class lifestyle they desired to be in danger. The rapid inflation of the 1970s had caused the buying power of the average middle-class family to shrink while taxes remained high.

Many Americans resented the taxes they had to pay for New Deal and Great Society programs when they themselves were losing ground economically. By the late 1970s, Americans had begun to rebel against these high taxes. In 1978 Howard Jarvis, a conservative activist, launched the first successful tax revolt in California with Proposition 13, a referendum on the state ballot that greatly reduced property taxes.

Anti-tax movements soon appeared in other states, and tax cuts became a national issue. For many Americans, the conservative argument that the government had become too big meant that taxes were too high. As conservatives began to call for tax cuts, middle-class Americans flocked to their cause.

The Religious Right Conservatism also drew people who feared American society had lost touch with its traditional values. Many Americans of deep religious faith were shocked by the events of the 1960s and 1970s. The Supreme Court decision in *Roe* v. *Wade,* which established abortion as a constitutional right, greatly concerned them. Other Supreme Court decisions that limited prayer in public schools and expanded the rights of people accused of crimes also drew criticism. 📖 *(See page 1006 for more information on* Roe v. Wade.)

The feminist movement and the push for the Equal Rights Amendment (ERA) further alarmed religious Americans because it seemed to represent an assault on the traditional family. The growing number of single mothers in the 1970s continued to increase in the 1980s. Many religious people were also shocked by the behavior of some university students in the 1960s, whose contempt for authority seemed to indicate a general breakdown in American values and morality. These concerns helped expand the conservative cause into a mass movement.

Religious conservatives included people of many different faiths. The number of these faiths had increased with the recent influx of immigrants. Still, the largest group within the social conservative movement was evangelical Protestant Christians. Evangelicals believe they are saved from their sins through conversion (which they refer to as being "born again") and a personal commitment to follow Jesus Christ, whose death and resurrection reconciles them to God.

Did You Know?

The initiative, referendum, and recall procedures created during the Progressive era offer voters a more direct form of democracy. People often confuse initiatives and referenda. An initiative allows citizens to introduce a bill into the legislature and requires the members to take a vote on it, while a referendum establishes a procedure by which voters cast ballots for or against a proposed law.

After World War II, a religious revival began in the United States. Protestant ministers such as **Billy Graham** and Oral Roberts built national followings. By the late 1970s, about 70 million Americans described themselves as "born again." Christian evangelicals owned their own newspapers, magazines, radio stations, and television networks.

Television in particular allowed evangelical ministers to reach a large nationwide audience. These **"televangelists,"** as they were nicknamed, included Marion "Pat" Robertson, who founded the Christian Broadcasting Network, and Jerry Falwell, who used his television show *The Old-Time Gospel Hour* to found a movement that he called the **"Moral Majority."** Using television and mail campaigns, the Moral Majority built up a network of ministers to register new voters who backed conservative candidates and issues. Falwell later claimed to have brought in 2 million new voters by 1980.

R

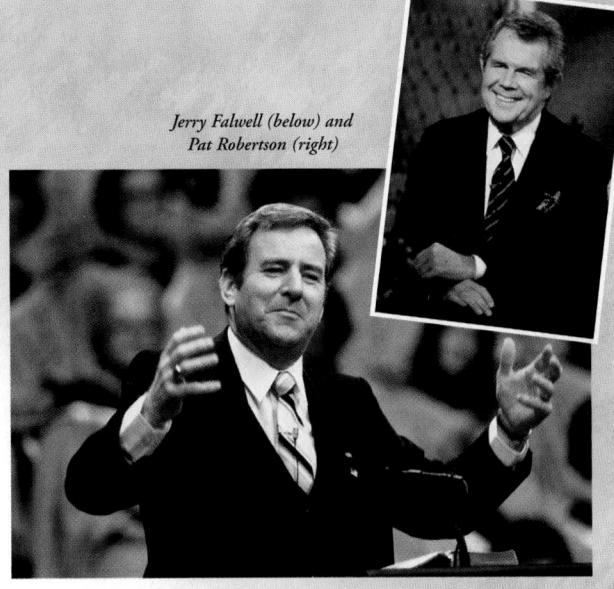
Jerry Falwell (below) and Pat Robertson (right)

A New Coalition By the end of the 1970s, the new conservative coalition of voters had begun to come together in the United States. Although the members of this coalition were concerned with many different issues, they were held together by a common belief that American society had somehow lost its way.

The Watergate scandal, high taxes, and special interest politics had undermined many Americans' faith in their government. Rising unemployment, rapid inflation, and the energy crisis had shaken their confidence in the economy. Riots, crime, and drug abuse suggested that society itself was falling apart. The retreat from Vietnam, the hostage crisis in Iran, and the Soviet invasion of Afghanistan made the nation look weak and helpless internationally. Many Americans were tired of change and upheaval. They wanted stability and a return to what they remembered as a better time. For some, the new conservatism and its most prominent spokesperson, Ronald Reagan, offered hope to a nation in distress.

Reading Check **Summarizing** Why did many Americans begin to support the conservative movement?

HISTORY Online **Study Central**

For help with the concepts in this section of *American Vision: Modern Times* go to tav.mt.glencoe.com and click on **Study Central**.

SECTION 1 ASSESSMENT

Checking for Understanding

1. **Vocabulary** Define: liberal, conservative, instance, televangelist.
2. **People and Terms** Identify: William F. Buckley, Sunbelt, Billy Graham, Moral Majority.
3. **Explain** why evangelical Protestant Christians began to support conservative issues.

Reviewing Big Ideas

4. **Describing** What kind of economy did conservatives want?

Critical Thinking

5. **Historical Analysis** **Analyzing** How did Christian evangelicals contribute to a growing conservative national identity? **CA HI1**
6. **Organizing** Use a graphic organizer similar to the one below to list conservative beliefs.

Conservative Beliefs

Analyzing Visuals

7. **Analyzing Maps** Study the map of the Sunbelt on page 889. What impact would the migration patterns shown have on representation in the U.S. House of Representatives?

Writing About History

8. **Persuasive Writing** Many conservatives believe that "government that governs least, governs best." Write a paragraph supporting or opposing this statement. **CA 11WS1.1**

CHAPTER 20   Resurgence of Conservatism   **891**

SECTION 1 ASSESSMENT ANSWERS

1. Content vocabulary is boldfaced and highlighted in yellow. Academic vocabulary is boldfaced.
2. William F. Buckley *(p. 888)*, Sunbelt *(p. 889)*, Billy Graham *(p. 891)*, Moral Majority *(p. 891)*
3. because they feared American society had lost touch with its traditional values
4. Conservatives wanted a free enterprise system.
5. The media supported conservative candidates.
6. free enterprise, emphasis on religious values, little government regulation of the economy
7. The population increase would give the Sunbelt more seats in the House of Representatives, and conservatives would likely be elected to fill those seats.
8. Students' paragraphs should express a clear point of view.

Scaffolding—Academic Vocabulary The word *register* was introduced in Chapter 16, Section 1. Ask a student to define the word. **BL**

ASSESS

Resources for page 891

Use these resources to assess student mastery.

📁 Section Quiz 20-1

📁 Reading Essentials and Study Guide 20-1

⊙ Interactive Tutor Self-Assessment CD-ROM

📁 California Standards Practice, Grade 11

Reading Check

Answer: They thought it would improve the economy, and they wanted to return to traditional values.

Study Central provides audio summaries, interactive games, and online graphic organizers to help students review section content.

CLOSE

Summary Writing Ask students to write a one-page summary of the events that occurred during the 1960s and 1970s that helped turn many Americans toward a more conservative political ideology. **OL** **CA 11WA2.4d**

891

FOCUS

BELLRINGER
SKILLBUILDER ACTIVITY

Project **Daily Focus Skills Transparency 20-2** and have students answer the question.

Guide to Reading

Understanding Vocabulary: Have students scan the section to see where the content vocabulary words and academic vocabulary words fall in relationship to the headings.

Answers to Graphic: Supply Side Theory: High taxes take away money that could be invested; Cutting taxes will generate capital to make new and larger businesses and new jobs; Larger supply of consumer goods will cause more spending.

Unpacking the Standards

Students will be able to:

• Explain Ronald Reagan's rise to the White House.

• Describe the Reagan economic recovery plan.

• Analyze Reagan's foreign policy, especially toward the Soviet Union.

Answers and Additional Support

SECTION 2 The Reagan Years

Guide to Reading

Connection
In the previous section, you learned about the rise of the new conservative coalition. In this section, you will discover how Ronald Reagan brought conservative ideals to the White House.

Main Idea
• President Reagan's experiences in Hollywood and as governor of California led to his successful campaign for presidency. (p. 893)
• Believing that government was part of the problem, President Reagan cut social service programs, sponsored tax cuts, and deregulated industry. (p. 894)
• President Reagan oversaw the largest peacetime buildup of the military in American history. (p. 896)

• President Reagan supported governments fighting communism, a policy known as the Reagan Doctrine. (p. 897)
• President Reagan's decision to place nuclear missiles in Western Europe triggered calls for a "nuclear freeze." (p. 898)

Content Vocabulary
supply-side economics, budget deficit, contra

Academic Vocabulary
exceed, offset, visible

People and Terms to Identify
Reaganomics, Sandra Day O'Connor, William Rehnquist, Geraldine Ferraro, Iran-Contra scandal, Oliver North, Mikhail Gorbachev

Reading Objectives
• **Explain** President Reagan's economic recovery plan.
• **Discuss** Reagan's policies toward the Soviet Union.

Reading Strategy
Organizing As you read about the Reagan presidency, complete the graphic organizer below by filling in the major points of the supply-side theory of economics.

Supply-Side Theory

Preview of Events

◆1980	◆1983	◆1986	◆1989

1980 — Reagan elected president

1983 — Terrorists bomb U.S. Marine barracks in Lebanon

1984 — Reagan reelected

1986 — Iran-Contra scandal breaks

1987 — Reagan and Gorbachev sign INF Treaty

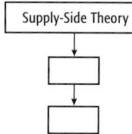

The following are the main History–Social Science Standards covered in this section.

11.8.4 Analyze new federal government spending on defense, welfare, interest on the national debt, and federal and state spending on education, including the California Master Plan.

11.9.4 List the effects of foreign policy on domestic policies and vice versa (e.g., protests during the war in Vietnam, the "nuclear freeze" movement).

11.9.5 Analyze the role of the Reagan administration and other factors in the victory of the West in the Cold War.

11.9.6 Describe U.S. Middle East policy and its strategic, political, and economic interests, including those related to the Gulf War.

11.11.2 Discuss the significant domestic policy speeches of Truman, Eisenhower, Kennedy, Johnson, Nixon, Carter, Reagan, Bush, and Clinton (e.g., with regard to education, civil rights, economic policy, environmental policy).

❧ The Big Idea ❧

International competition can lead to conflict and cooperation. President Reagan believed government policies were responsible for the country's economic and social problems. To combat the stagflation hindering the economy, he supported a policy of high interest rates and tax cuts. This policy became known as Reaganomics. He also proposed cuts to social programs and deregulation of oil and gas. Reagan's policies encouraged economic growth. In the 1984 election, he won in an overwhelming landslide. After his reelection, President Reagan focused on increasing military spending, believing that a strong military would foster peace. The combination of military spending and tax cuts, however, led to a large federal budget deficit. Reagan supported countries fighting against communism. By 1987 he had made great progress in ending the Cold War.

892 CHAPTER 20 Resurgence of Conservatism

SECTION RESOURCES

📁 Print Material
• Reproducible Lesson Plan 20-2
• Guided Reading Activity 20-2
• Reading Essentials and Study Guide 20-2
• Active Reading Note-Taking Guide 20-2

🖌 Transparencies
• Daily Focus Skills Transparency 20-2
• Section Graphic Organizer Transparency 20-2

Technology
💿 Interactive Tutor Self-Assessment CD-ROM
💿 ExamView® Pro Testmaker CD-ROM
💿 Presentation Plus! CD-ROM

The Road to the White House

Main Idea President Reagan's experiences in Hollywood and as governor of California led to his successful campaign for presidency.

Reading Connection How could being a movie star help someone be elected? Read on to learn more about the way that President Reagan's background shaped his conservatism.

Ronald Reagan grew up in Dixon, Illinois, the son of an Irish American shoe salesman. After graduating from Eureka College in 1932, Reagan worked as a sports broadcaster. In 1937 he won a contract from a Hollywood movie studio. Over the next 25 years, he made over 50 movies. Reagan learned how to speak publicly and how to project an image, skills that proved invaluable when he entered politics.

★ An American Story ★

In 1926 when he was 15 years old, Ronald Reagan earned $15 a week as a lifeguard at Lowell Park on the Rock River in Illinois. Being a lifeguard, Reagan later wrote, taught him quite a bit about human nature:

❝Lifeguarding provides one of the best vantage points in the world to learn about people. During my career at the park, I saved seventy-seven people. I guarantee you they needed saving—no lifeguard gets wet without good reason.... Not many thanked me, much less gave me a reward, and being a little money-hungry, I'd done a little daydreaming about this. They felt insulted. I got to recognize that people hate to be saved....❞

—quoted in *Where's the Rest of Me?*

The belief that people did not really want to be saved by someone else was one of the ideas that Ronald Reagan took with him to the White House. It fit with his philosophy of self-reliance and independence.

Moving to Conservatism In 1947 Reagan became president of the Screen Actors Guild—the actors' union. As head of the union, he testified about communism in Hollywood before the House Un-American Activities Committee. Reagan had been a staunch Democrat and supporter of the New Deal, but his experience in dealing with Communists in the union began shifting him toward conservative ideas.

In 1954 Reagan became the host of a television program called *General Electric Theater* and agreed to be a motivational speaker for the company. As he traveled around the country speaking to workers, secretaries, and managers, he became increasingly conservative. Over and over again, Reagan said later, he heard stories from average Americans about how high taxes and government regulations made it impossible for them to get ahead.

By 1964 Reagan had become such a popular national speaker that Barry Goldwater asked him to make a televised speech on behalf of Goldwater's presidential campaign. Reagan's speech greatly impressed several wealthy entrepreneurs in California. They convinced Reagan to run for governor of California in 1966 and helped finance his campaign. Reagan won the election and was reelected in 1970. Ten years later, he won the Republican presidential nomination.

The Election of 1980 Reagan's campaign appealed to Americans who were frustrated with the economy and worried that the United States had become weak internationally. Reagan promised to cut taxes and increase defense spending. He won the support of social conservatives by calling for a constitutional amendment banning abortion. During one debate with Carter, Reagan asked voters, "Are you better off than you were four years ago?" On Election Day, the voters answered "No." Reagan won nearly 51 percent of the popular vote and 489 electoral votes, easily defeating Carter in the Electoral College. For the first time since 1954, Republicans also gained control of the Senate.

✓ **Reading Check** **Describing** What event jumpstarted Ronald Reagan's political career as a conservative leader?

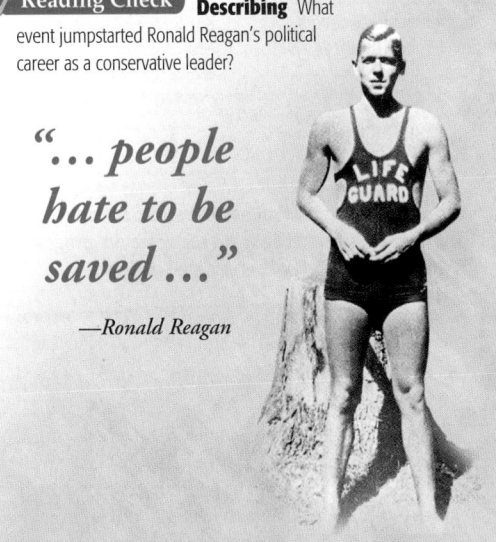

"*... people hate to be saved ...*"
—*Ronald Reagan*

CHAPTER 20   Resurgence of Conservatism   **893**

C **Critical Thinking**

Analyzing Primary Sources Reagan once said that "people hate to be saved." **Ask: How does this quote relate to the conservative political ideology?** *(Conservatives believe that people should rely more on themselves to solve problems, rather than expecting the government to fix their problems for them. They might think that people want to rely on their own choices rather than take charity and help from the government.)* **AL**

R₁ **Reading Strategy**

Activating Prior Knowledge In 1947 Ronald Reagan testified before the House Un-American Activities Committee. **Ask: What was the goal of HUAC?** *(to uncover evidence of Communist infiltration in the U.S. government)* **OL**

R₂ **Reading Strategy**

Connecting Jimmy Carter was the first incumbent president to lose a reelection bid since Herbert Hoover, but not the last. Ask students if they can name another incumbent president since then who lost his bid for reelection. *(George H.W. Bush)* **OL**

✓ **Reading Check**

Answer: A televised speech on behalf of Barry Goldwater's presidential campaign aided his political career as a conservative leader.

Resources for page 893

Have students read more about Ronald Reagan's first term in the Primary Source Reading 20-1.

Did You Know?

Ronald Reagan used his experience as an actor for his life in public office. Just as he had rehearsed his lines as an actor, he spent hours fine-tuning the wording and delivery of his speeches.

C Critical Thinking

Reading Primary Sources
President Carter and Governor Reagan present two very different views on the role of government in these excerpts. **Ask:** **How would you describe President Carter's view of the presidency?** *(It is a job that requires a firm belief in what is right and a willingness to hold true to that belief.)* **AL**

S Skill Practice

Comparing and Contrasting
Ask the class to read the two quotes from Ronald Reagan, one in the Different Viewpoints feature and the other at the bottom of the page. **Ask:** **What similar thought runs through both of Reagan's statements?** *(The role of the everyday individual is extremely important in American society.)* **OL** **CA HR2**

R Reading Strategy

Scaffolding—Academic Vocabulary The word *sustain* was introduced in Chapter 17, Section 2. Ask a student to define the word. **BL**

Answers and Additional Support

Different Viewpoints

Carter and Reagan on Government

As President Carter sought re-election in 1980, he had to deal with inflation, unemployment, and an energy crisis. He urged Americans to make sacrifices so that the government could solve these problems. His opponent, Ronald Reagan, disagreed. Reagan argued that Americans should trust themselves, not the government, to solve their problems.

President Jimmy Carter:

"[A] president cannot yield to the shortsighted demands, no matter how rich or powerful the special interests might be that make those demands. And that is why the president cannot bend to the passions of the moment, however popular they might be. And that is why the president must sometimes ask for sacrifice when his listeners would rather hear the promise of comfort.

. . . The only way to build a better future is to start with realities of the present. But while we Democrats grapple with the real challenges of a real world, others talk of a world of tinsel and make-believe.

. . . A world of good guys and bad guys, where some politicians shoot first and ask questions later.

No hard choices. No sacrifice. No tough decisions. It sounds too good to be true—and it is."

—from his acceptance speech at the Democratic National Convention, August 14, 1980

California governor Ronald Reagan:

"The American people, the most generous people on earth, who created the highest standard of living, are not going to accept the notion that we can only make a better world for others by moving backwards ourselves. Those who believe we *can* have no business leading the nation.

I will not stand by and watch this great country destroy itself under mediocre leadership that drifts from one crisis to the next, eroding our national will and purpose.

"Trust me" government asks that we concentrate our hopes and dreams on one man; that we trust him to do what's best for us. My view of government places trust not in one person or one party, but in those values that transcend persons and parties. The trust is where it belongs—in the people."

—from his acceptance speech at the Republican National Convention, July 17, 1980

Learning From History

1. **Historical Analysis** **Recognizing Ideologies** How do the two candidates differ regarding the role of government in solving the nation's problems? **CA HI2**

2. **Making Inferences** Ronald Reagan won the election of 1980. What part of his speech do you think may have had the most influence on voters? Why?

Reagan's Domestic Policies

Main Idea Believing that government was part of the problem, President Reagan cut social service programs, sponsored tax cuts, and deregulated industry.

Reading Connection Do you think cutting social programs is a good way to help the economy? Read on to learn more about Reagan's economic policies.

Ronald Reagan believed the key to restoring the economy and overcoming problems in society was to get Americans to believe in themselves again. He expressed this idea in his Inaugural Address:

"We have every right to dream heroic dreams. . . . You can see heroes every day going in and out of factory gates. Others, a handful in number, produce enough food to feed all of us. . . . You meet heroes across a counter. . . . There are entrepreneurs with faith in themselves and faith in an idea who create new jobs, new wealth and opportunity. . . . Their patriotism is quiet but deep. Their values sustain our national life."

—from Reagan's First Inaugural Address

Reagan also explained that Americans should not look to Washington for answers: "In this present

894 CHAPTER 20 Resurgence of Conservatism

Different Viewpoints

Answers:
1. Carter felt Americans should make sacrifices so government could solve problems. Reagan felt Americans should solve problems themselves.
2. Students' answer will vary, but students should support their choices with clear reasoning.
Ask: What words does Carter use to point the finger at Reagan's background as an actor? *(world of tinsel and make-believe)*

crisis, government is not the solution to our problem. Government is the problem."

Reaganomics Reagan's first priority was the economy, which was suffering from stagflation—a combination of high unemployment and high inflation. According to most economists, the way to fight unemployment was to increase government spending. Increasing spending, however, made inflation worse. Stagflation puzzled many economists, who did not expect inflation and high unemployment to occur at the same time.

Conservative economists offered two competing ideas for fixing the economy. One group, known as monetarists, argued that inflation was caused by too much money in circulation. They believed the best solution was to raise interest rates. Another group supported **supply-side economics.** They argued that the economy was weak because taxes were too high.

Supply-side economists believed that high taxes took too much money away from investors. If taxes were cut, businesses and investors could use their extra capital to make new investments, and businesses could expand and create new jobs. The result would be a larger supply of goods for consumers, who would now have more money to spend.

Reagan combined monetarism and supply-side economics. He encouraged the Federal Reserve to keep interest rates high, and asked Congress to pass a massive tax cut. Critics called his approach **Reaganomics** or "trickle-down economics." They believed Reagan's policy would help corporations and wealthy Americans, while only a little bit of the wealth would "trickle down" to average Americans. Reagan made deals with conservative Democrats in the House and moderate Republicans in the Senate. Eventually Congress passed a 25 percent tax rate cut.

Cutting Programs Cutting tax rates meant the government would receive less money. This would increase the **budget deficit**—the amount by which expenditures **exceed** income. To keep the deficit under control, Reagan proposed cuts to social programs. Welfare benefits, including the food stamp program and the school lunch program, were part of the cuts the president recommended. Medicare payments, student loans, housing subsidies, and unemployment compensation were also reduced.

After a struggle, Congress passed most of these cuts. The fight convinced Reagan that he would never get Congress to cut spending enough to balance the budget. He decided that cutting taxes and building up the military were more important than balancing the budget. He accepted the high deficit as the price of getting his other programs passed.

Deregulation Reagan believed that burdensome government regulations were another cause of the economy's problems by increasing costs for industries. His first act as president was to sign an executive order eliminating price controls on oil and gasoline. Critics argued that getting rid of controls would drive prices up, but in fact, they began to fall. The falling energy prices freed up money for businesses and consumers to spend elsewhere, helping the economy to recover.

Other deregulation soon followed. The National Highway Traffic and Safety Administration reduced its demand for air bags and higher fuel efficiency for

HISTORY Online

Student Web Activity Visit the *American Vision: Modern Times* Web site at tav.mt.glencoe.com and click on *Student Web Activities– Chapter 20* for an activity on the 1980s.

U Universal Access

Cooperative Learning Have students reread the passage about supply-side economics on this page. Then organize the class into three groups and ask each group to write a letter to President Reagan about the impact of his economic policies. One group should represent business owners, another group should represent workers in manufacturing industries, and the third group should represent people on fixed incomes. Have each group select a representative to read the group's letter to the rest of the class. **AL** **CA** 11WA2.1a

R Reading Strategy

Inferring President Reagan's pursuit of deregulation created concern among some critics. Have students identify industries in which Reagan eliminated or eased regulations. *(airlines and national media)* **Ask:** Who might have opposed deregulation in the areas of cable TV and the airlines? *(Consumers might have worried about rising prices.)* **OL**

The Attempt to Kill the President, March 30, 1981

Barely two months after the inauguration, on March 30, 1981, John Hinckley tried to kill President Reagan in a misguided attempt to impress actress Jodie Foster. Hinckley fired six shots as Reagan left a hotel in Washington, D.C. One bullet bounced off the president's rib and lodged near his heart. Another bullet seriously wounded press secretary Jim Brady. Reagan's recovery was long, but he stayed upbeat. His jaunty reply to his wife, "Honey, I forgot to duck," won the affection of many.

John Hinckley (center)

HISTORY Online

Objectives and answers to the student activity can be found in the **Web Activity Lesson Plan** at tav.mt.glencoe.com.

Did You Know?

Political opponents noted that Reagan, like Republican Calvin Coolidge, seemed rather detached from the process of government. Far from being insulted, Reagan reveled in the comparison. He hung Coolidge's portrait in a prominent place in the White House and regularly quoted Coolidge's philosophy on business and government.

S Skill Practice

Scaffolding—Historical Connections Have students discuss the impact the Reagan administration had on the make-up of the Supreme Court. *(more conservative justices were appointed; the Court was less willing to continue the reforms of the Warren Court era)* Encourage students to relate their discussion to current interest in the make-up of the Supreme Court and its conservative or liberal balance.

OL **CA HI1**

This **Historical Analysis** skill was introduced in Chapter 18.

U Universal Access

English Learners Ask students to read the text under the heading "Reagan Builds Up the Military" and then, working in pairs, summarize what they have just read. Remind them to include all the main ideas. **EL**

✔ Reading Check

Answer: Supply-side economics proposes low taxes as an incentive to generate more investment in business. In theory, this leads to new and larger businesses and more jobs. Under this theory more workers would have income with which to purchase the expanded production.

Answers and Additional Support

cars. The Federal Communications Commission abandoned efforts to regulate the new cable television industry. Carter had already begun deregulating the airline industry, and Reagan encouraged the process, which led to price wars, cheaper fares, and the founding of new airlines.

Reagan's Secretary of the Interior, James Watt, increased the amount of public land corporations could use for oil drilling, mining, and logging. Watt's decisions angered environmentalists, as did the Environmental Protection Agency's decisions to ease regulations on pollution control equipment and to reduce safety checks on chemicals and pesticides.

The Economy Booms In 1983 the economy finally began to recover. By 1984 the United States had begun the biggest economic expansion in its history up to that time. The median income of American families climbed steadily, rising 15 percent by 1989. Sales of goods and services shot upward. Five million new businesses and 20 million new jobs were created. By 1988 unemployment had fallen to about 5.5 percent, the lowest since 1973.

Shifting the Judicial Balance Reagan did not apply his conservative ideas only to the economy. He also tried to bring a strict constructionist outlook to the federal judiciary. Reagan wanted judges who followed the original intent and wording of the Constitution rather than those who interpreted and expanded its meaning. He also changed the face of the Supreme Court by nominating **Sandra Day O'Connor** to be the first woman on the Supreme Court.

In 1986 Chief Justice Warren Burger retired. Reagan chose the most conservative associate justice, **William Rehnquist,** to succeed him. He then named Antonin Scalia, also a conservative, to fill the vacancy left by Rehnquist. In 1987 Reagan's nomination of Robert Bork to the Court led to a bitter confirmation fight in the Senate. Liberals argued that Bork's opinions on issues were too extreme, and they managed to block his confirmation. Anthony Kennedy, a moderate, ultimately became the new associate justice.

Reagan Wins Reelection As the 1984 election approached, the growing economy made Reagan very popular. Democrats nominated Jimmy Carter's vice president, Walter Mondale. He chose as his running mate Representative **Geraldine Ferraro,** the first woman to run for vice president for a major party.

Instead of arguing issues with his opponent, Reagan emphasized the good economy. In an over-

896   CHAPTER 20   Resurgence of Conservatism

whelming landslide, he won about 59 percent of the popular vote and all the electoral votes except those from Minnesota and the District of Columbia.

✔ Reading Check   **Explaining** What is supply-side economics?

U Reagan Builds Up the Military

Main Idea President Reagan oversaw the largest peacetime buildup of the military in American history.

Reading Connection What was President Eisenhower's warning about the military as he left office? Read on to learn what President Reagan thought about the power of the military to defeat the Soviets.

Reagan did not limit his reforms to the domestic scene. He adopted a new Cold War foreign policy that rejected both containment and détente. Reagan called the Soviet Union "the focus of evil in the modern world" and "an evil empire." In his view, the United States should not negotiate with or try to contain evil. It should try to defeat it.

Peace Through Strength In Reagan's opinion, the only option in dealing with the Soviet Union was "peace through strength." The military buildup Reagan launched was the largest peacetime buildup in American history. It cost about $1.5 trillion over five years.

Reagan believed that the Soviets could not match the buildup. Any such attempt would require economic reform, or their economy would collapse. In 1982 Reagan told students at Eureka College that massive Soviet defense spending eventually would cause the Communist system to collapse:

❝The Soviet empire is faltering because rigid centralized control has destroyed incentives for innovation, efficiency, and individual achievement. But in the midst of social and economic problems, the Soviet dictatorship has forged the largest armed force in the world. It has done so by preempting the human needs of its people and in the end, this course will undermine the foundations of the Soviet system.❞

—quoted in *Ronald Reagan*

A Growing Deficit Reagan's military buildup drove the federal budget deficit higher and higher. At the same time, however, increased military spending helped expand the economy by providing jobs in

More Skill Practice

Reading Primary Sources Read aloud Reagan's quote on this page about the Soviet Union. **Ask: What did Reagan mean when he said the Soviets had achieved their military might by "preempting the human needs of its people"?** *(The Soviets had denied their citizens basic freedoms and provided no incentive for hard work.)* **OL**

More Skill Practice

Activating Prior Knowledge In contrast to Reagan's easy television demeanor, Walter Mondale appeared awkward and uncomfortable during the 1984 presidential election. **Ask: What other modern presidential election have you studied that hinged in part on television perceptions?** *(1960 election contest between Kennedy and Nixon)* **BL**

Profiles IN HISTORY

Justice Sandra Day O'Connor *1930–*

When a Supreme Court vacancy opened up in 1981, President Reagan decided to fulfill his campaign promise to name the first woman justice. He chose Sandra Day O'Connor, an Arizona appeals court judge.

When Reagan called O'Connor to ask to nominate her, she was surprised. "I was overwhelmed and, at first, speechless," O'Connor said. "After a moment I managed to tell him that I would be honored."

O'Connor grew up on the Day family's Lazy B Ranch in Arizona. Unlike most Supreme Court justices, she also had broad political experience. After earning a law degree in 1952, she found that most law firms would not hire a woman—except as a legal secretary. She went into public service, had three sons, and practiced law privately.

Appointed to a state senatorial vacancy in 1969, she successfully ran for the position and became its first woman majority leader in 1972. O'Connor won election as superior court judge in 1974 and was later appointed to the appeals court.

Her nomination to the Supreme Court had strong support from Justice William Rehnquist—a classmate at Stanford Law School—and Arizona senator Barry Goldwater. O'Connor's nomination was opposed by the Moral Majority because she had supported the Equal Rights Amendment (ERA) and refused to back an antiabortion amendment or criticize the *Roe* v. *Wade* decision. Others, however, praised her legal judgment and conservative approach to the law. As a moderate conservative, she quickly became an important swing-vote on the Court, between more liberal and more conservative justices.

defense industries. Originally, Reagan had hoped to **offset** the cost of the buildup by cutting other government programs. He also hoped, as supply-side economists had predicted, that the economic boom would lead to an increase in total tax revenue collected.

As the economy grew in the 1980s, the amount of money the government collected in taxes did rise steadily, but it was not nearly enough. With Congress unwilling to cut other programs, Reagan's defense spending pushed the annual budget deficit from $80 billion to over $200 billion.

✓ Reading Check) **Describing** How did Reagan's Cold War military policy affect the nation's economy?

The Reagan Doctrine

Main Idea President Reagan supported governments fighting communism, a policy known as the Reagan Doctrine.

Reading Connection What other presidents supported governments fighting communism? Read on to learn how President Reagan supported governments attempting to overthrow Communist regimes.

Building up the military was only part of Reagan's military strategy. He also believed the United States should support guerrilla groups around the world

who were fighting to overthrow Communist or pro-Soviet governments. This policy became known as the Reagan Doctrine.

Aid to the Afghan Rebels Perhaps the most **visible** example of the Reagan Doctrine was in Afghanistan. In late December 1979, the Soviet Union invaded Afghanistan to support a Soviet-backed government. The Soviets soon found themselves fighting Afghan guerrillas known as the *mujahadeen*.

President Carter sent about $30 million in military aid to the Afghan guerrillas. After taking office, President Reagan sent $570 million more. The Soviets were soon trapped in a situation similar to the American experience in Vietnam. They could not defeat the Afghan guerrillas. As casualties mounted, the war put additional strain on the Soviet economy. In 1988 the Soviets agreed to withdraw.

Nicaragua and Grenada Reagan was also concerned about Soviet influence and the spread of communism in Nicaragua. Rebels known as the Sandinistas had overthrown a pro-American dictator in Nicaragua in 1979. The Sandinistas set up a socialist government. They also accepted Cuban and Soviet aid and began supporting antigovernment rebels in neighboring El Salvador.

In response, the Reagan administration began secretly arming an anti-Sandinista guerrilla force

CHAPTER 20   Resurgence of Conservatism   **897**

Profiles IN HISTORY

known as the **contras,** from the Spanish word for "counterrevolutionary." When Congress learned of this policy, it banned further aid to the contras.

Aiding the contras was not Reagan's only action in Latin America. In 1983 radical Marxists overthrew the left-wing government on the tiny Caribbean island of Grenada. In October, Reagan sent in American troops. The Cuban and Grenadian soldiers were quickly defeated and a new anticommunist government was put in place.

The Iran-Contra Scandal Although Congress had prohibited aid to the Nicaraguan contras, individuals in Reagan's administration continued to illegally support the rebels. These officials secretly sold weapons to Iran in exchange for the release of American hostages being held in the Middle East. Profits from these sales were then sent to the contras.

News of the illegal operations broke in November 1986. One of the chief figures in the **Iran-Contra scandal** was Marine Colonel **Oliver North,** an aide to the National Security Council (NSC). He and other senior NSC and CIA officials testified before Congress and admitted to covering up their actions, including shredding documents to destroy evidence.

President Reagan had approved the sale of arms to Iran, but the congressional investigation concluded

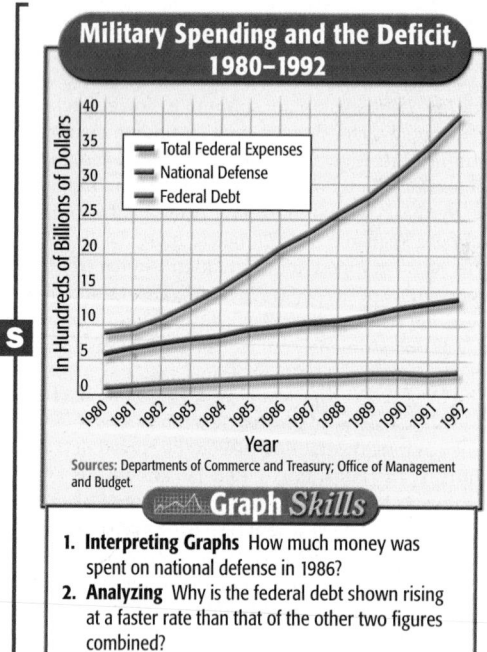

Military Spending and the Deficit, 1980–1992

- Total Federal Expenses
- National Defense
- Federal Debt

Sources: Departments of Commerce and Treasury; Office of Management and Budget.

Graph Skills

1. **Interpreting Graphs** How much money was spent on national defense in 1986?
2. **Analyzing** Why is the federal debt shown rising at a faster rate than that of the other two figures combined?

898 CHAPTER 20 Resurgence of Conservatism

that he had not been informed about the diversion of the money to the contras. To the end, Reagan insisted he had done nothing wrong, but the scandal tainted his second term in office.

✓ Reading Check **Identifying** What was the Reagan Doctrine?

U New Approaches to Arms Control

Main Idea President Reagan's decision to place nuclear missiles in Western Europe triggered calls for a "nuclear freeze."

Reading Connection How did President Eisenhower use brinkmanship to maintain peace after World War II? Read on to learn about President Reagan's opinion of "mutual assured destruction."

As part of the military buildup, Reagan decided to place nuclear missiles in Western Europe to counter Soviet missiles in Eastern Europe. This decision triggered a new peace movement. Tens of thousands of protesters pushed for a "nuclear freeze"—a halt to the deployment of new nuclear missiles.

Reagan offered to cancel the deployment of the new missiles if the Soviets removed their missiles from Eastern Europe. He also proposed Strategic Arms Reduction Talks (START) to cut the number of missiles on both sides in half. The Soviets refused and walked out of the arms control talks.

"Star Wars" Despite his decision to deploy missiles in Europe, Reagan generally disagreed with the military strategy known as nuclear deterrence, sometimes called "mutual assured destruction." This strategy assumed that as long as the United States and Soviet Union could destroy each other with nuclear weapons, they would be afraid to use them.

Reagan believed that mutual assured destruction was immoral because it depended on the threat to kill massive numbers of people. He also felt that if nuclear war did begin, there would be no way to defend the United States. In March 1983, Reagan proposed the Strategic Defense Initiative (SDI). This plan, nicknamed "Star Wars," called for the development of weapons that could intercept and destroy incoming missiles.

A New Soviet Leader In 1985 **Mikhail Gorbachev** became the leader of the Soviet Union and agreed to resume arms control talks. Gorbachev believed that the Soviet Union had to reform its economic system or it would soon collapse. It could not afford a new arms race with the United States.

Reagan and Gorbachev met in a series of summit meetings. The first of these were frustrating for both, as they disagreed on many issues. Gorbachev promised to cut back Soviet nuclear forces if Reagan would agree to give up SDI, but Reagan refused.

Reagan then challenged Gorbachev to make reforms. In West Berlin, Reagan stood at the Brandenburg Gate of the Berlin Wall, the symbol of divided Europe, and declared: "General Secretary Gorbachev, if you seek peace, if you seek prosperity for the Soviet Union and Eastern Europe . . . tear down this wall!"

Relations Improve By 1987 Reagan was convinced that Gorbachev did want to reform the Soviet Union and end the arms race. While some politicians distrusted the Soviets, most people welcomed the Cold War thaw and the reduction in the danger of nuclear war. In December 1987 the two leaders signed the Intermediate-Range Nuclear Forces (INF) Treaty. It was the first treaty to call for the destruction of nuclear weapons.

No one realized it at the time, but the treaty marked the beginning of the end of the Cold War. With an arms control deal in place, Gorbachev felt confident that Soviet military spending could be reduced. He pushed ahead with economic and political reforms that eventually led to the collapse of communism in Eastern Europe and in the Soviet Union.

With the economy booming, the American military strong, and relations with the Soviet Union rapidly improving, Ronald Reagan's second term came to an end. As he prepared to leave office, Reagan assessed his presidency: "They called it the Reagan

Picturing **History**

Superpower Summits During the 1980s, President Reagan and Premier Gorbachev met several times to discuss nuclear arms reductions. What Reagan defense proposal did Gorbachev want to eliminate before beginning arms reduction talks?

revolution. Well, I'll accept that, but for me it always seemed more like the great rediscovery, a rediscovery of our values and our common sense."

 Reading Check **Interpreting** What was the significance of the INF Treaty?

HISTORY Online **Study Central**

For help with the concepts in this section of *American Vision: Modern Times* go to tav.mt.glencoe.com and click on *Study Central.*

SECTION 2 ASSESSMENT

Checking for Understanding

1. **Vocabulary** Define: supply-side economics, budget deficit, exceed, offset, visible, contra.

2. **People and Terms** Identify: Reaganomics, Sandra Day O'Connor, William Rehnquist, Geraldine Ferraro, Iran-Contra scandal, Oliver North, Mikhail Gorbachev.

3. **List** the groups that Ronald Reagan appealed to in the 1980 presidential election.

Reviewing Big Ideas

4. **Explaining** What was President Reagan's stance on Foreign Policy?

Critical Thinking

5. **Forming an Opinion** Was the Iran-Contra affair a violation of the separation of powers? Explain.

6. **Organizing** Use a graphic organizer similar to the one below to list the ways that the Reagan doctrine was implemented.

Analyzing Visuals

7. **Analyzing Graphs** Study the graph on page 898 detailing the amount of money spent by the federal government from 1980 to 1992. What relationship do you see between military spending and the national debt?

Writing About History

8. **Expository Writing** Take on the role of a newspaper editorial writer during the Reagan administration. Write an article in which you present your opinion of Reagan's plans for a military buildup. **CA 11WA2.1a**

CHAPTER 20 Resurgence of Conservatism **899**

SECTION 2 ASSESSMENT ANSWERS

1. Content vocabulary is boldfaced and highlighted in yellow. Academic vocabulary is boldfaced.

2. Reaganomics (p. 895), Sandra Day O'Connor (p. 896), William Rehnquist (p. 896), Geraldine Ferraro (p. 896), Iran-Contra scandal (p. 898), Oliver North (p. 898), Mikhail Gorbachev

(p. 898)

3. social and economic conservatives

4. aggressive stance toward communism everywhere; military buildup to weaken Soviets

5. Students' answers will vary.

6. supported Afghan guerrillas and anti-Sandinista guerrillas in

Nicaragua, sent American troops to Grenada

7. Debt rose much faster due to interest charged on debt.

8. Students' articles will vary. Articles should express an opinion supported by fact.

ASSESS

Resources for page 899

Use these resources to assess student mastery.

- Section Quiz 20-2
- Reading Essentials and Study Guide 20-2
- Interactive Tutor Self-Assessment CD-ROM
- California Standards Practice, Grade 11

Picturing **History**

Answer: The Strategic Defense Initiative

Ask: What does this photograph evoke? *(possible answer— friendship)*

 Reading Check

Answer: It was the first treaty to call for the destruction of nuclear weapons. It marked the beginning of the end of the Cold War.

Study Central provides audio summaries, interactive games, and online graphic organizers to help students review section content.

CLOSE

Reading Primary Sources
Review Reagan's quote about the "Reagan revolution" at the end of the section. Discuss with students if they think it was really a revolution, and if so, in what sense. **OL**

Geography&History

FOCUS

History–Social Science Standards

This feature addresses the following standards:

11.11 Students analyze the major social problems and domestic policy issues in contemporary American society.

11.11.7 Explain how the federal, state, and local governments have responded to demographic and social changes such as population shifts to the suburbs, racial concentrations in the cities, Frostbelt-to-Sunbelt migration, international migration, decline of family farms, increases in out-of-wedlock births, and drug abuse.

TEACH

U Universal Access

Visual/Spatial Tell students to imagine that they are urban planners designing a new community that will use "smart-growth" ideas. Divide students into small groups in which they research possible smart-growth solutions. Then have them create rough sketches of plans for the new community. Each group should present its plan to the rest of the class. **AL** **CA HI5**

Answers and Additional Support

Urban America on the Move

Since the end of World War II, millions of Americans have abandoned older cities to find better lives—safer neighborhoods, bigger homes, better schools, and better jobs. Many found what they were seeking in the suburbs. Cities have grown into metropolitan areas that have continued to expand farther and farther into formerly rural regions.

The map at right shows patterns of recent population growth in the United States. The yellow and red areas represent growth since 1993, showing suburbs radiating out from the cities. A lot of growth has taken place in the Sunbelt states of the South and Southwest, helped by the spread of air-conditioning. The Atlanta region, for example, has more than doubled its population to 3.3 million in the last 30 years. It is now so big—and congested—that residents drive an average of 34 miles (55 km) per day.

Such rapid urban growth, or "sprawl," has brought a variety of cultural, social, and economic problems. In central cities and older suburbs, it has resulted in deteriorating infrastructure and a shortage of affordable housing. In the newer suburbs, growth has increased traffic and taxes and has resulted in declining air quality and a loss of open space.

Many city planners have mixed emotions about continued growth, and some—like those of San Francisco, California—have tried to curb it. Such efforts have been dubbed "smart growth." Proponents of smart growth seek to improve conditions in existing communities and to limit the spread of urbanization in outlying and rural areas. Specifically, they encourage developers to build housing and businesses in city centers rather than in the suburbs. They promote the preservation of undeveloped areas and parks near metropolitan regions. Smart growth advocates endorse expanding public transportation, combining residential and commercial areas, and building pedestrian-friendly communities as ways to reduce reliance on the automobile.

With smarter growth, cities can channel development in ways that maintain quality of life and make existing communities more inviting. Faced with long commutes on congested highways, some suburban residents are now opting to return to the cities that were so readily abandoned after the Second World War.

Existing development as of 1993
- Intense
- Moderate

Development since 1993
- Intense
- Moderate

Urban sprawl, traffic congestion, high ozone levels, and skyrocketing property taxes are part of the price Atlanta has paid for rapid growth.

LEARNING FROM GEOGRAPHY

1. Why did many Americans move to the suburbs after World War II?

2. In what parts of the country are cities growing fastest?

900

ANSWERS TO LEARNING FROM GEOGRAPHY

1. They sought safer neighborhoods, bigger homes, better schools, and better jobs.

2. Cities are growing fastest in the Sunbelt cities of the South and in the suburbs of major metropolitan areas.

AUSTIN
Like many Sunbelt cities, Austin, Texas (right), has experienced rapid growth in recent years, much of it fueled by an influx of high-tech companies. By 2010 its population—about 465,000 in 1990—is expected to reach 800,000.

Austin

Atlanta

R

ATLANTA
One of the fastest-growing regions in the country, metropolitan Atlanta, Georgia (right), is already larger in area than the state of Delaware. Atlanta's expansion into the surrounding counties since 1993 is shown at right in yellow and red.

CHAPTER 20   Resurgence of Conservatism   **901**

NATIONAL GEOGRAPHIC
Geography&History

R **Reading Strategy**
Predicting Have students study the map and the photographs on both pages. **Ask:** What problems do people experience as a result of urban sprawl? *(traffic congestion, increased exposure to pollution)* What benefits do people living in an urban area enjoy? *(access to fine dining, the arts and entertainment; more employment options)* Do you think the benefits outweigh the problems associated with urban sprawl? *(Answers will vary and will depend on the students' personal experiences.)* **OL**

ASSESS/CLOSE

Ask students to answer the Learning from Geography questions and discuss their answers with a classmate.

NGS **ONLINE**

Access National Geographic's Web site for current events, atlas updates, activities, links, interactive features, and archives at www.nationalgeographic.com.

More Skill Practice

Conducting a Survey Have students work in small groups to create a survey about local community development. In the process, students should research the topic, construct and test a hypothesis, and collect and evaluate the information. They should then write at least 10 survey questions with a range of responses; for example: Do you favor increased bus service? Responses could include Strongly Favor, Favor, Neutral, Oppose, and Strongly Oppose. Students should use their surveys to poll the opinions in their neighborhood and compare data with the entire class. **Ask:** Can you find significant differences between neighborhoods? **OL** **CA HR4**

Guide to Reading

Understanding Vocabulary: Ask students if they know what the word *yuppie* means. *(The text defines it as "young urban professionals.")* Discuss its meaning and whether it still applies to people today.

Answer to Graphic: AIDS, alcohol and drug abuse, crime, homelessness, Social Security, the environment, gay and lesbian rights

Unpacking the Standards

Students will be able to:

• Discuss the importance of money to the culture of the 1980s.

• Analyze the impact of the media on the era.

• Explain the growth in social activism during the decade.

Answers and Additional Support

SECTION 3 Life in the 1980s

Guide to Reading

Connection

In the previous section, you learned about the Reagan administration. In this section, you will discover what life in the United States was like during the 1980s.

Main Idea

• The economic recovery of the 1980s fueled the spending habits of young urban professionals. (p. 903)
• New technologies expanded music, video, and television capabilities. (p. 904)
• Social problems such as drug and alcohol abuse, crime, and the AIDS epidemic affected many people during the 1980s. (p. 905)

• Many groups became more politically active during the 1980s. (p. 906)
• As the nation sent out space shuttles and built space stations, it had to cope with several disasters. (p. 907)

Content Vocabulary

yuppie, space shuttle, space station

Academic Vocabulary

accumulate, via, orientation

Terms to Identify

AIDS, Sierra Club, American Association of Retired Persons

Reading Objectives

• **Discuss** the importance of money to the culture of the 1980s.
• **Explain** the growth in social activism during the decade.

Reading Strategy

Organizing As you read about life in the 1980s, complete a graphic organizer similar to the one below by listing the kinds of social issues that the United States faced in this decade.

Social Issues in the 1980s

Preview of Events

◆1981	◆1984	◆1987	◆1990
1981 MTV goes on the air	**1985** "Live Aid" rock concert benefit	**1986** Space shuttle *Challenger* explodes	**1988** More than 35,000 cases of AIDS diagnosed for the year.

The following are the main History–Social Science Standards covered in this section.

11.8.7 Describe the effects on society and the economy of technological developments since 1945, including the computer revolution, changes in communication, advances in medicine, and improvements in agricultural technology.

11.8.8 Discuss forms of popular culture, with emphasis on their origins and geographic diffusion (e.g., jazz and other forms of popular music, professional sports, architectural and artistic styles).

11.10.7 Analyze the women's rights movement from the era of Elizabeth Stanton and Susan Anthony and the passage of the Nineteenth Amendment to the movement launched in the 1960s, including differing perspectives on the roles of women.

11.11.3 Describe the changing roles of women in society as reflected in the entry of more women into the labor force and the changing family structure.

11.11.5 Trace the impact of, need for, and controversies associated with environmental conservation, expansion of the national park system, and the development of environmental protection laws, with particular attention to the interaction between environmental protection advocates and property right advocates.

11.11.7 Explain how the federal, state, and local governments have responded to demographic and social changes such as population shifts to the suburbs, racial concentrations in the cities, Frostbelt-to-Sunbelt migration, international migration, decline of family farms, increases in out-of-wedlock births, and drug abuse.

⌘ The Big Idea ⌘

Societies change over time. During the 1980s, the recovering economy encouraged spending. Profits for new discount retail stores soared. A transformation in the news and entertainment industry brought about the development of successful new television stations. Society, however, still faced several serious problems. Ongoing concerns about crime, drugs and alcohol, and the AIDS epidemic led to more politically active groups. Despite the strong conservative movement, liberal organizations and social activists continued to fight for their causes. NASA created the space-shuttle program and worked to develop space stations. The space-shuttle program, however, experienced several devastating losses.

902 CHAPTER 20 Resurgence of Conservatism

SECTION RESOURCES

📂 Print Material
• Reproducible Lesson Plan 20-3
• Guided Reading Activity 20-3
• Reading Essentials and Study Guide 20-3
• Active Reading Note-Taking Guide 20-3

🖌 Transparencies
• Daily Focus Skills Transparency 20-3
• Section Graphic Organizer Transparency 20-3

Technology
🖱 Interactive Tutor Self-Assessment CD-ROM
🖱 Exam*View*® Pro Testmaker CD-ROM
🖱 Presentation Plus! CD-ROM

S A Decade of Indulgence

Main Idea The economic recovery of the 1980s fueled the spending habits of young urban professionals.

Reading Connection Do you think it is important to have designer or brand name clothing and luxury goods? Read on to learn how consumerism dominated the 1980s.

Cultural commentators and the media in the 1980s portrayed American society as one of wealth and success. Stories emphasized the limousines, yachts, corporate jets, and designer gowns of the wealthy. Status symbols such as expensive watches and luxury cars became important. Popular television shows such as *Dallas* and *Dynasty* glamorized the lives of the very wealthy. By late 1983, the economy had revived after the 1981 recession. News stories described young stockbrokers, speculators, and real estate developers making multimillion-dollar deals.

★ An American Story ★

In the 1980s many young, ambitious professionals entered the heady world of finance. Julie Katzman, in her twenties, was on the fast track:

❝I constantly spent my time at the firm. I mean, all the time. I worked probably eighty hours a week. At the end of the summer, that Labor Day weekend, I got involved in another huge acquisition. That weekend I worked two and a half days without sleeping, and from that point until early December I didn't work a single week less than a hundred hours. You spend all your time working. You're kind of wiped out, but there's a lot of fulfillment. There's an incredible adrenaline rush. This is what you live on. You live on the highs.❞

—from *Sleepwalking Through History*

During this prosperous period, hundreds of companies were bought and sold. Real estate and stock values soared. Developer Donald Trump said: "I don't do it for the money. I've got enough, much more than I'll ever need. I do it to do it. Deals are my art form. Other people paint beautifully on canvas or write wonderful poetry. I like making deals, preferably big deals."

Yuppies The new moneymakers were young, ambitious, and hardworking. Journalists called them **yuppies**, from "young urban professionals." Many

worked in law or finance. They rewarded themselves with expensive stereo systems and luxury cars. They bought designer clothes and ate in upscale restaurants.

The rapid economic growth and emphasis on **accumulating** wealth in the 1980s was partly caused by the baby boom. By the 1980s, many baby boomers had finished college, entered the job market, and begun building their careers. Young people entering the workforce often placed an emphasis on acquiring goods and getting ahead in their jobs. Because baby boomers were so numerous, their concerns tended to shape the culture.

The strong economic growth of the 1980s benefited nearly everyone, but because much of it happened in industries that employed large numbers of middle and upper-class professionals, it shifted the distribution of the nation's income. From 1967 to 1986, the top 5 percent of Americans earned between 15.6 and 17.5 percent of the nation's total income. In the late 1980s, their share of the nation's income began to rise. By the mid-1990s, the top 5 percent of Americans earned well over 21 percent of the nation's income.

A Retail Revolution While news commentators in the 1970s and 1980s focused on inflation, the energy crisis, corporate mergers, and yuppies, several entrepreneurs worked on pioneering a new approach to retailing—or selling products to consumers—that greatly reduced prices for Americans.

This new type of retailing, known as discount retailing, began in the 1960s. Discount retailers sell large quantities of goods at very low prices, trying to sell the goods quickly so as to turn over their entire inventory in a short period of time. By selling a lot of products at low prices, they could make more money than traditional retailers who sold fewer products at

▼ *Finance traders at work*

CHAPTER 20   Resurgence of Conservatism   **903**

TEACH

S Skill Practice

Analyzing Information As students read this section, they may encounter text or information they do not understand. Point out to students they should adjust their reading strategies to increase their comprehension. Model how this is done by reading the section aloud. As you read, say things such as "What do I think the main focus of the 1980s was?" *(predicting)* Modeling how to read properly helps students think about skills they can use as they read independently. **BL**

W Writing Support

Expository Writing The 1980s was seen as a decade focused on personal wealth. **Ask:** Is society today less focused on gaining personal wealth than it was in the 1980s? Tell students to answer this question in a two-page paper, explaining their answer and providing examples to support their opinion. **OL**
CA 11WA2.4a

Resources for page 903

*Have students read more about social life in the 1980s in the **Primary Source Reading 20-2**.*

Did You Know?

While the 1980s is often seen as the decade of greed, the average American investor became more involved in the stock market in the 1990s. The Dow Jones Industrial Average closed over 3,000 in 1991, and reached its highest closing mark (11,722.98) in January 2000.

R Reading Strategy

Connecting Have students identify other retail giants that use the "superstore" concept to sell large quantities of goods at low prices. *(possible answers: Costco, Lowe's)* **Ask:** What was the key to the success of this business model? *(computerized inventory records to cut costs and lower prices)* **BL**

W Writing Support

Expository Writing The number of media outlets in the United States grew rapidly in the 1980s, due to government deregulation. Ask students to write a two-page paper detailing how many ways they can find entertainment in today's world. Encourage students to talk to their parents about how media services have expanded in the last few decades to make an accurate comparison. **OL**
CA 11WA2.4a

✓ Reading Check

Answer: young, urban professionals

---

higher prices. During the 1960s, many new discount retailers were founded, including K Mart, Woolco, Target, and Wal-Mart. Annual sales by discount stores grew from about $2 billion in the mid-1960s to nearly $70 billion by 1985.

The most successful discount retailer was Sam Walton, the founder of Wal-Mart. Walton grew up in poverty in the Dust Bowl of Oklahoma during the Great Depression. He was a plainspoken man who worked 16-hour days and stressed the importance of cost cutting and good customer service. He developed a system of distribution centers to rapidly resupply his stores, and he was one of the first retailers to use a computer database to track inventory and sales. By 1985 he was the richest person in the United States.

Others soon copied Walton's approach. By the late 1970s, retailers had begun to build huge "superstores" that enabled them to sell large quantities of goods very quickly at very low prices. One such entrepreneur was Arthur Blank, who grew up in a tiny one-bedroom apartment in Queens, New York. Blank studied accounting and worked hard as a manager. In 1978 he opened Home Depot, a chain of giant home-improvement stores. In 1983 Richard Schulze, a former air force officer, used his technical training

---

▼ *Robert Johnson, creator of Black Entertainment Television*

---

to found Best Buy, a huge discount retailer of consumer electronics. Dozens of other entrepreneurs started discount stores in other industries. Their innovations created millions of new jobs in the 1980s and helped fuel the era's rapid economic growth.

✓ Reading Check **Identifying** Who were yuppies?

Technology and the Media

Main Idea New technologies expanded music, video, and television capabilities.

Reading Connection What technological devices have become part of your everyday life? Read on to find out about the inventions of the 1980s.

In the 1980s, other entrepreneurs began transforming the news and entertainment industry. Until the late 1970s, television viewers were limited to three national networks and public television. In 1970 a 32-year-old businessman named Ted Turner used money from the billboard business he had inherited from his father to buy a failing television station in Atlanta, Georgia. Turner then pioneered a new type of broadcasting by creating WTBS in 1975. WTBS was the first "superstation"—a television station that sold low-cost sports and entertainment programs **via** satellite to cable companies throughout the nation.

Turner's innovation changed broadcasting and helped spread cable television across the country. Dozens of networks soon appeared. Many of the new networks specialized in one type of broadcasting, such as sports, movies, or news. In 1980 Turner himself founded the Cable News Network (CNN)—the first 24-hour all-news station in the nation.

Other new stations focused on a specific audience, such as churchgoers, shoppers, or minorities. In 1980 entrepreneur Robert Johnson created Black Entertainment Television (BET). Johnson was born into a poor family in rural Mississippi, the ninth of ten children. Hard work and determination enabled him to earn a master's degree from Princeton University. Johnson believed television had tremendous power to promote African American businesses and culture. In 1978, at age 32, he developed a plan to produce television programs for African Americans. His enthusiasm won him the support of several investors, and BET, the first and largest black-owned company on cable television, began broadcasting in 1980.

In 1981 music and technology merged, and Music Television (MTV) went on the air. MTV mixed songs

---

Did You Know?

Ted Turner first gained fame in 1977 after winning the prestigious *America's Cup* yacht race. After earning a fortune in the cable television and sports world, Turner announced in 1997 that he would give a total of $1 billion to programs sponsored by the United Nations.

and video images to create music videos. Music videos were like fast-moving short films, with costumes, makeup, and choreography. MTV was an instant hit, though its videos were often criticized for violence and sexual content. Many performers, such as Madonna and Michael Jackson, boosted their careers by producing videos with their new albums.

Rap music was another new sound of the 1980s. This musical style originated in local clubs in New York City's South Bronx. Emphasizing heavy bass and very rhythmic sounds, rap artists did not usually sing but rather spoke over the music and rhythmic beats. Rap's lyrics frequently focused on the African American experience in the inner city. While rap was initially popular among East Coast African Americans, it has grown in popularity, becoming a multimillion-dollar industry.

While the music industry was changing, new forms of entertainment also developed, including video games. The first video arcade game, called Pong, was released in 1972. In the early 1980s, sales reached about $3 billion with the release of games such as PacMan and Space Invaders. Video arcades became the new spot for young people to meet. By the mid-1980s, new technology allowed home video games to compete with arcade games in color and speed. Home video game sales rose dramatically in the 1990s.

✓ **Reading Check** **Describing** What forms of entertainment gained popularity in the 1980s?

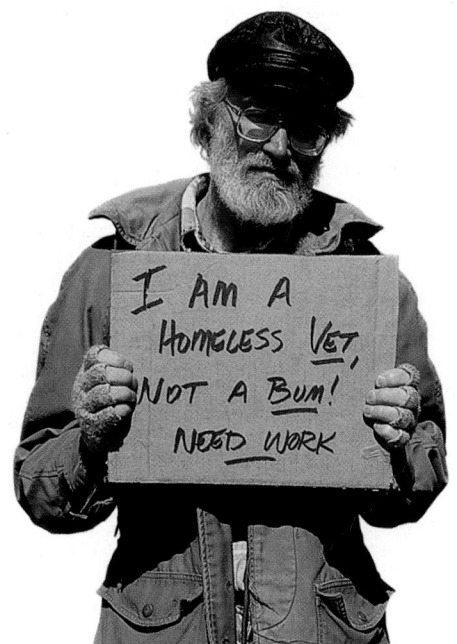

Picturing **History**

Homelessness During the 1980s, many people began living on the streets in makeshift shelters. A lack of low-income housing and care for the mentally ill added to the problem. How do you think the country's general prosperity influenced people to think about this problem?

A Society Under Stress

Main Idea Social problems such as drug and alcohol abuse, crime, and the AIDS epidemic affected many people during the 1980s.

Reading Connection Does your school have organizations such as Students Against Drunk Driving? Read on to learn more about attempts to limit teen alcohol abuse.

Although the 1980s were prosperous, many social problems continued to plague the nation and forced federal, state, and local governments to find resources to solve them.

Crime and Drugs Ongoing problems with drug abuse in the 1980s made many city neighborhoods dangerous. Drug users often committed crimes in order to get money for drugs, and dealers backed by street gangs fought to protect their territory. Cocaine use increased, especially a concentrated form, crack

cocaine, which made users hostile and aggressive. First Lady Nancy Reagan tried to discourage teen drug use with her "Just Say No" campaign. Many young people, however, continued to use drugs, especially marijuana and amphetamines. Drug use spread from cities to small towns and rural areas.

Problems With Alcohol Abuse of alcohol was also a serious concern. Teenagers with fake identification cards could easily buy alcoholic beverages. Although teen alcohol use declined during the 1980s, thousands of alcohol-related auto accidents involved young people. In 1980 Mothers Against Drunk Driving (MADD), a grassroots organization, was founded to look for effective solutions to underage drinking and drunk driving. In 1984 Congress cut highway funds to any state that did not raise the legal drinking age to 21. All states quickly complied.

A Deadly Epidemic In 1981 researchers identified a disease which caused seemingly healthy young men to become sick and die. They named it

CHAPTER 20 Resurgence of Conservatism **905**

R **Reading Strategy**

Connection Ask students how rap music has evolved since the late 1980s. *(Students' responses will vary but may include its increasing popularity among a broad cross-section of people. Hip hop music has developed into a separate genre.)* BL

C **Critical Thinking**

Analyzing Information The social issues of crime, drugs, and alcohol abuse reached a critical point in the 1980s. Have students research the attempts by interest groups and governments on the local, state, and national level to eliminate these issues. *(Students may identify programs such as "Just Say No" to drugs, MADD against drunk driving, and the Drug Enforcement Agency.)* OL

Review the Big Idea

Review the Big Idea for this section, "Societies change over time." Ask students to review the text under the heading "A Society Under Stress" and identify the most critical social problems of the decade. Discuss these choices as a class. OL

✓ **Reading Check**

Answer: Popular entertainment included listening to music such as rap music; watching movie videos, cable or satellite TV, and music videos; and playing video games.

Picturing **History**

Answer: The country's general prosperity might have influenced people to believe that some solution should be found for the problems of homeless people.
Ask: Is homelessness still a problem today? *(Students should recognize that although many groups have focused on resolving this problem, it still exists.)*

Resources for page 905

Have students read more about technological advances in the 1980s in the Linking Past and Present Activity 20.

Picturing **History**

Silent Witness The AIDS Quilt remembers those who have died from AIDS. Comprising more than 40,000 panels, it was first displayed near the Washington Monument. *What lesson do visitors take away from the enormous size of the quilt?*

"acquired immune deficiency syndrome," or **AIDS.** AIDS weakens the immune system, lowering resistance to illnesses such as pneumonia and several types of cancer. HIV, the virus that causes AIDS, is spread through bodily fluids. In the United States, AIDS was first noticed among homosexual men. Soon AIDS began to spread among heterosexual men and women. A few people got the disease from blood transfusions. Other victims included drug users who shared needles and, through them, infected blood. Many people were infected by sexual partners. By 1988 the Centers for Disease Control had identified more than 100,000 AIDS cases in the United States.

✓ Reading Check **Evaluating** What social problems did Americans face in the 1980s?

Social Activism

Main Idea Many groups became more politically active during the 1980s.

Reading Connection What political scandals affecting earlier administrations can you think of? Read on to discover the opposition to Secretary of the Interior James Watts's programs during the Reagan years.

AIDS increased the visibility of the country's gay and lesbian community, but some homosexuals had been defending their civil rights since the 1960s. On

June 27, 1969, New York City police raided a Greenwich Village nightclub called the Stonewall Inn. The police had a history of raiding the nightclub and targeting its patrons because of their sexual **orientation.** Frustration among the gay and lesbian onlookers led to a riot. The Stonewall riot marked the beginning of a gay activist movement. Soon after, organizations such as the Gay Liberation Front tried to increase tolerance of homosexuality and media coverage of gays and lesbians.

Although the 1980s witnessed the rise of a powerful conservative movement, liberal organizations and social activists continued to push their agenda as well, particularly on issues involving the environment and developing nations. In addition, elderly Americans began to organize politically for the first time.

Environmental Activism Grows Trying to promote environmental protection during the Reagan years was frustrating for environmental activists. Secretary of the Interior James Watt encouraged development on public lands, saying, "We will mine more, drill more, cut more timber." Congress, under pressure from environmental groups, blocked many of Watt's plans. Worried about Watt's program, many new members joined groups such as the **Sierra Club.**

906   CHAPTER 20   Resurgence of Conservatism

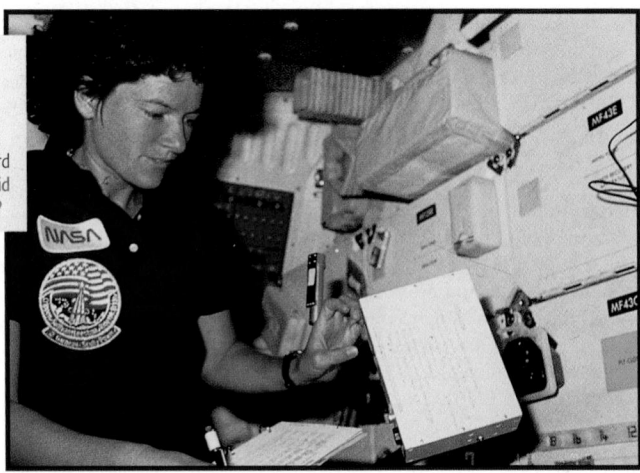

Picturing **History**

First Female Astronaut Dr. Sally Ride was accepted into the astronaut program in 1978. She became the first American woman to orbit the earth when she flew aboard the space shuttle Challenger in June 1983. What effect did Sally Ride's flight in space have on female astronauts?

The environmental movement born in the 1970s continued to grow in the 1980s. Environmentalists were active in protesting nuclear power plants and protecting fragile wetlands. Communities started recycling programs. Activists became concerned about the ozone layer and rain forests.

Artists Become Activists In the 1980s, ministers, politicians, and others targeted and criticized rock musicians as promoters of drug use and other negative behavior. Still, singers, actors, and other entertainers often organized benefit concerts to help others. In hits such as "Born in the USA," Bruce Springsteen sang about working-class Americans. A social activist, he gave concerts to benefit food banks and the homeless.

To help starving people in Ethiopia, Irish rocker Bob Geldof organized musicians in England to present "Band Aid" concerts in 1984. The next year, the event grew into "Live Aid." Musicians including Paul McCartney, Madonna, The Who, and Tina Turner participated in the musical benefits. Its theme song, "We Are the World," was a bestseller. The same year, country singer Willie Nelson organized "Farm Aid" to help American farmers going through hard times.

Other Groups Become Activists One noticeable political change in the 1980s was the stronger presence of senior citizens and immigrants. Decades of improvements in medicine had resulted in more Americans surviving to an older age. In addition, the birthrate had declined, so younger people represented a smaller proportion of the population. The fact that more Americans were receiving Social Security payments created budget pressures for the government. A dramatic increase in immigration during the 1980s and 1990s also altered voting patterns, increased cultural and religious diversity, and created a need for education reform to address the needs of bilingual students.

Older Americans became politically active, opposing cuts in Social Security or Medicare. Because they tended to vote in large numbers, senior citizens became an influential interest group. Their major lobbying organization was the **American Association of Retired Persons (AARP).**

✓ **Reading Check** **Summarizing** What issues did environmental activists focus on in the 1980s?

A New Era in Space

Main Idea As the nation sent out space shuttles and built space stations, it had to cope with several disasters.

Reading Connection Have you ever considered the dangers of space travel? Read on to find out more about one of the greatest disasters of the space program.

President Reagan, like many Americans, saw space as an exciting frontier. Improved technology and new exploration programs rekindled the nation's excitement for space exploration.

The Space Shuttle After Americans reached the moon, the National Aeronautics and Space Administration (NASA) began work on the **space shuttle**—a reusable spacecraft with wings that could rocket into space and then glide back to Earth. On April 12, 1981, the first space shuttle, *Columbia*, lifted off its launch pad in Florida. On board were two astronauts: John Young and Robert Crippen. John Young was a hero to many Americans. He had flown three times in

U **Universal Access**

Advanced Learners Tell students that while the *Challenger* explosion was tragic, NASA has had far more successes than failures in its history. Divide the class into groups of three to research the history of NASA. Each group should pick one event in the space agency's history and provide a multimedia presentation explaining the event, its importance, and its contribution to future NASA programs. **AL**

CA 11WA2.4b

W **Writing Support**

Persuasive Writing Critics of the space program have questioned its overall usefulness, while supporters see value in the science and achievements of space exploration. Have students research the space program's future goals and write a persuasive essay either supporting the continued funding of the space program or advocating a reduction. **OL** **CA** 11WS1.3

Answers and Additional Support

the 1960s and commanded the *Apollo 16* mission to the moon in 1972. After the shuttle landed successfully, Young remarked to the crowd: "We're really not too far, the human race isn't, from going to the stars."

Young and Crippen's flight demonstrated the shuttle's capabilities. Previously astronauts had been military pilots, but the shuttle could function as an orbiting laboratory, and civilians could now be astronauts. In 1983 Sally Ride became the first American woman in space, and after her flight, female astronauts became increasingly common.

In January 1986, disaster struck. The shuttle *Challenger* exploded after liftoff, killing everyone on board: Michael Smith, Dick Scobee, Judith Resnik, Ronald McNair, Ellison Onizuka, Gregory Jarvis, and Christa McAuliffe. Although Americans mourned the lost lives, President Reagan reminded everyone that the exploration of space is potentially dangerous and requires bravery:

> 66 The Challenger Seven were aware of the dangers, but overcame them and did their jobs brilliantly. . . . They had that special grace, that special spirit that says, 'Give me a challenge and I'll meet it with joy.' They had a hunger to explore the universe and discover its truths. . . . We've grown used to the idea of space, and perhaps we forget that we've only just begun. We're still pioneers. . . . [S]ometimes painful things like this happen. It's all part of the process of

exploration and discovery. It's all part of taking a chance and expanding man's horizons. The future doesn't belong to the fainthearted; it belongs to the brave. 99

—from *Speaking My Mind*

In June 1986, a presidential commission reported that defective seals in the rocket boosters had caused the explosion. Engineers fixed the problem, and in September 1988, the shuttle resumed operations.

W **A Home in Space** Between September 1988 and December 2002, the shuttle completed 87 missions. It placed many satellites in orbit, including the Hubble Space Telescope in 1990. This telescope gave astronomers the ability to look farther into space than ever before.

One reason NASA built the shuttle was to provide transportation to **space stations**—manned orbiting platforms in space that serve as a base of operations for space research. The United States had launched the space station *Skylab* in 1973, but it stayed in orbit only until 1979. In 1986 President Reagan announced that the United States would build a new space station to replace *Skylab*.

In the years following Reagan's announcement, the space station became an international project, and 16 nations helped create the International Space Station. Shuttle astronauts began assembling the station in December 1998, and the station's first crew

Profiles IN HISTORY

Franklin R. Chang-Diaz
1950–

Born in Costa Rica, Franklin R. Chang-Diaz dates his fascination with space to hearing about the *Sputnik* launching in 1957. His mother told him that a new star, made by humans, had been placed in the heavens. This convinced him, he said later, to become "a space explorer."

Chang-Diaz managed to save enough money—$50—to immigrate to the United States at the age of 18. He went to Hartford, Connecticut, where he had relatives. After completing high school and college, he went on to

earn a doctorate in applied plasma physics and fusion technology at MIT in 1977.

His goal of becoming an astronaut came true in 1980 when NASA selected him for the space shuttle program. In the following years, Chang-Diaz worked as part of the astronaut support crew and in early space station design studies.

His first spaceflight came in January 1986 on the space shuttle *Columbia*. In the late 1980s and 1990s, Chang-Diaz flew a number of shuttle missions.

Profiles IN HISTORY

Background: Chang-Diaz became director of the Advanced Space Propulsion Laboratory at the Johnson Space Center. He also is an adjunct professor of physics at Rice University and the University of Houston and has been instrumental in bringing astronauts and the scientific community closer together.

Ask: When did Chang-Diaz's fascination with space begin? *(He became interested in 1957 when he heard about* Sputnik.*)*

▲ *The space shuttle* Discovery

arrived in October 2000. By December 2002 the shuttle had completed 16 missions to the space station.

Seventeen years after the *Challenger* disaster, tragedy struck again. On February 1, 2003, the shuttle *Columbia* came apart while reentering the earth's atmosphere. All seven crew members were killed. As people around the world mourned, NASA began investigating the accident. Speaking to the nation, President George W. Bush proclaimed, "Mankind is led into the darkness beyond our world by the inspi-

 ration of discovery and the longing to understand." The president then promised that American space exploration would continue.

 Reading Check **Describing** How was the space shuttle different from previous spacecraft?

HISTORY Online **Study Central**

For help with the concepts in this section of *American Vision: Modern Times* go to tav.mt.glencoe.com and click on *Study Central.*

SECTION 3 ASSESSMENT

Checking for Understanding

1. **Vocabulary** Define: yuppie, accumulate, via, orientation, space shuttle, space station.
2. **Terms** Identify: AIDS, Sierra Club, American Association of Retired Persons.
3. **Summarize** the causes for which several musicians held concert benefits in the 1980s.

Reviewing Big Ideas

4. **Comparing** How do the social problems the United States faces today compare with those the nation faced in the 1980s?

Critical Thinking

5. **Analyzing** What new innovations occurred in the nation's space program in the 1980s? What would you invent for the space program?
6. **Organizing** Use a graphic organizer similar to the one below to list the changes in entertainment in the 1980s.

Changes in Entertainment

Analyzing Visuals

7. **Analyzing Photographs** Study the photo on page 905. Why does the man in the photo make a point of distinguishing himself as a veteran?

Writing About History

8. **Persuasive Writing** Choose one of the social problems of the 1980s. Write a letter to members of your favorite band asking them to perform a concert to benefit your cause. Your letter should include reasons the cause is important. **CA** 11WA2.2a

CHAPTER 20 Resurgence of Conservatism **909**

R **Reading Strategy**

Connecting Ask the class to spend 10 minutes writing about their thoughts on human-space travel when many believe that robots are capable of conducting space research at a lower cost. **AL** **CA** 11WS1.1

ASSESS

 Resources for page 909

Use these resources to assess student mastery.

📁 Section Quiz 20-3

📁 Reading Essentials and Study Guide 20-3

💿 Interactive Tutor Self-Assessment CD-ROM

📁 California Standards Practice, Grade 11

Reading Check

Answer: It was reusable.

HISTORY Online

Study Central provides audio summaries, interactive games, and online graphic organizers to help students review section content.

CLOSE

Summarizing Have students discuss attitudes toward money in the culture of the 1980s. **BL**

SECTION 3 ASSESSMENT ANSWERS

1. Content vocabulary is boldfaced and highlighted in yellow. Academic vocabulary is boldfaced.
2. AIDS *(p. 905),* Sierra Club *(p. 906),* American Association of Retired Persons *(p. 907)*
3. Band Aid and Live Aid aided famine victim in Ethiopia and elsewhere; Farm Aid helped American farmers.
4. Students should recognize that many problems are the same.
5. shuttle, space probe, and civilian and female astronauts
6. Changes included rap music; listening to music with portable cassette players; watching movie and music videos, cable or satellite TV; and video games.
7. He is hoping that this will encourage someone to trust him enough to get work.
8. Students' letters will vary but should use standard grammar and be persuasive.

FOCUS

History–Social Science Standards

This feature addresses the following standards:

11.8 Students analyze the economic boom and social transformation of post–World War II America.

11.8.2 Describe the significance of Mexican immigration and its relationship to the agricultural economy, especially in California.

Hunger of Memory is the story of Richard Rodriguez, a Mexican American who began school in California knowing little English. In his book Rodriguez recounts his personal struggles with his assimilation into mainstream American culture.

Read to Discover

Answer: They tease him.

Understanding Vocabulary

Before students begin reading, remind them to review **Read to Discover** and the **Reader's Dictionary.** This will help them better understand the literature excerpt.

Answers and Additional Support

American LITERATURE

from **Hunger of Memory**
by Richard Rodriguez

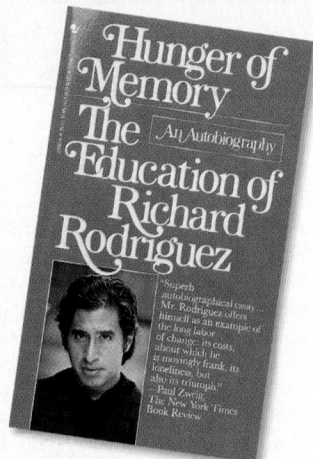

Richard Rodriguez

Hispanic Americans are the fastest-growing minority in the United States. Hispanics cherish their heritage, and many speak only Spanish among their friends and family. Most of their children's teachers, however, speak only English. As a result, Hispanic students often find school confusing and humiliating. Hispanic American Richard Rodriguez describes his struggle to become educated in his autobiography, *Hunger of Memory.*

In this excerpt, Rodriguez describes the difficulties he encountered at home after he became comfortable speaking English at school.

Read to Discover
What is the reaction of Richard's relatives to his reluctance to speak Spanish to them?

Reader's Dictionary
reticent: reluctant

anglicized: made to sound English

diminutive: shorter or more affectionate version

I grew up in a house where the only regular guests were my relations. For one day, enormous families of relatives would visit and there would be so many people that the noise and the bodies would spill out to the backyard and front porch. Then, for weeks, no one came by. . . .

In public, my father and mother spoke a hesitant, accented, not always grammatical English. And they would have to strain—their bodies tense—to catch the sense of what was rapidly said by *los gringos*. At home they spoke Spanish. The language of their Mexican past sounded in counterpoint to the English of public society. The words would come quickly, with ease. Conveyed through those sounds was the pleasing, soothing, consoling reminder of being at home.

During those years when I was first conscious of hearing, my mother and father addressed me only in Spanish; in Spanish I learned to reply. By contrast, English *(inglés),* rarely heard in the house, was the language I came to associate with *gringos.* I learned my first words in English overhearing my parents speak to strangers. At five years of age, I knew just enough English for my mother to trust me on errands to stores one block away. No more.

I was a listening child, careful to hear the very different sounds of Spanish and English. . . .

I was unable to hear my own sounds, but I knew very well that I spoke English poorly. My words could not stretch far enough to form complete thoughts. And the words I did speak I didn't know well enough to make into distinct sounds. . . . But it was one thing for *me* to speak English with difficulty. It was more troubling for me to hear my parents speak in public: their high-whining vowels and guttural consonants; their sentences that got stuck with 'eh' and

---

Reading Strategy > **ACTIVATING PRIOR KNOWLEDGE**

Adopted by California voters in 1996, Proposition 209 outlaws race-based and gender-based preferences by state and local governments. Critics claim it has severely weakened affirmative action efforts in the state. Supporters argue that it reestablishes an emphasis on merit. **Ask: Do you think race-based and gender-based preferences should be used to help redress social prejudices of the past?** *(Students' answers will vary but should be backed up with logical arguments.)* **OL** 'ah' sounds; the confused syntax; the hesitant rhythm of sounds so different from the way *gringos* spoke. I'd notice, moreover, that my parents' voices were softer than those of *gringos* we'd meet. . . .

But then there was Spanish. *Español:* my family's language. *Español:* the language that seemed to me a private language. I'd hear strangers on the radio and in the Mexican Catholic church across town speaking in Spanish, but I couldn't really believe that Spanish was a public language, like English. Spanish speakers, rather, seemed related to me, for I sensed that we shared—through our language—the experience of feeling apart from *los gringos.* . . .

Supporters of bilingual education today imply that students like me miss a great deal by not being taught in their family's language. What they seem not to recognize is that, as a socially disadvantaged child, I considered Spanish to be a private language. What I needed to learn in school was that I had the right—and the obligation—to speak the public language of *los gringos.* . . .

Three months. Five. Half a year passed. Unsmiling, ever watchful, my teachers noted my silence. They began to connect my behavior with the difficult progress my older sister and brother were making. Until one Saturday morning three nuns [from the Catholic school] arrived at the house to talk to our parents. . . .

With great tact the visitors continued, 'Is it possible for you and your husband to encourage your children to practice their English when they are home? Of course, my parents complied. What would they not do for their children's well-being? And how could they have questioned the Church's authority which those women represented? . . . The moment after the visitors left, the change was observed. '*Ahora,* speak to us *en inglés,*' my father and mother united to tell us.

At first, it seemed a kind of game. . . . In school, meanwhile, like my brother and sister, I was required to attend a daily tutoring session. I needed a full year of special attention. . . . Most of all I needed to hear my mother and father speak to me in a moment of seriousness in broken—suddenly heartbreaking—English. . . . Those *gringo* sounds they uttered startled me. Pushed me away. . . .

Again and again in the days following, increasingly angry, I was obliged to hear my mother and father: 'Speak to us *en inglés.*' (Speak.) Only then did I determine to learn classroom English. Weeks after, it happened: One day in school I raised my hand to volunteer an answer. I spoke out in a loud voice. And I did not think it remarkable when the entire class understood. That day, I moved very far from the disadvantaged child I had been only days earlier. The belief, the calming assurance that I belonged in public, had at last taken hold. . . .

. . . We remained a loving family, but one greatly changed. No longer so close; no longer bound tight

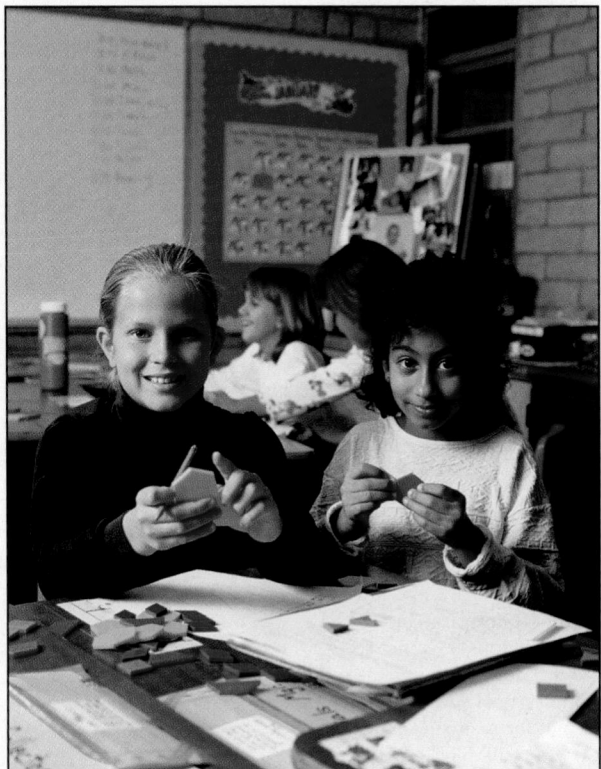
▲ *Children in a multi-ethnic classroom*

TEACH

R Reading Strategy

Inferring Ask the students to read Rodriguez's belief that Spanish was a private, personal language to be shared only among Spanish speakers. **Ask:** *What does this passage tell you about how Rodriguez viewed himself and his family at this time? (Students will likely infer that Rodriquez saw himself as outside American society.)* **OL**

U Universal Access

English Learners Ask students who learned English as a second language if they are willing to share some of their first experiences with English when they came to school. How did they feel? What were some obstacles they had to overcome? Are they still able to speak their native language today? **EL**

Reading Strategy EVALUATING

Bilingual education in California changed with the passage of Proposition 227 in 1998. Since the passage of Proposition 227, the percentage of students receiving bilingual education has declined and the percentage receiving varieties of English-only instruction has increased. Yet, a substantial number of English learners continue to receive bilingual instruction because parents are taking advantage of the law's "waiver" process to choose this option for their children. Have students research and evaluate the topic of bilingual education and use the evidence to either support or oppose it. **OL**

American LITERATURE

▲ *Hispanic American family gathering*

by the pleasing and troubling knowledge of our public separateness. Neither my older brother nor sister rushed home after school anymore. Nor did I. When I arrived home there would often be neighborhood kids in the house. Or the house would be empty of sounds. . . .

I grew up victim to a disabling confusion. As I grew fluent in English, I no longer could speak Spanish with confidence. I continued to understand spoken Spanish. And in high school, I learned how to read and write Spanish. But for many years I could not pronounce it. A powerful guilt blocked my spoken words; an essential glue was missing whenever I'd try to connect words to form sentences. . . .

When relatives and Spanish-speaking friends of my parents came to the house, my brother and sisters seemed reticent to use Spanish, but at least they managed to say a few necessary words before being excused. . . . I was cursed with guilt. Each time I'd hear myself addressed in Spanish, I would be unable to respond with any success. I'd know the words I wanted to say, but I couldn't manage to say them. I

would try to speak, but everything I said seemed to me horribly anglicized. My mouth would not form the words right. . . .

It surprised my listeners to hear me. They'd lower their heads, better to grasp what I was trying to say. They would repeat their questions in gentle, affectionate voices. But by then I would answer in English. No, no, they would say, we want you to speak to us in Spanish. . . . But I couldn't do it. *Pocho* then they called me. Sometimes playfully, teasingly, using the tender diminutive—*mi pochito*. Sometimes not so playfully, mockingly, *Pocho*. (A Spanish dictionary defines that word as an adjective meaning "colorless" or "bland." But I heard it as a noun, naming the Mexican-American who, in becoming an American, forgets his native society.) . . .

. . . I recount such incidents only because they suggest the fierce power Spanish had for many people I met at home; the way Spanish was associated with closeness. Most of those people who called me a *pocho* could have spoken English to me. But they would not. They seemed to think that Spanish was the only language we could use, that Spanish alone permitted our close association. . . .

For my part, I felt that I had somehow committed a sin of betrayal by learning English. . . . I felt that I had shattered the intimate bond that had once held the family close. . . .

Analyzing Literature

1. **Recall and Interpret** What does Richard mean by "public" and "private" language when he talks about English and Spanish? **CA** 11RC2.4; 11RC2.5

2. **Evaluate and Connect** Why did Richard's relatives nickname him *Pocho?* **CA** 11RC2.4

Interdisciplinary Activity

Journalism Interview a bilingual friend, relative, or classmate about when and where they use each of the languages they speak. Write a transcript of the interview.

Reading on Your Own

For other literature selections that relate to Americans from various ethnic backgrounds growing up and living in the United States, you might consider the following book suggestions.

Growing up Ethnic in America: Contemporary Fiction About Learning to Be American
Maria Mazziotti Gillan and Jennifer Gillan, editors

This collection of short stories by Native American, African American, Latino, Jewish, and other writers with ethnic roots examines what it means to become Americanized, to grow up as a minority, and to reflect on the heterogeneous culture of the United States.

The Joy Luck Club
by Amy Tan

Two differing world views of women who immigrated to the United States from China and their American-born daughters are explored. The younger generation eventually realizes the importance of preserving their culture.

Drink Cultura: Chicanismo
by José Antonio Burciaga

With his own life as a guide, Burciaga explores what it means to be Latino in American society.

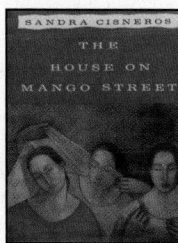

The House on Mango Street
by Sandra Cisneros

A young girl ponders her Hispanic Chicago neighborhood and evaluates her relationships with family and friends.

HISTORY Online

Refer to tav.mt.glencoe.com for additional Glencoe Literature titles, lesson plans, and study guides related to this unit.

TEACH

Cooperative Learning

Free-Form Mapping Divide students into groups and assign them additional reading on this topic. You can choose one of the titles from this list or select additional ones. After students have read the assignment, have each group create their own text representation with free-form mapping. Free-form maps use words and images to illustrate the content of the book. Each group must decide on the main ideas, themes, or concepts that they want to illustrate on their maps. Students should then use words, pictures, or diagrams to illustrate their ideas. Have groups present their maps to the class as a culminating activity. **OL**

GLENCOE BOOKLINK

Use **Glencoe BookLink** to create customized reading lists for your students' reading levels, interests and abilities.

Reading Strategy | REINFORCING READING SKILLS

To help students increase their comprehension of the reading selections, ask them to pause while reading and analyze the author's implicit and explicit assumptions and beliefs about the subject. Students can do this by asking: What is the main idea stated by the author? Does the author give specific examples that support or question the main point? **OL**

FOCUS

SKILLBUILDER ACTIVITY

Project **Daily Focus Skills Transparency 20-4** and have students answer the question.

Guide to Reading

Understanding Vocabulary
Ask students to explain the meaning of *perestroika* and *glasnost. (restructuring and openness)* Have them think of other foreign language vocabulary words they have encountered that are important to understanding U.S. history. *(laissez faire, détente)*

Answers to Graphic:
Soviet Union: cooperated with reform leader Gorbachev; China: halted arms sales and reduced diplomatic contact; Panama: invaded and seized dictator to help people hold elections and organize a new government; Middle East: imposed economic sanctions against Iraq and carried out Operation Desert Storm.

Unpacking the Standards

Students will be able to:

• Identify the events that brought an end to the Cold War.

• Explain the foreign policy and domestic policy challenges that the Bush administration faced.

SECTION 4

The End of the Cold War

Guide to Reading

Connection
In the previous section, you learned about life in the United States during the 1980s. In this section, you will discover how the Cold War ended.

Main Idea
• Since many Americans had benefited from the economic boom of the 1980s, they elected Republican George Bush as president in 1988. (p. 915)
• Reforms in the Soviet Union and the collapse of the Communist regime led to the end of the Cold War. (p. 916)

• Bush used his foreign policy expertise to deal with crises in China, Panama, and the Persian Gulf. (p. 917)
• To stimulate the economy, President Bush raised taxes, but lost the election to Bill Clinton. (p. 918)

Content Vocabulary
perestroika, glasnost, downsizing, capital gains tax, grassroots movement

Academic Vocabulary
revolution, relax, task

People and Terms to Identify
Boris Yeltsin, Tiananmen Square, Saddam Hussein, H. Ross Perot

Reading Objectives
• **Identify** the events that brought an end to the Cold War.
• **Explain** the domestic challenges facing the Bush administration.

Reading Strategy
Categorizing As you read about the administration of President Bush, complete a chart similar to the one below by describing U.S. foreign policy in each of the places listed on the chart.

Place	Foreign Policy
Soviet Union	
China	
Panama	
Middle East	

Preview of Events

♦1989	♦1990	♦1991	♦1992

May, 1989	November, 1989	August, 1990	January, 1991	December, 1991
Tiananmen Square protests begin	Berlin Wall falls	Iraq invades Kuwait	Persian Gulf War begins	Soviet Union collapses

The following are the main History–Social Science Standards covered in this section.

11.1.3 Understand the history of the Constitution after 1787 with emphasis on federal versus state authority and growing democratization.

11.8.4 Analyze new federal government spending on defense, welfare, interest on the national debt, and federal and state spending on education, including the California Master Plan.

11.9.5 Analyze the role of the Reagan administration and other factors in the victory of the West in the Cold War.

11.9.6 Describe U.S. Middle East policy and its strategic, political, and economic interests, including those related to the Gulf War.

11.11.7 Explain how the federal, state, and local governments have responded to demographic and social changes such as population shifts to the suburbs, racial concentrations in the cities, Frostbelt-to-Sunbelt migration, international migration, decline of family farms, increases in out-of-wedlock births, and drug abuse.

914 CHAPTER 20 Resurgence of Conservatism

～ *The Big Idea* ～

International competition can lead to conflict and cooperation. The economic boom of the 1980s convinced many Americans to elect another Republican president in 1988. While President George Bush's foreign policies were widely praised, his domestic policies were less popular. The need for economic reform in the Soviet Union and the collapse of its Communist regime led to the end of the Cold War and the start of tremendous change around the world. Bush used his experience in foreign policy to handle crises in China, Panama, and the Persian Gulf. In order to combat inflation and the economic slowdown at home, President Bush broke a major campaign promise by raising taxes. The country's recession and growing federal deficit led many Americans to elect Democratic presidential candidate Bill Clinton in the 1992 election.

SECTION RESOURCES

📁 **Print Material**
• Reproducible Lesson Plan 20-4
• Guided Reading Activity 20-4
• Reading Essentials and Study Guide 20-4
• Active Reading Note-Taking Guide 20-4

🖥 **Transparencies**
• Daily Focus Skills Transparency 20-4
• Section Graphic Organizer Transparency 20-4

Technology
⚙ Interactive Tutor Self-Assessment CD-ROM
⚙ Exam*View*® Pro Testmaker CD-ROM
⚙ Presentation Plus! CD-ROM

George Bush Takes Office

Main Idea Since many Americans had benefited from the economic boom of the 1980s, they elected Republican George Bush as president in 1988.

Reading Connection What type of background do you think presidents should have? Read on to find out the ways in which George Bush's background helped prepare him for the presidency.

When Ronald Reagan left office, few Americans were thinking about foreign policy. They wanted a continuation of Reagan's domestic policies—low taxes and less government action. Following the presidential election of 1988, however, the Persian Gulf War soon brought foreign policy to the forefront.

★ An American Story ★

On October 31, 1990, General Colin Powell, who was the chairman of the Joint Chiefs of Staff, Secretary of Defense Dick Cheney, and other high-ranking officials met with President George Bush. In August the country of Iraq had invaded neighboring Kuwait. American troops had been rushed to the Middle East in response. Now the president had to decide whether to go to war.

General Brent Scrowcroft, a close adviser to Bush, began the meeting: "Mr. President, we are at a Y in the road. Down one branch we can continue sanctions. . . . Down the other branch we . . . go on the attack." Powell then presented the plan for attacking Iraq. Several advisers gasped at the numbers, which called for over 500,000 American troops. "Mr. President," Powell began, "I wish . . . that I could assure you that air power alone could do it but you can't take that chance. We've gotta take the initiative out of the enemy's hands if we're going to go to war." Cheney later recalled that Bush "never hesitated." He looked up from the plans and said simply, "Do it."

—adapted from *Triumph Without Victory*
and *PBS Frontline Gulf War Interviews*

When George Bush accepted the Republican nomination in 1988, he too was more concerned about domestic issues. He reassured Americans with this promise: "Read my lips: No new taxes." The

Democrats hoped to regain the White House in 1988 by promising to help working-class Americans, minorities, and the poor. One candidate, civil rights leader Jesse Jackson, tried to create a "rainbow coalition"—a broad group of minorities and the poor—by speaking about homelessness and unemployment. He finished second in the primaries, the first African American to make a serious run for the nomination.

The Democrats' final choice was Massachusetts governor Michael Dukakis. The Bush campaign portrayed him as too liberal, unpatriotic, and "soft on crime." The Democrats questioned Bush's leadership abilities, but Bush had Reagan's endorsement, and with the economy still doing well, few Americans wanted to switch parties. Bush won 54 percent of the popular vote and defeated Dukakis 426 to 111 in the Electoral College. Democrats, however, kept control of Congress.

The war in the Persian Gulf was only one of many international crises that confronted President George Bush after his election in 1988. Fortunately, Bush's strength was in foreign policy. In the 1970s, he had served as ambassador to the UN and as the nation's first diplomatic envoy to the People's Republic of China. He then headed the CIA from 1976 to 1977 before becoming vice president in 1981.

✓ **Reading Check** **Describing** What kind of strategy did the Bush campaign use in the 1988 election?

▼ *Colin Powell*

TEACH

R₁ Reading Strategy

Using Context Clues Students can often determine the meaning of a word they do not know by using context—the words and sentences that surround an unfamiliar word. As they read the section and encounter words they do not know, they should use these clues to identify each word's meaning. Ask students to use clues to determine the definition of *rainbow coalition*. **BL**

R₂ Reading Strategy

Organizing Information The American Story on this page refers to several people who served in the Bush administration. Ask students to list each individual in a table, providing their role in 1990 and listing their role, if any, in today's government. Students may use library and Internet resources to find all relevant information. **OL**

✓ **Reading Check**

Answer: He promised no new taxes and the continuation of Ronald Reagan's domestic policies.

Did You Know?

Colin Powell served in the U.S. Army for 35 years, rising to the rank of 4-star General. During the Persian Gulf War he advised President Bush as the 12th Chairman of the Joint Chiefs of Staff, the highest military position in the Department of Defense.

Historical Interpretation
Review with students what they know about the Communist government of the Soviet Union during the last years of the Cold War.
Ask: Was the collapse of the Soviet Union inevitable?
(Students should recognize that events could have taken another direction depending upon the leaders or the sequence of events.) OL CA HI3; HI4

R Reading Strategy

Scaffolding—Academic Vocabulary The word *institute* was introduced in Chapter 15, Section 2. Ask a student to define the word. BL

✓ Reading Check

Answer: *Perestroika* was intended to save the Soviet economy by allowing some private enterprise and profit-making.

Answers and Additional Support

NATIONAL GEOGRAPHIC **Revolution in Eastern Europe, 1989–1993**

Geography *Skills*

1. **Interpreting Maps** Which Eastern European countries abandoned communism first?
2. **Applying Geography Skills** Why was the fall of communism in East Germany significant?

The Cold War Ends

S **Main Idea** Reforms in the Soviet Union and the collapse of the Communist regime led to the end of the Cold War.

Reading Connection What was the Berlin Wall? Read on to discover how it came down.

Almost immediately after taking office, President Bush had to draw on his foreign policy experience. With the help of Secretary of State James Baker, the president steered the United States through an era of sweeping change that resulted from the sudden end of the Cold War.

Gorbachev's Reforms As president, Bush continued Reagan's policy of cooperation with Soviet leader Mikhail Gorbachev. By the late 1980s, the Soviet economy was suffering from years of inefficient central planning and huge expenditures on the arms race. To

save the economy, Gorbachev instituted *perestroika*, or "restructuring," and allowed some private enterprise and profit-making.

The other principle of Gorbachev's plan was *glasnost*, or "openness." It allowed more freedom of religion and speech, allowing people to discuss politics openly.

Revolution in Eastern Europe Protests in Poland had led to the first independent trade union, Solidarity, in 1980. It was suspended a year later, but with Gorbachev's support, *glasnost* spread to Eastern Europe. In 1989 peaceful revolutions replaced Communist rulers with democratic governments in Poland, Hungary, Czechoslovakia, Romania, and Bulgaria. The spreading **revolution** soon reached East Germany, and at midnight on November 9, 1989, guards at the Berlin Wall opened the gates. Within days, bulldozers leveled the hated symbol of Communist repression. Within a year, East and West Germany had reunited.

The Soviet Union Collapses As Eastern Europe abandoned communism, Gorbachev faced mounting criticism from opponents at home. In August 1991, a group of Communist officials and army officers staged a coup—an overthrow of the government. They arrested Gorbachev and sent troops into Moscow.

In Moscow, Russian president **Boris Yeltsin** defied the coup leaders from the Russian Parliament. About 50,000 people surrounded the Parliament to protect it from troops. President Bush telephoned Yeltsin to express U.S. support. Soon afterward, the coup collapsed, and Gorbachev returned to Moscow.

The defeat of the coup brought swift change. All 15 Soviet republics declared their independence from the Soviet Union. Yeltsin outlawed the Communist Party in Russia. In late December 1991, Gorbachev announced the end of the Soviet Union. Most of the former Soviet republics then joined in a federation called the Commonwealth of Independent States.

✓ Reading Check **Explaining** Why did Mikhail Gorbachev institute the policy of *perestroika*?

Geography *Skills*

Answers:
1. Poland, Hungary, Bulgaria, and Romania
2. It was particularly significant because it meant that Germany could be reunified.

Geography Skills Practice
Ask: What happened to Czechoslovakia? *(In 1993 it was divided into two countries: the Czech Republic and Slovakia.)*

The "New World Order"

Main Idea Bush used his foreign policy expertise to deal with crises in China, Panama, and the Persian Gulf.

Reading Connection What student movements have been part of American history? Read on to learn about a student protest in China.

After the Cold War, the world became increasingly unpredictable. In a phrase made popular by President Bush, a "new world order" was developing. While trying to redefine American foreign policy, Bush faced crises in China, Panama, and the Middle East.

Tragedy in Tiananmen Square Despite the collapse of communism in Eastern Europe and the Soviet Union, China's Communist leaders were determined to stay in power. China's government had **relaxed** controls on the economy, but it continued to repress political speech and dissent. In May 1989, Chinese students and workers held demonstra-

tions for democracy. In early June, government tanks and soldiers crushed their protests in **Tiananmen Square** in Beijing—China's capital. Many people were killed and hundreds of pro-democracy activists were arrested. Many were later sentenced to death.

These events shocked the world. The United States and several European countries halted arms sales and reduced their diplomatic contacts with China. The World Bank suspended loans. Some congressional leaders urged even stronger sanctions, but President Bush resisted these harsher measures, believing that trade and diplomacy would eventually moderate China's behavior.

Panama While President Bush struggled to deal with global events elsewhere, a crisis developed in Panama. In 1978 the United States had agreed to give Panama control over the Panama Canal by the year 2000. Because of the canal's importance, American officials wanted to make sure Panama's government was both stable and pro-American.

By 1989 Panama's dictator, General Manuel Noriega, had stopped cooperating with the United

NATIONAL GEOGRAPHIC
MOMENT in HISTORY

A CITY REUNITED
Built in 1961, the Berlin Wall served to stem the mounting tide of immigration from Communist East Germany into the democratic western sector of the city. The wall also stood as a symbol of Cold War tensions between the world's superpowers. As reforms sparked by Mikhail Gorbachev swept through Eastern Europe, however, East German citizens began pressuring their government to open its borders. On November 9, 1989, the gates were thrown open, and East and West Berliners finally mingled freely. With great enthusiasm, they took hammers and chisels to the wall and tore down the hated symbol of division.

CHAPTER 20 Resurgence of Conservatism **917**

NATIONAL GEOGRAPHIC
MOMENT in HISTORY

The following events immediately preceded the wall's destruction: In October, East Germany celebrated its fortieth anniversary with a two-day visit by Mikhail Gorbachev. After Gorbachev left, the government arrested demonstrators who were protesting economic problems and the lack of democratic freedoms. Continued unrest forced President Erich Honecker, a hard-line Communist who had ruled East Germany since 1971, to resign. In November, the government opened its borders in an attempt to turn the tide of escaping citizens and convince them that leaving the country was unnecessary.

C Critical Thinking

Comparing and Contrasting
The overall control of the Communist Party weakened and failed in Eastern Europe and the Soviet Union in the late 1980s and early 1990s. However, communism remains strong in China. Ask the class to write a one-page paper that compares and contrasts the reactions of the Chinese Communist leaders to the reforms of Gorbachev. *(China allowed some economic freedoms but remained reluctant to increase freedom of speech and other personal freedom that Gorbachev allowed.)* **OL**

S Skill Practice

Visual Literacy The fall of the Berlin Wall was a strongly symbolic moment to people living in Germany in the late 1980s. **Ask: What emotions do you see in the faces of the people tearing down the Berlin Wall?** *(determination)* **What had the Wall come to represent for East Berliners?** *(oppression and a lack of freedom)* **BL** **CA HI3**

Review the Big Idea

Review the Big Idea for this section, "International competition can lead to conflict and cooperation." Ask the class to research the influence of U.S. policies on the democratic revolutions of 1989 to 1993 that ended Communist control of Eastern Europe. Students should focus on the close cooperation between President Bush and Mikhail Gorbachev. **OL**
CA CS1; HI1; HI2; HI4

S Skill Practice

Interpreting Events Some who favored military action against Saddam Hussein in 1991 compared his expansion to German actions prior to World War II. Opponents of the Persian Gulf War recalled the problems of the Vietnam War. Have students consider these arguments and decide whether the outcome of the war meant that one historical example was more fitting than the other. **AL** **CA** HR3; HR4

R Reading Strategy

Questioning Before students begin reading the text under the heading "Domestic Challenges," ask them to turn the heading and subheadings into questions that they will answer while reading. For instance, they might ask: **What domestic challenges did President Bush face?** Have students complete an outline based on their responses. **BL**

✓ Reading Check

Answer: American officials feared the invasion was only the first step and that Iraq's ultimate goal was to capture Saudi Arabia and its vast oil reserves.

Answers and Additional Support

918

▲ *Soldiers board a transport helicopter while preparing to liberate Kuwait*

States. He also aided drug traffickers, cracked down on opponents, and harassed American military personnel defending the canal. In December 1989, Bush ordered American troops to invade Panama. The troops seized Noriega, who was sent to the United States to stand trial on drug charges. The troops then helped the Panamanians hold elections and organize a new government.

S **The Persian Gulf War** President Bush faced perhaps his most serious crisis in the Middle East. In August 1990, Iraq's dictator, **Saddam Hussein,** sent his army to invade oil-rich Kuwait. American officials feared the invasion was only the first step and that Iraq's ultimate goal was to capture Saudi Arabia and its vast oil reserves.

President Bush persuaded other UN member countries to join a coalition to stop Iraq. Led by the United States, the United Nations first imposed economic sanctions on Iraq and demanded the Iraqis withdraw. The coalition forces included troops from the United States, Canada, Europe, and Arab nations. The UN set a deadline for the Iraqi withdrawal, or the coalition would use force to remove them. Congress also voted to authorize the use of force if Iraq did not withdraw.

Iraq refused to comply with the UN deadline, and on January 16, 1991, the coalition forces launched Operation Desert Storm. Dozens of cruise missiles and thousands of laser-guided bombs fell on Iraq, destroying its air defenses, bridges, artillery, and other military targets. After about six weeks of bombardment, the coalition launched a massive ground attack. Waves of tanks and troop carriers smashed through Iraqi lines and encircled the Iraqi forces defending Kuwait.

918 CHAPTER 20 Resurgence of Conservatism

The attack killed thousands of Iraqi soldiers. Many more surrendered. Fewer than 300 coalition troops were killed. Just 100 hours after the ground war began President Bush declared victory. "Kuwait is liberated," he announced. Iraq accepted the coalition's cease-fire terms. American troops returned home to cheering crowds celebrating the U.S. victory in the first large-scale war since Vietnam.

✓ Reading Check **Examining** Why did President Bush take action when Iraqi troops invaded Kuwait?

R Domestic Challenges

Main Idea To stimulate the economy, President Bush raised taxes, but lost the election to Bill Clinton.

Reading Connection How is your school and community designed to provide access for people who use wheelchairs? Read on to find out more about the Americans with Disabilities Act of 1990.

President Bush could not ignore domestic issues. He inherited a growing deficit and a slowing economy. As the Persian Gulf crisis began, the economy plunged into a recession and unemployment rose rapidly.

The Economy Slows The recession that began in 1990 was partly caused by the end of the Cold War. As the Soviet threat faded, the United States began reducing its armed forces and canceling orders for military equipment. Thousands of soldiers were released, and defense industry workers were laid off.

Companies began **downsizing**—laying off workers and managers to become more efficient. During the 1980s, many people moved from farms to cities to take advantage of the expanding job market. By 1990, however, jobs were being cut and less than two percent of the population still lived on farms. The nation's high level of debt made the recession worse. Americans had borrowed heavily during the 1980s and now faced paying off large debts.

In addition, the huge federal deficit forced the government to borrow money to pay for its programs. This borrowing kept money from being available to expanding businesses. The government also had to pay interest on its debt, money that might otherwise have been used to fund programs or jumpstart the economy.

Gridlock in Government Shortly after taking office, Bush tried to improve the economy. He called

Did You Know?

Iraqi leader Saddam Hussein liked to be called by his first name. When pronounced correctly, with the emphasis on the second syllable, *Saddam* means "leader" or "learned one." During the Persian Gulf Crisis, President Bush insisted on pronouncing the name with the emphasis on the first syllable. Pronounced this way, *Saddam* means "a boy who fixes or cleans shoes."

for a cut in the **capital gains tax**—the tax paid by businesses and investors when they sell stocks or real estate for a profit. Bush believed the tax cut would encourage businesses to expand and in turn create more jobs and stimulate the economy. Calling the idea a tax break for the rich, Democrats in Congress defeated it.

Aware that the growing federal deficit was hurting the economy, Bush broke his "no new taxes" campaign pledge. After meeting with congressional leaders, he agreed to a tax increase in exchange for cuts in spending. This decision turned many voters against Bush. They blamed him both for the tax increase, which he had promised not to do, and for trying to cut social programs.

Extending Rights Although President Bush and Democrats in Congress disagreed on economic issues, they cooperated on other legislation. One example was the Americans with Disabilities Act (ADA), signed by Bush in 1990. The legislation forbade discrimination in workplaces and public places against people who were physically or mentally challenged. The law had widespread effect. Access ramps were added to buildings, closed-captioned television became more commonplace, and wheelchair lifts were installed on city buses.

The 1992 Election Although the recession had weakened his popularity, President Bush won the Republican nomination. Bush promised to address voters' economic concerns, and he blamed congressional Democrats for the gridlock that seemingly paralyzed the nation's government and prevented change.

The Democrats nominated Arkansas governor Bill Clinton, despite stories that questioned his character and his failure to serve in Vietnam. Calling himself a "New Democrat" to separate himself from more liberal Democrats, Clinton promised to cut middleclass taxes and spending and to reform the nation's health care and welfare programs. His campaign repeatedly blamed Bush for the recession.

Many Americans were not happy with either Bush or Clinton. This enabled an independent candidate, billionaire Texas businessman **H. Ross Perot,** to make a strong challenge. Perot stressed the need to end deficit spending. His no-nonsense style appealed to many Americans. A **grassroots movement**—groups of people organizing at the local level—put Perot on the ballot in all 50 states.

Bill Clinton won the election with 43 percent of the popular vote and 370 electoral votes. The Democrats also retained control of Congress. Bush won 37 percent of the popular vote, while Perot received 19 percent—the best showing for a third-party candidate since 1912—but no electoral votes.

As the first president born after World War II, the 46-year-old Clinton was the first person from the "baby boom" generation to enter the White House. It was his **task** to revive the economy and guide the United States in a rapidly changing and increasingly technological world.

 Reading Check **Evaluating** Why did some people vote for H. Ross Perot in 1992? How successful was his election campaign as a third-party candidate?

HISTORY Online **Study Central**

For help with the concepts in this section of *American Vision: Modern Times* go to tav.mt.glencoe.com and click on *Study Central.*

SECTION 4 ASSESSMENT

Checking for Understanding

1. **Vocabulary** Define: *perestroika, glasnost,* revolution, relax, downsizing, capital gains tax, grassroots movement, task.

2. **People and Terms** Identify: Boris Yeltsin, Tiananmen Square, Saddam Hussein, H. Ross Perot.

3. **Describe** how Mikhail Gorbachev tried to reform the Soviet government.

Reviewing Big Ideas

4. **Explaining** How did the economy affect the 1992 election?

Critical Thinking

5. **Analyzing** How did the United States and its Western allies finally achieve victory in the Cold War?

6. **Organizing** Use a graphic organizer similar to the one below to list the causes of the recession of the early 1990s.

Budget Problems	Economic Problems	Foreign Developments

Analyzing Visuals

7. **Studying Maps** Examine the map on page 916. Which nations have significant oil resources?

Writing About History

8. **Descriptive Writing** Imagine that you are traveling in West Germany in 1989 when the Berlin Wall is being torn down. Write a letter back home to describe the event and the feelings of the German people. Also include your reaction to the situation and how you think it will affect the United States.
   CA 11WA2.1a; 11WA2.3a

CHAPTER 20 Resurgence of Conservatism **919**

SECTION 4 ASSESSMENT ANSWERS

1. Content vocabulary is boldfaced and highlighted in yellow. Academic vocabulary is boldfaced.

2. Boris Yeltsin *(p. 916)*, Tiananmen Square *(p. 917)*, Saddam Hussein *(p. 918)*, H. Ross Perot *(p. 919)*

3. Gorbachev wanted to allow some private enterprise and profit–making, and to allow more free-dom of speech and religion.

4. The recession hurt Bush's efforts to get reelected.

5. The West forced the Soviets to engage in an arms race they could not afford; Western powers also supported Gorbachev's reform ideas.

6. budget problems: tax increase; economic problems: recession; high consumer debt: federal deficit; foreign developments: fall of the Soviet Union, Persian Gulf war

7. Saudi Arabia, Kuwait, Iraq, and Iran

8. Students' letters will vary but should be descriptive and use standard grammar and punctuation.

 **Reading Strategy**

Connecting The ADA required that public facilities become wheelchair accessible. Since then, buildings have been retrofitted with access ramps and lifts. **Ask:** Can you identify places in your community where you have seen the effects of the ADA? Does your school provide full access? *(Responses will vary.)*
BL

ASSESS

Resources for page 919

Use these resources to assess student mastery.

📁 Section Quiz 20-4

📁 Reading Essentials and Study Guide 20-4

💿 Interactive Tutor Self-Assessment CD-ROM

📁 California Standards Practice, Grade 11

Reading Check

Answer: They did not like either Bush or Clinton. Perot had the best showing of a third-party candidate since 1912.

 HISTORY Online

Study Central provides audio summaries, interactive games, and online graphic organizers to help students review section content.

CLOSE

Summarizing Have students explain the domestic challenges facing the Bush administration.
OL

History–Social Science Standards

This feature addresses the following standards:

11.9 Students analyze U.S. foreign policy since World War II.

11.9.6 Describe U.S. Middle East policy and its strategic, political, and economic interests, including those related to the Gulf War.

Reading Connection

Tell students that crude oil is used in the production of fuels such as gasoline, diesel fuel, and heating oil. It is also used to make a wide assortment of products, including ammonia, bubble gum, crayons, deodorant, eyeglasses, and many others.

R Reading Strategy

Activating Prior Knowledge
Many students might not have heard of the Strait of Hormuz, but they likely have heard of other important waterways, either natural or artificial. Ask students to research other waterways and their significance and present the information in a chart. **OL**

Answers and Additional Support

Why It Matters

R Strait of Hormuz

The Strait of Hormuz is a narrow shipping lane between the Persian Gulf, the Gulf of Oman, and the Arabian Sea. Most of the crude oil produced in the Middle East passes through the Strait of Hormuz. In 1997 about 14 million barrels of crude oil passed through the Strait every day. Since the waterway is only about 40 miles (64 km) across at its widest point, it is possible that a country might block or hamper passage of ships. During the 1980s, the United States began escorting oil tankers through the Strait to protect them from Iranian attacks. If the passage were ever closed, oil would have to be shipped overland by pipeline—a much more expensive option.

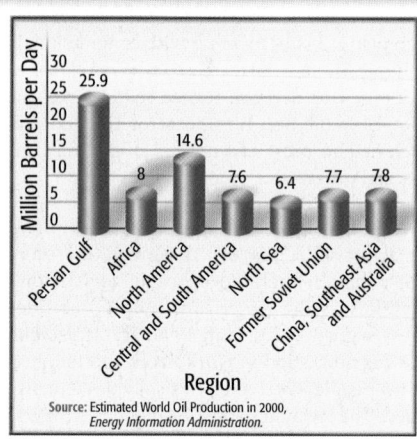

World Oil Production

Source: Estimated World Oil Production in 2000, *Energy Information Administration.*

The Persian Gulf countries consist of Saudi Arabia, Iran, Iraq, Kuwait, Qatar, and the United Arab Emirates. They may hold as much as 70 percent of the world's proven oil reserves.

EXTENDING THE CONTENT

New Fuel Alternatives As more of the world industrializes, the pressures on the limited fossil fuel resources of the planet have increased. This could lead to rising energy prices, including gasoline for automobiles. For this reason, more consumers are willing to consider purchasing vehicles that offer alternates to the traditional gasoline-powered internal combustion engine. Ask students to research new automobile designs such as electric cars or cars that use alternative fuels or fuel mixes. Students can begin their research on the Department of Energy Web site: www.eere.energy.gov/consumerinfo/energysmart_vehicles.html. **AL**

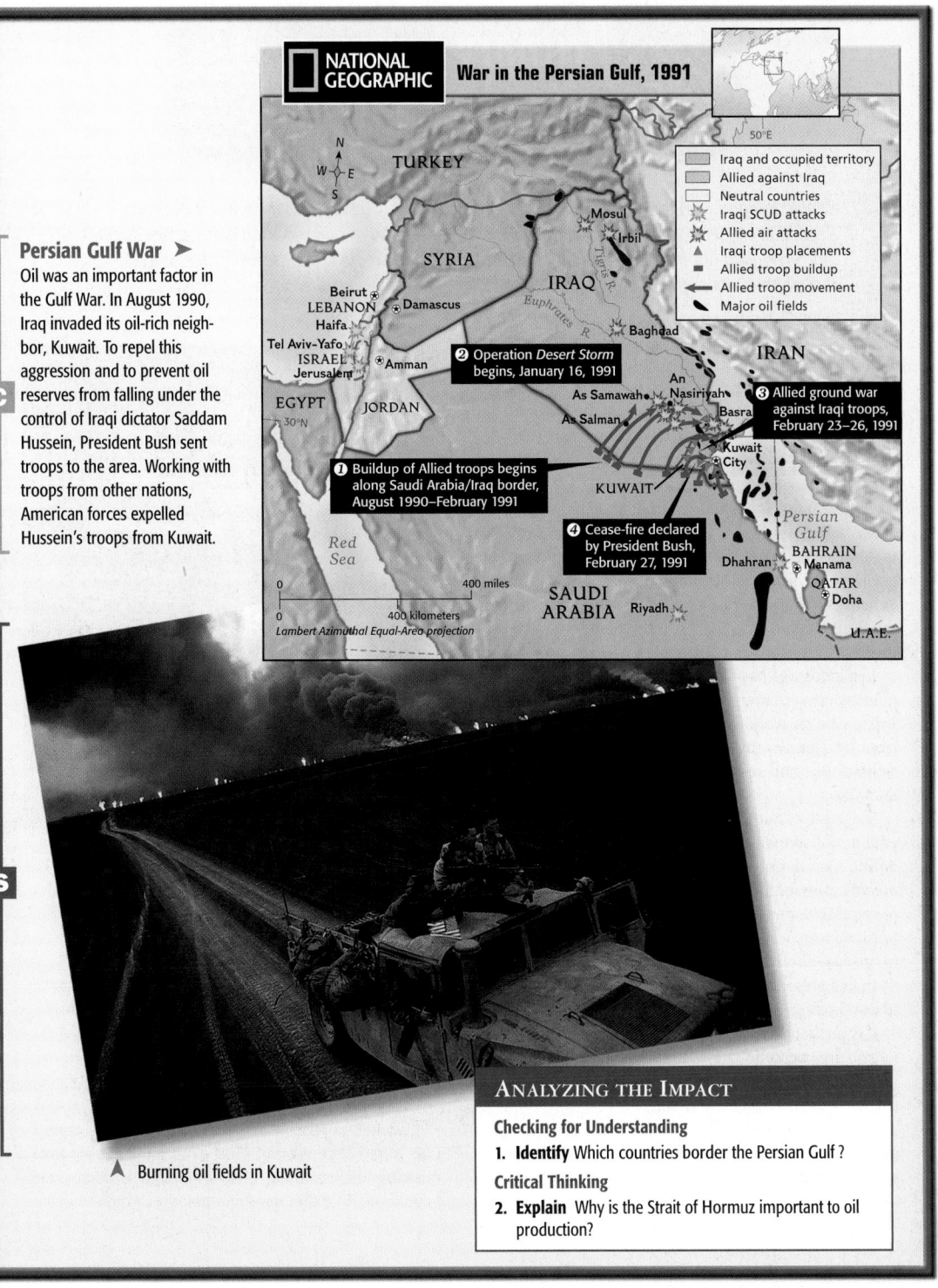

NATIONAL GEOGRAPHIC

War in the Persian Gulf, 1991

- Iraq and occupied territory
- Allied against Iraq
- Neutral countries
- ✳ Iraqi SCUD attacks
- ✳ Allied air attacks
- ▲ Iraqi troop placements
- ■ Allied troop buildup
- ← Allied troop movement
- Major oil fields

TURKEY

SYRIA

IRAQ

Mosul
Irbil

Beirut
LEBANON ⊕ Damascus
Haifa
Tel Aviv-Yafo
ISRAEL ⊕ Amman
Jerusalem
JORDAN

EGYPT

Baghdad

IRAN

An
Nasiriyah

As Samawah
As Salman

② Operation *Desert Storm* begins, January 16, 1991

Basra

③ Allied ground war against Iraqi troops, February 23–26, 1991

Kuwait City

KUWAIT

① Buildup of Allied troops begins along Saudi Arabia/Iraq border, August 1990–February 1991

④ Cease-fire declared by President Bush, February 27, 1991

Persian Gulf

BAHRAIN
⊕ Manama

Dhahran

QATAR
⊕ Doha

Red
Sea

0   400 miles
0   400 kilometers
Lambert Azimuthal Equal-Area projection

SAUDI
ARABIA   Riyadh

U.A.E.

Persian Gulf War ➤

Oil was an important factor in the Gulf War. In August 1990, Iraq invaded its oil-rich neighbor, Kuwait. To repel this aggression and to prevent oil reserves from falling under the control of Iraqi dictator Saddam Hussein, President Bush sent troops to the area. Working with troops from other nations, American forces expelled Hussein's troops from Kuwait.

▲ Burning oil fields in Kuwait

ANALYZING THE IMPACT

Checking for Understanding

1. **Identify** Which countries border the Persian Gulf?

Critical Thinking

2. **Explain** Why is the Strait of Hormuz important to oil production?

FOCUS

Understanding Vocabulary

Before students begin reading, point out that difficult or unfamiliar words are footnoted throughout the text.

TEACH

C Critical Thinking

Determining Cause and Effect
Inflation is an increase in the money supply, which results in price increases without corresponding increases in the supply of goods and services. Have students identify some of the effects of inflation that Reagan describes in his Inaugural Address. **OL**

CA HI6

Answers and Additional Support

Primary Sources
Eyewitness to History

Ronald Reagan won the presidential election of 1980 partly because of the weak economy. Reagan promised to solve economic problems by cutting taxes and reducing government spending. Struggling Americans hoped that this strategy would create rapid growth, while others thought that government no longer was considered the cure for all economic difficulties.

SOURCE 1:

President Ronald Reagan was a conservative Republican who had served two terms as governor of California. In his 1981 Inaugural Address, Reagan argued that government had created the nation's economic troubles.

C These United States are confronted with an economic affliction of great proportions. We suffer from the longest and one of the worst sustained inflations in our national history. It distorts our economic decisions, penalizes thrift, and crushes the struggling young and the fixed-income elderly alike. It threatens to shatter the lives of millions of our people.

Idle industries have cast workers into unemployment, causing human misery and personal indignity. Those who do work are denied a fair return for their labor by a tax system which penalizes successful achievement and keeps us from maintaining full productivity.

But great as our tax burden is, it has not kept pace with public spending. For decades, we have piled deficit upon deficit, mortgaging our future and our children's future for the temporary convenience of the present. To continue this long trend is to guarantee tremendous social, cultural, political, and economic upheavals. . . .

In this present crisis, government is not the solution to our problem. Government is the problem. . . .

It is no coincidence that our present troubles parallel and are proportionate to the intervention and intrusion in our lives that result from unnecessary and excessive growth of government. . . .

. . . It is time to reawaken this industrial giant, to get government back within its means, and to lighten our punitive tax burden. And these will be our first priorities; on these principles there will be no compromise.

▲ *President Regan visits a car assembly plant in Detroit, Michigan*

SOURCE 2:

Carl Stezko was a white male in his mid-50s who had been employed as a steelworker in Chicago. When steel mills closed in the 1970s and 1980s, he lost his job. Stezko described his experiences in a 1985 interview in **Rusted Dreams: Hard Times in a Steel Community.**

I worked at Wisconsin Steel for almost thirty years. I get a partial pension of $300 a month, that's all. No other benefits. Nothing. I had a hernia. The doctor said I could die if I didn't have an operation. I didn't have

---

UNIVERSAL ACCESS

Interpersonal Have students work in small groups to create three-column charts that identify the top three priorities of the Reagan administration, as described by Reagan in his 1981 Inaugural Address. Ask them to add the goals of each of these priorities in the second column and the possible effects—positive and negative—each might have on the economy in the last column. Have each group present their charts to the class. Then compare and contrast the different analyses of the effects of the Reagan economic policy on inflation. **OL** **CA HI6**

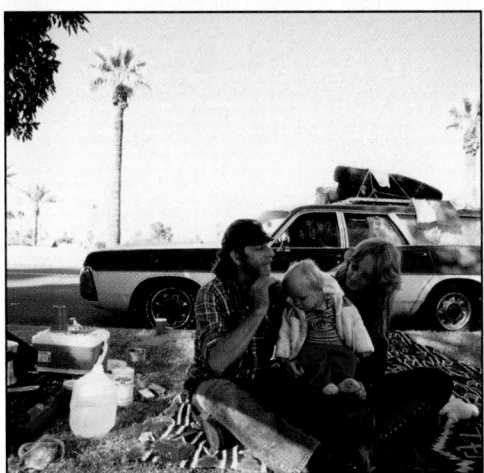

▲ *Homeless family in 1983*

any hospitalization, no money to pay for it. I tried to get a green card [Medicaid] to pay for it, but they said sell your house and car if you want it. I couldn't do that. Finally, my doctor says if you can get into the hospital, I'll do the operation. So I lied to the hospital, just went in there and told them I had insurance. I never could have imagined doing such a thing.

I've been everyplace looking for a job—White Castle, Burger King, McDonald's, Sears, K Mart. I've been to hospitals and cemeteries. I went to Jay's Potato Chips. They gave me a test and said, "You're overqualified." I said, "I'll tell you what, you said you're paying $5 an hour, well I'll work for $3." They still wouldn't take me. I'm a skilled electrician, plumber, a pipe fitter. But they ain't gonna hire a guy like me. I still go out every day and look.

My wife isn't healthy. She can't work. We have a two-flat, but the mortgage isn't paid off. I get $160 a month in rent on the other apartment. I'm paying $200 on the mortgage and $160 in gas bills. So you can't make ends meet. I only eat one meal a day. Food stamps turned me down. I don't know where to turn. I'm ashamed to ask for anything. I always swore I'd never go on pension—I'd work till the day I died.

I did go to the alderman for a year and a half trying to get a job. I was begging, pleading. I saw him at least twenty times. They kept telling me, "You're at the top of the list." . . . I pray every day. That's all I have faith in anymore.

SOURCE 3:

Michael J. Boskin, a Stanford University economist, wrote that Reagan had set the stage for a revival of the United States in his 1987 book, **Reagan and the Economy.**

[T]he prospect of sustaining the Reagan program beyond the President's personal popularity remains in doubt. Nevertheless, much has been accomplished. The Reagan economic program, while far from perfect, has created an *opportunity* for a much-improved economy for the balance of the century, by eliminating rising and **fluctuating**[1] double-digit inflation, explosive growth of nondefense government spending, . . . ever-growing government regulation, and outright government control through incomes policies or wage and price controls. It is worth recalling that these were serious problems as recently as 1980. . . .

. . . [T]he once popular notion that the government, especially the federal government, is the proper answer to *all* of society's economic problems has been dealt a serious blow. Following the terrible economic performance of the 1970s, the Reagan economic program seems to have accomplished the important but **intangible**[2] objective of discrediting this idea, making it more difficult for ill-advised policies to appear at the expense of the taxpayer and the economy. New spending programs will have to pass tougher tests for years to come, and that means less automatic budget growth in the future. Even if nothing else is done, the **repudiation**[3] of bad policies will stand as a major accomplishment.

[1]**fluctuating:** going up and down
[2]**intangible:** incapable of being defined
[3]**repudiation:** rejection

DBQ · Document-Based Questions

Historical Analysis · CA HI1; HI2

Source 1: According to Reagan, what is the reason for the nation's weak economy?

Source 2: What does Stezko describe as his main problems?

Source 3: Why does Boskin believe that Reagan has succeeded?

Comparing and Contrasting Sources
How does Stezko's unemployment illustrate the views of Reagan?

W Writing Support

Letter Writing Ask students to imagine themselves in the same circumstances as Carl Stezko—unemployed and without hope of finding work. Have students write letters to President Reagan from Stezko's point-of-view, explaining what his Inaugural Address meant to them and why it did or did not give them hope for their economic future. **OL**

U Universal Access

Advanced Learners Challenge students to write an essay in which they debate Boskin's belief that Reagan succeeded and argue instead that Reagan's economic strategy failed. Ask students to support their arguments with documented facts and examples. **OL** **CA** 11WA2.4d

ASSESS/CLOSE

Have students answer the Document-Based Questions.

DBQ · Document-Based Questions

1. "The longest and one of the worst sustained inflations in our national history" is the reason for the nation's weak economy.
2. Stezko's main problems include the loss of his job after 30 years; no money or health insurance to pay for health care; over-qualification for available, low-paying jobs; inability to pay mortgage, make ends meet, or qualify for basic government services such as food stamps.
3. He believes Reagan succeeded because his economic policies eliminated rising inflation, growth of government spending, and government control over wages and prices.

Comparing and Contrasting Sources: Stezko's unemployment illustrates the plight of unemployed American workers.

Resources for pages 924–925

Use the following resources to review, assess, and reteach the chapter.

- 📁 Chapter 20 Tests, Forms A and B
- 📁 Standardized Tests, Forms A and B
- 📁 Cumulative Authentic Assessment
- 💾 MindJogger Videoquiz
- 💿 Interactive Tutor Self-Assessment CD-ROM
- 💿 ExamView® Pro Testmaker CD-ROM
- 💿 Vocabulary PuzzleMaker CD-ROM
- 💿 Succeeding on . . .™ the California Standards: Grade 11 History–Social Science
- 📁 California Standards Practice, Grade 11

Reviewing Content Vocabulary

Students' answers will vary. The pages where the words appear in the text are shown in parentheses.

1. liberal *(p. 887)* **2.** conservative *(p. 887)* **3.** televangelist *(p. 891)* **4.** supply-side economics *(p. 895)* **5.** budget deficit *(p. 895)* **6.** contra *(p. 898)* **7.** yuppie *(p. 903)* **8.** space shuttle *(p. 907)* **9.** space station *(p. 908)* **10.** perestroika *(p. 916)* **11.** glasnost *(p. 916)* **12.** downsizing *(p. 918)* **13.** capital gains tax *(p. 919)* **14.** grassroots movement *(p. 919)*

Reviewing Academic Vocabulary

Students' answers will vary. The pages where the words appear in the text are shown in parentheses.

15. instance *(p. 888)* **16.** exceed *(p. 895)* **17.** offset *(p. 897)* **18.** visible *(p. 897)* **19.** accumulate *(p. 903)* **20.** via *(p. 904)* **21.** orientation *(p. 906)* **22.** revolution *(p. 916)* **23.** relax *(p. 917)* **24.** task *(p. 919)*

Reviewing Content Vocabulary

On a sheet of paper, use each of these terms in a sentence.

1. liberal
2. conservative
3. televangelist
4. supply-side economics
5. budget deficit
6. contra
7. yuppie
8. space shuttle
9. space station
10. *perestroika*
11. *glasnost*
12. downsizing
13. capital gains tax
14. grassroots movement

Reviewing Academic Vocabulary

On a sheet of paper, use each of these terms in a sentence that reflects the term's meaning in the chapter.

15. instance
16. exceed
17. offset
18. visible
19. accumulate
20. via
21. orientation
22. revolution
23. relax
24. task

Reviewing the Main Ideas

Section 1

25. Why did people in the Sunbelt tend to be conservative?

Section 2

26. What three steps did President Reagan take to improve the economy?

Section 3

27. What social issues did the United States face in the 1980s?

Section 4

28. What event triggered the Persian Gulf War?

29. What economic problems did President George Bush face during his administration?

Standards 11.1.3, 11.3.2, 11.8.4, 11.8.6, 11.8.7, 11.8.8, 11.9.3, 11.9.4, 11.9.5, 11.9.6, 11.10.7, 11.11.2, 11.11.3, 11.11.5, 11.11.7

Critical Thinking

30. **Reading Skill** **Comparing and Contrasting** Review the United States space program. Compare and contrast the program from its beginning up to the present. Use signal words to help the reader identify the similarities or differences.

31. **Civics** What responsibility does the federal government have to insure the welfare of its citizens? Write a persuasive essay reflecting either conservative or liberal perspectives on this issue.

32. **Synthesizing** How did conservatives gain political power in the 1980s?

33. **Organizing** Use a graphic organizer similar to the one below to list the domestic and foreign issues faced by the Reagan and Bush administrations.

Issues	Reagan Administration	Bush Administration
Domestic		
Foreign		

Writing About History

34. **Historical Analysis** **Analyzing Migration** Study the map and text on pages 900–901. Research and write a short essay on why some people choose to move to the suburbs and the problems associated with urban growth. Examine the urban patterns and changes in your area and include references in your essay. **CA CS3**

Chapter Summary

Resurgence of Conservative Politics

- The Cold War promotes a strong foreign policy and an emphasis on minimal government intervention in economics.
- Cold War fears of communism encourage religious Americans to turn to conservative ideas.
- Barry Goldwater wins the 1964 Republican presidential nomination.
- The growth of the Sunbelt increases conservative support.

Reagan's Agenda

- Supply-side economics emphasizes large tax cuts.
- Reagan's administration takes a strong anti-Communist stance in Latin America, the Caribbean, and the Middle East.
- Reagan and Gorbachev begin new nuclear arms reductions.
- Military spending drives the growing budget deficit to record levels.

The Bush Years

- Communism collapses in Eastern Europe and the Soviet Union.
- The uncertainty of a "New World Order" replaces the dualism of the Cold War.
- The Persian Gulf War drives Bush's popularity to its highest level.
- A domestic economic recession weakens Bush's re-election campaign.

Reviewing the Main Ideas

25. Their economy was expanding, and they did not want the government to interfere with their region's growth.

26. Reaganomics, cutting programs, and deregulation

27. They included AIDS, alcohol abuse, crime, drug abuse, homelessness, and Social Security.

28. Iraq's invasion of Kuwait and subsequent refusal to withdraw

29. George Bush faced the economic problems of recession, high consumer debt, and the federal deficit.

HISTORY Online

Self-Check Quiz

Visit the *American Vision: Modern Times* Web site at tav.mt.glencoe.com and click on *Self-Check Quizzes—Chapter 20* to assess your knowledge of chapter content.

35. **Big Idea** Write an article for the local newspaper that discusses the U.S. involvement in the Persian Gulf War. Why was the U.S. fighting? What were the results?

36. **Writing a Report** Research the status today of the independent republics formed from the Soviet Union. Find out about their political, social, and economic situations. Present your findings in a written report. **CA** 11WA2.4a; 11WA2.4d

DBQ Document-Based Questions

37. **Interpreting Primary Sources** President Reagan addressed the American people for the last time as president in 1988. The following is an excerpt from that address:

❝It's been quite a journey this decade, and we held together through some stormy seas.... The way I see it, there were two great triumphs, two things that I'm proudest of. One is the economic recovery, in which the people of America created—and filled—19 million new jobs. The other is the recovery of our morale. America is respected again in the world and looked to for leadership....

Common sense told us that when you put a big tax on something, the people will produce less of it. So, we cut the people's tax rates, and the people produced more than ever before. The economy bloomed....

Common sense told us that to preserve the peace, we'd have to become strong again after years of weakness and confusion. So, we rebuilt our defenses, and this New Year we toasted the new peacefulness around the globe....

[O]ne of the things I'm proudest of in the past eight years [is] the resurgence of national pride that I called the new patriotism. This national feeling is good, but it won't count for much, and it won't last unless it's grounded in thoughtfulness and knowledge....

An informed patriotism is what we want.... Let's start with some basics: more attention to American history and greater emphasis on civic ritual....❞

—from *Speaking My Mind*

a. What did Reagan believe were his greatest accomplishments as president? **CA** 11RC2.5

b. What did Reagan believe would promote patriotism in the nation? Do you agree with his belief? Why or why not? **CA** 11RC2.4

NATIONAL GEOGRAPHIC The Election of 1992

Presidential Election, 1992			
Candidate	Electoral Vote	Popular Vote	Political Party
Clinton	370	44,908,254	Democrat
Bush	168	39,102,343	Republican
Perot	0	19,741,065	Independent

Geography and History

38. The map above shows the results of the 1992 presidential election. Study the map and answer the questions below.
   a. **Interpreting Maps** How far short did President Bush fall in the race for Electoral College votes?
   b. **Applying Geography Skills** Bill Clinton won his strongest support in which region of the nation?

Standards Practice

Directions: Choose the phrase that best completes the following sentence.

39. The Strategic Defense Initiative (SDI) was proposed to strengthen the military by

A preventing the expansion of Communist countries.

B reemphasizing the use of infantry troops in future wars.

C developing weapons that would intercept and destroy incoming nuclear missiles.

D severely reducing the number of American troops stationed worldwide.

Standard 11.9.5: Analyze the role of the Reagan administration and other factors in the victory of the West in the Cold War.

HISTORY Online

Have students visit the Web site at tav.mt.glencoe.com to review Chapter 20 and take the Self-Check Quiz.

Writing About History

34. **Historical Analysis** Essays will vary. Students should address the desire to move to the suburbs and the problems with urban growth. References to any local issues should be addressed.

35. **Big Idea** Students' articles will vary. The articles should focus on the Persian Gulf War and provide specific details for reasons and results of the war.

36. Reports will vary but should include information about political, social, and economic conditions in the chosen country.

DBQ Document-Based Questions

37. **a.** Reagan was most proud of the economic recovery and the recovery of morale. **b.** Reagan thought attention to American history and to civic ritual would promote patriotism. Students' answers will vary.

Geography and History

38. **a.** 102 votes of the 270 needed in the Electoral College; **b.** Northeast and Pacific coast

Standards Practice

39. C

Bonus Question ?

Ask: What industries were deregulated during the Reagan years? *(oil and gas, automobile, cable television, and airline)*

Critical Thinking

30. **Reading Skill** Answers will vary. Students should use signal words to identify similarities and differences.

31. Students' essays will vary. Essays should clearly indicate conservative or liberal ideas.

32. They elected two presidents who reinforced conservative values and economic policies.

33.

Issues	Reagan Administration	Bush Administration
Domestic	stagflation growing deficit	recession unemployment growing deficit
Foreign	Soviet invasion of Afghanistan Grenada Iran-Contra Scandal	Eastern Europe collapse of Soviet Union Tiananmen Square

Chapter 21 Planning Guide

SECTION RESOURCES

MAIN IDEAS	📁 PRINT MATERIALS	TECHNOLOGY RESOURCES
Section 1: The Technological Revolution 1. A computer revolution changed how people communicate. 2. The 1996 Telecommunications Act increased competition among telephone companies. 3. A computer resource that linked government agencies quickly developed into the Internet. 4. Major developments in biotechnology spurred advances in medicine and improvement in agricultural technology.	• Daily Lecture and Discussion Notes 21-1 • Active Reading Note-Taking Guide 21-1 • Section Quiz 21-1 • Reading Essentials and Study Guide 21-1	📖 Daily Focus Skills Transparency 21-1 💿 Interactive Tutor Self-Assessment CD-ROM 💿 ExamView® Pro Testmaker CD-ROM 💿 Presentation Plus! CD-ROM 📖 California Standards Practice Transparencies
Section 2: The Clinton Years 1. Clinton took office with plans for improving health care, reducing the federal deficit, and strengthening gun control. 2. Republican victories in Congress set the stage for battles between the executive and legislative branches. 3. The economy helped Clinton win reelection in 1996. 4. During Clinton's second term, the U.S. became more involved in world events and the president's personal scandal.	• Daily Lecture and Discussion Notes 21-2 • Active Reading Note-Taking Guide 21-2 • Section Quiz 21-2 • Reading Essentials and Study Guide 21-2	📖 Daily Focus Skills Transparency 21-2 💿 Interactive Tutor Self-Assessment CD-ROM 💿 ExamView® Pro Testmaker CD-ROM 💿 Presentation Plus! CD-ROM 📖 California Standards Practice Transparencies
Section 3: An Interdependent World 1. Regional trade agreements, such as the North American Free Trade Agreement (NAFTA), became common in an increasingly interdependent world. 2. Concerns about nuclear proliferation and the environment led to efforts to reduce nuclear weapons and pollution.	• Daily Lecture and Discussion Notes 21-3 • Active Reading Note-Taking Guide 21-3 • Section Quiz 21-3 • Reading Essentials and Study Guide 21-3	📖 Daily Focus Skills Transparency 21-3 💿 Interactive Tutor Self-Assessment CD-ROM 💿 ExamView® Pro Testmaker CD-ROM 💿 Presentation Plus! CD-ROM 📖 California Standards Practice Transparencies
Section 4: America Enters a New Century 1. One of the closest and most contested races for the presidency led to a Supreme Court decision in favor of George W. Bush. 2. Bush focused on stimulating the economy, reforming education, and promoting strategic defense in the early months of his presidency.	• Daily Lecture and Discussion Notes 21-4 • Active Reading Note-Taking Guide 21-4 • Section Quiz 21-4 • Reading Essentials and Study Guide 21-4	📖 Daily Focus Skills Transparency 21-4 💿 Interactive Tutor Self-Assessment CD-ROM 💿 ExamView® Pro Testmaker CD-ROM 💿 Presentation Plus! CD-ROM 📖 California Standards Practice Transparencies
Section 5: The War on Terrorism 1. Terrorist attacks on September 11, 2001, changed American life. 2. The United States created the Department of Homeland Security and launched a war in Afghanistan. 3. Doubting the effectiveness of UN resolutions, the United States went to war with Iraq. 4. Despite obstacles in the war with Iraq, a divided nation reelected President Bush.	• Daily Lecture and Discussion Notes 21-5 • Active Reading Note-Taking Guide 21-5 • Section Quiz 21-5 • Reading Essentials and Study Guide 21-5	📖 Daily Focus Skills Transparency 21-5 💿 Interactive Tutor Self-Assessment CD-ROM 💿 ExamView® Pro Testmaker CD-ROM 💿 Presentation Plus! CD-ROM 📖 California Standards Practice Transparencies

PACING YOUR LESSONS

Chapter Introduction	Section 1	Section 2	Section 3	Section 4	Section 5	Chapter Assessment
½ Day	1 Day	2 Days	2 Days	1 Day	2 Days	½ Day

0:00 OUT OF TIME? 📁 Assign the Chapter 21 *Reading Essentials and Study Guide.*

Chapter 21 Planning Guide

Standards-Based Lesson Plan

 History–Social Science Standards Covered in Chapter 21

The standards covered in the chapter are listed below. Use the accompanying activity as you teach the chapter to ensure student mastery of these standards. This activity can be used in combination with the program's print and technology assessment materials.

Standard	Section 1	2	3	4	5
11.8.7 Describe the effects on society and the economy of technological developments since 1945, including the computer revolution, changes in communication, advances in medicine, and improvements in agricultural technology.	✔				
11.9.6 Describe U.S. Middle East policy and its strategic, political, and economic interests, including those related to the Gulf War.		✔			✔
11.9.7 Examine relations between the United States and Mexico in the twentieth century, including key economic, political, immigration, and environmental issues.			✔		
11.11 Students analyze the major social problems and domestic policy issues in contemporary American society.				✔	
11.11.2 Discuss the significant domestic policy speeches of Truman, Eisenhower, Kennedy, Johnson, Nixon, Carter, Reagan, Bush, and Clinton (e.g., with regard to education, civil rights, economic policy, environmental policy).		✔			

Cumulative Standards-Assessment Activity

The Cumulative Standards-Assessment Activity will help students organize and learn the important information from the chapter. Begin teaching the chapter with this activity, and have students complete it as they read the chapter.

CREATING A SUMMARY

Purpose Summarizing is an important reading skill. By writing effective summaries, students demonstrate that they have identified the key points in a text and that they can distill the most important information related to those points. Summarizing is also useful for committing important historical information to memory and gauging what students have learned and what they still need to learn.

Introduction to Summarizing

1. Review the steps in summarizing:
   - Distinguish main ideas from supporting details and focus on the main ideas.
   - Use your own words to describe the main ideas.
   - Ensure that summaries are short and focused.

2. Model how to summarize by reading the material under the first subheadings of Section 1 to help students see how they can reduce the information to a few sentences that convey the most important information.

3. Ask students to copy this diagram into their notebooks:

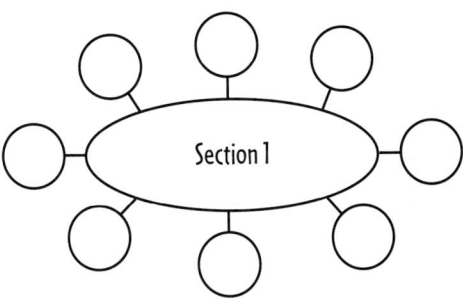

Suggest that students write key phrases in the web diagram as they read the section, then use their notes to write a summary of the section. They can do this exercise for each section in the chapter.

4. As you review the chapter, ask volunteers to read from their summaries. Encourage students to use their summaries as study aids.

Chapter 21 Planning Guide

READING SUPPORT

- Content Vocabulary Activity 21
- Academic Vocabulary Activity 21
- Reading Skills Activity 21
- Chapter 21 Active Reading Note-Taking Guide
- Chapter 21 Guided Reading Activities
- Chapter 21 Reading Essentials and Study Guide
- American Literature Readings, Unit 6
- *The American Vision: Modern Times* Video Program
- Vocabulary PuzzleMaker CD-ROM
- American History Primary Source Document Library CD-ROM

CRITICAL THINKING

- Critical Thinking Skills Activity 21
- Primary Source Reading 21
- Cause-and-Effect Transparency 21 Strategy and Activity
- Presentation Plus! CD-ROM

UNIVERSAL ACCESS

- Universal Access Activity 21
- English Learner Activity 21
- American Art Prints
- StudentWorks™ Plus CD-ROM
- American Music: Hits Through History
- School-to-Home Connection Activity 21

SKILL PRACTICE

- Map Overlay Transparency 21 Strategy and Activity
- Historical Analysis Skills Activity 21
- Time Line Activity 21
- Reading Skills Activity 21
- Reinforcing Skills Activity 21
- Linking Past and Present Activity 21
- Interpreting Political Cartoons 21
- Geography and History Activity, Unit 6
- Economics and History Activity, Unit 6
- MindJogger Videoquiz

WRITING SUPPORT

- Chapter 21 Active Reading Note-Taking Guide
- Writer's Guidebook
- High School Writing Process Transparencies

ASSESSMENT

- Chapter 21 Section Quizzes
- Chapter 21 Tests, Forms A and B
- Authentic Assessment Activity 21
- ExamView® Pro Testmaker CD-ROM
- Interactive Tutor Self-Assessment CD-ROM
- California Standards Practice, Grade 11
- Succeeding on . . .™ the California Standards: Grade 11 History–Social Science CD-ROM

- CD-ROM
- DVD
- Print Material
- Poster

- Transparency
- Music Program
- Videocassette

Chapter 21 Planning Guide

TECHNOLOGY

- StudentWorks™ Plus CD-ROM
- TeacherWorks™ CD-ROM
- ExamView® Pro Testmaker CD-ROM
- Interactive Tutor Self-Assessment CD-ROM
- Presentation Plus! CD-ROM
- Vocabulary PuzzleMaker CD-ROM
- American History Primary Source Document Library CD-ROM
- MindJogger Videoquiz
- *The American Vision: Modern Times* Video Program
- Professional Development in High School Social Studies Video Series
- Teach, Use, and Succeed With *The American Vision: Modern Times*
- American Music: Hits Through History
- Succeeding on . . .™ the California Standards: Grade 11 History–Social Science CD-ROM

SPANISH RESOURCES

- Spanish Activities and Assessment
  - Spanish Vocabulary Activities
  - Spanish Guided Reading Activities
  - Spanish Quizzes and Tests
  - Spanish Reteaching Activities
- Spanish Reading Essentials and Study Guide
- Spanish School-to-Home Connection Activities

TRANSPARENCIES

- Daily Focus Skills Transparencies
- Section Graphic Organizer Transparencies
- Map Overlay Transparencies
- Cause-and-Effect Transparencies
- Unit Time Line Transparencies
- Why It Matters Transparencies
- American Art and Architecture Transparencies
- High School Writing Process Transparencies
- California Standards Practice Transparencies

TEACHER PLANNING

- Daily Lecture and Discussion Notes
- English Learner Handbook
- Building Academic Vocabulary
- *The American Vision: Modern Times* Reading and Study Skills Foldables
- Reading Strategies and Activities for the Social Studies Classroom
- Universal Access for the American History Classroom
- NGS United States Desk Map
- NGS World Atlas
- Chapter 21 Reproducible Lesson Plans on TeacherWorks™ CD-ROM
- California Guide to Daily Intervention

PROFESSIONAL DEVELOPMENT

- Building Academic Vocabulary
- Strategies for Success
- Research-Based Strategies Used to Develop *The American Vision: Modern Times*
- Character Education in the High School Classroom
- Professional Development in High School Social Studies Video Series
- Teach, Use, and Succeed With *The American Vision: Modern Times*

MOMENTS IN TIME

The following resources can help you teach the content of this chapter.

- Unit 14 The Information Age (1977–2003)
- Unit 15 The War on Terrorism (1998–2001)

Chapter 21 Planning Guide

TEACHER'S CORNER

Index to National Geographic Magazine:

The following articles relate to this chapter:

- "Grand Staircase Escalante," July 1999
- "Rediscovering America," January 2000
- "Robot Revolution," July 1997
- "Unveiling the Universe," October 1999

National Geographic Society Products:

To order the following, call National Geographic at 1–800–368–2728

- *Branches of Government Series* (Video)
- *Democratic Government Series: The United States* (Video)
- *Historical Atlas of the United States* (Atlas)
- *National Geographic Atlas for Young Explorers–Classroom Library Edition* (Guide, Transparencies, Resource Masters)

NGS ONLINE

Access National Geographic's new dynamic MapMachine Web site and other geography resources at:

www.nationalgeographic.com

www.nationalgeographic.com/maps

Use our Web site for additional resources. All essential content is covered in the Student Edition.

You and your students can visit tav.mt.glencoe.com, the Web site companion to the **American Vision: Modern Times.** This innovative integration of electronic and print media offers your students a wealth of opportunities. The student text directs students to the Web site for the following options:

- **Chapter Overviews**
- **Self-Check Quizzes**
- **Student Web Activities**
- **Textbook Updates**

Answers to the student Web activities are provided for you in the **Web Activity Lesson Plans.** Additional Web resources and ePuzzles and games are also available.

MASTERING THE STANDARDS

The content and assessment in the Student Edition, Teacher Wraparound Edition, teacher planning materials, and the print and technology products are all standards-based. The use of these products during instruction leads to mastery of the standards.

PRACTICE
- California Standards Practice, Grade 11
- California Standards Practice Transparencies
- School-to-Home Connection

BENCHMARK ASSESSMENT
- Section Quizzes, Chapter Tests, and Authentic Assessment
- Exam*View*® Pro Testmaker CD-ROM
- Succeeding On . . . ™ the California Standards: Grade 11 History–Social Science CD-ROM

REMEDIATION
- California Guide to Daily Intervention
- Interactive Tutor Self-Assessment CD-ROM
- Exam*View*® Pro Testmaker CD-ROM
- California Standards Practice, Grade 11
- Reading Essentials and Study Guide

Dinah Zike's Foldables

Foldables are three-dimensional, interactive graphic organizers that help students practice basic writing skills, review key vocabulary terms, and identify main ideas. Every chapter has a foldable activity in the *Dinah Zike's Reading and Study Skills Foldables* booklet. You can use the foldables as they are presented or modify them to suit the needs of your individual class.

A variety of videotape programs are available from A&E Television and The History Channel to provide teaching assistance. To order, call Glencoe at 1-800-334-7344.

Chapter 21 Planning Guide

Reading List Generator CD-ROM

GLENCOE BOOKLINK

The Glencoe BookLink CD-ROM is a database that allows you to search more than 15,000 titles to create a customized reading list for your students.

- Reading Lists can be organized by students' reading level, author, genre, theme, or area of interest.
- The database provides Degrees of Reading Power™ (DRP) and Lexile™ readability scores for all selections.
- A brief summary of each selection is included.

Leveled reading suggestions for this chapter:

For students at a Grade 8 reading level:
- *Bill Clinton and His Presidency*, by Elaine Landau

For students at a Grade 9 reading level:
- *The Battle in Seattle*, by Margot Hornblower

For students at a Grade 10 reading level:
- *What's American About America?*, by Ishmael Reed

READING SUPPORT FROM JAMESTOWN EDUCATION

- *Timed Readings Plus in Social Studies* help students increase their reading rate and fluency while maintaining comprehension. The 400-word passages are similar to those found on state and national assessments.

- *Reading in the Content Area: Social Studies* concentrates on six essential reading skills that help students better comprehend what they read. The book includes 75 high-interest nonfiction passages written at increasing levels of difficulty.

- *Reading Fluency* helps students read smoothly, accurately, and expressively.

- *Jamestown's Reading Improvement,* by renowned reading expert Edward Fry, focuses on helping build your students' comprehension, vocabulary, and skimming and scanning skills.

- *Critical Reading Series* provides high-interest books, each written at three reading levels.

For more information about these products, see the Jamestown Ezducation materials in the Classroom Solutions in the front of this Teacher Wraparound Edition. To order these products, call Glencoe at 1-800-334-7344.

KEY for Using the Teacher Wraparound Edition

Use this key to help you identify the different types of prompts found in the Teacher Wraparound Edition.

R   Reading Strategies activities help you teach reading skills and vocabulary.

C   Critical Thinking strategies help students apply and extend what they have learned.

U   Universal Access activities provide differentiated instruction for students learning to speak English, along with suggestions for teaching various types of learners.

S   Skill Practice strategies help students practice historical analysis and geography skills.

W   Writing Support activities provide writing opportunities to help students comprehend the text.

Teaching strategies and activities have been coded for ability level appropriateness.

AL   Activities for students working above grade level
OL   Activities for students working on grade level
BL   Activities for students working below grade level
EL   Activities for English learners

FOCUS

History–Social Science Standards

This chapter addresses the following main standards:

11.9 Students analyze U.S. foreign policy since World War II.

11.11 Students analyze the major social problems and domestic policy issues in contemporary American society.

BELLRINGER
SKILLBUILDER ACTIVITY

Working in small groups, have students brainstorm changes that have occurred over the last decade. **Ask: How were things in the United States different ten years ago than they are now?** *(Students should include specific examples.)* After they have read Chapter 21, ask students to identify changes they did not include in their original list. **OL**

TEACH

Thinking About the Big Ideas

As you begin teaching each section, use these questions and activities to focus on the Big Idea.

Section 1
The Technological Revolution
Essential Question: Are the technological changes of the last 25 years truly a revolution? If so, in what ways? *(Students should agree that a communications revolution took place transforming society through such new devices as personal computers, fax machines, and*

CHAPTER 21
1992–present
Into a New Century
~ The Big Ideas ~

SECTION 1: The Technological Revolution
Societies change over time. *The introduction of the first electronic digital computer in 1946 launched a technological revolution.*

SECTION 2: The Clinton Years
Societies change over time. *Although President Clinton struggled with Republicans in Congress and faced impeachment, several major economic and social reforms were achieved during his presidency.*

SECTION 3: An Interdependent World
International competition can lead to conflict and cooperation. *As the world adjusted to a new era, it faced the advantages and disadvantages of growing economic globalization and saw the end of the U.S.-Soviet rivalry.*

SECTION 4: America Enters a New Century
Societies change over time. *The closest presidential election in American history served as the prelude to the new century. The new president initiated an ambitious program.*

SECTION 5: The War on Terrorism
The fate of nations is forever changed by monumental world events. *After suffering the worst terrorist attack in its history, the United States launched a massive effort to end international terrorism.*

The *American Vision: Modern Times* Video *The Chapter 21 video, "America's Response to Terrorism," examines how ordinary Americans responded to the terrorist attacks in New York City and Washington, D.C.*

United States PRESIDENTS
1991 • U.S. leads coalition of nations against Iraq in Operation Desert Storm
G. Bush 1989–1993
1993 • Mosaic, the first popular Web browser, is released
Clinton 1993–2001
1994 • U.S., Mexico, and Canada inaugurate NAFTA
1995 • Budget impasse shuts down federal government • Oklahoma City bombing
1996 • Bill Clinton reelected

1990 *1993* *1996*

World
1991 • Bosnia declares independence from Yugoslavia
1992 • Earth Day summit held in Rio de Janeiro, Brazil
1993 • Israeli-Palestinian peace accord signed • European Union launched
1994 • Multiracial elections held in South Africa; Nelson Mandela elected president
1995 • Cease-fire signed in Bosnian war

926

cell phones.) Tell students that as they read Section 1, they will learn about how the introduction of the first digital computer launched a technological revolution. **OL**

Section 2
The Clinton Years
Essential Question: What conditions does a president need for a successful domestic agenda? *(The president's party must influence*

Congress, or the president must cooperate with the opposing party to pass legislation.) In Section 2 students will find out how President Clinton worked with the Republican majority to achieve major economic and social reforms. **AL**

Section 3
An Interdependent World
Essential Question: How is the world growing more interconnected? *(global trade, the*

Internet, increased travel and tourism) Tell students that Section 3 will focus on the advantages and disadvantages of economic globalization. `OL`

Section 4
America Enters a New Century
Essential Question: How did the 2000 presidential election divide the country? *(accusations of voter fraud, popular vote winner lost electoral vote)* Tell students that in Section 4 they will study the 2000 election and President Bush's programs. `BL`

Section 5
The War on Terrorism
Essential Question: What is the goal of international terrorism aimed at the United States? *(to get the U.S. to change its policies around the world)* Tell students that in Section 5 they will learn about the events of September 11, 2001, and the efforts the United States has undertaken to combat terrorism. `AL`

January 20, 2001: George W. Bush is inaugurated as the nation's 43rd president.

1998
• House of Representatives impeaches President Clinton

1999
• Senate acquits Clinton

2000
• Electoral crisis delays naming of 43rd president

2001
• First map of the human genome published
• Terrorist attacks destroy World Trade Center and damage Pentagon

2002
• Winter Olympics held in Salt Lake City, Utah

G.W. Bush 2001–

1999

2002

1997
• Britain returns control of Hong Kong to China

2000
• Mexico's election of Vicente Fox ends 71 years of single-party rule

2001
• China chosen to be site of 2008 Olympic Games

HISTORY
Online

Chapter Overview
Visit the *American Vision: Modern Times* Web site at tav.mt.glencoe.com and click on *Chapter Overviews–Chapter 21* to preview chapter information.

927

Cultural Perspectives

With the development of more and faster communication technologies as well as the growth of international corporations, the world is becoming a seemingly smaller place. Have students work in small groups to brainstorm products they use or customs they practice that originated in another country. Then ask them to think of examples they have seen or heard of ways American culture has spread to other countries. **Ask:** What are the positive and negative effects of such globalization? Can distinct local societies coexist with a global society? `OL`

FOLDABLES™
Study Organizer

Dinah Zike's Foldables are three-dimensional, interactive graphic organizers that help students practice basic writing skills, review key vocabulary terms, and identify main ideas. Have students complete the foldable activity in the *Dinah Zike's Reading and Study Skills Foldables* booklet.

HISTORY
Online

Go to tav.mt.glencoe.com for student activities, lesson plans, and links to additional Web resources to help students learn about the presidencies of Bill Clinton and George W. Bush, technological changes, and the war on terrorism.

Reading Skill

Why It's Important

Students should monitor their reading and notice when something does not make sense. Then they can use clarification strategies like looking up new words or rereading a passage. These strategies enable students to become independent learners.

1. Introducing the Skill

Have students read the text about the 2000 election on pages 948–949. Ask them to discuss the length and complexity of the overall reading. They should then point out the steps they take to achieve reading clarification in a chart similar to the one below.
OL

Monitoring → Clarifying → Comprehending

If the meaning is <u>unclear</u>, then do one of the following:
a. _____
b. _____
c. _____

2. Extending the Skill

Have each student find a magazine or newspaper article about an unfamiliar topic. Ask students to read the article and jot down notes on how they used monitoring and clarifying to help them comprehend the article. Have them discuss their strategies with the class. **OL**

Answers and Additional Support

Reading Skill — Monitoring and Clarifying

Effective readers monitor their understanding of a text. This means that they notice when something they read makes sense and when it does not. When a portion of the reading is confusing, good readers use different strategies to gain a better understanding. They may look up new words, reread a passage, or read a bit further to locate additional explanations. When you use these strategies, this is called clarifying.

When you read a text, you should stop at the end of a paragraph or passage and ask yourself whether it made sense. If it did not, determine which parts were unclear. Find definitions for unfamiliar vocabulary words. You should then reread the passage or read further to better understand the passage. You can also look on the page for diagrams, maps, or pictures that might help you understand the passage.

Read the following paragraph on the election of 2000 and notice whether anything seems unclear to you.

The 2000 election turned into one of the closest in American history. Gore narrowly won the popular vote, 48.4 percent to 47.9 percent for Bush. To win the presidency, however, candidates have to win a majority of state electoral votes, not the overall popular vote.

Neither Gore nor Bush had the 270 electoral votes needed to win. The election came down to the Florida vote—both men needed its 25 electoral votes. (page 948)

MONITORING AND CLARIFYING

When a passage contains a lot of numbers, write them down in your notes. Organize them in charts or tables to help you understand the information they are conveying.

- Were any words unfamiliar to you? If so, look them up in a dictionary. You can look up any bold-faced or highlighted words in the glossary in the back of your textbook.

- Did you understand the distribution of electoral votes? Look at the map and chart on page 950 to help you understand the popular vote and the distribution of electoral votes.

- Can you determine the close margin in the percentage points of the popular vote? The difference is 0.5 percent (48.4% − 47.9%).

Apply the Skill

As you read through the chapter, stop at the end of each major passage to review the information and to determine if you understood everything you have just read. If not, use one of the strategies outlined above to help you clarify the information in each passage.

928

UNIVERSAL ACCESS

English Learners Read aloud the passage about the election of 2004. Create a word wall bulletin board for the section, listing words on the board whose meanings may be unclear to students. Have students list synonyms below each word on the word wall. **EL**

Historical Analysis Skill

Analysis Skill Standard CS4

Relating Current Events

Chronological and Spatial Thinking You should be able to relate current events to the physical and human characteristics of places and regions.

After the terrorist attacks of September 11, 2001, the citizens of the United States wanted to know why the attacks happened. Within a short period, a number of rumors, opinions, and unsubstantiated stories surrounding the cause of the attacks developed. As it became clear that al-Qaeda was responsible, U.S. citizens became increasingly interested in the characteristics of people who could commit such acts. One of the outcomes of the terrorist attack was that Americans have tried to more fully understand the physical and human characteristics that have resulted in the conflicts in the Middle East.

Read the following passage about the background of Middle East terrorism.

As oil became important to the American economy in the 1920s, the United States invested heavily in the Middle East oil industry. This industry brought great wealth to the ruling families in some Middle Eastern kingdoms, but most of the people remained poor. Some became angry at the United States for supporting the wealthy kingdoms and families.

The rise of the oil industry increased the Middle East's contact with Western society. As Western ideas spread through the region, many Muslims—followers of the region's dominant religion—feared that their traditional values and beliefs were being weakened. New movements arose calling for a strict interpretation of the Quran—the Muslim holy book—and a return to traditional Muslim religious laws.

These Muslim movements wanted to overthrow pro-Western governments in the Middle East and create a pure Islamic society. Muslims who support these movements are referred to as fundamentalist militants. Although the vast majority of Muslims believe terrorism is contrary to their faith, militants began using terrorism to achieve their goals. (pages 955–956)

In this passage you learn that the roots of Middle East terrorism reach far back into the early part of the previous century. U.S. policy at the time created ill feelings toward the United States among people in the Middle East. People there also were concerned about the erosion of their traditional values.

Apply the Skill

As you read this chapter, find other instances and events that had their roots in the past. Consider how these events might have been different if there had been different developments. For example, how might the history of computers have been different without the development of microprocessors?

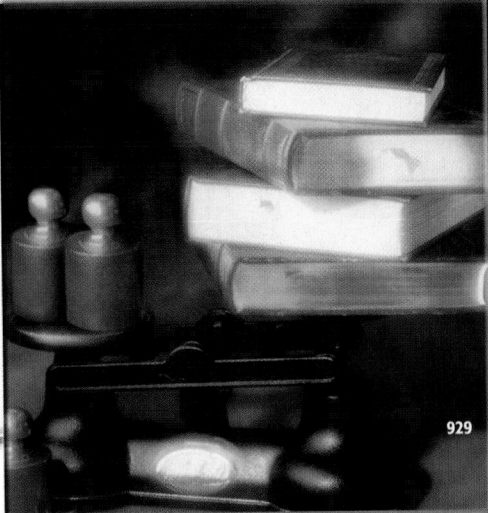

929

Historical Analysis

Why It's Important
Students need to understand the physical and human characteristics of places in order to understand current events that are impacted by these characteristics. This skill enables students to understand historical causality and the relationship between current events, history, and geography.

1. Introducing the Skill
Have students discuss with a partner what the terms "physical" and "human" characteristics of places and regions might mean.
Ask: What words can describe the physical characteristics of the Middle East? What words can describe human characteristics? Record students' answers in a chart similar to the one below.
OL **CA CS4**

Physical Characteristics	Human Characteristics

2. Extending the Skill
Have students construct posters through which they profile the physical and human characteristics of the place or region where they live. They should begin with a physical map of their community or county. For demographic data, they should research using the U.S. Census Bureau's American FactFinder Web page that provides fact sheets profiling communities and counties throughout the country. **OL**
CA CS4

UNIVERSAL ACCESS

Visual/Spatial Have student prepare an oral presentation on the Middle East. Students should collect pictures from old National Geographic magazines or other print sources and the Internet showing the physical and human characteristics of the region. The oral presentations should focus on the physical characteristics of the region as well as the various cultural characteristics of the people living there. **AL**

FOCUS

BELLRINGER
SKILLBUILDER ACTIVITY

Project **Daily Focus Skills Transparency 21-1** and have students answer the question.

Guide to Reading

Understanding Vocabulary: Have students choose one of the proper names from the section. Ask them to skim the text to find the word and write a brief explanation.

Answers to Graphic: Microprocessors: reduced computers' size, increased their speed and function; Apple II: first practical and affordable computer; Macintosh: popularized mouse and graphic icons; Windows: made Macintosh innovations widespread

Unpacking the Standards

Students will be able to:

• Describe the evolution of the computer from scientific tool to household appliance.

• Evaluate how the computer has revolutionized science, medicine, and communications.

Answers and Additional Support

SECTION 1 — The Technological Revolution

Guide to Reading

Connection
In the previous chapter, you learned about the Reagan and Bush administrations and the end of the Cold War. In this section, you will discover how a technological revolution changed American society.

Main Idea
• A computer revolution changed the workplace and the way people communicate. (p. 931)
• The 1996 Telecommunications Act increased competition among telephone companies. (p. 932)
• A computer resource that linked government agencies quickly developed into the Internet. (p. 933)

• Major developments in biotechnology spurred advances in medicine and improvements in agricultural technology. (p. 934)

Content Vocabulary
integrated circuit, microprocessor, software, telecommute

Academic Vocabulary
manipulate, protocol, sequence

People and Terms to Identify
ENIAC, Silicon Valley, Bill Gates, Internet, biotechnology, James Watson, Francis Crick, DNA

Reading Objectives
• **Describe** the evolution of the computer from scientific tool to household appliance.

• **Evaluate** how the computer has revolutionized science, medicine, and communications.

Reading Strategy
Categorizing As you read about the computer age, complete a chart similar to the one below to describe products that revolutionized the computer industry.

	How It Revolutionized Computer Industry
Microprocessors	
Apple II	
Macintosh	
Windows	

Preview of Events

◆1993	◆1996	◆1999	◆2002
1993 Mosaic, the first popular Web browser, introduced	**1996** Congress deregulates telephone companies	**1999** Over 86 million Americans own cell phones	**2001** Human Genome Project maps the human genome

The following are the main History–Social Science Standards covered in this section.

11.8.7 Describe the effects on society and the economy of technological developments since 1945, including the computer revolution, changes in communication, advances in medicine, and improvements in agricultural technology.

❧ The Big Idea ❧

Societies change over time. A computer revolution created competition and advancement in the technology industry. Computers became widely available and changed the way people communicated and worked. The use of the Internet expanded rapidly and led to a new "dot-com" economy. Other advances included breakthroughs in biotechnology. The use of computers helped scientists map the human genome.

SECTION RESOURCES

📁 Print Material
• Reproducible Lesson Plan 21-1
• Guided Reading Activity 21-1
• Reading Essentials and Study Guide 21-1
• Active Reading Note-Taking Guide 21-1

🖥 Transparencies
• Daily Focus Skills Transparency 21-1
• Section Graphic Organizer Transparency 21-1

Technology
🖴 Interactive Tutor Self-Assessment CD-ROM
🖴 ExamView® Pro Testmaker CD-ROM
🖴 Presentation Plus! CD-ROM

The Rise of the Compact Computer

Main Idea A computer revolution changed the workplace and the way people communicate.

Reading Connection What computer devices do you use regularly? Read on to learn about the beginnings of computer history.

The world's first electronic digital computer, called **ENIAC** (Electronic Numerical Integrator and Computer), went into operation in February 1946. ENIAC weighed over 30 tons and was the size of a small house. As the size of the computer decreased, so did the possibilities for its uses.

★ An American Story ★

After years as a magazine editor and television news commentator, Michael Kinsley jumped into the new technology of the Internet in 1996, by agreeing to edit an online magazine called *Slate*. "I was determined," Kinsley said, "to be on the next train to pull out of the station no matter where it was going—provided that I was the engineer."

Soon newspaper and print magazines were also developing Web resources. Television stations also used the Internet to update news stories, allowing consumers to access news when and how they wanted. As Kinsley explained:

❝Web readers *surf*. They go quickly from site to site. If they really like a particular site, they may visit it often, but they are unlikely to devote a continuous half-hour or more to any one site. . . . This appears to be in the nature of the Web and not something that is likely to change.❞

—from "*Slate* Goes Free," *Slate*, February 13, 1999

Long before computers and Internet use were common, the issues of weight and size needed to be solved. In early 1959, Robert Noyce designed the first **integrated circuit**—a complete electronic circuit on a single chip of silicon—which made circuits much smaller and very easy to manufacture. Noyce's company was located south of San Francisco. As new companies sprang up nearby to make products using integrated circuits, the region became known as **Silicon Valley.**

By 1968, Noyce and colleague Gordon Moore formed Intel, for "Integrated Electronics," a company that revolutionized computers by combining on a single chip several integrated circuits containing both memory and computing functions. Called **microprocessors,** these new chips further reduced the size of computers and increased their speed.

Computers for Everyone Using microprocessor technology, Stephen Wozniak and his 20-year-old friend Steven Jobs set out to build a small computer suitable for personal use. In 1976 they founded Apple Computer and completed the Apple I. The following year they introduced the Apple II, the first practical and affordable home computer.

Apple's success sparked intense competition in the computer industry. In 1981 International Business Machines (IBM) introduced its own compact machine, which it called the "Personal Computer" (PC). Apple responded in 1984 with the revolutionary Macintosh, a new model featuring a simplified operating system using onscreen graphic symbols called icons, which users could **manipulate** with a hand-operated device called a mouse.

Apple Founders In 1984 Apple president John Sculley (center), along with Steve Jobs (left) and Steve Wozniak, show off their new briefcase-sized Apple IIc computer. On what basic technology do personal computers rely?

TEACH

R₁ Reading Strategy

Activating Prior Knowledge Ask students to read and think about the first computer, known as ENIAC. **Ask:** What other inventions can you think of that started out in basic forms but were refined over time into more efficient, smaller designs? *(Students may mention the radio, television, or the telephone—all things that have grown smaller and more powerful over time.)* **OL**

S Skill Practice

Creating A Time Line Organize students into groups of four and have them create time lines illustrating the advances in technology during their lifetimes. Instruct students to start their time lines with the year the oldest member of the group was born and try to find a significant event or milestone for each year up until the present time (with a minimum of five). Students may also add events outlined in the section that occurred before they were born. As a class, review the time lines from each group and create a composite time line. **BL** **CA CS2**

R₂ Reading Strategy

Scaffolding—Academic Vocabulary The word *device* was introduced in Chapter 14, Section 3. Ask a student to define the word. **BL**

Resources for page 931

Have students read more about the computer's impact in:

📁 *Linking Past and Present Activity 21*

📁 *Primary Source Reading 21-1*

📁 *Moments in Time, Unit 14: The Information Age (1977–2003)*

Picturing History

Answer: microprocessor technology
Ask: How did Intel revolutionize computers? *(Intel combined several integrated circuits on a single chip containing both memory and computing functions.)*

R Reading Strategy

Using Context Clues Have students define the term "software" in their own words. **Ask: How does software differ from hardware?** *(Hardware is the comprehensive term for all of the physical parts of a computer, whereas software is the data it contains or operates on.)* **Which one is most important? Why?** *(Software is arguably more important because it is the "brains" of the computer.)* `OL`

Review the Big Idea

Review the Big Idea for this section, "Societies change over time." Divide the class into four equal groups and ask each group to discuss the changes brought about by the advances in computer technology and telecommunications. Have each group make a list of the changes. Ask a member of each group to present their lists to the class. `OL`

✓ Reading Check

Answer: The company purchased its original software rather than creating it from scratch.

Answers and Additional Support

HISTORY Online

Student Web Activity Visit the *American Vision: Modern Times* Web site at tav.mt.glencoe.com and click on *Student Web Activities–Chapter 21* for an activity on the technological revolution.

Bill Gates and Microsoft

As Jobs and Wozniak were creating Apple, 19-year-old Harvard dropout **Bill Gates** co-founded Microsoft to design PC **software,** the instructions used to program computers to perform desired tasks. In 1980 IBM hired Microsoft to develop an operating system for its new PC. Gates quickly paid a Seattle programmer $50,000 for the rights to his software, and with some refinements, it became MS-DOS (Microsoft Disk Operating System).

In 1985 Microsoft introduced the "Windows" operating system, which enabled PCs to use the mouse-activated, on-screen graphic icons that the Macintosh had popularized. Soaring sales and rising Microsoft stock values made Gates a billionaire at the age of 31. Compact computers soon transformed the workplace, linking employees within an office or among office branches. They became essential tools in virtually every kind of business. By the late 1990s, many workers used home computers and electronic

---

mail to **"telecommute,"** or do their jobs via computer without having to go to the office.

✓ Reading Check **Describing** How was Microsoft different from other computer companies?

The Telecommunications Revolution

Main Idea The 1996 Telecommunications Act increased competition among telephone companies.

Reading Connection What telecommunications inventions were developed at the end of the 1800s? Read on to find out more about the developments a century later.

A parallel revolution in communications coincided with the growing impact of computers. In the 1970s, 1980s, and 1990s, the government loosened telecommunications regulations, allowing more companies to compete in the telephone and television industries. In 1996 Congress passed the Telecommunications Act. This act allowed telephone companies to compete with each other and to send television signals, but it also permitted cable television companies to offer

---

TECHNOLOGY & History

Magnetic Resonance Imaging

One extension of computer technology is magnetic resonance imaging (MRI). An MRI allows physicians to diagnose certain diseases, abnormalities, and injuries without resorting to x-rays or surgery. An MRI unit is made up of a large cylindrical magnet, devices for transmitting and receiving radio signals, and a computer. *Why do you think physicians prefer MRIs over x-rays and surgery?*

1 A large **cylindrical magnet** with a magnetic field 30,000 times stronger than the earth's magnetic field surrounds the patient.

2 **Radio signals** are transmitted within the machine and pass through the patient's body.

3 **A computer** converts the radio signals into precise images of the body's internal structure.

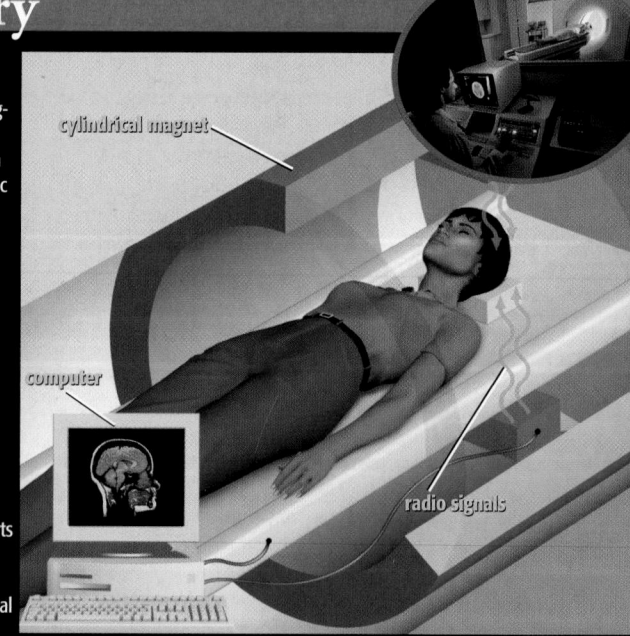

cylindrical magnet

computer

radio signals

TECHNOLOGY & History

Answer: Students might suggest that an MRI is safer than X rays or surgery and provides clearer images. **Ask: Why would a doctor use an X ray over an MRI?** *(The technology is much less expensive and/or the doctor may not need the detailed information provided by the MRI.)*

HISTORY Online

Objectives and answers to the student activity can be found in the Web Activity Lesson Plan at tav.mt.glencoe.com.

Profiles IN HISTORY

Jerry Yang
1968–

Jerry Yang was born in Taiwan in 1968 and immigrated with his family to San Jose, California, when he was 10 years old. Yang is a cofounder of Yahoo!, one of the world's best-known gateways to information and consumer goods on the Web. It is estimated that by the late 1990s, around 40 million people were visiting the Yahoo! Web site every month.

The company developed out of Yang's desire to be able to find good Web sites quickly. At Stanford University, he and cofounder David Filo were doctoral students sharing office space in a trailer. They also shared

information on their favorite Web sites, and Yang began compiling a list of them. He nicknamed the list "Jerry's Guide to the World Wide Web," and he posted it on the Internet.

Inquiries to the site boomed, and Yang and Filo concluded that they had found an untapped market. With the help of a loan from an imaginative venture capitalist, Yahoo! was born. Yang says they chose the name because it suggested the sort of "Wild West" character of the Internet. The mission for Yahoo! was not just to collect Web sites but to organize them into convenient categories, such as news, sports, games, and weather. Yahoo! became a popular gateway, or "portal," to the Web.

W Writing Support

Research Report Writing
The Internet and online search engines have transformed the way people conduct research. Ask students to use both library and Internet resources to review how research and literature searches were conducted prior to the Internet. Students may want to interview a librarian at their school to find out more information. Tell the class to write a three-page report discussing the changes they have uncovered.
AL **CA** 11WS1.6

telephone service. Such developments spurred the creation of new technologies such as Web-enabled cellular phones and other mixing of data-platforms.

✔ **Reading Check** **Explaining** How did deregulation affect the telecommunications industry?

The Rise of the Internet

Main Idea **A computer resource that linked government agencies quickly developed into the Internet.**

Reading Connection How do you evaluate whether a Web site is a wise choice for research or personal enrichment? Read on to discover how the World Wide Web began.

Digital electronics also made possible a new worldwide communications system. The **Internet** let computer users post and receive information and communicate with each other. It had its roots in a computer networking system that the U.S. Defense Department's Advanced Research Project Agency established in 1969. Known as ARPANET, this system linked government agencies, defense contractors, and scientists at various universities, enabling them to communicate with each other by electronic mail. In 1985 the National Science Foundation funded several supercomputer centers across the

country. This paved the way for the Internet, a global information system that operated commercially rather than through the government.

At first, Internet users employed different types of information. With the development of the hypertext transport **protocol** (http) and new software known as Web browsers, the Internet rapidly expanded. Users could now click on Internet links using their computer mouse and easily jump from Web site to Web site. Internet users could search for news, information, shop, and even meet new people. Internet use expanded by almost 300 percent between 1997 and 2000. As the Internet became more popular with consumers, more businesses and companies took advantage of the opportunity to increase advertising and sales through the Internet.

The Internet also spawned a "dot-com" economy (from the common practice of using a business name as a World Wide Web address, followed by ".com"). Seemingly rich with promise, a wide variety of dot.com companies made millions of dollars for stock investors without ever earning actual profit from operations. Internet-related stocks helped fuel the prosperity of the 1990s but dropped dramatically in 2000, raising questions about the ultimate profitability of online companies.

✔ **Reading Check** **Explaining** How did the Internet expand business opportunities?

CHAPTER 21   Into a New Century   **933**

U Universal Access

English Learners Ask students to compile an illustrated glossary of key Internet terms such as bookmark, browser, client, directory, domain, download, FTP, homepage, HTML, HTTP, newsgroup, search engine, server, URL, and World Wide Web. For each term have students write out a definition and draw a picture or provide an example that illustrates the function of the term in reference to the Internet. As students finish, place examples of each key Internet term on a bulletin board to form a Word Wall for reference and further study.
EL

✔ **Reading Check**

Answer: It created a global information system and encouraged the development of new software. It also spawned the "dot.com" economy.

Profiles IN HISTORY

Background: In addition to the Wild West connection, the name Yahoo! is an acronym for "Yet Another Hierarchical Officious Oracle." Ask students to look up these words and see if this acronym accurately defines the service that Yahoo! provides.

Ask: Before naming it Yahoo!, what did Yang call his site? *(Jerry's Guide to the World Wide Web)*

ASSESS

Resources for page 934

Use these resources to assess student mastery.

📁 Section Quiz 21-1

📁 Reading Essentials and Study Guide 21-1

💿 Interactive Tutor Self-Assessment CD-ROM

📁 California Standards Practice, Grade 11

✓ Reading Check

Answer: Computers made it possible to study and manipulate genes and cells at the molecular level.

HISTORY Online

Study Central provides audio summaries, interactive games, and online graphic organizers to help students review section content.

CLOSE

Summarizing Have students summarize Section 1 by working in pairs to create posters that retell the main ideas under each of the section subheadings. **EL**

Answers and Additional Support

934

Breakthroughs in Biotechnology

Main Idea Major developments in biotechnology spurred advances in medicine and improvements in agricultural technology.

Reading Connection Do you think everyone should have access to the findings of the Human Genome Project? Read on to discover the National Institutes of Health's answer to that question.

Computers greatly assisted scientists engaged in **biotechnology**—the managing of biological systems to improve human life. Computers made it possible for scientists to study and manipulate genes and cells at the molecular level for the first time. This improvement in scientific study and research made new advances possible. Through biotechnology, researchers developed new medicines, animal growth hormones, genetically engineered plants, and industrial chemicals.

Unraveling the Secrets of Life The first steps toward biotechnology came in 1953, when American molecular biologist **James Watson** and his British colleague, **Francis Crick,** deciphered the structure of deoxyribonucleic acid (DNA). **DNA** is the genetic material in cells that determine all forms of life. Crick and Watson began working on the structure of DNA in the fall of 1951. Their first attempt proved unsuccessful. Their second attempt in early March of 1953, however, was more successful. Their success in deciphering the structure of DNA opened the door for advances in biotechnology.

Once scientists learned how to read the message of DNA, their new knowledge improved medical research and provided law enforcement with new methods of identification for both victims and criminals. Further research in biotechnology created artificial genes and assisted genetic engineering for plants, animals, and humans.

The Human Genome Project For years scientists talked of mapping out the human genome by recording the DNA **sequence** of the human species. With the development of supercomputers, the Human Genome Project began in earnest at the National Institutes of Health (NIH) in 1990. NIH decided to place all of the Human Genome Project's data on the Internet to make it available to scientists all over the world, free of charge. Researchers hoped to prevent any single nation or private laboratory from controlling the outcome and limiting the use of genome findings. In February 2001, the project published its first map of the human genome. Researchers finished the sequence two years later. Scientists continue expanding their knowledge of DNA. Medical researchers expect that this information will help them determine which genes make people more susceptible to disease, thereby improving medical diagnoses and preventive medication and assisting in finding cures.

✓ Reading Check **Explaining** How did computers assist the development of biotechnology?

HISTORY Online **Study Central**

For help with the concepts in this section of *American Vision: Modern Times* go to tav.mt.glencoe.com and click on *Study Central.*

SECTION 1 ASSESSMENT

Checking for Understanding

1. **Vocabulary** Define: integrated circuit, microprocessor, manipulate, software, telecommute, protocol, sequence.
2. **People and Terms** Identify: ENIAC, Silicon Valley, Bill Gates, Internet, biotechnology, James Watson, Francis Crick, DNA.
3. **Explain** how scientific discoveries in biotechnology have improved people's lives.

Reviewing Big Ideas

4. **Describing** How have personal computers transformed the workplace?

Critical Thinking

5. **Historical Analysis** **Analyzing** How have advances in telecommunications and the rise of the Internet affected the standard of living in the United States? **CA HI1**
6. **Organizing** Complete a graphic organizer similar to the one below by listing developments that led to the technological revolution.

Technological Revolution

Analyzing Visuals

7. **Analyzing Photographs** Study the photograph of the Apple computer founders on page 931. How have computers changed since this picture in 1984?

Writing About History

8. **Descriptive Writing** Write two paragraphs describing the ways that you and your family use the Internet and how your way of life would be different without it. **CA 11WA2.1e**

934 CHAPTER 21 Into a New Century

SECTION 1 ASSESSMENT ANSWERS

1. Content vocabulary is boldfaced and highlighted in yellow. Academic vocabulary is boldfaced.
2. ENIAC *(p. 931)*, Silicon Valley *(p. 931)*, Bill Gates *(p. 932)*, Internet *(p. 933)*, biotechnology *(p. 934)*, James Watson *(p. 934)*, Francis Crick *(p. 934)*, DNA *(p. 934)*
3. led to artificial genes and assisted genetic engineering of plants, animals, and humans
4. linked employees, became essential in all kinds of business, and allowed people to telecommute
5. New technology, such as Web-enabled cell phones and the Internet, made a new communications system possible and spawned the "dot.com" economy.
6. deregulation of the telecommunications industry, microprocessors, Internet, personal computers, wireless technology
7. much more powerful, with larger monitors and separate processors
8. Students' paragraphs will vary.

SECTION 2 The Clinton Years

Guide to Reading

Connection

In the previous section, you learned about technological advances. In this section, you will find out about events during President Clinton's administration.

Main Idea

- President Clinton took office in 1992 with plans for improving health care, reducing the federal deficit, helping families, and strengthening gun control. (p. 936)
- Republican victories in Congress set the stage for battles between the executive and legislative branches. (p. 937)
- Riding the tide of economic prosperity, Clinton won reelection over Senator

Bob Dole and third-party candidate Ross Perot. (p. 938)
- Clinton tried to focus the domestic agenda on the needs of children, but personal problems marred his second term. (p. 939)
- During Clinton's second term, the United States became more involved in world events. (p. 940)

Content Vocabulary

perjury, ethnic cleansing

Academic Vocabulary

modify, stress, submit

People and Terms to Identify

AmeriCorps, Contract with America, Kenneth Starr, Dayton Accords

Reading Objectives

- **Describe** the difficulties and successes of Bill Clinton's two terms as president.
- **Discuss** the nation's involvement in world affairs during the Clinton presidency.

Reading Strategy

Taking Notes As you read about the administration of President Clinton, use the major headings of the section to create an outline similar to the one below.

The Clinton Years
I. Clinton's Agenda
   A.
   B.
   C.
   D.
II.

Preview of Events

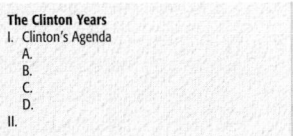

◆1993	◆1995	◆1997	◆1999

1993 Israeli-Palestinian peace accord

1994 Republicans win both houses of Congress

1995 Federal government shuts down during budget impasse

1998 House impeaches Clinton

1999 Senate acquits Clinton; NATO aircraft bomb Serbia

The following are the main History–Social Science Standards covered in this section.

11.9.6 Describe U.S. Middle East policy and its strategic, political, and economic interests, including those related to the Gulf War.

11.11.2 Discuss the significant domestic policy speeches of Truman, Eisenhower, Kennedy, Johnson, Nixon, Carter, Reagan, Bush, and Clinton (e.g., with regard to education, civil rights, economic policy, environmental policy).

11.11.3 Describe the changing roles of women in society as reflected in the entry of more women into the labor force and the changing family structure.

11.11.6 Analyze the persistence of poverty and how different analyses of this issue influence welfare reform, health insurance reform, and other social policies.

11.11.7 Explain how the federal, state, and local governments have responded to demographic and social changes such as population shifts to the suburbs, racial concentrations in the cities,

❧ The Big Idea ❧

Societies change over time. President Clinton was able to push through laws to help families and strengthen gun control, but he also raised taxes and failed to reform health care. During the 1994 mid-term elections, dissatisfied voters gave Republicans a majority in both houses of Congress. Although Congress and the president battled over the budget and legislation, they were able to approve reforms for health insurance and welfare. With a prospering economy, President Clinton won reelection in 1996. Personal scandal and impeachment, however, marred his second term. During this time, the president worked to end a crisis in Haiti, sent peacekeeping troops to Bosnia and Kosovo, and attempted to negotiate between Israeli and Palestinian leaders.

Frostbelt-to-Sunbelt migration, international migration, decline of family farms, increases in out-of-wedlock births, and drug abuse.

CHAPTER 21 Into a New Century **935**

FOCUS

BELLRINGER
SKILLBUILDER ACTIVITY

Project **Daily Focus Skills Transparency 21-2** and have students answer the question.

Guide to Reading

Understanding Vocabulary: Have students define the content vocabulary words for this section in their own words and then use each word in a sentence.

Answers to Graphic: Students should complete the outline by including all headings in the section.

Unpacking the Standards

Students will be able to:

- Describe the difficulties and successes of Bill Clinton's two terms as president.
- Discuss the nation's involvement in world affairs during the Clinton presidency.

SECTION RESOURCES

📖 Print Material
- Reproducible Lesson Plan 21-2
- Guided Reading Activity 21-2
- Reading Essentials and Study Guide 21-2
- Active Reading Note-Taking Guide 21-2

📄 Transparencies
- Daily Focus Skills Transparency 21-2
- Section Graphic Organizer Transparency 21-2

Technology
- Interactive Tutor Self-Assessment CD-ROM
- ExamView® Pro Testmaker CD-ROM
- Presentation Plus! CD-ROM

TEACH

R Reading Strategy

Organizing Information Have students create a chart similar to the one below to illustrate some of Clinton's domestic agenda. **OL**

	Issue	Action
Taxes		
Health Care		
Families		
Education		
Crime		
Gun Control		

W Writing Support

Narrative Writing Have students write a brief narrative explaining, in their own words, the problems the Clinton administration faced, the programs it proposed, and the success or failure of these programs. **OL**

CA 11WA2.3b

Answers and Additional Support

Clinton's Agenda

 Main Idea President Clinton took office in 1992 with plans for improving health care, reducing the federal deficit, helping families, and strengthening gun control.

Reading Connection Do you know anyone who has worked for Americorps? Read on to learn about the beginnings of this program.

President Clinton's first years in office were filled with grandiose plans and the difficult realities of politics.

★ An American Story ★

Bill Clinton was the third-youngest person ever to serve as president and the first of the "baby boom" generation to reach the Oval Office. Clinton brought with him a team of young, energetic advisers. In the early weeks of the administration, Clinton's team spent many hours at the White House adjusting to their new life. In early 1993, they began discussing plans for Clinton's new economic strategy for paying down the deficit and reducing interest rates. George Stephanopoulos, an aide to the president, remembers their inexperienced beginnings:

66 The president presided over the rolling Roosevelt Room meetings in shirtsleeves, with glasses sliding down the end of his nose. . . . Clinton let everyone have a say, played us off against one another, asked pointed questions, and took indecipherable notes. But the reminders of who we were and what we were doing was never far away. Late one night, we ordered pizzas. When they arrived, the president grabbed a slice with the rest of us . . . [b]ut just before he took his first bite, [a secret service] agent placed a hand on his shoulder and told him to put it down. The pie hadn't been screened. . . . 99

—quoted in *All Too Human*

 The new president put forth an ambitious domestic program focusing on five major areas: the economy, the family, education, crime, and health care.

Raising Taxes, Cutting Spending As he had promised in his election campaign, Clinton focused first on the economy. The problem, in the president's view, was the federal deficit. Under Reagan and

---

Bush, the deficit had nearly quadrupled, adding billions of dollars annually to the national debt. High deficits forced the government to borrow large sums of money to pay for its programs and helped to drive up interest rates.

Clinton believed that the key to economic growth was to lower interest rates. Low interest rates would enable businesses to borrow more money to expand and create more jobs. Low rates would also make it easier for consumers to borrow money for mortgages, car loans, and other items, which in turn would promote economic growth.

One way to bring interest rates down was to reduce the federal deficit. In early 1993, Clinton sent Congress a deficit reduction plan. In trying to cut the deficit, however, Clinton faced a serious problem. About half of all government spending went to entitlement programs, such as Social Security, Medicare, and veterans' benefits. Entitlement programs are very hard to cut because so many Americans depend on them.

Faced with these constraints, Clinton decided to raise taxes, even though he had promised to cut taxes during his campaign. Clinton's plan raised tax rates for middle- and upper-income Americans and placed new taxes on gasoline, heating oil, and natural gas. The tax increases were very unpopular, and Republicans in Congress refused to support them. Clinton pressured Democrats, and after many amendments, a **modified** version of Clinton's plan narrowly passed.

George Stephanopoulos ▼

Did You Know?

George Stephanopoulos first served as Bill Clinton's deputy campaign manager and communications director for the 1992 presidential campaign. After the election, he became a senior adviser for policy and strategy. Stephanopoulos left the White House staff in 1997 to work for the news media.

Stumbling on Health Care During his campaign, Clinton had promised to reform the U.S. health care system. An estimated 40 million Americans, or roughly 15 percent of the nation, did not have private health insurance. The president appointed a task force headed by his wife, Hillary Rodham Clinton—an unprecedented role for a first lady. The task force developed a plan that guaranteed health benefits for all Americans, but it put much of the burden of payment of these benefits on employers. Small-business owners feared they could not afford it. The insurance industry and doctors' organizations also opposed the plan.

Republicans opposed the plan as being complicated, costly, and reliant on government control. Congressional Democrats were divided. Some supported alternative plans, but no plan had enough support to pass. Faced with public opposition, Clinton's plan died without ever coming to a vote.

Families and Education Clinton did manage to push several major pieces of legislation through Congress. During his campaign, he had **stressed** the need to help American families. His first success was the Family Medical Leave Act. This law gave workers up to 12 weeks per year of unpaid family leave for the birth or adoption of a child or for the illness of a family member. Clinton also persuaded Congress to create the **AmeriCorps** program. This program put students to work improving low-income housing, teaching children to read, and cleaning up the environment. AmeriCorps volunteers earned a salary and were awarded a scholarship to continue their education.

Crime and Gun Control Clinton had promised to get tough on crime during his campaign. He had also strongly endorsed new gun-control laws. Despite strong opposition from many Republicans and the National Rifle Association (NRA), the Democrats in Congress passed a gun-control law known as the Brady Bill. The bill imposed a waiting period before people could buy handguns. It also required gun dealers to have police run a background check on a person's criminal record before selling them a handgun. The following year, Clinton introduced his first anticrime bill. The bill provided states with extra funds to build new prisons and put 100,000 more police officers on the streets.

✓ **Reading Check** **Explaining** Why did President Clinton's proposed health care plan fail?

Picturing **History**

High Hopes The Clintons entered the White House in 1993 determined to change the United States for the better. It took time for them to adjust to life in Washington, and many of their ambitious plans were defeated in Congress. *What legislative proposal was given to the First Lady to oversee?*

The Republicans Gain Control of Congress

Main Idea Republican victories in Congress set the stage for battles between the executive and legislative branches.

Reading Connection Have you ever refused to back down or give in when you believed you were right? Read on to find out how President Clinton's resolve led to better cooperation in Congress.

Despite his successes, Clinton was very unpopular by late 1994. Instead of cutting taxes, he had raised them, and he had not fixed health care. Although the economy was improving, many companies were still downsizing. Several personal issues involving President Clinton further weakened public confidence in him. These factors convinced many Americans to vote Republican in 1994.

The Contract With America As the 1994 midterm elections neared, congressional Republicans, led by Newt Gingrich of Georgia, created the **Contract with America**. This program proposed 10 major changes, including lower taxes, welfare reform, tougher anticrime laws, term limits for members of Congress, and

CHAPTER 21 Into a New Century **937**

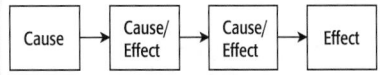

R **Reading Strategy**

Connecting Have students recall what they know about the current debate on health care issues in the United States. **Ask:** Are the issues surrounding health care similar to those described in the text? If not, how are they different? Students should recognize that universal health care is a topic that continues to be debated in Congress. **OL**

C **Critical Thinking**

Determining Cause and Effect Ask students to analyze the sequence of events that led to the Republicans gaining control of Congress in 1994, the budget battle of 1995, the cooperation between Clinton and the Republicans, and Clinton's eventual reelection in 1996. Have students create a flowchart that links the various actions taken by both the Republicans and the president to show the connections between cause and effect. The chain should follow the layout of the diagram below. *(Students' charts will vary.)* **OL**

| Cause | → | Cause/ Effect | → | Cause/ Effect | → | Effect |

Resources for page 937

*Have students read more about Clinton's effort to reform health care in the **Primary Source Reading 21-2**.*

✓**Reading Check**

Answer: Republicans said it was too costly and relied on federal control. Public opposition also was strong.

Picturing **History**

Answer: health care reform
Ask: What happened to health care reform? *(The plan died before a congressional vote.)*

Did You Know?

William Jefferson Blythe IV was born in Hope, Arkansas. While in high school, Blythe took his stepfather's last name of Clinton. After serving as attorney general and governor of Arkansas, Clinton ran for president in 1992. His campaign video was titled "A Man from Hope."

Review the Big Idea

Review the Big Idea for this section, "Societies change over time." Tell students to review the text about the electoral success of the Republicans during the first Clinton administration. **Ask: What were the goals of the Republicans once they gained the majority in Congress?** *(Students should describe the items in the Contract with America.)* **How would you assess their success?** *(The Senate defeated several proposals and Clinton vetoed some. Missteps during the budget battle of 1995 ended the momentum of House Republicans.)* **OL**

S Skill Practice

Conducting Research Have students gather data on the 1996 presidential election to determine how much of the popular vote and the electoral vote each of the three candidates garnered. Ask students to make a pair of circle graphs—one for the popular votes and one for the electoral votes—showing the results of the election. **OL** **CA HI1**

✓ Reading Check

Answer: They agreed on health insurance portability and welfare reform.

Answers and Additional Support

Picturing History

Republicans Triumphant As a result of the 1994 midterm congressional elections, the Republican Party gained control of the House and the Senate for the first time since the 1950s. Newt Gingrich (at podium) helped lead a group of young GOP congressional representatives in passing the Contract with America legislation. **How successful was the Contract with America legislation? Explain.**

a balanced budget amendment. Republicans won a stunning victory—for the first time in 40 years, they had a majority in both houses of Congress.

In their first 100 days in office, House Republicans passed almost the entire Contract with America, but they soon ran into trouble. The Senate defeated several proposals, including the balanced budget amendment, while the president vetoed others.

The Budget Battle In 1995 the Republicans lost more momentum when they clashed with the president over the new federal budget. Clinton vetoed several Republican budget proposals, claiming they cut into social programs too much. Gingrich believed that if Republicans stood firm, the president would back down. Otherwise, the entire federal government would shut down for lack of funds. Clinton, however, refused to budge.

By standing firm against Republican budget proposals and allowing the government to shut down, Clinton regained much of the support he had lost in 1994. The Republicans in Congress realized they needed to work with the president to pass legislation. Soon afterward, they reached an agreement with Clinton to balance the budget.

In the months before the 1996 election, the president and the Republicans worked together to pass new legislation. In August Congress passed the Health Insurance Portability Act. This act improved coverage for people who changed jobs and reduced discrimination against people with preexisting illnesses.

938 CHAPTER 21 Into a New Century

Later that month Congress passed the Welfare Reform Act, which limited people to no more than two consecutive years on welfare and required them to work to receive welfare benefits. Welfare reform had become a major issue by the mid-1990s because of growing evidence that welfare programs trapped people in poverty by giving them incentives to stay unemployed and to have children without getting married. Despite all the money spent on antipoverty programs, the percentage of Americans in poverty had changed very little. Both the Republican-led Congress and President Clinton agreed that the welfare system needed reforms to encourage people to go back to work.

✓ Reading Check Identifying

What two reforms did Clinton and Congress agree to support?

The 1996 Election

S **Main Idea** Riding the tide of economic prosperity, Clinton won reelection over Senator Bob Dole and third-party candidate Ross Perot.

Reading Connection How important is the unemployment rate during an election year? Read on to discover how low unemployment, inflation, and crime rates helped Clinton win the 1996 election.

As the 1996 campaign began, Clinton took credit for the economy. The economic boom of the 1990s was the longest sustained period of growth in American history. Unemployment and inflation fell to their lowest levels in 40 years. The stock market soared, wages rose, crime rates fell, and the number of people on welfare declined. With the economy booming, Clinton's popularity climbed rapidly.

The Republican Party nominated Senator Bob Dole of Kansas, the Republican leader in the Senate, to run against Clinton. Dole promised a 15 percent tax cut if elected and tried to portray Clinton as a tax-and-spend liberal.

H. Ross Perot also ran again as a candidate. This time he ran as the candidate of the Reform Party, which he had created. Once again Perot made the deficit the main campaign issue.

Picturing History

Answer: The Senate defeated several proposals, including the balanced budget amendment, while the president vetoed others.
Ask: Who was the leader of the Republicans who created the Contract with America?
(Newt Gingrich)

Did You Know?

Newt Gingrich was originally elected to the U.S. House of Representatives in 1978. He remained a representative until 1998, serving as the Speaker of the House from 1995 to 1998. Gingrich helped engineer the Republicans' success in gaining control of the House and Senate for the first time in almost a half century.

President Clinton won reelection, winning a little more than 49 percent of the popular vote and 379 electoral votes. Dole received slightly less than 41 percent and 159 electoral votes. Perot won about 8.4 percent of the vote—less than half of what he had received in 1992. Despite Clinton's victory, Republicans retained control of Congress.

✓ **Reading Check** **Explaining** Why do you think President Clinton won reelection in 1996?

Clinton's Second Term

Main Idea Clinton tried to focus the domestic agenda on the needs of children, but personal problems marred his second term.

Reading Connection What president in the 1800s was threatened with impeachment? Read on to learn about Clinton's impeachment trial.

During Clinton's second term, the economy continued its expansion. As people's incomes rose, so too did the amount of taxes they paid. At the same time, despite their differences, the president and Congress continued to shrink the deficit. In 1997, for the first time in 24 years, the president was able to **submit** a

balanced budget to Congress. Beginning in 1998, the government began to run a surplus—that is, it collected more money than it spent.

Putting Children First During his second term, Clinton's domestic agenda shifted toward children's issues. He began by asking Congress to pass a $500-per-child tax credit. He also signed the Adoption and Safe Families Act and asked Congress to ban cigarette advertising aimed at children. In August 1997, Clinton signed the Children's Health Insurance Program—a plan to provide health insurance for children whose parents could not afford it.

Clinton also continued his efforts to help students. "I come from a family where nobody had ever gone to college before," Clinton said. "When I became president, I was determined to do what I could to give every student that chance." To help students, he asked for a tax credit, a large increase in student grants, and an expansion of the Head Start program for preschoolers.

Clinton Is Impeached The robust economy and his high standing in the polls allowed Clinton to regain the initiative in dealing with Congress. By 1998, however, he had become entangled in a serious scandal that threatened to undermine his presidency.

The scandal began in Clinton's first term, when he was accused of arranging illegal loans for

C **Critical Thinking**

Comparing and Contrasting Ask students to examine the images of the Clinton impeachment shown on this page and in the media. Tell students to talk to someone who experienced the Watergate investigation of Richard Nixon's administration. They should ask what similarities and differences their interviewees see between the Watergate investigation and the Clinton impeachment proceedings. Tell students to present their interview results in a two-page written report. **OL**
CA 11WA2.3c

R **Reading Strategy**

Connecting Because of his poor family background, President Clinton wanted to help students by providing tax credits, increasing student grants, and expanding Head Start. **Ask:** If you were to become president, is there anything you would want to do to help others be successful? *(Students' answers will vary.)* **BL**

✓**Reading Check**

Answer: One possible answer: Clinton was reelected because the economy was booming.

Impeaching the President

The Constitution gives Congress the power to remove a president from office "upon impeachment for and Conviction of, Treason, Bribery, or other High Crimes and Misdemeanors." The House of Representatives has the sole power over impeachment—the formal accusation of wrongdoing in office. If the majority of the House votes to impeach the president, the Senate conducts a trial. A two-thirds vote of those present is needed for conviction. When the impeachment proceeding involves a president, the chief justice of the United States presides.

Chief Justice William Rehnquist being sworn in for the impeachment trial in the Senate

A somber President and Mrs. Clinton after the decision for impeachment was reached

Did You Know?

Bill Clinton joined Andrew Johnson as the only other president to be impeached by the U.S. Congress. Like Johnson, Clinton was acquitted of the impeachment charges and was not forced to resign from office. Johnson was acquitted by a single vote. Clinton faced two charges of impeachment, one of which was rejected by five votes in the Senate. The other charge resulted in a tied vote.

S Skill Practice

Evaluating Evidence Have students evaluate Clinton's foreign policy, especially his attempts to end conflicts in Haiti, Bosnia, and Kosovo. Ask them to explain how President Clinton used the power of the United States to combat international crises. Did he use a common strategy in more than one country? OL CA HR4

R Reading Strategy

Activating Prior Knowledge
Ethnic cleansing was the term used by the Serbs to justify their expulsion of certain ethnic groups from a geographic area in the 1990s. While ethnic cleansing begins as forcible emigration, it may turn into genocide—the deliberate killing of people based on their ethnicity, race, or religion. **Ask:** Are there other instances of ethnic cleansing or genocide you can recall from history? *(the Holocaust, the Armenian genocide, Cambodia under the Khmer Rouge, Rwanda)* AL

✓ Reading Check

Answer: allegations that Clinton had arranged illegal loans while he was governor of Arkansas; also allegations that he had perjured himself while testifying about his relationship with a White House intern

Answers and Additional Support

Whitewater Development—an Arkansas real estate company—while he was governor of that state. Attorney General Janet Reno decided that an independent counsel should investigate the president. A special three-judge panel appointed **Kenneth Starr,** a former federal judge, to this position.

In early 1998, a new scandal emerged involving a personal relationship between the president and a White House intern. Some evidence suggested that the president had committed **perjury,** or had lied under oath, about the relationship. The three-judge panel directed Starr to investigate this scandal as well. In September 1998, after examining the evidence, Starr sent his report to the Judiciary Committee of the House of Representatives. Starr argued that Clinton had obstructed justice, abused his power as president, and committed perjury.

After the 1998 elections, the House began impeachment hearings. Clinton's supporters charged that Starr's investigation was politically motivated. Clinton's accusers argued that the president was accountable if his actions were illegal.

On December 19, 1998, the House of Representatives passed two articles of impeachment, one for perjury and one for obstruction of justice. The vote split almost evenly along party lines, and the case moved to the Senate for trial. On February 12, 1999, the senators cast their votes. The vote was 55 to 45 that Clinton was not guilty of perjury, and 50–50 on the charge of obstruction of justice. Although both votes were well short of the two-thirds needed to remove the president from office, Clinton's reputation had suffered.

✓ **Reading Check** **Examining** What events led to the impeachment of President Clinton?

Clinton's Foreign Policy

S

Main Idea During Clinton's second term, the United States became more involved in world events.

Reading Connection When and why was NATO created? Read on to find out how the United States and NATO worked to resolve a crisis in southeastern Europe.

While attracting worldwide attention, the impeachment drama did not affect world affairs. The collapse of the Soviet Union virtually ended the struggle between communism and democracy, but small bloody wars continued to erupt around the world. On several occasions President Clinton used force to bring an end to regional conflicts.

The Haitian Intervention In 1991 military leaders in Haiti overthrew Jean Bertrand Aristide, the country's first democratically elected president in many decades. Aristide sought refuge in the United States. The new rulers of Haiti used violence, even murder, to suppress the opposition. Seeking to restore democracy, the Clinton administration convinced the United Nations to impose a trade embargo on Haiti. The embargo created a severe economic crisis in that country. Thousands of Haitian refugees fled to the United States in small boats, and many died at sea.

Determined to put an end to the crisis, Clinton ordered an invasion of Haiti. Before the troops arrived, however, former president Jimmy Carter convinced Haiti's rulers to step aside.

Peacekeeping in Bosnia and Kosovo The United States also was concerned about mounting tensions in southeastern Europe. During the Cold War, Yugoslavia had been a single federated nation made up of many different ethnic groups under a strong Communist government. In 1991, after the collapse of communism, Yugoslavia split apart.

In Bosnia, one of the former Yugoslav republics, a vicious three-way civil war erupted between Orthodox Christian Serbs, Catholic Croatians, and Bosnian Muslims. Despite international pressure, the fighting continued until 1995. The Serbs began what they called **ethnic cleansing**—the brutal expulsion of an ethnic group from a geographic area. In some cases, Serbian troops slaughtered the Muslims instead of moving them.

The United States convinced its NATO allies that military action was necessary. NATO war-planes attacked the Serbs in Bosnia, forcing them to negotiate. The Clinton administration then arranged peace talks in Dayton, Ohio. The participants signed a peace plan known as the **Dayton Accords.** In 1996 some 60,000 NATO troops, including 20,000 Americans, entered Bosnia to enforce the plan.

In 1998 another war erupted, this time within the Serbian province of Kosovo. Kosovo has two major ethnic groups—Serbs and Albanians. Many of the Albanians wanted Kosovo to separate from Serbia. To keep Kosovo in Serbia, Serbian leader Slobodan Milosevic ordered a crackdown. The Albanians then organized their own army to fight back. Worried by reports of Serbian violence against Albanian civilians, President Clinton convinced European leaders that NATO should again use force to stop the fighting. In March 1999, NATO began bombing Serbia. The bombing convinced Serbia to pull its troops out of Kosovo.

Did You Know?

Some presidents continue to be involved in international politics after they leave the White House. Since leaving the White House in 1980, Jimmy Carter has worked to negotiate many international conflicts around the world. The Carter Center, founded in 1982, helped to foster conflict resolutions in such countries as Haiti, Liberia, North Korea, Ecuador, Estonia, and many other nations.

Peacemaking in the Middle East

Despite the overwhelming defeat Iraq suffered in the Persian Gulf War, Iraqi President Saddam Hussein remained in power and continued to make threats against Iraq's neighbors. Hussein's threats eventually escalated into action. In 1996 Iraq attacked the Kurds, an ethnic group whose homeland lies in northern Iraq. To stop the attacks, the United States fired cruise missiles at Iraqi military targets.

Relations between Israel and the Palestinians were even more volatile. Many believed progress was being made in achieving peace. In 1993 Israeli Prime Minister Yitzhak Rabin and Palestine Liberation Organization leader Yasir Arafat reached an agreement. The PLO recognized Israel's right to exist, and Israel recognized the PLO as the representative of the Palestinians. President Clinton then invited Arafat and Rabin to the White House, where they signed the Declaration of Principles—a plan for creating a Palestinian government.

Opposition to the peace plan emerged on both sides. Radical Palestinians exploded bombs in Israel and in 1995 a right-wing Israeli assassinated Prime Minister Rabin.

In 1998 Israeli and Palestinian leaders met with President Clinton at the Wye River plantation in Maryland to work out details of the withdrawal of Israeli troops from the West Bank and the Gaza Strip. This agreement, however, failed to settle the status of Jerusalem, which both sides claimed.

In July 2000, President Clinton invited Arafat and Israeli Prime Minister Ehud Barak to reach an agreement, but these talks failed. Beginning in October, violence started to break out between Palestinians and Israeli soldiers. The region was as far from peace as ever.

Picturing **History**

Middle East Conflict The struggle over control of the Israeli/Palestinian areas intensified in the 1990s. Although President Clinton directed many negotiations to attempt to resolve the conflict, the region remained a very dangerous place. Which leaders agreed to a framework for peace in 1993?

Clinton Leaves Office

As he prepared to leave office, President Clinton's legacy was uncertain. He had balanced the budget and presided over the greatest period of economic growth in American history. Clinton's presidency was marred, however, by the impeachment trial, which had divided the nation and widened the divide between liberals and conservatives. In the election of 2000, that division would lead to the closest election in American history.

✓ **Reading Check** **Identifying** In what three regions of the world did Clinton use force to support his foreign policy?

Study Central

For help with the concepts in this section of *American Vision: Modern Times* go to tav.mt.glencoe.com and click on *Study Central.*

ASSESS

Resources for page 941

Use these resources to assess student mastery.

📁 Section Quiz 21-2

📁 Reading Essentials and Study Guide 21-2

⦿ Interactive Tutor Self-Assessment CD-ROM

📁 California Standards Practice, Grade 11

Picturing **History**

Answer: Yitzhak Rabin and Yasir Arafat

Ask: What did the Declaration of Principles accomplish? *(It created a plan for a Palestinian government.)*

✓ **Reading Check**

Answer: in southeastern Europe (Bosnia and Kosovo); in the Middle East (Iraq); was prepared to use force in Latin America (Haiti) but the crisis ended peacefully

Study Central provides audio summaries, interactive games, and online graphic organizers to help students review section content.

SECTION 2 ASSESSMENT

Checking for Understanding

1. **Vocabulary** Define: modify, stress, submit, perjury, ethnic cleansing.
2. **People and Terms** Identify: AmeriCorps, Contract with America, Kenneth Starr, Dayton Accords.
3. **Explain** why the federal government shut down in 1995.

Reviewing Big Ideas

4. **Evaluating** What government policies helped create the U.S. prosperity of the 1990s?

Critical Thinking

5. **Analyzing** Why was President Clinton able to win reelection in 1996?
6. **Categorizing** Complete a chart similar to the one below by explaining the foreign policy issues facing President Clinton in each of the areas listed.

Region	Issue
Latin America	
Southeastern Europe	
Middle East	

Analyzing Visuals

7. **Analyzing Photographs** Study the photographs on page 939 of Clinton's impeachment trial. What elements in the photograph reflect the seriousness of the occasion?

Writing About History

8. **Persuasive Writing** Take on the role of a member of Congress. Write a letter in which you attempt to persuade other lawmakers to vote either for or against the impeachment of President Clinton. Provide reasons for your position.
CA 11WS1.1

CHAPTER 21 Into a New Century **941**

CLOSE

Summary Writing Despite the Oslo agreement, violence escalated. Have students write three-page reports about the events since the agreement. **AL**
CA 11WS1.3

SECTION 2 ASSESSMENT ANSWERS

1. Content vocabulary is boldfaced and highlighted in yellow. Academic vocabulary is boldfaced.
2. AmeriCorps *(p. 937)*, Contract With America *(p. 937)*, Kenneth Starr *(p. 940)*, Dayton Accords *(p. 940)*
3. A budget impasse between Congress and Clinton led to a government shutdown.
4. a reduced federal deficit and lower interest rates
5. Americans' desire to continue the economic boom
6. Latin America: Haiti's democratically elected president overthrown; Southeastern Europe: ethnic cleansing in Bosnia and Kosovo; Middle East: tensions between Israel and the Palestinians, and Iraqi attacks on Kurds
7. Possible answers: people's somber expressions, Clinton's bowed head
8. Students' letters should express a clear point of view.

941

FOCUS

Project **Daily Focus Skills Transparency 21-3** and have students answer the question.

Guide to Reading

Understanding Vocabulary: Have students create a database for the academic vocabulary words and the content vocabulary words. Encourage them to enter additional words, terms, and names as they read this section.

Answers to Graphic: global warming, international trade, nuclear proliferation, terrorism, world economy

Unpacking the Standards

Students will be able to:

• Explain the development of regional economic blocs around the world.

• Assess environmental issues that have become important internationally.

SECTION **3** An Interdependent World

Guide to Reading

Connection
In the previous section, you learned about the Clinton administration. In this section, you will discover how the world became increasingly interdependent.

Main Idea
• Regional trade agreements, such as the North American Free Trade Agreement (NAFTA), became common in an increasingly interdependent world. (p. 943)
• Concerns about nuclear proliferation and the environment led to efforts to reduce nuclear weapons and pollution. (p. 945)

Content Vocabulary
trade deficit, euro, nuclear proliferation, global warming

Academic Vocabulary
currency, cite, phase

Terms to Identify
North American Free Trade Agreement, Kyoto Protocol

Reading Objectives
• **Explain** the development of regional economic blocs around the world.
• **Assess** environmental issues that have become important internationally.

Reading Strategy
Organizing Complete a graphic organizer like the one below to chart the major political and economic problems facing the world at the turn of the century.

Global Concerns

Preview of Events

♦1992	♦1995	♦1998	♦2001
1993 European Union launched	**1994** United States, Mexico, and Canada inaugurate NAFTA	**1995** Oklahoma City bombing	**1998** Terrorist bombings in Kenya and Tanzania	**2000** U.S. gives permanent trade status to China

The following are the main History–Social Science Standards covered in this section.

11.9.7 Examine relations between the United States and Mexico in the twentieth century, including key economic, political, immigration, and environmental issues.

11.11.5 Trace the impact of, need for, and controversies associated with environmental conservation, expansion of the national park system, and the development of environmental protection laws, with particular attention to the interaction between environmental protection advocates and property right advocates.

~ The Big Idea ~

International competition can lead to conflict and cooperation. Computer technology and the Internet played an important role in creating an interdependent world and a global economy. While the United States accumulated trade deficits, trade relations between countries became more important and trade agreements between countries more common. The United States entered into a major trade pact with Mexico and Canada and increased trade with China. Concerns about nuclear proliferation, ozone depletion, and global warming led to new legislation and international discussions.

Answers and Additional Support

SECTION RESOURCES

Print Material
• Reproducible Lesson Plan 21-3
• Guided Reading Activity 21-3
• Reading Essentials and Study Guide 21-3
• Active Reading Note-Taking Guide 21-3

Transparencies
• Daily Focus Skills Transparency 21-3
• Section Graphic Organizer Transparency 21-3

Technology
⊙ Interactive Tutor Self-Assessment CD-ROM
⊙ ExamView® Pro Testmaker CD-ROM
⊙ Presentation Plus! CD-ROM

The New Global Economy

Main Idea Regional trade agreements, such as the North American Free Trade Agreement (NAFTA), became common in an increasingly interdependent world.

Reading Connection Do you think tariffs directly affect you? Read on to learn about one alternative to tariffs.

In the latter part of the 1900s, American leaders became more concerned with many global issues. Economies around the world had become much more interdependent. Computer technology and the Internet played a big role in forging a global economy.

★ An American Story ★

It was an important breakthrough when President Clinton appointed Madeleine Albright in 1996 to be the first woman to serve as secretary of state. Born in Czechoslovakia, Albright immigrated to the United States as a young girl. She earned a Ph.D. in Russian studies from Columbia University. Her tough-talking approach as U.S. ambassador to the United Nations earned her the nation's top foreign policy job.

As secretary of state, Albright dealt with everything from peace negotiations in the Middle East to improving trade relations with China. She also championed women's rights in developing countries. Here, she expresses her views on women's rights:

❝[Halting violence against women] is a goal of American foreign policy around the world, where abuses range from domestic violence . . . to forcing young girls into prostitution. Some say all this is cultural, and there's nothing we can do about it. I say it's criminal, and we each have a responsibility to stop it.❞

—quoted in *Madeleine Albright and the New American Diplomacy*

Working on improved trade relations became an important task for Albright and other cabinet members. Selling American-made goods abroad had long been important to American prosperity. By the 1970s, however, serious **trade deficits** had mounted—Americans purchased more from foreign nations than American industry and agriculture sold abroad. The United States found it necessary to compete harder in the global marketplace by streamlining industry, using new technology, and opening new markets.

R From World War II to the present, Republican and Democratic administrations have both tried to lower barriers to international trade. They reasoned that the U.S. economy benefited from the sale of American exports, and that the purchase of imports would keep consumer prices, inflation, and interest rates low for Americans. Opponents warned that the global economy might cost the United States industrial jobs as manufacturing shifted to lesser-developed nations with few environmental regulations and cheap labor. By the 1990s, the debate between supporters of free trade and those who wanted to limit trade to protect industries had become an important part of American politics.

Regional Blocs One means of increasing international trade was to create regional trade pacts. In 1994 the **North American Free Trade Agreement** (NAFTA) joined Canada, the United States, and Mexico in a free-trade zone. With NAFTA in operation, exports of American goods to both Canada and Mexico rose dramatically. From 1993 to 2000, it is estimated that combined exports to those two countries rose from $142 to $290 billion, an increase of 104 percent.

Madeleine Albright ▼

CHAPTER 21 Into a New Century **943**

C Critical Thinking

Scaffolding—Analyzing Economic Behavior On January 1, 2002, the euro replaced the old national currencies of most EU states. Have students find the exchange rate of the U.S. dollar and the euro then and now and compare the two. **Ask:** What does the comparative value of the euro and the dollar tell you about the relative strength of the two regional economies? *(Students' answers should accurately interpret the data they uncover.)* **AL** **CA HI6**

This **Historical Analysis** skill was introduced in Chapter 8.

R Reading Strategy

Scaffolding—Academic Vocabulary The word *community* was introduced in Chapter 9, Section 3. Ask a student to define the word. **BL**

W Writing Support

Research Report Writing The World Trade Organization (WTO) has been the focal point for many protests against globalization. Have students research and write a two-page report showing the goals of recent WTO protests and assessing if these protests caused any changes in the behavior of the WTO member states. **OL** **CA 11WA2.4d**

Answers and Additional Support

One concern of many Americans was that industrial jobs would go to Mexico, where labor costs were lower. Although some jobs were lost to Mexico, unemployment rates in the United States fell during this period and wages rose. Many American businesses upgraded their technology, and workers shifted to more skilled jobs or to the service industry.

NAFTA faced competing regional trade blocs in Europe and Asia. In 1993 the European Union (EU) was created to promote economic and political cooperation among many European nations. The EU created a common bank and the **euro,** a common **currency** for member nations. The organization also removed trade barriers between its members and set policies on imports from nations outside the community.

EU rules tended to favor imports from the European nations' former colonies in Asia, Africa, and the Pacific over competing products from the United States. The EU also banned scientifically modified food, such as hormone-treated beef from the United States. American exporters argued that hormones were a safe way to accelerate livestock growth rates and produce leaner meat. They protested that European fears lacked a scientific basis.

The Asia Pacific Economic Cooperation (APEC) was an attempt to create a Pacific trade community to rival the European Union. APEC represented the fastest-growing region in the world and controlled 47 percent of global trade in 2001. APEC began as a forum to promote economic cooperation and lower trade barriers, but major political differences kept its members from acting together.

The World Trade Organization Central to the effort to promote a global economy was the World Trade Organization (WTO). The WTO administered international trade agreements and helped settle trade disputes. American supporters of the WTO **cited** benefits for U.S. consumers, including cheaper imports, new markets, and copyright protection for the American entertainment industry. On the other hand, the United States had no veto power in the WTO and poorer nations could outvote it.

Picturing **History**

A Busy Border NAFTA greatly increased trade across the Texas-Mexico border (below). It also led to the building of foreign-owned factories, known as *maquiladoras,* in Mexico near the American border to take advantage of low Mexican wages. The *maquiladora* pictured at right is located in Tijuana. How did NAFTA affect both the United States and Mexico?

Picturing **History**

Answer: U.S. unemployment fell and wages rose as workers shifted to more skilled jobs or to the service industry. U.S. exports to Mexico rose and Mexico gained jobs.
Ask: Why did Americans fear losing jobs to Mexico rather than to Canada? *(Possible answer: Workers feared that their jobs would be lost to low-wage workers in Mexico.)*

Resources for page 944

Have students read more about the mixing of cultures in the late twentieth century by assigning "My Native Costume" in the American Literature Readings 6.

NATIONAL GEOGRAPHIC
MOMENT in HISTORY

TERRORISM IN THE HEARTLAND

A couple comforts each other after placing flowers on one of the 168 chairs that form part of the Oklahoma City National Memorial. The site was dedicated on April 19, 2000—five years to the day after Timothy McVeigh detonated a massive bomb outside the Alfred P. Murrah Federal Building in downtown Oklahoma City. Most of the 168 killed and hundreds injured were government employees, but 19 children attending a day-care facility in the building also died in the blast. A jury found McVeigh guilty, and he was executed in 2001.

Trade With China China played an increasingly important role in world trade. Its huge population offered vast potential as a market for American goods. Many Americans, however, had strong reservations about China's record on human rights, and they worried about its threats to invade Taiwan. These Americans were wary of negotiating a trade agreement with China. Despite these concerns, President Clinton argued that regularizing trade with China would help bring it into the world community.

After negotiating a new trade agreement, Clinton pressed Congress to grant China permanent normal trade relation status. Those opposing the bill were an unusual coalition. Labor unions were concerned that inexpensive Chinese goods would flood U.S. markets; conservatives objected to China's military ambitions; and environmentalists worried about pollution from Chinese factories. Despite their opposition, the bill passed in late 2000.

Reading Check **Explaining** Why was the European Union (EU) created in 1993?

Issues of Global Concern

Main Idea Concerns about nuclear proliferation and the environment led to efforts to reduce nuclear weapons and pollution.

Reading Connection Are there groups in your school or area working to improve the environment? Read on to learn about efforts to reduce damage to the environment.

Although the end of the Cold War had reduced the threat of nuclear war between the United States and the Soviet Union, it increased fears that nuclear weapons might fall into the wrong hands. Equally worrisome were efforts by several nations, including Pakistan, North Korea, and Iraq, to acquire nuclear weapons and long-range missiles. In the 1980s, nations also began to be concerned about the environment.

Nuclear Proliferation During the Cold War, only a few nations had possessed nuclear weapons, and they tried to restrict the spread of nuclear technology

CHAPTER 21   Into a New Century   **945**

NATIONAL GEOGRAPHIC MOMENT in HISTORY

The Oklahoma City National Memorial includes 168 chairs, one for each victim, in 9 rows, one for each floor of the destroyed building. Each chair is made of bronze and stone and is on a lighted glass base etched with a victim's name.

ASSESS

Resources for page 946

Use these resources to assess student mastery.

📁 Section Quiz 21-3

📁 Reading Essentials and Study Guide 21-3

⦿ Interactive Tutor Self-Assessment CD-ROM

📁 California Standards Practice, Grade 11

✔ **Reading Check**

Answer: a layer of gas in the atmosphere; protects Earth from the sun's cancer-causing ultraviolet rays

HISTORY Online

Study Central provides audio summaries, interactive games, and online graphic organizers to help students review section content.

CLOSE

Summarizing Have students list the environmental issues that have become important globally.

BL

Answers and Additional Support

---

to other countries. When Russia agreed to reduce its nuclear arsenal, concerns arose that some of its nuclear weapons or radioactive material could be lost, stolen, or sold on the black market. In response, the United States provided funds to Russia to assist in the reduction of its nuclear stockpile.

Other measures followed to reduce the threat of **nuclear proliferation,** or the spread of nuclear weapons to new nations. Congress passed legislation that cut aid and imposed sanctions on nations seeking to acquire nuclear weapons. In 1996 President Clinton also signed the Comprehensive Nuclear Test Ban Treaty, but the U.S. Senate refused to ratify it fearing it would limit American nuclear research.

Concern About Ozone In the 1980s, scientists discovered that chemicals called chlorofluorocarbons (CFCs) had the potential to deplete the earth's atmosphere of ozone. Ozone is a gas in the atmosphere that protects life on Earth from the cancer-causing ultraviolet rays of the sun. At that time, CFCs were widely used in air conditioners and refrigerators. Many environmental activists began to push for a ban on CFC production. In the late 1980s, public awareness of the ozone issue increased dramatically when stories appeared documenting a large ozone "hole" over Antarctica. In 1987 the United States and 22 other nations agreed to **phase** out the production of CFCs and other chemicals that might be weakening the ozone layer.

Global Warming In the early 1990s, another global environmental issue developed when some scientists found evidence of **global warming**—an increase in average world temperatures over time. Such a rise in

temperature could eventually lead to more droughts and other forms of extreme weather. A furious debate is now underway among scientists over how to measure changes in the earth's temperature and what the results mean.

Many experts believe carbon dioxide emissions from factories and power plants cause global warming, but others disagree. Some question whether global warming even exists. The issue is very controversial because the cost of controlling emissions would affect the global economy. Industries would have to pay the cost of further reducing emissions, and those costs would eventually be passed on to consumers. Developing nations trying to industrialize would be hurt the most, but economic growth in wealthier nations would be hurt, too.

Concern about global warming led to an international conference in Kyoto, Japan, in 1997. Thirty-eight nations and the EU signed the **Kyoto Protocol** promising to reduce emissions, but very few put it into effect. President Clinton did not submit the Kyoto Protocol to the Senate for ratification because most senators were opposed to it. In 2001 President George W. Bush withdrew the United States from the Kyoto Protocol, citing flaws in the treaty. As the 2000s began, Americans struggled to balance economic progress with environmental concerns.

✔ **Reading Check** **Identifying** What is the ozone layer, and why is it important?

HISTORY Online — Study Central

For help with the concepts in this section of *American Vision: Modern Times* go to tav.mt.glencoe.com and click on *Study Central.*

SECTION 3 ASSESSMENT

Checking for Understanding

1. **Vocabulary** Define: trade deficit, euro, currency, cite, nuclear proliferation, phase, global warming.
2. **People and Terms** Identify: North American Free Trade Agreement, Kyoto Protocol.
3. **Describe** the international response to concerns about global warming.

Reviewing Big Ideas

4. **Explaining** Why was China an important factor in world trade?

Critical Thinking

5. **Analyzing** Do you think the new global economy has helped or hurt the United States?
6. **Organizing** Complete a graphic organizer similar to the one below by listing and describing the regional trade blocs that formed in the 1990s.

Regional Trade Blocs

Analyzing Visuals

7. **Analyzing Photographs** Study the photograph on page 945 of the Oklahoma City National Memorial. What do the empty chairs represent? How has the memorial helped relatives of the victims?

Writing About History

8. **Expository Writing** Decide which issue of global concern today is the most serious. In an essay, explain why you think it is the most serious problem, and provide some possible solutions.
   CA 11WA2.3a; 11WA2.3b

SECTION 3 ASSESSMENT ANSWERS

1. Content vocabulary is boldfaced and highlighted in yellow. Academic vocabulary is boldfaced.
2. North American Free trade Agreement (p. 943), Kyoto Protocol (p. 946)
3. The Kyoto Protocol pledged to reduce emissions, but the United States did not sign it. Few of the 39 countries that signed it have implemented any plans.
4. China's population provides a huge market for imported goods.
5. Students' answers will vary. Encourage students to provide reasons for their opinions.
6. NAFTA increased trade among Canada, Mexico, and the United States; EU promoted economic and political cooperation among European nations; APEC created a Pacific trade bloc.
7. bombing victims; answers should focus on the need to remember
8. Students' essays should clearly identify the issue.

SECTION 4

America Enters a New Century

Guide to Reading

Connection
In the previous section, you learned about the increasingly interdependent world. In this section, you will find out about the close presidential election of 2000.

Main Idea
• One of the closest and most contested races for the presidency led to a Supreme Court decision in favor of George W. Bush. (p. 948)
• Bush focused on stimulating the economy, reforming education, and promoting strategic defense in the early months of his presidency. (p. 950)

Content Vocabulary
chad, strategic defense

Academic Vocabulary
final

People to Identify
Al Gore, George W. Bush, Ralph Nader

Reading Objectives
• **Describe** the unusual circumstances surrounding the outcome of the 2000 presidential election.

• **Evaluate** the programs President George W. Bush initiated.

Reading Strategy
Organizing As you read about the 2000 presidential election, complete a graphic organizer similar to the one below by charting the key post-election events culminating in George W. Bush's victory.

☐ → ☐ → ☐ → Bush's Victory

Preview of Events

◆ Aug. 2000	◆ Dec. 2000	◆ Mar. 2001	◆ June 2001

August 2000
Republicans nominate Bush; Democrats nominate Gore

November 2000
Election takes place; recounts begin in Florida

December 2000
Gore concedes election to Bush

January 2001
George W. Bush inaugurated as president

June 2001
Bush signs tax cut bill into law

The following are the main History–Social Science Standards covered in this section.

11.11 Students analyze the major social problems and domestic policy issues in contemporary American society.

⌘ The Big Idea ⌘

Societies change over time. In the presidential election of 2000, Republican George W. Bush faced Vice President Al Gore and Green Party candidate Ralph Nader. The close election results in Florida led to a Supreme Court decision over a recount. While Gore won the popular vote, Bush became president based on the electoral votes. The president focused on cutting taxes and introducing health-care and education reforms. The government improved accounting regulations after a number of corporate scandals rocked the country. Bush also looked at ways to prepare the military for the post-Cold War world.

CHAPTER 21   Into a New Century   **947**

BELLRINGER
SKILLBUILDER ACTIVITY

Project **Daily Focus Skills Transparency 21-4** and have students answer the question.

Guide to Reading

Understanding Vocabulary:
Have students prepare a set of study cards with each content vocabulary term or academic vocabulary term on one side of the card and significant facts or definitions on the other side.

Answers to Graphic:
Recounts begin in Florida; Florida Supreme Court extends deadline for recount; U.S. Supreme Court rules in *Bush* v. *Gore* that recount in Florida is unconstitutional

Unpacking the Standards

Students will be able to:

• Discuss the outcome of the 2000 presidential election.

• Analyze the early goals of the George W. Bush administration.

SECTION RESOURCES

📖 Print Material
• Reproducible Lesson Plan 21-4
• Guided Reading Activity 21-4
• Reading Essentials and Study Guide 21-4
• Active Reading Note-Taking Guide 21-4

📄 Transparencies
• Daily Focus Skills Transparency 21-4
• Section Graphic Organizer Transparency 21-4

Technology
🖲 Interactive Tutor Self-Assessment CD-ROM
🖲 ExamView® Pro Testmaker CD-ROM
🖲 Presentation Plus! CD-ROM

TEACH

R₁ Reading Strategy

Scaffolding—Academic Vocabulary The word *perspective* was introduced in Chapter 12, Section 3. Ask a student to define the word. **BL**

R₂ Reading Strategy

Summarizing Ralph Nader ran in the 2000 election as the nominee of the Green Party. **Ask: What kinds of issues are important to the Green Party?** *(the environment, consumer rights, power of large corporations)* **Did Nader's candidacy affect the election?** *(He may have taken some votes away from Gore.)* **OL**

C Critical Thinking

Making Generalizations Ask students to use library and Internet resources to research other close elections in U.S. history. *(1800, 1877, and 1960)* **Ask: Can you identify any common characteristics between these presidential elections and the 2000 election?** *(Answers will vary; students may note that most of these elections were controversial.)* **AL**

Answers and Additional Support

948

A New President for a New Century

Main Idea One of the closest and most contested races for the presidency led to a Supreme Court decision in favor of George W. Bush.

Reading Connection Do you think the Electoral College needs to be modified or eliminated? Read on to find out how electoral votes affected the 2000 election.

The close election of 2000 was, in some ways, another legacy of Bill Clinton's years in power. Clinton's presidency had left the country deeply divided. Many people were pleased with the economy but disappointed with the president's personal behavior.

★ An American Story ★

The 2000 presidential election was very close. Two candidates battled over the Electoral College votes of one state—Florida. The election remained undecided for over a month. Though this election was a spectacle of demonstrations and ballot evaluations, some people tried to put it all in perspective. May Akabogu-Collins, an American citizen originally from Nigeria, contrasted the "turmoil" and "chaos" of the election with the transfer of power in other parts of the world:

❝America should be grateful that this election was as wild as it gets. Some of us originally came from places where heads would have rolled during a similar crisis. So far, not a gunshot has been heard on account of the balloting, and you call this 'wild'? An election held in Nigeria in 1993 led to the President-elect's being thrown in jail for trying to assume office and ultimately to his mysterious death. Going to court to decide who won this contest is, in my opinion, as civilized as it gets.❞

—quoted in *Time,* December 11, 2000

Long before the election, both Republicans and Democrats tried to find candidates who would appeal to a broad cross-section of society.

The 2000 Campaign Democrats nominated Vice President **Al Gore.** To demonstrate his independence, Gore chose as his running mate Senator Joseph Lieberman, who had been outspokenly critical of President Clinton's conduct in office. Republicans

selected Texas governor **George W. Bush,** son of the former president. To compensate for his inexperience in foreign and defense policy, Bush selected for his running mate former secretary of defense Richard Cheney.

The prosperity of the 1990s had turned the federal budget deficit into a large surplus in tax revenue. Both Bush and Gore promised to cut taxes, but Bush proposed a much larger tax cut than Gore. Instead of a large tax cut, Gore said he would set aside funds to strengthen Social Security. Both candidates pledged to improve public education and to support plans to help seniors pay for prescription drugs. In addition, Bush promised to restore dignity to the White House.

Frustrated by the similarities between Bush and Gore, well-known consumer advocate **Ralph Nader** entered the race as the nominee of the Green Party. Nader was critical of the power of corporations and accused both Bush and Gore of being dependent on campaign funds from large companies. Nader received less than 3 percent of the popular vote, but he still cut into Gore's margin in several states.

A Close Vote The 2000 election turned into one of the closest in American history. Gore narrowly won the popular vote, 48.4 percent to 47.9 percent for Bush. To win the presidency, however, candidates have to win a majority of state electoral votes, not the overall popular vote.

Neither Gore nor Bush had the 270 electoral votes needed to win. The election came down to the Florida vote—both men needed its 25 electoral votes.

The results in Florida were so close that state law required a recount of the ballots using vote-counting machines. Thousands of ballots were thrown out,

May Akabogu-Collins ▼

Did You Know?

Traditionally former presidents retain the title of "president." George W. Bush and his father, however, are both called President Bush. Some Bush family members affectionately call the men "41" and "43," because George Bush was the forty-first president and George W. Bush is the forty-third president.

A controversial punch ballot from West Palm Beach, Florida

The Florida Election, 2000

Bars represent the number of votes by which Bush led in Florida, in 15-minute intervals.

Gore has lead for 15 minutes. AP, networks call him winner of Florida.

Over next two hours, Bush lead builds to nearly 150,000 votes.

Florida called "undecided" around 10:30 P.M. Bush lead soon begins to shrink.

Networks call Bush winner in Florida—and president-elect—just after 2:15 A.M.

Bush's lead shrinks to **1,655 votes;** state again called a toss-up.

Gore declared winner
Winner undecided
Bush declared winner

Source: *Associated Press.*

---

however, because the counting machines were not able to read them accurately.

After the machine recount showed Bush slightly ahead, a battle began over a manual recount requested by Gore in several counties. Most Florida ballots required voters to punch a hole. The little piece of cardboard punched out of a ballot is called a **chad.** The problem for vote counters was how to count a ballot when the chad was still partially attached. On some, the chad was still in place, and the voter had left only a dimple on the surface of the ballot. Vote counters had to determine what the voter intended—and different counties used different standards.

When it became clear that the recount could not be finished in time to meet the deadline set by Florida law, Gore went to court to overturn the deadline. The Florida Supreme Court agreed to set a new deadline. Bush appealed to the U.S. Supreme Court. Meanwhile, on November 26, Florida officials certified Bush the winner by 537 votes.

Bush v. Gore Although Bush had been declared the winner in Florida, the state's supreme court ordered all Florida counties to begin a hand recount of ballots rejected by the counting machines. As counting began, the United States Supreme Court ordered the recount to stop until it had issued its ruling.

On December 12, in *Bush* v. *Gore,* the U.S. Supreme Court ruled 7–2 that the hand recounts in Florida violated the equal protection clause of the Constitution. The Court argued that because different vote counters used different standards, the recount did not treat all voters equally. The U.S. Supreme Court also ruled 5–4 that there was not enough time to conduct a manual recount. Federal law requires all electoral votes to be cast on a certain day. If Florida missed that deadline, its electoral votes would not count, and Gore would be the winner. This ruling left Bush the certified winner. *(See page 1004 for more information on Bush v. Gore.)*

Reading Check **Analyzing** Why did the U.S. Supreme Court stop the manual recounts in Florida?

S Skill Practice

Conducting Research Inform students that since the 2000 election and the problems with ballots, many states have moved toward electronic systems for voting, like the touch-screen system. Divide the class into four groups, and ask each group to collect information from multiple sources about new systems used for voting, including touch-screens and optical scanners. Students should evaluate their effectiveness and whether they are more reliable and less susceptible to fraud when compared to more traditional paper ballots. Have students prepare oral presentations to report their research and evaluations. **OL** **CA HR4**

R Reading Strategy

Connecting Tell students that some comedians joked after the 2000 election that Cuban leader Fidel Castro offered to send election observers to the next U.S. election. **Ask:** Why is that statement funny? *(Students may comment that the Communist government in Cuba does not have open elections; also election observers from the United States sometimes watch elections in countries where there is suspicion of fraud in order to keep the elections in those countries honest and fair.)* **AL**

Reading Check

Answer: The Supreme Court ruled that it violated the equal protection clause of the Constitution.

Picturing History

Answer: Florida
Ask: Approximately how large was Bush's lead at midnight? *(about 130,000 votes)*

Spatial Thinking Some analysts who examined the 2000 presidential election results argue that the nation is divided between the red states, in the South and the Great Plains, and the blue states, in the Northeast, upper Midwest, and West Coast. Have students examine the map of the 2000 election. **Ask:** Do you think division between the red states and blue states is true? What would explain such a division? *(Encourage students to present reasoned arguments; responses may indicate a belief in regional differences around issues concerning sex, religion, and morality.)* **OL** **CA** CS3; CS4

Review the Big Idea

Review the Big Idea for this section, "Societies change over time." Students should read the information on this page about the effects of the Bush administration's tax cut. Tell students to write a two-page report that describes how they think the tax cut was intended to work and that assesses its effectiveness. **AL** **CA** 11WS1.3

Bush Becomes President

Main Idea Bush focused on stimulating the economy, reforming education, and promoting strategic defense in the early months of his presidency.

Reading Connection Have the new policies in education affected the testing process in your school? Read on to learn about President Bush's education reforms.

On January 20, 2001, George W. Bush became the 43rd president of the United States. In his inaugural address, Bush promised to improve the nation's public schools, to cut taxes, to reform Social Security and Medicare, and to build up the nation's defenses.

Cutting Taxes After taking office, the president's first priority was to cut taxes to try to boost the economy. During the election campaign, the economy had begun to slow. The stock market dropped sharply, and many new Internet-based companies went out of business. Other businesses laid off thousands of workers. Despite opposition from some Democrats, Congress passed a large $1.35 trillion tax cut to be phased in over 10 years. In the summer of 2001, Americans began receiving tax rebate checks. The president hoped people would spend this money, thus putting about $40 billion back into the economy and preventing a recession.

The tax cuts did not stimulate the economy as greatly as the president had hoped. Also, while tax revenue declined, federal spending increased, which drained the economy until the budget surplus turned to a record-high deficit. This reduced the financial resources available to the federal government to deal with expanding demands on Social Security and Medicare as the large baby-boom generation began reaching retirement age.

Education and Health Reforms In both the Senate and the House of Representatives, Republicans and Democrats were almost evenly divided, and partisanship was intense. On many issues and nominations, Congress was stalemated. Still, the president did manage to score some legislative victories.

In education, President Bush wanted to allow parents to use federal funds to provide vouchers for private schools if their public schools were doing a poor job. Congress, however, refused to give federal funds to private schools. Bush was more successful in persuading Congress to vote in favor of annual reading and math tests in public schools for grades 3 through 8, a program known as "No Child Left Behind." Some members of Congress supported this program with the understanding that the government would increase funding to public schools to help them meet the new standards. They protested when budget deficits caused President Bush to cut funds for his own education programs.

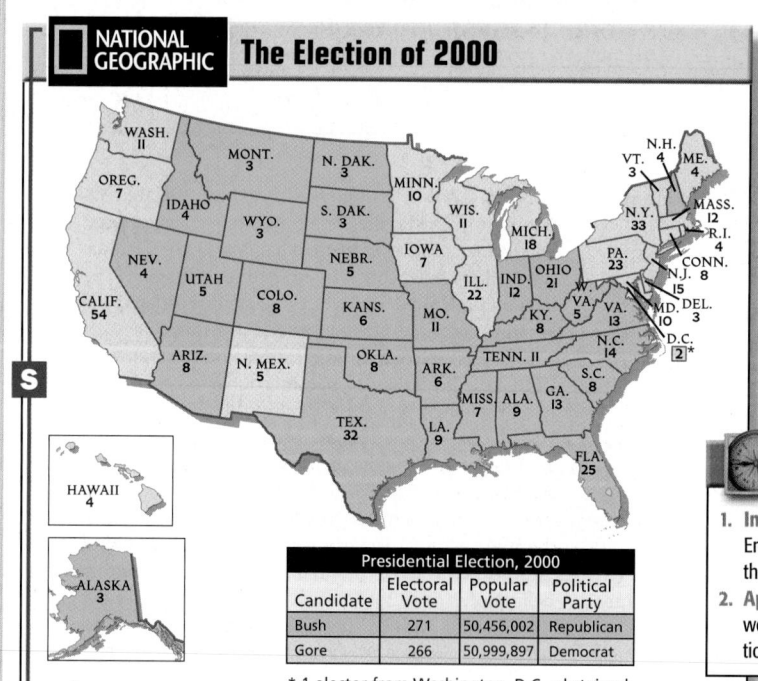

NATIONAL GEOGRAPHIC **The Election of 2000**

Presidential Election, 2000			
Candidate	Electoral Vote	Popular Vote	Political Party
Bush	271	50,456,002	Republican
Gore	266	50,999,897	Democrat

* 1 elector from Washington, D.C., abstained.

Geography *Skills*

1. **Interpreting Maps** Which single New England state did George W. Bush win in the election?
2. **Applying Geography Skills** Though Gore won less than half of the states, the election was extremely close. Why?

Answers and Additional Support

Geography *Skills*

Answers:
1. New Hampshire
2. There were a large number of electoral votes in the states Gore won.

Geography Skills Practice
Ask: Which candidate won the popular and electoral votes in Bush's home state of Texas and Gore's home state of Tennessee? *(Bush won both states.)*

In health care, the president endorsed legislation providing prescription drug benefits for senior citizens. The bill was mired in controversy until it was **finally** passed in November 2003. Passage of the bill by a single vote in the House of Representatives was a major achievement for the administration. The bill provided for the biggest overhaul of Medicare since its creation in 1965. Liberal critics of the plan argued that it made too many concessions to the pharmaceutical industry. They thought it restricted the government's ability to negotiate to buy medicines in bulk and individuals' ability to import cheaper prescription drugs from Canada. Some conservatives expressed dismay that the prescription drug bill had created another expensive entitlement program without a plan to pay for it.

Congress also reacted to a rash of corporate scandals. In one of the most flagrant cases, corporate leaders at the large energy trading company, Enron, cost investors and employees billions of dollars before the company went bankrupt. The federal government tightened accounting regulations and toughened penalties for dishonest executives.

Rethinking America's Defenses Shortly after taking office, President Bush asked for a comprehensive review of the nation's military. The president wanted to increase military spending, but he also wanted new military programs designed to meet the needs of the post–Cold War world.

His secretary of defense, Donald Rumsfeld, favored the use of light forces—small, mobile units that could be deployed swiftly as circumstances required. He believed that superior air power and missile strikes would reduce the need for large numbers of combat troops on the ground in potential conflicts in the future.

▲ *Secretary of Defense Donald Rumsfeld*

President Bush also favored **strategic defense**—the effort to develop missiles and other devices that could shoot down nuclear missiles. Bush argued that missile defense was needed because many unfriendly nations were developing the technology to build nuclear missiles.

The debate about the nation's military programs continued during the summer of 2001, until a horrific event changed everything. On September 11, 2001, terrorists crashed passenger jets into the World Trade Center and the Pentagon. A new war had begun.

 Reading Check **Explaining** What was President George W. Bush's first priority when he took office?

 Study Central

For help with the concepts in this section of *American Vision: Modern Times* go to tav.mt.glencoe.com and click on *Study Central.*

SECTION 4 ASSESSMENT

Checking for Understanding

1. **Vocabulary** Define: chad, final, strategic defense.
2. **People and Terms** Identify: Al Gore, George W. Bush, Ralph Nader.
3. **Reviewing Facts** What did the Supreme Court decide in *Bush v. Gore?*

Reviewing Big Ideas

4. **Explaining** What caused the vote-count controversy in Florida in the 2000 election?

Critical Thinking

5. **Forming an Opinion** Do you think the 2000 presidential election was decided fairly? Why or why not?
6. **Organizing** Complete a graphic organizer similar to the one below by listing President Bush's goals when he took office.

```
      ( )     ( )
         \   /
        ( Bush )
        ( Goals )
         /   \
      ( )     ( )
```

Analyzing Visuals

7. **Interpreting Graphs** Study the graph on page 949. By how many votes was Gore leading when news networks declared him the winner in Florida? What was Bush's lead when networks declared him to be the winner?

Writing About History

8. **Persuasive Writing** Take on the role of a Supreme Court justice. Write a statement explaining how you voted in *Bush v. Gore* and why you took this position.

CHAPTER 21   Into a New Century   **951**

ASSESS

 Resources for page 951

Use these resources to assess student mastery.

📁 Section Quiz 21-4

📁 Reading Essentials and Study Guide 21-4

⊙ Interactive Tutor Self-Assessment CD-ROM

📁 California Standards Practice, Grade 11

Study Central provides audio summaries, interactive games, and online graphic organizers to help students review section content.

CLOSE

Looking Back...

FOCUS

History–Social Science Standards

This feature addresses the following standards:

11.1 Students analyze the significant events in the founding of the nation and its attempts to realize the philosophy of government described in the Declaration of Independence.

11.1.1 Describe the Enlightenment and the rise of democratic ideas as the context in which the nation was founded.

TEACH

R Reading Strategy

Analyzing Tell students to examine the quotation of Thomas Paine at the bottom of this page. **Ask:** Do you believe that Paine's statement is correct? Is the right to vote the most fundamental right in a democracy, or is there something more basic? *(Students' answers will vary. Regardless of whether they agree with Paine or choose a more basic right, students should provide well-reasoned explanations of their choices.)* **OL**

Answers and Additional Support

952

Looking Back...

Representative Government

Why It Matters Bill Daley, the chairperson of Vice President Al Gore's presidential campaign, was frantically trying to reach the vice president. It was 2:00 A.M. on Wednesday morning, November 8, 2000, the day after the presidential election. The election had come down to the vote counts in one state—Florida—and the votes in Florida were showing George W. Bush as having a significant lead. Gore was preparing to publicly concede the election. Daley, however, had heard that the latest Florida counts showed Bush's lead shrinking to below one percent. There would have to be a recount. When Daley finally got Gore on the phone, Daley shouted, "Whatever you do, do not go out on the stage."

As the debate began in Florida over how to recount the ballots, Daley stressed that "technicalities should not determine the presidency of the United States; the will of the people should." The dispute over how to recount the ballots in Florida mattered deeply to both candidates and to the American people, because it involved one of the basic ideas of the American system of government—that officials are elected to represent the needs and wishes of the people.

Ballot box

Steps To . . . Representative Government

The United States has a representative government in which citizens elect representatives to speak for them on political matters. The roots of American representative government date back to the colonial era.

Virginia House of Burgesses The first representative body in colonial America was the Virginia House of Burgesses. The House was comprised of two elected representatives, or burgesses, from each of 10 of Virginia's settlements. The body had the power to pass laws for the colony. The Virginia Company, however, had the power to disallow laws passed by the Burgesses.

Despite this limitation on its authority, the House of Burgesses changed Virginia from a company-run colony into a partially self-governing colony where elected representatives made the laws. Later on, Virginia became a royal colony, ruled by a governor appointed by the king. To keep settlers' support, the king allowed the House of Burgesses to continue to meet. This established the tradition of representative government in the colonies.

R "The right of voting for representatives is the primary right by which other rights are protected. To take away this right is to reduce a man to [the] slavery . . . of being subject to the will of another. . . ."

—Thomas Paine, 1795

952

EXTENDING THE CONTENT

Redistricting The Constitution requires an official census of the United States every 10 years. One purpose of the census is to reallocate the number of seats in the House of Representatives based on current state populations. By basing the number of House seats on a state's population, the true representative nature of the American government is maintained.

THE FIRST LEGISLATIVE ASSEMBLY IN THE NEW WORLD, JAMESTOWN, VIRGINIA, JULY, 1619

Virginia House of Burgesses

The Mayflower Compact The Mayflower Compact was an agreement signed in November 1620 by the male passengers aboard the *Mayflower* before they came ashore at Plymouth. The signers agreed to form a civil government that represented the wishes of the majority. The compact called for government leaders to "enact, constitute, and frame such just and equal laws, ordinances, acts, constitutions . . . as shall be thought most meet and convenient for the general good of the colony. . . ."

Fundamental Orders of Connecticut The notion of representative government took another step forward in 1639 when several towns along the Connecticut River joined together to create a government. They laid out the structure of this government in the Fundamental Orders of Connecticut—the first written constitution in American history. The document, which consisted of a preamble and eleven orders, gave citizens the right to elect the governor, judges, and representatives to make laws. The Orders also introduced the idea of limited government. For example, citizens could call the legislature into session if the governor refused to do so. The legislature could also remove officials from power for misbehavior.

Colonial Assemblies By the time of the American Revolution, most British colonies in America had local assemblies elected by the people. Colonial governments were not truly rep-

resentative, however, because the king chose the governors and gave them the power to veto laws passed by the assemblies. Although the governors were powerful, the assemblies could control them by refusing to vote for new taxes. The American Revolution was partly caused by Britain's challenge to this system. When Britain began taxing the colonies directly, it endangered the power of the local assemblies. Americans insisted that taxation without representation violated their rights.

The U.S. Constitution These ideas of representative government and limited government would be bound together in the document that has governed the nation as a whole for more than 200 years: the U.S. Constitution. The Federalists, or those who supported the Constitution during its ratification process, strongly believed in representative government. Indeed, the authors of the *Federalist Papers,* the collection of famous essays written in support of the Constitution, preferred a government one step removed from the common people, whom they insisted "seldom judge or determine right." The fact that the Constitution placed political power "in the hands of the representatives of the people," the authors stated, "is the essential, and, after all, only efficacious security for the rights and privileges of the people."

Checking for Understanding

1. What is a representative government?
2. What was significant about the formation of the Virginia House of Burgesses?

Critical Thinking

1. Do you think a written constitution is preferable to a constitution based on tradition? Explain.
2. Would you rather live under a representative government or in a direct democracy, where people govern themselves by voting directly on all issues? Explain.

Checking for Understanding

1. A representative government is one in which citizens elect others to represent their own wishes and political opinions in government.
2. It was the first representative body in colonial America and could act on all tax laws and draft legislation.

Critical Thinking

1. Answers will vary. Some students will say a traditional constitution is more flexible and can change with the times. Others will say a written Constitution is a more reliable guide to what the Founders wanted and makes it easier to uphold the Constitution in court.
2. Answers may vary. Once students consider the large number of matters to be decided, many may support a representative democracy over a direct democracy.

FOCUS

BELLRINGER
SKILLBUILDER ACTIVITY

Project **Daily Focus Skills Transparency 21-5** and have students answer the question.

Guide to Reading

Understanding Vocabulary:
Have students write short paragraphs using all of the content vocabulary words found in this section.

Answers to Graphic:
U.S. support of wealthy countries and families that control Middle Eastern oil; the belief that western influence undermines Islamic values and beliefs; new strict fundamentalist religious movements that hope to establish a pure Islamic society; American support for Israel

Unpacking the Standards

Students will be able to:

• Describe the development of Middle East terrorism.

• Explain the response of the United States to the terrorist attacks on the World Trade Center and the Pentagon.

• Discuss the War in Iraq and the 2004 presidential election.

SECTION 5 The War on Terrorism

Guide to Reading

Connection
In the previous section, you learned about the election of George W. Bush. In this section, you will discover how a terrorist attack changed the United States.

Main Idea
• Terrorist attacks on the World Trade Center and the Pentagon changed American life. (p. 955)
• Support for the victims of the terrorist attacks showed American heroism and patriotism. (p. 957)
• The war on terrorism included cutting terrorists' access to funding, creating the Department of Homeland Security, and launching a war in Afghanistan. (p. 958)

• Doubting the effectiveness of UN resolutions, the United States went to war with Iraq. (p. 959)
• Despite obstacles in the war with Iraq, a divided nation reelected President Bush. (p. 960)

Content Vocabulary
terrorism, state-sponsored terrorism, anthrax

Academic Vocabulary
contrary, editor, inspector

People and Terms to Identify
Osama bin Laden, al-Qaeda

Reading Objectives
• **Describe** the development of Middle East terrorism.
• **Explain** the response of the United States to the terrorist attacks on the World Trade Center and the Pentagon.

Reading Strategy
As you read about America's war on terrorism, complete a graphic organizer similar to the one below to show the different reasons terrorists attack Americans.

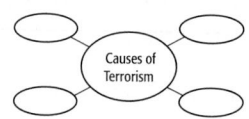

Causes of Terrorism

Preview of Events

♦1990	♦1995	♦2000	♦2005
1988 Al-Qaeda is organized	**1998** Bombs explode at U.S. embassies in Kenya and Tanzania	**2001** Attacks on the Pentagon and World Trade Center	**2003** War in Iraq begins

The following are the main History–Social Science Standards covered in this section.

11.9.6 Describe U.S. Middle East policy and its strategic, political, and economic interests, including those related to the Gulf War.

✂ The Big Idea ✂

The fate of nations is forever changed by monumental world events. On September 11, 2001, terrorists attacked the World Trade Center in New York City and the Pentagon in Washington, D.C. The attacks were traced to al-Qaeda, a Muslim terrorist organization under the leadership of Osama bin Laden. The administration responded by declaring a war on terrorism, creating a new Department of Homeland Security, and attacking targets in Afghanistan. A coalition led by the United States invaded Iraq over concerns about weapons of mass destruction. While U.S. troops fought terrorists in Iraq, the country remained politically divided in the 2004 presidential election. Voters chose to stay the course and reelected George W. Bush over his challenger Senator John Kerry.

954 CHAPTER 21 Into a New Century

SECTION RESOURCES

📁 **Print Material**
• Reproducible Lesson Plan 21-5
• Guided Reading Activity 21-5
• Reading Essentials and Study Guide 21-5
• Active Reading Note-Taking Guide 21-5

📊 **Transparencies**
• Daily Focus Skills Transparency 21-5
• Section Graphic Organizer Transparency 21-5

Technology
⦿ Interactive Tutor Self-Assessment CD-ROM
⦿ Exam*View*® Pro Testmaker CD-ROM
⦿ Presentation Plus! CD-ROM

September 11, 2001

Main Idea Terrorist attacks on the World Trade Center and the Pentagon changed American life.

Reading Connection What was the significance of the two sites chosen for the attacks? Read on to learn more about the events of September 11.

On September 11, 2001, the United States was faced with an event it had never before experienced. Terrorists attacked major buildings on the East Coast.

★ An American Story ★

At 8:45 A.M. Eastern Daylight Time on September 11, 2001, a Boeing 767 passenger jet slammed into the North Tower of the World Trade Center in New York City. As people below gazed in horror, a second plane collided with the South Tower. Soon afterward, a third plane crashed into the Pentagon in Washington, D.C. At 9:50 A.M., the South Tower collapsed in a billowing cloud of dust and debris. The North Tower fell about 40 minutes later. The falling towers killed thousands of people, burying them beneath a vast mound of rubble.

The airplanes did not crash accidentally. Hijackers deliberately crashed them into the buildings. Hijackers also seized a fourth airplane, United Airlines Flight 93, probably hoping to crash it into the White House or the Capitol. Many passengers on Flight 93 had cell phones. After hearing about the World Trade Center, four passengers—Todd Beamer, Thomas Burnett, Jeremy Glick, and Mark Bingham—decided to do something. An operator listening over a cell phone heard Todd Beamer's voice: "Are you ready, guys? Let's roll." Soon afterward, Flight 93 crashed in a field in Pennsylvania. At that moment, Vice President Dick Cheney was in a bunker under the White House. After hearing that Flight 93 had crashed, he said, "I think an act of heroism just took place on that plane."

—adapted from *Let's Roll: Ordinary People, Extraordinary Courage*

The attacks on the World Trade Center and the Pentagon were acts of terrorism. **Terrorism** is the use of violence by nongovernmental groups against civilians to achieve a political goal. Terrorist acts are intended to instill fear in people and to frighten their governments into changing their policies. The terrorist attacks on September 11, 2001, killed all 266 passengers and crewmembers on the four hijacked planes. Another 125 people died in the Pentagon. In New York City, nearly 3,000 people died. More Americans were killed in the attacks than died at Pearl Harbor or on D-Day in World War II.

Middle East Terrorism Although there have been many acts of terrorism in American history, most terrorist attacks on Americans since World War II have been carried out by Middle Eastern groups. The reason Middle Eastern terrorists have targeted Americans can be traced back to events early in the twentieth century.

As oil became important to the American economy in the 1920s, the United States invested heavily in the Middle East oil industry. This industry brought great wealth to the ruling families in some Middle Eastern kingdoms, but most of the people remained poor. Some became angry at the United States for supporting the wealthy royal families.

The rise of the oil industry increased the Middle East's contact with Western society. As Western ideas spread through the region, many Muslims—followers of the region's dominant religion—feared that their traditional values and beliefs were being weakened. New movements arose calling for a strict interpretation of the Quran—the Muslim holy book—and a return to traditional Muslim religious laws.

These Muslim movements wanted to overthrow pro-Western governments in the Middle East and create a pure Islamic society. Muslims who support

Todd Beamer ▼

CHAPTER 21   Into a New Century   **955**

TEACH

R **Reading Strategy**

Scaffolding—Recognizing Time and Sequence As students read the section, have them create a time line depicting Middle East terrorist events. They can include quotes, drawings, and photographs from magazines or other sources in addition to listing the events themselves. You may want to combine these time lines into group or whole class time lines as a culminating activity at the end of the section. **OL**

This `Reading Skill` was introduced in Chapter 10.

Review the Big Idea

Review the Big Idea for this section, "The fate of nations is forever changed by monumental world events." The attack on September 11, 2001, by Islamic terrorists changed the fate of the United States. Ask students to write a two-page paper that reviews the history of the Middle East and how actions and policies of Western nations have affected the region. **OL** **CA 11WA2.4d**

Resources for page 955

*Have students read more about the War on Terrorism in **Moments in Time, Unit 15: The War on Terrorism (1998–2001)**.*

More Skill Practice

Visual/Spatial Divide students into four equal groups. Tell each group to research the design competition for the 9/11 memorial and plans to replace the office buildings at the location of the destroyed World Trade Center. Have students research the architects involved and the final design chosen. Each group should critique the approved design. Then groups should come up with their own designs to illustrate, present, and display in the room. **OL**

NATIONAL GEOGRAPHIC — **Major Terrorist Attacks Affecting Americans, 1970–2003**

1. 1970 Terrorists hijack airplanes to Jordan
2. 1979 Fifty-two Americans held hostage in Iran for more than a year
3. 1983 Bombing of U.S. Marine barracks in Beirut, Lebanon, kills 241
4. 1985 TWA flight 847 hijacked; hostages held for 17 days in Beirut, Lebanon
5. 1986 Bombing at West Berlin dance club; kills 3, injures 150
6. 1988 Bomb on Pan Am flight 103 kills 270 in Lockerbie, Scotland
7. 1993 Bomb at World Trade Center kills 6
8. 1995 Truck bomb destroys a federal building in Oklahoma City; kills 168, injures more than 500
9. 1996 Bomb at U.S. complex in Dharan, Saudi Arabia, kills 19 American soldiers
10. 1998 Bombing at U.S. embassies in Kenya and Tanzania kills more than 200
11. 2000 Bomb kills 17 American sailors and injures 39 aboard USS *Cole*
12. 2001 Hijacked airliners crash into the World Trade Center, the Pentagon, and a field in Pennsylvania, killing thousands
13. 2002 Bombs in Indonesia kill over 200
14. 2003 Bombings in residential areas of Riyadh, Saudi Arabia, kill 8 Americans

these movements are referred to as fundamentalist militants. Although the vast majority of Muslims believe terrorism is **contrary** to their faith, militants began using terrorism to achieve their goals.

American support of Israel also angered many in the Middle East. In 1947 the UN divided British-controlled Palestine into two territories to provide a home for Jews. One part became Israel. The other part was to become a Palestinian state, but fighting between Israel and the Arab states in 1948 left this territory under the control of Israel, Jordan, and Egypt.

The Palestinians wanted their own nation. In the 1950s, they began staging guerrilla raids and terrorist attacks against Israel. Since the United States gave military and economic aid to Israel, it became the target of Muslim hostility. In the 1970s, several Middle Eastern nations realized they could fight Israel and the United States by providing terrorist groups with money, weapons, and training. When a government secretly supports terrorism, this is called **state-sponsored terrorism.** The governments of Libya, Syria, Iraq, and Iran have all sponsored terrorism.

A New Terrorist Threat In 1979 the Soviet Union invaded Afghanistan. In response, Muslims from across the Middle East headed to Afghanistan to join the struggle against the Soviets. Among them was 22-year-old **Osama bin Laden.** Bin Laden came from one of Saudi Arabia's wealthiest families. He used his wealth to support the Afghan resistance. In 1988 he founded an organization called **al-Qaeda** (al KY·duh), or "the Base." Al-Qaeda recruited Muslims and channeled money and arms to the Afghan resistance.

Bin Laden's experience in Afghanistan convinced him that superpowers could be beaten. He also believed that Western ideas had contaminated Muslim society. He was outraged when Saudi Arabia allowed American troops on Saudi soil after Iraq invaded Kuwait in 1991.

Operating first from Sudan and then from Afghanistan—then under the control of Muslim fundamentalists known as the Taliban—bin Laden dedicated himself and al-Qaeda to driving Westerners, and especially Americans, out of the Middle East. In 1998 he called on Muslims to kill Americans. Soon afterward, bin Laden's followers set off bombs at the

American embassies in Kenya and Tanzania. Over 200 people died in the attacks, including 12 Americans, and more than 5,400 were injured.

Shortly after these bombings, President Clinton ordered cruise missiles launched at terrorist facilities in Afghanistan and Sudan. The attacks did not deter bin Laden. In 1999 al-Qaeda terrorists were arrested while trying to smuggle explosives into the United States in an attempt to bomb Seattle. In October 2000, al-Qaeda terrorists crashed a boat loaded with explosives into the USS *Cole* while it was docked in Yemen.

✓ **Reading Check** **Explaining** What are the three main reasons some Muslims became angry with the United States?

America Unites

Main Idea Support for the victims of the terrorist attacks showed American heroism and patriotism.

Reading Connection Have you or anyone you know donated blood? Read on to learn how Americans responded to the tragedy after September 11.

The attack on the *Cole* and the attempted bombing of Seattle were overshadowed by the close presidential election of 2000. The new president, George W.

Bush, did not consider terrorism an imminent threat, although there were troubling signs of possible al-Qaeda activity within the United States. "The system was blinking red during the summer of 2001," CIA Director George Tenet later testified. Then, on September 11, 2001, terrorists struck again, hijacking four American passenger planes and executing the most devastating terrorist attack in history.

Citizens Respond to the Crisis The attacks on the World Trade Center and the Pentagon shocked Americans, but people responded rapidly to the crisis. Firefighters and medical workers from other cities headed to New York to help. Across the nation, Americans donated blood, raised money, and collected food, blankets, and other supplies. Americans did everything they could to help victims. Within weeks, they had donated over one billion dollars. From around the world came sympathy. "We are all Americans!" wrote one French journalist.

Across the nation, Americans put up flags to show their unity and resolve. They held candlelight vigils and prayer services as they searched for ways to help. If the terrorists had hoped to divide Americans, they failed. As the Reverend Billy Graham noted at a memorial service: "A tragedy like this could have torn our country apart. But instead it has united us and we have become a family."

Picturing **History**

Transcending Tragedy Although the destruction of the World Trade Center (lower right) and the attack on the Pentagon (right) shocked Americans, people responded rapidly to the crisis. Across the nation, images such as that of firefighters raising a flag in the ruins of the World Trade Center (left) inspired Americans. Many lined up to donate blood. Others raised money and collected food, blankets, and other supplies for the victims and rescue workers. On what date did the attacks occur?

A National Emergency The American government reacted quickly by grounding civilian airliners and alerting the armed forces. On September 14, President Bush declared a national emergency. Congress voted to authorize the use of force to fight the terrorists. Intelligence sources and the FBI quickly identified the attacks as the work of Osama bin Laden and the al-Qaeda network.

President Bush decided the time had come to end the threat of terrorism in the world. He issued an ultimatum to the Taliban regime in Afghanistan, demanding they turn over bin Laden and his supporters and close all terrorist camps. He also declared that although the war on terrorism would start by targeting al-Qaeda, it would not stop there. "It will not end," he announced, "until every terrorist group of global reach has been found, stopped, and defeated."

The president also announced that the United States would no longer tolerate states that aided terrorists. "From this day forward," he proclaimed, "any nation that continues to harbor or support terrorism will be regarded by the United States as a hostile regime." The war, President Bush warned, would not end quickly, but it was a war the nation had to fight:

> **R** 66Great harm has been done to us. We have suffered great loss. And in our grief and anger we have found our mission and our moment. . . . Our Nation—this generation—will lift a dark threat of violence from our people and our future. . . . 99
>
> —President George W. Bush, Address to Joint Session of Congress, September 20, 2001

✓ Reading Check **Explaining** How did American citizens respond to the terrorist attacks?

Airport Security Airline passengers, such as these at Denver International Airport, had to wait in long lines to go through checkpoints when American airports increased security measures after the terrorist attacks of 9/11.

A New War Begins

Main Idea The war on terrorism included cutting terrorists' access to funding, creating the Department of Homeland Security, and launching a war in Afghanistan.

Reading Connection Has your school or community made any plans for a response to bioterrorism or other attacks? Read on to learn of the national response to September 11.

Secretary of Defense Donald Rumsfeld warned Americans that "this will be a war like none other our nation has faced." The enemy, he explained, "is a global network of terrorist organizations and their state sponsors, committed to denying free people the opportunity to live as they choose." Military force would be used to fight terrorism, but other means would be used as well.

Fighting Terrorism at Home In an effort to protect the American people from further terrorist attacks, President Bush called on Congress to create the Department of Homeland Security to merge the dozens of federal agencies working to prevent terrorism. Among the organizations that the new department controls are the Coast Guard, the Border Patrol, the Immigration and Naturalization Service, the Customs Service, and the Federal Emergency Management Agency.

U President Bush also asked Congress to pass legislation to help law enforcement agencies track down terrorist suspects. Congress acted with unusual speed, and the president signed the antiterrorism bill—known as the USA Patriot Act—into law in October 2001. The new law allows secret searches to avoid tipping off suspects in terrorism cases. It also allows authorities to obtain a single nationwide search warrant that can be used anywhere. The law also makes it easier to wiretap suspects, and it allows authorities to track e-mail and seize voice mail. Although Congress has sought to balance Americans' rights with the need to increase security, civil libertarians worry that the new law erodes the Fourth Amendment's protection against unreasonable search and seizure.

Bioterrorism Strikes America As the nation tried to cope with the events of September 11, a new terrorist attack began. On October 5, 2001, a Florida newspaper **editor** died from anthrax. **Anthrax** is a type of bacteria. Several nations, including the United States, Russia, and Iraq, have used it to create biological weapons. Antibiotics can cure anthrax, but if left untreated, it can kill quickly.

Soon after appearing in Florida, anthrax was found at several news organizations in New York City. In Washington, D.C., a letter filled with anthrax arrived at Senator Tom Daschle's office. It became clear that terrorists were using the mail to spread anthrax. Several postal workers contracted anthrax, and two died. The FBI investigated the anthrax attacks, but no suspects were publicly identified.

War in Afghanistan On October 7, 2001, the United States began bombing targets in Afghanistan to attack al-Qaeda's camps and the Taliban's military forces. President Bush explained that Islam and the Afghan people were not the enemy, and he pledged food, medicine, and other supplies to Afghan refugees. The United States also sent aid to a coalition of Afghan groups known as the Northern Alliance, which had been fighting the Taliban.

The American bombing campaign quickly shattered the Taliban's defenses. The Northern Alliance then launched a massive attack on Taliban lines. By early December, the Taliban regime had collapsed. The United States and its allies then helped Afghan leaders create a new government. Meanwhile, thousands of American and allied troops began arriving in Afghanistan to act as peacekeepers and to hunt for bin Laden and other al-Qaeda terrorists.

Weapons of Mass Destruction The United States grew concerned that groups such as al-Qaeda might acquire nuclear, chemical, or biological weapons. These weapons of mass destruction could kill tens of thousands of people all at once.

In his state of the union speech in January 2002, President Bush warned that an "axis of evil," which he identified as Iraq, Iran, and North Korea, posed a grave threat to the world. Each of these countries had been known to sponsor terrorism and was suspected of trying to develop weapons of mass destruction. The president promised to take strong action: "The United States will not permit the world's most dangerous regimes to threaten us with the world's most destructive weapons."

Months later, North Korea announced that it had restarted its nuclear weapons program. The Bush

▲ *U.S. soldiers assist a young Afghani girl at a military medical tent.*

administration tried to use diplomatic pressure to persuade the North Korean government to stop the program. The North Koreans argued that they needed the weapons to protect themselves from a U.S. attack.

✓ Reading Check   **Outlining** What steps did the president take in response to the terrorist attacks?

Confronting Iraq

Main Idea **Doubting the effectiveness of UN resolutions, the United States went to war with Iraq.**

Reading Connection Do you think the UN is effective as a mediator in world affairs? Read on to learn about UN actions before the war with Iraq.

President Bush considered Iraq a more immediate threat than North Korea in developing and distributing weapons of mass destruction. Iraq's dictator, Saddam Hussein, had already used chemical weapons twice, once in Iraq's war against Iran in the 1980s and again in 1988 against the Kurds, an ethnic minority in northern Iraq who had rebelled against Hussein's

W Writing Support

Research Report Writing According to the Centers for Disease Control (CDC), anthrax is a disease caused by the bacterium *Bacillus anthracis.* Have students write a two-page paper that investigates the brief anthrax scare the country faced after September 11, 2001. In their papers, they should also discuss ongoing efforts to deal with other biological agents terrorists might use. Ask students to assess how prepared they believe the country is to combat a biological terrorist attack today. **AL** **CA** 11WA2.3b

R Reading Strategy

Scaffolding—Evaluating Have students speculate about what kinds of weapons qualify as "weapons of mass destruction." *(nuclear bombs, poison gas, "dirty bomb")* **Ask: Did not finding weapons of mass destruction in Iraq hurt President Bush's rationale for going to war with Iraq?** *(Students' responses will vary.)* **AL**

This Reading Skill was introduced in Chapter 18.

✓ Reading Check

Answer: He declared a national emergency; requested a $40 billion emergency aid package; formed an international coalition against terrorism; deployed American troops; and issued an ultimatum against terrorism and states sponsoring or aiding terrorism.

Did You Know?

The Taliban claimed to be Allah's followers desiring to bring a pure Islamic government to Afghanistan. Some of their earlier successes in ending corruption and dealing with cruel warlords won them much support in Afghanistan. However, as their control of the country became more complete, their regime became very repressive.

War in Iraq On April 9, 2003, just three weeks after the war in Iraq began, American troops reached the capital of Baghdad and helped Iraqis tear down a statue of former dictator Saddam Hussein.

regime. After the Gulf War in 1991, UN **inspectors** found evidence that Iraq had developed biological weapons and was working on a nuclear bomb.

Pressure on Iraq Also in the summer of 2002, President Bush increased pressure on Iraq, calling for a regime change in the country. In September he asked for a UN resolution demanding that Iraq give up its weapons of mass destruction. He made it clear, though, that the United States would act with or without UN support. He asked Congress to authorize the use of force against Iraq, and Congress granted his request.

During the congressional elections of 2002, Democrats focused on the nation's faltering economy, but Bush made national security his chief theme. His vigorous campaigning helped Republicans add seats in the House of Representatives and regain a slim majority in the Senate.

War and Its Aftermath Soon after the elections, the United Nations approved a new resolution that set a deadline for Iraq to readmit weapons inspectors. The inspectors returned to Iraq, but the Bush administration doubted their effectiveness. The administration believed that Saddam Hussein had hidden weapons of mass destruction that were ready or nearly ready for use. Bush also believed that Hussein had ties to al-Qaeda. Many of America's traditional allies in Europe, however, wanted to give the inspectors more time, and President Bush failed to achieve a declaration of war in the UN Security Council. The president argued

that Iraq posed such an imminent threat that it justified a preemptive war—a war launched to prevent rather than respond to an attack. The United States and Great Britain, with the support of about 30 other countries, prepared for war.

On March 20, 2003, the U.S.-led coalition forces attacked Iraq. Over the next six weeks, the Iraqi army dissolved as soldiers refused to risk their lives for Hussein. The coalition forces quickly seized control of the country, and on May 1, President Bush declared that the major combat was over. About 140 Americans, and several thousand Iraqis, had died. American troops captured Saddam Hussein by the end of the year.

Both the controversy over Iraq and the fighting, however, continued. No evidence was found that Iraq possessed weapons of mass destruction, nor was a serious link between Saddam Hussein and al-Qaeda ever uncovered. The United States also did not have sufficient forces in Iraq to stop the widespread looting that broke out after Hussein's government fell. The lawlessness that followed the war encouraged radical religious factions within Iraq and terrorists who entered the country to target American troops and consultants from coalition countries. More Americans died in Iraq after President Bush had declared the end of combat than during the war itself.

As casualties and costs mounted, President Bush sought help from the UN and other countries to stabilize and rebuild Iraq. "Iraqi democracy will succeed," he insisted, "and that success will send forth the news, from Damascus to Tehran, that freedom can be the future of every nation."

✓**Reading Check** **Summarizing** Why did President Bush decide to confront Iraq?

The 2004 Elections

Main Idea Despite obstacles in the war with Iraq, a divided nation reelected President Bush.

Reading Connection Have you ever participated in a school, local, or national election? Read on to learn about the 2004 presidential election.

The war on terrorism and the war in Iraq dominated the election of 2004. In the wake of the terrorist attacks, President Bush won widespread support for his firm determination to wage war on terrorism.

The Kerry Challenge President Bush and Vice President Cheney won nomination for a second term without challenge. After primary campaigns that

Did You Know?

The ground campaign of the 1991 Gulf War led by George H.W. Bush lasted a little more than four days. By contrast, the ground war of the 2003 war against Iraq led by President George W. Bush took approximately three weeks.

focused largely on the war in Iraq, Democrats nominated Massachusetts senator John Kerry and North Carolina senator John Edwards.

Kerry's nomination revived the Vietnam War as a campaign issue. Unlike President Bush, who served at home in the National Guard, and Vice President Cheney, whose student deferments had kept him from military service, John Kerry had enlisted in the navy. He fought in Vietnam, where he was decorated for valor. Kerry returned from Vietnam convinced of the futility of the war and became an outspoken critic.

Kerry's Vietnam experiences made him leery of sending American troops into combat. As a senator he opposed the first Gulf War, but he voted to authorize President Bush to use military force in Iraq. When no weapons of mass destruction were found in Iraq, Kerry called the war a "diversion" from the hunt for al-Qaeda.

A Choice for a Divided Nation In policies and personalities, Bush and Kerry offered the nation a sharp choice. As a conservative, President Bush pledged to continue cutting taxes and building a strong national defense. He opposed abortion and endorsed a constitutional amendment to ban same-sex marriages. His supporters saw him as someone who operated on fixed moral and religious principles, trusted his instincts, and steadfastly followed a course of action once he made a decision.

Senator Kerry criticized what he considered Bush's single-mindedness, insisting that a president must be able to focus on more than one issue at a time. He pledged to address domestic economic problems while pursuing the war on terrorism. As a liberal, Kerry promised to strengthen Social Security and to

raise taxes on the wealthiest individuals in order to fund health-care insurance for the millions of Americans who lacked health coverage. Although a Catholic, Kerry differed with church leaders on many social issues, including abortion.

W While the events of September 11, 2001, had united the nation emotionally, the country remained as divided politically as it had been during the 2000 election. President Bush drew his strength from the Southeast and Southwest, as well as from rural areas and outer suburbs. Senator Kerry's base was in the Northeast and on the West Coast, along with cities and inner suburbs. Both candidates devoted most of their campaigning to a few "battleground" states in the Midwest and in Florida, where voters' opinions were the most narrowly divided.

Bush Wins a Second Term Both parties saw voter turnout as the key to the victory. On election day the Republicans best succeeded in mobilizing their core supporters. President Bush took the lead in the popular vote and a majority in the Electoral College. His victory helped preserve the Republican majorities in the Senate and House of Representatives. Despite serious concerns about both foreign and domestic policy, voters felt safer in staying the course and asking President Bush to pursue the war on terrorism.

☑ **Reading Check** **Summarizing** Which issues divided the country during the 2004 presidential election?

HISTORY Online **Study Central**

For help with the concepts in this section of *American Vision: Modern Times* go to tav.mt.glencoe.com and click on *Study Central.*

SECTION 5 ASSESSMENT

Checking for Understanding

1. **Vocabulary** Define: terrorism, contrary, state-sponsored terrorism, editor, anthrax, inspector.
2. **People and Terms** Identify: Osama bin Laden, al-Qaeda.
3. **Explain** how the United States responded to the attacks on New York City and Washington, D.C.

Reviewing Big Ideas

4. **Making Inferences** Why does American foreign policy anger Islamic fundamentalists in the Middle East?

Critical Thinking

5. **Historical Analysis** **Interpreting** What factors have contributed to the rise of Middle Eastern terrorist groups? **CA HR4; HI2**

6. **Organizing** Use a graphic organizer similar to the one below to list the reasons why President Bush declared war on Iraq.

War on Iraq

Analyzing Visuals

7. **Examining Maps** Study the map on page 956 of terrorist attacks. In what region of the world did most of the attacks take place?

Writing About History

8. **Persuasive Writing** The attacks on New York City and Washington, D.C., convinced many Americans that more security was needed, even if it meant giving up some freedoms. Write a letter to a newspaper explaining why you are for or against increased security. **CA 11WA2.1a; 11WA2.1b**

CHAPTER 21 Into a New Century **961**

SECTION 5 ASSESSMENT ANSWERS

1. Content vocabulary is boldfaced and highlighted in yellow. Academic vocabulary is boldfaced.
2. Osama bin Laden (p. 956), al-Qaeda (p. 956)
3. Citizens donated money and supplies; the government vowed to end terrorism and targeted

al-Qaeda and the Taliban regime in Afghanistan.
4. U.S. support for Israel and for wealthy ruling families in some Middle Eastern countries angers Islamic fundamentalists.
5. increased contact with Western society; the growth of Islamic fundamentalism; and countries that

provide terrorists with money, weapons, and training
6. Iraq sponsored terrorism and had used chemical weapons; inspectors had found evidence of biological weapons and nuclear bomb making.
7. the Middle East
8. Students' letters will vary.

961

Summary Writing The election of 2004 showed a nation that was as strongly divided on political issues as it had been in 2000. Ask students to write a summary of the key issues that shaped the presidential election in 2004 and to assess what they believe to be the key reasons that swayed the close election for President Bush and helped the Republican Party succeed. **OL** **CA 11WA2.4a**

ASSESS

Resources for page 961

Use these resources to assess student mastery.

📂 Section Quiz 21-5

📂 Reading Essentials and Study Guide 21-5

💿 Interactive Tutor Self-Assessment CD-ROM

📂 California Standards Practice, Grade 11

☑ **Reading Check**

Answer: The nation was divided on the war in Iraq and defense issues, economic issues such as tax cuts, and views on abortion and same-sex marriage.

Study Central provides audio summaries, interactive games, and online graphic organizers to help students review section content.

CLOSE

Summarizing Have students explain the response of the United States to the terrorist attacks on the World Trade Center and the Pentagon. **OL**

FOCUS

History–Social Science Standards

This feature addresses the following standards:

11.9 Students analyze U.S. foreign policy since World War II.

11.9.6 Describe U.S. Middle East policy and its strategic, political, and economic interests, including those related to the Gulf War.

Understanding Vocabulary

Before students begin reading, point out that difficult or unfamiliar words are footnoted throughout the text.

TEACH

R Reading Strategy

Visualizing Divide the class into pairs. Have each pair write a slogan that addresses the issue of the U.S. battle with terrorism. Then have students create posters expressing their slogans. They may use photos, drawings, or other visuals to add impact to the slogans. Tell students that the slogans should be prominently displayed on the poster. **EL**

Answers and Additional Support

Primary Sources
Eyewitness to History

As the twentieth century ended and the twenty-first century began, the United States became the target of Islamic terrorists. Since the terrorist attacks came from small groups of people, no individual nation could be held responsible. Both Presidents Bill Clinton and George W. Bush struggled to respond to this new type of war.

SOURCE 1:

Retaliating for the August 7, 1998, terrorist bombings of the U.S. embassies in Kenya and Tanzania, the United States on August 20 used missiles to attack targets in Afghanistan and the Sudan. In a televised speech, President Bill Clinton linked the targets to the terrorists.

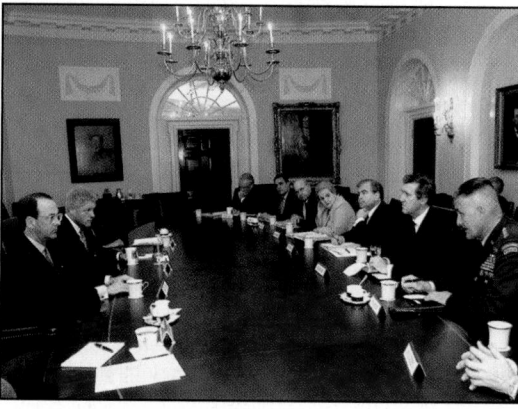

▲ *President Clinton meets with the National Security Council on August 20, 1998.*

And so, this morning, based on the unanimous recommendation of my national security team, I ordered our Armed Forces to take action to counter an immediate threat from the bin Laden network. Earlier today, the United States carried out simultaneous strikes against terrorist facilities and infrastructure in Afghanistan. Our forces targeted one of the most active terrorist bases in the world. . . .

Our forces also attacked a factory in Sudan associated with the bin Laden network. The factory was involved in the production of materials for chemical weapons.

I want you to understand, I want the world to understand, that our actions today were not aimed against Islam, the faith of hundreds of millions of good, peace-loving people all around the world, including the United States. No religion **condones**[1] the murder of innocent men, women, and children. But our actions were aimed at fanatics and killers who wrap murder in the cloak of righteousness; and in so doing, profane the great religion in whose name they claim to act.

My fellow Americans, our battle against terrorism did not begin with the bombing of our embassies in Africa; nor will it end with today's strike. It will require strength, courage and endurance. We will not yield to this threat. We will meet it, no matter how long it may take. This will be a long, ongoing struggle between freedom and fanaticism; between the rule of law and terrorism. We must be prepared to do all that we can for as long as we must.

America is and will remain a target of terrorists precisely because we are leaders; because we act to advance peace, democracy and basic human values; because we're the most open society on Earth; and because, as we have shown yet again, we take an uncompromising stand against terrorism.

SOURCE 2:

On the morning of September 11, 2001, terrorist attacks killed about 3,000 people and destroyed the two 110-story World Trade Center towers. On September 14, President George W. Bush delivered a speech in a ceremony at the National Cathedral in Washington, D.C., marking a National Day of Prayer and Remembrance.

[1] **condones:** excuses or ignores

UNIVERSAL ACCESS

Advanced Learners Ask students to write a poem about the September 11, 2001, terrorist attacks. Suggest that they write about what it might have been like to witness the terrorist attacks. Students may want to begin by giving overview of the event, including some objective facts, and then make the poem more personal by focusing on their own opinions or feelings. Invite volunteers to read their poems aloud to the class. **AL**

We are here in the middle hour of our grief. So many have suffered so great a loss, and today we express our nation's sorrow. We come before God to pray for the missing and the dead, and for those who love them. . . .

War has been waged against us by stealth and deceit and murder. This nation is peaceful, but fierce when stirred to anger. This conflict was begun on the timing and terms of others. It will end in a way, and at an hour, of our choosing. . . .

It has joined together political parties in both houses of Congress. It is evident in services of prayer and candlelight vigils, and American flags, which are displayed in pride, and wave in defiance.

Our unity is a kinship of grief, and a steadfast resolve to prevail against our enemies. And this unity against terror is now extending across the world.

America is a nation full of good fortune, with so much to be grateful for. But we are not spared from suffering. In every generation, the world has produced enemies of human freedom. They have attacked America, because we are freedom's home and defender. And the commitment of our fathers is now the calling of our time.

SOURCE 3:

In September 2002, the Bush administration changed the long-standing military policy of the United States. The new "National Security Strategy of the United States of America" stressed a commitment to human rights and claimed the right of preventive strikes against terrorists.

Today, the United States enjoys a position of unparalleled military strength and great economic and political influence. In keeping with our heritage and principles, we do not use our strength to press for **unilateral**[2] advantage. We seek instead to create a balance of power that favors human freedom: conditions in which all nations and all societies can choose for themselves the rewards and challenges of political and economic liberty. In a world that is safe, people will be able to make their own lives better. We will defend the peace by fighting terrorists and tyrants. We will preserve the peace by building good relations among the great powers. We will extend the peace by encouraging free and open societies on every continent. . . .

The gravest danger our Nation faces lies at the crossroads of radicalism and technology. Our enemies have openly declared that they are seeking weapons

[2]**unilateral:** one-sided

▲ *President Bush and staff discuss the attack on the Taliban in Afghanistan.*

of mass destruction, and evidence indicates that they are doing so with determination. The United States will not allow these efforts to succeed. . . . America will act against such emerging threats before they are fully formed. . . .

Finally, the United States will use this moment of opportunity to extend the benefits of freedom across the globe. We will actively work to bring the hope of democracy, development, free markets, and free trade to every corner of the world. The events of September 11, 2001, taught us that weak states, like Afghanistan, can pose as great a danger to our national interests as strong states. Poverty does not make poor people into terrorists and murderers. Yet poverty, weak institutions, and corruption can make weak states vulnerable to terrorist networks and drug cartels within their borders.

DBQ Document-Based Questions

Historical Analysis   CA HR4; HI3

Source 1: Why did Clinton order the bombings?

Source 2: According to Bush, what effect did the terrorist attacks have on the United States?

Source 3: How does the Bush administration plan to stop terrorism?

Comparing and Contrasting Sources:
In what ways do Clinton and Bush agree in their approaches to defeating terrorism?

Primary Sources
Eyewitness to History

W Writing Support

Narrative Writing Have students write one-page papers in which they describe how, or if, their lives have changed since the terrorist attacks of September 11, 2001. Tell them that they should focus on their own experiences rather than giving general facts about the attacks. Students should include descriptions about what had happened in their lives. Invite volunteers to take turns sharing their revised essays with the class. **OL**

CA 11WA2.1a; 11WA2.3a

R Reading Strategy

Predicting Divide the class into groups of five. Write the following question on the board: **Can the United States defeat terrorism?** Instruct groups to discuss President Bush's plans for defeating terrorism, and whether or not they believe that these plans will be effective. *(preemptive military power, homeland defense, efforts to cut off terrorist financing)* Ask a representative from each group to summarize the group's opinions for the rest of the class. Use students' responses to encourage a full-class discussion about the future threat of terrorism in the United States and around the world. **OL**

ASSESS/CLOSE

Have students answer the Document-Based Questions.

DBQ Document-Based Questions

Historical Analysis
1. Clinton ordered the bombings in retaliation for the August 7, 1998, terrorist bombings of the U.S. embassies in Kenya and Tanzania.
2. The terrorist attacks united Americans.
3. The Bush administration plans to use preemptive, or preventative, strikes against terrorists.

Comparing and Contrasting Sources
Answers will vary. Students should note that Presidents Clinton and Bush both believe that America should use force and refuse to yield in its battle with terrorism.

Reviewing Key Terms

Students' answers will vary. The pages where the words appear in the text are shown in parentheses.

1. microprocessor *(p. 931)* **2.** software *(p. 932)* **3.** telecommute *(p. 932)* **4.** Internet *(p. 933)* **5.** perjury *(p. 940)* **6.** ethnic cleansing *(p. 940)* **7.** trade deficit *(p. 943)* **8.** euro *(p. 944)* **9.** nuclear proliferation *(p. 946)* **10.** global warming *(p. 946)* **11.** chad *(p. 949)* **12.** strategic defense *(p. 951)* **13.** terrorism *(p. 955)* **14.** state-sponsored terrorism *(p. 956)*

Reviewing Key Facts

15. manipulate *(p. 931)* **16.** protocol *(p. 933)* **17.** sequence *(p. 934)* **18.** modify *(p. 936)* **19.** stress *(p. 937)* **20.** submit *(p. 939)* **21.** currency *(p. 944)* **22.** cite *(p. 944)* **23.** phase *(p. 946)* **24.** contrary *(p. 956)* **25.** editor *(p. 959)* **26.** inspector *(p. 960)*

Reviewing Key Terms

On a sheet of paper, use each of these terms in a sentence.

1. microprocessor
2. software
3. telecommute
4. Internet
5. perjury
6. ethnic cleansing
7. trade deficit
8. euro
9. nuclear proliferation
10. global warming
11. chad
12. strategic defense
13. terrorism
14. state-sponsored terrorism

Reviewing Academic Vocabulary

On a sheet of paper, use each of these terms in a sentence that reflects the term's meaning in the chapter.

15. manipulate
16. protocol
17. sequence
18. modify
19. stress
20. submit
21. currency
22. cite
23. phase
24. contrary
25. editor
26. inspector

Reviewing the Main Ideas

Section 1

27. How did compact computers transform the workplace?

Section 2

28. After his election in 1992, how did President Clinton propose to strengthen the nation's economy?

Section 3

29. What regional trade blocs were formed in the 1990s to increase international trade?

Section 4

30. Which state was significant in the 2000 presidential election?

Standards 11.8.7, 11.9.6, 11.9.7, 11.11, 11.11.2, 11.11.3, 11.11.5, 11.11.6, 11.11.7

Section 5

31. Who is Osama bin Laden, and what is al-Qaeda?

Critical Thinking

32. **Reading Skill** **Monitoring and Clarifying** Reread the text under the heading "Issues of Global Concern" on pages 945–946. Provide definitions for any unfamiliar words. Then write questions and answers clarifying the meaning of the text.

33. **Civics** Read what the Constitution of the United States says regarding impeachment. Refer to Article I, Section 2 and Section 3, and Article II, Section 4. What are the steps involved in the impeachment of a president? What vote is required to impeach the president? What vote is necessary to remove a president from office? Do you think impeachment is usually politically motivated? Explain your views.

34. **Categorizing** Complete the graphic organizer below by listing changes in communications, politics, the economy, and population that occurred in the United States by the end of the 1900s.

	Change
Communications	
Politics	
Economy	
Population	

Chapter Summary

The Technological Revolution

- Personal computers grow faster and more powerful.
- Communications deregulation expands cellular phone usage.
- The Internet provides a worldwide network of information.
- Biotechnology research increases knowledge of human genetics.

The Clinton Years

- A new global economy emerges based on regional trade blocs.
- The ozone layer and global warming become major environmental issues.
- Clinton and Congress cut spending; reform welfare and health care.
- U.S. economy grows rapidly; federal budget is balanced.
- U.S. tries to end violence in Haiti, the Middle East, and the Balkans.
- Scandal and impeachment tarnish the Clinton administration.

Bush Takes Office

- 2000 election results disputed in Florida; Supreme Court resolves dispute; George W. Bush becomes president.
- Bush focuses on cutting taxes, reforming education, and working on energy problems.
- Terrorists destroy the World Trade Center and attack the Pentagon.
- Bush organizes a global coalition and launches a new war on terrorism.
- War in Iraq ends the regime of Saddam Hussein.

Reviewing the Main Ideas

27. connected employees in offices together, modernized recordkeeping, increased productivity, and streamlined research avenues

28. by reducing the national deficit through cutting government spending and lowering interest rates

29. North American Free Trade Agreement, European Union, Asia Pacific Economic Cooperation

30. The outcome in Florida determined the winner of the election of 2000.

31. the leader of a radical Islamic terrorist group that is dedicated to eradicating Western influences (especially the United States) on the Middle East

Visit the American Vision: Modern Times Web site at
tav.mt.glencoe.com and click on *Self-Check Quizzes—
Chapter 21* to assess your knowledge of chapter content.

Writing About History

35. **Historical Analysis** **Relating Current Events** What effect did U.S. actions in the Middle East have on people's perceptions of the United States? How do these perceptions continue today? **CA CS4**

36. *Big Idea* Study the 2000 election map and chart on page 949. Then use library or Internet resources to research statistics on the 2004 presidential election. Using the 2000 election map and chart as a guide, create a similar map and chart of the 2004 election. Create questions about your map and chart that would help a classmate understand the data you have compiled.

DBQ **Document-Based Questions**

37. **Analyzing Points of View** Read the excerpt below about global warming, and then answer the questions that follow.

❝The world is getting warmer, and by the end of the 21st century could warm by another 6 degrees Celsius (10.8 degrees Fahrenheit). . . . And climate scientists at the heart of the research are now convinced that human action is to blame for some or most of this warming. . . .

Everywhere climatologists look—at tree-ring patterns, fossil successions in rock strata, ocean-floor corings . . . they see evidence of dramatic shifts from cold to hot to cold again. . . . None of these ancient shifts can be blamed on humans. . . . There is still room for argument about the precise role of the sun or other natural cycles in the contribution to global warming. . . . Richard S. Lindzen, a leading meteorologist at the Massachusetts Institute of Technology said . . . the picture of a consensus about global warming was 'misleading to the public and even to scientists. . . .' But most climate scientists . . . now believe that the climate is being influenced by human beings.❞

—from *World Press Review,* February 2001

a. According to the article, what two points of view exist about global warming? **CA 11RC2.4**

b. Why is the debate on global warming important?

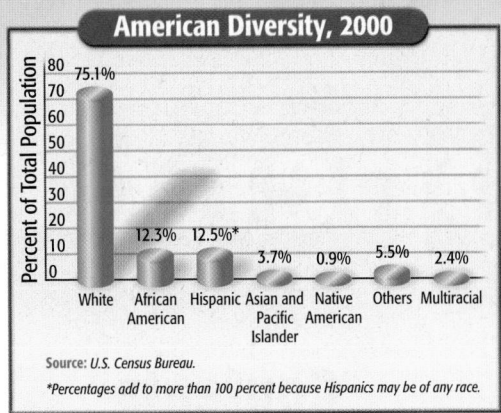

American Diversity, 2000

- White: 75.1%
- African American: 12.3%
- Hispanic: 12.5%*
- Asian and Pacific Islander: 3.7%
- Native American: 0.9%
- Others: 5.5%
- Multiracial: 2.4%

(Percent of Total Population)

Source: *U.S. Census Bureau.*

Percentages add to more than 100 percent because Hispanics may be of any race.

Geography and History

38. The graph above shows the diverse population of the United States at the beginning of the new century. Study the graph and answer the questions below.
   a. **Interpreting Graphs** Why is getting accurate data on the Hispanic population difficult?
   b. **Making Generalizations** How will population diversity affect government in the future?

Standards Practice

Directions: Choose the phrase that best completes the following sentence.

39. The Contract with America involved

A a commitment by Russia to eliminate land-based nuclear weapons.

B a campaign promise by President Clinton to create a national health-care system for all Americans.

C a legislative agenda promoted by the Republican Party in 1994.

D programs intended to increase the size and readiness of the military.

Standard 11.11: Students analyze the major social problems and domestic policy issues in contemporary American society.

Critical Thinking

32. **Reading Skill** Students' definitions should reflect the textbook content. Students' questions and answers will vary.

33. The House votes to determine if charges brought against a federal official is worthy of impeachment. The Senate then holds a trial. Students' opinions on impeachment will vary.

34. Communications: Internet, wireless technology; Politics: government shutdowns, impeachment; Economy: global economic blocs, Internet, and world economy; Population: racial diversity, aging, immigration

---

Online

Have students visit the Web site at tav.mt.glencoe.com to review Chapter 21 and take the Self-Check Quiz.

Writing About History

35. **Historical Analysis** American support for Israel and American investment in the oil industry in the Middle East led to the belief of some Muslims that American support of wealthy oil-producing countries increased Western influence and undermined traditional values and beliefs.

36. *Big Idea* Questions about the map will vary.

DBQ **Document-Based Questions**

37. a. Some scientists believe human activity causes global warming. Others think that natural factors may be involved. b. Global warming may alter the climate. If human activity is causing global warming, we may be able to stop it.

Geography and History

38. a. Students should note that some Hispanics would classify themselves in the Other or Multiracial categories. b. Students' answers will vary. Encourage students to give reasons for their answers.

Standards Practice

39. C

Bonus Question ?

Who were the Democratic and Republican presidential and vice presidential candidates in 2000? *(Democratic: Al Gore and Joseph Lieberman; Republican: George W. Bush and Richard Cheney)*

965

Appendix

Contents

Presidents of the United States

In this resource you will find portraits of the individuals who served as presidents of the United States, along with their occupations, political party affiliations, and other interesting facts.

**The Republican Party during this period developed into today's Democratic Party. Today's Republican Party originated in 1854.

1 George Washington

Presidential term: 1789–1797
Lived: 1732–1799
Born in: Virginia
Elected from: Virginia
Occupations: Soldier, Planter
Party: None
Vice President: John Adams

2 John Adams

Presidential term: 1797–1801
Lived: 1735–1826
Born in: Massachusetts
Elected from: Massachusetts
Occupations: Teacher, Lawyer
Party: Federalist
Vice President: Thomas Jefferson

3 Thomas Jefferson

Presidential term: 1801–1809
Lived: 1743–1826
Born in: Virginia
Elected from: Virginia
Occupations: Planter, Lawyer
Party: Republican**
Vice Presidents: Aaron Burr, George Clinton

4 James Madison

Presidential term: 1809–1817
Lived: 1751–1836
Born in: Virginia
Elected from: Virginia
Occupation: Planter
Party: Republican**
Vice Presidents: George Clinton, Elbridge Gerry

5 James Monroe

Presidential term: 1817–1825
Lived: 1758–1831
Born in: Virginia
Elected from: Virginia
Occupation: Lawyer
Party: Republican**
Vice President: Daniel D. Tompkins

6 John Quincy Adams

Presidential term: 1825–1829
Lived: 1767–1848
Born in: Massachusetts
Elected from: Massachusetts
Occupation: Lawyer
Party: Republican**
Vice President: John C. Calhoun

7 Andrew Jackson

Presidential term: 1829–1837
Lived: 1767–1845
Born in: South Carolina
Elected from: Tennessee
Occupations: Lawyer, Soldier
Party: Democratic
Vice Presidents: John C. Calhoun, Martin Van Buren

8 Martin Van Buren

Presidential term: 1837–1841
Lived: 1782–1862
Born in: New York
Elected from: New York
Occupation: Lawyer
Party: Democratic
Vice President: Richard M. Johnson

9 William H. Harrison

Presidential term: 1841
Lived: 1773–1841
Born in: Virginia
Elected from: Ohio
Occupations: Soldier, Planter
Party: Whig
Vice President: John Tyler

10 John Tyler

Presidential term: 1841–1845
Lived: 1790–1862
Born in: Virginia
Elected as V.P. from: Virginia
Succeeded Harrison
Occupation: Lawyer
Party: Whig
Vice President: None

11 James K. Polk

Presidential term: 1845–1849
Lived: 1795–1849
Born in: North Carolina
Elected from: Tennessee
Occupation: Lawyer
Party: Democratic
Vice President: George M. Dallas

12 Zachary Taylor

Presidential term: 1849–1850
Lived: 1784–1850
Born in: Virginia
Elected from: Louisiana
Occupation: Soldier
Party: Whig
Vice President: Millard Fillmore

13 Millard Fillmore

Presidential term: 1850–1853
Lived: 1800–1874
Born in: New York
Elected as V.P. from: New York
Succeeded Taylor
Occupation: Lawyer
Party: Whig
Vice President: None

14 Franklin Pierce

Presidential term: 1853–1857
Lived: 1804–1869
Born in: New Hampshire
Elected from: New Hampshire
Occupation: Lawyer
Party: Democratic
Vice President: William R. King

15 James Buchanan

Presidential term: 1857–1861
Lived: 1791–1868
Born in: Pennsylvania
Elected from: Pennsylvania
Occupation: Lawyer
Party: Democratic
Vice President: John C. Breckinridge

16 Abraham Lincoln

Presidential term: 1861–1865
Lived: 1809–1865
Born in: Kentucky
Elected from: Illinois
Occupation: Lawyer
Party: Republican
Vice Presidents: Hannibal Hamlin, Andrew Johnson

17 Andrew Johnson

Presidential term: 1865–1869
Lived: 1808–1875
Born in: North Carolina
Elected as V.P. from: Tennessee
Succeeded Lincoln
Occupation: Tailor
Party: Republican
Vice President: None

18 Ulysses S. Grant

Presidential term: 1869–1877
Lived: 1822–1885
Born in: Ohio
Elected from: Illinois
Occupations: Farmer, Soldier
Party: Republican
Vice Presidents: Schuyler Colfax,
Henry Wilson

19 Rutherford B. Hayes

Presidential term: 1877–1881
Lived: 1822–1893
Born in: Ohio
Elected from: Ohio
Occupation: Lawyer
Party: Republican
Vice President: William A.
Wheeler

20 James A. Garfield

Presidential term: 1881
Lived: 1831–1881
Born in: Ohio
Elected from: Ohio
Occupations: Laborer, Professor
Party: Republican
Vice President: Chester A.
Arthur

21 Chester A. Arthur

Presidential term: 1881–1885
Lived: 1830–1886
Born in: Vermont
Elected as V.P. from: New York
Succeeded Garfield
Occupations: Teacher, Lawyer
Party: Republican
Vice President: None

22 Grover Cleveland

Presidential term: 1885–1889
Lived: 1837–1908
Born in: New Jersey
Elected from: New York
Occupation: Lawyer
Party: Democratic
Vice President: Thomas A.
Hendricks

23 Benjamin Harrison

Presidential term: 1889–1893
Lived: 1833–1901
Born in: Ohio
Elected from: Indiana
Occupation: Lawyer
Party: Republican
Vice President: Levi P. Morton

24 Grover Cleveland

Presidential term: 1893–1897
Lived: 1837–1908
Born in: New Jersey
Elected from: New York
Occupation: Lawyer
Party: Democratic
Vice President: Adlai E.
Stevenson

25 William McKinley

Presidential term: 1897–1901
Lived: 1843–1901
Born in: Ohio
Elected from: Ohio
Occupations: Teacher, Lawyer
Party: Republican
Vice Presidents: Garret Hobart,
Theodore Roosevelt

26 Theodore Roosevelt

Presidential term: 1901–1909
Lived: 1858–1919
Born in: New York
Elected as V.P. from: New York
Succeeded McKinley
Occupations: Historian, Rancher
Party: Republican
Vice President: Charles W.
Fairbanks

27 William H. Taft

Presidential term: 1909–1913
Lived: 1857–1930
Born in: Ohio
Elected from: Ohio
Occupation: Lawyer
Party: Republican
Vice President: James S.
Sherman

28 Woodrow Wilson

Presidential term: 1913–1921
Lived: 1856–1924
Born in: Virginia
Elected from: New Jersey
Occupation: College Professor
Party: Democratic
Vice President: Thomas R.
Marshall

29 Warren G. Harding

Presidential term: 1921–1923
Lived: 1865–1923
Born in: Ohio
Elected from: Ohio
Occupations: Newspaper Editor,
Publisher
Party: Republican
Vice President: Calvin Coolidge

30 Calvin Coolidge

Presidential term: 1923–1929
Lived: 1872–1933
Born in: Vermont
Elected as V.P. from:
Massachusetts
Succeeded Harding
Occupation: Lawyer
Party: Republican
Vice President: Charles G. Dawes

31 Herbert C. Hoover

Presidential term: 1929–1933
Lived: 1874–1964
Born in: Iowa
Elected from: California
Occupation: Engineer
Party: Republican
Vice President: Charles Curtis

32 Franklin D. Roosevelt

Presidential term: 1933–1945
Lived: 1882–1945
Born in: New York
Elected from: New York
Occupation: Lawyer
Party: Democratic
Vice Presidents: John N. Garner,
Henry A. Wallace, Harry S
Truman

33 Harry S. Truman

Presidential term: 1945–1953
Lived: 1884–1972
Born in: Missouri
Elected as V.P. from: Missouri
Succeeded Roosevelt
Occupations: Clerk, Farmer
Party: Democratic
Vice President: Alben W.
Barkley

34 Dwight D. Eisenhower

Presidential term: 1953–1961
Lived: 1890–1969
Born in: Texas
Elected from: New York
Occupation: Soldier
Party: Republican
Vice President: Richard M.
Nixon

35 John F. Kennedy

Presidential term: 1961–1963
Lived: 1917–1963
Born in: Massachusetts
Elected from: Massachusetts
Occupations: Author, Reporter
Party: Democratic
Vice President: Lyndon B. Johnson

36 Lyndon B. Johnson

Presidential term: 1963–1969
Lived: 1908–1973
Born in: Texas
Elected as V.P. from: Texas
Succeeded Kennedy
Occupation: Teacher
Party: Democratic
Vice President: Hubert H. Humphrey

37 Richard M. Nixon

Presidential term: 1969–1974
Lived: 1913–1994
Born in: California
Elected from: New York
Occupation: Lawyer
Party: Republican
Vice Presidents: Spiro T. Agnew, Gerald R. Ford

38 Gerald R. Ford

Presidential term: 1974–1977
Lived: 1913–
Born in: Nebraska
Appointed as V.P. upon Agnew's resignation; succeeded Nixon
Occupation: Lawyer
Party: Republican
Vice President: Nelson A. Rockefeller

39 James E. Carter, Jr.

Presidential term: 1977–1981
Lived: 1924–
Born in: Georgia
Elected from: Georgia
Occupations: Business, Farmer
Party: Democratic
Vice President: Walter F. Mondale

40 Ronald W. Reagan

Presidential term: 1981–1989
Lived: 1911–2004
Born in: Illinois
Elected from: California
Occupations: Actor, Lecturer
Party: Republican
Vice President: George H.W. Bush

41 George H.W. Bush

Presidential term: 1989–1993
Lived: 1924–
Born in: Massachusetts
Elected from: Texas
Occupation: Business
Party: Republican
Vice President: J. Danforth Quayle

42 William J. Clinton

Presidential term: 1993–2001
Lived: 1946–
Born in: Arkansas
Elected from: Arkansas
Occupation: Lawyer
Party: Democratic
Vice President: Albert Gore, Jr.

43 George W. Bush

Presidential term: 2001–
Lived: 1946–
Born in: Connecticut
Elected from: Texas
Occupation: Business
Party: Republican
Vice President: Richard B. Cheney

Introduction

Have students complete the activities that follow to familiarize themselves with the types of primary sources.

Printed Publications

To help students analyze printed publications, instruct them to read the first two paragraphs under "Declaration of Natural Rights" in the Declaration of Independence (page 120). Discuss this passage in class, using questions such as: Is this a primary or secondary source? What is the main idea of the passage? What do you think this passage means?

Oral Histories

Work together with an English or Language Arts teacher to help students complete the following oral history activity. Have students interview a relative or friend who is much older than they are to see how his or her life was different from theirs when he or she was a teenager. Ask students to create a list of interview questions such as: What regular chores did you have to do? What did you and your friends talk about? What were your classes like in school?

Have students provide a transcript, or written record, of the interview and discuss their finding with the class.

Primary Sources Library

Using Primary Sources

Primary sources are written or artistic testimony to an era in history or to an important development. They can also be objects of daily life, reflecting how people lived and thought at a certain time. Perhaps a primary source represents the ideas of an industrial leader like Andrew Carnegie, who helped shape the American economy. Perhaps the source is a soldier's poem or the autobiography of a migrant worker.

Reading primary sources is important because it is an excellent way to understand how and why people believed and acted as they did in the past. While many people might have written down their stories or beliefs, the sources chosen here are from witnesses who were close to events or especially sensitive to them.

Opera glasses, late 1800s

Checking Your Sources

When you read primary or secondary sources, you should analyze them to figure out if they are dependable or reliable. Historians usually prefer primary sources to secondary sources, but both can be reliable or unreliable, depending on the following factors.

Time Span

With primary sources, it is important to consider how long after the event occurred the primary source was written. Generally, the longer the time span between the event and the account, the less reliable the account. As time passes, people often forget details and fill in gaps with events that never took place. Although we like to think we remember things exactly as they happened, the fact is we often remember them as we wanted them to occur.

Reliability

Another factor to consider when evaluating a primary source is the writer's background and reliability. First, try to determine how this person knows about what he or she is writing. How much does he or she know? Is the writer being truthful? Is the account convincing?

972

Teacher Notes

After studying the introduction to the Primary Sources Library, students should be able to meet the following objectives:

- explain how to interpret primary sources.
- explain the differences between primary sources and secondary sources.
- identify the different types of primary sources.
- understand that primary sources offer a unique view of people and events in a particular era.

Opinions

When evaluating a primary source, you should also decide whether the account has been influenced by emotion, opinion, or exaggeration. Writers can have reasons to distort the truth to suit their personal purposes. Ask yourself: Why did the person write the account? Do any key words or expressions reveal the author's emotions or opinions? You may wish to compare the account with one written by another witness to the event. If the two accounts differ, ask yourself why.

Interpreting Primary Sources

To help you analyze a primary source, use the following steps:

• **Examine the origins of the document.**
You need to determine if it is a primary source.

• **Find the main ideas.**
Read the document and summarize the main ideas in your own words. These ideas may be fairly easy to identify in newspapers and journals, for example, but are much more difficult to find in poetry.

• **Reread the document.**
Difficult ideas are not always easily understood on the first reading.

• **Use a variety of resources.**
Form the habit of using dictionaries, encyclopedias, and maps. These resources are tools to help you discover new ideas and knowledge, and they can be used to check the validity of various sources.

Primary Sources Library

Log book from Lewis and Clark expedition

Classifying Primary Sources

Primary sources fall into different categories:

Printed Publications

Printed publications include books such as biographies and autobiographies. Printed publications also include newspapers and magazines.

Songs & Poems

Songs and poems include works that express personal thoughts and feelings or political or religious beliefs of the writer, often using rhyming and rhythmic language.

Visual Materials

Visual materials include a wide range of forms: original paintings, drawings, and sculpture; photographs; film; and maps.

Oral Histories

Oral history collects spoken memories and personal observations through recorded interviews. In contrast, oral tradition involves stories that people have passed along by word of mouth from generation to generation.

Personal Records

Personal records are accounts of events kept by an individual who is a participant in or witness to these events. Personal records include diaries, journals, and letters.

Artifacts

Artifacts are objects such as tools or ornaments. Artifacts present information about a particular culture or a stage of technological development.

Primary Sources Library

Songs & Poems

Ask students to write a poem about a happy event in their lives. Suggest that the poem be in a standard form such as a limerick, haiku, or sonnet.

Visual Materials

Help students create a poster showing how your community or state changed during the 1900s. Students may use photographs or original drawings.

Personal Records

Ask students to describe what it might be like to witness an important public event. Provide the following guidelines: Write a journal entry describing the event. Begin by giving an overview of the event, including some objective facts. Then make the event personal by focusing on your own opinions or feelings.

Artifacts

To help students analyze artifacts, provide the following instructions: Find a primary source from your past such as a photograph, a report card, or a letter. Bring this source to class and explain what it shows about the time from which it comes.

Primary Sources Library **973**

Teacher Notes

Through the study of the selections in the Primary Sources Library and their accompanying questions, students should be able to:

• find main ideas in the selections.

• analyze information in a variety of written texts in order to make inferences and generalizations.

• provide an interpretation of the material in their own words.

FOCUS

History–Social Science Standards

This spread addresses the following main standards:

11.1 Students analyze the significant events in the founding of the nation and its attempts to realize the philosophy of government described in the Declaration of Independence.

11.2 Students analyze the relationship among the rise of industrialization, large-scale rural-to-urban migration, and massive immigration from Southern and Eastern Europe.

The three document excerpts represent three different time periods illustrating the loyalties that each author felt to the nation or to his region. Patrick Henry, a strong supporter of rebellion, is also quoted as saying "If this be treason, make the most of it." The song "Battle Cry of Freedom" followed another tune that has connections to the North and the South: The Confederate anthem "Dixie" was initially performed in Ohio before gaining Southern popularity. Andrew Carnegie demonstrated his love of country by donating about $350 million to libraries and other institutions.

TEACH

R₁ Reading Strategy

Using Context Clues Have students use the words *comport* and *unostentatious* in a sentence. **OL**

R₂ Reading Strategy

Analyzing Text Structure Write the indicated sentence on the board. Have students rewrite the sentence in their own words. **BL**

For use with Unit 1, "A Nation Is Born," and Unit 2, "Imperialism and Progressivism"

From the Beginnings to Progressivism

English colonists fought successfully against the English government for their rights. As the nation grew, so did feelings of nationalism—and sectionalism. A different sense of identity in the North and South contributed to the outbreak of the Civil War. In the latter part of the nineteenth century, change created many political and social problems, and Progressivism tried to solve them.

The first excerpt is from one of Patrick Henry's speeches. Known for his eloquence, Henry delivered this passionate plea at the second Virginia convention during a debate over whether to resist the English by force of arms.

The second set of excerpts relate to the Civil War. A Northerner wrote the "Battle Cry of Freedom," but the tune was so popular that a Confederate version was written as well. Both versions are shown against the background of an Augustus Saint-Gaudens sculpture honoring the 54th regiment of African American soldiers.

In the final excerpt, Andrew Carnegie presents his personal solution to the problem of a nation with both rich and poor citizens, a solution termed the "Gospel of Wealth." An immigrant himself, Carnegie became one of the nation's wealthiest industrialists and donors.

Reader's Dictionary

comport: to behave in a proper way

Dixie: nickname for the South, popularized in Daniel Emmett's song, "Land of Dixie"; term may derive from the French *dix* for "ten," referring to Louisiana ten-dollar bank notes

surplus wealth: in a capitalist system, the wealth remaining after labor and other costs are met

unostentatious: plain, not flashy or showy

"Give Me Liberty or Give Me Death" by Patrick Henry (1775)

The question before the House is one of awful moment. . . . For my own part, I consider it as nothing less than a question of freedom or slavery. . . . I have but one lamp by which my feet are guided, and that is the lamp of experience. . . . And judging by the past, I wish to know what there has been in the conduct of the British ministry for the last ten years to justify those hopes with which gentlemen have been pleased to solace themselves. . . . Ask yourselves how this gracious reception of our petition comports with those warlike preparations which cover our waters and darken our land.

They tell us, sir, that we are weak; unable to cope with so formidable an adversary. But when shall we be stronger? Will it be the next week. . . ? Will it be when we are totally disarmed. . . ? Gentlemen may cry, Peace, Peace—but there is no peace. . . . I know not what course others may take; but as for me, give me liberty or give me death!

"Battle Cry of Freedom"

Songs & Poems

Composer George F. Root wrote this song in 1862. It quickly became a favorite rallying song for Union soldiers. Composer H.L. Schreiner and W.H. Barnes adapted the tune for the South. The third verses of each are shown here.

"Gospel of Wealth" by Andrew Carnegie (1889)

Printed Publications

We start, then, with a condition of affairs under which the best interests of the race are promoted, but which inevitably gives wealth to the few. . . .

There are but three modes in which surplus wealth can be disposed of. It can be left to the families of the decedents; or it can be bequeathed for public purposes; or, finally, it can be administered during their lives by its possessors. . . .

The growing disposition to tax more and more heavily large estates left at death is a cheering indication of the growth of a salutary change in public opinion. . . . Of all forms of taxation, this seems the wisest. . . .

There remains, then, only one mode of using great fortunes: but in this way we have the true antidote for the temporary unequal distribution of wealth, the reconciliation of the rich and the poor. . . . Even the poorest can be made to . . . agree that great sums . . . gathered by some of their fellow-citizens and spent for public purposes, from which the masses reap the principal benefit, are more valuable to them than if scattered among them through the course of many years in trifling amounts.

This, then, is held to be the duty of the man of Wealth: First, to set an example of modest, unostentatious living, . . . ; to provide moderately for the legitimate wants of those dependent upon him; and . . . to consider all surplus revenues which come to him simply as trust funds . . . the man of wealth thus becoming the . . . trustee for his poorer brethren, . . . doing for them better than they would or could do for themselves.

Analyzing Primary Sources

1. What does Patrick Henry use to judge British intentions?
2. What is the main theme of the Union lyrics to "Battle Cry"?
3. What does Carnegie believe wealthy people should do with their excess money?
4. How does Carnegie think wealthy people should live? What are their other responsibilities?

Primary Sources Library

U **Universal Access**

Auditory/Musical Ask students to research other songs popularized during the Civil War era. Tell each student to write about one song that they selected in a one-page report. Students may perform the song to the class if they wish. **OL**

W **Writing Support**

Respond to Literature Writing Organize students into groups of four. Have students work together to write a short response to Carnegie. **Ask:** Are there only three ways to dispose of surplus wealth? *(Answers will vary, but students should respond accurately to what Carnegie wrote.)* **OL**

Resources for pages 974–975

- American History Primary Source Document Library CD-ROM

ASSESS/CLOSE

Tell students to answer the Analyzing Primary Sources questions.

Analyzing Primary Sources

1. He judges them based on his memory of British action over the previous ten years.
2. Men from any background can join the Union cause as long as they are loyal to the cause of freedom.
3. spend large amounts of it on public projects before their death
4. modestly, providing for the needs of those who depend on him, and spending the remainder for the good of the less fortunate

FOCUS

History–Social Science Standards

This spread addresses the following main standards:

11.5 Students analyze the major political, social, economic, technological, and cultural developments of the 1920s.

11.6 Students analyze the different explanations for the Great Depression and how the new Deal fundamentally changed the role of the federal government.

11.7 Students analyze America's participation in World War II.

During the 1920s American artists began to find their own style. Georgia O'Keeffe used Southwestern imagery and close-up techniques to create her signature style. The works of John Steinbeck and Audie Murphy illustrate the influence of the Depression and World War II on American life. *The Grapes of Wrath* won the 1939 Pulitzer Prize for Literature. Audie Murphy received 33 decorations, including the Medal of Honor and 5 decorations from France and Belgium.

TEACH

R Reading Strategy

Analyzing Text Structure Write *scuttle* on the board. Tell students to use the term in a sentence. **Ask:** How does this word's sound reflect its meaning? *(Answers will vary, but students should try to describe how the sound of something scuttling can be felt in the pronunciation of the word.)* **AL**

For use with Unit 3, "Boom and Bust," and Unit 4, "Global Struggles"

From Prosperity, through the Depression, to World War

Many artists and writers blossomed in the 1920s when the freer values of modern society took hold. Artists no longer tried to copy European models so much but instead created thoroughly American works. Art flourished during the Depression as well; at that time it often focused on the sorrows and hopes of the common people. Artists of the World War II era produced many works on themes of heroism and death.

Georgia O'Keeffe (1887–1986) created some of the most original images in the history of American art. A 1929 New Mexico trip powerfully influenced her style. Known for her strong sense of color, her most famous works are of single flowers.

John Steinbeck (1902–1968) is best known for his 1940 novel, The Grapes of Wrath. *It describes the Joad family's effort to find a new life in California after they have lost their Oklahoma farm. On the trip west, the Joads and thousands of others find solace at the makeshift camps they create along the way.*

The sacrifices that come with struggle are expressed in Audie Murphy's poetry on World War II. The son of a poor Texas sharecropper, Murphy is the most decorated U.S. combat soldier of that war.

Reader's Dictionary

scuttle: to run with short, shuffling steps

biomorphic: resembling or suggesting the forms of living organisms

---

The Grapes of Wrath
by John Steinbeck (1940)

 Printed Publications

The cars of the migrant people crawled out of the side roads onto the great cross-country highway, and they took the migrant way to the West. In the daylight they scuttled like bugs to the westward; and as the dark caught them, they clustered like bugs near to shelter and to water. And because they were lonely and perplexed, because they had all come from a place of sadness and worry and defeat, and because they were all going to a new mysterious place, they huddled together; they talked together; they shared their lives, their food, and the things they hoped for in the new country. Thus it might be that one family camped near a spring, and another camped for the spring and for company, and a third because two families had pioneered the place and found it good. And when the sun went down, perhaps twenty families and twenty cars were there.

In the evening a strange thing happened: the twenty families became one family, the children were the children of all. The loss of home became one loss, and the golden time in the West was one dream. And it might be that a sick child threw despair into the hearts of twenty families, of a hundred people; that a birth there in a tent kept a hundred people quiet and awestruck through the night and filled a hundred people with birth-joy in the morning. A family which the night before had been lost and fearful might search its goods to find a present for a new baby. In the evening, sitting about the fires, the twenty were one.

They grew to be units of the camps, units of the evenings and the nights. A guitar unwrapped from a blanket and tuned—and the songs, which were all of the people, were sung in the nights. Men sang the words, and women hummed the tunes.

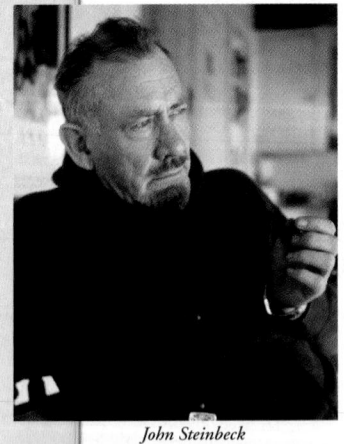
John Steinbeck

UNIVERSAL ACCESS

Visual/Spatial Point out that Steinbeck and Murphy create pictures with words, while O'Keeffe creates pictures with paint and canvas. Have students find examples of visual images in the works of Steinbeck and Murphy, and discuss other interpretations for the painting by O'Keeffe. *(Students' answers will vary but could include families' reactions to a baby's birth in Steinbeck's piece, or the dead sleeping on the field or marching on in Murphy's.)* **AL**

Georgia O'Keeffe's *Oriental Poppies* (1927)

Visual Materials

Georgia O'Keeffe's paintings of biomorphic flowers, rocks, and skulls are *abstract* paintings, meaning that they symbolize things other than what they actually are. *Oriental Poppies*, for example, could be seen as representing a cave-like enclosure.

Georgia O'Keeffe

"Alone and Far Removed" by Audie Murphy

Songs & Poems

Alone and far removed from earthly care
The noble ruins of men lie buried here.
You were strong men, good men
Endowed with youth and much the will to live
I hear no protest from the mute lips of the dead.
They rest; there is no more to give.

So long my comrades,
Sleep ye where you fell upon the field.
But tread softly please
March o'er my heart with ease
March on and on,
But to God alone we kneel.

Audie Murphy

Analyzing Primary Sources

1. According to Steinbeck, what binds the families of migrant people together?
2. How do you think Steinbeck feels about the migrants?
3. What is an abstract painting? How is it different from other paintings?
4. What is the main mood of Murphy's poem?

Primary Sources Library **977**

Analyzing Primary Sources

1. They are bound together by fear, desperation, and loneliness.
2. Although the migrants are struggling and desperate, Steinbeck sees them as extraordinarily human, showing a full range of human emotions.
3. Abstract paintings symbolize things other than what they actually show. Many other paintings are realistic, showing people and places as they are.
4. He feels sadness for the young men, his comrades, who lost their lives in battle.

FOCUS

History– Social Science Standards

This spread addresses the following standards:

11.8.2 Describe the significance of the Mexican immigration and its relationship to the agricultural economy, especially in California.

11.10.4 Examine the roles of civil rights advocates including the significance of Martin Luther King, Jr.'s "Letter from Birmingham Jail" and "I Have a Dream" speech.

Martin Luther King, Jr., used civil disobedience to force social change in the United States. His jailing generated more exposure for his efforts, especially when President Kennedy personally called his wife, Coretta Scott King, to assure her that Dr. King was safe in the Birmingham jail. Like African Americans, Mexican immigrants faced obstacles in American society. Elva Trevino Hart described her desire to overcome poverty and make a better life for herself.

TEACH

W Writing Support

Persuasive Writing Many of the people who participated in civil rights demonstrations were high school and college students. Tell students to imagine they were arrested in Birmingham. Students should write letters to their parents explaining why they participated in the demonstrations. Ask the students to anticipate some of their parents' arguments or fears and respond to them in the letters. **OL** **CA** 11WA2.1a

For use with Unit 5, "A Time of Upheaval," and Unit 6, "A Changing Society"

From Divisiveness to Diversity

American society took a sharp turn in the 1960s as a new generation sought to change some American values. Change became the challenge throughout the century as many new immigrants came to the United States to make it their home. By the year 2000, the nation was much more diverse. Hispanic Americans alone made up 12.5 percent of the population, approximately the same percentage as African Americans.

The 1960s were a breakthrough time for African Americans. Martin Luther King, Jr., persuaded many white Americans to acknowledge the need for more just laws for minorities. His "Letter from a Birmingham Jail" of April 16, 1963, makes the case that nonviolent resistance is not only moral, but is as American as the Boston Tea Party.

Elva Trevino Hart, born in southern Texas to Mexican immigrants, has a story that mirrors that of many immigrants. A migrant worker as a child, Hart eventually earned a master's degree from Stanford University. In this excerpt, she describes her father and his reaction to her graduation from high school.

Reader's Dictionary

conversely: reversed in order or action

civil disobedience: peaceful refusal to obey government demands as a means of forcing government concessions or changes in the law

admonish: to warn or express disapproval

macho: a strong sense of masculine pride

Letter from a Birmingham Jail by Martin Luther King, Jr. (1963)

 Personal Records

My dear fellow clergymen:
... Birmingham is probably the most thoroughly segregated city in the United States. On the basis of these conditions, Negro leaders sought to negotiate with the city fathers. ... As in so many past experiences, our hopes had been blasted. ... We had no alternative except to prepare for direct action, whereby we would present our very bodies as a means of laying our case before the conscience of the local and the national community. ...

You may well ask: ... Why sit-ins, marches and so forth? Isn't negotiation a better path?" ... Indeed, this is the very purpose of direct action. Nonviolent direct action seeks to create such a crisis ... that a community ... is forced to confront the issue. ...

... For years now I have heard the word "Wait!" It rings in the ear of every Negro with piercing familiarity. This "Wait" has almost always meant "Never." We must come to see, with one of our distinguished

Martin Luther King, Jr., (right) and Ralph Abernathy in Birmingham, Alabama

---

Reading Strategy — ANALYZING TEXT STRUCTURE

Ask students to carefully read Dr. King's letter, taking notes on its main points, the audience for which it is written, and the imagery that it uses. Tell students to compare these text themes to Dr. King's "I Have a Dream" speech, found in the textbook on p. 1002. Ask students to swap their notes with a classmate and compare their notes, discussing any differences they discover.
OL **CA** 11RC2.4; 11RL3.8

jurists, that "justice too long delayed is justice denied." . . . Perhaps it is easy for those who have never felt the stinging dark of segregation to say, "Wait." . . .

You express a great deal of anxiety over our willingness to break laws. . . . One may . . . ask: "How can you advocate breaking some laws and obeying others?" The answer lies in the fact that there are two types of laws: just and unjust. . . . One has not only a legal but a moral responsibility to obey just laws. Conversely, one has a moral responsibility to disobey unjust laws. . . .

Of course, there is nothing new about this kind of civil disobedience. . . . It was practiced superbly by the early Christians, who were willing to face hungry lions . . . rather than submit to certain unjust laws of the Roman Empire. . . . In our own nation, the Boston Tea Party represented a massive act of civil disobedience. . . .

. . . We will have to repent in this generation not merely for the hateful words and actions of the bad people but for the appalling silence of the good people. Human progress never rolls in on wheels of inevitability; it comes through the tireless efforts of men willing to be co-workers with God. . . .

I have heard numerous Southern religious leaders admonish their worshipers to comply with a desegregation decision because it is the law, but I have longed to hear white ministers declare: "Follow this decree because integration is morally right and because the Negro is your brother." . . . But even if the church does not come to the aid of justice, I have no despair about the future. . . . We will reach the goal of freedom . . . all over the nation, because the goal of America is freedom. . . . We will win our freedom because the sacred heritage of our nation and the eternal will of God are embodied in our echoing demands. . . .

Analyzing Primary Sources

1. Why does King say African Americans should not wait longer for change?
2. Who in ancient history practiced nonviolent resistance?
3. Why did Hart's father take his family so far to work in the summers?

Barefoot Heart
by Elva Trevino Hart

Printed Publications

"To get ahead, hijos (children). That's why we go a los trabajos (to work). When I first came from Mexico, I got paid dos reales al dia (two Spanish coins a day). I worked at building the railroad, . . . clearing land. . . . The only thing I would never do is strap on the contraption to burn brush with liquid fuel. Too dangerous. . . ."

I fingered the nickels in the pocket of my sun dress and tried to imagine Apa (Daddy) working for fifty cents a day. And I felt I understood why we had to go to Minnesota. Our family could make more money in the migrant fields than anywhere else. . . .

* * *

(My father) had only gone as far as the fourth grade in Mexico. . . . When I was in the fourth grade, I told my father that I wanted to go to college. . . .

On (high school) graduation night I delivered the valedictory speech, entitled "He Conquers who Conquers Himself." I wish now I had said "she," but it has remained the theme of my life nevertheless. Apa came up to me afterwards with big macho tears in his eyes. I had never seen him even close to crying before.

He pressed two thousand dollars in cash into my hand. "I have been saving this for you, mija (my daughter). It's your money to go to college." . . . I knew that this money would only be enough for about one semester, but I didn't tell him. Instead I hugged him, crying violently.

Primary Sources Library **979**

C Critical Thinking

Analyzing Information Ask students to read the excerpt from *Barefoot Heart*. **Ask:** What are the lessons that Elva Trevino Hart learned from her father? *(She learned that her education was very important to him even though he did not have much money and had not even finished grade school. She learned that working hard to support the family was very important.)* OL

R Reading Strategy

Analyzing Text Structure Hart states that her father had "big macho tears in his eyes" at her graduation. **Ask:** What does it mean to be macho? Ask students for examples of macho behavior. *(Student answers will vary but should reflect an understanding of the definition of the word, as used in the literature excerpt and as defined in the textbook.)* EL

Resources for pages 978–979

⊙ American History Primary Source Document Library CD-ROM

ASSESS/CLOSE

Tell students to answer the Analyzing Primary Sources questions.

Analyzing Primary Sources

1. In the past, waiting for change often meant change never came.
2. Christians who opposed unjust laws of the Roman Empire practiced nonviolent resistance.
3. He knew that the family could make more money in the migrant fields than anywhere else.

FOCUS

History–Social Science Standards

This spread addresses the following standards:

11.9 Students analyze U.S. foreign policy since World War II.

11.9.6 Describe U.S. Middle East policy and its strategic, political and economic interests, including those related to the Gulf War.

On September 11, 2001, millions of Americans watched the terrorist attacks on the World Trade Center and the Pentagon unfold on television. The attacks caused many Americans to feel unsafe in their country, similar to fears last felt during World War II and the early years of the Cold War. On September 20, 2001, President George W. Bush addressed Congress and the American people.

TEACH

R Reading Strategy

Using Context Clues In his speech, President Bush stated that terrorists practiced a "fringe form of Islamic extremism." Have students use the terms *fringe* and *extremist* in a sentence in a context not related to terrorism. **EL**

For use with Chapter 21, "Into a New Century"

The Challenges Ahead

With the onset of the twenty-first century, Americans faced the challenge of living in a more interconnected world. World trade expanded, but so too did awareness of potential threats from abroad. For most Americans, one event changed their view of the world: the terrorist attacks on the World Trade Center in New York City and on the Pentagon in Washington, D.C., on September 11, 2001. In these horrific attacks, thousands of people were killed.

Never before had Americans felt so unsafe on their own soil. In his address on September 20, President George W. Bush attempted to calm the nation's fears by announcing a new kind of war against terrorism. He also urged the American people to remain firm and united.

Reader's Dictionary

fringe: outside border; also, a group with extremist views

haven: harbor or port; also, a place of safety

pretense: professed claim rather than a real intention or purpose

terrorism: the political use of terror, especially on civilian populations, as a means of forcing an opponent to surrender or adopt different policies

---

Address to Joint Session of Congress by President George W. Bush, September 20, 2001

 Printed Publications

In the normal course of events, Presidents come to this chamber to report on the state of the Union. Tonight, no such report is needed. It has already been delivered by the American people.

We have seen it in the courage of passengers, who rushed terrorists to save others on the ground. . . .

We have seen the state of our Union in the endurance of rescuers, working past exhaustion. We have seen the unfurling of flags, the lighting of candles, the giving of blood, the saying of prayers. . . .

My fellow citizens, for the last nine days, the entire world has seen for itself the state of our Union—and it is strong. Tonight we are a country awakened to danger and called to defend freedom. Our grief has turned to anger, and anger to resolution. . . .

On September the eleventh, enemies of freedom committed an act of war against our country. Americans have known wars—but for the past 136 years, they have been wars on foreign soil, except for one Sunday in 1941. Americans have known the casualties of war—but not at the center of a great city on a peaceful morning. Americans have known surprise attacks—but never before on thousands of civilians. All of this was brought upon us in a single day—and night fell on a different world, a world where freedom itself is under attack.

Americans have many questions tonight. Americans are asking: Who attacked our country?

The evidence we have gathered all points to a collection of loosely affiliated terrorist organizations known as al-Qaeda. . . .

R The terrorists practice a fringe form of Islamic extremism that has been rejected by Muslim scholars and the vast majority of Muslim clerics—a fringe movement that perverts the peaceful teachings of Islam. The terrorists' directive commands them to kill Christians and Jews, to kill all Americans, and make no distinctions among military and civilians, including women and children.

UNIVERSAL ACCESS

Visual/Spatial Have students create posters that address the emotional themes to which President Bush refers in his speech: courage, endurance, and strength. Students may use photographs and quotations found in newspapers and magazines or relevant quotations from the president's address. Display the posters around the classroom. **BL**

President George W. Bush, center

This group and its leader—a person named Osama bin Laden—are linked to many other organizations in different countries. . . . There are thousands of these terrorists in more than sixty countries. They are recruited from their own nations and neighborhoods, and brought to camps in places like Afghanistan where they are trained in the tactics of terror. . . .

The leadership of al-Qaeda has great influence in Afghanistan, and supports the Taliban regime in controlling most of that country. In Afghanistan, we see al-Qaeda's vision for the world. Afghanistan's people have been brutalized — many are starving and many have fled. . . .

The United States respects the people of Afghanistan—after all, we are currently its largest source of humanitarian aid—but we condemn the Taliban regime. . . . The Taliban must act and act immediately. They will hand over the terrorists, or they will share in their fate. . . .

Americans are asking: Why do they hate us?

They hate what we see right here in this chamber—a democratically elected government. Their leaders are self-appointed. They hate our freedoms. . . . These terrorists kill not merely to end lives, but to disrupt and end a way of life. . . .

C We are not deceived by their pretenses to piety. We have seen their kind before. They are the heirs of all the murderous ideologies of the twentieth century. By sacrificing human life to serve their radical visions—by abandoning every value except the will to power—they follow in the path of fascism, and Nazism, and totalitarianism. And they will follow that path all the way, to where it ends: in history's unmarked grave of discarded lies.

Americans are asking: How will we fight and win this war? . . . . Americans should not expect one battle, but a lengthy campaign, unlike any other we have seen. . . . We will starve terrorists of funding, turn them one against another, drive them from place to place, until there is no refuge or rest. And we will pursue nations that provide aid or safe haven to terrorism. . . .

Our Nation has been put on notice: We are not immune from attack. We will take defensive measures against terrorism to protect Americans. . . . So tonight I announce the creation of a Cabinet-level position reporting directly to me— the Office of Homeland Security. . . . This is not, however, just America's fight. And what is at stake is not just America's freedom. This is the world's fight. This is civilization's fight. . . .

R I ask you to uphold the values of America, and remember why so many have come here. We are in a fight for our principles, and our first responsibility is to live by them. No one should be singled out for unfair treatment or unkind words because of their ethnic background or religious faith. . . .

After all that has just passed—all the lives taken, and all the possibilities and hopes that died with them—it is natural to wonder if America's future is one of fear. Some speak of an age of terror. I know there are struggles ahead, and dangers to face. But this country will define our times, not be defined by them. . . .

Great harm has been done to us. We have suffered great loss. And in our grief and anger we have found our mission and our moment. Freedom and fear are at war. The advance of human freedom—the great achievement of our time, and the great hope of every time—now depends on us. Our Nation—this generation— will lift a dark threat of violence from our people and our future. We will rally the world to this cause, by our efforts and by our courage. We will not tire, we will not falter, and we will not fail. . . .

Analyzing Primary Sources

1. Why does President Bush say that the American people themselves have already reported on the state of the nation?

2. What is so unusual about the attack that it makes Bush say that "night fell on a different world?"

3. To what "murderous ideologies" does Bush compare the terrorists?

Primary Sources Library **981**

Primary Sources Library

C Critical Thinking

Comparing and Contrasting
In his speech, President Bush refers to the totalitarian regimes of the World War II era. **Ask:** Do you believe it is accurate to compare the Taliban regime in Afghanistan to the groups mentioned here? *(Answers will vary, but students should recognize that the Taliban was an organization determined to impose its viewpoint on the Afghans.)* **AL**

R Reading Strategy

Activating Prior Knowledge
Ask students to think back and identify the time periods in the history of the United States where American citizens did single out others because of their ethnic background or religious faith. *(Answers will vary. Some possible answers include German Americans in World War I and Japanese Americans in World War II.)* **OL**

Resources for pages 980–981

● American History Primary Source Document Library CD-ROM

ASSESS/CLOSE

Tell students to answer the Analyzing Primary Sources questions.

Analyzing Primary Sources

1. He uses examples of the strong courage, compassion, and concern for others Americans have shown in the crisis as proof that the nation as a whole is strong.

2. This attack occurred within the United States and targeted civilians rather than military personnel.

3. He compares the terrorists to fascists, Nazis, and totalitarian dictators.

Documents of American History

TABLE OF CONTENTS

(above) Notes for Washington's Farewell Address

(right) Lincoln's drafts of the Gettysburg Address

Magna Carta

Why They Matter

Documents are often public statements by a president or an official body, such as a legislature, on an important issue. They have become documents because they define a particular issue so well that Americans continue to refer to them. Many documents here address fundamental American beliefs, such as the rights of the individual and the proper limits of government. Other documents, such as the Monroe Doctrine or the Truman Doctrine, address the nation's position and responsibilities in the world.

Documents matter because they are guides to American government and values. Sometimes people study them to learn how Americans came to believe in certain principles. Other times people read documents simply because these writings express certain principles passionately.

Signing the Mayflower Compact

Silver inkwell used in the signing of the Constitution

Documents That Shaped the American Republic

The first seven documents in this collection played an important role in shaping the American republic. Each contributed an essential building block for American political principles. Ultimately these principles were embodied in the Declaration of Independence, the Bill of Rights, and the Constitution.

Documents

DOCUMENT	WHY IT MATTERS
The Magna Carta In signing this charter in 1215, King John of England granted his subjects certain permanent liberties or rights, such as the right to a fair trial by a jury of their peers.	Over the centuries, English people believed that the Magna Carta gave them certain rights. They took this idea with them when they settled the American colonies. Some provisions of the Bill of Rights reflect ancient Magna Carta liberties.
The Mayflower Compact In 1620 the Pilgrims signed a compact while still aboard the *Mayflower.* This compact laid out a plan for self-government the Pilgrims would use once they landed in America.	This compact is the first plan for self-government put into effect in the English colonies. It reflected the idea that government should be based on a consensus of the entire community.
The Fundamental Orders of Connecticut Connecticut settlers agreed they would be governed according to a certain set of laws and through certain institutions. All citizens, not only those of a certain religion, could vote.	This document, the first written constitution drawn up in America, strengthened the colonists' beliefs about governing themselves.
The English Bill of Rights In 1689, after the Glorious Revolution, Parliament forced the king to accept this Bill of Rights guaranteeing basic civil rights.	This document clearly established that English subjects had certain rights and that the king could be removed from power for violating those rights.
Second Treatise of Government English philosopher John Locke wrote this document during the 1680s. One of his basic arguments was that government should be based on a contract between a ruler and those who are ruled. Rebellion is justified if a ruler violates the contract.	During the American Revolution, the colonists drew from Locke's theories of government and especially his ideas about the right to rebel.
The Virginia Statute for Religious Freedom This 1786 statute declared that the state of Virginia should not support Anglicanism or any other religious denomination.	The religious clauses of the Bill of Rights protecting the free exercise of religion and prohibiting an official religion were based on this statute.
The Federalist No. 10 In 1787 James Madison wrote this paper, one of a series arguing for stronger central government as reflected in the new Constitution.	The framework for American government today— a representative government with a strong federal government—was laid out in the Federalist Papers.

*Use the **American History Primary Source Document Library CD-ROM** to find additional primary sources about American heritage.*

The Magna Carta

The Magna Carta, signed by King John of England in 1215, marked a decisive step forward in the development of English constitutional government. Later it served as a model for the colonists, who carried the Magna Carta's guarantees of political rights to America.

John, by the grace of God, king of England, lord of Ireland, duke of Normandy and Aquitaine, and count of Anjou: to the archbishops, bishops, abbots, earls, barons, justiciaries, foresters, sheriffs, reeves, ministers, and all bailiffs and others his faithful subjects, greeting. . . .

1. We have, in the first place, granted to God, and by this our present charter, confirmed for us and our heirs forever that the English church shall be free. . . .

9. Neither we nor our bailiffs shall seize any land or rent for any debt so long as the debtor's chattels are sufficient to discharge the same. . . .

12. No scutage [tax] or aid shall be imposed in our kingdom unless by the common counsel thereof. . . .

14. For obtaining the common counsel of the kingdom concerning the assessment of aids. . . or of scutage, we will cause to be summoned, severally by our letters, the archbishops, bishops, abbots, earls, and great barons; we will also cause to be summoned generally, by our sheriffs and bailiffs, all those who hold lands directly of us, to meet on a fixed day . . . and at a fixed place. . . .

20. A free man shall be amerced [punished] for a small fault only according to the measure thereof, and for a great crime according to its magnitude. . . . None of these amercements shall be imposed except by the oath of honest men of the neighborhood.

21. Earls and barons shall be amerced only by their peers, and only in proportion to the measure of the offense. . . .

38. In the future no bailiff shall upon his own unsupported accusation put any man to trial without producing credible witnesses to the truth of the accusation.

39. No free man shall be taken, imprisoned, disseised [seized], outlawed, banished, or in any way destroyed, nor will we proceed against or prosecute him, except by the lawful judgment of his peers and by the law of the land.

40. To no one will we sell, to none will we deny or delay, right or justice. . . .

42. In the future it shall be lawful . . . for anyone to leave and return to our kingdom safely and securely by land and water, saving his fealty to us. Excepted are those who have been imprisoned or outlawed according to the law of the land. . . .

61. Whereas we, for the honor of God and the amendment of our realm, and in order the better to allay the discord arisen between us and our barons, have granted all these things aforesaid. . . .

63. Wherefore we will, and firmly charge . . . that all men in our kingdom shall have and hold all the aforesaid liberties, rights, and concessions . . . fully, and wholly to them and their heirs . . . in all things and places forever. . . . It is moreover sworn, as well on our part as on the part of the barons, that all these matters aforesaid will be kept in good faith and without deceit. Witness the above named and many others. Given by our hand in the meadow which is called Runnymede. . . .

The Mayflower Compact

*On November 21, 1620, 41 colonists drafted the Mayflower Compact while still aboard the **Mayflower**. It was the first self-government plan ever put into effect in the English colonies. The compact was drawn up under these circumstances, as described by Governor William Bradford:*

"This day, before we came to harbor, observing some not well affected to unity and concord, but gave some appearance of faction, it was thought good there should be an association and agreement that we should combine together in one body, and to submit to such government and governors as we should by common consent agree to make and choose, and set our hands to this that follows word for word."

In the Name of God, Amen. We, whose names are underwritten, the Loyal Subjects of our dread Sovereign Lord King James, by the Grace of God, of Great Britain, France, and Ireland, King, Defender of the Faith, etc.

Having undertaken for the Glory of God, and Advancement of the Christian Faith, and the honor of our King and Country, a Voyage to plant the first Colony in the northern Parts of Virginia, Do by these Presents, solemnly and mutually, in the Presence of God and one another, covenant and combine ourselves together into a civil Body Politick, for our better Ordering and Preservation, and Furtherance of the Ends aforesaid; And by Virtue hereof do enact, constitute, and frame, such just and equal Laws, Ordinances, Acts, Constitutions, and Offices, from time to time, as shall be thought most meet and convenient for the general Good of the Colony; unto which we promise all due Submission and Obedience. In Witness whereof we have hereunder subscribed our names at Cape Cod the eleventh of November, in the Reign of our Sovereign Lord King James of England, France, and Ireland, the eighteenth and of Scotland, the fifty-fourth. Anno Domini, 1620.

Signing of the Mayflower Compact

The Fundamental Orders of Connecticut

In January 1639, settlers in Connecticut, led by Thomas Hooker, drew up the Fundamental Orders of Connecticut—America's first written constitution. It is essentially a body of laws and a compact among the settlers.

Forasmuch as it has pleased the Almighty God by the wise disposition of His Divine Providence so to order and dispose of things that we, the inhabitants and residents of Windsor, Hartford, and Wethersfield are now cohabiting and dwelling in and upon the river of Conectecotte and the lands thereunto adjoining; and well knowing where a people are gathered together the Word of God requires that, to maintain the peace and union of such a people, there should be an orderly and decent government established according to God, . . . do therefore associate and conjoin ourselves to be as one public state or commonwealth. . . . As also in our civil affairs to be guided and governed according to such laws, rules, orders, and decrees as shall be made, ordered, and decreed, as follows:

1. It is ordered . . . that there shall be yearly two general assemblies or courts; . . . The first shall be called the Court of Election, wherein shall be yearly chosen . . . so many magistrates and other public officers as shall be found requisite. Whereof one to be chosen governor . . . and no other magistrate to be chosen for more than one year; provided aways there be six chosen besides the governor . . . by all that are admitted freemen and have taken the oath of fidelity, and do cohabit within this jurisdiction. . . .

4. It is ordered . . . that no person be chosen governor above once in two years, and that the governor be always a member of some approved congregation, and formerly of the magistracy within this jurisdiction; and all the magistrates freemen of this Commonwealth. . . .

5. It is ordered . . . that to the aforesaid Court of Election the several towns shall send their deputies. . . . Also, the other General Court . . . shall be for making of laws, and any other public occasion which concerns the good of the Commonwealth. . . .

7. It is ordered . . . that . . . the constable or constables of each town shall forthwith give notice distinctly to the inhabitants of the same . . . that . . . they meet and assemble themselves together to elect and choose certain deputies to be at the General Court then following to [manage] the affairs of the Commonwealth; . . .

10. It is ordered . . . that every General Court . . . shall consist of the governor, or someone chosen to moderate the Court, and four other magistrates, at least, with the major part of the deputies of the several towns legally chosen. . . . In which said General Courts shall consist the supreme power of the Commonwealth, and they only shall have power to make laws or repeal them, to grant levies, to admit of freemen, dispose of lands undisposed of to several towns or person, and also shall have power to call either Court or magistrate or any other person whatsoever into question for any misdemeanor. . . .

Connecticut settlers on their way to Hartford

The English Bill of Rights

In 1689 William of Orange (pictured at right) and his wife Mary became joint rulers of England after accepting a list of conditions that later became known as the English Bill of Rights. This document assured the English people of certain basic civil rights and limited the power of the English monarchy.

An act declaring the rights and liberties of the subject and settling the succession of the crown. Whereas the lords spiritual and temporal and commons assembled at Westminster lawfully fully and freely representing all the estates of the people of this realm did upon the thirteenth day of February in the year of our Seal of William and Mary Lord one thousand six hundred eighty-eight [-nine] present unto their majesties . . . William and Mary prince and princess of Orange . . . a certain declaration in writing made by the said lords and commons in the words following viz [namely]

Whereas the late king James the second, by the assistance of divers evil counsellors, judges, and ministers employed by him did endeavor to subvert and extirpate the protestant religion and the laws and liberties of this kingdom.

By assuming and exercising a power of dispensing with and suspending of laws and the execution of laws without consent of parliament. . . .

By levying money for and to the use of the crown by pretence of prerogative for other time and in other manner than the same was granted by parliament.

By raising and keeping a standing army within this kingdom in time of peace without consent of parliament and quartering soldiers contrary to law. . . .

By violating the freedom of election of members to serve in parliament. . . .

And excessive bail hath been required of persons committed in criminal cases to elude the benefit of the laws made for the liberty of the subjects.

And excessive fines have been imposed.

And illegal and cruel punishments inflicted. . . .

And thereupon the said lords spiritual and temporal and commons . . . do . . . declare that the pretended power of suspending of laws or the execution of laws by regal authority without consent of parliament is illegal. . . .

That levying money for or to the use of the crown . . . without grant of parliament for longer time or in other manner than the same is or shall be granted is illegal.

That it is the right of the subjects to petition the king and all commitments and prosecutions for such petitioning are illegal.

That the raising or keeping a standing army within the kingdom in time of peace unless it be with consent of parliament is against law. . . .

That election of members of parliament ought to be free. . . .

That excessive bail ought not to be required nor excessive fines imposed nor cruel and unusual punishments inflicted. . . .

The said lords . . . do resolve that William and Mary, prince and princess of Orange, be declared king and queen of England, France, and Ireland. . . .

Documents

Second Treatise of Government

English philosopher John Locke (above) wrote "Two Treatises of Government" in the early 1680s. Published in 1690, the "Second Treatise of Government" argues that government should be based on an agreement between the people and their ruler, and that if the ruler violates the agreement, a rebellion by the people may be justified.

Of the State of Nature

To understand Political Power right, and to derive it from its Original, we must consider what State all Men are naturally in, and that is, a State of perfect Freedom to order their Actions, and dispose of their Possessions, and Persons as they think fit, within the bounds of the Law of Nature, without asking leave, or depending upon the Will of any other Man. . . .

Of the Beginning of Political Societies

Men being, as has been said, by Nature, all free, equal and independent, no one can be put out of this Estate, and subjected to the Political Power of another, without his own Consent.

The only way whereby any one divests himself of his Natural Liberty, and puts on the bonds of Civil Society is by agreeing with other Men to joyn and unite into a Community, for their comfortable, safe, and peaceable living one amongst another, in a secure Enjoyment of their properties, and a greater Security against any that are not of it. This any number of Men may do, because it injures not the Freedom of the rest; they are left as they were in the Liberty of the State of Nature. . . .

Whosoever therefore out of a state of Nature unite into a Community, must be understood to give up all the power, necessary to the ends for which they unite into Society, to the majority of the Community. . . .

Of the Dissolution of Government

Governments are dissolved from within . . . when the Legislative is altered. . . . First, that when such a single Person or Prince sets up his own Arbitrary Will in place of the Laws, which are the Will of the Society, declared by the Legislative, then the Legislative is changed . . . . Secondly, when the Prince hinders the legislative from . . . acting freely, pursuant to those ends, for which it was Constituted, the Legislative is altered . . . . Thirdly, When by the Arbitrary Power of the Prince, the Electors, or ways of Election are altered, without the Consent, and contrary to the common Interest of the People, there also the Legislative is altered. . . .

In these and the like Cases, when the Government is dissolved, the People are at liberty to provide for themselves, by erecting a new Legislative, differing from the other, by the change of Persons, or Form, or both as they shall find it most for their safety and good. For the Society can never, by the fault of another, lose the Native and Original Right it has to preserve itself. . . .

The Virginia Statute for Religious Freedom

This statute, excerpted below, was the basis for the religion clauses in the Bill of Rights. Thomas Jefferson drafted the statute, and James Madison guided it through the Virginia legislature in 1786. The issue it addresses arose when the new state considered whether citizens should continue to support the Anglican Church, as they had in colonial times, or whether they should support any or all other denominations.

Whereas Almighty God hath created the mind free; that all attempts to influence it by temporal punishments . . . tend only to beget habits of hypocrisy and meanness, and are a departure from the plan of the Holy author of our religion; . . . that the impious presumption of legislators and rulers, civil as well as ecclesiastical, who being themselves but fallible and uninspired men, have assumed dominion over the faith of others, setting up their own opinions and modes of thinking as the only true and infallible, and as such endeavouring to impose them on others, hath established and maintained false religions over the greatest part of the world, and through all time; . . . that to compel a man to furnish contributions of money for the propagation of opinions which he disbelieves, is sinful and tyrannical; . . . that our civil rights have no dependence on our religious opinions, any more than our opinions in physics or geometry; that therefore the proscribing any citizen as unworthy the public confidence by laying upon him an incapacity of being called to offices of trust . . . unless he profess or renounce this or that religious opinion, is depriving him injuriously of those privileges and advantages to which in common with his fellow-citizens he has a natural right; that it tends only to corrupt the principles of that religion it is meant to encourage, by bribing with a monopoly of worldly honours and emoluments, those who will externally profess and conform to it. . . . :

Be it enacted by the General Assembly, That no man shall be compelled to frequent or support any religious worship, place, or ministry whatsoever, nor shall be enforced, restrained, molested, or burthened in his body or goods, nor shall otherwise suffer on account of his religious opinions or belief; but that all men shall be free to profess, and by argument to maintain, their opinion in matters of religion, and that the same shall in no wise diminish enlarge, or affect their civil capacities. . . .

Thomas Jefferson

The Federalist No. 10

James Madison (pictured at right) wrote several articles for a New York newspaper supporting ratification of the Constitution . In the excerpt below, he argues for the idea of a federal republic as a guard against factions, or overzealous parties, in governing the nation.

The latent causes of faction are thus sown in the nature of man; and we see them everywhere. . . . A zeal for different opinions concerning religion, concerning government, and many other points; . . . an attachment to different leaders ambitiously contending for pre-eminence and power . . . have, in turn, divided mankind into parties . . . disposed to vex and oppress each other than to cooperate for their common good. . . . But the most common and durable source of factions has been the various and unequal distribution of property. Those who hold and those who are without property have ever formed distinct interests in society. Those who are creditors, and those who are debtors, fall under a like discrimination. A landed interest, a manufacturing interest, a mercantile interest, a moneyed interest, with many lesser interests, grow up of necessity in civilized nations, and divide them into different classes, actuated by different sentiments and views. The regulation of these various and interfering interests forms the principal task of modern legislation and involves the spirit of party and faction in the necessary and ordinary operations of government. . . .

The inference to which we are brought is that the causes of faction cannot be removed and relief is only to be sought in the means of controlling its effects. . . .

By what means is this object attainable? Evidently by one of two only. Either the existence of the same passion or interest in a majority at the same time must be prevented, or the majority, having such coexistent passion or interest, must be rendered, by their number and local situation, unable to concert and carry into effect schemes of oppression. . . .

From this . . . it may be concluded that a pure democracy, by which I mean a society consisting of a small number of citizens, who assemble and administer the government in person, can admit of no cure for the mischiefs of faction. A common passion or interest will, in almost every case, be felt by a majority of the whole; a communication and concert results from the form of government itself; and there is nothing to check the inducements to sacrifice the weaker party or an obnoxious individual. Hence it is that such democracies have ever been spectacles of turbulence and contention. . . .

A republic, by which I mean a government in which the scheme of representation takes place, opens a different prospect and promises the cure for which we are seeking. . . .

The two great points of difference between a democracy and a republic are: first, the delegation of the government in the latter to a small number of citizens elected by the rest; secondly, the greater number of citizens and great sphere of country over which the latter may be extended.

The Federalist No. 51

The author of this Federalist paper is not known. It may have been either James Madison or Alexander Hamilton. The author argues that the Constitution's federal system and separation of powers will protect the rights of the people.

In order to lay a due foundation for that separate and distinct exercise of the different powers of government, which to a certain extent is admitted on all hands to be essential to the preservation of liberty, it is evident that . . . the great security against a gradual concentration of the several powers in the same department, consists in giving to those who administer each department the necessary constitutional means and personal motives to resist encroachments of the others. . . .

Ambition must be made to counteract ambition. . . . A dependence on the people is, no doubt, the primary control on the government; but experience has taught mankind the necessity of auxiliary precautions. . . . The constant aim is to divide and arrange the several offices in such a manner as that each may be a check on the other. . . . In the compound republic of America, the power surrendered by the people is first divided between two distinct governments, and then the portion allotted to each subdivided among distinct and separate departments. . . .

In a free government the security for civil rights must be the same as that for religious rights. It consists in the one case in the multiplicity of interests, and in the other in the multiplicity of sects. . . . In the extended republic of the United States, and among the great variety of interests, parties, and sects which it embraces, a coalition of a majority of the whole society could seldom take place on any other principles than those of justice and the general good. . . . It is no less certain than it is important . . . that the larger the society, provided it lie within a practical sphere, the more duly capable it will be of self-government.

The Federalist No. 59

In this Federalist paper, Alexander Hamilton explains why Congress, and not the states, should have the final say in how federal elections are conducted.

The natural order of the subject leads us to consider . . . that provision of the Constitution which authorizes the national legislature to regulate, in the last resort, the election of its own members. . . . Its propriety rests upon the evidence of this plain proposition, that every government ought to contain in itself the means of its own preservation. . . . Nothing can be more evident, than that an exclusive power of regulating elections for the national government, in the hands of the state legislatures, would leave the existence of the union entirely at their mercy. They could at any moment annihilate it, by neglecting to provide for the choice of persons to administer its affairs. . . .

It is certainly true that the state legislatures, by forbearing the appointment of senators, may destroy the national government. But it will not follow that, because they have a power to do this in one instance, they ought to have it in every other. . . . It is an evil; but it is an evil which could not have been avoided without excluding the states . . . from a place in the organization of the national government. If this had been done, it would doubtless have been interpreted into an entire dereliction of the federal principle; and would certainly have deprived the state governments of that absolute safeguard which they will enjoy under this provision. . . .

Washington's Farewell Address

Washington never orally delivered his Farewell Address. Instead, he arranged to have it printed in a Philadelphia newspaper on September 19, 1796. Designed in part to remove him from consideration for a third presidential term, the address also warned about dangers the new nation was facing, especially the dangers of political parties and sectionalism.

Friends and Fellow Citizens:

The period for a new election of a citizen to administer the executive government of the United States being not far distant . . . I should now apprise you of the resolution I have formed to decline being considered. . . .

The unity of government which constitutes you one people is . . . a main pillar in the edifice of your real independence; the support of your tranquility at home, your peace abroad; of your safety; of your prosperity in every shape; of that very liberty which you so highly prize. But as it is easy to foresee that, from different causes and from different quarters, much pains will be taken, many artifices employed to weaken in your minds the conviction of this truth. . . .

The name of American, which belongs to you, in your national capacity, must always exalt the just pride of patriotism more than any appellation derived from local discriminations. . . .

In contemplating the causes which may disturb our Union, it occurs as matter of serious concern that any ground should have been furnished for characterizing parties by geographical discriminations: Northern and Southern; Atlantic and Western; whence designing men may endeavor to excite a belief that there is a real difference of local interests and views. . . .

Let me now take a more comprehensive view and warn you in the most solemn manner against the baneful effects of the spirit of party generally. . . .

Washington preparing to leave office

The alternate domination of one faction over another, sharpened by the spirit of revenge natural to party dissension . . . is itself a frightful despotism. . . .

Of all the dispositions and habits which lead to political prosperity, religion and morality are indispensable supports. . . . A volume could not trace all their connections with private and public felicity. Let it simply be asked where is the security for property, for reputation, for life, if the sense of religious obligation desert the oaths, which are the instruments of investigation in courts of justice? And let us with caution indulge the supposition, that morality can be maintained without religion. Whatever may be conceded to the influence of refined education on minds of peculiar structure—reason and experience both forbid us to expect that national morality can prevail in exclusion of religious principle.

The great rule of conduct for us, in regard to foreign nations, is in extending our commercial relations to have with them as little political connection as possible. . . .

In offering you, my countrymen, these counsels of an old and affectionate friend, I dare not hope that they will make the strong and lasting impression I could wish. . . . But if I may even flatter myself that they may be productive of some partial benefit. . . .

The Kentucky Resolution

The Alien and Sedition Acts of 1798 made it easier for the government to suppress criticism and to arrest political enemies. This Federalist legislation inspired fierce opposition among Republicans, who looked to the state governments to reverse the acts. Two states, Kentucky and Virginia, passed resolutions stating their right to, in effect, disregard federal legislation. The resolutions laid the groundwork for the states' rights often cited during the Civil War. Thomas Jefferson wrote the Kentucky Resolution, excerpted below, which was adopted in 1799.

RESOLVED, . . . that if those who administer the general government be permitted to transgress the limits fixed by that compact, by a total disregard to the special delegations of power therein contained, annihilation of the state governments, and the erection upon their ruins, of a general consolidated government, will be the inevitable consequence; that the principle and construction contended for by sundry of the state legislatures, that the general government is the exclusive judge of the extent of the powers delegated to it, stop nothing short of despotism; . . . that the several states who formed that instrument, being sovereign and independent, have the unquestionable right to judge of its infraction; and that a nullification, by those sovereignties, of all unauthorized acts done under colour of that instrument, is the rightful remedy; . . .

Francis Scott Key

"The Star-Spangled Banner"

During the British bombardment of Fort McHenry during the War of 1812, a young Baltimore lawyer named Francis Scott Key was inspired to write the words to "The Star-Spangled Banner." Although it became popular immediately, it was not until 1931 that Congress officially declared "The Star-Spangled Banner" as the national anthem of the United States.

O! say can you see, by the dawn's early light,

What so proudly we hail'd at the twilight's last gleaming,

Whose broad stripes and bright stars through the perilous fight,

O'er the ramparts we watch'd, were so gallantly streaming?

And the Rockets' red glare, the Bombs bursting in air,

Gave proof through the night that our Flag was still there;

O! say, does that star-spangled Banner yet wave,

O'er the Land of the free, and the home of the brave!

Fort McHenry flag

The Monroe Doctrine

When Spain's power in South America began to weaken, other European nations seemed ready to step in. The United States was developing trade and diplomatic relations with South America, and it wanted to curb European influence there. The following is a statement President Monroe made on the subject in his annual message to Congress on December 2, 1823.

The occasion has been judged proper for asserting, as a principle in which the rights and interests of the United States are involved, that the American continents, by the free and independent condition which they have assumed and maintain, are henceforth not to be considered as subjects for future colonization by any European powers. . . .

. . . We owe it, therefore, to candor and to the amicable relations existing between the United States and those [European] powers to declare that we should consider any attempt on their part to extend their system to any portion of this hemisphere as dangerous to our peace and safety. With the existing colonies or dependencies of any European power we have not interfered and shall not interfere. But with the Governments who have declared their independence and maintain it, and whose independence we have, on great consideration and on just principles, acknowledged, we could not view any interposition for the purpose of oppressing them, or controlling in any other manner their destiny, by any European power in any other light than as the manifestation of an unfriendly disposition toward the United States. . . .

Our policy in regard to Europe, which was adopted at an early stage of the wars which have so long agitated that quarter of the globe, nevertheless remains the same, which is, not to interfere in the internal concerns of any of its powers; to consider the government de facto as the legitimate government for us; to cultivate friendly relations with it, and to preserve those relations by a frank, firm, and manly policy, meeting in all instances the just claims of every power, submitting to injuries from none.

The Seneca Falls Declaration

One of the first documents to call for equal rights for women was the Declaration of Sentiments and Resolutions, issued in 1848 at the Seneca Falls Convention in Seneca Falls, New York. Led by Lucretia Mott and Elizabeth Cady Stanton, the delegates at the convention used the language of the Bill of Rights to call for women's rights.

We hold these truths to be self-evident: that all men and women are created equal; that they are endowed by their Creator with certain inalienable rights; that among these are life, liberty, and the pursuit of happiness; that to secure these rights governments are instituted, deriving their just powers from the consent of the governed. Whenever any form of government becomes destructive of these ends, it is the right of those who suffer from it to refuse allegiance to it, and to insist upon the institution of a new government. . . .

The history of mankind is a history of repeated injuries and usurpations on the part of man toward woman, having in direct object the establishment of an absolute tyranny over her.

Now, in view of this entire disfranchisement . . . we insist that they have immediate admission to all the rights and privileges which belong to them as citizens of the United States. . . .

Lucretia Mott

The Emancipation Proclamation

On January 1, 1863, President Abraham Lincoln issued the Emancipation Proclamation, which freed all enslaved persons in states under Confederate control. The Proclamation was a significant step toward the passage of the Thirteenth Amendment (1865), which ended slavery in the United States.

Whereas, on the 22nd day of September, in the year of our Lord 1862, a proclamation was issued by the President of the United States, containing, among other things, the following, to wit:

That on the 1st day of January, in the year of our Lord 1863, all persons held as slaves within any state or designated part of a state, the people whereof shall then be in rebellion against the United States, shall be then, thenceforward, and forever free; and the executive government of the United States, including the military and naval authority thereof, will recognize and maintain the freedom of such persons and will do no act or acts to repress such persons, or any of them, in any efforts they may make for their actual freedom.

That the executive will, on the 1st day January aforesaid, by proclamation, designate the states and parts of states, if any, in which the people thereof, respectively, shall then be in rebellion against the United States; and the fact that any state or the people thereof shall on that day be in good faith represented in the Congress of the United States by members chosen thereto at elections wherein a majority of the qualified voters of such states shall have participated shall, in the absence of strong countervailing testimony, be deemed conclusive evidence that such state and the people thereof are not then in rebellion against the United States.

Now, therefore, I, Abraham Lincoln, President of the United States, by virtue of the power in me vested as commander in chief of the Army and Navy of the United States, in time of actual armed rebellion against the authority and government of the United States, and as a fit and necessary war measure for suppressing said rebellion, do, on this 1st day of January, in the year of our Lord 1863, and in accordance with my purpose so to do, publicly proclaimed for the full period of 100 days from the day first above mentioned, order, and designate as the states and parts of states wherein the people thereof, respectively, are this day in rebellion against the United States. . . .

And, by virtue of the power and for the purpose aforesaid, I do order and declare that all persons held as slaves within said designated states and parts of states are, and henceforward shall be, free; and that the executive government of the United States, including the military and naval authorities thereof, will recognize and maintain the freedom of said persons. . . .

And upon this act, sincerely believed to be an act of justice, warranted by the Constitution upon military necessity, I invoke the considerate judgment of mankind and the gracious favor of Almighty God. . . .

Abraham Lincoln

The Gettysburg Address

President Abraham Lincoln delivered the Gettysburg Address on November 19, 1863, during the dedication of the Gettysburg National Cemetery. The dedication was in honor of the more than 7,000 Union and Confederate soldiers who died in the Battle of Gettysburg earlier that year. Lincoln's brief speech is often recognized as one of the finest speeches in the English language. It is also one of the most moving speeches in the nation's history.

There are five known manuscript copies of the address, two of which are in the Library of Congress. Scholars debate about which, if any, of the existing manuscripts comes closest to Lincoln's actual words that day.

National monument at Gettysburg

Four score and seven years ago our fathers brought forth on this continent a new nation, conceived in liberty and dedicated to the proposition that all men are created equal.

Now we are engaged in a great civil war, testing whether that nation or any nation so conceived and so dedicated can long endure. We are met on a great battlefield of that war. We have come to dedicate a portion of that field as a final resting-place for those who here gave their lives that that nation might live. It is altogether fitting and proper that we should do this.

But in a larger sense, we cannot dedicate, we cannot consecrate, we cannot hallow this ground. The brave men, living and dead who struggled here have consecrated it far above our poor power to add or detract. The world will little note nor long remember what we say here, but it can never forget what they did here. It is for us the living rather to be dedicated here to the unfinished work which they who fought here have thus far so nobly advanced. It is rather for us to be here dedicated to the great task remaining before us—that from these honored dead we take increased devotion to that cause for which they gave the last full measure of devotion—that we here highly resolve that these dead shall not have died in vain, that this nation under God shall have a new birth of freedom, and that government of the people, by the people, for the people shall not perish from the earth.

The Pledge of Allegiance

Students in a New York City school reciting the Pledge of Allegiance

In 1892 the nation celebrated the 400th anniversary of Columbus's landing in America. In connection with this celebration, Francis Bellamy, a magazine editor, wrote and published the Pledge of Allegiance. The words "under God" were added by Congress in 1954 at the urging of President Dwight D. Eisenhower.

I pledge allegiance to the Flag of the United States of America and to the Republic for which it stands, one Nation under God, indivisible, with liberty and justice for all.

President Harrison on Hawaiian Annexation

An early expression of American imperialism came in the annexation of Hawaii. With the support of the American government, a small number of American troops overthrew the Hawaiian monarchy in January 1893. The excerpt below is from President Benjamin Harrison's written message to Congress. He sent the message along with the treaty for annexation to Congress on February 15, 1893.

I do not deem it necessary to discuss at any length the conditions which have resulted in this decisive action. It has been the policy of the administration not only to respect but to encourage the continuance of an independent government in the Hawaiian Islands so long as it afforded suitable guarantees for the protection of life and property and maintained a stability and strength that gave adequate security against the domination of any other power. . . .

The overthrow of the monarchy was not in any way promoted by this government, but had its origin in what seems to have been a reactionary and revolutionary policy on the part of Queen Liliuokalani, which put in serious peril not only the large and preponderating interests of the United States . . . but all foreign interests. . . . It is quite evident that the monarchy had become effete and the queen's government is weak and inadequate as to be the prey of designing and unscrupulous persons. The restoration of Queen Liliuokalani . . . is undesirable . . . and unless actively supported by the United States would be accompanied by serious disaster and the disorganization of all business interests. The influence and interest of the United States in the islands must be increased and not diminished.

Only two courses are now open—one the establishment of a protectorate by the United States, and the other annexation, full and complete. I think the latter course, which has been adopted in the treaty, will be highly promotive of the best interest of the Hawaiian people and is the only one that will adequately secure the interests of the United States. These interests are not wholly selfish. It is essential that none of the other great powers shall secure these islands. Such a possession would not consist with our safety and with the peace of the world. This view of the situation is so apparent and conclusive that no protest has been heard from any government against proceedings looking to annexation.

The American's Creed

In the patriotic fervor of World War I, national leaders sponsored a contest in which writers submitted ideas for a national creed that would be a brief summary of American beliefs. Of the 3,000 entries, the judges selected that of William Tyler Page as the winner. In a 1918 ceremony in the House of Representatives, the Speaker of the House accepted the creed for the United States.

I believe in the United States of America as a Government of the people, by the people, for the people, whose just powers are derived from the consent of the governed; a democracy in a republic; a sovereign Nation of many sovereign States; a perfect union, one and inseparable; established upon those principles of freedom, equality, justice, and humanity for which American patriots sacrificed their lives and fortunes.

I therefore believe it is my duty to my Country to love it; to support its Constitution; to obey its laws; to respect its flag, and to defend it against all enemies.

The Fourteen Points

On January 8, 1918, President Woodrow Wilson went before Congress to offer a statement of war aims called the Fourteen Points. They reflected Wilson's belief that if the international community accepted certain basic principles of conduct and set up institutions to carry them out, there would be peace in the world.

We entered this war because violations of right had occurred. . . . What we demand in this war, therefore, is . . . that the world be made fit and safe to live in. . . .

The only possible programme, as we see it, is this:

I. Open covenants of peace, openly arrived at, after which there shall be no private international understandings of any kind but diplomacy shall proceed always frankly and in the public view.

II. Absolute freedom of navigation upon the seas, outside territorial waters, alike in peace and in war. . . .

III. The removal, so far as possible, of all economic barriers and the establishment of an equality of trade conditions among all the nations. . . .

IV. Adequate guarantees given and taken that national armaments will be reduced to the lowest point consistent with domestic safety.

V. A free, open-minded, and absolutely impartial adjustment of all colonial claims, based upon a strict observance of the principle that in determining all such questions of sovereignty the interests of the populations concerned must have equal weight with the equitable claims of the government whose title is to be determined.

VI. The evacuation of all Russian territory and . . . opportunity for the independent determination of her own political development and national polity. . . .

VII. Belgium . . . must be evacuated and restored. . . .

VIII. All French territory should be freed and the invaded portions restored, and the wrong done to France by Prussia in 1871 in the matter of Alsace-Lorraine should be righted. . . .

IX. A readjustment of the frontiers of Italy should be effected along clearly recognizable lines of nationality.

X. The peoples of Austria-Hungary . . . should be accorded the freest opportunity of autonomous development.

XI. Rumania, Serbia, and Montenegro should be evacuated; occupied territories restored . . . the relations of the several Balkan states to one another determined by friendly counsel along historically established lines of allegiance and nationality. . . .

XII. The Turkish portions of the present Ottoman Empire should be assured a secure sovereignty. . . .

XIII. An independent Polish state should be erected which should include the territories inhabited by indisputably Polish populations. . . .

XIV. A general association of nations must be formed under specific covenants for the purpose of affording mutual guarantees of political independence and territorial integrity. . . .

Discussion of the Fourteen Points at the Versailles peace conference

The Four Freedoms

President Franklin D. Roosevelt delivered this address on January 6, 1941, in his annual message to Congress. In it, Roosevelt called for a world founded on "four essential human freedoms": freedom of speech and expression, freedom of worship, freedom from want, and freedom from fear.

Just as our national policy in internal affairs has been based upon a decent respect for the rights and dignity of all our fellow men within our gates, so our national policy in foreign affairs has been based on a decent respect for the rights and dignity of all nations, large and small. And the justice of morality must and will win in the end.

Our national policy is this:

First, by an impressive expression of the public will and without regard to partisanship, we are committed to all-inclusive national defense.

Second, by an impressive expression of the public will and without regard to partisanship, we are committed to full support of all those resolute peoples, everywhere, who are resisting aggression and are thereby keeping war away from our Hemisphere. . . .

Third . . . we are committed to the proposition that principles of morality and considerations for our own security will never permit us to acquiesce in a peace dictated by aggressors. . . .

Let us say to the democracies, "We Americans are vitally concerned in your defense of freedom. We are putting forth our energies, our resources, and our organizing powers to give you the strength to regain and maintain a free world. We shall send you, in ever increasing numbers, ships, planes, tanks, guns. This is our purpose and our pledge." In fulfillment of this purpose we will not be intimidated by the threats of dictators that they will regard as a breach of international

Caricature of President Roosevelt

law and as an act of war our aid to the democracies which dare to resist their aggression. . . .

In the future days, which we seek to make secure, we look forward to a world founded upon four essential human freedoms.

The first is freedom of speech and expression everywhere in the world.

The second is freedom of every person to worship God in his own way everywhere in the world.

The third is freedom from want, which, translated into world terms, means economic understandings which will secure to every nation a healthy peacetime life for its inhabitants everywhere in the world.

The fourth is freedom from fear—which, translated into world terms, means a worldwide reduction of armaments to such a point and in such a thorough fashion that no nation will be in a position to commit an act of physical aggression against any neighbor—anywhere in the world. . . .

The Truman Doctrine

President Harry S. Truman addressed a joint session of Congress on March 12, 1947, to request aid to fight Communist influence in Greece and Turkey. His message that communism had to be contained represents the central idea of American foreign policy during the Cold War.

The United States has received from the Greek Government an urgent appeal for financial and economic assistance. . . .

When forces of liberation entered Greece they found that the retreating Germans had destroyed virtually all the railways, roads, port facilities, communications, and merchant marine. More than a thousand villages had been burned. Eighty-five percent of the children were tubercular. Livestock, poultry, and draft animals had almost disappeared. Inflation had wiped out practically all savings. As a result of these tragic conditions, a militant minority, exploiting human want and misery, was able to create political chaos which, until now, has made economic recovery impossible.

Greece is today without funds to finance the importation of those goods which are essential to bare subsistence. Under these circumstances the people of Greece cannot make progress in solving their problems of reconstruction. Greece is in desperate need of financial and economic assistance to enable it to resume purchases of food, clothing, fuel and seeds. These are indispensable for the subsistence of its people and are obtainable only from abroad. Greece must have help to import the goods necessary to restore internal order and security, so essential for economic and political recovery. . . .

Meanwhile, the Greek Government is unable to cope with the situation. The Greek army is small and poorly equipped. It needs supplies and equipment if it is to restore the authority of the government throughout Greek territory. Greece must have assistance if it is to become a self-supporting and self-respecting democracy.

The United States must supply that assistance. We have already extended to Greece certain types of relief and economic aid but these are inadequate. There is no other country to which democratic Greece can turn. . . .

No government is perfect. One of the chief virtues of a democracy, however, is that its defects are always visible and under democratic processes can be pointed out and corrected. The Government of Greece is not perfect. Nevertheless it represents eighty-five percent of the members of the Greek Parliament who were chosen in an election last year. . . .

Greece's neighbor, Turkey, also deserves our attention. The future of Turkey as an independent and economically sound state is clearly no less important to the freedom-loving peoples of the world than the future of Greece. The circumstances in which Turkey finds itself today are considerably different from those of Greece. Turkey has been spared the disasters that have beset Greece. And during the war, the United States and Great Britain furnished Turkey with material aid. Nevertheless, Turkey now needs our support.

. . . . To ensure the peaceful development of nations, free from coercion, the United States has taken a leading part in establishing the United Nations. The United Nations is designed to make possible lasting freedom and independence for all its members. We shall not realize our objectives, however, unless we are willing to help free peoples to maintain their free institutions . . . against aggressive movements that seek to impose upon them totalitarian regimes. . . .

This is an investment in world freedom and world peace. . . . The seeds of totalitarian regimes are nurtured by misery and want. They spread and grow in the evil soil of poverty and strife. They reach their full growth when the hope of a people for a better life has died. We must keep that hope alive. . . . If we falter in our leadership, we may endanger the peace of the world—and we shall surely endanger the welfare of our own nation.

Brown v. Board of Education

On May 17, 1954, the Supreme Court ruled in **Brown v. Board of Education of Topeka, Kansas,** *that racial segregation in public schools was unconstitutional. This decision provided the legal basis for court challenges to segregation in every aspect of American life.*

These cases come to us from the States of Kansas, South Carolina, Virginia, and Delaware. They are premised on different facts and different local conditions, but a common legal question justifies their consideration together in this consolidated opinion.

In each of the cases, minors of the Negro race, through their legal representatives, seek the aid of the courts in obtaining admission to the public schools of their community on a nonsegregated basis. In each instance, they had been denied admission to schools attended by white children under laws requiring or permitting segregation according to race. This segregation was alleged to deprive the plaintiffs of the equal protection of the laws under the Fourteenth Amendment.

The plaintiffs contend that segregated public schools are not "equal" and cannot be made "equal," and that hence they are deprived of the equal protection of the laws. Because of the obvious importance of the question presented, the Court took jurisdiction. . . .

. . . Our decision . . . cannot turn on merely a comparison of these tangible factors in the Negro and white schools involved in each of the cases. We must look instead to the effect of segregation itself on public education.

In approaching this problem, we cannot turn the clock back to 1868 when the Amendment was adopted, or even to 1896 when *Plessy* v. *Ferguson* was written. We must consider public education in the light of its full development and its present place in American life throughout the nation. Only in this way can it be determined if segregation in public schools deprives these plaintiffs of the equal protection of the laws.

Today, education is perhaps the most important function of state and local governments. Compulsory school attendance laws and the great expenditures for education both demonstrate our recognition of the importance of education to our democratic society. . . . In these days, it is doubtful that any child may reasonably be expected to succeed in life if he is denied the opportunity of an education. Such an opportunity, where the state has undertaken to provide it, is a right which must be made available to all on equal terms.

Linda Brown

We come then to the question presented: Does segregation of children in public schools solely on the basis of race, even though the physical facilities and other "tangible" factors may be equal, deprive the children of the minority group of equal educational opportunities? We believe that it does.

. . . We conclude that, in the field of public education, the doctrine of "separate but equal" has no place. Separate educational facilities are inherently unequal. Therefore, we hold that the plaintiff and others similarly situated for whom the actions have been brought are, by reason of the segregation complained of, deprived of the equal protection of the laws guaranteed by the Fourteenth Amendment. . . .

"I Have a Dream"

On August 28, 1963, while Congress was debating broad civil rights legislation, Martin Luther King, Jr., led more than 200,000 people in a march on Washington, D.C. On the steps of the Lincoln Memorial, King gave a stirring speech in which he eloquently spoke of his dreams for African Americans and for the United States.

Martin Luther King, Jr., speaking at the march

Five score years ago, a great American, in whose symbolic shadow we stand, signed the Emancipation Proclamation. This momentous decree came as a great beacon light of hope to millions of Negro slaves who had been seared in the flames of withering injustice. It came as a joyous daybreak to end the long night of captivity.

But one hundred years later, we must face the tragic fact that the Negro is still not free. One hundred years later, the life of the Negro is still sadly crippled by the manacles of segregation and the chains of discrimination. . . .

There are those who are asking the devotees of civil rights, "When will you be satisfied?"

We can never be satisfied as long as the Negro is the victim of the unspeakable horrors of police brutality.

We can never be satisfied as long as our bodies, heavy with the fatigue of travel, cannot gain lodging in the motels of the highways and the hotels of the cities.

We cannot be satisfied as long as the Negro's basic mobility is from a smaller ghetto to a larger one.

We can never be satisfied as long as a Negro in Mississippi cannot vote and a Negro in New York believes he has nothing for which to vote.

No, no, we are not satisfied, and we will not be satisfied until justice rolls down like waters and righteousness like a mighty stream. . . .

I say to you today, my friends, that in spite of the difficulties and frustrations of the moment I still have a dream. It is a dream deeply rooted in the American dream.

I have a dream that one day this nation will rise up and live out the true meaning of its creed: "We hold these truths to be self-evident; that all men are created equal. "

I have a dream that one day on the red hills of Georgia the sons of former slaves and the sons of former slaveowners will be able to sit down together at the table of brotherhood.

I have a dream that one day even the state of Mississippi, a desert state sweltering with the heat of injustice and oppression, will be transformed into an oasis of freedom and justice.

I have a dream that my four little children will one day live in a nation where they will not be judged by the color of their skin but by the content of their character. . . .

When we let freedom ring, when we let it ring from every village and every hamlet, from every state and every city, we will be able to speed up that day when all of God's children, black men and white men, Jews and Gentiles, Protestants and Catholics, will be able to join hands and sing in the words of the old Negro spiritual, "Free at last! Free at last! Thank God Almighty, we are free at last!"

President Johnson's Message to Congress

In early August 1964, President Lyndon Johnson announced that on August 5 North Vietnamese torpedo boats had attacked American destroyers in the international waters of the Gulf of Tonkin off the coast of Vietnam. Johnson appealed to the American people and to Congress for their support of his Vietnam policies.

To the Congress of the United States:

Last night I announced to the American people that the North Vietnamese regime had conducted further deliberate attacks against U.S. naval vessels operating in international waters. . . .

These latest actions of the North Vietnamese regime have given a new and grave turn to the already serious situation in southeast Asia.

Our commitments in that area are well known to the Congress. . . .

. . . The North Vietnamese regime has constantly sought to take over South Vietnam and Laos. This Communist regime has violated the Geneva accords for Vietnam. It has systematically conducted a campaign of subversion, which includes the direction, training, and supply of personnel and arms for the conduct of guerrilla warfare in South Vietnamese territory. . . .

As President of the United States I have concluded that I should now ask the Congress on its part, to join in affirming the national determination that all such attacks will be met, and that the United States will continue in its basic policy of assisting the free nations of the area to defend their freedom. . . .

The Gulf of Tonkin Resolution

On August 7, 1964, Congress passed the Gulf of Tonkin Resolution, which stood as the legal basis for the Vietnam War. Later information raised doubts about the administration's description of actions in the Gulf of Tonkin. In December 1970, after war opposition had started to grow, Congress repealed the Gulf of Tonkin Resolution.

Resolved by the Senate and House of Representatives of the United States of America in Congress assembled,

That the Congress approves and supports the determination of the President, as Commander in Chief, to take all necessary measures to repel any armed attack against the forces of the United States and to prevent further aggression.

Section 2. The United States regards as vital to its national interest and to world peace the maintenance of international peace and security in southeast Asia. Consonant with the Constitution of the United States and the Charter of the United Nations and in

accordance with its obligations under the Southeast Asia Collective Defense Treaty, the United States is, therefore, prepared, as the President determines, to take all necessary steps, including the use of armed force, to assist any member or protocol state of the Southeast Asia Collective Defense Treaty requesting assistance in defense of its freedom.

Section 3. This resolution shall expire when the President shall determine that the peace and security of the area is reasonably assured by international conditions created by action of the United Nations or otherwise, except that it may be terminated earlier by concurrent resolution of the Congress.

Soldiers in Vietnam

Supreme Court Case Summaries

The following case summaries explain the significance of major Supreme Court cases mentioned in the text.

Abington School District v. Schempp (1963) struck down a Pennsylvania statute requiring public schools in the state to begin each school day with Bible readings and a recitation of the Lord's Prayer. The Court held that the Constitution's establishment clause leaves religious beliefs and religious practices to each individual's choice and expressly commands that government not intrude into this decision-making process.

Abrams v. United States (1919) upheld a conviction under the Sedition Act and Espionage Act of 1917. The Court ruled that freedom of speech could be limited if there was a threat to the country.

Baker v. Carr (1962) established that federal courts can hear suits seeking to force state authorities to redraw electoral districts. In this case, the plaintiff wanted the population of each district to be roughly equal to the population in all other districts. The plaintiff claimed that the votes of voters in the least populous districts counted as much as the votes of voters in the most populous districts.

Brown v. Board of Education (1954) overruled *Plessy v. Ferguson* (1896) and abandoned the separate-but-equal doctrine in the context of public schools. In deciding this case, the Supreme Court rejected the idea that equivalent but separate schools for African Americans and white students would be constitutional. The Court stated that the Fourteenth Amendment's command that all persons be accorded the equal protection of the law (U.S. Const. amend. XIV, sec. 1) is not satisfied by ensuring that African American and white schools "have been equalized, or are being equalized, with respect to buildings, curricula, qualifications, and salaries, and other tangible factors."

The Court then held that racial segregation in public schools violates the equal protection clause because it is inherently unequal. In other words, the separation of schools by race marks the separate race as inferior. The ruling in this case has been extended beyond public education to virtually all public accommodations and activities.

Bush v. Gore (2000) found that a manual recount of disputed presidential ballots in Florida lacked a uniform standard of judging a voter's intent, thus violating the equal protection clause of the Constitution. The Court also ruled that there was not enough time to conduct a new manual recount that would meet constitutional standards. The case arose when Republican candidate George W. Bush asked the Court to stop a hand recount. This decision ensured that Bush would receive Florida's electoral votes and win the election.

Chisholm v. Georgia (1793) stripped the immunity of the states to lawsuits in federal court. The Supreme Court held that a citizen of one state could sue another state in federal court without that state consenting to the suit. The Court's decision created a furor and led to the adoption of the Eleventh Amendment, which protects states from federal court suits by citizens of other states.

Dred Scott v. Sandford (1857) was decided before the Fourteenth Amendment. The Fourteenth Amendment provides that anyone born or naturalized in the United States is a citizen of the nation and of his or her state. In this case, the Supreme Court held that a slave was property, not a citizen, and thus had no rights under the Constitution. The decision was a prime factor leading to the Civil War.

Engel v. Vitale (1962) held that the establishment clause (U.S. Const. amend. I, cl. 1) was violated by a public school district's practice of starting each school day with a prayer which began, "Almighty God, we acknowledge our dependence upon Thee." The Supreme Court ruled that religion is a personal matter and that government should not align itself with a particular religion in order to prevent religious persecution.

Escobedo v. Illinois (1964) held that Danny Escobedo's right to counsel, as provided by the Sixth Amendment, had been violated. Throughout police questioning, Escobedo asked repeatedly, but unsuccessfully, to see his attorney. The Supreme Court reversed Escobedo's murder conviction, holding that an attorney could have assisted Escobedo in invoking his Fifth Amendment right against self-incrimination. This case served as a forerunner to *Miranda* v. *Arizona*.

Gibbons v. Ogden (1824) made it clear that the authority of Congress to regulate interstate commerce (U.S. Const. art. I, sec. 8, cl. 3) includes the authority to regulate intrastate commercial activity that relates to interstate commerce. Before this case, it was thought that the Constitution would allow a state to close its borders to interstate commercial activity. This ruling says that a state can only regulate internal commercial activity, but Congress can regulate commercial activity that has both intrastate and interstate dimensions.

Gideon v. Wainwright (1963) ruled that poor defendants in criminal cases have the right to a state-paid attorney under the Sixth Amendment. The ruling in this case has been refined to apply only when the defendant, if convicted, can be sentenced to more than six months in jail.

Griswold v. Connecticut (1965) overturned the conviction of two Planned Parenthood employees charged with violating an 1879 state law banning the use of contraceptives. In deciding this case, the Court went beyond the actual words of the Constitution to protect a right—the right to privacy—which is not listed in the Constitution. The case also served as a forerunner to the *Roe* v. *Wade* decision that legalized abortion on the same basis.

Heart of Atlanta Motel, Inc. v. United States (1964) upheld the Civil Rights Act of 1964, which prohibits racial discrimination by those who provide goods, services, and facilities to the public. The Georgia motel in the case drew its business from other states but refused to rent rooms to African Americans. The Supreme Court explained that Congress had the authority to prohibit such discrimination under both the equal protection clause (U.S. Const. amend. XIV, sec. 1) and the commerce clause (art. I, sec. 8, cl. 3). With respect to the commerce clause, the Court explained that Congress had ample evidence to conclude that racial discrimination by hotels and motels impedes interstate commerce.

Korematsu v. United States (1944) allowed the federal government's authority to exclude Japanese Americans, many of whom were citizens, from designated military areas that included almost the entire West Coast. The government defended the orders as a necessary response to Japan's attack on Pearl Harbor. Yet, in upholding the orders, the Court established that government actions that discriminate on the basis of race would be subject to strict scrutiny.

Loving v. Virginia (1967) ruled that state laws that outlaw interracial marriages are unconstitutional under the Fourteenth Amendment. The Court explained that such laws violated the equal protection clause and deprived "citizens of liberty without due process of law." The Court went on to say, "Marriage is one of the basic civil rights of man, fundamental to our very existence and survival."

Mapp v. Ohio (1961) established that evidence seized in violation of the Fourth Amendment could not be used by the prosecution as evidence of a defendant's guilt at the federal, state, or local level.

Marbury v. Madison (1803) established one of the most important principles of American constitutional law. The Supreme Court held that the Court itself has the final say on what the Constitution means. It is also the Supreme Court that has the final say whether or not an act of government—legislative or executive at the federal, state, or local level—violates the Constitution.

Martin v. Hunter's Lessee (1816) affirmed that the Supreme Court has the authority to review state court decisions and is the nation's final court of appeal. The Supreme Court ruled that section 25 of the Judiciary Act of 1789 was constitutional. This section granted the Supreme Court appellate jurisdiction over state courts in certain situations, such as a state court denying the authority of federal law.

McCulloch v. Maryland (1819) established the basis for the expansive authority of Congress. The Supreme Court held that the necessary and proper clause (U.S. Const. art. I, sec. 8, cl. 18) allows Congress to do more than the Constitution specifically authorizes it to do. This case holds that Congress can enact almost any law that will help it achieve the ends established by Article I, Section 8 of the Constitution. For example, Congress has the power to regulate interstate commerce; the necessary and proper clause permits Congress to do so in ways not specified in the Constitution.

Miranda v. Arizona (1966) held that a person in police custody may not be held unless reminded of his or her rights. These rights include: 1) the right to remain silent, 2) the right to an attorney (at government expense if the person is unable to pay), and 3) that anything the person says after acknowledging that he or she understands these rights can be used as evidence of guilt at a trial.

The Supreme Court explained that a person alone in police custody may not understand, even if told, that he or she can remain silent and thus might be misled into answering questions. The presence of an attorney is essential.

Morgan v. Virginia (1946) challenged racial segregation in the South. Irene Morgan was convicted for refusing to give up her seat on an interstate bus bound from Virginia to Maryland. The Court ruled that the Virginia law posed an undue burden on interstate commerce and struck down the statute. However, segregation on southern buses continued on an informal basis.

National Labor Relations Board v. Jones and Laughlin Steel Corp. (1937) upheld President Franklin Roosevelt's New Deal legislation, the National Labor Relations Act, which allowed workers to organize unions in businesses operating or affecting interstate commerce. Employers were prohibited from discriminating against their employees because of union membership. Prior to this case, the Supreme Court had ruled much New Deal legislation unconstitutional. This ruling came less than a week after Roosevelt's proposed court-packing plan. The president intended on "packing" the Supreme Court with additional justices in order to obtain a pro-New Deal majority on the Court.

New York Times Co. v. Sullivan (1964) extended the protections afforded to the press by the free press clause (U.S. Const. amend. I). In this case, the Supreme Court held that a public official or public figure suing a publisher for libel (i.e., defamation) must prove that the publisher published a story that he or she knew was false or published the story in "reckless disregard of its truth or falsity," which means that the publisher did not take professionally adequate steps to determine the story's truth or falsity.

Norris v. Alabama (1935) overturned the conviction of Clarence Norris, an African American sentenced to death for a crime in Alabama. The Supreme Court held that the grand jury and trial jury had systematically eliminated African American jurors. Thus, the Court reversed the conviction because it violated the equal protection clause of the Fourteenth Amendment.

Northern Securities Company v. United States (1904) dealt with the application of congressional antitrust legislation. The party involved held

three-fourths of the stock in two parallel railroad lines. By a narrow 5–4 decision, the Court upheld the application of the Sherman Antitrust Act. The Court ruled that the holding company clearly intended to eliminate competition between the two railroads, violating the constitutional right of Congress to regulate interstate commerce.

Plessy v. Ferguson (1896) upheld the separate-but-equal doctrine used by Southern states to perpetuate segregation after the Civil War officially ended law-mandated segregation. The decision upheld a Louisiana law requiring passenger trains to have "equal but separated accommodations for the white and colored races." The Court held that the Fourteenth Amendment's equal protection clause required only equal public facilities for the two races, not equal access. This case was overruled by *Brown* v. *Board of Education* (1954).

Regents of the University of California v. Bakke (1978) was the first Supreme Court decision to suggest that an affirmative action program could be justified on the basis of diversity. The Court explained that racial quotas were not permissible under the equal protection clause of the Fourteenth Amendment. However, the justices ruled that the diversity rationale was a legitimate interest that would allow a state medical school to consider an applicant's race in evaluating his or her application for admission. (Recent Supreme Court cases suggest that the diversity rationale is no longer enough to defend an affirmative action program.)

Reynolds v. Sims (1964) extended the one-person, one-vote doctrine announced in *Wesberry* v. *Sanders* to state legislative elections. The Court held that the inequality of representation in the Alabama legislature violated the equal protection clause of the Fourteenth Amendment.

Roe v. Wade (1973) held that women have the right under various provisions of the Constitution—most notably, the due process clause of the Fourteenth Amendment—to decide whether or not to terminate a pregnancy. The Court's ruling in this case was the most significant in a long line of decisions over a period of 50 years that recognized a constitutional right of privacy, even though the word *privacy* is not found in the Constitution.

Schechter Poultry Corporation v. United States (1935) overturned the conviction of the employers, who were charged with violating the wage and hour limitations of a law adopted under the authority of the

National Industrial Recovery Act. The Court held that because the defendants did not sell poultry in interstate commerce, they were not subject to federal regulations on wages and hours.

Schenck v. United States (1919) upheld convictions under the Federal Espionage Act. The defendants were charged under the act with distributing leaflets aimed at inciting draft resistance during World War I; their defense was that antidraft speech was protected under the First Amendment.

The Supreme Court unanimously rejected the defense, explaining that whether or not speech is protected depends on the context in which it occurs. Because the defendants' antidraft rhetoric created a "clear and present danger" to the success of the war effort, it was not protected.

Stone v. Powell (1976) reversed a Court of Appeals decision that evidence was seized illegally and should therefore be excluded. The Court ruled that the defendant was provided a fair and legal opportunity to claim a Fourth Amendment violation before a trial jury. The trial jury found that the search was constitutional and the evidence should not be excluded. The Court stated, "Where the state has provided an opportunity for full and fair litigation of a Fourth Amendment claim, a state prisoner may not be granted federal habeas corpus relief."

Swann v. Charlotte-Mecklenburg Board of Education (1971) established a new plan to ensure that public schools were not segregated. Many school systems were slow to desegregate after *Brown* v. *Board of Education* and used various tactics to appear to be resolving the problem. This case ordered that busing students, reorganizing school boundaries, and racial ratios all be used as methods to obtain desegregated public school systems.

Sweatt v. Painter (1950) held that it was unconstitutional for African Americans to be denied admission to the University of Texas Law School based on race. An inferior law school established for African Americans did not give the state justification to deny admission to the main school. This act was a violation of the Fourteenth Amendment.

Wabash v. Illinois (1886) held that states have no authority to regulate railroad rates for interstate commerce. The Supreme Court held that the commerce clause (U.S. Const. art. I, sec. 8, cl. 3) allowed states to enforce "indirect" but not "direct" burdens on interstate commerce. State railroad rates were ruled "direct" burdens and therefore could not be enforced by states. The decision created a precedent by establishing rate regulation of interstate commerce as an exclusive federal power.

Wickard v. Filburn (1942) indicated how far the Supreme Court had come in complying with President Franklin Roosevelt's economic philosophies. The Court upheld specific parts of the Second Agricultural Adjustment Act. In its ruling, the Supreme Court held that marketing quotas could be applied to wheat that never left the farm. Using the commerce clause (U.S. Const. art. I, sec. 8, cl. 3) as the basis for its decision, the Court ruled that wheat that never left the farm still had an effect on interstate commerce. Farmers growing their own grain depressed the overall demand and market price of wheat. The decision further extended the power of the commerce clause.

Worcester v. Georgia (1832) overturned the conviction of Samuel A. Worcester, a missionary among the Cherokee. Worcester was imprisoned under a Georgia law forbidding whites to reside in Cherokee country without taking an oath of allegiance to the state and obtaining a permit. The Supreme Court voided the state law, ruling that the Cherokee were an independent nation based on a federal treaty and free from the jurisdiction of the state. Georgia ignored the decision, and President Jackson refused to enforce it, instead supporting the removal of the Cherokee to the Indian Territory.

SKILLBUILDER

Introduction

The following **Skillbuilder Handbook** offers students the opportunity to practice critical thinking skills and research skills. Students can benefit in several ways from completing the lessons. First, being equipped with these skills makes students' reading more meaningful. Second, the lessons give students practice in using skills they will need to successfully complete the section and chapter assessments included in the text. Finally, the lessons help prepare students for standardized test taking since many of these skills are assessed on standardized tests.

The lessons are written and organized to correspond with the content of the text's chapters. They can be revisited as you review lessons for students who need extra practice.

SKILLBUILDER Handbook

Table of Contents

The exercises in the Glencoe Skillbuilder Handbook give you hands-on practice with the skills you need to study history and to master the content for United States history. The range of skills in this handbook reflect three major categories of skills: chronological and spatial thinking; historical research, evidence, and point of view; and historical interpretation.

Using these Skillbuilders will help you learn key history skills, such as interpreting points of view and distinguishing fact from opinion in historical interpretation. You will get the most from these Skillbuilders if you use them as you are studying each chapter. Each Skillbuilder has three parts:

- an explanation of why the skill is valuable
- step-by-step pointers for learning the skill
- an exercise to practice the skill that *uses the content of the chapter*

Critical Thinking SKILLBUILDER

Making Comparisons

For use with Chapter 1

Why Learn This Skill?

Suppose you want to buy a portable compact disc (CD) player, and you must choose among three models. You would probably compare characteristics of the three models, such as price, sound quality, and size to figure out which model is best for you. In the study of American history, you often compare people or events from one time period with those from a different time period. This helps you gain an understanding of how the past has affected the present.

Learning the Skill

When making comparisons, you examine two or more groups, situations, events, or documents. Then you identify any similarities and differences. For example, the chart on this page compares two documents with regard to the powers they gave the central government. The Articles of Confederation were passed and implemented before the United States Constitution, which took their place. The chart includes a check mark in each column that applies. For example, the entry *Protect copyrights* does not have a check under *Articles of Confederation.* This shows that the government under the Articles lacked that power. The entry is checked under *United States Constitution,* showing that the government under the Constitution does have that power.

When making comparisons, you first decide what items will be compared and determine which characteristics you will use to compare them. Then you identify similarities and differences in these characteristics.

Practicing the Skill

Analyze the information on the chart on this page. Then answer the questions.

❶ What items are being compared? How are they being compared?

The Articles of Confederation and the United States Constitution

Powers of the Central Government	Articles of Confederation	United States Constitution
Declare war; make peace	✔	✔
Coin money	✔	✔
Manage foreign affairs	✔	✔
Establish a postal system	✔	✔
Impose taxes		✔
Regulate trade		✔
Organize a court system		✔
Call state militia for service		✔
Protect copyrights		✔
Take other necessary actions to run the federal government		✔

❷ What are the similarities and differences of the documents?

❸ Which document had the most power regarding legal matters? How can you tell?

❹ Which document had the most power in dealing with other nations? How can you tell?

Applying the Skill

Making Comparisons On the editorial page of your local newspaper, read two columns that express different viewpoints on the same issue. Identify the similarities and differences between the two points of view.

 Glencoe's **Skillbuilder Interactive Workbook CD-ROM, Level 2,** provides instruction and practice in key social studies skills.

1009

TEACH

W Writing Support

Persuasive Writing After students make their predictions for the Applying the Skill activity, ask them to write an essay that attempts to persuade an audience that their prediction is likely to come true. Tell students that they may want to think of other possible predictions and address specific flaws in them. **OL**

CA 11WS1.3

Resources for page 1010

📁 Reinforcing Skills Activity 6

💿 Glencoe Skillbuilder Interactivity Workbook CD-ROM, Level 2

Critical Thinking
SKILLBUILDER

Predicting Consequences

For use with Chapter 2

Why Learn This Skill?

Did you ever wish you could see into the future? Although predicting future events is very difficult, you can develop skills that will help you identify the logical consequences of decisions or actions.

Learning the Skill

Follow these steps to help you accurately predict consequences:

- Review what you already know about a situation by listing facts, events, and people's responses. The list will help you recall events and how they affected people.

- Analyze patterns. Try to determine what the patterns show. Are some consequences more likely to occur than others?

- Use your knowledge and observations of similar situations. In other words, ask yourself, "What were the consequences of a similar decision or action that occurred in the past?"

- Analyze each of the potential consequences by asking, "How likely is it that this will occur?"

- Make a prediction.

Practicing the Skill

Candidates for public office often make campaign promises based on how they think voters will respond. Use the information in the chart on this page to help you predict what type of candidate would be elected president in 1848. Then answer the questions that follow.

❶ What event initially forced candidates to address the issue of slavery in new territories?

❷ Review the facts and events listed on the chart. Do you notice any patterns? What do the facts tell you about the 1840s?

Events of the 1840s	Results and Reactions
Victory in war with Mexico creates new territory in Southwest.	→ Americans torn over whether area should be free or slave territory.
Wilmot Proviso proposes ban on slavery in any area taken from Mexico.	→ Southerners are outraged.
Members of Congress try to avoid issue of slavery in territories.	→ Northerners and Southerners continue to angrily debate the issue.
Popular sovereignty lets settlers decide whether territories should be free or not.	→ Abolitionists argue against popular sovereignty; many Northerners support it.
Whig Party nomination of Zachary Taylor angers some party members.	→ Many Northern Whigs split and join with others to create the Free-Soil Party.

❸ What kind of president do you think Northerners would want? Southerners?

❹ How do you think the differences listed on this chart eventually will be resolved by Northerners and Southerners?

Applying the Skill

Predicting Consequences Read several newspaper articles about an event affecting your community today. Make an educated prediction about what will happen, and explain your reasoning. Write a letter to the editor, summarizing your prediction. You may want to check back at a later time to see if your prediction came true.

GO 💿 Glencoe's **Skillbuilder Interactive Workbook CD-ROM, Level 2,** provides instruction and practice in key social studies skills.

1010

Answers and Additional Support

ANSWERS TO PRACTICING THE SKILL

Possible answers:

1. the victory of the war with Mexico and the creation of the new territory in the Southwest

2. Although many in government tried to avoid the issue of slavery or make compromises, it continued to be hotly debated among the people; slavery was an important political issue in the 1840s and the people of the United States were divided into North and South

3. Northerners would want a president against slavery and Southerners would want one for slavery.

4. Civil War

Applying the Skill
Students' predictions will vary but should be based on reasonable assumptions based on facts. Encourage students to attach the newspaper articles to their letters.

Critical Thinking
SKILLBUILDER

Making Inferences

For use with Chapter 3

Why Learn This Skill?

Just as you are about to leave home to catch your school bus, you hear a radio report. Firefighters are battling a blaze near the bus garage. Your bus is late. Although no one told you, you know that the fire disrupted the bus schedule. You have made an *inference*. From the limited facts available, you formed a conclusion. By combining facts and general knowledge, you inferred that the fire trucks delayed your bus. The skill of making inferences can also be applied when studying history. Sometimes, a text or source does not provide all the information needed to draw a good conclusion, and you will need to make an inference.

Learning the Skill

Learning how to make inferences will help you draw conclusions about particular situations. To make accurate inferences, follow these steps:

- Read or listen carefully for stated facts and ideas.
- Review what you already know about the same topic or situation.
- Use logic and common sense to form a conclusion about the topic.
- If possible, find information that proves or disproves your inference.

Practicing the Skill

Read the following passage about early airplanes, and then answer the questions that follow.

On December 8, 1903, Samuel Langley was ready for his second attempt at flying a manned, self-propelled aircraft. This had never been done before.

Langley used a $50,000 U.S. government grant to build a plane based on unmanned aircraft designs, adding a very powerful engine. The plane broke apart on takeoff and crashed into the Potomac River.

In contrast, Wilbur and Orville Wright used a little more than $1,000 of their personal savings to build their aircraft. The brothers carefully studied the problems with

First flight at Kitty Hawk, December 17, 1903

previous planes and designed one with better wings, a more efficient propeller, and a strong but light engine. On December 17, 1903, these intrepid Americans made the first manned, powered flight in history on the sand dunes of Kitty Hawk, North Carolina.

❶ What are the facts regarding Langley's attempt?

❷ What are the facts regarding the Wright brothers' attempt?

❸ What inferences might you draw based on the success of the Wright brothers and failure of Langley?

Applying the Skill

Making Inferences Reread the American Story about Thomas Edison on page 244, then answer these questions.

1. What device did inventors struggle to develop for much of the 1800s?

2. Why did Edison want to develop this new device?

3. Based on these facts, what inference can you make about Thomas Edison's methods? What inference can you make about how his invention would affect the economy?

 Glencoe's **Skillbuilder Interactive Workbook CD-ROM, Level 2,** provides instruction and practice in key social studies skills.

Critical Thinking
SKILLBUILDER

TEACH

U Universal Access

English Learners Inferences can be made using non-verbal cues. Engage students in reading a picture book that tells a story without words. Ask them to use the bulleted list of steps under Learning the Skill to say or write a few sentences about what they were able to infer about the story that was not directly shown. Students may also try this exercise with comic strips or graphic novels. **EL**

 Resources for page 1011

📁 Reinforcing Skills Activity 9

💿 Glencoe Skillbuilder Interactivity Workbook CD-ROM, Level 2

Answers and Additional Support

ANSWERS TO PRACTICING THE SKILL

1. He used a large government grant to build a self-propelled aircraft plane; the plane broke apart on takeoff and crashed.

2. They studied previous designs, used their own savings to build their aircraft, and successfully flew on December 17, 1903.

3. A possible inference is that government grants cannot substitute for entrepreneurial initiative and the willing-ness to learn from mistakes.

Applying the Skill

1. the electric incandescent lamp or light bulb

2. Light bulbs would be cheaper, safer, and brighter than existing methods.

3. Answers will vary but may include that light bulbs would lead to an electrical industry and make candles and oil lamps obsolete.

TEACH

 Reading Strategy

Skimming Discuss with students how skimming can help them to decide what sources to spend time reading and what sources to bypass. Skimming Web sites can be as necessary as skimming print sources and may be the first step in evaluating a site. Before choosing the Web sites for the Applying the Skill activity, students should practice skimming the sites by reading the headings, glancing at the links, photos, and maps, and noting the colors and typefaces used. `OL`

Resources for page 1012

📂 Reinforcing Skills Activity 7

💿 Glencoe Skillbuilder Interactivity Workbook CD-ROM, Level 2

Technology SKILLBUILDER
Evaluating a Web Site

For use with Chapter 4

Why Learn This Skill?

The Internet has become a valuable research tool. It is convenient to use, and the information contained on the Internet is plentiful. However, some Web site information is not necessarily accurate or reliable. When using the Internet as a research tool, you will need to distinguish between quality information and inaccurate or incomplete information.

Learning the Skill

There are a number of issues to consider when evaluating a Web site. Most important is to check the accuracy of the source and content. The author and publisher or sponsor of the site should be credible and clearly indicated. The user must also determine the usefulness of the site. The information on the site should be current, and the design and organization of the site should be appealing and easy to navigate.

To evaluate a Web site, ask yourself the following questions:

- Are the facts on the site documented?
- Is more than one source used for background information within the site?
- Are the links within the site appropriate and up-to-date?
- Is the author credible and clearly identified?
- Does the site contain links to other useful resources?
- Is the information easy to access? Is it properly labeled?
- Is the design appealing?

Practicing the Skill

Visit the following Web site and answer the questions that follow.
  http://www.loc.gov/rr/hispanic/1898/

❶ Who is the author or sponsor of the Web site? Can you verify their credibility?

❷ What links does the site contain? Are they appropriate to the topic?

❸ What sources were used for the information contained on the site?

❹ Is the design of the site appealing? Why or why not?

❺ How is the home page organized?

Applying the Skill

Comparing Web Sites Locate two other Web sites about the Spanish-American War. Evaluate them for accuracy and usefulness, and then compare them to the site featured above. Be certain to go through the various links that the site includes so that you can do a thorough evaluation of the site. Share your findings with the class.

 Glencoe's **Skillbuilder Interactive Workbook, CD-ROM Level 2,** provides instruction and practice in key social studies skills.

1012

Answers and Additional Support

ANSWERS TO PRACTICING THE SKILL

1. Library of Congress, Hispanic Division; yes
2. many links internal to the Library of Congress; yes
3. scholarly works, manuscripts, maps, personal narratives; bilingual sources including books and periodicals
4. Answers will vary, but students should provide reasoning for their opinions.
5. graphic, quote, identification of author/sponsor of site, brief summary introduction, many links to more specific topics, acknowledgments

Applying the Skill
Answers will vary but should show that students used and understood the steps in evaluating a Web site.

Interpreting Political Cartoons

For use with Chapter 5

Why Learn This Skill?

Do you enjoy reading the comics section in the newspaper? Many people enjoy reading comic strips. Cartoons also appear on the editorial page. These cartoons express opinions on political issues. Political cartoons are good sources of historical information because they reflect opinions on current events.

Learning the Skill

Political cartoonists rely mostly on images to communicate a message. By using *caricatures* and *symbols,* political cartoonists help readers see relationships and draw conclusions about events. A caricature exaggerates a detail, such as a subject's features, in a drawing. Cartoonists use caricature to create a positive or negative impression of a subject. For example, if a cartoon shows one figure three times larger than another, it implies that the larger figure is more powerful than the smaller one or perhaps is a bully.

A symbol is an image or object that represents something else. For example, a cartoonist may use a crown to represent a monarch. Symbols often represent nations or political parties. The bald eagle and Uncle Sam are common symbols for the United States, a bear often stands for Russia, and a dragon might be used to represent China.

To analyze a political cartoon, first identify the topic and main characters. Then read labels and messages and note relationships between the figures and symbols. Review your knowledge of the cartoon's topic to determine the cartoonist's viewpoint and message.

Practicing the Skill

The political cartoon on this page, published in 1904, makes a statement about the Progressive era. Theodore Roosevelt took office in 1901 with a desire to offer the American public a "Square Deal." As part of the Square Deal, Roosevelt sought to break up trusts, or combinations of large corporations. Roosevelt thought that trusts hurt public interests. By breaking up large trusts, Roosevelt gained broad public support and earned the reputation of being a "trustbuster." Study the cartoon, and then answer the following questions.

❶ Why are the men in this cartoon portrayed as giants? Can you identify them? Why are they important?

❷ The man at the bottom of the cartoon is Theodore Roosevelt. What does he look like he wants to do?

❸ What does the size difference in the two opposing sides tell you about the type of resistance Roosevelt faced?

❹ Do you think that the artist who drew this cartoon is being supportive or critical of Roosevelt's actions toward large corporations? Explain.

Applying the Skill

Interpreting Political Cartoons Find a political cartoon in a newspaper or magazine. If an editorial appears with the cartoon, read that as well. Write a summary of the cartoon's message and explain whether or not you agree with this message.

 Glencoe's **Skillbuilder Interactive Workbook CD-ROM, Level 2,** provides instruction and practice in key social studies skills.

1013

Answers and Additional Support

ANSWERS TO PRACTICING THE SKILL

1. because they were leaders of large corporations; James J. Hill, Jay Gould, John D. Rockefeller, and John P. Morgan; these men formed large trusts
2. He looks determined to slay the giants.
3. Roosevelt faced much resistance in his fight against the trusts.
4. Answers may vary but should include that Roosevelt is made to look heroic.

Applying the Skill
Answers will vary but should show an understanding of how to interpret the cartoons. Make sure students attach the cartoons and editorials to their summaries.

TEACH

R **Reading Strategy**

Identifying the Main Idea and Supporting Details To help students learn the process of analyzing information, ask them to use the bulleted items under Learning the Skill to analyze a short newspaper or magazine article on a topic of personal interest. **BL**

Resources for page 1014

📁 Reinforcing Skills Activity 12

💿 Glencoe Skillbuilder Interactivity Workbook CD-ROM, Level 2

Answers and Additional Support

Critical Thinking
SKILLBUILDER

Analyzing Information

For use with Chapter 6

Why Learn This Skill?

The ability to analyze information is important in deciding your position on a subject. For example, you need to analyze a political decision to determine if you should support it. You would also analyze a candidate's position statements to determine if you should vote for him or her.

Learning the Skill

To analyze information, use the following steps:

- Identify the topic that is being discussed.
- Examine how the information is organized. What are the main points?
- Summarize the information in your own words, and then make a statement of your own based on your understanding of the topic and on what you already know.

Practicing the Skill

Read the following information taken from Henry Cabot Lodge's *On the League of Nations* speech. Use the steps listed above to analyze the information and answer the questions that follow.

I am as anxious as any human being can be to have the United States render every possible service to the civilization and the peace of mankind. But I am certain that we can do it best by not putting ourselves in leading strings, or subjecting our policies and our sovereignty to other nations. The independence of the United States is not only more precious to ourselves, but to the world, than any single possession.

I will go as far as anyone in world service that the first step to world service is the maintenance of the United States. You may call me selfish if you will, conservative or reactionary, or use any other harsh adjective

you see fit to apply. But an American I was born, an American I've remained all my life. I can never be anything else but an American, and I must think of the United States first. And when I think of the United States first in an argument like this, I am thinking of what is best for the world. For if the United States fails, the best hope of mankind fails with it. I have never had but one allegiance; I cannot divide it now. I have loved but one flag and I cannot share that devotion and give affection to the mongrel banner invented for a league. Internationalism, illustrated by the Bolshevik and by the men to whom all countries are alike, provided they can make money out of them, is to me repulsive. National I must remain and in that way I, like all Americans, can render the amplest service to the world.

The United States is the world's best hope, but if you fetter her in the interest through quarrels of other nations, if you tangle her in the intrigues of Europe, you will destroy her powerful good, and endanger her very existence. Leave her to march freely through the centuries to come, as in the years that have gone. Strong, generous, and confident, she has nobly served mankind. Beware how you trifle with your marvelous inheritance—this great land of ordered liberty. For if we stumble and fall, freedom and civilization everywhere will go down in ruin.

❶ What topic is being discussed?

❷ What are the main points of this excerpt from Senator Lodge's speech?

❸ Summarize the information in this excerpt, and then provide your analysis based on this information and your own knowledge.

Applying the Skill

Analyzing Information Find a short, informative piece of news, such as a political candidate's position paper or an editorial in a newspaper. Analyze the information and make a statement of your own.

 Glencoe's **Skillbuilder Interactive Workbook CD-ROM, Level 2,** provides instruction and practice in key social studies skills.

1014

ANSWERS TO PRACTICING THE SKILL

1. League of Nations
2. Independence of the United States is precious to us and the world; he cannot share his devotion to the United States with the League of Nations; getting involved in the intrigues of Europe will endanger the existence of the United States.
3. Students' answers will vary but should demonstrate an understanding of the material in the chapter.

Applying the Skill
Students should show that they used the three-step process to analyze the information.

Critical Thinking SKILLBUILDER

Synthesizing Information

For use with Chapter 7

Why Learn This Skill?

The authors of this book gathered information from many sources to present a story of how the United States came about and how the country's people lived. To combine the information into a logical story, the authors used a process called *synthesis*. Being able to synthesize information can be a useful skill for you as a student when you need to gather data from several sources for a report or a presentation.

Learning the Skill

The skill of synthesizing involves combining and analyzing information gathered from separate sources or at different times to make logical connections. Follow these steps to synthesize information:

- Select important and relevant information.
- Analyze the information and build connections.
- Reinforce or modify the connections as you acquire new information.

Suppose you need to write a research paper on the status of women in the 1920s. You would need to synthesize what you learn to inform others. You could begin by detailing the ideas and information you already have about the status of women in the 1920s. A graphic organizer such as the one on this page could help categorize the facts.

Then you could select an article about women in the 1920s, such as the following:

In 1923 the National Woman's Party first proposed an equal rights amendment to the Constitution. This amendment stated that "men and women shall have equal rights throughout the United States and every place subject to its jurisdiction." The National Woman's party pointed out that legislation discriminating against women existed in every state. . . .

Some progressive women reformers, however, opposed the goals of the National Woman's Party. These progressives favored protective legislation, which had brought shorter hours and better working conditions for many

Women's Status in the 1920s	
Economic:	Many more women worked in factories and other jobs outside the home.
Social:	Women had much more social freedom, including greater choices in clothing styles and public behavior.
Educational:	Many women had a high school education, and more than ever were attending college.

women. The efforts of the progressives helped defeat the equal rights amendment.

Practicing the Skill

Use the graphic organizer and the passage on this page to answer the following questions.

1. What information is presented in the table?
2. What is the main idea of the passage? What information does the passage add to your knowledge of this topic?
3. By synthesizing the two sources and using your own knowledge, what conclusions can you draw about the role of women in 1920s society?
4. Using what you have learned in your studies and from this activity, contrast women's roles in the 1920s with their roles today.

Applying the Skill

Synthesizing Information Find two sources of information on the same topic and write a short report. In your report, answer these questions: What kinds of sources did you use—primary or secondary? What are the main ideas in these sources? How does each source add to your understanding of the topic? Do the sources support or contradict each other?

 Glencoe's **Skillbuilder Interactive Workbook CD-ROM, Level 2,** provides instruction and practice in key social studies skills.

1015

Critical Thinking SKILLBUILDER

TEACH

C Critical Thinking

Making Generalizations Have students examine the front page stories of major newspapers for a week and take notes using the bulleted steps on this page. Afterward, have them write papers describing the types of stories that make the front page. OL

 Resources for page 1015

📁 Reinforcing Skills Activity 15

💿 Glencoe Skillbuilder Interactivity Workbook CD-ROM, Level 2

Answers and Additional Support

ANSWERS TO PRACTICING THE SKILL

1. status of women in the 1920s
2. An amendment dedicated to women's rights was proposed in 1923, but it was defeated with the help of women who opposed it.
3. Women pursued social freedom, entered the workforce, and made contributions in medicine, literature, and science.

4. Students' answers will vary but should address the greater social and economic freedoms women have today. Answers should also show students' successful synthesis of information.

Applying the Skill
Students' reports will vary. Students should correctly identify the sources they used as primary or secondary.

TEACH

Critical Thinking

Comparing and Contrasting

Have students find two stories on the same subject, one from the Internet and one from the daily newspaper. Students should identify the facts and opinions in each story using the description on this page under Learning the Skill. Then ask students to identify which story they believe to be more reliable. **BL** **CA HR1**

Resources for page 1016

📁 Reinforcing Skills Activity 16

🌐 Glencoe Skillbuilder Interactivity Workbook CD-ROM, Level 2

Answers and Additional Support

Distinguishing Fact From Opinion

For use with Chapter 8

Why Learn This Skill?

Imagine that you are watching two candidates for president debate the merits of the college loan program. One candidate says, "In my view, the college loan program must be reformed. Sixty percent of students do not repay their loans on time." The other candidate responds, "College costs are skyrocketing, but only 30 percent of students default on their loans for more than one year. I believe we should spend more money on this worthy program."

How can you tell who or what to believe? First, you must learn to distinguish a fact from an opinion. Then you will be better prepared to evaluate the statements that other people make.

Learning the Skill

A **fact** is a statement that can be proven. In the example above, the statement "Sixty percent of students do not repay their loans on time" may be a fact. By reviewing statistics on the number of student loan recipients who repay their loans, we can determine whether the statement is true or false. To identify potential facts, look for words and phrases indicating specific people, places, events, dates, amounts, or times.

An **opinion,** on the other hand, expresses a personal belief, viewpoint, or emotion. Because opinions are subjective, we cannot prove or disprove them. In the example above, most statements by the candidates are opinions. To identify opinions, look for qualifying words and phrases such as *I think, I believe, probably, seems to me, may, might, could, ought, should, in my judgment,* and *in my view.* Also, look for expressions of approval or disapproval such as *good, bad, poor,* and *satisfactory.* Be aware of superlatives such as *greatest, worst, finest,* and *best,* and notice words with negative meanings and implications such as *squander, contemptible,* and *disgrace.* Also, identify generalizations such as *none, every, always,* and *never.*

Practicing the Skill

For each pair of statements below, determine which is a fact and which is an opinion. Give a reason for each of your choices.

❶ **a.** President Harding was born in Ohio in 1865.

   b. Harding later became the most scandalous president in United States history.

❷ **a.** Harding's administration suffered numerous public scandals, including the Teapot Dome scandal.

   b. Calvin Coolidge was probably disgusted with Harding's poor performance in the White House.

❸ **a.** Harding stated that the United States needed a return to normalcy, but he did not do anything to help the country.

   b. Coolidge took over the White House after Harding's death and led the nation for the next several years.

❹ **a.** Henry Ford significantly lowered the price of the automobile with his mass production methods.

   b. Ford's Model T was the most significant invention of the 20th century.

❺ **a.** The Kellogg-Briand Pact was the most important foreign policy achievement of the Coolidge administration.

   b. Though ratified by 62 nations, the Kellogg-Briand Pact had no binding force.

Applying the Skill

Distinguishing Fact From Opinion In a newspaper, find a news article and an editorial on the same topic or issue. Identify five facts and five opinions from these sources.

 Glencoe's **Skillbuilder Interactive Workbook CD-ROM, Level 2,** provides instruction and practice in key social studies skills.

ANSWERS TO PRACTICING THE SKILL

Possible answers:

1. **a.** fact, it can be proven; **b.** opinion, expresses a viewpoint, includes the word *most*
2. **a.** fact, it can be proven; **b.** opinion, includes the word *probably*
3. **a.** opinion, expresses a viewpoint; **b.** fact, it can be proven

4. **a.** fact, it can be proven; **b.** opinion, expresses a point of view, includes the phrase *most significant*
5. **a.** opinion, expresses a viewpoint; **b.** fact, it can be proven

Applying the Skill
Students' lists will vary but should correctly identify five facts and five opinions.

Understanding Cause and Effect

For use with Chapter 9

Why Learn This Skill?

To understand past events, you should look for why or how an event or a chain of events took place. This process is using the skill of understanding causes and effects.

Learning the Skill

The stock market crash of 1929 caused investors to lose millions of dollars. The banking industry took a huge hit because banks had not only loaned money to stock speculators, but also invested depositors' money in the market. When the market collapsed, so did the banks. The stock market crash *caused* investors and banks to lose money. The failure of the bank system was the *effect*, or result. The chart below shows how one event—the **cause**—led to another—the **effect.**

Cause and Effect

Cause
• Stock market crashes

Effect
• Bank system fails

You can often identify cause-and-effect relationships in sentences from clue words such as the following:

because	therefore	produced
due to	thus	in order to
so that	led to	as a result

In a chain of events, an effect often becomes the cause of other events. The next chart shows the chain of events in the colonial rebellion.

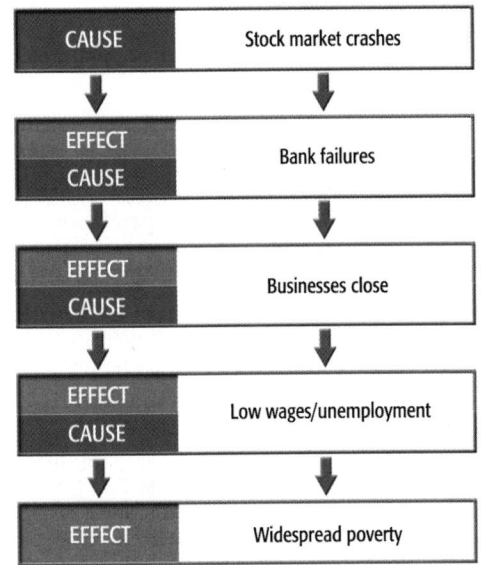

CAUSE	Stock market crashes
EFFECT / CAUSE	Bank failures
EFFECT / CAUSE	Businesses close
EFFECT / CAUSE	Low wages/unemployment
EFFECT	Widespread poverty

Practicing the Skill

Make a chart showing which events are causes and which are effects in the sentences listed in column 2.

❶ In September 1929, professional investors sold off holdings in order to protect their investments.

❷ Most American families could not afford to purchase the goods they produced.

❸ Some families, who lost their homes, moved to shantytowns.

❹ As people purchased fewer goods, companies had to cut production and lay off employees.

Applying the Skill

W **Understanding Cause and Effect** Read an account of a recent event in your community in a local newspaper. Determine at least one cause and one effect of that event. Show the chain of events in a chart.

 Glencoe's **Skillbuilder Interactive Workbook CD-ROM, Level 2,** provides instruction and practice in key social studies skills.

1017

TEACH

 Writing Support

Summary Writing To extend the Applying the Skill activity, have students write a summary of the cause-and-effect relationship that was explored in the activity. Ask the students to write a one-page paper that examines the significance of this relationship within the community. **OL**

Resources for page 1017

📁 Reinforcing Skills Activity 4

💿 Glencoe Skillbuilder Interactivity Workbook CD-ROM, Level 2

Answers and Additional Support

ANSWERS TO PRACTICING THE SKILL

Cause	Most American families could not afford to purchase the goods they produced.
Effect Cause	As people purchased fewer goods, companies had to cut production and lay off employees.
Effect	Some families, who lost their homes, moved to shantytowns.

Applying the Skill
Answers will vary but should correctly identify cause and effect. Remind students to attach the article to their chart.

TEACH

U Universal Access

Below Grade Level Some students may be able to learn this skill better if they can relate it to their own lives. Have students create a time line of their lives with five to six significant events. Then ask them to add four to five significant public events that occurred during their lifetimes. Some of these may be events they remember, but encourage them to do research if they cannot think of all four events from memory. **BL**

Resources for page 1018

📁 Reinforcing Skills Activity 1

💿 Glencoe Skillbuilder Interactivity Workbook CD-ROM, Level 2

Answers and Additional Support

Social Studies
SKILLBUILDER
Reading a Time Line

1929 Stock market crashes/ Depression begins

1932 FDR elected

1933 First New Deal begins

1935 Second New Deal begins

1941 Pearl Harbor attacked; U.S. enters World War II

The United States
1930   1935   1940   1945
The World

1931 German unemployment reaches 5–6 million

1933 Hitler becomes chancellor of Germany

1938 Hitler annexes Austria

1939 World War II begins

For use with Chapter 10

Why Learn This Skill?

When you read a time line, you see not only when an event took place but also what events took place before and after it. A time line can help you develop the skill of **chronological thinking.** Developing a strong sense of chronology—when and in what order events took place—will help you examine relationships among the events. It will also help you understand the causes or result of events.

Learning the Skill

A time line is a chart that lists events that occurred on specific dates. The number of years between dates is the **time span.** A time line that begins in 1910 and ends in 1920 has a 10-year time span. Some time lines are divided into centuries. The twentieth century includes the 1900s, the nineteenth century includes the 1800s, and so on.

Time lines are usually divided into smaller parts, or **time intervals.** On the two time lines below, the first time line has a 300-year time span divided into 100-year time intervals, and the second time line has a 6-year time span divided into 2-year time intervals.

1700   *1800*   *1900*   *2000*

1910   *1912*   *1914*   *1916*

Practicing the Skill

Sometimes a time line shows events that occurred during the same time period but in two different parts of the world. The time line above shows some events in the United States and in the rest of the world during the same time span. Study the time line, and then answer the questions.

❶ What time span and intervals appear on this time line?

❷ Who was elected as president of the United States in 1932?

❸ How many years after Hitler became chancellor of Germany did World War II begin?

❹ How many years were there between the beginning of the First New Deal and the beginning of the Second New Deal?

❺ How many years after World War II began did the United States enter the war?

Applying the Skill

Reading a Time Line Extend the time line on this page to include at least five additional events that took place in the United States between 1920 and 1930.

 Glencoe's **Skillbuilder Interactive Workbook CD-ROM, Level 2,** provides instruction and practice in key social studies skills.

ANSWERS TO PRACTICING THE SKILL

1. time span of 16 years; intervals of five years
2. Franklin D. Roosevelt
3. six years
4. two years
5. two years

Applying the Skill
Students' time lines should cover 1920 to 1930 and include five events.

Critical Thinking SKILLBUILDER

Making Generalizations

For use with Chapter 11

Why Learn This Skill?

Have you heard statements such as "Only tall people play basketball well," or "Dogs make better pets than cats"? Do you accept these statements at face value, or do you stop and consider whether or not they are valid?

Learning the Skill

The statements listed above are called *generalizations*, which are broad statements about a topic. To be valid, a generalization must be based on accurate information.

Let's examine the generalization, "Only tall people play basketball well." We can find many examples of tall basketball players, but there are also many shorter players who excel at this sport.

In this case, we began with a generalization and looked for facts to support or disprove it. In other cases, you will start with a group of facts about a topic and then make a generalization from these facts. To make a valid generalization, first collect information relevant to the topic. This information must consist of accurate facts, not opinions.

Suppose that you want to make a generalization about the relative danger of airplane travel compared to automobile travel. First, you would collect accident statistics involving airplanes and cars. Your next step would be to classify the information into categories. Then you would look for relationships between these categories. For example, you might put the airplane and automobile statistics in separate categories. You might also categorize the number of accidents and the number of fatalities. Finally, you should make a generalization that is consistent with most of the facts you gathered.

Practicing the Skill

Reread the passage about the Austrian *Anschluss* on page 543, and then answer these questions.

❶ What facts about the *Anschluss* are presented?

❷ Organize these facts into categories.

❸ How does the vote held in Austria relate to the other facts?

❹ What generalization can you make about Austria regarding the *Anschluss*?
Activity to assess your mastery of this skill.

❺ What does the fact that Hitler sent troops into Austria to force the *Anschluss* tell you about the type of diplomacy used by the Nazis?

Applying the Skill

Making Generalizations Review the information in your text about appeasement as it related to the countries of Czechoslovakia, France, and Britain. Write a generalization about Czechoslovakia's role in the appeasement policy. Support your generalization with at least five facts.

 Glencoe's **Skillbuilder Interactive Workbook CD-ROM, Level 2,** provides instruction and practice in key social studies skills.

1019

ANSWERS TO PRACTICING THE SKILL

1. Hitler demanded *Anschluss* on the basis of common language. He wanted to expand German territory and resources. He used threats and force to achieve it.
2. Possible categories: Hitler's actions, Austria's response
3. The vote was held after Hitler's troops were already in Austria.
4. Possible answers: Austrians could not have prevented the *Anschluss*; Austrians shared language and culture with Germans.
5. Hitler's diplomacy included intimidation and military enforcement.

Applying the Skill
Answers will vary. Students should have five facts supporting their generalizations.

TEACH

 Critical Thinking

Drawing Conclusions Bring in statistics about a topic that relates to World War II, such as employment figures for women and African Americans or the number of immigrants and their origin. Guide students in using the four steps to draw conclusions about the meaning of the statistics. Encourage class discussion on the meanings and how students arrived at their conclusions. **AL**

Resources for page 1020

📁 Reinforcing Skills Activity 9

🌐 Glencoe Skillbuilder Interactivity Workbook CD-ROM, Level 2

Answers and Additional Support

Interpreting Statistics

A Switching to Wartime Production					
Year	1941	1942	1943	1944	1945
Automobiles produced:	3,779,628	222, 862	139	610	70,001
Tanks produced:	4,203	23,884	29,497	17,565	11,184

For use with Chapter 12

Why Learn This Skill?

Often presented in graphs and tables, statistics are collections of data that are used to support a claim or an opinion. The ability to interpret statistics allows us to understand probable effects and to make predictions.

Learning the Skill

Use the following steps to help you interpret statistical information.

- **Scan** the graph or table, reading the title and labels to get an idea of what is being shown.
- **Examine** the statistics shown, looking for increases and decreases, similarities and differences.
- **Look** for a *correlation* in the statistics. Two sets of data may be related or unrelated. If they are related, we say that there is a correlation between them. In a positive correlation, as one number rises, so does the other number. In a negative correlation, as one number rises, the other number falls. For example, there is a positive correlation between academic achievement and wages, and there is a negative correlation between smoking and life expectancy. Sometimes, statistics may try to show a correlation when none exists. For example, a report that "people who go fishing are less likely to get cancer" may be statistically true but lack any real correlation.
- **Determine** the conclusions you can draw from the statistics.

Practicing the Skill

Study the table above, and then answer the following questions.

❶ What do these statistics tell you about American manufacturing during World War II?

❷ In what year was U.S. tank production the greatest? Why do you think tank production began to decrease after that year?

❸ Is the correlation between automobile production and tank production positive or negative? Explain.

Applying the Skill

Interpreting Statistics Create a survey with two questions for which you believe the answers will show a correlation. For example, you might ask, "How many hours of television do you watch per day?" and "How many hours of sleep do you usually get at night?" Organize your statistics in a chart or graph. Then, look for a correlation in your data and evaluate your results. Write a paragraph summarizing your evaluation.

 Glencoe's **Skillbuilder Interactive Workbook CD-ROM, Level 2,** provides instruction and practice in key social studies skills.

1020

ANSWERS TO PRACTICING THE SKILL

1. Manufacturing became focused on supplies for the war.
2. 1943; answers may vary but should include that the war began to turn in favor of the Allies after 1943.
3. Both: negative because automobile production went down as tank production increased; positive because factories were able to supply the military with needed equipment.

Applying the Skill
Answers will vary. Students should organize their data in a logical way, and their paragraphs should be supported by the data collected.

Interpreting Points of View

For use with Chapter 13

Why Learn This Skill?

Suppose you want to see a new movie, but your friends' opinions range from "terrific" to "boring." People often have different opinions about the same people, events, or issues because they look at them from different points of view.

Learning the Skill

A point of view results from one's own beliefs and values. Many factors affect an individual's point of view, including age, gender, racial or ethnic background, economic class, and religion. To judge the accuracy or the objectivity of an argument, you must first identify the speaker's point of view.

To interpret point of view in written material, gather background information on the author that might reveal his or her point of view. Identify aspects of the topic that the author chooses to emphasize or exclude. Look for emotionally charged words such as *charming, vicious, heartwarming,* and *drastic.* Also notice metaphors and analogies that imply an opinion, such as, "If this budget can work, then pigs can fly."

W Practicing the Skill

Read the following excerpts from diplomat George F. Kennan's "Long Telegram" regarding his views on Soviet Russia and how the United States should deal with communism. Then answer the questions.

(1) Our first step must be to apprehend, and recognize [it] for what it is, the nature of the movement with which we are dealing. We must study it with same courage, detachment, objectivity, and same determination not to be emotionally provoked or unseated by it. . . .

(2) We must see that our public is educated to realities of Russian situation. . . . It must be done mainly by Government, which is necessarily more experienced and better informed on practical problems involved. . . . I am convinced that there would be far less hysterical anti-Sovietism in our country today if realities of this situation were better understood by our people. . . .

(3) Much depends on health and vigor of our own society. World communism is like malignant parasite which feeds only on diseased tissue. This is point at which domestic and foreign policies meet. Every courageous and incisive measure to solve internal problems of our own society, to improve self-confidence, discipline, morale and community spirit of our own people, is a diplomatic victory over Moscow worth a thousand diplomatic notes and joint communiqués. . . .

(4) We must formulate and put forward for other nations a much more positive and constructive picture of sort of world we would like to see than we have put forward in past. . . .

(5) Finally we must have courage and self-confidence to cling to our own methods and conceptions of human society. . . .

George F. Kennan

❶ What did Kennan suggest the United States government do to better understand Russia?

❷ Why do you think Kennan suggests that the public be educated about Russia by the government and not by the press?

❸ What is Kennan's greatest fear in dealing with Russia?

Applying the Skill

Interpreting Points of View In a newspaper or magazine, find an editorial or letter to the editor that expresses a point of view on an issue. Write a paragraph analyzing the author's point of view. Compare it to your own and explain why you agree or disagree with the author.

 Glencoe's **Skillbuilder Interactive Workbook CD-ROM, Level 2,** provides instruction and practice in key social studies skills.

TEACH

W Writing Support

Summary Writing Ask students to write a one-page paper that summarizes George F. Kennan's argument in the excerpted text from the "Long Telegram." The papers should speculate on his particular point of view on this subject. OL CA 11RC2.5

Resources for page 1021

📁 Reinforcing Skills Activity 11

💿 Glencoe Skillbuilder Interactivity Workbook CD-ROM, Level 2

Answers and Additional Support

ANSWERS TO PRACTICING THE SKILL

1. study Russian communism with detachment and objectivity
2. The government is more experienced and better informed; it could more easily portray a cohesive picture than the press, which comes from many different sources.
3. The United States should solve its internal problems and aim for a positive world.

Applying the Skill
Answers will vary, but students' analyses should attempt to fairly identify the author's point of view. Have students attach the article to their assignment.

TEACH

 Critical Thinking

Comparing and Contrasting
Ask students to find three stories on the same subject from three different news sources, such as television, a newspaper, and the Internet. Using the three bullet points, students should compare and contrast the three stories and present their comparisons to the class. **OL**

Resources for page 1022

📁 Reinforcing Skills Activity 28

💿 Glencoe Skillbuilder Interactivity Workbook CD-ROM, Level 2

Answers and Additional Support

Analyzing News Media

For use with Chapter 14

Why Learn This Skill?

Every citizen needs to be aware of current issues and events in order to make good decisions when exercising citizenship rights. To stay informed, people use a variety of news sources, including print media, broadcast media, and electronic media. Whichever media source you use to gather information, it is important to analyze the source to determine its reliability.

Learning the Skill

To get an accurate profile of current events, you must learn to think critically about the news. The steps below will help you think critically.

C

- First, think about the source of the news story. Reports that reveal sources are more reliable than those that do not. If you know the sources, you can evaluate them.

- Many news stories analyze and interpret events. Such analyses may be more detailed than other reports, but they also reflect a reporter's biases. Look for biases as you read or listen to news stories.

- Ask yourself whether the news is even-handed and thorough. Is it reported on the scene or secondhand? Does it represent both sides of the issue? How many sources are used? The more sources cited for a fact, the more reliable it usually is.

Practicing the Skill

Follow the steps below to analyze two types of print media.

❶ Find two articles, one in a current newspaper and the other in a newsmagazine, on a decision made by the president or Congress on a topic such as Social Security, education, or taxes.

❷ What points were the articles trying to make? Were the articles successful? Can the facts be verified?

❸ Did either of the articles reflect a bias toward one viewpoint or the other? List any unsupported statements.

❹ Was the news reported on the scene or second-hand? Do the articles seem to represent both sides fairly?

❺ How many sources can you identify in the articles? List them.

Applying the Skill

Analyzing News Media Think of an issue in your community or in the nation on which public opinion is divided. Read newspaper features and editorials and monitor television reports about the issue. Can you identify any biases? Which reports more fairly represent the issue? Which reports are the most reliable?

 Glencoe's **Skillbuilder Interactive Workbook CD-ROM, Level 2**, provides instruction and practice in key social studies skills.

ANSWERS TO PRACTICING THE SKILL

Using questions two through five, students will analyze two types of print media related to a recent decision made by the president or Congress.

Applying the Skill
Students' analyses will vary. Encourage students to recognize bias on both sides of issues and to identify sources that provide fair representations of various points of view.

Critical Thinking SKILLBUILDER

Problem Solving

For use with Chapter 15

Why Learn This Skill?

Imagine you have just done poorly on a chemistry exam. You wonder why you cannot do better since you always go to class, take notes, and study. In order to improve your grades, you need to identify the specific problem and then take actions to solve it.

Learning the Skill

There are six key steps you should follow that will help you through the problem-solving process.

- Identify the problem. In the case listed above, you know that you are not doing well on chemistry exams.
- Gather information. You know that you always go to class and take notes. You study by yourself for about two hours each day for two or three days before the exam. You also know that you sometimes forget details or get confused about things as you are taking the exam.
- List and consider possible solutions. For example, instead of studying by yourself, you might try studying with a friend or a group. You might also study for shorter timespans to avoid overloading yourself with information.
- Consider the advantages and disadvantages of each solution.
- Now that you have listed and considered the possible options, you need to choose the best solution to your problem. Choose what you think is the right solution, and carry it out.
- Evaluate the effectiveness of the solution. This will help you determine if you have solved the problem. If you earn better scores on the next few chemistry tests, you will know that you have solved your problem.

Practicing the Skill

Reread the material in Section 1 on page 707 under the heading "Kennedy Struggles with

Congress." Use that information and the steps listed on this page to answer the following questions.

1. What problem did Kennedy encounter as he tried to pass domestic policy legislation through Congress?
2. Which of Kennedy's programs did Congress not support? What reasons did members of Congress give for not supporting Kennedy's domestic agenda?
3. What options were available to the president in facing this opposition? What were the advantages and disadvantages?
4. Explain the solution Kennedy implemented to solve his problem.
5. Evaluate the effectiveness of Kennedy's solution. Was it successful? How do you determine this?

Applying the Skill

Problem Solving The conservation club at your school has no money to continue its recycling project. The school district allocated money to the club at the beginning of the year, but that money has been spent. As a member of the club, you have been asked to join a committee to save the conservation club and its projects. Write an essay describing the problem, the list of options and their advantages and disadvantages, a solution, and an evaluation of the chosen solution.

 Glencoe's **Skillbuilder Interactive Workbook CD-ROM, Level 2,** provides instruction and practice in key social studies skills.

1023

Critical Thinking SKILLBUILDER

TEACH

U Universal Access

Interpersonal As a class, students should select a problem that the community is facing. Divide students into pairs and ask each group of two to use the six-step problem-solving process to identify the best solution. Have the class reach a consensus on the best solution. Submit the suggestion to local political leaders or other decision makers who may be working on the problem. AL

Resources for page 1023

📁 Reinforcing Skills Activity 23

💿 Glencoe Skillbuilder Interactivity Workbook CD-ROM, Level 2

Answers and Additional Support

ANSWERS TO PRACTICING THE SKILL

1. congressional resistance
2. health insurance for the elderly, Department of Urban Affairs, federal aid to education; too costly, too much federal power
3. He could push harder for all aspects of his agenda or reserve his bargaining power for only the issues that were truly important and winnable.
4. He chose to reserve his bargaining power.

5. Students' answers will vary. Students might mention that many of JFK's proposals were defeated, or that he lacked political leverage no matter what strategy he used.

Applying the Skill
Students' essays will vary. Encourage students to use the six steps on this page as they plan their essays.

TEACH

R Reading Strategy

Evaluating Ask students to look at the bibliography on this page and make observations about the sources, considering the following: Are the entries listed primary or secondary sources? Are they current or historical sources? What types of media are represented? Who is the intended audience? Do the sources cover a variety of author perspectives? Then tell students to consider how the quality and quantity of sources may affect the content of a report. **AL**

Resources for page 1024

📁 Reinforcing Skills Activity 24

💿 Glencoe Skillbuilder Interactivity Workbook CD-ROM, Level 2

Answers and Additional Support

Study and Writing
SKILLBUILDER

Preparing a Bibliography

For use with Chapter 16

Why Learn This Skill?

When you write research reports, you should include a list of the sources used to find your information. This list, called a *bibliography*, allows you to credit the sources you cited and supports the report's accuracy.

Learning the Skill

A bibliography is a list of sources used in a research report. These sources include books; articles from newspapers, magazines, and journals; interviews; and other sources.

There are two main reasons to write a bibliography. First, those who read your report may want to learn more about the topic. Second, a bibliography supports the reliability of your report.

A bibliography follows an established format. The entry for each source contains all the information needed to find that source, including the author, title, page numbers, publisher information, and publication date. You should document this information as you carry out your research. If you neglect this step early in your research, you must locate your sources again in order to credit them in your report.

You should arrange bibliographic entries alphabetically by the author's last name. The following are acceptable formats, followed by sample entries. Note that all lines after the first line are indented.

Books:

Author's last name, first name. *Full Title.* Place of publication: publisher, copyright date.

Hay, Peter. *Ordinary Heroes: The Life and Death of Chana Szenes, Israel's National Heroine.* New York: Paragon House, 1986.

Articles:

Author's last name, first name. "Title of Article." *Name of Periodical* in which article appears, volume number (date of issue): page numbers.

Watson, Bruce. "The New Peace Corps in the New Kazakhstan." *Smithsonian,* Vol. 25 (August 1994): pp. 26–35.

Other Sources:

For other kinds of sources, adapt the format for book entries as needed.

Practicing the Skill

Review the sample bibliography below from a report on Martin Luther King, Jr. Then answer the questions that follow.

Patrick, Diane. *Martin Luther King, Jr.* New York: Franklin Watts, 1990.

Franklin, John H. "Jim Crow Goes to School: The Genesis of Legal Segregation in Southern Schools." *South Atlantic Quarterly,* 57 (1956): pp. 225–235.

Washington, James Melvin, ed. *A Testament of Hope: The Essential Writings of Martin Luther King, Jr.* San Francisco: Harper & Row.

King, Jr., Martin Luther. Time for Freedom has Come. New York Times Magazine (Sept. 10, 1961).

❶ Are the bibliography entries in the correct order? Why or why not?

❷ What is missing from the second book listing?

❸ What features are missing from the second article listing?

❹ Why is it important to provide all bibliographical information for each source in a research paper? What are the consequences of not doing so?

Applying the Skill

Preparing a Bibliography Put together a bibliography of at least five sources that you could use for a report on the civil rights movement. Include books, periodicals, and any other sources you wish.

 Glencoe's **Skillbuilder Interactive Workbook CD-ROM, Level 2,** provides instruction and practice in key social studies skills.

ANSWERS TO PRACTICING THE SKILL

Possible answers:
1. No; they should be in alphabetical order using the last name of each author.
2. publication date
3. quotes around the title of the article, and italics for the name of the magazine
4. Bibliographical information gives credibility to a report and allows readers to verify information.

Incomplete information may make it difficult or impossible to locate the sources used.

Applying the Skill
Students' bibliographies will vary. Students should follow the guidelines on this page or other guidelines you provide.

Understanding the Parts of a Map

For use with Chapter 17

Why Learn This Skill?

Maps can direct you down the street or around the world. There are as many different kinds of maps as there are uses for them. Being able to read a map begins with learning about its parts.

Learning the Skill

Maps usually include a key, a compass rose, and a scale bar. The map key explains the meaning of special colors, symbols, and lines used on the map.

On a road map, for example, the key tells what map lines stand for paved roads, dirt roads, and interstate highways.

After reading the map key, look for the compass rose. It is the direction marker that shows the cardinal directions of north, south, east, and west. A measuring line, often called a scale bar, helps you estimate distance on a map. The map's scale tells you what distance on the earth is represented by the measurement on the scale bar. For example, 1 inch (2.54 cm) on the map may represent 100 miles (160.9 km) on the earth. Knowing the scale allows you to visualize the extent of an area and to measure distances.

Practicing the Skill

The map on this page shows the major U.S. and South Vietnamese troop movements during the Vietnam War. Look at the parts of the map, and then answer the questions.

1. What information is given in the key?
2. What body of water makes up South Vietnam's southeastern border?
3. What color is used to represent North Vietnamese supply lines?
4. What is the approximate distance, in miles, between the South Vietnamese capital of Saigon and the North Vietnamese capital of Hanoi?

NATIONAL GEOGRAPHIC   The Vietnam War

Map showing China, Dien Bien Phu, Hanoi, Haiphong, Laos, North Vietnam, Gulf of Tonkin, Thailand, Khe Sanh, Invasion of Laos Feb. 8–March, 1971, Quang Tri, Hue, Da Nang, Tam Ky, Chu Lai, My Lai Massacre March 16, 1968, Demilitarized Zone 17th Parallel, Ho Chi Minh Trail, Pleiku, Qui Nhon, Cambodia, South Vietnam, Invasion of Cambodia May 1–June 29, 1970, Ban Me Thuot, Nha Trang, Phnom Penh, Phoc Binh, Gulf of Thailand, Saigon, Long Binh, Mekong Delta, Can Tho, Khanh Hung, Quan Long, South China Sea, Miller Cylindrical projection

Key:
- Major U.S. and South Vietnamese troop movements
- Major North Vietnamese supply lines
- U.S. bases

0 — 150 miles
0 — 150 kilometers

Applying the Skill

Understanding the Parts of a Map Study the map of Indochina on page 774. Use the map to answer the following questions.

1. In what year did Burma gain independence?
2. What three countries border the Gulf of Thailand?
3. What countries form the western border of South Vietnam?

Glencoe's **Skillbuilder Interactive Workbook CD-ROM, Level 2**, provides instruction and practice in key social studies skills.

1025

TEACH

S Skill Practice

Using Geography Skills To really utilize a map effectively, students should be familiar with the different components and apparatus provided in a map. Before students answer the questions under Practicing the Skill, have them identify all the components of the map listed under Learning the Skill. Ask students to use the map scale to measure the distance from the demilitarized zone to Pleiku. **OL**

Resources for page 1025

📁 Reinforcing Skills Activity 27

💿 Glencoe Skillbuilder Interactivity Workbook CD-ROM, Level 2

Answers and Additional Support

ANSWERS TO PRACTICING THE SKILL

1. major U.S. and South Vietnamese troop movements, major North Vietnamese supply lines, and U.S. bases
2. South China Sea
3. red
4. just over 600 miles

Applying the Skill
1. 1948
2. Thailand, Cambodia, South Vietnam
3. Cambodia, Laos

TEACH

 Reading Strategy

Reading Primary/Secondary Sources Ask students to select one of the *An American Story* features from the book and focus on the quoted portion of the material, which is a primary source. Have students write down two or three things that they learn about a person, place, or event as a result of using the four steps to guide their study of the excerpt. **BL**

📖 **Resources for page 1026**

📁 Reinforcing Skills Activity 26

💿 Glencoe Skillbuilder Interactivity Workbook CD-ROM, Level 2

Answers and Additional Support

Analyzing Primary Sources

For use with Chapter 18

Why Learn This Skill?

To determine what happened in the past, historians do some detective work. They comb through bits of evidence from the past to reconstruct events. These bits of written and illustrated historical evidence are called *primary sources.* Examining primary sources can help you understand history.

Learning the Skill

Primary sources are records of events made by the people who witnessed them. They include letters, diaries, photographs, news articles, and legal documents.

Primary sources yield several important kinds of information. Often they give detailed accounts of events. However, the account reflects only one perspective. For this reason, you must examine as many perspectives as possible before drawing any conclusions. To analyze primary sources, follow these steps.

R
- Identify the author of the source. Note any biases or opinions expressed by the author or creator of the source.
- Identify when and where the document was written.
- Read the document for its content and try to answer the five "W" questions: Who is it about? What is it about? When did it happen? Where did it happen? Why did it happen?
- Determine what kind of information may be missing from the primary source.

Practicing the Skill

The primary source that follows is a small part of a United States legal document. Read the source, and then answer the questions.

Title IX, Education Amendments of 1972, Section 1684. Blindness or visual impairment; prohibition against discrimination

No person in the United States shall, on the grounds of blindness or severely impaired vision, be denied admission in any course of study by a recipient of Federal financial assistance for any education program or activity; but nothing herein shall be construed to require any such institution to provide any special services to such person because of his blindness or visual impairment.

➊ When was this document written?
➋ Who is affected by this legal document?
➌ What is the purpose of this legal requirement?
➍ Why do you think this document was written?

Applying the Skill

Analyzing Primary Sources Find a primary source from your past—a photo, a report card, an old newspaper clipping, or your first baseball card. Bring this source to class and explain what it shows about that time in your life.

 Glencoe's **Skillbuilder Interactive Workbook CD-ROM, Level 2,** provides instruction and practice in key social studies skills.

ANSWERS TO PRACTICING THE SKILL

Possible answers:
1. 1972
2. persons who are blind or visually impaired
3. to prevent discrimination against the blind or visually impaired in admission to an educational institution receiving federal funds
4. to prevent discrimination

Applying the Skill
Students' answers will vary. Give students time to present primary sources, answer the five "W" questions, and explain what they show about their lives at that time.

Critical Thinking SKILLBUILDER

Analyzing Secondary Sources

For use with Chapter 19

Why Learn This Skill?

This textbook, like many other history books, is a secondary source. Secondary sources draw from primary sources to explain a topic. The value of a secondary source depends on how its author uses primary sources. Learning to analyze secondary sources will help you figure out whether those sources are presenting a complete and accurate picture of a topic or event.

Learning the Skill

To determine whether an author uses primary sources effectively, ask these questions:

R

- Are there references to primary sources in the text, footnotes, or acknowledgments?
- Who are the authors of the primary sources? What insights or biases might these people have?
- Is the information from the primary sources interwoven effectively to support or describe an event?
- Are different kinds of primary sources considered? Do they represent varied testimony?
- Is the interpretation of the primary sources sound and logical?

Practicing the Skill

In the following excerpt from *The Cold War, 1945–1987,* author Ralph B. Levering discusses President Carter's China policy. Carter sent his national security adviser, Zbigniew Brzezinski, to China to encourage better relations and thus put pressure on the Soviets. As you read, identify the primary sources Levering uses to make his argument.

During his trip to Peking, Brzezinski did everything he could to please the Chinese leaders. . . . He stressed repeatedly the evil nature of the Soviet Union. . . . Upon his return, Brzezinski told a New York Times *reporter that the trip was intended to "underline the long-term strategic nature of the United States' relationship to China."*

. . . Soviet leaders were deeply concerned. An editorial in Pravda *on May 30, 1978, stated that Brzezinski*

President Nixon and First Lady Pat Nixon visiting the Great Wall of China during their historic 1972 trip.

"stands before the world as an enemy of détente." Pravda also blamed China, stating on June 17 that "Soviet-American confrontation . . . is the cherished dream of Peking." On the whole, U.S. officials were not displeased by the Kremlin's anger and concern: perhaps it would make Soviet leaders more anxious to conclude the SALT negotiations and more inclined to show restraint in the Third World.

❶ What kind of primary source does Levering use twice in this passage?

❷ Does the author use the primary source effectively to support or describe his point? Explain.

❸ Do you think this kind of primary source has any possible weaknesses?

❹ Would the use of government documents strengthen the author's argument? Why or why not?

Applying the Skill

Analyzing Secondary Sources Find and read an in-depth article in a newspaper. Then list the primary sources the article uses and analyze how reliable you think they are.

Glencoe's **Skillbuilder Interactive Workbook CD-ROM, Level 2,** provides instruction and practice in key social studies skills.

1027

Critical Thinking SKILLBUILDER

TEACH

R Reading Strategy

Reading Primary/Secondary Sources Ask students to research a topic in American history. Students should use library resources to select one secondary source on this topic. Have students evaluate the use of primary sources in their chosen secondary source using the five bullet points on this page. **OL** **CA** 11WA2.4b

Resources for page 1027

📁 Reinforcing Skills Activity 27

⚫ Glencoe Skillbuilder Interactivity Workbook CD-ROM, Level 2

Answers and Additional Support

ANSWERS TO PRACTICING THE SKILL

Possible answers:
1. an editorial in a newspaper
2. Students' answers will vary, but students should support their explanations with examples.
3. The reporter could be using the quote out of context. The *Pravda* editorials, as all editorials, are opinions.

Since the Soviet state ran *Pravda,* articles and editorials uniformly reflected government policy.
4. Students' answers will vary.

Applying the Skill
Students' answers will vary. Encourage students to attach the article to their analysis.

TEACH

Reading Strategy

Predicting Have students research current figures for the federal debt, national defense spending, and total federal expenses. Tell them to plot where current figures would end up if the line graph in the book was extended. Ask them to predict future spending of the administration based on what they know about the past and present. **OL**

Resources for page 1028

📁 Reinforcing Skills Activity 5

💿 Glencoe Skillbuilder Interactivity Workbook CD-ROM, Level 2

Answers and Additional Support

1028

Social Studies
SKILLBUILDER

Reading a Line Graph

For use with Chapter 20

Why Learn This Skill?

Line graphs are a way of showing numbers visually, making them easier to read and understand. Learning to read line graphs will help you compare changes over time or differences between places, groups of people, or related events.

Learning the Skill

Line graphs are often used to show changes in number or quantity over time. They show information in two dimensions. The horizontal axis (or x-axis) is the line along the bottom of the graph. If the graph shows information over time, this axis usually shows the time period. The vertical axis (or y-axis) is the line that runs up the side of the graph. This axis usually displays the quantity, or amount, of whatever is being measured in the graph.

Line graphs can be simple or complex. A single-line graph will show changes of only one item. More complex line graphs can combine information for two or more items on one graph. A double-line graph shows information for two related quantities. For example, such a graph may depict the growth of urban and rural populations in a state or community over a specific time period. A triple-line graph may record three related quantities. For instance, you and two of your friends might all record your running times over several different distances. Then, using a different color for each person, you could record that information on a graph. By looking at the varying heights of the three lines, you will be able to tell who was faster at each distance measured.

Before trying to understand any graph, be sure to read the title of the graph, the labels on both axes, and the key for each line. This will help you understand the information you should gain from the graph.

Military Spending and the Deficit, 1980–1992

In Hundreds of Billions of Dollars

- Total Federal Expenses
- National Defense
- Federal Debt

Year

Sources: Departments of Commerce and Treasury; Office of Management and Budget.

Practicing the Skill

Study the line graph and answer the following questions.

1. What kind of information does the graph compare?
2. What are the time intervals on the horizontal axis?
3. What quantity is measured on the vertical axis?
4. What trend does the graph seem to show?
5. What does this graph tell you about the spending practices of the government during the time span shown?

Applying the Skill

Reading a Line Graph Create a line graph comparing military spending deficit figures from 1995 to 2003. Compare your graph with the one on this page and write a summary of the differences you notice between the two.

 Glencoe's **Skillbuilder Interactive Workbook CD-ROM, Level 2,** provides instruction and practice in key social studies skills.

1028

ANSWERS TO PRACTICING THE SKILL

1. federal debt, national defense spending, and total federal spending
2. one year
3. money spent in hundreds of billions of dollars
4. As national defense spending and federal expenses rose, federal debt also increased but at a faster rate.
5. Government spending increased greatly.

Applying the Skill
Students' answers should display proper use of the graphs, and their summaries should show their ability to correctly interpret the graphs.

Critical Thinking SKILLBUILDER

Hypothesizing

For use with Chapter 21

Why Learn This Skill?

When you are reading new material, you may often encounter ideas and events that you do not immediately understand. One way to overcome this difficulty is to make educated guesses about what happened.

Learning the Skill

When you read things that you do not understand, you probably make guesses about what the material means. You may or may not have been able to prove these guesses, but you have taken a step toward deciphering the information. This step is called **hypothesizing.** When you hypothesize, you form one or more hypotheses, which are guesses that offer possible answers to a problem or provide possible explanations for an observation. When hypothesizing, follow these steps.

- Read the material carefully.

- Ask yourself what the material is actually saying. To do this, try to put the material in your own words.

- Determine what you might logically assume from your guesses. Then form one or more hypotheses.

- Test each hypothesis to determine whether or not it is correct. You can usually do this by asking yourself questions that relate to your hypothesis and then researching the answers.

- Based on your research, determine which hypothesis, if any, provides an explanation for the information that you originally read.

Hypotheses are only preliminary explanations. They must be accepted, rejected, or modified as the problem is investigated. Each hypothesis must be tested against the information gathered. Hypotheses that are supported by evidence can be accepted as explanations of the problem.

Practicing the Skill

Using the steps just discussed and your knowledge of recent history, test the following hypotheses and determine if they can be supported.

❶ Advances in telecommunications and the rise of the Internet have improved the standard of living in the United States.

❷ The economic boom of the 1990s was a major factor in President Clinton's reelection in 1996.

❸ The new global economy has hurt the United States economy.

❹ The oil industry has contributed to the rise of Middle Eastern terrorism.

❺ The United States is the only country in the world that has been affected by terrorist attacks in the past 30 years.

Students collaborating

Applying the Skill

Hypothesizing Read the material in your text about the rise of the Internet. Using the facts that you are given in this section, form at least two hypotheses that may explain what is being described. Test each hypothesis, then select the best one. Which hypothesis did you choose? Why?

Glencoe's **Skillbuilder Interactive Workbook CD-ROM, Level 2,** provides instruction and practice in key social studies skills.

1029

TEACH

R Reading Strategy

Predicting Have students choose a current problem in the United States and use the steps on this page to hypothesize a solution to the problem. As time goes on, discuss their hypotheses in light of any new information available in the news. As a class, revise the hypotheses as necessary. **OL** **CA HR4**

Resources for page 1029

📁 Reinforcing Skills Activity 10

💿 Glencoe Skillbuilder Interactivity Workbook CD-ROM, Level 2

Answers and Additional Support

ANSWERS TO PRACTICING THE SKILL

Answers will vary; students may determine that hypotheses one, two, and five are more easily supported than three and four.

Applying the Skill
Answers will vary. Students should follow the five steps outlined on page 1029 as they complete this assignment.

1029

Flag Etiquette

> **For Americans, the flag has always had a special meaning.
> It is a symbol of our nation's freedom and democracy.**

Rules and Customs

Over the years, Americans have developed rules and customs concerning the use and display of the flag. One of the most important things every American should remember is to treat the flag with respect.

- The flag should be raised and lowered by hand and displayed only from sunrise to sunset. On special occasions, the flag may be displayed at night, but it should be illuminated.

- The flag may be displayed on all days, weather permitting, particularly on national and state holidays and on historic and special occasions.

- No flag may be flown above the American flag or to the right of it at the same height.

- The flag should never touch the ground or floor beneath it.

- The flag may be flown at half-staff by order of the president, usually to mourn the death of a public official.

- The flag may be flown upside down only to signal distress.

- When the flag becomes old and tattered, it should be destroyed by burning. According to an approved custom, the Union (stars on blue field) is first cut from the flag; then the two pieces, which no longer form a flag, are burned.

Continental Colors
1775–1777

First Stars and Stripes
1777–1795

Betsy Ross Flag
c. 1790

15-Star Flag
1795–1818

20-Star Flag
1818

Great Star Flag
1818

35-Star Flag
1863–1865

38-Star Flag
1877–1890

48-Star Flag
1912–1959

50-Star Flag
1960

Glossary

This glossary includes all the content vocabulary words and academic vocabulary words from your text. Content vocabulary relates to history content. These words are boldfaced and highlighted in yellow in your text. Academic vocabulary will help you understand all of your school subjects. These words are boldfaced in your text and are shown with an asterisk in the glossary.

A

abolition the immediate ending of slavery (p. 188)

* **abstraction** an idea that is difficult for some to understand (p. 690)

* **academic** associated with higher learning at a scholarly institution (p. 188)

* **accompany** to be associated with (p. 675)

* **accumulate** to gain over time (p. 903)

* **acknowledge** to recognize or admit to (p. 866)

* **adapt** to change in order to meet the demands of a certain environment or circumstance (p. 238)

* **adequately** to complete a task without going above or beyond what is required (p. 387)

* **adjacent** sharing a common border (p. 198)

* **administration** a group of people meant to advise and assist the president (p. 778)

* **advocate** to propose a certain position or viewpoint (p. 334)

affirmative action an active effort to improve employment or educational opportunities for minorities (p. 825)

Agent Orange a chemical defoliant used to clear Vietnamese jungles during the Vietnam War (p. 782)

* **allocate** to set apart for something specific (p. 589)

* **alternative** something that is different from what is normal (p. 790)

* **ambiguous** to lack a definitive purpose (p. 181)

amendment a change to the Constitution (p. 128)

Americanization causing someone to acquire American traits and characteristics (p. 270)

amnesty the act of granting a pardon to a large group of people (p. 219)

amphtrac an amphibious tractor used to move troops from ships to shore (p. 603)

* **analogy** something that is common between two seemingly uncommon things (p. 724)

anarchist person who believes that there should be no government (p. 407)

annexation incorporating a territory within the domain of a country (p. 194)

anthrax a bacteria used to create biological weapons (p. 959)

* **anticipate** to predict an action before it happens (p. 547)

* **apparent** appearing to be fact as far as can be understood (p. 499)

appeasement accepting demands in order to avoid conflict (p. 544)

* **approximately** an estimation of a figure close to the actual figure (p. 599)

* **arbitrary** based on individual preference or convenience and not dependent on standards (p. 710)

arbitration settling a dispute by agreeing to accept the decision of an impartial outsider (p. 342)

armistice a temporary agreement to end fighting (p. 388)

* **aspect** refers to a portion of something with great influence or size (p. 410)

assembly line a production system with machines and workers arranged so that each person performs an assigned task again and again as the item passes before him or her (p. 450)

* **assign** to appoint to a position or duty (p. 581)

assimilate to absorb a group into the culture of a larger population (p. 242)

* **attain** to gain possession of something (p. 751)

* **attribute** to describe an effect by applying a cause (p. 858)

attrition the act of wearing down by constant harassment or attack (p. 209)

* **author** someone who creates original material (p. 428)

* **authorities** those who have control over determining and enforcing what is right or wrong (p. 394)

B

baby boom a marked rise in birthrate, such as occurred in the United States following World War II (p. 677)

bailiff minor officer of the courts (p. 475)

* **benefit** to be useful or profitable (p. 675)

* bias the presence of prejudice within someone's judgment (p. 815)

bilingualism the practice of teaching immigrant students in their own language (p. 829)

binding arbitration process whereby a neutral party hears arguments from two opposing sides and makes a decision that both must accept (p. 515)

black codes laws passed in the South just after the Civil War aimed at controlling freedmen and enabling plantation owners to exploit African American workers (p. 221)

black power the mobilization of the political and economic power of African Americans, especially to compel respect for their rights and to improve their condition (p. 760)

blitzkrieg name given to sudden violent offensive attacks the Germans used during World War II; "lightning war" (p. 545)

blue-collar jobs in the manual labor field, particularly those requiring protective clothing (p. 675)

blues style of music evolving from African American spirituals and noted for its melancholy sound (p. 428)

brinkmanship the willingness to go to the brink of war to force an opponent to back down (p. 653)

broker state role of the government to work out conflicts among competing interest groups (p. 525)

budget deficit the amount by which expenses exceed income (p. 895)

bull market a long period of rising stock prices (p. 470)

busing a policy of transporting children to schools outside their neighborhoods to achieve greater racial balance (p. 826)

C

cabinet a group of advisers to the president (p. 173)

* capacity an individual's ability to perform a specific task (p. 354)

capital gains tax a federal tax paid by businesses and investors when they sell stocks or real estate (p. 919)

caucus a meeting in which members of a political party choose their party's candidate for president or decide policy (p. 184)

censure to express a formal disapproval of an action (p. 648)

chad a small piece of cardboard produced by punching a data card (p. 949)

* channel to force through a preexisting pathway (p. 758)

charter a constitution (p. 616)

checks and balances the system in which each branch of government has the ability to limit the power of the other branches to prevent any from becoming too powerful (p. 128)

* circumstance a factor in a problem that determines its solution (p. 225)

* cite to point out as an example in an argument or debate (p. 944)

* civil relating to the citizens of a certain state or country (p. 540)

civilization a highly organized society marked by knowledge of trade, government, the arts, science, and, often, written language (p. 99)

* clause a distinct section in a written formal document (p. 174)

closed shop an agreement in which a company agrees to hire only union members (pp. 251, 667)

cloture a motion which ends debate and calls for an immediate vote, possible in the U.S. Senate by a vote of 60 senators (p. 754)

* code a signal or symbol used to represent something that is to be kept secret (p. 601)

* coincidental when two related things occur at the same time (p. 779)

Cold War the ideological and often confrontational conflict between the United States and the Soviet Union between 1946 and 1990 (p. 627)

* colleague a person who works in the same, or similar, profession (p. 478)

* commission to give authorization to perform a specific task (p. 260)

commission plan a plan in which a city's government is divided into different departments with different functions, each placed under the control of a commissioner (p. 329)

committee of correspondence committee organized in each colony to communicate with and unify the colonies (p. 115)

commune a group living arrangement in which members share everything and work together (p. 809)

* communicate to share information with people or groups (p. 115)

* community people with common characteristics living in the same area (p. 485)

* comprehensive to cover a broad range of topics (p. 755)

* **conceive** to create from nothing (p. 213)

concentration camp a camp where persons are detained or confined (p. 553)

* **concept** an abstract idea which can be put into practice (p. 249)

Confederacy nation declared to have been formed by the southern states that seceded from the Union in 1860–1861 (p. 201)

* **confine** to enclose or restrain (p. 726)

* **confirm** to give assurance of validity (p. 643)

* **conformity** to change in a way that fits a standard or authority (p. 692)

conscription requiring people to enter military service (pp. 209, 376)

consensus general agreement (p. 724)

* **consequence** the positive or negative result of an action (p. 835)

conservative a person who believes government power, particularly in the economy, should be limited in order to maximize individual freedom (p. 887)

* **constitute** to cause something to be necessary (p. 381)

* **consult** to ask for permission or advice (p. 575)

* **consumer** a person who buys what is produced by an economy (p. 451)

containment the policy or process of preventing the expansion of a hostile power (p. 633)

contra Spanish for counter-revolutionary, an anti-Sandinista guerrilla force in Nicaragua (p. 898)

contraband goods whose importation, exportation, or possession is illegal (p. 373)

* **contract** a binding legal document between two parties (p. 825)

* **contradict** to do the opposite of what is expected (p. 787)

* **contrary** to be in disagreement with (p. 956)

* **contribute** to give to a common cause (p. 485)

* **controversial** something that causes opposing views to be debated (p. 683)

convoy a group that travels with something, such as a ship, to protect it (p. 387)

convoy system a system in which merchant ships travel with naval vessels for protection (p. 584)

cooperative individualism President Hoover's policy of encouraging manufacturers and distributors to form their own organizations and volunteer information to the federal government in an effort to stimulate the economy (p. 458)

corporation an organization that is authorized by law to carry on an activity but treated as though it were a single person (p. 248)

cost of living the cost of purchasing goods and services essential for survival (p. 391)

cost-plus a government contract to pay a manufacturer the cost to produce an item plus a guaranteed percentage (p. 574)

counterculture a culture with values and beliefs different than the mainstream (p. 809)

covert not openly shown or engaged in (p. 654)

creationism the belief that God created the world and everything in it, usually in the way described in Genesis (p. 411)

credibility gap lack of trust or believability (p. 787)

* **crucial** something considered important or essential (p. 516)

* **culture** customs, religion, and social practices generally shared by a distinct group of people (p. 99)

* **currency** paper money used as a medium of exchange (p. 944)

customs duty a tax on imports and exports (p. 113)

de facto segregation segregation by custom and tradition (p. 741)

deficit spending government practice of spending borrowed money rather than raising taxes, usually an attempt to boost the economy (p. 511)

deflation a decline in the volume of available money or credit that results in lower prices, and, therefore, increases the buying power of money (p. 276)

* **demonstrate** to prove, or make clear, your beliefs (p. 521)

* **denote** to make reference to (p. 875)

deport to expel individuals from the country (p. 394)

* **derive** to gain something from a specific source (p. 811)

détente a policy which attempts to relax or ease tensions between nations (p. 855)

developing nation a nation whose economy is primarily agricultural (p. 654)

* **device** a scheme meant to deceive (p. 681)

* **devote** to assign for a specific task (p. 867)

Glossary

direct primary a vote held by all members of a political party to decide their candidate for public office (p. 330)

disco popular dance music characterized by hypnotic rhythm, repetitive lyrics, and electronically produced sounds (p. 874)

disfranchise to deprive of the right to vote (p. 577)

* **distribution** the act of shipping products from a central location to a vast amount of customers (p. 248)

* **diverse** being different from one another (p. 419)

dollar diplomacy a policy of joining the business interests of a country with its diplomatic interests abroad (p. 315)

* **dominant** one that takes control over all others (p. 652)

domino theory the belief that if one nation in Asia fell to the Communists, neighboring countries would follow (p. 775)

dove a person in favor of the United States withdrawing from the Vietnam War (p. 789)

downsizing reducing a company in size by laying off workers and managers to become more efficient (p. 918)

* **draft** to select a person at random for mandatory military service (p. 376)

due process a judicial requirement that laws may not treat individuals unfairly, arbitrarily, or unreasonably, and that courts must follow proper procedures and rules when trying cases (p. 710)

Dust Bowl name given to the area of the southern Great Plains severely damaged by droughts and dust storms during the 1930s (p. 476)

* **dynamic** the ability to grab the attention of an audience in order to express your goals (p. 349)

dynamic conservatism policy of balancing economic conservatism with some activism (p. 670)

E

* **editor** someone who arranges, alters, or corrects manuscript to be published in a book, newspaper, or magazine (p. 959)

* **element** the simplest principles of a system of thought or philosophy (p. 629)

* **eliminate** to get rid of (p. 557)

emancipation the act or process of freeing enslaved persons (p. 188)

embargo a government ban on trade with other countries (p. 865)

* **emerge** to be made known (p. 419)

* **emphasis** a special importance given to an object or idea (p. 369)

* **enhance** to improve or increase (p. 525)

Enlightenment movement during the 1700s that promoted science, knowledge, and reason (p. 112)

entrepreneur one who organizes, manages, and assumes the risks of a business or enterprise (p. 245)

enumerated powers powers listed in the Constitution as belonging to the federal government (p. 174)

* **environmental** having to do with the environment; the complex system of plants, animals, water, and soil (p. 344)

* **erode** to wear away at something until it fades (p. 372)

* **error** a misjudgment or miscalculation (p. 612)

espionage spying, especially to gain government secrets (p. 380)

* **establish** to create an organization or company (p. 351)

* **estate** a large amount of land, usually containing a large house (p. 655)

* **ethic** a set of moral values to live by (p. 411)

ethnic cleansing the expulsion, imprisonment, or killing of ethnic minorities by a dominant majority group (p. 940)

eugenics a pseudo-science that deals with the improvement of hereditary qualities of a race or breed (p. 408)

euro the basic currency shared by the countries of the European Union since 1999 (p. 944)

evolution the scientific theory that humans and other forms of life have evolved over time (p. 411)

* **evolve** to change depending on your physical environment (p. 266)

* **exceed** to go beyond what is required (p. 895)

executive privilege principle stating that communications of the executive branch should remain confidential to protect national security (p. 860)

* **explicit** to express without confusion of intent (p. 797)

* **exploit** a heroic act (p. 311)

* **exports** goods produced by one country which are sold and shipped to another (p.113)

extermination camp a camp where prisoners were sent to be executed (p. 554)

* **extract** to remove by force (p. 237)

F

fallout radioactive particles dispersed by a nuclear explosion (p. 649)

fallout shelter a shelter built with the intent to house and protect people from nuclear fallout (p. 649)

fascism a political system headed by a dictator that calls for extreme nationalism and racism and no tolerance of opposition (p. 537)

featherbedding practice of limiting work output in order to create more jobs (p. 667)

* **federal** refers to a strong central government (p. 825)

federalism political system in which power is divided between the national and state governments (p. 128)

feminism the belief that men and women should be equal politically, economically, and socially (p. 814)

filibuster an attempt to kill a bill by having a group of senators take turns speaking continuously so that a vote cannot take place (p. 754)

* **final** to be at the end of a process (p. 951)

* **finance** to provide money for a project (p. 513)

fireside chats radio broadcasts made by FDR to the American people to explain his initiatives (p. 502)

flapper a young woman of the 1920s who showed freedom from convention, especially in dress (p. 410)

flexible response the buildup of conventional troops and weapons to allow a nation to fight a limited war without using nuclear weapons (p. 715)

foreclose to take possession of a property from a mortgagor because of defaults on payments (p. 486)

fossil fuel a fuel formed in the earth from decayed plant or animal remains (p. 835)

* **foundation** the basis on which an action or idea is maintained (p. 357)

* **framework** a set of guidelines to be followed (p. 126)

franchise the right or license to market a company's goods or services in an area, such as a store of a chain operation (p. 676)

freedman person freed from slavery (p. 220)

Freedom Riders name given to a group of people who traveled to the South in 1961 to protest the South's refusal to integrate bus terminals (p. 750)

* **function** a specific task performed by a person, object, or group (p. 269)

* **fundamental** being of central importance (p. 505)

* **funds** money that is set apart for a specific purpose (p. 334)

* **furthermore** in addition (p. 543)

G

* **gender** term applied to the characteristics of a male or female (p. 814)

general strike a strike involving all the workers in a particular geographic location (p. 391)

* **generate** to cause a desired effect (p. 678)

* **generation** a classification of people who share the same experience throughout their lives (p. 794)

generation gap a cultural separation between parents and their children (p. 684)

glasnost a Soviet policy permitting open discussion of political and social issues and freer dissemination of news and information (p. 916)

global warming an increase in average world temperatures over time (p. 946)

graduated income tax tax based on the net income of an individual or business and which taxes different income levels at different rates (p. 277)

graft the acquisition of money in dishonest ways, as in bribing a politician (p. 261)

grandfather clause a clause that allowed individuals who did not pass the literacy test to vote if their fathers or grandfathers had voted before Reconstruction began; an exception to a law based on preexisting circumstances (p. 280)

grassroots movement a group of people organizing at the local or community level, away from political or cultural centers (p. 919)

Great Awakening movement during the 1700s that stressed dependence on God (p. 112)

greenback a piece of U.S. paper money first issued by the North during the Civil War (p. 209)

gross national product the total value of goods and services produced by a country during a year (p. 244)

* **guarantee** a statement of assurance (p. 830)

guerrilla armed band that carries out surprise attacks and sabotage rather than open warfare (pp. 368, 775)

guru a person with knowledge or expertise, especially a religious teacher and spiritual guide in Hinduism (p. 873)

Glossary

H

habeas corpus a legal order for an inquiry to determine whether a person has been lawfully imprisoned (p. 209)

hawk someone who believed the United States should continue its military efforts in Vietnam (p. 789)

hedgerow row of shrubs or trees surrounding a field, often on a dirt wall (p. 609)

hemispheric defense zone national policy during World War II that declared the Western Hemisphere to be neutral and that the United States would patrol this region against German submarines (p. 560)

* **hierarchy** classification based upon social standing within a group of people (p. 107)

hobo a homeless and usually penniless wanderer (p. 476)

Holocaust name given to the mass slaughter of Jews and other groups by the Nazis during World War II (p. 550)

homestead method of acquiring a piece of U.S. public land by living on and cultivating it (p. 240)

Hooverville nickname given to shantytowns in the United States during the Depression (p. 475)

horizontal integration the combining of competing firms into one corporation (p. 249)

I

* **ideology** a system of thought that is held by a individual, group, or culture (p. 501)

* **immigrate** entering and establishing oneself in a country other than that of their original nationality (p. 103)

immunity freedom from prosecution (p. 446)

* **impact** to make a lasting impression upon an individual or group (p. 430)

impeach to formally charge a public official with misconduct in office (pp. 222, 861)

imperialism the actions used by one nation to exercise political or economic control over a smaller or weaker nation (p. 295)

* **implement** to put into action (p. 550)

implied powers powers not specifically listed in the Constitution but claimed by the federal government (p. 174)

* **imply** to express indirectly (p. 655)

* **impose** to establish authority by force (p. 537)

impound to take possession of (p. 853)

* **incentive** something that motivates a person into action (p. 573)

income tax a tax based on the net income of a person or business (p. 355)

indentured servant an individual who contracts to work for a colonist for a specified number of years in exchange for transportation to the colonies, food, clothing, and shelter (p. 106)

individualism the thought that no matter what a person's background was, they could still become successful (p. 266)

* **induce** to cause a reaction in someone or something (p. 259)

industrial union an organization of common laborers and craft workers in a particular industry (p. 250)

* **inevitable** impossible to stop from occurring (p. 861)

inflation the loss of value of money (pp. 276, 864)

* **infrastructure** the basic facilities or services of a system or organization (p. 223)

* **inherent** to be characteristic of something by nature or habit (p. 742)

initiative the right of citizens to place a measure or issue before the voters or the legislature for approval (p. 330)

* **innovation** a new idea or method (p. 450)

* **inspector** an official placed in charge of critically examining something for evidence (p. 960)

installment buying an item on credit with a monthly plan to pay off the value of the good (p. 473)

* **instance** a specific occurrence or example (p. 888)

* **institute** to initiate or establish something (p. 717)

insubordination disobedience (p. 350)

insurrection an act of rebellion against the established government (p. 199)

* **integral** a part of something that has complete importance to the whole (p. 814)

* **integrate** to combine two previously separate things (p. 591)

integrated circuit a complete electronic circuit on a silicon chip which is small and easy to produced (p. 931)

* **integrity** a way of behaving that follows a strict moral code (p. 447)

* **intensify** to become more frequent and powerful (p. 584)

* **interact** to act on or communicate with one another (p. 875)

internationalism a national policy of actively trading with foreign countries to foster peace and prosperity (p. 540) *interpret to explain the meaning of complex material (p. 128)

*intervene to get involved in the affairs of another (p. 314)

*invest to put money into a company in order to gain a future financial reward (p. 470)

*investigate to systematically examine and make an official report (p. 540)

iron curtain the political and military barrier that isolated Soviet-controlled countries of Eastern Europe after World War II (p. 631)

isolationism a national policy of avoiding involvement in world affairs (p. 458)

*issue a matter of concern to a group of people (p. 344)

*item a distinct unit in a collection or series (p. 185)

jazz American style of music that developed from ragtime and blues and which uses syncopated rhythms and melodies (p. 428)

Jim Crow laws statutes or laws created to enforce segregation (p. 280)

jingoism extreme nationalism marked by aggressive foreign policy (p. 303)

joint-stock company form of business organization in which many investors pool funds to raise large amounts of money for large projects (p. 102)

judicial review power of the Supreme Court to determine whether laws of Congress are constitutional and to strike down those that are not (p. 175)

juvenile delinquency antisocial or criminal behavior of young people (p. 692)

kamikaze during World War II, a Japanese suicide pilot whose mission was to crash into his target (p. 605)

*labor an action that produces a good or service (p. 356)

labor union an organization of workers formed for the purpose of advancing its members' interests (p. 179)

laissez-faire policy that government should interfere as little as possible in the nation's economy (p. 245)

*legality a requirement to follow a specific law (p. 750)

*legislation a proposed law to be voted on by a governing body (p. 330)

*levy to use legal authority in order to enforce or collect (p. 355)

liberal a person who generally believes the government should take an active role in the economy and in social programs but that the government should not dictate social behavior (p. 887)

limited war a war fought with limited commitment of resources to achieve a limited objective, such as containing communism (p. 639)

linkage policy of improving relations with the Soviet Union and China in hopes of persuading them to cut back their aid to North Vietnam (p. 793)

*logic a system of thinking based upon likely or reasonable outcomes (p.112)

long drive driving cattle long distances to a railroad depot for fast transport and great profit (p. 239)

mandate authorization to act given to a representative (p. 214)

Manifest Destiny idea popular in the United States during the 1800s that the country must expand its boundaries to the Pacific Ocean (p. 193)

*manipulate to operate or arrange manually to achieve a desired effect (p. 931)

margin buying a stock by paying only a fraction of the stock price and borrowing the rest (p. 470)

margin call demand by a broker that investors pay back loans made for stocks purchased on margin (p. 470)

martial law the law administered by military forces that is invoked by a government in an emergency (p. 208)

Marxism theory of socialism in which a class struggle would exist until the workers were finally victorious, creating a classless society (p. 250)

mass media a medium of communication (as in television and radio) intended to reach a wide audience (p. 421)

mass production the production of large quantities of goods using machinery and often an assembly line (p. 450)

massive retaliation a policy of threatening a massive response, including the use of nuclear weapons, against a Communist state trying to seize a peaceful state by force (p. 652)

Glossary

Glossary

* **mediate** an attempt to resolve conflict between hostile people or groups (p. 525)

* **medium** a means of conveying information, communication, or entertainment (p. 705)

* **mental** having to do with mind and its thought processes (p. 872)

mercantilism the theory that a state's power depends on its wealth (p. 110)

* **method** to follow a plan of action in order to carry out a specific task (p. 553)

microprocessor a computer processor containing both memory and computing functions on a single chip (p. 931)

* **migrated** to move from one location to another (p. 379)

military-industrial complex an informal relationship that some people believe exists between the military and the defense industry to promote greater military spending and influence government policy (p. 657)

minutemen companies of civilian soldiers who boasted they were ready to fight on a minute's notice (p. 115)

missile gap belief that the Soviet Union had more nuclear weapons than the United States (p. 706)

* **modify** to make changes or alter (p. 936)

monopoly total control of a type of industry by one person or one company (p. 249)

moratorium a suspension of activity (p. 459)

muckraker a journalist who uncovers abuses and corruption in a society (p. 328)

multinational corporation large corporations with overseas investments (p. 675)

* **mutual** to share a common goal and take on equal responsibility (p. 635)

napalm a jellied gasoline used for bombs (pp. 613, 782)

nationalism loyalty and devotion to a nation (p. 369)

nativism a preference for native-born people and a desire to limit immigration (pp. 179, 257)

* **network** an interconnected system (p. 385)

* **nonetheless** expresses a view regardless of the circumstances surrounding it (p. 834)

* **norm** a standard by which people live (p. 864)

normalcy the state or fact of being normal (p. 445)

* **notion** a theory based upon experience (p. 854)

* **nuclear** a weapon whose power comes from a chain reaction of uranium or plutonium atoms (p. 648)

nuclear proliferation the spread of nuclear weapons to new nations (p. 946)

nullification theory that states have the right to declare a federal law invalid (p. 185)

* **obtain** to gain possession of (p. 859)

* **occupy** to take control or possession of a location (p. 775)

* **offset** to counteract an effect (p. 897)

Open Door policy a policy that allowed each foreign nation in China to trade freely in the other nations' spheres of influence (p. 313)

open range vast areas of grassland owned by the federal government (p. 238)

open shop a workplace where workers are not required to join a union (p. 454)

* **orientation** position relative to a standard (p. 906)

* **parallel** an imaginary line that circles the earth's surface to mark latitude (p. 638)

* **percent** one part of one hundred (p. 448)

perestroika a policy of economic and government restructuring instituted by Mikhail Gorbachev in the Soviet Union in the 1980s (p. 916)

periphery the outer boundary of something (p. 583)

perjury lying when one has sworn under oath to tell the truth (pp. 644, 940)

* **perspective** a way of looking at a situation that is unique to each individual (p. 587)

* **phase** a definite period of time over which a change is made (p. 946)

philanthropy providing money to support humanitarian or social goals (p. 267)

* **philosophy** the general beliefs, concepts, or attitudes of an individual (p. 458)

Pilgrim a Separatist who journeyed to the American colonies in the 1600s for religious freedom (p. 103)

placer mining method of extracting mineral ore by hand using simple tools like picks, shovels, and pans (p. 237)

pocket veto indirectly vetoing a bill by letting a session of Congress expire without signing the bill (p. 220)

police powers a government's power to control people and property in the interest of public safety, health, welfare, and morals (p. 413)

* **policy** a defined course of action that determines future response (p. 560)

political machine an organization linked to a political party that often controlled local government (p. 261)

poll tax a tax of a fixed amount per person that had to be paid before the person could vote (pp. 279, 755)

popular sovereignty government subject to the will of the people; before the Civil War, the idea that people living in a territory had the right to decide by voting if slavery would be allowed there (pp. 128, 196)

populism political movement founded in the 1890s representing mainly farmers, favoring free coinage of silver and government control of railroads and other large industries (p. 276)

* **pose** to act in a way as to require attention or consideration (p. 603)

* **potential** something that contains the possibility of becoming actual (p. 855)

poverty line a level of personal or family income below which one is classified as poor by the federal government (p. 689)

* **practice** to do something repeatedly so it becomes the standard (p. 245)

* **presume** to believe something without factual evidence (p. 445)

* **primary** first and most important (p. 562)

* **principal** an important or influential concept (p. 776)

* **principle** a system of thinking that follows a strict set of rules (p. 457)

* **prior** happening before an event (p. 238)

* **priority** a ranking of importance (p. 575)

progressivism a political movement that crossed party lines which believed that industrialism and urbanization had created many social problems and that government should take a more active role in dealing with these problems (p. 327)

* **prohibit** to make illegal by an authority (p. 550)

prohibition laws banning the manufacture, transportation, and sale of alcoholic beverages (p. 334)

propaganda the spreading of ideas about an institution or individual for the purpose of influencing opinion (p. 371)

* **proportion** a measurement of equality between two ratios (p. 788)

proprietary colony a colony owned by an individual (p. 105)

* **prospect** someone or something that has the potential of creating positive or negative consequences (p. 200)

* **prospective** to be likely to, or have intentions to, perform an act (p. 279)

protectorate a country that is technically independent but is actually under the control of another country (p. 295)

* **protocol** a standard for data that is transferred between two computers (p. 933)

* **psychological** relating to one's mental perception (p. 761)

public works projects such as highways, parks, and libraries built with public funds for public use (p. 483)

* **publication** a manuscript that has been printed and distributed (p. 834)

* **publish** to make a document available to the general public (p. 299)

quartz mining method of extracting minerals involving digging beneath the surface (p. 237)

racism prejudice or discrimination against someone because of his or her race (p. 758)

ratification formal approval (p. 129)

* **rational** the ability to use reason (p. 809)

rationing the giving out of scarce items on a limited basis (p. 592)

* **reaction** the response to a stimulus (p. 473)

reapportionment the method states use to draw up political districts based on changes in population (p. 710)

recall the right that enables voters to remove unsatisfactory elected officials from office (p. 330)

recession an economic slowdown (p. 126)

Reconstruction the reorganization and rebuilding of the former Confederate states after the Civil War (p. 219)

referendum the practice of letting voters accept or reject measures proposed by the legislature (p. 330)

* **regime** a form of government (p. 543)

* **region** a division of land based on geographic or political boundaries (p. 773)

Glossary

Glossary

* **register** to file personal information in order to become eligible for an official event (p. 746)

* **relax** to be made less strict or severe (p. 917)

relief aid for the needy, welfare (p. 485)

* **reluctant** not willing (p. 614)

reparations payment by the losing country in a war to the winner for the damages caused by the war (p. 389)

republic form of government in which power resides in a body of citizens entitled to vote (p. 125)

* **reside** to live in a particular location (p. 710)

* **resolve** to come to an agreement (p. 388)

* **resource** material used in the production process, such as money, people, land, wood, or steel (p. 303)

* **restoration** to rebuild something to resemble its original state (p. 395)

* **restrain** to keep under control, or limit freedom (p. 668)

* **retain** to keep in possession (p. 637)

revenue sharing federal tax money that is distributed among the states (p. 853)

* **reverse** for a situation to be completely changed (p. 458)

* **revise** to make changes to an original document (p. 128)

* **revolution** an uprising to overthrow a government and replace it with a new one (p. 916)

right-to-work law a law making it illegal to require employees to join a union (p. 667)

* **route** a specific course of action (p. 628)

safety net something that provides security against misfortune; specifically, government relief programs intended to protect against economic disaster (p. 525)

* **scheme** a plan of action (p. 349)

secede to leave or withdraw (p. 185)

secession withdrawal from the Union (p. 196)

* **sector** a subdivision of society based on economic or political lines (p. 729)

segregation the separation or isolation of a race, class, or group (p. 280)

self-determination belief that people in a territory should have the ability to choose their own government (p. 369)

separate-but-equal doctrine established by the 1896 Supreme Court case *Plessy v. Ferguson* that permitted laws segregating African Americans as long as equal facilities were provided (p. 741)

separation of powers government principle where power is divided among different branches (p. 128)

* **sequence** an arrangement when objects follow one after the other (p. 934)

* **series** a number of events that come one after another (p. 483)

settlement house institution located in a poor neighborhood that provided numerous community services such as medical care, child care, libraries, and classes in English (p. 269)

shantytown a poor section of town consisting of crudely built dwellings usually made of wood (p. 475)

sharecropper farmer who works land for an owner who provides equipment and seed and receives a share of the crop (p. 225)

siege a military blockade of a city or fortified place to force it to surrender (p. 212)

sit-down strike method of boycotting work by sitting down at work and refusing to leave the establishment (p. 515)

sit-in a form of protest involving occupying seats or sitting down on the floor of an establishment (p. 742)

slave code a set of laws that formally regulated slavery and defined the relationship between enslaved Africans and free people (p. 107)

smog fog made heavier and darker by smoke and chemical fumes (p. 834)

soap opera a serial drama on television or radio using melodramatic situations (p. 478)

Social Darwinism based on Charles Darwin's theories of evolution and natural selection, states that humans have developed through competition and natural selection with only the strongest surviving (p. 266)

socialism belief that business should be publicly owned and run by the government (p. 335)

software a computer program (p. 932)

* **sole** single, having no other (p. 646)

* **sought** to have gone in search of change (p. 427)

* **source** the point at which something is provided (p. 408)

space race refers to the Cold War competition over dominance of space exploration capability (p. 716)

space shuttle a reusable spacecraft designed to transport people and cargo between Earth and space (p. 907)

space station a large satellite designed to be occupied for long periods and to serve as a base for operations in space (p. 908)

speakeasy a place where alcoholic beverages are sold illegally (p. 413)

*** specific** to be referred to as belonging to a particular category (p. 745)

speculation investing money at great risk with the anticipation that the price will rise (p. 471)

sphere of influence section of a country where one foreign nation enjoys special rights and powers (p. 312)

spoils system practice of handing out government jobs to supporters; replacing government employees with the winning candidate's supporters (p. 184)

*** stability** being in a state of peace, free from social unrest (p. 367)

stagflation persistent inflation combined with stagnant consumer demand and relatively high unemployment (p. 865)

state-sponsored terrorism violent acts against civilians that are secretly supported by a government in order to attack other nations without going to war (p. 956)

*** status** the condition of something relative to what is normal (p. 760)

stock market a system for buying and selling stocks in corporations (p. 470)

strategic defense a plan to develop missiles and other devices that can shoot down nuclear missiles before they hit the United States (p. 951)

strategic materials materials needed for fighting a war (p. 562)

*** strategy** a plan or method for achieving a goal (p. 331)

*** stress** to place importance on something (p. 937)

*** structure** a system of organization that arranges something large into smaller portions to create order (p. 454)

*** submit** to put forward for consideration or judgment (p. 939)

*** subordinate** to be under the authority of a superior (p. 213)

*** subsidy** money granted by the government to achieve a specific goal that is beneficial to society (p. 670)

subsistence farming farming only enough food to feed one's family (p. 104)

subversion a systematic attempt to overthrow a government by using persons working secretly from within (p. 643)

*** successor** someone who takes the place of a ruler (p. 611)

suffrage the right to vote (p. 330)

*** sum** a specified amount of money (p. 471)

summit a meeting of heads of government (p. 855)

Sunbelt a new industrial region in southern California and the Deep South developing during World War II (p. 589)

*** supplement** an addition to something meant to make it complete (p. 853)

supply-side economics economic theory that lower taxes will boost the economy as businesses and individuals invest their money, thereby creating higher tax revenue (pp. 457, 895)

*** suspend** to temporarily stop an operation (p. 475)

*** sustain** to ensure the persistence of an action (p. 781)

*** symbol** something that stands for or suggests something else (p. 718)

syndicate a business group (p. 350)

*** task** an assigned job (p. 919)

teach-in an extended meeting or class held to discuss a social or political issue (p. 788)

*** technical** to have special understanding of mechanical or scientific knowledge (p. 693)

*** technique** a method of achieving a desired task (p. 479)

*** technology** the result of an improvement on an old or existing idea (p. 296)

telecommute to work at home by means of an electronic linkup with a central office (p. 932)

televangelist an evangelist who conducts regularly televised religious programs (p. 891)

temperance moderation in or abstinence from alcohol (pp. 187, 334)

*** temporary** lasting for only a short time (p. 629)

tenant farmer farmer who works land owned by another and pays rent either in cash or crops (p. 225)

tenement multi-family apartments, usually dark, crowded, and barely meeting minimum living standards (p. 260)

*** tension** unrest or strife over a situation (p. 314)

termination policy a government policy to bring Native Americans into mainstream society by withdrawing recognition of Native American groups as legal entities (p. 691)

terrorism the use of violence by non-governmental groups against civilians to achieve a political goal by instilling fear and frightening governments into changing policies (p. 955)

Glossary

* **theory** a hypothesis meant for argument or investigation (p. 719)

* **thereby** to be connected with or in reference to (p. 514)

Title IX section of the 1972 Educational Amendments prohibiting federally funded schools from discriminating against girls and young women in nearly all aspects of their operations (p. 817)

trade deficit the difference between the value of a country's imports versus its exports (p. 943)

transcendental meditation a technique of meditation in which a mantra is chanted as a way of achieving peak intelligence, harmony, and health (p. 873)

transcontinental railroad a railway system extending across the continent (p. 197)

* **transition** passing from one circumstance to another (p. 671)

* **transmit** to send information through a medium such as radio or internet (p. 582)

triangular trade a three-way trade route that exchanged goods between the American colonies and two other trading partners (p. 107)

* **trigger** to cause an action that causes a greater reaction (p. 341)

U-boat German submarine, term means *Unterseeboot* (undersea boat) (p. 373)

* **ultimate** the greatest or most intense characteristic of something (p. 793)

Underground Railroad a system that helped enslaved African Americans follow a network of escape routes out of the South to freedom in the North (p. 197)

unfair trade practices trading practices which derive a gain at the expense of the competition (p. 355)

* **unify** to bring a group together with a similar goal or thought pattern (p. 421)

union shop a business that requires employees to join a union (p. 667)

urban renewal government programs that attempt to eliminate poverty and revitalize urban areas (p. 689)

* **validate** to make something legal or official (p. 809)

vertical integration the combining of companies that supply equipment and services needed for a particular industry (p. 249)

veto power of the chief executive to reject laws passed by the legislature (p. 128)

* **via** to have come by or through (p. 904)

victory garden gardens planted by American citizens during war to raise vegetables for home use, leaving more for the troops (pp. 378, 592)

vigilance committee groups of ordinary citizens formed by local law enforcement officers and tasked with finding criminals and bringing them to justice (p. 238)

* **violate** to go against a previously set standard (p. 306)

* **virtual** nearly or almost entirely (p. 306)

* **visible** what can be seen (p. 897)

* **volume** refers to a considerable amount (p. 274)

war on poverty antipoverty program under President Lyndon Johnson (p. 725)

welfare capitalism system in which companies enable employees to buy stock, participate in profit sharing, and receive benefits such as medical care, common in the 1920s (p. 454)

white-collar jobs in fields not requiring work clothes or protective clothing, such as sales (p. 675)

* **widespread** having influence on or affecting a large group (p. 392)

yellow journalism type of sensational, biased, and often false reporting for the sake of attracting readers (p. 302)

yuppie a young college-educated adult who is employed in a well-paying profession and who lives and works in or near a large city (p. 903)

Este glosario incluye todas las palabras del contenido y vocabulario académico en tu texto. El vocabulario de contenido se relaciona con el contenido de historia. Estas palabras se encuentran en negrillas y están resaltadas en amarillo en tu texto. El vocabulario académico te facilitará la comprensión de todas las materias escolares. Estas palabras están en negrillas en tu texto y se muestran con un asterisco en el glosario.

A

abolition/abolición el final inmediato de la esclavitud (pág. 188)

*abstraction/abstracción** idea que es difícil de entender para algunas personas (pág. 690)

*academic/académico** asociado con aprendizaje universitario en una institución en el campo académico (pág. 188)

*accompany/acompañar** estar asociado con (pág. 675)

*accumulate/acumular** juntar con el tiempo (pág. 903)

*acknowledge/reconocer** admitir o hacer mención (pág. 866)

*adapt/adaptar** cambiar con el propósito de cumplir con las demandas de cierto ambiente o circunstancia (pág. 238)

*adequately/adecuadamente** completar una tarea sin ir más allá de lo que se requiere para completarla (pág. 387)

*adjacent/adyacente** que comparte una frontera común (pág. 198)

*administration/administración** grupo de personas cuyo propósito es aconsejar y asistir al presidente (pág. 778)

*advocate/propugnar** proponer cierta posición o punto de vista (pág. 334)

affirmative action/acción afirmativa un esfuerzo activo para mejorar las oportunidades educacionales y de empleo para las minorías (pág. 825)

Agent Orange/Agente Anaranjado defoliante que se usó para desbrozar los bosques vietnamitas durante la guerra de Vietnam (pág. 782)

*allocate/asignar** separar para algo específico (pág. 589)

*alternative/alternativo** algo que es diferente a lo que se considera normal (pág. 790)

*ambiguous/ambiguo** carecer de un propósito definido (pág. 181)

amendment/enmienda un cambio a la Constitución (pág. 128)

Americanization/americanización causar que una persona adquiera características y rasgos americanos (pág. 270)

amnesty/amnistía el acto de otorgar perdón a un número grande de personas (pág. 219)

amphtrac/*amphtrac* un tractor anfibio utilizado para mover tropas desde barcos a la orilla del mar (pág. 603)

*analogy/analogía** algo que es común entre dos cosas que aparentemente son poco corrientes (pág. 724)

anarchist/anarquista una persona que cree que no debe haber ningún gobierno (pág. 407)

annexation/anexión incorporar un territorio dentro del dominio de un país (pág. 194)

anthrax/ántrax bacteria que se usa para crear armas biológicas (pág. 959)

*anticipate/anticipar** predecir una acción antes de que ocurra (pág. 547)

*apparent/aparente** parecer que es un hecho en lo que se puede entender (pág. 499)

appeasement/apaciguamiento demandas aceptadas a fin de evitar conflictos (pág. 544)

*approximately/aproximadamente** un estimado o una cifra lo más cerca posible de la cifra real (pág. 599)

*arbitrary/arbitrario** que se basa en la preferencia o conveniencia del individuo y no depende de los estándares (pág. 710)

arbitration/arbitraje arreglar una disputa acordando aceptar la decisión de una persona imparcial (pág. 342)

armistice/armisticio acuerdo temporal de paz para terminar con una lucha (pág. 388)

*aspect/aspecto** se refiere a una parte de algo de gran influencia o tamaño (pág. 410)

assembly line/línea de montaje sistema de producción con máquinas y trabajadores arreglados para que cada persona haga su trabajo designado una y otra vez mientras el artículo pasa frente a ellos (pág. 450)

*assign/asignar** designar a una posición o deber (pág. 581)

assimilate/asimilar incorporar a un grupo dentro de la cultura de una población más grande (pág. 242)

*attain/lograr** obtener posesión de algo (pág. 751)

*attribute/atribuir** describir un efecto al aplicarle una causa (pág. 858)

attrition/atrición acto de desalentar por constantes ataques o acoso (pág. 209)

***author/autor** persona que crea material original (pág. 428)

***authorities/autoridades** aquéllos que tienen el control para determinar y hacer cumplir lo que está bien o lo que está mal (pág. 394)

baby boom/auge de nacimientos aumento marcado en la taza de natalidad, tal como ocurrió en Estados Unidos después de la Segunda Guerra Mundial (pág. 677)

bailiff/alguacil oficial en rango menor de las Cortes (pág. 475)

***benefit/beneficiar** ser de utilidad o rentable (pág. 675)

***bias/predisposición** prejuicio dentro del juicio de alguien (pág. 815)

bilingualism/bilingualismo la práctica de enseñar a estudiantes inmigrantes en su propio lenguaje (pág. 829)

binding arbitration/arbitraje obligatorio proceso por el cual un partido neutral escucha argumentos de dos partidos opositores y toma una decisión que ambos deben aceptar (pág. 515)

black codes/códigos negros leyes aprobadas en el Sur al terminar la Guerra Civil para controlar a los libertos y permitir a los dueños de plantaciones la explotación de los trabajadores afroamericanos (pág. 221)

black power/poder negro mobilización del poder económico y político de afroamericanos especialmente para imponer respeto por sus derechos y para mejorar sus condiciones (pág. 760)

blitzkrieg/guerra relámpago nombre dado a los ataques repentinos ofensivos violentos que los alemanes usaron durante la Segunda Guerra Mundial (pág. 545)

blue-collar/collar azul trabajos de mano de obra, particularmente aquellos que requieren ropa protectora (pág. 675)

blues/*blues* estilo de música que evolucionó de la música espiritual de los afroamericanos, distinguida por su sonido melancólico (pág. 428)

brinkmanship/política arriesgada la buena voluntad para ir al borde de guerra para forzar a un oponente a que se retracte (pág. 653)

broker state/estado intermediario el papel del gobierno para resolver conflictos entre grupos con intereses competitivos (pág. 525)

budget deficit/déficit del presupuesto la cantidad por la cual los gastos exceden los ingresos (pág. 895)

bull market/bolsa al alza largo período durante el cual los precios de acciones en la bolsa se incrementan (pág. 470)

busing/traslado obligatorio la política de transportar estudiantes a escuelas fuera de sus vecindarios para alcanzar un balance racial (pág. 826)

cabinet/gabinete grupo de consejeros al presidente (pág. 173)

***capacity/capacidad** la capacidad de un individuo de llevar a cabo una tarea específica sharing a common border (pág. 354)

capital gains tax/impuestos a las ganancias del capital impuesto federal pagado por inversionistas y negocios cuando ellos venden acciones y bienes raíces (pág. 919)

caucus/junta electoral reunión llevada a cabo por un partido político para escoger su candidato a la presidencia o para decidir políticas (pág. 184)

censure/censura expresar la desaprobación formal sobre una acción (pág. 648)

chad/agujereado pedazo pequeño de cartón producido taladrando una tarjeta de computadora (pág. 949)

***channel/encausar** forzar a lo largo de una ruta existente (pág. 758)

charter/carta de privilegio una constitución (pág. 616)

checks and balances/control y balances sistema en el cual cada ramo de gobierno tiene la habilidad para limitar el poder a los otros ramos para que ninguno vuelva a ser demasiado poderoso (pág. 128)

***circumstance/circunstancia** factor en un problema que determina su solución (pág. 225)

***cite/citar** hacer resaltar como ejemplo en un argumento o debate (pág. 944)

***civil/civil** relacionado con los ciudadanos de cierto estado o país (pág. 540)

civilization/civilización cultura sumamente desarrollada distinguida por un conocimiento de comercio, gobierno, las artes, las ciencias, y frecuentemente lenguaje escrito (pág. 99)

***clause/cláusula** sección bien diferenciada en un documento formal escrito (pág. 174)

closed shop/taller cerrado acuerdo en el que una compañía contrata solamente a miembros del sindicato (págs. 251, 667)

Spanish Glossary

cloture/clausura una moción que termina con el debate y requiere un voto inmediato, posible en el Senado de EE.UU. por un voto de 60 senadores (pág. 754)

*code/código señal o símbolo que se usa para representar algo que debe mantenerse en secreto (pág. 601)

*coincidental/fortuito cuando dos cosas relacionadas ocurren al mismo tiempo (pág. 779)

Cold War/Guerra Fría conflicto ideológico caracterizado por frecuentes confrontaciones entre Estados Unidos y la Unión Soviética entre los años 1946 y 1990 (pág. 627)

*colleague/colega persona que trabaja en la misma profesión o en una similar (pág. 478)

*commission/comisión autorizar a alguien para que realice una tarea específica (pág. 260)

commission plan/gobierno por comisión plan en el cual el gobierno municipal está dividido dentro de diferentes departamentos con diferentes funciones, cada uno bajo la dirección de un comisionado (pág. 329)

committee of correspondence/comité de correspondencia comité organizado en cada colonia para comunicar entre las colonias y unificarlas (pág. 115)

commune/comuna un arreglo de vivienda en el cual los miembros de un grupo trabajan juntos y comparten todo (pág. 809)

*communicate/comunicar compartir información con personas o grupos (pág. 115)

*community/comunidad gente con características comunes en la misma área (pág. 485)

*comprehensive/comprensivo cubrir una amplia gama de temas (pág. 755)

*conceive/concebir crear a partir de la nada (pág. 213)

concentration camp/campo de concentración un campamento donde personas están detenidas o encerradas (pág. 553)

*concept/concepto idea abstracta que puede ponerse en práctica (pág. 249)

Confederacy/Confederación nación formada por los estados sureños que se separaron de la Unión en 1860–1861 (pág. 201)

*confine/limitar encerrar o restringir (pág. 726)

*confirm/confirmar promesa de validez (pág. 643)

*conformity/conformidad cambiar de una manera que se amolda con un estándar o autoridad (pág. 692)

conscription/reclutamiento requerir que personas ingresen en el servicio militar (págs. 209, 376)

consensus/consenso acuerdo general (pág. 724)

*consequence/consecuencia el resultado positivo o negativo de una acción (pág. 835)

conservative/conservador una persona que cree que el poder del gobierno, particularmente en la economía, debe estar limitado para llevar al máximo la libertad individual (pág. 887)

*constitute/constituir hacer que algo sea necesario (pág. 381)

*consult/consultar pedir permiso o consejo (pág. 575)

*consumer/consumidor persona que compra lo que produce una economía (pág. 451)

containment/contención la política o proceso de prevenir la expansión de un poder hostil (pág. 633)

contra/contra contrarevolucionario, la fuerza guerrilla anti-Sandinista en Nicaragua (pág. 898)

contraband/contrabando artículos de los que la importación, exportación o posesión es ilegal (pág. 373)

*contract/contrato documento legal obligatorio entre dos partes (pág. 825)

*contradict/contradecir hacer lo opuesto de lo que se espera (pág. 787)

*contrary/contrario estar en desacuerdo con (pág. 956)

*contribute/contribuir dar a una causa común (pág. 485)

*controversial/polémico algo que causa opiniones opuestas a ser debatidas (pág. 683)

convoy/convoy un grupo que viaja junto con algo, tal como un barco, para protegerlo (pág. 387)

convoy system/sistema de convoy un sistema en el cual barcos mercantes viajan con buques navales para protección (pág. 584)

cooperative individualism/individualismo cooperativo política del Presidente Hoover para alentar a los manufactureros y distribuidores a formar sus propias organizaciones y pasar información voluntariamente al gobierno federal en un esfuerzo para estimular la economía (pág. 458)

corporation/sociedad anónima organización autorizada por ley a montar una actividad, tratada como si fuera una sola persona (pág. 248)

cost of living/costo de vida el costo de comprar artículos y servicios esenciales para la supervivencia (pág. 391)

cost-plus/costo más beneficio contrato del gobierno para pagar el costo de fabricación para producir un artículo más un porcentaje garantizado (pág. 574)

counterculture/contracultura una cultura con valores y creencias diferentes de los de la cultural principal (pág. 809)

covert/secreto no hecho o mostrado abiertamente (pág. 654)

creationism/creacionismo la creencia que Dios creó al mundo y todo lo que hay en él, usualmente como se describe en Génesis (pág. 411)

credibility gap/barrera de credibilidad falta de confianza (pág. 787)

*crucial/decisivo algo que se considera importante o esencial (pág. 516)

*culture/cultura costumbres, religión y prácticas sociales compartidas generalmente por un distinto grupo de individuos (pág. 99)

*currency/moneda papel moneda que se usa como medio de intercambio (pág. 944)

customs duties/derechos de aduana impuestos sobre importaciones y exportaciones (pág. 113)

de facto segregation/segregación de facto segregación por costumbre y tradición (pág. 741)

deficit spending/gastos déficits práctica del gobierno de gastar dinero prestado en vez de aumentar impuestos, usualmente una tentativa para levantar la economía (pág. 511)

deflation/deflación un decremento de la cantidad de dinero o crédito disponible el cual resulta en precios reducidos y por lo tanto aumenta el poder adquisitivo de la moneda (pág. 276)

*demonstrate/demostrar confirmar tus creencias o esclarecerlas (pág. 521)

*denote/denotar hacer referencia a (pág. 875)

deport/deportar expulsar del país a individuos (pág. 394)

*derive/derivar obtener algo de una fuente específica (pág. 811)

détente/détente una política que intenta relajar o borrar la tensión entre naciones (pág. 855)

developing nation/nación en desarrollo nación en donde la economía es principalmente agrícola (pág. 654)

*device/ardid plan cuyo objetivo es engañar (pág. 681)

*devote/dedicar asignar una tarea específica (pág. 867)

direct primary/elección primaria voto tomado por todos los miembros de un partido político para elegir a su candidato para un puesto público (pág. 330)

disco/música disco música popular para danza caracterizada por ritmo hipnótico, cantos repetitivos y sonidos producidos electrónicamente (pág. 874)

disfranchise/privación civil privar el derecho al voto (pág. 577)

*distribution/distribución el acto de repartir productos desde un lugar central a un gran número de clientes (pág. 248)

*diverse/diverso ser diferente a los demás (pág. 419)

dollar diplomacy/diplomacia del dólar política de juntar los intereses comerciales de un país con sus intereses diplomáticos en el extranjero (pág. 315)

*dominant/dominante aquél que toma el control por encima de los demás (pág. 652)

domino theory/teoría dominó la creencia que si una nación en Asia se derrumbara ante los comunistas, sus países vecinos hubieran caído en seguida (pág. 775)

dove/paloma persona a favor de que Estados Unidos se retirara de la guerra en Vietnam (pág. 789)

downsizing/reducción de personal reducción del tamaño de una compañía despidiendo gerentes y trabajadores para llegar a ser una empresa más eficiente (pág. 918)

*draft/reclutar ser seleccionado al azar para prestar servicio militar obligatorio (pág. 376)

due process/proceso justo requerimiento judicial de que las leyes no deben tratar individuos injusta, arbitraria, o irracionalmente y que las cortes deben de seguir procesos y reglamentos justos al jurar casos (pág. 710)

Dust Bowl/Cuenca Polvada nombre dado al área sureña de las Grandes Planicies severamente dañada por sequías y tormentas de polvo durante los años 1930 (pág. 476)

*dynamic/dinámico la capacidad de atraer la atención del público con el fin de expresar tus metas (pág. 349)

dynamic conservatism/conservatismo dinámico política de alcanzar un balance entre el conservatismo económico y algún activismo (pág. 670)

*editor/editor alguien que edita, altera o corrige manuscritos para ser publicados en libros, periódicos o revistas (pág. 959)

*element/elemento el principio más básico de un sistema de razonamiento o filosofía (pág. 629)

*eliminate/eliminar deshacerse de algo (pág. 557)

Spanish Glossary

emancipation/emancipación el proceso de liberar a personas esclavizadas (pág. 188)

embargo/embargo prohibición gubernamental contra el comercio con otros países (pág. 865)

*****emerge/surgir** dar o darse a conocer (pág. 419)

*****emphasis/énfasis** importancia especial que se le da a un objeto o idea (pág. 369)

*****enhance/acrecentar** mejorar o aumentar (pág. 525)

Enlightenment/Siglo Ilustrado movimiento durante los años 1700 que promovió el conocimiento, la razón, y las ciencias (pág. 112)

entrepreneur/empresario persona que organiza, dirige y asume el riesgo de un negocio o empresa (pág. 245)

enumerated powers/poderes enumerados poderes nombrados en la Constitución que pertenecen solamente al gobierno federal (pág. 174)

*****environmental/ambiental** relacionado con el ambiente; el complejo sistema de plantas, animales, agua y suelo (pág. 344)

*****erode/erosionar** desgastar algo hasta reducirlo (pág. 372)

*****error/error** juicio errado o cálculo equivocado (pág. 612)

espionage/espionaje espiar, especialmente para obtener secretos gubernamentales (pág. 380)

*****establish/establecer** crear una organización o compañía (pág. 351)

*****estate/propiedades** extensión grande de terreno, donde por lo general se halla una casa grande (pág. 655)

*****ethic/ética** conjunto de normas morales que rigen cómo se vive (pág. 411)

ethnic cleansing/purificación étnica expulsión, encarcelamiento o asesinato de minorías étnicas por un grupo mayoritario dominante (pág. 940)

eugenics/eugenesia seudociencia que trata con el perfeccionamiento de las cualidades hereditarias de una raza o especie (pág. 408)

euro/eurodólar moneda básica compartida por los países de la Unión Europea desde 1999 (pág. 944)

evolution/evolución teoría científica que los humanos y otras formas de vida se han evolucionado tras el tiempo (pág. 411)

*****evolve/evolucionar** cambiar según el ambiente físico (pág. 266)

*****exceed/exceder** ir más allá de lo que se requiere (pág. 895)

executive privilege/privilegio ejecutivo el principio de que las comunicaciones del ramo ejecutivo deben de permanecer confidenciales para proteger la seguridad nacional (pág. 860)

*****explicit/explícito** expresar claramente y sin confusión (pág. 797)

*****exploit/proeza** un acto heroico (pág. 311)

*****exports/exportaciones** bienes producidos por un país que se venden y se envían a otro país (pág. 113)

extermination camp/campo de exterminación campo donde los prisioneros eran enviados para ser ejecutados (pág. 554)

*****extract/extraer** eliminar por la fuerza (pág. 237)

fallout/caída radioactiva partículas radioactivas dispersadas por una explosión nuclear (pág. 649)

fallout shelter/refugio atómico un refugio construido para proteger a las personas de la caída radioactiva (pág. 649)

fascism/fascismo un sistema político encabezado por un dictador que pide por nacionalismo y racismo extremo y poca tolerancia de la oposición (pág. 537)

featherbedding/paro técnico práctica de limitar la producción con el fin de crear más trabajos (pág. 667)

*****federal/federal** se refiere a un gobierno central fuerte (pág. 825)

federalism/federalismo sistema político en el cual el poder está dividido entre los estados y el gobierno federal (pág. 128)

feminism/feminismo la creencia que los hombres y las mujeres deben ser iguales política, económica y socialmente (pág. 814)

filibuster/filibustero un atentado para acabar con un proyecto de ley hablando continuamente a turnos un grupo de senadores para que no pueda haber un voto (pág. 754)

*****final/final** estar al final de un proceso (pág. 951)

*****finance/financiar** proporcionar el dinero para un proyecto (pág. 513)

fireside chats/pláticas hogareñas emisiones de radio transmitidas por FDR al pueblo americano para explicar sus iniciativas (pág. 502)

flapper/*flapper* mujer jóven de los años 1920 que demostró libertad de las costumbres tradicionales especialmente en vestido (pág. 410)

flexible response/respuesta flexible formación de tropas y armas convencionales para permitir que un país entre en una guerra limitada sin usar armas nucleares (pág. 715)

foreclose/ejecutar una hipoteca tomar posesión de una propiedad por falta de pagos hipotecarios (pág. 486)

fossil fuel/combustible fósil un combustible formado en la tierra de los restos descompuestos de plantas o animales (pág. 835)

***foundation/cimiento** la base sobre la cual se mantiene una acción o idea (pág. 357)

***framework/estructura** conjunto de guías a seguir (pág. 126)

franchise/concesión derecho o licencia para vender los bienes o servicios de una compañía en un área tal como una cadena de tiendas (pág. 676)

freedman/liberto persona liberada de la esclavitud (pág. 220)

Freedom Riders/Jinetes de la Libertad nombre dado a un grupo de personas que viajaron al Sur en 1961 para protestar la negativa del Sur para integrar las terminales de autobuses (pág. 750)

***function/función** tarea específica que lleva a cabo una persona, objeto o grupo (pág. 269)

***fundamental/fundamental** que es de suma importancia (pág. 505)

***funds/fondos** dinero que se separa para un propósito específico (pág. 334)

***furthermore/además** a más de esto (pág. 543)

***gender/género** término que se aplica a las características masculinas o femeninas (pág. 814)

general strike/huelga general una huelga por todos los trabajadores de un lugar geográfico (pág. 391)

***generate/generar** causar el efecto deseado (pág. 678)

generation/generación clasificación de personas que comparten las mismas experiencias a lo largo de sus vidas (pág. 794)

generation gap/barrera generacional una separación cultural entre padres e hijos (pág. 684)

glasnost/glasnost política soviética que permitía discusión abierta de temas políticos y sociales y diseminación más libre de noticias e información (pág. 916)

global warming/calentamiento global aumento en la temperatura promedio mundial tras un período (pág. 946)

graduated income tax/impuesto graduado de utilidades impuesto basado en los ingresos netos de un individuo

o empresa en el cual la taza del impuesto se diferencia de acuerdo a diferentes niveles de salario (pág. 277)

graft/soborno adquisición de dinero de manera deshonesta tal como el sobornar a un político (pág. 261)

grandfather clause/cláusula de abuelo cláusula que permitió votar a los que no aprobaron el examen de leer si sus padres o sus abuelos habían votado antes de que empezara la Reconstrucción; excepción a una ley basada en circunstancias preexistentes (pág. 280)

grassroots movement/movimiento local grupo de personas que se organiza a nivel local y popular lejos de centros políticos o culturales (pág. 919)

Great Awakening/Gran Despertar movimiento durante los años 1700 que enfatizó la dependencia en Dios (pág. 112)

greenback/billete dorso verde billete de papel moneda de EEUU expedido por primera vez por el Norte durante la Guerra Civil (pág. 209)

gross national product/producto nacional bruto valor total de bienes y servicios producidos por un país durante un año (pág. 244)

***guarantee/garantía** un compromiso o garantía (pág. 830)

guerrilla/guerrilla banda armada que usa ataques sorpresas o sabotaje en vez de la guerra organizada (págs. 368, 775)

guru/gurú persona con conocimiento y experiencia, dicho especialmente de un maestro religioso y guía espiritual en el indoísmo (pág. 873)

habeas corpus/hábeas corpus orden legal para una encuesta para determinar si una persona ha sido encarcelada legalmente (pág. 209)

hawk/halcón persona que creía que Estados Unidos debía continuar sus esfuerzos militares en Vietnam (pág. 789)

hedgerow/seto fila de arbustos o árboles cercando un campo a menudo sobre un muro de tierra (pág. 609)

hemispheric defense zone/zona de defensa hemisférica política nacional durante la Segunda Guerra Mundial que declaró que el Hemisferio Oeste fue neutral y que Estados Unidos patrullaría esta región en contra de submarinos alemanes (pág. 560)

***hierarchy/jerarquía** clasificación basada en la posición social dentro de un grupo de individuos (pág. 107)

hobo/vagabundo persona errante sin hogar y usualmente sin dinero (pág. 476)

Spanish Glossary

Holocaust/Holocausto nombre dado a la exterminación masiva de judíos y otros grupos hecha por los nazis durante la Segunda Guerra Mundial (pág. 550)

homestead/posesionar método de adquirir una extensión de tierra pública de EEUU viviendo en ella y cultivándola (pág. 240)

Hooverville/*Hooverville* apodo dado a los barrios en Estados Unidos durante la Depresión (pág. 475)

horizontal integration/integración horizontal asociación de firmas competitivas en una sociedad anónima (pág. 249)

*ideology/ideología** sistema de razonamiento de un individuo, grupo o cultura (pág. 501)

*immigrate/inmigrar** entrar uno a un país diferente al país natal y establecerse en él (pág. 103)

immunity/inmunidad libertad de prosecución (pág. 446)

*impact/influir** hacer mella en un individuo o grupo (pág. 430)

impeach/acusar acusar formalmente a un oficial público de mala conducta en la oficina (págs. 222, 861)

imperialism/imperialismo acciones usadas por una nación para ejercer el control político o económico sobre naciones más pequeñas o débiles (pág. 295)

*implement/implementar** poner en acción (pág. 550)

implied powers/poderes implícitos poderes no nombrados específicamente en la Constitución pero reclamados por el gobierno federal (pág. 174)

*imply/dar a entender** expresar indirectamente (pág. 655)

*impose/imponer** establecer autoridad por la fuerza (pág. 537)

impound/confiscar tomar posesión de (pág. 853)

*incentive/incentivo** algo que motiva a una persona a tomar medidas (pág. 573)

income tax/impuesto de utilidades impuesto basado en el ingreso neto de una persona o empresa (pág. 355)

indentured servant/sirviente contratado individuo contratado para trabajar para un colono durante cierto número de años a cambio de transportación a las colonias, alimento, ropa y refugio (pág. 106)

individualism/individualism la idea de que fuere cual fuere el ambiente de una persona, ésta aún puede alcanzar el éxito (pág. 266)

*induce/inducir** causar una reacción en alguna persona o en algo (pág. 259)

industrial union/sindicato industrial organización de trabajadores comunes y obreros calificados en una industria (pág. 250)

*inevitable/inevitable** imposible de detener su ocurrencia (pág. 861)

inflation/inflación pérdida del valor del dinero (págs. 276, 864)

*infrastructure/infraestructura** las instalaciones o servicios básicos de un sistema u organización (pág. 223)

*inherent/inherente** característico de algo por naturaleza o hábito (pág. 742)

initiative/iniciativa derecho de los ciudadanos de poner una propuesta o tema ante los votantes o la legislatura para su aprobación (pág. 330)

*innovation/innovación** idea o método nuevo (pág. 450)

*inspector/inspector** funcionario encargado de examinar críticamente las pruebas (pág. 960)

installment/pago a plazos compra de un artículo a crédito con un plan de pago mensual para pagar el valor del artículo (pág. 473)

*instance/instancia** ocurrencia específica o ejemplo (pág. 888)

*institute/instituir** iniciar o establecer algo (pág. 717)

insubordination/insubordinación desobediencia (pág. 350)

insurrection/insurrección un acto de rebelión en contra del gobierno establecido (pág. 199)

*integral/íntegro** parte de algo esencial al todo (pág. 814)

*integrate/integrar** combinar dos cosas que antes estaban separadas (pág. 591)

integrated circuit/circuito integrado circuito completamente electrónico en una pastilla de silicio, el cual es pequeño y fácil de producir (pág. 931)

*integrity/integridad** manera de comportarse que sigue un código moral estricto (pág. 447)

*intensify/intensificar** que se hace más frecuente y poderoso (pág. 584)

*interact/interactuar** el acto de actuar o comunicarse con otro (pág. 875)

internationalism/internacionalismo política nacional de intercambio comercial activo con países extranjeros para promover la paz y la prosperidad (pág. 540)

*interpret/interpretar** explicar el significado de material complejo (pág. 128) *intervene/intervenir meterse en los asuntos de otro (pág. 314)

*invest/invertir poner dinero en una compañía con el fin de obtener una recompensa financiera futura (pág. 470)

*investigate/investigar examinar sistemáticamente e informar oficialmente (pág. 540)

iron curtain/cortina de hierro barrera política y militar que aisló a los países de Europa Oriental controlados por los soviéticos después de la Segunda Guerra Mundial (pág. 631)

isolationism/aislacionismo política nacional de evitar el involucramiento en asuntos mundiales (pág. 458)

*issue/cuestión tema de preocupación de un grupo de individuos (pág. 344)

*item/artículo unidad separada en una colección o serie (pág. 185)

jazz/jazz estilo de música americana que se desarrolló de ragtime y blues y que usa melodías y ritmos sincopados (pág. 428)

Jim Crow Laws/Leyes de Jim Crow leyes creadas para reforzar la segregación (pág. 280)

jingoism/patriotismo extremo nacionalismo marcado por la agresiva política extranjera (pág. 303)

joint-stock company/compañía por acciones forma de organización de negocios en la cual muchos inversionistas compran acciones para juntar grandes cantidades de dinero para grandes proyectos (pág. 102)

judicial review/revisión judicial derecho de la Suprema Corte para determinar si las leyes del Congreso son constitucionales y para derribar aquellas que no lo son (pág. 175)

juvenile delinquency/delincuencia juvenil comportamiento antisocial o criminal de los jóvenes (pág. 692)

kamikaze/kamikase durante la Segunda Guerra Mundial un piloto suicida japonés de quien la misión fue chocar en su objetivo (pág. 605)

*labor/mano de obra acción por medio de la cual se produce un bien o servicio (pág. 356)

labor union/sindicato organización de trabajadores formada con el propósito de promover los intereses de sus miembros (pág. 179)

laissez-faire/laissez-faire política que el gobierno debe interferir tan poco como sea posible en la economía del país (pág. 245)

*legality/legalidad requisito para seguir una ley especifica (pág. 750)

*legislation/legislatura propuesta de ley sometida a voto por un organismo gubernamental (pág. 330)

*levy/gravar usar la autoridad legal con el propósito de hacer cumplir o recaudar (pág. 355)

liberal/liberal persona que generalmente cree que el gobierno debe desempeñar un papel activo en la economía y programas sociales pero que el gobierno no debe dictar el comportamiento social (pág. 887)

limited war/guerra limitada guerra peleada con compromisos limitados de recursos para alcanzar un objetivo limitado, tal como la contención del comunismo (pág. 639)

linkage/enlace política de mejorar relaciones con la Unión Soviética y China con la esperanza de persuadirlas a que redujeran su ayuda a Vietnam del Norte (pág. 793)

*logic/lógica razonamiento basado en resultados probables o razonables (pág. 112)

long drive/manejo largo conducción de ganado por largas distancias a estaciones de ferrocarril para la transportación rápida y grandes ganancias (pág. 239)

mandate/mandato autorización dado a un representante (pág. 214)

Manifest Destiny/Destino Manifiesto idea popular en Estados Unidos durante los años 1800 de que el país debía extender sus fronteras hasta el Océano Pacífico (pág. 193)

*manipulate/manipular operar o arreglar manualmente para obtener el efecto deseado (pág. 931)

margin/margen comprar acciones pagando solamente una fracción del precio y pidiendo prestado el resto (pág. 470)

margin call/llamada de reserva demanda de un accionista a que los inversionistas paguen los préstamos hechos para la compra de acciones al margen (pág. 470)

martial law/derecho marcial derecho administrado por fuerzas militares que es invocado por un gobierno en una emergencia (pág. 208)

Marxism/marxismo teoría de socialismo en la cual una lucha de clases sociales existiría hasta que los trabajadores salieran finalmente victoriosos, creando una sociedad sin distinción de clases (pág. 250)

mass media/medios informativos medios de comunicación (como televisión y radio) con la intención de llegar a la audiencia extensa (pág. 421)

mass production/fabricación en serie producción de grandes cantidades de productos usando máquinas y a menudo una línea de montaje (pág. 450)

massive retaliation/represalia masiva una política que amenaza una respuesta masiva, incluyendo el uso de armas nucleares, contra un estado comunista que trata de captar un país pacífico por la fuerza (pág. 652)

*mediate/arbitrar intento que se hace para resolver un conflicto entre personas o grupos hostiles (pág. 525)

*medium/medio manera de proveer información, comunicar o entretener (pág. 705)

*mental/mental que tiene que ver con la mente y sus procesos de razonamiento (pág. 872)

mercantilism/mercantilismo teoría que el poder de una estado depende de su riqueza (pág. 110)

*method/método seguir un plan de acción con el fin de llevar a cabo una tarea específica (pág. 553)

microprocessor/microprocesador procesador de computadora que contiene memoria y funciones de computación en un solo chip (pág. 931)

*migrated/migrar trasladarse de un lugar a otro (pág. 379)

military-industrial complex/compejo militar industrial relación informal que algunas personas creen que existe entre lo militar y la industria de defensa para promover mayores gastos militares y para influenciar la política gubernamental (pág. 657)

minutemen/_minutemen_ compañías de soldados civiles que se jactaban de que podrían estar listos para tomar armas en sólo un minuto (pág. 115)

missile gap/diferencia de proyectiles creencia que la Unión Soviética tenía más armas nucleares que Estados Unidos (pág. 706)

*modify/modificar hacer cambios o alterar (pág. 936)

monopoly/monopolio control total de una industria por una persona o una compañía (pág. 249)

moratorium/moratoria suspensión de actividad (pág. 459)

muckraker/_muckraker_ periodista que revela abusos y corrupción en una sociedad (pág. 328)

multinational corporation/corporación multinacional grandes corporaciones de inversión extranjera (pág. 675)

*mutual/mutuo compartir una meta común y compartir equitativamente la responsabilidad (pág. 635)

napalm/_napalm_ gasolina gelatinosa utilizada para bombas incendiarias (págs. 613, 782)

nationalism/nacionalismo lealtad y devoción a una nación (pág. 369)

nativism/nativismo una preferencia para las personas oriundas y un deseo a limitar la inmigración (págs. 179, 257)

*network/red sistema interconectado (pág. 385)

*nonetheless/no obstante expresar un punto de vista sean cual sean las circunstancias que lo rodean (pág. 834)

*norm/norma estándar que se fijan las personas para vivir (pág. 864)

normalcy/normalidad estado de ser normal (pág. 445)

*notion/noción teoría basada en la experiencia (pág. 854)

*nuclear/nuclear arma cuya energía proviene de una reacción en cadena de los átomos de uranio o plutonio (pág. 648)

nuclear proliferation/proliferación nuclear distribución de armas nucleares a nuevas naciones (pág. 946)

nullification/anulación teoría que los estados tienen el derecho de declarar inválida una ley federal (pág. 185)

*obtain/obtener ganar acceso a (pág. 859)

*occupy/ocupar tomar control o posesión de un lugar (pág. 775)

*offset/compensar contrabalancear un efecto (pág. 897)

Open Door policy/política de Puertas Abiertas política que permitió a cada nación extranjera en China intercambiar libremente en las esferas de influencia de otras naciones (pág. 313)

open range/terreno abierto gran extensión de pastos propiedad del gobierno federal (pág. 238)

open shop/taller abierto lugar de trabajo donde los trabajadores no son requeridos de ser miembros del sindicato (pág. 454)

*orientation/orientación posición relativa a un estándar (pág. 906)

*parallel/paralelo línea imaginaria que circunda la superficie de la Tierra y la cual marca la latitud (pág. 638)

*percent/porcentaje una parte de cien (pág. 448)

perestroika/perestroika política de reestructuración económica y gubernamental instituida por Mikhail Gorbachev en la Unión Soviética en los años 1980 (pág. 916)

periphery/periferia frontera externa de algo (pág. 583)

perjury/perjurio mentir cuando uno ha jurado decir la verdad (págs. 644, 940)

*perspective/perspectiva manera de ver una situación y la cual es única a cada individuo (pág. 587)

*phase/fase período definido de tiempo a lo largo del cual se lleva a cabo un cambio (pág. 946)

philanthropy/filantropía proporcionar dinero para apoyar metas humanitarias o sociales (pág. 267)

*philosophy/filosofía las creencias, conceptos o actitudes generales de un individuo (pág. 458)

Pilgrim/peregrino Separatista que viajó a las colonias americanas durante los años 1600 para libertad religiosa (pág. 103)

placer mining/explotación de placeres método para extraer mineral a mano utilizando simples herramientas manuales como picos, palas y bateas (pág. 237)

pocket veto/veto indirecto vetar indirectamente un proyecto de ley permitiendo que una sesión del Congreso expire sin firmar el proyecto (pág. 220)

police power/fuerza policiaca poder gubernamental para controlar a personas y propiedades para la seguridad, salud, bienestar, y moral pública (pág. 413)

*policy/política curso de acción definido que determina una respuesta futura (pág. 560)

political machine/maquinaria política organización aliada con un partido político que a menudo controlaba el gobierno local (pág. 261)

poll tax/impuesto de capitación impuesto de cantidad fija por cada persona, el cual tenía que ser pagado antes de que una persona pudiera votar (págs. 279, 755)

popular sovereignty/soberanía popular teoría política de que el gobierno está sujeto a la voluntad del pueblo; antes de la Guerra Civil, la idea de que la gente que vivía en un territorio tenía el derecho de decidir votando si ahí sería permitida la esclavitud (págs. 128, 196)

populism/populismo movimiento político fundado en los años 1890 representando principalmente a los granjeros que favoreció libre acuñación de plata y el control gubernamental de ferrocarriles y otras industrias grandes (pág. 276)

*pose/posar actuar de una manera que requiere atención o consideración (pág. 603)

*potential/potencial que puede convertirse en realidad (pág. 855)

poverty line/línea de pobreza nivel de ingreso individual o familiar bajo del cual uno es clasificado por el gobierno federal como pobre (pág. 689)

*practice/practicar llevar a cabo alguna acción repetidamente de modo que ésta se convierte en el estándar (pág. 245)

*presume/dar por sentado creer algo sin tener pruebas reales (pág. 445)

*primary/principal primero y más importante (pág. 562)

*principal/principal concepto importante o esencial (pág. 776)

*principle/principio sistema de razonamiento que sigue un conjunto estricto de reglas (pág. 457)

*prior/previo que sucede antes de un evento (pág. 238)

*priority/prioridad orden de importancia (pág. 575)

progressivism/progresivismo movimiento político que cruzó las líneas partidarias que creyó que la industria y la urbanización habían creados muchos problemas sociales y que el gobierno debía tomar un papel más activo para resolver estos problemas (pág. 327)

*prohibit/prohibir declarar que algo es ilegal por una autoridad (pág. 550)

prohibition/prohibición leyes que prohibían la manufactura, transportación y venta de bebidas alcohólicas (pág. 334)

propaganda/propaganda diseminación de ideas sobre una institución o individuo con el propósito de influenciar la opinión (pág. 371)

*proportion/proporción medida de igualdad entre dos razones (pág. 788)

proprietary colony/colonia propietaria colonia propiedad de un individuo (pág. 105)

*prospect/expectativa algo o alguien que puede potencialmente crear consecuencias positivas o negativas (pág. 200)

*prospective/posible que puede llevar a cabo un acto o que tiene intención de hacerlo (pág. 279)

protectorate/protectorado país que es técnicamente independiente pero que en realidad queda bajo el control de otro país (pág. 295)

***protocol/protocolo** estándar para datos que se transfieren entre computadoras (pág. 933)

***psychological/psicológico** relativo a la percepción mental del individuo (pág. 761)

public works/obras públicas proyectos como carreteras, parques y bibliotecas construidos con fondos públicos para uso público (pág. 483)

***publication/publicación** manuscrito impreso y distribuido (pág. 834)

***publish/publicar** hacer un documento accesible al público en general (pág. 299)

Q

quartz mining/minería de cuarzo método para extraer minerales excavando debajo de la superficie (pág. 237)

R

racism/racismo prejuicio o discriminación en contra de alguien por su raza (pág. 758)

ratification/ratificación aprobación formal (pág. 129)

***rational/racional** capacidad de usar la razón (pág. 809)

rationing/racionamiento proporcionar escasos artículos de manera limitada (pág. 592)

***reaction/reacción** respuesta a un estímulo (pág. 473)

reapportionment/nueva repartición método usado por los estados para formar distritos políticos basados en los cambios de población (pág. 710)

recall/elección de revocación derecho que permite a los votantes quitar del cargo a los oficiales elegidos que son inadecuados (pág. 330)

recession/recesión retraso económico (pág. 126)

Reconstruction/Reconstrucción reorganización y reconstrucción de los estados de la ex-Confederación después de la Guerra Civil (pág. 219)

referendum/referéndum práctica de permitir a los votantes aceptar o rechazar medidas propuestas por la legislatura (pág. 330)

***regime/régimen** forma de gobierno (pág. 543)

***region/región** división de tierra de acuerdo con límites políticos o geográficos (pág. 773)

***register/registrar** archivar información personal con el fin de obtener idoneidad para un evento oficial (pág. 746)

***relax/relajar** hacer menos estricto o riguroso (pág. 917)

relief/asistencia pública ayuda para los necesitados; beneficencia (pág. 485)

***reluctant/renuente** que no desea hacer algo (pág. 614)

reparations/indemnización pago hecho por el país perdedor de una guerra al país ganador por los daños causados por la guerra (pág. 389)

republic/república forma de gobierno en el cual el poder reside en un cuerpo de ciudadanos con derecho al voto (pág. 125)

***reside/residir** vivir en un lugar en particular (pág. 710)

***resolve/resolver** llegar a un acuerdo (pág. 388)

***resource/recurso** material que se usan en los procesos de producción; por ejemplo: capital, mano de obra, tierra, madera o acero (pág. 303)

***restoration/restauración** reconstruir algo de modo se asemeje a su estado original (pág. 395)

***restrain/restringir** mantener bajo control o limitar la libertad (pág. 668)

***retain/retener** mantener el control o posesión de algo (pág. 637)

revenue sharing/participación en los ingresos fondos de impuestos federales que se distribuyen entre los estados (pág. 853)

***reverse/revocar** cambiar completamente una situación (pág. 458)

***revise/revisar** hacer cambios al documento original (pág. 128)

***revolution/revolución** insurrección para derrocar a un gobierno y reemplazarlo con uno nuevo (pág. 916)

right-to-work law/derecho a trabajar ley que hace ilegal la demanda que los trabajadores se unan a un sindicato (pág. 667)

***route/ruta** plan de acción específico (pág. 628)

S

safety net/red de seguridad algo que proporciona seguridad en contra de desgracias, específicamente, programas de beneficencia gubernamentales para proteger en contra del desastre económico (pág. 525)

***scheme/programa** un plan de medidas (pág. 349)

secede/separarse abandonar o retirar (pág. 185)

secession/secesión retiro de la Unión (pág. 196)

***sector/sector** subdivisión de la sociedad según delineamiento político o económico (pág. 729)

segregation/segregación separación o aislamiento de una raza, clase o grupo (pág. 280)

self-determination/autodeterminación creencia que las personas en un territorio deberían tener la habilidad para escoger su propio gobierno (pág. 369)

separate-but-equal/separados pero iguales doctrina establecida por la Suprema Corte en el caso *Plessy contra Ferguson* en 1896 que las leyes que segregaron a los afroamericanos fueron permitidas si facilidades iguales fueron proporcionadas (pág. 741)

separation of powers/separación de poderes principio de gobierno en el cual el poder está dividido entre diferentes ramos (pág. 128)

*sequence/sucesión arreglo en el cual los objetos se siguen uno detrás de otro (pág. 934)

*series/serie número de eventos que suceden uno después del otro (pág. 483)

settlement house/casa de beneficencia institución establecida en una vecindad pobre que proveía numerosos servicios comunitarios tal como cuidado médico, cuidado de niños, bibliotecas, e instrucción en inglés (pág. 269)

shantytown/villa miseria barrio pobre de un pueblo que consiste de viviendas mal construidas, normalmente hechas de madera (pág. 475)

sharecropper/aparcero agricultor que labra la tierra para un dueño que proporciona equipo y semillas y recibe una porción de la cosecha (pág. 225)

siege/sitio bloqueo militar de una ciudad o un recinto fortificado para forzarlo a rendirse (pág. 212)

sit-down strike/huelga de brazos caídos método de boicotear el trabajo por medio de sentarse en el lugar de trabajo y de rehusar a abandonar el establecimiento (pág. 515)

sit-in/plantón forma de protesta ocupando las sillas o sentándose en el piso de un establecimiento (pág. 742)

slave code/código de esclavos leyes aprobadas que regularon formalmente la esclavitud y definieron la relación entre los africanos esclavizados y la gente libre (pág. 107)

smog/*smog* niebla hecha más pesada y oscura por el humo y vapores químicos (pág. 834)

soap opera/novela drama en serie de radio o televisión utilizando situaciones melodramáticas (pág. 478)

Social Darwinism/darwinismo social idea basada en las teorías de Charles Darwin sobre la evolución y la selección natural. Establece que los humanos se han desarrollado a través de la competencia y la selección natural en las cuales sólo el más fuerte sobrevive (pág. 266)

socialism/socialismo creencia que los negocios deben ser propiedad del gobierno y dirigidos por él (pág. 335)

software/*software* programa de computadora (pág. 932)

*sole/único sólo, que no tiene otro de su especie (pág. 646)

*sought/buscado haber ido en busca de cambio (pág. 427)

*source/fuente el punto desde el cual se provee algo (pág. 408)

space race/carrera espacial se refiere a la competencia durante la Guerra Fría sobre el dominio de la exploración espacial (pág. 716)

space shuttle/puente espacial nave espacial diseñada para transportar personas y carga entre la tierra y el espacio la cual puede ser usada una y otra vez (pág. 907)

space station/estación espacial satélite grande diseñado para ser ocupado por largos períodos y para servir como base para operaciones en el espacio (pág. 908)

speakeasy/*speakeasy* lugar donde son vendidas clandestinamente bebidas alcohólicas (pág. 413)

*specific/específico que pertenece a una categoría específica o que se refiere a ella (pág. 745)

speculation/especulación acciones compradas con alto riesgo con la anticipación que los precios subirán (pág. 471)

sphere of influence/esfera de influencia sección de un país donde una nación extranjera tiene derechos y poderes especiales (pág. 312)

spoils system/sistema de despojos práctica de dar puestos gubernamentales a los partidarios; reemplazando a los empleados del gobierno con los partidarios del candidato victorioso (pág. 184)

*stability/estabilidad estar en estado de paz, libre de intranquilidad social (pág. 367)

stagflation/*stagflación* inflación persistente combinado con la demanda estancada y una taza de desempleo alta (pág. 865)

state-sponsored terrorism/terrorismo patrocinado por el estado actos violentos en contra de civiles que son secretamente apoyados por un gobierno con el motivo de atacar a otras naciones sin entrar en la guerra (pág. 956)

*status/estatus condición de algo en relación con lo normal (pág. 760)

stock market/bolsa de valores sistema para comprar y vender acciones de corporaciones (pág. 470)

strategic defense/defensa estratégica plan para desarrollar proyectiles y otras armas que pueden derribar proyectiles nucleares antes de que estos golpeen en Estados Unidos (pág. 951)

strategic materials/materiales estratégicos materiales necesarios para una guerra (pág. 562)

*****strategy/estrategia** plan o método para alcanzar una meta (pág. 331)

*****stress/acentuar** dar importancia a algo (pág. 937)

*****structure/estructura** sistema de organización que ordena algo grande en partes más pequeñas con el fin de crear orden (pág. 454)

*****submit/someter** presentar algo para ser considerado o juzgado (pág. 939)

*****subordinate/subordinado** que está bajo la autoridad de alguien de mayor rango (pág. 213)

*****subsidy/subsidio** dinero que concede el gobierno para alcanzar una meta específica que beneficia a la sociedad (pág. 670)

subsistence farming/agricultura de subsistencia labranza que sólo produce la cosecha que se necesita para alimentar a la familia de uno (pág. 104)

subversion/subversión intento sistemático para derrocar un gobierno utilizando personas que trabajan secretamente desde adentro (pág. 643)

*****successor/sucesor** aquél que toma el lugar del gobernante (pág. 611)

suffrage/sufragio derecho al voto (pág. 330)

*****sum/suma** cantidad específica de dinero (pág. 471)

summit/cumbre junta de jefes de gobiernos (pág. 855)

Sunbelt/Región Solada nueva región industrial en el sur de California y el Bajo Sur que se desarrolló durante la Segunda Guerra Mundial (pág. 589)

*****supplement/suplementar** añadir a algo para completarlo (pág. 853)

supply-side economics/economía de oferta teoría económica de que los impuestos bajos levantarían la economía invirtiendo su dinero los negocios y los individuos, así creando un alto ingreso del impuesto (págs. 457, 895)

*****suspend/suspenda** detener temporalmente una operación (pág. 475)

*****sustain/sostener** asegurar la perseverancia de una acción (pág. 781)

*****symbol/símbolo** algo que representa o sugiere algo más (pág. 718)

syndicate/sindicato grupo de negocios (pág. 350)

*****task/tarea** trabajo asignado (pág. 919)

teach-in/plantón educacional junta o clase extendida para discutir un asunto político o social (pág. 788)

*****technical/técnico** tener una comprensión especial de conocimientos mecánicos o científicos (pág. 693)

*****technique/técnica** método por medio del cual se completa una tarea deseada (pág. 479)

*****technology/tecnología** el resultado de una mejora a una idea existente o antigua (pág. 296)

telecommute/viajar electrónicamente trabajar en casa por medio de conexión electrónica con una oficina central (pág. 932)

televangelist/televangelista evangelista que transmite regularmente programas evangélicos por televisión (pág. 891)

temperance/templanza moderación o abstinencia del uso del alcohol (págs. 187, 334)

*****temporary/temporal** que dura sólo un corto tiempo (pág. 629)

tenant farmer/granjero arrendatario granjero que labra la tierra de un terrateniente y paga la renta ya sea con dinero efectivo o cosecha (pág. 225)

tenement/casa de vecindad apartamentos para varias familias, normalmente obscuros, apretados que apenas cumplen con los estándares mínimos de viviendas (pág. 260)

*****tension/tensión** desasosiego o conflicto acerca de una situación (pág. 314)

termination policy/política de terminación política gubernamental para traer a los Nativos Americanos dentro de la sociedad principal retirando el reconocimiento de los grupos Nativos Americanos como entidades legales (pág. 691)

terrorism/terrorismo el uso de violencia por grupos no del gobierno en contra de civiles para alcanzar una meta política impartiendo miedo y amenazando gobiernos para que cambien su política (pág. 955)

*****theory/teoría** hipótesis que se somete a argumento o investigación (pág. 719)

*****thereby/por eso** estar conectado con o en referencia a (pág. 514)

Title IX/Título IX sección de las Enmiendas Educacionales de 1972 prohibiendo que las escuelas que recibían fondos federales discriminaran contra niñas y mujeres jóvenes en casi todo aspecto de su operación (pág. 817)

trade deficit/déficit de intercambio diferencia entre el valor de las importaciones de un país y las exportaciones (pág. 943)

Spanish Glossary

transcendental meditation/meditación transcendental técnica de meditación en la cual una persona repite una palabra una y otra vez como manera de alcanzar la máxima inteligencia, armonía y salud (pág. 873)

transcontinental railroad/ferrocarril transcontinental sistema de ferrocarril que se extiende a través del continente (pág. 197)

*transition/transición que pasa de una circunstancia a otra (pág. 671)

*transmit/transmitir enviar información a través de un medio, como por ejemplo, la radio o Internet (pág. 582)

triangular trade/comercio triangular una ruta comercial de tres ramas para intercambiar productos entre las colonias americanas y otros dos asociados comerciales (pág. 107)

*trigger/activador acción que desencadena una reacción mayor (pág. 341)

U-boat/nave-U apodo inglés para submarino alemán, de Unterseeboot, término que significa barco submarino (pág. 373)

*ultimate/primordial la característica principal o más intensa de algo (pág. 793)

Underground Railroad/Ferrocarril Clandestino sistema que ayudó a los afroamericanos esclavizados a seguir una red de rutas de escape fuera del Sur hacia la libertad en el Norte (pág. 197)

unfair trade practices/prácticas comerciales injustas prácticas comerciales que ganan el beneficio perjudicando a la competencia (pág. 355)

*unify/unificar unir a un grupo con alguna meta o patrón de pensamiento (pág. 421)

union shop/taller sindicalizado comercio que requiere que los trabajadores se unan al sindicato (pág. 667)

urban renewal/renovación urbana programas gubernamentales que intentan eliminar la pobreza y revitalizar las áreas urbanas (pág. 689)

*validate/validar legalizar algo o hacerlo oficial (pág. 809)

vertical integration/integración vertical asociación de compañías que abastecen equipo y servicios necesarios a una industria particular (pág. 249)

veto/veto poder del jefe del ejecutivo de rechazar leyes aprobadas por la legislatura (pág. 128)

*via/vía medio de transmisión (pág. 904)

victory garden/huerto de victoria huertos plantados por ciudadanos americanos durante la guerra para cultivar vegetales para usar en casa así dejando más para las tropas (págs. 378, 592)

vigilance committee/comités de vigilancia grupos de ciudadanos comunes y corrientes formados por autoridades judiciales y policiales locales y cuya tarea es encontrar delincuentes y entregarlos a la justicia (pág. 238)

*violate/violar ir en contra de un estándar establecido con anterioridad (pág. 306)

*virtual/virtual a punto de o casi en su totalidad (pág. 306)

*visible/visible algo que se puede ver (pág. 897)

*volume/volumen se refiere a una cantidad considerable (pág. 274)

war on poverty/guerra contra la pobreza programa antipobreza bajo el Presidente Lyndon Johnson (pág. 725)

welfare capitalism/capitalismo de beneficencia sistema en el cual las compañías permiten a los trabajadores comprar acciones, compartir las ganancias, y recibir beneficios tal como atención médica, común en los años 1920 (pág. 454)

white-collar/collar blanco trabajos que no requieren ropa de protección o de trabajo, asi como los vendedores (pág. 675)

*widespread/difundido tener influencia o efecto sobre un grupo grande (pág. 392)

yellow journalism/periodismo amarillista tipo de reportaje sensacional, tendencioso, y a menudo falso con el propósito de atraer a los lectores (pág. 302)

yuppie/yuppie adulto joven educado en la universidad empleado en una profesión de buen salario y que vive y trabaja en o cerca de una ciudad grande (pág. 903)

Spanish Glossary

Italicized page numbers refer to illustrations. The following abbreviations are used in the index:
m = map; c = chart; p = photograph or picture; g = graph; crt = cartoon; ptg = painting; q = quote

Index

Index

Index

Index

bus boycott, 741, 744–45, *p744*; Montgomery Improvement Association, 744; *Morgan* v. *Virginia*, 741; movement begins, 741, 742; NAACP, 741, 752; Nation of Islam and, 761, 827; Native Americans and, 829–31; new civil rights legislation, 747; issues and approaches, 757–65; new political power, 742; nonviolent resistance, 760; *Norris* v. *Alabama*, 741; origins of, 741–42; *Plessy* v. *Ferguson*, 280, 741, 743; "Poor People's Campaign," 762; presidential policies, 751; protests, 743–55, 824–31; pupil assignment laws, 743; Rosa Parks, 744; Selma to Montgomery march, 755–56, *p755*; shift to economic rights, 759–60; sit-in movement, 742, 749; Southern Manifesto, 743; Stokely Carmichael, 760; struggle for voting rights and, 755–56; Student Nonviolent Coordinating Committee (SNCC), 750, 760; *Sweatt* v. *Painter*, 741; Thurgood Marshall, 742, 752; *University of California* v. *Bakke*, 826; violence during, 752, 753, *p753*, 755, 758, *p758*; Voting Rights Act of 1965, 756; Watts Riot, 759; Women's Political Council, 744. *See also* segregation; women's rights movement

Civil War, 206–15, *p220*, 238, 239, 245, 276; African Americans during, 211, 212, 215; Anaconda Plan, *c210*, 210; Appomattox courthouse, 215; battlefield medicine, 212, *p212*; beginnings of, 207–08; casualties of, 210, 211, 213, 214, *g214*; causes and effects of, *c200*, 238–39, 219–25, 244; conscription, 209; dissolution of Union, 199–201; Emancipation Proclamation, *c206*, 211–12, 219; European position on, 209; Gettysburg Address, 212–13; *Lee* v. *Grant*, 213–14; life during, 212; martial law, 208; military districts during, *m222*; new tariffs after, 245; opposing sides during, *c208*, 208–14; prisoners of war, 212; ranchers and the, 238–39, *m239*; Reconstruction and, 218–25, 238–39, 244; sectional conflicts, secession and, 199;

surrender, *c169*, 214–15; suspension of writs of habeas corpus, 209; technology and, 209, 210; turning points, 212–15; Vicksburg siege, 212; women during, 212, *p212*

Civil Works Administration (CWA), 506, *c506*, 507, *p507*, *q507*

Clarenbach, Dr. Kathryn F., 840, *p840*

Clark, Abraham, 123

Clark, George Rogers, 118

Clark, Jim, 756

Clarke, Edward Young, 408

Clarke, John H., 380

Clay, Henry, 183, 185, 186, 194, 196; Compromise of 1850, 196

Clay, Lucius, 635, *q635*

Clayton Antitrust Act, 356

Clean Air Act, 835

Clean Water Act, 835

Cleaver, Eldridge, 762

Clemenceau, Georges, 388

Clemens, Samuel, 265, 266, 267, 305–06

Clermont, 178

Cleveland, Grover, 273, 274, *crt274*, *q274*, 277, 278, 297, 302, 354; annexation of Hawaii and, 297; election of 1896, 278; Panic of 1893 and, 277

Clinton, Hillary Rodham, 937, *p937*, *p939*; health care reform and, 937

Clinton, William Jefferson, 919, *p926*, 935–41, *p937*, 962, *q962*, *p962*; agenda of, 936–37; Americorps, 937; balancing the budget, 937, 939, 941; Brady Bill, 937; children's issues, 939; Comprehensive Nuclear Test Ban Treaty, 946; Congress and, 937–38, 939; Contract with America, 937–38; crime and gun control, 937; domestic policies, 936–37, 939; economy and, 936, 938, 939; election of 1992, 919, *m925*; election of 1996, *c926*, 938–39; Family Medical Leave Act, 937; foreign policy, 940–41; government shut-down, *c926*, *c935*, 938; Haitian intervention, 940; health care reform, 937; Health Insurance Portability Act, 938; impeachment of, *c927*, *c935*, 939–40, *p939*;

intern scandal, 940; Kyoto Protocol, 946; legacy of, 941; peacekeeping in Bosnia and Kosovo, 940; peacemaking in the Middle East, 941; popularity of, 938, 939; response to Osama bin Laden, 957, 962, *q962*; second term, 939–40; Senate acquittal of, *c927*, *c935*, 940; trade with China, 945; Welfare Reform Act, 938; Whitewater, 939–40

closed shops, 251, 667

cloture, 754, 755

Clymer, George, 123

coal, 835, 836; disadvantages of, 836

Coal Strike of 1902, 342–43

Coast Guard, 958

Coercive Acts, *c114*, 115

Cold War, 622–57; after the fall of, 636–37; Alger Hiss, 644; American economic concerns and, 627–28; American policy during, 633; American society and, 642–49; America's nuclear arsenal, 652; armistice and, 639; Army-McCarthy hearings, *p647*, 647–48; Asia, spread of to, 636–37; atomic testing and weapons, 630, 643, 648, *p648*, *p649*, 652, *c653*; Bay of Pigs, 718–19; beginning of, 622–31; Berlin airlift, 633, *p633*, 634, 635; Berlin Blockade, 635; Berlin crisis, 634, 635; Berlin Wall, *p833*, 718; bombers and, 652; brinkmanship, 653, 654, 656; capitalism and, 633; causes and effects of, 629, 636, *c636*; China, 636, 637, 639; collapse of Soviet Union, 915; communist aggression and, 636, 643; conservatism and, 888; conspiracy and, 646–48; containment and, 633, 637–38, 639, 643, 648, 653–55, 657, 718; crisis in Iran and, 634; Cuban missile crisis, *p717*, 717–18; declaration of liberated Europe, 629; defense agreements and, 639; divided Europe, *m631*; economic causes of, 627, 629; Eisenhower and, 650–57, *q654*, *q65*; end of, 914–19; facing the bomb, 648–49; fall of Berlin Wall, 917, *p917*; fighting communism covertly, 654–56; free enterprise system, 628; Germany, 629, 634, 635; George H.W. Bush and, 914;

HUAC, 644, *p644*; Gorbachev's reforms and, 915; increasing world trade and, 627; Iran and Guatemala, 655; Iron Curtain, 631; Korean War, 637–39, *m638*, 653; life during, 648–49; Long telegram and, 633; loyalty review program, 643; Marshall Plan and, 634; massive retaliation and, 652; McCarran Internal Security Act and, 646–47; McCarthy and, 646, *q646*, 647–48; McCarthyism, 647, 649; NATO, 635–36, *m635*, 656; "New World Order" after, 916–17; origins of, 626–31; Poland and, 628–29; popular culture in, 649, *p649*; Potsdam conference and, 630, *p630*, 631; presidential policies and, 651–52; Project Venona, 645; Reagan and, *p833*, 898–99; Red Scare, 393–94, *p643*, 643–45, 646, 648; revolution in Eastern Europe, 915, *m915*; Rosenbergs, the, 644–45, *p644*; Soviet-American relations, 627, 630; Soviet security concerns and, 627, 646–47; space race, 652, *crt652*, 716–17; spies and, 643, 644, *p644*, 645, 646, 647, 651; Suez crisis, 654; Taiwan crisis, 653; trade and, 627; tragedy in Tiananmen Square, 917; Truman and, 629–31, 634, 639, *q639*; Truman Doctrine, 634, *q634*, 643; UN and, 638; uprising in Hungary, 655–56, *p655*; Vietnam War, 779; Warsaw Pact, *c635*, *m635*; West Germany and the, 635; Yalta Conference and, 628–29

"Cold Warrior," 705

Coleman, Bessie, 452, *p452*

Cole, Nat King, 685

Collier's magazine, 328, 344, 686

Collins, Michael, 716, *p716*

colonial assemblies, 953

colonies, American. *See* America; Middle Colonies; New England Colonies; Southern Colonies

Colorado, 195, 238, 331; women's voting rights and, 331

Colorado Museum of Natural History, 99

Colored Farmers' National Alliance, 279

Index

Faubus, Orval, 746–47

Faulkner, William, 479

FBI Domestic Security Investigation Guidelines, 861

featherbedding, 667

Federal Bureau of Investigation (FBI), 394, 643, 751, 959

Federal Campaign Act Amendments, 861

Federal Communications Commission (FCC), 896

federal courts, *c144*, 144

federal deficit, 918, 919, 936, 950

Federal Deposit Insurance Corporation (FDIC), 503, 506, *c506*

federal district courts, *c144*, 144

Federal Emergency Management Agency (FEMA), 958

Federal Emergency Relief Agency (FERA), 505, 506, *c506*, 511

Federal Farm Loan Act, 356

Federal Highway Act, *c663*, 671

federal income tax, 163, 165, 277, 355, 677

federalism, 128, 129, 138, 139, 174, 176, 518

Federalist Era, 174, 279

Federalist Papers, 953, *q953*

Federalist Party, 174, 176

Federalists, 129, 174, 953

Federalist, the, 129–30; national visions of, *c174*

"Federal Number One," 513

Federal Radio Commission, 453, 458

Federal Republic of Germany, 635. *See also* West Germany

Federal Reserve Act, 355

Federal Reserve Board, 445, 446, 485, 865, 895; actions of 1920s, 473; interest rates and, 473; 865, 895; mistakes of, 473

Federal Reserve System, 355, *c355*, *m355*, 457

federal revenue agents, 413

Federal Security Agency, 517. *See also* Social Security Administration

Federal Theater Project, 513

Federal Trade Commission (FTC), 355, 354, 487

Federal Writers' Project of the Works Progress Administration, 491

Feis, Herbert, 615, *q615*

Female Experience: An American Documentary, The, *q814*

Feminine Mystique, The (Friedan), *c802*, *p802*, *c813*, 815–16, *q815*, *p816*, 840

feminism, 814

feminist movement, 813–19, *c813*. *See also* women's rights movement

Ferdinand, Archduke Franz, 369, *p369*

Ferguson, John, H., 280

Ferguson, Patrick,

Ferraro, Geraldine, 896

fertility, 285

Fifteenth Amendment, 163, 222, 279, 331; debates over, 331; loophole in, 279

Fifteenth Regiment, 429

Fifth Amendment, *c141*, 145, 159–60; due process and, 145

Figgins, J.D., 99

Fight for Freedom Committee, 558

filibuster, 754, 755

Fillmore, Millard, 197, 198–99, 296; Japan, 296

film industry, 682; African American's roles in, 682; after the war, 682; Cinemascope, 682; television and, 682; women's roles in, 682

Filo, David, 933; Yahoo! and, 933

"final solution," 553–54

Finnerty, Joseph, T. , 285

Finney, Charles G., 187

fireside chats, 502

First Amendment, *c141*, 145, 146, 159, 378, 380, 381, 641, *c709*, 711; *Engel v. Vitale* and, 711; fundamental liberties and, 145, 425; ideas leading to, 641; school prayer and, 711; separation of church and state, 424, 711; violations of, 146

First American, The, *q99*

First Continental Congress, 115

"First Fig" (Millay), 420

first New Deal, 498–507

Fiske, John, 296, *q296*

fitness, aerobic, 875

Fitzgerald, F. Scott, *q419*, 420, *p422*, *q422*

"Five-Day Attack on Hastings Ridge," *q618*

fixed costs, 248–49

flapper, 414, *p414*, 415

Flappers, Bootleggers, "Typhoid Mary" and the Bomb, *q445*

Fletcher, Captain Luther, 609, *q609*

Fletcher v. Peck, *c177*

flexible response, 715

Flint, Michigan, 515

Florida, 113, 119, 177, 200, *c947*, 948–49, 952, 961; vote recount in election of 2000, *c947*, 948–49, 952

Florida Supreme Court, 949; election of 2000 and, 949

Floyd, William, 123

Foch, Ferdinand, 388

Folsom Dam, 506

Folsom, New Mexico, 99

Food Administration, 377, 469

Food and Drug Administration, *q382*

food safety, 336–38, *c340*, 344; false labeling and, 344; regulations on, 344

Foraker Act, 307

Forbes, Charles R., 445

Ford, Betty, *p866*

Ford, Gerald, 796, *p803*, *c846*, *p846*, *c847*, 860, 861, *q861*, *c863*, 866–67, *p866*, *q866*, 879, *p879*, *q879*; Cambodian seizure of the *Mayaguez*, 866–67; economic policies, 866; election of 1976, 867; foreign policy, 866–67; Helsinki Accords, *c847*, 866; Nixon pardon, 866, 879, *p879*, *q879*; South Vietnamese and, 796; 38th president, 861; vetoes of, 866; vice president, 860; Vietnam War, 796; WIN plan, 866

Ford, Henry, 450, *p450*, *q450*, 575; assembly lines, 450–51, *q450*, *p451*, *q451*, 575; social revolution and, 450; wartime production and, 575

Ford Motor Company, *c440*, 453

Fordney-McCumber Act, 455

Fordney-McCumber tariffs, 455

Ford's Theater, 215

Foreign Relations committee, 389

Fort Sumter, *c169*, 207

Fortune magazine, 479, 725

Forty-Niners, 196

For Whom the Bell Tolls (Hemingway), 420

fossil fuels, 835, 864

Founding Fathers, 126–31, 132–33, *p127*, *p129*, *p130*,

640–41; influence of classical thinkers on, 111, 112, 640; political philosophy of, 640–41

"Four Freedoms," 559

442nd Regimental Combat Team, 591–92

Four-Minute Men, 379

Fourteen Points, 388

Fourteenth Amendment, 145, 162–63, 280, 331, 221, 222, 226–27, *p226*, 331, 519, 710, 742; *Brown v. Board of Education*, 226, *c709*, *c736*, 742, 743, 744, 745, 746, 826; *Bush v. Gore*, 227; debates over, 331; due process and, 145; *Gideon v. Wainright*, 227; *Plessy v. Ferguson*, 226; using to apply Bill of Rights to states, 711

Fourth Amendment, *c141*, 145, 159, 958; USA Patriot Act and rights of, 958

France, 101, 113, 117, 312, 369, 449, 544, 545–46; appeasement, 544; division of Germany and, 629; French resistance, 609; Munich Conference, 544; Prussians and, 368; Vietnam and, 773, 774; withdrawal from Indochina, 776; World War II, 544, 545–46; 600–03, 609

franchises, 676

Franco, Francisco, 540

Franco-Russian Alliance, 369

Frank, Anne, 552

Frank, Otto, 552

Frankfurter, Justice, 745

Franklin, Benjamin, 110, *p110*, *q110*, 116, 123, 127, *q127*, 132, *q132*, 641, *q641*

Franklin D. Roosevelt: A Rendezvous with Destiny, 563, *q563*

Freed, Alan, 683, *q683*

freedmen, 220

Freedmen's Bureau, 220

Freedmen's school, *p223*

Freedom Bound, *q826*

freedom of assembly, 145, 146

freedom of religion, 141, 145, 425, *c709*; church and state, 424–25; Colonial beginnings of, 424; Constitutional guarantee of, 425; Warren Court and, *c709*

freedom of speech, 111, 139, 145, 146, 641, 731

freedom of the press, 139, 145, 641

Index

Index

Index

Index

Index

Index

Acknowledgments and Photo Credits

Acknowledgments

432 "The Negro Speaks of Rivers," "I, Too," "The Weary Blues," "Lenox Avenue: Midnight," "Aunt Sue's Stories," and "Mother to Son" from *The Collected Poems of Langston Hughes* by Langston Hughes. Copyright © 1994 by the Estate of Langston Hughes. Used by permission of Alfred A. Knopf, a division of Random House, Inc.

594 From *Farewell to Manzanar* by Jeanne Wakatsuki Houston and James D. Houston. Copyright © 1973 by James D. Houston. Reprinted by permission of Houghton Mifflin Company.

910 From *Hunger of Memory* by Richard Rodriguez (Boston: David R. Godine, Publisher, 1981). Copyright © 1981 by Richard Rodriguez. Reprinted by permission of Georges Borchardt, Inc., for the author.

976 From *The Grapes of Wrath* by John Steinbeck. Copyright © 1939, renewed 1967 by John Steinbeck. Used by permission of Viking Penguin, a division of Penguin Putnam, Inc.

977 "Alone and Far Removed" by Audie Murphy. Reprinted by permission of the Estate of Audie Murphy.

978 "Letter from Birmingham Jail" reprinted by arrangement with the Estate of Martin Luther King, Jr., c/o Writers House, Inc. as agent for the proprietor. Copyright Martin Luther King 1963, copyright renewed 1991 by Coretta Scott King.

979 From *Barefoot Heart: Stories of a Migrant Child* by Elva Trevino Hart. Reprinted by permission of Bilingual Press.

1002 From "I Have a Dream," reprinted by arrangement with the Estate of Martin Luther King, Jr., c/o Writers House, Inc. as agent for the proprietor. Copyright Martin Luther King 1968, copyright renewed 1996 by Coretta Scott King.

Glencoe would like to acknowledge the artists and agencies that participated in illustrating this program: Morgan Cain & Associates; Ortelius Design, Inc.; and QA Digital.

Photo Credits

Cover:(l to r, t to b) (fireworks, flag)CORBIS, (steam boat)Sean Sexton/CORBIS, (space shuttle)CORBIS, (covered wagon)David Muench/CORBIS, (Ellis Island)Bettmann/CORBIS, (gunboat)CORBIS, (assembly line)Bettmann/CORBIS, (Asian American with flag)Catherine Karnow/CORBIS, (marine)CORBIS, (Falling Water –Frank Lloyd Wright)Hedrich-Blessing Studio/CORBIS, (speed train)Reuters NewMedia Inc./CORBIS, (firemen raising flag)Thomas E. Franklin/Bergen Record/SABA/CORBIS, (immigrant)Bettmann/CORBIS, (naturalization ceremony)Bettmann/CORBIS, (child laborer)Lewis Hine/CORBIS, (F16)U.S. Air Force, (Edison in car)Bettmann/CORBIS, (Michael Phelps)Reuters/CORBIS, (Martin Luther King)Bettmann/CORBIS, (baseball player)Bettmann/CORBIS, (Mulberry Street) Bettmann/CORBIS, (Frederick Douglas)CORBIS, (Condoleezza Rice)AFP/CORBIS, (Liberty Bell)CORBIS, (Russell Means)Christopher Felver/CORBIS, (1957 Chevy) Richard Cummins/CORBIS, (train)CORBIS, (Iwo Jima)CORBIS, (others) PhotoDisc/Getty Images; viThe Valley Forge Historical Society; vii(t)Franklin D. Roosevelt Library, (b)Library of Congress; viii (t)Courtesy Baylor University/Wings Across America, (b)United Press International/CORBIS; ix(t)Thomas E. Franklin/Bergen Record/SABA/CORBIS, (b)CORBIS; xiDennis Brack/Black Star; xiiDigital Stock/CORBIS; xiiiHulton-Deutsch/CORBIS; xixCourtesy Ronald Reagan Library; xviCORBIS/Bettmann; 2(t)Image 100 Ltd., (b)Nik Wheeler/CORBIS; 3Lonely Planet Images; 4–5Masterfile; 6–7Panoramic Images; 8–9Panoramic Images; 10–11Getty Images; 12Ed Young/CORBIS; 13Panoramic Images; 14Lonely Planet Images; 16(t)Getty Images, (b) Panoramic Images; 39Museum of Fine Arts, Boston; 92Library of Congress; 92–93Lora Robins Collection of Virginia Art, Virginia Historical Society; 94Pilgrim Society; 94–95J. D. Bangs/Leiden American Pilgrim Museum; 95 (t)Colonial Williamsburg, (tr)Library of Congress, (b)White House Historical Association; 99Photo Archives, Denver Museum of Natural History; 100Richard A.Cooke III; 101The Oakland Museum; 102(t)Association for the Preservation of Virginia Antiquities, (b)Virginia State Library, Photographic Collection; 103Private Collection; 104Courtesy of The Massachusetts Historical Society; 105 Miriam & Ira D. Wallach Division of Art, Prints and Photographs, The New York Public Library, Astor Lenox and Tilden Foundation; 106Picture Research Consultants; 107Print Collection Miriam and Ira Wallach Division of Art, Prints and Photographs The New York Public Library Astor, Lenox and Tilden; 110 Harvard University Art Museum; 111Bettmann/CORBIS; 112National Portrait Gallery, London; 114American Antiquarian Society; 115 North Wind Picture Archives; 116 Library of Congress; 117 Virginia Historical Society; 119 The Valley Forge Historical Society; 121Yale University Art Gallery; 123unknown; 125National Museums & Galleries on Merseyside; 127 Fraunces Tavern Museum, New York; 128 Library of Philadelphia, Rare Books Room; 129 Library of Congress; 130 (l)Thomas Gilcrease Museum, Tulsa, (r)Courtesy Independence National Historic Park Collection; 132 Library of Virginia; 133 Smithsonian American Museum, Washington DC/Art Resource, NY; 136 PhotoDisc/Getty Images; 138(t)Stock Montage, (b)unknown; 139PhotoDisc/Getty Images; 145unknown; 146 AFP/Getty Images; 148 Sal di Marco/TimePix/Getty Images; 152 Dennis Brack/Blackstar; 168 White House Historical Association; 169 (t)Don Troiani, courtesy Historical Art Prints Southbury, CT, (cl)California State Capitol, (cr)Illinois State Historical Library, (b)White House Historical Association; 173National Museum of American History/Smithsonian Institution; 175Boston Public Library; 179 Courtesy Jack Naylor; 181 CORBIS/Bettmann; 183 West Point Museum Collections, 1822. United States Military Academy; 185Greenville County Museum of Art; 187Old Dartmouth Historical Society/New Bedford Whaling Museum; 189Collection of J. Paul Getty Museum; 190(t)National Museum of American History/Smithsonian Institution, (c)Ron Huntley, (b)Royalty-Free/CORBIS; 191 (t)Massachusetts Historical Society, (c)Mercer Museum/Bucks County Historical Society, (b)Picture Research Consultants; 193 Texas State Library and Archives Commission; 195 Bettmann/CORBIS; 196 American Antiquarian Society; 198 The Kansas State Historical Society, Topeka; 201 CORBIS; 202 203 Bettmann/CORBIS; 204 CORBIS; 205 Doug Martin; 207 Private Collection/Art Resources, NY; 211 The Cincinnati Historical Society; 212US Army Military History Institute; 213 216Library of Congress; 217 George Washington at Constitutional Convention by Junius Brutus Sterns; 219 Collection of William Gladstone; 220 221 Library of Congress; 223 Cook Collection/Valentine Museum; 224 Picture Research Consultants; 226 (t)Carl Iwasaki/TimePix/Getty Images, (b)CORBIS/Bettmann; 227 (t)Reuters NewMedia Inc./CORBIS, (b)Flip Schulke/Black Star; 228 CORBIS; 229 Getty Images; 232 (book) East Carolina University, (presidents)White House Historical Association; 233(l to r, t to b) Amistad Foundation/Wadsworth Atheneum, Library of Congress, Picture Research Consultants, (presidents) White House Historical Association; 233–234Brown Brothers; 237 U.S. Department of the Interior/Geological Survey; 239 (l)Thomas Gilcrease Institute, (r)Montana Historical Society, Helena; 240State Historical Society of Wisconsin; 241 Picture Research Consultants; 244 Library of Congress; 245 Bettmann/CORBIS; 246 (lightbulb)U.S. Dept. of the Interior/ National Park Service/Edison National Historic Site, (car)CORBIS/Bettmann, (others) National Museum of American History/Smithsonian Institution; 248The New York Historical Society; 250Library of Congress; 251The George Meany Memorial Archives; 252 (t)CORBIS, (c)Courtesy of the Rockefeller Archive Center, (b)CORBIS/Bettmann; 252–253 PhotoDisc/Getty Images; 253(l)E.O. Hoppe/CORBIS, (r)File photo; 255CORBIS/Bettmann; 257National Archives; 258Picture Research Consultants; 259(l)Museum of the City of New York/Gift of Mr. Shirley C. Burden, (r)Library of Congress; 260unknown; 262Chicago Historical Society; 263Mark Seider/National Geographic Society; 265Culver Pictures; 266Brown Brothers; 267United Charities Collection/Chicago Historical Society; 269(l)Brown Brothers, (r)Library of Congress; 270Lake County Museum/CORBIS; 272 Library of Congress; 273 Picture Research Consultant; 274 University of California at Berkeley, Bancroft Library; 275Nebraska State Historical Society; 276Private Collection; 277Kansas State Historical Society; 278 (l)Nebraska State Historical Society, (r)Ohio Historical Society; 279 Kansas State Historical Society; 280 Courtesy University of Chicago, Department of Special Collections; 281 282 283 Brown Brothers; 284 CORBIS; 285 Bettmann/CORBIS; 288 Collection of Colonel Stuart S. Corning. Photo by Rob Huntley/Lightstream; 288–289 West Point Museum/ Joshua Nefsky; 289Library of Congress; 290(tl)Courtesy US Naval Academy Museum, White House Historical Association; 290–291 Library of Congress; 291(l to r, t to b)Hawaii State Archives, Picture Research Consultants, (presidents)White House Historical Association, Hawaii State Archives, Library of Congress; 295 Hawaii State Archives; 297 National Portrait Gallery, Smithsonian Institution/Art Resource, N.Y.; 301 CORBIS/Bettmann; 302Picture Research Consultants; 305Culver Pictures; 306(l)Keystone-Mast Collection, UCR/California Museum of Photography, University of California, Riverside, (r)Library of Congress; 308 (l)Library of Congress, (r)Bettmann/CORBIS; 309Michael Ventura/Folio; 311 CORBIS/Bettmann; 313 Bettmann/CORBIS; 314CORBIS; 315 Bettmann/CORBIS; 316 (l)Picture Research Consultants, (r)CORBIS; 316–317Morton Beebe, S.R./CORBIS; 317Associated Press; 318AP Wide World Photos; 319Getty Images; 323White House Historical Association; 323 (t)CORBIS/Bettmann, (bl c)White House Historical Association, (br)Sagamore Hill National Historic Site; 327CORBIS; 328 Picture Research Consultants; 329CORBIS/Bettmann; 331Susan B. Anthony House; 332COR-

BIS/Bettmann; 333Library of Congress; 334Underwood & Underwood/CORBIS; 335 David J. & Janice L. Frent Collection/CORBIS; 336 Hulton-Deutsch Collections/CORBIS; 337 CORBIS; 338 Chicago Historical Society; 339 Doug Martin; 341 342 Library of Congress; 343 CORBIS; 345 Collection of the New York Historical Society; 347 (t)CORBIS/Bettmann, (b)Library of Congress; 349 White House Historical Association; 350 (l)Library of Congress, (c)Picture Research Consultants, (r)USDA Forest Service, Grey Towers, NHL, Milford, PA; 353 Collection of Janice L. and David J. Frent; 354 National Portrait Gallery/Smithsonian Institution/Art Resource; 355 John Skowronski/Folio; 356 358CORBIS; 359Hulton-Deutsch Collection/CORBIS; 362(l)White House Historical Association, (c)Library of Congress, (r)Courtesy Special Collections, Ellis Library, University of Missouri-Columbia; 363 (t)CORBIS/Bettmann, (bl)National Archives, (br)White House Historical Association; 367 CORBIS; 368 369 CORBIS/Bettmann; 372 CORBIS; 374 (t)Brown Brothers, (b)Picture Research Consultants; 376 377 National Archives; 378 Library of Congress; 381CORBIS/Bettmann; 382(t)Bettmann/CORBIS, (c)Brown Brothers, (b)Leon Gimple/Societe Francaise de Photographie/Life; 383 (Lenin) Culver Pictures, (others)Brown Brothers; 385 Colonel Stuart S. Corning Jr./Picture Research Consultants; 388 CORBIS/Bettmann; 391 Archives of Labor and Urban Affairs Wayne State University; 392 CORBIS/Bettmann; 394 Brown Brothers; 395(l)Library of Congress, (r)Culver Pictures; 396CORBIS; 397Bettmann/CORBIS; 398CORBIS/Bettmann; 400Picture Research Consultants; 400–401Whitney Museum of American Art, New York. Photo by Sheldan C. Collins, NJ; 401 National Portrait Gallery, Smithsonian Institution/Art Resource, N.Y.; 402 (l)White House Historical Association, (c)CORBIS/Bettmann, (r)White House Historical Association; 402–403 CORBIS; 403 (presidents)White House Historical Association, (book)Picture Research Consultants, Langston Hughes/National Portrait Gallery, (plane)National Air and Space Museum/Smithsonian Institution; 407File photo; 408Library of Congress; 410Bettmann/CORBIS; 411Getty Images; 412(l)Culver Pictures, (r)Getty Images; 414(t)Conde Nast Archive/CORBIS, (b)CORBIS; 415 (tl)Picture Research Consultants, (bl)National Museum of American History/Smithsonian Institution, (r)CORBIS/Bettmann; 416Collection of Janice L. and David J. Frent; 416–417(bkgd)Picture Research Consultants; 417(t)Picture Research Consultants, (b)CORBIS; 419(t)National Air and Space Museum/Smithsonian Institution, (b)Culver Pictures; 420 Art Institute of Chicago, Friends of American Art Collection; 421National Archives; 422(l)CORBIS/Bettmann, (r)Culver Pictures; 423(Lindberg)Culver Pictures, (others)Brown Brothers; 424CORBIS; 425The Metropolitan Museum of Art; 427Frank Driggs Collection; 428Yale Collection of American Literature, Beinecke Rare Book Room and Manuscript Library, Yale University; 429Donna Mussenden Van Der Zee. All rights reserved, (inset)Frank Driggs Collection; 430CORBIS; 431CORBIS/Bettmann; 432Langston Hughes/National Portrait Gallery; 433 Frank Driggs Collection; 434Bettmann/CORBIS; 435 Doug Martin; 436 CORBIS; 437 Bettmann/CORBIS; 440 (l)White House Historical Association, (cl)Collection of Janice L. and David J. Frent, (cr)White House Historical Association, (r)Culver Pictures; 441(t)Museum of the City of New York, (bl)CORBIS, (bc)National Museum of American History/Smithsonian Institution, (br)White House Historical Association; 445Brown Brothers; 446Culver Pictures; 447(l)Collection of Janice L. and David J. Frent, (r)CORBIS/Bettmann; 448Culver Pictures; 450Henry Ford Museum & Greenfield Village; 452(l)CORBIS, (r)Schlesinger Library, Radcliffe College; 453Frank & Marie-Therese Wood Print Collections/The Picture Bank; 457 Library of Congress; 458 CORBIS; 460 Schenectady Museum, Hall of Electrical History Foundation/CORBIS; 461CORBIS; 464(tl)Picture Research Consultants, (r)Museum of American Financial History, (bl)White House Historical Association; 465(t)AP/Wide World Photos, (bl)Chicago Historical Society, (br)White House Historical Association; 469 470CORBIS/Bettmann; 471National Portrait Gallery, Smithsonian Institution/Art Resource, N.Y.; 472 Collection of John P. Axelrod, Boston, MA; 473 CORBIS/Bettmann; 475Chicago Historical Society; 476 477 478Library of Congress; 480(l)San Diego Historical Society, (r)Brown Brothers; 481(t)MONOPOLY® & ©2004 Hasbro, Inc. Used with permission, (b)CORBIS/Bettmann; 483The Mahoning Valley Historical Society Collections; 485 Dorthea Lange Collection, The Oakland Museum of California. The City of Oakland. Gift of Paul S. Taylor. 486(t)St. Paul Daily News/Minnesota Historical Society, (r)AP/Wide World Photos; 487National Archives and Records Administration/AP/Wide World Photos; 489(t)US Department of the Interior/Bureau of Reclamation, (b)Robert Cameron/Getty Images; 490Bettmann/CORBIS; 491CORBIS; 494(l)White House Historical Association, (cl)CORBIS/Bettmann, (cr)Library of Congress, (r)White House Historical Association; 495 (t)Courtesy of Roosevelt Arts Project/photo Josh Nefsky, (b)Thomas Hart Benton, 'Steel', from America Today, 1930/AXA Financial, Inc. through its subsidiary The Equitable Life Assurance; 499 500Bettmann/CORBIS; 501Associated Press/Wide World Photo; 502CORBIS/Bettmann; 504Franklin D. Roosevelt Library; 505U.S. Forest Service; 507 CORBIS; 508 (l)Tennessee Valley Authority, (r)Picture Research Consultants; 509PhotoDisc/Getty Images; 511CORBIS; 512CORBIS/Bettmann; 514Franklin D. Roosevelt Library; 515CORBIS; 517Bettmann/CORBIS; 518CORBIS; 521AP/Wide World Photos; 522Franklin D. Roosevelt Library, (inset)Collection of Janice L. and David J. Frent; 523(l)Franklin D. Roosevelt Library, (r)CORBIS/Bettmann; 524The New Yorker Collection 1936 Peter Arno from Cartoonbank.com. All Rights Reserved.; 526 CORBIS; 527 Bettmann/CORBIS; 530 Collection of Chester Stott/Picture Research Consultants; 530–531 CORBIS; 531 National Portrait Gallery, Smithsonian Institution/Art Resource, N.Y.; 532 (t)Herbert Hoover Library, (c)White House Historical Association, (b)Picture Research Consultants; 533 (t)Hugo Jaeger/Stringer/TimePix/Getty Images, (bl)Private Collection, (bc)National Archives, (br)Hulton Getty; 537 Culver Pictures; 538 Hulton-Deutsch/Getty Images; 539 Archive Photos/Getty Images; 540 Archivo Iconografico, S.A./CORBIS; 541 CORBIS; 543 AP/Wide World Photos; 544 CORBIS; 546 Time Life Pictures/Getty Images; 547 Hulton Archive/Getty Images; 548 Library of Congress; 550 Courtesy University of Tennessee Press, (inset)U. S. Holocaust Memorial Museum, Washington, DC; 551 (l)Courtesy of the Leo Baeck Institute and U. S. Holocaust Memorial Museum, (r)National Archives, courtesy of USHMM Photo Archives; 552 (l)Yivo Institute for Jewish Research, (r)National Archives: Suitland, courtesy of the United States Holocaust Memorial Museum; 554 Library of Congress; 556 Picture Research Consultants; 557 US Army Museum of Hawaii; 558 Chicago Historical Society; 559 Thomas McAvoy/Life Magazine, Time Warner, (inset)Herbert Hoover Library; 562 Time Life Pictures/Getty Images; 564 Bettmann/CORBIS; 565Time Life Pictures/Getty Iamges; 568White House Historical Association; 569 (t)Digital Stock/CORBIS, (cl c)CORBIS, (cr)White House Historical Association, (b)John Launois/Black Star; 573CORBIS; 574–575CORBIS/Bettmann; 576 Courtesy The Smithsonian Institute; 577 CORBIS/Bettmann; 578Courtesy Baylor University/Wings Across America; 580U.S. Naval Institute; 581Digital Stock/CORBIS, (inset)Norm Avery; 584(l)Oscar White/CORBIS, (r)CORBIS; 585Hulton Archive/Getty Images; 587The Curtis Publishing Company; 588 National Archives; 590 CORBIS; 591 Toyo Miyatake Photograph; 592(l)CORBIS/Bettmann, (r)Stock Montage; 593Dr. Seuss Collection/Mandeville Special Collections Library/University of California, San Diego; 594 (l)Robert Scheer, (r)Digital Stock/CORBIS; 596 Seattle Post-Intelligencer Collection; Museum of History and Industry/CORBIS; 597 Doug Martin; 599 CORBIS; 600 Texas Military Forces Museum, 36th Infantry Division Gallery, Austin, Texas; 601CORBIS/Bettmann; 602–603 (bkgd)Digital Stock/CORBIS; 605 Digital Stock/CORBIS; 607 (t)CORBIS, (b)Cornelius Ryan Collection of World War II Papers, Alden Library, Ohio University, Athens OH 45701; 609 AP/Wide World Photos; 612 Digital Stock/CORBIS; 613 Digital Stock/CORBIS, (inset)Hulton Archive/Getty Images; 614 National Geographic Society; 614–615 National Geographic Society; 616 617 CORBIS; 618Bettmann/CORBIS; 619Hulton-Deutsch Collection/CORBIS; 622(l)White House Historical Association, (r)National Portrait Gallery, Smithsonian Institution/Art Resource, N.Y.; 622–623 AP/Wide World Photos; 623(l)White House Historical Association, (r)Smithsonian Institution; 627National Portrait Gallery, Smithsonian Institution/Art Resource, N.Y. Gift of Frances O. Tames; 628American Red Cross; 629John Florea/TimePix/Getty Images; 630Picture Research Consultants; 633 CORBIS/Bettmann; 637 National Archives; 640CORBIS; 643The Michael Barson Collection/Past Perfect; 644CORBIS/Bettmann; 645(l)Collection of Michael Barson, (r)CORBIS/Bettmann; 646CORBIS; 647Robert Phillips/Life Magazine/Time Warner; 648(l)Archive Photos/Getty Images, (c)Ralph Morse/TimePix, (r)Loomis Dean/TimePix; 649Getty Images; 651CORBIS; 652Ross Lewis Milwaukee Public Library; 654CORBIS/Bettmann; 655Time Life Pictures/Getty Images; 656(l)Time Life Pictures/Getty Images, (r)Smithsonian Institution; 657 Time Life Pictures/Getty Images; 658 659 Bettmann/CORBIS; 662 (l)Picture Research Consultants, (c)White House Historical Association, (r)CORBIS/Bettmann; 662 663 Superstock; 663(l)White House Historical Association, (c)FPG, (r)Natural Museum of American History/Smithsonian Instutution; 667CORBIS; 668Cornell Capa/TimePix; 669CORBIS/Bettmann; 670Getty Images, (inset)Time Life Pictures/Getty Images; 672(t)CORBIS, (c)Getty Images, (b)J R Eyerman/TimePix/Getty Images; 673 (t)Courtesy Wig Wam Motel, (b)CORBIS; 675 TimePix/Getty Images; 676B. Wiseman/from Hey, Can't You Forget Business? by Charles Preston, ©1953, E.P. Dutton & Co., Inc.; 678CORBIS; 681PhotoFest; 682Hulton Archive/Getty Images; 683Globe Photos; 684Elliot Erwitt/Magnum Photos, (inset)Picture Research Consultants; 685Photofest; 686(t)CORBIS/Bettmann, (bl)Archive Photos, (br)SuperStock; 687(l)CORBIS/Bettmann, (r)PopperFoto; 689CORBIS/Bettmann; 690Chicago Historical Society; 691AP/Wide World Photos; 692National Archives; 693Danny Lyon/Magnum Photos, Inc.; 694Time Lige Pictures/Getty Images; 695Bettmann/CORBIS; 698Picture Research Consultants; 698–699John Eastcott/Yva Momatiuk/Stock Boston; 699National Portrait Gallery, Smithsonian Institution, Washington, D.C./Art Resource N.Y.; 700(tl)Ohio Historical Society, (tr)AP/Wide World Photos, (bl)Art Resource, (br)White House Historical Association; 700–701Paul Schultzer/Life/Time Pix/Getty Images; 701Collection of Janice L. and David J. Frent; 705CORBIS/Bettmann; 706(l)Ohio Historical Society, (r)Bettmann/CORBIS; 707JFK Library/Sygma/CORBIS; 708Time Life Pictures/Getty Images; 710Bettmann/CORBIS; 711The Supreme Court of the United States Office of the Curator; 712 CORBIS/Bettmann; 713 (t)Ralph Morse/TimePix/Getty Images, (bl)AP/Wide World Photos, (br)Hulton-Deutsch Collection/CORBIS; 715Lynn Historical Society; 716 Bettmann/CORBIS; 717 AP/Wide World Photos;

719 John S. Boyer/National Geographic Society; 720 NASA; 721 (t)NASA, (c)Bill Ingalls/NASA, (b)Lockheed Martin Global Communication; 723 Chicago Historical Society; 724 725 AP/Wide World Photos; 726 (l)CORBIS/Bettmann, (r)Collection of Janice L. and David J. Frent; 728 Paul Conklin; 729 AP/Wide World Photos; 730 (t)Bridgeman Art Library Ltd., (b)National Portrait Gallery, Smithsonian Institution/Art Resource, NY; 732 CORBIS; 733 Bettmann/CORBIS; 736 (tl)Carl Iwaski/TimePix/Getty Images, (tr)CORBIS/Bettmann, (bl)White House Historical Association, (br)Art Resource; 736–737 Steve Schapiro/TimePix/Getty Images; 737 (tl)New York Public Library, (tr)Collection of Janice L. and David J. Frent, (bl)White House Historical Association, (br)CORBIS; 741 United Press International/CORBIS; 742 Carl Iwaski/Time Pix/Getty Images; 743 Library of Congress; 744 Dan Weiner/courtesy Sandra Weiner; 745 CORBIS; 746 AP/Wide World Photos; 749 Vic Colley/The Nashville Banner/The Nashville Public Library; 750 Bettmann/CORBIS; 751 CORBIS; 753 Charles Moore 1963/Black Star; 754 Steve Schapiro/Black Star, (inset)Francis Miller/TimePix/Getty Images; 755 New York Public Library; 758 CORBIS; 759 Jon Kennedy/Arkansas Democrat-Gazette; 760 AP/Wide World Photos; 761 CORBIS; 762 AP/Wide World Photos; 763 AP/Wide World Photos, (inset)Flip Schulke/Black Star; 764 765 Bettmann/CORBIS; 768 (t)AP/Wide World Photos, (bl br)White House Historical Association, (bc)Art Resource; 768–769 Diane Walker/TimePix/Getty Images; 769 (t)Picture Research Consultants, (c)Collection of Janice L. and David J. Frent, (b)White House Historical Association, (bl)White House Historical Association; 774 Paul Miller/Black Star; 775 Archive Photos/Getty Images; 776 Everette Dixie Reese, Courtesy of Alan Reese; 778 from The Living and The Dead by Paul Hendrickson; 779 780 AP/Wide World Photos; 782 Sp4 John Olson, U.S. Army; 784 CORBIS; 784–785 AP/Wide World Photos; 785 (t)AP/Wide World Photos, (b)CORBIS/Bettmann; 787 Photo by DeAlba/Washington Daily News/Lyndon Baines Johnson Library; 788 Bernie Boston; 790 Dick Swanson/TimePix; 793 CORBIS/Bettmann; 794 John Filo; 795 (l)Congressional Medal of Honor Society, (r)Picture Research Consultants; 796 Nik Wheeler/Black Star; 798 Time Life Pictures/Getty Images; 799 BLEIBTREU JASON/CORBIS SYGMA; 802 (l to r)White House Historical Association, Art Resource, White House Historical Association, Collection of Bettye Lane/Picture Research Consultants, White House Historical Association, Ken Regan, Camera 5; 802–803 Arthur Schatz/TimePix/Getty Images; 803 (t)AP/Wide World Photos, (b)White House Historical Association; 807 AP/Wide World Photos; 808 AP/Wide World Photo, (inset)Picture Research Consultants; 809 Lisa Law/The Image Works; 810 Tom Miner/The Image Works; 811 Tate Gallery, London/Art Resource, N.Y.; 812 Henry Diltz/CORBIS; 814 Red Book Magazine, August 30,1960; 815 CORBIS/Bettmann; 816 Schlesinger Library, Radcliffe College, (inset)Collection of Bettye Lane/Picture Research Consultants; 818 CORBIS/Bettmann; 819 Getty Images; 820 (l)Brown Brothers, (r)Idaho State Historical Society; 821 Archivo Iconografico, S.A./CORBIS; 822 Jerry Cooke/CORBIS; 823 Doug Martin; 825 826 AP/Wide World Photos; 827 Jacques M. Chenet/CORBIS; 828 (l)Arthur Schatz/TimePix/Getty Images, (r)Al Ransom/TimePix/Getty Images; 830 Bettmann/CORBIS; 831 Bob Daemmrich/The Image Works; 833 Alfred Eisenstaedt/TimePix/Getty Images; 834 Simon Fraser/Science Photo Library/Photo Researchers, (inset) Ken Regan, Camera 5; 835 Nathan Benn/CORBIS; 838 (t)Illustrations by David Kimble, (c)Molded Fiber Glass Companies, (b)Chevrolet communications; 839 (tl)Illustration by David Kimble, (tc)Jim Heafner, (tr)General Motors Corporation, (c)Used with permission, General Motors, GM, Chevrolet, Corvette & the Corvette Emblem are registered trademarks of GM Corp., (b)Paul Conklin/PhotoEdit/PictureQuest; 840 841 Bettmann/CORBIS; 844 Mark Ransom; 844–845 Nicole Bengiveno/NYT Pictures, The New York Times Company; 845 Charles Ommanney/SABA/CORBIS; 846 (l-c)White House Historical Association, (r)CORBIS/Bettmann; 846–847 Magnum Photos; 847 (t)Collection of Janice L. and David J. Frent, (bl)White House Historical Association, (br)Tom Ebenhoh/Black Star; 851 CORBIS; 853 AP/Wide World Photos; 854 Bettmann/CORBIS; 855 Ranan R. Lurie, Cartoonews International Syndicate, New York City; 856 Wally McNamee/CORBIS; 858 AP/Wide World Photos; 859 Dennis Brack/Black Star;

860 Fred Maroon/Folio; 861 (l)National Archives, (r)Alex Webb/Magnum Photos; 862 Chicago Tribune; 864 CORBIS/Bettmann; 865 Owen Franken/CORBIS; 866 Wally McNamee/CORBIS, (inset)Collection of Janice L. and David J. Frent; 867 CORBIS; 868 By permission of John L. Hart FLP and Creators Syndicate, Inc.; 869 Alain Mingam/Getty Images News Services; 870 Associated Press/AP Wide World Photo; 872 Picture Research Consultants; 873 (t)Hulton Archive/Getty Images, (b)Picture Rearch Consultants; 874 CORBIS/Bettmann; 875 Bettmann/CORBIS; 876 (l)Picture Research Consultants, (r)Lynn Goldsmith/CORBIS; 877 (tl)Collection of Hershenson-Allen Archives, (tr)Picture Research Consultant; (c b)Neal Preston/CORBIS; 878 Bettmann/CORBIS; 879 AP/Wide World Photos; 882 (t)File photo, (b)White House Historical Association; 882–883 Courtesy Ronald Reagan Library; 883 (l-c)File photo, (r)Dennis Brack/Black Star/PictureQuest; 887 Charles Geer Photography; 890 Associated Press, AP; 891 (t)Hoertel/Getty Images News Services, (b)CORBIS; 893 Courtesy Ronald Reagan Library; 894 AP/Wide World Photos; 895 (l)CORBIS/Bettmann, (r)Halstead/Getty Images News Services; 897 Dennis Brack/Black Star; 899 Joseph C. Marquette; 900 AP/Wide World Photos; 903 CORBIS; 904 Getty Images; 905 Bill Stormont/The Stock Market; 906 (l)Dennis Brack/Black Star/PictureQuest, (r)Ellen B. Neipris/Impact Visuals; 907 NASA; 908 Joe Skipper/Reuters; 909 Susan Greenwood/Gamma-Liaison; 910 (l)Copyright Robert Messick, Reproduced by permission of Robert R. Godine, Publisher, Inc., (r)Matt Meadows; 911 912 Getty Images; 913 Doug Martin; 915 Leif Skoogfors/CORBIS; 917 Alexandra Avakian, Contact Press Images; 918 Peter Turnley/CORBIS; 920 Timepix/Getty Images; 921 Bruno Barbey/Magnum Photos; 922 Bettmann/CORBIS; 923 Douglas Kirkland/CORBIS; 926 (l)file photo, (r)White House Historical Association; 926–927 AP/Wide World Photos; 927 (l)National Museum of American History/Smithsonian Institution, (c)Digital Art/CORBIS, (r)Official White House Photo by Eric Draper; 931 CORBIS; 932 R. Masonneuve/Publicphoto/Photo Researchers; 933 Reuters/Natalie Behring/Hulton Archive/Getty Images; 936 CORBIS; 937 Jeffrey Markowitz/Sygma/CORBIS; 938 Erik Freeland/Matrix; 939 Wally McNamee/CORBIS, (inset)Greg Gibson/AP/Wide World Photos; 941 Amit Shabi/Reuters/STR/Archive Photos/Getty Images; 943 Bureau of Public Affairs/U.S. Department of State; 944 (t)Annie Griffiths Belt/CORBIS, (b)Pablo San Juan/CORBIS; 945 Reuters Newmedia Inc./CORBIS; 948 Courtesy May Akabogu-Collin; 949 (t)Reuters New Media Inc./CORBIS, (b)AP/Wide World Photos; 951 Reuters/CORBIS; 952 CORBIS; 953 Jamestown-Yorktown Foundation; 955 AP/Wide World Photos; 957 (l)Thomas E. Franklin/Bergen Record/SABA/CORBIS, (tr)Tom Horan/AP/Wide World Photos, (br)Robert Clark/Aurora Quanta; 958 Steve Liss/CORBIS; 959 Cherie A. Thurlby/USAF/Getty Images; 960 AP/Wide World Photos; 962 Getty Images; 963 The White House/CORBIS; 967–971 White House Historical Association; 971 (George W. Bush) Official White House Photo by Eric Draper; 972 The Oakland Museum; 973 Bridgeman Art Library Ltd.; 974 The Wadsworth Atheneum; 977 AP/Wide World Photos; 978 Charles Moore/Black Star; 979 Library of Congress; 981 Getty Images; 982 Private Collection; 983 Independence National Historic Park Collection; 985 Private Collection; 987 988 The Bridgeman Art Library; 989 990 National Portrait Gallery, Smithsonian Institution/Art Resource, NY; 992 Chicago Historical Society; 993 (l)Maryland Historical Society, (r)Smithsonian Institution; 994 Picture Research Consultants; 995 Library of Congress; 996 (t)Andre Jenny/Focus Group/PictureQuest, (b)Bettman/CORBIS; 998 National Portrait Gallery, Smithsonian Institution, Washington, D.C./Art Resource. N.Y.; 999 Courtesy Franklin D. Roosevelt Library; 1001 Carl Iwaski/TimePix/Getty Images; 1002 Francis Miller/TimePix/Getty Images; 1003 LIFE Magazine c. Time Inc.; 1004 1005 PhotoDisc/Getty Images; 1006 unknown; 1007 Picture Research Consultants; 1011 Smithsonian Institution; 1012 Bob Daemmrich; 1013 Library of Congress; 1014 National Portrait Gallery, Smithsonian Institution/Art Resource, N.Y. Gift of the Hon. Henry Cabot Lodge; 1019 Bettmann/CORBIS; 1020 CORBIS; 1021 Bettmann/CORBIS; 1022 Matt Meadows; 1023 John F. Kennedy Library; 1026 David Brownell; 1027 CORBIS; 1029 Bob Daemmrich.

Photo Credits